The General Armory

of

England, Scotland, Ireland, and Wales

**COMPRISING A REGISTRY OF ARMORIAL BEARINGS
FROM THE EARLIEST TO THE PRESENT TIME**

❧ Volume 2 ❧

Sir Bernard Burke, C.B., LL.D.

ULSTER KING OF ARMS

AUTHOR OF *THE PEERAGE AND BARONETAGE; HISTORY OF THE LANDED GENTRY;
DORMANT AND EXTINCT PEERAGE; VICISSITUDES OF FAMILIES,* &C., &C.

HERITAGE BOOKS
2007

HERITAGE BOOKS

AN IMPRINT OF HERITAGE BOOKS, INC.

Books, CDs, and more—Worldwide

For our listing of thousands of titles see our website
at
www.HeritageBooks.com

A Facsimile Reprint
Published 2007 by
HERITAGE BOOKS, INC.
Publishing Division
65 East Main Street
Westminster, Maryland 21157-5026

Originally published

London:
Harrison, 59, Pall Mall,
Bookseller to the Queen and H. R. H. the Prince of Wales
1878

International Standard Book Number: 978-0-7884-3720-5

Fitzotho (WALTER, Castellan of Windsor Castle, and Warden of the Forests, co. Berks, *temp.* William the Conqueror, son of OTHO, a Baron of England in the 16th year of Edward the Confessor, who possessed numerous and extensive lordships in cos. Berks, Surrey, Buckingham, Dorset, Middlesex, Wilts, Somerset, and Hants. Descendants: I. FITZGERALD, *Duke of Leinster.* II. FITZGERALD, *Earl of Desmond.* III. OSBORN FITZGERALD, Lord of Ynysymaengwyn, co. Merioneth. IV. THE WHITE KNIGHT. V. THE KNIGHT OF GLYN. VI. THE KNIGHT OF KERRY. VII. FITZGERALD, bart., of Castle Ishen. VIII. CAREW, *Earl of Totnes.* IX. CAREW, bart., of Haccombe. X. CAREW, bart., of Anthony. XI. CAREW, of Hamworth. XII. CAREW, of Carew. XIII. CAREW, *Lord Carew.* XIV. FITZ-MAURICE, Lord of Kerry, *Marquess of Lansdowne.* XV. GRACE, feudal Barons of Courtstown and Lords of Graces country, now of Mantua House. XVI. GRACE, bart., of Grace Castle. Also tof the following branches: I. GERARD, bart., of Bryn. II. GERARD, Lord of Gerards Bromley. III. GERARD, of Brandon, *Earl of Macclesfield.* IV. GERARD, bart., of Fiskerton. V. GERARD, bart., of Flambards. VI. GERARD, of Crewe. VII. WINDSOR, *Lord Windsor, Earl of Plymouth.* VIII. WYNDSORE, feudal baron of Eston, or Estaines). Ar. a saltire gu. See FITZ-GERALD, *Duke of Leinster.*

Fitz-Ourse (co. Somerset). Ar. on a bend sa. three bears' heads erased ar. muzzled de the second.

Fitz-Ourse. Or, a bear pass. sa. *Crest*—An anchor and cable sa. and a sword az. hilt or, in saltire.

Fitz-Paine. Per pale ar. and sa. a fesse counterchanged.

Fitz-Patrick (*Lord Upper Ossory,* Chief of the Irish Sept of MacGillie Phadruig, created 1541, attainted 1691). Sa. a saltire ar. on a chief ar. three fleurs-de-lis or. *Crest*—A dragon reguard. vert, surmounted of a lion guard. sa. dexter paw resting on the dragon's head, tail extended sa. *Supporters*—Two lions sa. armed and langued gu. *Motto*—Ceart laidir a boo.

Fitz-Patrick (*Earl of Upper Ossory,* extinct 1818). Same *Arms* and *Crest.* *Supporters*—Two lions sa. collared, chained, and ducally crowned or. *Motto*—Fortis sub forte fatiscet.

Fitz-Patrick (Lisdoonvarna, co. Clare; Fun. Ent. 1637, DARBY FITZ-PATRICK, Esq., eldest son of FLORENCE FITZ-PATRICK, of the same place, descended from McGILLA PATRICK, Lord of Upper Ossory). Same *Arms.*

Fitz-Patrick (Akipe; Fun. Ent. 1674, THADY FITZ-PATRICK, M.D., son of TEIGUE OGE FITZ-PATRICK, grandson of DERMOT FITZPATRICK, of Ballyrellin, and great grandson of TEIGUE OGE McTEIGUE FITZPATRICK, |of Muindrihid). Sa. a saltire ar. on a chief of the last three pellets.

Fitz-Patrick (*Lord Castletown*). Sa. a saltire ar. on a chief az. three fleurs-de-lis or, within a bordure wavy of the second. *Crest*—A dragon on his back ppr. surmounted by a lion pass. sa. the whole debruised by a bendlet sinister wavy ar. *Supporters*—Two lions sa. ducally gorged and chained or, each charged on the shoulder with three fleurs-de-lis gold. *Motto*—Fortis sub forte fatiscet.

Fitz-Patrick. Az. six lions ramp. ar. three, two, and one.

Fitz-Payne (*Baron Fitz-Payne,* summoned to Parliament, 1299; abeyance, 1354). Gu. three lions pass. guard. in pale ar. over all a bend az.

Fitz-Payne. Ar. a hawk's lure gu.

Fitz-Payne (CHERETON FITZ-PAYNE; the heiress *m.* ·AUSBILL, co. Devon). Ar. two wings conjoined gu.

Fitz-Payne (co. Gloucester). Gu. two lions pass. in pale ar. over all a bend az. (another gobonated or and az.).

Fitz-Payne. Barry of six ar. and az. a bend gu.

Fitz-Pearce (Sir JAMES FITZ-PEARCE, knighted by Lord Mountjoy, Lord Deputy, at Dublin Castle, 1 May, 1600). Ar. a saltire gu. in chief a crescent sa.

Fitz-Peirs. Gu. three chevronels company ar. and az.

Fitz-Pen, alias Phippen (co. Cornwall, St. Mary Ottery, co. Devon, Weymouth, co. Dorset, Truro, co. Cornwall, and Ireland; monument in Truro Church to OWEN FITZ-PEN, of Ireland, eldest son of ROBERT FITZ-PEN, of Weymouth, and great grandson of HENRY FITZ-PEN, of St. Mary Ottery. Visit. Cornwall, 1620). Ar. two bars sa. in chief three escallops of the second. *Crest*—A bee volant in pale or, winged vert.

Fitz-Perewes, or Fitz-Perrens (co. Gloucester). Erm. three mascles in fesse gu.

Fitz-Piers (*Earl of Essex ;* passed to the BOHUNS, 1227. See MANDEVILLE, *Earl of Essex*). Quarterly, or and gu. a bordure vair.

Fitz-Piers. Gu. two chevrons chequy ar. and az. *Crest* —A bell az.

Fitz-Piers. Ar. a chief indented sa. fretty or.

357

Fitz-Piers. Gu. three lions ramp. or (another, a bordure engr. ar.).

Fitz-Piers. Erm. three fusils in fesse gu.

Fitz-Piers. Quarterly, or and gu. an inescutcheon sa.

Fitz-Pomery. Or, a lion ramp. gu. a bordure engr. sa. *Crest*—A serpent entwined round two hunting spears in pale ppr.

Fitz-Ralph (Nether-Whiteacre, co Warwick; RALPH FITZ-RALPH, Lord of that place, *temp.* King John, purchased lands in the Manor of Glascot, co. Warwick (*Dugdale*); ANNE FITZ-RALPH, *m.* THOMAS GLASCOTE, grandson of JOHN GLASCOTE, or GLASCOKE, 38 Henry III. Visit. Essex, 1614). Or, three chevronels gu. each charged with as many fleurs-de-lis or.

Fitz-Ralph (co. Berks). Barruly ar. and az.

Fitz-Ralph. Barry of six ar. and gu. in chief three buckles of the second. *Crest*—A square padlock az.

Fitz-Ralph (*temp.* Henry III.). Or, two bars az.

Fitz-Ralph. Or, three chevronels gu. fretty ar.

Fitz-Ralph. Barry of six ar. and az. three chaplets of roses gu. leaved vert.

Fitz-Randall. Az. a chief indented or.

Fitz-Randolf (Langton Hall, co. Notts, 1614, and Chesterfield, co. Derby; EDWARD FITZ-RANDOLF, 1640. Visit. Notts, 1614). Az. a chief indented az. *Crest*—On a chapeau or, turned up az. a wyvern of the last.

Fitz-Randolfe. Az. fretty or, a chief of the last.

Fitz-Randolph (co. Northumberland). Or, a chief indented az.

Fitz-Ranulph (cos. Derby and Nottingham, *temp.* Henry II.). Az. two chev. or.

Fitz-Raulf (co. Suffolk). Or, three chev. gu. each charged with as many fleurs-de-lis ar. (another, of the first).

Fitz-Raulf (co. Suffolk). Gu. a fesse vair.

Fitz-Raulf. See FITZ-RALPH.

Fitz-Raynard, or Fitz-Raynold. Gu. six lions ramp. ar. *Crest*—Two wings conjoined ppr.

Fitz-Raynold (co. Lancaster). Purp. three lions ramp. or.

Fitz-Raynold (co. Suffolk). Gu. three buglehorns or.

Fitz-Reand. Or, a fesse and two chev. gu. a canton of the last.

Fitz-Rery (Fun. Ent. Ulster's Office, 1682, ROBERT FITZ-RERY). Az. a lion ramp. az. crowned and armed or.

Fitz-Rice (Reg. Ulster's Office). Per pale sa. and erm. a fesse counterchanged.

Fitz-Richard (co. Lincoln). Az. on a fesse betw. three crosses crosslet fitchée ar. as many torteaux.

Fitz-Richard (Lord Mayor of London, 1260, 1261, and 1266). Quarterly, ermines and erm. a fesse counterchanged.

Fitz-Richard, or Fitz-Roand. Or, a fesse, chev. and canton gu. *Crest*—Two dolphins endorsed haurient ppr.

Fitz-Richard. Quarterly, or and gu. a bend sa.

Fitz-Richard. Per pale sa. and erm. a fesse counterchanged.

Fitz-Richard. Or, a cross gu. in the first quarter a lion ramp. sa.

Fitz-Rith (Colletrath, co. Dublin; impalement on Fun. Ent. of RICHARD LUTTERALL, of Sprickleston, same co., *d.* 1619, whose wife was ANNE, dau. of RICHARD FITZ-RITH). Ar. a lion ramp. az. crowned or, armed and langued gu.

Fitz-Robert (co. Northumberland, *temp.* King John). Or, two chev. gu.

Fitz-Roe (Reg. Ulster's Office). Ar. six crosses crosslet gu. three, two, and one, on a chief of the last a lion pass. of the first.

Fitz-Roger (co. Lincoln). Quarterly, or and gu. a bend sa.

Fitz-Ronard, or Fitz-Roward (co. Buckingham). Or, two chev. gu. in chief a lion pass. of the second.

Fitz-Ronard. Or, two chev. gu. on a canton of the second a lion pass. ar. *Crest*—A dove standing on a serpent nowed in a love-knot ppr.

Fitz-Routh. Or, a fesse, and in base a chev. gu. on a canton of the last a mullet of the first.

Fitz-Row (co. Waterford, Reg. Ulster's Office). Ar. six roses gu. three, two, and one.

Fitz-Row. Quarterly, per fesse indented az. and or.

Fitz-Rowe. Quarterly, or and az. in the second and third quarters a rose of the first.

Fitz-Roy (illegitimate son of Henry I.). Ar. on a canton gu. a lion pass. guard. or.

Fitz-Roy (*Duke of Richmond and Somerset,* K.G., illegitimate son of Henry VIII.; created 1525, extinct 1536). France and England, a bordure quarterly, erm. and company ar. and az. a baton sinister of the second, on an inescutcheon quarterly, gu. and vairé, or and vert, a lion ramp. ar. on a chief az. a castle betw. two bucks' heads cabossed ar.

Fitz-Roy (*Duke of Cleveland.* BARBARA VILLIERS, Mistress to Charles II., created *Duchess of Cleveland*, 1670, with remainder to two of her illegitimate sons by the King; extinct 1774). Royal arms of England, over all a baton sinister erm. *Crest*—On a chapeau gu. turned up erm. a lion statant guard. or, ducally crowned az. collared compony countercompony erm. and az. *Supporters*—Dexter, a lion guard. or, gorged with a collar compony countercompony erm. and az.; sinister, a greyhound collared as the dexter. *Motto*—Secundis dubusque rectus.

Fitz-Roy (*Duke of Southampton.* CHARLES FITZ-ROY, illegitimate son of Charles II.; so created 1674, extinct 1774). Same *Arms*, &c.

Fitz-Roy (*Duke of Northumberland.* GEORGE FITZ-ROY, illegitimate son of Charles II.; so created 1683, extinct 1716). Royal arms, &c., of England, debruised with a sinister baton compony erm. and az. *Crest*—On a chapeau gu. turned up erm. a lion statant guard. or, ducally crowned az. collared compony countercompony erm. and az. *Supporters*—Dexter, a lion guard. or, ducally crowned compony countercompony erm. and az.; sinister, a greyhound ar. collared compony countercompony erm. and az.

Fitzroy (*Duke of Grafton*). Quarterly, 1st and 4th, France and England, quarterly; 2nd, Scotland; 3rd, Ireland; the whole debruised by a baton in bend sinister compony of six pieces ar. and az. *Crest*—On a chapeau gu. turned up erm. a lion statant guard. or, crowned with a ducal coronet az. and gorged with a collar countercompony ar. and of the fourth. *Supporters*—Dexter, a lion guard. or, crowned with a ducal coronet az. and gorged with a collar countercompony ar. and of the second; sinister, a greyhound ar. gorged as the dexter. *Motto*—Et decus et pretium recti.

Fitzroy (*Baron Southampton*). Same *Arms*, a crescent for diff. *Crest*—On a chapeau gu. turned up erm. a lion statant guard. or, crowned with a ducal coronet az. and gorged with a collar countercompony ar. and of the fourth. *Supporters*—Dexter, a lion guard. or, crowned with a ducal coronet az. and gorged with a collar countercompony erm. and of the second; sinister, a greyhound ar. gorged as the dexter. *Motto*—Et decus et pretium recti.

Fitz-Roy (Kempston, co. Norfolk). Same *Arms*, a crescent for diff.

Fitz-Simmons. Sa. on a fesse betw. three crescents ar. another of the field. *Crest*—An eagle with wings expanded looking towards the sun all ppr.

Fitz-Simon (Simons Hide, co. Herts; Sir RICHARD FITZ-SIMON, Lord of that Manor, was one of the Founder Knights of the Garter, he occupied the 8th stall on the Sovereign's side, son of Sir HUGH FITZ-SIMON, grandson of Sir JOHN FITZ-SIMON, and great grandson of SIMON FITZ-ADAM, who was Lord of the same Manor, 1239). Ar. three inescutcheons, two and one gu.

Fitz-Simon. Sa. a fesse betw. three crescents ar.

Fitz-Simon (*temp.* Edward III.). Az. a lion ramp. erm. (another, with a label of four points gu.).

Fitzsimon (Ireland). Erm. on a chief gu. three mullets ar.

Fitz-Simon (Fun. Ent. of THOMAS FITZ-SIMON, of Dublin, Alderman, *d.* Jan. 1595). Sa. on a fess betw. three crescents ar. as many estoiles az.

Fitz-Simon (Ballymadraught, co. Dublin; Fun. Ent. of JOHN FITZ-SIMON, *d.* 21 Dec. 1614). Sa. three crescents ar. in chief a label of two points, and in fess another of one point of the last, the points issuant out of the crescents.

Fitz-Simond (Reg. Ulster's Office). Sa. a fess betw. three crescents ar. *Crest*—A dove ar.

Fitzsimond. Erm. a fesse chequy or and az.

Fitzsimonds. Gu. three escutcheons ar.

Fitzsimonds. Ar. on two bars sa. three crescents, two and one ar.

Fitz-Simons (Ireland). Ar. three escutcheons gu. *Crest*—A boar pass. reguard. pulling from his shoulder an arrow.

Fitz-Stephen (Norton, co. Devon). Gu. an eagle displ. with two heads ar. (another, or).

Fitz-Stephen. Az. three mullets or.

Fitz-Stevens (Ireland; Fun. Ent. of ROBERT FITZ-STEVENS, of Dublin, merchant, *d.* 24 Oct. 1598, Reg. Ulster's Office). Per pale erm. and gu. a saltire counterchanged. *Crest*—A wolf's head erased gu. holding in the mouth a snake ppr.

Fitz-Symon (Dublin). Sa. on a fesse betw three crescents ar. as many estoiles az. *Crest*—A demi parrot close vert, gorged with a collar gu. beaked of the last.

Fitz-Symon (co. Essex). Gu. three escutcheons ar.

Fitz-Symon (co. Hertford). Az. the field replenished with eagles displ. or.

Fitz-Symon. Ar. three eagles displ. vert.

Fitz-Symon (co. Hertford). Az. an eagle displ. or, a canton erm.

Fitz-Symon. Ar. three escutcheons gu. *Crest*—A dexter and sinister hand wielding a two-handed sword ppr.

Fitz-Symon. Gu. a chief or (another, tinctures reversed).

Fitz-Symon. Sa. a fesse betw. six crescents or (another, ar.).

Fitz-Symond (co. Lincoln). Az. a lion ramp. erm.

Fitz-Symond (cos. Norfolk and Northampton). Sa. a fesse betw. three crescents ar. *Crest*—A hand issuing from a cloud holding a club ppr.

Fitz-Symond. Same *Arms*, a chief of the second.

Fitz-Thomas (co. Essex). Az. five eagles displ. in cross or, a canton erm. (another, of the second). *Crest*—A dragon's head pierced through the neck with a spear in bend sinister ppr.

Fitz-Thomas (Lord Mayor of London, 1262 to 1265, inclusive, and 1269). Same *Arms*.

Fitz-Thomas, alias Fitz-Gerald (Ireland). Erm. a saltire gu. *Crest*—Out of a ducal coronet or, a sceptre entwined with a serpent betw. two wings ppr.

Fitz-Thomas. Ar. a griffin's head erased (another, couped) sa.

Fitz-Tiptoft, or De Gurney (co. Norfolk). Ar. a saltire engr. gu.

Fitz-Urse. Or, on a bend sa. three bears' heads couped ar. muzzled gold. *Crest*—Out of the top of a tower, issuing from the wreath, an arm in armour wielding a scymitar all ppr.

Fitz-Urse. Or, a bear pass. sa.

Fitz-Vrian. Same *Arms*. *Crest*—Two battle axes in saltire gu. and az. heads or, betw. the tops a bird sa.

Fitz-Vrian (Wales). Ar. a chev. betw. three martlets sa.

Fitz-Vrian (Wales). Same *Arms*, a bordure engr. gu.

Fitz-Vrian (Llangadock, co. Carmarthen; granted 20 Feb. 1526). Same *Arms*, a crescent of the field, a bordure engr. gu. bezantée.

Fitz-Vrith. Or, on a bend sa. three rams' heads couped ar.

Fitz-Wakelin. Barry of eight ar. and gu. a lion ramp. erm.

Fitz-Walker, or Fitz-Walter (co. Buckingham). Quarterly, or and gu. on a bend az. three fleurs-de-lis of the first.

Fitzwallen (co. Essex). Or, two bars and a canton gu.

Fitz-Walter (*Baron Fitz-Walter*; summoned to Parliament 1295, passed to the RATCLIFFE family 1432). Or, a fesse betw. two chevronels gu.

Fitz-Walter. Same *Arms*. *Crest*—A winged heart ppr.

Fitz-Walter (*Lord Fitz-Walter*). See BRIDGES.

Fitz-Walter. Ar. a fesse betw. two chev. gu.

Fitz-Walter (quartered by COPLESTONE). Ar. a chev. betw. three buckles gu.

Fitz-Walter. Quarterly, or and gu. a bend az.

Fitz-Walter. Gu. on a bend ar. three fleurs-de-lis az.

Fitzwarin. Gu. a fesse or, betw. six martlets ar.

Fitzwarin. Ar. on a bend az. three bezants, in the sinister chief a cross crosslet fitchée of the second.

Fitz-Warin (co. Dorset). Quarterly, per fesse indented gu. and erm.

Fitz-Warine (cos. Dorset and Somerset, *temp.* Edward III.). Per fesse indented erm. and gu. in the first quarter a fret of the last.

Fitz-Warine (*Baron Fitz-Warine;* summoned to Parliament 1295, passed to the BOUCHIER family 1429). Quarterly, per fess indented ar. and gu.

Fitz-Warine (*Baron Fitz-Warine;* summoned to Parliament 1342, abeyance 1414). Same *Arms*, in the first quarter a fret gu.

Fitz-Warren, or Fitz-Warine (co. Devon). Quarterly, per fesse indented or and gu. (another, ar. and sa.).

Fitz-Warren (co. Lancaster, *temp.* Henry III.). Quarterly, per fesse indented ar. and gu.

Fitz-Warren (co. Somerset). Quarterly, per fesse indented erm. and gu. *Crest*—A holy lamb reguard. ppr. with banner ppr.

Fitz-Warren (co. York). Gu. a bend ar. betw. six bezants.

Fitz-Warren. Gu. a fesse or, betw. six mascles (another martlets) ar.

Fitz-Warren. Quarterly, gu. and or, a chief indented counterchanged (another, or and gu.).

Fitz-Warren. Per pale sa. and ar. a chief indented counterchanged.

Fitz-Warren (Whittington, co. Salop). Quarterly, per fesse indented ar. and gu.

Fitz-Warren. Chequy or and az. (another, or and gu.).

Fitz-Waryne (descended from GUARINE, who, *temp.* the Conqueror, acquired by his good sword Whittington Castle, co. Salop. Sir WILLIAM FITZ-WARYNE was appointed Governor of Montgomery Castle 1330, was elected a Knight of the Garter *cir.* 1345, in the room of Sir SAUCHET D'ABRICHECOURT, the first of the Founder Knights who died). Quarterly, per fess indented erm. and gu. *Crest*—A wyvern ar. eared and langued or. *Another Crest*—A wivern, wings expanded gu.

Fitz-Water (co. Cumberland). Ar. a chev. sa. betw. three buckles gu.

Fitz-Water (co. Essex). Or (another, ar.) a fesse betw. two chevs. gu. (another, charges the fesse with a crescent ar.).

Fitz-Water (MILO FITZ-WATER, Constable of England *temp.* Henry I.). Gu. two bends, the upper or, the lower ar. *Crest*—A lion ramp. or.

Fitz-Water (co. York). Ar. a chev. betw. three chaplets sa.

Fitz-Water. Ar. on a chev. sa. betw. four roses gu. three square buckles or.

Fitz-Water. Quarterly, or and gu. on a bend az. three fleurs-de-lis ar.

Fitz-Water. Ar. a chev. sa. betw. three round buckles gu.

Fitz-Well (co. Buckingham). Paly of six ar. and gu.

Fitz-Werrey (Reg. Ulster's Office). Quarterly, indented ar. and sa.

Fitz-Wight. Gu. two bends engr. or. *Crest*—On a chapeau ppr. a lion pass. guard. az.

Fitz-Wight. Ar. three griffins pass. in pale ar.

Fitz-William (*Baron Fitz-William*; summoned to Parliament 1327, not summoned after). Lozengy ar. and gu.

Fitz-William (*Earl of Southampton*; created 1537, *d. s. p.* 1543). Same *Arms*, a mullet for diff.

Fitz-William (*Earl of Fitzwilliam*). Quarterly, 1st and 4th, lozengy ar. and gu.; 2nd and 3rd, sa. a chev. betw. three leopards' faces or. *Crests*—1st: Out of a ducal coronet or, a triple plume of ostrich feathers ar.; 2nd: A griffin pass. ar. *Supporters*—Two savage men, wreathed about the heads and waists with leaves, and in their exterior hands a tree eradicated, the top broken all ppr. *Motto*—Appetitus rationi pareat.

Fitz-William (Merrion, co. Dublin; Fun. Ent. of Sir RICHARD FITZ-WILLIAM, Knt., *d.* 5 March, 1595). Gu. on a bend cotised ar. three popinjays vert, beaked and legged gu. *Crest*—In front of a peacock's tail ppr. a greyhound's head erased ar. collared and spotted gu.

Fitz-William (Ballydongan, co. Dublin; Fun. Ent. 1635, NICHOLAS FITZ-WILLIAM, Esq.). Same *Arms*, a crescent for diff.

Fitzwilliam (*Viscount Fitzwilliam*; extinct 1833). Gu. on a bend cotised ar. three popinjays vert, beaked and legged gu. (These arms appear from various entries in Ulster's Office to have been the family arms of FITZ-WILLIAM, of Merrion, co. Dublin, but it appears from an entry in the Lords' Entries that the second *Viscount Fitz-William*, when created *Earl of Tyrconnel*, adopted the arms of FITZ-WILLIAM, of Sprotborough, which were used by the subsequent viscounts who succeeded after the earldom expired). *Crest*—In front of a peacock's tail ppr. a greyhound's head erased ar. spotted gu. plain collared or. *Supporters*—Two ostriches ar. each holding in the beak a horseshoe or. *Motto*—Deo adjuvante, non timendum.

Fitz-William (*Earl of Tyrconnel*; the second *Viscount Fitz-William* so created 1663, *d. s. p.* 1667). Lozengy or and gu. (N.B.—These arms appear on his Fun. Ent. in Ulster's Office).

Fitz-William (Jobstown, co. Dublin; Fun. Ent. of WILLIAM FITZ-WILLIAM, of that place, who *d.* of the plague at Merrion, co. Dublin, 23 Aug. 1605). Gu. on a bend cotised ar. three popinjays vert, beaked and legged of the field.

Fitz-William (co. Dublin; Fun. Ent. of CHRISTOPHER FITZ-WILLIAM, merchant, a natural son of the house of Jobstown, *d.* 14 Nov. 1620). Same *Arms*, a border gobony or and sa.

Fitz-William (Reg. Ulster's Office). Gu. a fesse betw. six escallops ar.

Fitz-William (Gainspark Hall, co. Essex, Milton, cos. Northampton and Lancaster, and Westminster). Same *Arms* and *Crest* as *Viscount Fitz-William*, of Merrion.

Fitz-William (co. Essex). Lozengy ar. and gu. a bordure az. bezantée.

Fitz-William (Chaworth, co. Lincoln). Lozengy erm. and gu. *Crest*—Out of a ducal coronet or, a double plume of feathers ar.

Fitz-William (Mablethorp, co. Lincoln). Lozengy ar. and gu. in fesse a fleur-de-lis of the second, a bordure sa. bezantée.

359

Fitz-William (Oldward, co. Surrey, and co. Lincoln, 1640). Lozengy ar. and gu. *Crest*—A tiger pass. sa. ducally gorged and lined ar.

Fitz-William. Ar. a chev. betw. three crosses crosslet sa. a bordure of the last bezantée. *Crest*—A phœnix az. beaked or, in flames gu.

Fitz-William. Lozengy ar. and gu. *Crest*—A trefoil stalked raguly and slipped ar.

Fitz-William. Ar. on a bend sa. three estoiles of the field.

Fitz-William. Barry of eight ar. and az. three chaplets gu.

Fitz-William. Quarterly, per fesse indented ar. and gu. in the first quarter a mullet of six points sa.

Fitzwilliams (co. Essex). Lozengy ar. and gu. a bordure az. charged with six bezants and as many fleurs-de-lis gold, alternately.

Fitzwilliams (co. Cornwall). Az. three bends or.

Fitzwilliams. Lozengy ar. and gu. in fesse a fleur-de-lis betw. the points of a crescent, both or.

Fitz-Williams (co. Lincoln). Ar. a cross engr. sa.

Fitz-With (co. Norfolk). Az. three griffins pass. or.

Fitz-With. Gu. two bends or.

Fitzwygram (Walthamstow, co. Essex, bart.). Ar. on a pale gu. three escallops or, over all a chev. engr. countercharged, on a chief waves of the sea, thereon a ship representing an English vessel of war of the 16th century, with four masts, sails furled all ppr. colours flying gu. *Crest*—On a mount vert a hand in armour in fesse couped at the wrist ppr. charged with an escallop and holding a fleur-de-lis erect or. *Supporters*—On either side an eagle, wings elevated ar. collared gu. and charged on the breast with a shamrock vert. *Motto*—Dulcis amor patriæ.

Fitzyay. Gu. a saltire or, on a chief of the last three mullets of the first.

Flacket (Dovebridge, co. Derby, 1611). Ar. on a fesse betw. three foxes' heads erased gu. as many lions' gambs erect and erased of the field. *Crest*—A fox's head erased gu. shot through the neck fesseways with an arrow sa. feathered ar.

Flaherty. See O'FLAHERTIE.

Flamank, or Flamock (Buscane, co. Cornwall; BERNARD FLAMANKE, descended from RICHARD FLAMANKE, of Bukian, *temp.* Henry VI. Visit. 1620). Ar. a cross betw. four mullets gu. pierced or, quartering PEVERELL. *Crest*—A Saracen's head ppr. banded round the temples or.

Flamank (PHILLIPPS-FLAMANK; exemplified to Rev. WILLIAM PHILLIPPS, upon his assuming, by royal licence, the additional surname of FLAMANK). Quarterly, 1st and 4th, ar. a cross gu. betw. four mullets of the last, each charged with a bezant, for FLAMANK; 2nd and 3rd, ar. a lion ramp. within an orle of saltires sa., for PHILLIPPS. *Crest*—A lion ramp. sa. semée of saltires ar. and holding betw. the paws an escarbuncle or. *Motto*—Virtus ad astra.

Flambert (cos. Cambridge and Essex). Gu. on a chev. engr. ar. three dolphins vert (another, az.).

Flambert. Gu. on a bend ar. three dolphins embowed vert.

Flamens. Gu. three mascles or.

Flammicke, or Flammyke. Ar. a cross betw. four mullets gu.

Flamsted (Ruston and Denton, co. Northampton). Or, three bars sa. on a chief of the second a lion pass. of the first. *Crest*—A talbot's head ar. erased gu. gorged with a bar gemelle or, eared of the last.

Flamvill (Aston, co. Leicester; Sir ROBERT FLAMVILL, Knt., 8 Edward III., 1334; his grandson, Sir WILLIAM FLAMVILL, left a dau. and heir, *m.* RICHARD TURVILL, of Normanton, same co. Visit. Leicester, 1619). Ar. a maunch az. (another, the maunch charged with three bezants; another, maunch gu.). *Crest*—Two battle axes endorsed saltireways ensigned by a dove all ppr.

Flanagan. See O'FLANAGAN.

Flanagan (Drumdoe, co. Roscommon). Ar. on a chev. gu. two lions ramp. or. *Crest*—A hand holding a dagger. *Motto*—Audaces fortuna juvat.

Flanders (Flandres, co. Warwick, *temp.* Richard II.; descended from HUGH DE FLANDERS, third son of GERARD DE ODINGSELLS, Baron of Makerstoke, co. Warwick, in right of his wife, BASILIA, dau. and heir of GEOFFREY, *Lord Lindsey*, Baron of Makerstoke, *temp.* Henry II. Visit. Leicester, 1619). Ar. a fesse gu. in chief three mullets sa.

Flanders. Or, a lion ramp. sa. over all a bend gu. *Crest*—A harp gu.

Flanders. Same *Arms*, a bordure engr. gu.

Flanders. Barry of six ar. and sa. in chief three mullets gu.

Flanders. Sa. fretty or.

Flanders. Gyronny of eight or and az. an inescutcheon gu.

Flanders. Ar. three mullets in chief pierced gu.

Flanders. Sa. a lion ramp. or.

Flanders, Earldom of (this was the fourth peerdom of France). Or, a lion sa. armed and langued gu.

Flandringham. Az. a fleur-de-lis ar. in chief a lion pass. of the last.

Flandringham, or Flandringe. Az. in chief a lion pass. guard. and in base a fleur-de-lis or.

Flanke. Sa. three flower pots ar.

Flarmey. Sa. a cinquefoil erm.

Flashman. Per pale or and az. two chevs. counterchanged. *Crest*—Out of a ducal coronet two arms from the elbows in saltire, each holding a scymitar in pale all ppr.

Flatesbury (Ireland, Reg. Ulster's Office). Ar. a chev. betw. three lozenges gu. *Crest*—On a mural coronet or, a stag sejant erm.

Flatesbury. Ar. a chev. embattled betw. three lions ramp. gu.

Flattesbury (Reg. Ulster's Office). Az. three lions ramp. or.

Flatterbury, Flattesbery, or Flatebury (Ireland; JAMES FLATTERBURY JOHNSON; Fun. Ent. Ulster's Office of ROBERT ASH, Esq., of Naas, *d.* 11 April, 1608, *m.* ELIZABETH, dau. of JAMES FLATTERBURY). Ar. a chev. betw. three lions ramp. gu.

Flaunders (Flaunders, co. Warwick; quartered by WHET-HILL, or WHEATLEY, of Shepey, co. Leicester. Visit. 1619. RICHARD WHETHILL, of that place, 1402, *m.* MARGARET, dau. and co-heir of JOHN FLAUNDERS). Ar. a fess gu. in chief three mullets sa.

Flaxal. Az. a chev. betw. three pheons or.

Flaxney (co. Oxford). Az. a fesse betw. two fleurs-de-lis or. *Crest*—On a mount vert a talbot sa. collared and lined or, the end of the line tied up in a knot.

Flay (THOMAS FLAY, of Exeter, Doctor of Physic, and ROBERT FLAY, of Chaldon, co. Devon. Visit. 1620). Erm. on a pale az. three birds ar. *Crest*—On a mural crown gu. a snake ppr.

Flecke (co. Surrey). Ar. two bars sa. each charged with three escallops of the first.

Fleeming (The Wergs, co. Stafford; settled there upwards of 400 years. MARY, only child of WILLIAM FLEEMING, Esq., and niece and sole heiress of JOHN FLEEMING, Esq., of the Wergs, *m.* 1794, RICHARD FRYER, Esq., M.P. for Wolverhampton). Erm. on a chev. engr. gu. betw. three crosses pattée fitchée sa. a Cornish chough betw. two crescents ar. *Crest*—On a mount vert a cross pattée fitchée or, thereon perched a Cornish chough ppr.

Fleet (co. Kent). Chequy or and gu. a canton ar.

Fleet (London). Ar. two bars sa. on the upper one as many escallops of the first. *Crest*—A sinister arm embowed, habited sa. puffed ar. holding in the hand ppr. a club of the second.

Fleet. Same *Arms*. *Crest*—A goat, holding in the mouth a trefoil ppr.

Fleet. Per pale gu. and sa. a lion ramp. ar.

Fleete (co. Kent). Ar. a lion ramp. gu. over all a bendlet sa.

Fleete (London; granted 13 May, 1691). Az. on a bend wavy or, betw. two dolphins embowed ar. three escallops gu. *Crest*—A sea-lion guard. erect, the upper part or, holding an escallop gu. the lower part ppr.

Fleets. Chequy or and gu. a sinister quarter ar.

Fleetwood (Calwick, co. Stafford, bart., extinct 1780; formerly of Penwortham, co. Lancaster; descended from HENRY FLEETWOOD, living 3 Henry VI., son of JOHN FLEET-WOOD, Lord of the Manor of Plumpton Parva, co. Lancaster, living *temp.* Edward III., whose descendant, RICHARD FLEETWOOD, Esq., of Calwick, was created a bart. 29 June, 1611). Per pale nebulée az. and or, six martlets counterchanged. *Crest*—A wolf pass. reguard. ar. charged on the breast with a trefoil vert.

Fleetwood (The Vache, co. Bucks; descended from Sir GEORGE FLEETWOOD, Knt., of the Vache, knighted 11 May, 1603, M.P. for Chipping-Wycombe, 28 Elizabeth; son of THOMAS FLEETWOOD, Esq., of The Vache, M.P. for Bucks, 5 Elizabeth, second son of WILLIAM FLEETWOOD, Esq., of Hesketh, co. Lancaster, great-grandson of JOHN FLEETWOOD, Esq., of Little Plumpton). Same *Arms*.

Fleetwood (Aldwinckle, co. Northampton; descended from Sir WILLIAM FLEETWOOD, of Cranford, co. Northampton, younger son of THOMAS HESKETH, Esq., of Hesketh. Of this family was GEORGE FLEETWOOD, colonel in the Parliament's service, one of King Charles's judges, and a Lord of Oliver Cromwell's other house; the celebrated General FLEET-

WOOD, Lord-Lieutenant of Ireland under the Protectorate; and GEORGE FLEETWOOD, pre-eminently distinguished in the service of Gustavus Adolphus of Sweden, by whom he was created a baron of that kingdom). Same *Arms*.

Fleetwood (Rossall, co. Lancaster; descended from EDMUND FLEETWOOD, Esq., of Rossall, youngest son of THOMAS FLEETWOOD, Esq., of Hesketh. The male line terminated with EDWARD FLEETWOOD, Esq., of Rossall, whose co-heiress, MARGARET, *m.* 16 Sept. 1733, ROGER HESKETH, Esq., of North Meols, co. Lancaster (a descendant of a younger branch of the HESKETHS of Rufford, co. Lancaster), and from this marriage descended the late Sir PETER HESKETH FLEET-WOOD, Bart., of Rossall). Same *Arms*. *Crest*—A wolf pass. reguard. ar.

Fleetwood (HESKETH-FLEETWOOD; Rossall Hall, co. Lancaster, bart., extinct 1866). Quarterly, 1st and 4th, per pale nebulée az. and or, six martlets, two, two, and two, counterchanged, a canton ar., for FLEETWOOD; 2nd and 3rd, ar. on a bend sa. three garbs or, a chief az. thereon an eagle displ. with two heads ppr. all within a bordure erm., for HESKETH. *Crests*—1st, FLEETWOOD: A wolf reguard. ar. charged on the breast with a trefoil vert; 2nd, HESKETH: A garb erect or, in front of an eagle displ. with two heads ppr. *Motto*—Quod tibi hoc alteri.

Fleetwood (HESKETH-FLEETWOOD; granted to the reputed son of the late Sir PETER HESKETH-FLEETWOOD, Bart., of Rossall Hall). Quarterly, 1st and 4th, per pale nebulée az. and or, six martlets, two, two, and two, counterchanged, a canton ar., for FLEETWOOD; 2nd and 3rd, ar. on a bend sa. three garbs or, a chief az. thereon an eagle with two heads displ. ppr. all within a bordure erminois, for HESKETH; the whole four quarters within a bordure wavy quarterly erm. and az. *Crests*—1st, FLEETWOOD: A wolf statant reguard. ar. charged on the breast with a trefoil vert, and on the body with a pale wavy az.; 2nd, HESKETH: A mount vert, thereon in front of an eagle with two heads displ. ppr. a garb or, banded gu. the whole debruised by a bendlet sinister wavy az. *Motto*—Quod tibi hoc alteri.

Fleetwood. Ar. on a chev. az. an escallop of the first.

Fleetwood (London). Per pale nebulée or and az. six martlets, three and three, counterchanged.

Fleetwood (Carrington Manor, co. Bedford; Fun. Ent. 1639, HESTER, *Lady Lambart*, dau. of Sir WILLIAM FLEET-wood, and widow of the first *Lord Lambart*). Same *Arms*.

Fleetwood (Sir MILES FLEETWOOD, knighted by Lord Mountjoy, Lord Deputy, 29 April, 1602). Same *Arms*.

Fleetwood (Reg. Ulster's Office). Same *Arms*. *Crest*—A wolf pass. reguard. ar.

Flegg (Bray, co. Berks). Per pale or and sa. a chev. counterchanged. *Crest*—Two lions' gambs in saltire sa. enfiled with two laurel branches in orle vert.

Flegg. Ar. a chev. engr. gu.

Fleggh. Per pale ar. and or, on a chev. (another, engr.) per pale sa. and az. a martlet of the second.

Flegh, or Flight (London). Ar. on a chev. engr. sa. betw. three pellets a fleur-de-lis betw. two conies of the first.

Fleming (*Lord Slane*, created 1537, dormant 1726). Vair a chief chequy or and gu. *Crest*—A mortar piece casting out a bomb with flames all ppr. chains and rings gold. *Supporters*—Two greyhounds ar. collared and armed gu. *Motto*—Bhear na Righ gan (Anglicé, May the king live for ever).

Fleming (*Viscount Longford;* the twenty-second *Lord Slan*, so created 1713, *d. s. p. m.* 1726). Same *Arms*, &c.

Fleming (Gernonstown, co. Meath; Fun. Ent., 1635, THOM-ASINE, wife of THOMAS FLEMING, second son of PATRICK FLEMING, descended from a younger son of the *Lords Slane*). Same *Arms*, a crescent for diff.

Fleming (JOHN FLEMING, Dublin, 1621; Fun. Ent. of his wife, KATHARINE WAFER). Same *Arms*, a martlet for diff.

Fleming (SEBASTIAN FLEMING, Drogheda, 1609: Fun. Ent. of his wife JANE, dau. of ROBERT BISSE, of Dublin). Same *Arms*, a border gu.

Fleming (THOMAS FLEMING, of Dublin, merchant: Fun. Ent. of his wife, 1639). Same *Arms*, an annulet sa. a bordure of the last.

Fleming (Visit. Cornwall, 1620. JOHN FLEMING, D.D., of Wadda' College, Oxford, and THOMAS FLEMING, Esq., of Landithe, co. Cornwall, grandsons of JOHN FLEMING, settled at Bristol, son of JOHN FLEMING, of the province of Munster, represented by NICHOLLS, of Trereife, near Penzance). Chequy or and gu

Fleming (Rydal, co. Westmoreland, bart.). Gu. a fret ar. *Crest*—A serpent nowed, holding in his mouth a garland of olive and vine all ppr. *Motto*—Pax, copia, sapientia.

Fleming (Beckermet, co. Cumberland). Same *Arms*.

Fleming (Wath, co. Cumberland). Az. two bars ar. on a chief of the second three lozenges gu.

Fleming (cos. Essex, Hants, Kent, and Salop). Gu. a chev. betw. three owls ar.

Fleming (co. Gloucester). Gu. fretty or. a fesse az.

Fleming (Stoneham and Southampton, co. Hants; confirmed 3 June, 1584, to the founder of the family, Sir THOMAS FLEMING, Knt., Lord Chief Justice of England, *temp.* James I.). Gu. on a chev. betw. three owls ar. an erm. spot **sa.** *Crest*—An eagle displ. sa. beaked, legged, and ducally gorged or.

Fleming (Sir THOMAS FLEMING, Lord Mayor of London. Visit. 1568). Same *Arms.*

Fleming (co. Lancaster; RICHARD FLEMING, Bishop of Lincoln 1420-31, founder of Lincoln College, Oxford). Barry of six ar. and az. in chief three lozenges gu.

Fleming (quartered by STANLEY, of Dalgarth and Awsthwaite. Visit. Cumberland, 1615). Same *Arms.*

Fleming (co. Lancaster). Ar. two bars sa. in chief three gadflies of the second.

Fleming (co. Salop and Wales). Gu. three crescents in fesse erm. betw. seven crosses crosslet fitchée ar. (another, or). *Crest*—A dexter hand in armour holding a sword all ppr.

Fleming (Eustow, co. Devon). Gu. a fret ar.

Fleming (Manchester). Same *Arms. Crest*—A serpent nowed ar. holding in the mouth a chaplet vert. *Motto*—Pax, copia, sapientia.

Fleming (Rayrigg and Belfield, co. Westmorland). Same *Arms. Crest*—A serpent nowed, holding in his month a garland of olives and vines all ppr. *Motto*—Pax, copia, sapientia.

Fleming (co. York). Barry of six ar. and az. in chief three water bougets gu.

Fleming (Brompton Park, co. Middlesex, bart., extinct 1763. Sir JOHN FLEMING, created bart. 1763, was son of ROBERT FLEMING, Esq., of Achonry, co. Sligo, by KATHARINE SPENCE, his wife; he *d. s. p. m.*; his dau. and heiress, JANE, *m.* the third *Earl of Harrington*). Az. two bars ar. on a double tressure flory counterflory of the last. *Crest*—A goat's head ppr.

Fleming (co. York). Az. two bars ar. on a chief of the second three cushions of the first tasselled or.

Fleming (co. York). Ar. a chev. betw. three fleurs-de-lis gu.

Fleming (Wales). Gu. three crescents erm. (another, semée of crosses crosslet or).

Fleming. Chequy or and gu. on a chief of the first three birds az.

Fleming. Or, a chev. az. betw. three bulls' heads sa. guttée d'or.

Fleming (Bratton Fleming, co. Devon, extinct *temp.* Henry VI.; the co-heirs *m.* BELLEW and DILLON). Vair a chief chequy or and gu.

Fleming (Stoke Fleming; LUCY, dau. and heir of SYMON A. FLEMING, *m.* MOHUN, *circ.* 1140). Vair a fess chequy ar. and gu. (sometimes a chief).

Fleming (granted to Sir FRANCIS FLEMING, Lieutenant of the Ordnance, 1549). Gu. a chev. betw. three owls ar. on a pile in chief or, a cannon az. discharged ppr.

Fleming. Barry of six az. and ar. in chief three lozenges or.

Fleming. Gu. a cinquefoil pierced erm.

Fleming. Az. a cinquefoil erm. charged with an annulet of the first.

Fleming. Az. three bars ar. on a chief of the last as many pair of wings conjoined gu.

Fleming (Cumbernauld; *Earl of Wigtoun;* title dormant since 1747). Quarterly, 1st and 4th, gu. a chev. within a double tressure flory counterflory ar., for FLEMING; 2nd, az. three frases ar., for FRASER. *Crest*—A goat's head erased ar. armed or. *Supporters*—Two harts ppr. attired with ten tynes or, each with a collar az. charged with three frases ar. *Motto*—Let the deed shaw.

Fleming (Ferme, bart., 1666). Quarterly, as the last, the chev. in the 1st and 4th quarters embattled for diff. *Crest*—A palm tree ppr. *Motto*—Sub pondere cresco.

Fleming (Borde, Scotland). Gu. a chev. betw. three frases ar. all within a double tressure flory counterflory of the second. *Crest*—A goat's head erased and attired or. *Motto*—Let the deed shaw.

Fleming (Barrochan, co. Renfrew). Or, a fesse chequy ar. and az. surmounted by a bend of the third. *Crest* and *Motto,* as the last.

Fleming (HUGHES-LE FLEMING, Rydal Hall, co. Westmorland; exemplified to GEORGE CUMBERLAND HUGHES, 1861, upon his assuming, by royal licence, the additional name of

LE FLEMING on succeeding to the estates of his kinswoman, ANNE FREDERICA ELIZABETH, widow of Sir DANIEL FLEMING, fifth bart. of Rydal). Gu. a fret. ar., for FLEMING, quartering HUGHES, quarterly, or and ar. a lion ramp. az. betw. three fountains ppr. *Crests*—A serpent nowed, holding in the mouth a wreath of olive and vine leaves all ppr., for FLEMING; a lion couchant the dexter paw resting on a fountain, for HUGHES. *Motto*—Pax, copia, sapientia.

Fleminge. Ar. a fesse engr. gu. in the dexter chief a rose of the last.

Flemyng (Shareston, co. York; granted by Flower, Norroy, 1571). Az. two bars ar. on a chief of the last three maunches gu. *Crest*—A dolphin ar. crowned az. and charged with six pellets.

Flemyng. See FLEMING.

Flemyngham. Sa. a chev. erm. betw. three covered cups or.

Flerior. Or, on a chief az. three fleurs-de-lis ar.

Fleshe. Ar. a fesse engr. gu. in chief an annulet of the last.

Fleshing. Ar. a fesse indented gu.

Fleshing. Or, two bars gemelles az.

Fleshing. Ar. a fesse per fesse indented gu. and or, double cotised az.

Fletchar (Cury and Nawgam, co. Cornwall; GODOLPHIN FLETCHAR, son of ROBERT FLETCHAR, Chaplain in Ordinary to Queen Elizabeth, and grandson of ROBERT FLETCHER, co. Leicester. Visit. 1620). Erm. a cross moline sa.

Fletcher (Hutton, co. Cumberland, bart., extinct 1712; descended through the sixth son, THOMAS FLETCHER, from HENRY FLETCHER, Esq., of Cockermouth, who entertained Mary Queen of Scots on her journey to Carlisle, 1568). Ar. a saltire engr. sa. betw. four pellets, each charged with a pheon of the field, points downwards.

Fletcher (Clea Hall, co. Cumberland, bart.). Sa. a cross engr. ar. betw. four plates, each charged with an arrow of the first. *Crest*—A horse's head ar. charged with a trefoil gu. *Motto*—Martis non Cupidinis.

Fletcher (Tarnbank, co. Cumberland). Same *Arms, Crest,* and *Motto.*

Fletcher (co. Chester). Same *Arms. Crest*—A pheon per pale erm. and sa. point upwards.

Fletcher (Kenward, co. Kent). Ar. a cross engr. sa. betw. four pellets, each charged with a pheon erect of the first. *Crest*—A horse's head erased ar. *Motto*—Martis non Cupidinis.

Fletcher (Lawneswood, co. Stafford; descended from the marriage of THOMAS FLETCHER, Esq., of Water Eyton, living *temp.* Elizabeth, with MARGARET, dau. and heiress of RALF ALPORT, of Cannock). Ar. a cross engr. sa. betw. four pellets, each charged with a pheon or, on a canton az. a ducal crown gold. *Crests*—1st: A horse's head erased ar. gorged with a ducal crown az.; 2nd: On a chapeau gu. a scaling ladder or. *Motto*—Sub cruce salus.

Fletcher (Moresby and Tallantire, co. Cumberland). Ar. a cross engr. sa. betw. four pellets charged with as many pheons of the field. *Crest*—A nag's head ar. charged with a trefoil gu. *Another Crest*—A horse's head erased ar.

Fletcher (co. Stafford). Sa. a cross flory betw. four escal lops ar.

Fletcher (St. Lawrence, London; Fun. Ent., Ulster's Office, 1643; WILLIAM FLETCHER, slain before Gloucester, and buried in the Collegiate Church there). Same *Arms,* impaling az. a chev. betw. three quatrefoils slipped ar., for VINCENT. *Crest*—A dexter arm in armour embowed, holding in the gauntlet all ppr. an arrow also ppr. headed or.

Fletcher (Swinford, co. Leicester, and Coventry, co. Warwick). Sa. a cross flory ar. surmounted of another of the first betw. four escallops of the second. *Crest*—A demi talbot ramp. az. eared or.

Fletcher (Chichester, co. Sussex; granted 15 Dec. 1767). Sa. on a cross flory betw. four escallops ar. a cross couped of the first, a canton erm. *Crest*—A talbot pass. ar. pellettée.

Fletcher (the Rev. JOHN KENDALL FLETCHER, D.D., of the University of Oxford, Chaplain to King George IV. and Vicar of Yarnscombe and Ashford, co. Devon). Sa. a cross flory ar. surmounted of a plain cross az. betw. four escallops of the second. *Crest*—A bloodhound ar. ducally gorged or. *Motto*—Dieu pour nous.

Fletcher (Steynesby, co. Derby; granted, in 1731, to JOHN FLETCHER, Esq., High Sheriff of the county in 1732, whose family had realized a fortune by the collieries). Ar. on a cross engr. sa. a compass dial in the centre betw. four pheons or, a chief gu. charged with a level staff betw. two double coal picks of the third. *Crest*—A horse's head couped ar. guttée de sang.

Fletcher (Peel Hall, near Bolton, co. Lancaster). Erm. a cross engr. betw. four escutcheons sa. each charged with a pheon ar. all within a bordure wavy az. *Crest*—Three arrows, two in saltire and one in fess ppr. diverging from each angle a fleur-de-lis az. and surmounted in the centre by a saltire wavy sa. *Motto*—Alta pete.

Fletcher (Mawgan, co. Cumberland). Erm. a cross moline sa.

Fletcher (London, and Woodstock, co. Oxford; granted 26 April, 1613). Gu. a chev. ar. betw. three laurel leaves of the second, on a canton per bend sinister vert and az. three fleurs-de-lis or, betw. eight bezants. *Crest*—A fleur-de-lis or, pellettée.

Fletcher (Condover, co. Salop). Sa. two pole axes in saltire ar. ducally crowned or.

Fletcher. Ar. a chev. betw. three mullets sa. *Crest*—Out of a ducal coronet or, a plume of three ostrich feathers az. banded gold.

Fletcher (granted to CALEB FLETCHER, Esq.). Az. two horses' heads erased erm. and in base an anchor with cable or, on a chief wavy of the last three hurts, each charged with a pheon ar. *Crest*—A dexter arm embowed in armour, the hand grasping an arrow, all ppr. behind the arm an anchor erect or. *Motto*—Nec quærere nec spernere honorem.

Fletcher (granted to GEORGE HAMILTON FLETCHER, Esq., of Barrow Hedges, co. Surrey). Az. three arrows in triangle, the barbs pointing to the centre or, on a chief ar. an anchor erect sa. betw. two dolphins respecting each other ppr. impaling WANSEY, or, a leopard's face betw. three dexter gloves gu. *Crest*—In front of a fernbrake a centaur ppr. wielding with the dexter hand a spear or. *Motto*—Droit comme ma flèche.

Fletcher. Quarterly, sa. and ar. a cross flory counterchanged.

Fletcher (Low Bashir, co. Westmeath; Reg. Ulster's Office, to BENJAMIN FLETCHER, son and heir of Col. BENJAMIN FLETCHER, Captain-General and Governor-in-Chief of the province of New York, province of Pennsylvania, and county of Newcastle, and Vice-Admiral of the same, who was son and heir of WILLIAM FLETCHER, Esq. (slain at Gloucester, 3 Sept. 1643), and of ABIGAIL VINCENT, his wife, dau. and heiress of HENRY VINCENT, Esq., London). Sa. a cross flory betw. four escallops ar. quartering VINCENT, viz., sa. a chev. betw. three quatrefoils slipped ar. *Crest*—An arm in armour embowed, holding in the gauntlet an arrow all ppr. point or. *Motto*—Per angustum.

Fletcher (Carrow, co. Cork, bart.). Sa. on a cross engr. erm. betw. four plates, each charged with a pheon erect az. a sword in pale ppr. on a canton or, a wreath of laurel vert. *Crest*—Out of a mural crown or, a horse's head erm. gorged with a wreath of laurel vert.

Fletcher (confirmed by Preston, Ulster, 1645, to ROBERT FLETCHER, an officer in His Majesty's train of artillery, descended from the FLETCHERS, of co. Chester). Sa. a cross engr. ar. betw. four plates, each charged with an arrow of the field. *Crest*—A pheon per pale erm. and sa. point upwards. *Motto*—Hic hodie cras urna.

Fletcher (Reg. Ulster's Office; descended from co. Chester). Same *Arms*, the plates charged with pheons. *Crest*—A horse's head erased ar. maned or. Same *Motto*.

Fletcher-Boughey. See BOUGHEY, Bart.

Fletcher-Vane. See VANE, Bart.

Fletcher (Saltoun, Scotland). Sa. a cross flory betw. four escallops ar. *Crest*—A demi bloodhound az. gorged with a ducal crown or. *Supporters*—Two griffins ppr. *Motto*—Dieu pour nous.

Fletcher (Aberlady, Scotland). Same *Arms*, within a bordure engr. ar. for diff. *Crest*—A demi lion ramp. az. holding in the dexter paw a cross crosslet fitchée ar. *Motto*—Fortis in arduis.

Fletcher (Ballinshoe, 1763). Sa. on a cross flory betw. four escallops ar. a crescent gu. *Crest* and *Motto*, same as Saltoun.

Fletcher (Dunans, co. Argyll). Sa. on a cross flory ar. betw. two escallops in dexter chief and sinister base of the last, and as many quivers filled with arrows in sinister chief and dexter base three crescents in pale vert. *Crest*—Two naked arms shooting an arrow out of a bow sa. *Motto*—Recta pete.

Fletchers, Company of (London). Az. a chev. betw. three arrows or, headed and feathered ar. *Crest*—A demi angel ppr. with wings endorsed or, vested and holding a bundle of arrows gold.

Flete. Ar. a chev. sa. in base a trefoil slipped of the second.

Fletewikes, or Flytewikes. Ar. two lions pass. guard. sa. *Crest*—An arm embowed, vested and cuffed ar. in the hand ppr. an arrow sa. headed and feathered of the first.

362

Fletham. Sa. three unicorns' heads ar.

Flett. Ar. a chev. betw. three trefoils sa.

Fletwick (co. Bedford). Ar. two lions pass. guard. sa. *Crest*—Two lions' gambs, supporting an escutcheon ar.

Fletwick. Ar. two lions pass. sa. and two bars of the second charged with as many escallops of the first.

Fletwick. Ar. a lion pass. guard. sa. tail forked.

Fletwicke. Sa. a lion ramp. guard. or.

Fleury (Ireland). Az. a saltire or, betw. four eels naiant wavy of the last. *Crest*—A lion pass. holding a crescent.

Flexney (Alderman of Oxford, *d.* 1578; St. Michael's, Oxford). Sa. a fesse betw. two fleurs-de-lis or.

Flinn. See O'FLINN.

Flint (Norwich). Az. on a chev. betw. three flint stones ar. two lions combatant gu.

Flint (Professor, St. Andrew's, Scotland). Vert a chev. betw. three flintstones ar. *Crest*—An estoile. *Motto*—Sine macula.

Flint. Sa. a chev. ar. betw. three crescents erm. *Crest*—A lion's gamb erect sa. holding a branch of laurel ppr.

Flint (the late Sir CHARLES WILLIAM FLINT, Knt.). Per chev. gu. and az. in chief two demi lions ramp. couped, in base a key paleways or. *Crest*—A flint ppr. thereon an estoile or.

Flint (granted by Clifford). Vert three flintstones ar.

Flint. Vert three leopards' faces ar.

Flint. Sa. a lion ramp. or, a bordure engr. of the last.

Flint. Sa. on a chev. engr. ar. betw. three crescents or, each charged with a mullet of the first, two lions combatant of the field.

Flintarne. Ar. a fesse gu. betw. three eagles displ. sa.

Flintham (Flintham, co. Notts; quartered by DRAPER, of that place; JOHN DRAPER, *temp.* Queen Elizabeth, *m.* ANNE, sister and heir of ROBERT HUSSEY, descended from Sir HUGH HUSSEY, Knt., of Flintham, *temp.* Henry IV. Visit. Notts, 1614). Ar. a fesse betw. six martlets sa.

Flitt. Or, on a pale az. three antique crowns of the first. *Crest*—On a mount a dove all ppr.

Flockart. Ar. a chev. sa.

Floelte. See FLOTE.

Flood (Bramber Hill, Honiton, co. Devon, Esq.). Or, on a chev. az. three cinquefoils of the field. *Crest*—A demi lion ramp. az. crowned or, holding a cinquefoil gold.

Flood (Flood Hall, Farmley, Paulstown Castle, and Viewmount, co. Kilkenny. The name of FLOOD is one of distinction in Ireland, and the high reputation, as patriot, orator, and statesman, of the Right Hon. HENRY FLOOD, of Flood Hall, and Farmley, has given it historic importance). Vert a chev. betw. three wolves' heads erased ar., confirmed *temp.* Elizabeth, to Sir THOMAS FLUDD, of the co. of Kent. *Crest*—A wolf's head, as in the arms. *Motto*—Vis unita fortior.

Flood (Newtown Ormonde, co, Kilkenny, and Banna Lodge, co. Wexford, bart., extinct 1824; FREDERICK FLOOD, younger brother of JOHN FLOOD, Esq., of Flood Hall, was created a bart. 1780, *d. s. p. m.*). Same *Arms*, *Crest*, and *Motto*.

Flood (SOLLY-FLOOD, Slaney Lodge, and Bromley, co. Wexford; exemplified, 1819, to FREDERICK SOLLY, Esq., maternal grandson of Sir FREDERICK FLOOD, Bart., of Banna Lodge and Slaney Lodge, co. Wexford, on his assuming, by royal licence, the additional surname of FLOOD). Quarterly, 1st and 4th, vert a chev. betw. three wolfs' heads erased ar.; 2nd and 3rd, ar. a chev. gu. betw. three sole fishes haurient ppr. within a bordure engr. sa. *Crest*—A wolf's head erased ar. *Motto*—Vis unita fortior.

Flood (LLOYD-FLOOD; granted, 1839, to WILLIAM LLOYD, Esq., of Farmley, co. Kilkenny, on his assuming, by royal licence, the additional surname of FLOOD, by the desire of JOHN FLOOD, Esq., of Flood Hall, Kilkenny). Vert a chev. betw. three wolves' heads erased ar. *Crest*—A wolf's head erased ar. *Motto*—Vis unita fortior est.

Flood. Or, a griffin segreant vert.

Flood. See FLUDD.

Florack. Ar. two chev. betw. three cinquefoils gu. (another, sa.).

Florence, Dukedom of. See TUSCANY.

Florence. Az. a cross flory ar. (another, or).

Florio (originally of Spain; granted 1614). Az. a heliotrope (or sunflower) or, issuing from the stalk, sprouting out of two leaves vert, in chief the sun in splendour ppr. *Crest*—A sun or.

Flory (co. Somerset). Az. a crescent betw. three fleurs-de-lis ar. seeded or.

Flory. Gu. a fleur-de-lis ar.

Floshing. Ar. a fesse indented point in point, or and gu. betw. two barrulets az.

Flote, or Floelte. Ar. a chev. sa. in base a trefoil slipped of the second. *Crest*—Out of a ducal coronet a reindeer's head ppr.

Flote (France). Ar. a bend lozengy gu. betw. six fleurs-de-lis az.

Flote. Or, a lion ramp. sa. over all a bendlet gu.

Flote. Ar. two bars sa. on each as many (another, three) escallops of the first.

Flote. Ar. a chev. betw. three trefoils slipped sa.

Flote, or Fleet. Ar. a lion ramp. gu. over all on a bend sa. three mullets or.

Flowde (co. Norfolk). Ar. on a cross sa. five crescents or. *Crest*—Out of a tower a greyhound's head erased ar. collared sa. in the mouth a hind's leg erased ppr.

Flower (*Viscount Ashbrook*). Ar. two chevronels betw. three ravens ppr. each holding in the beak an ᶜ ɪ. spot sa. betw. the chevronels three pellets. *Crest*—A raven, as in the arms. *Supporters*—Two tigers ppr. ducally gorged and chained or. *Motto*—Mens conscia recti.

Flower (Fun. Ent. 1674, Captain Thomas Flower, buried at Finglas, co. Dublin). Ar. on a chev. betw. three ravens, each holding an erm. spot in the beak all sa. three mullets of the first.

Flower (Fun. Ent. 1681, Sir William Flower, buried at Finglas, co. Dublin). Gu. three towers ar.

Flower (confirmed by St. George, Ulster, 1681, to Captain Thomas Flower, nephew to Sir William Flower, Colonel of one of His Majesty's Regiments of Guards). Quarterly, 1st and 4th, ar. two chevronels betw. three ravens, each holding in the bill an erm. spot all sa. betw. the chevronels three pellets; 2nd and 3rd, gu. three towers ar. *Crest*—A raven holding an erm. spot sa.

Flower (certified, 1655, by Carney, Ulster, as the arms of Lieut. Peter Flower; descended from Flower, of Estham, co. Kent). Erm. a cinquefoil vert, on a canton or, a cross crosslet fitchée gu. *Crest*—A boar statant az. armed, hoofed, and bristled or, langued gu.

Flower (Whitwell, co. Rutland; descended from William Flower, High Sheriff of the co. 10 Richard II. Her Visit. 1618). Ermines a cinquefoil erm. *Crest*—A flower erm. foliated vert.

Flower (Hucknall and Langer, co Notts.; Edward Flower, B.D., and Thomas Flower, kinsmen. Visit. Notts, 1614 and 1631). Erm. a cinquefoil ermines. *Crest*—A lion's head erased ar.

Flower (co. Brecon). Sa. a cinquefoil erm.

Flower, or Flowre (cos. Kent, Northampton, and York). Erm. a cinquefoil gu. *Crest*—A lion's head erased sa.

Flower (co. York; arms of William Flower, Norroy King of Arms, temp. Queen Elizabeth). Ermines a cinquefoil pierced ar. *Crest*—A lion's head erased ar. charged with a mullet gu.

Flower (Isle of Ely, co. Cambridge). Per fesse ar. and az. in chief two fleurs-de-lis gu. in base one or. *Crest*—A stork with wings elevated ppr. beaked and legged gu.

Flower (Park Hill, Croydon, co. Surrey). Or, two flaunches vert, in pale three escutcheons of the last, each charged with a fleur-de-lis of the field. *Crest*—Issuant from clouds a cubit arm erect, in the hand a rose and lily each slipped ppr. *Motto*—Flores curat Deus.

Flower (Lobb, co. Oxford, and Woodford, co. Essex, bart.). Per pale az. and gu. a unicorn or, on a chief invecked erm. three gillyflowers ppr. over the centre flower a sword in bend dexter also ppr. pommel and hilt gold, surmounted saltire-ways by a key of the last. *Crest*—A demi lion per pale erm. and erminois, gorged with a chain within a collar gemel or, in the dexter paw a gillyflower ppr. *Supporters*—Dexter, a unicorn or, collared az. therefrom pendent an escutcheon erm. charged with a key erect gold, holding in the mouth a gillyflower ppr.; sinister, a roebuck ppr. collared az. therefrom pendent an escutcheon erm. charged with the maze, representing that of the city of London erect or, in the mouth a gillyflower as the dexter. *Motto*—Persceverando.

Flower (co. Nottingham; granted 1681). Same *Arms* and *Crest* as Viscount Ashbrook.

Flower (Chilton, co. Wilts). Sa. a unicorn pass. or, on a chief ar. three pinks gu. stalked and leaved vert. *Crest*—A unicorn's head couped or.

Flower, or Flore. Az. a fleur-de-lis and a bordure or.

Flowerden (Hetherset, co. Norfolk). Per chev. invected ar. and sa. three sea lions counterchanged. *Crest*—A demi man habited az. wreathed about the temples ar. and sa. holding in the right hand a sprig of two roses gu. stalked and leaved ppr.

Flowerdew (co. Norfolk; Fun. Ent. Ulster's Office, of Thomas Flowerdew, Esq., d. 8 June, 1619). Per chev. engr. sa. and ar. three sea bears pass. counterchanged.

Flowerdew (impalement, Fun. Ent. Ulster's Office, 1674, Arthur Ward). Per fess ar. and sa. three sea bears counterchanged.

363

Flowerdue, or Flowerdew (Lopham, co. Norfolk). Per chev. engr. ar. and sa. three water bougets counterchanged. *Crest*—An arm couped at the shoulder, resting the elbow on the wreath in a maunch ppr.

Flowerdue. Per chev. engr. ar. and sa. three hinds tripping counterchanged.

Floyd (bart.). Sa. a lion ramp. reguard. ar. on a chief embattled or, a sword erect ppr. pommel and hilt gold, enfiled with an Eastern crown gu. betw. two tigers' faces also ppr. *Crest*—A lion ramp. reguard. ar. murally crowned gu. bearing a flag representing the standard of Tippoo Sultan flowing to the sinister ppr. *Motto*—Pations pulveris atque solis.

Floyd (co. Brecknock). Ar. a griffin segreant az.

Floyd. Ar. a cross sa. *Crest*—A griffin sejant az. holding in the dexter paw a garland of laurel vert.

Floyd (Ireland; descended out of Wales; impalement Fun. Ent. 1675, Doctor Cardiff, buried in Christ's Church, Dublin). Ar. three lioncels couchant gu.

Floyd (Reg. Ulster's Office). Vert a chev. betw. three wolves' heads erased ar. a crescent for diff.

Floyer (Floyer Hayes, co. Devon; John Floyer, of that place, m. Jane, dau. of John Carew, of Anthony, temp. Queen Elizabeth. Visit. 1620). Sa. a chev. betw. three arrows ar. *Crest*—A stag's head erased or, holding in the mouth an arrow ar.

Floyer (Metrith, co. Somerset) Same *Arms* and *Crest*.

Floyer (Martin Hall, co. Lincoln). Same *Arms*. *Crest*—A buck's head erased or, holding in the mouth an arrow ppr. *Motto*—Floret virtus vulnerata. *Quarterings*—Basshe; Croke; Martin; Loundres; Wadham, &c.

Floyer (West Stafford, co. Dorset). Same *Arms*. *Crest*—A buck's head erased or, holding in the mouth an arrow. *Motto*—Floret virtus vulnerata.

Floyer (Hints, co. Stafford). Ar. a chev. betw. three arrows sa.

Flud. Ar. on a cross sa. five crescents or (another, betw. four crescents sa.).

Fludd, or Flood (Millgate, co. Kent; granted 10 Nov. 1572, to Thomas Flood, Esq., of Millgate, co. Kent, son and heir of John Fludd, Esq., of Morton, co. Salop). Vert a chev. betw. three wolves' heads ar. *Crest*—Out of a ducal coronet ar. an ounce's head ppr.

Fludd (Fun. Ent. of Margaret, wife of Richard Fludd, of Dublin, d. 28 Jan. 1614). Vert a chev. erm. betw. three wolves' heads erased ar.

Fludd. Sa. three horses' heads erased ar.

Flude. Erm. a chev. betw. three crescents gu. *Crest*—An arm couped at the shoulder, embowed, and resting the elbow on the wreath, holding a sword in pale, enfiled with a Saracen's head couped ppr.

Fludyer (Trostry, co. Monmouth, bart., Lord Mayor of London, 1761). Sa. a cross patonce betw. four escallops ar. each charged with a cross patonce of the field, betw. two wings elevated ar. *Crest*—An escallop as in the arms, betw. two wings elevated ar.

Fly (co. Hants). Or, on a chev. engr. sa. betw. three pellets, each charged with a martlet of the field, as many fleurs-de-lis gold. *Crest*—A cubit arm in armour erect ppr. holding in the gauntlet a hawk's lure or, stringed gu.

Flye, or Flyght. Or, on a chev. engr. sa. betw. three pellets, each charged with a martlet of the field, a fleur-de-lis betw. two conies courant respecting each other ar.

Flygesthorpe. Vairé ar. and sa. a saltire gu.

Flyn. See O'Flyn.

Flynt (co. Norfolk). Sa. on a chev. engr. or, betw. three crescents erm. two lions combatant gu.

Flynt. Sa. a chev. ar. betw. three crescents of the second. *Crest*—A human heart purp. winged or.

Flynton (Laceby, co. Lincoln). Ar. a cross lozengy gu.

Foche (Wotton, co. Kent; granted by Cooke, Clarenceux, 1576). Gu. a fesse dancettée betw. six lozenges or.

Fochebury (co. Bedford). Erm. on a chev. gu. three roses ar.

Foden, or Fodon (co. Stafford). Ar. on a fesse az. betw. three crossbows strung sa. as many arrows or. *Crest*—Out of a ducal coronet or, a pike's head az.

Foden (Market Overton, co. Rutland). Same *Arms*. *Crest*—Upon a mount vert a unicorn sejant ramp.ar. armed, maned, and unguled or, supporting with the fore feet a crossbow sa.

Fodering, Fodringay, or Fodringhay. Quarterly, gu. and or, a cross lozengy ar. in the second quarter an eagle displ. of the third.

Fodringay. Same *Arms*, the eagle or. *Crest*—A crane ar. in the beak a bunch of clover vert.

Fodringay. Ar. a bend nebulée counter nebulée, betw. six crosses crosslet gu.

Foderinghay. Quarterly, or and gu. a cross lozengy ar.

Foderingshey (co. Dorset). Ar. three Saracens' heads couped at the shoulders sa.

Fodringham (co. York). Az. a bend ar. betw. six mullets of the last. *Crest*—A buck ppr.

Fogarty (Ireland, Reg. Ulster's Office). Az. two lions ramp. combatant supporting a garb or, in dexter base a crescent ar., and in the sinister, the harp of Ireland.

Foge, or Fogge (Turton and Entwisle Hall, co. Lancaster; Sir Marmaduke Constable's Roll, 1558). Ar. on a fess betw. three annulets sa. as many mullets of the field. See also ELLIOT (FOGGE-ELLIOT).

Fogelston, Foghelston, or Foulstone. Gu. on a chev. ar. three crescents sa.

Fogg, or Fogge (Richbury, co. Kent). Ar. (another, or) on a fesse betw. three annulets sa. as many mullets pierced of the first. *Crest*—A unicorn's head ar.

Fogg. Ar. on a fesse betw. six annulets sa. three mullets pierced of the first. *Two Crests*—1st: A unicorn's head couped ar.; 2nd: A unicorn's head couped ar. powdered with mullets sa.

Fogge. Ar. two bars sa. in chief three mullets of the last.

Fogo (Row, co. Perth, 1830). Ar. a fess sa. charged with three mullets of the field betw. two annulets in chief and two crosiers saltireways in base of the second, a bordure gu. *Crest*—A cross crosslet fitchée gu. *Motto*—Fuimus.

Fokeram, or Fokerham (co. Berks). Or (another, ar.) a bend engr. (another, lozengy) az. *Crest*—A long cross vert.

Fokeray, or Fokerhay (co. Devon). Chequy or (another, ar.) and az. a fesse vairé gu. and sa.

Fokeray, or Foukeray (co. Devon). Chequy or and gu. a fesse vair.

Fokeray, or Foulkeray (co. Devon). Chequy or and az. a fesse vairé ar. and sa.

Fokerey. Vair a fesse gu. charged with another wavy sa.

Fokerham (cos. Berks and Derby). Or, a bend lozengy az.

Fokesley. Gu. two bars ar.

Fokiston. Ar. a chev. gu.

Folborne (co. Cambridge). Or, a chev. sa. in chief two dragons respecting each other of the second.

Folborne. Or, a chev. betw. three dragons sa. *Crest*—A sinister hand couped fesseways ppr.

Folchard. Sa. a chev. betw. two covered cups or.

Folcher. Erm. on a bend gu. three bezants (another, plates).

Folcy (co. Worcester; granted to ROBERT FOLCY, of Stourbridge, by Walker, Garter, 12 Dec. 1671). Ar. a fesse engr. betw. three cinquefoils, all within a bordure sa. on a canton gu. a ducal coronet or. *Crest*—A lion sejant ar. holding betw. his feet a ducal coronet or.

Folebarne. Or, a chev. betw. three fish-wheels sa. *Crest*—Three holly leaves vert, banded gu.

Foleburne. Or, a chev. sa. two wiverns pass. displ. in chief, respecting each other, of the last.

Foleford. Az. three laurel leaves or.

Folehurst. Gu. a fret or, and a chief ar.

Folet. Gu. a bend ar. (another, or). *Crest*—On a chapeau ppr. an escallop or.

Foleville. Per fesse erm. and or, a cross moline gu.

Foley (*Baron Foley*). Ar. a fesse engr. betw. three cinquefoils sa. all within a bordure of the last. *Crest*—A lion ramp. ar. holding betw. the fore-paws an escutcheon charged with the arms. *Supporters*—Two lions ar. semée of cinquefoils sa. *Motto*—Ut prosim.

Foley (Halstead, co. Kent, bart., extinct 1782). Same *Arms*.

Foley (Ridgway, co. Pembroke. The FOLEYS possessed lands in that county from a very early period; 1383 is the date of the deed of feoffment, from ADAM HORTON, Bishop of St. David's, to JOHN FOWLEY, and ELLEN, his wife, in which the feoffee is styled "Constabularius castri nostri de Llewhawn et magister operum nostrorum"). Same *Arms, Crest*, and *Motto*, as *Lord Foley*.

Foley (co. Worcester; granted to ROBERT FOLEY, Esq., in 1671). Same *Arms*, with, on a canton gu. a ducal coronet or. *Crest*—A lion sejant ar. holding betw. his paws a ducal coronet or.

Foley (Prestwood, co. Worcester; Hon. EDWARD FOLEY, second son of THOMAS, third *Lord Foley, m.* ELIZA MARY, dau. and heiress of JOHN HODGETTS, Esq., of Shut End House, and Prestwood, March, 1790). Quarterly, 1st and 4th, same as *Lord Foley ;* 2nd and 3rd, HODGETTS, of Prestwood, viz., az. on a chev. betw. three doves in chief and a fleur-de-lis in base or. three crescents vert. *Crests*—1st, FOLEY : Same as *Lord Folcy ;* 2nd, HODGETTS : A horse's head erm. pierced through the neck with a broken spear ppr. *Motto*—Ut prosim.

Foley (Tetworth and Wistow, co. Huntingdon ; a branch of the noble family of FOLEY, represented by HENRY FOLEY, Esq., of Tetworth, son and heir of the late Major-Gen. RICHARD HENRY FOLEY). Ar. a fesse engr. betw. three cinquefoils sa. all within a bordure of the last. *Crest*—A lion ramp. ar. holding betw. the fore-paws an escutcheon charged with the arms. *Motto*—Ut prosim.

Foley, or Foyley. Ar. a fesse engr. betw. three cinquefoils sa.

Foley (Dublin; granted by Fortescue, Ulster, 1793, to JOHN FOLEY, Esq.). Gu. a chev. betw. three pheons points downwards ar. a border of the last, charged with eight roses of the first. *Crest*—A demi lion ramp. gu. holding in the dexter paw a pheon point upwards ar.

Folier (Scotland). Erm. a chev. az. betw. three mullets sa. on a chief of the last three boars' heads and necks erased ar.

Polifat, or Folifoot. Ar. a fesse betw. two lions pass. reguard. sa.

Foliot (co. Northampton, *temp.* Henry II.). Gu. a bend ar.

Foliot (*Baron Foliot ;* summoned to Parliament, 1295, abeyance, 1326). Same *Arms*.

Foliot (*Lord Foliot*). See FOLLIOTT.

Foliot (co. Norfolk). Same *Arms*.

Foliot (Bromyard, co. Worcester). Same *Arms*, a martlet sa. for diff. *Crest*—A battle axe ppr. *Motto*—Hope to come.

Foliot. Erm. two (another, three) bars nebulée gu.

Folishe, or Fonlish. Gu. a fret or, and chief ar. (another, the chief charged with three mullets pierced sa.

Foljambe (Walton, co. Derby, bart., extinct 1640, and Aldwarke, co. York; descended from Sir THOMAS FULJAMBE, Bailiff of the High Peak, Derbyshire, 1272; Sir FRANCIS FOLJAMBE was created a bart., 1622, *d. s. p. m.*, when the representation of this very ancient family devolved on his kinsman, PETER FOLJAMBE, Esq., of Streeton, ancestor of FOLJAMBE, of Osberton, co. Nottingham, and Aldwarke, co. York). Sa. a bend betw. six escallops or. *Crest*—A jambe unarmed, excepting the spur, quarterly, or and sa. In 1513, GODFREY FOLJAMBE, of Walton, had another crest granted to him, but it does not appear to have been adopted by his descendants, viz., a calopus or chatloup pass. or and sa. the horns quarterly in like manner. *Motto*—Soyez ferme.

Foljambe (Osberton, co. Notts, and Aldwarke, co. York; representative of FOLJAMBE, of Walton, descended from ROGER FOLJAMBE, Esq., of Linacre Hall, second son of HENRY FOLJAMBE, Esq., of Walton, *temp.* Henry VI.). Same *Arms, Crest*, and *Mottoes* as FOLJAMBE, bart., of Walton, with numerous quarterings.

Foljambe (Wakefield, co. York). Sa. a bend or, betw. six escallops ar. *Crest*—An armed leg couped at the thigh, quartered, or and sa. spurred gold.

Foljambe, or Foliambe (Croxdon, co. Stafford). Same *Arms*, within a border qu. a crescent for diff. *Crest*—A leg couped at the thigh, quarterly or and sa., spurred gold, charged with a fess indented gu. a crescent for diff.

Folke, or Fulke (co. Stafford). Ar. a fesse betw. three mullets sa.

Folkeray (Buckland Baron, co. Devon ; JOHANNA, sister and heir of GREGORY FOLKERAY, of that place, *m.* ROGER HOCKMORE, of Buckyate; she was sixth in descent from MICHAEL FOLKERAY, *temp.* Henry II., son of FULCHERIUS, mentioned in Domesday Book, quartered by HOCKMORE, of Buckland. Visit. 1620). Chequy ar. and sa. a fess vairé of the first and gu.

Folkes (Hillingdon, co. Norfolk, bart., extinct). Per pale vert and gu. a fleur-de-lis erm. *Crest*—A dexter arm embowed, vested per pale vert and gu. cuff erm. holding in the hand a spear ppr. *Mottoes*—Qui sera sera ; and, Principiis obsta.

Folkes (co. Middlesex ; granted 11 March, 1685). Same *Arms*. *Crest*—A dexter arm erect, habited per pale vert and gu. cuff turned up erm. the hand holding a javelin ppr.

Folkeston. Per pale gu. and ar. a fesse nebulée counterchanged.

Folkeworth. Ar. on a cross patonce gu. five escallops or. *Crest*—An ostrich holding in the mouth a broken tilting spear all ppr.

Folkingham (Barton, co. York). Ar. a chev. betw. three cinquefoils sa.

Folkingham. Sa. a bend betw. six escallops ar.

Folkstayn. Per bend nebulée ar. and gu. (another, gu. and ar.).

Follefait (quartered by RAWDON ; Fun. Ent. 1684, Sir GEORGE RAWDON, Bart., a Privy Councillor in Ireland). Ar. a fess betw. two lions pass. sa.

Foller. Ar. guttée de poix on a chief engr. gu. a lion pass. guard. of the field. *Crest*—A garb ppr.

Follett. Or, three palm branches vert. *Crest*—A wolf pass. reguard. transfixed with an arrow.

Follett (Sir WILLIAM WEBB FOLLETT, M.P., Her Majesty's Solicitor-General, son of BENJAMIN FOLLETT, Esq., of Topsham, near Exeter). Barry of twelve gu. and ar. a bend sa. *Crest*—A demi griffin segreant. *Motto*—Quo virtus ducit scando.

Folley (London. JOHN FOLLEY; his dau. and heir, SCISSELY, *m.* WILLIAM COOPER, of Thurgarton, co. Notts. Visit. Notts). Ar. on a chev engr. gu. betw. three martlets az. collared or, as many cinquefoils of the field.

Folliford. Az. three elm (or oak) leaves or.

Follingham. Sa. a bend ar. betw. three covered salts or.

Folliot (co. Northampton). Barry wavy of six erm. and gu. *Crest*—On a chapeau ppr. a wivern sejant vert.

Folliot (Pyrton, co. Worcester; claimed to descend from WILLIAM, brother of JORDAN, *Lord Foliot*, settled at Morton Foliot, *temp.* Henry I., and held lands at Pyrton, *temp.* Edward III. Visit. Worcester, 1569). Ar. a lion ramp. double queued purp. crowned or. (Nash says these are the arms of STURY, which FOLLIOTT adopted through an inter-marriage with that family).

Folliott (*Lord Folliot*, of Ballyshannon, extinct 1716; Right Hon. Sir HENRY FOLLIOT, son of THOMAS FOLLIOT, Esq., of Pyrton, by his second wife, was knighted by the *Earl of Essex*, Lord Lieutenant, 6 Feb. 1599, and was created a peer, 1619). Same *Arms*, a crescent for diff. *Crest*—A nag's head ar. issuing from a ducal coronet or. *Supporters*—Two lions ramp. purp.

Folliott (Hollybrooke, co. Sligo; descended from a common ancestor with the *Lords Folliot*). Gu. a bend ar. *Crest*—A lion ramp. per pale gu. and ar. double queued, murally crowned or. *Motto*—Quo virtus et fata vocant.

Folliott (Stapely House, co. Chester, and co. Londonderry; descended from co. York). Same *Arms*. *Crest*—A lion ramp. per pale ar. and gu.

Follsand (Scotland). Gu. a chev. ar.

Follye. Sa. a cross moline ar. *Crest*—An escallop or, betw. two olive branches ppr.

Follyoll (co. Dorset). Vert a canton az.

Folman. Ar. a fesse ermines betw. three crowns sa. *Crest* —A wolf courant per pale ar. and erm.

Folman. Gu. a chev. vair betw. three ducal coronets or.

Folnarby, or Folgnarby. Ar. three swans volant sa.

Folshurst (Crewe, co. Chester). Gu. a fesse or. *Crest*—A unicorn's head couped or.

Folton. Gu. two lions pass. erm. *Crests*—1st: Out of a ducal coronet a pair of wings or and ar.; 2nd: A stag lodged gu. ducally gorged and lined or, attired vert, at the top of each branch a bezant.

Folthorpe. Ar. a saltire engr. az.

Folunyll (co. Leicester). Vairé sa. and ar. a quarter gu.

Folvile (Ashby, cos. Buckingham and Huntingdon). Per fesse ar. and or, a cross moline gu.

Folvile, Fovell, or Folvill (co. Chester; granted by Camden, Clarenceux, 1599). Gu. a chief ar. over all a cross moline or. *Crest*—A garb per pale or and vert, the band counterchanged. *Motto* over—Fovendo foveo.

Folvile, or Folleville. Per fesse erm. and or, a cross sarcelly gu. *Crest*—A griffin's head erased, in the beak a sword ppr.

Folvile (Kersby, co. Durham). Barry nebulée of six ar. and sa. a canton gu.

Folvill (JOHN FOLVILL, *temp.* Edward I.; MABEL, his dau. and heir, *m.* JOHN WOODFORD, living 1335. Visit. Leicester, 1619). Same *Arms*, impaling per fess. erm. and or, a cross moline gu.

Folyott. Gu. a bend betw. six crescents ar.

Folyott. Az. six annulets or, three, two, and one.

Fondre. Quarterly, 1st and 4th, ar. a chev. voided sa. in the voidure three Moors' heads couped of the second; 2nd and 3rd, ar. on a chev. sa. three crosses crosslet of the field. *Crest*—A Moor's head ppr.

Fones. See FOWNES.

Fonlode. Ar. three leopards' faces sa. a lion pass. in chief gu.

Fonnder, or Fondrass (France). Gu. (another, az.) three bars ar. in chief a saltire engr. or.

Fonnereau (Edmonton, co. Middlesex, and Christ Church Park, co. Suffolk; descended from ZACHARY FONNEREAU, of La Rochelle, who came to England after the revocation of the Edict of Nantes). Gu. three chev. ar. on a chief az. a sun in splendour or. *Crest*—A sun in splendour or.

Fonnereau. Same *Arms*. *Crest*—A lion ramp. supporting a garb ppr.

Fontaine (London). Gu. a bend or, in the sinister chief a cinquefoil erm.

Fontaine. Ar. a chev. az. betw. three estoiles in chief and a crescent in base gu. *Crest*—An eagle's head erased ppr.

365

Fontaine, or Fontain. Same *Arms*. *Crest*—A raven's nest, with young ones ppr.

Fontall. Or, a cross sarcelly gu. a chief az.

Fonte (co. Galway; Reg. Ulster's Office). Ar crusily fitchée a lion ramp. sa. *Crest*—A demi lion sa.

Fonteghayne. Az. fretty or, on a canton of the last a lion's gamb erased of the field.

Fooge. Ar. on a fesse betw. three annulets sa. as many mullets of the field.

Fookes (Sir HENRY FOOKES, knighted by the *Earl of Essex*, Lord Lieutenant, 1599). Vert a fleur-de-lis ar. *Crest*—An arm in armour embowed vert, the hand grasping an arrow ppr.

Foord (Impalement Fun. Ent. of Lady FOORD, buried at St. Werburgh's Church, Dublin, 6 Feb. 1673). Az. three lions ramp. or.

Foord (Reg. Ulster's Office). Az. three lions ramp. crowned or. *Crest*—A demi lion ramp. crowned or, armed and langued gu. *Motto*—Noli iritare leonem.

Foord. Az. on a fesse ar. betw. three bezants as many cinquefoils gu. *Crest*—A flag displ. gu.

Foorth (London). Az. a rose betw. two martlets in pale or, and as many flaunches of the last, on each a rose gu.

Foorth (impaled by ST. JOHN on a monument at Longthorp). Gu. two bends ar. on a canton or, a greyhound courant issuing from the sinister sa.

Foot (Brentford, co. Middlesex; granted 14 Dec. 1769). Az. on a bend erm. cotised or, three leopards' faces ppr.

Foot, or Foote. Ar. on a chev. sa. betw. three trefoils slipped vert two trefoils of the field. *Crest*—A greyhound's head per fesse ar. and sa. collared gu.

Foot. Or, a chev. sa. in dexter chief a trefoil slipped ot the second. *Crest*—A demi griffin reguard. gu. winged or, holding a flag displ. of the first, charged with a crescent ar.

Foote (Tiverton, co. Devon). Same *Arms*. *Crest*—A naked arm erect ppr. holding a trefoil slipped sa.

Foote (London; Lord Mayor of London, 1651). Same *Arms*. *Crest*—An arm erect vested sa. cuff ar. in the hand ppr. a trefoil slipped sa.

Foote (Veryan, Lambesso in St. Clements, and Truro, co. Cornwall; of this family was SAMUEL FOOTE, the comedian and dramatist. The representative, when Lysons wrote, was HENRY FOOTE, Esq., of Wood, near Tavistock). Vert a chev. betw. three doves ar. *Crest*—A lion's head erased ar. charged with an erm. spot sa.

Foote (Cornwall, *temp.* Henry VI., and Charlton Place, co. Kent). Vert a chev. betw. three martlets ar. quartering, az. a sword in bend, point downwards ppr. betw. two mullets of six points pierced ar., for HATLEY. *Crest*—A lion's head erased ar. charged on the neck with an erm. spot sa. *Motto* —Pedetentim.

Foote (London). Gu. six lozenges ar. three, two, and one, a chief indented or.

Foote (co. Suffolk). Az. four mascles ar. in cross a chief indented of the second.

Foote, or Foots (London and co. Sussex). Same *Arms*. *Crest*—Out of a mural coronet or, a spear sa. headed ar. charged with three plates.

Foote (granted to HENRY WELLS FOOTE, Esq., of Harrington Square, London). Gu. two chevronels ar. betw. as many doves in chief and a cross pattée in base ar. *Crest*—Two crosses pattée fitchée in saltire gu. thereon a pelican in her piety ar. wings fretty gu. *Motto*—Excidit amor nunquam.

Foquett (Stride House and Newport, Isle of Wight). Ar. a squirrel sejant cracking a nut ppr. a bordure az. charged with eight fleurs-de-lis or. *Crest*—A horse's head ar. in mail az. on the head a plume of ostrich feathers of the first, bridled or.

Forbes (*Lord Forbes*). Az. three bears' heads couped ar. muzzled gu. *Crest*—A stag's head attired with ten tynes ppr. *Supporters*—Two bloodhounds ppr. collared gu. *Motto* —Grace me guide.

Forbes (Monymusk, co. Aberdeen, bart., 1628; generally designed "of Pitsligo" after 1781, when the fifth bart. became heir of line of the Pitsligo branch; arms borne by the first five barts.). Az. on a chev. ar. betw. three bears' heads couped of the last, muzzled gu. a man's heart ppr. *Crest*—A man's heart ppr. winged or. *Motto*—Spe expecto.

Forbes (Monymusk or Pitsligo; as recorded for Sir WILLIAM FORBES, sixth bart.). Quarterly, 1st and 4th, as the last; 2nd and 3rd, counterquartered, for FORBES, of Pitsligo, vir., 1st and 4th, az. three bears' heads couped ar. muzzled gu., for FORBES, 2nd and 3rd, az. three frases ar., for FRASER. *Crest*—Issuing out of a baron's coronet a nand holding a scymitar erected all ppr. *Supporters*—Two bears ppr. *Mottoes*—Above the crest: Nec timide nec temere; below the shield: Adversis major par secundis.

Forbes (Monymusk or Pitsligo; as recorded, 1865, for Sir JOHN HEPBURN STUART-FORBES, eighth bart.). Quarterly, 1st grand quarter, az. on a chev. ar. betw. three bears' heads couped of the last, muzzled gu. a man's heart ppr., for FORBES, of Monymusk; 2nd grand quarter, counterquartered, FORBES and FRASER, as in the last, for FORBES, of Pitsligo; 3rd grand quarter, counterquartered, 1st and 4th, or, a bend gu. surmounted of a fess chequy az. and ar. in chief a crescent of the third, for STUART, of Fettercairn, 2nd, or, three pallets gu. a chief vair, for BELSCHES, 3rd, ar. three piles in point gu., for WISHART; 4th grand quarter, counterquartered, 1st and 4th, gu. on a chev. ar. a rose betw. two lions combatant of the field, for HEPBURN, 2nd and 3rd, az. a cross pattée betw. three mullets, a double tressure flory counterflory or, for MURRAY, of Glendoick. *Crests*—1st, FORBES: Issuing out of a baron's coronet a hand holding a scymitar erected all ppr.; 2nd, STUART: A dexter hand grasping a sword ppr.; 3rd, HEPBURN: A horse's head couped ar. furnished gu. *Supporters*—Two bears ppr. *Mottoes*—FORBES: Nec timide nec temere; STUART: Avant; HEPBURN: I keep traist.

Forbes (Balfuig, co. Aberdeen). Az. on a chev. betw. three bears' heads couped ar. muzzled gu. a man's heart ppr. betw. two skenes of the first, pommelled or. *Crest*—A skene piercing a heart ppr. *Motto*—Non deest spes.

Forbes (Alford, co. Aberdeen, 1733). Same *Arms* and *Motto*. *Crest* —A hand issuing from a cloud holding an anchor all ppr.

Forbes (Colonel JONATHAN FORBES-LESLIE, of Rothie and Badenscoth, 1862). Quarterly, 1st grand quarter, counterquartered, 1st and 4th, ar. on a fess betw. a boar's head erased in chief and base az. three buckles or, for LESLIE, 2nd and 3rd, az. a fess chequy ar. and of the first betw. three boars' heads erased or, a bordure indented of the second, for GORDON: 2nd and 3rd grand quarters, az. a dirk in pale ar. hilted and pommelled or, surmounted of a wolf's head couped of the third betw. three bears' heads couped of the second, muzzled gu. on a chief also of the second and issuing out of the lower part thereof a demi otter sa. crowned with an antique crown of the fourth or, for FORBES. *Crests*—LESLIE: A griffin's head and neck erased ppr.; FORBES: A bear's head and neck couped and muzzled ppr. *Mottoes*—LESLIE: Grip fast; FORBES: Spe expecto.

Forbes (Prof. WILLIAM FORBES, of Glasgow, of the line of Corsindae, 1731). Az. three bears' heads couped ar. muzzled gu. within a bordure erm. a crescent of the second for diff. *Crest*—A book expanded ppr. *Motto*—Virtute me involvo.

Forbes (Robslaw, co. Aberdeen, 1678). Az. a skene in fess ar. hilted and pommelled or, betw. three boars' heads couped of the second, muzzled sa. *Crest*—A dove ppr. *Motto*—Virtute cresco.

Forbes (Corse, co. Aberdeen). Az. a cross pattée fitchée or, betw. three bears' heads couped ar. muzzled gu. *Crest*—A wreath of thorns ppr. *Motto*—Rosis coronat spina.

Forbes (Craigievar, co. Aberdeen, bart. 1630; eventually representative of Corse). Same *Arms*. *Crest*—A cock ppr. *Supporters*—Dexter, a knight in armour of the fifteenth century ppr., having the beaver of the helmet up, and leaning on a shield or, charged with the arms of Scotland; sinister, a bear ar. muzzled gu. *Motto*—Watch.

Forbes-Mitchell (Thainston, co. Aberdeen). Quarterly, 1st and 4th, az. a cross pattée fitchée betw. three bears' heads couped ar. muzzled gu. a bordure of the second; 2nd and 3rd, sa. a fess wavy betw. three mascles or, for MITCHELL. *Crests*—FORBES: A cock ppr.; MITCHELL: A phoenix rising from flames ppr. *Mottoes*—Watch; Nulla pallescere culpa.

Forbes (Balgownie, co. Aberdeen). Quarterly, 1st and 4th grand quarters, az. a cross pattée fitchée betw. three bears' heads couped ar. muzzled gu. a bordure of the second; 2nd and 3rd grand quarters, counterquartered, 1st and 4th, az. three frases ar., 2nd, or, a lion ramp. gu. debruised by a ribbon sa., 3rd, gu. a lion ramp. ar. all within a bordure az. charged with eight garbs or, for FRASER, of Fraserfield. *Crest*—A cock ppr. *Motto*—Watch.

Forbes (*Earl of Granard*). Az. three bears' heads couped ar. muzzled gu. *Crest*—A bear pass. ar. guttée de sang muzzled gu. *Supporters*—Dexter, a unicorn erminois, armed, maned, tufted, and unguled or; sinister, a dragon, wings expanded erm. *Motto*—Fax mentis incendium gloriæ.

Forbes (*Lord Forbes*, of Pitsligo; the Monymusk branch are heirs of line, and FORBES of Newe, claims to be heir male). Quarterly, 1st and 4th, az. three bears' heads couped ar. muzzled gu.; 2nd and 3rd, az. three frases ar., for FRASER. *Crest*—A hand holding a sword ppr. *Supporters*—Two bears ppr. *Motto*—Nec timide nec temere.

Forbes (Newe, co. Aberdeen, bart., 1823; arms as recorded 1833). Quarterly, as the last. *Crest*—A falcon ppr. *Supporters*—Two bears ar. *Motto*—Altius ibunt qui ad summa nituntur.

366

Forbes (Rires, co. Fife). Quarterly, 1st and 4th, or, a lion ramp. gu., for WEMYSS; 2nd and 3rd, az. three bears' heads couped ar. muzzled gu., for FORBES. *Crest*—A greyhound pass. ppr. *Motto*—Hinc delectatio.

Forbes (Tolquhon, co. Aberdeen; now FORBES-LEITH, of Whitehaugh). Quarterly, 1st and 4th, az. three bears' heads couped ar. muzzled gu.; 2nd and 3rd, ar. three unicorns' heads erased az., for PRESTON. *Crest*—A stag's head attired with ten tynes ppr. *Supporters*—Two greyhounds ppr. collared gu. *Motto*—Salus per Christum.

Forbes (Waterton, co. Aberdeen, 1672). Quarterly, as the last, on an escutcheon of pretence ar. a sword and key gu. as Constable of Aberdeen. *Crest*—An eagle displ. ppr. *Motto*—Virtuti inimica quies.

Forbes (Ballogie, co. Aberdeen). Per fess az. and ar. in chief three bears' heads couped of the second muzzled gu., in base as many unicorns' heads erased sa. *Crest*—A sheaf of arrows ppr. *Motto*—Concordia præsto.

Forbes (Auchredie). Quarterly, as Tolquhon, within a bordure chequy ar. and gu. *Crest*—A small sword in bend ppr. *Motto*—Scienter utor.

Forbes (Culloden, co. Inverness). Az. on a chev. betw. three bears' heads couped ar. muzzled gu. as many unicorns' heads erased sa. *Crest*—An eagle displ. or. *Motto*—Salus per Christum.

Forbes (Foveran, co. Aberdeen, bart., 1700). Quarterly, 1st and 4th, az. a cross pattée betw. three bears' heads couped ar. muzzled gu.; 2nd and 3rd, ar. three unicorns' heads erased sa., for PRESTON. *Crest*—A stag's head couped gu. attired ar. *Motto*—Cura et candore.

Forbes (Brux, co. Aberdeen). Quarterly, 1st and 4th, az. a martlet ar. betw. three bears' heads couped of the second, muzzled gu., for FORBES; 2nd and 3rd, or, three bars gu. within a bordure wavy vert, for CAMERON. *Crest*—A hawk's head erased ppr. *Motto*—Nec mons nec subtrahit aer.

Forbes (Skellater, co. Aberdeen, 1767). Quarterly, 1st and 4th, az. a martlet betw. three bears' heads couped ar. muzzled gu. a bordure of the last; 2nd and 3rd, az. a chev. betw. three boars' heads or, within a bordure counter-compony of the second and first, for GORDON. *Crest*—A hand holding a dagger erect, on its point a bear's head couped ppr. *Motto*—Solus inter plurimos.

Forbes (Echt, co. Aberdeen, earlier line). Az. a fess chequy ar. and gu. betw. three bears' heads couped of the second, muzzled of the third. *Crest*—A sandglass ppr. *Motto*—Fugit hora.

Forbes (Millbowie, co. Aberdeen). Az. a skene in pale ppr. with a wolf's head couped or, on the point betw. three bears' heads couped ar. muzzled gu. *Crest*—A bear's head muzzled as in the arms, within an orle of olive branches vert. *Motto*—Virtute non ferocia.

Forbesher. Erm. on a fesse engr. betw. three griffins' heads erased sa. a greyhound courant ar. *Crest*—On a chapeau the sun in splendour ppr.

Forbesher. Erm. on a chief sa. three unicorns' heads couped ar.

Forcer (Kelloe, co. Durham; granted by Flower, Norroy, in 1575). Sa. on a chev. engr. or, betw. three leopards' faces ar. as many annulets of the first. *Crest*—A fox sejant ppr. gorged with an arrow or, feathered ar.

Forcer. Ar. three bars gemelles gu.

Forcher. Erm. on a bend gu. three plates.

Ford (Ember Court, co. Surrey, bart.). Per pale gu. and or, two bends vair, on a canton of the second a greyhound courant sa. *Crest*—A greyhound's head sa. erased gu. muzzled or. *Motto*—Omnium rerum vicissitudo.

Ford (White Waltham, co. Berks). Ar. on a fesse dancettée sa. seven bezants, in chief a bear couchant of the second.

Ford (Islington, cos. Derby, Surrey, Sussex, and Wilts). Az. three lions ramp. ar. crowned or. *Crest*—A demi lion ramp. crowned or.

Ford (WILLIAM FORD, Esq., J.P., of Ellel Hall, co. Lancaster). Per fesse or and erm. a lion ramp. az. *Crest*—A demi lion ramp. *Motto*—Excitat.

Ford (Enfield Old Park, co. Middlesex). Same *Arms, Crest*, and *Motto*.

Ford (Abbey Field, co. Chester). Same *Arms*. *Crest*—A lion's head erased az.

Ford (Chagford, Ashburton, Bagtor, and Nutwell, co. Devon; supposed by Prince to be descended from FORDS, of Fordmore, in Moreton Hampstead. Visit. Devon, 1620). Per fesse ar. and sa. in chief a greyhound courant, in base an owl, a bordure engr. all counterchanged. *Crest*—A demi greyhound ramp. sa. charged with three acorns in bend betw. two bendlets or, betw. as many branches vert, fructed ar. *Another Crest*—A martlet or.

Ford, or Alford (Fordmore, co. Devon, temp, Edward I.).

Gu. a castle ar. crowned or, on the port a cross formée of the third

Ford (Frating, co. Essex). Ar. a wolf saliant sa.

Ford (Bexley, and Canterbury, cos. Gloucester and Kent). Gu. two bends vairé or and az. on a canton of the second an anchor sa. *Crest*—Out of a naval coronet ppr. a bear's head sa. muzzled gu.

Ford (London; RICHARD FORD, Lord Mayor of London, 1671). Gu. two bends vair, on a canton or, an anchor sa.

Ford (co. Suffolk). Gu. two bends vair, on a canton or, a greyhound courant az. *Crest*—A greyhound's head erased ar.

Ford. Gu. two bends vair, a canton or (another, on the canton three pellets).

Ford, or Forth. Gu. two bends ar. on a canton or, a greyhound issuant sa.

Ford (co. Middlesex). Az. a fesse dancettée betw. three lions ramp. or.

Ford (Ford, co. Devon). Sa. (another, gu.) a pomegranate branch slipped and fructed or (another, ppr.).

Ford. Gu. an eagle displ. and chief ar.

Ford de la Ford (quartered by POLE). Sa. a tree eradicated or.

Ford (Montrose, Scotland, 1804). Gu. two bends vairé ar. and sa. on a chief or, a greyhound courant sa. betw. two towers gu. *Crest*—A demi greyhound sa. holding in his paws an oak branch acorned ppr. issuing out of a tower gu. charged with an anchor ar. *Motto*—Persevere.

Ford (JONES-FORD): exemplified to Miss CECIL CLARE JONES, only child of JOHN CARSTAIRS JONES, Esq., of Gelli Gynan, co. Denbigh, by his first wife, upon her assuming the additional surname of FORD by royal licence). Quarterly, 1st and 4th, FORD, sa. two bendlets nebulée ar. betw. as many roses of the last, barbed and seeded ppr.; 2nd and 3rd, JONES, gu. on a chev. or, betw. three escutcheons ar. each charged with a boar's head couped of the first, an arrow palewise ppr.

Ford. See FOURDE.

Fordam, or Fordham. Barry wavy of six or and az. on a chief gu. two arrows in saltire betw. as many castles ar. *Crest*—On a mount vert a peacock ppr.

Fordayne. Az. three lions ramp. or, a label of as many points gu.

Forde (Ireland; Sir AMBROSE FORDE, knighted at Leixlip by Sir GEORGE CARY, Lord Deputy, 2 Aug. 1604). Az. two flaunches or, charged with three roses in fesse, the centre rose gold, the two exterior (on the flaunches) gu. betw. two martlets of the second. *Crest*—A demi lion ramp. crowned or, armed and langued gu. *Motto*—Lucrum Christi mihi.

Forde (Coolgreany, co. Wexford, and Seaforde, co. Down, originally of Welsh extraction). Same *Arms*. *Crest*—A martlet or. *Motto*—Incorrupta fides nudaque veritas.

Forde (Hadley, co. Suffolk). Or, four bends az.

Forde. Sa. six lions ramp. three, two, and one or, crowned gu.

Forde. Ar. three cocks gu. beaked and legged or.

Forde. Az. a fesse indented betw. three lions ramp. or.

Fordele (Wraxham). Gu. a griffin segreant ar.

Fordeor. Erm. a lion ramp. per fesse gu. and az. guttée d'eau.

Forder, or Fordore (co. Surrey). Erm. a lion ramp. per fesse az. and gu. fretty or. *Crest*—A hawthorn tree vert.

Fordesham. Ar. on a cross engr. sa. five mullets pierced or.

Fordham (Bishop of Ely, 1388). Sa. a chev. betw. three crosses patonce or.

Fordringham (co. York). Az. a bend betw. six mullets or.

Fordsham (co. Essex). Ar. on a cross engr. sa. five estoiles or.

Fordyce (Ayton, co. Berwick). Gu. a dagger paleways ppr. point upwards, betw. three bears' heads couped or, muzzled of the first. *Crest*—A camel's head couped at the neck ppr. *Motto*—Persevere.

Fordyce (DINGWALL-FORDYCE, Brucklay and Culsh, co. Aberdeen, as recorded, 1846). Quarterly, 1st and 4th, az. three bears' heads ar. muzzled gu., for FORDYCE; 2nd, az. a buck's head cabossed or, betw. three mullets pierced ar., for DINGWALL; 3rd, gu. a fess chequy ar. and az. in chief a mullet of the second, the base wavy of the third, a bordure engr. or, for LINDSAY. *Crests*—1st: An eagle volant ppr. holding in the claws an escroll with this *Motto*—Altius ibunt qui ad summa nituntur, for FORDYCE; 2nd : A stag lodged ppr. with *Motto*—In arduis fortis, for DINGWALL.

Forein. Gu. ten bezants, four, three, two, and one.

Forens. Sa. a pale engr. ar.

Forest (Merborne, co. Huntingdon). Ar. a fesse betw. three hinds' heads erased gu.

367

Forest. Ar. on a mount an oak tree all ppr. *Crest*—A grenade fired ppr.

Forest. Gu. a fesse counter-compony ar. and purp. betw. ten billets, four, three, two, and one, of the second. *Crest*—A squirrel sejant cracking a nut ppr.

Forest (France). Gu. an orle of eight martlets ar.

Forest. Gu. a dolphin in pale ar.

Forest. Ar. on a chev. sa. betw. three owls gu. a trefoil slipped of the first.

Forest. Ar. a fesse betw. three trefoils slipped az

Forest, or Forrest. Ar. three oak trees vert.

Forester (*Baron Forester*). Quarterly, 1st and 4th, quarterly, per fesse indented ar. and sa. in the 1st and 4th quarters a buglehorn of the last, garnished in or, for FORESTER ; 2nd and 3rd, az. a fesse nebuly betw. three crescents, two and one, erm., for WELD. *Crests*—1st, FORESTER : A talbot pass. ar. collared sa. and line reflexed or ; 2nd, WELD : A wyvern sa. guttée d'or, collared, wings elevated, and line reflexed over the back gold. *Supporters*—On either side a talbot ar. collared sa. therefrom pendent a buglehorn, as in the arms, line reflexed over the back or. *Motto*—Semper eadem.

Forester (Rev. TOWNSEND FORESTER, D.D., Prebendary of Worcester). Quarterly, per fesse indented ar. and sa. in the 1st and 4th quarters a buglehorn stringed of the last. *Crest* —A talbot pass. ar. collared and chained or.

Forester (co. York). Ar. a chev. gu. in chief two leopards' faces of the last, in base a buglehorn sa.

Forester. Az. a fer de moline betw. four crosses pattée or.

Foricell, or Ficaulte. Or, a cross moline gu. and chief ar. *Crest*—Two lions' gambs endorsed gu.

Forican. Same *Arms*. *Crest*—An elephant's head erased sa. eared and armed ar.

Foril. Gu. two bends vair, on a canton or, a demi greyhound sa.

Forington. Gu. three cinquefoils ar. *Crest*—A dragon sans wings, tail extended, per fesse vert and or.

Forington. Or, two bars gu. on a chief of the last a lion pass. of the first.

Forke (co. York). Ar. a saltire az.

Forkington. Sa. on a fesse ar. three leopards' faces gu. *Crest*—A demi greyhound sa. collared or.

Forlesse (Whatcombe, co. Berks; granted 26 June, 1637). Gu. eight estoiles in orle ar. on a canton of the second a lion ramp. sa. armed and langued of the first.

Forlington. Gu. three palets vair, a chief or.

Forlong (Reg. Ulster's Office). Gu. three palets ar.

Forman (Luthrie, co. Fife, Lyon King of Arms, 1555). Quarterly, 1st and 4th, sa. three camels' heads erased or, each with a bell ar. attached to a collar gu. about her neck, for FORMAN ; 2nd and 3rd, az. a chev. betw. three salmon haurient ar., for FISHER.

Forman, or Foreman (London and co. Leicester ; Lord Mayor of London, 1538). Barry wavy of six ar. and az. on a chev. sa. three martlets or, on a chief gu. a lion pass. betw. two anchors gold. *Crest*—A demi dragon ramp. vert.

Forman, or Freman. Az. three bars nebulée ar. on a chev. sa. as many martlets or, a chief gu. charged with a lion pass. guard. betw. two anchors gold.

Forman (co. Lincoln). Same *Arms*.

Forman, or Fornens (co. Norfolk). Sa. five fusils in pale ar.

Forman (co. Northumberland). Sa. five fusils in fesse ar.

Forman. Az. three bears' heads erased ar. collared gu. each charged with four bells or.

Formans (co. Northampton). Gu. a pile engr. ar.

Formby. Ar. a lion ramp. gu. on a chief az. two doves ppr. *Crest*—A dove ppr. *Motto*—Semper fidelis.

Fornam. Per pale or and az. three crescents counterchanged.

Fornars. Ar. a pile engr. sa.

Forneaulx, or Forneaux. Sa. (another gu.) a bend betw. six crosses crosslet or.

Forneaux (co. Devon). Or, a chief sa.

Forneaux (co. Norfolk). Sa. five fusils in fesse ar.

Forneche, or Fornech. Sa. a chev. embattled or, betw. three roses ar.

Forneux. Sa. a pile indented ar.

Forneys, or Fornens (co. Norfolk). Sa. a pile engr. ar. *Crest*—A wheel az.

Fornivall. Ar. three martlets gu.

Forrest. Ar. on a mount a grove of trees vert. *Crest*—A hand couped in fesse, holding a cross crosslet fitchée.

Forrest. Ar. on a mount in base three oak trees all ppr. *Crest*—An oak tree ppr. *Motto*—Vivant dum virent

Forrest. Gu. semée of martlets ar.

Forrest. Ar. three fleurs-de-lis sa

Forrest (Ireland, Reg. Ulster's Office). Sa. on a fess betw. three hinds' heads erased and erect ar. an oak tree ppr.

Forrest (Comieston, Mid Lothian. bart. 1838). Ar. three oak trees issuing out of the ground vert, on a chief gu. as many ears of rye slipped and barbed or, the whole within a bordure erm. *Crest*—An oak tree ppr. *Motto*—Vivunt dum virent.

Forrest (Leschenault, Australia, 1875). Ar. on a mount a forest of trees ppr. on a chief az. three stars of eight points of the first. *Crest*—A cubit arm erect, vested az. cuff ar. the hand ppr. holding a cross botonny fitchée in bend sinister of the second. *Motto*—Vivunt dum virent.

Forrester (*Lord Forrester*, of Corstorphine, Scotland; title now belongs to the *Earl of Verulam*. See GRIMSTON). Ar. a fess gu. betw. three hunting horns sa. garnished or, stringed gu. *Crest*—A ratchhound's head erased or, collared gu. *Supporters*—Dexter, a ratchhound or, collared gu. ; sinister, a greyhound ar. *Motto*—Hunter, blow the horn.

Forrester (Carden, co. Stirling, and Strathendry, co. Fife; heiress *m.* a son of DOUGLAS, of Kirkness, in the 17th century). Az. three hunting horns sa. garnished gu.

Forrester (ALEXANDER FORRESTER, cadet of Carden, 1680). Ar. a pellet betw. three hunting horns sa. garnished gu. *Crest*—A dexter hand holding a hunting horn, as in the arms. *Motto*—Its good to be loun.

Forrester (Sir ANDREW FORRESTER, 1680). Ar. a chev. betw. three hunting horns sa. garnished gu. *Crest*—A lily growing through and surmounting a bush of thorns ppr. *Motto*—Spernit pericula virtus.

Forrester (Carbeth, co. Stirling, 1874). Ar. on a fess wavy betw. three hunting horns sa. garnished and stringed vert two mullets of the field. *Crest*—A hunting horn, as in the arms. *Motto*—Hunter, blow the horn.

Forrester (Dundee, 1672). Ar. a ratchhound courant betw. three hunting horns sa. *Crest*—A greyhound with a leash ppr. *Motto*—Recreation.

Forrester. Quarterly, per fesse indented ar. and sa. in the first quarter a buglehorn of the last. *Crest*—A talbot statant ar. collared, lined, and ringed or.

Forrester. Ar. a buglehorn sa. stringed gu.

Forret. Sa. three boars' heads couped or.

Fors. Or, three fleurs-de-lis sa.

Forsan. Ar. on a bend cotised az. three roses or. *Crest*—A griffin's head per fesse az. and or.

Forse (co. Norfolk). Ar. a chief gu.

Forser (Kelboe and Harberhouse, co. Durham ; granted 1575). Sa. on a chev. engr. or, betw. three leopards' faces ar. as many annulets of the field. *Crest*—A fox sejant ppr. wounded in the neck by an arrow or, feathered ar.

Forset (Billingsley, co. Lincoln). Ar. on a bend sa. three bucks' heads cabossed of the field.

Forset, or Forsett (co. Middlesex, 1611). Or, a lion ramp. sa. over all a bend gobony ar. and gu. *Crest*—A demi lion sa. supporting a column gobony ar. and gu. the capital and base or.

Forsham. Chequy gu. and or, a chief ar. *Crest*—A talbot's head ar. eared gu. spotted sa.

Forsolder. Az. a cross sarcelly betw. four crosses formée or.

Forstall (Forstallstown, Rochestown, Ringville, &c., &c., co. Kilkenny; a family settled in that co. since the invasion of 1172 ; RICHARD FORSTALL was one of the Commissioners appointed, 1359, to collect armed horse and footmen from the Barony of Shillelogher, in that co.). Sa. three pheons ar. points down. *Crest*—A greyhound's head couped ar. collared and chained or. *Motto*—In corda inimicorum Regis.

Forstall (Carrigglony, co. Kilkenny, New Orleans, U.S. America, and the Island of Teneriffe. CHARLES EDWARD FORSTALL, of New Orleans, *b.* 1810, descended from PETER FORSTALL, ESQ., of Carrigglony, who got a grant of land in co. Clare, 30 June, 19 Charles II., 1666). Same *Arms*, *Crest*, and *Motto*.

Forstall (New Ross, co. Wexford, afterwards Edinburgh; descended from Carrigglony; JOHN FORSTALL, ESQ., of Broughton, Edinburgh, *d.* 1871, leaving three daus. his co-heirs; MARY FORSTALL, *m.* P. F. COMBER, ESQ., late of the Royal Mint, Melbourne, Australia; KATHERINE FORSTALL, *m.* HENRY VESEY COLCLOUGH, ESQ., Solicitor; and MARGARET FORSTALL). Same *Arms*, *Crest*, and *Motto*.

Forstall (Mullinahown, co. Kilkenny; allowed by Hawkins, Ulster, 1735, to MARCUS FORSTALL, of the Kingdom of Spain, fourth in descent from EDWARD FORSTALL, ESQ., of the former place). Same *Arms*, *Crest*, and *Motto*.

Forstall (Dublin; Fun. Ent., 1682, LUKE FORSTALL, of Dublin, merchant, descended from Forstallstown). Same *Arms*.

Forster (Alnwick, co. Northumberland). Ar. a chev. vert

betw. three buglehorns sa. stringed gu. *Crest*—A buck trippant ppr.

Forster (Bamborough Castle, co. Northumberland, bart. extinct 1623). Same *Arms*. *Crest*—A stag sa. attired gold guttée d'or. *Another Crest*—An arm in armour ppr. holding a broken tilting spear or.

Forster (Aldermaston, co. Berks, bart., extinct 1741 ; Sir GEORGE FORSTER, Knt., of Harpden, co. Oxford, descended from co. Northumberland, *m.* ELIZABETH, dau. and heir of JOHN DELAMERE, Esq., of Aldermaston, and was Sheriff, co. Berks, 1516). Sa. a chev. engr. betw. three arrows ar.

Forster (cos. Somerset and Warwick). Same *Arms*. *Crest*—A hind's head gu. ducally gorged and lined ar.

Forster, or Foster (Island of Jamaica, the Grange and Grove House, co. Buckingham, Brickhill, co. Bedford, &c., &c.). Same *Arms* and *Crest*.

Forster (JOHN FREDERICK FORSTER, ESQ., of the Priory, Lancaster, Chairman of Quarter Sessions at Salford, co. Lancaster, descended from the foregoing family). Same *Arms* and *Crest*.

Forster (JOHN FORSTER, Esq., Upper Charlotte Street, Fitzroy Square). Same *Arms*. *Crest*—An arm embowed in armour, holding in the hand a spear broken at the top all ppr.

Forster (Egham, co. Middlesex, and Battle, co. Sussex). Same *Arms*.

Forster (Westminster). Same *Arms*. *Crest*—A buck az. attired or.

Forster (co. Cumberland, and London ; Her. Off., London, c. 24). Ar. on a chev. vert betw. three buglehorns sa. stringed or, an escallop of the last. *Crest*—An arm in armour embowed ar. braced or, holding a broken tilting spear gold.

Forster (London). Ar. on a chev. betw. three buglehorns sa. a pheon ar. *Crest*—A dexter arm in armour embowed ar. purfled and braced or, round the arm a sash vert, holding in the hand ppr. an arrow of the third broken off at the head, barbed gold.

Forster (Lysways Hall, co. Stafford, bart.). Sa. on a chev. cotised betw. three pheons or, an annulet betw. two escallops of the first. *Crest*—In front of a stag's head erased ar. attired or, collared and line affixed thereto sa. two pheons also ar. *Motto*—Sit Fors ter felix.

Forster (Barton Green, co. Salop). Quarterly, per fesse indented ar. and sa., in the 1st and 4th quarters, a buglehorn of the last strung or, in the 2nd and 3rd, a pheon ar.

Forster (quartered by PERROTT, of Drayton, co. Oxford. Visit. 1574). Same *Arms*.

Forster (co. Salop). Ar. a buglehorn strung sa.

Forster (Battle, co. Sussex). Ar. on a bend engr. sa. three bucks' heads cabossed or. *Crest*—A talbot's head erased or, collared and ringed gu.

Forster (Trotton, cos. Sussex and Worcester). Sa. on a chev. ar. betw. three pheons or, as many escallops of the field. *Crest*—A stag's head erased ar. attired or, gorged with a collar and line gold.

Forster (co. Suffolk). Ar. on a chev. betw. three lions pass. sa. as many arrows in pale of the first. *Crest*—Out of a mural crown chequy ar. and sa. a stag's head ppr. attired or, holding in the mouth an arrow ar. *Motto*—Think on.

Forster. Sa. a buck trippant ar. betw. three plates, on each a pheon of the field, a bordure gobonated of the second and gu. *Crest*—An arm embowed, habited sa. charged with a pheon or, betw. two bezants in pale, holding in the hand a bow and arrow ar.

Forster. Sa. a chev. engr. betw. three arrows or, feathered ar.

Forster. Erm. a boar pass. az. on a chief or, two mullets pierced of the second. *Crest*—A demi boar az. armed and bristled or.

Forster (Coolderry, co. Monaghan, bart.). Sa. a chev. erm. betw. three pheons ppr. points down. *Crest*—An arm embowed in armour, the hand bare, grasping the butt end of a broken spear all ppr. *Motto*—Audaces fortuna juvat.

Forster (Killigh, co. Dublin. Visit. Dublin, 1607. Fun. Ent. of ELEANOR, dau. of JOHN FORSTER, Alderman and Mayor of Dublin, buried in St. John's Church, Aug. 1597). Sa. a chev. erm. betw. three pheons ar. points down.

Forster (Kilgreege, co. Dublin. Visit. Dublin, 1607). Erm. on a canton sa. an owl ar. a crescent for diff., quartering Ar. on a mount vert two lions ramp. combatant, supporting an oak tree growing out of the mount all ppr. and Az. a dexter hand couped at the wrist and erect ar. betw. an arrow in chief and a sword in base fessways of the last, pommel and hilt or. *Crest*—A hind's head couped ar. collared and chained or.

Forster (granted, 1812, to FORSTER HILL FORSTER, Esq., of

Forest, co. Dublin). Quarterly, 1st and 4th, sa. a chev. erm. betw. three pheons ar. a crescent for diff., for FORSTER; 2nd and 3rd, gu. a chev. erminois betw. three leopards' faces or, for HILL. Crests—1st: An arm in armour, holding a broken spear ppr., for FORSTER; 2nd: A talbot's head erased gu. collared or, for HILL. Motto—Vita potior libertas.

Forster (HAIRE-FORSTER; exemplified, 10 Aug. 1875, to Rev. ARTHUR NEWBURGH HAIRE, of Ballynure, co. Monaghan, son of Rev. HAMILTON HAIRE, of Mount Bailey, co. Louth, and CHARLOTTE FORSTER, his wife, on his assuming, by royal licence, the additional surname and arms of FORSTER). Quarterly, 1st and 4th, sa. on a chev. engr. betw. in chief two arrows, points downwards, and in base a rose ar. a crescent gu., for FORSTER; 2nd and 3rd, per pale or and gu. two bars counterchanged, a chief indented erm. thereon a cross crosslet gu., for HAIRE. Crests—1st, FORSTER: A hind's head erased gu. collared and chained or, in the mouth an arrow of the arms; 2nd, HAIRE: A demi lion ramp. couped ar. gorged with a collar dancettée gu. betw. the paws a cross crosslet of the arms. Motto—Odi profanum.

Forster. Az. a cross moline or, betw. four crosses pattée of the second.

Forsyth. Ar. a chev. betw. three griffins segreant gu. Crest—A cup gu.

Forsyth (that Ilk, Scotland). Ar. a chev. engr. gu. betw. three griffins segreant az. armed and membered sa. crowned or. Crest—A demi griffin vert. Motto—Instaurator ruinæ.

Forsyth (Tailzerton and Nydie, Scotland). Ar. a chev. engr. gu. betw. three griffins segreant vert, armed and membered of the second. Crest and Motto, as the last.

Forsyth (Scotland). Ar. a chev. engr. betw. three griffins segreant vert, armed and ducally crowned or. Crest—A demi griffin vert, armed and ducally crowned or.

Forsyth. Same Arms, chev. and griffins gu. Crest—A covered cup gu.

Forsyth (granted to THOMAS FORSYTH, Esq.). Ar. a chev. engr. betw. two gryphons segreant in chief az. and a sea-horse erect in base ppr. Crest—A gryphon segreant erm. supporting with the forepaws an anchor sa. Motto—Instaurator Ruinæ.

Fort (Read Hall, co. Lancaster). Quarterly, az. and gu. a castle with two towers ppr. a chief ar. thereon a bee volant also ppr. betw. two mullets sa. Crest—A rock ppr. thereon a lion sejant gu. bezantée gorged with a collar gemel or, in the dexter forepaw a cross crosslet fitchée sa. Motto—Fortis et audax.

Forte (co. Somerset). Ar. three mallets gu. (another, sa.) Crest—A cock gu. holding in the beak a daisy ppr.

Fortersley, or Fortryshey (co. Dorset). Ar. three Saracens' heads sa. wreathed of the field.

Fortescue (Winston, co. Devon; the senior line of the house of FORTESCUE, whose last male representative, EDMUND FORTESCUE, Esq., left five daus. co-heirs, MARY, m. the Right. Hon. WILLIAM FORTESCUE, Master of the Rolls; ELIZABETH, d. unm., 1768; SARAH, d. young, 1703; DOROTHEA, m. THOMAS BURY, Esq., son of Sir THOMAS BURY, Knt., of Exeter; and GRACE, d. unm., 1743. Of these daus. the only one to leave issue was DOROTHEA, wife of THOMAS BURY, Esq.; her dau. and heir, CATHERINE BURY, m. Rev. NATHANIEL WELLS, Rector of East Allington, co. Devon, and had, with other issue, a son EDMUND, who assumed the surname and arms of FORTESCUE). Az. a bend engr. ar. cotised or. Crest—An heraldic tiger pass. ar. armed, maned, and tufted or. Motto—Forte scutum salus ducum. The founder of the family, Sir RICHARD LE FORTE, protected William the Conqueror at Hastings, by bearing a shield before him, from which event the French word "escue" was added to the original word of "Forte;" and to the same circumstance the motto refers.

Fortescue (Fallapit, co. Devon, bart., extinct 1683. Sir EDMUND FORTESCUE, Knt., of Fallapit, was created a bart. 1664, d. s. p. m.). Same Arms, &c.

Fortescue (Earl Fortescue). Az. a bend engr. ar. plain cotised or. Crest—An heraldic tiger statant ar. armed, maned, and tufted or. Supporters—Two greyhounds ar. each ducally collared and lined gu. Motto—Forte scutum salus ducum.

Fortescue (Earl of Clinton, created 1746, extinct 1751). Same Arms, &c., as Earl Fortescue.

Fortescue-Aland (Lord Fortescue, created 1746, extinct 1781). Same Arms. Crest—A leopard pass. ppr. resting the dexter paw on a shield ar. Supporters—Two leopards ppr. murally gorged or. Motto—As Earl Fortescue.

Fortescue (Buckland Filleigh, co. Devon). Same Arms, Crest, and Motto, as Earl Fortescue.

Fortescue (Dromisken and Ravensdale, co. Louth; Sir

CHICHESTER FORTESCUE, Ulster King of Arms, 1788; derived from Sir FAITHFUL FORTESCUE, Knt., son of JOHN FORTESCUE, Esq., of Buckland Filleigh, by SUSANNAH, his second wife, sister of Sir ARTHUR CHICHESTER, Lord Deputy of Ireland). Same Arms, Crest, and Motto, as FORTESCUE, of Fallapit.

Fortescue (Earl of Clermont, created 1777, extinct 1806). Same Arms. Crest—A leopard pass. ppr. dexter paw resting on an escutcheon ar. Supporters—Two moose deer ppr. crined or, each gorged with a cellar of trefoils vert. Motto—Same as Earl Fortescue.

Fortescue (Viscount Clermont, extinct 1829). Az. a bend engr. ar. betw. two cotises or. Crest—A leopard pass. ppr. supporting with the dexter paw a shield ar. Supporters—Two moosedeer ppr. attired or, gorged with a chaplet of trefoils ppr. Motto—Forte scutum salus ducum.

Fortescue (Lord Clermont). Az. a bend engr. ar. cotised or. Crest—An heraldic tiger ppr. supporting with his forepaw a plain shield ar. Supporters—Two moose deer ppr. attired or, each gorged with a collar of trefoils also ppr. Motto—Forte scutum salus ducum.

Fortescue (PARKINSON-FORTESCUE, Lord Carlingford). Quarterly, 1st and 4th, az. a bend engr. ar. cotised or, a crescent for diff., for FORTESCUE; 2nd and 3rd, per chev. gu. and az. on a chev. engr. betw. three ostrich feathers erect of the third as many pellets, for PARKINSON. Crests—1st: An heraldic tiger ppr. supporting with his forepaw a plain shield ar. charged on the shoulder with a crescent sa. for diff., for FORTESCUE; 2nd: A falcon, wings addorsed ppr. belled or, and charged on the breast with a pellet, in the beak an ostrich feather ar. Mottoes—Forte scutum salus ducum; and, over the PARKINSON crest, Si celeres quatit pennas. Supporters—Same as Lord Clermont's, duly differenced.

Fortescue (Wood, co. Devon, bart., extinct 1686; descended from the marriage of Sir HENRY FORTESCUE, Chief Justice, Common Pleas, in Ireland, with JOAN, his first wife, heiress of Wood; the eventual heiress of this branch, ELIZABETH FORTESCUE, m. LEWIS FORTESCUE, Esq., of Preston; their descendant, PETER FORTESCUE, was created a bart., 1667, d. s. p. m.). Same Arms as FORTESCUE, of Fallapit.

Fortescue (Stapleford Abbots, co. Essex). Az. a bend engr. ar. cotised or. Crest—A leopard pass. guard. ppr.

Fortescue (Cookhill, co. Worcester, and Wethell, co. Warwick; derived from NICHOLAS FORTESCUE, groom porter to Henry VIII., illegitimate son of JOHN FORTESCUE, of Spirelston, co. Devon). Az. a bend engr. ar. betw. two cotises or, a border gobony of the second and first. Crest—A tiger pass. or.

Fortescue. Az. a bend engr. ar. cotised or, a bordure gu. (another, of the second).

Fortescue. Ar. fretty sa. on a chief of the first three roses gu. leaved vert.

Forth (London). Az. a rose betw. two martlets in pale betw. as many flaunches or, each charged with a rose gu. Crest—A hind's head couped vert guttée or, collared and lined of the last.

Forth (Butley Abbey, and Hadleigh, co. Suffolk). Gu. two bends vairé or and sa. on a canton of the second a demi greyhound couped courant of the third. Crest—A bear's head sa. muzzled gu.

Forth. Gu. a lion ramp. or, supporting a staff raguly of the last.

Forth (Rickmondsworth, co Herts; Reg. Ulster's Office, temp. William III., to Capt. SAMUEL FORTH, of Colonel Wolseley's regt. of horse). Erm. an Irish harp or, betw. three martlets gu. Crest—A cubit dexter arm embowed, naked, and encircled with a ducal coronet, the hand grasping a broken sword all ppr.

Forthingham (co. Southampton). Az. a bend betw. six mullets ar.

Fortibus (Seneschal, Poictou, and Aquitaine, temp. Henry III.). Ar. three mullets gu.

Fortibus (Earl of Albemarle, ODO, who m. a sister of William the Conqueror, was so created, extinct 1259). Ar. a chief gu.

Fortick (granted, 1775, to WILLIAM FORTICK, of the city of Dublin, descended from a family resident at Utrecht, Holland). Gu. two lions ramp. supporting a castle with two towers triple-towered ar. on a chief az. a sinister hand couped at the wrist appaumée betw. two estoiles or. Crest—A martlet sa. Motto—Foote.

Forton. Gyronny of eight or and gu.

Fortrose, Viscount (extinct 1781). See McKENZIE.

Fortyre. Ar. three boars' heads couped sa. langued or. Crest—A lion ramp. sustaining a spear ppr.

Forts, or De Fortibus. Gu. a cross patonce vair.

Forty. Or, a fesse embattled az. betw. three mullets gu.

Crest—On a ducal coronet a mullet betw. two branches of laurel in orle all ppr.

Forward (co. Lancaster). Sa. a chev. betw. three crosses pattée ar.

Forward (granted, 1780, to Hon. WILLIAM HOWARD, second son of RALPH, *Baron of Clonmore*, on his taking, by royal licence, the surname of FORWARD). Ar. a lion ramp. gu. on the shoulder an erm. spot or. *Crest*—A lion pass. gu. charged as the arms.

Fosbery (Clorane and Curragh Bridge, co. Limerick). Az. a saltire betw. four cinquefoils ar. *Crest*—A pheon supported by two bears' paws erased all ppr. *Motto*—Non nobis solum.

Fosbrooke, or Folbrooke (co. Northampton). Az. a saltire betw. four cinquefoils (another, roses) ar.

Fosbrooke (Shardlow Hall, and Ravenstone Hall, co. Derby). Same *Arms*. *Crest*—Two bears' gambs sa. supporting a spear erect ppr.

Foscot, or Foxcot (co. Berks, *temp.* Henry VI.) Ar. on a bend engr. az. three stumps of trees couped and eradicated of the first.

Foscott, or Foxcott. Same *Arms*. *Crest*—A dove on an olive branch ppr.

Foshaugh. Gu. three poleaxes erect in fesse ar. over all a fesse chequy of the first and second.

Foskett (Rosehill, Abbots Langley, co. Herts). Quarterly, erm. and gu. in the 1st and 4th quarters a lion ramp. of the second, over all an arrow in bend sinister, point upwards or. *Crest*—An arm embowed in armour, holding in the gauntlet a crossbow all ppr.

Foskett. Or, a bend chequy gu. and ar. betw. two cotises of the second. *Crest*—A broken spear in pale, the end hanging in bend ppr.

Fossard (Doncaster, co. York, *temp.* Richard I.). Or, a bend sa.

Fossard. Gu. six bends or.

Fosset. Ar. on a bend sa. three bucks' heads cabossed or, armed of the first.

Foster (co. York). Ar. a chev. betw. three buglehorns vert stringed or.

Foster. Ar. a chev. gu. betw. three buglehorns vert, on a chief of the second as many leopards' faces or. *Crest*—A stag's head, quarterly, sa. and ar. attired or.

Foster (Rev. JOHN FOSTER, Rector of Foxearth, near Sudbury, co. Suffolk). Same *Arms* as the last.

Foster. Ar. a chev. gu. betw. three buglehorns sa. stringed of the second. *Crest*—An arm embowed, holding a broken tilting spear ppr.

Foster (Copdock, co. Suffolk). Ar. three buglehorns stringed sa.

Foster. Ar. a chev. vert betw. three buglehorns, and a bordure sa. bezantée.

Foster (co. Berks). Ar. a chev. betw. three buglehorns stringed sa. *Crest*—A stag's head erased ppr.

Foster (Green Street, co. Kent, Watling Street and Sutton Maddox, co. Salop). Quarterly, per fesse indented ar. and sa. in the first and fourth quarter, a buglehorn of the second, garnished and stringed or. *Crest*—A talbot pass. ar. collared gu. lined or, nowed at the end.

Foster. Quarterly, per fesse indented ar. and gu. in the first quarter a buglehorn sa.

Foster (Brickhill, co. Beds, and The Bogue, co. Lancaster). Ar. a chev. vert betw. three bugles sa. stringed gu. *Crest*—An arm in armour embowed, holding in the hand the head of a broken tilting-spear ppr. *Motto*—Si fractus fortis.

Foster (The Bogue Estate, Jamaica, Egham, Kempstone, co. Beds; this family, long connected with the Island of Jamaica, is descended from the ancient house of FORSTER, or FOSTER, of Bamborough Castle, co. Northumberland). *Arms*, &c., same as the preceding.

Foster (co. Northumberland). Az. a chev. or, in chief two leopards' faces and in base a buglehorn of the last.

Foster (co. Northumberland). Ar. on a chev. vert three leopards' faces or.

Foster (co. Northumberland). Az. a chev. betw. three leopards' faces in chief and a crescent in base or.

Foster (Norwich, bart.). Ar. two bucks' heads erased ppr. betw. two chevronels az. the whole betw. three buglehorns sa. stringed gu. *Crest*—A buck ppr. the dexter forepaw resting on an inescutcheon az. charged with a castle ar. *Motto*—Virtute et labore.

Foster (Anstey Hall, co. Cambridge; granted to EBENEZER FOSTER, Esq.). Az. on a pile betw. two buglehorns in base stringed or, another buglehorn stringed of the field. *Crest*—A demi stag or, semée of pheons and holding betw. the legs a buglehorn az. *Motto*—Præmium honor.

Foster. Ar. on a bend sa. three bucks' heads cabossed or. *Crest*—A lion's head erased ar. collared gu.

370

Foster (co. Essex). Same *Arms*, the bend wavy.

Foster (Iden, co. Sussex; Fun. Ent., 1639, MARGARET, dau. of JOHN FOSTER, Esq., and wife of THOMAS HARDING, of Maryborough, Queen's Co.). Same *Arms*, the bend engr.

Foster (cos. Essex and Suffolk). Az. (another, gu.) a lion ramp. ar. guttée de sang (another, de l'armes).

Foster (co. Huntingdon). Sa. a chev. erm. betw. three pheons ar.

Foster (Lord Mayor of London, 1434). Same *Arms*.

Foster (cos. Lincoln and York). Sa. a chev. engr. erm. betw. three broad arrows or, feathered ar.

Foster (Wich, co. Worcester). Sa. on a chev. ar. betw three pheons or, as many escallops of the field. *Crest*—An antelope's head erased ar. attired, armed, and collared or, a line and ring flowing from the front of the collar gold.

Foster (Dowsby, co. Lincoln). Same *Arms* and *Crest*.

Foster (Barbadoes). Ar. on a chev. sa. betw. three lions pass. ppr. as many arrows of the field. *Crest*—Out of a mural crown chequy ar. and sa. a buck's head ppr. attired or, in the mouth an arrow of the first.

Foster. Az. a lion ramp. or.

Foster. Sa. (another, gu.) a chev. (another, engr.) betw. three pheons or.

Foster. Sa. a buck trippant ar. betw. three bezants, each charged with a pheon of the field.

Foster (London). Same *Arms*, a border gobony or and gu.

Foster. Az. a cross sarcelly betw. four crosses formée or.

Foster (Wadsworth Banks, and Heptonstall Slack, near Halifax). A bend or, betw. a demi unicorn erased in chief, and four crosses crosslet flory in base. *Crest*—A cubit arm erect, vested, holding in the hand a battle axe fesseways.

Foster (descendants of the late Rev. ROBERT FOSTER, Prebendary of the Cathedral Church of Wells). Per chev. embattled or and vert, three eagles displ. counterchanged. *Crest*—An eagle displ. or.

Foster. Vert a chev. betw. three butterflies volant ar.

Foster (Ireland; Reg. Ulster's Office). Sa. a chev. erm. betw. three pheons, points downwards ar.

Foster (Alderman JOHN FOSTER, Mayor of Dublin, from the Fun. Ent., 1640, of his dau. MARGARET, wife of CHRISTOPHER BISSE, Remembrancer of the Court of Exchequer). Same *Arms*, in chief a mullet ar. charged with another gu. for diff.

Foster (*Viscount Ferrard and Lord Oriel*). See SKEFFINGTON.

Foster-Skeffington (*Viscount Massereene*). See SKEFFINGTON.

Foster (Stonehouse, co. Louth, bart.). Ar. a chev. vert betw. three buglehorns sa. stringed gu. *Crest*—A stag pass. ppr. *Motto*—Divini gloria ruris.

Foster (Ballymacscanlan, co. Louth). Same *Arms*, *Crest*, and *Motto*.

Foster (granted to HENRY FOSTER, Esq., of Coomie Castle, co. Cavan). Ar. a chev. vert betw. three buglehorns sa. stringed gu. *Crest*—A stag pass. ppr.

Foston (co. York). Paly of six or and az. a chief gu.

Foston (arms of THOMAS FOSTON, in the chapel of University College, Oxford. Visit. 1574). Ar. on a chev. engr. sa. three crescents of the field. *Crest*—A gate az.

Fother, or Folcher (co. Derby). Erm. on a bend gu. three plates.

Fother. Gu. two chev. ar. on the first a fleur-de-lis of the field.

Fother, or Fodyr. Gu. a fesse dancettée or.

Fotherby (Burton, co. Lincoln, and Barham, co. Kent; granted, 28 Feb. 1605). Gu. a cross composed of nine lozenges, at each end a fleur-de-lis or. *Crest*—A falcon, wings expanded ppr. beaked or, holding in the mouth an acorn gold, leaved vert.

Fotherby. Gu. two chev. ar. on the first three fleurs-de-lis of the field.

Fothergill (Ravenstonedale, co. Westmoreland). Vert a buck's head couped or, a bordure engr. of the last.

Fothergill (Caerlcon, co. Monmouth; descended from FOTHERGILL, of Ravenstonedale). Same *Arms*. *Crest*—A talbot collared.

Fothergill. Same *Arms*. *Crest*—On a rock a lion ramp. ppr. collared and chained or, in the dexter paw an arrow sa.

Fotheringay. Quarterly, gu. and or, a cross fusily ar.

Fotheringham (Pourie, co. Forfar). Erm. three bars gu. *Crest*—A griffin segreant ppr. *Supporters*—Two naked men wreathed about the head and middle with laurel ppr. *Motto*—Be it fast.

Fotheringham (Lawhill, Scotland). Erm. three bars gu. on each bar a buckle or. *Crest*—A griffin's head couped ppr. *Motto*—Be it fast.

Fotheringham (Bandean, Scotland). Erm. three bars gu.

within a bordure of the second. *Crest*—A griffin's head erased ppr. *Motto*—Be it fast.

Fotherley (co. Lincoln). Gu. a fesse dancettée or. *Crest* —A lion's gamb erased or, grasping a wolf's head erased ar.

Fouachin, Fauchin, or Fashion (extinct in Guernsey). Or, on a fret sa. semée of plates, a bull's head erased of the field, the collar gu. charged with three bezants betw. four leopards' heads cabossed ar. *Crest*—An arm vested gu. holding a lynx or.

Foulcanley. Or, a cross (another, a chev.) engr. gu. a chief ar.

Foulchampe, or Foulgeham (co. Lincoln). Sa. a bend betw. six escallops or (another, ar.).

Foulchampe. Per pale sa. and az. six escallops ar. three, two, and one.

Fouler (Scotland). Az. a cross betw. a pelican in her nest in the first and fourth quarters, and a cinquefoil in the second and third ar. *Crest*—A stag's head gu. armed ar. *Motto*— Ne quid nimis.

Foulerton. Gu. on a fesse ar. three otters' heads sa. *Crest*—A Cornish chough sa.

Fouleshurst (cos. Chester, Essex, and Leicester). Gu. fretty or, a chief erm.

Foulhurst (co. Lancaster). Gu. a fret or, on a chief of the second three mullets of the first.

Foulion (co. Derby). Sa. a bend betw. six escallops or.

Foulis (Colinton, co. Edinburgh, bart. 1634). Ar. three laurel leaves slipped vert. *Crest*—A dexter hand couped, holding a sword in pale, supporting a wreath of laurel all ppr. *Motto*—Mente manuque præsto.

Foulis (Woodhall, co. Edinburgh; cadet of Colinton, succeeded eventually to the representation of that family). Ar. three laurel leaves slipped vert within a bordure erm. *Crest* —A flowerpot with a branch of laurel springing out of it. *Motto*—Non deficit.

Foulis (Ravelstoun, co. Edinburgh, bart.; attainted 1746). Ar. on a fesse betw. three laurel leaves vert a primrose or. *Crest*—A dove volant, holding a leaf in her beak ppr. *Motto* —Thure et jure.

Foulis (Ratho, Scotland). Ar. on a chev. betw. three laurel leaves vert, as many plates.—*Crest*—A dove holding in the beak an olive branch ppr. *Motto*—Pax.

Foulis (Edinburgh, 1672). Ar. a holly branch betw. three bay leaves slipped vert. *Motto*—I rise by industry.

Foulis (Ingleby Manor, co. York, bart.). Ar. three laurel leaves erect ppr. *Crest*—Out of a crescent ar. a cross formée fitchée sa. *Another Crest* — A demi unicorn winged.

Foulis (Heslerton, co. York; descended from Foulis, of Ingleby Manor, a branch of the Scotch house of Foulis, of Colinton). Same *Arms*. *Crests*—1st: A demi unicorn winged ppr.; 2nd: Out of a crescent ar. a cross formée fitchée sa.

Foulke (co. Stafford). Ar. a fesse betw. three mullets sa.

Foulke, or Fulke (Wickwonen, co. Worcester). Ar. on a chev. gu. betw. three owls sa. as many lozenges of the field, each charged with an erm. spot, on a chief az. three acorn branches or. *Crest*—A squirrel sejant az. bezantée gorged with a collar or, holding in the paws an acorn branch vert, fructed gold.

Foulke. Per pale indented or and gu. a bordure counterchanged.

Foulke. Gu. a fesse or, betw. six martlets ar.

Foulkes. Gu. crusily fitchée or, a lion ramp. ar. *Crest*—A lion's head erased and collared per pale ar. and sa. counterchanged.

Foulkeworth. Ar. on a cross flory gu. five escallops of the field.

Foulks. Ar. two sugar-canes in saltire ppr. surmounted by a fleur-de-lis gu. on a chief az. three plates, each charged with a mullet sa. *Crest*—Out of a tower ar. a demi eagle sa. beaked or, holding in the mouth a fleur-de-lis gu.

Foulkes (Eriviatt, or "Yr Eifiad," co. Denbigh; derived from Gronwy ap-Davydd, usually styled "Y Penwyn," one of the few Welsh chieftains who espoused the cause of Edward I., in his conquest of Wales. Gronwy, descended from Marchudd, living in the ninth century, head of one of the Fifteen Tribes of North Wales). Gu. three boars' heads erased ar. in pale, quartering Roberts, of Rhydonneu and Bryntangor, Jocelyn, of Stansteadbury, Salusbury, of Bryn-y-Barkit, and Wynne, of Maes-y-Coed. *Crest*—A boar's head, as in the arms. *Motto* (as used by some families of the name)—Jure non dono.

Foulkes (Rev. Henry Foulkes, D.D., Principal of Jesus College, Oxford, 1817). Or three boars' heads couped in pale sa. *Crest*—A boar's head, as in the arms.

Foulkes (Medland, co. Devon). Az. three lions pass. in pale ar.

Foulks (Cilan-yn-Edeirnion, co. Merioneth; derived through Morgan ap Robert, of Branas, from Rhys-ap-Ievan, Baron of Kymmer, Crogen, and Branas, in Edeirnion, ancestor of Hughes, of Gwerclas, *Baron of Kymmer-yn-Edeirnion*). *Arms*, those of Hughes, of Gwerclas, viz., ar. a lion ramp. sa. armed and langued gu.

Fouller. Sa. on a cross engr. or, five pellets. *Crest*—A greyhound's head erased sa. collared or.

Foulsherst (co. Lancaster). Gu. a fret or, on a chief of the second two mullets of the field.

Foulshurst (Crewe, co. Chester). Same *Arms*, the chief erm. *Crest*—A unicorn's head erminois attired or.

Foulson (Hunt-Foulson). Quarterly, 1st and 4th, gu. a chev. ar. in chief a mullet betw. two crescents and in base a crescent betw. two mullets or., for Foulston; 2nd and 3rd, az. an arrow in bend ppr. betw. two bendlets ar. the whole betw. six leopards' faces or., for Hunt. *Crests*—1st, Foulston : A demi lion gu. gorged with a collar and charged on the shoulder with five mullets saltirewise ar. holding in the mouth a crescent or.; 2nd, Hunt: A leopard's face az. in front of two arrows, points downwards, in saltire ppr. betw. two wings or. each charged with a cross potent az.

Foulston (co. Devon). Gu. a chev. betw. three crescents ar. *Crest*—A demi lion ramp. ar.

Foulthebury (co. Beds). Erm. on a chief gu. three roses or.

Foulthorpe. Ar. a cross moline sa.

Founder, or Foundaure. Ar. a bend betw. two lions ramp. az. *Crest*—Out of a ducal coronet a griffin's head betw. two wings all ppr.

Founders, Company of (London ; granted by Cooke, Clarenceux). Az. a laver pot (*i.e.* a vase) betw. two taper candlesticks or. *Crest*—A fiery furnace ppr. two arms of the last issuing from clouds on the sinister side of the first, vested az. holding in both hands a pair of closing tongs sa. taking hold of the melting pot in the furnace ppr. *Motto*— God the only founder.

Foundling Hospital. Per fesse az. and vert, in chief a crescent ar. betw. two mullets of six points or, in base an infant exposed, stretching out its arms for help ppr. *Crest*— A lamb pass. ar. holding in its mouth a sprig of laurel vert. *Supporters*—Two emblematical figures; the dexter, representing Nature, and the sinister Wisdom. *Motto*—Help.

Fountain, or Fountayne (Bawcombe and Stokenham, co. Devon; John Fountaine, of the latter place, aged 32. Visit. 1620). Ar. three bars gemels gu. on a canton az. a lion pass. guard. or. *Crest*—An eagle's head erased, holding in the beak a snake.

Fountain (Belchamp St. Paul, co. Essex ; granted 22 Feb. 1619). Gu. a bend or, in the sinister chief a cinquefoil ar. (another, erm.).

Fountain (Loch Hill, Scotland). Ar. on a fesse az. three bezants. *Crest*—An eagle rising ppr. *Motto*—Præclarius quo difficilius.

Fountaine (Narford Hall, co. Norfolk. Visit. Norfolk, 1563. Elizabeth Fountaine, sister and heiress of Sir Andrew Fountaine, the heiress of this family, which flourished in Norfolk, *temp.* Henry III., *m.* Col. Edward Clent ; her only dau. and heiress, Elizabeth Clent, *m.* Capt. W. Price, and left an only son, Brigg Price, Esq., of Narford, who assumed the name of Fountaine). Or, a fesse gu. betw. three elephants' heads erased sa. *Crest*—An elephant ppr. *Motto* —Vix ea nostra voco.

Fountaine-Wilson. See Wilson.

Fountains-Abbey (co. York). Gu. a cross betw. four lions ramp. ar. (another coat, az. three horseshoes or, two and one).

Fountavill. Az. three bends ar. an inescutcheon of the last.

Fountbery, Ferontbery, or Faukethbery (co. Bedford). Erm. on a chief gu. three roses or. *Crest*—A cross pattée az. enwrapped by a snake vert.

Fountinghien. Az. a fret or, on a canton of the second a lion's gamb erased and erect of the first.

Fourbins. Or, a chev. az. betw. three leopards' faces sa. a bordure gu. *Crest*—A sheaf of arrows ppr. banded gu.

Fourches. Gu. a lion ramp. ar. crowned or.

Fourde (Penshurst, co. Kent ; Margaret, eldest dau. and coheir of Richard Fourde, *m.* John Ashfield, of Esthorpe, co. Oxford, *cir.* Reg. Henry VI. Visit. Oxon. 1574). Sa. in chief two lions ramp. addorsed or, in base bendy wavy ar. and az.

Fourdes (co. Middlesex). Az. a fesse dancettée betw. three lions ramp. or.

Fournier. Az. a hawk volant ar. seizing a heron also volant or. *Crest*—A martlet per fesse az. and ar.

Fournivall. Ar. a bend gu. betw. six martlets sa.

Foutesherst. Ar. fretty sa. on a chief of the last two mullets of the first.

Fowbery (Bluntisham, co. Durham, and Newbald, co. York). Vert a stag pass. ar. attired or. *Crest*—A stag's head ar. attired or, charged on the neck with three trefoils slipped vert, one and two.

Fowbery (co. Huntingdon). Same *Arms*. *Crest*—A stag's head ar. attired or, charged on the neck with three trefoils slipped vert, one and two, holding in the mouth a rose gu. stalked and leaved vert.

Fowell (Fowell's Combe, co. Devon, bart., extinct 1692; an Anglo-Saxon family, stated to have existed at Fowell's Combe previously to the Conquest. Sir EDMOND FOWELL, of Fowell's Combe, Knt., M.P. for co. Devon, was created a baronet in 1661; his grandson, Sir JOHN FOWELL, of Fowell's Combe, the third and last baronet, M.P. for Totnes, *d.* in 1692, when the male representation of the family devolved upon his kinsman, WILLIAM FOWELL, Esq., of Black Hall and Diptford). Ar. a chev. sa. on a chief gu. three mullets pierced of the first. *Crest*—Out of a mural crown ppr. an antelope's head ar. attired gu. *Another Crest*—A griffin's head erased ar. struck through the breast with an arrow ppr. *Motto*—Non ostento sed ostendo.

Fowell (Black Hall and Diptford, co. Devon; descended from WILLIAM FOWELL, Esq., of Black Hall, *b.* 1556, second son of RICHARD FOWHILL, of Fowhill's Combe, grandfather of Sir EDMOND FOWELL, of Fowell's Combe, the first bart.). Same *Arms, Crest* and *Motto*.

Fowell (Plymouth and Harewood House, co. Cornwall; descended from JOHN FOWELL, Esq., barrister-at-law, town clerk of Plymouth, a younger son of RICHARD FOWELL, Esq., of Fowell's Combe, grandfather of Sir EDMOND FOWELL, the first bart.). Same *Arms, Crest,* and *Motto.*

Fowell (Corsham, co. Wilts; descended from RICHARD FOWELL, a younger son of FOWELL, of Black Hall). Same *Arms, Crest,* and *Motto.*

Fowey. Erm. on a chief gu. three cinquefoils ar.

Fowick. Ar. a fesse betw. three annulets gu.

Fowke (Lowesby, co. Leicester, bart.). Vert a fleur-de-lis ar. *Crest*—A dexter arm embowed, habited vert, cuff ar. holding in the hand an arrow or, barbed and flighted of the second, point downwards. *Motto*—Arma tuentur pacem.

Fowke (cos. Dorset, Stafford, and London). Same *Arms*. *Crest*—An Indian goat's head erased ar.

Fowke (Lord Mayor of London, 1653). Same *Arms* and *Crest.*

Fowke (Dublin; impalement on Fun. Ent. 1660, of Doctor TATE). Vert a fleur-de-lis or, betw. three escallops ar.

Fowke (Fun. Ent. Ulster's Office, 1666, Colonel JOHN FOWKE, buried at Ardee, co. Louth. He was son and heir of JOHN FOWKE, third son of ROGER FOWKE, third son of FOWKE, of Brewood, co. Stafford). Vert a fleur-de-lis ar. a mullet on a crescent or, for diff. *Crest*—Out of a ducal coronet or, a sword erect entwined with a serpent descending all ppr.

Fowke (Elmsthorpe, co. Leicester). Ar. a chev. gu. on a chief of the last three mullets pierced of the first.

Fowke (granted 1580). Az. a fleur-de-lis ar. on a chief indented of the last a lion pass. gu.

Fowkes (London). Sa. two bars ar. *Crest*—A golden fleece ppr.

Fowkes (Alderman FOWKES, of Dublin, Reg. Ulster's Office). Az. a fleur-de-lis or, betw. three escallops ar. *Crest*—A lion pass. az. charged on the shoulder with a fleur-de-lis or.

Fowkroy. Or, three lions pass. in pale sa. *Crest*—A lion's gamb holding an ostrich's feather ppr.

Fowlchampe. Sa. a bend betw. six escallops ar.

Fowle (Sandhurst, co. Kent, and Salhurst, co. Sussex). Ar. a chev. gu. on a chief of the last three mullets of the first. *Crest*—A griffin's head erased ar. pierced through the neck with an arrow gu. barbed of the first, vulned of the second.

Fowle (River Hall, co. Sussex). Gu. a lion pass. guard. betw. three roses or, barbed vert. *Crest*—Out of a ducal coronet or, an arm embowed in armour ppr. garnished gold, holding in the hand ppr. a battle axe also gold.

Fowle (Chute Lodge, co. Wilts). Same *Arms* and *Crest.*

Fowle (Market Lavington, co. Wilts). Quarterly, 1st and 4th, gu. a lion pass. guard. betw. three roses or, barbed and seeded ppr., for FOWLE; 2nd and 3rd, az. a stag's head cabossed ar. an annulet for diff., for LEGGE. *Crests*—1st, FOWLE: Out of a ducal coronet or, a dexter arm in armour embowed ppr. garnished and holding in the hand a battle axe gold. 2nd, LEGGE: Out of a ducal coronet or, a plume of feathers ar. and az. *Motto*—Boutez en avant.

Fowler (Ricott, co. Bedford). Az. on a chev. ar. betw. three lapwings or, as many crosses pattée sa. *Crest*—An owl ar. ducally gorged gu.

Fowler (St. Thomas, co. Stafford; descended from Sir RICHARD FOWLER, of Foxley, co. Buckingham, a Crusader, *temp.*

372

Richard I., who, by his extraordinary vigilance, having saved the Christian camp from a nocturnal surprise, received the honour of knighthood on the field from his sovereign, who, says tradition, caused the crest which Sir RICHARD then bore, a hand and lure, to be changed to the vigilant owl). Az. on a chev. (another, engr.) betw. three lions pass. guard. or, as many crosses formée (another, moline) sa. *Crest*—An owl ar. ducally gorged or. *Another Crest*—A cubit arm habited az. holding in the hand ppr. a lure vert, feathered ar. lined or, twisted round the arm.

Fowler (Harnage Grange, co. Salop, bart., extinct 1773; descended from WILLIAM FOWLER, second brother of BRIEN FOWLER, Esq., of St. Thomas). Same *Arms, &c.*

Fowler (Pendeford, co. Stafford; descended from JAMES FOWLER, youngest brother of BRIEN FOWLER, Esq., of St. Thomas). Same *Arms, &c.*

Fowler (Stonehouse, co. Gloucester; granted 13 March, 1606). Quarterly, az. and or, in the 1st quarter a hawk's lure and line of the second. *Crest*—An ostrich's head or, betw. two wings ar. holding in the beak a horseshoe az.

Fowler (co. Leicester). Gu. a chev. betw. three herons' heads erased ar.

Fowler (Islington, co. Middlesex, bart., extinct 1656, Sir THOMAS FOWLER, first bart., 1628, was descended from THOMAS FOWLER, Esq., owner of the Manor of Berners, or Barnersbury, Islington, 1548). Az. on a chev. ar. betw. three herons or, as many crosses formée gu.

Fowler (co. Oxford. In a glass window in Waterstoke Church, to WILLIAM FOWLER and CICELY, his wife. Visit. 1574). Ar. (another, or) three wolves' heads erased gu. a bordure of the last charged with eight castles or.

Fowler (co. Salop). Ar. three leopards' heads sa. in chief a lion pass. gu.

Fowler (Horton Hall, and Leek, co. Stafford). Az. (another, gu.) on a chev. ar. betw. three lions pass. guard. or, as many crosses pattée sa.

Fowler (granted 1693; EDWARD FOWLER, Bishop of Gloucester, 1697). Per pale gu. and sa. on a chev. or, betw. three lions pass. guard. erm. crowned gold, as many quatrefoils vert. *Crest*—A stork ar. membered gu. holding in the bill a cross formée fitchée or.

Fowler. Or, two wolves' heads erased gu. a bordure engr. of the last charged with eight escallops of the field.

Fowler. Ar. three cocks or, beaked and legged gu. collared az.

Fowler (granted to JOHN FOWLER, Esq., of Clifton, co. Gloucester). Quarterly, per pale indented az. and or, in the 1st and 4th quarters a hawk's lure, and in the 2nd and 3rd a lion pass. counterchanged. *Crest*—An ostrich's head couped or, in the beak a horseshoe sa. betw. two wings ar. each charged with two cinquefoils in pale az.

Fowler (Windlesham House, Bagshot, co. Surrey). Az. on a chev. ar. betw. three lions pass. guard. or, as many crosses pattée sa. *Crests*—1st, FOWLER: An owl ar. ducally crowned or; 2nd, ENGLEFIELD: An arm erect vested per pale az. and gu. cuff ar. the hand holding a branch of laurel ppr. *Motto*—Sapiens qui vigilat.

Fowler (Gunton Hall, co. Suffolk). Same *Arms*. *Crest*—A cubit arm vested az. grasping in the hand ppr. a hawk's lure vert, string twisted round the arm.

Fowler (Thornwood Lodge, Kensington, and Braemon, co. Ross). Quarterly, az. and sa. three crosses pattée betw. two chevronels or, in chief two lions pass. guard. of the last, and in base an owl ar. *Crest*—An owl ar. collared and charged on the breast with a cross pattée gu. wreathed about the head with ivy vert and resting his dexter claw upon a cross pattée or. *Motto*—Sapiens qui vigilat.

Fowler (Scotland). Az. a cross or, betw. a pelican of the second feeding her young in the 1st and 4th quarters, and a cinquefoil ar. in the 2nd and 3rd.

Fowler-Butler. See BUTLER.

Fowles. Ar. three laurel leaves erect vert. *Crest*—A crescent ar. betw. the horns a cross pattée fitchée sa.

Fowleshurst (co. Salop). Gu. fretty or, on a chief ar. two mullets pierced sa.

Fowliche. Gu. a fret or, and chief of the last.

Fowlinge (Ireland, Reg. Ulster's Office). Ar. on a chev. betw. three annulets gu. as many trefoils slipped or.

Fowlish. Gu. fretty or, on a chief of the second two mullets of the first.

Fowlthorpe (co. York). Ar. a cross moline, a crescent for diff.

Fowndowre. Ar. a bend betw. two lions ramp. az.

Fownes, or Fones (Plymouth, co. Cornwall; THOMAS FOWNES, descended from WILLIAM FONES, Esq., of Saxby, co. Worcester, *temp.* Henry V. Visit. 1620). Az. two eagles displ. in chief and a mullet in base ar.

Fownes (co. Devon; resident in that county for more than two centuries, previously of Saxby Saphy, co. Worcester). Same *Arms. Crest*—A stump of an oak, with a branch on each side ppr.

Fownes (co. Stafford). Same *Arms.*

Fownes. Az. three eagles displ. ar. *Crest*—A hawk holding in the dexter claw an ear of wheat ppr.

Fownes. See FOWNES-LUTTRELL.

Fownes (Woodstock, co. Kilkenny, bart., extinct *temp.* George III.; granted to WILLIAM FOWNES, Esq., Joint Ranger of the Phœnix Park, High Sheriff of Dublin, 1697, and Lord Mayor, 1708, created a bart., 1724: his great granddaughter, heiress of the family, SARAH FOWNES, *m.*, 1765, WILLIAM TIGHE, Esq., of Rossana, M.P.). Erm. a chev. gu. betw. two eagles displ. in chief az. armed or, and a mullet in base of the second. *Crest*—Out of a ducal coronet or, an eagle displ. az. armed gold.

Fox (*Lord Holland*, created 1762, extinct 1859; descended from Right Hon. Sir STEPHEN FOX, Lord Commissioner of the Treasury to King Charles II., *d.* 28 Oct. 1716; granted at Brussels by Sir Edward Walker, Garter, 30 Oct. 1658). Erm. on a chev. az. three foxes' heads erased or, on a canton of the second a fleur-de-lis of the third. *Crest*—On a chapeau az. turned up erm. a fox sejant or. *Supporters*—Dexter, a fox ar. gorged with a collar gobony gu. and of the first, thereon three roses of the second, and holding in the mouth a rose slipped and leaved ppr.; sinister, a fox ar. gorged as the dexter, chained or. *Motto*—Et vitam impendere vero.

Fox-Strangways (*Earl of Ilchester*). See STRANGWAYS.

Fox (Little Eppleton, co. Durham). Erm. on a chev. az. three foxes' heads erased or. *Crest*—On a chapeau az. turned up erm. a fox sejant or. *Motto*—Video et taceo.

Fox (Missenden, co. Bucks). Ar. a chev. sa. betw. three cocks gu. on a chief az. a fox courant or. *Crest*—A lion sejant guard. or, supporting with the dexter foot a book gold.

Fox (co. Lincoln). Or, two bends az. on a chief of the last a fox courant of the first.

Fox (Youlgrave, co. Derby). Or, a chev. gu. betw. three foxes' heads erased az. *Crest*—A fox pass. az.

Fox (cos. Hereford and Leicester; and Ludlow, co. Salop). Ar. a chev. betw. three foxes' heads erased gu. *Crest*—A fox pass. gu.

Fox (Greet, Yardley, and King's Norton, co. Worcester). Same *Arms* and *Crest.*

Fox (Osmaston Hall, co. Derby). Same *Arms.*

Fox (Ratcliff and Bosworth, co. Leicester. Visit. 1619. WILLIAM FOX, great-grandson of GEORGE FOX, of Market Bosworth). Same *Arms*, a mullet for diff.

Fox (London). Ar. a chev. betw. three foxes' heads erased gu. collared or. *Crest*—Out of a ducal coronet a greyhound's head or.

Fox. Ar. on a chev. az. betw. three foxes' heads erased gu. collared and ringed or, as many bezants. *Crest*—A fox's head erased gu. collared and ringed or.

Fox (London, and co. York). Erm. a chev. az. betw. three foxes' heads erased ppr. *Crest*—A fox's head as in the arms.

Fox (High Holborn, co. Middlesex; granted 12 June, 1632). Erminois a chev. betw. three foxes' heads erased gu. langued ar.

Fox (Chacombe, co. Northampton; ANNE, dau. of MICHAEL Fox, of that place, *m.* WALTER SAVAGE, of Clanfield, co. Oxford. Visit. Oxon, 1574). Gu. a chev. erminois betw. three lions' heads erased or, on a chief barry nebulée ar. and purp. a pale az. charged with a pelican of the third, all within a border of the same charged with ten hurts. *Crest*—A fox pass. reguard. per pale ar. and gu. in the mouth a rose branch flowered of the last, stalked and leaved vert.

Fox (co. Northampton). Gu. a chev. erm. betw. three lions' heads erased ar. on a chief of the second a fesse nebulée charged with a griffin's head of the first.

Fox. Gu. a chev. erm. betw. three lions' heads erased or, a chief per fesse wavy az. and gold.

Fox. Gu. a chev. betw. three lions' heads erased or, a chief ar. *Crest*—On a mount an oak tree growing among grass ppr.

Fox (co. Essex). Per pale vert and sa. a cross pattée ar. *Crest*—On a chapeau gu. turned up erm. betw. two crosses potent sa. and vert a fox pass. ar.

Fox (co. Essex). Quarterly, sa. and vert a cross crosslet ar.

Fox. Or, three foxes' heads erased ppr. a bordure ar. semée of eagles displ. sa. *Crest*—An eagle displ. sa.

Fox (Bramham Park, co. York). Quarterly, 1st and 4th, erm. a chev. sa. three foxes' heads erased gu., for Fox; 2nd and 3rd, ar. a lion ramp. gu. within a border sa. on a canton of the first a harp and crown or, for LANE.

Fox (Grove Hill, Falmouth, co. Cornwall; claiming descent from the noble family of Fox). Erm. on a chev. az. three foxes'

heads erased or, within a bordure flory of the second, and on a canton of the same a drinking cup of the third, bearing three fleurs-de-lis ppr. on the urn, and charged in the centre with a rose gu. The canton was granted to commemorate the descent of the Fox family from a branch of the CROKERS, of Lineham. *Crest*—A fox sejant or, collared flory az. the paw resting on a fleur-de-lis az. *Motto*—Faire sans dire.

Fox (EMBLETON-FOX). Quarterly, 1st and 4th, Fox, sa. on a fesse engr. betw. two foxes pass. ar. a fox pass. of the field; 2nd and 3rd, EMBLETON, erminois on a bend nebuly az. a fleur-de-lis betw. two crescents or. *Crests*—1st, FOX: A fox's head erased ar. gorged with a collar engr. sa. within a chain in arch or; 2nd, EMBLETON: Issuant from clouds ppr. a crescent ar. betw. the horns a fleur-de-lis or. *Motto*—Non immemor beneficii.

Fox (Malton and Thorpe under Willows, co. York). Gu. a chev. betw. three foxes' heads erased or.

Fox (EDWARD FOX, Bishop of Bath and Wells, 1492-94; of Durham, 1494-1501; and of Winchester, 1501-28; Lord Privy Seal and Counsellor to Henry VII. and VIII., obit 1528; Founder of Corpus Christi Coll., Oxon.). Az. a pelican in her piety or, vulned ppr.

Fox. Same *Arms*, a bordure or.

Fox (co. Cornwall, Brislington House, Bristol, &c.). Az. on a bend engr. erm. cotised or, three foxes' heads erased gu. a border of the second. *Crest*—A fox sejant gu. collared and chained or, supporting with the sinister paw a pennon, staff ppr. flag az. semée de lis gold. *Motto*—J'ay ma foi tenu à ma puissance.

Fox. Gu. on a chev. erm. a pale az. charged with a pelican vulning herself or, betw. three lions' heads erased of the last, within a bordure gold hurtée.

Fox. Or, three foxes' heads couped gu.

Fox. Ar. on a bend betw. two lions pass. az. three foxes' heads erased or.

Fox, or Sionnach (Kilcourcy, co. Tipperary). Ar. a lion ramp. and in chief two dexter hands couped at the wrist gu. *Crest*—An arm embowed in armour, holding a sword all ppr. *Motto*—Sionnach aboo.

Fox (Fox Hall, co. Longford; Fun. Ent. of Sir PATRICK FOX, Knt., of Moyvore, co. Westmeath, *d.* Jan. 1618; descended from the ancient Irish Sept of O'Sionach, Anglicé Fox). Az. a sceptre in bend betw. two regal crowns, and a chief or. *Crest*—A sceptre betw. two wings. *Motto*—Nec elatus nec dejectus.

Fox (Ireland; *Smith's Ordinary*). Same *Arms. Crest*—A fox sejant ppr.

Fox (Province of Munster, Reg. Ulster's Office). Ar. three foxes pass. in pale sa.

Fox (registered to Rev. SMYTH WHITELAW FOX, M.A., of Rathmines, co. Dublin, and of Cupidstown, co. Kildare). Quarterly, 1st and 4th, erm. on a chev. az. three foxes' heads erased or, a canton of the second, charged with a trefoil of the third, for Fox; 2nd, gu. three plates, on a chief ar. a lion pass. of the field, for MADDOCK; 3rd, sa. a chev. betw. three boars' heads fessways couped ar., for WHITELAW. *Crest*—On a ducal coronet ppr. a fox sejant or. *Motto*—Fortitudine et sapientia.

Fox (granted, 1840, to EDWIN FYDELL FOX, Esq., of Bath, and the other issue of EDWARD LONG FOX, Esq., M.D.). Az. on a bend engr. erm. cotised or, three foxes' heads erased gu. all within a border of the second. *Crest*—A fox sejant gu. collared and chained or, supporting by his sinister paw a flagstaff, thereon a banner az. semée of fleurs-de-lis or. *Motto*—J'ay ma foi tenu à ma puissance.

Foxall (London). Ar. a chev. az. betw. three foxes' heads erased gu. *Crest*—A griffin's head or, erased gu. ducally gorged of the last.

Foxall (London). Ar. two bars gu.

Foxall. Ar. a bend engr. az.

Foxall (Ireland; confirmed by Roberts, Ulster, 1649, to Lieut. THOMAS FOXALL, who served Charles I. in the regiment of foot under command of Col. Anthony Hungerford). Gu. a chev. chequy ar. and sa. betw. three foxes' heads erased of the second. *Crest*—A horse's head couped sa. pierced through the neck with the shiver of a lance gu.

Foxcote (co. Huntingdon). Or (another, ar.) on a cross az. five escallops of the field.

Foxcote. Ar. a bend engr. az.

Foxcott. Ar. on a bend az. three cronels reversed or.

Foxcroft (Halifax and Newgrange, co. York. Harl. M.S. 4360. For full pedigree of this family, see Poulson's "Beverlac"). Az. a chev. betw. three foxes' heads erased or.

Foxlay. Sa. three garbs ar. banded or, a chief of the second.

Foxley (co. Berks). Gu. two bars ar. *Crest*—A hawk's leg erased at the thigh sa. belled or.

Foxley (co. Northampton). Ar. a fesse engr. betw. three cinquefoils sa.

Foxley. Ar. a cross engr. betw. four cinquefoils sa.

Foxley (co. Dorset; granted by Camden, Clarenceux, to JOHN FOXLEY, Shaftesbury, co. Dorset, 1609). Ar. a saltire chequy or and sa. betw. four trefoils of the second.

Foxton (co. Cambridge and London). Ar. a chev. (another, engr.) gu. betw. three buglehorns sa. garnished or. Crest— A rose ar. barbed vert.

Foxwell. Per chev. vert and erm. in chief two leopards' faces or. Crest—A galley ppr.

Foxwest (London). Ar. a chev. betw. three crosses crosslet fitchée sa. Crest—A reindeer's head erased ppr.

Foy. Paly of eight sa. and ar. a crescent gu. Crest—An eel ppr.

Foy, or Le Foy. Ar. six pellets, three, two, and one.

Foyle (cos. Hants and Dorset, 1609). Ar. a cross counter-compony sa. and or, betw. four trefoils slipped of the second. Crest—A horse's head couped ar. crined gu. gorged with two bars compony or and sa.

Foyle (cos. Dorset and Stafford). Ar. a saltire betw. four trefoils slipped sa.

Foyle (co. Hants). Gu. a saltire chequy or and of the first, betw. four crosses crosslet fitchée ar. Crest—A cross crosslet fitchée ar. betw. two wings expanded chequy or and gu.

Foyle (Somerford-Keynes, co. Wilts). Gu. a saltire compony counter-compony or and az. betw four crosses crosslet fitchée ar. Crest—A cross crosslet ar. betw. two dragons' wings chequy or and az.

Foyle (Reg. Ulster's Office). Or, a rose az. barbed vert.

Foyster (granted to SAMUEL FOYSTER, Esq., of St. Pancras, co. Middlesex, by Heard, Garter, and Lock, Clarenceux, 28 June, 1784). Az. a chev. erminois betw. two buglehorns in chief and a stag's head erased in base or. Crest—A demi stag ppr. attired and unguled or, collared with a bar gemelle gu. thereto suspended a buglehorn gold, stringed of the third.

Fraigneau (St. James, Westminster; granted 1757). Or, on a chev. engr. gu. betw. two storks rising in chief az. beaked and membered of the second, and in base on a mount vert an ash tree ppr. three annulets of the first. Crest—A stork close ar. beaked and membered gu. holding in the beak a slip of ash tree ppr.

Framework Knitters, Company of (London). Ar. a knitting frame sa. garnished or, with work pendent in base gu. Supporters—Dexter, a student of the University of Oxford, vested ppr.; sinister, a woman ppr. vested az. hand-kerchief, apron, and cuffs to the gown ar., in the dexter hand a knitting-needle, and in the sinister a piece of worsted-knit gu. Motto—Speed, strength, and truth united.

Framham. Quarterly, ar. and az. four crescents counter-changed.

Framingham (co. Norfolk). Ar. a fesse gu. betw. three Cornish choughs ppr. Crest—A demi Moor, brandishing a scymitar, and therewith attacking a tiger issuing on the sinister side.

Framinghay. Sa. a chev. betw. three crescents erminois.

Framlingham, or Fremlin (Hartlip, co. Kent). Gu. a chev. betw. three close helmets ar. plumed or. Crest—An elephant or, armed gu. gorged with a chaplet vert.

Framlingham. Ar. a fesse gu. betw. three Cornish choughs sa. beaked and legged of the second. Crest— A lion's head erased guard. or, semée of hurts and torteaux.

Framlingham. Ar. a fesse sa. (another, az.) thereon another dancettée of the first (another or).

Frampton (Moreton, temp. Edward III., and Buckland, co. Dorset). Ar. a bend gu. cotised sa. Crest—A greyhound sejant ar. collared gu. ringed or. Motto—Perseverando.

Frampton (Upway, co. Dorset). Sa. three bars ar. in chief as many crescents or.

Frampton, or Framton. Sa. two lions' paws issuing out of the dexter and sinister base points chevronways ar. armed gu.

Frampton. Barry of six ar. and gu. on a chief of the second three crescents or.

Framsham (co. Warwick). Quarterly, ar. and az. four crescents counterchanged.

Framton. Gu. three bars ar. in chief as many crescents or.

Framyngham (co. Suffolk, 1584). Ar. a fesse gu. betw. three Cornish choughs ppr. Crest—A camel's head erased az. bezantée.

France, Kingdom of (ancient). Az. semée-de-lis or.

France, Kingdom of (modern, changed by Charles VI.). Az. three fleurs-de-lis or. Supporters—Two angels. Crest— A fleur-de-lis or.

France (Bostock Hall, co. Chester). Ar. on a mount in base

374

a hurst ppr. on a chief wavy az. three fleurs-de-lis or. Crest —A mount, thereon a hurst as in the arms, from the centre tree a shield pendent gu. charged with a fleur-de-lis or, strap az. Motto—Virtus semper viridis.

France. Ar. on a chief gu. three lions ramp. or. Crest—On a mount vert an ermine ppr.

France (Ystym Colwyn, Oswestry, co. Salop). Ar. on mount in base a hurst ppr. a chief wavy az. charged with three fleurs-de-lis or. Crest—A mount, thereon a hurst as in the arms, from the centre tree a shield pendent gu. charged with a fleur-de-lis or, strap az. Motto—Virtus semper viridis.

Franceis (Lord Mayor of London, 1400). Erm. on a canton sa. a harp ar. Crest—A hand issuing from a cloud seizing a stag by the horns all ppr.

Franceis (Gifford Hall, co. Suffolk). Gu. a chev. engr. erm. betw. three falcons displ. ar. beaked, legged, belled, and jessed or.

Franceis, Fraunceis, or Francis (Foremark, co. Derby, 1360; JANE, dau. and heiress of WILLIAM FRAUNCYS, Esq., of Foremark, m. Sir THOMAS BURDETT, Bart.). Ar. a chev. gu. betw. three eagles displ. sa. Crest—A falcon rising or, in its beak a vine branch fructed ppr.

Franceis (Coxliench, descended from Foremark). Same Arms and Crest.

Frances (co. Somerset). Ar. a chev. engr. betw. three mullets pierced gu.

Frances. Ar. a chev. betw. three eagles displ. gu. Crest— An eagle, wings endorsed or, standing on a branch of grapes reflexed over his head, fructed ppr. leaved vert.

Frances. Ar. a fesse betw. three eagles displ. with two heads gu.

Frances, or Francey. Ar. a chev. betw. three mullets gu. (another, sa.).

Frances (Scotland). Ar. a chev. betw. three eagles displ. az. Crest—The stump of an oak shooting forth a branch from the sinister vert.

Francey. Ar. two chev. betw. three mullets sa.

Franceys. Vert a fesse counterflory of fleurs-de-lis or.

Franch. Ar. a cross triparted sa.

Francham. Gu. three crescents ar. a chief erm.

Franche, or Franke (Bluemantle Pursuivant, temp. Henry VII.). Vert a saltire invecked or.

Franche. Sa. a cross triple-parted and fretted ar. Crest— A griffin segreant ppr. collared and lined or, the end of the line and ring turned off and held in the bill.

Francheville. Ar. on a chev. az. six billets of the field.

Francies. Erm. three bars sa.

Francis (cos. Derby and Essex). Gu. a saltire betw. four crosses formée or.

Francis (Cookmaines, co. Hertford). Ar. on a chev. wavy betw. three eagles displ. gu. as many estoiles of the first. Crest—On the trunk of a vine tree fructed an eagle, wings elevated all ppr.

Francis (co. Derby; granted 4 May, 1577). Per bend or and sa. a lion ramp. counterchanged. Crest—An eagle displ. erm. beaked and membered or.

Francis (co. Derby; Har. MS. 1400). Ar. a chev. betw. three eaglets gu.

Francis (granted, 1806, to Sir PHILIP FRANCIS, K.C.B., M.P. for Appleby, co. Westmoreland, son of Rev. PHILIP FRANCIS, D.D., Trin. Coll., Dublin). Per bend sinister sa. and or, a lion ramp. counterchanged, charged on the shoulder with a shamrock counterchanged of the field. Crest—Out of a ducal coronet or, a demi lion ramp. sa. charged on the shoulder with a shamrock or, holding in the paws a garb of the last.

Francis (granted to THOMAS JOHN FRANCIS, Esq., captain 16th (the Queen's) Regiment of Light Dragoons (Lancers), eldest son and heir of THOMAS FRANCIS, Esq., late of Ghwathodde, co. Glamorgan, and the Mall, Hammersmith, Middlesex). Ar. on a chev. betw. three eagles displ. gu. as many trefoils of the field. Crest—A falcon rising ppr. guttée de sang, in the beak a vine branch fructed also ppr. Motto—Ou le sort, Appelle.

Francis (Quy Hall, co. Cambridge). Per chev. or and vair, in chief two eagles displ. gu. Crest—Upon a mount vert, in front of three ears of wheat or, a dove ar. beaked and membered gu. in the beak a sprig of olive ppr.

Francis (RICHARD FRANCIS, one of the Gentlemen of the Ordnance in Ireland; Fun. Ent. of his wife, 1656). Per bend sa. and or, a lion ramp. counterchanged.

Francis (co. Derby). Per bend az. and ar. a lion ramp. counterchanged.

Francis, or Fraunces (co. Derby; ALICE, dau. and co-heir of Sir JOHN FRANCIS, Knt., wife of WILLIAM STAVELY, Esq., of Bignell, co. Oxford, d. 20 Oct. 1500. Visit. 1574). Ar. a chev. gu. betw. three eagles displ. sa.

Francis (co. Devon, and Combflory, co. Somerset). Ar. a chev. betw. three mullets gu. pierced of the field.

Francis (Colchester, co. Essex). Per fesse az. and or, a lion ramp. counterchanged.

Francis (co. Norfolk). Az. (another, gu.) a saltire betw. four crosses crosslet or.

Francis (co. Stafford). Ar. a chev. betw. three eagles displ. gu. *Crest*—Out of a ducal coronet or, a demi eagle displ. gu.

Francis (Gifford Hall, co. Suffolk). Gu. a chev. erm. betw. three falcons rising ar. legged, beaked, and belled or.

Francis. Gu. a chev. erm. betw. three doves volant ar. *Crest*—A dove, in the beak an olive branch ppr. *Motto*—Insontes ut columbæ.

Francis. Sa. on a bend gu. cotised of the same, three owls or.

Francis (granted to THOMAS JOHN FRANCIS, Esq., Capt. 16th Light Dragoons, eldest son and heir of THOMAS FRANCIS, late of Ghwathodde, co. Glamorgan, and the Mall, Hammersmith, Middlesex). Ar. on a chev. betw. three trefoils slipped as many trefoils of the field. *Crest*—A falcon rising ppr. guttée de sang, in the beak a vine branch fructed also ppr. *Motto* — Ou le sort appelle.

Francis, or Fraunces. Per chev. indented ar. and sa. three cocks, each charged on the neck with a bar gemellée all counterchanged.

Franck. Vert on a saltire engr. or, a lion's head erased gu. *Crest*—Out of a mural coronet or, a lion's head gu. betw. two wings erminois.

Franckcheney (co. Devon). Erm. on a chief gu. three lions ramp. ar.

Francke (Grimsby, co. Lincoln, *temp.* Richard II., and cos. Essex and Sussex). Ar. a bend engr. sa. betw. two Cornish choughs ppr. *Crest*—On a staff raguly fesseways or, a Cornish chough ppr.

Francke (cos. Derby and Lincoln). Vert a saltire engr. or.

Francke (Knighton, co. York). Gu. three hawks close ar. beaked and belled or.

Francke. Or, a bend engr. sa. in the sinister chief a Cornish chough ppr.

Francke. Ar. a bend dancettée sa. betw. two Cornish choughs ppr.

Francke (Fun. Ent. of JOHN FRANCKE, printer, some time Sheriff of Dublin, *d.* Oct. 1620). Sa. a bend dancettée or, betw. two martlets ar.

Francke. Gu. a saltire engr. or, a mullet for diff.

Francklin (Westlington, co. Bucks; GEORGE FRANCKLIN, Sheriff of Bucks, 1729; JOSEPH FRANCKLIN, Sheriff of Bucks, 1803). Ar. on a bend az. three dolphins embowed ppr.

Francklin (Moor Park, co. Herts, bart., extinct 1728; formerly Skipton, co. York). Ar. on a bend az. three dolphins naiant of the field.

Francklin (co. Devon). Az. a bend betw. two dolphins haurient, embowed or.

Francklin (Gonalston, co. Notts, and Great Barford, co. Bedford). Ar. on a bend engr. betw. two lions' heads erased gu. a dolphin haurient betw. two parrots or. *Crest*—A dolphin's head or, erased gu. betw. two olive branches vert. *Motto*—Sinceritate.

Franco (St. Catharine, Colman, London; granted 1760). In a landscape field a fountain, thereout issuing a palm tree all ppr. *Crest*—A dexter arm habited ppr. purfled and diapered or, cuff ar. holding in the hand ppr. a palm branch vert. *Motto*—Sub pace copia.

Francois. Gu. a pale vair. *Crest*—On the stump of a tree, shooting forth branches, a hawk, belled ppr.

Francois. Or, ten crescents gu. on each a hawk's bell ar.

Francois. Erm. three bars sa.

Frandolph, or Frandolfe. Or (another, ar.) two lions pass. in pale gu.

Frank (Alderton, co. Suffolk). Vert a saltire engr. or. *Crest*—A hawk close, belled ppr.

Frank (Boughtridge, Scotland). Vert on a saltire engr. ar. five fleurs-de-lis of the first. *Crest*—A lion saliant, tail forked ppr. *Motto*—Non nobis nati.

Frank (Campsal, co. York; granted to FREDERICK BACON FRANK, Esq.). Per saltire az. and vert on a saltire indented or, a falcon ppr. belled gold. *Crest*—A morion ppr. thereon a falcon also ppr. guttée de larmes and belled or. *Motto*—Esse quam videri.

Franke (co. Leicester; granted 6 Feb. 1689). Az. a bend embattled erm. betw. two dexter arms vambraced ar. garnished or. *Crest*—Out of a mural coronet or, a dexter arm vambraced, as in the arms, holding a falchion ar. hilt and pommel gold.

Frank (Knighton, co. York, 1665, and Campsall, co. York). Vert a saltire engr. or. *Crest*—A falcon ppr.

Franke. Vert a saltire or (another, fusily).

375

Franke (Pomfret). Gu. a lion ar. crowned or.

Frankford De Montmorency, Viscount. See MONTMORENCY.

Frankland (Thirkelby, co. York, bart.). Az. a dolphin naiant embowed or, on a chief of the second two saltires couped gu. *Crest*—A dolphin ar hauriant, and entwined round an anchor erect ppr. *Mottoes* — 1st: Libera terra, liberque animus; 2nd (assumed by the present bart.): A'lo hecho Pecho—What can't be cured must be endured.

Frankland-Russell (Thirkelby, co. York, bart., the seventh bart. assumed the additional name of RUSSELL, and *d. s. p. m.* 1849). Az. a dolphin naiant embowed or, on a chief of the second two saltires couped gu., quartering, RUSSELL, viz., ar. a lion ramp. gu. a chief sa. thereon three roses of the field. *Crests*—1st: A dolphin ar. haurient and entwined round an anchor erect ppr., for FRANKLAND; 2nd; A goat statant ar. gorged with a mural crown, armed and hoofed or, for RUSSELL. *Motto*—Libera terra, liberque animus.

Frankland (from the monumental inscription in Chichester Cathedral, for HENRY FRANKLAND, Vice-Admiral of the Red). Az. a dolphin or, on a chief of the last two saltires couped gu. *Crest*—An anchor erect sa. entwined by a dolphin ar.

Frankland (Rye, co. Hertford; granted 3 March, 1568). Az. a dolphin embowed or, on a chief of the second a bird of the first collared ar. betw. two saltires couped gu. *Crest*—An anchor sa. enfiled with a dolphin ar.

Frankland (co. York). Gu. a dolphin betw. two annulets in pale or, on a chief of the second a martlet sa. betw. two saltires couped of the first.

Frankland (London). Gu. a dolphin naiant ar. on a chief of the second three saltires couped az.

Franklin (Rainham, co. Norfolk). Ar. on a bend betw. two lions' heads erased gu. a dolphin embowed of the field betw. as many martlets close or, collared az. *Crest*—A conger eel's head erect or, erased per fesse gu. betw. two branches vert.

Franklin (late Governor of New Jersey). Same *Arms.* *Crest*—A dolphin's head in pale ar. erased gu. finned or, betw. two branches vert. *Motto*—Pro rege et patria.

Franklyn (co. Kent). Gu. on a bend betw two dolphins or, three lions' heads erased of the first (another, tinctures reversed).

Franklyn (Moore, co. Hertford, and co. Middlesex). Ar. on a bend az. three dolphins of the field. *Crest*—A dolphin embowed ppr. finned gu. pierced through the sides with two fishing spears in saltire or, tied at the top.

Franklin (Sir JOHN FRANKLIN, K.C.B., the Arctic voyager). Same *Arms* &c.

Franklin (Clemenstone, co. Glamorgan, and Baglan House, same co.). Same *Arms*, &c.

Franklyn, or Frankland (Beccles, co. Suffolk). Az. a dolphin embowed ar. a chief or. *Crest*—A dolphin ar. entwined round an anchor erect sa.

Franklin (granted, 1841, to Sir RICHARD FRANKLIN, Mayor of Limerick). Ar. a dolphin naiant in the sea ppr. on a chief gu. a trefoil slipped ar. betw. two saltires couped or. *Crest* —An anchor, the fluke upward in pale, entwined with a dolphin all ppr. *Motto*—Anchora labentibus undis.

Franklyn (co. York). Ar. on a bend engr. betw. three lions' heads erased gu. a dolphin betw. two birds or. *Crest* —A fish's head in pale or, erased gu. betw. two sprigs vert.

Franklyn. Az. on a bend betw. two dolphins embowed or, three lions' heads erased gu. *Crest*—A greyhound's head brown, collared or, betw. two wings ar.

Franklyn. Ar. on a bend betw. three lions' heads erased gu. two dolphins or.

Franklyn. Ar. on a pale gu. a dolphin hauriant of the first betw. two saltires engr. of the second, on a chief az. a lion ramp. of the first betw. two birds or. *Crest*—A hind's head erased or, charged with three pellets betw. two wings expanded vairé or and az.

Franks. Vert on a saltire or, a torteau. *Crest*—On the trunk of a tree a hawk ppr. charged on the breast with a torteau. *Another Crest*—On the stump of a tree ppr. a falcon or.

Franks (Woodhill Hatfield, co. Hertford). Same *Arms* and Crest. *Motto*—Sic vos non vobis.

Franks (Teddington, co. Middlesex). Ar. a bend betw. six lions ramp. sa. *Crest*—A stag's head erased ppr.

Franks (Carrig, co. Cork). Vert on a saltire or, a griffin's head erased gu. in the centre chief point a mullet of the second. *Crest*—Out of a mural crown or, a griffin's head gu. betw. two wings erminois, each charged with a mullet sa. *Motto*—Sic vos non vobis.

Franks (Ballyscaddane, co. Limerick; confirmed to JOHN

Franks, Esq., J.P., D.L.. eldest son of Sir JOHN FRANKS, Knt., Judge of the Supreme Court, Bengal). Same *Arms, Crest*, and *Motto*.

Frankton. Gu. on a chev. or, three mullets sa.

Frannes. Gu. a saltire betw. four crosses crosslet ar.

Fransham. Gu. three crescents ar. a chief erm.

Franshan, Fransham, or Francham. Per pale indented ar. and az. six martlets counterchanged.

Franton. Sa. two lion's paws in chev. ar. issuing from the base.

Fraser (Oliver Castle, co. Peebles; two co-heiresses in 14th century divided the property, who *m*. Sir PATRICK FLEMING, ancestor of the *Earls of Wigton*, and HAY, of Locherworth). Az. five frases ar. two, one, and two.

Fraser (*Lord Lovat*). Quarterly, 1st and 4th, az. three frases ar ; 2nd and 3rd, ar. three antique crowns gu. *Crest* —A buck's head erased ppr. *Supporters*—Two bucks ppr. *Motto*—Je suis prest.

Fraser (Inverallochy and Castle Fraser, co. Aberdeen; descended from a younger son of SIMON, eighth *Lord Lovat ;* on failure of heirs male these estates passed to the second son of the heir female, General ALEXANDER MACKENZIE FRASER, 1803, for whom are recorded the following arms). Quarterly, 1st and 4th, az. a crescent or, betw. three frases ar ; 2nd and 3rd, ar. three antique crowns gu. ; all within a bordure erminois. *Crest*—A stag's head ppr. *Motto*—Je suis prest.

Fraser (Strichen, co. Aberdeen ; descended from a second son of ALEXANDER, sixth *Lord Lovat ;* the representative of this branch became twelfth *Lord Lovat*). Quarterly, as *Lord Lovat*, within a bordure gu. *Crest*—A stag's head couped ppr. *Motto*—Vive ut vivas.

Fraser (Struy, co. Inverness; from a third son of HUGH, fifth *Lord Lovat*). Quarterly, as *Lord Lovat*, within a bordure or. *Crest*—A stag's head couped ppr. attired or. *Motto*— Amicum proba, hostem scito.

Fraser (Eskadale, a cadet of Struy). Quarterly, as *Lord Lovat*, within a bordure indented ar. charged with eight crescents gu. *Crest*—A stag's head erased ppr. attired or, charged with an increscent and a decrescent interlaced ar. *Motto*—Vel pax vel bellum.

Fraser (Belladrum, co. Inverness). Quarterly, as *Lord Lovat*, within a bordure engr. quarterly, ar. and gu. *Crest* —A stag starting ppr. attired or. *Motto*—Virtutis laus actio.

Fraser (Auchnagarne, co. Inverness). As Belladrum, the bordure charged with eight mullets counterchanged. *Crest* —A stag's head erased ppr. attired or, charged with a star of eight rays issuing from a crescent ar. *Motto*—Pace et bello paratus.

Fraser (Fingask). As Belladrum, the bordure charged with eight annulets counterchanged. *Crest*—As Auchnagarne. *Motto*—Ubique paratus.

Fraser (Farraline, co. Inverness). Quarterly, 1st and 4th, az. a bend engr. betw. three frases ar.; 2nd and 3rd, ar. three antique crowns gu. *Crest*—A sword ppr. hilted and pommelled or, and an olive branch also ppr. in saltire. *Motto*—Ready.

Fraser (Leadclune, bart., 1806). Quarterly, as Farraline, and in the 1st and 4th quarters a canton gyronny of eight or and sa. *Crest*—A buck's head erased gu. *Motto*—Je suis prest. *Supporters*—Two stags ppr. armed and unguled or, collared az. and pendent from each collar an escutcheon gyronny of eight or and sa. each supporter resting his foot on an anchor ppr.

Fraser-Tytler (Balnain). See TYTLER.

Fraser (Dr. WILLIAM M'KINNON FRASER, of Bath, 1798) Quarterly, 1st and 4th, az. a bend engr. betw. three frases ar.; 2nd and 3rd, gu. three antique crowns or. *Crest*—A stag's head erased ppr. on its neck the rod of Esculapius or. *Motto*—Je suis prest.

Fraser (Major CHARLES FRASER, brother of the last, 1803). As the last, with a crescent erminois in the centre of the quarters. *Crest*--A stag's head erased ppr. *Motto*—Je suis prest.

Fraser (PHILIP FRASER, Provost of Inverness, descended of FOYERS, 1692). Quarterly, 1st and 4th, az. a fess betw. three frases ar.; 2nd and 3rd, ar. three antique crowns gu. *Crest* A hand pointing upwards with the forefinger ppr. *Motto*— Estote semper parati.

Fraser (Col. AUGUSTUS SIMON FRASER, 1814). Quarterly, as *Lord Lovat*, all within a bordure embattled quarterly, az. and gu. in the centre of the shield pendent from a mural crown or, a representation of the gold cross conferred in testimony of his services at Vittoria, St. Sebastian, Nive, and Toulouse. *Crest*—A buck's head ppr. attired or. *Motto*—Je suis prest.

Fraser (Philorth, co. Aberdeen : before succeeding to the title of *Lord Saltoun*). Quarterly, 1st and 4th, az. three

frases ar., for FRASER; 2nd and 3rd, ar. a lion ramp. gu., for Ross. *Crest*—An ostrich's head, holding a horseshoe ppr. *Motto*—In God is all.

Fraser (*Lord Saltoun*). Quarterly, 1st and 4th, az. three frases ar., for FRASER; 2nd, gu. a lion ramp. ar., for Ross; 3rd, ar. three piles gu., for WISHART. *Crest*—An ostrich holding in his beak a horseshoe ppr. *Supporters*—Two cherubim with wings expanded and vested in long garments . or. *Motto*—In God is all.

Fraser (Fraserfield or Balgownie, co. Aberdeen ; from WILLIAM, second son of WILLIAM FRASER, eleventh *Lord Saltoun ;* now represented by FORBES, of Balgownie, as senior co-heir of line). Quarterly, 1st and 4th, az. three frases ar ; 2nd, or, a lion ramp. debruised by a riband sa., for ABERNETHY; 3rd, gu. a lion ramp. ar., for Ross, all within a bordure az. charged with eight garbs or. *Crest*—An ostrich ppr. holding in his beak a horseshoe az. *Supporters*—Two angels with wings displ. their habits az. fringed or. *Mottoes*—Above the crest: Quam sibi sortem; below the shield : In God is all.

Fraser (Tyrie, co. Aberdeen). Quarterly, 1st and 4th, az. three frases ar. ; 2nd and 3rd, gu. a lion ramp. ar. armed and langued sa. in the centre of the quarters a crescent ar. *Crest* —An ostrich holding in his beak a horseshoe ppr. *Motto*— In God is all.

Fraser (Broadlands, co. Aberdeen). Quarterly, as the last, and with a fleur-de-lis in the centre of the quarters. *Motto* —In God I trust.

Fraser (Findrack, co. Aberdeen, 1864, as representing DURRIS). Quarterly, 1st and 4th grand quarters, az. three frases ar., for FRASER; 2nd grand quarter, counterquartered, 1st, az. three boars' heads couped or, 2nd, or, three lions' heads erased ga., 3rd, or, three crescents within a double tressure flory counterflory gu., 4th, az. three frases ar. all within a bordure nebuly gu., for GORDON, of Invergordon; 3rd grand quarter, counterquartered, 1st and 4th, gu. a boar pass. or, for BAIRD, 2nd, az. a unicorn saliant ar. armed and unguled or, a bordure of the last, charged with eight half thistles ppr. and as many half roses gu. stalked and leaved ppr. conjoined paleways, for KINNOULL, 3rd, ar. three inescutcheons gu., for HAY. *Crest*—A stag's head erased ppr. *Supporters*—Two stags ppr. *Motto*—I am ready.

Fraser (Kirkton, co. Forfar). Quarterly, 1st and 4th, az. three frases ar.; 2nd, gu. a lion ramp. or, all within a bordure indented or. *Crest*—A bunch of strawberries ppr. *Motto*—Nosce teipsum.

Fraser (Hospitalfield, co. Forfar; heir of line of KIRKTON, paternally ALLAN, 1851). The same, with the addition of a canton erm. *Crest*—A talbot's head erased, holding in the mouth a bunch of strawberries ppr. *Motto*—Nosce teipsum.

Fraser (*Lord Fraser* of Muchalls, 1633, dormant or extinct since 1720). Az. three frases ar. *Crest*—A bunch of strawberries ppr. *Supporters*—A falcon and a heron ppr. *Motto* —All my hope is in God.

Fraser (Phopachy, co. Inverness; now represented by FRASER, of Torbreck). Az. three frases ar. within a bordure compony of the second and first. *Crest*—A phœnix ppr. *Motto*—Non extinguar.

Fraser (Ross Herald, 1680). Per pale az. and ar. three frases counterchanged. *Crest*—A winged globe surmounted of an eagle rising ppr. *Motto*—In virtute et fortuna.

Frater. Ar. two bars betw. nine martlets gu. three, three, and three.

Fratinge. Quarterly, gu. and or, a label of three points az.

Fraunceis (Fraunceis Court, co. Devon, *temp*. Edward II., afterwards of Combe Flory, co. Somerset ; one of the co-heirs *m*. PRIDEAUX, whose descendants bore the name of FRAUNCEIS, represented by GWYNN, of Forde Abbey). Ar. a chev. engr. betw. three mullets gu.

Fraunces (ISABEL, dau. and co-heir of JOHN PLESSINGTON grandson of Sir ROBERT PLESSINGTON, Treasurer of the Exchequer, *temp*. Edward III., *m*. Sir JOHN FRAUNCES, Knt., whose dau. and co-heir, ALICE, *m*. ROGER FLOWER, of Whitwell, co. Rutland. Her. Visit. 1618). Ar. a chev. betw. three eagles displ. gu.

Fraunceys (Lord Mayor of London, 1342 and 1355). Gu. a saltire betw. four crosses crosslet or.

Fraunceys (Lord Mayor of London, 1352 and 1353). Per bend sinister or and sa. a lion ramp. counterchanged.

Frauncis. See FRANCEIS.

Fraxines. Gu. a chev. betw three combs ar.

Fraybrough. Or, three human hearts betw. eight crosses crosslet gu.

Fraye. Erm. on a fesse sa. three beehives or. *Crest*—A stag pierced in the side with an arrow all ppr.

Frayle. Or, a fesse gu. on a canton of the second a cinque-foil of the first. *Crest*—A horse ramp. ar.

Fraynes (Reg. Ulster's Office). Barry of four gu. and ar. on a chief erm. a demi lion ramp. of the first.

Frear (London; granted Feb. 1602). Sa. on a chev. ar. betw. three dolphins or, as many castles of the first.

Freaston. Ar. on a chev. betw. three escallops sa. as many bezants.

Frebant (co. Buckingham). Gu. crusily a cross or.

Frebody (East Grinstead, co. Sussex; granted to JOHN FREBODY, of Udimore, co. Sussex, by St. George, Clarenceux, 1634). Gu. a chev. ar. betw. three human hearts or. *Crest*—A leopard sejant reguard. ar.

Freby. Ar. a chev. pierced with a bend gu. on a canton az. a fleur-de-lis or. *Crest*—A castle sa. ports and windows gu.

Freche. Ar. two chev. gu. on a canton az. a fleur-de-lis or.

Frechevile (Stavely, co. Derby). See FRESCHEVILLE.

Freckelton, or Freckleton (co. Huntingdon). Sa. a chev. betw. three covered cups or. *Crest*—A bear's head ar. muzzled or. *Another Crest*—A camel's head couped ar. bridled or.

Freckleton (Fun. Ent. of Sir FERDINANDO FRECKLETON, knighted at Dublin Castle, the coronation day of James I., 1603, d. 27 Feb. 1609). Same *Arms*.

Freckleton (co. Essex). Az. a chev. betw. three covered cups or.

Freckton, or Frekleton (co. Lancaster). Ar. a fleur-de-lis gu. (another, tinctures reversed).

Frederick (Westminster, since of Burwood House, co. Surrey, and Shawford House, co. Hants, bart.). Or, on a chief az. three doves ar. *Crest*—On a chapeau az. turned up erm. a dove as in the arms, in the beak an olive branch ppr. *Motto*—Prudens simplicitas beat.

Frederick (Hampton, co. Middlesex). Same *Arms*, *Crest*, and *Motto*.

Frederick (Sir CHARLES FREDERICK, installed Knight of the Bath, 26 May, 1761). Or, on a chief az. three doves, ppr. *Crest*—On a chapeau gu. turned up erm. a dove, holding in the beak a sprig of laurel all ppr. *Supporters*—Two men armed cap-à-pie, on their heads esquires' helmets with visors close, each man holding in his exterior hand a tilting spear all ppr. and each looking from the arms. *Motto*—Pretium et causa laboris.

Frederick (London). Ar. on a chief az. three martlets of the field.

Free. Vert three horses courant ar. bridled or. *Crest*—A fox's head ppr.

Freebairn (Scotland). Ar. on a chev. gu. betw. three martlets sa. an annulet or. *Crest*—The sun in splendour. *Motto*—Always the same.

Freebody. See FREBODY.

Freekby, or Freshby. Sa. on a bend betw. three leo-pards' faces or, as many oak leaves vert, a canton ar. charged with a cross formée gu.

Freeland (Gretham, co. Hants). Ar. a chev. ermines betw. three mullets gu. *Crest*—A leopard pass. ar. pellettée.

Freeland (Oaklands, co. Sussex). Same *Arms* and *Crest*. *Motto*—Libera terra liberque animus.

Freeland (Cornbrook Park, Manchester; confirmed to ROBERT FREELAND, Esq., of Cornbrook Park, and his descendants, and the descendants of his father, JOHN FREELAND, late of Westermains, co. Dumbarton). Az. a bend chequy or and gu. betw. two bears' heads couped ar. muzzled of the third. *Crest*—A bear's head couped ar. muzzled gu. gorged with a collar counter-compony or, and of the second betw. two mullets az. *Motto*—Res non verba.

Freeling (Ford and Hutchings, co. Sussex, bart.). Per fesse indented or and gu. three unicorn's heads, two and one, erased counterchanged. *Crest*—A unicorn's head erased per pale indented erm. and gu. armed, tufted, and crined or, *Motto*—Nunquam nisi honorificentissime.

Freeling (Bryanstone Square, London). Same *Arms, Crest*, and *Motto* (unicorns' heads couped).

Freeling. Gu. three unicorns' heads couped ar. maned, horned, and tufted or. *Crest*—A unicorn's head, as in the arms.

Freeman-Mitford (Baron Redesdale). See MITFORD.

Freeman (Castle Cor, co. Cork; representative of two ancient Irish families, DEANE, of Terrenure and Cromlin, co. Dublin, and FREEMAN, of Castle Cor). Quarterly, 1st and 4th, gu. three lozenges ar., for FREEMAN; 2nd and 3rd, ar. on a chev. gu. betw. three martlets sa. as many crosses pattée of the field, for DEANE. *Crests*—1st: A demi lion ramp. gu. holding a lozenge in his paws ar., for FREEMAN; 2nd: A tortoise displ., ppr., for DEANE. *Mottoes*—For

377

Freeman: Liber et auda; for DEANE: Ferendo non feriendo.

Freeman (confirmed to GEORGE ST. GEORGE FREEMAN, Esq., of Waterford, mayor of that city, 1873, eldest son of SAMUEL FREEMAN, Esq., of Enniscorthy, co. Wexford). Gu. a civic crown or, betw. three lozenges ar. *Crest*—A demi lion gu. holding betw. his paws a civic crown as in the arms. *Motto*—Nec temere nec timide.

Freeman (London, and Eberton, co. Worcester. Her. Visit.). Az. three lozenges in fesse or. *Crest*—A demi wolf ar. holding betw. his paws a lozenge ar.

Freeman (Battisford, co. Gloucester, and Emlode and Blockley, co. Worcester. Visit. Worcester, 1634). Same *Arms*, a mullet for diff.

Freeman (Springfield, co. Essex). Ar. on a pile az. three lozenges of the field. *Crest*—A demi lion ramp. gu. gorged with three lozenges in fesse ar.

Freeman (Pylewell Park, co. Hants, and Fawley Court, co. Oxford). Quarterly, 1st and 4th, az. three lozenges or, for FREEMAN; 2nd and 3rd, gu. a cave ppr. therefrom issuing a wolf at full speed reguard. ar., for WILLIAMS. *Crests*—1st: A demi lion gu. charged with a lozenge or, for FREEMAN; 2nd: a lion ramp. gorged with a chaplet of oak leaves ppr. crowned with a naval coronet or, for WILLIAMS. *Motto*—Libertas et natale solum.

Freeman (London, cos. York and Wilts). Az. three lozenges or. *Crest*—A demi lion ramp. erased gu. holding a cross flory or.

Freeman (Gaines, co. Hereford). Gu. three lozenges ar. *Crest*—A lion ramp. gu. holding a lozenge in the paws or.

Freeman (Housley, co. York; impaled by MACCLESFIELD, of Maer). Same *Arms*, a crescent for diff.

Freeman (co. Northampton). Az. three lozenges ar.

Freeman (Higham Ferrars, co. Northampton). Same *Arms*. *Crest*—A demi lion ramp. gu. charged with a lozenge ar.

Freeman (co. Northampton). Quarterly, erm. and az. three fusils in fesse or. *Crest*—Out of a ducal coronet az. a boar's head erect ar.

Freeman (Flower, co. Northampton). Erm. three lozenges conjoined in fesse sa. on the middle one a bezant. *Crest*—In a ducal coronet a wolf's head all ppr.

Freeman (Richmond). Az. three fusils or.

Freeman (Stratford-upon-Avon, co. Warwick). Ar. three lozenges sa. *Crest*—A demi lion ramp. holding betw. the paws a lozenge ga.

Freeman (co. York). Az. three lozenges in fesse or, (another, ar.). *Crest*—A demi fox ar. holding a lozenge ar.

Freeman. Same *Arms*, a bordure ar. *Crest*—A demi lion ramp. gu. holding a cross flory or.

Freeman. Gu. three lozenges or. *Crest*—A demi lion ramp. gu. charged with a lozenge or.

Freeman. Vert (another, az.) three fusils in fesse or.

Freeman. Gu. a cross betw. twelve crosses crosslet or.

Freeman. Or, on a chev. per pale ar. and gu. three fleurs-de-lis counterchanged.

Freemasons' Society, use the following *Arms, Crest*, and *Supporters*, viz. : Sa. on a chev. betw. three towers ar. a pair of compasses open chevronwise of the first. *Crest*—A dove ppr. *Supporters*—Two beavers ppr.

Freemasons (Gateshead-on-Tyne, 1671). Same *Arms*. *Crest*—A tower or. *Motto*—The Lord is our trust.

Freer (Stratford-upon-Avon, co. Warwick). Sa. a chev. ar. betw. three dolphins naiant ppr. *Crest*—A dolphin, as in the arms.

Freer (GEORGE FREER, Esq., of Glasgow). Ar. a saltire betw. in chief a mullet and in base a martlet az. *Crest*—A swan ppr. *Motto*—Sine non periculo.

Freer (Rev. RICHARD LANE FREER, Rector of Bishopstone, co. Hereford). Az. a chev. betw. three dolphins naiant ar. *Crest*—Out of a ducal coronet an antelope's head ppr.

Freere, or Fryer (co. Essex, and Charlton, co. Salop). Sa. a chev. betw. three dolphins ar. *Crest*—Out of a ducal coronet a hind's leg all ppr.

Freewood. Ar. on a chev. sa. an escallop of the field.

Freford, or Freeford. Gu. a bend masculy ar. *Crest*—Out of a ducal coronet an eagle's head all ppr.

Freford (co. Cornwall). Gu. five fusils in bend ar.

Freford (co. Leicester). Gu. five mascles in bend ar. in the sinister corner a martlet or.

Freford. Gu. a bend betw. six mascles ar.

Fregusius, or Tregusius (quartered by JAMES STEWARD, of Killymoon, co. Tyrone, 1783). Az. a lion ramp. ar. ducally crowned or.

Frehamton. Ar. on a bend gu. three cinquefoils or.

Freign, De. Erm. two bars gu. in chief a demi lion of the second.

Freigne (Carrig, co. Westmeath, Reg. Ulster's Office). Ar. a bend gu. over all a sinister bendlet or.

Freinde. Gu. a chev. ar. betw. three bucks' heads erm.

Freke (Ewern Courtney, co. Dorset; ROBERT FREKE, Auditor of Treasury, temp. Henry VIII. and Queen Elizabeth). Sa. two bars or, in chief three mullets of the last.

Freke (Hannington, co, Wilts; descended from RALPH FREKE, second son of Sir THOMAS FREKE, Knt., of Ewern Courtney). Same Arms.

Freke (West Bilney, co. Norfolk, bart., extinct 1764; descended from WILLIAM FREKE, third son of ROBERT FREKE, Esq., of Ewern Courtney, co. Dorset, Auditor of the Treasury, temp. Henry VIII. GRACE, sister and heiress of Sir JOHN REDMOND FREKE, bart., m. in 1741, the Hon. JOHN EVANS, second son of GEORGE, Lord Carbery). Same Arms. Crest— A bull's head couped sa. attired, collared, and lined or.

Freke (EVANS-FREKE, Baron Carbery). Quarterly, 1st and 4th, sa. two bars or, in chief three mullets of the last, for FREKE; 2nd and 3rd, ar. three boars' heads couped sa., for EVANS. Crests—1st, FREKE: A bull's head couped at the neck sa. collared and chained or; 2nd, EVANS: A demi lion ramp. reguard. or, holding betw. the paws a boar's head, as in the arms. Supporters—Two lions reguard. or, ducally crowned az. Motto—Libertas.

Freke (HUSSEY-FREKE; exemplified to AMBROSE DENIS HUSSEY-FREKE, Esq., of Hannington Hall, co. Wilts). Quarterly, 1st and 4th, sa. two bars and in chief three mullets or, and for distinction a canton of the last, for FREKE; 2nd and 3rd, barry of six erm. and gu. per pale counterchanged, on a canton of the second a cross patonce ar., for HUSSEY. Crests—1st, FREKE: A bull's head couped sa. collared and chained or, charged for distinction with a cross crosslet gold; 2nd, HUSSEY: A boot sa. spurred or, and turned over erm. surmounted by a heart ppr. supported by two arms embowed in armour, hands gauntleted also ppr.

Frekley. Gu. three bucks' heads cabossed ar.

Frelket. Ar. a crossbow betw. three martlets sa.

Fremantle (Baron Cottesloe). Vert three bars erm. surmounted by a lion ramp. gu. murally crowned or, in chief two plates. Crest—A demi lion gu. issuing out of a mural crown or, holding a banner, quarterly, ar. and vert, the staff gold, and charged on the shoulder with a plate. Supporters—On either side an eagle, wings expanded and inverted sa. Motto— Nec prece nec pretio.

Fremargan. Per pale gu. and az. a lion ramp. or.

Freme (Lippiat, co. Gloucester). Ar. a chev. sa. in chief a bar. engr. gu.

Fremingham. Ar. a fesse sa. betw. three Cornish choughs ppr.

Fremond. Per chev erm. and gu. three fleurs-de-lis or.

Frenband. Gu. a cross betw. twelve crosses crosslet or. Crest—A demi lion gu. holding in the dexter paw a trefoil slipped or.

Frenbingham. Sa. a fesse az.

French (Baron De Freyne). Erm. a chev. sa. Crest—A dolphin embowed ppr. Supporters—Dexter, an ancient Irish warrior habited, supporting with his dexter hand a battle axe head downwards, and bearing on his sinister arm a shield all ppr; sinister, a female figure, vested and scarf flowing ar. all ppr. Motto—Malo mori quam fœdari.

French (confirmed, 1811, to ARTHUR FRENCH, Esq., of Tyrone House, co. Galway). Same Arms and Crest.

French (Monivea Castle, co. Galway). Same Arms and Crest. Motto—Malo mori quam fœdari.

French (Cloonyquin, co. Roscommon). Same Arms and Crest.

French-Brewster. See BREWSTER.

French (Cranfield, co. Essex). Az. a bend or, betw. two dolphins embowed ar. Crest—A crescent per pale ar. and or, betw. the horns a fleur-de-lis counterchanged.

French Merchants' Company (incorporated by Edward IV.). Quarterly, az. and gu. in the 1st and 4th quarters a fleur-de-lis or; in the 2nd and 3rd quarters a lion pass. guard. of the last, over all a cross ar. Crest—A lion ramp. guard. or, supporting an anchor sa. beamed of the first. Supporters—Two dolphins ppr. ducally crowned and finned or.

French (co. Devon). Sa. a bend betw. two dolphins haurient, embowed ar.

French (Stream, co. Sussex). Gu. a bend betw. two dolphins ar.

French (Pershore, co. Worcester. Visit. 1634). Per bend sinister engr. or and sa. a lion ramp. counterchanged. Crest—A fleur-de-lis sa. seeded or.

French (Belturbet, co. Cavan, Ireland; granted in Ireland 26 July, 1682). Per bend sinister engr. or and sa. a lion ramp. betw. two fleurs-de-lis counterchanged. Crest—A fleur-de-lis or, charged with a trefoil vert.

878

French (Cuskinny, co. Cork). Vert three foxes. Crest—A dolphin. Motto—Veritas vincit.

French. Sa. a bend ar. betw. two dolphins naiant or. Crest—In a crescent ar. a fleur-de-lis sa.

French. Per pale sa. and ar. a wolf saliant counterchanged.

French. Ar. two bendlets betw. as many dolphins sa.

French. Per pale sa. and az. a wolf pass. ar.

French (Thornidikes and Frenchland, co. Berwick). Az. a chev. betw. three boars' heads erased or.

French (Bailliestown, co. Lanark). Az. a chev. betw. two boars' heads erased or, in chief, and a bezant in base. Crest— A ship in full sail ppr. Motto—Par commerce.

Frenche. Ar. a fesse engr. gu. in chief a rose of the last.

Frenchefoyle (co. Essex; ALICE FRENCHEFOYLE, heiress, m. John GLASCOTE, or GLASCOKE, temp. Henry III. Visit. Essex, 1614). Sa. a chev. betw. three cinquefoils ar.

Frend (co. Cambridge). Gu. a chev. erm. betw. three bucks' heads cabossed ar.

Frend. Same Arms. Crest—A beacon fired ppr.

Frend. Gu. a chev. betw. three bucks' heads cabossed erm.

Frend (Boskell, co. Limerick). Same Arms. Crest—A buck's head as in the arms. Motto—Aude et prevalibis.

Frend. Or, a chev. betw. three bulls' heads cabossed sa. (another, the bulls' heads gu.).

Frendband (co. Buckingham). Gu. a cross crosslet or.

Frende. Or, a chev. sa. betw. three bulls' heads cabossed gu. armed ar.

Frene (co. Hereford). Bendy of six az. and ar.

Frene. Same Arms. Crest—A physician's quadrangular cap ppr.

Frene (Nene-Sollers, co. Salop, and the Bower, co. Worcester, temp. Edward III.). Or, a lion ramp. gu. a bordure engr. sa.

Frene. Gu. two bars per fesse indented ar. and az.

Frene. Gu. a bend indented per bend indented or and az.

Frene. Gu. three bars vairé ar. and sa.

Freneland. Gu. semée of crosses crosslet a cross or.

Frenes (co. Hereford). Gu. two bends indented or.

Frenes. Bendy of six or and gu. (another, az. and or.).

Frennelly (co. Lancaster). Vert three harts' heads cabossed ar.

Frennes. Per bend az. and ar. two bends engr. counterchanged.

Frenney (Ireland, Reg. Ulster's Office). Or, a fleur-de-lis gu. a bordure of the last.

Frennoy. Gu. three pallets vairé ar. and gu.

Frenny. Or, a fleur-de-lis sa.

Freny, or Frenney. Same Arms, a bordure gu.

Frenye. Erm. four bars gu. in chief a lion ramp. of the last.

Frenye, or Freyne. Erm. two bars gu. in chief a lion ramp. of the second.

Frere (Roydon, co. Norfolk, and Finningham, co. Suffolk). Or, two leopards' faces in pale gu. betw. as many flaunches of the last. Crest—Out of a ducal coronet gu. an antelope's head ar. armed or. Mottoes—Traditum ab antiquis servare; and, Frere ayme frere.

Frere (Rt. Hon. Sir HENRY BARTLE EDWARD FRERE, Bart., G.C.B.). Same Arms, Crest, and Motto.

Frere (Water Eyton, co. Oxford, bart., extinct; WILLIAM FRERE, Esq., of the city of Oxford, J.P. Visit. 1574. FRERE, his son and heir, was created a bart. 1620, but d. s. p.). Or, an ear of barley betw. two bars humettée gu. two flaunches of the second each charged with an ear of barley of the first. Crest—Two arms embowed erect, holding a wheatsheaf.

Frere, Fryer, or Freer (The Blankets, Clains, co. Worcester). Sa. a chev. betw. three dolphins embowed naiant. ar. Crest—Out of a ducal coronet or, an antelope's head ar. armed, crined, and tufted gold.

Frescheville (Lord Frescheville, extinct 1682; Staveley, co. Derby, and cos. Devon and Nottingham, temp. Henry III. Sir RALPH FRESCHEVILLE, Knt., was summoned to Parliament as a Baron, 29 Edward I.; his descendant, JOHN FRESCHE-VILLE, was created Baron Frescheville, of Staveley, in 1664; his lordship left three daus., his co-heirs, CHRISTIAN, m. to CHARLES, Duke of Bolton; ELIZABETH, m. first to PHILIP WARWICK, Esq., and secondly, to CONYERS D'ARCY, second Earl of Holderness; and FRANCES, m. to Col. THOMAS COLE-PEPPER). Az. a bend betw. six escallops ar. Crest—A demi angel issuing from the wreath ppr. crined and winged or, on the head a cross formée of the last, vested ar., and the arms in armour ppr. holding in both hands an arrow in bend gold, feathered and headed also ar. Supporters—Two angels habited as in the crest, each holding an arrow.

Frescheville, or Freshwell. Same Arms. Crest—A gem ring or, stoned gu.

Frese. Erm. on a chev. sa. three withered branches ar.

Fresell, or Fresill. Sa. six roses ar. (another, or) three, two, and one. *Crest*—A hand issuing from the wreath plucking a rose from a bush ppr.

Fresell, or Fresill. Sa. six quatrefoils ar. (another, or) three, two, and one.

Freshfield (Moor Place, Betchworth, and Upper Gatton, co. Surrey). Per bend nebulée or and az. two bendlets betw. six escallops all counterchanged. *Crest*—A demi angel ppr. winged or, vested ar. the arms in chain mail holding a lance in bend point downwards also ppr. charged on the breast with a cross botonnée and on the head a like cross gu. *Motto* —Nobilitatis virtus non stemma character.

Freshford. Gu. a bend fusily ar.

Fresh. Ar. a fesse engr. gu. in chief an annulet sa. *Crest*— Out of a ducal coronet a horse's hind leg erect all ppr.

Fresh. Per pale sa. and az. a wolf saliant ar.

Fresh. Per pale sa. and gu. a leopard pass. ar.

Freshacre. Az. five fishes haurient or, three and two. *Crest*—A savage's head affrontée ducally crowned ppr. vested paly or and gu.

Freshe. Ar. a fesse engr. gu. betw. three annulets sa.

Freshe. Ar. a fesse engr. gu. in chief an annulet of the last.

Freshfield (co. Derby). Az. a bend betw. six escallops ar.

Freshfield. Same *Arms*. *Crest*—On a mount vert a stag lodged per fesse or and gu. attired of the last.

Freshfield (Moor Place, Betchworth, co. Surrey; descended from the ancient baronial family of FRESCHEVILLE). *Arms* and *Crest* as FRESCHVILLE, of Staveley. *Motto*—Nobilitatis virtus non stemma character.

Freshvill. Same *Arms* as FRESCHEVILLE.

Freshwater (Heybridge Hall, co. Essex). Az. a fesse erm. betw. two fishes ar. *Crest*—Two fishes (another, two arrows) in saltire ar. their tails in chief enfiled with a ducal coronet or

Fresill, or Freyshill. Ar. three roses gu.

Freskerell. Per bend ar. and gu. a lion ramp. counterchanged.

Fresley. Gu. three crescents or.

Fresmes. Az. a cross betw. twelve fleurs-de-lis or.

Fresmes, or Fresnes (France). Az. a cross ar. betw. twelve fleurs-de-lis or.

Freson (co. Cornwall). Gu. a bend lozengy ar.

Fressylles. Sa. nine crosses ar. three, three, two, and one.

Freston, or Freeston (Mendham, co. Norfolk). Az. on a fesse or, three leopards' faces gu. *Crest*—A demi greyhound ramp. sa. collared or.

Freston (Warmfield, co. York). Same *Arms*. *Crest*—A demi grayfriar ppr.

Freston (cos. Norfolk and Suffolk). Ar. on a chev. sa. three cinquefoils of the field.

Freston (Menham, co. Suffolk). Az. on a fesse or, three cinquefoils gu.

Freston (co. Suffolk). Ar. a chev. betw. six cinquefoils sa.

Freston (Altofts, co. York). Ar. a fesse dancettée betw. three mullets vert. *Crest*—A talbot's head erased gu. eared ar. the ears charged with three bars sa. gorged with a collar or.

Freston (co. York). Ar. on a fesse indented az. three mullets or.

Freswater (Fun. Ent. Ulster's Office, 1661). Gu. a dexter hand apaumée couped at the wrist betw. three cinquefoils ar.

Fretevile (RALPH FRETEVILE's arms in Brampton Church, co. Oxford. Visit. 1574). Ar. a chev. gu. betw. three Cornish choughs sa. beaked and legged or.

Frethorne. Quarterly, ar. and or, over all a cross engr. gu.

Freton. Ar. a bend gu. *Crest*—A unicorn's head ar. pellettée.

Frevil. Or, on a cross gu. a lozenge ar. betw. four lozenges vair, on the centre one a cross of the second.

Frevile, or Freville (co. Cambridge, and Tamworth Castle, co. Warwick). Gu. three crescents erm.

Frevile. Same *Arms*. *Crest*—Out of a ducal coronet or, an old man's head couped below the shoulders ppr. vested gu. turned back erm. on his head a cap of the third, tasselled gold.

Frevile (co. Worcester; Sir BALDWIN FREVILE; arms from his seal and Roll of Arms, *temp.* Edward II.). Or, on a cross pattée gu. five lozenges vair. *Crest*—Out of a ducal coronet a garb all ppr.

Frevile (Wickenford, co. Worcester; Sir ALEXANDER DE FREVILE, Roll of Arms, *temp.* Edward II.). Or, a cross masculy gu.

Frevile (co. Worcester). Ar. a cross lozengy vair.

Frevile. Or, a cross flory gu. *Crest*—On each side of a chapeau gu. turned up ar. a wing endorsed or.

Frevile. Ar. on a cross gu. betw. four lozenges vairé or and sa. five lozenges of the first, each charged with a cross of the second.

Frevill. Or, a maunch vairé ar. and gu.

Freville (*Baron Freville*, summoned to Parliament 1327, but never afterwards). Or, a cross patonce gu.

Freville (Tamworth, co. Warwick). Ar. on a cross gu. a cross lozengy vair.

Freville (Sir HUGH WILLOUGHBY, Knt., of Willoughby, co. Notts, *temp.* Henry VI., *m.* MARGARET, dau. and co-heir of Sir BALDWIN FREVILLE; she *m.* secondly Sir RICHARD BINGHAM, Chief Justice of the King's Bench. Visit. Notts, 1614). Or, a cross patoncée gu.

Freville. Or, a cross gu. betw. four lozenges vert.

Frewen (Northiam, co. Sussex, and Ilmer, co. Bucks; descended from RICHARD FREWEN, Bailiff of Worcester. Of this family was ACCEPTED FREWEN, Archbishop of York, d. in 1664). Erm. four bars az. a demi lion ramp. issuant in chief. *Crest*—A demi lion ramp. ar. langued and collared gu. bearing in the paws a caltrap az. *Motto*—Mutare non est meum.

Frewen (Brickwall House, Northiam, co. Sussex, and Cold Overton Hall, co. Leicester; a branch of FREWEN, of Northiam). Same *Arms*, *Crest*, &c.

Frewke. Vert a saltire engr. or. *Crest*—A goat's head erased sa. armed and bearded ar.

Frewod. Ar. on a chev. sa. an escallop of the first.

Freyne (co. Kilkenny). Erm. two bars gemelles gu. in chief a demi lion ramp. issuant of the last.

Freynes. Az. three bends embattled counter-embattled or.

Freysell. Sa. six cinquefoils ar. three, two, and one.

Freysell. Ar. six roses gu. three, two, and one.

Freysley. Or, three crescents gu.

Fribourg. Ar. a chev. betw. three demi fleurs-de-lis or. *Crest*—A unicorn's head erased erm. maned and horned or.

Frie. Vert a fleur-de-lis or, betw. three horses ar. bridled of the second.

Frie. Ar. (another, or) three bars vert.

Friend. Gu. a chev. erm. betw. three bucks' heads cabossed ar. *Crest*—A stag's head cabossed ppr.

Frier (St. Martin's, co. Stamford, and Baron, co. Lincoln). Sa. a chev. ar. betw. three dolphins embowed or, a canton erm. *Crest*—Out of a ducal coronet or, an antelope's head ppr.

Frier (Scotland). Az. a chev. betw. three dolphins naiant ar.

Friere. Or, three palets gu. on a canton az. a dart ar. *Crest*—Out of leaves vert five tulips or.

Fris, or Frise. Or, three bars vert.

Friskenny (co. Lincoln). Az. a saltire betw. four crosses crosslet or. *Crest*—A plume of five ostrich feathers, two ar. and three az. wreathed round the middle or and gu. with strings at each end.

Frisknay. Same *Arms* and *Crest*.

Friskney (JOHN FRISKNEY; his dau. *m.* ANTHONY CONNY, whose grandfather, ROBERT CONNY, of Bayonne, in France, came to England with Isabel, Queen of Edward II. Visit. Rutland, 1618). Az. a saltire betw. four crosses crosslet or.

Friskney. Ar. a chev. az. betw. three quatrefoils of the last, stalked and leaved vert.

Frisley, Fryteley, or Frytheby. Ar. three fleurs-de-lis gu.

Fristoke, or Frithelstoke-Priory (co. Devon). Vairé ar. and sa.

Frith (granted by Camden). Az. in chief two garbs in saltire or, in base a sickle fessways ar. handled of the second. *Crest* —Above a grove of trees ppr. the sun in splendour or, beneath clouds ppr.

Frith-Heatley. See HEATLEY.

Frobisher (co. Devon). Erm. on a fesse engr. az. betw. three griffins' heads erased sa. a greyhound courant ar.

Frobisher (Fumingley, co. Nottingham, originally of Doncaster, co. York). Erm. on a fesse engr. betw. three griffins' heads erased sa. a greyhound courant ar. gorged with a collar az. fimbriated or.

Frobyfar (Doncaster, co. York). Erm. on a fesse engr. betw. three griffins' heads erased sa. a talbot ar. collared and lined gu. line twisted into a hank at the end or.

Froddingham (Holderness). Az. a bend betw. six mullets or.

Frodham. Ar. on a cross sa. five lions pass. guard. or. *Crest*—A dexter hand holding a fleur-de-lis.

Frodingham (co. York). Az. a bend ar. betw. six mullets or.

Frodsham (Elton, co. Chester). Ar. on a cross engr. sa. five estoiles or. *Crest*—An escallop ar.

Frodsham, or Frodesham (co. Essex). Or, on a cross engr. sa. five mullets of the first.

Frogenhall (Feversham, co. Kent; depicted on the cloisters of Canterbury Cathedral). Ar. three bars sa.

Frogenhall, or Frognall. Sa. two bars or, a chief ar.

Frogg. Ar. a fesse engr. betw. four annulets sa. two in chief, and as many in base.

Froggat. Quarterly, az. and or, in the 1st and 4th quarters a mullet ar. *Crest*—A parrot feeding on a bunch of cherries ppr.

Froggatt (Fulmer Place). Az. three frogs ppr.

Froghall, or Frognall (co. Kent). Sa. two bars or, a chief ar.

Frogle. Sa. three lions' gambs couped and erect, the claws to the sinister side of the field or, armed gu.

Frogmer (Claynes, co. Worcester). Ar. a griffin segreant betw. three crosses crosslet sa. *Crest*—A demi griffin, wings endorsed ar. holding betw. the claws a cross crosslet sa.

Frogmorton. Gu. on a chev. ar. three bars gemelles sa. *Crest*—A falcon rising ar. jessed and belled or.

Frognall. Per pale az. and purp. a lion ramp. erm.

Frohock (London, and co. Cambridge ; granted 1764). Or, a chev. engr. ermines in base a lion ramp. gu. on a chief vert two garbs of the first. *Crest*—A stag ppr. charged on the shoulder with an estoile ar.

Frohock. Az. on a chev. betw. three leopards' faces or, as many trefoils slipped vert.

Froishe (Lord Mayor of London, 1394). Ar. a fesse engr. gu. in chief an annulet sa.

From. Az. on a fesse betw. three griffins segreant or, a cross crosslet gu. *Crest*—A demi griffin segreant or, holding in the dexter claw a cross crosslet gu.

Fromantrill. Erm. three bars az. a bend gu.

Frome (Kennet, co. Wilts). Ar. six martlets gu. three, two, and one. *Crest*—A greyhound couchant betw. two branches of laurel disposed in orle ppr.

Frome (Puncknoll, co. Dorset; borne by the lord of the manor). Quarterly, 1st and 4th, ar. a fesse betw. three griffins ramp. gu., for FROME; 2nd, quarterly, 1st and 4th, az. a lion ramp. betw. twelve crosses crosslet or, for DE BREWOSA, 2nd and 3rd, gu. two bars ar. in chief three plates, for DE MOELES; 3rd, az. a lion ramp. ar. in a chief three escallops of the second, for CLUTTERBUCK. *Crest*—A cross crosslet az. betw. two wings ar.

Fromond, or Fromount. Ermines a chev. betw. three fleurs-de-lis or. *Crest*—A dexter arm holding up an escallop.

Fromonds (Cheyham, co. Surrey, and Hadlow, co. Kent). Per chev. ermines and gu. a chev. betw. three fleurs-de-lis or. *Crest*—A tiger pass.

Frost (co. York). Ar. a chev. sa. betw. three trefoils slipped vert. *Crest*—An old man's head ppr. betw. two sprigs of laurel vert.

Frost (co. York). Ar. a chev. (another, a fesse) gu. betw. three trefoils slipped az.

Frost. Ar. on a chev. sa. betw. three owls gu. a quatrefoil or.

Frost (co. Suffolk). Ar. a fesse gu. betw. three trefoils az. *Crest*—A trefoil slipped betw. two wings erect az.

Frost (granted to ROBERT FROST, of Lambeth, co. Surrey). Ar. a chev. az. betw. two thistles slipped in chief and a hind's head erased in base ppr. *Crest*—A grey squirrel sejant ppr. semée of estoiles sa. collared and chained or, and holding betw. the paws a hazel branch fructed also ppr.

Frost (granted to the Rev. WILLIAM FROST, of Thorpe, co. Norfolk). Ar. a chev. sa. betw. two pellets, each charged with a trefoil or. *Crest*—A trefoil betw. two wings all az. *Motto*—E terra ad cœlum.

Frost (MEADOWS FROST, Esq., J.P., of St. John's House, co. Chester, and Meadowslea, co. Flint). Erm. three pelicans chevronwise betw. two chevronels gu. the whole betw. three trefoils az. *Crest*—Betw. two wings erm. each charged with a trefoil az. a mount vert, thereon a trefoil also az. *Motto*—E terra germino ad cœlum expando.

Frost (Sir THOMAS GIBBONS FROST, Knt., of Dolcorsllwyn, co. Montgomery). Ar. a pelican vulning betw. three trefoils slipped vert. *Crest*—On a mount vert betw. two wings erect az. each charged with a quatrefoil ar. a trefoil slipped of the second. *Motto*—E terra ad cœlum.

Frothingham (South Frothingham, co. York). Az. a bend ar. betw. six mullets or. *Crest*—A stag trippant ppr. attired gu. (In an ancient seal, the mullets of six points.)

Froud. Az. three lions ramp. or, ducally crowned gu. a bordure erm. *Crest*—A Saracen's head sa betw. two ostrich feathers ar.

380

Froude (Kingston, co. Devon; granted 1765). Vert a chev engr. erm. in chief two garbs or, in base a lion ramp. of the last. *Crest*—A stag reguard. ppr. attired, collared, and unguled or, in the mouth a sprig of oak vert, fructed ppr.

Frowicke (Wyley, co. Herts, and North Mims, co. Middlesex). Az. a chev. betw. three leopards' faces or (another, ar.)

Frowicke (Oldford, co. Surrey). Same *Arms.*

Frowicke (Lord Mayor of London, 1435 and 1444). Same *Arms*, a mullet for diff.

Frowicke (co. Middlesex). Same *Arms.* *Crest*—Two arms embowed vested az. holding a leopard's face or.

Froximore, or Froxmore (cos. Essex and Worcester). Sa. a griffin segreant betw. three crosses crosslet fitchée ar.

Froxmare (co. Essex). Sa. (another, az.) three griffins pass. in pale ar.

Froyle. Sa. three lions' paws erased or. *Crest*—A demi lion per pale gu. and az. collared ar.

Fructuozo (JOHN ANTHONY FRUCTUOZO, Esq., of Langham Place, London, m. 1815, JANE MARIA, eldest dau. of MANUEL ANTONIO NOGUEIRA, of Oporto, in the kingdom of Portugal). Ar. on a fesse wavy betw. three vine leaves vert as many bezants, each charged with a bee volant ppr. *Crest*—On a mount vert, in front of an orange tree fructed ppr. two Thyrsi in saltire also ppr. *Motto*—Fructus per fidem.

Fruen (London). Erm. three bars az. out of the uppermost a lion issuant sa. *Crest*—A demi lion ar. holding in the paws a caltrap az.

Fruiterers, Company of (London). Az. on a mount in base vert, the tree of paradise environed with the serpent betw. Adam and Eve all ppr. *Motto*—Arbor vitæ Christus, fructus per fidem gustamus.

Fry (Witheridge, co. Devon. Visit. 1620). Gu. three horses courant ar.

Fry (Exeter, co. Devon, and Tarrant Gunfold, co. Dorset). Vert three horses courant ar. bridled or. *Crest*—An arm embowed in armour, grasping a sword, enfiled with a Moor's head all ppr.

Fry. Gu. a fleur-de-lis or, betw. three horses courant ar. *Crest*—A demi horse saliant ar.

Fry. Ar. a fesse betw. three beehives sa. the field replenished with bees volant of the second.

Fry. Per pale vert and gu. three horses courant ar. bridled or.

Frye (Yartye, Deer-Parkwood, and Dulcis, co. Devon, *temp.* Edward IV.). Gu. three horses courant ar. *Crest*—A dexter arm embowed in armour, grasping in the hand ppr. a sword of the last, hilt and pommel or.

Frye (St. Winnion, co. Cornwall). Same *Arms* and *Crest.* *Motto*—In rebus arctis.

Fryer (Clan, co. Essex, London, and co. Worcester). Sa. a chev. betw. three dolphins embowed ar. *Crest*—Out of a ducal coronet or, an antelope's head ar. attired, crined, and tufted gold.

Fryer (Chatteris, Isle of Ely, co. Cambridge). Same *Arms* and *Crest.* *Motto*—Jamais arrière.

Fryer (London; granted 10 April, 1572). Same *Arms*, a canton erm. *Crest*—Out of a ducal coronet or, an antelope's head ar. armed, crined, and tufted gold.

Fryer (Lord Mayor of London, 1721). Same *Arms* and *Crest.*

Fryer, Frere, or Frear (London). Sa. on a chev. betw. three dolphins embowed ar. as many towers triple-towered of the first. *Crest*—On a tower sa. a cock or, the tower environed with a serpent ar. darting at the cock.

Fryer (Harleston, co. Norfolk). Or, a crescent betw. two leopards' faces in pale az. betw. as many flaunches gu.

Fryer (Thornes, co. Stafford). Or, two flaunches gu. as many bars humettée of the second, charged with three leaves of the first.

Fryer (the Wergs, co. Stafford, descended from FRYER, of Thornes). Or, semée of oak leaves vert betw. two flaunches az. each charged with a castle ar. *Crest*—A castle ar. entwined by a branch of oak fructed ppr. thereon a cock sa. combed and wattled gu. *Motto*—Mea fides in sapientiâ.

Fryer (Great Bloxwich, co. Stafford). Quarterly, 1st and 4th, same *Arms* as the preceding ; 2nd and 3rd, FLEMING, of the Wergs. See FLEMING, of the Wergs.

Fryer (Fyningham, co. Suffolk). Or, two leopards' faces in pale betw. as many flaunches gu.

Fryer. Az. (another, gu.) a chev. engr. ar. betw. three dolphins or, a canton erm. *Crest*—An heraldic antelope's head erased per fesse ar. and gu. gorged with a ducal coronet or, attired of the second.

Fryer. Ar. a chev. betw. three dolphins sa.

Fryer (co. Clare; Reg. Ulster's Office). Sa. a chev. ar. a canton erm. *Crest*—An heraldic tiger's head couped ar. crined and ducally gorged or.

Fryer (Reg. Ulster's Office, to HEYNALTE FRYER, of the Dublin Mountains). Per pale or and sa. two chevronels counterchanged, in the dexter chief a lion ramp. of the second.

Fryth (Thornes, Shenstone, co. Stafford; granted to THOMAS FRYTH, 1583). Sa. on a chev. embattled betw. three poleaxes or, the blades ar. as many annulets sa.

Fryton. Erm. on a fesse gu. three annulets or. *Crest*— An heraldic tiger's head ducally gorged and chained ppr.

Fryts, or Frys. Ar. three bars vert.

Fucourt, or Fuecourt (France). Ar. fretty gu.

Fuddie (Scotland). Ar. on a fesse betw. two mullets in chief gu. and a dove in base az. a mastiff's head couped of the field.

Fulborne, Fulbaron, or Fulbarron (co. York). Ar. on a fesse sa. three crescents or. *Crest*—Out of an antique coronet or, a demi lion az.

Fulchampe. Per pale gu. and az. six escallops or, three, two, and one.

Fulcher (co. Derby). Erm. on a bend gu. three plates. *Crest*—A demi lion holding an anchor ppr.

Fulcon. Ar. a cross sa.

Fulford (Great Fulford, co. Devon, written Folefort in Domesday Book; this family is one of the most ancient in the west of England). Quarterly, 1st, for FULFORD, gu. a chev. ar.; 2nd, for FITZURSE, ar. a bend betw. three bears' heads erased sa.; 3rd, for MORETON, ar. a chev. betw. three moorcocks sa.; 4th, for BILSTON, or, on a bend gu. three crosses formée ar.; 5th, for BOZOM, gu. three birdbolts ar.; 6th, for St. GEORGE, ar. a lion ramp. gu. a chief az.; 7th, for CANTILUPE, az. three leopards' faces jessant-de-lis or; 8th, for St. ALBYN, erm. on a cross gu. five bezants; 9th, for CHALLONS, gu. two bars and an orle of martlets ar. *Crest*—A bear's head erased sa. muzzled or. *Motto*—Bear up. (The arms, as above given, are cut in stone of an ancient date, and are over a fine gateway of the old mansion).

Fulford (co. Devon, and Pollard, co. Dorset; granted 1623). Sa. a chev. betw. three bears' heads erased ar. muzzled gu. *Crest*—A bear's head erased ar. muzzled sa.

Fulford. Ar. a chev. betw. three fishes' heads erased sa.

Fulham. Ar. a chev. sa. betw. three teazles stalked and leaved ppr. *Crest*—A greyhound's head ppr.

Fulham. Same *Arms*. *Crest*—On a mount vert a lion sejant or, supporting with the dexter foot an escutcheon ar. charged with a teazle, as in the arms.

Fuljames (Woodbrooke, co. Somerset; impaled by Sir JOHN COTTON, as appears from his monument in Minster, co. Cornwall, 1676). Az. a bend betw. six escallops or.

Fulke (*Earl of Anjou*). Gu. three roundlets vair, a chief or.

Fulke (*Talbois, Earl of Anjou*). Gu. two lions pass. guard. or.

Fulkeram, or Fulkroy. Chequy ar. and sa. (another, az.) a chief vairé of the first and gu.

Fulkney. Gu. a cross moline per pale or and erm.

Fulkworth. Ar. on a cross patteé gu. five escallops or. *Crest*—A dexter arm vested erm. in the hand ppr. a sword wavy az. headed or.

Fulkyn. Sa. billetteé ar. on a saltire of the last nine golpes.

Fulkyn, or Fulkin. Ar. on an inescutcheon sa. a crescent of the first, an orle of martlets of the second.

Fullam (Dublin; Reg. Ulster's Office). Ar. a cross sa. betw. four trefoils slipped vert, a border engr. az.

Fullarton (that Ilk, co. Ayr). Ar. three otters' heads erased gu. *Crest*—A camel's head and neck erased ppr. *Supporters*—Two savages wreathed about the head and middle with laurel, each holding in the exterior hand a club resting on the shoulder all ppr. *Motto*—Lux in tenebris.

Fullarton (Dreghorn. co. Edinburgh). Same *Arms*, with a crescent of the last in chief for diff. *Crest*—An otter's head erased gu. *Motto*, as the last.

Fullarton (Craighall, Scotland). Ar. a chev. betw. otters' heads erased gu. *Crest* and *Motto*, as FULLERTON, of that Ilk, co. Ayr.

Fullarton (Greenhill, Scotland). Ar. three otters' heads erased gu. on a chief of the last two croziers in saltire of the first. *Crest*—A camel's head and neck erased of the first. *Motto*—Ad summum emergunt.

Fullarton (Rosemount, Scotland). Ar. a stag's head betw. three otter's heads all erased gu. *Crest*—An otter's head erased gu. *Motto*—Lux in tenebris.

Fullarton (Kilmichael, co. Bute). Ar. a crescent betw. three otters' heads erased gu. *Crest*—A camel's head erased ppr. *Motto*—Lux in tenebris.

Fullarton (that Ilk, co. Forfar). Ar. on a chev. betw. three otters' heads couped gu. a crescent betw. two stars of the first.

Fullarton (Kinnaber, co. Forfar). Ar. on a fesse betw. three otters' heads erased gu. two mullets of the first. *Motto* —Mihi terraque lacusque.

Fullarton. Per fesse wavy or and sa. three tigers' heads couped, counterchanged. *Crest*—A tiger's head couped per fesse wavy or and sa. in the mouth a cinquefoil slipped vert.

Fuller (Hyde House and Germans, co. Bucks). Ar. three bars and a canton gu. *Crest*—On a mount vert a beacon erect fired ppr. *Motto*—Fermiora futura.

Fuller (Tanners Waldren, co. Sussex). Same *Arms*. *Crest* —Out of a ducal coronet gu. a lion's head ar. *Another Crest*—Out of a ducal coronet or, a lion's head ppr. (another, the lion's head gu.; another, or).

Fuller (Isle of Wight). Ar. three bars gu. on a canton of the second a castle or. *Crest*—A dexter arm embowed, vested ar. cuffed sa. holding in the hand ppr. a sword of the first, hilt and pommel or.

Fuller (co. Kerry; confirmed to JAMES FRANKLIN FULLER, Esq., F.S.A., only son of THOMAS HARNETT FULLER, Esq., of Glashnacree, by FRANCES DIANA, his wife, dau. of FRANCIS CHRISTOPHER BLAND, Esq., D.L., of Derriquin Castle, grandson of Captain EDWARD FULLER, of Sackville and Beechmount, by ELIZABETH, his wife, dau. of Rev. JOHN BLENNERHASSET, and great grandson of THOMAS FULLER, Esq., Treasurer of co. Cork, by ANNE, his wife, dau. of JOHN PURCELL, Esq., who was son of WILLIAM FULLER, Esq., of West Kerries, by JANE, his wife, dau. of WILLIAM HARNETT, Esq., of Ballyhenry, all in co. Kerry, in which county this family has been long settled. JOHN FULLER, Esq., of Ballybowler, co. Kerry, forfeited large estates in that county, as appears by the "Desmond Survey," 1583). Ar. three bars gu. on a canton of the second a mullet or. *Crest*—A horse pass. ppr. charged on the shoulder with a mullet or. *Motto*—Fortiter et recte.

Fuller (Dominion of Canada; Right Rev. THOMAS BROCK FULLER, D.D. and D.C.L., Bishop of Niagara, son of Major THOMAS RICHARD FULLER, 41st Regt., a descendant of FULLER, co. Kerry, by MARY ENGLAND, his wife, dau. of Captain ENGLAND, co. Clare). Ar. three bars gu. on a sinister canton of the last a tower or. *Crest*—A martlet ppr. *Motto* —Fidelitas in adversis.

Fuller (Lieut.-General Sir JOSEPH FULLER, G.C.B., *d.* 1841). Ar. three bars gu. on a chief embattled of the last, the representation of a castle with broken walls of the field, on a canton of the last a medal of Talavera or, suspended from a red ribbon with blue edges. *Crest*—Out of a mural coronet or, on a mount vert a beacon erect fired ppr. crossed by two swords in saltire ppr. hilts and pommels or. *Supporters*—On the dexter, a lion, and on the sinister, a horse, both reguard. ar. and murally gorged gu. the horse bridled sa. and the lion chained or. *Motto*—Semper paratus.

Fuller (granted to AUGUSTUS ELIOTT FULLER, Esq., of Rosehill Waldren and Ashdown House, co. Sussex, son and heir of JOHN TRAYTON FULLER, Esq., by ANNE, his wife, only dau. of the gallant defender of Gibraltar, GEORGE AUGUSTUS ELIOTT, *Lord Heathfield*). Quarterly, 1st, ar. three bars and a canton gu., for FULLER; 2nd, ar. on a bend gu. a close helmet ppr.; 3rd, gu. on a bend or, a baton of the first on a chief az. the fortress of Gibraltar ar. under it "Plus ultra"; 4th, ar. betw. two bars sa. the upper charged with a crescent betw. two plates, the lower with another plate, a lion pass. of the second, in chief three stags' heads cabossed, also of the second; 5th, az. fretty or, over all a fesse of the second, for PARKER, of Ratton. *Crests*— 1st: A horse pass. ppr.; 2nd: Out of a ducal coronet gu. a lion's head ar.; 3rd: A dexter hand in armour couped above the wrist, grasping a scimetar, all ppr. the wrist charged with a key sa. *Mottoes*—Over the 1st crest: Currit qui curat; over the 3rd: Fortiter et recte.

Fuller-Elliott-Drake, Bart. See DRAKE.

Fuller-Acland-Hood, Bart. See HOOD.

Fullerton (Thrybergh Park, co. York). Ar. a chev. betw. three otters' heads erased gu. *Crest*—A camel's head erased ppr. *Motto*—Lux in tenebris.

Fullerton (borne by GEORGE ALEXANDER DOWNING, Esq., of Ballintoy Castle, co. Antrim, and of Westwood, co. Hants, who assumed the surname and arms of FULLERTON, in lieu of his patronymic, DOWNING, having inherited estates from his great uncle, ALEXANDER FULLERTON, Esq., of Ballintoy Castle, descended from FERGUS FULLARTON, of Scotch ancestry, who settled in Ireland *temp.* James I.). Ar. three otters' heads erased gu. quartering DOWNING. *Crest*—A camel's head and neck erased ppr. *Motto* — Lux in tenebris.

Fulleshurst (Edlaston, co. Chester). Gu. fretty or, on a chief ar. two mullets pierced sa.

Fullford. Ar. a chev. betw. three millrinds sa.

381

Fulljames (Hasfield Court, co. Gloucester; descended from the family of FOLJAMBE, or FOLJAMBE, of Walton, co. Derby). Az. a bend betw. six escallops or. *Crest*—A stag, quarterly or and sa. attired gold and ar.

Fullumb. Ar. on a chev. sa. three crescents or.

Fullwood (Middleton, co. Derby, cos. Stafford and Warwick: confirmed 1579). Gu. a chev. betw. three mullets ar. *Crest* —A stag ppr. holding in the mouth an acorn branch vert, fructed or. *Another Crest*—A demi stag or.

Fullwood (co. Salop). Ar. three leopards' faces sa. in chief a lion pass. gu.

Fullwood. Gu. a chev. betw. three mullets or. *Crest*—A demi man in armour ppr. grasping a broken tilting spear or.

Fullwood. Gu. a chev. betw. three mullets pierced ar. a ':rdure or.

Fulmerston (granted to RICHARD FULMERSTON, of Thetford, co. Norfolk, by Dethick, 15 July, 2 and 3 Philip and Mary). Or, on a fesse betw. three sea-mewes az. a rose betw. two garbs of the first. *Crest*—A goat's head erased az. platée, horned and bearded or, in the mouth a branch of eglantine vert flowered ar.

Fulmerston (Lopham and Ormesby, co. Norfolk). Or, on a fesse betw. three doves az. a rose betw. two garbs of the first.

Fulmerston, or Fulmeston (Sir RICHARD FULMESTON, *temp.* Elizabeth). Same *Arms*. *Crest*—An heraldic antelope's head erased gu. platée armed or, holding in the mouth a branch with roses ppr.

Fulmerton. Or, on a chev. engr. betw. three doves az. as many fleurs-de-lis of the first.

Fulnetby, or Fulnesby (co. Lincoln, and Glenford, co. Suffolk). Gu. three crescents ar. a chief erm.

Fulrich. Ar. three Moors' heads erased sa. wreathed or and az. *Crest*—A tower, from the top thereof a plume of five ostrich feathers ppr.

Fulshurst (Crewe, co. Chester, *temp.* Edward III.). Erm. on a fesse gu. a fret or.

Fulsherst. Gu. a fret and chief or (another, the chief erm.).

Fulsherst. Gu. a fret or, on a chief ar. three mullets of six points sa.

Fulthorp (Tunstall, co. Durham). Ar. a cross moline sa. *Crest*—An eagle displ. ar. charged on the breast with a cross moline sa. *Another Crest*—A horse pass. az. bridled or.

Fulthorp. Sa. semée of annulets or, a lion ramp. ar.

Fulthorp. Erm. three fleurs-de-lis and a bordure engr. gu.

Fulthorpe. Sa. a lion saliant within an orle of annulets ar.

Fulthorpe. Ar. an inescutcheon sa.

Fulthurst (co. Chester). Or, a fretty gu. on a chief of the last three mullets of the first.

Fulton (exemplified to JOHN WILLIAMSON FULTON, of Braidujle House, Lisburn, co. Antrim, J.P., son of JOHN WILLIAMSON FULTON, Esq., by ANNE, his wife, dau. and co-heiress of ROBERT ROBERTSON, Esq.). Quarterly, 1st and 4th, ar. a lion ramp. az. a bend gobony erm. and gu. in the sinister chief point a mullet sa., for FULTON; 2nd and 3rd, gu. three wolves' heads erased ar. in the centre chief point a crescent or, a bordure engr. of the second, for ROBERTSON. *Crest*— A cubit arm erect grasping a broken javelin all ppr. the arm charged with a mullet sa. *Motto*—Vi et virtute.

Fulton (Inchinnan, co. Renfrew). Az. diapré or, semée of fleurs-de-lis of the second, on a fesse ar. a boar's head erased of the first. *Crest*—On a mount vert a stag lodged reguard. ppr. *Motto*—Quæ fecimus ipsi.

Fulton. Or, a lion ramp. az.

Fulton. Ar. (another, or) a lion ramp. az. a bend gobonated ar. and gu.

Fulton (Wimple Street, London, 1841). Ar. a lion ramp. az. a bend gobony erm. and gu.

Fulnetby. Sa. a chev. betw. three crescents ar. a chief erm.

Fulwar (Ringrone, co. Cork; granted 26 Feb. 1635, by Preston, Ulster, to Rev. THOMAS FULWAR, D.D., Chancellor of the Cathedral of St. Finbars, who was *b.* at Stebbing, co. Essex). Ar. three bars gu. on a canton of the second a book or. *Crest*—A pillar ar. crowned and based or, thereon a book gu.

Fulwer (London). Ar. three bars gu. a canton of the last. *Crest*—On a mount vert a beacon ar. fired ppr.

Fulwer (Tanbridge Court, co. Surrey). See FULLER.

Fulwer, or Fuller (co. Hants. Visit. 1634). Ar. three bars gu. on a canton of the last a tower or. *Crest*—A dexter arm embowed in armour sa. garnished, and holding in the gauntlet a sword ar. pommel and hilt or.

Fulwood (co. Lancaster, Middleton, co. Derby, Holborn, co.
382

Middlesex, Hemington, co. Leicester, and co. Hants). **Gu. a** chev. betw. three mullets pierced ar. *Crest*—A buck tripping, in the mouth an oakslip all ppr.

Fulwood (Foordehall, co. Warwick, Har. MSS. 6060). Ar. a chev. sa. betw. three mullets gu. pierced of the field.

Fulwood (Tamworth, co. Warwick, Har. MSS. 6060). **Az. a** fess or, three crescents ar.

Fulwood (confirmed to ROBERT FULWOOD, of Tamworth, twelfth in descent from ROBERT DE FULWOOD, of Sidenhall, also to ROBERT FULWOOD, of Alne, all in co. Warwick). Gu. a chev. betw. three mullets pierced or (another, ar.). *Crest*—A demi knight in armour ar. holding in the dexter hand a broken tilting spear or, in the helmet four feathers of the first and gu.

Fundin. Or, four bendlets gu.

Funeaux. Per chev. erm. and gu. in base a golden fleece. *Crest*—An arm from the elbow in armour holding up a caltrap ppr.

Funston (Wymondham). Ar. five crosses pattée in saltire gu.

Furbusher. Ar. a chev. sa. fretty or, betw. three gillyflowers ppr. *Crest*—Out of a ducal coronet gu. a griffin's head ar.

Furbusher. Erm. on a fesse engr. betw. three griffins' heads erased sa. each charged with an escallop or, a lion pass. ar. collared gu. lined and ringed gold. *Crest*—A unicorn's head erased az. armed ar. and ducally gorged or.

Furches. Gu. a lion ramp. ar. crowned or.

Furfar. Gu. three water bougets ar.

Furlong (Davidstown, co. Wexford; MATHEW FURLONG, of that place at Visit. 1618, fourth in descent from JOHN FURLONG, of the Barony of Forth, in same co.). Ar. on a mount in base vert an oak tree fructed ppr. in front thereof a boar pass. or.

Furlong. Ar. two bars betw. eight martlets sa. *Crest*—An eagle's head erased ppr. *Motto*—Liberalitas.

Furnace, or Furnese (Sandwich, co. Kent). Ar. a talbot sejant sa. a bordure of the last. *Crest*—A talbot sejant sa.

Furneaulx (Paignton and Buckfastleigh, co. Devon). Gu. a bend betw. six cross crosslets or. *Crest*—Round the stem of a tree erased at both ends in pale two serpents entwined all ppr.

Furneaux. Sa. a pale lozengy ar.

Furnes-Abbey (co. Lancaster). Sa. on a pale ar. a crozier of the first (another coat, sa. a bend compony ar. and az.).

Furnese, Furnes, and Furness. Ar. a talbot sejant sa. in chief three crescents gu. *Crest*—Out of a ducal coronet a lion's paw holding a lance all ppr.

Furnese (Waldershare, co. Kent, bart., extinct 1735. Alderman Sir HENRY FURNESE purchased the manor *temp.* William III., and was created a bart. 1707). Ar. a talbot sejant sa. a border of the last.

Furneus. Or, a label of three points az. a border indented gu.

Furneux. Gu. a bend betw. six martlets or.

Furney (Perristone, co. Hereford; seated there upwards of three hundred years. The heiress of JOHN FURNEY, Esq., of that place, *m.* in 1758, JOHN STRATFORD COLLINS, Esq., of Wythall Walford, co. Hereford, High Sheriff co. Hereford 1773). Ar. a fesse az. betw. three lions' heads erased gu. *Crest*—A lion's head erased gu.

Furnival (*Baron Furnival*, summoned to Parliament 1295, passed to the house of TALBOT, *Earls of Shrewsbury*, 1409, afterwards to the house of HOWARD, *Dukes of Norfolk*, in abeyance since 1777). Ar. a bend betw. six mascles gu.

Furnivall (co. Hertford, *temp.* Henry III.) Ar. a bend betw. six martlets gu.

Furnivall (co. York). Ar. three martlets gu.

Furnivall, or Furnival. Same *Arms*. *Crest*—An anchor with a cable and sword in saltire ppr.

Furnival (Blaysdon, co. Gloucester; Rev. WILLIAM BLACK, son of PATRICK BLACK, Esq., co. Perth, by EDITH, his wife, eldest co-heiress of PETER FURNIVAL, of Liverpool). Ar. on a chev. betw. three martlets' heads erased gu. as many mullets of the first.

Furnivall. Or, a bend betw. six martlets gu.

Furriers, Company of (Edinburgh). Erm. on a chief gu. three imperial crowns ppr.

Furrington. Sa. three unicorns in pale courant ar. armed or.

Fursdon (Fursdon, co. Devon, *temp.* Henry III. GEORGE FURSDON, of that place, at Visit. 1620, descended from WALTER FURSDON, of same place, *temp.* Edward I.). Az. a chev. az. betw. three fireballs sa. fired ppr. *Crest*—Out of a ducal coronet a plume of five feathers all ppr.

Furse (Furse, co. Devon, *temp.* Richard I., afterwards of

Halsdon in the same county). Gu. a chev. embattled counter-embattled betw. **six** halberts in pairs saltireways or. *Crest*—A tower ppr. *Motto*—Ne desit virtus.

Furse (Crokenwell, or Crediton, co. Devon; THOMAS FURSE, of that place. Visit. 1620. Descended from THOMAS FURSE and ALICE, his wife, *temp.* Edward III.). Same *Arms*.

Furse. Same *Arms*, a fleur-de-lis for diff. *Crest*—A lion sejant affrontée, holding in the dexter paw a dagger.

Furser, or Furzer. Gu. three mullets in chief ar. *Crest*—On a mount a stag lodged all ppr.

Fursland (Bekington and Kingstanton, co. Devon; JOHN FURSLAND, of the former place, aged 30. Visit. 1620). Or, a lion ramp. sa. betw. three crosses pattée fitchée gu.

Fursland. Same *Arms*. *Crest*—A savage's head affrontée couped at the shoulder ppr. vested paly of six sa. and ar.

Furtho (Furtho, co. Northampton). Gu. a lion ramp. ar. crowned or.

Fury (Westminster). Az. a bend in chief a mullet of six points or, issuing from the base three piles wavy of the last. *Crest*—A demi lion ramp. grasping a thunderbolt or.

Fuskenry. Gu. a cross moline per pale or and erm.

Fuskney. Gu. a cross sarcelly per pale ar. and erm.

Fusswell. Ar. a cross moline gu.

Fust (Hill Court, co. Gloucester, bart., extinct 1779). **Ar. on** a chev. betw. three forest bills' heads dimidiated per pale sa. as many mullets pierced of the first. *Crest*—A horse in full speed ar. *Motto*—Terrena per vices sunt aliena.

Fust (Sir HERBERT JENNER-FUST, Knt., of Chiselhurst, co. Kent). Quarterly, 1st and 4th, ar. on a chev. betw. three woodbills erect sa. as many mullets pierced of the field, for FUST; 2nd and 3rd, az. two swords erect chevronways, points meeting ar. pommels and hilts or, betw. three covered cups of the last, for JENNER. *Crest*—A horse courant ar.

utroye (Woodbridge House, co. Surrey). Erm. three elephants' trunks sa. on a chief engr. gu. a boar pass. betw. two fleurs-de-lis or. *Crest*—Two elephants' trunks issuing from the wreath sa. *Motto*—Tod (*i.e.*, Death).

Futter (co. Norfolk, and Stainton, co. Suffolk). Sa. betw. two flaunches or, as many swans in pale ppr. membered and beaked of the second. *Crest*—A goat's head erased or, attired sa. holding in the mouth a holly branch vert, fructed gu.

Fyan (Fun. Ent. of NICHOLAS FYAN, of Dublin, merchant, *d.* Oct. 1605). Per fess sa. and erm. on a chev. or, three trefoils slipped gu. in chief three covered cups of the third.

Fydell (Morcott, co. Rutland). Ar. two bars gemelles az. in chief an anchor sa. betw. two martlets respecting each other vert, and in base a lion pass. guard. gu. *Crest*—Issuing out of the rays of the sun gu. a demi lion ar. gorged with a collar flory counterflory, holding betw. the paws an escutcheon or, charged with an anchor sa. *Motto*—Esto fidelis, usque ad finem.

Fydell. Same *Arms*. *Crest*—A hind's head couped per chev sa. and erm.

Fydelow. Ar. three roses gu.

Fyers. Az. a cross ar. fretty gu. *Crest*—A goat pass. holding in the mouth a bunch of ivy.

Fyfe-Butler (Wedacre, co. Lancaster, 1664). Quarterly, 1st and 4th, or, a lion ramp. gu. on a chief of the second a crescent betw. two mullets of the first, for FYFE; 2nd and 3rd, az. a chev. betw. three covered cups or, for BUTLER. *Crest*—An eagle's head erased ppr.

Fyffe (Dron, co. Perth). Ar. a lion ramp. gu. on a chief of the last a crescent betw. two stars of the first. *Crest*—A demi lion ramp. gu. *Motto*—Decens et honestum.

Fyffe (JOHN FYFFE, Capt. R.N., 1816). Or, a lion ramp. gu. navally crowned az. holding betw. the paws a trident sa. *Crest*—Issuing out of a naval crown or, the rim encircled with a branch of laurel ppr. a demi lion gu. supporting in the dexter paw a sword erect ppr. pommel and hilt gold. *Motto*—Virtute et opera.

Fyfield. Quarterly, ar. and vert three acorns slipped counter-changed.

Fyfield (Har. MS. 1412). Erm. on a chief gu. two lions' heads affrontée or.

Fyler (descended from Rev. SAMUEL FYLER, M.A., Rector of Stockdon, co. Wilts, *b.* in 1629). Sa. three cinquefoils betw. nine crosses crosslet or. *Crest*—A dexter arm vested az. cuffed or, the hand ppr. holding a cross flory gold. *Motto*—Volonté de Dieu.

Fyler, or Philer (Heffleton, co. Dorset, and Woodlands, co. Surrey; descended from SAMUEL FYLER, Esq., of Dover Street, London, and of Twickenham, co. Middlesex, barrister-at-law, by MARY, his wife, dau. and sole heir of JOHN I'ANSON, Esq., and niece of Sir THOMAS BANKES I'ANSON, Bart., of Corfe Castle). Quarterly, 1st and 4th, sa. three cinquefoils **betw. nine** crosses crosslet **ar.**, for FYLER; 2nd and 3rd,

quarterly, az. **and** gu. a cross patonce and a chief or, for I'ANSON. *Crest*—A porcupine ppr. *Motto*—Volonté de Dieu.

Fylkin (Tattenhall, co. Chester). Ar. an inescutcheon within an orle of ten billets sa.

Fylkin. Or, on a saltire betw. twelve billets sa. nine plates. faces or.

Fylingley. Sa. a chev. engr. ar. betw. three leopard's faces or.

Fylkyn. Ar. within an orle a crescent sa. nine billets in orle of the second. *Crest*—A demi greyhound betw. two wings.

Fylloll. Vair a canton gu. *Crest*—A unicorn's head erased sa.

Fylloll. Or, on a fesse betw. two chev. gu. three trefoils slipped ar.

Fylsheal (co. Dorset). Or, an eagle displ. az.

Fyn. Gu. a swan pass. ppr.

Fynbaron. Ar. a fesse gu. betw. three bears pass. sa.

Fynbarow. Ar. on a fesse gu. betw. three mullets az. as many plates, each charged with a bear pass. sa.

Fynchfield. Ar. a fesse nebulée betw. four cotises gu.

Fynderne (Fynderne, co. Derby, a very ancient Derbyshire house, whose heiress *m.* HARPUR. See *Vicissitudes of Families*). Ar. a chev. (another, engr.) betw. three crosses formée fitchée sa. *Crest*—An ox yoke or.

Fynderne (Nuneaton, co. Warwick). Same *Arms*. *Crest*—An ox yoke or, chain pendent gu.

Fynes, or Fyneaux. Az. three lions ramp. or. *Crest*—A peacock's head erased az. crested or.

Fynes. Ar. a lion ramp. sa.

Fyneux (from a brass in Herne Church). Vert a chev. betw. three eagles displ. or. *Crest*—An eagle's head erased or, ducally crowned gu.

Fynmore, or Finmore. Ar. three mallets vert. *Crest*—A unicorn sejant, resting the dexter paw on a tree ppr.

Fynmore, or Finmore (North Hincksey, co. Berks). Erm. two chev. gu. *Crest*—A bull's head ar. couped sa. charged with two chev. gu.

Fynnee. Gu. a chev. betw. three martlets or.

Fynney (Fynney, co. Stafford). Vert a chev. betw. three eagles displ. or, armed and langued gu. *Crest*—A staff raguly or. *Motto*—Fortem posce animum.

Fynte. Gu. on a chev. betw. three martlets or, as many mullets sa. on a chief of the second three mascles of the first. *Crest*—A basilisk or.

Fynyng (Fun. Ent. of WILLIAM FYNYNG, of London, *d.* at Dublin, 4 Feb. 1611). Or, a griffin sejant sa. a border az.

Fyres. Ar. on a chev. gu. betw. two bombs sa. fired ppr. in chief, in base a salamander in flames also ppr. a portcullis with chains pendent betw. two falcons affrontée, belled or. *Crest*—A dexter hand holding a salamander in flames, head to the dexter all ppr. *Motto*—Ardet virtus non urit.

Fyshar (JOHN FYSHAR, Bishop of Rochester, 1515). Az. a dolphin embowed betw. three ears of wheat or.

Fyshe (co. Hertford, and Studshaw, co. Suffolk; confirmed 16 Nov. 1633). Chequy or and gu. on a pale sa. three mullets pierced of the first. *Crest*—A triangle ar. voided and sur-mounted on the top with an estoile or.

Fysher. (co. Bedford). Or, a kingfisher close gu.

Fysher (London, 1607). Same *Arms*, a mullet gu. for diff. *Crest*—A kingfisher ppr.

Fysher (Lydhamwicke, co. Wilts; granted 10 Oct. 1608). Ar. on a chev. cotised betw. three demi lions ramp. guard. gu. as many bezants. *Crest*—A demi lion ramp. guard. gu. holding a gauntlet ar.

Fyske (Studham and Hardings, co. Suffolk). Chequy ar. and gu. on a pale sa. three mullets or.

Fyske. Same *Arms*. *Crest*—On a chapeau a martlet all ppr.

Fytche (Eltham, co. Kent, bart., extinct 1736, descended from co. Essex). Vert. a chev. betw. three leopards' faces or.

Fyton. Az. three cinquefoils betw. nine crosses crosslet fitchée ar. three, three, two, and one.

Fyton. Erm. three annulets conjoined gu.

Fytton. Az. semée of crosses crosslet fitchée ar. three cinquefoils of the last.

Fytton (co. Chester). Ar. on a bend az. three garbs or, a canton gu.

G

GABB (Abergavenny, co. Monmouth). Barry of six or and and az. an inescutcheon ar. on a chief of the second a pile of the first charged with three pales also of the second. *Crest*—Out of a ducal coronet a harpy, wings expanded and ducally gorged all ppr. *Motto*—Nullius in verba.

Gabb (Shire Newton, co. Monmouth; descended from John Gabb, Esq., who was resident in co. Monmouth, *temp.* Queen Elizabeth). Quarterly, 1st and 4th, same *Arms*; 2nd and 3rd, ar. two chev. sa., for Ashe, being maternally descended from D'Esse, D'Essecourt, or Ashe, a family which was established in England at the Conquest, and from which derived the Ashes, of Clyst, Fornyson, Heytesbury, Freshfield, Langley, &c. Same *Crest* and *Motto.*

Gabb. Az. two swords in saltire, points upward ar. pommels and hilts or. *Crest*—A griffin's head betw. two wings holding in the beak a branch of palm all ppr.

Gabell (Winchester). Or, ten billets sa. four, three, two, and cne. *Crest*—A boar's head couped or.

Gabell. Ar. a chev. and chief vert. *Crest*—A savage wreathed about the middle, treading on a serpent all ppr.

Gabot (Acton Burnell, co. Salop; Robert Gabot, of that place, "had this banner given him by Maximilian, the Emperor, for his service." Visit. London, 1568). Gu. a griffin segreant or, holding in the claws a flag staff bendy ar. and sa. on it a flag of the third charged with a double-headed eagle displ. of the second.

Gabot. Ar. a chev. betw. three boars' heads couped sa.

Gabott (London, 1625). Same *Arms* as Gabot, of Acton Burnell.

Gabourel (Jersey). Ar. an anchor erect az. on a chief of the last three roses of the field. *Crest*—A greyhound's head couped ar. collared and chained or.

Gabriel, or Gabryell. Or, ten billets sa. four, three, two, and one. *Crest*—A demi savage reguard. ppr.

Gabriel (Edgcombe Hall, co. Surrey, bart.). Sa. on a pile or, ten billets, four, three, two, and one of the field. *Crest*—On a mount vert a boar's head erased sa. billetty or. *Motto* —In prosperis time in adversis spera.

Gace (London; granted 15 Oct. 1649). Gu. three swords in bend ar. hilts and pommels or, points upward. *Crest*—An arm embowed in armour ppr. grasping a broken falchion ar. hilt and pommel or.

Gacton. Or, ten billets gu. on a fesse az. three escallops ar.

Gadbery. Gu. a cross or, betw. four goats' heads erased ar.

Gaddes, or Gaddez. Ar. three gads sa. *Crest*—A stag's head ppr.

Gaddesden, or Gadesden (co. Hertford). Ar. two palets sa. in chief three mullets of the second. *Crest*—A wivern ppr. *Motto*—Decrevi.

Gaddy, or Gaddez (London). Ar. three billets sa.

Gadge (co. Kent). Per saltire az. and ar. a saltire gu.

Gadsby. Sa. a chev. erm. betw. three pheons ar. *Crest*— A stag pass. ar.

Gaff. Gu. on a chev. ar. three cinquefoils vert. *Crest*—A demi antelope or, collared gu.

Gaffard. Or, a cross lozengy sa.

Gage (*Viscount Gage*). Quarterly, 1st and 4th, gyronny of four az. and ar. a saltire gu., for Gage; 2nd and 3rd, az. the sun in splendour or, for St. Clere. *Crest*—A ram pass. ar. armed and unguled or. *Supporters*—Two greyhounds tenné each gorged with a coronet composed of fleurs-de-lis or. *Motto*—Courage sans peur.

Gage (Hengrave, co. Suffolk; Edward Gage, third, but second surviving son of Sir John Gage, first bart. of Firle, ancestor of the *Viscounts Gage*, was created a bart. 1662). Same *Arms* and *Crest* as *Viscount Gage*, without the quartering of St. Clere.

Gage (Rokewode-Gage, bart., dormant since 1867; Sir Thomas Gage, eighth bart. of Hengrave, and Sir Edward Gage, ninth bart. of Hengrave, both assumed the additional name and arms of Rokewode, but both *d. s. p.*). Quarterly, 1st and 4th, gyronny of four az. and ar. a saltire gu., for Gage; 2nd and 3rd, ar. six chessrooks, three, two, and one sa., for Rokewode. *Crests*—A ram pass. ar. armed or, for Gage; A chessrook sa. winged ar., for Rokewode. *Mottoes* —Over crests, 1st: Bon temps viendra; 2nd: Tout est Dieu.

Gage (Rands, co. Northampton, and co. Kent). Same *Arms* and *Crest* as Gage, bart. of Hengrave.

Gage (co. Devon). Or, on a fesse sa. five lozenges ar. (another, betw. three escallops sa.)

Gage (Hormead, co. Hertford). Per pale az. and gu. a saltire ar. *Crest*—A stag pass. ppr.

Gage (cos. Kent and Surrey). Quarterly, az. and ar. over all a saltire gu.

Gage. Per saltire ar. and gu. a cross or.

Gage. Gyronny of four ar. and az.

Gageworth, or Gagworth. Erm. on a chev. gu. three bezants.

Gahn (Sweden, 1781). Ar. a cross sa. in dexter chief point a lion ramp. of the last. *Crest*—A stag's head erased ppr. *Motto*—Si je puis.

Gaidon. See Geyton.

Gailie. Az. a cross moline lozengy pierced ar. *Crest*· Out of a mural crown a garb, thereon a bird all ppr.

Gaimes. Or, a bend cotised gu.

Gaine. Ar. two bars dancettée gu. *Crest*—A demi lion ramp.

Gaines. Barry of six vair and gu.

Gainsborough (Crowhurst, co. Surrey). Az. three chev. ar. a canton erm. *Crest*—A griffin's head erased az. charged with three chev. ar.

Gainsborough, Earl of. See Noel.

Gainsby. Gu. a fesse dancettée betw. six crosslets or. *Crest*—A sprig of laurel growing out of a mount vert.

Gainsford (Idbury, co. Oxford, and co. Kent). Ar. a chev. gu. betw. three greyhounds in full course sa. *Crest*—A demi woman, vested and crined or, in the dexter hand a chaplet vert, in the sinister a rose ppr.

Gair (Nigg, co. Ross). Ar. a fleur-de-lis sa. on a chief of the last a mullet of the first. *Motto*—Sero sed serio.

Gair (Capt. William Gair, 2nd regt.). Same *Arms*, the chief engr. *Crest*—A lion ramp. guard. gu. holding in his dexter paw an ox yoke ppr. Same *Motto.*

Gairdner (Scotland, 1761). Ar. on a fret of four pieces gu. as many hearts or, and in every interstice a rose of the second barbed vert, in chief a crescent az. *Crest*—A dove with an olive branch in his beak ppr. *Motto*—I mean no harm.

Gaire (Lord Mayor of London, 1647). Erm. a fleur-de-lis sa. a chief of the last.

Gairgrave. Lozengy or and sa. on a bend of the second three crescents of the first.

Gaisford. Ar. three bars sa. on a canton gu. a dagger of the first. *Crest*—A boar pass. per fesse or and gu. hoofed of the last, bristled of the first.

Gaisford (Offington, co. Sussex). Ar. a·chev. gu. betw. three greyhounds courant sa.

Gaitskill. Gu. a lion pass. ar. combatant with a snake, which entwines round his body ppr. a martlet or, for diff. on a chief embattled of the second a sword erect ppr. hilt and pommel gold, betw. two laurel branches ppr. inclining towards the sword. *Crest*—On a mountain an eagle reguard. wings expanded ppr. collared az. resting the dexter claw on a pellet.

Galaad. Ar. a cross gu. *Crest*—A demi greyhound ar.

Galaway. Az. a lion ramp. ar. crowned or.

Galborne. Ar. a cross patonce betw. four martlets gu.

Galbraith (Shanwally, Donegal, and Castlefin, Dublin, bart., extinct 1827). Per pale az. and gu. a trefoil slipped ar. betw. three bears' heads erased or, muzzled sa. *Crest*—A bear's head erased or, muzzled sa. in the mouth a trefoil slipped, as in the arms.

Galbraith (granted, 1813, to James Galbraith, Esq., of Shane Valley, co. Donegal, grandson of Samuel Galbraith, Esq., of Dunduffs Fort, co. Donegal, of Scottish descent). Per pale az. and gu. a trefoil slipped ar. betw. three boars' heads erased or. *Crest*—A boar's head, as in the arms. *Motto*—Quod cro spero.

Galbreath (Culcreuch, co. Dumbarton). Gu. three bears' heads erased ar. muzzled az.

Gale, or Gall (co. Cornwall, Dartmouth and Crediton, co. Devon, and Weveston, co. Suffolk). Az. a fesse ar. fretty of the field. *Crest*—A shankbone and palm branch in saltire ppr.

Gale (co. Cornwall). Same *Arms. Crest*—A horse's head erased bendy wavy of six or and sa.

Gale (Whitehaven, co. Cumberland). Ar. on a fesse betw. three saltires az. an anchor betw. two lions' heads erased or. *Crest*—A unicorn's head az. charged with an anchor or, betw. two palets ar.

Gale (Bardsea Hall, co. Lancaster; granted, 28 June, 1712, to John, Ebenezer, and Elisha Gale, all of Whitehaven). Ar. on a fesse betw. three saltires az. an anchor betw. two lions' heads erased or. *Crest*—A unicorn's head az. charged with an anchor or, betw. two palets ar.

Gale (Scruton, co. York; the heiress, Harriet, eldest dau. of Henry Gale, Esq., of Scruton Hall, *m.* Foster Lechmere Coore, Esq., of Firby, a lieut.-col. in the army). Az. on a fesse betw. three saltires ar. as many lions' heads erased of the field, langued az. *Crest*—Out of a ducal coronet ppr. a unicorn's head ar. and az. and or, armed gold.

Gale (Ashfield Hall, Queen's co). Same *Arms* and *Crest.*

Gale (co. Devon). Az. on a fesse ar. three saltires of the field (another, gu.).

Gale, or Galle (Stalbridge, co. Dorset). Sa. a fesse ar fretty engr. of the first betw. three greyhounds sejant of the second, collared gu. *Crest*—A horse's head, bendy wavy of six ar. and sa.

Gale, or Galle. Sa. a fesse or, fretty az. betw. three

greyhounds sejant of the second, collared of the third. *Crest*—A greyhound's head erased bendy wavy of six or and sa.

Gale. Gu. a griffin segreant or, a bordure gobony ar. and vert. *Crest*—A unicorn's head paly of six az. and or, the horns twisted of the second and first.

Gale. Az. a fesse ar. betw. three saltires or.

Gale-Braddyll. See BRADDYLL.

Galehault. Or, semée of estoiles a lion ramp. az.

Gales, or Gale. Gu. a fesse betw. two chev. or.

Gall. Ar. a bear sejant ramp. sa. muzzled gu. *Crest*—A ship ppr. her flags and pennant flying gu. *Motto*—Patientia vincit.

Gall. Quarterly, or and vair a cross gu. *Crest*—A lion sejant gu. holding a banner staff and spearhead ppr.

Gallagher (Ireland). See O'GALLAGHER.

Galland. Or, a lion ramp. betw. three crescents gu. *Crest*—A stag lodged per pale or and gu.

Gallard (Reg. Ulster's Office). Ar. a chev. betw. three cocks gu.

Gallard, or Galiard (Reg. Her. Office, London). Az. a bend ar. betw. three roses or, stalked and leaved vert. *Crest*—An arm embowed vested gu. holding in the hand ppr. a rose or, slipped and leaved vert.

Gallaway. Az. three lozenges in chief or.

Gallay, or Galley (Bath, co. Somerset). Sa. a fesse ar. fretty of the first betw. three greyhounds sejant of the second, collared or. *Crest*—A nag's head bendy wavy of six ar. and sa.

Galliard (London). Az. a bend betw. three roses or.

Galliers (Stapleton Castle, co. Hereford). Paly of six sa. and or, on a chief of the second three cocks of the first. *Crest*—An antelope pass. quarterly, sa. and ar.

Gallightly (Liverpool, 1800). Erminois a lion ramp. double-queued gu. issuing from an antique crown az. in chief two thistles ppr. *Crest*—A lion's head issuing gu. crowned with an antique crown or. *Motto*—Hactenus invictus.

Gallop. Ar. on a bend gu. a lion pass. or. *Crest*—A boar pass. sa. thrust through with a broken spear ppr. muzzled ar.

Gallot (France). Erm. three chev. the centre gu. the others sa.

Galloway (Lord Dunkeld). Ar. a lion ramp. az. *Crest*—A mound or, bespread with rays of the sun ppr. betw. two ears of corn in saltire and ensigned with a cross crosslet gold. *Supporters*—Two eagles volant ppr. *Motto*—Higher.

Galloway (Sandyhill, co. Lanark). Ar. a lion ramp. az. on a chief erm. three antique crowns of the second. Same *Crest* and *Motto*.

Galloway, Earl of. See STEWART.

Galloway, See of. Ar. St. Ninian standing and full-faced ppr. clothed with a pontifical robe purp. on the head a mitre, and in the dexter hand a crosier or.

Gally (a Huguenot family; took refuge in England at the revocation of the Edict of Nantes). Gu. on a chev. or, betw. two mullets in chief ar. and a cock in base of the same, beaked gold, a chain sa.

Gallyhalt. Or, semée of estoiles az. a lion ramp. gu.

Galton. Erm. a bend gu. a canton sa. *Crest*—A bull's head erased gu. ducally gorged or.

Galton (Claverdon Leys, co. Warwick; represented by DARWIN GALTON, Esq., of Claverdon Leys, J.P. and D.L., eldest son of the late SAMUEL TERTIUS GALTON, Esq., of Duddeston House, co. Warwick). Erm. on a fesse engr. betw. six fleurs-de-lis gu. an eagle's head erased ar. betw. two bezants. *Crest*—On a mount vert an eagle erm. looking up at the sun or, the dexter claw resting on a fleurs-de-lis gu. *Motto*—Gaudet luce videri.

Galton (Hadzor, co. Worcester). Same *Arms, Crest,* and *Motto*.

Galton (Warley Hall, co. Salop). Same *Arms, Crest,* and *Motto*.

Galtrim (Dublin and Dundalk; JOHN GALTRIM, son of WALTER GALTRIM. Visit. City of Dublin, 1607). Gu. two swords in saltire ar. pommels and hilts or, betw. four martlets of the last.

Galway, Viscount. See ARUNDEL.

Galwey (bart. extinct; descended from WILLIAM DE GALWEY, eldest son of Sir JOHN DE BURGO, alias DE GALWEY, d. 1400, younger brother of ULICK DE BURGH, ancestor of the noble house of CLANRICARDE. Sir GEOFFREY GALWEY, the head of the family, temp. James I., was created a Baronet of Ireland). Quarterly, 1st and 4th, or, on a cross gu. five mullets of the field; 2nd and 3rd, ar. the representation of Baal's Bridge, underneath, the date 1361. This second coat was granted by LIONEL, *Duke of Clarence*, to the first Sir JOHN DE GALWAY, for his signal services in defending Baal's Bridge, Limerick, against the great force of O'Brien, of Thomond

Galwey (Lota, co. Cork; descended from GEOFFREY DE GALWEY, younger son of Sir JOHN DE BURGO, alias DE GALWEY, d. 1400). Same *Arms. Crest*—A cat sejant ppr collared and chained or. *Mottoes*—Above the crest: Vinctus sed non victus; below the shield : Vincit veritas.

Gallwey (PAYNE-GALLWEY, Bart.). Quarterly, 1st and 4th, per fesse or and gu. in chief an eagle displ. sa. in base a castle ar., for GALLWEY; 2nd and 3rd, gu. a fesse betw. two lions pass. ar., for PAYNE. *Crests*—1st, GALLWEY : A cat pass. guard.; 2nd, PAYNE: A lion's gamb erased, holding the lower part of a tilting-lance in bend.

Gam (Wales). Ar. three cocks gu.

Gamach, or Gamage. Ar. a bend lozengy gu. on a chief az. three escallops of the first. *Crest*—A dexter hand holding a pen in pale ppr.

Gamack (Clerkenshiels, co. Edinburgh). Gu. a bend engr. ar.

Gamadge. See GAMAGE.

Gamage (Coyte and Royiade, co. Hertford). Ar. five fusils in bend gu. on a chief az. three escallops or. *Crest*—A griffin segreant or.

Gamage (Wales). Ar. a bend lozengy gu. on a chief az. three escallops of the field.

Gamage (Alderman ANTHONY GAMAGE, of London, son of WESENHAM, co. Norfolk, and grandson of JOHN GAMAGE, of Coytiff, co. Glamorgan. Visit. London, 1568). Same *Arms*, the escallops or, quartering HORNE.

Gamage. Ar. a bend lozengy gu. a chief az.

Gamage. Ar. on a bend az. three mascles of the first, a chief of the second charged with as many escallops or.

Gamage. Ar. a chev. betw. three mullets gu. a chief az.

Gambell, or Gamble. Gu. a fleur-de-lis or, a chief erm. *Crest*—A crane, in the beak a rose stalked and leaved all ppr.

Gambier (Lord Gambier, created 1807, extinct 1833). Erminois a fesse wavy az. betw. three starlings sa. beaked and legged gu. *Crest*—Out of a naval crown or, an eagle displ. erminois, charged on the breast with an anchor sa. *Supporters*—Dexter, a sailor, habited ppr. supporting a cross calvary gu.; sinister, a female figure, representing Hope, vested ar. zoned gu. mantle az. fringed or, on her breast the sun in splendour gold, her sinister hand resting upon an anchor sa. *Motto*—Fide non armis.

Gambier. Erminois a fesse wavy az. betw. three Cornish choughs ppr.

Gambon (cos. Devon, Dorset, Norfolk, and South Wales. Quartered by WYNDHAM and HUYSHE). Ar. a fesse betw. three men's legs couped at the thigh sa.

Gambone, or Gambon (Visit. Cornwall, 1620. HANNIBAL GAMON, or GAMBONE, Rector of Mawgan, great-grandson of JOHN GAMBON, or GAMON, Esq., of Gamon House, near Padstow, co. Cornwall). Same *Arms*, a crescent for diff.

Gambon, or Gamon. Ar. on a chev. gu. three mullets or, in chief an annulet sa. *Crest*—A torteau betw. two wings ppr.

Gambon, or Gamon. Az. three eagles' legs erased a la quise or.

Gamboun. Ar. on a chev. sa. three mullets or, pierced gu.

Gambow (Spain). Per pale vert and ar. on the first a wolf saliant ar. on the second three mulberry leaves vert, two and one.

Game (Minton, co. Salop, and of Wales). Sa. three spears' heads ar. embrued gu.

Game (Wales). Ar. three cocks gu. crested and jelloped or.

Game (Wales). Sa. three lozenges ar. on each a torteau. *Crest*—A cross crosslet fitchée and palm branch in saltire ppr.

Game. Sa. a chev. betw. three spears' heads ar. embrued gu.

Gamell, or Gammill. Or, three mallets sa. *Crest*—Two lions' heads addorsed gu.

Games, or Gaymes (Newton, co. Brecknock). Or, a lion pass. guard. gu.

Games (co. Leicester; granted 1614). Sa. a chev. erm. betw. three eagles close ar. *Crest*—An eagle's head or, betw. two wings erm.

Games. Or, a lion pass. gu.

Gamin. Gu. three bezants, each charged with a human head ppr. *Crest*—An armed arm embowed, grasping a sword, both ppr. round the arm a garland of laurel vert.

Gamlyn (Spalding, co. Lincoln). Sa. three mullets or. *Crest*—Out of a ducal coronet a trefoil slipped, betw. two wings expanded of the last, all or.

Gamme. Ar. three cocks ar. armed, crested, and jelloped or.

Gammell (Drumtochty, co. Kincardine). Ar. a chev. betw. three hearts fessways in chief gu. joined and pierced by a

chain az. and in base a branch of laurel ppr. and a sword of
the third, hilted and pommelled or, disposed saltireways.
Crest—A pelican with wings displ. pierced with an arrow from
behind all ppr. *Motto*—Moriens sed invictus.

Gammie (Shotover House). See MAITLAND.

Gammocke. Quarterly, or and gu. a cross erm.

Gamoll, or Gamull (co. Chester; Reg. Coll. of Arms,
London). Or, three mallets sa. *Crest*—A human heart
ppr. crowned or, betw. two wings displ. sa. purfled gold
(another, on a ducal coronet an estoile or, environed with
two snakes vert).

Gamoll, or Gamull (co. Chester). Or, a fesse betw. two
barrulets gu. over all three escutcheons vair.

Gamolle (*temp.* Edward III.). *Crest*—A barrulet betw. two bars
gemelles gu. over all three escutcheons vair.

Gamon (Minchenden House, co. Middlesex). Az. two chev.
betw. three human legs couped at the thigh ar. *Crest*—A
boar pass. ar. charged on body with a pale sa. thereon a
leopard's face or. *Motto*—Virtus in arduis.

Gamon (Byfield, co. Hereford). Ar. a fesse engr. betw.
three mullets gu.

Gams (Newton, co. Brecknock). Sa. a chev. betw. three
spears' heads embrued ppr.

Gamul (Buerton, co. Chester, *temp.* Edward IV.; the senior
male line became extinct by the death of Sir FRANCIS GAMUL
in 1654). Or, three mullets sa. *Crest*—Out of a ducal
coronet or, a trefoil slipped gold betw. two wings sa.

Gamul (Crabwall; descended from the foregoing family,
extinct in the male line, 1759, property vested in Faimer, of
Nonsuch Park, a maternal descendant). Same *Arms* and
Crest.

Gamull (Knitton, co. Stafford). Same *Arms,* &c.

Gamvill, or Gamuell (Storton). Ar. on a chief gu.
three trefoils slipped of the first.

Gamys. Sa. a fesse or, betw. three cinquefoils ar.

Gandey. Gu. three saltires ar. *Crest*—A saltire gu.

Gandolfi (Richmond, co. Surrey, Genoa, and Lombardy.
See HORNYOLD). Ar. in base a mount vert, thereon a
poplar tree betw. two lions ramp. combatant crowned
with counts' coronets all ppr. *Crest*—A demi lion gu.
crined or, holding in dexter gamb a dagger ppr.

Ganeston (co. Cornwall). Ar. six eagles displ. vert.

Ganeth (co. Cambridge). Or, a lion ramp. sa. billettée ar.

Ganfield. Or, three bars gu. a canton erm.

Ganfield (co. Leicester). Or, three bars gu. on a quarter ar.
a bend fusily gu.

Ganford, or Granford. Gu. a lion ramp. ar. a bordure
engr. sa.

Ganiboun. Ar. on a chev. sa. three mullets of the field.

Ganlard (France). Sa. a fesse betw. six martlets or. *Crest*
—A dexter hand brandishing a sabre ppr.

Gannocke (Lincoln, 1640). Erm. a fret gu. on a chief of the
second three crescents ar.

Gannoke (Libsey, co. Lincoln). Erm. a fret gu. on a chief of
the second three plates. *Crest*—A stag sejant ar. ducally
gorged or.

Gansell. Or, three bars gu. a quarter erm.

Gansell, or Gonsell. Paly of six ar. and gu. on a chief
az. a fesse dancettée or.

Gant (co. Lincoln). Barry of six or and gu. over all a
bend vair. *Crest*—A wolf's head or, gorged with a collar
vair.

Gant (*Earl of Lincoln, Baron Gant;* Earldom inherited from
the family of ROMARE, *temp.* King Stephen; Barony by
summons to Parliament, 1295, extinct 1297). Barry of six
or and az. a bend gu.

Gant, or Gaunt. Same *Arms. Crest*—A millrind ppr.

Gantlet (Netherampton, co. Wilts; granted 19 July, 1670).
Gu. a chev. betw. three gauntlets ar.

Gantlet. Az. a gauntlet ar. on a chief or, two roses gu.

Ganuble. Or, on a chief gu. three trefoils slipped ar. *Crest*
—A lion pass. tail extended ppr.

Ganuble (Spalding, co. Lincoln). Same *Arms,* debruised by
a sinister baton gobony ar. and sa.

Gape (St. Alban's, co. Hertford; granted 1684). Or, three
lions pass. in bend sa. betw. two bendlets vair. *Crest*—A lion
pass. reguard. or, pellettée, gorged with a collar vair.

Gapper. Az. on a chief ar. a lion pass. gu. *Crest*—Out of
an antique coronet or, a demi lion ramp. gu.

Gapper. (co. Somerset). Gu. a fesse betw. three crosses
crosslet fitchée in chief and a lion ramp. in base or. *Crest*—
A demi lion ramp. gu. holding in the dexter paw a cross
crosslet fitchée or.

Gar (Reg. Ulster's Office). Ar. a chev. betw. three stags'
heads cabossed sa.

Gar (Reg. Ulster's Office). Ar. an eagle displ. with two heads
sa. ducally crowned or.

Gara (co. Westmeath; Reg. Ulster's Office). Ar. three lions
ramp. az. on a chief gu. a demi lion ramp. or.

Gara. See O'GARA.

Garband. Az. a tilting spear and battle axe in saltire ar.
headed or, in chief an arrow barways of the second, feathered
and pointed of the third.

Garband (co. Lincoln). Barry of seven gu. and or, in
chief three bezants.

Garbed, or Gabit (Righton, co. Salop). Gu. a griffin
segreant or, supporting a standard ar. charged with an imperial eagle, the staff twisted of the third and sa. the foot
gold, head and tassels also of the third.

Garbett (ROBERT GARBETT, Exon of the Yeoman Guard in
1486; from whom derived FRANCIS GARBETT, Esq., of Huntington Park, co. Hereford, sheriff of co. Radnor, in 1790;
represented by WALSHAM, Bart., of Knill Court). Gu. a
griffin segreant or, supporting a knightly banner, flowing to
the dexter ar. and thereon an eagle with two heads displ. sa.
Crest—An imperial eagle as on the banner. *Motto*—Gare la
bête.

Garbitt (Acton Burnell, co. Salop). Same *Arms.*

Garbonell. Az. on a cross ar. five escallops gu.

Garbrand (Jamaica; granted 28 Oct. 1768). Or, a battle
axe in bend sinister, surmounted of a lance in bend dexter,
and in chief a dart barways pheoned and flighted all ppr.

Garbridge (Walsingham and Sparham, co. Norfolk). Sa. a
fesse betw. two chev. or. *Crest*—A bundle (or sheaf) of
reeds ppr. banded about the middle with a wreath ar.
and sa.

Garbyn, or Garbin (co. Cambridge). Ar. two bars sa.

Gard (co. Kent). Az. on a chev. ar. three birds vert membered
gu. on a chief or, three griffins segreant sa. *Crest*—A tower
ar. betw. two laurel branches vert.

Garde (Ballynecurra, co. Cork). Same *Arms. Crest*—A
demi griffin ramp. sa. *Motto*—Toujours fidèle.

Gardegrave. Lozengy ar. and sa. on a bend of the last
three crescents of the first.

Gardell. Az. a chev. engr. betw. three fleurs-de-lis ar.
(another, or).

Gardemow. Ar. on a chief sa. a lion pass. of the first.

Garden (co. Cambridge). Ar. two bars sa. a label gu.

Garden. Az. three baskets or. *Crest*—A mallard amongst
flags all ppr.

Garden (that Ilk). Ar. two chev. engr. gu.

Garden (that Ilk, co. Forfar). Ar. a boar's head erased sa.
armed or. *Crest*—Two dexter hands conjoined ppr. holding
a cross crosslet fitchée or. *Motto*—Cruciata cruce junguntur.

Garden (Troup, co. Banff, now GARDEN-CAMPBELL). Ar. a
boar's head erased sa. armed gu., now quartered with
CAMPBELL, of Glenlyon. See that name. *Crest*—A boar
pass. ar. *Motto*—Vires animat virtus.

Garden (Borrowfield, co. Forfar). Ar. a boar's head erased
sa. betw. three mullets gu. *Crest*—A dexter hand holding a
palm branch disposed in orle ppr. *Motto*—Vive le roi.

Garden (Leys, co. Forfar). Ar. a boar's head erased sa. betw.
three cross crosslets fitchée gu.

Garden (Minister of Balmerino, 1678). The same, within a
bordure counter compony sa. and ar. *Crest*—A rose slipped
ppr. *Motto*—Sustina et abstine.

Gardener (Himbleton, co. Worcester; granted by Cooke,
Clarenceux, 1592, to RICHARD GARDENER, Esq., of that place).
Ar. a chev. gu. betw. three pomegranates ppr. leaved vert.
Crest—Out of a mural crown or, an armed arm embowed
ppr. holding in the hand a flagstaff, thereon a split pennon
gu. flowing to the sinister, charged with two staves in
saltire, fired gold.

Gardener (Histon, co. Cambridge; Kokesforth, co. Norfolk; and Shrewsbury). Per fesse ar. and sa. a pale counterchanged, three griffins' heads erased of the second. *Crest*
—A griffin's head erased sa.

Gardener (Berwick-on-Tweed; granted 24 April, 1580). Sa.
a chev. erm. betw. three buglehorns ar. stringed or. *Crest*
—On a book sanguine, clasped and garnished or, a falcon
volant of the last.

Gardener (Calais). Or, on a chev. gu. betw. three griffins'
heads erased ar. two lions pass. respecting each other ar.

Gardener (Northall, co. Lincoln). Same *Arms,* the lions
gold. *Crest*—A Turk's head ppr. turban or and az.

Gardener. Sa. a chev. betw. three half spades ar.

Gardeners, Company of (London). The field a landscape, the base variegated with flowers, a man ppr. vested
round the loins with linen ar. digging with a spade, all of the
first. *Crest*—A basket of fruit all ppr. *Supporters*—Two
emblematical female figures with cornucopia, representing
plenty. *Motto*—In the sweat of thy brow shalt thou eat thy
bread.

Gardener (THOMAS GARDENER, citizen of London. Visit.

1568). Quarterly, gu. and az. in the second and third quarters a griffin segreant or, holding in the dexter claw a ring gemmed of the last, over all on a bend cotised of the last a leopard's face, holding in the mouth a round buckle betw. two fleurs-de-lis gu. *Crest*—A leopard pass. ar. pellettée, holding in the dexter paw a pine apple or, stalked and leaved vert.

Gardiner (*Earl of Blessington*, extinct 1829). Quarterly, 1st and 4th, or, a fesse chequy ar. and az. betw. three lions pass. sa.; 2nd and 3rd, or, a griffin pass. az. on a chief sa. three pheons' heads ar. *Crest*—An eagle's head erased betw. two wings. *Supporters*—Dexter, a man in complete armour garnished or, on his cap three feathers, two ar. and one gu.; sinister, a queen in her royal vestments gu. girded az. over all a mantle purp. doubled erm. her feet bare, hair dishevelled, and ducally crowned or. *Motto*—Nil desperandum.

Gardiner (WHALLEY-SMYTHE-GARDINER, Roche Court, near Farnham, co. Hants, bart.). Ar. on a chev. gu. betw. three griffins' heads erased az. two lions counterpass. of the field, quartering WHALLEY and SMITH. *Crest*—A Saracen's head couped at the shoulders ppr.

Gardiner (Bishop of Winchester; STEPHEN GARDINER, appointed 1531, deprived 1550, restored 1553, *d.* 1556). Az. on a cross or, betw. four griffins' heads erased ar. a cinquefoil pierced gu.

Gardiner (Bishop of Lincoln; JOHN GARDINER, appointed 1695, *d.* 1705). Or, a buck's head cabossed gu. betw. the attires a mullet of the last.

Gardiner (Rev. ROBERT BARLOW GARDINER, M.A., formerly Vicar of Wadhurst, co. Sussex). Same *Arms*, with a canton az. thereon a mitre of the first, labelled ar. *Crest*—A stag's head cabossed ppr. betw. the attires a mullet sa. pierced and pendent from a chain or.

Gardiner (cos. Berks and Buckingham). Gu. a chev. betw. three griffins' heads erased ar. a chief crenellée or. *Crest*—A griffin's head erased az. charged with three bends or.

Gardiner (Blandford, co. Dorset). Per fesse embattled az. and purp. on a chev. or, betw. three griffins' heads erased ar. as many escallops sa. *Crest*—A griffin's head erased bendy of six az. and purp.

Gardiner (Tollesbury, co. Essex). Ar. a griffin segreant sa. *Crest*—A griffin pass. reguard. sa.

Gardiner (Ivingsbury, co. Herts). Per pale or and gu a fesse betw. three hinds pass. counterchanged.

Gardiner (Cudsden, co. Oxford; Sir THOMAS GARDINER, Knt., Solicitor-General to Charles I.; *d.* Oct. 1652). Per pale gu. and or, a fesse betw. three hinds tripping counterchanged.

Gardiner (Thundridgbury, co. Herts). Per pale or and gu. on a fesse betw. three hinds pass. as many lozenges all counterchanged. *Crest*—Two halberts in pale, enwrapped round by a snake ppr.

Gardiner (London). Per pale or and gu. a fesse betw. three hinds trippant all counterchanged. *Crest*—A Saracen's head sidefaced ppr. erased at the shoulders gu. wreathed round the temples ar. and of the second.

Gardiner (Wigan, co. Lancaster). Or, on a chev. gu. betw. three griffins' heads erased az. two lions counter pass. of the field.

Gardiner (London). Same *Arms*. *Crest*—A man's head ppr. thereon a cap gu. turned up ar. crined and bearded sa.

Gardiner (Coombe Lodge, co. Oxford). Quarterly, 1st and 4th, same *Arms*, for GARDINER; 2nd and 3rd, gu. on a cross or, five mullets sa., for BODDAM. *Crest*—A griffin's head erased. *Motto*—Deo non fortunæ.

Gardiner (Lord Mayor of London, 1478). Purp. on a chev. ar. three escallops az. on a chief embattled of the third a cross potent or, betw. two griffins' heads erased of the second.

Gardiner (London, and Beccles, co. Norfolk). Gu. a chev. betw. three tigers' heads erased or. *Crest*—A rhinoceros pass. ar.

Gardiner (certified at the College of Arms, London, May, 1779). Quarterly, 1st and 4th, or, a griffin pass. with wings endorsed az. on a chief sa. three pheons ar.; 2nd and 3rd, gu. a fesse chequy ar. and az. betw. three lions ramp. or. *Crest*—A griffin's head or, gorged with a chaplet of laurel vert betw. two wings expanded az. *Motto*—Persevere.

Gardiner (co. Oxford, 1578). Az. a chev. erm. betw. three griffins' heads erased ar. (another, or). *Crest*—A stork ppr. *Another Crest*—A griffin sejant, resting his dexter foot on a book sa.

Gardiner (RICHARD GARDINER, D.D., and Canon of Christ Church, Oxford, *d.* 20 Dec. 1670). Sa. a chev. erm. betw. two griffins' heads erased in chief and a cross formée in base or.

387

Gardiner (Letherhead, co. Surrey). Sa. a chev. betw. three buglehorns stringed ar. on a pile in chief of the second a covered cup gu. a bordure or, charged with eight pellets. *Crest*—Out of a ducal coronet or, a goat's head gu. attired gold.

Gardiner (Haling and Peckham, co. Surrey). Az. a griffin pass. or.

Gardiner (*temp.* Henry VIII.). Per fesse ar. and sa. a pale and three goats' heads erased all counterchanged.

Gardiner (Reg. Ulster's Office, to Sir ROBERT GARDINER, Chief Justice of the King's Bench, 1586–1604). Gu. a chev. betw. three heraldic tigers' heads erased or.

Gardiner (Dublin; granted by Carney, Ulster, 1683, to WILLIAM GARDINER, of that city, merchant). Or, a griffin pass. wings expanded az. on a chief sa. three pheons points down ar. *Crest*—A griffin's head couped or, betw. two wings az. gorged with a chaplet vert. *Motto*—Honor rewards industry.

Gardiner (Madras, 1789). Ar. on a fret gu. a rose in every interstice of the second, barbed vert, betw. four hearts or, a bordure az. *Crest*—Out of a mural crown or, seven battle axes ppr. one in fess and the rest in bend dexter and bend sinister. *Motto*—Omnia superat virtus.

Gardinis. Ar. two bars sa. a label of five points gu.

Gardner (*Baron Gardner*). Or, on a chev. gu. betw. three griffins' heads erased az. an anchor erect betw. two lions guard. counter-pass. of the field. *Crest*—A demi griffin az. collared and lined, and supporting in the claws an anchor or. *Supporters*—Two griffins, wings elevated az. beaked, membered, and gorged with a naval coronet or, each resting the interior hind foot on an anchor, with cable sa. *Motto*—Valet anchora virtus.

Gardner (Chatteris House, Isle of Ely, co. Cambridge). Quarterly, 1st and 4th, ar. on a saltire betw. three griffins' heads erased, one in chief, two in fesse sa. and a woolpack in base az. another saltire, for GARDNER; 2nd and 3rd, az. on a chev. or, betw. two boars' heads erased in chief and a padlock in base ar. a lozenge gu. with two keys chevronwise sa., for DUNN. *Crests*—1st, GARDNER : A griffin's head erased ar. surmounted by two branches of laurel in saltire ppr.; 2nd, DUNN : Two swords in saltire, the points upwards ppr. pommels and hilts or, tied with a riband vert pendent therefrom a key sa. *Motto*—Fide et amore.

Gardner (Rev. LAURENCE GARDNER, D.D., Sansaw, Shrewsbury). Per fesse ar. and sa. a pale counterchanged three griffins' heads erased of the second. *Crest*—A griffin's head erased sa.

Gardner (cos. Lincoln and Salop). Same *Arms*. *Crest*—An elephant's head erm. eared sa. armed or.

Gardner (Lord Mayor of London; and of Suffolk). Per fesse or and sa. a pale counterchanged, and three griffins' heads erased of the second.

Gardner (Tunbridge Wells, co. Kent). Az. on a chev. betw. three griffins' heads erased ar. as many martlets sa. *Crest*—A griffin's head erased gorged with a mural coronet.

Gardner (co. Middlesex). Sa. a chev. betw. three buglehorns stringed ar. *Crest*—A reindeer's head ar. attired or.

Gardner (Kirkton, co. Lincoln). Az. a chev. betw. three buglehorns ar.

Gardner (co. Lincoln, and Wallbearswick, co. Suffolk). Quarterly, ar. and sa. in the 2nd and 3rd quarters a griffin's head erased or. *Crest*—An elephant's head couped erm.

Gardner, or Gardener (Wallingham and Bishop's Norton, co. Lincoln). Or, on a chev. gu. betw. three griffins' heads erased az. two lions combatant ar. *Crest*—A Saracen's head full faced ppr. erased at the neck gu. wreathed about the temples of the last and az. on his head a cap or.

Gardner, or Gardener (London). Per chev. ar. and purp. in chief three escallops az. in base a griffin's head erased or, on a chief of the second a cross formée betw. two griffins' heads erased of the first.

Gardner (co. Worcester). Per chev. az. and gu. on a chev. betw. three lions' heads erased ar. as many escallops sa.

Gardner (London). Gu. on a bend cotised or, a leopard's face betw. two fleurs-de-lis of the first.

Gardner (co. Somerset). Sa. a chev. betw. three spades ar.

Gardner (Stoke-Ash, co. Suffolk). Ar. on a chev. gu. betw. three griffins' heads erased az. two lions ramp. or.

Gardner (co. Herts; RICHARD GARDNER, Sergeant-at-Arms to Henry VIII., his brother, WILLIAM GARDNER, of Bermondsey Street, *d.* 1597; sons of WILLIAM GARDNER, co. Herts. Visit. London). Az. a griffin pass. or. *Crest*—On a ducal coronet or, a lion pass. guard. ar. (another, a demi unicorn erased ar. crowned and horned or, crined sa.).

Gardner (Bermondsey, co. Surrey). Same *Arms*. *Crest*—A demi unicorn erased or, crined and armed sa. ducally crowned or. *Another Crest*—On a ducal coronet or, a lion pass guard. ar.

Gardner. Or, a griffin pass. az. on a chief sa. three pheons ar. *Crest*—A griffin's head couped or, gorged with a chaplet vert betw. two wings az.

Gardner. Vert a griffin pass. and a chief or.

Gardner. Az. a griffin pass. or. *Crest*—A demi unicorn or, maned sa. crowned ar. horned gold.

Gardner (Ruspar, co. Sussex. Visit. 1634). Az. on a chev. ar. betw. three griffins' heads erased or, as many martlets sa.

Gardner. Per fesse gu. and ar. six pales wavy counterchanged.

Gardner. Per pale or and gu. on a fesse betw. three hinds two lozenges all counterchanged.

Gardner. Ar. a griffin's head erased sa.

Gardner (granted to ROBERT PANTING, Esq., upon his assuming, by royal licence, the name of GARDNER). Per fesse ar. and sa. a pale counterchanged three gryphons' heads erased of the second.

Gardner. Gu. a bend vair double cotised or.

Gardner (Torwoodhead, co. Stirling). Gu. on a fret of four pieces gu. as many hearts az. and in every interstice a rose of the second. *Crest*—A griffin's head erased ppr. *Motto*—In virtute et fortuna.

Gardner (Edinburgh, 1784). Same *Arms*, a crescent or, in chief for diff. *Crest*—A griffin's head erased ppr. charged with a crescent or. *Motto*—Virtute et fortuna.

Gardners. Purp. on a chev. ar. three escallops az. on a chief crenellée of the third a cross potent or, betw. two griffins' heads erased of the second.

Gardoyle, Garville, or Gardley. Paly of six or and az.

Gardyn. Ar. two bars sa. a label of five points gu.

Gardyne (Middleton, co. Forfar; BRUCE-GARDYNE, of Middleton, senior co-heir of line). Or, two chev. engr. gu. betw. three boars' heads erased sa.

Gare (co. Kent). Az. three lions ramp. ar. on a chief gu. a demi lion issuant or.

Garein, or Guarein. Chequy or and az. on a chief ar. a crescent gu.

Garen. Chequy or and az. a chief of the first. *Crest*—A cross crosslet fitchée gu.

Garenne. Chequy or and az.

Garfield (Kilsby, co. Northants, and Tuddington, co. Middlesex; BENJAMIN GARFIELD, Esq., of the latter place, grandson of RALPH GARFIELD, of the former. Visit. Middlesex, 1663). Or, three bars gu. on a canton erm. a cross of the second quartering, 1st, sa. on a chev. betw. three lions ramp. ar. an annulet gu.; 2nd, ar. on a chev. betw. three crosses crosslet gu. as many fleurs-de-lis or; 3rd, barry of six ar. and az. a lion ramp. gu. *Crest*—Out of a ducal coronet or, a cross calvary gu.

Garfield. Or, three bars gu. on a canton erm. a cross formée of the second. *Crest*—Out of a human heart a hand holding a sword all ppr.

Garfoote (Hyde, co. Essex, and Farnham, co. Suffolk, 1634). Sa. a bend betw. six goats saliant ar. attired or. *Crest*—Out of a mural crown sa. a goat's head ar. attired or.

Garforth (co. York). Sa. a bend betw. six goats pass. ar. *Crest*—Out of a ducal coronet or, a goat's head ar.

Garforth. Sa. a bend betw. three goats pass. ar. *Crest*—A wolf courant ppr.

Gargan (cos. Suffolk and Sussex). Ar. three lozenges gu. (another, fusils).

Gargate (Tournay, France). Gu. the field replenished with fleurs-de-lis or (another, within a border gobony ar. and sa.).

Gargate, or Gargat. Gu. two quartrefoils in chief, and a fleur-de-lis in base or. *Crest*—A lion poisson ramp.

Gargate. Per bend az. and or (another, ar. and az.) three fleurs-de-lis betw. two cotises counterchanged.

Garginton, or Garwinton. Sa. a chev. betw. three garlick heads ppr. *Crest*—A vine branch, fructed and leaved ppr.

Gargrave (co. Lancaster). Ar. on a chief indented gu. three crosses crosslet fitchée of the field.

Gargrave (Snapthorpe, co. York). Lozengy ar. and sa. on a bend gu. three crescents or. *Crest*—A falcon rising ar.

Gargrave (Nostel, co. York; descended from Sir JOHN GARGRAVE, Master of the Ordnance to Henry V. in France; the last male heir, Sir RICHARD GARGRAVE, Knt., Sheriff of co. York, 3 James I., dissipated in extravagance the whole of his great estates). Lozengy ar. and sa. on a bend of the second three crescents of the first. *Crest*—As the last.

Gargrave (co. York). Or, on a chief indented gu. three crosses crosslet fitchée ar.

Gargrave. Ar. on a bend betw. six lozenges sa. three cinquefoils or.

Gargrave. Or, on a fesse dancettée gu. three crosses cross let fitchée ar.

Garioch (Kinstair, co. Aberdeen). Az. a bend betw. a stag's head couped in chief attired or, and three crosses crosslet fitchée in base of the second. *Crest*—A palm tree growing out of a mount with a trefoil ppr. *Motto*—Concussus surgo.

Garioch (title of Lord *Garioch*, Scotland). Or, a fesse chequy az. and ar. betw. three open crowns gu.

Garland (Quatre Bras, co. Dorset). Paly of six or and gu. a chief per pale of the second and sa. in the dexter chief a chaplet ppr. in the sinister a demi lion ramp. issuant ar. *Crest*—Two lances saltirewise ar. interlacing a chaplet ppr.

Garland (Whitfield, Blacktorington, and Exeter, co. Devon. Visit. 1620). Or, three pales gu. on a chief per pale gu. and sa. a chaplet and a demi lion issuant ar.

Garland (Michaelstowe Hall, co. Essex, and Woodcote Grove, co. Surrey). Same *Arms. Crest*—On a mural crown or, a lion sejant reguard. ar. the dexter paw resting on an escutcheon of the second charged with a garland ppr. *Motto*—Libertas.

Garland (co. Lincoln). Gu. two bars or, in chief three bezants. *Crest*—A lion's paw erased, holding a battle axe ppr.

Garland (co. York). Same *Arms* and *Crest.*

Garland (Fun. Ent. of EDWARD GOUGH, Alderman of Dublin, d. 30 July, 1631, m. as second wife, ELLIS GARLAND). Ar. an eagle displ. with two necks sa. armed, beaked, and ducally gorged or.

Garland (Reg. Ulster's Office). Same *Arms. Crest*—A horse pass. ar. hoofed or.

Garlehampe (co. Middlesex). Sa. an estoile of six points or, charged with an annulet of the first betw. three covered cups of the second.

Garlick. Ar. three heads of garlick ppr. *Crest*—A dexter arm erect in armour, holding in the hand ppr. a cutlass of the last, also erect, pommel and hilt or.

Garling. Az. on a chev. gu. three mullets of the field, on a chief az. as many suns or. *Crest*—A fish's head erased per fesse ppr.

Garlington (co. Hereford). Sa. three gadbees volant ar.

Garlynape (co. Middlesex). Sa. three covered cups ar.

Garman, Garmon, or Germon. Ar. on a bend az. three escallops of the first. *Crest*—An oak tree, therefrom two weights pendent ppr.

Garmon. Ar. three bars (another, wavy) gu.

Garmston (co. Lincoln; granted 1758). Vert three flying fishes in pale ar. *Crest*—A shark's head reguard. couped ar. swallowing a Negro man ppr. *Motto*—Opera die mirifica.

Garmyn. Ar. a fesse betw. three crosses pattée sa.

Garnant. Ar. three pellets.

Garnatt, or Garnet (co. Essex, and Westminster). Az. three griffins' heads erased or. *Crest*—A squirrel sejant, holding in the forepaws a branch of hazel ppr.

Garnault. Per pale or and az. barry of six, and a chief charged with a pale, and its cantons divided, per bend, dexter and sinister respectively, all counterchanged, over all an escutcheon ar.

Garnegan (co. Suffolk). Ar. three fusils gu.

Garnegan. Barry of eight ar. and gu. over all a fleur-de-lis sa.

Garnegott. Or, two bars az. an eagle displ. gu.

Garneshe, or Garnishe (co. Suffolk). Ar. a chev. engr. az. betw. three escallops sa. *Crest*—A mermaid ppr.

Garnett (Quernmore, co. Lancaster). Gu. a lion ramp. ar ducally crowned, and a bordure nebulée or, on a canton of the last an eagle displ. with two heads sa. *Crest*—A demi lion ar. gorged with a wreath of oak ppr. holding betw. the paws an escutcheon gu. charged with a buglehorn or. *Motto*—Diligentia et honore.

Garnett (Wyreside, co. Lancaster). Gu. a lion ramp. ar. ducally crowned, and a bordure dovetail or, on a canton of the last a cross pattée fitchée of the field. *Crest*—A demi lion ar. gorged with a collar dovetail gu. holding betw. the paws an escutcheon or, charged with a cross pattée fitchée also gu.

Garnett. Same *Arms. Crest*—A dexter hand holding up a swan's head and neck erased ppr.

Garnett. Az. three griffins' heads erased or.

Garnett. Quarterly, 1st and 4th, az. three wolves' heads erased or; 2nd and 3rd (ancient coat), gu. a lion ramp. ar. ducally crowned or, a bordure engr. of the last.

Garnett-Botfield. See BOTFIELD.

Garneys, or Garnish (Laxfield, co. Suffolk, *temp.* King John, afterwards of Heveningham, Kenton, Mickfield, and Redesham, same county, and of Gelderton, co. Norfolk).

Ar. a chev. engr. betw. three escallops az. *Crest*—A cubit arm. erased grasping a scimetar embrued all ppr. hilt and pommel or. *Mottoes*—"Goddes grace governe Garneys," and "Flectar non Frangar."

Garnier (Weekham, co. Hants). Az. a sword in bend sinister, point downwards, betw. a fleurs-de-lis in chief and an oak branch acorned ar. in base. *Crest*—A griffin's head gu. betw. two wings ar. charged with a torteau.

Garnier (Rookesbury, co. Hants). Same *Arms*. *Crest*—A lion's head erased ar.

Garnier (granted to JOHN CARPENTER-GARNIER, Esq., of Mount Tavy, co. Devon, and Rookesbury, co. Hants). Quarterly, 1st and 4th, az. a sword bendwise, point downwards ppr., betw. in the sinister chief a fleur-de-lis and in the dexter base an oak branch or, a border embattled also or, for GARNIER; 2nd and 3rd, per pale indented or and az. an eagle displ. and in chief two pellets counterchanged, for CARPENTER. *Crest*—In front of a lion's head erased az. gorged with an oak wreath or, three fleurs-de-lis gold.

Garnon (Garnons, co. Herts, and Harnhill, co. Gloucester). Quarterly, 1st and 4th, gu. two lions pass. or; 2nd, sa. a chev. betw. three fleurs-de-lis ar.; 3rd, ar. a chev. betw. three dolphins embowed haurient az. *Crest*—A demi lion ramp. sa. crowned and ducally gorged or. *Motto*—Nid cyfoeth, ond boddlondeb.

Garnon (South Muskham and Carlton, co. Nottingham. Visit. Notts, 1614). Ar. a stag's head cabossed gu. a mullet for diff.

Garnon, or Gernon, alias Cavendish (Grimstead, co. Sussex). Ar. three piles wavy gu. the middle one issuant from the base. *Crest*—A wolf's head or, collared gu.

Garnon. Ar. a fesse betw. three crosses formée sa. (another, the tinctures reversed).

Garnon. Or, on a bend az. three escallops of the field.

Garnons (Colommendy, co. Denbigh; descended from RICHARD GARNONS, and CATHERINE, his wife, dau. and sole heiress of JOHN, second son of GRIFFITH VAUGHAN, Esq., of Coresgedol). Gu. two lions pass. or, a bordure az. quartering VAUGHAN, WYNNE, of Llanwnda, and WYNNE, of Leeswood. *Crest*—A demi lion ramp. ducally gorged and crowned or. *Motto* (Welsh)—Nid cyfoeth, ond boddlondeb; (English) —Not wealth, but contentment.

Garrad (London; granted 18 Dec. 1632). Az. two lions ramp. guard. addorsed or.

Garran. Ar. a sword in pale az. hilt and pommel or, surmounted on the point by a mullet gu. over all a saltire couped sa.

Garrard (Newberry, co. Berks, and Dorney, co. Buckingham, bart., extinct 1767; founded by Sir WILLIAM GARRARD, Knt., of Dorney, co. Buckingham, Lord Mayor of London in 1555, as was his son, Sir JOHN GARRARD, Knt., in 1601; descended from THOMAS GARRARD, Esq., of Sittingbourne, co. Kent. Visit. London 1568. Sir JOHN's son and heir, another Sir JOHN GARRARD, of Lamer, was raised to a baronetcy by King James I.). Ar. on a fess sa. a lion pass. of the first. *Crest*—A leopard sejant ppr.

Garrard (DRAKE-GARRARD, Lamer, co. Herts; JANE, dau. and heiress of Sir JOHN GARRARD, third bart. of Dorney, m. MONTAGUE DRAKE, Esq., of Shardeloes; their descendant assumed the additional name of GARRARD, 1767). Quarterly, 1st and 4th, ar. on a fesse sa. a lion pass. of the first; 2nd and 3rd, ar. a wivern with wings displ. and tail nowed gu. *Crests*—1st: A leopard sejant ppr.; 2nd: A naked dexter hand and arm erect, holding a battle axe sa. headed ar.

Garrard (London). Az. two lions combatant ar. *Crest*—A wivern, tail nowed ppr. pierced through the neck with a spear or, headed ar.

Garrard (Fellingham, co. Norfolk; granted by Camden, Clarenceux, to WILLIAM GARRARD). Az. in base out of waves of the sea ppr. a rock of the last, on either side a tun joined together by a chain passing through the sea all or. *Crest*—An heraldic tiger sejant ar. maned and tufted sa. resting the dexter paw on a tun or.

Garrard (Langford, co. Norfolk, bart., extinct 1728). Az. two lions ramp. guard. combatant ar.

Garrat (London). Az. a lion ramp. (another, pass.) betw. two flaunches ar. on a canton gu. a lion's head erased of the second. *Crest*—A hind sejant reguard. resting the dexter foot on a beehive ppr. *Motto*—Certe cruce salus.

Garratt (Bishops Court, co. Devon). Az. on a fesse sa. a lion pass. of the first. *Crest*—A lion pass. erm. resting the dexter paw on a fleur-de-lis or.

Garratt (JOHN GARRATT, Esq., Lord Mayor of London in 1824-25). Same *Arms* as GARRARD, of Dorney. *Crest*—A lion pass. erm. resting his dexter paw on a fleur de lis or.

Garraway. Az. a bend betw. three escallops ar. *Crest*—An escallop betw. two wings.

389

Garrene. Chequy or and az.

Garret. Ar. a saltire gu. *Crest*—A demi monk, in the dexter hand a lash.

Garrett. See GERROTTE.

Garrett (Fun. Ent. 1598, Ulster's Office, THOMAS GARRETT, Alderman and Mayor of Dublin). Ar. a saltire and a border gu. a crescent for diff.

Garrett (Kilgarron, otherwise Janeville, co. Carlow). Erm. on a fesse az. a lion pass. or. *Crest*—A lion pass. langued gu. resting the sinister paw on a trefoil. *Motto*—Semper fidelis.

Garrick (Hampton, co. Middlesex; borne by the celebrated DAVID GARRICK). Per pale or and az. on the dexter compartment a tower gu. and on the sinister on a mount vert a seahorse ar. mane, fins, and tail of the first, on a chief gold three mullets of the second. *Crest*—A mullet or.

Garrig. Chequy or and az. a chief of the first, charged in the dexter chief point with a crescent gu.

Garrow (Bolnore, Cuckfield, co. Sussex). Az. a bend betw. a buck's head erased in chief and three crosses crosslet fitchée in base all ar. *Crest*—On a mount vert a palm tree ppr. charged with three torteaux, two and one.

Garroway (co. Hertford, and Chichester, co. Sussex). Ar. a pile surmounted by a fesse betw. four leopards' faces gu. *Crest*—A griffin pass. or.

Garroway (East Sheen, co. Surrey). Same *Arms*. *Crest*—On a rock a Cornish chough ppr. beaked and legged gu.

Garselang (London). Az. three mascles ar. a bordure engr. gu.

Garsett (Norwich; confirmed by Camden to ROBERT GARSETT, Esquire of the body to James I., son of ROBERT GARSETT, Alderman of Norwich). Ar. a saltire betw. four mullets gu. *Crest*—A bow erect gu. stringed sa. with an arrow or, headed az. feathered ar.

Garsey. Az. a lion ramp. or.

Garshall, or Garshale (cos. Warwick and Leicester, *temp.* Edward I.). Quarterly, ar. and az. (another, gu.) on a bend gu. three fleurs-de-lis of the first.

Garside. Ar. a galley, her sails furled sa. flags gu. betw. three crosses crosslet fitchée of the last. *Crest*—Two daggers in saltire ppr.

Garstang, or Gorstang. Az. three mascles or, a chief ar. a bordure engr. gu.

Garstin. Ar. on a pale sa. a pike's head couped or. *Crest*—A dexter hand holding a broken hammer.

Garstin (Braganstown, co. Louth, and Coolderry, co. Monaghan; confirmed to Rev. ANTHONY GARSTIN, M.A., of those places, Rector of Mansfieldstown, diocese of Armagh, and to the other descendants of his ancestor, Captain SYMON GARSTIN, of Leragh Castle, co. Westmeath). Same *Arms*, in the dexter chief point a fleur-de-lis gu. *Crest*—Out of a ducal coronet or, a dexter arm in armour embowed, in the hand a dagger all ppr. the arm charged with a fleur-de-lis gu. *Motto*—Gladio et virtute.

Garstin (Dublin and Killiney, co. Dublin; JOHN RIBTON GARSTIN, Esq., J.P., descended from G..RSTIN, of Leragh). Same *Arms* and *Crest*.

Garston. Ar. on a fesse az. betw. two Cornish choughs ppr. in chief, and in base a lion pass. gu. crowned or, a fort of the first. *Crest*—Out of a mural coronet ar. a wivern or, charged on the breast with a fireball sa.

Garstyde (co. York). Per pale gu. and az. a chev. betw. three boars' heads couped or, a chief ar. *Crest*—A stag per pale gu. and sa. attired and hoofed or.

Garter (co. Norfolk). Or, on a cross quarterly pierced az. four caltraps of the field. *Crest*—A caltrap or, embrued on the upper point ppr.

Garter (Brigstock, co. Northampton; granted 2 July, 10 James I.). Same *Arms* and *Crest*.

Garter. Chequy erm. and or.

Garth (Morden, co. Surrey, and Headlam, co. Durham; a co-heir of this family, which has been located at Morden for three centuries and a half, ELIZABETH, second dau. of RICHARD GARTH, Esq., of Morden, m. WILLIAM LOWNDES STONE, of Brightwell, co. Oxford, and succeeded, at the decease of her elder sister without male issue, to the estate of Morden). Or, two lions pass. in pale betw. three crosses crosslet fitchée sa. *Crest*—An Indian goat ar. attired, eared, collared, and lined or.

Garth, or M'Grath (Galloway, Scotland). Quarterly, per pale and chev. ar. and gu.

Gartherne. Sa. a chev. betw. three spears' heads ar.

Garthside. Erm. a cross pattée az. *Crest*—Out of a ducal coronet or, a cross pattée az.

Garton (co. Kent). Chequy ar. and az.

Garton (co. Suffolk). On a chev. or, betw. two bezants in chief and a griffin's head erased in base of the second.

Garton (Woolavington, co. Sussex; descended from THOMAS

Garton, of London, merchant, living *temp.* Queen Elizabeth, by JOAN, his wife, dau. and heiress of Sir RICHARD BURFORD, Knt.; the heiress, MARY GARTON, *m.* ROBERT ORME, Esq.). Sa. nine tilting spears ar. in parcels, three in each, viz., one in pale and two in saltire, banded or. *Crest*—A leopard's head erased or, ducally gorged gu. on the head two straight horns of the last.

Garton (co. Sussex). Gu. a chev. ar. on a chief sa. a griffin's head erased or, betw. two bezants.

Garton (co. York). Per chev. sa. and gu. in chief two bezants.

Garton (co. York). Gu. a chev. or, betw. three bezants.

Garton. Per chev. gu. and sa. in chief two bezants, in base a griffin's head erased or.

Garton. Gu. billettée or, a chief indented of the last.

Garton. Chequy or and gu. on a fesse az. three escallops of the first.

Garton. Gu. a chev. ar. betw. two bezants in chief, and in base a griffin's head erased or.

Gartshore (that Ilk, co. Dumbarton). Ar. a saltire betw. four holly leaves vert. *Crest*—An eagle displ. ppr. *Motto* —I renew my age.

Gartshore (Alderston). See STIRLING, of Craigburnat.

Gartside (Rochdale, co. Lancaster, 1664). Ar. on a bend sa. three mullets of the field. *Crest*—A greyhound statant ar.

Garvagh, Baron. See CANNING.

Garvey (Aughnagonn, co. Down; PATRICK GARVEY, Esq., was Principal Secretary to Sir Henry Bagenal, Marshal of Ireland, *temp.* Queen Elizabeth; allowed by MacCulloch, Ulster, to his descendant, JAMES GARVEY, 1760). Erm. two chevronels betw. three crosses pattée gu. *Crest*—A lion pass. guard. gu. *Motto*—Mirior invictus.

Garvine (Edinburgh, 1674). Az. three garvine fishes naiant ar. *Crest*—A hand holding a fish ppr. *Motto*—Always helping.

Garvine (GEORGE GARVINE, writer, Irvine, 1674). Az. three garvine fishes fesseways in pale ar. the midmost looking to the sinister and the others to the dexter. *Motto*—Semper fidus.

Garway (Lord Mayor of London, 1640). Ar. a pile betw. four leopards' faces gu. over all a fesse of the second.

Garway (The Lea, co. Hereford). Same *Arms.*

Garway (co. Worcester; the heiress of this family *m.* Sir NIGIL BOVER GRESLEY, seventh bart. of Nether Seale). Gu. a pile betw. four leopards or, over all a fesse az.

Garway. Ar. a pile surmounted by a bend gu. betw. four leopards' faces of the last. *Crest*—A leopard's head erased thrust through the neck with an arrow in fesse ppr.

Garwinton. Ar. (another, or) a chev. betw. three leaves gu.

Garwinton. Sa. a fesse dancettée betw. three leopards' faces ar. (another, or.)

Garwinton. Sa. a chev. betw. three pomegranates pendent ar.

Garwynton. Or, on a chev. betw. three woodbine leaves gu. a ducal coronet of the first.

Gascoigne (Parlington, co. York). Quarterly, 1st and 4th, ar. on a pale sa. a demi lucy erect couped or, a canton gu., for GASCOIGNE; 2nd and 3rd, ar. a chev. sa. betw. two pellets in chief, and a fish in base gu., for OLIVER. *Crest*— Out of a ducal coronet or, a demi lucy erect of the last, charged with a pellet.

Gascoigne-Trench. See TRENCH.

Gascoigne (quartered by NEVILL, of Leversedge. Visit. 1612. Har. MS. 1487). Ar. on a pale sa. a conger eel's head couped or, in the dexter canton a cross crosslet fitchée of the second.

Gascoigne (co. Durham). Same *Arms.*

Gascoigne. Sa. three conger eels' heads couped and erect or.

Gascoine (Fun. Ent. of the wife of JOHN MILES, Sheriff of Dublin, whose maiden name was GASCOINE). Ar. on a fess sa. a lucy naiant or.

Gascoigne (Cardington, co. Bedford). Ar. on a pale sa. a demi lucy (or conger's head) erect couped or. *Crest*— A demi lucy's head erect or, betw. two ostrich feathers.

Gascoigne (Sir WILLIAM GASCOYNE, knighted in Ireland by ROBERT, *Earl of Essex,* Lord Lieutenant, 30 July, 1599). Same *Arms.*

Gascoyne, or Gascoigne (co. Norfolk, Kerby, co. Northampton, and Gawthrope, Lassingcroft, and Parlington, co. York). Same *Arms. Crest*—Out of a ducal coronet or, a demi lucy erect of the last.

Gascoyne (co. York). Az. (another, sa.) three lucies' heads couped or.

Gascoyne-Cecil (*Marquess of Salisbury*). See CECIL.

Gaselee (the late Sir STEPHEN GASELEE, Knt., one of the Judges of the Court of Common Pleas). Or, ten billets az. four, three, two, and one. *Crest*—An arm embowed in armour, holding in the hand ppr. a dagger ar. hilt and pommel or.

Gaskell (co. Lancaster). Erm. three bars vert. *Crest*—Out of waves of the sea a dexter arm issuant from the elbow, holding an anchor cabled all ppr., over the crest the *Motto* —Spea.

Gaskell (Kiddington Hall, co. Oxford, and Beaumount Hall, co. Lancaster). Barry of six per pale erm. and vert counterchanged a lion ramp. gu. betw. two fleurs-de-lis in chief and an annulet in base or, for GASKELL, quartering, gu. on a chief ar. a lion pass. guard. gu., for BROOKS. *Crest*—An arm in bend sinister entwined by a cable, and surmounted by a rainbow all ppr. *Motto*—Spes.

Gaskell (Thornes House and Lupset Hall, co. York). Quarterly, 1st and 4th, ar. on a pale sa. a conger eel's head couped and erect or, for GASKELL; 2nd and 3rd, az. on a chev. three windmill sails crossways or, a martlet for diff., for MILNES. *Crests*—1st: A stork ppr. collared or, pendent therefrom an escutcheon sa. charged with an annulet or, and the dexter foot resting on an escallop gu.; 2nd: A garb or, banded by a fesse dancettée az. charged with three mullets pierced gold, for MILNES. *Motto*—Scio cui credidi.

Gaskell. Gu. on a chev. betw. three falcons close ar. as many crosses crosslet fitchée of the first, a crescent for diff. on a chief erm. three spearheads sa. the points embrued ppr. *Crest*—On a mount vert under an oak tree ppr. a greyhound couchant sa. collared or, resting the dexter paw on an escutcheon or, charged with a fleur-de-lis az.

Gason (Ickham, co. Kent; granted in 1598). Az. a fesse erm. cotised ar. betw. three goats' heads erased of the third, attired or. *Crest*—On a chapeau az. turned up erm. a goat's head couped ar. bearded and attired or.

Gason (Richmond, Nenagh, co. Tipperary, formerly of Ickham, co. Kent; settled in Ireland in the year 1640). Same *Arms* and *Crest. Motto*—Fama semper vivit.

Gason (co. Kent; granted 10 June, 1547). Az. on a fesse engr. betw. three goats' heads couped ar. collared gu. attired or, a hurt charged with a sun ppr. betw. two mascles sa. *Crest*—A goat's head couped ar. armed or, gorged on the neck with three mascles sa.

Gason (co. Kent). Az. on a bend engr. ar. betw. three roebucks' heads couped or, collared gu. a hurt betw. two mascles sa. pierced of the third.

Gason. Az. a bend erm. cotised ar. betw. three goats' heads erased of the second, armed or. *Crest*—Out of a ducal coronet az. a goat's head couped ar.

Gaspar. Az. a star within a crescent or.

Gasselyn, or Gasselyne (co. Wilts). Or (another, ar.) ten billets az. four, three, two, and one. *Crest*—An eagle displ. sa.

Gesset (Norwich). Ar. a saltire betw. four mullets pierced gu.

Gastelyne (co. Hants). Or, billettée az. a bend gu.

Gasteneys. Sa. a lion ramp. ar. collared gu.

Gasterton. Ar. four lozenges in fess conjoined gu. each charged with an annulet or.

Gastinges. Ar. five lozenges in bend sa.

Gaston. Chequy ar. and gu. three escallops in bend or. *Crest*—An owl sa.

Gastrell (Shipton Moyne, and Setbury, co. Gloucester). Chequy ar. and sa. on a chief or, three bucks' heads couped of the second. *Crest*—A lion's head erased ppr. gorged with a chaplet vert.

Gastricke. Ar. a bend lozengy az.

Gatacre (Gatacre, co. Salop; a family seated at that place since the time of Henry III., which lands were held of the crown by military service, and acquired originally by grant from Edward the Confessor). Quarterly, gu. and erm. in the 2nd and 3rd quarters three piles of the first, over all on a fesse az. five bezants. *Crest*—A raven ppr.

Gataker (Mildenhall, co. Suffolk; descended from Rev. THOMAS GATACRE, rector of St. Edmund's, Lombard Street, London, younger son of WILLIAM GATACRE, of Gatacre, co. Salop). Quarterly, 1st and 4th, quarterly, gu. and erm., in the 2nd and 3rd quarters three piles issuing from the chief and pointing to the base of the first, over all on a fesse az. five bezants; 2nd, ar. a lion ramp. per fesse sa. and gu.; 3rd, ar. a cross pattée fleury, at the ends sa.

Gataker (WILLIAM GATAKER, Esq.). Quarterly, gu. and erm. a chief dancettée of the first.

Gatchell (co. Somerset). Erm. a garb. az. on a canton of the second an annulet or. *Crest*—Out of a mural crown ar. a dexter arm embowed, habited az. cuffed erm. holding in the hand a chaplet of wheat ppr.

Gateford (co. Salop). Sa. a bend betw. six goats climant ar.

Gateford. Sa. three goats pass. ar.

Gateford. Gu. three goats' heads erased or. *Crest*—A demi antelope ppr. collared or.

Gates (Colliton, co. Devon). Ermines three lions ramp. or.

Gates (co. Essex, and Semer, co. York). Per pale gu. and az. three lions ramp. guard. or. *Crest*—A demi lion ramp. guard. or.

Gates (Gosberton, co. Lincoln). Same *Arms.*

Gates, or Gate. Sa. bezantée, on a chief erm. three mascles gu.

Gates, or Gate. Sa. three swords in bend or.

Gatesby, or Getesbery. Gu. a cross or, betw. two goats' heads erased ar. in chief, and as many lozenges vair in base (another, the lozenges in chief and the goats' heads in base).

Gatesden (co. Warwick). Ar. two palets sa. in chief three mullets of the second. *Crest*—A dexter arm embowed, vested gu. cuffed ar. holding a tilting spear ppr.

Gatesden. Az. five lioncels ramp. three and two or.

Gatesford (co. Chester). See GATEFORD.

Gateshead, Trades of (charter of incorporation by JOHN COSIN, Bishop of Durham, 24 April, 1671).

    FREEMASONS. Sa. on a chev. betw. three towers or, a pair of compasses open chevronwise az.

    BRICKLAYERS and TILERS. Az. a chev. or, in chief a fleur-de-lis ar. betw. two brick axes palewise of the second, in base a bundle of laths of same. *Crest*—A dexter arm embowed vested per pale or and gu. cuffed ar., holding in the hand ppr. a brick axe or. *Motto*—In God is all our trust.

    GLAZIERS. Ar. two grazing irons in saltire betw. four closing nails sa. on a chief gu. a lion pass. guard. or. *Crest* —A lion's head couped betw. two wings expanded or. *Supporters*—Two naked boys ppr. each holding a long torch enflamed or.

    SCULPTORS. Gu. a chev. betw. two chipping axes in chief ar. and a mullet in base or. *Crest*—A dexter arm embowed az. cuffed ar. holding in the hand ppr. an engraving chisel or.

    PAPER STAINERS. Az. a chev. betw. three phœnix heads erased or. *Crest*—A phœnix close or, in flames ppr. *Supporters*—Two leopards ar. spotted sa. ducally crowned, collared, and chained or.

    PEWTERERS. Az. on a chev. or, betw. three antique limbecks ar. as many roses gu. *Crest*—Two arms embowed ppr. holding in both arms, erect, a dish ar. *Supporters*— Two sea horses or, tails ppr. *Motto*—In God is all my trust.

    PLUMBERS. Ar. on a chev. betw. a cross staff fesseways sa. inclosed by two plummets az. all in chief, and in base a level reversed of the second, two soldering irons in saltire or, betw. a cutting knife on the dexter and a shave hook on the sinister side of the first. *Crest*—A triple fountain ar. issuing water ppr. on the top an angel, holding in the dexter hand a sword and in the sinister a pair of scales all or.

    SADDLERS. Az. a chev. betw. three manage saddles complete or. *Crest*—A horse pass. and on his head a plume of three feathers ar. *Supporters*—Two horses ar. hoofed and bridled or.

Gatfield. Barry of six or and gu. on a canton erm. a cross of the second. *Crest*—On a ducal coronet or, a cross gu.

Gathwite. Gu. a chev. or. *Crest*—A mastiff ppr. chained and collared or.

Gatonby (Gatonby, co. York). Erm. a chev. gu. betw. three mullets az. *Crest*—Two swords in saltire ppr.

Gattie, Gattey, or Gatty. Or, a lion ramp. sa. in the dexter paw a torteau. *Crest*—A stork sleeping, in the foot a stone.

Gattiscombe. Purp. three eagles displ. ar.

Gatty. Az. two shinbones in saltire betw. four fleurs-de-lis or. *Crest*—A pheasant rising ppr.

Gatty (granted to the Rev. ALFRED GATTY, D.D., Sub-Dean of York, and Vicar of Ecclesfield, co. York (the historian), the Rev. ROBERT HENRY GATTY, of Buckden, co. Huntingdon, and to CHARLES HENRY GATTY, Esq., of Felbridge Park, East Grinstead, co. Sussex). Per fess sa. and az. in chief a demi cat issuant guard. ar. and in base a shin bone in bend, surmounted by another in bend sinister, betw. four fleurs-de-lis or. *Crest*—An embattled gateway, thereon a cock pheasant rising all ppr. *Motto*—Non cate sed caute.

Gatward (Reed, co. Hertford). Paly of six or and az. on a fesse dancettée sa. three mullets ar. pierced gu.

Gauden (JOHN GAUDEN, Bishop of Exeter 1660, and of Worcester 1662. Monument at Worcester). Az. a chev. erm. betw. three leopards' faces or, a border of the second.

Gauden. Gu. three talbots' heads erased ar. collared and ringed az. *Crest*—A peacock's head ppr.

Gaudge. Or, on a fesse paly of four gu. and ar. betw. three estoiles sa. a lion pass. betw. two fleurs-de-lis, each divided per pale counterchanged.

Gaudine (that Ilk). Ar. two chev. engr. gu. *Crest*—A savage's head couped ppr.

Gaughton. Ar. a bend gobony gu. and of the first betw. two hurts.

Gauldesborough. Az. a cross patonce ar. *Crest*—A pelican vulning herself ppr.

Gaulfield. Or, three bars gu. a canton erm. *Crest*—A dexter hand, vested gu. cuffed ar. holding up the sun ppr.

Gaunt (Highfield and Leek, co. Stafford; descended from JOHN GAUNT, Esq., of Rowley, co. Stafford, b. 1670, grandson of ROGER GAUNT, Esq., of Rowley, descended of a family who, by long tradition, claimed descent from the ancient *Earls of Lincoln*). Barry of six (sometimes of eight) or and az. a bend gu. *Crest*—A wolf's head or, gorged with a collar vair.

Gaunt (Canterbury). Barry of six or and gu. over all a bend vair. *Crest*—A wolf's head gorged with a collar vair.

Gaunt, De. Barry of eight or and az. a bend gu. *Crest*— A cross pattée fitchée sa.

Gaunt. Gu. three gauntlets ar.

Gauntlet, or Gauntlett. Quarterly, 1st and 4th, chequy gu. and ar.; 2nd and 3rd, sa. *Crest*—Out of a ducal coronet a bear's head muzzled all ppr.

Gausil. Ar. on a bend sa. three trefoils or.

Gaussen (Brookman's Park, co. Herts). Az. on a mount in base vert a lamb pass. ar. on a chief of the last three bees volant ppr. *Crest*—A hive with bees volant all ppr.

Gauston. Sa. three estoiles or, a bordure engr. of the last.

Gautier (Lorraine). Or, three pineapples vert, two and one, a bordure engr. gu.

Gautier (Jersey). Az. a chev. or, betw. three swords in pale ar. hilted of the first.

Gavell (Cobham, co. Surrey; granted 12 Aug. 1572). Sa. an eagle displ. ar. on a chief or, three pheons of the first. *Crest*—A demi buck reguard. or, vulned on the shoulder gu.

Gaven, or Gawen (co. Wilts). Erm. on a saltire engr. az. five fleurs-de-lis or. *Crest*—A dexter hand holding up a ducal coronet capped betw. two laurel branches all ppr.

Gavenor. Gu. a fox pass. or.

Gaveregan, or Gavergan (Gaveregan, co. Cornwall). Az. a goat pass. ar. horned or.

Gaveston (*Earl of Cornwall*; PIERS DE GAVESTON, the favourite of Edward II., beheaded 1314). Vert six eagles displ. or, beaked and membered gu.

Gavine (Langton, co. Berwick). Ar. a sword in pale az. ensigned with a mullet gu. surmounted by a saltire couped sa. *Crest*—In a sea a two-masted ship in full sail ppr. *Motto*—By industry we prosper.

Gawdy (Claxton, co. Norfolk, Stapleton and Ipswich, co. Suffolk). Vert a tortoise pass. ar. *Crest*—On a chapeau gu. turned up erm. two swords erect on their hilts ar. hilts and pommels or.

Gawdy (Harliston and West Herling, co. Norfolk, bart., extinct 1723). Same *Arms. Crest*—A wolf pass. per pale ar. and gu.

Gawdy (Crows Hall, co. Suffolk, bart., extinct at the death of the third bart.). Same *Arms* and *Crest*.

Gawdy (Wallington, co. Norfolk). Same *Arms*, tinctures reversed.

Gawdy (co. Norfolk). Or, on a fesse gobonated gu. and ar. betw. three estoiles sa. a demi lion ramp. and two fleurs-de-lis counterchanged.

Gawdy (cos. Lancaster and Hants, and Horsington, co Somerset). Erm. on a saltire engr. az. five fleurs-de-lis or.

Gawen. Ar. on a chief sa. three mullets pierced of the first.

Gawer. Gu. three lions ramp. ar. *Crest*—Out of a ducal coronet or, a boar's head erect sa. betw. two ostrich feathers ar.

Gawler. Gu. on a bend ar. three caltraps sa. *Crest*—A martlet sa. *Another Crest*—A mullet sa.

Gawler. Ar. a lion pass. in bend betw. two cotises gu. *Crest*—A hawk holding in the dexter claw an ear of wheat all ppr.

Gawsell (Wallington and Wiggenhall, St. Mary's, co. Nor. folk). Barry of six or and az. a canton erm.

Gawseworth. Ar. two chev. and a canton gu. *Crest*—A savage's head in profile ppr.

Gawthern (co. Nottingham). Ar. a bend compony gu. and az. betw. two pellets. *Crest* Out of a mural coronet or, a wyvern's head sa.

Gawtree (Boston, co. Lincoln). Ar. on a bend sa. three

cats-a-mountain, their tails betwixt their legs and over their loins of the field.

Gawyn. Gu. three crescents or, a bordure engr. ar.

Gay (Gouldesworth, co. Devon. The heiress of CURTOYS of Goldworthy, and a co-heiress of GAMOND, or GAMBON, m. into this family, which was originally of Hampton Gay, co. Oxford, and appears to have settled at Goldsworthy in 1420. JOHN GAY, the poet, was of this family. Visit. Devon, 1620). Or, on a fesse sa. betw. three escallops az. six lozenges conjoined ar.

Gay (co. Devon). Or, a chev. betw. three escallops az. Crest—On a chapeau gu. turned up erm. a lion pass. guard. or, charged on the breast with an escallop az.

Gay (Elmsted and Peckham, co. Kent). Gu. crusily or, three lions ramp. ar. Crest—A demi greyhound ramp. sa. collared or.

Gay (Alborough, co. Norfolk). Az. on a fesse per pale gu. and or, betw. three mullets of six points of the second, a demi lion ramp. betw. two fleurs-de-lis counterchanged. Crest—A fleur-de-lis or. Motto—Toujours gai.

Gay (Thurning Hall, and London Lode House, Upwell, co. Norfolk). Same Arms, Crest, and Motto.

Gay (Bath, co. Somerset). Sa. a chev. ar. betw. three escallops or. Crest—A greyhound courant ppr. Motto—Stat fortuna domus.

Gay. Az. a lion ramp. and a bordure or, a canton of the last.

Gay. Az. on a bend erm. (another, ar.) three mullets sa. (another, gu.).

Gay. Erm. on a chief gu. three cinquefoils ar.

Gay. Gu. a lion ramp. reguard. ar. Crest—A hand ppr. holding a sword ar. hilt and pommel or.

Gay. Az. on a chev. ar. betw. three leopards' faces or, as many fleurs-de-lis gu.

Gay (granted to WILLIAM GAY, Esq., son of the late WILLIAM GAY, Esq., of Falmouth, for 25 years Comptroller of the Post Office Packet Establishment at that port). Erm. on a pile betw. two escallops az. a falcon belled or. Crest—In front of a fir-tree ppr. a falcon ar. belled or, supporting with the dexter claw an arrow point downwards also ppr. and charged on its breast with an escallop az. Motto—Gwyr yn erbyn y byd.

Gayeon. Ar. a lion ramp. sa. surmounted by a bend gu. charged with three escallops or.

Gayer (Foxley, co. Berks). Ar. a fleur-de-lis sa.

Gayer (Trenbrace, co. Cornwall). Erm. a fleur-de-lis sa. Crest—A lion ramp. sa. supporting a spear.

Gayer. Or, on a bend cotised sa. three cinquefoils of the field.

Gayer. Ar. on a chief gu. three cinquefoils of the first.

Gayford (West Wretham, co. Norfolk; granted to FREDERICK GAYFORD, Esq., of West Wretham, 1855). Sa. three goats' heads erased ar. armed or. Crest—A goat's head, as in the arms.

Gaynor (cos. Meath and Longford; granted 21 Dec. 1666). Per pale gu. and vert a lion saliant betw. three trefoils or. Crest—A lion's head erased gu. charged with a trefoil or.

Gaynsford, or Gaynsforth. Gu. a lion pass. guard. ar. betw. three buckles or. Crest—A rose gu. slipped and leaved vert, and a spear ppr. in saltire.

Gaynsford. Or, three bars gu. a canton erm.

Gaynsford (Idbury, co. Oxford; JOHN GAYNSFORD, fourth in descent from Sir JOHN GAYNSFORD, Knt., of Crowhurst, co. Surrey. Visit. 1566). Ar. a chev. gu. betw. three greyhounds courant sa. collared or. Crest—A demi woman, vested and crined or, holding in the dexter hand a garland vert, charged with four roses gu. Another Crest—An anchor with double fluke and lined or.

Gaynsford (Cassolton, co. Surrey, and London. Her. Visit. 1568). Same Arms. Crest—A demi maiden couped below the waist, habited gu. crined or, holding in the dexter hand a wreath vert, and in the sinister a rose branch ppr.

Gaynsford (co. Kent) Same Arms.

Gaythinge. Ar. three pellets betw. two barrulets sa. all betw. three goats' heads erased gu. armed or.

Gaythold. Or, a bend sa. betw. two cotises engr. of the last.

Gayton. Ar. a fess betw. three fleurs-de-lis gu.

Gayton. Sa. an eagle displ. or. Crest—Three legs conjoined in armour, flexed at the knee and spurred all ppr.

Gayton. Ar. a fesse betw. six fleurs-de-lis gu.

Gaywood (London). Gu. three towers triple-towered ar.

Gealagh (allowed by Hawkins, Ulster, 1756, to SYLVESTER GEALAGH and his nephew, JAMES GEALAGH, both of Nantes, in France; descended from JOHN GEALAGH, son of Col. JOHN

O'NEILL, brother of ART O'NEILL, Prince of Tyrone, who d. 1519). Arms same as O'NEILL. Crest—A naked arm embowed, holding a sword all ppr. Motto—Hæc manus pro patria pugnando vulnera passa.

Geale (Ireland). Ar. three stocks of trees couped and eradicated sa. sprouting anew. Crest—Out of a ducal coronet or, a hand holding a fleur-de-lis ppr.

Geale-Brady. See BRADY.

Geare (Gillingham, co. Kent, and Heavitree, co. Devon). Gu. two bars or, on each three mascles az. on a-canton of the second a leopard's face of the first. Crest—A leopard's head az. ducally gorged or, betw. two wings gu.

Geare (co. Devon). Same Arms, leopard's face az.

Gearing (Winterton, co. Lincoln). Gu. two bars or, on each three mascles of the first, on a canton ar. a leopard's face of the first.

Geart. Or, two lions pass. betw. three crosses crosslet fitchée sa.

Geary (Polesden, co. Surrey, since of Oxonhoath, co. Kent, bart.). Quarterly, 1st and 4th, gu. two bars or, charged with three mascles az. two and one, on a canton ar. an anchor sa.; 2nd and 3rd, ar. a chev. voided betw. three fleurs-de-lis gu. a bordure of the last. Crest—Out of a naval crown a dexter hand and arm in a naval uniform all ppr. supporting a flag ar. charged with a cross couped gu. Motto—Chace.

Geary (co. Hertford). Gu. two bars ar. each charged with three mascles of the field, on a canton or, a leopard's face az. Crest—An antelope's head erased, quarterly ar. and sa. attired or, charged with three mascles, two and one, counterchanged.

Geary (co. Surrey). Gu. two bars ar. on each three mascles of the first, a canton erm. Crest—An heraldic antelope's head erased, quarterly ar. and sa. on the centre of the quartering a lozenge erm.

Geary-Salte (London; exemplified to WILLIAM GEARY, upon assuming, by royal licence, the name of SALTE in addition to that of GEARY, 1798). Az. on a chev. or. betw. three mullets per pale or and erm. three mascles gu. Crest—A demi lion per pale or and sa. charged on the shoulder with two mullets in fess counterchanged.

Gebes. Lozengy ar. and gu. on a bend az. a fleur-de-lis betw. two pairs of annulets interlaced of the first.

Ged (that Ilk). Az. three pikes haurient ar. Crest—A pike's head ppr. Motto—Durat, ditat, placet.

Geddes (Rachan, Scotland). Gu. an inescutcheon ar. betw. three pikes' heads couped or. Crest—A pike's head couped ppr. Motto—Capta majora.

Gedding (co. Norfolk). Gu. a chev. ar. betw. three griffins' heads erased or.

Gedding (Icklingham, co. Suffolk). Gu. a chev. betw. three eagles' heads erased or.

Gedding (co. Suffolk). Ar. three mullets gu.

Gedding. Chequy ar. and gu. on a fesse az. three buckles or. Crest—A demi savage holding a scimetar ppr.

Gedding, or Jenyns (granted, 1516, to WILLIAM JENYNS, Lancaster Herald, and allowed to his grandson, GALFRIDUS JENYNS, of Ipsley, co. Warwick. Visit. Warwick, 1619). Az. a chev. betw. three griffins' heads erased ar. on a chief or, a lion pass. gu. betw. two torteaux.

Gedeon. Az. a fleece ar. in chief six guttées d'eau.

Gedge. Az. three cinquefoils in bend or.

Geding (co. Suffolk). Ar. on a fesse az. three buckles of the field.

Gedinge. Gu. three chev. ar.

Gedney (Enderby, co. Lincoln). Ar. two fishes in saltire az. Crest—A bird perched on an oak plant ppr.

Gedney (Hudderley, co. Lincoln). Az. two lucies in saltire ar. Crest—Two lucies, as in the arms.

Gedney (co. Suffolk). Or, three eagles displ. sa.

Gedney. Or, on a fess betw. three leopards' faces gu. as many eagles displ. of the field.

Gedney (quartered by STAMFORD, of Rowley, co. Stafford). Or, on a fess gu. betw. three leopards' faces of the second, three eagles displ. of the field.

Gedon (Alderman of Dublin; Reg. Ulster's Office). Gu. a chev. betw. three roses ar.

Gedrinke, or Geding. Chequy or and gu. on a fesse az. three fleurs-de-lis or.

Gee (Rathley, co. Leicester; EUSTACE GEE, aged 30. Visit. 1619; seventh in descent from ALEXANDER GEE, of same place, temp. Henry V.). Gu. a sword in bend ar. hilt and pommel or. Crest—A dexter gauntlet erect ppr. grasping a sword, as in the arms.

Gee (London and co. York; originally of Rothley, co. Leicester). Same Arms and Crest.

Gee (Manchester). Same Arms.

Gee, or Ghee. Per pale gu. and ar. a sword in bend counterchanged.

Geekie (London). Ar. a chev. az. betw. two roses in chief gu. barbed ppr. and a bear's head erased sa. in base. *Crest*—A dexter hand holding a sickle ppr.

Geere (Kene, co. Devon; JOHN GEERE, of that place. Visit. 1620). Gu. two bars or, each charged with three mascles az. on a canton of the second a leopard's face of the third.

Geering. Gu. two bars ar. on each three lozenges of the first. *Crest*—A savage's head affrontée ducally crowned ppr.

Geff (Huborne, co. Berks; granted 1 April, 1579). Erm. on a canton sa. a saltire or, a martlet for diff. *Crest*—On a chapeau gu. turned up erm. a tiger couchant ar. tufted and maned sa. armed or, charged on the body with a martlet of the fourth.

Geffe, or Geffy. Ermines on a canton ar. a saltire engr. sa.

Geffery. Ar. three chev. sa.

Geffery (granted by Sir Edward Bysse, Clarenceux, 1676, to Sir ROBERT GEFFERY, Knt., then Sheriff of the City of London, and afterwards Lord Mayor). Ar. six billets sa. on a chief of the second a lion pass. or, armed and langued gu. *Crest*— A lion's head erased or, billettée sa.

Geffery (Lord Mayor of London, 1686; granted by Bysse, Clarenceux). Ar. six billets sa. on a chief of the second a lion pass. gu.

Geffry (co. Cornwall). Or, five billets in saltire sa.

Geffry. Az. a fret (another, fretty) or, on a chief ar. a lion pass. guard. gu. *Crest*—A lion's head erased ar. ducally crowned az.

Geffry. Gu. three lions pass. in pale ar.

Geffrys (co. Worcester). Or, three hawks' lures lined gu. on a chief crenellée of the last as many leopards' faces of the first. *Crest*—On a mount vert a sea-pye, wings expanded ppr. legged and beaked gu.

Geirveis (Benathleck, co. Cornwall; THOMAS GEIRVEIS, descended from JOHN GEIRVEIS, of Helston, 17 Edward II. Visit. 1620). Ar. a chev. betw. three garbs sa.

Geldart (Dr. GELDART, co. Cambridge). Vert a lion ramp. reguard. and ducally crowned az. *Crest*—A demi lion ramp. reguard. or, and crowned o' the last, holding an oak branch ppr.

Gelks. Erm. on three chev. az. betw. nine annulets gu. as many bezants.

Gell (Hopton, co. Derby, bart., extinct 1719. Sir JOHN GELL, of Hopton, the celebrated Parliamentary leader, was created a baronet in 1642; his grandson, Sir PHILIP GELL, of Hopton, the third bart., *d. s. p.* in 1719; his sister and heiress *m.* WILLIAM EYRE, of Highlow, and their second son, JOHN EYRE, inheriting the property, assumed the surname and arms of GELL; he was grandfather of PHILIP GELL, Esq., of Hopton, and of Sir WILLIAM GELL, Knt., the classical antiquary). Per bend az. and or, three mullets of six points in bend, pierced and counterchanged. *Crest*—A greyhound statant sa. collared or.

Gell (Westminster; granted 6 March, 1631). Per bend ar. and gu. a rose betw. two mullets of six points pierced in bend counterchanged.

Gell (Middleton and Wirk, co. Derby; granted in 1731). Same *Arms. Crest*—A greyhound sa.

Gell. Az. on a bend engr. betw. two lions' heads erased or, three cinquefoils gu.

Gellatly (Loughton, co. Essex, 1870). Erm. issuing from an antique crown or, a demi lion ramp. with two tails gu. holding in the dexter paw a thistle ppr. *Crest*—A lion's head erased crowned with an antique crown or. *Motto*—Hactenus invictus.

Gellatly (Uplands, co. Kent). Same *Arms*, a bordure gu. Same *Crest* and *Motto*.

Gelliat, or Gellyot (co. York). Erm. on a bend sa. three boars' heads (another, wiverns; another, fishes) erased ar.

Gellibrand (Paul's Cray, co. Kent, *temp.* Henry VIII., and Chorley Hall, co. Lancaster). Ar. two swords in their scabbards in saltire sa. hilts and chapes or.

Gellibrand (Peele, co. Lancaster, 1665). Same *Arms*, a canton gu.

Gellibrand (Ramsgreve, co. Lancaster). Same *Arms*, a cinquefoil in chief gu.

Gellie (Blackford, Scotland). Ar. an ark in the water ppr. ensigned by a dove with an olive branch in the beak vert. *Crest*—A man trampling on a serpent ppr. *Motto*—Divino robore.

Gelstable, Gelysale, or Gellisdale. Vert a hart trippant (another, saliant) or, attired ar. *Crest*—A dexter hand holding a sword in pale all ppr.

Genevill (co. Northumberland). Or, two bars az. betw. three coronets gu.

Genevill, Genevel, or Geneville. Same *Arms. Crest*—Out of a cloud a dexter hand brandishing a broken tilting spear all ppr.

Genevill (*Baron Genevill;* Ludlow Castle, co. Salop, and Trim Castle, Ireland, *temp.* Edward I; JOAN, dau. and heir of Sir PETER DE GEYNVILLE, *m.* in 1301, ROGER MORTIMER, *Earl of March*, in her right, Lord of Meath and Trim. Sir SIMON DE GEYNVILLE, Knt., younger brother of Sir PETER, was summoned as a Baron to Parliament in Ireland, 3 Edward II.). Az. three horses' bits or, on a chief erm. a demi lion issuant gu.

Genevill. Az. three barnacles in pale or, on a chief erm. a demi lion ramp. gu. crowned of the second.

Geney, Genney, or Jeny. Az. an inescutcheon ar. within an orle of eight martlets or. *Crest*—A hand issuing out of a cloud in fesse, holding a cross pattée fitchée ppr.

Geney. Or, a bordure az. charged with eight martlets of the field.

Geney. Gu. an eagle displ. ar. (another, or).

Genhaver. Ar. a cross betw. four lions ramp. gu.

Genkins (co. Chester). Sa. a lion pass. guard. tail turned betw. his legs and elevated over the back or.

Genn. Or, three piles meeting in point az. *Crest*—A Cornish chough rising betw. two spear heads in pale ppr.

Gennett. Ar. two chevronels gu. betw. six martlets sa. three, two, and one. *Crest*—A chevalier on horseback wielding a scymitar all ppr.

Genney (co. Norfolk). Paly of six or and gu. a chief erm.

Gennings (Fun. Ent. of STEPHEN GENNINGS, Clerk of Works in Ireland to Queen Elizabeth, buried 4 Nov. 1599). Az a chev. betw. three griffins' heads erased ar. on a chief or, a lion pass. guard. gu. betw. two torteaux.

Gennison (Fun. Ent. of NICHOLAS WHITE, Esq., of Dufferin, co. Down, *d.* 5 March, 1625, *m.* ELIZABETH GENNISON). Az. on a bend wavy betw. two swans ar. three roses gu. seeded of the second, leaved vert.

Gennys (HENN-GENNYS, Whitleigh, co. Devon; exemplified to EDWARD HENN, Esq., *m.* MARY, only dau. and heir of JOHN GENNYS, Esq., upon his assuming, by royal licence, 1802, the additional name of GENNYS). Quarterly, 1st and 4th, or and ar. a lion pass. guard. per pale az. and gu., for GENNYS; 2nd and 3rd, ar. a falcon sa. bezantée, belled or, in the beak a sprig of myrtle ppr., for HENN. *Crests*—GENNYS: An eagle per pale az. and gu. the wings elevated, each charged with a bezant, from the beak an escroll ar. thereon the words "Deo gloriâ;" HENN: A hen pheasant ppr.

Genon, or Genron. Az. a cross or, pierced of the field.

Genor. Sa. three cups or (another, ar). *Crest*—A dexter hand holding a baton gu. tipped or.

Gens (Antwerp; AGNES, dau. of SEBASTIAN GENS, of that place, *m.* Alderman JAMES HARVEY, of London. Visit. 1568). Or, three fleurs-de-lis sa. on a canton of the last three martlets ar. a border of the first.

Gensill (co. Sussex). Or, on a chief sa. two mullets ar.

Genslor, Genslwyr, or Genflor. Ar. three escallops gu. on a chief az. three crosses crosslet or.

Gent (Doddinghurst and Steeple Bumstead, co. Essex). Erm. on a chief indented sa. two eagles displ. or. *Crest*—Out of a ducal coronet or, a demi eagle displ. erm.

Gent (co. Essex). Erm. on a chief indented az. three eagles displ. or.

Gent (Norton and Muscott, co. Northumberland). Sa. a fesse counter-compony ar. and of the first betw. three lions' heads erased or. *Crest*—A demi griffin gu. wings endorsed or, holding a pink (or gillyflower) of the first, stalked and leaved vert. *Another Crest*—A griffin segreant or, holding in the beak a gillyflower gu. stalked and leaved vert.

Gent (Moyns, co. Essex. In the 15th century the family acquired the estate of Moyns, by the intermarriage of WILLIAM GENT, living 1468, with JOAN, dau. and heiress of WILLIAM LE MOYNS. The grandson of this marriage, Baron GENT, of the Court of Exchequer, is described "as a very considerable person in his time, and the glory and ornament of his family"). Erm. a chief indented sa. quartering MOYNE, viz., or, a cross engr. sa. a label of three points gu. on each three bezants. *Crest*—A demi eagle displ. erm.

Gentill (co. Lancaster). Or, on a chief sa. two mullets of six points ar. pierced gu. (another, three cinquefoils). *Crest* —Two lions' paws or, holding a bezant.

Gentill (co. Sussex). Or, on a chief sa. two mullets of the field (another adds, pierced gu.).

Gentle. Gu. three roses ar. a chief of the last. *Crest*—On a ducal coronet or, an estoile of twelve points.

Gentleman (Ballyhorgan and Mount Coal, co. Kerry; granted to GOODMAN GENTLEMAN, Esq., of those places).

Erm. two eagles displ. with two heads in chief sa. and an esquire's helmet in base ppr. a chief indented gu. *Crest*—A demi eagle displ. with two heads sa. on each wing a trefoil or. *Motto*—Truth, honour, and courtesy.

Gentleman-at-Arms, Corps of. Gu. two battle axes in saltire or, in chief a crown of the second, lined erm. *Motto*—Per tela per hostes.

Genton (co. Cumberland). Gu. a chev. betw. three escallops ar.

Genton (co. Warwick). Per bend ar. and sa. a staff raguly counterchanged (another, tinctures reversed).

Genton. Sa. a bend raguly ar.

Geoffrey. Erm. on a canton ar. a saltire engr. sa.

Geoffreys (Her. Off. London). Sa. a griffin segreant and a bordure engr. or.

Geoghegan (confirmed by Roberts, Ulster, 1646, to Lieut.-Col. BRYAN GEOGHEGAN, of Col. William Warren's regiment of foot, descended of an ancient family in Ireland). Ar. a lion ramp. sa. crowned and collared or, betw. two dexter hands couped gu. a crescent of the second charged with another of the first for diff. *Crest*—A greyhound pass. ar. collared vert, the collar studded with fleurs-de-lis or.

Geoghegan. See MAC-GEOGHEGAN.

Georg. Ar. a cross patonce sa.

George (Park Place, co. Middlesex, and St. Stephen's Green, co. Dublin, bart.). Ar. on a fesse engr. gu. betw. three falcons rising az. beaked, legged, and belled or, as many bezants, each charged with a lion's head erased sa. on a canton vert a harp gold, stringed of the first. *Crest*—A falcon, as in the arms.

George (Cirencester, co. Gloucester). Same *Arms*, without the canton.

George (Trenouth, co. Cornwall; SALATHIELL GEORGE, descended from Osmonton, co. Dorset, and Come, co. Gloucester. Visit. 1620). Ar. on a fess betw. three doves volant az. as many bezants, each charged with a lion's head erased sa. *Crest*—A demi talbot ramp. sa. gorged with a collar dancettée, and eared or, betw. two laurel branches vert.

George (Whittington, co. Worcester). Erm. a lion ramp. sa. a border engr. sa.

George (Scotland). Or, (another, ar.) a fess betw. three falcons rising az. membered gu. *Crest*—The sun shining on a sunflower ppr.

George. Ar. on a fesse engr. gu. betw. three parrots, wings expanded and addorsed az. as many bezants, each charged with a parrot's head erased sa.

George. Or, on a fesse betw. three falcons rising az. membered gu. as many bezants, each charged with a lion's head erased sa. *Crest*—A demi talbot sa. gorged with a collar indented and eared or, betw. two fir branches vert.

George (Bath, formerly of co. Norfolk). Ar. on a fesse engr. gu. betw. three doves volant az. beaked, belled, and legged or, three bezants, each charged with a lion's head erased sa. *Crest*—A demi lion ramp. ar. holding a staff raguly couped ppr.

Georges, or Gorge (Westminster and Hayes, co. Middlesex). Lozengy or and az. a chev. gu. *Crest*—A greyhound's head ppr.

Georges (Island of St. Christopher). Erm. on a saltire gu. a leopard's face or. *Crest*—A boar pass. az. armed and bristled or.

Georges. Gu. six lozenges or, three, two, and one.

Gepp (co. Essex, formerly co. Somerset). Per chev. az. and gu. a chev. engr. or, surmounted of a plain chev. sa. betw. three falcons close ar. beaked, legged, jessed, and belled of the third, collared gu. *Crest*—On a mount vert an eagle rising az. wings erminois, gorged with a collar, and in the beak a mascle or, the dexter claw supporting a sword erect ppr. pommel and hilt gold.

Gerald (Reg. Ulster's Office). Erm. a saltire engr. gu. a border of the last.

Gerard (Lord *Gerard*, of Gerards Bromley; created 1603, extinct 1707). Ar. a saltire gu. quartering Az. a lion ramp. erm. crowned or. *Crest*—A lion's gamb couped and erect erm. holding a hawk's lure gu. tasselled and garnished or.

Gerard (Earl of *Macclesfield* ; created 1679, extinct 1702). Ar. a saltire gu. a crescent for diff.

Gerard (Lord *Gerard* ; Sir ROBERT TOLVER GERARD, thirteenth bart. of Bryn, was so created 1876). Ar. a saltire gu. *Crest* —A lion ramp. erm. crowned or. *Supporters*—Two lions erm. ducally crowned or, gorged with a collar gemel gu. and supporting a tilting spear ppr. *Motto*—En Dieu est mon esperance.

Gerard (Ince, co. Lancaster; descended from the house of Bryn. Visit. Lanc. 1567). Az. a lion ramp. erm. crowned or, a crescent for diff., quartering INCE and HETTON. *Crest*—

A lion's gamb erect and erased erm. holding a lure gu. tasselled and lined or.

Gerard (Harrow-on-the-Hill, bart., extinct 1715; descended from the second son of WILLIAM GERARD, Esq., of Ince). Same *Arms* and *Crest*.

Gerard (Astley, co. Lancaster, 1567). Same *Arms*, a crescent on a crescent for diff. Same *Crest*, charged with a crescent on a crescent.

Gerard (co. Berks). Az. a chev. engr. erm.

Gerard (Crewood, co. Chester). Az. a lion ramp. erm. ducally crowned or, over all a bend gu.

Gerard (Etwall, co. Derby). Az. a lion ramp. erm. crowned or. *Crest*—Two wings expanded sa. *Another Crest*—A lion's gamb erect and erased erm. holding a lure gu. garnished and lined or, tasselled ar.

Gerard (co. Lancaster). Az. a lion ramp. erm.

Gerard (Sir WILLIAM GERARD, Lord Chancellor of Ireland, knighted by Sir Henry Sydney, Lord Deputy). Same *Arms*.

Gerard (Fisherton, co. Lincoln, bart., extinct). Ar. on a bend sa. three lions pass. guard. or.

Gerard. Gu. a lion pass. guard. ar. crowned or.

Gerard (Riddings, co. Chester. The heiress *m. circa* 1660, WM. DOMVILE, of Lymm). Az. a lion ramp. erm. ducally crowned or.

Gerard (Kingsley, co. Chester). Az. a lion ramp. ar. a bend gu.

Gerard (Hide). Az. a lion ramp. ar. crowned or, a bordure erm.

Gerard. Ar. a fesse betw. three mullets sa. pierced gu.

Gerard. Ar. (another, or) three chevronels gu.

Gerard. Gu. three inescutcheons erm.

Gerard. Erm. a fret of six sa. a chief gu.

Gerard. Per. fesse ar. and sa. a pale counterchanged, three negroes' head ppr.

Gerard. Ar. on a saltire gu. three crescents or.

Gerard. Ar. on a fesse az. three fleurs-de-lis or.

Gerard (Rochsoles, co. Lanark, 1807). Az. a lion ramp. or, on a chief embattled erm. a falchion in bend sinister ppr. hilted and pommelled or, surmounted by the Punja (one of the insignia borne before the Emperor Shah Allum) saltireways also ppr. *Crest*—Out of a mural crown ar. a lion's gamb erect erm. holding in bend sinister the Punja, as in the arms. *Motto*—Haud inferiora secutus.

Gerber. Erm. on a chief gu. three lozenges or.

Gerbrand. Gu. a fleur-de-lis or.

Gerbridge (Walsingham, co. Norfolk). Or, a fesse betw. two. chevronels az.

Gerbridge (co. Suffolk). Erm. on a chief gu. five lozenges or (another, lozenges of the field). *Crest*—A lion's paw holding a thistle ppr.

Gerbridge. Gu. three inescutcheons erm.

Gerby. Ar. a fret vert, on a canton sa. a stag at gaze ppr.

Gercom. Paly of six ar. and gu. *Crest*—A griffin segreant ppr. collared gu. in the mouth a line and ring or.

Gercomyle, or Gerconly. Quarterly, or and gu. (another, az.) in the first quarter a lion ramp. of the second.

Gerd, or Gird. Az. a chev. erm. betw. three lozenges or, each charged with an antelope's head erased ppr. attired of the third.

Gerdelley, or Gerdilley. Az. a chev. (another, engr.) betw. three fleurs-de-lis ar. *Crest*—A dexter hand brandishing a sword ppr.

Gerdston, or Gerdeston. Gu. a saltire lozengy ar.

Gere (Heavitree and Kenney, co. Devon, and Great Broughton, co. York. Dugdale, 1665). Gu. two bars or, on each three mascles az., on a canton of the second a leopard's face of the third.

Gere (co. Devon). Gu. a fesse erm. betw. six. mascles or.

Gere. Erm. a fleur-de-lis az.

Gerebzoff. Per pale two coats, 1st, ar. out of clouds, from the dexter an armed arm embowed issuant, the hand grasping a scymitar all ppr; 2nd, Or, a spread eagle dimidiated on the dexter sa. *Crest*—Out of a marquis's coronet ppr. a cross pattée or, surmounted by a human heart gu. flamant ppr. betw. two wings sa.

Geredot. Gu. three crescents ar.

Gerell. Sa. on a cross or, five pellets, a bordure engr. of the second.

Gergan, Gergand, or Geerewood. Per pale gu. and ar. three castles counterchanged (another, tinctures reversed).

Gergawd, or Gerwood. Per pale gu. and ar. three eagles counterchanged.

Gering (Winterton, co. Lincoln). Gu. two bars or, each charged with three mascles of the field, on a canton sa. a leopard's face of the second. *Crest*—An antelope's head erased, quarterly, ar. and sa. charged with four mascles counterchanged, attired or.

Gerlinge (Outwell, co. Norfolk, and co. York). Ar. on a bend gu. betw. two cotises sa. three fleurs-de-lis or. *Crest*—A unicorn's head erased ar. collared sa.

Gerlingham. Ar. three mascles gu.

Gerlington (Hakeford, co. York). Sa. three gadbees volant ar.

Gerlington (co. Lincoln). Same *Arms*, field gu. and a border engr. or.

Germain (*Duke of Dorset*, extinct 1843). See SACKVILLE-GERMAIN.

Germaine (Westminster, bart., extinct 1718). Az. a cross engr. or.

Germain, or Germyn. Sa. a crescent betw. two mullets in pale ar. *Crest*—A dexter arm couped and embowed resting on the elbow, holding a tilting spear in pale ppr.

German (Preston, co. Lancaster). Ar. a cross vairé gu. and or, in the 1st and 4th quarters an eagle displ. sa. *Crest*—A demi lamb ppr. supporting a flagstaff or, therefrom flowing a pennon ar. and charged with a rose also gu.

German (co. Cornwall). Paly wavy of six ar. and gu.

Germin (co. Essex). Ar. a stag's head cabossed gu.

Germin (EDWARD GERMIN, D.D., co. Hunts, 1613). Paly wavy of six erm. and gu. *Crest*—Three lilies ar. stalked vert.

Germin (Powershall). Ar. a chev. betw. three stags' heads cabossed sa.

Germingham (co. Suffolk). Ar. three lozenge buckles gu.

Germon (co. Kent). Barry nebulée of six ar. and gu.

Germy (co. Suffolk). Ar. a lion ramp. guard. gu.

Germyn, or Germin. Ar. a chev. betw. three harts' heads couped sa. *Crest*—A unicorn's head betw. two branches of laurel disposed orleways.

Germyn. Ar. three crosses pattée (another, patonce) sa.

Germyn. Erm. three piles in point gu.

Germyn. Gu. three escallops erm.

Germyn. Gu. a fesse embattled ar. betw. three leopards' faces or.

Germyn, or Germine. Gu. three inescutcheons erm.

Gernald. Ar. on a bend engr. sa. three buglehorns of the first.

Gernance. Sa. three covered cups ar.

Gernech, or Gernish. Ar. on a chev. az. betw. three escallops sa. as many annulets or.

Gernegan (Tanfield, Richmond). Barry of ten or and az. an eagle displ. gu.

Gernegan. Ar. three lozenges gu. *Crest*—An allerion displ. gu.

Gernegan. Barruly or and az. an eagle displ. of the first.

Gernegan. Ar. three bucks' heads gu.

Garnet (Speke, co. Lancaster; the heiress *m.* MOLYNEUX). Gu. a lion ramp. ar. crowned or, a bordure of the last.

Gerneth. Gu. three escallops or (another, ar.).

Gerney (co. Essex). Gu. a cross engr. gu. in the dexter chief quarter a cinquefoil az.

Gerney (co. Norfolk). Ar. a lion ramp. gu.

Gerney (co. Suffolk). Same *Arms*, the lion guard.

Gernon, Gernun, or Gernoun (co. Essex). Ar. three piles wavy gu. *Crest*—A hand issuing from a cloud in fesse, holding a club ppr.

Gernon (co. Hereford). Ar. three piles wavy gu. meeting in the base point and a bordure or.

Gernon (co. Hereford). Gu. two lions pass. ar. a bordure az.

Gernon, or Garnon (co. Nottingham). Or, a hart's head cabossed gu.

Gernon, alias Candishe. Ar. three piles wavy gu. *Crest*—A wolf's head couped az. collared and ringed or.

Gernon, alias Pike. Gu. three piles wavy ar.

Gernon (Bakewell, co. Derby). Paly wavy of six ar. and gu.

Gernon. Or, on a bend az. three escallops of the field.

Gernon. Ar. a chev. betw. three bucks' heads couped sa. (another, buck's heads gu).

Gernon. Ar. three harts' heads cabossed gu.

Gernon. Or, on a bend az. an escallop ar.

Gernon (Gernonstown and Killincoole, co. Meath; descended from ROGER DE GERNON, who went to Ireland with Strongbow, 1172. Fun. Ent. EDWARD GERNON, Ulster's Office, 1621). Ar. an eagle displ. sa. armed, beaked, and gorged with a chaplet or.

Gernon (Drogheda, Dublin, Bourdeaux, and Paris. Fun. Ent. of the wife of ROGER GERNON, of Dublin, Ulster's Office, 1620, and Reg. Ped.; descended from JOHN GERNON, second son of

395

Thomas Gernon, Esq., of Gernonstown, who *d.* 1517). Same *Arms*, a crescent for diff. *Crest*—A horse pass. ar. hoofed or.

Gernon (Athcarne Castle, co. Meath; descended from THOMAS GERNON, younger son of CHRISTOPHER GERNON, Esq., of Drogheda, and brother of RICHARD GERNON, living 1738, who settled at Bourdeaux). Same *Arms* and *Crest*. *Motto*—Parva contemnimus.

Gerondon-Abbey (co. Leicester). Gu. a cinquefoil erm. over all in bend a crozier or.

Gerow, or Gerrow. Ar. a cross gu. betw. four lions pass. respecting each other sa.

Gerrard (Harrow, co. Middlesex). Quarterly, 1st and 4th, ar. a saltire gu.; 2nd and 3rd, ar. a lion ramp. erm. crowned or.

Gerrard (Longhide, co. Somerset). Az. a lion ramp. ar. crowned or, a bordure erm.

Gerrare, or Greenere. Ar. three chalices sa.

Gerre (co. Hertford). Gu. two bars ar. on each three mascles az. on a canton of the last a leopard's face of the second. *Crest*—A lion's head guard. or, gorged with a collar gu. charged with three mascles gold betw. two wings displ. of the same.

Gerrey (co. Lancaster). Same *Arms*. *Crest*—A buck's head erased, quarterly, ar. and sa. charged with four mascles counterchanged.

Gerrotte (Fun. Ent. of THOMAS GERROTTE, Alderman and Lord Mayor of Dublin, buried at St. Audeons, 14 Feb. 1598). Ar. a saltire and a border gu.

Gerson (Gerson, co. Lancaster). Vert a cross engr. or. *Crest*—An arm in armour couped at the shoulder, in fesse from the elbow in pale, holding up a helmet all ppr.

Gertheston. Ar. on a fess sa. three crosses pattée or.

Gerton. Gu. twelve billets, five, four, two, and one, a chief indented or.

Gervais (Cecil, co. Tyrone; confirmed to FRANCIS JOHN GERVAIS, of that place). Az. a chev. or, betw. in chief two lions ramp. respectant ar. and in base a white rose leaved and slipped ppr. in the centre chief point a crescent of the third. *Crest*—A lion's head erased ar. charged with a fleur-de-lis az. *Motto*—Sic sustenta crescit.

Gervaise (Jersey). Ar. a chev. gu. betw. three escallops sa.

Gervays (Isle of Ely). Sa. a chev. engr. betw. three Cornish choughs ar.

Gervays. Az. three beacons with ladders or, fired gu. *Crest*—On a mural crown gu. a fire beacon betw. two wings ppr.

Gerveis. Gu. three greyhounds in full course in pale or.

Gerveis, or Gervais. Ar. a chev. gu. betw. three escallops sa.

Gerveys (Bonathlac, co. Cornwall; descended from JOHN GERVEYS, Esq., of Helston, living in 1329, and NICHOLIA, his wife, dau. and heiress of JOHN BONATHLAC, Esq., of Bonathlac; the heiress, ELIZABETH, only child of RICHARD GERVEYS, Esq., of Bonathlac, *m.* CHARLES GRYLLS, Esq., of Court, in Lanreath). Ar. a chev. betw. three garbs sa. quartering TREVANNION, of Tregaddar.

Gerveis, or Garvies (Pratling-Magna, co. Leicester). Gu. a lion ramp. ar.

Gervilance, Gerviland, or Gervylan. Ar. three saltires vert (another, the tinctures reversed).

Gervis (Isle of Ely, and co. Worcester). Sa. a chev. betw. three hawks ar. *Crest*—A tiger's head erased ar.

Gervis (Great Pettley, co. Leicester; granted by Camden, Clarenceux, May, 1614). Sa. a chev. erm. betw three hawks ar.

Gervis (co. Suffolk). Sa. three bechives or.

Gervis (Master of the Pipe Office, co. Essex; confirmed by Camden, Clarenceux, to ARTHUR GERVIS, Master of the Pipe Office). Quarterly, 1st and 4th, sa. on a chev. betw. three doves ar. a fleur-de-lis az.; 2nd and 3rd, gu. on a chev. betw. three trefoils slipped ar. as many pellets. *Crest*—A demi lion ramp. guard. or, supporting a banner, staff encircled with a coronet ppr. on the pennon ar. a cross gu.

Gervis (TAPPS-GERVIS, Hinton-Admiral, co. Hants, bart. See MEYRICK). Quarterly, 1st and 4th, ar. betw. six ostrich feathers sa. a cannon ball of the last, for GERVIS; 2nd and 3rd, az. on a fesse or, betw. three rhinoceroses ar. as many escallops gu., for TAPPS. *Crests*—1st, GERVIS: A plume of three ostrich feathers gu. and sa. bound by a wreath of laurel or, standing upon a mount ppr.; 2nd, TAPPS: A greyhound couchant per pale ar. and sa. charged on the body with two escallops fesseways counterchanged. *Motto*—Be just and fear not.

Gery (Bushmead Priory, co. Bedford; descended from THOMAS GERY, Esq., of Royston, co. Herts, Sheriff co. Cambridge, 1509. The last male heir, WILLIAM GERY, Esq., of Bushmead, *d.* 1802, leaving three daughters, his co-heirs,

viz., MARY SELINA, _m._ JOHN MILNES, Esq., of Beckingham Hall, co. Lincoln; ELEANOR, _m._ REV. THOMAS MILNES; and HESTER, _m._ Rev. HUGH WADE, who assumed, on his marriage, the surname and arms of GERY). Gu. two bars ar. each charged with three mascles of the field, on a canton or, a leopard's face az., quartering WADE. _Crest_—An antelope's head erased, quarterly ar. and sa., charged with four mascles counterchanged, attired or. _Motto_—Mentis honestæ gloria.

Gesors, or Gessors. Az. billettée and a lion ramp. or. _Crest_—A talbot sejant sa. collared ar.

Gesse. Ar. three dogfishes in pale sa.

Gethin (Peyton, co. Brecknock, and Southweld, co. Essex). Az. a buck saliant ar. crowned or. _Crest_—A buck sejant ar. crowned or, betw. two wings endorsed of the first.

Gethin (Gethinsgrott, co. Cork, and Percy Mount, co. Sligo, bart.). Vert a stag saliant ar. armed or. _Crest_—On a chapeau ppr. a stag's head erased ar. armed and ducally gorged or. _Motto_—Try.

Gethin (co. Salop). Per fesse sa. and ar. a lion ramp. counterchanged.

Gethin (Fedwdeg; descended from DAVID GOCH, Lord of Penmachno). _Arms_, those of DAVID GOCH, viz., sa. a lion ramp. ar. a bordure engr. or.

Gethinge. Ar. three pellets in fess betw. two bars sa. all betw. three goats' heads erased gu. attired or.

Gethyn. Ar. a chev. engr. az. betw. three birds rising sa. a bordure engr. of the second.

Gethyn (co. Montgomery; AMBROSE GETHYN, Esq., of Brithdir, the last male heir, _d. s. p._ 1803). Per fesse sa. and ar. a lion ramp. counterchanged.

Geton (Reg. Ulster's Office). Gu. a bend dancettée betw. two otlses ar.

Gettenes. Sa. a chev. betw. three fleurs-de-lis ar. _Crest_—A she-drake ppr.

Gettry (Reg. Ulster's Office). Az. fretty or, on a chief ar. a lion pass. guard. gu.

Gevill (quartered by CAVE, of Boroughdon, and ANDREWES, of Pisbrook. Visit. Rutland, 1618). Erm. on a chev. sa. three brocks' heads erased ar.

Geylslane. Chequy or and gu.

Geynes (Yolgrave, co. Derby). Gu. a bend vairé ar. and sa.

Geynes, or Gynes (co. Lancaster). Vairé or and az.

Geynes. Gu. a chief vair. _Crest_—A griffin's head erased ppr. in the beak a trefoil vert.

Geynton, or Geyton. Ar. a fesse betw six fleurs-de-lis gu. _Crest_—The sun in splendour or, at each ray a flame of fire ppr.

Geynville (_Earl of Ulster;_ arms in a window in Dorchester Church, co. Oxford. Visit. 1574). Az. three barnacles open or, on a chief erm. a demi lion ramp. gu.

Geyton, or Geiton (cos. Northumberland and Rutland). Ar. crusily az. three fleurs-de-lis of the last.

Geyton (Fun. Ent. of MARGARET GEYTON, widow of THOMAS USHER, and mother of HENRY USHER, Lord Primate of Ireland, _d._ Jan. 1597). Gu. a chev. betw. three cinquefoils pierced ar.

Ghest, Guest, or Geast (Row Heath, co. Worcester; descended from JOHN GHESTE, of Handsworth, co. Stafford, _temp._ Henry VII., represented by DUGDALE, of Merevale. Her. Visit. 1634). Az. a chev. or, betw. three swans' heads erased ppr. _Crest_—A swan's head erased ppr. betw. two ostrich feathers or.

Ghinucci. Erm. a serpent az. devouring an infant ppr. on a canton of the second a Catherine wheel ar.

Ghinucci (JEROME DE GHINUCCI, Bishop of Worcester, 1523-35). Vairé or and vert, a serpent in bend wavy ppr. within an annulet az. a quatrefoil ar. all within a border of the last.

Ghisnes (_Baron Ghisnes;_ summoned to Parliament, 1295). Barry of six vair and gu.

Ghisnes (Chokes, co. Northampton, 33 Henry III.). Same _Arms._

Ghrimes. Gu. on a cross ar. five mullets of the first, on a chief of the second three escallops of the field. _Crest_—A talbot sejant sa. collared ar.

Gib (Caribber, Scotland). Gu. a dexter hand holding a broken spear ar. betw. two spurs or, leathers of the second. _Motto_—Armis frango.

Gibb (granted to THOMAS A. GIBB, Esq.). Gu. a cubit arm erect grasping an arrow in bend sinister, point downwards, betw. four mullets in cross or. _Crest_—Issuant from a wreath of cinquefoils vert a stag's head or, couped gu. attired or.

Gibaut (Jersey). Az. a tower or, masoned sa. _Crest_—A tower, as in the arms.

Gibbard. Gu. on a bend cotised ar. a lion pass. az. _Crest_—

An arm couped, embowed, vested, and purfled at the shoulder, the part above the elbow in fesse, the hand in pale, holding a palm branch ppr.

Gibbe. Ar. three halberts in fesse sa. heads to the sinister. _Crest_—A Bengal tiger pass. guard. ppr.

Gibbens, or Gibbins. Ar. a lion ramp. gu. surmounted by a bend or, charged with three crosses pattée fitchée sa. _Crest_—A cubit arm holding a fish ppr.

Gibbes (Fackley, co. Oxford, bart.). Ar. three battle axes sa. _Crest_—An arm embowed, steel, in armour, garnished or, the hand in a steel gauntlet, grasping a battle axe, as in the arms. _Motto_—Tenax propositi.

Gibbes (co. Devon). Same _Arms._

Gibbes (Perrott, co. Dorset). Vert three cats pass. ar.

Gibbes. Or, on a chev. sa. two cats respecting each other ar. on a chief az. guttée d'or, a cross pattée gold, in base a holly branch fructed vert, leaved gu.

Gibbes. Az. three battle axes or. _Crest_—An arm armed or, holding a battle axe ar.

Gibbes. Same _Arms_, battle axes ar. _Crest_—An arm fesseways ppr. vested ar. cuffed and purfled at the shoulder sa. from the elbow in pale holding a palm branch of the first.

Gibbes. Paly bendy ar. and gu. on a bend az. two fleurs-de-lis of the first.

Gibbins, Gibbings, or Gibbins. Same _Arms_ as GIBBENS. _Crest_—On a ducal coronet or, the attires of a stag ppr.

Gibbings (Gibbings Grove, co. Cork; certified in Ulster's Office to that family). Ar. on a bend betw. three fleurs-de-lis two in chief and one in base az. a crescent or. _Crest_—A demi lion ramp. ppr. holding in his paws a fleur-de-lis az.

Gibbins. Or, a lion ramp. sa. over all on a bend gu. three escallops ar. _Crest_—A lion ramp. sa.

Gibbins. Or, a chev. az. betw. three leopards' faces az.

Gibbon (co. Dorset). Sa. a lion ramp. guard. crowned or, betw. three escallops ar.

Gibbon (Bishops Bourne, co. Kent). Same _Arms._ _Crest_—a demi lion ramp. guard. ar. ducally crowned or, holding betw. the paws an escallop gold.

Gibbon (Bolvenden, co. Kent; granted 6 April, 1629). Or, a lion ramp. sa. betw. three pellets. _Crest_—On a chapeau gu. turned up erm. an escarbuncle or.

Gibbon. Ar. a boar's head couped in pale az. in the mouth a garb or.

Gibbon. Ar. a griffin segreant sa. betw. three crescents gu.

Gibbon, or Guybon (Sheriff of Norfolk, 1513). Or, a lion ramp. sa. debruised by a bend gu. charged with three escallops ar.

Gibbon. Ar. a lion ramp. sa. depressed by a bend gu. charged with three escallops or.

Gibbon (cos. Lancaster and Suffolk). Or, a lion ramp. sa. over all two tilting spears in saltire gu. headed ar.

Gibbons (Stanwell Place, Middlesex, bart.). Gu. a lion ramp. or, debruised by a bend ar. charged with a torteau betw. two crosses pattée fitchee sa. _Crest_—A lion's gamb erased and erect gu. charged with a bezant, holding a cross pattée fitchée sa. _Motto_—Gratior est a rege pio.

Gibbons (Sittingbourne, co. Kent, bart.). Az. a lion ramp. in chief an escarbuncle betw. two escallops, and in base an escallop betw. two escarbuncles all or. _Crest_—A morion ppr. thereon an escarbuncle or. _Motto_—Fido Deo et ipse.

Gibbons (The Leasowes and Corbyns Hall, co. Stafford). Sa. a lion ramp. betw. three escallops ar. _Crest_—A demi-lion reguard. sa. betw. the paws an escallop ar.

Gibbons (co. Glamorgan, _temp._ Henpy VIII.). Or, a lion ramp. sa. armed gu. debruised by a bend of the last, charged with three crosses pattée fitchée ar.

Gibbons (Ditcley, co. Oxford, and New Hall, co. Warwick; THOMAS GIBBONS, grandson of JOHN GIBBONS, alias PAYNE, of Little Sutton, co. Warwick. Visit. Oxon, 1574). Gu. a lion ramp. or, over all on a bend ar. three crosses pattée sa. _Crest_—A lion's gamb erased gu. holding a cross pattée fitchée.

Gibbons (granted to Rev. BENJAMIN GIBBONS, of Poollands, Hartlebury, co. Worcester). Sa. a lion ramp. or, betw. three escallops ar. on a chief engr. of the last three crosses pattée gu. _Crest_—A demi lion reguard. or, gorged with a collar sa. pendent therefrom an escutcheon of the last, charged with a cross potent ar. betw. the paws an escallop, also ar. _Motto_—Fide et fortitudine.

Gibbons (Shrewsbury). Paly of six ar. and gu. on a bend sa. three escallops of the first. _Crest_—A demi lion ramp. sa. holding an escallop ar.

Gibbons. Bendy sinister of six ar. and gu. over all on a bend sa. three escallops of the first.

Gibbons. Gu. three lions pass or, a bend az.

Gibbons (Impalement Fun. Ent. 1632, of a dau. of JOHN GIBBONS, Alderman of Dublin, wife of FAGAN). Gu. a lion ramp. or, on a bend ar. three crosses formée sa.

Gibbons (recorded by Leveret, Athlone, to Captain GIBBONS, second Captain of the regiment under command of Col. Robert Tothill, which landed at Dublin, 3 May, 1649). Gu. a lion ramp. or, armed and langued az. on a bend ar. three crosses formée sa. *Crest*—A naked arm erect couped below the elbow, holding in the hand a salmon all ppr.

Gibbs (co. Derby, and Stoke, co. Suffolk). Ar. three battle axes in pale sa.

Gibbs (South Perrott, co. Devon). Same *Arms*, a bordure ermines. *Crest*—A leopard pass. guard. erm.

Gibbs (co. Hertford). Az. three poleaxes in pale ar. garnished or. *Crest*—An arm embowed in armour ppr. garnished or, holding in the gauntlet a poleaxe ar.

Gibbs (Elmestone, co. Kent). Ar. three battle axes sa. *Crest*—As the last.

Gibbs (Clifton Hampden, Oxon). Same *Arms*, a bordure nebuly sa. *Crest*—In front of a rock a dexter arm embowed in armour, the hand in a gauntlet ppr. holding a battle axe sa. *Motto*—Tenax propositi.

Gibbs (Tyntesfield, co. Somerset, and Clyst St. George, co. Devon). Same *Arms*, *Crest*, and *Motto*.

Gibbs (Honington, co. Warwick; confirmed by Camden's Deputies to Sir HENRY GIBBES, Knt., of Honington). Sa. three battle axes in pale ar. *Crest*—Three broken tilting spears or, two in saltire and one in pale, enfiled with a wreath ar. and sa.

Gibbs (Aldenham Park, Herts). Per fesse ar. and erm. three battle axes sa. *Crest*—An arm embowed in armour, garnished or, and charged with a cross couped gu. in the hand ppr. a battle axe, as in the arms. *Motto*—Tenax propositi.

Gibbs. Or, on a chev. sa. betw. three holly branches vert, fructed gu. two cats respecting each other ar. on a chief az. guttée d'or, a cross pattée of the last.

Gibbs. Lozengy ar. and gu. on a bend az. two fleurs-de-lis or, in the dexter chief point of which as many annulets conjoined of the first.

Gibbs. Ar. on a chev. betw. three filberts sa. two cats combatant of the field.

Gibbs. Ar. a chev. gu. betw. three leopards' faces az.

Gibbs (Derry, co. Cork, and Ballynoran and Inchigeelagh, in same co.; confirmed to JOHN GIBBS, Esq., son of JOHN GIBBS, Esq., of Ballynoran, co. Cork, son of Rev. JOHN GIBBS, of Inchigeelagh, co. Cork, second son of DANIEL GIBBS, of Derry, grandson of DANIEL GIBBS, of Cork, who bought Derry, co. Cork, in 1703, and to the other descendants of the said DANIEL GIBBS, the purchaser of Derry). Ar. three battle axes in pale sa. *Crest*—A griffin's head erased ar. pierced through the back of the neck with an arrow or, barbed and feathered of the first. *Motto*—Frapper au but.

Gibbs (The Yews, Sheffield, co. York; certified in Ulster's Office to JOHN GIBBS, of that place, only surviving son of JOHN GIBBS, Esq., of Ballynoran, co. Cork). Quarterly, 1st and 4th, ar, three battle axes erect in fess sa., for GIBBS; 2nd and 3rd, gu. betw. three demi lions ramp. erminois a plate, for BENNETT. *Crest*—A griffin's head erased ar. pierced through the back of the neck with an arrow or, barbed and feathered of the first. *Motto*—Frapper au but.

Gibeon (co. Essex). Paly of six ar. and gu. on a bend sa. three escallops of the first.

Gibion. Barry of eight ar. and gu. on a bend sa. three escallops or.

Gibon. Ar. a chev. sa. betw. three lions' heads erased gu. crowned or. *Crest*—Out of a ducal coronet or, a lion's head couped gu. bezantée.

Gibon. Az. a lion ramp. betw. three escallops ar. *Crest*—A demi wolf ramp. reguard. ar. collared gu.

Gibon. Ar. a fesse betw. three eagles' legs erased sa.

Gibon. Gu. a lion ramp. or, depressed by a bend ar. charged with three crosses pattée sa. *Crest*—A lion's paw holding a cross pattée or.

Gibon. Ar. a lion pass. sa. depressed by two battle axes in saltire, staves gu. headed of the first.

Gibon. Or, a chev. gu. betw. three lions' heads erased sa.

Gibons. Masculy ar. and gu. on a bend sa. two fleurs-de-lis or, an annulet for diff.

Gibons. Same *Arms* and *Crest* as GIBBON, of Rolvenden, Kent.

Gibons, or Gibus. Ar. a chev. gu. betw. three leopards' faces ar.

Gibraltar, See of. Ar. in base, rising out of waves of the sea a rock ppr. thereon a lion guard. or, supporting a passion cross erect gu. on a chief engr. of the last a crosier

in bend dexter, and a key in bend sinister or, surmounted by a Maltese cross ar. fimbriated gold.

Gibs (Sainthurst, co. Gloucester). Ar. three battle axes in pale sa.

Gibson-Maitland, Bart. See MAITLAND.

Gibson (cos. Cumberland, Essex, Northumberland, and London). Az. three storks rising ppr. *Crest*—Out of a ducal coronet or, a lion's gamb ppr. grasping a club gu. spiked gold. *Another Crest*—A stork rising ppr. in the beak an olive branch vert.

Gibson (Whelprigg, co. Westmoreland). Same *Arms*, quartering GODSALVE, of Rigmaden Hall, and MAWDESLEY, of Mawdesley Hall. *Crest*—A stork rising ppr.

Gibson (co. Kent). Per pale gu. and vert a tent or, on a chief of the third a fret betw. two crescents sa.

Gibson (Teede, co. Lancaster). Gu. two bars humettée ar. betw. three lions pass. in pale or.

Gibson (cos. Lancaster, York, and London), Barry of six erm. and sa. a lion ramp. or. *Crest*—A stork close ar. in the bill an oak leaf vert.

Gibson (London). Paly of six gu. and vert a tent ar. poled and garnished or, on a chief of the last a fret betw. two crescents sa. *Crest*—An arm embowed in armour, garnished or, holding a battle axe sa. (another, holding in the hand ppr. a maul or beetle sa. handled ar.).

Gibson (East Beckham and Thorpe, co. Norfolk; granted 1591). Paly of six ar. and sa. on a chief of the first a fret betw. two crescents of the second. *Crest*—A stork ar. beaked, legged, and ducally gorged gu.

Gibson (Saffron Walden, co. Essex, and Balder Grange, co. York). Paly of six ar. and az. on a chief erm. a fret gu. betw. two torteaux, quartering WYATT. *Crest*—On a mount vert a stork ar. beaked, membered, and gorged with a collar gu. pendent therefrom an escutcheon az. charged with a barnacle or. *Motto*—Recte et fideliter.

Gibson (Sandgate Lodge, co. Sussex). Gu. three keys fesseways in pale or, in chief a portcullis of the last. *Crest*—A pelican vulning herself and feeding her young ppr. gorged with a mural crown or. *Motto*—Cœlestes pandite portæ.

Gibson (Shalford, co. Surrey, and Sullington, co. Sussex ; of Scotch extraction). Gu. three keys fesseways in pale or, in chief a portcullis of the last. *Crest*—A pelican vulning herself and feeding her young ppr. gorged with a mural crown or. *Motto*—Cœlestes pandite portæ.

Gibson (Swindon, co. Wilts). Az. three storks, wings expanded ar.

Gibson (co. York). Paly of six ar. and gu. on a bend sa. three escallops of the first.

Gibson (Staveley, co. York; confirmed 16 Jan. 1655). Gu. a stork betw. three crescents ar. beaked and membered or.

Gibson (Coome Abbey, cos. Warwick and Worcester; Sir ISAAC GIBSON, knighted 1674. *d.* 1706, buried at Worcester). Same *Arms*.

Gibson (Yelland, co. Lancaster; settled in that country in the reign of James I., and, traditionally, derived from Scotland; the co-heirs, SARAH GIBSON, *d.* unm., leaving her property to GIBSON, of Myerscough; and ANNE GIBSON, *m.* WILLIAM WICKHAM, Esq., co. York). Az. three storks rising ppr. *Crests*—1st: A stork rising ppr. in his beak an olive branch vert; 2nd: Out of a ducal coronet or, a lion's gamb ppr. grasping a club gu. spiked gold.

Gibson (Myerscough and Quernmore Park, co. Lancaster). Same *Arms* and *Crest.*

Gibson (Barfield, co. Cumberland ; a younger branch of GIBSON, of Myerscough). Same *Arms.*

Gibson-Leadbitter. See LEADBITTER.

Gibson (Fun. Ent., 1641, RICHARD GIBSON, a Justice of the Peace, co. Carlow, third son of RICHARD GIBSON, Esq., of Arnwell, co. Notts). Az. three pelicans ar. wings elevated, beaked and legged gu. a martlet for diff.

Gibson (Fun. Ent. Major SEAFOUL GIBSON, buried in St. Peter's Church, Drogheda, 15 Jan. 1671). Barry of six erm. and sa. a. lion ramp. or, on a canton gu. a castle of the third.

Gibson-Carmichael (Skirling, co. Peebles, bart., 1628). Quarterly, 1st, ar. a fess wreathed az. and gu. within a bordure of the last, for CARMICHAEL; 2nd and 3rd, gu. three keys fessways in pale or, for GIBSON; 4th, erm. on a fess. sa. three crescents ar., for CRAIG. *Crests*—1st: An arm embowed, holding a broken lance top pendent ppr., for CARMICHAEL: 2nd : A pelican in her piety ppr., for GIBSON. *Motto*—Cœlestes pandite portæ.

Gibson-Craig. See CRAIG.

Gibson-Maitland. See MAITLAND.

Gibson-Wright (Cliftonhall, co. Linlithgow, and Kersie, co. Stirling, 1773). Quarterly, 1st and 4th, az. three keys paleways in fess or, wards downwards; 2nd and 3rd, az. a chev. betw. three battle axes or, all within a bordure of the last, for WRIGHT. *Crest*—A dexter arm in armour, issuing out of a cloud and grasping a scymitar ppr. *Motto*—Pro rege sæpe, pro republica semper.

Gibson (Durie, Scotland). Gu. three keys fesseways in pale or, the wards downward. *Crest*—A pelican in her nest feeding her young ppr. *Motto*—Pandite cœlestes portæ.

Gibson (Pentland, co. Edinburgh, bart.). Gu. three keys fessways in pale or, within a bordure vairé. *Crest* and *Motto*, as the last.

Gibthorp (co. Lincoln). Quarterly, 1st and 4th, chequy or and az.; 2nd and 3rd, erm.

Gibthorp, Gythorpe, or Gilthorpe. Ar. two bars gu. a bordure sa. *Crest*—A naked arm embowed, holding a dagger ppr.

Gibthorp. Quarterly, or and erm.

Gibthorpe (co. Lancaster). Quarterly, 1st and 4th, erm.; 2nd and 3rd, chequy or and gu.

Giddy (St. Erith, co. Cornwall; granted 11 June, 1770). Or, a fesse engr. vert, in chief a rose of the second betw. two torteaux, two and one. *Crest*—A lion pass. gu. in the dexter paw a banner az. thereon a cross or, the staff and point ppr.

Giddy (Tredrea, co. Cornwall, and Eastbourne, co. Sussex). Same *Arms* and *Crest*.

Gidersh, or Giderchs. Gu. a chev. betw. three martlets ar.

Gideon (Spalding, co. Lincoln, bart., extinct 1824). Per chev. vert and or, in chief a rose of the second betw. two fleurs-de-lis ar. in base a lion ramp. reguard. az. *Crest*—A stag's head erased ar. attired gu. gorged with a pallisado coronet or, in the mouth a slip of oak vert, fructed gold.

Gidion (London). Same *Arms* and *Crest*.

Gidley (Gidley, co. Devon. BARTHOLOMEW GIDLEY, of this family, was an officer in the service of King Charles II., and appears to have been in arms for the King before the Restoration, by a large silver medallion in the possession of his representative, who, at the time Lysons wrote, was GIDLEY, of Honiton; exemplified by Edward Bysshe, Clarenceux, in 1671). Or, a castle sa. a bordure of the second bezantée. *Crest*—An eagle issuant or, the wings sa. bezantée.

Gidley (Honiton, co. Devon). Same *Arms*. *Crest*—A griffin's head or, betw. two wings elevated sa. bezantée.

Giffard (*Earl of Buckingham;* William I. created, 1066, WALTER GIFFARD, the first earl of the kingdom. He was son of Osborne de Bolebec, by Aveline, his wife, sister of Gunnora, wife of Richard I., Duke of Normandy, father of Richard II., father of Robert *the Devil,* father of the Conqueror; extinct 1164). Gu. three lions pass. in pale ar.

Giffard (*Lord Giffard of Brimsfield;* Sir JOHN GIFFARD, descended from a brother of the first *Earl of Buckingham,* summoned to Parliament 8 Oct. 1311, attainted 1322). Gu. three lions pass. in pale ar. langued az.

Giffard (Chillington, co. Stafford; descended from Brimsfield). Quarterly, 1st and 4th, az. three stirrups with leathers or, two and one; 2nd and 3rd, gu. three lions pass. ar. *Crests*—1st: A tiger's head couped, full-faced, spotted various, flames issuing from his mouth ppr.; 2nd, granted 1513: A demi archer, bearded and couped at the knees, in armour ppr., from his middle a short coat paly ar. and gu. at his middle a quiver of arrows or, in his hands a bow and arrow drawn to the head or. *Motto*—Prenez haleine, tirez fort. (*Anglice,* Take breath and pull strong.)

Giffard. Gu. three bars engr. ar. *Crest*—A deer's head couped ppr. *Motto*—Spare not.

Giffard. Barry of six gu. and erm. in chief a lion pass. or.

Giffard (co. Leicester). Ar. a chev. betw. three roses az. a bordure gu.

Giffard (quartered by GRENVILE, of co. Cornwall. Visit. 1620). Az. three fleurs-de-lis or, each charged with three pellets.

Giffard (Jersey). Erm. a fesse betw. three lozenges in chief, and as many lions in base all sa.

Giffard (Aveton Giffard, and Weare Giffard, co. Devon, *temp.* Henry II., also of Halesbury and Brightley, in the same co.). Sa. three lozenges conjoined in fesse erm. *Crest* —A cock's head erased or.

Giffard (Kilcorrall, co. Wexford; representative of JOHN GIFFARL, eldest son of Col. JOHN GIFFARD, of Brightley, the distinguished Cavalier: of this line is Sir HARDINGE STANLEY GIFFARD, Q.C.). Same *Arms* and *Crest*.

Gifford (Tiverton and Halsworth, co. Devon). Same *Arms*. *Crest*—A cock's head erased or, holding in the beak a sprig of three leaves vert.

Gifford (Twyford, co. Bucks; Accott, co. Devon; Scotton, co. York; Battlebridge, co. Hunts; Stenes, co. Northampton; and Caswell Park, co. Oxford. Visit. Oxon, 1574).

Arms same as GIFFARD, *Earl of Buckingham*. *Crest*—An arm couped at the elbow vested or, charged with two bars wavy az. holding in the hand ppr. a buck's head cabossed gu.

Gifford, or Giffard (Burstall, co. Leicester; and Burton, co. Wilts; created a bart. 21 Nov. 1660, extinct 6 June, 1736; also St. James's Abbey, co. Northampton, and co. Oxford). Gu. three lions pass. in pale ar. *Crest*—An arm couped at the elbow, vested or, charged with two bars wavy az. cuffed ar. holding in the hand ppr. a buck's head cabossed gu.

Gifford (Claydon, co. Bucks). Ar. three lions ramp. in pale gu.

Gifford (co. Buckingham). Gu. three lions pass. reguard. erm.

Gifford (co. Worcester; Sir ALEXANDER GIFFORD, Knt., *d.* before 1279; Roll of Arms, Henry III. and Edward I.). Ar. ten torteaux, four, three, two, and one.

Gifford (GODFREY GIFFORD, Bishop of Worcester, younger brother of Sir ALEXANDER GIFFORD, consecrated 1268, *d.* 30 Edward I., 1302, when his nephew JOHN, son of WILLIAM GIFFORD, was found to be his heir). Same *Arms*.

Gifford (co. Worcester; Sir JOHN GIFFORD, Knt., Roll of Arms *temp.* Edward II., 1308). Same *Arms*.

Gifford (Itchell, co. Hants; Sir JOHN GIFFORD, Knt., of Itchell, Sheriff of the co. 2 Henry VI.; *d.* 10 June, 1444; Har. MS. 5865, f. 3). Same *Arms*.

Gifford (Castle Jordan, co. Meath, bart., extinct, descended from Itchell. Fun. Ent. of ELIZABETH, sister of Sir JOHN GIFFORD, Knt., of Castle Jordan, and wife of Sir WILLIAM COLLEY, Knt., of Edenderry, *d.* 24 March, 1629). Same *Arms*. *Crest*—A cubit arm erect, vested gu. slashed and cuffed ar. the hand ppr. holding four roses of the first seeded or, stalked and barbed vert. *Motto*—Mali mori quam fœdari.

Gifford (Northall, co. Middlesex, descended from Itchell; monument in West Twyford Church, Har. MSS.). Same *Arms*. *Crest*—A hand holding three gillyflowers all ppr.

Gifford (Aghern, co. Cork; Col. JOHN GIFFORD, eldest son of WILLIAM GIFFORD, and grandson of WILLIAM GIFFORD, Esq., of Northall, got grants in co. Cork, 28 Sept. 1666). Same *Arms* and *Crest*.

Gifford (Polemaloe, now Pilltown, co. Wexford, emigrated to Canada, 1822; JASPER GIFFORD, brother of Col. JOHN GIFFORD, of Aghern, got grants of Polemaloe, &c., 1660; Reg. Ulster's Office). Same *Arms*. *Crest*—A dexter arm in armour embowed, the hand holding a gillyflower all ppr. *Motto*—Potius mori quam fœdari.

Gifford (Ballysop, co. Wexford; descended from RAVENS-CROFT GIFFORD, second son of JASPER GIFFORD, the grantee of Polemaloe). Same *Arms*, *Crest*, and *Motto*.

Gifford (THEOBALD, son and heir of Sir BRYAN DE STANTON, Lord of Stanton, co. Notts, 6 Edward the Confessor, *m.* the dau. of Sir JOHN GIFFORD. Visit. Notts, 1569). Gu. ten bezants, a canton erm.

Gifford. Ar. a cross engr. sa. over all a gorge, or whirlpool, az.

Gifford (*Baron Gifford*). Az. a chev. betw. three stirrups with leathers or, a bordure engr. ar. semée of pellets. *Crest*—A panther's head couped affrontée betw. two branches of oak ppr. *Supporters*—Dexter, a bay horse ppr. charged on the shoulder with a portcullis or; sinister, a greyhound ar. charged on the body with three erm. spots in pale. *Motto* —Non sine numine.

Gifford (Elmdon, co. Warwick, and co. Stafford. Visit. Warwick). Az. three stirrups with leathers and buckles or.

Gifford (Roddinghurst, co. Wilts). Same *Arms*, a bordure engr. ar. pellettée.

Gifford. Ar. crusily sa. a lion ramp. gu.

Gifford. Erm. a fesse gu. on a chief of the second a lion pass. or.

Gifford. Or, a cross lozengy (another, engr.) sa.

Gifford. Chequy or and gu. a canton of the second.

Gifford. Erm. a saltire engr. ar.

Gifford (Yester, Scotland; ended in co-heiresses in the 15th century, the eldest the ancestress of the Tweeddale family). Gu. three bars erm.

Gifford (Sheriffhall, co. Edinburgh). The same, within a bordure engr. of the field.

Gifford (Busto, Shetland). Gu. three bars erm. within a bordure or. *Crest*—A hart's head erased ppr. armed or. *Motto*—Spare when you have nought.

Giffings. Az. fretty ar. on a chief or, two mullets gu.

Gigge, or Giggis (co. Suffolk). Sa. a fret erm. a chief chequy ar. and of the first. *Crest*—A lion statant sa.

Gigger (MACE-GIGGER, Reading; granted, by royal warrant, to JAMES MACE-GIGGER, Esq., of Reading, and his issue,

25 March, 1803). Per chev. gu. and erminois in chief two arrows erect or, points downwards, flighted and pheoned ppr. in base a cross crosslet fitchée of the first. *Crest*—A cubit arm ppr. in the hand a cross crosslet fitchée, surmounted of two arrows in saltire, as in the arms. *Motto*—Gratitude.

Giggins (Fun. Ent. of KATHERINE GIGGINS, *d.* 15 Oct. 1620), wife of HENRY FISHER, and mother of Sir EDWARD FISHER, Knt., of Fisher's Prospect, alias Courtown, co. Wexford). Quarterly, or and sa. a saltire engr. gu.

Gigon. Or, two chev. gu. a canton az. *Crest*—A dexter arm holding a swan's head erased ppr.

Gilbard (co. Sussex ; MARGERY, dau. of GILBARD, of that co., *m.* "AFFABEL PARTRIDGE, Esq., of London, Principal Goldsmith vnto our Sou'eyne Lady Quene Elizabeth." Visit. London, 1568). Ar. a talbot pass. sa. on a chief indented of the last three bezants.

Gilbard (co. Devon). Ar. on a chev. sa. three roses of the field. *Crest*—A squirrel cracking a nut ppr. (another, within a bordure gu.

Gilbard (co. Devon). Erm. on a chev. sa. three roses ar.

Gilberd (quartered by RICHARD WILKYNSON, citizen of London, grandson of JOHN WILKYNSON, of Goldhanger, co. Essex, by JANE, dau. and heir of JOHN GILBERD. Visit. London, 1568). Same *Arms*, the chev. engr.

Gilbert (The Priory, Bodmin, co. Cornwall). Ar. on a chev. gu. three roses of the field. *Crest*—A squirrel sejant on a hill vert feeding on a crop of nuts ppr. *Motto*—Mallem mori quam muture.

Gilbert (JOHN DAVIES GIDDY and his two daughters, who, by royal licence, dated 7 Jan. 1818, were authorised to take the surname and arms of GILBERT only). Ar. on a chev. gu. three roses of the field. *Crest*—A squirrel sejant gu. cracking a nut or.

Gilbert (Trelissick, co. Cornwall, and Eastbourne, co. Sussex ; JOHN DAVIES GILBERT, Esq., only son and heir of DAVIES GIDDY, Esq., and his wife, MARY ANNE, dau. and heiress of FRANCIS GILBERT, Esq., of Eastbourne, assumed, by royal sign manual, dated 10 Dec. 1817, the surname of GILBERT). Same *Arms*, with a canton gu. for diff. *Crest*—A squirrel sejant gu. cracking a nut or, charged on the shoulder with a cross crosslet gold for diff. *Motto*—Teg yw Heddwch.

Gilbert (co. Cornwall, Compton, Bridgerule, and North Petherwin, co. Devon, and Togenton and Bleckington, co. Sussex). Visit. Devon, 1620). Same *Arms*, a bordure gu., and *Crest*, without the cross crosslet.

Gilbert (Locko, co. Derby ; originally, at a very remote period, of Gilbert's Place, parish of Lullington ; subsequently of Barrow ; WILLIAM GILBERT, Esq., of that place, purchased Locko, *temp.* Elizabeth, and was ancestor of JOHN GILBERT, Esq., of Locko, who became possessed of Thurgarton Priory, co. Nottingham, by bequest from the COOPERS, and in consequence took the name and arms of COOPER in 1736). Sa. an armed leg couped at the thigh in pale betw. two broken spears ar. headed or. *Crest*—A dexter arm embowed in armour ppr. the hand darting a broken lance in bend sinister, the point ar. staff or.

Gilbert (Selby, co. Leicester ; WILLIAM GILBERT, son of HUGH GILBERT. Visit. Leicester, 1619). Same *Arms*, a mullet for diff. Same *Crest*.

Gilbert (cos. Hereford and Monmouth). Same *Arms*. *Crest* —An arm in armour embowed ppr. severed below the wrist, the hand dropping, grasping a broken spear or, headed ar. the point downwards. *Another Crest*—Out of a mural coronet or, a demi lion ramp. ducally crowned of the first, holding a battle-axe sa. headed ar.

Gilbert, alias Kniverton (Youlgreve, co. Derby, 1300 ; the heiress *m.* BARNESLY, *temp.* Charles I.). Gu. a bend vairé ar. and sa. *Crest*—Out of a ducal coronet or, a griffin's head gu. beaked of the first.

Gilbert (Savrart, co. Hertford, and Sandwich and Westbury, co. Kent ; granted 1593). Gu. a saltire or, on a chief erm. three piles of the field. *Crest*—A griffin's head az. beaked or, gorged with a collar erm.

Gilbert (Somerson, co. Suffolk, and London ; Sir ROBERT GILBERT, Knt., co. Suffolk, son of HENRY GILBERT, citizen of London, third son of RICHARD GILBERT, of the first place. Visit. London, 1568). Az. a chev. erm. betw. three eagles displ. or. *Crest*—An eagle displ. az.

Gilbert (Mayfield, Sussex). Same *Arms*. *Crest*—An eagle's head ppr. issuing out of rays or.

Gilbert (North Burlingham, co. Norfolk ; confirmed to THOMAS GILBERT, of that place, by Cooke, Clarenceux, 1576). Gu. two bars erm. in chief three fleurs-de-lis or. *Crest*— Out of a ducal coronet or, a stag's head erm. attired of the first.

Gilbert (WILLIAM HENRY GILBERT, Esq., of Cantley, co. Norfolk ; ROBERT GILBERT, Esq., of Postwick Hall, in the

same county ; and the Rev. JOHN GILBERT, of Chedgrave : sons of the late HENRY GILBERT, Esq., and grandsons of THOMAS GILBERT, Esq., of Chedgrave, *b.* in 1694). Same *Arms*, bars engr. *Crest*—A stag's head or, on the neck a fess engr. with plain cottises gu. *Motto*—Tenax propositi.

Gilbert (co. Salop). Gu. a bend vair. *Crest*—Out of a ducal coronet or, an eagle's head gu. beaked gold.

Gilbert (Brent Ely, co. Suffolk). Ar. on a chev. sa. betw. three leopards' faces az. as many roses or. *Crest*—On a mount vert a demi eagle displ. az. on the breast a mullet or.

Gilbert (Woodford, co. Essex). Same *Arms* and *Crest*, with a mullet for diff.

Gilbert (granted 26 Dec. 1759). Gu. an armed leg couped at the thigh or, betw. two broken spears of the last headed ar. on a chief of the second two eagles displ. sa. *Crest*—On a mount vert an arm embowed in armour or, grasping a broken spear of the last headed ar.

Gilbert. Ar. a chev. betw. three negroes' heads couped ppr.

Gilbert. Or, (another, ar.) on a fesse betw. three annulets gu. as many erm. spots of the first.

Gilbert. Barry of six or and az. a bend gu.

Gilbert. Ar. on a chev. gu. three cinquefoils of the first pierced of the second, a bordure engr. of the last.

Gilbert (Dublin ; Fun. Ent. of the wife of Mr. SHERIFF GILBERT, buried at St. Patrick's Cathedral, 17 June, 1651). Ar. a chev. engr. per pale gu. and or, betw. three Moors' heads erased ppr. wreathed about the temples of the second and third.

Gilbert (Reg. Ulster's Office, to Sir WILLIAM GILBERT, of Queen's co.). Ar. on a chev. sa. three roses of the first, quartering, 1st, CASTILLON, gu. a castle ar. issuing from the battlements a demi lion ramp. or, a canton erm. ; 2nd, POYTON, or, a bend sa. in sinister chief a rose gu. *Crest*—A squirrel sejant gu. holding betw. the paws a nut or.

Gilbert, or Giles. Or, on a cross sa. five plates.

Gilbert. Barry wavy of six ar. and az.

Gilbert (Scotland). Ar. on a chev. az. betw. three trefoils slipped vert as many fleurs-de-lis or.

Gilbertson. Gu. an armed leg couped at the thigh in pale betw. two broken spears ar. headed or. *Crest*—A snail in the shell ppr.

Gilborn. Ar. a cross flory betw. four birds close gu.

Gilborne (London). Az. on a chev. or, three roses gu. leaved vert. *Crest*—A tiger saliant ar. lined and collared or.

Gilborne (co. Kent). Same *Arms*, within a bordure of the second.

Gilby (Staynton, co. Lincoln). Az. a fesse wavy ar. betw. three estoiles or. *Crest*—A tower or, with a dragon's head issuing from the top and the tail out of the door ar.

Gilby. Ar. a fesse sa. in the dexter chief a square buckle gu.

Gilby. Ar. a fesse wavy betw. three estoiles az.

Gilchrist (Dr. JOHN GILCHRIST, afterwards BOTHWICK-GILCHRIST, Scotland, 1803). Az. the sun in his splendour or, betw. two crosses pattée fitchée in chief and a mullet in base ar. *Crest*—The sun rising out of a cloud ppr. *Motto*—I hope to speed.

Gilchrist (Dunoon, co. Argyll, 1874). Az. the sun in his splendour or, betw. two crosses pattée i.. chief and a water bouget in base ar. *Crest*—A lion ramp. ar. supporting in his forepaws a pennoncelle ppr. the flag az. charged with a horse pass. also ar. *Motto*—Mea gloria fides.

Gilchrist (Fun. Ent. Ulster's Office, 1657). Ar. a lion pass. sa. a chief az. charged on the dexter with a cross pattée and on the sinister with a covered cup both or.

Gildart (Liverpool, co. Lancaster ; granted 20 Dec. 1759). Vert a lion ramp. reguard. crowned or, betw. three arrows of the last. *Crest*—A demi lion ramp. reguard. or, crowned gold, holding in the dexter paw an oak branch ppr.

Gildford. Ar. two bars gemel sa.

Gildisburgh (quartered on the GATES Monument, in Broadwas Church). Ar. three piles in point gu.

Gildridge (Eastbourne, co. Sussex ; ELIZABETH GILDRIDGE, the heiress, *m.* in 1674, NICHOLAS EVERSFIELD, Esq., of Charlton Court, near Steyning). Chequy or and gu. on a chev. az. three annulets of the first. *Crest*—A sinister arm embowed in armour ppr. holding in the gauntlet a club in pale or, above the gauntlet a dexter hand ppr. couped gu. grasping the club.

Giles (Gilston, or Gilestoun, co. Glamorgan). Sa. a cross in saltire (or a Julian cross) ar., quartering, az. a chev. betw. three coronets or, another with two ostrich feathers ar.

Giles, or Gyles (Astley and Prickley, co. Worcester ; JOHN GYLES, of Prickley, aged 33, son of SAMUEL GYLES, of

Solhampton in Astley, aged 63. Visit. Worcester, 1683).
Gu. a cross betw. four chalices or, on a chief of the last three pelicans vulning themselves ppr. Crest—A chalice or, out of it three pansy flowers ppr.

Giles (Powick, co. Worcester). Same Arms, chief ar.

Giles (White Ladies, Aston, co. Worcester). Same Arms, the chief ar. charged with three eagles displ sa.

Giles (Bowden, co. Devon; Sir EDWARD GILES, Knt., of that place. Visit. 1620). Per chev. ar. and az. a lion ramp. counterchanged collared or. Crest—A lion's gamb erased and erect ppr. charged with a bar or, holding an apple branch vert fructed gold.

Giles (Kailzie, co. Peebles, 1850). Gu. on a cross betw. four chalices or, as many lions' heads full-faced ppr. on a chief of the second three pelicans sa. Crest—A chalice or, issuing therefrom three pansy flowers ppr. Motto—Pensez à moi.

Giles, or Gille. Per fesse gu. and az. on a bend ar. betw. two lions' heads erased and three crosses crosslet fitchée or, as many cinquefoils of the first. Crest—A squirrel sejant gu. bezantée holding betw. the paws an acorn branch leaved ppr.

Gilesburgh. Ar. three piles gu. over all a bend az.

Gilford (co. Kent). Or, a saltire sa. betw. four martlets az. Crest—An angel couped at the breasts ppr.

Gilham, or Gil'ham. Ar. a savage gu. holding a club over the shoulder vert. Crest—Three savages' heads conjoined in one neck, one looking towards the dexter, the other the sinister, and one upwards ppr.

Gill (co. Devon). Lozengy ar. (another, or) and vert a lion ramp. of the first.

Gill (Ward House, co. Devon). Same Arms, quartering CORNISH. Crest—A boar pass. resting its fore-paw on a crescent. Motto—In te, Domine, spes nostra.

Gill (Anstey, and of Wigill, co. Hertford, 1634). Lozengy or and vert a lion ramp. guard. gu. in chief a mullet for diff.

Gill (co. Hertford). Sa. two chev. ar. each charged with three mullets of the first, on a canton or, a lion pass. gu. Crest—A hawk's head az. betw. two wings or, fretty vert.

Gill (Sudbury, co. Northants, and London, 1633). Same Arms. Crest—A demi eagle ar. wings expanded fretty az.

Gill, or Gille (London; granted to ALEXANDER GILL, Head Master of St. Paul's School, London, 1614). Per pale or and ar. a chief dancettée sa. Crest—A salamander gu. issuant in flames of fire ppr.

Gill (London; granted about 1506). Ar. on a bend sa. three mullets pierced of the field, on a canton az. a lion pass. ar. Crest—A falcon's head couped az. betw. two wings or.

Gill. Sa. on a bend or, three mullets of the first, on a canton az. a lion pass. of the second.

Gill (Scraptoft, co. Leicester). Sa. a maunch erm. betw. four fleurs-de-lis ar. two and two, over all on a pale or, three bull's heads erased gu.

Gill (Wyrardisbury House and Remenham House, co. Buckingham). See GYLL.

Gill (Norton, co. Derby, temp. Elizabeth, and of Car House, near Rotherham; this family, from the similarity of arms, appears to be descended from the GELLS, of Hopton). Per bend ar and vert (sometimes az.) three mullets in bend counterchanged.

Gill (The Oaks, Norton, and Sheffield; a branch of the preceding family, whose heiress m. RICHARD BAGSHAW, ESQ., of Castleton). Same Arms.

Gill (Bickham Park, co. Devon; descended from a family of GILL, resident and possessed of landed property in the parish of Tavistock, since the reign of King Stephen). Erminois an eagle displ. with two heads sa. on a chief indented gu. a boar's head erased betw. two crescents ar. Crest—A boar pass. sa. the dexter forepaw resting on an increscent or. Motto—In te, Domine, spes nostra.

Gill (granted, 1803, to WILLIAM GILL, Esq., Lord Mayor of London). Sa. two chev. the upper one erm. the other ar. charged with three mullets of the field and in base a cinquefoil of the third, on a canton erminois a lion pass. guard. az. Crest—A falcon's head erased az. betw. two wings elevated vert fretty or.

Gill (granted to WILLIAM HENRY GILL, Esq., of Eshing House, co. Surrey). Sa. two chevronels erm. each charged with three mullets of the field, all betw. three lions pass. guard. ar. Crest—A falcon's head couped ar. charged with three mullets palewise sa. betw. two wings vair.

Gill (granted to ROBERT GILL, Captain Madras Army). Crest—Out of an Eastern crown a demi lion vert holding a sword ppr.

Gillam (co. Essex). Sa. on a chev. or, betw. three dolphins embowed ppr. as many bowers vert. Crest—Out of a ducal coronet or, a dragon's head ppr.

400

Gillam. Az. a fesse betw. two chev. or. Crest—A demi griffin vert, winged and beaked or.

Gilland, Gisland, or Gillesland (co. Northumberland). Chequy or and gu. Crest—A dexter arm embowed ppr. vested and cuffed az. holding up a covered cup or.

Gillbande. Ar. on a chev. sa. three cinquefoils of the first pierced of the second.

Gillbande. Ar. on a bend sa. three roses of the field.

Gillbanks (Whitefield House, co. Cumberland). Az. five hearts in saltire or, on a chief ar. a rose gu. betw. two trefoils slipped vert. Crest—A stag's head or. Motto—Honore et virtute.

Gille (London and co. Warwick). Lozengy or and vert a lion ramp. guard. ar. Crest—A demi parrot, wings expanded vert.

Gillers. Sa. on a chev. betw. three peweets' heads erased ar. as many annulets of the first.

Gilles. Per fesse gu. and or, on a bend engr. ar. betw. three lions' heads erased, two and one, in chief, and as many crosses crosslet, one and two, all counterchanged, as many cinquefoils of the first.

Gilles. Or, on a chev. engr. sa. betw. three crosses formée gu. as many martlets of the first.

Gilles. Ar. on a fesse engr. sa. three martlets or. Crest—A hand ppr. holding an escallop or.

Gillesborough. Or, three piles in point gu.

Gillespie (Scotland). Per fess or and az. a galley of the first with oars, mast, and flag gu. in dexter chief a hand couped holding a dirk in pale, and in sinister chief a cross crosslet of the third.

Gillespie (Newton, Scotland). Az. a chev. wavy ar. betw. three roses gu. slipped or. Crest—An anchor ppr. Motto—Tu certa salutis anchora.

Gillespie-Stainton (Biggarshiells, co. Lanark, and Bitteswell, co. Leicester, 1873). Quarterly, 1st and 4th, az. a three-masted ship, sails furled and flags flying in chief, a crosslet fitchée betw. a pelican in her piety, and a dexter arm fessways couped below the elbows, the hand holding a dagger erect all ppr., for GILLESPIE; 2nd and 3rd, az. on a chev. ar. betw. three boars' heads erased of the second, as many cinquefoils of the first, for STAINTON. Crests—A wild cat saliant ppr. for GILLESPIE; A fox saliant ppr. collared ar., for STAINTON. Mottoes—Qui me tanget pænitebit, for GILLESPIE; Moderata manent, for STAINTON.

Gillet, alias Chandler (Ipswich, co. Suffolk). Erm. on a bend engr. sa. three lucies' heads erased ar. collared with a bar gemel gu. Crest—A lucy's head erect and erased gu. collared with a bar gemel or.

Gillet, or Gillot (Broadfield, co. Norfolk). Same Arms, lucies' heads or. Crest—A lucy's head erased and erect or, collared as in the arms.

Gillett (Halvergate, co. Norfolk). Same Arms. Crest—A lucy's head erased and erect or, collared gu. Motto—Spes mea in Deo.

Gillett (Visit. Notts. 1614). Erm. on a bend sa. three lucies' heads erased ar. Crest—A lion ramp. holding in the dexter paw a battle axe ppr.

Gilliat (granted to JOHN SAUNDERS GILLIAT, Esq., of Paddington, co. Middlesex). Or, on a fess betw. four martlets, two and two, three ears of wheat of the field. Crest—On a mount vert in front of a garb or, two fronds of fern in saltire ppr.

Gillibrand (Chorley). Ar. two swords in saltire sa. hilted ar. points to chief.

Gillies (Jamaica, 1800). Az. a lymphad, oars, mast, tackling, and sail or, flagged ar. a bordure erminois, on a chief of the third two shepherds' crooks in saltire sa. betw. a dexter hand couped fessways, holding a dagger in pale in the dexter, and a cross crosslet fitchée in the sinister chief point gu. Crest—A cat courant ppr. Motto—Touch not the cat, but a glove.

Gillingham (Gillingham, co. Kent; borne by THOMAS, the last DE GILLINGHAM, one of whose two daus. and co-heirs m. JOHN DE GRENSTED). Quarterly, erm. and gu.

Gillingham. Az. a fesse or, betw. three swans ar. Crest—A dexter arm couped and embowed ppr. vested sa. cuffed ar. holding up a sword in pale enfiled with a leopard's face ppr.

Gilliot. Ar. on a fesse gu. betw. six martlets sa. three ears of wheat, stalked and leaved or. Crest—A garb or.

Gillis (Scotland). Per fesse engr. or and az. a galley of the first betw. a hand couped fesseways, holding a dagger in pale, and in the sinister canton a cross crosslet fitchée, all within a bordure gu. Crest—A cat courant ppr. Motto—Touch not the cat, but a glove.

Gillman (Foley, co. Hereford). Sa. a nag's head erased or, betw. three dexter hands couped ar.

Gillman (Curriheen, co. Cork, bart., extinct 1815; Sir JOHN ST. LEGER GILLMAN was so created 1 Oct. 1799). Sa. a dexter leg couped above the knee or. Crest—An eagle's head erased sa. holding in the beak a lion's gamb erased or. *Motto*—Non cantu sed actu.

Gillman (The Retreat, Clonakilty, co. Cork; confirmed to BENNETT WATKINS GILLMAN, of that place, second son of HERBERT GILLMAN, Esq., of Bennett's Grove). Same *Arms*, an annulet for diff. *Crest*—A griffin's head erased sa. charged with an annulet or, and holding in the beak a bear's paw of the last. *Motto*—Non cantu sed actu.

Gillock. Sa. a lion ramp. ar. on a chief of the second three roses of the first.

Gillon (Wallhouse, co. Linlithgow; granted 1676, and the supporters, 1824). Gu. on a saltire ar. five martlets volant of the first. *Crest*—A raven on the face of a rock ppr. *Supporters*—Two ravens ppr. *Motto*—Tutum refugium.

Gillon. Or, three fleurs-de-lis gu. *Crest*—A dexter hand holding up a bomb, fired ppr.

Gillow (Preston, co. Lancaster, and Lilystone Hall, co. Essex). Az. a lion ramp. ar. on a chief of the last three roses of the first. *Crest*—A horse pass. sa. saddled and bridled gu. *Motto*—Alis et animo.

Gillow. Gu. a lion ramp. or, on a chief of the last three fleurs-de-lis of the first.

Gillson. Vert on a pale ar. betw. two annulets or, a pile gu. *Crest*—A leopard's head erased erm. ducally gorged az.

Gillson (Reg. Ulster's Office). Or, on a bend sa. betw. two eagles displ. az. three crosses crosslet of the first, quartering, gu. a demi dragon ramp. or.

Gillum (Middleton Hall, co. Northumberland). Sa. on a chev. or, betw. three dolphins haurient ppr. as many castles. *Crest*—A dolphin, as in the arms.

Gilly (Hawkdon, co. Suffolk). Sa. on a bend ar. cotised erm. a rose ppr. betw. two annulets of the field. *Crest*—A demi griffin ramp. wings erect ar. holding in the dexter paw a saltire or, *Motto* over—Ab aquila.

Gilman (co. Norfolk). Ar. a man's leg couped at the thigh in pale sa. *Crest*—On a chapeau gu. turned up erm. a demi lion ramp. ar.

Gilman (co. Gloucester). Same *Arms*, tinctures reversed.

Gilman (Deptford-Strand, co. Kent). Ar. a man's leg couped at the thigh in pale sa. charged below the knee with a bar gemel or. *Crest*—A man's leg, as in the arms, issuing out of rays or, the foot in chief.

Gilmour (Craigmillar, co. Edinburgh, bart., 1688; the dau. and heir of the fourth and last bart. m. WILLIAM LITTLE, of Libberton). Az. a chev. betw. two fleurs-de-lis in chief or, and a writing pen full feathered in base ar. *Crest*—A garland of laurel ppr. *Motto*—Perseveranti dabitur.

Gilmour (LITTLE-GILMOUR, of Craigmillar and Libberton, 1811). Quarterly, 1st and 4th, as the last; 2nd, sa. a saltire ar. charged with a crescent gu., for LITTLE; 3rd, gu. three bears' heads erased ar. issuing out of the dexter base a lance, and out of the sinister base a Lochaber axe, both in pale and of the last, for RANKINE. Same *Crest* and *Motto*. *Supporters*—Two hawks rising ppr.

Gilmour (Townsend, co. Lanark, 1754). Az. a chev. ar. on a chief of the second a fleur-de-lis betw. a writing pen full feathered of the first in the sinister, and a bible sa. on the dexter, in base a trefoil vert. *Crest*—An old Gothic church window ppr. *Motto*—In limine ambulo.

Gilmour (South Walton, co. Renfrew, 1869). Ar. on a chev. betw. three trefoils slipped vert as many hunting horns stringed of the first. *Crest*—A dexter hand fessways couped, holding a writing pen ppr. *Motto*—Nil penna sed usus.

Gilmour (Eaglesham, co. Renfrew). As the last, with the chev. engr. for diff. Same *Crest* and *Motto*.

Gilpin (Hockliffe Grange, co. Bedford, bart.). Or, a boar pass. sa. in chief two roses gu. barbed and seeded ppr. *Crest*—In front of three tilting spears points upwards, one in pale and two in saltire ppr. as many mascles interlaced fessewise or.

Gilpin (Scaleby, co. Cumberland, and co. Westmoreland). Or, a boar pass. sa. *Crest*—A pine branch vert.

Gilpin (Bungay, co. Suffolk). Same *Arms*. *Crest*—Three halberts, two in saltire and one in pale ppr. tied with a ribbon, thereon the word Foy. *Motto*—Une foy mesme.

Gilpin. Or, a boar statant sa. *Crest*—A dexter arm embowed in armour, holding in the hand ppr. a sprig of laurel vert.

Gilsland. Vert a stag springing or. *Crest*—A dexter arm ppr. vested ar. cuffed az. holding up a caltrap of the first.

Gilson (Fun. Ent. of JOHN GILSON, d. in Dublin 22 April, 1610). Or, on a bend sa. betw. two eagles displ. az. armed and langued gu. three crosses crosslet of the first.

Gilstrap (Fornham Park, co. Suffolk). Ar. a chev. engr. vert betw. in chief two escutcheons gu. each charged with a galtrap of the field, and in base a talbot's head erased of the third. *Crest*—A cubit arm erect in armour ppr. grasping an

401

escutcheon gu. charged with a galtrap ar. *Motto*—Candide secure.

Giney (co. Norfolk). Chequy or and gu. a chief erm.

Ginger. Gu. on a pale ar. three pheons az. *Crest*—A savage's head affrontée ppr. betw. two branches of laurel vert.

Ginkell (*Earl of Athlone*, created 1692, extinct 1844). Ar. two bars dancettée sa. *Crest*—A pair of wings erect ar. charged with two bars dancettée sa. *Supporters*—Two griffins, wings expanded or. *Motto*—Malo mori quam foedari.

Ginsall. Vairé or and az.

Gipp, or Gypses (Welmetham and Horningsheath, co. Suffolk). Az. a fesse betw. six estoiles or. *Crest*—Out of a ducal coronet or, two wings expanded az. semée of estoiles gold.

Gipps (Newsham, co. Kent). Az. a fesse engr. betw. six estoiles or. *Crest*—Out of a mural coronet or, two wings elevated az. each charged with three estoiles in pale gold.

Gipps (Howlets, co. Kent). Same *Arms* and *Crest*.

Gipps. Same *Arms*. *Crest*—Out of a cloud a dexter arm holding up a wheatsheaf all ppr.

Girard (Jersey). Gyronny of six or and az. a chief of the first.

Girandot (Jersey; granted by the Parliament of Dijon). Quarterly, 1st and 4th, ar. a lion ramp. sa. armed and langued gu.; 2nd and 3rd, gu. a chev. ar. *Crest*—A lion ramp. sa. *Motto*—Nil desperandum.

Girardot (Allestrey, co. Derby; descended from an ancient French family). Same *Arms*.

Girardot (Car Colston, co. Nottingham, formerly of Allestree, co. Derby; descended from an ancient French family; now represented by the Rev. JOHN CHANCOURT GIRARDOT, M.A., incumbent and patron of Car Colston, co. Nottingham). Same *Arms*. *Crest*—A demi lion ramp. sa.

Girdler (co. Stafford). Az. a fesse erm. cotised or, betw. three goats' heads erased ar.

Girdler (Clarke, co. Wilts). Gu. a chev. erm. betw. three lozenges ar. each charged with a goat's head erased of the first.

Girdler. Az. on a chev. betw. three fleurs-de-lis ar. as many hurts. *Crest*—A hand issuing from the wreath pulling a rose from a bush ppr.

Girdlers, Company of (London). Per fesse az. and or, a pale counterchanged, three gridirons of the last, the handles in chief. *Crest*—A demi man ppr. representing St. Lawrence with glory round his head or, issuing out of clouds of the first, vested az. girt round the body with a girdle of the second, holding in the dexter hand a gridiron of the last, and in the sinister a book ar. *Motto*—Give thanks to God.

Girdlestone (SAMUEL GIRDLESTONE, Esq., of Chester Terrace, Regent's Park). Per pale gu. and az. a griffin segreant ar. on a fesse dancettée or, three crosses pattée of the first. *Crest*—A griffin's head erased az. in the beak two arrows in saltire, the pheons downwards gold, gorged with a collar dancettée or, thereon three crosses pattée gu.

Girflet. Or, a crequer plant of seven branches eradicated sa. *Crest*—An arm in armour embowed ppr. tied at the shoulder with a sash gu. and holding a club sa. spiked or.

Girgon. Gu. two bars ar. in chief three annulets of the second.

Girle. Gu. a cross engr. or. *Crest*—A garb or.

Girling (Stradbroke, co. Suffolk, and East Dereham, Twyford, Yaxham, Foulsham, Bintry, Foxley, Scarning, Gressenhall, Bradenham, and Holt, co. Norfolk). Ar. on a bend per bend gu. and az. betw. two cotises engr. sa. three fleurs-de-lis or. *Crest*—A demi griffin az. holding betw. the claws a fleur-de-lis gu.

Girlington, or Gerlinston (Girlington, co. York, and Thurland, co. Lancaster). Ar. a chev. betw. three bees (another, butterflies) volant sa. (another, tinctures reversed). *Crest*—A demi griffin, wings endorsed or, holding a bezant.

Girlington (co. Lincoln, 1640). Ar. a chev. betw. three butterflies volant sa.

Girvan (Achairne, Scotland, 1770). Az. three salmon naiant fessewa ys in pale ar. *Crest*—A dove holding in her beak an olive branch ppr. *Motto*—Home.

Gisborne (Yoxhall Lodge, co. Stafford, and Horwick House, co. Derby; granted 1741; descended from JOHN GISBORNE, Esq., of Derby, b. 1644). Erminois a lion ramp. sa. collared ar. on a canton vert a garb or. *Crest*—Out of a mural crown ar. a demi lion ramp. ermines collared dovetailed or.

Gisborne (Ireland). Or, on a fesse sa. betw. three hunting horns stringed gu. a greyhound courant ar. *Crest*—A horse's head az. bridled or.

Gisby (co. York). Lozengy or and az. a canton erm.

2 D

Gise (co. Gloucester). Barry of six indented ar. and sa.

Gise. Lozengy gu. and vair, on a canton or, a mullet pierced sa. *Crest*—A dexter hand couped fesseways, holding a rose branch with one rose all ppr.

Gise. Per fesse ar. and vert, in chief a demi lion ramp. gu.

Giseburn, or Gysburgh, Priory of (co. York). Ar. a lion ramp. az. d ebruised with a bend gu.

Gisland. Vert a stag springing or. *Crest*—A lion's head issuing from the w reath ppr.

Gislingham (Tuston, co. Suffolk). Az. a fesse or, betw. three swans ar. beaked and legged gu.

Gissing, or Gissinge. Ar. on a bend az. three eagles displ. reguard. or. *Crest*—An arm in armour brandishing a sword all ppr.

Gisors. Ar. a lion ramp. betw. ten billets sa.

Gist (Wormington Grange, co. Gloucester). Per pale gu. and sa. on a chev. engr. erminois betw. three annulets and necks erased erm. as many fleurs-de-lis az. *Crest*—A swan's head and neck erased erm. collared gu. betw. two palm branches vert.

Gist, or Gest. Sa. a chev. or, betw. three swans' necks erased ar. *Crest*—A swan's head and neck erased betw. two ostrich feathers ar.

Giustiniani (*Countess of Newburgh*). Quarterly, 1st grand quarter, gu. a tower ppr. on a chief or, an eagle displ. sa., for GIUSTINIANI; 2nd grand quarter, quarterly, 1st and 4th, or, a lion ramp. sa., 2nd, per pale ar. and gu. a lion ramp. sa., 3rd, ar. a chev. gu. betw. three snakes erect ppr , for MAHONY; 3rd grand quarter, chequy or and az. a fesse gu., for CLIFFORD; 4th grand quarter, ar. on a bend gu. betw. three gilliflowers slipped ppr. two and one, an anchor of the field, all within a tressure flory counterflory vert, for LEVINGSTONE. *Supporters*—Dexter, a wild man, wreathed about the temples and loins with oak ppr. ; sinister, a dapple grey horse, bridled and saddled gu.

Gladdish (WILLIAM GLADDISH, Esq., of Gravesend, J.P. co. Kent). Quarterly, az. and ar. on a fesse cotised erminois betw. three demi lions counterchanged of the field, as many eagles' heads erased sa. *Crest*—A mount vert, thereon an eagle rising reguard. or, holding in the mouth and dexter claw a tilting spear in bend sinister sa.

Gladstanes (that Ilk, co. Roxburgh) Ar. a savage's head couped, distilling drops of blood, thereon a bonnet composed of bay and holly leaves all ppr. within an orle of eight martlets sa. *Crest*—A demi griffin, holding in the dexter talon a sword ppr. *Motto*—Fide et virtute.

Gladstanes (Whitelaw). Same *Arms*, a bordure invecked gu. *Crest* and *Motto*, as the last.

Gladstanes (Edinburgh). The same as of that Ilk, a bordure indented gu. Same *Crest* and *Motto*.

Gladstone (Fasque and Balfour, co. Kincardine, bart.). Ar. a savage's head affrontée distilling drops of blood, about the temples a wreath of holly vert, within an orle fleury gu. all within eight martlets sa. *Crest*—Issuant from a wreath of holly vert a demi griffin sa. supporting betw. the claws a sword, the blade enfiled by a bonnet of holly and bay also vert. *Motto*—Fide et virtute.

Gladwin (Coldaston, *temp.* James I., afterwards of Edelston, 7 upton, and Stubbing, co. Derby; granted 1686). Erm. a chief az. over all on a bend gu. a sword ar. hilt and pommel or. *Crest*—On a mount ppr. a lion sejant ar. guttée de sang, holding in the dexter paw a sword erect or.

Glagg. Gu. on a bend ar. (another, or) three cinquefoils of the field.

Glanfield. Az. a lion ramp. ar.

Glanill (co. Suffolk). Az. semée of crosses crosslet three fusils in pale ar.

Glanton. Az. a chev. ar. betw. three crosses moline or.

Glantun. Gu. a chev. betw. three crosses patonce ar.

Glanvile (Launceston, co. Cornwall). Az. three saltires or. *Crest*—A buck pass. ppr.

Glanvile, Glanvill, or Glanville. Same *Arms*. *Crest*—Out of a maunch or, a dexter hand clenched ppr.

Glanvile, or Glanvill (co. Suffolk, and Broomhall, co. York). Ar. a chief indented az.

Glanvile. Az. on a chief or, a lion pass. gu.

Glanvile. Per pale az. and gu. three saltires ar.

Glanville (Halwell and Killworthy, co. Devon; reputed to have derived from the famed RANULPH DE GLANVILLE, Baron de Bromholme, co. Suffolk, *temp.* William the Conqueror, ancestor of the *Earls of Chester* and *Suffolk*). Az. three saltires or. *Crest*—On a mount vert, a stag trippant ppr.

Glanville (Tavistock, co. Devon; JOHN GLANVILLE, Justice of the Common Pleas, third son of JOHN GLANVILLE, of that place, d. 27 July, 1600. Visit. 1620). Same *Arms*, a mullet for diff. *Crest*—On a mount vert a buck statant ppr.

Glanville (Broadhinton, co. Wilts; descended from Sir

JOHN GLANVILLE, M.P. for Totnes, Speaker of the House of Commons, 1640, second son of the Judge; his grandson, JOHN GLANVILLE, Esq., sold Broadhinton, and *d. s. p.*). Same *Arms* and *Crest*, with due diff.

Glanville (Catchfrench, co. Cornwall, and Cleveancry, co. Wilts; derived from JOHN GLANVILLE, eldest son and heir of JULIUS GLANVILLE, Esq., Barrister-at-law, youngest son of Sir JOHN GLANVILLE, of Broadhinton, the Speaker.) Same *Arms* and *Crest*, with due diff.

Glanville (Visit. Oxon, 1574). Ar. a chief indented sa.

Glasbrook. Or, a lion pass. sa. on a chief gu. three fleurs-de-lis ar. *Crest*—A demi lion gu. ducally crowned or.

Glascock, Glascott, Glascote, Glascoke, or Glascok (co. Essex; originally from the Manor of Glascott, co. Warwick, Har. MSS., allowed at Visit. Essex, 1614, as the arms of JOHN GLASCOCK, Esq., of Highestre, co. Essex, eldest son of JOHN GLASCOKE, or GLASCOTT, eighth in descent from JOHN GLASCOTE or GLASCOKE, Esq., living 38 Henry III., A.D. 1253). Erm. a chev. betw. three cocks az. armed, crested, and jelloped or.

Glascock (Dyves Hall, and Chiche, co. Essex ; allowed to JOHN GLASCOCK, Esq., of Powers Hall, in Witham, eldest son of RICHARD GLASCOCK, brother of the foregoing JOHN GLASCOKE or GLASCOTT, of Highestre. Visit. Essex, 1614). Same *Arms*, a crescent for diff.

Glascock (Much Dunmow, Downe Hall, and Rokeswell, co. Essex; confirmed by Cooke, Clarenceux, 1571, to WILLIAM GLASCOCK, of the former place, and his brother, JOHN GLASCOCK, of the latter). Same *Arms*, on the chev. a mullet or, for diff. *Crest*—Out of a ducal coronet or, a dragon's head per pale ar. and vert.

Glascock (Duary, and Ballyroan, in the Queen's co., Music Hall, Kilbride, co. Dublin, and the city of Dublin; descended from Downe Hall. Visit. Essex, 1614. Reg. Ulster's Office). Same *Arms*. *Crest*—A cock az. armed, crested, and jelloped or, holding in the beak an annulet gu. *Motto*—Vigil et audax.

Glascock (Heyrons, Felstedbury, and Aldham, co. Essex, and Wormerley, co. Herts; confirmed by St. George, Clarenceux, to Sir WILLIAM GLASCOCK, Knt., of Wormerley, Master in Chancery, knighted 1661, and his son, Sir WILLIAM GLASCOCK, Knt., of Aldhamhow, Judge of the Admiralty of Ireland. Visit. Essex, 1634). Erm. on a chev. sa. betw. three cocks az. armed, crested, and jelloped or, a bezant. *Crest*—An antelope's head erased ar, attired, crined, and langued or, gorged with a collar vert, garnished gold.

Glascock (Hertshobury, Farnham, and Brices, co. Essex. Visit. Essex, 1664). Same *Arms*, a crescent for diff. *Crest*—An antelope's head erased ar. attired, crined, and langued or, gorged with a collar sa.

Glascott (Aldertown, co. Wexford, 1656 to 1810, descended from co. Essex; arms on the seal of JOHN GLASCOTT, Esq., of Aldertown, d. 1707, whose father settled at Aldertown, 1656, where his descendants resided until 1810, when JOHN GLASCOTT, Esq., of Aldertown, d. s. p.). Az. two eagles' legs barways erased a la quise ar. armed or. *Crest*—An eagle displ. with two heads gu. armed and beaked sa. *Motto*—Virtute decoratus.

Glascott (Killowen, co. Wexford, 1810; represented by JOHN HENRY GLASCOTT, Esq., J.P., an accomplished genealogist and herald, whose skill and learning have contributed largely to the production of this work; Mr. GLASCOTT is eldest son of JOHN GLASCOTT, Esq., of Killowen, d. 1871, the fifth son of JOHN GLASCOTT, Esq., of Killowen, d. 1841, who was nephew and residuary legatee of the last JOHN GLASCOTT, Esq., of Aldertown, d. 1810). Same *Arms*, impaling for Mrs. GLASCOTT, LOUISA REBECCA, dau. of JOHN McGUIRE, Esq., Tralee, the arms of McGUIRE, of Knockaninny. *Crest*—On a ducal coronet or, an eagle displ. with two heads gu. armed and beaked sa. *Motto*—Virtute decoratus.

Glasfurd (Borrowstounness, Scotland, 1672; now represented by Col. CHARLES GLASFURD, Bombay Staff Corps). Ar. a bend engr. betw. two spur rowels in chief gu. and a buglehorn in base of the second, stringed and garnished sa. *Crest*—A buglehorn, as in the arms. *Motto*—Mente et manu.

Glasgood. Ar. on a fesse betw. two bars gemels gu. three eagles' heads erased or.

Glasgow, Earl of. See BOYLE.

Glasgow (Scotland). Ar. a chev. az. betw. two fishes naiant in chief sa. and an oak tree growing out of a mount in base vert. *Crest*—A martlet sa. *Motto*—Lord, let Glasgow flourish.

Glasgow (Mountgreenan, co. Renfrew, 1807). Ar. a cocoanut tree fructed ppr. growing out of a mount in base vert, on a chief az. a shakefork, betw. a martlet on the dexter, and a salmon naiant on the sinister all ar. the last holding in the mouth an annulet or. *Crest*—A demi negro holding in the dexter hand a sugar cane all ppr. *Motto*—Parcere subjectis.

Glasgow, See of. Ar. on a mount in base vert an oak-tree ppr. the stem at the base thereof surmounted by a salmon on its back also ppr. with a signet ring in its mouth or, on the top of the tree a redbreast and in the sinister fess point an ancient hand-bell both also ppr.

Glasgow, City of. Same *Arms*. *Crest*—The half-length figure of St. Kentigern affrontée vested and mitred, his right hand raised in the act of benediction, and having in his left a crosier all ppr. *Supporters*—Two salmon ppr. each holding in its mouth a signet ring ppr. *Motto*—Let Glasgow flourish.

Glasier, Glasyer, or Glazier (co. Lancaster). Az. three pheons ar. a chief erm. *Crest*—A man's heart charged with a cinquefoil.

Glasier (co. Chester: Fun. Ent. of the wife of Sir THOMAS ASH, Knt., of Trim, co. Meath, *d.* Jan. 1632). Az. three pheons ar. a chief erm. a bordure engr. or.

Glasier (Lea, co. Chester). Az. three pheons ar. a chief erm. *Crest*—Out of a ducal coronet gu. a dragon's head and neck betw. two wings displ. or.

Glass (Sauchie, Scotland). Ar. a fleur-de-lis betw. three mullets within a bordure gu. *Crest*—A mermaid with mirror and comb ppr. *Motto*—Luctor, non mergor.

Glass, or Glas (East Indies; representative of Sauchie, 1812). Quarterly, 1st and 4th, ar. a fleur-de-lis betw. three mullets gu. a bordure of the last; 2nd and 3rd, ar. on a bend az. betw. two roses gu. barbed vert, three buckles or. *Crest*—As the last. *Supporters*—Two horses ar. saddled and bridled ppr. the housing gu. fringed or. *Motto*—Luctor, non mergor.

Glassford (that Ilk, co. Lanark). Ar. a bend engr. betw. two spur-rowels gu.

Glassford (Douglastoun, 1769). Ar. a bend engr. betw. two spur-rowels gu. *Crest*—Two hands conjoined issuing out of clouds, grasping a caduceus ensigned on the top with a cap of liberty all betw. two cornucopias all ppr. *Motto*—Prisca fides.

Glassford. See GLASFURD.

Glastenbury (co. Dorset). Ar. a bend lozengy sa.

Glastenbury. Or, a bend fusily sa. *Crest*—A griffin's head betw. two wings, each charged with three bezants.

Glastenbury. Or, a bend engr. sa.

Glaster (Glack, Scotland). Ar. a fleur-de-lis betw. three mullets gu. within a bordure of the last.

Glastings, or Glastinges. Ar. five fusils in bend sa. *Crest*—An arm in armour embowed ppr. holding a baton sa.

Glaston. Ar. (another, or) a saltire gu. on a chief of the second three leopards' faces or.

Glastonbury Monastery (co. Somerset). Vert a cross botonnée ar. on a canton of the last the Virgin Mary and her child ppr. (another coat, vert a cross botonnée ar. on the dexter chief quarter the Virgin Mary holding the infant in her dexter arm and in the sinister a sceptre all or, in each of the other quarters a ducal crown of the last).

Glatingbras. Ar. two (another, three) bends engr. gu.

Glavill (co. Suffolk). Az. three lozenges in pale ar.

Glaziers, Company of (London). Ar. two grazing irons in saltire sa. betw. four closing nails of the last on a chief gu. a lion pass. guard. or. *Crest*—A lion's head couped or, betw. two wings expanded az. *Supporters*—Two naked boys ppr. each holding a long torch inflamed of the last. *Motto*—Da nobis lucem, Domine. (The Company have sometimes used another motto, viz.—Lumen umbra Dei.)

Glaziers, Corporation of (Gateshead-on-Tyne, 1671). Az. two grazing irons in saltire betw. four closing nails sa. on a chief gu. a lion pass. guard. or. *Crest*—A lion's head couped betw. two wings expanded or. *Supporters*—Two naked boys ppr. each holding a long torch inflamed or.

Glazebrook (Glazebrook, and other parts of co. Lancaster, and Toronto, Canada). Or, a lion pass. sa. on a chief gu. three fleurs-de-lis ar. *Crest*—A demi lion ramp. gu. ducally crowned or. *Motto*—Dum spiro spero.

Gleadow (borne by Rev. THOMAS READER GLEADOW, of Froueslay, co. Salop, and by the other descendants of THOMAS GLEADOW, Esq., of Hull, *d.* in 1814). Per chev. or and az. in chief three crosses pattée gu. and in base a dove, wings expanded, of the first, beaked and legged of the third. *Crest* —A lion's head erased az. charged on the neck with a cross pattée or, betw. two wings of the last, each charged with a cross pattée of the first.

Gleane (Norwich and Hardwick, co. Norfolk, bart., extinct 1745). Erm. on a chief sa. three lions ramp. ar. *Crest*—A Saracen's head affrontée ppr. wreathed about the temples ar. and sa.

403

Gleave, or Gleaoe (High Leigh, co. Chester). Sa. three crescents or, (another, ar) *Crest*—Cupid holding in the hand a bow and arrow ppr.

Gledhill (Barkisland, Halifax; granted by St. George, Norroy, 1612, confirmed by Segar, Garter, 1632). Az. three lozenges in fess ar.

Gledstanes (exemplified in Ulster's Office, 1871, to MOD-TRAY VANCE GLEDSTANES, of Fardross, co. Tyrone, late lieut. 57th Regt., to ROBERT GLEDSTANES, Esq., junior, his brother, and to their father, ROBERT GLEDSTANES, Esq., senior, of Twickenham, King's co., on their taking, by royal licence, the surname of GLEDSTANES in lieu of that of HORNIDGE). Quarterly, 1st and 4th, per pale or and ar. within an orle of martlets sa. a savage's head couped, distilling drops of blood and wearing a bonnet composed of bay and holly leaves all ppr., for GLEDSTANES ; 2nd and 3rd, ar. on a chev. engr. betw. three buglehorns stringed gu. a trefoil slipped or, for HORNIDGE. *Crests*—1st, GLEDSTANES : A demi griffin sa. holding a spear ppr. transfixing a savage's head couped, distilling drops of blood and wearing a bonnet composed of bay and holly leaves, as in the arms ; 2nd, HORNIDGE : Out of park palings ppr. a demi huntsman affrontée, habited gu. belt and cap sa. winding a horn or, motto over, Virtutis laus actio. *Motto*—Under the arms : Fide et virtute.

Gleen. Erm. three mascles in fesse gu.

Gleg (Dr. THOMAS GLEG, Edinburgh, 1672). Sa. two lions counterpass. ar. collared gu. *Crest*—A falcon preying on a partridge all ppr. *Motto*—Qui potest capere capiat.

Glege, or Gleke (co. Chester). Gu. a sword in bend ar. (another, or).

Glege (Reg. Ulster's Office). Sa. a lion pass. ar.

Glegg (BASKERVILLE-GLEGG, Old Withington and Gayton Hall, co. Chester). Quarterly, 1st and 4th, sa. two lions counter-pass. in pale ar., for GLEGG ; 2nd and 3rd, ar. a chev. gu. betw. three hurts, for BASKERVILLE. *Crests*—1st, GLEGG : A hawk, wings expanded, preying on a partridge, all ppr.; 2nd, BASKERVILLE : A forester, vested vert, edged or, holding over the right shoulder a crossbow gold, and with the other hand, in a leash, a hound pass. ar. *Motto*—Qui potest capere capiat.

Glegg (Irbie and Blackford Hall, co. Chester). Quarterly, 1st and 4th, sa. two lions counterpass. in pale ar. a crescent within a crescent for diff., for GLEGG ; 2nd and 3rd, sa. three garbs or, a border ar., for BIRKENHEAD. *Crests*—1st, GLEGG : A hawk, wings expanded, preying on a partridge, all ppr.; 2nd, BIRKENHEAD : A goat saliant ar. attired or, resting the fore feet on a garb ppr.

Glegg. Sa. two lions pass. guard. ar. depressed by as many palets gu.

Gleig (Scotland). Ar. a bend engr. betw. a lion pass. in chie and a lion counterpass. in base gu. *Crest*—A rose gu. seeded or, barbed vert.

Glen. Ar. three martlets sa. *Crest*—An arm embowed vested sa., in the hand ppr. a heart gu.

Glen (Glasmount and Balmuto, co. Fife ; the heiress *m.* in 1400, Sir JOHN BOSWELL). Same *Arms*.

Glen (Bar, co. Renfrew, Scotland). Ar. a fesse gu. betw. three martlets sa. *Crest*—A martlet sa. *Motto*—Alta pete.

Glen (Stratton Audley Park, co. Oxford). Ar. a fess gu. betw. three martlets sa. *Crest*—A martlet sa. *Motto*—Alta pete.

Glendee (JOHN GLENDEE, B.D., Dean of Cashel, 1676-94). Ar. a cross betw. four bees sa. *Motto*—Pro rege et grege.

Glenden. Ar. three tilting spears sa. on each a banner gu.

Glendonwyn, or Glendinning (that Ilk, co. Roxburgh, and Partoun, co. Kirkcudbright; descended from ADAM DE GLENDONWYN of that Ilk, a person of rank, *temp.* Alexander III.; ended in co-heiresses, of whom the senior *m.* GORDON, of Letterfourie). Quarterly, ar. and sa. a cross parted per cross, indented and counterchanged of the same. *Crest*—The sleeve of a coat or, upon the point of a sword. *Motto*—Have faith in Christ.

Glendor. Or, a fesse betw. six crosses crosslet gu.

Glene (Glene, co. Leicester ; JOHN DE BELGRAVE, of Belgrave, 12 Edward IV., 1472, *m.* KATHERINE, dau. and co-heir of HUGH GLENE, of Glene. Visit. Leices. 1614). Erm. three mascles in fess sa.

Gleneagles (that Ilk). Ar. a saltire engr. sa. *Crest*—A eagle's head erased or. *Motto*—Suffer.

Glenelg, Baron (extinct 1866). See GRANT.

Glenester. Per fesse dancettée gu. and or, in chief a lion pass. ar. a crescent for diff. *Crest*—A boar pass. sa. charged with a gate ar. thereon a leopard's face ppr.

Glenfield (co. Leicester). Erm. three mascles in fesse gu.

Glenfield (co. Leicester). Erm. a fesse betw. three mascles gu.

Glengall, Earl of (extinct 1858). See BUTLER.

Glenham, Gleman, or Glemham (Glenham, co. Suffolk). Or, a chev. gu. betw. three torteaux. *Crest*—A hawk, wings expanded ar. beaked and legged gu. belled or.

Glenham. Ar. a chev. gu. betw. three torteaux.

Glenham. Or, a chev. gu. betw. three golpes.

Glenlyon, Baron. Merged in MURRAY, *Duke of Athole*.

Glenn, Glen, and Glene. Erm. three mascles in fesse sa. *Crest*—Out of a ducal coronet a hand holding a swan's head erased ppr.

Glennon (Tyrawley, co. Mayo). Gyronny of eight or and ar. four mullets pierced sa. *Crest*—A mullet pierced betw. two wings sa. *Motto*—Generosus et animosus.

Glennie (Brazil, 1859). Ar. three martlets sa. beaked and legged gu. on a chief of the last a pennon with a staff sa. and a claymore in saltire of the field, the former inscribed with the word "Bonnie." *Crest*—An eagle preparing to rise ppr. *Motto*—Eirich as a ghleannan.

Glenton (co. Warwick). Ar. (another, or) three piles az. a canton erm. *Crest*—A cubit arm erect ppr.

Glenton, or Glynton. Chequy az. and or.

Glindore. Per pale ar. and gu. a lion ramp. sa.

Glincester. Gu. on a chief dancettée or, a lion pass. sa.

Glinne (co. Cornwall). Ar. a chev. betw. three salmon spears sa.

Glisson (Rampisham, co. Dorset). Sa. on a bend ar. three mullets pierced gu.

Glisson, or Cliston (co. Somerset). Same *Arms*, with a crescent within an annulet for diff.

Gloag (LAKE-GLOAG, Edinburgh; exemplified 1866). Quarterly, 1st and 4th, or, a bend wavy az. betw. a lion pass. in chief sa. and a lion counter-pass. in base gu., for GLOAG; 2nd and 3rd, or, a chev. gu. betw. three lions' gambs erect and erased az., for AUSTIN; en surtout, sa. a bend betw. six cross crosslets fitchée ar., for LAKE. *Crest*—An eagle with wings expanded ppr. *Motto*—Nunquam senescit.

Glodrydd (one of the Royal Tribes of Wales). Quarterly, 1st and 4th, ar. three boars' heads couped sa.; 2nd and 3rd, gu. a lion ramp. reguard. ar.

Gloucester, City of. Vert on a pale gu. betw. two horseshoes, each horseshoe betw. three nails, two in chief and one in base, all meeting with their points to the shoe ar. a sword in a scabbard az. hilt, pommel, and studding of the scabbard or, on the point of the sword a cap of maintenance gu. turned up erm. on a chief per pale or and purp. a boar's head couped ar. betw. two demi roses, the dexter gu. barbed vert, the sinister of the third barbed vert, each issuing rays from its centre, pointing to the boar's head or. The arms for the Corporation by Sir RICHARD BELL, Knt., Alderman of the city of Gloucester, *temp.* Henry VIII., the original arms of the city being, or, three chev. gu. betw. ten torteaux, three, three, three, and one.

Gloucester. Earl of. See CLARE.

Gloucester and Bristol, See of. Az. two keys in saltire, the wards upwards or, for the *See of Gloucester*, impaling az. three ducal crowns in pale or, for the *See of Bristol*.

Gloucester Monastery. Az. two keys in saltire or, the wards in chief.

Gloucester, Dean of. Az. on a fess or, three crosses pattée fitchée of the first, on a quarter of the second the sun appearing in chief environed with a demi circle gu. on each side of the quarter a demi fleur-de-lis conjoined to the side of the first.

Gloucester (co. Gloucester). Ar. three lions gu. a bordure engr. az.

Gloucester. Gu. two bends or.

Gloucester. Gu. three fishes haurient ar.

Gloucester. Gu. a cross chequy or and sa.

Gloucester. Az. a fesse ar. in chief two leopards' faces or, in base a fish hauriant of the second.

Gloucester (Car Colston, co. Nottingham). Sa. a chev. betw. two martlets in chief and a cross botonnée fitchée in base ar.

Glover (Norwoods in Cudhams, co. Kent, and Tatsfield, co. Surrey). Sa. a fesse embattled erm. betw. three crescents ar. *Crest*—Out of a mural crown a demi lion ramp. holding betw. the paws a crescent.

Glover (co. Norfolk, 1611; granted by Camden, Clarenceux). Sa. a chev. erminites betw. three crescents ar. *Crest*—An eagle displ. ar. charged on the breast with three spots of erminites. *Another Crest*—A dragon pass. az.

Glover (Romney, co. Kent, and London). Same *Arms* and *Crest*.

Glover (Somerset Herald, *temp.* Queen Elizabeth). Same *Arms* and *Crest.*

Glover (confirmed to ALEXANDER GLOVER, of the Exchequer, by Camden, Clarenceux). Same *Arms*, with a fleur-de-lis or, for diff. *Crest*—A fleur-de-lis gu. betw. two wings sa.

Glover (London, 1604, Ashford, co. Kent, and Coventry, co. Warwick; granted by Camden, Clarenceux, 4 March, 1577). Sa. a chev. erm. betw. three crescents ar. *Crest*—A crossbow az. betw. two wings or.

Glover (THOMAS GLOVER, Esquire of the Body to James I., son of THOMAS GLOVER, of Coventry; confirmed by Camden, 17 Aug. 1606). Same *Arms* and *Crest*.

Glover (London; granted 1602, by Camden, Clarenceux, to Sir WILLIAM GLOVER, Sheriff of London, 1603). Same *Arms*, a bordure or. *Crest*—On a chapeau ppr. two wings gu.

Glover (Ambassador to the Turks, 1606). Sa. a chev. betw. three crescents ar. a bordure of the last.

Glover (co. Norfolk; granted 1611). Sa. a fesse embattled erm. betw. three crescents ar.

Glover (co. Oxon). Ar. four hounds gu. a bordure sa. charged with eight crescents or.

Glover. Sa. a bend ar. betw. three herons' heads erased of the second.

Glovers, Company of (London). Per fesse sa. and ar. a pale counterchanged, three rams saliant of the second, two and one, armed and unguled or. *Crest*—A ram's head ar. issuing from a basket of the last betw. two wings expanded gu.

Glovers and Skinners, United Company of (Exeter). Erm. on a chief gu. three regal or imperial crowns ppr. *Motto*—Soli Deo gloria.

Glowcester. Gu. on a chief dancettée or, a lion pass. sa.

Glubb. Gu. a water bouget ar. *Crest*—A demi lion az. bezantée.

Glyborne. Erm. on a chief indented az. two roses ar.

Glyn (Ewell, co. Surrey, bart.). Quarterly, 1st and 4th, ar. an eagle imperial displ. sa. guttée d'or; 2nd and 3rd, ar. three fiery brands sa. enflamed ppr. with an escutcheon of pretence ar. charged with a man's leg couped at the thigh sa. *Crest*—An eagle's head erased sa. guttée d'or, in the beak a brand ragulé fired. *Motto*—Pro libertate lege sancta.

Glyn (Gaunts, co. Dorset, bart.). Ar. an eagle displ. with two heads sa. guttée d'or. *Crest*—An eagle's head erased sa. guttée d'or, in the beak an escallop ar. *Motto*—Firm in my trust.

Glyn (*Baron Wolverton ;* GEORGE GRENFELL GLYN, eldest son of GEORGE CARR GLYN, fourth son of the first bart. of Gaunts, was so created 1869). Same *Arms* and *Crest*. **Supporters**—Two eagles, wings elevated sa. guttée d'or. *Motto*—Fidei tenax.

Glyn (Dursington House, Sheering, co. Essex). Ar. an eagle displ. with two heads sa. guttée d'or. *Crest*, as GLYN, bart.

Glyn. Ar. an eagle displ. with two necks sa. within a bordure of the last bezantée. *Crest*—A demi lion sa. charged with three bezants, one and two.

Glyn (Glyn, parish of Cardinam, co. Cornwall; NICHOLAS GLYN. Visit. 1620). Ar. three salmon spears sa. *Crest*—A demi talbot erm. eared or. *Motto*—Dry weres agan dew ny.

Glyn (Fairy Hill, Isle of Wight, and Boyton, co. Cornwall). *Arms, Crest,* and *Motto,* same as preceding

Glyndwrddwy (in Merioneth, Lords of; derived from, and eventually representatives of GRIFFITH MAELOR, Lord of Bromfield, eldest son of MADOC, last Prince of Powys-Fadoc. Descendants: I. OWEN AP GRIFFITH VYCHAN, last Lord of Glyndwrddwy, the memorable OWEN GLENDOWER; II. TUDOR AP GRIFFITH VYCHAN, Lord of Gwyddelwern, in Merioneth. See OWEN AP GRIFFITH VYCHAN, and TUDOR AP GRIFFITH). *Arms,* those of GRIFFITH MAELOR, Lord of Bromfield.

Glynn (Glynn, co. Cornwall; an ancient family extinct in the elder branch in the early part of the 14th century, when the heiress *m.* Sir JOHN CARMINOW; the younger branch became afterwards possessed, by purchase, of the seat of their ancestors, and from it derived the subsequent GLYNNS, of Glynn. The GLYNNS, of Boyton, Lanhydrock, Morvel, and Helston, bore the same *Arms*). Ar. three salmon spears, points downwards sa. *Crest*—A demi talbot erm. eared or.

Glynne (Hawarden Castle, co. Flint, bart., extinct 1874; KATHERINE, eldest sister of the last Bart., *m.* 1839, Right Hon. WILLIAM EWART GLADSTONE, First Lord of the Treasury, 1868-74). Ar. an eagle displ. with two heads sa. quartering, ar. three brands raguly sa. fired ppr. with an escutcheon of pretence ar. charged with a human leg couped at the thigh sa. *Crest*—An eagle's head erased, in the beak a brand raguly sa. fired ppr.

Glynne (Sir WILLIAM GLYNNE, knighted at Dublin Castle by Sir Arthur Chichester, Lord Deputy, 7 June, 1606). Ar. an eagle displ. gu.

Glysson. Sa. on a bend ar. three mullets pierced gu.

Goad (Cruxton). Gu. a chev. or, betw. three lions double queued ar.

Goadefroy. Gu. an anchor ar. stock or. *Crest*—An arm in armour embowed, holding in the gauntlet a sword all ppr.

Goarge (co. Worcester). Masculy or and az.

Goat, or Goate. Gu. a saltire ar. on a chief of the last three escallops of the first. *Crest*—A goat pass. ar. armed or.

Goater. Or, a fesse engr. betw. three crosses crosslet fitchée gu. *Crest*—A wolf sejant or, grasping a cross crosslet fitchée gu.

Goatham. Per fesse embattled gu. and ar. three goats pass. counterchanged. *Crest*—A hunting horn sa. garnished and stringed gu.

Goatley (Canterbury). Ar. a lion ramp. sa. over all on a saltire engr. gu. a crescent for diff. *Crest*—A sphinx couchant or, wing on the back ar. face and breast ppr.

Goband, or Gonband (co. Lincoln). Gu. two bars or, in chief three bezants.

Gobard (Coventry, co. Warwick; confirmed to JOHN GOBARD, of that place, son of PETER GOBARD, of Picardy, settled in England *temp.* Henry VIII.). Or, a bend betw. six martlets gu. *Crest*—A mermaid holding a dagger ppr.

Goband. Ar. three fishes, two and one, and a bordure sa.

Gobel. Paly of six az. and gu. on a chief ar. a wivern vert. *Crest*—A wivern vert.

Gobeon (Visit. Leicester, 1619; quartered by TURPEN). Quarterly, or, and barry of six ar. and gu. a border sa. charged with ten fishes naiant of the second.

Gobion (Gobion, co. Bedford; an heiress of this family *m.* Sir RALPH LE BOTELER, *circa. temp.* Edward I.). Quarterly, or, and barry of six ar. and gu. a bordure sa. charged with eight fish ar. (a second coat, barry of ten ar. and gu. a label of five points az.).

Gobion (co. York). Barry of eight ar. and gu. a label of three points sa.

Gobion, Gobyon, or Gobyns. Ar. three gudgeons haurient, and a bordure engr. sa. *Crest*—In water a swan swimming, with wings elevated ppr.

Gobion. Bendy of six or and az. a lion pass. guard. ar. on a chief gu. three saltires of the third.

Gobion. Barry of eight ar. and gu. on a bend sa. three escallops or.

Gobond (co. Lincoln). Gu. two bars or, in chief three bezants.

Gobotesley. Sa. a fesse componée gu. and or, betw. three crosses potent of the last.

Gobyan, or Gubyon. Paly of eight ar. and gu. on a bend sa. three escallops or.

Gobyns (co. York). Barry of ten (another, of eight) ar. and gu. on a bend sa. three escallops or.

Goch, or Goff (co. Devon). Ar. a cross fusily betw. four eagles displ. sa.

Goch (Wales). Per pale az. and sa. three fleurs-de-lis or.

Goche (co. Norfolk). Per pale sa. and ar. a chev. betw. three talbots pass. all counterchanged.

Godard. See GODDARD.

Godard (Alderman of London; confirmed 15 Aug. 1598). Erm. a cross patonce sa. in the first quarter an eagl. displ. gu.

Godard (Walpole, co. Norfolk). Gu. an eagle displ. or. *Crest*—An eagle's head betw. two wings or. *Another Crest*—An eagle's head erect or.

Godard. Gu. a lion ramp. ar. a bordure of the last, charged with nine escallops vert.

Godard. Quarterly, gu. and ar., in the second and third quarters an eagle displ. sa.

Godard. Per chev. gu. and sa. three falcons' heads erased ar.

Godard. Ar. a fesse betw. three horseshoes gu.

Godard, or Godherd. Gu. a fesse chequy or and az.

Godbold (Hatfield, co. Essex, and Westhall, co. Suffolk). Az. two bows strung in saltire or. *Crest*—An arm in armour ppr. wreathed about the arm or and az. with the ends flotant holding in the gauntlet an arrow sa. feathered and headed ar.

Godbold (Godalming, co. Surrey). Same *Arms. Crest*—An arm embowed in armour ppr. holding an arrow.

Godbow. Az. two bows strung or, one within the other in saltire. *Crest*—Out of a mural coronet or, a griffin's head betw. two wings gu.

Godby. Sa. a chev. ar. betw. three men's heads ppr. *Crest*—A tree. Seal of HUGH DE GONDEBY, of co. Sussex, 1 Henry IV.

Goddard (London, and East Wood Hay, co. Hants; granted by Barker, Garter, to WILLIAM GODDARD, 3 Dec. 1536. Visit.

405

1634). Az. five fusils in fesse betw. three eagles' heads erased or. *Crest*—A hawk's head or, holding in the beak a lure gu. capped vert, garnished of the first, stringed of the second.

Goddard (Cliffe Pypard, Upham, and Albourn, co. Wilts; an ancient Saxon family, settled at a very remote period in cos. Hants and Norfolk, and Wilts since the time of King John). Gu. a chev. vair betw. three crescents ar. *Crest*—A stag's head couped at the neck and affrontée gu. attired or. *Motto*—Cervus non servus.

Goddard (Swindon, co. Wilts; derived from THOMAS GODDARD, of Upham, second son of JOHN GODDARD, of Upham and Cliffe Pypard). Same *Arms*, &c., as the preceding.

Goddard (Purton, co. Wilts; a younger branch of GODDARD, of Cliffe Pypard, descended from the second son of FRANCIS GODDARD, Esq., of Standen Hussey and Cliffe Pypard; the heiress, MARGARET GODDARD, *m.* in 1792, ROBERT WILSONN, Esq., and had four daughters; the eldest *m.* to RICHARD MILES, Esq.). Same *Arms*, &c.

Goddard (Beeby, co. Leicester; WILLIAM GODDARD, of that place, *b.* 1583, great grandson of WILLIAM GODDARD, of the same place, who was descended from the co. Berks. Visit. Leicester, 1619). Az. on a fess betw. three hawks' heads erased or, five lozenges conjoined in fess vert.

Goddard (JOHN, Lord of Lynford, co. Berks, *temp.* Henry VIII., *m.* JOAN, dau. and heir of RICHARD GODDARD, Esq., of Upham, co. Wilts. Visit. Oxon, 1574). Gu. a chev. vair betw. three crescents erm.

Goddard. Erm. a cross pattée aa.

Goddart (Scotland). Gu. a chev. vair betw. three crescents ar. *Crest*—A stag's head affrontée couped gu. attired or.

Godden (Leyborn Castle, co. Kent; *Her. Off.*). Gu. two bars or, over all a bend ar. charged with three talbots' heads erased sa. *Crest*—On a garb lying fessways a bird close, in the beak an ear of wheat, all or.

Goddin (co. Kent). Sa. a chev. erm. betw. three leopards' faces or, a bordure of the third.

Goddinge. Gu. a chev. ar. betw. three griffins' heads erased or.

Goddiston (co. Essex). Ar. four crosses crosslet betw. three martlets sa.

Goderich. Ar. on a fesse betw. two lions pass. guard. sa. a fleur-de-lis betw. as many crescents or.

Goderidge (co. Devon; granted by Camden, Clarenceux). Ar. a fesse betw. three crosses crosslet fitché sa.

Godeston (sa. Essex). Ar. on a bend gu. three crescents or.

Godeston (co. Essex). Erm. a saltire engr. gu. *Crest*—A buffalo's head issuing sa.

Godewyn. Gu. three palets lozengy ar. and sa.

Godfray (Jersey). Ar. a griffin segreant sa. a border of the last bezantée. *Crest*—A demi griffin or. *Motto*—Deus est pax.

Godfrey (Hurst and Romney, co. Kent; in the reign of Charles II., a younger branch settled in Ireland). Sa. (sometimes az.) a chev. betw. three pelicans' heads or, vulning themselves ppr. *Crest*—A demi Saracen ppr. holding in the dexter hand a cross crosslet fitchée ar.

Godfrey (Lydd, Heppington, Hodiford, Norton Court, &c., co. Kent). Same *Arms* and *Crest*. *Motto*—Corde fixam.

Godfrey (co. Stafford, and Tamworth, co. Warwick; granted 1765). Sa. on a chev. betw. three pelicans' heads erased or, vulning themselves ppr. as many crosses crosslet gu. *Crest*—A pelican with wings endorsed or, gorged with an eastern coronet az. holding in the beak a cross crosslet fitchée gu.

Godfrey (co. Bedford, and Dartford, co. Kent). Ar. a griffin segreant sa.

Godfrey (Bolleyne). Az. a cross potence or, betw. four crosses pattée of the second.

Godfrey (co. Cornwall). Az. three bulls' heads erased and crowned or.

Godfrey (Wilmington, co. Kent). Az. three griffins pass. in pale or.

Godfrey (Basenes). Gu. an inescutcheon or, within an orle of eight cinquefoils ar.

Godfrey. Ar. a griffin pass. sa. within a bordure engr. az. bezantée. *Crest*—An eagle displ. sa.

Godfrey. Or, a cross gu. betw. four martlets sa. *Crest*—A leopard's head couped sa.

Godfrey. Barry wavy ar. and gu. on a bend sa. three bezants.

Godfrey (Bushfield, co. Kerry, bart.). Ar. a griffin pass. wings endorsed sa. betw. three lions' heads erased gu. *Crest*—A griffin pass. sa. holding in the dexter forepaw a sceptre or. *Mottoes*—God friend; and, Deus et libertas.

Godin. Sa. three ostrich feathers or. *Crest*—An ox yoke in bend sa. strapped az.

Goding (London). Gu. two bars or, over all on a bend ar. three lions' heads erased ppr. *Crest*—On a garb fessewise a bird close, in the beak an ear of wheat all or. *Motto*—Dominus providebit.

Godington. Or, two lions pass. guard. sa.

Godley (granted, 1810, to JOHN GODLEY, Esq., of Killigar, co. Leitrim, son of JOHN GODLEY, Esq., M.P. for Baltinglass, and grandson of Rev. WILLIAM GODLEY, Rector of Mullaghbrack, co. Armagh). Ar. three unicorns' heads erased sa. horned gu. two and one, and three trefoils slipped vert, one and two. *Crest*—A unicorn's head erased ar. horned gu. charged with three trefoils slipped vert. *Motto*—Sans Dieu rien.

Godman (granted, 1579, to THOMAS GODMAN, of Leatherhead, co. Surrey). Per pale erm. and ermines, on a chief indented or, a lion pass. vert. *Crest*—On a mount a black cock with wings displ. all ppr.

Godman (Park Hatch, co. Surrey, and Merston Manor Farm, co. Sussex). Same *Arms* and *Crest*. *Motto*—Cœlum quid quærimus ultra.

Godman, alias Bailey (Reg. Ulster's Office). Gu. on a cross or, four greyhounds' heads erased sa. in dexter chief a covered cup of the second.

Godmanston, or Goodmanston. Az. an eagle displ. or. *Crest*—A man's leg couped at the thigh ppr.

Godmonton. Ar. an eagle displ. az

Godolphin, Baron. See OSBORNE.

Godolphin (*Baron* and *Earl of Godolphin*, Earldom extinct 1766, Barony 1785; descended from JOHN DE GODOLPHIN, lord of the manor of Godolphin, co. Cornwall, *circa* Conquest; SYDNEY GODOLPHIN, Lord High Treasurer of England, was created *Baron Godolphin*, of Rialton, in 1664, and made *Earl of Godolphin* in 1706). Gu. an eagle with two heads displ. betw. three fleurs-de-lis ar. (Godolphin, in Cornish, signifies a white eagle, which was always borne in the arms of this family). *Crest*—A dolphin naiant embowed ppr. *Supporters*—Two eagles reguard. wings displ. ar. *Motto*—Francha Call Toge.

Godolphin (Trewarveneth, co. Cornwall, *temp.* Henry VIII.). Same *Arms* and *Crest*.

Godolphin (Sir WILLIAM GODOLPHIN, Knighted at Dublin Castle, by ROBERT, *Earl of Essex*, Lord Lieutenant, 13 July, 1599). Az. an eagle displ. ar. betw. three fleurs-de-lis or.

Godrevy (Godrevy in Gwithian, co. Cornwall; the heiress *m.* TREGENDAR). Ar. a chev. gu. betw. three blackamoors' heads in profile erased sa.

Godsal (Iscoyd Park, co. Flint). Per pale gu. and az. on a fesse wavy ar. betw. three crosses pattée or, as many crescents sa. *Crest*—A griffin's head erased paly of six indented ar. and sa. beaked or.

Godsall. Same *Arms*. *Crest*—A griffin's head erased paly of six indented ar. and sa.

Godsalve (Buckenham-Ferry, co. Norfolk). Per pale wavy gu. and az. three crosses formée in fesse or, betw. as many crescents ar

Godsalve (co. Suffolk). Per pale gu. and az. on a fesse wavy ar. betw. three crosses formée or, as many crescents sa. *Crest*—A griffin's head erased paly wavy of four ar. and sa. in the mouth a branch vert

Godsalve (EDWARD BLUNDEVILLE, Esq., of Newton Flatteman, co. Norfolk, *temp.* Henry VIII., *m.* ELIZABETH, dau. of THOMAS GODSALVE. Visit. Notts, 1614). Per pale gu. and az. on a fessa wavy ar. betw. three crosses pattée or, as many crescents sa.

Godschall (Lord Mayor of London, 1742). Az. three bends wavy ar.

Godschall. Or, a cross patonce sa. *Crest*—A lion's paw holding a crescent.

Godsell, Godsall, and Godseel. Sa. a cross botonnée or. *Crest*—An arm erect holding a spade ppr.

Godson. Gu. a fesse betw. six martlets or. *Crest*—An arm embowed in armour, the hand grasping a sword enfiled with a crown of thorns all ppr.

Godstone. Ar. three martlets in fesse betw. four crosses crosslet fitchée sa. *Crest*—On a chapeau ppr. a talbot's head issuing ar.

Godweston. Quarterly, ar. and sa. on a bend gu. three fleurs-de-lis of the first.

Godweston (quartered by PALMER, of Compton Scorphyn, co. Warwick. Har. MSS. 1100, 1167, and 1563, certified by Cooke, Clarenceux. Visit. of that co. 1619). Ar. four martlets sa. *Crest*—Out of a ducal coronet a plume of five ostrich feathers alternately ar. and sa.

Godwin (co. Dorset). Gu. a chev. erm. betw. three leopards' faces or.

Godwin. Or, three palets lozengy sa.

Godwin. Or, three lions ramp. sa. on a canton of the last three bezants.

Godwin. Sa. a chev. erm. betw. three leopards' faces or.

Godwin. Paly of six gu. and vair.

Godwyn (co. Kent). Or, two lions pass. sa. on a canton of the second three bezants.

Godwyn (co. Oxford). Or, a fesse betw. two chev. az.

Goff (Hale Park, Fordingbridge, co. Hants.; descended from a family formerly settled in cos. Waterford and Wexford; certified in Ulster's Office to JOSEPH GOFF, Esq.). Az. a chev. betw. two fleurs-de-lis in chief and a lion ramp. in base or. *Crest*—A squirrel sejant ppr. *Motto*—Fier sans tache.

Goff (Davis-GOFF, Horetown, co. Wexford; exemplified 7 May, 1845, to STRANGMAN DAVIS, Esq., on his assuming, by royal licence, the additional surname and arms of GOFF, in compliance with the testamentary injunction of his maternal uncle, JACOB WILLIAM GOFF, Esq., of Horetown). Quarterly, 1st and 4th, az. a chev. betw. two fleurs-de-lis in chief and a lion ramp. in base or, a crescent for diff., for GOFF; 2nd and 3rd, per pale gu. and ar. a chev. betw. three boars' heads couped counterchanged, for DAVIS. *Crest*—A squirrel sejant ar. *Motto*—Honestas optima politia.

Goff (Oakport, co. Roscommon; confirmed to THOMAS WILLIAM GOFF, Esq., of that place, M.P. for co. Roscommon, 1859). Az. on a chev. betw. two fleurs-de-lis in chief and a demi lion ramp. couped in base or, an annulet gu. *Crest*—A squirrel sejant ppr. charged on the shoulder with a fleur-de-lis or, and holding in its forepaws a nut also ppr. *Motto*—Honestas optima politia.

Goffe (Woodbury, co. Devon). Ar. a cross lozengy betw. four eagles displ. sa.

Gofton (Stockwell, co. Surrey; granted by Camden, Clarenceux.) Quarterly, az. and erm., in the 1st and 4th quarters a unicorn's head erased ar. ducally gorged or, armed and crined of the last. *Crest*—On a chapeau gu. turned up ar. a rose or, betw. two wings expanded az.

Goges. Gu. three estoiles ar.

Goghe (Reg. Ulster's Office). Gu. a chev. erm. betw. three plates, each charged with a fleurs-de-lis az. on a chief ar. a demi lion naissant of the field betw. two anchors in pale of the third.

Goghe, or Gough (Sir JAMES GOGHE, knighted by Sir George Carey, Lord Deputy, 29 Sept. 1603). Az. a chev. betw. two fleurs-de-lis in chief and a lion ramp. in base or.

Goghe. Az. a boar ar.

Gogill (Terrington, co. Norfolk). Or, on a bend sa. three crescents of the first.

Going (Traverston, co. Tipperary). Ar. on a mount vert a palm tree, therefrom a serpent descending ppr. *Crest*—An arm. embowed in armour charged on the fore-arm with three estoiles in pale gu. holding a palm branch all ppr.

Going (Ballyphilip, co. Tipperary). Same *Arms* and *Crest*. *Motto*—Dum spiro spero.

Gokin, or Gookeine (Ickham, co. Kent; granted in 1609, by Segar; the family occurs in the Kent Visit. of 1619 and in that of 1663). Gu. a chev. betw. three cocks ar. *Crest*—On a mural coronet ar. a cock or, beaked, barbed, and membered gu.

Golafer (Golafers, in Nafford and Berrow, co. Worcester). Barry wavy of six ar. and gu. on a bend sa. six bezants.

Golafre (Fyfield, co. Berks; in 1337 JOHN GOLAFRE was knight of the shire, and in 1389 Sir JOHN GOLAFRE was employed in an embassy to France; in the north aisle of Fyfield Church is the monument of Sir JOHN GOLAFRE, who died in 1442, with his arms depicted on the tomb). Ar. four bars wavy gu. over all on a bend sa. three bezants.

Goland. Gu. two bars or, in chief three bezants.

Golbore. Erm. on a chev. gu. three escallops ar.

Golborne (originally, at a very remote period, of Golborne David, and subsequently of Overton, co. Chester). Ar. a cross patonce gu. betw. four martlets of the second a label gu.

Golborne (co. Chester). Ar. a cross pattée betw. four martlets gu. *Crest*—A man's leg couped above the knee vert spurred or.

Golborne. Ar. a cross betw. four martlets gu.

Golborne. Ar. on a bend sa. three crosses patonce or.

Golcar, or Goldear. Gu. a cross patonce or.

Gold and Silver Wire Drawers, Company of (London). Az. on a chev. or, betw. two coppers in chief of the second, in base two points in saltire ar. a drawing iron betw. two rings (*i.e.* tools used by wire drawers) sa. *Crest*—Two arms embowed, vested gu. cuffed ar. holding betw. the hands ppr. an engrossing block or. *Supporters*—Dexter, an

Indian ppr. crowned with an eastern crown or, vested round the middle with feathers pendent alternately ar. and gu. holding over his shoulder a bar of silver; sinister, a man vested ppr. (called in the grant "a silk throwster") in his sinister hand a hank of silk ar. *Motto*—Amicitiam trahit amor.

Gold (quartered by PYNE, of Estdown, co. Devon. Visit. 1620). Gu. on a chev. betw. three roses or, as many roses of the field.

Gold (impaled by St. John, on a monument for his wife, MARY, dau. of Sir NATHAN GOLD, Knt., in Lenthorp Church). Or, on a chev. betw. three roses ar. three thistles slipped of the first.

Gold (co. Dorset). Ar. three roses gu. seeded or.

Gold (London). Gyronny of four az. and or, a lion ramp. guard. of the first.

Gold (co. Somerset). Or, on a chev. az. betw. three roses vert, as many bunches of grapes of the first.

Gold (Alarston, co. Wilts). Or, on a chev. betw. three roses az. as many pineapples of the first. *Crest*—An eagle's head erased az. in the beak a pine or. *Another Crest*—A demi lion ramp. or.

Gold. Gyronny of four az. and or, four lions ramp. counterchanged.

Gold. Gyronny of four az. and or, a lion ramp. guard. of the first, on a canton ar. two pot guns sa. (another, az.).

Gold (Reg. Ulster's Office). Or, on a chev. gu. betw. three roses slipped vert, seeded ar. as many bunches of grapes of the last.

Gold (Chief Justice of Munster; Reg. Ulster's Office). Ar. a chev. sa. betw. three goldfinches in chief and a rose in base vert.

Golde (Fun. Ent. Ulster's Office, 1656). Sa. semée of roses ar. seeded or, leaved vert, three goldfinches, two and one, in chief a fleur-de-lis, and another in base all of the second.

Golde (Reg. Ulster's Office). Gu. two bars ar. in chief three plates.

Goldacre. Az. a cross flory or.

Goldacre, or Gouldacre. Gu. a cross pattée or.

Golden (Gainsborough, co. Lincoln). Gu. a chev. ar. betw. three bezants. *Crest*—A dragon's head erased vert, collared and lined or.

Golden. Ar. three trefoils triple-fitched vert. *Crest*—A cinquefoil ppr.

Goldesborough, or Goldesbrough. Az. a cross pattée or. *Crest*—A dexter hand holding a trident ppr.

Goldesburgh (Chipping Ongar, co. Essex, and Goldesburgh, co. York). Az. a cross flory ar. *Crest*—A pelican, wings endorsed, vulning her breast ppr.

Goldesburgh (Lincoln's Inn). Az. a cross patonce ar. *Crest*—A demi lion ramp.

Goldesburgh (co. Kent). Az. a chev. erm. betw. three acorns or.

Goldfinch, or Gouldfinch (co. Kent). Paly of six ar. and az. on a chief or, a lion pass. guard. sa. *Crest*—A camel pass. ppr.

Goldford. Ar. four barrulets sa.

Goldfrap. Gu. on a chief ar. three crescents of the first. *Crest*—A wolf's head erm.

Goldie-Scot (Craigmuie, co. Kirkcudbright, 1868). Quarterly, 1st and 4th, or, on a bend betw. two griffins' heads erased az. a mullet betw. two crescents of the first, for SCOT; 2nd and 3rd, ar. a chev. gu. betw. three trefoils slipped vert, for GOLDIE; en surtout, ar. two bends sa. the upper one engr., for LEVER. *Crests*—1st, SCOT: A stag trippant ppr.; 2nd, GOLDIE: A garb or. *Mottoes*—1st, SCOT: Fideliter amo; 2nd, GOLDIE: Quid utilius.

Golding (Halstead, cos. Essex and Suffolk). Gu. a chev. or, betw. three bezants.

Golding (co. Essex, Cavendish and Postingford, co. Suffolk). Gu. a chev. ar. betw. three bezants. *Crest*—A dragon's head erased vert, collared and lined or. *Another Crest*—A garb or.

Golding (co. Kent). Sa. (another, gu.) a chev. betw. three wolves' heads erased ar.

Golding (co. Norfolk). Gu. a chev. or, betw. three bezants.

Golding (London). Gu. a chev. ar. betw. three bezants. *Motto*—Sparsa Coegi.

Golding. Ar. three mullets gu.

Golding. Sa. on a chev. betw. three wolves' heads erased ar. as many pellets.

Golding (Maiden Erlegh, co. Berks). Gu. a chev. or, betw. three bezants. *Crest*—A hind's head with an oak branch in the mouth all ppr. *Motto*—Pro Deo et Rege.

Golding (Colson Bassett, co. Notts, EDWARD GOLDING. Her. Visit. 1614). Gu. on a chev. ar. betw. three bezants a trefoil sa. *Crest*—A griffin's head erased gu. collared or.

Golding. Chequy or and ar. a cross az.

Golding (Fun. Ent. of WILLIAM GOLDING, of Dublin, merchant, d. 16 Feb. 1607). Az. six Cornish choughs or, three, two, and one.

Golding (The Grange, Portmarnock, co. Dublin; ANDREW GOLDING, son of RICHARD GOLDING, and grandson of WALTER GOLDING, all of same place. Visit Dublin, 1606). Az. five martlets in saltire or.

Golding (Reg. Ulster's Office). Barry of six erm. and sa. a griffin ramp. or. *Crest*—An arm in chain armour embowed, garnished at the wrist or, tied with ribbons ar. and sa. the hand ppr. holding an arrow gu. point gold.

Golding (Fun. Ent. 1607, WILLIAM GOLDING, of Dublin, merchant). Az. six goldfinches or, three, two, and one.

Goldingham (Barnham, co. Norfolk, and Balsted, co. Suffolk). Ar. a bend wavy gu. *Crest*—A lion's gamb erect and erased or.

Goldingham. Az. a cross engr. ar. betw. four fleurs-delis erm.

Goldingham. Barry nebulée of six gu. and ar.

Goldington (co. Bedford). Ar. two lions pass. az.

Goldington (co. Sussex). Barry nebulée of six ar. and gu.

Goldington. Or, a bend flory counterflory az. *Crest*—Out of a ducal coronet or, a cock's head ppr.

Goldington. Ar. on a bend az. a fleur-de-lis or.

Goldington. Gu. a chief nebulée erm.

Goldington. Gu. three lions ramp. ar.

Goldington. Ar. a bend az. semée-de-lis or.

Goldington. Or, on a bend az. five fleurs-de-lis of the first paleways.

Goldman (Sandford). Gu. a chev. or, betw. three marigolds of the last, stalked and leaved vert.

Goldney (Beechfield, Bradenstoke Abbey, and Rowden House, co. Wilts; GABRIEL GOLDNEY, the descendant of a family long settled in that co., and formerly at Bristol, M.P. for Chippenham since 1865). Per pale gu. and az. on a bend betw. two eagles displ. ar. three garbs sa. banded or. *Crest*—A garb. as in the arms, motto over, Si je puis. *Motto*—Honor virtutis præmium.

Goldoury (1528). Sa. a chev. ar. betw. three wolves' heads erased of the second.

Goldsbrough. Ar. (another, or) three piles gu.

Goldsbrough. Ar. three pales gu.

Goldsborough, and Goldbrough. See GOLDESBOROUGH, and GOLDESBURGH.

Goldsmid (St. John's Lodge, Regent's Park, co. Middlesex, bart.). Per saltire erminois and erm. on a chief gu. a goldfinch ppr. betw. two roses or, (being the family arms), over an escutcheon gu. charged with a tower gold, and ensigned by the coronet of a Baron of Portugal. *Crests*—1st: Out of the coronet of a Baron of Portugal ppr. a demi dragon, wings elevated or, holding in the claws a rose gu. slipped ppr.; 2nd: A demi lion ar. in the paws a bundle of twigs erect or, banded az. *Supporters*—Dexter, a lion ar. ducally crowned and charged on the shoulder with a rose gu.; sinister, a wyvern, wings elevated or, and charged on the shoulder with a rose gu. By royal licence, dated 6 June, 1846, the late Sir ISAAC LYON GOLDSMID, Bart., was authorized to accept and use in this country the title of Baron de Goldsmid and Da Palmeira, conferred upon him by the Queen of Portugal, in manifestation of the important services rendered by him on various occasions to the Portuguese nation, and as a public testimony of her royal munificence, and also to bear and use certain additional armorial bearings. The arms being the escocheon of pretence and coronet over. The first crest and the supporters were added to the family arms, and appertain to the title of baron conferred upon him by the Queen of Portugal. *Mottoes*—Over crests: Quis similis tibi in fortibus, Domine (Exod. xv. 11); under the arms: Concordiâ et sedulitate.

Goldsmith (Ireland; Fun. Ent. 1679). Az. on a chev. ar. betw. three goldfinches of the last as many crosses crosslet of the first, on a chief or, a lion pass. of the field.

Goldsmith (Exton, co. Hants). Gu. on a chev. ar. three crosses crosslet sa. on a chief or, a lion pass. gu. *Crest*—A stork sa. bezantée.

Goldsmith. Paly of six ar. and az. on a chief or, a lion pass. guard. sa.

Goldsmiths, Company of (city of Dublin; confirmed by Preston, Ulster, 1638). Quarterly, 1st and 4th, gu. a harp or, stringed ar.; 2nd and 3rd, az. a covered cup betw. two round buckles in fess or.

Goldston, or Goulston (co. Salop). Gu. on a chev. betw. three saltires ar. an annulet sa. *Crest*—A Minerva's head ppr.

Goldsworthy (Reg. College of Arms, May, 1779). Per pale or and ar. three mullets in bend sa. betw. two bendlets gu.

Crest—An eagle's head erased per pale or and ar. holding in the beak a holly leaf vert.

Goldsworthy. Ar. on a bend cotised sa. three martlets or. *Crest*—A griffin's head crased sa. holding in the beak a holly leaf vert.

Goldtrap (Dover, co. Kent; granted 1749). Az. two batons in saltire or, betw. as many anchors in fesse of the last the like number of boars pass. in pale ar. *Crest*—A lion's paw erased az. betw. two wings elevated or, holding a baton of the last.

Goldwell (Godinton, co. Kent, and co. Norfolk). Az. a chief or, over all a lion ramp. erm.

Goldwell. Az. a chief or, over all a baton ar. billettée sa. *Crest*—Out of a well or, a vine and two columbine branches ppr.

Goldwell. Az. a lion ramp. betw. seven billets ar. a chief or.

Goldwell. Az. a chief or, over all a lion ramp. ar. billettée.

Goldwell (Bridgham, co. Norfolk). Az. a chief or, over all a lion ramp. ar. guttée de poix.

Goldwell (arms in a window in the chapel of All Souls, Oxford, arms of Jacob Goldwell, Bishop of Norwich. Visit. 1574). Per fess or and az. a lion ramp. counterchanged.

Golever. Vairé ar. and gu. on a bend sa. three bezants.

Golever, or Golloner. Ar. a bend gu. betw. three griffins' heads erased sa.

Golever, or Goloner. Sa. a bend betw. three griffins' heads erased ar. *Crest*—A mermaid, with comb and mirror ppr.

Gollop (Strode, co. Dorset; descended from John Gollop, of North Bowood, and Temple, co. Dorset, living *temp.* Henry VIII.; and now represented by George Tilly Gollop, Esq., of Strode House). Gu. on a bend or, a lion pass. guard. sa. *Crest*—A demi lion bendy or and sa. holding in the dexter paw a broken arrow gu. *Motto*—Be bolde, be wyse.

Gollop (Berwick). Same *Arms*, &c.

Gollwin de Mochnant (Wales). Sa. a chev. betw. three roses ar.

Golofer (co. Oxford). Ar. four bars wavy gu. over all on a bend sa. three bezants.

Golofrey. Barry wavy of six ar. and gu. over all on a bend sa. three bezants.

Goloner, or Golover (co. Stafford). Az. a buck's head cabossed or. *Crest*—A demi griffin ppr. collared and sustaining an anchor az.

Golton (Ipswich, co. Suffolk). Or, two bars sa. in chief three fleurs-de-lis of the second.

Goltshed. Ar. on a mount in base vert a dove statant ppr. in chief two roses gu. *Crest*—Two wings conjoined or, thereon a dove statant ppr.

Gomblewhat (co. York). Sa. three bends erm.

Gomeldon. Ar. on a fesse wavy gu. three mullets or, on a canton az. a fleur-de-lis of the third. *Crest*—Out of a cloud an arm in armour embowed and gloved, wielding a spiked mace all ppr.

Gomeldon (Porton, co. Wilts; granted by Sir Edward Walker, Garter, 1662). Ar. on a fess wavy gu. three mullets or, on a canton az. as many fleurs-de-lis of the third. *Crest*—A demi griffin ar. holding betw. the claws a mullet or.

Gomeldon (Chiswick, co. Middlesex; descended from Roger Gomeldon, second son of William Gomeldon, Esq., of Porton. Visit. Middlesex, 1663). Same *Arms* and *Crest*.

Gomersall (London. Visit. 1568, by Dethick, Garter). Sa. a chev. engr. erm. betw. three dexter gauntlets ar. *Crest*—On a crescent or, a dexter gauntlet ar. grasping a battle axe gu. pointed and headed of the second.

Gomery, or Gourey (co. Bedford). Or, two lions pass. guard. in pale az. (another, the tinctures reversed).

Gomm (Clerkenwell, co. Middlesex; granted 24 Jan. 1761). Ar. a lion ramp. sa. on a chief gu. two seaxes (*i.e.* Saxon swords) in saltire of the first, hilts and pommels or. *Crest*—Two lions' gambs in saltire sa. erased gu. each holding a seax erect as in the arms.

Gomm (Field-Marshal Sir William Maynard Gomm, G.C.B). Same *Arms* and *Crest*. *Supporters* (granted 1859)—Dexter, an ancient warrior in armour ppr. mantle and surcoat ar. resting the exterior hand on a sword also ppr.; sinister, a female figure vested ar. holding in the dexter hand a passion cross, and in the sinister a book, both or. *Motto*—Per constanza e speranza.

Gomney, or Gomoney (co. Essex). Az. on a bend ar. three leopards' faces of the field, crowned or.

Gomonde (co. Hereford). Ar. a fesse betw. three mullets gu.

Gonerby. Erm. a griffin segreant gu. over all on a fesse az. two (another, three) bulls' heads cabossed or.

Gonerby, Gonorby, or Gonby. Erm. a griffin segreant gu. over all on a fesse az. three bucks' heads cabossed or.

Gonner. Az. a cross engr. ar.

Gonnor, or Guynor. Az. a saltire ar. guttée de sang. *Crest*—A stag's head ppr. in the mouth a five-leaved flower or, leaves vert.

Gonorey. Or, two lions pass. guard. az.

Gonowers, or Gonwers. Ar. a bull pass. gu. armed or.

Gonrany. Sa. a chev. betw. three bulls' heads cabossed or.

Gonsell, Gonsel, or Gonsley. Paly of six ar. and gu. a chief dancettée or.

Gonston (co. Devon). Ar. a fesse sa. betw. three pellets.

Gonston (co. Essex, and London). Ar. three bars wavy sa. each charged with as many plates, on a chief gu. a culverine betw. two anchors or. *Crest*—An antelope's head ar. guttée de sang.

Gonston, or Gunston (London). Ar. three hounds pass. sa. each charged with as many plates, on a chief gu. a gun betw. two anchors or.

Gonston. Barry of four az. and ar.

Gonton, Gorton, Gouton, or Gunton (Peterborough, co. Northampton). Gu. three bucks or. *Crest*—Out of an earl's coronet a black's head affrontée ppr.

Gonton. Gu. three round buckles or, points to the sinister.

Gonvill (Terrington and Rushworth, co. Norfolk, Founder of Gonvill College, Cambridge). Ar. on a chev. betw. two couple-closes indented sa. three escallops or. *Crest*—A dove ar. beaked and membered gu. holding in the beak, by the stalk, a flower gentle, stalked vert.

Gonvill and Caius College (Cambridge; founded in the year 1348, by Edmund Gonvill, Rector of Terrington and Rushworth, in Norfolk, who called it Gonvill Hall. Afterwards it was further amply endowed by the learned antiquary, Dr. John Caius, who obtained leave from Queen Mary to be a co-founder, whereupon it was called Gonvill and Caius College). Ar. on a chev. betw. two couple-closes indented sa. three escallops shells or, for Gonvill, impaling or, semée of flowers gentle, in the middle of the chief a sengreen resting upon the heads of two serpents in pale, their tails knit together, all proper colours, resting upon a square marble stone vert, for Caius, the whole within a bordure gobony ar. and sa. *Crest*—A dove ar. beaked and membered gu. holding in the beak by the stalk a flower gentle stalked vert.

Gonway, or Goneway. Ar. a chev. couped betw. three crosses formée fitchée sa.

Gonys. Quarterly, vair and gu.

Gooch (Clewer Park, co. Berks, bart.). Per pale ar. and sa. on a chev. betw. three talbots pass. two escallops counterchanged, on a chief engr. gu. a wheel betw. two leopards' faces or. *Crest*—A talbot per pale sa. and ar. gorged with a wreath of oak and resting the dexter forepaw on a wheel or. *Motto*—Fide et virtute.

Gooch (Brompton, co. Middlesex). Same *Arms* and *Motto*. *Crest*—A cubit arm erect vested per pale embattled or and gu. grasping in the hand ppr. a dragon's head erased also ppr.

Gooch (co. Norfolk). Paly of eight ar. and sa. a chev. of the first betw. three greyhounds of the second, spotted of the field. *Crest*—A talbot pass. ar. spotted and collared sa.

Gooche, Goche, or Goodge (Alvingham, co. Lincoln; Dr. Barnaby Gooche, Master of Magdalen College, Cambridge, 1614). Az. three boars ar. eared, tusked, and hoofed or. *Crest*—As Gooch, Brompton, co. Middlesex.

Gooche, or Goche (London, and Mettingham and Bungay, co. Suffolk). Same *Arms* and *Crest* as Gooch, bart.

Good (Fellow of Baliol College, ob. 1680). On a cross engr. five erm. spots.

Good (Girlby and Oneby, co. Lincoln). Gu. a chev. betw. three lions ramp. or. *Crest*—On a ducal coronet or, an otter pass. ar.

Good (Redmorley D'Abitot, co. Worcester. Visit. 1634). Gu. a chev. or, betw. three lions ramp. ar.

Goodall (Earlstonham, co. Suffolk; granted 1 March, 1612). Gu. an eagle displ. ar. armed or, on a canton of the second a chaplet gramine vert. *Crest*—An eagle displ ar. beaked and membered or, gorged with a chaplet gramine vert.

Goodall. Gu. two arrows in saltire ar. headed or, betw. four plates. *Crest*—A dexter arm embowed habited vert, holding in the hand ppr. two arrows in saltire ar. feathered or.

Goodbow. Az. two bows in saltire or, stringed sa.

Goodchepe. Per fesse or and sa. three rustres counterchanged.

Goodchild (Pallion, co. Durham). Ar. on a chev. sa. betw. three parrots vert beaked and legged gu. as many annulets or. *Crest*—A parrot, as in the arms. *Motto*—Vincit omnia veritas.

Goodchild (granted to THOMAS GOODCHILD, of London, and of Valetta, Malta, 29 Sept. 1808). Per pale erminois and erm. on a chev. az. betw. three parrots vert, beaked and legged gu. as many bezants. *Crest*—A pellet, thereon a parrot, as in the arms, in the beak an annulet gu.

Goodchild. Ar. on a chev. sa. three bezants.

Goodday (Terling, co. Essex). Ar. a fesse wavy betw. two leopards' faces sa. *Crest*—A greyhound sejant erm. collared and lined, reflexed over the back and tied in a knot or.

Gooddaye (Penlowe, co. Essex, Higham Ferrers, co. Northampton, and Kettlebaston, co. Suffolk). Ar. a fesse wavy betw. two leopards' faces in pale sa. *Crest*—A greyhound sejant erm. collared and lined or.

Goode (Whitstone, co. Cornwall; the heiress *m.* BADCOCK. Visit. Cornwall, 1621). Gu. on a chev. betw. three lions ramp. or, as many cinquefoils of the first. *Crest*—A talbot's head erased gu. ducally crowned or.

Goodere, or Goodyear (Burhope, co. Hereford, bart., extinct in 1776). Gu. a fesse betw. two chev. vair. *Crest*—A lion's head erased and crowned with an imperial crown ppr.

Goodden (Bower Hinton and Martock, co. Somerset, *temp.* Edward VI., and Over Compton, co. Dorset). Quarterly, 1st and 4th, az. on a bend betw. two demi lions ramp. erased or, three lozenges vairé ar. and gu.; 2nd and 3rd, ar. on a bend gu. betw. two demi lions ramp. couped sa. armed and langued of the second, three lozenges vairé ar. and az. *Crest*—A griffin's head erased or, with wings endorsed vairé ar. and gu. holding in its beak an olive branch ppr. *Motto* —Jovis omnia plena.

Goodenough (D.D., Bishop of Carlisle; consecrated 1807). Or, a chev. gu. betw. three guttées de sang. *Crest*—A demi wolf ramp. ppr. holding betw. the paws an escallop ar.

Goodenough. Ar. a chev. sa. betw. three pellets. *Crest* —A tower sa. inflamed at the top ppr.

Goodenough. Vert a lion ramp. or. *Crest*—On a chapeau gu. turned up erm. a lion crouching or.

Goodenough. Per chev. erm. and gu. on a chief ar. a lion's head erased az. *Crest*—A hand holding a dagger in pale all ppr.

Goodere (co. Gloucester). Gu. a fesse betw. two chev. vair. *Crest*—A partridge holding in the beak an ear of wheat all ppr. *Motto*—Possunt quia posse videntur.

Gooderick (Kirkby, co. Lincoln). Ar. on a fesse gu. betw. two lions pass. guard. sa. a fleur-de-lis betw. as many crescents or. *Crest*—A demi lion ramp. sa. collared or, supporting a battle axe ar. handled gu.

Goodfellow (Inner Temple, London; granted 16 April, 1665). Sa. three leopards' faces in fesse betw. two bars gemelles or.

Goodfellow. Sa. on a fesse double cotised or, three leopards' faces of the field. *Crest*—A horse ramp. gu.

Goodford (Chilton Cantelo, co. Somerset). Az. on a chev. betw. three boars' heads ar. langued and couped gu. as many pellets. *Crest*—A boar's head ar. langued gu. charged on the neck with a pellet.

Goodhall (Holywell, co. Lincoln). Or, a pile sa. on a canton ar. a saltire engr. ar. *Crest*—A boar's head erased and erect sa. plattée, ducally gorged or.

Goodhand (co. Lincoln and London). Chequy ar. and gu. on a fesse az. three sinister gauntlets of the first. *Crest*— An armed arm embowed ppr. holding a sword ar. hilt and pommel or.

Goodhand (Market-Raisen, co. Lincoln). Ar. three dexter hands couped and erect sa.

Goodhand (Fun. Ent. Ulster's Office, 1652). Az. three pheons or.

Goodhart (Langley Park, co. Kent). Gu. a buck trippant ar. in chief two stars volant or, on a chief nebulée of the third a cross of Lorraine of the field betw. two eagles displ. sa. *Crest*—A beehive or, betw. two bees within a rainbow terminating in clouds ppr. *Another Crest*—On a ducal coronet a lion pass. ppr.

Goodhugh (Scale, co. Kent). Gu. a chev. vairé betw. three talbots pass. ar.

Goodier. See GOODYER.

Gooding, Goodyng, or Godwyn (co. Lincoln). Ar. on three pales sa. as many spears' heads of the field.

Gooding, Gooden, or Goodwen (Whershed, Deback, and Cheffield, co. Suffolk, and co. Norfolk). Or, a fesse betw. six lions' heads erased gu. *Crest*—A griffin sejant, wings expanded or, guttée de sang, claws and beak sa.

Gooding. Same *Arms*. *Crest*—On a mount a hedgehog all ppr.

Goodinge (Henley, co. Oxford). Sa. two lions pass. or, on a chief of the second three pellets.

Goodison. Paly of six ar. and gu. on a chief az. three mullets of the first. *Crest*—A peacock's head ppr.

Goodlad (London). Per pale vert and erm. an eagle displ. or. *Crest*—A wing ar.

Goodlad. Per pale ar. and sa. a saltire engr. counter-changed, in chief a sword of the first, pommel gu. *Crest*—In a frame a globe ppr.

Goodlake (Letcomb Regis, co. Berks). Per fesse az. and or, a lion ramp. counterchanged. *Crest*—On a mount vert a woodwift, or wild man, ppr. holding up his club gold. *Motto* —Omnia bona desuper.

Goodlake (Wadley House, co. Berks). Same *Arms*, &c., quartering MILLS.

Goodlaw (Aspall, co. Lancaster; granted, 1581, by Flower, Norroy). Az. a chev. ar. betw. two leopards' faces in chief, and a cross pattée fitchée in base or. *Crest*—A griffin sejant ar. supporting with the dexter claw a column az.

Goodlegh (Reg. Ulster's Office). Ar. two bars az. on a canton gu. a mascle ar. bottony at each corner or.

Goodlet (Scotland). Or, a fesse gu. betw. two lions pass. guard. sa.

Goodlet (Empshaugh). Or, on a fesse gu. betw. two lions pass. guard. sa. a fleur-de-lis betw. as many crescents of the field.

Goodlock. Gu. a chev. engr. betw. three escallops ar. (another, or).

Goodmadam. Or, six torteaux, three, two, and one, on each a mullet of the field.

Goodman (Golborn, co. Chester, co. Hertford, and London). Gyronny of eight erm. and sa. an eagle displ. with two heads or. *Crest*— The battlement and upper part of a tower ar. thereon a woman couped at the knees, habited az. hair dishevelled or, in the dexter hand a rose gu. stalked and leaved vert.

Goodman (Chester, and Blazon, co. Leicester, 1619). Per pale sa. and erm. an eagle displ. with two necks ar.

Goodman (Ruthyn, co. Denbigh; granted 1572). Per pale erm. and sa. an eagle displ. with two heads or, on a canton az. a martlet of the third. *Crest*—Out of a ducal coronet or, a demi eagle displ. with two heads erm.

Goodman (Dean of Westminster, *d.* 1601). Per pale erm. and az. an eagle displ. with two heads or, on a canton of the second a martlet of the third.

Goodman. Per pale ermines and erm. an eagle displ. with two heads per pale ar. and sa.

Goodman (Reg. Ulster's Office). Sa. three demi grey-hounds courant in pale dexter, and as many mullets pierced, in pale sinister, ar.

Goodman (Loughlinstown, co. Dublin; ROSE, dau. of JAMES GOODMAN, and wife of JOHN WALSH, Esq., of Shanganagh, *d.* 25 July, 1609). Sa. on a chev. ar. betw. three bucks' heads cabossed or, as many trefoils slipped gu. on a chief dancettée of the second three hurts.

Goodmanston (co. Kent). Ar. three martlets betw. four crosses crosslet sa.

Goodmanston. Ar. an eagle displ. gu. membered or.

Goodneston (co. Kent). Ar. three martlets and four crosses crosslet sa. one, two, and one.

Goodreed (Ribstan, co. York). Gu. an anchor in pale ar. stock or.

Goodrich (Rev. CHARLES GOODRICH, Rector of Bittering Parva, co. Norfolk). Or, two lions pass. betw. ten crosses crosslet sa. *Crest*—A demi lion ramp. holding betw. the paws a cross crosslet sa.

Goodrich (Seling Grove, co. Essex). Az. semée of crosses crosslet a lion ramp. or. *Crest*—A demi lion ramp. couped ar. holding in the dexter paw a cross crosslet or.

Goodrick (Isle of Ely, and Stanmore, co. Middlesex). Ar. on a fesse gu. betw. two lions pass. guard. sa. a fleur-de-lis betw. wo crescents or. *Crest*—A demi lion ramp. sa. collared or, supporting a battle axe ar. handled gu.

Goodrick (East Kirkby, co. Lincoln). Ar. on a fesse betw. two lions pass. guard. sa. a fleur-de-lis betw. as many crescents or. Same *Crest* as the last.

Goodrick. Or, on a fesse gu. a fleur-de-lis betw. two crescents of the first, in chief three books of the second, leaves of the field, in base a leopard pass. sa.

Goodricke (Ribstone Hall, co. York, bart., extinct 1833; the sisters, and eventually co-heirs of Sir HENRY GOODRICKE, the sixth bart., were HARRIETT, wife of Sir THOMAS GOODRICKE, the eighth bart.; MARY, *m.* to CHARLES GREGORY FAIRFAX, Esq., of Gilling Castle, co. York; and ELIZABETH). Ar. on a fesse gu. betw. two lions pass. guard. sa. a fleur-de-lis betw. as many crescents or. *Crest*—A demi lion erm. armed and langued gu. issuing out of a ducal coronet or, holding in the paws a battle axe ppr. handled gold.

Goodricke (RICHARD GOODRICKE, Esq., of Stanware, *d.* 1562, nephew to THOMAS GOODRICKE, Bishop of Ely, 1534–54, and Lord Chancellor). Ar. on a fesse gu. betw. two lions pass. guard. sa. a fleur-de-lis or. *Crest*—A demi lion ramp. guard. sa. *Motto*—Fare wel til then.

Goodricke (HOLYOAKE-GOODRICKE, Ribstone Hall, co. York, bart.; FRANCIS HOLYOAKE, Esq., of Morton Bagot, co. Warwick, succeeded to those estates under the will of Sir HARRY JAMES GOODRICKE, seventh bart. of Bilstone, 1833, on condition that he should keep up the Quorn pack of hounds, and thereupon assumed the name of the testator). Quarterly, 1st and 4th, ar. on a fesse gu. betw. two lions pass. guard. sa. a fleur-de-lis ar. betw. two crescents or, a canton gu. for diff.; 2nd and 3rd, per pale or and gu. a buck's head cabossed betw. two crosses pattée in pale, all counterchanged. *Crests*—1st: Out of a ducal coronet or, a demi lion erm. holding in the paws a battle axe or, and charged on the shoulder with a cross crosslet gold for diff.; 2nd: On a mount vert an oak fructed ppr. around the lower part of the stem an escroll, thereon a cross pattée gu. betw. the words "Sacra quercus."

Goodridge (Totness, co. Devon; WALTER GOODRIDGE, of that place. Visit 1620). Ar. a fess sa. in chief three crosses crosslet fitchée of the last. *Crest*—A blackbird ppr.

Goodridge (Charlew, co. Gloucester). Ar. on a fesse gu. betw. three lions pass. guard. sa. a fleur-de-lis betw. two crescents of the field.

Goodrood. Gu. an anchor ar. stock or. *Crest*—A unicorn's head gu. collared or.

Goodsinging. Gu. semée-de-lis an eagle displ. ar.

Goodson. Erm. a chev. gu. betw. three quatrefoils or, stalked and leaved vert. *Crest*—A wolf's head erm. collared gu.

Goodwin, or Goodwyn (Upper Winchingdon, co. Bucks). Per pale or and gu. a lion ramp. betw. three fleurs-de-lis counterchanged. *Crest*—A demi lion ramp. ar. gorged with an heraldic coronet gu. *Motto*—De bon volore.

Goodwin (Stoneham Iva, co. Cambridge, and Diss, co. Norfolk). Or, three palets sa. on a chief gu. as many martlets of the field. *Crest*—Out of a ducal coronet ar. a nag's head or, maned and bridled of the first.

Goodwin (East Grinstead, co. Sussex. Dugdale's Visit. 1696). Ar. on a bend ragulée gu. a lion pass. of the field.

Goodwin (Rawmarsh, co. York. Visit. Dugdale, 1696; descended from the preceding). Same *Arms*.

Goodwin (Torrington, co. Devon, and co. Suffolk). Or, on a fesse betw. six lions' heads erased gu. an annulet of the field. *Crest*—A griffin sejant with wings expanded or, guttée de poix.

Goodwin (Pleintree, co. Hertford). Ar. on a bend gu. betw. two demi lions ramp. sa. three mascles vair. *Crest*—A griffin's head ar. wings endorsed vair.

Goodwin (London, and co. Lincoln, 1640). Or, a lion pass. guard. sa. on a chief gu. three lozenges vair. *Crest*—A lion sejant guard. sa. holding a lozenge vair.

Goodwin (Hinshleywood, co. Derby). Or, a fesse betw. six lions' heads erased gu. *Crest*—A griffin sejant with wings expanded or. *Motto*—Fide et virtute.

Goodwin (Hammersmith, co. Middlesex). Or, two bars betw. six lions' heads erased gu.

Goodwin, or Goodwyn (Dorking and Guildford, co. Surrey, and Lewes, co. Sussex). Gu. two bars or, betw. six lozenges ar. three, two, and one. *Crest*—An arm embowed, vested or, cuff ar. holding in the hand ppr. a lozenge gold.

Goodwin (Arlscot, co. Warwick). Or, a lion pass. guard. sa. on a chief gu. three mascles vair.

Goodwin. Or, two lions pass. guard. sa. on a canton of the last three bezants. *Crest*—A demi lion ramp. guard. sa. holding in the paws a bezant.

Goodwin (granted to GOODWIN CHARLES GOODWIN, Esq.). Quarterly, or and gu. a lion ramp. betw. two fleurs-de-lis in chief and a mascle in base all counterchanged. *Crest*—A demi lion ar. ducally gorged gu. charged on the body with three lozenges az. and holding betw. the paws a fleur-de-lis of the second.

Goodwin (Reg. Ulster's Office, 1698). Gu. a lion ramp. or, langued az. betw. three fleurs-de-lis of the second. *Crest*—Out of a ducal coronet or, a demi lion ramp. az. holding betw. the paws a fleur-de-lis gold. *Motto*—Lilia candorem pectus Leo nobile monstrat.

Goodwin (Reg. Ulster's Office). Or, a fess betw. six lions' heads erased gu. *Crest*—A griffin sejant, wings elevated or.

Goodwin (Ireland; Fun. Ent., Captain WILLIAM GOODWIN,

buried at Christ Church, Dublin, 4 May, 1597). Per pale ar. and gu. a lion ramp. betw. three fleurs-de-lis all counterchanged.

Goodwing (Fun. Ent., Ireland). Gu. an eagle reguard. wings endorsed standing on a mallard all ar.

Goodwing (Dublin; JOHN GOODWING, Sheriff of Dublin, 1597, son of WILLIAM, and grandson of MATTHEW GOODWING. Visit. city of Dublin, 1607). Gu. a falcon reguard. wings expanded ar. beaked, legged, and billed or, charged on the breast with a crescent gu. and holding in the claws a mallard gold. *Crest*—An ostrich ar. legged sa. charged on the breast with a crescent gu.

Goodwright. Ar. on a chev. gu. betw. two crescents in chief sa. and a dove with an olive branch in base or three bezants. *Crest*—A dove and olive branch ppr. *Motto*—Pro bona ad meliora.

Goodwyn (Kesgrave, co. Suffolk, and Torrington, co. Devon; HENRY GOODWYN, of the latter place. Visit. 1620). Or, a fesse betw. six lions' heads erased gu. an annulet for diff. *Crest*—A griffin sejant, wings ar. expanded guttée de poix.

Goodwyn (East Grinstead, co. Sussex; confirmed by Camden, Clarenceux, to JOHN GOODWYN, Esq.). Gu. two bars or, nine lozenges ar. three, two, and one. *Crest*—An arm embowed, vested gu. the hand ppr. resting on a lozenge ar.

Goodwyn (Wells, co. Somerset). Gu. a chev. erm. betw. three leopards' faces or.

Goodwyn (Winnington, co. Warwick. Her. Visit.). Gu. a chev. erm. betw. three lions' heads erased ar.

Goodwyn. Or, a fesse betw. six lions' heads erased gu.

Goodwyn. Lozengy vair and gu.

Goodyear (Hythorpe, co. Oxford, and Polesworth, co. War wick). Gu. a fesse betw. two chev. vair.

Goodyer, or Goodier (Windsor, co. Berks, cos. Middlesex and Oxford; granted 1579). Same *Arms*. *Crest*—A partridge holding in the beak three ears of wheat all ppr.

Goodyere (Cuddington Church, co. Oxford; WALTER GOODYERE, Parson of the Church, *d.* 1513. Visit. Oxon, 1574). Same *Arms*.

Googe. Az. three boars pass. ar. *Crest*—A rose stalked and leaved ppr. *Motto*—Audaces juvat.

Googe. Per pale sa. and ar. a chev. betw. three talbots pass. counterchanged on a chief gu. three leopards' faces or.

Googh, or Googe. Ar. a chev. betw. three cocks sa. armed gu.

Goold, or Gould (Fun. Ent. of Dr. JAMES FIELD, of Dublin, *d.* 25 Feb. 1623, *m.* MARY, dau. of JAMES GOULD, Chief Justice of Munster). Ar. a fess sa. betw. three goldfinches in chief vert and a cinquefoil in base of the last pierced or.

Goold (Old Court, co. Cork, bart.). Az. on a fesse or, betw. five goldfinches, three in chief and two in base ppr. three mullets gu. *Crest*—A demi lion ramp. or. *Motto*—Deus mihi providebit.

Goold (Dromadda and Rosbrien, co. Limerick; confirmed to Ven. FREDERIC FALKINER-GOOLD, Archdeacon of Raphoe and Rector of Raymochy, co. Donegal; descended from a branch of the family of GOOLD, Bart., of Old Court, co. Cork). Az. on a fesse or, betw. five mullets of the field, in the centre chief point a crescent of the second for diff. *Crest*—A demi lion ramp. or, charged on the shoulder with a crescent gu. *Motto*—Deus mihi providebit.

Goold (co. Dorset). Ar. on a chev. sa. betw. three roses gu. as many bunches of grapes ppr.

Goold. Per saltire or and az. a lion ramp. counterchanged. *Crest*—On a mount vert an ermine spot. ppr.

Goold, or Gould (Scotland). Ar. a chev. betw. three trefoils slipped gu. *Crest*—Within the horns of a crescent ar. a buckle or.

Gooseling. Ar. a chev. betw. three crescents or. *Crest*— A lion's paw erased gu. holding up a fleur-de-lis or.

Goosetrey, or Goosetree (co. Bucks). Ar. a chev. betw. three squirrels sejant gu. *Crest*—A stag's head erased or.

Gophill (co. Surrey). Ar. a chev. sa. surmounted of a cross pattée of the last. *Crest*—Out of a ducal coronet per pale az. and gu. a demi leopard ramp. guard. or, collared and lined of the second.

Gordane. Sa. three leopards' faces jessant de-lis or.

Gordnee. Sa. a chev. betw. three griffins' heads erased ar. *Crest*—On a mural coronet gu. a griffin's head, as in the arms.

Gordon (1445, *Earl*, and 1599, *Marquess of Huntly*, 1684, *Duke of Gordon*. On the death of the fifth duke in 1836, the dukedom became extinct, and the marquessate of *Huntly* passed to his kinsman, the *Earl of Aboyne*). Quarterly, 1st, az. three boars' heads couped or, for GORDON; 2nd, or, three lions' heads erased gu., for BADENOCH; 3rd, or, three crescents within a double tressure gu., for SETON; 4th, az. three cinquefoils ar., for FRASER. *Crest*—In a ducal coronet or, a stag's head and neck affrontée ppr. attired with ten tynes of the first. *Supporters*—Two deerhounds ar. each gorged with a collar gu. charged with three buckles or. *Motto* —Above the crest: Bydand; below the shield: Animo non astutia.

Gordon-Lennox (*Duke of Richmond, Gordon, and Lennox*). See LENNOX.

Gordon (*Earl of Aboyne*, 1660; the first earl was third son of the second *Marquess of Huntly*; the fifth earl succeeded to the marquessate of *Huntly*). Az. a chev. betw. three boars' heads couped or, within a double tressure adorned with fleurs-de-lis within and crescents without of the last. *Crest*—A demi lion ramp. gu. *Supporters*—Two chevaliers in complete armour, each holding in the exterior hand a halbert all ppr. *Motto*—Stant cætera tigno.

Gordon (Cluny, co. Aberdeen, bart., 1627; title extinct at death of first bart.; later GORDONS of Cluny do not belong to this branch). Quarterly, as *Marquess of Huntly*, with a crescent ar. in fess point. *Crest*—A boar's head couped gu, in the mouth four arrows gu. feathered and pheoned ar. *Motto*—Doe well and let them say.

Gordon (Gordonstown, co. Elgin, bart., 1625). Quarterly, 1st and 4th, the quartered coat of HUNTLY; 2nd and 3rd, gu. three mullets or, for SUTHERLAND; all within a bordure or. *Crest*—A cat-a-mountain saliant ar. armed az. *Supporters* —Dexter, a deerhound ar. with a collar gu. charged with three buckles or; sinister, a savage wreathed head and middle with laurel ppr. *Motto*—Sans crainte.

Gordon (Gight, co. Aberdeen; from a third son of the second *Earl of Huntly*). Quarterly, as *Earl of Huntly*, within a bordure quarterly, or and gu.

Gordon (Gight; paternally DAVIDSONS, the heiress was mother of *Lord Byron*). Quarterly, 1st and 4th, az. a star betw. three boars' heads couped or; 2nd and 3rd, az. on a fess engr. betw. three pheons ar. a buck's head erased of the field, for DAVIDSON. *Crest*—A buck's head and neck affrontée ppr. *Motto*—Bydand.

Gordon (Newton, co. Aberdeen; cadet of Gight). Az. a Moor's head couped ar. banded or, betw. three boars' heads erased or, a bordure engr. of the last. *Crest*—A dove with an olive branch in its beak ppr. *Motto*—I hope.

Gordon (Letterfourie, co. Banff; from a fourth son of the second *Earl of Huntly*. In 1806, the representative of this branch assumed the Gordonstown baronetcy; arms as recorded 1684). Quarterly, as *Earl of Huntly*, within a bordure indented ar. *Crest*—A stag at gaze ppr. *Motto*—Dum sisto vigilo.

Gordon (Glastirim, co. Banff). Quarterly, 1st and 4th, az. a frase ar. betw. three boars' heads couped or, for GORDON; 2nd and 3rd, or, three crescents within a double tressure flory counterflory gu., for SETON. *Crest*—A lion's head ppr. *Motto*—Divisa conjungo.

Gordon (Abergeldie, co. Aberdeen; from third son of the first *Earl of Huntly*; the heiress m. a son of GORDON, of Minmore, from whom the later GORDONS, of Abergeldie, descend). Quarterly, as *Earl of Huntly*, within a bordure quarterly, ar. and gu. *Crest*—A deerhound ar. *Motto*—God for us.

Gordon (Beldornie and Wardhouse, co. Aberdeen; descended from ADAM GORDON, Dean of Caithness, fourth son of the first *Earl of Huntly*). Quarterly, 1st and 4th, az. a lion ramp. ar. betw. three boars' heads couped or; 2nd and 3rd, az. three boars' heads erased ar. within a bordure engr. of the last. *Crest*—A cross crosslet fitchée gu. *Motto*—In hoc spes mea.

Gordon (Cadiz, 1790). Az. a lion ramp. ar. betw. three boars' heads couped or, in middle chief a star of the second. *Crest*—A cross calvary gu. *Motto*—Spero.

Gordon (Xeres le Frontera, 1835). Az. a lion ramp. ar. betw. three boars' heads couped or, in middle chief a covered cup of the last, all within a bordure of the second. *Crest*—A cross crosslet fitchée gu. betw. two wings expanded or. *Motto* —In hoc spes mea.

Gordon (South Carolina, 1776; descended from Beldornie). Quarterly, 1st, az. on a fess ar. betw. three boars' heads couped or, a wolf's head couped sa.; 2nd, or, three lions' heads erased gu., for BADENOCH; 3rd, or, three crescents within a double tressure flory counterflory gu., for SETON; 4th, az. three frases ar., for FRASER. *Crest*—A hart's head affrontée ppr. *Motto*—Animo

Gordon (Embo, co. Sutherland, bart., 1631; from JOHN

GORDON, of Drummoy, third son of ADAM GORDON, Dean of Caithness). Az. three boars' heads erased or. *Crest*—A boar's head, as in the arms. *Motto*—Forward without fear.

Gordon (Dalpholly and Invergordon, bart., 1705, also from JOHN GORDON, of Drummoy, son of the Dean of Caithness; heirs of line, the descendants of the sisters of the third bart., who m. the *Earl of Cromartie* and DUNDAS, of Arniston). Quarterly, as *Earl of Huntly*, within a bordure nebuly gu. *Crest* —A dexter hand issuing from a heart holding a flaming sword ppr. *Supporters*—Dexter, a greyhound; sinister, an antelope ppr. *Motto*—Corde manuque.

Gordon (Aberdeen, 1680). Quarterly, as *Earl of Huntly*, within a bordure sa. charged with eight bezants. *Crest*—In the sea a ship under sail ppr. *Motto*—Fertur discrimine fructus.

Gordon (Pitlurg, co. Aberdeen; now GORDON-CUMMING-SKENE; descended in common with the branches that follow from JOHN (" JOCK ") GORDON, of Scudargue, natural son or grandson of Sir ADAM GORDON, of that Ilk, whose dau. and heir was ancestress of the *Earls of Huntly*). Az. three boars' heads couped or, within a bordure of the last, quartered (1834), az. three garbs within a bordure or, for CUMMING; and az. three skenes ar. pommelled or, having on their points as many wolves' heads couped of the last, for SKENE. *Crest*—A dove ppr. *Supporters*—Dexter, a warrior holding in his dexter hand a shield, in his sinister a spear all ppr. ; sinister, a wild boar ppr. *Motto*—I hope.

Gordon (Faskine, co. Banff). Az. a roundle chequy or and of the first betw. three boars' heads of the second. *Crest*—A stag lodged ppr. *Motto*—Bydand to the last.

Gordon (Rothiemay, co. Banff; passed by heiress in 17th century to BARCLAY, of Towie). Az. a saltire ar. betw. three boars' heads couped or. *Motto*—Absit fraus.

Gordon (Park, co. Banff, bart., 1633; title extinct or dormant; DUFF-GORDON, of Park, the heir of line). Az. a dexter hand vambraced grasping a sword erect ar. hilted and pommelled or, betw. three boars' heads couped of the last. *Crest*—A sinister gauntlet ppr. *Motto*—Sic tutus.

Gordon (Glenbucket, co. Aberdeen). Az. a saltire betw. three boars' heads erased or, a bordure counter-compony of the second and first. *Crest*—A boar's head couped and erected within an adder disposed orleways ppr. *Motto*— Victrix prudentia.

Gordon (Edinglassie, co. Banff). Az. a cross moline betw. three boars' heads erased or. *Crest*—A boar's head erased, in his mouth a sword ppr. *Motto*—Aut mors aut vita decus.

Gordon (Avochie, co. Aberdeen). Az. on a chev. betw. three boars' couped or, a hand grasping a sheaf of arrows ppr.

Gordon (HAY-GORDON, of Avochie, as recorded 1858). Quarterly, 1st and 4th, as the last; 2nd and 3rd, counter-quartered, 1st and 4th, ar. three inescutcheons gu., 2nd and 3rd, az. three cinquefoils ar. a crescent gu. in the centre of the quarters, and all within a bordure of the last, for HAY, of Rannes. *Crest*—A stag's head cabossed within two branches of laurel conjoined at the top all ppr. *Motto*—Byde together.

Gordon (Tetachie, co. Aberdeen). Az. a sheaf of arrows or, betw. three boars' heads couped of the second. *Motto*— Ever faithful.

Gordon (Gordonbank, co. Berwick, 1700). Az. on a chev. betw. three boars' heads couped or, a hand grasping a sheaf of arrows ppr. a bordure of the second charged with eight crescents gu. *Crest*—A dexter hand issuing out of a cloud, grasping a sheaf of arrows all ppr. *Motto*—Legibus et armis.

Gordon (Lessmoir, co. Aberdeen; descended from WILLIAM, second son of JOHN GORDON, of Scudargue, bart. 1625, title dormant since 1839). Az. a fess chequy ar. and of the first betw. three boars' heads erased or. *Crest*—A hart's head couped ppr. *Supporters*—Dexter, a savage; sinister, a griffin both ppr. *Motto*—Bydand.

Gordon (Buthlaw, co. Aberdeen). As Lessmoir, with a mullet ar. in chief for diff. *Crest*—A Doric pillar or. *Motto* —In recto decus.

Gordon (Rothney, co. Aberdeen). As Lessmoir, within a bordure nebuly ar. *Crest*—A man presenting a gun all ppr. *Motto*—Vel pax vel bellum.

Gordon (Birkenburn, co. Banff). As Lessmoir, within a bordure ar. *Crest*—A hart's head couped ppr. and charged with a crescent ar. *Motto*—Bydand.

Gordon (Terpersie, co. Aberdeen). Az. a lion pass. guard. ar. betw. three boars' heads erased or. *Crest*—A hart at gaze ppr. *Motto*—Non fraude sed laude.

Gordon (Badenscoth, co. Aberdeen; co-heiresses *m*. FORBES, of Blackford, and LESLIE, of Rothie). As Lessmoir, within a bordure indented ar. *Crest*—A hart's head cabossed ppr. *Motto*—Still bydand.

Gordon (Lichiston, co. Banff). As Lessmoir, in middle chief a bear's head ar. for diff.

Gordon (Craig, co. Aberdeen; from a younger son of WILLIAM, second son of JOHN GORDON, of Scudargue). Az. three boars' heads erased or, within a bordure ar. *Crest*—A boar's head, as in the arms. *Motto*—Byde.

Gordon (Tilliangus, cadet of Craig). Az. three boars' heads couped or, a bordure wavy of the second charged with three unicorns' heads erased sa. and as many stags trippant ppr. *Crest*—A stag lodged ppr. *Motto*—Nunc mihi grata quies.

Gordon (Auchintoul, co. Banff). Az. a mullet betw. three boars' heads couped or, within a bordure of the last. *Crest*—A demi boar ppr. *Motto*—Bydand.

Gordon (Ardmealie, co. Banff; recorded 1700). Quarterly, 1st and 4th, az. three boars' heads erased or, within a bordure of the last charged with eight crescents gu.; 2nd and 3rd, ar. a demi otter issuing out of a bar wavy sa., for MELDRUM. *Crest*—A boar's head erased ppr. *Motto*—Byd bee.

Gordon (Haddo, bart., 1642; *Earl of Aberdeen*, 1682). Az. three boars' heads couped or, within a double tressure flowered and counterflowered alternately with thistles and fleurs-de-lis or. *Crest*—Two naked arms from the shoulder holding a bow ready to let fly an arrow ppr. *Mottoes*—Above the crest: Fortuna sequatur; below the shield: Ne nimium. *Supporters*—Dexter, a senator of the College of Justice in his robes ppr.; sinister, a minister of state in his robes also ppr.

Gordon (Nethermuir, cadet of Haddo). Az. three boars' heads couped or, within a bordure per fess ar. and or. *Crest*—A dexter hand issuing out of a cloud and throwing a dart all ppr.

Gordon-Oswald (Scotstown, co. Renfrew; descended from Auchlenchries, co. Aberdeen). Quarterly, 1st and 4th, az. a savage wreathed head and middle with laurel, having a quiver of arrows by his side and a bow in his sinister hand, the dexter hand pointing to a cornet in dexter chief point all ppr. within a bordure erm., for OSWALD; 2nd, az. three boars' heads couped or, within a bordure per fess ar. and of the second, and charged with three cushions pendent by the corners of the third, for GORDON; 3rd, counterquartered, 1st and 4th, ar. a saltire engr. sa., 2nd, ar. a saltire betw. four roses gu., 3rd, or, a bend chequy ar. and sa. all within a bordure wavy ar., for HALDANE. *Crests*—1st, OSWALD: A ship under sail ppr.; 2nd, GORDON: A dagger erect piercing a boar's head erased all ppr. *Mottoes*—1st, OSWALD: Non mihi commodus uni: 2nd, GORDON: Non astutia.

Gordon (Braco, cadet of Haddo). Az. three boars' heads couped or, within a bordure per pale ar. and or. *Crest*—A dexter hand holding a dart ppr. *Motto*—Sequor.

Gordon (Knockespock, co, Aberdeen; as recorded 1674). Az. a pheon betw. three boars' heads erased or. *Crest*—A stag's head ppr. attired or. *Motto*—Dum vigilo tutus.

Gordon (Northcourt, Isle of Wight; paternally GRANT, bart., 1818). Quarterly, 1st and 4th, az. a rose ar. betw. three boars' heads erased or, for GORDON; 2nd and 3rd, gu. a tilting spear betw. three antique crowns or, for GRANT; all within a bordure embattled quarterly ar. and or. *Crest*—Issuing from a mural crown ar. a dexter arm in armour embowed ppr. charged with a mullet gu. and garnished or, the hand grasping a falchion also ppr. transpiercing a boar's head erased and erected or. *Motto*—Animo non astutia.

Gordon (Sir WILLIAM GORDON, K.B., 1779). Az. a tilting spear in fess ar. the point to the dexter side betw. three boars' heads erased or. *Crest*—Out of a ducal coronet or, a cubit arm erect ppr. vested in armour also ppr. and holding in the hand a sword ar. hilted and pommelled or. *Supporters*—Two greyhounds ar. each gorged with a belt rimmed and buckled or, to each belt a shield pendent gu.

Gordon (Bailie of Banff, 1674). Az. a buckle betw. three boars' heads couped or. *Crest*—A ship under sail ppr. *Motto*—Nil arduum.

Gordon (Hallhead and Esslemont, co. Aberdeen; now WOL-RIGE-GORDON). Az. a fess betw. three boars' heads couped or. *Crest*—A hart's head ppr. *Motto*—Bydand.

Gordon (London, 1865). Az. three boars' heads couped or, on a chief ar. three stars of six points of the first. *Crest*—A stag's head erased ppr. *Motto*—Vigilando.

Gordon (Demerara, 1800). Az. three boars' heads couped or, in chief three frases az. *Crest*—A buck's head and neck affrontée erased ppr. attired or, gorged with a ducal coronet of the last. *Motto*—Truth prevails.

Gordon (Clu.., co. Aberdeen, 1753). Az. three boars' heads

couped or, within a bordure chequy of the first and last. *Crest*—A spreading oak tree gu. *Motto*—Sub tegmine.

Gordon (Tobago, 1788). Az. three buckles in fess betw. as many boars' heads couped or, a bordure chequy of the second and first. *Crest*—An oak tree ppr. *Motto*—Sub tegmine.

Gordon (Millrig, co. Ayr, 1807). Az. on a chev. erm. betw. three boars' heads erased or, a stag's head erased gu. *Crest*—A stag's head erased ppr. *Mottoes*—Above the crest: Bydand; below the shield: Dum vigilo tutus.

Gordon (Dr. JOHN TAYLOR-GORDON, 1837). Quarterly, 1st and 4th, az. three boars' heads erased or, within a bordure sa.; 2nd and 3rd, erm. on a chev. az. three escallops ar.; betw. as many anchors of the second, for TAYLOR. *Crests*—1st, GORDON: A spreading oak ppr.; 2nd, TAYLOR: A stork ppr. holding an anchor az. *Mottoes*—1st, GORDON: I byde; 2nd, TAYLOR: Dum spiro spero.

Gordon (Lochinvar, co. Kirkcudbright; *Viscount Kenmure;* title dormant since 1847). Az. a bend betw. three boars' heads couped or, afterwards changed to az. three boars' heads erased or. *Crest*—A demi savage head and middle with laurel. *Supporters*—Two savages ppr. *Motto*—Dread God.

Gordon (Culvennan, co. Kirkcudbright, cadet of Lochinvar; the heiress *m*. 1740, a younger son of Sir ALEXANDER GORDON, of Earlston; arms as recorded for her son). Az. a bezant betw. three boars' heads erased or, a bordure of the second charged with nine lozenges of the first. *Crest*—A dexter naked arm issuing out of a cloud and grasping a flaming sword all ppr. *Motto*—Dread God.

Gordon (Glasgow; descended from Culvennan, 1813). Az. three boars' heads erased or, within a bordure engr. ar. *Crest*—A palm tree ppr. *Motto*—Deo fidens.

Gordon (Earlston, co. Kirkcudbright, bart., 1706). Az. a bezant betw. three boars' heads erased or. *Crest*—A dexter hand holding a sword ppr. *Motto*—Dread God.

Gordon (Holm, co. Kirkcudbright). Az. three boars' heads erased or, within a bordure of the second charged with eight crescents of the third. *Crest*—A hand holding a writing pen ppr. *Motto*—Time Deum.

Gordon (Dingeuch, co. Kirkcudbright). Az. a bend engr. betw. three boars' heads erased or. *Crest*—A hand holding a baton erect ppr. *Motto*—Maneo non fugio.

Gordon (Shirmers, co. Kirkcudbright). Az. a bend betw. three boars' heads erased or, a bordure of the second. *Crest*—A demi savage holding in his right hand a baton erected on his shoulders, in his left an ear of wheat ppr. *Motto*—Tam pace quam prœlio.

Gordon (EVANS-GORDON, of Brockley, co. Suffolk). As the last, the bordure charged with four crescents az. for diff. Same *Crest* and *Motto*.

Gordon (Troquhan, co. Kirkcudbright). Az. a bend betw. three boars' heads couped or, armed and langued ar. a bordure of the second. *Crest*—A savage's head erased ppr. *Motto*—Fear God.

Gordon (Newark, 1674). Az. a billet betw. three boars' heads couped or. *Crest*—A crescent ar. *Motto*—Gradatim plena.

Gordon (London, 1680). Az. a chev. ar. betw. three boars' heads couped or. *Crest*—A dexter hand holding a dagger ppr. *Motto*—Time Deum.

Gordon (Aikenhead, co. Kirkcudbright, 1806). Az. three boars' heads erased or, a bordure engr. of the last charged with three escallops sa. *Crest*—A demi savage wreathed head and middle with laurel, holding a club over his shoulder all ppr. *Motto*—Dread God.

Gordon (Clifton, New Zealand, 1874). Az. a bend wavy ar. betw. three boars' heads erased or. *Crest*—A boar's head ppr. *Motto*—Maneo.

Gordon (MORE-GORDON, of Charlton, co. Forfar, 1863). Per chev. az. and erm. in chief two boars' heads couped or, in base a Moor's head ppr. banded and wreathed or and gu. *Crest*—A buck's head cabossed ppr. *Mottoes*—Above the crest : I byd my time ; below the shield : Deo favente.

Gordon (SMITH-GORDON, Bart., of Florida Manor, co. Down). Quarterly, 1st and 4th, per fesse az. and gu. two barrulets engr. erm. betw. three boars' heads erased or, for GORDON; 2nd and 3rd, az. on a bend cottised betw. two unicorns' heads erased az. three fusils or, on a canton gu. a sword erect ppr. pommel and hilt gold, the blade encircled by an Eastern crown of the last, for SMITH. *Crests*—1st, GORDON: Issuing from the battlements of a tower ar. a stag's head affrontée ppr. all betw. two palm branches vert; 2nd, SMITH (crest of augmentation): a representation of the ornamental silver centre piece of the service of plate presented to Lieut.-Gen. Sir LIONEL SMITH, G.C.B., by his European and native friends at Bombay, all ppr.; 3rd, SMITH : Out of an Eastern crown or, a dexter arm embowed in armour, encircled by a wreath of laurel, the hand grasping a sword all ppr.

Gordon-Moore. See MOORE.

Gore (co. Essex, and London; confirmed by Cooke, Clarenceux, to GERRARD GORE, Alderman of London, 1587). Gu. a fess betw. three crosses crosslet or. Crest—On a mount vert a tiger saliant ar. tufted and maned sa. ducally gorged or.

Gore (Manor Gore, co. Donegal, bart.). Gu. a fesse betw. three crosses crosslet fitchée or. Crest—A wolf ramp. ar. collared gu. Motto—Sola salus servire Deo.

Gore (Earl of Ross, sixth bart. so created 1772, d. s. p. 1802). Gu. a fess betw. three crosses crosslet fitchée or. Crest—A wolf ramp. ar. collared gu. Supporters—Two leopards ar. plain collared gu. Motto—Sola salus servire Deo.

Gore (Earl of Arran). Gu. a fesse betw. three crosses crosslet fitchée or, quartering, for SAUNDERS, of Saunders Court, co. Wexford, as representative of the senior line of that family in Ireland, ar. a chev. a chev. three elephants' heads erased sa. on a chief gu. betw. two plates a sword in pale, the blade broken ppr. point hanging down. Crest—A wolf ramp. ar. collared gu. Supporters—Two horses ar. Motto—In hoc signo vinces.

Gore (Lord Annaly; created 1766, extinct 1793). Same Arms (without the quartering), Crest, and Motto. Supporters—Dexter, a knight in complete armour, the dexter hand resting on the shield all ppr.; sinister, a horse ar.

Gore-Booth, Bart. See BOOTH.

Gore (ORMSBY-GORE, Baron Harlech). Quarterly, 1st and 4th, gu. a fesse betw. three crosses crosslet fitchée or, for GORE; 2nd and 3rd, gu. a bend betw. six crosses crosslet fitchée or, for ORMSBY. Crests—1st, GORE: An heraldic tiger ramp. ar. maned and tufted sa.; 2nd, ORMSBY: A dexter arm embowed in armour, holding in the hand a man's leg also in armour, couped at the thigh all ppr. Supporters—Dexter, an heraldic tiger ar. maned and tufted sa. ducally gorged or; sinister, a lion or. Motto—In hoc signo vinces.

Gore (KNOX-GORE, Belleek Manor, co. Mayo, bart., created 5 Dec. 1868). Quarterly, 1st and 4th, gu. a fesse betw. three cross crosslets fitchée or, all within a bordure ar., for GORE; 2nd and 3rd, gu. a falcon rising or, within an orle waved on the outer side and engr. on the inner side ar. a crescent for diff., for KNOX. Crests—1st, GORE: A wolf saliant or; 2nd, KNOX: A falcon close perched on a rest ppr. Motto—In hoc signo vinces.

Gore (Barrow Court, co. Somerset). Gu. a fesse betw. three cross crosslets fitchée or. Crest—A wolf's head saliant ar. collared gu. Motto—In hoc signo vinces.

Gore-Langton. See LANGTON.

Gore (Tyredagh Castle, co. Clare). Gu. on a fesse betw. three cross crosslets fitchée or, a trefoil slipped vert. Crest—An heraldic tiger saliant ar. collared. Motto—In hoc signo vinces.

Gore (Derrymore, co. Clare). Same Arms, &c.

Gore (VERNON-GORE; Derryluskan, co. Tipperary; descended from GORE, of Tyredagh Castle, co. Clare; exemplified to GEORGINA KATHERINE VERNON, widow of CHARLES VERNON, Esq., of Royal York Crescent, Clifton, co. Gloucester, upon her assuming, by royal licence, 1876, the additional name of GORE, in compliance with the testamentary injunction of Lieut.-Col. GEORGE GORE, 9th Queen's Royal Regt. of Lancers). Gu. on a fess betw. three crosses crosslet or, a trefoil slipped vert.

Gore (Enfield, co. Middlesex). Gu. a fesse betw. three crosses crosslet or, a crescent for diff.

Gore (Aldrington and Surrendon, co. Wilts). Or, three bulls' heads cabossed sa. Crest—A bull's head couped at the neck sa.

Gore. Az. three lions ramp. or, on a chief gu. a demi lion ramp. of the second.

Gore. Az. a chev. betw. three lions ramp. ar.

Gore. Or, three bars gu. in chief as many torteaux.

Gorey, Town of (co. Wexford; granted 24 Nov. 1623). Per saltire ar. or, az. and purp. in chief a cross of the last, in base a swan with an eel in its bill of the first, in dexter fesse point a lion pass. guard. of the second, and in the sinister a rose gu. seeded and barbed vert.

Gorge (Hillingdon, co. Middlesex and Ashton, co. Somerset; FERDINANDO GORGE, grandson of Sir FERDINANDO GORGE. Visit. Middlesex, 1663). Lozengy ar. and az. a chev. gu. Crest—A greyhound's head couped ar. collared az. studded or.

Gorges (Wraxall, Langford, &c. Sir THEOBALD RUSSELL, son and heir of Sir THEOBALD RUSSELL, by ELEANOR, his wife, sister and heiress of RALPH DE GORGES, assumed his maternal surname of GORGES, and also adopted the armorial bearings of the family, which occasioned a dispute, 2 Edward III., be-

413

tween him and WARBURTON, of Cheshire; and the latter gentleman, establishing his right to the arms in the court of Henry, Earl of Lancaster, Earl Marshal, GORGES had assigned to him—Lozengy or and az. a chev. gu.; which his posterity bore for some time, until they assumed again their ancient hereditary coat). Ar. a gurges (or whirlpool) az.

Gorges (Baron Gorges; summoned to Parliament, 1309-22, but not afterwards). Ar. a gurges (or whirlpool) az.

Gorges (quartered by CHICHESTER, of Rawleigh. Visit. Devon, 1620). Erm. a fess betw. three cinquefoils gu.

Gorges (Lord Dundalk; created 1620, extinct 1712). Lozengy or and az. a chev. gu. Crest—A greyhound's head couped ar. gorged with a bar gemels gu.

Gorges (Kilbrew, co. Meath). Same Arms.

Gorges (Bradpole). Lozengy or and az.

Gorgon. Sa. three leopards' faces or, jessant-de-lis of the second.

Gorham (Gorhambury, co. Herts; borne by the descendants of Sir HUGH DE GORHAM, temp. Richard II. Visit. Lincoln, 1562). Gu. three shackbolts conjoined in fess or.

Gorham (cos. Northampton and Lincoln). Same Arms.

Gorham (St. Neots, co. Huntingdon; a branch, it is supposed, of the Northampton family). Same Arms. Crest—A griffin's head couped betw. two wings all or. Motto—Ready and faithful.

Gorham. Same Arms. Crest—A sword in pale, supporting on the point a garland of laurel ppr.

Gorgys. Erm. a fesse betw. three cinquefoils gu.

Goring (Earl of Norwich; created 1646, extinct 1671). Ar. a chev. betw. three annulets gu.

Goring (Burton, co. Sussex, bart., extinct 1724). Same Arms.

Goring (Highden, co. Sussex, bart.). Ar. a chev. betw. three annulets gu. Crest—A lion ramp. guard. sa.

Goring (Kingston, and Frodley Hall, co. Stafford; derived from HENRY GORING, second son of GEORGE GORING, Esq., of Ovingdene, co. Sussex). Same Arms, &c.

Goring (Whiston Park, co. Sussex). Same Arms and Crest, quartering FAGG.

Goring, or Le Goring (Sussex). Same Arms and Crest.

Goringe. Ar. a fesse betw. three annulets gu.

Gorland. Ar. on a bend per bend az. and gu. cotised three lozenges, each charged with a fleur-de-lis, all counterchanged.

Gorland, or Goreland. Ar. three saltires vert.

Gorley, Gorely, or Goorlay (co. Kent). Erm. three martlets gu. Crest—A hand in armour holding a cross crosslet fitchée in pale all ppr.

Gorley (Sutton, co. York). Erm. three mullets gu.

Gorm (Scotland). Or, three cocks' heads erased az. Crest—An eagle's head erased sa. beaked or.

Gormagan (The Grange, co. Carlow; FARDAROUGHA GORMAGAN, of that place, whose dau. ELLEN, m. EDMOND BYRNE, Esq., of Ballycapell, co. Wicklow; impalement on his Fun. Ent. 1624). Gu. a talbot pass. ar. betw. three swords erect of the last, pommels and hilts or.

Gorman. Gyronny of eight erm. and sa. an eagle with two heads displ. or. Crest—A horse saddled ppr. at full speed.

Gorman. See O'GORMAN.

Gorman (granted to JOHN GORMAN, M.D., son of PATRICK MACGORMAN, late of Ballintapper, co. Monaghan). Az. a lion pass. erm. betw. three daggers erect, two and one, ar. hilted and pommelled or. Crest—A dexter armed arm embowed, the hand bare, grasping a sword, the blade wavy all ppr. Motto—Primi et ultimi in bello.

Gormanston, Viscount. See PRESTON.

Gornay (co. Suffolk). Ar. a saltire engr. gu.

Gornay. Or, a lion ramp. sa. a bordure gu.

Gornay, or Gornaye. Az. a bend or, betw. three fishes naiant ar.

Gorney, Gurnay, or Gurnard (Kendal, co. Westmorland). Paly of six or and az.

Gorney (cos. Devon, Essex, and London, 1622). Ar. a cross engr. gu. in the first quarter a cinquefoil az. Crest—On a chapeau gu. turned up erm. a lion pass. ar. resting the dexter paw on a cinquefoil or. The original Crest—On a chapeau gu. turned up erm. a fish in pale ar. the head in base.

Gorney (co. Essex). Az. on a bend cotised ar. three leopards' faces gu. crowned or.

Gorney (Malden, co. Essex, and co. Norfolk). Ar. a cross engr. gu.

Gorney (co. Norfolk). Ar. a cross engr. betw. four estoiles gu. (another, mullets of six points).

Gorney (WILLIAM HARDING, citizen of London, Visit. 1568, m. MARGARET, dau. of WILLIAM GORNEY). Ar. on a cross engr. betw. four mullets of six points pierced gu. a cross of the field.

Gorney. Ar. a cross engr. gu. betw. four mullets of the second. *Crest*—A merman ppr. holding a target or.

Gorran. Ar a sword in pale az. hilt and pommel or, surmounted on the top by a mullet gu. over all a saltire couped sa.

Gorrie, or Gorry (Scotland). Sa. a chev. betw. three mullets in chief and a lion ramp. in base or. *Crest*—An eagle's head sa.

Gort, Viscount. See VEREKER.

Gorton (Gorton, and other places, co. Lancaster). Gu. ten billets or, a chief indented of the last. *Crest*—A goat's head erased ar. ducally gorged or.

Gorwood, or Gurwood (originally from Savoy). Az. a chev. ar. *Crest*—A unicorn's head ppr. *Motto*—Pour jamais.

Gosell, or Goushill (Wallington, co. Norfolk). Barry of six or and az. a canton gules or, a talbot's head erm.

Gosell, or Goushill (co. Suffolk). Barry of six ar. and gu. a canton erm.

Gosewyn, or Goswyn. Chequy or and ar.

Gosford, Earl of. See ACHESON.

Gosfright. Ar. a bend gu. betw. three Cornish choughs ppr.

Goshall (co. Kent). Or, on a hart a cinquefoil pierced of the field, and on a chief indented az. two bezants, each charged with a cinquefoil pierced of the second.

Goshall. Az. a lion ramp. or, crowned gu. betw. ten crosses crosslet of the second. *Crest*—Out of a ducal coronet or, a lion's gamb erect gu. holding an arrow of the first, headed of the second.

Goshell, or Gowsley. Paly of six ar. and gu. a chief dancettée or.

Gosholme. Ar. three lions ramp. gu.

Goskar. Ar. a bend betw. three Cornish choughs ppr. on a chief sa. as many mullets of the field. *Crest*—A Cornish chough holding in the beak a mullet. *Motto*—Spes mea in Deo.

Goslett (Marshfield, co. Gloucester). Gu. a chev. betw. three pheons or. *Crest*—A stalk of wheat and a palm branch in saltire ppr.

Goslike, or Gostwyke. Ar. a bend gu. betw. six birds sa. on a chief or, three horses' heads couped az. bridled of the first. *Crest*—A griffin's head couped betw. two wings gu. platée.

Gosling, or Goselyn (London). Gu. a chev. betw. three crescents erm. *Crest*—An eagle's head erased sa. charged with a crescent erm.

Gosling (Hassobury, co. Essex). Vert on a chev. ar. betw. three crescents or, each charged with an erm. spot sa. a lion ramp. gu. betw. two crosses formée fitchée az. *Crest*—An eagle's head erased erm. on the neck a bezant charged with a cross formée ar.

Gosling. Gu. a chev. betw. three crescents or (another, crescents erm.).

Gosnall, or Gosnolde (Ipswich and Otley, co. Suffolk). Per pale crenellée or and az. *Crest*—A bull's head guard. couped at the neck per pale or and az.

Gosnall. Per pale crenellée or and az. two fleurs-de-lis of the first.

Gosnold (Beaconsfield, co. Buckingham). Per pale crenellée or and vert. *Crest*—A bull's head per pale or and vert, horns counterchanged.

Gosnold (second Justice of Munster, Reg. Ulster's Office). Per pale crenellée or and az.

Gosnold (Fun. Ent. Ulster's Office, 1658). Quarterly, 1st and 4th, per pale crenellée or and az ; 2nd and 3rd, ar. a fleur-de-lis sa. thereon three bezants.

Gospatric. Gu. a bezant.

Gospatrick (WILLIAM BIRD, Esq., of Pireth, 1295, *m.* EMME GOSPATRICK. Visit. Cumberland, 1615). Chequy ar. and gu. a chief az.

Gospatrick (quartered by TALBOT and LITTLETON). Gu. on a saltire ar. a martlet sa.

Gospatrick. Vair a pale sa.

Goss, or Gosse. Ar. nine mullets in saltire gu. *Crest*—A falcon, wings expanded and inverted ppr. ducally gorged or.

Gosse (Epsom, co. Surrey ; granted to HENRY GOSSE, Esq.). Or, fretty az. on a pile engr. sa. three pheons ar. *Crest*—A pheon sa. entwined by a branch of oak or, betw. two wings gold, guttée de sang.

Gosselin. Az. on a saltire ar. five guttées de sang.

Gosselin (Jersey, Guernsey, and the Priory, Ware, co. Herts). Gu. a chev. betw. three crescents erm. *Crest*—A negro's head ppr.

414

Gosset, or Gossett. Ar. three owls gu. a quarter az. *Crest*—A hand couped at the wrist erect, holding a dagger in pale all ppr.

Gosset (Jersey, and Northam, co. Devon). Az. a beanwreath or, leaved and fructed ppr. on chief ar. an eagle displ. sa. *Crest*—A greyhound's head erased ar. collared gu. ringed and garnished or.

Gossett (Eltham House, co. Kent). Az. an annulet and three bean-pods (*gousses*) leaved and stalked, proceeding therefrom and ranged *en pairle* or, on a chief ar. an eagle displ. sa. *Crest*—A greyhound's head erased ar. collared gu. ringed and garnished or.

Gossinge, or Gosson. Ar. on a bend gu. three eagles of the field.

Gossinton (Estevende, *temp.* Richard II.). Az. a rose pierced or.

Gossip (Hatfield, co. York ; the eldest branch of the GOSSIPS, of Thorp Arch). Per fesse indented ar. and sa. a pale counterchanged three goats' heads erased, two and one, and as many crosses pattée fitchée, one and two, of the first. *Crest*—Two goats' heads erased, addorsed, the dexter az. the sinister ar. ; quarterings, WILMER, THWENG, BRUCE, DE ARCHES, HATFIELD, &c.

Gossip (RANDALL GOSSIP, Esq., of Thorpe Arch, W.R. co. York). Same *Arms* and *Crest*. *Motto*—Prospice respice.

Gossip. Or, three double quatrefoils vert. *Crest*—A martlet sa.

Gost (London). Erm. on a pile sa. three pheons or. *Crest* —A pheon or, betw. two wings expanded ar.

Gostomes, or Goston (Stockwell, co. Surrey ; granted by Camden, Clarenceux, to Sir FRANCIS GOSTON, or GOSTOMES, Knt.). Quarterly, az. and erm. in the 1st and 4th quarters a unicorn's head erased ar. crined, armed, and ducally gorged or. *Crest*—On a cap gu. turned up ar. a rose or, betw. two wings az.

Gostwick (Willington, co. Bedford, bart., extinct 1766). Ar. a bend gu. cotised sa. betw. six Cornish choughs ppr. on a chief az. three mullets or. *Crest*—A griffin's head betw. two wings expanded gu.

Gostwick (co. Bedford, Master of the Horse to Henry VIII.). Ar. a bend gu. betw. six Cornish choughs sa. on a chief az. three horses' heads couped of the first, bridled or. *Crest*—A griffin's head betw. two wings expanded gu. pattée.

Gostwick (co. Cornwall). Ar. a bend cotised gu. betw. six martlets sa. on a chief or, three mullets of six points vert.

Gostwick (Fun. Ent. Ulster's Office, MARY GOSTWICK, buried at St. Patrick's Cathedral, 28 Feb. 1639, wife of Sir MAURICE WILLIAMS, Knt., of Dublin). Ar. a bend gu. betw. two Cornish choughs sa. beaked and legged of the second, on a chief or, three mullets az.

Gotesbury. Gu. a cross or, in the 1st and 4th quarters a lozenge vair, in the 2nd and 3rd, a goat's head erased ar.

Gotesby. Gu. a cross or, betw. two lozenges in chief vair and as many goats' heads erased in base ar.

Gotesley. Erm. three goats' heads erased gu.

Gotesley, or Gotysby (Har. MS. 1386). Ar. a lion ramp. sa. oppressed with a saltire engr. gu.

Gotham. Or (another, ar.) a bend sa.

Gotham. Erm. a bend sa. *Crest*—An eagle, wings endorsed, perched upon the stump of a tree ppr.

Gotham. Erm. a bend gu.

Gotham. Erm. on a bend gu. three barrulets wavy or.

Gothard (Newcastle). Gu. an eagle displ. or. *Crest*—Out of a ducal coronet or, a buck's head ppr. *Motto*—Aquila non captat muscas.

Gother (ante-chapel, New College, Oxford). Sa. on a fesse or, three mullets sa. in chief a lion pass. of the second, in base three fishes side by side haurient ar.

Gotley, or Gottelley. Erm. a goat's head erased gu. attired or. *Crest*—A demi lion ramp. holding a sword blade wavy all ppr.

Gotsan, Gotesham, or Goteshan. Az. a cross ar. betw. twenty billets or.

Gott (Battel, co. Sussex, and London). Per saltire ar. and sa. a bordure counterchanged. *Crest*—A griffin's head ermines betw. two wings expanded erm.

Gottes (Riborough, co. Cambridge). Vert a griffin segreant or. *Crest*—A greyhound's head erased ar. collared and lined or.

Gottington. Sa. two she-talbots pass. counterpass. ppr. the one surmounting the other. *Crest*—A horned owl ppr.

Gothers. Sa. guttée d'eau three open cups with handles ar.

Goucell. Or, two bars az. a canton erm. *Crest*—A unicorn pass. or.

Goudie (Scotland). Ar. a chev. betw. two trefoils slipped in chief vert and a tortoise in base gu. *Crest*—A garb or. *Motto*—Honestas.

Gouge (Wales). Az. three boars pass. ar. *Crest*—On a dexter gauntlet in fesse a hawk, wings expanded, all ppr.

Gouges. Ar. five annulets conjunct az.

Gough (*Viscount Gough*). Quarterly, 1st and 4th, gu. on a mount vert a lion pass. guard. or, supporting with the dexter paw the union flag ppr. and over the same, in chief, the words "China, India," in letters of gold; 2nd and 3rd, az. on a fesse ar. betw. three boars' heads couped or, a lion pass. gu. (being his family arms), in the centre chief point, pendent from a riband ar. fimbriated az. a representation of the badge of the Spanish Order of Charles III. ppr. and on a chief a representation of the east wall of the fortress of Tarifa, with a breach betw. two turrets, and on the dexter turret the British flag flying also ppr. *Crests*—In the centre, on a wreath, a boar's head couped at the neck or; on the dexter side, on a mural crown ar. a lion pass. guard. or, holding in the dexter paw two flag-staves in bend sinister ppr. the one bearing the union-flag of Great Britain and Ireland, surmounting the other, the staff thereof broken, with a triangular banner flowing therefrom, being intended to represent a Chinese flag, having thereon the device of a dragon, in an escroll, above the word "China;" on the sinister side, on a wreath, a dexter arm embowed, in the uniform of the 87th regiment, being gu. faced vert, the hand grasping the colour of the said regiment displ. and a representation of a French eagle reversed and depressed, the staff broken ppr. in an escroll above the word "Barrosa." *Supporters*—On the dexter side a lion reguard. or, gorged with an eastern crown gu. with chain reflexed over the back gold, the rim of the crown inscribed "Punjab", in letters also gold; on the sinister side a dragon (intended to represent the device upon a Chinese flag, granted to *Viscount Gough* in the crest of honourable augmentation) or, gorged with a mural crown sa. inscribed with the word "China," and chained gold. *Mottoes*—Over the family crest, "Faugh a Ballagh; " over the first crest, "China; " and over the third, " Barrosa;" under the arms, " Goojerat."

Gough (Bristol, co. Gloucester, cos. Radnor and Somerset). Ar. three boars' heads couped sa. armed or.

Gough (Oldfallings and Perry Hall, co. Stafford). Gu. on a fesse ar. betw. three boars' heads couped or, a lion pass. az. *Crest*—A boar's head couped ar. devouring a broken spear gu. *Motto*—Domat omnia virtus.

Gough (exemplified, 1845, to the Hon. FREDERICK GOUGH-CALTHORPE, on his taking the surname and arms of GOUGH only. The licence extended to his issue). Same *Arms* as GOUGH, of Perry Hall.

Gough (Marshe, co. Salop). Sa. three nags' heads erased ar.

Gough (Meriatt, co. Somerset). Gu. on a fesse or, betw. three boars' heads couped ar. a lion pass. of the field. *Crest* —A boar's head couped at the neck ar.

Gough (co. Warwick). Chequy or and az. a fesse erm.

Gough (co. Lincoln, 1640, and Wales). Az. three boars pass. ar. two and one.

Gough. Ar. on a chev. gu. three lions pass. guard. or.

Gough (Ireland; GARRETT GOUGH, settled in Ireland, 1530, Reg. Ulster's Office, by Carney, Ulster). Az. a chev. betw. two fleurs-de-lis in chief and a lion ramp. in base or. *Crest* —A wyvern, tail nowed ppr.

Gough (Kilmanahan, co. Waterford; allowed by Hawkins, Ulster, 1717). Same *Arms*.

Gough (Ballyorley, co. Wexford; CLEMENT GOUGH, Esq., of Ballyorley, *temp.* William III., descended from the preceding, *m.* MARY, dau. of RICKARD DONOVAN, of Clonmore, same co.). Same *Arms*.

Gough. See GOFF.

Gough (granted, 1816, to GEORGE GOUGH, Esq., of Woodstown, co. Limerick; descended from Right Rev. FRANCIS GOUGH, Bishop of Limerick). Az. on a fess ar. betw. three boars' heads couped or, a lion pass. gu. *Crest*—A boar's head couped at the neck or, tusked ar. *Motto*—Gradu diverso via una.

Goughton. Az. three bucks or.

Goughton, or Gowtheton. Ar. (another, or) a bend gobonated gu. and ar. betw. two pellets.

Gouie (Guernsey, extinct). Ar. a chev. gu. betw. three lions ramp. sa.

Gouis (Duntish, co. Dorset, *temp.* Edward II.). Ar. a lion ramp. sa.

Goulborne (Overton, co. Chester). Ar. a cross betw. four martlets gu.

Goulburn (Right Hon. HENRY GOULBURN, M.P., Chancellor of the Exchequer, and EDWARD GOULBURN, Esq., Serjeant-at-law, sons of MUNBEE GOULBURN, Esq., of Portland

Place, by SUSAN, his wife, dau. of the fourth *Viscount Chetwynd*). Ar. a cross betw. four doves gu. *Crest*—A dove with an olive branch in its beak all ppr.

Gould (Frome Bellett and Frampton, co. Glamorgan). Per saltire or and az. a lion ramp. counterchanged. *Crest*— An arm embowed, vested gu. cuffed or, holding in the hand ppr. a banner paly of six az. and gold, on a canton ar. a cross of the first, the staff also gold. *Motto*—Non nobis esti.

Gould (Exeter, *temp.* Edward III.; Combe in Staverton, *temp.* Elizabeth, and afterwards of Hayes and Downes, co. Devon; the elder branch became extinct at the decease of WILLIAM GOULD, Esq., in 1726; his co-heirs *m.* BULLER and TUCKFIELD; a younger branch was of Lew Trenchard). Per saltire az. and or, a lion ramp. counterchanged. *Crest*—A demi lion ramp. bezantée.

Gould (Lew Trenchard, co. Devon; the last male heir, EDWARD GOULD, Esq., of that place, *d.* in 1788, leaving a sister and heiress, MARGARET, wife of CHARLES BARING, Esq.). Per saltire or and az. a lion ramp. counterchanged, for GOULD, quartering BARING. *Crest*—A demi lion ramp. az. bezantée. *Motto*—Probitate et labore.

Gould (Dorchester and Edmonton, co. Middlesex). Per saltire az. and or, a lion ramp. counterchanged. *Crest*—An arm vested vert, holding in the hand ppr. a banner or, charged with three bars wavy az. on a canton ar. a rose gu.

Gould (Fleet House, co. Dorset). Same *Arms*. *Crest*—An arm embowed, vested gu. cuff or, holding in the hand ppr. a banner paly of six az. and of the second, on a canton ar. a cross of the first, the staff gold.

Gould (Upwey, co. Dorset; exemplified to HAMILTON LLE-WELLYN JACKSON, eldest surviving son of THOMAS JACKSON, Esq., of Fanningstown, co. Limerick, and grandson of THOMAS JACKSON, Esq., of same place, by BARBARA GOULD, his wife, dau. of WILLIAM READ, Esq., of Bradford, co. Wilts, and BARBARA, his wife, sister and heiress of JAMES GOULD, Esq., of Upwey, upon his assuming, by royal licence, 1871, the name of GOULD in place of JACKSON). Quarterly, 1st and 4th, per saltire az. and or, a lion ramp. counterchanged, for GOULD; 2nd and 3rd, ar. a greyhound courant ermines betw. three eagles' heads erased sa., for JACKSON. *Crest*— An arm embowed vested vert, holding in the hand a flagstaff ppr. therefrom flowing a banner or, charged with three barrulets wavy az. on a canton ar. a cross gu. *Motto*— Revirescat.

Gould. Az. a lion ramp. or, betw. three scrolls ar. *Crest*— A demi lion ramp. or, holding a scroll ar.

Gould (Admiral Sir DAVIDGE GOULD, G.C.B.). Same *Arms* and *Crest*. *Motto*—A Nilo Victoria.

Gould. Paly of six ar. and sa. six crosses crosslet or.

Gould (Ireland). Or, a lion ramp. gu. *Crest*—A martlet or.

Goulding (North Newherbar, co. Kent; confirmed 13 May, 1672). Ar. a cross voided betw. four lions pass. gu. *Crest*— A lion sejant sa. supporting with the dexter foot an escutcheon or.

Goulding (Ireland). Ar. a cross betw. four demi lions ramp. couped gu. *Crest*—A hawk ppr. jessed, belled, and hooded or.

Gouldingham (co. Norfolk). Ar. two bars wavy gu.

Gouldsmith (Nantwich, co. Chester). Gu. on a fesse or, betw. three martlets ar. as many fleurs-de-lis az.

Gouldsmith (Crayford, co. Kent). Gu. a chev. betw. three goldfinches ar. on a chief or, a lion pass. of the field. *Crest* —A Cornish chough ppr. guttée d'eau.

Gouldsmith (co. Kent). Gu. on a chev. betw. three goldfinches ar. as many roses sa. a baton of the third, on a chief of the second a lion pass. of the first.

Gouldwell (Wisbeach, co. Cambridge, and Bury St. Edmund's, co. Suffolk). Az. a chief or, over all a lion ramp. ar. billettée sa. *Crest*—Out of a well or, a branch of columbines stalked and leaved vert, flowered ppr.

Gouldwell (co. Kent). Gu. (another, az.) a lion ramp. ar. billettée sa. (A chief of the last sometimes added).

Gouldwell. Az. a chief or, over all a lion ramp. ar. billettée sa.

Goulston (quartered by PRIDEAUX). Ar. a fess betw. three pellets.

Goulston (MARGARET GOULSTON, heiress of Melton Mowbray, *temp.* Edward VI., *m.* THOMAS, son of JOHN DRAPER, co. Leicester. Visit. Notts, 1614). Gu. a chev. betw. three swans' heads erased ar.

Goulstone. Ar. two bars nebulée gu. over all on a bend sa. three plates. *Crest*—An ostrich's wing of five feathers alternately ar. and gu. charged with a bend, as in the arms.

Goulten (granted to THOMAS MORSE GOULTEN, Esq., of Aldmondsbury, co. Gloucester). Gu. two battle axes in saltire betw. as many anchors in pale and two mullets of six points in fesse all or. *Crest*—A cubit arm vested gu. cuffed ar. the hand ppr. holding a battle axe sa. suspended from the wrist by a chain an escutcheon or. charged with an anchor also sa. *Motto*—Animo et fide.

Goulton (co. York). Or, two bars sa. ni chief as many fleurs-de-lis of the last. *Crest*—A fleur-de-lis sa.

Gounery, or Gouneris. Gu. a chev. or.

Gouneys. Gu. a chev. erm.

Gouning (Mayor of Bristol; granted 22 Dec. 1662). Gu. three cannons barways in pale ar.

Goure, or Gower (arms in Aylworthes House, Tackley, co. Oxford. Visit. 1574). Az. a chev. betw. three wolves' heads erased or, (another, griffins' heads).

Gourlay (Kincraig, co. Fife). Sa. an eagle displ. ar. armed and beaked gu. *Old Arms*—Ar. three martlets gu. *Crest*—A demi eagle, as in the arms. *Motto*—Profunda cernit.

Gourlay (AUSTIN-GOURLAY, of Kincraig, 1865). Quarterly, 1st and 4th, as the last; 2nd and 3rd, or, on a chev. betw. three lions' gambs erect and erased gu. a crescent of the field, for AUSTIN. *Crests*—1st, GOURLAY: A demi eagle displ. ar. armed and beaked gu.; 2nd, AUSTIN: An eagle displ. with two heads per pale or and gu. on each wing a crescent counterchanged. *Supporters*—Two eagles ar. armed and beaked gu. *Mottoes*—1st, GOURLAY: Profunda cernit; 2nd, AUSTIN: Virtute non vi.

Gourlay (Dantzic, 1672). Sa. an eagle displ. ar. armed and beaked gu. a bordure engr. or. *Crest*—A salmon naiant ar. *Motto*—Ditat et alit.

Gournay (Feudal Baron of Yarmouth, co. Norfolk). The *Arms* are said to have been "pure sable," but paly of six or and az. has been attributed to them.

Gournay. Az. on a bend cotised ar. three leopards' faces (another, crowned) gu.

Gourney, or Gurney (Harpley, Westbarsham, Keswick, and Norwich, co. Norfolk, 28 Henry II.). Ar. a cross engr. gu.

Gourney. Ar. a cross engr. betw. four estoiles gu.

Gourney. Erm. a saltire engr. gu.

Gourney (co. Somerset, and Dartmouth, co. Devon; THOMAS GOURNEY, of the latter place. Visit. 1620). Ar. a cross engr. gu. in the first quarter a cinquefoil vert.

Gourney (confirmed by Camden, Clarenceux, to Sir THOMAS GOURNEY, Knt., High Sheriff co. Essex). Ar. a cross engr. gu. in the dexter chief a cinquefoil az. *Crest*—On a chapeau gu. turned up erm. a lion statant, tail extended ar. the right paw resting on a cinquefoil or.

Gousell, or Goushill. Paly of six ar. and gu. on a chief az. a barrulet indented or.

Gousell. Paly of six ar and gu. on a chief indented or, two barrulets wavy az.

Gouseton. Az. three roses or.

Goushill. Ar. a fess betw. six martlets sa.

Goushill (co. Essex). Barry of six or and az. a canton erm.

Goushill (co. Derby). Barry of six or and gu. a canton erm.

Gousley. Paly of six ar. and gu. in chief a bar indented or.

Gouston (co. Northumberland). Per saltire or and chequy of the first and gu.

Govan (Cardrona, co. Peebles). Gu. on a crescent ar. three stars az.

Govan (Scotland). Or, a sword in pale az. ensigned with a mullet gu. over all a saltire couped sa.

Gove. Ar. a cross lozengy betw. four eagles displ. sa. *Crest*—Out of a mural coronet or, a demi monkey sa.

Gover. Az. a saltire ar. *Crest*—In a maunch or, a dexter hand apaumée ppr.

Gover. Az. on a saltire ar. five guttées de sang.

Goverley. Erm. three martlets gu.

Govery (Stangod, co. Lincoln). Or, three bends erm.

Govis (London). Ar. three lions' heads erased gu. collared of the first.

Govis (London). Ar. a lion's head couped gu. *Crest*—A demi lady ppr. richly attired az. holding in the dexter hand a balance of the first.

Govis. Vair a bend lozengy gu.

Govis. Quarterly, gu. and vair a bend or.

Gow-Steuart (Little Colonsay, co. Argyll, 1864). Quarterly, 1st and 4th, or, a lion ramp. betw. three mullets az. over all a fess chequy ar. and of the third, all within a bordure of the third, for STEUART; 2nd and 3rd, vert on a fess ar. betw. a cat-a-mountain sejant guard. in chief, and a dexter hand couped holding a dagger erect in base ppr. three holly leaves of the first, for Gow. *Crests*—A demi lion holding in his dexter paw a Lochaber axe in pale ppr., for STEUART; a

dexter arm in armour embowed, holding a boar's head on a broadsword all ppr., for Gow. *Mottoes*—Firin, for STEUART; Caraid ann am fheum, for Gow.

Gowby. Gu. a chev. erm. betw. three woodbine leaves or.

Gowcell (Dinner, co. Norfolk). Or, two bars az. in chief a fleur-de-lis sa. a canton erm. *Crest*—A unicorn pass. or.

Gowcell. Barry of six or and az. a canton erm. in chief a ducal coronet sa.

Gowdie. Vert a tortoise pass. ar.

Gowe. Ar. a chev. betw. three ravens sa. each holding in the beak an erm. spot of the second.

Gower (SUTHERLAND-LEVESON-GOWER, *Duke of Sutherland*). Quarterly of eight, 1st, quarterly, 1st and 4th, barry of eight or and gu. over all a cross flory sa., for GOWER, 2nd and 3rd az. three laurel leaves ar, for LEVESON; 2nd, barry of eight ar. and gu. over all a cross patonce sa., for GOWER; 3rd, gu. three organ rests or suffiues or, for GRANVILLE, *Earl of Bath*; 4th, ar. a lion ramp. gu. betw. three pheons' heads sa., for EGERTON, *Duke of Bridgewater*; 5th, ar. on a bend az. three bucks' heads cabossed or, for STANLEY; 6th, gu. two lions pass. ar. for STRANGE, of Knockyn; 7th, barry of ten ar. and gu. over all a lion ramp. or, crowned per pale of the first and second, for BRANDON, *Duke of Suffolk*, on a canton chequy or and az. a fesse gu., for CLIFFORD, *Earl of Cumberland*; 8th, Royal arms, over all on an escutcheon of pretence, surmounted by an earl's coronet gu. three stars within a bordure or, charged with a double tressure flory counterflory of the field, being the arms of the ancient *Earls of Sutherland*. *Crests*—1st: A wolf pass. ar. collared and chained or, for GOWER; 2nd: A cat-a-mountain ppr., for SUTHERLAND. *Supporters*—Dexter, a wolf ar. collared and chained or; sinister, a savage, wreathed about the temples and waist with laurel, holding in the dexter hand a club resting on the shoulder ppr. and supporting with the sinister hand an antique shield charged with the arms of the ancient family of SUTHERLAND. *Motto*—Frangas non flectes.

Gower (LEVESON-GOWER, *Earl of Granville*). Quarterly, 1st and 4th, barry of eight ar. and gu. a cross flory sa., for GOWER; 2nd, az. three laurel leaves or, for LEVESON; 3rd, gu. three rests or, for GRANVILLE. *Crest*—A wolf pass. ar. collared and lined or. *Supporters*—Two wolves ar. plain collared and line reflexed over the back gold, and charged on the shoulder with an escutcheon gu. thereon a clarion or. *Motto*—Frangas non flectes.

Gower (Woodhall, Colemers Boughton, Droitwich, &c., cos. Worcester and Essex). Az. a chev. betw. three wolves' heads erased or. *Crest*—A wolf's head erased or.

Gower (Earl's Court, co. Worcester; JOHN GOWER, illegitimate son of ARNOLD GOWER, of the Woodhall family; his dau. and heiress carried Earl's Court to the INGRAM family. Har. MSS. 19816). Same *Arms* as GOWER, of Woodhall, with a sinister bendlet.

Gower (Visit. co. Worcester, 1533). Az. a chev. betw. three talbots pass. ar.

Gower (Durham). Az. a chev. betw. three talbots ar.

Gower (co. York). Ar. a fesse betw. three talbots pass. sa. *Crest*—A demi eagle or.

Gower (cos. Warwick and Worcester). Gu. a fesse erm. betw. six crosses crosslet fitchée ar.

Gower (Thorpe in Inkberrow, co. Worcester). Az. a chev. or, betw. two birds' heads erased ar. langued gu. and a mullet gold in chief, and two mullets with one bird's head in base.

Gower (ABEL ANTHONY GOWER, Esq., of Glandovan, co. Pembroke, who d. in 1837; his brother Admiral Sir ERASMUS GOWER, who d. in 1814, and their nephews and executors, ROBERT FREDERIC GOWER, Esq., of Glandovan, and ABEL LEWIS GOWER, Esq.). Same *Arms* and *Crest*, quartering or, a cross patonce gu. and three snakes nowed in triangle ar. *Motto*—Frangas non flectes.

Gower (Ireland). Barry of six ar. and gu. in chief three pallets. *Crest*—Two wings displ. or.

Gower (London). Tomb of the Poet GOWER). Ar. on a chev. az. three leopards' faces or. *Crest*—A talbot sejant.

Gower (Stanesby, co. York). Erm. a cross flory gu.

Gower (co. York). Ar. four bars gu. over all a cross crosslet sa.

Gowis. Ar. a lion's head erased gu.

Gowland (Durham; granted 1749). Per pale gu. and az. two bars or, betw. three bezants in chief and a pheon in base gu. *Crest*—A bezant charged with a mount vert, thereon a stag trippant ppr.

Gowland (co. Hereford; borne by JOHN SAMUEL GOWLAND, Esq., of Cagebrook, in that county). Same *Arms* and *Crest*.

Gowshell, or Goshall. Ar. a fesse betw. six martlets gu.

Gowtheton. Or, a bend gobony ar. and gu. betw. two pellets.

Goyler. Gu. billettée three mullets ar.

Goylin. Az. on a bend betw. two eagles displ. ar. three garbs vert, on a chief or, as many mullets sa. *Crest*—A greyhound's head per pale ar. and or, betw. two roses gu. stalked and leaved vert, a mullet sa. on the neck for diff.

Goylin. Per pale gu. and az. on a bend betw. two eagles displ. ar. three garbs vert, on a chief or, as many mullets pierced sa.

Goyling. Gu. on a fesse betw. three eagles ar. as many garbs vert.

Goyling. Per pale gu. and az. on a bend betw. two eagles displ. ar. three garbs vert.

Goylyn. Per fesse ar. and sa. a pale counterchanged three eagles displ. sa.

Goyter. Gu. billettée three cups with handles ar.

Graa, or Grey. Ar. on a bend betw. two cotises az. three griffins pass. or.

Graas (co. Devon). Erm. a fesse sa. betw. three cinquefoils gu.

Graas (quartered by COPLESTONE, of Coplestone. Visit. Devon, 1620). Erm. a fess betw. three cinquefoils gu.

Graben. Ar. a bend gu. *Crest*—An eagle displ. or, gorged with a chaplet of leaves vert.

Grabham (Bishops Lydiard and Enmore, co. Somerset, and Rochford, co. Essex). Per pale az. and gu. a lion pass. ar. vulned in the shoulder ppr. betw. three boars' heads erased or. *Crest*—On a mount vert a boar's head erased or, guttée de sang and entwined by a snake ppr. *Motto*—L'esperance du salut.

Grace (Barons of Courtstown, and Lords of Grace's country, co. Kilkenny). Gu. a lion ramp. per fesse ar. and or. *Crest* —A demi lion ramp. ar. *Supporters* (as they appear on the monument of Sir OLIVER GRACE, in Jerpoint Abbey, co. Kilkenny)—A demi lion and a talbot. *Mottoes*—En grace affle; and, Concordant nomine facta.

Grace (Ballylinch Castle, co. Kilkenny, and Shanagagh, now Gracefield, Queen's County). Same *Arms, Crest*, and *Motto*.

Grace (Mantua House, co. Roscommon; OLIVER DOWELL JOHN GRACE, Esq., J.P. and D.L., of Mantua House, co. Roscommon, and Gracefield, Queen's co., M.P. for the former co., chief of his house, and male representative of the ancient feudal Lords of Courtstown, bore a shield of nine quarterings). Gu. a lion ramp. per fesse ar. and or, quartering WINDSOR, BUTLER, SHEFFIELD, DOWELL, &c. *Crests*—1st: A demi lion ramp. ar.; 2nd: An arm embowed in armour, holding a dagger all ppr. *Mottoes*—En grace affic; and, Concordant nomine facta.

Grace (Grace Castle, co. Kilkenny, bart.). Quarterly, 1st, gu. a lion ramp. per fesse ar. and or, for GRACE (modern); 2nd, gu. a saltire ar. betw. twelve crosses crosslet or, for GRACE (ancient, *alias* WINDSOR); 3rd, or, a chief indented az. in bend three escallop shells counterchanged, for BUTLER, *Lord Dunboyne;* 4th, ar. a chev. betw. three garbs gu., for SHEFFIELD, *Duke of Buckingham and Normanby. Crests*—1st, for GRACE: A demi lion ramp. ar.; 2nd, for SHEFFIELD: A boar's head and neck erased or. *Mottoes*—Over the crests: En grace affie; under the arms: Concordant nomine facta.

Grace (Knole House, co. Sussex; as borne by SHEFFIELD GRACE, Esq., of that place, Barrister-at-law, LL.D., F.S.A., brother of Sir WILLIAM GRACE, Bart.). Same *Arms, Crest*, and *Motto*.

Grace (Ellington, co. Durham, cos. Somerset and Wilts). Gu. a lion ramp. or, within an orle of cinquefoils of the second. *Crest*—A lion pass. per fesse ar. and or.

Grace (London). Gu. semée of cinquefoils, a lion ramp. ar.

Grace. Or, a lion ramp. vert.

Grace. Az. three lions ramp. or, a chief ar.

Grace (Ellington, co. Hunts). Gu. semée of cinquefoils or, a lion ramp. per pale ar. and or.

Grace (Burley, Leeds). Gu. a lion ramp. per fess erm. and erminois betw. two roses ar. barbed and seeded ppr.

Grace. Az. three lions ramp. or, a chief of the first fretty ar.

Grace. Az. a fesse betw. three lions ramp. or (another, ar.).

Grace. Gu. a lion ramp. per fesse indented ar. and or. *Crest*—A demi lion ramp. ar.

Grace. Ar. a chev. sa. betw. three round buckles gu.

Gracedieu. Ar. a fesse dovetailed in base gu. betw. three torteaux.

Graden (Earnslaw, co. Berwick; heiress, in the 17th century *m.* JAMES DOUGLAS). Ar. on a chev. az. betw. three otters sa. each devouring a salmon of the second, as many pheons or. *Crest*—A demi otter erect sa. devouring a salmon, as in the arms. *Motto*—Ad escam et usum.

Gradock, or Gradocke. Ar. three boars' heads couped sa. *Crest*—A horseshoe az. betw. two eagles' wings ppr.

417

Gradwell (Dowth Hall, co. Meath; confirmed to RICHARD GRADWELL, Esq., J.P., of Dowth Hall aforesaid, and of Carlandstown, co. Westmeath, second son of GEORGE GRADWELL, Esq., J.P., of Preston, co. Lancaster, and grandson of JOHN GRADWELL, Esq., of Clifton, same county). Or, two foxes courant in pale ppr. in the centre chief point a rose gu. *Crest*—A stag trippant ppr. collared and chained or, charged with a rose gu. *Motto*—Nil desperandum.

Grady (Ireland). See O'GRADY.

Græme. See GRAHAM.

Græme (HAMOND-GRÆME, Holly Grove, co. Berks, bart.). Quarterly, 1st and 4th, or, three roses and a bordure gu. on a chief sa. three escallops of the first, for GRÆME; 2nd and 3rd, ar. on a chev. sa. betw. two pellets, each charged with a martlet of the first in chief, and in base a wreath of oak-leaves ppr. three escallops of the first, all within a bordure engr. vert, for HAMOND. *Crests*—1st, for GRÆME: Two arms erect, issuing from clouds, in the act of removing from a spike a human skull, above the skull a marquess's coronet, all betw. two palm branches ppr., motto over, "Sepulto viresco;" 2nd, for HAMOND: Out of a naval crown or, an eagle's head sa.

Grafford. Ar. two lions pass. sa. crowned or.

Grafton, Duke of. See FITZROY.

Grafton (Shrewsbury, Little Missenden, co. Bucks, co. Chester, and London). Per saltire sa. and erm. a lion ramp. or. *Crest*—On the trunk of a tree couped and eradicated or, an eagle volant gold.

Grafton (RALPH DE GRAFTON, of Grafton Flyford, Sheriff of Worcester, 10 Richard I., 1198). Sa. a fret ar. the field replenished with fleurs-de-lis or.

Grafton (Grafton Flyford, co. Worcester, and co. Stafford; RICHARD GRAFTON, of Grafton Flyford, "had many possessions in the cos. of Worcester, Stafford, and Salop." ROBERT GRAFTON, grandson of the above, was "Bayley of ye Citty of Worcester," *temp.* Edward IV.). Per saltire sa. and erm. a lion ramp. or, armed and langued gu. *Crest*—Same as the preceding (another, Har. MSS. 1450), on a tun lying fessways or, a falcon rising ar. supporting by the dexter claw a spear erect, the handle behind the tun.

Grafton (1605). Gyronny of four erm. and sa. a lion ramp. or. *Crest*—On a tun or barrel or, a falcon with wings expanded ar. holding in the claw a sceptre of the first.

Grafton. Or, a chev. gu. a canton erm.

Grafton (Grafton, co. Chester). See MILNETON.

Gragor, or Gregor. Or, three boars az. on a chief of the second a lion pass. of the first.

Graham (1458, *Lord Graham;* 1504, *Earl;* 1644, *Marquess;* and 1707, *Duke of Montrose*). Quarterly, 1st and 4th, or, on a chief sa. three escallops of the field, for GRAHAM; 2nd and 3rd, ar. three roses gu., for the title of MONTROSE. *Crest*— A falcon ppr. beaked and armed or, killing a stork ar. armed gu. *Supporters*—Two storks ppr. *Motto* — Ne oblie.

Graham (Braco, co. Perth; from the second son of the third *Earl of Montrose*, bart. 1625, extinct). Quarterly, 1st and 4th, or, on a chief engr. sa. three escallops of the field; 2nd and 3rd, ar. three roses gu., for MONTROSE. *Crest*—Two hands issuing out of a cloud, in each a sword, the dexter flourishing aloft, the sinister in a defensive posture. *Motto*—Defendendo vinco.

Graham, or Græme (Orchill, co. Perth; from the third son of the second *Earl of Montrose;* heiress *m.* DAVID GRAHAM, a cadet of Inchbrakie, and their line also ended in an heiress). Quarterly, 1st and 4th, or, a boar's head couped gu. on a chief sa. three escallops of the first; 2nd and 3rd, ar. three roses gu., for MONTROSE. *Motto*—Prosequor alis.

Graham (Killearn, co. Stirling; from WILLIAM GRAHAM, Rector of Killearn, son of the second *Earl of Montrose*). Quarterly, with MONTROSE, within a bordure quarterly gu. and sa. *Crest*—A falcon ppr. beaked and membered gu. *Supporters*—A falcon and a stork both ppr. *Motto*—Prædiæ memor.

Graham, or Græme (Inchbrakie, co. Perth; from a younger son of the first earl, and now the latest cadet of Montrose). Or, a wall fessways ar. broken down in some parts, in base a rose gu. on a chief sa. three escallops of the first. *Crest*—A dexter hand holding a garland ppr. *Motto*—A Deo victoria.

Graham (Bucklyvie, co. Stirling; cadet of Inchbrakie). Or, a stag courant betw. three roses gu. on a chief sa. as many escallops of the first. *Crest*—A stag lodged gu. *Motto*—Cubo at excubo.

Graham (Gorthie, co. Perth; cadet of Inchbrakie). Or, three roses within a bordure gu. on a chief sa. as many escallops of the field. *Crest*—Issuing from a cloud two arms erected and lifting up a man's skull encircled with two

2 B

branches of palm, and on the head a marquess's coronet all ppr. *Motto*—Sepulto viresco.

Graham (Græmeshall; cadet of Gorthie). Or, a lion ramp. az. betw. three roses gu. on a chief sa. as many escallops of the field. *Crest*—A lion couchant lying under a sword in pale ppr. *Motto*—Nec timide nec temere.

Graham (Breckness, co. Orkney). Or, a lion's paw erased and erected betw. three roses gu. on a chief sa. as many escallops of the field. *Crest*—A lion's paw, as in the arms, grasping a sword erected in pale ppr. *Motto*—Nec temere nec timide.

Graham-Stirling (Duchray; cadet of Inchbrakie, as recorded 1798). Quarterly, 1st and 4th, ar. on a bend engr. az. betw. two roses gu. three buckles or, for STIRLING; 2nd, or, a wall broken down in some parts az. betw. a crescent in the collar point and a rose in base gu. on a chief engr. sa. three escallops of the field, for GRAHAM; 3rd, ar. a saltire engr. az. on a chief of the last three stars of the field, for MURRAY. *Crest*—An eagle displ. ppr. in his dexter talon a sword, in his sinister a pistol of the last. *Supporters*—Two lions ar. crowned or. *Mottoes*—For right; and, Noctes diesque præsto.

Graham (Callendar, co. Stirling; descended from a younger brother of the first *Earl of Montrose*). Or, a man's heart gu. ensigned with an imperial crown ppr. on a chief sa. three escallops or. *Crest*—An escallop or. *Motto*—Spero meliora.

Graham (London, 1779). As the last, with the chief engr. for diff. *Crest*—An oak sprig with an acorn in the cup ppr. *Motto*—Alteri proses sæculo.

Graham (Dumblane, 1672). Ar. on a chief sa. three escallops or, for diff. a crescent of the second surmounted by a mullet of the third. *Motto*—Non oblie.

Graham (Fintry, co. Stirling, afterwards co. Forfar; descended from ROBERT, son of Sir WILLIAM GRAHAM, of Kincardine, by his second wife, the Princess MARY, dau. of Robert III.). Or, three piles sa. within a double tressure flory counterflory gu. on a chief of the second as many escallops of the first. *Crest*—A phœnix in flames ppr. *Motto*—Bon fin.

Graham (Claverhouse, co. Forfar; cadet of Fintry, 1688, *Viscount Dundee*, title extinct, 1700). Or, three piles wavy sa. within a double tressure flory counterflory gu. on a chief of the second as many escallops of the first.

Graham (Potento, co. Forfar). As the last, with the chief indented for diff. *Crest*—A flame of fire ppr. *Motto*—Semper sursum.

Graham (Duntroon, co. Forfar; became representative of Claverhouse, 1703, now paternally Stirling). As Claverhouse, with the chief engr. for diff. *Crest*—A flame of fire ppr. *Motto*—Recta sursum.

Graham, or Græme (Garvock, co. Perth; from a younger brother of the first laird of Fintry). Or, three piles gu. on a chief sa. as many escallops of the first. *Crest*—A lion ramp. gu. *Motto*—Noli me tangere.

Graham (Balgowan, co. Perth, 1814; *Baron Lynedoch;* title extinct 1843). Or, three piles sa. within a double tressure flory counterflory gu. on a chief of the second a rose betw. two escallops of the first. *Crest*—A dove ppr. afterwards an eagle ppr. *Supporters*—Dexter, a dapple grey horse reguard. bridled ppr.; sinister, a peasant of Andalusia, habited and bearing on the exterior shoulder a hoe ppr. *Motto*—Candide et secure.

Graham (MURRAY-GRAHAM, of Murrayshall). See MURRAY.

Graham (*Earl of Strathearn, Menteith, and Airth*. Earldom of Airth claimed by Mrs. BARCLAY ALLARDICE). Quarterly, 1st and 4th, or, on a chief sa. three escallops of the field; 2nd and 3rd, or, a fess chequy az. and ar. in chief a chevron gu., for STEWART, of Strathearn. *Crest*—A falcon's head ppr. *Supporters*—Two lions guard. gu. *Motto*—Rycht and reason.

Graham (Gartur, co. Stirling; descended from second son of second *Earl of Menteith*, eventually representative of the line, and now extinct). Quarterly, as the last. *Crest*—A dove rising with a twig of palm in her beak ppr. *Motto*—Peace and grace.

Graham (Gartmore, co. Stirling; bart. 1665, title extinct; claims to be heir male of the *Earls of Menteith*). Quarterly, 1st and 4th, or, a pale gu. charged with a crescent ar. on a chief sa. three escallops of the field; 2nd and 3rd, or, a fess chequy az. and ar. in chief a chevron gu. *Crest*—An eagle displ. in his dexter paw a sword in pale ppr. *Supporters*—Two lions guard. ppr. *Motto*—For right and reason.

Graham (*Viscount Preston;* peerage extinct). Quarterly, as *Earl of Menteith*, with a crescent gu. in the centre of the quarters. *Crest*—A demi lion ppr. *Supporters*—An eagle and a lion, both erm. armed gu. and crowned with ducal crowns or. *Motto*—Reason contents me.

418

Graham (Eske, co. Cumberland, bart., 1629). As the last but without the supporters.

Graham (Netherby, co. Cumberland, bart., 1783). As the last. *Crest*—A crown vallery or. *Motto*—Reason contents me.

Graham (Norton Conyers, co. York, bart., 1662). *Arms, Crest*, and *Motto*, as Eske.

Graham (Kirkstall, co. York, bart., 1808). Per pale indented erminois and sa. on a chief per pale of the last and or, three escallops counterchanged. *Crest*—Two armed arms issuing out of the battlements of a tower ppr. holding an escallop sa. *Motto*—Fideliter et diligenter.

Graham (Morphie, co. Kincardine. The present GRAHAMS, of Morphie, are paternally BARCLAYS, descended from a maternal aunt of the last of the old line). Sa. a chev. betw. three escallops ar.

Graham ("Master ROBERT GRAHAM, citizen in London and taylor to his Majestie, lineally and lawfully descended of the house and familie of MORPHIE, in the Kingdom of Scotland," 1680). Sa. on a chev. az. betw. three escallops or, a rose gu. barbed vert. *Crest*—A blade of thistle and a fig leaf ppr. in saltire. *Motto*—Hinc decus inde tegmen.

Graham (Airth, co. Stirling, 1730). Quarterly, 1st and 4th, or, on a chief sa. three escallops of the first; 2nd and 3rd, ar. a fess embattled betw. three roses gu. *Crest*—A dexter hand holding a sword in pale ppr. *Motto*—Non immemor.

Graham (Burntshields, co. Renfrew, 1854). Or, on a chief erm. three escallops of the field. *Crest*—A falcon ppr. beaked and armed, and killing a stork ar. armed gu. *Motto*—Ne oublie.

Graham (Glasgow, 1817). Or, on a chief ermines three escallops of the field. *Crest*—An eagle reguard. rising from the top of a rock all ppr. *Motto*—Souvenez.

Graham-Maxwell (Williamwood). See MAXWELL.

Graham (Meiklewood, co. Stirling). Or, on a chief embattled sa. three escallops of the field. *Crest*—A star ppr. *Motto*—Auxiliante resurgo.

Graham (Dougalstone, now GRAHAM-CAMPBELL, of Shirvan, co. Ayr). Or, a heron volant ppr. on a chief sa. three escallops of the field. *Crest*—An escallop or. *Motto*—Pignus amoris.

Graham (Newark). Or, on a chief sa. three escallops of the field, in base a boar's head erased of the second. *Crest*—A pelican's head couped ppr. *Motto*—Fides et amor.

Graham (Limekilns). Or, a buckle az. betw. three cinquefoils gu. on a chief engr. sa. three escallops of the field. *Crest*—A naked arm rising brandishing a spear both ppr. *Motto*—Pro rege.

Graham (monument in Elmley Castle Church, 1699; ELIZABETH, second wife of THOMAS, first *Earl of Coventry*, and dau. of RICHARD GRAHAM). Or, on a fess sa. three escallops of the field, a crescent gu. for diff.

Graham (granted to the co-heirs of ARTHUR GRAHAM, Esq., of Hockley Lodge, co. Armagh). Or, a bordure sa. on a chief of the second three escallop shells of the first.

Graham (Governor of Drogheda, Sir JAMES GRAHAM, Knt.; his only dau. and heiress, ELLEN, *m.* Sir ARTHUR RAWDON, second bart. of Moira; Fun. Ent. of Sir GEORGE RAWDON, first bart., *d.* 18 Aug. 1684). Ar. on a fess sa. three escallops of the field, a canton erm.

Graham (Drumgoon, co. Fermanagh, and Ballinakill, co. Galway; confirmed to ROBERT GRAHAM, of those places). Or, a rose gu. barbed and seeded ppr. on a chief sa. three escallops of the first. *Crest*—An arm embowed vested az. cuffed ar. the hand ppr. grasping a staff raguly gu. *Motto* —Ratio mihi sufficit.

Graham-Toler. See TOLER.

Graiden (Scotland). Ar. two chev. engr. gu.

Grailly (Sir JOHN DE GRAILLY, one of the Founder Knights of the Order of the Garter, Captal of Buch, a fort situate on a promontory fourteen leagues from Bordeaux, now called "La tête de Buch;" his Garter Plate remains in the Captals' Stall, third on the Sovereigns' side). Or, on a cross sa. five escallops ar. *Crest*—A man's head in profile with asses' ears ar.

Grainger (co. Essex). Gu. a pomegranate slipped and leaved or, seeded of the first.

Grainger, or Grave (London). Az. on a fesse betw. two pomegranates, stalked and leaved or, seeded gu. as many portcullises with chains of the third. *Crest*—A dexter arm couped az. purfled or, cuffed ar. hand ppr. holding by the chains gold a portcullis gu.

Grainger (co. Waterford; granted by Vanbrugh, Clarenceux, and Le Neve, Norroy, 1716, to JOHN GRAINGER, Teller of the Exchequer, son of RICHARD GRAINGER, of Waterford, and allowed by Hawkins, Ulster, 1780, to WILLIAM GRAINGER, of Liege, in Germany, grand nephew of said JOHN GRAINGER).

Az. on a fess betw. two pomegranates or, as many port-cullisses with chains gu. *Crest*—A dexter arm embowed, vested az. bezantée cuffed ar. the hand ppr. holding by the chains or, a portcullis gu.

Gramary. Gu. billettée or, a lion ramp. ar.

Grammer (Ware, co. Herts). Az. billettée ar. a lion ramp. of the second. *Crest*—A demi lion ramp. az. billettée or.

Grammer (London and co. Warwick). Gu. billettée or, a lion ramp. ar.

Gramore (co. York). Ar. three lozenges gu.

Grampound, Town of (co. Cornwall). The corporation seal represents a bridge of two arches over a river, the dexter end in perspective showing the passage over, at the sinister end a tree issuing from the base against the bridge, on the centre an escutcheon of the arms of the family of CORNWALL, viz., ar. a lion ramp. gu. within a bordure sa. bezantée.

Gramston. Paly of six ar. and az.

Granard, Earl of. See FORBES.

Grance, or Grancey. Gu. a lion ramp. ar. crowned or, within a bordure engr. of the third. *Crest*—A holly branch vert, fructed gu.

Grancester, or Grauncester. Erm. on a chief or, a lion pass. guard. gu.

Grancourt. Sa. (or gu.) semée-de-lis or.

Grancourt. Ar. a saltire gu.

Grand. Vairé or and az. a bend gu.

Grandall (co. York). Erm. a cross pattée gu.

Grandall, or Graundall. Erm. a cross engr. gu.

Granden. Ar. three chev. gu.

Grandeston (Exeter College; JOHN GRANDESTON, Bishop of Exeter 1328-69, and benefactor to the College. Visit. Oxon, 1574). Paly of six ar. and az. on a bend gu. a mitre betw. two eaglets displ. or.

Grandetoft (co. Lincoln). Sa. an eagle displ. ar.

Grandford. Gu. a lion ramp. within a bordure ar. *Crest*—A hawk perching on a fish ppr.

Grandford. Ar. two lions pass. gu. crowned of the first.

Grandford. Or, two lions pass. sa. crowned of the first.

Grandford. Ar. a saltire gu.

Grand-George, or Graundorge (Donington, co. Lincoln). Az. three ears of guinea-wheat couped and bladed or, two and one. *Crest*—A stag's head ar. gorged with a bar gemel gu. *Another Crest*—A stag's head couped per pale sa. and or, guttée counterchanged.

Grandin. Az. three mullets or.

Grandin. Az. six mullets or, three, two, and one.

Grandison (*Baron Grandison*, summoned to Parliament, 1299, and *d. s. p.*). Paly of six ar. and vert on a bend gu. three eagles displ. or.

Grandison(*Baron Grandison*, summoned to Parliament, 1299, in abeyance, 1374). Same *Arms*.

Grandison, or Grandson (co. Lancaster). Paly of six ar. and az. on a bend gu. three eagles displ. or.

Grandison (co. Lancaster). Paly of six ar. and az. on a bend gu. three escallops or.

Grandison, Grandeson, Grandson, and Granson. Paly of six ar. and az. a bend gu. *Crest*—A lady supporting a portcullis ppr.

Grandison, or Granson. Az. an eagle displ. or.

Grandison. Paly of six ar. and az. on a bend gu. three buckles (another, mullets) or.

Grandmesnill, or Grandmain. Gu. a pale or.

Grandoe. Or, a fesse betw. six crosses crosslet gu.

Grandon (co. Leicester). Ar. three chev. gu. (another adds a label vair). *Crest*—Out of a human heart a hand wielding a cutlass ppr.

Grandon (co. Warwick). Vairé ar. and sa. on a bend of the second three eagles displ. or.

Grandon. Vair on a bend gu. three eagles displ. or.

Grandon. Az. three mullets within a bordure engr. or.

Grandon. Ar. two chev. within a bordure gu.

Grandon. Az. six martlets ar. three, two, and one.

Grandorge. Az. three arrows or.

Grandvell. Sa. on a cross engr. or, five pellets, a bordure also engr. of the second. *Crest*—A greyhound's head sa. collared and ringed or.

Grane (co. York). Ar. on a fesse counter-embattled sa. betw. three pellets, on each a wolf's head erased or, a mart-let betw. two crescents of the third. *Crest*—A wolf pass. paly of four or and sa. holding in the mouth a pen of the first.

Grane. Per bend vert and gu. an eagle displ. or. *Crest*—A boar pass. sa. collared and lined ar.

Granell (France). Ar. on a chief gu. a lion ramp. of the first crowned or. *Crest*—A serpent entwined round a pheon shafted all ppr.

419

Grange (Bulbeck, co. Cambridge, and Swaffham, co. Norfolk) Per saltire or and sa. four griffins' heads erased counter-changed. *Crest*—A demi antelope or, attired, maned, armed and hoofed sa.

Grange (co. Warwick). Same *Arms*, a bordure az.

Grange (London). Gu. a pomegranate or. *Crest*—A lion's gamb erect and erased ppr. holding a bunch of pomegra-nates or.

Grange (Wolsingham, co. Chester, Bishops Auckland, co. Durham, and London; JOHN GRANGE, of the latter. Visit. 1568). Az. a chev. betw. three lions ramp. or, on a chief of the last as many escallops gu. a border compony of the second and last. *Crest*—A griffin's head erased sa. beaked and eared or, charged with three bezants.

Granger. Gu. a pomegranate in pale slipped or. *Crest*—A dexter arm couped and embowed, holding three ears of wheat all ppr.

Granger. Or, a crescent betw. two mullets in pale sa.

Granger (Tettenhall Regis, co. Stafford, as depicted on a deed, *temp.* Charles I.). Sa. a chev. erm. betw. three griffins ar. *Crest*—A griffin ar. *Motto*—Honestas optima politia.

Granlesse, or Grantz (Wales). Or, a lion ramp. sa. guttée d'eau.

Grannson (Exeter). Paly of six ar. and az. on a bend gu. three escallops or.

Granson (Chelsfield, co. Kent; Sir THOMAS DE GRANSON, descended from OTHO DE GRANSON, Lord of the fort and territory of Granson, in Burgundy, attended the *Duke of Lancaster* on his expedition to Calais, 1369, and was elected a Knight of the Garter same year). Paly of six ar. and az. on a bend gu. three eagles displ. or. *Crest*—Out of a ducal coronet gu. a plume of feathers ar.

Gransum. Paly of six ar. and az. on a bend gu. three round buckles or.

Grant (that Ilk and Freuchie; *s.* 1811, through maternal descent, to the earldom of *Seafield*, see OGILVIE). Gu. three antique or eastern crowns or. *Crest*—A burning hill ppr. *Supporters*—Two savages ppr. *Motto*—Stand fast. The hill of the crest is Craigeleachie (opposite Rothiemurchus), and the fire was lighted to call the whole clan together in Strathspey, the seat of the GRANTS in Morayshire. When drawn up in battle, the motto of the chief was "Stand fast," and the inferior chieftains re-echoed it to their troops, as "Stand firm," "Stand sure," &c.

Grant (Clarie, and Leaston). Gu. a lion pass. guard. ar. im-perially crowned ppr. betw. three antique crowns or. *Crest*—A boar's head couped ppr. *Motto*—Stabit conscius æqui.

Grant (Lurg). Gu. a lion ramp. or, in his dexter forepaw a crescent ar. betw. three antique crowns of the second. *Crest*—A hill, on the top of which is a forest all ppr. *Motto*—Stabilis.

Grant (Easter Elchies, co. Banff). Gu. a lion ramp. betw. three antique crowns or. *Crest*—A unicorn's head and neck ar. *Supporters*—Two griffins ppr. beaked and membered gu. collared and chained or. *Motto*—Audentior ito.

Grant (Rothiemurchus, co. Elgin). Quarterly, 1st and 4th, gu. three antique crowns or; 2nd, or, a fess chequy az. and ar. betw. three wolves' heads couped sa., for STEWART, of Athole; 3rd, az. a dexter hand vambraced holding a sword erected in pale az. hilted and pommelled or, betw. three boars' heads couped of the third, for GORDON, all within a bordure wavy or. *Crest*—A dexter hand and arm armed, holding a broad-sword ppr. *Mottoes*—Pro patria; and, In God is all my trust.

Grant (Ballindalloch, co. Elgin; later family, a branch of Rothiemurchus). Gu. a target ppr. betw. three antique crowns or. *Crest*—A dexter hand grasping a dirk ppr. *Motto*—Ense et animo.

Grant (MACPHERSON-GRANT, of Invereshie and Ballindalloch, bart., 1838). Quarterly, 1st and 4th, as the last; 2nd and 3rd, per fess or and az. a lymphad of the first, mast, oars, and tacklings ppr. ensigned gu. betw. a hand couped fessways, holding a dagger in pale in the dexter canton, and in the sinister a cross crosslet fitchée, a bordure gu., for MACPHER-SON. *Crest*—A dexter hand holding a dirk in pale. *Mottoes*—Above the crest: Ense et animo; and below the shield: Touch not the cat, but a glove.

Grant (Monymusk, co. Aberdeen, bart., 1705). Gu. three antique crowns within a bordure erm. *Crest*—A Bible displ. ppr. *Supporters*—Two angels ppr. *Mottoes*—Above the crest: Suum cuique; below the arms: Jehovah Jireh.

Grant (Prestongrange, co. Haddington; represented by Sir GEORGE GRANT-SUTTIE, Bart., and DUNDAS, of Arniston, as heirs of line. See GRANT-SUTTIE). Gu. three antique crowns or, within a bordure erm. on a canton ar. a demi otter issuing out of a bar waved sa. *Crest*—A Hercules' head ppr. *Motto*—Non inferiora secutus.

Grant (Corrimony, co. Inverness). Gu. three antique crowns or, within a bordure chequy of the second and first.—*Crest*—A demi savage ppr. *Motto*—I'll stand sure.

Grant (Shewglie and Redcastle). Gu. on a fess ar. betw. three antique crowns or, a lion pass. guard. of the first, imperially crowned ppr. *Crest*—A banyan tree ppr. *Motto*—Revirescimus.

Grant (*Baron Glenelg*). Gu. on a fesse betw. three antique crowns or, a lion pass. guard. of the field, imperially crowned ppr. betw. two cinquefoils also of the first. *Crests*—1st: A burning mount ppr.; 2nd: A banyan tree also ppr. *Supporters*—Dexter, a tiger; sinister, a stag, both ppr. the latter gorged with an eastern crown or. *Motto*—Stand fast.

Grant (Sir PATRICK GRANT, G.C.B., 1861). Gu. three antique crowns or, a bordure of the second charged with three wreaths of laurel vert. *Crest*—A burning mountain ppr. *Motto*—Stand fast.

Grant (Gartinbeg, 1672). Gu. three antique crowns or, a bordure engr. of the second. *Crest*—The trunk of an oak-tree sprouting out some leaves with the sun shining thereon ppr. *Motto*—Te favente virebo.

Grant (Dalvey, co. Elgin, bart., 1688). *Arms, Crest,* and *Motto,* as the last. *Supporters*—Dexter, a Highlander; sinister, a negro, both ppr.

Grant (Sir MAXWELL GRANT, K.C.B., 1816). Gu. three antique crowns within a bordure engr. ar. pendent from middle chief a representation of the cross conferred on him for his conduct in the Peninsula, the Pyrenees, Nivelle, the Nive, and Orthes, on a chief embattled ar. a tower of the first betw. a sword, hilt upwards, encircled with a garland of laurel all ppr. on the dexter, and on the sinister, the badge of the Ottoman order of the Crescent pendent by a ribbon all ppr. *Crest*—The stump of an oak tree sprouting forth fresh branches, the sun looking down thereon ppr. *Mottoes*—Above the crest: Te favente virebo; below the shield: Valour and loyalty.

Grant (Glenlochy, afterwards Kilgraston, co. Perth). Gu. a chev. erm. betw. three antique crowns or. *Crest*—A mountain in flames ppr. *Motto*—Ferte cito flammas.

Grant (Sir JAMES HOPE GRANT, G.C.B., 1861). As the last, within a bordure embattled or. Same *Crest* and *Motto*. *Also additional Crest*—A Roman fasces erect ppr., and *Motto* —Leges juraque serva.

Grant (Carron, co. Banff), Gu. a dove ar. holding in her beak an olive branch vert betw. three antique crowns or. *Crest*—An adder nowed, with the head erect ppr. *Motto*—Wise and harmless.

Grant (Ballindalloch, 1672). Gu. a boar's head couped betw. three antique crowns or. *Crest*—An oak tree ppr. *Motto*—Suo se robore firmat.

Grant (Wester Elchies, co. Banff, 1811). *Arms, Crest,* and *Motto,* as the last.

Grant (Dunlugas, co. Banff). The same, within a bordure or. *Crest*—A dexter hand, holding a branch of oak ppr. *Motto* —Radicem firmant frondes.

Grant (Auchernack, co. Aberdeen). Gu. a star of seven points wavy ar. betw. three antique crowns or. *Crest*—A burning hill ppr. *Motto*—Stand sure.

Grant (LEWIS GRANT, Adjutant of Chelsea College, 1780). Gu. a cross pattée fitchée ar. betw. three antique crowns or, a bordure invecked of the second. *Crest*—A two-handed sword in bend ppr. hilted and pommelled or, over a man's head of the first. *Motto*—Have at you.

Grant (Sir WILLIAM KEIR-GRANT, of Blackburn, Knt. of the Imperial Order of Maria Teresa, in Germany, 1794). Quarterly, 1st and 4th, gu. a cinquefoil ar. betw. three antique crowns or; 2nd, or, on a cross engr. sa. cantoned with four roses gu. three lozenges or, for KEIR; 3rd, ar. a saltire and chief gu. with a mullet in dexter chief, a bordure indented of the second, for BRUCE, of Wester Kinloch; en surtout, a medal or, charged with a profile of Francis II., Emperor of Germany, with legend, "Imp. Cæs. Franciscus II.; P. F. Aug." *Crest*—An arm in armour embowed grasping a sword all ppr. *Motto*—Fortitudine.

Gant (Aberlour, co. Banff, 1810). Gu. three antique crowns or, in fess point a dexter arm in armour fessways couped ppr. garnished or, holding a cross crosslet fitchée of the last. *Crest*—A burning mountain ppr. *Motto*—Stabit.

Grant (Litchborough). Gu. a fesse dancettée erm. betw. three crowns or. *Crest*—A conical hill fired at the summit ppr. issuant therefrom a cross calvary or. *Motto*—Stand sure.

Grant (Hillersdown House, co. Down). Gu. a boar's head couped in fesse betw. three eastern crowns or. *Crest*—An oak tree fructed ppr. *Motto*—Suo se robore firmat.

Grantbridge. Ar. a bordure sa. on a canton gu. a fleur-de-lis of the field.

Grantham (Goltho, co. Lincoln; JOHN GRANTHAM, Lord Mayor of London, 1328). Erm. a griffin segreant gu. *Crest* —A demi griffin ramp. gu. *Motto*—Honore et amore.

Grantham (Dunham, co. Lincoln). Erm. a griffin segreant coward gu. beaked and legged az. *Crest*—A Moor's head couped at the shoulders ppr. crined or.

Grantham (Sunbury, co. Middlesex; granted 27 July, 1711). Per pale erm. and ar. on the first a griffin ramp. gu. beaked and membered az. on the second upon a mount three pine trees all ppr. over all a chief of the fourth charged with as many crescents or. *Crest*—A mercurial cap placed above a scymitar, the edge downwards, and a caduceus saltireways, thereon a Turk's head full faced erased at the shoulders, ensigned with a turban all ppr.

Grantham. Sa. a fesse erm. in chief two covered cups ar.

Grantham, Town of (co. Lincoln). Chequy or and az. within a bordure sa. charged with eight trefoils slipped ar.

Grantham (Scotland). Gu. a target betw. three antique crowns or. *Crest*—A man's hand erect couped below the wrist, holding a dagger all ppr.

Grantley, Lord. See NORTON.

Grantmesnil, or Grantmains (Lord of Hinckley, temp. William the Conqueror, left five daus. co-heiresses). Gu. a pale or.

Granville, Earl of. See GOWER.

Granville, Earl of. See CARTERET.

Granville (Bideford, co. Devon, and Stow, co. Cornwall). Gu. three sufflues or organ rests or. *Crest*—On a cap of maintenance gu. turned up erm. a griffin or.

Granville (*Earl of Bath;* created 1661, extinct 1711). Same *Arms* and *Crest.* *Supporters*—Two griffins or.

Granville (*Lord Lanadownè;* created 1712, extinct 1734). Same *Arms, Crest,* and *Supporters. Motto*—Deo, patriæ, amicis.

Granville (Calwich Abbey, co. Stafford). Quarterly, 1st and 4th, gu. three sufflues or organ rests or, for GRANVILLE; 2nd and 3rd, or, three quatrefoils pierced gu. a chief vert. *Crest*—On a cap of maintenance gu. turned up erm. a griffin pass. or. *Motto*—Deo, patriæ, amicis.

Granville. Vert on a cross ar. five pellets. *Crest*—On a mural crown ar. a serpent nowed vert.

Grape (New Windsor, co. Berks; granted 1764). Vert talbot pass. in base or, in chief two pheons of the last. *Crest* —A stag erminois, collared gu. grazing on a mount vert.

Gras, or Grasse. Az. a fesse betw. three lions ramp. ar.

Grasay, or Grassey. Az. a lion ramp. or.

Grase (co. Devon). Erm. a fesse betw. three cinquefoils gu. *Crest*—An arm in armour embowed, holding a dagger ppr.

Grassall, or Grassell. Ar. a bend componée gu. and az. *Crest*—An arm in armour embowed, holding a dagger ppr.

Grasse. Az. three lions ramp. or, a chief ar.

Grasse (co. Suffolk). Az. five billets barways conjoined in fesse, three and two, gu. betw. three escallops or.

Grassell. Ar. a bend gobonated gu. and az.

Grassell. Gu. two bars engr. ar. (another, field sa. bars or).

Grattan. Quarterly, or and gu. a bordure az. *Crest*—A dove holding in the dexter claw a sceptre, and standing on a barrel all ppr.

Grattan (granted by Camden, Clarenceux, Feb. 1603). Gyronny of eight erm. and sa. a lion ramp. or. *Crest*—On a tun or, a falcon ar. wings elevated, holding in the dexter claw a sceptre gold.

Grattan (Enniskillen, co. Fermanagh; confirmed by Hawkins, Ulster, to Rev. CHARLES GRATTAN, Master of Portora School, fourth son of PATRICK GRATTAN, Senior Fellow, Trin. Coll., Dublin). Quarterly, 1st and 4th, per saltire erm. and sa. a lion ramp. or, for GRATTAN; 2nd and 3rd, ar. two bars sa., for BRERETON. *Crest*—On a tun or, a dove, wings elevated, holding in the dexter claw a sceptre all ppr.

Grattan (Tinnehinch, co. Wicklow; as borne by the Rt. Hon. HENRY GRATTAN, M.P.). Same *Arms* and *Crest. Motto*—Pro patriâ vivere et mori.

Grattan-Bellew. See BELLEW.

Gratton. Gu. a pale per saltire az. and or. *Crest*—On a human heart ppr. an eagle's leg.

Gratwich, or Grotwick. Or, a chev. engr. gu. betw. three pellets.

Gratwick (Ham, co. Surrey). Ar. a chev. betw. three hurts, each charged with a fret of the field.

Gratwick, or Grotwick (Forkington, co. Sussex). Or, three hurts, each charged with a fret of the field. *Crest*—An ostrich's head or, in the beak a horseshoe ar.

Graunge. Az. a chev. betw. three lions ramp. or, on a chief of the second three escallops gu. a bordure gobonated or and gu.

Graunsell (Reg. Ulster's Office). Ar. a saltire gu. a chief of the last, in the dexter chief a pheon point down of the first.

Graunt (Reg. Ulster's Office). Gu. a vine tree fructed ar. over all a bend erm.

Graunt (quartered by Sir THOMAS MONKE, Knt., of Potheridge, father of GEORGE, Duke of Albemarle; ELIZABETH, dau. and co-heir of WILLIAM GRAUNT, m. JOHN LE MONKE, living 17 Edward IV., 1487. Visit. Devon, 1620). Gu. on a fess betw. three crosses crosslet fitchée ar. a lion pass. az.

Graunte (Northbrokes, cō. Warwick. Har. MS. 6060). Erm. on a chev. gu. five bezants.

Gravatt (Her. Off. London). Az. a fesse embattled erm. (another, pean) betw. three wolves' heads eraśed ar. Crest—A wolf pass. per pale erminois and ar.

Grave (Hatfield, co. Berks; granted 17 Feb. 1773). Ar. a fesse az. betw. three escutcheons sa. each charged with a lion ramp. of the field. Crest—Within an annulet az. a like escutcheon, as in the arms.

Grave (Thanks, co. Cornwall, Westfirle, co. Sussex, and Heyton, co. York). Gu. an eagle displ. or, beaked, membered, and ducally crowned ar. Crest—A demi eagle erased or, beaked gu. environed round the body with a ducal coronet ar.

Grave (Reg. Ulster's Office). Gu. a lion ramp. ar.

Grave (Penrith, co. Cumberland). Gu. an eagle displ. ducally gorged or. Crest—Within a ducal coronet a demi eagle or.

Grave (London and York; granted 12 June, 1591). Gu. an eagle ar. wings expanded, ducally gorged or. Crest—A demi eagle erased or, beaked gu. environed with a ducal coronet ar.

Grave. Gu. a demi lion ramp. ar. crowned or.

Grave, or Grane. Per bend gu. and vert (another, vert and gu.) an eagle displ. or.

Grave (Ireland). Ar. on a fesse batelly counter-batelly sa. betw. three pellets, each charged with a talbot's head erased of the field, a martlet betw. two escallops or. Crest—A cock sa. combed and wattled gu.

Graveley (Graveley, co. Herts). Sa. a cross pointed ar. in the dexter chief point a mullet of the last.

Gravell, or Gravill. Gu. three buckles or. Crest—Out of a ducal coronet or, a demi eagle displ. or.

Gravene. Ar. a fesse componée or and gu. betw. three crosslets fitchée of the last.

Graves (Baron Graves). Gu. an eagle displ. or, ducally crowned ar. on a canton of the last an anchor ppr. Crest—A demi eagle displ. and erased or, encircled round the body and below the wings by a ducal coronet ar. Supporters—Two royal vultures, wings close ppr. Motto—Aquila non captat muscas.

Graves-Sawle, Bart. See SAWLE.

Graves (Mickleton and Poden in Church Honeybourne, co. Gloucester). Gu. an eagle displ. or, beaked, membered, and ducally crowned ar. betw. eight crosses crosslet of the second. Crest—A demi eagle erased or, environed with a ducal coronet gu. holding in the beak a cross crosslet fitchée of the last. Motto—Superna quærite. Other Mottoes (used at various times by the family)—Esse quam videri; Gravis dum suavis; and, Graves disce mores.

Graves (co. Salop). Or, a trefoil slipped vert.

Graves. Ar. a fesse ermines betw. three lions' heads erased sa. Crest—A squirrel sejant ermines.

Graves (confirmed to Very Rev. CHARLES GRAVES, D.D., Dean of the Chapel Royal, S.F.T.C.D., consecrated Bishop of Limerick, 1866, son of JOHN CROSBIE GRAVES, Esq., of Dublin, Barrister-at-law, by HELENA, his wife, eldest dau. and co-heiress of Rev. CHARLES PERCEVAL, Rector of Churchtown, co. Cork, and grandson of Very Rev. THOMAS RYDER GRAVES, Dean of Connor). Quarterly, 1st and 4th, per pale gu. and az. an eagle displ. ducally crowned or, in the dexter chief point a cross patonce of the last, for GRAVES; 2nd and 3rd, ar. on a chief indented gu. three crosses pattée of the field, a crescent for diff., for PERCEVAL (this quartering confirmed to the descendants of his father, JOHN CROSBIE GRAVES, Esq., only). Crest—A demi eagle displ. and erased or, encircled round the body below the wings with a ducal coronet gu. each wing charged with a cross patonce also gu. Motto—Aquila non captat muscas.

Graveshend (co. Kent). Or, three eagles displ. erm. a canton of the second.

Graveshend, or Gravesend (co. Kent). Erm. on a bend sa. three martlets or. Crest—A lion's gamb gu. charged with a bezant, and holding up a cross pattée fitchée or.

421

Gravett (Carrickfergus, co. Antrim; certified, 1719, by Hawkins, Ulster, to RICHARD GRAVETT, High Sheriff of Bristol, descended from JOHN GRAVETT, who served against the Earl of Clanricarde, 18 Queen Elizabeth, 1575). Ar. a leopard's face betw. two swords erect gu. Crest—An arm armed gu. the hand naked, holding a sword ppr. Motto—Per varios casus.

Gray (Baron Gray). Gu. a lion ramp. within a bordure engr. ar. Crest—An anchor (sans cable) in pale or. Supporters—Two lions guard. gu. Motto—Anchor, fast anchor.

Gray (Ballegarno, co. Perth). Gu. a lion ramp. ar. in his dexter paw an anchor or, a bordure engr. of the second. Motto—Anchor fast.

Gray (Warriestoun, 1672). Gu. a lion ramp. ar. in his dexter paw a stalk of wheat ppr. Crest—A lily slipped, seeded, and bladed ppr. Motto—Viget in cinere virtus.

Gray (Edinburgh, 1680, cadet of Schivas, co. Aberdeen). Gu. a lion ramp. ar. holding betw. his paws an anchor az. environed with an adder ppr. Motto—Secura quæ prudentes.

Gray (Haystoun, 1672). Gu. a lion ramp. ar. holding in his dexter paw a writing pen ppr. Crest—A fox reguard. ppr. Motto—Concussus surgo.

Gray (Dr. GEORGE GRAY, Calcutta, 1749). Same Arms, Crest, and Motto.

Gray (Carse, co. Forfar). Gu. a lion ramp. within a bordure wavy ar. Crest—An anchor fessways fastened to a cable ppr. Motto—Anchor fast.

Gray (Carntyne, formerly of Dalmarnock, co. Lanark; now represented by Mrs. ANSTRUTHER THOMSON, of Charlton, as heir of line). Gu. a lion ramp. betw. three cinquefoils ar. all within a bordure engr. of the last. Crest—An anchor cabled, stuck fast in the sea all ppr. Motto—Fast.

Gray (WILLIAM GRAY, Dingwall, Pursuivant, 1726). Gu. a lion ramp. ar. within a bordure engr. of the last, charged with eight thistles ppr. Crest—A heart ppr. Motto—Constant.

Gray (FRANCIS DELAVAL GRAY, Esq., 14th Light Dragoons, son and heir of the late JOHN GRAY, Esq., of Hartsheath Park, co. Flint, and, maternally, a descendant of the ancient family of DELAVAL). Quarterly, 1st and 4th, gu. within a bordure engr. a lion ramp. ar.; 2nd and 3rd, quarterly, 1st and 4th, erm. two bars vert; 2nd and 3rd, ar. a fesse az betw. an eagle displ. with two heads in chief and a lion ramp. in base sa. Crest—Out of a mural crown a phœnix in flames ppr. Mottoes—Over the crest : Clarior e tenebris; under the arms : Vixi liber et moriar.

Gray (WILLIAM GRAY, Esq., of York). Barry of six ar. and az. on a bend gu. three roses of the first. Crest—On a chapeau a wivern gu.

Gray (Bishopwearmouth, co. Durham). Vert a lion ramp. within a bordure engr. ar. Crest—An anchor erect or, the rope waved ppr. Motto—Anchor, fast anchor.

Gray (Dowland, co. Essex; granted 1634). Gu. a lion ramp. or, within a bordure engr. erm. a canton of the last. Crest—A ram's head couped ar.

Gray (co. Essex). Ar. a bend vert cotised indented gu.

Gray (co. Essex). Barry of six ar. and az. a bend gu.

Gray (Exeter). Or, on a bend az. three mullets of the first.

Gray (London; granted April, 1635). Barry of six ar. and az. on a bend gu. three chaplets or.

Gray (Gray's Inn, co. Middlesex). Gu. a lion ramp. ar. a bordure gobonated of the last and sa. bezantée.

Gray (Newcastle-upon-Tyne). Same Arms. Crest—On a ducal coronet or, a phœnix in flames ppr.

Gray (Martin and Tarbrook, co. Norfolk. Visit. 1634). Az. a fesse betw. two chev. or.

Gray (Ouchester). Ar. a lion ramp. gu. Crest—A scaling ladder of two rows, ensigned with a ram's head couped all ppr. Motto—De bon vouloir servir le Roy.

Gray. Barry of six ar. and az. in chief three torteaux depressed with a label of as many points erm. Crest—In a sun or, a unicorn pass. erm.

Gray (Farley Hill Place, co. Berks, and Crompton Fold, co. Lancaster). Az. a lion ramp. within an orle of annulets ar. a bordure indented erm. Crest—Upon a rock ppr. a bear's paw erect and erased sa. grasping a snake entwined around it also ppr. Motto—Tenebo.

Gray (East Bolton, co. Northumberland). Gu. in an orle of eight fleurs-de-lis a lion ramp. ar. the whole within a bordure engr. erm. Crest—A bear's paw grasping a snake.

Gray. Ar. a bend vert cotised gu.

Gray. Ar. three bars az. on a bend gu. as many leopards' faces or.

Gray. Barry of six ar. and az. on a bend gu. three escallops (another, fleurs-de-lis) or.

Gray (Charleville House, Rathmines, co. Dublin; granted to Sir JOHN GRAY, Knt., M.D., Chairman of the Waterworks

Committee, Dublin Corporation). Ar. an anchor erect sa. entwined by a ribbon az. with the word "Vartry" inscribed thereon in letters of gold (commemorative of the zeal and ability evinced by Sir John as Chairman of the [Vartry] Waterworks Committee of the Dublin Corporation), on a canton of the third a castle of the first flammant ppr. (as in the arms of the City of Dublin). *Crest*—An anchor erect sa. entwined, as in the arms, with a ribbon az. with the word "Vartry" inscribed thereon in letters of gold. *Motto* —Anchor, fast anchor.

Gray (granted, 1813, to James Gray, Esq., of Ballincor, King's co., son of Francis Gray, Esq., of Lehana, co. Cork). Ar. three closets az. in chief as many annulets gu. *Crest*— A demi lion ramp. or, holding in his mouth an annulet, as in the arms. *Motto*—Præstare et prodesse.

Gray-Archdall. See Archdall.

Graybow. Ar. a bend gu.

Graydon. Az. a cross betw. four mullets ar. *Crest*—Two lions' paws erect supporting an escutcheon.

Graydor, or Grayndor. Or, a fesse betw. six crosses crosslet gu.

Graye (Maldon, co. Essex). Ar. on a chev. betw. three storks' heads erased gu. as many roses of the field.

Grayhurst. Az. on a pale ar. three crescents gu. *Crest*— A dove az. in the beak an olive branch vert.

Grayne. Per bend gu. and vert an eagle displ. or.

Graynsly, or Gransby. Gu. a fesse dancettée betw. six crosses crosslet or.

Graytowyers. Erm. on a chev. betw. three squirrels gu. each with a nut branch fructed or, as many roses ar.

Grazebrook, or Greysbrook. Ar. an eagle displ. gu. beaked or, on a chief sa. three bezants, each charged with a fleur-de-lis az. *Crest*—A bear's head or, muzzled sa. charged on the neck with three fleurs-de-lis fesseways az.

Grazebrook (Audnam, near Stourbridge, Stourton Castle, co. Stafford, and Dallicott, co. Salop; borne by Michael Phillips Grazebrook, Esq., formerly of Audnam, but now of Hagley, co. Worcester, eldest son of the late Michael Grazebrook, Esq., J.P., D.L., of Audnam, who succeeded to the male representation of the family on the death *s.p.* of his cousin, the late Thomas Worrall Smith Grazebrook, Esq., of Dallicott House and Stourton, only son of Thomas Worrall Grazebrook, Esq., of Stourton Castle. This family is descended immediately from Michael Grasebrooke, or Greysbrooke, who settled at Stourbridge about the year 1640, younger son of John Greysbrooke, of Middleton, co. Warwick, who *d.* in 1636, by Mary, his wife, dau. of William Colmore, Esq., of Birmingham). Quarterly, 1st and 4th, ar. an eagle displ. gu. armed or, on a chief sa. three bezants, each charged with a fleur-de-lis az.; 2nd and 2rd, ar. three coneys gu., for Greysbrooke (ancient), quartering Worrall, Needs, &c. *Crest*—A bear's head or, muzzled sa. charged on the neck with three fleurs-de-lis in fesse az. *Mottoes*— Nec sinit case feros; and, Bear and forbear. See Greysbrooke.

Greame (Sewerby House, co. York). Or, on a chief sa. three escallops of the field. *Crest*—Two wings endorsed or.

Greame (Ireland, Fun. Ent. of Sir George Greame, Knt., of Castle Warning, *d.* 23 Dec. 1619). Same *Arms*, a crescent ar. on a martlet gu. for diff.

Greames (Lynnstown, Queen's co. Fun. Ent. of Sir Richard Greames, Knt., *d.* 7 Nov. 1626). Same *Arms*.

Greanhall. Ar. on a bend engr. sa. three buglehorns stringed of the first.

Great Grimsby, Town of (co. Lincoln). Ar. a chev. betw. three boars' heads couped sa.

Greathead. Erm. a martlet gu. *Crest*—On a chapeau gu. turned up erm. a martlet, wings endorsed sa.

Greatheed (Guy's Cliff House, co. Warwick). Az. on a saltire betw. four fleurs-de-lis or, a torteau, quartering the ensigns of Bertie. *Crest*—A fleur-de-lis or, upon a mount vert.

Greatheed (exemplified, 1826, to the Hon. Charles Percy, on his assuming, by royal licence, the names of Greatheed and Bertie, under the will of Bertie Bertie Greatheed, Esq., of Guy's Cliff). Az. on a saltire or, fimbriated ar. betw. four fleurs-de-lis of the second a torteau. Quartering for Bertie, ar. three battering rams barways in pale ppr. armed and garnished az. The said coats charged for distinction in the centre point with a fusil gu. *Crests*—1st, Greatheed: On a mount vert a fleur-de-lis or, the top of each leaf surmounted by a torteau, and the centre one charged for distinction with a fusil gu.; 2nd, Bertie: The bust of a man couped and affrontée ppr. ducally crowned or, the breast charged for distinction with a fusil or.

Greatrakes (Affane, co. Waterford. Fun. Ent. of the celebrated Valentine Greatrakes, of the reign of Charles II.,

d. at Affane, 28 Nov. 1613, buried in Lismore Church). Per pale sa. and gu. three leopards' heads erased or, pellettée, langued az.

Greaves (Greaves, *temp.* Henry III., Beeley and Stanton, co. Derby, and Mayfield, co. Stafford). Per bend vert and gu. an eagle displ. or, armed and langued of the second, quartering Allen, Ley, Newton, and Harthill. *Crests*— 1st: A demi eagle displ. or, winged and langued gu., for Greaves; 2nd: A king of the Moors armed in mail, crowned or, kneeling on his left knee and delivering up his sword, for Newton. *Mottoes*—Aquila non captat muscas; Superna quæro; and, Huic habeo, non tibi.

Greaves (Irlam Hall, co. Lancaster). Quarterly, 1st and 4th, per saltire vert and gu. an eagle displ. or, holding in the beak a cross crosslet fitchée ar., for Greaves, 2nd and 3rd, erm. two bars engr. one az. the other gu. in chief three roses of the last, on a canton of the same a lion pass. or, for Lancashire. *Crest*—Out of battlements ppr. a demi eagle displ. or, wings gu. the breast charged with a red rose, in the beak a cross crosslet fitchee ar. *Motto*—Spes mea in Deo.

Greaves (Kent, and St. Leonard's Forest, co. Sussex). Gu. an eagle displ. or, crowned ar. *Crest*, as Greaves, of Greaves.

Greaves. Ar. on a fesse gu. betw. three fetterlocks az. a mullet or. *Crest*—A dexter arm embowed in armour, thrusting a dagger ppr.

Greaves-Banning. Quarterly, 1st and 4th, per pale ar. and sa. two bars, both charged with as many roundels, on each an escallop all countercharged, for Banning; 2nd and 3rd, per saltire vert and gu. an eagle displ. or, in the beak a cross crosslet fitchée ar., and for distinction, a cross crosslet or, for Greaves. *Crests*—1st, Banning: Upon a key fesseways, wards downwards or, an ostrich ar. on the breast an escallop sa.; 2nd, Greaves: Out of battlements ppr. a demi eagle displ. or, wings gu. in the beak a cross crosslet fitchée ar. and on the breast a rose gu. the battlements charged (for distinction) with a cross crosslet also gu. *Motto*—A Deo non fortuna.

Greaves-Bagshawe. See Bagshawe.

Greaves (Page Hall, and Elmsall Lodge, co. York). Quarterly, 1st, quarterly, gu. and vert an eagle displ. in the beak a slip of oak fructed or, for Greaves; 2nd, ar. on a fesse gu. betw. three pellets as many bustards or, within a bordure engr. az., for Bustard; 3rd, ar. a chev. engr. betw. three trefoils slipped sa., for Clay; 4th, sa. three bars engr. betw. ten elm leaves erect or, for Elmsall. *Crest*—On a mount vert a stag trippant or, in the mouth a slip of oak ppr. *Motto*—Deo non fortunâ.

Greaves (Kingsnorton, co. Worcester). Or, a mullet gu. on a chief sa. three escallops of the first.

Greaves, Greves, or Grevis (Mosley Hall, co. Worcester; Sir Richard Greves, Knt., of Mosley, High Sheriff of Worcester 8 James I., 1609. Visit. 1634). Ar. on a fesse az. betw three pellets, each charged with a lion's head erased of the field a griffin pass. betw. two escallops or. *Crest*—An eagle with two heads displ. sa. beaked and membered or (another, a squirrel holding betw. the paws an escallop or).

Greaves (The Cliff, co. Warwick). Same *Arms* and *Crest*.

Grebell (Canterbury). Sa. a cross engr. within a bordure or, *Crest*—A greyhound's head erased at the neck ar. pellettée, collared and ringed or.

Greby (co. Northampton). Erm. two flaunches az. each charged with three ears of wheat couped or. *Crest*—A demi eagle holding in the dexter claw a branch of laurel vert.

Greby. Ar. a fesse sa. on a canton of the second a mullet of the first.

Greby, or Greyby. Erm. two flaunches az. each charged with three arrows or.

Greby, or Greyby. Ar. six lions ramp. gu. three, two, and one.

Grechanton, and Grechmerton. Ar. a fesse sa. in chief three crosses pattée gu.

Gredon (Gredon, co. Berwick). Or, on a fesse sa. betw. three bears' heads gu. as many escallops of the first.

Greeke (granted by Camden, Clarenceux, to Thomas Greeke, Baron of the Exchequer, 1576). Or, a trefoil slipped betw. two chevronels sa. *Crest*—The trunk of a tree eradicated and sprouting branches ppr. pendent from the trunk a circular shield or, thereon a sun az.

Greeke (London, 1611). Or, a trefoil slipped betw. two chev. sa. *Crest*—A trunk of a tree couped at the top and erased at the root ppr. towards the top two branches vert, thereon hung on a belt gu. a Grecian target or, embellished with a star az.

Greek School (Cambridge). Per chev. ar. and sa. in chief the Greek letters A Ω; in base a grasshopper of the first, on a chief gu. a lion pass. guard. or, charged on the side with the letter G of the second.

Green (Marass, co. Kent, bart., extinct 1825). Per chev. vert and ar. in chief two castles of the second, in base another, surrounded by a fortification ppr. over all a chev. or, charged with three torteaux. *Crest*—Out of a mural .rown gu. a horse's head ar. maned or.

Green (Milnrow, co. York, bart., extinct 1831). Or, three leopards pass. ppr. on a chief sa. a demi griffin segreant betw. two cinquefoils erm. holding a key also ppr. *Crest*—A griffin's head erased sa. langued gu. doubly collared or, betw. the collars a cinquefoil, as in the arms, holding in the beak a key or. *Motto*—Æquam servare mentem.

Green (Sampford, co. Essex, bart., extinct 1676). Per fess sa. and ar. a lion ramp. counterchanged.

Green (Leventhorp, co. York; granted as a 'quartering to CHARLES CHADWICK, of Healey Hall). Ar. on a bend vert three fleurs-de-lis or.

Green (ARAUNAH GREEN, Esq., of Chiddingly, co. Sussex, who, upon his marriage, changed his patronymic, VERRAL, for the name of GREEN). Quarterly, 1st and 4th, vert three stags trippant, two and one, betw. two crosses crosslet in chief and one in base or, for GREEN; 2nd and 3rd, gu. a fesse company or and az. betw. three mullets, two in chief and one in base ar., for VERRAL *Crests*—1st, GREEN: In front of a spear erect ppr. therefrom pendent a buglehorn sa. stringed gu. a stag statant or; 2nd, VERRAL: A mount vert, thereon an antelope erm. horned or, the dexter forefoot resting on a hurt charged with a cross crosslet gu.

Green-Price, Bart. See PRICE.

Green (Poulton Hall, co. Chester). Az. three bucks trippant erminois, on a chief or, three crescents sa. *Crest*—A demi buck springing per fesse or and az. charged with two crescents counterchanged.

Green (JOHN GEORGE GREEN, Esq., of Buckden, grandnephew of the late Dr. JOHN GREEN, Bishop of Lincoln, descended from an old and respectable Yorkshire family). Az. three stags trippant or.

Green. Ar. on a fesse wavy gu. betw. two torteaux in chief, each charged with a bull's head couped of the field, and in base a ship in full sail ppr. a griffin pass. betw. two escallops or. *Crest*—On a mount vert a squirrel sejant ppr. holding an escallop az.

Green (Abingdon, co. Berks, and London). Az. a pheon betw. three bucks trippant or. *Crest*—A stag's head erased and attired or, charged on the neck with a pheon sa. underneath which are three guttées de sang.

Green (Great Kingshill, co. Buckingham; granted 13 Dec. 1768). Az. a chev. engr. ar. guttée de sang timbriated or, in base an estoile of the second, on a chief embattled gold, two leopards' heads vert, *Crest*—Out of a mural crown ar. a demi lion ramp. purp. in the dexter paw a slip of laurel vert.

Green (Boys' Hall, co. Essex, and co. Oxford; confirmed by Camden). Az. three bucks trippant (another, courant) or.

Green (Bristol, and Barnet, co. Herts). Az. three bucks trippant or, a crescent for diff. *Crest*—A buck's head erased erm. attired or.

Green (Samford, co. Essex). Gu. a lion ramp. ar. crowned or, a bordure engr. of the third.

Green (co. Essex). Per fesse sa. and ar. a lion ramp. counterchanged, a bordure engr. gu.

Green (co. Essex). Ar. on a cross engr. gu. an annulet or. *Crest*—A lion sejant per pale or and sa.

Green (Gurlingham). Ar. a buglehorn betw. three griffins' heads erased sa.

Green (Dunsby, Spelding, co. Lincoln, and Great Caddesden, co. Herts). Az. three bucks trippant or. *Crest*—Out of a ducal coronet a buck's head all ppr.

Green (cos. Hertford and Nottingham, and Awkeley Hall, co. York). Ar. on a fesse az. betw. three pellets, each charged with a lion's head erased of the first, a griffin pass. betw. two escallops or. *Crest*—A woodpecker picking a staff couped, raguled, and erect, all ppr.

Green (co. Kent). Gu. a cross crosslet erm. a bordure gobonated ar. and sa.

Green (co. Leicester, and Drayton, co. Northampton). Ar. a cross engr. gu.

Green (London and Norwich). Az. a chev. embattled betw. three bucks or. *Crest*—A buck's head erased or, attired ar. murally gorged and chained of the last.

Green (Milton-Chevsdon, co. Somerset; granted 1529). Ar. a fret az. charged with nine bezants, on a chief sa. a stag trippant or, betw. two mullets of the last pierced gu. *Crest*—A cubit arm erect, vested vert, cuffed or, holding in the hand a bunch of holly ppr. fructed gu.

423

Green (co. Norfolk). Az. a chev. betw. three bucks trippant or.

Green (co. Norfolk, and Wilby). Per pale az. and gu. a chev. betw. three bucks trippant or. *Crest*—A stag's head erased az. attired or.

Green (Knapton, co. Norfolk). Az. a fret engr. ar. betw. three bucks pass. or. *Crest*—A dragon without wings pass. per fesse or and vert.

Green (co. Norfolk). Ar. on a cross engr. gu. five crescents of the field.

Green (co. Northampton). Az. three bucks pass. or (another, ppr.).

Green (co. Northumberland). Az. three bucks pass. ar.

Green (co. Oxford, 1605). Az. three bucks or, a mullet for diff. *Crest*—A buck's head or, charged on the neck with a mullet sa.

Green (Newby, co. York). Ar. a chev. betw. three fleurs-de-lis sa.

Green (Stock Newton). Same *Arms*. *Crest*—A demi greyhound.

Green (co. Suffolk). Vert a chev. or, betw. three bezants.

Green (co. Suffolk). Or, a cross engr. gu.

Green (Wykin, co. Warwick, and Rolleston, co. Leicester). Az. three bucks trippant, within a bordure or, quartering PELL, FORTREY, JOCELYN, BARDOLF, &c. *Crest*—Out of park pales, in a circular form, a stag's head erased or.

Green (Stanleche, co. Wilts, and co. York). Ar. on a cross engr. gu. five crescents or, a chief az. charged with three bezants. *Crest*—A griffin's head erased, quarterly, or and sa. in the beak a trefoil slipped of the last.

Green (Horsforth Green, co. York). Ar. on a chev. betw. three fleurs-de-lis sa. as many escallops of the field.

Green (granted by Le Neve, 1725). Gu. on a lion ramp. within a bordure engr. ar. a boar's head couped sa. *Crest*—A rose gu. barbed vert, seeded or, environed by two laurel branches of the second.

Green. Ar. three griffins' heads erased sa.

Green. Gu. a demi lion ramp. ar. crowned or.

Green. Ar. fretty sa. on a canton of the second a buck pass. or.

Green. Az. a fesse betw. three catharine wheels ar.

Green. Chequy or and ar. (another, or and az.) within a bordure gu.

Green. Ar. a fesse dancettée betw. three leopards' faces sa.

Green (Thundercliffe Grange, Sheffield; granted by Richard St. George, 6 Oct. 1612, to THOS. GREEN, of Cawthorn, co. York, father of JAMES GREEN, of Thundercliffe). Az. three demi lions ramp. erased erminois. *Crest*—Out of a mural crown gu. a demi lion ramp. erminois.

Greene (Bancke, co. York, 1666). Same *Arms* and *Crest*.

Green (Little Sandford, co. Essex). Gu. a lion ramp. per fesse ar. and erm. crowned or.

Green. Ar. three bars az. on a bend gu. as many bezants.

Green. Per chev. az. and gu. three bucks in full course or.

Green (Poulton Hall, co. Chester). Az. three stags trippant or, on a chief of the last three crescents sa. *Crest*—A demi stag per fesse or and az. charged with two crescents counterchanged. *Motto*—Virtus semper viridis.

Green (Alkley, co. Nottingham). Ar. on a fesse az. betw. three pellets, each charged with a lion's head erased of the field, a griffin pass. betw. two escallops or. *Crest*—A woodpecker, with his beak against the trunk of a tree ppr.

Greenacre (co. Lancaster). Gu. a saltire engr. or.

Greenacre. Sa. three covered cups ar.

Greenaker. Vert (another, sa.) a chev. betw. three garbs ar.

Greenaker. Ar. a torteau betw. three cups covered sa.

Greenaway (Barrington Grove, co. Gloucester, and Burford Priory, co. Oxford). Gu. a chev. betw. three covered cups or, on a chief ar. three griffins' heads erased az. beaked gold. *Crest*—A griffin's head erased az. pendent from the beak an annulet or.

Greenall (Grappenhall Hall, co. Chester; borne by EDWARD GREENALL, Esq., J.P.). Ar. on a bend sa. three buglehorns or, stringed of the field. *Crest*—A buglehorn betw. two wings ar. *Motto*—Alta pete.

Greenall (Linholm, Keswick, co. Cumberland; JAMES FENTON GREENALL, Esq., J.P., Lieut.-Colonel 9th Lancashire Rifle Volunteers). Same *Arms, Crest,* and *Motto.*

Greenall (Walton Hall, co. Lancaster, bart.; GILBERT GREENALL, Esq., M.P., was so created 1876). Or, on a bend nebuly plain cotised vert three buglehorns stringed of the first. *Crest*—Betw. two wings or, a pomme surmounted by a buglehorn, as in the arms. *Motto*—Alta peto.

Greene (Lichfield). Az. three stags trippant or, quartering, ar. a cross wavy sa. in the dexter chief quarter an eagle displ. of the last, for WEBB, and, or, a torteau betw. four saltires hummetée gu., for JEVON. *Crest*—A stag's head erased or.

Greene (confirmed by Camden, Clarenceux, to Sir WILLIAM GREENE, co. Oxford, 1603). Az. three stags trippant or, a mullet for diff. *Crest*—A buck's head couped or, charged with a mullet for diff.

Greene (quartered by VERNEY, of Compton, co. Warwick. Har. MS. 1167). Az. three stags trippant within a border or.

Greene. Chequy or and az. a bordure gu.

Greene (Navestock, co. Essex). Az. a stag trippant or. *Crest*—A stag's head or.

Greene (Mitcham, co. Surrey; granted Jan. 1663). Per pale az. and sa. three bucks trippant or.

Greene (Slyne, co. Lancaster, *temp.* James I., an ancient family now represented by THOMAS GREENE, of Slyne, near Lancaster, and of Whittington Hall, Burton, co. Westmoreland, Esq., M.P.). Vert on a fesse invecked or, betw. in chief two pheons ar. and in base a buglehorn ar. stringed gu. three fleurs-de-lis of the last. *Crest*—A stag ppr. gorged with a collar invecked vert, a shield suspended therefrom or, charged with a rose gu.

Greene (Alderman of Chester, 1602). Gu. a lion ramp. per fesse ar. and sa. crowned or, langued az. charged on the shoulder with a trefoil vert.

Greene (Greene's Norton, co. Northampton). Az. three bucks trippant or.

Greene (New England; descended from JOHN GREENE, a descendant of the GREENES, of co. Northampton, who emigrated to New England in 1635; was a companion of ROGER WILLIAMS, and a party to the Providence Purchase from the Indians; his descendant, GARDINER GREENE, Esq., of Boston, *m.* ELIZABETH CLARKE COPLEY, sister of *Lord Lyndhurst*). Same *Arms* *Crest*—A buck's head or.

Greene (Kilmanahan Castle, near Clonmel, Ireland). Az. three bucks trippant or. *Crest*—Out of a ducal coronet a buck's head or. *Motto*—Nec timeo nec sperno.

Greene (Kilranalagh, co. Wicklow). Az. three bucks trippant or. *Crest*—A buck's head or. *Motto*—Nec timeo nec sperno.

Greene (Wexford; Reg. Ulster's Office). Vert three stags trippant or.

Greene (Kilmainham; Reg. Ulster's Office). Ar. on a chev. az. betw. three pomeis, each charged with a stag trippant or, a horse's bit betw. two stirrups of the last.

Greene (Greeneville, co. Kilkenny). Az. three stags trippant or. *Crest*—Out of a ducal coronet a stag's head or. *Motto*—Nec timeo nec sperno.

Greenfield, or Greenville. Vert on a cross ar. five torteaux.

Greenfield (Rhyddgaer, co. Anglesey, and Brynderwen, co. Monmouth; granted in 1839). Per saltire gu. and vert three clarions or. *Crest*—A gryphon with wings elevated or, resting its dexter claw on a clarion gu. *Motto*—Injussi virescunt.

Greenfield. Gu. three clarions or, a crescent for diff. *Crest* —On a chapeau gu. turned up erm. a griffin statant ar. beaked and membered or.

Greenford. Quarterly, or and az. a lion ramp. counterchanged.

Greenford. Per fesse vert and or, a lion ramp. counterchanged.

Greenford (Levanton, co. Kent). Gu. a chev. erm. betw. three squirrels or. *Crest*—Out of a ducal coronet or, a boar's head and neck az. betw. two wings ar. *Motto*—Fide sed cui vide.

Greenhalgh (Greenhalgh, Brandlesome, &c., co. Lancaster, 1664). Ar. on a bend sa. three buglehorns of the first stringed or. *Crest*—A buglehorn sa. stringed or.

Greenhalgh, or Greenow. Same *Arms*, &c.

Greenham (Impalement Fun. Ent. 1661, Ulster's Office). Barry of ten ar. and gu. on a chief of the last three cinquefoils pierced or.

Greenham. Ar. a chev. betw. two crosses formée in chief and a saltire in base sa.

Greenhaugh. See GREENHALGH.

Greenhill (London; granted 1698). Vert two bars erm. in chief a leopard pass. or. *Crest*—A demi griffin gu. powdered with thirty-nine mullets, in commemoration of his being the thirty-ninth child of one father and mother.

Greenhill (Greenhill, co. Middlesex). Vert two bars ar. in chief a leopard pass. or. *Crest*, as the last. *Motto*—Honos alit artes.

Greenhill. Same *Arms*. *Crest*—A demi griffin segreant ar. (another, or).

424

Greening. Ar. a cross engr. gu. *Crest*—A nag's head ar.

Greenland. Ar. three saltires vert. *Crest*—A dexter arm couped and embowed, holding up a bomb fired all ppr.

Greenlaw (that Ilk, co. Berwick). Ar. a fleur-de-lis betw. three mullets gu. within a bordure of the last.

Greenlees (Dr. ROBERT GREENLEES, Scotland, 1750). Ar. a fleur-de-lis vert betw. three mullets gu. within a bordure engr. of the last. *Crest*—A sprig growing out of a mount ppr. *Motto* —Viresco.

Greenly (Titley Court, co. Hereford). Vert a chev. per pale, erm. and erminois betw. three stags trippant, each per pale as the chev. *Crest*—A demi stag springing per fesse erm. and erminois, on the shoulder an escallop az. *Motto*—Fal y Gallu (Anglice) As I can: the device of the WILLIAMSES, of Cwmdû, maternal ancestors of this family.

Greenough (Regent's Park, London). Ar. on a bend engr. az. three buglehorns ar., for GREENHOUGH, quartering, ar. a chev. gu. betw. two fleurs-de-lis in chief and as many in base az., for BELLAS. *Crests*—1st: A sun in splendour ppr. enclosed by a buglehorn az. stringed gu. rimmed and mounted or; 2nd: A stag's head erased per fesse indented ar. and gu. attired or, holding in the mouth a fleurde-lis az.

Greenough. Ar. on a bend engr. sa. three buglehorns stringed of the field.

Greenould (co. Nottingham). Ar. on a chev. sa. three bulls pass. of the field.

Greenow. See GREENHALGH.

Greensill. Ar. three griffins' heads erased sa.

Greensmith (Steeple Grange, co. Derby; granted 1714; in the following year, ROBERT GREENSMITH, Esq., was High Sheriff of the county). Vert on a fesse or, betw. three doves close ar. beaked and legged gu. each with an ear of wheat in the bill of the second, as many pigs of lead az. *Crest*—A dove as in the arms, standing on a pig of lead.

Greenstreet (Sittingbourne, co. Kent, 1451). Barry of eight ar. and az. on a canton of the second a martlet or.

Greenstreet (Milton-by-Sittingbourne, co. Kent, 1614). Ar. five bars az. on a canton of the first a martlet sa.

Greenstreet (Linsted, co. Kent ; LAURENCE GREENSTREET, gent., *d.* 1451, Har. MSS. 3917). Barry of eight ar. and az. on a canton of the second a martlet or.

Greenstreet (Selling, co. Kent; quartered by ADDISON, or Newark House, near Maidstone; WILLIAM ADDISON, *m.* MARY, dau. of PETER GREENSTREET, ob. 1733, of Selling, by ANNE, dau. of the Rev. HENRY DERING, Vicar of Thurnham, Kent). Same *Arms*.

Greenstreet (Faversham, co. Kent; JOHN, ROBERT, and MICHAEL GREENSTREET, Mayors of Faversham). Same *Arms*.

Greenstreet (Ospringe, co. Kent; confirmed in 1642, to PETER GREENSTREET, of Ospringe, ob. 1644). Same *Arms*, canton charged with a double-headed eagle or.

Greenway (co. Warwick). Gu. a chev. betw. three covered cups or, on a chief of the last as many griffins' heads az., quartering, ar. three scaling ladders in bend gu., for KELYNGE. *Crests*—1st: A griffin's head erased az., for GREENWAY; 2nd: A lion sejant or, holding in the dexter paw a scaling ladder gu.

Greenway (cos. Berks and Bucks). Gu. a fesse or, in chief three griffins' heads erased of the second, within a bordure gobonated ar. and az.

Greenway (Raynefords House, co. Oxford. Visit. 1574). Gu. a fesse or, on a chief of the last three birds vert, legged of the first, a border gobony ar. and sa.

Greenway (co. Devon). Gu. a chev. betw. three covered cups or, on a chief ar. as many griffins' heads erased az. *Crest*—A griffin's head erased az. holding in the mouth an anchor gu.

Greenway, or Grenway. Ar. a chev. fracted sa. betw. three crosses crosslet fitchée of the last.

Greenway. Barry of four or and gu. in chief five birds vert, membered of the second, within a bordure gobonated ar. and sa.

Greenwell (Greenwell Ford, co. Durham). Or, two bars az. betw. three ducal coronets gu. *Crest*—An eagle's head ar. beaked gu. gorged with a chaplet of laurel vert.

Greenwell (Greenwell Hill, co. Durham). Same *Arms*. *Crest*—A crane's head couped ar. beaked gu. gorged with a wreath of laurel vert. *Motto*—Viresco.

Greenwell (Broomshields, co. Durham). Same *Arms*. *Crest*—A crane's head couped ar. beaked gu. with an olive branch round the neck vert.

Greenwood (cos. Derby and York). Sa. a chev. erm. betw. three saltires ar. *Crest*—A demi lion or, holding betw. the paws a saltire ar.

Greenwood (Brookwood Park, co. Hants). Same *Arms* and *Crest.*

Greenwood (co. Lancaster). Sa. a chev. erm. betw. three crosses pattée ar.

Greenwood (Norwich and co. York, 1594). Ar. a fesse betw. three mullets in chief and as many ducks in base all sa. *Crest*—A mullet betw. a pair of duck's wings expanded sa. *Motto*—Ut prosim.

Greenwood (Burgh Castle, co. Suffolk). Sa. a chev. erm. betw. three saltires ar. *Crest*—A lion sejant sa. holding a saltire ar.

Greenwood (Castleton, Greenwood, and Norton Bruin, co. Oxford). Same *Arms* and *Crest.*

Greenwood. Per chev. sa. and ar. a chev. erm. betw. three escallops or. *Crest*—A tiger sejant or.

Greenwood (Swarcliffe Hall, co. York). Per chev. sa. and ar. a chev. betw. three saltires couped counterchanged. *Crest*—A tiger sejant or.

Greenwood. Or, on a fesse gu. betw. three leaves vert as many escallops ar.

Greer. Gu. a pale erm. charged with a bend az. *Crest*—A hand vested gu. cuffed or, holding a trefoil vert.

Greer (The Grange, MacGregor, and Tullylagan, co. Tyrone, and Sea Park, co. Antrim; confirmed to the Irish family of GREER, claiming descent from the clan MACGREGOR, in Scotland). Az. a lion ramp. or, armed and langued gu. betw. three antique crowns of the second, on a canton ar. an oak tree eradicated, surmounted by a sword in bend sinister, ensigned on the point with a royal crown all ppr. *Crest*—An eagle displ. ppr. charged on the breast with a quadrangular lock ar. *Motto*—Memor esto.

Greet (cos. Hereford and Salop). Ar. a saltire engr. az. within a bordure also engr. or. *Crest*—A cock's head erased or.

Greete (Stavely, co. York; confirmed 1655). Erm. on a chief gu. three bucks' heads cabossed or. *Crest*—A demi greyhound ar. collared az.

Gretham. Gu. three mullets or, one and two. *Crest*—Two hands issuing holding a two-handed sword ppr.

Grethead. Az. a saltire or, betw. four fleurs-de-lis ar. *Crest*—A fleur-de-lis, as in the arms.

Greeve. Ar. a fesse indented, three leopards' faces in chief sa.

Greeve, or Grive. Ar. a fesse indented betw. three leopards' faces sa.

Greffy, or Greffry (co. Warwick). Per fesse sa. and erm. in chief an eagle with two necks or (another, the field per chev.).

Grefield. Ar. on a bend gu. four lozenges of the first.

Greg (Norcliffe Hall, co. Chester, and Coles Park, co. Hertford, 1875). Quarterly, 1st and 4th, ar. out of a mount in base vert a fir tree surmounted by a sword bendwise ppr. on a canton az. an antique crown also ppr., for GREG; 2nd and 3rd, az. on a pale engr. or, betw. two mullets in chief of the second, and as many crescents in base ar. a lion ramp. gu., for LIGHTBODY. *Crest*—A dexter arm in armour embowed, the hand grasping a scymitar ppr. *Motto*—An oak doe and spair not; also, S'Rioghal mo dhream.

Gregg (Gropenhall, co. Chester). Or, three trefoils slipped betw. two chevronels sa. *Crest*—Out of a ducal coronet or, a stork's head and neck per pale ar. and sa. holding in the beak a trefoil slipped of the second.

Gregg (Ilkeston, co. Derby; descended from the preceding family). Same *Arms* and *Crest.*

Gregg (Hapsford and Bradley, co. Chester). Same *Arms.* *Crest*—A stork's head and neck ppr. in the mouth a trefoil slipped vert.

Gregg (co. Derby; granted 25 June, 1725; and Hammersmith, co. Middlesex). Or, three trefoils slipped betw. two chevronels sa. in the dexter chief point an eagle reguard. wings expanded of the last. *Crest*—Out of a ducal coronet or, an eagle's head and neck per pale ar. guttée de sang and sa. holding in the beak a trefoil slipped of the last.

Gregg (Wallington, co. Surrey). Same *Arms and Crest.*

Gregg (Middle Temple, London; granted by patent 25 June, 1725). Or, three trefoils slipped betw. two chevronels sa. in the dexter chief point an eagle's leg erased of the second. *Crest*—Out of a ducal coronet or, an eagle's head and neck per pale erm. and sa. holding in the beak a trefoil slipped of the last.

Gregg. Ar. three lions pass. guard. in pale az. *Crest*—A lion pass. guard. az.

Gregge-Hopwood (Hopwood Hall, co. Lancaster). Quarterly, 1st and 4th, paly of six ar. and vert; 2nd and 3rd, or, three trefoils betw. two chevronels sa. *Crest*—Out of a ducal coronet or, a griffin's head per pale ar. and sa. holding in the beak a trefoil vert.

425

Gregor. Ar. three boars pass. az. a chief of the last. *Crest*—A hind's head erased gu.

Gregor. Or, three boars az. on a chief of the second a lion pass. of the first.

Gregor (Trewarthenick, co. Cornwall; ancient). Ar. a chev. gu. betw. three partridges ppr. the word "Gregor" signifying "partridge" in Cornish. *Crest*—A garb or.

Gregor (Trewarthenick, co. Cornwall; modern). Erm. a chev. gu. betw. three partridges ppr. a chief of the second, thereon two escutcheons or, each charged with an eagle displ. vert. *Crest*—A Saracen's head affrontée surmounting a javelin in bend all ppr.

Gregorie (Pliston, co. Devon). Az. within three increscents or, as many mullets ar.

Gregorie (Lenton, co. Nottingham). Gu. on a chev. betw. ten crosses crosslet or, three crosses crosslet of the first. *Crest*—A garb or, banded gu.

Gregorie (Dunkirk, 1783). Ar. a fir tree upon a mount in base ppr. surmounted of a sword in bend also ppr. hilted and pommelled or, supporting on the point an imperial crown in dexter chief point of the last. *Crest*—The trunk of an old fir tree fallen, from which issues a vigorous shoot ppr. *Motto*—Non deficit alter.

Gregory (WELBY-GREGORY, Denton Hall, Lincoln, bart.) Quarterly, 1st and 4th, gu. on a chev. betw. ten cross crosslets, six in chief and four in base or, three cross crosslets of the field, a canton for distinction, for GREGORY; 2nd and 3rd, sa. a fesse betw. three fleurs-de-lis ar., for WELBY. *Crests*—1st, GREGORY: Three garbs or, banded gu. the centre one charged with a cross crosslet sa. for distinction; 2nd, WELBY: A cubit arm in armour issuing in bend sinister from clouds, holding a sword, pommel and hilt or, over flames of fire issuant from the wreath ppr. *Motto*—Per ignem per gladium.

Gregory (Styvechall, co. Warwick; confirmed, with five quarterings, by Camden's deputies, to JOHN GREGORY, Esq., of Styvechall, grandson of THOMAS GREGORY, Esq., of Asfordby, and thirteenth in descent from JOHN GREGORY, Lord of Freseley). Or, two bars az. in chief a lion pass. of the last armed and langued gu. *Crest*—A demi boar ramp. sa. collared and crined or. *Motto*—Vigilanter.

Gregory (co. Kent; derived from a Leicestershire branch of the family of GREGORY, of Styvechall, co. Warwick, and now represented by the Rev. FRANCIS T. GREGORY, M.A., Vicar of St. Mary, Platt, in Wrotham). Same *Arms.* *Crest*—A demi boar ramp. sa. langued gu. unguled, crined, and collared or. *Motto*—Vigilanter (another, Γρηγορεῖτε).

Gregory (High-Hurst, co. Lancaster, and Rodington, co. Salop. Visit. 1567). Per pale ar. and az. two lions ramp. endorsed counterchanged. *Crest*—Two lions' heads endorsed and erased ar. and az. collared counterchanged.

Gregory (Harlaxton Manor, co. Lincoln, Rempstone Hall, co. Nottingham, and elsewhere; GEORGE GREGORY, Esq., of Nottingham, who derived his descent through a younger branch from a family long seated at High-Hurst, co. Lancaster, and whose father obtained a grant of armorial bearings at the Visit. of Notts in 1662, m. SUSANNA, sister and co-heir of JOHN WILLIAMS, Esq., of Rempstone Hall, co. Nottingham, and was father of GEORGE GREGORY, Esq., of Rempstone Hall, who acquired a considerable estate in Lincolnshire, through his marriage with ANNE, sole dau. and heir of JOHN ORTON, Esq., of the city of London, by ELIZABETH, his wife, dau. and heir of DANIEL TYRWHITT, Esq., who was son and heir of SCROOP TYRWHITT, Esq., and ELIZABETH, his wife, eldest dau. and eventual co-heir of Sir DANIEL DE LIGNE, Knt., of Harlaxton, co. Lincoln; the last male heir, GEORGE GREGORY, Esq., of Harlaxton, d. s. p. in 1860, and was succeeded, under the entail of the will of his uncle, GEORGE DE LIGNE GREGORY, Esq., by the late JOHN SHERWIN SHERWIN, Esq., of Bramcote, co. Nottingham, who assumed in consequence the name and arms of GREGORY, by royal licence). Gu. on a chev. betw. ten crosses crosslet or, three crosses crosslet of the first. *Crest*—Three garbs or, banded together gu. *Motto*—Crux scutum.

Gregory (Normanton). Gu. on a chev. betw. ten crosses crosslet or, three crosses crosslet of the first. *Crest*—Three garbs or, banded together gu.

Gregory (Greenwich, co. Kent, and Westminster, co. Middlesex). Or, two bars az. in chief a lion pass. of the last, ducally crowned gu. *Crest*—Out of a mural coronet per pale or and az. a demi boar saliant ar. crined and armed of the first, collared of the second, vulned in the breast gu. with an arrow gold feathered of the third.

Gregory (Stockwith, co. Lincoln). Or, two bars az. in chief a lion ramp. of the second. *Crest*—Out of a ducal coronet or, a maiden's head ppr. vested gu.

Gregory (Lord Mayor of London, 1451). Per pale ar. and az. two lions ramp. guard. endorsed counterchanged.

Gregory (Lastingham, co. York). Or, two bars az. in chief a lion pass. of the second crowned of the first.

Gregory (Capt. WILLIAM FILMER GREGORY, R.N., of Hanbury Mount, co. Worcester). Per. pale ar. and az. on a pale betw. two lions ramp. addorsed three cross crosslets ar. all countercharged. *Crest*—Two lions' heads erased and addorsed az. semée of cross crosslets ar. in front of a garb fessewise or. *Motto*—Nil desperandum crux scutum.

Gregory (Ashfordby, co. Leicester; WILLIAM GREGORY, b. 1570, descended from RICHARD GREGORIE, Lord of Freseley and Ashfordby, d. 20 Edward I., 1291. Visit. Leices. 1619). Or, two bars az. in chief a lion pass. of the last, quartering, 1st, ar. a saltire engr. sa.; 2nd, az. a lion ramp. ar. crowned or, debruised by a bend gu.; 3rd, erm. a fess paly of six or and gu.; 4th, sa. two lions pass. in pale ar. crowned or; 5th, vair a fess gu. fretty or. *Crest*—A demi boar ramp. couped sa. collared or.

Gregory (Reg. Ulster's Office, to Sir HENRY GREGORY). Barry of eight or and az. on a chief of the last a lion pass. of the first. *Crest*—A lion's head erased, collared or.

Gregory (Dr. JOHN GREGORY, Scotland, 1766). Ar. a fir tree growing out of a mount in base vert surmounted by a sword in bend, ensigned by a royal crown in the dexter chief point all ppr., in the sinister chief and dexter base a lion's head erased or. *Crest*—A sphere ppr. *Motto*—Altius.

Gregson (Murton and Burdon, co. Durham). Ar. a saltire gu. a canton chequy or and az. *Crest*—An arm couped at the elbow, vested bendy wavy of six, and environed round the wrist with a ribbon ar. and gu. holding in the hand ppr. a battle axe or, handled sa.

Gregson (Moor House, Hawkhurst, co. Kent). Same *Arms*. *Crest*—A cubit arm in armour charged with three bendlets wavy sa. holding in the gauntlet a battle axe of the last, headed or.

Gregson (Lowlyn, co. Durham). Ar. a saltire gu. recercellée engr. az. a canton chequy erminois and of the last. *Crest*—A cubit arm couped ar. charged with a bendlet wavy az. betw. two others gu. tied round the wrist with a riband of the same colours and holding in the hand ppr. a battle axe or, the staff sa. entwined with a wreath of oak fructed also ppr.

Gregson (granted to Rev. WILLIAM GREGSON, M.A., Rector of Whinburgh with Westfield, Norfolk). Gu. two bars erm. each charged with as many crosses pattée fitchée, at the foot of the first in chief three annulets ar. *Crest*—A griffin's head couped chequy ar. and sa. encircled by an annulet or.

Gregson (Liverpool, co. Lancaster; borne by the late MATTHEW GREGSON, Esq., F.S.A., author of the " Portfolio of Lancashire Fragments," &c.). Quarterly, 1st and 4th, ar. a saltire gu. a canton chequy or and az., for GREGSON; 2nd, paly of six erm. and az.; 3rd, per chev. gu. and or, three gates counterchanged, for YATES. *Crest*—An arm couped at the elbow, vested bendy wavy of six ar. and gu. holding by the head in the hand ppr. a battle axe erect or, handled sa. environed round the wrist with a ribbon. *Motto*—Virtute et labore.

Gregson (co. Lancaster). Ar. a saltire gu. over all three bars sa. a canton chequy or and az.

Grehan (Mount Plunkett and St. John's, co. Roscommon; confirmed to PATRICK GREHAN, Esq.) Or, a trefoil slipped vert, on a chief sa. three escallops of the first. *Crest*—A demi lion gu. gorged with three escallops or. *Motto*—Ne ublies.

Grehan (Ireland). Ar. a tree growing out of the base vert, betw. two daggers paleways in base ppr. *Crest*—A demi bull issuing sa. armed or.

Greiby. Erm. two flaunches az. on each three ears of wheat or.

Greig (Ballingrie, co. Fife). Gu. three dexter hands couped and disposed bendways ar. two and one, within a bordure engr. of the second. *Motto*—Signantur cuncta manu.

Greig (Eccles, co. Berwick, 1820). Gu. three dexter hands couped and disposed erect ar. within a bordure or. *Crest*—A dexter arm in armour embowed, brandishing a scimetar ppr. *Motto*—Strike sure.

Greig (Lethangie, co. Kinross, 1846). Gu. three dexter hands erect couped or, within a bordure of the last charged with as many martlets sa. *Crest*—A martlet sa. *Motto*—Nec sorte nec fato.

Greig (Glencarse, co. Perth, 1856). Gu. a cross moline or, square pierced of the field betw. three dexter hands erect couped ar. *Crest*—A falcon riding ppr., jessed, belled, and ducally gorged or. *Motto*—Certum pete finem.

Greike. Or, two chev. sa.

Greilly. Or, on a cross sa. five escallops ar.

426

Greinvile (Stow and Aldercombe, co. Cornwall; Sir GEORGE GREINVILE, Knt., of Stow, and THOMAS GREINVILE, Esq., of Aldercombe. Visit. 1620). Gu. three clarions or. *Crest*—A demi griffin or.

Greiseley (co. Stafford). Vairé gu. and erm.

Greisty. Ar. a chev. sa. betw. three escutcheons gu. each charged with a griffin segreant or.

Greive. Ar. a fesse engr. voided gu. betw. three square padlocks of the second. *Crest*—An arm in armour brandishing a scymitar ppr. *Motto*—Hoc securior.

Greive (co. Northumberland). Ar. on a fesse gu. betw. three fetterlocks az. a mullet betw. two crescents or. *Crest*—A martlet sa. *Motto*—J'ai la clef.

Grelley, or Grayley (co. Lancaster). Gu. three sinister bendlets enhanced or. *Crest*—A hand holding a fish ppr.

Grelley. Vairé ar. and gu.

Grelley. Gyronny of ten ar. and sa.

Grely. Ar. on a chief sa. five escallops or.

Greman. Gu. two bars or, in chief three griffins' heads erased of the second, a bordure ar. (another, a bend gobonated ar. and sa.).

Gremer. Vert three eagles displ. ar.

Gremiston. Paly of six ar. and az. on a bend sa. three round buckles ar. *Crest*—Out of a crescent ar. a lion's face sa. crowned with an antique crown or.

Grenald. Ar. on a bend engr. sa. three buglehorns of the field.

Grenald. Gu. a cinquefoil betw. eight crosses crosslet ar.

Grenalder. Or, a fesse betw. five crosses crosslet gu.

Grendall (St. Bright's, co. Cornwall). Az. a cross quarterly erm. and or, betw. four Cornish choughs of the last, collared ar.

Grendall (co. Huntingdon). Ar. on a cross az. five garbs or. *Crest*—A lion pass. guard. or, sustaining with the dexter paw a flag ar. staff sa.

Grendon (Grendon, co. Warwick, *temp.* King Stephen). Ar. two chev. gu. *Crest*—A decrescent or.

Grendon (*Baron Grendon*, summoned to Parliament 1299; abeyance *temp.* Edward III.). Same *Arms*.

Grendon (co. Gloucester). Same *Arms*.

Grendon (Sarsdon House, co. Oxford. Visit. 1574). Same *Arms*.

Grene. Ar. fretty az. on each joint a bezant, on a chief gu. a buck trippant betw. two mullets or, pierced.

Grene. Ar. a fess dancettée and in chief three leopards' faces sa.

Greneham. Barry of twelve ar. and az. on a chief gu. three six-foils pierced or.

Greney. Ar. on a fesse dancettée sa. three leopards' faces or.

Grenfeld (co. Wilts). Vert a lion ramp. or.

Grenfell (Taplow House, co. Buckingham). Gu. three organ rests or. *Crest*—On a chapeau gu. turned up erm. a griffin pass. or.

Grenford. Per fesse vert and or (another, ar.) a lion ramp. counterchanged. *Crest*—A hunting-horn gu. viruled or.

Grenford. Gu. a chev. erm. betw. three wolves or, the two in chief combatant.

Grenford, or Grensted. Gu. a chev. erm. betw. three squirrels sejant or.

Grenfylde. Ar. on a bend gu. four lozenges of the field.

Grenill. Gu. three round buckles or.

Grenker. Ar. a cross voided gu.

Grentemaisnill (Hinckley, co. Leicester; Lord High Steward of England, *temp.* Henry I.). Gu. a pale or.

Grentmesnell. Same *Arms*. *Crest*—A plume of ostrich feathers ar.

Grenville (London). Vert on a cross or, five torteaux. *Crest*—A sinister arm couped and embowed, extended towards the sinister ppr. vested gu. holding a bow bent sa.

Grenville (TEMPLE-NUGENT-BRYDGES-CHANDOS-GRENVILLE, *Duke and Marquess of Buckingham and Chandos*). Quarterly, 1st and 6th, vert on a cross ar. five torteaux, for GRENVILLE; 2nd, quarterly, 1st and 4th, or, an eagle displ. sa., for LEOFRIC; 2nd and 3rd, ar. two bars sa. each charged with three martlets or, for TEMPLE; 3rd, erm. two bars gu., for NUGENT; 4th, ar. on a cross sa. a leopard's face or, for BRYDGES; 5th, or, a pile gu., for CHANDOS. *Crests*—1st, GRENVILLE: A garb vert; 2nd, TEMPLE: On a ducal coronet a martlet or; 3rd, BRYDGES: The bust of an old man in profile, couped below the shoulders ppr. habited paly of six ar. and gu. semée of roundles counterchanged, wreathed round the temples of the second and az.; 4th, CHANDOS: A Saracen's head couped at the shoulders and affrontée ppr. wreathed about the temples ar. and sa. *Supporters*— Dexter, a lion per fesse embattled or and gu.; sinister, a horse ar. semée of eaglets sa. *Motto*—Templa quam dilecta!

Grenville (*Baron Grenville*, of Wotton-under-Bernewood, co. Buckingham; extinct 1834). Quarterly, 1st and 4th, vert on a cross ar. five torteaux, for GRENVILLE: 2nd, or, an eagle displ. sa., for LEOFRIC, *Earl of Mercia;* 3rd, ar. two bars sa. each charged with three martlets or, for TEMPLE. *Crest*—A garb vert. *Supporters*—Dexter, a lion per fesse embattled gu. and or; sinister, a horse ar. semée of eaglets sa. each collared ar. banded vert, charged with three torteaux. *Motto*—Repetens exempla suorum.

Grenville (*Lord Glastonbury;* created 1797, extinct 1826). Same *Arms* and *Crest* as the *Duke of Buckingham and Chandos. Supporters*—Dexter, a lion per pale embattled or and gu.; sinister, a horse ar. semée of eaglets sa. both plain collared. *Motto*—Uni æquus virtuti.

Grenwell (granted by Camden, Clarenceux). 'Or, two bars az. betw. three ducal coronets gu. *Crest*—A swan's head and neck couped ar. beaked gu. gorged with a branch of laurel vert.

Greshall. Quarterly, ar. and az. on the second three cinquefoils of the first, over all a bend gobonated of the second and gu.

Greshall, or Grassell. Quarterly, ar. and az. on a bend gobonated gu. and of the second six cinquefoils of the first.

Gresham (Gresham, co. Norfolk, *temp.* Edward III.; subsequently of Holt, in the same co., of Osterley Park, co. Middlesex, and Titsey, co. Surrey; of this family was Sir THOMAS GRESHAM, Founder of the Royal Exchange, fourth in descent from JAMES GRESHAM, Esq., of Gresham. Visit. London, 1568). Ar. a chev. ermines betw. three mullets pierced sa. *Crest*—On a mount vert a grasshopper ppr.

Gresham (Limpsfield, co. Surrey, bart., extinct 1801; MARMADUKE GRESHAM, son of Sir EDWARD GRESHAM, Knt., of Titsey, was created a bart. 1660). Same *Arms* and *Crest.*

Gresham (Lord Mayor of London, 1547). Ar. a chev. ermines betw. three mullets pierced sa. on a chief or, a trefoil slipped vert betw. two griffins' heads erased sa. collared gold.

Gresham (London). Ar. a chev. ermines betw. three mullets pierced sa. on a chief gu. a pelican and two griffins' claws couped ar (another, two hinds' heads erased or).

Gresham (JOHN, Sheriff of London. Augmentation granted 1537). Ar. a chev. ermines betw. three mullets sa. pierced of the field, on a chief or, a cinquefoil (in picture a trefoil slipped) az. betw. two hinds' heads erased sa. about their necks a bar gemelle az. on each erasure a bezant langued gu. *Crest*—A grasshopper ppr. about the neck a gemelle gold, holding in the mouth a pawnce flower ppr.

Gresham (Walsingham, co. Norfolk). Sa. a chev. erm. betw. three mullets ar.

Gresham. Ar. a chev. betw. three mullets pierced sa. on a chief or, a trefoil slipped gu. betw. two foxes' heads erased of the second.

Gresham College. Ar. a chev. erm. betw. three mullets pierced sa. *Crest*—On a mount vert a grasshopper or.

Gresley (*Baron Gresley;* summoned to Parliament 1308, extinct 1347). Vairé erm. and gu.

Gresley (co. Derby, *temp.* William the Conqueror). Same *Arms.*

Gresley (Drakelow, co. Derby, bart., and also of Nethersale Hall, co. Leicester). Same *Arms. Crest*—A lion pass. erm. armed, langued, and collared gu. *Motto*—Meliore fide quam fortuna.

Gresley (DOUGLAS-GRESLEY, High Park, co. Worcester; ROBERT ARCHIBALD DOUGLAS, Lord of the Manor of Salwarpe, co. Worcester, assumed, 1830, the name of GRESLEY, in compliance with the will of PHILIP GRESLEY, Esq.). Quarterly, 1st and 4th, vairé erm. and gu. a canton vert for distinction, for GRESLEY; 2nd and 3rd, DOUGLAS. *Crests*—1st, GRESLEY: A lion pass. ar. gorged for distinction with a collar vairé erm. and gu.; 2nd, DOUGLAS, motto over, Jamais arrière. *Motto*—Meliore fide quam fortunâ.

Gresley (arms in Ricote Church, co. Oxford, Visit. 1574; also in Thame Church; impaled by QUATREMAINE). Vairé or and gu.

Gresnore (Yeton). Sa. a cross patonce ar.

Gresque (Lasby, co. Lincoln). Vairé ar. and gu. guttée de sang. *Crest*—A lion pass. ar. guttee sa. collared gu.

Gresque. Sa. three cinquefoils ar. on a chief of the second a demi buck gu. attired or.

Gressall. Ar. a bend componée gu. and az.

Gressall. Quarterly, ar. and az. on a bend gobony gu. and of the second six cinquefoils of the first.

Gressey. Ar. sa. betw. three inescutcheons gu. each charged with a griffin segreant or. *Crest*—A talbot sejant sa. collared and lined or.

Gressingham. Ar. a buglehorn betw. three griffins' heads erased sa.

Gresson. Or, a bend chequy ar. and sa.

Gressy. Erm. on a chief sa. an imperial eagle or.

Grestingthorpe. Erm. a maunch gu.

Greswolde (Yardley, co.Worcester, and Solihull and Malvern Hall, co. Warwick; an ancient family recorded in Visits. cos. Warwick and Worcester, direct male line extinct). Ar. a fess gu. betw. two greyhounds courant sa. No *Crest* appears to be registered to this family in Coll. of Arms, but a greyhound pass. was sometimes used.

Greswolde (London. Visit. London, 1568. DOROTHY, dau. and heir of ROGER GRESWOLDE, of London, third son of RICHARD GRESWOLDE, of Solihull, *m.* JOHN WELD). Same *Arms.*

Greton. Quarterly, or and gu. a bordure az.

Grevalder. Ar. a fesse betw. six crosses crosslet gu.

Greve (Shinley, co. Hertford, and co. York; granted 1523). Ar. on a fesse az. betw. three pellets, each charged with a lion's head erased of the first, a griffin pass. betw. two escallops or. *Crest*—A squirrel sejant sa. charged with two bends sinister ar. holding an escallop or.

Greves. Per chev. ar. and gu. three fig leaves counterchanged.

Grevill, or Greville (Campden, co. Gloucester, Milcote, Beauchamp Court, and Warwick Castle, co Warwick; confirmed, with five quarterings, by Camden's Deputies, to Sir EDWARD GREVILE, Knt., of Milcote, eighth in descent from WILLIAM GREVILL, of Campden). Sa. on a cross engr. or, five pellets, a border engr. of the second. *Crest*—A greyhound's head erased sa. bezantée, gorged with a collar ar. charged with three pellets.

Grevill. Sa. on a cross engr. or, five pellets, in the first quarter a mullet of the second, on a chief chequy gold and az. a griffin pass. erm.

Grevill. Ar. six lions ramp. gu.

Grevill. Ar. on a cross sa. five bezants within a bordure engr. or.

Greville (*Earl of Brooke and Warwick*, now head of the house of GREVILLE). Quarterly, 1st and 4th, sa. on a cross engr. or, five pellets, a bordure engr. of the second, for GREVILLE; 2nd, or, fretty az., for WILLOUGHBY; 3rd, gu. a fesse betw. six crosses crosslet or, for BEAUCHAMP. *Crests*—1st: Out of a ducal coronet gu. a swan, wings expanded and elevated ar. beaked of the first; 2nd: a bear sejant ar. muzzled gu. collared and chained or, supporting a ragged staff of the first. The bear and ragged staff belongs to the Saxon *Earls of Warwick*, derived from the chivalrous GUY. It was adopted by the NEWBURGHS, the first *Earls of Warwick*, after the Conquest. *Supporters*—Two swans, wings addorsed ar. legged, beaked, and ducally gorged gu. *Motto*—Vix ea nostra voco.

Greville (GREVILLE-NUGENT, *Lord Greville*). Quarterly, 1st and 4th, erm. two bars gu. and a canton of the last for diff., for NUGENT; 2nd and 3rd, sa. on a cross engr. or, five pellets, a bordure of the last, for GREVILLE. *Crests*—1st, NUGENT: A cockatrice ppr. wings elevated and charged on the breast with a pellet for diff.; 2nd, GREVILLE: Out of a ducal coronet gu. a demi swan, wings expanded and elevated ar. *Supporters*—Dexter, a swan, wings inverted ar. ducally gorged gu. charged on the breast with a pellet; sinister, a cockatrice, wings elevated and endorsed vert, gorged with an antique Irish crown or, combed and wattled gu. *Mottoes*—Over the 1st crest: Decrevi; under the arms: Vix ea nostra voco.

Greville (Arle's Court, near Cheltenham. Visit. Worcester, 1634). Same *Arms* as GREVILLE, *Earl of Warwick*, border plain.

Grevis, or Greves. See GREAVES.

Grey (*Lord Grey of Codnor;* summoned to Parliament 1299, abeyance 1495). Barry of six ar. and az. in chief three torteaux.

Grey (*Lord Grey of Wilton;* summoned to Parliament 1295, attainted 1603: descended from CODNOR). Same *Arms*, with a label of three points ar. *Crest*—On a hand lying fessways couped at the wrist ar. bracelet or, a falcon of the last wings expanded. *Supporters*—Dexter, a wyvern or; sinister, a lion ar. ducally crowned or.

Grey (*Lord Grey of Ruthyn;* summoned to Parliament 1322, descended from WILTON, abeyance 1868). Same *Arms* as GREY, of Codnor. *Supporters*—Dexter, a wyvern or; sinister, a lion ramp. reguard. gu.

Grey (*Earl and Lord Grey of Kent;* the fourth *Lord Grey of Ruthyn* created earl 1465, the twelfth earl created duke 1710, extinct 1741). Same *Arms* as GREY, of Codnor. *Crest*—On a chapeau gu. turned up erm. a wyvern or. *Supporters*—Two wyverns or. *Motto*—Foy est tout.

Grey (*Lord Grey of Groby, Marquess of Dorset,* and *Duke of Suffolk;* attainted 1554; summoned to Parliament 1449, the third lord created marquess 1475, third marquess created duke 1551; descended from Ruthyn). Same *Arms* as GREY, of Codnor, with a label of three points erm.

Grey (*Lord Grey of Groby,* and *Earl of Stamford* and *Warrington;* male heir and representative of the house of GREY; descended from Groby). Barry of six ar. and az. *Crest*— A unicorn pass. erm. armed, maned, tufted, and unguled or, in front of a sun in splendour. *Supporters*—Two unicorns erm. armed, maned, tufted, and unguled or. *Motto* —A ma puissance.

Grey (*Lord L'Isle,* and *Viscount L'Isle;* created 1483, extinct 1512; descended from Groby). Same *Arms* as GREY, of Codnor, with a label of three points ar.

Grey (*Viscount Graney;* created 1535, attainted 1541; descended from Groby). Same *Arms* as GREY, of Codnor, with a label of three points erm.

Grey (*Lord Grey of Rotherfield;* summoned to Parliament 1297; JOHN, second lord, was one of Founder Knights of the Garter, title passed to the *Viscounts Lovel,* attainted 1487; descended from Codnor). Same *Arms* as GREY, of Codnor, with a bend gu.

Grey (*Lord Grey of Powis;* summoned to Parliament 1482; *Earl of Tankerville,* in Normandy, abeyance 1552). Gu. a lion ramp. and a border engr. or.

Grey (*Lord Grey of Werke,* and *Earl of Tankerville;* created 1642 and 1695, extinct 1706; descended from Powis). Same *Arms* as GREY, of Powis.

Grey (*Lord Grey of Howick,* and *Earl Grey;* descended from Powis). Gu. a lion ramp. within a bordure engr. ar. *Crest* —A scaling ladder or. *Supporters*—Dexter, a lion guard. purp. ducally crowned or; sinister, a tiger guard. ppr. *Motto*—De bon vouloir servir le roy.

Grey (Falloden, bart.; descended from Howick). Same *Arms,* a mullet for diff. *Crest*—A scaling ladder in bend sinister or, hooked and pointed ar. *Motto*—De bon vouloir servir le roy.

Grey (Chillingham, co. Northumberland, bart., extinct 1706; descended from Sir THOMAS GREY, Knt., of Heton, brother of Sir JOHN GREY, who was created *Earl of Tankerville* in Normandy by Henry V., 1418). Same *Arms* as GREY, of Powis.

Grey, or Gray (Segenhoe, co. Bedford, Essex, and Pellham, co. Hertford). Ar. a bend vert cotised dancettée gu. *Crest*—A demi woman couped at the waist ppr. hair flotant or, holding in each hand a sprig of laurel vert.

Grey (Norton, near Stockton-on-Tees). Same *Arms, Crest,* and *Motto,* as Earl Grey.

Grey (Southwick, co. Durham; Sir ARTHUR GREY, of Wilton, *temp.* Elizabeth). Barry of six ar. and az. *Crest*— Upon a sinister glove lying fesseways ar. a falcon rising or, encircled with a band of honeysuckle ppr.

Grey (Morwick, co. Northumberland; a branch of GREY, of Howick. JOHN GREY, Esq., of Morwick, Major-General in the army, C.B.). Same *Arms, Crest,* and *Motto,* as Earl Grey.

Grey (Sir CHARLES EDWARD GREY, Knt., K.C.H., of the Oaks, co. Surrey, appointed one of the Judges of the Supreme Court at Madras in 1820, son of RALPH WILLIAM GREY, Esq., of Backworth, co. Northumberland, by ELIZABETH BRANDLING, his wife). Barry of six ar. and az. on a bend gu. three bezants or.

Grey (co. Derby, and Broadgate, co. Lincoln). Barry of six ar. and az. in chief three torteaux, and a label of five points of the second.

Grey (Jofard, co. Lincoln, and Barton, co. York). Barry of six ar. and az. over all a bend gobony or and gu.

Grey (co. Essex). Ar. a bend az. betw. two cotises wavy gu.

Grey (co. Hereford). Ar. two bars az. on a bend gu. three chaplets or. *Crest*—On a mount vert a bar or.

Grey (Langley and Donnington, co. Leicester). Barry of six ar. and az. a bordure gobony counterchanged, on a canton quartered or and gu. a boar pass. of the first within a bordure sa. bezantée. *Crest*—Out of a ducal coronet az. a demi peacock in pride ppr.

Grey (Ilchester, co. Norfolk). Az. a fesse betw. two chev. or. *Crest*—A dragon's head or.

Grey (Merton, co. Norfolk). Same *Arms,* chev. erm.

Grey (Chillingham and Berwick, co. Northumberland, *temp.* Henry V.). Gu. a lion ramp. ar. a bordure engr. of the last. *Crests*—1st: A scaling ladder ar.; 2nd: A ram's head ar.

Grey (Horton, co. Northumberland), Ar. two bars az. on a bend gu. a bezant.

Grey (Whittington, Envil or Enville, and Kinver, co.

428

Stafford). Barry of six ar. and az. in chief three torteaux, a label of as many points erm.

Grey (Thrandeston, co. Suffolk). Gu. a lion ramp. erm. double queued ar. a bordure engr. of the last. *Crest*—A unicorn pass. gu. bezantée, crined, armed, hoofed, and ducally gorged or.

Grey (Wolbeding, co. Sussex, and Barton, co. York). Barry of six ar. and az. a bend gobonate or and gu. *Crest*—Out of a ducal coronet per pale or and gu. a demi eagle, wings elevated ar.

Grey (Kingston Mereward). Barry of six ar. and az. a label of five points gu. on each three bezants. *Crest*—A badger ppr.

Grey (Beverley, co. York, 1666). Barry of six ar. and az. as many fleurs-de-lis or, three, two, and one. *Crest*—On a chapeau gu. turned up erm. a wyvern or.

Grey. Barry of six ar. and az. on a bend gu. three leopards' faces (another, jessant-de-lis) or.

Grey. Barry of six ar. and az. over all a bend fleur-de-lis or.

Grey. Sa. three lions' heads erased ar.

Grey. Gu. seven lozenges or, three, three, and one, joined together, over all a bend gobonated ar. and az.

Grey. Quarterly, ar. and az. a label of three points gu. on each as many bezants.

Grey Tauyers, Company of (London). Erm. on a chev. sa. betw. three squirrels ppr. with beads and chains of gold about their necks, three roses ar. *Crest*—A squirrel sejant ppr. as in the arms.

Grey, or Gray (Ireland; Patent 1612). Ar. three bars az. in chief as many annulets gu. *Crest*—A griffin's head erased ar. beaked or, holding in the beak an annulet gu.

Grey (Impalement Fun. Ent. 1607, MARY GREY, buried at St. Katharine's, Dublin, wife—1st, of JOHN JENNINGS ; 2nd, of WILLIAM PIGOTT, Mayor of Dublin; and, 3rd, of GILES ALLEN, also Mayor of Dublin). Barry of six ar. au point en point vert and sa.

Greybe. Ar. a fesse dancettée betw. three leopards' faces sa.

Greyby. Or, a fret sa. on a canton of the second a buck pass. of the first.

Greyfield, or Grefield. Ar. on a bend gu. four lozenges of the field.

Greyley. Vairé ar. and gu. a bordure sa. bezantée.

Greynald, or Grenald. Ar. on a bend engr. sa. three buglehorns of the field.

Greyndour. Or, a fesse betw. six crosses crosslet gu. *Crest*—A squirrel sejant holding in the paws a nut all ppr.

Greynor. Vert a chev. betw. three garbs ar.

Greys. Quarterly, ar. and az. over all on a bend sa. three mullets or.

Greysbrooke, or Greisbrooke (Shenstone, co. Stafford, and Middleton, co. Warwick; as tricked in the Harl. MS. 1563, and as represented on the seal of ROBERT GREYSBROOKE, gent., of Middleton, 1668. This family was originally of Gresbroke (*hodie* Greasbrough), co. York. The first of the family who settled in co. Stafford was BARTHOLOMEW DE GRESBROKE, who purchased an estate in Shenstone from Roger de Grendon in the reign of Henry III. The elder line continued at Shenstone until 1728, when, on the death *s. p.* of ROBERT GREISBROOKE, of that place, the estates were sold by GREISBROOKE CRAMP, his nephew and heir. A junior branch established itself at Middleton early in the 16th century. JOHN GREYSBROOKE, of Middleton, son of ROBERT and grandson of ALURED, all of Middleton, the then representative of this branch, *d.* intestate in 1636, and administration of his effects was granted to MICHAEL, his son, lineal ancestor of the present MICHAEL PHILLIPS GRAZEBROOK, Esq., of Hagley, co. Worcester. The other children of JOHN were ROBERT, of Middleton, 1668, who *d.* without male issue, JOHN, who *d. s. p.* in 1640, and GEORGE, who appears also to have *d.* issueless). Ar. three coneys gu.

Greystock (*Lord Greystock;* summoned to Parliament 1295; abeyance 1569). Barry of six ar. and az. three chaplets gu.

Greystock. Barry of six ar. and az. three chaplets of roses gu. leaved vert. *Crest*—A lion pass. guard. or. *Motto*—Volo non valeo.

Greystock. Gu. three lozenges ar.

Greyve. Ar. a fesse dancettée betw. three leopards' heads sa.

Greywith. Az. a griffin segreant or.

Grice (Iver, co. Bucks, and Littleton, co. Middlesex). Ar. on a bend sa. three boars pass. of the first.

Grice (Brokedish, co. Norfolk). Quarterly, gu. and az. on a bend ar. three boars pass. sa. armed or. *Crest*—A boar pass. sa. ducally gorged or.

Grice. Or, a chev. gu. betw. three boars' heads erased at the neck ppr. *Crest*—Betw. two wings or, a blackamoor's head couped sa. ear-rings or, and ducally gorged of the last.

Grice (Impalement Fun. Ent. 1675, Alderman DANIEL HUTCHINSON, Lord Mayor of Dublin, 1651). Quarterly, gu. and az. on a bend ar. three boars pass. sa.

Gridley, Gredley, or Grelley. Gu. three bendlets enhanced or (same as GRELLEY or GREDLEY, Barons, of Manchester). *Crest*—Out of a ducal coronet a demi lion ramp. or, holding betw. the paws a pheon ppr. *Motto*—Devant si je puis.

Grierson (Lagg, co. Dumfries, bart., 1865). Gu. a fesse or, betw. three quadrangular locks (or fetterlocks) ar. (an earlier coat was gu. a saltire and chief ar. the latter charged with three cushions of the first). *Crest*—A lock, as in the arms. *Motto*—Hoc securior.

Grierson (Snowdown Herald, Scotland, 1672). Ar. a fir tree growing out of the middle base vert, surmounted of a sword in bend, bearing upon the point an imperial crown ppr. within a bordure gu. charged with four fetterlocks of the first *Crest*—A branch of fir ppr. *Motto*—Spem renovat anni.

Grierson (Milton Park, co. Kircudbright, 1875). Gu. on a fess betw. two fetterlocks in chief or, and a boar's head erased of the last in base a mullet az. *Crest*—A fetterlock or. *Motto*—Hoc securior.

Griesdale (London). Erm. on a bend engr. az. betw. a dolphin in chief and an anchor cabled in base all ppr. three crosses flory or. *Crest*—A dexter hand fesseways couped and frilled, holding a sword in pale ppr.

Grieve (Dr. JOHN GRIEVE, Russia, 1784). Ar. on a fess gu. betw. three fetterlocks az. a mullet or, a border of the third. *Crest*—A dexter arm armed holding a dagger ppr. *Motto*—Quia fidem servasti.

Grieve (Moscow, 1784). Same *Arms*, *Crest*, and *Motto*, bordure engr.

Grieves. Ar. three hurts, a chief embattled gu. *Crest*—A pelican's head erased vulning ppr.

Grieveson (granted to HENRY JOHN GRIEVESON, Esq., J.P., of Nevill Holt, co. Leicester). Per pale or and az. two wings conjoined in lure and elevated betw. four escallops saltirewise all counterchanged. *Crest*—An escallop or, surmounted by a mascle az. betw. two wings also az. each charged with an escallop gold. *Motto*—Celeriter sed certe.

Griffeth. Erm. a lion ramp. gu. *Crest*—A griffin's head e"ased or (another, ppr.). *Motto*—Non crux sed lux.

Griffeth. Az. a fesse betw. three lozenges ar.

Griffeth. Gu. six escallops ar. three, two, and one, a chief embattled of the second.

Griffies-Williams, Bart. See WILLIAMS.

Griffin (*Lord Griffin of Braybroke*; created 1688, extinct 1742). Sa. a griffin segreant ar. beak and forelegs or.

Griffin (*Lord Braybrooke*). Quarterly, 1st and 4th, sa. a griffin segreant ar. beaked and forelegged or, for GRIFFIN; 2nd and 3rd, quarterly, 1st and 4th, gu. on a saltire ar. a rose seeded and barbed ppr., for NEVILLE, 2nd and 3rd, or, fretty sa. on a canton per pale erm. and gold, a galley with sails furled of the second, also for NEVILLE. Badges: on the dexter a rose gu. seeded or, barbed vert, on the sinister a portcullis or. *Crests*—1st: A talbot's head erased sa., for GRIFFIN; 2nd : A bull ar. pied sa. armed gold, and charged on the neck with a rose gu. barbed and seeded ppr. *Supporters*—Two lions ramp. reguard. ar. maned and tufted sa. gorged with a chaplet of laurel vert. *Motto*—Ne vile velis.

Griffin (Bartherton, co. Chester). Ar. two bars gu. a griffin segreant sa.

Griffin (London ; one of the six clerks of the Court of Chancery). Sa. a chev. betw. three fleurs-de-lis ar. *Crest*—Out of a ducal crown or, a demi griffin erm. membered or.

Griffin, or Griffith (co. Stafford). Gu. on a fesse dancettée betw. three griffins segreant or, as many martlets sa. *Crest*—A woman's head couped at the breast ppr. hair flotant or.

Griffin (cos. Stafford and Suffolk). Gu. on a fesse dancettée ar. betw. six lions pass. or, three martlets sa.

Griffin (Penrith, Wales). Gu. on a fesse betw. three lozenges or, each charged with a fleur-de-lis of the first, a demi rose betw. two griffins segreant of the field.

Griffin (co. York). Erm. a bend gu. cotised or.

Griffin. Gu. three griffins' heads, two in chief couped ar. and one in base erased or.

Griffin. Gu. a lion ramp. or, within a bordure invecked ar.

Griffin. Az. three eagles displ. or.

Griffin (Violet Hill, Bray, co Wicklow; confirmed to EDWARD LYSAGHT GRIFFIN, Esq., Barrister-at-Law, second son of the late Right Rev. HENRY GRIFFIN, D.D., Bishop of Limerick, by JANE EYRE, his wife, dau. and co-heiress

of EDWARD LYSAGHT, Barrister-at-law). Quarterly, 1st and 4th, ar. on a chev. betw. three bucks' heads erased gu. an annulet betw. two fleurs-de-lis or, for GRIFFIN; 2nd and 3rd, ar. three spears erect in fess gu. on a chief az. a lion pass. guard. or, a crescent for diff., for LYSAGHT. *Crest*—A demi griffin segreant ar. charged on the shoulder with a fleur-de-lis az. *Motto*—Fide et fortitudine.

Griffin-Stonestreet. See STONESTREET.

Griffith (Munster Grillagh, co. Londonderry, bart.) Quarterly, 1st and 4th, az. on a fesse betw. a trefoil slipped vert, for GRIFFITH; 2nd and 3rd, gu. a chev. erm. betw. three Englishmen's heads in profile, couped at the neck and bearded ppr., for GRIFFITH, of Penrhyn. *Crest*—On a ducal coronet a griffin segreant or, charged on the shoulder with a trefoil vert. *Motto*—Jovis omnia plena.

Griffith (Bristol; granted 1 November, 1623). Barry of six ar. and sa. three griffins segreant or. *Crest*—A wolf's head couped sa. semée d'estoiles or.

Griffith (Penrhyn, co. Carnarvon). Gu. a chev. erm. betw. three old men's heads in profile, couped at the neck ppr.

Griffith (Woodhouse and Barrow-Super-Soar, co. Leicester ; FRANCIS GRIFFITH, aged 16, Visit. 1619, grandson of FRANCIS GRIFFITH, Page to HENRY GREY, *Duke of Suffolk, temp.* Henry VIII.). Per chev. ar. and gu. three stags' heads cabossed counterchanged.

Griffith (Wales). Ar. a chev. betw. three fleurs-de-lis gu.

Griffith (Wales). Gu. a chev. ar. betw. three stags' heads cabossed per pale of the second and or.

Griffith (co. York). Erm. a bend gu. cotised or.

Griffith (Burton Agnes, co. York, bart., extinct 1656; Sir HENRY GRIFFITH was so created in 1627 ; his dau. and eventual heiress, FRANCES, m. Sir MATTHEW BOYNTON, of Boynton and Barmston, bart.). Gu. on a fesse dancettée ar. betw. six lions ramp. or, three martlets sa.

Griffith (Wichnor, co. Stafford). Same *Arms*.

Griffith. Same *Arms*. *Crest*—A woman's head couped at the shoulders ppr. hair or.

Griffith (WILLIAM GRIFFITH, Esq., co. Gloucester). Same *Arms*. *Crest*—A female head affrontée ppr. and over it the *Motto*—A fin.

Griffith. Or, a lion ramp. sa. *Crest*—A lion ramp. sa.

Griffith. Gu. a chev. ar. betw. two Saracens' heads in chief couped or, wreathed az. and sa. in base one of the same erased of the second, haired and bearded of the third. *Crest*—A buck's head cabossed per pale or and ar.

Griffith. Az. a fesse betw. three fusils (another, lozenges) ar.

Griffith. Gu. on a fesse indented betw. six griffins segreant or, three martlets sa.

Griffith. Sa. three crosses pattée or, a label ar.

Griffith. Sa. a chev. betw. three fleurs-de-lis ar. *Crest*—A stag's head erased holding in the mouth a sprig of oak ppr.

Griffith (JOHN GRIFFITH GRIFFITH, Esq., of Bangor, co. Carnarvon). Paly of eight gu. and sa. a lion ramp. or, a bordure nebulée of the last. *Crest*—Upon a mount vert a lion statant, tail extended erm. charged on the body with three crosses pattée in fesse gu.

Griffith (JOHN GRIFFITH, Esq., of Llwynduris, co. Cardigan; registered in the College of Arms). Per chev. gu. and ar. two chevronels counterchanged betw. as many men's heads in profile, armed in helmets, vizors up ppr. garnished or, in chief, and a lion ramp. reguard. sa. in base, for GRIFFITH; quarterly, vert and erm. in the 2nd and 3rd quarters a trefoil slipped ppr. on a bend wavy ar. a cinquefoil gu. base two caltraps sa., for SANDHAM. *Crest*—GRIFFITH: A griffin reguard. sa. wings elevated or, in the mouth an arrow, the barb downwards ppr. the dexter fore-claw resting upon a man's head in profile armed in a helmet, as in the arms. *Motto*—Le bon temps viendra.

Griffith. Gu. a cross ar.

Griffith, or Griffon. Sa. a griffin segreant or.

Griffith, Ap-. Or, a lion ramp. gu. *Crest*—A buck's head cabossed per pale or and ar.

Griffith Maelor (*Lord of Bromfield*, eldest son of MADOC AP MEREDITH, last Prince of Powys-Fadoc. Descendants: I. OWEN AP GRIFFITH VYCHAN, Lord of Glyndwrdwy, celebrated as OWEN GLENDOWER; II. TUDOR AP GRIFFITH VYCHAN, Lord of Gwyddelwern). Paly of eight ar. and gu. over all a lion ramp. sa.

Griffith ap Cynan (King of North Wales, Founder of the I. Royal Tribe of Wales, derived from ANARAWD, King of North Wales, eldest son of RHODRI MAWR, King of Wales. Descendants: I. Princes of North Wales ; II. DAVID GOCH AP DAVID, Lord of Penmachno; III. RODERICK, AP OWEN GWYNEDD, Lord of Anglesea). Gu. three lioncels pass. in pale ar. armed az.

Griffith ap Jenkyn (Wales; quartered by GLYNNE MYTTON, Esq., of Pontyscowred and North Cleobury, co. Salop). Sa. a chev. or, betw. three owls ar.

Griffith ap Nicholas (co. Herts). Ar. a chev. sa. betw. three Cornish choughs of the last, beaked and membered gu.

Griffith (Garn, co. Denbigh; derived from MADOC DDU, of North Wales, a descendant of EDWIN, Lord of Tegengl). Paly of six ar. and sa.

Griffith (Caer Rhun, co. Carnarvon, Brongain, co. Montgomery, &c.; descended from IDNERTH BENVRAS, Lord of Maesbrook, descended from EDWIN, Lord of Tegengl). Ar. a cross flory engr. sa. betw. four Cornish choughs ppr. on a chief az. a boar's head couped ar. tusked or, and langued gu.

Griffith (Rev. THOMAS GRIFFITH, M.A., Prebendary of St. Paul's, son of BENJAMIN GRIFFITH, by his wife, the dau. and co-heir of RICHARD JACKMAN, Esq.). Or, on a bend gu. betw. two griffins segreant az. three mullets pierced ar. quartering, JACKMAN, viz., Per saltire ar. and sa. two eagles displ. of the last. Crest—A griffin's head erased sa. guttée d'or.

Griffith (arms in the Crown Inn, Aylesbury, co. Bucks. Visit. Oxon, 1574). Sa. a wyvern or.

Griffith (Prince of Upper Powys). Or, a lion's gamb erased in bend gu.

Griffith, ap, Sir Howel, Knt. Gu. a chev. or, betw. three stars of the second.

Griffith ap Rhys (Gloddoeth, in Cryddyn, whose dau. and heiress, MARGARET, m. in 1640 HOWEL AP EVAN VYCHAN, ancestor of MOSTYN, Bart., of Mostyn, co. Flint). Gu. a chev. ar. betw. three plates.

Griffith (Llwyndegrust, North Wales; derived from Sir GRIFFITH LLOYD, Knt., of co. Carnarvon, living in 1322). Arms as LLOYD, of Llyn.

Griffith (co. Warwick). Sa. a griffin segreant ar. a crescent for diff.

Griffith (Penprompren, co. Cardigan, and Trevalyn Hall, co. Denbigh; an ancient family in that county, of which was JOHN GRIFFITH, Esq., High Sheriff of the county in 1757). Ar. a lion pass. sa. betw. three fleurs-de-lis gu. Crest —A lion pass. sa.

Griffith ap Llewellin (son of HWLKYN AP HOWELL AP YERWORTH, which HOWELL altered his paternal coat of arms. He was descended from HWVA AP KYNDDELW, "one of ye 15 Tribes in accompt amongst ye Brittaines"). Gu. a lion pass. ar.

Griffith Goch (Lord of Ross and Rhyvoniog; lineally descended from MARCHUDD AP CYNAN, Founder of the VIII. Noble Tribe of North Wales). Descendants: I. CONWAY, of Bryn Eirin; II. HUGHES, of Cefen Garlley; III. LEWIS, of Llwyn Gwren; IV. LLOYD, of Dolin Ederion). Or, a griffin segreant gu.

Griffith (Fun. Ent. of JUDGE GRIFFITH, buried in Christ Church, Dublin, 2 Nov. 1666). Sa. semée of roses and a lion ramp. ar.

Griffiths (Chwaen, Isle of Anglesea). Gu. a chev. betw. three lions ramp. or.

Griffiths (Thorn Grove Park, near Worcester). Or, a lion ramp. gu. Crest—A demi lion ramp. gu.

Griffiths. Gu. a chev. betw. three Saxons' heads in profile, two in chief couped ar. charged with an erm. spot sa. the one in base erased per fesse of the last. Crest—A stag's head cabossed per pale gu. and az. betw. the attires or, an estoile of eight points gold.

Griffiths (co. Hereford). Ar. on a fesse dancettée gu. volded of the field three blackbirds ppr. in chief a griffin segreant betw. two crickets of the second. Crest—A wolf's head sa. semée d'estoiles or. Motto—Firmitas et sanitas.

Griffiths (HENRY ST. GEORGE GRIFFITHS, Esq.). Ar. two bars dancettée gu. betw. in chief a griffin segreant betw. two grasshoppers, and in base three ravens sa.

Griffiths (Dinthill, co. Salop; of whom were SAMUEL GRIFFITHS, Esq., Sheriff, 1759, and JOSEPH GRIFFITHS, Esq., Sheriff, 1771. The late representative, LEIGHTON DELAMORE GRIFFITHS, Esq., sold the estate). Ar. three boars' heads couped sa.

Griffiths-Jermyn. See JERMYN.

Griffon (Reg. Ulster's Office). Gu. three escallops ar. in chief three piles of the last.

Griffyn. Per pale or and sa. a chev. betw. six martlets all counterchanged.

Grigby. Erm. on a fesse betw. three mullets gu. a bull pass. or. Crest—An ounce's head erased ppr. collared ar. charged with two mullets gu. the edges of the collar dovetailed.

Grigg (granted to JOHN GRIGG, Esq.). Gu. a chev. betw. three griggs (or young eels) with tails in the mouth az. Crest—A horse's head erased ar. Motto—Ut prosim.

Grigg (co. Kent). Ar. a trefoil betw. two chev. sa.

Grigg (Bealing Parva, co. Suffolk). Ar. three lions pass. in pale az. a bordure of the last.

Grigg. Ar. two chev. sa. Crest—Out of a ducal coronet a dexter hand holding up a swan's head all ppr.

Grigge. Gu. a fleur-de-lis ar.

Griggs. Gu. three ostrich feathers ar. Crest—A sword in pale enfiled with a leopard's face ppr.

Grigson. Gu. two bars ar. on a chief of the last three mullets of the first. Crest—A ram's head erased ppr.

Grigson (Saham Toney, co. Norfolk; borne by Rev. WILLIAM GRIGSON, M.A., of Saham Toney). Gu. two bars in chief three annulets ar. Crest—Out of a ducal coronet or, a griffin's head chequy ar. and sa.

Griles. Per fesse gu. and az. on a bend engr. betw. two lions' heads erased ar. as many crosses crosslet fitchée or, a crescent of the second.

Griles (Tavistock, co. Devon; WILLIAM GRILES, of that place. Visit. 1620). Or, three bends enhanced gu. Crest—A hedgehog ar.

Grill. Sa. a cross couped and pierced ar. Crest—A demi chevalier in armour, holding a scymitar ppr.

Grills, or Grylls (Launceston, Calstock, and Laurethoe, co. Cornwall; SAMPSON GRILLS of the former, MARK GRILLS of the second, and JOHN GRYLLS of the latter. Visit. 1620). Or, three bendlets enhanced gu. Crest—A porcupine pass. ar.

Grimbald (co. Leicester). Barry ar. and az. a bordure gu.

Grime. Az. three crosses tau or.

Grimes (London; granted, 1575, by Cooke, Clarenceux, to THOMAS GRYMES, of London). Or, on three bars gu. as many martlets of the first, on a chief of the second two bars nebulée ar. Crest—A martlet vert.

Grimes (Bonchurch, near Newport, Isle of Wight). Or, a bordure engr. az. on a chief sa. three escallops ar. Crest— A pair of wings addorsed or.

Grimes (HENRY GRIMES, Esq., of Cotton House, near Rugby, co. Warwick, J.P. and D.L.). Same Arms and Crest.

Grimes. Sa. a horse's head erased or, betw. three mullets ar. Crest—A horse's head couped or, betw. two wings expanded ar.

Grimes. Barry of six ar. and gu. on the second bar a boar's head couped of the first, over all the trunk of an oak in bend, leaved ppr. a bordure engr. sa.

Grimond (Scotland, 1866). Gu. a chev. or, betw. two camels' heads erased of the second, collared of the first, and campaned ar. in chief and a wolf's head also erased of the last in base. Crest—A camel's head, as in the arms. Motto—Gaudet patientia duris.

Grimsbie (Brachlowe, co. Leicester, temp. Henry VIII.). Barry nebulée of six sa. and or, on a chief ar. three birds of the first. Crest—A demi ram saliant sa.

Grimsby (Drakelow, co. Leicester; WILLIAM GRIMSBY, of that place, 38 Henry VI., 1459; his only dau. and heir, ANNE, m. 1st, ROBERT VINCENT, of Messingham, co. Lincoln; and 2nd, RICHARD WATERTON. Visit. Leicester, 1619). Barry nebulée of six sa. and or, on a chief ar. three birds of the first.

Grimsby. Per chev. az. and ar. in chief two chevronels of the second.

Grimsby. Per chev. sa. and ar. two chevronels counterchanged.

Grimscot (Grimscott in Launcells, co. Cornwall; the heiress m. LANGDON, of Keverell). Sa. three swords in pale ar. hilted or.

Grimsdith (Grimsditch, co. Chester, temp. Henry III., extinct in the chief line in 1726). Vert a griffin or, armed gu. seizing on a man, in complete armour, lying on his back ppr.

Grimsditch (Dublin; Fun. Ent. of JOAN, widow of RALPH GRIMSDITCH, Farmer of the Customs of the Port of Dublin, d. 25 April, 1607, and of her son, GEORGE GRIMSDITCH, Customer of the Port of Dublin; d. 26 April, 1616). Same Arms.

Grimsditch (arms in Tarven Church). Ar. a wolf pass. sa.

Grimshaw (Grimshaw, co. Lancaster). Ar. a griffin segreant sa. beaked and legged or. Crest—Two lions' heads erased, collared and endorsed ppr.

Grimshaw (NICHOLAS GRIMSHAW, Esq., of Preston, co. Lancaster). Same Arms. Crest—A griffin, as in the arms.

Grimshaw (The New House, in the Forest of Pendle, co. Lancaster). Same Arms.

Grimshaw (Andershaw Lodge, co. Lancaster). Same Arms.

Grimsted, or Grimstead. Gu. two bars vair. Crest —A dexter arm couped, resting on the elbow, holding a bow towards the sinister ppr.

Grimsted (co. Dorset). Gu. two bars vairé, vert and or.

Grimsteed (co. Dorset). Ar. three bars vert.

Grimston (Grimston Garth and Kilnwick, both in the East Riding co. York). Ar. on a fesse sa. three mullets of six points or, pierced gu. *Crest*—A stag's head, with a ring round the neck, ar. *Motto*—Faitz proverount.

Grimston (Bradfield, co. Essex, bart., extinct 1700. MARY, sister of the last bart., m. Sir CAPEL LUCKYN, Bart., of Messinghall, whose grandson, WILLIAM LUCKYN, assumed the surname of GRIMSTON, and was ancestor of the *Earls of Verulam*). Ar. on a fesse sa. three mullets of six points pierced or, in the dexter chief point an erm. spot. *Crest* —A stag's head erased ppr. attired or. *Motto*—Mediocria firma.

Grimston (*Earl of Verulam*). Quarterly, 1st and 4th, ar. on a fesse sa. three mullets of six points pierced or, in the dexter chief point an erm. spot, for GRIMSTON; 2nd, sa. a fesse dancettée betw. two leopards' faces or, for LUCKYN; 3rd, ar. three buglehorns sa., for FORRESTER. *Crest*—A stag's head erased ppr. attired or. *Supporters*—Dexter, a stag reguard. ppr. attired or; sinister, a griffin reguard. or. *Motto* —Mediocria firma.

Grimston (co. Devon). Ar. a chev. betw. three boars' heads sa.

Grimston (quartered by HILLERSDON, of Memland, co. Devon. Visit. 1620). Ar. a chev. betw. three boars' heads couped sa.

Grimwood. Az. a pale ar. surmounted by a chev. or, charged with three mullets of the field. *Crest*—On the top of a tower, an eagle issuing, wings endorsed, holding in the beak an acorn slipped all ppr.

Grimwood (exemplified to JEFFREY GRIMWOOD GRIMWOOD, Esq., of Woodham Mortimer Lodge, co. Essex). Quarterly, 1st and 4th, az. a chev. engr. erm. betw. three mullets in chief fessways and a saltire couped in base ar.; 2nd and 3rd, or, on a chev. gu. betw. three wolves' heads erased sa. as many oval buckles of the first. *Crests*—1st: A demi wolf ramp. collared, holding betw. the paws a saltire; 2nd: A lion's gamb erased and erect sa. charged with a cross crosslet ar. and holding in the paw a buckle or. *Motto*— Auxilio divino.

Grindal, or Grindall (co. York). Gu. a cross moline or. *Crest*—A dexter arm in armour embowed, the hand holding by the blade a sword, point downwards, all ppr.

Grindall. Or, a cross quarterly erm. and az., in the 1st and 4th quarters a dove az. collared ar.; in the 2nd and 3rd, a dove of the last collared of the third. *Crest*—A demi lion ramp. per pale or and az.

Grindall (20 Dec. 1759). Quarterly, or and az. (another, ar. and az.) a cross quarterly erm. and of the first betw. four pea-hens collared, all counterchanged, of the second and ar.

Grindall. Erm. a cross patonce gu.

Grindall. Barruly ar. and gu. a cross flory sa.

Grindlay. Quarterly, or and az. a cross quarterly erm. and of the first, betw. four pheons counterchanged of the field. *Crest*—A pea-hen ppr. *Motto*—Non degener.

Grindley. Az. a cross betw. four pheons or. *Crest*—A buffalo's head erased gu.

Grindoure (Forest of Denn, co. Gloucester). Per pale or and vert twelve guttées in pale counterchanged, four, four, and four.

Grisewood (London, and Daylesford, co. Worcester). Ar. a lion pass. environed with a laurel vert, betw. three garbs az. banded or. *Crest*—A demi lion guard. ar. environed with laurel vert, holding a garb, as in the arms. *Motto*—Nil desperandum.

Grisley (Manchester, co. Lancaster). Gu. a bend with two bendlets enhanced.

Grisley, Grely, and Grelley. Gu. a bend or, in chief a bar gemelle of the last. *Crest*—A dexter hand ppr. holding a lozenge or.

Grisley. Gu. on a bend ar. three crosses flory sa.

Grismund (Worcester, Monument in St. Martin's Church, to RICHARD GRISMUND, and ELIZABETH, his wife). Or, a bend compony of the first and gu.

Grissell (Norbury Park, co. Surrey). Or, two barrulets dancettée gu. betw. as many greyhounds courant sa. *Crest*—A greyhound's head erased sa. round the neck a double chain or, pendent therefrom an escutcheon gold charged with a bugle stringed sa.

Gritton. Or, a bend sa. betw. two lions' heads erased gu. *Crest*—A lion's face betw. two wings ppr.

Grizzlehurst (Grizzlehurst). Ar. three boars statant, bones in their mouths, all ppr.

Grobber, and Grobbere. Sa. a fesse ar. in chief three lozenges of the last.

431

Grobham (Bishop's Liddiard, co. Somerset, and Wishford Magna, co. Wilts. Ped. Ent. Visit. 1623. Arms granted by Camden, 1599). Gu. a lion pass. erm. wounded in the shoulder gu. *Crest*—A boar's head couped or.

Grobham (Sir RICHARD GROBHAM, Knt., descended from the preceding, d. 5 July, 1629; Fun. Ent. Coll. of Arms). Same *Arms*, impaling for WHITMORE, vert fretty or, a mullet ar. for diff.

Grogan (Johnstown, co. Wexford; granted by Hawkins, Ulster, 1757, to JOHN GROGAN, Esq., and son of her of COR-NELIUS GROGAN, and grandson of JOHN GROGAN, all of same place, with an escutcheon of pretence for his wife, KATHERINE, dau. and heir of MAJOR ANDREW KNOX, of Rathmacknee, co. Wexford). Barry of six or and sa. on a chief az. a lion pass. of the first, an escutcheon of pretence gu. a falcon rising or, within an orle ar. the inner rim engr. the outer wavy. *Crest*—A lion's head erased sa. *Motto*—Honor et virtus.

Grogan (Harcourt Street, Dublin, bart.; Sir EDWARD GROGAN, M.P. for Dublin, 1841–65, male heir of GROGAN of Johnstown). Barry of six or and sa. on a chief engr. az. a lion pass. of the first. *Crest*—A lion's head erased sa. charged with a mullet or. *Motto*—Honor et virtus.

Grogan-Morgan (Johnstown Castle, co. Wexford; exemplified to HAMILTON KNOX GROGAN, Esq., of Johnstown, upon his assuming, by royal licence, 1828, the additional name of MORGAN, in compliance with an injunction in the will of his kinsman, SAMUEL MORGAN, Esq., of Waterford). Quarterly, 1st and 4th, or, a griffin segreant sa., for MORGAN; 2nd and 3rd, barry of six or and sa. on a chief az. a lion pass. of the first. *Crests*—1st, MORGAN: A reindeer's head cabossed or; 2nd, GROGAN: A lion's head erased sa., motto over—Honor et virtus. *Motto*—Fidus et audax.

Grome (Rattlesden, co. Suffolk). Or, three piles gu. on a chief az. two helmets close of the first. *Crest*—A dexter arm in armour ppr. garnished or, holding in the hand a gauntlet ppr..

Grono Llwyd-y-Penwyn (derived through Idhon, third son of Idnerth-ap-Edryd, from Marchudd, Founder of the VIII. Noble Tribe of North Wales and Powys. GRONO was a distinguished military leader, and was instrumental in obtaining for Edward I. the sovereignty of Wales: Descendants: 1. VAUGHANS, of Plas-Neuadd, in Llanvair; 2. WYNNS, of Melai; 3. WYNNES, of Garthewin). Gu. three boars' heads in pale erased ar.

Grono (Wales). Gu. on a garb or, three martlets sa.

Grooby (Rev. JAMES GROOBY, Vicar of Swindon, co. Wilts). Gu. seven mascles, three, three, and one, or. *Crest*—Out of a ducal coronet or, an eagle displ.

Groom. Erm. three piles az. each charged with a cross pattée fitchée or, on a chief gu. two helmets close ppr. *Crest*—A dexter arm embowed in armour ppr. garnished or, holding in the hand a gauntlet, both ppr. suspended from the wrist by a pink riband a shield gold, thereon a pile gu. charged with a cross pattée fitchée ar.

Groom, or Groome. Ar. three piles in point gu. a chief az. *Crest*—On the top of a torteau winged gu. an eagle standing, with wings displ. or.

Groome (Kimenhall; Greswolde Monument, Yardley Church, co. Worcester). Or, three piles meeting in base gu. on a chief indented az. two helmets close of the first.

Groombridge. Ar. three inescutcheons or, bordured gu. *Crest*—Out of a mural coronet a garb, and thereon perched a crow all ppr.

Grosby. Ar. a maunch sa. (another, gu.).

Grose (Richmond, co. Surrey; granted 1756; the arms of FRANCIS GROSE, F.S.A., the antiquary). Or, on a mount betw. two lesser ones vert a lamb sa. holding with the dexter foot a banner erm. charged with a cross clechée gu. *Crest*—On a mount vert a lamb holding a banner, as in the arms.

Grosett (Logie, co. Clackmannan). Az. three mullets in fess ar. and in base as many bezants.

Groset (Lisbon). Az. three mullets in fesse ar. and as many bezants in base, in chief an acorn of the second. *Crest*—A dexter hand holding a sword ppr. *Motto*—Pro patriâ.

Grossett-Muirhead. See MUIRHEAD.

Gross. Sa. on a fesse betw. three mullets pierced ar. as many crosses crosslet gu. *Crest*—On a ducal coronet or, a talbot pass. ppr. collared and lined gold.

Grosse (co. Norfolk). Quarterly, ar. and az. on a bend sa. three martlets or.

Grosse (Camborne, co. Cornwall; the heiress m. BULLER, of Shillingham). Quarterly, ar. and az. (another, or and az.) on a bend sa. three martlets or.

Grosse. Sa. a fesse betw. six crosses crosslet ar.

Grosse. Quarterly, ar. and az. on a bend sa. three mullets or. *Crest*—Out of a ducal coronet or, a hand holding a dagger ppr.

Grosset, or Grossett. Ar. nine trefoils in cross vert. *Crest*—Four arrows points downwards and a strung bow in saltire all ppr.

Grossome. Or, a bend chequy ar. and sa.

Grosvenor. Az. a garb or. In the time of Richard II. a protracted litigation arose between Sir ROBERT LE GROS-VENOR and Sir Richard le Scrope, relative to the bearing "Az. a bend or," which both used. The dispute, known as the SCROPE and GROSVENOR Controversy, was decided in favour of SCROPE. *Crest*—A talbot statant or. *Supporters*—On each side a talbot ramp. reguard. or, gorged with a plain collar az. *Motto*—Nobilitatis, virtus, non stemma character.

Grosvenor (*Duke of Westminster*). Quarterly, 1st and 4th, az. a portcullis with chains pendent or, on a chief of the last in pale, the arms of King Edward the Confessor betw. two united roses of York and Lancaster, being the arms of the city of Westminster, granted to the duke's ancestors as a coat of augmentation; 2nd and 3rd, az. a gar'; or, the family arms of GROSVENOR. *Crest*—A talbot statant or. *Supporters*—On each side a talbot ramp. reguard. or, gorged with a plain collar az. *Motto*—Virtus non stemma.

Grosvenor (*Baron Ebury*). Az. a garb or, a mullet for diff. *Crest*—A talbot statant or. *Supporters*—On either side a talbot reguard. or, gorged with a plain collar az. charged on the shoulder with a mullet of the second. *Motto* —Virtus non stemma.

Grosvenor (co. Chester). Quarterly, ar. and sa. a cross flory counterchanged.

Grosvenor (co. Dorset). Az. a garb or. *Crest*—A horse courant, saddled and bridled all ppr.

Grosvenor (Leek, co. Stafford). Paly of ten gu. and or, a cross moline ar. betw. four crows sa.

Grosvenor (co. Stafford). Gu. a bend or, a bordure erm.

Grosvenor (Bushbury, co. Stafford. Visit. Stafford, 1583). Az. a garb or, betw. three bezants. *Crest*—A talbot statant or, collared gu.

Grosvenor (Sutton Coldfield, co. Warwick. Visit. Warwick, 1619). Same *Arms* and *Crest*.

Grocvenor, or Gravenor (High Grosvenor, Whitmore, Bridgnorth, and Dallicott, co. Salop, &c. The heiress of the GROSVENORS, of Dallicott, SARAH, only child of WILLIAM GROSVENOR, of that place, *m.* in 1709, EDWARD SMITH, son of JOHN SMITH, Esq., of Hilton, and was buried at Claverley in 1763, leaving issue WILLIAM SMITH, Esq., of Dallicott House, who *m.* ELIZABETH, dau. and co-heir of SAMUEL HURTLE, Esq., of Sutton, and *d.* in 1792, aged 80, leaving issue a dau. and heir, MARY, *m.* to ROBERT WILKES, Esq., by whom she had issue (with sons who *d.* issueless), a dau. and heir, ELIZABETH, *m.* in 1805 to THOMAS WORRALL GRAZE-BROOK, Esq., of Stourton Castle, co. Stafford. Mr. GRAZE-BROOK *d.* in 1816, and was *s.* by his only son, the late THOMAS WORRALL SMITH GRAZEBROOK, Esq., of Dallicott and Stourton, on whose decease *unm.* in 1846, the Dallicott and Stourton estates devolved upon his only sister, ELIZA-BETH, wife of GEORGE MCKENZIE KETTLE, Esq., now of Dalli-cott *jure uxoris*). Az. a garb or, betw. three bezants. *Crest*—A talbot pass. or, collared gu.

Grosvenor. Sa. a cross patonce ar.

Grosvenor (Wade's Mill, co. Herts). Az. a garb or, betw. three bezants.

Grosvenor (co. Leicester). Az. a fesse betw. three garbs or, banded gu.

Grote (GEORGE GROTE, Esq., formerly M.P. for the city of London, eldest son of GEORGE GROTE, Esq., Sheriff of Kent in 1809). Ar. on a mount vert three pine trees ppr. a dexter side or. *Crest*—A pine tree betw. two elephants' probosces erect ppr. *Motto*—Prodesse quam conspici.

Grout (granted to JOSEPH GROUT, Esq., of Hackney, co. Middlesex). Per chev. ar. and or, on a chev. gu. betw. two tigers' faces in chief ppr. and an eagle displ. in base sa. a boar's head erased of the second, betw. two spear heads erect of the first. *Crest*—On a mount vert a dexter arm embowed in armour ppr. garnished or, the hand grasping a javelin in bend sinister, point downwards, surmounted by two branches of oak also ppr.

Grovall. Gu. a chief dancettée or.

Grove (Grove Place, co. Bucks, and London). Erm. on a chev. engr. gu. three escallops ar.

Grove (Agmondesham, co. Bucks). Same *Arms*.

Grove (Walbury, co. Essex). Same *Arms*. *Crest*—A talbot pass. sa. collared ar.

Grove (co. Wilts). Same *Arms*. *Crest*—A talbot pass. **sa.** collared ar.

Grove (Groveshot). Same *Arms*.

Grove (Ferne, co. Wilts, bart.). Erm. on a chev. engr. gu. three escallops, the centre one or, the other two ar. *Crest*— A talbot statant sa. collared ar. *Motto*—Ny dessux ny dessoux.

Grove (Rev. CHARLES GROVE, and HENRY THOMAS GROVE, Esq., of Oldstock, near Salisbury). Erm. on a chev. engr. gu. three escallops or. *Crest*—A talbot pass. sa. collared ar. *Motto*—Ni dessus ni dessous.

Grove (Nuneham-Courteney Church. Visit. Oxon. 1566). Gu. a chev. betw. three pineapples or (another, tinctures reversed). *Crest*—A hand holding a thistle ppr.

Grove (Dunhead, co. Wilts). Erm. on a chev. engr. gu. an escallop or, betw. two others ar. *Crest*—A talbot pass. sa. ducally collared or.

Grove (Shenston Park, co. Stafford). Ar. a chev. engr. gu. betw. three stumps of trees eradicated and erased ppr. quartering, ar. on a chev. betw. three martlets gu. as many estoiles or. *Crest*—On a mount vert a dragon statant ppr. collared and chained or, charged on the shoulder with an estoile gu. *Motto*—Laudo manentem.

Grove. Ar. a sun gu.

Grove. Ar. (another, or) a bend engr. az.

Grove. Per bend vert and gu. an eagle displ. or.

Grove (Rowley Regis, co. Stafford. Monument at Aldridge). Ar. three leaves vert on a canton gu. three crescents of the field.

Grove (Fun. Ent. Ireland, 1597). Ar. on a chev. az. betw. three cocks vert as many roses or.

Grove (co. Donegal; Fun. Ent. 1681, THOMAS GROVE, of that co., buried in St. John's Church, Dublin). Ar. on a chev. engr. gu. three escallops of the field.

Grove (Dublin; Fun. Ent. 1597). Ar. on a chev. betw. three cocks az. as many roses or.

Grove (Castle Grove, co. Donegal; Reg. Ulster's Office). Erm. on a chev. gu. three escallops ar. *Crest*—A lion ramp. gu. *Motto*—Gloria finis.

Grover. Per bend gu. and or, a pale vair. *Crest*—Out of a cloud, in the sinister, an arm embowed holding a garland of flowers all ppr.

Grovyll. Gu. a chief indented or.

Groze. Gu. a cross or, in the dexter chief quarter a lion ramp. supporting an anchor cabled all gold.

Grubb (North-Mims Parsonage, co. Herts). Erm. on a chief embattled gu. three roses or. *Crest*—A griffin's head erased per pale ar. and gu. charged with a rose counterchanged.

Grubb (Horsendon, co. Bucks). Quarterly, 1st and 4th, erm. on a chief embattled gu. three roses or, for GRUBB; 2nd and 3rd, ar. two bendlets engr. sa. surmounted by a label of three points gu., for RATCLIFFE.

Grubb (Potterne, co. Wilts). Vert on a chev. ar. betw. three demi lions ramp. or, as many crosses crosslet sa. *Crest*—A lion's head az. ducally crowned or.

Grubb (co. Wilts). Same *Arms*. *Crest*—A lion's gamb a. holding a rose gu. stalked and leaved vert.

Grubbam. Gu. a lion ramp. erm. vulned on the shoulder ppr. *Crest*—A cock ppr.

Grubham (Bishop's Lediard). Same *Arms*. *Crest*—A rose gu. stalked and leaved vert.

Gruffe (Wales). Chequy or and az. on a fesse gu. three leopards' faces of the first.

Gruffeth (Wicknor, co. Stafford, and Wigmore, co. Warwick). Gu. on a fesse indented ar. betw. six lions ramp. or, three martlets sa. *Crest*—A demi woman habited gu. face ppr. hair or.

Gruffith ap Kadwgan. Or, a lion ramp. az. langued gu.

Grull, or Grall (Grace Court; Reg. Ulster's Office). Quarterly, gu. and vert a lion ramp. erm.

Grumley (Reg. Ulster's Office). Ar. on a fess cotised az. betw. three pelicans ppr. a mural crown or.

Grumley (Ireland). Vert a bend or, betw. two anchors ar. *Crest*—A vine branch ppr.

Grumstead. Ar. on a fesse betw. two bars nebulée sa. a lion pass. of the field. *Crest*—An antelope's head couped ar. attired or.

Grundie (Turgarton, co. Nottingham). Ar. on a cross engr. betw. four lions pass. guard. gu. five martlets or. *Crest* — A demi leopard ramp. guard. sa. bezantée.

Grundy (The Oaks, co. Leicester). Same *Arms*. *Crest*—A demi leopard affrontée ppr. bezantée. *Motto*—In Deo solo salus.

Grungfield (Tressenfield, co. Suffolk). Or, on a chief az. three dexter gauntlets of the first. *Crest*—A gauntlet or.

Grushill. Ar. a fesse betw. six martlets sa.

Gry. Sa. a crescent betw. two mullets in pale ar.

Gry. Ar. a fesse sa. betw. three mullets purp.

Gryce (co. Norfolk). Quarterly, or and az. on a bend sa.

three boars pass. or. *Crest*—A boar ar. ducally gorged, hoofed and armed or.

Gryffith. Az. a boar ar. betw. ten trefoils slipped of the second.

Gryffithe. Erm. a bend gu. cotised or.

Gryffydd (Bach-y-saint, co. Carnarvon, and Tan-y-bwlch, co. Merioneth; MARGARET, only dau. and heiress of EVAN GRIFFITH, Esq., High Sheriff of Merioneth in 1770, *m*. WILLIAM OAKLEY, Esq.). Ar. on a chev. sa. three mullets pierced of the field.

Gryffyth ap Cynan (*Prince of North Wales*). Gu. two lions pass. in pale ar. armed and langued az.

Grylls (Rev. RICHARD GERVEYS GRYLLS, of Helston, co. Cornwall. In the confirmation to WILLIAM GRYLLS, Esq., of Tavistock, of the crest, dated 13 June, 1557, occur the following remarks: "I, Robert Cooke, Clarenceux Roy d'Armes, being required of WILLIAM GRYLLS, of Tavistocke, co. Devon, Arm. to make searche in the registers and recordes of myne office, for the aunciente arms and create belonging to the name and family, whereof he is descended; wh'upon at his requeste, I have made search accordingly, and doe finde that he maie lawfully beare, as *his ancestors heretofore have borne*, hereafter following," &c. &c.). Or, three bendlets enhanced gu., quartering, BEERE, GERVEYS, BONATHLACK, TREVELYOS, TREVANION, GLYNN, POLKINGHORNE, &c. *Crest*—A porcupine pass. ar. *Motto*—Vires agminis unus habet.

Grylls (Tavistock, co. Devon. Visit. 1620). Az. three bends enhanced or.

Gryme (Authingham, co. Norfolk). Az. three crosses tau or.

Gryme (Reg. Ulster's Office). Same *Arms*.

Gryme. Ar. three pilgrims' staves in pale gu. *Crest*—A Roman fasces ppr.

Gryme. Az. five crosses patonce or.

Gryme. Ar. on a cross az. five crescents of the first, on a chief of the second three bezants.

Grymer. Vert three eagles displ. or.

Grymes, or Grymelles. Or, on a cross gu. five mullets of six points pierced of the field.

Grymes (Sir GEORGE GRYMES, knighted at Dublin Castle by Sir George Carey, Lord Deputy, 1603). Gu. a sword ar. pommel and hilt or, surmounting a battle axe of the last, headed of the second in saltire, on a chief of the second three escallops of the last. *Crest*—A griffin's head crased sa. semée of escallops or.

Grymesby. Ar. three chev. sa.

Grymesby, or Grensby (co. Essex). Per chev. sa. and ar. in chief three cinquefoils of the second. *Crest*—A sinister hand holding a bow ppr.

Grymsby. Per chev. sa. and ar. in chief two chev. or. (another, the chev. ar.).

Grymsby. Per chev. ar. and sa. two chev. counterchanged.

Grymsby. Gu. a fesse dancettée betw. six crosses crosslet or.

Grys (Wakefield, co. York). Quarterly, gu. and az. on a bend ar. three boars pass. sa. armed or, a bordure of the last.

Grys. Quarterly, gu. and az. on a bend ar. three boars pass. sa. armed or. *Crest*—A lion sejant sa. collared and lined or.

Gryse (co. Norfolk). Quarterly, gu. and az. on a bend ar. three boars sa.

Guales. Quarterly, or and gu. four lions pass. counterchanged.

Guay. Or, a lion ramp. reguard. sa.

Gubbay (granted to MOSES GUBBAY, of Poona, East India). Gu. three keys erect or, on a chief ar. a rose gu. slipped, leaved, surmounted by a branch of palm and a branch of willow, saltirewise all ppr. *Crest*—A pelican ar. standing on a rose branch slipped ppr. and charged on the wing with a key gu. *Motto*—Probitas fons honoris.

Gubbins. Vert a fesse erm. betw. six bezants. *Crest*—An arm from the elbow vested, holding a holly branch.

Gube. Gu. a chev. erm. betw. three pine apples or.

Gubyon. Or, a lion ramp. sa. depressed by a bend gu. charged with three escallops ar. *Crest*—A demi lion ramp. sa. charged with three escallops ar.

Gubyon. Gu. a cross pattée ar. over all a label az.

Gueriet. Az. an eagle displ. or, debruised by a ribbon gu.

Guerin (a noble French family, established at Champaign, Isle of France, and Auvergne, from which derived the Rev. J. GUERIN, of Norton Fitz-Warren, near Taunton). Or, three lions ramp. sa. langued, armed, and crowned gu.

Guerin (Guernsey). Lozengy ar. and sa. a cross gu.

Guest (Dowlais, co. Glamorgan, bart.). Az. on a chev. or, betw. three swans' heads erased ppr. as many crosses moline sa. *Crest*—A swan's head erased ppr. gorged with a collar or, and underneath charged with a cross moline, as in the

433

arms, betw. two ostrich feathers gold. *Motto*—Ferro non gladio.

Guest. Az. a chev. or, betw. three swans' heads erased ppr. *Crest*—A swan's head erased ppr. betw. two ostrich feathers or.

Guest (Sir LIONEL GUEST, knighted at Leixlip, co. Dublin, by Sir George Carey, Lord Deputy, 5 May, 1604; Fun. Ent., 1608, Ulster's Office). Ar. on a fess sa. three cross crosslets of the field.

Guest, or Gheast. Az. a chev. or, betw. three shovellers' heads erased ppr.

Guevera (co. Lincoln; granted 1617). Quarterly, 1st and 4th, or, three bends erm.; 2nd and 3rd, gu. five watercress leaves in saltire ar. *Crest*—Four feathers, the two outside ones or, the others gu.

Guevera (co. Lincoln; descended from Spain). Quarterly, 1st and 4th, or, three bends erm.; 2nd and 3rd, gu. five watercress leaves pendent in saltire ar. all within a bordure inscribed, La mayor, victoria de ellas es el bien mere cellas. *Crest*, as the last.

Guiana, See of. Ar. a cross az. charged in the centre with a passion cross or, on a chief gu. a lion pass. guard. holding in the dexter paw a crosier erect, all of the third.

Guid (Scotland). Ar. on a chev. gu. three bezants, in base a dove with an olive branch in the beak.

Guidott (co. Hants). Per saltire nebulée or and az. in pale two crescents gu. on a chief az. a lion pass. guard. betw. three fleurs-de-lis or, one and two. *Crest*—A falcon with wings endorsed ppr. holding a laurel branch stalked and leaved vert, fructed or.

Guidott (descended from ANTONIO GUIDOTTI, a noble Florentine, who settled in England in the 16th century. In 4 Edward VI. he received a grant of the following augmentation : On a chief sa. a lion pass. (" peditans ") betw. three fleurs-de-lis or. *Crest*—A gerfalcon ppr. wings elevated, beaked and membered or, in the beak a branch of olive vert, fructed or, in allusion to his services in promoting a peace. *Motto*—Pax optima rerum.

Guildeford (Sir RICHARD GUILDFORD, K.G. 1500, *d.* 28 Sept. 1506, and Sir HENRY GUILDEFORD, K.G. 1526, *d.* 1532). Or, a saltire betw. four martlets sa.

Guilford. Az. a lion pass. betw. three fleurs-de-lis ar. *Crest*—A dragon's head. *Motto*—Animo et fide.

Guilford, Earl of. See NORTH.

Guilford. See GULDEFORD.

Guilford. Or, a saltire betw. four martlets sa. on a canton gu. a pomegranate gold. *Crest*—A tree raguly, couped at the top or, flamant gu. *Another Crest*—On a chapeau gu. turned up erm. and charged with an escallop or, an ostrich's feather erect gold.

Guilford, or Guldeford, Town of (co. Surrey). Sa. on a mount vert a castle with two towers embattled, on each tower a spire, surmounted with a ball from the battlements, betw. the towers a tower triple-towered all ar. and charged with an escutcheon, quarterly, of France and England under the battlements of the castle two roses in fesse or, the port ppr. charged on the centre with a key and portcullised both gold, on the mount before the port a lion couchant guard. of the fourth, on each side the castle, in fesse, a woolpack of the third paleways, the base of the field water ppr.

Guillam. Ar. on a chev. sa. betw. three dolphins naiant embowed ppr. as many towers of the field. *Crest*—A dolphin hauriant embowed ppr.

Guillamore, Viscount. See O'GRADY.

Guille (Bailly of Guernsey, 1511). Az. a chev. betw. three mullets of eight points or. *Crest*—A mullet of seven points or, betw. two wings ar. *Motto*—Raptim ad sidera tollar.

Guille (Jersey). Az. a chev. betw. three stars of seven points or. *Crest*—A star, as in the arms. *Motto*—E cœlo lux mea.

Guillim (Westbury and Minsterworth, co. Gloucester, 1571). Ar. a lion ramp. erm. gorged with a collar or. *Crest*—An arm embowed in armour, holding a broken sword all ppr.

Guillim (Langston, co. Herts). Sa. a horse's head erased or, betw. three gauntlets ar.

Guillim (Newry, co. Down; Fun. Ent. of PARR GUILLIM, drowned near Ringsend, Dublin Harbour, 2 April, 1618). Ar. a lion ramp. guard. sa. armed and langued gu. a martlet for diff.

Guinness (granted, 1814, to Rev. HOSEA GUINNESS, LL.D., Rector of St. Werburgh's, and Chancellor of St. Patrick's, Dublin, grandson of RICHARD GUINNESS, Esq., of Celbridge, co. Kildare). Per saltire gu. and az. a lion ramp. or, a chief erm. a dexter hand couped at the wrist gu. *Crest*—A boar pass. quarterly or and gu. *Motto*—Spes mea in Deo.

Guinness (GRATTAN-GUINNESS, Beaumont, co Dublin; exemplified 1856, to Rev. WILLIAM SMYTH GRATTAN-GUINNESS,

M.A., of Beaumont, on his assuming, by royal licence, the additional surname and arms of GRATTAN). Quarterly, 1st and 4th grand quarters, quarterly, 1st and 4th, GUINNESS, per saltire gu. and az. a lion ramp. or, on a chief erm. a dexter hand couped at the wrist of the first, 2nd and 3rd, GRATTAN, quarterly or and gu. in the 1st quarter a trefoil slipped vert, all within a bordure az.; 2nd and 3rd grand quarters, LEE, ar. on a fess betw. three crescents sa. a trefoil slipped or, a canton gu. charged with a lion ramp. of the first, and a chief of the same, thereon a mullet az. betw. two torteaux, the said canton being borne in commemoration of descent from the family of SMYTH. Crests—1st, GUINNESS: A boar pass. quarterly or and gu.; 2nd, GRATTAN: On a mount vert a falcon, wings elevated, holding in the dexter claw a sceptre all ppr., motto over, Esse quam videri. Motto—Spes mea in Deo. Quartering and crest of LEE, granted to the above Rev. WILLIAM SMYTH GRATTAN-GUINNESS and his younger brothers, viz., ar. on a fess betw. three crescents sa. a trefoil or. Crest—On a pillar ar. encircled by a ducal coronet or, an eagle preying on a bird's leg erased ppr.

Guinness (Ashford, co. Galway, bart.). Quarterly, 1st and 4th, GUINNESS, per saltire gu. and az. a lion ramp. or, on a chief erm. a dexter hand couped at the wrist of the first, a crescent for diff.; 2nd and 3rd, LEE, ar. on a fesse betw. three crescents sa. a trefoil or. Crests—1st, GUINNESS: A boar pass. quarterly or and gu. a crescent for diff.; 2nd, LEE: On a pillar ar. encircled by a ducal coronet or, an eagle preying on a bird's leg erased ppr. Supporters (granted, by royal warrant, May, 1867, to Sir BENJAMIN LEE GUINNESS, Bart., and the heirs male of his body, upon whom the dignity of a Baronet shall descend in virtue of the limitations of the patent of the 15th April, 1867)—On either side a stag gu. attired and gorged with a collar gemel or, pendent therefrom by a chain gold, an escutcheon, that on the dexter charged with the arms of GUINNESS, and that on the sinister with the arms of LEE. Motto—Spes mea in Deo.

Guise (Elmore, co. Gloucester, bart., extinct 1783; an ancient family descended from Sir WILLIAM GYSE, who came to England with William I.). Gu. seven lozenges vair, three, three, and one. N.B. These are the arms of DE BURGH. ANSELME GYSE m., temp. Henry II., MAGOTTA DE BURGH, dau. of HUBERT, Earl of Kent, and got with her the Manor of Elmore, when he assumed her family arms. The previous arms of the family were, erm. a chevronel gu.

Guise (Highnam, co. Gloucester, bart.). Gu. seven lozenges vair, three, three, and one, on a canton or, a mullet pierced sa. Crest—Out of a ducal coronet or, a swan rising ppr. collared and chained gold. Supporters—(granted by royal warrant, dated 12 July, 1863, to Sir JOHN W. GUISE, Bart., G.C.B., and the heirs male of his body, to whom the dignity of a baronet shall descend, under the patent of creation)—Dexter, a swan ar. crusily and langued gu. beaked and membered sa. collared and chained or; sinister, a bear sa. billety collared and chained or, langued and armed gu. The warrant for these supporters recites that Her Majesty has been pleased to grant her special licence for their use, "in order to give a testimony of her approbation of the services of the aforesaid Sir JOHN W. GUISE." Motto—Quo honestior eo tutior.

Guise, or Gwyse (co. Gloucester). Lozengy gu. and vair, on a canton or, a mullet of six points sa.

Guise. Lozengy, couped per fesse ar. and sa.

Guise. Ar. an ink moline gu.

Guising. Ar. on a bend az. three eagles displ. or.

Gulby. Az. a chev. or, betw. three crosses moline ar. Crest—A naked arm embowed, thrusting with a sword, point downwards ppr.

Gulby. Az. a chev. or, betw. three crosses sarcelly ar.

Guldeford (Hemsted Place, co. Kent, temp. Richard I., bart., created 1685, d.s.p. The dau. and heiress of Sir EDWARD GULDEFORD, Knt., Lord Warden of the Cinque Ports, and Constable of Dover Castle, m. JOHN DUDLEY, Duke of Northumberland, the male line of the family being continued by GEORGE GULDEFORD, Esq., of Hemsted, Sir EDWARD'S younger brother). Or, a saltire betw. four martlets sa. on a canton ar. a pomegranate ppr. seeded gu. Crest—A fire-brand flamant ppr.

Guldeford (cos. Cumberland and Northumberland). Ar. two bars, each cotised sa.

Guldes (Scotland). Az. a chev. ar. betw. three tadpoles or.

Gulford, or Guildeford (cos. Stafford and York). Or, two bars gemelles sa.

Gulion (co. Bedford). Gu. a cross formée ar. a label sa.

Gull (Brook Street, Hanover Square, London, bart. In consideration of the great skill and unremitting attention evinced by Sir W. W. GULL during the dangerous illness of

H.R.H. the Prince of Wales, he was created a baronet 8 Feb. 1872, and granted by Her Majesty in the same year an augmentation to his arms). Az. a serpent nowed or, betw. three sea gulls ppr. with the following honourable augmentation, viz., a canton erm. thereon an ostrich feather ar. quilled or, enfiled by the coronet which encircles the badge or plume of the Prince of Wales gold. Crests—1st (of honourable augmentation): A lion pass. guard. or, supporting with the dexter paw an escutcheon az. thereon an ostrich feather ar. quilled or, enfiled with a like coronet; 2nd: Two arms embowed, vested az. cuffs ar. the hands ppr. holding a torch or, fired also ppr. Motto—Sine Deo frustra.

Gull (Sandwich, co. Kent). Paly of six or and sa. (another, az. and ar.) a chief of the first. Crest—A dexter arm in armour, couped at the shoulder, lying fesseways, embowed and erect from the elbow, holding in the hand all ppr. a battle axe ar. handled or.

Gull (co. Kent). Paly of six ar. and az. a chief or.

Gull (RICHARD BIRD, of Pinchbeck, co. Lincoln, temp. Henry VI., m. LUCY, dau. and heiress of ROBERT GULL. Visit. Cumberland, 1615). Paly of six sa. and ar. a chief or.

Gullan (Scotland). Gu. a chev. ar. betw. three fleurs-de-lis or.

Gullat, or Gullet. Or, a cross botonnée gu.

Gulline. Gu. on a chev. ar. betw. three fleurs-de-lis or, a mullet of the first. Crest—A falcon belled ppr.

Gullon. Gu. on a saltire ar. five martlets volant of the first. Crest—A rock with a blackbird sitting in a cavity all ppr. Motto—Tutum refugium.

Gully (Major WILLIAM SLADE GULLY, of Trevennen, co. Cornwall, grandson of SAMUEL CORYN GULLY, Esq., by MARY SLADE, his wife, heiress of Trevennen, and great-grandson of JOHN GULLY, Esq., by SUSANNA, his wife, dau. and co-heir of JOHN CORYN, Esq., of Trevorder). Quarterly, 1st and 4th, ar. a chev. gu. betw. three crosses crosslet sa., for GULLY; 2nd and 3rd, ar. three nags' heads erased sa. a chief gu., for SLADE, quartering also POWNE, CORYN, &c. Crest—Two keys in saltire. Motto—Nil sine cruce.

Gulston (Wymondham, co. Leicester; granted by Camden, Clarenceux, to JOHN GULSTON, of Gray's Inn, and THEODORE GULSTON, sons of WILLIAM GULSTON, Esq., of Wymondham). Ar. two bars nebulée gu. over all on a bend sa. three plates. Crest—An ostrich's wing erect, feathers alternately ar. and gu. on a bend sa. three plates.

Gulston (Gray's Inn, co. Middlesex, and co. Herts). Same Arms and Crest.

Gulston (Dirleton and Derwydd, co. Carmarthen). Same Arms and Crest.

Gulston (exemplified to FREDERICK BIGG, Esq., of West Clandon, co. Surrey, who, by sign manual, assumed the surname and arms of GULSTON). Quarterly, 1st and 4th, barry nebulée of six ar. and gu. on a bend sa. three plates, for GULSTON; 2nd and 3rd, per pale erm. and az. a lion pass. gu. crowned or, within a bordure engr. of the third, charged with eight fleurs-de-lis or, for BIGG. Crest—An ostrich's wing, the feathers alternately ar. and gu. charged with a bend, as in the arms.

Gulway. Az. three lozenges or, a chief of the last.

Gumars, or Gunas (Witham, co. Essex). Ar. a chev. betw. three lions' heads erased sa.

Gumbleton (Chiswick, co. Middlesex). Ar. on a fesse wavy gu. three mullets or, on a canton az. a fleur-de-lis of the third. Crest—A demi griffin, wings endorsed, ar. beaked and legged gu. holding a mullet or.

Gumbleton (Glanatore, co. Cork). Same Arms. Crest—A demi griffin with wings endorsed ar. beaked and legged gu. holding a mullet or. Motto—Memento mori.

Gumley (Isleworth, co. Middlesex). Erm. on a bend engr. gu. betw. three fleurs-de-lis az. as many escallops or.

Gumley. Erm. on a bend engr. gu. three escallops ar.

Gun (Fethard, co. Tipperary; granted by Hawkins, Ulster, 1768, to WILLIAM GUN, Esq., of that place, descended from an ancient family of the name in Munster). Gu. on a chev. or, three mullets az. on a chief of the second two flint muskets full cock in saltire ppr. a border erm. Crest—Two swords in saltire, points upwards ppr. pommels and hilts or. Motto—Dum spiro spero.

Gun (Rattoo, co. Kerry). Ar. three cannon barrels fessways ppr. Crest—A dexter hand couped at the wrist erect ppr. Motto—Vincit amor patriæ.

Gun-Cuninghame. See CUNINGHAME.

Gun-Monro. See MONRO.

Gunby. Ar. a lion ramp. az.

Gundry. Or, two lions pass. guard. in pale az. Crest—A demi lion holding in the dexter paw a sword all or.

Gunman (JAMES GUNMAN, Esq., of Dover). Vert an eagle

displ. with two heads ar. ducally gorged gu. *Crest*—Out of a naval coronet ar. an anchor erect sa. cable or.

Gunsmiths, Company of (London). Ar. two guns in saltire ppr. in chief the letter G, in base the letter Y sa. each crowned with a regal crown, on the dexter side in fesse a barrel, and on the sinister three balls all of the second.

Gunn (Irstead, co. Norfolk). Gu. three lions ramp. ppr. on an escutcheon of pretence erm. on a bend az. three escallops ar. within a bordure or. *Crest*—A lion ramp. ppr. holding a bezant.

Gunn (Sutherland). Ar. a galley of three masts, her sails furled and oars in action sa. flags gu. within a bordure az. on a chief of the third a bear's head of the first, muzzled of the second betw. two mullets of the field. *Crest*—A dexter hand wielding a sword ppr. *Motto*—Aut pax aut bellum.

Gunn (co. Caithness). Ar. a ship under sail in a sea in base all ppr. on a chief gu. three mullets of the field.

Gunner. Az. a saltire ar. guttée de sang. *Crest*—A lion's head erased or.

Gunning (Eltham, co. Kent, bart.), afterwards of Horton, co. Northampton). Gu. on a fesse erminois betw. three doves ppr. as many crosses formée per pale of the first and a az. *Crest*—A dove holding in the dexter claw a caduceus ppr. *Motto*—Imperio regit unus æquo. The first bart., as a Knight of the Bath, bore for *Supporters*— Dexter, a stag ppr. collared pily; sinister, a fox ppr. collared as the dexter. *Motto*—Imperio regit unus æquo.

Gunning (Castle Coote, co. Roscommon; derived from the GUNNINGS, of Kent; the last male heir in the direct line, General JOHN GUNNING, left an only dau. and heiress, *m.* Major JAMES PLUNKETT. General GUNNING's sisters were— MARY, *Countess of Coventry;* ELIZABETH, *Baroness Hamilton,* wife successively of the *Dukes of Hamilton* and *Argyll;* and CATHERINE, *m.* to ROBERT TRAVIS, Esq.). Gu. on a fesse erm. betw. three doves ar. ducally crowned or, as many crosses pattée of the first.

Gunning (cos. Kent, Somerset, and Gloucester; the Kentish branch, of which was the Right Rev. PETER GUNNING, Bishop of Ely, who *d. unm.* in 1684; arms on the Bishop's Tomb in his Cathedral). Gu. on a fesse betw. three doves ar. as many crosses pattée of the field.

Gunning (Swainswick, co. Somerset; granted 1765). Gu. on a fesse ar. betw. three doves ppr. a barnacle az. betw. two crosses pattée of the field. *Crest*—An ostrich holding in the beak a horseshoe all ppr. charged on the breast with a cross pattée, as in the arms.

Gunning (co. Kent). This family originally bore . . . three billets in fesse . . . but on 9 May, 1670, the son of Bishop GUNNING obtained from Walker a grant of the following :— Gu. on a fesse betw. three doves ar. as many crosses pattée of the field. *Crest*—A dove ar. supporting with the dexter paw a crozier.

Gunter (Racton, co. Sussex, of Welsh extraction; FRANCES CATHERINE, only dau. of Sir CHARLES GUNTER NICHOLL, K.B., *m.* WILLIAM LEGGE, second *Earl of Dartmouth*). Gu. three dexter gauntlets ar. *Crest*—A stag's head couped per pale gu. and sa. the attires counterchanged.

Gunter (co. Brecon). Sa. a chev. betw. three gauntlets, fingers clenched or. *Crest*—A stag's head per pale gu. and sa.

Gunter (Chichester and Emley, co. Sussex). Sa. three gauntlets ar. within a bordure or. *Crest*—A stag's head erased per pale sa. and gu. attired or.

Gunthorpe (THOMAS GUNTHORPE, of Tuxford-in-the-Clay; monument in the church there. Visit. Notts). Gu. a bend and border gobony ar. and az. the former charged with two lions' heads erased of the second betw. three leopards' faces or.

Gunthorpe. Gu. a bordure and bend gobonated ar. and az. on the bend betw. two lions' heads erased of the second three leopards' faces or. *Crest*—A lion's head erased, gorged with a plain collar.

Gunton (co. Northampton). Gu. three round buckles or.

Gunvill. Ar. on a chev. sa. three escallops or.

Gurdon (Assington Hall, co. Suffolk). Sa. three leopards' faces jessant-de-lis or. *Crest*—A goat climbing a rock, with a sprig issuing from the top ppr. *Motto*—Virtus viget in arduis.

Gurdon (Letton, co. Norfolk). Same *Arms,* &c.

Gurdon. Or, a fleur-de-lis gu. (another, az.).

Gurlin. Ar on a bend per bend gu. and az. betw. two cotises counterchanged three fleur-de-lis of the first. *Crest*— On a mural coronet gu. an eagle with wings endorsed or, in the beak an acorn, stalked and leaved ppr.

435

Gurlyn (co. Cornwall). Per bend ar. and gu. two bendlets betw. three fleurs-de-lis all counterchanged.

Gournay, or Gurnay (*temp.* William the Conqueror, and Henry III.). Paly of six or and az.

Gurnay. Or, three piles (another, pales) gu.

Gurnay. Sa. a chev. betw. three bulls' heads or.

Gurnay. Paly of six ar. and az. a bend gu.

Gurney (West Barsham, co. Norfolk). Ar. a cross engr. gu. *Crests*—1st: On a chapeau gu. turned up erm. a gurnet fish in pale, with the head downwards; 2nd: A wrestling collar or.

Gurney (Norwich, Keswick, Earlham, North Runcton, &c., co. Norfolk). Same *Arms,* &c., as the last.

Gurney (North Runcton, co. Norfolk). Same *Arms* and *Crest.*

Gurney, or Gurnard (Sir RICHARD GURNEY, Lord Mayor of London, was created a bart. 1641, *d. s. p.* 1647). Paly of six or and az. per fesse counterchanged. *Crest*—A lion's head erased or, gorged with a palisado coronet, composed of spear heads az.

Gurney, or Gurnard (London; granted 26 July, 1633; Her. Off. London, c. 24). Same *Arms* and *Crest.*

Gurney (Causton and Aylesham, co. Norfolk). Ar. a cross engr. gu. in the dexter quarter a crescent az.

Gurney (Reg. Ulster's Office). Az. on a chev. betw. two cotises ar. three leopards' faces gu. crowned or.

Gurnut. Az. three griffins' heads erased or.

Gurteen (granted to STEPHEN HUMPHREYS GURTEEN, Esq., of Bleane, co. Kent). Per chev. sa. and or, in chief two bulls' heads cabossed, and in base a lion ramp. counterchanged. *Crest*—A demi heraldic antelope sa. armed, hoofed, and crined or, supporting betw. the legs a tilting spear gold.

Gurwood. Az. a chev. ar. *Crests*—1st: A unicorn's head issuant; 2nd: Out of a mural coronet a castle ruined in the centre, and therefrom an arm in armour embowed, holding a scymetar all ppr.

Gushill. Ar. a fesse betw. six martlets sa.

Guson (London). Paly of six ar. and az. on a bend gu. three round buckles or.

Gussand. Az. five lozenges in bend or (another, ar.).

Gusset. Ar. two guttées de poix.

Gussey (Woodland, co. Devon). Ar. a fesse sa. betw. three lions ramp. gu.

Gusthart (ROBERT GUSTHART, Esq., M.D., 1750). Ar. three passion nails pileways in point embrued. *Crest*—An eagle displ. sa. pierced through with an arrow bendwise ar. *Motto*—Avitos novit honores.

Guston. Barry of four az. and ar. on a chief of the second three hurts. *Crest*—A demi wolf gu.

Guthrie (that Ilk, co. Forfar). Quarterly, 1st and 4th, or, a lion ramp. gu.; 2nd and 3rd, az. a garb. or. *Crest*—A dexter hand issuing, holding a drawn sword ppr. *Supporters*—Two chevaliers in full armour, with batons in the dexter hands, the visors of their helmets up ppr. *Motto*— Sto pro veritate.

Guthrie (Carsbank, Scotland). Quarterly, 1st and 4th, ar. a cross sa.; 2nd and 3rd, az. three garbs or, all within a bordure engr. gu. *Motto*—Pietas et frugalitas.

Guthrie (Kingedward, co. Banff, bart.). Quarterly, 1st and 4th, or, a lion ramp. reguard. gu. holding in the dexter paw a cross crosslet fitchée az.; 2nd and 3rd, az. three garbs or. *Crest*—A lion's paw issuant, grasping a twig of a palm branch ppr. *Motto*—Sto pro veritate.

Guthrie (Halkertoun, co. Kincardine). Quarterly, 1st and 4th, or, a lion ramp. reguard. gu.; 2nd and 3rd, az. three garbs or, all within a bordure indented az. *Crest*—A falcon, wings erected, standing on a dexter hand in fess couped behind the wrist ppr. *Motto*—Ad alta.

Guthrie (Provost of Forfar, 1672). Quarterly, 1st and 4th, or, a lion ramp. reguard. gu.; 2nd and 3rd, az. three garbs or, all within a bordure indented ar. *Crest*—A cross crosslet fitchée az. *Motto*—Ex unitate incrementum.

Guthrie (Lunan, co. Forfar). Quarterly, 1st and 4th, ar. a lion ramp. gu.; 2nd and 3rd, az. three garbs or.

Guthrie (Craigie, co. Forfar). Quarterly, 1st and 4th, ar. a cross sa.; 2nd and 3rd, az. three garbs or, banded gu. all within a bordure waved gu. *Crest*—A demi lion ramp. gu. holding in his dexter paw a cross crosslet fitchée gu. *Mottoes*—Above the crest: Sto pro veritate; below the shield : Nec tumidus nec timidus.

Guthrie (*Baron Oranmore;* arms of GUTHRIE, of the Mount, co. Ayr; borne under the limitations of an entail as his only arms). Quarterly, 1st and 4th, or, a lion ramp. gu. armed and langued az. surmounted of a fess ar charged with a mount betw. two edock leaves vert; 2nd and 3rd, az. three garbs or. *Crest*—A dexter hand erect holding a sword in

2 F 2

bend all ppr. and over the crest an escroll, with the motto, " Sto pro veritate." *Supporters*—Dexter, a knight in chain armour ppr. holding in the exterior hand a battle axe, and on the other arm a shield gu. charged with two lions pass. guard. or; sinister, a like knight, the armour covered by a surcoat ar. and hanging from the sinister arm a shield ar. thereon the arms of BROWNE, viz., barry of eight or and az. an eagle displ. with two heads sa. surrounded by an orle of martlets gu. *Motto*—Fortiter et fideliter. *Crest* of BROWNE (formerly used)—A griffin's head erased ppr.

Guthrie (Rev. R. R. LINGARD-GUTHRIE, of Taybank, co. Forfar, 1871). Quarterly, 1st and 4th grand quarters, counterquartered, 1st and 4th, ar. a cross sa., 2nd and 3rd, az. three garbs or, banded gu. all within a bordure indented of the last for diff., for GUTHRIE; 2nd and 3rd grand quarters, barry of six or and vair on a bend engr. sa. four escallops ar., for LINGARD. *Crest*—A demi lion ramp. gu. holding in his dexter forepaw a cross crosslet fitchée az. *Mottoes*—Above the crest: Sto pro veritate; below the shield: Nec tumidus nec timidus.

Gutteridge, or Guttridge. Ar. a cross gu. betw. four mullets pierced sa. *Crest*—A swan pass. crowned with an antique crown all ppr.

Guttyns (co. Salop). Gu. on a fesse betw. three goats' heads erased ar. as many pellets.

Guven. Gu. a chev. ar. betw. three fleurs-de-lis or.

Guy, or Guise (Dunsley, co. Herts). Gu. seven lozenges vair, three, three, and one.

Guy (Oundle, co. Northampton, and co. Wilts). Az. on a chev. ar. betw. three leopards' faces or, as many fleurs-de-lis gu. *Crest*—A lion's head az. betw. two wings expanded or, collared ar.

Guyan (Danes Hall, co. Essex). Ar. three bends az. on a canton sa. a lion pass. guard. or. *Crest*—A demi lion ramp. guard. or, gorged with a collar per pale ar. and sa.

Guyernon. Chequy or and az. a chev. erm.

Guylemin (co. Hertford, and Troyle, co. Anglesey, Wales). Ar. a man's leg in pale sa. couped at the thigh gu. gartered or. *Crest*—An eagle's head erased sa. beaked gu. in the mouth a lion's gamb or, erased of the second.

Guyling. Barry of ten ar. and az. a lion ramp. gu. *Crest* —An arm embowed ar. holding a scymitar of the last, pommelled or, hand ppr.

Guynes. Vairé or and az. a quarter erm.

Guyon (granted to JOHN GUYON, Esq., of Richmond, co. Surrey). Per pale az. and gu. on the dexter side two lions ramp. or, supporting a tower ar. in base a scymetar, the pommel and hilt towards the sinister betw. two other scymetars, the pommels and hilts towards the dexter ppr. and on the sinister side on a bend of the third betw. three fleurs-de-lis ar. six pellets, all within a bordure also of the third. *Crest*—Out of a mural crown ar. charged with three pellets a demi lion ppr.

Guyreon, or Guyrien. Per fesse or and az. a lion ramp. gu.

Guyse. Ar. an ink moline gu.

Guythold. Or, a bend engr. cotised sa.

Gwaethvoed (King of Cardigan, and by marriage, Prince of Gwent, head of one of the Royal tribes of Wales). Or, a lion ramp. sa.

Gwatkin (co. Cornwall). Erm. three harvest flies gu. *Crest*—A garb or.

Gwatkin (Townhope, co. Hereford, and Nonsuch House, Chippenham). Erm. three bees volant ppr.

Gwavas (Gwavas, in Sithney, originally HICKS, assumed the name of GWAVAS, temp. Elizabeth: the co-heiress m. VEALE, and CARLYON). Ar. three battle axes ppr.

Gweirydd ap-Rhys Goch (Lord of Tal Ebolion in Anglesey; from GWEIRYDD, derived the FOULKES's of Gwernygran, co. Flint). Ar. on a bend sa. three lions' heads cabossed of the first.

Gwerry. Erm. two bars gu. on a canton of the last a mullet or.

Gwerystan (Prince of Powys). Az. a lion ramp. ar. head, feet, and tip of tail gu.

Gwillawne (Plompon, co. York). Az. five lozenges in fesse ar. each charged with an escallop gu. *Crest*—An eagle perched ppr.

Gwilliam (Wales). Az. three bucks' heads cabossed or.

Gwilliam (Wales). Az. on a cross sa. five crescents or, in the dexter chief quarter a spear's head erect sa.

Gwillim (Brainge Court, co. Hereford, there before 1500; the heiress m. JAMES COLLINS, Esq., of Drybridge House, co. Hereford). Ar. a lion ramp. ermines collared or, quartering RAVENHILL, MAUDE, and others.

436

Gwillim (Whitchurch, co. Hereford; WILLIAM GWILLIM, Esq., was Sheriff co. Hereford, 1692). Same *Arms*.

Gwillim (Langstone Court, co. Hereford, of whom was the learned JOHN GWILLIM, author of "The Display of Heraldry"). Sa. a horse's head erased or, betw. three gauntlets couped ar.

Gwillym (Bewsey Hall, co. Lancaster; now represented by THOMAS LITTLETON, fourth Lord Lilford). Sa. a horse's head erased or, betw. three gauntlets ar.

Gwilt (originally of co. Montgomery, and subsequently of co Surrey, and also of Westminster; granted, 1826, to GEORGE and JOSEPH GWILT (the latter an architect). The second crest was granted to JOSEPH GWILT in 1828. Both crests are derived from the bearings of SMITH, of Camden, co. Gloucester). Ar. a lion ramp. sa. on a chief dancettée of the last three saltires couped or. *Crest*—A dexter cubit arm couped ppr. holding a saltire, as in the arms, surmounted by a fleur-de-lis sa. *Second Crest*, borne by the Westminster family—On a saltire or, interlaced by two amphisbœnæ az. langued gu. a rose of the last barbed and seeded ppr.

Gwilt. Per pale gu. and az. on a chev. embattled betw. three estoiles or, as many lozenges sa.

Gwilt. Per fesse gu. and ar. on a pale engr. erminois betw. four unicorns' heads erased counterchanged a key sa. betw. two crosses pattée of the first.

Gwilt (originally of co. Montgomery, and subsequently or Icklingham, co. Suffolk). Az. a pale engr. erminois betw four unicorns' heads erased ar. horned, maned, and tufted or. *Crest*—From rays of the sun a unicorn's head, as in the arms, collared gu. ringed or. *Another Crest*—From a mount vert the sun rising in its splendour ppr. therefrom issuant a unicorn's head couped sa. armed and crined or, in the mouth a cross pattée fitchée gold.

Gwine. Or, a bordure vair.

Gwinnell. Or, a fesse vert betw. three mural crowns gu. *Crest*—An arm couped at the shoulder, vested gu. embowed, and resting the elbow on the wreath, the hand towards the sinister holding a bow ppr.

Gwinnet (Moreton Hall, co. Hereford, and Penlline Castle, co. Glamorgan). Az. a chev. betw. three spear heads ar. embrued ppr. within a bordure or. *Crest*—A horse's head sa. gorged with a wreath of oak or, in the mouth a broken spear in bend sinister, point downwards, embrued ppr.

Gwinnett (Cheltenham, and Brockhampton Park, co. Gloucester). Az. a chev. ar. betw. three spear heads ppr. embrued gu. *Crest*—A horse's head couped sa. holding in the mouth a spear in bend, head downwards, and embowed ppr.

Gwinnett (Wistaston). See TYLER.

Gwrgyn (Lord of Bryn, co. Denbigh). Ar. three grey hounds courant in pale sa. collared or.

Gwriad (King of the Isles). Ar. three fusils conjoined in fesse gu. each charged with an eagle displ. or.

Gwyn (Brecon; Sonning, co. Berks, 1688; and St. Martin's-in-the-Fields, 1768). Same *Arms* as GWYNNE, of Trecastle. *Crest*—A dexter arm embowed in armour ppr. the gauntlet grasping a sword below the hilt in bend sinister ar. pommel and hilt or. *Motto*—Gogoniant yr clethaf (glory to the sword).

Gwyn (Baron's Hall, co. Norfolk). Gu. a chev. betw. three lions ramp. or. *Crest*—A lion ramp. or.

Gwyn (Garth, co. Brecon). Ar. three boars' heads sa.

Gwyn (Dyffryn, co. Glamorgan). Sa. a fesse or, betw. two swords, the point of that in chief upwards, the other downwards, both in pale ar. hilted of the second. *Crest*—A hand ppr. holding a dagger erect ar. hilted or, thrust through a boar's head couped of the second. *Motto*—Vim vi repellere licet.

Gwyn (Llandovery, co. Caermarthen). Same *Arms*. *Crest*— A gauntlet, holding a sword ar. the point through a dragon's head erased or, vulned ppr.

Gwyn (Wadham College, co. Oxford, d. 20 Sept. 1683). Sam- *Arms* and *Crest*.

Gwyn (Pont-y-corred, co. Brecon). Same *Arms*. *Crest*—A sword erect in pale ppr. point downwards, pierced through a boar's head sa.

Gwyn (Glazbury and Newton, co. Brecon). Same *Arms*, field ar. swords gu.

Gwyn (Maeslech, co. Brecon). Sa. a lion ramp. reguard. or.

Gwyn (co. Derby). Az. a bend lozengy ar.

Gwyn (Fakenham, co. Norfolk). Gu. a chev. betw. three lions saliant or.

Gwyn (Abercrave, co. Brecon, and Baglan House, co. Glamorgan). Sa. a fesse or, betw. two swords, that in chief point upwards, the other downwards, both in pale ar. hilted of the second. *Crest*—A hand ppr. holding a dagger ar. hilted or, thrust through a boar's head couped of the second. *Motto*—Vim vi repellere licet.

Gwyn. Or, a bordure vair. *Crest*—A cannon mounted ppr.

Gwyn. Or, on a chev. couched sinister betw. three birds sa. five mullets ar. *Crest*—A stag's head erased ppr. betw. the attires a cross crosslet fitchée.

Gwyn. Gu. a lion ramp. within a bordure engr. or.

Gwyn (Ford Abbey, co. Devon). Quarterly, 1st and 4th, per pale az. and gu. three lions ramp. ar., for GWYN; 2nd, ar. a chev. sa. in chief a pile of three points gu., for PRIDEAUX; 3rd, ar. a chev. betw. three mullets pierced gu., for FRAUNCEIS. *Crests*—GWYN: A lion ramp. ar.; FRAUNCEIS: A pine tree ppr. *Motto*—Expectes et sustineas.

Gwyn (registered by Hawkins, Ulster, 1701, to Right Hon. FRANCIS GWYN, a Privy Councillor in Ireland and State Secretary to LAWRENCE, first *Earl of Rochester*, Lord Lieutenant of Ireland; FRANCIS GWYN's ancestors bore the surname of HERBERT *temp.* Henry VIII.). Per pale az. and gu. three lions ramp. ar., an escutcheon of pretence, quarterly, 1st and 4th, ar. a chev. sa. in chief a label of three points gu.; 2nd and 3rd, ar. a chev. betw. three mullets gu. *Crest*—A lion ramp. ar.

Gwynbourne (arms in a window in Lincoln College. Visit. Oxon, 1574` Gu. semée of cross crosslets three boars' heads couped ar.

Gwynn (allowed by Hawkins, Ulster, 1698, to JOHN GWYNN, of Cork, grandson of JOHN GWYNN, of Welshpool, co. Montgomery, who came to Ireland *temp.* Queen Elizabeth). Ar. three nags' heads erased gu.

Gwynne (JOHN GWYNNE, of Gwynne Vale House, Crickhowell, South Wales). Same *Arms* and *Crest* as GWYN, of Llandovery.

Gwynne (Trecastle, Hay, co. Brecon, and Glanbrane Park, co. Caermarthen). Sa. a fesse or, betw. two swords, the one in chief pointing upwards, the one in base downwards, blades ar. hilts and pommels of the second. *Crest*—A hand couped at the wrist ppr. holding a dagger, blade ar. hilt or, thrust through a boar's head erased sa. *Note*—The ancient crest was a dragon's head erased vert, on the point of a sword.

Gwynne (Garth, co. Brecon). Gu. a lion ramp. reguard. or. *Crest*—A lion ramp. reguard. supporting betw. the forepaws a boar's head all or.

Gwynne. See VAUGHAN.

Gwynne (Ireland). Az. a bend lozengy ar. and gu. *Crest*—A dolphin naiant az.

Gwyrdyr (Wales). Az. three crowns, two and one, or, on an inescutcheon sa. a lion ramp. ar.

Gwys (Wiston, co. Brecknock). Gu. a chev. erm.

Gwythold. Or, a bend sa. betw. two cotises engr. of the second.

Gybbes. Paly bendy sinister ar. and gu. on a bend az. two fleurs-de-lis or.

Gybbon (co. Dorset). Sa. a lion ramp. ar. crowned or, betw. three escallops of the second. *Crest*—A demi lion ar. crowned or, holding in the paw an escallop of the first.

Gybbons, or Guybon (Stratchet, co. Norfolk). Or, a lion ramp. sa. over all a bend gu. charged with three escallops ar. *Crest*—A demi lion ramp. sa. charged with three escallops in pale ar.

Gybons (co. Lancaster, and Darsham, co. Suffolk). Ar. a lion pass. sa. over all two tilting spears in saltire gu. headed of the second.

Gybons, or Gibbons (co. Glamorgan, Ditley, co. Oxford, and Newhall, co. Warwick). Gu. a lion ramp. or, over all on a bend ar. three crosses formée sa. *Crest*—A lion's gamb erect and erased gu. holding a cross formée fitchée sa.

Gybons. Ar. two partisans in saltire gu. headed sa. over all a lion pass. or.

Glyde (Stout's Hall, co. Gloucester). Az. on a chev. betw. three fleurs-de-lis or, as many mullets pierced of the field. *Crest*—Out of an earl's coronet or, four plumes issuant, two on the dexter gold, those on the sinister gu.

Gye. Az. on a chev. ar. betw. three leopards' faces or, as many fleurs-de-lis gu.

Gyhewe. Ar. a chev. gu. betw. two mullets in chief sa. and a cinquefoil pierced of the second in base.

Gyles (Bowden, co. Devon; Sir EDWARD GYLES, Knt., son of JOHN GYLES. Visit. 1620). Per chev. ar. and az. a lion ramp. counterchanged, collared or. *Crest*—A lion's gamb erased and erect ppr. charged with a bar or, holding an apple branch vert, fructed gold.

Gyles (Ireland; impalement on the Fun. Ent., 1652, of Mrs. FRANCIS GYLES, wife of RICHARD FRANCIS, one of the Gentlemen of the Ordnance in Ireland). Per chev. sa. and or, a lion ramp. counterchanged.

Gyles (co. Kent). Per pale az. and gu. a griffin pass. or.

Gyles (London; granted 28 July, 1579). Gu. a cross betw.

four uncovered cups or, on a chief ar. three pelicans with wings elevated sa. vulning their breasts ppr.

Gyles. Per fesse gu. and az. on a bend engr. ar. three cinquefoils of the second.

Gyles. Per fesse gu. and az.

Gyles. Per pale gu. and az. a griffin pass. or.

Gyles. Ar. on a fesse engr. sa. betw. three crosses formée gu. as many martlets or.

Gyles. Or, on a cross sa. five plates.

Gyles (London). Per fesse gu. and az. on a bend engr. ar. betw. two lions' heads erased, each holding in the mouth a cross crosslet or, three cinquefoils of the second.

Gyll (Barton, co. York. Dugdale's Visit. 1666). Sa. a pale betw. four fleurs-de-lis or, a canton ar. *Crest*—The head of an eastern king couped at the shoulders in profile ppr. crowned and collared, a chain passing from the rim of the crown behind to the back of the collar, all or.

Gyll (Haughton le Skerne, co. Durham; derived from THOMAS GYLL, of Thriscrosse, Knaresborough, co. York, living in the 16th century; the sisters and co-heirs of THOMAS GYLL, Esq., Barrister-at-law, of Barton, who *d.* in 1780, were ANNE, wife of FRANCIS HARTLEY, Gent., of Middleton Tyas, co. York; JANE, *m.* to THOMAS BUCKTON, of Dalton Gales, co. York; ELIZABETH, MARY, and ALICE, *m.* to RALPH HOBSON, of Kneeting). Sa. a pale betw. four fleurs-de-lis or. *Crest* —The head of an eastern king couped at the shoulders in profile ppr. crowned and collared, a chain passing from the rim of the crown behind to the back of the collar all or.

Gyll (co. Essex). Ar. a chev. betw. three escallops sa.

Gyll (granted, about 1586, to RALPH GYLL, "Keeper of the Queene's lyons at the Tower of London;" four generations of this family, viz., I. THOMAS, II. RALPH, III. ROBERT, and IV. WILLIAM, were Lion Keepers at the Tower). Ar. on a bend sa. three mullets pierced of the field, on a canton az. a lion pass. or. *Crest*—A falcon's head az. winged or.

Gyll (Wyddial Hall, co. Hertford, and Wyrardisbury, co. Buckingham; originally from co. Cambridge, in which county the family was resident from the reign of Richard II. until about the year 1455, when JOHN GYLL, Esq., of Buckland, *m.* a lady of that place, and removed thither. His grandson, JOHN GYLL, *m.* MARGARET, dau. and heiress of GEORGE CANON, Esq., of Wyddial·Hall, and, dying in 1546, left a son and heir, GEORGE GYLL, Esq., grandfather of Sir GEORGE GYLL, Knt., direct ancestor of the present family). Sa. two chev. ar. each charged with three mullets of the field, in base a cinquefoil of the second, on a canton or, a lion pass. guard. gu.; quartering, for FLEMYNG, quarterly, 1st and 4th, gu. a chev. within a double tressure flory counterflory ar.; 2nd and 3rd, az. three cinquefoils ar. all within a bordure or, charged with eight fleurs-de-lis az. *Crest*—A hawk's head az. betw. two wings fretty vert. *Motto*— Virtutis gloria merces.

Gyll (co. York). Sa. a fesse betw. four fleurs-de-lis or.

Gyll (co. Hertford). Sa. a bend or, over all a chev. ar. charged with three mullets of the first, on a canton of the second a lion ramp. gu.

Gylle. Lozengy or and vert a lion ramp. guard. ar.

Gylles, or Gyles. Ar. on a fesse engr. sa. betw. three crosses pattée gu. as many martlets of the first. *Crest*—A dexter hand holding a spiked club ppr. spikes or.

Gylver (co. Hants). Per pale gu. and sa. a griffin segreant ar.

Gylwike. Ar. a chev. betw. three martlets az.

Gymber (London, 1520). Sa. on a bend ar. cotised of the last three chevronels gu. *Crest*—A dexter arm in armour, holding in the hand ppr. a spiked club or.

Gynes. Vairé or and az.

Gynn (co. Hertford). Az. a griffin segreant or, on a chief indented erm. three pellets. *Crest*—On a garb or, a bird close az.

Gynney (co. Norfolk). Chequy or and gu a chief erm.

Gynney. Paly of six or and gu. a chief erm.

Gyrlyn (Wellingham, co. Norfolk). Az. on a bend per bend of the first and gu. betw. two cotises engr. on the outside sa. three fleurs-de-lis or. *Crest*—A demi griffin az. wings, beak, and legs or, holding a fleur-de-lis per pale of the first and gu.

Gyrlyn. Ar. on a bend cotised az. three fleurs-de-lis of the first.

Gysors (Lord Mayor of London, 1245, 1246, 1249, 1311, and 1314). Az. a lion ramp. ar. within an orle of billets and a bordure engr. or.

Gyssard. Gu. two bars erm. in chief a lion pass. or.

Gysse (co. Bucks). Gu. six lozenges vair, three, two, and one, on a canton ar. a mullet of the field.

Gysseling (Algorley, co. Lincoln). Vair guttée counterchanged. *Crest*—A lion pass. erm. collared gu.

Gyssinge, Gyslyng, or Gymsying. Ar. on a bend az. three eagles displ. or. *Crest*—A lion ramp. az. winged or.

Gyssors. Or, a lion ramp. az.

Gytties (Elmeston, co. Kent). Ar. three battle axes sa. *Crest*—An arm embowed in armour ppr. garnished or, holding a battle axe ar.

Gyttings (co. Salop). Gu. on a fesse betw. three goats' heads erased ar. as many pellets. *Crest*—Two tilting spears in saltire.

H

HABERDASHERS, COMPANY OF (London). · See LONDON, Principal Corporate Companies of.

Haberdashers, Company of (Exeter). Same as the HABERDASHERS COMPANY OF LONDON.

Haberiam (Haberiam-Eurs, co. Lancaster). Ar. three crosses couped sa.

Habert (cos. Norfolk and Northumberland). Erm. two flaunches sa.

Habgood. Or, on an anchor betw. three fishes naiant az. *Crest*—A sword and quill in saltire ppr.

Habileyne. Or, on a cross sa. five eagles ar.

Habingdon (Hindlip and Wichenford, co. Worcester, and Brockhampton, co. Hereford; of the Hindlip family was THOMAS HABINGDON, the antiquarian collector for the History of co. Worcester). Ar. on a bend gu. three eagles displ. or. *Crest*—An eagle displ. or, ducally crowned az. (Granted 1577).

Habingdon (Dowdeswell, co. Gloucester, of the Wichenford line). See ABINGDON (Dowdeswell).

Hable, or Habley. Ar. a chev. canton and bend gu.

Hacche (*Baron Hacche*, summoned to Parliament 1299, *d.* 1336). Or, a cross engr. gu.

Hacclut (co. Gloucester). Ar. on a bend cotised gu. three mullets or.

Haccombe (Haccombe, co. Devon, temp. Henry III., the heiress *m.* ERCEDEKNE). Ar. three bends sa. *Crest*—A dexter arm from the shoulder, holding a bow and arrow all ppr.

Haccombe (Smith's Ordinary). Lozengy az. and sa. *Crest* —A dragon's head erased vert sealed or.

Hacebellow (Reg. Ulster's Office). Sa. on a fess ar. an annulet of the field.

Hach (co. Devon). Gu. three demi lions pass. guard. or.

Hachatt. Ar. a fesse gu. in chief a bar indented of the second.

Hache (Hache and North Aller, co. Devon). Gu. two demi lions pass. guard. in pale or.

Hacher. Az. a chev. betw. six escallops ar. three, two, and one.

Hachet, or Hanchet. Per fesse gu. and ar. on a chief of the second another indented of the first.

Hachet. Ar. on a bend sa. cotised gu. three fleurs-de-lis or.

Hack (co. Essex). Quarterly, ar. and sa. a cross betw. four escallops counterchanged.

Hackebecke. Or, two bars az.

Hacker (HEATHCOTE-HACKER, East Bridgford, Old Hall, co. Nottingham). Quarterly, 1st and 4th, erm. three pomeis, each charged with a cross or, for HEATHCOTE; 2nd and 3rd, sa. a cross vair betw. four mullets or, pierced of the field, for HACKER. *Crests*—1st: On a mural c. vn az. a pomeis charged with a cross or, betw. two win₀ displ. erm., for HEATHCOTE; 2nd: A woodpecker standing on the top of a tree eradicated ppr., for HACKER.

Hacker (Trowell and Flintham, co. Nottingham). Az. a cross vairé or, and of the first betw. four mullets pierced of the second. *Crest*—On the trunk of a tree fesseways a moorcock ppr.

Hacker. Ar. three wolves pass. gu.

Hacket (co. Buckingham and London). Ar. three fleurs-de-lis in bend betw. two cotises gu. *Crest*—A demi panther ar. spotted az. or and gu. holding a branch vert flowered of the fourth.

Hacket (Scotland). See HALKET.

Hacket. Az. three fishes haurient ar.

Hackett (St. John's, Worcester). Ar. two bends gu.

Hackett (Sir WALTER HACKETT, one of the Knts. of co. Notts, temp. Edward I.). Ar. two bends gu.

Hackett, or Halkett. Sa. three piles meeting in the base ar. on a chief gu. a lion pass. guard. or. *Crest*—A demi eagle with two heads displ. per pale gu. and or, wings counterchanged, each head ensigned with a crown.

Hackett (Dublin; confirmed by Carney, Ulster, 1688, to Sir

438

THOMAS HACKETT, Lord Mayor of Dublin; descended from an ancient family long settled in Ireland). Gu. three hake haurient in fesse ar. on a chief or, three trefoils slipped ppr. *Crest*—Out of a mural crown ar. an eagle displ. with two heads sa. *Motto*—Spes mea Deus.

Hackett (Moor Park, King's co., and Riverstown, co. Tipperary; confirmed to THOMAS HACKETT, Esq., and the de scendants of his grandfather). Sa. three piles pointing to the base ar. the centre one charged with a trefoil slipped vert, on a chief gu. a lion pass. guard. or. *Crest*—A demi panther ar. spotted az. collared gu. charged on the shoulder with a trefoil slipped vert, and holding in the dexter paw a branch of the last. *Motto*—Virtute et fidelitate.

Hackett (Hackettstown, co. Carlow). Az. three hake fishes haurient in fesse ar. on a chief of the second three shamrocks ppr. *Crest*—An eagle displ. with two heads ppr. issuing from a ducal coronet, surmounted by a tiara resting on two snakes. *Motto*—Fortitudine et prudentia.

Hackett, alias Hay (Reg. Ulster's Office). Ar. on a saltire engr. sa. nine plates, each charged with an erm. spot.

Hackett (Killedmond, co. Tipperary; Fun. Ent. of JOHN HACKETT, *d.* 15 April, 1639). Gu. three plumbers' hammers or hacketts ar. *Crest*—An eagle displ. with two heads per pale az. and gu. betw. the heads a trefoil slipped vert. *Motto*—Spes mea Deus.

Hackett (co. Waterford; Sir JOHN HACKETT was Ambassador for Henry VIII., Ulster's Office). Same *Arms*, with a chief or, charged with a rose gu. betw. two estoiles az.

Hackford. Chequy or and vert. *Crest*—A swan with wings endorsed ar. standing on a trumpet or.

Hackford. Ar. two bends nebulée sa.

Hacklet, Hackluyt, or Hacklute (cos. Gloucester and Salop). Ar. on a bend cotised gu. three mullets pierced or.

Hacklet, or Hackluit (co. Salop). Ar. on a bend cotised wavy gu. three mullets or. *Crest*—A hand holding a hunting-horn ppr.

Hacklet (co. Salop). Gu. a bend dancettée ar. cotised or.

Hacklet. Ar. three shoemakers' knives gu.

Hackluit. Ar. three battle axes erect, two and one gu.

Hackluyt, or Hackvill (Yetton, co. Hereford and co. Salop). Gu. three hatchets or.

Hackon (co. Norfolk). Sa. two bars vair.

Hackshaw (Hutton, co. Salop). Or, a chev. betw. three herons' heads erased gu. *Crest*—A heron's head erased ar. gorged with a ducal coronet gu.

Hackwell. Or, an ass's head erased sa.

Hackwill, or Hakewill (Totness and Exeter, co. Devon; WILLIAM HACKWILL, Solicitor to Anne, Queen of James I., and Rev. GEORGE HACKWILL, D.D., Chaplain to Charles, Duke of York, afterwards Charles I. Visit. Devon, 1620). Or, a bend betw. six trefoils slipped purp. *Crest*—A trefoil slipped purp. betw. two wings expanded or. *Another Crest*— A human heart gu. betw. two wings displ. or.

Hackwill (co. Lincoln). Same *Arms* and *Crest*.

Hackworthy (co. Devon). Ar. two bends wavy sa.

Hacon (Ipswich, co. Suffolk, and Whiteacre, co. Norfolk; granted 2 June, 1536). Sa. two bars vairé ar. and vert, in chief a falcon close or, betw. two bezants. *Crest*—A falcon barry of six ar. and vair.

Hacon (Toperoft, co. Norfolk). Sa. two barrulets vairé ar. and vert, in chief a martlet or, betw. two plates.

Haoote. Ar. on a bend az. three lions ramp. or. *Crest*— On a ducal coronet a martlet all ppr.

Hadd, or De la Hadd (Canterbury, co. Kent). Gu. three bucks' heads cabossed or, on each a cross crosslet fitchée ar. *Crest*—On a mount vert a talbot sejant ar. eared sa. ducally gorged gu. on the dexter side of the mount a laurel branch ppr.

Hadd (co. Kent). Vert on a fesse betw. three crosses crosslet fitchée or, as many bucks' heads cabossed az.

Hadd. Gu. three stags' heads cabossed ar. betw. the attires of each a cross formée of the last.

Hadden (Lanerick). Quarterly, 1st and 4th, ar. a saltire engr. sa.; 2nd ar. a saltire engr. betw. four roses gu.; 3rd, or, a bend chequy ar. and sa. in the centre over the quarterings, a crescent ar. *Crest*—An eagle's head erased or. *Motto*—Suffer.

Hadden. Ar. three roses gu. a chief of the last. *Crest*—An arm embowed brandishing a scymetar ppr.

Hadderwick (Pitcullo). Gu. a lion pass. guard. chequy ar. and az. betw. three pheons of the second. *Crest*—A dexter arm from the elbow, holding a roll of paper ppr. *Motto*— Ne timeas recte facienulo.

Haddington, Earl of. See HAMILTON.

Haddock (co. Lancaster). Ar. a cross sa. in the first quarter a fleur-de-lis of the last. *Crest*—A dexter hand holding a fish all ppr.

Haddon. Or, a man's leg couped at the thigh az. *Crest*—A man's leg couped in the middle of the thigh in armour ppr. garnished and spurred or, embowed at the knee, the foot upwards, the toe pointing to the dexter side.

Haden (Haden Hill, co. Stafford). Or (sometimes, ar.) a human leg embowed, couped at the thigh az.

Hadeswell. Ar. a fesse betw. three boars pass. sa.

Hadfield. Erm. on a chev. sa. three cinquefoils or. *Crest*—An arm embowed, habited az. holding in the hand ppr. a trefoil slipped or.

Hadfield. Ar. a pale gu. in fesse three cinquefoils counter-changed. *Crest*—An escallop or.

Hadham. Ar. a bend betw. six buckles az.

Hadiswell. Gu. three wells ar. masoned sa. *Crest*—A demi lion ramp. gu. holding in the paws a battle axe az.

Hadley (co. Hereford, and London; granted 1685). Gu. two chevrons betw. three falcons ar. beaked, legged, and belled or. *Crest*—A falcon ar. beaked, legged, and belled or, holding in the mouth a buckle of the last.

Hadley (co. Somerset). Gu. three round buckles ar.

Hadley (co. Herts). Gu. a chev. betw. three falcons ar.

Hadley (London). Az. a chev. and fesse ar. in chief three annulets or.

Hadley (Lord Mayor of London, 1379 and 1393). Az. a chev. betw. three annulets or, over all on a fesse of the second as many martlets gu.

Hadley (Cranbrook Park, co. Essex; granted to SIMEON CHARLES HADLEY, Esq., Alderman and Sheriff of London). Gu. three chevronels or, betw. as many falcons belled ar. in the centre chief point a buckle, the tongue erect of the second. *Crest*—Upon a mount vert a falcon belled ar. supporting in the dexter claw a buckle, as in the arms, and holding in the beak three ears of wheat or. *Motto*—God is my help.

Hadley. Ar. a pair of compasses, and in base an annulet sa.

Hadley. Gu. on a chev. or, three crosses patonce of the first.

Hadley. Gu. a chev. ar. betw. three plates, over all a fesse az.

Hadley. Az. a chev. surmounted of a fesse betw. three annulets or.

Hadley (Reg. Ulster's Office). Gu. three oval buckles ar. tongues fessways.

Hadlow. Ar. a lion ramp. az. guttée d'or.

Hadnam (cos. Oxford and Lincoln). Ar. three fleurs-de-lis az.

Hadnoll (co. Hants). Or, a maunch sa.

Hadokes. Ar. a cross sa. in the first quarter a fleur-de-lis of the second. *Crest*—A talbot's head erased sa. collared ar.

Hadowie (Scotland). Ar. three hunting horns sa. stringed gu.

Hadringdon. Erm. a cross voided gu.

Hadshall. Or, a cross engr. gu.

Hadsley (co. Essex). Az. on a chev. or, three crosses potent sa.

Hadson (co. Cambridge). Sa. a chev. betw. three hawks volant or. *Crest*—On a ducal coronet or, a lion ramp. gu.

Hadsor (Middle Temple, London). Gu. three bars erm. betw. ten crosses formée or, three, three, three, and one, a canton of the last. *Crest*—Out of a ducal coronet gu. a dragon's head or, holding in the mouth leaves vert.

Hadsor (Drogheda; Fun. Ent. 1620, ELIZABETH, dau. of NICHOLAS HADSOR, and wife of CHRISTOPHER FITZ-WILLIAM, of Dublin, merchant). Sa. two bars ar. on a bend gu. three crosses crosslet fitchée of the second.

Hadstock (co. Suffolk). Or, a chev. gu. pierced with a bend erm.

Hadstocke. Or, a chev. gu. and canton erm.

Hadwen (granted to SIDNEY JOHN WILSON HADWEN, Esq., Dean House, Sowerby, co. York). Per pale az. and sa. a stag's head caboshed ar. on a chief or, two setter dogs' heads erased respecting each other ppr. *Crest*—A rock overgrown with heath, thereon a grouse, a thistle all ppr. *Motto*—Had on and win.

Hadwick (Scotland). Ar. three hunting-horns sa.

Hadys. Barry of eight az. and ar. on a canton gu. a lion ramp. or.

Haffenden (Homewood, co. Kent, and Clearwell Court, co. Gloucester). Chequy ar. and sa. on a bend az. three mullets or.

Haffenden (exemplified to Rev. JOHN WILSON, of Stillington, co. York, on assuming the name of HAFFENDEN, by royal licence, 1872). Quarterly, 1st and 4th, chequy ar. and sa. a bend az. three escutcheons of the first, each charged with a

439

mullet of the second, for HAFFENDEN; 2nd and 3rd, sa. a wolf saliant or, collared of the field, in chief a cross pattée betw. two estoiles and in base an estoile of the second, for WILSON. *Crests*—1st, HAFFENDEN: A gryphon's head erased sa. pendent from the beak an escutcheon ar. charged with a mullet sa.; 2nd, WILSON: A demi wolf or, guttée de sang holding betw. the paws a cross pattée gu.

Haffey (confirmed to HENRY HAFFEY, Esq., of Bath, formerly of Armagh). Ar. a lion ramp. gu. on a chief az. two crosses pattée or. *Crest*—A demi lion ramp. az. armed and langued gu. grasping in the dexter paw a cross pattée or. *Motto*—Avise la fin.

Hagan (confirmed to ROBERT HAGAN, Esq., Capt. R.N., son of JOHN HAGAN, Esq., late of Magherafelt, co. Londonderry). Ar. two sea lions ramp. gu. supporting an anchor in pale sa. in base a salmon naiant in waves of the sea all ppr. *Crest*—Out of a naval crown or, a demi negro affronteé with broken manacles depending from each wrist, grasping in the dexter hand the Union Jack displ. on a flagstaff, and in the sinister hand on a similar staff the cap of liberty all ppr. *Motto*—Vota vita mea.

Hagar (Bourne, co. Essex; granted 1605). Or, on a bend sa. three lions pass. ar.

Hagar (Baynecast, co. Cambridge). Ar. on a bend sa. three lions pass. of the first.

Hagar. Gu. on a bend or, three lions pass. sa.

Hagar. Or, three chevronels vert, each charged with a mullet ar.

Hagart (Eastbury Manor, co. Surrey, late of Bantaskine, co. Stirling, 1814). Per bend az. and or, on a bend sa. betw. two estoiles of sixteen points, counterchanged, a lion pass. ar. betw. as many crosses moline of the second. *Crest*—A lion ramp. ppr.—*Motto*—Sans peur.

Hagell. Erminois a pile gu. *Crest*—An olive branch slipped ppr.

Hagelle. Gu. two bars or, in chief an escutcheon of the last.

Hagen (Bermondsey). Az. a chev. or, betw. two doves close in chief ar. and in base an oak tree ppr. *Crest*—A dove rising ar.

Hagen. Or, a fesse betw. three cramp-irons sa. *Crest*—A stork's head erased ppr.

Haggar (Bourne, co. Cambridge, and co. Essex). Ar. on a bend sa. three lions pass. of the first. *Crest*—On a mount vert a talbot pass. or, collared and lined gu.

Haggard. Az. a mullet of six points ar.

Haggard (WILLIAM MEYBOHM RIDER HAGGARD, Esq., J.P., D.L., of West Bradenham, co. Norfolk; the representative of an ancient family which came from co. Perth, temp. James I.) Quarterly, 1st, az. a mullet of six points ar., for HAGGARD; 2nd, erm. on a chief indented az. three martlets or, each holding in the beak a trefoil slipped ar., for RIDER; 3rd, vert a chev. betw. three garbs or, for AMYAND; 4th, ar. on a mount a man in armour holding a tree growing from the mount all ppr., for MEYBOHM. *Crests*—1st: A mullet of six points, as in the arms, for HAGGARD, motto over, Micat inter omnes; 2nd: Out of a mural crown per pale or and az. a snake erect ppr. holding in the mouth a trefoil slipped vert. *Motto*—Modeste conabor.

Haggatt, or Haget (co. Somerset; temp. Henry VI.). Ar. two bends gu.

Hagger. Vert a lion ramp. within an orle ar. *Crest*—A demi lion gu. supporting a long cross az.

Haggerston (Haggerston Castle, co. Northumberland; bart.). Az. on a bend cotised ar. three billets sa. *Crest*—A lion pass. ar.

Haggerston. Same *Arms.* *Crest*—A talbot erm.

Haggerstone. See *Supplement.*

Haggitt. See WEGG-PROSSER.

Hagley (Hagley, co. Worcester; arms from the seal of HENRY DE HAGGELEY, Extreator of co. Worcester, 1395; the coat seems to be that of MORTIMER). Per pale or and az. three bars counterchanged, in chief two palets, and as many cantons also counterchanged, an inescutcheon ar. *Crest*—A dexter arm in armour embowed, holding in the gauntlet a battle axe all ppr.

Hague (Micklegate, co. York; descended from a Berkshire family of that name). Per chev. or and ar. two mullets az. in chief and a crescent gu. in base. *Crest*—A griffin's head erased ar.

Hague (Stanley Hall, near Wakefield). Ar. a bend az. on a chief gu. three martlets of the field. *Crest*—A martlet ar.

Haidon (co. Devon). Ar. three bars gemelles az. on a chief gu. a wivern or.

Haig, or Haigh. Az. a saltire betw. in chief a crescent reversed, in dexter fess a decrescent, in sinister fess an increscent, and in base a crescent ar. *Crest*—A demi savage holding over the dexter shoulder a hammer.

Haig (Bemerside, co. Roxburgh). Az. a saltire cantoned with two stars in chief and base, and with as many crescents addorsed in the flanks ar. *Crest*—A rock ppr. *Motto*—Above the crest: Tyde what may; and below: Sola virtus invicta.

Haig (cadet of Bemerside, 1672). As the last, charging the saltire with a primrose slipped ppr. for diff. *Motto*—Jam transit hyems.

Haigh (Grainsby Hall, co. Lincoln) Az. a saltire cantoned with a star in chief and in base, and with two crescents addorsed in the flanks ar. *Crest*—A rock ppr. *Mottoes*—Sola virtus invicta; and, Tyde what may.

Haighton (Chaigeley, co. Lancaster). Ar. on a bend engr. sa. three bulls' heads cabossed of the field. *Crest*—Out of a ducal coronet or, a bull's head ar.

Hailard. Ar. three bars betw. ten fleurs-de-lis az. four, three, two, and one.

Haine (co. Devon). Ar. a chev. gu. betw. three martlets sa.

Haines (co. Berks). Ar. a fesse az. bezantée betw. three annulets of the second.

Haines. Gu. three crescents paly wavy ar. and az. *Crest*—On a crescent an arrow in pale all ppr.

Haines. Or, on a fesse gu. three bezants in chief a greyhound courant az. collared ar. *Crest*—An eagle displ. az. semée of estoiles ar.

Hains. Ar. on a fesse betw. three annulets gu. as many ducal coronets or.

Hair (Scotland). Ar. a chief sa.

Haire (Armagh Manor, co. Fermanagh; confirmed to JAMES HAIRE, Esq., son and heir of ROBERT HAIRE, Esq., Q.C., and grandson of JAMES HAIRE, of Armagh, and their descendants). Gu. two bars or, on a chief indented ar. a thistle ppr. *Crest*—A lion ramp. ar. supporting the Roman fasces ppr. *Motto*—In te Domine speravi.

Haire-Forster. See FORSTER.

Hairsnet. Az. two bars dancettée erm. betw. six crosses crosslet or, three, two, and one.

Hairstans (Craigs, Scotland). Quarterly, 1st and 4th, az. a chev. or, betw. three keys fesseways ar.; 2nd and 3rd, ar. a savage's head couped, distilling drops of blood, thereon a bonnet composed of bay and holly leaves all ppr. within an orle of eight martlets sa., for GLADSTANES. *Crest*—A dexter arm holding a key ppr. *Motto*—Toujours fidèle.

Haitlie (Mellarstanes, Scotland). Or, on a bend az. three boars' heads erased of the first.

Haitlie. Az. a sword bendways ppr. hilt in chief or, betw. two mullets of the last. *Crest*—A hand holding four arrows, points downwards all ppr.

Haize, or De la Haize (London; originally of France, 1757). Erminois a saltire gu. on a chief of the last three escallops or. *Crest*—A wolf's head ppr. erased gu. charged on the neck with an escallop or.

Hake (co. Devon). Ar. a chev. betw. three hakes haurient gu.

Hake. Az. three hake-fishes haurient ar.

Hake (Peterborough, co. Northampton). Gu. a bend betw. two boars' heads erased bendways or. *Crest*—A sword erect ar. hilt and pommel or, enfiled with a boar's head couped az.

Hake. Az. three bars or, a bordure engr. ar.

Hakebeche, or Hakbeech. Or, two bars az.

Hakebeche (Emneth, co. Norfolk). Or, on two bars az. three ducal coronets of the field.

Hakeford (co. Gloucester). Or, an eagle displ. sa. collared ar.

Hakeford. Or, an eagle displ sa. a bend ar.

Hakehed (Reg. Ulster's Office). Gu. three hakes haurient fessways ar.

Hakeluyt (co. Gloucester). Ar. on a bend cotised gu. three mullets of the field (another, or).

Haket, or Hacket (co. Kent, temp. Henry III.). Sa. crusily and three hake fish haurient ar.

Haket (co. Salop). Gu. three polexnes or.

Hakewood. Az. a chev. betw. three escallops ar. *Crest*—On a chapeau a garb all ppr.

Haampton. Ar. on a bend gu. three eagles displ. or.

Halanton. Az. a bend ar. betw. three eagles displ. or.

Halaton. Gu. three bucks' heads or.

Halbayne (co. Devon). Ar. a chev. sa. betw. two flaunches of the last.

Halbecke. Or, two bars gu.

Halberdyn. Ar. a chev. betw. three halberts ar. staves or. *Crest*—A wolf ramp. reguard. ppr.

Halcro (Scotland). Quarterly, 1st and 4th, ar. a mountain

vert issuing from the base; 2nd and 3rd, erm. on a fesse gu. three crescents ar. *Crest*—Two hands holding a sword in pale ppr.

Haldane (DUNCAN-HALDANE, *Earl of Camperdown*). See DUNCAN.

Haldane. Ar. a bend engr. gu. a chief sa. *Crest*—A globe ppr.

Haldane (that Ilk, co. Peebles). Gu. two leopards ar.

Haldane (Gleneagles, co. Perth). Quarterly, 1st and 4th, ar. a saltire engr. sa., for HALDANE; 2nd, ar. a saltire cantoned with four roses gu., for LENNOX; 3rd, or, a bend chequy sa. and ar., for MENTEITH. *Crest*—An eagle's head erased or. *Motto*—Suffer.

Haldane (Lanrick, co. Stirling). Same *Arms*, with a crescent gu. in the centre for diff.

Haldane-Oswald. See OSWALD.

Halden (Halden, co. Kent). Ar. a chief sa. (another, az.) over all a bend engr. gu.

Haldenby (Haldenby, co. York). Vert a fesse betw. three covered cups or. *Crest*—A swan close ar. beaked and legged gu. in the beak a sprig of laurel vert.

Haldenby. Az. five cinquefoils in cross ar.

Haldimand. Gu. a chev. betw. three annulets or. *Crest*—A sea-lion sejant ppr.

Haldon (Haldon, Scotland). Gu. two lions pass. guard. ar.

Hale (Sir FRANK VAN HALE, eighth son of FREDERICK DE HALLE, stated to have been a natural son of ALBERT, King of the Romans, was among the followers of the *Earl of Derby* into Gascony, 1344, and was elected a Knight of the Garter, 1359). Gu. a wyvern, wings elevated and crowned or, pendent from the neck an escutcheon of the field, thereon an eagle displ. with two heads ar. all within a border az. charged with six lioncels ramp. and as many fleurs-de-lis alternately of the second. *Crest*—On the battlements of a castle ar. a wyvern sa. wings addorsed guttée d'or, gorged with a ducal coronet, therefrom a chain reflexed over the back all gold, in the dexter claw a sword erect az.

Hale (Somerton Hall; granted to JOSEPH EATON HALE, Esq.). Ar. on a chev. engr. betw. three escutcheons az. each charged with a cinquefoil of the field three towers of the last. *Crest*—Upon a rock a tower ppr. surmounted by a sun in splendour or, and resting upon the battlements a scaling ladder in bend sa. *Motto*—Turris fortis mihi Deus.

Hale (Alderley, co. Gloucester; of this family was the celebrated Sir MATTHEW HALE). Ar. a fesse sa. in chief three cinquefoils of the last. *Crest*—A heron's head erased ar.

Hale (King's Walden, co. Hertford). Az. a chev. embattled and counter-embattled or. *Crest*—A serpent ppr. entwined round five arrow-shafts or, headed sa. feathered ar. one in pale, four saltirewise. *Motto*—Vera sequor.

Hale. Ar. on a pale fusily gu. a leopard's head or.

Hale (granted to the Venerable Archdeacon HALE). Per pale az. and gu. on a chev. betw. three arrows, points downward or, a cross patée of the second, all within a bordure erm. *Crest*—An arm embowed, vested az. fretty ar. cuffed or, the hand ppr. grasping two arrows also ppr. *Motto*—Cum principibus.

Haleighwell. Or, on a bend gu. three goats pass. ar. armed or.

Halengton. Az. a bend ar. betw. three eagles displ. or.

Halep (Lamorran, co. Cornwall; a family of consideration in the 14th and 15th centuries). Or, three bendlets sa.

Hales (Woodchurch, co. Kent, also of Hales' Place, Canterbury, bart., extinct 1802). Gu. three arrows or, feathered and barbed ar. *Crest*—A dexter arm embowed at the elbow in armour ppr. garnished or, and bound about with a ribbon gu. holding an arrow, as in the arms.

Hales (Beaksbourne, co. Kent; since of Brymore, co. Somerset, bart.; extinct 1824). Same *Arms* and *Crest*. *Motto*—Vis unita fortior.

Hales (Coventry, co. Warwick, bart., extinct ante 1812). Same *Arms*.

Hales, or Hals (co. Devon). Ar. a fesse betw. three griffins' heads erased sa. *Crest*—A griffin sejant ar.

Hales (Hackbendon, co. Kent). Gu. on a saltire ar. betw. four demi lions ramp. or, a cross of the first pierced vert.

Hales (Coventry, and Tunstall, co. Kent). Gu. three broad arrows or, feathered and headed ar. *Crest*—An arm embowed in armour ppr. garnished or, holding in the hand ppr. an arrow ar. headed gold, round the arm a scarf vert.

Hales (Holt, co. Norfolk). Gu. three arrows or, feathered and barbed ar., quartering, sa. a chev. betw. three fers-demoline erm. on a chief ar. a lion pass. gu., for TURNER; and ar. three torteaux and a chief gu., for BASELEY. *Crest*—A dexter arm embowed in armour ppr. garnished or, and bound round about with a ribbon gu. holding in the hand ppr. an arrow, as in the arms.

Hales (granted to Edward Hales, Esq.,North Frith, co. Kent). Per chev. engr. or and gu. in chief two arrows erect, points downwards sa. and in base a griffin's head couped of the first. Crest—Upon a mount a garb vert, in front thereof a shield or, charged with a griffin's head couped sa. Motto— Vis unita fortior.

Hales (Mychurch, co. Somerset). Sa. a chev. betw. three lions ramp. ar.

Hales (co. Stafford). Ar. three broad arrows az.

Hales. Az. a chev. embattled ar. (another, or).

Hales. Sa. a fret and canton ar.

Hales. Barry of eight az. and ar. on a canton gu. a lion pass. or.

Hales. Ar. on a chev. sa. betw. three annulets gu. as many estoiles ar (another, the estoiles of the first).

Hales. Sa. a chev. betw. three lions pass. ar.

Hales. Ar. three battle axes in pale barways sa.

Hales. Gu. three arrows ar. points downward, barbed or.

Hales. Quarterly, gu. and ar. in the first quarter three arrows or, feathered of the second, in the second quarter a lion ramp. sa. within a bordure engr. of the same.

Hales. Ar. a bend engr. vert.

Hales, or Hailes, Abbey of (co. Gloucester). Ar. in bend dexter a crosier gu. surmounted with a lion ramp. of the last, all within a bordure sa. bezantée.

Hales (confirmed by Camden, Clarenceux, 1616). Sa. on a fess or, betw. two chevronels ar. a cinquefoil gu. a border erm.

Hales-Owen-Abbey (co. Salop). Az. a chev. ar. betw. three fleurs-de-lis or.

Haleston. Paly of six ar. and sa. on a chev. gu. a cross crosslet or.

Haley (London, and Edgware-Bury, co. Middlesex). Az. three goats pass. ar. a chief of the last. Crest—A goat's head erased ar. gorged with a chaplet gu.

Haley (Eartham, co. Sussex). Or, on a cross az. a cinquefoil betw. four mascles of the field. Crest—On a crescent ar. a cross patonce gu.

Halfacre (Whiston, co. Cornwall). Erm. on a chev. vert betw. three lions' heads erased gu. as many acorns or.

Halfehide (granted 1560). Ar. two chev. conjoined in fesse sa. Crest—A greyhound sejant or, collared az. garnished and ringed of the first.

Halford (Wistow, co. Leicester, bart., extinct 1780). Ar. a greyhound pass. sa. on a chief az. three fleurs-de-lis or.

Halford (Welham, co. Leicester, bart., extinct). Same Arms.

Halford (Paddock House, near Canterbury, a branch of the preceding). Ar. a greyhound statant sa. collared or, on a chief az. three fleurs-de-lis of the third. Crest—A demi greyhound sa. collared or. Motto—Virtus in actione consistit.

Halford (Wistow Hall, co. Leicester, bart.; Sir Henry Vaughan was created a bart. 1809; he was son of James Vaughan, Esq., M.D., by Hester Halford, his wife, cousin of Sir Charles Halford, last bart. of Wistow, and assumed the surname of Halford 1814). Ar. a greyhound pass. sa. on a chief az. three fleurs-de-lis or. By royal warrant of augmentation, in 1837, a rose ar. was substituted for the centre of the fleurs-de-lis; and as further augmentation, on a canton erm. a staff entwined with a serpent ppr. and ensigned by a coronet composed of crosses pattée and fleursde-lis or. Crests—1st (of augmentation) : A staff entwined by a serpent ppr. and ensigned by a coronet composed of crosses pattée and fleurs-de-lis: 2nd : A greyhound's head couped at the neck sa. collared or. Motto—Mutas inglorius artes (To exercise, unambitious of praise, the silent arts). This motto is an elegant quotation from Virgil's description of the physician Iapis. Supporters—Two emeus ppr. each gorged with a coronet composed of crosses pattée and fleurs-de-lis or.

Halfpenny. Chequy ar. and sa. on a chief or, a rose gu. leaved vert, seeded of the third. Crest—A lion sejant ppr. holding in the dexter paw a cross crosslet fitchée or, resting the sinister on a triangle gu.

Halfpenny. Ar. a mullet gu. pierced of the first.

Halgate, or Holgate (Helsworth, co. York). Barry of four ar. and gu. a bend or, betw. two bulls' heads sa.

Halghton. Or, two bars gu. on a chief ar. three open bowls of the second, the insides of the third.

Halghwell, or Halwell (Halwell, co. Devon; extinct about the year 1500; the co-heiresses were six sisters—the eldest m. to Bray; the second to Brooke, Lord Cobham; the third to Verney, and afterwards to Oatsbby; the fourth to Pecham: the fifth to Bruges; and the sixth to Lifield). Ar. on a chev. gu. three annulets ar.

Halhead. Erm. five bars gu. over all three escutcheons

441

or, two and one. Crest—A falcon with wings expanded ar. beaked and belled or.

Haliburton. See Halyburton.

Haliday (Carnmoney, co. Antrim; confirmed to Alexander Henry Haliday, Esq., eldest son and heir of William Haliday, Esq., and their descendants). Ar. a sword paleways, the pommel within a crescent in base gu. on a canton az. a St. Andrew's cross of the first. Crest—A boar's head couped ar. langued and tusked or. Motto—Virtute parta.

Haliers. Quarterly, ar. and az. a bend gu.

Halke (Selling, near Feversham, co. Kent). Gu. a fesse betw. three hawks belled or. Crest—A dexter arm embowed in armour, holding in the hand a battle axe all ppr.

Halkerston (Rathillet, co. Fife). Or, three falcons' heads erased gu. Crest—A falcon's head, as in the arms. Supporters—Two falcons ppr. hooded and belled or. Motto—In ardua nitor.

Halkett (Pitfirrane, co. Fife, bart., 1662 and 1697 ; only the latter baronetcy belongs to the present family, who are heirs of line, and paternally Wedderburns). Sa. three piles conjoined in base ar. on a chief gu. a lion pass. or. Crest—A falcon's head erased ppr. Supporters—Two falcons close ppr. jessed and belled or. Mottoes—Over the crest: Fides sufficit; under the arms : Honeste vivo.

Halkett (Hall Hill and Dumbarnie, co. Fife). Arms, &c., as those of Hackett, Bart., quarterly with Craigie, of Dunbarnie.

Halkett (Gen. Sir Colin Halkett, G.C.H., &c., &c., Col. 31st Foot, eldest son of the late Major-General Frederick Halkett, a scion of the Halketts, of Hall Hill, co. Fife). Sa. three piles ar. on a chief gu. a lion pass. or. Crest—A falcon's head erased ppr. Supporters—On the dexter, a horse ar. gorged with a chaplet of laurel vert, therefrom suspended the Peninsula medal, inscribed in an escroll beneath, "Vento del poso ; " on the sinister, a lion reguard. gu. gorged with a chaplet of laurel or, pendent therefrom the Waterloo medal and ribbon. Motto—Fides sufficit.

Halkett, Baron (Hanover). Quarterly, 1st and 4th, three piles conjoined in base ar. on a chief gu. a lion pass. guard. or, for Halkett : 2nd, or, three crescents, within a double tressure flory counterflory gu., for Seton ; 3rd, ar. a fesse wavy sa. issuant therefrom a demi otter of the last, ducally crowned gu., for Meldrum. Crest—A falcon's head erased ppr. Supporters—On either side a falcon ppr. gorged with a wreath of laurel vert and murally crowned or. Motto—Fides sufficit.

Hall (Middleham, co. Bedford). Ar. a cross moline sa. in the dexter chief a fleur-de-lis gu.

Hall (Horton Hall, co. Bucks, and of London). Ar. on a chev. betw. three talbots' heads erased az. a bezant.

Hall (Lord Llanover ; extinct 1867). Per pale ar. and or, on a chev. betw. three talbots' heads erased, their necks encircled with mural crowns, three hawks' lures ppr. Crest—A griffin's head or, with a hawk's lure ppr. in the mouth and a palm branch vert behind. Motto—Turpiter despe ratur.

Hall (Warnham, co. Sussex, and London. Visit. London, 1589). Ar. semée of crosses crosslet and three talbots' heads erased sa.

Hall (Banbury, co. Oxford. Visit. 1634. Anthony Hall, of that place, great grandson of Richard Hall, of Stoarford, in same co., Judge of Assize, temp. Henry VII.). Ar. an eagle displ. gu.

Hall, or Hull (co. Cambridge). Az. an eagle displ. or.

Hall (Haninsley, co. Cambridge). Ar. a chev. gu. fretty of the first, betw. three demi lions ramp. az. on a chief of the second as many chaplets or.

Hall (Barton Hall, and Hollybush, co. Derby; Lorenzo O'Toole, Esq., of Ballyfod, co. Wexford, m. Harriett, dau. and heir of Thomas Hall, Esq., of Hollybush, and had a son, Lorenzo Kirkpatrick O'Toole, who assumed, by royal licence, the name and arms of Hall). Az. three talbots' heads erased sa. betw. eight cross crosslets gu.

Hall (co. Devon). Sa. a chev. betw. three talbots' heads erased or.

Hall (co. Devon). Az. a chev. ar. betw. three chaplets or.

Hall (co. Devon). Gu. a bend vair betw. six crosses crosslet ar.

Hall (co. Devon). Ar. four lozenges in pale ~~.~~ on each a leopard's face or.

Hall (co. Devon). Ar. a broad arrow gu. feathered or, betw. three harts' horns of the third.

Hall (Brittly, co. Durham). Ar. a chev. sa. fretty or, betw. three demi lions pass. az. on a chief gu. as many annulets of the first.

Hall (Streatham, in the Isle of Ely) Ar. a chev. gu. fretty cf the first betw. three demi lions ramp. az. on a chief of the second as many chaplets or.

Hall (Newsham, co. Durham). Ar. a chev. engr. az. betw. three talbots' heads sa. on a chief of the second as many mullets of the first. *Crest*—A talbot's head erased ar. gorged with a collar chequy or and az.

Hall (co. Essex). Or, four bars sa. on three escutcheons ar. as many church bells of the second, clappers of the first.

Hall (co. Essex). Sa. a lion ramp. ar.

Hall (Exeter; granted 20 March, 1684). Sa. three talbots' heads erased ar. collared gu. with rings on the collars or. *Crest*—A talbot's head erased sa. eared ar. gorged with a chaplet or, garnished with roses gu.

Hall (Banbury, co. Oxford; ANTHONY HALL, great grandson of RICHARD HALL, of Swarford, same co. Visit. 1634). Ar. an eagle displ. gu.

Hall (High Meadow, co. Gloucester). Ar. a chev. betw. three talbots' heads erased sa.

Hall (Kennington, co. Kent). Az. three halberts in pale or. *Crest*—A horse's head sa. in armour ppr. bridled and armed or, on the head two feathers, one az. the other gold.

Hall (co. Lancaster). Ar. a chev. sa. fretty or, betw. three lions ramp. of the second, on a chief gu. as many roses of the third, barbed and seeded vert.

Hall (co. Leicester). Gu. a lion ramp. guard or, crowned ar.

Hall (cos. Lincoln and Middlesex, and Middle-Walton, co. York). Ar. a chev. sa. fretty or, betw. three demi lions ramp. az. on a chief gu. as many chaplets of the third. *Crest* —A dragon's head couped az. collared or.

Hall (Grantham, co. Lincoln; Sir HENRY SUTTON, Knt., of Averham, co. Notts, *temp.* Henry VIII., m. ALICE, dau. of FRANCIS HALL. Visit. Notts). Ar. three talbots' heads erased sa.

Hall (Spalding, co. Lincoln). Ar. a chev. engr. betw. three talbots' heads erased sa. a bordure gu.

Hall (Grantham, co. Lincoln). Ar. on a chev. betw. three talbots' heads erased sa. as many estoiles or. *Crest*—A talbot's head erased or, pellettée.

Hall (Grantham, co. Lincoln). Sa. three talbots' heads erased ar.

Hall (Gretford, co. Lincoln). Ar. a chev. engr. betw. three talbots' heads erased sa. *Crest*—Out of a ducal coronet or, a plume of feathers ar. thereon a demi lion ramp. of the first.

Hall (co. Lincoln, 1640). Ar. on a chev. engr. betw. three lions' heads erased sa. an estoile or.

Hall (co. Lincoln). Vert on a saltire engr. ar. five mullets gu.

Hall (co. Lincoln). Same *Arms*, tinctures reversed, mullets or.

Hall (Walton-on-the-Hill, co. Surrey). Ar. three talbots' heads erased sa. langued gu. betw. nine cross crosslets of the last. *Motto*—Esto quod esse videris.

Hall (Cilgwyn, co. Cardigan, and Greville House, co. Middlesex, lineally descended in direct line from the noble family of FITZWILLIAM, by the branch FITZWILLIAM, of the Hall (hence the name), settled at the Hall Place, co. Norfolk). Quarterly, 1st and 4th, barry of eight gu. and erm. over all three escutcheons ar.; 2nd and 3rd, gu. on a chev. ar. betw. three talbots' heads ppr. collared or, and langued gu. as many blue bells also ppr. *Crest*—A demi lion ramp. holding a flaming sword imbrued all ppr. *Motto*—Vive ut vivas. Some ancestors of the family bore in the 1st and 4th quarters, barry of twelve, five shields, and a talbot's head for crest.

Hall (Greatford Hall, co. Lincoln, Skelton Castle, co. York, and Wratling Park, co. Cambridge; of the FITZWILLIAMS, of Cliseby). Ar. on a chev. engr. sa. betw. three talbots' heads erased of the second an estoile or. *Crest*—A talbot's head erased sa. spotted or.

Hall (Arrow's Foot, co. York, a branch of the HALLS, of Greatford Hall). Same *Arms* and *Crest*. *Motto*—Remember, and forget not.

Hall (Blacklands Park, co. Wilts). Ar. on a chev. betw. three talbots' heads erased sa. an estoile or. *Crest*—A talbot's head erased sa. spotted or. *Motto*—Esse quam videri.

Hall (Ashford, co. Kent; granted, 1583, by Cooke, Clarenceux). Ar. three halberts in fesse headed ppr. handles or. *Crest*— A horse's head couped sa. maned ar. bridled silver, tasselled gold, upon the head armour ppr. with a spike upon the forehead or, and therefrom issuant two ostrich feathers, the dexter gu. the sinister gold.

Hall (Skipton, co. York; EDWARD HALL, citizen of London. Visit. 1568). Ar. a fess betw. two greyhounds courant sa. *Crest*—Out of a ducal coronet or, a demi greyhound sa. collared gold.

Hall (Sawforth and Harborough, co. Lincoln). Ar. a chev.

---

betw. three demi lions ramp. gu. on a chief of the last as many chaplets or. *Crest*—A greyhound's head erased gu. collared or.

Hall (Ore, co. Sussex). Gu. three talbots' heads erased ar.

Hall (Rev. GEORGE HALL, D.D., Master of Pembroke College, Oxford). Ar. a chev. betw. three talbots' heads erased sa. *Crest*—A talbot's head, as in the arms.

Hall. Ar. a chev. sa. fretty or, betw. two columbines ppr. *Crest*—A dove, in the beak an olive branch all ppr.

Hall (co. York). Ar. a chev. betw. three talbots' heads couped sa. *Crest*—A talbot's head, as in the arms.

Hall (cos. Berks and Oxford). Erm. five barrulets gu. over all three escutcheons or, a mullet for diff.

Hall (Whatton Manor, co. Nottingham). Az. a bend betw. three talbots' heads erased ar. on a chief of the first, barbed and seeded ppr. *Crest*—A crescent ar. surmounted by a griffin's head erased sa. in the beak three ears of wheat or. *Motto*—Persevere.

Hall (Costock, co. Nottingham). Ar. a chev. engr. az. betw. three talbots' heads erased sa.

Hall (London; granted 18 May, 1768). Or, on a chev. sa. betw. three demi lions pass. az. five barrulets ar. on a chief gu. three chaplets of the fourth. *Crest*—A mural crown ar. thereout issuing a dexter arm embowed, habited az. fretty of the first, cuffed or, in the hand ppr. a dagger of the last, hilt and pommel gold.

Hall (London). Or, on a chief sa. a cross moline fitchée of the field. *Crest*—A demi lion gu. supporting a cross moline fitchée or.

Hall and Laventhorpe, co. York). Ar. a fesse betw. two greyhounds courant sa. collared or. *Crest*—On a chapeau gu. turned up ar. a greyhound sejant erm.

Hall (London). Ar. a chev. sa. betw. three talbots' heads erased pean.

Hall (London). Ar. three talbots' heads erased sa. collared or, betw. five crosses crosslet gu.

Hall (Hoxton, co. Middlesex; granted April, 1613). Az. on a chief erm. a lion pass. guard. of the field.

Hall (co. Middlesex, and Northale and Kynersley, co. Salop; Har. MS. 1404). Gu. a wivern or, within a bordure az. charged with a verdoy of fleurs-de-lis, interlaced with an enurny of lions pass. of the second. *Crest*—On the stump of a tree couped or, a wivern, wings endorsed sa. collared, ringed, and lined of the first, the line reflexed over the back, grasping in the dexter claw a sword ar. hilt and pommel gold.

Hall (co. Norfolk). Sa. a chev. ar. betw. three chaplets or. *Crest*—A demi buck saliant sa. attired or, gorged with a collar of the last charged with three chaplets of the first.

Hall (Salisbury). Ar. on a chev. betw. three columbines az. stalked and leaved vert, a mullet of six points ar.

Hall (Henwick, co. Worcester, Rotherhithe, &c. Visit. Leicester, 1619). Ar. three talbots' heads erased sa. betw. nine cross crosslets az. *Crest*—A dragon's head couped az. collared ar.

Hall (Mathon, co. Worcester. Visit. Leicester, 1619). Same *Arms* and *Crest*.

Hall (Redcriff, near London. Visit. Leicester, 1619). Same *Arms* and *Crest*, a crescent for diff.

Hall (Bishop of Bristol, 1691–1710). Sa. three talbots' heads erased betw. nine cross crosslets ar.

Hall (Warnham, co. Sussex, Goldings, co. Herts, London, &c.). Ar. three talbots' heads erased sa. betw. nine cross crosslets gu.

Hall (Wilsborough, co. Kent; granted 27 June, 1599. Visit. Kent, 1619). Gu. three poleaxes in pale or. *Crest*—"A horshead coupe sables armed with Shafferon and brydeled argent, purfiled or plumed gould and goules."

Hall (co. Salop). Sa. billettée two bars erm. in chief a hound's head erased betw. two chaplets or. *Crest*—A buck's head armed or, collared sa.

Hall. Same *Arms*. *Crest*—A demi buck saliant or, eared sa. gorged with a fesse wavy betw. two cotises of the last.

Hall (co. Salop). Ar. on a chev. cotised gu. three chaplets or.

Hall (Hermitage, co. Chester). Ar. three talbots' heads erased sa. *Crest*—A talbot's head sa.

Hall (co. Somerset). Az. a chev. erm. betw. three chaplets or.

Hall (South Newington and Banbury, co. Oxford, and co. Warwick). Ar. an eagle displ. gu. *Crest*—A demi eagle with wings endorsed sa. collared or.

Hall (Moundesmere, co. Southampton; granted 1767). Paly of four or and az. on a bend ar. three human hearts ppr. each pierced with two arrows saltireways of the first. *Crest* —A demi wolf ar. in the dexter paw a heart, as in the arms.

Hall (Warnam, co. Sussex, and London; JOHN HALL, Citizen. Visit. 1568). Ar. semée of crosses crosslet three talbots' heads erased sa.

Hall (Captain JAMES HALL, R.N.). Ar. on a bend engr. az. betw. two anchors sa. three talbots' heads erased of the field. Crest—A dexter cubit arm in bend, vested az. semée of escallops ar. grasping a dagger sheathed, point downwards ppr. Motto—Always ready.

Hall (Ipswich, co. Suffolk; confirmed 8 Feb. 1587). Erm. five barrulets gu. over all three escutcheons or.

Hall (Coggeshall, co. Essex, and co. York). Same Arms.

Hall (Coventry, co. Warwick). Ar. a chev. sa. betw. three columbines slipped ppr.

Hall (Bradford, co. Wilts). Sa. three poleaxes ar. Crest—An arm embowed in armour ppr. garnished or, holding a poleaxe ar.

Hall (co. York). Sa. a chev. betw. three dexter hands couped ar.

Hall. Gu. a lion ramp. crowned or.

Hall. Per pale ar. and sa. a chev. betw. three dolphins embowed all counterchanged.

Hall. Gu. a lion ramp. or, crowned az.

Hall. Az. an eagle displ. or, ducally gorged ar.

Hall. Ar. three lozenges in pale gu.

Hall. Az. a chev. betw. three covered cups or.

Hall. Vert a chev. ar.

Hall. Per bend vert and or.

Hall. Ar. three piles sa.

Hall. Ar. three crosses crosslet fitchée in bend az. betw. two bendlets gu. Crest—A dove and olive branch ppr.

Hall. Or, on a bend sa. three chevronels of the first betw. two lions ramp. of the second.

Hall. Ar. a chev. and bend gu. on a canton of the second a crescent of the first.

Hall. Gu. a dragon displ. ar. on his breast an escutcheon purp. a bordure az. verdoy of fleurs-de-lis or.

Hall (Clifton, co. York, and the Grange Hall, co. Chester; descended from the ancient family of Clifton, co. York, resident at Leeds, 1700; Scarborough, 1750; and Manchester; the late JOHN HALL, Esq., of Mersey Bank House, Heaton Norris, and Manchester, co. Lancaster, a magistrate for that county and the borough of Stockport, who represented this family, and d. 1 Oct. 1843, was eldest brother of the present Vice-Chancellor HALL, present representative). Sa. on a chev. betw. three dexter hands couped and erect, each within an annulet ar. a wreath of laurel vert betw. two roses barbed and seeded ppr. Crest—A tilting spear erect surmounted by a sword and laurel branch saltirewise all ppr. Motto—Aut pax aut bellum.

Hall. Ar. four bars humettée gu. on the second a leopard's head or.

Hall, or Hull. Erm. three lozenges gu.

Hall, or Hull. Az. three eagles displ. ar.

Hall. Vert a griffin ramp. ar.

Hall. Ar. a chev. sa. fretty or, betw. three lions ramp. az. Crest—A dragon's head couped az. collared or.

Hall (Sir JOHN HALL, K.C.B., M.D., Inspector-General of Hospitals, and Chief of the Medical Staff of the Army, son of late JOHN HALL, Esq., of Littlebeck, Westmoreland). Or, on a pile betw. two battle axes erect sa. three talbots' heads couped of the field. Crest—On a wreath the battlements of a tower, thereon a cock entwined by a snake all ppr. Motto—Perseverantiā et curā quies.

Hall (Westbank House, co. Chester). Barry of six erm. and vert on a chief az. a talbot's head erased betw. two martlets or. Crest—A demi buck ppr. collared or.

Hall (Newsham and Great Chilton, co. Durham; descended from the HALLS of Greatford). Ar. a chev. engr. betw. three talbots' heads erased az. on a chief of the second as many mullets or. Crest—A talbot's head erased sa. (The junior branches of London, &c. bore the crest, collared counter-compony or and az. and the mullets in the arms ar.).

Hall (Birtley, Conset, and Framwellgate, co. Durham, subsequently of Dublin, and of co. Antrim; afterwards of Bishop Wearmouth). Or, a chev. sa. fretty of the first betw. three demi lions pass. az. on a chief gu. as many chaplets ar. a martlet for diff.

Hall (Greencroft; descended from ROBERT HALL, living in the fifteenth century). Same Arms.

Hall (Narrow Water, co. Down). Ar. a chev. engr. betw. three talbots' heads erased sa. Crest—A bear's head muzzled ppr.

Hall (Mainwarra, co. Galway, and Merville, co. Dublin). Same Arms, &c.

Hall (Ramelton, co. Donegal, and Barbadoes; allowed by Betham, 1810; granted to WILLIAM HALL, Esq., of Sully,

co. Donegal). Vert a chev. or, betw. three storks' heads erased ar. all within a bordure of the second charged with eight trefoils slipped of the first. Crest—On a mount a stork ar. holding in her dexter claw a pellet. Motto—Cura quietem.

Hall (Dunglass, co. Haddington, bart., 1687). Az. a chev. ar. betw. three storks' heads erased at the neck or. Crest—A stork standing on a mount in a watching posture ppr. Motto—Dat cura quietem.

Hall (London, cadet of Dunglass, 1787). Az. a chev. engr. ar. betw. two storks' heads erased in chief and a saltire couped in base or, a bordure of the second. Crest—A demi griffin ppr. Motto—Per ardua ad alta.

Hall (Fullbar, co. Renfrew, Scotland). Az. a fesse chequy or and gu. betw. three herons' heads erased ar.

Hall-Dare. See DARE.

Hallam (Hallam, co. York). Ar. a lion ramp. az. guttée d'or.

Hallam (West Hallam, Kirk Hallam, and Hallam Parva, co. Derby). Same Arms.

Hallam. Sa. a cross erm. Crest—On a mount vert a bull gu.

Halle. Erm. two bars gu. the first charged with two, the other with one escutcheons ar.

Halle, or Hale. Az. a chev. counter-embattled or.

Halleley, Hallely, or Halliley (Hackney, co. Middlesex). Az. a chev. flory counterflory ar. betw. three martlets or.

Hallep (co. Cornwall). Or, two bends sa.

Halles (London; granted by Camden, Clarenceux, 1603). Az. a chev. embattled counter-embattled or. Crest—Five arrows, one in pale, the others saltireways or, flighted ar. encircled by a serpent ppr.

Halles (Upwimborne, co. Dorset). Gu. three greyhounds' heads erased ar.

Halles, Hale, or Hales. See HALE.

Halles. Az. a chev. betw. three covered cups or.

Halles. Gu. three arrows or, barbed and feathered ar.

Hallesfield. Ar. two bends wavy sa.

Hallestowe. Paly of six ar. and sa. on a chev. gu. a crosslet or.

Hallet (Higham, near Canterbury). Or, a chief engr. sa. over all on a bend engr. gu. three bezants. Crest—Out of a ducal coronet or, a demi lion ar. holding in the paws a bezant.

Hallet (Stedcombe, in Axmouth, co. Devon, purchased 1691; originally from Barbadoes). Same Arms and Crest.

Hallet (Cannons, co. Middlesex). Same Arms. Crest—Out of a ducal coronet or, a demi lion.

Hallet (Whitchurch, co. Middlesex; certified at the College of Arms, London, May, 1799). Same Arms, a crescent for diff. Crest—Out of a ducal coronet or, a demi lion ramp. ar. holding betw. the paws a bezant.

Hallet (Crockhorn, co. Somerset). Same Arms. Crest—A demi lion holding a bezant.

Halleton. Sa. a chev. or, betw. three garbs ar.

Hallett. Same Arms as HALLET. Crest—A dexter hand holding a key ppr.

Hallewell (co. Devon). Ar. on a bend sa. three bezants.

Hallewell. Ar. on a chev. sa. three bezants.

Hallewell. Ar. on a chev. sa. three annulets of the field. Crest—A boar's head erect sa. betw. two ostrich feathers ar.

Hallewton. Gu. a lion ramp. ar. crowned or.

Halley (London). Az. a chev. betw. three annulets or, over all on a fesse of the last as many martlets gu.

Halliday (cos. Wilts and Somerset, Yard House, near Taunton, Iford Park, Wilts, Chapel Cleeve, co. Somerset, and Westcombe Park, co. Kent, Warminster, &c.). Sa. three helmets ar. garnished or, a border engr. of the second. Crest—A demi lion ramp. or, holding an anchor az. Motto—Quarta saluti.

Halliday (Rodborough, co. Gloucester; derived from EDWARD, second son of HENRY HALLIDAY, of Minchin Hempton, son of WALTER HALLIDAY, the minstrel. Of this branch was Sir LEONARD HALLIDAY, Lord Mayor of London in 1605). Same Arms, Crest, and Motto.

Halliday (Tullibole, co. Kinross). Ar. a sword erected in pale ppr. hilted and pommelled or, the pommel within a crescent, in base gu. a canton az. charged with a saltire of the first. Crest—A boar's head couped ar. armed or. Motto—Virtute parta.

Halliday (Castledykes, co. Kirkcudbright, 1779). Ar. a sword erected in pale ppr. hilted and pommelled or, the pommel within a crescent in base gu. a chief erm. and a dexter canton az. charged with a saltire of the field. Crest—A dexter arm armed, couped below the shoulder ppr.

grasping a dagger also ppr. hilted and pommelled or, and distilling drops of blood from the point. *Motto*—Merito.

Halliday (Sir ANDREW HALLIDAY, K.G.H., Deputy Inspector of Army Hospitals, &c.). Same as HALLIDAY of Tullibole, the field being erm. and the additions of a mural crown above the point of a sword, a wreath on either side of the same. *Crest*, as Tullibole, transpiercing the boar's head with a sword.

Halifax, Viscount. See WOOD.

Halifax, or Halyfax (co. York; granted 9 Oct. 1573). Or, on a pile engr. sa. betw. two fountains three crosses crosslet of the first.

Hallifax (Waltham Lodge, Chelmsford, co. Essex). Same *Arms*. *Crest*—A moor-cock, wings expanded, per bend sinister sa. and gu. combed and wattled of the last, ducally gorged and charged on the breast with a cross crosslet or.

Hallifax (Chadacre Hall, co. Suffolk; descended from the WATERHOUSES, through a younger branch which took the name of "DE HALIFAX," from the place of their abode). Quarterly, 1st and 4th, or, on a pile engr. sa. betw. two fountains three cross crosslets of the first, for HALIFAX; 2nd and 3rd, ar. on a bend sa. three owls of the field, for SAVILE. *Crest*—A moor-cock, wings expanded, combed and wattled ppr. ducally gorged and charged on the breast with a cross crosslet or.

Halligwell (Holwell; Sir RICHARD HALLIGWELL, of Holwell, *m.* ANNE, dau. and heir of Sir JOHN NORBURY, Knt., by ELIZABETH, eldest sister and co-heir of RALPH BOTELER, *Baron Sudley*, and had a dau. and heiress, JANE, mother, by her husband, EDMUND BARON BRAYE, of a son and heir, JOHN BARON BRAYE). Or, on a bend gu. three goats ar. attired of the first.

Halliley (Hackney and London; granted by Hawley, Clarenceux, 15 March, 5 Edw. VI.). Az. a chev. flory counterflory ar. betw. three martlets or, a lily gu. stalked and leaved vert. *Crest*—An arm couped, vested az. the shirt apparent, holding in the hand a flagon gold.

Hallington (co. Cambridge) Ar. on a bend gu. three eagles displ. of the field.

Hallington, or Hallowton. Gu. a lion ramp. ar. crowned or. *Crest*—Out of a ducal coronet or, a greyhound's head sa.

Hallington. Az. a bend ar. betw. three eagles displ. or.

Hallington. Ar. a bend gu.

Halliford, or Hallirard. Ar. on a fesse sa. three crescents or.

Hallis. Gu. a fesse embattled counter-embattled or, betw. three leopards' faces ar.

Halliwell. Or, on a bend gu. three goats trippant ar. attired of the field.

Halliwell (Pike House, co. Lancaster). Ar. on a bend gu. three antelopes pass. of the first, attired or. *Crest*—A griffin pass. wings expanded ar. beaked and legged gu.

Hallman (co. Devon, 1607). Vert a chev. ar. guttée de sang betw. three pheons or. *Crest*—A crossbow erect or, betw. two wings gu.

Hallom (co. Northumberland). Sa. two bars vairé ar. and vert.

Hallom. Sa. a cross engr. erm. *Crest*—A hand gu. holding a grenade fired ppr.

Hallom. Sa. a cross ar. guttée de poix.

Hallop (Trewonwall, co. Cornwall; MAUD, dau. and co-heir of LAWRENCE HALLOP, *temp.* Henry VI., *m.* RICHARD BOSCAWEN. Visit. Cornwall, 1620). Or, three bends sa.

Halloran (co. Kent). See O'HALLORAN.

Hallow. Gu. three crescents ar. a bordure engr. or (another, ar.). *Crest*—An eagle displ. reguard. or, holding in the dexter claw a sword in pale ppr.

Halloway (London). Gu. a fesse erm. betw. three crescents ar. *Crest*—A demi lion ramp. guard. purp.

Hallowes (originally of Hallowes in Dronfield, subsequently of Dethic, and of Glapwell, co. Derby). Az. on a fesse ar. betw. three crescents of the second as many torteaux. *Crest*—A demi griffin ramp. sa. winged ar.

Hallpenny (Reg. Ulster's Office). Ar. a pelican az. betw. three crosses formée sa.

Halls (co. Salop). Ar. two piles issuing from the dexter and sinister chief points sa.

Halls. Ar. four lions pass. guard. in bend sa. betw. two double cotises of the last.

Hallusby. Sa. a saltire or.

Hallwell (Halwel, co. Devon). See HALYWEL.

Hallys. Sa. a chev. betw. three lions ramp. ar.

Halnaby. Ar. a fesse betw. six fleurs-de-lis sa.

Halnesby. Sa. a cross sarcelly or.

Halowton (JOHN DE HALAUGHTON, or HALTON, Bishop of Carlisle, 1292-1524). Gu. a hand erect ar.

444

Halpeny, or Harpeny (Fun. Ent. of MARY, wife of ANTHONY HALPENY, or HARPENY, *d.* 18 Feb. 1681). Vert three tortoises displ. or.

Halperton. Gu. three crescents or, a label of five points componée of the last and az.

Halperton, or Haperton. Gu. crescent or, a label of three points az. on each an estoile of the second.

Halpin. Ar. fretty sa. a fleur-de-lis gu. *Crest*—Out of a tower ar. a demi griffin sa.

Halram. Gu. fretty ar. a fesse or.

Hals (Beauford and Hardwick, co. Devon; PHILIP HALS, son of THOMAS HALS, of Hardwick, in same co. Visit. Devon, 1620). Ar. a fess betw. three griffins' heads erased sa.

Halsall (Halsall, co. Lancaster, 1567). Or, three dragons' heads erased az.

Halsall (Melinge, co. Lancaster, 1600). Ar. three heraldic tigers' heads erased az.

Halsam (co. Lincoln). Ar. a chev. betw. three leopards' faces gu.

Halsby (co. Leicester). Ar. a lion ramp. az. billettée of the field.

Halse (Fentongollan and Tresawsen, co. Cornwall; derived from JOHN HALS, appointed one of the Judges of the Common Pleas in 1423, who built the ancient mansion of Kenedon, in Devon. His direct descendant, Sir NICHOLAS HALS, purchased Fentongollan, the seat of the CARMINOWS, in 1600. JOHN HALSE, Bishop of Lichfield and Coventry, *d.* 1490, was of this family. From a younger branch, of which was WILLIAM HALS, the historian, derived JAMES HALSE, Esq., late M.P. for St. Ives). Ar. a fesse betw. three griffins' heads erased sa.

Halse (Kenedon and Efford, co. Devon; originally from co. Cornwall, settled at Kenedon, *temp.* HENRY HALS. The daus. and co-heirs of MATTHEW HALS, Esq., of Efford, in the reign of Charles II. *m.* ELFORD and TRELAWNY). Ar. a fesse betw. three griffins' heads erased sa. *Crest*—A griffin sejant, wings endorsed ar.

Halsoll (Sir CUTHBERT HALSELL, knighted in Dublin, 22 July, 1599). Ar. three lucies' heads couped and erect az.

Halsey (co. Devon). Or, a fesse betw. three griffins' heads erased sa.

Halsey (Gaddesden Park, co. Hertford). Ar. on a pile sa. three griffins' heads erased of the first. *Crest*—A dexter hand ppr. sleeved gu. cuffed ar. holding a griffin's claw erased or. *Motto*—Nescit vox missa reverti.

Halsey (co. Hertford). Ar. three boars' heads couped in pale sa. *Crest*—A sword erect ar. hilt or, on the blade a boar's head couped sa.

Halsey (co. Surrey). Ar. guttée de poix on a pile az. three griffins' heads erased of the first ducally gorged or. *Crest*—On a garb lying fesseways or, a griffin's head sa. guttée d'eau ducally gorged ar.

Halsey (Henley Park, co. Surrey). Ar. three boars' heads erased in pale sa. *Crest*—On a sword erect ppr. pommel and hilt or, a boar's head erased transfixed sa.

Halsey. Ar. on a fesse betw. three griffins' heads erased gu. a mullet of the first.

Halshall. Ar. three snakes' heads az.

Halsham (co. Suffolk). Ar. a chev. engr. betw. three leopards' faces gu.

Halson (co. York). Or, a fesse chequy ar. and az. in chief a lion pass. gu.

Halsted, Town of (co. Essex). Az. a coronet composed of one fleur-de-lis and two leaves or.

Halsted (Sunning, co. Berks, and London; granted 10 May, 1687). Gu. an eagle displ. erm. beaked and legged or, a chief chequy of the last and az. *Crest*—Out of a ducal coronet chequy or and az. a demi eagle issuant erm. beaked gold.

Halsted (Rowley). Gu. an eagle displ. erm. beaked and legged or, a chief chequy or and az.

Halsted (London). Gu. an eagle. displ. erm. a chief chequy ar. and az.

Halsted. Gu. two bars ar. in chief three plates.

Halstow. Paly of six ar. and az. on a chev. gu. three crosses crosslet of the first.

Halswell (Halswell and Wells, co. Somerset). Az. three bars wavy ar. over all a bend gu.

Halswell. Gu. a cross betw. twelve crosses formée fitchée ar. *Crest*—An ounce sejant ppr. resting the forepaw on a shield gu.

Halswell. Gu. a cross betw. twelve crosses crosslet fitchée ar.

Halswell (NICHOLAS HALSWELL; arms in a window of the Cloister of All Souls College, Oxford. Visit. 1574). Barry wavy az. and ar. a bend gu.

Halthom (Fun. Ent. Ulster's Office, buried in St. Werburgh Church, Dublin, 1668). Ar. three bars sa.

Haltemprise-Priory (co. York). Sa. a cross patonce quarterly ar. and gu. (another coat, sa. a cross fleury ar.).

Haltoft, or Holtoft. Ermines three lozenges erm. meeting in the fesse point.

Haltofte (co. Norfolk). Ar. three lozenges ermines a bordure engr. sa.

Haltofts. Ar. three lozenges in triangle ermines (another, tinctures reversed).

Haltom, or Haltun. Ar. on a chev. sa. three hammers of the field.

Halton (Samford, co. Essex, bart., extinct 1823). Per pale az. and gu. a lion ramp. ar. *Crest*—A lion sejant ar. holding in the dexter paw a broken lance ppr.

Halton (Greenthwaite Hall, co. Cumberland, *temp.* Richard II.). Per pale gu. and az. a lion ramp. or. *Crest,* as the preceding.

Halton (South Winfield, co. Derby). Per pale gu. and az. a lion ramp. or.

Halton (Bristol). Per pale az. and gu. a lion ramp. ar. charged on the shoulder with an escarbuncle of the second.

Halton (co. Lancaster). Ar. a lion ramp. gu. crowned or.

Halton (co. Lincoln, 1640). Per pale gu. and vert a lion ramp. ar.

Halton (co. York). Gu. a saltire engr. or.

Halton. Ar. a griffin pass. (another, segreant) wings displ. sa. armed gu. *Crest*—Out of a ducal coronet gu. a griffin's head sa. betw. two wings, the dexter or, the sinister az.

Halton (Halton Craven, co. York). Ar. two bars az.

Halton. Ar. two bars az. on each as many escallops or.

Halton. Gu. a lion ramp. or, depressed by a bend erm.

Halton. Az. two bars ar. in chief three escallops or.

Halton. Sa. a chev. or, betw. three garbs ar.

Halton. Sa. a cross engr. erm.

Haltridge (confirmed, 1707, by Hawkins, Ulster, to JOHN HALTRIDGE, Esq., High Sheriff, co. Down, 1699). Or, a stag's head cabossed betw. three hearts, one and two, gu. *Crest*— An ostrich ppr.

Halxton. Gu. in a crescent or, a mullet of the second, a label of three points az. *Crest*—A dexter hand holding a dagger in pale, embrued at the point all ppr.

Halxton, or Halperton. Gu. a crescent or, a label of three points az. each charged with a mullet of the second.

Haly (Ballyhally, co. Cork, formerly of co. Limerick; allowed by Hawkins, Ulster, 1775). Vert three bars wavy ar. in chief a mullet pierced or. *Crest*—A mermaid with comb and mirror all ppr. *Motto*—Sapiens dominabitur astris.

Halyburton (that Ilk, co. Berwick). Or, on a bend sa. three mascles of the first.

Halyburton (*Lord Dirleton ;* ended in co-heiresses in the 16th century). Quarterly, 1st and 4th, as the last; 2nd, or, three bars gu., for CAMERON; 3rd., ar. a bend gu., for VAUX. *Crest*—A Moor's head ppr. banded ar. *Supporters*—Two naked Moors ppr. banded head and middle with ar. *Motto* —Watch weel.

Halyburton (Pitcur, co. Forfar). Or, on a bend az. betw. three boars' heads erased sa. as many lozenges of the first. *Crest*—A negro's head and neck in profile couped at the shoulders and armed with a helmet ppr. *Supporters*—Two cats ppr. *Motto*—Watch weel.

Halyburton (Egliscairnie, co. Haddington). Or, on a bend wavy az. three lozenges of the first. *Crest*—A boar's head couped and erect ppr. *Motto*—Majores sequor.

Halyburton (Newmains, co. Roxburgh). Or, on a bend az. three mascles and in the sinister canton a buckle of the first. *Crest*—A stag at gaze ppr. *Motto*—Watch weel.

Halyburton (cadet of Egliscairnie, 1672). Or, on a bend the upper side waved and the under side engr. az. three lozenges of the first. *Crest*—A boar's head couped and erect ppr. *Motto*—Majores sequor.

Halys. Barry of fourteen ar. and az. on a canton or, a lion pass. gu.

Halywell. Ar. on a chief sa. three bezants.

Ham, or Hame. Vert three salmon naiant. *Crest*—On a chapeau a unicorn's head erased ppr.

Ham. Az. a lion ramp. guard. ar. armed gu.

Hamberbras. Chequy or and gu. a chief ar.

Hambert (Rye, co. Sussex). Gu. a bend erm.

Hambey (1575). Quarterly, 1st, sa. three esquires' helmets or; 2nd, per pale or and sa. three mullets counterchanged; 3rd, ar. a cross engr. sa. ; 4th, ar. a chev. betw. eight crosses crosslet sa. five in chief and three in base.

Hambl-y, or Hambly. Sa. on a pale ar. three torteaux. *Crest*---A dolphin hauriant ar.

Hamborough. Gu. a tower ar. within an orle of crosses

crosslet or, and guttées d'or, alternately. *Crest*—On a mount vert a horse courant ar.

Hamborough. Ar. a tower sa. within an orle of crosses crosslet of the last and guttée de sang alternately. *Crest,* as the last.

Hamborough. Gu. a castle or, betw. eight guttées d'eau.

Hamborough (Steephill Castle, Isle of Wight, and Pipewell Hall, co. Northampton, of Hanoverian origin). Quarterly, 1st and 4th, ar. semée of cross crosslets az. and guttée de sang a tower sa., for HAMBOROUGH ; 2nd and 3rd, sa. on a fesse betw. two chev. erm. two covered cups az., for HOLDEN. *Crest*—On a mount vert a horse courant ar. powdered with cross crosslets az. and guttées de sang, motto over: Foresight. *Motto*—Honestum utili præfer.

Hambrois. Sa. on a bend ar. three escallops gu.

Hambury. Az. a chev. or, in chief a lion pass. guard. ar.

Hamby (co. Lincoln; granted 12 March, 1568). Az. three close helmets or. *Crest*—A hawk volant ppr. beaked, legged, and inside of the wings or.

Hamden (FRANCIS HAMDEN, *temp.* Henry VIII., left an only dau. and heiress, *m.* Sir JOHN BRANCHE, Knt., Alderman and Mayor of London. Visit. London, 1568). Ar. a saltire gu. betw. four eagles displ. az. quartering or, three piles wavy meeting in base gu. a chief of the last.

Hamden, or Hampden (Hartwell, co. Bucks, and Rothwell, co. Northampton). Ar. a saltire gu. betw. four eagles displ. az. *Crest*—An eagle's head erased az. *Another Crest* —A talbot pass. erm. collared and lined gu. the end of the line tied in a bow-knot and reflexed over the back.

Hamden (London). Sa. a fesse betw. two. chev. erm.

Hame (co. Cornwall). Vert two salmon hauriant ar.

Hamelden (Sir JAMES HAMILTON, one of the knights who jousted at the tournament held at Dunstable, 1308, 2 Edward II.). Ar. fretty of eight pieces gu. each charged in the midst with a fleur-de-lis or.

Hamelin. Chequy or and sa.

Hamell (co. Buckingham). Az. a chev. dancettée or.

Hamell, or Hamel. Az. a fesse betw. three griffins pass. or. *Crest*—A crescent or.

Hamelton (co. Suffolk). Ar. fretty and the field replenished with fleurs-de-lis gu.

Hamelyn (co. Cambridge). Gu. semée-de-lis fretty or.

Hamelyn, Hamelen, Hamelin, Hamelyng, and Hamelyne. Ar. three bulls pass. sa. *Crest*—A hand pulling a rose from a bush ppr.

Hamelyn (Reg. Ulster's Office). Gu. a lion ramp. erm. ducally crowned or.

Hamelyn. Ar. fretty gu. on a chev. of the second a fleur-de-lis or.

Hamelyn (quartered by BERKELEY, of Wymondham Ley; descended from Sir THOMAS BERKELEY, co. Leicester, brother of MAURICE, second *Lord Berkeley.* Visit. Leices. 1619). Gu. a lion ramp. erm. ducally crowned or.

Hamelyne (co. Leicester, *temp.* Edward III.). Same *Arms.*

Hamelyng. Gu. fretty ar. the field replenished with fleurs-de-lis or. *Crest*—A seahorse couchant, resting the dexter paw on a cross pattée ar.

Hamend. Az. three attires of a stag in pale or.

Hamer (Hamer, co. Lancaster). Sa. a bend or, betw. two lions ramp. ar.

Hamer. Gu. a cock or. *Crest*—On a chapeau az. turned up erm. a lion's head ar.

Hamersley (Lord Mayor of London, 1687; Pyrton Manor, co. Oxford, and co. Stafford; granted 1614). Gu. three rams' heads couped or. *Crest*—A demi griffin or, holding a cross crosslet fitchée gu.

Hamersley (co. Stafford and London; granted by Camden, Clarenceux, 1614, to HUGH HAMERSLEY, of London, son of RICHARD HAMERSLEY, Esq., co. Stafford). Gu. three goats' heads. *Crest*—A demi griffin segreant or, holding betw. the claws a cross crosslet fitchée gu.

Hamerton (Preston-Jacklyn, co. York, 1666). Ar. on a chev. betw. three hammers sa. a trefoil for diff. or.

Hamerton (Hamerton, Wigglesworth, and Hellifield Peel, co. York). Ar. three hammers sa. *Crest*—A greyhound couchant. *Motto*—Fixus adversa sperno.

Hamerton. Same *Arms.* *Crest*—A hand holding a broken hammer ppr.

Hamerton (co. Stafford). Ar. a chev. betw. three hammers sa. *Crest*—A swan issuant, wings addorsed and distended ar.

Hamerton (co. York). Ar. a fesse betw. three lions ramp. sa. tails forked.

Hamerton. Quarterly, ar. and sa. (another, ar. and vert).

Hames (Fun. Ent. of MARGARET, dau. of WILLIAM HAMES, co. Leicester, and wife of JAMES WATSON, Sheriff of Dublin.

d. Nov. 1630). Sa. on a fess or, betw. three cinquefoils pierced ar. a lozenge of the field.

Hameston. Erm. a saltire chequy or and gu. betw. four bezants.

Hamey (St. Luke's, Chelsea). Gu. a fesse betw. a roebuck courant in chief or, and three estoiles in base ar.

Hamey. Gu. a fesse or, in chief a buck courant of the last, and in base three mullets ar. two and one.

Hamfield, or Hanfield (co. Essex). Or, a chev. sa.

Hamford (co. Lincoln). Gu. a bend ar. betw. six mullets of the second.

Hamigston. Ar. on a chev. engr. sa. betw. three demi lions erased vert as many trefoils slipped erm. *Crest*—A dragon's head erased gu. ducally gorged ar.

Hamill (Ireland). Az. two bars erm. *Crest*—On a ducal coronet a leopard sejant ppr.

Hamill-Stewart. See **Stewart.**

Hamilton (Cadzow, co. Lanark; *Earls of Arran, Marquesses* and *Dukes of Hamilton, Earls, Marquesses, and Duke of Abercorn, Dukes of Chatellerault* in France, &c., &c.; present heir male, James, *Duke of Abercorn,* K.G. See *post*). Quarterly, 1st and 4th, gu. three cinquefoils pierced erm., for Hamilton; 2nd and 3rd, ar. a ship with sails furled and oars sa., for the *Earls of Arran. Crest*—Out of a ducal coronet or, an oak, fructed and penetrated transversely in the main stem by a frame-saw ppr. the blade inscribed with the word "Through," the frame gold. *Supporters*—Two antelopes ar. horned, ducally gorged, chained, and hoofed or. *Mottoes*—Through; and, Sola nobilitat virtus. The origin of the crest and motto of the Hamiltons is thus narrated: Sir Gilbert Hamilton, the founder of the family, having slain John de Spencer in a rencounter, fled from the Court of Edward II. of England, and sought safety in Scotland. Being, however, closely pursued, he and his attendant changed clothes with two woodcutters, and taking their saws, were in the act of cutting through an oak tree when his pursuers passed by. Perceiving his servant notice them, Sir Gilbert hastily cried out " Through," which word, with the oak and saw through it, he took for a crest, in commemoration of his deliverance. The legendary crest appears for the first time on the seal of the first *Earl of Arran.* Prior to the 16th century the crest was a boar's head. The *Earls of Arran* quartered gu. three cinquefoils erm. (or sometimes, ar.), for Hamilton; with ar. a galley, sails furled sa., for Arran.

Hamilton (*Duke of Hamilton and Brandon.* In terms of the patent of 1643, the dukedom of *Hamilton* descended to the dau. of the first duke, the Duchess Anna, wife of Lord William Douglas; and, since 1761, the *Duke of Hamilton* has been heir male of the Angus branch of the house of Douglas). Quarterly, four grand quarters, viz., 1st and 4th, quarterly, 1st and 4th, gu. three cinquefoils pierced erm., for Hamilton, 2nd and 3rd, ar. a ship with her sails furled sa., for Arran; 2nd and 3rd, quarterly, 1st, az. a lion ramp. ar. crowned or, for Galloway, 2nd, or, a lion ramp. gu. debruised by a bendlet sa., for Abernethy, 3rd, ar. three piles gu., for Wishart, of Brechin, 4th, or, a fesse chequy az. and ar. surmounted with a bend gu. charged with three buckles of the first, for Stewart, of Bonkill. Over these feudal quarterings of Douglas an escutcheon, charged with the arms of Douglas, viz., ar. a man's heart gu. imperially crowned ppr. on a chief az. three stars of the field. *Crest*—Out of a ducal coronet or, an oak tree fructed and penetrated transversely in the main stem by a frame-saw ppr. the frame or. *Supporters*—Two antelopes ar. ducally gorged and chained or, armed and hoofed of the last. *Motto*—Through.

Hamilton (*Earls, Marquesses, and Duke of Abercorn, Marquess of Hamilton, Viscount Strabane, Baron Paisley,* &c., &c.; present head and male line of the house of Hamilton, and representative of the male line of the Regent James, second *Earl of Arran,* and first *Duke of Chatellerault*). Quarterly, 1st and 4th, gu. three cinquefoils pierced erm., for Hamilton; 2nd and 3rd, ar. a ship with sails furled and oars sa., for Arran; in the point of honour over all an escutcheon az. charged with three fleurs-de-lis or, and surmounted by a French ducal coronet, for Chatellerault. *Crest*—Out of a ducal coronet or, an oak fructed and penetrated transversely in the main stem by a frame-saw ppr. the blade inscribed with the word "Through," the frame gold. *Supporters*—Two antelopes ar. horned, ducally gorged, chained, and hoofed or. *Mottoes*—Through; and, Sola nobilitas virtus.

Hamilton (*Earl of Ruglen;* title, which was bestowed, 1697, on the fourth son of the Duchess Anna, went to her heirs female, and was extinct at the death of the fourth *Duke of Queensberry*). Quarterly, Hamilton and Arran, as above; en surtout, Ar. a heart gu. imperially crowned

448

ppr. on a chief az. three stars of the first, for Douglas. *Crest* and *Motto*, as *Duke of Hamilton. Supporters*—As *Duke of Hamilton,* except being gorged with an earl's coronet.

Hamilton (*Earl of Orkney;* title, bestowed 1696, on the fifth son of Anna, Duchess of Hamilton, has passed by female succession to the Fitzmaurice family; arms borne by the first earl). Quarterly, 1st, az. a ship or, sails furled of the last, flags flying gu., for Orkney; 2nd and 3rd, quarterly, Hamilton and Arran; 4th, Douglas. *Crest*—Issuing out of a ducal coronet an oak tree penetrated by a frame-saw ppr. on the tree a martlet ar. *Motto*—Through. *Supporters* —An antelope and a stag ar. each attired and unguled or, gorged with a ducal coronet and chained of the last.

Hamilton (Baldoon, co. Wigtown; from the sixth son of Anna, Duchess of Hamilton, and the granddau. and heiress of Sir David Dunbar, of Baldoon. This branch, in 1744, *s.* to the earldom of Selkirk, see under Douglas). Quarterly, 1st and 4th, counterquartered, Hamilton and Arran; 2nd, Douglas; 3rd, gu. a lion ramp. ar. within a bordure of the second, charged with ten roses of the field, for Dunbar. *Crest* and *Motto*, as *Duke of Hamilton. Supporters*—Two lions guard. ar. each with a rose slipped gu. in one of his forepaws.

Hamilton (*Lord Bargeny;* from a legitimated son of the first *Marquess of Hamilton;* title dormant or extinct since 1736, when the estates went to the Dalrymples, of North Berwick, heirs of line of the second lord). Quarterly, Hamilton and Arran, within a bordure compony ar. and az. the former charged with hearts gu. the latter with mullets of the first. *Crest*—A crescent gu. *Supporters*— Dexter, an antelope ar. armed and unguled or, with a collar gu. charged with three cinquefoils erm.; sinister, a savage ppr. with a shoulder-belt gu. charged with three cinquefoils ar. wreathed head and middle with laurel vert, and holding in his sinister hand a garb or. *Motto*—J'espère.

Hamilton (Samuelston, co. Haddington; from Sir John Hamilton, of Clydesdale, natural son of the first *Earl of Arran*). Gu. a roundle chequy ar. and az. betw. three cinquefoils of the second. *Crest*—A mascle or. *Motto*—I'll deceive no man.

Hamilton (Gilkerscleugh, co. Lanark; descended from Sir James Hamilton, of Finnart, natural son of the first *Earl of Arran*). Gu. three cinquefoils erm. within a double tressure flory counterflory gu. *Crest*—Issuing out of a ducal coronet or, an oak tree fructed and penetrated transversely by a frame-saw all ppr. *Mottoes*—Above the crest: Through; below the arms: In arduis fortitudo. *Supporters*—Two antelopes ar. horned and hoofed or, each gorged with a collar gu. charged with three cinquefoils ar. with a chain reflexed over its back of the second.

Hamilton (Blair; from John Hamilton, of Broomhill, natural son of St. St. Andrews, natural son of the first *Earl of Arran*). Quarterly, Hamilton and Arran, within a bordure compony of eight pieces ar. and gu. charged alternately with a saltire of the second and a buckle of the first. *Crest*—An oaken plant ppr. *Motto*—Dum in arborem.

Hamilton (*Lord Belhaven and Stentom*; first lord descended from John Hamilton, of Broomhill, natural son of James, Lord Hamilton, and the heiress of Hamilton, of Udstone; same arms borne by the second lord, husband of the first lord's granddaughter, who was of the Raploch line, *v. infra*, and by the subsequent lords of the Wishaw line, who succeeded as heirs male of the second lord). Gu. a sword in pale az. hilted and pommelled or, betw. three cinquefoils of the second. *Crest*—A horse's head and neck ar. bridled gu. *Supporters*—Two horses ar. bridled gu. *Motto*—Ride through.

Hamilton (Silverton Hill, co. Lanark, bart., 1646: from a younger brother of James, *Lord Hamilton*). Gu. a gilleflower stalked and leaved ppr. betw. three cinquefoils erm. all within a bordure or. *Crest*—A horse's head and neck couped ar. maned or. *Motto*—Stimulis majoribus ardens.

Hamilton (Cobairdy, co. Aberdeen; from Silvertonhill). Gu. three cinquefoils ar. within a bordure of the second charged with four saltires couped, alternating with as many mullets of the first. *Crest*—A cinquefoil ar. *Motto*—Non mutat genus solum.

Hamilton (Westport, co. Linlithgow; descended from Silvertonhill, and now represented by the Ferrier-Hamiltons, of Kirkland, co. Renfrew, as heirs of line). Gu. three cinquefoils erm. within a bordure ar. charged with eight martlets of the first. *Crest*—Two branches of oak crossed in saltire and fructed ppr. *Motto*—Addunt robur stirpi.

Hamilton (Orbiston, co. Lanark; from Gavin Hamilton, Provost of the Collegiate Church at Bothwell, younger brother of James, *Lord Hamilton,* and of the first Alexander of Silvertonhill). Gu. an annulet or, betw. three cinquefoils erm. *Crest*—An antelope's head ppr. armed and unguled or. *Motto*—Quis accusabit.

Hamilton (Dalzell, co. Lanark; cadet, and eventually representative of Orbiston; acquired Rosehall, co. Lanark, by marriage with the dau. and heiress of Sir ARCHIBALD HAMILTON). Quarterly, 1st and 4th, as the last; 2nd and 3rd, gu. a mullet ar. betw. three cinquefoils erm. on a chief of the second a rose of the first, for HAMILTON, of Rosehall. *Crest*—An antelope ppr. armed and unguled or. *Supporters*—Dexter, an antelope ppr. gorged with an open crown and a chain hanging thereto or; sinister, a savage ppr. wreathed head and middle with laurel, holding a club over his shoulder or. *Motto*—Quis occursabit.

Hamilton (Kilbrackmont, co. Fife, cadet of Orbiston). Quarterly, 1st and 4th, gu. three cinquefoils ar.; 2nd and 3rd, ar. on a bend sa. three escallops or, for DISHINGTON. *Crest*—A hand pulling up a cinquefoil ppr. *Motto*—Et neglecta virescit.

Hamilton (Haggs, co. Lanark, bart., 1671). Gu. a salmon's head couped ar. with an annulet through the nose or, betw. three cinquefoils of the second. *Crest*—A salmon hauriant ar. having an annulet through the nose or.

Hamilton (Raploch, co. Lanark; from the eldest son of THOMAS HAMILTON, of Darngaber, younger brother of Sir JAMES HAMILTON, of Cadzow). Gu. a heart betw. three cinquefoils ar.

Hamilton (*Earl of Clanbrassil;* descended from Raploch; title extinct; *Baron Dufferin* the heir of line; HAMILTON, of Killyleagh, co. Down, the male representative). Gu. three cinquefoils ar. on a chief or, a lion pass. guard. of the first holding in his dexter hand a caltrap az. *Crest*—A demi antelope ar. armed or, supporting a heart ppr. *Supporters*—Dexter, a lion gu. gorged with the royal tressure or; sinister, an antelope ar. gorged with the royal tressure gu. *Motto*—Qualis ab incepto.

Hamilton (Barnes, co. Dumbarton, cadet of Raploch). Gu. a man's heart or, betw. three cinquefoils erm. a bordure indented of the second. *Crest*—A man's heart gu. charged with a cinquefoil ar. *Motto*—Faithful in adversitie.

Hamilton (CLAUD HAMILTON HAMILTON, paternally BROWN, 1865). Quarterly, 1st and 4th, gu. a man's heart or, betw. three cinquefoils erm. a bordure indented per pale of the second and third; 2nd and 3rd, az. a chev. chequy ar. and sa. betw. three fleurs-de-lis of the second, for BROWN. *Crest*—A man's heart gu. charged with a cinquefoil ar. *Motto*—Fidelis in adversis.

Hamilton (Udstone, co. Lanark; from JOHN HAMILTON, of Neilsland, youngest son of the third laird of Raploch, and the heiress of HAMILTON, of Udstone, of the Bruntwood line, *v. infra*). Quarterly, 1st and 4th, gu. a mullet ar. betw. three cinquefoils erm., for HAMILTON, of Bruntwood; 2nd and 3rd, gu. a man's heart shadowed or, betw. three cinquefoils erm. as his paternal coat. *Crest*—A boar's head erased ppr. *Motto*—Ubique fidelis.

Hamilton (Barncleuth, co. Lanark, from a second son of Udstone, circa 1690). Quarterly, 1st and 4th, gu. a mullet ar. betw. three cinquefoils erm., for HAMILTON, of Udstone; 2nd and 3rd, counterquartered, 1st and 4th, the same coat repeated, 2nd and 3rd, gu. a man's heart shadowed or, betw. three cinquefoils erm., these two coats for HAMILTON, of Udstone. *Crest*—A sphere ppr. *Motto*—Dat decus origini.

Hamilton (Presmennan, co. Haddington, 1672, father of the second *Lord Belhaven*). Gu. three cinquefoils erm. within a bordure quartered vairy and countercomponed both ar. and of the first. *Crest*—A dexter hand holding a writing pen ppr. *Motto*—Tam virtute quam labore.

Hamilton (Pencaitland, co. Haddington, younger brother of the second *Lord Belhaven*, through whose granddaughter the Belhaven estates passed to heirs female). Gu. a chev. betw. three cinquefoils erm. *Crest*—An arm issuing out of a cloud holding a pen ppr. *Motto*—Tam virtute quam labore.

Hamilton (CHRISTOPHER-NISBET-HAMILTON, of Dirleton, heir of line of Presmennan, 1855, and inheritor of the Belhaven estates). Quarterly, 1st and 4th, gu. a sword paleways ar. hilted and pommelled or, betw. three cinquefoils of the second, for HAMILTON; 2nd ar. on a chev. gu. betw. three boars' heads erased sa. as many cinquefoils of the first, the chev. ensigned with a thistle ppr., for NISBET; 3rd, ar. a chev. gu. betw. three pineapples ppr. a chief sa., for CHRISTOPHER. *Supporters*—Two horses ar. bridled gu. *Motto*—Ride through.

Hamilton (Wishaw, co. Lanark; from a third son of Udstone, 1690; this branch eventually became *Lords Belhaven*). Quarterly, 1st and 4th, gu. a mullet ar. betw. three cinquefoils erm.; 2nd and 3rd, gu. a man's heart shadowed

or, betw. three cinquefoils erm. all within a bordure &c. *Crest*—A dexter hand holding a sword indented on the back like a saw and a quill crossing each other saltirewise ppr. *Motto*—Tam virtus quam honos.

Hamilton (Newton, a younger son of Wishaw, 1740). Quarterly, as the last, with a martlet ar. in the centre for diff. *Crest*—A dexter hand holding a sword indented on the back like a saw ppr. *Motto*—Fideliter.

Hamilton (Neilsland; from a younger son of JOHN HAMILTON, of Neilsland, and the heiress of Udstone). Gu. three cinquefoils erm. within a bordure quarterly engr. ar. and invecked .az. *Crest*—An oak tree fructed ppr. *Motto*—Obsequio non viribus.

Hamilton (Capt. FREDERICK HAMILTON, cadet of Millburn, 1672). Gu. a man's heart or, betw. three cinquefoils erm. a bordure embattled of the second charged with six crescents of the first. *Crest*—Two twigs of oak in saltire ppr. *Motto*—Fortiter qui fide

Hamilton (Torrance, co. Lanark; from the second son of THOMAS HAMILTON, of Darngaber, younger brother of Sir JAMES HAMILTON, of Cadzow). Gu. a mullet betw. three cinquefoils ar.

Hamilton (Aikenhead, afterwards Holmhead, co. Renfrew, cadet of Torrance). Gu. a hunting horn betw. three cinquefoils ar. *Crest* A hand holding an oaken slip ppr. *Motto*—Virebo.

Hamilton (Westburn, co. Lanark, cadet of Torrance; afterwards HAMILTON-DUNDAS, of Duddingston; as recorded 1672). Gu. three cinquefoils erm. a bordure potent counterpotent of the second and first. *Crest*—A hand grasping a lance in bend sinister ppr. *Motto*—Et arma et virtus. See also under DUNDAS.

Hamilton (ARCHIBALD HAMILTON, cadet of Westburn, 1774). As the last, with a castle ar. masoned sa. in the centre for diff. Same *Crest* and *Motto*.

Hamilton (GILBERT HAMILTON; Glasgow, 1787). As Westburn, with a holly leaf or, in fess point. *Crest*—A dexter hand grasping a lance in bend sinister ppr. the hand charged with a star gu. *Motto*—Et arma et virtus.

Hamilton (Bourtreehill, co. Ayr, cadet of Torrance; heiress *m.* the twenty-first *Earl of Crawford*). Gu. a fleur-de-lis or, betw. three cinquefoils ar. *Crest*—A saw placed across the trunk of an oak tree both ppr. *Motto*—Saw through.

Hamilton (Sundrum, co. Ayr; from a brother of Bourtreehill). Gu. three fleurs-de-lis or in fess betw. as many cinquefoils ar. *Crest*, as the last. *Motto*—Through.

Hamilton (Ardoch, co. Ayr, now Craighlaw, co. Wigtown, cadet of Torrance). Gu. a mullet betw. three cinquefoils ar. within a bordure wavy of the last. *Crest*—A dolphin pursuing another fish in the water ppr. *Motto*—Honestum pro patria.

Hamilton (Dr. ALEXANDER HAMILTON, Edinburgh, 1785; descended of Kinkell, a cadet of Torrance). Gu. a star or, betw. three cinquefoils ar. a bordure of the last charged with four fleurs-de-lis vert, alternating with as many crescents az. *Crest*—A fir tree with a frame-saw across the trunk ppr. *Motto*—Through.

Hamilton (Woodhall, co. Lanark; heiress *m.* CRAWFORD, of Jordanhill). Gu. three holly leaves conjoined at the stalk or, betw. as many cinquefoils ar. *Crest*—A dexter hand holding a holly leaf ppr. *Motto*—Semper virescens.

Hamilton (Fairholm, co. Lanark; from youngest son of HAMILTON. of Darngaber; elder co-heiress *m.* 1866, JAMES STEVENSON of Braidwood, who takes the name of STEVENSON-HAMILTON). Quarterly, 1st and 4th, gu. a mullet ar. betw. three cinquefoils erm. a bordure of the last, for HAMILTON; 2nd and 3rd, ar. a chev. betw. three fleurs-de-lis gu. on a chief sa. three mullets of the field, for STEVENSON. *Crests*—HAMILTON: A hawk rising ppr. belled or, holding in the dexter foot a sword also ppr. hilted and pommelled or; STEVENSON: A dexter hand issuing from a cloud and holding a wreath of laurel all ppr. *Mottoes*—Thankful, for HAMILTON: Cœlum non solum, for STEVENSON.

Hamilton (Inverdovat, co. Fife, 1700; descended from GEORGE HAMILTON, of Borland, co. Ayr, second son of Sir DAVID HAMILTON, of Cadzow, and JONETTA KEITH; the representative of this branch *m.* the heiress of INGLIS, of Mardiestoun, and took her name. See under INGLIS). Quarterly, 1st and 4th, gu. a crescent ar. betw. three cinquefoils erm. a bordure embattled or; 2nd and 3rd, ar. on a chev. sa. betw. three boars' heads erased gu. armed of the second, a crescent of the first, for ELPHINSTONE of Inverdovat. *Crest*—The trunk of an oak tree sprouting ppr. *Motto*—Iline orior.

Hamilton (Olivestob, co. Haddington; also from Borland, present heir of line, JAMES GIBSON STARKE). Gu. a martlet betw. three cinquefoils ar. a bordure embattled or. *Crest*—

An antelope's head gorged and attired gu. *Motto*—Invia virtuti pervia.

Hamilton (Blantyrefarm, co. Haddington; also from Boreland). Gu. three cinquefoils erm. within a bordure counter-indented ar. and of the first. *Crest*—A trunk of an oak couped in pale sprouting out two branches ppr. *Motto*—Non deficit alter.

Hamilton (Bruntwood and Udstone, co. Lanark; from ANDREW, fourth son of Sir DAVID HAMILTON, of Cadzow, and JONETTA KEITH; line ended in an heiress, who *m.* successively HAMILTON, of Neilsland, and HAMILTON, of Broomhill). Gu. a mullet ar. betw. three cinquefoils erm.

Hamilton (Little Earnock, co. Lanark, cadet of Bruntwood). Gu. a mullet ar. betw. three cinquefoils erm. a chief embattled of the second. *Crest*—A boar's head erased ppr. *Motto*—Non metus.

Hamilton (Bangour, co. Linlithgow, from Little Earnock). Gu. a mullet betw. three cinquefoils ar. a chief of the second. *Crest*—A ship in distress ppr. *Motto*—Littora specto.

Hamilton (Dr. THOMAS HAMILTON, brother, of Bangour, 1672). As the last, with a martlet gu. on the chief for diff. *Crest*—A ship in distress ppr. *Motto*—Per varios casus.

Hamilton (Sir WM. HAMILTON, Lord Justice Clerk, 1672). As Bangour, with an annulet gu. on the chief for diff. *Crest*—A ship in distress ppr. *Motto*—Littore sistam.

Hamilton (Bardowie, co. Lanark; from JOHN, younger son of DAVID HAMILTON, of Cadzow, and JONETTA KEITH; heiress *m.* BUCHANAN, of Spittal and Leny; arms as recorded, 1810). Gu. on a chev. betw. three cinquefoils ar. a boar's head couped of the first, in the middle chief an annulet or. *Crest* —Issuing out of a ducal coronet an oak tree fructed and penetrated transversely in the stem by a frame-saw ppr. the frame or.

Hamilton (Cambuskeith, afterwards Grange, co. Ayr; from WALTER, younger brother of DAVID HAMILTON, of Cadzow, the husband of JONETTA KEITH). Gu. a lion ramp. ar. betw. three cinquefoils erm. *Crest*—An oak tree ppr. *Motto*—Viridis et fructifera.

Hamilton (Sorne and Sanquhar, co. Ayr; from Cambuskeith). Gu. three cinquefoils within a double tressure flory counterflory or.

Hamilton (Colquhot, co. Peebles, from Sanquhar). Gu. three cinquefoils betw. two flasques ar. *Crest*—Cupid with his bow, quiver, and arrows ppr. *Motto*—Quos dedit arcus Amor.

Hamilton (Innerwick, co.Haddington; from JOHN, second son of Sir WALTER FITZ-GILBERT, and the heiress of Sir ROGER DE GLAY). Gu. a fess chequy ar. and az. betw. three cinquefoils erm. in chief a buckle of the second.

Hamilton (*Earl of Haddington;* from Innerwick). Quarterly, 1st and 4th, gu. on a chev. betw. three cinquefoils ar. a buckle az. betw. two erm. spots, all within a bordure or, charged with eight thistles vert, for HAMILTON; 2nd and 3rd, ar. a fess wavy betw. three roses gu., for the title of *Earl of Melrose*, which was afterwards exchanged for *Earl of Haddington*. *Crest*—Two dexter hands issuing out of clouds joined fessways and holding a branch of laurel. *Supporters* —Two spaniels ar. collared gu. *Motto*—Præsto et persisto. Since 1859, the arms are borne quarterly, 1st and 4th, counter-quartered, HAMILTON and MELROSE, as above; 2nd and 3nd, BAILLIE, of Jervieswoode, (*q.v.*) and the crest and motto of BAILLIE, of Jervieswoode, are borne in addition to those above given.

Hamilton (Redhouse, co. Haddington; from Sir ANDREW HAMILTON, brother of the first *Earl of Haddington*). Gu. on a chev. betw. three cinquefoils erm. a buckle az. all within a bordure embattled or, charged with eight thistles vert, flowered gu. *Crest*—Two dexter hands issuing out of clouds joined fessways, and holding two branches of laurel disposed in orle ppr. *Motto*—Perstando præsto.

Hamilton (Little Preston, co. Fife, and Fala, co. Edinburgh; from PATRICK, brother of the first *Earl of Haddington;* the heiress *m.* Sir JOHN DALRYMPLE, Bart., of Cousland, ancestor of the present *Earl of Stair*). Gu. on a chev. betw. three cinquefoils ar. as many buckles az. *Crest*—A greyhound's head couped ppr. collared gu. garnished or. *Motto*—Fidèle.

Hamilton (Easter Binning, co. Linlithgow, cadet of Innerwick). Gu. on a chev. betw. three cinquefoils ar. a buckle az. betw. two erm. spots all within a bordure of the second, charged with eight trefoils slipped vert. *Crest*—The trunk of an oak sprouting forth a new twig ppr. *Motto*--Through God revived.

Hamilton (Preston, co. Haddington, and Fingalton, co. Renfrew, bart., 1673, the oldest cadet of the house of HAMILTON). Gu. three cinquefoils within a bordure ar. *Crest*--A demi man brandishing a sword aloft ppr. *Motto*—Pro patria.

448

Hamilton (Cairnes). Gu. on a fess betw. three cinquefoils ar. a man's heart ppr. *Crest*—A Bible expanded ppr. *Motto* —Credo, lego.

Hamilton (Mount Hamilton, co. Armagh, cadet of Cairnes, bart., 1682, title extinct). Gu. three cinquefoils erm. within a bordure per pale ar. and or. *Crest*—Within an adder disposed in a circle a cock in a guarding posture all ppr. *Motto* —Adest prudenti animus.

Hamilton (Riseland, Tobago, 1800). Gu. a spur rowel or, betw. three cinquefoils ar. all within a bordure engr. erminois. *Crest*—Issuing from a ducal coronet an oak tree with a saw across it all ppr. on the iron part of the latter the word " Through," as motto.

Hamilton (Dr. JAMES HAMILTON, London, 1825). Gu. three cinquefoils within a bordure erm. on a canton ar. in front of three arrows in bend a Roman fasces surmounted by a bow in bend sinister all ppr. *Crest*—Betw. two cornucopias or, filled with fruits and grain ppr. a hand holding a dagger erect also ppr. hilted and pommelled or. *Mottoes*—Above the crest: Through; below the arms: Ser libre o morir.

Hamilton (Minard, co. Argyll, 1863). Gu. three cinquefoils ar. *Crest*—An oak tree ppr. crossed by a frame-saw ar. *Motto*—Through.

Hamilton (Fahy, co. Galway; descended from JAMES HAMILTON, eldest son, by his first wife, of Sir WILLIAM HAMILTON, Knt., of Manor Ellerston, son of Sir GEORGE HAMILTON, second son of first *Lord Paisley :* allowed by Bryan, then Deputy Ulster, 1768, to PATRICK HAMILTON, Colonel in the service of Her Imperial Majesty Maria Teresa). Gu. three cinquefoils pierced erm. *Crest*—Out of a ducal coronet or, an oak tree transfixed by a frame-saw all ppr. *Motto*—Through.

Hamilton (Woodbrooke, co. Tyrone, bart.; descended from Sir WILLIAM HAMILTON, Knt., of Manor Ellerston, same co., son of Sir CLAUDE HAMILTON, second son of first *Lord Paisley*, by his second wife, by BEATRIX CAMPBELL). Quarterly, 1st and 4th, gu. three cinquefoils pierced erm.; 2nd and 3rd, ar. a lymphad sa. over all on a chief of honourable augmentation ar. a mount, thereon a castle, a Spanish flag flowing from the battlements all ppr. beneath inscribed, "Alba. de Tormes." *Crests*—1st, of augmentation: A mount, thereon a castle, as in the arms, motto over, Alba de Tormes; 2nd : Out of a ducal coronet or, an oak tree transversed with a frame-saw all ppr., motto over, Through. *Supporters*—Two antelopes ar. ducally gorged, chained, and hoofed or. *Motto* —Sola nobilitas virtus.

Hamilton-Russell (*Viscount Boyne;* descended from Hon. FREDERICK HAMILTON, youngest son of first *Lord Paisley*). Quarterly, 1st and 4th, ar. betw. two chevronels a cinquefoil, all betw. three crosses crosslet fitchée gu., for RUSSELL; 2nd and 3rd, gu. three cinquefoils pierced erm., for HAMILTON. *Crests*—1st, RUSSELL: A goat pass. ar. collared gemell, and charged on the body with an escallop sa.; 2nd, HAMILTON: Out of a ducal coronet or, an oak tree transversed with a frame-saw all ppr. *Motto* over—Through. *Supporters*—Two mermaids ppr. hair dishevelled or, each holding in the exterior hand a mirror gold. *Motto*—Nec timeo nec sperno.

Hamilton (The Mount, co. Middlesex, bart.; descended from Hon. WILLIAM HAMILTON, brother of JAMES, second *Earl of Abercorn*). Quarterly, 1st and 4th, gu. three cinquefoils ar.; 2nd and 3rd, ar. a lymphad with her sails furled sa. *Crest*—Out of a ducal coronet or, an oak tree fructed and transversed with a frame-saw ppr. the frame gold. *Motto*— Through.

Hamilton (Trebinshun House, co. Brecon, bart.; descended from Sir EDWARD HAMILTON, K.C.B., second son of the first Bart. of the Mount). Quarterly, 1st and 4th, gu. three cinquefoils erm.; 2nd and 3rd, ar. a lymphad with her sails furled sa. *Crest*—Out of a ducal coronet ar. an oak tree ppr. fructed or, transversed with a frame-saw also ppr. *Motto* —Through.

Hamilton (*Baron Glenawley*, extinct 1680; descended from HUGH HAMILTON, second son of MALCOLM HAMILTON, Archbishop of Cashel, *d.* 1628, whose second son, HUGH HAMILTON, was so created 1660; Fun. Ent. Ulster's Office, of the Archbishop and his elder brother, Sir CLAUD HAMILTON, Knt., of Castlecroome, co. Antrim, *d.* 1640). Gu. three cinquefoils erm. pierced vert. *Crest*—On a mount vert an oak tree transversed with a frame-saw both ppr.

Hamilton (*Barons* and *Counts Hamilton*, of the Kingdom of Sweden; descended from Captain JOHN HAMILTON, third son of MALCOLM HAMILTON, Archbishop of Cashel, *d.* 1628). Same *Arms* and *Crest* as *Lord Glenawley*.

Hamilton (Castle Hamilton, co. Cavan; exemplified, 1776, to ARTHUR CECIL, Esq., of Salisbury, upon his assuming the name of HAMILTON, as nephew and heir of Sir FRANCIS

HAMILTON). Quarterly, 1st and 4th grand quarters, quarterly, 1st and 4th, gu. three cinquefoils erm., for HAMILTON, 2nd and 3rd, ar. a chev. chequy gu. and of the first betw. three bugles sa. garnished or, for TEMPLE; 2nd and 3rd grand quarters, barry of ten ar. and az. over all six escutcheons, three, two, and one sa., each charged with a lion ramp. of the first. *Crest*—A sheaf of seven arrows or, headed and feathered ar. banded gu. surmounted by a morion ppr.

Hamilton (Fun. Ent. Major ROBERT HAMILTON, buried in St. Michael's Church, Dublin, 3 May, 1666). Gu. a fesse counter-compony az. and ar. betw. three cinquefoils of the last.

Hamilton (*Earl of Clanbrassil and Viscount Claneboye*, extinct 1675; Sir JAMES HAMILTON, Knt., of Killyleagh, co. Down, eldest son of Rev. HANS HAMILTON, Vicar of Dunlop, co. Ayr, was created *Viscount Claneboye* in the Peerage of Ireland, 1622; his successor was created *Earl of Clanbrassil*, 1647, the second earl *d. s. p.* 1675. The representation of the family eventually devolved on JAMES HAMILTON, Esq., of Neilsbrook, co. Antrim, whose dau. and eventual heir, ANNE HAMILTON, *m.* HANS STEVENSON, Esq.; their only son, JAMES STEVENSON, had an elder dau. DORCAS STEVENSON, *m.* Sir JOHN BLACKWOOD, Bart., of Ballyleidy, co. Down, and was created, 1800, *Baroness Dufferin* and *Claneboye*, a peerage enjoyed by her descendant, FREDERICK TEMPLE, *Earl of Dufferin* and fifth *Baron Dufferin* and *Claneboye*, K.P., senior heir-general of the HAMILTONS, *Earls of Clanbrassil*). Gu. three cinquefoils pierced erm. on a chief or, a lion pass. of the field. *Crest*—A demi antelope erect and affrontée erm. horned and unguled or, holding betw. the hoofs a human heart gu. *Supporters*—Dexter, a lion gu. armed and langued az. gorged with a double tressure flory counterflory or; sinister, an heraldic tiger erm. armed, langued, and gorged with a double tressure flory counterflory gu. *Motto*—Qualis ab incepto.

Hamilton (Killyleagh, co. Down; descended from GAWIN HAMILTON, brother of JAMES HAMILTON, Esq., of Neilsbrook). Gu. three cinquefoils pierced erm. on a chief or, a human heart of the field. *Crest*, same as the *Earl of Clanbrassil*.

Hamilton (Ballygally, co. Londonderry, and The Curragh, co. Kildare; descended from GAWIN HAMILTON, third son of the Vicar of Dunlop). Same *Arms*, *Crest*, and *Motto*, as Killyleagh, a crescent for diff.

Hamilton (Monella and Hamilton's Bawn, co. Armagh, bart., extinct 1730; HANS HAMILTON, eldest son of JOHN HAMILTON, Esq., of Coronary, co. Cavan, was so created 1662). Same *Arms*, &c., as Killyleagh.

Hamilton (Bailieborough, co. Cavan, Carlow, and Summer Hill, Dublin; descended from JAMES HAMILTON, Esq., of Bailieborough, second son of JOHN HAMILTON, Esq., of Coronary). Same *Arms*, &c., as Killyleagh, with a mullet for diff.

Hamilton (Sheephill, now Abbotstown, co. Dublin; descended from JAMES HAMILTON, Esq., of Sheephill, second son of JAMES HAMILTON, Esq., M.P. for Carlow). Same *Arms*, &c., as the last, the mullet charged with a crescent for diff.

Hamilton (Ballymacoll, co. Meath, Fitz-William Place, Dublin, Dunboyne Castle, &c., &c.; cadets of Sheephill). Same *Arms*, &c., as Sheephill.

Hamilton (Tullybrick, co. Armagh, and Rock Hamilton, co. Down; descended from FRANCIS HAMILTON, Esq., of Tullybrick, third son of JOHN HAMILTON, Esq., of Coronary). Same *Arms*, &c., as Bailieborough.

Hamilton (Newcastle and Bangor, co. Down; descended from WILLIAM HAMILTON, Esq., of Newcastle, fourth son of the Vicar of Dunlop, now represented through the co-heirs, the daus. of JAMES HAMILTON, Esq., of Bangor, by *Viscount Bangor*, and the *Earl of Carrick*). Same *Arms*, &c., as Killyleagh, with a martlet for diff.

Hamilton (Erinagh and Tollymore, co. Down; descended from WILLIAM HAMILTON, Esq., of Erinagh, third son of WILLIAM HAMILTON, Esq., of Newcastle, *m.* ELLINOR, dau. of PHELIM MCGENIS, of Tollymore, and heiress of her brother, buried at Downpatrick, Jan. 1680; Fun. Ent. Ulster's Office). Same *Arms*, &c., as Newcastle.

Hamilton (*Earl of Clanbrassil and Viscount Limerick*: extinct 1798; JAMES HAMILTON, Esq., of Tollymore, grandson of WILLIAM HAMILTON, Esq., of Erinagh, by ELLINOR MCGENIS, his wife, heiress of Tollymore, was raised to the Irish Peerage 1756; the eventual heiress of the family, Lady ANNE HAMILTON, *m.* ROBERT, first *Earl of Roden*). Quarterly, 1st and 4th, as the former *Earls of Clanbrassil*, quartering, vert a lion ramp. or, on a chief ar. a dexter hand apaumée couped at the wrist gu., for McGENIS. Same *Crest* and *Motto* as the former *Earls of Clanbrassil*. *Supporters*—Dexter, a lion gu. armed and langued az. gorged with a double tressure flory counterflory

or; sinister, an antelope ar. crined and unguled or, gorged with a double tressure flory counterflory gu.

Hamilton (Dundonald, Granshaw, and Mount Collier, co. Down; descended from PATRICK HAMILTON, youngest son of the Vicar of Dunlop). Same *Arms*, &c., as Killyleagh, with an annulet for diff.

Hamilton (Cornacassa, co. Monaghan; confirmed to JAMES HAMILTON, Esq., of Cornacassa, J.P., High Sheriff 1830, son and heir of the late DACRE HAMILTON, of Cornacassa, and grandson of Sir JAMES HAMILTON, Knt., of Monaghan, and their descendants). Gu. a chev. betw. three cinquefoils erm. on a canton or, three holly leaves conjoined vert. *Crest*—Out of three cinquefoils in fess conjoined or, an oak tree fructed and penetrated transversely in the main stem by a frame-saw ppr. frame and handles gold. *Motto*—Semper virescens.

Hamilton (confirmed to ROBERT HAMILTON, M.D., of Clifton Mount, Jamaica, eldest son of Rev. ARCHIBALD HAMILTON, M.A., and grandson of ROBERT HAMILTON, Esq., of Hill, Curragh, co. Kildare; and their descendants). Gu. a crescent ar. betw. three cinquefoils pierced erm. on a chief or, a heart of the first. *Crest*—A demi antelope affrontée ar. armed and unguled or, charged with a crescent gu. holding betw. the forelegs a heart, as in the arms. *Motto*—Qualis ab incepto.

Hamilton (confirmed to Sir WILLIAM OSBORNE HAMILTON, K.H., formerly Governor of Heligoland). Gu. on a chev. erm. betw. three cinquefoils ar. a sword in pale, the blade passing through a wreath of laurel all ppr., on a canton or, an eagle displ. with two heads sa. *Crest*—Out of a mural crown or, an oak tree ppr. the trunk thereof transfixed with a sword in fess, the blade wavy ar. pommel and hilt or; over the crest the motto, Through.

Hamilton (granted to Lieut.-Col. JOHN HAMILTON, Capt. Coldstream Guards, grandson of PATRICK HAMILTON, of Garrison, co. Fermanagh). Quarterly, 1st and 4th, gu. a trefoil or, betw. three cinquefoils erm.; 2nd and 3rd, ar. an ancient ship of three masts with sails furled sa. over all a cross counterchanged. *Crest*—Out of a ducal coronet or, charged with three bombs fired ppr. an oak tree transfixed with a framed saw ppr. in a scroll above the crest the word "Through." *Motto*—Through.

Hamilton (Saint Peter Port, Guernsey; confirmed to WILLIAM HENRY HAMILTON, Esq., son of WILLIAM HENRY HAMILTON, Esq., of Saint Peter Port, by RACHEL, his wife, only surviving dau. of ELIAS BLANCHEMAIN, of Saint Peter Port, and grandson of JOHN HAMILTON, a native of Ireland). Quarterly, 1st and 4th, gu. three cinquefoils pierced erm.; 2nd and 3rd, ar. a lymphad with her sails furled sa. over all in the centre chief point a mullet counterchanged. *Crest*—Out of a ducal coronet or, an oak tree fructed ppr. and penetrated transversely in the main stem by a frame-saw, frame and handles or, suspended from the tree by a blue ribbon an escutcheon quarterly ar. and gu. charged with a mullet counterchanged.

Hamilton (granted to Sir JAMES HAMILTON, Knt., of Belfast, J.P., formerly Chairman of the Belfast Harbour Commissioners, second son of Rev. GEORGE HAMILTON, of Armagh and Carrickfergus, by ANNE, his wife, dau. of THOMAS CAMPBELL, of Armagh). Per pale indented az. and gu. a boar's head erased or, betw. three cinquefoils pierced ar. *Crest*—On a mount vert an oak tree ppr. the trunk surmounted of a shield gyronny or and sa. *Motto*—Virtus acquirit honorem.

Hamilton (Fyne Court, co. Somerset; JOHN HAMILTON, Esq., of that place, and of Howden, co. Devon, eldest son and heir of ANDREW CROSSE, Esq., of Fyne Court, by MARY ANNE, his wife, eldest dau. of Captain JOHN HAMILTON, of Garrison, co. Fermanagh, representative in the male line of the family of CROSSE, assumed the name and arms of HAMILTON by royal licence, long resident in co. Somerset). Quarterly, 1st and 4th, HAMILTON, per chev. ar. and gu. three cinquefoils within a bordure nebuly all counterchanged; 2nd and 3rd, CROSSE, quarterly, ar. and gu. in the first quarter a cross crosslet of the second. *Crests*—1st, HAMILTON: On a mount vert betw. two wings ar. an oak tree, penetrated transversely by a frame-saw ppr.; 2nd, CROSSE (held under a grant from Camden, Clarenceux, setting forth that the said crest is assigned to the "ancient arms of Sir ROBERT CROSSE, Knt., a son of WILLIAM CROSSE, of Charlenge, co. Somerset, descended of a house long bearing arms"): A cross pattée fitchée gu. betw. two wings ar, each charged with a cross crosslet of the first. *Motto*—Se inserit astris.

Hamilton (Sir LAWRENCE HAMILTON, one of the knights who jousted at the Tournament held at Dunstable, 2 Edward II., 1308). Ar. fretty of eight pieces gu. each charged in the midst with a fleur-de-lis or,

Hamley (Halwyn, co. Cornwall; traceable to the 13th century, and extinct in 1427, when the heiress *m.* CHAMPER-NOWNE. A younger branch settled at Treblethick, *temp.* Henry VII., and was represented, when Lysons wrote, by RICHARD HAMLEY, of St. Colomb). Ar. three talbots pass. az.

Hamley (quartered by TREVILIAN, of Yarnscombe, co. Devon. Visit. 1620). Ar. three talbots pass. sa. (another, quartered by MONK, of Powdridge, talbots az.).

Hamley. Same *Arms. Crest*—A garb lying fesseways.

Hamley (Fun. Ent. 1683, Ulster's Office, JANE HAMLEY, wife of Captain ROGER BRETTRIDGE, of Castle Magner, co. Cork). Gu. three esquires' helmets or.

Hamley. Gu. three crescents ar.

Hamlin. Gu. a lion ramp. erm. crowned with an antique crown or. *Crest*—Seven arrows, points upward ppr.

Hamlin (Hamlinstown; Reg. Ulster's Office). Ar. a chev. betw. three spaniels sejant gu.

Hamlin (co. Leicester). Gu. a lion ramp. erm. ducally crowned or.

Hamlin. Ar. two bars indented gu.

Hamline (Impalement Fun. Ent. of ROLAND ST. LAWRENCE, Alderman of Drogheda, *d.* 9 July, 1633, *m.* ALSON, dau. of Alderman THOMAS HAMLINE, of same place). Ar. a chev. betw. three lions sejant gu.

Hamlyn (Paschoe and Leawood, co. Devon, 1611). Sa. two swords in saltire, the points upwards, hilted and pommelled or, quartering CALMADY and POLLEXFEN [*which see*]. *Crest*—A griffin guard. *Motto*—Caute sed strenue.

Hamlyn (Clovelly Court, co. Devon, bart.). Or, a falcon sa. belled gu. betw. three roses of the last leaved vert. *Crest* —A swan ar. collared gu. wings endorsed, beaked and legged or, holding in the beak a birdbolt sa.

Hamlyn-Fane. See FANE.

Hamme (Suffolk). Vert two lucies endorsed in pale or.

Hamme. Az. on a bend or, three demi lions of the field.

Hamme. Erm. three crescents chequy gu. and az.

Hammencourt. Ar. three mallets sa.

Hammer. Vert two dolphins haurient endorsed ar.

Hammersley (Pall Mall, London). Gu. three rams' heads couped or. *Crest*—A demi griffin segreant or, holding in the dexter claw a cross crosslet fitchée gu.

Hammersley. Same *Arms. Crest*—Two lions' gambs holding up a crescent.

Hammes, Hamme, or Hames. Az. a chev. betw. three demi lions or. *Crest*—On a ducal coronet a lion pass. ppr.

Hammet (granted 1803). Per fesse ar. and gu. a pale counterchanged, over all a lion ramp. erminois, on a canton of the second five fleurs-de-lis or. *Crest*—From the battlements of a castle of three towers ppr. a demi lion double queued issuant erminois, betw. the paws a pellet.

Hammick (Cavendish Square, London, bart.). Paly of four or and vert, a bordure erm. charged with seven hurts, on a chief az. a lion pass. ar. *Crest*—A demi lion per pale or and vert holding in the dexter paw an escarbuncle gold. *Motto*—Laudari a laudato.

Hammington, or Hamigston (Dover, co. Kent). Ar. on a chev. sa. betw. three demi lions ramp. erased vert as many trefoils erm. *Crest*—A dragon's head erased sa. ducally gorged ar. charged on the breast with three guttées d'eau in fesse.

Hammil (Roughwood, co. Ayr). Quarterly, 1st, gu. a mullet or; 2nd, az. a crescent ar.; 3rd, ar. a shakefork sa.; 4th, gu. a fleur-de-lis or. *Crest*—A fleur-de-lis or. *Supporters*— Two serpents.

Hammok. Ar. a cross gu. betw. four mullets pierced of the second.

Hammon, (Ellingham, co. Norfolk). Or, on a chev. sa. three Cornish choughs ar. *Crest*—An elephant's head ar. ducally gorged and eared or.

Hammon. Az. three tilting spears bendways or.

Hammon. Per pale az. and or. a chev. gu.

Hammon. Erm. three buglehorns stringed gu.

Hammond (*Baron Hammond*). Ar. on a chev. pean betw. three mullets sa. a sun in splendour or. *Crest*—Betw. a stag's attires a falcon rising ppr. each wing charged with a mullet or. *Supporters*—On either side a falcon, wings elevated ppr. gorged with a chain or, pendent therefrom an escocheon ar. charged with a mullet sa. *Motto*—Per tot discrimina rerum.

Hammond (co. Kent; certified May, 1779). Az. a fesse erm. betw. three lions' heads erased or. *Crest*—An eagle, wings expanded ar. beaked and legged or, betw. two stags' horns ppr.

Hammond (Cheam, co. Surrey). Gu. three demi lions pass. or.

Hammond (cos. Bucks and Kent). Per pale or and az. three demi lions pass. counterchanged. *Crest*—A wolf's head erased per pale indented or and az.

Hammond (St. Alban's Court, near Wingham, co. Kent; descended from THOMAS HAMMOND, who purchased, in 1551, the manor of St. Alban's). Ar. on a chev. sa. betw. three pellets, each charged with a martlet of the field, as many escallops or, a bordure engr. vert. *Crest*—An eagle's head erased sa. enfiled with a rose gu. the rose issuing rays or. *Motto*—Pro rege et patria.

Hammond (Wistaston Hall, co. Chester). Per chev. engr. gu. and ar. three oxenheads ppr. *Crest*—A boar pass. ppr.

Hammond (General Sir FRANCIS THOMAS HAMMOND, of Plumpton, co. Suffolk, G.C.H., Lieut.-Governor of Edinburgh Castle). Same *Arms* and *Crest* as HAMMOND, of St. Alban's Court.

Hammond. Quarterly, or and gu. on a bend sa. a cross pattée fitchée of the first.

Hammond (Fun. Ent. of Col. HAMMOND, buried in Christ Church, Dublin, 19 Oct. 1654). Ar. five crescents in cross az. a crescent for diff.

Hammond (Mount Hanover, co. Wexford, extinct; Mount Hanover sold to the ancestor of GLASCOTT, of Killowen. Fun. Ent. of NATHANIEL HAMMOND, of Dublin, merchant, *d.* 12 Oct. 1622, *m.* SUSAN, dau. of RICHARD PROUDFOOT). Or, on a chev. sa. three martlets ar. in chief a cross crosslet fitchée of the second.

Hammy. Az. a chev. or, betw. three half elm leaves of the last.

Hammys, or Hammye. Sa. a fesse or, betw. three cinquefoils ar. (another, erm.).

Hamnell. Gu. a crescent or, in chief a label az. charged with an estoile on each point of the second.

Hamner. Az. a chev. betw. three demi lions ramp. or.

Hamon (co. Kent). Az. two bends az. a bordure engr. sa.

Hamon. Ar. a lion ramp. az.

Hamon. Per pale az. and or, a chev. gu.

Hamon. Az. three tilting spears in bend or, headed ar.

Hamon (Seigneurs of Samare's, Jersey). Az. a lion ramp. guard. or. *Crest*—A lion, as in the arms. *Motto*—En tout loyal.

Hamon (arms of WILLIAM HAMON, a Monk Prior, of Cogges, co. Oxford, set up in the church there. Visit. Oxon, 1574). Ar. a chev. gu. a chief az.

Hamond (Windingham and Pampisford Hall, co. Cambridge, co. Herts, Tuddington, co. Middlesex, Haling House, co. Surrey, and co. York). Per pale gu. and az. three demi lions pass. guard. or. *Crest*—A wolf's head erased quarterly or and az.

Hamond (co. Hants). Or, five crescents in cross az.

Hamond (Isle of Wight). Same *Arms*, tinctures reversed.

Hamond-Græme, Bart. See GRÆME.

Hamond (Holly Grove, co. Berks, bart.). Ar. on a chev. sa. betw. two pellets, each charged with a martlet ar. in chief and an oak wreath ppr. in base three escallops or, a bordure engr. vert. *Crest*—Out of a naval crown or, the sails ar. an eagle sa. *Motto*—Paratus et fidelis. *Supporters* —Dexter, an eagle reguard. sa.; sinister, a stork ppr. each navally gorged with a line reflexed over the back or.

Hamond (co. Kent). Az. three demi lions pass. guard. or. *Crest*—A wolf's head erased quarterly per fesse indented or and az.

Hamond (co. Kent). Per pale az. and or, three demi lions pass. guard. in pale az.

Hamond (West Acre, High House, South Wotton, and Swaffham, co. Norfolk). Az. three doves (another, martlets) betw. two chev. ar. *Crest*—On a rocky mount ppr. a dove rising ar. holding in the beak a slip of olive vert.

Hamond (Chertsey, co. Surrey; granted to JOHN HAMOND, M.D., "physician to HENRY, *Prince of Wales*," by St. George, Norroy, 1607). Or, five crescents in cross az. on a canton of the last an ostrich's feather in pale ar. *Crest*—A crescent ar. within an annulet az. charged with eight estoiles or.

Hamond (Over Dinsdale Hall, co. York). Ar. a chev. betw. three mullets sa.

Hamond (Tuddington, co. Middlesex ; LEONARD HAMOND, grandson of LEONARD HAMOND, Esq., of Royston, co. Herts. Visit. Middlesex, 1663). Per pale az. and gu. three demi lions pass. guard. or, quartering three roses or. *Crest*—A wolf's head erased quarterly or and az.

Hamond (Brasted, co. Kent). See HAYMON and HEYMAN.

Hamond. See HAMMOND.

Hamound (co. Salop). Ar. on a chev. engr. gu. betw. three cinquefoils az. as many martlets or.

Hampden (Great Hampden, co. Bucks; arms of JOHN HAMPDEN, twenty-third Hereditary *Lord of Great Hampden*, *d.* 1754, who left his estates to Hon. ROBERT TREVOR, fourth

Lord Trevor, created, 1776, *Viscount Hampden*, son of THOMAS, first *Lord Trevor*, who was second son of Sir JOHN TREVOR, Knt., of Trevallyn, by RUTH, his wife, dau. of JOHN HAMPDEN, *Lord of Great Hampden*. Of the diverging branches are the HAMPDENS, of Kembell, Wycomb, Brails, Hartwell, and Prestwood, co. Bucks, Emington, co. Oxford, and Abingdon, co. Berks). The original *Arms* were—Ar. a raven croaking ppr.; but they were changed at a very early period by Sir REGINALD HAMPDEN to the following:—Ar. a saltire gu. betw. four eagles displ. az. *Crest*—A talbot statant erm. collared, ringed, and lined gu. the end of the line tied in a knot over his back. *Motto*—Vestigia nulla retrorsum.

Hampden (*Earl of Buckinghamshire*). See HOBART.

Hampden (*Viscount Hampden*). See TREVOR.

Hampden. Same *Arms*. *Crest*—A peacock's head couped az.

Hampden (Bishop of Hereford, 1849). Ar. four bendlets in saltire interlaced sa. betw. four eagles displ. az.

Hampden. Erm. on a chev. engr. sa. three cinquefoils or.

Hampnes. Az. a lion ramp. or.

Hampson (Taplow, co. Bucks, bart.) Ar. three hempbrakes sa. *Crest*—Out of a mural crown ar. a greyhound's head sa. collared of the first, rimmed or. *Motto*—Nunc aut nunquam.

Hampsted (co. Norfolk). Gu. a bend chequy or and az.

Hampsted. Gu. a chief ar.

Hampsted, or Hamsted. Az. on a bend ar. betw. three fleurs-de-lis or, as many escallops gu.

Hampton (co. Gloucester). Gu. a fesse chequy or and az. a bordure ar.

Hampton (Henllys, co. Anglesey, A.D. 1460, previously settled in co. Lancaster). Gu. on a fesse or, betw. a mullet in chief and an escallop in base ar. three martlets az. *Crest*—A wivern vert in bullrushes ppr. *Motto*—A Deo et rege.

Hampton (London; descended from co. Stafford, and of Norwood, co. Middlesex). Ar. a chev. gu. betw. three cinquefoils az. *Crest*—A wolf's head erased ar.

Hampton (Wolverhampton, co. Stafford). Ar. on a chev. gu. betw. three cinquefoils az. as many bezants. *Crest*—A wolf's head ar.

Hampton (Blechingly, co. Surrey; granted 6 Aug. 1662, to Rev. WILLIAM HAMPTON, Rector of that place). Gu. a fesse chequy ar. and sa. a bordure or. *Crest*—A demi eagle displ. or.

Hampton (Wales). Gu. a fesse ar. and label of five points of the second.

Hampton (Archbishop of Armagh. Fun. Ent. of CHRISTOPHER HAMPTON, Lord Primate of all Ireland, d. 3 Jan. 1624). Gu. a fess erm. in chief a label of five points or.

Hampton. Ar. a chev. componée az. and purp. betw. three martlets gu. *Crest*—A greyhound sejant holding in his mouth a hare.

Hampton (quartered by DRAKE, of Ashe and Otterton; JOHN DRAKE of the latter, *temp.* Henry V., *m.* CHRISTIAN, dau. and co-heir of JOHN BILLET, by ALICE, his wife, dau. and co-heir of WARREN HAMPTON. Visit. Devon, 1620). Gu. on a fess ar. two mullets sa.

Hampton (Norwood, co. Middlesex; ROBERT HAMPTON, Esq., grandson of FRANCIS HAMPTON, Esq., co. Stafford. Visit. Middlesex, 1663). Ar. a chev. gu. betw. three cinquefoils az. *Crest*—A tiger's head erased ar.

Hampton. Per fesse gu. and or, three cinquefoils counterchanged.

Hampton. Ar. a fesse chequy or and az. betw. six martlets gu.

Hampton. Per fesse gu. and ar. three roses counterchanged barbed and seeded vert and or.

Hampton (Lord Mayor of London, 1472). Gu. a fesse componée or and sa. a bordure ar.

Hampton. Gu. a fesse ar.

Hampton. Gu. on a fesse ar. a mullet sa.

Hamptonne (Hamptonne, St. Lawrence, Jersey). Gu. three mullets pierced or.

Hamste. Sa. a fesse betw. three cinquefoils or.

Hamsted. Az. on a bend fimbriated ar. betw. three fleurs-de-lis or, as many escallops of the first.

Hamton (Rockbere, co. Devon, whose heiress *m.* BILLET, of Ashe, co. Devon). Gu. on a fesse ar. two mullets sa.

Hamwell (impaled by LATIMER, of Duntish). Az. a fess dancettée betw. three martlets or.

Hanacre, De. Ar. on a chief gu. two mullets of six points pierced or.

Hanam, Hanham, or Hannam. Quarterly, or and gu. over all on a bend sa. three crosses pattée ar. *Crest*—A demi griffin ar. holding betw. the paws a helmet az.

Hanbere. Az. a chev. ar. in chief a lion pass. guard. or.

451

Hanbury (co. Stafford). Or, on a bend engr. gu. cotised sa. three bezants.

Hanbury (Wolverhampton, and Norton Hall, co. Stafford; granted by Dugdale, 23 April, 1664, to FRANCIS HANBURY, of Wolverhampton, gent.). Same *Arms*, the bend purp.

Hanbury. Az. a chev. or, in chief a lion pass. guard. of the second.

Hanbury. Or, a bend vert cotised sa.

Hanbury (Hanbury, co. Worcester; seated there from a remote period). Or, a bend engr. vert plain cotised sa. *Crest*—Out of a mural crown sa. a demi lion ramp. or, holding in the paws a battle axe of the first helved gold.

Hanbury (Colebrooke, co. Monmouth; a branch of HANBURY, of Pont-y-pool). Same *Arms*, &c.

Hanbury (Holfield-Grange, Great Coggeshall, co. Essex). Or, a bend engr. az. cotised sa. *Crest*—Out of a mural crown gu. charged with two estoiles or, a demi lion ramp. guard. erm. holding in the dexter paw a battle axe ppr.

Hanbury (granted to D. B. HANBURY, Esq., Clapham, co. Surrey). Or, a bend engr. vert cotised sa. a bordure engr. of the second charged with four trefoils slipped of the first. *Crest*—Out of a mural crown sa. a demi lion or, charged on the shoulder with three trefoils slipped, one and two, and gorged with a collar gemel vert, holding in the dexter paw a battle axe, staff sa. head gold.

Hanbury (BATEMAN-HANBURY, *Lord Bateman*). Quarterly, 1st and 4th, or, a bend engr. vert, plain cotised sa. in chief a crescent on a crescent for diff., for HANBURY; 2nd and 3rd, or, on a fesse sa. betw. three Muscovy ducks ppr. a rose of the field, for BATEMAN. *Crests*—1st, HANBURY: Out of a mural crown sa. a demi lion or, holding in the dexter paw a battle axe sa. headed gold; 2nd, BATEMAN: A duck's head and neck betw. two wings ppr. *Supporters*—Two lions ar. gorged with plain collars, each charged with a rose betw. two fleurs-de-lis or, and chains of the latter affixed to each collar, and reflexed over the back. *Motto*—Nec preece, nec pretio.

Hanbury-Tracy (*Baron Sudeley*). See TRACY.

Hanbury-Leigh (Pontypool, co. Monmouth; CAPEL HANBURY-LEIGH, Esq., of Pontypool Park, Lord-Lieutenant, co. Monmouth, assumed the additional surname and arms of LEIGH in right of his descent, through the TRACYS, from THOMAS, first *Lord Leigh* of Stoneleigh). Quarterly, 1st and 4th, or, a bend engr. vert plain cotised sa., for HANBURY; 2nd and 3rd, gu. a cross engr. ar. in the first quarter a lozenge of the second, for LEIGH. *Crests*—1st, HANBURY: Out of a mural crown sa. a demi lion ramp. or, holding in the paws a battle axe sa.; 2nd, LEIGH: A unicorn's head erased ar. armed and crined or. *Motto*—Nec preece, nec pretio.

Hanby (co. Lincoln). Ar. a cross engr. gu. in the dexter chief quarter an annulet of the second.

Hanby. Az. three goats couchant ar. attired or. *Crest*—Two arms in armour embowed, holding a heart all ppr.

Hanby. Az. a bend ar. betw. six mullets of the second.

Hanchet (Hinkworth, co. Herts). Sa. three dexter (another, sinister) hands couped at the wrist ar.

Hankford. Sa. a chev. barry nebulée ar. *Crest*—A demi cupid holding in the dexter hand a torch ppr.

Hankwood. Ar. on a chev. sa. three escallops of the field. *Crest*—On the stump of a tree sprouting anew ppr. a shield of the arms pendent.

Hancloo. Ar. a lion ramp. az. guttée d'eau, crowned or.

Hanclow, Hancler, or Haneler. Ar. on a chev. sa. three garbs or.

Hancock (co. Leicester). Gu. a plate, on a chief ar. three cocks of the first. *Crest*—A cock's head erminois, combed, wattled, beaked, and ducally gorged gu.

Hancock (London, 1635). Erminois on a pile sa. a gauntlet or. *Crest*—A cock or, combed and wattled gu. armed sa. supporting a palm branch vert.

Hancock. Or, a chev. cotised betw. three griffins' heads couped sa. the two in chief respecting each other.

Hancocke (Combe Martin, co. Devon; granted 1588). Gu. on a chief ar. three cocks of the field. *Crest*—A demi griffin ar. armed or.

Hancocks (Wolverley Court, and Woodfield, co. Worcester, and Fairfield and Marston, co. Hereford). Per chev. az. and gu. in chief betw. two cocks respecting each other in base, a lion ramp. or. *Crest*—On a mount vert a cock gu. holding in the dexter claw an ear of wheat. *Motto*—Redeem time.

Hancoke (Gregory Stoke, co. Somerset). Sa. a chev. betw. three cocks ar. combed, legged, and wattled gu.

Hancombe, or Hantombe (co. Cornwall). Ar. three bendlets sa.

Hancott. Erm. on a bend gu. three mullets or.

Hancre. Az. two bends ar.

Hand. Ar. a chev. az. betw. three dexter hands gu. *Crest*—A stag trippant ppr.

Hand (Dublin; SYMOND HAND, merchant; Fun. Ent. 1640, of his dau. ELLENOR, wife of ROBERT JORDAN, Esq., of Barbestown, co. Dublin). Chequy ar. and sa. a lion ramp. az. armed and langued gu. holding betw. the paws a dexter hand couped at the wrist ppr.

Handacres, or Handesacres. Erm. three cronels gu.

Handasyd, or Handyside (Gains Park, co. Huntingdon, and Scotland). Ar. a lion ramp. sa. on a chief az. three mullets of the first. Crest—A dexter hand couped at the wrist and erect ppr. Motto—Munifice et fortiter.

Handby. Az. five cinquefoils, two and one, and three crosses crosslet fitchée, one and two, ar.

Handchett. Sa. three hands in gauntlets ar.

Handchicke. Sa. three dexter hands couped ar. over all fretty or.

Handcock (Portleek, co. Westmeath). Erm. on a chev. sa. a dexter hand betw. two cocks ar. armed, crested, and jelloped gu. Crest—A demi lion ramp. az. holding betw. the paws a fusil ar. charged with a cock gu.

Handcock (Viscount, now Baron Castlemaine). Same Arms and Crest. Supporters—Dexter, a lion guard. az. ; sinister, a cock ppr. Motto—Vigilate et orate.

Handcock (Waterstown, co. Westmeath; a branch of the Castlemaine family). Same Arms and Crest.

Handcock. Sa. a chev. betw. three cocks ar. combed, legged, and wattled gu. Crest—Out of the sea an arm embowed, holding a bait spade.

Handcock (Cole Hill House, co. Longford). Ar. a fesse gu. betw. three goats pass. sa. bearded, unguled, and armed or. Crest—A goat, as in the arms. Motto—Perseverando.

Handcock (Dublin; Alderman MATHEW HANDCOCK, Mayor of Dublin; Fun. Ent. of his son-in-law, Alderman JOHN SHELTON, 1603). Gu. a dexter hand couped and erect ar. on a chief of the last three cocks of the first. Crest—A cock gu.

Handcock (Dublin; Reg. Ulster's Office). Ar. issuing out of the sinister base an arm fessways vested az. cuffed of the first, hand ppr. thereon standing a cock gu. combed and wattled ar.

Handcome (1634, granted by St. George, Clarenceux, to HANDCOME, of London, and co. Warwick). Gu. a cross ar. in the chief quarters two estoiles or. Crest—A lion sejant or, collared gu. thereon two estoiles of the first.

Handeloe (Williamstrip, co. Gloucester). Ar. a lion ramp. az.

Handen. Ar. a fesse embattled counter-embattled gu. betw. three escallops of the second.

Handerside. Ar. a chev. az. betw. three lions' heads erased gu. a bordure engr. of the second.

Handfield (Ashford, co. Kent). Ar. a lion ramp. sa. betw. nine crosses crosslet of the last. Crest—An eagle's head couped, wings elevated and ducally crowned.

Handford (co. Somerset). Ar. two bends wavy sa.

Handish. Sa. three arms armed ar.

Handish. Sa. three hands with gauntlets ar.

Handle, or Hanillo (Borstall, co. Oxford; arms on an impalement in the Manor House of Chadlington. Visit. Oxon, 1574). Ar. a lion ramp. az. bezantée, crowned or.

Handley, or Hanley. Or, a fret gu. Crest—A sceptre in pale ppr.

Handley. Erm. on a chief gu. three bucks' heads ar. (another, or).

Handley (Newark, and Muskham Grange, co. Notts, Pointon House, co. Lincoln, Culverthorpe Hall, co. Lincoln, granted 1614). Ar. a fesse gu. betw. three goats pass. sa. bearded, unguled, and armed or. Crest—A goat, as in the arms.

Handley (Bramcote, co. Notts; granted by Segar, Garter, 21 June, 1612). Ar. a fess gu. betw. three goats courant sa. armed and unguled or. Crest—A goat, as in the arms.

Handley (London, 1738). Gu. a fess or, betw. six mascles of the second.

Handley. Gu. a bend or, betw. six mascles of the second. Crest—A hand holding a bunch of quills ppr. Motto—Equity.

Handlo. Ar. two chev. gu. on a canton of the last a crescent of the first.

Handlow (co. Kent). Gu. three crescents ar.

Handlow (co. Oxford). Ar. a lion az. guttée d'eau crowned or.

Handsard (Sir RICHARD HANDSARD, knighted 11 Oct. 1604 ; Fun. Ent. of his wife, 1619). Gu. three mullets pierced ar.

Handshall. Ar. a fesse betw. six martlets gu.

Handvile (Ulcombe, co. Kent). Ar. a lion ramp. sa. the field semée of crosses pattée of the second. Crest—An eagle's head erm. ducally crowned or, betw. two wings ppr.

452

Handy. Ar. on a saltire gu. betw. four lions' heads erased sa. five mullets of the field. Crest—Two arms in armour embowed, holding a battle axe all ppr.

Handyside (Scotland, 17th century). Ar. a lion ramp. sa. within a bordure engr. of the last.

Handyside (London, from Scotland, 1680). Ar. a lion ramp. sa. on a chief az. three mullets of the first. Crest—A dexter hand appaumée ppr. Motto—Munifice et fortiter.

Hanercroft (confirmed by Roberts, Ulster, 1646, to Captain WILLIAM HANERCROFT, who commanded a troop of horse in the service of Charles I.). Vert a fess betw. three lions saliant ar. armed and langued gu. collared sa. Crest—A demi lion ramp. gu. collared sa. holding betw. the paws an open book ppr. Motto—Vita more fide.

Haners (London, and co. Norfolk, 1634). Or, on a fesse sa. three millrinds ar.

Hanett. Ar. on a cross sa. five plates.

Hanford (Watton, co. Lincoln). Gu. three mullets ar. Crest—A cubit arm erect, vested or, cuffed ar. holding in the hand ppr. an estoile gold.

Hanford (Wollashill; one of the knightly families of co. Worcester, recorded in the first edition of Mr. SHIRLEY'S work, Noble and Gentle Men of England). Sa. a star of eight rays ar. Crest—On a chapeau gu. turned up erm. a wivern of the first, wings expanded ar. Motto—Memorare novissima.

Hanford (co. Chester). Same Arms.

Hanford (co. Lincoln). Gu. a bend betw. six mullets ar.

Hanford (co. Somerset). Ar. two bends wavy sa.

Hangefield (co. Essex). Or, a chev. sa.

Hanger (Baron Coleraine ; created 1762, extinct 1824). Erm. a griffin segreant per fesse or and az. Crest—A demi griffin segreant or, holding betw. the paws an escarbuncle gold. Supporters—Two griffins az. beaked and forelegged ar. armed and langued gu. Motto—Artes honorabit.

Hanginside, or Hanoreshaw (Scotland). Ar. a lion ramp. within a bordure engr. sa.

Hangrest. Ar. on a cross gu. five escallops or.

Hanham (Dean's Court, near Winbourne, co. Dorset, and Newston Park, co. Wilts, bart.). Quarterly, or and gu. on a bend engr. sa. three crosses pattée fitchée of the first. Crest—A griffin's head erased or, ducally gorged.

Hanham. Quarterly, or and gu. on a bend sa. three crosses formée ar.

Hanillo (Borstall). See HANDLE.

Haningfield. Or, a chev. sa.

Hanington. Ar. on a chev. engr. sa. betw. three demi lions ramp. vert. three plates, each charged with as many erm. spots.

Hanke (Mayor of Chester; granted 6 Sept. 1580). Gyronny of eight az. and gu. a wolf ramp. or, armed sa. langued of the second.

Hankepenny. Chequy az. and or, a chief or.

Hankes. Bendy of six az. and or, a chief erm.

Hankey (Churton, co. Chester; granted, 14 Elizabeth, to HENRY HANKEY, Esq., Mayor of Chester). Per pale gu. and az. a wolf saliant ar.

Hankey (Sir HENRY HANKEY, Alderman of London, d. in 1736: from whom derived HANKEY, of East Bergholt, co. Suffolk, of London, and Fetcham Park, co. Surrey). Per pale gu. and az. a wolf saliant erminois, vulned on the shoulder of the first. Crest—A demi wolf erminois.

Hankford (co. Devon). Sa. on a chev. ar. another wavy gu.

Hankford (Exeter College; RICHARD HANKFORD, Knt., " of the blood and consanguinity of the Founder." Visit. 1574). Ar. two bends nebulée sa.

Hankford (quartered by GREINVILE, co. Cornwall, brought in by MARY, d. 1623, dau. and heir of Sir JOHN ST. LEGER, m. Sir RICHARD GREINVILE. Visit. 1620). Sa. a chev. vairé ar. and gu.

Hankford. Gu. billettée a fesse ar.

Hankins (Greenhouse, co. Gloucester). Quarterly, 1st and 4th, ar. on a lion pass. gu. in base three bars wavy sa. on a chief az. three bezants, for HANKINS; 2nd and 3rd, gu. a fesse vair betw. three pelicans' heads erased or, for MACHEN. Crest—A Moor frontfaced, with a bow hung over the left shoulder, and a quiver of arrows, and holding in the hands extended a snake all ppr.

Hankinson (co. Middlesex). Ar. a fesse gu. fretty or, betw. three ducks sa. Crest—A demi phœnix, wings elevated or, issuant from flames. Motto—Vi et animo.

Hanley (co. Buckingham). Az. a fesse dancettée betw. three hawks or.

Hanley (co. Devon). Ar. a buckle lozengeways sa.

Hanley (co. Devon). Ar. fretty gu. a canton of the first.

Hanley (cos. Devon and Cornwall). Az. three goats ar attired or.

Hanley. Ar. a mascle depressed by a fesse sa.

Hanley. Ar. a lion ramp. sa. crowned or, within a bordure az.

Hanley. Ar. three talbots pass. az.

Hanlon (co. Kent). Gu. three crescents ar.

Hanlon. Gu. three plates.

Hanlon. See O'HANLON.

Hanlow. Ar. a lion ramp. az.

Hanly. See O'HANLY.

Hanmalyn. Gu. a lion ramp. or, guttée sa.

Hanmer (Hanmer, co. Flint, bart., extinct 1746; Sir JOHN DE MACCLESFIELD, Constable of Carnarvon Castle, *temp.* Edward I., assumed the name of HANMER from his mother's family, she being heiress of that place. The family is now represented by *Lord Hanmer*). Ar. two lions pass. guard. az. armed and langued gu. *Crest*—On a chapeau az. turned up erm. a lion sejant guard. ar. *Motto*—Gardez l'honneur.

Hanmer (*Baron Hanmer*). Ar. two lions pass. guard. az. armed and langued gu. *Crest*—On a chapeau az. turned up erm. a lion sejant guard. ar. *Supporters*—Dexter, a swan ar.; sinister, a stork ppr. each holding in the beak a rose ppr. leaves vert. *Motto*—Gardez l'honneur.

Hanmer (Holbrook Hall, co. Suffolk; a branch of HANMER, of Hanmer). Same *Arms, Crest,* and *Motto.*

Hanmer (Beachfield, co. Salop). Same *Arms* and *Crest.*

Halmer (Porkington, co. Salop). Az. a lion pass. guard. coward or. *Crest*—Out of a mural coronet or, a cubit arm erect, vested quarterly ar. and az. cuffed erm. on the hand ppr. a falcon close of the first, beaked, winged, and legged of the third, belled gold.

Hanmer (Elweny Maptis, co. Salop). Sa. three goats pass. ar.

Hanmer. Vert two dolphins endorsed or, (another, ar.).

Hannam. Quarterly, or and gu. on a bend sa. three crosses formée fitchée ar.

Hannam. See HANAM.

Hannay, or Ahannay (Sorbie, co. Wigtown). Ar. three roebucks' heads couped az. collared or, with a bell gu. pendent from each collar.

Hannay (Mochrum, co. Kirkcudbright, bart., 1630, heir male of Sorbie). Ar. three roebucks' heads couped az. collared or, a bell pendent from each collar. *Crest*—A cross crosslet fitchée, issuing out of a crescent sa. *Supporters*—Two roebucks ppr. *Motto*— Per ardua ad alta.

Hannay (cadet of Sorbie). Ar. three roebucks' heads couped az. with a mullet in the collar point for diff. *Crest*— A cross crosslet fitchée issuing out of a crescent sa. *Motto*— Per ardua ad alta.

Hannell. Ar. a bend gu. a bordure erm.

Hannell. Ar. on a cross sa. five plates.

Hannes (co. Oxford; granted 3 Dec. 1641). Per pale gu. and az. on a fesse dancettée betw. three mullets ar. as many crosses crosslet sa.

Hanney, or Haney. Az. a chev. betw. three demi lions ramp. or. *Crest*—A stag's head ppr. collared or, betw. the attires a cross pattée gu.

Hannill. See HANNYLE.

Hanning (Dillington House, co. Somerset). Erm. on a chief gu. three bucks' heads cabossed or. *Crest*—A stag's head erased ppr.

Hanningfield, or Havingfield (co. Cornwall). Or, a chev. sa.

Hannyle (co. Buckingham). Az. a fesse dancettée betw. three griffins pass. or.

Hanrott (London). Ar. an eagle displ. with two heads sa. gorged with an antique crown or, on the breast a human heart ppr. holding in the dexter claw a dagger and in the sinister claw a chaplet of laurel all ppr. *Crest*—An eagle displ. with two heads sa, a motto over, Perseverando. *Motto*— Humani nihil alienum.

Hansard (co. Lancaster). Gu. three martlets ar.

Hansard (cos. Lincoln, Suffolk, and York). Gu. three mullets ar.

Hansard (co. Sussex). Gu. a crescent betw. three mullets ar.

Hansard (THOMAS CORNWALLIS, of London, merchant, 2 Richard II., A.D. 1377, *m.* JANE, dau. and heiress of WILLIAM HANSARD. Visit. Notts). Gu. a crescent betw. three mullets ar.

Hansard (co. Westmoreland). Gu. a bend ar. a mullet for diff.

Hansard. Gu. a bend ar. *Crest*—An antique crown or.

Hansard. Gu. three estoiles or.

Hansard. Gu. an estoile of eight points ar.

Hansard. Gu. a bend betw. six mullets ar.

Hansard (Fun. Ents. of ANNE MARBURY, Lady HANSARD, *d.* 8 Oct., and of her husband, Sir RICHARD HANSARD, *d.* 5 Oct. 1619). Gu. three mullets pierced ar.

Hansard (Lifford, co. Donegal, Reg. Ulster's Office). Gu. three mullets ar. *Crest*—An arm in armour embowed holding in the gauntlet a broken sword all ppr. *Motto*—Fractus pugnatu.

Hansby, or Hans (St. Giles, Beverley, and New Malton, co. York; granted 10 Oct. 1582). Az. three sheldrakes close ar. a chief erm. *Crest*—A pheon or.

Hansby (Fun. Ent. Ulster's Office). Quarterly, erm and az. on a cross or, five pellets.

Hanslape (Thorp, co. Warwick. Har. MSS. 6060). Ar. two bars gu. over all a cross in pale az.

Hanslop, or Hanslap (cos. Northampton and Warwick). Ar. a cross crosslet fitchée az. betw. two bars gu. *Crest*—A leopard sejant ppr.

Hanslore. Sa. billettée or, a cross flory of the last.

Hansom (Fun. Ent., Ulster's Office, Mrs. HANSOM, buried in St. John's Church, Dublin, 24 Oct. 1667). Erm. on a canton sa. a fleur-de-lis or.

Hanson (Abingdon, co. Berks, and London; Sir ROBERT HANSON, Lord Mayor of London 1675). Ar. three mascles (another, lozenges) sa. on a chief of the second as many lions ramp. of the first. *Crest*—A lion ramp. sa. holding a mascle ar.

Hanson (Gilstead Hall, near Brentwood, co. Essex). Or, a chev. chequy ar. and az. betw. three martlets of the last. *Crest*—On a ducal coronet or, a dove close, holding in the beak a sprig of olive all ppr.

Hanson (Peckham, co. Surrey, and Rastricke and Woodhouse, co. York). Or, a chev. counter-componée ar. and az. betw. three martlets sa. *Crests*—On a chapeau az. turned up ar. a martlet, wings endorsed sa.

Hansted (co. Northumberland). Gu. a bend chequy or and az.

Hansted, or Hasted (cos. Northampton and Northumberland). Gu. a chief chequy or and az.

Hansted. Gu. a chev. chequy or and az. surmounted by a bend erm.

Hantevill (co. Devon). Sa. semée of crosses botonnée, a lion ramp. az.

Hantevill (*temp.* Edward I.) Sa. a lion saliant ar. within an orle of crosslets of the second.

Hantey. Gu. an inescutcheon ar. within an orle of plates.

Hantom. Ar. a cross formée sa. betw. six lions ramp. of the last.

Hantvile, or Handville (cos. Devon and Kent). Ar. semée of crosses crosslet fitchée sa. a lion ramp. of the second. *Crest*—An eagle's head erm. ducally crowned or, betw. two wings.

Hantvill. Sa. a lion ramp. ar. within an orle of eight crosses crosslet of the second. *Crest*—An ox-yoke in pale gu. bows to the sinister or.

Hanvill (co. Bucks). Az. a fesse indented betw. three griffins ramp. or.

Hanvill (co. Bucks.) Az a fesse indented betw. three martlets or.

Hanwood, or Hamwood. Ar. a chev. quarterly, sa. and gu. embattled counter-embattled az. billettée of the field, betw. three ravens' heads erased of the second.

Hanway (impalement on Fun. Ent. 1661, CHARLES, first *Earl of Mountrath,* whose second wife was the dau. of Sir ROBERT HANWAY, Bart., Scotland). Quarterly, 1st and 4th, ar. three roebucks' heads erased az. attired or; 2nd and 3rd, ar. three crescents sa. issuant from each a cross crosslet fitchée of the last. *Crest*—A demi lion ramp. holding a cross crosslet fitchée. *Motto*—True to the end.

Hanynton (co. Kent). Ar. on a chev. betw. three lions ramp. vert as many trefoils slipped erm.

Hanyton. Gu. on a fesse ar. three mullets sa. pierced of the second.

Happen (co. Oxford). Ar. a mullet pierced gu.

Hara, or O'Hara (Coolany, co. Sligo; granted, 1635, by Preston, Ulster, to KEAN O'HARA, Esq., of Coolany). Vert on a pale radiant or, a lion ramp. sa. armed and langued gu. *Crest*—A demi lion ramp. pean, armed and langued gu. holding in the paws a chaplet of oak leaves ppr. *Motto*— Virtute et claritate.

Haradon. Ar. on a chev. gu. betw. three eagles' heads erased sa. as many crescents or.

Harbe, or Harbey (Asby, co. Northampton). Sa. a fesse indented erm. betw. eight billets ar. *Crest*—An eagle's head erased or, betw. two wings sa. bezantée.

Harberton, Viscount. See POMEROY.

Harbin (Somerset; granted in 1618 to ROBERT HARBIN, Esq., of Newton, co. Somerset). Az. a saltire voided betw. four cronels or. *Crest*—A gauntleted hand, couped above the wrist az. holding a spur or, leathered sa.

Harbord (*Baron Suffeld*). Quarterly, 1st and 4th, quarterly, az. and gu. an imperial crown or, betw. four lions ramp. ar., for HARBORD; 2nd and 3rd, ar. a fleur-de-lis gu., for MORDEN. Crest—On a chapeau gu. turned up. erm. a lion couchant ar. Supporters—Dexter, a lion ramp. or, collared and chained az.; sinister, a leopard guard. ppr. collared and chained or. Motto—Æquanimiter.

Harborne (cos. Chester and Middlesex). Gu. a fish naiant ar.

Harborne (Yarmouth, co. Norfolk, and co. Middlesex. Visit. London, 1568). Gu. on a fess ar. three bezants a lion pass. sa. Crest—A bezant betw. two lions' gambs sa.

Harborne (granted 1582). Same Arms and Crest. Another Crest—On a chapeau gu. turned up. erm. an eagle displ. or.

Harborne (Thackley, co. Oxford; JOHN HARBORNE, High Sheriff of the co., 1632. Visit. Oxon, 1634). Gu. a lion pass. or, betw. three bezants. Crest—A lion sejant or, resting the dexter paw on a bezant. Motto—Deus industriam beat.

Harborne (Sheen Lane, co. Middlesex; granted by Camden, Clarenceux, 1613). Az. a lion pass. or, betw. three bezants. Crest—On the stump of a tree couped and eradicated ppr. an eagle displ. or, beaked and legged gu.

Harborough, Earl of. See SHERARD.

Harbotell (co. Northumberland). Or, three escallops gu.

Harbottell (Basingthorpe, co. Lincoln, and Eglington, co. Rutland; descended from ROGER HARBOTTELL, Lord of Harbottell, temp. Henry I. Visit. Rutland, 1618). Az. three icicles bendways or.

Harbottle (co. Brecon). Same Arms (another, the icicles ar.). Crest—A dexter arm embowed, vested az. cuff ar. holding in the hand ppr. a club or.

Harbottle (co. Suffolk). Same Arms, a bordure cngr. erm. Crest—A demi falcon or, with wings expanded, barry wavy of six ar. and az.

Harbred (co. York). Gu. a cross vair betw. four lions ramp. or.

Harbright (Reg. Ulster's Office). Gu. three leopards' faces or.

Harbron (co. Chester). Gu. a hawk ar.

Harbron. Gu. a fish naiant ar. Crest—A hand holding an anchor ppr.

Harby (Aldenham, co. Herts, Adston and Astley, co. Northampton). Gu. a fesse dancettée erm. betw. ten billets ar. four in chief and six in base. Crest—A demi eagle erased, wings expanded sa. bezantée.

Harby (Aldenham, co. Herts, bart., extinct 1674, originally from cos. Northampton and Cambridge). Same Arms.

Harby, or Harvy (Lord Mayor of London, 1272 and 1273). Ar. two bars wavy sa. on a chief of the second three crosses pattée fitchée or.

Harby (Atweston, co. Northampton; granted 1599). Gu. a fesse erm. betw. ten billets ar. four, three, and three, Crest—A heron's head erased or, betw. two wings expanded sa.

Harbye (Canons Ashby, cos. Northants and Cambridge, and London. Her. Visit. 1568). Gu. a fesse dancettée erm. betw. ten billets ar. four in chief, three, two, and one, in base. Crest—A heron's head erased or, beaked sa. betw. two wings expanded of the last bezantée.

Harbyn. See HARBIN.

Harcarse (that Ilk, co. Berwick). Sa. a chev. betw. three fleurs-de-lis ar.

Harcla (Earl of Carlisle; created by Charter 1322, forfeited same year). Ar. a cross gu. in the first quarter a martlet sa.

Harcourt (Stanton Harcourt and Nuneham Courtenay, co. Oxford, originally from Harcourt in Normandy, correctly styled by Collins "an ancient and illustrious family;" its representative at the opening of the eighteenth century was Sir SIMON HARCOURT, Lord Chancellor of England, temp. George I., who was created Baron and Viscount Harcourt: his grandson SIMON, second Viscount, was advanced to an earldom 1749, and was Lord Lieutenant of Ireland 1772. At the death of his lordship's last surviving son, Field Marshal WILLIAM, third Earl Harcourt, G.C.B., in 1830, the Peerage honours became extinct, but the estates devolved on EDWARD VERNON, Archbishop of York, nephew of SIMON, first Earl Harcourt, and are now enjoyed by by his Grace's grandson, EDWARD WILLIAM HARCOURT, Esq., of Stanton Harcourt and Nuneham Courtenay). Gu. two bars or. Crest—On a ducal coronet or, a peacock close ppr. Supporters (of the Lords Harcourt)—Two lions or, each gorged with a bar gemel gu. Mottoes—Le bon temps viendra; also, Gesta verbis prævenient.

Harcourt (Cadby and Dadlington, co. Leicester. Visit. Leicester, 1619). Same Arms as the Earl Harcourt, a mullet

for diff. Crest—On a ducal coronet or, a peacock close ppr.

Harcourt (Ankerwycke, co. Bucks; descended from PHILIP HARCOURT, Esq., brother of the first Viscount, and son of Sir PHILIP HARCOURT, of Stanton Harcourt, co. Oxford, by ELIZABETH, his second wife, dau. and heiress of JOHN LEE, Esq., of Ankerwycke). Same Arms, Crest, and Motto, as HARCOURT, Earl Harcourt.

Harcourt (Winsham, co. Chester). Same Arms, a mullet for diff.

Harcourt. Or, two bars gu. in chief three escallops of the second.

Harcourt. Or, two bars and a chief gu.

Harcourt (Ellenhall, co. Stafford. Visit. 1583). Gu. two bars or.

Hard. Or, a chev. engr. az. betw. three hedgehogs sa.

Hardacre. Sa. two boars' heads erased in chief ar. Crest—On a rock an eagle rising reguard. all ppr.

Hardbeane (co. Lincoln). Ar. three bean-cods vert.

Hardby. Gu. billettée a fesse and chev. ar.

Hardcastle. Sa. on a chev. betw. three castles ar. as many leopards' faces gu. Crest—A lady attired az. holding in the dexter hand the sun, and in the sinister the moon ppr.

Hardcastle (Netherhall, co. Suffolk, and The Lodge, Holt, co. Norfolk). Sa. on a chev. betw. three castles ar. as many leopards' faces gu. Crest—A castle ar. Motto—Deus mihi munimen.

Hardde. Vert a lion ramp. or.

Harde, or Hardy. Ar. a cross engr. az. betw. four hedgehogs sa.

Hardehill, Hardeshall, or Hardshall (co. Leicester). Or, a cross engr. gu. a martlet vert for diff.

Hardel (Lord Mayor of London, 1215). Vert a fesse flory counterflory or.

Hardeley. Ar. on a bend betw. two lions' heads erased sa. three crosses crosslet or. Crest—A soldier firing a gun ppr.

Hardell. Or, a bend az. cotised gu.

Hardewick. Gu. a saltire engr. ar. betw. four mullets or.

Hardey (London). Ar. on a bend engr. gu. a crescent betw. two leopards' faces of the first, a chief az. charged with three catharine wheels or. Crest—A cock's head bendy ar. and sa. betw. two wings, the dexter or, the sinister gu. holding in the mouth a sceptre of the last.

Hardfeild. Chequy or and gu. on a bend ar. three horseshoes az.

Hardgrave (co. Lincoln). Az. a fesse or, fretty gu. betw. three hinds trippant ar.

Hardgrave. Ar. a griffin segreant az. (another, gu.).

Hardgrave. Ar. a griffin segreant sa. forelegs gu. armed or.

Hardgrave, or Hardgrove. Ar. a griffin segreant per fesse gu. and sa. armed or. Crest—A water bouget gu.

Hardhill. Ar. a cross engr. gu. in the first quarter a martlet az.

Hardie (Scotland). Gu. a dexter hand fesseways, holding a dagger ar. point downwards, betw. two mullets or.

Hardiman, or Hardyman. Ar. three chev. gu. a canton sa. Crest—On a serpent nowed a hawk perched all ppr.

Harding (King's Newton, co. Derby; granted 3 July, 1711). Gu. on a chev. ar. fimbriated or, three escallops az. Crest—A mitre gu. banded and stringed or, charged with a chev. ar. fimbriated of the second, thereon three escallops az. Motto—Audax omnia perpeti.

Harding (co. Kent). Per pale ar. and sa. two wolves and three cinquefoils counterchanged, a bordure per pale gu. and or.

Harding (Lieut.-Col. HARDING, Upcott House). Ar. on a bend az. three martlets or. Crest—A falcon displ. ppr.

Harding (Baraset, co. Warwick). Erm. a fesse chequy or and az. Crest—On a chapeau az. turned up erm. a boar pass. or.

Harding (Comb Martin and Upcot, co. Devon; the learned THOMAS HARDING, D.D., Fellow of New College, Oxford, the antagonist of JOHN JEWELL, Bishop of Salisbury, born at Comb Martin, was a son of this family). Ar. on a bend az. three martlets or. Crest—A falcon, wings expanded.

Harding (Conley, co. Gloucester, and Rockfields, co. Monmouth). Gu. three greyhounds in pale courant or, collared az. Crest—A demi leopard ramp. erased erm. attired and gorged with a chain or.

Harding (Houldingfield, co. Durham). Gu. three greyhounds courant in pale or, collared az. (another, ar.).

Harding (WILLIAM HARDING, citizen of London. Visit. 1568). Gu. three greyhounds courant in pale or, collared az. Crest—A demi leopard ramp. erm. gorged with a collar az bezantée, chained or.

Harding (London; granted 30 Aug. 1568). Or, on a bend

az. three martlets ar. a sinister canton of the second, charged with a rose of the first, betw. two fleurs-de-lis of the third. *Crest*—A demi buck ppr. attired or, holding an anchor of the last.

Harding (Newtowne, co. Wilts). **Ar.** on a bend az. three martlets or.

Harding. Vert three acorns or.

Harding. Ar. a saltire engr. az.

Harding-Nott. See NOTT.

Harding (ROBERT HARDING, Treasurer's Remembrancer in Ireland, 1655. Fun. Ent. of his dau. 1660). Or, on a bend az. three martlets ar.

Harding (allowed by Betham, Ulster, 1820, to HENRY HARDING, Esq., of the Treasury). Ar. on a bend sa. betw. two annulets gu. three martlets or. billettée gu.

Harding (Reg. Ulster's Office). Ar. on a bend az. three martlets or, a canton ermines.

Harding (Maryborough, Queen's co.; Fun. Ent. of MARGARET (*d.* 1639), wife of HUGH HARDING, of Dublin, third son of THOMAS HARDING, of the former). Ar. on a bend sa. three martlets or.

Hardinge (granted to Rev. HENRY SIRRE HARDINGE, of Monkstown, co. Dublin). Ar. a bend betw. two mascles gu. on a canton or, a fleur-de-lis az. *Crest*—A raven rising ppr. *Motto*—Non melior patribus.

Hardinge (Boundes Park, co. Kent, bart.). Gu. on a chev. ar. fimbriated or, three escallops sa. and as an honourable augmentation, on a chief wavy of the second a dismasted French frigate with her colours struck, towed by an English frigate all ppr. *Crest*—Of augmentation, on a wreath a hand fessewise, couped above the wrist, habited in naval uniform, holding a sword erect, surmounting a Dutch and French flag in saltire, on the former inscribed "Atlanta," on the latter, "Piedmontaise," the blade of the sword passing through a wreath of laurel near the point, and a little below, through another of cypress, with the motto "Postera laude recens." *Family Crest*—A mitre gu. charged with a chev. as in the arms. *Motto*—Postera laude recens.

Hardinge (*Viscount Hardinge*). Gu. on a chev. ar. fimbriated or, three escallops sa. *Crest*—A mitre gu. thereon a chev. ar. fimbriated or, charged with three escallops sa. *Supporters*—On either side a lion ppr. that on the dexter murally crowned or, and supporting a flagstaff ppr. therefrom flowing to the dexter a flag or, and that on the sinister crowned with an eastern crown and supporting a like staff, therefrom flowing to the sinister a flag also or. *Motto*—Mens æqua rebus in arduis.

Hardington, or Harrington (co. York). **Or, a fesse** betw. three escallops gu.

Hardishall (quartered by COLEPEPER. Fun. Ent. 1610, of ELIZABETH COLEPEPER, widow of HENRY DILLON). Ar. a chev. betw. three martlets sa.

Hardishall. Or, a cross engr. vert, in the first quarter a martlet of the last.

Hardishull (co. Warwick). Ar. a chev. sa. betw. ten martlets, six and four, gu.

Hardisty (co. York). Az. a lion ramp. betw. three fleurs-de-lis or, a chief vair. *Crest*—A boar's head couped ppr. pierced through by an arrow.

Hardles (Lord Mayor of London, 1254 to 1258 inclusive). Or, a bend betw. two cotises sa.

Hardly (London). Az. a chev. betw. three annulets or. debruised by a fesse gu.

Hardly. Gu. a chev. ar. betw. three plates, over all a fesse az.

Hardman. Per bend gu. and or, on a chief ar. three lions gu. betw. two fleurs-de-lis az. *Crest*—A hand issuing, pulling a rose ppr.

Hardman (Liverpool and Rochdale, co. Lancaster). Ar. on a fesse engr. gu. betw. three crosses patonce of the second as many crescents of the field. *Crest*—A naked arm embowed, couped at the shoulder, holding a mill-pick ppr.

Hardness (co. Kent). Erm. a lion ramp. az.

Hardres (Hardres, co. Kent, bart., extinct 1764; descended from PHILIP DE HARDRES, living *temp.* King John and Henry III. According to tradition, the gates of Boulogne were at Hardres Court, having been given by Henry VIII. to a member of the family who attended him at the siege). Gu. a lion ramp. erm. debruised with a chev. or, (denoting the tenure of Hardres by knight's service of the castle of Tunbridge, co. Kent, the ancient seigniory of the *Earls of Gloucester*, who bore or, three similar chev. gu.). *Crest*—A buck's head couped or and erm. attired gu. and az.

Hardres (co. Kent). Gu. a lion ramp. erm. tail forked, depressed with a chev. or.

Hardres. Per chev. or and az. three cups counterchanged.

455

Hardreshall, or Hardresham. Az. a fesse gu. in chief three leopards' heads or, in base as many fishes haurient and six crosses crosslet fitchée of the last.

Hardrishall (Fun. Ent. Ireland). Ar. a chev. betw. three martlets sa.

Hardware (Peel and Bromborough, co. Chester). Sa. a chev. ar. betw. three hands erect, couped at the wrist of the second. *Crest*—Out of a ducal coronet or, a cubit arm az. cuffed ar. holding in the hand ppr. an oak branch of the last fructed or.

Hardwick, or Hardwicke (Hardwick, co. Derby). Ar. a saltire engr. az. on a chief of the second three cinquefoils (another, roses) of the first. *Crest*—On a mount vert a stag courant ppr. gorged with a chaplet of roses ar.

Hardwick (WILLIAM HARDWICK, Esq., of Diamond Hall, Bridgenorth, co. Salop). Same *Arms*, a crescent for diff. *Crest*—On a mount vert a stag courant gorged with a chaplet of roses all ppr. a crescent for diff. *Motto*—Cavendo tutus.

Hardwick (Lindley, co. Leicester, 3 Henry VIII.). Gu. a saltire engr. betw. four mullets or, quartering LANGHAM, of Gopsall.

Hardwick (Sheffield). Same *Arms*.

Hardwick. Gu. a saltire engr. betw. four mullets pierced ar.

Hardwicke, Earl of. See YORKE.

Hardwike. Ar. a saltire engr. az. on a chief of the second three cinquefoils of the first. *Crest*—An ostrich's feather enfiled with a ducal coronet all ppr.

Hardworth. Ar. a bend sa.

Hardy (bart., extinct; Admiral Sir THOMAS MASTERMAN HARDY, G.C.B., was captain of the "Victory," at Trafalgar, and was created a bart. 1806, *d. s. p. m.*). Pean on a chev. betw. three escallops ar. as many dragons' heads ppr. *Crest*—Out of a naval crown or, a dragon's head, as in the arms.

Hardy (Toller Wilmer, co. Dorset; Hatchment, Sir THOMAS HARDY, Knt., 1732). Sa. on a chev. betw. three escallops or, as many dragons' heads erased of the first. *Crest*—A dexter arm embowed in armour, holding in the hand ppr. a dragon's head erased sa.

Hardy (London). Ar. on a bend engr. gu. a crescent betw. two leopards' faces of the first, on a chief az. three catharine wheels or. *Crest*—An eagle's head, bendy of four ar. and sa. betw. two wings, the dexter or, the sinister gu. in the beak a pansy flower ppr. stalked and leaved vert.

Hardy, or Hardye. Same *Arms*. *Crest*—A heart within a fetterlock gu.

Hardy. Sa. on a chev. erm. betw. three escallops ar. as many griffins' heads erased of the field. *Crest*—An arm embowed in armour, gauntlet ppr. garnished or, holding a griffin's head, as in the arms.

Hardy (Wetwang, co. York, 1665). Ar. a cross engr. az. betw. four boars pass. sa. *Crest*—A demi eagle ar. wings displ. gu. charged on the breast with two bendlets sa. in the beak a rose branch.

Hardy (Letheringsett Hall, co. Norfolk). Quarterly, 1st and 4th, per chev. ar. and or, in chief two bomb shells fired, and in base an eagle's head erased ppr., for HARDY; 2nd and 3rd, per pale az. and gu. on a pile or, a lion ramp., for COZENS. *Crests*—1st, HARDY: A dexter arm embowed ppr. charged with a pellet betw. two chevronels or, and grasping an eagle's head fesseways also ppr.; 2nd, COZENS: A lion ramp. or, guttée de sang and fretty gu. *Motto*—Fear one.

Hardy (Guernsey). Az. a chev. potent counter-potent or and sa. in middle chief point a crescent ar. on a chief of the first a lion pass. gu. *Crest*—An ostrich feather or.

Hardy (Dunstall Hall, co. Stafford, bart.). Ar. on a bend invected plain cotised gu. three catharine wheels or, on a chief of the second as many leopards' faces of the third. *Crest*—A dexter arm embowed in armour ppr. garnished or, entwined by a branch of oak vert charged with two catharine wheels, the one above and the other below the elbow gu. the hand grasping a dragon's head erased ppr. *Motto*—Armé de foi hardi.

Hardy (Chilham Castle, co. Kent). *Arms*, &c., as the preceding.

Hardy (Hemsted Park, co. Kent). *Arms*, &c., as HARDY, of Dunstall Hall.

Hardy. Ar. on a bend gu. a leopard's face betw. two crescents of the field, on a chief of the second three catharine wheels of the first.

Hardy (confirmed to PHILIP DIXON HARDY, Esq., of Greenfields, co. Dublin). Per pale gu. and az. on a chev. ar. betw. three griffins' heads erased or, three escallops of the first. *Crest*—A griffin's head erased or, charged with an escallop gu. *Motto*—Spes in Domino.

Hardy (Reg. Ulster's Office). Ar. on a bend gu. three catharine wheels or, on a chief gu. a crescent of the third betw. two leopards' faces of the first.

Hardyshill, or Hardyshull. Ar. a chev. sa. within an orle of martlets gu.

Hare (*Earl of Listowel*). Gu. two bars or, a chief indented of the last. *Crest*—A demi lion couped ar. ducally gorged or. *Supporters*—Two dragons erm. armed and langued gu. wings elevated and endorsed. *Motto*—Odi profanum.

Hare (*Lord Coleraine; created 1625, extinct with the third lord*). Gu. two bars or, a chief indented of the last. *Crest*—A demi lion ramp. ar. ducally gorged gu. *Supporters*—Two dragons erm.

Hare (Stow Bardolph, co. Norfolk, bart., extinct 1764). Gu. two bars and a chief indented or. *Crest*—A demi lion ramp. ar. holding a cross crosslet fitchée gu. *Motto*—Non videri sed esse.

Hare (Stow Hall, co. Norfolk, bart.; THOMAS LEIGH, Esq., of Stow Hall, son of THOMAS LEIGH, Esq., of Iver, co. Bucks, and grandson of THOMAS LEIGH, Esq., of London, by MARY HARE, his wife, sister of the last bart. of Stow Bardolph, assumed the surname of HARE, and was created a bart. 1818). Same *Arms*. *Crest*—A demi lion ramp. ar. ducally gorged or. *Motto*—Non videri sed esse.

Hare (Docking Hall, co. Norfolk; a younger branch of HARE, of Stow). Same *Arms* and *Crest*.

Hare (co. Norfolk). Same *Arms*. *Crest*—A demi lion ar. holding a cross patonce fitchée gu. *Another Crest*—A demi lion ramp. ar. gorged with a naval coronet gu.

Hare (Walsoken, co. Norfolk). Ar. a chev. engr. sa. betw. three griffins' heads erased az. on a chief gu. a mullet betw. two martlets or.

Hare (co. Norfolk). Or, two bars gemelles gu. a chief indented ar. *Crest*—A demi lion ar.

Hare (Court Grange, co. Devon). Gu. two bars or, a chief indented ar. *Crest*—A demi lion ramp. ducally gorged. *Motto*—Odi profanum.

Hare (Scotland). Az. two bars and a chief indented or.

Hare (co. Suffolk). Gu. two bars or, a chief indented ar. *Crest*—A lion ramp. ar.

Hare. Ar. on a chev. engr. sa. two martlets or, in chief three griffins' heads erased gu.

Hare. Ar. three Cornish choughs ppr.

Hare (CHARLES JOHN HARE, Esq., M.D., of Beeston, co. York, and Etchingham, co. Sussex). Or, eight arrows interlaced saltirewise and banded gu. on a chief sa. three mullets ar. a canton of the last, thereon a gate of the third, the whole within a bordure erm. *Crest*—A demi lion ar. semée of mullets gu. supporting a flagstaff ppr. therefrom flowing towards the sinister a pennon gu. charged with a mullet ar. *Motto*—By watchfulness, by steadfastness.

Harebread (co. York; confirmed by St. George, Norroy, 1603). Gu. a cross vair betw. four lions pass. or. *Crest*—An ostrich's feather in pale ar.

Hareford (Bosbury, co. Hereford). Sa. two bends ar.

Hareford. Az. two bars or, on a chief sa. three harts' heads of the second.

Hareward. Sa. on a chief ar. three falcons' heads erased of the first.

Hareware (co. Warwick). Az. a bend wavy betw. two bucks' heads erased or.

Harewedon. Ar. on a bend gu. five lozenges of the field (another, a lozenge or).

Harewell (Blakenham, co. Suffolk, and Besford and Wotton-Shottrey, co. Worcester). Ar. on a fesse nebulée sa. three hares' heads couped or (another, the heads erased ar.). *Crest* —A hare's head erased or.

Harewell. Ar. on a fesse wavy sa. three hares' heads erased bendways ar.

Harewell. Sa. two lions pass. crowned or.

Harewell. Ar. two lions pass. guard. sa.

Harewood, Earl of. See LASCELLES.

Harewood. Sa. on a chief ar. three harts' heads erased of the field.

Hareworth, or Harworth (Boyntonhall, co. Norfolk). Az. a fesse gobonated ar. and gu. betw. three owls of the second.

Harfe. Ar. three lozenges sa. each charged with an escallop or.

Harfett (co. Kent; granted 9 May, 1564). Az. three mullets or, a canton of the last, a bordure counter-componée of the second and first. *Crest*—A demi dolphin erect ppr. (another, a dolphin embowed ppr.).

Harfield (co. Bucks). Per pale ar. and gu. three lions' paws erased counterchanged.

Harfleet, or Hartfleet. Az. three escallops or.

Harford (co. Devon). Ar. a fesse fusily gu. a lion pass. in chief sa.

Harford (Bosbury, co. Hereford; descended from JOHN HARFORD, of Bosbury, Esq., by ANNE. his wife, dau. of RICHARD SCROPE, Esq., of Castlecombe). Sa. two bends ar. on a canton (the arms of SCROPE) az. a bend or. *Crest*—Out of flames ppr. a phœnix or, wings az. fire issuing from the mouth.

Harford (Blaise Castle, co. Gloucester). Same *Arms* and *Crest*.

Harford (Sirhowy House, co. Monmouth). Same *Arms* and *Crest*.

Harford (Falcondale, Lampeter, co. Cardigan). Same *Arms* and *Crest*.

Harford. Az. a bend cotised ar. betw. six lions ramp. or.

Harford. Sa. an estoile of eight points ar.

Harford (HENRY HARFORD, Esq.). Paly of six or and sa. a bend counterchanged. *Crest*—Out of a ducal coronet or, two flags, the one gold the other sa. both staves of the first.

Harforth (Reg. Ulster's Office). Ar. on a fess. az. three bucks' heads cabossed or.

Hargest. Or, a griffin ramp. az.

Hargevill. Vert three annulets ar.

Hargil (Clementhorp, co. York). Gu. three mullets or, a canton erm. *Crest*—Out of a ducal coronet gu. a lion's head or.

Harglas (Reg. Ulster's Office). Ar. a stag trippant gu. attired vert.

Hargonell. Ar. three annulets vert.

Hargost. Ar. a griffin segrant az. armed or (another, armed gu.).

Hargrave (co. Lincoln). Az. a fesse ar. fretty gu. betw. three stags in full course or, attired of the second. *Crest*—A stag's head erased per fesse or and az. attired ar. *Another Crest*—A buck's head erased per fesse or and gu. fretty az. attired of the second.

Hargrave (co. Chester). Ar. a griffin segreant per fesse gu. and sa. beak and claws or.

Hargraves. Az. a fesse betw. three stags courant or. *Crest*—Out of a ducal coronet two branches of laurel in orle ppr.

Hargreaves (co. Lancaster). Quarterly, or and vert on a fesse erm. betw. three stags courant counterchanged a fret gu.

Hargreaves (Bank Hall, co. Lancaster). Per pale nebuly or and az. a fesse erm. fretty gu. betw. three bucks courant counterchanged. *Crest*—A buck's head erased az. attired or, gorged with a collar ar. fretty gu. in the mouth a sprig of heath ppr. *Motto*—Vincit amor patriæ.

Hargreaves (Broad Oak, co. Lancaster). Quarterly, or and vert on a fesse erm. betw. three stags courant counterchanged a fret gu. *Crest*—A buck's head erased vert, attired or, with a collar ar. charged with a fret gu. in the mouth a sprig of oak ppr. *Motto*—Fortitudine et prudentia.

Harhun (Reg. Ulster's Office). Ar. on a bend sa. three mullets pierced of the field.

Haringell. Gu. three mullets or, a quarter erm.

Harington (*Baron Harington; summoned to Parliament, 1324, attainted 1554*). Sa. a fret ar.

Harington (*Baron Harington, of Exton; created 1603, extinct 1614*). Same *Arms*.

Harington (Ridlington, co. Rutland, bart.). Same *Arms*. *Crest*—A lion's head erased or, round the neck a thong buckled, and the end hanging down gu. *Motto*—Nodo firmo.

Harington. Sa. a fret ar. a bordure componée of the second and vert.

Harington (co. Derby). Or, a chief gu. on a bend az. an annulet or.

Harington (co. Leicester). Gu. a chief or, a bordure az.

Harington. Or, a bend az. a chief gu. *Crest*—A lion's paw holding a thistle.

Harington (Glaston, co. Rutland. Visit. Rutland, 1618). or, a chief az. over all a bend gu.

Harington. Or, a chief gu. a bordure sa.

Hariot (Lord Mayor of London, 1481). Per pale ermines and Or, erminois three crescents counterchanged.

Haris (co. Devon). Sa. three crescents ar. a bordure or.

Harison. Az. on a fesse or, betw. six crosses pattée ar. three estoiles gu. all within a bordure engr. of the second, charged with eight pellets.

Harison (citizen of London. Visit. 1568). Gu. an eagle displ. and a chief or. *Crest*—A snake vert entwined around a broken column or.

Harison (JOHN HARISON. Visit. Notts, 1614). Ar. a fess flory counterflory gu. betw. three anchors az. quartering ar. a fess gu. betw. two cotises engr. sa.

Harken. Or, two bars dancettée gu.

Harkeyn. Or, two bars az.

Harkness (confirmed to Rev. ROBERT HARKNESS, Rector of Stowey, co. Somerset, son of WILLIAM HARKNESS, of Dublin, merchant). Gyronny of eight or and erm. each piece charged with a crescent alternate gu. and az. over all a lion ramp. sa. *Crest*—A dove close per pale or and vert, holding in the beak an olive branch of the second fructed of the first. *Motto*—Hope in God.

Harlakenden (Woodchurch and Tunstall, co. Kent, and Earl's Colne, co. Essex). Az. a fess erm. betw. three lions' heads erased or. *Crest*—Betw. the attires of a stag or, an eagle reguard. wings expanded ar.

Harland (Sproughton, co. Suffolk, bart.). Or, on a bend wavy betw. two sea-lions sa. three bucks' heads cabossed ar. *Crest*—A sea-lion sa. supporting an anchor ppr. *Motto*—Per juga per fluvios.

Harland. Or, on a bend betw. two sea-lions erect on their tails az. three stags' heads cabossed of the first. *Crest*—A sea-lion, as in the arms, ducally crowned or, holding betw. his paws an anchor gold, fluked sa.

Harland. Sa. a cross patonce or.

Harland (Sutton Hall, near York). Quarterly, 1st and 4th, ar. on a bend sa. cotised az. three bucks' heads cabossed or, in the sinister chief point an escallop gu., for HARLAND ; 2nd and 3rd, quarterly, sa. and gu. an eagle displ. with two heads ar. a bordure invected counterchanged, for HOARE. *Crests*—1st, HARLAND : A demi seahorse ppr. charged on the shoulder with an escallop gu. and holding in the claws a buck's head cabossed or ; 2nd, HOARE : An eagle's head erased sa. charged on the neck with an erm. spot or, pendent from the lower member of the beak an annulet gold. *Motto* —Constantia in ardua.

Harlaw. Sa. three inescutcheons ar. each charged with a lion ramp. az. *Crest*—A Moor's head ppr.

Harle. Ar. three piles meeting in the base point sa.

Harlegh. Or, a bend cotised sa.

Harlen. Gu. three crescents ar.

Harleshall. Sa. three stars or.

Harleston (South Kendon, co. Essex). **Ar. a fesse erm.** betw. two bars gemelles (another, barrulets) sa. *Crest*—Out of a ducal coronet a stag's head browsing a hawthorn all ppr. berried or.

Harleston. Ar. a saltire gu. betw. four fleurs-de-lis az.

Harleston. Or, a chev. sa. in dexter chief a bird of the last.

Harleston. Az. an inescutcheon or, (another, ar.).

Harleston. Ar. a bordure az.

Harleston. Ar. a fesse erm.

Harlewin (co. Devon). Az. a fesse ar. in base three apples of the last. *Crest*—A tower, on the top thereof a crescent.

Harlewin. Sa. a chev. or, betw. three garbs ar.

Harlewin. Az. semée of fleurs-de-lis ar.

Harlewyn. Ar. three lions ramp. gu. crowned or.

Harlewyn. Az. fretty and semée-de-lis or.

Harley (*Barl of Oxford ;* created 1711, extinct 1853). Or, a bend cotised sa. *Crest*—A castle triple-towered ar. out of the middle tower a demi lion issuant gu. *Supporters*—Two angels ppr. habited and wings displ. or. *Motto*—Virtute et fide.

Harley (THOMAS HARLEY, Bishop of Hereford, 1553-54, arms in the west window of Magdalen College, Oxford. Visit. Oxon, 1574). Or, on a bend double cotised sa. a fleur-de-lis of the field, a border engr. gu.

Harley. Ar. three piles sa.

Harley. Ar. two palets sa.

Harling (co. Devon). Az. semée-de-lis ar.

Harling (co. Suffolk). Az. nine fleurs-de-lis ar. three, three, two, and one.

Harling (co. Suffolk). Ar. a unicorn sejant sa. armed and ungued or.

Harling, or Harlingham (co. Suffolk). **Ar.** a unicorn climant sa. armed and ungued or. *Crest*—A bombshell inflamed ppr.

Harling. Az. a fesse dancettée betw. three martlets or.

Harling. Ar. a saltire engr. az.

Harling. Gu. a fesse vair, in chief a unicorn courant or, betw. two mullets of the last, a bordure engr. of the third.

Harlow (co. Essex). Sa. three inescutcheons ar. on each a lion ramp. gu.

Harlow (Gray's Inn, London, and Preston, co. Northampton; granted 1629). Gu. a fesse vair betw. six billets or. *Crest* —A cinquefoil or, issuing from betw. the horns of a crescent vairé.

Harlow. Per saltire or and az. two martlets in pale and as many cinquefoils in fess all counterchanged.

Harlow. Per saltire or and az. on a chief of the first a martlet of the second, charged with a cinquefoil gold.

457

Harlston (co. Essex). **Ar.** a fesse erm. *Crest*—A cannon mounted ppr.

Harlston (Hardwick, co. Kent). Paly of six or and az.

Harlston. Ar. a chev. sa. in the dexter point a bird of the last.

Harlston. Sa. a cross erm. betw. four crescents or.

Harlstone (South Ossenden, co. Essex). Ar. a fesse erm. cotised sa. *Crest*—Out of a ducal coronet or, a stag's head erm. attired of the first, bearing betw. the attires a hawthorn bush fructed ppr.

Harlstone (Secretary to the Master of the Rolls, 1640). Same *Arms* and *Crest*.

Harlwyn. Ar. three human legs couped at the thigh sa.

Harlyston (arms in the Library, Ball. Coll. Oxford. Visit. Oxon, 1574). Az. three fleurs-de-lis erm. quartering, quarterly or, and paly of six of the last and gu. in the 1st and 4th quarters a lion ramp. az.

Harlyston. Paly of six or and sa.

Harman (co. Dorset). Quarterly, or and gu. on a bend sa. three crosses formée fitchée or.

Harman (co. Kent). Ar. a chev. sa. betw. three perukes ppr.

Harman (Taynton, co. Oxford ; EDMOND HARMAN, grandson of PAULE HARMAN, of Ipswich, co. Suffolk, who was son of PETER HARMAN, of the Stilyard. Visit. 1574). Sa. three currycombs ar. *Crest*—An arm erect, vested ar. cuffed or, holding in the hand ppr. a halbert gold, handled gu.

Harman (JOHN HARMAN, *alias* VESEY, Bishop of Exeter, Magdalen College, Oxford, son of WILLIAM HARMAN, Esq., of Sutton Coldfield, co. Warwick, *b.* 1455, *d.* 1555, aged 100 years, buried at Sutton Coldfield, where a monument was erected to him; having been educated by a man named VOYSEY or VESEY, he sometimes was known by that name ; appointed Bishop of Exeter, 1519. Visit. 1574). Ar. on a cross sa. a buck's head cabossed and four martlets of the first, on a chief az. a cross flory betw. two roses or.

Harman (Moore Hall, co. Warwick; confirmed by Dethick, Garter. Visit. 1619). Ar. on a cross sa. a buck's head cabossed betw. four martlets of the field. *Crest*—Out of a ducal coronet sa. a buck's head ar.

Harman (Harman Hall, co. Sussex). Quarterly, ar. and gu. on a bend az. three roses of the first. *Crest*—Out of a ducal coronet or, an arm embowed in armour ppr. garnished of the first, grasping two sprigs of roses ar. stalked and leaved vert, seeded gold.

Harman (Rendlesham and Mulford, co. Suffolk). Az. a chev. betw. six rams accosted counter-tripping, two, two, and two, ar. attired or. *Crest*—A demi old man ppr. beard and hair ar. wreathed about the head with leaves vert, in the dexter hand the stump of a tree erased of the last, fructed or, chained round the body, with the end of the chain in the sinister hand, gold.

Harman (Antigua, West Indies). Same *Arms*, quartering CAHUSAC, per pale or and az. a fesse counterchanged. *Crest* —A demi man ppr. crowned with an eastern coronet or, chained round the waist, and holding the end in the sinister hand of the last, the dexter hand holding a withered tree torn up by the root ppr.

Harman (cos. Carlow and Longford; Fun. Ent. of Sir THOMAS HARMAN, Knt., M.P., Carlow and Kildare, buried at Christ's Church Cathedral, 14 Dec. 1667). Sa. a chev. betw. three rams pass. ar. armed and ungued or.

Harman (Belenacarrig, co. Cavan; descended from WILLIAM HARMAN, brother of Sir THOMAS HARMAN). Same *Arms*.

Harman (Palace, co. Wexford; descended from HENRY HARMAN, youngest brother of Sir THOMAS HARMAN). Same *Arms*. *Crest*—Out of a ducal coronet or, a dexter arm in armour, couped at the elbow, erect ppr. doubled down ar. the hand grasping two roses ar. and gu. stalked and leaved vert. *Motto*—Dieu défend le droit !

Harman (granted to LAWRENCE PARSONS, Esq., of New-castle, co. Longford, created *Barl of Rosse*, 1806, by Fortescue, Ulster, 26 Aug. 1792, upon his taking the name of HARMAN, in compliance with the will of his maternal uncle, Very Rev. CUTTS HARMAN, Dean of Waterford). Quarterly, 1st and 4th, sa. a chev. betw. three rams pass. ar. attired or, for HARMAN; 2nd, gu. three leopards' faces ar., for PARSONS; 3rd, sa. a fess betw. three talbots pass. or, each holding an arrow in his mouth ar., for SHEPPARD. *Crest*—Out of a ducal coronet or, a dexter arm armed erect in pale, couped at the elbow, doubled down ar. grasping two slips of roses gu. and ar. stalked, seeded, and leaved ppr.

Harman (Ayres, co. Kent; descended from HENRY HARMAN, Clerk of the Council to Henry VII. Har. MSS.). Ar. a chev. purp. betw. three ostrich feathers sa.

Harmantle. Or, two bars az.

Harmanvill. Or, two bars gu.

Harme (co. Surrey). Az. a sphere or.

Harme (Reg. Ulster's Office). Ar. a maunch gu.

Harmer. Ar. on a chev. betw. three annulets gu. an annulet of the first.

Harmer. Sa. three chev. interlaced ar. on a chief or, a lion ramp. gu. *Crest*—A book expanded ppr.

Harmlyn. Gu. a lion ramp. or, guttée de poix.

Harmon (Reg. Ulster's Office). Ar. in base a crescent gu. issuant therefrom a rose branch vert, flowered az.

Harmon (co. Gloucester; granted 1615). Quarterly, per fesse indented or and sa. on a bend of the last three lozenges of the first. *Crest*—An arm vested sa. cuff ar. holding in the hand ppr. two rose branches vert, one arching to the right, and flowering on the top with a white rose, the other to the left, in like manner, with a red rose.

Harnage (Belswardyne, co. Salop, bart.). Quarterly, 1st and 4th. ar. six torteaux, three, two, and one, for HARNAGE; 2nd and 3rd, erm. three lions ramp. ar. a bordure or, semée of crescents az., for BLACKMAN. *Crests*—1st, HARNAGE: Out of a ducal coronet a lion's gamb holding a torteaux, motto over, Deo duce decrevi; 2nd, BLACKMAN; A demi griffin or, semée of crescents az. collared gu., motto over, Fide et fiduciâ.

Harnage (Shenton and Shrewsbury, co. Salop). Ar. six torteaux, three, two, and one. *Crest*—Out of a ducal coronet a lion's paw ppr. holding up a torteau. *Motto*—Deo duce decrevi.

Harne (Reg. Ulster's Office). Erm. a water bouget gu.

Harnehull (Harnehull, co. Gloucester. Har. MSS. 1566, quartered by WALSH, of Shelsby, co. Worcester.). Or, three roses gu.

Harnett (Ballyhenry, co. Kerry). Az. a fess or, betw. two lions' heads erased in chief and a crescent in base ar.

Harnett. Ar. a pale sa. surmounted by a saltire gu. a chief az. *Crest*—A hornet fly, wings elevated ppr.

Harneys, or Harnous (co. Bedford). Ar. a chev. sa. guttée d'or. *Crest*—A stag's head sa. guttée d'or, attired gold.

Harnge. Gu. a bend betw. three trefoils ar.

Harnie (Alrick). Gu. a fesse or, betw. three mullets in chief ar. and a mascle in base of the second.

Harnoys. Ar. on a chev. sa. three guttées or (another adds, a crescent in chief gu.).

Harokins. Or, on a chev. betw. three cinquefoils az. as many escallops ar. on a chief per pale gu. and sa. a griffin pass. erm. *Crest*—A griffin's head chequy ar. and sa. betw. two wings, dexter or, sinister gu.

Harold (WALTER HAROLD). Fun. Ent. of his dau., ROSE, wife of EDWARD BEE, Sheriff of Dublin, d. 12 April, 1614). Gu. an escarbuncle or, betw. three estoiles ar.

Harold, or Harould (co. Salop). Vert a fesse flory counterflory or. *Crest*—A hawk's lure ppr.

Harold (co. Suffolk). Gu. an escarbuncle betw. two estoiles or.

Harold. Gu. a fesse ar. betw. three estoiles or.

Harold. Gu. an escarbuncle betw. three estoiles or.

Harold. Gu. a cross moline (another, three crosses moline) erm.

Harold. Or, two bars (another, bends) gu.

Harow (co. Essex). Vert on a fesse cotised or, three crescents gu.

Harowden. Ar. guttée de poix a fesse wavy sa.

Harowden. Gu. a lion ramp. bendy wavy of eight ar. and az.

Harowdon. Gu. two bars erm. a canton of the last.

Harowdon, or Harwedon. Ar. on a bend gu. five lozenges or.

Harows. Or, a bend betw. ten billets sa.

Harpden (co. Gloucester). Ar. a mullet of six points pierced sa. *Crest*—A hind's head or.

Harpden (co. Oxford). Ar. a mullet gu. (another, pierced sa.; another, an estoile gu.).

Harpeny. See HALPENY.

Harper (co. Bedford). Az. on a fesse or, betw. three eagles displ. ar. a fret betw. two martlets gu.

Harper (confirmed to JOHN HARPER, Treasurer of Christ's Hospital, and Alderman of the city of London, son of JOHN HARPER, of Walton, co. Lancaster, by William Segar, Garter, and borne by the late TRISTRAM HARPER, Esq. quartering STRACHEY and ROBERTS, whose heiress m. JOHN SHEPHERD, Esq., of Kensington). Per fesse ar. and or, a lion ramp. per fesse gu. and az. all within a bordure gobonated of the second and third. *Crest*—A lion's head erased per fesse or and gu. collared of the last, lined of the first.

Harper (co. Essex). Ar. a lion ramp. gu. a bordure engr. sa.

Harper (Amerly, co. Hereford). Sa. a chev. ar. and canton erm.

458

Harper (co. Kent). Ar. a lion ramp. sa. *Crest*—A boar pass. or, ducally gorged and crined gu.

Harper (co. Kent; Sir GEORGE HARPER, Knt., of Sutton, Sheriff of Kent, 1547, 2nd Edward VI.). Sa. a lion ramp. or, a bordure engr. of the second.

Harper (Sir WILLIAM HARPER, Mayor of London. Visit. 1568). Az. on a fess betw. three eagles displ. or, a fret betw. two martlets of the first. *Crest*—Upon a crescent or, charged with a fret betw. two martlets az. an eagle displ. of the last.

Harper (London). Per fesse ar. and sa. a lion ramp. counterchanged, a bordure gobonated or and gu.

Harper (Bambury). Ar. on two bars az. three greyhounds' heads erased or.

Harper. Erm. a cinquefoil az. on a chief gu. a lion pass. guard. or.

Harper. Or, a chev. gu. a chief vair.

Harper (Swarkeston and Bridsall, co. Derby, and New Ross, Ulster). Per bend sinister ar. and sa. a lion ramp. counterchanged, a border gobony or and gu. *Crest*—A lion's head erased per pale or and gu.

[Note: There is text about "dau. of THOMAS, son of BASIL HARPER, of New Ross, and wife of PHILIP WALSH, then residing in France)." embedded in the above]

Harper (Cambusnethan, Scotland, 1673). Ar. a lion ramp. sa. holding in his dexter paw a harp az. a bordure engr. of the second. *Crest*—A boar pass. ar. *Motto*—Et suavis et fortis.

Harper (Edinburgh, 1870). Ar. a fess az. betw. three harps sa. stringed or. *Crest*—A harp, as in the arms. *Motto*—Te Deum laudamus.

Harpetre (Harpetre, co. Somerset, 1138). Ar. a saltire couped and flory at the ends gu.

Harpfield, or Harpsfield (London). Ar. three harps sa. stringed or.

Harpham (North Chapel, co. Lincoln). Gu. a mullet ar. betw. three fleurs-de-lis or.

Harpham (Marfleet, co. York; confirmed 9 July, 1657). Sa. a harp ar. stringed or.

Harpur (Calke, coss. Derby, Devon, and Stafford, bart., now CREWE, Bart., of Calke; Sir HENRY HARPUR, seventh bart., assumed that surname, 1808). Ar. a lion ramp. and a bordure engr. sa. *Crest*—A boar pass. or, ducally gorged and crined gu.

Harpur (Berianherbert, co. Devon; NICHOLAS HARPUR, of that place, Visit. 1620, grandson of JOHN HARPER, a younger brother of HARPER, of Swarkeston, co. Derby). Same *Arms*, a crescent for diff. *Crest*—A boar pass. or, chained and collared gu.

Harpur (Chilvers Coton, co. Warwick, and Burton Hall, co. Northampton). Ar. a lion ramp. and a bordure engr. sa. *Crest*—On the battlement of a tower masoned ppr. a boar's head erased fesseways.

Harpur. Ar. two bars az. each charged with a lion's head erased or.

Harrance (Foot's Cray Place, co. Kent). Vert a herring haurient ar. *Crest*—A stork ppr. in the beak a herring ppr.

Harres. Ar. a lion ramp. gu. debruised with a chev. or.

Harreys (Guernsey). Gu. a chev. betw. three hares' heads erased ar. *Crest*—A hare couchant ar. betw. two bushes ppr.

Harriard (co. Hants). Gu. three leopards pass. ar.

Harries, or Harris. Ar. a lion ramp. gu. over all a chev. or. *Crest*—An oak tree growing out of a mount among long grass ppr.

Harries (Tregwint, co. Pembroke; settled there for several centuries). Az. three mullets pierced or. *Crest*—A mullet pierced or.

Harries (Priskilly, co. Pembroke). Same *Arms* and *Crest*. *Motto*—Integritas semper tutamen.

Harries (Llanunwas, co. Pembroke). Same *Arms*.

Harries (Cruckton and Tong Castle, co. Salop, bart., extinct; Sir THOMAS HARRIES, of Tong Castle, a learned lawyer, was created a bart. 1623; his only dau. and heiress, ELIZABETH, m. WILLIAM PIERREPONT, Esq., of Thoresby. From ARTHUR HARRIES, Esq., of Prescot, third son of JOHN HARRIES, Esq., of Cruckton, co. Salop, and brother of Sir THOMAS, of Tong, descended the family of HARRIES, of Cruckton). Barry of eight erm. and az. over all three annulets or. *Crest*—A hawk ar. beaked and belled or, preying on a pheasant of the first.

Harringham. Gu. three fishes haurient ar.

Harrington, Earl of. See STANHOPE.

Harrington (Kelston, co. Somerset; granted 12 Feb. 1568). Sa. a fret hunettée ar. a bordure chequy of the first and second.

Harrington (co. Somerset). Sa. a fret ar. a bordure counter-componée ar. and sa.

Harrington (co. Cumberland, Hornby, Wickham, co. Essex, and Ridlington, co. Rutland). Sa. a fret ar.

Harrington (Worden, co. Devon). Same *Arms.*

Harrington (co. Essex). Sa. a fret or.

Harrington (Honington-Sibble, co. Essex). Sa. a fret ar. charged with nine fleurs-de-lis gu.

Harrington (Hayton, co. Lancaster). Sa. fretty ar. over all a label of three points or. *Crest*—A lion's head erased or, gorged with a belt buckled gu. (another, a lion's face sa.).

Harrington (Bangworth, co. Leicester). Sa. a fret ar. and crescent or.

Harrington (Hanwell, co. Middlesex). Sa. a fret ar. *Crest*—A leopard's head couped ppr.

Harrington (Stepney, co. Middlesex). Sa. a fret ar. and label of three points throughout gu.

Harrington (Bishton, co. Salop). Sa. a fret ar. on a chief of the second three trefoils slipped vert. *Crest*—A lion's head erased or, gorged with a collar gu. betw. two trefoils slipped vert, to the collar a line and ring ar.

Harrington (Sir HENRY HARRINGTON, knighted at Christ's Church, Dublin, 24 April, 1574. Fun. Ent. 1612). Sa. a fret ar.

Harrington. Sa. a fret ar. *Crest*—A lion's head erased or, collared gu.

Harrington. Quarterly, 1st and 4th, sa. a fret ar. over all a label of three points gu. charged with nine bezants; 2nd and 3rd, ar. a cross patonce sa. *Crest*—A lion's head erased or, gorged with a label of three points gu. charged with nine bezants.

Harrington. Ar. on a bend gu. three eagles displ. or.

Harrington. Or, a cross gu. voided ar.

Harrington. Ar. a chev. gu. betw. three leopards' faces sa.

Harrington (Sir JOHN DE HARRINGTON, Knt., co. Notts, *temp.* Edward I.). Ar. a chief gu. and a bend az.

Harrington (co. Notts). Same *Arms.*

Harringwell (Frickley). Ar. on a bend sa. three martlets of the field.

Harringworth. Gu. six plates, three, two, and one. *Crest* —An antique crown or.

Harris (*Earl of Malmesbury*). Az. a chev. erminois betw. three hedgehogs or, on a chief ar. the eagle of Prussia displ. sa. beaked, legged, and langued gu. on the breast the cipher F. R., and over it the electoral cap, in the dexter claw a sceptre, and in the sinister a mound all gold, and on each wing a trefoil ar. *Crest*—A hedgehog or, charged on the side with three arrows, one in pale and two in saltire ar. and across them barways a key az. *Supporters*—Dexter, the Prussian eagle, wings elevated sa. crowned and charged on the breast and wings as that on the chief of the arms; sinister, a reindeer ppr. *Mottoes*—Over the crest, on an orange-coloured label: Je maintiendrai, the motto of the House of Nassau; under the shield: Ubique patriam reminisci.

Harris (*Baron Harris*). Vert upon a chev. embattled erminois betw. three hedgehogs or, as many bombs sa. fired ppr. upon a chief of augmentation ar. the gates and fortress of Seringapatam, the draw-bridge let down, and the Union flag of Great Britain and Ireland hoisted over the standard of Tippoo all ppr. *Crest*—On a mural crown or, a royal tiger pass. guard. vert, striped or spotted gold, pierced in the breast with an arrow of the last, vulned gu. charged on the forehead with a Persian character for Hyder, and crowned with an Eastern coronet, both of the first. *Supporters*—Dexter, a grenadier soldier of the 73rd regiment, in his regimentals ppr. supporting with the exterior hand a staff, thereon hoisted the Union flag of Great Britain and Ireland, over that of the standard of Tippoo Sultan, and beneath the tri-coloured flag entwined, inscribed with the word "Republique;" sinister, a Malay soldier in his uniform ppr. supporting a like staff, thereon hoisted the flag of the E. I. Co., ar. striped barwise gu. with a canton over the standard of Tippoo Sultan, with the tri-coloured flag entwined beneath, as on the dexter, inscribed with the word "Française" all ppr. *Motto*—My prince and my country.

Harris (Cherston, co. Devon; Sir EDWARD HARRIS, Chief Justice of Munster, and his cousin, ARTHUR HARRIS, grandsons of WALTER HARRIS, co. Monmouth. Visit. Devon. 1620). Sa. an antelope saliant ar. armed and crined or. *Crest*—A demi antelope, as in the arms.

Harris (Radford, co. Devon and Lanrest, co. Cornwall. Visit. Devon, 1620). Sa. three crescents ar. *Crest*—An eagle displ. or.

Harris (co. Cornwall). Visit. Cornwall, 1620). Same *Arms*, with a border ar.

Harris (Boreatton, co. Salop, bart., extinct 1685; Sir THOMAS HARRIS, of Boreatton, Master in Chancery, created a bart. in 1622). Or, three hedgehogs az. *Crest*—A hedgehog or.

Harris (Hayne, co. Devon, bart., extinct 1686; WILLIAM HARRIS, *temp.* Edward IV., descended from HARRIS, of Radford, *m.* THOMASINE, dau. and heiress of WALTER HAYNE, Esq., of Hayne). Sa. three crescents ar. a border of the last.

Harris (Kenegie, co. Cornwall). Same *Arms.*

Harris (Windsor, co. Berks). Erm. on a bend az. three hedgehogs or. *Crest*—A demi pegasus gu. wings endorsed or.

Harris (cos. Chester and Devon). Ar. on a fesse betw. three Moors' heads couped at the shoulders sa. as many martlets of the field.

Harris (co. Cornwall, Eyston, co. Devon, and co. Hertford). Sa. three crescents and a bordure ar. *Crest*—On a stump of a tree raguly, lying fesseways vert, a falcon rising erm. beaked and legged or. *Another Crest*—On the stump of a tree lying fesseways a hawk, wings expanded ppr. beaked, membered, and belled or.

Harris (co. Cornwall). Gu. fretty ar. a canton of the second.

Harris (cos. Devon and Monmouth). Sa. an antelope saliant ar. attired, tufted, and maned or. *Crest*—A demi antelope, as in the arms, saliant and erased.

Harris (Cricksey, co. Essex). Or, on a bend engr. az. three cinquefoils ar. pierced of the field. *Crest*—A demi hare saliant ppr.

Harris (Maldon, co. Essex). Or, on a bend az. three cinquefoils pierced of the field. *Crest*—A talbot sejant or. *Another Crest*—A buck's head chequy ar. and az. attired or.

Harris (granted to GEORGE DAVID HARRIS, Esq., of the Bahamas). Sa. on a fesse wavy betw. three sea dogs courant or, as many Cornish choughs ppr. *Crest*—In front of a rock ppr. a demi sea dog or, gorged with a collar gemel sa. and grasping a Cornish chough also ppr. *Motto*—True and fast.

Harris (co. Salop; granted by Camden, Clarenceux, 1604, to Sir THOMAS HARRIS, Serjeant-at-law). Barry of eight erm. and az. three annulets or. *Crest*—An eagle preying on a cock ppr.

Harris, or Harries (Loughton, co. Essex, and Prickwell, co. Sussex). Ar. on a chev. engr. betw. three wolves' heads erased sa. a lozenge or, betw. two fishes of the first.

Harris (co. Hants). Erm. five bars gu.

Harris (co. Kent). Erm. on a chev. az. betw. two anchors in chief and a crescent in base gu. a cinquefoil betw. two escallops or.

Harris (London). Sa. three crescents and a bordure ar. *Crest*—A winged heart gu. imperially crowned or.

Harris (co. Essex). Ar. on a chev. engr. sa. betw. three hounds gu. a trefoil or, betw. two fusils of the field.

Harris (Middle Temple, London; granted 10 April, 1671). Ar. on a bend engr. sa. three cinquefoils of the first.

Harris (Abcot, co. Salop). Az. a chev. erm. betw. three hedgehogs or. *Crest*—A hedgehog or. *Another Crest*—A pelican in her piety ppr. (another, a demi pelican ppr.) *Motto*—Ubique patriam reminisci.

Harris (Stockton, co. Salop). Az. a chev. ar. betw. three hedgehogs or. *Crest*—A hedgehog or.

Harris (co. Surrey). Sa. a chev. betw. three hedgehogs ar.

Harris. Ar. a chev. erminois betw. three hedgehogs or, a label for diff. *Crest*—A hedgehog or, charged on the side with a key in pale az. *Motto*—Ubique patriam reminisci.

Harris (Cousland). Ar. a' thistle vert flowered gu. betw. three hedgehogs sa.

Harris. Ar. a lion ramp. gu. over all a chev. or.

Harris. Erm. on a bend az. three urchins or.

Harris (Cusgarne, co. Cornwall; quartered by WILLIAMS, of Tregullow, bart.). Sa. a tilting spear fesswise betw. three crescents ar.

Harris (Rosewarne, in Camborne, co. Cornwall). Quarterly, 1st and 4th, per pale sa. and az. on a fesse engr. betw. three crescents or, as many crosses fitchée sa.; 2nd, sa. three crescents ar.; 3rd, gu. three paschal lambs ar., for ROWE. *Crest*—A falcon rising erm. belled and spurred or.

Harris (Ratcliffe Hall, co. Leicester; JOHN DOVE HARRIS, Esq., M.P. for Leicester). Az. on a pile betw. two cinquefoils in base ar. a cinquefoil of the field. *Crest*—A fernbrake ppr. therefrom rising a dove reguard. az. beaked and membered gu. in the beak a trefoil vert. *Motto*—Virtute et opera.

Harris (Ireland; Fun. Ent. of Sir THOMAS SOUTHWELL, Knt., of Polenelony, co. Cork, *d.* 1626, *m.* ANNE, dau. of Mr. Serjeant HARRIS, and sister of Sir EDWARD HARRIS, one of the Justices of the Court of Chief Pleas in Ireland). Sa. three crescents ar. in chief three plates.

Harris (Sir EDWARD HARRIS, Judge of the King's Bench in Ireland. Fun. Ent. of his wife, 1637). Sa. three crescents ar. in chief as many plates.

Harris (Impalement Fun. Ent., 1666, Judge GRIFFITH). Barry of eight erm. and az. three annulets or.

Harris (Lakeview, Blackrock, co. Cork; confirmed to WILLIAM PRITTIE HARRIS, Esq., of that place (of the family of HARRIS, of Assolas, co. Cork), son of the late WILLIAM HARRIS, of Kilbarny, and grandson of RICHARD HARRIS, of Lisgriffin Castle, co. Cork, and their descendants). Az. a chev. betw. three hedgehogs or, on a chief ar. as many cinquefoils pierced gu. Crest—A demi lion ramp. or, holding betw. the paws a cinquefoil pierced gu. Motto—Industria veritas et hospitalitas.

Harrison (co. Essex). Az. two bars erm. betw. six estoiles or, three, two, and one. Crest—A stork, wings expanded ar. beaked and membered or.

Harrison (Reisby and Burton-Stath, co. Lincoln). Same Arms.

Harrison (FISKE-HARRISON, Copford Hall, co. Essex). Quarterly, 1st and 4th, az. two bars erm. betw. six estoiles, three, two, and one ar.; 2nd and 3rd, ar. three crescents barry undée az. and gu. Crest—A stork, wings expanded ar. beaked and membered or. Motto—Ferendo et feriendo.

Harrison (Hurst and Finchampstead, co. Berks; granted 1623). Or, on a chief sa. three eagles displ. of the field. Crest —Out of a ducal coronet or, a talbot's head of the last guttée de poix.

Harrison (Reading, co. Berks). Same Arms. Crest—Out of a ducal coronet or, a talbot's head ppr. collared gu. Motto—Amicitia permanens et incorrupta.

Harrison (Linethwaite, co. Cumberland). Per pale gu. and az. an eagle displ. or, murally gorged of the first, betw. two pheons in fesse ar. a chief indented erminois. Crest—The fasces fessewise ppr. banded gu. surmounted by an anchor erect entwined by a cable all or.

Harrison (Snelston Hall, co. Derby). Az. three demi lions or, a canton ar. Crest—A demi lion or, supporting a chaplet of roses vert.

Harrison (Galligreaves Hall, Blackbourne, co. Lancaster). Az. a demi lion couped betw. three pheons or. Crest—Within a wreath or and az. a talbot's head erased of the last, collared gold. Motto—Not rashly nor with fear.

Harrison (Downe Hill, co. Kent). Az. two bars erm. betw. six estoiles ar. three, two, and one. Crest—A chapeau gu. turned up erm. on either side a wing expanded ar.

Harrison (Gouldhurst, co. Kent). Sa. three lozenges conjoined in fesse erm. Crest—A demi lion ramp. ppr. holding in the paws a lozenge erm.

Harrison (Atcliff, co. Lancaster, and Elkington, co. Northampton; granted 10 Sept. 1616). Or, on a cross az. five pheons of the field. Crest—An arm vested az. purfled or, cuffed ar. holding in the hand a broken dart ppr. pheoned gold. Another Crest—A snake vert entwined round a broken column ar. (another, or).

Harrison (Poulton-le-Fylde, co. Lancaster). Or, a cross sa. Crest—An arm embowed in armour ppr. garnished or, holding a broken spear, the head dependent ppr.

Harrison (Lincoln's Inn Fields). Same Arms. Crest—An arm erect, couped below the elbow, habited az. cuffed ar. the hand holding an arrow ppr. barbed or.

Harrison (London; descended from Durham). Az. an eagle displ. or, ducally gorged or. Crest—On a chapeau az. turned up and indented erm. a bird with wings endorsed sa.

Harrison (co. Lancaster). Or, on a cross az. four pheons or.

Harrison (London). Per fesse or and ar. an anchor erect in pale sa. Crest—Out of a crown or, a plume of ostrich feathers of the last and ar.

Harrison (London). Az. an eagle displ. or, a chief erm. Crest—On a chapeau az. turned up erm. an eagle, wings expanded, sa.

Harrison (London; Her. Off.). Az. an eagle displ. gorged with a ducal coronet or, a chief erm.

Harrison (Norton Place, co. Lincoln; quartered by Sir MONTAGUE CHOLMELEY, Bart., 1840). Az. on a chief or, three eagles displ. sa.

Harrison (Tydd St. Mary, co. Lincoln). Az. a fleur-de-lis or. Crest—An ostrich with a serpent in its mouth. Motto—Deo non fortunâ.

Harrison (London; confirmed to JOHN HARRISON, of London, by Cooke, Clarenceux, 5 May, 1578). Gu. an eagle displ. and chief or. Crest—A snake vert entwined round a broken column or.

Harrison (Newcastle). Same Arms and Crest.

Harrison, or **Haryson** (co. Norfolk; granted by Barker,

460

Garter, A.D. 1549, to RYCHARDE HERYSON, alias HERS, of Great Plumstead, co. Norfolk). Ar. an eagle displ. sa. on a chief az. three crosses pattée fitchée or. Crest—Out of a ducal coronet or, a harpy ppr. crined sa. gorged with a laxe gold.

Harrison (Caister, by Yarmouth, co. Norfolk). Same as last, quartering HARGRAVE and FLIGHT. Crest—Same as last. Motto—Virtus in arduis.

Harrison (Great Yarmouth, co. Norfolk, Melbourne, Australia, and Burgh Castle, co. Suffolk). Same Arms and Crest. Motto—Le culte en difficulté.

Harrison (London, and North Riding co. York; granted 1574). Or, on a chief gu. three eagles displ. of the field. Crest—Out of a ducal coronet a talbot's head or, guttée de poix.

Harrison (Acaster, Caton, and Flaxby, co. York). Az. three demi lions ramp. or. Crest—A demi lion ramp. ar. holding a laurel branch vert.

Harrison (Greenbank, Ambleside, co. Westmoreland). Az. three demi lions ramp. or. Crest—A demi lion ramp. ar. Motto—Vincit qui patitur.

Harrison (Hendon, co. Middlesex, and of the City of Westminster: Bluemantle Pursuivant of Arms, 1767; Windsor Herald, 1774; Norroy King of Arms, 1784; and Clarenceux King of Arms, 1803). Az. three demi lions ramp. erased or, each crowned with an Eastern crown ar. Crest—Out of a mural crown az. a demi lion ramp. or, crowned with an Eastern crown ar. in the paws a laurel garland adorned with four damask roses ppr. Motto—Absque virtute nihil.

Harrison (ROGERS-HARRISON; exemplified to GEORGE HARRISON ROGERS-HARRISON, Esq., Blanche Lion Pursuivant Extraordinary, now Windsor Herald). Quarterly, 1st and 4th, HARRISON, az. three demi lions ramp. erased or, each crowned with an Eastern crown ar.; 2nd and 3rd, ROGERS, or, three stags trippant ppr. in the centre chief point on an inescutcheon gu. a lion ramp. ar. (in allusion to his office of Blanche Lion Pursuivant). Crests—1st, HARRISON: Out of a mural coronet az. a demi lion issuant or, crowned, as in the arms, and holding betw. the paws a chaplet of roses ppr.; 2nd: On a ducal coronet or, a lion ramp. ar. (also an allusion to his office); 3rd, ROGERS: On a chapeau gu. turned up erm. a stag trippant ppr. gorged with a coronet of a King of Arms, therefrom a chain passing betw. the fore legs or. The following Crest was subsequently granted, in token of his maternal descent—Out of a coronet composed of trefoils gold a plume of five ostrich feathers alternately ar. and or.

Harrison (ROGERS-HARRISON, Hendon, co. Middlesex). Quarterly, 1st and 4th, az. three demi lions ramp. erased or, each crowned with an Eastern crown ar., for HARRISON; 2nd and 3rd, or, a crown vallery gu. betw. three stags trippant ppr., for ROGERS. Crests—1st, HARRISON: Out of a mural crown az. a demi lion ramp. or, crowned with an Eastern crown ar. in the paws a laurel garland adorned with four damask roses; 2nd, ROGERS: On a crown vallery or, a stag trippant ppr. charged on the shoulder with a trefoil vert. Motto—Absque virtute nihil.

Harrison (Ripley, co. Surrey; granted, 31 March, 1819, to ROBERT HARRISON, Esq., of Ripley, and exemplified, 14 May following, to ROBERT STEERE, second son of LEE-STEERE STEERE, Esq., by SARAH his wife, eldest dau. of the said ROBERT HARRISON, Esq., who assumed, by sign manual, the surname and arms of HARRISON). Per pale az. and sa. three demi lions ramp. erm. each gorged with a collar gemellée gu. Crest—A demi lion ramp. erminois erased gu. holding betw. the paws a garland of laurel ppr. encircling a mascle of the second.

Harrison (Winscales and Stainburn, co. Cumberland, exemplified to JOHN FALCON, Esq., of Whitehaven, upon his assuming, by royal licence, the name of HARRISON). Quarterly, 1st and 4th, ar. two bars gemelles sa. betw. three hares courant ppr., for HARRISON; 2nd and 3rd, erm. two chevrons engr. paly az. and sa. betw. three falcons belled or, for FALCON. Crests—1st, HARRISON: Upon a mount vert a stag courant reguard. sa. semée of quatrefoils, attired and unguled or, holding in the mouth an arrow in bend sinister ppr.; 2nd, FALCON: On a fret sa. a falcon rising ppr. belled or, and holding in the beak a lure of the last. Motto—Vite, courageux, fier.

Harrison-Broadley. See BROADLEY.

Harrison. See SLATER-HARRISON.

Harrison (granted to WILLIAM HARRISON, Esq., F.S.A.). Az. a demi lion ramp. couped betw. three pheons or. Crest—A talbot's head erased as. collared or, within a wreath gold and of the first.

Harrison (Fun. Ent. 1630. PETER HARRISON, Cursitor and a Six Clerk in Chancery). Ar. on a chev. engr. gu. betw. three hares saliant ppr. as many bezants, a mullet for diff. *Crest*—A coney holding betw. the paws three ears of wheat all ppr.

Harrison (Reg. Ulster's Office). Vert a lion ramp. and a chief or.

Harrison (confirmed by Roberts, Ulster, 1648, to WILLIAM HARRISON, of Dublin, Gent., descended from an ancient family in England). Ar. two bends gu. on a chief sa. an eagle displ. or. *Crest*—A demi eagle displ. murally gorged or.

Harrold (Limerick; Reg. Ulster's Office). Gu. a pall fiory ar. betw. three plates, one and two, each charged with an estoile of eight points of the field. *Crest*—A demi angel ppr. vested gu. crined and winged or.

Harrold (Ireland). Gu. an escarbuncle of eight rays or, betw. three mullets ar. a label of three points of the last.

Harrow. Erm. three harrows conjoined in the nombril point of the escutcheon gu. with a wreath ar. and of the second, toothed or. *Crest*—A hand vested gu. cuffed or, holding a baton az.

Harrowby, Earl of. See RYDER.

Harrowdin (co. Chester). Ar. guttée de poix a fesse wavy sa.

Harrowdon. Ar. on a bend gu. five lozenges or.

Harrower (America). Az. a fesse betw. three harrows or, teethed gu. *Crest*—A garb ppr. *Motto*—Sedulo numen.

Harrower (Enzievar). Az. a chev. betw. three harrows or. *Crest*—A garb ppr.

Harry, alias Henry (Poston, co. Hereford). Ar. a fesse betw. three lozenges az. a bordure of the last. *Crest*—An angel's head couped below the breast ppr., wings expanded, vested az.

Harryson. Gu. an eagle displ. or, a chief of the second. *Crest*—A serpent entwined round a broken pillar or.

Harryson. Ar. a chev. gu. betw. three escallops sa. a bordure engr. of the last.

Harsack, or Harseck (co. Norfolk). Or, a chief indented sa.

Harsetongue. Ar. on a fesse betw. three chev. gu. two escallops of the first.

Harsick (co. Norfolk). Ar. a chief indented sa.

Harsick, or Hartsick (co. Suffolk). Per fesse indented sa. and or.

Harsnet (co. Sussex). Az. two bars dancettée erm. betw. nine crosses crosslet or. *Crest*—A dexter hand holding a sword, blade wavy ppr.

Harsnet (SAMUEL HARSNET, Bishop of Chichester, 1609-19, and of Norwich 1619-28, Archbishop of York 1628-31; granted by Camden, Clarenceux, 1613). Az. two bars dancettée erm. betw. six crosses crosslet or, three, two, and one.

Harst. Ar. (another, erm.) a sun in splendour gu.

Harswell (Basford, co. Warwick; allowed, with nine quarters, by Glover, Somerset). Ar. on a fess wavy sa. three conies' heads couped of the field. *Crest*—Out of a ducal coronet a conie's head couped or.

Hart (Lullingstone Castle, co. Kent; originally of Westmill, co. Hereford, where STEPHEN HART was seated, *temp.* Edward III. JOHN HART, Esq., of the Middle Temple, m. ELIZABETH, only sister and heiress of Sir JOHN PECHE, of Lullingstone, a Knight Banneret, and Lord Deputy of Calais, and had a son and heir, Sir PERCYVAL HART, Knt., of Lullingstone, ancestor of the HARTS, of Lullingstone, whose eventual heiress, ANNE, only dau. and heiress of Sir PERCYVAL HART, Knt., of Lullingstone, M.P. for Kent 9 and 12 Queen Anne, m. first, JOHN BLUET, Esq., of Holecomb Regis, co. Devon, by whom she had no issue; and, secondly, Sir THOMAS DYKE, Bart., of Horeham, co. Sussex). Per chev. az. and gu. three harts trippant or. *Crest*—A lion's head couped erm. ducally crowned gu.

Hart (Yarnacombe, co. Devon; seated there prior to 1640). Gu. a bend betw. three fleurs-de-lis ar. quartering PROWSE, sa. three lions ramp. ar. langued and armed gu. *Crest*—A fleur-de-lis ar. issuing from a cloud ppr. *Motto*—Deo adjuvante vincam.

Hart (Chester Herald, d. 16 July, 1572). Gu. a fesse betw. three fleurs-de-lis ar.

Hart (Boston, co. Lincoln). Ar. three lozenges az. each charged with an escallop or. *Crest*—A stag's head erased, with an oak branch in the mouth all ppr.

Hart (Lord Mayor of London, 1589). Sa. a chev. ar. betw. three fleurs-de-lis or.

Hart (London). Gu. on a chief indented or, three human hearts of the first.

Hart (co. York). Sa. a chev. or, betw. three fleurs-de-lis ar.

Hart (London). Per chev. az. and gu. in chief two bucks drinking ar. attired or, in base a well of the third.

Hart (Highgate, co. Middlesex). Gu. a bend betw. three fleurs-de-lis ar.

Hart (Hampton-Wick, co. Middlesex). Sa. a bend engr. betw. three fleurs-de-lis or. *Crest*—A buck pass. ppr.

Hart (Grimmons). Gu. on a chief ar. three harts of the field. *Crest*—A hart's head ppr. *Motto*—Via una, cor unum.

Hart. Per chev. gu. and az. three bucks or. *Crest*—A lion's head erased erm. ducally crowned or.

Hart. Per chev. az. and gu. in chief a fountain, in base two hearts counter-trippant or.

Hart. Ar. three bucks' heads couped sa.

Hart (Fun. Ent. of Mrs. ROSE LEGGE, *alias* HART, widow of ROBERT LEGGE, buried at St. Michael's, Dublin, March, 1607). Gu. a bend betw. three fleurs-de-lis ar.

Hart (Fun. Ent. of Capt. PIERCE HART, buried at St. John's Church, Dublin, 9 Sept. 1664). Gu. a chev. erm. betw. three fleurs-de-lis or.

Hart (Kilderry, co. Donegal). Ar. a bend betw. three fleurs-de-lis gu. *Crest*—A heart inflamed issuant out of a castle triple-towered ar. *Motto*—Cœur fidèle.

Hart (Scotland). Vert on a saltire or, a trefoil gu. on a chief of the second a crescent betw. two stars of the first.

Hart (Baltully, co. Fife). Gu. on a chief ar. three hearts ppr. *Crest*—A dexter arm grasping a spear all ppr.

Hart (Edinburgh, 1773). Ar. two hearts inflamed ppr. *Crest*—A dexter arm grasping a scymitar ppr. *Motto*—Fide et amore.

Harte (co. Kent). Sa. a fesse or, voided of the field betw. four mullets of the second.

Harte (Melton Mowbray, co. Leicester). Sa. a bend engr. betw. three fleurs-de-lis or. *Crest*—A stag ppr.

Harte (Fulham, co. Middlesex, and Wallpoole, co. Norfolk, 1634). Ar. three lozenges sa. charged with as many escallops or. *Crest*—A stag's head erased sa. attired ar. in the mouth a flower of the last stalked and leaved vert.

Harte. Sa. a fesse or, betw. three cinquefoils of the last.

Harte. See O'HART.

Hartelowe. Ar. a cross gu. a label of five points az.

Harter (granted to JAMES COLLIER HARTER, Esq., of Broughton Hall, near Manchester). Ar. a lion ramp. double-queued betw. three mullets of six points az. pierced of the field. *Crest*—A stag springing from a fernbrake ppr. and gorged with a collar az. *Motto*—Deo omnia.

Hartery. Ar. a saltire fiory gu.

Harteshill. Ar. a chev. sa. betw. six mullets gu.

Harteshorn. Az. a chev. betw. three bucks' heads cabossed ar.

Hartfleet (co. Kent). Az. three escallops or.

Hartford (co. Bedford). Or, two bars undée az. on a chief sa. three bucks' heads of the field.

Hartford (co. Chester). Ar. a squirrel sejant gu. cracking a nut or.

Hartford (co. Huntingdon, and London; JOHN HARTFORD, citizen, Visit. London, 1589, son of THOMAS HARTFORD, Gent.). Barry nebulée of six or and az. on a chief sa. three stags' heads cabossed of the first. *Crest*—A dexter arm erect couped at the elbow, vested per pale ar. and gu. holding in the hand ppr. a stag's horn sa.

Hartford. Az. three chevronels betw. as many harts' heads cabossed or. *Crest*—A parrot's head gu. betw two wings vert.

Hartford. Gu. a chev. betw. three bucks' heads or.

Hartford. Az. two bars or, on a chief sa. three harts' heads couped or.

Hartford. Ar. on a fesse sa. three bucks' heads cabossed or.

Hartford. Gu. on a fesse ar. three bucks' heads couped sa.

Hartford. Gu. three eagles displ. or (another, ar.).

Hartford. Sa. a bend lozengy ar.

Hartford. Sa. two bends ar.

Hartgift. Ar. three harts' heads couped sa. attired or.

Hartgill (Kilmington, co. Somerset). Ar. three bucks' heads cabossed sa.

Hartgrave (Bollingbroke, co. Lincoln). Az. a fesse ar. fretty gu. betw. three hinds courant or. *Crest*—A demi man in armour, wielding a scymitar in the sinister hand and regally crowned ppr.

Hartgull. Ar. three bucks' heads cabossed sa. *Crest*—A buck's head erased sa. attired or.

Hartham (co. Leicester). Sa. a chev. erm. betw. three talbots of the second.

Harthell. Barry of six ar. and vert.

Harthill. Ar. on a mount ppr. a stag lodged gu.

Harthill. Per pale or and sa. two bars vert.

Hartigan. See O'HARTIGAN.

Hartigan. Az. a lion ramp. ar. brandishing betw. the forepaws a sword ppr. *Crest*—A hand in armour couped below the wrist erect ppr. holding a sword of the last.

Hartington. Or, a stag's head cabossed gu.

Hartington. Gu. a fesse betw. three bucks' heads cabossed ar. attired or.

Hartland, Baron. See MAHON.

Hartland (The Oaklands, co. Devon). Ar. on a bend **sa.** three bucks' heads erased or, quartering DIXON. *Crest*—A buck's head erased or.

Hartley (Manchester, co. Lancaster. Visit. Lancaster, 1664). Ar. on a cross gu. pierced of the field four cinquefoils or, in the 2nd and 3rd quarters a martlet sa. *Crest*—A martlet sa. holding in the beak a cross crosslet fitchée or.

Hartley (Bucklebury House, co. Berks; representative of the WINCHCOMBES, of that place). Same *Arms* and *Crest*. *Motto*—Vive ut vivas.

Hartley (Gillfoot, near Whitehaven). Same *Arms*, &c.

Hartley (Wheaton Aston, co. Stafford). Erm. on a cross engr. gu. four quatrefoils or, in the 1st and 4th quarters a martlet sa. *Crest*—Upon a mount vert a martlet sa. in the beak a cross pattée fitchée or. *Motto*—Sub hoc signo vinces.

Hartley (granted to JOHN HARTLEY, Esq., of Catteral Hall, Giggleswick, co. York). Gu. a cross erm. on a chief ar. three hearts of the field. *Crest*—A heart, as in the arms, ensigned with a crown vallery or, betw. two wings barry of six az. and or.

Hartley (Settle, Giggleswick, co. York). Same *Arms*, a canton erm. for diff. *Crest*—A heart, as in the arms, ensigned with a crown vallery or, betw. two wings barry of six az. and or, the heart charged with an erm. spot gold, for diff.

Hartley (Middleton Lodge, near Richmond, co. York). Or, a chev. betw. three annulets gu. over all a fesse ar. *Crest*—A stag couchant reguard. ar.

Hartley (Beech Park, Clonsilla, co Dublin; confirmed to RICHARD WILSON HARTLEY, Esq., and the other descendants of his grandfather). Ar. on a cross gu. pierced of the field four cinquefoils or, in the 1st and 4th quarters a martlet sa. and in the 2nd quarter a rose of the second barbed and seeded ppr. *Crest*—Out of a mural crown or, a stag's head ppr. holding in the mouth a rose gu. barbed and seeded ppr. *Motto*—Spectemur agendo.

Hartman. Quarterly, 1st and 4th, sa. a demi man in armour couped at the thighs ppr. garnished or, vizor open, brandishing a poleaxe of the first; 2nd and 3rd, gu. on a bend wavy betw. two decrescents ar. three estoiles pierced sa. *Crest*—Out of a ducal coronet or, a demi man, as in the arms, betw. two wings, each charged at the second quartering in the arms.

Hartop (Little Dalby, co. Leicester). Sa. a chev. erm. betw. three otters ar. *Crest*—Out of a ducal coronet or, a pelican ar. vulning herself ppr.

Hartop (Buckminster, co. Leicester; granted by Segar, Garter). Sa. a chev. betw. three otters pass. ar. *Crest*—Out of a ducal coronet or, a demi pelican, wings endorsed ar. vulning her breast gu.

Hartop (co. Kent). **Sa. a** chev. betw. three falcons' heads couped ar.

Hartop. Sa. a chev. erm. betw. three tigers ar. *Crest*—Out of a ducal coronet a pelican or, vulning herself gu.

Hartopp (Freathby, co. Leicester, bart., extinct 1762). Sa. a chev. betw. three otters pass. ar. *Crest*—Out of a ducal coronet or, a demi pelican, wings endorsed ar. vulning herself gu.

Hartopp (CRADOCK-HARTOPP, Freathby, co. Leicester, bart.). Quarterly, 1st and 4th, sa. a chev. ar. betw. three otters pass. ar., for HARTOPP; 2nd and 3rd, per saltire gu. and ar. crusily, and three boars' heads, two and one, couped, counterchanged, for CRADOCK. *Crest*—An arm in armour couped at the elbow, lying fessewise, the hand holding **a** sword erect, transfixed with a boar's head, and out of a ducal coronet or, a pelican ar. vulning herself ppr.

Hartopp (Cambridge and Leicester; granted 18 May, 1596). Sa. a chev. erm. betw. three otters pass. of the second (another, ar.). *Crest*—Out of a ducal coronet or, a demi pelican ar. vulning herself ppr.

Hartpole (Sir WILLIAM HARTPOLE, knighted by Sir George Carey, Lord Deputy of Ireland, 2 Oct. 1603). Gu. a chev. ar. on a chief of the last a lion's head erased betw. two torteaux.

Hartpole (Shrewl, Queen's co.; Fun. Ent. of GEORGE HARTPOLE, Esq., of Grange, in same co., d. Feb. 1632). Gu. a chev. embattled ar. on a chief of the last a torteaux betw. two lions' heads erased sa.

Hartree (granted by Young, Garter, 1855). Gu. a demi stag couped betw. three mullets of six points pierced or. *Crest*—A stag's head erased ppr. in front of a saltire engr. gu. *Motto*—De quo bene speratur.

Hartridge (co. Kent, and Tyshurst, co. Sussex). Or, on **a** chev. sa. three hawks' heads couped ar. *Crest*—On a portcullis sa. lined and studded ar. a lion pass. also ar.

Hartrow (confirmed 19 March, 1579). Or, a mascle **sa.** betw. three pellets.

Hartshill. Or, a chev. sa. betw. six martlets gu.

Hartshorn (granted to WILLIAM HARTSHORN, Captain half-pay 24th Foot). Per fesse dovetailed ar. and gu. in chief two stags' heads cabossed of the last, and in base a bugle of the first, garnished and stringed or. *Crest*—A demi wolf ppr. gorged with a collar, therefrom pendent a bugle or, and supporting a sword, point downwards also ppr. *Motto*—Fortiter in angustis.

Hartshorne. Ar. a chev. gu. betw. three bucks' heads cabossed ar. *Crest*—A buck's head erased sa.

Hartstronge (exemplified to MATHEW WELD, Esq., of Dublin, on his assuming, by royal licence, 2 Feb. 1811, the surname and arms of HARTSTRONGE in lieu of those of WELD, in compliance with the will of JOHN HARTSTRONGE, of Brackendstown, co. Dublin). Per chev. invected or and sa. in chief three pellets, in base a stag trippant of the first. *Crest*—A demi savage ppr. capped ar. holding in his dexter hand a sword hilted or, point downwards, and in his sinister hand a battle axe or, hilt ppr. *Motto*—Sub libertate quietem.

Hartstrong (South Repps, co. Norfolk). Per chev. engr. or and sa. in chief three ogresses, in base a hart trippant of the first.

Hartswell. Ar. three pheons sa.

Hartsyde (Scotland). Or, a saltire betw. three hearts gu. on a chief ar. three crescents sa.

Hartwell (cos. Kent and Northumberland, and Preston, co. Northampton). Sa. a buck's head cabossed ar. betw. the attires a cross formée or. *Crest*—A beetle pass. gu. wings endorsed sa. horns ar.

Hartwell (Dale Hall, Essex, bart.). Sa. a buck's head cabossed ar. attired or, betw. the attires a cross pattée fitchée of the last, in chief a lion pass. guard. per pale of the second and third, on a canton erm. two bars per fesse az. and gu. *Crest*—On a mount vert, surrounded with seven pales, the second and fifth charged with a spear's head sanguinated ar. a hart lodged, the dexter foot on a well of the last and in the mouth a sprig of oak vert. *Motto*—Sorte suâ contentus.

Hartwell (co. Cornwall). Ar. on a fesse wavy sa. three hares' heads erased of the first.

Hartwell (co. Northumberland). Sa. a hart's head cabossed, in base betw. the attires a cross formée fitchée ar. in chief two harts or.

Hartwell. Sa. a buck's head cabossed ar. attired or, betw. the horns a cross pattée, fitched at the foot, of the last. *Crest*—In a park paled or, a stag lodged ar.

Hartwell. Sa. two lions pass. ar. crowned or.

Hartwell. Gu. three lozenges ar.

Harty (Birchington, co. Kent). Or, on a fesse sa. three falcons volant of the field. *Crest*—A falcon's head erased ppr. betw. two wings expanded or.

Harty (Prospect House, Roebuck, co. Dublin, bart.; granted to ROBERT WAY HARTY, Esq., Lord Mayor of Dublin, created a bart. 1831). Or, on a fess sa. betw. three trefoils slipped vert as many falcons volant of the first. *Crest*—Betw. two wings erect or, each charged with a hurt, a falcon's head erased ppr. charged on the neck with a trefoil slipped vert. *Motto*—Malo mori quam fœdari.

Harvage. Ar. a lion ramp. gu. tail forked, in chief three torteaux.

Harvage. Ar. six torteaux, three two, and one.

Harvedon. Ar. on a bend gu. five lozenges or.

Harvell. Ar. on a chev. gu. five bezants.

Harvey (Cambridge and Storbrook, co. Suffolk). Or, **a** chev. gu. in chief two leopards' heads of the last. *Crest*—A demi leopard ar. spotted sa. holding betw. the paws an increscent erm.

Harvey (Langley Park, co. Buckingham, bart.). Gu. on a bend engr. ar. three trefoils slipped vert, all within a bordure wavy erm. *Crest*—A lion reguard. ppr. supporting an escutcheon ar. charged with a bat's wing sa. *Motto*—Probitas verus honos.

Harvey (Ailsbeare, co. Devon; RICHARD HARVEY, of that place, Visit. 1620, great grandson of THOMAS, fourth son of THOMAS, second son of JOHN HARVEY, Esq., of Thurley, co. Bedford). Same *Arms* as HERVEY, Marquis of Bristol, viz., gu. on a bend ar. three trefoils slipped vert.

Harvey (ENOCH HARVEY, Esq., of Aigburth, Liverpool).

Erm. a chev. engr. betw. three leopards' faces gu. *Crest*—A leopard pass.

Harvey (granted to Capt. HARVEY, R.N., C.B.). Az. on a pale ar. betw. two eagles displ. or, each surmounted by an anchor erect of the last, a trident sa. entwined by two branches of laurel ppr. *Crest*—Betw. a branch of oak and another of laurel a dexter cubit arm erect ppr. the hand holding a trident or, on the staff a flag hoisted az. thereon the word "Rosario" in letters of gold. *Motto*—Dieppe.

Harvey (cos. Devon and Suffolk). Gu. on a bend ar. three trefoils slipped vert. *Crest*—A leopard sa. bezantée collared and lined or, holding in the dexter paw a trefoil slipped gold.

Harvey (London; WILLIAM HARVEY, Comptroller for the Sheriff of London, grandson of WILLIAM HARVEY, of same place; certified by Camden, Clarenceux). Or, on a chev. betw. three leopards' faces gu. as many trefoils ar. *Crest*—A leopard pass. ar. ducally gorged and chained or, charged on the shoulder with a trefoil vert.

Harvey (co. Essex and London). Or, a chev. betw. three leopards' faces gu. *Crest*—A leopard ar. ducally gorged and lined or.

Harvey (Alvington, Isle of Wight, and Wormersley. co. York; granted 1688). Same *Arms*, chev. engr. *Crest*—A leopard pass. ppr. gorged with a collar engr. gu.

Harvey (Eastry, co. Kent; descended from the HARVEYS, of Eythorne, settled there in the fifteenth century; from the same stock spring the HARVEYS, of Cowden). Ar. on a chev. embattled gu. betw. three bears' gambs erased and erect ermines as many crescents erminois. *Crest*—Two bears' gambs, the paws supporting a crescent as in the arms.

Harvey (JOHN SPRINGETT HARVEY, Esq., Accountant-General of the Court of Chancery, son of the Rev. RICHARD HARVEY, of Eastry, by CATHERINE, his wife, only child of JOHN SPRINGETT, Esq.). Same *Arms* and *Crest*, on the arms a canton gu. charged with an eagle displ. ar. ducally crowned or, standing on a serpent nowed in fret ppr.

Harvey (co. Kent; borne by Admiral THOMAS HARVEY, son of Admiral Sir HENRY HARVEY, K.B., of Walmer, a descendant of HARVEY, of Eastry). Az. on a chev. embattled betw. two bears' paws erased in chief and an anchor erect in base or, a bomb on fire accompanied by two crescents sa. on a canton of the second a slip of oak fructed ppr. grasping a crescent or.

Harvey (St. Lawrence, Ramsgate, co. Kent). Same *Arms* and *Crest*.

Harvey (Ickwell Bury, co. Bedford; a younger branch of the HARVEYS, or HERVEYS, of Thurley, co. Bedford, and Finningley Park, co. York). Or, on a chev. gu. betw. three leopards' heads, as many trefoils ppr. *Crest*—A leopard pass. bezantée, gorged with a ducal coronet and chained or, holding in his dexter paw a trefoil slipped ppr. *Motto*—Recte faciendo neminem timeas.

Harvey (Sir JAMES HARVEY, Lord Mayor of London, 1582, son of WILLIAM HARVEY, Gent., of Cotwalton, co. Stafford; his son, Sir SEBASTIAN HARVEY, Lord Mayor of London, 1618). Or, on a chev. betw. three leopards' heads gu. a crescent of the field. *Crest*—A leopard pass. ar. spotted sa. ducally gorged and chain reflexed over the back or.

Harvey (co. Middlesex). Or, on a chev. betw. three leopards' faces gu. as many trefoils slipped ar. *Crest*—A leopard pass. ar. spotted sa. ducally collared and chained or, on the shoulder a trefoil slipped of the first.

Harvey (Tonbridge and Cowden, co. Kent). Sa. a fesse wavy, and in chief three crosses formée ar.

Harvey (co. Suffolk). Sa. on a bend ar. three trefoils slipped vert, in chief a fleur-de-lis erm. *Crest*—A demi leopard sa. bezantée, holding in the paw a trefoil vert.

Harvey (Thorpe, co. Norfolk). Erminois on a chief indented gu. three crescents ar. *Crest*—Over a dexter cubit arm erect ppr. a crescent ar. betw. two branches of laurel also ppr. *Motto*—Alteri sic tibi.

Harvey (Crown Point, co. Norfolk, bart.). Erminois on a chief indented gu. a representation of the gold medal presented to Sir ROBERT JOHN HARVEY for his services at the battle of Orthes, pendent from a ribbon gu. fimbriated az. beneath the word "Orthes," betw. two crescents ar. a canton erm. thereon a representation of a badge of the Order of the Tower and Sword. *Crest*· Out of a mural crown or, a dexter cubit arm erect ppr. above a crescent ar. betw. two branches of laurel also ppr. *Motto*—Alteri sic tibi.

Harvey (Wormersley, co. York). Erminois a chev. engr. betw. three leopards' faces gu. *Crest*—A leopard pass. ppr. gorged with a collar engr. gu.

Harvey. Gu. on a chev. erminois six trefoils slipped vert (the erm. and trefoils inclining the same way as the chev.) on a chief or, a stag's head cabossed az. betw. two mullets of the field. *Crest*—Issuant from a crescent or, charged with a

stag's head cabossed az. a cubit arm erect, holding a trefoil slipped ppr.

Harvey. Az. on a bend betw. two mullets in chief and a mascle in base ar. three trefoils slipped vert. *Crest*—A cubit arm holding a trefoil slipped and erect ppr.

Harvey. Ar. three trefoils slipped vert.

Harvey, or Harvy. Ar. three lions' heads erased sa.

Harvey (Chigwell, co. Essex; WILLIAM HARVEY, M.D., so famed for the discovery of the circulation of the blood, was of this family; the last male heir, Admiral Sir ELIAB HARVEY, G.C.B., of Rolls Park, Chigwell, *d.* in 1830, leaving six daus. his co-heirs, viz., LOUISA, *m.* to WILLIAM LLOYD, Esq., of Aston, co. Salop; EMMA, *m.* to Lieut.-General WILLIAM CORNWALLIS EUSTACE, K.C.H.; MARIA, *m.* to the Rev. WILLIAM TOWER, of Weald, co. Essex; GEORGIANA, *m.* to WILLIAM DRUMMOND, Esq.; ELIZA. *m.* to THOMAS WILLIAM BRAMSTON, Esq., M.P., of Skreens; and MARY, *m.* to R. G. C. FANE, Esq.). Or, on a chief indented sa. three crescents ar. *Crest*—A dexter hand couped at the wrist and erect ppr. over it a crescent reversed ar., motto over, Temeraire. *Supporters* (granted to Admiral Sir ELIAB HARVEY, G.C.B.)—Dexter, a Triton, holding over the dexter shoulder a trident, laurel entwining it, all ppr.; sinister, a horse ar. gorged with a naval crown or, on the rim the word "Trafalgar" sa. hanging to it by a white ribbon with two blue stripes the Trafalgar medal or. *Motto*—Redoubtable et fougueux.

Harvey (Comb-Nevile, co. Surrey; descended from DANIEL HARVEY, fourth son of THOMAS HARVEY, of Folkestone, and brother of Dr. HARVEY, the celebrated physician). Same *Arms* and *Crest*,.

Harvey (Rev. RICHARD HARVEY, Vicar of Eastry, co. Kent, *d.* 1778). Same *Arms*.

Harvey (Bargy Castle, co. Wexford, originally of Bosworth, co. Leicester; settled in the former county as early as 1590). Or, on a chief indented sa. three crescents ar. *Crest*—A dexter arm embowed in armour, grasping a sword ppr. pommel and hilt or. *Motto*—Semper idem.

Harvey (Kyle, co. Wexford; descended from the eldest son of the Rev. WILLIAM HARVEY, of Bargy Castle, by his second wife, DOROTHEA, dau. and heiress of CHRISTOPHER CHAMPNEY, Esq., of Kyle). Same *Arms* and *Motto*. *Crest*—A dexter hand couped at the wrist and erect ppr. above which a crescent reversed ar.

Harvey (Mintiagho, Innishowen, co. Donegal, and Goldington Hall and Bolnhurst, co. Bedford). Gu. on a bend ar. three trefoils slipped vert. *Crest*—A lion pass. guard. ppr. holding in the dexter paw a trefoil slipped vert.

Harvey (Fun. Ent. Ulster's Office, Captain GEORGE HARVEY, Constable of the Fort of Maryborough, *d.* 1 Oct. 1599). Gu. on a bend ar. three trefoils slipped az.

Harvey (confirmed by St. George, Ulster, 1665, to Sir PETER HARVEY, Knt., one of the farmers of His Majesty's Customs in Ireland). Ar. three lions ramp. sa. on a chief indented az. as many crescents or. *Crest*—A demi lion ramp. sa. holding in the dexter paw a crescent or.

Harvey (granted to ROBERT HARVEY, Esq., of Killiane Castle, co. Wexford, grandson of Rev. JAMES HARVEY by MARTHA, dau. of JOHN BEAUCHAMP, Esq., of Ballyloughane, co. Carlow, in token of his descent from the BEAUCHAMP family, then extinct). Gu. a fesse betw. six trefoils slipped or. *Crest*—A bear ramp. supporting himself on a staff raguly all ppr.

Harvey. Ar. on a mount vert a hare saliant ppr.

Harvey (Elrick, co. Aberdeen). Gu. a fesse or, betw. three mullets in chief and a mascle in base ar.

Harvey (Broadley, co. Aberdeen). Az. on a bend or, three trefoils vert. *Crest*—A trefoil vert. *Motto*—Delectat et ornat.

Harvey (Castle Semple, co. Renfrew). Gu. on a bend erminois three trefoils slipped vert, on a chief ar. a buck's head cabossed sa. betw. two mullets of the first, and in the sinister chief point a cross pattée of the fourth. *Crest*—Out of a crescent or, charged with a buck's head, as in the arms, a cubit arm ppr. the hand grasping a trefoil slipped, erect vert. the arm charged with an erm. spot or. *Motto*—Omnia bene.

Harvey (Sir GEORGE HARVEY, President of the Royal Scottish Academy, 1871). Az. on a bend ar. three trefoils slipped vert. *Crest*—A dexter hand ppr. holding a trefoil slipped vert. *Motto*—Delectat et ornat.

Harvey. See HERVEY.

Harvie. Az. a fesse betw. three martlets or. *Crest*—A boar's head and neck issuing sa.

Harvie. Az. a fesse or, betw. two martlets in chief and a catharine wheel in base ar.

Harvy (Hale, parish of Linkinhorn, co. Cornwall; BALDWYN,

son of JOHN HARVY. Visit. 1620). Ar. a chev. betw. three harrows sa.

Harvy (London). Az. on a chev. embattled or, three leopards' faces sa.

Harvy (London). Sa. on a chev. betw. three leopards' faces or, a crescent gu.

Harvy, or Harvey (cos. Norfolk and Suffolk). Ar. three saddles sa. *Crest*—A lion couchant gu.

Harvy. Ar. two bars nebulée sa. on a chief of the last three crosses pattée fitchée or.

Harvye (Brockley, co. Somerset). Sa. a fesse or, betw. three squirrels sejant ar. cracking nuts of the second. *Crest*—A squirrel sejant ar. tail or, cracking a nut gold.

Harvys. Ar. on a chev. sa. three guttées d'or.

Harward (Hayne, co. Devon; settled there for more than three centuries; the last male heir, CHARLES HARWARD, Dean of Chichester, left an only dau. and heiress, who *m*. the Rev. CHARLES BLAKE, of Woodstock, who took the name and arms of HARWARD, in 1816). Gu. on a cross crosslet ar. betw. four guttées d'eau, five annulets az. *Crest*—A leopard statant erm. collared or, surmounting a cross crosslet fitchée sa. from the collar a chain or, reflexed and attached to the cross.

Harward (cos. Cornwall and Worcester). Chequy or and az. on a bend gu. three eagles displ. of the first.

Harward (Little Chelsea, co. Middlesex). Az. on a chev. ar. betw. three doves ppr. as many acorns of the last.

Harward, or Herward (Alborough, Pensshoppe, and Guessnore, co. Norfolk). Az. a fesse paly of six gu. and vert betw. three owls ar.

Harward (co. Dorset; Fun. Ent. of MILLICENT, wife of HENRY HARWARD, of that co., *d.* in Dublin, 5 March, 1633). Sa. a fess paly of six cr and gu. betw. three owls ar. a mullet for diff.

Harward (Merrow, co. Surrey). Az. a lion ramp. ar. over all on a fesse or, three roses gu. *Crest*—A demi stag ramp. erm. ducally gorged and attired gu.

Harward. Sa. on a chief ar. three birds' heads erased of the first.

Harward. Az. a fesse gobonated gu. and ar. betw. three owls of the third.

Harware (Stoke, co. Warwick). Quarterly, 1st and 4th, az. a fess wavy betw. two stags' heads couped or ; 2nd and 3rd, az. on a fess or, betw. three owls ar. as many pallets vert. *Crest*—Out of pallisadoes or, a stag's head gu. attired of the first, and gorged with a wreath or and az.

Harwedon (Harwedon, co. Northampton). Ar. a bend gu. surmounted by a bend fusilly or.

Harwedon. Ar. a bend counter-componée or and gu.

Harwedon (co. Chester). Ar. guttée de poix a fesse wavy sa.

Harwell. See HAREWELL.

Harwich, Borough of (co. Essex). Gu. a portcullis with chains pendent or, nailed and pointed az. *Crest*—An antique ship with one mast or, in water ppr. on the head and stern towers ar. one also fixed near the top of the mast, on the sinister side the sail furled, and on the mast-head a split pennon flotant gu.

Harwine (London). Or, three trefoils slipped vert. *Crest*—A hatchet.

Harwood, Herwood, Horwode, and Whorwood (of Saxon origin, seated at a very remote period in cos. Lincoln and Cambridge; from this ancient line derived the families of the name seated at Compton, Sandwell, and Stourton Castle in the co. of Stafford, at Halton, co. Oxford, and in the cos. of Berks, Salop, Hants, &c.). Chequy or and az. on a bend gu. three eagles displ. ar.; borne by Sir ROBERT HERWOOD, co. Cambridge, *temp.* Edward l.; the cos. Stafford and Berks HARWOODS altered this ancient bearing for "ar. a chev. betw. three stags' heads cabossed sa. (sometimes gu.);" but at what period has not been ascertained.

Harwood (exemplified to HENRY HARWOOD PENNY, Esq., of Cromarty House, Porchester Terrace, Hyde Park, Barrister-at-law, son of the Rev. HENRY PENNY, M.A., of Chessington Hall, Surrey, by SARAH, his wife, only child of JOHN HARWOOD, Esq., on his assuming, by royal licence, the surname of HARWOOD). Ar. on a chev. betw. three stags' heads cabossed gu. as many eagles displ. or. *Crest*—A stag's head cabossed gu. holding in the mouth a slip of oak ppr. fructed or, betw. the attires a buglehorn stringed also gu. *Motto*—Suaviter.

Harwood (Hagbourn and Streatley, co. Berks, and Crick-heath and Tern, co. Salop; descended from the ancient Saxon house of HARWOOD). Ar. a chev. betw. three stags' heads cabossed gu. *Crest*—A stag's head cabossed gu. holding in its mouth an oak bough ppr. acorned or.

Harwood (Deane, co. Hants). Az. a chev. erm. betw. three martlets ar.

Harwood, alias Whorwood (co. Salop). Or, a chev. betw. three stags' heads cabossed sa. each holding in the mouth a sprig of oak ppr. fructed of the firs*:*

Harwood (Newmarket, co. Cambridge, Exning Hall, co. Suffolk). Az. a fesse compony ar. and gu. betw. three owls of the second. *Crest*—An owl ar.

Harwood (The Cloisters, Bath). Ar. on a chev. betw. two stags' heads cabossed in chief and a lion ramp. in base gu. three mullets or. *Crest*—A stag's head cabossed gu. betw. the attires a fret ar. and on either side a palm branch ppr. *Motto*—Generosus et paratus.

Harwood. Az. a fesse gobony gu. and ar. betw. three owls of the last. *Crest*—An owl ar.

Harwood. Az. a chev. erm. betw. three martlets ar. *Crest* —Out of a ducal coronet or, a triple plume of twelve ostrich feathers, three, four, and five.

Harwood. Gu. a fesse humettée betw. two lions pass. (another, pass. guard.) or.

Hasard (co. Gloucester). Gu. four bars ar. on a chief or, three escallops of the first. *Crest*—A bear's head and neck sa. muzzled or.

Hasard (Syngleton, co. Essex, *temp.* Edward III.). Or, three chev. gu. over all a lion ramp. of the last.

Hasbrough, or Hasburgh. Or, a lion ramp. gu.

Hascalerton. Ar. three lions ramp. gu. crowned or.

Hase (Berkhampstead, co. Hertford). Gu. a hare saliant ar. *Crest*—From a bush a hare courant all ppr.

Hase (Lord Mayor of London, 1614). Erminois three lions' heads erased sa.

Hase (Great Melton, co. Norfolk; granted 1750). Erm. a fesse engr. or, betw. three lions ramp. or. quartering az. two combs in fesse betw. a broken lance barways or, one piece in chief, the head respecting the dexter side, the other half towards the dexter base point, for LOMBE. *Crest*—A falcon rising erminois belled ar. charged on the breast with an estoile of sixteen points also ar. in the centre an erm. spot. *Another Crest*—For LOMBE, two lances in saltire or, each charged with a small pennant gu.

Hase. Erm. a fesse engr. ar. betw. three lions ramp ppr. *Crest*—A falcon volant erm. belled ar. charged on the breast with an estoile of the last.

Hase. Sa. a chev. ar. betw. three leopards' faces or.

Hase, or Hayes. Ar. on a pale sa. betw. two palets engr. az. three bulls' heads couped or.

Haselday (co. Cambridge). Ar. a cross flory sa.

Haselden (Goldington, co. Bedford). Same *Arms*.

Haselden (Stamford, co. Lincoln). Gu. a cross patonce or, on a chief az. three round buckles of the second. *Crest*—A talbot's head ar.

Haselden, or Carter. Gu. a cross flory or, on a chief az. three round buckles of the second. *Crest*—A talbot's head ar. charged on the neck with a mullet gu.

Haselerton (Great Grimsby, co. Derby). Gu. six lions ramp. ar. crowned or, three, two, and one. *Crest*—A flag az. charged with a cross ar.

Haselerton. Same *Arms*. *Crest*—A sword in pale ensigned with a cross pattée gu.

Haseley, Hasley, or Hassely (co. Suffolk). Ar. a fesse gu. betw. three hazel nuts or, husks and stalks vert. *Crest*—A leopard's face or.

Haselfoot (Boreham Manor, co. Essex). Quarterly, 1st and 4th, quarterly, az. and or, four lozenges conjoined in cross counterchanged ; 2nd and 3rd, gu. on a fess engr. or, three bezants, each charged with a peacock's head erased az. as many mascles of the field. *Crest*—A demi peacock or, wings expanded az. holding in the beak a snake twined round the neck ppr.

Haselfoot (PASKE-HASELFOOT; exemplified to THEOPHILUS PASKE, Esq., of Wandsworth, co. Surrey, on his assuming, by royal licence, the surname of HASELFOOT). Quarterly, 1st and 4th, HASELFOOT, quarterly, az. and or, four lozenges in cross counterchanged , 2nd and 3rd, PASKE, quarterly, sa. and ar. in the 1st and 4th quarters three fleurs-de-lis of the second. *Crest*—A demi peacock or wings expanded az. in the beak a snake twined round the neck ppr.

Haselin. Ar. on a bend sa. three roses or.

Hasell (Dalemain, co. Cumberland). Or, on a fesse az. betw. three hazel slips ppr. as many crescents ar. *Crest*—A squirrel sejant cracking a nut betw. two oak branches all ppr

Hasellfoot (London, 1656). Per pale or and az. four lozenges meeting in the fesse point counterchanged. *Crest*—A demi peacock with wings expanded az. in the beak a snake ppr. entwined round the neck.

Haselrigg (Noseley, co. Leicester, THOMAS HASELRIGGE, living at Visit. Leicester, 1619; descended from SIMON DE

Haslrigg, Lord of Wotteslade and West Brunton, co. North-umberland, to whom Edward I. gave the Manor of Yetham Corbet, 1280). Ar. a chev. sa. betw. three hazel leaves vert. *Crest*—A maiden's head couped at the shoulders ppr. hair dishevelled or.

Haselrigg (Sutton Bonnington, co. Notts; descended from Haselrig, co. Leicester. Visit. Notts. 1569). Same *Arms*, a crescent for diff. *Crest*—On a chapeau gu. turned up erm. a man's head in profile ppr. crined and bearded or.

Haselrigg (Weteslade and West Brunton, co. Northumber-land). Same *Arms*.

Haselwall (Haselwall, co. Chester). Az. a chief or.

Haselwood, or Hasselwood (co. Suffolk). Ar. on a chev. gu. betw. three leopards' faces sa. as many lozenges erm. a chief az.

Haselwood (Maidwell, co. Northants, Wickwarren, co. Worcester, and co. Oxford). Ar. on a chev. gu. betw. three owls sa. as many lozenges erm. on a chief az. three hazel branches or. *Crest*—A squirrel sejant az. collared or, charged with three bezants in pale, holding a hazel branch ppr. fructed gold.

Haselwood (Belton, co. Rutland. Visit. 1618). Ar. a chev. betw. three hazel leaves vert.

Haskell. Vairé ar. (another, or) and sa. *Crest*—On a mount an apple tree fructed ppr.

Haskins (Oxted, co. Surrey). Per chev. gu. and az. a chev. engr.. or, betw. three lions ramp. ar. *Crest*—A lion's head erased ppr.

Haskins. Same *Arms*. *Crest*—Two hands issuing from clouds conjoined and supporting a heart inflamed ppr.

Haslack. Sa. a chev. erm. (another, or) betw. three catha-rine wheels ar.

Haslam (confirmed by Roberts, Ulster, 1647, to Captain Francis Haslam, descended from co. Oxford). Ar. a cross betw. four hazel leaves slipped ppr. a crescent for diff. *Crest*—On a mount in front of a hazel tree a lamb couchant all ppr.

Haslatine. Gu. a cross patonce or, on a chief az. three round buckles of the second. *Crest*—A talbot's head couped ar.

Haslefoote. Per pale az. and ar. a cross lozengy counter-changed.

Haslefoote. Per pale or and az. a cross lozengy counter-changed. *Crest*—Two wings endorsed erm.

Hasler (Aldingbourne and Barkfold, co. Sussex). Per chev. gu. and sa. three lions ramp. ar. each charged on the shoulder with a cross pattée az. *Crest*—A squirrel sejant cracking a nut ppr. collared gemel az. betw. two branches of palm also ppr. *Motto*—Qui nucleum vult, nucem frangat.

Haslett (granted by William Haslett, Esq., of London-derry, and Summerhill, co. Donegal, only son of William Haslett, Esq., of Derrymount, co. Derry). Ar. on a bend az. betw. two lions' heads erased gu. three round buckles or, on a canton sa. as many candlesticks of the last. *Crest*—A talbot's head couped sa. gorged and chained or. *Motto*—Semper fidelis.

Haslewood (Oldington and Newton, and of Bridgenorth, co. Salop). Or, on a chev. gu. betw. three owls sa. as many lozenges erm. on a chief az. three hazel branches or. *Crest*—A squirrel sejant az. collared or, charged with three bezants in pale, holding a hazel branch ppr. fructed or. *Motto*—Quod me mihi reddit amicum.

Haslewood (descended from Thomas Haslewode, Esq., of Oldington, co. Salop, temp. Henry V.). Same *Arms* and *Crest* as last. *Motto*—Quod me mihi reddit amicum.

Hasling (Mepham, co. Kent). Gu. a fesse embattled erm. betw. three talbots pass. or. *Crest*—An ostrich, in the mouth a broken tilting spear ppr.

Haslington. Gu. three mullets or.

Haspurg. Gu. a fesse ar.

Hassal (Hassal, co. Chester). Per chev. ar. and or, three pheons sa. *Crest*—An arm embowed, couped at the elbow, vested or, turned down at the wrist ar. holding a dart with the point downwards or, feathered ar. barbed sa.

Hassall (Hankelow and Nantwich, co. Chester). Same *Arms* and *Crest*.

Hassard (borne by the late General Hassard, Royal Engineers). Ar. three bars az. in chief three escallops of the second. *Crest*—An escallop. *Motto*—Vis en espoir.

Hassard (Gardenhill, co. Fermanagh). Gu. two bars ar. on a chief or, three escallops of the first. *Crest*—An escallop or, motto over, Vive en espoir. *Motto*—Fortuna viam ducit.

Hassard (Glenville, co. Waterford). Same *Arms*, *Crest*, and *Mottoes*.

Hassell. Vert three adders erect ar. *Crest*—A dexter arm erect, habited vert, cuffed or, holding in the hand a branch of laurel all ppr.

465

Hassell (Robert Prous Hassell, Esq., of Wraysbury). Same *Arms* and *Crest*.

Hassell (John Hassell, Esq., of St. Giles's-in-the-Fields, co. Middlesex). Same *Arms* and *Crest*.

Hassell, or Hassall. Per chev. or and sa. three pheons counterchanged. *Crest*—Out of a ducal coronet a hand holding three arrows, points downward.

Hassell (Fun. Ent. Ulster's Office, 1600). Same *Arms*.

Hassell. Vairé ar. and sa.

Hassenhull. Erm. a mullet of six points pierced gu.

Hasset. Ar. a chev. erm. betw. three dolphins naiant az.

Hassey (Normandy). Erm. a chev. az. betw. three holly leaves vert.

Hast (Wyndham, co. Norfolk). Per chev. or and gu. three greyhounds in full course counterchanged. *Crest*—A stag's head erased gu. attired ar. ducally gorged or (another, collared ar.).

Hast. Ar. a sun gu.

Hastake. Gu. a chev. erm. betw. three catharine wheels or.

Hastaline. Gu. a cross patonce or, on a chief az. three round buckles of the second. *Crest*—A talbot's head couped ar.

Hastang (co. Stafford). Az. a chief gu. over all a lion ramp. or.

Hastang (Leamington and Newbold, co. Warwick, temp. Henry II.). Same *Arms*.

Hastang (Baron Hasting; summoned to Parliament 1311, abeyance temp. Edward III.). Same *Arms*.

Hastang. Per fesse gu. and az. a lion ramp. or.

Hastang. Az. a chief gu. over all a lion ramp. or, depressed by a bend ar.

Hastange (Sir Robert de Hastange, co. Stafford; MS. arms from Visit. Stafford, 1583). Az. a lion ramp. double queued or, a chief gu.

Hastange (Sir John de Hastange, co. Stafford; MS. arms from Visit. Stafford, 1583). Az. a lion ramp. or, on a chief gu. a label of three points ar.

Hastday (Saltwood, co. Kent). Az. a griffin segreant ar. a chief of the last. *Crest*—On a mount vert a hare sejant ppr.

Hasted (Sunnings, co. Berks; descended from Rowley, co. Lancaster; Reg. Ulster's Office, Smith's Ordinary). Gu. an eagle displ. erm. a chief chequy or and az. *Crest*—Out of a mural crown az. an eagle displ. erm. beaked or.

Hasted. Gu. a chief chequy or and az. *Crest*—A wheel ppr.

Hasted. Erm. a mullet of six points gu. pierced or.

Hastie (Scotland). Or, on a ground in base vert, a lion saliant of the last, royally crowned az.

Hastings (Baron Hastings; summoned to Parliament 1264, title passed to Grey of Ruthin, 1391). Or, a maunch gu.

Hastings (Earl of Pembroke; the fourth Baron Hastings was so created 1339, extinct 1391). Same *Arms*.

Hastings (Baron Hastings, of Gressing Hall; summoned to Parliament, 1342, vested in Astley, Bart. See Astley, Lord Hastings). Same *Arms*.

Hastings (Earl of Huntingdon). Ar. a maunch sa. *Crest*—A bull's head erased sa. crowned, gorged with a ducal coronet and armed or. *Supporters*—Two man tigers affrontée or, their manes resembling the human face ppr. *Mottoes*—In veritate victoria; and, Honorantes me honorabo.

Hastings (Lord Hastings of Loughborough; created 1558 and 1643, extinct 1666). Same *Arms* as the Earl of Huntingdon.

Hastings (Elford, co. Oxford; Sir Edward Hastings, Knt., descended from Sir Miles Hastings, Knt., of Delsford, co. Worcester. Visit. Oxon, 1574). Same *Arms*, a crescent for diff.

Hastings (Rawdon-Hastings, Marquess of Hastings; extinct 1868). Quarterly, 1st and 4th, ar. a maunch sa., for Hastings; 2nd and 3rd, ar. a fesse betw. three pheons sa., for Rawdon. *Crests*—1st, Hastings: A bull's head erased sa. armed and ducally gorged or; 2nd, Rawdon: On a mural crown ar. a pheon sa. with a laurel branch issuant thereout ppr. *Supporters*—Two bears ar. muzzled gu. chains affixed to the muzzles and reflexed over the back or, and fastened by a staple to a trunk of a tree erect ppr. held betw. the fore-paws. *Motto*—Et nos quoque tela sparsimus.

Hastings (Abney-Hastings, Earl of Loudoun). Quarterly, 1st and 4th, Hastings, ar. a maunch sa.; 2nd and 3rd, Abney, or, on a chief az. a demi lion issuant ar. *Crests*—1st, Hastings: A bull's head erased ermines attired and ducally gorged ar.; 2nd, Abney: A demi lion or, the sinister paw resting upon an antique shield, charged with the arms of Hastings. *Supporters*—Dexter, a chevalier in armour, holding a spear in the right hand ppr. and plumed on the head with three feathers gu.; sinister, a lady nobly

2 H

dressed, plumed on the head with three feathers ar. and holding in the left hand a letter of challenge. *Motto*—I bide my time.

Hastings (ABNEY-HASTINGS, Willesley Hall, co. Leicester, bart., extinct). Quarterly, 1st and 4th, ar. a maunch sa. a bordure engr. of the last, for HASTINGS; 2nd and 3rd, or, on a chief gu. a demi lion ramp. ar., for ABNEY. *Crests*—1st: A buffalo's head erased erminois, armed and ducally gorged or, for HASTINGS; 2nd: A demi lion ramp. or, resting the left paw on an antique shield, charged with a maunch as above, for ABNEY. *Motto*—In veritate victoria.

Hastings (Agmondesham, co. Bucks, and cos. Dorset and Leicester). Ar. a maunch sa. *Crest*—A bull's head erased sa. attired ar. ducally gorged or.

Hastings (Cambridge). Erm. on a chief az. two mullets ar.

Hastings (co. Derby, Dringham, co. Norfolk, co. Oxford, and Fennick, co. York). Or, a maunch gu.

Hastings (co. Gloucester). Barry of twelve ar. and az. over all an inescutcheon or, charged with a maunch gu.

Hastings (co. Gloucester). Or, a maunch gu. over all a bendlet az.

Hastings (Billesby, co. Lincoln). Ar. a maunch sa. in the middle chief point a trefoil slipped.

Hastings (Hinton, co. Northampton; granted 10 July, 1685). Erm. three lozenges in bend betw. two bendlets az. *Crest*—A demi panther guard. ppr. supporting a lozenge or.

Hastings (co. Nottingham). Or, a maunch gu. with a label of three points az.

Hastings (co. Northumberland). Ar. a fesse gu. betw. three maunches sa.

Hastings (co. Oxford). Ar. a maunch sa. *Crest*—A demi mermaid, in her hands a comb and mirror all ppr.

Hastings (co. Oxford). Or, a fesse betw. two mullets gu.

Hastings (co. Oxford). Or, a lion pass. gu. a label az.

Hastings (Scotland). Or, a maunch gu. *Crest*—A bull's head couped or, armed gu.

Hastings (Somerset Herald, *temp.* Henry VIII.). Or, a fesse and two mullets in chief gu.

Hastings (co. Stafford). Az. a lion ramp. or, tail forked, a chief gu.

Hastings (co. York). Ar. three maunches sa.

Hastings. Per fesse vert and or, a bull counterchanged.

Hastings. Barry of ten ar. and az. on an inescutcheon or, a maunch gu., an orle of martlets of the last.

Hastings. Ar. a fesse betw. three lozenges az.

Hastings. Ar. a fesse lozengy az.

Hastings. Ar. a chief or, over all a lion ramp. gu.

Hastings. Gu. a bend or.

Hastings. Or, three maunches gu.

Hastings (Daylesford, co. Worcester; borne by WARREN HASTINGS, Governor General of India). Or, a maunch gu. *Crest*—A bull's head gu. armed or. *Motto*—Mens æqua in arduis.

Hastlehill. Ar. a mullet of six points gu. pierced or.

Hastolph. Quarterly, 1st, quarterly, or and az.; 2nd, az. a fret or; 3rd, sa. a cross patonce or; 4th, a bend betw. six crosses crosslet fitchée sa. *Crest*—A crow volant, in the beak an oak branch acorned all ppr.

Haswell (Scotland). Per fesse dancettée sa. and ar. in chief three mullets, and in base a boar's head couped all counterchanged.

Hasswell. Or, on a bend gu. three goats ar. attired of the first.

Hatband Makers, Company of (London). Az. on a chev. betw. three hatbands or, as many merillions sa.

Hatbeane (impalement Fun. Ent. Ulster's Office, 1654). Ar. a crescent gu. betw. three beanpods slipped vert.

Hatch (co. Devon). Gu. two demi lions pass. guard. or. *Crest*—A lion's head cabossed or.

Hatch (Windsor, co. Berks). Gu. two demi lions pass. guard. couped or. *Crest*—A boar's head.

Hatch. Or, a cross engr. gu. (another, the tinctures reversed). *Crest*—A flag in bend.

Hatch. Gu. a cross engr. or.

Hatch. Sa. two demi lions pass. guard. or.

Hatch (Busuistock, co. Cornwall; CHRISTOPHER HATCH, descended from JEFFREY HATCH, *temp.* Edward III. Visit. 1620). Gu. two demi lions pass. or.

460

Hatch (Sutton, co. Surrey). Gu. two demi lions pass. guard. couped in pale or, quartering the arms of CLIFFE, viz., quarterly, 1st and 4th, ar. on a fesse betw. three wolves' heads erased sa. as many mullets or; 2nd, ar. on a bend cotised sa. three mullets of the first; 3rd, az. fretty ar. a bordure engr. or. *Crest*—A demi lion ramp. or, betw. the paws a sphere, a cross pattée fitchée stuck therein.

Hatch (quartered by BERRY of Croscombe and Chittle-hampton, co. Devon. Visit. 1620). Gu. two lions pass. guard. ar. a border engr. or.

Hatch, or Hacche (Hatch, co. Devon; a co-heiress of ROBERT HATCH, Esq., of Saterleigh Park, co. Devon; the representative of this family *m.* JOHN DRAKE, Esq., of Barn-staple, ancestor of ROBERT HACCHE DRAKE, Esq., Com-mander R.N., and ZACHARY HAMMETT DRAKE, Esq., of Springfield, co. Devon). Gu. two demi lions pass. guard. or. *Crest*—A lion's head cabossed ar.

Hatch (Auler and Chittlehampton, co. Devon; THOMAS HATCH, Esq., of Auler, *m.* the dau. of Sir JOHN CHICHESTER, Bart., of Raleigh. Visit. Devon, 1620). Gu. two demi lions pass. guard. or.

Hatch (Ardee Castle, co. Louth; confirmed to WILLIAM HATCH, M.D., grandson of THOMAS HATCH, Esq., and descendants). Gu. two demi lions pass. guard. couped in pale or, on a chief ar. a cannon mounted ppr. *Crest*—A demi lion ramp. or, armed and langued gu. charged on the breast with a pile of shot ppr. and holding in the paws a staff also ppr. thereto affixed a flag ar. charged with a cross of the second. *Motto*—Fortis valore et armis.

Hatcher (Carby and Bytham, co. Lincoln). Az. a chev. betw. six escallops ar. *Crest*—An arm embowed vested as charged with three bars ar. holding in the hand ppr. a branch of olives vert.

Hatchet, or Hatchett. Ar. nine annulets in saltire interlaced, five gu. and four az. *Crest*—A thunderbolt ppr.

Hatcliff. Az. two bars or, over all a lion ramp. gu. *Crest*—A lion ramp. ar. guttée sa.

Hatcliffe (Hatcliffe, co. Lincoln). Az. three quatrefoils slipped ar. *Crest*—A lion pass. gu. holding in the dexter paw a cutlass erect ar. hilt and pommel or.

Hatcliffe (co. Sussex). Az. three cinquefoils or.

Hatecliffe (co. Lincoln). Az. three quatrefoils slipped or.

Hateley (Scotland). Or, on a bend az. cotised gu. three boars' heads erased of the field. *Crest*—An otter's head erased sa.

Hateringdon. Erm. a cross gu. surmounted of another ar.

Haterington. Sa. a cross or, voided of the field.

Hatfeild (Hatfeild Hall, co. York). Erm. on a chev. sa. three cinquefoils ar. *Crest*—A buffalo's head erased or.

Hatfeld. Ar. ten crosses crosslet gu. four, three, two, and one.

Hatfield (Willoughby, co. Notts; THOMAS HATFIELD, *temp.* Henry VIII. Visit. Notts, 1614). Erm. on a chev. sa. three cinquefoils or.

Hatfield. Paly of six gu. and ar. on a chev. or, two bars gemel, a bordure sa. and a chief quarterly erm. and az.

Hatfield (Thorpe Arch, co. York). Quarterly, 1st and 4th, erm. on a chev. engr. sa. three cinquefoils or, for HATFIELD; 2nd and 3rd, per fesse indented ar. and sa. a pale counter-changed, three goats' heads erased, two and one az. and as many crosses pattée fitchée, one and two, of the first, for GOSSIP. *Crests*—1st, HATFIELD: A dexter cubit arm vested sa. cuffed ar. the hand ppr. holding a cinquefoil slipped or; 2nd, GOSSIP: Two goats' heads erased addorsed, the dexter az., sinister ar. *Motto*—Pax.

Hatfield. Sa. on a chev. or, betw. three lions ramp. ar. a mullet of the field.

Hatfield (Carlton, Norwell, and Willoughby, co. Notting-ham). Erm. on a chev. gu. three mullets or.

Hatfield. Erm. on a chev. sa. three cinquefoils ar.

Hatfield, or Hitfield. Ar. a chev. engr. betw. three cinquefoils sa. *Crest*—An ostrich's feather enfiled with a ducal coronet or.

Hatfield (ALEXANDER HATFIELD, Esq., of Twickenham, co. Middlesex). Erm. on a chev. engr. sa. three cinquefoils or. *Crest*—An arm erect couped below the elbow, habited sa. cuffed ar. holding in the hand ppr. a cinquefoil slipped or.

Hatfield (confirmed by Carney, Ulster, to RIDGELEY HAT-FIELD, Lord Mayor of Dublin). Erm. on a chev. sa. three cinquefoils ar. quartering ar. on a bend az. three fusils of the field, each charged with a pheon point downwards gu. *Crest*—A talbot's head erased ar. collared or.

Hatherfield. Az. a lion ramp. guard. or.

Hatherley, Baron. See WOOD.

Hatherley (London and Bristol, 1442). Ar. on a bend gu.

betw. two lions' heads erased sa. three crosses pattée of the field.

Hatherton, Baron. See LITTLETON.

Hathersage, or Hathersege. Paly of six ar. and gu. on a chief az. a fesse dancettée or.

Hatheway (Rewardine, in the Forest of Dean, co. Gloucester). Sa. a buglehorn garnished and rimmed, stringed ar.

Hatheway (co. Gloucester). Sa. a buglehorn garnished ar.

Hatheway, or Hathaway. Same *Arms.* *Crest*—A demi lion ramp. gu. holding in the dexter paw a fleur-de-lis.

Hatheway. Paly of six ar. and sa. on a bend or, three pheons of the second.

Hathey (co. Devon). Sa. three birds ar. membered gu.

Hathorn (Overairies, co. Wigtoun). Quarterly, 1st and 4th, ar. a chev. gu. betw. three hunting horns vert, stringed of the second; 2nd and 3rd, or, a fesse chequy az. and ar. surmounted by a bend engr. gu. all within a double tressure of the last, in chief a buckle of the second, for STEWART. Crest —A lion ramp. gu. armed and langued az. grasping a hawthorn tree fructed, and in the dexter paw a scimetar defending the same ppr. *Mottoes*—Above the crest: Fidelitate et amore; below the arms: Suffibulatus majores sequor.

Hathorne. Or, on a bend sa. three mullets ar.

Hathorpe. Sa. a chev. betw. three owls or.

Hathorpe. Sa. a chev. engr. ar. (another, or).

Hatley (Aylesbury, co. Buckingham, Coxton, co. Cambridge, and St. Ede's, co. Huntingdon). Az. a sword in bend ar. hilt and pommel or (the hilt to the dexter chief point), betw. two mullets of six points pierced of the third. *Crest*—Out of a ducal coronet an antelope's head or, armed, tufted, and maned sa. pierced through the neck with a broken spear gu.

Hatsell (co. Middlesex; granted, 1708, to Sir HENRY HATSELL, Knt., a Baron of the Exchequer). Erm. three vipers' heads erect and erased ppr. *Crest*—On a mount vert a like viper's head, holding in the mouth a branch of rue ppr.

Hatt (co. Berks, Orsett, co. Essex, and London). Quarterly, ar. and gu. on a bend sa. three chaplets or. *Crest*—A falcon's head quarterly ar. and gu. betw. two wings expanded sa.

Hatt, or Hatte. Ar. a chev. sa. betw. three annulets az.

Hatter. Paly of six ar. and gu. on a chief of the second a griffin pass. ar.

Hattley (Brecon). Az. a sword in bend ar. pommelled and hilted or, the point downwards betw. two mullets of the second.

Hatton (Hatton, co. Chester; *temp.* William the Conqueror. In 35 Edward I., MATILDA, sole dau. and heiress of JOHN HATTON, Esq., m. RALPH VERNON, of Shipbrooke; the VERNONS held the lands of Hatton until *temp.* Henry IV. or V., when PETRONILLA, dau. and co-heir of RALPH VERNON, of Hatton, m. HUGH DUTTON. The estate was sold by DOROTHY DUTTON and JOHN MASSIE, of Coddington, her husband, *circa* 1699; from HUGH HATTON, of Great Aldersey, of this family, descended Sir CHRISTOPHER HATTON). Az. a chev. betw. three garbs or. *Crest*—A hind statant or.

Hatton (*Viscount Hatton;* created 1682, extinct in 1762). Az. a chev. betw. three garbs gu. *Crest*—A doe pass. or. *Supporters*—Two horses ar. bridled sa. *Motto* (sometimes inscribed on the reins " Gwillim ")—Quid ni tandem.

Hatton (Long Stanton, co. Cambridge, bart., extinct 1812). Same *Arms* as *Viscount Hatton*, a mullet for diff.

Hatton (FINCH-HATTON, *Earl of Winchilsea*). Quarterly, 1st and 4th, az. a chev. betw. three garbs or; 2nd and 3rd, ar. a chev. betw. three griffins pass. wings endorsed sa. *Crests*— 1st: A griffin pass. segreant sa.; 2nd; A pegasus courant ar. winged, maned, and hoofed or, ducally gorged of the last. *Supporters*—Dexter, a pegasus ar. wings, mane, and hoofs or, ducally gorged of the last; sinister, a griffin, wings endorsed sa. ducally gorged or. *Mottoes*—Nil conscire sibi; Virtus tutissima cassis.

Hatton (cos. Cambridge, Chester, Gloucester, and Northampton, Shrewsbury, co. Salop, and Harringham, co. Warwick). Az. a chev. betw. three garbs or. *Crest*—A hawk close ar. holding in the beak an ear of wheat or. *Another Crest*—A hind trippant or.

Hatton (Cambridge). Ar. three hurts each charged with a bend of the first, on a chief vert an eagle displ. or.

Hatton (London). Same *Arms*. *Crest*—A demi bear ramp. sa.

Hatton (Holderness). Erm. six mascles gu. three, two, and one.

Hatton (co. Northampton). Sa. a cross engr. erm. within a bordure ar. *Crest*—A hind pass. or.

Hatton. Quarterly, 1st, sa. a cross engr. erm.: 2nd, ar.

467

---

five cinquefoils in cross ar.; 3rd, ar. three bendlets sa. on a canton of the last a tower of the first; 4th, ar. on a chief gu. three fleurs-de-lis or.

Hatton (Archdeacon of Ardagh. Fun. Ent. of Ven. EDWARD HATTON, J.P., cos. Monaghan and Fermanagh, d. 1 Oct. 1632). Az. on a chev. betw. three garbs ar. a trefoil slipped of the field betw. two mullets gu.

Hatton (Clonard, co. Wexford; confirmed to VILLIERS LL TOUCHE HATTON, Esq., Lieut. Col. in the Army, and the descendants of his great-grandfather, JOHN HATTON, Esq., of Clonard). Az. on a chev. betw. three garbs or, an annulet gu. *Crest*—A hind statant or, charged with an annulet, as in the arms. *Motto*—Virtus tutissima cassis.

Hatton. Sa. a chev. engr. erm. a bordure ar.

Hatton. Sa. a cross engr. erm.

Hatton. Ar. a bend gu. charged with three bars indented or.

Hatton. Lozengy gu. and erm.

Hatworth. Ar. three hats sa. *Crest*—A hat sa. ornamented with a cinquefoil or.

Hauckford (arms in Exeter College, Oxford, of Sir RICHARD HAUCKFORD, Knt., "of the blood and consanguinity of the Founder." Visit. Oxon. 1574). Ar. two bends nebulée sa.

Haugherne. See O'HAUGHERNE.

Haughton (Haughton, co. Chester). Sa. three bars ar. *Crest*—A bull's head couped ar. charged on the neck with three bars sa.

Haughton (cos. Chester and Lancaster). Barry of six sa. and ar.

Haughton (Beckbury, co. Salop). Ar. a cross sa. in the first and last quarters an owl ppr.

Haughton. Sa. three bars and a canton ar. *Crest*—A pelican's head and neck vulning itself ppr.

Haughton. Ar. three bars sa. on a chief of the second two mullets of the first.

Haughton. Ar. three bars gu. in chief three covered cups of the second.

Haughton. Ar. a cross sa. in the chief dexter quarter an owl gu.

Haule (Wye, co. Kent). Erm. on a pale sa. three martlets or.

Hault (Maidstone, co. Kent; granted 23 Nov. 1584). Or, on a saltire sa. five mullets of the first. *Crest*—An ermine pass. ducally gorged or.

Hault (co. Norfolk). Sa. four lozenges erm. a bordure engr. ar.

Haundsart (Reg. Ulster's Office). Sa. a saltire betw. four annulets ar.

Hausellynn (co. Nottingham; *temp.* Henry I.). Ar. on a bend sa. three roses or.

Hausted (*Baron Hausted ;* summoned to Parliament 1332, extinct). Gu. a chief componée or and az.

Hauterill. Gu. semée of crosses crosslet a lion ramp. ar.

Hautevill (co. Devon). Sa. semée of crosses botonnée a lion ramp. ar.

Hautten (co. Oxford; granted 1566). Or, on a fesse cotised gu. betw. three asses' heads erased sa. a unicorn in full course ar. *Crest*—An ass's head erased betw. two sprigs of thistles ar. stalked and leaved vert.

Havard (Devyncock, co. Brecon). Ar. a bull's head cabossed betw. three mullets gu. *Crest*—A bull's head, as in the arms.

Havard. Or, a bull's head cabossed gu. betw. nine mullets of the second.

Havelock (Sir HENRY HAVELOCK, K.C.B., the famous General in the Indian Mutiny, d. at Dilkooska, near Lucknow, 24 Nov. 1857; his son, Sir HENRY MARSHMAN HAVELOCK, V.C., was created a bart. 22 Jan. 1858). Vert a castle ar. betw. two fleurs-de-lis in chief and a cross crosslet fitchée in base or. *Crest*—A lion ramp. gu. powdered with erm. spots, and charged on the shoulder with a castle ar. sustaining a Danish battle axe ppr. *Motto*—Fideliter.

Havenell. Sa. a cross ar.

Haverfordwest, Town of (co. Pembroke). The arms are generally said to be an old man's head couped at the neck. The seal represents a castle triple-towered on a mount, from the centre a man blowing a horn, on each of the other towers a flag, the tower supported by two heraldic tigers.

Havering (co. Dorset). Ar. a lion ramp. tail queued gu. collared of the first.

Havering (co. Wilts). Ar. semée of crosses crosslet a lion ramp. tail queued gu.

Havering (quartered by POLE, of Colcombe, co. Devon; JOHN POLE, *temp.* Henry VI , m. ELIZABETH, dau. and heir of JOHN HAVERING. Visit. 1620). Ar. a lion ramp. gu.

2 H 2

Havering. Ar. a lion ramp. sa. tail forked. *Crest*—A lion ramp. holding a spear flagged gu.

Havering. Ar. a griffin segreant gu. a bordure az.

Havering. Ar. a lion ramp. double-queued gu. within an orle of crosslets of the last.

Haverington. Sa. a fret of eight ar. a label of three points or.

Havers (Thelton Hall, co. Norfolk; descended from JOHN HAVERS, of Winfarthing, Steward of the HOWARD family, whose son, THOMAS HAVERS, of Winfarthing, purchased Thelton in 1592. The present representative of the family is THOMAS HAVERS, Esq., of Thelton Hall. Arms granted 1668). Or, on a fesse sa. three chessrooks of the field. *Crest* —A griffin sejant ar. beaked and forelegs or, ducally collared and lined gold.

Havers. Same *Arms*. *Crest*—A griffin sejant erm. ducally gorged and chained gu.

Haversage. Paly of six or and gu. a chief of the first.

Haversedge. Paly of six or and gu. a chief of the last.

Haversham. Az. a fesse betw. six crosses pattée ar. *Crest* —On a ducal coronet or, a mullet sa.

Haversham. Az. a fesse betw. six crosses crosslet ar. (another, the crosslets or).

Haversham (quartered by WILLOUGHBY, of Willoughby, co. Notts. Visit. Notts, 1569). Az. a fess betw. six cross crosslets ar.

Havert (Wales). Ar. a bull's head cabossed betw. three mullets gu.

Havilland (de Havilland Manor, in Guernsey, since 1176; originally of the fief of Haverland, in the Coutantin, Normandy ; a branch of this family settled in co. Dorset, *circ.* 1480, of the Isle of Purbeck in trust. co. Challoner's Ord. of Arms, 1583 ; arms with ped. in Visit. Gloucester, 1623, as of Hawkesbury. Visit. co. Somerset, 1672, as of Charlinch, and Langford-Budville. Modern pedigree recorded in the College of Arms, London, 1866). Ar. three towers triple-towered sa. portcullised gu. *Crest*—Out of a crest coronet sa. a tower triple-towered ar. portcullised gu. *Motto*— Dominus fortissima turris.

Haw, or Haugh. Ar. a chev. betw. ten crosses crosslet gu. *Crest*—A poplar-tree growing out of a mount ppr.

Haward (co. Cornwall). Chequy or and az. on a bend gu. three eagles displ. ar.

Haward (Isle of Hartry, co. Kent). Or, a bull's head cabossed betw. three mullets sa. *Crest*—An arm vested sa. turned up or, holding in the hand ppr. a human heart gu.

Haward (confirmed by Camden, Clarenceux, 1616). Ar. two bendlets and a border gu. impaling ar. a greyhound statant sa. collared or. *Crest*—On a stump of a tree couped and eradicated ppr. a falcon alighting also ppr. belled or.

Haward. Quarterly, ar. and sa. a saltire engr. counterchanged.

Haward. Ar. a bull's head gu. betw. three mullets sa.

Haward, or Hawerd. Gu. a lion ramp. ar. crowned or.

Haward. Gu. a bend ar.

Haward. Quarterly, az. and ar. a saltire engr. counterchanged.

Hawarden. Viscount. See MAUDE.

Hawarden (Appleton and Wolston, co. Lancaster). Ar. guttée sa. a fesse nebulée of the second.

Hawarden (Widnes, co. Lancaster, 1665). Quarterly, sa. and ar. a cross flory counterchanged, a bordure erm. *Crest* —Out of a ducal coronet or, a stag's head erm. horned of the first.

Hawberk. Barry nebulée of six or and vert.

Hawberke (co. Leicester). Ar. on a bend sa. three gem-rings conjoined or.

Hawberke. Ar. on a bend sa. nine annulets or, interlaced in threes. *Crest*—A hand holding a dart ppr.

Hawborgh. Gu. gutté d'eau a castle or.

Hawborough. Gu. a cross crosslet or, betw. eight guttées d'eau.

Hawdenby, or Hoodenby. Vert a fesse ar. betw. three covered cups or.

Hawe (Basingham and Helgay, co. Norfolk; granted 15 Nov. 1559). Sa. a fesse humettée erm. betw. three griffins' heads erased of the last. *Crest*—A griffin's head erased erm. collared and lined or.

Hawe, or Hagh. Ar. a chev. gu. betw. ten crosses crosslet of the last.

Hawe. Ar. on a bend az. three lions ramp. or.

Haweis (Treworgy and Kelliow, co. Cornwall; originally from co. Suffolk). Ar. a fesse wavy betw. three lions pass. or, armed and langued gu.

Hawerk. Barry nebuleé of six or and vert.

Hawes (Wimborne, co. Dorset). Sa. three greyhounds'

458

heads erased ar. *Crest*—A goat's head sa. in the mouth a holly branch vert. *Another Crest*—A greyhound's head sa. ducally collared and lined or.

Hawes (Lord Mayor of London, 1574). Az. on a chev. or, three cinquefoils gu. on a canton ar. a lion pass. guard. within a bordure engr. sa.

Hawes (London, Ipswich, and Belstead, co. Suffolk, and Tadworth Court, co. Surrey, 1623). Az. a fesse wavy betw. three lions pass. or. *Crest*—Out of a mural coronet az. a lion's head or.

Hawes (Sir JAMES HAWES, Knt., Lord Mayor of London. Visit. 1568). Az. on a chev. or, three cinquefoils pierced purp. a canton erm. *Crest*—Out of a ducal coronet or, a stag's head ar. attired gold.

Hawes, or Hawys (London and Walsham, co. Suffolk. *temp.* Edward III.). Az. a fesse wavy betw. three lions pass or, armed and langued gu.

Hawes (London). Az. on a chev. or, three cinquefoils gu. a canton erm. *Crest*—Out of a ducal coronet or, a stag's head ppr. holding in the mouth a sprig of laurel vert.

Hawes (London). Az. on a chev. ar. three cinquefoils gu. a canton erm.

Hawes (London). Sa. a chev. betw. three leopards' faces ar.

Hawes, or Hawse (London). Az. on a chev. ar. three cinquefoils purp. a quarter of the second charged with a lion pass. within a bordure engr. gu.

Hawes (Weston and Stoke Albany, co. Northampton, cos. Stafford and Warwick). Sa. a chev. ar. betw. three leopards' faces or.

Hawes. Az. on a chev. or, three cinquefoils gu. a canton ar. charged with a lion pass. of the third betw. two steel gads ppr. *Crest*—A buck's head erased ppr. attired or, in the mouth an oak branch vert fructed gu.

Hawes. Az. on a chev. ar. three cinquefoils purp. on a canton of the last a lion ramp. per pale gu. and sa.

Hawes. Per chev. ar. and gu. three fleurs-de-lis counterchanged.

Hawes. Az. on a chev. or, three cinquefoils purp. on a canton ar. a lion pass. sa.

Hawes. Ar. a chev. betw. ten crosses crosslet gu.

Hawes. Gu. three bulls' heads couped or.

Hawford (co. Cambridge). Az. on a fesse betw. three fleurs-de-lis ar. a greyhound courant sa.

Hawford (co. Leicester). Sa. three fleurs-de-lis in chief and a greyhound pass. in base ar.

Hawkborne. Ar. a cross moline or, betw. four acorns gu. husks and stalks vert, on a chief az. a mitre or, betw. two birds.

Hawke (*Baron Hawke*). Ar. a chev. erminois betw. three pilgrims' staves purp. *Crest*—A hawk rising erm. beaked, belled, and charged on the breast with a fleur-de-lis or. *Supporters*—Dexter, Neptune, his mantle of a sea-green colour edged ar. crowned with an eastern coronet or, his dexter arm erect darting downwards his trident az. headed silver, resting his sinister foot on a dolphin also sa.; sinister, a sea-horse or, sustaining in his fore fins a banner ar. the staff broken ppr. *Motto*—Strike.

Hawke (Treriven and Altenon, co. Cornwall; NICHOLAS HAWKE. Visit. 1620). Bendy of six az. and or, a chief erm.

Hawke. Ar. a chev. erminois betw. three flagstaves ppr. *Crest*—A falcon rising ppr. charged on the breast with a fleur-de-lis or.

Hawke. Per pale az. and gu. a wolf saliant or, vulned in the shoulder of the second.

Hawkeford. Gu. billettée a fesse ar.

Hawkepenny. Chequy ar. and sa. a chief or.

Hawker (co. Essex). Sa. on a trestle a hawk ar. belled or.

Hawker (co. Wilts). Sa. a hawk standing on a perch ar. beaked and legged or. *Crest*—A hawk's head erased or.

Hawker (Long Parish House, co. Hants). Same *Arms* and *Crest*, quartering RYVES and RANESTON. *Motto*—Accipiter prædam non gloriam.

Hawker. Same *Arms*. *Crest*—A dexter hand ppr. holding a hawk's lure or.

Hawker. Az. a cross vairé or and of the first betw. four mullets of the second pierced of the field. *Crest*—On the stump of a tree lying fesseways a hawk ppr.

Hawkeridge (Hawkworthy, co. Devon). Gu. a bend wavy ar. in the sinister chief point a falcon standing on a perch or.

Hawreridge (co. Devon). Gu. a bend wavy sa. an arm issuing from the sinister of the last, on a glove of the first a hawk or.

Hawkes (Manor of Edon, co. Notts. Her. Visit.). Gu. bezantée a lion ramp. ar.

Hawkes (co. Stafford). Az. three bends or, a chief erm. *Crest*—On a chapeau ppr. an owl with wings expanded ar.

Hawkesford. Sa. two bars or, in chief three martlets ar. *Crest*—A griffin pass. sa.

Hawkeston (co. Chester, *temp.* Henry IV.). Erm. a fesse gu. fretty or.

Hawkestone (Hawkestone, co. Salop; GEORGE HAWKE-STONE, Esq., of Hawkstone, was Sheriff, 1416). Erm. a fesse gu. fretty or, a bordure engr. of the last.

Hawkesworth (Hawkesworth, co. York, bart., extinct 1735). Sa. three falcons close ppr.

Hawkesworth, or Hawksworth. Same *Arms.* *Crest*—A sinister hand in fesse issuing from a cloud in the dexter, reaching to a serpent ppr.

Hawkeworth (Burhope Hall, co. Hereford). Or, a cross crosslet gu. *Crest*—A cubit arm erect, vested or, cuffed ar. holding in the hand ppr. a cross crosslet gu.

Hawkewood. Ar. on a chev. sa. three escallops of the first. *Crest*—A hawk's head or.

Hawkewood. Az. a chev. betw. three escallops ar.

Hawkewood. Ar. two bendlets nebulée sa.

Hawkey. Gu. three thistles or. *Crest*—A hand couped holding a curling stone.

Hawkings (co. Salop, and Rushall, co. Stafford). Ar. a hawk ppr. beaked and legged or, standing on a trunk of a tree vert. *Crest*—A lion's paw gu. charged with a chev. or.

Hawkins (Nash Court, co. Kent; the co-heirs of THOMAS HAWKINS, Esq., of Nash Court, d. 1800, were 1st, BRIDGET, *m.* Lord *Teynham;* 2nd, MARY, *m.* Sir EDWARD KNATCH-BULL, Bart.; 3rd, ANNE, *m.* Lieut.-Colonel WOODROFFE, of Poyle Park, co. Surrey; 4th, ELEANOR, *m.* HENRY GOOLD, brother of Sir GEORGE GOOLD, 2nd bart. Colonel WOODROFFE left an only dau. and heiress, MARY THERESA, *m.* FRANCIS HAROLD DUNCOMBE, of H.M. 74th regt.). Ar. on a saltire sa. five fleurs-de-lis or, quartering, a chev. betw. three demi lions ramp. or, for HAMES. *Crest*—On a mount vert a hind lodged or.—"In Edward the Third's reign," says Barnes, "when the French King, John, was a prisoner in England, the King of Navarre declared war against the kingdom of France, and collected men-at-arms from all parts, for he paid them largely out of the treasures he had amassed. The Navarrois took the towns and castles of Creil-upon-Oise, Herielle, and Mauconseil; after the taking of the Castle of Mauconseil, it was garrisoned with three hundred men, under the command of RABIGOIS, of Derry, an Irishman; FRANKLYN and HAWKINS, two squires of England, A.D. 1358." The origin of the arms is derived, most likely, from this expedition, the saltire being used as a scaling ladder, and the fleurs-de-lis being on the standard of France, which was taken from the castle of Mauconseil.

Hawkins (The Gaer, co. Monmouth, and Tredunnock, same co.). Ar. on a saltire sa. five fleurs-de-lis or. *Crest*—On a mount vert a hind lodged or. *Motto*—Toujours pret.

Hawkins (Kelston, co. Somerset, bart.). Ar. on a saltire engr. sa. five fleurs-de-lis or. *Crest*—On a mount vert a hind lodged or. *Motto*—Pro Deo et rege.

Hawkins (Trewithan, co. Cornwall, bart., extinct 1829). Per saltire or and ar. on a saltire sa. five fleurs-de-lis of the first, a bordure gobony or and of the third. *Crest*—A cubit arm erect vested ar. charged with two fleurs-de-lis in pale az. holding in the hand ppr. a baton or, tipped sa.

Hawkins (Pennans, co. Cornwall). Per pale ar. and or, on a saltire **sa.** a lozenge charged with a fleur-de-lis gu. betw. four others or.

Hawkins (Plymouth; borne by Sir JOHN HAWKINS, the naval commander, *temp.* Queen Elizabeth; granted by Harvey, Clarenceux, anno 8 Elizabeth, 1565: Sir JOHN HAWKINS was *b.* in 1520, the son of WILLIAM HAWKINS, Esq., of Plymouth, and grandson of JOHN HAWKINS, Esq., of Tavistock). Sa. on a point wavy a lion pass. or, in chief three bezants: in 1571 an addition was granted by Cook, Clarenceux, viz., on a canton or, an escallop betw. two palmers' staves sa. *Crest* (granted with the first of these coats, in token of a remarkable victory over the Moors)—A demi Moor ppr. bound and captive, with annulets on his arms and ears or.

Hawkins (THOMAS HAWKINS, Esq., of Sharpham Park, co. Somerset, great-great-grandson of the Rev. NATHANIEL HAWKINS, Vicar of Ashill, who is presumed to have been of the family of the great naval commander, Sir JOHN HAWKINS). Same *Arms* and *Crest.*

Hawkins (Norton, co. Devon; descended from the family of Sir JOHN HAWKINS, the navigator). Same *Arms,* &c.

Hawkins (Lewell, co. Dorset). Sa. on the waves of the sea ppr. a lion pass. **or,** in chief three bezants. *Crest*—A demi naked man ppr. wreathed about the temples ar. and az. the hands extended and manacled at each arm, with a rope passing behind his back all also ppr.

Hawkins (co. Devon). Az. a chev. erm. betw. three oak slips or.

Hawkins (co. Kent). Sa. a lion pass. or, in chief three bezants.

Hawkins (co. Gloucester, and Sherington, co. Hereford). Or, on a chev. betw. three cinquefoils az. as many escallops ar. on a chief per pale gu. and sa. a griffin pass. erm. *Crest*—A falcon's head chequy ar. and sa. beaked or, betw. two wings expanded gu.

Hawkins (co. Berks). Or, on a chev. betw. three cinquefoils az. as many escallops ar. on a chief gu. a griffin pass. of the field. *Crest*—A demi eagle ar.

Hawkins. Per pale or and az. a chev. betw. three lions ramp. counterchanged.

Hawkins (Marsham, co. Berks). Or, on a chev. betw. three cinquefoils az. as many escallops ar. on a chief gu. a griffin pass. of the third.

Hawkins (monument of ISAAC HAWKINS and ANN, his wife, *d.* 1727, in church of Burton-upon-Trent). Or, on a chev. gu. betw. three cinquefoils sa. three escallops ar. on a chief of the second a greyhound courant of the last, impaling WATSON, barry of six ar. and gu. three crescents, two and one, erm. on a chief of the second two lances in saltire, the heads broken off or.

Hawkins, Edge (co. Salop). Ar. a hawk ppr. beaked and legged or, standing on a staff couped and raguled vert.

Hawkins, alias Fisher (Hawkesnest, co. Warwick). Gu. a fesse vair betw. two falcons volant in chief and a dolphin embowed in base ar. a bordure engr. of the last. *Crest*—A dexter arm couped at the shoulder fesseways and erect from the elbow, habited vair, in the hand ppr. a falcon perched ar. beaked, legged, and belled or.

Hawkins-Dempster (Dunnichen). See DEMPSTER.

Hawkins (Enniscorthy Castle, co. Wexford; granted to ANTHONY HAWKINS, Esq., of that place). Per chev. ar. and vert a trefoil counterchanged betw. three hinds trippant ppr. a bordure gu. *Crest*—A falcon, wings addorsed gu. charged on the breast with a trefoil slipped or, and standing on a lure az. stringed gold.

Hawkins (Fun. Ent. 1680, Alderman WILLIAM HAWKINS, of Dublin). Per chev. ar. and vert three hinds trippant ppr.

Hawkins (Rathfriland, co. Down, descended from Alderman WILLIAM HAWKINS; of this family were JOHN HAWKINS, Ulster King of Arms, and his sons, JAMES HAWKINS, Bishop of Raphoe, and Sir WILLIAM HAWKINS also Ulster). Same *Arms.* *Crest*—A falcon ppr. rising, belled or, perched on a lure gold. *Motto*—Providence with adventure.

Hawkins (impalement Fun. Ent. Ulster's Office, 1669). Ar. on a saltire sa. five fleurs-de-lis or.

Hawkirke. Barry nebulée of six or and vert.

Hawks. Erm. two bars vert. *Crest*—In the sea a column ppr.

Hawkshaw (Sir JOHN HAWKSHAW, F.R.S., C.E., of Great George Street, Westminster). Az. in chief two hawks rising, belled or, and in base upon a mount a hurst ppr. *Crest*—Issuant from the battlements of a tower sa. a hawk's head or, gorged with a collar gemel also sa. *Motto*—My lure is truth.

Hawkshaw (granted to Rev. WILLIAM HAWKSHAW, Rector of Fermonamorghan, diocese of Derry, grandson of Rev. JOHN HAWKSHAW, of Kilmarron, co. Monaghan). Ar. a chev. gu. betw. three hawks' heads erased ppr. each gorged with a ducal coronet or. *Crest*—A hawk's head erased and gorged, as in the arms. *Motto*—Perseverance.

Hawksworth (Hawksworth). Sa. three falcons close ppr.

Hawksworth (cos. Gloucester and York). Sa. three falcons close ar. beaks and bells or.

Hawkwood. Ar. on a bend sa. three escallops of the field.

Hawkworthy (quartered by ACLAND, of Acland, co. Devon; ROBERT ACLAND, *temp.* Richard II., *m.* CICELY, dau. and co-heir of RICHARD HAWKWORTHY. Visit. 1620). Ar. two bends wavy.

Hawle. Per bend or and vert. *Crest*—Out of a ducal coronet or, a mullet gu. betw. two laurel branches orleways vert.

Hawle. Or, two chevronels gu. on a canton of the second a crescent ar.

Hawles (Isle of Wight). Sa. three goats' heads erased ar.

Hawles (Oregresing, co. Sussex). Sa. three greyhounds' heads erased ar. *Crest*—A greyhound's head sa. ducally gorged, ringed and lined or.

Hawleston. Ar. on a fesse gu. three martlets or.

Hawley (Leybourne Grange, co. Kent, bart.). Vert a saltire engr. ar. *Crest*—A dexter arm in armour ppr. garnished or, holding in the hand a spear in bend sinister, point downwards also ppr.

Hawley (co. Devon). Ar. a barbed arrow in pale, feathered or, betw. three buglehorns sa.

Hawley (*Lord Hawley;* extinct 1772; descended from the HAWLEYS of cos. Somerset and Dorset; created 1646). Vert a saltire engr. ar. *Crest*—An Indian goat's head, holding a three-leaved sprig of holly all ppr. *Motto*—Suivez moi.

Hawley (WILLIAM HENRY TOOVEY HAWLEY, Esq., of West Green House, near Hartford Bridge, co. Hants; descended from ROBERT HAWLEY and SUSAN, Lady Erle, his wife, dau. of WILLIAM FIENES, third *Viscount Saye and Sele;* this ROBERT HAWLEY is supposed to have been a son of FRANCIS, Lord *Hawley,* so created in 1646). Same *Arms.* *Crest*— A thunderbolt ppr.

Hawley (co. Lincoln). Vert a saltire engr. ar. betw. four mullets or.

Hawley (Clarenceux King of Arms, *d.* 22 Aug. 1577). Vert a cross invecked ar.

Hawley. Per bend or and vert. *Crest*—A falcon with wings endorsed.

Hawley. Ar. a saltire engr. sa.

Hawley (Brentford, co. Middlesex). Erm. a cross engr. gu.

Hawley. Or, a cross engr. gu.

Hawley. Vert on a cross engr. ar. five mullets gu.

Hawley (Dartmouth, co. Devon; quartered by COPLESTONE; ELIZABETH, dau. and heir of JOHN HAWLEY, by EMMA, his wife, dau. of Sir ROBERT TREVILYAN, *m.* JOHN COPLESTONE, Esq., of Coplestone. Visit. Devon, 1620). Or, three buglehorns sa. stringed gu. with an arrow in pale of the second through that in base, point downward, barbed and feathered ar. betw. two mullets in fess of the second.

Hawley (Buckland, co. Somerset, bart., extinct 1774). Vert a saltire engr. ar.

Hawley. Az. three goats couchant ar. attired or.

Hawley (Ore, co. Sussex). Gu. three talbots' heads erased ar.

Hawleys. Sa. a fret and canton ar. *Crest*—An arm embowed, throwing a dart ppr.

Hawling. Barry of ten ar. and az. a lion ramp. gu. *Crest*—An arm embowed ar. holding a scymitar, blade of the last, pommelled or, hand ppr.

Hawmes (co. Suffolk). Vert two fishes endorsed in pale ar.

Haworth (Haworth, co. Lancaster). Az. a bend betw. two stags' heads couped or. *Crest*—A stag's head couped gu. attired or, around the neck two twisted cords ar.

Haworth. Same *Arms.* *Crest*—A wolf pass. collared, holding in the dexter paw a trefoil.

Haworth (Hullbank House, and Rowlston Hall, co. York; a branch of the family settled at Barham Wood, co. Herts. The present BENJAMIN B. HAWORTH-BOOTH, Esq., of Hullbank, has taken, by royal licence, his additional surname. See BOOTH). Same *Arms.* *Crest*—A stag's head gu. attired or, gorged with a laurel wreath ar. *Motto*—Quod ero spero.

Haworth (Thurcroft, co. Lancaster). Az. a bend or, cotised ar. betw. three stags' heads couped of the second.

Haworth (Manchester). Az. a bend or betw. three bucks' heads couped ar.

Haworth (Highercroft, co. Lancaster). Az. a bend cotised betw. two stags' heads couped or. Same *Crest* as HAWORTH, of Haworth, twisted cords or.

Haworth (Parkhead and Dunscar, co. Lancaster). Same *Arms* and *Crest,* a mullet for diff.

Hawrobyn. Ar. a fesse nebulée sa.

Haws, or Hawse. Gu. a fret ar. a canton of the second. *Crest*—A sphinx statant, wings expanded.

Haws. Per chev. ar. and gu. three fleurs-de-lis counterchanged.

Hawsted (co. Northampton). Gu. a chief chequy or and az.

Hawtayne (The Ley, co. Oxford. Visit. Oxon, 1574). Or, on a fess cotised gu. betw. three asses' heads erased sa. a unicorn courant ar. *Crest*—An ass's head erased or, betw. two sprigs of thistles ar. sprigged and leaved vert.

Hawte (Hawland, co. Sussex). Sa. three talbots' heads erased ar.

Hawte. Or, a cross engr. ar. *Crest*—A dragon's head and wings per pale or and gu. on the breast a cinquefoil.

Hawte. Gu. an inescutcheon ar. betw. eight cinquefoils in orle or.

Hawte. Ar. on a bend az. three lions ramp. or.

470

Hawten (Leigh or Ley, co. Oxford; JOHN HAWTEN. Visit. 1574). Or, on a fess cotised gu. betw. three asses' heads erased sa. a unicorn courant ar. *Crest*—An ass's head erased or, betw. two sprigs of thistles ar. sprigged and leaved vert.

Hawten (Colthrope, co. Oxford; THOMAS HAWTEN, Visit. 1634, grandson of GERRARD HAWTEN, younger brother of JOHN HAWTEN, Esq., of Leigh or Ley). Same *Arms* and *Crest.*

Hawthorn (Castlewig, co. Wigtown, 1769). Ar. a chev. betw. two cinquefoils in chief gu. and a hawthorn tree vert, flowered ppr. growing out of a mount in base of the third. *Crest*—A hawthorn tree ppr. *Motto*—Stabo.

Hawthorn (Overairley). See HATHORN.

Hawton, or Haughton (London, Her. Off. c. 24). Ar. three bars sa. in chief two mullets pierced of the second, a crescent for diff. *Crest*—A bull's head erased ar. armed sa.

Hawtre (co. Bedford). Per bend az. and ar. a cross moline per bend or and of the first.

Hawtre (co. Bedford). Sa. three lions pass. in bend betw. four cotises ar. crowned or.

Hawtre (co. Bucks). Ar. three lions ramp. in bend betw. four cotises sa.

Hawtre. Ar. on a bend cotised sa. four lions pass. guard. of the first.

Hawtrey (Ascott, co. Middlesex). Ar. three lions pass. in bend sa. betw. two bendlets of the last.

Hawtrey (Bodicot, co. Oxford. Visit. 1636). Ar. three lions pass. guard. in bend betw. four bendlets sa. *Crest*—A lion's head erased or, fretty sa.

Hay (*Earl of Erroll.* "In the reign of Kenneth III.," says Douglas, "about 980, the Danes having invaded Scotland, were encountered by that King near Loncarty, in Perthshire; the Scots at first gave way, and fled through a narrow pass, where they were stopped by a countryman of great strength and courage, and his two sons, with no other weapons than the yokes of their ploughs; upbraiding the fugitives for their cowardice, he succeeded in rallying them; the battle was renewed, and the Danes totally discomfited. It is said that after the victory was obtained, the old man lying on the ground, wounded and fatigued, cried 'Hay, Hay;' which word became the surname of his posterity; the King, as a reward of that signal service, gave him as much land in the Carse of Gowrie as a falcon should fly over before it settled; and a falcon being accordingly let off, flew over an extent of ground six miles in length, afterwards called Errol, and lighted on a stone, still called Falcon-stone; the King also assigned three shields or escutcheons for the arms of the family, to intimate that the father and the two sons had been the three fortunate shields of Scotland." This legend, first told by Hector Boece, was invented to explain the arms, which are at least as old as 1292, and in turn suggested the crest, motto, and supporters). Ar. three escutcheons gu. *Crest*—A falcon rising ppr. *Supporters*—Two men in country habits, each holding an ox-yoke over the shoulder ppr. *Motto*—Serva jugum.

Hay (Fudie, co. Aberdeen). Ar. a chev. sa. betw. three inescutcheons gu.

Hay (Seafield, co. Aberdeen). Ar. a chev. betw. three inescutcheons gu. *Crest*—An increscent ppr. *Motto*—Donec impleat orbem.

Hay (Dalgety and Ardendraght, co. Aberdeen; descended from a second brother of the first *Earl of Erroll;* heiress *m.* CUTHBERT, of Castlehill). Ar. a cinquefoil az. betw. three inescutcheons gu.

Hay (Sir DAVID HAY, physician; descended of Dalgety, 1692). Ar. three inescutcheons gu. within a bordure az. charged with six frases ar. *Crest*—An ox-yoke with a serpent entwined round it all ppr. *Motto*—Fortius dum juncta.

Hay (Letham; from Dalgety, 1693). Ar. three inescutcheons gu. within a bordure indented az. charged with three frases of the field. *Crest*—An ox-yoke entwined with laurel and olive ppr. *Motto*—Fert laurea fides.

Hay (Cardenie; from Dalgety). Ar. a fess nebuly betw. three inescutcheons gu. *Crest*—An ox-yoke erected in pale gu. *Motto*—Hinc honor et opes.

Hay (Park, co. Wigtown, bart., 1663). Ar. three inescutcheons within a bordure gu. *Crest*—A falcon displ. ppr. *Motto*—Serva jugum.

Hay (DALRYMPLE-HAY, of Park Place, bart.). See DALRYMPLE.

Hay (Leys, co. Perth; from a younger son of the first WILLIAM DE HAYA, of Erroll). Erm. three inescutcheons gu. *Crest*—A stag's head caboosed ppr.

Hay (PATERSON-BALFOUR-HAY, of Leys and Randerson, 1872). Quarterly, 1st and 4th, as the last; 2nd, or, on a chev.

sa. betw. two trefoils vert in chief, and a garb in base of the last, banded of the first, an otter's head erased sa., for BALFOUR; 3rd, ar. three pelicans feeding their young ppr. in nests vert, on a chief gu. three crescents of the first, for PATERSON. *Crest*—A Lowland Scots countryman, demi figure vested grey, waistcoat gu. bonnet az. and feather ppr. bearing on his right shoulder an ox-yoke ppr. broken at one extremity. *Motto*—Primus e stirpe.

Hay (Megginch, co. Perth, cadet of Leys). Ar. an acorn ppr. betw. three inescutcheons gu.

Hay (Pitfour, co. Perth, cadet of Megginch). Ar. three inescutcheons gu. within a bordure chequy of the first and last.

Hay (Newhall, as recorded 1773; afterwards became representative of Pitfour). As the last, with a crescent az. in fess point. *Crest*—A naked arm in pale, holding three stalks of wheat ppr. betw. the hand and the wheat ears an ox-yoke in fess gu. *Motto*—Diligentia fit ubertas.

Hay (Seggieden, co. Perth, cadet of Pitfour; as recorded, 1809; the heiress m. 1859, Col. H. M. DRUMMOND, youngest son of Admiral Sir ADAM DRUMMOND, of Megginch). Quarterly, 1st and 4th. ar. a bull's head betw. three inescutcheons gu. a bordure chequy of the second and first; 2nd and 3rd, per fess sa. and ar. on a chaplet four quatrefoils counterchanged, for NAIRNE. *Crest*—A demi countryman, holding over his shoulder an ox-yoke or, the bows gu. *Motto*—Diligentia fit ubertas. *Supporters*—Dexter, a countryman ppr. holding over his shoulder an ox-yoke or, the bows gu.; sinister, a talbot ppr.

Hay (*Earl of Kinnoull*). Quarterly, 1st and 4th grand quarters, counterquartered, 1st and 4th, az. a unicorn saliant ar. armed, maned, and unguled or, a border of the last charged with eight demi thistles vert impaled with as many demi roses gu., for augmentation, 2nd and 3rd, ar. three escutcheons gu., for HAY; 2nd grand quarter, counterquartered, 1st and 4th, or, three bars wavy az. surmounted of a scymitar in pale ar. hilted and pommelled of the field, for DRUMMOND, 2nd and 3rd, or, a lion's head erased within a double tressure flory counterflory gu. a coat of augmentation, likewise for DRUMMOND. *Crest*—An aged Lowland Scots countryman couped at the knees, vested in grey, waistcoat gu. bonnet az. bearing on his shoulder an ox-yoke ppr. *Supporters*—Two young Lowland Scots countrymen habited as the crest, the dexter holding over his shoulder the coulter of a plough, the sinister a paddle, both ppr. *Motto*—Renovate animos.

Hay (E. W. AURIOL HAY, Lyon Clerk, 1824). Quarterly, 1st, az. a unicorn saliant ar. armed, maned, and unguled or, within a bordure of the last charged with eight half thistles vert impaled with as many half roses gu.; 2nd, or, a lion's head erased within a double tressure flory counterflory gu.; 3rd, ar. three inescutcheons gu.; 4th, or, three bars wavy gu. surmounted of a scymitar in pale ar. hilted and pommelled of the field, all within a bordure gu. *Crest and Motto*, as *Earl of Kinnoull*.

Hay (ROBERT WILLIAM HAY, Commissioner for Victualling the Navy, 1824). Quarterly, as the last, within a bordure erm. Same *Crest and Motto*.

Hay (Lochloy, co. Elgin). Ar. three inescutcheons gu. within a bordure of the last. *Crest*—An ox-yoke erected in pale or, with bows gu. *Motto*—Serva jugum.

Hay (Strowie, co. Perth). As the last, the bordure charged with eight crescents ar. for diff. *Crest*—An ox-yoke gu. in pale ensigned with a crescent ar. *Motto*—Cresco sub jugo.

Hay Paris, co. Perth, 1778). Ar. a falcon's head erased betw. three inescutcheons gu. a bordure of the last. *Crest*—A plough ppr. *Motto*—Nil desperandum.

Hay (Woodcockdale, co. Linlithgow, 1672; the family afterwards adopted the name of BRUCE on marrying the heiress of KINNAIRD). Ar. a fess wavy betw. three inescutcheons gu. a bordure of the last. *Crest*—A demi arm ppr. holding an ox-yoke or, with bows gu. *Motto*—Hinc incrementum.

Hay (Carriber, co. Linlithgow, 1720). As the last, the fess charged with an otter's head erased ar. for diff. *Crest*—A dexter arm holding the bow of a plough ppr. *Motto*—Laboranti palma.

Hay (Monkton, 1672; the heiress m. MITCHELSON, of Middleton). Ar. three inescutcheons gu. within a bordure engr. az. powdered with frases of the field.

Hay (Naughton, co. Fife, earliest cadet of Erroll; the property through two female descents came afterwards to HAYS of the Megginch branch). Ar. three inescutcheons gu. within a bordure indented of the last.

Hay (Locherworth, co. Peebles; *Earl and Marquess of Tweeddale*). Quarterly, 1st and 4th, az. three cinquefoils ar., for FRASER; 2nd and 3rd, gu. three bars erm., for GIFFORD.

of Yester; over all upon an escutcheon ar. three escutcheons gu., for the paternal coat of HAY. *Crest*—A goat's head erased ar. armed or. *Supporters*—Two bucks ppr. attired and unguled or, each gorged with a collar az. charged with three cinquefoils ar. *Motto*—Spare nought.

Hay-Newton (Newton, co. Haddington). Quarterly, 1st and 4th, the quartered coat of TWEEDDALE, in the centre a mullet gu. for diff.; 2nd and 3rd, vert a lion ramp. or, on a chief of the last three roses gu., for NEWTON. *Crest*—A demi lion ramp. or, brandishing a scymitar ppr. hilted and pommelled of the first. *Motto*—Pro patria.

Hay (now BAIRD-HAY, of Belton, co. Haddington). Quarterly, 1st and 4th, the quartered TWEEDDALE coat within a bordure eng.; 2nd and 3rd, per pale gu. and or, a boar pass. counterchanged, for BAIRD. Same *Crest and Motto* as *Marquess of Tweeddale*.

Hay (Drummelzier). As *Marquess of Tweeddale*, quartering the arms of SETON, *Viscount Kingston* (q.v.). *Crest and Motto*, as *Marquess of Tweeddale*.

Hay (Linplum, co. Haddington). Quarterly, as *Marquess of Tweeddale*, within a bordure ar. *Crest*—A goat's head erased ar. armed or, and charged with a crescent az. *Mottoes*—Above the crest: Spare nought; below the arms: Malum bono vince.

Hay (Smithfield and Haystoun, co. Peebles, bart. 1683). Quarterly, as *Marquess of Tweeddale*, within a bordure vert charged with unicorns' heads couped alternating with mullets ar. *Crest*—An ox-yoke in bend or, with bows gu. *Motto*—Pro patria. *Supporters*—Dexter, a countryman ppr. holding over his shoulders an ox-yoke or, the bows gu.; sinister, a royal stag ppr.

Hay (Craignethan, co. Peebles, cadet of Haystoun). Quarterly, 1st and 4th, az. three frases ar., for FRASER; 2nd, gu. three bars erm., for GIFFORD; 3rd, vert a unicorn's head erased ar. en surtout ar. three inescutcheons gu, for HAY.

Hay (Monkton, co. Haddington; heiress m. Sir ALEXANDER HAY, of Whitburgh, descended of Lochloy, v. supra). Ar. three inescutcheons gu. within a bordure engr. az. charged with eight frases of the field.

Hay (Edinburgh, 1672). Quarterly, as *Marquess of Tweeddale*, differenced by a mullet charged with a crescent in the centre. *Crest*—A buck's head cabossed ppr. *Motto*—Venter and gain.

Hay (Alderston, co. Haddington, bart. 1703). Quarterly, as *Marquess of Tweeddale*, in the centre a key fessways wards downwards sa. *Crest*—A goat's head erased ar. horned or. *Motto*—Spare nought.

Hay (Rannes, co. Aberdeen, 1764; represented by LEITH-HAY, of Leith Hall, as heir of .line ; GORDON, of Avochie, the heir male). Quarterly, 1st and 4th, ar. three inescut cheons gu.; 2nd and 3rd, az. three cinquefoils ar., for FRASER; in the centre a crescent for diff. *Crest*—A goat pass. ar. armed and unguled or. *Motto*—Spare nought.

Hay (Faichfield and Cocklaw; as recorded for CHARLES HAY, a judge of the Court of Session, under the title of *Lord Newton*, 1806). Quarterly, 1st and 4th, ar. three inescutcheons gu.; 2nd and 3rd, az. a chev. erm. betw. three pheons ar. a bordure indented of the third, for MUDIE; in the centre of the quarters a crescent gu. *Crest*—A goat pass. ar. armed and unguled or. *Motto*—Spare nought.

Hay (Laxfirth, Shetland). Ar. a mullet az. betw. three inescutcheons gu. a bordure of the second. *Crest*—A goat's head ar. horned or, charged on the neck with a mullet az. *Motto*—Malum bono vincitur.

Hay (London, 1672). Ar. three inescutcheons gu. within a bordure counter-compony of the last and first. *Crest*—A dexter hand holding an ox-yoke ppr. with bows gu. *Motto*—Valet et vulnerat.

Hay (Leith, 1685). Ar. three inescutcheons gu. each charged with a garb or, banded of the second. *Crest*—An ox-head couped ppr. *Motto*—Nec abest jugum.

Hay (Königsberg, 1807). Ar. three inescutcheons gu. within a bordure engr. sa. charged with eight annulets or. *Crest*—Two arms from the shoulders embowed vested in russet, grasping an ox-yoke or, the bows gu. *Motto*—Pro patria.

Hay. Gu. on a fesse betw. six martlets ar. two martlets sa. *Crest*—A hand holding an annulet or.

Hay. Ar. a bend sa. an orle of martlets counterchanged.

Hay. Ar. a fesse sa. in chief three martlets gu.

Hay. Ar. three escallops in bend sa. cotised gu.

Hay, or De la Hay. Ar. a pile wavy gu.

Hay (*Earl of Carlisle*; created 1622, extinct 1660). Ar. three escutcheons gu.

Hay (Robertsbridge, co. Sussex, temp. Edward IV., and of Glynbourne, in the same county; the last male heir, THOMAS HAY Esq., Lieut-Colonel of the Sussex Militia, and M.P. for

Lewes, *d. unm.* in 1786; the LANGHAMS, of Cottesbrooke, co. Northampton, now represent the HAY family). Ar. on a fesse gu. betw. six martlets sa. two martlets or.

Hay (Tacumshane and Ballinkeele, co. Wexford, a family settled in that co. for several centuries. Visit. 1618). Ar. three inescutcheons gu. *Crest*—A falcon ar. wings expanded ppr. belled or.

Hay (St. Malo; confirmed by 'Hawkins, Ulster, 1723, to EDWARD HAY, Esq., of St. Malo, fourth in descent from ROBERT HAY, eldest son of MATTHEW HAY, Esq., of Tacumshane). Same *Arms*. *Crest*—A falcon ar. wings expanded ppr. belled or. *Motto*—Serva jugum.

Hay (Castlebarne, co. Longford; Fun. Ent. of WILLIAM HAY, of that place, *d.* March, 1634). Same *Arms*, a mullet for diff.

Haycock. Erminois an elephant statant az. on a chief of the last the sun in splendour betw. two beehives ppr. *Crest*—An heraldic antelope sejant erminois, collared gu. the dexter foot resting on a beehive or.

Haycock. Az. two garbs in chief and a mullet in base or. *Crest*—On a ducal coronet per pale gu. and or, a lion pass. per pale counterchanged.

Hayday (Weston, co. Hereford). Gu. on a bend or, three leopards' faces vert.

Hayday (London). Same *Arms*, bend ar.

Hayden (Sir JOHN HAYDEN, knighted by ROBERT, *Earl of Essex*, Lord Lieutenant of Ireland, 5 Aug. 1599). Barry of twelve ar. and az. on a chief gu. a bar dancettée or.

Haydock (Haydock, co. Lancaster; descended from HUGH DE EYDOCK, mentioned in the "Testa de Nevill." The eventual heiress, JOAN, dau. of GILBERT HAYDOCK, *m.* Sir PETER LEGH, of Lyme, co. Chester). Ar. a cross sa. in the dexter chief quarter a fleur-de-lis of the second.

Haydock, Haidocke, or Heydock (Greywell, co. Hants. Visit. 1612) Same *Arms*. *Crest*—A demi swan with wings expanded ar. ducally gorged, lined, and beaked gu.

Haydock (Banyton, co. Oxford; THOMAS HAYDOCK, living at Visit. 1574). Same *Arms*, quartering ar. a goat's head erased sa. betw. three cocks gu. *Crest*—A swan rising ar. beaked or, ducally gorged and lined gu.

Haydock, or Heydock (cos. Lancaster and Oxford). Ar. three sparrow hawks close gu.

Haydoke (CHRISTOPHER HAYDOKE, Esq., Alderman of Preston in 1562). *Arms* and *Crest*, same as HAYDOCK, co. Lancaster.

Haydon (Bowood or Boughwood, Epford, and Cadhay, co. Devon; ROBERT HAYDON, Esq., of Bowood, tenth in descent from ROBERT HAYDON, of Boughwood, living 19 Edward I., 1290. Visit. Devon, 1620). Ar. three bars gemels az. on a chief gu. a fess dancettée or. *Crest*—A lion ar. seizing on a bull courant sa.

Haydon, or Haidon (JOHN HAIDON, mercer, Sheriff of London, *d.* 1583; descended from Boughwood). Same *Arms* and *Crest*. *Motto*—Ferme en foy.

Haydon (Woodbury, co. Devon, London, and co. Surrey). Same *Arms*.

Haydon (ADAM HAYDON, illegitimate son of ROGER HAYDON, of Nether Stowford, 7 Edward II., who was son of ROBERT HAYDON, of Boughwood, 19 Edward I. Visit. London, 1568). Same *Arms*, a border compony gu. and or.

Haydon (Grove, Watford, and Oxley, co. Herts). Quarterly, ar. and az. a cross engr. counterchanged. *Crest*—A talbot statant az.

Haydon. Same *Arms*, a bordure gobonated or and az.

Haydon (Baconstrope, co. Norfolk). Quarterly, ar. and gu. a cross engr. counterchanged. *Crest*—A talbot ar. spotted sa.

Haydon (co. Worcester). Quarterly, ar. and az. a cross engr. counterchanged, in the first quarter a Cornish chough sa.

Haye (co. Salop). Az. three mullets or, on a chief ar. as many pellets.

Haye (Monkes Hall and Chorlton Hall, co. Lancaster, 1664). Az. a demi man in armour ppr.

Haye, or Hay (Battel, co. Sussex). Ar. on a fesse gu. betw. six martlets sa. two martlets or.

Haye (granted 1628). Erm. on a chief az. two martlets or. *Crest*—A dexter arm embowed, vested gu. turned up and indented ar. holding in the hand ppr. a scythe in bend or, the blade arching to the right.

Haye (Halnaked, co. Sussex, *temp.* Henry I.). Ar. a fesse, and in chief three martlets sa.

Haye. Ar. on a chief sa. a griffin's head erased betw. two mullets pierced or.

Haye, or Hay. Ar. a mullet gu.

Haye. Gu. a lion ramp. or, crowned ar.

Haye. Az. three mullets or (another, ar.).

472

Hayeby. Az. three storks ar. a chief erm. *Crest*—A pheon or.

Haye, De la. Ar. three escallops in bend gu. cotised sa.

Hayse (Westminster, co. Middlesex, bart.). Quarterly, 1st and 4th, ar. a chev. az. betw. three escutcheons gu. each charged with a leopard's face or; 2nd and 3rd, ar. a lion ramp. gu. betw. three pheons az. *Crest*—On a perch ppr. a falcon, wings expanded or, an escutcheon pendent from the beak, as in the arms. *Motto*—Nil desperandum.

Hayes (Windsor, co. Berks, and London; granted 13 May, 1662). Ar. a chev. betw. three tigers' heads sa. erased and langued gu.

Hayes (Wardrobe and Litley, co. Chester; granted 1615). Sa. on a chev. ar. betw. three leopards' faces or, a crescent gu. *Crest*—A demi lion holding a pheon ar. staff or.

Hayes (co. Devon). Az. on a pale or, three bulls' heads of the field.

Hayes (co. Devon). Az. on a pale betw. two endorses or, three bulls' heads couped of the field.

Hayes (Rockingdon, co. Essex). Ar. on a chev. gu. betw. three dragons' heads erased vert as many bezants.

Hayes (co. Essex). Ar. on a chev. gu. betw. three boars' heads erased and erect vert as many bezants.

Hayes (Nowton and Kettleburgh, co. Suffolk; granted 1703) Ar. on a chev. sa. betw. three escutcheons gu. as many leopards' faces of the first. *Crest*—A demi leopard ramp. reguard. collared and chained or, supporting an escutcheon gu.

Hayes (confirmed by Camden, Clarenceux, 1613, to Sir THOMAS HAYES, of London). Quarterly, 1st and 4th, erminois three lions' heads erased sa.; 2nd and 3rd, ar. a fess embattled gu. in chief three martlets sa. *Crest*—A fox pass. erminois.

Hayes (Wardrop, granted by Camden, Clarenceux, 1615). Sa. on a chev. ar. betw. three leopards' faces or, a crescent of the field. *Crest*—A demi lion ramp. or, holding in the paws a flagstaff gold, pennon ar.

Hayes (Hayes, co. Hants). Sa. a chev. ar. betw. three boars' heads couped or.

Hayes (co. Hertford). Erm. three lions' heads erased sa. *Crest*—A leopard's head sa.

Hayes (Great Badgebury, co. Kent; granted 8 May, 1689). Erm. three escutcheons gu. *Crest*—A falcon volant ppr. jessed and belled or, gorged with a ducal coronet per pale of the last and gu.

Hayes (Hadley, co. Middlesex). Az. on a pale or, three bulls' heads couped sa.

Hayes (London, 1613). Erminois three wolves' heads erased sa. *Crest*—A wolf pass. erminois.

Hayes. Az. on a chev. ar. betw. three boars' heads erased ermines as many ewers gu.

Hayes. Gu. a fesse or, betw. two bezants.

Hayes. Ar. a chev. sa. betw. three dragons' heads of the last erased per fesse gu.

Hayes (Drumboe Castle, co. Donegal, bart.). Ar. a chev. betw. three griffins' heads erased sa. *Crest*—A griffin's head erased. *Motto*—Dieu me conduise.

Hayes (granted to HENRY HAYES, Esq., of Stratford, Rathgar, co. Dublin, son of ANDREW HAYES, Esq., of Dublin). Per pale gu. and sa. on a chev. ar. betw. three leopards' faces or, a pheon of the second. *Crest*—A demi lion ramp. or, holding in his paws a flagstaff, therefrom a pennon gu. and charged on the shoulder with a pheon sa. *Motto*—Renovate animos.

Hayhurst (Parkhead, co. Lancaster; depicted on a window in Whalley Church). Ar. a chev. az. charged with a sun or, betw. three hay-rakes ppr.

Hayle. Ar. eight bars gemelles az. on a canton gu. a lion pass. or.

Hayles. Gu. a fesse or, betw. two chevronels ar. *Crest*—A hand ppr. holding a torteau.

Hayles. Sa. a fesse or, chev. ar. and bordure erm.

Hayles. Sa. a fesse or, betw. two chev. a bordure erm.

Hayles. Ar. a chev. gu. in chief three roses of the second.

Hayley (co. Salop; granted 1701, to WM. HAYLEY, of Cleobury Mortimer). Or, on a cross az. a cinquefoil betw. four mascles of the first. *Crest*—A crescent ar. charged with a cross pattée gu.

Hayley. Or, a fret gu. *Crest*—A demi boy ppr.

Haylis. Or, a chev. sa. on a chief of the second three roses gu.

Haylis. Or, a chev. sa. betw. three roses of the second, a chief of the last.

Haylord, or Haylard. Ar. three bars betw. ten fleurs-de-lis az. three, three, three, and one.

Hayman. Gu. three cocks' heads erased or. *Crest*—A scymitar and caduceus in saltire, ensigned with a round hat.

Hayman (Myrtle Grove and South Abbey, Youghal, co. Cork; a branch of a Somersetshire family, derived from the younger of two brothers, SAMUEL HAYMAN, who went to Ireland in the suite of the *Duke of Ormonde*, Lord Lieutenant 1662, and settled in the town of Youghal, where he purchased, in 1670, part of the estates of Sir Walter Raleigh). Ar. on a chev. engr. az. betw. three martlets sa. as many cinquefoils pierced or. *Crests*—1st: A demi Moor, full-faced, wreathed round the temples, holding in the dexter hand a rose slipped and leaved all ppr.; 2nd: A martlet sa. *Motto*—Cœlum non solum.

Hayne (Hayne, co. Devon; the heiress *m*. HARRIS). Ar. a chev. gu. betw. three martlets sa.

Hayne (granted to JOHN HAYNE, Esq., of Gloucester Square, Hyde Park). Erm. on a fess nebuly gu. three quatrefoils ar. in chief a greyhound courant sa. *Crest*—On a tortoise ppr. an eagle displ. bendy of six sa. and ar. in the beak a rose also ar. slipped ppr. *Motto*—Labore et honore.

Hayne (Dorchester). Quarterly, 1st, or, on a fess gu. three bezants, in chief a greyhound courant ppr.; 2nd, quarterly, 1st and 4th, gu. a crescent or, 2nd and 3rd, erm. a chief dancettée gu. over all on a fesse az. four bezants; 3rd, sa. a chev. or, betw. three leopards' faces ar.; 4th, barry of six sa. and gu. a chief paly of six or and sa. an escutcheon of pretence erm. *Crest*—On a tortoise ar. an eagle displ. or. The crest confirmed to THOMAS HAYNE, of Fryer Waddon, co. Dorset, by William Segar, Garter, 1607.

Hayne (Dartmouth, Honiton, co. Devon; granted 1702). Or, on a fesse invecked az. a rose ar. seeded of the first, barbed vert betw. two. plates, in chief a greyhound courant sa. *Crest* —A tortoise ar. thereon an eagle displ. ppr. beaked and legged gu. having upon each wing a plate, and on the breast a rose of the first.

Hayne (Fryer Waddon, co. Dorset; granted 4 Sept. 1607). Or, on a fesse gu. three plates, in chief a greyhound courant az.

Hayne (Haddon, Jamaica, and Burderop Park, near Marlborough, co. Wilts). Ar. a chev. gu. betw. three martlets sa. *Crest*—An eagle, wings expanded and distended, preying on a tortoise all ppr.

Hayne, or Haynes. Ar. on a fesse nebulée betw. three annulets gu. six bezants.

Haynelles (co. Norfolk). Gu. a chev. or, betw. three fleurs-de-lis ar.

Haynes (Reading, co. Berks). Gu. three crescents paly wavy ar. and az.

Haynes (co. Berks). Ar. on a fesse wavy az. betw. seven bezants three annulets or.

Haynes (Chelsea, co. Middlesex). Erminois on a fesse sa. a greyhound courant ar. on a canton gu. a leopard's face jessant-de-lis or.

Haynes (Hackney, co. Middlesex; confirmed 1578). Ar. three crescents barry wavy az. and gu.

Haynes (co. Salop). Ar. on a fesse gu. betw. three demi greyhounds courant az. as many bezants.

Haynes (Thimbleby Lodge, Northallerton, co. York). Quarterly, 1st and 4th, ar. three crescents paly wavy gu. and az.; 2nd and 3rd, gu. two billets ar. *Crest*—A stork, wings displ. ppr. in the beak a serpent of the last.

Haynes, or Heynes (co. Surrey). Chequy or and gu. a bend az. a griffin's head erased betw. two falcons ar. a canton erm.

Haynes. Or, on a fesse gu. three bezants, in chief a greyhound courant sa. collared of the second. *Crest*—An eagle displ. az. semée of estoiles or.

Haynes, or Hayne. Ar. a fesse nebulée az. betw. three annulets gu. (another, of the second).

Hayns. Ar. on a fesse az. betw. three crescents of the last, as many fleurs-de-lis of the first. *Crest*—Three Moors' heads conjoined in one neck, facing the dexter sinister and upwards.

Hays (Dallamore, co. Devon). Gu. a fesse or, betw. three bezants, quartering TREVY and HELE. *Crest*—A swan's head ppr.

Hays (co. Dorset). Or, a sun gu.

Hays, or Hayes (London). Ar. on a pale betw. two palets engr. sa. three bulls' heads couped or.

Hays. Erm. a fesse engr. or, betw. three lions ramp. ppr. *Crest*—A hawk, wings displ. erminois.

Hays. Ar. a lion ramp. betw. three mullets sa. *Crest*—A monkey pass. ppr. collared round the loins and chained or.

Hays. Erm. on a chev. az. three roses or. *Crest*—An arm embowed in armour or, wielding a scymitar ppr.

Haystacke. Or, a chev. gu. pierced by a bend erm.

Haytefeld. Erm. a chev. engr. betw. three cinquefoils sa.

Hayter (Salisbury). Az. three bulls' heads couped or. *Crest*

—A bull's head couped or, pierced through the neck with a broken spear ar.

Hayter (East Creech, co. Dorset). Az. an escallop betw. two annulets ar. and as many flaunches guttée de poix.

Hayter (Southill Park, Berks, bart.). Az. an escallop betw. three bulls' heads couped or. *Crest*—A bull's head erased sa. semée of escallops or, and pierced through the neck with a broken spear in bend sinister, point upwards, ppr. *Motto*—Via vi.

Haytfield. Erm. on a chev. sa. (another, engr.) three cinquefoils (another, trefoils) ar.

Hayton (WILLIAM CHUTE HAYTON, Esq., of Moreton Court, near Hereford). Sa. a cross engr. or. *Crest*—A cock gu. combed, wattled, and legged or, holding in the beak a heart's-ease slipped ppr.

Hayton (co. Essex). Vert a bend ar.

Hayton. Ar. on a bend sa. three bucks' heads cabossed of the field. *Crest*—A buck's head, as in the arms.

Hayton. Ar. three church bells sa. *Crest*—A hand holding a sickle ppr.

Hayton. Ar. three bulls pass. sa.

Hayverd, or Haverd. Or, a fesse sa. in chief a cross crosslet gu.

Hayvills. Gu. a chev. or, betw. three fleurs-de-lis ar.

Hayward (Quedgeley House, co. Gloucester). Ar. on a bend sa. three fleurs-de-lis or, on a chief of the second a lion pass. of the third. *Crest*—Out of a mural crown or, a demi lion ramp. sa. holding in the dexter paw a fleur-de-lis or.

Hayward (Sir JOHN HAYWARD, the historian, *temp.* Elizabeth). Ar. guttée de sang a fesse nebulée gu.

Hayward (Dewes Grove, Sandhurst, co. Gloucester; granted 1750). Ar. on a bend betw. two roses gu. barbed and seeded ppr. another rose betw. as many fleurs-de-lis or, on a chief of the second a lion pass. of the fourth. *Crest*—A mural crown or, thereon a demi lion ramp. sa. charged on the shoulder with a rose, holding in the dexter paw a rose of the second, barbed and seeded ppr.

Hayward (co. Hereford). Or, three lions ramp. gu. over all a bendlet sa.

Hayward (Acton Round, co. Salop; granted 15 Feb. 1560). Or, a bull's head betw. three mullets gu. on a chief sa. a lion pass. erm. betw. two crosses crosslet fitchée of the field. *Crest*—Two crosses crosslet fitchée or, saltireways, enfiled with a bull's head cabossed sa.

Hayward, Haward, or Heyward (Brocton, co. Salop). Gu. a lion ramp. ar. ducally crowned or.

Hayward, or Heyward (of the North). Same *Arms*. *Crest*—A unicorn courant ppr.

Hayward (Tandridge Hall, co. Surrey). Sa. two bars ar. in chief a talbot pass. of the second. *Crest*—A talbot's head ar. collared sa. a ring of the first to the front of the collar.

Hayward. Ar. a bull's head gu. betw. three mullets sa.

Haywell (Fellwell, co. Norfolk). Gu. a chev. or, betw. three fleurs-de-lis ar.

Haywood (co. Stafford). Ar. on a bend cotised gu. three plates.

Haywood (co. Stafford). Ar. a firepan sa. inflamed ppr. a crescent for diff.

Haywood, or Heywood. Ar. three torteaux in bend betw. two cotises gu. a bordure of the second. *Crest*—On the stump of a tree a falcon rising ppr.

Haywood (Sillins, co. Worcester; EDWARD WALDRON HAYWOOD, Esq., of Sillins, High Sheriff co. Worcester, 1875). Same *Arms* and *Crest*.

Haywood. Ar. on a fesse engr. gu. betw. three martlets sa. collared or, as many cinquefoils erm.

Haywood. Ar. two bends gu. a bordure of the last. *Crest* —A tiger's head ar. armed and maned or, pierced through the neck with a broken spear sa. headed gold, vulned gu.

Haywood. Barry of six ar. and sa. three cotton hanks or.

Haywood. Ar. on a bend engr. gu. three plates, a bordure of the second.

Hazard. Az. two bars ar. on a chief or, three escallops gu. *Crest*—An escallop gu.

Hazard. Az. a garb or. *Crest*—On the top of an anchor in the sea, a dove holding in the beak an olive branch all ppr.

Hazlerigg (Nosely Hall, co. Leicester, bart.). Ar. a chev. betw. three hazel leaves vert. *Crest*—On a chapeau gu. turned up erm. a Scot's head ppr. *Motto*—Pro aris et focis.

Hazlewood (Belton, co. Rutland). Ar. on a saltire az. betw. three owls sa. as many lozenges ar. each charged with an erm. spot, on a chief az. three branches of hazel or. *Crest*—A squirrel sejant az. bezantée, cracking a nut.

Heacock (Newington, co. Middlesex; granted 1746). Erminois an elephant az. on a chief of the second the sun in splendour betw. two beehives or. *Crest*—A hind sejant reguard. erminois, collared gu. reposing the dexter foot on a beehive or.

Head (Hermitage, co. Kent, bart.). Ar. a chev. ermines betw. three unicorns' heads couped sa. *Crest*—A unicorn's head couped ermines. *Motto*—Study quiet.

Head (bart.; MOSES MENDEZ, of London, m. ANN GABRIELLE, dau. of Sir FRANCIS HEAD, fourth bart. of Hermitage; his second son was brother of Sir FRANCIS HEAD, Governor of Canada, who assumed the name and arms of HEAD, and was created a bart. 1837). Same *Arms, Crest,* and *Motto.*

Head (Seaton, co. Devon). Sa. a chev. betw. three unicorns' heads erased ar. *Crest*—A unicorn's head erased ar.

Head (co. Berks, and London). Same *Arms* and *Crest.*

Headfort, Marquess of. See TAYLOR.

Headlam (Kexby, co. York, 1665). Gu. a chev. or, betw. three lambs' heads erased ar. *Crest*—A demi griffin segreant holding a spear all ar.

Headley, Baron. See WINN.

Headworth. Ar. two bars gu. on a canton of the second a cross moline or.

Heald. Ar. on a chev. betw. three bombs sa. fired ppr. as many bezants, a chief of the second. *Crest*—A sword and key in saltire ppr.

Heald (JAMES HEALD, Esq., of Par's Wood, Didsbury, co. Lancaster). Quarterly, gu. and az. in the 1st and 4th quarters an eagle, wings border or, in the 2nd and 3rd, a fret of the last, over all a fesse ar. thereon, betw. two crosses pattée a rose of the first, barbed and seeded ppr. *Crest*—On a mount vert a bundle of arrows fesseways, the points towards the dexter ppr. bound gu. thereon an eagle, wings elevated erminois, in the beak a sprig of oak also ppr. the dexter claw resting on a cross pattée, as in the arms. *Motto*—Mea gloria crux.

Heale (Highfield, co. Herts; descended from WILLIAM HELE, Esq., of South Hele, co. Devon, *temp.* Henry V.). Same *Arms,* &c., as HELE, of South Hele.

Healing. Ar. on a chev. betw. two couple closes sa. three escallops or.

Healinge. Or, on a chief az. two mullets ar.

Healy, or Healey. Az. three boars' heads couped in pale ar. *Crest*—On a chapeau gu. turned up erm. a lion statant guard. ppr. ducally gorged or.

Heane (Ruardeane, co. Gloucester; arms from a brass plate taken out of the church of the monastery of Abergavenny, in memory of Sir JOHN ATTE HENE, Knt., of Esme, co. Surrey, *d.* 1432). Per fesse or and ar. a lion ramp. issuant therefrom a demi lion ramp. gu.

Heanton (Old Port, co. Devon; the heiress *m.* SOMASTER). Vert a bend or.

Heaps. Ar. a chev. betw. two crescents in chief and a dexter arm embowed couped fesseways, wielding a sword all gu. *Crest*—A cross crosslet fitchée betw. two branches of palm in orle ppr.

Heapy. Ar. three peahens close ppr. *Crest*—A cubit arm erect vested, holding in the hand a lamb ppr.

Heard (co. Somerset; Sir ISAAC HEARD, Garter King of Arms; granted 1762). Ar. a Neptune crowned with an Eastern crown of gold, his trident sa. headed or, issuing from a stormy ocean, the sinister hand grasping the head of a ship's mast appearing above the waves, as part of the wreck all ppr. on a chief az. the Arctic polar star of the first betw. two water bougets of the second. *Crest*—A swan, wings elevated ar. beaked and membered sa. charged on the breast with a rose gu. barbed and seeded ppr. ducally crowned, collared, and chained or.

Heard (Manchester, 1868). Ar. three hearts in chief gu. in base a demi otter issuing out of water all ppr. *Crest*—A swan with wings expanded ppr. *Motto*—Recte et sapienter.

Hearing (Eye, co. Suffolk). Or, on a pale betw. two palets gu. three eagles displ. of the first. *Crest*—A griffin segreant, wings expanded ar. ducally gorged.

Hearle. Ar. a pale surmounted by a maunch gu. *Crest*— A hand holding a crosier in bend sinister.

Hearne (Sir WILLIAM HEARNE, Knt., of Maidenhead, co. Berks, Sheriff of London, 1797; descended from Alderman RICHARD HERNE, Sheriff of London, 1618). Sa. a chev. erm. betw. three herons ar. *Crest*—A heron's head ducally gorged all ppr. *Motto*—Leges, juraque servat.

Hearne, or Hearn. Per fesse ar. and az. three chaplets counterchanged. *Crest*—On a mount vert a horse at full speed, saddled and bridled ppr.

Hearon (W. H. HEARON, Lord Mayor of York in 1827). *Arms,* &c., same as HERON, of Shacklewell, co. Middlesex.

Hearon (Sir NICHOLAS HEARON, knighted at Drogheda by Sir HENRY SYDNEY, Lord Deputy, 1566). Gu. a chev. erm. betw. three herons ar. beaked and legged or.

Heart. Gu. on a chief ar. three human hearts ppr. *Crest*—

474

Out of a ducal coronet or, a demi lion ar. holding in the dexter paw a heart gu.

Heartston. Gu. a chev. ar. guttée de poix betw. three leopards' faces of the second.

Heatcock, alias Arras (co. Bucks). Ar. on a cross sa. five fleurs-de-lis ar.

Heath (Little Eden, co. Durham, Twickenham, co. Middlesex, and Lynn, co. Norfolk. Visit. Lond. 1568). Per chev. or and sa. in chief two mullets of the second, in base a heathcock of the first, combed and wattled gu. *Crest*—A cock's head erased or, combed and wattled gu.

Heath (Mile End, co. Middlesex; granted 21 June, 1707). Per chev. embattled sa. and ar. in chief two mullets of six points or, pierced gu. and in base a heathcock of the first, combed and wattled ppr.

Heath. Per chev. crenellée sa. and ar. in chief two estoiles of the last, in base a heathcock sa. combed and wattled gu. *Crest*—A cock's head sa. crested and jelloped gu. betw. two branches vert.

Heath (Shelwell, co. Oxford; THOMAS HEATH, Esq., of that place, son of ROBERT HEATH, of the same, and grandson of RICHARD HEATH, of the city of Oxford, by DOROTHY, his wife, dau. and co-heir of Sir JOHN CORNWALL, Knt., of Shelwell. Visit. Oxon, 1574). Erm. a chev. sa. betw. three moorcocks gu., quartering CORNWALL, viz., erm. a lion ramp. gu. a border engr. sa. bezantée. *Crest*—A tower ar. flammant ppr.

Heath (Tidderington, co. Chester; confirmed by Carney, Ulster, 1695, to SAMUEL HEATH, Esq., son of WILLIAM HEATH, Esq., of Land, co. Stafford, descended from Bradstad, co. Kent, by ANNE WORTH, his wife, dau. of PETER WORTH, Esq., of Tidderington, whose male issue having failed on the death of his grandson, JOHN WORTH, in 1695, the estates devolved on the above SAMUEL HEATH). Quarterly, 1st and 4th, gu. a cross engr. ar. betw. twelve billets or, for HEATH; 2nd and 3rd, ar. a cross ragulée couped sa., for WORTH. *Crest*—A heathcock holding in the beak a branch of heath all ppr.

Heath (Kepyer, co. Durham; granted 4 Aug. 1558; the HEATHS, of Kepyer, derived from JOHN HEATH, of London, Warden of the Fleet, *d.* 1591, son of JOHN HEATH, of Twickenham, and grandson of JOHN HEATH, of Heath, co. Middlesex; the eventual heiress of the family, ELIZABETH, only dau. and heir of JOHN HEATH, Esq., of Old Durham, *m.* JOHN TEMPEST, Esq.). Same *Arms.* *Crest*—A heathcock's head erased sa. wattled gu. *Motto*—Espere mieux.

Heath (co. Hertford). Az. a bend per pale gu. and or, a bordure counterchanged.

Heath (Eatonbridge, co. Kent). Ar. a saltire engr. betw. twelve billets gu.

Heath (Brasted, co. Kent, Lyndsfeild and Tanridge, co. Surrey; from the Surrey family derived Sir ROBERT HEATH, Lord Chief Justice of the Common Pleas). Ar. a cross engr. betw. twelve billets gu. *Crest*—A wolf's head erased per pale sa. and or, ducally gorged ar. holding in the mouth a broken spear of the second, headed of the third.

Heath (Pedingham, co. Sussex). Same *Arms,* quartering COMBER.

Heath (NICHOLAS HEATH, Bishop of Rochester, 1540-44; Bishop of Worcester, 1544-55; Archbishop of York, 1555-60; Lord President of the Marches of Wales, 1553-56. Har. MSS. 12,443). There are four coats ascribed to this prelate, viz., 1st, vert a chev. engr. ar. betw. three plates, each charged with a Cornish chough with a bird's claw in the beak sa., for CLIVE; 2nd, per chev. sa. and ar. in chief two mullets and in base a heathcock counterchanged, for BEDFORD; 3rd, ar. three pellets, two and one, the first charged with a cross of the field, for COLE; 4th, az. a chev. engr. or, betw. three plates, each charged with a martlet sa.

Heath (Ford Hall, co. Warwick). Vert on a chief ar. three cinquefoils az.

Heath (co. Stafford). Ar. a chev. engr. sa. betw. three moorcocks of the last.

Heath (co. Suffolk). Ar. three pellets, on each a cross crosslet of the first.

Heath (Fordall, co. Warwick). Vert on a chief or, three mullets sa.

Heath. Vert on a chief ar. three cinquefoils az.

Heath (Fun. Ent. of HEATH, Searcher of the Customs for the Port of Dublin, *d.* 1 Dec. 1619). Gu. on a bend or, cotised ar. three moorcocks ppr. an annulet for diff.

Heathcoat-Amory, Bart. See AMORY.

Heathcote (Chesterfield, co. Derby, *temp.* Edward IV.; descended from GILBERT HEATHCOTE, Alderman of Chester, *d.* 1690; the baronets of Normanton (now *Lords Aveland*) and Hursley derive from this stock). Erm. three pomeis, each charged with a cross or. *Crest*—On a mural crown az. a pomeis as in the arms, betw. two wings displ. erm.

Heathcote (*Baron Aveland*). See WILLOUGHBY.

Heathcote (Normanton, co. Rutland, Stamford, co. Lincoln, and Durdans, Epsom, co. Surrey). Quarterly, 1st and 4th, erm. three pomeis, each charged with a cross or; 2nd and 3rd, az. a saltire engr. erm. *Crest*—On a mural crown az. a pomeis, as in the arms, betw. two wings displ. erm.

Heathcote (Hursley Park, co. Hants, bart.). Erm. three pomeis, each charged with a cross or. *Crest*—On a mural coronet az. a pomeis charged with a cross or, betw. two wings displ. erm.

Heathcote (Brampton and Cutthorp, co. Derby, A.D. 1614; the late CORNELIUS HEATHCOTE, Esq., of Brampton, assumed, on inheriting the estates, the name and arms of RODES, of Barlborough [*see that name*]. Same *Arms* as HEATHCOTE, of Chesterfield.

Heathcote (Connington Castle, co. Huntingdon). Erm. three pomeis, each charged with a cross or. *Crest*—On a mural crown az. a pomeis, as in the arms, betw. two wings displ. erm.

Heathcote (Longton Hall, co. Stafford). Quarterly, 1st and 4th, same *Arms* as the last; 2nd and 3rd, ar. a chev. betw. three horseshoes sa., for EDENSOR. *Crest*, same as HEATHCOTE, of Chesterfield.

Heathcote (Apedale Hall, co. Stafford). Erm. three pomeis, each charged with a cross or, quartering the arms of GRESLEY, Mr. HEATHCOTE being (through his mother, who eventually became co-heiress) a co-representative of the elder branch of the GRESLEYS, of Drakelow. *Crest*—On a mural crown az. a pomeis, as on the arms, betw. two wings displ. erm.

Heathe. Ar. on a cross sa. five crosses crosslet or.

Heather (cos. Derby and Surrey). Paly of six az. and or, on a chief of the second a fesse dancettée gu. *Crest*—A lion's paw. sa. holding up a heart gu.

Heathfield. Az. three garbs ar. *Crest*—An arm embowed, vested vert, and cuffed ar. holding in the hand ppr. a sword of the last ppr.

Heathorn (Charlton Park, co. Gloucester). Az. on a cross wavy ar. betw. four pigeons' heads erased or, five hurts. *Crest*—A mount vert, thereon a hawthorn tree ppr. pendent therefrom by a riband gu. an escutcheon az. charged with a pigeon's head gold.

Heatley (FIRTH-HEATLEY; exemplified to JOHN FIRTH, Esq., of the city of Waterford, on his assuming, by royal licence, 1848, the surname and arms of HEATLEY, in compliance with the will of his maternal uncle, CHARLES HEATLEY, Esq., of Rockview, co. Waterford). Vert on a bend ar. betw. two boars' heads erased or, three mullets of the field. *Crest*—A sword erect entwined by two snakes all ppr.

Heatley. Or, on a bend vert three boars' heads erased sa.

Heaton (Plas Heaton, co. Denbigh). Ar. on a bend engr. sa. three bucks' heads of the field. *Crest*—A buck's head, as in the arms.

Heaton, or Heton (Grovelay Hall, co. Worcester, Winkell, co. Lincoln, and London). Ar. six trefoils slipped vert, two and one, two and one. *Crest*—A pelican or, legged sa. vulning herself ppr.

Heaton (Claremont, Leeds). Ar. two bars sa. betw. a de-crescent and increscent in chief and an increscent in base az.

Heaton. Gu. three nags' heads erased ar. *Crest*—A nag's head erased ar.

Heaton (Mount Heaton, King's co.; confirmed by Hawkins, Ulster, 1715, to FRANCIS HEATON, son of Very Rev. RICHARD HEATON, Dean of Clonfert, and grandson of FRANCIS HEATON, Esq., of Morehouse, co. York). Vert a lion ramp. ar. *Crest*—A lion ducally crowned, plain collared and chained all ppr.

Heaven, or Hevyn (quartered by BLOUNT). Az. three boars' heads couped close or, betw. nine crosses crosslet fitchée ar.

Hebborn. Gu. on a chev. ar. a cinquefoil betw. two lions counter pass. of the first.

Hebborne (Hebborne, co. Northumberland). Ar. three un-covered cups (sometimes described as lamps) sa. in each a flame of fire ppr. The origin of these arms appears to have been this: the summit of Ros Hill, which immediately overlooks the little Peel of Hebborne, was the station of the chief beacon for the East and West Marches. The flaming lamp is, therefore, the blazing crescent of a border beacon.

Hebborne (Hardwick, co. Durham). Same *Arms*, a label of five points gu. quartering gu. a chev. betw. three trefoils slipped ar., for HOTON, of Hardwick.

Hebbs (Corton, co. Dorset). Sa. on a chev. or, betw. three swans close ar. as many lions' heads erased gu. *Crest*—A lion's head erased or, gorged with a chaplet of roses gu.

Hebden, or Hepden (Hebden, Craven, co. York; the co-heirs *in.* Sir PIERS TEMPEST, of Bracewell, Knt., and Sir

THOMAS DYMOK). Erm. five fusils in fesse gu. *Crest*—A triton holding in the dexter hand a trident all ppr.

Hebden (formerly of Easthope Park, and now of Appleton, co. York; an ancient family in the North Riding of that county). Erm. on a chief az. three crescents or. *Crest*—A demi lion ramp. az. supporting betw. the paws a crescent or. *Motto*—Re e merito.

Hebdon (co. Oxford). Erm. on a chief indented az. three crescents or. *Crest*—Out of a ducal coronet or, a leopard's face betw. two wings az.

Heber (Marton, co. York ; confirmed by Dethick and Camden, in 1569, to REGINALD HEBER, Esq., of Marton; the last male heirs of this family were RICHARD HEBER, Esq., of Hodnet and Morton, *d.* 1833, and his brother, REGINALD HEBER, Bishop of Calcutta, *d.* 1826). Per fesse az. and gu. a lion ramp. or, in the dexter chief point a cinquefoil ar. *Crest*—Out of a ducal coronet or, a lady's head and shoulders in profile ppr. crined or. *Motto*—Prest d'accomplir.

Heber-Percy (Hodnet Hall, co. Salop; ALGERNON CHARLES PERCY, Esq., of Hodnet, co. Salop, assumed the additional surname and arms of HEBER, on his marriage with EMILY, dau. and co-heir of REGINALD HEBER, Bishop of Calcutta). Quarterly, 1st and 4th grand quarterings, 1st and 4th, quarterly, 1st and 4th, or, a lion ramp. az., for BRABANT, 2nd and 3rd, gu. three lucies haurient ppr., for LUCY, 2nd and 3rd, az. five fusils in fesse or, for PERCY; 2nd and 3rd grand quarterings, per fesse az. and gu. a lion ramp. or, in the dexter chief point a cinquefoil az. a cross crosslet for diff., for HEBER; an escutcheon of pretence—HEBER, without the diff. *Crests*—1st, PERCY : On a chapeau gu. turned up erm. a lion statant az. tail extended ; 2nd, HEBER : Out of a ducal coronet or, a lady's head and shoulders ppr. in profile crined or. *Motto*—Esperance en Dieu.

Heber. Same *Arms*. *Crest*—A lion's gamb holding a palm branch ppr.

Heberden (St. James's, Westminster; granted 1752). Erminois four lozenges conjoined in fess vert, on a chief az. an annulet betw. two suns or. *Crest*—On a mount vert a tiger sejant reguard. erminois, collared of the first, holding in the dexter paw an escutcheon az. charged with two suns in chief and an annulet in base or.

Heberden (London). Same *Arms*, with five lozenges in fess. *Crest*—A wolf sejant erminois, collared vert, holding in the dexter paw an escutcheon az. charged with two suns in chief ppr. and an annulet in base or.

Hebert. Gu. a cross ar. surmounted by a bend az. *Crest*—A fish naiant ppr.

Heberton. Or, on a fesse gu. betw. three mullets sa. as many trefoils slipped ar.

Heblethwayte (Sedbergh and Malton, co. York ; descended from JAMES HEBLETHWAYTE, of that place, *temp.* Henry VI.). Ar. two palets az. on a canton or, a mullet pierced sa. *Crest*—Out of a ducal coronet or, a demi wolf ramp. ermines.

Heblethwayte (co. Norfolk). Ar. two palets vert, on a canton or, a mullet gu.

Heborne (co. Chester). Gu. on a chev. ar. a cinquefoil betw. two lions pass. counter-pass. of the first. *Crest*—A round buckle or, the point of the tongue in chief.

Hebrew School (Cambridge). Ar. the Hebrew letter ⌐ sa. on a chief gu. a lion pass. guard. or, charged on the side with the Hebrew letter, as in the arms, of the second.

Hecnedon. Or, a fesse dancettée betw. nine mullets, four, three, and two, gu.

Hechins (Hole, co. Cornwall). Ar. a cross patonce, quarterly gu. and az. betw. four lions' heads erased sa. *Crest*—A lion's head or, issuing from the centre of a rose gu. barbed vert.

Hector. Ar. three bends gu. on the centre the sun or. *Crest*—Out of a mural coronet ar. masoned sa. a demi lion az. holding a palm branch vert.

Hector. Ar. three bends gu. an estoile az.

Hedd (MOLWYNOG, Lord of Uwch Aled, Founder of the IX. Noble Tribe of North Wales and Powys; descendants, LLOYDS, of Havodunos, co. Denbigh; LLOYD, of Llwyn y Maen, co. Salop ; IOLO GOCH, the celebrated bard of Owen Glen-dower). Sa. a hart pass. ar. attired or.

Hedd (HENRY HEDD, Sheriff of London ; his dau. MARY, m. RICHARD ALLEN, of London, gentleman, *temp.* Henry VII., Visit. London, 1568). Sa. a chev. erm. betw. three unicorns' heads erased ar.

Hedderwick (Pitcullo, Fife, 1672). Gu. a lion pass. guard. chequy ar. and az. betw. three pheons of the second. *Crest*—A dexter arm from the elbow, the hand holding an escroll by one end ppr. *Motto*—Ne timeas recte faciendo.

Hede, or Hedesa (co. Kent, and London). Sa. a chev. erm. betw. three unicorns' heads couped ar. *Crest*—An escallop or, betw. two branches vert.

Hedges (London; granted 25 Nov. 1687). Az. three swans' heads erased ar. *Crest*—A swan's head erased ppr.

Hedges (Alderton, co. Wilts). Same *Arms* and *Crest*.

Hedges (Romney, co. Hants). Sa. on a chief or, three mascles of the first.

Hedges (Finchley, co. Middlesex). Az. three swans' heads erased or.

Hedges-White (*Earl of Bantry*). See WHITE.

Hedingham. Erm. a bend engr. gu. guttée d'eau, on a chief az. a buck's head couped or.

Hedingham-Nunnery (co. Essex). Ar. a billet in pale az. surmounted of another in fesse gu.

Hedisham. Ar. a bend engr. betw. two crescents sa.

Hedlam (Stainton, co. Durham). Gu. a chev. or, betw. three lambs' heads couped az.

Hedley, or Headley (co. Huntingdon). Gu. on a chev. betw. three falcons ar. membered and belled or, a cross crosslet fitchée sa. *Crest*—A martlet or.

Hedley (Newcastle-on-Tyne). Gu. a chev. betw. three falcons ar. beaked and legged or. *Crest*—An arm embowed habited, holding in the hand a spear.

Hedley (co. Salop). Ar. on a bend az. three leopards' faces or.

Hedney, or Hedeney. Az. an estoile or.

Hedon (Morton, Holderness). Ar. a chev. betw. three mens' heads sidefaced, couped at the shoulders sa.

Hedry. Paly of six az. and or.

Hedworth (Harraton, co. Durham). Ancient arms, on a bend three quatrefoils; since the match with DARCY the family has borne ar. an inescutcheon sa. within an orle of cinquefoils gu. *Crest*—A female's head affrontée couped at the breast ppr. hair flowing or, wreathed about the temples with a garland of cinquefoils gu. pierced gold.

Hedworth (Durham). Ar. three chev. braced in base sa. *Crest*—A lion couchant sa. against an oak ppr.

Hedworth (co. Lincoln). Ar. an inescutcheon and orle of cinquefoils gu.

Heeley, or Heely. Gu. a chev. ar. betw. three lions ramp. or. *Crest*—A dexter hand brandishing a scymitar all ppr.

Heende (Lord Mayor of London, 1391 and 1404). Ar. on a chev. az. three escallops of the field, on a chief of the second a lion pass. of the first.

Heeper, or Heper. Sa. a chev. or, and canton erm. *Crest*—A leopard couchant guard. ppr.

Heesee, Le. Ar. a fess sa. betw. three lions ramp. gu.

Heete (co. Hereford). Per pale gu. and or, a bend and border counterchanged.

Hegens (Scotland). Ar. a saltire betw. a cross-gate in chief and in base, and a crescent in each flank gu.

Hegerty. See O'HEGERTY and O'HAGERTY.

Hegham. Sa. a fesse componée or and az.

Hegliffe. Ar. on a chev. or, a demi lion ramp. gu.

Heglise. Erm. on a chief or, a demi lion ramp. issuant vert.

Heglise (arms in a window in Queen's College, Oxford. Visit. 1574). Erm. on a chief or, a demi lion ramp. vert.

Heiford. Ar. a chev. sa. betw. three bucks trippant gu.

Heigh (Cheshire). Ar. a cross sa. on the dexter chief a fleur-de-lis of the second.

Heigham (Hunston Hall, co. Suffolk, 1577). Sa. a fesse chequy or and az. betw. three nags' heads erased ar. *Crest* A nag's head, as in the arms.

Heigham (co. Bedford). Paly of six ar. and az. on a chief gu. three escallops or. *Crest*—An escallop or, charged with a mullet gu.

Heigham. Az. a cross flory betw. six herrings or.

Heighington (Graystone and Mesbett, co. Durham). Erm. on a chev. betw. three wolves' heads erased az. as many crosses crosslet fitchée or.

Heigine, or Higgins (Craigforth, co. Stirling; the heiress *m.* JOHN BURN-MURDOCK, Esq., of Gartincaber). Az. a saltire betw. a unicorn's head in chief and base ar. armed gu. in the dexter flank a decrescent, in the sinister an increscent of the second. *Crest*—On a rock a dove with an olive branch in the beak all ppr. *Motto*—Firme dum fide.

Heingrave. Ar. a chief indented gu. *Crest*—A dragon's head erased gu. collared or.

Heire. Gu. a chev. lozengy or and az.

Heire. Ar. a fesse vairé gu. and of the first.

Heisham. Ar. a bend engr. betw. two crescents sa. *Crest* —A lion ramp. holding in the dexter paw a battle axe all ppr.

Heiton (co. Lancaster). Ar. on a bend engr. sa. three bulls' heads cabossed of the first. *Crest*—Out of a ducal coronet or, a bull's head armed of the first.

Heken, or Heking. Sa. a griffin segreant ar.

476

Heland (co. York). Gu. a bend betw. six martlets or.

Helbert (granted to JOHN HELBERT HELBERT, Esq., of Gloucester Place, Portman Square). Gu. a lion ramp. or, supporting a battle axe ppr. in chief three roses ar. *Crest*— A mount vert, thereon a stag trippant ppr. in the mouth a rose gu. slipped of the first, the dexter forefoot resting on an escutcheon gu. charged with three arrows, one in pale and two in saltire, the pheons downwards also ppr.

Helborne (co. Durham). Ar. three pots sa. fire issuant ppr. a label of as many points gu. *Crest*—A fiend's head couped ppr. winged or.

Heldersham (co. Suffolk). Gu. a chev. ar. betw. three crosses crosslet or.

Hele (co. Dorset). Gu. a bend fusily erm. *Crest*—On a chapeau gu. turned up erm. an eagle ar.

Hele (Hele, in the hundred of Harwidge, &c., co. Devon; WALTER HELE, of that place. Visit. 1620; descended from Sir ROGER HELE, Knt., of Hele, *temp.* Henry III.). Ar. five fusils in pale gu. the middle one charged with a leopard's face or. *Crest*—On a chapeau gu. turned up erm. an eagle close or.

Hele (Cornwood, co. Devon; THOMAS HELE. Visit. Cornwall, 1620). Same *Arms.*

Hele (Holwell, co. Devon; descended from JOHN HELE, Esq., of Holberton, second son of NICHOLAS HELE, Esq., of Hele; the daus. and co-heirs of the last ROGER HELE, Esq., of Holwell were: JULIANA, *m.* first, to PEREGRINE, third *Duke of Leeds;* secondly, to CHARLES, second *Earl of Portmore;* and CHARITY, wife of the Right Hon. GEORGE TREBY, of Plympton). Same *Arms.*

Hele (Fleet Damarel, co. Devon, bart., extinct 1677; descended from THOMAS HELE, Esq.. of Fleet, High Sheriff of the county in 1601, eldest son of NICHOLAS HELE, Esq., of Hele, by MARGERY, his second wife, dau. of RICHARD DOWNE, Esq. Sir THOMAS HELE, of Fleet, was created a bart. in 1627). Same *Arms.*

Hele (Wembury, co. Devon; derived from Sir JOHN HELE, Knt., Serjeant-at-law, fourth son of NICHOLAS HELE, Esq., of Hele, by MARGERY DOWNE, his second wife; the heiress of the Wembury branch *m.* Sir EDWARD HUNGERFORD, K.B. From this line, maternally, descends Sir WARWICK HELE TONKIN). Same *Arms.*

Hele, or Heale (Bovey Tracey, co. Devon; ELLIS HEALE, of that place, Visit. 1620, grandson of NICHOLAS HELE, Esq., of Hele). Gu. five fusils in bend erm. *Crest*—On a chapeau gu. turned up erm. an eagle, wings expanded or, beaked and legged or.

Helebeke. Gu. six annulets or, three, two, and one, a border engr. ar.

Helers. Quarterly, ar. and az. a bend gu.

Helesby. Or, a saltire sa.

Heley (Heley, co. Lancaster). Gu. four lozenges engr. in bend erm.

Helfordes. Az. a chev. betw. three lozenges ar.

Helias. Ar. three bends gu. in chief a label sa. *Crest*—A leg in armour, couped at the thigh, the knee bent ppr. garnished and spurred or.

Heligan (co. Cornwall). Gu. on a bend or, three bucks' heads of the field.

Heligan. Paly of six or and gu. a chief az.

Helinbridge (co. Gloucester). Chequy ar. and sa. a bend gu.

Helingsale, or Heligsal. Gu. three bars humettée ar.

Helion. Ar. three stags' heads (three quarter) couped at the neck sa.

Helion. Ar. a buck's head sa.

Helion (Asseriston, co. Devon; extinct *temp.* Edward I.). Ar. on a bend sa. three martlets or.

Helisbe (co. Chester). Ar. a saltire sa.

Heliston. Ar. a chev. engr. betw. three leopards' faces gu.

Hell (Hellcourt, co. Kent). Erm. three lozenges gu.

Hellam. Vair a bend gu. *Crest*—On a mural coronet or, an eagle, wings endorsed, in the beak an oak branch acorned all ppr.

Hellard (co. Cornwall, and Mitcham, co. Surrey). Sa. a bend flory ar.

Hellard, alias Highlord (London; granted 26 May, 1630). Same *Arms.*

Hellard, and Helard. Sa. a bend betw. two cotises flory counterflory ar. *Crest*—A demi Hercules ppr.

Hellenes (cos. Hereford and Salop). Sa. on a bend cotised or, three stags' heads cabossed ar.

Heller (Lostwithiel, co. Cornwall). Gu. a chev. vair betw three ducal coronets or. *Crest*—A Cornish chough erm *Another Crest*—An eagle, wings endorsed or, preying on a snake nowed ppr.

Hellerd (Bridlington, co. York; granted 1470). Sa. a bend cotised ar. betw. six fleurs-de-lis of the last.

Hellers. Quarterly ar. and gu. a bend az.

Helles. Sa. a bend and chief ar.

Helles (Helles Court, co. Kent; arms in the Cloisters of Canterbury Cathedral). Erm. three lozenges gu.

Helles, Gilbert de (Helles Court, Sheriff of Kent, 30 Edward III.; Cloisters of Canterbury Cathedral). Sa. a bend ar. This coat was probably derived from ANTINGHAM, of Antingham, co. Norfolk, who bore the same arms.

Helles, or Hilles (co. Kent; quartered by WILDYOS and HORDAY, who m. heiresses. Berry's and Hasted's Kent). Az. a chev. betw. three fleurs-de-lis ar.

Hellias. Ar. three hands gu. in chief a label sa.

Helliar (Exeter). Az. a chev. ar. betw. three mullets or.

Helliard. Or, a chev. betw. three mullets az.

Hellier (Woodhouse, co. Stafford; confirmed 1763 to Sir SAMUEL HELLIER, High Sheriff, co. Stafford, d. s. p. 1784, and bequeathed his estates to Rev. THOMAS SHAW). Az. a chev. ar. guttée de sang betw. three mullets or. Crest—A cock ar. guttée de sang, combed and wattled gu. Motto—Pro republicâ semper.

Hellier (exemplified to Rev. THOMAS SHAW, of Woodhouse, co. Stafford, who assumed the name and arms of HELLIER, by royal licence, 1786, in compliance with the will of Sir SAMUEL HELLIER). Quarterly, 1st and 4th, az. a chev. ar. guttée de sang, betw. three mullets or, for HELLIER; 2nd and 3rd, or, a chev. invected pean betw. three eagles displ. sa., for SHAW. Crests—1st, HELLIER: A cock ar. guttée de sang, combed and wattled gu.; 2nd, SHAW: A hind's head quarterly ar. and or, pierced through the neck with an arrow, headed az. the feather broken and dropping ar.

Hellis. Per pale ar. and gu. a lion pass. or.

Hellis. Sa. a fesse counter-embattled betw. three leopards' faces or.

Hellis, or Hallis. Same Arms, field gu. fesse or, and charges ar.

Hellis. Sa. (another, gu.) a bend and chief ar. Crest—A hand holding an ear of wheat ppr.

Hellis. Sa. a fesse battellée ar. betw. three leopards' faces or.

Hellis. Sa. a fesse crenellée betw. three leopards' faces or.

Hellord, or Highlord (Woodbury, co. Devon). Sa. a bend flory counterflory ar. Crest—An escarbuncle of eight points ar.

Hellyon. Gu. fretty ar. a fesse or.

Helman. Ar. three bendlets az. a bordure gu.

Helme (co. Worcester). Ar. on a bend sa. three pheons of the first. Crest—A pheon az.

Helme (Standish House, near Stroud). Or, on a pile az. betw. two griffins segreant respecting each other gu. an esquire's helmet ppr. garnished or. Crest—On a mount vert a demi dragon az. holding in the dexter claw a cross crosslet fitchée or, and supporting with the sinister an escutcheon gold, charged with an esquire's helmet ppr. Motto—Cassis tutissima virtus.

Helmebridge (co. Gloucester). Chequy sa. and ar. a bend gu.

Helps (the late Sir ARTHUR HELPS, K.C.B., Clerk of the Privy Council, and his sons, Rev. C. L. HELPS, and EDMUND HELPS, Esq.). Per saltire erm. and az. in chief and in base a lion ramp. gu. and in each flank three cross crosslets fitchée or. Crest—An eagle's head erased ppr. in front of two cross crosslets fitchée or, the points meeting in saltire or. Motto—Auxilia auxiliis.

Helsby (Helsby, co. Chester). Or, a saltire sa. quartering 2nd, HATTON; 3rd, CRISPIN; 4th, ACTON; 5th, FRODSHAM; 6th, CHOLMONDELEY; 7th, KINGSLEY; 8th, KINGSLEY; 9th, SYLVESTER; 10th, STOURTON; 11th, STANLEY; 12th, AUDLEY; 13th, BAMVILLE; 14th, SYLVESTER; 15th, STOURTON; 16th, HOOTON; 17th, LEFTWICH; 18th, HAUGHTON; 19th, GROSVENOR; 20th, MOBBERLEY; 21st, DOWNES; 22nd, PULFORD; 23rd, HARINGTON; 24th, FLEMYNG; 25th, CANCEFIELD. Crest—A demi lion ramp. or, holding in his dexter paw a plain cross gu. and in his sinister paw a saltire sa. Motto—En Dieu est mon esperance.

Helsham. Ar. a fesse engr. betw. three leopards' faces gu. Crest—An esquire's helmet ppr.

Helsham (Legatts Rath, co. Kilkenny; confirmed to GUSTAVUS HELSHAM, Esq., of St. Mary's Hall, King's Lynn, co. Norfolk, grandson of JOHN HELSHAM, Esq., of Kilkenny; descended from Capt. ARTHUR HELSHAM, grantee under the Act of Settlement of the castle and lands of Legatts Rath). Ar. on a chev. engr. betw. three leopards gu. a crescent or. Crest—An esquire's helmet ppr. charged with a crescent gu. Motto—Cassis tutissimus virtus.

477

Helstowe. Ar. seven lozenges conjoined sa. three, three, and one, each charged with an erm. spot of the first.

Helton (co. York). Sa. three annulets ar. a chief of the last fretty of the field. Crest—On a chapeau gu. turned up erm. a sinister wing ppr. charged with a chev. of the first.

Helton. Vert a lion ramp. ar.

Helton. Ar. on a bend engr. sa. three bulls' heads cabossed of the first.

Helwell, or Hellwell. Ar. on a chev. sa. three bezants, a bordure engr. gu.

Helwell (quartered by SHERARD, of Stapleford, co. Leicester. Visit. 1619. THOMAS SHERARD, temp. Henry VIII., m. MARGARET, dau. and heir of Sir JOHN HELWELL, Knt.). Ar. on a chev. sa. three bezants, a border engr. gu.

Helwish (Worleby). Or, a fesse az. over all a bend gu.

Hely, or Helly. Ar. on a chev. betw. three leopards' faces gu. guttée d'or, a sun of the last. Crest—An arm in armour holding a broken tilting spear ppr.

Hely-Hutchinson (Earl of Donoughmore). See HUTCHINSON.

Hely. Vert flory ar. a lion ramp. or.

Helyar (Coker Court, co. Somerset, originally from co.Devon). Az. a cross flory ar. betw. four mullets pierced or. Crest—A cock sa. beaked, legged, combed, and wattled gu. standing against a cross flory fitchée or.

Helyard, or Hyldeyard. Az. a chev. ar. betw. three mullets or. Crest—A cock sa. combed and wattled gu.

Helyen, or Helion. Or, a hart's head cabossed sa.

Helyon. Or, a buck's head couped at the neck sa.

Hemans (GEORGE WILLOUGHBY HEMANS, Esq., eldest surviving son of the late Capt. HEMANS, of the 4th Regt. of Infantry, by FELICIA DOROTHEA HEMANS, his wife, the poetess, elder sister of Sir THOMAS HENRY BROWNE, of Bronwylfa, co. Flint. The family of HEMANS was of Danish or German extraction, and became connected by marriage with the WYNNES, of Garthewin, co. Flint, and with a branch of the WILLOUGHBYS, of Parham). Or, fretty az. over all the bust of a man, couped at the shoulders and affrontée ppr. Crest—A lion pass. guard. ppr. Motto—Verité sans peur.

Hemenford, or Hemford (Estocke, co. Somerset). Ar. a chev. betw. three drakes sa. collared gu.

Hemenhall, or Hemnall (co. Norfolk). Or (another, ar.) on a fesse betw. two chev. gu. three escallops ar.

Hemenhall, or Henninghall (THOMAS DE HEMENHALL, or HENNIBALL, Bishop of Norwich, 1336). Or, on a fesse betw. two chev. gu. three escallops ar. Crest—A bear's scalp sa.

Hemerford. Ar. on a fesse gu. three martlets of the field.

Hemery (Jersey). Sa. a crescent betw. five mullets of six points pierced or, two, two, and one. Crest—A stag's head ar. Motto—Flecti non frangi.

Hemgrave. Ar. on a fesse betw. two chev. gu. three escallops ar. Crest—A bear's scalp sa.

Hemgrave. Ar. a chief indented gu.

Heming, or Hemming. Ar. a water bouget sa. Crest—On a chapeau gu. turned up erm. a lion statant guard. az. crowned and gorged with a ducal coronet or.

Heming (Hanbury and Evesham, co. Worcester. Har. MSS. 5814). Barry wavy of six ar. and az. on a chief gu. (another, sa.) three bezants.

Heminge (co. Hertford). Gu. on a fesse betw. three mascles or, as many escallops of the field, on a bordure engr. of the second eight torteaux.

Hemingham (co. Norfolk). Ar. a chief indented gu.

Hemington, or Hemmington. Barry of eight ar. and az. a bend fusily gu.

Hemming (Bentley and Springrove, co. Worcester). Ar. on a chev. engr. az. betw. three lions' heads erased gu. an ostrich, wings endorsed of the first, in the beak a key betw. two pheons or. Crest—An eagle, wings expanded ar. charged on the breast with a pheon sa. and supporting with the dexter claw an escutcheon erm. thereon a pale az. charged with three leopards' faces or.

Hemmingway. Sa. on a fesse wavy betw. three awans close ar. as many mullets gu. Crest—A swan's head and neck couped ppr.

Hemphill (Rathkeany, co. Tipperary). Or, on a fesse gu. betw. two chev. and a star az. for diff. three escallop shells ar. Crest—A greyhound courant ppr. collared gu. Motto—Constanter ac non timide.

Hempnall, or Hennall (temp. Edward II.). Ar. on a fesse betw. two chev. gu. three escallops of the first.

Hemsted, or Hemstead. Gu. a fesse ar. on a chief of the second three mullets of the first. Crest—The top of a halbert issuing from the wreath.

Hemsworth (Hemworth, co. York). Per saltire ar. and or, a leopard's face sa. Crest—A dexter arm embowed in armour, the gauntlet grasping a sword all ppr. transfixing a leopard's face sa.

Hemsworth (Shropham Hall, co. Norfolk; descended from Hemsworth). Same *Arms* and *Crest.* *Motto*—Manus hæc inimica tyrannis.

Hemsworth (Abbeyville, co. Tipperary; granted to THOMAS HEMSWORTH, Esq., and his brother, HENRY HEMSWORTH, of Shropham Hall, co. Norfolk, and the descendants of their grandfather). Same *Arms, Crest,* and *Motto.*

Hemy (Hooton). Ar. on a bend az. three stars or.

Hemyngton, or Henyngton (co. Chester). Barry of six or and az. a bend lozengy gu.

Henbury. Ar. six cinquefoils sa. three, two, and one. *Crest*—A primrose ppr.

Henchman, or Hinchman (co. Northampton). Ar. a chev. betw. three buglehorns sa. stringed gu. on a chief of the second three lions ramp. guard. of the first. *Crest*—A buffalo's head erased gu.

Henckell (GEORGE HENCKELL, Esq., of Welbeck Street, Cavendish Square, London). Ar. three bars enarched in the middle gu. *Crest*—Out of a ducal coronet or, two proboscides of an elephant, contrary, embowed.

Hend, or Hende. Az. a lion pass. betw. three escallops ar.

Hendy, or Hinde (co. Lancaster). Ar. on a chev. az. three escallops of the first, on a chief of the second a lion pass. of the field. *Crest*—A lion's head erased ar.

Henden. Az. a lion pass. betw. three escallops or. *Crest*—A greyhound courant in front of a tree ppr.

Hender (Botreaux Castle and Veriam, co. Cornwall; JOHN HENDER, of the former, d. 1611, leaving four daus. and co-heirs, EDWARD HENDER, of the latter, signed Visit. 1620). Az. a lion ramp. within an orle of escallops or. *Crest*—A sword erect ar. the blade wavy, guttée de sang, with flames of fire ppr. issuing from the sides and top, hilt and pommel or.

Hender (co. Cornwall). Az. three broad arrows gu.

Henderson (Randalls Park, Surrey, 1865). Gu. three piles issuing from the sinister or, a chief engr. erm. *Crest*—A cubit arm erect ppr. holding in the hand a star of eight points wavy, ensigned with a crescent ar. *Motto*—Sola virtus nobilitat.

Henderson (Fordell, co. Fife, bart., 1664; title extinct or dormant; heir of line, G. W. HENDERSON-MERCER, Esq., of Fordell). Gu. three piles issuing out of the sinister side ar. on a chief of the last a crescent az. betw. two erm. spots. (An older blazon is, per pale indented sa. and ar. on a chief of the second a crescent vert betw. two erm. spots.) *Crest*—A cubit arm ppr. the hand holding a star or, ensigned with a crescent az. *Supporters*—Two mertrixes erm. *Motto*—Sola virtus nobilitat.

Henderson (Chesters, co. Haddington). As FORDELL, old blazon, with a rose gu. in fess for diff.

Henderson (St. Laurence, Scotland, 1672). Per pale indented sa. and ar. two attires of a hart counterchanged, on a chief gu. a crescent or, betw. two erm. spots. *Crest*—A wheel. *Motto*—Sic cuncta caduca.

Henderson (Eildon Hall, co. Roxburgh, 1825). Per pale indented or and sa. three roundles in fess counterchanged. *Crest*—A dexter hand ppr. holding a star of six points wavy or, ensigned with a crescent az. *Motto*—Virtus nobilitat.

Henderson (Glasgow, 1872). Ar. three piles issuing from the sinister sa. on a chief wavy az. an anchor betw. two crescents of the first. *Crest*—A lion ramp. supporting in his forepaws a trident ar. *Motto*—Secure amid perils.

Hendis. Ar. a bend cotised gu.

Hendley (Hendley, co. Lancaster). Az. on a mount vert a hind lodged (another, grazing) ar.

Hendley (Ireland, Reg. Ulster's Office). Same *Arms,* a mullet for diff. *Crest*—An heraldic antelope's head erased ppr. horned and collared or.

Hendley. Az. on a mount vert a stag reguard. ar. *Crest*—A column entwined with woodbine ppr.

Hendley (Cuckfield, co. Sussex, and Courseom, co. Kent, bart., extinct in 1675). Paly bendy gu. and az. an orle of eight martlets or. *Crest*—A martlet rising or.

Hendley (Gore Court, co. Kent; descended from JOHN HENDLEY, brother of Sir WALTER HENDLEY, Bart., of Cuckfield). Same *Arms* and *Crest.*

Hendmarsh (co. Kent). Ar. a lion ramp. guard. vert, tail queued, crowned or.

Hendmarsh. Or, a lion ramp. crowned vert. *Crest*—An oak tree ppr. appendent thereon an escutcheon gu.

Hendon (co. Kent). Az. a lion pass. betw. three escallops or.

Hendrick (granted by Hawkins, Ulster, 1703, to JOHN HENDRICK, Sheriff of the City of Dublin, descended from a

478

family of that name in Brabant). Az. three leopards' faces or. *Crest*—Out of a ducal coronet or, a crescent gu.

Hendrie, or Hendry. Bendy of eight erm. and gu. *Crest*—A demi cupid, holding in the dexter hand a torch ppr.

Hendscombe (quartered by PYNE, of Estdown, co. Devon Visit. 1620). Ar. a chev. sa. betw. three birds' legs gu.

Hendy, or Hendey. Ar. a bend vert, cotised gu. *Crest*—The stump of a holly bush shooting forth new leaves ppr.

Hendy. Bendy lozengy az. and gu. an orle of martlets or.

Hene. Per fess or and ar. a fesse sa. in chief a demi lion ramp. issuing gu.

Heneage (Hainton, co. Lincoln. Or, a greyhound courant sa. betw. three leopards' faces az. a bordure engr. gu. *Crest*—A greyhound courant sa.

Heneage (WALKER-HENEAGE, Compton Basset, co. Wilts). Or, a greyhound courant sa. betw. three leopards' faces az. a bordure engr. gu. on a mullet a crescent for diff., quartering, Az. a chev. engr. erm. betw. three plates, each charged with a trefoil slipped ppr., for WALKER. *Crests*—1st, HENEAGE: A greyhound courant sa. differenced as the arms; 2nd, WALKER: A demi heraldic tiger saliant, per pale indented ar. and sa. armed and langued gu. maned and tufted ar.

Hengham. Gu. on a fesse or, three hurts. *Crest*—Among clouds a globe ppr.

Hengott, or Henscott (co. Devon). Ar. on a chev. sa. betw. three ogresses, each charged with a leopard's face or, two pales gold. *Crest*—A savage's head affrontée, couped at the shoulders, vested and ducally crowned.

Hengrave (co. Suffolk). Ar. a chief dancettée gu.

Hengrave, or Hempgrave. Ar. a chief indented gu. *Crest*—Out of a mural coronet a leopard's face ducally gorged.

Hengscot (co. Devon). Erm. on a chev. betw. three leopards' faces az. four plates.

Hengscott. Ar. on a chev. betw. three leopards' faces az. as many bezants, each charged with a pellet. *Crest*—A stag's head erased and attired or, charged on the neck with two nails in saltire sa. betw. four pellets.

Henhull. Quarterly, ar. and sa. a stag's head cabossed or, over all a bendlet gu.

Henhull (Henhull, co. Chester; Har. MSS. 1535). Gu. a fesse per fesse indented az. and ar. betw. three leopards' heads affrontée erased of the last.

Hening (London; descended from co. Worcester). Or, on a chev. sa. betw. three lions' heads erased of the second as many pheons ar. *Crest*—On a chapeau az. turned up erm. a lion sejant of the last.

Heningfield (Essex, temp. Edward I.). Or, a chev. az.

Heningham, or Heveningham (cos. Norfolk, Stafford, and Suffolk). Quarterly, or and gu. on a bordure sa. eight escallops ar. *Crest*—An old man's head in profile ppr. habited round the shoulders gu. on the head a cap or, turned up erm. the cap charged with three guttées de sang (another, the cap az. guttée d'or).

Heningham. Ar. a fesse betw. two chev. sa.

Henkelagh (Reg. Ulster's Office). Per pale dancettée ar. and gu.

Henkeney, or Henkney. Per pale indented or and gu.

Henkley, or Henkely. Per pale indented ar. and gu.

Henley (Henley, co. Somerset, bart., extinct 1740; ROBERT HENLEY, Esq., of Henley, was High Sheriff for the co. 1613, his great grandson was created a bart. 1660). Az. a lion ramp. ar. crowned or, a border of the second semée of torteaux.

Henley (Earl of Northington; created 1764, extinct 1786). Az. a lion ramp. ar. ducally crowned or, a border of the second charged with eight torteaux, quartering Az. three battering rams ppr. armed and garnished ar., for BERTIE.

Henley (Baron Henley). Quarterly, 1st and 4th. gu. on a chev. ar. betw. three garbs or, banded vert, as many escallops sa., for EDEN; 2nd and 3rd, az. a lion ramp. ar. crowned or, a bordure of the second charged with eight torteaux, for HENLEY. *Crest*—A dexter arm in armour couped at the shoulder ppr. and grasping a garb or, banded vert. *Supporters*—Dexter, a lion ar. semée of torteaux, ducally crowned or, having a plain collar of the last, rimmed az. on the collar three escallops sa. and pendent therefrom a shield gold, charged with an eagle displ. with two heads sa.; sinister, a stag ar. attired and hoofed or, semée of torteaux, and collared as the lion. *Motto*—Si sit prudentia.

Henley-Ongley (Baron Ongley). See ONGLEY.

Henley (Northington, co. Hants). Az. a lion ramp. ar.

crowned or, within a bordure of the second charged with eight torteaux. *Crest*—A lion's head erased ar. charged with hurts, ducally crowned or.

Henley (co. Somerset, 1612). Same *Arms* and *Crest* (another, the bordure charged with pellets).

Henley (The Right Hon. JOSEPH WARNER HENLEY, of Waterpery, co. Oxford, M.P. for that shire). Az. a lion ramp. ar. supporting a rudder or, on a chief of the second an anchor sa. betw. two trefoils ppr. *Crest*—An eagle, wings displ. or, holding in the dexter claw an anchor and cable sa. and in the beak a trefoil ppr. *Motto*—Perseverando.

Henley (co. Kent, and Rotherhithe, co. Surrey). Fusily az. and gu. an orle of eight martlets or. Same *Crest* as the last.

Henley (co. Kent). Ar. a saltire pean betw. four ogresses, on a chief az. a hind couchant or.

Henley (co. Salop). Quarterly, 1st and 4th, gu. three pales ar. (another, paly of eight gu. and ar.); 2nd and 3rd, or.

Henly, alias Hendley (Forshorne, co. Kent). Paly bendy az. and gu. an orle of eight martlets or. *Crest*—A martlet with wings endorsed or.

Henlington (co. Gloucester). Ar. a label of five points az.

Henlock, or Herlock. Az. six garbs or, three, two, and one. *Crest*—A demi lion ramp. gu. maned and armed or, holding a mullet az.

Henlyon. Or, three bucks' heads couped sa. attired of the first.

Henn, or Hene (Wingfield, co. Berks, bart., extinct *cir.* 1700; HENRY HENN was so created 1642). Vert a chev. or, in chief three lions ramp. of the second. *Crest*—A demi lion ramp. guard. holding a battle axe ar.

Henn (Paradise, co. Clare; confirmed to THOMAS RICE HENN, Esq.). Gu. a lion ramp. ar. on a canton of the last a wolf pass. sa. langued of the first. *Crest*—On a mount vert a hen pheasant ppr. *Motto*—Gloria Deo.

Henneber. Per chev. az. and or, on a chief engr. of the second an eagle displ. sa.

Henneker, or Henniker (Newton Hall, co. Essex; granted 1765). Or, on a chev. gu. three estoiles ar. in chief two crescents az. in base an escallop of the last. *Crest*—An escallop or, charged with an estoile gu.

Hennessy (Ballymacmoy, co. Cork). Gu. a boar pass. ppr. *Crest*—An arm embowed in armour, holding in the hand a battle axe all ppr. *Motto*—Vi vivo et armis.

Hennessy (Cognac, France; a branch of the Ballymacmoy family). Same *Arms*, *Crest*, and *Motto*.

Hennidge. Or, a greyhound courant sa. betw. three leopards' faces az. a bordure engr. gu. *Crest*—An eagle's head erased ppr. *Motto*—Deo duce.

Henniker-Major (*Baron Henniker*). Quarterly, 1st and 4th, or, a chev. gu. betw. two crescents in chief, and in base an escallop az., for HENNIKER; 2nd and 3rd, az. three columns or pillars of the Corinthian order, on the top of each a ball or, for MAJOR. *Crests*—1st, MAJOR: A dexter arm embowed, habited gu. cuffed ar. charged on the elbow with a plate and holding in the hand ppr. a baton or; 2nd, HENNIKER: An escallop or, charged with an estoile gu. *Supporters*—Dexter, a stag ar. gorged with a chaplet of oak leaves ppr. therefrom pendent a shield gu. charged with an escallop or; sinister, an otter az. ducally gorged or, pendent therefrom a shield of the arms of MAJOR. *Motto*—Deus major columna.

Henniker (Newton Hall, co. Essex, bart.). Same *Arms* and *Crest*. *Motto*—Deus major columna.

Henniker-Wilson. See WILSON.

Henning (Poxwell, co. Dorset; granted 20 May, 9 James I., 1610). Barry wavy of six ar. and az. on a chief gu. three plates. *Crest*—A seahorse ar. enclosing in his paws a plate.

Henning (Wolveton, co. Dorset). Same *Arms*. *Crest*—A seahorse ramp. ar. holding in the paws a plate.

Henning. Gu. on a fesse betw. three mascles or, as many escallops of the field, on a bordure engr. of the second semée of torteaux.

Henningfield (co. Suffolk). Or, a chev. sa.

Henningham. Quarterly, or and gu. a bordure sa. charged with escallops ar.

Henraghty (Ireland). Az. a griffin pass. or. *Crest*—On an esquire's helmet a dolphin naiant.

Henrie, or Henry. Az. a fesse betw. three pelicans ar. vulned ppr. *Crest*—A pelican's head erased vulning itself ppr. *Motto*—Fideliter.

Henry (Kylemore Lodge, Letterfrack, co. Galway, and Strathcden House, Knightsbridge, co. Middlesex; confirmed to MITCHELL HENRY, Esq., now M.P. for Galway, and the descendants of his grandfather). Per pale indented ar. and

479

gu. on the dexter side a rose of the second, a chief az. charged with a lion pass. of the first. *Crest*—Out of a crown ppr. a demi lion ramp. ar. holding betw. the paws a ducal coronet or. *Motto*—Vincit veritas.

Henryllis. Paly of six ar. and az. a fesse gu.

Henscot (co. Devon). Erm. a chev. componee az. and or, betw. three leopards' faces of the second.

Henscot (co. Devon). Ar. on a chev. componée or and az. betw. three leopards' faces of the third as many hurts.

Henscot (Fun. Ent. Ulster's Office). Erm. a chev. paly of six ar. and az. betw. three leopards' faces of the last.

Henscott (quartered by BURNBY, of Bratton, co. Devon; JOHN BURNBY, *temp.* Edward IV., m. WILMOT, dau. and heir of HENSCOTT. Visit. 1620). Erm. on a chev. ar. four pellets betw. three leopards' faces az.

Henscott. Erm. on a chev. betw. three leopards' faces az. four plates.

Henshall. Or, two chev. vert on a canton gu. a lion's head erased ar. *Crest*—Out of a ducal coronet or, a hand vested ar. cuffed gu. holding a sun ppr.

Henshaw (Henshaw, co. Chester; the heiress of the elder branch m. THORNYCROFT). Ar. a chev. sa. betw. three heronshaws or moor hens sa. *Crest*—A falcon belled, wings elevated, preying on a mallard's wing ar. guttée de sang.

Henshaw (Bassets Fee and Billinghurst, co. Sussex; descended from co. Chester). Same *Arms*.

Henshaw (co. Chester; granted 20 Dec. 1565). Quarterly, ar. and az. a cross charged with five crescents all counterchanged, in the dexter chief and sinister base points a fleur-de-lis of the second, in the sinister chief and dexter base a dolphin embowed of the first. *Crest*—A griffin's head couped per pale ar. and az. charged on the neck with three bars counterchanged, in the beak an olive branch vert, fructed or.

Henshaw (Great Marlow, co. Essex, and London). Ar. a chev. erm. betw. three cocks sa. beaked and legged gu. *Crest*—A falcon or, ducally gorged and belled az. preying on a wing gold, guttée de sang.

Henshaw (Gloucester; quartered by STAMFORD, of Rowley, co. Stafford). Gu. on a chev. betw. three lozenges ar. as many bells sa. (MS. Pedigree of Stamford).

Henshaw (GEORGE HENSHAW, 1597; Fun. Ent. of his dau. MARGARET, wife of CHRISTOPHER BISSE, Second Remembrancer in Ireland). Quarterly, 1st and 4th, ar. a chev. gu. betw. three shovellers sa.; 2nd and 3rd, quarterly, or and az. a cross betw. four fleurs-de-lis all counterchanged.

Henshawe. Gu. on a chev. betw. three lozenges ar. as many church bells sa.

Hensley. Gu. a tree growing out of the base or. *Crest*—A beech tree ppr.

Henslow (co. Hants). Ar. on a cross gu. five lions' heads erased or. *Crest*—An eagle with wings expanded, supporting a standard ppr. flag gu.

Henslowe (Visit. Surrey, 1623; borne by PHILIP HENSLOWE, Gentleman Sewer of his Majesty's Chamber). Gu. a lion statant guard. or, a chief az. semée-de-lis of the second.

Henson. Gyronny of twelve ar. and gu.

Henston (co. Lancaster). Ar. a lion ramp. sa.

Hentington. Ar. a file of five lambeaux in chief az.

Hentley. Ar. a chev. betw. three bucks' heads couped sa.

Henville. Sa. a chev. betw. eight crosses crosslet ar. *Crest*—An eagle's head erased betw. two wings or. *Motto*—Virtus vera nobilitas.

Henville (Looke). Same *Arms*, *Crest*, and *Motto*.

Henzell, or Henzey (Hamblecote, co. Stafford; a noble refugee family from Lorraine, which settled in England *temp.* Queen Elizabeth, and for several generations carried on the glass trade in the neighbourhood of Stourbridge, co. Worcester, and at Newcastle-upon-Tyne). Gu. three acorns slipped or, two and one. *Crest*—A "ffire-boulte and ffireball" or. *Motto*—"Seigneur, je te prie garde ma vie." (From an old painting upon vellum of the arms of "Mr. JOSHUA HENZELL, of Hamblecott (Amblecott, near Stourbridge) co. Stafford, gentleman, who was the sonne of ANNANIAS HENZELL, de la maison de Henzell, tout pré la village de Darnell, en la Pie (pays) de Lorraine." The said JOSHUA HENZEY was buried at Oldswinford, April 14, 1660).

Hepborne, or Hebborne (Hardwick, co. Durham). Ar. a lamp sa. fired ppr. a label of three points gu.

Hepborne, alias Richardson (Tottenham High Cross, co. Middlesex, 1608). Gu. on a chev. ar. a cinquefoil betw. two lions counterpass. of the first, in the dexter quarter an annulet or. *Crest*—A round buckle or, the point of the tongue upwards, charged with an annulet gu.

Hepburn (HAILES, *Earl of Bothwell* and *Duke of Orkney*).

Quarterly, 1st. gu. on a chev. ar. a rose betw. two lions countercombatant of the first, for HEPBURN; 2nd, az. a ship or, her sails furled ar. within a double tressure flory counterflory of the second, as *Duke of Orkney;* 3rd, erm. three chevronels gu., for SOULIS; 4th, or, a bend az., for VAUX. *Crest*—A horse furnished and tied to a tree ppr. *Supporters*—Two lions guard. gu. *Motto*—Keep traist.

Hepburn (BUCHAN-HEPBURN, Smeaton, co. Haddington, bart.). Quarterly, 1st and 4th, gu. on a chev. ar. a rose betw. two lions pass. combatant of the field, for HEPBURN; 2nd and 3rd, ar. three lions' heads erased gu., for BUCHAN. *Crests*—1st, HEPBURN: A horse ar. furnished gu. tied to a yew tree ppr.; 2nd: A sunflower in full blow towards the sun in the dexter all ppr. *Supporters*—Dexter, a lion gu.; sinister, a heron with a snake in its beak ppr. *Mottoes*—Keep tryst; and, Non inferiora secutus; below the shield: Domum antiquam redintegrare.

Hepburn-Stuart-Forbes-Trefusis (*Baron Clinton*). See TREFUSIS.

Hepburn (Whitsome, co. Berwick). Gu. on a chev. ar. a rose betw. two lions combatant of the field, in base a buckle or.

Hepburn (Riccarton, co. Kincardine). Gu. on a chev. ar. a rose betw. two lions combatant of the field, in base a buckle ar.

Hepburn (Keith). Same *Arms*, with a crescent ar. in chief. *Crest*—An anchor pendent in pale ppr. *Motto*—Expecto.

Hepburn (Blackcastle, co. Haddington). Gu. on a chev. ar. a rose betw. two lions combatant of the first, in base a buckle in shape of a heart of the second. *Crest*—A horse's head couped ppr. garnished gu. *Motto*—Keep traist.

Hepburn-Belshes (Blackcastle and Invermay, 1804). Quarterly, 1st and 4th, as the last; 2nd, or, three pallets gu. a chief vair, for BELSHES: 3rd, az. a cross pattée betw. three mullets, all within a double tressure flory counterflory gu., for MURRAY. *Crest*—A horse's head couped ar. furnished gu. *Supporters*—On a compartment consisting of the trunk of an oak tree eradicated, with leaves sprouting out ppr. two lions ppr. collared and chained or, each collar charged with three torteaux. *Mottoes*—Above the crest: Keep tryst; below the arms: Reviresco.

Hepburn (Bearford, co. Haddington). Gu. on a chev. ar. a rose betw. two lions counterpass. of the field, in base three cannets of the second.

Hepburn (Clerkington, co. Haddington). Gu. on a chev. ar. a rose betw. two lions counterpass. of the first, all within a bordure erm. *Crest*—A horse furnished and tied to a tree ppr. *Motto*—Keep tryst.

Hepburn (Humbie, co. Haddington). Quarterly, 1st and 4th, gu. on a chev. ar. a rose betw. two lions combatant of the first; 2nd and 3rd, ar. three laurel leaves vert, for FOULIS. *Crest*—An oak tree ppr. and a horse pass. saddled and bridled gu. *Motto*—Keep tryst.

Hepburn (Nunraw, co. Haddington). Gu. on a chev. a rose betw. two lions counterpass. of the first, within a bordure engr. of the second.

Hepburn (Waughton, co. Haddington). Quarterly, 1st and 4th, gu. on a chev. ar. a rose betw. two lions combatant of the first; 2nd and 3rd, an orle gu. in chief ar. three martlets sa., for RUTHERFORD.

Hepburn (Dr. GEORGE HEPBURN, Edinburgh, 1672). Gu. on a chev. ar. a rose betw. two lions counterpass. of the first, in base a starstone ppr. *Crest*—A mort's head overgrown with moss ppr. *Motto*—Virtute et prudentia.

Hepburne-Scott (*Baron Polwarth*). See SCOTT.

Hepden (Burwash, co. Sussex). Erm. five fusils in fesse gu. *Crest*—A lion pass. or, coming out of a mountain cave ppr.

Hepell (co. Northumberland). Erm. an inescutcheon and a bordure engr. gu.

Hepell (co. Northumberland). Erm. a bordure engr. gu.

Hepenstal (DOPPING-HEPENSTAL; exemplified to RALPH ANTHONY DOPPING, Esq., of Derrycassan, co. Longford, on his assuming, by royal licence, 1859, the additional surname and arms of HEPENSTAL). Quarterly, 1st and 4th, per chev. erm. and ar. on a chev. gu. betw. in chief a cross crosslet of the third, and in base an eagle displ. sa. three cinquefoils of the second, for HEPENSTAL; 2nd and 3rd, gu. a chev. erm. in base a plate, a chief chequy az. and az. a bordure engr. or, for DOPPING. *Crests*—1st, HEPENSTAL: A pelican in her piety ppr. on the breast a cross crosslet gu.: 2nd, DOPPING: A talbot's head ar. chained or, and gorged with a collar engr. gu. thereon three bezants. *Motto*—Virescit vulnere virtus.

Heppell (co. Northumberland; borne by WILLIAM HEPPELL, Esq., R.N.). Erm. an orle within a bordure engr. gu. *Crest* —A man-of-war in full sail ppr.

Hepstall. Quarterly, gu. and sa. in the second and third quarters a fleur-de-lis or, over all a bend of the last.

Hepton. Gu. a chev. ar. in chief two leopards' faces of the second.

Hepworth. Erm. three cinquefoils az. *Crest*—Out of a mural coronet a demi lion ramp. holding up a palm branch all ppr.

Hepworth (Pontefract, co. York). Ar. a bend sa. betw. two lions ramp. gu. *Crest*—A wyvern vert issuing out of a ducal coronet or. *Motto*—Loyal à mort.

Herald (co. Hereford). Ar. a fesse gu. betw. three stars of six points sa.

Heralds' Office, or College of Arms. Ar. a cross gu. betw. four doves, the dexter wings expanded and inverted az. *Crest*—On a ducal coronet or, a dove rising az. *Supporters*—Two lions ramp. guard. ar. ducally gorged or. The three principal officers of the College have arms of office, which they bear impaled on the dexter side, viz., GARTER KING OF ARMS, ar. a cross gu. on a ducal coronet encircled with a garter betw. a lion pass. guard. on the dexter, and a fleur-de-lis on the sinister, all or; CLARENCEUX, ar. a cross gu. on a chief of the second a lion. pass. guard. or, crowned of the last; NORROY, ar. a cross gu. on a chief of the second a lion pass. guard. crowned of the first betw. a fleur-de-lis on the dexter, and a key on the sinister, of the last. Each of the above has a coronet which he may bear over his arms.

Herault (Bailly of Jersey, 1611). Ar. on a mound a palm tree vert, a bordure gu.

Herben. Erm. on a fesse gu. three fleurs-de-lis or.

Herberiour. Gu. a fesse betw. three horseshoes or.

Herbert (*Earl of Pembroke and Huntingdon*, and *Baron Herbert* of Herbert, summoned to Parliament as a baron 1481, created *Earl of Pembroke* 1468, title changed to *Huntingdon* by charter, 1472, earldom extinct 1491; *Barony of Herbert* vested in the *Duke of Beaufort;* Lady ELIZABETH HERBERT, only dau. and heir of WILLIAM, second *Earl of Pembroke*, afterwards *Earl of Huntingdon,* m. Sir CHARLES SOMERSET, *Earl of Worcester;* his descendant, the fifth earl, was created *Marquis of Worcester*, and the third marquis was created, 1682, *Duke of Beaufort*). Per pale az. and gu. three lions ramp. ar.

Herbert (Colebrook, co. Monmouth; borne by Sir RICHARD HERBERT, of that place, son of Sir WILLIAM HERBERT AP THOMAS, of Raglan Castle, co. Monmouth, and youngest brother of WILLIAM, first *Earl of Pembroke* of the original creation. Sir RICHARD was ancestor of the HERBERTS, of Colebrook, whose male line terminated at the decease, in 1709, of Sir JAMES HERBERT, whose only dau. and heir, JUDITH, m. Sir THOMAS POWELL, Knt.; the *Lords Herbert*, of Chirbury; of the HERBERTS, *Earls of Powis;* of the HERBERTS, of Tintern; and of the HERBERTS, of the co. Kerry). Per pale az. and gu. three lions ramp. ar. armed and langued or. *Crest*—A bundle of arrows or, headed and feathered ar. six in saltire, one in pale, girt round the middle with a belt gu. buckle and point extended gold.

Herbert (*Lord Herbert*, of Castle Island, and of Chirbury; created 1629, extinct 1691). Per pale az. and gu. three lions ramp. or. *Crest*—A bundle of seven arrows, six in saltire and one in pale or, headed and feathered ar. banded gu. *Supporters*—Dexter, a lion ramp. gu. armed and langued az. bezantée; sinister, a lion az. semée of fleurs-de-lis or, armed and langued gu.

Herbert (Ribbesford, co. Worcester, descended from Sir HENRY HERBERT, brother of EDWARD, *Lord Herbert*, of Chirbury. Her. Visit. 1634). Same *Arms* as HERBERT, *Earl of Pembroke and Huntingdon.* The visitation erroneously adds a border gobony. Through the WALKERS, of Wootton, co. Salop, the representation of this branch of the HERBERTS appears to be vested in the SALWAYS, of Moor Park.

Herbert (*Lord Herbert*, of Chirbury; created 1694, extinct 1738). Per pale az. and gu. three lions ramp. ar. armed and langued or. *Crest*—Seven arrows erect or, headed and feathered ar. banded gu. buckle and studs gold. *Supporters* —Dexter, a lion or, semée of cinquefoils gu.; sinister, a lion az. semée of fleurs-de-lis or. *Motto*—Constantia et fortitudine.

Herbert (*Earl of Torrington;* created 1689, extinct 1716). Same *Arms*, a mullet for diff.

Herbert (*Earl of Powis;* created 1748, extinct 1801). Same *Arms*. *Crest*—A wyvern, wings expanded vert, holding in the mouth a sinister hand couped at the wrist gu. *Supporters*—Dexter, a lion ar. semée of roses, armed and langued gu.; sinister, a lion az. semée of fleurs-de-lis or. *Motto*—Fortitudine et prudentia

Herbert (*Earl of Powis;* EDWARD CLIVE, second *Earl* y

Powis, K.G. assumed, by royal licence, the surname and arms of HERBERT). Per pale az. and gu. three lions ramp. **ar.** *Crest*—A wyvern vert, holding in the mouth a sinister hand couped at the wrist gu. *Supporters*—Dexter, an elephant; sinister, a griffin, wings expanded, both ar. the latter gorged with a ducal coronet gu. and charged with five mullets in saltire sa. *Motto*—Audacter et sincerè.

Herbert (Llanarth, co. Monmouth; derived immediately from HOWELL AP GWILLIM, third son of WILLIAM AP JENKIN, *alias* HERBERT, of Werndu, near Abergavenny, and elder brother of Sir THOMAS AP GWILLIM, Knt., father of the celebrated Sir WILLIAM AP THOMAS, Knt., of Raglan, ancestor of the HERBERTS, of Raglan, represented by the *Duke of Beaufort* as heir general). Per pale az. and gu. three lions ramp. ar. *Crest* (as borne at present)—A blackamoor's head couped sa. wreathed about the temples ar. and gu.; but on the monument of Sir WILLIAM AP THOMAS, of Raglan, co. Monmouth, nephew of HOWELL AP GWILLIM ancestor of the family of Llanarth, the crest appears to be "a Saracen's head affrontée ppr. three annulets suspended from each ear or, turbaned ar. and gu." *Motto*—Asgre lân diogel ei pherchen; literally, A pure conscience is a safeguard to its possessor.

Herbert (Clytha, co. Monmouth). Same *Arms*, &c., as HERBERT, of Llanarth.

Herbert (Muckruss, co. Kerry; descended from Sir WILLIAM HERBERT, son of Sir MATTHEW HERBERT, of Colebrook, and now represented by HENRY ARTHUR HERBERT, Esq., of Muckruss, M.P., heir male of the family of HERBERT, of Raglan Castle). Same *Arms* and *Crest* as HERBERT, of Colebrook.

Herbert (*Earl of Pembroke and Montgomery*). Per pale az. and gu. three lions ramp. ar. *Crest*—A wyvern, wings elevated vert, holding in the mouth a sinister hand couped at the wrist gu. *Supporters* — Dexter, a panther ramp. guard. ar. spotted of various colours, fire issuing out of the mouth and ears, ducally gorged az.; sinister, a lion ar. gorged with a ducal coronet gu. *Motto*—Ung je serviray.

Herbert (*Marquis of Powis;* created 1687, extinct 1748). Same *Arms*, *Crest*, *Supporters*, and *Motto* as the preceding, with a crescent for diff.

Herbert (*Earl of Carnarvon*). Per pale az. and gu. three lions ramp. ar. *Crest*—A wyvern, wings elevated vert, holding in the mouth a sinister hand couped at the wrist gu. *Supporters*—Dexter, a panther guard. ar. semée of torteaux and hurts, flames issuant from the mouth and ears ppr.; sinister, a lion ar., each ducally gorged per pale az. and gu. and chained or, and charged on the shoulder with an erm. spot sa. *Motto*—Ung je serviral.

Herbert (Durrow, in King's Co.; Sir GEORGE HERBERT, created a bart. 1630, extinct 1712; Fun. Ent. of Sir EDWARD HERBERT, Knt., of Durrow, *d.* 3 Oct. 1629; descended from the *Earls of Pembroke*). Per pale az. and gu. three lions ramp. ar. a border gobony of the last and sa. and a cinquefoil in chief pierced of the second.

Herbert (Troy, in Wales, and Rathkeale, co. Limerick). Per pale az. and gu. three lions ramp. ar. a border gobony or and of the second, in every alternate compartment of the bordure two bezants. *Crest*—Same as that of the *Earl of Pembroke and Montgomery*.

Herbert (Conington, co. Hunts). Per pale az. and gu. three lions ramp. ar. a bordure gobony of the second and sa. in every second division of the bordure a bezant.

Herbert (KENNEY-HERBERT; exemplified to JOHN KENNEY, Esq., of Lockarrig, co. Cork, on his taking, by royal licence, 1842, the additional surname and arms of HERBERT, in compliance with the desire of JOHN HERBERT, Esq., of Castle Island, co. Kerry). Quarterly, 1st and 4th, per pale ar. and sa. three lions ramp. two and one, counterchanged, armed and langued gu., for HERBERT; 2nd and 3rd, per pale or and az. a fleur-de-lis betw. three crescents, two and one, counterchanged, for KENNEY. *Crests*—1st: A bundle of twelve arrows in saltire or, headed and feathered ar. belted gu. and buckled gold, for HERBERT; 2nd: A dexter cubit arm erect, vested gu. cuffed ar. the hand grasping a paper scroll ppr., for KENNEY. *Motto*—Ung je serviral.

Herbert. Ar. three pales gu. on a chief of the first as many lapwings' heads erased az.

Herbert. Ar. a cinquefoil az. on a chief gu. a lion pass. or.

Herbert. Or, three chevronels gu. a chief vair.

Herbert (Middleton Qhernhow, co. York, 1665). Per pale az. and gu. three lions ramp. ar. a bordure compony gu. and or.

Herbertstone (Brachnie, Scotland, 1672). Ar. on a bend betw. three goats' heads erased az. a crescent betw. two cinquefoils of the field. *Motto*—Deus spes mea.

Herbottyll. Ar. three bears sa. muzzled or.

481

Herbright. Gu. three leopards' faces ar. *Crest* On a tower ppr. a flag flotant to the sinister gu. staff sa.

Herbright (Reg. Ulster's Office). Gu. three leopards' heads erased reguard. ar.

Herbright. Ar. three cocks in bend betw. two cotises sa.

Hercold. Vert a fesse flory counterflory or.

Hercy (Grove, co. Nottingham). Gu. a chief ar. quartering, 1st, erm. a chief az., for ARCHES; 2nd, ar. on a saltire engr. sa. nine annulets or, for LEKE; 3rd, sa. a castle or, for SOMERS; 4th, ar. a chev. betw. three lozenges sa., for STAVELEY; 5th, ar. semée of crosses crosslet fitchée three fleurs-de-lis gu., for TALBOT; 6th, erm. two bars gu. in chief a demi lion of the second. *Crest*—Out of a ducal coronet or, a man's head ppr. wreathed about the temples.

Hercy (Cruchfield, co. Berks). Same *Arms*, *Crest*, &c.

Hercy (Oxford; JOHN HERCY, aged 30, 1634, sixth in descent from Sir HUMPHREY HERCY, Knt., of Grove, co. Notts. Visit. 1636). Gu. a chief ar. *Crest*—Out of a ducal coronet or, a Saracen's head couped ppr. encircled with a wreath ar. hair sa.

Hercy. Or, three hedgehogs pass. in pale gu. (another, sa.).

Hercy. Erm. on a chev. engr. sa. three cinquefoils or.

Hercy (HUGH HERCY, *temp.* Richard II.). Ar. a chief gu.

Hercy. Gu. a chief ar. a bordure gobony of the last and az.

Herd (London). Ar. a chev. gu. betw. three water bougets sa. *Crest*—A demi goat saliant ppr. attired or, ducally gorged gold.

Herdbon, Herdban, or Herbon (co. Lincoln). Erm. on a fesse gu. three fleurs-de-lis or.

Herdby, or Herdeby. Gu. a fesse dancettée betw. ten billets ar. three, two, three, and two.

Herdby. Gu. a fesse dancettée betw. nine billets ar. four above and five below.

Herdson (co. Kent). Ar. semée-de-lis gu. a cross engr. sa. *Crest*—A demi leopard ramp. ducally gorged and chained ppr.

Herdson (London; GEORGE STODDARD, of London, Visit. London, 1568, *m.* ANNE, dau. of HENRY HERDSON, of same place). Ar. a cross sa. betw. four fleurs-de-lis gu.

Here. Ar. the trunk of an oak tree sprouting afresh sa. *Crest*—Out of a ducal coronet or, two dexter wings az.

Hereford, Viscount. See DEVEREUX.

Hereford, Earl of. See CLARE.

Hereford, See of. Gu. three leopards' faces reversed jessant-de-lis or.

Hereford (Sufton Court, co. Hereford). Gu. three eagles displ. ar. *Crest*—An eagle displ. ar.

Hereford (The Lowe and Moore, co. Worcester). Same *Arms*, eagles erm.

Hereford. Or, on a chief indented az. three annulets ar. *Crest*—An arm from the elbow ppr. holding an annulet or.

Hereford. Sa. five fusils in bend or.

Hereford. Ar. five mascles in fesse gu. each charged with a martlet of the first, in chief a lion pass. sa. collared of the second.

Hereford. Sa. a lion ramp. ar.

Hereford, City of. Gu. three lions pass. guard. in pale ar. on a bordure az. ten saltires of the second. *Crest*—A lion pass. guard. ar. holding in the dexter paw a sword erect ppr. hilt and pommel or. *Supporters*—Two lions ramp. guard. ar. each gorged with a collar az. charged with three buckles or. *Motto*—Invictæ fidelitatis præmium.

Hereford-Priory (co. Pembroke). Gu. a wivern or, on a chief az. three mullets pierced of the second.

Herenden (London, co. Rutland, and Maidstone, co. Kent; JOHN HERENDEN, 23 Henry VII., *m.* the dau. and heir of STRICKLAND. Visit. Rutland, 1618). Ar. a raven sa. beaked or, quartering STRICKLAND.

Hereward (Sheriff of Norfolk, 1300). Chequy or and az. on a bend gu. three eagles ar.

Herey, or Hery. Gu. a chev. chequy or and az.

Herford, Hereford, or Hurford (co. Devon). Ar. a fess lozengy gu. a lion pass. guard. in chief sa. *Crest*—A demi lion ramp. guard. sa. four drops of blood on breast and flank.

Hergest (Shenston, co. Hereford). Ar. a griffin segreant sa.

Hergreve. Ar. a griffin segreant per fesse gu. and az.

Herham. Paly wavy of six ar. and gu. (another, or, three palets wavy gu.).

Herice, or Heriz. Or, three hedgehogs sa.

Herick (London, 1605). See HERRICK.

Heriet (London). Per pale erm. and ermines three crescents counterchanged.

Heriet, Herriot, or Herriott. Per pale erm. and gu. three crescents counterchanged. *Crest*—A hind's head couped or.

Herile (co. Kent). Lozengy gu. and ar. eight martlets in orle or.

Hering. Gu. on a bend ar. a cinquefoil betw. two lions pass. of the field.

Hering. Az. six herrings hauriant ppr. three, two, and one.

Hering (Owsley-Minor, co. Warwick, *temp.* Henry VII.). Vert on a bend ar. a cinquefoil betw. two lions pass. guard. gu.

Hering (Island of Jamaica). Same *Arms.*

Heringaud. Gu. three herrings hauriant ar.

Heringaud (co. Sussex). Az. semée of crosses crosslet, six herrings in pale or.

Heringdon. Or, a chief gu. over all a bend sa.

Heringe (co. Salop, and Owsley-Minor, co. Warwick). Az. semée of crosses crosslet, six herrings or, three, two, and one (another, three herrings ar.). *Crest*—A bull's head sa. ducally gorged and crowned or.

Heringham. Gu. three herrings in pale ar. *Crest*—On a chapeau a dolphin hauriant all ppr.

Heringham, or Herringham. Az. semée of crosses crosslet, six herrings hauriant ar.

Heringrave. Ar. a chief indented gu.

Heriot (Trabrown, Scotland) Ar. on a fesse az. three cinquefoils of the field.

Heriot (Jeweller to King James VI.) Ar. on a fesse transposed az. a crescent betw. two stars of the first.

Heriot (Ramornie, co. Fife, now MAITLAND-HERIOT). Ar. on a fess vert betw. three escallops az. three cinquefoils of the field. *Crest*—A demi man in complete armour brandishing a sword ppr. *Supporters*—Dexter, a chevalier in complete armour holding in his hand a lance or spear all ppr.; sinister, an eagle with wings expanded also ppr. *Motto*—True and trusty.

Heriot. Quarterly, erminois and ermines, three crescents counterchanged, two and one. *Crest*—An arm embowed in armour ppr. garnished or, holding in the hand a dagger of the first, hilt and pommel of the second.

Heriot. Ar. a mullet az. on a chief of the last three roses of the first.

Heris. Az. a fesse betw. three hedgehogs ar. *Crest*—On a mount vert a crane holding in the dexter claw a stone ppr.

Heris. Or, three boars pass. in pale sa.

Heris. Or, on a bend az. three cinquefoils of the first.

Heritage (Byrton-Dassett, co. Warwick; confirmed to JOHN HERITAGE, of that place). Bendy of six ar. and sa. on a chief gu. three crosses crosslet or.

Heritage. Ar. a fesse gu. in chief two mullets of the second. *Crest*—A bear's head muzzled and parted per chev. ar. and sa. betw. two wings parted per fesse of the last and first.

Heriz (South Wingfield, co. Derby, and Gonalston, co. Nottingham, 27 Edward I.). Az. a fesse betw. three hedgehogs ar. (another, az. three urchins or).

Heriz (co. Leicester). Az. three hedgehogs or.

Heriz, alias Smith (Withcock, co. Leicester, *temp.* Henry VII.). Az. a fesse betw. three hedgehogs ar. quartering SMITH, of Withcock, co. Leicester.

Heriz. Az. a chev. erm. betw. three hedgehogs or.

Herize (Sir JOHN HERIZE, *temp.* King John, and Sir MORRIS HERIZE, Chamberlain to RICHARD, *Earl of Cornwall*, King of the Romans. Visit. Notts, 1614). Az. three hedgehogs or.

Herland. Or, on a bend wavy betw. two sea lions ramp. az. three bucks' heads cabossed of the first. *Crest*—On sea ppr. a sea lion ramp. az. ducally crowned or, holding an anchor sa.

Herland. Sa. a cross formée or.

Herle (Prideaux, co. Cornwall; descended from JOHN HEARLE, of West Hearle, co. Northumberland. Visit. 1620). Gu. a fess or, betw. three shovellers ppr. *Another Coat*—Gu. three escallops and a border ar.

Herle, or Hearle (Penryn in Trelissock, co. Cornwall; a younger branch of the preceding family; the co-heiresses *m.* FRANCIS RODD, Esq., of Trebartha Hall, Captain WALLIS, and Rev. HENRY HAWKINS TREMAYNE, of Sydenham, co. Devon). Same *Arms*, &c., as the preceding.

Herle (Grammond, co. Cornwall). Sa. a fesse or, betw. three shovellers ar.

Herle (co. Devon). Gu. a chev. or, betw. three shovellers ar.

Herle (Welford, co. Northampton). Gu. a fesse betw. three shovellers ar.

Herle (Wyard, co. Oxford; JOHN HERLE, *alias* VYTHAM, *temp.* Queen Elizabeth; his dau. ETHELRED, *m.* EDMOND

482

Molyneux, Esq., of Thorpe, near Newark-upon-Trent, co. Nottingham. Visit. Notts, 1614). Gu. a garb or, thereon three birds sa.

Herley. Gu. a chev. ar. betw. three owls ppr.

Herlington. Ar. a lion ramp. sa. crowned or.

Herman (co. Buckingham). Quarterly, indented ar. and sa. on a bend of the second betw. three martlets of the first as many fleurs-de-lis of the last.

Herman (Middleton-Stoney, co. Oxford; confirmed 10 Dec. 1630). Vert a lion pass. or, armed and langued gu. betw. three annulets ar. *Crest*—A lion couchant guard. or, under a palm tree ppr.

Herman. Ar. a chief indented gu.

Herman. Gu. a bend ar. (another, or).

Hermentall. Or, two bars az.

Hermon. Or, on a chev. gu. betw. three falcons rising a crescent. *Crest*—An arm holding a dagger ar.

Hermon (Preston, co. Lancaster, and Wyfold Court, Checkendon, co. Oxford). Or, on a pale engr. az. betw. two fleurs-de-lis in fesse of the last a shuttle in pale, the thread pendent of the first. *Crest*—In front of two palm trees ppr. a lion couchant guard. erminois, resting the dexter paw upon a bale of cotton ppr. *Motto*—Fido non timeo.

Herne (BURCHELL-HERNE, Bushy Grange, co. Herts). Quarterly, 1st and 4th, ar. a chev. ermines betw. three herons sa., for HERNE; 2nd and 3rd, ar. on a chev. betw. three cross crosslets fitchée sa. as many fleurs-de-lis of the first, for BURCHELL. *Crests*—1st, HERNE: Out of a ducal coronet ar. a heron's head ppr.; 2nd, BURCHELL: A lion ramp. az. supported by a tree vert. *Motto*—Usque ad astra.

Herne, or Heron (Panfield Hall, co. Essex, London, and Shacklewell, co. Middlesex, 1600). Sa. a chev. erm. betw. three herons close ar. *Crest*—A heron's head erased ar. ducally gorged and beaked or.

Herne (Godmanchester, co. Huntingdon). Gu. a chev. erm. betw. three herons ar. *Crest*—A heron or.

Herne. Sa. a chev. engr. betw. three herons ar.

Herne (Sir THOMAS HERNE, of Haveringland, Sheriff co. Norfolk, 1620). Or, three bars gemel gu. on a canton of the last five lozenges in saltire of the first.

Herne. See HEARNE.

Hernshill (co. Chester; the dau. and heir of Sir JOHN HERNSHILL *m.* Sir JOHN STONER, living 34 Edward III., 1359. Visit. Oxon, 1566). Or, three roses gu.

Hernway. Ar. three herons' heads erased sa.

Heron (*Baron Heron;* summoned to Parliament 1371, extinct with first Baron). Gu. a chev. betw. three herons ar.

Heron (*Baron Heron;* summoned to Parliament 1393, extinct 1404). Same *Arms.*

Heron (Ford Castle, co. Northumberland, *temp.* Edward I.). Same *Arms*. *Crest*—A heron, as in the arms.

Heron (Bokenfield, co. Northumberland). Gu. three herons ar. *Crest*—Out of a ducal coronet or, a heron's head ppr.

Heron (Newark-upon-Trent, co. Notts, since of Stubbers, co. Lincoln, bart., extinct 1854). Quarterly, 1st and 4th, same *Arms* as HERON, of Bokenfield; 2nd and 3rd, same *Arms* as HERON, of Ford Castle. *Crests*—1st: Same as HERON, of Ford Castle; 2nd: Same as HERON, of Bokenfield. *Motto*—Ardua petit ardea.

Heron (Chipchase, co. Northumberland, bart., extinct 1801). Gu. three herons ar. *Crest*—A heron close ppr. holding in the bill a standard staff, the banner flotant, thereon the word "Hastings." *Motto*—Nil desperandum.

Heron (General PETER HERON, of Moor, co. Chester). Same *Arms* and *Crest*, as HERON, of Bokenfield. *Motto*—Ardua petit ardea.

Heron (Applyndon, co. Durham). Ar. three herons az.

Heron (East Thickley, co. Durham, 1575). Gu. on a chev. betw. three herons ar. a cinquefoil sa. *Crest*—Out of a ducal coronet or, a heron's head and neck ppr.

Heron (cos. Essex and Northumberland, and Ipswich, co. Suffolk). Az. three herons close ar. *Crest*—A heron ar.

Heron (cos. Essex and Stafford). Ar. three herons az.

Heron (co. Northumberland, and Scotland). Sa. a heron ar.

Heron (Croydon, co. Surrey). Gu. a chev. engr. betw. three herons close ar. *Crest*—A heron close ar. *Another Crest*—Out of a ducal coronet or, a heron's head ppr.

Heron (that Ilk, co. Kirkcudbright; heiress *m.* Sir JOHN MAXWELL, of Springkell; arms and supporters now borne by their second son, who succeeded his mother). Ar. two lions ramp. affrontée supporting betw. their forepaws a rose gu. stalked and leaved vert. *Crest*—A demi lion ar. holding in his dexter paw a cross crosslet fitchée gu. *Supporters*—Two herons ppr. *Mottoes*—Above the crest: Par valeur; above the shield: Ad ardua tendit.

Hero) (co. Stafford). Gu. three herons ar.

Heron (co. Surrey). Per pale gu. and az. on a chev. betw. three herons ar. as many cinquefoils sa. Crest—A heron's head erased ar. ducally gorged or.

Heron. Sa. two chev. or, betw. three herons ar.

Herondon. Ar. a heron volant in fesse az. membered or.

Herondon. Same Arms, betw. three escallops sa.

Heronvile. Az. three herons ar.

Heronville (Wednesbury, co. Stafford. Pedigree of Comberford. Hist. of Wednesbury). Sa. two lions pass. ar. crowned or.

Herovill. Sa. two lions pass. ar. crowned or, on each shoulder a fleur-de-lis az.

Herper. Erm. a cinquefoil az. on a chief gu. a lion pass. guard. or. Crest—A griffin statant ducally gorged ppr.

Herpingham. Vert an inescutcheon within an orle of martlets ar.

Herrays (co. Lancaster). Ar. a chev. betw. three boars pass. gu.

Herren (Sylington, Scotland). Gu. on a bend ar. a rose betw. two lions pass. of the first.

Herrer. Az. three hedgehogs or.

Herrick, or Eyrick (Beaumanor, co. Leicester, seated at Streton, in that county, in the 11th century). Ar. a fesse vairé or and gu. Crest—A bull's head erased ppr. semée of annulets or, in the mouth a pear tree branch eared sa. gorged with a chaplet of roses ppr. Motto—Virtus omnia nobilitat.

Herrick (Rev. SAMUEL HERRICK, Rector of Brompton, co. Northampton, representative of ROBERT HERRICK, Esq., M.P., for Leicester, elder brother of the first Sir WILLIAM HERRICK, Knt., of Beaumanor). Same Arms, Crests, and Motto.

Herrick (PERRY-HERRICK, Beaumanor Park, co. Leicester). Quarterly, 1st and 4th, ar. a fess vairé or, and gu., for HERRICK; 2nd and 3rd, barry of six or and gu. on a bend indented ar. three lions pass. sa. two flaunches erm., for PERRY. Crests—1st, HERRICK; 2nd, PERRY: A hind's head erased ppr. semée of annulets or, in the mouth a pear tree branch slipped ppr. fructed or. Motto—Virtus omnia nobilitat.

Herrick (Shippool, co. Cork; descended from JOHN HERRICK, Esq., born in 1612, who is presumed to have been seventh son of Sir WILLIAM HERRICK, the purchaser of Beaumanor). Arms, &c., as HERRICK, of Beaumanor.

Herries (Lord Herries, of Terregles. See also MAXWELL). Ar. three urcheons sa. Crest—A buck's head or, attired with ten tynes ar. Supporters—Two savages with clubs over their shoulders ppr. Motto—Dominus dedit.

Herries (Rotterdam; second son of Halldykes, 1747). Ar. a crescent betw. three urcheons sa. Same Crest and Motto.

Herries (third son of Halldykes, 1787). Ar. three urcheons sa. within a bordure wavy gu. Crest—A buck's head erased gu. attired vert. Motto—Dominus dedit.

Herries (Mabie). As Lord Herries, with a crescent az. in chief.

Herring (Archbishop of Canterbury, 1750). Gu. three lucies haurient ar. betw. nine crosses crosslet or.

Herring (Lethendy, co. Perth). Quarterly, 1st and 4th, gu. on a bend ar. a rose betw. two lions ramp. of the field; 2nd and 3rd, az. a chev. or.

Herring (Carsewell). Gu. on a fesse ar. a rose betw. two lions ramp. of the first.

Herring. Az. semée of crosslets, three herrings ar. Crest—A boar's head couped in fesse, pierced through the snout with four arrows ppr.

Herring (Gilmerton, co. Edinburgh). Gu. on a bend ar. a rose betw. two lions pass. of the field.

Herring, or Herringham (co. Dorset; quartered, through WILLIAMS, by THOMAS C. H. D'OYLEY, of the E.I.C.S.) Gu. three herrings haurient in fesse ar.

Herring (Winterbourne, Herrington). Same Arms.

Herring. See HERING.

Herris (Woodham Mortimer, co. Essex). Or, on a bend gu. three cinquefoils of the field. Crest—A talbot sejant or.

Herris (Sandon, co. Essex). Erm. (another, or) on a bend engr. az. three cinquefoils or. Crest, as the last.

Herrys (Cryxsey, co. Essex; confirmed 19 Nov. 1578). Or, on a bend az. three cinquefoils pierced of the field, a mullet for diff.

Herschel (Collingwood House, co. Kent, bart.). Ar. on a mount vert a representation of the forty-feet reflecting telescope with its apparatus ppr. a chief az. thereon the astronomical symbol of Uranus, or the Georgium Sidus, irradiated or. Crest—A demi terrestrial sphere ppr. thereon an eagle, wings elevated or. Motto—Cœlis exploratis.

Hersett (co. Norfolk). Or, a chief indented sa.

Hersewell. Sa. three estoiles ar.

Hersey (co. Kent). Gu. on a chief ar. a label of three points az.

483

Hersey. Gu. a chev. ar. Crest—A stag sejant ppr.

Hersey. Gu. a chev. ar. betw. thr ee owls ppr.

Herst. Ar. an estoile of sixteen points gu.

Herst. Quarterly, or and az. four suns counterchanged.

Herst, alias Grove. Ar. a star of eight points az. Crest—A grove of trees ppr.

Herst, alias De La Hay (arms in glass at Malvern; quartered by POPLESHAM). Ar. the sun ppr.

Hert (Bovy-Tracy, co. Devon). Sa. a bend betw. three fleurs-de-lis ar.

Hertford, Marquess of. See CONWAY.

Hertford (co. Hertford). Gu. three eagles displ. ar. (another, or).

Hertford, or Herford (co. Worcester). Az. (another, sa.) five fusils in bend or.

Hertford, or Hartford. Gu. three eagles displ. ar. (another, erm.). Crest—A parrot's head gu. betw. two wings vert.

Hertford. Gu. on a fesse or (another, ar.) three bucks' heads cabossed of the first.

Hertford, Town of. Ar. on a mount vert a stag couchant gu.

Hertford College, Oxford. No Arms. Seal—Represented in a landscape a hart stooping down his head as going to drink at a ford, all within a ribbon, on which was the Motto—Sicut cervus anhelat ad fontes aquarum.

Herthale (co. Derby). Ar. two bars vert.

Herthall. Ar. two bars vert, over all a bendlet gu.

Herthall, or Herthull. Or, two bars vert.

Hertham (co. Northumberland). Or, an orle az. (another, purp.).

Hertham. Paly of six ar. and gu.

Herthey, or Hertley. Or, a bend betw. two cotises sa.

Herthull (Herthull and Ballidon, co. Derby, Pooley in Polesworth, co. Warwick, &c., &c.; the heiress m. COKAYNE, of Ashbourne, co. Derby, temp. Henry IV.). Ar. two bars vert, quartering EDNESOR, ROSSINGTON, DEYVILLE, SAVAGE, &c.

Herthull (Sir RICHARD DE HERTHULL, Knt., co. Notts, temp. Edward I.). Ar. two bars vert.

Hertington. Ar. a hart pass. sa. Crest—A stag's head or, collared gu. betw. the attires a cross pattée az.

Hertington. Az. two lions pass. or.

Hertington. Vert a fesse betw. three stags' heads cabossed ar.

Hertington. Erm. a lion ramp. gu. crowned or.

Hertland-Abbey (co. Devon). Ar. a crozier in pale or, enfiled with a stag's head cabossed sa. (another coat, gu. a bend betw. three pears or).

Hertland (co. Devon). Ar. on a bend sa. three harts' heads or.

Hertlaw (co. Northumberland). Ar. a cross gu.

Hertlaw. Ar. a cross gu. in the first quarter a martlet sa.

Hertley (co. Suffolk). Ar. a cross gu. in the dexter canton a martlet.

Hertley. Or, a bend cotised sa.

Hertley, or Hetley. See Supplement.

Hertlington. See Supplement.

Hertog. See Supplement.

Herton. See Supplement.

Hertslet (EDWARD HERTSLET, Esq., C.B., Librarian and Keeper of the Papers, Foreign Office). Barry dancettée of eight az. and or, impaling, Gu. a lion ramp. ar. langued az. debruised by a fess sa. in chief a ducal coronet or. Crest—A demi lion ramp. ppr. crowned with an Eastern diadem or, and resting the sinister paw on a closed book sa. clasped and hinged gold. Motto—Fato fortior virtus.

Hervesell. Or, an orle sa.

Hervey (Marquess of Bristol). Gu. on a bend ar. three trefoils slipped vert. Crest—An ounce pass. sa. bezantée, ducally collared and chain reflexed over the back or, holding in the dexter paw a trefoil slipped vert. Supporters—Two ounces sa. bezantée, ducally collared and chain of each reflexed over the back or. Motto—Je n'oublieray jamais.

Hervey (Lord Hervey, of Ross and Kidbrooke, created 1620 and 1628, extinct 1642; descended from a common ancestor with the Marquess of Bristol). Same Arms and Crest. Supporters—Two leopards or, pellettée.

Hervey-Bathurst (Lainston, co. Southampton, bart.). Quarterly, 1st and 4th, gu. on a bend ar. three trefoils slipped vert, for HERVEY; 2nd and 3rd, sa. two bars erm. in chief three crosses formée or, for BATHURST. Crests—1st, HERVEY: An ounce sa. bezantée, collared and lined or, holding in the dexter paw a trefoil slipped vert; 2nd, BATHURST: A dexter arm embowed, habited in mail, grasping in the hand ppr. a club with spikes or. Motto—Je n'oublierai jamais.

Hervey (Thurley, co. Bedford). Gu. on a bend ar. three trefoils slipped vert.

Hervey (Kidbrooke, co. Kent, bart., extinct 1642). Same *Arms.*

Hervey (cos. Cornwall and Somerset). Sa. a fesse or, betw. three squirrels sejant ar. *Crest*—A squirrel sejant ar. tail or, cracking nuts.

Hervey (Tiddington, co. Oxford). Az. three pack-saddles sans stirrups or.

Hervey. Gu. on a chev. betw. three leopards' faces or, as many trefoils slipped vert.

Hervey (Killiane Castle, co. Wexford). Gu. on a bend ar. three trefoils slipped vert. *Crest*—A cat-a-mountain ppr. holding in the dexter paw a trefoil slipped vert. *Motto*—Je n'oublierai jamais.

Hervieu (VICTOR ALEXANDRE HERVIEU-DUCLOS, M.D., son of NICOLAS HERVIEU-DUCLOS, of Normandy, by JEANNE, his wife, dau. of PIERRE FRANCOIS LENTAINGE, an officer in the French army; Dr. HERVIEU was Lieut. Commandant of a company of grenadiers, in the Royal Volunteers of Calvados, at Bayeux, in 1815, and *d.* in Dublin, 1831). Az. three acorns or. *Crest*—A wolf ramp. or.

Hervy. Vert a lion pass. guard. ar. *Crest*—An ox-yoke in bend gu. bows or.

Hervy. Or, a chev. betw. three leopards' faces gu.

Hervyll (Her. Visit. 1533). Sa. two lions pass. in pale ar. ducally crowned or.

Herward (co. Salop, and Odiham, co. Hants. See HARWOOD). Chequy or and az. on a bend gu. three eagles displ. with two heads ar.

Herward (co. Norfolk). Az. a fesse componée sa. and or, in the first quarter a mullet pierced ar.

Herward. Ar. a cross crosslet gu.

Herwell. Ar. a lion coward pass. sa. *Crest*—A dexter hand holding up a boar's head erect couped ppr.

Herwell. Ar. two lions pass. coward sa.

Herwesell. Or, an inescutcheon sa.

Herwill. Az. two lions pass. ar. crowned or.

Herwille. Sa. two lions pass. ar. ducally crowned or, charged on the shoulders with a fleur-de lis az.

Herwood (impaled on Fun. Ent. of Capt. PHILIP CARPENTER, Principal Serjeant-at-Arms of Ireland, *d.* 1675). Gu. a fess humettée betw. two lions pass. ar.

Herworth (Epplin, co. Devon). Ar. three bucks' heads couped sa. collared of the first. *Crest*—A cubit arm erect ppr. holding a snake.

Hesding. Chequy or and az. a chev. erm. *Crest*—A dexter hand holding a pistol ppr.

Hese, or Hesey. Ar. three human legs gu.

Heseltine. Gu. a bull's head caboosed ar. *Crest*—A swan, wings endorsed ar. crowned with an antique crown or.

Hesill. Ar. a chev. sa. betw. three trefoils vert. *Crest*—On a chapeau gu. turned up ar. a flame ppr.

Hesill, or Hesyll. Ar. a chev. sa. betw. three trefoils slipped gu.

Hesilrigge (Nosely, co. Leicester, bart.). Ar. a chev. betw. three hazel leaves vert. *Crest*—On a chapeau gu. turned up erm. a man's head in profile, couped at the shoulders ppr. *Supporters*—Dexter, a stag ppr.; sinister, a talbot ar. pied sa. and gorged with a plain collar gu. *Motto*—Pro aris et focis.

Hesketh (Rufford Hall, co. Lancaster, bart.). Ar. on a bend sa. three garbs or. *Crest*—A garb or, banded az.

Hesketh (FERMOR-HESKETH; exemplified to Sir THOMAS GEORGE HESKETH, Bart., and Lady ANNA MARIA ARABELLA FERMOR, his wife, eldest dau. of THOMAS WILLIAM, fourth *Earl of Pomfret*, and sister of GEORGE WILLIAM RICHARD, last *Earl of Pomfret*, and also to THOMAS GEORGE HESKETH, their second son, upon their assuming, by royal licence, 1867, the surname of FERMOR, in addition to and before that of HESKETH). Quarterly, 1st and 4th, ar. on a bend sa. three garbs or, for HESKETH; 2nd and 3rd, ar. a fesse sa. betw. three lions' heads erased gu., for FERMOR. *Crests*—1st, HESKETH: A garb or, banded az.; 2nd, FERMOR: Out of a ducal coronet or, a cock's head gu. combed and wattled or.

Hesketh-Fleetwood. See FLEETWOOD.

Hesketh (Gwyrch Castle, co. Denbigh). Or, on a bend sa. betw. two torteaux three garbs of the field, quartering BAMFORD and LLOYD. *Crests*—1st: A garb or, charged with a cross pattée; 2nd: A rose ar.; 3rd: A dexter arm couped at the shoulder, and embowed in armour, holding a scythe all ppr. *Motto*—In Deo mea spes.

Hesketh (co. Lancaster). Ar. a cross flory sa.

Hesketh (co. Lancaster). Ar. on a bend sa. three garbs or.

Hesketh. Gu. a chev. betw. three leopards' faces or. *Crest*—Out of a ducal coronet or, two arms embowed in

armour, the hands ppr. supporting a leopard's face, as in the arms.

Hesketh. Ar. on a bend sa. three garbs or, a bordure gu.

Hesketh (North Meols, co. Lancaster). Ar. on a bend sa. three garbs or, a chief az. thereon an eagle with two heads displ. ppr. all within a bordure erminois, quartering FLEETWOOD and BOLD.

Hesketh (Aughton, co. Lancaster, 1664). Ar. on a bend sa. cotised gu. three garbs or. *Crest*—A garb or, banded az.

Hesketh (Preston, co. Lancaster, 1664). Ar. on a bend sa. three garbs or, a canton az. *Crest*—A garb or, banded sa.

Hesketh (Poulton, co. Lancaster, 1664). Same *Arms.* Crest —A garb or, banded az.

Heskett (Lancaster Herald, 1713). Erm. on a bend sa. three garbs or, in the sinister chief a rose gu. *Crest*—A garb or, charged with a rose gu. the stalk and leaves twisting round the garb.

Heslerton (Rotford, Heslarton, and Waverthorpe, co. York). Gu. six lions ramp. ar. crowned or.

Hesse. Ar. on a fesse wavy betw. two birds (swallows) volant in chief, and on a mount in base a wolf pass. az. a bezant betw. two mullets. *Crest*—A demi wolf betw. two wings.

Hester. Ar. on a bend sa. three swans close of the field. *Crest*—A parrot gu. holding in the beak a ring or.

Hetherfield, or Hethersett. Az. a lion ramp. ar (another, guard. or). *Crest*—A sinister wing charged with a chev. gu.

Hetherfield. Az. three leopards segreant or.

Hetherington, and Hetherton. Per pale ar. and sa. three lions ramp. counterchanged. *Crest*—A lion's head erased gu. within a chain ar. both ends issuing from the wreath in orle.

Hetherington (RICHARD HETHERINGTON, Esq., Governor of Tortola, and of Burton, in Lune Vale). Sa. a fret ar. *Crest*— A leopard's face.

Hetherington (Tuble, King's Co.; Fun. Ent., GEORGE HETHERINGTON, *d.* 29 Dec. 1619). Per pale ar. and gu. a lion ramp. counterchanged, armed and langued az.

Hetherington (Fun. Ent. of MARGARET, wife of DAVID HETHERINGTON, Esq., of Ballyroan, in the Queen's co., *d.* 8 May, 1618). Same *Arms.* *Crest*—Out of a ducal coronet or, a tower, quarterly ar. and gu.

Hetherington (Ballyroan, Queen's co.; granted by Roberts, Ulster, 1648, to ARTHUR HETHERINGTON, son of FERGUS HETHERINGTON, Esq., of that place, descended from an ancient family of that name in England). Same *Arms*, with a canton of the second for diff. *Crest*—A castle with four towers per fess or and gu.

Hethersall. A lion ramp. ar. pellettée.

Hetherset. Az. a lion ramp. guard. or.

Hetley (Bulbridge House, co. Wilts). Gu. on a chev. ar. betw. three sparrow-hawks ppr. a cross crosslet fitchée sa. *Crest*—On the stump of a tree a sparrow-hawk all ppr.

Heton (co. Lancaster). Ar. on a bend engr. sa. three bulls' heads caboosed of the first,

Heton. Vert a lion ramp. ar. (another, a bordure engr. ar.).

Heton. Gu. a lion pass. ar.

Heton. Vert billettée or, a lion ramp. of the second within a bordure gu.

Heton. Ar. on a saltire az. five water bougets or, (another, of the field) a bordure gu.

Heton. Erm. on a chev. gu. three mullets or.

Heton (Winkell, co. Lincoln, and London; FRANCIS HETON, citizen and goldsmith, of London, younger son of GEORGE HETON, of the former place. Visit. London, 1568). Same *Arms, &c.*, as HEATON, of Groveley.

Heuband (co. Warwick). Sa. three leopards' faces jessant-de-lis ar.

Heubright. Ar. two bendlets betw. three cocks sa.

Heuer. Quarterly, gu. and vert on a chev. betw. three cats pass. guard. or, as many garbs of the first. *Crest*—A cat sejant ar. in the mouth a goldfinch ppr.

Heugh (Holmwood Park, Kent, 1865). Az. a fess betw. three arrows paleways, points downwards or. *Crest*—A unicorn's head ar. *Motto*—Per ardua.

Heusch (CHARLES HEUSCH, Esq., of Bedford Square). Az. on a bend betw. a cross crosslet in chief and a trefoil slipped in base, all within a bordure or, a talbot's head erased sa. *Crest*—A trefoil slipped or. betw. two wings ar.

Heuxton (co. Bedford). Gu. a chev. betw. three leopards' faces ar.

Hevell. Ar. a fesse gu. betw. six martlets sa. *Crest*—A lion ramp. ppr. supporting an anchor reversed az.

Heven (Heven, co. Hereford). Az. crusily fitchée three boars' heads couped or.

Heveningham. Per saltire or and gu. on a bordure engr. sa. eight escallops ar.

Heveningham (co. Norfolk). Quarterly, or and gu. on a bordure engr. sa. eight escallops ar.

Hever (Cuckfield, co. Surrey; descended from the HEVERS, of Hever Wood, co. Surrey, *temp.* Henry VIII.). Quarterly, gu. and vert on a chev. betw. three leopards pass. or, as many garbs of the first. *Crest*—A leopard sejant or.

Hever, or Heuer. Gu. a cross ar. *Crest*—A phœnix in flames ppr.

Heverley. Or, on a bend az. three escallops of the field.

Heverston, Haverston, or Haverton. Or, on a fesse gu. betw. three mullets sa. a cross botonnée ar.

Heverton. Or, on a fesse gu. betw. three mullets sa. as many crosses botonnée fitchée ar.

Hewar (London, 1687). Sa. two talbots' heads couped or, betw. as many flaunches erm.

Hewar (Emneath, co. Norfolk). Same *Arms*, talbots' heads erased.

Heward.

Heward (Sir SIMON HEWARD, Knt., M.D., of Carlisle). Or, two swords in saltire ppr. pommels and hilts sa. betw. two cinquefoils in fesse, another in base, and three hearts in chief gu. all within a bordure az. *Crest*—A dexter arm embowed in armour ppr. garnished or, entwined by a serpent, the hand in a gauntlet, holding a sword also ppr. pommel and hilt gold, the blade piercing a heart, as in the arms.

Heward (confirmed by Molyneux, Ulster, 1617, to NICHOLAS HEWARD, Chief Chamberlain of the Exchequer in Ireland). Per fess paly of six gu. and sa. counterchanged, three wings ar. *Crest*—A swan's leg couped a la quise with wing displ. conjoined ar.

Heward (Boton). Az. a fess gobonée ar. and gu. betw. three owls of the second.

Heward (Alburgh). Az. a fess gobonée ar. and vert betw. three owls of the second.

Hewarde, or Hayward (London, and Tonbridge Court, co. Surrey). Sa. two bars ar. in chief a talbot pass. of the last.

Heware (Marshland). Az. two talbots' heads erased or, betw. as many flaunches erm.

Hewatt, or Hewat (Scotland). Az. a chev. ar. surmounted by another gu. betw. three owls of the second. *Crest*—The sun rising out of a cloud ppr. *Motto*—Post tenebras lux.

Heway (co. Devon). Ar. fretty gu. a canton of the second. *Crest*—A wolf reguard. ppr.

Hewe. Gu. betw. two bendlets indented ar. three chessrooks erm.

Hewer (Oxborough, co. Norfolk). Sa. two talbots' heads erased in pale or, betw. as many flaunches erm. *Crest*—A demi dragon az. wings endorsed or, collared and lined gold, holding the line in his forelegs.

Hewes, or Hues (Bromham, co. Wilts). Ar. a lion ramp. reguard. sa.

Hewes. Ar. two bars betw. seven crescents sa. three in chief, the like number in fesse, and one in base.

Hewes. Ar. on a fesse gu. two gadbees or. *Crest*—A peacock's head erased az.

Hewes. Gu. fretty ar. a canton of the last.

Hewes (WILLIAM HEWES, and his next brother, JAMES, citizen and grocer of London, Visit. 1568, sons of JOHN HEWES, gent., of Donyvord, co. Somerset). Ar. on a bend sa. three fish naiant of the field, fins and tails or, a mullet gu. for diff. *Crest*—An elephant's head couped az. bezantée, eared and crowned ar. a mullet or, for diff.

Hewes (Fun. Ent. of Mrs. HEWES, alias EDWARDS, buried in Christ's Church Cathedral, 1654). Ar. on a chev. betw. three leopards' faces sa. as many plates.

Hewester (London). Ar. a pale within a bordure (another, engr.) az.

Hewet (Ampthill). Sa. a chev. counter-embattled betw. three owls ar.

Hewet (London). Gu. a chev. erm. betw. three owls ar.

Hewet (Hedley Hall, co. York). Gu. a chev. engr. betw. three owls ar. *Crest*—The stump of a tree ppr. thereon a falcon close ar. *Motto*—Ne te quæsiveris extra.

Hewet. Ar. a chev. betw. three owls, sa. *Crest*—A cross pattée betw. the horns of a crescent gu.

Hewetson. Az. three plumes of ostrich feathers ar. two and one. *Crest*—A serpent nowed, the head in pale or, holding in the mouth a garland of laurel vert.

Hewetson (Thomastown, co. Kilkenny; Fun. Ent. Rev. CHRISTOPHER HEWETSON, Rector of Howth, and Treasurer of Christ Church Cathedral, *d.* 5 April, 1633). Per pale erm.

and gu. an eagle displ. or, charged on the breast with a crescent sa. *Crest*—A coney sejant sa. collared ar. *Another Crest*—A talbot pass. ar. holding in the mouth a sword ppr. *Motto*—Ambo dexter.

Hewett (Netherseale, co. Leicester, bart.). Gu. on a chev. embattled betw. three owls ar. on the head of each an Eastern crown or, as many bombs, fired ppr. *Crest*—Out of a mural crown or, the stump of an oak tree with branches, thereon a hawk ppr. gorged with an Eastern coronet, and belted of the first. *Supporters*—Dexter, a buffalo; sinister, a tiger ppr. on the shoulder of the tiger a trefoil. *Motto*—Ne te quæseveris extra.

Hewett (Headley Hall, co. York, bart., extinct 1822). Gu. a chev. engr. betw. three owls close ar. *Crest*—On the stump of a tree ppr. a falcon close or. *Motto*—Ne te quæsiveris extra.

Hewett (Pishiobury, co. Hertford, extinct 1689). Same *Arms*.

Hewett (Viscount *Hewett*; the second bart. of Pishiobury was so created in the peerage of Ireland, 1689, and *d. s. p.* same year). Same *Arms*.

Hewett (Heckfield, co. Hants; CHARLES HEWET; impalement Fun. Ent., 1626, of his son in-law, RICHARD FORSTER, Mayor of Dublin). Ar. on a chev. sa. betw. three owls ppr. a rose slipped or, betw. two cinquefoils of the last.

Hewett (Tir Mab Ellis, Llantrissant, co. Glamorgan; descended from HEWETT, Bart., of Headley Hall, co. York). *Arms* and *Crest*, same as HEWETT, of Headley Hall. *Motto*—Une pure foi.

Hewett (Lord Mayor of London, 1559). Az. on a fesse flory counterflory betw. three lions pass. guard. or, as many birds sa.

Hewett (London). Gu. three lions' paws erased and erect erm.

Hewett (London, and co. York). Az. on a fesse flory betw. three lions pass. or, as many magpies ppr.

Hewett (Sir EDWARD OSBORNE, Knt., clothworker, and Mayor of London, Visit. 1568, *m.* the dau. of HEWETT, and impaled her arms). Az. on a fesse flory counterflory betw. three lions pass. ar. as many lapwings ppr. *Crest*—A lapwing ppr.

Hewgill (Smeaton and Hornby Grange, co. York). Sa. two battle axes in saltire ar. *Crest*—A nag's head erased sa.

Hewham. Az. an estoile of six points or.

Hewick, or Hewike. Gu. on a chev. or, three crosses crosslet flory sa.

Hewick, or Hewikes. Gu. bezantée a lion ramp. ar.

Hewike, or Hewicke. Vert six bezants, three, two, and one.

Hewis. Gu. a fret ar. *Crest*—On a chapeau ppr. a water bouget sa.

Hewis. See HUVIS.

Hewish (co. Cornwall). Gu. fretty ar. a canton of the second.

Hewish (co. Devon). Ar. on a bend sa. three pikes haurient of the field.

Hewit (co. Derby). Az. on a chev. flory or, betw. three lions pass. of the second as many lapwings ppr.

Hewit (co. Stafford). Sa. a chev. engr. betw. three owls ar.

Hewit. Sa. a chev. or. *Crest*—A demi huntsman ppr. coat gu. firing a gun of the first.

Hewitt (Viscount *Lifford*). Gu. a chev. engr. betw. three owls ar. *Crest*—On a stump of a tree, with one branch growing thereon, an owl all ppr. *Supporters*—Dexter, a vulture or, wings inverted ar. gorged with a plain collar az. thereon three bezants; sinister, a griffin or, wings elevated ar. gorged as the dexter. *Motto*—Be just and fear not.

Hewitt (Burgatia, Roscarberry; monument at Bodmin, 1861). Gu. a chev. engr. betw. three owls. *Crest*—An owl perched on the trunk of a tree all ppr. *Motto*—Be just and fear not.

Hewitt (Ireland; EPHRAIM HEWITT, Esq., of Ballylane, co. Wexford, *m.* MARY, dau. of THOMAS HARMAN, Esq., of Palace, same co., and *d.* 1823, leaving an only dau., DEBORAH HEWITT, *m.* Rev. WILLIAM HINSON, Rector of Rosdroit, same co.). Same *Arms* and *Crest*. *Motto*—After darkness comes light.

Hewitt (London, 1586). Or, on a pile gu. three escallops of the first. *Crest*—A falcon close upon a lure ar. lined and ringed or.

Hewitt (Alveston, co. Warwick; granted 1764). Gu. a chev. engr. betw. three owls ar. *Crest*—On the trunk of an old tree, from which spring fresh branches, a horned owl all ppr.

Hewitt (LUDLOW-HEWITT, Littleton-on-Severn, co. Gloucester; exemplified to THOMAS ARTHUR LUDLOW, Esq., on his assuming, by royal licence, the additional surname of HEWITT). Ar. two chevronels indented gu. betw. three owls ppr. *Crest*—The trunk of a tree fessewise eradicated ppr. therefrom rising a falcon belled or, fretty gu. in the beak an acorn slipped also ppr.

Hewlet. Sa. on a fesse ar. three roses gu. *Crest*—On a mount vert, semée of weeds, an oak tree ppr.

Hewlett, or Howlett (Dublin ; assigned by Carney, Ulster, 1662, to GEORGE HEWLETT, Lieut. of the City of Dublin Militia, and High Sheriff of the same city). Sa. on a fess betw. three owls' heads erased and affrontée ar. as many roses gu. *Crest*—An owl's head erased and affrontée ar. ducally gorged or.

Hewley (co. York). Ar. a pile issuing from the chief and two from the base gu.

Hewling. Erm. three roses per pale or and gu.

Hewmarche. Sa. an inescutcheon ar. charged with a fesse lozengy gu. within an orle of martlets of the second.

Heworth, or Hepworth. Ar. a saltire betw. four mullets gu.

Hewscott (co. Devon). Ar. on a chev. betw. three leopards' faces az. as many palets of the first.

Hewse (granted 10 Dec. 1573). Gu. a Saracen's head erased ppr. hair and beard or, round the temples a fillet nowed ar. and az. on a chief of the fourth three roses of the second.

Hewson (Hunter Street, Brunswick Square, London). Quarterly, gu. and erm. an eagle displ. or, in the first quarter a lion pass. guard. ar. *Crest*—A bull's head couped ar. armed or, in the mouth a torch of the last emitting flames of fire ppr.

Hewson (Fun. Ent. of the wife of Col. JOHN HEWSON, Governor of Dublin, buried in Christ Church Cathedral, 15 Jan. 1652). Quarterly, gu. and erm. an eagle displ. or, in the dexter chief quarter a lion pass. ar.

Hewson (London; WILLIAM HEWSON, *temp.* James I.; his dau. KATHERINE *m.* JOHN WOOD, Esq., of Lumley, co. Nottingham. Visit. Notts, 1614). Az. three chev. interlaced or, a chief of the last and a border compony ar. and gu.

Hewster. Sa. a fesse dancettée or, in chief three fleurs-de-lis ar. *Crest*—Out of a coronet ar. an ostrich's head and wings of the same, holding a horseshoe ar.

Hewster. Ar. a pale engr. az. a bordure of the last.

Hewston (Wigtoft, co. Lincoln). Az. three chev. fretty in base or, on a chief of the second a crescent sa. charged with a mullet ar.

Hexstall (Hexstall, co. Warwick, and co. Stafford). Quarterly, gu. and sa. a bend betw. two fleurs-de-lis ar.

Hext (Trenarren, co. Cornwall ; originally of Kingston, co. Devon). Or, a tower triple-towered betw. three battle axes sa. *Crest*—On a tower sa. a demi lion ramp. or, holding in the dexter paw a battle axe of the first.

Hext (Stavton, co. Devon; JOHN HEXT and his brother, WILLIAM HEXT, of Constentin, co. Cornwall. Visit. 1620). Same *Arms.*

Hext. Same *Arms. Crest*—A stag's head cabossed, ducally gorged or.

Hextall. Quarterly, gu. and sa. in the 2nd and 3rd quarters a fleur-de-lis ar. over all a bend of the last.

Hexton. Sa. (another gu.) a chev. betw. three leopards' faces ar. *Crest*—A leopard's face ar. jessant a fleur-de-lis or.

Heycock (East Norton, co. Leicester). Or, a cross sa. in the first quarter a fleur-de-lis.

Heydon, or Headon (cos. Hertford and Lincoln). Quarterly, ar. and az. a cross engr. counterchanged. *Crest* —A talbot pass. ar. spotted sa.

Heydon (co. Norfolk). Quarterly, ar. and gu. a cross engr. counterchanged.

Heydon. Quarterly, ar. and gu. in the first quarter a buglehorn sa.

Heydon. Gu. three bezants, a label of as many points ar.

Heydon. Ar. on a bend az. three eagles displ. or.

Heydon (Reg. Ulster's Office). Sa. four mullets, two in pale and two in fess ar. a canton erm.

Heydon (Fun. Ent. Ulster's Office, 1656, of PETER HEYDON, son of JOHN HEYDON, and grandson of RICHARD HEYDON). Quarterly ar. and gu. a cross engr. counterchanged, in dexter chief a martlet of the second, and in the sinister a crescent of the first.

Heyes (Ratington, co. Essex; granted 2 Aug. 1563). Ar. on a chev. az. betw. three snakes erect and erased vert, as many bezants. *Crest*—A snake's head erect and erased vert, ducally gorged or.

Heyford, and Heyforde. Gu. a maunch or. *Crest*— Out of a ducal coronet two branches orleways all ppr.

Heyford. Ar. a chev. sa. betw. three bucks springing gu. attired or.

Heyforde (Lord Mayor of London, 1477). Ar. a chev. sa. betw. three bucks trippant gu.

Heygate (Southend, co. Essex, bart.). Gu. two bars ar. on a bend or, a torteau betw. two leopards' faces az. *Crest*—A wolf's head erased gu. *Motto*—Boulogne et Cadiz.

Heygeys. Ar. a chev. gu. betw. three demi dragons couped and erect vert.

Heyham. Paly of six ar. and az.

Heyhurst (Parkhead, co. Lancaster). Ar. on a chev. az. betw. three hayrakes ppr. a sun or.

Heyland (co. Suffolk). Az. a lion ramp. ar. a bend gu.

Heyland (co. Suffolk). Ar. a bend gu.

Heyland (co. York). Gu. a bend betw. six martlets or. *Crest*—On a chapeau gu. a martlet sa.

Heyland (Glendaragh, co. Antrim, and Tamlaght, co. Derry ; confirmed to ALEXANDER CHARLES HEYLAND, of the Bengal Civil Service, late Judge of Ghazeepore, India, second son of LANGFORD ROWLEY HEYLAND, of Glendarragh, co. Antrim, and Tamlaght, co. Derry, and grandson of ROWLEY HEYLAND, of Castle Roe, co. Derry, and the descendants of his said grandfather). Az. a lion ramp. ar. armed and langued gu. surmounted by a bend of the last, charged with a tower ppr. *Crest*—Out of battlements of a tower ppr. charged with a cross crosslet gu. a nag's head ar. *Motto*—Faveat fortuna.

Heylin (Alderton, co. Salop). Sa. three nags' heads erased ar. *Crest*—A bear pass. sa. gorged with a collar and bell or.

Heyliston, or Heylston (London). Ar. a chev. engr. betw. three leopards' faces gu.

Heylyn (co. Surrey). Ar. three horses' heads erased sa. *Crest*—Out of a ducal coronet or, a demi lion ramp. sa.

Heylyon, or Helion. Gu. fretty ar. a fesse or.

Heyman (Somerfield, co. Kent, bart., extinct 1808, a very ancient family in that co. ; Tenterden Free School was founded by a HEYMAN near 400 years ago. RALPH HEYMAN purchased the Manor of Haringe *temp.* Henry VII. His grandson, PETER HEYMAN, *m.* ELIZABETH, only dau. of WILLIAM TILDE, Esq., of Somerfield, who brought that place to her husband ; HENRY HEYMAN, fourth in descent from them, was created a bart. 1641). Ar. on a chev. engr. az. betw. three martlets sa. as many cinquefoils or. *Crest*—A Moor fullfaced, wreathed round the temples, holding in the dexter hand a rose slipped and leaved all ppr.

Heyman. Ar. on a chev. engr. sa. betw. three martlets of the last as many cinquefoils or.

Heynault (Reg. Ulster's Office). Per pale or and sa. two chevronels, in the dexter chief a lion ramp. all counterchanged.

Heynes (Turston, co. Bucks). Or, a chev. betw. three arrows sa. on a chief crenellée az. as many mullets of the first. *Crest*—An eagle's head erased erm. ducally gorged or.

Heynes (Wilden Hall, co. Suffolk ; confirmed 20 Sept. 1575). Same *Arms.*

Heynes, or Eynes (Dorchester, Charlebury, co. Oxford, and co. Salop). Or, on a fesse gu. three bezants, in chief a greyhound courant sa. collared of the second. *Crest*—1st: An eagle displ. standing on a tortoise ; 2nd: An eagle displ. az. semée d'estoiles or.

Heynes (London). Ar. three crescents paly wavy of six gu. and az.

Heynes. Ar. on a fesse gu. betw. three demi hinds couped az. as many bezants.

Heynes. Gu. semée of crosses crosslet a cinquefoil or.

Heynes. Ar. a fesse wavy (another, nebulée) az. betw. three annulets gu.

Heynes. Ar. a chev. gu. betw. three demi lizards couped vert.

Heyngrave. Ar. a chief indented gu.

Heyre. Ar. a fesse vairé or and gu.

Heyrick (WILLIAM HEYRICK, Esq., of Thurmaston Lodge, co. Leicester). Ar. a fesse vairé or and gu. *Crest*—A bull's head erased ar. gorged with a chaplet of roses ppr.

Heyrick (Manchester, co. Lancaster, 1664 ; descended from Sir WILLIAM HEYRICK, of Beaumanor, co. Leicester). Ar. a fesse vairé or and gu. *Crest*—A bull's head couped ar. round the neck a garland of laurel vert, horned or, tipped sa. the ears and mouth of the last.

Heys (Woodside, co. Renfrew, 1875). Ar. a fesse betw. three inescutcheons az. *Crest*—A demi lion ramp. az. supporting in its paws a banner ar. *Motto*—Invictus maneo.

Heys. Ar. a fesse sa. betw. three lions ramp. gu.

Heysham (London). Gu. an anchor in pale or, on a chief of the last three torteaux.

Heysham. Same *Arms. Crest*—A stag's head cabossed ensigned with a ducal coronet.

Heysham (Stagenhoe Park, co. Herts ; as borne by ROBERT THORNTON HEYSHAM, Esq., of that place). Same as the preceding.

Heytesbury, Baron. See A'COURT and HOLMES.

Heytesbury (co. Wilts). Per pale indented gu. and vert a chev. or

Heytesbury, Town of (co. Wilts). *Arms* on seal, viz., a long cross mounted on three degrees, ensigned on the top with a fleur-de-lis, on each side of the cross an escutcheon, thereon a chief and two chev.

Heyth, or Hythe (co. Kent). The corporation seal represents an antique vessel with one mast, two men in the vessel, one blowing a horn, and two men lying on the yard-arm.

Heyton (Birchley, co. Lancaster; the heiress *m.* GERARD, of Ince, *circa* 1550). Ar. on a bend engr. sa. three stags' heads cabossed of the field, a crescent for diff.

Heyton (co. Lancaster; WILLIAM HEYTON, citizen and tailor of London, eldest son of BRYAN HEYTON, of the former place. Visit. London, 1568). Ar. on a bend engr. sa. three bulls' heads couped of the field. *Crest*—Out of a ducal coronet gu. a bull's head ar.

Heyton (Heyton; RICHARD HEYTON, *temp.* Henry VIII.; his dau. MARGARET, *m.* WILLIAM PENDOCK, Esq., of Gotherton, co. Gloucester, from whom PENDOCK, of Tollaston, co. Nottingham. Visit. Notts, 1614). Ar. six trefoils, three, two, and one, vert.

Heyton (Heyton). Az. three arrows in pale and a chief or.

Heyton (co. Lancaster). Vert a lion ramp. guard. ar.

Heyton. Vert a lion ramp. ar.

Heyton. Vert a lion ramp. within a bordure engr. ar.

Heyward (Middle Temple, London; granted 1 Dec. 1768). Az. a chev. per pale or and erm. betw. three garbs of the second. *Crest*—A dexter arm embowed, habited gu. holding in the hand ppr. a tomahawk of the last.

Heyward (Middle Temple, London, and co. Norfolk, 1611). Ar. on a pale sa. three crescents of the field. *Crest*—On a wing ar. a pale sa. charged with three crescents of the first.

Heyward (Wenlock, co. Salop). Per chev. gu. and az. a lion ramp. erm. ducally crowned or. *Crest*—An ibex pass. erm. armed, crined, and tufted or.

Heyward (co. Salop). Gu. a lion ramp. or, crowned ar.

Heywarde (Lord Mayor of London, 1570). Gu. a lion ramp. guard. ar. crowned or.

Heywick. Gu. a lion ramp. ar. betw. nine plates.

Heywood (cos. Lancaster and Middlesex, 1594). Ar. three torteaux betw. two bendlets gu. all within a bordure of the last. *Crest*—A falcon on the stump of a tree with wings displ. all ppr.

Heywood (Maristow, co. Devon). Same *Arms* and *Crest.*

Heywood (Claremont, co. Lancaster, bart.). Ar. three torteaux in bend betw. two bendlets gu. on a canton of the last a cross pattée or. *Crest*—On a mount vert the trunk of a tree with two branches sprouting therefrom, and entwined by ivy, thereon a falcon with wings displ. ppr. *Motto*—Alte volo.

Heywood (Heywood, co. Lancaster, 1664). Ar. three torteaux betw. two bendlets gu. *Crest*—On a mount vert a trunk of a tree, thereon a sparrow-hawk perched ppr.

Heywood (Stanley Hall, Wakefield). Ar. three torteaux in bend betw. two bendlets gu.

Heywood (Hope End, co. Hereford). Ar. three torteaux in bend betw. two bendlets gu. on a canton of the last a cross pattée or. *Crest*—On a mount vert the trunk of a tree, with two branches sprouting therefrom, and entwined by ivy, thereon a falcon with wings displ. ppr. *Motto*—Alte volo.

Heywood (Little Lever, co. Lancaster). Ar. three torteaux betw. two bendlets gu. on a canton of the last a cross pattée or. *Crest*—On a mount vert the stump of a tree branched, perched upon the sinister branch a falcon, wings expanded all ppr.

Heyworth (Lichfield). Az. a saltire or, within a bordure of the last charged with eight mitres of the field.

Heyworth (Yewtree, co. Lancaster; granted to LAWRENCE HEYWORTH, Esq., of Yewtree, in the parish of West Derby, co. Lancaster, at one time M.P. for Derby). Erm. two barrulets wavy az. betw. three bats sa. *Crest*—A crescent az. issuant therefrom fire ppr. betw. two bats' wings sa. *Motto*—Nil dimidium est.

Hiatt. Az. a lion ramp. ar. *Crest*—A lion's paw erased, holding a broken spear all ppr.

Hibbens, or Hibbyns (Weo, co. Salop). Or, on a chev. embattled betw. three castles gu. as many guttes of the first.

Hibbens. Same *Arms. Crest*—A lion's head erased ducally crowned, all betw. two ostrich's feathers ppr.

Hibberd. Ea. an estoile of six points or, betw. two flaunches erm.

Hibbert (Portland Place, London). Erm. on a bend sa. three crescents ar. *Crest*—An arm erect couped below the

Hibbert. Barry of eight and a pale counterchanged *Crest* —A hand holding a millrind ppr.

Hibbert (THOMAS HIBBERT, Esq., of Birtles Hall, co. Chester). *Arms*, &c., same as HIBBERT, of Portland Place, London.

Hibbert (Bucknell Manor, co. Oxford). *Arms*, &c., as HIBBERT, of Birtles Hall.

Hibbert (Chalfont Park, co. Bucks). *Arms*, &c., as HIBBERT, of Birtles Hall.

Hibbert (Braywick Lodge, co. Berks). *Arms*, &c., as preceding.

Hibbert (HOLLAND-HIBBERT, Munden House, Watford, co. Herts; exemplified to ARTHUR HENRY HOLLAND, Esq., second son of Sir HENRY THURSTAN HOLLAND, Bart., upon his assuming, by royal licence, the additional surname of HIBBERT). Quarterly, 1st and 4th, erm. on a bend nebuly sa. three crescents ar. in the sinister chief point a cross bottonée fitchée of the second, for HIBBERT; 2nd and 3rd, per pale ar. and az. semée-de-lis a lion ramp. guard. counterchanged, debruised by a bendlet engr. gu. *Crests*— 1st, HIBBERT: In front of a dexter cubit arm erect ppr. vested az. cuff erm. holding in the hand a crescent ar. a demi catharine wheel also ar.; 2nd, HOLLAND: Out of a crown vallery or, a demi lion guard. per bend ar. and az. charged with a bendlet engr. counterchanged and holding in the dexter paw a fleur-de-lis ar.

Hibbert-Ware. See WARE.

Hibbins (Redmarley, co. Worcester, and co. Hereford; confirmed by Segar, Garter). Or, a chev. betw. three castles triple-towered gu.

Hibbottes (Sir THOMAS HIBBOTTES, Chancellor of the Exchequer in Ireland; impalement Fun. Ent. of Lady HIBBOTTES, *d.* 16 Oct. 1620). Sa. three leopards' faces jessant-de-lis ar.

Hibbs (Tunbridge Wells, co. Kent). Az. a chev. engr. betw. three salmons ar. on a chief gu. as many storks of the second ducally crowned or. *Crest*—A demi stork, wings expanded, ducally crowned or, holding in the beak a salmon ar.

Hiccocks (London; granted 1707). Vert a garb or. *Crest* —On a mural coronet ar. a sun in splendour ppr.

Hiccox (EDWARD HICCOX, Esq., of Stratford-on-Avon, co Warwick). Quarterly, vert and or, in the 1st and 4th quarters a garb of the last.

Hicham. Gu. on a chief or, three torteaux, a crescent for diff. *Crest*—On a mount vert a stag springing ar. attired and unguled or, on the dexter part of the mount a branch of laurel of the first.

Hichcoke. Ar. on a cross az. five fleurs-de-lis or, within a bordure engr. of the second. *Crest*—In a tower gu. embattled or, a lion's head of the last.

Hiche. Per fesse or and ar. three estoiles sa.

Hiching. Sa. a fesse chequy or and az. betw. three horses heads erased ar. *Crest*—An anchor in pale sa.

Hichins (co. Cornwall). Ar. a cross formée quarterly, quartered az. and gu. betw. four lions' heads erased sa. langued of the second.

Hichins (London). Sa. a castle triple-towered ar.

Hickcombe. Az. three broad arrows or, a chief of the second.

Hicke. Per fesse or and sa. three estoiles counterchanged.

Hickes (Shipston-on-Stour, co. Worcester; confirmed by Anstis, Garter, 1722, to HENRY HICKES, Esq., of St. Paul's, Covent Garden, son of HENRY HICKES, Esq., of Stretton-super-Foss, co. Warwick, and grandson of WILLIAM HICKES, Esq., of Shipton). Az. a fess wavy betw. three fleurs-de-lis or. *Crest*—A hart's head couped ar. attired or.

Hickes. Gu. a chev. erm. betw. three clarions or.

Hickes (Silton Hall, co. York). Gu. a fesse wavy betw. three fleurs-de-lis or. *Crest*—A buck's head couped at the shoulder or, gorged with a chaplet vert. *Motto*—Tout en bon heure.

Hickes (Luxulion, co. Cornwall; WILLIAM HICKES, Visit. 1620, *d.* 1636. Monument in the church there). *Arms*, same as HEXT, of Stavton and Constentin.

Hickey. Gu. a lion ramp. ar. on a chief erm. a saltire engr. az. *Crest*—A dexter arm embowed in armour ppr. garnished or, holding in the hand a truncheon of the second.

Hickey (Dublin; Fun. Ent., WILLIAM HICKEY, Doctor of Physic, buried in St. James's Church there, 9 Sept. 1677). Gu. a lion pass. or, on a chief ar. a saltire engr. az.

Hickey (Ireland). Gyronny of eight sa. and or, on the first four acorns, and on the last as many oak leaves counterchanged. *Crest*—A lamb reguard. holding over the dexter shoulder a flag, charged with an imperial crown.

Hickey. Gu. a lion pass. or, a chief of the last. *Crest*—A wivern with wings expanded, holding in the mouth a human hand ppr.

Hickford, or Huckford. Vert a chev. betw. three bucks' heads cabossed or. *Crest*—A demi swan, wings endorsed ppr.

Hickford (co. Worcester). Az. on a fess betw. three leopards' faces ar. as many pellets.

Hickie (Billing, co. Northampton). Gu. a lion pass. or, on a chief ar. a saltire engr. az. charged with a lion pass. guard. of the third. *Crest*—A lion's head erased ar. pierced through the mouth with a cross crosslet fitchée gu.

Hickie (Kilelton, co. Kerry). Gu. a lion pass. or, on a chief ar. a saltire engr. az. *Crest*—A dexter arm embowed in armour ppr. garnished or, holding in the hand a truncheon gold. *Motto*—Honor virtutis præmium.

Hickie (granted by Carney, Ulster, 1688, to MICHAEL HICKIE). Gu. a lion pass. or, on a chief ar. a saltire engr. az. *Crest*—A lion's head couped ar. betw. two palm branches vert. *Motto*—Virtus sub pondere crescit. The following additions were confirmed by Vanbrugh, Clarenceux, 1712, to the said MICHAEL HICKIE, then of Billing, co. Northampton, viz., A lion pass. guard. ar. to be borne in the centre of the saltire in his arms, and the lion's head in his crest to be pierced through the mouth with a cross crosslet fitchée gu.

Hickinson (Fun. Ent. Ulster's Office, ISABEL HICKINSON, wife of LUKE NIGHTINGALE, Esq., of Ballycran, co. Wexford, buried in St. John's Church, Dublin, March, 1631.) Ar. two bars gu. each charged with three martlets of the field.

Hickling (Green's Norton, co. Northampton). Az. three bars or, in chief as many lions' heads erased of the second. *Crest*—A leopard's head erased or, pellettée.

Hickling. Ar. three bars az. in chief as many lions' heads erased of the second.

Hickman (Gainsborough, co. Lincoln, bart., extinct 1781; descended from ROBERT FITZ-HICKMAN, lord of the manors of Bloxham and Wickham, co. Oxford, 56 Henry III., 1272; WILLOUGHBY HICKMAN, Esq., of Gainsborough, his descendant, was created a bart. in 1643). Per pale indented ar. and az. *Crest*—A talbot couchant ar. collared and lined az. at the end of the line a knot. *Motto*—Toujours fidèle.

Hickman (Oaken, co. Stafford; granted to NATHAN HICKMAN, of Oaken, and the descendants of RICHARD HICKMAN, his grandfather, by St. George, Garter, and Le Neve, Norroy, 1708). Per pale indented or and az. two fleurs-de-lis in fesse counterchanged. *Crest*—A talbot couchant ar. spotted sa. collared gu.

Hickman (co. Clare; impalement Fun. Ent. 1683, HUGH PERCEVAL, Esq., of Gortvadroma, same co., whose wife was RHODA HICKMAN). Per pale indented ar. and az. on the dexter side three roses in pale gu. and on the sinister as many in pale of the first.

Hickman (Fenloe, co. Clare). Per pale indented ar. and az. *Crest*—A talbot sejant ar. collared and chained gu. *Motto*—Per tot discrimina rerum.

Hicks (Beverston, co. Gloucester, bart., now HICKS-BEACH). See BEACH.

Hicks (Campden, co. Gloucester, bart., extinct 1629; *Viscount Campden;* BAPTIST HICKS, youngest brother of Sir MICHAEL HICKS, Knt., of Beverston, the ancestor of Sir MICHAEL HICKS-BEACH, Bart., was created a bart. 1620, and in 1628 was raised to the Peerage, with special remainder to his son-in-law, Sir EDWARD NOEL, d. next year, when the Peerage passed according to the limitation. See NOEL, *Earl of Gainsborough,* extinct 1798). Gu. a fess wavy betw. three fleurs-de-lis or. *Crest*—A buck's head couped at the neck, gorged with a wreath of laurel ppr.

Hicks, or Hickes (Rickols, co. Essex, and London). Gu. a fesse wavy betw. three fleurs-de-lis or. *Crest*—A buck's head or, gorged with a chaplet of cinquefoils of the last leaved vert.

Hicks (Wilbraham Temple, co. Cambridge). Quarterly, 1st and 4th, gu. a fesse betw. three fleurs-de-lis or, for HICKS; 2nd and 3rd, per bend sinister or and sa. a lion ramp. counterchanged, holding between the paws a gauntlet az., for SIMPSON. *Crests*—1st, HICKS: A buck's head couped or, gorged with a chaplet of roses leaved vert; 2nd, SIMPSON: An ounce's head ppr. erased and ducally crowned gu. charged on the neck with a gauntlet or. *Motto*—Tout bien ou rien.

Hicks (Trevitick, in Alternon, and Luxilion, co. Cornwall). Ar. a tower triple-towered betw. three poleaxes sa.

Hicks (London, and Beccles, co. Norfolk). Az. two palets betw. nine fleurs-de-lis or. *Crest*—A griffin sejant az. gorged

with a collar embattled counter-embattled or, beaked, legged, and holding in the dexter foot an arrow gold.

Hicks (Kilmacanoge, co. Wicklow, and Mount Anville, co. Dublin: granted to RICHARD JOHN HICKS, Esq., and the descendants of his great-grandfather). Quarterly, gu. and or, a fess wavy, quarterly erm. and sa. *Crest*—A stag's head couped ar. attired gu. gorged with a chaplet of trefoils vert. *Motto*—Donner et pardonner.

Hickson (Kent, and Williats, South Mims, co. Middlesex). Or, two eagles' legs erased a la quise in saltire sa.

Hickson (Fermoyle, co. Kerry; originally from co. Cambridge, settled for a considerable time in Kerry, where members of the family have for more than a century filled the highest county offices; confirmed to ROBERT CONWAY HICKSON, of that place, High Sheriff co. Kerry, 1855-56, grandson of ROBERT HICKSON, and the descendants of the said ROBERT HICKSON). Or, two eagles' legs erased à la quise in saltire sa. in the centre chief point a trefoil vert. *Crest*—Out of a ducal coronet or, a griffin's head sa. beaked of the first, charged with a trefoil gold. *Motto*—Fide et fortitudine.

Hickson (Dingle and Ballintaggart, co. Kerry; descended from HICKSON, of Fermoyle). *Arms, Crest,* and *Motto,* as the preceding.

Hickton. Or, three eagles displ. sa.

Hide. See HYDE.

Hide-Abbey (co. Hants). Ar. a lion ramp. sa. on a chief of the last two keys adorsed and conjoined in the bows in pale of the first.

Hide (Albury, co. Hertford, bart., extinct 1665; BRIDGET, only dau. and heir of Sir THOMAS HIDE, of Albury, bart., who d. in 1665, m. PEREGRINE OSBORNE, *Duke of Leeds*). Ar. a chev. betw. three lozenges az. on a chief gu. an eagle displ. or.

Hide (Reg. Ulster's Office). Az. a chev. betw. three lions pass. or.

Hidon (co. Devon). Gu. three bezants.

Hiet. Ar. a lion ramp. sa. a chief indented of the second.

Hifferman. Per fesse vert and gu. on a fesse betw. three crescents in chief ar. a lion pass. guard. az. *Crest*—An arm in armour erect, holding in the gauntlet a broken sword ppr. hilt and pommel or.

Higate, or Highgate (Fun. Ent. Ulster's Office, 1661). Vert a gate or.

Higden. Per pale az. and vert a chev. betw. three bucks heads erased or. *Crest*—On a chapeau gu. turned up erm. a phœnix in flames ppr.

Higden. Per pale az. and vert a chev. betw. three bucks' heads or, on a chief ar. a torteau betw. two leopards' faces of the first (another adds, on the torteau a lion's head erased ar.).

Higford (co. Salop). Az. three bucks' heads cabossed or.

Higford (co. Worcester). Vert on a chev. betw. three bucks' heads or, as many mullets sa.

Higford, or Hickford (Twining, co. Gloucester). Vert on a chev. betw. three bucks' heads cabossed or, as many mullets gu.

Higgat (co. Suffolk). Gu. two bars ar. over all on a bend or, three leopards' faces sa. *Crest*—An anchor az. betw. two wings endorsed or.

Higgens (Bury, co. Somerset). Ar. guttée de poix on a fesse sa. three towers of the first. *Crest*—Out of a tower gu. a lion ramp. issuant ar. *Another Crest*—A castle gu.

Higginbotham, or Higgenbottom. Ar. a rose gu. barbed vert, seeded or. *Crest*—A dexter and sinister arm shooting an arrow from a bow all ppr.

Higginbotham (Glasgow, 1869). Same *Arms,* on a chief of the second two Cornish choughs ppr. *Crest*—A sinister and a dexter arm shooting an arrow from a bow all ppr. *Motto*—By aim and by effort.

Higgins, or Higgons (co. Hereford, and Shrewsbury). Vert three cranes' heads erased ar. *Crest*—A griffin's head erased or, gorged with a collar gu.

Higgins (co. Salop). Ar. guttée de poix a fesse sa.

Higgins (Moreton Jeffreys, and Thing Hill, Withington, co. Hereford). Per fesse vert and ar. a pale counterchanged three cranes' heads erased of the second, and as many lobster claws erased sa. *Crest*—A gryphon's head erased or, gorged with a collar sa. charged with a lozenge ar. betw. two plates, in the beak a lobster's claw erased gu. *Motto*—Faithful and true.

Higgins (Worcester; JOHN HIGGINS, Mayor, 1654, and JAMES HIGGINS, Mayor, 1680). Ar. a chev. vairé of the first and gu. betw. three hurts, each charged with a lion's gamb erased of the field.

Higgins (Skellow Grange, co. York). Erm. on a fesse sa. three towers ar. *Crest*—Out of a tower sa. a lion's head ar

Higgins (Turvey Abbey, co. Bedford). Vert three cranes' heads erased ar. *Crest*—A griffin's head erased or, gorged with a collar gu.

Higgins (Eastnor, co. Hereford; borne by the late Rev. JOSEPH HIGGINS, Rector of Eastnor and Pixley, J.P. for the counties of Hereford, Worcester, and Gloucester, the representative of an ancient family derived immediately from the marriage, in 1561, of EDWARD HIGGINS, Esq., with MARY, dau. of THOMAS CLYNTON, Esq., of Castleditch, by MARGARET, his wife, dau. of RICHARD TRACY, Esq., of Toddington, co. Gloucester). Paly of six or and az. on a chev. cotised erm. three crosses pattée gu., quartering, for CLYNTON, paly of six or and az. a chev. erm. per pale dancettée az. and or; and for YONGE, ar. on a bend sa. three griffins' heads erased or. *Crest*—A garb ppr. charged with two crosses pattée gu. *Motto*, allusive to the crest—Patriam hinc suśtinet.

Higgins (London). Ar. guttée de poix on a fesse of the second three towers double-towered or. *Crest*—Out of a tower double-towered sa. a demi griffin ar. holding in the dexter paw a sword of the last, hilt and pommel or.

Higgins (Glenary, co. Waterford; granted to JOSEPH NAPIER HIGGINS, Esq., Q.C.). Per chev. ar. and vert, a crescent betw. three cranes' heads erased counterchanged. *Crest*—A griffin's head erased or, charged with a crescent gu. and gorged with a collar of the last, thereon three bezants. *Motto*—Pro patriâ et virtute.

Higgins (Scotland). See HEIGINE.

Higginson (Saltmarshe, co. Hereford). Per fesse or and ar. on a fesse per pale sa. and gu. a tower of the second betw. two bezants, quartering BARNEBY and LUTLEY. *Crest*—A tower, as in the arms, in front of the portal thereof, pendent by a riband az. an escutcheon gu. charged with three bezants, two and one, for HIGGINSON, and the crest of BARNEBY.

Higginson (granted, 1764, to JOSEPH HIGGINSON, Esq., of Mile End, co. Middlesex). Vert a chev. quarterly or and gu. betw. two garbs in chief and a sun in base of the second. *Crest*—A dexter hand erect betw. two stalks of wheat flexed in saltire issuing from a human heart all ppr. in the hand a book shut sa. garnished or.

Higginson (Lisburn, co. Antrim; granted to HENRY THEOPHILUS HIGGINSON, Esq., of Lisburn, Registrar to the Bishop of Down and Connor, grandson of Rev. THOMAS HIGGINSON, Rector of Lisburn). Sa. three towers in fess ar. betw. six trefoils slipped, three in chief and three in base or. *Crest*—Out of a tower ppr. a demi griffin segreant vert armed and beaked or. *Motto*—Malo mori quam fœdari.

Higgs (Collesborne, co. Gloucester). Ar. a chev. betw. three bucks couchant gu. *Crest*—A buck's head gu. attired or, pierced through the neck with an arrow headed gold, feathered ar.

Higgs (Charlton Kings, co. Gloucester). Quarterly, 1st and 4th, ar. a chev. betw. three bucks couchant gu.; 2nd and 3rd, gu. a dexter arm embowed, vambraced or.

Higham (Higham, co. Chester). Chequy or and sa. on a chief of the last a lion pass. guard. of the first. *Crest*—An arm embowed in mail, grasping in the hand all ppr. a sword ar. hilt and pommel or, round the arm a scarf gold.

Higham (co. Bedford). Paly of six ar. and az. on a chief gu. three escallops or, (another, of the first).

Higham (Stannard, co. Berks, cos. Essex and Suffolk). Sa. a fesse componée or and az. betw. three horses' heads erased ar. *Crest*—A horse's head erased ar.

Higham (Eastham, co. Essex, Sutton, in the Isle of Ely, cos. Norfolk and Suffolk). Sa. a fesse counter-componée or and az. betw. three horses' heads erased ar. *Crest*—A nag's head erased ar.

Higham (Cooling, co. Suffolk). Or, a chev. sa. over all a bend engr. ar. *Crest*—A talbot pass. sa. collared and lined or, at the end of the line a coil or knot of the same.

Higham (co. Norfolk). Per pale or and vert, a fer-de-moline in cross gu.

Higham-Ferrars, Town of (co. Northampton). The corporation seal, which is very ancient, represents in chief a dexter hand, couped at the wrist, the little finger and the next doubled in, the others pointing to the dexter side, under the hand nine men's heads in profile couped at the neck, five in the upper row, the centre head looking to the dexter side, all the other eight looking to the centre of the seal.

Higham (Echingham, co. Sussex). Paly of six or and az. on a chief sa. a lion pass. guard. of the first. *Crest*—An arm embowed in armour ppr. holding a broken sword ar. hilt or, tied round the arm with a sash of the first and gu.

Higham. Ar. a lion ramp. sa. an orle of crosses crosslet fitchée gu.

Higham. Az. a bend cotised ar.

Highfield (co. Suffolk). Gu. a chev. ar. betw. three acorns or.

Highfield (co. York). Gu. a chev. betw. three buckles, the tongues pendent or.

Highfield (co. Chester; impaled by BEDELL, of Hamerton). Az. a chev. betw. three oak slips acorned or.

Highgate (Hayes, co. Middlesex, and Rendlesham, co. Suffolk). Gu. two bars ar. on a bend or, a torteau betw. as many leopards' faces az. *Crest*—A wolf's head erased gu.

Highmore (Armathwaite, co. Cumberland,· *temp.* Henry IV.). Erm. a crossbow bent, point downwards, betw. three moorcocks sa. *Crest*—A moorcock ppr.

Highmore (Harby-brow, co. Cumberland, *temp.* Edward IV., and Strickland, co. Dorset; a branch probably of the HIGHMORES, of Armathwaite). Ar. a crossbow pointed upwards betw. four moorcocks sa. beaked and membered gu. *Crest* (granted in 1683)—An arm in armour ppr. brandishing a falchion ar. hilt and pommel or, betw. two pike staves gu. headed gold.

Highmore (Sherborne). Same *Arms*. *Crest*—A talbot's head couped at the neck.

Higson. Ar. three boars' heads couped in fesse gu. *Crest*—A hand couped in fesse charged with an eye ppr.

Hiklinge. Ar. three bars az. on a chief of the last as many lions' heads erased or.

Hilary. Ar. three fleurs-de-lis az. an orle of eight crosslets fitchée sa.

Hilary. Ar. a fesse componée or and sa.

Hilborne (Kingsdon, co. Somerset; granted 1708). Per saltire gu. and or, two garbs in pale of the last, in fesse as many roses ppr. *Crest*—On a mount vert a sunflower ppr. betw. two ears of wheat, stalks interlaced or.

Hildersham (co. Cambridge). Sa. a chev. betw. three crosses formée flory (another, patonce) or.

Hildersham (Molton, co. Suffolk). Sa. a chev. engr. or, betw. three cinquefoils of the last, charged in the middle with a torteau.

Hildersham (co. Suffolk). Sa. a chev. betw. three crosses crosslet or. *Crest*—A swan devouring a fish ppr.

Hildesley (Cromers Gifford; WILLIAM HILDESLEY, grandson of WILLIAM HILDESLEY, Esq., of Benam, co. Berks; descended from WILLIAM HILDESLEY, living at Byneham, 50 Edward III., 1375. Visit. Oxon, 1566). Or, two bars gemelles sa. in chief three pellets. *Crest*—On a mural crown a griffin's head betw. two wings expanded ar.

Hildyard (Wynestead, co. York, and East Horseley, co. Surrey; an ancient and eminent family, co. York). Az. three mullets ar. (and sometimes ar.) a chev. betw. three mullets ar. *Crest*—Originally, a reindeer ppr.; subsequently, a cock sa. beaked, legged, and wattled gu. The latter crest was granted to this family for the valour shown by members of it at the battle of Towton, between the Houses of York and Lancaster, when Sir ROBERT HILDYARD was slain, commanding under the banner of Lancaster.

Hildyard (Patrington, co. York, bart., extinct 1814; ROBERT HILDYARD, Esq., of Patrington, was created a bart. 1660, he was youngest son of Sir CHRISTOPHER HILDYARD, Knt., of Wynestead). Same *Arms* and *Crest*.

Hildyard (Flintham, co. Notts; exemplified to THOMAS BLACKBORNE THOROTON-HILDYARD, Esq., of Flintham, J.P. and D.L., High Sheriff of Notts in 1862). Sa. a chev. betw. three mullets or. *Crest*—A game-cock beaked, legged, and wattled gu.

Hilicke. Ar. a chief indented (another, dancettée) sa.

Hiling. Or, a mullet within a bordure sa. bezantée.

Hill (Hillsborough, co. Down; Fun. Ent. of Sir MOSES or MOYSES HILL, who accompanied the *Earl of Essex* to Ireland, 1573, ancestor of the *Marquess of Downshire*, d. Feb. 1629). Sa. on a fess betw. three leopards pass. guard. or, spotted of the field, as many escallops gold.

Hill (*Marquess of Downshire*). Quarterly, 1st, same *Arms*, for HILL; 2nd, per bend sinister erm. and ermines a lion ramp. or, for TREVOR; 3rd, gu. a cinquefoil or, for ROWE; 4th, ar. a chev. az. betw. three trefoils slipped per pale gu. and vert, also for ROWE. *Crest*—A reindeer's head couped gu. attired and plain collared or. *Supporters*—Dexter, a leopard or, spotted sa. ducally gorged and chained gu.; sinister, a reindeer gu. attired, unguled, and plain collared or. *Mottoes*—Per Deum et ferrum obtinui; and, Ne Tentes aut Perfice.

Hill (Buntingdale and Court of Hill, co. Salop; the daus. and co-heirs of the last THOMAS HILL, Esq., of Court of Hill, were LUCY, m. first, in 1780, to THOMAS HUMPHREY LOWE, Esq., of Bromsgrove, and secondly, in 1809, to THOMAS FOWLER, Esq., of Abbey Cwmhir, co. Radnor; and ANNA MARIA, m. in 1787, ᴸᴼ THEᴼᴾʜILUS RICHARD SALWEY, Esq., of the Lodge, co. Salop). Erm. on a fess sa. a tower triple-towered ar.

Hill (*Viscount Hill*). Same *Arms*. *Crest*—A tower ar. surmounted with a garland of laurel ppr. *Supporters*—Dexter, a lion ar. murally crowned or, gorged with a wreath of oak fructed ppr. ; sinister, a horse ar. bridled and saddled ppr. murally gorged gu. *Motto*—Avancez.

Hill (NOEL-HILL, *Baron Berwick*). Quarterly, 1st and 4th, Same *Arms*, on a canton gu. a martlet or, for HILL; 2nd, or, fretty gu. a canton erm., for NOEL; 3rd, or, a chev. betw. three stags' heads cabossed gu., for HARWOOD. *Crests*—1st, HILL: A stag statant ar.; 2nd, NOEL: On the battlements of a tower ppr. a hind statant ar. collared and chained or; 3rd, HARWOOD: A stag's head cabossed sa. in the mouth a sprig of oak ppr. *Supporters*—Dexter, a pegasus ar. gorged with a plain collar sa. thereon a martlet or; sinister, a stag ar. attired or, gorged with a plain collar sa. thereon a leopard's face gold, and a chain reflexed over the back also gold. *Motto*—Qui uti scit, ei bona.

Hill (Standish Hall, near Wigan, co. Lancaster). Same *Arms, Crest*, and *Motto* as Lord Hill.

Hill (co. Bedford). Sa. on a fesse betw. three cats pass. or, as many crosses moline of the field.

Hill (co. Berks). Same *Arms.*

Hill (co. Berks). Sa. on a fesse ar. betw. three ounces pass. guard. or, as many escallops gu.

Hill (co. Berks.) Sa. on a fesse ar. betw. three cats pass. guard. or, a cross moline betw. two escallops gu. *Crest*—A goat's head per pale indented gu. and az. collared and armed or.

Hill (Heligan, co. Cornwall, Visit. 1620 ; Hill's Court, co. Devon, cos. Hants, Lincoln, and Somerset; the HILLS, of Heligan, descended from Sir JOHN HILL, of Kenston, co. Somerset). Gu. a saltire vair betw. four mullets ar. *Crest*—A demi leopard ar. spotted of all colours, ducally gorged or.

Hill (OLIVER HILL, of Shilston, co. Devon; and RICHARD HILL, of Truro, co. Cornwall, sons of ROBERT HILL, of the former. Visit. Cornwall, 1620). Ar. a chev. betw. three water bougets sa. *Crest*—A dove ar. in the beak an olive branch vert.

Hill (Hillstope, co. Cornwall; WILLIAM HILL, descended from ROBERT HILL, of Hill Top, who came into England with the Conqueror. Visit. 1620.) Gu. a chev. erm. betw. three garbs or.

Hill (Sir ROBERT HILL, one of the Judges of the Common Pleas, *temp.* Henry VI.). Ar. a chev. betw. three water bougets sa. *Crest*—A dove ar. in the beak an olive branch vert.

Hill (Ashborne, co. Derby; granted 1615). Per chev. ar. and sa. three cinquefoils counterchanged.

Hill (RICHARD HILL, Serjeant to the Cellar to Henry VIII. Visit. Hants, 1634). Gu. a saltire vair betw. four mullets ar.

Hill (co. Gloucester). Sa. on a chev. betw. three owls ar. as many mullets pierced gu. a bordure engr. erm.

Hill (granted to Capt. HENRY HILL, of Knutsford, co. Chester). Az. a chev. paly of six ar. and sa. betw. two horses' heads erased in chief of the second and in base as many swords in saltire ppr. pommels and hilts or. *Crest*—Betw. two branches of palm ppr. a boar's head couped or, in the mouth a trefoil vert. *Motto*—Auxilio divino.

Hill (co. Worcester; granted to WILLIAM HILL, Esq., F.R.A.S., of Worcester, descended from HUMPHREY HILL, Esq., of Little Witley, co. Worcester, living 1712. WILLIAM HILL's son, by ELIZABETH, his wife, dau. of THOMAS ROWLEY, Esq. of Stourport, is THOMAS ROWLEY HILL, Esq., of St. Katherine's Hill, co. Worcester, M.P., High Sheriff of that county, 1870). Erm. a chev. chequy or and az. in base on a mount vert a Cornish chough ppr. *Crest*—On a mount in front of a fernbrake ppr. a talbot or, collared az. resting the dexter foot on three annulets interlaced gold. *Motto*—Avancez.

Hill (Hill's End, co. Hertford, London and Finchley, co. Middlesex). Per chev. embattled ar. and sa. three cinquefoils counterchanged. *Crest*—On a mount a branch vert, with three cinquefoils ar.

Hill (Lewisham, co. Kent). Vert three talbots pass. ar. *Crest*—A stag's head erased ppr. holding in the mouth an acorn branch vert, fructed or.

Hill (co. Kent). Az. a chev. betw. three fleurs-de-lis ar.

Hill (co. Kent, and London). Sa. a chev. betw. three lions pass. guard. erm.

Hill (Wye, co. Kent). Sa. on a fesse betw. three leopards pass. ar. as many escallops gu. *Crest*—A stag's head erased ppr.

Hill (co. Lincoln). Per chev. ar. and sa. three cinquefoils counterchanged.

490

Hill (Lord Mayor of London, 1484). Sa. a chev. erm. betw. three lions pass. guard. ar.

Hill. Gu. three barrulets erm. in chief a lion pass. guard. or. *Crest*—A fleur-de-lis az.

Hill (Sir ROWLAND HILL, Lord Mayor of London, 1549, a descendant of HUMPHREY HILL, of Court of Hill; his niece and co-heiress, ALICE BARKER, m. Sir THOMAS LEIGH). Gu. two bars or, on a canton sa. a chev. betw. three pheons of the fourth, charged with a wolf's head erased betw. two mullets gu.

Hill (London, 1616). Sa. a chev. erm. betw. three talbots' heads erased ar. *Crest*—A talbot's head erased ar. betw. two laurel branches vert.

Hill (London). Ar. an eagle displ. with two heads sa. on a chief of the second three roses of the first.

Hill (London). Az. two bars or, a canton sa.

Hill (London). Az. two bars ar. on a canton sa. a chev. betw. three pheons of the second.

Hill (London; quartered by AUSTREY, co. Hunts). Per chev. embattled three cinquefoils counterchanged.

Hill (JOHN HILL, gentleman, of London, whose ancestors were of the North. Visit. London, 1568). Sa. a fess erm. betw. two cats-a-mountain pass. guard. ar.

Hill (London). Ar. on a chief sa. three roses of the first.

Hill (Tuddington, co. Middlesex). Sa. a chev. erm. betw. three leopards' faces ar. *Crest*—A talbot's head couped sa. guttée d'eau, gorged with a collar gu. rimmed and studded or.

Hill (co. Middlesex, and Bromsgrove, co. Worcester). Erm. a chev. chequy or and sa. *Crest*—A talbot pass. or, collared gu.

Hill (Hales, co. Norfolk). Gu. two bars erm. in chief a lion pass. per pale or and ar. *Crest*—A boar's head and neck sa. in the mouth a broken spear ppr. headed ar.

Hill (Yarmouth and Lynn, co. Norfolk). Gu. two bars erm. in chief a lion pass. or. *Crest*—On a chapeau gu. turned up erm. a demi lion pass. or, betw. two dragons' wings expanded of the first, each charged with as many bars of the second.

Hill, or Hull (Silvington, co. Salop). Or, on a chief vert three bulls' heads couped of the first. *Crest*—On the horns of a crescent vairé or and az. a bull's head erased gold.

Hill, alias Hule (Parva-Drayton, co. Salop). Az. an eagle displ. ar. over all a bend gu.

Hill (Bridgwater, co. Somerset). Gu. a chev. engr. betw. three garbs or.

Hill (Taunton, co. Somerset). Gu. a chev. erm. betw. three garbs or. *Crest*—A dove with wings expanded, in the beak an olive branch all ppr.

Hill (Denham Place, co. Bucks). Same *Arms.*

Hill (Pounsford, co. Somerset). Gu. a chev. betw. three garbs or, a bordure ar. *Crest*—An eagle, wings expanded ppr. in the beak an acorn slipped vert, fructed or.

Hill (Rothwell, co. Northampton ; quartered by COKAYNE). Gu. a chev. vair betw. three garbs or.

Hill (Taunton, co. Somerset). Az. three dolphins embowed or, on a chief of the last as many hurts. *Crest*—A squirrel sejant ar. collared and lined or.

Hill, alias Hull (Littlepipe, co. Stafford ; granted 1560). Az. a chev. betw. three fleurs-de-lis or, a canton of the last. *Crest*—A lion ramp. ar. pierced through the breast with a broken spear in bend ppr. the head guttée de sang.

Hill (Bury St. Edmunds, co. Suffolk). Gu. two bars erm. in chief a lion pass. or. *Crest*—A boar's head couped sa. in the mouth an acorn or, leaved vert, another acorn as the last stuck upon the head.

Hill. Sa. on a fesse ar. betw. three cats pass. guard. or, a cross moline betw. two cocks gu. *Crest*—A buck's head per pale gu. and az. on the nose or, collared of the last.

Hill. Az. two bars ar. on a quarter sa. a chev. betw. three pheons of the second, charged with a wolf's head erased betw. two mullets gu. *Crest*—A wolf's head erased az. thereon two bars ar. in the mouth a trefoil slipped vert.

Hill. Erm. a chev. componée ar. and gu. *Crest*—A talbot pass. ppr. collared gu.

Hill. Ar. a fesse betw. six martlets gu.

Hill. Gu. on a chev. engr. erm. betw. three garbs ar. a cinquefoil of the first.

Hill. Erm. a chev. lozengy gu. and or.

Hill. Az. a chev. ar. betw. three goats' heads erased of the second, armed or.

Hill. Ar. a chev. gu. betw. three lozenges sa.

Hill (Dennis Park, co. Stafford, and Blaenavon, co. Monmouth). Gu. two bars erm. in chief a lion pass. per pale or and ar. *Crest*—A fleur-de-lis ar. *Motto*—Esse quam videri.

Hill (Alveston, co. Gloucester). Az. on a chev. betw. three owls ar. three mullets sa. a bordure erm.

Hill (co. York). Sa. a chev. engr. erm. betw. three leopards' faces ar. *Crest*—A talbot's head and neck couped sa. eared and semée of cinquefoils ar. gorged with a collar gu. edged, ringed, and studded or.

Hill (Ditton). Sa. on a chev. engr. erm. betw. in chief two garbs or, and in base on a mount vert a garb, also or, betw. two reaping hooks erect ppr. three palets gu. each charged with an erm. spot of the third. *Crest*—Upon a mount vert betw. two ears of wheat or, a tower triple-towered ppr. charged with a passion cross or.

Hill (Castle-Morton, co. Worcester, Oakhill, co. Hereford, Pepper Hill, co. Salop, and Stallington Hall, co. Stafford; Sarah, only child and heiress of Richard Clarke Hill, Esq., of Stallington Hall, *m.* 28 Jan. 1835, Sir Smith Child, Bart., of Newfield, co. Stafford, M.P.). Sa. a chev. or, betw. three wild cats pass. guard. ppr. *Crest*—A hawk ppr. belled or.

Hill (Weston Coyney, co. Stafford; Walter William Hill, Esq., *m.* Mary Catherine, dau. and heir of Edward Coyney, Esq., of Weston Coyney, and took her name, 1788). See Coyney.

Hill (Honiley, co. Warwick). Vert six talbots pass. ar.

Hill (granted to Edward Smith Hill, Esq.). Gu. a saltire betw. two martlets in pale and as many garbs in fesse or. *Crest*—A demi leopard ppr. gorged with a collar gemel or, holding betw. the paws a star of eight points ar. *Motto*—Par negotiis neque supra.

Hill (John David Hay Hill, Esq., J.P., Gressenhall Hall, co. Norfolk). Gu. two bars erm. in chief a lion pass. or. *Crest* —A boar's head erased ppr. holding in the mouth a trefoil vert. *Motto*—Spe labor levis.

Hill (Henry Edward Hill, Esq., Oxford). Vert three talbots pass. ar. *Crest*—A buck's head erased, in the mouth an oak sprig ppr.

Hill (Very Rev. John Hill, Dean of Kilmore; Fun. Ent. of his wife, Ulster's Office, 1634). Vert on a chev. betw. three talbots pass. ar. armed and langued gu. a mullet of the last.

Hill (Hacketstown, co. Carlow; granted by Roberts, Ulster, 1648, to Arthur Hill, formerly of Winter's Park, Oxenhall, co. Gloucester, and descended from Hill, of Hillhouse, in same co.). Sa. on a chev. invected betw. three bears' heads erased ar. as many pellets. *Crest*—A greyhound sejant ar. collared az.

Hill (Brooke Hall, co. Londonderry, bart.). Sa. a chev. erminois betw. three leopards' faces ar. *Crest*—A talbot's head couped sa. guttée d'eau, collared gu. studded and ringed or. *Motto*—Ne tentes aut perfice.

Hill (St. John's, co. Wexford). Ar. two bars ermines, in chief a lion pass. gu. *Crest*—A demi lion gu. *Motto*—Candide me fides.

Hill (Graig, Doneraile, co. Cork; settled there for upwards of two centuries, having been previously of Kilmallock, co. Limerick; granted 1560). Az. a chev. betw. three fleurs-de-lis or, a canton of the last. *Crest*—A lion ramp. ar. pierced through the breast by a broken spear in bend ppr. the head guttée de sang. *Motto*—Ne tenta, vel perfice.

Hill (Lambhill, Scotland, 1676). Az. a mount or, with the sun arising and appearing over the top in his splendour ppr. *Crest*—A Bible expanded ppr. *Motto*—Veritas superabit montes.

Hill (Merrylee, co. Renfrew, 1865). Same *Arms*, within a bordure erm. Same *Crest* and *Motto*.

Hill (James Matthew Hill, Edinburgh and Bengal, 1858). Az. a mount ar. with the sun arising and appearing over the top in his splendour ppr. on a chief or, a wolf's head erased of the first betw. two eastern crowns gu. *Crest*—A dexter arm in armour embowed, the hand grasping a dagger all ppr. *Motto*—Esse quam videri.

Hill (Joseph Hill, London, 1858). As the last, within a bordure gu. Same *Crest* and *Motto*.

Hillarey, and St. Hillary. Sa. three leopards' faces jessant-de-lis ar. betw. nine crosslets fitchée of the second.

Hillarie. Ar. semée of crosslets sa. three fleurs-de-lis of the last. *Crest*—A griffin's head holding in the beak a key ppr.

Hillary (Danbury Place, co. Essex, afterwards of Rigg House, co. York, bart., extinct 1855). Ar. three fleurs-de-lis sa. betw. six crosses crosslet az. a bordure of the second. *Crest*—Out of a mural crown gu. a cubit arm armed ppr. garnished and the joints embattled or, the gauntlet holding a chevaltrap of the last, round the arm a scarf vert. *Supporters*—Two lions ar. each gorged with a collar or, fimbriated sa. charged with a fleur-de-lis betw. two crosses crosslet of the last. *Motto*—Virtuti nihil invium.

491

Hillary (co. Leicester) Sa. crusily three fleurs-de lis and a bordure engr. ar.

Hillary (Daver, co. Norfolk). Ar. a fesse chequy or and sa. (another, of the first and sa.) in chief a mullet of the third.

Hillary (co. Norfolk). Ar. a fesse counter-componée or and gu.

Hillary (Hadley, co. Suffolk). Same *Arms*, a mullet sa. for diff.

Hillary. Sa. three crosses crosslet, two and one, and five fleurs-de-lis ar. one, two, and two.

Hillary. Ar. six crosses crosslet fitchée sa. three, two, and one.

Hillas (exemplified to George William Webb, Esq., sometime of Zurich, Switzerland, and Esther Henrietta, his wife, dau. of Robert William Hillas, of Rutland Square, Dublin, and Seaview House, co. Sligo, on their assuming, by royal licence, 1846, the name of Hillas, in lieu of that of Webb). Per saltire ar. and sa. in fess two mullets pierced of the second, in the chief and base points two crescents ar. within an annulet or, a mullet pierced sa. *Motto*—Per ferrum obtinui.

Hille (Spraxton, co. Oxford; arms of John Hille, in Exeter College. Visit. Oxon, 1566). Gu. a lion ramp. or, debruised by a bend erm.

Hillersdon (originally of Hillersdon, in Collumpton, co. Devon, settled at Membland *temp.* Henry VI.). Ar. on a chev. sa. three bulls' heads cabossed of the first. *Crest*—A squirrel sejant ppr. collared and cracking a nut or.

Hillersdon (Membland, co. Devon; Richard Hillersdon, of that place. Visit. 1620). Ar. on a chev. sa. three bulls' heads cabossed of the field.

Hillersdon (Hoclyfe, co. Bedford; granted 1596). Ar. on a chev. within a bordure engr. sa. three bulls' heads cabossed of the first. *Crest*—A squirrel sejant ppr. collared and cracking a nut or.

Hilles (quartered by Browne, of London, Her. Visit. 1568, through Margaret, dau. of John Lucas, Esq., of Halden). Az. a fess betw. three stags statant.

Hilley. Ar. a fesse sa. betw. six martlets gu.

Hilliar, or Hillyar. Quarterly, erm. and gu. on the 1st and 4th a crescent of the second. *Crest*—A harp or.

Hilliard (co. Durham). Az. a chev. ar. betw. three mullets of the second. *Crest*—A cock sa. combed, legged, and beaked gu.

Hilliard (Marlborough, and of Holderness). See Hildyard.

Hilliard, or Hillary (co. Warwick, and Maringe, co. York). Ar. three fleurs-de-lis az. betw. six crosses crosslet fitchée sa. a crescent gu. for diff. *Crest*—A cubit arm erect in armour ppr. holding in the gauntlet a caltrap ar. round the arm a sash vert.

Hilliard (co. York). Sa. a chev. betw. three mullets of six points ar.

Hilliard. Ar. a cross moline betw. four mullets or. *Crest* —An arm embowed in armour, grasping in the hand a spear all ppr.

Hilliard. Ar. a cross crosslet fitchée sa. betw. three fleurs-de-lis gu.

Hilliard (Caherslee, co. Kerry). Az. three mullets or. *Crest*—A cock ppr.

Hilling, or Hiling. Or, a mullet sa. pierced, a bordure of the second bezantée.

Hilling. Or, on a mullet sa. an annulet of the first, a bordure of the second bezantée.

Hillinge. Paly of six sa. and or, two lozenges in pale counterchanged.

Hillion (co. Essex). Or, three lions ramp. sa.

Hillion. Gu. a fess betw. two frets ar. (another, the fess or).

Hillis. Per pale or and gu. a lion pass. ar.

Hillman. Gu. on a bend cotised or, three roses of the field, seeded of the second, barbed vert. *Crest*—A demi eagle, wings displ. or, holding in the beak a rose gu. stalked and leaved vert.

Hillock, or Hillick. Ar. a chief indented sa. *Crest*—A pheon az. betw. two wings ppr. out of the pheon a branch of laurel vert.

Hillon. Ar. on a canton sa. three ducal coronets in bend or.

Hills (late Astell, of Colne Parke, co. Essex). Erm. on a fesse sa. a tower with two turrets ppr. *Crest*—A tower, as in the arms.

Hills. Ar. a cross betw. four crescents az. a chief of the last. *Crest*—A horse courant gu. in the mouth a broken spear's head sa.

Hills (Chelsea, co. Middlesex, and the Isle of Sheppey, co. Kent; granted in 1784). Vert three hillocks ar.

Hills (Right Rev. GEORGE HILLS, Bishop of British Columbia, 1859). Ar. a chev. betw. three martlets sa.

Hillson. Ar. a cross couped betw. four pheons az. *Crest*—A bull's head erased. *Motto*—Courage.

Hillton (co. Sussex). Ar. two bars az. *Crest*—Moses's head affrontée couped at the shoulders, illumined ppr. *Motto*—Tant que je puis.

Hillyard. Az. three mullets or.

Hillyer (cos. Devon and Oxford). Ar. a bordure engr. gu. on a chief az. three mullets or.

Hilmingham (co. Suffolk). Az. a saltire erm. betw. four eagles displ. ar. *Crest*—A leopard sejant erm. collared.

Hiltoft (Boston, co. Lincoln). Or, on a chev. gu. betw. three fleurs-de-lis vert as many martlets ar.

Hiltoft, or Hiltofte. Ar. an eagle rising sa. armed or.

Hilton (Hilton, co. Durham; one of the great baronial families of the Palatinate Barons of the Bishopric. Of this ancient house were ROBERT DE HILTON, of Hilton, and ALEXANDER DE HILTON, of Hilton, who both had summons to Parliament, the former in 1295, the latter in 1332. The last male heir of the *Palatine Barons of Hilton* was JOHN HILTON, Esq., M.P. for Carlisle in 1727, *d. unm.* 1746, leaving his three sisters his co-heirs, namely, ANNE, *m.* Sir RICHARD MUSGRAVE, fourth bart., of Hayton Castle; ELIZABETH, *m.* THOMAS YOUNGHUSBAND, Esq., of Budle; and CATHERINE, *m.* to JOHN BRISCOE, D.D., of Crofton, co. Cumberland : ELEANOR, only dau. and heiress of Sir RICHARD MUSGRAVE HYLTON, fifth bart., and grand-daughter and heir of ANNE, Lady MUSGRAVE, *m.* WILLIAM JOLLIFFE, Esq., M.P. for Petersfield, whose grandson, Sir WILLIAM GEORGE JOLLIFFE, Bart., of Merstham, was created *Lord Hylton,* 1866). Ar. two bars az. *Crest*—On a close helmet, Moses's head in profile, glorified, adorned with a rich diapered mantle all ppr. *Another Crest or Cognizance*—A stag couchant ducally gorged and chained or. *Supporters*—Two lions az. ; anciently two conies and two stags were used as supporters.

Hilton (*Baron Hilton ;* summoned to Parliament 1332; passed to the WIDDRINGTONS, Lords Widdrington, attainted 1716). Same *Arms* and *Crest.*

Hilton (South Shields, co. Durham, co. Sussex, London, co. Leicester, and the Island of Jamaica; descended from HENRY HILTON, younger son of Sir WILLIAM HILTON, of Hilton, by ANNE, his wife, dau. of Sir JOHN YORKE). Same *Arms* and *Crest.*

Hilton (WILLIAM HILTON, Baron of the Exchequer in Ireland; Fun. Ent. of his dau. MARGARET, wife of Capt. ANDREW WILSON, brother of Sir JOHN WILSON, Knt., of Wilson's Fort, co. Donegal, *d.* 15 Nov. 1639). Same *Arms,* a crescent for diff.

Hilton (Rea Hall, co. Stafford, claiming descent from HILTON, of Hilton Castle, co. Durham). Same *Arms, &c..*

Hilton (Dyons, co. Durham). Gu. on a bend ar. cotised or, three martlets sa.

Hilton (cos. Lancaster and York). Ar. a lion ramp. gu. crowned or.

Hilton (Millwood, co. Lancaster; descended from HILTON, of Hilton, co. Westmoreland, 1664). Sa. three annulets ar. in chief two saltires couped of the second.

Hilton (Swyne, co. Durham ; a branch of Hilton, of Hilton, which adopted the arms of the family of LASCELLES, whence they maternally descended; the daus. and co-heirs of Sir ROBERT HILTON, Lord of Swyne, *d.* 1431, were ISABEL, wife of ROBERT HILDYARD, Esq., and ELIZABETH, wife of JOHN MELTON, Esq.). Ar. three chaplets gu.

Hilton (co. Westmoreland). Sa. three mullets in base and two saltires in chief ar.

Hilton. Az. two bars ar. *Crest*—A hand vested barry ar. and sa. holding a holly branch ppr.

Hilton. Or, a chief counter-componée erm. and az.

Hilton. Sa. three saltires ar.

Hilton. Az. two bars ar. in chief as many mullets or.

Hilton (arms in Bletchingdon Church, co. Oxford, of EDWARD HILTON, B.D., *d.* 14 July, 1530. Visit. Oxon, 1566). Sa. in chief two saltires couped, and in base three annulets ar.

Hilton (Reg. Ulster's Office). Sa. a lion's head cabossed ar.

Hinchley. Or, two piles gu. *Crest*—A leopard couchant ppr.

Hinchley. Ar. two piles vert, a chief sa.

Hinchley. Paly of six or and gu.

Hinchliff (London). Or, a wivern betw. three fleurs-de-lis vert.

Hinchman. Ar. a chev. betw. three buglehorns sa. stringed gu. on a chief of the second as many lions ramp. of the first.

434

Crest—A demi lion ramp. ar. holding a buglehorn, as in the arms.

Hinchud. Sa. a fesse chequy or and az. betw. three horses' heads erased ar.

Hinckes, Hincks, or Hinks. Paly of six or and az on a chief of the last three annulets of the first. *Crest*—A hand holding a scorpion all ppr.

Hincks (Chorlton, co. Chester). Gu. a lion ramp. erm. an orle of bezants and plates alternately. *Crest*—A demi lion gu. guttée de larmes, gorged with a collar dancettée ar. the sinister paw resting on an annulet or. *Motto*—In cruce et lachrymis spes est.

Hincks (confirmed to Rev. THOMAS DIX HINCKS, LL.D., Professor of Hebrew at the Belfast Institution). Sa. a lion ramp. ar. an orle of six bezants. *Crest*—A demi lion ramp. ar. the sinister jamb resting on a bezant.

Hind (Kent). Ar. on a chev. gu. betw. three goats' heads az. collared and attired or, as many lozenges of the first, on a chief sa. a lion pass. guard. of the fourth. *Crest*—A griffin's head couped betw. two wings, collared and charged on the breast with an escallop.

Hind (London). Ar. on a chev. sa. three escallops of the first, on a chief az. a lion pass. of the field. *Crest*—A hind's head couped ppr. collared or, holding in the mouth a rose gu. stalked and leaved vert.

Hind (Mayor of Calais, 1557). Ar. on a chev. gu. betw. three talbots pass. sa. collared or, as many bezants. *Crest*—A demi talbot ar. collared sa. holding betw. the paws a key or, ward upwards.

Hind. Gu. a chev. betw. three hinds or. *Crest*—A cockatrice or, on the trunk of a tree raguled or.

Hind. Same *Arms.* *Crest*—An ensign in full dress, with cocked hat, holding the union standard of Britain all ppr.

Hind. Az. a fesse betw. three lozenges ar.

Hinde (Bishopwearmouth, co. Durham). Ar. a chev. betw. three escallops az. on a chief of the second a lion pass. of the first. *Crest*—A demi pegasus ar. maned or, holding a sword of the first, hilt and pommel gold. *Motto*—Tutum te robore reddam.

Hinde (co. Lancaster). Same *Arms* and *Crest.*

Hinde (Hodgeworth, co. Bucks ; granted 1583). Gu. a chev. betw. three hinds trippant or. *Crest*—Out of a ducal coronet ar. a cockatrice volant or.

Hind (Laxton, co. Nottingham). Same *Arms* and *Crest.*

Hinde (co. Cambridge). Sa. three hinds' heads erased ar.

Hinde (co. Cambridge). Ar. a chev. betw. three lozenges or, on a chief of the second a lion pass. erm.

Hinde (co. Cambridge). Ar. on a chev. gu. betw. three goats' heads erased az. attired and collared or, as many lozenges of the last, on a chief sa. a lion pass. guard. erm.

Hinde (London). Gu. on a chev. betw. three hinds trippant or, a lion's head erased az. betw. two hurts, each charged with a fleur-de-lis of the second.

Hinde (London). Per chev. or and sa. three pheons counter-changed.

Hinde (Evelith, co. Salop). Ar. on a chev. betw. three escallops az. as many escallops of the first, a chief of the second charged with a lion pass. of the field. *Crest*—A lion's head erased ar.

Hinde. See HODGSON-HINDE.

Hinde, or Hynde. Sa. a pelican in her nest feeding her young ar.

Hindeston (co. Devon). Gu. a naked arm couped ppr. holding a battle axe ar.

Hindley (Hindley, co. Lancaster, 6 Henry VII.). Az. a stag lodged (sometimes at gaze) ar. (Quartered by CULCHETH). *Crest*—An arm in armour erased fesseways, holding a scymitar in pale, enfiled with a boar's head couped.

Hindmarch. Gu. on a mount vert a hind couchant ar.

Hindmarsh, or Hendmarsh (co. Kent). Ar. a lion vert, tail double queued, crowned or.

Hindmarsh, Hendmarsh, or Hyndmarsh (Scotland). Same *Arms.* *Crest*—A demi lion ramp. *Motto*—Nil nisi patria.

Hindmarsh. Ar. a lion ramp. guard. vert, crowned or.

Hindsey. Gu. an inescutcheon voided ar.

Hine (granted to JOHN HINE, Esq., of Dartmouth, co. Devon). Ar. on a fesse engr. az. three anchors or, in chief a greyhound courant sa. *Crest*—On a tortoise ar. an eagle rising, holding in the beak a sprig of heath, and gazing on the sun all ppr.

Hine (Bristol). Or, three hinds' heads erased sa.

Hingenson (co. Buckingham). Gu. a naked arm embowed, issuing from the sinister, holding a battle axe erect all ppr. *Crest*—A squirrel sejant cracking a nut all ppr.

Hingham (co. Norfolk). Per fesse or and vert a millrind

gu. *Crest*—A horse's head furnished with cart harness ppr.

Hingham (co. Suffolk). Quarterly, or and gu. a bordure engr. sa. semée of escallops ar.

Hingham. Per pale or and vert a cross fourchée gu.

Hingham. Ar. a leopard coward pass. reguard. sa. betw. six crosses crosslet fitchée gu.

Hingston (Holbeton, co. Devon). Gu. an arm in armour ppr. holding a Danish battle axe ar. *Crest*—A hind's head couped or, holding in the mouth a holly slip ppr.

Hinkley (co. Chester). Gu. a chev. engr. per pale erm. and az.

Hinkley, or Hinckley. Per pale indented ar. and gu. *Crest*—On a ducal coronet or, a star of twelve points ppr.

Hinkly. Gu. a pale or.

Hinkpenn. Gu. two bars gemelles or, a chief indented erm.

Hinks, or Hincks (London). Or, a saltire gu. on a chief of the second three lions' heads erased ar. *Crest*—A lion's head erased or, betw. two wings ar.

Hinsham (London). Az. on a saltire engr. ar. five martlets sa.

Hinshaw (Scotland, 1871). Ar. a lion ramp. sa. within a bordure engr. per pale of the second and gu. *Crest*—A fox's head holding in the mouth an olive branch ppr. *Motto*—Vigilantia.

Hinson (Fordham, co. Cambridge, Tavistock, co. Devon, and Hunts Court, co. Gloucester; descended from WILLIAM HINSON, Esq., of Fordham, 23 Henry VII., A.D. 1507. Visit. Middlesex, 1663). Az. a chev. betw. three suns or.

Hinson (Fulham, co. Middlesex, and of Dublin; granted by Preston, Ulster, 1644, to THOMAS HINSON, of Dublin and Fulham, son of RICHARD HINSON, second son of THOMAS HINSON, Esq., of Fordham, for service done in Ireland. Reg. Her. Coll. London. Same *Arms*, a bordure erm. *Crest* —A fleur-de-lis per pale erm. and az.

Hinson, alias Powell (Pengethley, co. Hereford, bart.; WILLIAM HINSON, second son of THOMAS HINSON, of Dublin, by ANNE, dau. of EDWARD POWELL, Esq., of Fulham, *s.* to the estate of his maternal uncle, Sir EDWARD POWELL, Bart., of Pengethley, on condition of his calling himself POWELL, *alias* HINSON, and was created a bart. 1661, *d. s. p. m.* 1681). Same *Arms* and *Crest*.

Hinstoke. Sa. a chev. erm. betw. three lions ramp. ar. crowned or.

Hintinge. Az. ten plates, four, three, two, and one.

Hinton (Hinton). Per fesse indented sa. and ar. six fleurs-de-lis counterchanged.

Hinton (South Denchworth and Kingston-Lisle, co. Berks, and co. Salop). Same *Arms*. *Crest*—An eagle's leg erased, encircled by a serpent ppr.

Hinton (co. Cumberland). Per pale indented sa. and or, six fleurs-de-lis counterchanged ar. and sa.

Hinton (co. Derby, and Deverel-Langbridge, co. Dorset). Vert a bend or.

Hinton (co. Essex). Vert a bend ar.

Hinton (co. Salop). Ar. on a bend sa. three martlets of the field. *Crest*—The paschal lamb ar. glory or, carrying a banner of the first, charged with a cross gu.

Hinton (Ringwardine, co. Salop). Same *Arms* as HINTON, of co. Salop, with a crescent in chief.

Hinton (Rushton, co. Chester). Az. on a bend sa. betw. two poppies gu. stalked vert, three martlets ar.

Hinton (quartered by STANLEY, of Dalgarth and Awsthwaite. Visit. Cumberland, 1615). Per fess indented or and sa. a fleur-de-lis counterchanged.

Hinton. Erm. on a chev. sa. five martlets ar.

Hinton. Gu. on a bend ar. cotised or, three martlets sa.

Hinton. Per fesse indented sa. and or, on a chief ar. two fleurs-de-lis of the first.

Hinton. Per fesse indented sa. and or, in chief three fleurs-de-lis ar.

Hinton (co. Salop; ANNE, dau. and co-heir of GRIFFITH HINTON, of that place, *m.* THOMAS CLUDDE, of Orleton, in same co., 30 Henry VIII., 1538. Visit. Notts, 1614). Ar. in chief two estoiles, and in base three arrows, two in saltire and one in pale ppr. flighted of the field, barbed az. banded gu.

Hinton (Halstone, co. Wexford; confirmed to THOMAS HINTON, Esq., of that place). Ar. on a bend az. cotised gu. betw. six trefoils slipped vert three doves close of the first. *Crest*—A mount vert, thereon an eagle's leg erased, the claw pressing down the neck of a serpent entwined around the limb all ppr. *Motto*—Assurgam.

Hinxman (Little Durnford, co. Wilts; granted to EDWARD HINXMAN in 1549). Or, a chev. betw. three buglehorns sa. stringed gu. on a chief gu. three lions ramp. or. *Crest*—A

cubit arm quarterly or and vert, hand ppr. holding a buck's horn or.

Hipkiss. Per fesse nebulée gu. and ar. three martlets counterchanged. *Crest*—A sphinx guard. wings endorsed ppr.

Hippisley (Camely, co Somerset, and Stanton, co. Wilts; granted 1564). Sa. three mullets pierced betw. two bendlets or. *Crest*—Out of a ducal coronet ppr. a hind's head erased or, gorged with a collar sa. charged with three mullets of the first.

Hippisley (Warfield Grove, co. Berks, bart.). Sa. three mullets pierced in bend betw. two bendlets and as many annulets or. *Crest*—Out of a ducal coronet or, a hind's head erased sa. gorged with a collar gold. *Supporters*— Two eagles reguard. sa. wings expanded pean, beaked and membered or, on the breast of each, pendent by a chain from the neck gold a shield, thereon the arms of Wirtemburg, viz., or, three stags' horns barways sa. *Motto*— Amicitiæ virtutisque fœdus : the inscription of the great Order of Wirtemburg. The *Family Motto* is—Non mihi, sed patriæ.

Hippisley (Lamborne Place, co. Berks; descended from RICHARD HIPPISLEY, Esq., who received large grants of land in co. Somerset from John-o'-Gaunt, *Duke of Lancaster*, *temp.* Edward III.). Sa. three mullets pierced in bend betw. two bendlets or. *Crest*—A hind's head erased ppr. gorged with a collar sa. and or, surcharged with three mullets pierced.

Hippisley (Ston Easton, co. Somerset). Sa. three mullets pierced in bend betw. two bendlets or. *Crest*—A hind's head erased ppr. gorged with a collar sa. charged with three mullets pierced or.

Hippisley (Shobrooke Park, co. Devon). Same *Arms* and *Crest*.

Hippon (Featherstone). Az. three keys erect, one and two, betw. as many fleurs-de-lis, two and one, all or.

Hipsley (Hackney and Bushy Park, co. Middlesex). Or, three mullets betw. two bendlets sa. *Crest*—A hind's head or, gorged with a bar gemelle sa.

Hird (Low Moor House, co. York). Az. a fess betw. three stags trippant or.

Hird (Bradford, co. York). Same *Arms*. *Crest*—A buck's head erased gu horned, or.

Hirme (Heveringland, co. Norfolk). Or, three bars gemelles gu. on a canton sa. five lozenges in saltire of the second. *Crest*—A talbot pass. sa. collared and lined or, the line coiled at the end.

Hirst, or Hirste. Gu. on a chief indented ar. three annulets az. *Crest*—A hand cutting a feather with a scymitar engr. on the back.

Hirst (Rotherham, co. York). Ar. a sun in splendour gu.

Hirst (Howarth, co. York). Ar. a sun in splendour gu. on a chief az. a rose ar. betw. two sinister hands spaunée or. *Crest*—A hurst of trees ppr. pendent therefrom a shield ar. charged with a cinquefoil vert. *Motto*—Efflorescent.

Hirst (Clough House, co. York; granted 28 Oct. 1820). Ar. a sun in splendour gu. on a chief az. a rose ar. betw. two sinister hands couped or. *Crest*—A hirst of trees, upon which hangs a shield charged with a cinquefoil.

Hirward. Ar. a cross crosslet gu.

Hislop (Tothill, co. Devon, bart., extinct; Lieut-Gen. Sir THOMAS HISLOP, G.C.B., Royal Artillery, was so created, 1813, *d. s. p. m.*). Ar. on a mount a buck couchant under a tree all ppr. and for honourable augmentation, on a chief az. a mount vert, thereon a lion in the act of tearing the standard of the Mahratta Prince, Holkar, and beneath the word "Madripore." *Crests*—1st, of augmentation : A soldier of the 22nd Light Dragoons mounted and in the position of attack ppr. ; 2nd : Out of a mural coronet a buck's head couped ppr. attired gold. *Motto* (over the first crest)—Deckan.

Hitch (co. Worcester). Per fesse or and sa. three estoiles counterchanged.

Hitch (cos. Worcester, Berks, and Gloucester). Quarterly, 1st and 4th, or, a bend vair betw. two cotises indented sa.; 2nd and 3rd, per fesse or and sa. three estoiles counterchanged. *Crest*—An antelope's head erased sa. tufted, armed, and maned or, vulned through the neck with a birdbolt gold, feathered ar. holding the end in his mouth. *Motto* —Avi numerantur avorum.

Hitch (Wendlebury, co. Oxford; WILLIAM HITCH, Esq., of that place, son of JOHN HITCH, of Kemston, co. Beds, and grandson of ROGER HITCH, of the same place, who was second son of JOHN HITCH, of Hardwick, in same co., the son and heir of THOMAS HITCH, of Ingleton Fells, co. York. Visit. Oxon, 1566). Ar. a bend vair betw. two cotises indented gu. *Crest*—An antelope's head erased sa. horned and vulned through the neck with an arrow or, holding the end in the mouth.

Hitcham (confirmed, 1604, to Sir ROBERT HITCHAM). Gu. on a chief or, three torteaux.

Hitchcock (Preshute, co. Wilts). Ar. on a cross az. five fleurs-de-lis or, in the dexter chief quarter a lion ramp. gu. *Crest*—A lion's head erased or, in the mouth a round buckle ar.

Hitchcock. Gu. a chev. betw. three alligators ar. *Crest*—An alligator ppr.

Hitchins (co. Oxford). Sa. a castle ar. *Crest*—A castle ar. *Another Crest*—Out of a mural coronet a garb, on the top a bird perched ppr.

Hitchins. Ar. a cross flory, quarterly gu. and az. betw. four lions' heads erased sa. *Crest*—On an heraldic rose placed horizontally gu. barbed vert, a lion's head erased or.

Hitford. Vert a chev. betw. three bucks' heads cabossed or.

Hiwis, or Hewis (Stowford, co. Devon; the heiress *m.* HAWLEY; quartered by COPLESTONE, of Coplestone, co. Devon. Visit. 1620). Gu. fretty and a canton ar.

Hixon (co. Cambridge, and Greenwich, co. Kent; confirmed 1617). Or, two eagles' legs erased in saltire sa.

Hizam. Ar. a lion pass. reguard. sa. betw. six crosses pattée fitchée of the second.

Hizard. Ar. a lion pass. coward sa. in chief a cross formée fitchée gu.

Hoadly (granted, 1715, to Rev. BENJAMIN HOADLY, D.D., successively Bishop of Bangor, Hereford, Salisbury, and Winchester). Quarterly, az. and or, in the first quarter a pelican of the second vulning herself ppr. *Crest*—Upon a terrestrial orb or, a dove, wings expanded, holding an olive branch in the beak ppr. *Motto*—Veritas et patria.

Hoar (GEORGE HOAR, Esq., of Twyford, co. Hants). Quarterly, sa. and gu. over all an eagle displ. with two heads ar. a bordure invecked counterchanged. *Crest*—An eagle's head erased ar. charged with three erm. spots, pendent from the beak an annulet.

Hoar. Same *Arms* as HOARE, of Gloucester. *Crest*—A fox courant ppr.

Hoard. Per fesse or and ar. in chief a Cornish chough sa. *Crest*—A lamb ppr. holding a flag gu. charged with a saltire ar.

Hoare (London; derived from Sir RICHARD HOARE, M.P., Lord Mayor of London 1713, and now represented by HENRY HOARE, Esq., of Staplehurst, co. Kent). Sa. an eagle displ. with two heads ar. charged on the breast with an erm. spot of the first, within a bordure engr. of the second. *Crest*—An eagle's head erased ar. charged with an erm. spot sa. *Motto*—In ardua.

Hoare (Stourhead, co. Wilts, bart.). Sa. an eagle displ. with two heads ar. charged on the breast with an erm. spot, a bordure engr. of the second. *Crest*—An eagle's head erased ar. charged with an erm. spot. *Motto*—In ardua.

Hoare (Annabelle, co. Cork, bart.). Sa. an eagle displ. with two necks, within a bordure engr. ar. *Crest*—A deer's head and neck ppr. erased ar., motto over, Venit hora. *Motto*—Dum spiro spero.

Hoare (Factory Hill, co. Cork; a branch of HOARE, of Annabelle). Same *Arms*, &c.

Hoare, or Hore (co. Gloucester). Sa. an eagle displ. within a bordure engr. ar. *Crest*—An eagle's head erased sa. gorged with a bar gemelle or.

Hoare, or Hore (Trenouth, co. Cornwall; RICHARD HORE. Visit. 1620). Az. on a bend or, three torteaux.

Hoare, or Hoar (co. Middlesex). Ar. an eagle displ. with two necks, within a bordure engr. sa. *Crest*—A deer's head erased.

Hoast (London). Az. a bull's head couped ar. winged and armed or.

Hobart (*Earl of Buckinghamshire*). Sa. an estoile of eight rays or, betw. two flaunches erm. *Crest*—A bull pass. per pale sa. and gu. bezantée, in the nose a ring or. *Supportors*—Dexter, a stag; sinister, a talbot, both ppr. and reguard. each gorged with a collar radiant and lined or. *Motto*—Auctor pretiosa facit.

Hobart (Blickling and Intwood, co. Norfolk). Sa. an estoile of eight points or, betw. two flaunches erm. *Crest*—A bull pass. per pale sa. and gu. bezantée, in the nostrils an annulet or. *Another Crest*—A bull's head couped sa. semée of estoiles or.

Hobart (Dromore, co. Waterford). Same *Arms*, &c.

Hobart (co. Suffolk). Sa. an estoile of six points or, betw. two flaunches erm.

Hobart. Sa. three fleurs-de-lis ar.

Hobberthorne (co. Lincoln; Lord Mayor of London,

1546). Sa. a mascle within a double tressure flory counter flory ar.

Hobbes (Sarum, co. Wilts). Sa. on a chev. or, betw. three swans ar. as many lions' heads erased of the field. *Crest*—Betw. the horns of a crescent ar. an estoile or, all betw. two wings gu.

Hobbins (Redmarsley, co. Hereford). Or, a chev. betw. three castles triple-towered gu. *Crest*—A stag's head issuant ppr.

Hobbs (West Wickham, co. Buckingham). Ar. a three-legged trivet sa.

Hobbs (co. Middlesex). Gu. a chev. engr. betw. three fishes naiant ar. on a chief of the second as many herons sa. membered and beaked of the first. *Crest*—A demi heron volant ar.

Hobbs (Stoke-Gursy, co. Somerset). Sa. three escutcheons or, each charged with an eagle displ. of the field. *Crest*—A demi tiger az. armed, maned, and tufted ar. pierced through the body with a broken spear or, headed of the second, vulned on the shoulder gu. the spear entering the breast and coming out at the shoulder.

Hobbs (Tooting, co. Surrey). Ar. a bend wavy az. betw. two falcons close ppr. beaked, legged, and belled or. *Crest*—On a dexter glove lying fesseways ar. a falcon, as in the arms.

Hobbs (Quedgely, co. Gloucester). Same *Arms* and *Crest*.

Hobbs (Weybridge, co. Surrey, 1634). Sa. on a chev. or, betw. three swans ppr. as many lions' heads erased of the field.

Hobby (co. Hereford). Ar. on a chev. embattled betw. three hawks az. as many roses or.

Hobby (co. Kent; granted 6 June, 1580). Ar. a fesse sa. betw. three hawks ppr. belled and jessed or. *Crest*—A tiger ramp. reguard. ar.

Hobby (Hailes, co. Gloucester). Ar. a fesse betw. three martlets sa.

Hobeck (Wickingham, co. Norfolk; granted June, 1613). Ar. on a saltire vert seven escallops of the first.

Hoberd, or Hobert. Ar. three fleurs-de-lis sa. *Crest*—A demi lion gu.

Hobhouse (co. Somerset). Az. three crescents ar. betw. the horns of each a mullet of six points of the last. *Crest*—A griffin sejant ppr.

Hobhouse (Westbury College, co. Gloucester, and Chantry House, co Wilts, bart.). Per pale az. and gu. three crescents ar. issuant therefrom as many estoiles irradiated or. *Crest*—Out of a mural crown per pale az. and gu. a crescent and estoile, as in the arms. *Motto*—Spes vitæ melioris.

Hobhouse (*Baron Broughton*, of Broughton Gyfford; extinct 1869; Sir JOHN CAM HOBHOUSE, second bart. of Westbury, was so created 1851, *d. s. p. m.*). Same *Arms*, *Crest*, and *Motto*. *Supporters*—Two horses sa. each charged on the shoulder with an estoile radiated or.

Hobhouse (Hadspen House, co. Somerset; descended from HENRY, younger brother of JOHN HOBHOUSE, Esq., of Westbury College, co. Gloucester). Same *Arms*, *Crest*, and *Motto*.

Hobilder, or Hobildod. Ar. on a bend gu. three martlets or, a bordure of the second.

Hobillion (London). Ar. three hop-poles sustaining their fruit ppr.

Hoble. Az. on a fesse betw. six acorns or, as many roses gu.

Hobleday (Thornton, co. Warwick; allowed by Camden's Deputies). Ar. on a bend gu. three martlets or, a border engr. sa. *Crest*—Out of a ducal coronet or, a demi lion ramp. bezantée.

Hoblethorne. See HOBBERTHORNE.

Hoblethwayte (Sedberg, co. York). Ar. two pales az. on a canton or, a mullet sa. pierced gu. *Crest*—Out of a ducal coronet or, a demi wolf erm.

Hoblyn (Bodreyn and Nanswhyden, co. Cornwall; THOMAS HOBLYN, Visit. 1620, and THOMAS HOBLYN, of Nanswhyden, settled at the former place five generations before 1620). Az. a fesse or, betw. two flaunches erm. *Crest*—A tower ar.

Hoblyn (Colquite, co. Cornwall). See PETER-HOBLYN.

Hobson (Merington, co. Durham; confirmed 16 Jan. 1657). Ar. a chev. az. betw. three hurts, a chief of the second. *Crest*—A griffin's head couped ar. betw. two wings elevated az. *Motto*—Fortitudine.

Hobson (co. Lincoln). Sa. a cinquefoil ar. a chief chequy or and az.

Hobson (Cambridge, 1676). Ar. on a fess betw. two chev. sa. three billets ar. *Crest*—A lion's head erased or, issuing from a ducal coronet chequy or and sa.

Hobson (Wingwood, Isle of Wight). Ar. on a chev. engr. az. betw. three torteaux as many cinquefoils of the field, a chief chequy or and az.

Hobson (Spalding, co. Lincoln). Sa. a cinquefoil erm. a chief chequy or and az. *Crest*—A panther's head erased and guard. ppr. fire issuing from the mouth and ears, gorged with a collar chequy or and az.

Hobson (Marylebone Park, co. Middlesex. Visit. co. Hants, 1634). Ar. on a chev. az. betw. three torteaux as many cinquefoils of the first, a chief chequy or and of the second. *Crest*—A griffin pass. per pale erm. and or, beaked, membered, and holding in the beak a key gold.

Hobson (co. Middlesex, 1633). Ar. on a chev. az. betw. three torteaux three cinquefoils or, a chief vairé or and az. *Crest*—A lion's head affrontée ar. charged with three torteaux.

Hobson (Chichester, co. Sussex). Ar. on a chev. engr. az. betw. three torteaux as many cinquefoils of the field. *Crest*— A leopard's head ar. semée of torteaux.

Hobson (Shipley, co. Sussex). Ar. a chev. betw. three leopards' faces az.

Hobson. Ar. a chev. engr. az. betw. four lozenges gu. each charged with a cross or.

Hobson. Ar. on a chev. az. betw. three torteaux as many cinquefoils or.

Hoburne. Gu. semée of crosses crosslet ar. a lion ramp. or.

Hobury. Gu. a lion pass. or, betw. eight crosses crosslet fitchée ar.

Hobury. Gu. a lion ramp. within an orle of crosses crosslet fitchée ar.

Hobush. Gu. three fusils in fesse ar. *Crest*—Out of a ducal coronet or, a savage's head affrontée couped at the shoulders ppr. vested gu. on the head three ostrich feathers ar.

Hoby (Bisham, co. Berks, and co. Kent, bart., extinct 1766; descended from Sir THOMAS HOBY, Knt., of Bisham, Ambassador to the Court of France in 1566. Visit. Worcester, 1569). Ar. a fess sa. betw. three hobies ppr. This family frequently used as its paternal coat one of its quarterings, BADLAND, viz., ar. three fusils upon slippers in fess gu. threaded or. *Crest*—A hoby rising, beaked, legged, and belled or. *Another Crest*—On a chapeau gu. turned up erm. an heraldic tiger ramp. ar.

Hoby, or Hobby (Neath Abbey, co. Glamorgan, and Ewler, co. Worcester). Ar. three fusils upon slippers gu. *Crest*— On a chapeau gu. turned up erm. a tiger ramp. ar.

Hoby (co. Leicester). Az. a bend (another, a pale) betw. six mullets or.

Hoby (co. Radnor, 1561). Ar. a fesse betw. three hoby birds close sa. *Crest*—A hoby-bird, wings elevated sa.

Hoby (Sir THOMAS POSTUMOUS HOBY, knighted by Sir William Fitz-William, Lord Deputy, 1593). Ar. three fusils in fess gu. *Crest*—Out of a ducal coronet a fish's head ppr.

Hobyn. Ar. a hart pass. ppr. attired or.

Hocid (Scotland). Gu. a dexter hand couped fesseways betw. two mullets pierced in fesse of six points ar.

Hockenhull (Hockenhull, co. Chester). Ar. an ass's head erased sa. *Crest*—A buck's head and neck erased per fesse ar. and or, pierced through the nostrils with a dart in bend gold, feathered also ar. barbed az.

Hockenhull (Duddon). Same *Arms*, with a canton gu.

Hockin (Lydford, co. Devon; granted 1764). Per fesse wavy gu. and az. a lion pass. guard. or, beneath the feet a musket lying horizontally ppr. semée of fleurs-de-lis of the third. *Crest*—On a rock a seagull rising all ppr. *Motto*—Hoc in loco Deus rupes.

Hockin. Ar. a lozenge buckle tongue in fesse sa.

Hocklay. Or, a fesse betw. three lozenges gu.

Hockleton (co. Salop). Vert a lion ramp. ar.

Hockley. Or, a fesse betw. three mascles gu.

Hockly (Wickwar, co. Gloucester; granted 23 Oct. 1772). Ar. on a fesse az. betw. three mullets pierced sa. as many crescents or. *Crest*—A demi griffin segreant pean, wings endorsed, holding in the claws a mullet gu.

Hockmore (Buckyate and Buckland Baron, co. Devon; WILLIAM HOCKMORE, of those places, descended from RICHARD HOCKMORE, *temp.* Richard II., *m.* AGNES, dau. and co-heir of JOHN BUCKYATE, of Buckyate. Visit. 1620). Per chev. sa. and or, in chief two pairs of reaping hooks endorsed and entwined, blades az. handles of the second, and in base a moorcock of the first, combed and wattled gu. quartering BUCKYATE, Az. a buck's head cabossed ar. armed or, with three arrows feathered of the second, shafts of the third, one in pale passing through the head, and two in base. *Crest*—An eagle close, seizing and preying on a moorcock all ppr.

Hocknell (co. Chester). Ar. an ass's head erased sa.

Hocknell (Duden, co. Chester). Same *Arms*, with a canton of the last.

495

Hocknell. Same *Arms*. *Crest*—A dexter hand holding a sugar-cane ppr.

Hockn◌ll (co. Chester). Ar. three asses' heads erased sa.

Hodbonell, or Hodbonille (*temp.* Edward I.). Per pale or and az. a saltire counterchanged.

Hodby (co. Lincoln). Az. three doves ppr.

Hoddar, or Hodder. Ar. three halberts sa. headed az. *Crest*—An angel in a praying posture ppr. betw. two laurel branches vert.

Hodder (Ringabella, co. Cork). Ar. three pole-axes erect in fess ppr. *Crest*—A fire ship in full sail ppr. *Motto*— Igne et ferris vicimus.

Hodder (MOORE-HODDER, Hoddersfield, co. Cork). Quarterly, 1st and 4th, ar. three pole-axes erect in fesse ppr., for HODDER; 2nd and 3rd, az. on a chief indented or, three mullets pierced gu., for MOORE. *Cre ts*—1st, HODDER: A fire-ship with her courses set, fire issuing from below the rigging all ppr.; 2nd, MOORE: Out of a ducal coronet or, a Moor's head in profile all ppr. *Motto*—Per ignem ferris vicimus.

Hoddenet. Quarterly, per fesse indented ar. and gu. a label of five points az.

Hoddy (co. Devon). See HODY.

Hoddy, or Hody. Chequy az. and or, on a canton sa. a bird ar. *Crest*—A trout naiant ppr.

Hodge (Scotland and Sunderland, co. Durham). Az. a chev. ar. betw. three annulets or. *Crest*—A garb entwined with two serpents ppr.

Hodge. Or, a chev. gu. surmounted by a pale sa. *Crest*— An eagle rising, looking at the sun ppr.

Hodge (impalement Fun. Ent. of JAMES TAYLOUR, Sheriff of Dublin, *d.* 20 Dec. 1605, *m.* ISABEL HODGE). Ar. three chevronels az. in chief three inescutcheons gu.

Hodges (Shipton Moyne, co. Gloucester; the late Rev. WALTER HODGES, D.D., Provost of Oriel College, Oxford). Az. a fesse betw. three crescents ar. *Crest*—Out of clouds az. a crescent ar. betw. the horns a star of six points or. *Motto*—Dant lucem crescentibus orti.

Hodges (cos. Dorset and Gloucester). Or, three crescents sa. on a canton of the second a ducal coronet of the first. *Crest*—Out of a ducal coronet or, an heraldic antelope's head ar. horned and tufted gold.

Hodges (Broadwell, co. Gloucester). Sa. three crescents or, on a canton gu. a ducal coronet of the second.

Hodges (Hanwell, co. Middlesex; HENRY HODGES, son of WILLIAM HODGES, Esq., of Rigton, co. Salop. Visit. Middlesex, 1663). Same *Arms*. *Crest*—An antelope's head couped or.

Hodges (co. Middlesex). Or, three crescents sa. on a canton ar. as many bars az. over all an anchor in pale of the second.

Hodges (Hemsted, co. Kent). Same *Arms* and *Crest*.

Hodges (Hanworth, co. Middlesex, and London, 1610). Same *Arms*. *Crest*—On a ducal coronet or, a crescent sa. *Another Crest*—Out of a ducal coronet an antelope's head or.

Hodges (Spickington, co. Somerset). Same *Arms*. *Crest*— An antelope's head erased or, ducally gorged gu. *Another Crest*—On a chapeau gu. turned up erm. a crescent ar. betw. two wings or.

Hodges (Overne, co. Leicester). Gu. a chev. erm. betw. three talbots' heads or, each issuing out of a mural coronet az. *Crest*—A talbot's head ar. guttée de sang, gorged with a collar gu. rimmed and ringed or, charged with three bezants.

Hodges (Burton and Sison, co. Leicester; FRANCIS HODGES, aged 31. Visit. 1619). Same *Arms*, a mullet for diff. *Crest* —A talbot's head couped or, guttée de sang, collared and ringed gu. *Motto*—Fundamentum gloriæ humilitas.

Hodges (Broadway, co. Worcester; arms confirmed and crest granted by Camden, Clarenceux, 1610). Or, three crescents sa. on a canton of the second a ducal coronet of the first. *Crest*—Out of a ducal coronet or, a crescent sa.

Hodges (Sulgrave, co. Northampton). Same *Arms*. *Crest* —An antelope's head erased or, ducally gorged gu.

Hodges (co. Somerset). Or, three crescents sa. on a canton of the second a crescent of the first.

Hodgeson (WILLIAM HODGESON, merchant, of London, son of THOMAS HODGESON, gent., co. York. Visit. London, 1568). Gu. three scynitars in pale ar. hilted or, points of the first and third to the dexter, point of the second to the sinister, a border engr. of the second pelletée. *Crest*—A dexter arm erect, couped at the elbow, habited bendy sinister of four ar. and gu. holding in the hand ppr. a covered cup or.

Hodgetts (Dudley, Elm Lodge, Hagley, co. Worcester). Per fesse az. and gu. on a chev. engr. betw. three doves in chief and a fleur-de-lis in base or, three annulets gold.

Crest—An eagle, wings expanded ppr. in the beak an annulet. *Motto*—Confido conquiesco.

Hodgetts (exemplified in 1867, to WILLIAM THOMAS HODGETTS CHAMBERS, Esq., upon his assuming by royal licence, the surname of HODGETTS, in lieu of that of CHAMBERS). Same *Arms* and *Crest*.

Hodgetts (Prestwood, co. Stafford; granted 6 Oct. 1768). Az. on a chev. betw. three doves in chief and a fleur-de-lis in base or, three crescents vert. *Crest*—A horse's head erm. pierced through the neck with a spear, the staff broken ppr.

Hodgkins, or Hodgskins (co. Gloucester, and Hammersmith, co. Middlesex). Ar. a cross quarterly pierced betw. five cinquefoils vert. *Crest*—An eagle rising looking towards the sun ppr.

Hodgkinson (Preston, co. Lancaster, 1664). Or, a cross quarter pierced betw. five cinquefoils vert. *Crest*—A cinquefoil or, betw. two bats' wings vert.

Hodgkinson (co. Middlesex). Or, on a cross couped and quarterly pierced betw. four cinquefoils vert, a cinquefoil az. *Crest*—A cinquefoil or, betw. two dragons' wings displ. vert. *Motto*—Sans Dieu rien.

Hodgkinson (London). Or, on a cross couped betw. four cinquefoils vert, a cinquefoil or. Same *Crest*.

Hodkinson (Overton Hall, Ashover, co. Derby; the heiress ANNE, only dau. of WILLIAM HODGKINSON, Esq., of Overton, *m.* JOSEPH BANKS, Esq., and was grandmother of the celebrated Sir JOSEPH BANKS, Bart.). Or, on a cross couped betw. four cinquefoils vert, a cinquefoil of the first. *Crest*—A garb or, betw. two wings expanded vert.

Hodgson (Boston, co. Lincoln). Quarterly, 1st and 4th, gu. three cutlasses barways in pale, the points toward the sinister part of the shield ar. hilts and pommels or, for HODGSON; 2nd, lozengy ar. and gu., for FITZWILLIAM; 3rd, az. a chev. betw. three cotton-hanks ar., for COTTON. *Crest*—A dexter cubit arm, holding in the hand a broken and bloody hanger, the pommel and hilt or, point gu.

Hodgson (co. Chester; granted 1717). Gu. a garb or, betw. three cutlasses erect ar. hilts and pommels of the second. *Crest*—On a mount vert a falcon, wings close ppr. beaked, legged, and belled or, collared dancettée ar. and pierced through the breast with a sword of the last, hilt gold, vulned ppr.

Hodgson (Newby Grange, co. Cumberland). Per chev. engr. or and az. three martlets counterchanged. *Crest*—A dove az. winged or, beaked and membered gu. holding in the mouth an olive branch ppr.

Hodgson (Houghton House, co. Cumberland). Sa. a chev. betw. three martlets or. *Crest*—A dove close ar. holding in his beak a sprig of laurel ppr. *Motto*—Dread God.

Hodgson (Newcastle-on-Tyne). Per chev. embattled or and sa. three martlets counterchanged.

Hodgson (co. Cumberland). Gu. three escutcheons ar. betw. nine bezants.

Hodgson (Elswick House, co. Northumberland; descended from a family whose name occurs among the records of that town, in the reign of Edward I.). Per chev. embattled or and az. three martlets counterchanged. *Crest*—On a rock a dove az. winged or, in the beak an olive branch ppr.

Hodgson (co. Essex; granted 1631). Per chev. engr. or and az. three martlets counterchanged. *Crest*—A dove az. winged or, beaked and membered gu. holding in the mouth an olive branch ppr.

Hodgson (Bascodyke, co. Cumberland, and co. Middlesex). Same *Arms* and *Crest*.

Hodgson (Wormanby, Dover, Scotby, London, Liverpool, &c.; quartered by BADLEY, of Caldbeck, with STUDHOLME, of Rickerby, near Carlisle, and Westminster; from the seal of Field-Marshal HODSON). Per chev. embattled or and az. three martlets counterchanged.

Hodgson (Highthorne, co. York). Per chev. embattled or and sa. three martlets counterchanged. *Crest*—A dove close ar. in the beak an olive branch ppr.

Hodgson-Hinde (Stella Hall, and Acton House, co. Northumberland). Per chev. embattled or and az. three martlets counterchanged. *Crest*—On a rock a dove az. winged or, in the beak an olive branch ppr. *Motto*—Miseris succurrere disco.

Hodgson (Hebborne, co. Durham; derived from RICHARD HODGSON, Mayor of Newcastle, 1555, 1566, and 1580). Same *Arms*. *Crest*—A martlet az. wings or, in the beak a laurel sprig vert.

Hodgson (Manor House, Lanchester, co. Durham). Same *Arms*.

Hodgson (Lincoln's Inn, London). Same *Arms*. *Crest*—A dove with an olive branch in the beak all ppr.

Hodgson (Tooting and Buckland, co. Surrey). Az. three

496

scymitars in pale ar. hilts amd pommels or, the points to the sinister.

Hodgson (Framfield, co. Sussex; granted by Segar in 1628). Erm. on a chief gu. three cutlasses erect ar. hilts or. *Crest*—A griffin's head erased, devouring a hand erased at the wrist gu.

Hodgson (cos. York and Norfolk). Gu. three cutlasses in fesse ar. hilts and pommels or. *Crest*—A cubit arm erect, in coat of mail, holding in the hand all ppr. a broken falchion gu.

Hodiam. Gu. on a bend erm. three chevronels of the first. *Crest*—A lion's head erased az.

Hodiam. Sa. on a bend erm. three chevronels gu.

Hodilow, Hoddylowe, or Hoddelow (Relden, co. Essex, *temp.* Elizabeth; Grafton-Underwood, co. Northampton, 1618, pedigree recorded that year; Hampstead, co. Middlesex, 1696; cos. Leicester, Chester, Stanty, co. Denbigh, in Wales, Radwell, co. Hertford, Wenham, co. Suffolk, London; originally of Ely, co. Cambridge). Gu. a cross pattée fitchée at the foot ar. a bordure engr. or. *Crest*—A dragon's head sa. collared or.

Hoding, or Hodding. Vair on an inescutcheon gu. a bend of the first.

Hodington (Hodington, co. Worcester; descended from RICHARD DE HODINGTON, of Hodington; who held a hide of land there 27 Edward I., 1298). Ar. a saltire gu. a border az. bezantée; this coat was allowed to RUSSELL as a quartering at Visit. 1569, but Visit. 1533 gives, ar. a saltire gu. a border sa. charged with mullets pierced or. *Crest*—On a tower ar. a bird volant or.

Hodisham (co. Suffolk). Ar. a bend engr. sa. cotised of the last.

Hodisham. Ar. a bend engr. betw. two (another, three) crescents sa.

Hodiswell (co. York). Gu. three wells ar. water az. *Crest*—A well gu.

Hodkinson. Ar. on a saltire betw. four mullets gu. five estoiles or. *Crest*—A shankbone and palm branch in saltire ppr.

Hodleston. See HUDDLESTON.

Hodlington. Ar. three crescents sa.

Hodnell, Hodvell, Hodwell, or Hole. Az. a fesse betw. three fleurs-de-lis or.

Hodnet. Quarterly, per fesse indented or and az.

Hodney. Az. an estoile of six points or.

Hodsall. Az. a fesse betw. three wells ar. *Crest*—A well ar.

Hodsdon (Hodsdon, co. Herts). Ar. a bend wavy gu. betw. two horseshoes of the field. *Crest*—A man's head couped at the shoulders ppr. vested ar. on the head a cap or.

Hodsdon (Edgeworth, co. Middlesex; SIMON, son of THOMAS HODSDON, descended from HODSDON, of Hodsdon, co. Herts. Visit. London, 1568). Ar. a bend wavy gu. betw. two horseshoes az. *Crest*—A man's head ppr. couped at the shoulders, vested az. collared or, on the head a chapeau gu. turned up erm.

Hodsoll (London, and Hollywell and South Ash, co. Kent). Az. a fesse wavy betw. three stone fountains ar.

Hodsoll. Az. a fesse wavy betw. three wells ar. *Crest*—A well, as in the arms.

Hodson (co. Cambridge; granted 1590). Sa. a chev. betw. three falcons volant or. *Crest*—A unicorn courant reguard. ar. gorged with a chaplet vert.

Hodson (Hollybrooke House, co. Wicklow, bart.). Sa. a chev. betw. three martlets or. *Crest*—A dove close az. beaked and membered or, holding in the beak an olive branch ppr.

Hodson, Hudson, or Hudgeson (co. Middlesex). Per pale or and vert, a chev. betw. three martlets counterchanged.

Hodson. Ar. a bend wavy gu. betw. two horseshoes az.

Hodstoke. Or, a chev. gu. pierced with a bend erm.

Hody (Nethewey, co. Devon; descended from Sir JOHN HODY, Chief Justice of the King's Bench, son of Sir JOHN HODY, of Stowell, co. Somerset, by the heiress of COLE, of Nethewey; from this family derived the HODYS, of Nothover, co. Somerset, and of Pillesden, co. Dorset). Ar. a fesse indented point in point vert and sa. betw. two cotises, that in chief of the last, and that in base of the second. *Crest*—A bull pass. sa.

Hody (Pillesden, co. Dorset). Quarterly, 1st and 4th, same *Arms*, for HODY; 2nd, a bull pass. sa. a bordure of the last bezantée, for COLE; 3rd, ar. a chev. betw. three Moors' heads couped sa., for JEWE. *Crest*—A bull pass. sa.

Hodye, or Hudny (Hamon, co. Dorset). Ar. a fesse per fesse indented vert and or, cotised of the third.

Hodysham. Ar. a bend engr. betw. two crescents sa.

Hoe (co. Bedford). Quarterly, sa. and ar. a bend or. See Hoo.

Hoe (Fun. Ent. Ulster's Office). **Ar.** an eagle displ. with two heads az.

Hoe. Ar. on a chief indented sa. three mullets or.

Hoese (*Baron Hoese;* summoned to Parliament 1295; descendants not summoned since 1349). Barry of six erm. and gu.

Hoese (*Baron Hoese*, of Beechworth; summoned to Parliament 1348: extinct 1361). Same *Arms.*

Hoet (London; granted 22 March, 1663). Ar. on two bars sa. three fleurs-de-lis or.

Hoey (Dunganstown, co. Wicklow: Fun. Ent. Ulster's Office, JOHN HOEY, Serjeant-at-Arms, *d.* 2 April, 1612). Chequy or and gu. a lion ramp. ar. armed and langued az. *Crest—* Out of a ducal coronet or, a dexter and sinister arm in armour, the hands grasping a sword all ppr. pommel and hilt gold.

Hoey (exemplified to JOHN BAPTIST CASHEL-HOEY, Esq., of the Middle Temple, Barrister-at-law). Quarterly, 1st and 4th, chequy or and az. over all a lion ramp. erm. crowned with an Irish crown gu., for HOEY; 2nd and 3rd, gu. a lion pass. ar. gorged with a collar sa., for CASHEL. *Crest—* A unicorn sejant ar. armed and unguled or, gorged with an Irish crown gu. *Motto—*Iterum iterumque.

Hoffman. Erm. three lozenges gu. *Crest—*Issuing out of the top of a tower a demi lady ppr. attired az. holding in the dexter hand a garland of laurel vert.

Hoffmann (granted to JAMES RIX HOFFMANN, Esq., of York Terrace, Regent's Park, *d.* June, 1838). Per bend or and az. a bend gobony of three, gu. ar. and gu. in chief a demi lion double queued of the second, and in base a sun in splendour ppr. *Crest—*A demi lion double queued az. betw. two elephants' proboscies erect, the dexter per fesse gu. and ar., the sinister per fesse or and az. holding betw. the paws a sun in splendour ppr. *Motto—*Over the crest: Tiens a la verité.

Hofner. Or, a demi lion ramp. couped gu. *Crest—*The hind parts of a lion couped in the middle of the back, the legs towards the dexter and sinister, the tail erect.

Hog (Harcarse, Scotland). Ar. three boars' heads erased az. armed or. *Crest—*An oak tree ppr. *Motto—*Dat gloria vires.

Hog (Cammo, Scotland). Ar. a crescent betw. three boars' heads erased az. *Crest* and *Motto*, as the last.

Hog (Newliston, Scotland; representative of Harcarse). Ar. three boars' heads erased az. *Crest* and *Motto*, as the last. *Supporters—*Two boars ppr.

Hog (Bleridryn, Scotland, 1693). Ar. three boars' heads erased az. armed and langued or, distilling drops of blood gu. *Crest—*A dexter hand couped gu. *Motto—*Dant vires gloriam.

Hogan (London). Ar. on a fesse az. betw. three crosses crosslet sa. as many escallops or. *Crest—*On a chapeau gu. an escallop or, betw. two wings ppr.

Hogan (Wales). Ar. on a chief sa. three martlets of the field.

Hogan. Ar. a chev. engr. vairé or and gu. betw. three hurts of the third, each charged with a lion's paw erased of the second.

Hogan (East Bradnam; EDMOND HOGAN, citizen and mercer of London, fifth son of ROBERT HOGAN. Visit. 1568). Ar. a chev. engr. vairé or and gu. betw. three hurts, each charged with a lion's paw erased in bend of the field, an annulet for diff. *Crest—*A lion's paw couped and erect ar. holding in the claw an annulet gu. charged with an annulet for diff.

Hogan (Reg. Ulster's Office). Gu. three lions pass. in pale or, each holding betw. the forepaws an esquire's helmet ppr. *Crest—*A dexter arm in armour embowed, the hand grasping a sword all ppr.

Hogard. Az. an estoile of sixteen points or.

Hogarth, or Howgart (Scotland). Az. a star of six points or, on a chief of the last three spears' heads of the first. *Crest—*A pegasus's head or, winged ar. *Motto—* Candor dat viribus alas.

Hogelinton. Ar. three crescents sa.

Hogesdon, or Hogsdon. Ar. three bars sa.

Hogg (Bishopwearmouth, co. Durham). Ar. three boars' heads erased sa. *Crest—*A boar statant sa. pierced in the side with an arrow sa. against an oak tree vert, fructed gu.

Hogg. Ar. three boars' heads couped sa. *Crest—*An oak tree fructed ppr.

Hogg (Chesham Place, London, bart.). Ar. three boars' heads erased az. langued gu. betw. two flaunches of the second, each charged with a crescent of the field. *Crest—*Out of an eastern crown ar. an oak tree fructed ppr. and pendent therefrom an escutcheon az. charged with a dexter arm

437

embowed in armour, the hand grasping an arrow in bend sinister, point downwards also ppr. *Motto—*Dat gloria vires.

Hogg (Norton House, co. Durham). Quarterly, 1st, ar. three boars' heads couped sa., for HOGG; 2nd, az. a fret ar. on a chief of the last three leopards' faces gu., for JEFFERSON; 3rd, or, on a mount vert a lion ramp. az., for JONES; 4th, ar. a wolf statant sa. on a chief az. three crosses formée of the first, for EWER. *Crest—*A boar statant ppr. pierced in the side with an arrow or, against an oak tree ppr. fructed or. *Motto—*Dat gloria vires.

Hogg. Ar. three boars' heads erased ppr. *Crest—*An oak tree fructed ppr.

Hogg. Ar. two bends gu.

Hogg (Edinburgh, 1761). Ar. a pheon betw. three boars' heads erased az. langued gu. armed or. *Crest—*An oak tree fructed ppr. *Motto—*Dat gloria vires.

Hoggart (Old Broad Street, London). Ar. a chev. vair betw. three hearts gu. each charged with a lion's gamb erased in bend sinister of the first. *Crest—*A lion's gamb erased and erect, grasping a similar gamb all ppr.

Hoggart (Tooting, co. Surrey). Ar. a chev. vairé or and gu. betw. three hearts of the third, each charged with a lion's gamb erased in pale, paw downwards, of the second. *Crest—*A lion's gamb couped and erect, grasping another erased in bend sinister ppr.

Hoggeson (co. York). Gu. three cutlasses or hangers ar. hilted or, two points to the sinister and one betw. to the dexter side of the escutcheon. *Crest—*A swallow volant sa.

Hoggeson, or Hoggson. Same *Arms*, field az. *Crest—* A hand couped below the wrist or, the hand ppr. holding a broken cutlass ar. hilted of the first, the broken piece fallen from the other.

Hogglington (quartered by CLIFFORD; arms in a window at Great Malvern). Ar. three crescents sa.

Hogh (co. Chester). Ar. on a chev. sa. three crescents of the field.

Hogh. Ar. a chev. gu. betw. ten crosses crosslet of the same.

Hogh. Ar. a bend sa.

Hoghahad, or Hoghahed. Vairé ar. and gu. a bordure sa.

Hoghe (co. Chester). Ar. on a chev. sa. three crescents of the first. *Crest—*A lion's paw ppr. holding a cross pattée or.

Hoghton (Hoghton Tower, co. Lancaster, bart.). Sa. three bars ar. with the augmentation of the rose of England and the thistle of Scotland impaled in a canton or, quarterly with the arms of BOLD, viz., ar. a griffin segreant sa. *Crest* —A bull pass. ar. (A more ancient crest, a bull's head ar. collared with three bars sa.). *Supporters—*Over the gates of Hoghton Tower, put up in the beginning of the reign of Elizabeth, two bulls ar. *Motto—*Malgré le tort.

Hoghton (Park Hall, co. Lancaster; four descents registered in the Visit. 1613). Barry ar. and sa. a bordure gu. *Crest—* A bull pass ar. horned and hoofed sa. collared or.

Hoghton (Park Hall, co. Lancaster, 1613 and 1664). Sa. three bars ar. a bordure engr. gu. *Crest—*A bull pass. ar. collared or, armed and unguled sa.

Hogillington, or Hoglington. Ar. six crescents sa.

Hogington. Ar. three crescents sa.

Hogshagg, or Hogshead. Vairé ar. and gu. a bordure sa. bezantée.

Hogue (Scotland). Ar. a cross crosslet sa. betw. three boars' heads erased az. *Crest—*An oak tree ppr. *Motto—*Dat gloria vires.

Hokele. Ar. two chev. betw. three oak leaves vert.

Hokeley. Or, on a fesse betw. three mascles gu. **as many** plates. *Crest—*A bee volant reversed sa.

Hokeley. Or, a fesse betw. three mascles gu.

Hokeley. Ar. a fesse betw. three fusils gu.

Hokelley. Ar. a saltire engr. betw. four cinquefoils az.

Hokenhull, or Hokenell (Hokenhull, Penton, and Tranmere, co. Chester). Ar. an ass's head erased sa.

Hokenhull. Sa. a star of sixteen points ar.

Hoker. Ar. a fesse betw. three mascles gu.

Hokes. Az. a fesse betw. three fleurs-de-lis ar.

Holand. See HOLLAND.

Holand. Per fesse az. and gu. three fleurs-de-lis ar.

Holand. Or, two bars az. in chief three escallops gu. *Crest* —An arm ppr. holding an arrow ar. feathered or.

Holand. Per pale indented or and az.

Holbaron. Ar. on a fesse sa. three crescents or.

Holbe. Az. a bend betw. six mullets pierced ar.

Holbeach, or Holigh. Ar. a chev. engr. sa.

Holbeame (Holbeame and Coffinswell, co. **Devon;** the

2 K

heiress _m._ MARWOOD). Ar. a chev. enarched sa. _Crest_—A cross crosslet gu. betw. two palm branches.

Holbeame. Ar. two bars and a chev. in chief sa.

Holbech, or Holbeach (Farnborough, co. Warwick, and Mollington, co. Oxford, originally of Holbech, co. Lincoln; derived from Sir LAWRENCE HOLBECH, living 1351, descended from OLIVER HOLBECH, of Holbech, living in 1223; confirmed by the Deputies of Camden, Clarenceux, to THOMAS HOLBECH, Esq., son of WILLIAM HOLBECH, who was eldest son of THOMAS HOLBECH, of Fillongley, seventh in descent from Sir LAWRENCE HOLBECH, and to WILLIAM HOLBECH, of Birchley Hall, grandson of THOMAS HOLBECH, the second son of THOMAS HOLBECH, of Fillongley; AMBROSE HOLBECH, fifth in descent from the said THOMAS HOLBECH, of Fillongley). Quarterly, 1st and 4th, vert six escallops, three, two, and one ar.; 2nd, sa. a bend engr. betw. six billets ar.; 3rd, ar. a lion ramp. gu. a bordure engr. sa. bezantée. _Crest_—A maunch vert, semée of escallops ar.

Holbeche, or Holbeame (Stow, co. Lincoln; granted 1586). Or, on a chief az. three lions' heads erased of the field. _Crest_—Out of a ducal coronet or, a pelican's head gold, vulned gu.

Holbeche. Ar. a chev. engr. sa.

Holbeck (Whitingham; confirmed June, 1613). Ar. on a saltire vert five escallops of the first. _Crest_—A demi griffin or, winged gu. holding in the dexter claw an escallop ar.

Holbert. Az. a bend betw. six mullets ar.

Holberton (granted to WILLIAM HOLBERTON, Esq., of Tor House, co. Devon). Per fesse or and az. a pale counterchanged, over all on a plain fesse with cotices engr. erm. betw. three mascles, as many boars' heads erased gu. _Crest_—On a mount vert in front of two tilting spears in saltire ppr. a boar's head erect couped gu. _Motto_—Ora et labora.

Holbiche (co. Suffolk). Az. on a chev. or, three magpies ppr.

Holbiche. Ar. a chev. engr. sa. _Crest_—A peacock's head erased az.

Holbiche. Vert six escallops ar. a bordure az. charged with eight fleurs-de-lis or.

Holbourne. Ar. a fesse betw. three crescents gu.

Holbroake. Gu. a chev. betw. ten crosses crosslet or.

Holbrokes. Or, a fesse betw. six crosslets gu.

Holbrook (co. Suffolk). Ar. a chev. betw. ten crosses crosslet gu. _Crest_—A lion pass. guard. tail extended ppr.

Holbrook. Or, a chev. betw. ten crosses crosslet gu.

Holbrooke (Newington, co. Kent). Az. a cross or, fretty of the first, betw. four mullets of the second.

Holbrooke (co. Suffolk). Or. a chev. gu. surmounted with a cross formée fitchée at the foot of the second. _Crest_—A lion's head erased sa. charged with a chev. or, as in the arms.

Holbrooke (co Suffolk). Or, crusily gu. a bend of the second.

Holbrooke (co. Suffolk). Ar. a chev. betw. three crosses crosslet gu.

Holbrow. Ar. a chev. betw. six crosses crosslet in chief and four in base gu.

Holbry. Az. on a bend sa. a mullet pierced ar.

Holburne (Menstrie, co. Edinburgh, bart., 1706). Quarterly, 1st and 4th, gu. a fesse couped betw. three crescents or; 2nd and 3rd, or, an orle gu. _Crest_—A demi lion holding in the dexter paw a mullet ar. _Motto_—Decus summum virtus.

Holbush. Gu. three fusils in fesse ar.

Holby. Az. a fret ar. a chief of the second.

Holcam, and Holcan. Az. two bars wavy (another, nebulée) erm.

Holchief, or Holdchiefe. Az. a garb or, banded gu.

Holcombe (Hull, co. Devon; seven descents are recorded in the Visit. of 1620). Az. a chev. ar. betw. three men's heads in profile, couped at the shoulders or, wreathed about the temples sa. and of the second. _Crest_—A man's head fullfaced, couped at the breast ppr. wreathed round the temples or and az.

Holcombe (co. Pembroke, an ancient family in that co.; HARCOURT FORD HOLCOMBE, Esq., Lieut.-Col. Royal Artillery, and C.B., descended from a younger branch of HOLCOMBE, of Hull, settled in co. Pembroke nearly two centuries ago). Same _Arms_ and _Crest._

Holcombe, or Holcomb. Same _Arms._ _Crest_—A serpent nowed, holding in the mouth a garland of laurel ppr.

Holcot (arms in a window in Kidlington Church, co. Oxford. Visit. Oxon, 1566). Ar. a chev. betw. three buckles sa.

Holcott. Lozengy ar. and gu. a bordure az. _Crest_—On the point of a sword a stag's head cabossed all ppr.

Holcott, or Hulcott. Lozengy or and gu. a bordure az.

498

Holcrew, or Holgrave. Vert a chev. betw. three owls ar.

Holcroft (Holcroft, co. Lancaster). Ar. a cross and bordure engr. sa., quartering CULCHETH. _Crest_—A raven, wings elevated, holding in the dexter claw a sword all ppr.

Holcroft (Vale Royal, co. Chester). Same _Arms_ and _Crest._

Holcroft, alias Henley. Ar. a cross within a bordure engr. sa. _Crest_—An eagle, wings expanded sa. holding in the dexter claw a sword ar. hilt and pommel or.

Holcroft (Balkerton, co. Nottingham). Ar. on a cross engr. sa. a fleur-de-lis or, a bordure engr. of the second. _Crest_—An eagle gu. holding in the dexter claw a sword in pale ar. hilt and pommel or, charged on the breast with a fleur-de-lis of the last.

Holcroft. Sa. four quatrefoils ar.

Holcroft. Ar. a cross engr. sa. a bordure of the last.

Holcroft. Ar. a fesse and a bordure engr. sa.

Holcroft. Ar. a cross and bordure gu.

Hold. Erm. on a chief az. a garb or.

Holde. Ar. a fesse betw. two chev. sa.

Holden (Holden, co. Lancaster). Ar. six allerions gu. three, two, and one, in the centre an escutcheon of the last. _Crest_—1st: A double-headed allerion gu.; 2nd: A moorcock sa. winged or.

Holden (Erdington, co. Warwick; SIMON HOLDEN, _temp._ Queen Elizabeth, was ninth in descent from WILLIAM HOLDWIN, son of HOLDWIN, _temp._ King John). Vert a bar erminois betw. two pheons erect in chief, and a buglehorn strung in base or.

Holden (Reedly House and Palace House, co. Lancaster; HENRY HOLDEN, Esq., is son and heir of JOHN GREENWOOD, Esq., of Palace House, J.P., by ELIZABETH, his wife, dau. of HENRY ASPINALL, Esq., of Reedly House, which lady obtained a royal licence, bearing date 28 July, 1840, authorizing her and her children to take the name and arms of HOLDEN. The HOLDENS, of Holden and Palace House, are an ancient family in co. Lancaster, and their pedigree appears on record in the Heralds' Visitations). Sa. a fesse betw. two chev. erm. betw. the fesse and upper chev. a covered cup or. _Crest_—A moorcock ppr. charged on the breast with a cinquefoil or. _Motto_—Nec tempore nec timide.

Holden (Aston, co. Derby; derived from ROBERT HOLDEN, Esq., of Aston, _d._ 1746; ROBERT HOLDEN, Esq., the last male heir of the elder branch, _d._ 1746; his heiress, MARY HOLDEN, _m._ JAMES SHUTTLEWORTH, Esq., of Gawthrop, co. Lancaster, whose second son took the name and arms of HOLDEN, but dying _s. p._ was succeeded by his next surviving brother, the Rev. CHARLES SHUTTLEWORTH, who likewise assumed his maternal surname and arms). Sa. a fesse engr. erminois or, betw. two chev. erm. quartering SHUTTLEWORTH, viz., ar. three weavers' shuttles sa. topped and furnished with quills of yarn, the threads pendent or. _Crests_—1st, HOLDEN: On a mount vert a moorcock rising sa. winged or; 2nd, SHUTTLEWORTH: A cubit arm in armour ppr. grasping a gauntlet a shuttle, as in the arms.

Holden (Darley Abbey, co. Derby, and Nuttall Temple, co. Notts, a younger branch of HOLDEN, of Aston; the representative of the family, WILLIAM DRURY HOLDEN, Esq., assumed by royal licence, the name and arms of LOWE, of Locko, _which see_). Per pale erm. and sa. a fesse betw. two chev. counterchanged. _Crest_—A moorcock sa. combed and wattled gu.

Holden (co. Worcester; descended from a family formerly resident at Wednesbury, co. Stafford). Vert a fess erminois betw. two pheons erect in chief and a buglehorn strung in base or. _Crest_—A dexter cubit arm vested sa. hand ppr. holding a cross crosslet fitchée or, from the wrist a pile erm. the arm charged with a buglehorn strung gold. _Motto_—Et teneo et tenecr. These arms were granted to WILLIAM HOLDEN, gentleman, on the 10th Feb. 1791, and were confirmed, and the crest granted, 19 July, 1827, to his grandson, the Rev. WILLIAM ROSE HOLDEN, M.A. The Rev. WILLIAM LUCAS HOLDEN, son of the before-named WILLIAM HOLDEN, assumed the surname of ROSE in 1785, and quartered the above arms with the arms of ROSE. The present head of the HOLDEN family is WILLIAM ROSE HOLDEN, Esq., of Weymouth, who has one brother, the Rev. OSWALD MANOIR HOLDEN, M.A., B.C.L., Vicar of Gailey-cum-Hatherton, co. Stafford.

Holden (Hockridge, co. Kent; granted 20 May, 1663). Erm. on a chief az. three pears or.

Holden (Cruttenden). Az. on a chev. or, betw. three spurrowels ar. five guttes sa. in chief a crescent of the third. _Crest_—An antelope's head issuing ppr.

Holden. Ar. a bend engr. gu. a chief az. _Crest_—An eagle's leg erased at the thigh ppr.

Holden. Ar. a chief sa. over all a bend engr gu

Holden. Ar. three escallops gu.

Holden. Sa. a chev. erm. in base a covered cup ar.

Holden. Per fesse sa. and ar. a bend engr. gu.

Holden. Gu. a chev. betw. three crosses crosslet or, on a chief of the second a lion pass. of the first.

Holden (Aston, co. Warwick). Gu. a chev. betw. three crosses crosslet or.

Holdenby (cos. Northampton and Nottingham). Az. five cinquefoils in cross ar.

Holdenby. Az. five cinquefoils in saltire ar.

Holder (co. Cambridge). Az. a fesse dancettée betw. three griffins pass. wings endorsed or. Crest—On a ducal coronet gu. a lion sejant or.

Holder (South Wheatly, co. Notts). Sa. a chev. betw. three anchors ar.

Holder. Az. three griffins segreant or. Crest—Out of a five-leaved ducal coronet gu. a lion sejant or.

Holderman. Sa. a chev. erm. betw. three cats pass. ar.

Holdernes. Ar. on a bend gu. betw. six mullets of the last a cross formée of the first.

Holderness (co. York). Barry of six or and az.

Holderness. Ar. three cinquefoils gu. a chief of the last. Crest—Betw. the horns of a crescent or, a cross pattée gu.

Holdesheife, or Holdesheaff. Az. a garb ar.

Holdich, or Holdiche. Az. on a chev. or, three martlets sa. a chief ar. Crest—An arm in armour embowed ppr. holding in the gauntlet a scymitar all ppr.

Holdich. Az. on a chev. or, (another, ar.) three birds sa.

Holdich (granted 1824, to the Rev. Thomas Holdich, of Maidwell Hall, Rector of Maidwell, co. Northampton). Or, on a chev. sa. cotised gu. three martlets of the field, a chief vair. Crest—A martlet sa. in front of a cross pattée fitchée betw. two branches of palm or.

Holdiche, or Holditch (Raworth, co. Norfolk). Az. on a chev. or, three magpies (another, seapies) ppr.

Holding (co. Middlesex). Or, a cock standing on a bugle-horn ppr. Crest—A buglehorn ppr.

Holdip (London and Southampton; granted 5 June, 1725). Erm. on a bend az. a griffin's head erased betw. two spears' heads or. Crest—On a chapeau az. turned up ar. a griffin's head erm. collared of the first, beaked sa. holding in the beak a broken spear or.

Holdon. Ar. three escallops sa.

Holdsheffe. Ar. a bend vert betw. three garbs az.

Holdston. Ar. fretty gu.

Holdsworth (co. Warwick). Ar. the stem of a tree couped and eradicated in bend ppr.

Holdsworth (Widecombe, co. Devon, originally from Halifax, co. York; Arthur Holdsworth, Esq., of Wide-combe, represented Dartmouth in Parliament). Same Arms.

Holdwayt. Sa. fretty erm.

Hole (Ebberly House, near Great Torrington, co. Devon). Az. an annulet ar. betw. three lozenges or, quartering Gu. two bars or. Crest—Out of a mural coronet or, an arm in armour embowed, holding a battle axe all ppr. Motto—Honor virtutis præmium.

Hole (co. Salop). Quarterly, ar. and sa. a cross engr. betw. four escallops all counterchanged. Crest—An escallop sa. betw. two wings ar.

Hole. Az. an annulet betw. three lozenges ar. Same Crest.

Holebrooke (co. Suffolk). Or, a chev. betw. three crosses crosslet gu.

Holebrooke. Or, a chev. betw. ten crosses crosslet gu. Crest—Two dolphins in saltire az.

Holeman. Erm. a fesse counter-componée or and az. betw. three crescents gu.

Holeway (co. Devon). Gu. a fesse betw. three crescents ar.

Holford (Holford, co. Chester, temp. Edward II.; the direct male line of the family became extinct about the year 1600, when the heiress brought Holford to the Cholmondeleys. The Holfords, of Weston Birt, are a branch of this ancient house). Ar. a greyhound pass. sa. Crest—A greyhound's head sa.

Holford (Weston Birt, Tetbury, co. Gloucester). Ar. a greyhound pass. sa. Crest—A greyhound's head couped sa.

Holford (co. Lancaster). Same Arms.

Holford (Davenham, co. Chester). Same Arms, a canton sa.

Holford. Quarterly, 1st and 4th, ar. on a mount vert a greyhound pass. sa. collared or, for Holford; 2nd and 3rd, sa. a fesse.

Holford (co. Rutland). Az. on a fesse ar. betw. three fleurs-de-lis or, a greyhound courant sa.

Holford (co. York). Ar. a greyhound in full course sa.

Holford (Lieut.-Colonel James Price Gwynne Holford, of Buckland, near Brecknock, eldest son of John Josiah Hol-

499

Ford, Esq., of Kilgwyn, co. Carmarthen, who m. in 1830, Anna Maria Eleanor, dau. of Thynne Howe Gwynne, Esq., of Buckland, and assumed in consequence, the following year, the additional name and arms of Gwynne). Quarterly, 1st and 4th, ar. on a mount vert a greyhound pass. sa. collared or, for Holford; 2nd and 3rd, sa. a fesse cotised or, betw. two swords ar. hilts and pommels gold, the one in chief pointing upwards, the one in base downwards. Crests—1st: From the sun in splendour or, rising from behind a hill vert a greyhound's head issuant sa.; 2nd: A dexter arm in armour ppr. issuant from a crescent ar. holding a sword erect also ppr. hilt and pommel gold, enfiled by a boar's head or, erased and vulned ppr. Mottoes—Over the crest: Vim vi repellere licet; under the arms: Toujours fidèle.

Holford. Ar. a chev. betw. three text T's (old English characters) sa.

Holgate (Walden, co. Essex). Or, a bend betw. two bulls' heads couped sa. Crest—Out of a mural coronet ar. a bull's head sa. gorged with a collar of the first, charged with two bends gu. (another, collared bendy of six gu. and ar.).

Holgill. Ar. three cinquefoils in pale betw. two martlets in fesse gu. on a chief az. a pelican vulning herself betw. two combs paleways or.

Holgrave or Holgreve (co. Chester). Ar. an inescutcheon gu. within an orle of martlets sa.

Holgrave, Holgreve, or Hulgrave. Erm. an inescutcheon gu. Crest—A hand holding a thunderbolt in pale ppr.

Holgrave. Vert a lion ramp. betw. three owls ar.

Holgrave. Paly of six erm. and az.

Holinshed. Ar. a cross sa. Crest—A bull's head and neck sa.

Holinshed. Ar. on a cross sa. a mullet or, a canton ermines.

Holker (London; granted 1 Jan. 1770). Per chev. embattled or and az. three lions ramp. counterchanged. Crest—A lion ramp. per chev. embattled or and az.

Holkham. Az. two bars wavy erm.

Holl (Malton, co. Norfolk). Or, on a chev. sa. three unicorns' heads erased ar. Crest—A sea lion sejant or, guttée de sang.

Holl (Pimlico). Same Arms and Crest. Motto—Integritas tuta virus non capit.

Holland (Baron Holland, extinct 1859). See Vassall-Fox.

Holland (Holland, co. Lancaster, temp. King John). Az. a lion ramp. guard. betw. six fleurs-de-lis ar.

Holland (Denton, co. Lancaster: a branch of the preceding). Same Arms.

Holland (Robert de Holland, summoned to Parliament, 8 Edward II., his descendant, Sir Thomas, first Earl of Kent, m. the Lady Joan Plantagenet, "the Fair Maid of Kent," and was one of the Founder Knights of the Garter). Az. semée de fleurs-de-lis a lion ramp. ar.

Holland (Earl of Kent ; Sir Thomas, second earl, was elected a Knight of the Garter 1375–76, in the room of John, Lord Mohun, one of the Founder Knights). The arms of England within a border ar.

Holland (Duke of Exeter ; John, third son of Thomas de Holland, Earl of Kent, by Joan Plantagenet, "the Fair Maid of Kent," was so created 1387. In 1381, he was elected a Knight of the Garter, beheaded and attainted 1400). England, within a bordure or, semée-de-lis az. Crest—On a chapeau the royal lion, gorged with a collar az. charged with a fleur-de-lis and ducally crowned.

Holland (Sir Otho, or Otes Holland, brother of Thomas, first Earl of Kent, was one of the Founder Knights of the Garter). Az. semée de fleurs-de-lis a lion ramp. guard. ar.

Holland (Weare, Shipwash, and Upcott Avenel, co. Devon, descended from the marriage of John de Holland, a younger son of Robert, Baron Holland, with Elinor, dau. and heiress of Sir Andrew Metsted, Lord of Shipwash, 1314 ; the last male representative of the family, William Holland, Esq., of Upcott Avenel, left at his decease two daus., viz., Mary, m. Stephen Coham, Esq., of Coham, co. Devon; and Margaret, m. John Coham, Esq., of Bovacott, co. Devon). Az. semée-de-lis a lion ramp. ar. (sometimes or).

Holland (Conway, co. Sussex). Az. semée-de-lis a lion ramp. guard. ar. Crest—Out of a flame ppr. an arm issuant, habited in a close sleeve sa. the fist ppr. holding a lion's gamb barwise erased or, the talons to the sinister side. Motto—Fiat pax, floreat justitia.

Holland (Albert, Count of Holland, third son of Lewis, Emperor of Bavaria, elected a Knight of the Garter 1397). Quarterly, 1st and 4th, bendy lozengy ar. and az. for Bavaria ; 2nd and 3rd, or, four lions ramp., 1st and 4th, sa. 2nd and 3rd, gu., for Holland.

Holland (Hendre Vawr or Plas Cadwgan, North Wales).

2 K 2

Az. a demi lion ramp. guard. betw. seven fleurs-de-lis ar.

Holland (Ely, co. Cambridge, Boston, co. Lincoln, and West Angmering, co. Sussex). Az. a lion ramp. guard. betw. eight fleurs-de-lis ar. *Crest*—A cubit arm erect ppr. issuing out of rays or, and grasping a lion's gamb erased of the last. *Another Crest*—A wolf pass. sa.

Holland (Sandlebridge, co. Chester, bart.). Per pale ar. and az. semée-de-lis a lion ramp. guard. counterchanged, debruised by a bendlet engr. gu. *Crest*—Out of a crown vallery or, a demi lion guard. per bend ar. and az. charged with a bendlet engr. counterchanged, holding in the dexter paw a fleur-de-lis also ar.

Holland (co. Chester). Per fesse az. and gu. (another, gu. and az.) three fleurs-de-lis ar.

Holland (co. Devon). Az. a lion saliant guard. betw. five fleurs-de-lis ar.

Holland (Ely, in the Isle of Ely). Az. semée-de-lis a lion ramp. within a bordure all ar. *Crest*—A wolf pass. sa.

Holland (co. Lancaster). Sa. a cross pattée or.

Holland (Stevington, co. Lincoln, and Kinton, co. Nottingham). Per pale indented or and gu. quartering Az. semée of fleurs-de-lis a lion ramp. guard. ar. *Crest*—A sinister wing or.

Holland (Siston, co. Gloucester). Per pale or and gu.

Holland (co. Lincoln). Barry bendy of eight gu. and or.

Holland (co. Lincoln). Per pale indented gu. and or (another, gu. and ar.).

Holland (Henry Holland, M.D., of Brook Street, Grosvenor Square, London). Az. semée-de-lis a lion ramp. ar. over all a bend gu. *Crest*—Out of a ducal coronet or, a demi lion ramp. guard. tail fourchée ar. collared gu.

Holland (Quidenham and Harleston, co. Norfolk, bart., extinct 1729). Az. semée-de-lis a lion ramp. guard. ar. *Crest*—A wolf pass. sa. charged on the breast with a mullet for diff.

Holland (Wittenham, co. Berks, bart., extinct 1811; Nathaniel Dance, Esq., lord of the manor of Wittenham, assumed the name of Holland by sign manual, and was created a bart. 1800, d. s. p.). Per pale az. and gu. a lion ramp. erm. betw. eight fleurs-de-lis alternately ar. and or.

Holland (granted to Thomas Lindsey Holland, Esq., of Cornwall Terrace, Regent's Park, co. Middlesex). Az. semée-de-lis a lion ramp. guard. ar. on a bend gu. an ostrich feather of the second betw. two bezants. *Crest*—Out of a crown pallisado or, the rim charged with three torteaux, a demi lion guard. ppr. holding in the dexter paw a plume of three ostrich feathers ar.

Holland (Denton, co. Lancaster, 1567). Az. semée-de-lis a lion ramp. guard. ar. over all a bend gu. *Crest*—Out of a ducal coronet or, a demi lion ramp. guard. ar. collared gu. holding in the dexter gamb a fleur-de-lis also ar.

Holland (Clifton, co. Lancaster, 1567 ; descended from Holland, of Denton). Az. a lion ramp. guard. betw. six fleurs-de-lis ar. depressed by a bend gu. charged with a crescent or. *Crest*—A wolf pass. sa.

Holland (Sutton, co. Lancaster, 1567). Same *Arms*, a mullet betw. the points of the crescent. *Crest*, 1664—Out of a ducal coronet or, a demi lion ar. holding betw. the paws a fleur-de-lis of the second.

Holland (Heaton, co. Lancaster, 1664). Az. semée-de-lis and a lion ramp. guard. ar. *Crest*—Out of a ducal coronet or, a demi lion ramp. guard. ar. holding in the dexter paw a fleur-de-lis gold.

Holland (Dumbleton, co. Gloucester, formerly of Mobberley, co. Chester; Edward Holland, M.P. for Evesham, High Sheriff, co. Gloucester, 1842). Az. crusily a lion ramp. ar.

Holland (Burwarton, Charlecot, and Pickthorne, co. Salop). Az. a lion ramp. guard. ar. betw. ten plates, all within a bordure of the second. *Crest*—A demi lion ramp. guard. grasping a fleur-de-lis az.

Holland (co. Surrey; William Holland, citizen and merchant of London, Visit. London, 1568, grandson of Richard Holland, gent.). Az. a lion ramp. guard. betw. four crosses pattée ar.

Holland (Benhall Lodge, co. Suffolk). Az. a lion ramp. within an orle of trefoils ar. *Crest*—Out of a ducal coronet or, a demi lion ramp. ar. *Motto*—Vincit qui se vincit.

Holland (Bognor, co. Sussex). Az. a lion ramp. within an orle of trefoils ar. *Crest*—Out of a ducal coronet or, a demi lion ramp. ar.

Holland (co. Westmoreland). Sa. a cross flory or.

Holland. Sa. a bordure of escallops a lion ramp. or.

Holland. Quarterly, ar. and sa. on a bend of the second three eagles displ. or, in the second and third quarters two chev. of the last.

Holland. Gu. three leopards' faces or, a bordure of the last.

Holland. Gu. three leopards pass. in pale and a bordure ar.

Holland. Gu. two leopards pass. or, depressed with a bend az. a bordure of the third semée of escallops ar.

Holland. Gu. two leopards pass. in pale or, a bend az. within a bordure of the third, semée of fleur-de-lis of the second.

Holland. Az. semée of cinquefoils a lion ramp. guard. ar.

Holland. Gu. three lions pass. guard. in pale or, a bordure ar.

Holland. Sa. a bordure engr. ar.

Holland Priory (co. Lincoln). Az. a lion ramp. guard. betw. eight fleurs-de-lis ar. over all on a bend gu. three keys, the wards upwards or.

Hollenshed. Ar. three bars and a canton gu.

Hollery (co. Norfolk). Ar. a fesse chequy or and sa.

Holles, or Hollis (Grimsby, co. Lincoln, and Haughton, co. Nottingham; descended from the marriage of William Holles, of Haughton (second son of Sir William Holles, Lord Mayor of London in 1540) with Anne, dau. and heiress of John Denzell, Esq., of Denzell, co. Cornwall; the grandson of this alliance, John Holles, of Haughton, was created Baron Haughton in 1616, and Earl of Clare in 1624 ; the last inheritor of which honours, John Holles, fourth Earl of Clare, was created Duke of Newcastle; his Grace left an only child, Henrietta, wife of Edward, Lord Harley, and mother of Margaret, Duchess of Portland). Erm. two piles in point sa. *Crest*—A boar pass. az. bristled or.

Holles (Duke of Newcastle 1694, Earl of Clare, 1624, extinct 1711). Erm. two piles in point sa. *Crest*—A boar pass. az. tusked and bristled or. *Supporters*—Dexter, a lion : sinister, a tiger, both or. *Motto*—Spes audaces adjuvat.

Holles (Lord Holles, of Ifield, created 1661, extinct 1694; derived from Denzill, second son of John, first Earl of Clare). Same *Arms* and *Motto*. *Crest*—A Moor's head couped below the shoulders ppr. wreathed around the neck and temples ar. and sa. *Supporters*—Dexter, a lion or, ducally crowned ppr.; sinister, a tiger sa. gorged with a plain collar or.

Holles (Winterborne, co. Dorset, bart., extinct 1694; Francis Holles, eldest son of the first Lord Holles, of Ifield, was created a bart. 1660). Same *Arms*, with a file of three points.

Holles (Pelham-Holles, Duke of Newcastle, created 1715, extinct 1768). Quarterly, 1st and 4th, az. three pelicans ar. vulning themselves in the breast gu., for Pelham; 2nd and 3rd, erm. two piles in point sa., for Holles. *Crest*—A peacock in his pride ar. *Supporters*—Dexter, a bay horse; sinister, a bear ppr., each collared or, gorged with a belt ar. buckles and studs gold. *Motto*—Vicit amor patria.

Holles. Same *Arms*. *Crest*—A Moor's head couped and wreathed about the temples ar. and az.

Holles. Same *Arms*. *Crest*—A lion's paw erased or, holding a heart gu.

Holles, or Hollys (co. Norfolk). Sa. on a bend betw. two talbots pass. and a dolphin embowed ar. three annulets gu.

Holles, or Holleis. Az. on a bend or, betw. a talbot courant in chief and a dolphin embowed in base ar. three torteaux.

Holles. Sa. on a bend betw. a greyhound courant in chief and a dolphin embowed in base ar. three roses gu.

Hollet, or Holiffe (co. Gloucester). Az. a chev. or, betw. three crescents ar.

Holleys (Lord Mayor of London, 1539). Sa. on a bend ar. betw. a talbot courant in chief and a dolphin embowed in base of the second three torteaux. *Crest*—An arm embowed, vested bendy of six ar. and sa. cuffed or, holding in the hand ppr. a branch of holly vert, fructed gu.

Holliam. Or, on a bend sa. three mullets pierced ar. *Crest*—A harrow gu.

Holliam. Or, on a bend sa. three mullets ar. pierced gu.

Holliard. Sa. a chev. betw. three estoiles ar.

Holliche. Ar. a chev. engr. sa.

Holliday (London). See Halliday.

Holliday (Bromley, co. Middlesex; descended from Sir Leonard Holliday, Lord Mayor of London, 1605. Visit. Middlesex, 1663). Sa. three helmets ar. garnished or, a border of the last. *Crest*—A demi lion ramp. guard. resting the paws on an anchor all ppr.

Hollier. Or, a buck's head cabossed az. *Crest*—A dexter hand holding a fish ppr.

Hollier (London; borne by Thomas Hollier, of London, surgeon, d. 1690; monumental tablet and Har. MSS.). Same *Arms*. *Crest*—On a mural crown a buck's head cabossed holding in the mouth a bear's paw erased ar. *Another Crest*—A bear's paw erect and erased erm. holding a sceptre with a fleur-de-lis gu.

Holligan (granted to James Holligan, Esq., of Barbadoes).

Per pale az. and gu. on a chev. engr. ar. betw. three lions' heads erased erminois as many holly leaves slipped vert. *Crest*—A demi lion az. gorged with a collar gemel or, and charged on the shoulder with a bezant, holding in the dexter paw a branch of holly ppr.

Hollingbury. Ar. a fesse sa. in chief three pheons gu. in base a buck's head cabossed of the last. *Crest*—A buck's head, as in the arms.

Hollingshed (Hollins, in the township of Sutton, co. Chester; the heiress of Sir HUGH HOLLINSHEAD, the last of the elder branch, at an early period, *m.* into the family of Ravenscroft; the next line was HOLLINSHEAD, of Cophurst, whose representative was RALPH HOLINSHED, the historian, whose sister and heir *m.* CORBET; and from the Cophurst family descended HOLLINSHEAD, of Bug Lawton and Heywood, &c.). Ar. a cross sa. a canton ermines. *Crest*—A bull's head gorged with a ducal coronet.

Hollingshed (co. Stafford). Ar. a cross sa. charged with a trefoil slipped of the first, a canton ermines.

Hollingsworth (York Herald, *temp.* Richard III.). Az. on a bend ar. three leaves slipped vert. *Crest*—A stag couchant ar.

Hollingsworth (Surrey and Hartlepool, co. Durham). Ar. a chev. erm. betw. three stags trippant ppr. *Crest*—A crescent ar. *Motto*—Lumen accipe et imperti.

Hollington (Alvechurch, co. Worcester). Sa. a fret ar.

Hollingworth (Hollingworth, co. Chester). Az. on a bend ar. three holly leaves vert. The family name was formerly spelt HOLLYNWORTHE, and is evidently derived from the holly tree, called in Cheshire " Hollyn Tree," with which the estate abounded. *Crest*—A stag lodged ppr. *Motto*—Disce ferenda pati.

Hollins (Moseley, co. Stafford). Ar. a chev. az. in chief four crosses formée fitchée of the second. *Crest*—A dexter hand pointing with two fingers to a star ppr.

Hollinshed (Hollinshed Hall, co. Lancaster). Quarterly, 1st and 4th, per bend ar. and erm. on a cross sa. a cross crosslet fitchée or, in the dexter chief point an escallop az. for distinction, for HOLLINSHED; 2nd and 3rd, az. a brock or, betw. three bezants, two and one, for BROCK. *Crests*—1st, HOLLINSHED: A heron ar. in the beak a cross crosslet fitchée sa. behind the heron an arrow and bow in saltire ppr. the heron charged on the breast with an escallop az. for distinction; 2nd, BROCK: A boars' head couped or, betw. two bucks' horns sa. *Motto*—Nemo me impune lacessit.

Hollis (cos. Devon and Nottingham). Sa. on a bend betw. a talbot pass. in chief and a dolphin embowed in base ar. three torteaux.

Hollis (Winchester, co. Hants). Erm. two piles issuing out of the dexter and sinister chief points and meeting in the centre of the escutcheon sa. *Crest*—A Saracen's head couped at the shoulders, wreathed round the temples sa.

Hollis (Stoke, near Coventry, co. Warwick). Same *Arms*. *Crest*—A blackamoor's head couped at the shoulders in profile ppr. bound about the temples and tied in a knot ar. and az.

Hollis (Ereby, co. Lincoln, and Nottingham; granted 24 May, 1550). Sa. a bend betw. two talbots pass. ar. *Crest*—A dexter arm embowed in armour, garnished or, holding in the gauntlet a holly branch with berries all ppr.

Hollis (Shire Newton House, co. Monmouth). Same *Arms* and *Crest.*

Hollis (co. Middlesex). Ar. on a chev. az. betw. three holly branches vert, fructed ppr. as many doves of the last.

Hollis (Flincham, co. Norfolk). Sa. on a bend betw. a lion saliant in chief and a dolphin in base ar. three torteaux.

Hollis (co. Nottingham). Sa. a chev. betw. two talbots ar.

Hollis. Az. on a bend or, three torteaux.

Hollist (exemplified to ANTHONY CAPRON, Esq., of Midhurst, co. Sussex, who assumed the surname of HOLLIST, 1833, by royal licence). Sa. on a bend betw. a greyhound courant bendways in chief and a dolphin haurient in base ar. three torteaux, on a chief of the second three sprigs of strawberry fructed ppr. *Crest*—Betw. two sprigs of strawberry, as in the arms, a dexter arm embowed in armour, the hand within a gauntlet holding a sprig of holly all ppr. *Mottoes*—Currendo; over the crest: Gardez le Capron.

Holliwell (Reg. Ulster's Office). Az. a chev. engr. or, betw. three hawks ar.

Hollon. Per pale gu. and az. a lion ramp. guard. or.

Holloway (CHARLES HOLLOWAY, of the Inner Temple, London, Barrister-at-law, and JOHN HOLLOWAY, of Oxford, sons of JOHN HOLLOWAY, of Oxford, gent. Visit. Oxon, 1634). Gu. a fess betw. three crescents ar. a canton erm. *Crest*—A goat's head erased and horned ar. collared and lined gu. on the collar three crescents of the first.

Holloway (Maydenhatch, co. Berks). Gu. a fesse ar. cotised or, betw. three crescents of the second.

Holloway (London). Gu. a fesse erm. betw. three crescents ar. *Crest*—A demi lion ramp. guard. purp.

Holloway (Fellow of New College, Oxford, *d.* 1632). Gu. a fesse betw. three crescents ar. a canton erm. *Crest*—A goat's head ar. gorged with a collar gu. charged with three crescents of the first, lined of the second.

Holloway. Gu. a fesse betw. three crescents ar. *Crest*—Out of a mural coronet ar. a lion's head or, charged with a torteau.

Holloway. Same *Arms*, the fesse cotised.

Holloway (Kensington, co. Middlesex). Paly of six az. and or, a fesse gu. betw. three crescents ar. a canton erm. *Crest*—Out of a crescent or, an antelope's head gu. attired, collared, and chained gold. *Motto*—A Deo lux nostra.

Holloway. Sa. three goats pass. ar. attired or. *Crest*—A goat's head erased ar. attired or, a rose in its mouth slipped and leaved ppr.

Hollowell. Or, on a bend gu. three goats pass. ar. *Crest*—A goat pass. ar. attired or.

Hollowell, or Holwell. Per chev. gu. and erm. three chessrooks counterchanged.

Hollybarne. Ar. on a fesse sa. three crescents or.

Hollyday. See HALLIDAY.

Hollywood, or Holywood. Az. a chev. engr. betw. three martlets ar.

Holm. Ar. a cross botonnée gu.

Holman (co. Devon; granted June, 1608). Vert a chev. ar. guttée de sang betw. three pheons or.

Holman (London). Vert a chev. or, betw. three pheons ar. *Crest*—On a chapeau gu. turned up erm. an ostrich's head ar.

Holman (Banbury, co. Oxford). Same *Arms*. *Crest*—A bow and arrow, the bow erect, bent and strung, the arrow fesseways on the bow all or.

Holman. Same *Arms*. *Crest*—On a chapeau az. turned up erm. an ostrich's head couped at the neck ar.

Holman (Godeston, co. Surrey). Vert a chev. betw. three pheons or. *Crest*—A bow and arrow drawn, the arrow fesseways betw. two wings all or.

Holman. Vert on a chev. or, betw. three pheons ar. a fleur-de-lis gu.

Holman. Vert a chev. betw. three roses ar.

Holmden, or Holmeden (Tenchleys, co. Surrey; granted 20 June, 1577). Sa. a fesse betw. two chev. erm. *Crest*—An otter's head couped (another, erased) or.

Holmden (Crowle, co. Worcester ; LYDIA, dau. and heir of JOHN HOLMDEN, *m.* RICHARD AMPHLETE, Esq., of Hadsor). Same *Arms*, the chev. each charged with three crosses crosslet of the field.

Holmden (THOMAS LEE, second son of THOMAS LEE, gent., of Enfield, co. Stafford, *m.* MARY, dau. of JOHN HOLMDEN. Visit. London, 1568). Sa. a fess betw. two chev. erm.

Holme, or Hulme (Hulme, co. Lancaster). Barry of eight or and az. on a canton ar. a chaplet gu. *Crest*—A lion's head erased gu. langued az. ensigned with a cap of maintenance. *Motto*—Fide sed cui vide. The canton and the chaplet are stated to have been an augmentation granted to Sir WILLIAM DE HULME, Knt., of Hulme, for his services under the Black Prince, in France.

Holme (Up Holland House, co. Lancaster ; descended from WILLIAM HULME, second son of HULME, of Hulme. Visit. Cheshire, 1566). Same *Arms* and *Motto*. *Crest*—The Up-Holland branch has latterly borne, apparently without authority, a griffin's head betw. two wings.

Holme (co. Lancaster). Barry of six or and az a canton ar.

Holme, or Hulme (Overhulme, co. Stafford). Barry of six or and az. on a canton erm. a chaplet gu. *Crest*—On a ducal coronet or, a chaplet gu. therein a garb of the first.

Holme-Cultram Abbey (co. Cumberland). Az. a cross moline or, impaling or, a lion ramp. sa.

Holme-Sumner (Hatchland Park, near Guildford, co. Surrey). See SUMNER.

Holme (Beverley, co. York). Ar. a stag trippant ppr. attired and unguled or.

Holme (Huntington, co. York). Ar. a chev. az. betw. three chaplets gu.

Holme (THOMAS HOLME, citizen of London, son of HUGH HOLME, gent., of Codington, co. Chester. Visit. London, 1568). Barry of eight or and az. on a canton ar. a chaplet gu. *Crest*—A lion's head couped or, crowned with a chapeau az. turned up erm,

Holme (co. York). Ar. a stag trippant gu. attired and unguled or.

Holme (Stapleton, co. Gloucester). Ar. a chev. az. a bordure engr. sa. *Crests*—1st: A demi ostrich gu. holding in the beak a horseshoe ar.; 2nd: A lion's head couped or, thereon a cap of maintenance az. turned up erm.

Holme. Ar. a buck az. attired or.

Holme. Sa. a lion ramp. ar. charged with three bendlets gu.

Holme. Sa. a lion ramp. ar. debruised with a bend gu.

Holme. Sa. a lion ramp. barry of six ar. and gu.

Holme. Or, three fleurs-de-lis az.

Holme. Or, two bars az. on a canton ar. a chaplet of laurel ppr. *Crest*—A griffin's head couped az. betw. two wings or.

Holme (Tranmere, co. Chester). Barry of six or and az. on a canton erm. a rose gu. seeded or, barbed vert. *Crest*—An arm couped and embowed, vested barry of six or and az. cuffed erm. grasping a rose branch ppr.

Holme (Paull-Holme, co. York, *temp.* Conquest). Barry of six or and az. on a canton ar. a chaplet gu. *Crests*—1st: A holly tree fructed ppr.; 2nd (granted to Sir BRYAN HOLME, of Paull-Holme, in 1346, on the taking of the King of the Scots prisoner): Out of a mural coronet gu. a hound's head erased or. *Motto*—Holme semper viret.

Holmede (Coddington, co. Chester). Barry of seventeen or and az. on a canton ar. a laurel crown gu.

Holmede (co. Chester). Barry of five or and az. on a canton erm. a rose gu.

Holmes (Gawdy Hall, co. Norfolk). Barry of six or and az. on a canton gu. a chaplet ar. *Crest*—A holly tree vert, fructed gu.

Holmes. Barry of six or and az. in chief a mullet of the second, on a canton gu. a cinquefoil ar.

Holmes (Brook Hall, co. Norfolk). Barry of eight or and az. a bordure nebulée erm. on a canton of the second a chaplet of roses ppr. *Crest*—Out of a crown vallery or, the rim charged with three annulets in fesse az. a stag's head erm. attired gold.

Holmes (Scole House, co. Norfolk). Barry of eight or and az. on a canton gu. three garlands ppr. *Crest*—A lion's head erect or. *Motto*—Ora et labora.

Holmes (*Lord Holmes*, of Kilmallock; created 1760, extinct 1764). Barry wavy of six or and az. on a canton gu. a lion pass. guard. of the first.

Holmes (*Lord Holmes*; Rev. LEONARD TOUGHEAR, nephew of *Lord Holmes*, of Kilmallock, assumed the name of HOLMES, and was created a peer 1797, extinct 1804). Same *Arms.*

Holmes (WORSLEY-HOLMES, Pidford House and Newport, co. Hants, bart., extinct 1825). Quarterly, 1st and 4th, barry wavy of six or and az. on a canton gu. a lion pass. guard. of the first, for HOLMES; 2nd and 3rd, ar. a chev. betw. three hawks sa., for WORSLEY. *Crests*—1st, HOLMES: Out of a naval crown or, a dexter arm in armour embowed, holding a trident ppr. pointed gold; 2nd, WORSLEY: A wolf's head erased or.

Holmes (A'COURT-HOLMES, *Baron Heytesbury*). Quarterly, 1st and 4th, barry wavy of six or and az. in a canton gu. a lion of England pass. guard. or, for HOLMES; 2nd and 3rd, per fesse or, and paly of six erminois and az. in chief an eagle displ. sa. beaked and membered gu. charged on the body with two chevronels ar., for A'COURT. *Crests*—1st, HOLMES: Out of a naval crown or, an arm embowed in armour, the hand ppr. grasping a trident az. headed or; 2nd, A'COURT: An eagle displ. sa. charged with two chevronels, beaked and legged gu. holding in the beak a lily slipped ppr. *Supporters*—On either side an eagle, wings elevated sa. beaked and membered gu. each holding in the beak a lily slipped ppr. *Motto*—Grandescunt, aucta labore.

Holmes (Retford, co. Nottingham). Barry wavy of six or and az. on a canton gu. a lion pass. of the first. *Crest*—Out of a naval crown or, a dexter arm embowed in armour, holding a trident ppr. spear gold. *Motto*—Justum et tenacem propositi.

Holmes (Berowe, co. Cambridge). Barry of six or and gu. on a canton of the second a chaplet of the first.

Holmes (Coddington, co. Chester). Barry of eight az. and or, on a canton ar. a chaplet gu. (another, the chaplet sa.).

Holmes (co. Lancaster). Barry of six or and az. on a canton ar. three roses gu.

Holmes (North Mymes, co. Herts). Sa. on a lion ramp. ar. three bends gu.

Holmes (Hampoll. Visit. York, 1585). Sa. a lion ramp. ar. charged with three bendlets gu. *Crest*—A demi griffin az. guttée d'or, holding in the dexter claw a sword erect az. pommel and hilt or.

Holmes (co. York). Barry of six ar. and az. on a canton gu. a chaplet of the first.

502

Holmes (co. York). Sa. a lion ramp. ar. semée of crosses crosslet of the field.

Holmes (impalement Fun. Ent. Ulster's Office, 1608, CICELY HOLMES, wife of RICHARD FAGAN, Alderman of Dublin). Az. a lion ramp. erm. armed and langued gu.

Holmes (Fun. Ent. Ulster's Office, GEORGE HOLMES, buried in St. Michael's Church, 14 Nov. 1675). Ar. a lion ramp. vert.

Holroyd (*Earl of Sheffield*). Quarterly, 1st, az. on a fesse dancettée ar. betw. three griffins pass. wings endorsed or, as many escallops gu.; 2nd, az. five cinquefoils in saltire ar., for HOLROYD; 3rd, erm. on a chief gu. a demi lion ramp. issuant or, for ELWOOD; 4th, az. on a fesse or, betw. three swans' heads erased ar. ducally gorged of the second, as many cinquefoils gu., for BAKER. *Crest*—A demi griffin segreant, wings endorsed sa. holding betw. the claws a ducal coronet or. *Supporters*—Dexter, a lion reguard. ppr.; sinister, a horse bridled ppr. *Motto*—Quem te Deus esse jussit.

Holroyd (one of the Judges of the Court of King's Bench). Az. five spur-rowels in saltire or. *Crest*—A demi griffin or.

Holsall (Holsall). Ar. three dragons' heads erased, fire issuing from their mouths ppr.

Holsheff. Az. a garb ar. banded gu.

Holstock (Orsett, co. Essex). Or, on a bend engr. sa. betw. two lions saliant az. three bezants. *Crest*—A demi man ppr. chained round the middle and holding the chain in his sinister hand or, in the dexter a club raguly ar.

Holston (Hynnamhall, co. Suffolk). Gu. a saltire countercompony or and erm. in chief a key, sinister a martlet, base a dolphin embowed, and dexter a ragged staff all ar. on a chief or, betw. a squirrel sejant and a bull's head couped sa. a pellet charged with a talbot sejant ar.

Holt (Aston Hall, co. Warwick, bart., extinct 1782; Sir THOMAS HOLT, Sheriff of the co. 1597, was created a bart. 1612; he was descended from JOHN ATTE HOLTE, *temp.* Edward II.). Az. two bars or, in chief a cross formée fitchée of the last. *Crest*—A squirrel sejant or, holding a hazel branch slipped and fructed all ppr.

Holt (Erdington Hall, co. Warwick). Same *Arms* and *Crest.* *Motto*—Exaltavit humiles.

Holt (Swaston, co. Cambridge). Ar. on a bend sa. three fleurs-de-lis of the field. *Crest*—A pheon sa.

Holt (Brereton, co. Chester). Ar. a chev. betw. three saltires engr. gu.

Holt (co. Lancaster, and London; granted 18 June, 1582). Ar. on a bend engr. sa. three fleurs-de-lis of the field. *Crest*—A dexter arm embowed in armour ppr. garnished or, holding in the gauntlet a pheon sa.

Holt (Twyford and Portsmouth, co. Hants; a branch of HOLT, of co. Lancaster. Visit. Hants, 1634). Same *Arms* and *Crest.*

Holt (granted to WILLIAM HOLT, Esq., of Bishham Hall, Billinge Higher End, co. Lancaster). Ar. on a bend engr. betw. two fers-de-moline in bend sa. three fleurs-de-lis of the field. *Crest*—In front of a cubit arm in armour the hand in a gauntlet ppr. holding a pheon sa. a fer-de-moline fesseways of the last.

Holt (Shevington and Ince). Ar. on a bend engr. sa. three fleurs-de-lis of the field.

Holt (Stubley, co. Lancaster; ELLEN, dau. of JAMES HOLT, of that place, *m.* JOHN NICOLLS, of London, Comptroller of the Works at London Bridge at Visit. 1568). Ar. on a bend engr. sa. three fleurs-de-lis of the field. *Crest*—A pheon sa.

Holt (Gristlehurst, co. Lancaster, 1567). Ar. on a bend engr. sa. three fleurs-de-lis of the field, a crescent for diff.

Holt (Bridge Hall, co. Lancaster, 1664). Ar. on a bend engr. cotised sa. three fleurs-de-lis of the field.

Holt (Ashworth, co. Lancaster, 1664). Ar. on a bend sa. three fleurs-de-lis of the field. *Crest*—A pheon sa.

Holt, or Holte (co. Suffolk). Ar. on a bend engr. sa. (another, az.) three fleurs-de-lis or. *Crest*—An arm erect couped at the elbow, habited per pale az. and gu. in the hand ar. a pheon sa.

Holt. Or, a fleur-de-lis az.

Holt. Ar. a chev. betw. three fleurs-de-lis gu.

Holt. Per pale az. and gu. two bars or.

Holt. Ar. a chev. betw. three squirrels gu. cracking nuts or.

Holt, or Holte. Or, three fleurs-de-lis gu.

Holt, or Holte. Per fesse az. and gu. two bars or.

Holte. Az. three fleurs-de-lis ar.

Holtby (Tryton, co. York). Az. fretty ar. a chief of the second.

Holte (Stoke Lyne, co. Oxford. Visit. Oxon, 1566. WILLIAM HOLTE, *d.* 7 Jan. 1682; monument, Stoke Lyne Church). Ar. on a bend engr. sa. three fleurs-de-lis of the first.

Crest—An arm holding a baton with a pheon on the top of it.

Holte. Az. two bars or, betw. the bars a barrulet environed with an annulet of the last, in chief a cross pattée fitchée of the second.

Holte (Fun. Ent. Ulster's Office, 1596, ANNE HOLTE, wife of Capt. HENRY PIERS). Az. two bars or, in chief a cross formée fitchée of the last.

Holteby. Az. a fret ar. a chief of the second.

Holthens. Vairé or and az.

Holtoft (co. York). Az. a cross sarcelly ar.

Holtoft. Sa. three fishes' heads erased haurient ar.

Holtofte (Flintham, co. Notts; WALTER HOLTOFTE, of that place. Visit. 1614). Sa. three conger eels' heads couped and erect ar.

Holton. Az. on a bend or, three eagles displ. gu. *Crest*—A map ppr.

Holton. Quarterly, az. and gu. a lion ramp. ar.

Holton. Sa. three saltorels ar.

Holtost. Sa. three dragons' heads erased and erect ar.

Holway (Watton in Stoke Gabriel, co. Devon. Visit. 1620. The co-heirs *m.* BLACKMORE and WINDSOR). Sa. two swords in saltire, hilts and pommels in chief all ar. the dexter surmounted by the sinister.

Holway. Gu. a fesse betw. three crescents ar. *Crest*—Out of a ducal coronet or, a greyhound's head sa.

Holwell. Or, a bend sa.

Holwell. Per chev. gu. and erm. in chief three chessrooks of the last.

Holworthey. Or, a chev. betw. three trefoils slipped sa. *Crest*—A greyhound collared and lined.

Holworthey (Palsgrave, co. Norfolk). Or, on a chev. betw. three trefoils slipped sa. as many mullets of the field.

Holy Spirit, College of the (Isle of Cumbrae, N.B.; granted 30 Nov. 1874, by George Burnett, Lyon). Quarterly, 1st and 4th grand quarters, az. St. Columba in a boat at sea, on his sinister hand a dove, and in dexter chief a blazing star all ppr.; 2nd and 3rd grand quarters, counterquartered, 1st and 4th or, an eagle displ. with two heads gu. armed and beaked az., 2nd and 3rd, parted per bend embattled gu. and ar.; in an escutcheon of pretence in the centre of the 2nd and 3rd grand quarters or, three stags' horns gu.

Holyday (Archdeacon of Oxford, *d.* 2 Oct. 1661). Sa. three helmets sidefaced and close within a bordure engr. ar.

Holyfe (co. Gloucester). Az. a chev. or, betw. three crescents ar.

Holyland. Per pale ar. and sa. in chief two mullets and in base a cinquefoil all counterchanged. *Crest*—A demi calvary entwined by a serpent all ppr.

Holyland, or Hollyland. Per pale ar. and sa. a cinquefoil betw. three mullets counterchanged. *Crest*—A demi savage handcuffed ppr.

Holyman. Ar. two bars, the first engr. on the upper side, the second on the under side az. betw. three roses gu. stalked and leaved vert, betw. the two roses in chief as many martlets of the third.

Holyngworthe (Holyngworthe Hall, co. Chester). Sa. on a bend or, three holly-leaves vert. *Crest*—A stag lodged ppr. *Motto*—Disce ferenda pati.

Holyoake (Tettenhall, co. Stafford, and Studley Castle, co. Warwick). Per pale or and gu. a buck's head caboossed betw. two crosses pattée in pale all counterchanged. *Crest*—On a mount vert an oak fructed ppr. around the lower part of the stem an escroll, thereon a cross pattée gu. betw. the words " Sacra quercus."

Holyoake-Goodricke, Bart. See GOODRICKE.

Holyoke. Az. a chev. ar. cotised or, betw. three crescents of the second. *Crest*—A cinquefoil. Another *Crest*—A cubit arm erect, habited gu. cuffed ar. holding in the hand ppr. an oak branch vert, fructed or.

Holywood (Dublin, Herbertstown, co. Meath, and Cartain, co. Kildare; Fun. Ent. of RICHARD HOLYWOOD, of Dublin, *d.* 24 March, 1609). Az. a chev. engr. betw. three falcons close ar. beaked, legged, and belled or.

Holyworth. Sa. three falcons ar. armed, jessed, and belled or.

Homan, or Howman, alias Feckenham (last Abbot of Westminster, *d.* 1585). Gu. a cross fusily ar.

Homan (Dunlum, co. Westmeath, bart.). Vert a chev. or, betw. three pheons, points downwards ar. *Crest*—A lion's head erased or, on the head a chapeau gu. turned up. erm. *Motto*—Homo sum.

Home (that Ilk, co. Berwick). Quarterly, 1st and 4th, vert a lion ramp. ar.; 2nd and 3rd, three popinjays vert, beaked and membered gu. *Crest*—A popinjay's head ppr.

Home (*Earl of Home*). Quarterly, 1st and 4th, vert a lion ramp. ar. armed and langued gu., for HOME; 2nd and 3rd,

503

ar. three popinjays vert, beaked and membered gu., for PEPDIE, of Dunglas; over all an escutcheon or, charged with an orle az., for LANDELL. *Crest*—A lion's head erased ar. on a chapeau gu. turned up erm. *Supporters*—Two lions ar. *Mottoes*—Over the crest: A Home, a Home, a Home; under the arms: True to the end.

Home (Eccles, Scotland). Quarterly, 1st and 4th, HOME; 2nd, PEPDIE; 3rd, three escutcheons vert, for HUME, of Broxmouth. *Crest*—A lion's head erased and fullfaced. *Motto*—True to the end.

Home (FERGUSSON-HOME, of Bassendean, co. Berwick; as recorded 1860). Per bend vert and ar. in chief a lion ramp. ar. in base three papingoes of the first, on a chief or, a buckle betw. two boars' heads couped az. *Crest*—On a chapeau gu. doubled erm. a lion's head erased vert. *Mottoes* —A home, a home; and, True to the end.

Home (Ayton, co. Berwick; descended from GEORGE, second son of ALEXANDER, first *Lord Home*). The quartered arms of HOME and PEPDIE, charged in the centre with a rose gu.

Home (West Reston, cc. Berwick; cadet of Ayton). Quarterly, as Ayton, within a bordure gu. *Crest*—A lion's head erased ar. collared gu. charged with three roses of the first. *Motto*—True to the end.

Home (Wedderburn, co. Berwick). Quarterly, 1st and 4th, HOME; 2nd, PEPDIE; 3rd, ar. a cross engr az., for SINCLAIR. *Crest*—A unicorn's head and neck ar. gorged with a coronet, maned and horned or. *Motto*—Remember.

Home (Renton, bart., 1698). Quarterly, 1st and 4th, HOME; 2nd, PEPDIE; 3rd, ar. three hunting horns sa. stringed gu., for FORRESTER; 4th, gu. a pelican feeding her young ar. vulned ppr., for ELLEM. *Crest*—A pelican's head ppr.

Home (Kames; represented by HOME-DRUMMOND, of Blair Drummond, as heir of line). Quarterly, as the last, within a. bordure engr. gu. *Crest*—A pelican's head couped ppr.

Home (Blackadder, co. Berwick, bart., 1671). Quarterly, 1st and 4th, vert a lion ramp. ar. within a bordure erm.; 2nd and 3rd, az. on a chev. ar. three roses gu., for BLACKADDER. *Crest*—A lion's head erased ar. collared erm. *Motto*—True to the end.

Home, or Hume (Crossrigg; cadet of Blackadder). Quarterly, as BLACKADDER, within a bordure or. *Crest*—A lion's head erased ar. collared gu. *Motto*—True to the end.

Home (Kimmerghame, co. Berwick). Quarterly, 1st and 4th, vert a lion ramp. ar. within a bordure engr. or, charged with eight roses gu.; 2nd, ar. three piles engr. gu., for POLWARTH; 3rd, ar. a cross engr. sa., for SINCLAIR, of Herdmanston. *Crest*—A lion's head erased ar. with a collar or, powdered with roses and fleurs-de-lis gu. *Motto*—True to the end.

Home (*Earl of Marchmont*, Ninewells, Whitfield, &c.). See HUME.

Home (Well Manor Farm, co. Southampton, bart., 1813). Vert a lion ramp. betw. two piles engr. issuing from the chief ar. all within a bordure engr. of the last, charged with six popinjays of the field, beaked and membered gu. *Crest*—A lion's head erased ppr. thereon a label of three points ar. the middle point charged with a fleur-de-lis az. the others with the cross of St. George gu. *Supporters*—Two lions ramp. reguard. ar.

Home (Blackadder, co. Berwick, bart., 1671). Quarterly, 1st, az. on a chev. ar. three roses gu., for BLACKADDER; 2nd, vert a lion ramp. ar., for HOME; 3rd, ar. three popinjays vert, for PEPDIE; 4th, ar. a cross engr. az., for SINCLAIR, of Hermandston. *Crest*—An adder sa. in pale, holding in its mouth a rose gu. leaved and stalked vert. *Supporters*—Dexter, an otter; sinister, a falcon, both ppr. *Motto*—Vise à la fin.

Home (East Grinstead, co. Suffolk). Gu. a fesse vairé or and az.

Homell, or Honell (co. Suffolk). Sa. a cross ar.

Homer (West Town, Backwell, co. Somerset). Erm. a fesse gu.

Homer. Ar. a crossbow unbent sa. betw. four cocks gu. *Crest* —A lion's gamb holding up a cross pattée.

Homes. Or, a fesse dancettée betw. three griffins' heads erased az. *Crest*—An antelope pass. ppr.

Homes (Southampton). Same *Arms*, a bordure of the last bezantée.

Homffrevylle (quartered by AYSCOUGH, Nuthall, co. Notts. Visit. Notts 1631). Gu. a cinquefoil within an orle of crosses crosslet or.

Homfray (The Hyde, co. Stafford; Wollaston Hall, Broadwaters House, and Red Hill House, co. Worcester; Cowerth Park, co. Berks; Penny Darren Place, Rhonda House, and Llandaff House, co. Glamorgan; Great Yarmouth, co. Norfolk; and co. York; derived from FRANCIS HOMFRAY, Esq., of Aston, co. York, supposed to have been killed at the siege of Clonmel, under Cromwell). Quarterly, 1st and 4th, gu. a cross botonnée erm.; 2nd, quarterly, ar. and sa.; 3rd, sa. four palets erm. *Crests*—1st : An otter pass. wounded in the sinister shoulder with a spear all ppr., motto over, Vulneror non vincor; 2nd: Out of a ducal coronet or, a dragon's head vert; 3rd : A dragon's head vert, holding in his mouth a sinister hand couped at the wrist gu. *Motto*— L'homme vrai aime son pays.

Homfray (Penllyne Castle, co. Glamorgan). Quarterly, 1st, gu. a cross bottony erm.; 2nd, quarterly, ar. and sa.; 3rd, sa. four pales erm.; 4th, ar. three bars gemelles sa. *Crest*—An otter ppr. wounded in the shoulder with a spear. *Motto*—Vulneratur non vincitur.

Homfray (The Place, Stradishall, co. Suffolk). Gu. a cross bottony erm. *Crest*—An otter ppr. wounded in the shoulder with a spear.

Homfray-Addenbrooke (Wollaston Hall, co. Worcester). Quarterly, az. and ar. a fesse wavy or, betw. three crescents counterchanged, quartering the three coats, as in HOMFRAY, of the Hyde. *Crest*—On the banks of a river ppr. an otter pass. ppr. ar. and sa. charged with two crescents counterchanged. *Motto*—Vincit qui patitur.

Homfray (Wales and Rotherham, co. York, 1674). Gu. a cross botonnée erm. *Crest*—An otter ppr. wounded in the shoulder with a spear.

Homill, or Hummell (Scotland). Ar. a bend betw. two crescents gu.

Homyll (Scotland). Ar. a bend betw. a crescent in chief gu. and a fleur-de-lis in base az.

Homyngford. Erm. on a chief az. seven bezants, four and three.

Honchach, or Honychurch. Az. on a bend or, (another, ar.) a boar's head betw. two mullets gu.

Honde. Sa. three pickaxes ar.

Hondesacre. Erm. three chess rooks gu.

Hondon (Lincoln). Gu. a chev. betw. three crosses crosslet or, in chief a lion pass. of the second.

Hondon. Gu. a chev. betw. three crosses crosslet or, on a chief of the second a lion pass. guard. of the first.

Hone (Ottery, co. Devon). Ar. two bars wavy betw. three honestones az.

Hone (co. Devon). Ar. two bars wavy betw. three billets sa. *Crest*—A sword in pale ppr. ensigned with a cross pattée.

Hone (the Spa, co. Gloucester). Per pale indented az. and or, two lions ramp. combatant, holding a crescent all counterchanged. *Crest*—An arm embowed in armour, holding a scymitar ppr.

Hone (Ireland). Az. two bars betw. six billets or. *Crest*— On a mount, overgrown with rye grass, a birch tree ppr.

Honede. Az. a chev. betw. three lozenges ar.

Honell (Ashboking, co. Suffolk). Sa. a cross betw. four water bougets ar.

Honell (co. Suffolk). Sa. three crescents ar.

Honeypott (quartered by WINGFIELD, of Tickencote. Visit. Huntingdon, 1613, and Visit. Rutland, 1619). Ar. ten torteaux, four, three, two, and one.

Honeywill. Ar. a chev. embattled counter-embattled per chev. and per pale sa. and az. counterchanged, betw. three hawks' heads erased of the last. *Crest*—A bechive with bees volant ppr.

Honford. Ar. a chev. betw. three mascles gu.

Honford. Sa. an estoile of eight points ar. radiated. *Crest*—On a chapeau az. turned up erm. a dragon pass. gu.

Hongbrigg (co. York). Ar. a bend betw. two cocks sa.

Hongebrigg (co. York). Ar. three cocks in bend cotised sa.

Hongon (East Bradenham, co. Norfolk; granted by Thos. Hawley, Clarenceux, 20 May, 1546). Ar. a chev. engr. vairé or and gu. betw. three hurts, each charged with a lion's gamb ar. *Crest*—A lion's gamb az. gripping a lion's paw erased gu.

Honing (Carleton, co. Suffolk). Quarterly, gu. and vert a lion ramp. ar.

Honingham (co. York). Ar. two crosses formée in fesse sa.

Honner, or Honnere. Erm. on a bend gu. a cinquefoil in the chief point or.

Honners. Or, on a bend az. betw. three hawks' heads erased sa. as many cinquefoils of the first.

Honnyloe (WALTER HONNYLOE, of Dundalk; Fun. Ent. 1614, of his dau. MARION, wife of WILLIAM BROWNE, Sheriff of Dublin). Ar. two bars az. on a chief sa. three trefoils slipped of the field.

Honnyton. Ar. a fesse betw. two chev. sa. *Crest*—A hand holding a dart point upwards all ppr.

Honor, or Honnor. Ar. a chev. betw. three quatrefoils az. stalked vert. *Crest*—A serpent nowed sa. spotted or.

Honor (Honorsborough, *alias* Maddam, Barony of Carbery, co. Cork; granted by Carney, Ulster, 1666, to Lieut.-Col. JOHN HONOR, who went to Ireland with Oliver Cromwell in 1649). Ar. on a bend betw. two eagles' heads erased gu. three cinquefoils or. *Crest*—An eagle displ. ppr. guttée de sang, charged on the breast with a cinquefoil or. *Motto*— Altiora videnda.

Honston. Ar. a lion saliant sa.

Hontbark. Per chev. engr. or and az. in chief an eagle displ. sa.

Honte. Ar. a bordure gu. bezantée.

Honte. Per pale ar. and sa. a saltire counterchanged.

Honte. Sa. a fesse betw. three cinquefoils or.

Honte. Az. a chev. betw. three martlets ar.

Hontsacre, Hondsacre, or Hondisacre. Erm. three chess-rooks gu.

Hontston (co. Lincoln). Ar. a lion ramp. sa. armed az.

Honychurch (Honychurch, *temp.* Henry III.). Az. on a bend ar. a dragon's head erased betw. two mullets gu.

Honychurch (Tavistock and Aveton-Gifford, co. Devon. Visit. 1620). Gu. on a bend ar. a dragon's head erased betw. two mullets of the field.

Honychurch. Az. (another, gu.) on a bend ar. a boar's head betw. two mullets gu.

Honyman (Armadale, Orkney, bart., 1804). Ar. a bend engr. voided gu. *Crest*—An arrow paleways point downwards ppr. feathered ar. *Supporters*—Two lions ramp. guard. ppr. *Motto*—Progredere ne regredere.

Honyngton. Ar. a fesse and chev. sa.

Honyngton. Ar. a fesse betw. two chev. sa.

Honypot. Ar. seven torteaux, two, two, two, and one.

Honyton. Per fesse az. and ar. a pale counterchanged, three kingfishers of the second.

Honywood (Pette, and Send-Newington, near Hythe, co. Kent; granted by patent 10 Nov. 1576). Ar. a chev. betw. three falcons' heads erased az. beaked or.

Honywood (Evington, co. Kent, bart.). Ar. a chev. betw. three hawks' heads erased az. *Crest*—A wolf's head couped erm. *Motto*—Omne bonum desuper.

Honywood (Mark's Hall, Coggeshall, co. Essex, Elmested, and Sibton, near Folkestone, co. Kent). Ar. a chev. betw. three eagles' heads erased az. *Crest*—A wolf's head erased erm.

Honywood (co. Kent). Ar. a chev. quarterly sa. and gu.

Honywood. Ar. a chev. per pale sa. and az. battelly counter-battelly betw. three hawks' heads erased of the third.

Honywood. Ar. a chev. az. betw. three birds, wings expanded sa.

Honywood. Ar. a chev. quarterly sa. and gu. battelly counter-battelly betw. three hawks' heads erased az. billettée of the field.

Honywood. Ar. a chev. betw. three talbots pass. gu.

Hoo. Ar. three circles of chains sa.

Hoo. Ar. on a fesse betw. three goats' heads erased sa. armed or, each having an annulet in the mouth of the last, a fret betw. two birds of the third.

Hoo, or Hoe. Az. a fret ar. and chief sa.

Hoo. Ar. on a fesse dancettée sa. three mullets or.

Hoo, or Hoe. Ar. on a chief indented sa. three mullets or, (another, pierced gu.).

Hoo (*Baron Hoo*; extinct 1453: descended from ROBERT DE Hoo, of Hoo, co. Bedford, and Knebworth, co. Hertford, living *temp.* Edward I. Sir THOMAS H·o, a distinguished soldier in France in the reign of Henry III., was summoned to Parliament as *Baron Hoo*. His daus. and co-heirs were ALEANORE, *m.* Sir JAMES CAREW, Knt., of Bedington, co. Surrey; JANE, *m.* Sir ROGER COPLEY, Knt. ; and ELIZABETH, *m.* Sir JOHN DEVENISH, Knt.). Quarterly, sa. and ar. ; quarterly, ar. and sa. ; quarterly, or and gu. ; quarterly, sa. and ar. within a bordure erminois; and quarterly, sa. and ar. a bend or, were used at various times, and by various branches. *Crests*, at different periods, borne on a chapeau, were—1st: A griffin segreant; 2nd : A hand holding a hautboy ; 3rd : A bull pass. quarterly ar. and sa.

Hoo (co. Stafford; borne by JOHN Hoo, Serjeant-at-law, *temp.* George II.). Quarterly, sa. and ar. a bordure erminois. *Crest*—Within a ring of gold a maiden's head ppr.

Hood (FULLER-ACLAND-HOOD, Bart., St. Audries, Somerset). Quarterly, 1st and 4th, quarterly, 1st and 4th, az. a fret ar. on a chief sa. three crescents or, for HOOD, 2nd, chequy ar. and sa. a fesse gu., for ACLAND, 3rd, ar. three bars and a canton gu., for FULLER; 2nd, Hood; 3rd, PERIAM, gu. a chev. engr. betw. three leopards' faces or. *Crests*—1st, Hood: A Cornish chough holding an anchor on the dexter side in bend sinister ppr.; 2nd,

Acland: A man's hand couped at the wrist in a glove lying fessewise, thereon a falcon perched all ppr. *Motto—* Zealous.

Hood (*Viscount Hood*). Quarterly, 1st and 4th, erminois three cats-a-mountain pass. guard. in pale az. each charged on the body with an erm. spot or, for **Tibbets**; 2nd and 3rd, **az.** a fret ar. on a chief or, three crescents sa., for **Hood**. *Crests*—1st, **Tibbets**: A demi cat-a-mountain guard. az. gorged with a collar gemel, and charged on the body with three erm. spots, two and one or; 2nd, **Hood**: A Cornish chough sa. in front of an anchor in bend sinister or. *Supporters*—Dexter, a merman, in his exterior hand a trident; sinister, a mermaid, in her exterior hand a mirror all ppr. *Motto*—Ventis secundis.

Hood (*Viscount Bridport*). Az. a fret ar. on a chief or, three crescents sa. *Crest*—A Cornish chough ppr. supporting with the dexter claw an anchor or. *Supporters*—Dexter, Neptune ppr. mantled vert, supporting with the left arm a trident, and resting the right upon an anchor or; sinister, a sea-lion ar. supporting with the sinister paw an anchor or. *Motto*—Steady.

Hood (Tidlake, co. Surrey, since of Wootton, co. Somerset, bart.). Az. a fret ar. on a chief sa. three crescents or. *Crest*—A Cornish chough holding an anchor on the dexter side in bend sinister ppr. *Motto*—Zealous.

Hood (Cockburn-Hood, Stoneridge, co. Berwick). Quarterly sa. and ar. a bend or, on a chief of the second a lion's head erased betw. two cocks gu. *Crest*—A demi archer, clothed and accoutred ppr. *Mottoes*—Over the crest: Swift and sure; below the arms: Olim sic erat.

Hood (Nettleham Hall, co. Lincoln). Az. a fret ar. on a chief sa. three crescents or. *Crest*—A hooded crow, in the beak a Scotch thistle, in the dexter claw a sword all ppr. *Motto*—Esse quam videri.

Hood, or Hoods (Rector of Lincoln College, co. Oxford, of Ickford, near Brille, co. Buckingham, *d.* 3 Aug. 1668). Az. a fret ar. on a chief sa. three crescents or. *Crest*— A Cornish chough sa. beaked and membered gu.

Hood (Bardon Park, co. Leicester; originally settled at Wilford, near Nottingham). Az. a fret ar. on a chief sa. three crescents or, quartering **Snell, Harrison, Fiennes**, &c. *Crest*—A demi talbot ppr. collared and lined or. *Motto* —Manners maketh man.

Hoode. Chequy or and gu. a canton sa.

Hoogan (Castleacre, co. Norfolk). Ar. a chev. vairé or and gu. betw. three hurts, each charged with a lion's gamb erased of the field.

Hook (Sir **Richard Hook**, Knt., co. York, served in Scotland and elsewhere under Edward I. Visit. York, 1584). Az. a fess betw. three fleurs-de-lis or.

Hooke (**Richard Hooke**, Esq., of Alway. Visit. Gloucester, 1583 and 1623). Sa. a fess betw. six fleurs-de-lis ar. *Crest*— A demi eagle displ. gu. ducally gorged or.

Hooke (**Richard Hooke**, Esq., of Bramshott. Visit. Hants, 1575 and 1633). Quarterly, ar. and sa. a cross betw. four escallops all counterchanged. *Crest*—An escallop sa. betw. two wings ar. (Same *Arms*, with the escallop of the crest issuing out of a ducal coronet, were confirmed to **John Hooke**, Esq., of Bramshott, 20 Oct. 1660).

Hooke (Hanchford, co. Surrey, and Chichester, co. Sussex). Same *Arms* and *Crest*.

Hooke (Drogheda; **John Hooke**, Sergeant-at-law, 1703). Same *Arms* and *Crest*, a crescent for diff.

Hooke. Ar. on a cross (another, engr.) gu. five water bougets or.

Hooke (Norton Hall, co. Worcester; descended from Hooke, of Crooke's Park, co. Gloucester). Gu. a fess betw. three fleurs-de-lis ar. *Crest*—A demi eagle displ. gu. charged on the breast with a ducal coronet or.

Hooke, or Hoke. Quarterly, ar. and sa. a cross (another, engr.) betw. four escallops counterchanged. *Crest*—An escallop sa. betw. two wings ar.

Hooker, alias Vowell (Exeter, co. Devon). Ar. a fesse vair betw. two lions pass. guard. sa. *Crest*—A hind pass. or, in the mouth a branch, leaved vert, flowered ar.

Hooker. Sa. a fesse betw. six fleurs-de-lis ar. *Crest*—A demi eagle displ. gu. charged on the breast with a ducal coronet or.

Hooker. Gu. on a fesse engr. ar. betw. three cinquefoils or, two fleurs-de-lis az.

Hooker. Gu. a fesse engr. betw. three roses ar.

Hooker (Fun. Ent. Ulster's Office, 1667). Or, a chev. vair betw. three lions pass. guard. sa.

Hookham. Vert an eagle with two heads displ. ar. *Crest*— A covered cup ar.

Hooklay. Or, on a fesse betw. three mascles gu. as many plates. *Crest*—An arm embowed, vested gu. cuffed ar.

holding in the hand ppr. a branch of oak vert, acorned also ppr.

Hookley. Ar. on a fesse betw. three mascles gu. as many plates.

Hoole (**Henry Elliott Hoole**, Esq., of Sheffield). Per fesse or and gu. on a pale two roses all counterchanged. *Crest*—An eagle displ. per fesse or and gu. each wing charged with a rose per fesse counterchanged, surmounted by a rainbow ppr. *Motto*—Spes mea Deus.

Hoole (Edgefield, Bradfield, co. York). Barry of six or and gu. in bend as many roses counterchanged. *Crest*—An eagle displ. gu. each wing charged with two roses and transfixed through the mouth by a tilting spear palewise or. *Motto*— Flectas non franges.

Hooley (Woodthorpe, co. Nottingham). Barry of six or and gu. *Crest*—A rose gu. barbed vert, seeded or.

Hooley. Az. a bend betw. three mullets or. *Crest*—Out of a mount vert a tree ppr.

Hooper (Linkinghorne, co. Cornwall). Ar. on a fesse gu. betw. three mullets of the last as many annulets of the first. *Crest*—A demi lion holding a ring betw. the paws.

Hooper (London, Stanmore Cottage, co. Middlesex, and Sarum, co. Wilts). Or, on a fesse betw. three boars pass. **az.** as many annulets of the first. *Crest*—A boar's head erased at the neck az. bezantée, armed and crined or.

Hooper (Hendford, Yeovil, co. Somerset). Gyronny of eight erm. and az. over all a tower ar. *Crest*—A demi wolf couped, holding in the dexter paw an oak branch fructed, all ppr.

Hooper (Grimley, co. Worcester; **George Hooper**, *b.* 1640, Bishop of St. Asaph, 1703-4, and of Bath and Wells, 1704-27). Gyronny of eight or and erm. a tower triple-towered sa.

Hooper (**John Hooper**, Bishop of Gloucester, 1550-54, burned at Gloucester, 9 Feb. 1555). Or, on a fess dancettée betw. three flames of fire gu. proceeding from clouds ar. a lamb couchant betw. two estoiles of the last.

Hooper. Or, on a fesse gu. betw. three falcons close az. as many bezants.

Hoops. Gu. a fesse erm. betw. three lions' heads erased ar. *Crest*—On a plate a Cornish chough ppr.

Hoops. Same *Arms*, within a bordure az. charged with two crescents in chief and a mullet in base or. Same *Crest*. *Motto*—Amo.

Hoord (Parkbromage, co. Salop). Ar. on a chief or, a hawk sa. *Crest*—A nag's head ar. maned or.

Hoorne. Gu. a fret vair.

Hoote, or Hottot (co. Gloucester). Az. a chev. or, betw. three crescents ar.

Hooton (Hooton, co. Chester). Ar. on a bend vert three mullets or. *Crest*—A chevalier holding his horse by the bridle with the dexter hand ppr.

Hooton. Ar. on a bend sa. three mullets or.

Hopcot (co. Cornwall). Ar. on a chev. betw. three boars pass. sa. armed or, as many roses of the last, barbed vert. *Crest*—A fox's head erased ppr.

Hopcroft. Ar. a cross engr. gu. within a bordure engr. of the last. *Crest*—A steel cap.

Hope (Craighall and Pinkie, co. Edinburgh, bart., 1628). Az. a chev. or, betw. three bezants. *Crest*—A broken globe surmounted of a rainbow with clouds at each end ppr. *Supporters*—Two females vested vert, winged or, on their heads garlands of roses ppr. each sustaining in her exterior hand an anchor az. *Motto*—At spes infracta.

Hope (Kerse, Scotland, bart., 1672). Az. on a chev. or, betw. three bezants a roebuck courant of the first. Same *Crest*. *Motto*—Spes tamen infracta.

Hope (Granton, co. Edinburgh, Cupbearer to Charles I.). Az. on a chev. or, betw. three bezants a rose gu. Same *Crest* as Craighall. *Motto*—Spero suspiro donec.

Hope (*Earl of Hopetoun*). Az. on a chev. or, betw. three bezants a laurel leaf slipped vert. *Crest*—A broken globe under a rainbow with clouds at each end all ppr. *Supporters*—Two ladies in loose garments, hair dishevelled, each holding an anchor in her exterior hand as the emblem of Hope all ppr. *Motto*—At spes infracta.

Hope (Rankeillor, Scotland). Same *Arms* as of Craighall, within a bordure or, for diff. Same *Crest* and *Motto*.

Hope-Vere (Craigiehall, co. Linlithgow). Quarterly, 1st and 4th, as *Earl of Hopetoun;* 2nd, ar. on a fess az. three mullets of the first, for **Vere** or **Weir**, of Blackwood; 3rd, or, an anchor in pale gu., for **Fairholm**. *Crests*—Dexter, as *Earl of Hopetoun;* sinister, on a chapeau gu. turned up erm. a lion statant az. armed or. *Mottoes*—At spes non fracta; and, Vero nihi verius.

Hope (Balcomy, co. Fife, bart.. 1698). Az. on a chev. ar. betw. three bezants as many palets gu. *Crest*—A broken

505

globe surmounted by a rainbow ppr. *Motto*—At spes solamen.

Hope (Deepdeene, co. Surrey; a branch of the ancient family of HOPE, of Craighall, long established at Amsterdam; the late representative of the family was HENRY THOMAS HOPE, Esq., of Deepdene, co. Surrey, eldest son and heir of the late THOMAS HOPE, Esq., of Deepdene, the celebrated author of "Anastasius," and an eminent patron of the Arts, by the Hon. LOUISA BERESFORD, his wife, youngest child of the Right Rev. *Lord Decies*, Archbishop of Tuam). Same *Arms, Crest*, and *Motto*, as HOPE, of Craighall.

Hope (BERESFORD-HOPE, Bedgebury Park, co. Kent, and Beresford Hall, co. Stafford; ALEXANDER JAMES BERESFORD-HOPE, Esq., third son of THOMAS HOPE, Esq., of Deepdene, assumed the additional name of BERESFORD, by royal licence, 1854). Same *Arms*, &c.

Hope (OLIVER HOPE, Rotterdam, 1767). Az. on a chev. or, betw. three bezants a crescent gu. charged with an annulet of the second. *Crest*—A broken globe surmounted of a rainbow ppr. *Motto*—At spes infracta.

Hope (Grangefield, co. Derby; traceable to the reign of James I.). Ar. a chev. engr. sa. betw. three Cornish choughs ppr. *Crest*—A Cornish chough rising ppr.

Hope (Rev. CHARLES STEADE HOPE, Rector of All Saints, co. Derby). Ar. a chev. engr. sa. betw. three Cornish choughs ppr. *Crest*—A Cornish chough with wings expanded ppr.

Hope (Northall Court, co. Middlesex). Erm. two chev. engr. az. betw. three escallops gu.

Hope (Llandriendred). Ar. three storks sa. quartering MUDDLETON, of Chirk.

Hope (WILLIAM WILLIAMS HOPE, Esq., of London). Az. a chev. or, betw. three bezants, a bordure of the second, quartering WILLIAMS, viz., Ar. a greyhound courant sa. betw. three Cornish choughs ppr. a bordure engr. az. charged with four crosses crosslet or, and as many bezants alternately. *Crests*—1st, HOPE: A globe fractured ppr. charged with an anchor sa. over the globe a rainbow; 2nd, WILLIAMS: A cubit arm erect, habited sa. charged with a cross crosslet or, cuffed gold, the hand holding two sprigs of oak in saltire ppr. acorned also gold, on the hand a Cornish chough statant also ppr.

Hope (Northall Court, co. Middlesex). Erm. two chevronels engr. az. betw. three escallops gu.

Hope (Mullingar, co. Westmeath; Fun. Ent. of THOMAS, son of WALTER HOPE, of that place, *d.* 26 Feb. 1611). Ar. a pile engr. ermines betw. two lions' heads erased gu. langued az. a chief vair, a border vert. *Crest*—A palm tree ppr.

Hopkins (Oving House, co. Bucks, and Coventry, co. Warwick). Sa. on a chev. betw. three pistols or, as many roses gu. *Crest*—A tower per bend indented ar. and gu. flames issuing from the top and windows ppr.

Hopkins (Newland, co. Gloucester, and Lincoln's Inn, London; granted 1734). Erm. on a fesse gu. a lion pass. guard. ar. a canton of the second charged with a rose or. *Crest*—An ostrich's head couped erm. holding in the beak a key az.

Hopkins (Arundel, co. Sussex). Same *Arms* and *Crest*.

Hopkins (Tidmarsh House, co. Berks). Sa. on a chev. betw. three pistols or, as many roses gu. *Crest*—A castle in flames ppr. *Motto*—Inter primos.

Hopkins (exemplified, 20 Jan. 1773, to BOND, of Hackney, on taking, by sign manual, the name and arms of HOPKINS). Quarterly, 1st and 4th, sa. on a chev. erminois betw. three pistols or, as many roses gu. barbed and seeded ppr., for HOPKINS; 2nd and 3rd, ar. on a chev. pean three bezants, for BOND. *Crests*—1st, HOPKINS: A castle in flames ppr. charged with two pellets in fesse; 2nd, BOND: A lion sejant erm.

Hopkins (Athboy, co. Meath, bart., extinct; confirmed by Fortescue, Ulster, 1789, to FRANCIS HOPKINS, Esq., who was created a bart. 1795, and *d. s. p.*). Sa. on a chev. betw. three dexter gauntlets ar. as many roses gu. seeded gold. *Crest*—A tower ar. flammant ppr.

Hopkins (Maryland; granted 1764). Sa. on a chev. betw. two pistols in chief or, and a silver medal, with the French king's bust, inscribed Louis XV., tied at the top with a red ribbon in base, a laurel chaplet in the centre, a scalp on a staff on the dexter, and a tomahawk on the sinister all ppr. a chief embattled ar. *Crest*—A rock, over the top a battery in perspective, thereon the French flag hoisted, an officer of the Queen's Royal American Rangers on the said rock, sword in hand, all ppr.; round the crest this *Motto*—Inter primos.

Hopkinson (Bonsol, co. Derby). Az. on a chev. ar. betw. three estoiles or, as many lozenges gu. a bordure of the third.

506

Hopkinson (Alford, co. Lincoln; granted *temp.* Elizabeth, and now borne by FRANCIS HOPKINSON, Esq.). Az. on a chev. ar. betw. three estoiles or, as many lozenges gu. a bordure of the third. *Crest*—A demi lion ramp. sa. armed and incensed gu.

Hopkinson (Lofthouse, co. York). Vert three pillows erm.

Hopkinson. Az. on a chev. betw. three trefoils ar. as many lozenges gu. a bordure of the third.

Hopkirk (Dalbeth, co. Lanark). Gu. a saltire engr. ar. betw. four fleurs-de-lis or. *Crest*—An arm in armour ppr. pointing with one finger to a crescent in dexter chief ar. *Motto*—Spero procedere.

Hopley (granted to GEORGE AUGUSTUS HOPLEY, Esq., of Charlestown, South Carolina, U.S., son of JOSEPH HOPLEY, Esq., sometime Governor of St. Vincent). Ar. on a fess gu. cotised wavy sa. three crescents or, all betw. as many pheons of the third, in the centre chief point a lion ramp. of the second. *Crest*—Out of a mural crown gu. a garb or, issuant therefrom a serpent ppr. *Motto*—In copia cautus.

Hopley (Liverpool). Per fesse gu. and sa. a gryphon segreant ar. betw. two flaunches vair. *Crest*—A stag's head affrontée erased ppr. gorged with a collar gemel az. betw. two ears of wheat or. *Motto*—Semper vigilans.

Hoppe. Vert a swan, wings endorsed ar. *Crest*—A demi swan, wings endorsed ppr.

Hopper (Hermitage, co. Durham). Gyronny of eight sa. and erm. over all a tower triple-towered ar. masoned of the first. *Crest*—A tower, as in the arms. *Motto*—Subditus fidelis regis et salus regni.

Hopper (Silksworth, co. Durham). Gyronny of eight sa. and erm. over all a tower triple-towered ar. masoned of the first. *Crest*—A tower, as in the arms.

Hopper (co. Devon). Gyronny of eight or and erm. over all a tower triple-towered ar.

Hopper-Williamson (Recorder of Newcastle-upon-Tyne). Quarterly, 1st and 4th, gyronny of eight sa. and erm. over all a tower triple-towered ar. masoned of the first; 2nd and 3rd, ar. three annulets, and in chief two saltires gu. Same *Crest* as the last.

Hopper (Scotland). Ar. three roses gu.

Hopperton (near Wakefield). Gu. a crescent or, in chief a label of three points ar. points or, each charged with a mullet az.

Hoppey. Paly of six ar. and az. a chief or. *Crest*—A stag's head cabossed gu. betw. the attires a cross crosslet fitchée of the last.

Hoppey. Same *Arms*. *Crest*—A dexter hand ppr. holding a fleur-de-lis in pale az.

Hopson (exemplified to WILLIAM ONGLEY, Esq., of Minster, in the Isle of Sheppey, co. Kent, Captain in the 7th Garrison Battalion, on his assuming, by sign manual, dated 27 Feb. 1824, the surname and arms of HOPSON). Per pale ar. and or, on a chev. engr. az. betw. three torteaux as many cinquefoils of the first, a chief engr. chequy of the second and third. *Crest*—A mount vert, thereon a griffin pass. or, wings elevated, chequy of the last and az. the dexter claw resting upon a cinquefoil vert.

Hopson. Ar. on a chev. az. betw. three torteaux as many roses of the first, a chief counter-componé of the second and or. *Crest*—A stag lodged ppr.

Hopton (Hopton, co. Salop, *temp.* King Stephen). Gu. semée of crosses pattée fitchée a lion ramp. or.

Hopton (Canon Frome, co. Hereford). Same *Arms*. *Crest*—Out of a ducal coronet or, a griffin's head ar. in the beak a bleeding hand ppr.

Hopton (Hopton, co. Hereford). Gu. semée of crosses crosslet a lion ramp. or. *Crest*—On a lion's head erased or, a bend gu. charged with three crosses crosslet of the first.

Hopton (co. Somerset, and Blithbon, co. Suffolk). Erm. two bars sa. on each three mullets or. *Crest*—A griffin pass. ar. holding in the dexter claw a stone sa.

Hopton (*Lord Hopton*, of Stratton; created 1643, extinct 1652). Same *Arms*.

Hopton (Ermeley Hall). Ar. two bars sa. on each three mullets pierced of the first.

Hopton (co. Gloucester, *temp.* Edward I.). Gu. a lion ramp. or, within an orle of crosses crosslet of the last.

Hopton (co. Gloucester). Ar. crusily fitchée sa. a lion ramp. az.

Hopton (co. Suffolk). Ar. a chev. az. and label of three points of the second, each charged with five bezants.

Hopton (Armly Hall, co. York). Ar. a fesse sa. in chief three martlets gu.

Hopton (co. York). Ar. two bars sa. each charged with three mullets of six points or.

Hopton (co. York). Ar. two bars sa. on each three mullets or.

Hopton. Ar. a chev. az. (another adds a label of three points erm.).

Hopton. Gu. a demi lion erect in a tun ar.

Hopton. Az. a bend cotised ar. betw. six crosses pattée or, within a bordure engr. gu. platée.

Hopwell (co. Devon). Ar. three hares playing on bag-pipes gu. two and one.

Hopwood (Hopwood, co. Lancaster). Barry of six ar. and vert, on the second an escallop of the first.

Hopwood (Chopwood). Paly of six ar. and vert. Crest— Out of a ducal coronet or, a griffin's head per pale ar. and sa.

Hopwood (Droitwich and Milton, co. Hereford). Or, a pile az.

Hopwood (co. Salop). Or, a pile az.

Hopwood (Blackburn, co. Lancaster). Paly nebuly of six or and vert, on a canton sa. a millrind in pale of the first. Crest—A dexter hand fessewise couped at the wrist ppr. holding an escallop or. Motto—Gradatim.

Horan (co. Galway ; Reg. Ulster's Office). Vert three lions ramp. or. Crest—A demi lion ramp. or.

Horbyn, or Horbon (co. York). Barry of eight ar. and az.

Hord (Hord's Park, and Walford, co. Salop). Az. on a chief or, a raven sa. Crest—A nag's head couped ar. maned or.

Horde. Az. on a chief ar. a fleur-de-lis of the field.

Hordeby. Gu. a fesse dancettée ar. betw. ten billets of the last, four in chief, and three, two, and one in base.

Horden (co. Kent). Per pale ar. and sa. two wolves pass. betw. three quatrefoils in pale within a bordure all counter-changed.

Horden. Per pale ar. and sa. two wolves betw. three cinquefoils in pale counterchanged within a bordure per pale gu. and or. Crest—A demi wolf quarterly sa. and ar. holding in the dexter foot a quatrefoil quarterly of the second and first.

Hordentyn. Or, a bend betw. six billets az.

Hordern (Oxley House, co. Stafford, and Dunstal Hall). Gu. on a cross raguly ar. an arrow in pale, the pheon upwards sa. in the first and fourth quarters a wolf's head erased erminois. Crest—An ox's head cabossed gu. armed or, surmounting two arrows in saltire of the last, barbed and flighted ar. Motto—Fortiter ac sapienter.

Hore (Pole Hore, co. Wexford; descended from Sir WILLIAM LE HORE, one of the Norman knights who invaded Ireland in 1170. Visit. Wexford, 1618). Ar. an eagle displ. az. Crest—A demi eagle az. Motto—Constanter.

Hore (Shandon, co. Waterford; the daus. and co-heirs of the last MATTHEW HORE, Esq., of Shandon Castle, were, MABELLA, m. JOHN DONELLAN, Esq., of Ballydonellan, co. Galway; MARY, m. 1756, Sir PATRICK BELLEW, Bart. ; and HONORA, m. 1765, MICHAEL AYLMER, Esq., of Lyons). Same Arms, &c., with the due mark of diff.

Hore (Killsallaghan, co. Dublin, a branch of HORE, of Pole Hore; Fun. Ent. of MARY, dau. of PHILIP HORE, of that place, d. 3 July, 1627). Same Arms.

Hore (Ballyshelan, co. Wexford; a branch of HORE, of Pole Hore; Fun. Ent. of PHILIP HORE, d. 24 Feb. 1630). Same Arms, eagle charged with a crescent ar. for diff.

Hore (Harperstown, co. Wexford; MATTHEW LE HORE, temp. Edward III., m. AGATHA, dau. and heir of PHILIP LE HARPER, Lord of Harperstown. Visit Wexford, 1618). Same Arms and Crest, a crescent for diff. Motto—Constanter.

Hore (Cadiz, in Spain; certified 1767, by Hawkins, Ulster, to HYACINTH HORE, Esq., of that place, descended from the house of Harperstown, co. Wexford). Same Arms, Crest, and Motto.

Hore-Ruthven (Devon Ruthven). See RUTHVEN.

Hore (Risford, parish of Chagford, co. Devon; JOHN HORE, of that place; Visit. 1620, eighth in descent from ROBERT HORE, temp. Edward III., m. ALICE, dau. of ROWLAND DE RIFFORD). Sa. an eagle with two heads displ. and a border engr. ar.

Hore (confirmed to Sir JOHN HORE, co. Warwick; EDITH, dau. and heir of JOHN HORE, temp. Henry VII., m. ROWLAND PUDSEY, ancestor of PUDSEY, of Ellesfield, co. Oxford. Visit. Oxon, 1634). Sa. three cinquefoils ar. pierced gu.

Hore, or Horem (Trenowth, co. Cornwall). Az. on a bend ar. three torteaux.

Hore, or Horem. Same Arms. Crest—A hand holding a sickle ppr.

Hore (cos. Devon and Norfolk). Sa. a bend or.

Hore. Vert a stag's head cabossed ar. betw. the attires a cross formée of the last.

507

Horell (co. Lancaster). Sa. on a fesse battelly ar. three torteaux.

Horevill, or Horvill. Ar. on a chev. gu. three (another, five) bezants.

Horkesley (Horkesley, co. Essex). Erm. on a chief indented az. three lions ramp. or.

Horley. Ar. a chev. az. betw. three magpies ppr.

Horley. Sa. a fret erm.

Horman. Az. a bend ar. betw. two pelicans' heads erased or. Crest—A lizard guard. sa.

Hormiston (Hormiston, Scotland). Ar. three pelicans vulning themselves gu.

Horn (Bishopwearmouth, co. Durham). Gu. three herons ar. Crest—A heron close ppr. holding in the bill a standard staff, the banner flotant, thereon the word "Hastings." Motto—Nil desperandum.

Horn (Germany). Or, three buglehorns sa.

Horn (co. Norfolk). Gu. on a chev. engr. betw. three herons ar. a cinquefoil of the first.

Horn (co. Salop). Gu. a fesse vair. Crest—An owl ppr.

Horn (co. Sussex). Gu. a fret vair.

Horn. Ar. a lion ramp. guard. az.

Horn (Westhall, co. Aberdeen ; heiress m. DALRYMPLE, of Drummore. See DALRYMPLE). As recorded 1685—Ar. a fesse wavy cotised az. betw. three unicorns' heads couped in chief and a buglehorn in base, garnished of the first, stringed of the third. Crest—A buglehorn az. garnished and stringed ar. Motto—Monitus munitus. Altered, 1725, to or, three hunting horns ay. Crest—Two horns conjoined, parted per fess or and sa. Motto—Moneo et munio.

Horn (Edinburgh, 1855). Az. a fess or, betw. two hunting horns in chief of the second and a bear's head in base erased ar. muzzled sa. Crest—A hunting horn or, stringed az. Motto—Monitus munitus.

Hornacot (Hornacot, co. Cornwall). Gu. a buglehorn stringed or.

Hornbrook (Tavistock, co. Devon). Ar. two bars wavy betw. six crescents, three, two, and one, ar.

Hornby (Dalton Hall, co. Lancaster). Or, two chevronels betw. three buglehorns, the mouths to dexter sa. on a chief of the last three eagles' legs erased of the first; this family also bore: Or, a chev. betw. three buglehorns, mouths to sinister sa. Crest—A buglehorn of the arms stringed, and below the string a pheon gu.

Hornby (Ribby Hall, co. Lancaster). Ar. a chev. vert in base a buglehorn stringed sa. on a chief of the second two buglehorns of the field. Crest—A buglehorn stringed sa. and passing through the knot in fesse an arrow, point towards the sinister or. Motto—Crede cornu.

Hornby (Liverpool). Same Arms, &c.

Hornby (co. Lincoln). Gu. on a fesse erm. betw. three buglehorns stringed ar. as many boars' heads erased or.

Hornby (Newcastle-upon-Tyne). Ar. on a fesse betw. three buglehorns sa. stringed gu. as many fleurs-de-lis of the field.

Hornby. Ar. a chev. betw. three buglehorns sa. (another, stringed gu.). Crest—A leopard pass. ppr.

Hornby. Ar. a chev. betw. three buglehorns sa. Crest—A Roman soldier in full armour ppr.

Hornby. Ar. three buglehorns stringed gu.

Hornbye. Sa. fretty ar. a label of three points gu.

Horncastle (Dublin; granted by Carney, Ulster, 1683). Erm. a chev. gu. on a chief vert two towers ar. Crest—A unicorn's head erased vert, armed and maned or, charged on the neck with a trefoil gold.

Horncastle. Per chev. erm. and vert, on a chief gu. three towers ar. Crest—On a chapeau a serpent nowed all ppr.

Hornden (co. Kent). Ar. a buglehorn garnished and stringed sa.

Horndon (Pencrebar, co. Cornwall). Ar. a heron volant in fesse az. membered or, betw. three escallops sa.

Horne. Ar. two bars vair.

Horne (Saresden House, co. Oxford. Visit. Oxon, 1566). Ar. on a chev. engr. gu. betw. three unicorns' heads erased az. a crescent or.

Horne (THOMAS DARRELL, Esq., Scotney, temp. Henry VII., m. ELIZABETH, dau. and heir of JAMES HORNE, Esq., of Bethersden, co. Kent. Visit. Notts, 1614). Ar. on a chev. gu. betw. three hunting horns sa. stringed or, as many mullets of the last.

Horne (Wesenham, co. Norfolk; THOMASINE, dau. and co-heir of EDWARD HORNE, m. WILLIAM, son of JOHN GAMAGE, of Coytiff, co. Glamorgan. Visit. London, 1568). Gu. fretty vair.

Horne (co. Cambridge, Lord Mayor of London, 1487). Gu. on a chev. betw. three talbots pass. ar. a buglehorn sa.

Horne (co. Kent). Ar. on a chev. betw. three buglehorns sa. as many estoiles of six points (another, mullets) or.

Horne (co. Kent). Sa. on a chev. ar. betw. three buglehorns or, as many mullets pierced gu. *Crest*—A hand gu. holding a hawk's lure ar.

Horne (Sir WILLIAM HORNE, Q.C., a Master in Chancery, knighted when Solicitor-General, 24 Nov. 1830). Ar. on a chev. engr. gu. betw. three buglehorns sa. stringed of the second, as many mullets of the field. *Crest*—A bull's head couped ar.

Horne (London). Ar. on a chev. engr. gu. betw. three buglehorns sa. as many mullets pierced of the first.

Horne, or Horn (co. Oxford). Gu. three chev. or. *Crest* —A unicorn's head erased az. semée of mascles or.

Horne (Stoke, co. Warwick; confirmed by the Deputies of Camden, Clarenceux, to REGINALD HORNE, grandson of REGINALD HORNE, Esq., co. Salop). Gu. a fess vair.

Horne (Auld's Arnold, cos. Salop and Sussex.). Same *Arms.*

Horne. Sa. three buglehorns ar. *Crest*—A buglehorn, as in the arms.

Horne (co. Stafford). Az. three chevronels ar.

Horne. Sa. on a chev. betw. three talbots pass. ar. a buglehorn of the field, stringed gu. *Crest*—A talbot sejant ar. collared and lined or.

Horne. Erm. three bulls pass. or. *Crest*—A bull's head couped or.

Horne. Gyronny of eight or and az. on a bend counterembattled erm. three unicorns' heads couped sa.

Horne. Ar. a leopard ramp. gu.

Horne. Ar. three buglehorns in pale sa.

Horne (EDWARD HORNE, Esq., of the Leasowes, Hales Owen, co. Salop, Sheriff 1780). Gu. three chevronels or.

Horneby. Or, three hunting horns gu. stringed sa.

Hornbey (Reg. Ulster's Office). Az. a chev. betw. three hunting horns ar. stringed sa.

Horneck (St. Margaret's, Westminster; granted June, 1772). Ar. three buglehorns, one in chief and two in base, counterembowed az. adorned, stringed, and garnished or. *Crest*—A trunk of a tree couped ppr. from the sinister chief corner a fresh branch sprouting vert.

Horner (co. Dorset.) Sa. on a bend betw. six crosses formée ar. three buglehorns or.

Horner (Caleford, co. Somerset; granted 1584). Sa. three talbots pass. ar. *Crest*—A talbot sejant ar. collared and lined or.

Horner. Sa. on a bend betw. six crosses pattée fitchée ar. three buglehorns stringed of the first.

Horner. Ar. three buglehorns sa. garnished or.

Horner (Mells, co. Somerset). Quarterly, 1st, sa. three talbots pass. ar., for HORNER (granted 1584); 2nd, gu. a horse armed or, bridled and saddled of the first, with a plume on his head and trappings, and on his shoulder a cinquefoil of the last, on his hip an escutcheon charged with a cross, all betw. three garbs of the second, for MALT; 3rd, az. a bend engr. ar. cotised or, for FORTESCUE; 4th, sa. three mullets pierced in bend betw. two bendlets and two annulets or, for HIPPISLEY. *Crest*—A talbot sejant ar. collared and lined or. *Motto*—Tyme tryeth troth.

Hornes. Ar. three buglehorns in pale gu. *Crest*—A griffin sejant ppr. resting the foot on a shield of the arms.

Hornesey (co. Lincoln, 1640). Or, a fess barry wavy ar. and az. in chief two annulets sa. and a pellet in base.

Hornhill. Or, three roses gu.

Hornibrooke (granted 16 Dec. 1663). Barry wavy of six ar. and az. over all three crescents sa.

Hornley, Hornly, or Horneley. Or, three buglehorns gu.

Hornsby, or Hornesby (Grantham). Gu. a bend betw. six crosses crosslet or. *Crest*—A demi bear ramp. sa.

Hornsey. Or, on a fesse per pale ar. and sa. a fesse wavy counterchanged betw. three annulets of the third. *Crest*— A rock ppr. *Motto*—Semper eadem.

Hornsey. Gu. a bend betw. six crosses crosslet ar.

Hornsley. Gu. a bend betw. six crosses crosslet (another, fitchée) ar.

Hornyold (Blackmore Park and Hanley Castle, co. Worcester; name anciently written DE HORNINGWOLD, HORNYNGWOLD, and HORNWOLD, supposed to be of Saxon origin, one of the five remaining Worcestershire families which entered their arms at the first Visitation of the county in 1533. The then head of the family was JOHN HORNYOLD, of Standon, Herts, and Hanley, co. Worcester, Knight of Malta, Governor of Calais, and Auditor of the Exchequer. He was the grantee of Blackmore Park). Az. on a bend embattled counterembattled ar. a wolf pass. betw. two escallops sa. *Crest*—A demi unicorn gu. crined, hoofed, and armed or. *Motto*—Fidem tene.

508

Hornyold (Bredon, co. Worcester). Az. on a bend embattled counter-embattled betw. two fishes in bend ar. a greyhound courant betw. two escallops sa. all within a bordure or, charged with ten torteaux.

Horold. Gu. three crosses moline erm.

Horon (Sir GERARD). Ar. a lion ramp. guard. gu.

Horrell. Ar. three torteaux in bend cotised gu. a chief sa. *Crest*—A crow feeding ppr.

Horrocks (Preston, Lark Hill, co. Lancaster). Or, a fret az. on a chief of the last a bee volant betw. two shuttles in pale of the first. *Crest*—On a rock an eagle with wings elevated and endorsed ppr. pendent from the beak a shield gu. charged with a hank of cotton ar.

Horrocks. Or, a fret az. on a chief of the last two bees volant of the first. *Crest*—On a mount a hawk with wings endorsed ppr. *Motto*—Spe.

Horsby. Ar. two horses courant in pale gu.

Horscote. Ar. a cross sarcelly betw. four roses or. *Crest*— A chevalier in full armour, holding in the dexter hand a scymitar all ppr.

Horsburgh (that Ilk). Az. a horse's head couped ar. *Crest*—A horse's head. *Motto*—Ægre de tramite recto.

Horsefall (Staresgall, co. York; granted 1612). Gu. a bezant betw. three horses' heads couped ar. bridled az. *Crest* —A horse's head couped erm.

Horsefall. Gu. three horses' heads couped ar. *Crest*—On a ducal coronet or, a swan with wings endorsed ar. ducally gorged gu.

Horsefield, or Horsford. Az. on a chev. ar. three lions' heads erased of the first. *Crest*—Out of a ducal coronet a demi pegasus.

Horseley. Az. a fesse or, betw. three horses' heads erased ar. bridled gu. within a bordure gobonated of the third and vert.

Horseman (Ripon, co. York). Ar. three dexter hands in pale sa.

Horseman (granted 1590). Or, three caltraps gu. *Crest*— Flames of fire ppr. issuing from a cup or.

Horseman. Az. a horse barnacle or, betw. three plates, on a chief per fess indented of the first and purp. two estoiles of sixteen points of the second, in the centre of each a rose ar.

Horsemonden. Gu. a saltire or, over all a fesse az. charged with three leopards' faces or.

Horsenail (Worvill, co. Berks; granted 17 Feb. 1740). Ar. a cross dovetailed betw. four mullets az. *Crest*—Out of a mural crown ar. a horse's head, dun colour, maned sa. gorged with a collar dovetailed az.

Horsey, de Horsey (Great Glemham, co. Suffolk; borne by Rear-Admiral ALGERNON DE HORSEY, Melcombe House, West Cowes). Az. three horses' heads couped or, bridled ar. *Crest*—A horse's head couped ar. armed up to the neck and face down to the nose, with a spike in the forehead or, bridled ar. with three plumes of feathers or, az., and gu. gu.

Horsey (co. Berks). Ar. a fesse sa. betw. three lions ramp. gu.

Horsey (Clifton, co. Dorset, and co. Somerset). Az. three horses' heads couped or, bridled gu.

Horsey (co. Dorset). Az. three horses' heads couped at the neck or, bridled ar.

Horsey (Diggeswell, co. Hertford, and Mortine, co. Wilts). Az. three horses' heads couped in armour or. *Crest*—A horse's head in armour ar. bridle and reins or.

Horsey (Honington, co. Warwick; confirmed by the Deputies of Camden, Clarenceux, to HANIBAL HORSEY, son of JOHN HORSEY, Esq., co. Wilts). Az. three horses' heads couped ar. bridled or. *Crest*—A horse's head couped and bridled ar. plumed az.

Horsfall (granted to JAMES HORSFALL, of Birmingham, 19 June, 1861). Quarterly, gu. and az. a millrind fessways or, betw. three horses' heads erased ar. *Crest*—On the stem of a tree leaved vert, a horse's head erased ar. a collar gemel gu.

Horsfall (Bishop of Ossory, 1886-1609; Right Rev. JOHN HORSFALL, a native of co. York; Fun. Ent. Ulster's Office, 1635, of his son-in-law, HENRY MAINWARING, Master in Chancery). Gu. three horses' heads couped ar. bridled or.

Horsham. Az. two bends ar. (another, or) on each three mullets gu.

Horsham. Az. three bendlets or, on each as many mullets gu.

Horsham. Az. three bends or, on the middle bend as many mullets pierced gu.

Horsham. Az. three bends or, each charged in the centre with a mullet gu.

Horsham, Town of (co. Sussex). Az. a lion ramp. ar. resting the dexter hind foot on the letter H.

Horske. Ar. three adders' heads erased in pale az. stings gu.

Horsley (Horsley, co. Northumberland). Gu. three horses' heads erased ar. *Crest*—A horse's head erased ar.

Horsley-Beresford (*Baron Decies*). See BERESFORD.

Horsley (Little Hellingbury, co. Hertford). Gu. three horses' heads couped ar. bridled or. *Crest*—A horse's head couped ar. bridled or.

Horsley (co. Northampton). Ar. a chief gu.

Horsley (Sherpenbeck, co. York). Sa. three cinquefoils within a bordure engr. ar.

Horsley (co. York; ROBERT HORSLEY, *temp.* Richard II.). Gu. three horses' heads erased ar. bridled sa.

Horsley. Az. a fesse or, betw. three horses' heads erased ar. bridled gold, within a bordure gobonated of the second and first (another, of the third and vert).

Horsley. Az. on a cross quarterly pierced betw. four escallops or, as many escallops of the first.

Horsley. Az. a cross pierced betw. four escallops ar.

Horsman, or Horseman (Sleaford, co. Lincoln). Az. a pair of barnacles in pale or. *Crest*—A horse's head in armour bridled and plumed ppr.

Horsman (Kensington, co. Middlesex). Or, three sinister gauntlets sa. *Crest*—A castle on fire ppr.

Horsman (cos. Norfolk and Sussex). Az. a pair of barnacles or, betw. three plates, on a chief indented per fesse of the first and purp. three roses ar.

Horsman (co. Sussex). Az. bezantée a pair of barnacles or, on a chief of the first three quatrefoils pierced ar.

Horspoole (SIMON HORSPOOLE, citizen and Draper of London, son of JOHN HORSPOLE, of London. Visit. London, 1568). Sa. on a chev. ar. three lions' heads erased of the field. *Crest*—A demi pegasus erased, wings expanded erm. girded round the loins with a ducal coronet or.

Hort (Castle Strange, co. Middlesex, and Hortland, co. Kildare, bart.). Az. a cross or, in the first quarter a rose ar. *Crest*—An eagle reguard. wings expanded ppr. in the beak a chaplet vert.

Hortford (co. Huntingdon; JOHN HORTFORD, citizen of London, eldest son of ROBET HORTFORD, of the former county. Visit. London, 1568). Barry nebulée of six or and az. on a chief sa. three stags' heads cabossed of the first. *Crest*—A dexter arm erect, couped at the elbow, vested per pale ar. holding in the hand a stag's horn sa.

Horton (Chadderton, co. Lancaster, bart., extinct 1821). Gu. a lion ramp. ar. charged on the breast with a bear's head couped az. a bordure engr. of the second. *Crest*—A red rose seeded and barbed ppr. surrounded with two laurel branches vert. *Motto*—Pro rege et lege.

Horton (Howroyde, co. York). Quarterly, 1st and 4th, same *Arms*; 2nd and 3rd, per bend sinister erm. and sa. a lion ramp. ar. Same *Crest* as the last.

Horton (Tatternall, co. Bedford). Ar. a stag's head cabossed sa.

Horton (Howle, co. Chester). Sa. a stag's head cabossed or.

Horton (Catton, co. Derby; seated there more than four hundred years). Sa. a stag's head cabossed ar. attired or. *Crest*—On waves of the sea ppr. a spear erect or, headed ar. enfiled with a dolphin also ppr.

Horton (WILMOT-HORTON, Bart., of Osmaston and Catton, co. Derby; exemplified to Sir ROBERT WILMOT, third bart., on his assuming the additional name of HORTON). 1st and 4th, HORTON, viz.: sa. a stag's head cabossed ar. attired or; 2nd and 3rd, WILMOT, viz.: sa. on a fess or, betw. three eagles' heads couped az. as many escallops gu. the whole within a bordure engr. of the third. *Crests*—1st, HORTON: Out of waves of the sea ppr. a tilting spear erect or, headed and enfiled with a dolphin ar. finned gold; 2nd, WILMOT: An eagle's head couped ar. gorged with a collar engr. az. holding in the beak an escallop gu.

Horton (The Holt, co. Northampton). Per fesse az. and sa. a stag's head cabossed in base and in chief three roses ar. *Crest*—A dolphin naiant ar. in front of a tilting spear erect and two spears saltirewise or. *Motto*—Perseverantia palmam obtinebit.

Horton (co. Kent). Per pale ar. and sa. three cinquefoils and two otters counterchanged.

Horton (Hullington, co. Somerset, and Ilford, co. Wilts). Ar. on a fesse az. betw. two wolves pass. in chief and a crossbow in base gu. three martlets or. *Crest*—A cubit arm erect, vested gu. cuffed ar. holding in the hand ppr. an arrow az. feathered and barbed or.

Horton (co. Somerset). Ar. a stag's head cabossed sa. attired or.

Horton (Wales). Sa. three bends engr. a canton or.

Horton. Or, a chev. az. betw. two wolves pass. in chief gu.

and a crossbow of the last in base. *Crest*—An arm gu. couped at the elbow, holding in the hand ppr. an arrow az. feathered and barbed or, point downwards of the third, and a branch of roses erect ar. leaved vert, a crescent of the fourth on the arm.

Horton. Gu. a lion ramp. within a bordure engr. ar. *Crest*—A cinquefoil gu. within two branches of laurel disposed orleways ppr.

Horton (WILLIAM HORTON "DE FOREST," co. Cumberland). Gu. a fesse sa. betw. three pillows ar.

Horton (Southwark, Albert Square, Lambeth, co. Surrey, and of Ystrad, co. Carmarthen). Per saltire or and gu. two stags' heads cabossed in pale, and as many bugles stringed in fesse counterchanged. *Crest*—A demi stag gu. semée of cinquefoils or, resting the sinister foot upon a millrind gold. *Motto*—Vigilo et spero.

Horton (quartered by OSBALDESTON, through WENTWORTH). Ar. a cross formée fitchée sa.

Horton. Ar. three bars sa. in chief two mullets of the last.

Horwood (co. Huntingdon). Sa. three bars erm. cotised or. *Crest*—A crow, wings expanded, pierced through the breast with an arrow point upwards.

Horwood (co. Stafford). Ar. on a chev. betw. three bucks' heads cabossed sa. a crescent or.

Horwood. Erm. four bars gemelles componée or and sa.

Hose (Kentish Town, co. Middlesex; granted 3 Feb. 1806). Erm. on a mount vert a beaver ppr. a chief az. charged with an anchor erect, cabled or, betw. two eagles' heads erased ar. beaked gold. *Crest*—A reindeer's head couped ppr. attired or, gorged with a collar erminois, fimbriated ar.

Hose. Ar. three legs couped at the thigh gu. *Crest*—A lion's head erased.

Hose, de la. Ar. three men's hose gu.

Hoseason (Jamaica, originally of Zetland; recorded 1808). Quarterly, 1st and 4th, ar. an arm in armour, holding a pair of balances az. and in base a sword and Roman fasces in saltire all ppr., for HOSEASON; 2nd and 3rd, or, on a saltire gu. a mullet of the first, a chief of the second, for BRUCE. *Crest*—An eagle reguard. rising from a rock ppr. *Motto*—In recto decus.

Hosier (Croukton, co. Salop). Per bend sinister erm. and ermines a lion ramp. or. *Crest*—On a chapeau az. turned up or, a talbot sejant.

Hosier (impalement Fun. Ent., HENRY CHESHIRE, Sheriff of Dublin, *d.* 5 Oct. 1622, *m.* MARGARET HOSIER). Quarterly, or and sa. a cross, each end terminating in two eagles' heads quarterly gu. and of the first.

Hosken (Carines and Ellenglaze, co. Cornwall). Per pale gu. and az. on a chev. or, betw. three lions pass. ar. as many cinquefoils of the first. *Motto*—Vis unita fortior.

Hosken (monument in Bodmin Church, Rev. ANTHONY HOSKEN, 1791). Per pale az. and gu. a chev. betw. three lions ramp. ar.

Hoskins (co. Monmouth; granted by Segar). Barry of six or and vert, a bordure erm. *Crest*—Two limbs of a tree raguled and couped in saltire ar. the sinister surmounting the dexter.

Hoskins (Higham, co. Cumberland). Per pale gu. and az. a chev. engr. or, betw. three lions ramp. ar. *Crest*—A cock's head erased or, pellettée, combed and wattled gu. betw. two wings expanded of the first. *Motto*—Virtute non verbis.

Hoskins (North Perrott Manor, co. Somerset). Per pale gu. and az. a chev. engr. or, betw. three lions ramp. ar. *Crest*—A cock's head erased or, pellettée, combed and wattled gu. betw. two wings expanded of the first. *Motto*—Finem respice.

Hoskins (Oxted, co. Surrey). Per pale gu. and az. a chev. engr. or, betw. three lions ramp. ar. *Crest*—A cock's head erased or, pellettée, combed and wattled gu. betw. two wings expanded of the first.

Hoskins. Barry of six or and vert, a bordure gu.

Hoskins (Fun. Ent. Ulster's Office, 1666). Gu. a chev. engr. or, betw. three lions ramp. ar.

Hoskyns (Harewood, co. Hereford, bart.). Per pale az. and gu. a chev. betw. three lions ramp. or. *Crest*—A lion's head erased or, issuing out of a ducal coronet, flames of fire from the mouth ppr. crowned of the first.

Hoskyns (WREN-HOSKYNS, Wroxhall Abbey, co. Warwick; exemplified to CHANDOS HOSKYNS, second son of Sir HUNGERFORD HOSKYNS, Bart., of Harewood, who assumed, on marrying, in 1837, THEODOSIA ANNE MARTHA, dau. and heir of CHRISTOPHER WREN, Esq., of Wroxhall Abbey, the additional surname and arms of that family, descended in direct line from the celebrated Sir CHRISTOPHER WREN). Same *Arms* as Hoskyns, Bart., quartering Wren, viz., ar. a chev. betw. three lions' heads erased az. on a chief gu. three crosses crosslet or, a canton of the first. Crests—1st, as Hoskyns, Bart., a crescent az. for distinction; 2nd, Wren: A lion's head erased ar. (formerly the head was borne az.) pierced by a broken spear, broken off on the dexter, cuspated on the sinister, collared gu. with a cross crosslet of the last for distinction. Mottoes—Vincula da linguæ, vel tibi lingua dabit, for Hoskyns; Numero, pondere, et mensurâ, for Wren, ancient; Virtuti fortuna comes, Wren, modern.

Hoskyns (Bemenster). Per pale az. and gu. a chev. betw. three lions or.

Hosse, or Hossey (co. Berks). Ar. a fesse betw. three lions ramp. gu.

Host (London, 1634). Az. a bull's head affrontée, couped at the neck ar. attired or, betw. two wings of the last. Crest—Two wings endorsed or, charged with a crescent gu.

Host, or Hoost (Middleburgh, Zealand, and Sandringham, co. Norfolk). Same Arms. Crest—Two wings endorsed or.

Hoste, Bart. Az. a bull's head affrontée, couped at the neck ar. betw. two wings or; and, as an honourable augmentation, in chief a naval crown, pendent therefrom by a ribbon a representation of the gold medal given to the first bart. by the Prince Regent, for his distinguished conduct on 13 March, 1811, subscribed "Lissa." Crests—1st, of augmentation: Out of a naval crown, the rim encircled with a branch of laurel, an arm embowed, vested in naval uniform, grasping a flag-staff, flowing therefrom a flag, inscribed "Cattaro." 2nd, Family Crest: Two wings addorsed or. Motto—Fortitudine.

Hospital, Bethlehem (founded as a Priory in 1247, established as an hospital for lunatics in 1446, and refounded by Edward VI. in 1546). Ar. two bars sa. a label of five points throughout gu. on a chief az. an estoile of sixteen points or, charged with a plate, thereon a cross of the third betw. a human skull in a cup on the dexter side, and a basket of bread, i.e., wastell cakes, all of the fifth, on the sinister side.

Hospital, Sutton's, or Charterhouse. Or, on a chev. betw. three annulets of the second as many crescents of the first.

Hosterly. Barry of six ar. and sa.

Hoston. Ar. an inescutcheon gu.

Hostot (co. Bedford). Az. a cross patonce erm. betw. four roses or.

Hotchkis (Hoxwood, co. Salop). Per pale gu. and az. a chev. engr. or, betw. three lions ramp. ar. Crest—A cock's head erased or, betw. two wings displ. pellettée.

Hotensill. Or, on a fesse gu. three plates.

Hotham (Baron Hotham). Barry of ten ar. and az. on a canton or, a Cornish chough ppr. Crest—A demi seaman issuing out of the water ppr. holding in the dexter hand a flaming sword ar. hilt and pommel or, on the sinister arm a shield of the arms of Hotham. Supporters—Two seamen habited, each holding a sword, the point resting on the ground all ppr. Motto—Lead on.

Hotham, or Hutham (co. York). Or, on a bend sa. three mullets ar. pierced gu.

Hotham (co. York.) Ar. three bars sa.

Hotham. Barry of six ar. and az. a chief ermines and a canton of the first (another, or).

Hotham. Per fesse battelly ar. and az. on a canton or, a martlet sa.

Hotham. Az. two bars or, (another, ar.) a chief per fesse indented erm. and ar. a canton or.

Hotham. Ar. on a bend sa. three mullets or (another, gu. a pale lozengy ar.; another, barry of eight ar. and az. on a canton sa. a martlet ar.).

Hothe. Per chev. (another, per fesse) or and vert, three mullets counterchanged.

Hothersell (St. Bride's, London, 1615). Az. a lion ramp. or.

Hothum (Hothum, co. York, temp. Edward II.). Ar. four bars az. a canton gu.

Hothwayt, or Hothwarte. Sa. a fret erm.

Hotie. Az. a chev. or, betw. three crescents ar.

Hotoft (Flintham, co. Nottingham). Sa. three dragons' heads erect and erased ar. Crest—A lion's gamb holding up a human heart ppr.

Hotoft, or Hostetoft. Az. a cross pattée erm. betw. four roses or, (another, az. a cross sarcelly ar.).

Hotoft. Sa. a boar's head erect couped ar. (another, az. a chev. ar. betw. three bezants; another, sa. three congers' heads erased and erect ar.).

Hoton (co. Gloucester). Az. a chev. or, betw. three crescents ar. Crest—A seahorse couchant ar. ducally gorged sa. sustaining an anchor az.

Hoton (co. York). Ar. a fesse betw. three cushions sa. (another, az. a cross ar. betw. four roses or; another, gu. a fesse betw. three cushions ar.).

Hoton, or Hooton. Ar. on a bend vert three mullets or.

Hotost. Sa. three firebrands ar.

Hotoste, or Hotofte. Az. a cross moline ar.

Hotot. Az. on a chev. or, betw. three crescents ar. two bars gemelles sa.

Hotott (co. Gloucester). Az. (another, gu.) a chev. or, betw. three crescents ar.

Hotton (co. Cumberland). Gu. on a canton ar. a martlet sa. Crest—A martlet rising ppr.

Hotton. Erm. on a chev. gu. three mullets or.

Hotton. Ar. a lion ramp. gu. crowned or.

Hotton. Erm. five fusils in fesse gu.

Hottot. Az. on a chev. cotised or, betw. three crescents ar. two bars gemelles of the first.

Houblon (Hallingbury Place, co. Essex, and Culverthorpe, co. Lincoln). Quarterly, 1st and 4th, ar. the base vert issuing therefrom three hop poles sustaining their fruit all ppr., for Houblon; 2nd and 3rd, quarterly, 1st and 4th, erm. a cross sa., for Archer, 2nd and 3rd, ar. on a chev. sa. three quatrefoils or, for Eyre. Crests—1st, Houblon: A lion's head erased ar.; 2nd, Archer: A wivern ar.; 3rd, Eyre: A leg in armour couped at the thigh ppr. garnished and spurred or.

Houblon. Az. three fishes naiant ppr. Crest—A dexter hand holding up a book expanded ppr.

Houburke. See Huband.

Hough (Layton, co. Chester). Ar. a bend sa. Crest—A wolf's head erased sa.

Hough (impalement Fun. Ent., Alderman John Marfen, d. April, 1652). Quarterly, 1st and 4th, ar. a bend sa.; 2nd and 3rd, ar. a wolf's head erased sa.

Hougham (Hougham, Wedington, and Barton House, co. Kent; Solomon Hougham, Esq., of Barton House, Sheriff co. Kent 1696; descended from Robert de Hougham, of Hougham, temp. Richard I.). Ar. five chevronels sa., borne by Robert de Hougham, at the siege of Acon, in Palestine, temp. Edward I.; the family sometimes bore, or, on a chev. betw. three elephants' heads erased gu. as many mullets ar. Crest—On a chapeau gu. turned up erm. a falcon ar. with wings expanded or, beaked and belled of the last.

Hougham (London; descended from Richard Hougham, Esq., of Wedington, d. 1606). Same Arms, &c.

Houghbrig. Ar. on a bend fimbriated three cocks reguard.

Houghford. Ar. two bends nebulée sa.

Houghton, or Haughton (Haughton, co. Chester, Petersfield, co. Hants, cos. Lancaster and Sussex). Sa. three bars ar. Crests—1st: A bull's head sa. attired ar. charged on the neck with three bars of the last; 2nd: A bull pass. gu.

Houghton (co. Lancaster). Ar. three bars sa. Crest—A bull's head couped gu. horned or.

Houghton (Alderman of London, d. 31 Dec. 1596). Sa. three bars ar. Crest—A bull pass. ar.

Houghton (London). Ar. three bars sa. in chief two mullets pierced of the last, the horns barry of the first and second.

Houghton (King's Clyff, co. Northampton, and of co. Rutland). Sa. three bars ar. in chief a rose or. Crest—A bull's head ar. attired or, gorged with three bars sa. on the centre one a rose of the second.

Houghton (Gunthorp, co. Norfolk). Ar. on a bend sa. three eagles displ. or. Crest—A demi eagle displ. or, guttée de sang.

Houghton (Beckbury, co. Salop). Ar. a cross sa. in the dexter chief and sinister base an owl ppr.

Houghton (co. York). Erm. a cross engr. sa. Crest—A scymitar erect ar. hilt and pommel downwards or.

Houghton. Erm. a chev. (another, two chevronels) engr. sa.

Houghton. Ar. a cross sa. betw. four owls gu.

Houghton. Gu. four leopards' faces jessant-de-lis, two and two, or, a canton erm.

Houghton (Ballyanne and Kilmannock, co. Wexford; represented by Houghton, of Glashare, co. Kilkenny; the late George Powell Houghton, Esq., of Kilmannock, left three daus. his co-heirs, viz., Anne Coote, m. Sir John Marcus Stewart, Bart.; Alice, m. Captain Edward Webber Smith; and Charlotte, m. Standish O'Grady, Esq.; at the death of G. P. Houghton, Esq., his first cousin, George Henry Houghton, Esq., of Glashare, became heir male of the family. Impalement Fun. Ent., Valentine Savage, 1670, whose wife was Mary, dau. of Thomas Houghton, Esq., of Ballyanne). Ar. three bars sa.

Houison. See HOWISON.

Houlder (Isle of Ely). Az. a fesse dancettée betw. three griffins pass. or. *Crest*—Out of a ducal coronet gu. a lion sejant or.

Houlditch. Az. a chev. or, betw. three seagulls ar.

Houldsworth (Gonaldston, co. Nottingham, and Coltness, co. Lanark). Erm. the trunk of a tree in bend raguly, eradicated at the base ppr. betw. three foxes' heads erased gu. *Crest*—A stag's head erased gu. attired and collared or, the attires bound within a hank of cotton ar. *Motto*—Honos præmium industriæ.

Houldsworth (WILLIAM HOULDSWORTH, Glasgow, 1868). Same *Arms*, within a bordure gu. Same *Crest* and *Motto*.

Houldsworth (JOSEPH H. HOULDSWORTH, Glasgow, 1868). Same *Arms*, within a bordure engr. gu. Same *Crest* and *Motto*.

Houldsworth (Cranstonhill, co. Lanark, 1869). As Gonaldston, within a bordure az. for diff. Same *Crest* as Gonaldston. *Motto*—Flecti non frangi.

Houldsworth (JOHN MUIR HOULDSWORTH, Glasgow, 1869). Same *Arms*, with the bordure engr. Same *Crest* and *Motto* as the last.

Houldsworth (W. T. HOULDSWORTH, Glasgow). Same *Arms* as Gonaldston, within a bordure invecked az. Same *Crest* and *Motto* as Cranstonhill.

Houlton. Ar. on a fesse wavy betw. three talbots' heads az. as many bezants. *Crest*—A ferret pass. ppr.

Houlton (Farley Castle, co. Somerset). Same *Arms*. *Crest*—A talbot's head erased ppr. gorged with a collar wavy or, charged with three torteaux. *Motto*—Semper fidelis.

Houndgate. Gu. a chev. (another, engr.) betw. three talbots sejant ar.

Houndsmore. Ar. three talbots' heads erased sa.

Hounslow Priory (co. Middlesex). Gu. a lion ramp. guard. per fesse or and ar. betw. three plates, each charged with a cross of the first. *Another Coat*—Gu. a lion ramp. guard. per fesse or and ar.

Hounston (Boston, co. Lincoln). Sa. a cross erm. betw. four lozenges of the last, a bordure engr. ar. *Crest*—A nag's head or, in the mouth a holly branch vert, fructed gu.

Hounston. Sa. three lozenges erm. a bordure engr. ar.

Housden. Ar. a fesse betw. two chevronels sa.

House. Vert a cross ar. *Crest*—Two hands issuing from a cloud in chief, holding an anchor in the sea ppr.

Housson, or Howson (London, 1605). Quarterly, ar. and sa. in the 1st and 4th quarters a pellet, in the 2nd and 3rd a plate. *Crest*—Out of clouds ppr. a bull's head az. semée of estoiles or.

Houstar. Sa. a fesse indented betw. three fleurs-de-lis ar.

Houston (BLAKISTON-HOUSTON; exemplified, 1844, to RICHARD BAYLEY BLAKISTON, Esq., of Orangefield, co. Down, on his assuming, by royal licence, the additional surname of HOUSTON, in compliance with the injunction of his father-in-law, JOHN HOLMES HOUSTON, Esq.). Quarterly, 1st and 4th, or, a chev. chequy sa. and ar. betw. three martlets of the second, for HOUSTON; 2nd and 3rd, ar. two bars and in chief three cocks gu. an annulet az. for diff., for BLAKISTON. *Crests*—1st, HOUSTON: A sandglass ppr., motto over, Time; 2nd: A cock statant gu. charged with an annulet or; over the crests the motto, In Time. *Motto*—Do well and doubt not.

Houstoun (that Ilk, co. Renfrew, bart., 1668; family now represented by HOUSTON, of Johnstone, same co.). Or, a chev. chequy az. and ar. betw. three martlets sa. beaked gu. *Crest*—A sandglass ppr. *Supporters*—Two hinds ppr. *Motto*—In time.

Houstoun (Culreoch, co. Wigtoun, and Calderhall, co. Edinburgh; now HOUSTON-BOSWALL, Bart.). Quarterly, 1st and 4th, ar. on a fesse sa. betw. two thistles in chief and a garb in base ppr. three cinquefoils of the first, for BOSWALL; 2nd and 3rd, or, a chev. chequy sa. and ar. betw. three martlets of the second, for HOUSTOUN. *Crests*—1st, BOSWALL: A cubit arm grasping a sword ppr.; 2nd, HOUSTOUN: A sandglass winged ppr. *Supporters*—Two greyhounds ppr. collared and chained or. *Mottoes*—Over the BOSWALL crest: Fortiter; over the HOUSTOUN crest: In time.

Hout. Per pale or and sa. a saltire counterchanged of the second and ar.

Houtlane (Reg. Ulster's Office). Gu. three pheons points down ar.

Houton. Or, a fesse cotised gu. betw. three hinds' heads sa. *Crest*—A fox courant.

Hoveden (Ireland; granted 1585). Chequy sa. and ar. on a bend gu. three lions' heads erased or. *Crest*—A dragon's head vert issuing out of flames ppr.

Hoveden. Chequy ar. and sa. on a bend gu. three lions' heads erased or.

Hovell (Hillington, co. Norfolk). Sa. a crescent

Hovell (co. Suffolk). Sa. a cross or, on a chief wavy erm. three fleurs-de-lis gu.

Hovell (Ashfield, co. Suffolk). Sa. a cross or. *Crest*—A greyhound couchant or, collared and lined sa.

Hovell, or Hoovill (co. Suffolk). Sa. a cross flory or.

Hovell (co. Sussex). Sa. a cross ar.

Hovell. Sa. a cross ar. on a chief wavy erm. three fleurs-de-lis gu. *Crest*—On a ducal coronet or, a leopard sejant ppr.

Hovell, or Hovile. Sa. a fleur-de-lis or.

Hovell. Paly of six or and az. on a fesse gu. three mullets of six points of the first.

Hovenell. Ar. a chev. betw. three water bougets sa.

Hovered. Az. a chev. betw. three lozenges or.

Hovile. Ar. a bend az.

How (co. Kent). Gu. on a chev. or, three crescents sa.

How (RICHARD How, son of Sir RICHARD How, Knt., Alderman of London; granted 1691). Ar. a fesse engr. sa. guttée or, betw. three wolves' heads erased of the second, collared gu. *Crest*—A wolf's head erased pean.

How (London). Same *Arms*. *Crest*—A wolf's head sa. in the mouth a rose gu. stalked and leaved vert.

How, or Howe (London). Ar. a fesse wavy betw. three wolves' heads erased sa.

How (Herse, co. Somerset). Ar. a fesse betw. three wolves' heads couped sa. *Crest*—Out of a ducal coronet or, a demi wolf sa.

How (cos. Essex and Suffolk). Ar. a chev. betw. three wolves' heads couped sa. *Crest*—Out of a ducal coronet or, a unicorn's head gu. attired and crined of the first.

How. Quarterly ar. and sa.

Howard (co. Norfolk; Sir WILLIAM HOWARD, Chief Justice of the Common Pleas, *temp.* Edward I., the immediate founder of the noble house of HOWARD, was son of JOHN HOWARD, and grandson of ROBERT HOWARD, or HERWARD "*filius* HAWARDI," *temp.* King John). Gu. a bend betw. six crosses crosslet fitchée ar.

Howard (*Lord Howard;* Sir ROBERT HOWARD, fourth in descent from Sir WILLIAM HOWARD, the Chief Justice, was summoned to Parliament 1476. He *m.* Lady MARGARET MOWBRAY, dau. of THOMAS, Duke of Norfolk, and was ancestor of the illustrious house of HOWARD, Dukes of Norfolk; the Barony is in abeyance betw. the Lords Stourton and Petre since 1777). Gu. a bend betw. six cross crosslets fitchée ar.

Howard (*Duke of Norfolk*, Earl Marshal of England). Quarterly, 1st, gu. on a bend betw. six cross crosslets fitchée ar. an escutcheon or, charged with a demi lion ramp. pierced through the mouth by an arrow within a double tressure flory counterflory of the first, for HOWARD; 2nd, gu. three lions pass. guard. in pale or, in chief a label of three points ar., for BROTHERTON; 3rd, chequy or and az., for WARREN; 4th, gu. a lion ramp. or, for FITZALAN; behind the shield two gold batons in saltire enamelled at the ends sa. (the insigna of Earl Marshal). *Crests*—1st: Issuant from a ducal coronet or, a pair of wings gu. each charged with a bend betw. six cross crosslets fitchée ar.; 2nd: On a chapeau gu. turned up erm. a lion statant with tail extended or, gorged with a ducal coronet ar.; 3rd: On a mount vert a horse pass. ar. holding in the mouth a slip of oak fructed ppr. *Supporters*—Dexter, a lion; sinister a horse, both ar. the latter holding in his mouth a slip of oak vert, fructed ppr. *Motto*—Sola virtus invicta. THOMAS, *Earl of Surrey* (afterwards *Duke of Norfolk*), who achieved the victory of Flodden over James IV. of Scotland, had a special grant from Henry VIII. of an honourable augmentation of his arms to him and the heirs male of his body, viz., "On the bend of the original HOWARD coat, in an escutcheon or, a demi lion ramp. pierced through the mouth with an arrow, within a double tressure flory counterflory gu," being the tressure of the Royal Arms of the Scottish monarch.

Howard (FITZALAN-HOWARD, *Lord Howard*, of Glossop). Same as HOWARD, *Duke of Norfolk*, with a crescent for diff.

Howard (Greystoke, co. Cumberland; HENRY HOWARD, Esq., of Greystoke Castle, co. Cumberland, son and heir of the late *Lord Henry Thomas Howard Molyneux Howard*, and nephew of BERNARD EDWARD, twelfth *Duke of Norfolk*). Same *Arms* (with the distinction for the second house) as those usually borne by the *Dukes of Norfolk*, viz.: 1st, HOWARD; 2nd, BROTHERTON; 3rd, WARREN; and 4th, MOWBRAY; with the additional quarterings of, 5th, DACRE, gu. three escallops ar.; and 6th, GREYSTOKE, barry of six ar. and az. three chaplets ppr. *Crest* and *Motto*, same as those of the *Duke of Norfolk*.

Howard (*Earl of Stafford;* created 1640, extinct 1762). Arms same as the *Duke of Norfolk*, with a crescent for diff.

Crests—1st: On a chapeau gu. turned up erm. a lion statant, tail extended or, gorged with a ducal coronet ar. charged with a crescent for diff., for HOWARD; 2nd: Out of a ducal coronet per pale sa. and gu. a demi swan rising ar. beaked of the first, for STAFFORD. *Supporters*—Dexter, a lion ar. (HOWARD) with a crescent for diff. ; sinister, a swan, wings expanded ar. beaked and membered sa. gorged with a ducal coronet per pale gu. and of the second (STAFFORD). *Motto*—Abstulit qui dedit.

Howard de Walden, Lord. See ELLIS.

Howard (*Earl of Suffolk and Berkshire*). Quarterly, 1st, gu. a bend betw. six cross crosslets fitchée ar. on the bend an escutcheon or, charged with a demi lion ramp. pierced through the mouth with an arrow, within a double tressure flory counterflory gu., for HOWARD; 2nd, gu. three lions pass. guard. in pale or, and a label of three points ar., for BROTHERTON; 3rd, chequy or and az., for WARREN; 4th, gu. a lion ramp. ar., for MOWBRAY; in the centre of the shield a crescent for diff. *Crest*—On a chapeau gu. turned up erm. a lion statant guard. tail extended or, ducally gorged ar. and charged on the body with a crescent for diff. *Supporters*—Two lions ar. each charged on the breast with a crescent sa. *Mottoes*—Nous maintiendrons ; and, Non quo, sed quo modo.

Howard (*Lord Howard*, of Escrick; created 1628, extinct 1715). Same *Arms*, *Crest*, and *Supporters* as the *Earl of Suffolk and Berkshire*, charged with a mullet on a crescent for diff.

Howard (*Earl of Carlisle*). Quarterly of six, 1st, HOWARD, gu. on a bend betw. six cross crosslets fitchée ar. an escutcheon or, charged with a demi lion ramp. pierced through the mouth with an arrow, within a double tressure flory counterflory of the first, a mullet for diff.; 2nd, BROTHERTON, gu. three lions pass. guard. in pale or, in chief a label of three points ar. ; 3rd, WARREN, chequy or and az. ; 4th, MOWBRAY, gu. a lion ramp. ar. armed and langued az. ; 5th, DACRE, gu. three escallops ar.; 6th, GREYSTOCK, barry of six ar. and az. three chaplets gu. *Crest*—On a chapeau gu. turned up erm. a lion statant guard. the tail extended or, ducally gorged ar. a mullet sa. for diff. *Supporters*—Dexter, a lion ar. a mullet for diff. ; sinister, a bull gu. armed, unguled, ducally gorged and lined or.

Howard (*Baron Lanerton*). Same *Arms*, *Crest*, and *Motto* as the *Earl of Carlisle's*, a crescent for diff. *Supporters*—Dexter, a lion ar. charged on the shoulder with a mullet sa. ; sinister, a bull gu. hoofed, armed, ducally gorged, and line reflexed over the back or, both charged on the body with a crescent gold.

Howard (*Corby Castle*, co. Cumberland). Gu. on a bend betw. six cross crosslets fitchée ar. an escutcheon or, charged with a demi lion ramp. pierced through the mouth with an arrow within a double tressure flory counterflory of the first, quartering BROTHERTON, WARREN, MOWBRAY, DACRE, and GREYSTOKE. *Crest*—On a chapeau gu. turned up erm. a lion statant guard. tail extended or, ducally crowned ar. gorged with a label of three points of the last. *Motto*—Sola virtus invicta.

Howard (*Earl of Northampton; created 1604, extinct 1614*). Gu. on a bend betw. six crosses crosslet fitchée ar. an escutcheon or, charged with a demi lion ramp. pierced through the mouth with an arrow, within a double tressure flory counterflory of the first, a crescent for diff.

Howard (*Viscount Bindon; created 1559, extinct 1610*). Same *Arms*.

Howard (*Earl of Nottingham; created 1596, extinct 1681*). Same *Arms* and *Crest* as the *Duke of Norfolk*, with a mullet for diff. *Supporters*—Two lions ar. *Motto*—Desier na repos.

Howard (*Earl of Effingham*). Gu. on a bend betw. six cross crosslets fitchée ar. an escutcheon or, charged with a demi lion ramp. pierced through the mouth with an arrow, within a double tressure flory counterflory of the first. *Crest*— On a chapeau gu. turned up erm. a lion statant guard. tail extended or, gorged with a ducal coronet ar. *Supporters*—Two lions ar. on the shoulder of each a mullet for diff. *Motto*—Virtus mile scuta.

Howard (Dublin; confirmed by Hawkins, Ulster, 1708, to Doctor RALPH HOWARD, son of JOHN HOWARD, and father of ROBERT HOWARD, Bishop of Elphin, ancestor of the *Earls of Wicklow*). Gu. a bend betw. six crosses crosslet fitchée ar.; in 1713 the following augmentation was granted, viz.: on a canton az. a sun in splendour or. *Crest*—On a chapeau gu. turned up erm. a lion statant guard. tail extended or, ducally gorged gu. and pierced through the mouth with an arrow ppr.

Howard (*Earl of Wicklow*). Quarterly, 1st and 4th, gu. a

bend. betw. six cross crosslets fitchée ar. ; 2nd and 3rd, ar. a lion ramp. gu. *Crest*—On a chapeau gu. turned up erm. a lion statant guard. or, ducally gorged gu., holding in the mouth an arrow ppr. *Supporters*—Two stags ppr. ducally gorged, each charged on the shoulder with a cross crosslet fitchée ar. *Mottoes*—Inservi Deo et lætare; and, Certum pete finem.

Howard (Bushy Park, co. Wicklow, bart.; extinct 1873). Gu. a bend betw. six crosses crosslet fitchée ar. *Crest*—On a chapeau gu. turned up erm. a lion pass. guard. or, holding in the mouth an arrow in fesse ppr. *Motto*—Inservi Deo et lætare.

Howard (Castle Rising, co. Norfolk; exemplified to Col. Hon. FULKE GREVILLE UPTON, of Castle Rising, and Levens, co. Westmoreland, second son of CLOTWORTHY, first *Lord Templetown*, who assumed the name and arms of HOWARD, on his marriage with MARY, dau. and heiress of RICHARD HOWARD, Esq., of Castle Rising, *d.* 1846). *Arms*—HOWARD, quarterly with UPTON. *Crest*—HOWARD.

Howard (Broughton Hall, co. Flint). Gu. on a bend indented or, three escallops of the first betw. six cross crosslets fitchée ar. *Crest*—A lion's head affrontée or, three crescents of the first betw. two wings, a cross crosslet fitchée issuing from the head. *Motto*—Virtus sine metu.

Howard (St. Andrew's, Holborn; granted 1756). Gu. on a bend engr. betw. six crosses botonnée fitchée or, three crescents of the first. *Crest*—A lion couchant erm. holding in the dexter paw a cross botonnée fitchée of the second.

Howard-Vyse (The Manor Cottage, Old Windsor). Quarterly, 1st and 4th, VYSE, ar. a buck's head cabossed sa. betw. the attires a cross of the last; 2nd and 3rd, HOWARD, gu. on a bend betw. six crosses crosslet fitchée ar. an escutcheon or, charged with a demi lion pierced through the mouth with an arrow, within a double tressure flory counterflory gu. a mullet sa. charged with a crescent or, for diff. *Crest* —HOWARD: On a chapeau gu. turned up erm. a lion statant guard. the tail extended or, ducally crowned, and charged on the neck with a label of three points ar. a mullet sa. charged with a crescent or, for diff. *Motto*—Virtus mille scuta.

Howard-Vyse (Stoke Place, co. Bucks, and Boughton, co. Northampton). Same *Arms*, &c.

Howard (co. Lancaster). Gu. on a bend betw. six crosses crosslet ar. an annulet for diff. *Crest*—A lion ramp. ar. holding betw. the paws a cross crosslet fitchée of the first.

Howard (London). Gu. on a bend ar. betw. six crosses crosslet fitchée or, a mullet betw. two cinquefoils of the first. *Crest*—A demi wolf ppr. holding betw. the paws a cross crosslet fitchée or, collared gu. thereon a mullet betw. two cinquefoils gold.

Howard (Hackney, co. Middlesex). Gu. a bend or, betw. six crosses flory fitchée ar. on a canton of the second a hind's head erased ppr. *Crest*—On a chapeau gu. turned up erm. a demi hind saliant ppr. charged on the shoulder with a cross flory fitchée ar.

Howard (Beinnington Hall, co. Chester). Barry of six or and az. on a bend erm. betw. two crosses botony gu. a shuttle ppr. *Crest*—In front of a cross botony fitchée gu. a lion couchant or, charged on the shoulder with an estoile gu. *Motto*—Per fidem omnia.

Howard. Gu. a bend vairé or and az. betw. six crosses crosslet fitchée of the second. *Crest*—Two wings expanded gu. each charged with a bend vairé or and az. betw. six crosses crosslet of the last.

Howard. Gu. a bend betw. six crosses crosslet fitchée ar. *Crest*—Out of a ducal coronet or, two wings expanded gu. each charged with a bend betw. six crosses crosslet, as in the arms.

Howard. Gu. a bend betw. six crosses crosslet fitchée ar. *Crest*—A lion's head erased collared.

Howard, Same *Arms*. *Crest* On a chapeau gu. turned up. erm. two wings endorsed of the first, each charged with a bend betw. six crosses crosslet, as in the arms.

Howard. Per chev. az. and gu. a lion saliant erm. (another, the lion crowned).

Howard, or Howart. Quarterly, ar. and az. a saltire counterchanged (another, the saltire engr.).

Howard, or Hayward. Ar. a bull's head gu. betw. three mullets sa.

Howard (Toronto, Canada; JAMES SCOTT HOWARD, Esq., of Toronto, J.P. and Treasurer of the united counties of York and Peel, in Upper Canada, son of the late JOHN HOWARD, by MARY, his wife, dau. of JAMES SCOTT, of Bandon, descends from a Huguenot family, named OUWARD, which fled from France at the revocation of the Edict of Nantes, and became established at Innishannon, co. Cork, where they acquired property, and founded a flourishing and extensive business in silk and cotton manufactures. In more propitious times, NICHOLAS HOWARD, the grandfather of the present representative, returned to France, and succeeded in recovering a portion of his ancestral property). Az. a fesse ar. betw. in chief a passion cross of the last betw. two fleurs-de-lis or, and in base a catharine wheel of the second. Crest—A catharine wheel ar. betw. on the dexter side, a branch of palm, and on the sinister a branch of cypress ppr. Motto—Pro fide.

Howarth (co. Stafford). Az. a bend betw. two stags' heads couped or.

Howat (Glasgow, 1872). Per pale sa. and gu. a chev. betw. three owls or. Crest—The sun in his splendour rising out of a cloud ppr. Motto—Post tenebras lux.

Howay (Howay, co. Devon). Gu. a fesse betw. three crescents ar.

Howberiam (Howberiam-Eves, co. Lancaster). Ar. three crosses sa.

Howbridge, or Howghbrige (co. York). Ar. two bendlets betw. three cocks sa.

Howden. Or, on a bend sa. three mullets ar.

Howdenby. Vert a fesse ar. betw. three covered cups or.

Howdon, or Houdon. Gu. a chev. betw. three crosses crosslet or, on a chief of the second a lion pass. of the first. Crest—A dragon's head spouting fire ppr. Motto—Ferio, tego.

Howe (CURZON-HOWE, Earl Howe). Quarterly, 1st and 4th, or. a fesse betw. three wolves' heads erased sa., for Howe; 2nd and 3rd, ar. on a bend sa. three popinjays or, beaked and legged gu., for CURZON. Crests—1st, HOWE: Out of a ducal coronet or, a plume of five ostrich feathers az.; 2nd, CURZON: A popinjay rising or, collared gu. Supporters—Dexter, a Cornish chough; sinister, a cockatrice, wings elevated, or, tail nowed, with a head at the end thereof. Motto—Let Curzon holde what Curzon helde.

Howe (Langar, co. Nottingham, and Emble, co. Somerset). Or, a fesse betw. three wolves' heads couped sa. Crest—A gauntlet lying fesseways ppr. lined gu. holding a falchion ar. hilt or, the middle part of the blade debruised by a wolf's head couped sa.

Howe (Viscount Howe; extinct 1814, created 1701). Or, a fess betw. three wolves' heads couped sa. Crest—Out of a ducal coronet or, a plume of five ostrich feathers az. Supporters—Two Cornish choughs ppr. beaked and membered gu. Motto—Utcunque placuerit Deo.

Howe (Earl Howe; extinct 1799, created 1788). Same Arms. Crest, &c., as Viscount Howe, the fourth viscount being so created.

Howe (Compton, co. Gloucester, bart.; extinct 1814, created 1660). Or, a fess betw. three wolves' heads erased sa. langued gu. Crest—Out of a ducal coronet or, a plume of five ostrich feathers az.

Howe (Cold Barwick, co. Wilts, bart., extinct 1735; descended from a brother of the first bart. of Compton). Same Arms, a crescent for diff.

Howe (Lord Chedworth; extinct 1804, created 1741). Or, a fess betw. three wolves' heads couped sa. a crescent for diff. Crest—A dexter arm in armour erased below the elbow, lying fessways, and holding in the hand a scymitar all ppr. pommel and hilt or, pierced through a boar's head couped sa. Supporters—Dexter, a lion ar. pellettée, armed and langued gu.; sinister, an angel ppr. face in profile, hair brownish, habited crimson, under garments az. wings ar. pinioned of the fourth. Motto—Justus et propositi tenax.

Lowe (Emble, co. Somerset; granted 10 Dec. 1625). Same Arms as How, Compton, co. Gloucester.

Howe (co. Somerset). Ar. on a fesse betw. three foxes' heads erased sa. an escallop of the field. Crest—An arm erect ppr. vested ar. charged with two bends wavy gu. holding a bunch of broom vert.

Howe, or How (London). Ar. a fesse engr. betw. three wolves' heads couped sa. Crest—Out of a ducal coronet or, a demi wolf ramp. sa.

Howel-Coedmor (Gwyder in Llanrwst, co. Denbigh; derived from DAVID GOCH, of Penmachno). Az. a chev. betw. three javelin points ar. embrued gu.

Howeldon. Gu. an inescutcheon betw. six eagles displ. ar.

Howeldon, or Howedon. Ar. an inescutcheon betw. six eagles displ. gu.

Howell, or Powell (St. Alban's, co. Hertford). Sa. three roses ar. barbed vert. Crest—Out of a ducal crown or, a rose ar. stalked and leaved vert, betw. two wings endorsed sa.

Howell (co. Kent, Stratford and Haley, co. Norfolk, and co. Sussex). Ar. two lions conjoined with one head ramp. guard. per pale gu. and sa.

513

Howell (Prinknash Park, co. Gloucester). Quarterly, 1st and 4th, sa. a chev. betw. three fleurs-de-lis ar., for HOWELL; 2nd and 3rd, ar. a chev. sa. betw. three boars' heads couped ppr., for JONES. Crests—1st: A stag lodged sa. in the mouth a leaf ppr.; 2nd: Out of a ducal coronet or, a lion's head sa. gutté d'eau.

Howell (Prince of Caerleon-upon-Uske, co. Monmouth). Gu. three towers triple-towered ar.

Howell, or Hovell (Soulgrave, co. Northampton, co. Suffolk, and Pack, co. Warwick). Sa. a cross or. Crest—A griffin sejant ar. beaked, legged, and winged az. pierced through the breast with a broken tilting spear ppr. and holding the bottom part of the broken spear in the sinister claw.

Howell (Eynsham, co. Oxford; WILLIAM HOWELL, Esq. Visit. 1574). Sa. a cross or, a crescent for diff. Crest—A griffin segreant az. holding a broken spear sa. Motto—Virtus in arduo.

Howell, Howel, Hovell, and Hovel. Same Arms. Crest—A camel ppr.

Howell. Ar. two lions pass. reguard. in pale sa. Crest—A beaver pass. ppr.

Howell. Gu. a chev. betw. three mullets ar.

Howell. Gu. three towers triple-towered ar.

Howell. Az. a wolf saliant ar.

Howell. Quarterly, per fesse indented gu. and ar.

Howell. Gu. on a chief or, a lion pass. sa.

Howell ap Bennet. Ar. a lion ramp. sa. depressed with a fesse gu.

Howell ap Griffith (co. Montgomery). Ar. on a fesse az. three boars' heads couped close or, in chief a lion pass. gu.

Howell Ddu (North Wales). Gu. three lions pass. in pale or, armed and langued sa.

Howen (co. Sussex). Gu. a chev. erm. betw. three old men's heads couped ar.

Howenden (Killeban, Queen's co.; registered by Hawkins, Ulster, on a certificate from Cooke, Clarenceux, 1585). Chequy ar. and sa. on a bend gu. three lions' heads erased or. Crest—Out of flames ppr. a dragon's head issuant ar. Motto—Virtute et prudentia.

Howes. Ar. five piles sa. three issuing from the chief and two from the base, each charged with a plate. Crest—A demi youth ppr. vested az. holding in the dexter hand a heart gu.

Howes. Same Arms. Crest—A passion nail gu. betw. two wings ppr.

Howes, or Howse (Morningthorpe, co. Norfolk). Ar. a chev. cotised betw. three griffins' heads erased and a bordure indented sa. Crest—Three ostrich feathers or, therefrom issuant a unicorn gu. collared, armed, and crined or. Motto—Stat fortuna domûs.

Howes (co. Essex; JOAN HOWES, heiress of the family, temp. Henry VIII., m. JOHN GLASCOTE, or GLASCOKE. Visit. Essex, 1614). Or, a fess betw. three wolves' heads erased sa. Crest—A dexter hand erect, holding an ear of wheat all ppr.

Howghten. Quarterly, az. and ar. in the 2nd and 3rd quarters a chev. sa. charged with three mullets of the first, over all on a bend sa. as many eagles displ. ar.

Howghten. Ar. on a bend sa. three eagles displ. or.

Howitts. Ar. a chev. betw. three lapwings sa.

Howison (Braehead, co. Midlothian; now represented by HOWISON CRAUFURD, of Craufurdland, co. Ayr, and of Braehead, co. Midlothian). Ar. a man's heart gu. on a chief az. three fleurs-de-lis or. Crest—A dexter hand couped apaumée ppr. Motto—Sursum corda.

Howison (Holmfoot, co. Lanark, 1783). Same Arms. Crest—An eagle rising ppr. Motto—Nulla temerata nube.

Howison (Ireland). Quarterly, ar. and sa. six roundles counterchanged, three, two, and one. Crest—An antelope pass. gu.

Howland (co. Cambridge, London, and Streatham, co. Surrey; granted 1584). Ar. two bars sa. in chief three lions ramp. of the second. Crest—A leopard pass. sa. ducally gorged or.

Howland. Az. crusily a lion ramp. ar.

Howlatsone (Gardenston Rigg, Scotland). Ar. a treble violin az. stringed or, betw. two fleurs-de-lis in chief and a man's heart in base gu. Motto—Dulcedo capior.

Howlestock (co. Essex). Ar. on a bend engr. sa. betw. two lions pass. az. three plates.

Howlett (Sydenham, co. Kent; granted 1559). Per chev. or and sa. in chief two triple-towers of the second, in base a ship in full sail of the first. Crest—An owl ar. ducally gorged or, holding in the dexter claw a rose gu. slipped and leaved vert.

Howlett (Ireland). See HEWLETT.

Z L

Howley. Vert a saltire ar.

Howley (Archbishop of Canterbury, 1828). Az. an eagle displ. erminois, on the breast a plain cross gu.

Howlison (Scotland). Ar. a man's heart gu. on a chief az. three fleurs-de-lis or.

Howly. Or, on a canton gu. a crescent ar.

Howman (granted by Dugdale and St. George, 5 May, 1684, to ROGER HOWMAN, M.D., of the city of Norwich). Gu. a rose ar. seeded or, barbed vert, a chief erm. *Crest*—On a mount ppr. a pegasus volant sa. *Motto*—Labile quod opportunum.

Hownd, or Hound (Callis, co. Cambridge, and co. Hereford). Ar. on a chev. gu. betw. three hounds pass. sa. collared or, as many bezants. *Crest*—A demi talbot ar. collared sa. holding a key or.

Howndhile, Howndhill, or Hounhill. Vert six talbots pass. ar. three, two, and one. *Crest*—A Saracen's head issuing ppr. wreathed round the temples or and gu.

Hownhill, Hounehill, or Howndhill. Vert a chev. betw. three hounds pass. ar. *Crest*—A lion's gamb erased, holding a tilting spear in bend tasselled all ppr.

Hownillyard (co. Devon). Sa. a chev. betw. three water bougets ar.

Hownyll. Ar. a chev. betw. three water bougets sa.

Howood. Ar. a chev. betw. three talbots pass. gu.

Howorth (Howorth, co. Lancaster). Az. a bend betw. two stags' heads couped or. *Crest*—A stag's head gu. attired or, gorged with a wreath ar.

Howorth (Thurcroft, co. Lancaster, 1664). Az. a bend or, cotised ar. betw. two stags' heads couped of the second. *Crest*—A stag's head couped gu. collared ar. attired or.

Howper, or Hooper (co. Devon). Gyronny of eight or and erm. over all a tower triple-towered sa. *Crest*—A demi wolf erm. holding a pine branch vert, fructed or.

Howsdon. Or, a fesse betw. two chev. sa.

Howse. See HOWES.

Howson (Bishop of Durham; confirmed 1605). Quarterly, ar. and sa. in the 1st and 4th quarters a pellet, and in the 2nd and 3rd a plate.

Howson. Sa. a fesse betw. three birds' legs erased, those in chief fesseways, the claws to the centre, that in base paleways, the claw in chief. *Crest*—A falcon belled ppr. *Motto*—Ad finem fidelis.

Howson. Gu. a chev. sa. guttée d'eau betw. three leopards' faces ar.

Howson (co. Lincoln, 1640). Sa. a fess betw. three eagles' legs erased a-la-quise or.

Howster (London). Sa. a fesse dancettée betw. three fleurs-de-lis ar.

Howth, Earl of. See ST. LAWRENCE.

Howton (co. Oxford). Or, on a fesse cotised gu. betw. three hinds' heads erased sa. a unicorn courant ar. *Crest*—A hind's head erased or, betw. two branches of roses, flowered ar. stalked and leaved vert.

Howtred (co. York). Gu. on a cross flory or, five mullets of the field.

Howxley (co. Chester). Erm. on a bend cotised gu. three crescents ar.

Hoxton (Sutterton Hoxton, co. Suffolk). Gu. a chev. ar. guttée de poix betw. three leopards' faces of the second. *Crest* A tower ppr. ensigned with a flag az. flotant to the sinister, staff sa.

Hoy (Harold's Park, co. Essex). Chequy or and gu. a lion ramp. ar.

Hoy (Midanbury, co. Hants, Sheriff of London, 1812–13). Chequy or and gu. a lion ramp. ar. *Crest*—A dexter arm embowed, couped above and near the elbow, holding in the hand a sword all ppr. pommel and hilt or.

Hoy (granted to ISAAC A. HOY, Esq., of Higham Lodge, co. Suffolk). Vert on a fesse dancettée betw. four lions' heads erased, three in chief and one in base or, three doves az. *Crest*—A griffin sejant sa. holding in the dexter claw a sword erect ppr. pommel and hilt or.

Hoy, or Hoye. Or, a unicorn ramp. sa. *Crest*—A demi lion gu. supporting a long cross or.

Hoyland, or Holland (co. Lancaster). Per pale indented gu. and or. *Crest*—A dexter hand in fesse issuing from a cloud in the sinister, and pointing towards a crosier in pale, issuing ppr.

Hoyland (co. Lincoln). Barry pily of eight or and gu.

Hoyland. Sa. a cross patonce or.

Hoyle. Ar. two lions combatant sa. *Crest*—A demi lion ramp. reguard. or, holding betw. the paws a shield az. charged with a sun gold.

Hoyle (Upper Swift Place, Ripponden, co. York, and Denton, co. Northumberland). Erm. a mullet or.

Hoyle (Eastwood Lodge, Rotherham, co. York; confirmed

514

to FRETWELL WILLIAM HOYLE, Esq., eldest son and heir of WILLIAM FRETWELL HOYLE, Esq., of Ferham House, co. York, and their descendants). Per pale or and erm. a mullet sa. *Crest*—An eagle's head erased ppr. charged on the neck with a mullet sa. and holding in the beak a white rose slipped ppr. *Motto*—Facta non verba.

Hoyle (confirmed by Hawkins, Ulster, 1715, to Doctor RICHARD HOYLE, eldest son of JOHN HOYLE, Captain of a Company of Foot in the army of Charles II., descended from HOYLE, of Light Hazell, co. York). Ar. a fess az. betw. three mullets sa. *Crest*—A lion couchant or, charged on the shoulder with a mullet sa.

Hozier (Newlands, co. Lanark, 1824). Vair on a chief gu. three bezants, a chief chequy or and sa. *Crest*—A bloodhound sejant ppr. *Motto*—Aye ready.

Huband (Ipsley, co. Warwick, bart., extinct 1730; descended from Sir HENRY HUBANT, who held a knight fee in Ipsley, 20 Henry III.). Sa. three leopards' faces jessant-de-lis ar.

Huband (co. Dublin). Same *Arms*. *Crest*—A wolf pass. or. *Motto*—Cave lupum.

Huband. Sa. three fleurs-de-lis ar.

Huband (co. Oxford; JOHN HUBAND, son of NICHOLAS HUBAND; confirmed at Visit. 1566). Sa. a chev. ar. betw. three leopards' faces reversed jessant-de-lis or.

Hubard, or Hauberke (quartered by SHERRARD, of Whitsundyne. Visit. Rutland, 1618). Ar. on a bend sa. nine annulets interlaced in threes or.

Hubard, or Hubbard (Barleythorpe, co. Rutland). Same *Arms*.

Hubart, Hubert, or Hubberd (Birchanger, co. Essex: granted May, 1578). Quarterly, ar. and sa. on a bend gu. three lions pass. or. *Crest*—A boar's head couped gu. collared, ringed, and lined ar. in the mouth a spear sa. headed of the second.

Hubart (Calais). Az. a chev. ar. betw. three swans' necks erased of the second, ducally gorged gu.

Hubaud, or Hubald (Twiford, co. Derby). Sa. three leopards' heads jessant-de-lis ar. *Crest*—A wolf pass. gu.

Hubbald (Stoke, co. Surrey; granted 1707). Gu. two ostrich feathers in saltire ar. betw. four leopards' faces or. *Crest*—A leopard's face or, jessant three like feathers, the centre one az. the other two gu.

Hubbard (Durham). Sa. in chief a crescent ar. and in base an estoile of eight points or, betw. two flaunches erm. *Crest*—A wolf pass. or.

Hubbard (Freeby, co. Leicester). Gu. on a bend ar. three leopards' faces sa. *Crest*—A Saracen's head ppr.

Hubbard (Wyfordby, co. Leicester). Gu. on a bend sa. three annulets or. *Crest*—A wolf's head erased.

Hubbard (Barleythorpe, co. Rutland. Visit. Rutland, 1618). Ar. on a bend sa. nine annulets, three, three, and three, interlaced or.

Hubbard. Vert a chev. betw. three eagles' heads erased ar. ducally gorged gu.

Hubbard, or Hubert. Quarterly, ar. and sa. on a bend gu. three lions ramp. or.

Hubbert (Cork, Ireland, and Isle of Teneriffe). Az. a talbot ar. *Crest*—A boar's head sa.

Hubblethorn (co. York). Sa. a mascle, a tressure flory ar.

Huberk (quartered by CALVELLY). Ar. on a bend sa. three mascles or.

Hubersted (cos. Westmoreland and York). Vert a fesse or, betw. three moles sa.

Hubert (Sunbury, co. Middlesex). Quarterly, or and sa. on a bend gu. three lions ramp. of the first. *Crest*—On a chapeau gu. turned up erm. a lion's head erased or, charged with three estoiles in fesse of the first.

Hubert (extinct in Guernsey). Quarterly, or and sa. on a bend gu. three lions ramp. of the field. *Crest*—On a cap of maintenance a lion's head or.

Hubert (Burghe, co. Kent). Lozengy gu. and vair.

Hubert-Marshall. Barry of six ar. and sa. on a chev. engr. gu. three pheons or. *Crest*—A demi heraldic tiger sa. guttée d'or, armed, crined, tufted, and gorged with a collar gemel gold, resting the sinister paw upon an escutcheon gu. charged with a pheon also gold. *Motto*—Ducit amor patriæ.

Hubey, or Hulbey. Per pale ar. and sa. a chev. betw. three dolphins all counterchanged.

Huckbush. Az. ten plates, four, three, two, and one.

Huckel. Ar. a chev. betw. three oak leaves slipped vert.

Huckford. Or, an eagle displ. sa. collared ar.

Huckle. Per chev. embattled ar. and gu. three lions ramp. counterchanged.

Huckley, or Hukeley. Ar. two chevronels betw.

three oak leaves vert. *Crest*—A dexter hand supporting the German imperial crown ppr.

Huckling, Hurting, or Hurtynge. Ar. ten hurts, four, three, two, and one.

Huckmore, or Hugmore (Buckland Baron, co. Devon; the last heir male of this ancient family, Sir GREGORY HOCK-MORE, *d.* in 1678, leaving a dau. and heiress, *m.* into the GOULD family). Per chev. sa. and or, in chief four scythes conjoined two and two ar. the handles of the second, in base a moorcock of the first. *Crest*—A falcon ppr. preying on a moorcock sa. combed and wattled gu.

Huckmore (Bokeyt, co. Devon). Per chev. or and sa. in chief two pairs of sickles conjoined ar. handles or, in base a moorcock, bill and wattles gu. *Crest*—A falcon ppr. seizing on a moorcock, as in the arms.

Hucks. Ar. a chev. betw. three owls az. *Crest*—On a ducal coronet or, a fleur-de-lis ar.

Hucks (quartered by GIBBS, of Aldenham,' co. Herts, and Tyntesfield, co. Somerset). Ar. two chevronels betw. three owls az.

Hucksam (co. Devon). **Ar.** on a fesse sa. three crosses crosslet or, a bordure az.

Huckvile (co. Devon). Or. a bend betw. six trefoils slipped purp.

Huddesfield. Ar. a fesse betw. three boars sa. *Crest*—A boar pass. or.

Huddesdon, or Hudson (Gyles-Clift, co. Warwick, and Henvill, co. Sussex; confirmed by Cooke, Clarenceux, to THOMAS BEAUFOE, as the arms of WILLIAM HUDSON, or HUDDESON, of Guy's Cliff). Gu. a chev. ar. betw. six annulets or, two, two, and two, linked together paleways. *Crest* —An eagle's leg sa. joined at the knee to a sinister wing or.

Huddie (quartered by PRIDEAUX, of Throwborough, co. Devon. Visit. 1620). Ar. a fess indented per fess sa. and vert betw. two cotises of the second.

Huddleston (originally, before the Conquest, of Hodelston, co. York, and subsequently of Millum Castle, co. Cumberland; derived immediately from the marriage, *temp.* Henry III., of Sir JOHN DE HODELSTON, Knt., with JOAN, dau. and heir of ADAM DE BOIVILL, Lord of Millum; the heiress of this, the chief line of the family, was ELIZABETH, only child of WILLIAM HUDLESTON, Esq. of Millum, *m.* in 1748 to Sir HEDWORTH WILLIAMSON, Bart.). Gu. a fret ar. *Crest*— Two arms, dexter and sinister, embowed, vested ar. holding in their hands a scalp ppr. the inside gu.

Huddleston (Hutton John, co. Cumberland, a younger branch of the HUDDLESTONS, of Millum). *Arms*, &c. as the preceding.

Huddleston (Sawston, co. Cambridge; derived from Sir WILLIAM HODLESTON, Knt. (youngest son of Sir JOHN HODLEston, Lord of Millum, Sheriff of Cumberland, 35 Henry VI.), by the Lady ISABEL, his wife, fifth dau. and eventually co-heir of JOHN NEVILL, *Marquess of Montacute*). *Arms* and *Crest*, as the preceding. *Motto*—Soli Deo honor et gloria.

Huddleston (exemplified to Rev. GEORGE JAMES CROFT, of Upwell Hall, co. Cambridge, eldest son of the late GEORGE CROFT, Esq., who assumed in 1819 the name and arms of HUDDLESTON only, in pursuance of the will of GEORGE HUDDLESTON, Esq., of Croydon). Erm. a fret gu. in chief a lion pass. guard. sa. *Crest*—Two arms, dexter and sinister, embowed, vested erm. cuff gu. the hands supporting a dexter gauntlet erect ppr. encircled by a chaplet of roses gu.

Huddon. Quarterly, 1st and 4th, or, a man's leg couped above the knee az.; 2nd and 3rd, ar. on a fesse gu. five bezants, three and two.

Huddy (Stewel, co. Dorset). Ar. a fesse per fesse vert and sa. betw. two cotises counterchanged.

Huddy (co. Devon; granted 13 Feb. 1570). Ar. a fesse indented paly vert and sa. cotised of the second. *Crest*—A bull pass. sa. attired or, collared and lined ar.

Huddy (Hithway, co. Devon). Ar. a fesse indented per fesse sa. and vert betw. two cotises counterchanged of the fesse.

Huddy (Langnam, co. Somerset). Ar. a fesse indented paly vert and sa. *Crest*—A bull pass. sa. attired or.

Hudelston. Gu. fretty ar. a bordure or.

Hudelton (co. Chester). Ar. four erm. spots in cross sa.

Hudenett. Quarterly, per fesse indented or and gu. a label of five points az.

Hudleston. See HUDDLESTON.

Hudleston. Gu. fretty ar.

Hudson (Melton Mowbray, co. Leicester, bart., extinct). Per chev. embattled ar. and gu. three escallops counterchanged. *Crest*—A griffin's head erased ar. gorged with a mural crown gu. charged with three escallops of the first.

Hudson (Wanlip, co. Leicester, bart.; Sir CHARLES•THOMAS

HUDSON, second bart., assumed the surname of PALMER by royal licence, 1813. See PALMER, Bart., of Wanlip). Per chev. embattled or and az. three martlets counterchanged. *Crest*—A martlet or.

Hudson (London). Quarterly, per fesse embattled or and sa. three martlets counterchanged. *Crest*—A dexter hand erect, holding with the thumb and forefinger a bezant ppr.

Hudson (London). Per chev. embattled or and vert three martlets counterchanged. *Crest*—A martlet vert winged or.

Hudson (Park Crescent, Portland Place). Or, on a fesse betw. three boars' heads couped gu. as many lions ramp. of the field. *Crest*—A lion's head erased or.

Hudson. Gu. on a fesse or, betw. three boars' heads erased ar. as many lions ramp. sa. *Crest*—A lion holding a boar's head erased betw. the forepaws all ppr.

Hudson (Preston, co. Lancaster). Same *Arms*, the boars' heads couped. *Crest*—A lion ramp. or, holding betw. the paws a boar's head couped sa.

Hudson. Per chev. embattled or and az. three martlets-counterchanged. *Crest*—A martlet sa. wings or. *Another Crest*—On a rock ar. a martlet or (another, on a tower ar. a martlet az.).

Hudson (DONALDSON-HUDSON, Cheswardine Hall, co. Chester; exemplified to CHARLES DONALDSON, Esq., second son of JOHN DONALDSON, and grandson of ALEXANDER DONALDSON, by ELIZABETH HUDSON, his wife, upon taking the additional name and arms of HUDSON, by royal licence, 30 Jan. 1862, on succeeding to the estates of his great uncle, THOMAS HUDSON, Esq.). Quarterly, 1st and 4th, on a fesse dancettée sa. two boars' heads couped in chief and a lion ramp. in base gu. two martlets of the field, for HUDSON; 2nd and 3rd, ar. a lymphad sa. betw. three dolphins naiant az., for DONALDSON. *Crest*:— 1st: Upon a mill-rind fesseways sa. a lion's head erased or, gorged with a bar gemel indented gu., for HUD-ON; 2nd: In front of a saltire az. a cubit arm erect grasping a dagger and charged with a thistle slipped both ppr., for DONALDSON.

Hudson (granted 10 April, 1766, to ELIZABETH HUDSON, dau. and heir of THOMAS WILSON, of Burlington, co. York, merchant, relict of BENJAMIN HUDSON, of Burlington, eldest son of WILLIAM HUDSON, of the same place, merchant; the arms of HUDSON to be borne by the descendants of WILLIAM, and the arms of WILSON by her descendants as a quartering). Per chev. embattled or and az. three martlets counterchanged, two and one, those in chief charged on the breast with a fret of the first, and that in base with a fret sa. *Arms* of WILSON —Sa. a wolf saliant or, plain collared az. in chief three estoiles ar.

Hudson. Ar. a cross moline betw. two lozenges in chief and a boar's head couped in base sa. armed or.

Hudson (WILLIAM HUDSON, Esq., of Frogmore Lodge, co. Herts.) Gu. on a fesse betw. three boars' heads erased ar. as many lions ramp. sa. *Crest*—A lion ramp. holding a boar's head erased all ppr.

Hudson (co. York, now of Low Hall, Scarborough). Gu. three falchions ar. hilts and pommels or. *Crest*—A cubit arm erect in coat of mail, holding in the hand all ppr. a broken falchion gu. The family now quarter az. a maunch or, through a marriage with a CONYERS, co. York.

Hudson's Bay Company (incorporated 21 Charles II., 1670). Ar. a cross gu. betw. four beavers pass. ppr. *Crest* —On a chapeau gu. turned up erm. a squirrel sejant ppr. *Supporters*—Two bucks ppr. *Motto*—Pro pelle cutem.

Hudwel (co. Devon). Ar. a fesse betw. three bears pass. sa.

Hue (Jersey). Ar. three bears' heads cabossed sa.

Hue (Normandy, after of Jersey). Az. an eagle displ. or, in chief two mullets of the second.

Huet. Gu. a pale erm. *Crest*—A crow rising ppr.

Huge. Ar. on a chief gu. two mullets or, pierced vert.

Huger (South Carolina; granted 1771). Ar. a human heart emitting flames betw. two laurel branches fructed saltire-ways in chief, and an anchor erect in base all ppr. betw. two flaunches az. each charged with a fleur-de-lis or. *Crest*—A sprig, thereon a Virginian nightingale all ppr. *Motto*—Ubi libertas ibi patria.

Hugesson (The Paddock, co. Kent; granted to HUGHE HUGESSINE by the *Duke of Vandomme*, and subsequently confirmed to his descendants in England, by a grant in 1624 from Sir William Segar). Ar. on a mount vert in base an oak tree ppr. betw. two boars combatant sa. armed and tusked or. *Crest*—A tree, as in the arms, betw. two wings az.

Hugesson (Linsted, co. Kent). Or, on a mount an oak tree ppr. betw. two boars combatant az. *Crest*—An oak tree betw. two wings erect.

Hugessen (Norton, co. Kent). Ar. on a mount vert an oak tree ppr. betw. two boars erect sa. armed or.

Hugford. Az. three harts' heads cabossed or. *Crest*—A lion's paw resting upon a shield.

Hugford, Hugforde, or Hukeford (co. Gloucester, *temp.* Edward I.). Or, an eagle displ. sa.

Hugford, or Huggeford. Vert on a chev. or, betw. three bulls' heads cabossed of the second as many mullets pierced gu.

Hugford. Gu. three bucks' heads cabossed ar.

Hugford (Dicklestone, *alias* Dixton, co. Gloucester, Wollas Hall, co. Worcester, and co. Warwick; confirmed to JOHN HUGFORD, of Henwood, seventh in descent from ROBERT HUGFORD, of Edmondscott). Vert on a chev. betw. three bucks' heads cabossed or, as many mullets gu. *Crest*—A stag's head or, gorged with a chaplet of laurel vert.

Huggard. Az. an estoile or.

Huggen. Or, on a fesse betw. three crosses crosslet sa. as many escallops of the field.

Hugget (co. Kent). Gu. a chev. betw. three bucks' heads cabossed or.

Huggins (London). Erm. a chev. vair betw. three lozenges az. on each a lion's gamb erect and erased ar. *Crest*—A sword in pale, enfiled with a leopard's face.

Huggins (granted 15 June, 1725, to JOHN HUGGINS, Esq., Warden of the Fleet Prison, London). Erm. a chev. vaire or and gu. betw. three lozenges az. each charged with a lion's gamb erased and erect ar.

Hugh (co. Lincoln). Az. a saltire erm. betw. four fleurs-de-lis or.

Hugh. Az. a chev. engr. betw. three leopards' faces or, langued ar.

Hugham. Ar. two chevronels sa. *Crest*—A fox's head ar. semée of torteaux.

Hughan (Airds, co. Kirkcudbright, 1862). Ar. on a fess sa. betw. two cross crosslets in chief of the second and in base a demi lion gu. issuing out of a bar wavy az. three escallops or. *Crest*—An escallop or. *Motto*—E mari.

Hughes (Gwerclas, in Edeirnion, co. Merioneth; derived from OWAIN BROGYNTYN, Lord of Edeirnion, Dinmael, and Abertenant, in Powys-Fadoc). Ar. a lion ramp. sa. armed and langued gu. *Crests*—1st, HUGHES, of Gwerclas: A demi lion ramp. sa. issuing out of a ducal coronet; 2nd, ROGERS, of Bryntangor: A boar pass. fretty gu.; 3rd: On a chapeau az. turned up erm. a dragon gu. gorged with an ancient regal crown, cognizance of the ancient Princes of Wales. *Supporters*—Dexter, a lion sa.; sinister, a dragon gu. *Motto* — Kymmer-yn-Edeirnion.

Hughes (Plas yn Diserth and Llewerllyd, co. Flint; derived by uninterrupted male succession from CADWALLADR, second son of GRIFFITH AP CYNAN, King of North Wales, and his second wife DYDDGY, dau. of MEREDITH AP BLEDDYN AP CYNFYN, Prince of Powys). Gu. two lions pass. and a rose in chief ar. *Crest* (granted by St. George, Norroy, 1620, to WILLIAM HUGHES, Esq., of Llewerllyd)—Out of a coronet or, a demi lion ar. holding a rose gu. stem and leaves vert.

Hughes (Kinmel Park, co. Denbigh. The present representative, HUGH ROBERT HUGHES, Esq., of Kinmel, Lord-Lieut. co. Flint, is nephew of WILLIAM LEWIS, first Lord Dinorben, and grandson of Rev. EDWARD HUGHES, A.M., of Kinmel Park, by MARY LEWIS, his wife, niece and heiress of WILLIAM LEWIS, Esq., of Llysdulas, co. Anglesea). Gu. two lions pass. and a rose in chief ar. *Crest*—Out of a ducal coronet or, a demi lion ramp, ar. holding betw. the paws a rose gu. slipped ppr. *Motto*—Heb Dduw heb ddim, Duw a digon.

Hughes (Tregib, co. Carmarthen). Gu. a lion ramp. or, in a true love knot ar. betw. four fleurs-de-lis, their stalks bending towards the centre of the second.

Hughes (Alltlwyd, co. Cardigan). Ar. a chev. betw. three fleurs-de-lis az. on a chief of the last a mullet pierced of the field. *Crest*—On a chapeau gu. turned up erm. a demi lion ramp. holding in the dexter paw a fleur-de-lis. *Motto*—Y cyflawn sydd hy megis Llew.

Hughes (Plâs Côch, co. Anglesea). Ar. a chev. erm. betw. three Cornish choughs ppr. each holding in the beak an erm. spot. *Crest*—A Cornish chough ppr. *Motto*—Duw a ddarpar i'r brain.

Hughes (Plâs-yn-Llangoed, co. Anglesea). Same *Arms*, &c.

Hughes (Bodwryn, co. Anglesea). Ar. an eagle with two heads displ. sa. *Crest*—An eagle's head erased sa. in the beak a brand raguly of the same fired gu. *Motto*—A fynno Duw, derfyd.

Hughes (Ystradd, co. Denbigh). Or, three lions couchant sa. *Crest*—A lion couchant sa.

Hughes (Brecon). Sa. a chev. betw. three fleurs-de-lis or. *Crest*—An arm in armour ppr. holding a fleur-de-lis ar.

516

Hughes (Trostrey, co. Monmouth; borne by ROBERT HUGHES, Esq., of Cheltenham). Sa. a chev. betw. three fleurs-de-lis ar. *Crest*—A hand in armour ppr. couped above the wrist lying fesseways, and holding in the hand a fleur-de-lis ar.

Hughes (East Bergholt, co. Suffolk, bart.). Az. a lion ramp. or. *Crest*—A lion couchant or.

Hughes (Wells, co. Somerset). Same *Arms* and *Crest*.

Hughes (Donnington Priory, co. Berks). Quarterly, 1st and 4th, sa. a fesse cotised betw. three lions' heads erased ar.; 2nd, az. three arrows, points downwards or. on a chief of the second three Moors' heads couped sidefaced sa.; 3rd, ar. a chev. erm. betw. three unicorns' heads capped sa.

Hughes (Rev. HUGH HUGHES, of Nuneaton, co. Warwick). Erm. a lion ramp. gu. a bordure sa. fretty or. *Crest*—In front of a griffin's head erased sa. a fret or.

Hughes (WILLIAM HUGHES HUGHES, Esq., of Clapham Common, co. Surrey, and Ryde. Isle of Wight, M.P. for Oxford in four Parliaments, eldest son of JOHN HEWITT, Esq., of Clapham, by SOPHIA his wife, only child of the late WILLIAM HUGHES, Esq., of Clapham). Ar. on a pile engr. az. betw. two escallops in fesse gu. a lion ramp. of the field. *Crest*—In front of a staff raguly fesseways ppr. and thereon a lion couchant az. holding betw. the paws an escallop, as in the arms, a tilting spear erect or. *Motto*—Semper vigilans.

Hughes (Sherdley Hall, co. Lancaster). Gu. two lions pass. in pale and a rose in chief ar. *Crest*—Out of a ducal coronet or, a demi lion ramp. ar. holding betw. the paws a white rose ppr. *Motto*—Heb Dduw heb ddim, Duw a digon.

Hughes (Maidstone, co. Kent). Gu. on a bend ar. three fleurs-de-lis, in chief a demi lion ramp. *Crest*—On a chapeau gu. turned up erm. a demi eagle with wings elevated.

Hughes (Middleton Stoney, co. Oxford; MICHAEL HUGHES, son of JOHN HUGHES, descended from co. Carnarvon. Visit. 1634). Gu. on a bend betw. two demi lions ramp. ar. three fleurs-de-lis sa. *Crest*—A heron ar. beaked gu.

Hughes (co. Northampton). Ar. on a bend gu. betw. two demi lions ramp. couped ppr. three fleurs-de-lis or.

Hughes. Ar. a chev. betw. three fleurs-de-lis gu. *Crest*—A lion ramp. or, holding a thistle slipped ppr.

Hughes. Gu. a fret ar. on a canton or, a pheon of the field.

Hughes. Ar. fretty gu. a canton erm.

Hughes (Archerstown, co. Tipperary). Gu. on a chev. ar. betw. three griffins' heads erased or, three mullets az. *Crest*—A demi griffin or. *Motto*—Non sibi sed patriæ.

Hughes (confirmed to Sir FREDERIC HUGHES, Knt., K.L.S., eldest surviving son of ROBERT HUGHES, Esq., of Ely House, co. Wexford, and the other descendants of his grandfather). Or, on a chev. sa. betw. three griffins' heads erased ar. a fleur-de-lis betw. two mullets of the field. *Crest*—A griffin's head erased gu. holding in the beak a fleur-de-lis or. *Motto*—Verus amor patriæ.

Hughes (Reg. Ulster's Office). Gu. a chev. betw. three lions ramp. or. *Crest*—A lion ramp. ar.

Hughson. Quarterly, gu. and erm. in the 1st quarter a lion ramp. or, over all an eagle displ. of the last.

Hughton (Scotland). Ar. three piles issuing from a chief sa.

Hugo (co. Devon). Az. on a bend engr. ar. three trees eradicated vert. *Crest*—A lion ramp. holding in the paws a standard ar. charged with a cross gu.

Hugo. Ar. a lion ramp. az. crowned or, a bordure az.

Hugo. Gu. fretty or, a bordure az.

Hugo de Grandmesnil. Gu. a pale or.

Hugon. Ar. on a chev. vairé or and gu. betw. three hurts, a hurt charged with a lion's head erased of the field.

Hugworthy (quartered by PRIDEAUX, of Throwborough, co. Devon. Visit. 1620). Ar. a fess gu. betw. three pellets.

Huish (Gosport and Portsmouth). Ar. on a fesse sa. a lion pass. ar. *Crest*—Out of a ducal coronet or, a plume of feathers ar. These arms are entered in the Alphabet of Arms, Heralds' Office, as "HUISH, HUSEY, or HUSSEY, of Nottingham."

Huish. See HUYSH.

Huish (Sand-in-Sidburie, co. Devon, London. and Doniford, co. Somerset; ROWLAND HUISH, of Sand. Visit. 1620). See HUYSHE.

Huitson (Cleaseby, co. York). Az. an estoile of sixteen points or.

Hulbat (Farnham, co. Surrey). Sa. a cross betw. four leopards' faces jessant-de-lis or.

Hulbert (granted March, 1639). Quarterly, ar. and sa. in the sinister chief and dexter base a lion ramp. or, over all a bend gu. charged with three annulets of the third.

Hulbert. Az. a bend erm. betw. six nullets ar.

Huleys. Az. three eagles displ. or, over all a bend engr. gu.

Hulford (co. Gloucester). Ar. an eagle displ. sa.   *Crest*—A dexter hand holding an oak branch ppr.

Hulghton. Gu. a lion pass. ar.

Hulgrave (co. Chester). Ar. a bend betw. six martlets gu. *Crest*—A hand holding a thunderbolt ppr.

Hulgrave. See HOLGRAVE.

Hulgreve, or Hulgreeve (Minshull Vernon, co. Chester). Erm. an inescutcheon gu.

Hulin, or Hulyn (Lord Mayor of London, 1459). Ar. a chev. az. a bordure engr. sa.

Hulke. Per chev. crenellée ar. and gu. three lions ramp. counterchanged.

Hulkeford (co. Gloucester). Ar. an eagle displ. sa. ducally gorged of the field (another, or, an eagle displ. sa. collared ar.).

Hull, Town of (co. York). Az. three ducal coronets in pale or.

Hull (co. Buckingham, Larkbeare, co. Devon, Osterley, co. Durham, Battersea, co. Surrey, and London, 1616). Sa. a chev. erm. betw. three talbots' heads erased ar. *Crest*—A talbot's head erased ar. betw. two laurel branches ppr. united at the top.

Hull (Battersea, co. Surrey; confirmed 25 Jan. 1624). Same *Arms* and *Crest*. *Another Crest*—A talbot's head erased ar. collared gu.

Hull (St. Leonard's, co. Cornwall, and Oxford). Sa. a chev. betw. three talbots' heads erased ar.

Hull (co. Cornwall). Ar. a chev. gu. betw. three water bougets sa.

Hull (co. Devon). Az. a chev. ar. betw. three chaplets or.

Hull (Child-Ockford, co. Dorset, *temp.* Henry III.). Or, a bull pass. sa. collared and belled gold.

Hull (co. Durham). Per pale az. and gu. a chev. or, betw. three fleurs-de-lis ar. *Crest*—A cubit arm grasping a fleur-de-lis ar.

Hull, alias Hill (Olneston, co. Gloucester). Az. on a chev. betw. three owls ar. as many mullets sa. a bordure engr. erm.

Hull (Hammersmith, co. Middlesex). Sa. a chev. embattled betw. three talbots' heads erased ar.

Hull (co. Stafford). Ar. a chev. gu. (another, sa.) betw. three water bougets sa.

Hull (Hameldon, co. Surrey). Ar. on a chev. az. betw. three demi lions ramp. gu. as many plates (another, bezants).

Hull (co. Surrey). Ar. on a chev. az. betw. three demi lions gu. as many bezants, on a chief sa. two piles of the field. *Crest*—A dragon's head couped ar. eared gu. collared or, charged with three torteaux, on the neck a pale ar. betw. four plates.

Hull, or Hall. Az. an eagle displ. or. *Crest*—A hunting horn az. garnished ar.

Hull. Per fesse or and ar. three suns sa. (another, ar. a pale lozengy gu. on the second a mullet or ; another, or, three roses gu.; another, erm. three fusils gu.; another, per pale ar. and sa. a chev. betw. three dolphins naiant counterchanged.

Hull (impalement Fun. Ent. Ulster's Office, 1662). Ar. on a chev. az. betw. three demi lions ramp. gu. as many bezants, a chief point en point sa. and of the first.

Hull (Clonakilty, co. Cork; Fun. Ent. 1637, HENRY HULL, brother of Sir WILLIAM HULL, Knt., sons of HENRY HULL, Esq., of Exeter, co. Devon; descended from a second son of HULL, of Larkbeare, in same co.). Sa. a chev. erm. betw. three talbots' heads erased ar. *Crest*—A talbot's head couped ar.

Hull. See HILL.

Hullcott. See HOLCOTT.

Hullers. Az. an eagle displ. ar.

Hullers. See HULLEYS.

Hulles, Hulse, Hulsey, Huls, or Howes (Newbury, co. Berks and Betherden, co. Kent). Ar. three piles, one issuing out of the chief betw. two others, reversed sa. *Crest*—A buck's head couped ppr. attired or, betw. the attires a sun of the last.

Hulles (co. Berks). Sa. two piles ar.

Hulles (co. Chester). Ar. two (another, three) piles sa.

Hulles, or Hulls. Az. a chev. betw. three fleurs-de-lis or.

Hulles, or Hulse (Sutton Courtenay, co. Berks; MALLYN, dau. of ANDREW HULLES, or HULSE, of that place, *m.* JAMES YATE, Esq., of Stanlake, co. Oxford. Visit. Oxon, 1574). Ar. three piles from the chief sa.

Hulles. Az. an eagle displ. ar. membered or.

Hulles, or Hules. Az. a chev. ar. betw. three fleurs-de-lis or.

Hullewell. Ar. on a chev. sa. three bezants.

Hulleys, or Hullers (co. Cambridge). Az. an eagle displ. ar. a baton in bend gu.

Hulley, Hullies, and Hullys. Same *Arms*. *Crest*—Out of a ducal coronet or, a unicorn's head gu.

Hulleys, or Hullies. Az. three eagles displ. or, over all a bend engr. gu.

Hulling, or Hullingey. Erm. three roses gu. *Crest*—A demi savage holding over the shoulder a tree eradicated, and bound round the waist and temples with leaves ppr.

Hullock (Barnard Castle, co. Durham; borne by Sir JOHN HULLOCK, Baron of the Exchequer, 1825). Ar. a chev. vair betw. three Moors' heads couped at the neck in profile ppr. *Crest*—An ostrich's head couped ar. betw. two ostrich wings gu. in the mouth a horseshoe or.

Hulls. See HULLES.

Hullys. See HULLEYS.

Hulme (MICHAEL HULME, brother to WALTER HULME, and heir to JAMES HULME, his nephew, *temp*. William the Conqueror, ancestor of Sir MICHAEL MANNOURS, Knt., 39 Henry III. Visit. Notts, 1631). Ar. six annulets, two, two, and two sa.

Hulme (Hulme, co. Lancaster). Barry of eight or and az. on a canton or, a chaplet gu.

Hulme (Reddish, co. Lancaster). Same *Arms*.

Hulme (Ball-Hay House, near Leek, co. Stafford). Ar. a chev. ermines betw. three crosses crosslet fitchée sa.

Hulme. See HOLME.

Huls (Norbury, co. Chester; granted 1566). Same *Arms* as HULLES. *Crest*—A stag's head ppr. attired sa. gorged with a chaplet vert, betw. the horns a sun or.

Hulse (Breamore House, co. Hants. bart.). Ar. three piles, one issuing from the chief betw. the others reversed sa. *Crest*—A buck's head couped ppr. attired or, betw. the attires a sun of the last.

Hulse (Rethersden, co. Kent). Same *Arms*.

Hulse (Norbury, co. Chester). Ar. three piles, one issuant from chief and two from base sa. *Crest*—A buck's head couped ppr. collared or, betw. the horns a sun of the last.

Hulse (Mobberley, co. Chester). Ar. three piles in point sa.

Hulse, and Hulsey. See HULLES.

Hulson (London and co. York; granted 10 Feb. 1577). Ar. on a canton sa. three cronels (another, ducal crowns) in bend or. *Crest*—A lion ramp. sa. holding a shield ar. within a carved bordure.

Hulston. Same *Arms*. *Crest*—A lion ramp. sa. holding an escutcheon ar. betw. his forepaws.

Hulston. Ar. fretty gu.

Hulton (Hulton, co. Lancaster). Ar. a lion ramp. gu. armed and langued az. *Crest*—Out of a ducal coronet or, a hart's head and neck cabossed ar. betw. two branches of hawthorn ppr. *Motto*—Mens flecti nescia. The following grant of the crest was made to the family by Dalton, Norroy, 1561: "Know ye that I, Norrey Kynge of Arms above-said, considering that ADAM HYLTON, of Hylton, in the county of Lancaster, and hys ancestors, have long continued in noblynes, bearing arms, which be sylver, a lyon ramp. gewles armed and langued asure, quartered with sylver, a lyon ramp. gewles crouned gold, armed and langued asuré, which he beareth for ALYCE, daughter and sole heire to JOHN HYLTON, of Farnworth. Yet wanting a crest, badge, or cognizance, hath desired me, &c. that is to say, upon a helmet, on a wreathe gewles, a crowne golde, thereout issuing a hart's head and necke, cabowshed sylver, horned golde, betwene two branches of hawthorn ppr."

Hulton-Harrop (Bardsley, co. Lancaster). Quarterly, 1st and 4th, per chev. ar. and sa. three eagles displ. collared and charged on the breast with a fleur-de-lis all counterchanged, for HARROP; 2nd and 3rd, ar. a lion ramp. gu., for HULTON. *Crests*—1st, HARROP: In front of a saltire or, an eagle displ. sa. crusily ar.; 2nd, HULTON: In a ducal crown or, a stag's head with two branches of fructed hawthorn ppr. *Motto*—Terrena pericula sperno.

Hulton (Farnworth, co. Lancaster, 1567). Or, an eagle displ. gu. beaked and membered az.

Hulton (EDWARD HORNE HULTON, Esq., eldest son of the late HENRY HULTON, Esq., of Bevis Mount, co. Hants, Barrister-at-law, and Recorder of King's Lynn, brother of THOMAS HULTON, Esq., of Wroxham Hall, co. Norfolk, who assumed the surname and arms of PRESTON, by sign manual, in 1805, and was created a bart. in 1814). Quarterly, 1st and 4th, ar. a lion ramp. double queuéd gu.; 2nd, az. a lion ramp. barruly ar. and gu.; 3rd, quarterly, sa. and or, in the first quarter a lion pass. of the second, for BOWDEN. *Crest*—Out of a ducal coronet or, a hart's head ppr. attired of the first betw. two branches also ppr. each bearing three roses gu.

Hulton (Donington, co. Linc., & Parke). Ar. a lion ramp. gu.

Hulton. Az. a lion ramp. barry of six ar. and gu.

Hulton. Az. a lion ramp. vairé ar. and gu.

Hulton. Gu. a lion ramp. ar. fretty az.

Humberston (Walkerne, co. Herts, and co. Norfolk). Ar. three bars sa. in chief as many. pellets. *Crest*—A griffin's head erased ar. charged with three pellets in pale.

Humberston (Mollington Banastre, co. Chester, formerly of Gwersyllt Park, co. Denbigh). Same as last.

Humble (Stratford, co. Essex, and London, 1634). Sa. a buck trippant or, a chief indented of the last. *Crest*—On a chapeau an owl rising all ppr.

Humble (London, bart. ; extinct 1745, created 1660). Same *Arms*. *Crest*—A demi buck gorged with a wreath of laurel ppr.

Humble (Kensington; created a bart. 1687, extinct 1705). Same *Arms* and *Crest*.

Humble (Cloncoskoran, co. Waterford, bart.). Quarterly, 1st and 4th, sa. a stag trippant or, on a chief dancettée ar. a trefoil vert, for HUMBLE; 2nd and 3rd, erm. two bars gu. a fleur-de-lis for cadency, for NUGENT. *Crest*—A demi stag ppr. horned or, charged on the breast with a trefoil vert. *Motto*—Decrevi.

Humby (granted to GEORGE HUMBY, Esq., of Bedford Row, in the parish of St. Andrew, co. Middlesex). Gu. an eagle displ. in chief three bees or. *Crest*—An eagle displ. gu. charged on the breast and on either wing with a bee or.

Hume (Castle-Hume, co. Fermanagh, bart., extinct 1750; the heiress m. LOFTUS). Quarterly, 1st and 4th grand quarters, quarterly, 1st, vert a lion ramp. ar., for HUME, 2nd, ar. three piles engr. gu., for POLWORTH, 3rd, ar. a cross engr. az., for SINCLAIR, 4th, ar. three popinjays vert, beaked and legged gu., for PEPDIE; 2nd and 3rd grand quarters, quarterly, 1st and 4th, gu. three cinquefoils pierced erm., for HAMILTON, 2nd and 3rd, ar. a lymphad sa., for ARRAN. *Crest*—An heraldic tiger's head erased ar. *Motto*—True to the end.

Hume (exemplified to NICHOLAS LOFTUS, Esq., of Loftus Hall, by Hawkins, Ulster, 1736, upon his marriage with MARY HUME. only dau. and heir of Sir GUSTAVUS HUME, Bart., of Castle-Hume, when he adopted the surname of HUME). Quarterly, 1st, vert a lion ramp. ar., for HUME; 2nd, sa. a chev. engr. betw. three trefoils ar., for LOFTUS; 3rd, gyronny of eight ar. and sa. a saltire engr. betw. four fleurs-de-lis, the ends converging towards the centre all counterchanged, also for LOFTUS; 4th, or, a chev. gu. betw. three buglehorns sa. stringed az., for CREWKERN. On an escutcheon of pretence the arms of HUME, Bart., of Castle-Hume, as above. *Crest* and *Motto* same as LOFTUS, Earl of Ely.

Hume (*Earl of Marchmont*). Quarterly, 1st grand quarter counterquartered, 1st and 4th, vert a lion ramp. ar. armed and langued gu., for HUME, 2nd and 3rd ar. three popinjays vert, beaked and membered gu., for PEPDIE; 2nd, ar. three piles engr. gu. issuing from the chief, for POLWORTH; 3rd, ar. a cross engr. az., for ST. CLAIR; 4th, as the first; over all in the centre an escutcheon ar. charged with an orange ppr. stalked and slipped vert, ensigned with an imperial crown ppr. *Crest*—Out of a human heart a dexter arm erect, holding a scymitar all ppr. *Supporters*—Two lions reguard. ar. armed and langued gu. *Motto*—True to the end.

Hume (Ninewells, co. Berwick; lands now owned by the heir female, paternally a Ross). Vert a lion ramp. ar. within a bordure or, charged with eight fountains barry wavy of the first and second. *Crest*—A lion's head erased ar. gorged with a collar gu. charged with fountains as the bordure. *Motto*—True to the end.

Hume (Whitfield, co. Edinburgh; cadet of Ninewells). Quarterly, 1st and 4th, as NINEWELLS; 2nd, PEPDIE; 3rd, ar. a stag's head erased gu. betw. the attires a cross crosslet fitchée of the last, for CAIRNCROSS. *Crest*—A lion's head erased ar. gorged with a collar or, charged with three mullets gu. *Motto*—True to the end.

Hume (Harries, 1802). Vert a lion ramp. az. armed and langued or, within a bordure engr. erminois, on a chief of the second three pepingoes of the first, beaked and membered gu. *Crest*—A lion's head ppr. *Motto*—True to the end.

Hume (Auchindolly, co. Kirkcudbright, 1867). Per fess vert and ar. a lion ramp. counterchanged. *Crest*—A lion's head erased gu. *Motto*—True to the end.

Hume (other branches of the family). See under HOME.

Humerston. Erm. a saltire componée or and gu. betw. four bezants.

Humet (Sandford, co. Lincoln, Constable of Normandy, *temp.* Henry II.). Ar. a bordure gu. bezantée.

Humffreys (Llwyn, co. Montgomery; descended paternally from IDNERTH BENVRAS, Lord of Maesbrook, and, by an

518

heir female, from OSBORNE FITZGERALD, a scion of the house of DESMOND, who settled in Wales in the 13th century, having migrated from Ireland to support the cause of Prince Llewellyn, with whom he was a favourite). Quarterly, 1st and 4th, ar. a cross flory engr. sa. betw. four Cornish choughs ppr. on a chief az. a boar's head couped ar. tusked or, langued gu.; 2nd and 3rd, erm. a saltire engr. gu. thereon a crescent or. *Crest*—On a chapeau a boar pass. ar. fretty gu. more usually described and depicted as "a boar in a net."

Humfines. Ar. three lions pass. gu.

Humfray (Reg. Ulster's Office). Sa. two palets erm.

Humfreston (co. Hants). Ar. an eagle displ. with two heads sa. over all on a chev. gu. three roses or.

Humfreston (Humfreston, co. Salop). Ar. an eagle displ. vert, over all on a chev. gu. three roses of the field.

Humfrevile. Az. billettée a cinquefoil within a bordure ar. charged with a horseshoe sa.

Humfrevyle (JOHN HUMFREVYLE, *temp.* Edward I. m. MARGARET, dau. of Sir WILLIAM HARBOTTLE, Knt., co. Northumberland. Visit. Rutland, 1618). Gu. a cinquefoil or, surmounted by a bend az.

Humfrey (Truro, co. Cornwall). Gu. a cross botonnée ar. charged with four escallops sa. *Crest*—On a mount vert a Cornish chough ar. wings expanded, beaked and legged gu. gorged with a bar gemelle or.

Humfrey (Chaldon-Humfrey, co. Dorset). Gu. a cross botonée ar. quarter pierced of the field, charged with twelve escallops sa. *Crest*—A leopard pass. or, embrued at the mouth gu.

Humfrey (cos. Gloucester and Northampten). Gu. on a cross botonée ar. five pellets. *Crest*—A cross botonée ar. charged with five pellets.

Humfrey (Rottendon, co. Essex). Quarterly, 1st and 4th, gu. a cross botonée ar. charged with five pellets; 2nd, ar. on a chev. betw. three rooks' heads erased sa. as many mullets of the first; 3rd, ar. three bars gemel sa., for CABSWELL. *Crest*—A dexter arm in armour, holding in the hand all ppr. a cross botonée fitchée ar. charged with four pellets.

Humfrey (Leicester and Barton, co. Northampton). Same *Arms* as Chaldon Humfrey, co. Dorset). *Crest*—A harpy ar. face ppr. crined or, wings expanded of the last.

Humfrey (London; granted 20 June, 1562, by Hervey, Clarenceux, to WILLIAM HUMFREY, "Saye Master to the Queen's Mint"). Sa. a chev. engr. or, betw. three bezants, on a chief of the second a rose gu. betw. two fleurs-de-lis az. *Crest*—A horse's head or, pellettée betw. two wings barry wavy of six ar. and az.

Humfrey (London). Same as HUMFREYS, London and Wales.

Humfrey. Or, on a chev. betw. three fleurs-de-lis sa. as many bezants.

Humfrey. Quarterly, ar. and sa.

Humfrey (Wroxham House, co. Norfolk). Quarterly, 1st and 4th, gu. a lion ramp. and above the head a ducal coronet or, with a canton of the last for distinction, for HUMFREY; 2nd and 3rd, ar. a chev. betw. three garbs sa. within a bordure of the last, thereon eight fleurs-de-lis of the first, for BLAKE. *Crests*—1st, HUMFREY: On a ducal coronet an eagle. wings elevated, holding in the dexter claw a sceptre or, and charged on the breast, for distinction, with a cross crosslet gu.; 2nd, BLAKE: On a morion a martlet ppr. *Motto*—Cœlestem spero coronam.

Humfrey, or Humphrey. Sa. four palets erm.

Humfrey (Dublin; confirmed 26 Jan. 1638). Gu. a lion ramp. or, surmounted by a ducal coronet of the last, armed and langued az. *Crest*—On a ducal coronet an eagle with wings extended, holding in the dexter hand a broken spear all or.

Humfrey (Cavanacor, co. Donegal). Gu. on a cross botonée ar. five pellets. *Crest*—A sphinx sejant. *Motto*—Sic olim.

Humfrey (Fun. Ent. of KATHERINE, dau. of Alderman JOHN HUMFREY, of Dublin, and wife of Sir THADY DUFFY, Lord Mayor of Dublin, d. 3 March, 1622). Or, on a bend gu. three leopards' faces of the field.

Humfrey (Rishangles, co. Suffolk; confirmed 26 Jan. 1638). Same *Arms* and *Crest* as of Dublin.

Humfrey, or Humphrey (Holbroke and Dunkstone, co. Suffolk). Same *Arms* and *Crest* as of Dublin.

Humfreys, Humphreys, Humfrey, or Humfry (London and Wales; granted 22 April, 1717). Sa. three nags' heads erased ar. *Crest*—A lion sejant or, reposing the dexter foot upon a nag's head couped ermines.

Humphery (Penton Lodge, Andover, Surrey, bart.). Az. on a chev. or, betw. three gryphons' heads erased ar. a chaplet of oak vert, a chief of the second, thereon three martlets gu. *Crest*—A unicorn pass. ar. armed, crined, and hoofed or, the dexter foot supporting a Roman fasces in bend of the last. *Motto*—Deus protector meus.

Humphrey, Humphrie, or Humphry. Sa. three ostrich feathers ar. *Crest*—A demi griffin, wings endorsed, holding betw. the claws a ducal coronet ppr.

Humphrey (Swebston, co. Leicester, and Barton, co. Northampton. Visit. Leicester, 1619). Quarterly, 1st and 4th, az. a bend betw. four leopards' faces or; 2nd and 3rd, gu. a cross patonce ar. quarter pierced of the field, charged with four escallops sa. *Crest*—A harpy ar. crined or, wings displ. gold.

Humphrey (Barton, co. Northampton, and Shipson, co. Leicester; RICHARD HUMPHREY, of the former, and Sir THOMAS HUMPHREY, of the latter, Visit. Leicester, 1619, sons of WILLIAM HUMPHREY, fifth in descent from Sir PETER HUMPHRY, Knt., of Cirencester, co. Gloucester). Gu. a cross botonée ar. quarter pierced of the field, charged on each end with three escallops sa. *Crest*—A harpy ar. crined or, wings displ. gold.

Humphreys (Bishop of Bangor, 1697). Gu. a lion ramp. ar.

Humphreys. Gu. a cross patonce erm. *Crest*—A badger ppr.

Humphreys (London, bart.; extinct 1737; Sir WILLIAM HUMPHREYS, Knt., Lord Mayor of London, 1 George, 1714, was created a baronet same year). Sa. three nags' heads erased ar.

Humphreys (THOMAS HUMPHREYS, Esq., of Bodelwyddan, co. Flint, 1660). Ar. on a bend sa. three leopards' faces or.

Humphries (JAMES HUMPHRIES, Esq., of Ham Frith, co. Essex). Ar. a lion pass. guard. sa., quartering sa. three nags' heads erased ar. *Crest*—A nag's head erased ar.

Humphrys, Humphreys, Humphries, Humphris, and Humphryes. Ar. a lion pass. guard. sa. *Crest*—Three legs conjoined at the thigh flexed at the knee and spurred ppr.

Humphrys (Ballyhaise House, co. Cavan: granted to WILLIAM HUMPHRYS, Esq., J.P., D.L.). Gu. a lion ramp. superintending his head a ducal coronet or, in a canton ar. a trefoil slipped ppr. *Crest*—On a ducal coronet an eagle, wings endorsed or, armed and membered gu. in the dexter claw a broken spear head of the first. *Motto*—Optima sperando spiro.

Hun, or Hunne (cos. Essex and Kent; granted 8 Sept. 1572). Az. a lion ramp. guard. ar. *Crest*—A demi lion ramp. ar. ducally gorged or.

Hun. Az. a leopard ramp. (another, pass. ar.).

Hunden. Ar. a fesse embattled betw. three escallops gu.

Hundfield, or Hunfield. Quarterly, or and gu. in the 2nd and 3rd quarters each three plates.

Hundscot, or Hundescot. Erm. a bordure gu.

Hunesdon. Ar. a fesse counter-embattled betw. three escallops gu.

Hungate, or Hungatt (Saxton, Sandhutten, Burnby, and North Dalton, co. York, bart.; extinct 1749). Gu. a chev. engr. betw. three talbots sejant ar. *Crest*—A hound sejant ar.

Hungate. Gu. on a chev. engr. betw. three talbots ramp. ar. a mullet. *Crest*—On a mount vert a talbot pass. sa.

Hunger. Sa. two bars ar. betw. three plates. *Crest*—Two sickles interlaced ppr.

Hungerford (*Baron Hungerford*, Farley Castle, co. Somerset; Sir WALTER DE HUNGERFORD, K.G., of Farley Castle, Lord Treasurer, was summoned to Parliament as a baron in 1426; he was grandson of Sir WALTER DE HUNGERFORD, by ELIZABETH, his wife, dau. and heir of Sir ADAM FITZ-JOHN, Knt., of Chevill, co. Wilts, who was the grandson of WALTER DE HUNGERFORD, co. Berks, who m. MAUD, dau. and heir of JOHN DE HEYTESBURY, co. Wilts; vested in the *Earl of London*. The HUNGERFORDS appear to have borne for arms the coats of the heiresses with whom they intermarried; ROBERT, third *Baron Hungerford*, bore, quarterly, 1st, per pale indented gu. and vert a chev. or, HEYTESBURY; 2nd, sa. two bars ar. in chief three plates, FITZ-JOHN; 3rd, barry of six erm. and gu., HUSSEY; 4th, gu. three garbs ar. banded of the field, a chief of PEVERELL; 5th, ar. three toads erect sa., BOTREAUX; 6th, sa. on a chief ar. three lozenges gu., MOLINES. *Crest*—Out of a ducal coronet or, a garb betw. two sickles ppr. *Motto*—Et Dieu mon appuy. *Supporters*—Dexter, a griffin sa.; sinister, a bird with a long bill, wings expanded and chained sa.

Hungerford (*Baron Hungerford*, of Heytesbury; WALTER HUNGERFORD, brother of THOMAS, fourth *Lord Hungerford*, was summoned to Parliament 1536, attainted 1541). Same *Arms*, &c.

519

Hungerford (Down Ampney and Winrush, co. Gloucester; descended from Sir EDMUND HUNGERFORD, second son of WALTER, first *Lord Hungerford*). Sa. two bars ar. in chief three plates. *Crest*—Out of a ducal coronet or, a pepper garb of the first betw. two sickles erect ppr. *Motto*—Et Dieu mon appui.

Hungerford (GEORGE WALKER HUNGERFORD, Esq., of Calne, co. Wilts, whose only dau. m. JOHN, second *Lord Crewe*). Sa. two bars ar. in chief three plates, quartering HEYTESBURY, per pale indented gu. and vert a chev. or. *Crest*, as the last.

Hungerford. Or, on a chev. sa. betw. two chevronels gu. three martlets of the field, a chief vair. *Crest*—Out of a ducal coronet a garb or, betw. two sickles ppr. *Another Crest*—A martlet sa. betw. two palm branches or, in front of a cross formée fitchée of the last.

Hungerford. Az. a cross or, ringed at the ends, with a ring linked to each betw. four bezants, on a chief ar. a griffin pass. sa.

Hungerford. Gu. a chev. betw. three crosslets fitchée or.

Hungerford. Per pale indented or and vert a chev. gu.

Hungerford (Dingley, co. Northampton; exemplified to HENRY HUNGERFORD HOLDICH, Esq., of Dingley Park, High Sheriff in 1828, who succeeded to the estates of the late JOHN PEACH HUNGERFORD, Esq., M.P., and assumed the additional surname of HUNGERFORD). Quarterly, 1st and 4th, as HUNGERFORD, of Farley Castle; 2nd and 3rd, or, on a chev. sa. cotised gu. three martlets of the field, a chief vairé, for HOLDICH. *Crests*—1st, HUNGERFORD: As Farley Castle; 2nd: A martlet sa. in front of a cross pattée fitchée betw. two branches of palm or. *Motto*—Et Dieu mon appui.

Hungerford (confirmed by Roberts, Ulster, to Colonel ANTHONY HUNGERFORD, who arrived in Dublin with his regiment, 30 April 1647, son and heir of HENRY HUNGERFORD, Esq., of Marson, co. Wilts, and grandson of HENRY HUNGERFORD, Esq., of same place, the second son of Sir JOHN HUNGERFORD, Knt., of Down Ampney, co. Wilts). Sa. two bars ar. in chief three plates, a crescent sa. charged with another or, for diff. *Crest*—Out of a ducal coronet or, a garb gold betw. two sickles ppr.

Hungerford (Inchodony, or The Island, co. Cork; descended from Sir EDMUND HUNGERFORD, Knt., of Down Ampney, co. Gloucester. The connection of the Irish with the English house is traced by the will of JOHN HUNGERFORD, of Lincoln's Inn, 1729). Same *Arms* and *Crest*. *Motto*—Et Dieu mon appuy.

Hungerford (Cahirmore, co. Cork; a younger branch of HUNGERFORD, of The Island). Same *Arms*, *Crest*, and *Motto*.

Hungford (*temp.* Edward I.). Gu. three stags' heads cabossed ar. horned or.

Hungham. Ar. six chevronels sa. *Crest*—A dexter hand holding a pair of compasses, points upward, ppr.

Hunhulton. Ar. on a pale sa. three eagles displ. of the field.

Huning. Quarterly, az. and gu. over all a lion ramp. ar.

Huning (Huning, co. Fermanagh; URSULA, dau. of HENRY HUNING, of that place, m. HENRY FLOWER, Esq., then of Langer, co. Notts; CORDELL SAVILLE, of Clerkenwell, London, 1623, m. KATHERINE, dau. of EDWARD HUNINGS, of Aye, co. Suffolk. Visit. 1614). Quarterly, gu. and vert a lion ramp. ar.

Huninges (Chester, and Carsam, co. Suffolk). Quarterly, vert and gu. a lion ramp. ar. *Crest*—A lion's head erased ar. collared sa.

Huninges. Az. a lion ramp. ar. a chief or.

Hunke (Sir THOMAS HUNKE, knighted at Dublin Castle, by Sir ARTHUR CHICHESTER, Lord Deputy, 1605). Ar. three mullets sa. a bordure gu. bezantée.

Hunkerville. Vert three hatchets, or poleaxes, erect or.

Hunkes (co. Warwick. Harl. MSS. 6060). Ar. three mullets sa. a bordure gu. bezantée.

Hunkes, or Huncks (cos. Buckingham, Gloucester, Norfolk, Warwick, and Worcester). Gu. an inescutcheon ar. charged with three mullets sa. within an orle of eight bezants. *Crest*—A greyhound courant erm. collared and ringed sa.

Hunkin (Gatherley, co. Devon; JOHN HUNKIN, descended from WILLIAM HUNKYN, Esq., of Southkimbare, co. Cornwall, 27 Henry VI. Visit. 1620). Ar. a mascle sa. over all a fess of the last.

Hunkin (South Kimber and Liskeard, co. Cornwall). Same *Arms*.

Hunlock (London; granted 1587). Az. on a fesse betw. three tigers' heads erased or, as many mullets of the field. *Crest*—On a chapeau az. turned up erm. a cockatrice ppr.

Hunloke (Wingerworth, co. Derby, bart.). Az. a fesse betw. three tigers' heads erased or. *Crest*—On a chapeau az. turned up erm. a cockatrice, wings expanded ppr. combed, beaked, and wattled or.

Hunnis (co. Middlesex; granted 14 Feb. 1568). Bendy of six or and az. a unicorn ramp. vert, armed ar. *Crest*—Betw. two honeysuckles ppr. a unicorn's head couped or, charged with two bendlets az.

Hunsley. Sa. a fesse betw. three cinquefoils ar.

Hunsted. Gu. a chief chequy or and az.

Hunsten (Boston, co. Lincoln). Sa. four lozenges in cross erm. a bordure engr. ar.

Hunster, Hunt, or Huniste (cos. Bedford and Kent). Sa. a fesse betw. three cinquefoils or (another, ar.).

Hunston (Walpole, co. Norfolk; granted by patent, dated 6 Feb., 3 and 4 Philip and Mary). Sa. four lozenges, one, two, and one, erm. a bordure engr. or, quartering DENVERS and HALTOFT. *Crest*—A hind's head couped or, holding in the mouth a holly slip vert, fructed gu.

Hunt (Longnor, co. Salop, 1623). Per pale ar. and sa. on a saltire a crescent all counterchanged. *Crest*—A hind's head couped ar. wounded on the breast with a pheon sa. dropping blood ppr.

Hunt (Boreatton, co. Salop). Per pale ar. and sa. a saltire counterchanged. *Crest*—A talbot sejant sa. collared or, lined az. the line tied to a halbert in pale of the second, headed of the last.

Hunt (ROWLAND HUNT, Esq., of Lincoln's Inn). Per pale ar. and vert a saltire counterchanged, a canton erm.

Hunt (RICHARD BURGES HUNT, Esq.). Or, on a bend sa. betw. two water bougets az. a chev. betw. three pheons of the field, a chief gu. thereon three leopards' faces gold. *Crest*—A mount vert, thereon a talbot sejant or, gorged with a collar vair, attached by a ribband az. to a spear erect ppr. therefrom a banner flowing towards the sinister sa. charged with a pheon, as in the arms.

Hunt (HUSEY-HUNT, Comp'on Pauncefoot, co. Somerset). Quarterly, 1st and 4th, HUNT, az. two chevronels erm. betw. three martlets ar. a canton ar. for distinction; 2nd and 3rd, HUSEY, barry of six erm. and gu. a canton ar. for distinction. *Crests*—1st, HUNT: An arm embowed vested az. cuffed or, in the hand a slip of trefoil in blossom ppr.; 2nd, HUSEY: A boot sa. spurred or, topped erm. surmounted by a heart supported by two hands issuant from clouds ppr. and on an escroll above the words "Cor nobyle cor immobyle."

Hunt (Chalderston, co. Bedford). Ar. on a chev. within a bordure gu. an annulet or.

Hunt (Ashover, co. Derby, *temp.* Henry III., and Aston, same co., *temp.* Henry VIII.). Ar. a buglehorn sa. stringed vert, on a chief gu. three mullets pierced of the field (another, on a chief three roses or). *Crest*—A buglehorn, as in the arms.

Hunt (Chudleigh, co. Devon; traced in the Visit. of 1620 to the year 1500). Az. on a bend betw. two water bougets or, three leopards' faces gu. *Crest*—On a mount vert against a halbert erect in pale gu. headed ar. a talbot sejant or, collared and tied to the halbert of the second.

Hunt (Exeter, co. Devon; NICHOLAS HUNT, of that place, Visit. 1620, great-grandson of THOMAS HUNT, three times Mayor of Exeter). Same *Arms* and *Crest.*

Hunt (Stockgrave, co. Devon, and of Worcester). Gu. on a fesse betw. three cinquefoils or, a lion pass. of the field. *Crest*—A boar's head erect betw. two ostrich feathers sa.

Hunt (Romford, co. Essex). Per pale ar. and vert a saltire counterchanged, a canton erm. *Crest*—A talbot sejant sa. collared or, lined az. the line tied to a halbert in pale of the second, headed of the last.

Hunt (Hoggesback, co. Hereford). Sa. a fesse or, in chief two cinquefoils of the last.

Hunt (Lincoln's Inn). Az. a bend betw. six leopards' faces or. *Crest*—A stag's head erased ppr.

Hunt (Kilderveston, co. Norfolk). Per pale ar. and sa. a saltire counterchanged betw. four horseshoes gu.

Hunt (Hermyngtoft, co. Norfolk, and co. Suffolk). Vert a saltire or. *Crest*—A lion sejant erm.

Hunt (Lyndon and Hindon, co. Rutland, and Gayton, co. Stafford). Az. a bend between six leopards' faces or. *Crest*—A leopard's face betw. two wings expanded ar.

Hunt (Stoke Lindon and Barradon, co. Rutland; granted by Cooke, Clarenceux, 20 July, 1585, to JOHN HUNT, Esq., of Lindon and Stoke Aubeney, descended from JOHN LE HUNT, 40 Edward III., great-grandson of GILBERT DE STOKE, called the Forester, and MATILDA, his wife, dau. and heir of JOHN RIDOL, of Ramesthorpe and Ashley. Visit. Rutland, 1618). Az. a bend betw. six leopards' faces or, quartering RIDOL. *Crest*—A leopard's face between two wings expanded of

520

Hunt (Longnor, co. Salop), Per pale ar. and sa. a saltire counterchanged. *Crest*—A lion's head erased per pale ar. and sa. collared gu. lined and ringed or.

Hunt (Speckington, co. Somerset). Az. two chevronels betw. three martlets ar. (another, a chev. voided).

Hunt. Az. on a bend or, betw. six leopards' faces of the second three water bougets sa. *Crest*—On a chapeau gu. turned up erm. a talbot statant ar.

Hunt. Az. on a fesse ar. betw. three cinquefoils or, a lion pass. gu. *Crest*—A boar's head couped and erect betw. two ostrich feathers.

Hunt. Quarterly, or and sa. a cross lozengy counterchanged.

Hunt. Per pale ar. and sa. a saltire counterchanged, on a canton of the second a lion pass. of the first.

Hunt. Per pale ar. and sa. a saltire counterchanged, in chief a lion pass. guard. per pale of the second and first.

Hunt. Az. a chev. (another, engr.) betw. three martlets ar.

Hunt. Gu. a talbot pass. betw. three pheons or, a bordure engr. ar. pellettée.

Hunt. Ar. a bordure gu. bezantée.

Hunt. Ar. on a chev. within a bordure gu. five bezants.

Hunt. Gu. an inescutcheon ar. within an orle of bezants (another, of crescents or).

Hunt. Sa. on a fesse or, betw. three cinquefoils of the second a lion pass. gu.

Hunt (co. Norfolk). Gu. three mullets ar. on a bordure eight torteaux.

Hunt. Gu. a hind springing ar. betw. three pheons or, a bordure of the last pellettée.

Hunt. Gu. a hind trippant betw. three pheons or, within a bordure of the second (another, the bordure engr. ar.) pellettée.

Hunt-Foulston. See FOULSTON.

Hunt (Lanhydrock, co. Cornwall), Per pale ar. and sa. a saltire counterchanged, quartering, ar. a talbot sa. sejant, collared and chained or, and fastened to a stake.

Hunt (Reg. Ulster's Office to Captain HUNT, of Col. Chidley Cootes' Regiment, the brother of the first *Earl of Mountrath*). Sa. a chev. betw. six leopards' faces or, on a chief of the last a lion pass. gu. holding in the dexter paw a snake ppr. *Crest*—Out of a ducal coronet or, an arm erect gu. the hand grasping the pommel and hilt of a broken sword gold.

Hunt (Fun. Ent. Ulster's Office, 1677). Az. on a bend betw. three water bougets or, as many leopards' faces gu.

Hunt (Curragh, co. Limerick, bart., now DE VERE; confirmed by Fortescue, Ulster, 1797, with an augmentation of the Castle of Limerick, as a memorial, SIR VERE HUNT, the first bart., having raised the 135th or Limerick Regiment of Infantry). Az. on a bend betw. two water bougets or, three leopards' faces gu., and for augmentation, on a chief of the third a castle or port betw. two towers ar. masoned sa. with the Union Jack of England displ. from a flagstaff erect ppr., and in a canton of the field an Irish harp of the second, stringed of the fourth. *Crest*—A castle, as in the arms.

Huntbach (co. Stafford). Gu. upon a fess or, fretty of the field betw. three talbots' heads erased ar. *Crest*—A talbot's head erased ar. collared gu. fretty or.

Hunter (Hunterston, co. Ayr; sometimes styled "of that Ilk, Præfectus Venatorum Regiorum in Cuninghame;" ancient arms as reverted to in 1865, by ROBERT HUNTER, of Hunterston, heir of line of the family). Or, three hunting horns vert, garnished and stringed gu. *Crest*—A greyhound sejant ppr. gorged with an antique crown or. *Supporters*—Two greyhounds ppr. gorged with antique crowns or. *Motto*—Cursum perficio. [At and prior to the commencement of the 17th century we find this family bearing, "Vert three dogs of chase argent, on a chief of the second three hunting horns of the first bandressit gules." The present HUNTER of Hunterston submitted his claims to the Lord Lyon, who "ratified, maintained, and confirmed to him" the original arms, with crest, motto, and supporters as above detailed.]

Hunter (DAVID HUNTER, Calcutta, heir male of Hunterston, 1826). Vert three greyhounds courant ar. collared or, on a chief wavy of the second three hunting horns of the first, stringed gu. *Crest*—A greyhound sejant ar. collared or. *Supporters*—Two greyhounds ar. collared or. *Motto*—Cursum perficio.

Hunter (Restennet, co. Forfar, 1672). Vert three greyhounds courant ar. collared or, on a chief engr. of the second three hunting horns of the first, stringed gu. *Crest*—A fir tree ppr. *Motto*—Jucunditate afficior.

Hunter (St. Lucar, 1775). Vert two greyhounds courant in pale ar. on a chief engr. of the last a boar's head erased sa.

betw. two hunting horns of the first, stringed gu. *Crest*—An anchor ppr. *Motto*—Raised again.

Hunter (Polmood, co. Peebles). Ar. three hunting horns vert, stringed gu.

Hunter (Ballagan, co. Dumfries). Ar. a crescent az. betw. three hunting horns vert, stringed gu.

Hunter (DAVID HUNTER, cadet of Polmood, 1738). Ar. a chev. wavy az. betw. three hunting horns vert, stringed gu. *Crest*—A dexter and sinister hand and arm holding a bow and arrow in full draught ppr. *Motto*—Fortuna sequatur.

Hunter (Ayr, 1680). Vert three collars or, on a chief indented ar. as many hunting horns of the first, garnished and stringed gu. *Crest*—A greyhound in full course ar. collared or. *Motto*—Expedite.

Hunter (Barjarg, co. Dumfries). As the last, within a bordure ar. charged with four roses or, barbed vert. *Crest*—A stag's head crased ppr. *Motto*—Vigilantia robur voluptas.

Hunter (Thurston, co. Haddington). Vert three hunting horns ar. garnished gu. on a chief of the second two boars' heads couped of the third. *Crest*—A stag's head erased ppr. *Motto*—Vigilantia robur voluptas.

Hunter (Hafton, co. Argyll). Vert three hunting horns ar. garnished gu. and stringed or, within a bordure of the last. *Crest*—An anchor in pale ppr. *Motto*—Spero.

Hunter (Glencarse, co. Perth, 1792). Vert three greyhounds in pale in full speed ar. collared gu. within a bordure or, on a chief wavy of the second a fleur-de-lis az. betw. two hunting horns of the field, garnished of the fourth and stringed of the third. *Crest*—A greyhound's head and neck ar. collared gu. *Motto*—Dum spiro spero.

Hunter (Burnside, co. Forfar). Ar. a man's heart ppr. betw. three hunting horns vert, stringed gu. *Crest*—A hunting horn, as in the arms. *Motto*—Spero.

Hunter (Manchester, 1866). Per fess ar. and vert three hunting horns counterchanged, garnished and stringed gu. *Crest*—A greyhound's head erased ppr. *Motto*—Dum spiro spero.

Hunter (Dean Burn, co. Roxburgh, 1875). Per fess wavy or and az. in chief two hunting horns vert, garnished and stringed gu. in base an anchor ar. *Crest*—A dexter and a sinister arm shooting an arrow from a bow all ppr. *Motto*—Far and sure.

Hunter-Blair. See BLAIR.

Hunter (Mortimer Hill, co. Berks, bart., Lord Mayor of London, 1811-12). Or, a lion ramp. gu. betw. eight crosses pattée fitchée sa. *Crest*—A demi lion holding betw. the paws a cross pattée fitchée, as in the arms.

Hunter (co. Durham). Gu. on a fesse or, betw. three stags' heads erased of the second as many buglehorns stringed sa. *Crest*—A buglehorn vert, garnished or, stringed gu.

Hunter, alias Perry (Wotton-under-Edge, co. Gloucester). Ar. on a chev. az. betw. three lions ramp. gu. as many buglehorns or.

Hunter (Medolmsley, co. Durham). Gu. on a chev. or, betw. three bucks' heads erased of the second as many buglehorns stringed sa. *Crest*—A deer's head. *Motto*—Vigilantia robur voluptas.

Hunter (Croyland, co. Lincoln; descended from JAMES HUNTER, fourth son of ROBERT HUNTER, of Hunterston, living in 1674). Same *Arms* as HUNTER, of Hunterston, co. Ayr, quartering ORBY, HOWARD, and GERARD. *Crest*—A greyhound's head and neck couped ar.

Hunter (granted to WILLIAM HENRY HUNTER, Esq.). Per pale vert and gu. a sun in splendour or, betw. three greyhounds courant, two and one ar. collared of the second, a chief engr. erminois, thereon a cross crosslet fitchée also gu. betw. two buglehorns stringed az. *Crest*—A mount vert, thereon a greyhound's head erased or, collared gu. betw. two thistles issuant ppr.

Hunter (Upper Grosvenor Street, London). Quarterly, 1st and 4th, or, on a mount vert a tree ppr. on a chief gu. a crescent betw. two mullets ar. all within a bordure gobony of the first and fourth; 2nd and 3rd, gu. three arrows lying fesseways in pale ar. the points towards the dexter. *Crest*—A demi lion.

Hunter (Rev. JOSEPH HUNTER, F.S.A.). Or, a stag's head cabossed sa. on a chief indented of the second three crosses pattée of the first.

Hunter. Or, a lion ramp. gu. an orle of crosses pattée fitchée sa.

Hunter. Ar. three buglehorns in bend gu. stringed vert.

Hunter (Straidarran, co. Londonderry). Ar. three buglehorns bendways gu. garnished and furnished vert. *Crest*—A stag's head cabossed ppr. *Motto*—Arte et marte.

Huntercombe (*Baron Huntercombe;* summoned to Parliament 1295, extinct 1312). Erm. two bars gemels gu.

Huntercombe. Erm. two bars gemels gu. *Crest*—A sword in pale enfiled with a man's head couped and wreathed about the temples.

Huntercombe. Az. a chief or, over all a lion ramp. of the second.

Huntercombe (Woodborough, co. Nottingham). Erm. billettée gu. two bars gemels of the last.

Hunting, or Hurting. Ar. ten hurts, four, three, two, and one. *Crest*—A dexter hand ppr. holding up a shield az.

Hunting. Ar. eighteen hurts, nine, four, three, and two.

Huntingdon, Earl of. See CLINTON.

Huntingdon, Earl of. See HASTINGS.

Huntingdon, Town of. A landscape, on the centre a tree, on the dexter of which is a bird perched, on the sinister side of the tree a huntsman blowing a horn, in his sinister hand a bow and arrow, on the dexter side a stag courant, pursued by two dogs all ppr.

Huntingdon (Winchley Hall, co. Essex). Ar. fretty sa. on a chief gu. three mullets or.

Huntingdon, or Huntington. Or, billettée a lion ramp. az. *Crest*—A crosier ar.

Huntingdon. Gu. a fesse betw. three buglehorns ar.

Huntingdon. Ar. fretty sa. on a chief of the second three mullets or.

Huntingfield (*Baron Huntingfield;* summoned to Parliament 1294, abeyance 1377). Or, on a fess gu. three plates.

Huntingfield (*Baron Huntingfield;* summoned to Parliament 1362-69, but never after). Same *Arms*.

Huntingfield, Baron. See VANNECK.

Huntingfield. Quarterly, or and gu. a label of three points sa. on each as many plates.

Huntingfield (cos. Bedford and Hertford). Gu. on a bend ar. three lions ramp. sa.

Huntingfield (co. Hereford, *temp.* Edward I.). Same *Arms*.

Huntingfield (co. Kent). Quarterly, or and gu. a bordure (another, engr.) sa.

Huntingfield (Huntingfield, co. Suffolk, *temp.* Henry II.). Or, on a fesse gu. three plates.

Huntingfield. Same *Arms*. *Crest*—A dagger and sword in saltire ppr.

Huntingfield. Quarterly, gu. and or, on a bend ar. three lions ramp. of the first.

Huntingfield. Quarterly, or and gu. a label of five points sa.

Huntingfield. Quarterly, or and gu. a label of five points az. bezantée.

Huntingfield. Or, a cross az.

Huntingfield. Gu. a bend betw. six crosses formée fitchée ar.

Huntingfield. Or, on a bend gu. three plates.

Huntingfield (GEORGE HUNTINGFIELD, Esq., of Castle Waring, co. Down; implacement Fun. Ent. 1619, of his son-in-law, Sir GEORGE GREAME, Knt.). Or, on a fess gu. three plates, a crescent for diff.

Huntingford (GEORGE ISAAC HUNTINGFORD, Bishop of Gloucester, 1802-15, and of Hereford, 1815-32; the descendant of a family whose representative, *temp.* William and Mary, was possessed of a good landed estate at Tillington, co. Sussex). Per fesse sa. and erminois fretty gu. a fesse per fesse nebulée of the second and first, in chief three crosses pattée fitchée at the foot ar. *Crest*—A griffin's head erased or, wings elevated fretty gu. holding in the beak a cross pattée fitchée at the foot ar.

Huntington (co. Devon). Erm. three water bougets in bend sa. two cotises gu.

Huntington. Ar. billettée a lion ramp. az.

Huntington. Ar. three lions ramp. purp.

Huntisdon, or Hunsdon. Gu. a fesse betw. three buglehorns or.

Huntley (Treowen, co. Monmouth, *temp.* Edward III.). Sa. on a chev. betw. three bucks' heads cabossed ar. as many bugles stringed of the first. *Crest*—A buck's head cabossed ar. betw. the horns a bugle stringed sa.

Huntley (Boxwell, co. Gloucester). Ar. on a chev. betw. three stags' heads erased sa. as many buglehorns stringed of the field. *Crest*—A talbot ppr. collared and lined or.

Huntley (Dorking, co. Surrey, and of Wales). Ar. on a chev. betw. three bucks' heads erased sa. as many bugle-horns or, (another, the horns ar.).

Huntley. Ar. (another, erm.) a chev. betw. three bucks' heads couped sa.

Huntley. Erm. a chev. couped sa.

Huntly, Marquess of. See GORDON.

Hunton (co. Wilts; granted 1578). Sa. a chev. erm. betw. three talbots pass. ar. *Crest*—A demi talbot ramp. and erased ar.

Hunton (East Knoyle, co. Wilts). Ar. on a chev. per pale gu. and az. betw. three talbots pass. sa. as many stags' heads cabossed or. *Crest*—A demi talbot gu. collared and eared or, holding betw. the paws a stag's head cabossed of the last.

Hunton, or Hutton (co. Cambridge). Ar. three hurts, each charged with a martlet of the field, on a chief vert an eagle displ. or, all within a bordure engr. gu.

Huntsman (Attercliffe, co. York; granted to FRANCIS HUNTSMAN, Esq.). Gu. three escutcheons ar. each charged with a buglehorn sa. garnished or, and stringed of the field. *Crest*—A mount vert, thereon a fernbrake in front of two spears in saltire ppr. therefrom pendent a buglehorn garnished and stringed, as in the arms. *Motto*—Esto vigilans.

Hurd. Vert a bend erm. betw. three escallops ar. *Crest*—A bear's head sa. muzzled gu. betw. two wings or.

Hurding (co. Dorset). Gu. two bars wavy erm.

Hurlblatt (Farnham, co. Surrey. Visit. Hants, 1634). Sa. a cross betw. four leopards' faces jessant-de-lis or. *Crest*—Out of a ducal coronet or, a talbot's head ar. eared gu. collared of the last, ringed and studded of the first.

Hurlebert. Quarterly, ar. and sa. in the 2nd and 3rd quarters a lion ramp. or, on a bend gu. three annulets of the third. *Crest*—An arm bent couped at the shoulder gu. holding a battle-axe, staff of the last, blade and gauntlet ar. at the wrist a ribbon tied in a knot of the first.

Hurleston (Hurleston, and Newton, co. Chester). Ar. four ermines' tails in cross sa. *Crest*—An ermine pass. ar.

Hurleston (Picton, co. Chester). Ar. four erm. spots in cross sa.

Hurlestone. Quarterly, 1st and 4th, ar. a cross of four erm. spots sa.; 2nd, ar. a bend and demi bend both engr. sa.; 3rd, ar. a chev. betw. three stone bows sa. *Crest*—A goat's head ar. bearded and attired or, on the neck four erm. spots in cross.

Hurlestone. Ar. a chev. betw. three bows sa.

Hurley. Ar. a crescent betw. three trefoils az. *Crest*—Out of a ducal coronet a peacock ppr.

Hurley (Province of Munster, Reg. Ulster's Office). Ar. on a cross gu. five frets or.

Hurlston (Canington, co. Bedford). Ar. a fesse ermines betw. two bars gemelles az.

Hurlston, or Horleston (Hurlston, co. Lancaster). Ar. four erm. spots in cross sa. the heads meeting in the centre point. *Crest*—An ermine pass. ppr.

Hurlston. Sa. a cross betw. four crescents erm.

Hurlstone (Walton Hall, Wakefield). Ar. a cross couped az. betw. four pheons of the last, a crescent for diff.

Hurly (Tralee, co. Kerry; confirmed to ROBERT CONWAY HURLY, Esq., eldest son of JOHN HURLY, Clerk of the Crown, J.P.). Az. on a fess betw. three crosses crosslet or, a dexter hand couped betw. two mullets gu. *Crest*—Out of an antique Irish crown or, a naked arm embowed ppr. holding a cross crosslet gold. *Motto*—Dextra cruce vincit.

Hurrell, Hurell, or Hurle. Ar. a chev. betw. three crossbows unbent az. *Crest*—A lion ramp. ppr. holding a flag displ. gu. charged with a cross in the dexter chief ar.

Hurry (NICHOLAS HURRY, Esq., Liverpool, descended from a Norfolk family). Ar. a lion ramp. gu. and in base two mullets az. pierced of the field. *Crest*—A harpy, wings expanded and inverted ppr. *Motto*—Nec arroge nec dubite.

Hurry (Scotland). Ar. in chief a lion ramp. gu. in base two mullets az. *Crest*—A lion's gamb. *Motto*—Sans tache.

Hurse (Sterford, co. Hertford). Ar. the sun in splendour gu. *Crest*—In a wood ppr. the sun or.

Hurst (Sabridgeworth, co. Hertford). Same *Arms* and *Crest*, a crescent for diff.

Hurst (Welbery, co. Hertford; granted 1715). Quarterly, erm. and or, a sun gu. *Crest*—A sun or, rising from behind a castle ppr. standing on a mount vert.

Hurst (Hinckley, co. Leicester; granted 1763). Quarterly, az. and gu. over all a sun or, in the 1st and 4th quarters two fleurs-de-lis fesseways, in the 2nd and 3rd a lion pass. guard. of the third. *Crest*—A dragon, wings elevated ar. resting the dexter foot on a cross crosslet or, charged on the shoulder with a fleur-de-lis az.

Hurst (Horsham Park, co. Sussex). Quarterly, erm. and or, over all a sun gu. *Crest*—An oak tree ppr.

Hurst (Barrowby, co. Lincoln). Ar. an estoile of twelve points gu.

Hurst (co. Salop). Ar. six billets az. fretty, three in fesse and as many in pale.

Hurst (Hurst, co. Lancaster). Ar. the sun in his splendour gu. *Crest*—Upon a mount vert a hurst or group of trees ppr. *Motto*—Pro Deo et rege.

Hurt (Alderwasley, co. Derby; Ashborne, at the time of the Visitation of 1611). Quarterly, 1st, a fesse betw. three

cinquefoils or, for HURT; 2nd, gu. a wolf pass. ar., for LOWE, of Alderwasley; 3rd, az. a hart trippant ar., for LOWE, of Denby and Alderwasley ; 4th, ar. a buglehorn betw. three crescents sa. each charged with a bezant or, for FAWNE, of Alderwasley. *Crest*—A hart pass. ppr. horned, membered, and hurt in the haunch with an arrow or, feathered ar. *Motto*—Mane prædam vesperi spolium.

Hurysse. Ar. a chev. gu. betw. three hinds' heads cabossed of the second.

Husband. Ar. on a fesse voided az. betw. three martlets sa. a mallet gu. *Crest*—A demi griffin holding in the claws a ducal coronet ppr.

Husband (Gesley). Ar. on a fesse voided az. betw. three martlets sa. as many mullets gu. fimbriated of the second.

Husband. Ar. on a fesse cotised betw. three martlets gu. as many mullets of the field.

Husdell (Monkwearmouth, co. Durham). Per fesse or and sa. a pale counterchanged, three fleurs-de-lis gu. *Crest*—A demi lion ppr.

Huse. Ar. a leg in bend sinister, couped at the thigh sa. betw. two cinquefoils gu. *Crest*—A dexter hand ppr. holding a cross pattée in pale or.

Husee, Hussee, and Hussy. Ar. a cross vert. *Crest*—A leopard pass. guard. ppr.

Husey. Or, on a fesse sa. a lion pass. ar.

Huskisson (the late Rt. Hon. WILLIAM HUSKISSON, M.P., of Earth, Petworth, co. Sussex). Gu. a chev. or, betw. three elephants' heads erased ppr. *Crest*—An elephant's head erased ppr. tusked ar. *Motto*—Ut secura quies.

Huskisson (TILGHMAN-HUSKISSON, Easham, co. Sussex). Quarterly, 1st and 4th, gu. on a chev. nebulée betw. three elephants' heads erased ar. as many torteaux, for HUSKISSON; 2nd and 3rd, per fesse sa. and ar. a lion ramp. reguard. counterchanged, crowned or, for TILGHMAN. *Crests*—1st, HUSKISSON: An elephant's head erased ar. guttée de sang, and pierced in the neck by an arrow ppr.; 2nd: A demi lion sejant sa. crowned or. *Motto*—Spes alit agricolam.

Huskisson (MILBANKE - HUSKISSON, Halnaby, co. York, bart.). Quarterly, 1st and 4th, gu. on a chev. nebuly betw. three elephants' heads erased ar. as many torteaux, for HUSKISSON; 2nd and 3rd, gu. a bend erm. on a canton or, a lion's head erased of the first, for MILBANKE. *Crests*—1st, HUSKISSON: An elephant's head erased ar. guttée de sang, and pierced in the neck with an arrow ppr.; 2nd, MILBANKE: A lion's head couped gu. charged with a bend erm. *Motto*—Resolute and firm.

Huson (Tenterden, co. Kent). Quarterly, gu. and erm. an eagle displ. or. *Crest*—A ram's head erased ar. horned or.

Huson (NARCISSUS EDMOND HUSON, Esq., of Springfield, Major Wexford Militia; certified by Sir Alexander Erskine, Bart., Lyon King of Arms, 16 May, 1702, to Rev. BENJAMIN HUSON, Secretary to Narcissus Marsh, Archbishop of Dublin, of Scotch parentage, descended from the house of HOWISON) Ar. a heart gu. on a chief engr. az. a fleur-de-lis of the first. *Crest*—A harp az. stringed or. *Motto*—Sursum corda.

Husse. Ar. three legs couped at the thigh gu. spurred or.

Hussey (*Baron Hussey;* JOHN HUSSEY, of Sleford, was summoned to Parliament 1534, attainted 1537). Or, a cross vert.

Hussey (Honington, co. Lincoln, bart., extinct 1734; descended from Sir ROBERT HUSSEY, brother of JOHN, first Lord Hussey). Same *Arms*, quartering barry of six erm. and gu.

Hussey (Caythorpe, co. Lincoln, bart., extinct 1734; CHARLES HUSSEY, third son of the first bart. of Honington, was created a bart. 1661). Same *Arms*.

Hussey (cos. Dorset, Essex, Salop, Suffolk, Sussex, and Wilts). Barry of six erm. and gu. *Crest*—A boot sa. spurred or, topped erm.

Hussey (Nash Court, Marnhull, co. Dorset). Same *Arms* and *Crest*.

Hussey (AMBROSE HUSSEY, Esq., of Salisbury; derived from the same ancestry as the HUSSEYS, of Nash Court). Same *Arms* and *Crest*.

Hussey (Scotney Castle, co. Sussex). Quarterly, 1st and 4th, or, a cross vert charged with a mullet or; 2nd and 3rd, barry of six erm. and gu. quartering LAKE, LUCAS, BERKELEY, CALOW, BRIDGE, JEMMET, &c. *Crest*—A hind lodged under an oak tree ppr. ducally gorged and chained or.

Hussey (Upwood and Wood Walton, co. Hunts; the late Admiral Sir RICHARD HUSSEY HUSSEY, K.C.B. and G.C.M.G., of Wood Walton, co. Huntingdon, father of the present RICHARD HUSSEY HUSSEY, Esq., of Upwood, and second son of the late ROBERT MOUBRAY, Esq., of Cockairny, co. Fife, assumed, in 1832, by sign manual, on in-

heriting Wood Walton, the present surname and arms).
Quarterly, per a cross of pearls or and gu. in the 1st
and 4th quarters a cross az., in the 2nd and 3rd three
lions pass. guard. two and one, gold, on the centre chief
point (as an honourable augmentation) a plate charged with
the turban of an Omrah of the Mogul empire ppr. *Crest*—
A hind trippant ppr. gorged with a ducal coronet and
chained or. *Supporters* (by royal licence, dated 1835,
personal to the late Sir R. H. Hussey)—On the dexter,
a soldier of the E. I. C. Artillery habited ppr. the exterior
hand supporting a flag flying to the sinister az.; on the
sinister a soldier of the Native Artillery of Bengal, also
habited ppr. and holding a flag flying to the dexter gu. both
inscribed with the word " Hindostan " in letters of gold.

Hussey (Moslerton, and Bredy, near Barton Bradstock,
co. Dorset). Barry of six erm. and gu. per pale counterchanged, on a canton of the second a cross patonce ar.
Crest—A boot sa. spurred or, turned over erm. surmounted
by a heart ppr. supported by two arms embowed in armour,
hands gauntleted also ppr. *Motto*—Cor immobile.

Hussey (Marnhull, co. Dorset). Barry of six erm. and gu.
Crest—A boot sa. spurred or, topped erm.

Hussey (co. Dorset. Hador, Gowthorp, and Linwood, co.
Lincoln, and co. Wilts). Or, a cross vert. *Crest*—On a mount
vert a hind couchant reguard. against a hawthorn tree ppr.
ducally gorged and lined or.

Hussey (Phineas Hussey, Esq., of Wyrley Grove, near
Lichfield, co. Stafford). Barry of six erm. and gu. quartering,
vert a fleur-de-lis ar., for Foulke; ar. a chev. gu. betw. three
cinquefoils az., for Wyraston; and az. a fesse embattled
betw. three cocks' heads erased ar., for Jesson. *Crest*—A
leg couped above the knee, booted sa. top erm. spurred.

Hussey (Rathkenny, co. Meath). Barry of six erm. and gu.
on a canton of the last a cross or. *Crest*—A stag under an
oak tree all ppr.

Hussey (Sir Hugh Hussey, Knt., of Flintham, co. Notts,
temp. Henry V.; the heiress, Anne, dau. of John Hussey,
temp. Queen Elizabeth, *m.* John Draper, of Melton Mowbray. Visit. Notts, 1631). Or, on a fesse sa. a lion pass.
guard. ar.

Hussey (Henington, co. Lincoln). Ar. a cross vert.

Hussey (cos. Nottingham and Wilts). Or, on a fesse sa. a
lion pass. ar.

Hussey (co. York). Or, on a cross vert a mullet of the first.

Hussey (co. York). Or, on a cross vert a label gu.

Hussey, or Husey. Erm. a chev. az. betw. three holly
leaves vert.

Hussey. Or, three boots sa.

Hussey. Ar. three fleurs-de-lis gu.

Hussey. Gu. a fesse betw. two chevronels erm.

Hussey. Sa. three bears' heads erased ar. muzzled or.

Hussey (Feudal *Baron of Galtrim* ; descended from Sir Hugh
Hussey, who went to Ireland 17 Henry II.). Barry of six
erm. and gu. on a canton of the last a cross or. *Crest*—A
hind pass. ar. on a mount vert and under a tree ppr.
Motto—Cor immobile.

Hussey (*Earl of Beaulieu ;* created 1784, extinct 1802;
descended from the Barons of Galtrim. The earl
having *m.* Lady Isabella Montagu, dau. and co-heir of the
Duke of Montagu, assumed at the Duke's death, 1749, his
grace's name and arms). Same *Arms* as the Barons of Galtrim. *Crest*—A griffin's head couped or, beaked and winged
sa. *Supporters*—Two stags ppr. ducally gorged and chained
or, chains reflexed over backs. *Motto*—Spectemur agendo.

Hussey (Dingle, co. Kerry; exemplified to Eugene
Finnerty, Esq., M.D., Surgeon H.E.I.C.S., on his assuming,
by royal licence, 1847, the name of Hussey, in lieu of
Finnerty, in compliance with the desire of his maternal
uncle, Edward Hussey, Esq., of Dingle). Barry of six gu.
and erm. on a canton az. an eastern crown or. *Crest*—Under
an oak tree ppr. a hind pass. gu. *Motto*—Ubi fides ibi
vires.

Hussey (Westown, co. Dublin, and Mullafin and Balrath,
co. Meath ; confirmed to Anthony Strong Hussey,
Esq., only son and heir of Gerald Hussey, formerly
Gerald Strong (fourth son of John Strong, of Mullafin,
co. Meath, by Mabel, his wife, eldest dau. of Sir Andrew
Aylmer, Bart., of Balrath), who took the surname of Hussey
by Act of Parliament, 51 Geo. III.). Barry of six erm. and
gu. on a canton of the last a cross or. *Crest*—On a mount
vert a hind pass. ar. beneath a tree ppr. *Motto*—Cor immobile.

Hustler (Acklam, co. York). Ar. on a fesse az. betw. two
martlets sa. three fleurs-de-lis or. *Crest*—A talbot sejant
ar. gorged with a collar az. charged with three fleurs-de-lis or.

Hustock, or Hustoke. Sa. a chev. erm in chief a lion
pass. ar. crowned or.

523

Huston (co. Cornwall). Sa. a lion pass. gu. crowned or.

Hustwayte (co. Lincoln. Harl. MSS. 1550. Visit. co.
Lincoln, 1564-1572). Paly of six or and az. on a chief ar. a
lion pass. sa.

Hutaker, or Huttaker. Ar. on a chev. sa. three garbs
or.

Hutchens. Sa. a tower ar. *Crest*—A lion's head erased
or, gorged with a mural coronet az.

Hutcheon (Scotland). Ar. a fesse vert surmounted of
three arrows, the middlemost in pale, the other two bend
dexter and sinister wise, points meeting in base gu. in chief
a boar's head erased sa.

Hutcheson (Drummalig, co. Down, and Clifton, co. Gloucester; descended from an ancient Scotch family, of whom
was Francis Hutcheson, D.D., Professor in the University
of Glasgow, an eminent writer, who *d.* 1746; William
Hutcheson, Esq., of Clifton, *m.* Sarah Kyrle, the heiress of
John Kyrle, called "The Man of Ross," and the dau. *m.,* in
1787, Philip Jones, Esq., of Cleve, co. Hereford). Gu. three
arrows, points upward, or, on a chief vert a boar's head
couped of the second. *Crest*—An arrow, pointed upwards,
ppr.

Hutcheson (Scotland). Ar. on a fess vert betw. three
boars' heads erased sa. as many pheons of the first.

Hutchinge (co. Devon). Ar. a cross patonce quarterly
az. and gu. betw. four leopards' faces az.

Hutchings. Erm. on a pale vert betw. two *daggers*, points
downward, az. hilted or, three elephants' proboscos of the
last. *Crest*—Out of a mural coronet a demi lion, holding in
the dexter paw a branch of palm vert.

Hutchings (co. Somerset). Gu. a tower embattled or.
Crest—A lion's head erased gu. ducally crowned or.

Hutchings (James Hutchings, of Telscombe, co. Sussex).
Purp. on a saltire ar. an arch betw. four crosses crosslet
fitchée sa. *Crest*—A lion's head erased ar. gorged with a
collar sa. thereon three arches, and in the mouth a cross
crosslet fitchée or.

Hutchinson (Hely-Hutchinson, *Earl of Donoughmore*).
Quarterly, 1st and 4th, per pale gu. and az. a lion ramp. betw.
eight cross crosslets ar., for Hutchinson; 2nd, az. a fesse betw.
three stags' heads erased in chief ar. and a demi lion ramp.
in base or, for Hely; 3rd, az. a garb or, betw. three wolves'
heads erased ar., for Nixon. *Crest*—Out of a ducal coronet
or, a demi cockatrice, wings elevated az. *Supporters*—Two
cockatrices, wings elevated or, collared sa. combed and
wattled gu. and each charged on the breast with a wreath of
laurel vert. *Motto*—Fortiter gerit crucem.

Hutchinson (Synge-Hutchinson, Castle Sallah, co. Wicklow, bart.). Quarterly, 1st and 4th, per pale az. and gu. a
lion ramp. erm. betw. nine cross crosslets or ; 2nd and 3rd,
quarterly, 1st and 4th, az. three millstones ar., 2nd and 3rd,
ar. an eagle displ. with two heads sa. *Crests*—1st: A
cockatrice issuing out of a ducal coronet all ppr.; 2nd : An
eagle's talon issuing from a ducal coronet all ppr. *Mottoes*
—Non sibi, sed toti, for Hutchinson; Cœlestia caninus,
for Synge.

Hutchinson (Bishopwearmouth, co. Durham ; descended
of the Hutchinsons, of co. Cumberland, *temp.* Charles I.).
Per pale gu. and az. a lion ramp. ar. betw. eight crosses
crosslet or. *Crest*—A cockatrice, wings expanded az.
combed, wattled, and membered or. *Another Crest*—A
demi lion ramp. *Motto*—Cunctanter tamen fortiter.

Hutchinson (cos. Essex and York). Same *Arms.*

Hutchinson (Owthorpe, co. Notts; Thomas Hutchinson,
fifth in descent from Thomas Hutchinson, of same place.
Visit. Notts, 1614). Per pale gu. and az. semée of cross
crosslets or, a lion ramp. guard. ar. *Crest*—A cockatrice az.
combed and legged or.

Hutchinson-Lloyd-Vaughan. See Vaughan.

Hutchinson (Dublin; granted by St. George, Ulster, 1676,
to Daniel Hutchinson, Alderman of Dublin). Az. semée of
crosses crosslets or, a lion ramp. ar. on a chief of the last
three trefoils slipped vert. *Crest*—A demi lion ramp. az.
charged on the shoulder with a trefoil slipped or.

Hutchinson (Skirsgill and Crossfield House, co. Cumberland, and afterwards of Newbiggin Hall and Appleby, co.
Westmoreland). Per pale gu. and az. crusily or, a lion ramp.
ar. and a canton erm. *Crest*—Out of a ducal coronet or, a
cockatrice, wings endorsed az. beaked, combed, and wattled
gu.

Hutchinson (Whitton, co. Durham). Per pale gu. and az.
semée of crosses crosslet and a lion ramp. or. *Crest*—Out of
a ducal coronet or, a cockatrice az. *Motto*—Nihil humani
alienum.

Hutchinson (co. Lincoln; borne by Bingham Hutchinson,
Esq., descendant of William Hutchinson, who emigrated,
in 1633, from the neighbourhood of Boston, co. Lincoln and

became one of the founders of Boston in America, where the family continued, holding offices of trust and importance until the American revolution in 1776, when the great-grandfather of the present BINGHAM HUTCHINSON, being Governor of Massachusetts, lost, through his fidelity to the crown, all his estates in America, and the family returned to England). Per pale gu. and az. semée of crosses crosslet or, a lion ramp. ar. armed and langued of the third. *Crest*—A cockatrice az. crested, jelloped, and armed gu. issuing out of a ducal crown or.

Hutchinson (granted to Lieut.-Gen. Sir WILLIAM HUTCHINSON, Knt., K.C.H., Governor of Carrickfergus, Equerry to H.R.H. the *Duke of Sussex*). Per pale az. and gu. semée of cross crosslets or, a lion ramp. ar. on a canton of the fourth a mural coronet of the second. *Crest*—On a mural coronet or, a cockatrice ar. combed and wattled gu. gorged with a wreath of laurel or. *Motto*—Perseverando.

Hutchison (Rockend, co. Dumbarton, 1856). Ar. a fess az. surmounted of three arrows, points downwards, meeting in base counterchanged, in chief a boar's head erased sa. in base two escallops ermine. *Crest*—A stag's head erased gu. attired or. *Motto*—Memor esto.

Hutchison (Carlowrie, co. Linlithgow, 1870). Ar. three arrows, points downwards, meeting in base ppr. surmounted of a fesse az. charged with a fox courant also ppr. *Crest*—A stag's head erased ppr. collared or. *Motto*—Scientiæ laborisque memor.

Hutchison (Edinburgh). As the last, within a bordure az. Same Crest and Motto.

Hutchon. Ar. on a fesse vert three pheons of the field, in chief a lion pass. guard. gu. crowned with an antique crown or. *Crest*—A stag's head erased at gaze. *Motto*—Fortis est veritas.

Hutetoft. Az. a cross pattée erm. betw. four roses or.

Huth (granted to C. F. HUTH, Esq., Tokenhouse Yard, London). Ar. two chevronels gu. in chief a human heart of the last and in base a bat sa. with ostrich feathers ppr. *Crest*—Three sprigs of oak erect ppr. each bearing one acorn or.

Huthorne. Or, on a bend sa. three mullets of the field (another, ar.).

Huttolfe (co. Essex). Az. a chev. or, betw. three bezants.

Huttoft. Erm. three bars gu. on a canton az. a cross engr. ar. betw. four pheons or. *Crest*—A whale's head erect and erased az. gorged with a mural coronet or, thereon three pellets, to the collar a chain and ring gold.

Huttoft. Erm. three bars gu. on a canton az. a cross engr. ar.

Huttofts (co. Bedford). Az. a cross formée erm. betw. four cinquefoils or.

Huttofts (co. Hants, and Salisbury, co. Wilts). Erm. three bars gu. on a canton az. a cross engr. ar. betw. four pheons or.

Hutton (Hutton John, co. Cumberland; traceable to the reign of Edward III.; one of the co-heirs *m.* HUDDLESTON). Gu. a fesse or, betw. three cushions ar. tasselled of the second, each charged with a fleur-de-lis of the field, on a canton az. a falchion of the third, hilt and pommel gold. *Crest*—Two eagles' heads erased in saltire, endorsed sa. enfiled with a coronet or.

Hutton (Bishopwearmouth, co. Durham). Gu. on a fesse or, betw. three cushions erm. tasselled of the second a fleur-de-lis sa. *Crest*—A man ppr. wreathed round the temples and loins vert, holding in the hand three leaves of the last. *Motto*—Pax.

Hutton (cos. Durham and Lancaster). Same *Arms. Crest* —A man ppr. banded round the waist ar. holding in the hand three leaves vert. *Another Crest*—An American ppr. wreathed round the middle vert, holding in the dexter hand a tobacco leaf ppr.

Hutton (co. Cambridge). Ar. three hurts, on each a martlet of the field, on a chief az. an eagle displ. or.

Hutton (Forrest, co. Cumberland). Erm. on a fesse gu. three bucks' heads cabossed ar.

Hutton (Thorpensty, co Lancaster, 1664). Gu. on a fesse or, betw. three cushions erm. two fleurs-de-lis of the first.

Hutton (Gate Burton, co. Lincoln). Ar. on a fesse sa. three stags' heads cabossed or. *Crest*—A stag's head, as in the arms. *Motto*—Spero.

Hutton (Penrith, co. Cumberland; Sir RICHARD HUTTON, Knt., a judge, brother of Sir RICHARD HUTTON, Knt., of Penrith; descended from JOHN DE HOTTON, *temp.* Henry VI. Visit. Cumberland, 1615). Ar. on a fess sa. three stags' heads cabossed or.

Hutton (Gale and Hutton Hall, co. Cumberland, and Goldsborough, co. York; granted 5 June, 1599). Ar. on a fesse sa. three bucks' heads cabossed or. *Crest*—Three broad

524

arrows, two in saltire and one in pale sa. enfiled with a ducal coronet or.

Hutton (Overthwaite, co. Westmoreland). Same *Arms*, quartering MOLYNEUX. *Crest*—Issuant from a tower ppr. arrows sa.

Hutton (Westmorland). Gu. on a fesse betw. three cushions or, tasselled of the last, each charged with a fleur-de-lis of the field, a martlet sa. *Crest*—An eagle displ. or, beaked and legged sa. betw. two branches of laurel vert.

Hutton (granted to MATTHEW HUTTON, D.D., Dean of York, July 20, 1584, by Dethick, Garter). Gu. on a fesse betw. three cushions ar. tasselled or, a cross humettée betw. two fleurs-de-lis of the first.

Hutton (Hemwick, co. Durham). Vert an eagle displ. or, armed sa. *Crest*—An ostrich's head betw. two ostrich wings expanded ar. holding in the mouth a horseshoe or.

Hutton (cos. Lincoln and York; as borne by HENRY HUTTON, Esq., of Lincoln). Ar. on a fesse sa. three bucks' heads cabossed or. *Crest*—A buck's head, as in the arms.

Hutton (Houghton le Spring, co. Durham; derived from the HUTTONS, of· Priest Hutton, co. Lancaster, described by Glover as "familia antiqua in Lancastriensi Palatinatu nobilibus satis parentibus oriunda." The last male heir of the direct line, the Rev. JOHN HUTTON, M.A., of Houghton le Spring, co. Durham, and of Tenterden Hole, eo. Kent, *d. s. p.*). Gu. a fesse or, betw. three cushions erm. are the arms assigned to the family in *Surtees' History of Durham;* but other authorities give the following: Gu. on a fesse or, betw. three lozenge-shaped cushions ern. fringed and tasselled of the second, as many fleurs-de-lis sa. *Crest*—A blackamoor wreathed about the temples and waist and holding in the dexter hand a trefoil slipped vert.

Hutton (Marske, co. York). Gu. on a fesse betw. three cushions ar. fringed and tasselled or, as many fleurs-de-lis of the field. *Crest*—On a cushion gu. placed lozengeways an open book, the edges gilt, with the words "Odor vitæ" inscribed. *Motto*—Spiritus gladius.

Hutton (co. York). Az. three bars humettée ar.

Hutton. Ar. a lion ramp. gu. betw. three arrows ppr. on a chief of the second as many bezants. *Crest*—A serpent emitting fire out of its mouth and nostrils all ppr.

Hutton. Sa. a chev. betw. three bucks' heads cabossed or.

Hutton. Erm. five fusils in fesse gu. (another, the fusils pierced).

Hutton. Gu. on a canton ar. an eagle, wings expanded and inverted sa.

Hutton. Ar. three hurts, on each a martlet of the first, on a chief vert an eagle displ. or.

Hutton. Ar. a fesse sa. betw. three bucks' heads cabossed or. *Crest*—Three double pointed darts sa. feathered and pointed ar. in a ducal crown or.

Hutton (Glasion, co. Rutland. Visit. 1618). Vert an eagle displ. or.

Hutton (that Ilk, co. Berwick). Or, three annulets gu.

Hutton (Dr. JOHN HUTTON: Scotland, 1692). Or, a lion ramp. az. betw. three arrows, points downwards, two and one ppr. headed and feathered ar. on a chief gu. as many bezants. *Crest*—A serpent catching at the finger of a man's hand issuing from a cloud all ppr. *Motto*—Deus quia contra.

Huxham (quartered by BAMFIELD, of Poltimore, co. Devon. Visit. 1623. WILLIAM HUXHAM, of Harberton, same co., disclaimed in Totness, 26 Aug. 1620, at the Visit.). Ar. a lion ramp. sa.

Huxham (Plymouth, co. Devon, and of London; granted Nov. 1750). Ar. a lion ramp. ermines, on a chief gu. a cinquefoil betw. two crosses crosslet or. *Crest*—A demi lion ramp. ermines holding in the paws an escutcheon ar. charged with a cross crosslet gu.

Huxham (co. Devon). Ar. a lion ramp. sa.

Huxley (Huxley, co. Chester). Ar. on a bend. cotised gu. three crescents ar. *Crest*—A snake ppr.

Huxley (Edmonton, co. Middlesex). Same *Arms. Crest*— Out of a ducal coronet or, a demi lion ramp. erm. collared of the first, holding betw. the paws a crescent of the last.

Huxley. Erm. on a bend cotised gu. three crescents ar. *Crest*—A wolf's head erased sa. gorged with a collar or, charged with three crescents gu. *Motto*—In Deo omnia.

Huyde, or Hyde. Az. a chev. betw. three lozenges or, a file of three points in chief gu.

Huysh (confirmed by Cooke, Clarenceux, 32 Elizabeth, 1589, to SYLVESTER HUYSH, Esq., of Donyford; WILLIAM HUYSH, Esq., of Dunster; ROWLAND HUYSH, Esq., of Southbrente, all in co. Somerset; and RICHARD HUYSH, of New Inn, co. Middlesex, gent., kinsmen). Ar. on a bend sa. three lucies of the first *Crest*—An elephant's head couped ar. ducally crowned and tusked or.

Huyshe, Hiwis, Huish, Hewish (Lod Hiwis, Lynch, Doniford, Aller, and Taunton, co. Somerset; Sand and Clisthydon, co. Devon: cos. Derby and Nottingham; descended from RICHARD DE HYWIS, of L..d Hywis, living *temp.* King John). Ar. on a bend sa. three roches ppr., taken on the marriage of OLIVER HYWISH, *temp.* Edward III. with the heiress of DE LA ROCHE. *Ancient Arms*—A chev. betw. three roundles; also, a chev. on a chief three leaves. *Crest*—An elephant's head couped ar. crowned and tusked or.

Huyshe (RICHARD HUYSHE, Esq., Founder of the Hospital bearing his name at Tauriton, who *d.* 1615, as appears by his monument in St. Mary Magdalene's Church). Quarterly, 1st and 4th, ar. on a bend sa. three lucies of the first, HUYSHE; 2nd and 3rd, ar. five fusils in fesse sa. betw. two cottises gu., AVENELL. *Crest*—An elephant's head couped ar. crowned and tusked or.

Huystock. Sa. a chev. erm. betw. two lions pass. ar. crowned or.

Hwatacre. Ar. on a chev. sa. three garbs or.

Hwfa ap Cynddelw (founder of the 1st Noble Tribe of North Wales and Powys. Descendants: OWENS, of Bodeon, co. Anglesey, and Orielton, co. Pembroke; OWENS, of Bodsilin; and OWENS, of Penrhos, co. Montgomery). Gu. a chev. betw. three lioncels ramp. or.

Hwitle (Sion Hill, Wolverley, co. Worcester; borne by JOHN HWITLE, Esq., High Sheriff co. Worcester, 1774). Az. a fesse embattled betw. three lions ramp. or.

Hyatt. Ar. a lion ramp. sa. a chief per fesse indented of the first and second. *Crest*—A demi lion ramp. ppr. *Another Crest*—A tower gu. out of the battlement a demi lion ramp. sa. *Motto*—Fac et spera.

Hybbinge. Paly of six sa. and or, two lozenges in pale counterchanged.

Hyde (*Earl of Clarendon;* created 1661, extinct 1743; Lady ANNE HYDE, dau. of the first earl, was first wife of James II., and mother of Mary II. and Queen Anne). Az. a chev. betw. three lozenges or. *Crest*—An eagle, wings expanded gu. *Supporters*—Two eagles, wings endorsed sa. ducally crowned and charged on the breast with a cross or. *Motto*—Deus nobis hæc otia fecit.

Hyde (*Earl of Rochester;* created 1682, merged in the earldom of Clarendon 1723, extinct with it). Same *Arms* and *Crest*, with a crescent for diff. *Supporters*—Two storks ar. beaked and membered gu. *Motto*—Soyez ferme.

Hyde (Hydon, co. Dorset). Or, a chev. betw. three lozenges az. on a chief gu. a saltire engr. betw. two birds of the field. *Crest*—A cock's head erased az. crested and jelloped gu. bezantée, in the mouth a pansy flower of the last.

Hyde (Denton, co. Lancaster. Visit. 1567). Ar. three lozenges sa. *Crest*—An eagle's head erased or, beaked sa.

Hyde (Ormston, co. Lancaster, 1567; descended from HYDE, of Norbury, co. Chester). Az. a chev. betw. three lozenges or, in fesse point a crescent. *Crest*—A raven or crow rising.

Hyde (London; Reg. Her. Office, London). Az. a saltire or, betw. four bezants, a chief erm. *Crest*—A unicorn's head erased ar. armed and maned or, collared vair.

Hyde (HENRY ELWIN HYDE. Esq., J.P., East Dereham, co. Norfolk). Gu. two chevronels ar. on the upper one a mullet of the first. *Crest*—A stag's head erased gu.

Hyde (co. Nottingham). Gu. a saltire or, betw. four bezants, a chief erm. *Crest*—A unicorn's head gorged with a collar componée.

Hyde. Gu. on a saltire engr. or, five torteaux, a chief erm.

Hyde. Az. a chev. betw. three lozenges or, on a canton gu. a lion ramp. betw. two crosses crosslet fitchée of the second.

Hyde. Ar. a chev. betw. two mullets in chief and a cinquefoil in base gu.

Hyde (co. Norfolk). Or, a chev. betw. three lozenges az. on a chief gu. a saltire engr. betw. two martlets fessways of the first. *Crest*—A cock's head erased az. combed purp. on the neck a lozenge or, betw. four bezants, in the beak a pansy flower ppr. stalked and leaved vert.

Hyde (Hyde, co. Bedford and co. Dorset; arms confirmed by Cooke, Clarenceux, 1571). Az. a chev. betw. three lozenges or. *Crest*—A raven volant sa. mantled gu. doubled ar.

Hyde (South Denchworth and Kingston Lisle, co. Berks; an ancient and distinguished family, of which was Sir GEORGE HYDE, of Kingston Lisle, Knight of the Bath, *temp.* James I., whom a pedigree, Harl. MSS. 1535, states to have been sixth in descent from the first of the family who settled at Denchworth). Gu. two chevronels ar. *Crest*—A lion's head erased sa. bezantée.

525

Hyde (Pangborne, co. Berks). Same *Arms* as HYDE, of South Denchworth. *Crests*—1st: A spear ppr. with a pennon gu.; 2nd, as HYDE, of South Denchworth.

Hyde (Romsey, co. Hants; descended from HYDE, of Denchworth. Visit. Hants, 1634). Gu. two chev. ar. on the upper a fleur-de-lis az.

Hyde (Norbury and Hyde, co. Chester). Az. a chev. betw. three lozenges or. *Crest*—An eagle, wings endorsed sa. beaked and membered or.

Hyde, or Hide (Ireland; Fun. Ent. 1656). Same *Arms*, on each lozenge a fleur-de-lis gu. a crescent for diff.

Hyde (Castle Hyde, now of Creg, co. Cork; allowed by Betham, then Deputy Ulster, to JOHN HYDE, Esq., Esquire to the *Earl of Shannon*, at his installation as a Knight of St. Patrick, 29 June, 1809). Gu. two chevronels ar. the upper one charged with an erm. spot. *Crest*—A leopard's head erased sa. bezantée. *Motto*—De vivis nil nisi verum.

Hyde (Reg. Ulster's Office). Purp. a chev. betw. three lions pass. or.

Hyde (Great Hadham, co. Herts, and co. Salop). Same *Arms*.

Hyde (London). Per pale or and az. on a chev. engr. betw. three lozenges all counterchanged, on the dexter side as many guttées d'eau, and in the sinister three erm. spots. *Crest*—Seven arrows, six in saltire and one in pale, az. feathered and headed ar. enfiled with an Eastern coronet or.

Hyde (St. Katharine's, co. Middlesex; confirmed 5 Aug. 1637). Az. on a chev. betw. three lozenges or, as many fleurs-de-lis gu.

Hyde (Whetstone, co. Middlesex; granted 1691). Erm. an eagle displ. ermines, debruised with a chev. engr. or, charged with three lozenges az. *Crest*—A demi eagle displ. and erased az. gorged with a collar ar. charged with three lozenges or.

Hyde (co. Stafford). Sa. a fesse betw. six martlets ar.

Hyde (co. Stafford). Or, a chev. gu. betw. three mullets pierced az.

Hyde. Az. a chev. betw. three lions ramp. ar. (another, or).

Hyde (Stoke Bliss, co. Hereford; Har. MSS. 1043). Ar. on a chev. betw. three fleurs-de-lis sa. as many crescents of the field.

Hydon (quartered by HALS, of Beauford, co. Devon. Visit. 1620). Gu. three bezants.

Hydon (quartered by HARINGTON, Bart., of Ridlington, through SAPCOTE, of Burleigh; Sir JAMES HARINGTON, first bart., *m.* FRANCES, dau. and co-heir of ROBERT SAPCOTE. Visit. Rutland, 1618). Gu. three bezants, a label of three points az.

Hyelt. Ar. a lion ramp. sa. a chief per fesse indented of the first and gu.

Hyende. Gu. a chev. betw. three lozenges ar. on a chief of the first a lion pass. of the second.

Hyer (London). Gu. a porcupine ar. collared or.

Hyett (Wotton, co. Somerset, 1573). Ar. a lion ramp. gu. a chief per fesse indented of the first and sa. *Crest*—A demi pegasus sa. crined or, wings endorsed, of the last.

Hyett. Same *Arms*. *Crest*—A dexter hand, holding a thistle in pale ppr.

Hyett (Brampton, co. Hereford; RICHARD HYETT, Esq., was Sheriff co. Hereford, 1601). Ar. a lion ramp. sa. in chief a fesse of the second, a crescent for diff.

Hyett (co. Gloucester). Ar. a lion ramp. sa. a chief indented of the last. *Crest*—A tower gu. out of the battlements a demi lion ramp. sa.

Hyett (Painswick House, co. Gloucester). Quarterly, 1st and 4th, ar. a lion ramp. az. on a chief dancettée sa. two roses ar., for HYETT; 2nd and 3rd, erm. three cats pass. in pale az., for ADAMS. *Crests*—1st: A castle ppr. charged with four pellets, issuing therefrom a lion's head sa. in the mouth a rose slipped gu., for HYETT; 2nd: A greyhound's head erased erm., for ADAMS. *Motto*—Cor immobile.

Hygate. Gu. two bars ar. on a bend or, a torteaux betw. as many leopards' faces az.

Hyggins (Nook). Ar. a saltire az. betw. a mullet in chief and base, and an increscent and decrescent in the flanks gu.

Hygham. Sa. a fesse componée or and az.

Hygham, or Hyham. Az. a bend betw. two herons ar.

Hyghlord, alias Hellard (co. Devon, and Mitcham, co. Surrey). Sa. a bend flory ar. *Crest*—A ship in full sail in a sea all ppr.

Hyghmore (Femethwayt, co. Cumberland). Erm. a crossbow bent betw. three moorcocks sa. *Crest*—A moorcock ppr.

Hyham. Az. a bend betw. three lapwings ar.

Hylton. See HILTON, Hilton Castle.

Hymerford. Ar. a chev. sa. betw. three shovellers ppr.

Hymor (co. Northumberland). Or, a crossbow sa. betw. four cocks gu.

Hympen, or Hympden (co. Hertford). Gu. three bars gemels erm. a chief indented of the second.

Hynd (Hesore, co. Bucks; granted 1583). Gu. a chev. betw. three hinds or.

Hynd (London). Gu. on a chev. betw. three hinds trippant or, a lion's head erased az. betw. two hurts, each charged with a fleur-de-lis of the second. *Crest*—A hand gu. holding an eagle's claw ppr.

Hynde (certified by Roberts, Ulster, 1647, to OBADIAH HYNDE, descended from co. Lancaster, who served for four years in the Netherlands, and arrived in Ireland in April, 1647, as Lieut. in the Parliament Army). Ar. on a chev. az. three escallops of the first, on a chief of the second a lion pass. of the field, armed and langued gu. all within a border or. *Crest*—A demi pegasus ramp. ar. maned or, grasping with the paws a sword ppr. pommel and hilt gold.

Hynde. Same *Arms. Crest*—A hind's head couped ppr. collared or, holding in the mouth a rose gu. leaved vert.

Hynde. Az. on a chev. gu. betw. three goats' heads erased az. attired and collared or, as many lozenges of the first, on a chief sa. a lion pass. guard. of the fourth. *Crest*—A griffin's head az. collared and charged with an escallop or, betw. two wings of the first guttée d'eau.

Hynde (Sir JOHN HYNDE, Chief Justice of Common Pleas, *d.* 1550). Ar. on a chev. az. betw. three goats' heads erased sa. horned and collared or, as many lozenges of the last, on a chief of the third a lion pass. guard. erm. *Crest*—A demi eagle az. guttée de larmes, beaked or, collared ar. and charged upon the breast with an escallop gold. *Motto*—Miserere mei Deus.

Hynde. Sa. a lion pass. ar. betw. three escallops of the second, each charged with a lozenge az. *Crest*—An ostrich's head couped chequy ar. and sa. in the mouth a horseshoe az.

Hynde (Hedsore, co. Buckingham; ROWLAND HYNDE, eldest son of AUGUSTIN HYNDE, Alderman and Sheriff of London, 1551. Visit. Notts, 1614). Gu. a chev. betw. three hinds or. *Crest*—On a ducal coronet or, a cockatrice gold, combed and legged gu.

Hynde (Laxton, co. Nottingham; AUGUSTINE and RICHARD HYNDE, sons of AUGUSTINE HYNDE, of the Inner Temple, second son of AUGUSTIN HYNDE, Sheriff of London, 1551. Visit. Notts, 1614). Same *Arms* and *Crest*, a crescent for diff.

Hynde. Gu. three hinds' heads erased ar.

Hyndfield. Ar. a fesse betw. three boars pass. sa.

Hyndford, Earl of. See CARMICHAEL.

Hyndley. Ar. an eagle, wings expanded sa. preying on a child in swaddling clothes, the face ppr. clothes gu. and binding or.

Hyndman. Az. a saltire or. *Crest*—A sundial and the sun shining thereon all ppr. *Motto*—True as the dial to the sun.

Hyndstoke. Sa. a chev. or, in chief two lions ramp. of the second.

Hynell. Sa. a fleur-de-lis or. *Crest*—An angel in a praying posture ppr.

Hyslop (Scotland). Ar. a stag ppr. lodged under a holly tree growing out of the base vert.

Hyslop (ARCHIBALD HYSLOP, Stationer, Edinburgh, 1678). Ar. a stag ppr. lodged under a holly tree growing out of the base vert, on a chief of the third a book bound or, betw. two stars of the first. *Crest*—A bookbinder's folding stick and polishing iron crossing each other saltireways ppr. *Motto*—His parva crescunt.

Hyslop-Maxwell (Glengaber). See MAXWELL.

Hytte (co. Worcester). Vert six talbots pass. three, two, and one, ar. armed and membered sa. a crescent for diff.

I

I'ANON. Quarterly, az. and or, a cross patonce gu. a chief ar.

I'ans (Whitstone; descended from ROBERT I'ANS, Esq., Master of the Ordnance to Queen Elizabeth, and one of Her Majesty's Privy Council in Ireland). Gu. on a bend ar. three Cornish choughs sa.

I'anson (originally of cos. Westmoreland and York, subsequently of co. Northampton, and finally of co. Dorset; derived through JAMES I'ANSON, of Hawkeswell, Richmond, captain of a man-of-war, *temp.* Henry VIII. from a noble family in France; the last male heir, JOHN BANKES I'ANSON,

526

Rector of Corfe Castle, *d.* 28 Oct. 1799, when the representation of the family devolved on his first cousin, the dau. of his uncle, JOHN I'ANSON, Esq., MARY, wife of SAMUEL FYLER, Esq.). Quarterly, az. and gu. a cross patonce and a chief or. *Crest*—A griffin's head betw. two wings ppr.

Ibbetson (Leeds, co. York, bart.). Gu. on a bend cotised ar. betw. two toisons d'or, three escallops of the field. *Crest*—A unicorn's head erased per fesse ar. and gu. charged with three escallops, two and one, counterchanged. *Motto*—Vixi liber et moriar.

Ibbetson (SELWIN-IBBETSON, Down Hall, co. Essex, bart.; Sir JOHN THOMAS IBBETSON, sixth bart., assumed the name of SELWIN in lieu of IBBETSON, 1825, on inheriting Down Hall; his son, Sir HENRY JOHN SELWIN-IBBETSON, seventh bart., resumed his paternal surname after SELWIN). Quarterly, 1st and 4th, gu. on a bend cotised ar. betw. two toisons d'or, three escallops of the field, for IBBETSON; 2nd and 3rd, ar. on a bend cotised sa. three annulets or, for SELWIN. *Crests*—1st, IBBETSON; A unicorn's head ar. powdered with escallops, horned, maned, and erased gu.; 2nd, SELWIN: Two lions' gambs erased ar. supporting a torch in pale or, fired ppr. *Motto*—Vixi liber et moriar.

Ibbotson (granted to CHARLES IBBOTSON, Esq., of Crofton Hall, co. York). Az. on a bend cotised betw. two unicorns' heads erased ar. armed and crined or, an estoile betw. two escallops sa. *Crest*—A unicorn's head, as in the arms, charged on the neck with an escallop gu. betw. four estoiles az.

Ibbott (quartered by COPLESTONE, of Bicton, through REIGNEY. Visit. Devon, 1620). Sa. a fess betw. three trees ar.

Ibgrave (co. Hertford). Per pale ar. and gu. on a cross moline betw. two lozenges in fesse a lozenge betw. four mullets all counterchanged. *Crest*—A dexter arm embowed, vested bendy of six or and az. cuffed ar. holding in the hand ppr. a cross crosslet fitchée sa.

Ibgrave (co. Suffolk). Per fesse or and gu. a fer-de-moline betw. four lozenges counterchanged.

Ibyneworth, or Ibenworth. Ar. a chev. betw. three lozenges gu.

Icham. Sa. a chev. betw. three hawks ar. belled or.

Ichingham, or Echingham. Az. fretty ar. *Crest*—A demi dragon, wings expanded vert.

Ickam (Canterbury). Ar. on a chev. sa. three keys ensigned with a coronet or.

Ickworth. Sa. a lion saliant ar. armed and langued gu. a bordure gobony of the first and second.

Ideche (co. Suffolk). Ar. a fesse betw. two chevronels gu.

Ideley (co. Oxford; arms from a stone in Dorchester Church. Visit. Oxon, 1574). Erm. a fess per fess dancettée or and gu.

Iden. See EDEN.

Idio (Wyllt, Wales). Sa. a chev. betw. three spears' heads ar. embrued gu.

Idle. Gu. a fesse or, in chief two helmets ppr. garnished of the second. *Crest*—A helmet, as in the arms.

Idle. Per pale gu. and az. a chev. erminois betw. three helmets ppr. *Crest*—A leopard pass. reposing the dexter foot on a helmet all ppr.

Idnerth-Benfras (Lord of Masebrook, *jure uxoris* EVA, dau. and heir of CADWGAN VYCHAN, of Masebrook-Idnerth, derived from EDWYN, Lord of Tegaingle. Descendants of IDNERTH: I. BROMFIELDS, of Mortyn; II. LLOYDS, of Glantanad Uch; III. WYNNS, of Abercynlleth; IV. OWENS, of Woodhouse, Condover, Llynloedd, Rhain, and Wilcock; V. WYNNS, of Llangywer; VI. GRIFFITHS, of Brongain and Broniarth; VII. HUMPHREYS, of Meardy Gwyddelwern; VIII. LLOYDS, of Mathruval; IX. LEWIS, of Cil; and others). Ar. a cross engr. flory sa. betw. four choughs ppr. on a chief az. a boar's head couped close of the first, armed or, langued ar.

Idwal (King of Wales). Az. a cross pattée fitchée betw. four martlets or.

Ievan ap Iorwerth (Llanwyllin, co. Merioneth; derived from SANDDE HARDD, Lord of Burton). *Arms*, those of SANDDE HARDD, vert semée of broom-slips a lion ramp. er.

Ifield. Az. a chev. betw. three acorns or. husked vert. *Crest*—Out of a ducal coronet or, a dolphin's head az.

Iggulden (Deal, co. Kent, and Russell Square, London). Quarterly, erm. and az. in the second and third quarters a vine branch and bunch of grapes ppr. over all on a bend gu. three stags' heads caboshed ar. *Crest*—Two arms in armour embowed, placing a savage's head in profile on the point of a pheon all ppr.

Ihones (London, and co. Salop, 1610). Az. a lion pass. betw. three crosses formée fitch ée or, a chief of the second. *Crest*—A lion ramp. or, supporting an anchor az. stock of the first.

Iilsey. Ar. three molehills ppr.

Ikeling, or Ikling. Az. a chief chequy ar. and gu. (another, or and gu.).

Ikensale, or Iskensale (co. Suffolk). Gu. a fesse betw. two chevronels or, a canton erm.

Ikensale. Az. a fret or.

Ilam (London). Ar. a fesse engr. betw. six cinquefoils sa. (another has the fess charged with three crosses crosslet of the field).

Ilam, or Ilamy. Ar. a fesse betw. six escallops sa. *Crest*—A peacock's head betw. two wings or, holding in the beak a serpent, the tail twisted round the neck ppr.

Ilam, or Ilamy. Ar. a fesse betw. six escallops sa.

Ilard. Az. three mullets or.

Ilbert (Bowringsleigh, and Horswell House, co. Devon; settled prior to 17th century at Rill, in the parish of Buckfastleigh). Or, two chevronels engr. vert betw. three roses gu. seeded and barbed ppr. quartering ROOPE. *Crest*—A cock pheasant ar. combed and wattled gu. *Another Crest*—A demi wivern issuing vert, collared or. *Motto*—Nulla rosa sine spinis.

Ilbery (Biscaya, Spain, and Reading, co. Berks; borne by JAMES ILBERY, Esq., of London and Calcutta). Ar. a chev. sa. betw. three herons ppr. *Crest*—A demi dragon vert, wings and belly flesh-colour, holding in the claws a lozenge az. charged with a fleur-de-lis or.

Ilchester, Earl of. See FOX-STRANGWAYS.

Ilchester, Town of (co. Somerset). In a crescent an estoile of sixteen points.

Ilcombe (quartered by PYNE, of Estdown. Visit. Devon, 1620). Gu. two lions pass. guard. ar. a bordure engr. sa.

Ilderton (Ilderton, co. Northumberland). Ar. three water bougets gu.

Ilderton (co. York). Or, three water bougets sa. *Crest*—Out of a ducal coronet or, a battle-axe broken in the handle ppr.

Ilderton. Ar. two bars sa.

Ile. Or, a chev. gu. (another, or, a fesse betw. two chevronels sa.).

Iles (co. York). Ar. a fesse engr. sa. in chief three fleurs-de-lis of the last.

Iles. Per pale az. and or, on a canton ar. a lion ramp. gu. *Crest*—A wolf collared and lined ppr.

Ilesley. Az. three bars ar.

Iley. Ar. a fesse engr. betw. six fleurs-de-lis sa. *Crest*—A cubit arm erect, vested ar. holding in the hand ppr. a fleur-de-lis sa.

Iliff (WILLIAM TIFFIN ILIFF, Esq., of Newington Butts). Sa. a lion ramp. ar. collared gu. betw. three crosses pattée or. *Crest*—A demi lion ramp. ar. collared gu. *Motto*—Vive ut vivas.

Ilinn. Ar. a horse's head erased sa. bridled or. *Crest*—A wolf's head erased gu.

Illeigh (co. Northumberland). Erm. two chev. sa.

Illey (co. Lincoln). Gu. an eagle displ. or, a bendlet of the field.

Illey (co. Suffolk). Same *Arms.*

Illey, Iley, and Ilney. Erm. a chev. sa. *Crest*—A hand erect holding a cross crosslet fitchée in pale.

Illey, Illes, or Ilys. Az. a cross or, guttée de sang betw. four doves ar. (another, martlets).

Illey, or Isley. Erm. a fesse gu.

Illidge (JOHN ILLIDGE, Esq., of Brixton, co. Surrey). Erm. on a chev. engr. sa. three bezants, in chief two eagles' heads erased of the second. *Crest*—An eagle's head erased sa. in front of a saltire couped or. *Motto*—Aquila non capit muscas.

Illing. Per pale sa. and or, three lozenges in pale counterchanged.

Illingworth (co. Leicester). Erm. on a bend gu. three chaplets or.

Illingworth, or Illingsworth (co. Surrey). Ar. a fesse flory gu. betw. three escallops sa. *Crest*—Within a crescent ar. a cock crowing sa.

Ilsake. Sa. a bend or, on a sinister canton ar. a leopard's face of the second.

Ilsley (Ilsley, co. Berks). Or, two bars gemels sa. in chief three pellets.

Ilsley, or Illsley. Same *Arms. Crest*—Betw. two serpents disposed orlewaya, tails in saltire, a cock ppr.

Image (Whepstead and Bury, co. Suffolk). Az. on a cross flory ar. five guttes de sang, on a canton of the second a fusil of the field. *Crest*—A wolf's head erased az. gorged with a collar ar. charged with three roundels, holding in the mouth a cross crosslet fitchée.

Imbort. Or, billettée a lion rump. sa.

Imbrie (Crubie, Scotland, 1672). Barry of eight sa. and ar.

527

over all three fusils counterchanged. *Crest*—A plough ppr. *Motto*—Evertendo fæcundat.

Imhoff. Ar. three buffaloes' heads couped sa.

Immins. Gu. on a fesse betw. three lozenges or, as many escallops of the first, a bordure engr. also of the first, charged with eight plates. *Crest*—A dragon's head couped.

Impey (Hammersmith, co. Middlesex). Gu. on a chev. betw. three leopards' faces or, as many cinquefoils of the field.

Impey (Yarmouth, co. Norfolk). Gu. on a chev. or, three crescents of the first. *Crest*—A leopard's face sa. betw. two wings or.

Impey. Vert a unicorn's head erased ar. *Crest*—An ostrich, wings endorsed, holding in the beak a horseshoe ppr.

Inbell. Sa. a bend ar. betw. three trefoils of the second.

Ince (Ince, co. Lancaster). Ar. three torteaux in bend betw. two cotises sa. *Crest*—On a mount vert a horse sejant against an oak tree ppr.

Ince (city of Chester, 1613). Same *Arms*, a fleur-de-lis or, on a mullet of the second for diff. *Crest*—A tree fruited or.

Ince, or Inch (co. Lincoln). Ar. three torteaux in bend betw. two bendlets sa.

Incent (co. Oxford; arms in Chyner Church. Visit. Oxon, 1574). Ar. on a bend engr. gu. a woman recumbent of the field, holding a rose ppr. in chief a martlet of the second.

Inchiquin, Baron. See O'BRIEN.

Inckell. Sa. a bend ar. betw. six martlets (another, mullets) or.

Inckpen (Golaker, co. Hants). Gu. two bars gemels or, a chief erm.

Inckpen, or Inckpeny (Whitehouse, co. Hants). Gu. two bars gemels or, a chief indented erm. *Crest*—A dexter hand holding a club ppr.

Incledon (Incledon, in Braunton, co. Devon; traceable by records from the time of Edward III.; the heiress *m.* P. R. WEBBER, Esq. The representative of a younger branch and heir male of the family is INCLEDON, of Yeotown House, in Goodleigh, co. Devon). Ar. a chev. engr. betw. three tuns sa. fire issuing from the bungholes ppr. *Crest*—A falcon ppr. beaked and belled or.

Infant. Gu. three boys' heads couped ar. crined or.

Ingaldesthorp (co. Norfolk). Gu. a cross engr. ar.

Ingaram. See INGERHAM.

Inge (co. Bedford). Or, a chev. vert.

Inge (Thorpe Constantine, co. Stafford; descended from RICHARD INGE, Esq., co. Leicester, by JANE, his wife, dau. and co-heiress of Alderman WILLIAM IVES, co. Leicester, who purchased Thorpe in 1631). Or, on a chev. vert three leopards' faces ar. (another, or). *Crest*—Two battle axes in saltire ppr. enfiled with a ducal coronet or.

Inge. Or, on a chev. vert three leopards' faces of the field. *Crest*—A hand holding a glove ppr.

Inge (temp. Edward I.). Or, a chev. vert.

Ingefield, or Ingefeld. Barry of fourteen gu. and ar. on a canton of the first a mullet of the second.

Ingeham. Gu. three bars vair.

Ingelram. Quarterly, 1st and 4th, vair two bars gu.; 2nd and 3rd, gu. a fesse az.

Ingelton. Ar. a chev. betw. three crescents sa. flammant gu.

Ingerham (co. Warwick; confirmed to Sir ARTHUR INGARAM). Gu. on a chev. betw. three lions pass. or.

Ingerham, or Ingerhall. Or, two palets gu.

Ingerham. Barry of twelve az. and ar.

Ingerland. Ar. a fesse az. betw. three hawks' heads erased sa. *Crest*—On a plate a thistle ppr.

Ingersalem. Ar. seven bars gemels az.

Ingham (Baron *Ingham ;* OLIVER DE INGHAM, of Ingham, co. Norfolk, was summoned to Parliament 1328, *d.* 1344, leaving two daus. his co-heirs). Per pale or and vert a cross moline gu.

Ingham (co. Norfolk). Per pale or and vert a cross moline gu. *Crest*—On a chapeau gu. turned up erm. an owl ppr. sitting in holly leaves vert.

Ingham (Marton in Craven, co. York). Quarterly, or and vert a cross moline counterchanged, on a chief ar. a maunch sa. *Crest*—Two arms embowed, vested, and holding betw. the hands a maunch. *Motto*—In veritate victoria.

Ingham-Abbey (co. Norfolk). Ar. a cross pattée per saltire gu. and az.

Ingham (cos. Kent and Norfolk). Quarterly, or and vert, a cross engr. gu.

Ingham (co. Leicester). Erm. a cross patonce gu.

Ingham (co. Norfolk). Quarterly, or and vert a cross moline gu.

Ingham, or Inge (co. Stafford). Or, a chev. vert.

Ingham, or Hugham. Ar. a chev. sa. betw. three pellets, on a chief gu. a lion pass. reguard. or.

Ingham, or Ingeham. Per pale erm. and vert a cross pattée gu. Crest—An arm in armour embowed issuing from a cloud in the sinister, holding a sword ppr.

Ingham. Or, on a fesse gu. three escallops of the first.

Ingham. Vert on a fesse ar. three escallops per fesse or and gu.

Ingilbert. Gu. a bend or, cotised ar.

Ingleby (23 Edward III. Visit. Yorkshire, Harl. MSS. 1420, f. 240). Sa. an estoile ar. Crest—A boar's head couped ar. armed or.

Ingleby (Lankland Hall, co. York). Same Arms. Crest—A boar's head erect ar. Motto—Mon droit.

Ingleby (Austwick, co. York: borne by CHRISTOPHER INGLEBY, Esq., of that place). Same Arms, Crest, and Motto as last.

Ingilby (AMCOTTS-INGILBY, Kettlethorpe Park, co. Lincoln, and Ripley Castle, co. York, bart., extinct 1854; JOHN INGILBY, illegitimate son of Sir JOHN INGLEBY, sixth bart. of Ripley, was created a bart. 1781). Quarterly, 1st and 4th, sa. an estoile of six points ar. within a bordure engr. compony gu. and or, for INGILBY; 2nd and 3rd, ar. a tower triple-towered betw. three covered cups az., for AMCOTTS. Crests—1st: A boar's head couped and erect ar. tusked or, issuant out of the mouth an estoile of the last, for INGILBY; 2nd: A squirrel sejant gu. cracking a nut, and collared or, for AMCOTTS.

Ingilby (Ripley, co. York, bart.). Sa. an estoile ar. a bordure engr. gobony or and gu. The marriage in 1502 of Sir WILLIAM INGLEBY, of Ripley, with CICELY, sister and co heiress of GILBERT, Lord Talboys, of Kyme, brought in numerous brilliant quarterings. Crest—A boar's head couped and erect ar. tusked or, in the mouth an estoile of the last. Motto—Mon droit.

Ingilton. Ar. a chev. sa. betw. three griffins' heads erased az. and five crosses crosslet fitchée of the second.

Ingle. Ar. two chevronels sa. on a chief of the second a lion pass. of the first. Crest—A hand erect issuing out of a cloud holding a sword blade waved ppr.

Inglebert. Gu. a bend cotised or. Crest—A greyhound courant towards a tree vert.

Inglebert, or Ingleberd. Gu. on a fesse or, cotised ar. a crescent sa.

Inglebert (quartered by NEVILL, of Holt. Visit. Leicester, 1619). Bendy of eight or and vert a chev. erm.

Ingleby (Ripley, co. York, bart., extinct 1772, created 1642; Sir JOHN INGLEBY, sixth bart. d. s. p. 14 July, 1772). Sa. an estoile of six points ar. Crest—A boar's head ar. tusks or.

Ingleby (co. Worcester). Same Arms.

Ingleby (quartered by PENISTON, of Bampton, co. Oxford. Visit. Oxon, 1566). Ar. an estoile pierced gu.

Ingleby (co. Chester). Sa. a star of eight points ar.

Ingleby (co. Norfolk). Sa. an estoile of sixteen points ar.

Ingleby (co. York). Sa. an estoile erm.

Ingleby. Sa. five fleurs-de-lis ar. two, one, and two.

Ingleby. Sa. a fleur-de-lis ar.

Ingleden. Az. a fesse dancettée or, betw. three guttées d'or.

Ingleden (Newcastle-on-Tyne and co. York). Ar. on a chev. gu. betw. three flames of fire ppr. as many mullets of the field. Crest—A phœnix ppr. Motto—Ex flamma lux.

Ingledew. Ar. a chev. betw. three mullets gu. Crest— A dexter arm embowed fesseways issuing from a cloud in the sinister, reaching forth a garland of laurel.

Inglefield (co. Berks). Barry of eight ar. and gu. on a chief or, a lion pass. az.

Inglefield (co. Warwick). Gu. two bars ar. on a chief or, a lion pass. az. Crest—An arm embowed habited per pale gu. and or, cuffed ar. grasping in the hand ppr. a branch vert.

Inglefield. Barry of ten ar. and gu. on a canton of the second a mullet of the first.

Inglefield. Ar. four bars gu. a canton of the first.

Inglefield. Closetted gu. and ar. on a chief or, a lion pass. sa.

Inglefield (Fun. Ent. Ulster's Office, 1673. KATHERINE INGLEFIELD, wife of CHRISTOPHER KENNEDY, of Dublin). Barry of six gu. and ar. on a chief or, a lion pass. az. an annulet for diff.

Inglethorp, or Inglethorpe (co. Norfolk). Gu. a cross engr. ar.

Inglethorpe (co. Worcester; RICHARD INGLETHORPE, Mayor of Worcester, 1610). Same Arms.

Inglethorpe. Ar. on a canton gu. a rose or.

Ingleton, or Incleden (Brampton, co. Devon). Ar. a chev. engr. sa. betw. three tuns of the last, from the bung-

hole of each a flame issuing ppr. Crest—A hand issuing from a cloud in fesse pointing to a serpent ppr.

Inglett (Allington, co. Devon). Sa. a bend ar. betw. six escallops or. Crest—A lion's head erased gu.

Ingley (1535). Or, a fesse chequy ar. and az.

Inglis (Murdieston, co. Lanark). Az. a lion ramp. ar. in chief three stars of the second.

Inglis (Murdieston, 1734; paternally HAMILTON). Quarterly, 1st and 4th, as the last; 2nd, gu. three cinquefoils erm. within a bordure embattled or, for HAMILTON, of Inverdovat; 3rd, ar. on a chev. sa. betw. three boars' heads erased gu. armed of the second, a crescent of the first, for ELPHINSTONE. Crest—A demi lion ar. grasping in his dexter paw an oak branch slipped ppr. Motto—Invictus maneo.

Inglis (Manner and Mannerhead, co. Peebles). Az. a lion ramp. ar. in chief three stars of the second. Crest—A demi lion ramp. ar. Motto—Nobilis est ira leonis.

Inglis (JOHN INGLIS, Advocate, 1672). As Manner, within a bordure gu. Same Crest. Motto—Recte faciendo securus.

Inglis (Newtounleys, co. Haddington). Az. a lion ramp. ar. on a chief engr. of the second three stars of the first. Crest—A star environed with clouds ppr. Motto—In tenebris lucidior.

Inglis (Cramond, co. Edinburgh, bart., 1687. title extinct or dormant; C. HALKETT CRAIGIE INGLIS, of Cramond, heir of line). Az. a lion saliant ar. on a chief or, three mullets of the first. Crest—A demi lion ramp. ar. holding in the dexter paw a mullet or. Motto—Nisi Dominus frustra.

Inglis (Mauldslie, co. Lanark, afterwards Milton-Bryan, co. Bedford, bart., 1801, title extinct). Az. a lion ramp. ar. within a bordure of the second, on a chief or, three stars of six points of the field. Crest—A demi lion ramp. ppr. in the dexter paw an estoile or. Mottoes—Above the crest: Nobilis est ira leonis; under the arms: Recte faciendo securus.

Inglis (Gen. Sir WILLIAM INGLIS, K.C.B., 1815). Az. a lion ramp. ar. within a bordure of the last, on a chief or, three mullets of the field. Crest—A demi lion ar. Motto—Nobilis est ira leonis.

Inglis (S. B. INGLIS, Captain in the German Legion, 1815). Az. a lion ramp. ar. in chief a frigate under sail or, betw. two mullets of the second. Crest—Out of a mural crown or, a demi lion ramp. ar. Supporters—Dexter, a sailor, vested blue, trousers white, holding in his dexter hand a French flag, somewhat lowered; sinister, a lion ramp. guard. ar. collared az. the collar charged with three mullets also ar.

Inglis (Glencorse, co. Edinburgh; Lord Justice General of Scotland, 1867). Az. a lion ramp. ar. on a chief of the last three mullets sa. Crest—A demi lion ramp. holding in his dexter paw a mullet ar. Crest—Recte faciendo securus.

Inglis (Broomhill, co. Lanark, 1873). Az. a lion ramp. ar. on a chief or, three arrows banded together, points downward, betw. two mullets of the third. Crest—A demi lion ramp. ar. holding in his dexter paw a mullet gu. Motto— Recte faciendo securus.

Inglis (Edinburgh). Az. a lion ramp. ar. on a chief or, three mullets of the field. Crest—A demi lion holding a mullet. Motto—Invictus maneo.

Inglish (co. Norfolk). Gu. three bars gemels or, on a canton ar. six billets sa.

Inglish (co. Suffolk). Gu. three bars gemels or, on a canton ar. five billets sa.

Inglish. Quarterly, or and gu. in the first quarter a lion ramp. of the second. Crest—An ear of wheat and a palm branch in saltire ppr.

Inglish. Erm. a bend az.

Inglos, or Inglosse (the dau. of INGLOSSE m. CHARLES HOSKYNS, Visit. London, 1568, son of THOMAS HOSKYNS, co. Monmouth). Barry of six or and az. on a canton ar. five billets in saltire of the field.

fngloys (co. Norfolk). Gu. two bars gemels or, a canton ar. billettée sa.

Ingo, or Ingoe (co. Essex). Ar. three roses gu. seeded or, barbed vert.

Ingo (co. Essex). Az. three cinquefoils pierced or. Crest— Out of a ducal coronet or, a dragon's head and wings gu.

Ingoldsby, or Ingoldsby (Lethenborough, Waldridge, co. Buckingham, and Newbottle, co. Northampton, bart., extinct 1726, derived from Sir ROGER INGOLDSBY, Lord of Ingoldsby, co. Lincoln, in 1230. Of this family were Sir RICHARD INGOLDSBY, K.B., the celebrated Parliamentary General, and Sir HENRY INGOLDSBY, of Lethenborough, created a baronet in 1661, sons of Sir RICHARD INGOLDSBY, Knt., of Lethenborough, by ELIZABETH, his wife, dau. of Sir OLIVER CROMWELL, K.B.). Erm. a saltire engr. sa. Crest— Out of a ducal coronet or, a demi lion gu. charged on the shoulder with an estoile gold. *Motto* (Reg. Ulster's Office) —Fiducia creat fidem.

Ingoldsby (co. Lincoln). Sa. a chev. betw. three estoiles ar. a bordure engr. or.

Ingoldsby (co. York). Sa. an estoile of six points ar. a bordure or.

Ingoldesthorpe (co. Norfolk, 1223). Gu. a cross engr. ar.

Ingon (France). Vert a cross crosslet fitchée in the foot or.

Ingowville (Jersey). Ar. a cross gu. betw. four eagles displ. sa. *Crest*—A lion ramp. ppr.

Ingpen (Galaker, co. Hants; descended from THOMAS INGPEN, of that place, 27 Edward III. Visit. Hants, 1634). Gu. two bars gemels ar. a chief indented erm.

Ingram (*Viscount Irvine*, extinct 1778; HENRY INGRAM, Esq., of Temple Newsom, co. York, was so created in the Peerage of Scotland, 1661; CHARLES, tenth Viscount, *d.* without male issue, 27 June, 1778, leaving five daus., his co-heirs). Erm. on a fesse gu. three escallops or. *Crest*—A cock ppr. *Supporters*—Dexter, a griffin ppr.; sinister, an antelope ppr. horned, maned, tufted, and unguled or, ducally gorged gu. *Motto*—Magnanimus esto.

Ingram (MEYNELL-INGRAM, Temple Newsom and Hatfield, co. York, and Hoar Cross, co. Stafford; HUGO CHARLES MEYNELL, eldest son of HUGO MEYNELL, Esq., of Hoar Cross, by Hon. ELIZABETH INGRAM, his wife, dau. and co-heir of CHARLES, tenth and last *Viscount Irvine*, assumed the surname of INGRAM). Quarterly, 1st and 4th, erm. on a fesse gu. three escallops or, for INGRAM; 2nd and 3rd, vairé ar. and sa., for MEYNELL, *Crests*—1st, INGRAM: A cock or; 2nd, MEYNELL: A horse's head erased ar. *Motto*—Virtute vici.

Ingram (Halstead, co. Essex, cos. Hereford, Warwick, Worcester, Wilts, and London). Erm. on a fesse gu. three escallops or. *Crest*—A griffin's head quarterly, gu. and ar. *Another Crest*—A cock ppr.

Ingram (JAMES INGRAM, D.D., President of Trinity College, Oxford; descended from JOHN INGRAM, of Codford, co. Wilts, who *d.* there in 1653). Same *Arms.*

Ingram (Upper House, in Clifton-on-Teme, and Ticknell, Bewdley, co. Worcester; descended from JOHN INGRAM, Esq., of Upper House, 1614). Same *Arms.*

Ingram (Earls Court, St. John's, co. Worcester; descended from INGRAM, of Little Wolford, co. Warwick. Visit. Worcester, 1569 and 1634). Same *Arms*, quartering, az. a fess gu. over all a lion ramp. or, for HOSTANG. *Crests*—1st: A griffin's head, quarterly gu. and ar.; 2nd: A cock ppr.

Ingram (ARCHIBALD INGRAM, Provost of Glasgow, 1763). Erm. on a fesse gu. three escallops or, all within a bordure engr. az. charged with eight bees ppr. *Crest*—A phœnix in flames all ppr. *Motto*—Ad sidera vultus.

Ingram. Az. a chev. betw. three lions pass. or. *Crest*—A cock ppr.

Ingram. Per fesse vert and ar. a pale, in chief a bull's head erased, and in base two garbs all counterchanged. *Crest*—A bull's head erased.

Ingram. Or, two pales gu.

Ingstubbs (co. Cambridge). Ar. a fesse gu. in chief a mullet of the second.

Ingwardby (Willesley, co. Derby; a co-heiress *m.* ABNEY, about A.D. 1400). Or, on a chief gu. a lion pass. ar.

Inhoff (Germany). Ar. a lion poisson, or sea-lion.

Inians. Az. three fleurs-de-lis ar.

Inkepenne. Barry of eight gu. and or, on a chief per pale of the second and first a lion pass. ar.

Inkersall (cos. Hertford and Middlesex; Her. Coll.). Gu. a fesse dancettée erm. betw. six trefoils slipped or. *Crest*—A griffin's head gu. gorged with a fesse dancettée erm. betw. two wings displ. or.

Inkledon, or Inkleton (Buckland, co. Devon). Ar. a chev. betw. three tuns sa. flames issuing from the bungs ppr. *Crest*—An ibex pass. or.

Inkpen. Gu. two bars gemels or, a chief invected erm.

Inman. Vert on a chev. or, three roses gu. slipped and leaved of the first. *Crest*—On a mount vert a wivern ppr. ducally gorged and lined or.

Inner, or Junor. Ar. on a cross az. five fleurs-de-lis of the first a bordure engr. of the second.

Innes (that Ilk, co. Elgin, bart., 1625, now represented by the *Duke of Roxburgh*). *Crest*—Within an adder disposed circleways a castle triple-towered ppr. *Supporters*—Two greyhounds ar. each with a collar charged with three stars of the first. *Motto*—Prudentia et vi.

Innes (Balveny, bart., 1628). Ar. three stars in chief az. *Crest*—A dexter arm armed, couped at the elbow, holding a broadsword in pale ppr. *Supporters*—Two greyhounds ar. *Motto*—Pro patria.
529

Innes (Edingight, co. Banff). Ar. three stars az. within a bordure chequy of the second and first. *Crest*—A branch of palm slipped ppr. *Motto*—Ornatur radix fronde.

Innes (Raemoir, co. Aberdeen). As Edingight, with a crescent az. in the fess point for diff. *Crest and Motto*, as Edingight.

Innes (Learney, co. Aberdeen, 1875). Quarterly, 1st and 4th, as Edingight, with a crescent az. in the fess point for diff.; 2nd and 3rd, or, a fess erm. betw. three griffins' heads erased vert, langued gu., for BREBNER. *Crest and Motto* for INNES, as the last. *Crest*—BREBNER: A cubit arm in armour the hand bare, holding a dart point downwards all ppr.

Innes (Lochlash, co. Ross, and Coxton, co. Moray, bart., extinct 1831). Quarterly, 1st and 4th, ar. three stars of six points az., for INNES; 2nd and 3rd, or, on a chief sa. three escallops of the field, for GRAHAM. *Crest*—A boar's head erased ppr. langued gu. *Mottoes*—Be traist; and. Exempla suorum. *Supporters*—Two greyhounds ppr. the dexter gorged with a collar az. charged with three stars of six points az. the sinister gorged with a collar sa. charged with three escallops or, both with chains reflexed over the back of the last.

Innes (Blairtoun, Lyon Depute). Ar. a fesse betw. three stars az. *Crest*—A primrose ppr. thereon a bee sucking the same or. *Motto*—E labore dulcedo.

Innes (Blairtoun, Scotland; as altered 9 Nov. 1688). Erm. three stars az. *Crest*—A thistle ppr. thereon a bee sucking the flower thereof. *Motto*, as the last.

Innes (Edinburgh, 1672). Ar. a cross pattée betw. three stars az. *Crest*—Two hands joined fesseways, grasping a sword all ppr. *Motto*—Ditat servata fides.

Innes (ROBERT INNES, Parson of Gamrie, 1680). Ar. a fess engr. betw. three stars az. *Crest*—A bee ppr. *Motto*—E labore dulcedo.

Innes (GEORGE INNES, Parson of Belhelvie, 1680). Ar. a fess wavy betw. three stars az. Same *Crest* and *Motto.*

Innes (THOMAS INNES, cadet of Benwall, 1680). Ar. a fess counter-embattled betw. three stars az. Same *Crest* and *Motto.*

Innes (Towie, co. Aberdeen, 1685). Ar. a water bouget sa. betw. three stars az. *Crest*—A bee volant ppr. *Motto*—Provide qui laboriosa.

Innes (Reidhall, co. Banff, 1693). Ar. a torteaux betw. three stars az. *Crest*—A bee flying upwards ppr. *Motto*—Non sevit sed laborat.

Innes (Lichnet, co. Banff, 1693). Ar. a fusil fessways betw. three stars az. *Crest*—A bee volant ppr. *Motto*—Provide qui laboriose.

Innes (Dunkinty, co. Elgin). Ar. a chev. betw. three stars az. *Crest*—A star az. *Mottoes*—Virtus ad astra; and, Sub tigno salus.

Innes (Jamaica, 1753). Ar. a crescent betw. three stars az. *Crest*—A crescent az. *Mottoes*—Consilio et labore; and, Virtus tollit ad astra.

Innes (JAMES INNES, of Chelsea, 1722; his dau. JANE, *m.* THOMAS PITT, Esq., of Blandford, grandfather of THOMAS, Lord Camelford, and WILLIAM, Earl of Chatham). Quarterly, 1st and 4th, ar. three stars az. within a bordure of the second; 2nd and 3rd, gu. three swords in point conjoined in the middle chief ar. hilted and pommelled or. *Crest*—A dexter hand and arm from the shoulder vambraced ppr. holding a banner disveloped gu. *Motto*—Pro patria.

Innes (Edinburgh, 1733). Ar. a chev. waved betw. three stars of six points az. *Crest*—A star of twelve points ar. *Motto*—Me duce.

Innes (Gifford Vale, co. Haddington, 1803). Ar. three star of six points az. within a bordure engr. gu. *Crest*—A Scotch thistle with a bee sucking thereof ppr. *Motto*—E labore dulcedo.

Innes (MITCHELL-INNES, of Parson's Green, co. Edinburgh, 1848). Quarterly, 1st and 4th, ar. three stars of six points az. within a bordure az. charged with eight bezants, for INNES; 2nd and 3rd, sa. on a fess betw. three mascles or, as many mullets gu., for MITCHELL. *Crests*—1st, INNES: An increscent ppr.; 2nd, MITCHELL: A hand holding a garland of laurel all ppr. *Mottoes*—1st, INNES: Je recois pour donner; 2nd, MITCHELL: Deo favente.

Innes (Thursiter, co. Caithness). Ar. three stars of five points within a bordure indented az. *Crest*—A star of six points or, environed with clouds all ppr. *Motto*—Dum spiro, cælestia spero.

Innholders, Company of (London). Az. a chev. per pale and per chev. gu. and ar. counterchanged betw. three garbs or, on a chief ar. a St. Julian's cross sa. *Crest*—An estoile of sixteen points or, issuing from clouds in base ppr. *Supporters*—Two horses reguard- ar. *Motto*—Hinc

2 M

spes affulget. (The original motto was, Come, ye blessed, when I was harbourless ye lodged me.)

Inns of Court and Chancery:

BERNARD's. Per pale indented arm. and sa. a chev. gu. fretty or.

CHESTER, or STROUD. Az. on a bend gu. three garbs or, all within a bordure of the second.

CLEMENT's. Ar. an anchor erect without a stock ppr. environed on the centre with the letter C, or.

CLIFFORD's. Chequy or and az. a fesse gu. all within a bordure of the last, charged with eight bezants.

CURSITOR's. Gu. on a chief ar. two mullets sa. a bordure compony or and az.

FURNIVAL's. Ar. a bend betw. six martlets gu. all within a bordure az.

GRAY's. Sa. a griffin segreant or.

KIDDERMINSTER, or SIX CLERKS' OFFICE. Az. on two chev. betw. three plates eight pellets.

LINCOLN's (Gwillim). Az. fifteen fer-de-molines or, on a canton of the second a lion ramp. purp.

LINCOLN's. Or, a lion ramp. purp.

LION's. Chequy or and ar. over all a lion ramp. sa.

NEW, or OUR LADY's. Vert a flower-pot ar. with gilliflowers gu. leaved vert.

SERJEANTS' (Fleet Street). Gu. two garbs in saltire or, banded az.

SERJEANTS' (Chancery Lane). Or, a stork ppr.

STAFFORD's (Office of the Remembrancer of the Exchequer). Or, a chev. gu. a canton erm.

STAPLE's. Vert a woolpack ar. corded of the last.

TEMPLE, INNER. Az. a pegasus saliant or.

TEMPLE, MIDDLE. Ar. on a cross gu. a paschal lamb or, carrying a banner ar. charged with a cross gu.

THAVIES. Ar. on a bend gu. two garbs or, on a chief sa. the letter T of the first.

Innynge. Ar. a chev. betw. three hinds trippant sa. on a canton or, two palets gu.

Inreys, Inrys, or Inereis. Ar. a chev. betw. three measuring yards gu.

Inverarity (Rosemount, co. Forfar, 1840). Gu. on a chev. or, betw. six arrows in chief, three and three, the points upwards, two saltireways and one in pale, plumed and banded ar. and in base a hunting horn stringed of the third, an elephant's head sa. Crest—A rose bush ppr. Motto—Semper floreat.

Inverness, Duchess of. See UNDERWOOD.

Inwardby. Ar. a saltire engr. sa. on a chief of the last two mullets of the first.

Inwood (Cobham, co. Surrey). Vert a griffin pass. or, on a chief of the second three laurel leaves of the first. Crest—A demi lion ramp. or, holding a battle axe az.

Inwyne. Ar. three holly leaves pendent ppr.

Inyng, or Junyng (co. Devon). Or, a fesse betw. two doves sa. a canton quarterly or and gu.

Inyng (co. Devon). Ar. a fesse betw. two hinds' heads sa. a chief paly of four or and gu.

Inyr (styled Earl of Hertford). Az. three crowns or, on an inescutcheon of the first a lion ramp. per fesse or and ar. within a bordure of the last.

Inyr (King of Gwent). Per pale or and az. a tree eradicated ppr. supported on the sinister by a lion ramp. or.

Inyr-ddu (King of Gwent). Per pale az. and sa. three fleurs-de-lis or.

Inys. Ar. three torteaux in bend cotised gu. Crest—On a mount vert a rabbit ppr. against a tree of the first, fructed or.

Iorwerth Goch (Lord of Mochnant, younger son of MEREDITH AP BLEDDYN, Prince of Powis). Descendants: KYNASTONS, of Otley Park, co. Salop, and the KYNASTONS, of Hardwick, extinct family. Az. a lion ramp. sa.

Ipers. Ar. a chev. betw. three bulls' heads couped gu.

Ipgrave. Sa. on a fer-de-moline ar. five mullets gu.

Ipre (Earl of Kent; extinct 1162; creation of King Stephen, 1141). Gyronny of eight or and az. an escallop gu. over all a baton az.

Ipre. Barry lozengy sa. and or. Crest—On a mount vert a leopard couchant guard. gu. ducally crowned or.

Ipres (co. Lancaster). Ar. a chev. betw. three bulls' heads cabossed gu. Crest—A unicorn's head or, collared gu.

Ipstans. Ar. a chev. betw. three mullets gu.

Ipstans, Ipstanes, and Ipstones (Ipstans or Ipstones, co. Suffolk). Ar. a chev. betw. three crescents gu.

Ipstones (Ipstonea; the heiress m. RANDLE BRERETON, of Malpas, co. Chester). Ar. a chev. betw. three crescents gu.

Ipswich, Town of (Suffolk; confirmed in 1561). Per pale gu. and az. in the dexter a lion ramp. guard. or, on the sinister three demi hulks of ships joined to the impaled line

of the last. Crest—A demi lion ramp. or, holding in the paw a ship of three masts, the sails all furled, and round the top of the third, on the maintop mast-head a pennon. Supporters—Two seahorses ppr. finned and maned or.

Irball (co. Lancaster). Ar. a chief chequy or and gu. Crest—Two halberts erased and endorsed sa.

Irbill. Sa. a bend betw. three trefoils slipped ar.

Irby (Baron Boston). Ar. fretty sa. on a canton gu. a chaplet or. Crest—A Saracen's head in profile ppr. wreathed about the temples ar. and sa. (The ancient crest was a tiger's head ar. erased, maned and collared gu.). Supporters—Two antelopes gu. each gorged with a chaplet or. Motto—Honor fidelitatis præmium.

Irby (co. Lincoln; temp. 2 Elizabeth). Ar. fretty sa. Crest—A wivern's head ar. gorged with two bars gemels gu.

Irby (temp. Richard II.). Ar. two quatrefoils and a quarter gu.

Irbye. Ar. a fretty sa. on a canton gu. a cinquefoil (another, a mullet) or.

Irdis, or Irish. Ar. a fesse az. a bendlet gu.

Irebill. Sa. a bend betw. three trefoils ar.

Ireby (cos. Cambridge and Cumberland). Ar. a fret sa. on a canton of the second a mullet of the first. Crest—A sword in pale enfiled with a savage's head ppr.

Ireby (Ireby, co. Cumberland). Ar. a fret gu. a canton az.

Ireby. Ar. fretty gu. a canton sa. Crest—An antelope pass. ppr.

Ireford (London). Ar. on a chev. sa. betw. three fleurs-de-lis az. as many goats' heads erased of the field.

Ireland, Kingdom of. Az. a harp or, stringed ar. The ancient arms of the kingdom after the invasion of 1172 were, "Az. three crowns or." This was the coat of St. Edmund, and it is possible the Anglo-Norman invaders, who were arrayed under the banners of St. George and St. Edmund, introduced the bearings of the latter saint as the ensigns of their new conquest. When Richard II. created ROBERT DE VERE, Earl of Oxford, Duke of Ireland, he gave him as a coat of augmentation the arms of Ireland, viz., "Az. three crowns or." Henry VIII. relinquished the old arms for the "harp" when he declared himself King of Ireland, from an apprehension, it is said, that the three crowns might be taken for the triple tiara of the Pope. Since James I. introduced the arms of Ireland among the quarterings of the Royal achievement, the bearing has been "Az. a harp or, stringed ar." From a MS. in the handwriting of Sir William Le Neve, Clarenceux, it appears on the authority of Sir William Segar, Garter, that "Ye three crowns are ye antient arms of Ireland, the harp but an ancient badge," and "In ye tyme of Edward ye IVth a commission being to enquire the arms of Ireland it was returned yt ye 3 crownes were the armes." The same bearing appears on the reverse of ancient Irish coins. Another ancient coat, as recorded in Ulster's Office, is, Sa. a king sitting on his throne cross-legged, holding in his right hand a lilly or. Crest—A tower triple-towered or, from the portal a hart springing ar. attired and hoofed gold. The badge, as settled at the Union with Great Britain, is the harp ensigned with the imperial crown. A MS. in the British Museum, Add. MSS. 4814, f. 8, exhibits a banner on either side of the shield, viz., dexter, sa. a king enthroned in his chair of state with a sceptre in his right hand and his left leaning on a cushion all ar.; sinister, gu. a house triple-chimneyed, smoke issuant or, a stag in the port of the first, and a tree on the dexter side of the second.

Ireland (Hutt and Hale, co. Lancaster; descended from Sir JOHN DE IRELAND, temp. William I.; the last male heir in the direct line, Sir GILBERT IRELAND, M.P. for Liverpool, son and heir of Sir JOHN DE IRELAND, Knt., of Hutt and Hale, d. 1675, leaving his two sisters his co-heirs, m. GREEN and ASPINWALL, now represented by BLACKBURNE, of Hale). Gu. six fleurs-de-lis, three, two, and one ar. Crest—A dove and olive branch ppr. Motto—Amor et pax.

Ireland (Robbinstown, co. Kildare; a branch of the IRELANDS, of the Hutt and Hale; derived from WILLIAM IRELAND, son of GEORGE IRELAND, who is said to have been brother of Sir JOHN DE IRELAND, the father of the great Sir GILBERT IRELAND, of the Hutt and Hale). Same Arms, Crest, and Motto.

Ireland (Lydiate, co. Lancaster; descended from THOMAS, second son of Sir JOHN DE IRELAND, of Hutt and Hale). Gu. a spear in bend or, headed ar. the head pointing to the sinister base point, at the other end a pennon pendant of the third betw. six fleurs-de-lis of the last, all within a bordure engr. of the second pellettée.

Ireland (cos. Hertford and Salop; granted 1601). Gu. three fleurs-de-lis ar. on a chief indented of the last a lion pass. of the first. Crest—A fleur-de-lis ar. entwined with a snake reguard. vert perforating the middle leaf of the fleur.

Ireland (Owsden Hall, co. Suffolk). Gu. six fleurs-de-lis, three, two, and one or. Crest—A dove and olive branch ppr.

Ireland (co. Surrey). Ar. a chev. erm. betw. three mullets gu.

Ireland (granted 1601). Gu. three fleurs-de-lis ar. a chief indented erm.

Ireland. Or, three crowns az.

Ireland. Gu. a fleur-de-lis ar.

Ireland. Ar. on a chev. sa. three helmets close or.

Ireley, or Irelled. Quarterly, per fesse indented or and az.

Iremonger (cos. Lancaster and Salop). Sa. a chev. vairé or and gu. betw. three boars' heads ar. couped of the third. *Crest*—A boar's head ar. collared vairé or and gu.

Iremongers (granted to the "honurable crafte and fellasship of the ffraunchised men of Iremongers of the citie of London," by Lancaster King of Arms, 1 Sept. 34 Henry VI., 1455). Ar. on a chev. gu. betw. three gads of steel az. three swivels or. *Crest*—Two lizards ramp. combatant coupled with gowlys ppr.

Iremonger (Wherwell, co. Hants; borne by Lieut-Col. WILLIAM IREMONGER, of that place, son of JOSHUA IREMONGER, Esq., of Wherwell, by ANNE, his wife, dau. and heiress of Colonel JOSEPH DUSSAUX, and grandson of JOSHUA IREMONGER, Esq., of London, by DELICIA, his wife, dau. of Sir JOHN FRYER, Bart.). Sa. on a chev. or, betw. three boars pass. ar. as many falcons' heads erased of the field, quartering FRYER, sa. a chev. betw. three dolphins naiant ar. a canton erm. *Crest*—A phœnix or, wings expanded.

Irenhampton. Ar. a fesse sa.

Ireton (Little Ireton, co. Derby, and Attenborough, co. Nottingham; nine descents are recorded in the Visit. of the former county, A.D. 1611. Gen. HENRY IRETON, representative of the family, so notorious in the civil wars, was born at Attenton, in 1610 : he m. BRIDGET, dau. of OLIVER CROMWELL, and dying in 1651, when Lord Deputy of Ireland under the Usurpation, left one son, HENRY, who d. s. p., and four daus. ; first, ELIZABETH, m. to THOMAS POLHILL, Esq., of Otford, co. Kent; second, JANE, m. to RICHARD LLOYD, Esq. ; third, BRIDGET, m. to THOMAS BENDYSH, Esq., of Southtown, co. Sussex; and fourth, m. to Mr. CARTER, a wealthy merchant of Yarmouth). Erm. two bends gu. *Crest*—A squirrel sejant cracking a nut ppr. *Motto*—Fay ce que doy, advienne que pourra.

Ireton (JOHN IRETON, Lord Mayor of London, 1659, brother of Gen. IRETON). Ar. two bends gu.

Ireton. Erm. (another, ar.) a bend voided gu.

Ireton (co. Oxford; arms in the Church of Queen's Coll. Visit. Oxon, 1574). Per saltire or and gu.

Ireton. Gyronny of four erm. and gu.

Ireton. Per saltire or and gu. (another, erm. and gu.).

Ireton (Reg. Ulster's Office). Erm. two bendlets gu. *Crest*—A squirrel sejant ppr.

Ireton. Ar. a fesse and three mullets in chief gu.

Irish, or Ireys (Ireys, co. Dorset). Az. a fesse ar. over all a bend gu. *Crest*—In an oak tree eradicated and erect ppr. a dragon or, pierced through the breast with a sword of the first, hilt of the second.

Irishe. Sa. a cross flory ar. betw. twelve billets of the second.

Irland (Baruban, Scotland). Ar. two bars gu. on the uppermost three mullets or, in chief a boar's head couped az.

Irland (Scotland). Gu. two bars ar. in chief three mullets and in fesse a boar's head erased of the last.

Irland. Erm. a fesse gu. fretty ar.

Irmynges. Az. a chev. betw. four birds' heads erased or.

Irnynge. Ar. a fesse betw. two hinds sa. a chief paly of four or and gu. *Crest*—A child's head issuing ppr.

Ironmongers, Company of. See LONDON, Corporate Companies of.

Ironmonger (co. Lincoln, 1640). Ar. a chev. vair betw. three boars' heads couped sa.

Irons. Or, a fesse indented quarterly gu. and az. *Crest*—A cross moline lozengy pierced ar.

Ironside (Houghton-le-Spring, co. Durham). Per pale az. and gu. a cross patonce or. *Crest*—A cross crosslet. *Motto*—In hoc signo vinces.

Ironside (Bishop of Hereford, 1679). Per pale az. and gu. a cross flory counterflory or.

Ironside (co. Lincoln). Sa. a fesse dancettée ar. in chief two chaplets or.

Ironside. Quarterly, gu. and az. a cross patonce or. *Crest*—A dexter hand in fesse couped, holding a sword in pale, surmounted by a laurel crown all ppr.

Ironside. Or, a cross formée fitched at the foot az.

Ironside (cos. Durham and Dorset). Quarterly, az. and gu. a cross flory or patoncé or.

Irrell. Quarterly, per fesse indented or and az.

531

Irton. Ar. (another, erm.) two bends gu.

Irton (Irton, co. Cumberland; settled there previously to the Conquest. Visit. Cumberland, 1615). Ar. a fesse sa. in chief three mullets gu. *Crest*—A Saracen's head ppr. *Another Crest*—A demi lion sa. collared ar. holding in the dexter paw a mullet gu. *Motto*—Semper constans et fidelis.

Irvine (now FORBES-IRVINE, Drum, co. Aberdeen; descended from WILLIAM DE IRWIN, whom Robert Bruce appointed his armour-bearer). Ar. three small sheaves or bundles of holly, two and one, each consisting of as many leaves slipped vert, banded gu. *Crest*—A sheaf of nine holly leaves vert. *Supporters*—Two savages, wreathed about the head and middle with holly, each carrying in their hands a baton all ppr. *Motto*—Sub sole, sub umbra, virens.

Irvine (Fedderet, co. Aberdeen). As Drum, within a bordure engr. vert. *Crest*—A sheaf of six holly leaves vert, banded gu. *Motto*—Ope solis et umbræ.

Irvine (Artamfoord; a cadet who eventually succeeded to Drum). As Drum, within a bordure indented vert. *Crest*—Two holly leaves in saltire vert. *Motto*—Sub sole viresco.

Irvine (Murthill, co. Aberdeen). Ar. a sheaf of arrows gu. betw. three sheaves of holly, each of as many leaves vert, banded of the second. *Motto*—Sub sole, sub umbra, crescens.

Irvine (Beildside, co. Aberdeen). As the last, within a bordure vert for diff. *Crest*—Three holly leaves conjoined in one stalk ppr. *Motto*—Moderata durant.

Irvine (Kingcausie, co. Aberdeen). Quarterly, 1st and 4th, as Drum, within a bordure chequy vert and ar. ; 2nd and 3rd, ar. an eagle displ. sa. armed gu. within a bordure of the second, for RAMSAY. *Crest*—A decussis like the letter X, within a circle sa. *Motto*—Deo, regi, et patriæ.

Irvine (Burleigh, 1735). As Drum, with a crescent gu. in fess point. *Crest*—A dexter hand holding a holly branch consisting of three leaves ppr. *Motto*—Sub sole, sub umbra, virens.

Irvine (Lairney, co. Aberdeen). As Drum, within a bordure vert charged with six holly leaves slipped ar. *Crest*—A sheaf of holly and a lily both slipped in saltire ppr. *Motto*—Condide et constanter.

Irvine (Cairnfield, co. Banff). Quarterly, 1st and 4th, the same *Arms* as of Drum, within a bordure engr. vert; 2nd and 3rd, gu. three crescents ar., for OLIPHANT. *Crest*—A cross crosslet fitchée gu. and a branch of holly slipped vert in saltire. *Motto*—Feréndo feres.

Irvine (Lenturk, co. Aberdeen). As Drum, within a bordure vert. *Crest*—A sheaf of holly of seven leaves, banded gu. *Motto*—Fideque perennat.

Irvine (Gottenburg, 1757). As Drum, within a bordure nebuly vert. *Crest*—A dexter hand holding two holly branches of three leaves each crossways ppr. *Motto*—Color fides que perennis.

Irvine (Dublin, 1797). As Drum, within a bordure gu. *Crest*—A dexter gauntleted hand lying fessways and holding a thistle erected in pale all ppr. *Motto*—Sub sole, sub umbra, virens.

Irvine (Bonshaw, co. Dumfries). Ar. three holly leaves slipped vert. *Crest*—An arm gauntleted, the hand holding a branch of holly consisting of seven leaves ppr. *Motto*—Haud ullis labentia ventis.

Irvine (Dr. CHRISTOPHER IRVINE, 1672). Ar. three holly leaves vert, a chief of the last. *Crest*—A hand holding a bay rod adorned with nine leaves ppr. with the chemical letters of Terra, Aqua, Ignis, Sal Spiritus, Sulphur, Sol, Venus, Mercurius, or. *Motto*—Auspice summo numine.

Irvine (Auchinbedridge, co. Dumfries, 1771). Ar. a hunting horn stringed sa. voided or, betw. three holly leaves vert. *Crest*—A hand holding a branch of holly, whereon are five leaves ppr. *Motto*—Nil mihi tollit hyems.

Irvine (Inchray, Scotland). Ar. a chev. betw. three holly leaves vert. *Crest*—Two holly branches in saltire ppr. *Motto*—Sequitur vestigia patrum.

Irvine (Castle Irvine, co. Fermanagh; descended from the IRVINES, of Bonshaw). Ar. a fesse gu. betw. three holly leaves ppr. *Crest*—A dexter arm in armour fessways issuant out of a cloud, grasping ppr. holding a thistle also ppr. *Motto*—Dum memor ipse mei.

Irvine (Lowtherstown, co. Fermanagh, bart., extinct 1690; confirmed by Erskine, Lord Lyon, 1673, to Lieut.-Col. GERRARD IRVINE, of Castlefartagh, second son of CHRISTOPHER IRVINE, Esq., of Castle Irvine, who was created a bart. 1677). Ar. a fess gu. betw. three holly leaves vert. *Crest*—A gauntlet issuing out of a cloud holding a thistle all ppr. *Motto*—Dum memor ipse mei.

Irvine (Killadeas, co. Fermanagh; descended from JOHN

2 M 2

Irvine, *d.* 1716, brother of CHRISTOPHER IRVINE, Esq., of Castle Irvine). Same *Arms* and *Crest*. *Motto*—Sub umbra, sub sole, virescens; and over the crest, Dum memor ipse mei.

Irvine (MERVYN-D'ARCY-IRVINE; exemplified to HENRY IRVINE, Esq., of Castle Irvine, co. Fermanagh, eldest son and heir of WILLIAM D'ARCY IRVINE, Esq., of Necarne Castle, same co., on his assuming, by royal licence, 1861, the surnames of MERVYN and D'ARCY before that of IRVINE). Quarterly, 1st and 4th, ar. a fess gu. betw. three holly leaves vert., for IRVINE; 2nd, az. semée of cross crosslets and three cinquefoils ar., for D'ARCY; 3rd, or, a chev. sa., for MERVYN. *Crests*—1st, IRVINE: A gauntlet issuing out of a cloud and holding a thistle all ppr., an escroll above, motto over, Un Dieu, un Roy; 2nd, D'ARCY: On a chapeau gu. turned up erm. a bull pass. sa. armed or; 3rd, MERVYN: A squirrel sejant ppr. cracking a nut gu., motto over, De Dieu est tout. *Motto*—Dum memor ipse mei.

Irving (Woodhouse, co. Dumfries, bart., 1809). Ar. three holly leaves vert, in chief a mullet gu. *Crests*: 1st: A chapeau gu. turned up erm. wreathed round the crown with holly or; 2nd: A dexter arm armed and embowed ppr. charged with a mullet gu. holding a branch of three holly leaves vert, banded gu. *Supporters*—Two savages wreathed head and middle with laurel, each holding a club over his shoulder all ppr. *Mottoes*—Haud ullis labentia ventis; and, Sub sole, sub umbra, virens.

Irving (Newton, co. Lanark). Ar. on a fess az. betw. three small sheaves of holly, each containing as many leaves vert, banded gu. three mullets of the first. *Crest*—Three arrows ppr. points upwards, two saltireways and one in pale, plumed ar. banded gu. *Motto*—Sub sole, sub umbra, virens.

Irving (Hyde Park Square; granted to CLARKE IRVING, Esq.). Ar. on a chev. gu. betw. three holly leaves vert as many mullets of six points of the field, a bordure of the second, upon a chief az. a fleece or, betw. two emus respectant ppr. *Crest*—A cornucopia fesseways ppr. in front of an arm embowed in armour also ppr. holding a holly leaf vert. *Motto*—Sub sole, sub umbra, virens.

Irwin (Calder Abbey and Justustown, co. Cumberland). Ar. three holly leaves ppr. *Crest*—A dove holding an olive branch in its beak. *Motto*—Haud ullis labentia ventis.

Irwin (Derrygore, co. Fermanagh; confirmed to EDWARD IRWIN, Esq., only surviving son of ACHESON IRWIN, and grandson of GEORGE IRWIN, Esq., all of Derrygore, and their descendants). Ar. a mural crown gu. betw. three holly leaves ppr. *Crest*—A mailed arm fessways holding in the hand a thistle and a holly leaf all ppr. and charged on the arm with a crescent gu. *Motto*—Nemo me impune lacessit.

Irwin (exemplified to JAMES DANIEL NOLAN, Esq., on his assuming by royal licence, 1867, the name and arms of IRWIN in lieu of NOLAN). Per pale ar. and or, on a fess gu. betw. three holly|leaves vert as many martlets of the first. *Crest*—A dexter arm in armour fessways issuant out of a cloud, the hand holding a sword erect enwreathed with a thistle all ppr. the arm charged with a cross pattée gu. *Motto*—Dum memor ipse mei.

Irwine (Lieut.-Gen. Sir JOHN IRWINE, K.B., installed 19 May, 1779). Ar. three bunches of holly of as many leaves each vert, tied gu. the strings flotant, on the centre a crescent for diff. *Crest*—An arm *couped* above the wrist in armour ppr. lying fesseways, holding in the gauntlet a bunch of holly, as in the arms, on the arm a crescent for diff. *Supporters*—Two savages wreathed about the head and loins with holly leaves, each holding in the exterior hand a club erect all ppr. each club enfiled with a ducal coronet az. *Motto*—Sub sole, sub umbra, virens.

Isaac (Buriatt, in Atherington, co. Devon, temp. Henry III. Visit. Devon, 1620). Per pale az. and purp. a cross flory or.

Isaac (Boughton, co. Worcester). Sa. a bend or, on a sinister canton of the last a leopard's face sa. *Crest*—A dexter arm embowed in armour, the hand holding a sword, the blade enfiled with a leopard's face, the point downwards resting on the wreath all ppr.

Isaack (Exeter and Heavitree, co. Devon, originally from co. Kent). Sa. a bend or, on a canton ar. a leopard's face gu. *Crest*—A leopard's head erased or, pellettée and ducally collared gold. *Motto*—Florescat.

Isaackson (Fifield, co. Essex). Or, on a pile betw. two escallops az. a lion ramp. ar. *Crest*—A demi lion ar. holding betw. the paws an escallop az.

Isaacson. Or, on a pile betw. two escallops az. a lion ramp. ar. *Crest*—A demi lion ramp. ar. holding betw. the paws an escallop az. *Another Crest*—Two lions' gambs issuing sa. holding up a bezant.

Isack (Brakesborne, co. Kent). Sa. a bend or, in the sinister chief point a leopard's face of the second.

Isack. Quarterly, or and purp. a cross pattée fitched at each foot, betw. four lambs ar. each gorged with a rope az and pendent in front.

Isall. Az. two bars ar. over all a bend gu. a bordure engr. gobony of the second and third.

Isbery, or Isbury. Ar. three bends wavy (another, nebulée) sa.

Isely (co. Kent). Erm. a bend gu.

Isely, or Isley. Quarterly, erm. and ar. a fesse gu. in the 2nd and 3rd quarters a bend of the third. *Crest*—A hand holding a roll betw. two branches of laurel in orle all ppr.

Isham (Bramston, co. Northants, and London; GREGORY ISHAM and JOHN ISHAM, Visit. London, 1568, third and fourth sons of EASEBY ISHAM, son and heir of WILLIAM ISHAM, of Pitesley, heir male of the house of ISHAM, of Isham, in same co.). Gu. three piles meeting in base or, over all a fess of the last. *Another Coat*—Gu. three piles meeting in the fess point and a fess wavy ar. *Crest*—A demi swan, wings endorsed ar. guttée de larmes.

Isham (Lamport, co. Northampton, bart.). Gu. a fesse wavy and in chief three piles also wavy, points meeting in fesse ar. *Crest*—A demi swan with wings displ. ar. beaked sa. *Motto*—Ostendo non ostento. *Another Motto*—On things transitory resteth no glory.

Isham (co. Kent and London). Gu. three piles wavy or, over all a fesse of the second.

Isham, or Ipsam (co. Kent). Gu. a fesse or, in chief three piles wavy of the last.

Isham (co. Somerset). Vert three piles ar. in chief a fleur-de-lis or.

Isham. Per fesse wavy gu. and ar. three piles in chief of the second.

Isherwood (Windsor, co. Berks; granted 1764). Erm. two bars gemels az. on a chief gu. a leopard (another, a lion) pass. guard. or, spotted sa. *Crest*—A wolf's head per pale ermines and erminois erased gu.

Isherwood (Marple Hall, co. Chester, and Bradshaw Hall, co. Lancaster). Quarterly, 1st and 4th, ISHERWOOD, ar. a fesse dancettée az. on a chief az. a lion pass. or; 2nd and 3rd, BRADSHAW, ar. two bendlets sa. betw. as many martlets of the last. *Crests*—1st, ISHERWOOD: A wolf's head erased ppr. issuant out of a crescent az.; 2nd, BRADSHAW: On a mount vert a stag at gaze ppr. under a vine branch also ppr. fructed or. *Motto*—Bona benementi benedictio.

Isles, See of the (Scotland). Az. the figure of St. Columba in a boat at sea, on his sinister hand a dove, in dexter chief a blazing star all ppr.

Isley (Souldridge, co. Kent). Erm. a fesse sa.

Isley (co. Kent). Erm. a fesse vair (Har. MSS. 4108).

Isley. Gu. a bend vair betw. two fleurs-de-lis or.

Islip (SIMON ISLIP, Archbishop of Canterbury, 1349-66). Gu a cross pattée co.

Ismay (granted to THOMAS HENRY ISMAY, Esq., of Waterloo, co. Lancaster). Or, on a bend wavy az. betw. two anchors erect of the last, a mullet betw. two crescents ar. *Crest*—On waves of the sea a seahorse reguard. betw. two coral branches all ppr. *Motto*—Naturæ lex processus.

Ismaye. Az. a chev. or, betw. two bezants in chief and a cross crosslet fitchée in base or.

Isoed (granted by Cooke, Clarenceux). Ar. six leopards' faces vert, three, two, and one.

Ispal (co. Surrey, temp. Edward I.). Az. a chev. or.

Isprod, or Ispord. Or, a rose gu. on a chief sa. an eagle displ. of the first.

Isprid. Ar. a rose gu. on a chief sa. a demi lapwing displ. or

Israel. Gu. on a pile ar. three cinquefoils of the field. *Crest*—A sun rising from behind a cloud ppr.

Isted (Ecton, co. Northampton, originally of Framfield, co Sussex). Gu. a chev. vair betw. three talbots' heads erased or. *Crest*—A buck's head erased ppr. attired and ducally gorged or.

Itchingham. See ECHINGHAM.

Ithel-Anwyl (Englefield, in North Wales. Descendants. I. LLOYD, of Maes y Groes, Halkin, Argoed, and Abergele; II. RONDLE, of Argoed). Per pale gu. and or, in pale a hymoc (mound of earth) ppr. betw. two lions ramp. addorsed counterchanged of the field.

Ithel-Velyn (Yale, in Denbighland; eldest son of LLEWELYN AUB DORCHOG, but took a different coat of arms. Descendants: I. WYNN, of Mallwyd and Llandyrnog; II. PRICE, of Gwernfield; III. NICHOLAS, of Yale; IV. EDWARDS, of Hendre Bippa; V. HUGHES, of Abergele; VI. GRIFFITH, of Bryn Eglwys; VII. EDWARDS AP ROGERS, of Kymono; VIII. LLOYD, of Llangollen Vachan, &c.). Sa. a chev. betw. three goats' heads erased or.

Ithel (Lord of Bryn, co. Denbigh). Ar. three greyhounds courant sa. in pale, collared ar.

Ithell (co. Cambridge, and Billesden, co. Leicester). Ar. a cross engr. (another, raguly) flory betw. four Cornish choughs sa. *Crest*—On a ducal coronet or, a Cornish chough, wings expanded sa. beaked and legged gu.

Ivan. Ar. three fleurs-de-lis sa. (another, az. a lion ramp. or).

Ivatt, or Ivat (London; confirmed 27 June, 1626). Ar. on a cross gu. five fleurs-de-lis of the field (another, the tinctures reversed). *Crest*—Out of a mural coronet an armed cubit arm holding in the gauntlet all ppr. a fleur-de-lis or.

Ive. Sa. a fesse betw. three goats pass. ar. attired or. *Crest*—An arm in armour couped and embowed, resting the elbow on the wreath, holding a sword all ppr.

Ive. Az. a cross pattée betw. four martlets or.

Iveagh, Viscount of. See McGennis.

Iver (Sheriff co. Berks, 1759). Ar. a fess betw. three lions ramp. sz.

Iverach (Wideford, co. Orkney). Quarterly, 1st and 4th, quarterly, or and gu. on a fess engr. sa. three crosses crosslet fitchée ar.; 2nd and 3rd, counter-quartered, 1st and 4th, gyronny of eight or and sa., 2nd, ar. a dexter hand couped in fess grasping a dagger erect gu., 3rd, ar. a galley, sails furled and oars in action sa. the whole within a bordure ar. charged with three cushions gu. *Crest*—A boar's head couped ar. *Motto*—Nunquam obliviscas.

Iverby. Ar. a saltire engr. sa. in chief two mullets gu.

Ivers, or Jevers. Ar. on a bend az. three fleurs-de-lis or. *Crest*—A demi lion ramp. or, collared sa.

Ivers (Reg. Ulster's Office). Quarterly, or and gu. on a bend sa. three fleurs-de-lis ar.

Ivery, or Every (from a monument in the chapel of Ford Abbey, co. Devon). Ar. three chevronels gu.

Ivery (Dungate, co. Somerset). Ar. on a bend gu. three oak leaves of the first.

Ives (co. Northampton). Sa. on a fesse betw. three goats pass. ar. attired, bearded, and unguled or, as many crescents gu. *Crest*—Out of a ducal coronet gu. an Indian goat's head ar. guttée de sang, attired or.

Ives, Town of (co. Cornwall). Ar. an ivy branch overspreading the whole field vert.

Ives (Bradwell, co. Norfolk). Ar. a chev. sa. betw. three blackamoors' heads couped ppr. *Crest*—A boar pass. ppr. collared and chained or.

Ives, or Ivys. Ar. three torteaux betw. two bendlets gu.

Iveson (Hedon, near Hull, co. York). Ar. a chev. betw. three Moors' heads in profile, erased at the neck sa. *Crest*—A Moor's head, as in the arms.

Ivett. Ar. a bend sa. betw. three ivy branches ppr.

Ivett. Ar. on a cross flory gu. five fleurs-de-lis of the field.

Ivey (Exeter). Gu. a lion ramp. or. *Crest*—A demi lion ramp. or, supporting a staff raguly vert.

Ivie (city of Oxford; Thomas Ivie, Visit. Oxon, 1634, son and heir of Sir George Ivie, Knt., of Westhingham, co. Wilts, fourth in descent from Thomas Ivie, Esq., of Sodbury). Ar. a lion ramp. gu.

Ivis, Iwis, or Iwys. Ar. a chev. sa.

Ivor ap Cadifor Vawr (Wales). Or, a griffin segreant sa.

Ivor ap Bledvi ap Cadifor Vawr (Lord of Eloed, co. Carmarthen). Or, a griffin segreant sa.

Ivory. Ar. a bend vert betw. three mullets gu. *Crest*—A lion sejant affrontée gu. holding in the dexter paw a sword ar. pommel and hilt or, and in the sinister a fleur-de-lis gold.

Ivye (co. Oxford, and West Keynton, co. Wilts). Ar. a lion ramp. gu. quartering ar. a fesse embattled gu. betw. three annulets sa. *Crest*—A lion ramp. ar. supporting a staff raguly gu.

Ivyn (Tudington, co. Gloucester). Sa. six plates, three, two, and one, on a chief ar. a demi lion ramp. gu.

Iwardby (Mapledurham, co. Oxford). Ar. on a saltire engr. sa. a rose of the field, on a chief of the second two mullets pierced of the first.

Iwardby (co. Oxford; arms in the Divinity School, Oxford. Visit. Oxon, 1574). Ar. a saltire engr. sa. on a chief of the last a mullet of the first.

Izacke (Exeter). Sa. a bend or, on a canton ar. a leopard's face of the field. *Crest*—A leopard's face erased sa. ducally gorged or.

Izod (Tudington and Stainton, co. Gloucester). Ar. six leopards' faces vert, three, two, and one. *Crest*—A man's head sidefaced ppr. in armour or, on the head a plume of feathers gu. and ar.

533

Izod (Chapelizod House, co. Kilkenny). Same *Arms* and *Crest*.

Izon. Ar. on a pale sa. three antique crowns or. *Crest*—A dexter hand fesseways, couped ppr. holding a cross crosslet fitchée in pale sa.

Izzard. Ar. six leopards' faces vert, three, two, and one. *Crest*—A dolphin embowed ppr.

J

JACK (England). Per saltire ar. and sa. two oak leaves in pale vert, and as many acorns in fesse or. *Crest*—A pear tree vert, fructed or.

Jack (Scotland). Ar. a chev. sa. betw. two crescents in chief gu. and in base an armed arm of the second, holding a sword ppr. hilt and pommel or.

Jack (Woodhall, Scotland). Ar. three demi holly leaves divided fesseways vert.

Jack. Ar. on a fesse sa. three escallops gu. *Crest*—A horse's head erased, holding in the mouth a broken tilting spear.

Jacket, or Jaket. Per chev. sa. and erm. in chief two estoiles or. *Crest*—Out of a cloud a dexter hand ppr. holding a cross pattée fitchée in pale or.

Jackman (cos. Buckingham and Durham, Hornchurch, co. Essex, cos. Hereford and Huntingdon; granted 1561). Per saltire ar. and sa. in pale two eagles displ. of the second. *Crest*—A griffin's head erased sa. guttée d'or.

Jackman (Hackman, in the Liberties of Havering, co. Essex; Edward Jackman, grandson of Alderman Edward Jackman, Sheriff of London, 1564. Visit. London, 1568). Same *Arms* and *Crest*.

Jackson (Bromfield, co. Middlesex; John Jackson, gent., son of Joseph Jackson, merchant. Visit. Middlesex, 1663). Gu. a greyhound courant ar. betw. three pheons or. *Crest*—A demi greyhound saliant ar. collared or, holding betw. the paws a pheon sa.

Jackson (Beach Hill, co. Surrey, bart., extinct). Gu. a fesse betw. three shovellers, tufted on the head and breast ar. each charged with a trefoil slipped vert. *Crest*—A shoveller, as in the arms, motto over, Innocentiæ securus. *Motto*—Malo mori quam fœdari.

Jackson (The Manor House, Birkenhead, and Portland Place, London, bart.). Az. a fesse betw. two goats' heads couped in chief and a fleur-de-lis in base ar. two flaunches of the last. *Crest*—Upon a ragged staff sa. a goat's head couped ar. semée of trefoils vert. *Motto*—Fortiter, fideliter, feliciter.

Jackson (Doncaster, co. York). Per pale gu. and az. on a fess erm. cotised ar. betw. three shovellers of the last a cross crosslet betw. two annulets of the field. *Crest*—A demi griffin gu. collared and chain reflected over the back or, holding in the dexter claw a shoveller's head erased ar. *Motto*—Strenue et honeste.

Jackson (arms of Anne, wife of Hawkshaw, eldest surviving dau. of Rev. James Jackson, late of Green Hammerton par Whixley, W.R. co. York). Gu. two horses counter-courant in pale ar. guttée de sang.

Jackson (Arlsey, co. Bedford, bart.). Ar. on a fesse betw. a goat's head couped in chief gu. and a ship in full sail in base ppr. a greyhound courant betw. two pheons or. *Crest*—A goat's head couped ar. guttée de sang, armed and bearded or, gorged with a collar gu. charged with three bezants, ringed and line reflexed over the back gold.

Jackson (co. Cumberland, and Combhay, co. Devon). Or, (another, ar.) on a chev. sa. betw. three eagles' heads erased az. as many cinquefoils ar. *Crest*—A horse courant ar. guttée de sang.

Jackson (Keswick, co. Cumberland, and co. Oxford). Erm. a spear's head in pale az. embrued gu. *Crest*—A sun or, in flames ppr.

Jackson. Ar. on a fess gu. betw. three hawks' heads erased sa. a greyhound courant ar. betw. two pheons or, a bordure sa. bezantty.

Jackson, alias Lascelles (Gauthorpe, co. York, 1584). Sa. a cross patonce or, a bordure of the last. *Crest*—A bear's head erm. muzzled and collared gu. the collar ringed or.

Jackson (London; Francis Jackson, citizen of London, Visit. 1568, great grandson of John Jackson, the second son of William Jackson, Esq., of Sugthall, co. York). Gu. a fess ar. betw. three jackdaws ppr.

Jackson (Chester Herald, temp. Henry VIII.). Vert on a fesse or, three magpies ppr.

Jackson (West Chester). Ar. on a fesse gu. a greyhound courant betw. two pheons or, in chief a goat's head couped of the second, a bordure of the last. *Crest*—A goat's head az. attired or.

Jackson (cos. Derby and Stafford). Ar. a lion pass. gu. on a chief of the second three battle axes of the first.

Jackson (co. Hereford). Ar. on a chev. sa. betw. three hawks' heads erased az. as many cinquefoils or. *Crest*—On a five-leaved coronet or, a hawk's head and neck erased gu. charged on the breast with a cross pattée fitchée gold. *Motto*—Scuto amoris divini.

Jackson (Claines, co. Worcester; PHINEAS JACKSON, High Sheriff of the county, 3 Queen Anne, 1703). Ar. on a fess gu. betw. three cocks' heads erased sa. a greyhound courant betw. two pheons of the field, a border engr. az. bezantée.

Jackson (WARD-JACKSON, Greatham Hall, co. Durham). Ar. a fesse erm. betw. three sheldrakes ppr. *Crest*—A sheldrake ppr.

Jackson (Sunderland, co. Durham). Ar. on a chev. sa. betw. three hawks' heads erased of the second as many cinquefoils pierced of the first. *Crest*—A horse at full speed ar. guttée de sang.

Jackson (co. Kent). Or, on a fesse betw. three pheons az. a lion pass. of the first. *Crest*—A demi lion ramp. or, holding betw. the paws a pheon az.

Jackson (Southgate, co. Middlesex). Gu. a greyhound courant in fesse ar. betw. three pheons or. *Crest*—A greyhound pass. sa. collared or, resting the dexter foot on a pheon gold.

Jackson (London). Same *Arms*. *Crest*—A hand ppr. holding a boar's head erased and erect sa.

Jackson (Newcastle-on-Tyne, co. Northumberland). Gu. a fesse betw. three shovellers ar.

Jackson (Bishop of Oxford, 1812). Same *Arms*.

Jackson (co. Northampton; granted 1689). Ar. a greyhound courant ermines betw. three eagles' heads erased sa. *Crest*—A demi horse ar. guttée de sang.

Jackson (co. Nottingham; Right Rev. JOHN JACKSON, D.D., Bishop of Lincoln, 1853). Sa. a cross pattée betw. three pheons or.

Jackson (co. Oxford, 1790). Sa. a spearhead ar. a canton or, a label for diff. *Crest*—An eagle rising ppr.

Jackson (co. Rutland). Ar. guttée de sang a spearhead in pale az. embrued gu. *Crest*—A sun rising ppr.

Jackson (Lochhouse, Scotland). Barry of eight or and gu. a lion ramp. ar.

Jackson (Scotland). Barry of ten ar. and az. over all a lion ramp. gu.

Jackson (Hickleton, co. York, bart., extinct 1727 ; descended from Sir JOHN JACKSON, Knt., *temp.* Queen Elizabeth, whose grandson, JOHN JACKSON, Esq., of Hickleton, was created a baronet in 1660). Gu. a fesse betw. three sheldrakes ar.

Jackson (Harraton, co. Durham; Sir JOHN JACKSON, Knt., Lieutenant-Colonel in the service of Charles I., eldest son of THOMAS JACKSON, Esq., of Harraton, *d.* 1673). Or, a chev. indented gu. betw. three eagles' heads erased sa.

Jackson (Bath, co. Somerset). Gu. a greyhound courant in fesse ar. collared az. betw. three pheons or, on the shoulder a torteau. *Crest*—A dove close, in the beak an olive branch ppr. on the breast a torteau.

Jackson (Christ Church, co. Surrey; granted 16 Oct. 1700). Az. on a chev. betw. three covered cups ar. as many cinquefoils gu. *Crest*—A horse pass. ar. semée of cinquefoils gu.

Jackson (Bedale, co. York; granted 1563). Ar. on a chev. sa. betw. three hawks' heads erased of the second as many cinquefoils of the first. *Crest*—A horse in full speed ar. guttée de sang.

Jackson (Kelwood's Grove, co. York). Gu. three suns or, a chief erm. *Crest*—The sun or, betw. two branches in orle vert. *Another Crest*—A naked arm embowed, grasping a poniard all ppr.

Jackson (co. York). Ar. on a chev. sa. betw. three eagles' heads erased az. as many cinquefoils of the field, on a chief or, two anchors in cross of the third betw. as many trefoils slipped of the last, each charged with twelve bezants.

Jackson (Normandy Hall, co. York). Az. a fesse erm. betw. three sheldrakes ppr. *Crest*—A sheldrake ppr.

Jackson (co. York). Gu. a fesse betw. three falcons close ar.

Jackson (Duddington, co. Northampton). Ar. a greyhound courant ermines betw. three eagles' heads erased sa. *Crest*—A demi horse ar. guttée de sang, maned and hoofed sa.

Jackson (Bubnell, co. Derby; three generations described in the Visitation of 1662). Ar. a lion pass. gu. on a chief of the last three battle axes of the first. *Crest*—An arm in armour embowed, holding a battle axe all ppr.

Jackson. Quarterly, 1st and 4th, ar. a lion pass. gu. on a chief of the last three battle axes of the first; 2nd and 3rd, or, three bars wavy az. on a canton gu. a lion pass. guard. ar. *Crest*—An arm in armour embowed, holding a battle axe all ppr.

534

Jackson. Sa. a pheon, point down ar. a canton or. *Crest*—An eagle close ppr.

Jackson. Ar. on a chev. betw. three daws' heads erased az. as many cinquefoils or. *Crest*—A horse courant ar. guttée de sang.

Jackson. Ar. on a fesse betw. three cocks' heads erased sa. a greyhound betw. two pheons or, a bordure az. platée.

Jackson. Az. a lion ramp. ar. billettée gu.

Jackson. Ar. a chev. gu. betw. three Cornish choughs ppr.

Jackson. Vert a fesse or, betw. three magpies ppr.

Jackson (RICHARD JACKSON, Esq., of Preston, co. Lancaster; the representative of a family originally of co. Chester). Ar. on a chev. sa. betw. as many falcons' heads erased az. three cinquefoils pierced of the field. *Crest*—A falcon's head. *Motto*—Malo mori quam foedari.

Jackson. Ar. a lion pass. betw. three martlets or.

Jackson (Coleraine, co. Londonderry ; Fun. Ent. 1688, WILLIAM JACKSON, son of Rev. RICHARD JACKSON, of Whittington, co. Lancaster, by DOROTHY OTWAY, his wife, dau. of Sir JOHN OTWAY, Knt., of Ingmire). Gu. a fesse betw. three cormorants ar.

Jackson (Enniscoe, co. Mayo; confirmed to General Sir JAMES JACKSON, K.C.B., Colonel 6th Dragoon Guards, third son of GEORGE JACKSON, M.P., and to the descendants of his grandfather). Ar. on a chev. sa. betw. three hawks' heads erased az. as many trefoils slipped or. *Crest*—A horse pass. ar. charged on the shoulder with a trefoil slipped vert. *Motto*—Celer et audax.

Jackson (Fanningstown, co. Limerick). Ar. a greyhound courant ermines betw. three eagles' heads erased sa. *Crest*—A demi horse ramp. ar. guttée de sang, maned and hoofed sa.

Jackson (Ahanesk, co. Cork). Ar. a lion pass. gu. on a chief of the last three battle axes of the first. *Crest*—An arm in armour embowed, in the hand a battle axe all ppr.

Jackson (Glanbeg, co. Waterford). Same *Arms*. *Crest*—An arm in armour embowed holding a battle axe all ppr.

Jackson (Forkhill, co. Armagh). Gu. three shovellers tufted on the head and breast ar. each charged with a trefoil vert. *Crest*—A shoveller, as in the arms. *Motto*—Malo mori quam foedari.

Jackson (Torphin, Scotland). Gu. three suns in splendour or, a bordure az. a chief erm. *Crest*—A dexter arm in armour embowed, holding a battle axe ppr. *Motto*—Devant si je puis.

Jacob (Dover, co. Kent; descended from JOHN JACOB, of Dover, *d.* 1627, whose grandson, Sir ABRAHAM JACOB, Governor of Walmer Castle, was knighted at Windsor Castle, June, 1663). Or, on a canton gu. an eagle displ. of the field. *Crest*—A lion ramp or, supporting a cross crosslet fitchée gu.

Jacob (Tolpiddle, co. Dorset; descended from WILLIAM JACOB, Esq., of Tolpiddle, *temp.* Henry VI.). Same *Arms* and *Crest*.

Jacob (Sir ROBERT JACOB, Attorney-General for Ireland, knighted at Christ Church, 5 Nov. 1601, second son of ROBERT JACOB, Esq., of Bockhampton, co. Dorset, who was second son of WILLIAM JACOB, Esq., of Tolpiddle). Same *Arms* and *Crest*, a crescent for diff.

Jacob (Bromley and Bow, co. Middlesex, bart., extinct, and of Gamlingay, co. Cambridge ; Sir JOHN JACOB was created a bart. 1665, with remainder, in default of male issue, to the male issue of his brother, ROBERT JACOB, in reward for his great loyalty to Charles I. ; he had an estate of £3,000 per annum, but adhering to his sovereign he was deprived of all he had by Oliver Cromwell; he was grandson of ROBERT JACOB, Esq., of Gamlingay, by KATHERINE, his wife, dau. of WILLIAM ABRAHAM, of London, and his wife JANE, dau. of ROBERT BOSTOCK, co. Chester. The last male descendant of Sir JOHN JACOB, the first bart., Sir HILDEBRAND JACOB, Bart., *d. s. p.* 1790, when the title devolved on his kinsman, Sir CLEMENT BRYDGES JACOB, as fifth bart., who also *d. s. p.*). Ar. a chev. gu. betw. three heraldic tigers' heads erased ppr. maned and tusked or. *Crest*—An heraldic tiger pass. ppr. maned and tusked or. *Motto*—Tantum in superbos.

Jacob (Sigginstown, Temple Shannon, and Woodbrook, co. Wexford, Ballinakill and Maryborough, Queen's co., and Llanfawr, co. Anglesey ; descended from Lieut. WILLIAM JACOB, who got a grant of Sigginstown and other lands in co. Wexford, 1667. JOHN JACOB, his eldest son and successor, disinherited his own eldest son, whose family then removed to the Queen's co.; of this senior line was the late ARTHUR JACOB, Esq., M.D., of Ely Place, Dublin, the eminent surgeon-oculist). Same *Arms*, *Crest*, and *Motto*.

Jacob (Newhall, co. Oxford). Same *Arms*, *Crest*, and *Motto*.

Jacob (Wootton Basset, co. Wilts; descended from JOHN

JACOB, *m.* ante 1573, SYBIL, dau. and heiress of THOMAS THORNE, Esq., of Wootton Basset, and settled in co. Wilts ; arms confirmed 1633. Visit. Wilts, 1674). Or, on a canton sa. an heraldic tiger's head erased of the field, langued gu. *Crest*—An heraldic tiger pass. sa. resting the foot on an escutcheon or.

Jacob (Shillingstone, co. Dorset, and Salisbury, co. Wilts ; descended from Rev. THOMAS JACOB, Vicar of Enford, co. Wilts, 1670). Same *Arms* and *Crest*. *Motto*—Dum spiro spero.

Jacob (Canterbury, Woolavington, Waldershare, Whitfield, and Sextries, co. Kent ; descended from AMOS JACOB, Esq., of Barrow Hill, co. Kent, *d.* 1688 ; of this line was HERBERT JACOB, Major-General Bombay Army, and his brother, JOHN JACOB, C.B., Col. Bombay Artillery, Brigadier-General, and the renowned commander of the Scinde Irregular Horse ; also Sir GEORGE LE GRAND JACOB, Knt., Commander of the Star of India and C.B.). Quarterly, 1st and 4th, or, guttée de sang a bordure gu. on a canton of the last an eagle displ. of the field, for JACOB ; 2nd and 3rd, per fesse ar. and sa. a lion ramp. within an orle of crosses pattée and crosses crosslet alternately, all counterchanged, for LONG. *Crest*—On a mount vert a lion ramp. per fesse or and gu. supporting a cross crosslet botony fitchée also gu. *Motto*—Non nobis solum.

Jacobs. Ar. a greyhound courant sa. a canton ermines. *Crest*—An arm in armour embowed grasping a sword by the blade all ppr.

Jacobs (Ripple, co. Kent). Quarterly, dancettée sa. and or, in the first quarter a pelican of the last.

Jacomb (Burton Lazers, co. Leicester ; granted 20 April, 1672). Per chev. az. and erm. in chief two lions' heads erased ar. *Crest*—A hand holding two branches of palm in orle ppr.

Jacomb. Per chev. az. and erm. in chief two lions' heads erased of the second. *Crest*—A lion's head erased barry of six ar. and az.

Jacques. See JAQUES.

Jacson (Barton, co. Lancaster ; CHARLES ROGER JACSON, Esq., of Barton, J.P. and D.L., eldest surviving son of the late GEORGE JACSON, who purchased the Barton estate, and grandson of Rev. ROGER JACSON, patron and rector of Bebington, who succeeded to Somersale in 1806, at the decease of his aunt, FRANCES FITZHERBERT. The family of JACSON was settled at an early period in co. Derby). Gu. a fesse betw. three sheldrakes ar. *Crest*—A sheldrake rising ppr.

Jadewin (London ; confirmed 21 Sept. 1629). Sa. ten plates, four, three, two, and one, a chief or. *Crest*—An oak tree vert fructed or, supported by two lions' paws erased gold, entwined with a scroll, inscribed with the *Motto*—Robur in vita Deus.

Jadis (Rev. JOHN JADIS, Vicar of Humbleton, co. York). Ar. a chev. betw. three eagles displ. with two heads az. *Crest*—Out of a ducal coronet or, a demi eagle displ. with two heads az.

Jaduyn. Sa. ten bezants, four, three, two, and one, on a chief ar. a demi lion issuant gu.

Jaffray (King's Wells, co. Kincardine). Paly of six ar. and sa. on a fesse of the first three mullets of the second. *Crest*—The sun beaming through a cloud ppr. *Motto*—Post nubila Phœbus.

Jaffray (Dilspro, Scotland, 1672). As the last, with a crescent for diff. Same *Crest* and *Motto*.

Jaffray (Edinburgh, 1672). As King's Wells, with a mullet for diff. Same *Crest* and *Motto*.

Jaffrey (Portsmouth, New England, America ; descended from Hon. GEORGE JAFFREY, Speaker of the Assembly of New Hampshire. The family, an influential one in New Hampshire, ended in three co-heiresses, one of whom *m.* DAVID JEFFRIES, of Boston). Paly of six ar. and sa. surmounted by a fesse of the first charged with three stars of the second. *Crest*—The sun shining through a cloud ppr. *Motto*—Post nubila Phœbus.

Jager. Az. a cross pattée throughout or, cantoned with four fleurs-de-lis gu. *Crest*—Out of a ducal coronet a hand holding a sword ppr.

Jago ap Idwall (*Prince of Powys*). Gu. three lions pass. ar.

Jago (Trejago). Or, a chev. betw. three crosses crosslet sa.

Jago (St. Erme and Helston, cc Cornwall, *circa* 1500 ; a branch of JAGO, of Trejago ; from the JAGOS, of St. Erme, derived THOMAS JAGO, M.P., of Launceston ; SAMUEL JAGOE, of Ennis, in St. Erme ; and the JAGOES, of co. Warwick, now extinct, ancestors of the poet). Same *Arms*.

Jago. Or, a greyhound courant in bend sa. in the dexter chief a hunting horn stringed of the last. *Crest*—Issuing

from clouds two dexter hands, both seizing the stump of an old tree sprouting anew all ppr.

Jakeman. Per chev. gu. and erm. in chief two eagles displ. or. *Crest*—Out of a ducal coronet or, an eagle's head ppr. (sometimes sa.).

Jakes (co. Leicester). Ar. on a fesse gu. three escallops or.

Jakes (London). Ar. on a fesse engr. sa. three escallops of the field. *Crest*—A horse's head couped ar. maned or, struck in the breast with a tilting spear of the last.

Jakys. Or, two bars tortile of eight az. and gu.

Jalabert (granted by Hawkins, Ulster, 1748, to ISRAEL JALABERT, of the city of Dublin, merchant, descended from an ancient family in France). Ar. a British private ship of war at anchor ppr. on a chief az. two garbs or. *Crest*—Ceres ppr.

Jalfou (granted to ISAAC JALFOU, Esq., of Hackney, co. Middlesex). Ar. on a mount vert an oak tree ppr. fructed or, a chief az. thereon three esquires' helmets gold. *Crest*—On a mount vert a greyhound courant ar. holding in the mouth a sword in pale, point downwards ppr. pommel and hilt gold.

Jalmes. Ar. three martlets sa. *Crest*—Out of a ducal coronet or, five ostrich feathers, the three middle ones sa. and two outside ones ar.

Jamare (co. Hants, *temp.* Edward III.). Gu. two lions pass. guard. in pale ar.

Jamerdeston (co. Suffolk). Az. two bars ar. on a chief gu. a lion pass. guard. or.

James (Langley Hall, co. Berks, bart.). Gu. a dolphin embowed or. *Crests*—1st : An ostrich ppr. beaked and legged or ; 2nd : Out of a ducal coronet or, two laurel branches in saltire vert, environed with a snake ppr. *Motto*—J'aime à jamais.

James (Dublin, bart., Lord Mayor of Dublin, 1822). Quarterly, vert and gu. a cross ar. charged with a ship in full sail ppr. betw. four anchors erect az. in the 1st and 4th quarters a dolphin naiant of the third betw. three crosses crosslet or ; in the 2nd and 3rd a lion pass. guard. of the last betw. three trefoils slipped of the third *Crest*—Out of a ducal coronet or, a swan ppr. beaked gu. holding in the beak a dart gold, feathered ar. point towards the breast, motto over, A jamais. *Motto*—Pro Deo, Patria, et Rege.

James (Presteign, co. Radnor). Az. a lion ramp. betw. two castles triple-towered in chief and a scaling-ladder in base ar. a bordure or, charged with four roses gu. and as many spear heads alternately sa. *Crest*—A lion ramp. ar. collared and holding betw. the forepaws a rose gu. the dexter hind-paw resting on an escutcheon ar. charged with a spear head, as in the arms. *Motto*—Duw a Digon.

James (Washington and Hetton Le Hole, co. Durham ; WILLIAM JAMES, Bishop of Durham, 1606-17). Quarterly, 1st and 4th, sa. a dolphin embowed ar. ; 2nd and 3rd, erm. on a chief gu. three crosses crosslet or. *Crest*—A bull's head couped sa. armed or. These arms, which are, perhaps, borrowed from FITZJAMES, of co. Dorset (viz., az. a dolphin embowed ar. betw. three cinquefoils or), are carved in wood over a mantelpiece in a house in the North Bailey, Durham, the property of THOMAS HOPPER, Esq., which is said to have been the residence of FRANCIS JAMES, Esq., the Bishop's younger son.

James (Denford, co. Berks, and Newport, Isle of Wight. Visit. Hants, 1634). Gu. a dolphin embowed or. *Crest*—An ostrich ar. beaked and legged or. *Another Crest*—On a ducal coronet or, two laurel branches in saltire vert, environed with a snake ppr.

James (Slangeler, co. Carmarthen) Gu. a dolphin naiant embowed or.

James (Wyke House, Gillingham, co. Dorset). Az. a dolphin embowed ar.

James (co. Dorset). Az. a fesse betw. three dolphins or.

James (co. Kent). Sa. a dolphin in fesse ar. finned or. *Crest*—A buffalo courant sa. attired or.

James (Barrow Court, co. Somerset ; confirmed by Camden, Clarenceux). Sa. a dolphin naiant betw. three crosses crosslet or. *Crest*— A dolphin naiant ppr.

James (Michbarrow, co. Somerset). Sa. a dolphin embowed betw. three crosses botonnée or. *Crest*—A demi bull or, wreathed round the middle with a chaplet of laurel vert.

James (Pantalson, co. Pembroke). Same *Arms*. *Crest*—A demi bull ramp. sa. langued gu. armed and hoofed or.

James (co. Stafford). Sa. a dolphin embowed within an orle ar.

James (Barrock, co. Cumberland, Burnville Lodge, near Tavistock, and Finch House, near Liverpool). Az. a dolphin embowed ppr. *Crest*—A buffalo pass. ppr. *Motto*—Vincit amor patriæ.

James (Cathedine, co. Brecon). Gu. from behind bushes

vert a stag courant ar. on a chief ar. three castles of the field, one and two.

James (Shwynbred, co. Brecon). Sa. a chev. betw. three gauntlets clenched or.

James (co. Cambridge). Per pale or (another, ar.) and az. on a chev. betw. three lions pass. guard. as many escallops all counterchanged. *Crest*—A dove ar. standing upon two palm branches in saltire vert.

James (co. Cornwall). Ar. a lion ramp. az. betw. three escallops gu. *Crest*—Two lions' gambs erased sa. supporting an escallop ar. charged with a crescent az. *Motto*—Nosce teipsum.

James (cos. Worcester and Gloucester). Same *Arms.*

James (Upminster, co. Essex, and co. Kent; granted by Camden, Clarenceux, 18 Nov. 1611). Ar. a chev. betw. three fer-de-molines fesseways sa. *Crest*—A garb ar. banded vert.

James (co. Gloucester). Az. on a chev. or, betw. three lions pass. guard. of the second as many purses sa.

James (Haughton Hall, Hanover, Jamaica). Az. on a chev. betw. three lions pass. guard. erm. as many escallops gu. quartering HAUGHTON, HALTON, FISHER, FOWLER, DRAYNER, and PARSON. *Crest*—A demi lion ramp. erm. holding an escallop gu. *Motto*—Malgré le tort.

James (Park Farm Place, Eltham, co. Kent, extinct 1792). Az. on a chev. betw. three lions pass. guard. or, ducally crowned of the last, three grenades sa. fired ppr. *Crest*—In a naval coronet or, a tower with two portholes in front gold, fire issuing from the portholes and top ppr. on the tower a flagstaff of the last, thereon a flag flotant to the sinister gu. in a position of striking, being half down the staff. *Motto*—Victor.

James (Wellsborough, co. Kent, and Riegate, co. Sussex). Quarterly, 1st, and 4th, ar. two bars crenellée gu.; 2nd, ar. three fer-de-molines barways sa.; 3rd, barry wavy of six ar. and az. on a chief or, three swallows volant sa. *Crest*—Out of a ducal coronet or, a demi swan with wings expanded ar. beaked gu.

James (Creshall, co. Essex, bart., extinct 1741; descended from ROGER JAMES, third son of JACOB VAN HAESTRECHT, who removed from the neighbourhood of Utrecht, and settled in England, *temp.* Henry VIII.). Ar. two bars embattled gu.

James (GREVIS-JAMES, Ightham Court, co. Kent; WILLIAM JAMES, Esq., third son of ROGER JAMES, son of JACOB VAN HAESTRECHT, purchased the manor of Ightham Court, *temp.* Elizabeth; DEMETRIUS GREVIS, Esq., eldest son of CHARLES GREVIS, Esq., formerly of Moseley Hall, co. Worcester, by ELIZABETH, his wife, dau. of Colonel DEMETRIUS JAMES, third son of WILLIAM JAMES, Esq., of Ightham Court, assumed the additional surname and arms of JAMES, by royal licence, 1817). Quarterly, 1st and 4th, ar. two bars embattled gu., for JAMES; 2nd and 3rd, ar. on a fesse az. betw. three pellets, each charged with a lion's head erased of the first, a griffin pass. betw. two escallops or, for GREVIS. *Crests*—1st, JAMES : Out of a ducal coronet or, a demi swan, wings expanded ar. beaked gu.; 2nd, GREVIS : A squirrel holding betw. the paws an escallop shell or. *Motto*—Fide et constantiâ.

James (granted to Right Hon. Sir WILLIAM MILBOURNE JAMES, Knt., Lord Justice of Appeal). Or, a chev. vair betw. three lions' heads erased gu. *Crest*—A cock gu. gorged with a collar gemel or, the dexter claw resting on a portcullis gold. *Motto*—GWNA A DDYLED DOED A DDEL.

James (Stoke, co. Surrey). Per chev. gu. and ar. three unicorns' head couped and counterchanged.

James (co. Surrey). Quarterly, ar. and az. a cross sarcelly counterchanged.

James (Otterburn Tower, and Rodchester, co. Northumberland). Sa. on a chev. ar. betw. three dolphins embowed erminois as many cross crosslets gu. *Crest*—A buffalo pass. gu. armed ppr. the dexter forefoot resting on an escutcheon ar. charged with a pheon az. *Motto*—Deo semper confide.

James (co. Worcester). Sa. on a bend or, betw. two bezants three martlets of the field.

James (co. Worcester). Az. a dolphin embowed ar.

James (co. Worcester). Ar. a chev. betw. three millrinds sa. *Crest*—A garb ar. banded vert.

James (Astley, co. Worcester; HUGH JAMES, Groom of the Privy Council to Henry VII. Visit. Worcester, 1634. Pedigree registered 1683. HIGGINS JAMES, Esq., of Astley, was High Sheriff of the county 13 William III., *d.* 1709). Az. on a chev. betw. three lions pass. reguard. or, as many escallops sa. *Crest*—Out of a mural coronet az. a demi lion reguard. or, collared also az. holding betw. the paws an escallop sa. (N.B. These are the arms recorded at the two visitations referred to above, but on the tablet to HIGGINS JAMES, at Astley, these arms are given, viz. : Per chev. gu.

536

and ar. three unicorns' heads couped counterchanged, impaling PYTTS).

James (Forfield Court, co. Worcester. HENRY JAMES, Esq., of Forfield, left four daus. co-heiresses, ELIZABETH *m.* HUMPHREY PERROTT, Esq., of Bell Hall; DOROTHY, *m.* HENRY GRESWOLD, Esq., of Yardley; ANNE, *m.* THOMAS RUDYARD, Esq., of Rudyard, *d.* 1626; MARTHA, *m.* JOHN PERROTT, Esq., Worcester). Same *Arms* and *Crest.*

James (Rowley, co. Stafford; descended from WALTER JAMES, brother of HENRY JAMES, Esq., of Forfield). Same *Arms* and *Crest.*

James (Pool Court, co. Worcester). Az. on a chev. or, betw. three lions pass. ar. as many escallops sa.

James (cos. Worcester and Gloucester). Ar. a lion ramp. az. betw. three escallops gu.

James (cos. Salop and Stafford). Az. on a chev. betw. three lions pass. guard. or, as many escallops sa. *Crest*—A demi lion ramp. or, holding betw. the paws an escallop sa.

James (Lord Mayor of London, 1479). Same *Arms* and *Crest.*

James. Az. on a chev. betw. three leopards' heads or, as many escallops sa.

James (the Close, Exeter). Gu. a water bouget within an orle of eight annulets ar. on a chief of the second a fesse per fesse indented vert and sa. betw. two barrulets, the upper of the last, and the lower of the third. *Crest*—On a mount vert a bull erm. armed, hoofed, tufted, and collared or, the dexter forefoot supporting a water bouget, and charged on the body with two annulets, as in the arms.

James (Roseinvale). Ar. a lion ramp. az. betw. three escallop shells gu.

James (Reg. Ulster's Office). Ar. a bend gu. a border sa.

James (Reg. Ulster's Office). Az. on a bend betw. three lions pass. or, as many escallops of the first.

Jameson (granted to JOHN JAMESON, Esq., of Windfield, co. Galway, eldest son of JAMES JAMESON, Esq., of Windfield, and Mont Rose, co. Dublin, and grandson of JOHN JAMESON, Esq., Sheriff and Clerk of co. Clackmannan). Az. a saltire or, cantoned in chief and flanks by Roman galleys ppr. and a buglehorn in base of the second. *Crest*—A Roman galley ppr. the sail gu. charged with a lion pass. guard. or. *Motto*—Sine metu.

Jameson (Scotland). Az. a saltire or, cantoned with four ships under sail az.

Jameson. Ar. two arrows in saltire, points in chief az. cantoned with four cinquefoils of the last. *Crest*—An antelope trippant or, horned gu.

Jamieson (Glasgow, 1864). Ar. a fess wavy vert betw. three anchors sa. *Crest*—A ship under sail ppr. *Motto*—Ad littora tendit.

Jamieson (Croy, co. Dumbarton, 1865). Ar. a fess wavy az. betw. three anchors sa. *Crest* and *Motto*, as the last.

Jamieson (Glasgow, 1869). Ar. a fess wavy vert betw. three anchors sa. a bordure of the second. *Crest* and *Motto*, as the last.

Jamy (Wells, co. Somerset). Ar. a fesse engr. vert betw. three escallops sa.

Jandrell. Sa. three buckles, the tongues pendent ar.

Jane, or Jeane. Az. an eagle displ. or. *Crest*—A swan, wings endorsed, devouring a trout all ppr.

Janes, or James (Kirtling, co. Cambridge, and Botalock, co. Cornwall). Ar. a lion ramp. az. betw. three escallops gu. *Crest*—Out of a ducal coronet or, a demi lion az. holding an escallop gu.

Janes, or J'anes. Az. a chev. erm. betw. six annulets, two, two, and two, linked together or.

Janes, or Janns (JAMES JANES, Mayor of Dublin, 1593, son of ROBERT JANES, or JANNS, Master of the Ordnance in Ireland, 1592. Visit. city of Dublin, 1607). Gu. on a bend ar. three Cornish choughs sa. beaked and legged of the first.

Janiville, or Jamvile. Az. three pairs of barnacles or, on a chief erm. a demi lion ramp. gu.

Janns (DUDLEY-JANNS; exemplified to Rev. SHELDON FRANCIS DUDLEY on his assuming, by royal licence, 1874, the additional surname and arms of JANNS, in compliance with the will of his kinsman, CHARLES JAMES JANNS, Esq., of Ennis, Commander R.N.). Quarterly, 1st and 4th, per pale gu. and az. on a bend engr. ar. three Cornish choughs sa. beaked and membered of the first, for JANNS; 2nd and 3rd, or, two lions pass. az. betw. in chief a rose gu. seeded of the field and barbed vert, and in base a trefoil slipped of the last, a bordure engr. of the second, for DUDLEY. *Crests*—1st, JANNS : A lion ramp. sa. collared gemelle ar. holding betw. the paws an escallop of the last; 2nd, DUDLEY : A lion ramp. double queued az. holding betw. the paws a rose gu. entwined with a trefoil slipped and leaved vert, motto over, Mori quam fœdari. *Motto*—Honor virtutis præmium.

Janson (co. Kent; granted 1605). Quarterly, az. and gu. a cross patonce and a chief or. *Crest*—On a mount vert a hind ppr. collared gu.

Janson. Ar. two bundles of reeds in fesse paleways vert. *Crest*—An arm from the elbow vambraced, holding a falcon's lure all ppr

Janson (Ashby Ledgers, co. Northampton). Quarterly, az. and gu. a cross patonce and a chief or. *Crest*—A cubit arm erect, vested or, cuffed ar. holding a cross patonce of the first.

Janssen (Wimbledon, co. Surrey, bart., extinct 1777; THEODORE JANSSEN, grandson of THEODORE JANSSEN DE HEEZ, youngest son of the *Baron de Heez*, Governor of Brussels at the period of the *Duke of Alva's* persecution, was so created 1714). Quarterly, 1st, ar. two bundles of reeds in fesse vert; 2nd, per fesse or and az. two swans close in fesse ppr.; 3rd, per fesse or and az. a swan in fesse ppr.; 4th, ar. a bundle of reeds vert. *Crest*—A quatrefoil (another, a trefoil) stalked and leaved vert.

Janvim (Jersey). Az. a chev. ar. betw. two bezants in chief and a fleur-de-lis of the second in base. *Crest*—A griffin's head betw. two eagles' wings. *Another Crest*—A dolphin embowed ppr. *Motto*—Labor ipse voluptas. *Another Motto* —Pour mon Roy.

Jaques (co. Middlesex, bart., extinct 1650 ; Sir JOHN JAQUES, Gentleman Pensioner *temp.* Charles I., was so created 1628, and *d. s. p.*). Ar. on a fesse gu. three escallops or.

Jaques (Easby Abbey, and Silton, co. York). Sa. on a fesse engr. ar. a lion pass. of the first. *Crest*—A lion's head erased gu. wounded through the neck with a sword ar. hilted and pommelled or.

Jaques (co. York; descended from Sir ROGER JAQUES, of Elvington, Lord Mayor of York in 1639, who was knighted by Charles I.). Sa. on a fesse engr. ar. betw. three escallops or, a lion pass. gu. *Crest*—A lion's head erased gu. wounded through the neck with a sword ar. hilted and pommelled or.

Jaques, Jeex, or Jacques (co. Middlesex). Ar. on a fesse engr. az. three escallops or. *Crest*—A horse's head couped ar. maned or, struck in the breast with a tilting spear of the last.

Jaques. Or, on a fer-de-moline sa. five estoiles ar.

Jaques. Or, on a bend sa. three bezants. *Crest*—A bezant charged with a lion's head erased ppr. collared or.

Jarberd. Or, a fesse betw. two chev. sa. (another, the tinctures reversed).

Jarden. Ar. six mascles gu.

Jardine (Applegirth, co. Dumfries, bart., 1672). Ar. a saltire and chief gu. the last charged with three mullets of the field. *Crest*—A spur-rowel of six points ar. *Supporters*—Dexter, a horse at liberty ar.; sinister, a man in armour having a scymitar at his side all ppr. *Motto*—Cave adsum.

Jardine (Sir HENRY JARDINE, Knt., King's Remembrancer in the Exchequer of Scotland). Ar. a saltire gu. on a chief of the last two wings conjoined and inverted erm. betw. as many spur-rowels of the first. *Crest*—A dexter hand holding up a spur-rowel or. *Motto*—Cave adsum.

Jardine (Edinburgh, 1672). Ar. on a saltire gu. five bezants, on a chief of the second three mullets or. *Crest*—A hand holding a bezant all ppr. *Motto*—Ex virtute honos.

Jareddur (Lord of Llechwerdd Ucha, co. Carnarvon). Descendants: I. COETMORES, of Coetmore; II. LLOYDS, of Rowtyn; III. OWENS, of Garth in Abergeley; IV. WYNNS, of Penheskin; and V. JONES, of Beaumaris). Gu. a chev. betw. three stags' heads caboshed ar. attired or.

Jarman. Or, three bendlets gu. *Crest*—An eagle's leg erased in bend sinister, grasping a feather in bend dexter.

Jarrat, Jarratt, or Jarrett. Sa. a lion ramp. ar. ducally crowned or, collared gu. *Crest*—An eagle, wings expanded ppr.

Jarrerd, or Jarrard. Quarterly, per fesse indented or and az.

Jarrett. Ar. a lion pass. betw. two flaunches purp. *Crest*—A lion pass. as in the arms, resting the dexter forepaw on a fleur-de-lis or.

Jarrett. Az. a lion ramp. ducally crowned or. *Crest*—A lion's head erased and ducally crowned or, collared gu.

Jarrett (granted 19 May, 1696, to JAMES JARRETT, son of WILLIAM JARRETT, of London, merchant). Az. a lion ramp. ar. guttée de poix, collared gu. and ducally crowned or. *Crest*—A lion's head erased ar. guttée de poix, collared gu. ducally crowned or.

Jarrett (Camerton Court, co. Somerset). Quarterly, 1st and 4th, az. a lion ramp. erm. ducally crowned or, for JARRETT; 2nd, gu. a sword erect ppr. betw. three mullets

at., for STEPHENS; 3rd, ar. on a mount vert a bull statant gu. armed or, charged on the shoulder with a plain cross ar., for RIDLEY. *Crest*—A lion's head erased or, ducally crowned and collared gu.

Jarveis (Pratling, co. Leicester). Sa. a chev. erm. betw. three hawks ar.

Jarvis (Doddington Hall, co. Lincoln). Sa. on a chev. engr. betw. three martlets ar. as many cinquefoils pierced of the first, on a chief of the second a fleur-de-lis betw. two escallops of the field. *Crest*—A unicorn's head ar. gorged with a collar charged with three cinquefoils.

Jarvice (Patling, co. Cambridge). Sa. on a chev. engr. betw. three doves ar. as many cinquefoils pierced of the first, on a chief of the second a fleur-de-lis betw. two escallops of the field.

Jarvie (Glasgow and Singapore, 1856). Ar. on a chev. gu. betw. two goshawks belled in chief sa. and a demi lion of the second issuant out of the base wavy az. an elephant's head couped or, betw. two bezants. *Crest*—An eagle rising ppr. *Motto*—Ad littora tendo.

Jarvill. Paly of six or and az.

Jarvis, or Jarveis. Az. six ostrich feathers ar. three two, and one. *Crest*—A lion ramp. gu.

Jarvis. Ar. six ostrich feathers sa. three, two, and one.

Jarvis. Sa. a chev. betw. six (another three) lapwings ar.

Jary (St. Andrew's House, Burlingham, co. Norfolk). Gu. on a pile erm. betw. two lions ramp. respecting each other or, three roses, two and one, of the field. *Crest*—Out of clouds two arms embowed in armour ppr. the hands also ppr. supporting a rose, as in the arms. *Motto*—Mens conscia recti.

Jason (Broad Somerford, co. Wilts, bart., extinct 1738, and Enfield, co. Middlesex). Az. a toison d'or within a double tressure flory counterflory gold. *Crest*—On a chapeau gu. turned up erm. a pegasus saliant, with wings endorsed, having in the mouth a burr ppr.

Jason. Az. a lion pass. or, on a canton ar. a cross gu.

Jasper (London). Ar. an anchor sa. on a chief wavy gu. three escallops of the first. *Crest*—A standard issuing from the wreath ar. charged with a cross gu.

Jasper. Ar. a bordure az. charged with eight martlets or.

Jaudrill. Ermines three round buckles ar. tongues pendent. *Crest*—A demi antelope gu. holding betw. the paws an escutcheon or.

Jawderill (co. Cambridge, Sutton, Isle of Ely, and Stoughton, co. Huntingdon; confirmed by Lee, Clarenceux, to ROBERT JAWDERILL, Esq., of Wycham, Isle of Ely, 2 July, 1597). Ar. three round buckles sa. tongues pendent. *Crest* —An antelope's head ar. gorged with a belt and buckle.

Jawdrell. Sa. three annulets ar.

Jay (co. Devon). Ar. a chev. az. betw. three jays ppr.

Jay. Gu. on a bend ar. three roses of the field. *Crest*—On a ducal coronet or, a griffin sejant az. resting the dexter foot on an escutcheon gu.

Jay (Selston, co. Nottingham). Same *Arms*.

Jay (Sheriff of Norfolk, 1678). Same *Arms*, bend engr.

Jay (Scotland). Az. three dolphins naiant or. *Crest*—A lion's paw holding a thistle ppr.

Jay. Az. a lion saliant and a canton or, a bordure engr. of the second.

Jay. Ar. three Midas' heads erased sa. crowned or.

Jay (Holme). Gu. four chains fixed to an annulet in fess saltireways az.

Jaye (London, and co. Norfolk; granted by Camden, Clarenceux, to Alderman HENRY JAY, 1601). Gu. on a bend engr. ar. three roses of the field seeded or, leaved ppr. *Crest* — An otter pass. ppr.

Jaye (Dorking, co. Surrey). Sa. three leopards' heads erased ar. crowned or (another coat bears, or, three leopards' heads erased and crowned sa.). *Crest*—Out of a ducal coronet or pale or and az. a camel's head sa. bezantée.

Jeaffreson (Dullingham, co. Cambridge; seated there since the year 1656). Az. a fret ar. on a chief of the last three leopards' faces gu. *Crest*—A talbot's head erased ar. eared gu.

Jeanes. Ar. a lion ramp. betw. three escallops az.

Jebb (Trent Place, bart., extinct 1787; RICHARD JEBB, M.D., Physician to George III., son of SAMUEL JEBB, M.D., of Nottingham, and of Stratford, co. Essex, was so created 1778, but *d. unm.* 1787; he had three uncles: I. RICHARD JEBB, Esq., of Drogheda, grandfather of RICHARD JEBB, Judge of the King's Bench in Ireland, and of JOHN JEBB, D.D., Bishop of Limerick; II. JOSHUA JEBB, Alderman of Chesterfield, grandfather of JOSHUA JEBB, Esq., of Walton, co. Derby, and RICHARD JEBB, Esq., of Tapton Grove, in the same county; III. JOHN JEBB, D.D., Dean of Cashel, father of the learned JOHN

Jebb, M.D., F.R.S.). Quarterly, vert and or, in the 1s quarter a falcon close ar. belled of the second, in the 4th a hawk's lure of the third.

Jedburgh, Borough of. Gu. on a horse saliant ar. furnished az. a chevalier armed at all points, in the right hand a Jedburgh staff ppr. *Motto*—Strenue et prospere.

Jee (Hart's Hill, co. Warwick). Gu. a sword in bend ar. pommelled or. *Crest*—A gauntlet ar. garnished at the wrist or, holding a sword of the first, hilt and pommel gold. *Motto* —Deus fortitudo meo.

Jee (co. York; Fun. Ent. Ulster's Office, 1668, RICH, fourth dau. of Col. THOMAS JEE). Gu. a sword bendways, point upwards ar. pommel and hilt or.

Jefery (Langly). Ar. a fesse betw. three escallops sa.

Jeffcott, or Jephcott (cos. Worcester and Northampton, also the Middle Temple, London). Erm. three crescents az. on a canton gu. four crosses crosslet fitchée. *Crest*—A boar pass.

Jefferay (Malling, co. Sussex; descended from SIMON JEFFE-RAY, living *temp.* HENRY VI.; of this family was Sir JOHN JEFFERAY, Knt., Lord Chief Baron of the Exchequer, who *d.* at Chiddingley, in 1573). Az. fretty or, on a chief ar. a lion pass. guard. gu. *Crest*—A lion's head erased ar. ducally crowned az.

Jefferay. Az. a fret or, on a chief ar. a lion pass. gu.

Jefferey. Sa. a lion saliant betw. three scaling ladders or.

Jefferis. Sa. a chev. ar. betw. three spears' heads of the last. *Crest*—A lion ramp. sa.

Jefferson (London, and Ripon, co. York). Az. on a saltire or, betw. four bezants a leopard's face of the field. *Crest*—A demi griffin az. collared or, holding a bezant.

Jefferson (Thicket Priory, co. York). Quarterly, 1st and 4th, gu. a griffin sejant, wings endorsed ar. a border engr. of the last charged with eight pellets, for JEFFERSON: 2nd and 3rd, paly of six ar. and az. on a chief gu. a bezant betw. two annulets or, for DUNNINGTON. *Crests*—1st, JEFFERSON: A griffin, as in the arms, gorged with a collar gemel az. in the beak a lily slipped ppr.; 2nd, DUNNINGTON: A horse courant ar. gorged with a collar gu. charged with a bezant betw. two annulets or. *Motto*—A cruce salus.

Jefferson (Ven. JOSEPH JEFFERSON, M.A., F.A.S., Archdeacon of Colchester, *d.* 1821). Az. a saltire or, betw. four bezants. *Crest*—A demi griffin segreant az. holding betw. the claws a bezant.

Jeffery (London). Ar. six billets sa. three, two, and one, on a chief of the second a lion pass. or, armed and langued gu.

Jefferv. Erm. two lions pass. guard. gu. *Crest*—A demi lion ramp. holding a scymitar ppr.

Jefferyes (Brecon and Abercywieg, co. Brecon). Ar. a lion ramp. sa. a canton chequy or and az.

Jefferyes (Little Bursted, co. Essex; confirmed 20 Feb. 8th James I.). Az. a fret or, on a chief of the second a lion pass. of the first. *Crest*—Out of a mural crown or, a lion's head az. ducally crowned gold.

Jefferyes (London). Ar. a chev. gu. betw. three spears' heads ppr.

Jefferyes (Earl's Croom, co. Worcester, which manor was granted by Edward VI. to WILLIAM JEFFERYES, Cofferer to Henry VII.; the heiress of the family *m.* Sir ROBERT BARK-HAM, second bart. of Wainflete). Per fesse embattled gu. and or, in chief three leopards' faces, in base as many hawks' lures, lined and ringed, counterchanged. *Crest*—On a mount vert a sea-pie ash colour, wings expanded, beaked and legged gu.

Jefferyes, or Geffreys (Clifton and Corncastle, co. Worcester, 1569). Sa. a lion ramp. or, betw. three scaling ladders of the second. *Crest*—On a rock ar. a castle with two towers or, towers domed. *Another Crest*—On a mount vert a castle ar.

Jeffrey (co. Suffolk). Gu. fretty or, on a chief ar. a lion pass. guard. gu.

Jeffrey. Erm. on a canton sa. a saltire engr. ar.

Jeffrey. Sa. a lion ramp. or, betw. three scaling ladders of the second. *Crest*—On a ducal coronet or, a martlet ppr.

Jeffrey (Edinburgh, 1869). Paly of six ar. and az. on a fess erm. an annulet betw. two mullets sa. *Crest*—The sun rising from a cloud ppr. *Motto*—Post nubila Phœbus.

Jeffreys (Acton, co. Denbigh; descended from TUDOR TREVOR, and represented in 1796 by Dr. JEFFREYS, Rector of Whiteford, co. Flint). Erm. a lion ramp. sa. a canton of the last.

Jeffreys (Lord *Jeffreys*, of Wem, extinct 1703. Sir GEORGE JEFFREYS the Infamous, Judge JEFFREYS of the reign of James II., younger son of JOHN JEFFREYS, Esq., of Acton, co. Denbigh, by MARGARET, his wife, dau. of Sir THOMAS IRELAND, Knt., of Bewsey, co. Lancaster, and was created a Peer, 1685; his son, JOHN, second and last Lord *Jeffreys*, left an only dau. and heiress, *m.* to THOMAS, first *Earl of Pomfret*)

538

Same *Arms*, a mullet for diff. *Crest*—A demi lion or, jessant a laurel wreath ppr. *Supporters*—Two lions reguard. sa. ducally crowned or. Quarterings: 1st, az. a lion ramp. or; 2nd, gu. a fess or, betw. horses' heads erased az.; 3rd, az. a lion pass. guard. or; 4th, erm. a lion ramp. az.; 5th, gu. three chevronels ar.

Jeffreys (Slywell, co. Brecon). Sa. a chev. embattled betw. three spear heads ar. embrued gu.

Jeffreys (co. Dorset). Gu. three pillars ar. garnished or.

Jeffreys (Blarney Castle, co. Cork; Fun. Ent. 1666, Lady JEFFREYS). Erm. a lion ramp. sa. a canton chequy or and gu.

Jeffries. See JEFFERYES.

Jeffries (Boston, New England, America; descended from DAVID JEFFRIES, son of DAVID JEFFRIES, *b.* in England 1658, emigrated to New England 1677). Sa. a lion ramp. or, betw. three scaling ladders of the second. *Crest*—A castle with two towers or. *Motto*—Fac recte et nil time.

Jeffry (London and co. Worcester). Or, three hawks' lures gu. on a chief embattled of the second three leopards' faces of the first. *Crest*—On a mount vert a bird, wings expanded ar.

Jeffry. Az. billettée and a lion ramp. or.

Jeffryes (Priory, co. Brecon). Sa. a chev. betw. three spear heads ar. embrued gu. *Crest*—On the stump of a tree coupof and shooting out new branches vert a stork ar. *Another Crest*—A lily and holly branch in saltire ppr.

Jeffryes (London; Lord Mayor of London, 1686). Ar. six billets, three, two, and one, sa. on a chief of the second a lion pass. guard. or. *Crest*—A lion's head erased ar. charged with three billets sa. two and one.

Jeffryes (Chiddingley, co. Sussex). Az. fretty or, on a chief ar. a lion pass. gu. *Crest*—A lion's head erased ar.

Jeffryes, or Jeffereys. Erm. a lion ramp. sa. a canton of the last. *Crest*—A demi lion ramp. or, holding betw. the paws a chaplet vert.

Jeffs. Erm. on a canton gu. a saltire or. *Crest*—A pelican's head erased, vulning itself ppr.

Jeffson, or Jephson (London). Az. a fesse embattled or, betw. three cocks' heads erased ar. combed and wattled of the second. *Crest*—An arm couped at the elbow and erect, habited paly of four ar. and az. cuffed of the first, thereon a bend gu. holding in the hand a bunch of roses ppr. stalked and leaved vert.

Jegon. Az. a chev. betw. three pelicans or, vulning themselves ppr. *Crest*—A pelican, as in the arms.

Jegon. Or, two chev. gu. a canton az.

Jegon, or Jeggins. Ar. two chev. gu. on a canton az. an eagle, wings inverted or. *Crest*—An eagle with wings expanded or, beaked ar.

Jehangier (granted to COWASJEE JEHANGIER). Az. within an orle of eight mullets the sun in splendour or, on a canton ar. the rose of England and the lotus of India in saltire ppr. *Crest*—On a mount vert a low pillar, the base and capital masoned, flames of fire issuing therefrom all ppr. *Motto*—Burning I shine.

Jehibenod. Ar. two swords in saltire sa. hilts and pommels in base az.

Jejeebhoy (granted 14 April, 1842, to Sir JAMSETJEE JEJEEBHOY, of Bombay, Justice of the Peace at that Presidency, a distinguished and benevolent Parsee merchant, who received knighthood, by patent, in 1842, was created a bart. in 1857, and was presented, by command of Her Majesty, with a gold medal, inscribed "To Sir JAMSETJEE JEJEEBHOY, Knt., from the British Government, in honour of his munificence and his patriotism"). Az. a sun rising above a representation of the Ghautz mountains, near Bombay, in base, and in chief two bees volant all ppr. *Crest*—A mount, thereon amidst wheat a peacock, in the beak an ear of wheat all ppr. *Motto* —Industry and liberality.

Jeken, or Jekin (Dover; granted 16 July, 1803). Ar. a lion pass. reguard. ermines betw. two cinquefoils in chief vert and an escallop in base gu. *Crest*—A demi lion reguard. erm. powdered with crescents gu. holding betw. the paws a pheon sa.

Jekyl (Castle Hedingham, co. Essex, 1670). Or, a fesse betw. three hinds trippant sa. *Crest*—A horse's head couped ar. maned and bridled sa. studded and tasselled or.

Jekyll (Bocking, co. Essex, and cos. Lincoln, Middlesex, and Nottingham). Same *Arms* and *Crest*.

Jekyll (New Street, Spring Gardens, London, and Dalington Manor House, near Northampton). Same *Arms* and *Crest*.

Jekyll (co. Middlesex). Per pale ar. and or, a fesse wavy gu. betw. three hinds trippant sa. *Crest*—A horse's head paly wavy ar. and sa. bridled or.

Jelberd. Per pale ar. and sa. a fesse nebulée (another, wavy) betw. three garbs all counterchanged.

Jelf (Oaklands Park, co. Gloucester). Per chev. engr. az. and erm. in chief two doves ar. beaked and legged gu. in base three cinquefoils, two and one, of the last. *Crest*—A stork, wings elevated ar. beaked and legged gu. in the beak a trefoil slipped vert, on the breast a cross pattée of the second, the dexter paw supporting a fleur-de-lis or.

Jelibrand. Ar. two swords in saltire sa. hilted gu.

Jelley, or Jelly. Erm. a chev. sa. *Crest*—A garb entwined by two snakes ppr.

Jellicoe. Az. on a bend ar. three mullets gu. a chief or. *Crest*—A cherub or.

Jelter. Per pale gu. and vert, on a chev. betw. three cats pass. guard. or, as many garbs of the field. *Crest*—A cat sejant guard. or.

Jemmet (Ashford). Per chev. gu. and az. three unicorns' heads couped ar. *Crest*—A unicorn's head erased.

Jemyn. Per chev. gu. and ar. three unicorns' heads couped and counterchanged.

Jencote, Jenicot, or Jenycote (Gascoygne). Ar. a bend sa. on a chief of the second a leopard's face or.

Jenery (Fun. Ent. Ulster's Office, 1682, ELIZABETH, Lady SANTRY, dau. of HENRY JENERY, Esq., and wife of RICHARD BARRY, second *Lord Santry*). Az. a cross pattée fitched at the foot ar. betw. four fleurs-de-lis or.

Jeney, Jenney, or Geney. Az. an inescutcheon within an orle of eight martlets or.

Jenico. Barry nebulée of six gu. and ar.

Jenicot. Ar. a bend sa. on a chief gu. three leopards' faces or.

Jenings. Az. a chev. or, betw. three bezants. *Crest*—A dove volant az. legged ar.

Jenins (granted by Wriothesley, Garter, to WILLIAM JENINS, of London, and confirmed to his grandson, WALTER JENYNS, by the Deputies of Camden, Clarenceux). Az. a chev. betw. three griffins' heads erased ar. on a chief, a lion pass. gu. betw. two torteaux. *Crest*—A cat's head erased guard. gu. bezantée, holding in the mouth a cross formée fitchée ar.

Jenison (Walworth, co. Durham; descended from THOMAS JENISON, of Yokeflete, co. York, *temp.* Henry VI.). Az. a bend betw. two swans ar. *Crest*—Out of a ducal coronet or, a dragon's head az.

Jenison (Elswick, co. Northumberland; descended from RALPH JENISON, Mayor of Newcastle-on-Tyne, 1597, third son of ROBERT JENISON, of Yokeflete; the heiress of this branch, MARY, sister and heiress of RALPH JENISON, of Elswick and Walworth, M.P. co. Northumberland, and Master of the Buckhounds to George II., m. ROBERT SHAFTO, Esq., of Benwell, co. Northumberland). Same *Arms* and *Crest*.

Jenison (Nesham Abbey and Husworth; another branch of JENISON, of Walworth). Same *Arms* and *Crest*.

Jenison, or Jenyson (Marncham, co. Notts; THOMAS JENISON, Esq.; his dau. MARGARET, m. LEONARD LAYCOCK, co. Lincoln, son of THOMAS LACOCK, of Stourton, co. Notts, who served Henry VIII. in his French wars. Visit. Notts, 1614). Same *Arms*.

Jenison (co. Lincoln, Itheston, co. Northampton, co. York, and Wales). Same *Arms*, the bend wavy. *Crest*—Out of a ducal coronet or, a dragon's head az.

Jenken (Wales). Or, a fesse sa. in chief three mullets gu.

Jenkens, or Jenkyns. Per bend sinister erm. and ermines, a lion ramp. or. *Crest*—A wivern gu. standing on a tilting spear, without bar or vamplet, and broken off at the point or, and bearing in the mouth the remaining part of the shaft, armed ar.

Jenkes (Wolverton, co. Salop; granted 2 May, 1582). Or, three boars' heads couped sa. a chief indented of the last. *Crest*—A dexter arm embowed, habited sa. cuffed ar. enfiled with a ducal coronet or, grasping in the hand ppr. a sword of the second, hilt and pommel gold.

Jenkes. Az. two bars or, each charged with a martlet betw. as many fleurs-de-lis of the first, on a chief of the second a rose gu. seeded gold, barbed vert, betw. two fleurs-de-lis of the field.

Jenkin (Folkestone, co. Kent; descended from JENKINS of the North). Ar. a lion ramp. reguard. sa. *Crest*—On a mural coronet ar. a lion pass. reguard. sa.

Jenkin (Minster, co. Kent). Same *Arms*. *Crest*—A lion sejant ar.

Jenkin (Stowling Court, co. Kent, and Warbleton and Burwash, co. Sussex; descended from THOMAS JENKIN, Esq., of Stowling, co. Kent). Same *Arms* and *Crest*, the lion ramp.

Jenkin (Higher St. Columb, co. Cornwall). Or, a lion ramp. reguard. sa. *Crest*—A lion ramp. reguard. sa. *Another Crest*—On a mural coronet sa. a lion pass. reguard. or.

539

Jenkins (Sir RICHARD JENKINS, G.C.B., of Bicton Hall, co. Salop, eldest son and heir of RICHARD JENKINS, Esq., of Bicton, and great-grandson of RICHARD JENKINS, Esq., son and heir of THOMAS JENKINS, Esq., of the Abbey Foregate, co. Salop). Or, a lion ramp. reguard. sa., quartering BAGOT and MUCKLESTON. *Crest*—On a mural crown ppr. a lion pass. reguard. or. *Motto*—Perge sed caute.

Jenkins (Cairleon, co. Monmouth). Per chev. sa. and or, a chev. engr. betw. in chief two escarbuncles, and in base a lion pass. counterchanged. *Crest*—A lion sa. charged with two fleurs-de-lis or, and the dexter paw on an escarbuncle also gold. *Motto*—Fidus ad finem.

Jenkins (Rev. RICHARD JENKINS, D.D., Master of Baliol College, Oxford). Az. on a saltire engr. four crosses pattée fitchée, points downwards sa. *Crest*—Seven arrows, one in pale, the rest saltireways, encircled with an annulet or.

Jenkins (Charlton Hill, co. Salop). Or, a lion ramp. reguard. sa. *Crest*—On a mural crown sa. a lion pass. reguard. or. *Motto*—Perge sed caute.

Jenkins (Wales). Per pale az. and sa. three fleurs-de-lis or. *Crest*—A battle axe, handled or, headed ppr.

Jenkins. Sa. a chev. betw. three fleurs-de-lis ar. *Crest*—A lion's gamb erased, holding a bezant all or.

Jenkins. Ar. three martlets in pale betw. two flaunches sa. each charged with a lion pass. of the first.

Jenkinson (Hawkesbury, co. Gloucester, bart.). Az. a fesse wavy ar. charged with a cross pattée gu. in chief two estoiles or. *Crest*—A sea-horse assurgent ar. maned az. supporting a cross pattée gu. *Motto*—Pareo non servio.

Jenkinson (*Earl of Liverpool*; extinct 1851. Sir CHARLES JENKINSON, seventh bart. of Hawkesbury, was created *Lord Hawkesbury* 1786, and was raised to the earldom 1796; the third earl d. s. p. m. 1851, when the baronetcy devolved on the heir male). Az. a fesse wavy ar. charged with a cross pattée gu. in chief two estoiles or, and, as an honourable augmentation, upon a chief wavy of the second a cormorant sa. beaked and legged of the third, holding in the beak a branch of seaweed (called laver) inverted vert, being the arms of LIVERPOOL. *Crest*—A seahorse assurgent ar. maned az. supporting a cross pattée gu. *Supporters*—Two hawks, wings elevated and inverted ppr. beaked, legged, and belled or, charged on the breast with a cross pattée gu. *Motto*—Palma non sine pulvere.

Jenkinson (Walton, co. Derby, bart., extinct 1739; PAUL JENKINSON, Esq., of Walton, son of RICHARD JENKINSON, merchant, was created a baronet 17 Dec. 1685). Az. two barrulets or, in chief three suns ppr. *Crest*—A seahorse's head couped az. crined or, gorged with two barrulets gold.

Jenkinson (Walcot, co. Oxford; confirmed 16 James I.). Az. on a fesse wavy ar. a cross pattée gu. in chief two estoiles or. *Crest*—A seahorse assurgent or, maned az. supporting a cross pattée gu.

Jenkinson. Az. a fesse erm. in chief three suns or. *Crest*—Out of a ducal coronet az. a demi lion ramp. ar. holding a palm branch vert. *Another Crest*—A seahorse's head couped ar. crined gu. gorged with a fesse az.

Jenkinson (co. Lincoln; granted 14 Feb. 1568). Az. a fesse wavy ar. three estoiles in chief or. *Crest*—A seahorse ppr.

Jenkinson (London; ANTHONY JENKINSON, citizen of that city. Visit. London, 1568). Same *Arms*. *Crest*—A seahorse assurgent per pale or and az. crined gu.

Jenkinson (Tunstal, co. Norfolk, and Oulton, co. Suffolk; confirmed by Harvey, Clarenceux, 8 Nov. 1563). Or, two bars gemelles gu. betw. three boars' heads erased at the neck sa. *Crest*—A bull's head ar. crined sa. the horns twisted or and of the second.

Jenkinson (Norwich; granted 1687). Or, two barrulets gu. betw. three horses' heads erased sa. *Crest*—A seahorse's head couped ar. finned and gorged with two barrulets or.

Jenks. Sa. a chev. betw. three fleurs-de-lis ar.

Jenks. Vert a griffin segreant or. *Crest*—Out of a ducal coronet or, a griffin's head ppr.

Jenkyn. Az. a bend ar. betw. six mullets or.

Jenkyn (Trekening, in St. Columb, co. Cornwall; the co-heirs m. ST. AUBYN, SLAMING, TRELAWNEY, and CARY). Or, a lion ramp. reguard. sa. *Crest*—On a ducal coronet sa. a lion ramp. reguard. or.

Jenkyns (York City, and Rusby, co. York). Same *Arms*, &c.

Jennence, or Jennins (Bosmangan, co. Cornwall, and co. Salop). Erm. a lion ramp. gu.

Jennens (Acton, co. Suffolk). Ar. a chev. gu. betw. three griffins' heads erased, each having a plummet pendent in their beaks sa. *Crest*—A griffin's head couped betw. two wings inverted ppr. in the beak a plummet pendent sa.

Jenner (co. Essex). Az. a cross flory (another, potent) betw. four fleurs-de-lis or. *Crest*—A greyhound sejant ar.

Jenner (London; granted 1684). Az. (another, sa.) two swords chevronways ar. hilts and pommels or, betw. three covered cups of the last. *Crest*—A covered cup or, standing betw. two swords in saltire ar. hilts and pommels gold. *Motto*—In pretium persevero.

Jenner (Harley Street, London, bart.). Per chev. az. and or, in chief two estoiles of the last, in base a serpent nowed ppr. a bordure engr. erm. *Crest*—On a mount vert a lamp with three branches ar. suspended by three chains or, fired ppr. *Motto*—Fide et labore.

Jenner-Fust (Hill Court, co. Gloucester). Quarterly, 1st and 4th, quarterly, 1st and 4th, ar. on a chev. betw. three forest bills sa. as many mullets of the field pierced, for FUST, 2nd and 3rd, az. betw. three covered cups or, two swords chevronwise ar. hilts and pommels of the second, for JENNER; 2nd grand quarter, or, a fesse betw. three crescents sa. flammant ppr., for POE; 3rd, ar. on a chev. gu. betw. three buglehorns stringed sa. as many crosses crosslet fitchée of the first, for BIRT. *Crests*—1st, FUST: A horse at full speed ar., motto over, Swift and true; 2nd, JENNER: A covered cup or, betw. two swords saltirewise ar. hilt and pommels gold. *Motto*—Terrena per vices sunt aliena.

Jennet (Norgrove, co. Worcester). Ar. two chevronels gu. betw. six martlets sa. three, two, and one. *Crest*—Out of a ducal coronet or, a dexter arm embowed in mail ppr. holding in the hand a sword ar. pommel and hilt gold.

Jenney (Bredfield House, co. Suffolk; representative of the JENNEYS, of Knodishall, who are supposed to have accompanied William I. to England, and settled in co. Suffolk temp. Edward III.). Erm. a bend gu. cotised or. *Crest*—On a glove in fesse ar. a hawk or falcon close or, jessed and belled gold.

Jenney, or Jenny (co. Lincoln, Tottenham, co. Middlesex, and Fennerton, co. Suffolk). Erm. a bend cotised gu. *Crest*—On a glove ar. a hawk or, belled of the last.

Jenney (Great Cressingham, co. Norfolk). Erm. a bend cotised sa. (sometimes gu.). *Crest*—A falconer's hand within a glove in fesse ppr. bearing a falcon perch thereon or.

Jenney (Frisby Hall, co. Derby; descended from a family of the name of JENNY, or GYNEY, circa 1563). Erm. a bend cotised gu. *Crest*—On a falconer's glove lying fessewise ar. a hawk ppr. belled or. *Motto*—Deus mihi providebit.

Jenney (quartered by SKEFFINGTON, of Skeffington, co. Leicester. Visit. Leicester, 1619). Ar. three Cornish choughs sa.

Jenning. Ar. a chev. betw. three hinds sa. a quarter paly of four or and gu.

Jenning (granted to the Rev. JOHN JENNING, of St. Peter's, Westminster). Paly of six ar. and az. on a fesse engr. betw. plain cotisos gu. a cross pattée or, betw. two bezants. *Crest* -On a mount vert a wolf pass. erm. in front of a cross calvary gu.

Jenninges. Az. a chev. or, betw. three bezants, on a chief erm. three cinquefoils gu. *Crest*—A jay ppr.

Jennings (Harlington, co. Bedford). Erm. a lion ramp. gu.

Jennings (Oldcastle, co. Chester, and co. Salop). Ar. a fesse gu. betw. three plummets sa. *Crest*—A wolf's head erased per pale ar. and vert.

Jennings (co. Devon). Or, on a fesse vert betw. three battle axes gu. a rose betw. two demi fleurs-de-lis or.

Jennings (co. Cornwall. Visit. Cornwall, 1620). Erm. a lion ramp. gu.

Jennings (WILLIAM JENNINGS, Lancaster Herald, 2 May, 1526, grandfather of JEFFREY JENNINGS, Esq., of Ipsley, co. Warwick). Az. a chev. betw. three griffins' heads erased or, a chief of the last.

Jennings (Lord Mayor of London, 1508, and co. York). Ar. a chev. gu. betw. three plummets sa. *Crest*—A wolf's head erased per pale ar. and vert (another, and sa.). *Another Crest*—An eagle's head couped ppr. holding in the beak a plummet sa.

Jennings (Harwich, co. Essex). Same *Arms*. *Crest*—A bull's head gu. corned ar. *Motto*—Virtus basis vitæ.

Jennings (St. John's, Westminster, co. Middlesex; granted 1760, to ROBERT JENNINGS, Esq.). Erminois three battle axes erect az. two and one, on a chief gu. three bendlets az. *Crest*—A demi dragon erminois, wings endorsed gu. erased of the last, holding a battle axe erect az. *Motto*—Il buon tempo verra.

Jennings (Burton, co. Somerset, and Pynsent, co. Devon). Az. a chev. or, betw. three bezants, on a chief erm. as many cinquefoils gu. *Crest*—A redbreast sitting on a morion.

Jennings (Ripon and Lilesden, co. York; granted 1641) Ar. a chev. betw. three plummets sa. *Crest*—A griffin's head couped ber. two wings inverted ppr. in the beak a plummet pendent sa.

Jennings (Hayes, co. Middlesex). Ar. on a fesse gu. three bezants (another, or, on a fesse gu. three plates). *Crest*—A demi lion ramp. or, holding the upper part of a spear-shaft of the last.

Jennings. Az. a chev. betw. three griffins' heads erased ar. *Crest*—A cat's head erased guard. gu. bezantée, holding in the mouth a cross pattée fitchée ar.

Jennings (The Shrubbery, Dover). Az. a chev. engr. erm. betw. three toisons or. *Crest*—A dragon pass. vair, wings or, the dexter claw resting on a shield az. charged with a toison gold. *Motto*—Conservabo ad mortem.

Jennings (confirmed to WILLIAM DAVID JENNINGS, Esq., Procurator-General in the Arches Court of Canterbury, son of DAVID JENNINGS, Esq., of Dublin). Ar. a lion ramp. gu. holding in the paws a battle axe ppr. on a chief az. three ducal coronets or. *Crest*—Out of a ducal coronet or, a demi lion ramp. sa. holding in the paws a battle axe ppr.

Jennins (Milford, co. Hants). Ar. a chev. betw. three plummets sa. *Crest*—A demi griffin ppr. in the beak a plummet sa.

Jennins. Az. a chev. or, betw. three bezants, on a chief erm. as many cinquefoils gu. *Crest*—A griffin pass. gu. holding a buckle or.

Jennor. Or, on a cross az. four fleurs-de-lis of the first, a bordure engr. of the second.

Jenny (cos. Norfolk and Suffolk). Paly of six ar. and gu. a chief erm. (another, the chief ar.).

Jenny. Paly of six ar. and az. an orle of martlets or. *Crest*—Out of a ducal coronet or, an arm in armour brandishing a scymitar all ppr.

Jennyng. Ar. on a fesse gu. three bezants.

Jennyns (Ipsley, co. Warwick. Visit. Warwick, 1619). Az. a chev. betw. three griffins' heads erased ar. on a chief or, a lion pass. gu. betw. two torteaux. *Crest*—A leopard's head erased and guard. gu. bezantée, holding in the mouth a cross formée fitchée ar.

Jennyns (co. Middlesex). Az. a chev. betw. four griffins' heads erased or, three and one.

Jennyns (co. Middlesex). Quarterly, per fesse indented az. and ar., in the first quarter a lion pass. of the second.

Jennyns, or Jennings (Fun. Ent. 1599, STEPHEN JENNYNS, Clerk of Her Majesty's Works in Ireland). Az. a chev. betw. three griffins' heads erased ar. on a chief or, a lion pass. guard. gu. betw. two torteaux.

Jenoure (Much Dunmow, co. Essex, bart., extinct 1755; WILLIAM JENOURE, was of Stowham Aspall, co. Suffolk, temp. Edward IV.; his descendant, KENELEN JENOURE, was created a bart. 1628. Visit. Essex, 1634). Az. a cross patonce betw. four fleurs-de-lis or.

Jenynge (co. Hants, and Hesse, co. Middlesex). Ar. on a fesse gu. three bezants. *Crest*—A demi lion erased and ramp. or, supporting a spear erect gold, headed az.

Jenynges (co. Devon). Ar. a fesse betw. two hinds sa. a canton paly of four or and gu.

Jenynges (London). Ar. a chev. gu. betw. three fishes' heads erased sa.

Jenynges (London). Ar. a chev. betw. three demi estoiles couped per fesse gu. rays in base.

Jenynges (co. Suffolk). Or, on a fesse vert betw. three halberts az. staves gu. a fleur-de-lis betw. two demi roses paleways ar. seeded of the field. *Crest*—A demi savage sa. collared round the neck or, wreathed round the temples gold and vert, holding in the dexter hand a halbert az. staff gu.

Jenynges, or Jenninges. Az. a chev. betw. three griffins' heads erased or.

Jenynges. Ar. three torteaux in fesse.

Jenyns (Bottisham Hall, co. Cambridge). Ar. on a fesse gu. three bezants. *Crest*—A demi lion erased and ramp. or, supporting a spear erect gold, headed az.

Jenyson (impalement Fun. Ent. Ulster's Office, 1624, NICHOLAS WHITE, of Dufferin, co. Down, whose wife was ELIZABETH JENYSON). Az. on a bend wavy betw. two swans ar. three roses gu. seeded of the second, leaved vert.

Jenysonn (Burnham West Gate, co. Norfolk). Az. on a bend wavy or, betw. two swans ar. three roses gu.

Jeoffry (London). Or, three leopards' lures gu. on a chief embattled of the second three leopards' faces of the first.

Jephcott (Evesham, co. Worcester; Rev. JOHN JEPHCOTT, D.D., was Rector of All Saints, Evesham, 1681). Az. on a chev. betw. three stars of eight points ar. as many cocks' heads erased gu.

Jephson (Froyle, co. Hants, temp. Henry VIII.; of which

family was the Right Hon. Sir JOHN JEPHSON, of Froyle, a Major-General, M.P. for the county, who m. ELIZABETH, dau. and heir of Sir THOMAS NORREYS, Lord President of Munster, son of HENRY, Lord Norreys of Bicote, and thus acquired the estate of Mallow, co. Cork, Ireland. Visit. Hants, 1577). Erm. three buglehorns sa.; but Sir JOHN JEPHSON registered, ar. on a chev. sa. betw. three lions' heads gu. bezantée a sun in glory. Since the Protectorate, the family has used the arms of JESSON, viz., az. a fesse embattled or, betw. three cocks' heads ar. wattled ppr.

Jephson (Spring Vale, co. Dorset, bart.). Az. a fesse embattled or, betw. three cocks' heads erased ar. wattled gu. Crest—A cubit arm vested paly ar. and az. cuffed of the second, surmounted of a bend gu. in the hand a pansy or heartsease ppr. Motto—Veritas magna est.

Jephson. Ar. two bars az. betw. nine mullets, three in chief, three in fesse, and three in base.

Jephson (Sir JOHN JEPHSON, knighted at Dublin Castle, 18 Dec. 1605). Ar. on a chev. betw. three lions' heads erased gu. bezantée the sun in his glory or.

Jephson (Fun. Ent. Ulster's Office, 1625, JOHN JEPHSON, Attorney of the Common Pleas). Az. a fess embattled or, betw. three cocks' heads erased ar. combed and wattled gu.

Jephson (impalement Fun. Ent. 1657, Sir JOHN GIFFORD, Knt., of Castle Jordan, co. Meath, whose wife was ELIZABETH, dau. of Sir JOHN JEPHSON, Knt.). Ar. a chev. embattled betw. three cocks' heads erased gu.

Jephson (Mallow, bart.). See NORREYS.

Jephson (Reg. Ulster's Office, 1809, to LORENZO HICKEY JEPHSON, Esq.). Quarterly, 1st and 4th, gu. a lion pass. or, on a chief ar. a saltire engr. az.; 2nd and 3rd, az. a fess embattled or, betw. three cocks' heads erased ar. combed and wattled gu. Crest—A lion's head erased ar. betw. two palm branches vert. Motto—Virtus sub pondere crescit.

Jepine (1634). Vert three pineapples or. Crest—A lion's head erased or, billettée sa. and ducally crowned gold.

Jeppe (Sutton's Court, co. Somerset). Az. a chev. betw. three falcons close ar. Crest—An eagle displ. ppr.

Jerard (Pamford, co. Somerset). Ar. a chev. gu. betw. three erm. spots sa. Crest—An eagle displ. with two heads or, charged with a saltire sa.

Jerard. Quarterly, per fesse indented or and az.

Jerball (cos. York and Sussex). Ar. a chief chequy or and gu.

Jerbert. Sa. a fesse betw. two chev. or.

Jerbridge. Erm. an annulet sa. on a chief gu. three lozenges of the first.

Jeremy. Ar. three maunches gu. Crest—An arm in armour embowed, gauntleted, wielding a battle-axe all ppr.

Jereys. Ar. a chev. betw. three blackamoors' heads couped sa. caps vert, fretty or.

Jerires. Ar. a chev. betw. three delves gu.

Jerkanvile. Quarterly, or and az. in the first quarter a lion ramp. gu.

Jermain (Westminster). Vert a cross engr. or. Crest—A gillyflower ppr.

Jermin (Wickham Bishop, co. Essex; granted 9 Aug. 1664). Ar. two bars gemels betw. three bucks' heads caboosed sa. Crest—A buck's head cabossed sa. betw. two wings expanded ar.

Jermin (Exeter). Paly wavy of six erm. and az.

Jermy, or Jermyn (Antingham, Merlingforth, and Wyton, co. Norfolk, and Brightwell and Stutton, co. Suffolk). Ar. a lion ramp. guard. gu. Crest—A griffin, wings expanded gu.

Jermy. Ar. a leopard saliant guard. gu. Crest—A griffin pass. gu.

Jermy. Gu. three escutcheons erm.

Jermyn (Earl of St. Alban's and Baron Jermyn; earldom extinct 1683, barony 1703). Sa. a crescent betw. two mullets in pale ar. Crest—A talbot pass ar. ducally gorged or. Supporters—Two greyhounds or, collared and ringed az. each collar charged with three fleurs-de-lis gold.

Jermyn (Baron Jermyn, of Dover, extinct 1708; HENRY JERMYN, brother of THOMAS, second Lord Jermyn of St. Edmondsbury, was so created 1685). Same Arms, Crest, and Supporters, with a crescent for diff.

Jermyn (Debden, Hesset, and Rushbrook, co. Suffolk, 1400). Same Arms. Crest—A greyhound's head sa. gorged with a bar gemel or. Another Crest—Out of a ducal coronet or, a greyhound's head ppr. collared gold (another, a talbot pass. ppr. ducally gorged gold). Motto—Nec ab oriente nec ab occidente.

Jermyn (Exeter, co. Devon, and Lordington, co. Sussex). Paly of six erm. and gu. Crest—A tiger's (sometimes a dragon's) head erased gu.

541

Jermyn. Ar. a lion ramp. gu.

Jernegan, or Jerningham (Cossey, co. Norfolk, and Somerleton, co. Suffolk). Ar. three buckles lozengy gu. Crest—Out of a ducal coronet or, a demi falcon displ. ar.

Jerningham (Baron Stafford). Quarterly, 1st and 4th, ar. three lozenge-shaped arming-buckles gu. tongues fesseways, for JERNINGHAM; 2nd and 3rd, or, a chev. gu., for STAFFORD. Crests—1st, JERNINGHAM: Out of a ducal coronet or, a demi falcon, wings expanded ppr.; 2nd, STAFFORD: Out of a ducal coronet per pale gu. and sa. a demi swan rising, wings elevated, ar. beaked gu. Supporters—Dexter, a lion ramp.; sinister, a swan ar. beaked and legged sa. ducally gorged per pale gu. and of the second. Motto—Virtus basis vitæ.

Jerningham (Longridge Towers, co. Northumberland, descended from EDWARD JERNINGHAM, Esq., of Costessy, Gloucester, third son of Sir WILLIAM JERNINGHAM, sixth bart. of Costessy, and brother of Sir GEORGE WILLIAM, Lord Stafford). Ar. three lozenge-shaped arming buckles gu. tongues fessways, quartering, 1st, HOWARD, Viscount Stafford; 2nd, PLANTAGENET (of Woodstock) Duke of Gloucester; and 3rd, STAFFORD, Lord Stafford. Crest—Out of a ducal coronet or, a demi falcon rising, wings expanded ppr. Motto—Virtus basis vitæ.

Jernouthe. Or, guttée de sang a bend gu.

Jernyngham. Ar. on a chev. gu. fimbriated engr. sa. three escallops of the first.

Jersey, Earl of. See VILLIERS.

Jersey, or Jercy. Per pale az. and gu. an eagle displ. ar. Crest—A phœnix ppr.

Jersey, Deanery of. Ar. three bends gu.

Jersey (arms of the Bailiwick). A seal superseding on all writs or contracts requiring authentication, the Great Seal of England, was presented to the islands of Jersey and Guernsey by Edward I., in the seventh year of his reign (1279), by letters patent. This seal bore the royal arms, and was surmounted by the legend, S. Ballivie Insularum pro Rege Anglie ✝. Between 1291 and 1315, each island attained to the dignity of a separate Bailly, and the legend around the seal, in the case of Jersey, was altered to its present reading, S. Ballivie Insule de Ierseye.

Jerveis (co. Worcester). Sa. a chev. betw. three pheasants ar. Crest—A tiger's head sa.

Jervile, De (co. Norfolk). Paly of six or and az.

Jervis (Earl of St. Vincent; extinct 1823; Sir JOHN JERVIS, Admiral R.N., was so created 1797, as a reward for the victory he achieved over the Spanish fleet off Cape St. Vincent; in 1801 he was created Viscount St. Vincent, with special remainder to the issue of his sister MARY, wife of WILLIAM HENRY RICKETTS, and d. s. p. 1823). Sa. a chev. erm. betw. three martlets ar. Crest—Out of a naval crown or, enwrapped by a wreath of laurel vert, a demi pegasus ar. maned and hoofed gold, winged az. charged on the wing with a fleur-de-lis also gold. Supporters—Dexter, an eagle, wings elevated and endorsed, holding in the sinister claw a thunderbolt all ppr.; sinister, a pegasus ar. maned and hoofed or, wings az. charged with a fleur-de-lis gold. Motto—Thus. This motto is a graceful and seamanlike allusion implying perfect rectitude. "Thus" is the word of direction given to the steersman by the quartermaster when the ship is going in a perfectly correct course. For instance, if he wish the vessel to proceed to the right, he says "Starboard;" if to the left, "Port;" but if the ship be going quite as it ought to do, he says "Keep thus," or "Thus" simply, corrupted in nautical pronunciation into "Theis."

Jervis (Viscount St. Vincent). Sa. a chev. erm. betw. three martlets ar. Crest—Out of a naval crown or, enwrapped by a wreath of laurel vert a demi pegasus ar. maned and hoofed of the first, winged az. charged on the wing with a fleur-de-lis gold. Supporters—Dexter, an eagle, wings elevated and endorsed, holding in the sinister claw a thunderbolt all ppr.; sinister, a pegasus ar. maned and hoofed or, wings az. charged with a fleur-de-lis gold. Motto—Thus.

Jervis (Darlaston, co. Stafford). Same Arms, quartering, 1st, per chev. sa. and ar. in chief three leopards' faces of the last, for SWINFEN; 2nd, az. a cross pattée ar.; 3rd, gu. on a fesse betw. three leopards' faces ar. as many cinquefoils of the field. Crest—An eagle's head erased betw. two wings ar. Motto—Virtute et amicitiâ.

Jervis (Sir HUMPHRY JERVIS, Knt., twice Lord Mayor of Dublin; Fun. Ent. ELIZABETH, Lady JERVIS, d. 11 Jan. 1687). Sa. a chev. erm. betw. three martlets ar.

Jervis (WHITE-JERVIS, Bally Ellis, co. Wexford, bart.) Quarterly, 1st and 4th, sa. a chev. erm. betw. three martlets or, for JERVIS; 2nd and 3rd, gu. a chev. vair betw. three lions ramp. or, for WHITE. Crests—1st: A martlet ar.; 2nd: Three arrows, one in fesse and two in saltire, gu. flighted ppr. Motto—Venale nec auro.

Jervis (Exbridge and Exeter, co. Devon). Ar. six ostrich feathers, three, two, and one, sa.

Jervis (Petling, co. Leicester; granted by Camden). Sa. a chev. erm. betw. three hawks close ar. *Crest*—A hawk's head or, betw. two wings expanded erm.

Jervis (Chatculme, or Chatkyll, in the parish of Eccleshall, co. Stafford; supposed to be descended from ROBERT JERVAYS DE CHATCULME, 18 Edward III.). Sa. a chev. erm. betw. three martlets or.

Jervoise (THOMAS JERVOISE was Lord of Northfield and Weoley, *temp.* Mary I.; the eventual heiress of the family *m.* 1729, SAMUEL CLARKE, Esq., of Westbromwich, co. Stafford). Sa. a chev. betw. three eagles close ar. *Crest*—A tiger's head couped sa.

Jervoise (CLARKE-JERVOISE, Idsworth Park, co. Hants, bart.). Quarterly, 1st and 4th, sa. a chev. betw. three eaglets close ar., for JERVOISE; 2nd and 3rd, az. three escallops in pale or, betw. two flaunches erminois, each charged with a cross pattée fitchée gu., for CLARKE. *Crests*—JERVOISE: A griffin's head sa.; CLARKE: Within a gold ring, set with a diamond ppr. a roundlet per pale gu. and az. charged with a pheon ar.

Jervoise (Herriard, co. Hants). Quarterly, 1st and 4th, a chev. betw. three eagles close ar., for JERVOISE; 2nd and 3rd, az. three stirrups or, for PUREFOY. *Crest*—An heraldic tiger's head sa.

Jervys (Letheringsett, co. Norfolk). Az. a chev. betw. three beehives or.

Jervys. Sa. three beehives or. *Crest*—A hand ppr. holding an eagle's leg erased at the thigh gu.

Jerwerth Goch (son of MEREDITH, Prince of Powys, from whom KYNASTON, of Hordley, &c.). Ar. a lion ramp. sa.

Jerwerth Voel (Lord of Mechain, in Wales, derived from MAEL MELIENYDD. Descendants: I. OWEN, of Llan-y-Meiched; II. MAURICE, of Llansaintffraid). Ar. a fesse betw. three fleurs-de-lis sa.

Jerworth (Penryn, Wales). Gu. three boars' heads erased in pale ar.

Jerworth. Az. on a fesse or, betw. three lions ramp. of the last as many crosses pattée fitchée sa. *Crest*—A crane's head couped ppr.

Jesore. Az. a lion ramp. or, within an orle of billets ar. a bordure engr. of the second.

Jesse (Llanbedr Hall, co. Denbigh). Ar. three demi seadogs pass. in pale sa. *Crest*—A lion sejant supporting an escutcheon gu.

Jesson (Coventry, co. Warwick). Ar. a fesse embattled sa. betw. three cocks' heads erased gu. *Crest*—A dexter arm ppr. vested gu. charged with a bend ar. cuffed or, holding a red rose, stalked and leaved vert.

Jesson (co. Lincoln). Or, on a bend cotised sa. three crosses moline of the first.

Jesson. Az. a lion ramp. betw. three billets or.

Jesson (London, and Hill Park, Westerham, co. Kent; granted 1635). Az. a fesse crenellée betw. three cocks' heads erased ar. beaked, wattled, and combed gu. *Crest*—A cubit arm erect, habited paly of four ar. and az. charged with a bend gu. cuffed ar. holding in the hand a marigold slipped and leaved ppr.

Jesson (Oakwood, co. Stafford; descended from an ancient family long settled at West Bromwich, co. Stafford. Az. on a fesse embattled counter-embattled ar. betw. three cocks' heads erased of the last, beaked, combed, and wattled gu. two roses of the last. *Crest*—A cubit arm erect, vested az. charged with a bend embattled counter-embattled, and cuffed ar. in the hand a rose gu. slipped ppr. *Motto*—Consilii taciturnitas nutrix.

Jessope (Gillingham, Chilcomb, Chickwell, and East Chequerell, co. Dorset). Ar. (another, or) two bars gu. in chief three leopards' faces of the last. *Crest*—A cockatrice vert with wings displ. ppr. combed and wattled gu. *Another Crest*—A man on horseback at a charge, holding a broken tilting spear ppr.

Jessop (Doory Hall, co. Longford). Or, two bars gu. in chief three leopards' faces of the second; some families of JESSOP, in Ireland, have used, ar. a fesse betw. three leopards' faces gu. *Crest*—A dove with an olive branch in the beak all ppr. *Motto*—Pax et amor.

Jessop (Butterley Hall, co. Derby; descended from the same parent stock as JESSOP, of Doory Hall). Same *Arms*. *Crest* —A cockatrice's head erased purp. combed gu. winged ppr.

Jessop (exemplified to ROBERT BOMFORD, Esq., of Mount Jessop, co. Longford, on his assuming, by royal licence, the surname and arms of JESSOP in lieu of those of BOMFORD, in compliance with the will of his maternal uncle, Rev. THOMAS

542

Jessop, LL.D., of Mount Jessop). Ar. two bars gu. on a chief of the last three leopards' faces of the first. *Crest*—A cockatrice's head ppr. combed and wattled, wings displ. gu. each charged with a trefoil slipped ar.

Jessope (Bromehall, co. York; granted 13 July, 1575). Barry of six ar. and az. on the first nine mullets gu. three, three, and three. *Crest*—A turtle dove standing on an olive branch ppr.

Jestyn ap Gwrgant (Tributary Prince of Glamorgan, founder of the Fifth Royal Tribe of Wales). Gu. three chevronels ar.

Jesus' College, Oxford (founded by Queen Elizabeth, 1571). Az. three stags trippant ar. being the arms of HUGH PRICE, Doctor of Laws, who contributed largely to the building.

Jesus' College, Cambridge (founded by JOHN ALCOCK, Chancellor of England, 1497). Ar. on a fesse betw. three cocks' heads erased sa. crested and jelloped gu. a mitre or, all within a border of the third, charged with eight ducal coronets of the fourth. *Crest*—On a ducal coronet or, a cock sa. crested and jelloped gu.

Jett (London). Ar. on a cross gu. five fleurs-de-lis of the field, in the dexter quarter a trefoil slipped vert, in the sinister a portcullis az. *Crest*—Out of rays of the sun or, a demi swan, wings elevated sa. in the beak an arrow ar.

Jetter (Bayton, Ellowe, and Lowestoft, co. Suffolk). Az. (another, sa.) a fesse betw. three bats displ. ar. *Crest*—Out of a ducal coronet or, a cubit arm erect in mail, holding in the hand all ppr. the blade of a broken sword ar.

Jeune (Jersey). Sa. a stag trippant or, attired ar. *Crest*—The attires of a stag ar. *Motto*—Faire sans dire.

Jeune (Bishop of Peterborough, 1864). Sa. a buck trippant ar.

Jevan Voell (Penkelly, Wales). Az. a chev. betw. three cocks ar., armed, crested, and jelloped or.

Jevon (co. Stafford). Or, a torteau betw. three saltires gu.

Jew (Whitfield, co. Devon). Ar. a chev. betw. three Jews' heads couped at the shoulder ppr.

Jew (Evesham, co. Worcester). Same *Arms*.

Jewardby. Ar. a saltire engr. sa. on a chief of the last two mullets of the first.

Jewe (Cotleigh, co. Devon). Vert a lion ramp. erm. over all a fesse gu.

Jewell (Salisbury, co. Wilts). Az. three gillyflowers ar.

Jewell, or Jule (Bowden, co. Devon; of this family was JOHN JEWELL, Bishop of Salisbury, 1560-71). Or, on a chev. az. betw. three gillyflowers gu. stalked and leaved vert, a maiden's head of the field, ducally crowned of the third, on a chief sa. a hawk's lure double stringed betw. two falcons ar. beaked and legged of the first. *Crest*—A cubit arm vested az. cuffed ar. holding in the hand ppr. a gillyflower, as in the arms.

Jewell (quartered by THOMAS LOVETT, Esq., of Astwell, co. Northants, whose dau. ELIZABETH, was wife of Sir WILLIAM CHESTER, Knt., Mayor of London 1559. Visit. London, 1568). Per pale or and az. a chev. erm.

Jewell, or Jule (Scotland). Or, a chev. az. betw. three gillyflowers gu. slipped and leaved vert, on a chief of the third a hawk's lure betw. two popinjays of the field. *Crest*—A dexter hand holding a gillyflower ppr.

Jewkes (Wolverley, co. Worcester). Az. three eagles' heads erased ar.

Jex (Lowestoft, co. Suffolk). Ar. on a fesse engr. sa. three escallops of the field. *Crest*—A horse's head ar. maned or, holding in his mouth a broken spear gold.

Jex (JEX-BLAKE, Swanton Abbots, co. Norfolk). Quarterly, 1st and 4th. ar. a chev. betw. three garbs sa. a bordure of the last, charged with eight fleurs-de-lis of the field, for BLAKE; 2nd and 3rd, ar. on a fesse engr. sa. betw. two plain cottises gu. three escallops of the field, for JEX. *Crests*—1st, BLAKE: A morion ppr. thereon a martlet ar.; 2nd, JEX: A horse's head ar. maned or, erased gu. in the mouth a broken tilting spear gold. *Motto*—Bene præparatum pectus.

Jeys. Sa. a fesse or, betw. three cinquefoils erm. *Crest*—A horse pass. ar.

Joanes (Taplow, co. Buckingham). Ar. three cocks gu. combed and wattled or.

Joanes (London, and co. Worcester; granted 1634). Quarterly, 1st and 4th, ar. a lion ramp. vert, mouth bloody; 2nd and 3rd, gu. a bend or, over all a label of three points sa. a martlet for diff. *Crest*—A sun in splendour or.

Joanes (Walpole, co. Norfolk). Or, a chev. engr. betw. three swallows sa. a bordure az. bezantée.

Joanes (Brimsey, co. Somerset). Or, on a mount in base vert a lion ramp. az. *Crest*—A tiger's head erased or.

Joanes (Wales). Vert a lion ramp. or, betw. five ears of wheat of the last, two, two, and one.

Joass (Collinwort, co. Banff). Vert a sandglass running, ar. and in chief the Holy Bible expanded ppr. *Crest*—A sandglass winged. *Motto*—Cogit amor.

Jobber (Aston, co. Salop). Vert a fesse erm.

Jobber (co. Stafford). Vert a chev. erm. *Crest*—A fox sejant ppr.

Jobling (Newton Hall, co. Northumberland). Gu. a lion ramp. ar. on a chief or, three mullets pierced az. *Crest*—A demi lion ramp. ar. holding a battle axe ppr. *Motto*—For my country.

Jobson (Ilford, co. Essex; granted *temp.* Edward VI.). Paly of six ar. and az. a chev. erm. betw. three eagles displ. or, armed gu.

Jobson (Snayth, co. York). Gu. five escallops in cross (another, in saltire). *Crest*—On a hand extended ar. a falcon close or.

Jobson. Per pale az. and or, an eagle displ. counterchanged, on a chief gu. three escallops ar.

Jobson (Windsor, co. Berks, *temp.* Queen Elizabeth). Az. three leopards' faces or.

Jobson (London: Fun. Ent. Ulster's Office, 1625, KATHERINE JOBSON, *m.* first, Capt. HENRY MALBY, co. Roscommon; and second, Sir RALPH SYDLEY, Knt.). Paly of six ar. and az. a chev. erm. betw. three eagles displ. or.

Joce (co. Suffolk). Ar. on a chev. per pale az. and gu. three escallops of the first.

Joce. Sa. on a fesse ar. three cinquefoils of the first. *Crest* —An antelope pass. ppr.

Joce, or Joos. Ar. on a bend gu. three water bougets or.

Joce. Ar. a fesse betw. three (another, six) crosses formée sa. (another, ar. a chev. betw. three lions ramp. gu.; another, ar. three torteaux in bend betw. two cotises; another, ar. betw. three holly leaves gu.; another, sa. on a fesse ar. three wilks lying fesseways gu.).

Jocelyn (*Earl of Roden*). Az. a circular wreath ar. and sa. with four hawks' bells conjoined thereto in quadrangle or. *Crest*—A falcon's leg erased à la cuisse ppr. belled or. *Supporters*—Two falcons ppr. wings inverted, belled or. *Motto* —Faire mon devoir.

Jocelyn, or Jocelyne (Sawbridgeworth, co. Herts). Same *Arms.*

Joceys. Ar. an eagle displ. sa. over all a bendlet gu. (another, az.).

Jodrell (Sall Park, co. Norfolk, bart.). Erm. a trefoil slipped or, betw. three round buckles, tongues pendent ar. *Crest*—A demi cock, wings erected or, combed and wattled gu. issuant out of a wreath of roses of the last, seeded gold. *Motto*—Non sibi, sed patriæ natus.

Jodrell (Yeardsley Hall, co. Chester; settled there *temp.* Edward III. WILLIAM JAUDRELL served under Edward the Black Prince in the French wars; his lineal descendant, FRANCIS JODRELL, Esq., of Yeardsley, High Sheriff of Cheshire in 1716, was *s.* by his granddau. FRANCES, elder dau. of his son, FRANCIS JODRELL. She *m.*, 1775, JOHN BOWER, Esq., who took the surname and arms of JODRELL). Sa. three buckles ar. *Crest*—A cock's head and neck couped or, wings elevated ar. combed and wattled gu.

Jodrell (Duffield, co. Derby). Sa. a trefoil slipped or, betw. three round buckles, tongues pendent ar. *Crest*—A cock's head and neck couped, wings erect or, combed and jelloped gu. issuant out of a chaplet of roses, barbed and seeded ppr.

Jodrell (London, and Lichfield, co. Stafford; granted 10 July, 1707). Ermines a trefoil slipped or, betw. three round buckles, tongues pendent ar.

Jodrell (co. Stafford). Sa. three chaplets ar.

Jodrell. Sa. an estoile ar.

Joel. Lozengy gu. and ar. a chief erm. *Crest*—A hare lodged among grass ppr.

John (Penzance, co. Cornwall; formerly of Phillack, same co.). Ar. two bars sa. on a chief of the last as many bezants. *Crest*—An arm in armour embowed, grasping a sword.

John. Ar. a chev. betw. three Cornish choughs sa. beaked and membered gu. a bordure engr. of the second. *Crest*— Two battle axes in saltire ppr. blades or, thereon standing a Cornish chough, as in the arms.

John. Sa. a chev. betw. three wilk shells ar. *Crest*—A demi lion ramp. ppr.

John. Sa. a chev. betw. three trefoils slipped ar.

John-ap-Rhys (South Marchog-yn-Eideirnion, co. Merioneth; derived from GRIFFITH GOCH, son of RHYS-AP-IEVAN, *Baron of Kymmer, Crogen, and Blanas,* in Eideirnion, ancestor of the HUGHES's of Gwerclas, *Barons of Kymmer-yn-Eideirnion;* MARGARET (heiress of Saeth Marchog), dau. and heiress of JOHN-AP-RHYS, *m.* THOMAS VAUGHAN SALUSBURY, Esq., of Ponty-go, third son of

543

PYERS SALUSBURY, Esq., of Rug-yn-Eideirnion). Same *Arms* as HUGHES, of Gwerclas, viz., Ar. a lion ramp. sa. armed and langued gu.

John-ap-William (*Lord of Mawddwy,* son of WILLIAM, Lord of Mawddwy, living 17 Edward I., fourth son of OWEN CYFEILIOC, *Prince of Higher Powys,* afterwards called Powys-Wenwynwyn). *Arms,* those of BLEDDYN-AP-CYNFYN, King of Powys.. viz., Or, a lion ramp. gu. langued az.

Johnes (Llanvairclydoge and Hafodychtryd; descended from JAMES JOHNES, Esq., of Llanbadarn-fawr, co. Cardigan, Sheriff 1586, third son of Sir THOMAS JOHNES, Knt., of Albermarles, co. Carmarthen). Ar. a chev. sa. betw. three ravens ppr. a bordure invected gu. bezantée. *Crest*—Two battleaxes saltireways sa.

Johnes (Dolau Cothy, co. Carmarthen; a younger branch of JOHNES, of Hafodychtryd, descended from JOHN, second son of THOMAS JOHNES, Esq., of Dolau Cothy, grandson of THOMAS JOHNES, Esq., of Llanvairclydoge, M.P. for co. Cardigan 1713-22; the late JOHN JOHNES, Esq., of Dolau Cothy, *d.* 1876, leaving two daus. and co-heirs, CHARLOTTE, widow of CHARLES CÆSAR COOKMAN, Esq., of Monart, co. Wexford, and ELIZABETH). Same *Arms* and *Crest. Motto*—Deus pascit corvos.

Johnes (London). Az. a lion ramp. betw. three crosses formée fitchée or, a chief of the last. *Crest*—A lion ramp. or, supporting an anchor az. fluke gold.

Johnes (co. Monmouth, 1573). Ar. on a chev. betw. three birds sa. a lion's head erased of the field betw. two trefoils slipped vert, a bordure engr. plattée. *Crest*—Two battle axes in saltire ppr. handles or.

Johnes. Az. a lion pass. betw. three crosses pattée fitchée or, a chief of the last.

Johns (Trewince, co. Cornwall). Ar. three Cornish choughs sa. *Crest*—Two battle-axes in saltire ppr.

Johns (Procurator Fiscal of Glasgow, 1672). Per bend az. and gu. in chief three stars and in base as many pheons or. *Crest*—A crow ppr. *Motto*—Semper sic.

Johns. Az. a lion ramp. or, on a chief of the last three crosses pattée of the first. *Crest*—On a mural coronet a serpent nowed vert.

Johns. Az. crusily or, a lion ramp. erm.

Johns (BELDAM-JOHNS, Windmill Lodge, Bishops Stortford, co. Hertford; exemplified to FREDERICK MEADOWS NASH-WOODHAM, Esq., upon his assuming, by royal licence, 1867, the surnames of BELDAM-JOHNS, in the place of those of NASH-WOODHAM). Vert three garbs chevronwise betw. as many dexter hands couped at the wrist or. *Crest*—Upon a mount vert a garb banded or, pendent from the band by a ring also or, an escocheon vert charged with a dexter hand, as in the arms. *Motto*—Dat Deus incrementum.

Johnson (New York and Twickenham, co. Middlesex, bart.). Gu. on a chev. betw. three fleurs-de-lis ar. three escallops of the field. *Crest*—An arm couped at the elbow erect, holding an arrow ppr. *Supporters*—Two Indians wreathed about the waist with foliage, quivers over their left shoulders, bows in their exterior hands, and plumes on their heads all ppr. *Motto*—Deo regique debeo. Subsequently to this registration, a pedigree of JOHNSON, Bart., of New York and Twickenham, deducing the family from THOMAS O'NEILL, called MACSHANE or JOHNSON, son of JOHN O'NEILL, Esq., of Dungannon, who was grandson of Sir TIRLOUGH O'NEILL, was placed on record by Betham, Ulster, in the Office of Arms, Dublin Castle, and the coat of O'NEILL was allowed, viz.—Ar. two lions counter-ramp. supporting a dexter hand gu. in chief three estoiles of the last, and in base a salmon naiant in water ppr. *Crest*—An arm gu. encircled with a ducal crown or, the hand grasping a sword ppr. pommel and hilt gold. *Motto*—Nec aspera terrent.

Johnson (Bath, bart.). Per pale sa. and az. on a saltire ar. betw. three towers or, fired ppr. one in chief and two in fesse, and two tilting-spears saltirewise in base of the second, five cooks of the first. *Crest*—A tower ar. on the battlements a cock ppr. *Supporters*—Dexter, a grenadier habited and accoutred and arms ordered ppr.; sinister, a light-infantry man habited and accoutred and arms trailed ppr. supporting with his exterior hand a flag-staff also ppr. therefrom flowing a banner gu. inscribed "New Ross " in letters of gold. *Mottoes*—Above the crest: Vicisti et vivimus; below the shield : Nunquam non paratus.

Johnson (Milton Bryant, co. Bedford; granted to NICHOLAS JOHNSON by St. George, Clarenceux, 1632). Ar. on a pile az. three ounces' heads erased of the first. *Crest*—On a chapeau gu. turned up erm. an ounce's head erased ar.

Johnson (Olney, Bucks). Same as last.

Johnson (Wytham-on-the-Hill, co. Lincoln; descended from JOHNSON, of Olney, co. Bucks, a branch of JOHNSON, of Milton Bryant). Ar. on a pile az. three ounces'

heads erased of the field, langued gu., quartering for ROBERT JOHNSON, B.D., Archdeacon of Leicester, the founder, in 1548, of the school at Uppingham, and subsequently of that at Oakham : Ar. a chev. sa. betw. three lions' heads couped gu. langued az. and crowned gold. Crest—On a chapeau gu. turned up erm. an ounce's head, as in the arms. Motto—Qui vit content tient assez.

Johnson (Goldington, co. Bedford). Az. a chev. or, in chief two eagles volant, in base a sun of the second.

Johnson (co. Bedford and London). Az. a chev. betw. three eagles rising or.

Johnson (Beaconsfield, co. Bucks). Per pale az. and gu. a cross flory or, a chief of the last. Crest—A cubit arm habited or, grasping in the hand ppr. a cross flory of the first.

Johnson (co. Chester). Quarterly, per fesse indented or and az. in the first quarter an eagle, wings expanded sa. Crest—On a ducal coronet or, an eagle, as in the arms.

Johnson (co. Chester). Ar. nine pheons meeting in point, six in chief and three in base sa. Crest—An arm in armour, holding in the hand all ppr. an arrow ar. with a pheon's head or.

Johnson (Kittlesworth, co. Durham ; granted 20 May, 1569). Per pale sa. and az. on a saltire ar. betw. three towers of the last flammant ppr. and two spears saltireways in base or, five cocks of the field. Crest—A dexter arm embowed in armour firing a pistol all ppr.

Johnson (Worcester; BENJAMIN JOHNSON, Sheriff co. Worcester, 1763). Ar. a fess lozengy betw. three lions' heads erased gu. Crest—Out of a ducal coronet or, a nag's head sa.

Johnson (Hanley Castle, co. Worcester; monument, St. Martin's Church, Worcester, of WILLIAM JOHNSON, d. 1711, aged 63). Ar. a cross sa. on a chief gu. three cushions or.

Johnson (Bowden, co. Wilts; from the hatchment of JAMES JOHNSON, Bishop of Worcester, 1759-74, grandson of GEORGE JOHNSON, a Welsh Judge). Ar. a bend sa. on a chief of the last three cushions of the first. Crest—A goat's head ar. erased gu. horned sa.

Johnson (Bricklehampton Hall, co. Worcester; R. W. JOHNSON, Esq., was High Sheriff, 1867). Quarterly, per fess indented or and az. in the 1st quarter an eagle, wings expanded sa. Crest—On a ducal coronet or, an eagle, as in the arms. Motto—Vigilans.

Johnson (co. Worcester). Az. on a chev. ar. three pheons gu. in dexter chief the sun in splendour ppr.

Johnson (Twyzell, co. Durham ; the last male heir, MICHAEL JOHNSON, Esq., d. 1714, leaving three daus. and co-heirs, of whom the eldest, MARY, m. first, JOHN BROCKHOLES, Esq., of Claughton, co. Lancaster, by whom she was mother of CATHARINE, wife of CHARLES, tenth Duke of Norfolk; and secondly, RICHARD JONES, Esq., of Caton, co. Lancaster). Sa. on a bend or, betw. two shackelbolts ar. three pheons gu. Crest—A leopard's face per pale az. and sa. bezantée, from the mouth and ears flames of fire ppr. Another Crest—A tiger's head couped sa. bezantée.

Johnson (co. Essex). Ar. on a chev. sa. an estoile of sixteen points or, betw. three lions' heads erased gu.

Johnson (Winford, co. Gloucester, and Tunbridge, co. Kent). Ar. a fesse lozengy betw. three lions' heads erased gu. Crest—Out of a ducal coronet or, a nag's head sa.

Johnson (co. Hants). Erm. on a chief az. three bezants.

Johnson (Nethercourt and Margate, co. Kent). Quarterly, per fesse indented sa. and or, in the dexter chief quarter a pelican vulning herself of the second.

Johnson (co. Kent, 1605). Quarterly, az. and gu. over all a cross patonce or, a chief of the last. Crest—An arm erect habited per pale az. and or, holding in the hand ppr. a cross patonce of the second.

Johnson (granted to WILLIAM JOHNSON, B.D.). Ar. a chev. az. betw. three pheons gu. on a chief of the second an open book, representing the Holy Bible ppr. edged and sealed or, thereon inscribed " Proverbs, chap. xxii. v. 6," betw. two crosses flory of the last. Crest—A pheon, as in the arms, surmounted by a star of eight points or.

Johnson (Warrington, co. Lancaster, 1741). Or, a lion pass. reguard. az. on a chief dovetailed vert three acorns slipped and leaved of the last.

Johnson (Withcot, co. Leicester; granted 1727). Ar. on a bend gu. three pheons or, a canton erm. Crest—A demi griffin gu. collared erm. holding betw. the claws a pheon or.

Johnson (Gainsborough, co. Lincoln; granted 7 May, 1579). Ar. on a bend sa. three erm. spots of the first. Crest —A leopard pass. guard. sa. plattée and bezantée.

Johnson (Stamford, co. Lincoln). Ar. three boars' heads sa. couped gu.

Johnson (Thwate, co. Lincoln, Blackwall, co. Middlesex, and co. Norfolk). Or, a water bouget sa. on a chief of the

second three bezants. Crest—Out of a ducal coronet per pale ar. and az. two wings expanded counterchanged.

Johnson (Ayscoughfee Hall, Spalding, co. Lincoln). Or, a water bouget sa. on a chief of the last three annulets of the first. Crest—Out of a ducal coronet or, two wings erect sa. Motto—Onus sub honore.

Johnson (Pinchbeck, co. Lincoln). Ar. a chev. betw. three lions' heads erased gu. crowned or.

Johnson (Preston, originally of Walsh Whittle, co. Lancaster). Ar. a lion pass. gu. on a chief or, three acorns slipped vert.

Johnson (Sarre Court, co. Kent, and Temple Belwood, co. Lincoln; exemplified to JOHN WILLIAM DENNE JOHNSON, Esq., J.P., son of the Rev. JOHN DENNE HILTON, by ELIZABETH FRANCES, his wife, sister of ROBERT POPPLEWELL JOHNSON, Esq., of Temple Belwood). Quarterly, 1st and 4th, ar. a lion pass. gu. on a chief vert three acorns leaved and slipped or, for JOHNSON; 2nd and 3rd, erm. two bars az. in chief an annulet betw. two saltires of the last, for HILTON. Crest— 1st, JOHNSON : On a mount vert a wolf pass. sa. in the mouth a branch of woodbine ppr.; 2nd, HILTON : Moses' head affrontée betw. two bullrushes ppr.

Johnson (Tower, London; granted June, 1604). Gu. three spears' heads ar. a chief erm. Crest—A spear's head ar. betw. two branches of laurel vert, crossing each other over the spear's head.

Johnson (London, and co. York, 1634). Az. on a chev. ar. three pheons gu. in the dexter chief quarter a sun or. Crest—A cock ar. combed and wattled or, on the body three guttées de sang.

Johnson (London ; granted to THOMAS JOHNSON, Esq., Lord Mayor of the city 1841). Az. on a chev. ar. three pheons gu. in the dexter chief a sun in splendour ppr., in base two swords, points upwards in saltire, encircled with a double chain all or. Crest—A cock ar. combed and wattled or, standing upon the fasces gold.

Johnson (London; Her. Coll.). Ar. a pheon az. betw. three mascles gu. Crest—A tiger's head erminois, maned ar.

Johnson (London). Erm. on a chev. az. three bezants, a mullet for diff. Crest—Out of a ducal coronet a swan's neck or.

Johnson (London). Az. a cross betw. four pheons or.

Johnson (London). Ar. on a chev. sa. betw. three lions' heads erased gu. bezantée an estoile of eight points or.

Johnson (Long Melford, co. Suffolk ; granted 1663). Ar. a bend sa. on a chief gu. three woolpacks or. Crest—A spear or, strap gu. betw. two wings gold.

Johnson (Bury, Saxmundham, and Bildeston, co. Suffolk). Sa. on a fesse betw. two double manacles ar. three pheons gu. on a chief or, a demi lion ramp. betw. two lozenges az. Crest—A leopard's head erased ppr. collared or. Motto— Fortiter in re, suaviter in modo.

Johnson (Deanery, co. Durham). Gu. on a chev. ar. betw. three savages' heads ppr. as many pheons sa. Crest— A savage's head, couped at the shoulders, bearded, and wreathed about the temples all ppr. Motto—Nil admirari.

Johnson (cos. Northumberland and Durham). Per chev. gu. and sa. on a chev. engr. ar. betw. three men's heads affrontée ppr. as many pheons sa. Crest—In front of a man's head affrontée, couped at the shoulder ppr. wreathed about the temples ar. and gu. two pheons or.

Johnson (London). Ar. on a pile az. three wolves' heads erased of the field.

Johnson (Limehouse, co. Middlesex). Gu. on a chief indented or, four human hearts of the first, over all on a bend of the second three peas, slipped, stalked, and leaved vert, the pea pendent. Crest—A triangular harrow or.

Johnson (Great Yarmouth, co. Norfolk ; granted 10 Sept. 1660). Ar. a fesse embattled counter-embattled betw. three lions' heads erased gu. ducally crowned or. Crest—Out of a ducal coronet or, a leopard's head and neck gu.

Johnson (co. Northampton). Az. on a bend raguly betw. two cocks ar. crested and jelloped or, a snake vert.

Johnson (co. Northumberland). Az. on a bend betw. two towers ar. three pheons gu. on a chief or, a lion pass. betw. two lozenges az.

Johnson (Luffenham, co. Rutland; granted 1592). Ar. a chev. betw. three lions' heads couped gu. ducally crowned or. Crest—A lion's head couped gu. ducally crowned or betw. two ostrich feathers ar. Another Crest—Out of a ducal coronet ar. a leopard's head or.

Johnson (ROBERT JOHNSON, B.D., Archdeacon of Leicester, 1591-1625). Same Arms. Crest—A lion's head couped gu. langued az. ducally crowned or, betw. two ostrich feathers ar.

Johnson (cos. Stafford and Suffolk). Per bend ar. and sa. three trefoils slipped counterchanged. Crest—On a mount vert an ibex sejant erm. ducally gorged, crined, and tufted or, attired ar.

Johnson (granted to Rev. CROXTON JOHNSON, Rector of Wilmslow, co. Chester). Gu. on a saltire ar. betw. three towers or, fired ppr. one in chief and two in the flanks, and two tilting spears saltireways in base of the second, five game cocks of the first. *Crest*—A dexter arm embowed in armour firing a pistol all ppr. *Motto*—Fugite fures omnes.

Johnson (Tyldesley, co. Lancaster; Lord Mayor of London, 1545; represented by ORMEROD, of Tyldesley). Ar. a saltire sa. on a chief gu. three cushions or. *Crest*—A spur erect, betw. two wings or, straps and buckles gu.

Johnson (Runcorn, co. Chester; borne by JOHN JOHNSON, Esq., son of JOHN JOHNSON, whose father, RICHARD, son of PETER JOHNSON, was son of RICHARD JOHNSON, who settled at Higher Runcorn, at an early period). Or, a saltire vair betw. two cocks' heads erased in pale sa. combed and wattled gu. and two pheons in fesse of the third. *Crest*—A crescent or, issuant therefrom a pheon, the whole betw. two wings sa. *Motto*—Servabo fidem.

Johnson. Az. on a bend embattled ar. betw. two cocks of the second, crested and jelloped or, a snake vert. *Crest*—On a mount vert a talbot couchant ar. collared and chained or.

Johnson. Erm. on a chev. az. three bezants. *Crest*—Out of a mural coronet gu. a cubit arm erect, vested or, turned up ar. holding in the hand ppr. a scymitar of the third, hilt of the second.

Johnson. Ar. a lion pass. gu. in chief three oak sprigs fructed all ppr. *Crest*—A wolf pass. holding in the mouth a sprig of woodbine in full blossom all ppr.

Johnson. Per pale. or and az. a fesse counterchanged. *Crest*—A mermaid, holding in the dexter hand a sceptre, and in the sinister a mirror all ppr.

Johnson (Yaxham and Welborne, co. Norfolk; borne by the Rev. JOHN BARHAM JOHNSON, M.A., Rector of Welborne). Gu. on a saltire ar. five crosses moline of the first. *Crest*—A wolf's head erased per pale crenellée ar. and gu.

Johnson (Ulverscroft and Burleigh Field, co. Leicester; GEORGE WILLIAM LILLINGSTON, Esq., of Burleigh Field, only son of Rev. GEORGE LILLINGSTON, M.A., Incumbent of Southend, co. Essex, by BARBARA ANNE, his wife, only dau. of HENRY SPOONER, Esq., of Gracechurch-street, London, and heiress of her mother, ANN JANE, third dau. of NATHANIEL PALMER JOHNSON, Esq., of Burleigh Field, assumed by royal licence, 22 March, 1859, the surname and arms of JOHNSON, in compliance with the will of his grand-uncle, the Rev. NATHANIEL PALMER JOHNSON, M.A., Rector of Aston-upon-Trent, co. Derby). Ar. two chevronels betw. as many griffins' heads erased in chief, and a palmer's scrip in base gu. *Crest*—A griffin's head erased per fesse ar. and gu. holding in the beak a palmer's scrip of the last.

Johnson (Bowden Park, co. Wilts, 1679). Ar. a bend sa. on a chief of the last three cushions of the first.

Johnson (Blackwall, co. Middlesex; HENRY JOHNSON, grandson of HENRY JOHNSON, Esq., of Alborough, co. Suffolk; descended out of co. Norfolk. Visit. Middlesex, 1663). Or, a water bouget sa. on a chief of the last three bezants. *Crest*—Out of a ducal coronet per pale ar. and az. two wings erect counterchanged.

Johnson (Walton House, co. Cumberland). Ar. on a saltire sa. five bezants, on a chief gu. an Eastern crown betw. two woolpacks or. *Crest*—An estoile within a spur erect betw. two wings elevated or.

Johnson. Sa. on a fesse or, betw. a nag's head and two buglehorns in chief and another in base ar. garnished of the second, a demi lion ramp. betw. two pheons ar.

Johnson. Az. a woolpack ar. (another, ar. on a cross raguly betw. four pheons gu. five bezants; another, ar. a chev. gu. betw. three lions pass. sa.; another, per pale az. and gu. on a chev. ar. betw. three fleurs-de-lis or, as many escallops of the second; another, per bend ar. and sa. three cinquefoils pierced all counterchanged; another, gu. three greyhounds courant in pale ar. collared or; another, gu. on a chief indented or, four body hearts of the field, over all a bend vert; another, az. on a saltire ar. five trefoils slipped vert; another, or, three fusils in fesse sa.; another, az. a fesse engr. erm. betw. three escallops or; another, per pale and per bend or and ar.).

Johnson (Rockenham, co. Cork; confirmed to NOBLE JOHNSON, Esq., of that place, son of WILLIAM JOHNSON, Esq., of Rockenham, High Sheriff, co. Cork, 1815, and to the other descendants of his grandfather, NOBLE JOHNSON, Esq., Mayor of Cork, 1809). Ar. a saltire sa. betw. a lymphad in chief of the second and a tower in base gu. on a chief engr. of the last three cushions or. *Crest*—On a mural crown ppr. a spur erect or, betw. two wings expanded ar. each charged with an annulet gu. *Motto*—Nunquam non paratus.

Johnson (Woodlands, Vóstersoeg, co. Cork, as borne by WILLIAM JOHNSON, Esq., J.P. and D.L., of that place,

brother of NOBLE JOHNSON, Esq., of Rockenham). Same *Arms*, &c.

Johnson (Reg. Ulster's Office). Gu. on a chev. betw. three fleurs-de-lis ar. as many escallops of the field.

Johnson (granted to Sir WILLIAM GILLELAND JOHNSON, Knt., Mayor of Belfast, in commemoration of the Queen's first visit to that town). Ar. a saltire sa. betw. in chief a pile chequy or and gu. a chief vair, being part of the arms of Belfast, two sinister hands couped, one in dexter, the other in sinister fess points of the fourth, and in base a cushion of the fourth, thereon the municipal mace of Belfast in fess of the third, on a chief of the fourth a royal crown of England betw. St. George's and St. Patrick's ensigns displ. all ppr. *Crest*—An arm embowed in armour grasping a sword ppr. betw. two wings erect az. *Motto*—Nunquam non paratus.

Johnson-Walsh (Bart). See WALSH.

Johnson (Edinburgh). Ar. a saltire sa. betw. an increscent and decrescent in the flanks az. and a palm branch in base vert, on a chief of the second three cushions of the first. *Crest*—A winged spur ppr. *Motto*—Nunquam non paratus.

Johnsonn. Ar. on a chev. sa. betw. three lions' heads erased gu. bezantée an estoile or. *Crest*—A greyhound's head couped vert, collared or.

Johnston (Johnston and Caskieben, co. Aberdeen, bart., 1625¹. Quarterly, 1st and 4th, ar. a saltire sa. and on a chief gu. three cushions or, for JOHNSTON; 2nd and 3rd, az. on a bend betw. three harts' heads erased ar. attired or, in chief, and as many crosses crosslet fitchée of the second in base. *Crest*—A phœnix in flames ppr. *Supporters*—Two Indians ppr. wreathed about the head and middle with laurel vert. *Motto*—Vive ut postea vivas.

Johnston (Major JAMES JOHNSTON, 61st Foot; cadet of Caskieben, 1774). Ar. a saltire sa. cantoned with two bucks' heads erased in chief and base ppr. attired or, and as many cross crosslets fitchée in flanks az. *Crest*—A phœnix in flames ppr. *Motto*—Vive ut vivas.

Johnston (Holly Park, co. Down). Ar. a saltire sa. on a chief gu. three cushions or. *Crest*—A winged spur. *Motto*—Nunquam non paratus.

Johnston (Knappagh and Glenaule, co. Armagh). Ar. a saltire sa. on a chief az. three cushions or. *Crest*—An arm in armour embowed, holding a sword. *Motto*—Nunquam non paratus.

Johnston (granted to CHARLES BOLTON JOHNSTON, Esq., of Dublin, son of CHARLES OLIVER JOHNSTON, Esq.). Sa. a bend and in sinister chief a tower ar. all within a border gobony ar. and az. *Crest*—A horse trippant per fess ar. and sa. *Motto*—Festina lente.

Johnston (cos. Armagh and Dublin, and the city of Dublin; confirmed to Rev. RICHARD JOHNSTON, M.A., Rector of Kilmore, Diocese of Armagh, descended from WILLIAM JOHNSTON, who served at the siege of Londonderry, 1689, and to the other descendants of the said WILLIAM JOHNSTON). Ar. a saltire sa. betw. in chief a trefoil slipped vert, and in base a heart ensigned with an imperial crown ppr. on a chief gu. three cushions or. *Crest*—An arm in armour embowed, the hand grasping a sword all ppr. charged on the elbow with a spur-rowel gu. *Motto*—Nunquam non paratus.

Johnston (confirmed to the issue of the aforesaid Rev. RICHARD JOHNSTON, M.A., Rector of Kilmore, co. Armagh (fourth son of ANDREW JOHNSTON, Esq., of Barn Hill, Dalkey, and Temple Street, Dublin, by SOPHIA, his wife, only dau. and heiress of GEORGE CHENEY, Esq., of Hollywood, co. Kildare), and of AUGUSTA SOPHIA HAMILTON, his late wife, last surviving child of Rev. GEORGE HAMILTON, M.A., one of the sons of the Rt. Rev. HUGH HAMILTON, D.D., Lord Bishop of Ossory). Quarterly, 1st and 4th, JOHNSTON, ar. a saltire sa. betw. in chief a trefoil slipped vert, and in base a heart ensigned with an imperial crown ppr. a chief gu. thereon three cushions or; 2nd, CHENEY, az. six lions ramp. three, two, and one, ar. armed and langued gu. a canton erm. charged with a bull's scalp ppr.; 3rd. HAMILTON, quarterly, gu. and ar. in the 1st and 4th quarters three cinquefoils pierced erm. and a canton of the second charged with a trefoil slipped vert, in the 2nd and 3rd quarters a lymphad, sails furled, oars in action sa. *Crest*—An arm in armour embowed, the hand grasping a sword all ppr. charged on the elbow with a spur-rowel gu. *Motto*—Nunquam non paratus.

Johnston (exemplified to Rev. ALEXANDER MONTGOMERY, of Beaulieu, co. Louth, on his assuming, by royal licence, 1813, the surname and arms of JOHNSTON in lieu of MONTGOMERY, in compliance with the will of his wife's brother, ARTHUR JOHNSTON, Esq., of Little Mount, co. Fermanagh). Ar. a saltire sa. betw. three shamrocks slipped, and in base a human heart ensigned with an imperial crown ppr on a chief gu. three cushions or. *Crest*—A winged spur or, leathered gu. *Motto*—Nunquam non paratus.

Johnstone (Johnstone, co. Dumfries, *Earl of Hartfell and Marquess of Annandale;* title dormant since 1792, and claimed by Sir F. J. W. JOHNSTONE, Bart., of Westerhall, J. J. HOPE JOHNSTONE, of Annandale, and others). Quarterly, 1st and 4th, ar. a saltire sa. on a chief gu. three cushions or; 2nd and 3rd, ar. an anchor gu., for FAIRHOLM, of Craigiehall. *Crest*—A winged spur or. *Supporters*—Dexter, a lion ramp. ar. armed and langued az. crowned with an imperial crown or; sinister, a horse ar. furnished gu. *Motto*—Nunquam non paratus.

Johnstone (Westerhall, co. Dumfries, bart., 1700). Ar. a saltire sa. on a chief gu. three cushions or, in base a man's heart ensigned with an imperial crown ppr. *Crest*—A spur with wings or, leather gu. *Motto*—Nunquam non paratus.

Johnstone (Hackness Hall, co. York, bart., 1705). Quarterly, 1st and 4th, JOHNSTONE, ar. a saltire sa. in base a human heart ensigned with a regal crown ppr. on a chief gu. three cushions or; 2nd and 3rd, VANDEN-BEMPDE, per fesse, the chief or, the base per pale gu. and vert, a demi eagle with two heads displ. issuing in chief sa. the dexter base charged with a tower, the sinister with five towers in saltire gold, the gate and portcullis of each ppr. *Crests*—1st: A spur erect, rowel upwards, with wings elevated or, leather gu. buckle ppr.; 2nd: Issuing from the battlements of a tower ppr. a demi eagle with two heads displ. sa. wings or, about the neck a pearl collar, therefrom a diamond pendant on the breast, a sword fesseways ppr. pommel and hilt gold. *Motto*—Nunquam non paratus.

Johnstone (Hiltoun, co. Berwiek; now represented by General F. JOHNSTONE). Ar. a saltire engr. sa. on a chief also engr. gu. three cushions or. *Crest*—A sword and dagger ppr. hilted or, crossing each saltireways with points upwards. *Motto*—Paratus ad arma.

Johnstone (Graitney, co. Dumfries). Ar. a saltire sa. betw. a mullet of the last in chief and base, on a chief gu. three cushions or. *Crest*—An armed man on horseback brandishing a sword ppr. *Motto*—Cave paratus.

Johnstone (Elphinstone, co. Haddington, bart.). Quarterly, 1st, or, three crescents within a double tressure flory counterflory gu., for SETON; 2nd, ar. a saltire sa. on a chief of the last three cushions of the field, for JOHNSTONE; 3rd, az. three garbs or; 4th, ar. a chev. sa. betw. three boars' heads couped gu. armed ar., for ELPHINSTONE.

Johnstone (Clanchrie, co. Dumfries). Ar. a saltire invecked sa. betw. two. pellets in base on a chief gu. three cushions or. *Crest*—A star issuing out of clouds ppr. *Motto*—Appropinquat Dies.

Johnstone (Gormack, Scotland). Ar. a saltire and chief nebulée sa. the last charged with three cushions of the first. *Crest*—A spur-rowel within two branches of palm in orle ppr. *Motto*—Securior quo pariatior.

Johnstone (Poltoun, co. Edinburgh). Ar. a saltire sa. on a chief wavy of the last three cushions or. *Crest*—A spur ppr. betw. two wings ar. *Motto*—Sic pariatior.

Johnstone (Wardmilnes, Scotland). Ar. a saltire sa. betw. two escallops in fesse gu. on a chief of the second three cushions of the first. *Crest*—A hand ppr. holding an escallop gu. *Motto*—Sine fraude fidus.

Johnstone (Warristoun). Ar. a saltire engr. sa. on a chief gu. three cushions or.

Johnstone (Edinburgh, 1672). Ar. a saltire wavy sa. on a chief engr. gu. three cushions or. *Crest*—A dexter hand ppr. holding a bezant. *Motto*—Ex sola virtutes honos.

Johnstone (Galabank, co. Dumfries; descended from NEWBY; now Fulford Hall, co. Warwick). Ar. a saltire sa. betw. a mullet in chief and a rose in base gu. and in flanks two garbs vert, on a chief of the third three cushions or. *Crest*—A spur ppr. winged or. *Motto*—Nunquam non paratus.

Johnstone (Lathrisk, co. Fife). Ar. a saltire sa. within a bordure engr. az. on a chief gu. a spur-rowel of the field betw. two cushions or. *Crest*—A spur placed upright, the rowel in chief or, winged ar. and leathered gu. *Motto*—Semper paratus.

Johnstone (Netherwood, co. Dumfries). Ar. a saltire sa. betw. two stars in chief and an anchor in base gu. all within a bordure az. on a chief of the third three cushions or. *Crest*—A spur with wings or, feathered gu. *Motto*—Caute et sedule.

Johnstone (Pitkelrie, co. Fife, 1775). Ar. a saltire sa. on a chief gu. three cushions or, a bordure wavy vert charged with three bezants. *Crest*—A winged spur or. *Motto*—Assiduitate.

Joiners, Company of (London). Gu. a chev. ar. betw. two pairs of compasses in chief extended at the points, and a sphere in base or, on a chief of the last a pale az. betw. two roses gu. seeded of the third, barbed vert, on the pale an

escallop shell of the second. *Crest*—A demi savage ppr. wreathed about the head and waist with leaves vert, holding in the dexter hand, over the shoulder, a tilting spear or, headed ar. *Supporters*—Two naked boys ppr. the dexter holding in the hand an emblematical female figure, crowned with a mural coronet sa. the sinister holding in the hand a square. *Motto*—Join truth with trust.

Jokes (London). Ar. on a fesse engr. sa. three escallops or. *Crest*—On a ducal coronet or, a cockatrice displ. gu.

Joles (Lord Mayor of London, 1615). Ar. (another, or) a cinquefoil gu. betw. three pheons sa.

Joley. Gu. a fesse erm.

Jolles, or Joyles (London). Or, a cinquefoil gu. betw. three pheons sa. *Crest*—Out of a mural coronet a nag's head or.

Jolley, or Jollye (co. Lancaster). Ar. on a pile vert three dexter hands couped of the field. *Crest*—A cubit arm habited vert, charged with a pile ar. holding in the hand ppr. a sword of the second, hilt and pommel or.

Jolley (Fun. Ent. 1602, JOLLY, Her Majesty's Gunner in Ireland). Lozengy or and sa. a lion ramp. guard. ar.

Jollie. Ar. three gillyflowers ppr. *Crest*—A hand holding a scymitar ppr.

Jolliffe (Cofton Hall, co. Worcester, Leek, co. Stafford, and Buglawton, co. Chester). Ar. on a pile vert three dexter hands couped at the wrist and erect of the field. *Crest*—A cubit arm erect, vested vert and cuffed, and the sleeve charged with a pile ar. the hand grasping a sword ppr.

Jolliffe (London, and Botham and Carswell Castle, co. Stafford). Same *Arms*, the pile az.

Jolliffe (*Baron Hylton*). Quarterly, 1st and 4th, ar. on a pile vert three dexter hands couped of the first, for JOLLIFFE; 2nd and 3rd, ar. two bars az., for HYLTON. *Crest*—A cubit arm erect, couped, vested vert, cuffed and the sleeve charged with a pile ar. the hand grasping a sword in bend ppr. *Supporters*—Two lions guard. az. each charged on the shoulder with three annulets, two and one or. *Motto*—Tant que je puis.

Jolliffe (Ammerdown, co. Somerset; descended from JOHN JOLLIFFE, Esq., third son of BENJAMIN JOLLIFFE, Esq., of Crofton Hall). Same *Arms*, quartering TWYFORD, viz., ar. two bars sa. on a canton a cinquefoil. *Crest*—A cubit arm in armour, holding in the gauntlet a scymitar all ppr. *Motto*—Tant que je puis.

Jolly, or Jolley (Hatton Garden, London; granted 1692). Az. a lion pass. guard. or, in chief three sinister hands ar. *Crest*—A demi eagle displ. or. *Another Crest*—A demi eagle displ. or, holding in the beak a sinister hand ar.

Jolly (London). Ar. three stags lodged gu.

Jolly (Scotland, 1690). Ar. an ark in the water ppr. surmounted by a dove az. standing thereon and holding in the beak an olive branch vert, all betw. three gillyflowers gu. stalked and leaved of the fourth. *Crest*—A dove holding an olive branch, as in the arms. *Motto*—Lætavi.

Jolly. Ar. a mullet gu. betw. three pheons sa.

Jollye (Leek, co. Stafford; confirmed 27 Aug. 1614). See JOLLIFFE.

Jollyffe. Sa. an eagle with two heads displ. ar. on a chief gu. a lion pass. or. *Crest*—An eagle's head erased sa. beaked or.

Joly. Ar. a mullet gu. betw. two mullets in chief and a pheon in base sa.

Jolys. Ar. three pheons sa. a mullet gu. for diff.

Jonas. Az. on a cloud extending along the chief ar. the rays of the sun illumined or. *Crest*—On a tower ppr. a crescent or.

Jones (*Viscount Ranelagh*). Az. a cross betw. four pheons, points downwards, or. *Crest*—A dexter arm embowed in armour, the hand in a gauntlet ppr. grasping a dart or. *Supporters*—Two griffins erminois. *Motto*—Cœlitus mihi vires.

Jones (*Earl of Ranelagh*; extinct 1711; RICHARD, third Viscount Ranelagh, was so created 1674, *d. s. p. m.*). Az. on a cross betw. four pheons or, five mullets gu. *Crest*—A dexter arm embowed in armour, holding a dart all ppr. *Supporters*—Two griffins per fesse vert and or. *Motto*—Cœlitus mihi vires.

Jones (Boultibrook, co. Hereford, bart., extinct). Ar. a chev. betw. three crows sa. in chief a star of the Order of the Crescent. *Crest*—A crow sa. holding in the dexter claw the star of the Order of the Crescent. *Motto*—Deus pascit corvos.

Jones (Foy, co. Hereford; descended from Rev. WILLIAM JONES, *m.* ELIZABETH, second dau. and co-heir of Rev. GEORGE ABRAHALL, of Foye, about 1690). Erm. a bend sinister gu. over all a lion ramp. or. *Crest*—A hedgehog pass. ppr.

Jones (Stanley Hall, co. Salop, bart.). Quarterly, 1st and 4th, ar. a lion ramp. vert, vulned in the mouth ppr., for

Jones; 2nd and 3rd, gu. three lapwings (or peewits) or, for TYRWHITT. *Crests*—1st, JONES: The sun in splendour, each ray inflamed or; 2nd, TYRWHITT: A savage ppr. wreathed and cinctured vert, in the dexter hand a club ppr. *Motto*—Esto sol testis. See TYRWHITT, Bart.

Jones (Cranmer Hall, co. Norfolk, bart.). Az. on a fesse or, three grenades fired ppr. in chief a castle, and in base a lion couchant ar. *Crest*—In front of a castle ar. a lion couchant or. *Motto*—Marte et arte.

Jones (Littlington, co. Bedford). Az. a cross betw. four pheons or. *Crest*—On a chapeau az. turned up or, an armed arm embowed, tasselled gu. holding in the hand ppr. a spear, staff of the fourth, armed of the second.

Jones (Glan Helen, co. Carnarvon). Sa. on a chev. betw. three spearheads ar. two staves of Æsculapius chevronwise, each entwined by a serpent ppr. *Crest*—A dexter arm embowed in armour ppr. garnished or, surmounted by two branches of laurel in saltire vert, the hand grasping a javelin in bend sinister, point downwards of the first, from the wrist pendent by a ribbon an escutcheon gu. charged with a scymitar also ppr. pommel and hilt gold. *Motto*—Integritate et fortitudine.

Jones (Sir WILLIAM JONES, K.C.B., Lieut.-Gen., Col. 32nd Regt.). Same as JONES, of Glan Helen.

Jones, or Johnes (Caton, co. Lancaster). Quarterly, 1st, erm. a chev. couped sa., for JOHNES, or JONES; 2nd, sa. on a bend or, betw. two shacklebolts ar. three pheons gu., for JOHNSON, of Twyzell, co. Durham; so blazoned in the Visit. of Durham, A.D. 1664; in some authorities, for the shacklebolts two turrets are substituted; 3rd, quarterly, or and gu. on a bend sa. three escallops ar., for EURE, or EVRES; 4th, az. a bend or, for SCROPE. *Crest*—Out of a ducal coronet or, a plume of feathers az. *Motto*—Vince malum bono.

Jones (Chiswick, co. Middlesex; JOHN JONES, son of THOMAS JONES, of same place. Visit. Middlesex, 1663). Or, five fusils in fess sa. each charged with a fleur-de-lis ar. *Crest* —A lion's head erased sa. collared or, studded gu.

Jones (Stratford, Bow, co. Middlesex; JOHN JONES, gent., grandson of JOHN JONES, of Bristol, co. Devon. Visit. Middlesex, 1663). Or, on a mount vert a lion ramp. az. *Crest*—A wolf's head erased or.

Jones (Buckland, co. Brecon). Vert a chev. betw. three wolves' heads or.

Jones (Sunningwell, co. Berks, Chastleton, co. Oxford, and co. Worcester). Gu. a lion ramp. and a bordure indented or. *Crest*—A demi lion ramp. or, holding betw. the paws a mullet gu.

Jones (co. Salop, and London; granted Nov. 1610). Az. a lion pass. betw. three crosses formée fitché or, a chief of the last.

Jones (co. Berks). Same *Arms*. *Crest*—A lion ramp. or, grasping an anchor in pale sa.

Jones (Tredustan, co. Brecon). Ar. a stag trippant, with wings attached to the buttocks and hind legs ppr. betw. the attires a rose or.

Jones (co. Brecknock). Sa. a fesse embattled erm. betw. three boars' heads couped or. *Crest*—A boar's head erect and erased or.

Jones (co. Carmarthen). Ar. three bulls' heads cabossed sa.

Jones (Abermarles, co. Carmarthen, bart., extinct; descended from JOHN AP THOMAS, of Abermarles, sixth son of THOMAS AP GRIFFITH AP NICHOLAS, whose elder son, Sir RHYS AP THOMAS, K.G., was ancestor of *Lord Dynevor*. ELIZABETH dau. and heir of Sir HENRY JONES, Bart. of Abermarles, m. Sir FRANCIS CORNWALLIS, Knt.). Ar. on a cross ragulée az. betw. four pheons gu. five bezants.

Jones (ROBERT JONES, Esq., of Hafod, co. Flint, whose dau. SYDNEY, m. Captain EDWARD PIERSE, co. Meath; Fun. Ent. Ulster's Office, 1655). Ar. a crescent gu. betw. three boars' heads sa. langued and couped of the second, a border engr. of the third.

Jones (SAMUEL THOMAS JONES, Esq., of Glanmere House, Forest Hill, co. Kent). Az. a stag statant ar. betw. three roses of the last barbed and seeded ppr. *Crest*—Upon a mount betw. two roses ar. slipped ppr. a stag lodged also ppr. collared az. *Motto*—Ex vero decus.

Jones (Castle March). Ar. a chev. az. betw. three nags' heads erased sa.

Jones (Penrose, co. Cornwall, and co. Wilts). Chequy or and sa. on a fesse gu. three leopards' faces jessant-de-lis of the first. *Crest*—A dragon's head erased vert.

Jones (co. Denbigh). Ar. a lion ramp. vert, vulned on the shoulder gu. *Crest*—The sun ppr. at the end of each ray a flame of fire of the first.

Jones, or Johnes (Grothkenan, co. Denbigh; of this line

547

was INIGO JONES, the architect). Per bend sinister erm. and ermines a lion ramp. within a bordure engr. or. *Crest*—A lion's head erased per pale ar. and sa.

Jones (Archdeacon of Hereford, d. 1823). Per bend sinister erm. and ermines, a lion ramp. or, within a bordure engr. per bend sinister ar. and sa. *Crest*—A lion ramp. or.

Jones (co. Hereford, and Rowe, co. Middlesex). Or, on a mount vert a lion ramp. az. *Crest*—A tiger's head erased or.

Jones (The Bower Park, co. Worcester. Visit. 1683). Gu. a cross crosslet on three grieces or.

Jones (Lanvayre, co. Denbigh). Same *Arms*.

Jones (Edvin Loach, co. Worcester. Visit. 1683). Or, a lion ramp. and a bordure sa.

Jones (Lulsley, co. Worcester). Gu. a lion ramp. betw. six trefoils slipped ar. a border of the last.

Jones (Worcester; granted 1602, by Dethick, Garter, to WALTER JONES, of the city of Worcester, son of JOHN JONES, the second son of JOHN JONES, of Greysmund, co. Monmouth, "with ye consent of ye Rt. HONBLE GILBERT, *Earl of Shrewsbury*, who beareth ye same arms"). Gu. a lion ramp. and a border engr. or. *Crest*—A demi lion ramp. or, holding betw. the forepaws a mullet gu.

Jones (Abberley, co. Worcester). Quarterly, 1st and 4th, az. on a cross raguly ar. betw. in the 1st and 4th quarters a pheon, and in the 2nd and 3rd a cross moline or, five mullets gu., for JONES; 2nd and 3rd, sa. three bars ar., for LEES. *Crest*—A stag lodged and reguard. ppr. semée of acorns vert, in the mouth a fern branch also ppr. *Motto*—Deo adjuvante.

Jones (Wateringbury Place, co. Kent). Gu. three lions ramp. or, on a chief of the second a fret of the first. *Crest*—A talbot's head couped ar. chained round the neck or.

Jones (Barrow and Filmingham, co. Lincoln). Or, a chev. engr. betw. three Cornish choughs sa. *Crest*—A cubit arm erect, vested purp. cuffed ar. holding in the hand ppr. a branch of marigolds also ppr. stalked and leaved vert.

Jones (Lord Mayor of London, 1620). Az. a lion pass. guard. betw. three crosses crosslet fitchée or, a chief of the last.

Jones (London; granted Sept. 1604). Az. on a cross or, betw. four pheons of the second five estoiles gu. *Crest*—An arm in pale vested or, thereon three estoiles in pale gu. in the hand ppr. a pheon erect ar.

Jones (Marshal of the King's Bench, London). Erm. on a bend az. a rose betw. two annulets or, in chief a sword in pale ppr. hilt and pommel gold, crossed by another, the hilt towards the dexter side of the escutcheon. *Crest*—A demi lion ramp. ppr.

Jones (London). Per pale az. and gu. three lions ramp. ar. a mullet for diff. *Crest*—A buck's head erased sa. attired or, holding betw. the horns a bugiehorn of the first.

Jones (London). Sa. a fesse ar. betw. two daggers, one in chief erect, and one in base pendent of the second, hilts and pommels az. *Crest*—A gauntlet barways or, holding a sword erect ar. hilt of the first, pierced through a boar's head erased vert.

Jones (London). Or, a lion ramp. az. charged on the shoulder with a bezant, in chief two martlets sa.

Jones (co. Merioneth). Or, a lion ramp. within a bordure az. *Crest*—A lion ramp. az. holding a shield or, within a carved bordure (another, the shield az.).

Jones (Dol-yn-Edeirnion, co. Merioneth; derived from JESTYN AP GWRGANT, Lord of Glamorgan, whose last descendant in the direct male line, seated at Llanrhaiadr Dyffryn Clwyd, d. in the beginning of the 17th century, and was buried in the parish church, where there is a monument to his memory). Same *Arms*.

Jones (Chiswick, co. Middlesex). Az. three nags' heads erased ar. a canton of the last.

Jones (Ratcliffe, co. Middlesex). Ar. a chev. sa. betw. three crows ppr. a bordure of the second charged with eight bezants.

Jones (co. Monmouth). Ar. on a chev. betw. three birds sa. a lion's head erased betw. two trefoils slipped or, a bordure of the second platée.

Jones (co. Monmouth). Sa. a stag standing at gaze ar. attired and unguled or. *Crest*—On a chapeau gu. turned up erm. a stag ar. attired vert.

Jones (co. Monmouth). Sa. a spearhead betw. three scaling ladders ar. on a chief gu. a tower triple-towered of the second.

Jones (Walpole and Marshland, co. Norfolk). Or, a

2 N 2

chev. engr betw. three Cornish choughs sa. a bordure az. bezantée. *Crest*—A battle axe and spear in saltire, handles gu. heads ar. mounted or.

Jones (Fakenham, co. Norfolk). Gu. a lion couchant ar. a canton or. *Crest*—A lion couchant sa.

Jones (Esthall, co. Oxford; RICE JONES, Visit. Oxon, 1634, grandson of JOHN JONES, of Kenioke, co. Flint, who was grandson of GRIFFITH AP DAVID GOCH, *alias* JONES, 1465). Sa. a buck pass. ar. attired or. *Crest*—A buck pass. ar.

Jones (Chilton and Shrewsbury, co. Salop; granted 16 June, 1607). Ar. a lion ramp. vert, vulned in the breast gu. *Crest*—A sun in splendour or.

Jones (co. Somerset, 1645). Vert a chev. betw. three wolves' heads erased ar.

Jones (co. Salop, Lord Mayor of London). Ar. a lion pass. betw. three crosses pattée fitchée gu. a chief az.

Jones (Wales). Sa. a chev. betw. three spear heads ar *Crest*—A cubit arm erect in armour ppr. holding in the gauntlet a spear of the first, headed ar. embrued gu.

Jones (EDWARD JONES, a native of co. Montgomery, was consecrated Bishop of Cloyne, 1683, and translated to St. Asaph, 1692, *d.* 1703). Sa. three horses' heads erased ar.

Jones (Revell, co. Wilts). Ar. a lion pass. sa. langued gu. armed or, on a chief of the second a ducal coronet of the last. *Crest*—Out of a ducal coronet or, a demi lion ramp. sa. langued gu. armed of the first.

Jones (Llanarth and Treowen, co. Monmouth; the senior branch of the great house of HERBERT, derived immediately from HOWELL AP GWILLIM, third son of WILLIAM AP JENKIN, *alias* HERBERT, of Werndu, near Abergavenny, and elder brother of Sir THOMAS AP GWILLIM, Knt., father of the celebrated Sir WILLIAM AP THOMAS, of Raglan, Knt., ancestor of the HERBERTS, of that place). See HERBERT, of Llanarth.

Jones (Uppingham, co. Rutland). Or, a lion ramp. az. *Crest*—A paschal lamb ppr.

Jones (exemplified to JOHN HENRY WHITMORE, Esq., on his assuming the surname and arms of JONES, Chastleton House, co. Oxford). Quarterly, 1st and 4th, gu. a lion ramp. within a border indented or, a canton erm.; 2nd and 3rd, vert fretty or, for WHITMORE. *Motto*—Incorrupta fides.

Jones (Badsworth Hall, co. York). Or, a lion ramp. az., quartering LONGUEVILLE. *Crest*—A talbot's head couped at the shoulders gu. gorged with a collar dancettée erm. *Motto* —Till then thus.

Jones (Shackerley Hall, co. Salop). Ar. a lion ramp. vert, wounded in the breast gu. *Crests*—1st: The sun in splendour or; 2nd: On an eastern crown or, a dragon pass. guard. gu. *Mottoes*—Ovner na ovno angau; and, Esto sol testis.

Jones (Kelston Park, co. Somerset). Erm. a lion ramp. az.

Jones (Larkhill, West Derby, co. Lancaster). Quarterly, 1st and 4th, or, a lion ramp. az.; 2nd and 3rd, gu. a fesse dancettée erm. betw. six crosses crosslet ar. *Crest*—A talbot's head couped at the shoulders gu. collared dancettée ar. *Motto*—Till then thus.

Jones (Ystrad, co. Carmarthen; a branch of JONES, of Llansadaial). Ar. a chev. flory gu. betw. three stags' heads cabossed ppr. *Crest*—A stag's head ppr. *Motto*—Heb Dduw heb ddim.

Jones (Trewythen, co. Montgomery; descended from CADWGAN, Lord of Nannau, in Merioneth, younger son of BLEDDYN AP CYNFYN, King of Powys. The senior male line terminated in an heiress, MARY, *m.* BOWEN JONES, Esq., of Cefn Penworth, descended from JONES, of Trewythen). Quarterly, or, a lion ramp. gu. langued and armed of the first; 2nd and 4th, sa. three nags' heads ar. *Crest*—A lion ramp. as in the arms. *Motto*—Frangas non flectes.

Jones (Derry Ormond, co. Cardigan). Ar. a chev. betw. three boars' heads couped sa. *Crest*—The sun in splendour ppr.

Jones (Gwynfryn, co. Cardigan). Ar. a cross flory sa. betw. four Cornish choughs ppr. *Crest*—A demi lion ramp. ppr. *Motto*—Mors mihi lucrum.

Jones (Llanio, co. Cardigan; descended from DANIEL JONES, of Llanio, who took the name of JONES in 1693, son of JOHN AP GRIFFITH GOCH, and grandson of GRIFFITH GOCH). Or, a lion ramp. reguard. sa. a bordure engr. gobony ar. and az.

Jones (Plympton, co. Devon; descended from THOMAS JONES, Esq., of Llanio, High Sheriff of Cardigan in 1739). Same *Arms.*

Jones (Llanerchrugog, co. Denbigh; descended from BLEDDYN

548

AP CYNFYN, Founder of the III. Royal Tribe of North Wales and Powis, seventh in descent from RHODRI MAWR, or the Great, King of Wales). Quarterly, 1st, ar. a lion ramp. sa. armed and langued gu. on a chief az. three garbs or, for JONES, of Glyn Arthur; 2nd, or, a lion ramp. gu., for BLEDDYN AP CYNFYN; 3rd, az. the Three Men of Kent guard. in fesse ppr. wreathed and cinctured vert, bearing clubs also ppr. and shields ar. charged with crosses gu., for WOOD, of Goodnestone, co. Kent; 4th, gu. a chev. betw. three falcons rising or, for SMALLMAN; 5th, ar. a bull pass. sa. armed and unguled or, for BWLA; 6th, sa. three nags' heads erased ar., for JONES, of St. George; 7th, gu. a lion ramp. within a bordure engr. or, for TALBOT; 8th, per bend sinister erm. and ermines a lion ramp. or, armed and langued gu., for TREVOR; 9th, az. a wolf pass. ar. armed and langued gu., for GELLYN AP BLAIDD RHUDD. *Crest*—A garb or. *Motto*—Look to the past.

Jones (Hartsheath, co. Flint). As originally borne—Ar. a chev. betw. three boars' heads couped gu. *Crest*—A boar's head couped gu. *Motto*—Heb nevol nerth, nid sicr saeth: Without help from above, the arrow flies in vain.

Jones (Fitzroy Square, London, and Clifton, co. Gloucester). Or, a lion ramp. az. *Crest*—A buck at gaze ppr.

Jones (Goodrich, co. Hereford, originally of Bwlch Gwent, co. Carmarthen). Gu. three arrows or, barbed and bearded ar. *Crest*—A hand and dart ppr.

Jones (Nass, near Lydney, and Hay Hill, near Newnham, co. Gloucester; seated at the former place since the reign of Queen Elizabeth). Ar. a lion ramp. gu. *Crest*—A Cornish chough ppr.

Jones (Sugwas, Poulstone, Cleve, and Mountcraig, co. Hereford; claiming descent from BLEDDYN AP CYNFYN, King of Powis, and settled in co. Hereford more than 300 years, descended of the family of JONES, of Lanwarne, co. Hereford, to whom Dethick granted arms, 10 June, 1566. These arms were borne by PHILIP JONES, Esq., High Sheriff, co. Hereford, 1811, by EDMUND JONES, Esq., M.D. and J.P., of Mountcraig, and others). Or, on a mount vert a lion ramp. az. *Arms*, now used, recorded in Herald's College— Gu. on a bend engr. ar. betw. two stags' heads erased erminois three trefoils slipped vert. *Crest*—A gauntlet lying fesseways, holding a spear enfiled with a boar's head erased ppr.

Jones (Maes-y-Gannedd; descended from IEVAN, of Maes-y-Gannedd, son of IEVAN AP IEVAN, Constable of Harlech Castle, *temp.* Henry VI., from OSBORNE FITZGERALD, Lord of Ynysymaengwyn). *Arms*, those of OSBORNE FITZGERALD, viz.: Erm. a saltire gu.

Jones (Fonmon Castle, co. Glamorgan). Quarterly, 1st, sa. a chev. ar. betw. three spear heads ar. the points embrued with blood (borne as descended from BLEDDIN AP MAENARCH, the last Lord of Brecon); 2nd, ar. a wyvern's head erased vert, holding in the mouth a dexter hand gu., for the Lords of Monmouth; 3rd, gu. a chev. erm., for PHILIP GWYS, Lord of Wiston, co. Pembroke; 4th, ar. a stag couchant gu. the horns and hoofs or, and holding in the mouth a branch vert, for MALLT, or MATILDA, dau. and sole heiress of LLEWELLYN YCHAN AP LLEWELLYN, a large proprietor in Gower, co. Glamorgan. This quartered coat is taken from a pedigree compiled at the Heralds' College, 1654, attested by George Owen, York Herald. *Crest*—A cubit arm erect in armour ppr. in the gauntlet a spear of the first headed ar. embrued gu.

Jones (Lancych, or Blaencych, co. Pembroke; descended maternally from CADIFOR VAWR, Lord of Blaencych). Quarterly, 1st and 4th, or, a lion ramp. reguard. sa. armed and langued gu., for JONES; 2nd and 3rd, sa. three scaling ladders ar. and betw. the two uppermost a spear's head of the last, the point embrued ppr. on a chief gu. a tower triple-towered of the second, for LLOYD, of Ffoeshelig, co. Cardigan, and Lancych, co. Pembroke). *Crest*—A lion ramp. reguard. sa. armed and langued gu. *Motto*—Sine numine nihilum.

Jones (Pant-glas, co. Carmarthen). Ar. on a mount vert a representation of a Pembroke ox statant ppr. a chief gu. thereon a falcon ar. belled betw. two stags' heads erased or. *Crest*—A mount vert, thereon a representation of a Pembroke ox's head in profile erased ppr. bezantée. *Motto*—Da-ei-fydd.

Jones (Gellicynan, co. Denbigh; descended from COWRYD AP CADVAN, a chieftain of Duffryn Clwyd, and now represented by JOHN CARSTAIRS JONES, Esq., of Gellicynan and Hartsheath, co. Flint, eldest son of the late WILSON JONES, Esq., of Hartsheath, Cefn Coch, and Gellicynan, M.P. for Denbigh). Gu. on a chev. or, betw. three escocheons ar. each charged with a boar's head couped of the first, an arrow palewise ppr. *Crest*—On a mount vert a boar's head couped gu. in front of an arrow palewise ppr. *Motto*—Heb nevol nerth nid sicr sacth.

Jones (granted to VALENTINE JONES, Esq., Captain 10th Light Dragoons, only son and heir of VALENTINE JONES, Esq., late of Bailbroote House, co. Somerset, and grandson of VALENTINE JONES, of Belfast). Per bend sinister erm. and ermines a lion ramp. within a bordure engr. or. *Crest*—A boar's head erased per bend sinister erm. and ermines.

Jones (Beaver Hill, co. Derby; granted to HENRY CADMAN JONES, Esq.). Ar. a cross indented gu. betw. four spear heads az. each betw. two laurel branches ppr. *Crest*—In front of a spear betw. two laurel branches ppr. a cross pattée gu. *Motto*—Esto fidelis usque ad mortem.

Jones. Gu. a chev. az. betw. three nags' heads erased ar. *Crest*—A nag's head, as in the arms.

Jones. Quarterly, sa. and gu. a cross ar. in the 1st and 4th quarters three lance-rests or, in the 2nd and 3rd as many cockatrices of the last.

Jones (granted to MORGAN JONES, Esq., son of JACOB JONES, Esq., of Kilwendeage, co. Pembroke, a descendant of the families of MORGAN, JONES, and TRENCH, a branch of the TRENCHES of Ireland). Ar. on a chev. betw. two bulls' heads erased in chief and a lion pass. in base az. a tower ensigned by a ducal coronet or, betw. two boars' heads couped of the field. *Crest*—A boar's head erased az. tusked or, in front of a dexter arm embowed in armour ppr. garnished gold, the hand within a gauntlet in the attitude of striking with a scymitar also ppr. the hilt of the second. *Motto*—Pro patriâ et rege.

Jones-Brydges, Bart. See BRYDGES.

Jones (Sir ELLIS JONES, knighted at Reban, co. Kildare, 12 March, 1603). Vert a cross crosslet or.

Jones (Sir ROGER JONES, knighted at Drogheda, 24 March, 1606). Az. on a cross betw. four pheons, points down or, five estoiles gu. *Crest*—An arm couped at the elbow erect, vested or, the hand holding a pheon, point upwards ar.

Jones (Vintnerstown, co. Londonderry; Fun. Ent. 1623, Sir BAPTIST JONES). Ar. a cross ragulée gu. on a chief sa. two pheons, points down or.

Jones (CHARLES JONES, Esq., 1683; Fun. Ent. of his sister, ANNE, wife of Sir THOMAS HARMAN, Knt., of Athy). Sa. a buck trippant ar. horned or.

Jones (confirmed by Roberts, Ulster, 1647, to BRYAN JONES, Esq., Dublin; descended from an ancient Welsh family). Gu. three lioncels ramp. guard. or, on a canton of the second a fret of the first. *Crest*—A talbot's head couped ar. langued and chained gu. *Motto*—Deus fortitudo mea.

Jones (Bealanamore and Headford, co. Leitrim; descended from BRYAN JONES, Esq., of the city of Dublin, Auditor of War, the descendant of an ancient family in Wales, who had a grant of lands 1662, and was great-grandfather of THEOPHILUS JONES, Esq., of Bealanamore, co. Dublin, and afterwards of Headford, co. Leitrim, whose grandson, Right Hon. THEOPHILUS JONES, of Headford, a Privy Councillor in Ireland, was M.P. for the county of Leitrim, and subsequently for the borough of Coleraine). Gu. two lioncels ramp. guard. or, armed and langued az. on a canton of the second a fret of the first. *Crest*—A talbot's head couped ar. langued and chained gu. *Motto*—Deus fortitudo mea.

Jones (confirmed by Carney, Ulster, 1683, to EDWARD JONES, Esq., co. Wexford, son and heir of Ven. RICHARD JONES, of Croiswyan, co. Flint, Archdeacon of Ferns). Az. a chev. ermines betw. three boars' heads erased sa. armed or, langued gu. *Crest*—A boar's head erased and erect ermines. *Motto*—Pawb yn ol ei arfer.

Jones (Fun. Ent. Ulster's Office, 1651). Quarterly, 1st, or, a lion ramp. gu.; 2nd, per pale or and sa. three fleurs-de-lis counterchanged; 3rd, sa. three nags' heads erased ar.; 4th, vert a stag trippant ar. attired or.

Jones (Fun. Ent. Ulster's Office, JEREMIAH JONES, d. in Dublin 1661). Per bend sinister erm. and ermines a lion ramp. or, a border engr. of the last. *Crest*—A wolf statant ar. resting the dexter paw on a human head erased ppr.

Jones (Fun. Ent. AMBROSE JONES, Bishop of Kildare, 1667-78). Gu. three boars' heads erased in pale ar.

Jones (Fun. Ent. Ulster's Office, 1674). Gu. on a cross betw. four mullets or, a pheon with broken staff, point downwards, of the field.

Jones (Fun. Ent. Ulster's Office, 1676, Alderman JONES, of Dublin). Sa. a fess embattled counter-embattled erm. betw. three boars' heads couped ar.

Jones (Fun. Ent. Ulster's Office, 1677, the wife of Rev. Doctor JONES). Per fess indented or and az. a lion ramp. counterchanged.

Jones (Fun. Ent. Ulster's Office, 1678, Captain JONES). Gu. a cross crossed on three greices or.

549

Jones (Benada Castle, co. Sligo; Reg. Ulster's Office). Gu. on a chev. betw. four mullets pierced or, a broken spear, pheon downwards. *Crest*—A wing gu. semée of estoiles or.

Jones (Reg. Ulster's Office, to Alderman JONES, of Dublin). Par saltire ar. and az. two garbs in pale gu. and as many pheons, points down, in fess or.

Jones (confirmed to Sir LEWIS TOBIAS JONES, K.C.B., Admiral, retired list, and to the other descendants of his grandfather, LEWIS JONES, Esq., of the family of JONES, of Ardnaglass, co. Sligo). Per bend sinister erm. and ermines a lion ramp. or, armed and langued gu. a bordure engr. of the third. *Crest*—A lion ccuchant or, armed and langued gu. charged on the shoulder with a trefoil slipped vert. *Motto*—Periculum ex alus facito.

Jones (Walsall, co. Stafford; granted to WILLIAM JONES, Esq., of that place). Per chev. az. and vert, in chief three suns in splendour, and in base a lion ramp. reguard. or. *Crest*—Issuant from a sun rising in splendour ppr. a lion's head vert semée of bezants. *Motto*—Diligentia.

Jones (New South Wales; granted to HENRY JONES, Esq.). Az. a goat statant ar. horned, crined, and unguled or, in chief three stars of eight points of the last. *Crest*—A stag or, collared, with line reflexed over the back sa. resting the dexter foot on a shield az. charged with a star, as in the arms. *Motto*—Perseverantia ad finem optatum.

Jones (MARSHAM-JONES, Hayle Cottage, co. Kent; exemplified to HENRY SHOVELL MARSHAM, Esq., upon his assuming, by royal licence, the additional surname of JONES). Quarterly, 1st and 4th, gu. two lioncels ramp. guard. or, armed and langued az. on a canton of the second a fret of the first, in chief a cross crosslet for distinction, for JONES; 2nd and 3rd, ar. a lion pass. gu. betw. two bendlets az., for MARSHAM. *Crests*—1st, JONES: A talbot's head couped ar. langued and chained gu. charged on the neck, for distinction, with a cross crosslet also gu.; 2nd, MARSHAM: A lion's head erased gu. langued az.

Jonetson (co. Worcester). Sa. a bend ar. betw. two fleurs-de-lis or.

Jope (Merryfield, co. Cornwall; JOHN JOPE, son and heir of ROGER JOPE. Visit. Cornwall, 1620). Ar. two pheons in chief an annulet in base sa. *Crest*—An antelope sejant erm. supporting with the dexter foot a shield per pale or and ar.

Jopling, or Joppling. Ar. a decrescent gu. betw. three mullets az. *Crest*—A dexter hand ppr. holding up an escallop or.

Jopp (Cotton, co. Aberdeen, 1796). Gu. a garb or, on a chief ar. a ship in full sail in the sea ppr. *Crest*—On a garb lying fessways a cock crowing all ppr. *Motto*—Sic donec.

Jorcey, or Jorge. Ar. a fesse betw. three lions ramp. sa. *Crest*—A hand ppr. holding a swan's head and neck erased ar. beaked gu.

Jorcey. Per pale gu. and az. three eagles displ. ar.

Jorcey, or Jorcie. Ar. on a bend az. three water bougets or.

Jorcy. Per pale az. and gu. an eagle displ. ar. armed or.

Jordaine (Windsor Forest, co. Berks, *temp.* Edward II.). Sa. three mullets of six points pierced ar. a border erm.

Jordan (co. Pembroke; of Anglo-Norman origin; the first settler in Wales having been JORDAN DE CANTINGTON, one of the companions of Martin de Tours in his conquest of Kemmes, *temp.* William I. At the close of the 14th or beginning of the 15th century, LEONARD JORDAN m. the heiress of Dompledale; the family, which was once widely dispersed over co. Pembroke, is now extinct in the male line; FRANCES, fourth dau. and co-heir of the late BARRET BOWEN JORDAN, Esq., of Neeston, co. Pembroke, by MARTHA, his wife, youngest dau. of JOHN ADAMS, Esq., of Whitland, co. Carmarthen, m., in 1807, JOHN HILL HARRIES, Esq., of Priskilly). Ar. a chev. betw. three greyhounds courant gu.

Jordan (co. Dorset). Az. semée of crosses crosslet a lion ramp. or.

Jordan (GILES JORDAN, of Loughborough, co. Leicester, arms from his tomb; *d.* 1415). Quarterly, 1st and 4th, ar. three mullets gu., JORDAN; 2nd and 3rd, sa. a chev. or, betw. three garbs ar.

Jordan (co. Somerset, and Chittern Whistley, co. Wilts, 1604). Az. a lion ramp. betw. eight crosses crosslet fitchée or, a chief of the second (another, the lion charged with a crescent gu.). *Crest*—A mount or, over it a scroll with this motto, Percussa resurgo. *Another Crest*—A football ppr.

Jordan (Catwick and Charlwood, co. Surrey). Three coats and crests. First, *temp.* Edward I., viz., az. semée of crosses crosslet, a lion ramp. or. *Crest*—A lion sejant or, sustaining a cross crosslet fitchée: this crest was granted 1629. Second, sa. an eagle betw. two bendlets ar. on a chief or, three almond leaves vert. *Crest*—An almond tree ppr. fructed or. Third, sa. an eagle displ. in bend betw. two cotises ar. a chief or. *Crest*—A demi lion or, issuant, resting on the sinister foot, and holding in the dexter an eagle's head erased sa. Note.—This alteration in the arms and crest by grant 2 June, 1631.

Jordan (Mountfield, co. Sussex). Sa. an eagle displ. in bend betw. two cotises ar. a sinister canton or. *Crest*—A lion sejant or, holding in his dexter foot an eagle's head erased sa.

Jordan (Pigeonsford, co. Cardigan). Gu. a lion ramp. betw. eight cross crosslets fitchée or, a chief of the second.

Jordan (co. Wilts). Per pale az. and or, a chev. betw. three lozenges all counterchanged, on a chief gu. three martlets of the second.

Jordan (co. Lancaster). Az. a cinquefoil erm. betw. three serpents nowed or, a border engr. of the second. *Crest*—A crescent or, issuing therefrom a plume of five feathers az. entwined by a serpent gold. *Motto*—Arte non vi.

Jordan (co. Worcester). Gu. a fess betw. three lions' heads erased ar.

Jordan, or Jerdon (co. Worcester). Gu. a fret or, charged with three mullets sa.

Jordan (Aldridge, co. Stafford; monument in the church). Sa. an eagle displ. betw. two cotises ar.

Jordan. Ar. a cross patonce betw. four martlets gu. (another, az. nine lozenges, three, three, and three; another, ar. three mullets gu.). *Crest*—A martlet with wings displ. gu.

Jordan (Fun. Ent. Ulster's Office, 1634, CHRISTOPHER JORDAN, of Dublin). Ar. on a fess sa. a mullet of the field, in chief issuant from the fess two demi lions ramp. gu.

Jordan (Rosleven Castle, co. Mayo). Gu. a lion ramp. betw. three cross crosslets or. *Motto*—Percussus resurgo.

Jordayne (London). Ar. on a fesse betw. three towers triple-towered gu. a lion pass. guard. or. *Crest*—On a chapeau gu. turned up erm. a hawk or, inside of the wings of the second.

Jordayne (co. Somerset). Sa. an eagle displ. in bend betw. two cotises ar. on a chief or, three oak leaves vert (another, three escallops).

Jorden (Welynton, co. Salop). Ar. a chev. betw. three greyhounds courant gu. *Crest*—A demi talbot gu.

Jorden (EDWARD JORDEN, Esq., of Priors Lee, co. Salop, Sheriff of the co., 1720). Sa. an eagle displ. in bend ar. betw. two cotises or, in the sinister chief quarter a canton of the third.

Jordon. Az. a lion ramp. betw. three crosses crosslet or. *Crest*—Out of a mural coronet a hand ppr. vested az. brandishing a sword waved of the first.

Jorney. Ar. three gillyflowers slipped ppr.

Jorwerth-Drwrdwn (Wales). Sa. a lion ramp. or, a bordure engr. of the last.

Joseph (JOSEPH JOSEPH, F.S.A. and J.P., co. Brecon). Per chev. az. and vert, in chief three garbs, and in base two chevronels or. *Crest*—A garb or. *Motto*—Cas ni charo y wlad a'i mago.

Joskin, or Joskyn. Gu. three sheaves of arrows points upward ar. *Crest*—An antelope's head ar. collared gu. armed sa.

Joslin, or Josceline (Mount Tregamenian, co. Cornwall). Az. three escallops or.

Josselyn. Gu. three escarbuncles ar.

Josselyne (co. Essex). Chequy gu. and az. on a fesse of the first an annulet or. *Crest*—A bear's head and neck sa. muzzled or.

Jossey (Westpans, co. Haddington). Ar. a fesse betw. two stars in chief az. and a hunting-horn in base sa. garnished gu. *Crest*—An eye ppr. *Motto*—Je voy.

Jossey (Edinburgh, 1672). Ar. a fesse wavy betw. two stars, &c., as the last. *Crest*—As the last. *Motto*—Manuque.

Josue. Per bend sinister or and gu. a bat displ. sa.

Joubere (Jersey). Gu. an escarbuncle or.

Joulby (Treyes, co. Cornwall). Ar. a mullet betw. three broad arrows sa. in chief another mullet of the same.

Joule. Ar. a fesse betw. three martlets sa. *Crest*—Out of a ducal coronet or, a stag's head affrontée ppr.

Jourdan. Gu. three mural coronets ar. masoned sa. *Crest*—Two anchors in saltire ppr.

Journeaulx (Jersey). Az. a lobster in fesse or.

Jousey, or Jossey (Scotland). Ar. a chev. betw. two roses in chief and a hunting-horn in base sa.

Jove. Ar. on a chev. per pale vert and gu. three escallops of the first (another, ar. three lions ramp. sa.).

Joweles (cos. Kent and Surrey). Ar. a tower triple-towered gu. betw. three pheons sa. *Crest*—A tower gu. surmounted with three broad arrows falling at the top, four and four, fretty in bend dexter and sinister ar.

550

Jowers (Ipswich, co. Suffolk). Az. the sun or, betw. three bezants.

Jowett, or Jowitt. Az. a three-masted galley, sails furled or, flags gu. *Crest*—A demi pegasus reguard. wings endorsed ar. holding a flag gu.

Jowett (Ashton-under-Lyne, Bredbury, co. Chester, and Lower Hall, Mellor, co. Derby). Same *Arms* and *Crest*. *Motto*—Animo et prudentiâ.

Jowett. Or, a chev. gu. betw. three lions' heads erased sa.

Jowitt (Eltofts Thorner, co. York). Az. on a chev. ar. betw. two chaplets of oak in chief, and a lion sejant guard. in base or, three buglehorns stringed sa. *Crest*—A lion sejant guard. gu. the dexter forepaw supporting an escutcheon of the arms.

Jowles (Alkham, co. Surrey; granted 1620). Same *Arms* and *Crest* as JOWELES.

Jowsie (Scotland). Ar. a chev. az. betw. two roses in chief gu. and a hunting-horn in base sa. stringed of the third.

Joy (London). Or, a chev. vert guttée d'eau betw. three vine leaves of the second. *Crest*—A falcon standing on a cinquefoil betw. two vine branches all ppr.

Joy (co. Worcester). Gu. on a bend engr. az. three roses of the field.

Joy. Vert a lion ramp. ar. a fesse gu. *Crest*—A demi lion ramp. *Motto*—Pro patriâ ejusque libertate.

Joy (Hartham Park. co. Wilts). Az. a chev. ar. in chief three fleurs-de-lis or, and in base a lion ramp. ppr. quartering, 1st, gu. three battle-axes in fesse or, HALL; 2nd, or, on a chev. betw. three vine leaves vert, five guttes d'eau, JOYE, of Benefield, co. Northampton, granted 1738; 3rd, ar. on a chev. engr. betw. three talbots' heads erased sa. an estoile or. *Crest*—Out of a ducal coronet or, a plume of five feathers ar. *Motto*—Vive la joye.

Joyce (Burton Joyce, co. Nottingham; descended from ROBERT DE JORTZ, Lord of Burton, co. Nottingham, temp. Henry II.; the last heir, WILLIAM DE JOYCE, of Burton Joyce, d. s. p. temp. Henry VI.). Paly of six or and gu. on a bend sa. three water bougets ar.

Joyce, Joice, or Joys. Ar. three torteaux in bend betw. two bendlets gu. *Crest*—A demi chevalier in armour brandishing a scymitar all ppr.

Joyce. Gu. a chev. betw. three pine leaves slipped ar.

Joyce (Galway; settled in that co. for many years; originally from Wales. Reg. Ulster's Office). Ar. an eagle displ. gu. charged on the breast with a bar gemel erm. *Crest*—A demi wolf ducally gorged ppr.

Joye (Benefield, co. Northampton; granted 1738). Or, on a chev. betw. three vine leaves vert, five guttes d'eau. *Crest*—A trunk of a vine with two branches, thereon a dove standing all ppr.

Joye (West Kington, co. Wilts). Ar. a lion ramp. gu. *Crest*—A lion ramp. ar. supporting a ragged staff or.

Joye, or Joyer. Per pale az. and gu. an eagle displ. ar. membered or.

Joyliff (Eastover, co. Dorset; granted 28 March, 1664). Ar. a fesse embattled betw. three pheons sa.

Joyner (London, and co. Sussex; granted 1591). Az. on a bend ar. an eagle displ. sa. *Crest*—A dexter arm embowed in armour, holding in the gauntlet a battle axe, handle or, headed ar.

Joyner (Norroy King of Arms, temp. Henry VIII.). Ar. on a cross az. four fleurs-de-lis of the first, within a border of the second.

Joyner. Az. a cross flory betw. four fleurs-de-lis or (another, ar. on a cross az. five fleurs-de-lis of the first, a border engr. of the second; another, or, on a cross engr. within a bordure az. five fleurs-de-lis ar.; another, ar. a pale az.; another, vert a pile ar. issuing out of the dexter quarter, on a chief or, a rose gu. seeded of the third, barbed of the first; another, per chev. vert and erm. in chief a pelican or, vulning her breast ppr.).

Joyner (confirmed by Molyneux, Ulster, 1607, to LAWRENCE JOYNER, Deputy Vice-Treasurer of His Majesty's Revenue in Ireland). Ar. on a cross engr. az. five fleurs-de-lis or, in the 1st quarter an escallop charged with a mullet for diff. *Crest*—A demi lion az. langued gu. holding betw. the paws a fleur-de-lis or, charged with a mullet also gu.

Joynes, or Geynes. Gu. a chief vair.

Joynson (Liscard, co. Chester). Az. an eagle's head erased or, betw. four roses ar. *Crest*—On a mount vert an eagle displ. with two heads az. semée of roses ar. *Motto*—Ad honorem industria ducit.

Joynt (granted to CHRISTOPHER JOYNT, M.D., son of HENRY JOYNT, Esq., of Ballina, co. Mayo, by ELEANOR, his wife, dau. of WILLIAM JOHNSON, of Molaugh, co. Mayo, and grandson of HENRY JOYNT, Esq., of Kinnaird House, co. Mayo, and to their descendants). Az. on a saltire or, betw. in chief a spur of the second winged ar. and three fleurs-de-lis, two in the flanks, and one in base of the second, a trefoil slipped vert. *Crest*—On a mount vert a boar passant ppr. resting the foreleg on an escutcheon az. charged with a fleur-de-lis or. *Motto*—I hope.

Joynt (granted to WILLIAM LANE JOYNT, Esq., of Grange Abbey, Baldoyle, co. Dublin, Queen's Clerk for co. Dublin, an Alderman and afterwards Lord Mayor of Dublin, only son of WILLIAM JOYNT, of Limerick, merchant). Az. an eagle's head erased betw. three saltires couped ar. *Crest*—Issuant out of a chaplet of oak leaves vert, two eagles' heads conjoined, the dexter gu. the sinister az. *Motto*—Nec degenero.

Joyre. Or, a lion ramp. az. depressed with a bend gu.

Juatt. Ar. on a cross gu. five fleurs-de-lis of the first. *Crest*—An armed arm ppr. holding a fleur-de-lis or.

Juba. Ar. three pheons az. on a chief sa. as many martlets or. *Crest*—An antelope sejant ar. tufted, maned, and armed or, resting the dexter foot on an escutcheon per pale of the second and first.

Jubbs. Ar. on a chev. engr. betw. three bears pass. sa. a mullet of the field.

Jubell, or Inbell. Sa. a bend ar. betw. three trefoils of the second.

Juchen, or Van Juchen. Vert in water in base ppr. a swan, wings endorsed, naiant ar. *Crest*—Two wings expanded ppr.

Juckes (quartered by CLIFTON). Ar. a chev. gu. betw. three bluebottles (the flower) slipped ppr. *Crest*—An arm embowed in armour ppr. holding a tilting-spear erect ar. headed and tasselled or, thereto affixed the Holy Standard of the Trinity, "per fesse ar. and sa. the device of the Trinity or," fringed gold, the ends of the streamer forked, and floating behind the spear to the dexter.

Judd (London; Sir ANDREW JUDD, Knt.; his dau. ALICE, *m.* THOMAS SMYTH, Collector of the Queen's Tonnage and Poundage, and Farmer of the Customs, *temp.* Queen Elizabeth. Visit. London, 1568). Gu. a fess ragulée betw. three boars' heads couped ar., quartering, Az. three lions ramp ar. a border of the last.

Judd (Tunbridge, co. Kent; Lord Mayor of London, 1550). Gu. a fesse ragulée betw. three boars' heads couped ar. *Crest* —On a ducal coronet or, a cockatrice, wings displ. ppr.

Judd (JOHN PHILLIPS JUDD, Esq., J.P. and D.L., Rickling, co. Essex). Az. a chev. paly of eight erm. and vert betw. three garbs or, each charged with a fleur-de-lis of the third. *Crest*—A griffin's head erased per chev. or and vert, charged with three fleurs-de-lis counterchanged, in the beak an ear of wheat gold. *Motto*—Et mea messis erit.

Jude (co. Bedford). Or, a chev. vert.

Jude (co. Hants). Gu. a fesse engr. sa. betw. three boars' heads couped ar. holding in their mouths apples ppr. eared and tusked of the field.

Jude (London, 1592). Ar. on a chev. betw. three fleurs-de-lis gu. as many mullets of the first. *Crest*—A ferret pass. ppr. collared and lined ar.

Judge. Or, a chev. vert.

Judge. See BREHON.

Judge (Mosstown, co. Meath; allowed by Hawkins, Ulster, 1774, as the arms of POYNTZ JUDGE, great-grandson of ARTHUR JUDGE, Esq., of Mosstown). Sa. a chev. erm. betw. three escallops ar. *Crest*—An escallop or. *Motto*—Totum est providentia.

Judith. Az. a chieftain's head couped ar. betw. two swords transposed barways or.

Judkin (Heyford, co. Northampton). Ar. two bars gu. in chief three mullets of the second.

Judkin-FitzGerald, Bart. See FITZGERALD.

Juds. Gu. a bend betw. six lozenges or.

Judson, or Judgson (Scotland). Per saltire az. and erm. four lozenges counterchanged. *Crest*—Out of a ducal coronet or, two dexter arms in saltire, vested gu. holding two scymitars in pale ppr.

Judson. Or, a chev. purp. betw. three dragons' heads erased vert.

Jue. Sa. a fesse betw. three goats pass. ar. armed or. (another, per chev. sa. and ar. three elephants' heads erased counterchanged, crowned or).

Juers. Ar. on a bend az. three fleurs-de-lis of the field.

Jues, or Jewes. Ar. a chev. sa. betw. three blackamoors' heads couped ppr.

Jues. Ar. on a bend cotised az. three mullets or.

Juet. Ar. on a cross gu. five fleurs-de-lis of the field.

Juge (co. Leicester). Or, on a chev. vert three leopards' faces of the first. *Crest*—Two battle axes in saltire, handles gu. headed ppr. enfiled with a ducal coronet or.

Jugg (London). Per pale gu. and vert an escarbuncle of eight rays flory or, an orle of cinquefoils ar.

Jugg. Ar. three roses gu. seeded or. *Crest*—An oak leaf vert.

Juggell. Sa. a bend ar. betw. six martlets or.

Jugler (Reigate, co. Surrey). Or, two bars az. on a canton sa. five billets ar. *Crest*—Two swords in saltire ppr. surmounted by a cross crosslet sa.

Juis, or Jues. Ar. a chev. sa.

Jule. See JEWELL.

Julius (Richmond, co. Surrey). Ar. a fesse az. betw. three estoiles gu. *Crest*—An estoile ar.

Julian, or Julion (York's Union of Honor, 1640). Ar. a St. Julian's cross sa. *Crest*—On a chapeau gu. turned up erm. a salamander in flames ppr.

Julien. Az. a lion ramp. ar. wielding a sword ppr. *Crest*—A lion's paw erased holding the hilt of a broken sword ppr.

Jump (granted to HENRY JUMP, Esq., of Woodlands, Little Woolton, co. Lancaster). Az. a cross parted and fretty or, in the 1st and 4th quarters a stag's head, and in the 2nd and 3rd a rose ar. *Crest*—A demi stag reguard. ppr. charged on the shoulder with three roses chevronwise ar. supporting a passion cross or. *Motto*—Fortiter et fideliter.

Jumper. Ar. two bars gemels sa. betw. three mullets gu. *Crest*—A demi lion ppr. supporting a long cross gu.

Jumper (granted by Bysshe, 24 Feb. 1651, to WILLIAM JUMPER, of London). Ar. two bars gemels sa. betw. three mullets of six points gu. *Crest*—A wing ar. charged with two bars gemels sa. Le Neve doubts the validity of this grant, as it was made during Oliver Cromwell's usurpation, and all Bysshe's grants during that period (and also Ryley's) were declared void.

Junor (London). Az. a chev. or, betw. three bezants, on a chief of the second as many cinquefoils gu.

Juon (Harlston). Ar. a fesse erm. cotised sa.

Juon (North Wales). Ar. three fleurs-de-lis sa.

Jurden. Per pale or and az. a chev. betw. three lozenges counterchanged, on a chief gu. as many martlets ar.

Jurdon (Wolverton). Az. semée of crosses crosslet or, a lion ramp. ar. on the breast a fleur-de-lis sa.

Jurney. Az. three gillyflowers ar.

Jupp. Ar. a chev. betw. three eagles' heads erased az. *Crest*—A griffin pass. ppr. holding a buckle or.

Jury. Az. three portcullises or. *Crest*—A cubit arm in armour, holding a caltrap all ppr.

Just (Monkwearmouth, co. Durham). Sa. a chev. betw. three pigeons' heads erased ar. *Crest*—A swan's head erased ar. betw. two ostrich feathers erect of the first.

Justice (East Crichton, co. Edinburgh). Az. a sword in pale ppr. supporting a pair of balances or, within a bordure of the last. *Crest*—A sword ppr. *Motto*—Non sine causa.

Justice (Coventry; granted by Camden, Clarenceux), Sa. a fess erm. betw. three crescents or. *Crest*—On a garb or, a cock gu.

Justice (Knighton, co. Stafford). Vert (another, az.) a bend erm. cotised or, betw. two falcons rising of the third.

Justice. Gu. a chev. betw. three leopards' faces or. *Crest* —A cat sejant ramp. ppr.

Justice. Gu. on a cross couped ar. five mullets sa.

Justine, or Justyne. Gu. three chev. ar. *Crest*—A stag's head erased affrontée or.

Justyne. Barry of six az. and ar. in chief three torteaux.

Juxon (WILLIAM JUXON, Bishop of London, 1633-60, Archbishop of Canterbury, 1660-63; d.1663, leaving his nephew, Sir WILLIAM JUXON, Bart., his heir. The representation of the family eventually vested in that of HESKETH). Or, a cross gu. betw. four blackamoors' heads couped at the shoulders ppr. wreathed about the temples of the field.

Juxon (Albourne, co. Sussex, bart., extinct 1740). Same Arms. *Crest*—An Ionic pillar on a base ar.

Juxton (London). Ar. on a fesse dancettée betw. five herons sa. beaked and legged gu. eight bezants, four and four.

Juyce (co. Worcester). Gu. three laurel leaves slipped ar. in the fess point a crescent or.

Juys. Ar. three torteaux betw. two cotises gu.

K

KADRAD. Ar. two foxes saliant counter-saliant in saltire, the sinister surmounting the dexter gu. *Crest*—Two anchors in saltire az.

Kadivor Vawr. See CADIVOR.

Kedivor ap Dynawall. See CADIVOR.

Kadrodhard, or Kadrohard (Wales). Ar. two foxes counter-saliant gu. *Crest*—A griffin's head erased sa.

Kadwale, or Kadwalyder (Wales). Az. a cross formée fitchée or.

Kadwall. Az. a cross formée fitchée betw. eight estoiles or. *Crest*—A cock's head ar. combed, wattled, and beaked gu. betw. two wings expanded sa. holding in the beak a cross formée fitchée or.

Kadwall, or Kadwell (Wales). Sa. (another, az.) a cross formée fitchée or.

Kadye. See CADYE.

Kadyow (Scotland). Ar. a chev. sa. betw. two roses in chief and a holly leaf in base gu.

Kaer. Gu. a cross gringolée erm. heads or. *Crest*—Issuing out of a crescent two eagles' heads endorsed.

Kagg. Az. a pile issuing from the base in bend sinister or. *Crest*—A falcon reguard. resting the dexter claw upon a laurel crown all ppr.

Kahl. Ar. three demi lions ramp. couped gu. *Crest*—A camel's head ar.

Kaines (co. Leicester). Barry of six or, az. and gu.

Kaines. Or, on a fesse gu. three garbs of the field. *Crest*—A wolf courant gu.

Kairnie (Scotland). Or, three birds az. on a chief gu. an acorn betw. two mullets of the field.

Kaloway. Ar. on a chev. betw. three leopards' faces sa. as many annulets of the field.

Kane (confirmed to WILLIAM FRANCIS DE VISMES KANE, Esq., of Drumreaske, co. Monaghan). Gu. three fishes haurient ar. in the centre chief point an estoile or. *Crest*—A naked arm embowed ppr. charged with an estoile gu. and holding in the hand a sword also ppr.

Kane. Gu. three trouts in fesse ppr. betw. as many estoiles or. *Crest*—An arm embowed in armour, holding a sword ppr.

Karadoc (Wales). Az. a lion ramp. per fesse or and ar. a bordure of the last.

Karben. Az. a fleur-de-lis ar. on a chief or, a demi lion ramp. gu. *Crest*—Out of a ducal coronet or, an arm from the elbow vested gu. cuffed gold, holding up the sun ppr.

Karblen. Az. a fleur-de-lis ar. on a chief of the last a lion pass. gu.

Karbyll. Az. on a chief ar. a demi lion ramp. gu. *Crest*—A stag lodged or.

Kardoyle, or Kardaile. Gu. six annulets ar. three, two, and one. *Crest*—An antelope trippant erm. armed gu.

Kardoyle. Gu. six annulets ar. two, two, and two (another, tinctures reversed).

Karedig (Wales). Sa. a lion ramp. ar. incensed gu.

Karkenton, or Karkington. Gu. three bars ar. *Crest*—Out of an antique crown or, a demi lion ramp. gu.

Karkettle (Scotland). Ar. a bend gu.

Karnabye (co. Northumberland). Ar. two bars az. in chief three hurts. *Crest*—A triton holding in the dexter hand a trident.

Karnabye. Same *Arms*, adding, on a canton of the second a lion ramp. of the first.

Karr (Zair, Scotland). See KER.

Karricke, or Carricke (co. Gloucester). Sa. three cinquefoils ar. *Crest*—A dexter arm embowed ppr. vested gu. cuffed or, holding a covered cup gold.

Karvell (co. Norfolk). Gu. a chev. betw. three leopards' faces ar.

Karvell, or Karwell (Wiggen Hall, co. Norfolk). Ar. a fesse betw. three fleurs-de-lis gu.

Karvell, or Kervell (Watlington, co. Norfolk). Sa. three leopards' faces jessant-de-lis ar. *Crest*—On a ducal coronet or, a wivern gu.

Kassye, or Kayre (co. Northumberland). Gu. on a chev. ar. three estoiles sa. *Crest*—A dexter hand pointing with two fingers gu.

Kater (originally from Lippy in Germany). Az. on a bend engr. or, betw. two fleurs-de-lis ar. an eagle with two heads displ. sa. *Crest*—A cat-a-mountain ppr. betw. two elephants' trunks or.

Katheram. Or, on a bend sa. three leopards' faces ar. *Crest*—An arm in armour resting on the elbow and holding a club all ppr.

Katherler, Kateler, or Kateller. Az. three catharine wheels or. *Crest*—On a chapeau ppr. a lion's head erased az. ducally crowned gu.

Katherley, or Katerley. Or, three piles sa. *Crest*—A hind's head ppr.

Katyng, Kating, Katting, and Katlyng. Ar. a saltire betw. four pineapples (in base) gu. *Crest*—A demi angel holding in the dexter hand a griffin's head erased ppr.

Katz (Germany). Quarterly, 1st, or, a lion ramp. az.; 2nd, az ; 3rd purp. on a mount vert a tree ppr.; 4th, ar. on a mount in base vert a fox springing ppr.

552

Kavanagh (Ireland; descended from DONEL CAOMHANAGH, or "The Handsome," son of DERMOT McMURROGH, last King of Leinster, *d.* 1171; ART OGE KAVANAGH, seventh in descent from DONEL CAOMHANAGH, is called in "The Annals of the Four Masters" King of Leinster. He *d.* 1416, having divided Leinster between his two sons, DONEL MORE KAVANAGH, styled King of Leinster, and GERALD KAVANAGH, Lord of Ferns, the ancestor of DONEL SPANIAGH KAVANAGH, of Clonmullen, *d.* 1631, and the house of Borris; from DONEL MORE KAVANAGH, King of Leinster, descended KAVANAGH, of Garryhill, co. Carlow, the chief of whom, DONEL OGE KAVANAGH, of Garryhill, was executed for rebellion, leaving MAURICE and MOROUGH KAVANAGH both living in 1630. N.B.—The line of DONEL MORE KAVANAGH retained possession of the ancient crown of Leinster, and though deprived of their lands, and often in want, and tempted with large sums of money by the junior and more wealthy branches, always refused to part with this remnant of royalty, which, unfortunately, was subsequently lost during the French Revolution in the last century). Ar. a lion pass. gu. in base two crescents of the last. *Arms* of McMURROGH, Kings of Leinster—Sa. three garbs or.

Kavanagh (DONEL SPANIAGH KAVANAGH, Chief of the Clonmullen line of this Sept, sixth in descent from GERALD KAVANAGH, Lord of Ferns, 1431 ; the second son of ART OGE KAVANAGH *d.* 1416; impalement Fun. Ent. 1619, ARTHUR EUSTACE, Esq., of Ballyminry, co. Carlow, whose wife was OWNY, dau. of DONEL SPANIAGH KAVANAGH). Ar. a lion pass. gu. in base two crescents of the last.

Kavanagh (Nantes, in the Kingdom of France; allowed by Hawkins, Ulster, 1768, to NICHOLAS KAVANAGH, eldest son of IGNATIUS KAVANAGH, Captain in the Irish Brigade in France, who was great-grandson of DONEL SPANIAGH KAVANAGH, of Clonmullen). Same *Arms*. *Crest*—Issuant from the horns of a crescent gu. a garb of the last. *Motto*—Virtus sola nobilitat.

Kavanagh (Borris, co. Carlow; descended from ART BUOY KAVANAGH, of St. Molin's, who was eldest son of DERMOT KAVANAGH, the eldest son and successor of DERMOT KAVANAGH LAMHDEARG, second son of GERALD KAVANAGH, Lord of Ferns, 1431, now represented by ARTHUR McMURROGH KAVANAGH, Esq., of Borris, M.P., co. Carlow). Ar. a lion pass. gu. in base two crescents of the last. *Crest*—Issuant from the horns of a crescent gu. a garb or. *Motto*—Siothchain agus fairsinge (Peace and plenty).

Kavanagh (*Baron Ballyanne; CAHIR MAC ART KAVANAGH*, eldest son of ART BUOY KAVANAGH, of St. Molin's, and the direct ancestor of KAVANAGH, of Borris, was so created *for life*, 1554). Same *Arms*, &c., as the last.

Kavanagh (Ballyleigh and Templeudigan, co. Wexford, and Bohemia; allowed by Hawkins, Ulster, 1774, to JOHN BAPTIST KAVANAGH, Baron of Gniditz in Bohemia, son of BRYAN NA STROIC KAVANAGH, of Drummond, co. Carlow; descended from MAURICE KAVANAGH, brother of ART BUOY KAVANAGH, of St. Molin's, the ancestor of the house of Borris). Same *Arms* as KAVANAGH, of Borris. *Crest*—Issuant from the horns of a crescent gu. a garb or. *Motto*—Mea gloria fides.

Kavanagh (Coolgreany, co. Wexford; registered by Hawkins, Ulster, 1717, to THOMAS KAVANAGH, Esq., of that place). Ar. in dexter chief a lion pass. guard. gu., in sinister chief a lizard pass. vert, and in base a dexter hand apaumée couped at the wrist of the second. *Crest*—A dexter arm embowed, vested purp. holding in the hand ppr. a sword ar. pommel and hilt or.

Kavanagh (Austria and Bath; allowed by Betham, Ulster, 1825, to JOHN KAVANAGH, in the service of the Emperor of Austria, son of NATHANIEL KAVANAGH, of Bath, who was grandson of DENIS KAVANAGH, of Dublin, gent., son of JOHN KAVANAGH, of the stock of Borris). Same *Arms, Crest*, and *Motto*, as KAVANAGH, of Borris.

Kavanagh (Baron of Elinton; Fun. Ent. of JOHN KAVANAGH, *d.* 8 Oct. 1682). Ar. six annulets, three, two, and one, sa. on a chief gu. three mullets of the field.

Kavanagh (Fun. Ent. of BRIAN KAVANAGH, son of MORGAN MAC BRIAN KAVANAGH, *d.* 1 Dec. 1662, buried next day in St. James's Church, Dublin). Ar. six pellets, three, two, and one, on a chief az. three mullets pierced of the field.

Kavanagh. See CAVANAGH.

Kavanagh. Vert a cross crosslet or, within an orle of cross crosslets of the last.

Kawn (co. Chester). Az. three bars ar.

Kawston, or Kawson. Ar. (another, or) a bend betw. six crosses crosslet sa. *Crest*—Out of a mural coronet a hand ppr. vested paly of six ar. and sa. holding a mullet of the first.

Kay (Bass Lane House, co. Lancaster; granted to JOHN

ROBINSON **KAY**, Esq.). Az. two bendlets ar. betw. as many stags trippant or. *Crest*—A demi stag supporting a cornucopea ppr. and gorged with a collar gemel az. *Motto*—In via recta celeriter.

Kay (East Sheen, co. Surrey, bart.). Ar. on a bend engr. az. betw. two griffins' heads erased gu. an annulet betw. two crescents or. *Crest*—A griffin's head erm. collared az. charged with three crescents or, holding in the beak a key gold. *Motto*—Fidem parit integritas.

Kay (Edith-Weston, co. Rutland, and Woodsome, co. York). Ar. two bendlets sa. *Crest* (granted by Flower, Norroy, 22 Oct. 1564)—A goldfinch ppr.

Kay (Glatton, co. Huntingdon). Same *Arms* and *Crest*, a mullet for diff.

Kay (Milshaw, Dalton, and The Heath, co. York). Same *Arms*, a mullet for diff. *Crest*—A griffin's head erased ar. beaked gu. charged with a martlet sa. holding in the beak a key or.

Kay (Newhall, co. York). Same *Arms*, with same diff.

Kay. Ar. on a fesse betw. a stag's head erased in chief and a sheaf of arrows in base az. three fleurs-de-lis or. *Crest*—A martlet volant. *Motto*—In Deo solo spes mea.

Kay (granted to JAMES PHILLIPS KAY, of Battersea, co. Surrey, LL.D.). Ar. three erm. spots in bend betw. two bendlets sa. the whole betw. two crescents az. *Crest*—On a crescent or, a goldfinch ppr.

Kay (granted to JAMES OPENSHAW KAY, Esq., of the Elms, Bedhampton, co. Southampton). Az. on a pile betw. two lions ramp. or, a greyhound's head erased sa. *Crest*—A demi griffin, wings elevated sa. holding in the claws three arrows, one in pale and two in saltire ppr. surmounted in the centre by an escutcheon az. charged with an annulet or.

Kay (Sunderland, co. Durham, and North Shields, co. Northumberland). Ar. a bend sinister sa. betw. an annulet in chief gu. and a griffin's head erased in base of the second, in the beak a key az. *Crest*—A griffin's head, as in the arms.

Kay (Fun. Ent. Ulster's Office, 1640, PETER KAY, a Pursuivant of the Realm of Ireland, second son of ARTHUR KAY, Esq., of Escomb, co. Kent, Purveyor to James I.: descended from KAY, of Woodsett, co. York). Ar. two bendlets sa. a martlet charged with a crescent for diff.

Kay (Cornhill, co. Lanark, 1874). Or, a fess gu. betw. two torteaux in chief, and in base a griffin's head erased vert. *Crest*—A griffin's head erased vert, in the beak a key or. *Motto*—In Deo solo spes mea.

Kay-Shuttleworth, Bart. See SHUTTLEWORTH.

Kayble. Ar. a mound gu., on a canton sa. a lion pass. or.

Kayble. Same *Arms*, the lion ramp. *Crest*—An arm from the elbow ppr. vested erm. cuffed, indented gu. holding an escarbuncle of the last.

Kaye (Woodesham or Woodsome, co. York, bart., extinct 1810. JOHN KAYE, Esq., of Woodsome, descended from Sir JOHN KAYE, Knt., living temp. William I., and his wife, the dau. and heiress of Sir JOHN WOODESHAM, Knt., of Woodesham, was created a bart. 1641; the fifth bart. *d. unm.* 1789, and bequeathed his estates to JOHN LISTER, who assumed the surname of KAYE, and was created a bart. 1812). Ar. two bends sa. *Crests*—1st: A griffin's head erased ar. holding in the beak a key or; 2nd: A goldfinch ppr. *Motto*—Kynd Kynn Knawne Kepe.

Kaye (LISTER-KAYE, Denby Grange, co. York, bart., created 1812). Quarterly, 1st and 4th, ar. two bendlets sa., for KAYE; 2nd and 3rd, erm. on a fesse sa. three mullets or, for LISTER; the whole within a border wavy az. *Crests*—1st, KAYE: A goldfinch ppr. charged on the breast with a rose gu.; 2nd, LISTER: A buck's head ppr. erased wavy or, attired sa., in the mouth a bird-bolt bendways of the third, flighted ar. *Motto*—Kynd Kynn Knawne Kepe.

Kayle (co. Cornwall). Quarterly, battelly counter-battelly ar. and sa. *Crest*—A demi talbot ducally gorged.

Kayle, or Kele (Visit. London, 1568). Quarterly, embattled ar. and sa. in the 1st quarter a mullet of the last. *Crest*—A wyvern ar. wings expanded or.

Kayle. Quarterly, ar. and sa. billettée counterchanged. *Crest*—On a chapeau gu. turned up ar. a greyhound pass. of the last.

Kaynell, or Keynell (Bridestone, co. Wilts). Ar. a fesse flory counterflory gu.

Kaynes, or Caignes (Lord of Midleton, co. Notts. The heiress MARGARET, dau. of ROBERT KAYNES, granddau. of JOHN KAYNES, aged 26, 43 Henry III., 1258, fourth in descent from ROBERT DE CAIGNES or KAYNES, Lord of Middleton, *m.* PHILIP AYLESBURY, of co. Bucks, living 23 Edward III., 1348. Visit. Notts). Vair two bars gu.

503

Kaynes (ROBERT DE CAIGNES or KAYNES, Lord of Middleton, co. Nottingham, *temp.* King John. Visit. Notts, 1614). Vair two bars gu.

Kaynille. Ar. a fesse gu.

Kaynton. Ar. a pale nebulée sa. *Crest*—A mountain ppr.

Kayre. Sa. a chev. ar.

Kays. Per chev. gu. and sa. three keys or, wards to the sinister.

Kayville. Ar. a fess flory counterflory gu.

Kean (exemplified to JAMES MEARA, Esq., of Dublin, on his assuming by royal licence, 1824, the surname and arms of KEAN). Ar. an oak tree eradicated ppr. in chief two lions combatant az. supporting a ducal coronet gu. and in base a salmon naiant ppr. *Crest*—A cat-a-mountain ramp. per fess az. and gu. *Motto*—Inclyta virtus.

Keane (Cappoquin House, co. Waterford, bart.). Gu. three salmons naiant in pale ar. *Crest*—A cat sejant ppr. supporting in the dexter paw a flag-staff, thereon a union jack ppr. *Motto*—Felis demulcta mitis.

Keane (*Baron Keane*). Gu. three salmons naiant in pale ar. on a chief of honourable augmentation a representation of the fortress of Ghuznee all ppr. *Crests*—1st: A representation of the Cabool gate of the fortress of Ghuznee all ppr., and on an escroll above, the word "Ghuznee;" 2nd: A cat sejant ppr. supporting in his dexter paw a flagstaff, thereon a union jack ppr. *Supporters*—Dexter, a mounted Beloochee soldier; and sinister, a mounted Affghan soldier, both ppr. *Motto*—Deus mihi providebit.

Keane (Belmont, co. Waterford; confirmed to JOHN KEANE, Esq., of that place). Gu. three trout ar. *Crest*—A cat-a-mountain sejant ppr. holding in his dexter paw a staff displaying a banner of the union of Great Britain. *Motto*—Virtute.

Keane (Hermitage, co. Clare; confirmed to FRANCIS NICHOLAS KEANE, Esq., J.P., eldest surviving son of ROBERT KEANE, Esq., J.P., of Beech Park, in same co., and grandson of CHARLES KEANE, Esq., of Corbally, in same co., and to the other descendants of the said CHARLES KEANE). Quarterly, gu. and or, in the 1st and 4th quarters a salmon naiant ar., in the 2nd and 3rd a tree vert. *Crest*—A wild cat ramp. guard. ppr. gorged with an antique Irish crown or, charged on the shoulder with a trefoil vert. *Motto*—Felis demulcta mitis.

Keane (Beech Park, co. Clare). Quarterly, gu. and or, in the 1st and 4th quarters a salmon naiant ar., in the 2nd and 3rd quarters a tree vert. *Crest*—A wild cat ramp. guard. ppr. gorged with an antique Irish crown or, and charged on the shoulder with a trefoil vert. *Motto*—Felis demulcta mitis.

Kearney. See CARNEY and O'CARNEY.

Kearney (Ballinknockane, co. Tipperary; confirmed by Preston, Ulster, 1635, to MICHAEL KEARNEY, son of PATRICK KEARNEY, Esq., of that place). Ar. three lions ramp. gu. on a chief az. an arm couped above the wrist lying fessways, vested or, une hand ppr. holding a dagger erect of the field, pommel and hilt of the fourth betw. two pheons, points downwards of the last. *Motto*—Sustine et abstine.

Kearney (St. Louis and St. Germains, in France; allowed by Hawkins, Ulster, 1771, to FREDERICK LAURENCE KEARNEY, of St. Louis, descended from KEARNEY, of Fethard and Knockanglass, co. Tipperary). Ar. three lions ramp. gu. on a chief az. a gauntleted hand lying fessways, holding a dagger erect ppr. pommel and hilt or, betw. two crosses crosslet fitchée of the field. *Crest*—A gauntleted hand lying fessways ppr., holding a dagger erect ar. pommel and hilt or.

Kearney (Blanchville, co. Kilkenny). Ar. three lions ramp. gu. on a chief az. betw. two pheons or, a gauntleted hand in fesse of the last, holding a sword ppr. pommel and hilt gold. *Crest*—A gauntleted hand or, holding a dagger ar. *Motto*—Sustine et abstine.

Kearney (Ballyvary, co. Mayo). Sa. on a chev. ar. three garbs vert; 2nd, ar. three lions ramp. gu. on a chief az. betw. two pheons or, a gauntleted hand in fesse of the last holding a dagger ppr. pommel and hilt gold. *Crests*—1st: A ruined castle in flames; 2nd: A gauntleted hand or, in fesse, holding a dagger ar. *Motto*—Sustine et abstine.

Kearney (Ballinvilla, co. Mayo; descended from KEARNEY, of Knockanglass, co. Tipperary). Quarterly, 1st and 4th, KEARNEY, sa. on a chief ar. three wheatsheaves vert; 2nd. ar. three lions ramp. gu. on a chief az. betw. two pheons or, a gauntleted hand in fesse ppr. holding a dagger ppr. pommel and hilt gold; 3rd, KELLY, gu. on a mount vert two lions supporting a tower ar. *Crests*—1st: A ruined castle in flames ppr.; 2nd: A gauntleted hand in fesse holding a dagger, as in the arms. *Motto*—Sustine et abstine.

Kearney (ROBERT CECIL KEARNEY, *Count Kearney*, **of the** Papal States, by patent dated Nov. 1868, third son of the late ROBERT KEARNEY, Esq., of Ballinvilla). Same *Arms, Crest,* and *Motto.*

Kearney (CUTHBERT-KEARNEY; exemplified to THOMAS CUTHBERT, Esq., of Garrestown, co. Cork, on his assuming, by royal licence, 1832, the additional surname and arms of KEARNEY). Quarterly, 1st and 4th, ar. three lions ramp. two and one gu. on a chief az. an armed arm in fess couped below the elbow, the hand bare, grasping a dagger erect ppr. betw. two pheons of the first, for KEARNEY; 2nd and 3rd, vert a fess engr. betw. four mullets or, surmounting an arrow in pale, the point downwards ppr., for CUTHBERT. *Crests*—1st, KEARNEY: A dexter armed arm couped below the elbow in fess, the hand bare, grasping a dagger erect all ppr.; 2nd, CUTHBERT: A demi lion ramp. or, debruised by an arrow, point downwards gu. *Motto*—Semper fidelis.

Kearney (AYLWARD-KEARNEY; exemplified to JAMES AYLWARD, Esq., of Shankhill Castle, co. Kilkenny, D.L., son and heir of NICHOLAS AYLWARD, Esq., of Shankhill, by ELIZABETH KEARNEY, his wife, eldest dau. of JAMES KEARNEY, Esq., of Blanchville, in same co., upon his assuming, by royal licence, dated 28 March, 1876, the additional name of KEARNEY). Quarterly, 1st and 4th, ar. three lions ramp. gu. on a chief az. betw. two pheons or, a gauntleted hand in fess of the last, holding a dagger of the first, pommel and hilt gold, for KEARNEY; 2nd and 3rd, az. a fleur-de-lis betw. two estoiles in dexter bend and as many increscents in sinister bend or, for AYLWARD. *Crests*—1st, KEARNEY: A gauntleted hand fessways or, holding a dagger ar. pommel and hilt gold; 2nd, AYLWARD: Out of a ducal coronet or, an arm embowed vested az. cuffed ar. the hand ppr. grasping an anchor gold, motto over, Verus et fidelis semper. *Motto*—Sustine et abstine.

Kearney (BUTLER-KEARNEY; exemplified to CHARLES JAMES BUTLER, Esq., of Drom, co. Tipperary, Lieut. 104th regt., grandson of Rev. THEOBALD BUTLER, of Drom, by ANNE KEARNEY, his wife, second dau. of JAMES KEARNEY, Esq., of Blanchville, co. Kilkenny, upon his assuming, by royal licence, dated 20 April, 1876, the additional surname of KEARNEY). Quarterly, 1st and 4th, ar. three lions ramp. gu. on a chief az. betw. two pheons or, a gauntleted hand in fess of the last holding a dagger of the first, pommel and hilt gold, for KEARNEY; 2nd and 3rd, or, a chief indented az. three escallops in bend counterchanged, for BUTLER. *Crests*—1st, KEARNEY: A gauntleted hand fessways or, holding a dagger ar. pommel and gilt gold; 2nd, BUTLER: Out of a ducal coronet or, a plume of five ostrich feathers ar. issuant therefrom a demi falcon also ar., motto over, Timor Domini fons vitæ. *Motto*—Sustine et abstine.

Kearsley (co. Lancaster, and London; granted by Bysshe, Clarenceux, 1662, to HENRY KEARSLEY, of the Liberty of the Tower of London, gent., son of OLIVER KEARSLEY, of Dean, co. Lancaster. Visit. Middlesex, 1663). Or, two bars sa. betw. six lions' heads couped gu. three, two, and one. *Crest*—A demi eagle erm. winged or.

Keate (The Hoo, co. Herts, bart., extinct 1657). Ar. three mountain cats pass. in pale sa.

Keate (Woodford, co. Essex, and Grovehurst, co. Kent). Same *Arms.* *Crest*—A mountain cat pass. sa.

Keating (Kilcoan, co. Wexford. Visit. Wexford, 1618). Ar. a saltire gu. betw. four nettle leaves vert. *Crest*—A boar statant gu. armed and hoofed or, holding in the mouth a nettle leaf vert.

Keating (Rosetown, co. Wexford. Visit. Wexford, 1618). Same *Arms* and *Crest.*

Keating (Baldwinstown, co. Wexford. Visit. Wexford, 1618). Same *Arms* and *Crest.*

Keating (Brittany, in France, settled there after the revolution of 1688; allowed by Hawkins, Ulster, 1784, to CHARLES KEATING, of Brittany, great-grandson of THOMAS KEATING, Esq., of Baldwinstown). Same *Arms* and *Crest.*

Keating (Clonoghinthe, co. Carlow; Fun. Ent. 1619, REDMOND KEATING, of that place). Same *Arms.*

Keating (Narraghmore, co. Kildare; Fun. Ent. 1683, MAURICE KEATING, of that place). Same *Arms.*

Keating (Baybush, co. Limerick; allowed by Bryan, Deputy Ulster, 1767, to VALENTINE KEATING, Esq., of that place, descended from KEATING, of Kilcoan). Same *Arms* and *Crest.* *Motto*—Fidelissimus semper.

Keating (Kilmandan; Reg. Ulster's Office). Quarterly, 1st and 4th, same *Arms;* 2nd and 3rd, az. a lion ramp. ar. over all in middle point a cross pattée of the first. *Crest*—A boar pass. gu. in front of a bunch of nettles ppr. *Motto*—Providentia divina.

Keats (borne by Admiral Sir RICHARD GOODWIN KEATS, G.C.B., of Dorrant House, Dover, Governor of Greenwich

554

Hospital). Pean three mountain cats pass. in pale ar. on a canton ar. a fesse gu. surmounted by an anchor of the third, encircled by a wreath of laurel vert, for KEATS; quartering or, a lion pass. guard. sa. on a chief gu. three lozenges vair, for GOODWIN. *Crest*—On a naval coronet or, a tiger statant guard. ppr. charged on the body with an anchor sa. *Supporters*—Dexter, a triton in the act of blowing a conc shell all ppr. a ribbon round his neck white, edged blue, therefrom pendent a gold medallion representing Victory crowning Britannia; sinister, a sea lion ppr. gorged with a collar az. rimmed or, thereon the word "Superb" in letters of gold, beneath the collar the ribbon and medallion as the dexter.

Keats (cos. Berks and Gloucester). Ar. three mountain cats pass. in pale sa. *Crest*—A mountain cat, as in the arms.

Kebbell, or Kebyll (London). Ar. a chev. az. on a chief of the second three mullets or, pierced sa.

Kebell (Homerston, co. Leicester; HENRY KEBELL, son of FRANCIS KEBELL, and grandson of WALTER KEBELL, all of that place, d. 9 May, 1571, leaving two daus., ELIZABETH, aged 11, and MARGARET, aged 10. Visit. Leicester, 1619). Barry nebulée of six ar. and sa. on a canton gu. a crescent of the first, quartering, Gu. a chev. betw. three eagles displ. ar. *Crest*—A demi eagle, wings displ. ar. gorged with a bar gemellée.

Kebill. Ar. a chev. engr. gu. on a chief az. three escallops of the field.

Keble (Lord Mayor of London, 1510; confirmed as the arms of KEBLE, of co. Warwick). Ar. a chev. engr. gu. on a chief az. three mullets or.

Keble (West Creting, Old Newton, and Stowmarket, co. Suffolk). Ar. three bars nebulée sa. a canton gu. *Crest*—A demi eagle displ. ar.

Keble, or Kebell (co. Suffolk). Barry nebulée of six ar. and az. a canton of the first.

Keble (Sir HENRY KEBLE, Knt., temp. Henry VIII., whose dau. ALICE m. WILLIAM BROWNE, son and heir of Sir JOHN BROWNE, Knt., Mayor of London. Visit. London, 1568). Ar. a chev. engr. gu. on a chief az. three mullets or.

Keble. Sa. a chev. engr. or, on a chief ar. three mullets of the field. *Crest*—An elephant's head couped.

Keborne. Ar. a chev. betw. ten crosses pattée sa.

Kebyll. Ar. (another, or) a fesse wavy gu. on a canton sa. a lion pass. of the field.

Keck (Staughton Grange, co. Leicester, and Bank Hall, co. Lancaster; ANTHONY JAMES, Esq., assumed the name of KECK, 1737, as devisee of his maternal grandfather, ANTHONY KECK, Esq.). Sa. a bend erm. betw. two cotises flory counterflory or. *Crest*—Out of a mural crown gu. a maiden's head erm. purfled or, hair dishevelled and flotant gold, adorned with a chaplet vert, garnished with roses ppr.

Keck (POWYS-KECK, Staughton Grange, co. Leicester; Hon. HENRY LITTLETON POWYS, fifth son of THOMAS, second Lord Lilford, by HARRIET LEGH, his wife, dau. and co-heir of PETER LEGH, Esq., of Lyme, and cousin of GEORGE ANTHONY LEGH-KECK, Esq., of Staughton, assumed the additional surname of KECK, Feb. 1861, upon inheriting the Staughton estates). Same *Arms* and *Crest.*

Kedale. Ar. on a bend az. three mullets or.

Kedall, or Keydall (co. Cornwall). Ar. a chev. betw. three dolphins sa.

Kedall, or Kiddall. Sa. a saltire counter-embattled ar.

Kedmarston (co. Suffolk). Ar. three war-bells gu. *Crest*—A demi lion ramp. ar.

Kedslie. Gu. three palets ar. on a chief of the second as many torteaux. *Crest*—An eagle displ. with two heads ppr. charged on the breast with a mullet ar. *Motto*—Veritas omnia vincit.

Kedwelley (Hartley and Winchfield, co. Hants; descended from IEVAN ISCOD, of co. Glamorgan; MARGERY, dau. and heiress of LAWRENCE KEDWELLEY, Esq., of Hartley, m. JAMES RUDYERD, and was mother of the celebrated Sir BENJAMIN RUDYERD, M.P.). Or, a fesse indented gu.

Keeble (East Leach, co. Gloucester). Or, a chev. engr. gu. on a chief sa. three mullets ar.

Keefe. See O'KEEFE.

Keel (London). Quarterly, crenellée ar. and sa. in the first quarter a crescent of the second.

Keeling (co. Worcester, and Southill, co. Beds; WILLIAM KELYNGE, co. Worcester, was father of JOHN KELYNGE, who, by ALICE his wife, dau. of GREGORY WATERHOUSE, Esq., had a son, Sir JOHN KEELING, Knt., of Southill, Chief Justice of King's Bench, 1665, d. 1671). Ar. three scaling ladders in bend gu. *Crest*—A lion sejant or, supporting a scaling ladder gu.

Keeling, Kellyng, Kelyng, or Kelynge. Same *Arms. Crest*—A sword in pale enfiled with a Saracen's head affrontée all ppr.

Keeling (co. Essex). Sa. a lion ramp. or, holding an escocheon ar. charged with a cross crosslet fitchée gu. *Crest* —Out of a mural crown a demi lion as above.

Keelinge (Sedgley Park, co. Stafford, and Bewarsley. Visit. 1663. Sir JOHN KEELINGE was Chief Justice of the King's Bench; MARY, only dau. and heiress of WILLIAM KEELINGE, Esq., of Sedgley Park, *m.* 1738, THOMAS FLETCHER, Esq., of Cannock). Gu. betw. two lions ramp. or, a bend engr. of the second charged with three scaling ladders of the field.

Keen (North Cove and Thanderston, co. Suffolk; granted 3 May, 1562;). Az. a talbot pass. or, on a chief indented az. three crosses flory sa. *Crest*—A hind's head erased sa. bezantée.

Keen (Scotland). See KEIN.

Keen (Reg. Ulster's Office). Erm. a cross patoncée ermines. *Crest*—Five arrows, one in pale and four in saltire, heads down or, headed ar. banded gu.

Keene. Gu. a cross crosslet ern.

Keenlyside. Ar. three battle axes paleways, two and one sa. *Crest*—A beacon lighted ppr.

Keep. Or, a bend gu. on a canton ar. a galley, her oars in action, of the second. *Crest*—A weaver's shuttle in pale gu. threaded ppr.

Keet (Canterbury; granted 1745). Erm. a fesse invecked az. betw. two bees volant in chief ppr. and a damask rose in base gu. barbed vert. *Crest*—A dexter erm embowed couped at the shoulder, habited az. cuffed ar. holding in the hand ppr. a battle axe of the second, staff or, entwined with a serpent vert.

Keete (Chellesburne, co. Dorset). Az. a chev. betw. three kites' heads erased or. *Crest*—A unicorn's head erased ar. collared gu. buckled and garnished and armed or.

Kefford (co. York). Gu. a fesse embattled betw. three bees volant or.

Keigans (confirmed by Roberts, Ulster, to CORNELIUS KEIGANS, descended from KEIGAN, of co. Westmeath, a captain in Col. William Warren's Regt., under the command of EDWARD, *Earl of Glamorgan*). Gu. a lion saliant ducally crowned and holding in the dexter paw a crescent all ar.

Keighley. Ar. a fesse sa. *Crest*—A dragon's head erased ar. charged on the breast with a mullet sa.

Keigwin (Mousehole, co. Cornwall; of Welsh origin, descended from JENKIN KEIGWIN, of Mousehole, who was slain in 1595, in an attack made by some Spanish galleys on the towns of Mousehole, Newlyn, and Penzance). Vert a chev. betw. three greyhounds courant ar.; these arms, evidently from the name Keigwin, or Ker gwyn, which signifies in Cornish " white dog," have been used by the family for full two centuries; but a manuscript in the Heralds' Office gives a lion ramp. crowned, as the arms of KEIGWIN, of Penzance. *Crest*—A greyhound's head erased ar.

Keiling (Newcastle-under-Lyne, co. Stafford). Sa. a lion ramp. or, holding an escutcheon ar. charged with a cross formée fitchée gu. *Crest*—A demi lion ramp. or, holding an escutcheon, as in the arms.

Kein, or Keen (Cadisley, co. Roxburgh). Gu. a gauntlet in fesse or, on a chief ar. three stars of the first.

Keines (co. Somerset). Az. a bend wavy cotised ar.

Keinsham (co. Bedford). Per pale ar. and az. three cinquefoils counterchanged.

Keir (The Carse, co. Stirling). Ar. a cross engr. sa. betw. four roses gu.

Keir (Calcutta; descended from WHITMORE, co. Berwick, 1768). Ar. on a cross engr. sa. four lozenges or, betw. four roses gu. *Crest*—A mahout, or Indian elephant driver, upon an elephant all ppr. *Motto*—Cum grano salis.

Keir-Grant. See GRANT.

Keirie (Gogar, co. Edinburgh). Ar. a fesse counter-embattled betw. two cinquefoils in chief and a cross crosslet fitchée in base gu. *Crest*—A hand holding a rose slipped ppr. *Motto*—Virtute viget.

Keirll (Croft Castle, co. Hereford). Sa. a chev. erminois, on a chief indented ar. an estoile betw. two mullets az. *Crest* —A horse's head erased ar. in the mouth a palm branch ppr.

Keitelby (co. Gloucester). Per pale gu. and sa. a lion ramp. crowned ar.

Keith (*Earl Marischal;* the junior branches of this ancient and distinguished race were the KEITHS of Galstoun, of Ludquhairn and Innerugie; of Northfield, of Auquhorsk, of Garvock, of Uras, of Dunottar, and Ravelstoun, &c. JAMES, the celebrated Field-Marshal KEITH, so distinguished in the wars of Frederick the Great, was second son of WILLIAM,

ninth *Earl Marischal*). Ar. on a chief gu. three palets or. *Crest*—A hart's head erased ppr. armed with ten tynes or. *Supporters*—Two harts ppr. attired as in the crest. *Motto*— Veritas vincit: behind the shield two batons gu. semée of thistles, ensigned on the top with an imperial crown or, placed saltireways as badges of the office of Great Marischal of Scotland.

Keith, Baroness. See ELPHINSTONE.

Keith-Falconer (*Earl of Kintore*). Quarterly, 1st and 4th, gu. a sceptre and sword in saltire, with an imperial crown in chief, within an orle of eight thistles or, as a cont of augmentation; 2nd and 3rd, ar. on a chief gu. three pallets or, for KEITH. *Crest*—A demi woman richly attired, holding in the dexter hand a garland of laurel ppr. *Motto*— Quæ amissa salva.

Keith (*Lord Altrie*, Scotland). Quarterly, 1st and 4th, or, a saltire and chief gu.; 2nd and 3rd, ar. on a chief three pallets or. *Crest*—A rock ppr. *Supporters*—Dexter, a unicorn ar. horned and unguled or; sinister, a deer ppr. *Motto* —Watch the temptation.

Keith (*Lord Dingwall*, Scotland). Quarterly, 1st and 4th, ar. on a chief gu. three palets or; 2nd and 3rd, gu. a lion ramp. ar. *Crest*—A stag's head couped ppr. *Motto*—Memento creatorem.

Keith (Ravelston, co. Edinburgh, and Dunnottar, co. Kincardine; as recorded 1737). Ar. a lymphad sa. on a chief gu. three pallets or. *Crest*—A dexter arm grasping a dagger ppr. *Motto*—Pro veritate. The principal arms and supporters of the family were recorded for ALEXANDER KEITH, of Ravelston and Dunnottar, as heir male of the *Earls Marischal* in 1801. The heiress *m.*, in 1833, Sir WILLIAM MURRAY, of Ochtertyre, Bart.

Keith (Auquhorsk, co. Aberdeen). Ar. on a chief gu. three pallets or, differenced by a buckle of the third. *Crest*—A hand holding a writing pen ppr. *Motto*—Et loquor et taceo.

Keith (Craig, co. Kincardine). Ar. on a chief embattled gu. three pallets or, a bordure also embattled of the second. *Crest*—A stag standing at gaze under a hollybush ppr. *Motto*—Fortiter qui sedulo.

Keith (Craig; as recorded 1769, for ROBERT KEITH, Ambassador to the Courts of Vienna and St. Petersburgh). Quarterly, 1st and 4th, as the last; 2nd and 3rd, or, a fetterlock sa. on a chief az. three stars ar., for MURRAY. *Crest*—An ermine ppr. *Supporters*—Two roebucks ppr. attired and unguled or, both collared, that on the dexter gu. charged with three pallets or, that on the sinister az. with three stars ar. having chains affixed thereto passing betw. their forelegs and reflexed over their backs or. *Motto*—Ex candore decus.

Keith (Montrose, descended of Craig, 1737). Ar. an anchor in pale az. on a chief embattled gu. three pallets or, a bordure also embattled of the third. *Crest*—A hand holding a thunderbolt winged or. *Motto*—Fortiter qui sedulo.

Keith (Ostend, descended of Crichie, 1791). Ar. a heart gu. within a bordure az. on a chief of the second three pallets or, charged with a star of the third. *Crest*—A demi lion ramp. ppr. *Motto*—Recta sequor.

Keith (Harthill, co. Aberdeen). Or, a cross crosslet fitchée az. betw. two crescents in chief and a fusil in base gu.

Keith (Innerugie, co. Aberdeen). Ar. a chief paly of six or and gu. within a bordure engr. sa.

Keith (Ludquhairn, co. Aberdeen). Ar. a cross crosslet fitchée and an escallop az. in fesse, on a chief gu. three palets or. *Crest*—A dexter hand casting an anchor in the water. *Motto*—Remember thy end.

Keith (Arthur House, co. Kincardine, 1672). Ar. a saltire gu. on a chief of the last three pallets or, all within a bordure compony az. and of the first. *Crest*—A dexter hand holding a pike erect ppr. *Motto*—Justa sequor.

Keith (Ravenscraig, co. Aberdeen). Ar. on a chief gu. three palets or, quartering or, three cushions gu. within a double tressure counterflowered of the last, for RANDOLPH.

Keith (Tillygone, co. Kincardine). Parted per fesse or and ar. on the first three demi palets gu. and in base a man's heart of the last. *Crest*—A lure ppr. *Motto*—Venit ab astris.

Kekebourne. Ar. a chev. betw. ten crosses crosslet sa. *Crest*—On a ducal coronet or, a lion sejant, holding a sword in pale ppr.

Kekewich (Peamore, co. Devon, originally of co. Lancaster; settled about the middle of the 16th century in Cornwall, in consequence of a marriage with the heiress of Talcarne). Ar. two lions pass. in bend sa. *Crest*—Two bendlets gu. *Crest*—A leopard's head and neck affrontée.

Kekewich (Ketchfrench, co. Cornwall; WILLIAM KEKEWICH, Visit. Cornw., 1620, grandson of GEORGE KEKEWICH, of same place). Ar. two lions pass. in bend sa. betw. two bendlets gu. *Crest*—A leopard's head and neck affrontée sa.

Kekitmore. Gu. three text S's or, two and one.

Kelden. Per bend gu. and or, a pale vair.

Keldon. Gu. a pale reversed erm.

Kele (London). See KAYLE.

Kele (London). Or, two bars gu. each charged with three martlets ar. betw. as many billets fesseways of the second. *Crest*—A demi woman ppr. hair dishevelled or, on the head a chaplet vert.

Keleman. Gu. a bend betw. two talbots pass. ar.

Keleyne. Ar. a saltire betw. four trefoils slipped vert.

Kelford. Gu. on a chev. ar. three mullets of the first, in chief two bucks' heads erased of the second, attired or, in base a cat pass. of the second.

Kelham (Bleasby Hall, co. Nottingham). Quarterly, 1st and 4th, per pale gu. and az. a chief engr. of the last as many estoiles sa., for KELHAM; 2nd, az. three covered cups or, for KELHAM (ancient); 3rd, sa. a chev. betw. three estoiles ar., for LANGDALE. *Crest*—A demi eagle displ. with two heads az. semée of erm. spots or, on each wing a covered cup gold. *Motto*—Beneficiorum memor.

Kelhull. Gu. three palets ar. a chief az.

Keling (Hackney, co. Middlesex; granted 30 April, 1632). Sa. a lion ramp. or, holding in the paws an escutcheon ar. charged with a cross pattée fitchée as the foot gu. *Crest*—Out of a mural crown a demi lion or, holding an escutcheon, as in the arms.

Kelk (Bentley Priory, Stanmore, and Lancaster Gate, co. Middlesex, bart.). Per pale az. and gu. on a bend engr. flory counterflory ar. three escallops of the second. *Crest*—A wolf sejant sa. collared or, holding betw. the paws a leopard's face ppr. jessant-de-lis ar. *Motto*—Lætus sorte vives sapienter.

Kelk (Walsoken House, co. Norfolk). Quarterly, ar. and gu. three escallops counterchanged. *Crest*—A wolf sejant ppr.

Kelke (Kelke, co. Lincoln). Sa. a bend cotised flory or. *Crest*—A wolf sejant ppr.

Kelke (Barnaby, co. Lincoln). Ar. three escallops gu.

Kelke. Sa. a plain bendlet or, betw. two bendlets flory counterflory of the last.

Kelkefield, or Kelkfeld. Ar. a cross engr. sa.

Kell. Or, on a chev. vert betw. a lion pass. in chief and two mullets in base gu. three garbs or.

Kellall. Paly of six ar. and gu. a chief az.

Kellam, or Killome (Danby, co. York). Az. three covered cups or. *Crest*—A cross crosslet fitchée and palm branch vert in saltire.

Kellam. Gu. a double-bodied lion guard. crowned or, a bordure ar.

Kellam. Gu. two lions ramp. or, crowned az. a bordure of the second.

Kellam. Gu. three lions ramp. or, with wreaths on their heads az.

Kelland (Painsford, in Ashprington, co. Devon; the last male representative, JOHN KELLAND, Esq. of Painsford, d. in 1712; his co-heirs m. STAFFORD, COFFIN, and COURTENAY). Sa. a fesse ar. in chief three fleurs-de-lis of the last. *Crest*—A demi tiger saliant or, maned ar.

Kellaway, or Kelloway (Stowford, co. Devon). Ar. two glaziers' snippers in saltire betw. four pears sa. *Crest*—A tiger pass. reguard. sa.

Kellawaye (Sherborne, co. Dorset). Same *Arms*, a border engr. of the last. *Crest*—A cock ar. combed and wattled az.

Kelle (co. Cornwall). Ar. a chev. betw. three billets gu.

Kelle (London). Per bend crenellée ar. and sa. *Crest*—A boar's head erased az. ducally gorged or.

Kellet (Ripley, co. Surrey; confirmed 1 Oct. 4 Edward VI.). Ar. on a mount vert a wild boar sa. chained and armed or. *Crest*—A cubit arm habited sa. cuffed ar. puffed of the last, holding in the hand a roll of parchment ppr.

Kellet, or Kellett. Vert a saltire ar. in chief a cinquefoil or. *Crest*—A demi wolf ramp. sa.

Kellett (Lota, co. Cork, bart.). Quarterly, 1st and 4th, ar. on a mount vert a boar pass. sa.; 2nd and 3rd, ar. a cross gu. in the first quarter a fleur-de-lis of the last. *Crest*—An armed arm embowed, in armour, garnished or, holding in the hand a baton gold. *Motto*—Feret ad astra virtus.

Kelley (Torrington, co. Devon). Sa. a lion ramp. or, betw. three fleurs-de-lis erm. *Crest*—A seahorse in water ppr. holding in the paws a spiked ball.

Kelley. Ar. on a chev. betw. three leopards' faces sa. as many annulets or.

Kelley. Quarterly, crenellée ar. and sa. in the first quarter a crescent of the second.

Kullie-McCallum See McCALLUM.

556

Kellingworth. Ar. three cinquefoils sa. pierced or.

Kellio (Kellio in Cornely, co. Cornwall; extinct in the fifteenth century, when the heiress m. TREDENHAM). Or, a chev. betw. two cinquefoils in chief and a mulet in base sa.

Kello (Scotland). Gu. a fesse or, betw. two lilies slipped in chief ar. and an annulet in base of the second.

Kellobery. Gu. a bend or (another, ar.).

Kellowey (co. Hants. Visit. 1634). Ar. five grosing irons in saltire sa. betw. four Kelway pears ppr. a border en.gr. of the second. *Crest*—A cock ar. comb, wattles, beak, and spurs az.

Kelloway (Roborough, co. Devon). Ar. five grosing-irons in saltire sa. betw. four Kelway pears ppr. within a bordure engr. of the second.

Kelloway. Ar. a saltire sa. betw. four pears pendant gu *Crest*—A barnacle bird ar.

Kellum, or Kelhull. Paly of six gu. and ar. a chief az.

Kelly (Kelly, co. Devon; settled in that co. from a remote period; derived from KELLY, of Kelly, temp. Richard I.). Ar. a chev. betw. three billets gu. *Crest*—Out of a ducal coronet gu. an ostrich's head ar. holding in the beak a horseshoe or.

Kelly (Castle Kelly, co. Galway). Az. two lions ramp. combatant ar. chained or, supporting a tower triple. turretted of the second. *Crest*—An enfield vert. *Motto*—Turris fortis mihi Deus.

Kelly (Newtown, co. Galway). Gu. two lions ramp. combatant supporting a tower triple-towered ar. *Crest*—An enfield pass. vert. *Motto*—Turris fortis mihi Deus.

Kelly (confirmed to ROBERT HUME KELLY, Esq., of Glencara, co. Westmeath). Az. two lions ramp. combatant ar. chained or, supporting a tower of three turrets of the second, in the centre chief point a mullet of the third. *Crest*—An enfield vert charged on the shoulder with a mullet, as in the arms. *Motto*—Turris fortis mihi Deus.

Kelly. See O'KELLY.

Kelly (Sir FITZROY KELLY, Lord Chief Baron of the Exchequer). Az. two lions ramp. or, supporting a castle ppr. *Crest*—On a chapeau gu. turned up erm. an enfield vert. *Motto*—Turris fortis mihi Deus.

Kelly (Scotland). Or, a saltire, sa betw. four fleurs-de-lis az.

Kelly-(WILLIAM HENRY KELLY, Esq., of Porchester Terrace, Paddington, co. Middlesex). Or, a lion ramp. az. betw. two flaunches of the last, each charged with a castle of the first. *Crest*—In front of two anchors in saltire sa. a castle or. *Motto*—Justum perficito nihil timeto.

Kelly, Kelley, or Keylley. Or, on two bars sa. betw. three billets gu. two and one, five martlets, three or two (another, mullets) of the first. *Crest*—A boar pass. or, wounded by an arrow ppr.

Kelsall (THOMAS KELSALL, Esq.). Erm. a bend engr. sa. *Crest*—An eagle's head erased. *Motto*—Meliora sequentur.

Kelsall (Kelsall, in Tarvin, co. Chester; extinct at an early period). Erm. a bend. engr. sa.

Kelsall (Bradshaw and Heathside, co. Chester; a younger branch of KELSALL of Kelsall). Same *Arms*.

Kelsall(Boston, co. Lincoln, and co. Middlesex). Same *Arms*.

Kelsey (Ripley, co. Surrey; WILLIAM KELSEY, of Ripley, m. temp. Edward III. Maud, dau. and heir of Sir Richard Willoughby. His grandson, THOMAS KELSEY, of Ripley, left an only dau. and heiress, LUCIA, who m. cir. 1390, Sir NICHOLAS CAREW, of Beddington, Keeper of the Privy Seal). Gu. a cross moline ar. surmounted of a bend az. charged with three plain crosses couped of the second.

Kelsey (Chelmsford and Thorp, co. Essex; granted 24 June, 1634). Sa. on a pale betw. two palets or, three escutcheons gu. *Crest*—Two cubit arms erect, vested sa. cuffed or, holding in the hands ppr. an escutcheon gold.

Kelsham, or Kilsham (co. Kent). Sa. a fesse engr ar. betw. three garbs or.

Kelso (Kelsoland, co. Ayr; descended from HUGO DE KELSO, called the founder of the KELSOS, of Kelsoland, living 1296. JOHN KELSO, of Kelsoland, alienated that property in 1676; and his second son, WILLIAM KELSO, Esq., acquired the lands of Dankeith, co. AYR, which is now the family estate, and possessed by its present representative). Sa. a fesse engr. erm. betw. three garbs or. *Crest*—A garb or. *Motto* (over the crest)—Otium cum dignitate.

Kelston. Sa. a saltire engr. ar. (another, or).

Kelt (quartered by FLOWER, of Langar, co. Nottingham. Visit. Notts, 1614). Sa. on a bend cotised flory or, an erm. spot (another, the bend ar., Har. MSS. 1400).

Kelton (co. Salop). Erm. three cinquefoils in fesse sa. pierced ar. *Crest*—A lion pass. per pale erm. and ermines.

Kelverdon (co. Essex). Gu. a pale erm.

Kelverton. Gu. a bend vairé or and az. betw. two eagles' heads couped ar. *Crest*—An eagle's head couped ar gorged with a chaplet of roses ppr.

Kelway. Ar. two thigh-bones in saltire sa. betw. four pears or, a bordure engr. of the second.

Kelwich. Ar. two lions ramp. in bend betw. as many bendlets sa. *Crest*—A lion's head guard. sa.

Kelyng. Sa. on a chev. betw. three annulets or, as many spearheads az.

Kellyng, Kelyng, and Kelynge. See KEELING.

Kemble (Wydell, co. Wilts, and Lamborne, co. Berks). Sa. on a bend erm. three leopards' faces of the first. *Crest* —A wolf's head trunked and embrued or.

Kemble (co. Gloucester). Ar. a chev. betw. three mullets sa. a border of the last.

Kemble. Az. on a bend or, cotised ar. a rose gu. betw. two leopards' faces sa. *Crest*—Betw. a branch of laurel on the d'exter side and one of palm on the sinister ppr. a boar's head and neck sa. erased gu. charged with an estoile ar.

Kemble (Fun. Ent. Ulster's Office, 1660). Ar. a chev. betw. three mullets sa.

Keme. Gu. a cross engr. ar.

Kemelicke. Per fesse indented or and gu.

Kemes (Wales). Ar. three pheons sa.

Kemeys (Cefn Mably, co. Glamorgan, bart., extinct 1735, derived directly from the marriage of DAVID KEMEYS, third son of JEVAN KEMEYS, of Began, A.D. 1447. Sir NICHOLAS KEMEYS, of Cefn Mably, M.P. for co. Glamorgan, was created a bart. 1642. The eventual heiress, JANE, sister of Sir CHARLES KEMEYS, of Cefn Mably, fourth bart., *m.* Sir JOHN TYNTE, Bart., of Halswell, co. Somerset, and Cefn Mably, co. Glamorgan). Vert on a chev. ar. three pheons sa. *Crest* —On a mount vert a unicorn sejant az. armed and crined or. *Motto*—Ddw-Dy-Ras.

Kemiell (Kemiell in St. Paul's, co. Cornwall). Ar. three dolphins sa.

Kemis (Wickwick, co. Gloucester). Vert on a chev. ar. three pheons sa. (sometimes in base a rose of the second).

Kemish, or Kemiche (co. Lancaster). Ar. two lions pass. in bend betw. two cotises sa.

Kemishe. Barry of six vair and gu.

Kemor, or Kemur (cos. Gloucester, Kent, Middlesex, Gissing, co. Norfolk, cos. Suffolk and Sussex). Gu. a chief or. *Crest*—A lion's head erased or, pierced through with an arrow sa.

Kemp (Gissing, co. Norfolk, bart.). Gu. three garbs and a border engr. or. *Crest*—On a garb or, a pelican vulning herself ppr. *Motto*—Lucem spero.

Kemp (Inner Temple, London; LEONARD KEMPE and BARTHOLOMEW KEMPE, sons of FRANCIS KEMPE, and grandsons of FRANCIS KEMPE, second son of BARTHOLOMEW KEMPE, gent., of Gissing, co. Norfolk. Visit. Middlesex, 1663). Same *Arms*. *Crest*—A falcon ppr. hooded gu. beaked and belled or. *Another Crest*—On a garb or, a pelican rising gold, vulning herself ppr.

Kemp (Westbroke, co. Norfolk, and South Malling, co. Sussex). Gu. a fesse erm. betw. three garbs or, all within a bordure of the second. *Crest*—On a garb lying fesseways or, a falcon with wings endorsed erm.

Kemp (Comistoun, Scotland). Gu. two hands holding a two-handed sword in bend sinister, broken near the top ar.

Kemp. Ar. a lion ramp. gu. on a chief sa. three escallops of the field. *Crest*—A goat statant ar.

Kemp. Gu. three garbs within a border engr. or, entoyre of pomeis. *Crest*—On a mount vert a pelican or, charged on the breast with a pomeis, picking at a garb gold.

Kemp (co. Devon). Gu. a bend vair betw. three (another, six) escallops ar.

Kemp (granted to GEORGE BROOKES KEMP, Esq., of Goodyers, Hendon, co. Middlesex). Per pale az. and gu. a mascle betw. three garbs or, a border nebulée of the last. *Crest*— A garb fesseways or, thereon feeding her young a pelican, wings elevated sa. vulned ppr., charged on the breast with three annulets interlaced, and gorged with a collar gemel or.

Kemp (HINCHIN-KEMP; exemplified to FREDERICK WILLIAM HINCHIN, Esq., of Hawley Square, Margate, co. Kent, upon his assuming the additional surname of KEMP by royal licence, 13 June, 1868). Per pale az. and gu. a mascle betw. three garbs or, a border nebulée of the last. *Crest*—On a garb fesswise or, a pelican feeding her young, wings elevated sa. vulned ppr. charged on the breast with three annulets interlaced, and gorged with a collar gemel gold. *Motto*— Honestas et veritas.

Kempe (Olantigh, co. Kent; a very ancient family, of which were Cardinal JOHN KEMPE, Archbishop of Canterbury, who d. in 1454, and THOMAS KEMPE. Bishop of London, who d. 4 Henry VII. The daus. and co-heirs of Sir

557

**THOMAS KEMPE, Knt., of Olantigh, who d. in 1607, were MARY, *m.* to Sir DUDLEY DIGGES, Knt.; ANNE, *m.* to Sir JOHN CUTTS, Knt.; DOROTHY, *m.* to Sir JOHN CHICHELE; and AMY, *m.* to Sir HENRY SKIPWITH. One branch of the KEMPES of Olantigh is now represented by THOMAS READ KEMP, Esq., of Kemp Town, Brighton; and from another, settled at Lavethan, co. Cornwall, descend the KEMPES of that county, from whom derive WILLIAM KEMPE, Esq., of Teign Villas, co. Devon, formerly of Roath Castle, co. Glamorgan, son of the late SAMUEL KEMPE, Esq., of Rosteage, co. Cornwall; and the Rev. CHARLES TREVANION KEMPE, son of the late Admiral ARTHUR KEMPE). Gu. three garbs within a bordure engr. or. *Crest*—On a garb lying fesseways or, a falcon, wings endorsed ppr. The Cornish KEMPES bear the falcon without the garb.

Kempe (Slindon, co. Sussex; the heiress, BARBARA, dau. of ANTHONY KEMPE, Esq., of Slindon, *m.* JAMES BARTHOLOMEW, third *Earl of Newburgh*). Same *Arms*, &c.

Kempe (Spain's Hall, co. Essex, and co. Suffolk). Ar. a chev. engr. gu. betw. three estoiles az. *Crest*—An arm couped at the elbow vested ar. charged with two bends wavy az. cuffed of the first, holding in the hand ppr. a chaplet vert.

Kempe (Pentlow, co. Essex, bart., extinct 1667; descended from GEORGE KEMPE, sixth son of WILLIAM KEMPE, Esq., of Spain's Hall). Same *Arms*, &c.

Kempe (Dover, co. Kent; granted 1641). Az. a fesse betw. three garbs or, a border engr. of the last. *Crest*—A demi griffin or, winged gu. holding a garb of the first.

Kempe (cos. Kent and Suffolk). Gu. a bend engr. betw. three garbs or.

Kempe (co. Norfolk). Or (another, erm.) on a saltire engr. gu. five fleurs-de-lis of the field.

Kempe (co. Norfolk). Az. a bend engr. betw. three garbs or.

Kempe (co. Oxford; arms in Merton Hall Coll. Visit. Oxon, 1574). Gu. three garbs or, a border engr. of the last (another, in the Divinity School, Oxford, the border ar.).

Kempe (London; EDWARD KEMPE, Mercer, fourth son of BARTHOLOMEW KEMPE, Esq., of Gissing, co. Norfolk. Visit. London, 1568). Quarterly, gu. and ar. in the 1st and 4th quarters three garbs or, a border of the last, a martlet for diff.

Kempe (Cavendish, co. Suffolk). Ar. on a chev. engr. gu. betw. three estoiles az. an annulet or.

Kempenfelt (Admiral KEMPENFELT, lost in the "Royal George"). Ar. on ground in base vert a man in complete armour, standing with his sinister arm embowed, the dexter arm holding a sword above his head all ppr. *Crest*—A demi man, as in the arms, betw. two wings erect.

Kempley, or Kemsey (co. Salop). Gu. three scythes in pale ar.

Kempsing (Kempsing, co. Kent). Ar. a fesse and chev. interlaced sa.

Kempson, or Kempston (Walsall, co. Stafford, and Hilbarow, co. Warwick; confirmed by the Deputies of Camden, Clarenceux, to LEONARD KEMPSON, Esq., of Hilbarow, grandson of THOMAS KEMPSON, Esq., of Walsall). Or, three bars vert, in chief as many mullets az. *Crest*—A demi lion az. gorged with a collar or, charged with three mullets of the first.

Kempster. Az. a bend erminois, in chief a thistle ar. *Crest*—A lion's paw holding a thistle all ppr.

Kempston, or Kempton. Quarterly, ar. and gu. on a bend vert cotised or, three towers of the first.

Kempstone. Ar. a chev. sa. in the dexter point a cinquefoil of the second.

Kempt. Gu. three garbs ar. *Crest*—A hedgehog or.

Kempt (Lieut.-Gen. Right Hon. Sir JAMES KEMPT, G.C.B., Quarterly, 1st and 4th, gu. two naked arms issuant from the sinister base, grasping a sword broken in the centre of the blade all ppr.; 2nd and 3rd, gu. three cinquefoils ar. betw. the two coats in chief the badge of British military merit suspended by a red ribbon with blue edges from a mural coronet ar. the whole within a border crenellée of the last. *Crest*—Out of the battlements of a tower ar. a demi lion erminois, grasping in both paws a battle axe, blade and handle ar. spearhead or. *Supporters*—Two eagles sa. that on the dexter gorged with a chaplet of laurel or, suspended therefrom the medal, as in the arms; that on the sinister collared or, with the ribbon and medal of Waterloo pendent. *Motto* —Promptus.

Kempthorne (Morestow, co. Cornwall). Ar. a chev. betw. three bears' heads couped and bendways sa. muzzled or.

Kempthorne (co. Cornwall). Ar. three pine trees ppr.

Kempthorne (Ven. RICHARD KEMPTHORNE, M.A., Rector

of Elton, co. Hunts, formerly Archdeacon of St. Helena).
Same *Arms*. *Crest*—A lion sejant.

Kempton (Morden, co Cambridge, and London; granted
1577). Az. a pelican, wings elevated, vulning her breast
betw. three fleurs-de-lis or. *Crest*—A goat erm. horns and
hoofs or, collared and lined sa. the collar charged with three
bezants, with a ring at the end of the line.

Kempton (co. Cambridge, Hadley, co. Middlesex, and London). Az. a fesse or, in chief three fleurs-de-lis of the
second *Crest*—Out of a ducal coronet or, a garb ar.

Kemyell (co. Cornwall). Ar. (another, or) three dolphins
naiant in pale sa.

Kemyng (co. Somerset). Erm. three crescents gu. *Crest*—
A unicorn's head sa. semée of plates.

Kemys. Vair three bars gu.

Kemyston. Ar. on a saltire sa. a cinquefoil in the dexter
chief of the first.

Kenah (granted to THOMAS KENAH, Esq., Lieut.-Col. 58th
Foot, C.B., and the other descendants of his grandfather,
WILLIAM KENAH, of Castle Martyr). Barry of eight per pale
indented ar. and gu. counterchanged three fleurs-de-lis two
and one az. on a chief vert betw. two bezants a representation of the badge of a military C.B. *Crest*—A horse's head
erased ar. charged on the neck with a fleur-de-lis az. *Motto*
—Fidelis.

Kenan (Dumfries, 1680). Per bend sa. and az. three bars
or. *Crest*—A lion ramp. az. *Motto*—Nostra quæ fecimus.

Kendall (co. Bedford). Ar. a bend vert, a label of three
points gu. (another, five points).

Kendall (Twicresse, co. Leicester and Smithsby, co. Derby;
HENRY KENDALL, Visit. Leicester, 1619, great-grandson of
WILLIAM KENDALL, eldest son of BARTHOLOMEW KENDALL, of
Twicresse, *temp.* Henry VII.). Gu. a fesse chequy or and
az. betw three eagles displ. of the second.

Kendall (Blaby, co. Leicester; HUMPHREY KENDALL, Visit.
Leicester, 1819, grandson of CHRISTOPHER KENDALL, second
son of above BARTHOLOMEW KENDALL). Same *Arms*, a
crescent for diff.

Kendall (Basingborne, co. Essex). Same *Arms*.

Kendall (Stourbridge, co. Worcester; arms on the tomb of
EDWARD KENDALL, *b.* 1684, in Oldswinford Churchyard).
Same *Arms*. *Crest*—An eagle displ. or (sometimes with two
heads).

Kendall (Austrey, co. Warwick; confirmed by the Deputies
of Camden, Clarenceux, to HENRY KENDALL, Esq., of Aldes-
trie, third in descent from JOHN KENDALL, a younger son of
KENDALL, of Smithsby). Same *Arms*.

Kendall (Pelyn, co. Cornwall: THOMAS KENDALL, Visit.
Cornwall, 1620, grandson of NICHOLAS KENDALL, of Pelyn;
LAWRENCE KENDALL, of Pelyn, was father of WALTER KEN-
DALL, of same, Inq. Post. Mort. 1 Edward VI., who had a
son and heir, NICHOLAS KENDALL, then aged 36 years). Ar.
a chev. betw. three dolphins naiant embowed sa. *Motto*—
Virtus depressa resurget.

Kendall (Medrose, co. Cornwall: descended from RICHARD
KENDALL, third son of NICHOLAS KENDALL, of Pelyn. Visit.
Cornwall, 1620). Same *Arms*.

Kendall (Treworgie, co. Cornwall; descended from Pelyn.
Visit. Cornwall, 1620). Same *Arms*.

Kendall (Kingsbridge and Exeter, co. Devon; GEORGE
KENDALL, Visit. Devon, 1620, great-grandson of THOMAS
KENDALL, of Treworgie). Same *Arms*, a crescent for
diff.

Kendall (co. Devon). Ar. a bend vert. *Crest*—A hand
holding a sheaf of arrows, points downward all ppr.

Kendall (Ripon, co. York). Per bend dancettée ar. and sa.

Kendall (Thorpthules, co. Durham, 1575; descended from a
younger son of KENDALL, of Ripon; granted 1666). Same
Arms, in the sinister canton a mullet gu. pierced of the
first. *Crest*—A wolf's head erased ar.

Kendall. Per chev. ermines and gu. three pelicans' heads
erased ar. vulning themselves, on a chief az. three fleurs-de-
lis or. *Crest*—A demi pelican ar. vulning herself ppr.

Kendall (Exeter). Ar. a chev. betw. three dolphins embowed sa. *Crest*—A lion statant, tail passed betw. his legs
and over his back gu.

Kendall (co. Hertford). Ar. a bend dancettée vert cotised
gu.

Kendall. Gu. seven annulets conjoined in pale ar.
(another, gu. a bend chequy ar. and az.; another, chequy sa.
and ar. a bend gu.; another, gu. a fesse counter-componée
or and az.; another, per fesse indented or and gu.;
another, ar. fretty gu. on a chief az. three escallops of the
first; another, ar. two bars gu. on a canton of the last a
lion pass. or; another, or, a cross vert.)

Kendiffe. Vert an ant ar.

Kendlemarsh, or Kendlemarch. Per fesse erm.

558

and ermines a lion ramp. counterchanged. *Crest*—Two
lions' gambs chevronways ermines, armed gu.

Kendolph (Wallingford, co. Berks). Gu. on a cross ar. five
horseshoes sa.

Kendrick (Reading, co. Berks). Erm. a lion ramp. sa.

Kendrick (Warrington, co. Lancaster). Same *Arms*.
Crest—On a sheaf of arrows a falcon jessed and belled all ppr.
Motto—Virtue is honour.

Kendrick (Suckley, co. Worcester). Ar. five palets sa.
Crest—A hawk's.head erased jessed and belled all ppr.

Kene (Starston, co. Norfolk). Ar. a talbot pass. sa. eared
and collared or, to the collar a ring of the second, on a
chief indented az. three crosses crosslet of the third. *Crest*—
A hind's head erased ar. gorged with a collar gu. charged
with three bezants, to the collar a ring or.

Kene (co. Suffolk). Ar. a talbot pass. sa. charged on the
shoulder with a trefoil slipped or, on a chief indented
az. three crosses crosslet of the third. *Crest*—A hind's
head erased ar. pellettée, charged with a trefoil or.

Kene (Ipswich, co. Suffolk). Az. a talbot pass. or, on a chief
ar. three crosses crosslet sa. *Crest*—A hind's head or,
pellettée.

Kene. Erm. a cross flory sa.

Kenell (co. Kent). Or, two chevronels gu. a canton of the
last.

Kenell. Barry nebulée (another, wavy) of six az. and ar.

Kenelworth. Gu. a bend betw. six estoiles ar.

Keneram, or Keveram. Or, a chief bendy of six ar.
and gu.

Kenerby. Per fesse or and gu. three lions pass. counterchanged. *Crest*—A wolfs head erased erm.

Keney, or Keny. Az. on a fesse betw. two chevronels or,
three eagles displ. gu.

Keniam. Sa. a chev. engr. or, betw. three crosses crosslet
ar.

Keningham, or Kenyngton. Sa. a pale betw. two
cinquefoils pierced ar.

Kenisham (Semford, co. Bedford; granted 14 Nov. 1570).
Per pale ar. and az. three cinquefoils counterchanged.
Crest—A greyhound's head couped az. charged on the neck
with three bars wavy as many guttées d'or.

Kenley (Drogheda; Reg. Ulster's Office). Ar. on a bend
sa. three escallops of the field.

Kenley Per bend indented (another, embattled) ar. and
sa.

Kenmare, Earl of. See BROWNE.

Kenmure, Viscount. See GORDON.

Kenn (Langford, co. Somerset). Erm. three crescents gu.
Crest—Three crescents interwoven ar.

Kennard (Hordle Cliff, co. Hants). Per chev. gu. and az.
a chev. engr. ar. betw. two keys in chief or, and a sword
erect in base ppr. pommelled and hilted gold. *Crest*—A cubit
arm erect in armour ppr. holding a key and broken sword
in saltire or. *Motto*—At spes non fracta.

Kennard. Or, a fesse gu. betw. three mullets az. *Crest*—
A lion's gamb erased vert.

Kennaway (Escot, co. Devon, bart.). Ar. a fesse az.
betw. two eagles displ. in chief, and in base, through an
annulet gu. a slip of olive and another of palm in saltire
ppr. *Crest*—An eagle rising ppr. from the beak an
escutcheon pendent az. charged with the sun in splendour
gold. *Motto*—Ascendam.

Kennaway. Ar. a fesse betw. three eagles displ. gu.
Crest—A phœnix ppr.

Kenne (Kenne, co. Somerset). *Ancient Coat*—Ar. three
crescents gu. *Crest*—Three crescents interlaced or. *Later.
Coat* (granted 1561)—Erm. three crescents gu. *Crest*—A
unicorn's head az. bezantée, maned or, horned of the last.
and sa.

Kenne (Hutton and Clevedon, co. Somerset). Same *Arms*
and *Crest*, a mullet for diff.

Kenne (co. Somerset, Reg. Ulster's Office). Same *Arms*
and *Crest*.

Kenne. Gu. a chev. betw. six crescents or.

Kenneday. Ar. on a fesse az. three mullets of the field.
Crest—An arm erect grasping a belt all ppr.

Kennedy (England). Sa. three esquires' helmets ar. *Crest*
—On a rock a goose ppr.

Kennedy. See O'KENNEDY, or O'CINNEIDIGH.

Kennedy (Tombrechan, co. Tipperary; Fun. Ent. JAMES
KENNEDY, son and heir of WILLIAM KENNEDY, grandson of
DONOGH KENNEDY, and great-grandson of RORY KENNEDY, all
of the same place, killed at Borris, co Tipperary, by Kean
O'Carroll, 14 May, 1640). Sa. three esquires' helmets ar.
garnished or. *Crest*—An arm erect couped below the elbow,
the hand holding an oak branch fructed all ppr.

Kennedy (HUGH KENNEDY, of Dublin, merchant, son of

Lawrence Kennedy. Visit. City of Dublin, 1607). Same *Arms. Crest*—A *d*emi eagle displ. sa. bezantée, holding in the bill a cross formée fitchée gu.

Kennedy (Robert Kennedy, Alderman of Dublin, son of the foregoing. Visit. Dublin, 1607). Same *Arms* and *Crest*, a mullet for diff.

Kennedy (Dublin; Fun Ent. 1595, Ulster's Office). Sa. a fleur-de-lis betw. three esquires helmets ar. garnished or.

Kennedy (confirmed by Molyneux, Ulster, 1628, to Robert Kennedy, Chief Chamberlain of the Exchequer in Ireland). Sa. an escallop or, betw. three helmets ar. garnished of the second. *Crest*—A naked hand holding a hon. betw. two oak leaves ppr.

Kennedy (Hill Foot, Ireland). Sa. on a fess ar. betw. three esquires' helmets close ppr. a greyhound courant ppr. *Crest*—An arm in armour embowed, the hand holding an oak branch acorned all ppr. *Motto*—Adhæreo virtuti.

Kennedy (Johnstown-Kennedy, co. Dublin, bart.; granted to John Kennedy, Esq., of Johnstown, co. Dublin). Sa. on a fess betw. three helmets close ar. a fox courant ppr. *Crest*—An armed arm embowed ppr. the hand grasping a branch of oak also ppr. fructed or. *Motto*—Adhæreo virtuti.

Kennedy (granted to George Crookshank Kennedy, Esq., of Londonderry). Ar. a chev. gu. betw. three crosses crosslet fitchée sa. *Crest*—A dolphin naiant ppr. *Motto*—Avise la fin.

Kennedy-Baillie. See Baillie.

Kennedy (Bargany and Ardstinchar, co. Ayr). Quarterly, 1st and 4th, ar. a chev. gu. betw. three cross crosslets fitchée sa., for Kennedy; 2nd and 3rd, az. three fleurs-de-lis or, the arms of France, borne for the aid given by Sir Hugh Kennedy in the French wars with England.

Kennedy (Kirkhill, representative of Bargany, 1678). Quarterly, as the last. *Crest*—A hand grasping a dagger ppr. *Motto*—Fuimus.

Kennedy (Bennane, co. Ayr, representative of Bargany, 1837). Quarterly, as the last. *Crest*—A fleur-de-lis or, issuing out of two oak leaves ppr. *Supporters*—Dexter, a lady attired in the costume of the 16th century; sinister, a wyvern, both ppr. *Motto*—Fuimus.

Kennedy (Clowburn, co. Ayr). Quarterly, 1st and 4th, ar. on a fesse az. three mullets of the first, for Weir; 2nd and 3rd, quarterly, 1st and 4th, ar. a chev. gu. betw. three cross crosslets fitchée sa. all within a double tressure flory counter-flory of the second, for Kennedy, 2nd and 3rd, France, as in the arms of Kennedy, of Bargany. *Crest*—A dexter hand holding a military girdle, on it the words " Vires veritas." *Motto*—Below the shield : Non fallo.

Kennedy (Auchtyfardell, co. Lanark, 1752). Ar. on a chev. gu. betw. three cross crosslets fitchée sa. a fleur-de-lis ar. *Crest*—A dexter hand holding a dagger ppr. *Motto*—Avise la fin.

Kennedy (*Earl of Cassilis*, and *Marquis of Ailsa*). Ar. a chev. gu. betw. three cross crosslets fitchée sa. all within a double tressure flory counterflory of the second. A dolphin naiant ppr. *Supporters*—Two swans ppr. beaked and membered gu. *Motto*—Avise la fin.

Kennedy (Blairquhan, co. Ayr). Quarterly, 1st and 4th, ar. a chev. gu. betw. three cross crosslets fitchée sa.; 2nd and 3rd, az. a lion ramp. ar. crowned or, for Macdowall.

Kennedy (Girvanmains, co. Ayr). Ar. on a chev. gu. betw. three crosses crosslet fitchée sa. a boar's head erased of the first, and in the middle chief point a man's heart of the second. *Crest*—A dolphin naiant ppr. *Motto*—Avise la fin.

Kennedy (Kirkmichael, co. Ayr). Ar. a chev. gu. betw. two crosses crosslet fitchée in chief, and a boar's head erased sa. in base. *Crest*—A palm branch slipped vert. *Motto*—Malim esse probus quam haberi.

Kennedy (Kirmucks, co. Aberdeen). Ar. two keys saltire-ways gu. and in base a cross crosslet fitchée sa.

Kennedy (Ardmillan, co. Ayr). Ar. a chev. ensigned with a man's heart gu. betw. three cross crosslets fitchée sa.

Kennedy (Col. Alex. Kennedy, C.B., K.C.H., 1839). Ar. a chev. gu. betw. three cross crosslets fitchée sa. and in middle chief point a fleur-de-lis az., and for an augmentation, on a chief erm. the representation of a French ensign and flag, with the inscription " L'Empereur Napoleon, au 105me Regiment," &c., thereon, and a sword displ. saltireways, and over the same the word "Waterloo." *Crests*—Dexter : A soldier of the 1st Royal Dragoons, holding in his right hand a sword ppr., and in his left a French eagle with a tricolored flag, having thereon the number 105; sinister: A dolphin az. *Motto*—Avise la fin.

Kennedy (Underwood, co. Ayr, 1850). Ar. on a chev. gu. betw. three cross crosslets fitchée sa. a mullet pierced betw. two lions counter-pass. or. *Crest*—A dolphin hauriant ppr. *Motto*—Vincit vim virtus.

559

Kennedy (Cultra, co. Down). Ar. a chev. gu. betw. three cross crosslets fitchée sa. within a double tressure flory counterflory of the second. *Crest*—A dolphin naiant ppr. *Motto*—Avise la fin.

Kennell. Barry wavy of eight az. and ar. *Crest*—Two lions' heads erased and endorsed, one or, the other gu.

Kennerley. Vert a fesse betw. two crosses pattée ar. *Crest*—A lion's gamb, holding a laurel branch ppr.

Kennet (Coventry, co. Warwick; granted by Dethick, Garter, to Sir Thomas Kennet, Alderman of Coventry). Ar. a chev. betw. three demi lions pass. az. ducally gorged and ringed or, tasselled of the first.

Kennet. Ar. a bend within a bordure engr. sa. *Crest*—Two branches of palm in orle.

Kennedy (Brackley Kennett, Esq., Lord Mayor of London, 1780). Quarterly, or and gu. a label of three points in chief sa. each point charged with three bezants in pale. *Crest*—Out of a ducal coronet or, an arm embowed in armour ppr. the hand in a gauntlet holding an esquire's helmet ppr.

Kennett (The Manor House, co. Oxford). Quarterly, 1st and 4th, or and gu. over all a label of three points sa., for Kennett; 2nd and 3rd, ar. three chevronels gu. a label of three points az., for Barrington. *Crest*—1st, Kennett: Out of a ducal coronet an arm embowed in armour, holding in the gauntlet a helmet erect all ppr.; 2nd, Barrington: A capuchin friar couped at the breast, black hair, vested paly or and gu. on the head a cowl hanging behind of the last. *Mottoes*—1st, Kennett: Audi alteram partem; 2nd, Barrington: Honesta quam splendida.

Kenney (marshalled for Nicholas Kenney, of Dublin, gent., by Narbon, Ulster, 6 March, 1571). Quarterly, 1st and 4th, per pale or and az. a fleur-de-lis betw. three crescents counterchanged, for Kenney; 2nd, quarterly, 1st and 4th, or, a cross engr. gu., 2nd and 3rd, per pale az. and gu. a lion ramp. erm., for Hassan; 3rd, ar. on a chev. sa. betw. three columbines az. stalked vert an estoile or, for Hay. *Crest*—A demi arm erect, vested gu. cuffed ar. the hand holding a roll of parchment all ppr.

Kenney (Fun. Ent. 1617, Edward Kenney, eldest son of Nicholas Kenney, Escheator). Per pale or and az. a fleur-de-lis counterchanged.

Kenney (Fun. Ent. 1599, the wife of John Young). Per pale or and az. a fleur-de-lis betw. three crescents, and a border all counterchanged.

Kenney (co. Wexford; Fun. Ent. 1682, Richard Kenney, Esq.). Per pale or and az. a fleur-de-lis betw. three crescents, all counterchanged.

Kenney (Kilclogher, co. Galway; Reg. Ulster's Office, 6 March, 1571, and confirmed to James Christopher Fitzgerald-Kenney, Esq., J.P., of that place, Clogher House, co. Mayo, and Merrion Square, Dublin, eldest surviving son and heir of Lieut.-Col. James Fitzgerald Kenney, J.P., of Kilclogher, &c., by his wife Jane Olivia Nugent, only sister of Anthony Francis, ninth *Earl of Westmeath*, and grandson of William Kenney, Esq., of Kilclogher, Keelogues, &c., co. Galway, Ballytarnsney, co. Wexford, and Longwood, co. Meath (direct descendant and representative of Nicholas Kenney, Esq., of Kenney's Hall, and Edermine, co. Wexford, a junior of Kenne, co. Somerset, Feodary General of all Ireland, *temp.* Queen Elizabeth and James I.), by Bridget Fitzgerald, his wife, dau. and heiress of John Daly, Esq., of Dalybrook, co. Kildare, and Julia, his wife, dau. and, in her issue, heiress of Gerald Fitzgerald, Esq., of Rathrone, co. Meath, by his wife Clare, only dau. of Sir John Bellew, Bart., of Bellewstown and Barmeath). Per pale or and az. a fleur-de-lis betw. three crescents all counterchanged, quartering Kenne (ancient), erm. three crescents gu. a fleur-de-lis az. for diff. *Crest*—Out of an earl's coronet or, (indicative of his representation of the Rathrone and Ticroghan lines of the noble house of Kildare), a cubit arm erect, vested gu. cuffed ar. the hand grasping a roll of parchment ppr. *Motto*—Teneat luceat floreat. This family also quarters the arms of Hay, Hassan, Kenney of Newcastle, Taylor of Swords, O'Kelly of Kilclogher, Daly of Dalybrook, Hope of Hopestown, Ledwich of Carrick and Grange, Fitzgerald of Rathrone, Fitzgerald of Ticroghan, and Carey of Fort Lester.

Kenney (confirmed to James Louis Lionel Kenney, Lieutenant in the Imperial Navy of France, and Knight of the Legion of Honour, and St. Stanilaus, of Russia, son of Thomas Henry Kenney, Esq., of Ballyforan, co. Roscommon, younger brother of Lieut.-Col. James Fitzgerald Kenney, of Kilclogher). Same *Arms, Crest*, and *Motto*.

Kenney-Herbert. See Herbert.

Kenny. See Kingsmill.

Kenning, or Kennings (co. Norfolk). Az. a fesse engr. betw. three escallops ar.

Kenning (co. Northumberland). Az. a fesse betw. three escallops ar. *Crest*—A yew tree growing out of a mount semée of trefoils ppr.

Kennion (Liverpool, co. Lancaster). Sa. a chev. engr. erm. betw. in chief two crosses patonce, and in base an anchor erect or. *Crest*—A demi lion ramp. ppr. holding in the paws an anchor erect or. *Mottoes*—Ventis secundis; and, Deo juvante.

Kennis. Barry of six vair and gu.

Kenny. Ar. on a saltire purp. five hearts or. *Crest*—A demi lion ramp. guard. holding a fleur-de-lis or.

Kenrick (Lord Mayor of London, 1652). Erm. a lion ramp. sa. *Crest*—On a sheaf of arrows fesseways or, feathered and headed ar. a hawk close also ar. beaked and belled gold. *Another Crest*—Three arrows, one in pale and two in saltire, bound with a ribbon ppr. thereon a hawk statant sa.

Kenrick (Whitley, co. Berks, bart., extinct in 1699). Same *Arms* and *Crest*.

Kenrick (Stock and Bradley, co. Worcester). Same *Arms* and *Crest*.

Kenrick (Sutton, co. Northants). Same *Arms* and *Crest*.

Kenrick (co. Lancaster). Same *Arms* and *Crest*.

Kenrick (co. Surrey; descended from the marriage of EDWARD KENRICK, Esq., with SUSANNAH CRANMER, grandniece of Archbishop CRANMER). Same *Arms*, &c. *Motto*—Virtue is honour.

Kenrick (Woore Manor, co. Salop). Same *Arms*. *Crest*—A sparrowhawk ar. standing on five arrows or.

Kensey (co. Hertford). Erm. on a bend gu. cotised az. three escallops ar. *Crest*—A demi griffin erased erm. holding betw. the paws a mullet or.

Kensing. Ar. a chev. betw. three squirrels sejant gu. cracking nuts or. *Crest*—A stag springing ppr.

Kensington, Baron. See EDWARDS.

Kensington. Gu. five crescents in saltire or. *Crest*—Out of a ducal coronet a demi eagle displ. ppr.

Kensit (THOMAS GLOVER KENSIT, Esq., of Skinner's Hall, London). Per chev. or and erm. on a chev. az. betw. a lion pass. guard. in chief and the Roman fasces erect in base ppr. three fleurs-de-lis of the first. *Crest*—The Roman fasces fesseways ppr. thereon an eagle rising reguard. or, holding in the mouth a tilting spear, resting on the fasces in bend sinister also ppr.

Kent-Egleton (Fornam St. Genevieve, co. Suffolk, bart., extinct 1848). Gu. three roses erm. *Crest*—A lion's head erased or, collared gu.

Kent (Thatcham, co. Berks). Az. a lion pass. guard. or, a chief erm. *Crest*—A lion's head erased erminois, collared, lined, and ringed az. *Another Crest*—A lion's head erased or, collared and armed sa.

Kent (cos. Berks, Gloucester, Lincoln, and Warwick, Duvis, co. Wilts, and co. York; granted by Richard St. George). Same *Arms* and *Crests*.

Kent (cos. Suffolk and Wilts). Gu. three cinquefoils erm.

Kent. Quarterly, gu. and or, on a label of three points sa. nine bezants.

Kent. Per fesse or and sa. a pale and three water bougets counterchanged (another, ar. a fesse gu.; another, gu. a chief ar.).

Kent (Daneston; BARTHOLOMEW KENT, Esq., of that place; Fun. Ent. of his wife, Ulster's Office, 1621). Sa. three lions pass. guard. two and one ar.

Kent (Reg. Ulster's Office). Gu. three cinquefoils pierced erm.

Kentbury. Sa. a chev. betw. three eagles displ. or.

Kenthorpe. Ar. a fesse betw. three escallops gu.

Kentish, Kentishbey, Kentlesber, or Kentisbury (co. Somerset). Gu. a pair of wings conjoined ar. over all a bendlet az. *Crest*—A demi ostrich, wings endorsed sa. holding in the beak a horseshoe or.

Kenton (Kenton Hall, co. Suffolk). Sa. two bars, in chief th ee cinquefoils or.

Kenton. Ar. a fret az. over all on a fesse gu. three mullets or. *Crest*—A dexter hand couped fesseways gu. holding a fleur-de-lis or.

Kenton. Same *Arms*. *Crest*—On a chapeau gu. turned up or, a lion pass. guard. ar. ducally crowned or.

Kenton. Sa. a chev. betw. three cinquefoils or.

Kentwood (co. Berks). Ar. (another, or) on a bend betw. six (another, three) crosses crosslet fitchée sa. three cinquefoils or.

Kentwood. Or, on a bend betw. three crosses pattée fitchée at the foot sa. as many cinquefoils of the first.

Kenward (Yalding, co. Kent). Az. on a bend or, betw. three crosses crosslet fitchée ar. as many roses gu.

Kenwick. Gu. on a bend engr. ar. three roses of the field.

Kenwick. Ar. three martlets gu. on a chief of the second as many martlets of the first. *Crest*—An arm in armour, holding up an esquire's helmet all ppr.

Kenworthy. Ar. a fesse counter-componée or and gu. betw. three eagles displ. sa.

Kenwricke. See KENRICK.

Kenyam. Sa. a chev. engr. or, betw. three crosses patonce ar.

Kenyon (Lord Kenyon). Sa. a chev. engr. or, betw. three crosses flory ar. *Crest*—A lion sejant ppr. resting the dexter paw on a cross flory ar. *Supporter*.—Dexter, a female figure representing Truth, vested ar. her head irradiated, on her breast a sun, and in her dexter hand a mirror, all ppr.; sinister, Fortitude, represented by a female figure, vested in a corslet of mail, robe or, sash gu. on her head a casque plumed, in her dexter hand a branch of oak, and her sinister arm resting on a pillar ppr. *Motto*—Magnanimiter crucem sustine.

Kenyon. Sa. a cross lozengy ar. over all a bend gobonated or and gu. *Crest*—On a rock a dove and olive branch all ppr.

Kenyon (Peele, co. Lancaster, 1664). Sa. a chev. engr. or, betw. three crosses patonce ar.

Kenyon (Easthall, co. Oxford, and London; WILLIAM KENYON, Visit. Oxon, 1634, son of THOMAS KENYON, of London). Sa. a cross lozengy ar. in sinister chief an eagle displ. of the last. *Crest*—A demi lion ramp. ppr. holding a halbert gu. headed or.

Keogh (Kilbride, co. Carlow). Ar. a lion ramp. gu. betw. a dexter hand apaumée in the dexter, and a crescent in the sinister chief point, both of the second. *Crest*—A boar pass. ppr. *Motto*—Resistite usque ad sanguinem.

Keogh (Ireland). See MACKEOGH.

Keppel (Earl of Albemarle). Gu. three escallop shells ar. *Crest*—Out of a ducal coronet or, a swan's head and neck ar. *Supporters*—Two lions ducally crowned or. *Motto*—Ne cede malis.

Keppel (Viscount Keppel, of Elvedon, extinct 1786; Hon. ARTHUR KEPPEL, second son of WILLIAM, second Earl of Albemarle, was so created 1782, d. unm.). Same *Arms*, &c., a crescent for diff.

Keppoke (Reg. Ulster's Office). Ar. on a chev. sa. betw. three escallops az. five martlets or, on a chief of the third three crosses formée of the fourth.

Keppyng. Lozengy or and az. on a chief gu. a lion pass. or, betw. two bezants, each charged with a fleur-de-lis of the second.

Kepwith (co. Warwick). Ar. three bars gu. in chief a greyhound courant sa. collared or.

Ker (Cessford, co. Roxburgh, sixteenth century). Az. on a chev. ar. three mullets sa., sometimes quartered with gu. three mascles or, probably for ST. MICHAEL.

Ker (Duke of Roxburghe). Quarterly, 1st and 4th, vert on a chev. betw. three unicorns' heads erased ar. armed and maned or, as many mullets sa., for KER; 2nd and 3rd, gu. three mascles or. *Crest*—A unicorn's head erased ar. armed and maned or. *Supporters*—Two savages wreathed about the head and waist with oak leaves, each holding with the exterior hand a club resting upon the shoulder all ppr. *Motto*—Pro Christo et patriâ dulce periculum.

Ker (Earl of Ker, extinct 1804; ROBERT, second Duke of Roxburgh, was raised to the Peerage of England in this title, vita patris: his successor, JOHN, second Earl and third Duke, d. unm.). Same *Arms*, *Crest*, *Supporters*, and *Motto*.

Ker (Earl of Lothian, of the Cessford branch). Quarterly, 1st and 4th, az. the sun in his splendour ppr., as a coat of augmentation; 2nd and 3rd, per fesse gu. and vert, on a chev. betw. three mascles in chief or, and a unicorn's head erased in base ar. as many mullets of the field. *Crest*—A sun, as in the arms. *Supporters*—Two angels ppr.

Ker (Faldonside, co. Roxburgh). Quarterly, 1st and 4th, vert on a chev. ar. betw. three unicorns' heads erased of the last as many stars gu.; 2nd and 3rd, or on a bend az. three mascles of the first, for HALYBURTON.

Ker (Littledean, co. Roxburgh). Quarterly, 1st and 4th, vert on a chev. ar. three mullets gu. in base a unicorn's head erased of the second; 2nd and 3rd, az. three crosses moline ar., for AINSLIE, of Dolphington.

Ker (Moristoun, co. Roxburgh). Quarterly, as Littledean, within a bordure ar. *Crest*—A unicorn's head couped ar. collared az. charged with three crosses moline of the first. *Motto*—Dulce pro patria periculum.

Ker (Greenhead, co. Roxburgh bart., 1637). Gu. on a chev. ar. three mullets of the first, a buck's head erased in base, in chief a crescent of the second.

Ker (Chatto, co. Roxburgh). As Greenhead, within a bordure az. *Crest*—The sun ppr. *Motto*—Regulier et vigoureux.

SCOTT-KERR, of Chatto, the heir of line, quarters this coat with, or, on a bend az. a star of six points betw. two crescents of the field, in the sinister chief a rose gu. stalked and barbed ppr. surmounted of a martlet ar. *Crest*—For SCOTT: A stag trippant armed with ten tynes ppr. *Motto*—Pacem amo.

Ker (Sheriff Clerk of Linlithgow, 1672). Vert on a chev. embattled betw. a unicorn's head erased in chief and a stag's head couped in base ar. three mullets sa. *Crest*—A pelican volant ppr. *Motto*—Deus meum solamen.

Ker (Ferniehurst, ço. Roxburgh, sixteenth century). Az. on a chev. ar. three mullets sa. in base a stag's head erased or.

Ker (*Lord Jedburgh*). Gu. on a chev. ar. three mullets of the first. *Crest*—A stag's head erased or. *Supporters*—Two stags ppr. *Motto*—Forward.

Ker (*Earl of Ancrum*). Quarterly, 1st and 4th, erm. on a chief per pale ar. and gu. a lion pass. counterchanged; 2nd and 3rd, gu. on a chev. ar. three mullets of the first. *Crest*—A stag's head and neck couped ar. collared gu. charged with three mullets of the first issuing out of an open crown or. *Supporters*—Two stags ppr. collared as the crest. *Motto*—Tout droit.

Ker (*Marquess of Lothian*). Quarterly, 1st and 4th, az. the sun in splendour ppr., a coat of augmentation for the title of LOTHIAN; 2nd and 3rd, gu. on a chev. ar. three mullets of the field, for KER. *Crest*—The sun, as in the arms. *Supporters*—Dexter, an angel ppr. vested az. surcoat vert, winged and crined or; sinister, a unicorn ar. armed, maned, and unguled or, gorged with a collar gu. charged with three mullets ar. *Motto*—Sero sed serio.

Ker (Abbotrule, co. Roxburgh). Same *Arms* as the *Marquess of Lothian*, with a unicorn's head erased ppr. in the centre of the quarters for diff. *Crest*—The sun rising out of a cloud ppr. *Motto*—J'avance.

Ker (Feniclee, co. Selkirk). Vert on a chev. ar. three stars gu. and in base a pelican vulning herself or.

Ker (Zair, afterwards Sunderland Hall, co. Roxburgh). Gu. on a chev. ar. three stars of the first, in base a stag's head erased or, guttée de sang ppr. all within a bordure invecked of the second. *Crest*—A dexter hand holding a dagger ppr. *Motto*—Abest timor.

Ker (Knock, co. Banff, afterwards Blackshiells, co. Haddington). Vert on a chev. betw. two holly leaves in chief ppr. and a unicorn's head erased of the second attired, or in base, three mullets gu. *Crest*—A unicorn's head erased ar. *Motto*—Virescit in arduis virtus.

Ker (Samuelstoun, co. Roxburgh). Ar. a unicorn saliant sa. horned or.

Ker (*Viscount of Rochester* and *Earl Somerset*). See CARR.

Ker (Cavers). See CARRE.

Ker (Mantalto, co. Down). Vert on a chev. ar. three mullets sa. *Crest*—A unicorn's head erased ar. armed and maned or.

Kerby. Ar. on a fesse gu. three crosses crosslet or. *Crest*—A hand in armour holding a pheon ppr.

Kerby. Ar. on a fesse vert three crosses pattée or.

Kercher (co. Norfolk; confirmed April, 1606, by Camden, Clarenceux). Or, three crosses crosslet az. on a chief of the last as many bezants. *Crest*—A cross botonnée az. betw. two wings inverted saltireways or.

Kercher (co. Norfolk, KERCHER of the North). Ar. three crosses crosslet sa. on a chief az. as many bezants.

Kerchinall (Parwell, co. Northampton). Gu. three horses courant ar. *Crest*—A demi bay horse ppr. armed and bridled gold, on his head three feathers az., or, and ar.

Kerchivall (Nether Dunsforth, co. York, and Orston, co. Nottingham; descended from JOHN KERTCHIVALL, Master of the Horse to Anne of Bohemia, wife of Richard II.). Sa. three horses courant ar. maned or. *Crest*—A demi horse of a roan colour in complete armour ppr. studded and bridled or, having upon the head a plume of feathers of divers colours.

Kercy, or Kersey. Ar. guttée de poix a saltire gu. *Crest*—A boar's head couped or.

Kercy. Gu. on a chief ar. a crescent of the first.

Kerdeston (*Baron Kerdeston; ROBERT DE KERDESTON* was summoned to Parliament 1332-37, in abeyance *temp.* Edward III.). Gu. a saltire engr. ar.

Kerdeston (cos. Norfolk and Suffolk, *temp.* Edward I.). Gu. a saltire engr. ar.

Kerdiff (Reg. Ulster's Office). Ar. a chev. betw. three escallops sa.

Kerdiffe (Fun. Ent. Ulster's Office, 1609, NICHOLAS KERDIFFE, Serjeant-at-Law). Ar. three blackamoors' heads in profile couped sa.

Kerdiffe. Az. a fesse or. *Crest*—A hind sejant reguard. rising ppr. the dexter foot on a mount vert.

Kerdiffe. Az. a fesse betw. six mullets (another, martlets) or. *Crest*—Out of a tower ppr. a lion ramp. or.

Kerdiffe. Ar. a chev. betw. three door-staples sa.

Kerdiston (co. Norfolk). Gu. a saltire engr. ar. (another, or). *Crest*—Out of a tower a demi griffin ppr. *Another Crest*—A dexter hand apaumée couped fesseways ppr.

Keresforth (Keresforth, co. York). Az. two millrinds fesseways in pale ar. *Crest*—A demi lion ramp. gu. holding in the paws a millrind paleways ar.

Keresforth. Ar. a fesse embattled sa. betw. three butter-flies gu.

Kerey, or Kercey. Ar. a saltire gu. betw. twelve guttées sa.

Keriell, and Kerioll. See CRIOLL.

Kerifford (Reg. Ulster's Office). Ar. a fess embattled sa. betw. three butterflies gu. *Crest*—A demi lion ramp. sa. holding betw. the paws a cross moline or.

Kerkbonell. Ar. a chev. betw. three crosses crosslet sa.

Kerkbride, or Kerkbrigg. Ar. a saltire engr. vert.

Kerkby (Reg. Ulster's Office). Ar. a cross gu. a border sa.

Kerkeby. Sa. two lions pass. or.

Kerkele. Gu. two bars or, in chief three keys ar. wards upward.

Kerle. See KYRLE.

Kernaby. Ar. a demi lion ramp. az. a canton of the last. *Crest*—A cubit arm ppr. holding a crescent sa.

Kernby, or Kernaby. Ar. two bars az. in chief three hurts.

Kerne (Truro, co. Cornwall). Sa. a saltire couped and crossed ar. betw. four crescents or. *Crest*—On a mount vert a grey-hound courant per pale or and ar. collared gu.

Kerne. Vert six doves ar. three, two, and one.

Kerne. Ar. a chev. betw. three lobsters' claws gu.

Kerney. Vert on a chev. ar. three pheons sa. *Crest*—A unicorn sejant sa. armed and maned or.

Ker (Northampton, 1787). Gu. on a chev. betw. a fleur-de-lis in chief and a martlet in base ar. three mullets of the first. *Crest*—A stag's head erased or. *Motto*—Deus solamen.

Kerr (Col. JAMES KERR, E.I.C.S., 1806). Same *Arms*, with the chev. embattled. Same *Crest* and *Motto*.

Kerr (Bughtrigg, co. Roxburgh, 1787). Gu. on a chev. ar. three mullets of the field, all within a bordure of the second. *Crest*—The sun in splendour ppr. *Motto*—A Deo lumen.

Kerr (Gallowhill, co. Renfrew, 1867). Gu. on a chev. ar. two mullets az. in base a fusil of the second. *Crest*—A stag's head erased ppr. *Motto*—Ingenio ac labore.

Kerrich (Geldeston Hall, co. Suffolk, a family of considerable antiquity, the name appearing in the rolls of the borough of Dunwich. co. Suffolk, as early as 1581; JOHN KERRICHE was M.P. for the borough at Westminster, 2 Edward II., 1308). *Arms* (granted 17 June, 1630, to Capt. KERRICH, a distinguished diplomatist in the reign of Charles I.)—Sa. on a pile ar. a galtrap of the first. *Crest*—On a mount ppr. a galtrap sa. *Motto*—Nunquam non paratus.

Kerrison (Breccles, co. Norfolk). Or, on a pile az. three galtraps of the field. *Crest*—On a mount vert a tiger pass. ppr. collared and lined or, the dexter forepaw resting on a galtrap, as in the arms. *Motto*—Rien sans Dieu.

Kerrison (Hoxne and Brome, co. Suffolk, bart.). Or, on a pile az. three galtraps of the field; the augmentation following: out of a crest embattled erm. a wreath of laurel encircling a sword erect ppr. pommel and hilt gold, betw. on the dexter, pendent from a ribbon gu. fimbriated az. a representation of the gold medal presented to Sir EDWARD KERRISON for his services at the battle of Orthes, beneath it the word "Orthes" in letters sa., and on the sinister, pendent from the like ribbon, a representation of the silver medal presented to him in commemoration of his services at the battle of Waterloo, beneath it the word "Waterloo" in letters sa. *Crests*—1st, of augmentation: Out of a mural crown or, a dexter arm embowed in armour, entwined by a branch of laurel, holding in the hand a flagstaff ppr. therefrom flowing a banner forked gu. fringed or, inscribed "Peninsula" in letters gold; 2nd: Upon a mount vert a tiger pass. ppr. collared and lined or, the dexter forepaw resting upon a galtrap, as in the arms. *Supporters*—Dexter, a horse sa. caparisoned, thereon mounted a hussar of the 7th regiment; sinister, a bay horse caparisoned, thereon mounted a dragoon of the 14th regiment, both habited and armed, their swords drawn all ppr. *Motto*—Rien sans Dieu.

Kerrison (Birkfield Lodge, Ipswich, co. Suffolk; exemplified by and registered in the Herald's Coll., dated 12 Aug. 1806.) Quarterly, gu. and sa. a lion ramp. betw. three annulets or, for Sir ROGER KERRISON and his descendants; and for Dame

Mary Ann Kerrison and her descendants, quarterly, or and sa. on a bend inverted gu. three foxes' heads erased ar. *Crest* —A bundle of sugar canes ppr. thereon a dove ar. wings or, in the beak an olive branch ppr.

Kerry (Binweston and Wortham, co. Salop). Per saltire erm. and az. *Crest*—A beehive sa. with bees volant or.

Kerry, Earl of. See Fitz-Maurice, *Marquess of Lands-downe.*

Kerryll. Ar. a bend gu. and a canton sa. *Crest*—A lion ramp. gu. holding a sword in pale ppr.

Kersa. Gu. a chief ar.

Kershaw (Savile Green, co. York; granted to William Kershaw, Esq.). Ar. three crosses crosslet sa. on a chief az. three bezants, the centre one charged with a cross gu. *Crest*— The stump of an oak eradicated and sprouting fesseways ppr. thereon a pheasant, in the beak a sprig of oak also ppr.

Kershaw. Gu. a chev. erm. betw. three cinquefoils or, stalked and leaved vert. *Crest*—A ram pass. ppr.

Kershaw. Gu. a sword in pale ar. hilt and pommel or, in base a serpent nowed vert, on a chief of the third three martlets sa.

Kershaw (Heskin Hall, co. Lancaster). Ar. three crosses crosslet sa. on a chief az. as many bezants. *Crest*—A pheasant ppr.

Kerslake (Barmer Hall, co. Norfolk). Ar. a mullet vert pierced of the field betw. three trefoils of the second. *Crest* —On the stump of a tree, with one branch sprouting therefrom, a falcon close all ppr. *Motto*—Ad fincm fidelis.

Kersteman (Canewdon; this family came into England from Upres, in the Netherlands, 1564-66). Az. three fishes naiant in pale or. *Crest*—A demi man affrontée in armour ppr. vizor up, plumed ar. holding in the dexter hand an arrow palewise or, barbed and flighted az.

Kervill (King's Lynn, co. Norfolk). Gu. three leopards' faces reversed or, jessant-de-lis sa.

Kervill, or Carvill (co. Norfolk). Gu. a chev. or, betw. three lions' faces ar.

Kervyle (Wallington, co. Norfolk). Gu. three leopards' faces ar. jessant-de-lis sa. *Crest*—Two lion's gambs erect ar. holding betw. their claws a cone reversed gu.

Kervyle (Wiggenhall, co. Norfolk). Gu. a chev. or, betw. three leopards' faces ar. *Crest*—A goat pass. sa. attired and bearded or.

Keryell (co. Kent). Ar. a bend and sinister canton gu. *Crest*—An arm in armour embowed, couped at the shoulder, the part above the elbow in fesse, resting on the wreath, the hand in pale holding a close helmet all ppr.

Kerysae (Reg. Ulster's Office). Ar. a boar pass. sa. tusked, bristled, and hoofed or.

Kesackes. Per pale or and az. a fesse counterchanged.

Kesakes, and Kesale. Same *Arms.*

Kessall, or Kessell. Ar. five lozenges in cross gu.

Kestell (Kestell, in Egloshayle, co. Cornwall; traceable to the time of King John). Ar. a chev. sa. betw. three falcons rising or. *Crest*—A tower ar.

Kestell (Kestell, in Manaccan, co. Cornwall; the heiresses *m.* Langford and Penrose). Or, three castles gu. *Crest*— A demi bull erm. attired, unguled, collared, and lined sa.

Kestell (Pendevy, Bokedock, Bodman, Boturnell, and formerly of Kestell, al' in co. Cornwall; Thomas Kestell, Esq., of Pendevy. Visi/ Cornwall 1620, descended from Peter Kestell, of Kest/ t, temp. Edward I., son and heir of John Kestell, Lord o' Kestell, to whom his father, William Kestell, made a deed of Kestell sealed with the arms of the family). Ar. a chev. sa. betw. three falcons close ppr.

Keston. Az. a fesse erm. betw. three leopards' faces per pale or and ar.

Ketching. Ar. on a chev. gu. betw. three cormorants sa. as many bezants.

Kete (St. Colomb, co. Cornwall; Ralph Kete, Visit. Cornwall, 1620, son of Ralph Kete, of Whaddon, near Salisbury, co. Wilts, and grandson of William Kete, of Hugborne, co. Berks). Ar. three cats pass. in pale sa.

Kete (confirmed as the arms of Kete, co. Warwick). Ar. billettée vert three torteaux, two and one.

Ketelby. Az. a saltire embattled counter-embattled betw. four martlets ar.

Keteridge (London; granted 1593). Sa. a lion ramp. or. *Crest*—Out of a mural coronet a lion's head or.

Keterton. Ar. a chev. betw. three cinquefoils sa.

Ketford (co. Gloucester). Gu. a chev. betw. three bulls' heads ar. attired or.

Ketford. Gu. on a chev. ar. three mullets of the first, in chief two bucks' heads erased of the second, attired or. *Crest*—A stag's head erased affrontée, as in the arms.

Ketford. Gu. on a chev. or. betw. two bucks' heads erased

---

ar. in chief and a cat pass. in base or, as many mulletr pierced of the first.

Kethall. Paly of six gu. and ar. a chief az.

Kethe. Ar. on a chief gu. three palets or.

Ketsford. Ar. a bend lozengy sa.

Ketson (co. Lancaster and London). Sa. three fishes haurient ar. on a chief or, a lion ramp. gu. betw. two pellets, each charged with an anchor of the third.

Ketson (London). Sa. three fishes haurient ar. on a chief or, a pellet charged with an anchor of the third betw. two torteaux.

Ketson. Sa. three fishes haurient ar. on a chief or, as many pellets. *Crest*—A lion's head erased, in the mouth a trefoil slipped all ppr.

Kett (Brooke House and Suthing Hall, co. Norfolk, where the family has been established as landed proprietors since the time of King John). Or, on a fesse betw. three leopards' heads erased and cabossed az. a lion pass. guard. ar. *Crest*—A leopard's head erased, as in the arms.

Kett (Kellsall, co. Suffolk; granted 1756). Or, a lion ramp. guard. gu. betw. three leopards' heads erased and cabossed sa. *Crest*—On a mount vert a peacock ppr. *Motto*—Rara avis in terris.

Kettell (co. Chester. Har. MSS. 1535). Ar. a boar pass. sa. betw. three trefoils vert.

Kettelby. Az. a saltire embattled counter-embattled betw. four birds ar. *Crest*—A lion's head erased gu. in the mouth an arrow az. feathered ar.

Kettle (London). Az. a bend betw. two bucks' heads erased or. *Crest*—A bundle of five arrows ppr. buckled or, banded gu.

Kettle (Dallicott House, Claverly, co. Salop; borne by George McKenzie Kettle, Esq., *m.* Elizabeth, only sister and sole heiress of the late Thomas W. J. Grazebrook, Esq., of Dallicott). Az. on a fesse erm. betw. two bucks' heads erased in chief and a lion pass. in base or, three cinquefoils gu.; on an escutcheon of pretence, the arms of Grazebrook, quartering Wilkes, Smith, and Grosvenor. *Crest*—A reindeer's head erased ppr. collared and chained or. *Motto*—Bono vince malum.

Kettleby (cos. Gloucester and Lincoln, and Steple, co. Salop). Ar. two chev. sa. a file of three points gu. *Crest*— A lion's head erased gu.

Kettleby (Steeple, co. Salop. Add. MSS.). Same *Arms.*

Kettleby. Az. a saltire raguly betw. four martlets ar. (another or).

Ketton. Ar. three leopards' faces sa. *Crest*—A boar's head couped in fesse betw. two branches of laurel disposed in orle ppr.

Ketton. Az. six garbs or, three, two, and one.

Ketyn. Ar. a saltire gu. betw. four leaves vert.

Keux. Az. two keys barways in pale, the ward of the one in chief to the dexter, and that in base to the sinister ar. *Crest* —A mound crossed and banded ppr.

Kevelioc, or Keveliok. Az. six garbs or, three, two, and one.

Kevell. Ar. a fesse flory sa.

Keverdale (co. Lancaster). Quarterly, ar. and sa. four leopards' faces counterchanged.

Keverdon (Keverdon, co. Lancaster). Per bend sinister az. and or, a griffin segreant counterchanged, within a bordure engr. and gobonated ar. and sa. *Crest*—A buck's head per pale ar. and az. attired counterchanged.

Keverell (Keverell, co. Cornwall). Sa. two lions pass. in pale or.

Keverell (co. Warwick). Ar. a chev. sa. betw. three mullets gu.

Kevermond. Gu. an eagle displ. or.

Kevett (Coventry, co. Warwick; granted 1558). Ar. a chev. betw. three demi lions ramp. purp. *Crest*—A demi lion ramp. purp. murally gorged ar. lined and ringed or.

Kevill. Sa. a chev. or, on a chief of the third three mullets gu.

Kew (co. York). Az. six garbs or, three, two, and one. *Crest*—A demi lion or, holding betw. the paws a garb az.

Kextmell. Ar. a leopard's face betw. three mullets gu.

Key (Thornbury, co. Gloucester, bart.). Per chev. dovetailed ermines and gu. three keys erect, the wards upwards and to the sinister or. *Crest*—A mount vert, thereon a hart lodged full-faced ppr. charged on the body with three mullets fesseways ar. *Motto*—In Domino confido.

Key. Ar. two bends sa. *Crest*—A greyhound's head ar. charged with three roundles sa.

Key. Sa. a chev. flory at the point ar.

Keybell. Barry nebulée of six ar. and sa. a canton erm. (another, gu.).

Keydesby. Sa. a fesse ar. betw. two chev. or.

Keye (Milcomb, co. Oxford; granted 1688). Ar. two bendlets humettée purp. *Crest*—A griffin's head couped at the breast, wings endorsed ar. holding in the beak a key or.

Keyes (co. Kent). Gu. a chev. erm. three leopards' faces ar. (another, or). *Crest*—A griffin's head betw. two wings, holding a palm branch ppr.

Keyes (Cavanacor, co. Donegal; granted to THOMAS JOHN HUDLESTON KEYES, Esq., Major Madras Army, and CHARLES PATTON KEYES, Esq., C.B., Lieut.-Col. Madras Staff Corps, only surviving sons of THOMAS KEYES, Esq., Asst. Surg. Madras Army, by MARY ANNE, his wife, dau. of WILLIAM PATTON, Esq., of Croghan, cq. Donegal). Per chev. gu. and sa. three keys or, the wards of the two in chief facing each other, and of the one in base to the sinister, on a canton ar. a lion ramp. of the first. *Crest*—An open hand couped at the wrist ppr. holding betw. the forefinger and thumb a key or. *Motto*—Virtute adepta.

Keyfield. Gu. a fleur-de-lis erm.

Keyle. Or, on two bars sa. six martlets ar. betw. three billets longways gu. *Crest*—A woman's head and shoulders az. face ppr. hair dishevelled, and chaplet on the head or.

Keymer (Chelborough, co. Dorset). Ar. three wolves courant in pale az. a bordure of the last.

Keymer. Ar. three wolves courant in pale az. a bordure of the last. *Crest*—An ass pass. ppr.

Keyne (Cretingham, co. Suffolk). Ar. a talbot pass. sa. ears and collar or.

Keyne (Rowlesby, co. Norfolk). Same *Arms*, a crescent for diff.

Keyne (co. Suffolk). Ar. a talbot pass. sa. eared and collared ar. on a chief indented az. three crosses crosslet of the third (another, three crosses botonnée). *Crest*—Six arrows in saltire ppr. feathered ar. barbed or, tied with a ribbon sa.

Keynes, or Keyneto (Tarent, co. Dorset, temp. Henry I.). Vair three bars gu.

Keynes (Milton Keynes, co. Bucks). Same *Arms*.

Keynes, or Keignes. Gu. bezantée, a chief erm. *Crest* —A cross crosslet fitchée gu. betw. two palm branches vert.

Keynes, or Keignes. Az. bezantée, a chief erm. *Crest*—A talbot pass. sa. collared ar.

Keynes, or Keignes (Winckley Keynes, co. Devon, temp. Henry II., removed into co. Somerset about 1600). Az. a bend wavy cotised ar.

Keynion (co. Lancaster). Sa. a chev. engr. or, betw. three crosses flory ar. *Crest*—A lion sejant ppr. resting the dexter paw on a cross flory ar.

Keyrs. Sa. a chev. ar.

Keys. Quarterly, or and az. four crescents counterchanged. *Crest*—Minerva's head ppr.

Keys (granted to Rev. ROGER KEYS, and THOMAS KEYS, his brother, who had been engaged in the works of Eton Coll., temp. Henry VI.). Per chev. gu. and sa. three keys or, the wards of the two in chief facing each other.

Keys (impalement Fun. Ent. Ulster's Office, 1622, HENRY STANIHURST, whose wife was SYBELL, dau. of Captain Keys). Sa. a chev. betw. three keys erect or, wards to the dexter.

Keys. Gu. a cross crosslet or.

Keyt (Ebrington, co. Gloucester, bart., extinct 1784; descended from WILLIAM KEYT, Esq., of Ebrington, High Sheriff of Worcester, 1632, whose grandson, JOHN KEYT, was created a baronet in 1660). Az. on a chev. betw. three kites' heads erased or, as many trefoils slipped gu. *Crest*—A kite's head erased or. The family of KEYT appear, however, to have borne the chev. uncharged, and thus the coat occurs on the monument of WILLIAM KEYT, of Ebrington, A.D. 1632.

Keyte (Chesselborne, co. Dorset, London, and co. Worcester). Same *Arms*. *Crest*—A unicorn's head erased ar. armed and collared gu.

Kibble (Whiteford, co. Renfrew). Ar. two bars sa. in chief an eagle's head and neck couped ppr. on a canton gu. a crescent or. *Crest*—A demi eagle rising ppr. *Motto*—Illæso lumine solem.

Kibrow. Gu. a bend betw. two lions ramp. or.

Kichard. Or, billettée a lion ramp. az.

Kidd. Vert a saltire engr. erm. betw. four mullets of six points or, a chief paly of six ar. and az. *Crest*—Out of a crescent az. a pineapple ppr. *Motto*—Nil sine magno labore.

Kidd (co. Norfolk). Az. a fesse betw. three lozenges ar.

Kidd. Az. two goats saliant combatant ar. *Crest*—A martlet, wings endorsed ppr.

Kidd (Farnworth, co. Lancaster). Same *Arms*. *Crest*—A goat's head erased ar. attired or. *Motto*—Nil admirari.

Kidd (Scotland). See KYD.

Kiddall (co. Cornwall). Ar. a chev. betw. three dolphins sa.

Kiddall (South Ferreby, co. Lincoln). Sa. a saltire raguly

ar. *Crest*—A goat's head erased ar. ducally gorged, attired, and bearded or.

Kiddell, alias Benner (Camden, co. Gloucester). Paly of six or and gu. on a chief az. three lions ramp. of the first. *Crest*—A talbot's head ar. gorged with a collar az. studded and rimmed or.

Kidder (RICHARD KIDDER, Bishop of Bath and Wells, 1691-1703). Ar. a saltire embattled counter-embattled sa.

Kidder (Maresfield, co. Sussex, temp. Henry VII.). Vert three crescents or. *Crest*—A hand couped below the elbow, vested az. holding in the hand ppr. a packet, thereon the word "Standard."

Kidder (Aghaboe, Queen's co., co. Lancaster, and London; allowed by Betham, Deputy Ulster, 1811, to THOMAS KIDDER, Esq., then of London, son of THOMAS KIDDER, Esq., who settled in co. Lancaster, the grandson of VINCENT KIDDER, of Aghaboe, a Major in Oliver Cromwell's Army). Same *Arms*. *Crest*—An arm erect couped at the elbow, vested az. studded on the cuff or, the hand ppr. holding a sheet of paper, thereon the word "Standard." *Motto*—Boyne.

Kidderminster. Az. two chev. or, betw. three bezants. *Crest*—A greyhound's head ar. gorged with a fesse dancettée ar. charged with three bezants.

Kidley, alias Poynter (co. Devon). Gu. three pales or, on a chief of the second as many pellets. *Crest*—A turbot naiant az.

Kidney (London, and Market Harborough, co. Leicester; granted 1765). Az. on a chev. or, betw. two lambs in chief and a ram in base ar. three lambs' kidneys gu. *Crest*—On a mount vert an eagle reguard. rising ppr. in the beak a kidney, as in the arms.

Kidson (Bishopwearmouth, co. Durham). Sa. three salmon erect ar. two and one, a chief or. *Crest*—A unicorn's head ar. attired and maned or, environed with palisadoes gold. *Motto*—Pro rege et lege.

Kidston (Glasgow, 1871). Sa. three salmon hauriant ppr. in fess, on a chief or, three goats' heads erased of the first. *Crest*—A unicorn's head erased ar. *Motto*—Pro rege et lege.

Kidson. Ar. a chev. engr. betw. three leaves pendent.

Kidwall, or Kinwold. Ar. a mullet sa. over all a bend sinister gu.

Kidwall, or Kidwalley. Or, a fesse dancettée gu.

Kidwally. Az. a wolf ramp. ar. collared and chained gu.

Kidwell (Wales). Az. a wolf saliant or, collared az. bezantée. *Crest*—A peacock's head couped ppr.

Kiffin (co. Essex). Gu. a lion ramp. ar.

Kiffin (Knolyrante, co. Salop). Per fesse ar. and sa. a lion ramp. counterchanged. *Crest*—On a garland of laurel orleways a lion pass. ppr.

Kiffin (co. Salop). Ar. a chev. gu. betw. three pheons sa. two in chief, lying fesseways, point to point, and one in base erect.

Kiffin (Fun. Ent. 1597, MAURICE KIFFIN, Esq., Controller of the Musters in Ireland). Per fesse sa. and ar. a lion ramp. counterchanged.

Kift. Az. on a bend or, betw. two lions pass. ar. three escallops of the first. *Crest*—A lion's head erased, ducally crowned.

Kighley (cos. Chester and York). Ar. a fesse and bordure sa.

Kighley (Gray, co. Essex, and co. York). Ar. a fesse sa. *Crest*—A dragon's head couped (another, erased) sa.

Kighley (London; THOMAS KIGHLEY, whose dau. BRIDGET, m. HUMPHREY FAIRFAX, citizen of London, Visit. London, 1658, son of JOHN FAIRFAX, co. Lincoln, descended from co. York). Ar. a fess sa. in dexter chief an annulet gu.

Kighley, or Kightley (co. Lancaster, South Littleton, co. Worcester, and Keighley, co. York. Visits. 1569 and 1634). Ar. on a fesse sa. a mullet of the field. *Crest*—A dragon's head couped sa. (sometimes vert), with three tongues gu. and charged with a mullet or.

Kighly (Reg. Ulster's Office). Ar. a fess sa.

Kihford. Per bend ar. and sa. a lion ramp. counterchanged.

Kikington, alias Colbrooke. Ar. a lion ramp. sa. on a fesse or, three crosses crosslet fitchée of the second.

Kilburne (Hawkehirst, co. Kent, and London). Ar. a chev. az. betw. three bald coots close sa. heads ar. beaks tawny. *Crest*—A bald coot ppr.

Kilby (JOHN KILBY, chosen Alderman of York, 1803). Ar. three boars az. in chief as many annulets of the last.

Kilby. Ar. three torteaux in fesse betw. two barrulets az. *Crest*—A hand issuing from a cloud in fesse, pointing to a crosier in pale all ppr.

Kilche. Sa. a lion ramp. ar.

Kilchech (Kilcheck, co. Lancaster), Quarterly, 1st and

4th, ar. an eagle sa. seizing on a child, face ppr. wrapped gu. swaddled or; 2nd and 3rd, ar. a griffin segreant sa.

Kilcheche. Ar. an eagle sa. seizing on a child, the face ppr. wrapped gu. swaddled or.

Kildahl (granted to SOBIESKI KILDAHL, Esq., of the city of Dublin, descended of a family formerly of Christiana, Norway). Vert a chev. ar. betw. three dolphins embowed or. *Crest*—A demi lion gu. holding betw. his paws a decrescent az. *Motto*—Infirmis opitulare.

Kildare, See of. Ar. a saltire engr. gu. on a chief az. an open Bible ppr. garnished and clasped or, thereon the words in gold, "The Law was given by Moses, but grace and truth came by Jesus Christ."

Kilderbee (co. Suffolk). Erm. on a bend cotised betw. two crosses pattée gu. three escallops or. *Crest*—A demi cockatrice or, charged on the breast with an escallop, and on each wing with a cross pattée gu.

Kilfenora, See of. Ar. a red rose ppr. on a chief sa. three mullets or.

Kilgour (Scotland). Ar. a dragon, wings displ. within a bordure inwardly circular sa. charged with three crescents of the first. *Crest*—A crescent ar.

Killala, See of. Gu. a crozier in pale or, suppressed by an open book ppr. garnished and clasped gold.

Killaloe, See of. *Ancient Arms*—Ar. a cross az. betw. four trefoils slipped vert, on a chief of the second a key in pale or. *Modern Arms*—Ar. a cross gu. betw. twelve trefoils slipped vert, on a chief az. a key in pale or.

Kilham. Or, a morion gu.

Kilkenny, Earl of. See BUTLER.

Kilkenny, City of. Ar. a castle of three towers, the middle one the tallest and topped with a spire, on each of the others a man issuant, with a bow charged with an arrow all ppr. in base on a mount vert a lion pass. guard. gu.

Killegrave. Ar. on a chev. sa. betw. three pellets as many bezants.

Killegrew (Killegrew and Arwennick, co. Cornwall, *temp.* Richard II., bart., extinct 1704; the dau. of the last bart. m. RICHARD ERESEY, Esq., of Eresey; her descendant, the *Earl of Kimberley*, represents the families of WEST, ERESEY, and KILLEGREW). Ar. an eagle displ. sa. a bordure of the second bezantée. *Crest*—A demi lion sa. charged with three bezants in pale (another, in bend).

Killegrew (co. Cornwall). Ar. on a chev. sa. betw. three torteaux as many annulets of the field (another, three bezants).

Killegrew (co. Devon). Gu. three mascles or.

Killegrew. Per pale gu. and az. an eagle displ. with two heads ar. within a bordure of the last.

Killesson, or Kyllmessane. Sa. three swans ar.

Killicke. Ar. a chev. betw. three pickaxes sa. *Crest*—A swan, wings endorsed ar.

Killikelly (Bilbil, in Spain; allowed by Hawkins, Ulster, 1772, to BRIAN or BERNARD PAUL KILLIKELLY, of that place, fourth in descent from MORTOGH KILLIKELLY, of Castle Lydican, co. Galway). Vert two lions ramp. combatant, supporting a tower triple-towered or, all betw. three crescents ar. *Crest*—Out of a ducal coronet or, an arm in armour embowed, the hand grasping a spear all ppr.

Killingbeck (Leeds, co. York). Ar. on a chev. sa. betw. three unicorns' heads couped az. as many annulets or.

Killinghall (Middleton St. George, co. Durham; seated there 1390, represented by the ALLANS, of Blackwell and Blackwell Grange, co. Durham). Gu. a bend raguly ar. betw. three garbs or.

Killinghall (co. Cumberland). Gu. a bend raguly ar. betw. two garbs or.

Killingmarch (co. Oxford; arms in the church of Queen's Coll. Visit. Oxon, 1574). Per. fess erm. and ermines a lion ramp. counterchanged.

Killingworth, or Kilingworth (Killingworth, co. Northumberland, and Sibble, co. Essex). Ar. three cinquefoils pierced sa. *Crest*—A seahorse az. ducally gorged or.

Killingworth. Ar. three scaling ladders bendways gu.

Killiowe (Lansallos, co. Cornwall; JOHN KILLIOWE, Visit. co. Cornwall, 1620, son of JOHN KILLIOWE, d. 1602, and grandson of THOMAS KILLIOWE, all of same place). Or, a chev. betw. two roses in chief and a mullet in base sa.

Killiowe (quartered by WILLIAM BASTARD, Recorder of Totness. Visit. Devon, 1620). Same *Arms*, a crescent for diff.

Killowe (Dale, co. Cornwall). Or, a chev. sa. in chief two cinquefoils, in base a mullet of the second. *Crest*—Two hands issuing from clouds in chief sustaining an anchor all ppr.

Killuhurst, or Killuhust (co. York). Ar. on a chev.

betw. three crosses crosslet fitchée sa. on the dexter side three fleurs-de-lis, and on the sinister as many martlets or.

Kilmaine, Baron. See BROWNE.

Kilmarnock, Earl of. See BOYD.

Kilmerux (Reg. Ulster's Office). Ar. three battle axes az. (another bears a chev. betw. the battle axes).

Kilmesham (Reg. Ulster's Office). Sa. three swans or.

Kilminthwch (Lord of Glynllwon, in Arvon). Ar. in the 1st and 4th quarters an eagle displ. with two heads; in the 2nd and 3rd quarters three ragged staves gu.

Kilmore, See of. *Ancient Arms*—Ar. on a cross sa. a pastoral staff surmounted of a mitre sa. *Modern Arms*—Ar. a cross gu. in each quarter five trefoils in saltire slipped vert.

Kilmore. Az. three standing cups or. *Crest*—A demi eagle with two heads, wings displ. sa. ducally gorged or.

Kilmorey, Earl and Viscount of. See NEEDHAM.

Kilnore. Sa. an eagle displ. ar. armed gu.

Kilpec (Kilpec Castle, co. Hereford, *temp.* King John; the heiress m. PHILIP MARMYON, Lord of Tamworth Castle, co. Warwick, Baron of Scriveslby, co. Lincoln, and hereditary King's Champion, *temp.* Henry III.). Ar. a sword in bend sa.

Kilpeck (quartered by WILLOUGHBY, Bart., of Wollaton, co. Nottingham. Visit. Notts, 1614). Sa. a sword, point downwards, ar. pommel and hilt or.

Kilrenny, Burgh of (Scotland). Az. an open boat in the sea rowed by four mariners on each side, the pilot at the helm, a hook suspended from the side of the boat near the stern, the rays of the sun issuing from a cloud in chief all ppr. *Motto*—Semper tibi pendeat hamus.

Kilrington. Ar. a lion ramp. gu. depressed by a fesse or, charged with three crosses pattée fitchée sa.

Kilsyth, Viscount of. See LIVINGSTONE.

Kilton. Or, three eagles displ. gu.

Kiltra (Scotland, 16th century). Az. a mullet or, betw. two crescents ar.

Kiltra. Az. two crescents and a mullet in pale ar.

Kilwarby. Ar. on a bend gu. three eagles displ. of the field.

Kilvington. Ar. a fesse gu. betw. three erm. spots. *Crest*—Out of a cloud a hand holding a sealed letter all ppr.

Kimbell. Ar. a fesse within a bordure engr. sa.

Kimber. Ar. three Cornish choughs sa. beaks and legs gu. on a chief of the second as many mullets of the first. *Crest*—A bull's head affrontée ppr. *Motto*—Frangas non flectes.

Kimberley, Earl of. See WODEHOUSE.

Kimberley. Ar. an oak tree eradicated vert, fructed or.

Kimperley. Az. on two bars ar. three mullets gu., two and one.

Kimpton. Sa. a saltire arg. on a chief of the second a lion pass. of the first. *Crest*—A crescent per crescent or and gu.

Kimpton (Monken Hadley, co. Middlesex; granted by Cooke, Clarenceux, 3 April, 1574). Az. a pelican betw. three fleurs-de-lis or. *Crest*—A demi goat ermines, horned and hoofed gold, a collar and chain about his neck sa.

Kinahan (granted to Rev. JOHN KINAHAN, M.A., Rector of Knock Breda, co. Down). Per bend az. and gu. on a cross couped ar. a fleur-de-lis sa. *Crest*—A demi lion ramp. sa. holding in his paws a battle axe ppr. and charged on the shoulder with a cross or. *Motto*—Deo fidens persistas.

Kinarby. Ar. a fesse sa. betw. three crescents gu. *Crest*—A flag gu. flotant to the sinister.

Kinardesley (co. Salop). Gu. crusily a lion ramp. ar.

Kinardisley. Az. semée of crosses crosslet or, a lion ramp. ar. langued and armed gu.

Kinardsly. Az. a lion ramp. ar. within an orle of crosslets of the second.

Kinardsly (Brailsford, co. Derby; JOHN KINARDSLY, of this place, *temp.* Queen Elizabeth, descended from JOHN KINARDSLEY, Esq. of Loxley, co. Warwick, *temp.* Edward III. Visit. 1611). Ar. a fesse vairé or and gu. betw. three eagles displ. of the last.

Kinardsly (Warde End, co. Warwick; confirmed by the Deputies of Camden, Clarenceux, to JOHN KINARDSLY, grandson of JOHN KINARDSLEY, Esq., of Brailsford, *temp.* Queen Elizabeth). Same *Arms*. *Crest*—On a mount vert a greyhound sejant ar. collared or, under a holly tree ppr. fructed gu.

Kinaston (Ruyton, co. Salop; a branch of KYNASTON, descended from Sir THOMAS KYNASTON, Knt., the eldest son of Sir ROGER KYNASTON, Knt., was Sheriff of co. Salop, 1462). Ar. a lion ramp. sa., quartering erm. a chev. gu.

Kincaid (that Ilk, co. Stirling). Gu. a fess erm. betw. two mullets in chief or, and a castle triple-towered in base ar.

masoned sa. Crest—A castle, as in the arms, and issuing therefrom a dexter arm embowed, grasping a swcrd ppr. Supporters—Two Highlanders armed with cuirasses, each grasping a Lochaber axe all ppr. Motto—I'll defend.

Kincaid (Lord Provost of Edinburgh, 1776). Gu. on a chev. ar. three stars of the field, in chief two spur-rowels or, and in base a castle of the second, masoned sa. Crest—A dexter arm from the elbow holding a drawn sword ppr. Motto—I will defend.

Kincaid-Lennox. See LENNOX.

Kincaid (THOMAS KINCAID, surgeon, Edinburgh, 1685). ᴜu. on a fesse erm. betw. two mullets in chief or, and a castle triple-towered in base, masoned sa. a lozenge of the first. Crest—A dexter hand holding a chirurgeon's instrument, called bistoury, ppr. Motto—Incidendo sano.

Kinchant (Park, co. Salop; JOHN QUINCHANT, as the name was then written, a native of France, was brought into England whilst a child in arms by his mother, the only part of the family who escaped from his own country, temp. Louis XIV. JOHN QUINCHANT entered the British army, became a captain in General Pulteney's regiment of foot, and fell at the battle of Fontenoy. His grandson, JOHN CHARLTON KINCHANT, Esq., of Park, was High Sheriff of co. Salop, 1775). Az. three lions' heads, two and one, erased ar. crowned or.

Kincraigie (Scotland). Sa. a fesse erm. betw. three crescents ar.

Kindelan (Ballinakill, co. Meath, and Spain; certified by Hawkins, Ulster, 1749, to VINCENT KINDELAN, then in the service of the King of Spain, and his brothers, descended from Ballinakill). Az. a lion pass. betw. three stars of eight points or. Crest—An arm in armour holding a sword all ppr.

Kinder (Harrytown Hall, co. Chester). Quarterly, 1st and 4th, or, a column gu. betw. three Cornish choughs ppr.; 2nd and 3rd, sa. three lozenges in fess ar. betw. as many bucks' heads ppr. Crests—1st: On a column or, a Cornish chough sa. beaked and legged gu.; 2nd: A buck's head ppr. couped at the neck.

Kinder, or Kynder (Ely, co. Cambridge, and co. Nottingham). Or, a column gu. betw. three Cornish choughs ppr. Crest—On a column or, a Cornish chough sa. beaked and legged gu.

Kinderton. Az. two bars ar.

Kindon, or Kingdon (Ar. a chev. sa. betw. three Cornish choughs ppr. Crest—An eagle's head erased ppr.

Kine. Ar. two chev. sa.

Kinerby. Ar. three lions pass. in pale gu. Crest—On a chapeau gu. turned up erm. a lion pass. of the first.

Kinersley (North Cleobury and Badger, co. Salop, and co. Stafford). Az. crusily a lion ramp. ar. Crest—On a mount vert a greyhound sejant ar. collared or, under a holly tree of the first, fructed gu.

King (Baron King; the eighth baron, was created, 1838, Earl of Lovelace). Sa. three spears' heads erect ar. embrued gu. on a chief or, as many poleaxes az. their edges to the sinister. Crest—A dexter arm erect, couped at the elbow, vested az. thereon three erm. spots in fesse or, cuffed ar. hand ppr. grasping a truncheon sa. the top broken off, the bottom couped of the field. Supporters—Two English mastiffs reguard. ppr. each gorged with a plain collar gu. Motto—Labor ipse voluptas.

King-Noel (Earl of Lovelace; exemplified to the earl upon his assuming by royal licence, 1860, the additional surname of NOEL). Quarterly, 1st and 4th, NOEL, or, fretty gu. a canton erm.; 2nd and 3rd, KING, sa. three spears' heads erect ar. the points sanguine, on a chief or, three pole-axes az. their edges to the sinister. Crests—1st, NOEL: A buck at gaze ar. attired or; 2nd, KING: A dexter arm erect couped at the elbow, vested az. adorned with three erm. spots in fesse or, the cuff turned up, grasping a truncheon of a spear, the head silver. Supporters—On either side a mastiff dog reguard. ppr. collared gu. Motto—Pensez a bien.

King (granted to CHARLES FRANCIS KING, Esq., of Broomfield, co. Essex). Vert a chev. or, surmounted by another erm. charged with three woolpacks ppr. betw. two lambs pass. in chief ar. and in base a golden fleece. Crest—In front of a lion couchant gu. a woolpack, as in the arms.

King (DASHWOOD-KING, West Wycombe, co. Bucks, bart.; the third bart. assumed the additional name of KING by Act of Parliament 1742, d. 1793). See DASHWOOD.

King (Ashby Hall, co. Lincoln). Sa. on a chev. engr. ar. three escallops of the field. Crest—A talbot's head erased sa. collared and ringed gu. eared or.

King (Belleone, co. Kent, bart.). Sa. a lion ramp. erm. betw. three crosses pattée fitchée or. Crest—A lion's gamb erased

and erect sa. grasping a cross pattée, as in the arms. Motto—Jamais sans espérance

King (Charlestown, co. Roscommon, bart.). Sa. a lion ramp. double queued or. Crest—A scallop shell gu. Motto—Spes tutissima cœlis.

King (Corrard, co. Fermanagh, and Dublin, bart.). Az. on a fesse ar. betw. a lion's head erased in chief and a mullet in base or, three buckles erect gu. and, as an honourable augmentation, on a chief erm. an imperial crown within a chaplet of trefoils both ppr. Crest—A dexter cubit arm erect, holding a dagger in pale all ppr. surmounted by a scroll, inscribed "17 Aug. 1821," in allusion to the period in which, as Lord Mayor of Dublin, he had the honour of receiving George IV. on His Majesty's visit to the capital of his Irish dominions. Motto—Audaces fortuna juvat.

King (Staunton Park, co. Hereford). Quarterly, ar. and az. in the 2nd and 3rd quarters a mullet of six points or, pierced of the field, over all a bend barry of six of the second and gu. charged with a cinquefoil of the third Crest—A lion ramp. bendy of or and az. supporting two branches composed of two roses gu. and three cinquefoils vert, slipped and leaved of the last.

King (Highbury Crescent, co. Middlesex; granted to JOHN THOMAS KING, Esq.). Per pale or and az. a cross patée fitchée betw. three lions' heads erased countercharged. Crest—A lion sejant per chev. engr. or and az. supporting with the dexter paw a spear erect gold, enfiled with a gauntlet also az. Motto—Altiora peto.

King (co. Bucks). Sa. a lion ramp. or, tail double queued.

King (co. Devon, and Towcester, co. Northampton). Sa. a lion ramp. betw. three crosses crosslet or, ducally crowned ar. Crest—Out of a ducal coronet or, a demi ostrich ar. wings endorsed, beaked gold.

King (Bickenhill, co. Warwick; granted by Dugdale, Garter, to THOMAS KING, Alderman of Coventry; descended from co. Kent). Sa. a lion ramp. double queued crowned or, in chief three billets ar. Crest—A demi lion double queued or, billettée ar. ducally crowned gold, holding in the dexter paw a sword ar.

King (Pyrland Hall, co. Somerset; descended from JOHN MEADE, Esq., of Lyng, in same co., living 1600, assumed in 1830, in compliance with the will of RICHARD KING, Esq., of the Rectory, North Petherton, the additional surname and arms of KING). Quarterly, 1st and 4th, ar. a lion ramp. betw. three crosses crosslet sa. and as many escallops gu., for KING; 2nd and 3rd, gu. on a chev. ar. betw. three leopards' faces or, two arrows in saltire az. barbed and flighted ppr. betw. two bows chevronwise of the fourth, stringed of the field, for MEADE. Crests—1st, KING: A mount vert, thereon an arm in bend dexter couped at the elbow, the hand supporting a tilting spear erect, the head broken, the arm surmounting a branch of oak fructed in bend sinister, all ppr.; 2nd, MEADE: A demi griffin az. wings elevated erm. in the dexter claw a fleur-de-lis or. Motto—Cadenti porrigo dextram.

King (Exeter; granted 1691). Sa. two flaunches erm. a lion ramp. betw. three ducal coronets or. Crest—Out of a mural coronet ar. a lion's head and neck sa. charged with three ducal coronets or.

King (co. Hants). Or, on a pale az. three regal crowns of the first. Crest—An esquire's helmet ppr. garnished or.

King (co. Hereford). Ar. a lion ramp. az.

King (Bromley, co. Kent). Sa. a lion ramp. guard. erm. betw. three crosses pattée fitchée at the foot or. Crest—A lion's gamb erect and erased sa. holding a cross pattée fitchée or.

King (Eltham, co. Kent; granted 14 June, 1707, to DANIEL KING, Esq., of Eltham). Per fesse indented gu. and sa. a lion or, ducally crowned ar. betw. three crosses crosslet fitchée of the last. Crest—An ostrich's head couped ar. ducally gorged or, betw. two ostrich feathers ppr.

King (co. Leicester). Sa. on a chev. ar. three escallops of the field. Crest—A lion pass. erm. ducally crowned or.

King (co. Lincoln). Gu. a chev. betw. ten crosses crosslet fleury or.

King (London). Sa. on a chev. erm. three escallops gu. Crest—A talbot's head erased sa. collared and eared or.

King (London; granted by Camden, Clarenceux). Sa. on a chev. betw. three crosses crosslet or, as many escallops of the field. Crest—A dexter arm embowed in armour, holding a broken spear all ppr.

King (Loxwood House, co. Sussex). Same Arms and Crest.

King (Towcester, co. Northampton). Same Arms.

King (Midhurst). Same Arms. Crest—An ostrich's head ar. ducally gorged or.

King (co. Middlesex). Ermines, on a chief ar. three escallops sa.

King (co. Oxford). Per fesse gu. and ar. three roses counter-changed.

King (granted 1611). Sa. a lion ramp. betw. three crosses formée fitchée or. *Crest*—A greyhound's head couped, ducally gorged.

King (co. Wilts). Sa. on a chev. engr. ar. three escallops of the field. *Crest*—A talbot's head couped sa. collared or.

King. Sa. a fesse wavy betw. three escallops ar. *Crest*—A lion sejant ppr. holding an escallop ar.

King. Sa. a chev. erm. betw. three fishes ar. *Crest*—A demi griffin or.

King. Ar. on a chev. gu. three lions pass. guard. or.

King. Or, a fesse betw. two ducal coronets sa.

King. Sa. a lion ramp. or, crowned ar. betw. three crescents of the second.

King (borne by Rev. W. KING, D.D., 1730-1740). Sa. on a chev. ar. three escallops az. on a chief or, a demi dragon gu. betw. two battle axes, the heads to the dexter of the second, and in base a cross pattée fitchée of the same. *Crest* —A dexter arm couped below the elbow erect, habited and cuffed, the hand holding a roll.

King (London; Sir JOHN KING, Knt. Visit. London, 1568). Sa. a lion pass. or, a label of three points ar. *Crest*—On a ducal coronet a lion ramp. or, holding in the dexter paw a lance ar. on the point thereof an annulet gold.

King (Coventry, co. Warwick, 1682). Sa. a lion ramp. queue furché or, ducally crowned of the last, in chief three billets ar. *Crest*—A demi lion ramp. queue furché az. billettée and ducally crowned or, holding in the dexter claw a sword ar.

King (Umberslade, co. Warwick, and Hungrill, co. York). Sa. a lion ramp. betw. three crosses crosslet or. *Crest*—A demi lion ramp. issuing out of a ducal coronet or.

King (Skellands, co. York, from which descended WALKER KING, D.D., Bishop of Rochester). Sa. a lion ramp. betw. three cross crosslets or.

King (Chadshund, co. Warwick). Same *Arms* and *Crest*.

King (Preston Candover, co. Hants). Same *Arms* and *Crest*.

King (Fun. Ent. 1637, Sir JOHN KING, Knt., of Abbey, Boyle, co. Roscommon, Muster-Master-General of Ireland, and a Privy Councillor). Gu. two lions ramp. combatant supporting with the forepaws a dexter hand couped at the wrist all ar.

King (Baron Kingston, extinct 1761; Sir JOHN KING, elder brother of Sir ROBERT KING, ancestor of the *Earls of Kingston*, was so created 1660. The fourth baron left an only dau. and heiress, MARGARET, wife of RICHARD FITZ-GERALD, Esq., of Mount Offaly, and had an only dau. and heiress, who m. her cousin, ROBERT, second Earl of King-ston). Gu. two lions ramp. supporting a dexter hand couped at the wrist, erect ar., quartering BLOUNT, BLAYNEY, and GORE. *Supporters*—Two lions per fess ar. and gu. ducally crowned of the last.

King (Earl of Kingston). Gu. two lions ramp. combatant supporting a dexter hand couped at the wrist and erect ar. quartering GORE, BLAYNEY, BLOUNT, FITZGERALD, FENTON, THE WHITE KNIGHT, &c., &c. *Crest*—Out of a five-leaved ducal coronet or, a dexter hand erect, the third and fourth fingers turned down ppr. *Supporters*—Two lions per fesse ar. and gu. ducally crowned of the last. *Motto*—Spes tutissima coelis.

King (Viscount Lorton ; Hon. ROBERT EDWARD KING, second son of ROBERT, second Earl of Kingston, was so created 1806. His son, ROBERT, second Viscount Lorton, s. his cousin JAMES, fifth Earl of Kingston, as sixth Earl, when the viscounty of Lorton merged in the earldom). Same *Arms*, *Crest*, and *Supporters* as the Earl of Kingston, each charged with a crescent for diff.

King (impalement Fun. Ent. Ulster's Office, 1632, JOHN BURNET, Esq., of Ballylack, co. Monaghan, whose wife was KATHERINE KING). Sa. on a chev. ar. three crescents of the field, in middle chief a mullet of the second.

King (Clontarf, co. Dublin. Visit. Dublin, 1606. GEORGE KING, High Sheriff co. Dublin, son of JOHN KING, Esq., of Clontarf, by MARY, his wife, dau. of Sir HENRY COLLEY, Knt., of Edenderry, and grandson of MATHEW KING, Muster-Master of the Army in Ireland, who was a native of the North of England). Gu. a lion ramp. or, betw. two flaunches erm.

King (Fun. Ent. Ulster's Office, 1680). Sa. a lion ducally crowned betw. three crosses crosslet or.

King (granted by Carney, Ulster, 1690, to WILLIAM KING, Bishop of Derry). Az. on a chev. ar. betw. three estoiles or, as many escallops sa. *Crest*—A dexter hand couped at the wrist erect ppr. holding a cross crosslet fitchée gu.

566

King (Clontarf, co. Dublin; Reg. Ulster's Office). Az. three fusils or.

King (Ballylin, King's co.). Sa. a lion ramp. double queued or. *Crest*—An escallop gu. *Motto*—Spes tutissima coelis.

King (Mount Pleasant, co. Waterford; confirmed 1809, by Betham, then Deputy Ulster, to THOMAS KING, Esq., and the descendants of his grandfather, WILLIAM KING). Gu. a lion ramp. betw. three trefoils, two and one ar. and as many crescents, one and two or. *Crest*—Out of a ducal coronet or, a dexter hand, third and fourth fingers az. *Motto*—Medio tutissimus ibis.

King (Barra, co. Aberdeen; Lord Ythan). Az. on a fesse ar. three round buckles gu. in chief a lion's head erased, and in base a mullet of the second.

King (Newmilne, co. Elgin). Same *Arms*. *Crest*—A hand holding a dagger ppr. *Motto*—Audaces fortuna juvat.

King (Rev. S. KING, Rector of Saxlingham, co. Norfolk, 1845 and 1867). Az. on a fess ar. betw. a lion's head erased of the last and a water bouget or, three round buckles gu. *Crest*— A demi lion ramp. gu. crowned with an antique crown or, and holding in his dexter paw a rose ppr. *Motto*—Richt do and fear na.

King (Campsie, co. Stirling, 1869). Az. on a fess ar. betw. a lion's head erased in chief and two billets in base or, three round buckles of the field. *Crest*—A dexter hand ppr. *Motto*—Honos industriæ præmium.

Kingan (granted to SAMUEL KINGAN, of Finaghy House, Dun-murray, Belfast, son of WILLIAM KINGAN, formerly resident at White Abbey, Belfast). Az. a fess indented ar. betw. an antique crown in chief or, and in base two dexter hands clasped and conjoined, that on the dexter ringed on the third finger with a royal signet all ppr. *Crest*.—Two dexter hands clasped and conjoined, as in the arms, the third finger of that on the dexter side also ringed, as in the arms, thereon a lion ramp. guard. or. *Motto*—A favore regis nomen.

Kingbude, or Kingsbed. Ar. a saltire engr. vert.

Kingdom. Ar. a chev. betw. three birds sa.

Kingdom. Az. three banners bendways in pale flotant to the sinister or. *Crest*—Out of a ducal coronet or, a griffin's head gu. holding in the beak a key gold.

Kingdon (Launcells, co. Cornwall, and Compton Hall, other-wise Castle Hartley, co. Devon). Quarterly, 1st and 4th, ar. a chev. sa. betw. three magpies ppr., for KINGDON ; 2nd and 3rd, sa. three crescents or, for BOUGHTON. *Crest*—An eagle displ. with two heads sa. *Motto*—Regis donum gratum bonum.

Kingdon (confirmed by Carney, Ulster, 1684, to LEMEUEL KINGDON, a Privy Councillor in Ireland). Az. a chev. erm. betw. three dolphins embowed or. *Crest*—A dolphin embowed or.

Kinge (Sherborne, co. Dorset; granted 10 April, 1641). Sa. a fesse wavy betw. three escallops ar. *Crest*—A lion sejant ppr. resting the forepaw on an escallop ar.

Kinge (co. Essex). Az. on a bend cotised or, three escallops sa.

Kinge (co. Essex). Az. a bend engr. erm. betw. three eagles displ. or.

Kinge (Gainsborough, co. Lincoln). Sa. a chev. betw. three escallops ar. *Crest*—A talbot's head sa. eared gu. collared and ringed or.

Kinge (co. Lincoln). Sa. on a chev. engr. ar. three escallops of the field.

Kinge (London ; granted 1591). Sa. on a chev. erm. three escallops gu. *Crest*—A talbot's head erased sa. eared and collared or.

Kinge (London). Az. (another, gu.) a bend betw. two eagles displ. with two necks or.

Kinge. Sa. on a chev. betw. three crosses crosslet ar. as many escallops of the field. *Crest*—An armed arm, couped at the elbow ppr. garnished or, holding in the gauntlet a broken spear of the second, headed ar. and girt round the arm with a scarf of the last.

Kinge. Az. on a bend ar. three fermails of the field (another, gu.).

Kinge. Ar. a fesse dancettée betw. three eagles displ. sa.

Kingescot. Erm. in the dexter chief an inescutcheon gu. charged with a mullet or.

Kingeston. Az. a cross or, betw. four leopards' faces ar. *Crest*—On a mount vert a goat ar. horned or, leaping against a tree of the first.

Kingestone. Gu. three eagles displ. or, betw. two bend-lets ar.

Kingfield, Kingsfield, and Kingsford. Gu. two bends erm.

Kingford (Youlkston, co. Cornwall; granted 1691). Az. three bars wavy erm. in chief an eagle displ. betw. two ducal coronets or. *Crest*—An eagle displ. per fesse gu. and az. crowned or, holding in the beak a rose ar. slipped and barbed vert, seeded gold.

Kingford. Ar. a chev. betw. three ravens ppr. *Crest*—A raven, the body to the sinister and the head reguard.

Kinghan (granted to WILLIAM KINGHAN, Esq., of Silverstream, Greenisland, co. Antrim, son of the late JOHN KINGHAN, of Drumadoney and Ballymacarn, co. Down). Az. a fess wavy ar. betw. an antique crown in chief or, and in base two dexter hands clasped and conjoined, that on the dexter ringed on the third finger with the royal signet all ppr. *Crest*—Two dexter hands clasped and conjoined as in the arms, the third finger of that on the dexter side also ringed as in the arms, thereon a lion ramp. or. *Motto*—A favore regis nomen.

Kinglake (Saltmoor, parish of Stoke St. Gregory, co. Somerset; descended from WILLIAM KINLOCH, or KINGLAKE, M.D., a younger son of the Scottish family of KINLOCH, who changed his name of KINLOCH to KINGLAKE upon settling in England). Az. a boar's head erased ar. betw. three mascles or. *Crest*—An eaglet perched looking up to the sun in its splendour. *Motto*—Non degener.

Kingley. Or (another, ar.; another, erm.) a close helmet gu. *Crest*—A cross crosslet fitchée sa and sword ppr. in saltire. *Another Crest*—A cock's head betw. two wings ppr.

Kingsale, Lord. See DE COURCY.

Kingsbury (confirmed by Hawkins, Ulster, 1742, to Doctor THOMAS KINGSBURY, Fellow of the King and Queen's College of Physicians, Ireland, son of THOMAS KINGSBURY, Esq.; descended from co. Dorset). Az. a chev. or, betw. two doves in chief ppr. and a serpent in base nowed of the last. *Crest*—A wyvern vert. *Motto*—Prudens et innocuus.

King's College, Cambridge (founded in 1441, by Henry VI., who granted thereto the following). Sa. three roses ar. barbed vert, seeded or, on a chief per pale az. and gu. a fleur-de-lis on the dexter or, and a lion pass. guard. on the sinister of the last.

Kingscote (Kingscote, co. Gloucester; ROBERT NIGEL FITZ-HARDING KINGSCOTE, Esq., of Kingscote, C.B., Lieut-Col. in the army, A D.C. to the late *Lord Raglan* in the Crimea, and M.P. for co. Gloucester; the representative of a family which claims Saxon descent; NIGELL FITZ-HARDING, son of ANGERUS the Saxon, living A.D. 985, m. ADEVA, dau. of ROBERT FITZ-HARDINGE, by EVA, his wife, niece of William I.; as her dower he got the manor of Kingscote. His son, ADAM DE KINGSCOTE, had a confirmation of the manor 1188). Ar. ten escallops four, three, two, and one, on a canton gu. a mullet pierced or. *Crest*—An escallop sa.

Kingsey, or Kynsey (co. Chester). Ar. a chev. betw. three squirrels sejant gu. cracking nuts or, stalked and leaved vert.

Kingsford. Erm. in the dexter chief quarter a cross couped gu. *Crest*—The branch of a rose bush bearing roses ppr.

Kingshamed. See KINGSMEAD.

Kingsley (Kingsley, co. Chester, *temp.* Henry II., hereditary Forester of Delamere under the Norman earls palatine; its representative in the female line is HELEN KATHERINE, Countess of Haddington, wife of GEORGE, eleventh *Earl of Haddington*, dau. and only child of Sir JOHN WARRENDER, fifth bart. of Lochead, by his second wife, the Hon. FRANCES HENRIETTA ARDEN, eldest sister of RICHARD PEPPER, third and last *Lord Alvanley*). Vert a cross engr. erm.; and on an honorary escutcheon of pretence, ar. a bugle strung sa., the escutcheon is sometimes borne as an additional cost.

Kingsley (Canterbury). Sa. a cross engr. erm. in the 1st quarter a mullet or. *Crest*—A goat's head couped ar.

Kingsley (Sorrett, co. Hertford). Vert a cross engr. ar. (another, erm.). *Crest*, as the last.

Kingsley. Ar. a buglehorn stringed sa.

Kingsley. Ar. a fesse sa.

King's Lynn, or Lynn-Regis, Borough of (co. Norfolk). Az. three conger eels' heads erased and erect or, in the mouth of each a cross crosslet fitchée of the last.

Kingsman (co. Essex). Per pale ar. and az. three saltires counterchanged.

Kingsmead, or Kingsmede. Barry of six or and az. on a bend ar. three escallops gu.

Kingsmill (Sidmanton, co. Hants, and Aston, co. Gloucester, bart., extinct 1823; descended from JOHN KINGSMILL, Judge of Common Pleas, *d.* 1504). Ar. semée of crosses crosslet fitchée sa. a chev. erm. betw. three fers-de-moline of the second, a chief of the third. *Crest*—A cubit arm erect vested ar. holding in the hand ppr. a millrind sa. *Motto*—Do well, doubt not.

Kingsmill (Sir JOHN KINGSMILL, Knt., of Hermitage, near Lucan, co. Dublin, who m. 1824, ELIZA CATHERINE, only dau. and heiress of Sir ROBERT KINGSMILL, Bart., of Sidmanton, co. Hants). Same *Arms*.

567

Kingsmill (Millbrook, co. Hants). Ar. crusily fitchée sa. a chev. ermines betw. three millrinds of the second, a chief of the third. *Crest*—A cubit arm erect, vested ar. cuff sa. holding in the hand ppr. a millrind of the second.

Kingsmill (co. Hants). Same *Arms*. *Crest*—A Moor's head in profile couped at the shoulders ppr. wreathed about the temples or and gu.

Kingsmill (co. Warwick). Ar. a chev. ermines betw. three millrinds sa. a chief of the second.

Kingsmill (exemplified to THOMAS NUGENT KENNEY, Esq., of Correndoo Park, co. Galway, and of Hermitage Park, co. Dublin, and to his wife, ISABEL AUGUSTA BRUCE, only child and heiress of Sir JOHN KINGSMILL, Col. Battle Axe Guard, by ELIZABETH CATHERINE, his wife, dau. and heiress of Sir JOHN KINGSMILL, Bart., of Sidmanton, co. Southampton, on his assuming, by royal licence, 18 Jan. 1866, the surname of KINGSMILL, in lieu of that of KENNEY). Quarterly, 1st and 4th, ar. semée of cross crosslets fitchée sa. a chev. ermines betw. three fers-de-moline pierced of the second, a chief of the second charged with a Maltese cross or, for distinction, for KINGSMILL; 2nd and 3rd, per pale or and az. a fleur-de-lis betw. three crescents all counter changed, a crescent for diff., for KENNEY; an escocheon of pretence, in the 1st and 4th quarters the arms of KINGSMILL, without the Maltese cross, in the 2nd and 3rd the arms of BRICE, otherwise BRUCE, viz.: Or, a saltire gu. a chief of the last, thereon in the dexter chief point a mullet of the first. *Crests*—1st : A cubit arm erect, vested ar. cuffed ermines, in the hand ppr. a fer-de-moline, as in the arms, the arm charged with a Maltese cross gu., for distinction, for KINGSMILL; 2nd: Out of an earl's coronet or, a cubit arm erect, vested gu ruffed ar. the hand grasping a roll of parchment ppr. the arm charged with a crescent ar. for diff., for KENNEY.

Kingston, Earl of. See KING.

Kingston, Viscount of. See SETON.

Kingston (co. Bedford). Sa. a lion ramp. or.

Kingston (co. Berwick). Same *Arms*, the lion's tail double queued.

Kingston (Wendover, co. Buckingham). Same *Arms*.

Kingston (co. Derby). Az. three swords fessways in pale ar.

Kingston (cos. Gloucester and Leicester). Az. a cross or, betw. four leopards' faces ar.

Kingston (Grimslye and Bassingham, co. Lincoln). Same *Arms*. *Crest*—A goat saliant ar. against a tree vert.

Kingston (London). Sa. guttée d'eau a lion ramp. or. *Crest*—Out of a mural coronet counter-componée or and sa. a unicorn's head az. crined ar. horn gobonée of the second and first.

Kingston (co. York). Ar. a bend wavy cotised gu.

Kingston (*temp.* Richard II.). Ar. a steel cap ppr. in the front thereof a feather gu.

Kingston. Az. three swords in pale ar. hilted or, two erect upwards and one betw. downwards.

Kingston. Sa. three leopards' faces ducally crowned ar.

Kingston. Chequy or and gu. a bend erm.

Kingston. Ar. a bend wavy gu. betw. two bendlets of the last.

Kingston. Ar. guttée de sang, on a chief az. three crowns or.

Kingston. Gu. on a chev. or, betw. three cinquefoils of the second three mullets az.

Kingston (*temp.* George III.). Per pale az. and gu. guttée d'eau a lion ramp. double queued erminois.

Kingston (Mosstown, co. Longford; granted to ALEXANDER KINGSTON, Esq., of that place, one of the Governors of the co. Longford). Per pale ar. and gu. a chev. counterchanged betw. a thistle slipped in dexter chief ppr. and a trefoil in sinister chief or, in dexter base a trefoil slipped vert, and in sinister a thistle slipped of the fourth. *Crest*—A swan holding in its beak a thistle slipped ppr. *Motto*—Dei gratia.

Kingston, or Kynston. Gu. a chev. vair.

Kingston-upon-Thames, Town of (co. Surrey). Three salmons hauriant in pale ar.; the common seal is a tun, over it in chief a Saxon K, the whole encircled with two olive branches.

Kingswell (co. Hants). Gu. a saltire betw. four lions' heads erased or. *Crest*—A parrot gu. in the mouth an annulet or.

Kington (Charlton House, co. Somerset). Ar. guttée de sang, on a chief wavy per pale gu. and vert three ducal coronets or. *Crest*—On a crescent az. five guttées d'or betw. two sprigs of myrtle ppr.

Kingthorp, or Kingsthorp. Ar. a fesse betw. three escallops gu.

Kinkeny. Ar. a saltire sa. within a bordure engr. of the last.

Kinkley. Gu. a chev. engr. ar.

Kinley. Ar. on a bend sa. three escallops of the first.

Kinloch (that Ilk, and Nevay, co. Forfar, bart.). Az. a boar's head erased betw. three mascles or. *Crest*—A young eagle perching and looking up to the sun in its splendour ppr. *Motto*—Non degener,

Kinloch (Aberbothrie, co. Forfar, 1672). Az. a boar's head erased betw. three mascles or. Same *Crest* and *Motto* as the last.

Kinloch (Gourdie, co. Forfar). Az. on a chev. betw. three mascles a boar's head erased of the field, in chief a fleur-de-lis of the second. *Crest*—An eagle soaring aloft ppr. *Motto*—Yet higher.

Kinloch (Kilrie, co. Forfar, 1764). Az. on a chev. ar. a mullet gu. betw. two mascles in chief of the second and a boar's head erased in base or. *Crest*—An eagle reguard. wings endorsed sa. armed gu. looking at the sun ppr. *Motto*—Altius tendo.

Kinloch (Kinloch, co. Perth, bart., 1873). Quarterly, 1st, az. a boar's head erased betw. three mascles or, a crescent of the second in chief for diff., for KINLOCH; 2nd, gu. a chev. embattled betw. three crescents ar., for OLIPHANT; 3rd, per fess ar. and sa. a chev. betw. three cinquefoils counterchanged, for BALNEAVES; 4th, counter-quartered, 1st, gu. a broken spear and a standard saltireways ar. the last charged with a cross of the second and fringed or, 2nd, az. a cat saliant ar., 3rd, ar. on a saltire sa. nine mascles of the first, a bordure az., 4th, or, three bars wavy gu. each charged with an escallop of the field, all for SMYTH. *Crest*—A young eagle perched, looking up to the sun in his splendour all ppr. *Motto*—Non degener.

Kinloch (Gilmerton, co. Edinburgh, bart., 1686; as recorded 1829). Quarterly, 1st and 4th, az. a boar's head erased betw. three mascles or; 2nd and 3rd, ar. a fess betw. a boar's head erased in chief and two mullets in base az., for ROCHEAD. *Crest*—An eagle rising ppr. *Motto*—Altius tendo.

Kinmarton. Ar. a chev, betw. three escallops gu.

Kinnaird (Inchture, co. Perth, before elevation to the Peerage). Quarterly, 1st and 4th, gu. a saltire betw. four crescents or, for KINNAIRD; 2nd and 3rd, gu. three stars ar., for KIRKALDY. *Crest*—A garland of laurel ppr. *Motto*—Qui patitur vincit.

Kinnaird (*Baron Kinnaird*). Quarterly, 1st and 4th, or, a fesse wavy betw. three mullets gu. as a coat of augmentation; 2nd and 3rd, gu. a saltire betw. four crescents or. *Crest*—A mullet betw. the horns of a crescent or, issuing out of a cloud within two branches of palm in orle ppr.; over the crest the motto, Phœbo lux. *Supporters*—Two savages wreathed about the head and middle with oak leaves, their hands which support the shield in chains hanging down to their feet, in their other hands a garland of laurel all ppr. *Mottoes*—Errantia lumina fallunt; and, Certa cruce salus.

Kinne. Gu. a chev. ar.

Kinnear (that Ilk, co. Fife). Sa. on a bend or, three canary birds ppr. *Crest*—Two anchors saltireways ppr. *Motto*—I live in hope.

Kinnear (Edinburgh, 1818). Quarterly, 1st and 4th, as KINNEAR, of that Ilk, within a bordure or; 2nd and 3rd, ar. on a fret of four pieces gu. as many hearts or, in every interstice a rose of the second barbed vert, for GARDINER. *Crest*—An anchor ppr. *Motto*—Spem fortuna alit.

Kinner. Gu. a chief dancettée or.

Kinneram. Or, on a chief ar. three bends gu.

Kinnersby (co. Salop). Az. semée of cross crosslets a lion ramp. ar.

Kinnersley (Binfield Manor, co. Berks). Per pale az. and sa. a lion ramp. erm. holding betw. the paws a cross pattée fitchée or, within an orle of eight cross crosslets of the last. *Crest*—A mount vert, thereon before an oak tree fructed ppr. a greyhound sejant erm. collared or, the dexter forepaw supporting a cross crosslet, as in the arms. *Motto*—Timor omnis abesto.

Kinnersley. Ar. a chev. engr. betw. three mullets sa.

Kinnerton. Ar. a chev. gu. betw. three mullets sa.

Kinninmond (that Ilk, co. Fife; the heiress *m.* Sir WILLIAM MURRAY, of Melgund). Az. a chev. ar. in chief three fleurs-de-lis of the second. *Crest*—An oak tree vert. *Motto*—Stabo.

Kinnoull, Earl of. See HAY-DRUMMOND.

Kinnyman, or Kinsman. Gu. a bull's head cabossed ar. armed or.

Kinross (Scotland). Gu. two swords in saltire ar. hilted or, betw. four hands couped apaumée ppr.

Kinross (Scotland). Gu. a chev. chequy or and az. betw. three swords paleways ar. hilts and pommels or.

Kinsellagh. See O'CINSALLAGH.

Kinsellagh (Smith's Ordinary, Ulster's Office). Ar. a fess gu. betw. two garbs in chief and a lion pass. in base sa.

Kinsellagh (confirmed by Roberts, Ulster, 1647, to EDMUND KINSELLAGH, gent., of the city of Dublin). Vert two lions ramp. combatant or, armed and langued gu. on a chief quarterly of the second and sa. an eft or lizard pass. ppr. *Crest*—A demi eft or lizard saliant ppr.

Kinsey. Ar. a tower gu. *Crest*—Out of the top of a tower ppr. an arm embowed, vested vert, the hand holding a spear fessways all ppr.

Kinsey (quartered by WELBY, of Woodhead, co. Rutland. Visit. Rutland, 1618). Or, pellettée, an eagle displ. with two heads sa.

Kinsey (Blackden Hall, co. Chester; allowed at Visit. co. Chester). Ar. a chev. betw. three squirrels sejant gu.

Kinsey (Knutsford, co. Chester). Same *Arms*.

Kinsman, or Kynnesman (Loddington, Pipwell-Abbey, and Broughton, co. Northampton). Per pale az. and gu. three saltires ar. *Crest*—A buck ppr. lodged in fern vert.

Kinthorpe. Ar. a fesse betw. three escallops gu.

Kintore (that Ilk, co. Aberdeen). Or, a chev. betw. three castles gu.

Kintore, Earl of. See KEITH.

Kinver. Per chief indented or and gu.

Kinveton, alias Gilbert (co. Derby). Gu. a bend vairé ar. and sa.

Kinwelmarch, or Kilmarch. Per fesse erm. and ar. a lion ramp. sa.

Kippen (Glasgow, 1819). Ar. a saltire within a bordure engr. purp. *Crest*—An eagle, wings expanded, issuing out of a tower all ppr.

Kipping (Tewdley, co. Kent). Lozengy or and az. on a chief gu. a lion pass. of the first.

Kirby, or Kirkby (Hawthorn, co. Durham, and Kirkby Thore, co. Westmoreland). Ar. on a fesse vert three crescents or. *Crest*—An anchor gu. entwined with a serpent vert.

Kirby, or Kirkby. Same *Arms*. *Crest*—A flaming heart gu. betw. two branches of palm in orle vert.

Kirby (co. Kent). Az. six lions ramp. ar. three, two, and one, on a canton or, a mullet gu.

Kirby (Meophams-Bank, Tunbridge, co. Kent, Sheriff of London, 1816-17). Ar. two bars gu. on a canton of the second a lion's head erased or. *Crest*—Out of a ducal coronet per pale or and ar. an elephant's head erased or. eared of the second, tusked of the first.

Kirby (granted to RICHARD CHARLES KIRBY, Esq., C.B., of Blandford Square, co. Middlesex). Ar. a chief embattled gu. over all a bend sa. charged with three greyhounds' heads erased of the first. *Crest*—A dexter arm embowed in armour grasping a scymitar, and in front thereof a chaplet of roses all ppr. *Motto*—Firm.

Kirby. Ar. two bars gu. on a canton of the second a cross moline of the first. *Crest*—On a chapeau purp. turned up erm. a cross moline ar. within a circular wreath of the last and gu.

Kirby (London). Ar. on a fesse vert three crosses formée.

Kirby (co. Nottingham, temp. Elizabeth). Ar. two bars and a canton gu.

Kirby. Az. a lion ramp. or on a canton ar. a mullet gu. (another, gu. three crosses crosslet or; another, a cross within a bordure engr. sa.; another, ar. on a fesse gu. three crosses crosslet or.

Kirch. Ar. a stag saliant gu. armed or. *Crest*—A talbot's head sa. collared and lined gu.

Kirch. Ar. a stag saliant ppr. armed or. *Crest*—On a pillar ar. a heart gu.

Kircham, or Kirkham. Erm. three lions ramp. gu. a bordure engr. of the last.

Kirdeston. Gu. a saltire engr. ar.

Kirhile, or Kirhir (co. Devon). Or, an eagle displ. sa.

Kiriel (co. Leicester). Ar. two chev. and a canton gu.

Kirk (Retford, co. Nottingham). Ar. a chev. betw. three boars' heads erased sa. *Crest*—A boar's head erect and erased sa.

Kirk (Scotland). Gu. a crosier or, and sword ar. saltireways, on a chief of the second a thistle vert.

Kirk (Aberfoil, Scotland). Same *Arms*, a bordure indented ar. *Crest*—A crosier and dagger in saltire. *Motto*—Optimum quod primum.

Kirkaldie (Inchture, co. Perth). Gu. three stars ar.

Kirkaldie (Grange, Scotland, bart., 1664). Gu. a chev. betw. three stars in chief and a crescent in base or. *Crest*—A man's head, with the face looking upwards ppr. *Motto*—Fortissima veritas.

Kirkaldie (Scotland, 1672). Gu. a chev. invecked ar. betw. two stars in chief and a crescent in base or.

Kirkaldy, Burgh of (Scotland). Az. an abbey of three pyramids, each ensigned with a cross pattée or. *Motto*—Vigilando maneo.

Kirkbrid (Kirkbridge, co. Cumberland). Sa. a cross engr. ar.

Kirkbridge (Ellerton in Hesket, co. Cumberland; descended from ODARD, Baron of Wigton). Ar. a cross engr. vert.

Kirkbridge (co. Northumberland). Ar. a saltire vert.

Kirkbryd (quartered by DALSTON, of Dalston, co. Cumberland. Visit. Cumb. 1615). Ar. a cross engr. vert betw. four annulets sa.

Kirkby (Kirkby, co. York; WILLIAM KIRKEBY, whose dau., JOAN, *m.* HENRY LUDYNGTON, father of NICHOLAS LUDYNGTON, citizen of London. Visit. London, 1568). Ar. two bars gu. on a canton of the last a cross patonce or.

Kirkby (Kirkby, co. Lancaster, 1664). Same *Arms*.

Kirkby (Kirkby Hall, co. Lincoln). Same *Arms*.

Kirkby (Uprawcliffe, co. Lancaster, 1567). Same *Arms*, a crescent for diff.

Kirkby (Stainbridge, co. Hants). Per pale ar. and gu. on a chief sa. a lion pass. or.

Kirkby (co. Leicester). Per pale gu. and sa. a lion ramp. ar.

Kirkby (co. Leicester). Ar. a cross betw. two annulets vert.

Kirkby (co. Kent; Sir JOHN KIRKBY, Knt., *temp.* Henry IV.; his dau. and heir, ALICE, *m.* THOMAS STONER, Esq., of Stoner, co. Oxford. Visit. Oxon, 1566). Az. six lions ramp. or, on a canton of the last a mullet gu.

Kirkby (Kirkby-in-Ashfield, co. Nottingham). Az. a fesse betw. two chev. erm.

Kirkby (quartered by MITFORD through WHARTON. Visit. Durham, 1613). Ar. two bars gu. on a canton of the second a cross flory of the first.

Kirkconnel (that Ilk, co. Dumfries; the heiress *m.* AYMER MAXWELL, younger brother of the first *Lord Maxwell*). Az. two croziers in saltire adossée, and in chief a mitre.

Kirke (The Eaves, co. Derby). Ar. a chev. betw. three boars' heads erased sa. *Ancient Arms*—Per fesse or and gu. a lozenge counterchanged. *Crest*—A wild boar pass. sa.

Kirke (Eastham, co. Essex). Per fesse or and gu. a lozenge counterchanged, on a canton az. a lion ramp. or, supporting a cutlass blade ar. chained and collared gold. This canton was granted as an augmentation to Sir DAVID KIRKE, Governor of Newfoundland; to LEWIS KIRKE, Governor of Canada; and to Captain THOMAS KIRKE, Vice-Admiral of the English Fleet, for their victory over the French, and the capturing of Canada. *Crest*—A dexter arm embowed in armour ppr. garnished or, holding a cutlass ar. hilt and pommel gold.

Kirke (Markham, co. Notts). Ar. a chev. betw. three boars' heads couped sa. *Crest*—A boar's head erect couped sa.

Kirke (co. York). Or, a chev. az.

Kirke. Per fesse or and gu. a bend erm. (another, a lion ramp. counterchanged).

Kirke (Edinburgh, 1682). Gu. on a saltire ar. a thistle vert, on a chief of three second three cushions az. *Crest*—A temple ppr. *Motto*—Conamine.

Kirkebridge. Ar. a saltire engr. vert.

Kirkeby (co. Derby). Ar. on a fesse vert three crescents or.

Kirkeby (co. Lincoln). Gu. a fesse betw. two chev. erm.

Kirkeby. Ar. on a chev. betw. three martlets gu. five lozenges erm. a bordure engr. vert.

Kirkeby. Sa. a lion ramp. supporting a garb ar.

Kirkeby. Ar. a chev. az. betw. three cocks gu.

Kirkeby. Sa. two lions pass. in pale or.

Kirkebyrd. Ar. a cross engr. vert.

Kirkefton. Gu. two bars ar.

Kirkeland. Ar. a saltire engr. vert.

Kirkelord. Sa. three mullets ar. and a bordure engr. or.

Kirkenton, Kirkton, or Kerton (Kirton, co. Lincoln). Gu. three bars erm. *Crest*—A fox pass. ppr.

Kirketon, or Kerketon (Kirketon, co. Lincoln, *temp.* Edward II.). Barry of six gu. and ar.

Kirketon (*Baron Kirketon*, extinct; THOMAS DE KIRKETON summoned to Parliament 1342, but never after). Same *Arms*.

Kirketon (*Baron Kirketon*, extinct 1367; JOHN DE KIRKETON was summoned to Parliament 1362-63, *d. s. p.*). Same *Arms*.

Kirketon. Or, three eagles displ. sa.

Kirketon. Ar. a fesse gu.

Kirketon, or Kirkton. Az. three martlets ar.

Kirketon, or Kirton. Az. three water bougets ar.

Kirketot (co. Suffolk, *temp.* Henry III.). Az. on a cross ar. five escallops gu.

Kirkham (Ashcombe, *temp.* Henry III., and Blagdon, co. Devon, *temp.* Edward I.; Sir WILLIAM KIRKHAM, Knt., Visit. Devon, 1620, sixth in descent from ROBERT KIRKHAM, living 5 Henry V., A.D. 1416; the heiress *m.* Sir GEORGE BLOUNT, co. Oxford). Erm. three lions ramp. gu. a bordure engr. sa. *Crest*—A lion's head erased ar.

Kirkham (Pinhoe, co. Devon; descended from Blagdon). Same *Arms* and *Crest*.

Kirkham (Fynnshed and Cutterstock, co. Northampton). Ar. on a fesse gu. three bezants. *Crest*—A Saracen's head fullfaced ppr. couped at the shoulders, gorged with a ducal coronet or, wreathed about the temples ar. and sa. *Another Crest*—A popinjay vert, beaked and collared gu.

Kirkham. Ar. three lions ramp. gu.

Kirkhill (co. Devon). Or, an eagle displ. sa.

Kirkhoven (*Earl of Bellomont* in Ireland, and *Baron Wotton* in England, extinct 1683). Ar. three hearts gu. *Crest*—A demi negress couped at the waist in profile ppr. wreathed around the temples az. and ar. winged of the last. *Supporters*—Dexter, a dragon sans wings vert; sinister, a buck erm. armed and winged or.

Kirkhoven. Or, three hearts gu. *Crest*—A beacon fired ppr.

Kirkland (Kirkland, co. Cumberland, Kirkland, co. Lancaster, Brampton, co. Derby; founded by GAMEL, *Lord of Kirkeland*, co. Cumberland, *temp.* William I.; now represented in the senior line by WALTER KIRKLAND, Esq., of Wirksworth, co. Derby, and Eastbourne, co. Sussex). Sa. three mullets ar. within a bordure engr. or, quartering, KIRKLAND (ancient), sa. three mullets or. *Crest*—On a ducal coronet a falcon jessed and belled all ppr., KIRKLAND.

Kirkland (Ashby-de-la-Zouch, co. Leicester; settled there at Ashby early in the last century; the last male representative, THOMAS SMITH KIRKLAND, Esq., M.D., *d.* 1869). Sa. three mullets ar. within a bordure engr. or. *Crest*—Out of a ducal coronet or, a falcon close belled ppr. *Motto*—Facta non verba.

Kirkland (co. Lancaster). Ar. a bend engr. sa. (another, ar. a saltire engr. vert).

Kirkland. Ar. on a mount in base vert an oak tree ppr. debruised by a fesse gu. charged with three owls ar. *Crest*—An owl, as in the arms.

Kirkland, Kirkeley, Kirklay, Kirklayne, or Kirkaton. Ar. three bars gemels sa. (another, the tinctures reversed). *Crest*—A church environed with trees ppr.

Kirkley (co. York). Ar. two bars engr. sa.

Kirkley. Gu. two bars or, in chief three keys ar. (another, gu. a chev. erm.; another, or).

Kirkman. Sa. two crosiers in saltire or, on a chief concave az. three mitres ar. garnished gu. *Crest*—A crosier and sword in saltire ppr. *Motto*—In Deo confido.

Kirkman. Ar. two bars sa. in chief as many palets of the second. *Crest*—A demi lion ramp. ar.

Kirkpatrick (Closeburn, co. Dumfries, bart., 1685). Ar. a saltire and chief az. the last charged with three cushions or. *Crest*—A hand holding a dagger in pale distilling drops of blood. *Motto*—I make sure.

Kirkpatrick (Culloch, co. Kirkcudbright, 1791). Ar. a saltire az. betw. one star in chief and two in flanks gu. on a chief of the second three cushions or. *Crest*—As Closeburn. *Motto*—I mak sicker.

Kirkpatrick-Howat (Mabie, co. Kirkcudbright, 1861). Ar. a saltire az. betw. one star in chief, two in flanks, and in base an owl gu. on a chief of the second three cushions or, a bordure of the third. *Crest*—A dexter armed hand holding a dagger in pale distilling drops of blood ppr. *Motto*—I mak sicker.

Kirkpatrick (Allanshaw, co. Lanark, 1872). Per saltire or and ar. on a saltire az. betw. two cinquefoils in flank vert a martlet of the second, on a chief of the third three cushions of the first. *Crest*—As the last. *Motto*—I'se mak sicker.

Kirkpatrick (England). Ar. a saltire az. on a chief of the last a cushion of the first. *Crest*—A stag's head ar.

Kirkpatrick (Liverpool). Ar. a saltire az. on a chief engr. of the last three cushions or. *Crest*, and *Motto*, the same as of Closeburn.

Kirkslow, Kirkstowe, or Kirstow (co. Lancaster). Gyronny of twelve or and sa. on a canton gu. a covered cup of the first.

Kirkstall-Abbey (co. York). Az. three swords ar. points in base, hilts and pommels or.

Kirkswold. Per fesse gu. and az. a griffin ar. armed or, seizing on a dragon vert, holding a plume of the third.

Kirkton, or Kirton. Ar. three eagles displ. sa. *Crest*—An arm couped, resting the elbow on the wreath, holding three ears of wheat ppr.

Kirkton (quartered by NICHOLAS KERDIFFE, Sergeant-at-Law, 1609). Az. three water bougets or.

Kirkton (Fun. Ent. Ulster's Office, 1596). Same *Arms.*

Kirktot (co. Suffolk). Az. a cross ar. charged with five escallops gu.

Kirkwood (Scotland). Per fesse az. and ar. on the first a demi savage issuing, wielding a wooden mallet ppr. on the second three branches of oak vert.

Kirkwood (Scotland, 16th century). Gu. three fetterlocks or, on a chev. of the second three pheons of the first.

Kirkwood (Woodbrook, co. Roscommon; confirmed to JAMES KIRKWOOD, Esq., J.P., High Sheriff of that co. 1848, son of THOMAS KIRKWOOD, Esq., of same place, J.P., High Sheriff 1808, and grandson of JAMES KIRKWOOD, J.P., and to the other descendants of the said last-mentioned JAMES KIRKWOOD). Gu. on a chev. or, betw. three fetterlocks ar. a pheon betw. two mullets pierced sa. *Crest*—A pheon sa. charged with a mullet or. *Motto*—Spes mea in Deo.

Kirkyn. Ar. a fesse az. *Crest*—A demi griffin ppr. holding in the claw an escallop or.

Kirlington. Ar. a lion ramp. gu. depressed by a fesse or, charged with three crosses pattée fitchée sa.

Kirriell. Or, two chev. gu. a canton of the last.

Kirsopp (The Spital, co. Northumberland). Gu. a saltire erm. betw. two cranes in pale ar. and two garbs in fesse or. *Crest*—A mount vert, thereon a crane, as in the arms, the dexter claw resting on an escutcheon ar. charged with the letter K sa. *Motto*—Credo.

Kirstowe (co. Lancaster). Gyronny of twelve or and az. on a canton sa. a covered cup of the first, on a chief gu. three covered cups gold.

Kirton (co. Lancaster). Gyronny of twelve or and az. on a canton gu. a covered cup of the first.

Kirton (co. Lincoln). Barry of eight erm. and gu.

Kirton (Thorp Mandevil, co. Northampton). Quarterly, 1st, ar. a fesse and a chev. in chief gu.; 2nd, ar. a crescent within a bordure invecked sa.; 3rd, per pale or and gu. a fesse betw. three leopards' faces counterchanged; 4th, ar. a fesse betw. three hawks' hoods gu. *Crest*—A falcon, wings expanded ar. beaked, jessed, and belled or, resting the dexter claw on a hawk's hood gu. *Ancient Crest*—A hawk close ppr. hooded gu. beaked and legged or.

Kirton (co. Westmoreland). Ar. a fesse and a chev. in chief gu.

Kirton (co. Wilts). Or, a fesse and chev. in base gu.

Kirton. Ar. a chev. gu. betw. three mullets sa. (another, ar. a fesse gu.; another, sa. a fesse erm. in chief four fleurs-de-lis or, in base three pikes ar.; another, ar. a chev. betw. three crosses crosslet gu.; another, ar. six eagles displ. sa. three, two, and one).

Kirvill (co. Cornwall). Sa. three lions' heads jessant, as many fleurs-de-lis ar.

Kirwan. See O'QUIRIVAN.

Kirwan (Cregg, co. Galway; WILLIAM KIRWAN d. in Galway, 1499; Reg. Ulster's Office). Ar. a chev. sa. betw. three Cornish choughs ppr. *Crest*—A Cornish chough ppr. *Motto*—Mon Dieu, mon Roi, et ma patrie.

Kirwan (Blindwell, co. Galway; settled at Tober Keagh, Anglice Blindwell, prior to the reign of Henry VII.). Same *Arms, Crest,* and *Motto.*

Kirwan (Castle Hacket, co. Galway; descended from Cregg). Same *Arms* and *Crest*. *Motto*—J'aime mon Dieu, mon Roi, et mon pays.

Kirwan (Stowe Lodge, co. Galway; descended from Cregg). Same *Arms* and *Crest.*

Kirwan (late of Moyne, co. Galway; JOHN STRATFORD KIRWAN, Esq., late of Moyne, m. 1859, Lady VICTORIA MARY RAWDON HASTINGS, third dau. of GEORGE, second *Marquess of Hastings,* and co-heiress of her brother HENRY, fourth *Marquess of Hastings, Baron Hastings, Hungerford, Grey de Ruthyn,* &c., &c.). Same *Arms* and *Crest.* *Motto*—J'aime mon Dieu, mon Roi, et ma patrie.

Kirwan (The Island of Martinique; allowed by Hawkins, Ulster, 1745, to MICHAEL KIRWAN, grandson of PIERSE KIRWAN, who left Galway in 1652, and settled at Martinique). Same *Arms* and *Crest.*

Kirwan (Burdigala, in France; allowed by Bryan, Deputy Ulster, 1766, to MARCUS KIRWAN, of that place, great-grandson of NICHOLAS KIRWAN, Esq., of Ballintobber, co. Mayo, the son of RICHARD KIRWAN, Governor and M.P. of Galway). Same *Arms* and *Crest.* *Motto*—J'aime mon Dieu, mon Roi, et mon pais.

Kirwan (England). Gu. three crescents ar. *Crest*—A hand erect issuing from a cloud, holding a broken spear all ppr.

Kitchen. Per chev. ar. and sa. three water bougets counterchanged. *Crest*—An arm in armour embowed, issuing from a cloud in the sinister, holding a sword all ppr.

Kitchener. Erm. a chief wavy az. *Crest*—A bull's head sa. betw. two flags az. charged with a cross or.

Kitchin (Meales, co. Lancaster). Gu. a chev. paly of four ar. and sa. betw. three bezants, each charged with a lapwing of the third.

Kitchin (London). Ar. on a pile az. betw. two crosses crosslet gu. an eagle displ. of the field. *Crest*—A pelican's head erased az. beaked or, vulned gu.

Kitchiner. Ar. on a chev. quarterly, gu. and sa. betw. three bustards of the second, as many bezants. *Crest*—A buck's head erased, pierced throug't the neck by an arrow in bend all ppr.

Kitching (co. Hereford). Ar. a chev. betw. three bustards gu. *Crest*—On a ducal coronet or, a wivern vert.

Kitchingham. Ar. on a chev. quarterly, gu. and sa. three bezants.

Kitchingman (Helmesley, co. York; granted by Camden, April, 1616). Ar. on a pile sa. betw. two crosses crosslet fitchée gu. three lozenges of the field.

Kite, or Keyte (Cheselborne, co. Dorset, and co. Worcester, Lord Mayor of London, 1767). Az. a chev. betw. three kites' heads erased or. *Crest*—A unicorn's head erased gu. armed and collared gu.

Kite, or Keyte (Ebrington, co. Gloucester). Az. on a chev. betw. three kites' heads erased or, as many trefoils slipped gu. *Crest*—A kite's head erased or.

Kitesford (co. Somerset). Ar. a bend lozengy sa.

Kitson (Hengrave, co. Suffolk). Sa. three lucies nauriant ar. a chief or. *Crest*—A unicorn's head ar. attired and maned or, environed with palisadoes gold. *Another Crest* —On a mount or, in flames ppr. a unicorn's head az. This coat was granted 13 Feb. 1568, by Dethick, Garter, to THOMAS KITSON, Esq., of Hengrave, being an alteration from the coat borne by his ancestors, which was confused, and greatly needed correction. The older coat (granted to THOMAS KITSON, 14 April, 1527) was, sa. three lucies in pale ar. on a chief or, a lion ramp. of the first guttée d'or betw. two pellets, the dexter charged with a martlet, and the sinister with an anchor or.

Kitson. Paly of six ar. and az. on a chief gu. three bezants.

Kittermaster (Meriden, formerly of Coleshill, co. Warwick, granted by Segar, Garter, to THOMAS KITTERMASTER, of Coleshill, co. Warwick, and Lincoln's Inn, London; confirmed to WILLIAM KITTERMASTER, son of THOMAS KITTERMASTER, who was great-grandson of WILLIAM KYDERMASTER, of Coleshill, co. Warwick, and Romsey, co. Salop). Az. a chev. erminois betw. three bezants. *Crest*—On a chapeau az. turned up erm. an eagle, wings expanded erminois.

Kittleby, or Kittelby (Steple, co. Salop). Ar. two chev. sa. *Crest*—A lion's head erased gu (another, or).

Kittleby. Az. a saltire embattled betw. four martlets or.

Kivellioc. Az. six garbs or, three, two, and one. *Crest*—An Indian goat's head ar.

Klere, or Kleere. Ar. (another, or) a cross betw. four estoiles gu.

Klokefield (co. Norfolk). Az. a cross chequy ar. and gu.

Knaplock (Winchester, 1601). Az. a fesse betw. two chev. gobony erm. and gu. *Crest*—A boar's head couped or, the mouth embrued with blood.

Knaplod. Barry of six or and az. a bend gu.

Knapman (Throwleigh, co. Devon; WILLIAM KNAPMAN, of that place, Visit. Devon, 1620, great-grandson of WILLIAM KNAPMAN, of the same place). Or, on a cross gu. betw. four Cornish choughs ppr. five blocks of tin ppr. marked with the letter W sa.

Knapman. Ar. three lions ramp. in fesse gu. *Crest*—A sword in pale enfiled with a Saracen's head couped ppr.

Knapp (Tuddenham, co. Norfolk, Needham and Washbroke, co. Suffolk). Or, in chief three close helmets sa. in base a lion pass. of the last. *Crest*—An arm embowed in armour ppr. garnished or, the hand also ppr. grasping by the blade a broken sword ar. hilt and pommel gold, with a branch of laurel vert.

Knapp (Little Linford Hall and Shenley, co. Bucks). Same *Arms.*

Knapp (HAMBLY-KNAPP). Or, a lion pass. in base and in chief three esquires' helmets sa., quartering gu. a lion ramp. ar. crowned or, for HAMBLY. *Crest*—Same as Tuddenham.

Knapp. Ar. a cross gu. betw. four roses ppr.

Knappe (Woodcot, co. Oxford; granted 2 Sept. 1669). Sa. a lion pass. in chief three helmets ar.

Knapton. Or, a cross sa. charged with a cross calvary crossed at the top ar. *Crest*—Out of a ducal coronet or, two arms dexter and sinister, in saltire, each holding a scymitar in pale ppr.

Knapton (quartered by FEILDING, of Newnham, co. Warwick. Har. MSS. 1167). Erm. on a fess vert three escallops or.

Knapton (Boldre, Hants). Gu. a chev. dancettée erm. betw. three chaplets or. *Crest*—A garland gu. floreated or, about a lance ar. *Motto*—Pretium victoribus coronæ.

Knaresburgh (Knaresbrough, co. York). Ar. a lion ramp. gu. ducally crowned or, within a bordure sa. charged with eight bezants.

Knaresborough, Town of (co. York). Seal of the Corporation represents a castle in base, on an escroll four letters, viz., E R Q R, over the castle, on a wreath, a dexter hand in armour couped at the wrist, holding a branch of acorns, the date 1611.

Knaresborough-Abbey (co. York). Ar. a lion ramp. gu. within a bordure of the last bezantée.

Knatchbull (Mersham Hatch, Kent, bart.). Az. three cross crosslets fitchée betw. two bendlets or. *Crest*—On a chapeau az. turned up erm. a leopard statant ar. spotted sa. *Motto*—In crucifixa gloria mea.

Knatchbull (Fun. Ent. Ulster's Office, 1635, VINCENT KNATCHBULL, son and heir of REGINALD KNATCHBULL, Esq., of Mersham, co. Kent, *d.* at Kellagh, co. Kilkenny). Az. three crosses crosslet fitchée in bend betw. two bendlets or.

Knatchbull (co. Kent; granted 1574). Az. three crosses crosslet in bend betw. two bendlets engr. or. *Crest*—As the last.

Knatchbull (Babington, co. Somerset). Az. three crosses crosslet fitchée betw. two bendlets or. *Crest*—On a chapeau az. turned up erm. a leopard statant ar. spotted sa. *Motto*—In crucifixa gloria mea.

Knatchbull-Huggessen. See HUGGESSEN.

Kneford. Az. a chev. betw. ten mullets or, six in chief and four in base.

Kneland (that Ilk, Scotland). See CLELAND.

Knell (cos. Oxford and Gloucester). Gu. crusily a lion ramp. or. *Crest*—A demi lion or, holding in the dexter paw a cross crosslet fitchée az.

Knell. Gu. semée of cross crosslets fitchée a lion ramp. or, crowned and langued az.

Knell. Gu. a chev. betw. three roses ar.

Knell, or Knelly. Ar. on a chev. sa. three mullets of the field.

Kneller (co. Wilts.) Quarterly, 1st, ar. two escutcheons, each charged with a rose ppr. in base a point charged with a fleur-de-lis; 2nd, sa. on a chev. three covered cups ar. a rose gu.; 3rd, sa. two bars engr. ar. on a chief or, a lion pass. betw. two fleurs-de-lis of the first; 4th, or, an eagle's leg couped contourne, and a sinister wing in fesse. *Crest*—On a mount vert a stag standing beside a vine tree all ppr.

Knevet (co. Norfolk, and Escrick, co. York). Ar. a bend within a bordure engr. of the second.

Knevet. Ar. a bend betw. three trefoils sa. within a bordure engr. of the last. *Crest*—A nest with young birds ppr.

Knevet. Ar. three chaplets gu. *Crest*—In the sea a ship in full sail ppr.

Knevet. Ar. on a bend sa. three trefoils of the first within a bordure engr. of the second.

Knevett, or Knevit (Rosemaryn, co. Cornwall, cos. Norfolk and Suffolk). Ar. a bend within a bordure engr. sa. *Crest*—A dragon's head betw. two wings expanded sa.

Knevett (co. Norfolk). Ar. a bend sa. within a bordure engr. az.

Kneysworth, or Knesworth (Lord Mayor of London, 1505; cos. Cornwall and Stafford). Erm. a chev. wavy gu. betw. three greyhounds in full course sa.

Kneysworth, or Knesworth. Or, a chev. wavy gu. between three greyhounds in full course sa. *Crest*—A buffalo's head erased gu.

Kneysworth. Erm. a chev. embattled (another, wavy) gu. between three greyhounds courant sa. collared or.

Knife. Az. three knives in pale ar. hafts or. *Crest*—A dove reguard. holding in the beak an olive branch all ppr.

Knife. Paly of six ar. and az. on a chief sa. two swords in saltire of the first, hilts or.

Knifton (co. Derby). Gu. a bend vair.

Knight (*Earl of Catterlough* and *Baron Luxborough*, extinct 1772). Ar. three bendlets gu. on a canton az. a spur, rowel down, leathered, all or, quartering, quarterly, 1st and 4th, gu. a lion reguard. or; 2nd and 3rd, ar. three boars' heads couped sa. langued gu. *Crests*—A spur, rowel up, leathered, all or, betw. two wings displ. gu. *Supporters*—Dexter, a lion reguard. or; sinister, a boar sa. langued gu. ducally gorged and chained gold.

Knight (Charwerton and Rowington, co. Northants; granted 1613). Same *Arms* and *Crest*.

571

Knight (Banbury, co. Oxford). Same *Arms*, a border of the second.

Knight (The Manor House, Glen Parva, co. Leicester). Paly ar. and gu. on a canton of the second a spur or, a bordure engr. sa. *Crest*—Betw. two wings a spur or, rowel downwards, leathered and buckled gold.

Knight (quartered by the Right Hon. Sir JAMES LEWIS KNIGHT BRUCE, Knt.). See BRUCE.

Knight (Congresbury, co. Somerset, *temp.* Queen Elizabeth, and Tythegston, co. Glamorgan; ROBERT KNIGHT, eldest son of Sir JOHN KNIGHT, Knt. of Congresbury, *m.* 1708, CECIL, dau. and heiress of EDWARD TURBERVILLE, of Sutton, and granddau. and heiress of RICHARD LOUGHOR, Esq., of Tythegston). Ar. three palets gu. within a bordure engr. az. on a canton of the second a spur or. *Crest*—On a ducal coronet an eagle displ. all or. *Motto*—Gloria calcar habet.

Knight (Ruscombe, co. Berks). Ar. three palets gu. on a canton of the second a spur, with the rowel downwards, leathered or, within a bordure engr. sa.

Knight (arms in New Coll., Oxford; granted by the Emperor Maximilian to WILLIAM KNIGHT, Fellow of this Coll. Letters Patent, 20 July, 1514. Visit. Oxon, 1574). Per fess or and gu. a demi sun and a demi rose conjoined counterchanged, on the top of the demi rose two eagles' heads issuant sa. and from each side an eagle's wing displ. of the last.

Knight (Kingerby, co. Lincoln). Ar. three bendlets gu. on a canton az. a spur with rowel downwards of the first.

Knight (co. Buckingham). Sa. a griffin segreant erm. beaked and armed gu. a bordure of the second.

Knight (cos. Gloucester and York). Sa. a griffin segreant or. *Crest*—A talbot's head erased sa. bezantée.

Knight (Norroy King of Arms, *d.* 1593). Vert a bend lozengy or.

Knight (Chester Herald, *d.* 1618). Same *Arms*, a crescent for diff.

Knight (Clopton and Althorpe, co. Northampton; granted, 1546, by Barker, Garter, to THOMAS KNIGHT, of Hol, co. Northampton). Ar. on a fesse betw. three bulls' heads erased sa. armed and ringed at the nose or, a fret betw. two doves of the field. *Crest*—A dexter arm embowed, vested bendy wavy sinister of four or and gu. supporting with the hand a sword in pale, the point resting on the wreath, the pommel surmounting a pair of spurs all ppr.

Knight (co. Hants; granted 1523). Ar. three palets gu. on a canton of the second a spur or, a bordure engr. az. *Crest*—On a ducal coronet gu. an eagle displ. or.

Knight (co. Norfolk). Same *Arms*.

Knight (co. Hants). Or, on a chev. sa. three griffins segreant of the first.

Knight (Baldock and Weston, co. Hertford, and Betsford, co. Nottingham). Sa. on a fesse ar. three quatrefoils of the field, in chief a nag's head erased of the second. *Crest*—A goat's head erased per fesse gu. and or, attired gold, holding in the mouth a laurel sprig vert.

Knight (Chawton, co. Hants; granted 1738). Vert a bend lozengy or, in base a cinquefoil ar. *Coat*—A demi grayfriar ppr. holding in the dexter hand a cinquefoil slipped ar. from the sinister wrist a bracelet of beads pendent as.

Knight (Rowington, co. Warwick; confirmed to WILLIAM KNIGHT, of that place. Her. Visit.). Same *Arms* and *Crest* as KNIGHT, *Earl of Catterlough*.

Knight (Godmersham, co. Kent). Same *Arms*, a canton gu., quartering or, a chev. gu. betw. three lions' gambs erect sa., for AUSTEN. *Crest*—A demi grayfriar ppr. holding in the dexter hand a cinquefoil slipped ar. and in the sinister a cross sa. suspended from the wrist, the breast charged with a rose gu. *Motto*—Suivant St. Pierre.

Knight (London). Same *Arms*, a crescent for diff. *Crest*—A demi friar ppr. vested and hooded ar. having an upper mantle or, holding in the dexter hand a lanthorn, purfled of the third, in the sinister hand a paternoster gu. with a crucifix pendent at the end.

Knight, alias Brother (London and Clerkenwell, co. Middlesex; granted 25 July, 1664). Ar. a fesse gu. fretty or, betw. three bulls' heads erased sa. attired of the third.

Knight (Westerham, co. Kent; granted 20 Feb. 1662). Per chev. engr. sa. and ar. three griffins pass. counterchanged.

Knight (co. Middlesex). Quarterly, 1st and 4th, vert a bend lozengy or; 2nd and 3rd, per chev. ar. and sa. three cinquefoils counterchanged, over all, as an augmentation of honour, an escutcheon ar. charged with a cross of St. George.

Knight (co. Northampton, 1613; exemplified, 1772, to JANE DAVIES, of St. Mary-le-bone, co. Middlesex, on her taking the name and arms of KNIGHT). Ar. three bends gu. on a canton az. a spur with buckle and leathers or.

Knight (Sir ARNOLD JAMES KNIGHT, M.D. of Sheffield,

knighted 1841). Same *Arms.*   *Crest*—A spur, as in the arms.

Knight (Brockhole, co. Northampton). Paly of six or and gu. a canton erm.

Knight (Piddington, cos. Northampton and York). Gu. two bars ar. in chief three wolves' heads erased of the second.

Knight (Shrewsbury and Bashchurch, co. Salop; eight descents of this family are given in *Vincent's Salop*). Ar. three palets gu. a bordure engr. az. on a canton of the second a spur or. *Crest*—On a spur lying fesseways or, an eagle per fesse ar. and az. wings expanded gold, beaked and legged gu.

Knight (Wolverley, co. Worcester). Ar. three palets gu. within a bordure engr. az. on a canton of the second a spur or. *Crest*—On a spur lying fesseways or, an eagle per fesse ar. and az. wings expanded gold, beaked and legged gu.

Knight (Downton Castle, co. Hereford, Simons Bath, co. Devon, and Wolverley, co. Worcester; descended from RICHARD KNIGHT, of Downton, who acquired, about a century ago, a large fortune by the Iron Works). Same *Arms*, &c.

Knight (granted by Hawley, Clarenceux, 4 Edward VI., to WILLIAM KNIGHT, Collector of the Subsidies for Southampton. Visit. Hants, 1634). Per chev. engr. ar and sa. three griffins pass. counterchanged. *Crest*—A griffin’ ad erased gu. beaked and dexter ear ar. the sinister sa. gorged with a collar or.

Knight. Az. on a fesse or, betw. three fishes haurient ar. as many roses gu. *Crest*—An arm couped, habited bendy of four or and az. holding in the hand ppr. the lower half of a fish couped in the middle of the second.

Knight. Or, on a chev. sa. three griffins segreant of the field. *Crest*—Out of a ducal coronet or, an eagle displ. erm.

Knight. Ar. on a canton gu. a spur or, within a bordure sa. (another, of the second).

Knight. Az. three fishes naiant in pale ar. against their heads as many guttées d'or, on a chief of the last three torteaux.

Knight (Langold, co. York, 1666). Or, on a chief sa. three griffins segreant of the field). *Crest*—An eagle displ or.

Knight. Ar. on a fesse betw. three bucks' heads erased sa. attired or, a fret betw. two martlets of the third.

Knight. Gu. three palets ar. a bordure engr. sa. on a canton of the last a spur and leather, rowel downwards or.

Knight. Per chev. ar. and sa. three trefoils (another, cinquefoils) counterchanged.

Knight. Az. three Cornish choughs in fesse ar. on a chief or, as many torteaux.

Knight. Ar. on a canton gu. a spur leathered or, rowel downwards, within a bordure sa.

Knight. Or, three palets gu. on a canton sa. a spur-rowel of the field within a bordure engr. of the third.

Knight. Per chev. or and sa. three cinquefoils counterchanged.

Knight. Or, on a chief sa. three griffins segreant of the field.

Knight. Or, a bordure engr. sa.

Knight. Ar. two palets az. on a canton gu. a spur, buckle and strap or.

Knight. Ar. a helmet gu.

Knight (London; granted by letters patent, dated 14 July, 1514, to WILLIAM KNIGHT, Prothonotary of the Apostolical seat (and Ambassador from King Henry VIII. to the Emperor Maximilian), afterwards made Bishop of Bath and Wells, *d.* 1547). Per fesse or and gu. an eagle with two heads displ. sa. having on its breast a demi rose and a demi sun conjoined into one, counterchanged of the field.

Knight (Danestown, co. Dublin; Reg. Ulster's Office). Gu. a chev. betw. three oval buckles or.

Knight (Reg. Ulster's Office). Ar. a chev. gu. on a canton of the last a spur with leathers, rowel down, all or.

Knight (confirmed to RICHARD GOOLD KNIGHT, of Santa Cruz, in the West Indies, Planter, late Member of the Colonial Office, now of Cloncorrich Castle, co. Leitrim, grandson of JOSEPH KNIGHT, of Kilcorby, co. Cavan). Ar. two roses in fess gu. seeded or, barbed vert, on a canton az. a spur of the third. *Crest*—Ar. spur or, betw. two wings ar. each charged with a rose, as in the arms. *Motto*—Virtus sibi aureum.

Knight (Oldtoun Corsby; Provost of Ayr, 1672). Ar. on a fess betw. three mullets az. a boar's head erased of the first. *Motto*—Fortis et verus.

Knight (Jordinstoun and Dundee, 1772). Ar. a griffin se-

greant ppr. armed and langued gu. in chief two stars az. *Crest*—A ship under sail in a sea ppr. *Motto*—Darien.

Knight (BOUGHTON-KNIGHT; exemplified to ANDREW JOHNES ROUSE BOUGHTON, Esq., of Downton Castle, co. Hereford, second son of Sir WILLIAM EDWARD ROUSE BOUGHTON, tenth bart. of Lawford, by CHARLOTTE, his wife, dau. of THOMAS ANDREW KNIGHT, Esq., of Downton Castle, upon his assuming, by royal licence, 1857, the name of KNIGHT, on inheriting the estates of his maternal grandfather). Quarterly, 1st, ar. three pallets gu. and a border indented az. on a chief of the last three spurs erect or, for KNIGHT; 2nd, ar. on a chev. betw. three cross crosslets fitchée sa. as many bucks' heads cabossed or, vulned in the forehead ppr. on a chief gu. a goat pass. of the field, and a crescent of the same for diff., for BOUGHTON; 3rd, sa. three crescents or, for BOUGHTON; 4th, sa. two bars engr. ar., for ROUSE. *Crests*—1st, BOUGHTON: A stork's head erased chevronny of four sa. and ar. holding in the beak or, a snake ppr. ; 2nd, KNIGHT; On a spur fessways or, an eagle rising ppr. holding in the beak a spear erect gold; 3rd, ROUSE: The bust of a man couped at the shoulders ppr. hair beard, and whiskers sa. the head surrounded and crossed by a riband knotted at the top, and the ends flowing from either temple ar. *Motto*—Eques sit semper æquus.

Knight-Bruce. See BRUCE.

Knight-Erskine. See ERSKINE.

Knight (registered to HENRY EDMUND KNIGHT, Esq., Alderman of the City of London). Or, three bendlets az. on a chief gu. a civic wreath betw. two spurs of the first. *Crest*—On a Roman fasces lying fessewise or, a spur, as in the arms, betw. two wings az. each charged with a civic wreath gold. *Motto*—Virtute et labore.

Knightbridge (Chelmsford, co. Essex). Ar. two bars sa. three garbs or.

Knightley (Fawsley Park, co. Northampton, bart.). Quarterly, 1st and 4th, erm.; 2nd and 3rd, paly of six or and gu Crest—A buck's head couped ar. attired or. *Supporters*— Two falcons ppr. *Motto*—Invita fortuna.

Knightley (Offchurch, co. Warwick, bart., extinct 1608; descended from EDWARD KNIGHTLEY, younger brother of Sir RICHARD KNIGHTLEY, Knt., of Fawsley, *temp.* Henry VIII). Same *Arms.*

Knightley (Shuston, 15 Ric. II.). Same *Arms*, a bordure engr. az.

Knightley (Knightley and Gnowsall). Same *Arms* as KNIGHTLEY, of Shuston, a bend engr. az. in place of the border.

Knightley (co. Stafford). Quarterly, 1st and 4th, paly of six or and gu.; 2nd and 3rd, erm.

Knightley (Kingston-upon-Thames, co. Surrey; granted by Camden, 1623, to WILLIAM KNIGHTLEY, Esq.). Quarterly, 1st and 4th, erm.; 2nd and 3rd, paly of six or and gu. on a bend az. a tilting-spear of the second. *Crest*—A stag's head ar. attired or, charged upon the neck with a trefoil vert.

Knightly (Chorley, co. Lancaster). Vert a cross engr. erm. in the 1st quarter a mullet pierced. *Crest*—A goat's head ar. charged with a mullet for diff.

Knightly (co. Stafford). Paly of six or and gu.

Knightly (co. Worcester). Ar. on a fesse sa. a mullet of the field. *Crest*—A dragon's head sa. with three tongues gu.

Knightly. Az. a hart's head cabossed or (another, ar.).

Knighton (Carlston, co. Dorset, and of Blendworth Lodge, co. Hants, bart.). Barry of eight per pale az. and or, counterchanged a bend erminois, on a chief gu. a dragon's head erased betw. two annulets of the second. *Crest*—Out of a ducal coronet or, two dragons' heads in saltire couped at the shoulders, the dexter gu. sinister or, wreathed about the neck with a chain of the last.

Knighton (co. Hertford). Ar. two bars az. on a canton of the second a tun or.

Knighton (Bayford, co. Herts). Barry of eight ar. and az. *Crest*—Out of a ducal coronet or, two dragons' heads and necks in saltire ppr.

Knighton (co. Suffolk). Barry of eight ar. and az. on a canton or, a tun paleways gu. *Crest*, as the last.

Knighton (JOHN KNIGHTON, Visit. London, 1568, whose dau. DIONISE, *m.* EDMOND BURTON, citizen of London, son and heir of JOHN BURTON, Esq., of Stapleforth, co. Notts, descended from BURTON, of co. York). Same *Arms*, quartering ar. six annulets gu. three, two, and one. *Crest*—Two dragons' heads and necks twisted in each other az. in a ducal coronet gu.

Knighton. Ar. a bend nebulée gu. betw. two bendlets of the last.

Knighton. Vert two lions ramp. in fesse or.

Knilegh, or Kilegh. Az. a buck's head or.

Knill (Knill, co. Hereford; now represented by Sir JOHN WALSHAM, Bart., of Knill, the twenty-sixth in lineal descent from Sir JOHN DE KNILL, Knt., Lord of Knill, in the twelfth century). Gu. crusily fitchée a lion ramp. or. *Crest*—Out of a ducal coronet or, a plume of ostrich feathers ar.

Knipe (London; granted 16 Nov. 1616). Gu. two bars ar. in chief three wolves' heads couped of the second. *Crest*—A wolf's head ar. transfixed through the breast with a broad arrow or, flighted and pointed of the first.

Knipe (co. Lancaster, and Westminster). Same *Arms* and *Crest*.

Knipell. Az. on two bars or, three mullets gu. *Crest*—A tiger's face or, betw. two laurel branches vert.

Knite, or Knight. Gu. two bars ar. in chief three wolves' heads erased of the second.

Kniveton (Bradley, co. Derby). Gu. a bend vair betw. six crosses formée or.

Kniveton (Mercaston, co. Derby, bart., extinct in 1706; derived from NICHOLAS DE KNIVETON, of Mercaston, *d.* 46 Edward III.; Sir WILLIAM KNIVETON, of Mercaston, M.P. for Derby 1 James I., and twice High Sheriff of the county, was created a baronet, 1611). Gu. a chev. vairé ar. and sa. *Crest*—An eagle's head betw. two wings all ppr.

Kniveton, alias Gilbert. Gu. a bend vairé ar. and sa.

Knienton. Gu. a chev. vair.

Knoles. Az. crusily a cross moline voided throughout or.

Knoll (ELIAS DE KNOLL, Lord of Knollsmere, Wigglesworth, and Hellifield Peel, co. York, whose daus. and co-heirs were, I. KATHARINE, *m.* to ADAM DE HAMERTON, Lord of Hamerton, co. York; and II. ANASTASIA, who *m.* Sir JOHN DE HALTON, Knt., of Halton, co. York). Gu. a chev. betw. three roses ar.

Knolle, or Knolls. Gu. a chev. ar. betw. three annulets pierced ar.

Knolles (co. Chester). Ar. on a chev. gu. three roses of the field.

Knolles (Little Hampston, co. Devon). Or, a falcon sa. preying on a moorcock ppr. on a chief of the second three birdbolts ar.

Knolles. Gu. on a chev. ar. three roses of the field.

Knolles (co. Hants). Or, three demi lions pass. guard. gu. *Crest*—A griffin segreant or.

Knolles. Or, a cross couped gu. *Crest*—On a cloud a sphere ppr.

Knolles (from ped. of Sir ROBERT KNOLLES, K.G., lord of the manor of Scouthorpe, co. Norfolk, a "very valyant captayne" in the wars in France, *temp.* Edward III. and Richard II., who *d.* 17 Aug. 1407, 8 Henry IV.). Gu. on a chev. ar. three roses of the field barbed ppr.

Knolles (JOHN KNOLLES, settled in co. Hants *temp.* Henry VIII.; descended of a younger branch of Sir ROBERT KNOLLES, K.G., *temp.* Edward III.; confirmed by St. George, Clarenceux, 1633). Same *Arms*, differenced with a canton erm.

Knolls, or Knowls (co. Chester, Chisping, co. Lancaster, Chipping and Harpley, co. Norfolk). Gu. on a chev. ar. three roses barbed and seeded of the field. *Crest*—A ram's head ar. attired or.

Knollys (Grove Place, co. Hants). Gu. on a chev. ar. three roses of the field, a canton erm.

Knollys (*Earl of Banbury*, extinct; WILLIAM KNOLLYS, descended from the renowned Sir ROBERT KNOLLYS, K.G., the companion in arms of the Black Prince, who was created *Baron Knollys* 1603, *Viscount Wallingford* 1616, and raised to the Earldom 1626, *d.* 1632; NICHOLAS KNOLLYS, alias VAUX, claimed the titles and seat as *Earl of Banbury* in the Convention Parliament, 1660, as did his descendants, until the House of Lords declared the Peerage extinct in 1813). Gu. on a chev. ar. three roses of the field; also, az. semée of crosses crosslet a cross moline or, voided throughout of the field. *Crest*—An elephant ar.

Knollys (Thame, co. Oxford, bart., extinct 1772; descended from Sir FRANCIS KNOLLYS, Knt., of Reading Abbey, younger brother of the *Earl of Banbury*). Same *Arms*, quartering gu. on a chev. ar. three roses of the field, a canton erm. *Crest*—An elephant ar. *Motto*—In utrumque paratus.

Knomley. Or, three stars ga.

Knomly, Knowles, or Knonvile (co. Gloucester). Ar. three mullets gu.

Knot (Whitchurch, co. Southampton; granted 15 April, 1632). Sa. a key erect in pale or, betw. two palets erminois. *Crest*—A lion's head erased gu.

Knotford. Ar. four fusils in fesse sa.

Knotsford (Studley, co. Warwick). Ar. a fess lozengy sa.

573

Knotsford (Great Malvern, co. Worcester; JOHN KNOTSFORD, Serjeant-at-Law, High Sheriff Worcester 1 Queen Elizabeth, A.D. 1558). Sa. on a cross engr. ar. an annulet of the field.

Knotshull. Sa. a chev. embattled betw. three crescents ar. *Crest*—A dexter hand issuing from a cloud, holding a broken spear all ppr.

Knotshull. Az. guttée d'eau a chev. raguly betw. three crescents ar.

Knotsworth. Ar. four lozenges in fesse sa.

Knott (co. Suffolk). Az. guttée d'or a chev. of the last betw. three crescents ar.

Knott (co. Sussex). Az. guttée d'or a chev. betw. three crescents of the last. *Crest*—A unicorn's head ar. armed and crined or.

Knott. Same *Arms*. *Crest*—A wolf collared and chained ppr.

Knottisford. Ar. two bars within a bordure engr. gu.

Knotton. Ar. a fret az. on a fesse gu. three mullets of the field.

Knotwood (co. Norfolk). Ar. (another, or) three cinquefoils gu.

Knotwood. Ar. three cinquefoils gu. *Crest*—A boar reguard. sa. seizing an arrow fixed in his shoulder.

Knovill (*Baron Knovill*, extinct; BOGO KNOVILL was summoned to Parliament 1295-1307, *d.* that year, leaving a son, BOGO KNOVILL, then aged 30 years, of whom, or his descendants, if any, nothing is known). Ar. three estoiles gu.

Knowler (Stroud, co. Kent). Ar. on a bend betw. two cotises sa. a lion pass. guard. of the field crowned or. *Crest*—A demi heron ppr. volant issuing out of reeds also ppr. *Another Crest*—Out of a ducal coronet or, a demi heron issuing erm.

Knowles (Lovel Hill, co. Berks, bart.). Quarterly, 1st and 4th, az. crusily of crosslets a cross moline voided or; 2nd and 3rd, gu. on a chev. ar. three roses of the first *Crest*—An elephant statant ar. *Motto*—Semper paratus.

Knowles, or Knoell (Sanford Oreas, co. Dorset, and co. Somerset). Gu. on a bend ar. three escallops sa.

Knowles (Aylesham, co. Norfolk). Gu. on a chev. ar. three roses of the field, in chief a crescent or, charged with a mullet sa. *Crest*—A ram's head ar. attired or.

Knowles (Cole Ashby, co. Northampton, and Walton, co. Suffolk; granted 1580). Gu. on a chev. ar. three roses vert, barbed and seeded of the field, on a canton of the second a fleur-de-lis of the first. *Crest*—Out of a ducal coronet gu. an elephant's head ar.

Knowlys (Heysham Hall, co. Lancaster, and Stockwell, co. Surrey). Same *Arms* and *Crest*. *Motto*—Lento sed certo et recto gradu.

Knowles. Az. a hawk seizing a partridge ar. on a chief of the last three bird bolts of the first.

Knowles (Downton and Winchester. Visit. Hants, 1634). Or, three demi lions pass. guard. gu. *Crest*—A griffin segreant or.

Knowling (anciently KNOLLING, of Exeter and Harburton, co. Devon, subsequently of Lower Washbourne, same co.; PETER KNOWLING, Esq., of Lower Washbourne, *d.* 1796, leaving two daus. his co-heirs; of these, only one had issue, viz., SARAH, the younger, wife of Rev. JOHN DIGBY FOWELL, of Blackhall and Diptford, co. Devon, and mother by him of JOHN DIGBY FOWELL, Esq., who, with his sisters, inherited the KNOWLING estates). Erm. three bends gu. *Crest*—A falcon with wings displ. ppr.

Knowlys. Ar. a cross couped and pierced sa. a chief gu. *Crest*—A unicorn ramp. ppr.

Knows (Scotland, 16th century). Gu. on a chev. ar. three roses of the first.

Knowsley. Az. a pale engr. erminois betw. two lions ramp. ar. *Crest*—A leopard's head couped ppr., collared and lined, with a ring at the end of the line or.

Knowton. Ar. a chev. gu. betw. three crowns sa.

Knowyl (co. Gloucester). Ar. three mullets gu.

Knox (Ranfurly, co. Renfrew). Gu. a falcon volant or, within an orle engr. ar.

Knox. Quarterly, gu. and ar. an orle counterchanged, in the centre an eagle volant sa. *Crest*—A griffin's head betw. two wings or, each charged with a torteau.

Knox. Ar. two keys in saltire gu. *Crest*—A demi lion ar. holding in the dexter paw a key gu.

Knox (Reg. Ulster's Office; descended of Ranfurly, 1693). Gu. a falcon volant or, within an orle waved in the outer and engr. in the inner side ar. *Crest*—A falcon close on a perch all ppr. *Motto*—Moveo et proficior.

Knox (Rathmacnee, co. Wexford; descended from ANDREW KNOX, Bishop of Raphoe, 1611-32, second son of UCHTER

Knox, of Ranforley, co. Renfrew; arms confirmed 1757, on an escutcheon of pretence to JOHN GROGAN, Esq., of Johnstown, co. Wexford, who m. KATHERINE, only dau. and heir of ANDREW KNOX, Esq., of Rathmacnee). Same *Arms.*

Knox (Prehen, co. Londonderry; descended from ANDREW KNOX, Bishop of Raphoe, 1611-32; ANDREW KNOX, Esq., of Derry, fourth in descent from the Bishop, m. HONORIA, dau. and co-heir of ALEXANDER TOMKINS, Esq., of Prehen, co. Londonderry, by whom he got that estate). Same *Arms.*

Knox (confirmed to THOMAS KNOX, son of THOMAS KNOX, descended from KNOX, of Ranforley, Scotland). Gu. a a falcon volant or, within an orle engr. wavy on the outer edge ar. *Crest*—A perch, thereon a falcon close all ppr. *Motto*—Moveo et proficior.

Knox (*Earl of Ranfurly*). Gu. a falcon volant or, within an orle wavy ar. *Crest*—A falcon perched ppr. *Supporters*—Two falcons, wings expanded ppr. ducally gorged, chained, beaked, and taloned or. *Motto*—Moveo et propitior.

Knox (Moyne and Rappa Castle, co. Mayo). Gu. a falcon, wings expanded, within a bordure engr. or, on a canton of the same a fesse chequy ar. and az. *Crest*—A falcon close on a perch all ppr.

Knox-Gore (Belleek Manor, co. Sligo, bart.; descended from JAMES KNOX, second son of FRANCIS KNOX, Esq., of Rappa). See GORE.

Knox (Netley Park, co. Mayo; descended from HENRY KNOX, third son of FRANCIS KNOX, Esq. of Rappa). Gu. a falcon, wings expanded, within an orle wavy engr. or, on a canton of the same a fesse chequy ar. and az. *Crest*—A falcon close on a perch ppr.

Knox (Castlerea, co. Mayo, and Woodstock, co. Wicklow; descended from ARTHUR KNOX, younger son of FRANCIS KNOX, Esq., of Moyne). Same *Arms* and *Crest.*

Knox (Mount Falcon, co. Mayo; descended from JOHN KNOX, second son of JOHN KNOX, Esq., of Castlerea). Same *Arms* and *Crest.*

Knox-Browne. See BROWNE.

Knoyle. Gu. on a bend ar. three escallops sa.

Knyffe. Paly of six ar. and az. on a chief sa. two swords in saltire of the first, hilts or.

Knyfton, or Kniveton (Uphill Lodge, co. Somerset; descended from KNIVETON, of Mercaston, co. Derby). Gu. a chev. vairé ar. and sa. *Crest*—An eagle's head erased or, betw. two wings displ. sa. *Motto*—In Domino confido.

Knyfton. Barry of six ar. and gu. on a bend sa. three mullets or.

Knyll. See KNILL, of Knill Court.

Knypersley (co. Stafford). Az. three spades or, handles ar.

Knyple. Az. on two bars or, three mullets pierced gu.

Knyston. Sa. a lion ramp. double queued or.

Knyvet. Ar. on a bend engr. sa. three trefoils slipped of the first, a bordure engr. of the second.

Knyvett (Buckenham, co. Norfolk; descended from OTHOMARUS DE KNYVET, Lord of the Castle and Borough of Launceston before the Conquest; ELIZABETH KNYVETT, heiress of KNYVETT, of Ashwellthorpe, m. HENRY WILSON, Esq., of Didlington, and conveyed to that family her right to the barony of Berners. The male heir of the KNYVETS of Funden Hall, co. Norfolk, CHARLES KNYVETT, Esq., of Sonning, near Reading, was descended from WILLIAM KNYVETT, second son of EDMUND KNYVETT, younger son of Sir EDMUND KNYVET, Knt., of Buckenham). Ar. a bend sa. a bordure engr. of the last. *Crest*—A demi dragon, wings az.

Knyvett (Buckenham, co. Norfolk, bart., extinct 1699; PHILIP KNYVETT, Esq., of Buckenham, great-grandson of Sir EDMUND KNYVETT, Knt., of Buckenham, M.P. Norfolk, 1545, was created a bart. 1611; the second bart., Sir ROBERT KNYVETT, *d. s. p.*). Same *Arms,* &c.

Knyvett (*Baron Knyvett*, extinct 1622; Sir THOMAS KNYVETT, Knt., second son of Sir HENRY KNYVETT, knighted by Queen Elizabeth, 1574, younger brother of Sir EDMUND KNYVETT, M.P. Norfolk, 1545, was summoned to Parliament, 1607, *d. s. p.*). Same *Arms,* &c.

Knyvett (Ashwell Thorpe, co. Norfolk; descended from EDMUND KNYVETT, Serjeant Porter to Henry VIII., who acquired the manor of Ashwell Thorpe in right of his wife, JANE BOURCHIER, dau. and heir of Sir JOHN BOURCHIER, second *Lord Berners.* EMMA HARRIETT, Baroness *Berners* in her own right, wife of Sir HENRY THOMAS TYRWHITT, third bart. of Stanley Hall, is heir-general of this family). Same *Arms,* &c.

Knyvett (Rosemaryn, co. Cornwall; THOMAS KNYVET, Visit. Cornw. 1620, grandson of HENRY KNYVET, second son of Sir THOMAS KNYVET, Knt., of Ashwell Thorpe, co. Norfolk). Same *Arms,* a crescent for diff.

574

Knyvett. Az. three knives ar. with crooked (or bent) hafts gu. *Crest*—A sword and ear of wheat in saltire ppr.

Knyvett. Ar. a chev. gu. betw. three stags' heads couped ppr.

Kocker. Ar. two squirrels sejant in pale gu.

Kocking. Per pale ar. and sa. a fesse nebulée counterchanged.

Koehler. Or, three coulters of a plough fesseways in pale az. *Crest*—Two coulters endorsed paleways az.

Kognose (co. Northumberland). Gu. a fesse ar. in chief three lozenges of the second. *Crest*—A cock sa. combed and wattled gu. beaked and legged or.

Koke. Az. three cocks ar. armed, crested, and jelloped or, (another, armed gu.).

Kokes. Sa. three bends ar.

Kokesatton. Ar. fretty gu.

Koking (co. Hereford). Per pale wavy ar. and sa.

Kokington. Gu. three cocks ar. *Crest*—A unicorn's head erased ar.

Kokyrham. Ar. on a bend sa. three leopards' faces or.

Kragg, Krag, Krog, or Kroge. Az. a plough in fesse ar. *Crest*—A dexter hand holding up a garland of laurel vert. *Motto*—Juvat dum lacerat.

Kramer (Reg. Ulster's Office, to Col. BALTHAZAR KRAMER, born in Germany, who was twenty-two years Serjeant-Major of a regiment of foot in the city of Steinbargen, settled in Ireland, and was made a free denizen; afterwards Colonel of regiment of foot raised for the protection of the city of Dublin, 1641). Per fess indented az. and or, in chief two fleurs-de-lis of the last, a canton erm. *Crest*—A fleur-de-lis betw. two wings expanded or, penned ar. *Motto*—Inevitabile fatum.

Krampton. Ar. a chev. betw. three martlets sa. *Crest*—A dexter hand vested az. holding a branch of palm ppr.

Kronton. Ar. a chev. gu. betw. three mullets sa.

Krowton. Ar. on a chev. gu. betw. three crows ppr. as many crescents ar. *Crest*—An arm holding a broken spear ppr. top pendent.

Kroye. See KRAGG.

Kuckfield. Barry of four or and az. a lion counterchanged.

Kudford. Az. a chev. betw. nine mullets or, four, two, one, and two.

Kuelley, or Kewley. Ar. on a chev. sa. two mullets of the field. *Crest*—The head of a seahorse issuant from waves ppr.

Kuerden (Preston, co. Lancaster, 1664). Per bend sinister or and az. a griffin segreant counterchanged. *Crest*—A stag's head couped quarterly or and az.

Kukefield. Sa. a fleur-de-lis erm. *Crest*—A demi lion ramp. sa. brandishing a scymitar or.

Kulcheth, or Culcheth (Culcheth, co. Lancaster). Ar. an eagle sa. preying on a child ppr. swaddled gu. banded or.

Kullingwike. Per chev. or and az. in chief two roses gu. stalked, leaved, and barbed vert, seeded of the first, in base an ostrich feather ar. *Crest*—A cubit arm erect, vested sa. cuffed erm. holding in the hand ppr. a chaplet of laurel vert.

Kullingwike. Ar. a chev. gu. betw. three fleurs vert.

Kullingworth. Ar. a chev. gu. betw. three pots vert.

Kumer. Gu. a chief indented or.

Kumerson. Ar. a chev. betw. three mullets gu. *Crest*—A griffin's head erased or.

Kutchin. Ar. on a chev. per pale gu. and sa. betw. three pheons of the second as many crescents or. *Crest*—A crane's head erased ar.

Kyan (Ballymurtagh, co. Wicklow, and formerly of Mount Howard, co. Wexford; confirmed to Rev. WILLIAM EDWARD KYAN, of the former place, eldest son of JOHN HOWARD KYAN, Esq., of same, grandson of JOHN HOWARD KYAN, Esq., of same and Mount Howard, and great-grandson of HOWARD KYAN, Esq., of same places, who *d.* 1766, who claimed descent from the O'CAHANS, Princes of Derry). Gu. an antique Irish crown or, betw. three fishes haurient ar. *Crest*—A wild cat ramp. ppr. gorged with an antique Irish crown or.

Kychard. Or, a lion ramp. sa. within an orle of billets of the second. *Crest*—A wolf's head or, collared gu. in the mouth a trefoil vert.

Kyd (Scotland). Ar. a tree eradicated vert, pendent on the branches a bugelhorn or, on a chief az. three mullets of the field. *Crest*—An increscent ppr. *Motto*—Donec impleat orbem.

Kyd (Craigie, Scotland). Ar. a pine tree eradicated ppr. with a hunting-horn pendent from a branch or, stringed gu. on a chief az. three mullets of the third. *Motto*—Quem non torret hyems.

Kyd (Woodhill, Scotland). Same *Arms*, with a crescent for diff. *Motto*—Donec impleat orbem.

Kydale, or Kendale. Ar. a chev. betw. three dolphins naiant sa.

Kyddy. Sa. a lion ramp. ar. armed and langued gu.

Kydermaster (Lincoln's Inn, London, and Coushall, co. Warwick). Az. two chev. erminois betw. three bezants. *Crest*—On a chapeau az. turned up erm. a cockatrice erminois, wings elevated and endorsed.

Kydermaster (co. Sussex). Az. two chev. Ar. betw. three bezants. *Crest*—On a chapeau gu. turned up erm. an eagle ar. wings endorsed.

Kydwalley. Or, a fesse dancettée gu.

Kyerkwald. Per fesse gu. and or, in chief a griffin pass. ar. in base a wolf pass. reguard. vert, holding in the mouth a fish of the third.

Kyffin (Bodfach, co. Montgomery; derived, through JOHN KYFFIN, Esq., of Bodfach, son of WILLIAM AP MEREDITH, of Mochnant-yn-Rhaiadr, from EINION EFELL, Lord of Cynllaeth. ELIZABETH, dau. and heiress of WILLIAM KYFFIN, Esq., of Bodfach, *m.* ADAM PRICE, Esq., of Glan Miheli). *Arms*, those of EINION EFELL, viz., Per fess sa. and ar. a lion ramp. counterchanged, armed and langued gu.

Kyffin (Glascoed; derived, through MEREDITH AP HOWEL, of Glascoed, from EINION EFELL, Lord of Cynllaeth. MARGARET, dau. and heiress of WATKIN KYFFIN, Esq., of Glascoed, *m.* Sir WILLIAM WILLIAMS, Bart., paternal ancestor of the present Sir WATKIN WILLIAMS WYNN, Bart.). Same *Arms*.

Kyffin (Maenan, co. Carnarvon; derived, through MORRIS KYFFIN, of Maenan, from EINION EFELL, Lord of Cynllaeth. The male heir terminated with Sir JOHN KYFFIN, Knt., of Maenan, who left three daus. and co-heiresses: 1. ELIZABETH, *m.* WILLIAM JOAN LENTHALL, Esq., of Bessels Leigh, co. Berks, father of KYFFIN JOHN WILLIAM LENTHALL, Esq., of Bessels Leigh and Maenan Hall; 2. ANNE, *m.* the Rev JOHN NANNEY, of Maes-y-Neuadd, co. Merioneth; 3. ERMINA, *m.* RICHARD HUGHES KENRICK, Esq., of Nantclwyd, co. Denbigh, and left, with other issue, a younger son, HENRY, who assumed the name of KYFFIN in compliance with the will of his aunt, Mrs. NANNEY (under which he succeeded to the estate of Belmont, co. Denbigh). Same *Arms*.

Kyffin (Belmont, co. Denbigh). Per fesse indented sa. and ar. a lion ramp. counterchanged, charged on the shoulder with three erm. spots in chev.

Kyffin. Ar. on a chev. gu. betw. three pheons sa. a mullet of the first.

Kyffyn, alias Waghan (co. Salop). Per fesse sa. and ar. a lion ramp. counterchanged. *Crest*—A lion ramp. per fesse ar. and sa.

Kyghley. Ar. a fesse sa.

Kylahy. Ar. two chev. sa.

Kylche. Ar. a lion ramp. az.

Kylchiche. Sa. a griffin segreant, wings elevated ar.

Kyle (Scotland). Or, three candlesticks sa.

Kyle (Scotland). Ar. two candlesticks in chief sa. and a mullet in base gu. *Crest*—An anchor and cable ppr.

Kyle. Or, three candlesticks within a bordure ar. *Crest*—A deer's head ppr. *Motto*—Providentia me committo.

Kyle (confirmed to Right Rev. SAMUEL KYLE, D.D., Bishop of Cork, whose family were long seated at Kyle, N.B., and whose immediate ancestors settled at Camnish, co. Derry). Per fess sa. and or, three altar candlesticks counterchanged. *Crest*—A lion ramp. per fess sa. and or, supporting in his paws a cross formée fitchée ar. *Motto*—Tibi soli.

Kyllingbeck (Talworth, Heningham, and Leeds, co. York). Ar. on a chev. sa. betw. three unicorns' heads erased az. as many annulets or.

Kyllingbeck (Chappell-Allerton, co. York). Ar. on a chev. sa. betw. three unicorns' heads couped az. as many annulets or. *Crest*—On a ducal coronet a talbot collared and lined all ppr.

Kylom, alias Draper. Ar. on a fesse engr. betw. three annulets gu. as many covered cups or. *Crest*—A buck's head couped gu. attired or, charged on the neck with a fesse gold, betw. three annulets gu.

Kymbell, and Kymberley. Ar. a fesse and bordure engr. sa.

Kymber (ELIZABETH KYMBER, heiress of her father, *m. temp.* Edward IV., HENRY KELLY, Esq., of Kelly; her dau. ALICE KELLY, *m.* RICHARD WEEKS, and their dau. and heir, JOHN, *m.* THOMAS HAYDON, Esq., of Bowood and Epford. Visit. London, 1568). Ar. two chevronels gu. a bordure engr. of the last.

Kymberlee, or Kymberley. Ar. an oak tree eradicated vert fructed or. *Crest*—A cock reguard. gu.

Kymberlee. Ar. a chev. sa. a bordure engr. of the second.

Kymble. Ar. on a bend gu. three leopards' faces of the first.

Kyme (Kesteven, co. Lincoln, *temp.* Henry II.). Gu. a chev. betw. ten crosses crosslet or (another, nine; another, six).

Kyme (*Baron Kyme*, extinct 1338; PHILIP DE KYME was summoned to Parliament 1295-1313; his son, WILLIAM, second *Baron Kyme*, summoned 1323-36, *d. s. p.*). Same *Arms*.

Kyme. Ar. a chev. betw. three quatrefoils az. stalked and leaved vert. *Crest*—A polecat ppr.

Kyme. Gu. a chev. vert.

Kyme. Or, two chev. sa.

Kyme. Az. a chev. betw. three crosslets or.

Kymer (West Shelburgh, co. Dorset). Ar. three cats pass. in pale az. a bordure of the last bezantée. *Crest*—A cat's head couped az.

Kymes. Ar. a chev. betw. three quatrefoils az. stalked and leaved vert. *Crest*—On a mount vert a tortoise ppr.

Kympton (Weston, co. Hertford). Az. a pelican betw. three fleurs-de-lis or. *Crest*—A demi goat erm. attired and hoofed or, collared and lined sa.

Kympton. Az. a fesse betw. three fleurs-de-lis or.

Kymyell (Kymyell, co. Cornwall). Ar. three dolphins embowed in pale sa.

Kynansley. Ar. a fesse vairé or and az. betw. three eagles displ. gu.

Kynardby. Ar. a fesse sa. betw. three crescents gu. a bordure engr. of the second.

Kynardesley (Braylford, co. Derby, cos. Somerset, Stafford, and Ward-End, co. Warwick). Ar. a fesse vairé or and gu. betw. three eagles displ. sa. *Crest*—On a mount vert a greyhound sejant ar. collared or, under a holly tree of the first, fructed gu.

Kynardesly (co. Salop, *temp.* Edward I.). Az. a lion ramp. ar. within an orle of crosses crosslet of the second.

Kynardsley, or Keynardsley (co. Kent). Vert a chev. betw. three leopards' faces or. *Crest*—A leopard's face or, in the mouth a sword ppr.

Kynaston (Hardwick, co. Salop, bart., created 1818, extinct 1866; descended from IORWERTH GOCH, Lord of Mochnant, younger son of MEREDITH, Prince of Powys). Quarterly, 1st and 4th, erm. a chev. gu.; 2nd and 3rd, as derived from MEREDITH AP BLEDDYN, ar. a lion ramp. sa. The origin of the first coat, erm. a chev. gu., is thus narrated: Sir ROGER KYNASTON was a Yorkist, and as a soldier was reckoned one of the most able and illustrious heroes of his time. He was present, mounted on his white charger (Ar ei gwrser gwyn) at the battle of Bloreheath, near Drayton, co. Salop, 22 Sept. 1459, under the command of the *Earl of Salisbury*. At this battle *Lord Audley*, the Lancasterian leader, fell, according to the family tradition, by the hand of ROGER KYNASTON. Two years after the battle, when the *Earl of March* ascended the throne under the title of Edward IV. he not only knighted the squire of Hordley, but also assigned to him the confiscated arms of the fallen AUDLEY as an honorary addition to his own, which were borne in the 1st quarter of the KYNASTON shield.

Kynaston (Oteley Park, co. Salop; descended from KYNASTON, Bart., of Hardwick; MARY, sister and co-heiress of EDWARD KYNASTON, Esq., of Otley, *m.* JAMES MAINWARING, of Bromborough, co. Chester, one of the Barons of the Exchequer). Ar. a lion ramp. sa. *Crest*—A lion's head erased sa. guttée d'or.

Kynaston (Poole, co. Dorset; descended from KYNASTON, Bart., of Hardwick). Same *Arms*.

Kynaston (Hordley, co. Salop). Erm. a chev. gu. *Crest*—A dexter arm embowed in armour ppr. holding a sword ar. hilt or, all against a sun of the last.

Kynaston, or Kynerston (Ryton Stokes, Shrewsbury, Woodhouse and Shotter, co. Salop; granted 19 April, 1569). Ar. a chev. engr. betw. three mullets sa. *Crest*—An eagle's head erased sa. ducally gorged ar. in the beak a sprig of laurel vert.

Kynaston (Thorington, co. Essex). Same *Arms*, a martlet for diff.

Kynaston (confirmed by Roberts, Ulster, to Col. JOHN KYNASTON, third son of Rev. RALPH KYNASTON, B.D., Chaplain to James I., and grandson of ROGER KYNASTON, Esq., of Morton, co. Salop). Ar. a lion ramp. sa. armed and langued gu. a crescent charged with a mullet for diff. *Crest*—An armed arm in armour embowed, the hand holding a sword within a sun all ppr. *Motto*—Honor potestate honorantis.

Kynaston (exemplified to Rev. WALTER CHARLES EDWARD OWENS, Incumbent of St. John's, Huddersfield, co. York.

on assuming the name of KYNASTON, by royal licence, 1868). Erm. a chev. gu., and for distinction a canton of the last. *Crest*—In front of a sun in splendour a dexter arm embowed in armour, the hand grasping a sword all ppr. the arm charged above the elbow (for distinction) with a cross crosslet gu. *Motto*—Deus est nobis sol et ensis.

Kyndall. Erm. on a bend gu. three chevronels or.

Kyndwell. Az. a wolf saliant ar. collared and chained or.

Kyne, or Kynes. Az. a bend wavy cotised ar.

Kyner. Gu. a chief indented or.

Kynerby. Ar. three lions pass. gu. *Crest*—On a chapeau gu. turned up ar. charged with four fleurs-de-lis or, a lion pass. of the second.

Kynerston. Ar. a chev. betw. three mullets gu. (another, the mullets sa.).

Kyneston, or Kyngeston. Ar. a bend wavy betw. two cotises gu.

Kyngarby. Ar. on a fesse sa. betw. three crescents gu. two crosses crosslet fitchée or, a bordure engr. of the second.

Kyngesley. Vert on a cross engr. erm. an annulet sa. *Crest*—Out of a ducal coronet gu. a goat's head ar.

Kyngeston. Ar. on a bend az. three crosses crosslet or.

Kynn. Ar. two chev. sa. *Crest*—An eagle's head couped or.

Kynnelmarch. Per fesse ar. and sa. a lion ramp. per fesse az. guttée ar. and erm. *Crest*—Two lions' gambs conjoined at the bottom, guttée ar. and sa. holding a wolf's head erased sa.

Kynnersley (Leighton, co. Salop; some historians derive this family from co. Hereford; there is, however, no doubt they adopted their surname from Kinnersley on the Wildmoors (anciently written Kinardsey), co. Salop. JOHN DE KYNARDESEYE, the first recorded ancestor of this family, was nephew of Sir JOHN DE KYNARDESEYE, clerk of THOMAS PLANTAGENET, *Earl of Lancaster*, grandson of Henry III.). Az. crusily a lion ramp. ar. *Crest*—On a mount vert a greyhound sejant ar. collared or, under a holly tree of the first, fructed gu.

Kynnersley (Loxley, co. Stafford; THOMAS SNEYD, Esq., of Loxley Park, assumed in 1815 the additional surname of KYNNERSLEY at the decease of his kinsman, CLEMENT KINNERSLEY, Esq.). Az. a lion ramp. ar. within an orle of crosses crosslet of the second; quartering SNEYD [*which see*]. The original arms of KYNNERSLEY were, az. a lion ramp. ar.; the crosses were added *temp.* Henry III. by HUGO DE KYNNARDSLEYE, who accompanied Prince Edward, afterwards Edward I., to the Holy Land. *Crests*—1st: On a mount vert a greyhound sejant ar. collared or, under a hawthorn tree ppr., for KYNNERSLEY; 2nd: SNEYD. *Motto*—Nec opprimere, nec opprimi.

Kynnesman (Knaptoft, co. Leicester). Gu. a fesse chequy or and az. betw. six cross crosslets of the second.

Kynns (Send, co. Gloucester). Az. on a fesse cotised or, three martlets gu.

Kynvrig ap Rhiwallon (Lord of Bromfield, co. Denbigh. Descended from KYNVRIG: I. ROBERTS, of Havod Hwch and Plas Newydd in Llanvair; II. BROUGHTON, of Plas Issa; III. WYNN, of Garwyavawr and Bersham; IV. SONNLLI, of Stanley, Bron Deg; V. ELLIS, of Alrhey; VI. PICILL; VII. CLAY; VIII. MAIN; IX. POWELL, of Alrhey; X. ERTHIG, of Erthig; XI. EDWARDS, of Bron Deg; XII. EYTON, of Erbistock; XIII. LLOYD, of Plasmadock). Erm. a lion ramp. sa.

Kynvrig Vychan (Gwepra, Wales). Vert a stag pass. reguard ar. attired or.

Kynynmound (that Ilk). See KINNINMOND.

Kynynmound (ELLIOT-MURRAY-KYNYNMOUND, *Earl of Minto*). See ELLIOT.

Kyrby, or Kyrkby (co. Essex). Sa. a lion ramp. ar. holding in the paw a garb or.

Kyrby, or Kyrkby (co. Kent). Az. five lions ramp. or, on a canton ar. a mullet gu.

Kyrby, or Kyrkby (co. Lincoln). Az. a fesse betw. two chev. engr. erm.

Kyrby. Ar. two bars gu. on a canton of the second a lion's head erased or (another, a cross crosslet or). *Crest* Out of a ducal coronet per pale or and ar. an elephant's head gu. eared of the second, tusked gold.

Kyrby, or Kyrkby. Per pale gu. and sa. a lion ramp. ar.

Kyrell (Sutton, co. Kent). Or, two chev. gu. a canton of the last. *Crest*—A bull's head cabossed sa. *Another Crest* —A talbot's head erased ar.

Kyrham (co. Devon). Ar. three lions ramp. gu.

Kyriell. Or, two chev. gu. on a canton of the second a lion pass. guard. of the first.

Kyrkalon. Ar. three bars gemels sa.

Kyrkbryn (Norwich). Or, a cross engr. vert.

Kyrkby. Ar. on a fesse vert three crescents or.

Kyrkby. Ar. two bars gu. on a canton of the second a cross moline or.

Kyrke. Per fesse or and gu. a lion ramp. reguard. counterchanged.

Kyrkeby. Az. six lions ramp. or, on a canton of the second a mullet gu.

Kyrkeby. Az. a fesse betw. two chev. engr. or.

Kyrkelorde. Sa. three mullets ar. a bordure engr. or. *Crest*—An antique lamp or, flammant ppr.

Kyrkeshagh (co. Lancaster; quartered by CHADWICK, also by NEWALL). Or, on a chief per pale gu. and sa. three bezants.

Kyrkton. Gu. three bars erm.

Kyrktot, Kribitot, or Kribtot (co. Suffolk). Az. on a cross ar. five escallops gu. *Crest*—A dexter hand holding a sword in pale all ppr.

Kyrkyn. Chequy gu. and ar. a cross az.

Kyrle (co. Hereford; descended from ROBERT CRUL, of Altone, or Old Town, near Ross, who resided, in 1295, at Homme, now Hom Green, in the same vicinity. THOMAS KYRLE, Esq., of Walford Court, co. Hereford, was living *temp.* Henry VII., and left nine sons and four daus. ; of the former, WALTER, the eldest, was ancestor of the KYRLES of Walford Court, and of JOHN KYRLE, the celebrated "*Man of Ross* "). Vert a chev. betw. three fleurs-de-lis or. *Crest*— On a mount vert a hedgehog or. *Motto*—Nil moror ictus: *i.e.*, I care not for blows.

Kyrle (Ross, co. Hereford; JOHN KYRLE, called the "*Man of Ross*," High Sheriff of co. Hereford, 1683). Same *Arms* as KYRLE, a crescent for diff.

Kyrle (Walford and Ross, co. Hereford; VANDERVORT KYRLE, son of THOMAS KYRLE, Esq., seventh son of JAMES KYRLE, Esq., of Walford Court, co. Hereford, was devisee representative of JOHN KYRLE, called the "*Man of Ross :*" his granddau. and heiress *m.* WILLIAM HUTCHINSON, Esq., of Clifton, co. Gloucester). Same *Arms*, with numerous quarterings.

Kyrle (Much Marcle, co. Hereford, bart., extinct 1680 ; descended from THOMAS KYRLE, fourth son of THOMAS KYRLE, Esq., of Walford, in same co., *temp.* Henry VII.). Same *Arms*.

Kyrle (MONEY-KYRLE, Much Marcle, co. Hereford). Quarterly, 1st and 4th, vert a chev. betw. three fleurs-de-lis or, for KYRLE; 2nd and 3rd, chequy ar. and gu. on a chief sa. three eagles displ. or, for MONEY. *Crests*—1st: On a mount vert a hedgehog or, for KYRLE; 2nd: An eagle's head sa. erased ar. collared gemel, holding in the beak a fleur de-lis or, for MONEY. *Motto*—Nil moror ictus.

Kyrslow. Gyronny of twelve or and sa. on a canton gu. a covered cup of the first.

Kyrton (STEPHEN KYRTON, Alderman of London, whose dau. GRISILD, *m.* NICHOLAS WOODROOFF, Alderman of London, son of DAVID WOODROOFF, Sheriff of the city in 1554. Visit. London, 1568). Ar. a fess and in chief a chev. gu., quartering, 1st, ar. a crescent and a border sa.; 2nd, per pale or and gu. a fess betw. three leopards' faces counterchanged; 3rd, ar. a fess betw. three hawks' lures gu.

Kyrton. Sa. three fishes naiant in pale ar. a chief per fess of the field and erm. on the first as many fleurs-de-lis or.

Kyrtun. Az. on a fesse betw. two chev. ar. three crescents gu.

Kytchyn (Belper, co. Derby, and Islington, co. Middlesex; granted 12 Feb. 1578). Ar. on a pile az. betw. two crosses crosslet gu. a dove volant ar. beaked and membered of the third.

Kyte. Az. on a chev. betw. three kites' heads erased or, as many tulips flowered gu. leaved vert.

Kyveliok (HUGH DE KYVELIOCK, *Earl of Chester ;* extinct 1232. See MESCHINES, *Earl of Chester*.) Az. six garbs or.

Kyverdale (quartered by MITFORD through OSBALDESTON and MOLYNEUX. Visit. York, 1666). Quarterly, ar. and sa. on each a leopard's face counterchanged.

L

LA BARTHE (Smith's Ordinary, Ulster's Office). Gu. three cinquefoils ar. *Crest*—A cinquefoil ar.

Labere. Az. a bend ar. cotised or, betw. six martlets of the last.

Labey (Jersey). Ar. a St. Andrew's cross vert.

Labibard. Or, a chief chequy of the first and gu.

Laborer. Ar. on a bend sa. three annulets of the first, a trefoil slipped of the second.

Laborer. Or, two bars gemels gu. in chief two crosses couped of the second.

Laborer, or Labruer. Or, two bars gemels gu. in chief a cross of the second. *Crest*—A hand couped fesseways charged with an eye both ppr.

Laborne. Chequy ar. and gu. on a chief or, a demi lion ramp. sa.

Laborne. Ar. on a bend betw. three trefoils slipped gu. as many annulets of the field.

La Brion. Az. a cross moline or.

Lace. Ar. a pale gu. in fesse three mullets counterchanged. *Crest*—A talbot's head sa.

Lace (Ingthorpe Grange, co. York, formerly of the Isle of Man). Or, a lion ramp. betw. three demi eagles displ. purp. *Crest*—A demi eagle, as in the arms, issuing out of a wreath of oak or, in the beak an ear of wheat ppr. *Motto*—Dum exspiro spero.

Lacer. Ar. on a chief gu. five roses of the field.

Lacer. Or, on a cross az. five roses ar.

Lacester. Az. a fesse betw. three fleurs-de-lis or.

Lacey. Az. three bendlets erm. *Crest*—A bear's paw erased holding a rose branch ppr. leaved vert.

Lachault. Ar. two harts' horns in saltire sa.

Lackerstein (granted by Betham, Ulster, to JOHN LACKERSTEIN, of the city of Calcutta). Ar. on the sea an East India merchant ship under sail with colours displ. all ppr. on a chief az. a bee volant in pale or, betw. two clasps of arrows banded ar. *Crest*—A Latin cross in pale or, surmounted by an anchor sa. cabled ar. *Motto*—Deo et virtute.

La Cloche (Jersey). Az. three church bells or. *Crest*—An eastern crown or.

Lacock (Stourton and Burton, co. Nottingham; PHILIP LACOCK, Counsellor-at-law, son and heir of GEORGE LACOCK, of Burton, Clerk of the Peace for the county, who was grandson of THOMAS LACOCK, of Stourton, served Henry VIII. in his wars in France; certified by St. George, Norroy, 1613. Visit. Notts, 1614). Ar. a dexter gauntlet sa. garnished or. *Crest*—A cock ar. wattled, jelloped, and legged gu. resting the dexter claw on a gauntlet, as in the arms. *Motto*—Verus honor honestas.

Lacock (Southwell, co. Nottingham; confirmed 12 Nov. 1613). Ar. a gauntlet sa. studded or, a crescent for diff. *Crest*—A cock ar. combed, jelloped, and legged gu. supporting with the dexter foot a gauntlet sa. purfled or.

Lacon (Willey and Kinlet, co. Salop; derived from JOHN LAKEN, Lord of Laken, temp. Edward III., fifth in descent from Sir ROBERT DE LAKYN; ANNE LACON, dau. and heiress of ROWLAND LACON, Esq., of Kinlet, m. Sir WILLIAM CHILDE, LL.D. See p. 193). Quarterly, per fesse indented az. and erm. in the 1st quarter a hawk belled and jessed ar.

Lacon (Audley, co. Essex, Ryby, co. Lincoln, and London). Same *Arms* and *Crest*.

Lacon (Great Yarmouth, co. Norfolk, bart.). Quarterly, per fesse indented erminois and az. in the 2nd quarter a wolf's head erased ar. *Crest*—A mount vert, thereon a falcon ppr. beaked and belled or, charged on the breast with a cross flory and gorged with a collar gu. *Motto*—Probitas verus honos.

Lacon (Llanddyn and Porkington, co. Salop; derived from OWEN GWYNEDD, Prince of North Wales; the dau. of WILLIAM WYNNE LACON, of Llanddyn and Porkington, m. Sir WILLIAM MORRIS, of Clennenneu). *Arms*, those of OWEN GWYNNED, viz.: Vert three eagles displ. in fess or.

Lacon: Sa. a saltire or, betw. four crosses formée or.

Lacy (co. Cambridge). Ar. an inescutcheon gu. over all a bend sa.

Lacy (co. Cornwall). Az. (another, gu.) three shovellers' heads erased ar. (another, or).

Lacy (co. Hereford, temp. Edward I.). Or, a fesse gu. in chief three martlets of the second.

Lacy (Melton Mowbray, co. Leicester, Cromwell and Beverley, co. York; JOHN LACY, son of WILLIAM LACY, of that place, who was living 1563, the grandson of RICHARD LACY, of Halifax, co. York. Visit. Leicester, 1619). Ar. six pellets, three, two, and one. *Crest*—A fret-knot ar. and purp.

Lacy (Stamford, co. Lincoln). Ar. on a saltire engr. az. betw. four lions pass. gu. five bezants (another, the lions ramp. and four bezants). *Crest*—A demi lion ramp. gu.

Lacy (London). Gu. two bends wavy erm.

Lacy (Longworth, co. Lancaster, 1664). Ar. six pellets, three, two, and one.

577

Lacy (Skipton-under-Whichwood, co. Oxford. Visit. Oxon, 1634). Gu. two bars wavy erm. *Crest*—Out of a ducal coronet or, a lion sejant erm.

Lacy, alias Hedges (London, cos. Oxford and Wilts). Az. five swans' necks erased ar.

Lacy (Enfield, co. Middlesex). Gu. two bars wavy erm. *Crest*—Out of a ducal coronet or, a lion sejant erm.

Lacy (cos. Northampton and Northumberland). Barry nebulée of six erm. and gu.

Lacy (Walsham-in-the-Willows, co. Norfolk, and co. Suffolk). Quarterly, ar. and sa. on a bend gu. three martlets or, over all a label of five points of the last, each charged with an erm. spot of the second. *Crest*—Out of a ducal coronet gu. a demi eagle, wings expanded or, in the beak an arrow of the first, headed and feathered ar.

Lacy (Beverley, co. York). Ar. a chev. betw. three bucks' heads cabossed sa. *Crest*—A buck's head cabossed per pale ar. and or, the horns counterchanged.

Lacy (co. York). Or, a lion ramp. gu. a bordure of the first and second charged with eight bezants.

Lacy (Lane House, Feckenham, co. Worcester). Ar. on a bend gu. three martlets or, a bordure engr. sa. *Crest*—On a ducal coronet or, a demi lion ramp. ar.

Lacy. Or, a lion ramp. gu. *Crest*—A lion's face looking out of a bush ppr.

Lacy. Or, three chev. gu. in chief two lions ramp. sa. (another, ar. on a bend sa. three plates; another, ar. two bends erm.; another, or, on a cross az. five cinquefoils pierced ar.; another, ar. on a fesse gu. four pales wavy of the field betw. three leopards' heads erased az.; another, ar. a fesse and three martlets in chief gu.; another, gu. a bordure ar. over all a bendlet sa.; another, ar. a fesse betw. three crescents sa.).

Lacy. Ar. on a saltire engr. az. betw. four lions pass. guard. gu. five bezants. *Crest*—A demi lion ramp. gu.

Lacy. Gu. a fesse erm. betw. three boars' heads couped or.

Lacy. Ar. nine pellets, three, three, and three.

Lacy (Lord of Meath and Earl of Ulster). See DE LACY.

Lacy (Ballingarry, co. Limerick; a branch of the great Anglo-Norman family of DE LACY). Or, a lion ramp. purp. armed and langued gu. *Crest*—An eagle rising or. *Motto*—Meritis augentur honores.

Lacy, or De Lacy (allowed by Hawkins, Ulster, 1756, to PATRICK DE LACY, Colonel in the service of the Emperor of Germany, descended from LACY, of Ballingarry; this PATRICK became afterwards Count of the Holy Roman Empire, President of the Aulic Council, and Field-Marshal) *Arms, Crest,* and *Motto*, same as LACY, of Ballingarry.

Lacy (Bruff and Rathcahill, co. Limerick; another branch of the Anglo-Norman family of DE LACY; to this branch belonged the Russian General MAURICE DE LACY, of Grodno, and also EDMOND LACY, of Milltown, from whom descended, in the female line, the late British General Sir DE LACY EVANS, G.C.B.). *Arms, &c.,* same as LACY, of Ballingarry.

Ladbroke (Lord Mayor of London, 1748). Az. a chev. erm. *Crest*—An arm couped at the elbow and erect, vested gu. cuffed ar. holding in the hand ppr. five quatrefoils in cross, stalked of the second, pierced of the first.

Ladbrook, or Ladbrooke. Az. a chev. ar. *Crest*—A hawk rising ppr. ducally gorged and belled or.

Ladd. Or, a fesse wavy betw. three escallops sa.

Ladde, alias Baker (Terrington, co. Norfolk). Or, on a fesse wavy az. betw. three escallops sa. as many shelldrakes ar.

Ladde, or Ladd. Or, on a fesse wavy sa. betw. three escallops of the last as many shelldrakes ar. *Crest*—On a cloud a crescent ensigned with a star, all betw. two branches of palm disposed in orle ppr.

Lade (Barham, co. Kent). Ar. a fess wavy betw. three escallops sa. *Crest*—A panther's head guard. sa. spotted or.

Lade (Nash Court, co. Kent). Same *Arms*. *Crest*—A leopard's face ppr.

Lade (Warbleton, co. Sussex, bart., extinct 1746; THOMAS LADE, second son of VINCENT LADE, Esq., of Barham, was so created 1730). Same *Arms*. *Crest*—Out of a ducal coronet or, a leopard's head reguard. sa. bezantée.

Lade (Gray's Inn, London). Ar. a fesse wavy betw. three escallops sa. *Crest*—A panther's head guard. sa. spotted or.

Lade (Boughton House, co. Kent). Same *Arms*.

Lade (Glasgow, 1867). Sa. a chev. or, betw. three escallops in chief and a lion ramp. in base ar. *Crest*—A panther's head erased guard. ppr. *Motto*—Constant et ferme.

Ladkin (co. Herts). Sa. three mullets or, on a chief of the

2 F

second a lion issuant gu. *Crest*—A **savage's** head crowned with a garland of laurel ppr.

Laffan (Cobham, co. Kent, bart.; granted by Betham, Ulster, to JOSEPH DE COURCY LAFFAN, M.D., sometime physician to the *Duke of Kent*, son of WALTER LAFFAN, of Cashel, co. Tipperary). Or, a lion ramp. sa. holding in the dexter forepaw a fleur-de-lis az. *Crest*—Out of a ducal coronet or, an eagle displ. sa. semée-de-lis or. *Motto*—Vincit omnia veritas.

Laffer. Erm. on a bend az. three billets paleways ar. each charged with a torteau. *Crest*—An eagle rising, with the dexter claw resting on a flintstone ppr.

Laffhan (impalement Fun. Ent. Ulster's Office, 1677). Or, on a chief indented az. three plates.

Laffull, or Luffull. Gu. three helmets ar. plumed or.

La Font (Hinxworth, co. Herts; descended from an ancient family, a branch of LA FONT, de la Roche des Arnauldes, and connected with the houses of Vitrolles and of Toulouse de Lautrec, Viscomtes de Lautrec, which fled from France on the revocation of the Edict of Nantes, A.D. 1685; of this branch was JOHN LA FONT, a merchant of London, in 1760). Quarterly, 1st, sa. a rock, the sea in base and the sky in chief ar.; 2nd, sa. a cross moline betw. the fragments of a broken lance ar., for LA FONT; 3rd, ar. a fesse betw. three crescents gu., for OGLE; 4th, or, an orle az., for BERTRAM. *Crest*—A bull's head or, armed az. ducally gorged gu. *Motto* —Prenez en ire.

Laforey (Whitby, co. Devon, bart., extinct). Quarterly, 1st and 4th, ar. on a chev. az. three mullets or, in chief two fleurs-de-lis of the second, in base an anchor sa.; 2nd and 3rd, ar. a cross engr. sa. betw. four torteaux. *Crest*—A lion ramp. reguard. in the dexter paw a firebrand all ppr. *Motto*—Loyal au mort.

La Foy. Ar. six pellets, three, two, and one.

La Full (co. Norfolk). Gu. three helmets ar. garnished or.

Lagage. Az. two bars dancettée ar. in chief three covered cups or.

Lagenham. Ar. a cross betw. four lions pass. az. *Crest*— Out of a ducal coronet or, a serpent erect nowed vert.

Lagenham. Ar. a cross betw. four lions pass. (another, ramp.) gu.

Lagford (co. Northumberland). Paly of six or and gu. a bordure ar. *Crest*—A dexter arm gu. holding a sabre in pale az. hilted or.

Lagherne (co. Cornwall). Az. a chev. betw. three escallops or.

Laidlaw (Scotland). Sa. three bezants.

Laing. Per pale sa. and or, a chief dancettée az. *Crest*— On a chapeau az. turned up ar. a cock gu.

Laing (Morisland, Scotland, 1672). Per pale engr. ar. and sa. a chief indented counterchanged. *Motto*—Honeste.

Laing-Weir. See WEIR.

Laing. Az. three piles in chief ar.

Laing. Per pale ar. and sa. a chief indented counterchanged.

Lainham. Quarterly, ar. and sa. in the 1st quarter a fleur-de-lis gu., in the 4th an erm. spot of the second.

Lainson (granted to Alderman JOHN LAINSON, of Euston Square, Sheriff of London, 1835). Ar. on a fesse gu. cotised dancettée betw. two fleurs-de-lis in chief az. and in base a civic wreath vert, three mullets or. *Crest*—In front of a rock surmounted by a castle a ship in full sail all ppr.

Laird (Glenhuntly, co. Renfrew, 1777). Ar. a chev. gu. betw. two boars' heads erased ppr. in chief and a crescent in base of the second. *Crest*—A buck's head issuing ppr. *Motto*—Spero meliora.

Lake (*Viscount Lake*, extinct 1848). Sa. a bend betw. six crosses crosslet fitchée ar., on a chief of augmentation of the last a representation of the fish of Mogul barways per pale or and vert, banded vert and gu. pierced with a shaft erect headed with a crescent and by other shafts in saltire, headed variously with golden balls, an annulet, &c., granted in 1807 for services in the Mahratta war. *Crest*—A horse's head couped ar. charged on the neck with a bar gemel gu. *Supporters*—Dexter, a grenadier soldier of the 60th Regiment supporting with the exterior hand a musket all ppr.; sinister, a Malay soldier with his musket also ppr.

Lake (Smarden, co. Kent; THOMAS LAKE, M.D., *d.* 1595). Sa. a bend betw. six crosslets fitchée ar., quartering BISHOP, ar. on a bend sa. cotised gu. three bezarls.

Lake (Edmonton, co. Middlesex, bart.). Quarterly, 1st, for a coat of augmentation, granted to EDWARD LAKE, Chancellor of the Diocese of Lincoln, by Charles I., for services at Edge Hill, to be borne in the 1st quarter, gu. a dexter arm embowed in armour, issuing from the sinister side of the shield, holding in the hand a sword erect all ppr. thereto affixed a banner ar. charged with a cross betw. sixteen es-

cutcheons of the first, on the cross a lion pass. guard. or; 2nd, sa. on a bend betw. six crosses crosslet ar. a mullet for diff.; 3rd, ar. a chev. betw. three boars' heads couped sa.; 4th, quarterly, ar. and sa. on a bend of the last three fleurs-de-lis of the first. *Crests*—1st: A chevalier in complete armour on a horse courant ar. bridle and trappings all ppr. in the dexter hand a sword embrued gu. holding the bridle in his mouth, the sinister arm hanging down useless, round his body a scarf in bend of the last; 2nd: A seahorse's head ar. finned or, gorged with three bars gu. *Motto*—Un Dieu, un roy, un cœur.

Lake (Welston and Buckland, cos. Bucks, Hertford, and Stafford). Quarterly, or and az. four crescents counterchanged. *Crest*—A cross formée fitchée in a crescent, all within an annulet or.

Lake (co. Devon). Ar. on a chief gu. two annulets braced or, over all a bend engr. az.

Lake (co. Hants). Or, on a saltire engr. az. nine annulets ar. on a canton gu. a tower of the third. *Crest*—A cannon mounted ppr.

Lake (Sir THOMAS LAKE, Clerk of the Signet. Visit. London, 1568). Sa. on a bend betw. six crosses crosslet fitchée ar. a mullet of the field, quartering, Quarterly, ar. and sa. on a bend gu. three mullets ar. a martlet or, for diff.

Lake (STEPHEN LAKE, of London, Doctor of the Civil Law; impalement Fun. Ent. Ulster's Office, 1627, WILLIAM CROE, whose wife was ELIZABETH, dau. said STEPHEN LAKE). Sa. a bend betw. six crosses crosslet hée ar.

Lakebourne. Ar. a chev. betw. th. .e crosses crosslet sa.

Lakemore. Ar. three stags' heads cabossed gu. armed or.

Lakenlyche. Ar. a chev. sa. betw. three chapeaus of the same turned up gu. *Crest*—A harp or.

Lakin, or Laking. Quarterly, per fesse indented erm. and az. *Crest*—A dexter arm ppr. vested sa. holding a palm branch vert.

Lakington (Washbourne, co. Devon). Or, three bars wavy sa. *Crest*—A pelican in her piety ppr.

Laleed, or Lallee (co. Hereford). Ar. a cross chequy or and az.

Lalerion (co. Devon). Sa. three chev. ar.

Lally (Tullindally, co. Galway, originally O'MULLALY; the direct descendant of this ancient Sept was the gallant and ill-fated THOMAS ARTHUR LALLY, *Count Lally Tollendal*, Peer of France, and Commander-in-Chief of the French army in India, beheaded 1766). Ar. three eagles displ. gu. two and one, each holding in the beak a sprig of laurel ppr. betw. as many crescents, one and two az. *Crest*—An eagle, as in the arms.

Lalor (recorded by Carney, Ulster, 1659, as an impalement to HEWITSON). Or, a lion ramp. guard. gu.

Lalor (confirmed to THOMAS LALOR, Esq., of Cregg. co. Tipperary, and the descendants of his great-grandfather, JOHN LALOR, Esq., of Long Orchard, same co.). Vert a lion ramp. or, armed and langued gu. *Crest*—An arm embowed, vested gu. cuffed vert, the hand ppr. grasping a short sword also ppr. *Motto*—Fortis et fidelis.

Lalor (POWER-LALOR; exemplified by Betham, Ulster, to EDMOND JAMES POWER, Esq., of Long Orchard, co. Tipperary, son of EDMOND POWER, Esq., of Gurteen, co. Waterford, by ANASTATIA PHELAN LALOR, his wife, dau. and sole heir of JOHN LALOR, of Cranagh, co. Tipperary, on his assuming, by royal licence, 1853, the additional surname of LALOR). Quarterly, 1st and 4th, or, a lion ramp. guard. gu. armed and langued az., for LALOR; 2nd, ar. a chief indented sa., for POWER; 3rd, or on a chief gu. three escallops of the first. *Crests*—1st: A demi lion ramp. guard. gu. armed and langued az., for LALOR (this crest was subsequently found to be incorrect, and the following was granted as the proper crest for LALOR—An arm embowed, vested gu. cuffed vert, the hand ppr. grasping a sword also ppr.); 2nd: A stag's head affrontée or, betw. the horns a crucifix ppr., for POWER. *Mottoes*—Under the arms: Fortis et fidelis; over the second crest: Per crucem ad coronam

Lalynde. Ar. a cross engr. gu. *Crest*—A maiden's head affrontée, couped at the breasts ppr. attired az.

Lalynde. Az. a decrescent or.

Lamare. Ar. a lion ramp. gu.

Lamb (*Viscount Melbourne*, extinct 1853). Sa. on a fesse erminois betw. three cinquefoils ar. two mullets of the field. *Crest*—A demi lion ramp. gu. holding betw. the paws a mullet sa. *Supporters*—Two lions gu. collared and chained or, on each collar two mullets sa. *Motto*—Virtute et fide.

Lamb (late BURGES, of Burville, co. Berks, bart.). Quarterly, 1st and 4th, per pale wavy ar. and erminois a chev. betw. three lambs pass. sa., for LAMB; 2nd, per fesse ar. and erm.

a fesse lozengy or and az. in chief three mascles of the last, a bordure of the fourth bezantée, in a dexter canton gu. a bend of the first charged with the bâton of Knight-marshal, for BURGES; 3rd, az. a fleur-de-lis or, betw. three crescents in chief and three mullets in base ar., for MONTOLIEU. Crests —1st: A lamb pass. sa. charged on the body with a bezant, threon a trefoil slipped vert, for LAMB; 2nd: A camel's head ppr. bezantée, erased gu., for BURGES. Supporters—Two eagles ppr. Motto—Levius fit patientiâ.

Lamb (WARREN MAUDE LAMB, Esq., of Newcastle-on-Tyne). Gu. on a fesse betw. three cinquefoils ar. two mullets of the field. Crest—A paschal lamb ppr. Motto—Palma non sine pulvere.

Lamb (Barham, co. Suffolk; granted 3 July, 1559). Sa. a fesse or, betw. three cinquefoils erm. charged with a lion pass. gu. betw. two mullets of the field. Crest—A demi lion gu. collared or, holding in the dexter paw a mullet sa.

Lamb (Kennington, co. Kent). Same Arms and Crest, without the lion on the fesse.

Lamb (Colston, co. Wilts). Sa. on a fesse or, betw. three cinquefoils erm. two mullets of the field. Crest—On a mount vert a lamb ar.

Lamb (Rye, co. Sussex). Same Arms, the cinquefoils ar.

Lamb. Az. on a fesse wavy or, betw. two lions ramp. in chief ar. and a paschal lamb in base ppr. three crosses pattée. Crest—On a mount vert a gate surmounted of a paschal lamb, the staff of the banner entwined with laurel all ppr.

Lamb. Ar. a chev. engr. gu. betw. three paschal lambs pass. sa. Crest—A lion ramp.

Lamb. Az. (another, gu.) three paschal lambs pass. ar. the banners charged with a cross gu.

Lamb. Sa. on a fesse betw. three cinquefoils erminois two mullets vert. Crest—A demi lion ramp. erminois, holding in the dexter paw a mullet vert.

Lamb. Sa. on a fesse or, betw. three cinquefoils erm. a lion pass. betw. two mullets of the first.

Lamb (West Denton, co. Northumberland). Sa. on a fesse erm. betw. three cinquefoils ar. two mullets of the field. Crest—A paschal lamb ppr. Motto—Palma non sine pulvere.

Lamb (AUDOUIN-LAMB; exemplified to GEORGE AUDOUIN-LAMB, Esq., of East Hill, co. Wicklow, on his assuming, by royal licence, 1801, the additional surname of LAMB, by the desire of his uncle, HALL LAMB, Esq., of Dublin). Quarterly, 1st and 4th, ar. on a pale or, four bendlets sa., for AUDOUIN; 2nd and 3rd, gu. three holy lambs pass. ar. each bearing a banner of the second charged with a cross gu., for LAMB. Crest—A stag's head erased ppr. Motto—Chassé pour foi.

Lambale. Per fesse dancettée ar. and gu.

Lambard (Lord Mayor of London, 1531). Ar. on a chev. engr. gu. betw. three eagles sa. an annulet or.

Lambard, or Lambarde. Gu. a chev. vair betw. three lambs ar. Crest—A garb lying fesseways ppr.

Lambard. Same Arms. Crest—A horse's head erased or, bridled gu.

Lambard (Sevenoaks, co. Kent. Visit. 1663. WILLIAM LAMBARD, topographer of co. Kent). Gu. a chev. vair betw. three lambs ar. Crest—A reindeer's head erased sa. Motto—Deo, patriæ, tibi.

Lambard (granted by Hawley, Clarenceux, 1551, to JOHN LAMBARD, of Ledbury, co. Hereford, then Sheriff of London). Gu. a chev. vair betw. three lambs pass. ar. unguled sa. Crest—A trogodice's head erased az. maned or, eared and horned ar. langued gu.

Lambarde (Beechmont, co. Kent). Quarterly, 1st, LAMBARDE, gu. a chev. vair betw. three lambs ar.; 2nd, HORNE, of Lindon; 3rd, DEANE, of Halling; 4th, WHITE, of Beverley. Crest—A reindeer's head erased ar. Motto—Deo patriæ tibi.

Lambarton (co. Cornwall). Sa. three chev. ar.

Lambart (Earl of Cavan). Gu. three narcissuses ar. pierced of the field. Crest—On a mount vert a centaur ppr. drawing his bow gu. arrow or. Supporters—Two men in armour to the waist sa. garnished or, short trousers gu. fringed of the second, faces, arms, knees, and swords ppr. each having a steel cap, adorned with six ostrich feathers alternately ar. and the third. Motto—Ut quocunque paratus.

Lambart (Beau Parc, co. Meath; descended from Hon. OLIVER LAMBART, of Painstown, second son of CHARLES, first Earl of Cavan). Gu. three narcissuses ar. pierced of the field. Crest—On a mount vert a centaur ppr. drawing his bow gu. arrow or. Motto—Ut quocunque paratus.

Lambart (co. York). Gu. a chev. ar. a chief chequy or and az.

Lambe (Troston, co. Suffolk). Erm. a lion ramp sa.

Lambe (Stoke Pogeis, co. Bucks). Sa. on a fesse or, betw. three cinquefoils erm. a leopard's face gu. betw. two mullets pierced of the field.

Lambe (Fun. Ent. Ulster's Office, 1601, DOROTHY LAMBE, wife of ROWLAND ARGALL, Secretary to the Earl of Sussex, Lord Lieutenant of Ireland). Sa. on a fess betw. three cinquefoils pierced erm. two mullets pierced of the field.

Lamberby. Per chev. sa. and ar. in chief two suns or. Crest—On a ducal coronet a stag sejant ppr.

Lambert (London, bart.). Ar. on a mount ppr. an oak tree vert and a greyhound courant gu. Crest—Out of a ducal coronet or, three ostrich feathers gu. ar. and az Motto—Sequitando si giunge.

Lambert (Pinchbeck, co. Bucks). Gu. a chev. ar. a chief chequy or and az. Crest—A lion's head erased ar. gorged with a fesse chequy or and az.

Lambert (Stockton, co. Durham). Gu. a chev. erminois betw. three lambs pass. ar. Crest—A demi lamb ramp. ar. holding a shield erminois.

Lambert (co. Buckingham, Hull and Owton, co. York). Gu. a chev. betw. three lambs pass. ar. a chief chequy or and az. Crest—A sphinx pass. guard. or, face ppr. holding in the dexter foot a rose gu. seeded and leaved vert.

Lambert (Lyston Hall, co. Essex). Gu. three cinquefoils pierced ar. Crest—A centaur ppr. bow gu. arrow or. Motto —Ut quocunque paratus.

Lambert (Lord Mayor of London, 1532; and Malden Bradley, co. Wilts. Visit. Hants, 1634). Ar. a chev. engr. gu. betw. three Cornish choughs ppr.

Lambert (London and Paris). Ar. on a mount vert an oak tree ppr. on the mount a greyhound pass. gu.

Lambert (Lord Mayor of London, 1741). Gu. three cinquefoils and a canton or.

Lambert (London and co. Surrey; granted 1737). Gu. three narcissus flowers ar. a canton or. Crest—On a mount vert a centaur pass. reguard. the human parts ppr. the other erm. girt about the waist with a laurel garland of the first, drawing a bow and arrow gu.

Lambert (co. York). Gu. a chev. betw. three lambs pass. ar.

Lambert. Gu. a chev. betw. three fleurs-de-lis or. Crest— A lion ramp. ar.

Lambert. Gu. a chev. betw. three lambs ar. Crest—Two lobsters' claws erect gu. holding in each a fish or.

Lambert (granted to JAMES LAMBERT, Esq., of Brixton, co. Surrey). Per pale or and az. a chev. betw. two bees volant in chief and a cinquefoil in base all counterchanged. Crest— In front of a gate or, a stag's head couped ppr. attired gold, in the mouth a slip of oak vert, fructed or, the neck charged with a bend az. thereon three acorns also gold.

Lambert (RICHARD LAMBERT, Alderman of London, and JOHN LAMBERT, citizen of same, sons of JOHN LAMBERT, second son of RICHARD LAMBERT, gentleman, of Kirton, co. Lincoln. Visit. London, 1568). Ar. on a bend engr. betw. two lions ramp. sa. three annulets of the first.

Lambert (Boyton, co. Wilts; descended from RICHARD LAMBERT, Esq., of Kirton, co. Lincoln, who purchased the estate of Boyton in 1572). Ar. on a bend engr. betw. two lions ramp. sa. three annulets or. Crest—A demi pegasus, wings expanded erm.

Lambert (Castle Lambert, Kilquain, and Castle Ellen, co. Galway). Gu. three cinquefoils pierced or. Crest—A centaur ppr. bow gu. arrow or. Motto—Ut quocunque paratus.

Lambert (Waterdale, formerly of Creg Clare, co. Galway, 1630, a branch of LAMBERT, of co. York; WALTER MAC-CLELLAN LAMBERT, Esq., of Waterdale). Quarterly, 1st and 4th, gu. three cinquefoils pierced ar., for LAMBERT; 2nd and 3rd, ar. two chev. sa., for STAUNTON. Crest—A centaur ppr. bow. gu. arrow or. Motto—Ut quocunque paratus.

Lambert (Carnagh, co. Wexford; HENRY LAMBERT, Esq., of Carnagh, D.L., descended from LAMPORTE, of Ballyhire, and now the representative of that ancient Anglo-Irish family; granted by Carney, Ulster, 1683, to PATRICK LAMBERT, Esq., of Dunmain, High Sheriff co. Wexford). Quarterly, 1st and 4th, vert a lamb ambulant ar.; 2nd and 3rd, erm. an eagle displ. gu. Crest—A sagittarius pass. per pale gu. and ar. charged with a trefoil vert, bow and arrow or. Motto—Deus providebit.

Lambert (confirmed to ALEXANDER CLENDINNING LAMBERT, Esq., of Brook Hill, and Cong Abbey, co. Mayo, and the descendants of his grandfather). Gu. a cross crosslet or, betw. three cinquefoils pierced ar. Crest—A centaur ppr. charged on the shoulder with a cross crosslet or. Motto— Ut quocunque paratus.

Lambie (Scotland). See L'AMY.

Lamborn, or Lamborne (Lambourn, co. Cornwall; the

nciress m. ARUNDELL, of Lanherne). Ar. a fesse betw. two chevronels sa. *Crest*—A demi lion ramp. gu. supporting the rudder of a ship sa.

Lamborne (co. Essex). Or, two chev. sa.

Lamborne (*temp.* Henry VI.). Erm. on a bend cotised sa. three lions' heads erased or.

Lamborne. Ar. two chev. sa. *Crest*—Out of a tower ppr. a lion's head or, collared sa.

Lamborne. Ar. on a bend sa. cotised gu. three lions' heads erased or.

Lamport. Ar. on a bend az. three bucks' heads couped or.

Lambrand, or Lambrund. Ar. on a bend sa. cotised gu. three dragons' head erased close or.

Lambrine. Ar. on a chief gu. three boars' heads of the field.

Lambroke (co. Somerset). Paly wavy of six or and sa. on a chief of the second three crescents ar.

Lambton (*Earl of Durham*). Quarterly, 1st, sa. a fesse betw. three lambs pass. ar., for LAMBTON; 2nd, ar. a fesse gu. betw. three popinjays vert, collared of the second, for LUMLEY; 3rd, ar. an inescutcheon sa. within an orle of cinquefoils gu., for HEDWORTH; 4th, ar. three cinquefoils gu., for D'ARCY. *Crests*—1st, LAMBTON : A ram's head cabossed ar. attired sa.; 2nd, HEDWORTH : A woman's head affrontée, couped at the breast ppr. hair flowing or, wreathed about the temples with a garland of cinquefoils gu. pierced of the second; 3rd, D'ARCY : Out of a ducal coronet or, an antelope's head issuant, winged ar. attired and barbed of the first. *Supporters*—Two lions, the dexter gu. the sinister az. each ducally gorged and supporting a staff or, therefrom banners of the second, the dexter banner charged with a cross patonce and the sinister with a lion pass. guard. of the third. *Motto*—Le jour viendra.

Lambton (co. York). Sa. a fesse betw. three lambs ar. *Crest*—A ram's head cabossed ar. attired sa.

Lambton. Gu. a fesse betw. three lambs' heads couped ar.

Lamburne. Ar. on a bend sa. (another, cotised gu.) three wolves' heads erased or.

Lame (co. Kent). Sa. on a fesse or, betw. three cinquefoils erm. a crescent betw. two mullets of the first.

Lamelin (Lamelin, co. Cornwall; the heiress m. TRELAWNY). Ar. a bull pass. sa. (a bordure of the second bezantée is sometimes added).

Lamelyne, or Lamlyn (co. Bedford). Ar. a fleur-de-lis sa.

Lamere. Gu. three fishes sa.

Lamesey, or Lambsey. Ar. a lion pass. gu. betw. three trefoils slipped vert. *Crest*—A savage's head ppr. wreathed round the head ar. and az.

Lamford, or Lambford. Paly of six or and gu. a bend ar. *Crest*—A dexter hand ppr. brandishing a scymitar ar.

Lamingham. Ar. a fesse az.

Lamkyn. Barry of six ar. and az. on a chief gu. a lion pass. guard. or.

Lamkyn. Gu. a stag's head and neck couped or.

Lammin, or Lamming (co. Lincoln; as borne by WILLIAM HENRY LAMMIN, Esq., of Shorrolds, Fulham, Middlesex). Sa. a fesse ar. betw. three paschal lambs pass. of the last. *Crest*—A paschal lamb, as in the arms. *Motto*—Agnus Dei mihi salus.

Lamois, or Kamois. Gu. a chief indented or.

Lamon, and Lanam. Per chev. gu. and ar. in base an annulet of the first.

Lamont (that Ilk, co. Argyll). Az. a lion ramp. ar. *Another Coat*—Az. a mound ensigned with a cross or. *Crest*—A hand couped ppr. *Motto*—Ne parcas nec spernas.

Lamorat. Purp. semée of crosses crosslet a lion ramp. or.

Lamorle (co. York). Per fesse gu. and ar. three crescents counterchanged.

Lamorley, or Lammorle (cos. Norfolk and York). Per fesse gu. and ar. in chief three crescents of the second. *Crest*—On a naval coronet or, a lion ramp. gu.

Lamote. Vair a bend gu. a label of four points ar.

Lamott (London, formerly of Flanders, 1633). Ar. three bars humettée sa.

Lampard. Ar. on a bend engr. betw. two lions ramp. sa. three plates. *Crest*—A cinquefoil az.

Lampay. Or, a water bouget sa. a bordure of the last bezantée.

Lampen (Paderda in Linkinhorne, co. Cornwall; showing seven descents before 1620). Ar. on a bend engr. sa. three rams' heads cabossed of the field, attired or. *Crest*—A ram's head cabossed ar. attired or.

Lampen (Lampen and Pardardaye, co. Cornwall; JOHN LAMPEN, of the latter place, son of JOHN LAMPEN, of the

former. Visit. Cornwall, 1620). Ar. on a chev. engr. sa. three rams' heads cabossed of the first, attired or.

Lampergy. Sa. a chev. betw. three talbots pass. ar.

Lampet (co. Suffolk). Ar. on a cross engr. gu. betw. four escallops sa. five bezants.

Lampet (co. Suffolk). Ar. on a bend engr. sa. three goats' heads couped of the field.

Lampet, or Lampeth (co. Suffolk). Ar. on a bend engr. sa. three rams' heads of the field, attired or. *Crest*—A Doric pillar ar. entwined with a laurel branch vert, on the top a flame ppr.

Lampkyn. Barry of six ar. and az. a chief gu.

Lamplogh. Ar. a chev. betw. three lions' heads erased sa.

Lamplow, or Lampelaw. Ar. three lamps sa. (another adds a label gu.).

Lamplow. Az. a cross flory or.

Lamplugh (Lamplugh Hall, co. Cumberland; descended from Sir ROBERT DE LAMPLUGH, Lord of Lamplugh, *temp.* Henry II.; of this family was THOMAS LAMPLUGH, D.D., Archbishop of York, *d.* 1691; JOHN LAMPLUGH, Visit. Cumberland, 1615, son of Sir JOHN LAMPLUGH, Knt., of Lamplugh, who was great-grandson of JOHN LAMPLUGH, of same place). Or, a cross flory sa., quartering, 1st, per fess ar. and gu. six martlets counterchanged; 2nd, barry of six ar. and gu. on a canton of the last a cinquefoil or. *Crest*—A goat's head couped sa. attired and bearded or.

Lamplugh (RAPER-LAMPLUGH; the last male heir of this old family, the Rev. THOMAS LAMPLUGH, of Lamplugh, Rector of Copgrove, *d. s. p.* in 1783, and was *s.* by his nephew, JOHN RAPER, Esq., of Abberford and Lotherton, co. York, whose eldest son and heir, JOHN LAMPLUGH RAPER, Esq., assumed in 1825 the name and arms of LAMPLUGH). Or, a cross flory sa. *Crest*—A goat's head ar. attires and beard or (another, a goat's head erased ar. attired or). *Motto*—Providentia Dei stabiliuntur familiæ.

Lampson (Rowfant, co. Sussex, bart.). Per saltire ar. and gu. two gryphons' heads erased in fesse and as many escarbuncles in pale counterchanged. *Crest*—A gryphon's head erased gu. charged with an escarbuncle ar. betw. two wings paly of four ar. and gu. *Motto*—Persevera et vince.

Lampt. Per pale ar. and gu. a saltire engr. counterchanged.

Lampton (co. Kent). Gu. a chev. betw. three lambs' heads cabossed ar.

Lampuric. Or, a cross pattée fitchée sa.

L'Amy (now RAMSAY-L'AMY, Dunkenny, co. Forfar). Quarterly, 1st and 4th, az. three crosiers paleways in fess or, in base a saltire couped ar., for L'AMY; 2nd and 3rd, ar. an eagle displ. sa. beaked and membered gu. charged in the breast with an inescutcheon of the last, a bordure of the second. *Crest*—A dexter hand erect ppr. holding a crosier or. *Supporters*—Two savages wreathed head and middle with laurel, holding oak batons over their shoulders ppr. *Motto*—Per varios casus.

Lanacre (co. York). Ar. a chev. betw. three fleurs-de-lis ar.

Lanbrun. Ar. on a bend sa. cotised gu. three dragons' heads erased or. *Crest*—Two lions' heads issuing addorsed ppr. collared or.

Lancashire. Ar. on a bend sa. three martlets of the field, on a sinister canton gu. two bendlets or, the uppermost engr. *Crest*—A demi lion ramp. ar. gorged with a chaplet vert, holding in the paws an escutcheon charged as the canton.

Lancashire (Polefield, Prestwich, co. Lancaster). Erm. two bars engr. one az. the other gu. in chief three roses of the last, on a canton of the same a lion pass. or.

Lancashire. Erm. on a bend sa. three mullets ar. a sinister canton gu. charged with two bends or.

Lancaster (*Baron Lancaster*, extinct 1334 ; JOHN DE LANCASTER, summoned to Parliament 1299, *d. s. p.*). Ar. two bars gu. on a canton of the second a lion pass. guard. or.

Lancaster (WILLIAM LANCASTER, of Cokbridge, whose dau. and heir m. HUGH LOWTHER, of Lowther, co. Westmoreland, living *temp.* Henry VI. Visit. Rutland, 1615). Or, two bars gu. on a canton of the last a mullet of the first.

Lancaster, Duke of. The ancient arms of England, viz., quarterly, 1st and 4th, az. semée-de-lis or ; 2nd and 3rd, gu. three lions pass. guard. in pale or, a label ar.

Lancaster, Town of. Per fess vert and az. in chief a castle quadruple-towered ar. in base a lion pass. or.

Lancaster (arms in a window in the Church of Queen's College, Oxford. Visit. Oxon, 1566). Ar. two bars gu. on a canton of the last a mullet of the first.

Lancaster (Crackhouse, co. Cumberland, and Rainhill, co. Lancaster). Same *Arms*. *Crest*—A lion's head erased ar. charged with a crescent gu. *Another Crest*—A seahorse ppr.

Lancaster (Stockbridge, co. Westmoreland). Ar. two bars gu. on a canton of the second a mullet of the first.

Lancaster (Richmond, co. York). Ar. two bars gu. on a canton of the second a cinquefoil of the first (another, or).

Lancaster. Ar. on a chief gu. a lion ramp. guard. or (another, gu. a leopard ramp. or, collared az.; another, gu. a lion ramp. guard. or).

Lancaster (Fun. Ent., Ulster's Office, 1598, MARGERY LAN-CASTER, wife of THOMAS LAWTON, of Dublin). Ar. two bars gu. on a canton of the last a lion pass. guard. or.

Lancaster, De. Ar. two bars gu. on a canton of the second a lion pass. guard. of the first. *Crest*—A lion couchant or.

Lance. Gu. a fesse or.

Lancedale. Ar. three torteaux, a quarter gu.

Lancelin. Ar. a fleur-de-lis gu.

Lancell, Lancelin, or Lancelyn. Ar. on a fesse az. three mullets of the field.

Lancellyn, Lancelin, Lamelyng, or Lamlin (co. Bedford). Ar. a fleur-de-lis sa. (another, tinctures reversed).

Lancelot (co. Leicester). Ar. three bends gu. *Crest*—An astrolabe.

Lancelot. Or, on a chief az. three fusils of the field.

Lancher. Or, six pellets, three, two, and one.

Lanching. Vert a saltire engr. ar.

Land. Gyronny of eight or and sa. a bend gu. *Crest*—A church environed with trees ppr.

Landawarnick (Landawarnick, Duloe, co. Cornwall). Ar. two bars sa. in chief a griffin segreant az.

Landawre, Landawrey, or Landwrey. Gu. a bend betw. two cotises indented or.

Landel (that Ilk, co. Berwick; the heiress *m.* the first *Earl of Home*). Or, an orle az.

Landel (Coull, co. Fife). Or, an orle indented on the inner side az. *Motto*—Olim florebat.

Landell (Southwark, co. Surrey). Or, an orle az. betw. four taws az. *Crest*—On a mount vert a garb or, thereon an escutcheon sa. charged with a taw gold.

Landen (co. Lincoln, 1641). Gu. a lion ramp. or, a canton per bend sinister erm. and sa. *Crest*—A dexter hand apaumée ppr. *Motto*—Ero quod eram.

Landener, Landomer, or Landew. Gu. a fesse ar. charged with a fesse wavy sa. betw. three boars' heads couped of the second.

Lander (St. Ives, co. Cornwall). Per bend or and vert.

Lander. Paly of eight sa. and or, a fesse gu. *Crest*—A hand issuing from a cloud holding a sword wavy all ppr.

Landesduke. Az. a chev. or, fretty sa. betw. three crosses moline ar.

Landeth, or Londeth. Erm. on a chief gu. a lion pass. or. *Crest*—A winged heart ppr.

Landles. Az. three orles or.

Landon (Cheshunt, co. Herts). Gyronny of eight or and az. an inescutcheon ar. *Crest*—A lizard ppr. *Motto*—Ma force d'en haut.

Landon. Or, a chev. sa. betw. three bustards vert. *Crest*—A demi pegasus reguard. ar. supporting a pennon gu. tasselled or.

Landon. Ar. a chev. sa. betw. three cameleons vert.

Landonthorp, or Landorthorpe. Gu. three lions ramp. erm.

Landor (Rugeley, co. Stafford, Ipsley Court, co. Warwick, and of Llanthony Abbey, co. Monmouth; granted 8 June, 1687). Ar. two bends gu. each charged with a bendlet indented or. *Crest*—A hand and arm erect, habited bendy of six or and gu. cuffed ar. in the hand ppr. a fleur-de-lis az.

Landres. Az. (another, sa.) a lion ramp. or, a bordure erm.

Landsleydown (co. Cornwall). Sa. three chevronels ar.

Landstroder. Erm. a chev. sa.

Landwath. Gu. three bends vair. *Crest*—A demi pegasus ar. guttée de poix.

Lane (Wycombe, co. Bucks, Allhallow-Gussing, cos. Dorset, and Hereford; Lord Mayor of London, 1695; Courteen Hall, Hanler, Twinden, Horton, and Walgrave, co. Northampton, and cos. Somerset and York). Per pale az. and gu. three saltires couped ar. *Crest*—Two eagles' heads issuant out of a crescent or, the dexter gu. the sinister az. (Some bear the dexter head az. and the sinister gu.).

Lane (co. Gloucester). Same *Arms* and *Crest.*

Lane (King's Bromley, co. Stafford, and Lily Hill, co. Berks; originally of Hyde and Bentley, Staffordshire). Per fesse or and az. a chev. gu. betw. three mullets counterchanged,

on a canton of the third the royal lions of England, being the augmentation granted to the family for "the great and signal service performed by JOHN LANE, Esq., of Bentley, in the county of Stafford, in his ready concurring to the preservation of King Charles II. after the battle of Worcester." *Crests*—1st: A strawberry roan horse saliant, couped at the flanks, bridled sa. bitted and garnished or, supporting betw. the feet an imperial crown ppr.; 2nd: Out of a ducal coronet or, a pair of wings endorsed ppr. *Motto*—Garde le Roy.

Lane (Cottesbroke, co. Northants). Per pale gu. and az. three saltires couped ar., impaled by BEDELL, of Hamerton.

Lane (Stratford, co. Warwick. Visit. Warwick). Sa. a chev. betw. three arrows ar.

Lane (co. Kent). Or, on a chief az. two mullets of the field.

Lane (Badgemore, co. Oxford). Per pale az. and gu. three saltires couped ar. *Crest*—Two griffins' heads, one gu. the other az. issuing out of a crescent or. *Motto*—Nec degenero.

Lane (London). Gu. on a fesse wavy betw. three swans ppr. membered or, as many crosses pattée sa. on each four bezants.

Lane (London). Gu. on a fesse wavy betw. three swans ar. as many crosses formée or.

Lane (Twickenham, co. Middlesex). Or, on a fesse gu. betw. three torteaux a trefoil slipped betw. two mullets or. *Crest*—A demi griffin ar.

Lane (co. Northampton). Per chev. or and az. a lion ramp. counterchanged.

Lane (Great Yarmouth, and co. Northumberland). Per pale az. and ar. three saltires couped counterchanged.

Lane (Hyde and Bentley, co. Stafford). Or, a chev. gu. betw. three mullets pierced az.

Lane (Ipswich, co. Suffolk). Ar. three chevronels sa. *Crest*—A demi lion ramp. gu. bezantée holding betw. the paws a bezant.

Lane (Bridgetown, co. Warwick; confirmed by the Deputies of Camden, Clarenceux, to RICHARD LANE; Her. Visit.). Az. three fireballs or, flammant ppr.

Lane. Or, a chev. ermines betw. three mullets pierced az. *Crest*—A dexter arm vested ermines, turned up and indented ar. holding in the hand ppr. a mullet az.

Lane. Per pale ar. and sa. a saltire purp. betw. four fleurs-de-lis counterchanged.

Lane. Ar. a fesse betw. six crosses crosslet fitchée gu.

Lane. Gu. a lion pass. guard. betw. three saltires couped or.

Lane (Ryelands, co. Hereford, representative of RODD, of the Rodd). Per pale az. and gu. three saltires couped ar., quartering RODD. *Crest*—Out of a crescent or, two griffins' heads addorsed, one gu. the other az. *Motto*—Celeriter.

Lane (Moundsley Hall, Kingsnorton, co. Worcester). Per pale az. and gu. three saltires couped or. *Crest*—Two eagles' heads addorsed, one gu. the other az. issuing out of a crescent or.

Lane (Coffleet, co. Devon). Per pale az. and gu. three saltires couped ar., quartering VEALE, on a bend sa. three calves pass. of the first; and TOTHILL, ar. on a bend sa. cotised of the same a lion pass. guard. of the first. *Crest*—Two eagles' heads addorsed issuing out of a crescent or, dexter gu. sinister az.

Lane (Sir RALPH LANE, knighted by Sir WILLIAM FITZ-WILLIAM, Lord Deputy of Ireland, 1588-94). Quarterly, 1st and 4th, per pale az. and gu. three saltires couped ar.; 2nd, quarterly, 1st and 4th, ar. two bars az. a border engr. sa., 2nd and 3rd, or, three water bougets sa.; 3rd, gyronny of eight or and sa. on a canton gu. a covered cup ar.

Lane (Sir WILLIAM LANE, of Horton, co. Northampton, knighted at St. Patrick's Cathedral, Dublin, 27 March, 1597, by Sir WILLIAM RUSSELL, Lord Deputy). Per pale az. and gu. three saltires couped, that in the dexter chief az., that in sinister of the first, and that in base per pale of the third and first.

Lane (Tulske, co. Roscommon; Fun. Ent. Ulster's Office. 1631, MABEL, wife of RICHARD LANE). Or, on a bend betw. two fleurs-de-lis gu. a lion pass. of the field.

Lane (*Viscount Lanesborough*, extinct 1724). Ar. a lion ramp. sa. a border sa. on a canton az. a crown or.

Lane-Fox (*Baron Bingley*, extinct 1772; GEORGE FOX, eldest son of HENRY FOX, Esq., by Hon. FRANCES LANE, his wife, sister of the last *Viscount Lanesborough*, assumed the surname of LANE on inheriting his maternal uncle's estates, and was created a peer 1762). Quarterly, 1st and 4th, same as the preceding, for LANE; 2nd and 3rd, ar. a chev. betw. three foxes' heads erased gu., for Fox. *Crest*—Out of a ducal coronet or, a demi griffin segreant sa. winged az. *Supporters*—Two bears ar. *Motto*—Inconcussa virtus.

Lane (Reg. Ulster's Office to Sir GEORGE LANE). Or, on a bend gu. betw. two fleurs-de-lis sa. a lion pass. of the first. *Crest*—A mermaid holding a cup.

Lane (Roscommon, Ireland; granted 6 April, 1661). Ar. a lion ramp. gu. armed az. a bordure sa. *Crest*—Out of a ducal coronet or, a demi griffin sa. winged ar.

Lane-Fox. See FOX.

Laneham (quartered by NEVILL, of Holte, co. Leicester. Visit. Leicester, 1619). Quarterly, ar. and sa. in the 1st quarter a fleur-de-lis of the last, and in the 4th quarter an erm. spot.

Lanesborough, Earl of. See BUTLER.

Laney (Pulham). Sa. a chev. erm. betw. three catharine wheels ar.

Lanfaunt. Ar. on an inescutcheon within an orle of martlets gu. a crescent of the first.

Lanfret, or Landfret. Ar. an eagle displ. gu.

Lang. Sa. on a fesse betw. two cinquefoils in chief ar. and on a mount in base three oak sprigs vert, acorned or, the text letters A, B, C, D, E, F, of the field. *Crest*—Three oak sprigs acorned.

Langave, or Landgave. Gu. (another, az.) semée of crosses crosslet or, a fesse dancettée of the last.

Langborne. Ar. two chev. gu.

Langdale, Baron. See BICKERSTETH.

Langdale (Langdale, co. York). Sa. a chev. betw. three estoiles ar. *Crest*—An estoile ar.

Langdale (Baron Langdale, extinct 1777). Same *Arms* and *Crest*. *Supporters*—Two bulls sa. armed, crested, and unguled ar.

Langdale (Houghton, co. York; the senior branch of the noble family of LANGDALE; the late PHILIP LANGDALE, of Houghton, devised his estates to Hon. CHARLES STOURTON, third son of the 16th *Lord Stourton*, by MARY, his wife. dau. and co-heiress of *Lord Langdale*, who thereupon assumed the name and arms of LANGDALE in 1815, and was father of the present CHARLES LANGDALE, Esq., of Houghton). *Arms*, &c., as the preceding.

Langdale (Whilbistrond, co. York). Or, a chev. betw. three mullets sa.

Langdale. Paly of six or and gu. a bend of the first (another, az.).

Langdall (Langdall, co. York; ISABELL, dau. of LANGDALL, of Langdall, *temp.* Edward IV., *m.* GEORGE PERROTT, of Haverfordwest, co. Pembroke, son of OWEN PERROTT, third son of PERROTT, of Narberth Castle, same co. Visit. Oxon, 1566). Sa. a chev. betw. three estoiles ar.

Langdole. Ar. on a fesse sa. betw. three spears' heads az. a tower betw. two roses or.

Langdon (Keverell, co. Cornwall; WALTER LANGDON, son of RICHARD LANGDON, and grandson of JOHN LANGDON, of Bicton, same co. Visit. Cornwall, 1620). Ar. a chev. betw. three lizards' heads sa.

Langdon (Langdon, co. Cornwall. Visit. Cornwall, 1620). Ar. a chev. betw. three bears' heads erased sa.

Langdon (Wolterton, co. Norfolk). Ar. a chev. cotised betw. three bears' heads erased barways sa. muzzled of the field. *Crest*—On a mount vert a lynx of the last gorged with two bars or.

Langeford. Paly of six ar. and gu. on a chief az. a lion pass. guard. or.

Langesford (Bratton, co. Devon; MOSES LANGESFORD, aged 44 years at Visit. Devon, 1620, grandson of RICHARD LANGESFORD, of same place). Paly of six ar. and gu. on a chief ar. a lion pass. sa. a crescent for diff.

Langfford (Sir JOHN DE LANGFFORD, one of the knights of co. Nottingham, *temp.* Edward I. Visit. Notts, 1614). Paly of six or and gu. a bend ar.

Langfield. Ar. on a chev. sa. betw. three crosses botonnée fitchée of the second, as many covered cups of the field.

Langford, Baron. See ROWLEY.

Langford (Alington; confirmed by Segar, Garter). Gu. a wild goose close ar. a crescent for diff.

Langford (Selford, co. Bedford; granted March, 1607). Paly of six ar. and gu. on a bend of the first three eagles displ. of the second. *Crest*—In a row of partridge feathers of divers colours three chibbals or and ar.

Langford (cos. Wilts and Berks). Paly of six ar. and gu. on a chief az. a lion pass. or.

Langford (Langford Hill, co. Cornwall; seven descents in Visit. Cornwall, 1620; the heiress *m.* WOLLACOMBE). Paly of six ar. and gu. on a chief az. a lion pass. guard. or.

Langford (Hallatrow, co. Somerset, 1620; descended from the LANGFORDS of co. Wilts). Same *Arms*.

Langford (Trungle and Penzance, co. Cornwall). Same *Arms.*

Langford (co. Worcester). Paly of six or and gu. (sometimes az.) a bend ar.

Langford (arms in the Manor House of Sarsden, co. Oxford; EDWARD LANGFORD, with THOMAS STONOR, and RICHARD HARCOURT, granted the Manor of Tackley, co. Oxford, to JOHN NEWERS, and CLEMENTIA, his wife, 1 Edward IV., 1461. Visit. Oxon, 1566). Paly of six ar. and gu. on a chief az. a lion pass. or.

Langford (Sir JOHN LANGFORD, *temp.* Edward II.; his sister *m.* EDWARD PIERPOINT, Esq., of Holm Pierpoint, ancestor of the extinct *Dukes of Kingston*. Visit. Notts, 1614). Quarterly, ar. and gu.

Langford (Langford Hill, Poundstock, Liskerd, and Tromade, all in co. Cornwall; descended from LANGFORD. of Langford, co. Devon. Visit. Cornwall, 1620). Paly of six ar. and gu. on a chief az. a lion pass. guard. or, a mullet for diff.

Langford (cos. Derby, Nottingham, and Salop). Paly of six or and gu. over all a bend ar. *Crest*—A tiger pass. coward gu. maned and tufted or.

Langford (Bratton, co. Devon). Paly of six ar. and gu. on a chief of the first a lion pass. sa.

Langford (co. Leicester). Paly of six ar. and gu. a bend of the first.

Landford, or Langeford (London and co. Middlesex). Gu. a shoveller, wings close ar. a crescent for diff. *Crest*— A demi shoveller, wings displ. ar. charged with a crescent for diff.

Langford (London). Per pale ar. and gu. three mullets counterchanged.

Langford (co. Northumberland). Paly of six or and gu. a bordure ar.

Langford (Muckmaire, co. Antrim; impalement Fun. Ent. Ulster's Office, 1630, Sir HUGH CLOTWORTHY, Knt., whose wife was MARY, dau. of ROGER LANGFORD, from whom descend maternally *Viscount Massereene* and *Ferrard*, and *Lord Langford*). Paly of six sa. and or, on a chief vert a lion pass. of the field.

Langford (Kilmackedret, co. Londonderry, bart., extinct; Sir HERCULES LANGFORD was created a bart. 1667, *d.* 18 June, 1683, and was *s.* by his son, Sir ARTHUR LANGFORD, who *d. s. p.*, leaving his sister, MARY LANGFORD, his heiress; she *m.* Sir JOHN ROWLEY, ancestor of *Lord Langford ;* Fun. Ent. Ulster's Office). Paly of six sa. and or, on a chief vert a lion pass. guard. of the second. *Crest*—A demi lion ramp. holding in the dexter paw a truncheon all or.

Langford. Quarterly, gu. and ar. (another, gu. fretty engr. erm.).

Langford-Nibbs (Island of Antigua; granted 1759). Az. a chev. engr. erm. on a chief ar. two stags' heads cabossed gu. *Crest*—A stags' head cabossed gu. stricken in the scalp with an arrow or, feathered ar.

Langham (Cottesbrooke Park, co. Northampton, bart.). Ar. three bears' heads erased sa. muzzled or. *Crest*—A bear's head erased, as in the arms. *Motto*—Nec sinit esse feros.

Langham (co. Essex). Ar. a fesse gu. a label az.

Langham (co. Leicester). Az. a chev. embattled betw. three cinquefoils ar.

Langham, or Langholme (Coinsholme, co. Lincoln). Az. a chev. embattled betw. three cinquefoils or. *Crest*—A hare's head erased ar.

Langham (Gopsall, co. Leicester; ROBERT LANGHAM, living 19 Richard II., 1395, son of REGINALD LANGHAM, and grandson of ROBERT LANGHAM; the eventual heiress of the family, the dau. of EDWARD LANGHAM, *m.* RICHARD EVERARD, Esq., of Shenton, co Leicester, who *d.* 1556. Visit. Leicester, 1619). Ar. three bears' heads couped sa. muzzled or.

Langham (co. Northampton, and Pailton, co. Warwick. Visit. Warwick). Ar. on a fesse betw. three bears' heads erased sa. muzzled or, as many bezants.

Langham. Ar. a fleur-de-lis betw. three bears' heads erased sa. muzzled gu. *Crest*—Out of a coronet gu. a bear's paw sa. holding a sword ar. pommelled or.

Langham. Barry of six or and az. on a bend gu. three cinquefoils ar.

Langham. Ar. a fesse gu.

Langharne (Tregavethan, co. Cornwall; STEPHEN LANGHARNE. Visit. Cornwall, 1620). Az. a chev. betw. three escallops or.

Langhergy (co. Cornwall). Ar. a fesse ermines betw. three greyhounds' heads ar. collared gu.

Langherne (Tregavethan, near Truro, and St. Erme, co. Cornwall). Az. a chev. betw. three escallop shells or.

Langholme. Az. a chev. embattled or, betw. three cinquefoils of the last. *Crest*—A paschal lamb ppr. standard gu. *Motto*—In cruce salus.

Langhorn, or Langhorne (co. Bedford; granted 20 Jan. 1610). Sa. a cross ar. on a chief of the second three buglehorns of the field stringed gu. *Crest*—A buglehorn sa. stringed gu. betw. two wings expanded ar.

Langhorne (London, bart., extinct 1714). Same *Arms.*

Langland. Per pale ar. and or, a cockatrice sa. combed gu.

Langlands (that Ilk). Ar. on a chev. gu. three mullets of the first. *Crest*—An anchor in pale placed in the sea ppr. *Motto*—Spero.

Langlee. Ar. a fesse sa. in chief three escallops of the last (another, ar. on a fesse sa. three escallops of the first).

Langley (Langley, co. Durham, and Sheriff Hutton, co. York). Paly of six ar. and vert. *Crest*—In a ducal coronet or, a plume of five ostrich feathers, three ar. and two vert.

Langley (Higham Gobion, co. Bedford, bart. extinct; WILLIAM LANGLEY, descended from LANGLEY, of Langley, co. Durham, and Sheriff Hutton, co. York, was so created 1641. Sir HENRY LANGLEY, sixth bart., *d. s. p.*). Same *Arms.*

Langley (co. Chester). Ar. a cockatrice sa. membered gu.

Langley (co. Essex). Gu. a chev. engr. or, betw. three escallops ar.

Langley (Bristow and Mangerfield, co. Gloucester). Gu. a saltire or. *Crest*—A dexter gauntlet lying fesseways, holding a sword erect all ppr. the blade enfiled with a dragon's head sa. couped at the neck gu.

Langley (cos. Gloucester, Salop, and Warwick). Ar. a fesse sa. in chief three pellets (another, hurts). *Crest*—On a garb lying fesseways or, a dove close ar. beaked and legged gu. *Motto*—Beare and forbeare.

Langley (co. Kent). Quarterly, per fesse indented or and az. (another, az. and or).

Langley (co. Lancaster, Eye, co. Suffolk, Ousethorpe and Dalton, co. York). Ar. a cockatrice volant sa. crested, membered, and beaked gu. *Crest*—A cock ar. combed, legged, and wattled gu.

Langley (co. Lincoln). Quarterly, 1st and 4th, ar. a cockatrice sa. crested, beaked, and membered gu.; 2nd and 3rd, gu. a mermaid with comb and glass ar.

Langley (co. Lincoln, London, and co. Salop). Ar. a fesse sa. in chief three pellets, a bordure of the second. *Crest*—A cockatrice sa. beaked or, combed and wattled gu.

Langley (Agecroft, co. Lancaster, 1567). Ar. a cockatrice, wings endorsed and tail nowed sa. beaked or.

Langley (THOMAS LANGLEY and JOHN LANGLEY, Aldermen, both of London, sons of ROBERT LANGLEY, Esq., of Althorp, co. Lincoln, and grandsons of JOHN LANGLEY, Esq., co. York. Visit. London, 1568). Erm. on a bend vert three leopards' faces or. *Crest*—A cockatrice sa. combed and wattled gu.

Langley (Lincoln's Inn, London; granted 20 Jan. 40 Elizabeth). Same *Arms* and *Crest.*

Langley (London; confirmed 4 June, 1632). Per pale ar. and or, a cockatrice, wings expanded sa. beaked of the second, crested, wattled, and legged gu.

Langley (Golden, co. Salop; of whom was THOMAS LANGLEY, Esq., of Golden, Sheriff 1743, whose great-grandson, JOHN LANGLEY, sold the estate, 1820). Paly of six ar. and vert.

Langley (Brokley, co. Salop). Same *Arms*, on a canton gu. a pheon or. *Crest*—A pheon or, betw. two laurel sprigs vert.

Langley (Studington, co. Warwick). Ar. a fesse sa. in chief three escallops of the second.

Langley (co. Warwick). Quarterly, per fesse indented as. and or.

Langley (Rathorpe Hall, Dalton, co. York). Ar. a cockatrice, wings endorsed and tail nowed, at the end thereof a dragon's head all sa.

Langley (co. York). Per pale ar. and or, a cockatrice sa. combed gu.

Langley (Wickham Abbey, Malton, co. York). Quarterly, 1st and 4th, or, a fesse betw. three crescents gu.; 2nd and 3rd, paly of six ar. and vert. *Crest*—Out of a ducal coronet five feathers ar.

Langley. Per chev. gu. and or, a lion ramp. barry nebulée ar. and az.

Langley. Quarterly, or and gu. a bend sa. (another adds, a label of three points ar.)

Langley. Ar. a fesse betw. three oak leaves gu.

Langley. Ar. a bend az. betw. three mullets gu.

Langley. Quarterly, per fesse indented or and gu. in the 1st a lion pass. guard. ar.

Langley (Coalbrook, co. Tipperary). Ar. a fesse sa. in

chief three hurts. *Crest*—A cockatrice, wings addorsed sa. combed and wattled gu. *Motto*—Fide sed cui vide.

Langley (confirmed to HENRY LANGLEY, Esq., J.P. and D.L., of Queen's Gate Terrace, Kensington, late 2nd Life Guards, eldest son of HENRY LANGLEY, Esq., of Brittas Castle, co. Tipperary, and grandson of OLIVER LANGLEY, second son of HENRY LANGLEY, Esq., of Priestown, co. Tipperary, by MARGARET, his wife, dau. and heiress of OLIVER GRACE, Esq., of Brittas Castle). Quarterly, 1st and 4th, ar. a fess sa. charged with a crescent or, in chief three hurts, for LANGLEY; 2nd and 3rd, gu. a lion ramp. per fess ar. and or, for GRACE. *Crest*—A cockatrice, wings addorsed sa. combed, wattled, and spurred gu. charged on the breast with a crescent or. *Motto*—Fide sed cui vide.

Langlois (Hamptonne, Jersey). Az. a chev. or, betw. three crescents ar. on a chief gu. as many mullets of six points pierced of the second. *Crest*—A rock ppr.

Langlond. Ar. a wivern displ. sa.

Langlond. Ar. a chev. cotised gu.

Langman (RALPH LANGMAN, York Herald, *temp.* Queen Elizabeth). Ar. on a pile betw. two water bougets sa. a portcullis of the first.

Langman (arms of ROGER LANGMAN, in Hart's Hall, Oxford. Visit. Oxon, 1574). Ar. on a chev. betw. three water bougets sa. a crescent of the field.

Langmead (co. Devon). Gu. a lion ramp. ar. on a chief wavy of the last a leopard's face betw. two cinquefoils of the first. *Crest*—A boar's head and neck erased gu. gorged with a chaplet of oak ppr.

Langmore, or Longmore. Sa. a chev. or, and canton erm. *Crest*—On a chapeau a greyhound statant all ppr.

Langriche, or Langrithe (London). Quarterly, 1st and 4th, ar. six billets sa. three, two, and one; 2nd and 3rd, gu. a lion ramp. or, preying on a dragon reversed of the last.

Langrige, or Langrich. Ar. six billets sa. three, two, and one.

Langrish (West Ashling, co. Sussex). Quarterly, sa. and or, four covered cups countercharged.

Langrishe (Knocktopher, co. Kilkenny, bart.). Quarterly, sa. and or. four covered cups countercharged. *Crest*—A demi lion ramp. ar. *Motto*—Medio tutissimus ibis.

Langriplover. Or, a cross flory sa.

Langrith. Ar. six billets sa.

Langsdale. Paly of six or and gu. a bordure az.

Langsford (co. Cornwall). Paly of six or and sa. on a chief vert a lion pass. of the first.

Langstaff. Az. a bend or, betw. three cocks ar.

Langstaff (granted to JOSEPH LANGSTAFF, Esq., of Newcastle). Ar. on a bend az. betw. two pheons sa. a leopard's face betw. two escallops or, a chief engr. gu. thereon an estoile betw. two fleurs-de-lis gold. *Crest*—On a serpent nowed or, in front of two palm branches in saltire vert, a stork rising ppr.

Langston, or Langstone. Or, a chev. gu. in chief two (another, three) roses ppr. in base a dolphin embowed of the last. *Crest*—A lion ramp. gu. supporting a pillar ppr.

Langston (Sedgeberrow and Malvern, co. Worcester. Visit. Worcester, 1634. HENRY LANGSTONE was patron of Sedgeberrow Church, 1551). Same *Arms*, roses of the second, dolphin az.

Langston (co. Worcester). Az. three fleurs-de-lis in pale betw. two palets engr. or.

Langston (quartered by WAYNEHAM, of Witney, co. Oxford. Visit. Oxon, 1566). Or, a chev. az. betw. in chief three roses gu. and in base a dolphin embowed of the second.

Langston (Cavershill, co. Bucks; JOHN LANGSTON; his dau. and heiress, JANE, *m.* THOMAS GIFFORD, 12 Edward IV., 1472. Visit. Oxon, 1569). Gu. a chev. erm. betw. three hinds or.

Langston (Sarsden, co. Oxford). Or, on a chev. betw. two roses in chief gu. and a dolphin in base ppr. three crosses crosslet of the first.

Langston (seal to will of HONOR SPRY, *née* LANGSTON, impaled by SPRY, dated 1689). Ar. a chev. sa. betw. in chief three torteaux and in base a dolphin embowed of the second.

Langstone. Quarterly, az. and ar. a bend or.

Langthorne. Az. six cinquefoils gu. three, two, and one. *Crest*—A beer butt sa. in the bunghole three roses gu. stalked and leaved vert.

Langthorne. Ar. six annulets sa.

Langton (Langton, co. Leicester). Az. an eagle displ. with two heads or, a bend gu.; described by Burton to be engraved on the monument of THOMAS DE LANGTON, at Church Langton. The brisure by a bend denotes these arms to have belonged to a cadet of the family.

Langton (West Langton, co. Leicester). Vair.

Langton (*Baron of Newton*, co. Lancaster. The first of this family who settled in co. Lancaster was JOHN DE LANGETON, son of ROBERT DE LANGETON, lord of the manor of West Langton, co. Leicester; he bore for arms a shield vair, as appears by his seal; he *m.* ALESIA, dau. of JAMES BANASTRE, and sole heiress of his father, Sir ROBERT BANASTRE, *Baron of Newton*, and Lord of Walton-in-the-Dale, co. Lancaster; his brother, JOHN DE LANGETON, was Bishop of Chichester, 1305–37, and Chancellor of England, *d.* 1337; Sir ROBERT DE LANGETON, Knt., son of JOHN DE LANGETON, bore three chev. (the arms of BANASTRE) within a bordure vair, but RALPH DE LANGETON, *Baron of Newton*, grandson of Sir ROBERT DE LANGETON, abandoned the bordure, as appears by his seal, 1364. According to the Visit. 1567, the later LANGTONS, *Barons of Newton*, bore: Quarterly, 1st and 4th, for LANGTON, ar. three chev.; 2nd and 3rd, for BANASTRE, ar. a cross patonce sa. *Crest*—The head of a maiden affrontée couped below the shoulders ppr. vested gu. cap and necklace or. The barony of Newton descended to the FLEETWOODS by an heir female, *temp.* James I., on the death of Sir THOMAS LANGTON, K.B. Through the LANGTONS of Broughton Tower, a younger branch of this family, are descended, WILLIAM LANGTON, Esq., of Liverpool, SKINNER ZACHARY LANGTON, Esq., of Barrow House, Derwentwater, and WILLIAM LANGTON, of Manchester, who represent the three remaining branches of that family; their arms are: Ar. three chev. gu. a canton vair. *Crest*—An eagle displ. with two heads vert, charged on the breast with a trefoil or. *Motto*—Loyal au mort.

Langton (Broughton Tower, co. Lancaster; of the same lineage). Per pale ar. and or, three chev. gu. *Crest*—A talbot sejant reguard. sa. his ears ar., as allowed by William Ryley, Norroy, 25 June, 1657. The arms were altered by Sir William Dugdale at the Visit. of 1664, to the following: Ar. three chev. gu. a canton vair. *Crest*—An eagle displ. with two heads vert, charged on the breast with a trefoil or. *Motto*—Loyal au mort.

Langton (co. Herts; ANNE LANGTON, descended from co. York, *m.* THOMAS EGERTON, of London, Mercer. Visit. London, 1568). Ar. three chevronels gu.

Langton (Winyard, co. Durham). Ar. a lion ramp. sa. a bordure engr. gu.

Langton (Herton, co. Cumberland; JAMES LANGTON was aged 63, 1591, sixth in descent from Sir ROBERT LANGTON, Knt., of Newton, *temp.* Richard II., the grandson of Sir THOMAS LANGTON, of Walton, co. Lancaster. Visit. Cumberland, 1615). Ar. three chevronels gu. in dexter chief a fleur-de-lis sa.

Langton (Lowe, in Hindley, co. Lancaster; descended from Sir ROBERT LANGTON, second son of the second *Baron of Newton*). Quarterly, 1st and 4th, ar. an eagle displ. with two heads vert; 2nd and 3rd, ar. three chevronels gu. *Crest*—An eagle displ. as in the arms.

Langton (Langtonwick, co. Berks). Quarterly, or and gu. a bend sa.

Langton (Windsor, co. Berks). Or, a lion ramp. sa.

Langton (Berwick). Ar. three leopards' faces gu.

Langton (STEPHEN LANGTON, Archbishop of Canterbury 1207-28). Per pale az. and gu. a bend ar.

Langton (Walton, co. Chester). Ar. three chev. gu.

Langton (Ledall, co. Lancaster). Ar. three chev. gu. *Crest*—A man's head sidefaced ppr. hair flotant or, on his head a cap sa. turned up erminois, couped below the shoulders and in armour gu.

Langton (Langton, co. Lincoln; a family long seated in that co.). Quarterly, sa. and or, a bend ar. *Crest*—An eagle or, and a wivern vert, their necks entwined reguard.

Langton (GORE-LANGTON, Newton Park, co. Somerset). *Arms and Crest* same as last, quartering GORE.

Langton (Stanton and Stanmore, co. Middlesex; granted 7 Dec. 1577). Az. two palets engr. betw. three fleurs-de-lis in chief or. *Crest*—Out of a ducal coronet gu. a demi lion ramp. or, holding in the paws a battle axe ar.

Langton (Hudleston, *temp.* Henry VI.). Az. a chev. erm. betw. three lions ramp. or.

Langton. Or, on a cross quarterly az. and gu. five roses ar.

Langton. Ar. a chev. betw. three leopards' faces vert.

Langton, or Langham. Ar. a chev. betw. three cinquefoils gu.

Langton. Ar. a chev. sa. betw. three lizards vert.

Langton. Per fesse or and az. a cross moline gu. over it a bend sa.

Langton. Or, six annulets sa. three, two, and one.

Langton. Quarterly, or and az. a cross flory gu.

581

Langton. Per pale or and az. a cross flory gu. (another, moline gu. over all a bend sa.)

Langton. Or, a saltire gu.

Langton. Barry of six ar and gu. a bend ar.

Langton (Danganmore, co. Kilkenny; confirmed to HENRY MICHAEL FAUSTINUS LANGTON, Esq., of Danganmore, son of MICHAEL THEOBALD LANGTON, Esq., of Bath, by MARY, his wife, eldest dau. and coheiress of JEREMIAH RYAN, of Newtown, co. Waterford). Quarterly, 1st and 4th, LANGTON, ar. three chevronels gu.; 2nd, RYAN, quarterly, 1st and 4th, gu. on a bend ar. six ears of rye sa., 2nd and 3rd, az. a chev. betw. three griffins' heads erased ar.; 3rd, COMERFORD, az. a buglehorn ar. stringed gu. betw. three mullets or. *Crest*—A heart gu. betw. two wings ar. *Motto*—Sursum corda.

Langtree (Langtree, co. Lancaster, 1567). Sa. a chev. ar. a canton erm. *Crest*—A saker, wings expanded gu. membered or.

Langtree (Langtree, co. Lancaster). Erm. three chev. sa.

Langtrey (co. Lancaster, and Howlett, co. Northampton). Quarterly, 1st and 4th, erm. three chev. sa.; 2nd and 3rd, erm. three bars sa.

Languilles, or Langvilles. Ar. a bend betw. six crosslets sa.

Langworth. Ar. three dragons' heads couped sa. vulned in the neck ppr.

Langworthy (Bath). Sa. three greyhounds courant in pale ar. *Crest*—A demi stag ppr.

Langworts, or Langworth (Langworth, co. Lancaster). Ar. three dragons' heads couped sa.

Lanham. Ar. a fesse gu. three lambeaux depending in chief az.

Lanham, or Landham. Az. a chev. betw. three roses or.

Lanherne (originally PINCERNA, extinct *temp.* Edward I; the heiress *m.* ARUNDEL). Az. three covered cups or.

Lanhorgy (co. Cornwall). Az. three greyhounds ar.

Lanhorne (London). Sa. on a cross ar. five fleurs-de-lis gu. on a chief of the second three buglehorns of the field, stringed of the third.

Lanigan. See LENIGAN.

Lanine (co. Cornwall). Sa. a castle ar. standing on the waves ppr. on the same a falcon hovering, with bells or.

Lanisdale (Reg. Ulster's Office). Barry of six gu. and ar. on a canton erm. a cross of the first.

Lankin. Barry of six ar. and az. on a chief gu. a lion pass. or. *Crest*—Two wings endorsed ar. one on each side of a chapeau ppr. issuing from the rim.

Lanleyron, Lanlairon, or Langlaron (co. Cornwall). Sa. three chev. ar.

Lann. Ar. on a fesse betw. six crosses crosslet fitchée sa. three cinquefoils of the first.

Lanncelot. Or, on a chief az. a lion ramp. of the field.

Launcelot. Ar. a pale and three bendlets gu.

Lannde (co. Sussex). Erm. a cross chequy or and gu. in the first quarter a lion ramp. (another, pass.) sa.

Lannde. Az. three trefoils slipped ar. a chief indented gu.

Launndie (Fun. Ent. Ulster's Office, 1610, KATHERINE LANNDIE, wife of GEORGE GRIMSDICH). Az. three trefoils slipped ar. a chief gu.

Lannoy (Bletsoe, co. Bedford). Az. three fleurs-de-lis or. *Crest*—A chevalier's head armed with a helmet and plume all ppr.

Lannoy (Hammersmith). Az. a chev. betw. two swans in chief and a pair of shears in base ar.

Lanphier (granted by Betham, Ulster, to THOMAS LANPHIER, Esq., of Parkstown, co. Tipperary, Lieut.-Colonel 86th Regiment, and to the descendants of his grandfather). Paly of six gu. and ar. on a chief az. a lion pass. of the second. *Crest*—A demi lion ramp. gu. *Motto*—Virtute et fidelitate.

Lansdowne, Marquess of. See FITZ-MAURICE.

Lanselatt. Or, on a chief az. three fusils of the first.

Lansford. Az. a chev. betw. three bucks' heads couped or. *Crest*—A savage's head couped ppr.

Lansford. Ar. crusily fitchée sa. three greyhounds in pale of the last.

Lansladron (co. Cornwall). Az. three chev. sa.

Lant (cos. Devon, Northampton, and Stafford). Quarterly, 1st and 4th, per pale ar. and gu. a cross engr. counterchanged, in the dexter chief a cinquefoil of the second; 2nd and 3rd, gu. a saltire or, surmounted by another vert. *Crest*—A dove ar. beaked and legged gu. standing on a serpent nowed ppr.

Lant (Thorp Underwood, co. Northampton). Same *Arms*. *Crest*—On a serpent nowed az. a dove ar. on the breast a mullet of the first. *Motto*—Prudentia et simplicitate.

Lant. Gu. on a fesse wavy betw. three swans with wings endorsed ar. as many crosses pattée sa. each charged with five bezants. *Crest*—A swan's neck couped bendy of six ar. and sa. thereon a rose or, on each side of the crest a branch of rose tree leaved vert.

Lant. Or, a cross engr. gu.

Lante (Exeter, co. Devon; JOHN LANTE, Visit. Devon, 1620, grandson of WILLIAM LANTE, who "came out of ye North"). Per pale ar. and gu. a cross engr. counterchanged.

Lante. Same *Arms. Crest*—A serpent nowed vert.

Lanvoys. Ar. (another, or) two bars betw. eight cinquefoils gu. four, three, and one.

Lanwall. Az. a bend ar.

Lanway. Or, a water bouget ar. a bordure of the second bezantée.

Lanwe, or Lanwo. Sa. a pair of wings conjoined ar.

Lanwray (co. Somerset). Sa. a fesse or, betw. three fleurs-de-lis ar.

Lany (co. Leicester, and London). Ar. on a bend betw. two fleurs-de-lis gu. a lion pass. or. *Crest*—A merman ppr. tail ar. fins and hair or, tied round the temples with two ribbons ar. and az. holding in his hand a hawk's bell hung to two strings of the second and third.

Lany (Ipswich, co. Suffolk, Newark, co. Leicester, and Berwick, co. Northumberland; sons of JOHN LANY, of Cratfield, co. Suffolk. Visit. Leicester, 1619). Same *Arms*, quartering 1st, ar. a chev. engr. betw. three cinquefoils gu. on a chief of the last a lion pass. or; 2nd, gu. a crescent erm. within an orle of martlets or. *Crest*—A mermaid ppr. wreathed about the temples ar. and az. holding in the dexter hand a hawk's bell of the first attached to a string vert, at the end a silver tassel.

Lany (Dublin; JOHN LANY, High Sheriff, 1607. Visit. Dublin, 1607). Or, on a chev. engr. betw. three mullets pierced az. as many torteaux.

Lanyon (Lanyon, co. Cornwall; JOHN LANYON, eldest son of RICHARD LANYON, Esq., of Lanyon. Visit. Cornw. 1620). Gu. on waves of the sea az. a square castle in perspective, with a tower at each corner or, in the courtyard of the field a falcon ppr. rising from a mount vert. *Crest*—On a mount vert within a castle with four towers ar. a falcon standing on waves of the sea az. as above, volant ppr.

Lanyon (Wynyard, co. Cornwall; WILLIAM LANYON, son of EDWARD LANYON, the second son of RICHARD LANYON, Esq., of Lanyon. Visit. Cornw. 1620). Same *Arms*, with due diff.

Lanyon (Camborne, co. Cornwall). Same *Arms. Crest*—A falcon rising, wings extended, belled.

Laon. Chequy ar. and az. three pales gu. a chief of the first.

La Porest. Ar. a chief sa. *Crest*—A unicorn sejant ar. armed, crined, and tufted or.

Lapp (Darnford, co. Wilts). Or, a mermaid, comb, glass, and hair ppr.

Lapp. Same *Arms. Crest*—A demi mermaid issuing ppr. in her dexter hand a purse gu. in her sinister a comb or.

Lappeslode (co. Devon). Sa. a chev. betw. three goats' heads erased ar.

Lapslie (Rev. JAMES LAPSLIE, Campsie, co. Stirling, 1797). Or, an eagle displ. gu. beaked and membered sa. surmounted by a fesse engr. az. charged with a bezant betw. two buckles of the field. *Crest*—A passion cross gu. *Motto*—Corona mea Christus.

Lapthorne. Ar. on a fesse sa. three plates. *Crest*—A lion's head erased or, collared vair.

Lapworth (co. Cambridge). Vair on a saltire gu. five fleurs-de-lis or. *Crest*—A stork ppr. resting the dexter foot on a fleur-de-lis or.

La Rache. Gu. three lions crowned or.

Larayne, or Lareyn. Quarterly, sa. and ar. a cross counterchanged. *Crest*—Out of a cloud a hand holding a garland of laurel ppr.

Larbalestier (Jersey). Erminois a cross-bow drawn, charged with an arrow all ar.

Larcom (Heathfield, Fareham, co. Hants, bart.). Ar. on a mount a hawthorn bush ppr. and in chief an eagle displ. gu. *Crest*—On a cap of maintenance az. turned up erm. a martlet sa. with a fleur-de lis in its beak or. *Motto*—Le roy la loy.

Lardener. Gu. a fesse ar. surmounted of another nebulée sa. betw. three boars' heads couped of the second, tusked or.

Larder (Upton Pyne, co. Devon; HUMPHREY LARDER, Esq., left an only dau. and heir, m. ANTHONY COPLESTONE, living at Visit. Devon, 1620, nephew of HUMPHREY COPLESTONE, Esq., of Instow, in same co.). Ar. three piles sa. each

585

charged with as many bezants. *Crest*—A woman's head couped at the shoulders ppr. habited gu. garnished or, hair of the last.

Larder (Loders, co. Dorset; a younger branch of the co. Devon family, extinct in 1766; the co-heiresses m. BROWN, WALROND, and BRAGGE). Erm. three piles sa. on each as many bezants. *Crest*—An elephant's head sa. armed and ducally crowned or.

Lardner. Gu. on a fesse betw. three boars' heads couped ar. a bar wavy sa. *Crest*—On a chapeau a bull all ppr.

Larendon, or Laringdon. Gu. three cinquefoils ar.

Large. Ar. a bend az. betw. three mullets gu. *Crest*—A demi savage holding a sheaf of arrows in the dexter hand, and pointing with the sinister to a ducal coronet all ppr.

Large, or Lorge. Ar. a bend az. betw. six mullets gu.

Large (Fun. Ent. Ulster's Office, 1608, JOHN LARGE, born in Picardy). Ar. a chev. vert, over all a lion ramp. sa. armed and langued gu.

Largriph (London). Ar. six billets sa. three, two, and one.

Lark, or Larke. Or, on a chev. sa. betw. three pellets, each charged with a lark ar. an estoile of sixteen points pierced of the field. *Crest*—A hand issuing from a cloud in fesse, lifting a garb ppr.

Larke (co. Lincoln). Same *Arms. Crest*—A lark with wings endorsed.

Larkan, or Larken. Or, on a fesse gu. three quatrefoils ar. *Crest*—A greyhound sejant az.

Larke. Or, on a chev. sa. betw. three torteaux, each charged with a martlet ar. an estoile of the first, on a chief gu. a lion pass. of the third.

Larkin, or Larkins (cos. Cambridge, Hereford, and Frinsbury, co. Kent). Erm. three leopards' faces sa. *Crest*—A lark, wings endorsed, holding in the beak a columbine all ppr.

Larkin. Erm. three leopards' faces or, on a chief gu. a lion pass. guard. of the second.

Larkin. Chequy gu. and ar. a cross az.

Laroche (Over, co. Gloucester, bart.; extinct in 1805. PETER CROTHAIRE, of Bordeaux, accompanied Prince George of Denmark to England, and assumed the name of LAROCHE, by desire of the Prince; his grandson, created a bart. 1776, d. s. p.). Quarterly, 1st and 4th, or, a raven ppr.; 2nd and 3rd, ar. on a mount vert an eagle close looking at the sun in his glory in the dexter chief point. *Crest*—A raven, as in the arms.

Laron (Sir FRANCIS LARON, knighted at Dublin Castle 13 July, 1599, by ROBERT, *Earl of Essex*, Lord Lieutenant). Quarterly per fess indented erm. and az.

Larpent (*Baron de Hochepied*, in the kingdom of Austria). A military shield erect per pale, divided perpendicularly into equal parts, on the dexter side on a field ar. a chev. acute angular erect gu., above which two crescents, and below one; on the sinister side on a field az. a right hand, the fingers and palm spread open, below two fetters with chains broken ppr. as a true and faithful memorial of Christian charity displayed by the liberation of many unhappy Christians lingering in Turkish servitude, and for services rendered in the negotiations which terminated in the peace of Carlowitz in Jan. 1699. *Crest*—Two military helmets craticulated or, open, with royal diadems, the one with a crescent sa. the other with a right hand extended ppr. "Hochepied," name given in falconry to the first bird that strikes the hawk in its flight. *Motto*—Optivo cognomine crescit.

Larpent (Roehampton, co. Surrey, bart.). Quarterly, 1st and 4th, gu. a saltire or, betw. four plates, each charged with a hurt, on a chief erm. a fleur-de-lis az., for LARPENT; 2nd and 3rd, per pale ar. and az. on the dexter a chev. gu. betw. three crescents sa. and on the sinister a dexter hand expanded issuant from the sinister in bend, and beneath a pair of manacles, the chains broken ppr., for DE HOCHEPIED. *Crests*—1st : A unicorn's head ar. crined or, the neck charged with a fleur-de-lis and beneath four annulets conjoined az., for LARPENT: 2nd: Out of a ducal coronet or, a crescent sa.; 3rd: Out of a ducal coronet or, a dexter hand issuant ppr., both for DE HOCHEPIED. *Motto*—Optivo cognomine crescit.

Lascels, or Lascells (Easton, cos. Nottingham and York, temp. Edward I.). Ar. three chaplets gu. *Crest*—Out of a ducal coronet or, a griffin's head vert.

Lascels (*Baron Lascels*, abeyance since 1297; ROBERT DE LASCELS, summoned to Parliament 1295, left four daus. his co-heirs). Ar. three chaplets gu.

Lascelles (*Baron Harewood*, extinct 1795; EDWIN LASCELLES, Esq., of Harewood, was so created 1790, d. s. p. and was s. by his heir-at-law, EDWARD LASCELLES, Esq., afterwards first *Earl of Harewood*). Sa. a cross flory or, a border of the last.

Lascelles (*Earl of Harewood*). Sa. a cross patonce within a bordure or. *Crest*—A bear's head couped at the neck erm. muzzled gu. buckled or, collared of the second, rimmed and studded gold. *Supporters*—Dexter, a bear erm. muzzled and collared gu. buckled and chained, the chain reflexed over the back or, the collar studded and rimmed gold, and pendent therefrom a shield also or, charged with a cross patonce sa; sinister, a bull az. armed, unguled, and semée of mullets or, collar, chain, and shield as the dexter. *Motto*—In solo Deo salus.

Lascelles (Woodhouse, co. Leicester; SAMUEL LASCELLES, Visit. Leicester, 1619, son of HENRY LASCELLES, of Normanton, co Notts). Ar. three chaplets gu., quartering, 1st, az. two bars or, each charged with three martlets gu.; and 2nd, ar. a chev. betw. three talbots' heads erased gu. *Crest*—Out of a ducal coronet or, a griffin's head vert, beaked gold.

Lascelles, alias Jackson. See JACKSON.

Lascelles (Sturton and Gaytford, co. Notts; Sir GEORGE LASCELLS, Knt., Visit. Notts 1614, descended from Sir RICHARD LASCELLS, Knt., of Eastkrick, co. York, temp. King John). Ar. three chaplets gu. with seven quarterings. *Crests*—1st: A buck's head ar.; 2nd : Out of a ducal coronet or, a griffin's head vert, beaked gold, charged on the neck with a mullet for diff.; 3rd : Out of a ducal coronet or, an eagle's head betw. two wings sa.

Lascells (Elston, co. Notts; GEORGE LASCELLES, Esq., Visit. Notts, 1614, son and heir of JOHN LASCELLS, by ELIZABETH METHLEY, his wife, dau. and heir of BARTHOLOMEW METHLEY, Esq., of Elston, descended from GALFREY LASCELLES, *temp.* Henry II.). Same *Arms* and *Crest*, a mullet for diff.

Lascells (Lascells, Sowerby, Brakerberg, and Northallerton, co. York). Sa. a cross patonce or. *Crest*—A bear's head couped erminois, muzzled gu.

La Serre (Guernsey). Or, a mountain vert issuant from the base, on a chief invecked az. three estoiles of the field. *Crest*—A stag ppr. attired or, semée of estoiles of the same, resting the right forefoot on a bezant. *Motto*—L'Eternel regne. (Ancient arms—Az. a fesse and three mullets in chief ar.; another, a stag trippant in base ar.).

Lascye (co. Lincoln, *temp.* Edward I.). Ar. a lion ramp. ppr.

Lasey. Ar. six gun-stones sa.

Lashaw (London). Gu. a lion pass. guard. betw. three gauntlets or.

Laslett (Abberton Hall, co. Worcester). Ar. on a fess sa. three buckles or. *Crest*—A demi lion ramp. sa. charged with five bezants. *Motto*—Finem respice.

Lashmar. Az. two dolphins naiant in pale or. *Crest*—A boar's head erased and erect sa.

Lasman, or Larman. Or, on a chev. az. three mascles of the field. *Crest*—A squirrel sejant or, holding betw. the paws a laurel branch vert.

Lason (London and Osworth, in the Bishopric of Durham; borne by the six sons of WILLIAM LASON, of Osworth. Visit. London, 1563). Per pale ar. and sa. a chev. counterchanged. *Crest*—Out of clouds ppr. two arms embowed, vested erm. holding in the hands also ppr. a sun in splendour or.

Lasonby, or Lasinby (co. York). Gu. a fesse betw. three cushions ar. tasselled or, over all a bend sa. guttée d'or.

Lassells (co. Norfolk). Gu. three helmets ar. plumed or.

Lassells (cos. Nottingham and York). Ar. six cinquefoils gu.

Lassells. Gu. a saltire ar. a chief of the last.

Lassells. Ar. six roses gu.

Lassells. Ar. a pale fusily gu. within a bordure az. bezantée.

Lassey, Lassew, or Lassow. Sa. a cross flory ar. (another, or).

Latch (Woodhouse, co. Leicester, and Elston, co. Nottingham). Ar. on a fesse wavy az. betw. three escutcheons gu. as many lozenges or. *Crest*—A lion's head or, gorged with a fesse wavy az.

Late. Ar. a cross chequy or and az.

Lateward (London). Ar. on a fesse gu. betw. three cinquefoils per pale of the first and az. a hind trippant betw. two pheons or. *Crest*—A demi hawk, wings expanded sa. on the head two horns bent or.

Latham (Papworth-Agnes, co. Cambridge, and Northokenham, co. Essex). Or, on a chief indented az. three **plates** within a bordure gobonated ar. and of the second.

Latham (Hanley, co. Worcester). Same *Arms* as LATHOM, of Latham, chief dancettée.

Latham (Bradwall, co. Chester). Erminois on a chief indented az. three bezants, over all a bend gu. *Crest*—On a rock ppr. an eagle, wings elevated erminois, preying on an infant ppr. swaddled az. banded ar. *Mottoes*—Expertus fidelem; and, Secunda alite.

Latham (from the monument of NICHOLAS LATHAM, of Brigstock Great Park, in Church of Barnwell, St. Andrew, 1620). Or, on a chief indented az. three plates. *Crest*—A pelican in her nest or.

Latham (Weaste, Pendleton, co. Lancaster, from co. Chester, represented by ARTHUR GEORGE LEATHAM, Esq., of Weaste). Same *Arms* as last. *Crest*—On an oak branch lying fessways, truncated and leaved vert, an eagle rising or. *Motto* —Æquanimitate.

Latham. Quarterly, 1st and 4th, az. two chev. or; 2nd and 3rd, gu. a fesse dancettée betw. six billets or.

Latham. Quarterly, 1st and 4th, az. two chev. or; 2nd and 3rd, ar. an inescutcheon within an orle of eight cinquefoils pierced sa.

Latham. Sa. six annulets or, three, two, and one.

Latham (Smith's Ordinary, Ulster's Office). Quarterly, 1st and 4th, or, on a chief az. three plates; 2nd and 3rd, gu. a fess dancettée betw six crosses crosslet or.

Lathberge (co. Derby; the heiress of the family m. WILLIAM CHAMBERS, of Gadesby, co. Leicester, living temp. Henry VIII. Visit. Leicester, 1619). Barry of six ar. and az. on a canton sa. a cinquefoil or.

Lathbroke. Az. a chev. ar. (another, or).

Lathbury (co. Derby). Paly of six ar. and az. on a canton or, a crescent sa.

Lathbury (cos. Lancaster and Leicester). Barry of six ar. and az. on a canton of the second a martlet or.

Lathbury (Holme, co. Derby. Visit. 1611). Ar. two bars and a canton az. charged with a martlet or (another, ar.).

Lathebury. Ar. three bars az. on a canton of the second a martlet or.

Lathom (Lathom, co. Lancaster; represented, in the female line, by the *Earl of Derby*). Or, on a chief indented az. three plates (but occasionally three bezants, as in Sir Harris Nicolas's Tournament Roll, temp. Edward III.). *Crest*—An eagle reguard. or, rising from a child's cradle gu., depicted in ancient windows of Astbury Church. Harl. MSS. 2157. In an old Visitation of the county of Lancaster, in the College of Arms, it is stated that a child was found in an eagle's nest upon the estate, and adopted by one of the LATHAMS: this, it is assumed, was the origin of the crest.

Lathom (Parbold and Allerton, co. Lancaster. Visit. 1664). Same *Arms* as LATHOM, of Lathom. *Crest*—An oak branch fesseways truncated and leaved ppr. thereon a heron rising or.

Lathom (Moosborough, Ormskirk, co. Lancaster. Visit. 1613). Same *Arms* as LATHOM, of Lathom, a mullet for diff. *Crest*—On a chapeau gu. turned up erm. an infant ppr. swaddled gu. banded ar. thereon an eagle preying or.

Lathom (Irlam, co. Lancaster). Same *Arms* as LATHOM, of Lathom, differenced by bezants in chief in Visit. 1613, and by a bend gu. over all, in the Visit. 1664.

Lathom (Whiston, co. Lancaster, 1664). Same *Arms* as LATHOM, of Lathom, over all a bendlet gu.

Lathom (Astbury, co. Chester). Same *Arms* as LATHOM, of Lathom, over all a bendlet gu., sometimes dexter, sometimes sinister.

Lathum. Az. two chev. or.

Latimer (*Baron Latimer, of Danby*, passed to the NEVILLS 1380, now vested in *Lord Willoughby de Broke*: WILLIAM DE LATIMER summoned to Parliament 1299). Gu. a cross patonce or. *Crest*—A plume of feathers or.

Latimer (*Baron Latimer, of Braybrooke*, passed to the GRIFFINS; THOMAS LATIMER, son of JOHN DE LATIMER, brother of WILLIAM, first *Baron Latimer*, of Danby, by the heiress of the BRAYBROOKES, was summoned to Parliament 1299). Same *Arms*, &c.

Latimer (co. Devon). Gu. a cross patonce or, charged with five escallops sa. a bordure az.

Latimer (co. Dorset). Gu. on a cross patonce or, five torteaux (another, with a border engr. az.).

Latimer (co. Suffolk). Az. a chev. ar. in chief a cinquefoil of the second pierced, in base three crosses crosslet or.

Latimer (co. York, temp. Edward I.). Gu. on a cross patonce or, four escallops sa.

Latimer. Ar. on a chief gu. four crosses crosslet or. *Crest*—An eastern crown gu.

Latimer. Gu. a cross moline or, in the 1st quarter a crescent of the last. *Crest*—On a mount vert a hind sejant ar. collared and chained or, under a tree ppr.

Latimer (HUGH LATIMER, Bishop of Worcester, 1535-39; arms in a window at Hartlebury Castle, co. Worcester). Gu. a cross patonce or, over all a bend az. semée-de-lis of the second.

Latimer. Ar. two bars gu. on a canton of the last a cross couped or.

Latimer, or Latymer. Gu. on a cross patonce or, five maunches of the field (another, seven pellets).

Latimer. Gu. a cross patonce or, on a bordure az. three fleurs-de-lis of the second.

Latimer. Gu. a'saltire ar. charged with an annulet.

Latimer. Gu. on a fesse betw. six crosses crosslet sa. three cinquefoils ar.

Latin, or Layton. Sa. on a bend ar. three escallops gu.

Latinbras (Reg. Ulster's Office). Or, a bend engr. az.

Laton (co. Somerset). Or, a cross moline gu.

Laton. Ar. a fesse betw. three lozenges sa. Crest—Out of a ducal coronet or, a stork's head ar.

Laton. Ar. on a fesse betw. six crosslets fitchée sa. three cinquefoils of the field.

Laton. Or, on a bend az. three greyhounds' heads erased of the field collared ar.

Laton. Ar. a fesse betw. seven crosses crosslet sa. three, two, and two.

Laton. Ar. a fesse betw. three fusils sa.

Laton. Or, a fret vair.

La Touche (England). Gu. a chev. ar. in chief three bezants. Crest—A hand in armour couped in fesse, holding a scymitar enfiled with a boar's head couped.

La Touche (Dublin, Marlay, co. Dublin, Harristown, co. Kildare, and Bellevue, Glen of the Downs, co. Wicklow; descended from DAVID DIGGES LA TOUCHE, a Huguenot officer in Colonel La Caillemot's regiment of French refugees at the Battle of the Boyne). Ar. a pomegranate slipped in pale ppr. on a chief gu. two mullets of the first. Crest—A mullet or. Motto—Quid verum atque decens curo et rogo.

Latter. Az. three wedding favours, single bowed and ribbons pendent ppr. a chief ar. Crest—Out of a foreign coronet of sixteen balls (nine visible), a greyhound's head ar. collared and chained or. Motto—Pour trois. Another, over the crest—A tôt bien estrainz.

Lattin (Upton, co. Berks, and Esher, co. Surrey; descended, according to family pedigrees, from Stutcville, co. Berks). Per pale ar. and sa. a saltire engr. ermines and erm. Crest —A crossbow or.

Lattin (Morristown Lattin, co. Kildare; a branch of DE LATTON, of co. Wilts, settled in Ireland, temp. King John; confirmed by MacCullagh, Ulster, 1763, to GEORGE LATTIN, Esq.; the heiress m. MANSFIELD). Per fess in chief per pale ar. and sa. a chev. engr. per pale ermines and erm., for DE LATTON; in base ar. three crescents gu. a border or, for LATTIN. Crest—An eagle's leg erased ar. charged with a crescent gu.

Lattin (Naas, co. Kildare; Fun. Ent. Ulster's Office, 1618, ELIZABETH, dau. of JOHN LATTIN, and wife of GILBERT SUTTON, of Ardress, same co.). Per pale sa. and erm. a saltire engr. counterchanged.

Latton. Sa. on a bend ar. three escallops gu.

Latymer (Freston, co. Suffolk). Az. a chev. ar. betw. a cinquefoil pierced and three crosses crosslet in chief and four in base of the last.

Laud (WILLIAM LAUD, Archbishop of Canterbury, beheaded in 1644). Sa. on a chev. or, betw. three estoiles of six points of the second as many crosses pattée fitchée gu.

Laudeles. Az. an orle or.

Lauder (Bass, Scotland). Gu. a griffin segreant within a double tressure flowered and counter-flowered ar. Crest—A solan goose sitting on a rock ppr. Motto—Sub umbra alarum tuarum. Supporters—Two angels ppr.

Lauder (Belhaven and Westbarnes; descended from LAUDER, of Bass). Arms, the same as of Bass, charging the griffin's breast with a heart ensigned with an imperial crown all ppr. for diff. Crest—The trunk of an old tree budding ppr. Motto—Repullulat.

Lauder (Hatton, Scotland). Ar. a griffin segreant sa.

Lauder (Newington, ancestor of Fountainhall, 1672). Gu. a griffin segreant sa. in the dexter canton a tower or. Crest—A balance equilibrated or. Motto—Mediocria firma.

Lauder (now DICK-LAUDER, Fountainhall, co. Haddington, bart., 1688). Quarterly, 1st and 4th, gu. a griffin segreant within a bordure ar., for LAUDER; 2nd and 3rd, a fess wavy az. betw. three mullets gu., for DICK. Crests— For LAUDER: A tower embattled ar. thereon a man in a watching posture full-faced, his head and shoulders only appearing ppr.; for DICK: A stag's head erased ppr. attired or. Supporters. Two lions ar. Mottoes. For LAUDER: Turris prudentia custos; for DICK: Virtute.

587

Lauder (Winepark, Scotland, 1745). Gu. a griffin segreant ar. within a bordure of the last charged with four hearts ensigned with imperial crowns ppr. and as many crescents gu. Crest—A dexter hand holding a scymitar, and on the point thereof a Saracen's head all ppr.

Lauderdale, Earl of. See MAITLAND.

Lauderdale (Scotland). Sa. fretty or.

Laudermonie (Scotland). Ar. on a bend gu. two crosses couped of the first.

Laudham. Az. a chev. betw. three roses or.

Laugharne. Per chev. gu. and ar. a pale counterchanged. Crest—Out of a cloud a hand erect pointing with one finger to the sun all ppr.

Laugher. Gyronny of eight or and sa. a chief gu. Crest— A plough ppr.

Laughlin (quartering on Fun. Ent. Ulster's Office, FORSTER, of Kilgreege, co. Dublin; WALTER FORSTER, of that place, temp. Henry VI., m. MARY, dau. and heiress of LAUGHLIN. Visit. Dublin, 1607). Az. a dexter hand apaumée couped at the wrist, betw. in chief an arrow, and in base a sword barways, points to the dexter ar. pommel and hilt or.

Laughton. Ar. on a bend sa. three mullets or.

Lauginger (Germany). Sa. an eagle's leg and wing conjoined in fesse and elevated gu.

Launce (Penair, co. Cornwall, and co. Suffolk). Or, on a chief indented sa. three cinquefoils of the field. Crest—A demi bull erm. attired or, pierced through with a broken spear sa. headed ar. vulned guttée de sang.

Launce (Hallesworth, co. Suffolk ; granted 8 Nov. 1580). Or, on a fesse indented sa. three cinquefoils of the field, on a canton of the second a lion ramp. of the first. Crest—A hand in armour ppr. lying fesseways grasping a lance or, headed ar.

Launce. Or, a chief gu.

Launceston, or Dunheved (" the swelling hill "), Town of. Gu. a triple circular tower in a pyramidical form or, the first battlements mounted with cannon of the last, all within a border az. charged with eight towers domed ar. Crest—In a ducal coronet or, a lion's head gu. betw. two ostrich feathers ar.

Launceston-Priory (Cornwall). Ar. guttée de sang a cock gu. on a chief of the last three roses or.

Laundeles. Az. an orle or.

Launder (New Hall, co. Lancaster; granted 19 June, 1687). Sa. three mullets of six points in bend ar. betw. two cotises indented or. Crest—A demi unicorn sa. attired, unguled, and crined or, the body charged with three mullets of six points bendways ar.

Launder (Elton, co. Nottingham). Per saltire sa. and gu. three mullets of six points in bend or, betw. two bendlets dancettée of the last.

Laune (Penneare, co. Cornwall; ROBERT LAUNE, Visit. Cornwall, 1620, son of JOHN LAUNE, both of same place). Or, on a fess dancettée sa. three roses of the field.

Laungton (Wilford, co. Wilts). Ar. a saltire gu. on a chief of the last three boars' heads couped or. Crest—A dexter arm in armour embowed, brandishing a sword all ppr.

Launslin, or Launcelyn. Ar. on a fesse sa. three mullets of the field.

Laurence (Sherdington, co. Gloucester, 1682). Ar. a cross raguly gu. Crest—A demi fish erect, tail upwards, per pale ar. and gu.

Laurence (co. Lancaster, 1566). Ar. a cross raguly gu.

Laurence (MATHEW LAURENCE, second son of Sir OLIVER LAURENCE; his dau., ELIZABETH, m. MARTIN FREEMAN, of London. Visit. London, 1563). Ar. a cross ragulée gu., quartering WASHINGTON, viz., ar. two bars, in chief two mullets gu.

Laurence (certified by Betham, Ulster, to WALTER LAURENCE, Esq., of Lisreaghan, co. Galway). Quarterly, 1st and 4th, ar. a cross raguly gu., for LAURENCE; 2nd and 3rd, sa. a catharine wheel betw. two crescents in chief and a trefoil in base or, for SCOTT. Crest—A demi turbot, tail erect ppr. Motto—Pro rege sæpe, pro patria semper.

Laurie, or Lawrie (Maxwelton, co. Dumfries, bart.). Sa. a cup ar. with a garland betw. two laurel branches all issuing out of the same vert. Crest—A garland of laurel betw. two branches of the same ppr. Motto—Virtus semper viridis.

Laurie, or Lawrie (Plainstones, Bailie, Portsburgh, Scotland, 1674). Per fesse gu. and sa. a cup ar. with a garland issuing out of the top betw. two laurel branches vert. Crest—The trunk of an oak sprouting out ppr. Motto—Repullulat.

Laurie (Redcastle, co. Kirkcudbright, 1722). As Maxweltown, within a bordure ar. charged with eight boars' heads erased gu. Crest—The trunk of an oak tree sprouting ppr. above the same a cross pattée fitchée gu. Motto—Benedictio Dei ditat.

Laurie (CRAIG-LAURIE, of Redcastle, 1857). Quarterly, 1st and 4th, as the last; 2nd and 3rd, erm. a saltire engr. gu. betw. a mullet in chief of the second and a boar's head erased in base az. the saltire being surmounted of a fess ar. charged with three crescents sa., for CRAIG. *Additional Crest* for CRAIG—A chevalier on horseback in full career grasping a broken lance in bend ppr. *Motto* for CRAIG— Vive Deo ut vivas.

Laurie (Polmont, co. Linlithgow, Lord Provost of Edinburgh, 1774). Az. a laurel wreath betw. two slips of the same ppr. issuing out of a cup ar. in the dexter and sinister chief points two cross crosslets fitchée ppr. *Crest*—A dexter arm holding a slip of laurel ppr. *Motto*—Virtutem coronat opus.

Laurie (granted to JOHN LAURIE, Esq., major of artillery in the service of the East India Company). Ar. on a pile sa. a cup of the first issuant therefrom two branches of laurel ppr. *Crest*—Out of a mural crown or, the stump of an oak tree sprouting out leaves ppr.

Laurin. Ar. a lion pass. guard. sa. a bordure engr. gu. *Crest*—On a chapeau ppr. an eagle's head az.

Lauriston. Erm. a fesse betw. three cocks gu. *Crest*—A dexter arm in armour embowed holding a scymitar all ppr. *Motto*—Justitia et veritas.

Lautour (Hexton House, Hitchin, co. Herts). Erminois a fesse embattled cotised gu. in chief a tower triple-towered sa. *Crest*—A dexter arm in armour embowed to the sinister ppr. garnished or, supporting with the gauntlet a shield erminois charged with a fesse embattled cotised gu.

Lauty (Scotland). Sa. three piles ar. on a fesse surmounting the exterior one, and debruised by the centre one gu. two crescents of the second. *Crest*—A dexter hand holding a spear in pale ppr.

Lauty (Scotland). Sa. three piles in point ar. surmounted of a fesse gu. charged with as many crescents or.

Lauzon. Ar. three serpents embowed biting their tails ar. *Crest*—A mermaid with mirror and comb all ppr.

Lavache (co. Oxford). Gu. three lions ramp. ar. crowned or. *Crest*—A bull's head reversed erm.

Lavache. Gu. three lions ramp. crowned or.

Lavall. Or, on a cross gu. five escallops ar. (another, az. a bend ar. (another, gu.); another, barry of six erm. and gu.; **another,** az. two bars or, within a bordure engr. gu.).

Lavalling, or Lavelin. Ar. a fleur-de-lis az.

Lavelis (Castleharnock, co. Cornwall). Ar. three calves' heads couped gu. *Crest*—A tower triple-towered or.

Lavell (co. Oxford). Ar. a lion ramp. within an orle of eight crosses crosslet fitchée az.

Lavell, or Lanall. Or, on a cross gu. betw. twelve eagles displ. vert five escallops ar.

Lavell. Or, on a cross gu. five escallops ar. *Crest*—A fox courant ppr.

Laven (Auchenland, Scotland). Or, six lozenges gu.

Laven (Quarlewood). Ar. (another, or) six lozenges gu.

Lavender (Felmersham, co Bedford). Per fesse gu. and ar. a pale and three gem rings counterchanged.

Lavender (co. Hertford, and London). Per fesse gu. and ar. a pale counterchanged, three fountains. *Crest*—A demi horse ar. gorged with a chaplet of lavender.

Lavender (cos. Hereford and Middlesex, and London; confirmed 7 May, 1628). Per fesse gu. and ar. a pale counterchanged, three plates.

Lavenham, or Lavingham (co. Essex). Az. three eagles displ. ar. armed or.

Lavenham. Quarterly, per fesse indented gu. and vert, in chief a wyvern volant, tail extended or.

Lavenses. Ar. a bend betw. six billets gu.

Laver. Or, on a cross gu. a lion ramp. ar. *Crest*—A talbot's head erased gu. ducally crowned or.

Laver. Sa. three boars' heads or.

Lavering. Ar. two chevronels sa. in chief as many harts' heads cabossed gu. *Crest*—A shepherd's flute in pale ppr.

Lavering. Ar. two chevronels sa. betw. three harts' heads cabossed gu.

Lavering. Ar. a lion pass. sa. a bordure engr. of the last.

Laverock, Laverick, or Laverike. Erm. on a fesse engr. gu. a mullet az. *Crest*—Two lions' gambs erased ppr. supporting a pillar or.

Laverock, Laverike, or Leverike. Erm. a fesse engr. gu.

Laverock, or Lesterock. Erm. on a cross gu. five laverocks or larks or.

Laverye. Az. a fleur-de-lis or, in the 1st quarter a leopard's face of the second. *Crest*—A savage's head affrontée ppr.

Laverye. Or, a cross gu. a chief vert.

Lavider. Per fesse gu. and or (another, **ar.**) a pale counterchanged.

Lavie. Or, a hind's head erased gu. betw. three crosses pattée fitchée az. *Crest*—Out of a ducal coronet or, a lion's paw holding a cross crosslet fitchée az.

Laville. Erm. a bend sa.

Lavington. Ar. a saltire gu. on a chief of the last three boars' heads erased of the first. *Crest*—A covered cup ar.

Lavington (Bassishaw, Scotland). Ar. a saltire gu. in chief a crescent sa. on a chief of the second three boars' heads couped.

Lavyder. Per fesse gu. and or, a pale counterchanged, three gem rings of the second, stoned az.

Law (*Lord Ellenborough*) Erm. on a bend engr. betw. two cocks gu. three mullets pierced or. *Crest*—A cock gu. chained round the neck and charged on the breast with a mitre or. *Supporters*—Two eagles, wings elevated sa. the dexter chained round the neck, and pendent therefrom on the breast a mitre all or, the sinister with a like chain, and pendent therefrom a covered cup also or. *Motto*—Compositum jus fasque animi.

Law (*Earl of Ellenborough*, extinct 1871; EDWARD, second Lord Ellenborough, was created *Earl of Ellenborough* and *Viscount Southam*, 1844, *d. s. p.*). Same *Arms, Crest, Supporters,* and *Motto*.

Law (Cannon Hill, Maidenhead, co. Berks). Erm. on a bend engr. betw. two cocks gu. three mullets or.

Law (Bishop of Carlisle, 1769). Ar. on a bend betw. two cocks gu. three mullets of the field.

Law (Stanmore and Newington, co. Middlesex). Gu. on a chief indented ar. two wolves' heads erased of the field, a wolf's head erased gu. ducally gorged or.

Law (Archdeacon of Rochester). Ar. an eagle displ. with two heads vert, armed **gu.** *Crest*—A dove, in the beak an olive branch all ppr.

Law (Anstruther, Fife, 1672). Erm. a bend betw. a cock in chief and two mullets in base gu. *Motto*—Trusty and kind.

Law (Burntoun, Fife). Erm. a bend betw. two cocks gu. *Crest*—A unicorn's head ppr. *Motto* — Nec obscura nec ima.

Law (Cameron, Scotland). Erm. a bend betw. two cocks within a bordure engr. gu. *Motto*—Non obscura.

Law (Easter Kinevie, Scotland). As Burntoun, within a bordure gu. *Crest*—A unicorn's head erased ppr. charged with a crescent or. *Motto*—Non obscura nec ima.

Law (Newton, Scotland). Erm. a bend raguly betw. two cocks gu. *Crest*—A cock's head erased ppr. *Motto*—Nec obscura nec ima.

Law School of Cambridge. Purp. a cross moline ar. on a chief gu. a lion pass. guard. of the second charged on the side with the letter L sa.

Law (Lauriston, co. Edinburgh ; Count of the Empire of France). Erm. a bend betw. two cocks gu. a bordure invecked of the last. *Crest*—A unicorn's head ppr. *Motto*—Non obscura nec ima.

Laward, or Lawarre (Estercombe, co. Somerset; granted 1756). Gu. a lion ramp. betw. eight crosses crosslet fitchée ar. *Crest*—Out of a ducal coronet or, a griffin's head az. beaked gold.

Laward, alias Lord. Ar. on a fesse gu. betw. three cinquefoils az. a hind pass. betw. two pheons or. *Crest*—A demi bird sa. on the head two small horns or, wings expanded, the dexter outside gu. inside ar., the sinister outside of the last, inside of the third.

Laward. Barry nebulée of six sa. and ar.

Laware. Ar. a fesse dancettée sa.

Lawday (Exeter, bart., extinct). Per saltire gu. and sa. a griffin segreant or.

Lawder (Mough House, co. Leitrim). Gu. a griffin segreant with a double tressure flory counterflory ar. *Crest*—A solan goose standing on one leg on a rock ppr. *Motto*—Sub umbrâ alarum tuarum.

Lawdey (Exeter, bart., extinct or dormant since 1648 ; Sir RICHARD LAWDEY, Knight Banneret, slain in the civil wars *temp.* King Charles, was so created 1642). Per saltire gu. and sa. a griffin segreant or.

Lawe (Preston, co. Lancaster, 1664). Ar. an eagle displ. with two heads vert.

Lawes (Rothamsted Manor House, co. Hertford). Or, on a chief az. three estoiles of the field, quartering BENNET, gu. a bezant betw. three demi lions ramp. ar., and WITTEWRONGE, ar. three bendlets gu. on a chief sa. a bar dancettée or. *Crest*—On a ducal coronet or, an ermine pass. ppr.

Lawston (Laweston, Scotland). Ar. three mullets gu.

Laweston. Az. three crescents or.

Lawford. Az. seven crescents ar. three, three, and one.

Crest—An arrow point downwards and palm branch in saltire all ppr.

Lawford (the late Admiral Sir JOHN LAWFORD, K.C.B.). Quarterly, gu. and erminois on a band wavy cotised ar. an anchor sa. betw. two estoiles gu. *Crest*—A demi lion ramp. erm. holding a naval crown or, in the mouth a laurel branch ppr. *Motto*—In utrumque paratus.

Lawford (EDWARD LAWFORD, Esq.). Az. three lions ramp. ar. ducally crowned or, a mullet for diff. *Crest*—A lion ramp. ppr. ducally crowned, as in the arms. *Motto*—In Deo confido.

Lawfull. Gu. three bars humettée ar. *Crest*—A cornucopia or, flowers and fruit ppr. and a trident az. in saltire.

Lawkin, or Lawkyn. Sa. three mullets ar. on a chief of the second a demi lion ramp. gu.

Lawler (England). Ar. a chev. betw. three leopards' faces az. *Crest*—On a dexter hand couped in fesse a falcon rising ppr.

Lawles. Az. three covered cups or, a chief indented ar.

Lawless (*Baron Cloncurry*). Ar. on a chief indented sa. three garbs or. *Crest*—Out of a ducal coronet or, a demi man in armour in profile, visor closed, holding in the right hand a sword all ppr. the helmet adorned with a plume of three feathers, the exterior two gu. the centre one ar. *Supporters*—Dexter, a bull sa. armed and horned ar.; sinister, a ram ar. *Motto*—Virtute et numine.

Lawless (Reg. Ulster's Office). Or, on a chief az. three covered cups of the field.

Lawless (Reg. Ulster's Office). Ar. on a chief dancettée sa. three garbs or. *Crest*—A man's head in an esquire's helmet, visor up all ppr. plumed ar. and sa.

Lawlesse. Gu. a saltire betw. four boars' heads couped ar.

Lawley (*Baron Wenlock*). Quarterly, 1st and 4th, per fesse ar. and sa. a fesse embattled betw. three falcons belled all counterchanged, for THOMPSON; 2nd and 3rd, ar. a cross formée throughout chequy sa. and or, for LAWLEY. *Crests* —1st: An arm embowed, quarterly or and az. grasping the truncheon of a tilting spear or, for THOMPSON; 2nd: A wolf statant sa., for LAWLEY. *Supporters*—On either side a wolf sa. gorged with a plain collar or, pendent therefrom an escutcheon ar. charged with a chev. of the first betw. three Moors' heads opposite ppr. *Motto*—Je veux de bonne guerre.

Lawley (co. Gloucester). Ar. a fesse sa. in chief three escallops of the last.

Lawndaur. Gu. a bend ar. cotised indented or.

Lawnde. Az. three trefoils ar. a chief indented gu. *Crest* —A hand in armour couped, holding a cross crosslet fitchée gu.

Lawne. Chequy ar. and az. on a chief of the first three palets gu.

Lawne. Per pale gu. and az. three lions pass. guard. in pale or.

Lawrance (Foxhall, co. Gloucester). Ar. a cross raguly gu. in the 1st quarter a lion pass. of the last. *Crest*—A wolf's head ppr. charged on the neck with a crescent or.

Lawrance (co. Hants). Ar. a cross betw. four cinquefoils gu. *Crest*—On a chapeau gu. turned up erm. a talbot sejant of the first.

Lawrence (Ashton Hall and Washington, co. Lancaster, Fisbury, co. Wilts, and St. James's, co. Suffolk; descended from Sir ROBERT LAWRENCE, of Ashton Hall, who accompanied Richard I. to the Holy Land). Ar. a cross raguly gu. *Crest*—A demi turbot ar. tail upwards. *Another Crest*—Two laurel branches vert, forming a chaplet. *Another Crest*— A wolf's head couped ppr.

Lawrence (Sevenhampton and Sandywell Park, co. Gloucester, Crich Grange, co. Dorset; in Har. MSS. 891, a curious badge is recorded as belonging to this family, attached to the coat of LAWRENCE, quartering WASHINGTON). Same *Arms*. *Crest*—The tail and lower part of a fish erected and couped ppr.

Lawrence (Sandywell Park, co. Gloucester; WALTER LAWRENCE LAWRENCE, Esq., assumed the name and arms of LAWRENCE, in lieu of his patronymic MORRIS, by desire of his maternal grandfather, WALTER LAWRENCE, Esq., of Sevenhampton, descended in a direct line from Sir ROBERT LAWRENCE, who acquired the arms in Palestine in 1191). Same *Arms*, a crescent for diff. *Crest*—The tail and lower part of a fish erect and couped ppr.

Lawrence (Iver, co. Buckingham, bart., extinct 1714). Same *Arms*, on a chief of the second a lion pass. guard. or. *Crest*—A stag's head erased sa. plattée, attired or, ducally gorged ar.

Lawrence (St. Ive's, co. Huntingdon, bart., extinct 1756). Same *Arms*.

Lawrence (Cowsfield House, co. Wilts, Mossley Hall, co.
589

Lancaster, and Fairfield, in Jamaica; JOHN LAWRENCE settled in Jamaica 1676, a younger son of HENRY LAWRENCE, Esq., of St. Ives, co. Huntingdon). Same *Arms*, without the chief. *Crest*—A demi turbot, tail erect ppr. *Motto*— In cruce salus.

Lawrence, or Lawrance (Delaford, Chertsey, and Chelsea, co. Middlesex). Ar. a cross raguly gu. on a chief az. three leopards' faces or. *Crest*—A demi turbot, tail erect gu.

Lawrence (co. Devon). Chequy or and az. on a bend gu. three escallops ar.

Lawrence, Bart. Erm. on a cross raguly gu. an eastern crown or, on a chief az. two swords in saltire ppr. pommels and hilts gold, betw. as many leopards' faces ar. *Crest*— Out of an eastern crown or, a cubit arm entwined by a wreath of laurel and holding a dagger all ppr. *Motto*—Never give in.

Lawrence (*Baron Lawrence*). Same *Arms* and *Crest*. *Supporters*—Dexter, an officer of the Guide cavalry (irregulars), of the Pathan tribe, in the province of Peshawar, habited and accoutred ppr.; sinister, an officer of the Sikh irregular cavalry, also habited and accoutred ppr. *Motto*—Be ready.

Lawrence (Ealing Park, co. Middlesex, bart.). Erm. a cross raguly gu. in the 1st and 4th quarters a serpent nowed ppr. *Crest*—A gryphon's head couped ar. in front thereof a serpent nowed ppr. *Motto*—Mente et labore.

Lawrence (Westbourne Terrace, Middlesex, bart.). Erm. on a cross raguly gu. betw. in the 1st and 4th quarters a fasces erect, surrounded by a wreath of oak leaves ppr. a pair of compasses extended or. *Crest*—On a wreath of the colours a wolf's head erased ar. crusily, charged with a pair of compasses extended sa. *Motto*—Per ardua stabilis.

Lawrence (ROBERT JOHN GREWS LAWRENCE, Esq., of Montagu Square, d. 1838). Erm. a cross raguly gu. on a chief of the last a lion pass. or, and canton erm. *Crest*—A lion ramp. *Motto*—Fortiter gerit crucem.

Lawrence (confirmed, 1559, by Harvey, Clarenceux, to LAWRENCE, Sheriff of Rugby). Az. on a chev. engr. betw. three griffins' heads erased or, a fleur-de-lis of the field betw. two roses gu. *Crest*—A lion's paw erased or, holding a branch of dates vert, fructed or, husks ar.

Lawrence (granted to JOHN LAWRENCE, of London, and JAMES and ABRAHAM, his brothers, sons of ABRAHAM LAWRENCE, by Bysshe, Clarenceux, 1664). Erm. a cross raguly gu. and a canton ermines. *Crest*—A saltire raguly ar. encircled with two branches of laurel vert.

Lawrence (granted to RICHARD LAWRENCE, Esq., of Foxcote, co. Gloucester, by Dethick, Garter, 1598). Ar. a cross raguly, in the 1st quarter a lion pass. gu. *Crest*—A fox's head ppr. charged with a bezant.

Lawrence (Seaborow, co. Dorset, 1634). Ar. on a cross raguly gu. a fleur-de-lis of the field. *Crest*—A demi turbot erect, tail upwards ar.

Lawrence (London, 1634). Ar. on a cross raguly gu. five crescents or, on a chief az. three lions' faces of the last. *Crest*—A dolphin naiant ppr.

Lawrence (London; granted 18 Nov. 1652). Ar. a cross raguly gu. a canton ermines. *Crest*—Two trunks of a tree raguly in saltire, environed with a chaplet vert.

Lawrence (West Stocklands, co. Leicester). Sa. three lozenges ar. each charged with a saltire gu.

Lawrence. Gu. two swords in saltire ppr. betw. four cinquefoils ar. *Crest*—A sea lion parted per fesse ar. and ppr. *Motto*—Que pensé.

Lawrence. Sa. a chev. betw. three broken swords ar. on a chief embattled of the second as many martlets gu.

Lawrence (Cirencester, co. Gloucester). Gu. two chev. ar. *Crest*—A griffin's head erased.

Lawrence (Studley Park, co. York). Ar. a cross raguly gu. quartering AISLABIE, viz., Gu. three lozenges in fesse ar. *Crest*—A wolf's head az. charged on the neck with a crescent or.

Lawrence (Scotland). Ar. a cross gu. on a chief of the second a lion pass. guard. or. *Crest*—An acorn slipped and leaved vert.

Lawrence. Az. three martlets or, a border of the last, charged with eight chess-rooks az.

Lawrence (Lisreaghan, co. Galway; claiming descent from LAWRENCE, of Ashton Hall, co. Lancaster). Quarterly, 1st and 4th, ar. a cross raguly gu., for LAWRENCE; 2nd and 3rd, sa. a catharine wheel betw. two crescents in chief and a trefoil in base or, for SCOTT. *Crest*—A demi turbot, tail erect ppr. *Motto*—Pro rege, et pro patriâ, semper.

Lawrens (co. Dorset and Winchester. Visit. Hants, 1634). Ar. a cross betw. four cinquefoils gu. *Crest* On a chapeau gu. turned up erm. a talbot sejant of the first.

Lawrie. See LAURIE.

Lawrie (The Moss, co. Stirling, and Ceylon, 1873). Per pale sa. and gu. a cup ar. and issuing therefrom a garland betw. two branches of laurel vert. Crest—The stump of an oak tree with a branch sprouting from either side ppr. Motto—I'll be wary.

Lawrie (England). Az. on a fesse ar. betw. three plates a cross pattée gu. Crest—A monk, holding in the dexter hand a crucifix, and in the sinister a rosary.

Lawrus (Picardy). Sa. three broad arrows in pale or.

Lawryn. Ar. a lion pass. sa. a bordure engr. of the last.

Laws. Gu. a fesse or.

Lawse, or Lawes (cos. Kent and Norfolk; granted 1584). Or, on a chief az. three estoiles of the field. Crest—On a ducal coronet or, an ermine pass. ppr.

Lawselin (co. Chester). Ar. on a fesse sa. three mullets of the first.

Lawson (Brough Hall, co. York, bart., extinct 1834; Sir HENRY LAWSON, sixth and last bart., d. s. p., when his estates passed to his nephew, WILLIAM WRIGHT, son of JOHN WRIGHT, Esq., of Kelvedon Hall, co. Essex, by ELIZABETH LAWSON, his wife, second dau. of Sir JOHN LAWSON, fifth bart., who assumed the name of LAWSON, and was created a bart. 1841). Ar. a chev. betw. three mascles or. Crest (granted 1592)—On a chapeau gu. turned up erm. a martlet sa.

Lawson (Brough Hall, co. York, bart.). Ar. a chev. betw. three martlets sa. Crest—Two flexed arms ar. supporting the rising sun ppr. Motto—Leve et reluis.

Lawson (Longhirst, co. Northumberland; descended from ROBERT LAWSON, of Longhirst, whose will bears date 1610). Same Arms and Crest.

Lawson (Nesham Abbey, co. Durham; descended from THOMAS LAWSON, d. 1499, m. the heiress of CRAMLINGTON, of Cramlington). Same Arms and Crest. Motto—Rise and shine.

Lawson (Little Osworth, co. Durham; confirmed 1558) Same Arms and Crest.

Lawson (Popleton and Moreby, co. York; descended from Sir GEORGE LAWSON, Knt., Treasurer of Berwick-upon-Tweed, temp. Henry VIII., and Lord Mayor of York in 1530; represented by LAWSON, of Aldborough Lodge and Boroughbridge Hall, co. York). Paly of four gu. and vert, on a chev. or, a greyhound's head erased sa. betw. two cinquefoils az. on a chief of the third an ogress, thereon a demi lion ramp. ar. betw. two crescents of the fourth, on each three plates. Crest—A wolf's head erased ppr. charged on the neck with three bezants, one and two, betw. the bezants a collar vert. Motto—Loyal, secret; Loyal, confidential—adopted by Sir GEORGE LAWSON, Knt., on his appointment as Treasurer of Berwick-upon-Tweed.

Lawson (co. York). Paly of six gu. and vert, on a chev. ar. three wolves' heads erased sa. on a chief or, as many ogresses.

Lawson (Ushworth). Per pale sa. and ar. a chev. counterchanged.

Lawson (Isell, co. Cumberland, bart., extinct 1806; descended from JOHN LAWSON, Lord of Fawlesgrave, temp. Henry III.; WILFRED LAWSON, Esq., of Isell, was created a bart. 1688; Sir WILFRED LAWSON, tenth bart., d. s. p., and bequeathed the estates to THOMAS WYBERGH, son of THOMAS WYBERGH, Esq., of Clifton Hall, co. Westmoreland, by ISABELLA HARTLEY, his wife, sister of ANNE, the wife of Sir WILFRID, he d. s. p. 1812, and was s. by his brother, WILFRID WYBERGH, Esq., of Brayton, co. Cumberland, who assumed the name of LAWSON, and was created a bart. 1831). Per pale ar. and sa. a chev. counterchanged.

Lawson (Brayton, co. Cumberland, bart., created 1831). Per pale ar. and sa. a chev. counterchanged, a canton sa. charged with two bars or. Crest—Out of clouds ppr. two arms embowed, vested erminois, cuffs sa. holding a sun also ppr. Motto—Quod honestum utile.

Lawson (Longhirst, co. Northumberland). Ar. a chev. betw. three martlets sa. Crest—Two arms embowed couped at the elbow, vested erm. cuffed ar. supporting in the hands ppr. the sun in splendour gold.

Lawson (Cramlington, co. Northumberland). Quarterly, 1st and 4th, quarterly, 1st and 4th, ar. a chev. betw. three martlets sa., for LAWSON, 2nd and 3rd, ar. two chev. betw. three trefoils vert, for DE CARDONNEL (granted to MANSFELDT DE CARDONNEL, Esq., of Chirton, co. Northumberland); 2nd and 3rd grand quarters, HYLTON, of Hylton Castle, co. Durham. Crests—1st: Two arms embowed supporting a sun ppr., motto over, Rise and shine, for LAWSON; 2nd: A dove ppr., for DE CARDONNEL. Motto—Tant que je puis.

Lawson (London). Per pale ar. and sa. a chev. counterchanged, in chief an escallop of the second.

590

Lawson (Boghall and Cairnmuir, co. Peebles). Ar. a saltire and chief sa. on the last three garbs or.

Lawson (Humbie, co. Haddington). Az. two crescents ar. in chief and a star in base or.

Lawson (Halheriot, co. Edinburgh, Lord Provost of Edinburgh, 1863). Per saltire ar. and sa. a saltire gu. in chief az. three garbs or. Crest—A garb or. Motto—Dominus providebit.

Lawson, or Lewson. Ar. on a bend betw. two trefoils slipped sa. three mascles or.

Lawton (Lawton, co. Chester; settled there temp. Henry V.). Ar. on a fesse betw. three crosses crosslet fitchée sa. as many cinquefoils of the field. Crest—A demi wolf saliant reguard. ar. vulned in the breast gu.

Lawterham (Bowden, co. Devon; STEPHEN LAWTERHAM, temp. Edward VI., left an only dau. and heir, m. JOHN STONE; their dau. and heir, ELIZABETH STONE, m. WALTER COPLESTONE, Esq., of Yakhampton, co. Devon, third son of JOHN COPLESTONE, Esq., of Coplestone. Visit. Devon, 1620). Sa. a lion ramp. ar.

Lawtrell, or Lowtrell. Az. a fesse betw. six mullets ar.

Lawyne. Gu. semée of billets or, a fesse ar.

Lax (St. Ibbs, co. Herts). Barry of six erminois and gu. on a chief az. three catharine wheels or. Crest—On a mount vert a catharine wheel or.

Laxton (Lord Mayor of London, 1544). Ar. a chev. componée erm. and sa. betw. three griffins' heads gu. guttée d'or.

Laxton (Sir WILLIAM LAXTON. Visit. London, 1563. His brother, JOHN LAXTON, had a dau., JOANE, heir to her uncle, m. THOMAS WANTON, citizen of London). Erm. a chev. engr. betw. three griffins' heads erased gu.

Laxton (London). Gu. a fesse betw. three conies ar.

Laxton (co. York). Barry of six ar. and gu. on a chief az. three catharine wheels or.

Laxton (co. York). Gu. a chev. betw. three hedgehogs ar.

Laxton. Paly of six ar. and sa. on a chief gu. a lion pass. guard. or. Crest—Out of a tower ppr. a demi griffin or.

Laxton (Fun. Ent. Ulster's Office, 1677, Lady HAY, wife of Sir JAMES HAY, Bart.). Ar. a chev. chequy sa. and erm. betw. three griffins' heads erased gu. guttée d'or.

Lay, or Ley. Gu. on a chev. ar. three torteaux. Crest—An escallop or, charged with a saltire gu. all betw. two wings gold.

Lay (granted to HORATIO NELSON LAY, Esq., Inspector-General of Customs in China). Gu. two stags' heads cabossed fesswise or, on a chief engr. of the last a cross patonce sa. betw. two estoiles az. Crest—A demi unicorn ar. collared vair, resting the sinister foot on a cross patonce sa. Motto—Through.

Layard (St. George's, Westminster; recorded in the Coll. of Arms, 1779). Quarterly, 1st and 4th, gu. a chev. or, in chief two mullets of six points of the last, the edges issuing rays pierced of the field, in base a crescent ar. on a chief az. three mullets gold, for LAYARD; 2nd gu. a cross or, in the dexter chief quarter a lion ramp. supporting an anchor cabled all of the second, for BALAIRE. 3rd, vert three doves volant ar., for BALAIRE. Crest—Out of a ducal coronet or, a mullet, as in the arms. Motto—Juvante Deo.

Layard. Gu. two bars erm. on a canton sa. a millrind ar.

Laycock (Sleaford; EDMOND LAYCOCK, Esq., M.D., 1770-1820). Ar. a chev. betw. three cocks sa. Crest—A cock ar. resting the dexter claw on a gauntlet ppr.

Layer (Norwich, co. Norfolk). Per pale ar. and sa. a unicorn courant sa. betw. three crosses crosslet all counterchanged. Crest—A unicorn's head erased az.

Laer (co. Essex, Cringleford and Norwich, co. Norfolk, and Booton, co. Suffolk). Same Arms. Crest—A mullet of six points gu.

Layer (Cringleford, co. Norfolk). Same Arms.

Layfield (Archdeacon of Essex; confirmed 1639). Or, on a chev. betw. three demi lions gu. as many trefoils slipped of the field. Crest—A bull's head cabossed sa.

Layford, or Layforth. Ar. a bend dngr. cotised gu.

Layland. Ar. three staves raguly sa. flammant at the top ppr. Crest—On a terrestrial globe a ship sailing ppr.

Layland. Ar. a bend gu. cotised sa.

Layman. Per chev. gu. and ar. three annulets counterchanged (another, three annulets in chief of the second). Crest—A demi bull ramp. ppr.

Layman. Ar. on a fesse gu. three annulets or.

Laynne. Ar. three wool cards sa. the back parts outward.

Layston. Vert three falcons or.

Layton (Delemain, co. Cumberland, *temp.* Henry III.). Sa. on a bend ar. three escallops gu. *Crest*—A lion's head erased **ar.** gorged with a collar sa. charged with three bezants.

Layton (co. Lincoln, Kirkby, Laton, Saxay, and Weston, co. York). Ar. a fesse betw. six crosses crosslet fitchée sa. *Crest*—Out of a mural coronet two wings expanded ar. each charged with a cross crosslet fitchée sa.

Layton (co. Somerset). Ar. a fesse az. in chief a cross crosslet fitchée sa.

Layton (co. York). Gu. a chev. betw. three crosses formée or.

Layton. Ar. on a fesse betw. three crosses crosslet fitchée sa. a cinquefoil or (another, three cinquefoils of the field).

Layton. Sa. two bars or, on a bend ar. three escallops gu.

Layton, or Laton. Or, a cross gu.

Layton, or Latin. Gu. a cross pattée or, on a bend az. three fleurs-de-lis of the second.

Layton, or Leighton. Gu. on a bend ar. three escallops of the field (another, tinctures reversed).

Layton. Ar. a ram sa. armed or.

Layworth (co. Oxford). Vair on a saltire gu. five fleurs-de-lis or. *Crest*—A lapwing ppr. laying his talon on a fleur-de-lis.

Lea (Halesowen Grange, co. Worcester; granted by Anstis, Garter, and Knox Ward, Clarenceux, to WILLIAM LEA, Esq., 1740, whose ancestor, WILLIAM LEA, Esq., of Halesowen, bore same arms when High Sheriff co. Worcester, *temp.* William III.). Ar. on a pale betw. two leopards' faces sa. three crescents or. *Crest*—A unicorn ar. guttée de poix, gorged with a double tressure flory and counterflory gu. *Motto*—Contentus paucis.

Lea (*Baron Dudley*, 1740-51; in abeyance since 1757; FERDINANDO DUDLEY LEA, fifteenth *Baron Dudley*, son of WILLIAM LEA, Esq., of Halesowen Grange, by FRANCES WARD, only dau. and, in her issue, sole heiress of EDWARD, thirteenth *Baron Dudley*, and WILLIAM, fourteenth *Baron Dudley*, succeeded to the Barony of Dudley on the death of his maternal uncle, 20 May, 1740, but dying *unm.* on 21 Oct. 1757, the title fell into abeyance among his sisters, and his estates passed to his nephew, FERDINANDO SMITH, Esq., grandfather of the present FERDINANDO DUDLEY LEA-SMITH, Esq., of Halesowen Grange, senior co-heir to the barony). Same *Arms*. *Supporters* (granted 19 Nov. 1740)—Two lions double queued vert, armed and langued gu. each gorged with a ducal coronet, thereto a cordon passing betw. the forelegs and reflexed over the back or. *Motto*—In seipso totus teres.

Lea, or Lee (co. Buckingham). Ar. a fesse gu. betw. three leopards' faces az.

Lea (co. Cornwall). Ar. three pine trees ppr.

Lea, or Lee (co. Cumberland). Az. two bars **ar.** a bend gobony of the last and gu.

Lea (Lea, co. Lancaster). Sa. three bars ar.

Lea (co. Salop). Vert a fesse flory counterflory **or.**

Lea (Astley Hall, co. Worcester). Erm. a fess dancettée vert flory counterflory or, betw. in chief two lions pass. sa. and in base a stag lodged ppr. collared and chain reflexed over the back of the third. *Crest*—A beaver ppr. semée-de-lis or, holding in the mouth a branch of willow also ppr. *Motto*—Spe vitæ melioris.

Lea (Dublin; impalement Fun. Ent. Ulster's Office, 1623, Sir BAPTIST JONES, Knt., of Vintnerstown, co. Londonderry, whose wife was ELIZABETH, dau. of ROBERT LEA). Az. on a fesse or, betw. two barrulets ar. three torteaux.

Lea (Kildare; Captain THOMAS LEA; impalement Fun. Ent. Ulster's Office, 1619, of his sœin-in-law, NORTON). Ar. on a fess az. betw. three unicorns' heads couped sa. armed or, as many lilies of the last.

Lea (THOMAS LEA, Keeper of the Council Chamber, Dublin, Fun. Ent. Ulster's Office, *d.* 7 Feb. 1673). Ar. on a fess betw. three crescents sa. a fleur-de-lis or.

Leach (co. Devon). Ar. on a chief sa. three crowns or.

Leach (Stoke Climsland, co. Cornwall; NICHOLAS LEACHE, son of JOHN LEACHE, Chancellor of the Church of Exeter. Visit. Cornwall, 1620). Erm. on a chief indented gu. three ducal coronets or. *Crest*—Out of a ducal coronet or, a dexter forearm grasping a serpent all ppr.

Leach, or Leache. Same *Arms*. *Crest*—Out of a ducal coronet or, a lion's gamb holding a cross crosslet fitchée sa.

Leach (Crediton, co. Devon; extinct in 1708, at the decease of Sir SIMON LEACH, K.B.). Same *Arms*.

Leach (quartered by AMHURST, through EVERING and MORRIS. Visit. Kent, 1619). Erm. on a chief indented gu. an annulet betw. two crowns or.

Leach (Fun. Ent. Ulster's Office, 1666, Mrs. WETHERS, *alias* LEACH). Erm. on a chief indented gu. three ducal coronets or.

Leachveake. Gu. a saltire ar. a crescent for diff.

Leadbitter (Deptford, near Sunderland, co. Durham). Gu. on a chev. ar. betw. as many plates three crosses pattée sa. *Crest*—Out of a mural coronet gu. a demi unicorn erminois erased of the first, armed and crined or.

Leadbitter (GIBSON-LEADBITTER, Warden House, near Hexham, co. Northumberland). Quarterly, 1st and 4th, gu. on a chev. or, betw. three bezants as many crosses patoncé of the field, in the centre chief point a cross crosslet of the second for distinction, for LEADBITTER; 2nd and 3rd, per pale indented az. and sa. three water bougets chevronways betw. as many storks rising ar., for GIBSON. *Crests*—1st, LEADBITTER: A griffin's head sa. erased gu. pierced through the mouth by an arrow fessways or, and charged on the neck with a cross crosslet gold for distinction; 2nd, GIBSON: In front of a stork rising ar. holding in the beak an olive branch ppr. betw. two ears of wheat or, a water bouget sa. *Motto*—Fidelis.

Leader (Much Stoughton, co. Huntington, *temp.* Henry VIII.; Sir OLIVER LEADER, knighted by Mary I.). Or, on a fess betw. three ogresses sa. each charged with an escallop ar. a lion's head erased betw. two boars' heads couped of the field, a bordure engr. az. *Crest*—An arm embowed, habited vert, with two pallets gu. the hand ppr. holding a sprig of rose-mary flowered ppr.

Leader (Buntingford, co. Herts, and of Moor End, Sheffield, originally of co. Essex). Or, on a fess betw. three escallops within as many annulets sa. a lion's betw. two boars' heads all erased of the field, a bordure nebulée of the second. *Crest* —An arm embowed issuing from an annulet and vested or, charged with two pallets engr. sa. the hand ppr. holding a sprig of three roses also ppr. *Motto*—Virtus salus ducum.

Leader (confirmed to THOMAS LEONARD LEADER, Esq., of Ashgrove, co. Cork, son of THOMAS LEADER, of Spring-mount, co. Cork). Ar. on a fess sa. betw. three ogresses of the second, each charged with an escallop of the first, a lion's head erased betw. two boars' heads also erased or, a bordure wavy gu. *Crest*—An arm embowed, habited paly wavy of six vert and gu. the hand grasping a branch of three roses barbed and leaved all ppr. *Motto*—Probum non pœnitet.

Leaf (Park Hill, Streatham). Az. on a chev. betw. three staff tree leaves slipped or, as many bees volant ppr. *Crest* —A dove rising ppr. resting the dexter claw on a staff tree leaf or.

Leahy (confirmed to FRANCIS ROBERT LEAHY, Esq., of Shan-akiel House, co. Cork, and to the descendants of his grand-father). Gu. a lion ramp. or, armed and langued az. in chief two sceptres in saltire of the second. *Crest*—Out of a mural crown ppr. a demi lion ramp. grasping in the dexter paw a sceptre all or, and charged on the shoulder with a tower ppr. *Motto*—Tout vient de Dieu.

Leake (STEPHEN MARTIN LEAKE, of Thorp Hall, co. Essex, and Mile End, co. Middlesex, Garter King of Arms, *d.* 1773). Quarterly, 1st and 4th, or, on a saltire engr. az. eight annulets ar. on a canton gu. a castle triple-towered of the third, for LEAKE; 2nd and 3rd, paly of six or and az. on a chief gu. three merlins of the first, for MARTIN. *Crest*—A ship gun carriage, on it a piece of ordnance mounted all ppr. *Motto*—Pari animo.

Leake (London). Ar. on a saltire engr. az. nine annulets or, on a canton gu. a castle of the third. *Crest*—A cannon mounted on a carriage all ppr.

Leake (Southwark, London, originally from Germany). Or, a saltire flory, in chief a lion pass. sa.

Leake. Sa. a bend betw. three crosses botonnée fitchée ar.

Leal, Leale, or Lealle. Gu. six crescents ar. three, two, and one, a bend gobonated or and az. *Crest*—Out of a ducal coronet a sceptre entwined with a serpent betw. two wings all ppr.

Lealle. Gu. six crescents ar. three, two, and one.

Lealle, or Leall (co. Kent). Gu. a bend or, betw. six crescents ar.

Lealle. Gu. a bend or, betw. six annulets ar.

L'Archier (extinct in Guernsey). Gu. three arrows barwise, points dexter or.

Lear (Lindridge, co. Devon, bart., extinct 1740; PETER LEAR was so created 1660; MARY, only child of Sir JOHN LEAR, third bart., *m.* Sir THOMAS TIPPING, bart.). Az. a fesse raguly betw. three unicorns' heads erased or.

Lear (London). Az. a fesse embattled counter-embattled betw. three unicorns' heads erased or. *Crest*—Two hands issuing from clouds, grasping the trunk of an oak tree ppr.

Leardlaw. Az. three mascles or.

Learmonth (Balcomie, co. Fife). Quarterly, 1st and 4th, or, on a chev. sa. three mascles of the first; 2nd and 3rd, az. on a bend ar. three roses gu., for BALCOMIE. *Crest*—A rose slipped ppr. *Motto*—Spero.

Learmonth (LIVINGSTONE-LEARMONTH, London, 1870). Quarterly, 1st and 4th, or, on a chev. sa. three lozenges of the first, for LEARMONTH; 2nd and 3rd, ar. a mascle az. betw. three gillyflowers slipped gu. a double tressure flory counterflory vert, for LIVINGSTONE; the whole within a bordure az. Crests—1st, LEARMONTH: A dove holding in the beak an olive branch ppr.; 2nd, LIVINGSTONE: A dexter hand holding a sabre ppr. Mottoes—Dum spiro spero, for LEARMONTH; Si possim, for LIVINGSTONE.

Learmonth (LIVINGSTONE-LEARMONTH, of Parkhall, co. Stirling). As the last, but the bordure engr. ar. Same Crest and Motto.

Leary. See O'LEARY.

Leash (Scotland). Sa. on a fesse betw. three mullets in chief as many mascles in base ar. a cross crosslet fitchée gu. Crest—A demi lion gu. holding in the dexter paw a thistle ppr. and in the sinister a fleur-de-lis or.

Leask (that Ilk). Sa. a fesse betw. three mullets in chief and as many mascles in base ar. Crest—A crescent ar. Motto—Virtute cresco.

Leatham (High Hall, Hemsworth, co. York). Quarterly, 1st and 4th, ar. on a chief indented az. three plates, for LEATHAM; 2nd and 2rd, ar. a chev. betw. three crescents sa. Crest—An eagle with wings elevated, preying on an infant ppr. swaddled az. banded ar. Motto—Virtute vinces.

Leatham (Hemsworth Hall, co. York). Per saltire erm. and or, on a chief engr. az. three bezants, each charged with a saltire gu. Crest—Upon a nest an eagle, wings elevated or, the nest and wings fretty vert. Motto—Virtute vinces.

Leathersellers, Company of (London). Ar. three bucks trippant reguard. gu. attired and unguled sa. Crest—A demi buck gu. attired and unguled sa. Supporters—The dexter, a buck or, attired sa.; sinister, a ram ar. attired or. Motto—Deo honor et gloria.

Leather (Leventhorpe Hall, co. York). Ar. on a bend sa. cotised compony or and of the last a fountain betw. two mullets of six points of the third. Crest—A demi lion ramp. sa. charged on the shoulder with three mullets of six points, two and one or, holding between the paws a fountain. Motto —Nil nisi quod honestum.

Leather, or Leatherland. Ar. on a bend cotised three mullets or.

Leathes (Herringfleet Hall, co. Suffolk; CARTERET MUSSENDEN, Esq., M.P., took the name and arms of LEATHES, as heir to his maternal uncle, WILLIAM LEATHES, Esq., many years Minister at the Courts of Brussels and the Hague. The family of MUSSENDEN descended from Sir WILLIAM DE MUSSENDEN, Grand Admiral of England, temp. Henry III., and Founder of the Abbey of Great Missenden). Arms of LEATHES—Az. on a bend betw. three fleurs-de-lis or, as many mullets pierced gu. Crest of LEATHES—A demi griffin segreant or, armed and langued gu. Motto of LEATHES— In ardua virtus. Arms of MUSSENDEN—Or, a cross engr. gu. in the dexter chief a Cornish chough ppr. Crest of MUSSENDEN—A dove with an olive branch in its beak all ppr. Legend over Crest—Tending to Peace.

Leathes (Leathes and Dalehead, co. Cumberland; seated at the former place shortly after the Conquest; the last male heir, THOMAS LEATHES, Esq., d. in 1806, and was s. by his nephew, THOMAS STRANGER, Esq., who assumed the additional name and arms of LEATHES). Same Arms as LEATHES, of Herringfleet. Crest—A buck's head affrontée ppr.

Leathes (Reg. Ulster's Office, to Capt. ROBERT LEATHES, of Belfast). Az. on a bend betw. three fleurs-de-lis or, as many mullets pierced gu. Crest—A demi griffin segreant or.

Leaton (Whick, co. Durham). Ar. a fesse betw. six crosses crosslet fitchée sa. Crest—A lion ramp. or. Motto—Dieu defende le droit.

Leatt (London; granted 13 Dec. 1616). Ar. on a fesse gu. betw. three crescents sa. from each flames of fire ppr. a lion pass. or. Crest—On a mural crown or, a beacon sa. fired ppr. betw. two wings az.

Leaver, or Lever. Ar. two bends engr. gu. Crest—An arm embowed holding a club ppr.

Leaver, or Lever. Sa. three bears' heads couped or.

Leaves (Kensington, co. Middlesex). Or, two pheons in chief gu. in base a garb vert, a chief dovetailed az.

Leband (co. Essex). Gu. three keys or.

Lebaret (France). Ar. three rustres az.

Le Bailly (Jersey). Az. a fortress ar. maçonnée sa. Crest— A demi lion ppr. Motto—Deus fortissima turris.

Le Blanc (Charterhouse Square, co. Middlesex, and Rouen, Normandy; granted 1753). Az. a chev. betw. three cinquefoils or, on a chief of the second an eagle displ. sa. ducally crowned gold. Crest—An eagle displ. sa. ducally crowned or, charged on the breast with a cinquefoil of the last. Motto—Sans tache.

Leblount (co. Warwick). Gu. a fesse betw. six martlets or.

Lebnefe (co. Buckingham) Gu. three lions pass. ar.

Le Bon. Ar. a chev. betw. three quatrefoils slipped gu. Crest—Out of a ducal coronet or, a plume of ostrich feathers ppr. Motto—Confido.

Le Boutillier (GEORGE LE BOUTILLIER, of Grouville, Jersey). Az. seven chevronels ar. in base a stag trippant of the second. Crest—A cubit arm gu. cuffed ar. holding in the hand a sprig of oak fructed ppr. Motto—Pro rege.

Le Brent. Gu. a wyvern, wings erect ar.

Le Breton (Jersey and London). Az. two chevronels or. Crest—A rose slipped and leaved vert.

Le Brett. Gu. a lion pass. guard. or.

Le Brion (co. Kent). Az. a fer-de-moline ar.

Le Broog (Jersey). Az. a fleur-de-lis or, on a chief ar. a lion pass. guard. gu.

Le Carrant (co. Wilts). Ar. three hurts, each charged with as many chev. or.

Lecawell. Ar. three sails of ships gu. Crest—A unicorn ar. horned gu.

Le Cerf (Jersey). Az. a fesse betw. three stags trippant ar.

Lecester. Az. a fesse gu. fretty or, a bordure ar.

Leche (Chatsworth, co. Derby). Erm. on a chief indented gu. three ducal coronets or. The origin of the crowns in the arms is thus recorded in an old pedigree: "One of this auncient family living in Barkshire, near Windsor, in ye time of King Edward III. entertained and feasted three Kinges in his house, one ye King of England, ye King of France, and ye King of Scotts, which two kings were at that time prisoners to King Edward; which King Edward, to requite his good entertainment and other favours, gave him three crowns on his chief indented gu. ye field ermine; which coate is borne by the name and family, dispersed into many other countays, as Bedford, Nottingham, York, Chester, and Lancaster." Crest—Out of a ducal coronet or, an arm erect ppr. grasping a leech or snake environed round the arm vert.

Leche (Carden, co. Chester, originally from co. Derby; descended from the marriage temp. Henry IV. of JOHN LECHE, with LUCY, second dau. and co-heir of WILLIAM DE CAWARDEN, of Carden). Same Arms, &c.

Leche. Same Arms. Crest—Two lions' gambs erased sa. holding up a crescent ar.

Lecheche. Chequy ar. and az. two bars gu.

Lechford (Shelwood, co. Surrey). Sa. a chev. betw. three leopards' faces ar. Crest—A leopard's face per pale ar. and sa. betw. two wings expanded counterchanged. Another Crest (confirmed by Segar, Garter, 1605)—A unicorn's head erased ar. maned and horned or, and bearing on the horn a serpent ppr.

Lechingham (co. Bedford, and Wendover, co. Bucks). Sa. three boars' heads couped ar. a bordure engr. of the last. Crest—A ram's head cabossed or.

Lechmere (Lechmere's Place, Hanley Castle, co. Worcester, temp. William I.; represented by CHARLTON, of Ludford, co. Hereford). Gu. a fess or, in chief two pelicans vulning themselves of the last. Crest—A pelican az. vulning herself ppr.

Lechmere (Baron Lechmere, extinct 1727; NICHOLAS LECHMERE, second son of EDWARD LECHMERE, Esq., of Hanley Castle, was raised to the peerage 1721, d. s. p.). Quarterly, 1st and 4th, gu. a fess, and in chief two pelicans or, vulning themselves of the first, for LECHMERE; 2nd, vert fretty or, for WHITMORE; 3rd, ar. a chev. engr. betw. three chess-rooks sa., for ROOK. Crest—Out of a ducal coronet a pelican or, vulning herself ppr. Supporters—Two leopards reguard. or, ducally gorged.

Lechmere (Fownhope Court, co. Hereford; descended from SANDYS LECHMERE, of Fownhope, Esq., second son of Sir NICHOLAS LECHMERE, of Hanley Castle, co. Worcester, appointed a Baron of the Exchequer at the Revolution). Quarterly, 1st, gu. a fesse or, in chief two pelicans ar., for LECHMERE; 2nd, vert fretty or, for WHITMORE; 3rd, ar. a chev. engr. sa. betw. three chess-rooks of the last, for ROOK; 4th, gu. three stirrups leathered and buckled or, for SCUDAMORE. Crest—A pelican az. vulning herself ppr.

Lechmere (The Rhyd, co. Worcester, bart.). Gu. a fesse or, in chief two pelicans vulning themselves of the last. Crest— A pelican az. vulning herself ppr. Motto—Christus pelicano.

Lechmere (Allensmore, co. Hereford; quartered by PATESHALL, of that place). Same Arms.

Leck (Hollybush, co. Ayr, 1876). Ar. a chev. gu. betw. two roses of the second in chief and a holly bush ppr. in base. Crest—A wolf's head erased ppr. Motto—Virtutis præmium.

Leckennfeld. Ar. a bull's head couped at the neck sa. horned or, a bordure engr. of the second.

Leckey (granted by Betham, Ulster, to JOHN HARTPOLE LECKEY, Esq., of Craigavoran, Queen's co., descended of a Scottish family). Gu. a chev. betw. three roses ar. *Crest*—An anchor in pale ppr. cabled or and gu. surmounted by a boar's head erased and erect az. *Motto*—Gubernat navem Deus.

Leckie (Scotland). Ar. on a fess vert three cinquefoils of the first (another, roses).

Lecky, or Leckie (England). Gu. three crescents ar. *Crest*—An arm embowed holding a club ppr.

Lecky (Castle Lecky, co. Derry, and Ballyholland House, co. Down). Az. a chev. betw. three mullets or. *Crest*—A wild boar's head erased ppr. *Motto*—Semper paratus.

Lecky (BROWNE-LECKY; exemplified to RAYMOND SAVILLE BROWNE, Esq., of Aughentaine, co. Tyrone, on his assuming by royal licence, 1871, the additional surname of LECKY, in compliance with the will of his grand-uncle, CONOLLY McCAUSLAND LECKY, of the city of Londonderry). Quarterly, 1st and 4th, ar. on a chev. betw. three roses gu. a trefoil slipped or, for LECKY; 2nd and 3rd, per chev. gu. and az. a mullet betw. three fleurs-de-lis, or, for BROWNE. *Crests* —1st: A boar's head erased ppr. charged with a rose gu., for LECKY; 2nd: A lion ramp. or, resting the forepaw on a shield gu. charged with a fleur-de-lis gold, for BROWNE. *Motto*—Utere dum potes.

Lecky (BROWNE-LECKY; exemplified to CONOLLY WILLIAM LECKY BROWNE, Esq., of Aughentaine Castle, co. Tyrone, on his assuming by royal licence, 1874, the additional surname of LECKY, in compliance with the will of his grand-uncle, CONOLLY McCAUSLAND LECKY, Esq., of Londonderry). Same *Arms*, *Crest*, and *Motto*.

Le Cocq (Jersey, Guernsey, and Alderney). Az. three cocks or. *Crest*—A cock crowing, wings extended sa.

Lecpon (Wilborne, co. Lincoln). Ar. on a bend cotised gu. three cinquefoils or. *Crest*—A savage's head couped at the shoulders affrontée ppr wreathed round the temples gu. and or.

Le Couteur (St. John la Hougue Boëte, Jersey). Ar. three owls sa. *Crest*—On an ivy wreath erect or, an owl sa. *Mottoes*—La vita il fin e'l di loda la sera; over the crest: Boni virtutis amore.

Le Couteur (Bellevue, Jersey). Ar. three bendlets az. *Crests*—1st: A dove holding in the beak an olive branch all ppr. (ancient); 2nd: A sword and sprig of laurel in saltire ppr. *Motto*—Toujours prest.

Le Cronier (Jersey). Or, on a chev. az. betw. three mullets of seven points sa. *Crest*—A mastiff ppr. *Motto*—Je garde ma foy.

Ledbrooke. Az. a chev. or (another, erm.).

Leder, or Leader (Great Stoughton, co. Hants). Ar. on a fesse sa. betw. three ogresses, each charged with an escallop of the field, a lion's head erased betw. two boars' heads couped or, a bordure engr. az. *Crest*—A dexter hand holding a sheaf of arrows ppr.

Leder. Same *Arms*, field or. *Crest*—A cubit arm habited bendy sinister of six gu. and vert, holding in the hand ppr. a bunch of leaves of the second.

Le Despencer, Baroness. See STAPLETON.

Ledet (Braybroke, co. Northampton). Ar. a fesse dancettée betw. six crosses crosslet gu.

Ledet (West Wardon, co. Northampton, *temp.* King John). Or, a bend gu. a bordure of the last bezantée.

Ledger. Per saltire or and gu. three pallets counterchanged. *Crest*—An escarbuncle az.

Lediard (Cirencester). Gu. on a fesse betw. three wolves' heads erased or, five lilies slipped and inverted pean. *Crest* —A wolf's head erased per pale pean and gu.

Ledlie. Sa. three plates. *Crest*—A ram's head couped ar. attired or, behind the head a crosier in bend sinister ppr.

Ledred (co. Somerset). Ar. a chev. betw. three talbots' heads erased gu.

Ledsam (Hawarden, co. Flint, Northfield, co. Worcester, and Cloughjordan, co. Tipperary). Quarterly, sa. and ar. four leopards' faces counterchanged. *Crest*—A Cornish clough ppr. *Motto*—Fac et spera.

Ledsham. Quarterly, ar. and sa. four leopards' faces counterchanged.

Ledwich (allowed by Betham, Ulster, Smith's Ordinary). Ar. a fess betw. three eagles displ. gu. *Crest*—An eagle displ., as in the arms.

Ledwich (allowed by Betham, Ulster, Smith's Ordinary). Az. three caps of maintenance or, turned up erm. *Crest*— A lion ramp. gu.

Lee (Lee and Darnhall, co. Chester, *temp.* Henry III.; of

this family the *Earls of Lichfield* were a branch; the chief line removed from Lee to Darnhall *temp.* Charles I., and became extinct in the male line at the decease of General CHARLES LEE, the American General; the heiress, FRANCES, dau. of NATHANIEL LEE, Esq., of Darnhall, *m.* JOHN TOWNS-HEND, Esq., of Hem, co. Denbigh). Ar. a chev. betw. three leopards' faces sa. *Crest*—On a ducal coronet or, a leopard's face sa.

Lee (Dynas Powis, co. Glamorgan). Same *Arms*, chev. engr. a crescent for diff. *Crest*—Out of a ducal coronet or, a leopard's face sa. *Motto*—Fortiter sed suaviter.

Lee (Quarendon, co. Bucks, and Ditchley, co. Oxford; descended from BENEDICT LEE, younger son of JOHN LEE, of Lee Hall, co. Chester; granted to Sir ROBERT LEE, Knt., 1513). Ar. on a fess. az. three unicorns' heads erased sa. as many columbines or. *Crest*—A falcon or, wings close az. preying on an eagle's leg lying fessways az.

Lee (Sir HENRY LEE, of Quarendon, elected a K.G. 23 April, 1597, and installed 24 May following, *d.* 12 Feb. 1611; descended from ROBERT LEE, eldest son of RICHARD LEE, Esq., of Quarendon, who altered the original bearing of his arms). Ar. a fess betw. three crescents sa.

Lee (*Earl of Lichfield;* extinct 1766; descended from BENE-DICT LEE, second son of RICHARD LEE, Esq., of Quarendon). Same *Arms*. *Crest*—Out of a marquess's coronet or, a demi stone column ar. on its capital an eagle's leg erased at the thigh preyed on by a falcon all ppr. *Supporters*—Two lions guard. erm. each collared with a plain collar ar. charged with three crescents sa. *Motto*—Fide et constantia

Lee (London; THOMAS LEE, second son of THOMAS LEE, gent., of Enfield, co. Middlesex. Visit. London, 1563). Same *Arms*, a crescent or, for diff.

Lee (RICHARD LEE, Clarenceux King of Arms, 1594-7). Same *Arms*, a fleur-de-lis for diff.

Lee (Binfield, co. Bucks, *temp.* James I.). Same *Arms*, a mullet for diff.

Lee (Wincham, co. Chester). Ar. a fesse betw. three leopards' faces sa. *Crest*—Out of a ducal coronet or, a leopards' face sa.

Lee (Stamford, co. Lincoln). Az. on a fesse cotised or, three leopards' faces gu. a bordure gobony erm. and sa.

Lee (Stamford, co. Lincoln). Az. (another, vert) on a fesso cotised or, three leopards' faces gu.

Lee (Pinhoe, co. Devon; RICHARD LEE, Mayor of Totness, 1620, and WILLIAM LEE, sons of WILLIAM LEE, Esq., of Pinhoe. Visit. Devon, 1620). Az. on a fess cotised or, three leopards' faces of the field.

Lee (Southwell co. Nottingham). Same *Arms*. *Crest*—A demi Moor vested gu. the sleeves ar. holding in the dexter hand a gem ring, and having round the neck a collar or, entwined round the temples with a wreath of the second and az.

Lee (EDWARD LEE, Archbishop of York, 1531-44; arms in the east window, Founder's Chamber, Magdalen College, Oxford. Visit Oxon, 1566). Az. on a fess cotised or., three leopards' faces gu.

Lee (North Aston, co. Oxford; GEORGE LEE, baptised 1 March, 1569, son and heir of EDWARD LEE, Esq., of North Aston, who was son and heir of THOMAS LEE, Fellow of Magdalen College, Oxford. Visit. Oxon, 1574). Ar. a fess. betw. two crescents in chief and a lion's face in base sa.

Lee (Hartwell, co. Bucks, bart., extinct 1827). Az., two bars or, a bend chequy of the last and gu. *Crest*—A bear pass. sa. muzzled, collared, and chained ar. *Motto*—Verum atque decens.

Lee (Hartwell, co. Bucks; JOHN FIOTT, son of JOHN FIOTT, Esq., by HARRIETT LEE, his wife, *d.s.u.* of WILLIAM LEE, Esq., of Totteridge, the son of Sir WILLIAM LEE, Lord Chief Justice of England, second son of the second bart. of Hartwell, *s.* to the estates by the will of the sixth bart., and assumed the name and arms of LEE). Quarterly, 1st and 4th, az. two bars or, a bend chequy of the last and gu for LEE; 2nd and 3rd, az. on a chev. betw. three lozenges or, an anchor sa., for FIOTT. *Crests*—1st, LEE: A bear pass. sa. muzzled and chain reflexed over the back ar.; 2nd, FIOTT; A demi horse ramp. ar. charged on the shoulder with a fleur de-lis for diff. *Motto*—Verum atque decens.

Lee (co. Buckingham). Ar. a fesse az. betw. three unicorns' heads erased sa. charged with as many lilies or.

Lee (co. Buckingham). Ar. a fesse betw. three leopards' faces sa.

Lee (Bagley, co. Chester). Az. three muscles or.

Lee, or Lea (cos. Chester and Leicester). Ar. a fleur-de-lis sa.

Lee (co. Devon, and London). Ar. a fesse counter-compouncée az. and or, betw. six billets sa. a bordure engr. gu.

Lee (Fishburn, co. Durham). Or, a chev. chequy of the first and az. a crescent for diff. *Crest*—An antelope's head erased ar. pellettée, maned, tufted, and attired sa. holding in the mouth a white lily slipped ppr.

Lee (Ebford, co. Devon; granted 1759). Gu. two bars or, over all a bend engr. vair, in chief an eagle displ. of the second. *Crest*—A bear sejant ppr. muzzled and chained or.

Lee (Plaistow, co. Essex, and Ratcliffe, co. Leicester). Az. two bars ar. over all a bend gu. *Crest*—An arm embowed, habited gu. cuffed ar. holding in the hand ppr. a sword erect of the second, hilt or, on the blade a snake entwined vert.

Lee (Coldrey, co. Hants). Or, on a chief embattled sa. three bezants. *Crest*—On a mount vert a bear pass. ppr. muzzled and chained ar.

Lee (co. Hereford). Ar. on a cross gu. five leopards' faces of the field.

Lee (co. Herts). Ar. on a cross gu. five wolves' heads erased of the field.

Lee, or Lea (St. Julian's and Sopwell, co. Herts). Per chev. or and gu. in chief two lions ramp. combatant sa. armed and langued of the second. *Crest*—A dexter arm embowed in armour, holding a sword ar. hilt and pommel or, from the blade flames of fire issuing ppr.

Lee (Delce, co. Kent, and Lanfoist, co. Monmouth; an old family in Kent, deriving from Sir RICHARD LEE (grandson of SYMON LEE, co. Worcester), twice Lord Mayor of London, *temp.* Henry VI. The daus. and co-heirs of the last RICHARD LEE, Esq., of Great Delce, co. Kent, and Clytha, co. Monmouth, MARY, *m.* JOHN JONES, Esq., of Lanarth; ELIZABETH, *d. unm.*; and APPOLONIA, *m.* 1792, ROBERT BERKELEY, Esq., of Spetchley). Az. on a fesse cotised or, three leopards' faces gu. *Crest*—A dexter arm vested gu. rimmed round the collar with two bars or, tied round the waist with a ribbon ar. wreathed about the head of the last and second, holding in the dexter hand a gem ring of the third.

Lee (The Abbey, Knaresborough). Sa. three crowns or. *Crest*—An arm in armour, holding a battle axe all ppr. *Motto*—Dum spiro spero.

Lee (Grove Hall, co. York). Same *Arms* and *Crest. Motto* Aut nunca aut nunquam.

Lee (Lady-hole, co. Derby; Dugdale's Visit.; the heiress *m.* THOMAS GRESLEY, Esq., of Nether Seale). Az. three ducal coronets or, a border ar. *Crest*—An arm in armour, embowed ppr. bandaged or, gauntleted az. holding in the hand a battle axe ppr. staff gold.

Lee (Holborough Court, co. Kent). Az. two bars erminois. *Crest*—A bear statant ppr. muzzled gu. collared and chained ar. *Motto*—Verum atque decens.

Lee (London). Az. two bars erminois, over all a bend counter-compony of the second and gu. *Crest*—A bear statant ppr. muzzled gu. collared and chained ar. charged on the shoulder with a bezant.

Lee (Isle of Wight). Ar. on a chev. embattled sa. three bezants.

Lee, or Leigh (Bilsley, co. Warwick, Lord Mayor of London, 1602; granted 20 Dec. 1593). Ar. a fesse sa. in chief two pellets, in base a martlet of the second. *Crest*—A talbot's head ar. collared az. to the collar a ring and line nowed of the last.

Lee (London; descended from co. Chester; confirmed 25 Oct. 1583). Ar. on a chev. engr. betw. three leopards' faces sa. a crescent or.

Lee (co. Middlesex; granted 1592). Gu. three chevronels or. *Crest*—A cock ar. combed and wattled or, beaked and legged gu.

Lee (North Aston, co. Oxford). Ar. a fesse sa. betw. in chief two crescents, in base a leopard's face of the second.

Lee (Langley, co. Salop, bart., extinct 1660; descended from RICHARD LEE, High Sheriff of Salop, 1479). Gu. a fesse counter-componé or and az. betw. eight billets ar. *Crest*— On a staff raguly a squirrel cracking a nut, from the dexter end of the staff an oak branch fructed all ppr.

Lee (Coton, co. Salop, a branch of LEE, Bart., of Langley). Same *Arms*, &c.

Lee (Fitchworth, co. Sussex). Az. a lion ramp. guard. ar. *Crest*—A stag's head erased or.

Lee (Lee, co. Sussex). Same *Arms*, lion or, tail forked.

Lee, or Lea (co. Wilts). Or on a chief embattled sa. three plates.

Lee (granted to ROBERT COOPER LEE BEVAN, Esq., of Fosbury, co. Wilts, as a descendant and representative of ROBERT COOPER LEE, of Bedford Square, co. Middlesex, to be borne as a quartering with his paternal arms). Az. three bars engr. or, a bend lozengy ar. and gu.

Lee. Ar. a cross betw. four fleurs-de-lis sa. *Crest*—Out of a ducal coronet a ram's head issuing, in the mouth a branch all ppr.

594

Lee. Or, on a chev. sa. three lions ramp. ar.

Lee. Sa. a lion pass. ar. crowned or.

Lee. Ar. on a fesse az. betw. three unicorns' heads erased sa. as many leopards' faces or.

Lee. Ar. a scythe, handle sa. the blade upwards ppr.

Lee (confirmed to JOHN LEE, Esq., M.D., of Tralee, co. Kerry, by Hawkins, Ulster, 1785). Ar. a chev. engr. betw. three leopards' faces sa. *Crest*—On a ducal coronet or, a lion ramp. sa. holding in the dexter paw a sword ppr. pommel and hilt gold. *Motto*—Fide et fortitudine.

Lee (granted by Betham, Ulster, to Rear-Admiral RICHARD LEE, only son of JOHN LEE, of Londonderry, formerly of Patna, East Indies). Ar. a lion ramp. gu. navally crowned az. on a canton of the last pendent by a ribbon ar. fimbriated of the canton a representation of the golden medal presented by George III. to Rear-Admiral LEE for his services as Capt. of the *Courageux*, off Cape Ortegall, 1805). *Crest*—A demi lion ramp. erminois, navally crowned az. holding betw. the paws a sceptre sa. *Motto*—Courageux.

Lee (Barna, co. Tipperary). Ar. a fesse betw. three crescents sa. *Crest*—On a column ar. encircled with a ducal coronet or, a falcon close ppr. standing on a bird's leg az, erased gu. *Motto*—Fide et constantia.

Lee (DILLON-LEE, *Viscount Dillon*). See DILLON.

Lee-Norman. See NORMAN.

Lee (Sir THEOPHILUS LEE, Knt., whose grandfather assumed the surname of M'CLELLAN, in addition to that of LEE. Paternally, Sir THEOPHILUS LEE derived from M'CLELLAN, *Lord Kirkcudbright*). Quarterly, 1st and 4th, az. a fesse of Lee and Darnhall; 2nd and 3rd, or, two chev. sa., for M'CLELLAN. *Crests*—1st, on a ducal coronet or, a leopard's face sa.; 2nd: a cubit arm erect ppr. holding a sword also ppr. hilt and pommel or, on the point a Moor's head. *Motto*—Dum spiro spero.

Lee (Dr. JAMES LEE, Scotland and Calcutta, 1868). Gu. a fess chequy ar. and sa. betw. three billets in chief and a crescent in base or. *Crest*—The upper part of a column, thereon a falcon preying on a heron's leg erased ar. *Motto*—Fide et constantia.

Leech (cos. Lincoln, Kent, and Surrey). Erm. on a chief dancettée gu. three ducal coronets or.

Leech (city of Chester, 1613). Same *Arms*, a mullet charged with a crescent for diff.

Leech (confirmed to Rev. JOHN LEECH, M.A., Chaplain of Kingston College, Mitchelstown, co. Cork, grandson of JOHN LEECH, of Rathroan, co. Mayo, and of Dublin, Deputy Governor of Sligo, and to the descendants of his said grandfather). Erm. a trefoil vert, on a chief intended gu. three ducal coronets or. *Crest*—Out of a ducal coronet or, charged with a trefoil vert, an arm erect ppr. grasping a snake environed about the arm also vert. *Motto*—Virtute et valore.

Leech (Nestaling, Scotland). Ar. a fesse fusily sa.

Leech (Scotland). Ar. a fesse wavy sa.

Leechford. Sa. a chev. betw. three leopards' faces ar.

Leechford. Ermines a chev. betw. three leopards' faces ar.

Leechford (Shelwood, co. Surrey; confirmed by William Segar, Garter, 22 Nov. 1604). Sa. a chev. betw. three lions' faces ar. *Crest*—A unicorn's head erased ar. maned, bearded, and horned or, bearing on the horn a serpent twined ppr.

Leechman, or Leeshman (Scotland). Gu. three pelicans ar. *Crest*—A pelican ppr. *Motto*—Industriæ munus.

Lee, or Leeds, (co. Berks, Molscroft, co. Lincoln, Lincoln's Inn, co. Middlesex, and North Milford, co. York). Ar. a fesse gu. betw. three eagles displ. sa. *Crest*—On a staff raguly vert a cockatrice. wings endorsed or, combed and wattled gu.

Leeds (Croxton Park, co. Cambridge, bart.). Same *Arms*, a bordure wavy of the second. *Crest*—A staff raguly fesseways vert, thereon a cock gu. wings expanded. *Motto*— Vigilate.

Leedes (co. York). Ar. a fesse betw. three eagles displ. gu.

Leeds, Duke of. See OSBORNE.

Leeds, Town of (Town seal, 1662). Az. a fleece or, on a chief of the last three mullets az. *Crest*—An owl ppr. *Supporters*—Two owls ducally crowned.

Leeds, Priory of (co. Kent). Or, a cross voided gu.

Leegh (quartered by ROUSE, of co. Devon. Visit. Devon, 1620). Or, on a bend gu. a fish naiant ar.

Leek. Az. on a saltire engr. sa. nine annulets of the first. *Crest*—A demi lion guard. holding a fleur-de-lis.

Leeke (Longford, co. Salop; descended from RALPH LEEKE, Esq., of Ludlow, same co. 1334). Ar. on a chief gu. a fleur-de-lis or, over all a bend engr. az. *Crest*—A human leg

couped at the thigh ar. charged with two fleurs-de-lis. *Motto*
—Agendo gnaviter.

Leeke (Newark-on-Trent, co. Nottingham). Ar. on a saltire engr. sa. nine annulets or. *Crest*—A peacock's tail erect, the plume displ. ppr. supported by two eagles with wings expanded ar.

Leeke (Hallom, co. Nottingham; WILLIAM LEEKE, Visit. Notts, 1614, great-grandson of JOHN LEEKE, Esq., eldest son of WILLIAM LEEKE, Esq., *d.* 1493, both of same place). Ar. on a saltire engr. sa. five annulets or, quartering COOPER and SMITH.

Leeke (Normanton, co. Nottingham; WILLIAM LEEKE, Visit. Notts, 1614, son of WILLIAM LEEKE the elder, son of ALEXANDER LEEKE, second son of WILLIAM LEEKE, Esq., of Hallom, *d.* 1493). Same *Arms*, without the quarterings.

Leeke (Balderton, co. Nottingham; JAMES LEEKE, Visit. Notts, 1614, grandson of THOMAS LEEKE, second son of ALEXANDER LEEKE, the second son of WILLIAM LEEKE, Esq., of Hallom, *d.* 1493). Same *Arms*.

Leeke (co. Leicester). Per pale gu. and sa. a lion ramp. ar.

Leeke (Edmonton, co. Middlesex). Or, on a saltire sa. five annulets of the field. *Crest*—A human leg couped at the thigh ar. gartered below the knee az.

Leeke (Gray's Inn, co. Middlesex; descended from co. Salop). Ar. a chief gu. over all a bend engr. az. a fleur-de-lis in the sinister corner of the chief or, for diff. *Crest*—A human leg. ar. couped at the thigh, gartered az. passing through several blades of grass vert.

Leeks. Gu. two bars betw. six martlets or. *Crest*—A tree ppr.

Leeme (*temp.* Edward II.). Or, a saltire engr. vert.

Lees. (Lees, co. Lancaster). Sa. three bars ar.

Lees (granted to JOHN FREDERICK LEES, Esq., of Werneth, Oldham, co. Lancaster). Per fesse or and gu. a fesse dovetail per fesse embattled betw. two falcons belled in chief and a lion ramp. in base all counterchanged. *Crest*—A lion ramp. gu. supporting a flag of the arms, the staff entwined by a wreath of oak fructed ppr.

Lees (Blackrock, co. Dublin, bart.). Az. a fesse chequy ar. and sa. betw. six cross crosslets fitchée, three in the chief and three in the nombril points or, and three billets, two in the honor and one in the base points of the second. *Crest*—A dexter hand couped above the wrist and erect ppr. grasping a crescent or. *Motto*—Exegi.

Lees (Scotland). Gu. a fesse chequy ar. and sa. betw. nine billets, three, two, three, and one, of the second.

Leeson (*Earl of Milltown*). Gu. a chief ar. on the lower part a cloud, the rays of the sun issuing therefrom ppr. *Crest*—A demi lion ramp. gu. holding betw. the paws the sun or. *Supporters*—Dexter, a horse; sinister, a talbot both ar. *Motto*—Clarior e tenebris.

Leeson (Whitfield, co. Northampton). Gu. rays of the sun or, issuing from a chief nebulée ar.

Leeson (co. Northampton). Ar. a cross sa. guttée d'or.

Leet (Eversden and Kingston), co. Cambridge, and Southoe, co. Huntingdon). Ar. a fesse gu. betw. two rolls of matches sa. kindled ppr. *Crest*—On a ducal coronet an antique lamp or, fire ppr.

Leete (Bury St. Edmunds, co. Suffolk). Same *Arms*, a martlet for diff. *Crest*—A demi bull issuing gu. gorged with a chaplet of laurel vert.

Leeth. Ar. on a bend betw. three fleurs-de-lis az. as many mullets or, a bordure wavy gu. *Crest*—A demi griffin segreant gu. winged az. charged on the body with two fleurs-de-lis or.

Leeves (Tortington, co. Sussex; granted 1738, to WILLIAM LEEVES, of Tortington Place, and examplified 1839, to WILLIAM FOWLER (fourth son of THOMAS FOWLER, Esq., of Walburton, by MARY, his wife, dau. of RICHARD LEEVES, Esq.) on his taking the name of LEEVES). Gu. a fesse dancettée erminois betw. three garbs or. *Crest*—On a mount vert a swan ar. wings elevated, ducally crowned or, gorged with a ducal coronet, thereto a chain reflexed over the back gold, charged on the breast with three pellets, two and one, beaked and numbered sa.

Leeys. Sa. on a chev. betw. three lilies or, two scythes, blades crossing each other at the points az.

Le Febvre (Guernsey). Az. a fleur-de-lis in chief, and in base two mullets pierced or (another, az. a greyhound springing ar. collared gu. garnished or, in chief a label of three points of the second).

Le Febvre (Seigneur of Vinchelez-de-Bois, Jersey, 1393). Gu. three escallops or, in chief a label of three points ar. *Crest*—An escallop or.

Le Feuvre (St. Peter, Jersey). Ar. a chev. gu. betw. three mullets pierced **sa.** *Crest*—A triple-eared stem of corn ppr.

595

Le Feuvre (Jersey and Southampton). Ar. a chev. gu. betw. three mullets pierced sa. a bordure of the last. *Crest*—A lion pass. couchant, cowarded ppr. *Motto*—Toujours.

Lefever, or Lefevre. Az. a pile erm. betw. three cinquefoils or. *Crest*—The trunk of a tree couped and eradicated in fesse, betw. the branches a fleur-de-lis.

Lefevre (Stepney, co. Middlesex). Sa. a chev. betw. three trefoils in chief and an orb and cross in base all or. *Crest*—A trefoil or.

Lefevre (granted 7 July, 1789, to JOHN LEFEVRE, Esq. of Old Ford, co. Middlesex). Sa. a chev. ar. betw. two trefoils slipped in chief or, and in base a bezant, therefrom issuant a cross pattée of one third. *Crest*—Six arrows interlaced saltirewise, three and three ppr. within an annulet or.

Lefevre (SHAW-LEFEVRE; exemplified to Right Hon. CHARLES SHAW-LEFEVRE, of Heckfield, co. Hants, Speaker of the House of Commons, son of CHARLES SHAW, Esq., who, on his marriage with HELENE LEFEVRE, assumed the name and arms of that family). Quarterly, 1st and 4th, sa. a chev. ar. betw. two trefoils slipped in chief or, and in base a bezant, therefrom issuant a cross pattée of the third, for LEFEVRE; 2nd and 3rd, sa. a chev. erm. on a canton or, a talbot's head erased gu., for SHAW. *Crest*—Six arrows interlaced saltireways, three and three ppr. within an annulet or. *Motto*—Sans changer.

Lefevre (*Viscount Eversley ;* the foregoing Right Hon. CHARLES SHAW LEFEVRE, Speaker to the House of Commons for 18 years, was so created 1857). Sa. a chev. ar. betw. two trefoils slipped in chief or, and a bezant in base, therefrom issuant a cross pattée of the third. *Crest*—Six arrows interlaced saltirewise, three and three ppr. within an annulet or. *Supporters*—On either side a talbot, that on the dexter gu., on the sinister sa., each charged on the shoulder with a mace erect gold. *Motto*—Sans changer.

Lefevre (co. Southampton). Ar. two bars gu. in chief three cinquefoils sa. *Crest*—A lion couchant, tail extended or.

Lefevre. Az. a fleur-de-lis and a mullet or, in pale.

Lefitz. Vair on a chief gu. two mullets ar.

Le Forest. Ar. a chief sa. *Crest*—A unicorn sejant ar. armed, crined, and tufted or.

Lefroy (confirmed to Right Hon. THOMAS LANGLOIS LEFROY, of Carrickglass, co. Longford, Lord Chief Justice of Ireland, eldest son of ANTHONY LEFROY, Esq., Lieut.-Col. 9th Dragoons, and grandson of ANTHONY LEFROY, Esq. of Leghorn, by ELIZABETH, his wife, sister of BENJAMIN LANGLOIS, Esq., M.P., former Under Secretary of State, and the descendants of his grandfather. Quarterly' 1st and 4th, vert fretty of eight pieces ar. on a chief of the second a hood or cap (allusive to the badge assumed by the party opposed to the *Duke of Alva*) betw. two wyverns gu., for LEFROY ; 2nd and 3rd, az. a chev. or, betw. three crescents ar. on a chief gu. three mullets of the third, for LANGLOIS. *Crest*—A demi wyvern gu. langued and armed az. *Motto*—Mutare sperno.

Lefroy (Ewshot House, co. Hants). Same *Arms*, *Crest* and *Motto*.

Lefroy (Westham, near Basingstoke; borne by CHRISTOPHER EDWARD LEFROY, formerly for ten years British Commissary Judge at Surinam for the suppression of the slave trade, brother of the late Rev. JOHN HENRY GEORGE LEFROY, of Ewshot House). Same *Arms*, *Crest* and *Motto*.

Leftwich (Leftwich, co. Chester ; descended from ROBERT DE WYNINGTON, son of LYUPH DE TWEMLOWE, who m. MATILDA; dau. of Sir RICHARD DE WILBRAHAM, and his wife, MATILDA, dau. and co-heir of WARIN VERNON, *Baron of Shipbrook*. The son of ROBERT DE WYNINGTON and MATILDA, RICHARD, took the name of LEFTWICH In 1618, ELIZABETH, dau. and heiress of RALPH LEFTWICH, *m.* WIILLAM OLDFIELD, fourth son of PHILIP OLDFIELD, Esq., of Bradwall). *Ancient Arms*—Ar. an escutcheon voided within an orle of eight martlets sa. within the escutcheon a cross pattée gu. for diff., for WINNINGTON. *Modern Arms*—Ar. on a fesse engr. az. three garbs or. *Crest*—Five leaves conjoined at base vert.

Leftwich (co. Salop). Same *Arms* as the modern in the preceding.

Leg, or Legg. Gu. a cross engr. ar. a bordure of the last. *Crest*—A fountain of three raisings playing ppr.

Le Gallais (Jersey). Gu. a crescent betw. six roses or, three in chief and three in base. *Crest*—A cock statant, the dexter foot uplifted. *Motto*—Jamais chancelant.

Legard (Ganton, co. York, bart.). Ar. on a bend betw. six mullets pierced gu. a cross pattée or. *Crest*—A greyhound or, collared sa. studded ar. *Motto*—Per crucem ad stellas.

Legard (co. Leicester ; CHRISTOPHER LEGARD, Visit. Leicester, 1619, thirteenth in descent from JOHN LEGARD , living *temp.* Henry III.). Same *Arms*, cross or, quartering, 1st, ar. on a bend gu, three crescents of the field ; 2nd, gu. a bend or; and 3rd, ar, three water bougets sa. *Crest*—A greyhound statant, collared or, studded gu.

Legat (Edinburgh). Ar. a cross cavalry on three degrees gu. *Crest*—A cherub ppr. *Motto*—Jesus hominum salvator.

Legat (cos. Essex, Kent, and Norfolk). Erm. a lion ramp. gu. *Crest*—Two lions' gambs erect gu. supporting a mitre or.

Legat, or Legethe (co. Norfolk). Ar. on a saltire engr. az. an escallop or.

Legat (Pondhall, co. Suffolk, *temp.* Henry IV., represented by D'OYLY, of Shottisham, co. Norfolk, and the East Indies). Ar. a saltire engr. az.

Legatt (Hornchurch, co. Essex). Per. chev. engr. sa. and ar. three greyhounds' heads erased and counterchanged, collared gu. *Crest*—A sea-lion sejant ar.

Legborne (Legborne, co. Notts, *temp.* Edward II.; the heiress *m.* JOHN ATWELL. Visit. Notts, 1614). Sa. two lions' gambs erased in saltire ar.

Legborne (co. Lincoln). Sa. two lions' gambs erased in saltire ar.

Legcroft. Az. a saltire erm. over all a cross gu.

Legeard (co. York). Lozengy or and az. a chev. gu.

Legem. Az. a fesse engr. or, betw. three women's heads couped ppr. crined of the second.

Leger. Per fesse or and az. three lions' heads erased countercharged. *Crest*—A pheon with a piece of the shaft sticking therein.

Legett. Erm. a lion ramp. gu. *Crest*—Two lions' paws supporting the royal crown all ppr.

Le Geyt (Jersey). Erm. a lion ramp. gu. *Crest*—A lion's head couped ppr. *Motto*—Quo fata vocant.

Legg (London). Barry wavy of ten or and az. three torteaux, in chief as many fleurs-de-lis gu.

Legg. Gu. a cross engr. ar. a bordure of the last.

Legg (ROWAN-LEGG; exemplified to WILLIAM ROWAN, Esq., of Carrickfergus, on his assuming by royal licence, 1864, the additional surname of LEGG). Quarterly, 1st and 4th, per pale az. and gu. a stag's head cabossed ar. in the centre chief point a mullet or, for LEGG ; 2nd and 3rd, a vert fess chequy or and gu. betw. a trefoil slipped in chief, and in base three cross crosslets fitchée issuant from as many crescents of the second, for ROWAN. *Crests*—1st, LEGG: Out of a mural crown ppr. five ostrich feathers, alternately ar. and az. the centre feather charged with a mullet gu., motto over, Cresco per crucem ; 2nd, ROWAN: A dexter hand and arm couped at the elbow ppr. grasping a dagger also ppr. *Motto*—Gaudet tentamine virtus.

Leggat, or Leggatt (England). Quarterly, ar. and or. a saltire gu. *Crest*—An arm erect couped at the elbow, vested counter-componée gu. and or, holding a millrind sa.

Legge (*Earl of Dartmouth*). Az. a buck's head cabossed ar. *Crest*—Out of a ducal coronet or, a plume of five ostrich feathers, three ar. two az. *Supporters*—Dexter a lion ar. semée-de-lis sa. ducally crowned or, issuing thereout five ostrich feathers, as in the crest; sinister, a buck ar. semée of mullets sa. *Motto*—Gaudet tentamine virtus.

Legge (*Baron Stawell*; extinct 1820). Quarterly, 1st and 4th, same as last; 2nd and 3rd, az. a demi rose ar. on the dexter side impaled with a demi pomegranate on the sinister or, leaved vert. Same *Crest* as last. *Supporters*—Two tigers ar. human faces ppr. armed with satyrs' horns, maned and tufted or. *Motto*—En parole je vis.

Legge (co. Cambridge). Ar. a cross flory sa. *Crest*—A unicorn's head erased ar. crined, armed, and ducally gorged or.

Legge (co. Wilts). Az. a buck's head cabossed ar. an annulet for diff.

Legge (co Kent; quartered by BEEBEE, of Willey Court. Of this family long seated at Legges, near Tunbridge, was THOMAS LEGGE, Lord Mayor of London in 1345; his descendant, WILLIAM LEGGE, settled in Ireland, and *m.* ANN, dau. of *Lord Athenry*). Or, two lions pass. counter-pass. az. *Crest*—A man's leg couped at the middle of the thigh, standing on a triple tower all ppr.

Legge (Fun. Ent. Ulster's Office, 1607, JOAN, widow of ROBERT LEGGE). Sa. a lion pass. or, armed and langued gu. betw. three torteaux.

Legget (Scotland). Az. on a bend ar. three human hearts gu. on a chief of the second as many martlets sa.

Leggey. Az. a buck's head cabossed and attired or, on a chief ar. five lozenges of the first, all within a bordure of the third.

Leggy (Lord Mayor of London, 1347 and 1354). Ar. a buck's head sa. on a chief gu. three crosses flory or.

Legh (East Hall, High Legh, co. Chester; descended from
596

OSWALD DE LEGA, of East Hall). Ar. a lion ramp. gu. *Crest*—A demi lion ramp. gu. collared or. *Motto*—La vie durante.

Legh (Bechton, co. Chester; son of JOHN LEGH, of Booths; his daus. and co-heirs *m.* FITTON and DAVENPORT). Az. two bars ar. over all on bend gu. three dart heads ar.

Legh (Ridge, co. Chester). Gu. on a cross engr. ar. a mullet sa.

Legh (Knutsford Booths, co. Chester; descended from Sir WILLIAM VENABLES, Knt., of Bradwall (second son of Sir WILLIAM VENABLES, *Baron of Kinderton*) who was living A.D. 1300, and husband to AGNES, dau. and heiress of RICHARD DE LEGH, of West Hall, in High Legh. Their son, JOHN DE LEGH, purchased Knutsford Booths before 28 Edward I. From this family descend LEGH, of Isall; LEGH, of Bechton; TOWNELEY, of Towneley ; LEGH, of Adlington, Annesley, Eggington, Lyme, Birch, Ridge, Rushall, Longborow, Adelstrop, Stoneleigh, Newnham Regis, Stockwell; LEGH, of Baggilegh, ; RADCLIFFE, of Ordsall; and SHAKERLEY. The last heiress, RUTH, who *d.* 1715-16, *m.* THOMAS PENINGTON, of Chester, whose son assumed the name of LEGH). Az. two bars ar. over all a bend gu. *Crest*—An arm embowed, couped at the shoulder, vested gu. hand ppr. holding a sword erect ppr. a snake twisting round the same ar.

Legh (now of Norbury Booths Hall and Knutsford Booths, co. Chester; THOMAS PENNINGTON, Esq., son of THOMAS PENNINGTON and RUTH LEGH, as above, assumed the surname and arms of LEGH). Az. two bars ar. over all a bend gu. *Crest*—An arm embowed, couped at the shoulder, vested gu. hand ppr. holding a sword erect also ppr. a snake twisting round the same ar. *Motto*—Prudens, fidelis et audax.

Legh (Adlington, co. Chester; derived from ROBERT DE LEGH, second son of JOHN LEGH, Esq., of Booths, by ELLEN, his wife, dau. and heiress of THOMAS DE CORONA, of Adlington). Az. two bars ar. over all a bend componée gu. and or. *Crest*—A unicorn's head couped ar. maned and armed or, on the neck a cross patonce gu. The LEGHS of Adlington bore anciently the coat of CORONA of Adlington, differenced, viz., az. within a border ar. three ducal coronets or, in the centre point a plate.

Legh (Baguleigh, or Baggiley, co. Chester). Az. two bars ar. over all a bend sa. *Crest*—On a wreath a bear pass. chained or.

Legh (GERARD LEGH, author of the "Accedence of Armorie," who *d.* 1563; descended from an illegitimate son of RANDAL LEGH, second son of Sir EDMUND LEGH, of Bagulegh, co. Chester). Quarterly, 1st, LEGH, of Bagulegh, az. a bend sa. surmounted by two bars ar. (in his father's arms the bend was placed over the bars); 2nd, BAGULEGH, or, three lozenges az. ; 3rd, DE CORONA, erm. a fesse gu. on a chief indented of the second three crowns or; 4th, LEVENSHULME, ar. a fleur-de-lis sa. over all a label of three points gu. *Crest*—A bear pass. ppr. chained or.

Legh (Bruche, near Warrington, co. Lancaster, 1664 and 1727). Az. two bars ar. a bend gobony or and gu. and sometimes three crowns in chief or.

Legh (Lyme, co. Chester ; derived from Sir PETER LEGH, of Lyme, Knight Banneret, who died of wounds received at Agincourt, eldest son of Sir PIERS LEGH, Knt., younger son of ROBERT LEGH, of Adlington, *d temp.* Richard II. The last male heir, Colonel THOMAS PETER LEGH, of Lyme, *d. unm.* in 1797. Colonel LEGH's sister and heiress in blood, MARTHA AMIE LEGH, *m.* LAWRENCE ORMEROD, Esq., of Ormerod). Gu. a cross engr. ar. *Crest*—Out of a ducal coronet or, a ram's head ar. attired of the first, in the mouth a laurel sprig vert.

Legh (now of Lyme, co. Chester). The following grants of the arms, each bearing a varied difference, were given to THOMAS LEGH, Esq. : gu. a cross engr. ar. in the chief point on an inescutcheon sa. samée of estoiles ar. an arm in armour embowed of the second, the hand ppr. holding a pennon silver, the whole within a bordure wavy ar. ; to WILLIAM LEGH, his next brother, the same within a bordure wavy or; to PETER, his youngest other, the same within a bordure erm. ; to MARIA, elde sister, the same within a bordure ar. charged with four roses gu. ; to MARGARET, second sister, the same within a bordure ar. charged with four trefoils vert; to EMMA, third sister, the same within a bordure ar. charged with four quatrefoils gu. ; to MARY, fourth sister, the same within a bordure ar. charged with four cinquefoils az. *Crest*—Issuant out of a ducal coronet or, a ram's head ar. armed or, in the mouth a laurel slip vert, over all a pallet wavy gu. ; to WILLIAM, the same, with the pallet az. ; to PETER, the same, with the pallet vert.

Legh (The Limes, Lewisham, co. Kent; representative of the LEGHS of Ridge, co. Chester, derived from JOHN LEGH,

Escheator of co. Chester, 12 Henry VI., second son of Sir PIERS LEGH, of Lyme). Same *Arms* as LEGH, of Lyme.

Legh (afterwards MACCLESFIELD, of Macclesfield, co. Chester). Gu. a cross engr. erm.

Legh (Preston, co. Lancaster, 1664). Gu. a cross engr. ar. a canton or. *Crest*—Out of a ducal coronet or, a ram's head ar. holding a sprig of laurel vert, charged on the neck with a trefoil gu.

Legh (co. Cumberland). Ar. a fesse sa. in chief three mullets of the second.

Legh (co. Devon, and Wells, co. Somerset). Ar. on a chev. gu. three martlets or, on a chief of the second a culverin dismounted of the third. *Crest*—A demi hound sa. holding a stag's head ar. attired or.

Legh, or Leigh. Gu. on a cross engr. ar. betw. four lions' heads erased or, five hurts.

Legh, or Leigh. Erm. on a chev. sa. three bezants.

Legham, or Leigham (co. Berks). Sa. six fleurs-de-lis or, three, two, and one. *Crest*—An arm couped at the shoulder, the part above the elbow in fesse, the hand erect holding a bombshell fired ppr.

Legham, or Leigham. Gu. a swan ar. membered or.

Legide. Az. three fleurs-de-lis or, over all a bendlet gu.

Legoos (Crostwight, co. Norfolk). Quarterly, ar. and az. on a bend sa. three martlets or.

Legot, or Lazor (Lord Mayor of London, 1345). Erm. a lion ramp. sa.

Legrand. Ar. a bend betw. four mullets gu. within a bordure gobonated of the first and az.

Le Grice (Treriefe, co. Cornwall). Quarterly, gu. and az. on a bend ar. three boars pass. sa. *Crest*—A boar pass. sa. collared or.

Le Grice, or Le Grys (co. Norfolk). Quarterly, az. and gu. on a bend ar. three boars pass sa. *Crest*—A boar sa. armed or.

Le Gros (Scoley, co. Norfolk, 1440, and co. Suffolk). Quarterly ar. and az. on a bend sa. three martlets (another, mullets) or.

Le Gros (Greffier of Jersey, 1875). Az. three lions ramp. or, a chief ar. *Crest*—A dexter arm embowed ppr. vested gu. holding by the blade a sword, point downwards ar. hilted or. *Motto*—In Deo confido.

Legros. Gu. a cross patonce vair.

Legryle (Brockdish, co. Norfolk). Quarterly, gu. and az. (another az. and or.) on a bend ar. three boars sa. *Crest*—A boar pass. sa.

Leguard. Ar. on a bend betw. six mullets gu. a cross pattée or. *Crest*—A greyhound statant or, collared and ringed gu.

Le Hardy (St. Peter, Jersey). Sa. on a chev. betw. three escallops or, as many griffins' heads of the field. *Crest*—A dexter arm embowed in armour ppr. garnished or, holding a griffin's head, as in the arms, motto over, Le hardy ne querre pas querelle. *Motto*—Sic Donec.

Le Hert (WALTER LE HERT, Bishop of Norwich ; arms in the Divinity School, Oxford. Visit. Oxon, 1566). Ar. a bull pass. sa. armed or, a border of the second bezantée.

Lehoop, or Lehook (London). Sa. a chev. erm. betw. three beehives ppr.

Lehoop. Gu. three beehives betw. nine bees volant or. *Crest*—A rose ppr.

Le Hunt (BAINBRIGGE-LE HUNT ; PETER BAINBRIGGE, Esq., of Burgh, co. Lincoln, and Ashbourn, co. Derby, fourth in descent from WILLIAM BAINBRIGGE, Esq., of Lockington, co. Lincoln, assumed the additional surname and arms of LE HUNT. by royal licence, 1832). Quarterly, 1st and 4th, az. a bend betw. six leopards' faces or, on a canton of the first a gauntlet of the second, for LE HUNT ; 2nd and 3rd, az. a chev. embattled betw. three battle axes sa., for BAINBRIGGE ; quartering PARKER, gu. a chev. betw. three leopards' faces or. *Crest*—On a hill vert a goat sa. collared, horned, and hoofed ar. *Motto*—Deus mihi providebit.

Le Hunte (Little Bradley, co. Suffolk, and Huntshall, co. Essex). Vert a saltire ar. *Crest*—Out of a baron's coronet or, pearls ar. a dexter hand holding a cutlass all ppr.

Le Hunte (Artramont, co. Wexford ; descended from Col. RICHARD LE HUNTE, M.P. for Cashell in 1661, Captain of Cromwell's Guard, youngest son of Sir GEORGE LE HUNTE, Knt., of Little Bradley, Sheriff of Suffolk in 1610). Same *Arms*. *Crest*—A lion sejant ar. *Motto*—Parcere prostratis.

Leiborne. Or, six lions ramp. sa. (another, az. five lions ramp. ar. a canton erm. ; another, az. six lions ramp. or ; another, within a bordure or).

Leicester, Borough of (the arms and town seals of the borough confirmed and enlarged by James I., to NICHOLAS GILBERT, Mayor. Visit. 1619). A cinquefoil pierced erm. quartering the arms of England, a label of three points, the

shield surmounted by a ducal coronet. *Crest*—A dragon wings displ. and tail nowed erm. *Seals*, five in number, viz. : 1st: A cinquefoil pierced erm. with the legend "Sigillum : Communitatis : Leyrcestrie : " 2nd : Issuant from clouds a sheaf of three arrows, points downwards, one in pale and two in saltire, on the dexter side a scroll, thereon inscribed " In anti trinitarios," on the sinister a cinquefoil pierced erm., legend, "Sigill. : hospitalis : s'etæ : trinitatis : in : novo : opere ; " 3rd : A cinquefoil pierced erm., legend, "Sigillum : Statut : Burgi : Llicestrie ; " 4th : A cinquefoil pierced erm., legend, " Villa. Leic. Tarlat. ; " 5th : The Virgin crowned, holding a sceptre in the dexter hand and a naked child in the sinister seated under a canopy with finals below them, on a small shield a cinquefoil pierced erm., legend, "Sigill ; Mioratus. Viste : Leicestre."

Leicester, Earl of. See COKE.

Leicester (Tabley, co. Chester, bart., extinct 1742 ; MERIEL LEICESTER, only dau. and heir of Sir FRANCIS LEICESTER, third and last bart. of Tabley, m. as her 2nd husband, Sir JOHN BYRNE, Bart., of Timogue, Queen's co., and her son, Sir PETER BYRNE, assumed the name and arms of LEICESTER, and was father of the first *Lord de Tabley*). Az. a fess betw. three fleurs-de-lis or.

Leicester (*Lord de Tabley*). Same *Arms*. *Crest*—A swan's head and neck couped ar. guttée de sang. *Supporters*—Dexter, a bay horse caparisoned ppr. collared and chained or, supporting a standard of the King's Regiment of Chester Yeomanry, viz., gu. charged with the letters K. Ry. C. Yy. and fringed or ; sinister, a swan ar. guttée de sang, charged on the body with five fleurs-de-lis in saltire ar. *Motto*—Tu domine gloria mea (another, Pro rege et patriâ). See also WARREN, *Lord de Tabley*.

Leicester. Same *Arms*, a bordure ar.

Leicester. Per pale indented ar. and gu.

Leicester. Bendy sa. and or.

Leicester, Earls of (ROBERT DE BELLAMONT, or BEAUMONT, so created by Charter 1103, extinct 1204). Gu. a cinquefoil erm.

Leicester (Westbury, co. Salop). Quarterly, 1st and 4th, az. a fesse betw. three fleurs-de-lis or ; 2nd and 3rd, gu. a fret or. *Crest*—A swan's head ar. guttée de sang.

Leicester College (Newark, co. Nottingham). Gu. three lions pass. guard. or, overall a label of three points throughout ar. charged with nine fleurs-de-lis.

Leicester (Toft, co. Chester ; impalement Fun. Ent. Ulster's Office, 1633, Sir BASIL BROOKE, Knt., of Donegal, whose wife was ANNE, dau. of THOMAS LEICESTER, Esq.). Az. a fess betw. three fleurs-de-lis or.

Leicester (Kilcarmick, King's co. ; Fun. Ent. Ulster's Office, 1684, JOHN LEICESTER). Same *Arms*.

Leich (Scotland). Ar. a fesse wavy sa.

Leich (Grafton). Erm. on a chief indented gu. three crowns or.

Leids. Ar. a fesse gu. betw. three eagles close sa. *Crest*—An Eagle's head gu. betw. two wings or.

Leigh (*Baron Leigh*, created 1839 ; descended from ROWLAND LEIGH, Esq., of Adlestrop, co. Gloucester, eldest son of Sir THOMAS LEIGH, Knt., Lord Mayor of London, 1558). Gu. a cross engr. ar. in the 1st quarter a lozenge of the second. *Crest*—A unicorn's head erased ar. armed and crined or. *Supporters*—On either side a unicorn ar. armed, maned, tufted, and unguled or, gorged with a ducal coronet gu. pendent therefrom an escutcheon charged with the arms of BRYDGES, viz., ar. a cross sa. thereon a leopard's face or. *Motto*—Tout vient de Dieu.

Leigh (*Baron Leigh*, of Stoncleigh, extinct 1806; created 1643 ; descended from Sir THOMAS LEIGH, Bart., of Stoneleigh, second son of Sir THOMAS LEIGH, Knt., Lord Mayor of London, 1558). Gu. a cross engr. ar. in the 1st quarter a lozenge of the second. *Crest*—A unicorn's head erased ar. armed and crined or. *Supporters*—On either side a unicorn ar. armed, maned, tufted, and unguled or. *Motto*—Tout vient de Dieu.

Leigh (*Earl of Chichester*, extinct 1667 ; descended from Sir WILLIAM LEIGH, Knt., of Newnham Regis, co. Warwick, third son of Sir THOMAS LEIGH, Knt., Lord Mayor of London, 1558). Gu. a cross engr. ar. in the 1st quarter a lozenge of the second.

Leigh (Charlestown, South Carolina, bart.). Or, a lion ramp. gu. *Crest*—A cubit arm erect habited, grasping a tilting spear in fesse all ppr.

Leigh (Whitley, co. Lancaster, bart.). Gu. a cross engr. ar. betw. four lozenges erm. *Crest*—A demi lion ramp. gu. holding a lozenge erm.

Leigh (West Hall, in High Leigh, co. Chester ; descended from THOMAS DE LEIGH, of the West Hall, Lord of a moiety of Lymme in 1305, eldest son of RICHARD DE LYMME, by

AGNES, his wife, dau. and heir of RICHARD DE LEIGH). Or, a lion ramp. gu. *Crest*—A cubit arm, vested paly of five pieces or and sa. cuffed ar. hand ppr. grasping the upper and lower fragments of a broken tilting spear, point downwards. *Another Crest*—A demi lion ramp. or, holding a pennon displ. az. charged with two bars or, inscribed "Force avec vertue;" and with a shield of the arms of LEIGH, of West Hall, in High Leigh, co. Chester, on which are three escutcheons of pretence, with the arms of the three husbands of AGNES DE LEIGH, of West Hall, &c., viz., LYMME, VENABLES, and HAYWARDEN.

Leigh (Oughtrington, co. Chester; a branch of LEIGH, of the West Hall, in High Leigh). Quarterly, 1st and 4th, or, a lion ramp. gu.; 2nd and 3rd, ar. a bend lozengy sa. *Crest*—A cubit arm erect, vested paly of six or and sa. cuff ar. holding in the hand ppr. a broken tilting spear of the third.

Leigh (Hindley Hall, co. Lancaster, bart., extinct 1843; ROBERT HOLT LEIGH, Esq., M.P. for Wigan, son of HOLT LEIGH, Esq., of Whitley Hall, by his wife, MARY, dau. and co-heir of THOMAS OWEN, Esq., of Bispham, was created a bart. 1815, d. *unm.* 21 Jan. 1843. His estates devolved on his nephew, the Right Hon. THOMAS PEMBERTON, Chancellor of the Duchy of Cornwall, who assumed the surname of LEIGH, and was created, 1858, *Lord Kingsdown*). Gu. a cross engr. ar. betw. four lozenges erm. *Crest*—A demi lion ramp. holding in the paws a lozenge ar. charged with a rose of York and Lancaster.

Leigh (PEMBERTON-LEIGH, *Lord Kingsdown*, extinct 1867). Quarterly, 1st and 4th, gu. a cross engr. ar. betw. four lozenges erm., for LEIGH; 2nd and 3rd, erm. an estoile or, betw. three buckets sa. hoops and handles gold, for PEMBERTON. *Crests*—1st, LEIGH : A demi lion ramp. gu. holding in the paw a lozenge ar. charged with a rose of the first; 2nd : A dragon's head erm. erased gu. ducally gorged or, and transfixed by an arrow fessways ppr. *Supporters*—Dexter, a lion gu. charged on the shoulder with a lozenge ar. thereon a rose of the first; sinister, a wyvern erm. ducally gorged or, and charged on the shoulder with an estoile gu. *Motto*—Ut tibi sic alteri.

Leigh (Standishgate, near Wigan, co. Lancaster; granted to RICHARD LEIGH, Esq.). Ar. two bars az. a saltire betw. two mascles in pale and as many lozenges in fesse gu. *Crest*—A cubit arm erect, grasping a serpent entwined about the arm ppr. betw. two antlers gu. *Motto*—Hæc manus inimica tyrannis.

Leigh, or Lee (Abingdon, co. Berks, and co. Derby). Az. three ducal crowns or, within a bordure ar. *Crest*—An armed man couped at the shoulder or, enwrapped with a scarf az. grasping a halbert ppr.

Leigh (co. Chester). Az. platée three ducal crowns or.

Leigh (co. Chester). Ar. a cross fiory sa

Leigh, or Lee (co. Cumberland). Erm. three bezants.

Leigh (cos. Cumberland and Lancaster). Erm. on a chev. sa. three bezants (another, plates).

Leigh (co Derby). Az. a plate betw. three ducal crowns or.

Leigh (Eggington, co. Derby; the heiress *m.* EVERY). Same *Arms*, a bordure ar. *Crest*—A unicorn's head ar. crined or, armed gobony gu. and gold. *Another Crest*—An armed arm couped at the shoulder or, enwrapped with a scarf az. grasping a halbert ppr.

Leigh (Borough of Northam, co. Devon; derived from LEIGH, of High Leigh; the co-heiresses *m.* BASSET and BURY). Ar. a lion ramp. gu. on a sinister canton of the second an escallop or. *Crest*—A demi lion ramp. erminois holding an escallop ar.

Leigh (Clinkford, co Essex). Ar. a fesse sa. in chief two pellets, in base a martlet of the second.

Leigh (Northcourt, Isle of Wight; descended from Sir JOHN LEIGH, Knt., of Northcourt, in Shorwell, living 1619, son of BARNABAS LEIGH, Esq., of Stoke, co. Somerset; the daus. and co-heirs of the last JOHN LEIGH. Esq., of Northcourt, were AMELIA, *m.* first, General THOMAS GOLDIE, and secondly, the Rev. DAVID LLOYD, Chaplain to Greenwich Hospital; CATHERINE, *m.* CHALONER ARCEDECKNE, Esq., of Glevering Hall, co. Suffolk; JOHANNA, *m.* first, RICHARD BENNETT LLOYD, Esq., and, secondly, FRANCIS LLOYD LEIGH, Esq., of Basing Park, co. Hants; ELIZABETH, *m.* ALEXANDER STEWART, Esq. : and MARY, *m.* JAMES STRACHAN, Esq.). Ar on a chief embattled gu. three plates. *Crest*—A hind pass. ar.

Leigh (Belmont, co. Chester). Gu. a cross engr. ar. in the 1st quarter a lion ramp. or, and in the 2nd a lozenge of the second. *Crest*—A lozenge gu. charged with a unicorn's head ccuped ar. armed and crined or. *Motto*—Leges juraque servo.

Leigh (Woodchester Park, co. Gloucester). Same *Arms* and *Crest*.

Ř98

Leigh, or Lea (Bradley, co. Lancaster). Ar. two bars az. over all a bend gobonated of the second and gu. *Crest*—A dexter arm embowed, vested gu. cuffed ar. holding in the hand ppr. a sword of the second, hilt and pommel or, environed with a snake vert.

Leigh (Barton, co. Lancaster, 1664). Ar. a lion ramp. sa.

Leigh (Singleton Grange, co. Lancaster, 1664). Same *Arms*.

Leigh (Lord Mayor of London, 1602). Ar. a fesse betw. two pellets in chief and a martlet in base sa.

Leigh (Ridware, co. Stafford). Gu. a cross engr. ar. in the dexter canton a lozenge or. *Crest*—A unicorn's head or.

Leigh (granted to ROGER LEIGH, Esq., of Barham Court, co. Kent). Gu. a cross engr. ar. betw. four lozenges erm., for distinction a canton or. *Crest*—A demi lion gu. holding betw. the paws a lozenge ar. charged with a rose gu. and charged on the shoulder for distinction with a cross pattée or.

Leigh (Wells, co. Somerset). Ar. on a chev. gu. three martlets or, on a chief of the second a culverin dismount d of the third. *Crest*—A demi greyhound sa. holding a stag s head cabossed ar.

Leigh (co. Somerset). Or, three fusils az.

Leigh (Rushall, co. Stafford). Gu. a cross engr. ar. in the dexter quarter an escutcheon of the second, charged with two bars az. and a bend of the field. *Crest*—A unicorn's head erased sa. armed or, crined and collared ar.

Leigh (Addington, co. Surrey, 1609). Or, on a chev. sa. three lions ramp. ar. in the dexter quarter an annulet of the second. *Crest*—On a mount vert a lion couchant guard. ar. charged on the breast with an annulet sa.

Leigh (Stockwell, co. Surrey, and Couldray, co. Hants; Derived from LEIGH, of Ridge. Visit. Hants, 1634). Gu. a cross engr. ar. and a bordure also engr. ar. *Crest*—A cockatrice az. combed and wattled gu.

Leigh (co. Warwick). Gu. a cross engr. ar. a bordure of the second, in the dexter quarter a lozenge or.

Leigh (Bilsley, co. Warwick; Har. MSS. 6060). Ar. a fess betw. in chief three pellets, and in base a martlet sa.

Leigh (Preston, co. York). Az. two bars or, over all a bend of the last.

Leigh. Ar. a cross pattée sa. (another, sa. a lion pass. ar. crowned or; another, ar. a culverin dismounted in fesse sa. ; another, ar. a fesse sa. in chief three mullets of the second, the middle one pierced ; another, or, on a chev. betw. three annulets sa. as many lions ramp. ar.).

Leigh (London; Sir THOMAS LEIGH, Lord Mayor 1558. Visit. London, 1563). Gu. a cross engr. ar. in dexter chief a lozenge or. *Crest*—A unicorn's head couped or.

Leigh (WALTER LEIGH, *m.* MARY, dau. of JOHN HAYDON, Sheriff of London, *temp.* Henry VIII. Visit. London, 1563). Ar. a billet fessways sa. in chief a crescent of the last.

Leigh (Visit. Cornwall, 1620). Ar. a lion ramp. gu.

Leigh (Leigh, co. Cornwall; ROBERT LEIGH, of Leigh, *temp.* Henry IV., and NICHOLAS LEIGH, of Leigh, *temp.* James I. Visit. Cornwall, 1620). Or, on a bend gu. a lucie ar.

Leigh. Or, three fusils az. (another, az. three mascles or).

Leigh, or Lea. Per chev. ar. and gu. in chief two lions combatant sa.

Leigh. Vert on a fesse cotised or, three leopards' faces gu. (another, az. two bars ar. on a bend or, three pheons gu.; another, ar. a fleur-de-lis sa. ; another, ar. a chev. sa. a label of three points gu.).

Leigh (Leatherlake House, Runnymead, co. Surrey ; descended from Rev. THOMAS LEIGH, M.A., third son of the Rev. PETER LEIGH, M.A., of the West Hall). *Arms*, &c., as LEIGH, of West Hall in High Leigh.

Leigh (Southwell, co. Nottingham; GERVOIS LEIGH, *alias* LEE, Visit. Notts, 1614, grandson of GEOFFREY LEIGH, of same, descended from LEE, of co. Kent). Az. on a fess cotised or, three leopards' faces gu. *Crest*—A demi Moor vested gu. sleeves ar. holding in the dexter hand a gem ring and round the neck a collar or, wreathed round the temples of the second and gu.

Leigh (quartered by LARDER, of Upton Pine, co. Devon. Visit. Devon, 1620). Vert three covered cups or.

Leigh (Asfordsby, co. Leicester; GILBERT LEIGH and JAMES LEIGH, Visit. Leicester, 1619, sons of ROBERT LEIGH, of same place, the son of GILBERT LEIGH, of Asfordsby, descended from the LEIGHS, of co. Chester). Az. two bars ar. over all on a bend gu. a mullet or, for diff., quartering, 1st, or, three lozenges az.; 2nd, erm. on a chief indented gu. three ducal coronets or; 3rd, ar. a fleur-de-lis sa. a mullet for diff.

Leigh (Scarlets Wargrave, co. Berks). Gu. a cross engr.

ar. in the dexter chief point a lozenge of the second. *Crest* —A unicorn's head couped or.

Leigh (Ridge, in Bishop's Morchard, co. Devon; ten descents given in Visit. 1620). Ar. two bars az. over all a bend compony or and gu.

Leigh (Bardon, co. Somerset, 1595; a younger branch of LEIGH, of Ridge). Same *Arms*. *Crest*—A demi lion ramp. or, armed and langued gu. *Motto*—Legibus antiquis.

Leigh (Leigh, near Tiverton, and East Allington, co Devon. Visit. 1620). Vert a saltire betw. four eagles displ. or.

Leigh (Quithiock, co. Cornwall). Ar. a bend lozengy sa.

Leigh (Middleton). Ar. two bars sa. over all a bend gu.

Leigh (Sir HENRY LEIGH, knighted at Dublin Castle, 20 April, 1603, by CHARLES, Lord Mountjoy, Lord Lieutenant). Barry of six ar. and az. a bend compony counter-compony or and gu.

Leigh (Fun. Ent. Ulster's Office, 1608, Capt. EDMUND LEIGH, Commander of the Army in co. Tyrone). Az. on a chev. betw. three ducal coronets or, as many hurts, a crescent for diff.

Leigh (Drogheda; JOHN LEIGH and JAMES LEIGH, *temp.* George II., sons of THOMAS LEIGH, of same place, descended from LEIGH, of Elsmore, co. Salop. Reg. Ped. Ulster's Office). Ar. a lion ramp. gu. armed and langued az. charged on the shoulder with a mullet or, for diff. *Crest*— Out of a ducal coronet a demi lion holding in the paws a sceptre surmounted of a fleur-de-lis all gu. armed and langued az.

Leigh (Rathbride, co. Kilbride; Fun. Ent. Ulster's Office, 1612; JOHN LEIGH, or LY, of that place, claiming descent from MCLAEGHIS, of Leix, Interpreter to Queen Elizabeth, who, like Sir PATRICK MACCROSSAN, *alias* CROSBIE, and many others of the Irish, about 1585, Anglicised his Celtic surname of MCLAEGHIS, and took the appellation of LY, LYE, or LEIGH; his descendant, FRANCIS LEIGH, Esq., of Rathbride, M.P. for Kildare, and Escheator-General of Leicester, forfeited all his estates by his adhesion to James II.). Ar. two bars az. over all a bend compony counter-compony or and gu. *Crest* (Reg. Ulster's Office)—A dexter arm embowed vested compony counter-compony or and gu. the hand holding a sword ppr. pommel and hilt gold.

Leigh (Rosegarland, co. Wexford; ROBERT LEIGH, second son of JOHN LEIGH, Esq., of Rathbride, having attended Charles II. abroad, and served him faithfully during his exile, was rewarded after the Restoration with a grant of the Lordship, Manor, Castles, &c., of Rosegarland, co. Wexford; he *m.* MARGARET, sister and heir of Sir CÆSAR COLCLOUGH, Bart., of Tintern Abbey, and dying *s.p.* 1695, bequeathed the Manor of Rosegarland to his nephew, ROBERT LEIGH, eldest son of his brother, FRANCIS LEIGH, who forfeited Rathbride 1690; he dying *unm.* 1724, was *s.* by his brother, FRANCIS LEIGH, direct ancestor of the present FRANCIS AUGUSTINE LEIGH, Esq., of Rosegarland, D.L.). Same *Arms*. *Crest* (borne by the present Mr. LEIGH)—A hand lying fessways couped above the wrist, cuffed or, holding a sword erect impaling three gory heads all ppr. pommel and hilt of sword gold.

Leight, alias Toderleigh (co. Hants). Erm. two flames in saltire gu. *Crest*—A wolf pass. gu.

Leight. Gu. three swans close ar.

Leighton (RANDOLPH DE LEIGHTON, 20 Edward I., 1330). Ar. three eagles' heads erased sa.

Leighton (Watlesborough, co. Salop, bart.). Quarterly, per fesse indented or and gu. *Crest*—A wyvern, wings expanded sa. *Motto*—Dread shame.

Leighton (Bausley, or Ballesley, co. Montgomery, and of Shrewsbury; Rev. FRANCIS KNYVETT LEIGHTON, descended from DANIEL LEIGHTON, Lieut.-Col. in Gen. Evans' horse, younger son of Sir EDWARD LEIGHTON, first bart.). Same *Arms*, &c.

Leighton. Quarterly, indented or and gu. in the 2nd and 3rd quarters six (another, three) boars' heads of the first, three and three.

Leighton (Sir BRYAN LEIGHTON, *temp.* Henry VIII.). Sa. on a bend ar. three escallops gu.

Leighton. Ar. a buglehorn betw. three crescents sa.

Leighton. Sa. two bars or, on a bend ar. three escallops gu.

Leighton (Ulishaven, co. Forfar). Ar. a lion ramp. gu. *Crest*—A palm tree vert. *Motto*—Per adversa virtus.

Leighwood (London). Ar. a chev. az. betw. three tigers vert. *Crest*—A banyan tree ppr.

Leike. Ar. on a saltire engr. sa. an annulet or.

Leinhams. Quarterly, ar. and sa in the 1st quarter a fleur-de-lis gu.

Leinster, Province of. Vert an Irish harp or, stringed ar.

Leinster, Duke of. See FITZGERALD.

Leister (Reg. Ulster's Office). Az. a fess betw. three fleurs-de-lis or, a border of the last.

Leir, or Lear (Ditcheat, co. Somerset, and Jaggard's House, co. Wilts; descended from RICHARD LEIR, B.A. of Exeter, presented to the rectory of Charlton Musgrave in 1617. Az. a fesse raguly betw. three unicorns' heads erased or. *Crest* —A demi unicorn ramp. holding betw. the legs a staff raguly.

Le Ireys GEOFFREY LE IREYS, son of THOMAS LE IREYS, *temp.* Henry III.). Az. on a fess ar. three escallops of the first, over all a bend gu.

Leitch (Scotland). Gu. on a bend engr. or, betw. six fusils of the second, three escutcheons az. *Crest*—A hand holding a serpent ppr.

Leith (Burgh St. Peter's, co. Norfolk, bart.). Or, a cross crosslet fitchée sa. betw. three crescents in chief and as many lozenges in base gu. *Crest*—A lion pass. gu. charged on the body with three mullets in fesse or. *Motto*—Trusty to the end.

Leith (Restalrig, co. Edinburgh). Ar. five fusils in fess sa.

Leith (Leith Hall, co. Aberdeen; now LEITH-HAY, of Rannes and Leith Hall). Or, a cross crosslet fitchée sa. betw. three crescents in chief and as many fusils in base gu.; now quartered with HAY of Rannes [*which see*]. *Crest*—A cross crosslet fitchée sa. *Motto*—Trustie to the end.

Leith (Freefield and Glenkendy, co. Aberdeen). Quarterly, 1st and 4th, or, a cross crosslet fitchée sa. betw. three crescents in chief and as many fusils in base gu. a bordure az.; 2nd and 3rd, az. a hart trippant or, attired and unguled gu., for STRACHAN. *Crest*—A hart at gaze ppr. *Motto*— Trusty to the end.

Leith (Craighall, Scotland). Or, a cross crosslet fitchée sa. betw. two crescents in chief gu. and in base three fusils az. two and one, all within a bordure of the third. *Motto*— Trusty and bydand.

Leith (Over-Barns, Scotland). Or, a chev. betw. three fusils az. *Crest*—A turtle dove ppr. *Motto*—Semper fidus.

Leith (Hearthill, Scotland). Or, a cross crosslet fitchée az. betw. two crescents in chief and a fusil in base gu.

Leith (Whitehaugh, co. Aberdeen; now FORBES-LEITH, the heiress having *m.* FORBES, of Tolquhon). Ar. a fess fusily sa. (or, ar. five fusils in fess sa.). *Crest*—A dove with an olive branch in her beak ppr. *Motto*—Fidus ad extremum.

Leitrim, Earl of. See CLEMENTS.

Leke (Sutton, co. Derby). Ar. on a saltire engr. sa. nine annulets of the field. *Crest*—Two eagles ar. supporting a garb or.

Leke (*Earl of Scarsdale*, extinct 1736; Sir FRANCIS LEKE, Knt., of Sutton, was created *Baron Deincourt* 1624, and raised to the earldom 1645). Same *Arms*. *Crest*—A peacock's tail erect ppr. supported by two eagles' wings expanded ar. *Supporters*—Two angels ppr. upper garments purp. under garments, wings, and hair or. *Motto*—Gloria Deo in excelsis.

Leke (Newark-on-Trent, co. Nottingham, bart., extinct 1682). Same *Arms*.

Leke, or Leake (Southwark). Or, a saltire flory sa. in chief a lion pass. of the last.

Leke. Ar. on a saltire engr. sa. nine annulets or. *Crest*—A peacock's tail erect, the plume displ. ppr. supported by two eagle's wings expanded ar. *Another Crest*—A garb or, banded gu.

Leke. Sa. six annulets or, three, two, and one.

Leke, or Leake. Sa. a bend betw. six annulets or (another, a bend engr. sa. a chief gu.).

Leke, Leake, or Leyke (co. Lincoln). Ar. a chief (another, a chev.) gu. over all a bend engr. az. (another, sa.).

Lekeborne (co. Lincoln). Ar. a chev. betw. three crosses crosslet sa.

Lekeborne. Ar. a chev. sa. (another, sa. three fusils ar.).

Lekesworth (co. Suffolk). Chequy ar. and gu. on a bend az. three lions ramp. of the first.

Lekyborne. Ar. crusily sa. a chev. of the last.

Lelam (Bricksworth, Chawsham, co. Northampton, co. York). Ar. a saltire sa. *Crest*—On a mount vert a cock gu. combed, wattled, and legged or, charged on the breast with a saltire of the last.

Leland. Gu. on a saltire ar. three palets az. a chief or. *Crest*—A crow rising, transfixed with an arrow.

Leland. Ar. a bend gu. cotised sa.

Leley. Gu. three lilies ar.

Lello (co. Hereford). Erm. on a canton gu. a cross moline or. *Crest*—A gem ring or, entwined and fretted with a serpent ppr.

Lelly (1680). Ar. a fesse betw. three roses gu. in chief a crescent for diff.

Lelly. See LELY.

Lelon, or Lellow (co. Buckingham). Ar. two bars gu. in chief three wolves' heads erased of the second. *Crest*—On a rock a fort in flames ppr.

Lelon, or Lelow. Ar. on two bars gu. three hounds courant of the field, in chief as many wolves' heads erased of the second.

Lelon, or Lelow. Gu. three wolves pass. ar.

Lely (Sir PETER LELY, of the Piazza, Covent Garden, Kew Green, Surrey, and Greetwell, co. Lincoln, the Court Painter, knighted by Charles II.). Ar. a fesse betw. three roses gu. *Crest*—A cornucopia ppr.

Lely (Framlingham Hall, co. Norfolk, and Cawthorpe, co. Lincoln; BRIDGET LELY, granddau. of JOHN LELY, son of Sir PETER LELY, the Court Painter, *m.* WILLIAM OSTLER, Esq., of Barton, and their son, WILLIAM OSTLER, Esq., *m.* his cousin, LYDIA ANNE, dau. and heiress of DAVID LELY, Esq.). Ar. a fesse betw. three roses gu. *Crest*—A cornucopia ppr.

Lem. Ar. on a bend gu. three lions pass. or.

Le Maire (London; DAVID LE MAIRE, Visit. London, 1563, son of JAMES LE MAIRE, of Tournay). Ar. three Moors' heads couped ppr. *Crest*—A Moor's head couped ppr. *Motto*—Tempera te tempori.

Le Maistre (Jersey). Ar. a chev. gu. in base a marigold (locally termed "la fleur du Maistre") closed ppr. on a chief az. three estoiles or. *Crest*—A dexter arm embowed in armour ppr. holding in the hand a rose wreath (another, a laurel wreath) all ppr. *Motto*--Ferme et fidèle.

Leman, or Lemmon (Northaw, co. Herts, bart., extinct 1762; Sir JOHN LEMAN, was Lord Mayor of London, 1616). Az. a fesse betw. three dolphins hauriant ar. *Crest*—In a lemon tree ppr. a pelican in her nest or, feeding her young ppr.

Leman (co. Norfolk). Ar. a fesse between three dolphins naiant gu.

Leman (Brampton Hall, co. Suffolk). Az. a chev. or, betw. three owls ar. legged of the second. *Crest*--Out of a ducal coronet an owl's leg erect or.

Leman (Fun. Ent. Ulster's Office, 1671, of the wife of NATHANIEL STOUGHTON, of Dublin, merchant). Az. a fess betw. three dolphins embowed ar.

Lemarch. Barruly ar. and az. a lion ramp gu. *Crest*—An arm in armour embowed, striking with a dagger all ppr.

Lemarchand (granted to MICHAEL JOSEPH LEMARCHAND, Esq., of Ghazepoor, Bengal). Per chev. embattled gu. and ar. in chief two lions' heads erased of the last, in base a ship under sail at sea, in the centre chief point a bee volant all ppr. *Crest*—Out of an eastern crown or, a horse's head ar. charged with a bee, as in the arms.

Le Marchant (Guernsey). Az. a chev. or, betw. three owls ar. legged of the second. *Crest*—Out of a ducal coronet gu. an owl's leg erect or. *Supporters*—(as shown by the seal of PIERRE LE MARCHANT, Seneschal of the Priory of St. Michel du Valle, Guernsey, in 1388)—Two griffins ppr. *Motto*—Me Minerva lucet.

Le Marchant (Chobham Place, Surrey bart.). Az. a chev. or, betw. three owls ar. legged of the second. *Crest*—Out of a ducal coronet an owl's leg erect or.

Le Master (granted to WILLIAM LE MASTER, of Cambridge, by Dethick, Garter, 17 Nov. 1587). Or, on a fess az. betw. three pheons gu. two lions pass. of the first. *Crest*—A lion's head affrontée or, pierced with a pheon in pale issuant from the mouth.

Lementon. Az. fretty or, on a chief of the last a lion ramp. betw. two mullets gu.

Le Merchant. Gyronny of eight erm. and az. a bordure engr.

Lemesey (co. Warwick). Gu. an eagle displ. or, membered az.

Le Mesurier, or Le Messurier (Guernsey). Ar. a chev. betw. three dexter hands gu. *Crest*—A hawk ppr. wings extended or.

Le Mière (Jersey). Az. a chev. betw. three escallops or.

Le Milliere. Gu. three roses ar. barbed and seeded ppr.

Leming (Colchester, co. Essex, co. Lancaster, and co. York). Erm. a cross patonce az.

Leming. Erm. a cross crosslet az.

Lemington, or Lenington (Lemington, co. York'. Ar. (another, or) a saltire gu. on a chief of the second three boars' heads couped or.

Lemington. Ar. a chev. sa. in chief three crescents, and in base a buglehorn of the last.

Lemington (ROBERT LEMINGTON, of Loughborough, *d.* 1512; arms from his tomb). Ar. on a chev. engr. az. betw. three cranes gu. a chevronel or.

Lemitare, or Lemitaire (Westminster; descended from Normandy; confirmed 14 June, 14 James I.). Per chev. sa. and ar. three catharine wheels counterchanged. *Crest*—A demi griffin sa. holding a catharine wheel ar.

Lemming (co. Essex). Ar. fifteen guttées de sang, five, four, three, two, and one.

Lemmington, or Lennington. Ar. a buglehorn betw. three crescents sa. *Crest*—A savage's head erased affrontée ppr.

Lemmington, or Lennington. Az. a buglehorn sa.

Lemon (Carclew, co. Cornwall, bart.). Ar. on a chev. betw. three mullets gu. an eagle displ. of the field. *Crest*—A lion pass. gu. charged with three mullets or.

Lemon, or Lemmon. See LEMAN.

Le Montais (Jersey). Sa. four fusils in fesse or, in chief an increscent of the last.

Lemosy, or Lymesey (co. Warwick). Gu. an eagle displ. or, armed sa.

Lemosy, or Lymesey (co. Warwick). Or, an eagle displ. gu. a bordure sa.

Le Mottée (Guernsey). Ar. a boar pass. sa. a bordure of the last. *Crest*—A boar's head sa.

Lempreur (Normandy, &c.). Or, a double-headed eagle displ. sa. in chief a sun in splendour gu.

Lemprew, or Lempreur. Gyronny of twelve ar. and gu. on a chief az. an eagle with two heads displ. ar.

Lemprière (Seigneurs of Rozel, Jersey). Gu. three eagles displ. or. *Crest*—An eagle rising ppr. *Supporters*—Two knights fully armed, visors raised ppr. *Motto*—Timor Dei nobilitas.

Lempy. Ar. a lion pass. sa.

Lemsels, or Lomsels (co. Cornwall). Az. a wolf's head erased or.

Lemster (London). Ar. on a fesse betw. three lions' heads erased gu. as many crescents or, each charged with a mullet of the second.

Lemster. Ar. on a fesse betw. three crescents gu. as many mullets or. *Crest*—A demi cupid issuing, in the dexter hand an arrow, in the sinister a bow bent all ppr.

Lemuses, or Lennuses (De Tourney). Gu. a bend or, betw. six roses ar.

Lenale. Sa. three boars' heads couped ar.

Lenall. Ar. eleven billets sa. four, three, three, and one.

Lench (Wych, co. Worcester; RANDOLPH DE LENCH, High Sheriff, *temp.* Henry II. Visit. Worcester, 1533 and 1634). Ar. two bars engr. az. each charged with three cinquefoils or, quartering, Ar. on a chev. az. three crosses pattée or, for BEAUFO. *Crest*—A tiger sejant or, collared gu. resting the forepaw on a shield per chev. of the second and first.

Lenche (Dowdeswell). Ar. two bars engr. vert, on each three cinquefoils of the first.

Lend (Caule, Scotland). Or, an orle indented on the inner edge az.

Lendrum (confirmed to GEORGE LENDRUM, Esq., of Jamestown, co. Fermanagh, son of JAMES LENDRUM, of same place, and grandson of GEORGE LENDRUM, Esq., of Moorfield, co. Tyrone, and the descendants of his said grandfather). Gu. three garbs or, on a chief ar. three woolpacks sa. *Crest*—On a mount vert a dove close, in the beak an olive branch all ppr. *Motto*—La Paix.

Lenenholme (co. Lancaster). Ar. three fleurs-de-lis sa.

Le Neve (Tivetshall, co. Norfolk, and co. Suffolk, *temp.* Henry IV.; confirmed to WILLIAM LE NEVE, Clarenceux King of Arms). Ar. on a cross sa. five fleurs-de-lis of the field. *Crest*—Out of a ducal coronet or, a lily ar. stalked and leaved vert, barbed and seeded ppr.

Le Neve (London). Ar. on a cross az. five fleurs-de-lis of the field betw. two tortoises gradient vert, one in the 1st quarter, the other in the 4th. *Crest*—On a mount vert three silver lilies in one stalk, leaved and seeded all ppr.

Lenhorgy (co. Cornwall). Az. three greyhounds pass ar.

Lenigan (Castle Fogerty, co. Tipperary; WILLIAM LANIGAN, Esq., *m.* ELIZABETH, only dau. (and eventual heiress to her brother JAMES) of THOMAS FOGERTY, Esq., of Castle Fogerty). Quarterly, 1st, az. on a palet ar. betw. two lions ramp regarding each other or, each betw. three fleurs-de-l' two and one of the second, three trefoils in pale vert to LENIGAN; 2nd, az. in chief two lions ramp. regarding each other, supporting a garb all or, in the dexter base a crescent, and in the sinister an Irish harp, both gold, stringed ar., for FOGARTY (ancient); 3rd, vert a fesse ar. betw. three garbs or, for FOGARTY (modern); 4th, ar. a chief vert, for MYLER. *Crests*—1st: A lion ramp. or, leaning on a sword ar. hilted gold; 2nd: An arm embowed in armour ppr. garnished or, holding a dagger ar. hilted gold.

Lenihan (Limerick; granted to MAURICE LENIHAN, Esq., J.P. of that city, son of JAMES LENIHAN, Esq., of Waterford, and their descendants). Ar. on a mount vert a buck trippant gu. attired or, in the mouth a trefoil slipped of the second, a chief az. charged with a castle having on each tower an obtuse spire surmounted by a weathercock, and on an arch over the curtain wall a cross flory all of the field. Crest—A buck trippant gu. attired or, holding in the mouth a trefoil slipped vert, and resting the forefoot on an escutcheon of the BURKE arms, viz., or, a cross gu. in the 1st quarter a lion ramp. sa. and in the 2nd a hand of the last. Motto—Patriæ infelici fidelis.

Lennard (Chevening and Knoll, co. Kent, and Bell House, co. Essex). Or, on a fesse gu. three fleurs-de-lis of the field. Crest—Out of a ducal coronet or, a tiger's head ar. Another Coat (said to have been borne by this family. See Vincent's Small Barony)—Or, on a fesse gu. betw. three eagles' heads erased sa. a lion's pass. betw. two fleurs-de-lis of the field. Crest—A demi lion ramp. ar. ducally gorged or, holding in the dexter paw a rose gu.

Lennard (Earl of Sussex and Baron Dacre; earldom extinct 1715, barony is now vested in THOMAS, twenty-second Lord Dacre; SAMPSON LENNARD, Esq., eldest son of JOHN LENNARD, Esq., of Chevening and Knole, m. MARGARET FIENNES, Baroness Dacre in her own right, sister and heiress of GEORGE, tenth Lord Dacre: she conveyed the barony to her husband's family; THOMAS, fifteenth Lord Dacre, was created Earl of Sussex 1674, d.s.p.m.). Or, on a fess gu. three fleurs-de-lis of the field. Crest—Out of a ducal coronet or, an heraldic tiger's head ar. maned and tufted gold. Supporters—Dexter, a wolf ar. gorged with a spiked collar, chain reflexed over back or; sinister, a bull gu. armed, ducally gorged and chain reflexed over back or. Motto—Pour bien desirer.

Lennard (Wickham Court, co. Kent, bart., extinct 1727; descended from Sir SAMUEL LENNARD, Knt., of Wickham, younger brother of SAMPSON LENNARD, Esq., of Chevening, ancestor of the Lords Dacre and Earls of Sussex). Or, on a fesse gu. three fleurs-de-lis of the field, a crescent for diff. Crest—Out of a ducal coronet or, a tiger's head ar.

Lennard. Same Arms. Crest—A lion ramp. gu. semee of estoiles or, issuing from clouds ppr., Motto over—Inter nubus resplendeo. (The crest granted to LENNARD, Herald of Arms, afterwards Bluemantle Pursuivant of Arms).

Lennard. Per pale gu. and az. three demi lions pass. or. Crest—A tiger's head quarterly or and az.

Lennard (BARRETT-LENNARD, Bellius, co. Essex, bart.). Quarterly, 1st and 4th, or, on a fesse gu. three fleurs-de-lis of the first; 2nd and 3rd, per pale ar. and gu. barry of four counterchanged, for BARRETT, all within a bordure wavy sa. Crest—Out of a ducal coronet or, an Irish wolf-dog's head per fesse ar. and erm. charged with an escallop barways nebulée gu. and sa. Mottoes—La loi le veut, et moi ni mot; Pour bien désirer; and, La bondad para la medra.

Lennie, or Leny (Scotland). Sa. on a chev. betw. three bears' heads ar. muzzled gu. as many cinquefoils of the last. Crest—A dexter arm ppr. holding up a covered cup or.

Lennon (Reg. Ulster's Office). Ar. on a mount in base vert a buck browsing ppr. Crest—On a mount vert a buck browsing ppr. Motto—Prisco stirpe Hibernico.

Lennos, or Lenos. Az. three fleurs-de-lis ar. on a bordure of the last eight roses gu. Crest—A pennant parted per pale gu. and or, tasselled of the last.

Lennock. Ar. guttée de poix, a fesse sa.

Lennox (GORDON-LENNOX, Duke of Richmond, Lennox, and Gordon). Quarterly, 1st and 4th, France and England, quarterly; 2nd, Scotland; 3rd, Ireland (being the arms of Charles II.), all within a bordure compony ar. and gu. charged with eight roses of the second, barbed and seeded ppr., over all an escutcheon of pretence gu. charged with three buckles or, for the Dukedom of Aubigny. Crests—1st: On a chapeau gu. turned up erm. a lion statant guard. or, crowned with a ducal coronet gu. and gorged with a collar, as the bordure in the arms; 2nd: A demi lion ramp. or. Supporters—Dexter, a unicorn ar. armed, maned, and unguled or; sinister, an antelope ar. armed and hoofed or, each supporter gorged with a collar compony, as the bordure in the arms. Motto—En la rose je fleurie.

Lennox (Scotland; ancient Earls of Lennox, extinct). Ar. a saltire gu. cantoned with four roses of the last.

Lennox (Woodhead, Scotland, now LENNOX-KINCAID). Ar. a saltire gu. betw. four roses of the last, barbed vert, now quartered with KINCAID, of that ilk [which see]. Crest—Two broadswords in saltire behind an imperial crown all ppr. Supporters—Two savages, wreathed head and middle with oak, holding in their hands clubs erect all ppr. Motto—I'll defend.

601

Lenosey. Gu. an eagle displ. with two heads or, a baton ar.

Lens (Norwich). Az. on a chev. betw. three martlets or, three trefoils slipped of the field.

Lenstofte. Or, a lion ramp. per fesse gu. and sa.

Lent (WILLIAM LENT, temp. Edward III., quartered by BURY, of Culham, co. Oxford. Visit. Oxon. 1574). Quarterly, ar. and or, a cross engr. gu.

Lent. Vert a chev. erm. betw. three leaves or. Crest—A horse pass. ar.

Lentaigne (Tallaght, co. Dublin; JOHN FRANCIS LENTAIGNE, Esq., C.B., J.P. cos. Dublin and Monaghan, Inspector-General of Prisons, and Commissioner of National Education in Ireland, represents the Irish branch of an ancient family of Normandy, where the head of the elder branch, GUSTAVE, Count Lentaigne de Logicière, resides on his estate of De Beauvoir, near Livarot, Calvados. The Irish branch descends from JEAN FRANCOIS LENTAIGNE, b. 1699, d. 1780, fifth son of RICHARD LENTAIGNE, Sieur de la Croix, d. 1720, the common ancestor of both houses). Quarterly, 1st and 4th, or, on a chev. az. betw. three martlets sa. a fleur-de-lis of the field, on a chief of the second three mullets ar., for LENTAIGNE; 2nd, ar. two lions ramp. combatant, supporting a dexter hand couped at the wrist gu. in chief three estoiles of the last, in base, in waves of the sea a salmon naiant all ppr., for O'NEILL; 3rd, sa. a bend ar. in chief a tower of the last, for PLUNKETT. Mr. LENTAIGNE, C.B., bears on an escutcheon of pretence, in right of his wife, MARY, dau. and co-heir of FRANCIS MAGAN, Esq., of Emoe, co. Westmeath, az. a chev. betw. three boars pass. az. Crest—A dove ppr. charged on the breast with a mullet ar. holding in the beak a fleur-de-lis or. Mottoes—Over the crest: Profide, rege, et patria pugno; under the arms: Dieu ayde.

Lentally. Quarterly, per fess indented erm. and ermines.

Lenthall (Leynthall, and Hampton Court, co. Hereford, Lachford, Great Haseley, Burford Priory, and Yelford Hastings, co. Oxford, and Besselsleigh, co. Berks; derived from Sir ROWLAND LENTHALL, Knt., of Hampton Court, Master of the Robes to Henry IV., and one of the Commanders at Agincourt; WILLIAM LENTHALL, Speaker of the House of Commons temp. Charles I. was immediate ancestor of the LENTHALLS of Burford Priory, co. Oxford, and of Besselsleigh, co. Berks). Ar. on a bend cotised sa. three mullets or. Crest—A greyhound saliant sa. collared or.

Lenthall (Lachford, co. Oxford; WILLIAM LENTHALL, of Latchford. Visit. Oxon. 1574, great-grandson of THOMAS LENTHALL, the son of JOHN LENTHALL, of Lenthall). Ar. on a bend cotised sa. three mullets pierced or, quartering sa. a bend fusily ar., another coat of LENTHALL, also BADLEY, PYPARD, and WILLIE.

Lenthall (Besselsleigh Manor, Abingdon). Ar. on a bend cotised sa. three mullets or. Crest—A greyhound saliant sa. collared or. Motto—Azincourt.

Lenthall (Monkton, co. Devon; PETER LYTHALL, of that place, at Visit. Devon, 1620, grandson of EDWARD LENTHALL, a younger son of LENTHALL, of Lachford, who left the co. Oxford, and settled at Monkton). Same Arms and Crest.

Lenthall (co. Dorset). Same Arms. Crest—A greyhound in full course sa. collared or.

Lenthall. Ar. two bars sa. each charged with three mullets or.

Lenther. Ar. on a bend cotised sa. three mullets or.

Lenthorne. Gyronny of eight or and sa. an eagle displ. ar.

Lenthorp, Lenthrop, or Leventhorp (co. Essex, and Shingley Hall, co. Herts). Ar. a bend gobonated gu. and sa. (another, az.) cotised of the second. Crest—A lady standing ppr. richly attired vert.

Lenton (co. Buckingham, and Aldwinkle, co. Northampton; granted 21 March, 1584). Ar. a bend erm. betw. two dolphins embowed and bendways or. Crest—A tiger's head erased az. tufted, armed, collared, and ringed or.

Lenton (Fun. Ent. Ulster's Office, 1623, EDWARD LENTON, Esq., of Kilmainham, Provost-Marshal of Ireland). Az. a bend erm. betw. two dolphins embowed bendways or.

Lenton-Priory (co. Nottingham). Quarterly, or and az. over all a cross calvary on three grieces or steps sa. fimbriated of the first.

Lentston. Ar. a lion ramp. sa.

Lenysis. Gu. a bend betw. six crosses botonnée or.

Leon (co. Norfolk). Or, a saltire engr. vert.

Leon (arms in Dedington Church, co. Oxford. Visit. Oxon. 1566). Ar. a lion ramp. sa.

Leonard (Reg. Ulster's Office). Per fess dancetté ar. and az. a fess gu.

Leonard (Chevening; allowed at the funeral of Mrs. LEONARD, of Knole). Or, on a fess gu. three fleurs-de-lis of the first.

Leonard, Lenor, or Lenorey. Az. three garbs or.

Leonard. Or, on a fesse az. three fleurs-de-lis ar. *Crest*—Out of a ducal coronet or, a tiger's head ar.

Pe Lelley (Seigneurs of the Island of Sark). Or, a chev. gu. on a chief of the second three mascles of the first.

Lepla (Isle of Ely, co. Cambridge). Ar. a lion ramp. gu. a bordure componée or and vert.

Leple. Erm. an inescutcheon gu. a bordure engr. of the last.

Le-Poer-Trench (*Earl of Clancarty*). See TRENCH.

Leport. Az. three towers domed or, gates sa.

Leppington (Louth, co. Lincoln, and Haverstock Hill, co. Middlesex). Per chev. or and az. in chief two annulets, and in base a billet counterchanged. *Crest*—Upon a mount vert a garb or, banded az. within a chain in arch gold. *Motto*—A vito non sine honore.

Lepton (Kepwick, co. York). Barry of six ar. and gu. on a chief az. three catharine wheels or.

Lepton (co. York). Ar. on a chief az. three catharine wheels or. *Crest*—Issuing from a castle triple-towered a demi lion ppr.

Le Quesne (Jersey). Ar. a lion pass. gu. *Motto*—Suis ducibus ubique fidelis.

Lermouth. Ar. a chev. betw. three mascles (another, lozenges; another, fusils) sa.

Le Roulx, or Le Poitevin-dit-le Roulx (Jersey). Az. a bend or, in chief a falcon close, and in base a lion ramp. ar. *Crest*—A falcon rising ppr.

Le Roy (Guernsey). Gu. a bend, and in the middle chief point a crescent, both ar.

Lerrier (Lieut.-Bailly of Jersey, 1875). Ar. a fesse sa. in chief the sun is splendour ppr. betw. two crosses pattée vert, in base a cottage also ppr., the whole within a bordure engr. az. *Crest*—A chapel ppr. *Mottoes*—Pugna pro aris; Bonus, justus, et utilis.

Le Ruez (St. Ouen, Jersey). Gu. three arrows in fesse or, points in base. *Crest*—A lion ramp. gu. *Motto*—Vi et virtute.

Lescher (granted to JOSEPH SAMUEL LESCHER, Esq., of Boyles, co. Essex, and his cousin, WILLIAM JOSEPH LESCHER, Esq., of Upton, co. Essex, grandsons of LAWRENCE LESCHER, of Kertzfild, in Alsace). Or, a cross gu. on a chief az. a stork ar. beaked and legged of the second. *Crest*—In front of a buglehorn sa. a dexter arm embowed in armour ppr. garnished or, entwined by a serpent, the hand grasping a dagger fesseways, the point towards the dexter also ppr. pommel and hilt gold. *Motto*—Singulariter in spe.

Le Scot (*Earl of Chester, d.s.p.* 1237). Or, three piles gu. *Crest*—Two battle axes in saltire az. hilted sa.

Lesington (co. York). Ar. three saltorels engr. sa.

Lesk (that Ilk). Sa. a fesse betw. three mullets in chief and as many mascles in base all or.

Leskesworth (co. Suffolk). Chequy ar. and gu. a bend sa.

Leslie (that Ilk, co. Aberdeen). Ar. on a bend az. three buckles or, within a double tressure flory counterflory gu. *Crest*—A griffin's head ppr. *Motto*—Grip fast.

Leslie (*Earl of Rothes;* now borne by the *Countess of Rothes* in a lozenge). Quarterly, 1st and 4th, ar. on a bend az. three buckles or, for LESLIE; 2nd and 3rd, ar. a lion ramp. gu. debruised by a ribbon sa., for ABERNETHY. *Crest*—A demi griffin ppr. *Supporters*—Two griffins ppr. beaked, armed, and winged or. *Motto*—Grip fast.

Leslie (*Lord Lindores*). Quarterly, 1st and 4th, ar. on a bend az. three buckles or; 2nd and 3rd, or, a lion ramp. gu. debruised by a ribbon sa. by way of surtout an escutcheon gu. charged with a castle triple-towered ar. masoned sa., for the title of LINDORES. *Crest*—A demi angel with wings or, holding in the dexter hand two greyhounds' heads erased ppr. *Motto*—Stat promissa fides.

Leslie (*Lord Newark*). As Lord Lindores, with a crescent gu. in chief. *Crest, Motto,* and *Supporters,* as *Lord Lindores.*

Leslie (Findrassie, co. Elgin; heiress m. 1794, Sir JOHN LESLIE, of Wardis). Quarterly, as *Earl of Rothes,* within a bordure chequy gu. and or. *Crest*—A buckle ar. *Motto*—Firma durant.

Leslie (Burdsbank, Scotland). The quartered *Arms* of the *Earl of Rothes,* within a bordure parted per pale chequy and counter-componée gu. and or. *Crest*—A buckle or. *Motto*—Keep fast.

Leslie (Torry, co. Forfar). The quartered coat of ROTHES, within a bordure indented and parted per pale az. and ar. *Crest*—A buckle or. *Motto*—Hold fast.

Leslie (Balquhain, co. Aberdeen). Ar. on a fesse az. three

buckles or. *Crest*—A griffin's head erased ppr. *Motto*—Grip fast.

Leslie (Kincraigie, co. Aberdeen). Ar. on a fesse betw. two crosses crosslet fitchée az. three buckles or. *Crest*—A griffin's head couped ppr. charged with a cross crosslet fitchée ar. *Motto*—Firma spe.

Leslie (Glasslough, co. Monaghan, bart.; a branch of Balquhain). Quarterly, 1st and 4th, ar. on a bend az. two holly leaves vert three buckles or; 2nd and 3rd, or, a lion ramp. gu. debruised by a ribbon sa. *Crest*—A griffin's head erased gu. *Motto*—Grip fast.

Leslie (JAMES LESLIE, Advocate, of the family of New Leslie, co. Aberdeen, 1694). Ar. on a fesse buckles or, within a bordure of the second charged with as many stars of the first. *Crest*—A griffin ppr. winged or, holding in the dexter talon a buckle of the last. *Motto*—Probitas et firmitas.

Leslie (Kininvie, co. Aberdeen). Ar. on a fess az. three buckles or, within a bordure indented of the second. *Crest*—A griffin ppr. holding in the dexter talon a buckle ar. *Motto*—Quæ juncta firma.

Leslie-Melville (*Earl of Leven and Melville*). Quarterly, 1st, az. a thistle slipped ppr. ensigned with an imperial crown or, as a coat of augmentation to the arms of LESLIE; 2nd, ar. on a bend az. three buckles or, for LESLIE; 3rd, ar. a fesse gu.; 4th, gu. three crescents within a bordure ar. charged with eight roses of the first, both for MELVILLE. *Crest,* of LESLIE: A demi chevalier in complete armour, holding in the dexter hand a dagger erect ppr. pommel and hilt or; of MELVILLE: The head of a ratch-hound erased sa. *Supporters*—1st: Two chevaliers completely armed, each holding in the exterior hand the banner of Scotland, for LESLIE; 2nd: Dexter, a ratch-hound; sinister, an eagle ppr., for MELVILLE. *Mottoes*—Pro rege et patria, for LESLIE; and, Denique cœlum, for MELVILLE.

Leslie (Pitcaple, co. Aberdeen). Ar. on a bend az. betw. two mullets gu. three buckles or.

Leslie (Wardis, co. Aberdeen, and Findrassie, co. Moray, bart., 1625). Ar. on a bend az. betw. two holly leaves vert three buckles or; quartered with LESLIE, of Findrassie. *Crest*—A demi griffin ppr. *Motto*—Grip fast.

Leslie (Warthill, co. Aberdeen). As LESLIE, of Wardis, without the Findrassie quarter. *Crest*—A griffin's head erased ppr. *Motto*—Grip fast.

Leslie (Tulloch, co. Aberdeen). Ar. on a fesse az. three buckles or, betw. as many fleurs-de-lis of the second. *Crest*—An eagle's neck with two heads erased sa. *Motto*—Hold fast.

Leslie (Colpnay-Shiels, co. Aberdeen). Ar. on a fess az. three buckles or, within a bordure invecked of the second, charged with eight crescents of the first. *Crest*—A buckle issuing out of a crescent ar. *Motto*—Connanine augeor.

Leslie (Oustens, Scotland, 1672). Ar. on a bend az. betw. three oak branches slipped vert, acorned ppr. as many buckles or. *Crest*—A man holding a writing pen ppr. *Motto*—Soli Deo gloria.

Leslie (GEORGE LESLIE, Bailie of Aberdeen, 1672). Ar. on a bend embattled az. three buckles or. *Motto*—Deus providebit.

Leslie (Aberdeen, 1672). Ar. a pair of wings inverted conjoined ppr. surmounted of a fesse az. charged with three buckles or. *Motto*—God guide all.

Leslie (Powis, co. Aberdeen). Quarterly, 1st and 4th, ar. on a bend az. three buckles or, within a bordure gu.; 2nd and 3rd, az. three frases ar. within a bordure quartered or and of the second, the first charged with three antique crowns gu. the last with as many cinquefoils ar. *Crest*—A crescent ar. *Motto*—Crescat Deo promotore.

Leslie (Dunlugas, co. Banff, 1814). Quarterly, as *Earl of Rothes* within a bordure az., en surtout, per fess ar. and az. in chief two bears' paws crossing saltireways ppr. and in base three cinquefoils, two and one ar., for GRÖN, of Christiansand, in Norway. *Crest*—A demi griffin ppr. holding in his paws a buckle or. *Motto*—Grip fast.

Leslie (Colonel JONATHAN FORBES LESLIE, of Rothie, co. Aberdeen, 1862). Quarterly, 1st and 4th grand quarters, counter-quartered, 1st and 4th, ar. on a fess betw. two boars' heads erased az. in chief and base three buckles or, for LESLIE, 2nd and 3rd, az. a fess chequy ar. and of the first betw. three boars' heads erased or, a bordure indented of the second, for GORDON, of Badenscoth; 2nd and 3rd grand quarters, az. a dirk in pale ar. hilted and pommelled or, on its point a wolf's head couped of the third, betw. three bears' heads couped of the second, muzzled gu. a chief also of the second and issuing from its base a demi otter sa. crowned with an antique crown of the fourth, for FORBES. *Crests*—A griffin's head [and neck erased ppr., for LESLIE ; a bear's head and neck couped and muzzled ppr., for FORBES. *Mottoes*—Grip fast, for LESLIE; Spe expecto, for FORBES.

Leslie (Nethermuir, co. Aberdeen, 1872). Per pale ar. and or, on a bend az. betw. two crosses flory gu. three buckles of the third. *Crest*—A demi griffin ppr. *Motto*—Grip fast.

Leslie (Ballybay, co. Monaghan; confirmed by Hawkins, Ulster, 1708, to Ven. HENRY LESLIE, of Hillsborough, D.D., Archdeacon of Down, son of JAMES LESLIE, Esq., of the same place, and grandson of HENRY LESLIE, Bishop of Meath). Quarterly, 1st and 4th, ar. on a chev. az. three round buckles or; 2nd and 3rd, ar. a lion ramp. sa. *Crest*—An angel ppr.

Leslie (exemplified to FRANCIS CHARLES BEERS, Esq., of Ballyward Lodge, co. Down, on his assuming, by royal licence, 1850, the surname of LESLIE in lieu of BEERS, in memory of his maternal uncle, Rev. JOHN LESLIE, of Kincraigie Castle, co. Donegal). Ar. on a fess, betw. two cross crosslets fitchée az. three buckles or, a crescent gu. for diff. *Crest*—A griffin's head couped ppr. charged with a cross crosslet fitchée ar. *Motto*—Firma spe.

Leslie (exemplified to MARTIN LESLIE HAWORTH, Esq., son of MARTIN EDWARD HAWORTH, Esq., of Balham Wood, co. Herts, by Lady MARY LESLIE, his wife, eldest surviving sister of the eleventh *Earl of Rothes*, and now heiress presumptive to that peerage, upon his taking the name and arms of LESLIE, instead of that of HAWORTH, by royal licence). Ar. on a bend az. three buckles or. *Crest*—A demi griffin segreant ppr.

Lesone (Wheatfield and Soulgrave, co. Northampton). Gu. a chief ar. on the lower part thereof the sun's resplendent rays issuant thereout ppr. *Crest*—The sun or, rising out of clouds ppr.

Lesone (arms confirmed and crest granted by Hawkins, Ulster, 1701, to JOSEPH LESONE, fourth son of HUGH LESONE, of Stephen's Green, Dublin, descended from the co. Northampton). Gu. a chief ar. on the lower part thereof a cloud the rays of the sun issuing therefrom all ppr. a martlet for diff. *Crest*—A demi lion ramp. gu. holding betw. the paws the sun rising out of clouds ppr. *Motto*—Clarior e tenebris.

Le Spring (co. Durham). Sa. an orle ar.

Lesque. Ar. (another, or) a chev. betw. three calves pass. sa.

Lessingre (co. Middlesex). Gu. a blade of a sword-fish ar. crowned or.

Lessingham. Sa. three boar's heads couped and a bordure engr. ar. *Crest*—A martlet sa.

Lessington. Gu. three porches of churches with double doors expanded ar. (some say gu. three ports ar.). *Crest*—On a baron's coronet or, a lion ramp. gu.

Lester (co. Chester). Ar. a fesse az. betw. three fleurs-de-lis gu. *Crest*—A demi griffin segreant gu.

Lester (Wimborne Minster, co. Dorset). Gu. a fess betw. two fleurs-de-lis or, in chief and the caduceus ar. in base. *Crest*—A demi griffin ar. holding the caduceus.

Lester (Sir GEORGE LESTER, knighted at Dublin Castle, 6 Aug. 1599. Az. a fess. betw. three fleurs-de-lis or.

Lester (Wimborne Minster, co. Dorset; exemplified to LESTER GARLAND, Esq., upon his assuming by royal licence, the surname of LESTER only). Gu. a fesse erminois betw. two fleurs-de-lis in chief ar. and a caduceus in base ppr. thereon the cap of Mercury of the third. *Crest*—A demi gryphon, wings elevated erm. beaked and membered or, in the claws a trident erect az. headed gold. *Motto*—Favente Deo.

Leston. Vert ten bezants, four, three, two, and one. *Crest*—A lion pass. az. ducally gorged and chained or.

Le Strange (Hunstanton, co. Norfolk, bart., extinct, 1760; derived from HAMON LE STRANGE, *temp.* Edward II., to whom his brother, JOHN, sixth *Lord Strange of Knockyn*, gave the lands of Hunstanton. SIR NICHOLAS LE STRANGE of Hunstanton, *temp.* Charles I., eldest brother of the celebrated Sir ROGER LE STRANGE, was created a baronet in 1629; the sisters and co-heirs of the last baronet, Sir HENRY LE STRANGE, were, ARMINE, wife of NICHOLAS STYLEMAN, Esq., of Snettisham, co. Norfolk, and LUCY, wife of Sir JACOB ASTLEY, Bart.). Gu. two lions pass. guard. ar. *Crest*—A lion pass. guard. or.

L'Estrange (Moystown, King's co.; Fun. Ent. Ulster's Office, 1686, ANNE, dau. of HENRY L'ESTRANGE, and wife of EDMOND MALONE, Esq., of Ballynahown, co. Westmeath; descended from RICHARD L'ESTRANGE, second son of Sir THOMAS L'ESTRANGE, Knt., of Hunstanton, Sheriff of Norfolk). Same *Arms*, &c. *Motto*—Memento mei.

Le Strange (Knockyn, co. Salop; quartered by D'OYLY, of

603

Shottisham, co. Norfolk, and the East Indies, through DE DUNSTON, and by that family through NOEL, which last family acquired divers lands by marrying MARGARET, dau. of GUY, and sister and co-heiress to the lands of RALPH LE STRANGE, *temp.* Henry II.). Same *Arms*. *Badge*—Two hands conjoined in pale, the upper or, the other gu. *Motto*—Sans changer ma verité.

Le Strange (Sir NICHOLAS LE STRANGE, knighted by Sir WILLIAM FITZ-WILLIAM, Lord Deputy of Ireland). Gu. two lions pass. in pale ar. over all a bendlet of the last. *Crest*—A dexter and sinister hand couped at the wrist clasped ppr.

Lesturmy. Gu. a chev. betw. three estoiles or.

Lestwiche (Lestwiche, co. Chester). Ar. an orle betw. ten martlets sa. *Crest*—A still ar.

Le Sueur (Grouville, Jersey). Az. a chev. betw. two crescents in chief and a rose in base or. *Crest*—A bezant charged with a rose gu. *Motto*—Sure.

Lesume. Barry of ten ar. and az. three torteaux on the first bar.

Le Taylor (Lidgate and Stechworth, co. Suffolk ; JOHN LE TAYLOR, Esq., great-great-grandson of THOMAS LE TAYLOR, Esq., of Corlehill, co. Cumberland. Visit. London, 1563). Sa. a lion pass. ar., quartering, 1st, or, a lion ramp. guard. gu. collared or; 2nd, ar. a chev. gu. betw. three eagles displ. sa. *Crest*—A lynx ppr.

Letch. Gyronny of eight ar. and gu. an annulet counterchanged. *Crest*—A harp gu.

Lete, or Light (cos. Huntingdon and Suffolk). Ar. on a fesse gu. betw. two matches sa. rolled and fired ppr. a martlet or. *Crest*—Out of a ducal coronet or, a lamp of three branches of the same fired ppr.

Letebrooke. Az. a chev. erm.

Letemps. Vert an anchor in pale ar. *Crest*—Time passing with his scythe over his shoulder all ppr.

Letford (co. Gloucester). Gu. on a chev. ar. betw. two stags' heads erased of the second, armed or, in chief and a talbot pass. in base of the last, three mullets of the field, pierced gold.

Letham, or Lethem. Gu. a cross erm. *Crest*—A griffin's head betw. two wings, holding in the beak a feather all ppr.

Letham. Quarterly, ar. and ermines, in the 1st quarter a fleur-de-lis gu.

Lethbridge (Sandhill Park, co. Somerset, bart.). Ar. over water ppr. a bridge of five arches turreted gu., in chief an eagle displ. sa. *Crest*—Out of a mural crown or, a demi eagle displ. ppr. motto over, Truth. *Motto*—Spes mea in Deo.

Lethbridge (co. Devon). Sa. two bars gemelles betw. six roses ar. three, two, and one. *Crest*—A stag's head erased per fesse ar. and sa. attired or, in the mouth a rose of the first, stalked and leaved vert.

Lethieullier, or Lethulier (Acton, co. Middlesex). Ar. a chev. gu. betw. three parrots' heads couped vert, beaked of the second. *Crest*—A parrot ppr.

Lethieullier, or Lethulier (Alderstock, co. Essex). Ar. a chev. gu. betw. three parrots' heads erased vert. *Crest*, as the last.

Leton. Ar. two bars gu. in chief three wolves' heads couped of the second.

Le Touzel (Jersey). Gu. a fesse or, betw. three roses ar. on a chief az. three fleurs-de-lis of the second. *Crest*—Out of a ducal coronet or, a demi rose gu. and a demi fleur-de-lis gold conjoined. *Motto*—Deus ab inimicis me defendit.

Letsler. Gu. a lion ramp. ar. a bordure of the second, a mullet for diff.

Letster. Gu. a lion ramp. betw. three crescents ar.

Lett. Gu. a saltire or, on a chief of the last a crescent betw. two mullets sa. *Crest*—Three organ pipes, two in saltire surmounted by the third in pale banded vert.

Letterington. Gu. on a bend ar. three bears sa.

Lettice. Gu. on a chev. ar. three trefoils sa.

Letton, or Lytton (co. Hertford). Ar. two bars betw. three bears' heads erased gu. *Crest*—A dexter hand fesseways couped gu. holding up a cross crosslet fitchée az.

Letwood, alias Saracole (co. Lancaster, and London. Visit. London, 1633-4). Same *Arms* as SOROCOLD.

Leukenor. Az. three chevronels ar. *Crests*—1st : A unicorn's head couped az. platée, horned or; 2nd : A hawk's lure az. fringed ar.

Levall. Gu. a bend or, betw. six crescents ar. *Crest*—Out of the top of a tower issuing a Cornish chough, wings expanded all ppr.

Levall. Sa. three rams' heads couped ar. (another, ar. ten-billets sa. four, three, two, and one; another, gu. six crescents ar.; another, az. a bend ar.).

Levant, or Turkey Merchants, Company (incorporated by Queen Elizabeth, 1579). Az. on a sea in base ppr. a ship with three masts in full sail or, betw. two rocks of the second, all the sails, pennants, and ensigns ar. each charged with a cross gu. a chief engr. of the third, in base a seahorse ppr. *Crest*—A demi seahorse saliant. *Supporters*—Two seahorses. *Motto*—Deo reip et amicis.

Le Vavasour (co. York). Or, a fesse dancettée sa. *Crest*—A dog sa.

Leveale. See LEVELIS.

Leveland (co. Kent). Sa. three boars' heads couped bendways ar. two and one. *Crest*—A dexter hand holding a dagger in pale with a garland of laurel pendent therefrom ppr.

Levelis (Trewoof, co. Cornwall; ARTHUR LEVELIS, Visit. Cornwall, 1620, sixth in descent from THOMAS LEVELIS, of Castle Horneck, in same co., settled there since *temp.* William I.). Ar. three calves' heads couped gu. *Crest*—A tower masoned sa.

Leven, Earl of. See LESLIE.

Levens (WILLIAM LEVENS, Alderman, and five times Mayor of the city of Oxford, *d.* 12 April, 1616, aged 100 years; descended from LEVYNZ, of Levynz Hall, co. Westmoreland. Visit. Oxon. 1574). Ar. a hazel branch ppr. surmounted by a bend sa. charged with three escallops of the field. *Crest*—A squirrel sejant ppr. within a wreath of hazel leaves vert.

Leventhorpe (Shingey Hall, co. Herts, bart., extinct 1800). Ar. a bend gobony gu. and sa.

Leventhorpe (co. Kent). Ar. a bend gobony gu. and sa. betw. two cotises of the second.

Lever (Arlington, co. Lancaster). Ar. two bendlets sa. the under one engr. *Crest*—On a trumpet lying fesseways a cock all ppr.

Lever (Lever, co. Lancaster), Same *Arms*, a crescent gu. *Crest*—On a trumpet a cock, wings expanded all ppr. *Another Crest*—A hare ppr.

Lever (co. Lancaster). Ar. a chev. gu. betw. three harts trippant sa.

Lever. Sa. three boars' heads couped or (another, bears' heads).

Leverage. Ar. a chev, betw. three matchlocks sa. *Crest*—A leopard's face ppr.

Leveret (Fun. Ent. Ulster's Office, 1618, WILLIAM LEVERET, Athlone Herald, Leveret, also Athlone Herald). Quarterly, 1st and 4th, ar. in chief three battle axes erect sa., for LEVERET; 2nd and 3rd, gu. three chevronels vair, for TURVILE. *Crest*—A dove ar. holding in the beak an olive branch vert.

Leverett (Great Chelsea, 1662). Ar. a chev. betw. three leverets courant sa.

Leverett. Gyronny of eight or and sa. over all an eagle volant gu.

Leverick. Erm. on a fesse engr. sa. three mullets pierced or.

Leverington. Gu. (another, az.) three hares in pale ar.

Levermore (Lanlivery, co. Cornwall). Gu. three estoiles sa.

Levermore (Exeter, co. Devon). Ar. a fesse (another, cotised) sa. betw. three tufts of grass vert. *Crest*—An arm embowed holding a scymitar in pale ppr.

Leveroy. Ar. on a chev. sa. three leopards' faces or.

Leverpoole. Quarterly, gu. and or, a cross potence az.

Leversage (Leverseck, Whelock, Kinderton, and Bechton, co. Chester. Leversage of Whelock was acquired by a marriage, *temp.* Henry VI., with AGNES, dau. and heiress of THOMAS WORTH, who *m.* ELIZABETH, dau. of THOMAS WHELOCK, the male line of WHELOCK failing in 1439). Ar. a chev. betw. three ploughshares erect.sa. *Crest*—A leopard's face jessant-de-lis or.

Leversage. Gu. three lions' heads erased ar. in the centre a matchlock or. *Crest*—A leopard's head erased guard. ppr.

Leversedge (co. Essex). Gu. a chev. betw. three lions' heads erased or (another, ar.).

Leversedge (Vallis, co. Somerset). Sa. a chev. or, betw. three dolphins ar. *Crest*—A leopard's face jessant-de-lis or.

Leversedge. Gu. a cross engr. ar. (another, betw. four crescents or).

Leversedge (quartered by NEVILL, of Leversedge. Har. MSS. 1487). Lozengy ar. and sa.

Leversege. Sa. three bills' heads ar.

Leversege. Ar. a chev. betw. three matchlocks sa.

Leverton (Purley House, Croydon, co. Surrey). Gu. three

604

estoiles or, a canton erm. *Crest*—A pelican ar. vulning herself ppr.

Leverton. Vert a fesse wavy betw. three pelicans or vulning themselves ppr. *Crest*—A pelican ppr.

Leverton. Az. three hares ar. *Crest*—A hare sejant ar.

Leverton. Gu. two estoiles ar. a canton erm. (another estoiles with eight points or).

Leveryke. Erm. a fesse engr. gu.

Levesco. Per fesse ar. and sa. in base three bezants.

Levesey. See LIVESEY.

Levesey (cos. Kent and Lancaster). Ar. a lion ramp. guard gu. betw. three estoiles vert. *Crest*—A lion's paw issuing ppr. supporting an escutcheon gu.

Levesey (co. Lancaster). Sa. a lion ramp. within an orle of crosses formée fitchée ar.

Levesey, or Leviesey. Ar. a lion pass. gu. betw. three trefoils slipped vert. *Crest*—A lion's paw gu. holding a cluster of six trefoils vert.

Levesholme. Ar. a fleur-de-lis sa.

Leveson (Willenhall, co. Stafford; RICHARD DE LEVESON, of that place, *temp.* Edward I., had three sons: RICHARD LEVESON, *d. s. p.*; ROBERT LEVESON, of Wolverhampton ancestor of LEVESON, of that place, whose heiress, SARAH LEVESON, *m.* CHARLES FOWLER, Esq., of Pendeford: and JOHN LEVESON, Esq., of Willenhall, ancestor of LEVESON, of Lilles hall, co. Salop, and Haling, co. Kent; represented by the *Duke of Sutherland*). Az. three holly leaves or. *Crest*—A goat's head erased erm. attired or.

Leveson, or Lewson (Wolverhampton, co. Stafford *temp.* Edward I.). Quarterly, az. and gu. three sinister hands couped at the wrist and erect ar. *Crest*—An arm embowed in armour ppr. garnished or, holding in the gauntlet a battle axe, handle gu. blade ar.

Leveson-Gower (*Duke of Sutherland*). See GOWER.

Leveson-Gower (*Earl of Granville*). See GOWER.

Leveson (co. Warwick). Az. a fesse wavy ar. betw. three leaves or.

Leveson (London; NICHOLAS LEVESON, gent. Visit. London 1563). Az. a fess nebulée ar. betw. three leaves or quartering ar. a chev. gu. betw. three cinquefoils pierced sa. *Crest*—A goat's head erased ar. attired or.

Levet (Sherborn, co. Dorset). Sa. a fesse raguly betw. three lions' heads erased ar.

Levet, or Levett. Paly of six ar. and az. over all a bend paly of six gu. and or. *Crest*—A gadfly, wings endorsed ppr.

Levethrope. Ar. a bend componée sa. and gu. betw. two cotises of the last.

Levett (Wychnor Park, co. Stafford; granted to JOHN LEVETT, Esq.). Ar. a lion ramp. betw. three crosses crosslet fitchée sa. a bordure engr. az. charged with four crosses crosslet fitchée and four fleurs-de-lis alternately or. *Crest*—A demi lion ar. ducally crowned or, gorged with a collar az. in the dexter paw a cross crosslet fitchée sa. the sinister paw resting on an escutcheon of the third, charged with a fleur-de-lis gold.

Levett (Packington Hall). Same *Arms* and *Crest*.

Levett (Milford, co. Stafford; derived from Sir RICHARD LEVETT, Lord Mayor of London in 1700, son of WILLIAM LEVETT, Esq., of Savernake, Page to Charles I.). Ar. a lion ramp. sa. murally crowned or, and two crosses crosslet fitchée in pale betw. two piles issuing from the dexter and sinister chief sa. each pile charged with three crosses crosslet fitchée of the third. *Crest*—A demi lion ar. entwined in a sprig of laurel vert, and supporting a cross crosslet fitchée sa.

Levett (Salehurst, co. Sussex; granted by patent, 21 Dec 1607). Ar. a semée of crosses crosslet fitchée, a lion ramp sa. *Crest*—A demi lion ramp. ar. crowned or, holding a cross crosslet fitchée of the first.

Levett (Normanton, co. Nottingham. List of Knights, co. Notts). Sa. a fess embattled betw. three wolves' heads erased ar.

Levett (Normanton, co. Nottingham. Visit. 1614, Har. MSS. 1555). Ar. two chev. sa.

Levett (Fun. Ent. Ulster's Office, 1619, WILLIAM LEVETT, Citizen of Dublin). Ar. a chev. engr. paly of the first and gu. betw. three shovellers sa. beaked and legged of the second.

Levilloigne. Ar. three inescutcheons az. on each as many mullets of the field.

Leving, or Levinge. Per chev. vert and or, three escallops counterchanged. *Crest*—A sword and sheaf of wheat in saltire ppr.

Leving, or Living (Woolwich and Bridgen, co. Kent). Ar. on a bend az. three escallops erminois.

Levinge (High Park, now Knockdrin Castle, co. Westmeath, bart.). Quarterly, 1st, vert a chev. or, in chief three escallops ar., for LEVINGE; 2nd, az. on a chief or, three ravens ppr., for CORBYN: 3rd, vert three bucks trippant crowned or, for GREENE; 4th, sa. an escallop shell or, betw. three helmets close ar. garnished of the second, for KENNEDY. *Crest*—An escallop ar. within a garland ppr. *Motto*—Vestigia nulla retrorsum.

Levings, or Leving (cos. Derby and Warwick; granted 10 Sept. 1611; confirmed by the Deputies of Camden, Clarenceux, to THOMAS LEVING, of Baddesley, co. Warwick. Visit. Warwick). Vert a 'chev. or, in chief three escallops ar. *Crest*—Within a chaplet vert an escallop ar.

Levington (Levington, co. Cumberland, *temp.* Henry I.). Or, a saltire gu. on a chief of the second three boars' heads couped of the first.

Levington (Saltcoats, co. Haddington). Ar. a bend betw. two otters' (or boars'?) heads erased gu.

Levington. Ar. a saltire gu. on a chief of the second three bears' heads couped or.

Levins (co. Cambridge). Ar. a chev. gu. in chief three escallops of the second. *Crest*—A bull's head issuing sa. charged with a crescent gu.

Levins (co. Essex). Gu. billettée or, a fesse of the last.

Levins. Ar. on a chief indented sa. three martlets of the first.

Levinston. Ar. three pinks slipped gu. within a double tressure flory counterflory vert.

Levinz (London, cos. Northampton and Oxford). Ar. a vine with leaves and fruit ppr. over all on a bend sa. three escallops of the first. *Crest*—A squirrel sejant in a vine garden all ppr.

Levinz. Ar. on a bend sa. three escallops erm. *Crest*—On a torteau a squirrel sejant ppr.

Lew. Az. a cross couped ar. a chief nebulée gu. rayonée alternately wavy and straight or. *Crest*—A dexter arm holding a roll of vellum ppr.

Leward. Sa. a lion ramp. or, holding betw. the paws a mullet ar. *Crest*—A demi lion ramp. or, holding betw. the paws a mullet ar.

Lewcar. Ar. a chev. sa. betw. three horses' heads couped gu.

Lewcell (co. Wilts). Ar. four fusils in pale gu. a bordure sa. (another, az.) bezantée.

Lewellyn, or Llewellyn. Per pale or and ar. three lions pass. in pale gu. *Crest*—A pheon ppr.

Lewellin (confirmed by Hawkins, Ulster, 1775, to EDWARD LEWELLIN, son of ROBERT LEWELLIN, Esq., of Silvermines, co. Tipperary). Same *Arms*. *Crest*—Out of a ducal coronet or, a man's head couped at the shoulders and affrontée ppr. *Motto*—Virtus et nobilitas.

Lewen (Siston. co. Leicester). Or, a bend raguly sa. betw. two trefoils slipped vert. *Crest*—The moon in her complement ar.

Lewer. Ar. on a bend sa. three ewers of the first.

Lewes (Llysnewydd, South Wales). Gu. three serpents conjointed in triangle ar. *Crest*—An eagle displ. with a serpent embowed round the body ppr. *Motto*—Sine dolo.

Lewes (Lord Mayor of London). Quarterly, 1st and 4th, or, three serpents conjoined in triangle vert; 2nd and 3rd, ar. a lion ramp. sa. *Crest*—An eagle displ. sa. the feet resting on the wreath, in the beak and enwrapped round the body a serpent ppr.

Lewes (Norwich). Ar. a chev. betw. three trefoils slipped sa.

Lewes (co. Glamorgan). Sa. a lion ramp. ar. a bordure gobonated of the second and first.

Lewes (Wales). Chequy or and az. on a fesse gu. three leopards' faces jessant-de-lis of the first.

Lewes. Sa. a chev. betw. three trefoils slipped ar.

Lewes (List of Knights, temp. Cos. Derby and Nottingham). Sa. a bend erm. betw. six owls ar.

Lewes, Earl of. See NEVILL, *Marquess of Abergavenny*.

Lewes, Town of (co. Sussex). Chequy ar. and az. on a sinister canton of the first a lion ramp. of the second betw. eight crosses crosslets sa.

Lewesholme. Ar. a fleur-de-lis sa.

Lowhite (Bromham, co. Wilts). Az. a fesse betw. three garbs or.

Lewin (co. Hertford). Per pale gu. and az. three bucks' heads erased at the neck or. *Crest*—A buck trippant quarterly or and az.

Lewin (Sir GREGORY ALLNUTT LEWIN, Knt., Barrister-at-Law, son of RICHARD LEWIN, Esq., of Eltham, co. Kent). Same *Arms*, &c.

Lewin. Per fesse embattled or and az. three stags' heads cabossed counterchanged.

Lewin (Northbourne Court, co. Kent). Or, on a chev. betw. three elephants' heads erased gu. as many mullets ar.

Lewin (The Hollies, Bexley, co. Kent). Per pale gu. and or, three bucks' heads counterchanged. *Crest*—A buck trippant quarterly or and az. *Motto*—Dieu sait tout.

Lewin (Ottrington, co. Kent). Per pale gu. and az. three bucks' heads couped or. *Crest* – A buck trippant or, gorged with a chaplet vert.

Lewin (co. Kent). Or, a chev. engr. az. in chief three escallops gu. in base a bucks' head of the last. *Crest*—A sea lion ppr. tail nowed, holding in the paws a shield gu. charged with an escallop or.

Lewin. Or, six martlets gu. three, two, and one.

Lewin, or Lewins. Or, a bend counter-embattled betw. two trefoils slipped sa. *Crest*—A demi lion ramp. sa. holding a lozenge or, charged with a trefoil slipped vert.

Lewin (Cloghans, co. Mayo). Ar. a bend engr. sa. betw. two trefoils slipped vert. *Crest*—A demi lion sa. holding betw. the paws a trefoil slipped vert. *Motto*—Spes mea in Deo.

Lewin. See ROSS-LEWIN.

Lewis (Harpton Court, co. Radnor, bart.). Ar. a cross double parted and fretty sa., in the 1st and 4th quarters an eagle displ. gu.. and in the 2nd and 3rd a lion ramp. of the second, ducally crowned or. *Crest*—On a cap of maintenance an heraldic tiger statant or. *Motto*—Expertus fidelem.

Lewis (Brecon). Ar. a dragon's head and neck erased vert, holding in the mouth a bloody hand ppr.

Lewis (Bristol and London). Sa. a chev. erm. betw. three spears' heads ar.

Lewis (Canterbury). Or, on a chief sa. three estoiles of the field. *Crest*—An ermine pass. ppr.

Lewis (Doncaster; confirmed 22 Oct. 1586). Sa. a chev. betw. three trefoils slipped or.

Lewis (Stoke, co. Dorset, and co. Somerset). Erm. on a fesse az. three boars' heads couped ar. *Crest*—An antelope's head erased sa. armed, attired, maned, tufted, and ducally gorged or.

Lewis (cos. Essex, Hertford, and York). Sa. a chev. betw. three trefoils ar. *Crest*—Out of a ducal coronet or, a plume of five ostrich feathers ar.

Lewis (Rossenden-in-Bleane, co. Kent). Ar. a chev. gu. betw. three beavers' tails erect ppr. *Crest*—A demi beaver ppr.

Lewis (St. Pierre, co. Monmouth; descended through PHILIP LLEWELLEN-AP-IVOR, second son of LLEWELLEN, Lord of St. Clair and Tredegar, from CADIVOR, Prince of Divet, co. Pembroke, *temp.* William I.). Or, a lion ramp. guard. sa. *Crest*—A griffin segreant sa. *Motto*—Ha persa la fide ha perso l'honore.

Lewis (The Van, co. Glamorgan; derived from IVOR AP MEURIG, known in Welsh history as IVOR BACH, living *temp.* Henry II. The eventual heiress, ELIZABETH, only dau. of THOMAS LEWIS, Esq., of The Van, m. OTHER, *Earl of Plymouth*). Sa. a lion ramp. ar. *Crest*—A lion sejant ar. *Motto*—Patriæ fidus.

Lewis (Lanishen Court, co. Monmouth, and Lanishen House, co. Glamorgan ; both originally from LEWIS, of Van). Same *Arms*, *Crest*, and *Motto*.

Lewis (Green Meadow, co. Glamorgan). Quarterly, 1st, sa. a lion ramp. ar ; 2nd, sa. a chev. betw. three spear heads ar. embrued gu. ; 3rd, sa. a chev. betw. three fleurs-de-lis or; 4th, or, on a quarter gu. two lions pass. guard. of the first. *Crests*—1st, LEWIS; A lion sejant ar. 2nd, PRICE: A paschal lamb glorified or, bearing a pennon of St. George. *Mottoes*—Patriæ fidus ; and, Ofner na ofno angau.

Lewis (Gilfach, co. Carmarthen). Quarterly, 1st and 4th, az. a stag trippant ar. unguled and attired and bearing betw. his horns an imperial crown or ; 2nd and 3rd, az. a chev. betw, three eagles' heads erased or. *Crest*—A stag and an eagle's head, as in the arms.

Lewis (Llanarchayron, co. Cardigan). Gu. on a mount in fesse vert three towers triple-towered ar. betw. three scaling ladders or. *Crest*—Out of a mural coronet gu. a demi wolf saliant ar. *Motto*—Libertas.

Lewis (Gwynfe, Wales). Quarterly, 1st and 4th, gu. a griffin segreant or, for LEWIS, of South Wales ; 2nd and 3rd, sa. three nags' heads ar., for LLOYD. *Crest*—A demi griffin segreant couped or.

Lewis (Pengwerne, co. Merioneth). Erm. a saltire gu.

Lewis (co. Monmouth). Chequy or and sa. on a fesse gu. three leopards' faces jessant-de-lis of the first.

Lewis (Sutton Magna, co. Salop). Gu. a griffin segreant or. *Crest*—A demi griffin or.

Lewis (Malvern Hall, co. Warwick). Gu. three serpents nowed in triangle ar. within a bordure engr. or.

Lewis, or Lewys (Ledstone Hall and Marre, co. York, bart,; extinct). Sa. a chev. betw. three trefoils or. *Crest*, 1674—Out of a ducal coronet a plume of five ostrich feathers, two or and three sa. charged with a chev. of the first. *Motto*—Spe tutiore armis.

Lewis. Vert a lion ramp. or. *Crest*—On a mount vert a greyhound couchant gu. collared or.

Lewis. Az. a wolf ramp. ar. *Crest*—A demi wolf ramp. ar.

Lewis (Stanford, co. Nottingham). Ar. on a fesse az. three boars' heads couped or, in chief a lion pass. gu. *Crest*—Out of a mural coronet or, a boar's head erect erm. langued gu.

Lewis. Paly of six ar. and gu on a chief az. a lion pass. ar. ducally crowned or. *Crest*—On a chapeau gu. turned up erm. a greyhound sa. collared or.

Lewis. Per pale indented az. and ar. three trefoils slipped counterchanged.

Lewis, or Lewes. Ar. on a fesse az. three boars' heads couped or, in chief a lion pass. gu.

Lewis. Per fesse gu, and az. three bucks' heads couped at the neck or.

Lewis (Clynfiew, co. Pembroke). Gu. three serpents nowed in triangle ar. within a bordure engr. or. *Crest*—A nag's head couped, bridled ppr. *Motto*, in English—Be wise as a serpent, harmless as a dove.

Lewis (Festiniog, co. Merioneth; derived, through IEVAN, of Maes-y-Gammedd, son of DAVID AP IEVAN, Constable of Harlech Castle, *temp.* Henry VI., from OSBORNE FITZ-GERALD, Lord of Ynys-y-Maengwyn). Same *Arms* as OS-BORNE FITZGERALD.

Lewis (HAMPTON-LEWIS, Bodior and Henllys, co. Anglesey). Quarterly, 1st and 4th, quarterly, 1st and 4th, ar. a chev. sa. betw. three Cornish choughs ppr. in the beak of each an erm. spot, for LEWIS, 2nd and 3rd gu. on a chev. betw. three bucks' heads cabossed ar. a crescent of the field for diff., for ROBERTS, of Bodior; 2nd and 3rd quarters, HAMPTON, gu. on a fesse or, betw. a mullet in chief and an escallop in base ar. three martlets sa. *Crests*—1st, LEWIS: A Cornish chough ppr. in the dexter claw a fleur-de-lis az.; 2nd, HAMPTON: A wivern amidst bulrushes ppr. *Motto*—A Deo et rege.

Lewis (Lampeter Velfry, co. Pembroke). Az. a chev. erm. betw. three garbs. *Crest*—An arm embowed holding an arrow. *Motto*—Sors est contra me.

Lewis (THOMAS LEWIS, Dublin; impalement Fun. Ent. Ulster's Office, 1656, of his son-in-law, WALTER CARWARDEN). Sa. three scaling ladders ar. in chief an eagle displ. of the last.

Lewis (JOHN LEWIS, Esq., of Prescoed, whose only dau. and heir *m.* Col. MARCUS TREVOR, created 1662, *Viscount Dungannon;* impalement Fun. Ent. Ulster's Office of *Lord Dungannon, d.* Jan. 1669). Az. a chev. betw. three lions ramp. or.

Lewis (confirmed to ARTHUR GAMBELL LEWIS, Esq., of Sea-town, co. Dublin, and Clanamully, co. Monaghan). Sa. on a chev. erm. betw. three spear heads ar. a crescent gu. *Crest*—Out of a ducal coronet ppr. a plume of five ostrich feathers alternately and az. charged with a chev. or, thereon a crescent gu. *Motto*—Bidd llu hebb llydd.

Lewis (Kilcullen, co. Kildare, and Grosvenor Street, Gros-venor Square, London). Same *Arms*, a mullet gu. *Crest*—Out of a ducal coronet ppr. a plume of five ostrich feathers alternately gu. and az. charged with a chev. or. *Motto*—Bidd llu hebb llydd.

Lewiston (Lewiston, co. Dorset, cos. Durham and Hun-tingdon). Gu. three battle axes ar.

Lewkenor. Gu. three bucks' heads couped ar.

Lewkenor (co. Kent). Gu. three bucks' heads cabossed or.

Lewknor (West Dean, co. Sussex, and co. Worcester). Az. three chev. ar. (another, or). *Crest*—A greyhound courant ar. collared or. *Another Crest*—A unicorn's head erased az. benzantée, horned and maned or.

Lewknor. Sa. six doves ar. three, two, and one.

Lewley. Ar. a chev. sa. betw. three herons' heads of the second, beaked gu.

Lewne. Erm. on a bend gu. three escallops or.

Le Wright. Per pale or and gu. a lion ramp. purp. charged on the shoulder with a cross ancrée sa.

Lews (co. Norfolk). Or, a saltire engr. vert.

Lewsell. Ar. a pale fusily gu. within a bordure az. bezantée. *Crest*—An antelope's head guard. or, attired sa.

Lewsell. Ar. a pale lozengy within a bordure az. bezantée.

Lewson (co. Warwick). Az. a fesse wavy or, betw. three trefoils of the second.

Lewson, or Leveson. Az. a fesse per fesse nebulée or and sa. betw. three laurel leaves erect of the second. *Crest*—A goat's head erased erm. attired or.

Lewston (co. Dorset). Gu. three battle axes pale or, edged ar.

Lewthwaite (Broadgate, co. Cumberland, Adel Rectory, near Leeds, and Whitehaven). Erm. a cross flory az. fretty or. *Crest*—A garb or, banded by a serpent ppr. holding in the mouth a cross crosslet fitchée gu. *Motto*—Tendens ad æthera virtus.

Lewyne. Erm. on a bend gu. three escallops or.

Lewyres (co. Kerry; Reg. Ulster's Office). Ar. on a fess az. three bears' heads couped fessways of the first, in chief a lion pas:. ppr.

Lewys (Wales). Or, a chev. betw. three lions ramp. gu.

Lewys. Sa. a chev. betw. three trefoils slipped ar.

Lexham. Sa. three fleurs-de-lis or.

Lexinton (Tuxford, co. Nottingham; ROBERT DE LEXING-TON, Chief Justice of Common Pleas, 26 Henry III., 1241, eldest son of JOHN DE LEXINTON, Lord of Tuxford, *d. s. p.;* his sister and co-heir *m.* ROWLAND SUTTON, ancestor of the extinct *Lords Lexinton, of* Aram. Visit. Notts, 1614). Ar. a cross patoncée az.

Lexinton (co. York). Sa. three saltires engr. ar. *Crest*—A demi lady betw. two branches of palm disposed in orle, holding in her hand a thistle ppr.

Lexsinton, or Lesenton. Ar. three saltires engr. sa. in chief a crescent of the second.

Lexton. Ar. on a chief az. three catherine wheels or. *Crest*—Issuing from a castle triple-towered a demi lion ppr.

Ley (Ley, co. Devon; HENRY LEY, of Ley, captain of a com-pany of foot, served against the Western rebels, *temp.* Edward VI., and against Sir Thomas Wyatt, *temp.* Mary I., sold all his ancient lands in cos. Devon and Cornwall, and purchased the Manor of Teffont-evias, Wilts, *d.* 7 June, 1574, leaving three sons surviving; he was descended from HENRY DE LEY, living 20 Richard II., 1396, who was the descendant of WILLIAM DE LEIGH, living 24 Edward I., 1295, the sixth known possessor of a house and land called Leigh or Ley, in the hundred of Rowburgh, co. Devon). Ar. a chev. betw. three bears' heads couped bendways sa. langued gu. *Crest*—A lion sejant or.

Ley (*Earl of Marlborough,* extinct 1679; Sir JAMES LEY (third son of the above HENRY LEY, Esq.), Chief Justice of the King's Bench in Ireland, and Lord President of the Council, was created a bart. 1619, a baron 1622, and raised to the earldom 1626). Same *Arms, Crest* and *Motto. Supporters*—Dexter, a lion ar. semée of trefoils slipped vert; sinister, a lion gu. bezantée.

Ley (Kempthorne and Tonacombe, co. Cornwall; JOHN LEY, of the latter, Visit. Cornwall, 1620, descended from LEY, of Ley, co. Devon). Same *Arms* and *Crest.*

Ley (Trevorgan Vean, in St. Erme, co. Cornwall). Ar. three pine trees vert.

Ley, or Leys (co. Huntingdon). Sa. a chev. or, betw. three sinister hands couped ar.

Ley (co. Stafford). Ar. a bend lozengy gu.

Ley or Lea (co. Warwick). Ar. on a chief sa. two (another, three) scythe blades point to point ar. (another, or).

Ley (co. Wilts. and Kenn, co. Devon). Ar. a chev. betw. three seals' heads (sometimes bears' heads) couped sa. *Crest*—A lion sejant or, the dexter forepaw raised. *Motto*—Vincendo victus.

Ley (Combe Martin and Ley House, Marwood, co. Devon). Same *Arms, Crest,* and *Motto.*

Ley. Ar. a chev. betw. three birds' heads couped sa.

Ley. Ar. on chief sa. three plates.

Ley, or Lea. Or, a saltire sa. on chief gu. three martlets of the field.

Ley, or Lea. Ar. on a chief sa. three bezants.

Ley. Per chev. or and gu.

Ley (Reg. Ulster's Office). Sa. a fleur-de-lis ar.

Leybock. Ar. six lions ramp. gu.

Leyborn. Ar. on a bend sa. three annulets of the first, in the sinister chief a trefoil slipped of the second.

Leyborne (co. Kent, Cunswicke, co. Westmorland, and Caveswick, co. York). Az. (another, gu.) six lions ramp. ar. three, two, and one (another coat, trefoils reversed; another, a border engr. or). *Crest*—An eagle reguard. with wings expanded az. beaked and legged or.

Leyborne (impalement Fun. Ent. Ulster's Office, 1633, JOHN SHEE, Mayor of Kilkenny, whose wife was LUCY LEYBORNE). Same *Arms, Crest* and gu.

Leybourn. Ar. on a chief gu. two buck's heads cabossed or. *Crest*—A buck's head erased ppr.

Leybourns. Sa. two lions' paws erased in saltire and inverted erm. armed or.

Leyburn (*Baron Leyburne*, extinct, 1369; Sir ROGER DE LEIBURN, summoned to Parliament 1299). Az. six lioncels ramp. ar.

Leyburne (arms in a window in Dorchester Church, co. Oxford. Visit. Oxon, 1566). Az. six lions ramp. ar. three, two, and one.

Leycester (*Lord de Tabley*). See LEICESTER.

Leycester. Or, a fesse az. betw. three fleurs-de-lis gu. *Crest*—A demi lion ramp. sa. holding a fleur-de-lis.

Leycester (Nether Tabley, co. Chester; a family of great antiquity, descended from the marriage, *temp.* Henry III., of NICHOLAS DE LEYCESTER with MARGARET DE DUTTON, of Nether Tabley; the eventual representative, MURIEL, dau. and heir of Sir FRANCIS LEYCESTER, Bart., *m.* 1st, FLEETWOOD LEIGH, Esq., and 2nd, Sir JOHN BYRNE, Bart., of Timogue, ancestor of the *Lords de Tabley*). Az. a fess betw. two fleurs-de-lis or. *Crest*—A swan's head and neck couped ar. gutté de sang.

Leycester (Toft, co. Chester; descended from RALPH LEYCESTER (a younger brother of LEYCESTER, of Tabley), living *temp.* Richard II., by JOAN, his wife, dau. and heir of ROBERT TOFT, Esq., of Toft; as granted by Sir Gilbert Dethick, Norroy, to Sir RAFE LEYCESTER, Knt., of Toft, 15 May, 2 Edward VI.). Sa. on a fesse engr. betw. three falcons volant ar. beaked and legged or, a lion's face az. langued and eared ppr. two covered cups gu. *Crest*—A roebuck trippant per pale or and gu. horned of the second, holding in his mouth an acorn branch vert. N.B.—Sir PETER LEYCESTER, the Cheshire antiquary, writing of this coat, says: "I wonder that he should seek for a coat, as being ignorant of the one due to him."

Leycester (Worleston, co. Chester). Same *Arms* as LEYCESTER, of Nether Tabley, a crescent for diff. *Crest*—A fleur-de-lis per fesse or and az.

Leycester (Poole, co. Chester; descended from RANDAL LEYCESTER, son of the first RALPH LEYCESTER, of Toft, the last male whereof was RICHARD LEYCESTER, Mayor of Chester, *d.* 1658; his youngest sister and eventual heiress, *m.* RANDAL MINSHULL, of Hampton. Same *Arms*, &c., as LEYCESTER, of Toft.

Leycester (White Place, near Maidenhead, co. Berks). Az. a fesse or, fretty gu. betw. two fleurs-de-lis of the second. *Crest*—A roebuck statant per pale or and gu. attired of the second, holding in his mouth an acorn branch ppr. *Motto*—Dominus illuminatio mea.

Leycester (co. Chester). Az. a fess gu. between three fleurs-de-lis or, and a bordure ar.

Leycester (co. Chester). Ar. a chev. betw. three T's sa. (Also borne by TOFT, of co. Chester).

Leycroft. Erm. a cross pattée throughout gu. *Crest*—A hand erect vested az. holding in the hand ppr. a chaplet gu.

Leyke. Ar. on a saltire engr. sa. five annulets of the field.

Leyland (Morley, co. Lancaster; ANNE, dau. and heir of THOMAS LEYLAND, *m.* EDWARD TYLDESLEY, of Tyldesley). Ar. on a fess sa. a lion pass. betw. two escallops of the field, in chief nine ears of barley gu. three, three, and three, each placed one in pale and two in saltire, and banded with a string or. *Crest*—A demi dove ar. wings endorsed az. in the beak three ears of wheat or.

Leyland (The Grange, Hindley, near Wigan, co. Lancaster; JOHN LEYLAND, Esq., fifth in descent from JAMES LEYLAND, Esq., *d.* 1679, seized of an estate in Ashton-in-Makerfield, same co.). Per fess sa. and barry wavy of six ar. and az. in chief nine ears of wheat or three, three, and three, banded gu. *Crest*—On a mount vert amid flags a corn-crake all ppr. in the beak three ears of wheat or. *Motto*—God feedeth ye land.

Leyland (co. Lancaster). Quarterly, 1st and 4th, or, on a bend sa. a lion pass. ar. in chief three roses gu.; 2nd and 3rd, ar. two swords in saltire sa.

Leyland (co. Lancaster). Ar. on a fesse sa. a lion betw. two crescents of the field.

Leyley or Lilly. Gu. three lilies ar. stalked vert.

Leyll (Scotland). Gu. a fret or.

Leyneshelme. Ar. a fleur-de-lis sa.

Leynham. Quarterly ar. and sa., in the 1st quarter a fleur-de-lis gu., on the 2nd a fleur-de-lis erm.

Leynham (co. Berks). Sa. six fleurs-de-lis or, three, two, and one.

Leynys. Az. a fesse nebulée charged on each nebulé with a torteau betw. six oak leaves or. *Crest*—A hand holding an oak branch acorned or.

Lezers, or Leyzers. Paly of six or and gu. a fesse az.

Liall (co. Kent). Gu. six crescents ar. three, two, and one, over all a bend gobonated or and az.

607

Liall. Az. a bend betw. six crosses crosslet fitchée or.

Liall. Gu. six crescents ar. three, two, and one.

Liard (co. Norfolk). Ar. a bull pass. coward sa. within a bordure of the last bezantée. *Crest*—An antelope trippant ppr. collared or.

Libberton (that Ilk, co. Edinburgh). Vert a leopard's face or.

Libby. Erm. a lion ramp. az. *Crest*—Oat of a paling or, a dexter arm ppr. vested gu. holding a baton az. tipped of the first.

Liberton (England). Vair on a pale gu. three leopards' heads guard. erased or. *Crest*—A stag's head couped az.

Lichfield, Earl of. See ANSON.

Lichfield, City of. Or, a cross quarter pierced erm. betw. five chev. gu. M.S., Coll. of Arms, "Arms of Towus." N.B. At various times five or six different coats have been given for this city. The above having the authority of Robert Cooke, Clarenceux, who *d.* 1592, is selected as the oldest.

Lichfield, Corporation Seal of. The common seal of the Corporation, made about the year 1620, represents three slain kings in armour, with crowns, broken swords, and weapons lying near them. From the rudeness of the execution it appears to be the copy of a much older seal, probably that of the guild of St. Mary. Gwillim blazons the arms of the city, "On a landscape proper several martyrs in divers manners massacred."

Lichfield, See of. Per pale gu. and ar. a cross potent quadrat in the centre betw. four crosses pattée all counterchanged. Anciently the arms were blazoned, "Per pale gu. and ar. a cross potent quadrat in the centre per pale of the last and or, betw. four crosses patée, those on the dexter ar. those on the sinister or." These arms are also used by the Dean and Chapter.

Lichfield (co. Oxford). Per chev. sa. and ar. in chief three leopards' faces or. *Crest*—An arm embowed vested ar. holding in the hand ppr. a bow or, strung gu.

Lichfield. Same *Arms*. *Crest*—On a chapeau gu. turned up erm. a garb. ppr.

Lichfield. Per chev. sa. and ar. three leopards' faces counterchanged.

Lichfield. Az. two bends ar.

Lichford. Sa. a chev. betw. three leopards' faces ar.

Lichinfield. Per chev. sa. and ar. three leopards' faces in chief or.

Lickton. Gu. a chev. engr. or, betw. three cinquefoils ar.

Lidcott. (Rushcombe, co. Berks: CHRISTOPHER LIDCOTT, Esq., son of JOHN LIDCOTT, Esq. Visit. Oxon, 1574). Vairé ar. and sa. two bars or, on a chief of the last three dovecotes gu., quartering, for BURLEY, ar. a chief sa. over all three titling spears erect counterchanged. *Crest*—A catharine wheel or, surmounted with a boar's head couped sa. ringed gold.

Lidcott (Checkendon, co. Oxford: LEONARD LIDCOTT, second son of CHRISTOPHER LIDCOTT, Esq., of Rushcombe. Visit. Oxon, 1574). Same *Arms* and *Crest*.

Liddell (Halkertoun, co. Kincardine). Gu. on a bend ar. three mullets sa.

Liddell (Edinburgh, 1672). Gu. on a bend betw. a cross crosslet fitchée in chief and a fleur-de-lis in base ar. three spur-rowels of the first. *Crest*—A rose slipped ppr. *Motto*—Hinc odor et sanitas.

Liddell (*Earl of Ravensworth*). Ar. fretty gu. on a chief of the last three leopards' faces or. *Crest*—A lion ramp. sa. billetée and crowned with an Eastern crown or. *Supporters*—Two leopards or. semée of golps, and gorged with mural crowns purp. *Motto*—Fama semper vivit.

Liddell (*Baron Ravensworth*, extinct 1749; Sir HENRY LIDDELL, fourth bart. of Ravensworth Castle, was so created 1747, *d. s. p.* and was *s.* in the baronetcy by his nephew, Sir HENRY GEORGE LIDDELL, fifth bart., ancestor of the *Earl of Ravensworth*). Same *Arms*, &c.

Liddell (cos. Durham and Northumberland). Same *Arms* (leopards' faces or), *Crest*, and *Motto*.

Lidderdale (St. Mary Isle, co. Kirkcudbright). Az. a chev. erm. *Crest*—An eagle's head erased ppr. *Motto*—Foresight is all.

Lidderdale (London; from Scotland, 1685). Same *Arms*, within a bordure engr. ar. *Crest*, as the last. *Motto*—Per belle qui prævidet.

Liddiard, alias Stratton (Rockley, co. Wilts). Quarterly, 1st and 4th, erm. on a chev. or, three mullets pierced gu.; 2nd and 3rd or, on a chief inder red az. three escallops of the first. *Crest*—A demi lion ra np. ar. holding in the dexter paw a mullet gu.

Liddiat (Humley and Walsall. co. Stafford, and Wollaston, co. Worcester). Gu. a fesse ermincis betw. three wolves' heads couped or. *Crest*—A wolf's head erased per pale erminois and gu.

Liddle. Gu. a fesse wavy betw. three boars' heads erased ar. *Crest*—Two lions' gambs erased supporting a column ppr.

Lidel. Ar. fretty gu. on a chief of the second three leopards' faces or. *Crest*—Two hands conjoined in fesse, each hand united to a wing at the wrist.

Lidgbird (Plumstead, co. Kent, and Rougham, co. Suffolk; granted 1740). Quarterly, gu. and az. a chev. erm. in chief two eagles displ. ar. in base a lion pass. or. *Crest*—A mural crown, therein a trunk of a tree ppr. sprouting vert, surmounted with a pelican of the third, vulning herself of the fourth ducally crowned az.

Lidsel (co. Essex). Gu. three garbs ar.

Lidsey (London). Gu. a fesse chequy or and az. in chief a trefoil slipped betw. two mullets of the second. *Crest*—A demi griffin segreant az. beaked and legged gu. in the dexter claw a trefoil slipped or.

Lidwall (Bathebar, Scotland). Per fesse gu. and ar. a fesse wavy az. with spikes on each side counterchanged, an escutcheon surtout or.

Lidwall (Dromard, Clonmore, and Cormackstown, co. Tipperary). Ar. fretty gu. on a chief of the second three leopards or. *Crest*—A lion ramp. sa. crowned or. *Motto*—Vis unita fortior.

Lie (co. Chester). Ar. a bend fusily, in the sinister chief a crescent sa.

Lie. Sa. a chev. or, betw. three hawks' lures ar.

Lienis, or Lyenys. Az. a fesse nebulée ar. guttée de sang betw. six leaves or. *Crest*—An arm couped at the elbow and erect, vested ar. holding in the hand ppr. a bunch of acorns vert, fructed or.

Lieubenrood (Prospect Hill, near Reading, co. Berks). Ar. three bends sa. on a chief gu. a demi buck saliant, issuant ar. attired and unguled or. *Crest*—Out of an eastern coronet gu. two antelopes' horns ar. round each a ribbon twisted vert.

Lievre (Rev. JOHN STURGE LIEVRE, A.M.). Az. a chev. or, betw. two roses in chief ar. barbed and seeded ppr. and an eagle displ. with two heads in base of the same. *Crest*—A hare courant ppr., motto over, Il y a de ma vie. *Motto*—Gardez bien.

Life. Or, on a fesse betw. three martlets sa. as many harts of the field.

Lifelde, or Lifield (co. Surrey). Or (another, erm.) on a chev. betw. three demi lions gu. as many trefoils slipped of the field. *Crest*—A bull's head cabossed ar. armed or, charged on the forehead with three erm. spots, one and two.

Lifford, Viscount. See HEWITT.

Ligen (Harlackston, co. Lincoln, formerly of Hainault; granted 20 Jan. 1619). Or, a chief chequy ar. and az. over all a bend gu.

Liggen, or Ligney. Chequy ar. and az. a fesse gu.

Ligh (co. Cornwall). Vert a saltire betw. four eagles displ. or.

Ligh. Ar. a bend lozengy betw. two crosses crosslets fitchée sa.

Ligham. Barry of six or and az. a bend gu.

Lighes, Leighes, or Lees Priory (co. Essex). Az. three plates, each charged with three piles wavy gu.

Light (Lites Cary, co. Somerset). Gu. a chev. betw. three swans rising ar. *Crest*—A plume of three ostrich feathers, the external ones gu. the centre one ar. issuing from behind a demi swan rising ppr.

Light (Horley, co. Oxford; CHRISTOPHER LIGHT, of that place, was buried there 16 Aug. 1546; CHRISTOPHER LIGHT was of the same place. Visit. Oxon, 1574). Same *Arms* and *Crest*, each charged with a crescent for diff.

Light. Vert a saltire betw. four eagles displ. or.

Light Gu. three swans ar.

Lightbody (Glasgow, 1786). Az. on a pale or, betw. two mullets in chief and as many crescents in base ar. a lion ramp. gu. *Crest*—A star issuant from a cloud ppr. *Motto*—Clarior e tenebris.

Lightbody (Liverpool, 1767). Az. on a pale engr. or, betw. two mullets in chief of the second and as many crescents in base ar. a lion ramp. gu. *Crest*—A star issuing from a cloud ppr. *Motto*—Clarior e tenebris.

Lightborne (Manchester; granted 1662). Az. six lions ramp. three, two, and one ar. on a bordure of the second ten hurts. *Crest*—An eagle displ. az. ducally gorged, beaked and membered or.

Lightborne (co. Somerset). Same *Arms*, bordure engr. or.

Lightborne, or Likeborne. Sa. three lozenges ar.

Lightfoot (Ashford, co. Kent). Barry of six or and gu. on

a bend sa. three escallops ar. *Crest*—A human heart pierced with a passion-nail in bend.

Lightfoot (London). Same *Arms*, escallops of the first.

Lightford. Az. a pale rayonée or.

Lightlie. Ar. on a fesse sa. an annulet of the field.

Lightolres (co. Lancaster). Vert a lion ramp. or, charged with caltraps sa.

Lighton (Merville, co. Dublin, bart.). Barry of eight ar. and vert, over all a lion ramp. crowned with an eastern crown or, armed and langued az. a canton of Ireland. *Crest*—A lion's head erased, crowned with an eastern crown or, langued az. *Motto*—Fortitudine et prudentia.

Ligo (Burcot, Weston Turville, and Stoke Mandeville, co. Buckingham). Or, on a pale sa. three estoiles of the field. *Crest*—On a chapeau az. turned up ar. an estoile betw. two wings expanded or.

Ligon (Upton, St. Leonard's, co. Gloucester, and Madresfield, co. Worcester). Ar. two lions pass. in pale gu. (another, sa.). *Crest*—A Saracen's head ppr. wreathed about the temples ar. and gu. *Another Crest*—An old man's head ppr. hair and beard sa.

Ligon. Chequy ar. and az. a fesse gu.

Ligonier (*Earl of Ligonier* and *Viscount Ligonier*, of Clonwell, earldom extinct 1770, viscounty 1782; Sir JOHN LIGONIER, of an ancient French family, was created a viscount 1757, got a new patent, with remainder to his nephew, 1762, and was created an earl 1766, *d. s. p.*). Gu. a lion ramp. or, on a chief ar. a crescent betw. two mullets az. *Crest*—Out of a mural coronet or, a demi lion erminois holding in the dexter paw a palm branch vert. *Supporters*—Two lions reguard. erminois, murally gorged gu. each supporting in the interior paw a tilting spear ppr. headed or, thereon a banner of the arms fringed and tasselled gold. *Motto*—A rege et victoria.

Ligonier (London, and Cobham, co. Surrey). Gu. a lion ramp. or, on a chief ar. a crescent betw. two annulets az. *Crest*—A demi lion ramp. erminois issuing out of a mural coronet gu. holding in the dexter paw a palm branch vert.

Lihou (Guernsey). Ar. a heart in chief and a crescent in base gu.

Lilborne. Ermines a chev. betw. three crescents or.

Lilburne, or Lilborne (Thickley, Pincherdon, co. Durham). Ar. three water bougets sa. *Crest*—A dexter arm in armour ppr. holding a truncheon or. *Another Crest*—A castle triple-towered ppr. flagged sa. *Motto*—Vis viri fragilis.

Lile (co. Middlesex). Erminois, on a chief az. three lions ramp. or.

Lilford, Baron. See POWYS.

Lilgrave, or Lillgrave (co. York). Ar. on a chev. betw. three water bougets sa. as many estoiles or.

Lill, or Lioll (co. Kent). Gu. a bend gobonated or and az. betw. six crescents ar.

Lill (Fun. Ent. Ulster's Office, 1629, ELIZABETH, wife of WILLIAM LILL, buried in the Church of Trim, co. Meath). Ar. a fess sa. betw. six mullets of six points gu.

Lillburn. Sa. three lozenges ar.

Lille (co. Rutland). Ar. on a fesse betw. two chev. sa. three roses ar.

Lille, or Lile. Ar. a fesse betw. six estoiles pierced gu. *Crest*—On a chapeau ppr. a lion couchant or.

Lilleborne. Per pale ar. and sa. a chev. counterchanged.

Lillegrane (co. York). Or, on a chev. betw. three water bougets sa. as many stars of the field.

Lillie (England). Per chev. ar. and gu. three lilies counterchanged. *Crest*—A rose gu. betw. the attires of a stag or.

Lillie (Drimdoe Castle, co. Roscommon). Az. three lilies ar.

Lilling. Gu. three pikes naiant in pale, a bordure engr. az.

Lilling (impalement Fun. Ent. Ulster's Office, 1620, THOMAS RUSSELL, Sheriff of Dublin). Same *Arms*, border plain pellettée.

Lilling (co. Norfolk). Same *Arms* (another, the bordure plain).

Lillinge. Gu. three salmons naiant in pale ar., a bordure erm.

Lillington (co. Dorset). Chequy ar. and vert.

Lillingston (Ferriby Grange, co. York, supposed to be of German extraction; the heiress m. SPOONER). A bugle stringed between three crescents.

Lilly, or Lighly (Newhall, co. York). Ar. on a fesse sa. a fleur-de-lis or. *Crest*—A dexter hand apaumée gu.

Lilly, or Lisley (cos. Northampton and York). Or, another, ar.) on a fesse betw. two chev. sa. three roses ar.

Lilly (Stoke Prior and Bromsgrove, co. Worcester; NICHOLAS LILLY was fined for not taking knighthood at the coronation of Charles I.). Gu. three lilies slipped ar. *Crest*—A swan head erased ar. *Another Crest*—A heart gu. winged or, charged with a fleur-de-lis gold.

Limbery, or Lymbrey (co. Dorset). Per pale ar. and gu. a chev. betw. three lions ramp. counterchanged. *Crest*— A unicorn pass. gu. crined, armed, and hoofed or.

Limborne. Ar. an inescutcheon sa. within an orle of martlets gu. *Crest*—A dexter hand holding a hunting horn sans strings ppr.

Limborne. Ar. a chev. sa. within an orle of nine martlets gu.

Limbury (Limehouse, co. Middlesex). Per pale ar. and gu. a chev. betw. three lions ramp. counterchanged.

Limbury. Ar. six cinquefoils sa. three, two, and one.

Lime. Gu. three lozenges in pale ar.

Limerick, Earl of. See PERY.

Limerick, See of. Az. in the dexter chief a crosier, in the sinister a mitre labelled, and in base two keys indorsed saltirewise all or.

Limerick, City of. Quarterly, 1st and 4th, gu. a castle, on each tower an obtuse spire with a weathercock, on an arch over the curtain wall a cross flory ar.; 2nd and 3rd, gu. three lions of England or.

Limesey (Long Iching, co. Warwick). Gu. three eagles displ. or.

Limesie. Ar. two bars gu. *Crest*—A rose bush bearing roses ppr.

Limpenie (Her. Office). Per pale sa. and gu. a mountain cat betw. three roses ar.

Limsey (Arley, co. Warwick, *temp.* Henry III.). Gu. an eagle displ. or, armed sa.

Limsey. Gu. three allerions displ. or.

Limsey. Or, an eagle displ. gu. a bordure of the second charged with eight cinquefoils ar.

Linacre (Linacre Hall, co. Derby; twenty descents of this ancient family recorded in Vincent's Derbyshire Peds.). Sa. a chev. betw. three escallops ar. on a chief or, three greyhounds' heads erased of the first. *Crest*—A greyhound's head erased quarterly ar. and sa. charged with four escallops counterchanged.

Linacre. Sa. a chev. betw. three escallops ar. a chief or. (another, the chief charged with a bear's head muzzled sa.).

Linaker (Fun. Ent. Ulster's Office, 1620, ROBERT LINAKER, some time Sheriff of Dublin). Per pale ar. and az. an eagle's head betw. two escallops counterchanged.

Linarce (co. York). Az. a chev. betw. three fleurs-de-lis ar.

Linarce. Ar. on a fesse az. five estoiles or.

Linbury, or Limburgh. Ar. six cinquefoils sa. pierced gu. three, two, and one.

Linch. Sa. three lynxes saliant ar. *Crest*—A lynx pass. ar.

Lincoln, See of. Gu. two lions pass. guard. or, on a chief az. the Holy Virgin and Child sitting crowned and bearing a sceptre of the second.

Lincoln College (co. Oxford; founded 1429, by Hugh Fleming, then Bishop of Lincoln). The escutcheon divided paleways into three parts, the centre ar. thereon the arms of the see of Lincoln, ensigned with a mitre all ppr., on the dexter side the arms of RICHARD FLEMING, Bishop of Lincoln, viz.: barry of six ar. and az. in chief three lozenges gu. the sinister side vert three stags trippant, two and one ar. attired or; being the arms of THOMAS SCOTT, otherwise ROTHERHAM, who first was Bishop of Rochester, afterwards Bishop of Lincoln, then Archbishop of York, and Chancellor of England, under the title of Sancta Cæcilia. He finished the college, and in 1479 refounded and liberally endowed it.

Lincoln, City of. Ar. on a cross gu. a fleur-de-lis or. The city seal is a castle with five towers with the above arms placed over the port.

Lincoln. Ar. on a cross vert an estoile pierced or.

Lincoln (impalement Fun. Ent. Ulster's Office, 1678, WILLIAM BARON). Ar. a lion ramp. sa.

Lincolne (cos. Dorset and Somerset, *temp.* Richard I.). Quarterly, per pale indented or and gu., in the 1st and 4th quarter a cross of five lozenges of the second.

Lincolne. Ar. a lion ramp. sa. ducally gorged or. *Crest*— A lion ramp., as in the arms.

Lincolne. Gu. a lion ramp. or. *Crest*—Out of a ducal coronet or, a demi lion ppr. crowned with an antique crown of the first.

Lincolne. Or, a leopard ramp. sa. armed ar.

Lincolne. Or, on a cross gu. five estoiles ar.

Lincolne. Ar. on a cross az. five mullets or.

Lincolne (Dublin; granted by Carney, Ulster, 1689, to Alderman NICHOLAS LINCOLNE). Or, a lion ramp. sa.

609

langued gu. betw. three trefoils slipped vert, a chief az. *Crest*—A leopard's head erased ar. spotted sa. betw. two oak branches vert, acorned or. *Motto*—Non vi sed mente.

Lind (Gorgie, co. Edinburgh, and Isle of Wight). Gu. two spears in saltire betw. a mullet in chief and a crescent in base all ar. within a bordure of the last, charged with four fleurs-de-lis and as many annulets alternately az. *Crest*— Two sprigs of laurel in saltire pp. *Motto*—Semper virescit virtus.

Lind (Poland, 1769). As the last, within a bordure invecked or, charged with four fleurs-de lis and as many annulets alternately ar. Same *Crest* and *Motto*.

Lind (Sir JAMES LIND, K.C.B., 1815). As Gorgie, within a bordure engr. ar. charged with four fleurs-de-lis and as many annulets alternately az. Same *Crest* and *Motto*.

Linde (co. Dorset). Gu. three buck's heads couped ar.

Linde. Sa. three leopards' faces ar.

Lindesay. See LINDSAY.

Lindesay-Bethune, Bart. See BETHUNE.

Lindesci, or Lindsey (co. Warwick, *temp.* Henry III.). Gu, three eagles displ. or.

Lindesey. Or, semée of crosses crosslet gu. an orle vert.

Lindear (granted by St. George, Ulster, 1668, to JOHN LINDEAR, citizen of Dublin, and then High Sheriff of the city). Per pale ar. and vert. an eagle displ. with two heads charged on the breast with a trefoil slipped betw. three escallops all counterchanged. *Crest*—On a mount a stag statant charged on the shoulder with a trefoil slipped all ppr.

Lindley (Skigby, co. Notts; extinct in the male line in 1758, on the death of JOHN LINDLEY, Esq., of Skigby). Ar. on a chief sa. three griffins' heads erased of the field. *Crest*— A griffin's head erased ar. gorged with a bar gemelle sa.

Lindley (Sir HENRY LINDLEY, knighted at Offaley, 30 July, 1599, at the rising of the camp immediately after the battle). Sa. on a chief ar. three eaglets displ. of the field.

Lindley (Middleton Castle, co. York; impalement Fun. Ent. Ulster's Office, 1680, EDWARD LOFTUS, *Viscount Loftus*, of Elge, whose wife was JANE, dau. and co-heir of JOHN LINDLEY, Esq.). Ar. on a chief sa. three griffins' heads erased of the first.

Lindores. Gu. a castle ar.

Lindow (Ingwell, co. Cumberland). Erm, on a chev. dovetailed betw. three sinister hands couped at the wrist gu. as many fountains. *Crest*—A lion ramp. gu. semée of buckles or, and holding betw. the paws a fountain. *Motto*—Vi et virtute.

Lindow (BURNS-LINDOW, Irton Hall, co. Cumberland; JONAS LINDOW BURNS-LINDOW, only surviving son of ISAAC BURNS, Esq., of Whitehaven, by AGNES LINDOW, his wife, sister of SAMUEL LINDOW, Esq., of Ingwell, co. Cumberland). Same *Arms, Crest,* and *Motto.*

Lindsay (Scotland; earliest arms). Gu. an eagle displ. or.

Lindsay (*Earl of Crawford and Balcarres*). Quarterly, 1st and 4th, gu. a fesse chequy ar. and az., for LINDSAY; 2nd and 3rd, or, a lion ramp. gu. debruised of a ribbon in bend sa., for ABERNETHY. *Crest*—An ostrich ppr. holding in his mouth a key or. *Supporters*—Two lions sejant guard. gu. *Motto*—Endure fort.

Lindsay (*Lord Spynie;* title extinct or dormant; heir of line H. A. LINDSAY-CARNEGIE, of Spynie, paternally a FULLERTON). Quarterly, 1st and 4th, gu. a fesse chequy ar. and az. with a label of three points ar. in chief; 2nd and 3rd, ABERNETHY, as above. *Crest*—An ostrich's head erased ppr. with a label of three points ar. above the neck, holding in the beak a horseshoe or. *Supporters*—Two lions sejant guard. gu. armed or, with a label of three points above the neck or. *Motto*—Toujours loyal.

Lindsay (Edzell, co. Forfar). Quarterly, as *Earl of Crawford,* within a bordure ar.

Lindsay (*Earl of Balcarres;* the sixth *Earl of Balcarres* became, *de jure, Earl of Crawford,* and the right of the seventh Earl to that title was recognised by the House of Lords). Quarterly, as *Earl of Crawford,* within a bordure az. charged with fourteen stars or. *Crest*—A tent az. fringed and semée of stars or, ensigned with a pennon gu. *Supporters*—Two lions sejant guard. gu. each with a collar az. charged with three stars or. *Motto*—Astra castra numen lumen munimen.

Lindsay (Deerpark, co. Devon, 1871). Quarterly, 1st, 2nd, and 4th, as in the arms of the *Earl of Crawford;* 3rd, counterquartered, 1st and 4th, gu. a bend betw. six cross crosslets fitchée ar., for HOWARD; 2nd and 3rd, ar. a lion ramp. gu., for FORWARD. *Crest* and *Motto,* as *Earl of Crawford.*

Lindsay (Sir COUTTS LINDSAY, of Balcarres and Westville, *s.* in 1837 to baronetcy conferred on his maternal grandfather, Sir COUTTS TROTTER, in 1821). Quarterly, 1st and 4th, the quartered coat of the *Earl of Balcarres;* 2nd and 3rd, counter-quartered, 1st and 4th, ar. a crescent gu. on a chief indented az. three mullets pierced of the field, for TROTTER, 2nd and 3rd, gu. a lion ramp. ar. crowned or, with a crescent of the first on the lion's shoulder, for MOWBRAY; these two coats within a bordure erm. *Crest*—As *Earl of Balcarres*. *Supporters*—Dexter, a white horse ppr.; sinister, a lion ar. armed and langued az. *Motto*—Astra castra numen lumen munimen.

Lindsay (Balgawies, co. Forfar). Quarterly, as *Earl of Crawford*, within a bordure ar. a crescent or, in the centre for diff.

Lindsay (Evelick, co. Perth, bart., 1666). Quarterly, as *Earl of Crawford*, within a bordure az. *Crest*—A sword erect, on the point a pair of balances all ppr. *Motto*—Recta vel ardua.

Lindsay (Kilspindie, co. Perth). As the last, charging the bordure with eight roses ar. for diff. Same *Crest* and *Motto*.

Lindsay (Pitcarlies and Cairn, co. Forfar). Quarterly, 1st and 4th, gu. a fess chequy ar. and az. within a bordure counter-compony of the second and third; 2nd and 3rd, or, a lion ramp. gu. debruised of a ribbon in bend sa., for ABERNETHY. *Crest*—Two stalks of wheat bladed and eared, disposed in saltire ppr. *Motto*—Non solum armis.

Lindsay (Dowhill, co. Kinross). Gu. a fess. chequy ar. and az. in dexter chief a mullet of the second, the base barry wavy of the second and third. *Crest*—A castle ppr. *Motto*—Firmus maneo.

Lindsay (Culsh, co. Aberdeen; now represented by DINGWELL-FORDYCE, of Bruckley, heir of line). As the last, within a bordure engr. or. *Crest*—A tower ppr. ensigned on the top with a crescent ar. *Motto*—Firmiter maneo.

Lindsay (Cavill, co. Kinross). Quarterly, as *Earl of Crawford*, within a bordure quarterly or and gu. charged with eight martlets counterchanged. *Crest*—An ostrich head erased ppr. *Motto*—Sis fortis.

Lindsay (Lord *Lindsay*, of the Byres; title dormant since 1808, now claimed by Sir J. T. LINDESAY-BETHUNE, Bart., of Kilconquhar). Gu. a fess chequy ar. and az. in chief three mullets of the second. *Crest*—A griffin's head ar. beaked gu. *Supporters*—Two griffins gu. armed and membered or. *Motto*—Je ayme.

Lindsay (*Viscount Garnock*). Quarterly, 1st and 4th, az. three crosses pattée or, for BARCLAY; 2nd and 3rd, gu. a fess chequy ar. and az., for LINDSAY; en surtout, gu. a fess erm., for CRAWFORD. *Crest*—A stag's head erased ppr. betw. the attires a cross pattée fitchée gu. *Supporters*—Dexter, a Highlander ppr. with a shield gu. in his exterior hand, charged with a fess erm.; sinister, a greyhound ppr. collared erm. *Motto*—Hinc honor et salus.

Lindsay (Kirkforther, co. Fife). Gu. a fess chequy ar. and az. betw. three mullets in chief and a hunting horn in base of the second.

Lindsay (Pyetstone, co. Fife; the branch to which the historian LINDSAY, of Pitscottie, belonged). Gu. a fess chequy ar. and az. betw. three mullets in chief and a mascle in base of the second.

Lindsay (Wormistone, co. Fife). Gu. a fess chequy ar. and az. betw. three mullets in chief of the second and an annulet in base or. *Crest*—An Ostrich ppr. *Motto*—Patientia vincit.

Lindsay (The Mount, co. Fife: as borne by Sir DAVID, Lyon King of Arms). Gu. a fess chequy ar. and az. betw. three mullets in chief and a man's heart in base of the second. *Crest*—A man's heart in flames gu. *Motto*—Je ayme.

Lindsay (Covington, co. Lanark). Gu. a fess chequy ar. and az. in base a mascle or.

Lindsay (Wauchopedale, co. Dumfries). Gu. a fess chequy ar. and az. in chief a label of three points of the second.

Lindsay (Dunrod, co. Renfrew, representative of Craigie, co. Ayr). Gu. a fess chequy ar. and az. betw. three stars of the second. *Crest*—A duck with wings expanded ppr. *Supporters*—Two unicorns sejant.

Lindsay (Blacksolme, co. Renfrew). Gu. a fess chequy ar. and az. in chief a label of three points of the second. *Crest*—A withered branch of oak sprouting forth green leaves ppr. *Motto*—Et mortua virescunt.

Lindsay (Linbank, co. Lanark). Gu. a fess chequy ar. and az. betw. two mullets in chief and a hunting horn in base of the second.

Lindsay (Corsbasket, co. Lanark). Gu. a fess chequy ar. and az. betw. two mullets in chief and a cinquefoil in base of the second.

Lindsay (Turin Castle, co. Mayo). As Dunrod. *Crest*—A two-headed eagle gu. *Motto*—Endure fort.

Lindsay (Bonhill, co. Dumbarton). Quarterly, as *Earl of Crawford*, in the centre of the quarters a rose gu.

Lindsay (Broadlands, co. Kincardine). Gu. a fess chequy ar. and az. in chief a fleur-de-lis of the second.

Lindsay (Pitscandlie, co. Forfar). Gu. a fess chequy ar. and az. a mullet of the second in chief and a dirk paleways ppr. in base.

Lindsey, Earl of. See BERTIE.

Lindsey (Cumberland). Or, an eagle displ. purp. membered gu.

Lindsey (co. Huntingdon). Vair an orle ar. on a bordure gu. eight crosses crosslet or.

Lindsey (London, and Bucksted, co. Sussex; confirmed 20 June, 1608). Or, an eagle displ. sa. armed and membered az. a chief vair.

Lindsey (co. Warwick). Gu. three eagles displ. or, membered az.

Lindsey. Ar. on a chief sa. three griffins' heads erased of the field.

Lindsey. Or, an eagle displ. sa. charged on the breast with ten plates in cross.

Lindsey (Hollymount House, co. Mayo). Gu. a fesse chequy ar. and az. betw. three mullets of the second. *Crest*—An eagle displ. with two necks.

Linesley (Linesley, co. Lancaster). Sa. a lion ramp. betw. eight crosses pattée fitchée ar. *Crest*—An arm in armour embowed holding in the gauntlet a sabre all ppr.

Linford. Quarterly, gu. and or, on the 1st and 4th an escallop ar. *Crest*—A talbot pass. ar.

Lingard (Curdworth, co. Warwick; confirmed by the Deputies of Camden, Clarenceux, to EDWARD LINGARD. Visit. Warwick, 1619). Barry of six or and az. on a bend sa. three escallops ar. *Crest*—A wolf's head erased sa.

Lingard-Guthrie (Tay Bank, Dundee). Barry of six or and vair, on a bend sa. four escallops ar., quartering GUTHRIE. See GUTHRIE.

Lingard. Or, a fesse bendy of eight sa. and ar. betw. three rests gu. *Crest*—A stag's head affrontée gorged with a ducal coronet ppr.

Linge (Reg. Ulster's Office). Az. a chev. or, betw. three lings' heads fessways erased ar.

Lingen, or Lingeyne (Lingen Castle, and Sutton, co. Hereford; a family of great antiquity in that co., in which they held estates, *temp.* Henry III.). Barry of six or and az. on a bend gu. three roses ar. *Crest*—Out of a ducal coronet or, a garb vert.

Lingen, or Lingayne (cos. Derby, Gloucester, Northampton, Salop, and Worcester). Barry of six or and az. on a bend gu. (another, az.) three roses ar. *Crest*—Out of a ducal coronet or, a garb vert.

Lingen (Penlanole, co. Radnor; a branch of the LINGENS, of Lingen Castle). Same *Arms* and *Crest*.

Lingen (co. Northumberland). Paly of six or and az. on a bend gu. three chaplets ar.

Lingen, Liggen, or Ligney. Chequy ar. and az. a fesse gu. *Crest*—A dexter arm embowed in armour brandishing a scymitar fastened to the wrist all ppr.

Lingham. Bendy of six sa. and or, a chief gu. *Crest*—Two branches of oak in saltire ppr.

Linghooke, or Lynlooke (Terrington, co. Norfolk). Paly of four az. and gu. a fesse dancettée betw. three bulls' heads erased or. *Crest*—A griffin's head erased gu. gorged with a collar dancettée or, in the beak a violet az. stalked and leaved vert.

Lingwood (Braintree, co. Essex). Az. on a saltire betw. four fleurs-de-lis or, five annulets gu. *Crest*—A talbot's head or, pellettée, gorged with a mural coronet of the first.

Lingwood. Same *Arms.* *Crest*—An antelope's head erased erm.

Lingwood (granted to ROBERT MAULKIN LINGWOOD, Esq., of Christ's College, Cambridge). Az. a saltire engr. erminois betw. four fleurs-de-lis or. *Crest*—A talbot's head erminois erased and eared sa. gorged with a mural crown gu.

Linisey. Gu. an eagle displ. or, membered az.

Linlithgow, Town of (Scotland). Az. the figure of the Archangel Michael, with wings expanded, treading on a serpent with its tail nowed fessways in base all ar. the head of which he is piercing with a spear in his dexter hand, grasping in his sinister an escutcheon charged with the arms of Scotland. *Motto*—Collocet in cœlo nos omnes via Michaelis.

Linlithgow, Earl of. See LIVINGSTONE.

Linne (London). Sa. a trefoil or, charged with a German text ℟.

Linnet. Sa. a chev. betw. three bears' heads couped ar.

Crest—Out of a ducal coronet or, a double plume of ostrich feathers ar. five and four.

Linnet. Sa. a chev. betw. three boars' heads erased ar. muzzled gu.

Linnett. Ar. semée of crosses crosslet a lion ramp. sa.

Linque, or Linq (co. Lincoln; descended of a family of LINQUE, in the province of Hainault). Or, a chief chequy ar. and az. over all a bend gu. *Crest*—On a mount vert a lion sejant guard. or, reposing his foot on a caltrap az.

Linsey. Or, an eagle displ. sa. charged with seven plates in pale (another, tinctures reversed, without the plates).

Linsey (Reg. Ulster's Office). Ar. on a chief sa. three griffins' heads erased of the first.

Linskill. Or, an eagle displ. with two heads purp. beaked and membered gu. a chief nebulée az. *Crest*—A demi eagle displ. with two heads or, holding in the beak a scroll with this *Motto*—Victor.

Lint. Ar. three battle axes gu. *Crest*—A dexter hand gu. holding a cross crosslet fitchée sa.

Linton (co. Cambridge). Ar. on a cross gu. five roses of the field. *Crest*—A griffin's head erased.

Linton (Drumerick, Scotland). Gu. a cross crosslet ar. betw. four crescents or.

Linton (Scotland). Gu. an eagle displ. ar. on a chief of the last three roses of the first. *Crest*—An eagle's head erased, holding in the beak an acorn stalked and leaved all ppr.

Linton. Vairé or and az.

Linwood. Gu. a hind betw. three pheons or. *Crest*—A demi talbot holding in the mouth an arrow ppr.

Linwood. Same *Arms*, within a bordure engr. pelletée.

Lion (Lord Mayor of London, 1554). Az. on a fesse engr. or, betw. three bezants, each charged with a griffin's head erased sa. a lion pass. guard. betw. two cinquefoils gu.

Lionnel. Ar. three bars az. betw. eight estoiles sa. one, three, three, and one. *Crest*—An antique crown.

Lions. Per pale or and az. a chev. (another, a fesse) erm.

Lions (Reg. Ulster's Office). Sa. a chev. betw. three lions sejant guard. ar. (another, the field ar. chev. az. and lions gu.).

Lippincot (Stoke Bishop, co. Gloucester, bart., extinct 1829; descended from co. Devon). Quarterly, 1st and 4th, per fesse embattled gu. and sa. three talbots statant guard. ar.; 2nd and 3rd, sa. a chev. ar. betw. three mermaids ppr. crined and combed or. *Crest*—Out of a mural coronet gu. a plume of six ostrich feathers in one row, alternately ar. and az. *Motto*—Secundis dubiisque rectus.

Lippingcott (Lippingcott and Wybbery, co. Devon; PHILIP LIPPINGCOTT, Visit. Devon, 1620, son of JOHN LIPPINGCOTT, of Lippingcott, who was grandson of JOHN LIPPINGCOTT, of same place, by JANE WYBBERY, his wife, dau. of JOHN WYBBERY, of Wybbery, and co-heir of her brother, WILLIAM WYBBERY). Quarterly, 1st and 4th, per fesse embattled gu. and sa. three leopards pass. ar., for LIPPINGCOTT; 2nd and 3rd, sa. a chev. betw. three mermaids ar.

Lisbone, or Lisborne. Sa. three lozenges ar. *Crest*—A boar pass. or.

Lisburne, Earl of. See VAUGHAN.

Lisk (Scotland). Ar. three mascles az. on a chief gu. as many mascles of the field.

Liskerett, or Liskerd, Town of. Seal of the Mayor and Burgesses, re-incorporated 6 July, 29 Queen Elizabeth, 1576. A fleur-de-lis betw. two beds, inscribed Sigillum, commun. burgi. de. Liskertt.

L'Isle (JOHN L'ISLE, Visit. Warwick, twelfth in descent from WILLIAM DE INSULA, 21 Henry III., 1236, Dugdale). A r. three eaglets displ. gu. a border sa.

L'Isle (*Baron Lisle*, of Rougemont; dormant or extinct 1399; ROBERT DE LISLE was summoned to Parliament 1311). Or, a fess betw. two chevronels sa.

L'Isle (*Baron de L'Isle*, abeyance temp. Henry VI.). Gu. a lion pass. ar. crowned or.

Lisle, Baron. See LYSAGHT.

Lisle, or Lisley (Wilbraham, co. Cambridge, 1632). Or, a fesse betw. two chev. sa.

Lisle (Wodyton, Thruxton, and Moyles Court, co. Hants; descended from JORDAN DE INSULA, temp. Henry I. The sisters and co-heirs of the last CHARLES LISLE, Esq., of Wodyton and Moyles Court, were MARY, *m.* to Rev. CHRISTOPHER TAILOR, D.D.; SUSAN, *m.* THOMAS MARCH PHILLIPPS, Esq., of Garendon Park, co. Leicester; CATHERINE, *m.* first, JOHN MANLEY, Esq., and secondly, J. TAILOR, Esq., of Reading; and ELIZABETH, *d.* young; AMBROSE LISLE MARCH PHILLIPPS, Esq., of Garendon Park, grandson of the second co-heiress, SUSAN LISLE, assumed the surname and arms of DE LISLE. Of the family of LISLE, of Moyles Court,

611

was ALICE, the widow of JOHN LISLE, Esq., of Moyles Court, who was beheaded, at the age of 80, by Judge JEFFRIES, 1685). Or, on a chief az. three lions ramp. of the first. *Crest*—A stag trippant ppr. attired or.

Lisle (St. Martin's-in-the-Fields, co. Middlesex). Erminois (another, or) on a chief az. three lions ramp. or. *Crest*—A lion's gamb ar. holding an escallop or.

Lisle (Brackley, co. Northampton, and Felton, co. Northumberland. Gu. a lion pass. guard. ar. crowned or.

Lisle (Yorwell, co. Northampton, and co. Warwick). Ar. three eagles displ. with two heads gu. (another, the eagles with one head).

Lisle (co. Surrey). Or, on a chev. betw. three demi lions ramp. gu. as many trefoils ar.

Lisle. Per pale or and gu. a point in point erm. over all a cross Tau az.

Lisle. Or, a fesse betw. two chev. sa. *Crest*—A millstone ar. in the centre a millrind sa.

Lisle. Or, a lion ramp. az. tail forked.

Lisle. Or, a fret gu.

Lisle, or Lile. Ar. a lion ramp. az.

Lisle. Ar. a fesse betw. six martlets gu.

Lisle. Or, a chev. betw. three leaves gu.

L'Isle (Rugemont, co. Bedford, temp. Henry III.). Gu. a lion pass. guard. ar. crowned or.

L'Isle (Kingston Isle, co. Berks). Same *Arms*.

L'Isle (Isle of Wight, temp. Henry III.). Same *Arms*.

L'Isle (Fun. Ent. Ulster's Office, 1664). Erm. a lion ramp. az.

Lisle de. Same *Arms*, semée of crosslets or.

Lisley (confirmed by the deputies of Camden, Clarenceux, to JOHN LISLEY, of Moxhull, co. Warwick. Visit. Warwick). Ar. three eagles displ. gu.

Lisley (quartered by SKEFFINGTON, of Skeffington, co. Leicester. Visit. Leices. 1619). Gu. an eagl. displ. or.

Lismore, Viscount. See O'CALLAGHAN.

Lisse. Paly of six ar. and az. a fesse gu.

Lister (Burwell Park, co. Lincoln; the senior line of LISTER, of co. York, of which was Sir MARTIN LISTER, the celebrated physician, temp. Charles I.; the representative is, through the DYMOKES, one of the co-heirs to the ancient barony of Kyme). Erm. on a fesse sa. three mullets or, quartering BANCROFT, or, on a bend betw. six crosses crosslet az. three garbs of the field. *Crest*—A stag's head erased ppr.

Lister (Little Chester, co. Derby, and Manningham, co. York). As the preceding.

Lister (Hirst Priory, co. Lincoln). Erm. on a fesse sa. three mullets or. *Crest*—A stag's head issuing from a ducal coronet. *Motto*—Retinens vestigia famæ.

Lister (impalement in Sarsdon Manor House, with the names "R. BLOUT and E. LISTER" written over. Visit. Oxon, 1566). Az. on a cross betw. four doves ar. five torteaux, each charged with an estoile of the second, quartering gu. semée of crescents or, a lion ramp. ar., another coat of LISTER.

Lister (Gisburne, co. York; *Baron Ribblesdale*). Erm. on a fesse sa. three mullets or. *Crest*—A stag's head erased per fesse ppr. and gu. attired or, differenced with a crescent. *Supporters*—Dexter, a stag reguard. sa. attired and hoofed or, charged on the body with an eagle displ. of the last, gorged with a collar of SS. and portcullises gold; sinister, a bay horse, bridled, saddled, and supporting a staff ppr. headed or, with a banner vert, fringed, and charged with the letters Y. L. D. gold, meaning York Light Dragoons. *Motto*—Retinens vestigia famæ.

Lister (Armitage Park, co. Stafford; a branch of LISTER, of Gisburne). Same *Arms* and *Crest*.

Lister (New Windsor, co. Berks). Vert on a cross ar. five torteaux, each charged with a mullet or.

Lister (cos. Derby and Westmorland, and Wydopp, co. York). Erm. on a fesse sa. three mullets or. *Crest*—A buck's head erased ppr.

Lister (Finchley, co. Middlesex, and co. Essex). Az. on a cross ar. five torteaux, each charged with a mullet or.

Lister (London; granted 20 April, 1602). Erm. on a fesse cotised sa. three mullets or. *Crest*—A stag's head erased per fesse ppr. and or, attired of the last.

Lister (Rowton, co. Salop). Erm. on a fesse sa. three mullets ar. *Crest*—A buck's head erased ppr.

Lister (Shipden Hall, co. York; on the roof of Halifax church). Erm. on a fesse sa. three mullets ar. a canton gu. *Crest*—A stag's head erased ppr. charged on the neck with a trefoil slipped gu. *Motto*—Justus propositi tenax.

Lister (Scotland). Same *Arms* and *Crest*. *Motto*—Meal mori quam fœdari.

Lister. Gu. semée de mullets a lion ramp. ar.

Lister-Kaye (bart., created 1812). See KAYE.

Liston (Scotland). Gu. two gillyflowers in pale slipped ppr. a chief raguly ar. *Crest*—Two hands conjoined and couped ppr.

Liston (Sir ROBERT LISTON, G.C.B., 1817). Gu. on a cross raguly ar. two gillyflowers slipped ppr. *Crest*—An antique plough ppr. *Motto*—Poco a poco.

Liston. Gu. a cross raguly or.

Liston. Ar. a bend dancettée sa.

Liston. Vert six (another, ten) bezants.

Liston-Foulis, Bart. See FOULIS.

Listowel, Earl of. See HARE.

Litchfield. Or, a sword in pale az. surmounted by a crescent sa. all betw. two crosses crosslet fitchée gu. *Crest*— An arm in armour embowed, holding a sword ppr. *Motto* —Semper pugnare paratus.

Litcott. Or, two bars vairé ar. and sa. *Crest*—An old man's head ppr. vested sa. and ducally crowned or.

Litelcot. Gu. a cross erm.

Litham (Redborne, co. Rutland ; quartered by TOOKE, of South Luffenham. Visit. Rutland, 1619). Ar. a fess gu. over all a bend sa.

Lithgow (Drygrange, Scotland). Ar. a demi otter sa. issuing out of a loch in base ppr.

Litle. Vert six lions ramp ar.

Litle. Sa. a saltire ar. (another, or).

Litlebury. Ar. three lions pass. in pale gu.

Litler (Tathwell, co. Lincoln). Ar. two bars az. in chief a griffin pass. gu. all within a bordure engr. sa.

Litler (London). Ar. a chev. sa. betw. three squirrels sejant gu. *Crest*—A filbert tree ppr. the trunk raguly, on each side a squirrel saliant gu.

Litlington (London). Quarterly, ar. and gu. on the 2nd and 3rd quarters a fret or, over all a bend az. charged with three fleurs-de-lis of the third.

Litster (co. Lincoln, 1640). Erm. on a fesse sa. three mullets ar. *Crest*—An anchor and cable sa. *Motto*—Sine Deo nihil.

Litster. Az. on a cross ar. betw. four magpies or, five torteaux, on each an estoile of the third. *Crest*—A stag at gaze ermines, ducally gorged and attired or.

Littell, or Little (Bray, co. Berks). Per chev. ar. and sa. in chief three fleurs-de-lis of the last, in base a tower of the first.

Littell. Same *Arms.* *Crest*—Two daggers in saltire ppr.

Littell (Harsted and Little Keney, co. Essex, and co. Norfolk). Sa. a pillar ducally crowned or, betw. two wings expanded and joined to the base, of the last. *Crest*—A cock standing on an arrow or, combed and wattled gu.

Littell. Az. a saltire engr. or, in chief a mullet of the last.

Littlman, or Littleman (Scotland). Or, a chev. sa. betw. a cross pattée in chief of the last and a heart in base gu.

Little (Meikledale and Langholme, Dumfries). Sa. a saltire engr. .ar. *Crest*—A tiger's head affrontée ppr. *Motto*— Magnum in parvo.

Little (Libberton, co. Edinburgh). Sa. on a saltire ar. a crescent gu. *Crest*—A leopard's head or. *Motto*—Magnum in parvo.

Little. Ar. six lions ramp gu. (another, sa.) three, two, and one.

Little (Llanvair Grange, co. Monmouth). Sa. a chev. engr. ar. *Crest*—A leopard's head ppr. *Motto*—Magnum in parvo.

Little-Gilmour. See GILMOUR.

Littleborne. Per pale ar. and sa. three chev. counterchanged.

Littleborne. Ar. three water bougets sa.

Littleboys (Wickham, co. Bucks, and Ashburnham, co. Sussex). Sa. two hands, one dexter and one sinister, couped in the wrist in fesse ar. the fingers downward.

Littlebury (Fillingham, co. Lincoln). Ar. two lions pass. guard. in pale gu.

Littlebury (Stensby and Winsby, co. Lincoln). Gu. two lions pass. guard. in pale ar. *Crest*—A man's head couped at the shoulders, armed in mail all ppr.

Littlebury. Same *Arms.* *Crest*—A lion's paw per fesse gu. and az. holding a spear sa. point or.

Littlebury (co. Lincoln). Or, two lions pass. guard. gu.

Littlebury. Ar. on a bend vert betw. two lions pass. gu. three eagles displ. or.

Littlebury. Sa. three wicker baskets with handles ar.

Littledale (Bolton Hall, co. York). Ar. a lion pass. gu. on a chief az. three cross crosslets of the field. *Crest*—A demi lion gu. gorged with a collar gemelle ar. holding in the dexter paw a cross crosslet of the second. *Motto*—Fac et spera.

Littledale (Scarlets). Same *Arms, &c.*

Littlefield. Vert on a chev. ar. betw. three garbs or, as many boys' heads couped ppr. *Crest*—On a garb or, a bird ar. in the beak an ear of wheat vert.

Littlejohn (Woodston, Scotland, 1761). Ar. three arrows gu. two in saltire and one in pale and banded vert. betw. six trefoils slipped of the last, two in chief, two in fesse, and two in base. *Crest*—Two naked arms issuing out of a cloud, holding a bow in full bent to let fly an arrow all ppr. *Motto* —Ferio.

Littlejohn (Scotland). Ar. a crescent betw. three roses gu.

Littler (Wallerscote, co. Chester). Ar. a chev. sa. betw. three squirrels sejant gu.

Littler (co. Middlesex). Ar. a chev. sa. betw. three squirrels, sejant gu. *Crest*—A squirrel sejant eating a nut ppr.

Littler (as granted to Col., afterwards Gen. Sir JOHN HUNTER LITTLER, G.C.B., claiming descent from LITTLER, of Vale Royal, co. Chester, settled in that co. since Edward I.). Vert two bars erm. betw. a griffin pass. in chief and an Eastern crown in base or, in the fesse point a sword fesseways, the point to the dexter ppr. pommel and hilt gold, all within a bordure engr. of the last. *Crest*—Two crescents interwoven, in front of a palm tree, an elephant statant ppr. the trappings gu. fimbriated or, and charged with a sun in splendour, the girth az. also fimbriated gold, the trunk grasping a lotus flower slipped also ppr. *Motto*—Astra et castra.

Littleton (Pillaton Hall, co. Stafford, bart., extinct 1812 ; descended from RICHARD LYTTLETON, second son of Sir THOMAS LYTTLETON, Knt., of Frankley (see LYTTELTON, *Lord Lyttelton*), which RICHARD LYTTELTON *m.* ALICE, dau. and heir of WILLIAM WINESBURY, Esq., of Pillaton Hall). Az. a chev. betw. three escallops sa.

Littleton (*Baron Hatherton* : descended from MORETON WALHOUSE, Esq., of Hatherton, co. Stafford, by FRANCES LITTLETON, his wife, only sister of Sir EDWARD LITTLETON, fourth and last bart. of Pillaton ; the grandson of this marriage, EDWARD JOHN WALHOUSE, Esq., assumed, 1812, the name and arms of LITTLETON, and was created a peer, as *Baron Hatherton*, 1835). Same *Arms.* These, with the motto, " Ung Dieu et ung roy," were the identical ensigns of the great author of " The Tenures," and are scrupulously preserved by the family. *Crest*—A stag's head caboshed sa. attired or, betw. the attires a buglehorn gold, hanging by a bend gu. *Supporters*—Dexter, a stag ppr. gorged with a collar or, therefrom pendent an escutcheon ar. charged with a bugle or, therefrom pendent an escutcheon, charged as the dexter, stringed sa. ; sinister, a lion gu. gorged with a ducal coronet. *Motto*—Ung Dieu et ung roy.

Littleton (Stoke Milburgh, co. Salop, bart., extinct, 1710 ; descended from a younger son of THOMAS LYTTLETON, Esq., of Spetchley, co. Worcester, third son of Sir THOMAS LYTTLETON, Knt., of Frankley (see LYTTELTON, *Lord Lyttelton*). Same *Arms.*

Littleton. Ar. two lions pass. gu.

Littleton (co. Leicester). Ar. a bend betw. two cotises sa. within a bordure engr. gu. charged with eight bezants.

Littleton. Ar. a chev. betw. three escallops within a bordure sa.

Littlewood. Az. a bull's head erased or. *Crest*—On a mount vert a peacock ppr.

Litton (Knebworth). See LYTTON.

Litton. Erm. a chief dancettée az.

Litton (confirmed to EDWARD LITTON, Q.C., of Altmore, co. Tyrone, a Master in Chancery, Ireland, grandson of THOMAS LITTON, Esq., of Oldtown, co, Kildare, and their descendants). Erm. a crescent gu. on a chief indented az. three ducal coronets or. *Crest*—Out of a ducal coronet or, an ermine's head erm. *Motto*—Prudentia gloriam acquirit.

Litton (Ardavilling, co. Cork). Same *Arms.*

Liverpole. Quarterly, gu. and or, a cross pattée ar.

Liverpool, Earl of. See JENKINSON.

Liverpool, Town of. Ar. a cormorant sa. beaked and legged gu. holding in the beak a branch of sea-weed, called lauer, inverted vert. *Crest*—A cormorant with wings endorsed sa. beaked and legged gu. in the beak a sprig of lauer vert. *Supporters*—Dexter, a figure of Neptune, holding a banner of the arms; sinister, a merman blowing a shell and holding a banner charged with a ship. *Motto*—Deus nobis hæc otia fecit.

Livesey (Livesey, co. Lancaster. Visit. co. Lancaster, 1664). Ar. a lion ramp. gu. betw. three trefoils slipped vert. *Crest* —A lion's gamb erased gu.

Livesey (East Church, co. Kent, bart., extinct, 1660 ; descended from LIVESEY, of Livesey. MICHAEL LIVESEY was so created 1627; was one of those who signed the warrant for the murder of Charles I., *d. s. p. m.* before the Restoration). Same *Arms.*

Livesey (Sutton, co. Lancaster, 1664). Same *Arms* and *Crest*, a bordure az.

Livesey, or Livesay (Stourton Hall, co. Lincoln, formerly of Livesey, co. Lancaster). Same *Arms* and *Crest.*

Ligie (Montague Square). Or, a chev. betw. two mascles in chief and a boar's head in base az.

Livingstone (that Ilk). Ar. three cinquefoils (or gilliflowers) gu. pierced of the field.

Livingstone (*Earl of Linlithgow*). Quarterly, 1st and 4th, ar. three cinquefoils gu. within a double tressure flory counterflory vert; 2nd and 3rd, sa. a bend betw. six billets or, for CALLENDAR ; over all, on a escutcheon az. a tree growing out of the base or, within a bordure ar. charged with eight cinquefoils gu., for the title of LINLITHGOW. *Supporters*—Two savages wreathed round the head and middle with laurel ppr. and holding in their exterior hands batons erect or. *Crest*—A demi savage ppr. holding a baton or club erect in his dexter hand, and round the sinister arm a serpent twined vert. *Motto*—Si je puis.

Livingstone (*Earl of Callendar*). Quarterly, as the last, without the escutcheon of pretence. *Crest*—A dexter hand holding a sword ppr. *Motto*—Et domi, et foris.

Livingstone (Westquarter, co. Stirling, bart., 1699; arms confirmed to FENTON LIVINGSTONE, of Westquarter, the heir of line in 1854). Quarterly, LIVINGSTONE and CALLENDAR, all within a bordure quartered or and gu. *Crest*—A savage's head wreathed about with laurel. *Motto*—Si possim.

Livingstone (Dunipace, co. Stirling, bart., 1625). Ar. three cinquefoils within a double tressure counterflory gu.

Livingstone (Aberdeen, 1672). Ar. two gillyflowers in chief, and an escallop in base, all within a bordure engr. gu. *Crest*—A boar's head couped, holding in the mouth a pair of balances ppr. *Motto*—Fortis et æquus.

Livingstone (Baldron, co. Stirling). Same *Arms*, the bordure indented. *Crest*—A gillyflower slipped ppr. *Motto*—Nativum retinet decus.

Livingstone (Counteswells, co. Aberdeen). Ar. three cinquefoils within the royal tressure flory counterflory vert, in the centre a cross crosslet fitchée sa. *Crest*—A demi Hercules, wreathed about the head and middle, holding in the dexter hand a club erect, and in the sinister a serpent all ppr. *Motto*—Si je puis.

Livingstone (Glentirran, co. Stirling). Same *Arms*, a bordure componée, and on each of the last a boar's head couped. *Crest*—A dexter hand brandishing a sword ppr. *Motto*—Ut possim.

Livingstone (KINNAIRD, *Earl of Newburgh*). Ar. on a bend betw. three gillyflowers gu. an anchor of the first, a double tressure flory counterflory vert. *Crest*—A Moor's head couped ppr. banded gu. and ar. with pendles ar. at his ears. *Supporters*—Exeter, a savage wreathed head and middle with laurel ppr. : sinister, a horse ar. furnished gu. *Motto*—Si je puis.

Livingstone (*Viscount Kilsyth*). Ar. three gillyflowers slipped gu. within a double tressure flory counterflory vert. *Crest*—A demi savage wreathed about the head and middle with laurel all ppr. *Supporters*—Two lions gu. *Motto*—Spe expecto.

Livingstone (*Viscount Tiviot*). Quarterly, 1st and 4th, az. three oranges slipped ppr, within an orle of thistles or ; 2nd and 3rd, ar, three cinquefoils gu. within a double tressure flory counterflory vert. *Supporters*—Dexter, a horse ar. furnished gu. ; sinister, a savage wreathed head and middle with laurel, holding in his left hand a baton with its head downwards or. *Crest*—A demi man holding a baton upwards or.

Livingstone (Parkhall, co. Stirling ; paternally MITCHELL, 1766). Ar. a mascle az. betw. three gillyflowers slipped gu. a double tressure flory counterflory vert. *Crest*—A dexter hand grasping a sabre ppr. *Motto*—Si possim.

Livingstone-Learmonth (Parkhall). See LEARMONTH.

Livington, or Levington (Saltcoats, co. Haddington). Ar. a bend betw. two otters' heads couped gu. (another Ar. a bend engr. gu. in chief a bear's head erased az. muzzled of the second).

Livington. Ar. a bend engr. gu. in chief a bear's head erased az. muzzled of the second.

Livius. Vert on a chev. in point embowed or, another chev. of like form gu. betw. three pomegranates slipped and leaved ppr.

Llandaff, See of. Sa. two crosiers in saltire or and ar. on a chief az. three mitres labelled gold.

Llandaff, City of. Sa. two crosiers in saltire or, on a chief az. three mitres of the second.

Llewellyn ap Griffith (Prince of North Wales, derived

613

from GRIFFITH AP CYNAN, King of North Wales [*see that name*]. LLEWELLYN, who was slain 10 Dec. 1282, by the forces of Edward I. *m.* 3 Oct. 1278, ELEANOR, dau. of SIMON DE MONTFORD, *Earl of Leicester*, by ELEANOR, second dau. of King John, and left an only dau. and heiress, CATHERINE, mother, by her husband, PHILIP AP IVOR, Lord of Iscoed, in Cardigan, of a dau. and heiress, ELEANOR, who *m.* THOMAS AP LLEWELLYN, last Lord of South Wales, and had two daus. and co-heirs : I. ELEANOR, *m.* GRIFFITH VAUGHAN, Lord of Glyndwrdwy, co. Merioneth ; II. MARGARET, *m.* SIR TUDOR AP GRONO, Knt., and had a son, MEREDITH AP TUDOR, father of OWEN TUDOR, progenitor of Henry VII. and the Royal House of Tudor). *Arms*, those of the principality of North Wales, viz., quarterly, or and gu. four lions pass. guard. counterchanged.

Llewellyn ap Madoc (Baron of Cryniarth-yn-Edeirnion, co. Merioneth. Bishop of St. Asaph, 3 Edward III. (1357) ; derived from ELLIS, living 22 Edward I. (1284), second son of IORWERTH, Lord of Half-Edeirnion, ancestor of the HUGHES's, of Gwerclas, Barons of Kymmer-yn-Edeirnion. LLEWELLYN AP MADOC *d.* in 1335, leaving seven sisters and co-heirs., viz., I. LLEIKI, *m.* GRONO LLWYD-Y-PENWYN, of Melai, in Denbighland ; II. ANGHARAD, of Vaerdre, *m.* MADOC AP GRIFFITH, Vir Goch of Newedd wen-yn-Llandderfel ; III. EFA, *m.* GRIFFITH AP LLEWELLYN, of Cors-y-Gedol, co. Merioneth ; IV. MYFANWY, *m.* IEVAN VYCHAN, styled Y Crach, of Llanwydelyn ; V. MARGARET, *m.* ITHEL AP GWERGENEU VYCHAN, of Rhiwaedog, co. Merioneth ; VI. NEST, *m.* IEVAN AP Y MOELWRCH ; VII. MALI, *m.* LLEWELYN AP MADOC, of Vaerdre in Edeirnion). Same *Arms.*

Llewellyn ap Ynyr (Lord of Yale, in Denbighland, second son of HOWEL AP MORIDDIG AP SANDDE HARDD, Lord of Mostyn, in Denbighland. LLEWELYN greatly distinguished himself at the battle of Corwen, and his valour was rewarded by his Prince, Gryffyd ap Madoc, Lord of Dinas Bran, under the following circumstances. While conversing with the Prince after the fight, LLEWELYN accidentally drew his left hand, smeared with blood, across his sword, leaving four blood stains upon it, which the Prince observing, ordered him to bear those marks henceforth on his shield, at the same time conferring upon him, as a substantial recognition of his services, the lordship of Gelligynan. The grant is dated in Yale, on the vigil of St. Egidius (probably Eligius, as remarked by Sir Sam. Meyrick in his edition of " Dunn's Visitations," the festival falling on December 1) in the year 1256. Descendants : I. LLOYDS, of Yale, Trowyn and Noelvodig, and three branches, LLOYD, of Bodidris, in Yale, bart., now extinct in the male line ; LLOYD, of Gloster, King's co., extinct in the male line, the last of this line, Col. HARDRESS LLOYD, *d. unm.*, and is now represented by VAUGHAN, of Golden Grove ; II. ELLISES, of Brondeg and Groes Newydd). Paly of eight ar. and gu ; some authorities say or, instead of ar. [Authorities : Reynold's " Display of the Heraldry of North Wales, 1739," Pennant's " Tour in Wales," vol. 1, p. 406, &c. The first edition of the Armory makes the battle that of Crogen, but Reynolds says it was Corwen; and it is simply impossible it could have been Crogen, which was fought nearly a century before the grant made to LLEWELYN. Besides LLEWELYN was certainly contemporary with Gryffyd, Lord of Dinas Bran, whose grandfather, Gryffyd Maelor, a distinguished chief, took part, along with Owen Brogyntyn, at the battle of Crogen, and died 30 years later, in 1191, the date of Crogen being 1165.]

Llewellyn Voelgrwn (Main, in North Wales. Descendants : I. MATTHEWS, of Trefanney ; II. PARRY, of Main ; III. GRIFFITHS, of Main: IV. MORRICE, of Bryn y Gwalie : IV. DAVIES, of Peniarth). Ar. a lion pass. sa. a bordure indented gu.

Llewellyn Aurdorchog (Golden Torques, in Yale). Az. a lion pass. or.

Llewellyn (EDWARD TURBERVILLE LLEWELLYN, ESQ.) Quarterly, 1st and 4th, gu. three chev. ar. ; 2nd and 3rd, TURBERVILLE, chequy or and gu. a fesse erm. *Crest*—A lamb bearing a banner charged with a cross of St. George, a glory round the head. *Motto*—Vincit qui patitur.

Llewellyn (King of Powys). Or, a lion ramp. gu.

Llewellyn (Peterstone-super-Ely-Coedriglan, and Stockland, co. Glamorgan). Gu. three chev. ar. *Crest*—A lamb bearing a banner charged with a cross of St. George, a glory round the head.

Llewellyn (DILLWYN-LLEWELLYN, Penllergare, co. Glamorgan.) Gu. on a chev. ar. three trefoils slipped of the first. *Crest*—A stag's head couped ppr. *Motto*—Craignez honte.

Llowarch (Holbwrch) Treasurer of Griffith ap Llewellyn, Prince of North Wales, and ancestor of the family of CAER VALWCH YE LLANYNTS). Vert a stag trippant ar. attired or.

Llowarch ap Bran (Founder of the II. Noble Tribe of North Wales and Powys). Ar. a chev. betw. three crows sa. with erm. in their bills.

Lloyd (Plymog, co. Denbigh; Gwerclas and Kymmer-yn-Edeirnion, co. Merioneth; and Bashall Hall, co. York. This family, one of the most distinguished in the Principality, derives, in common with the Royal House of Tudor, from MARCHUDD, Lord of Abergelleu, and Brynffenigl, in Carnarvon, Founder of the VIII. Noble Tribe of North Wales and Powys, living in the middle of the 9th century. *Arms*, those of EDNYFED VYCHAN, viz., Gu. a chev. erm. betw. three Englishmen's heads in profile ppr., quartering the bearings of; 1. IWFA AP KENDRIG, Lord of Christionydol; 2. RHYS AP GRIFFITH, derived from YNYR, Lord of Yale; 3. DAVIES, of Denbigh, derived from EDNOWAIN BENDEW, Lord of Tegaingle, Founder of the XIII. Noble Tribe of North Wales and Powys; 4. HUGHES, of Gwerclas, Barons of Kymmer-yn-Edeirnion [*see that name*]; 5. WALMESLEY, of Coldcoates Hall, co. Lancaster, and Bashall Hall [*see that name*]. *Crests*—1st, LLOYD, of Plymog: an Englishman's head in profile couped ppr.; 2nd HUGHES, of Gwerclas: A demi lion sa. issuing out of a ducal coronet; 3rd, WAL-MESLEY, of Coldcoates Hall and Bashall Hall: A lion statant guard. ducally crowned gu.; 4th, TALBOT, of Bashall: A talbot pass. sa. *Motto*—Heb Dduw heb ddym a Duw a digon.

Lloyd (Forest, North Wales; derived from WILLIAM LLOYD, Esq., of Forest, descended from RHYS, third son of EDRYD, fourth in descent from MARCHUDD AP CYNAN). *Arms*, those of MARCHUDD, viz., Gu. a Saracen's head erased at the neck ppr. wreathed about the temples sa. and ar.

Lloyd (LLOYD-MOSTYN, *Baron Mostyn*). See MOSTYN.

Lloyd (Dolglessyn in Edeirnion, co. Merioneth; derived from IEVAN, second son of DAVID AP RHYS, Baron of Kymmer-yn-Edeirnion, ancestor of the HUGHESES, of Gwerclas, Barons of Kymmer-yn-Edeirnion). *Arms*, those of HUGHES, of Gwerclas, viz., ar. a lion ramp. sa. armed and langued gu.

Lloyd (Crogen-yn-Edeirnion, co. Merioneth; derived from GRIFFITH, of Crogen, and Branas, second son of RHYS AP IEVAN, Baron of Kymmer-yn-Edeirnion, Crogen, and Branas, ancestor of the HUGHESES, of Gwerclas, Barons of Kymmer-yn-Edeirnion). Same *Arms*.

Lloyd (Baron of Hendwr in Edeirnion, co. Merioneth; derived from MADOC, second son of GRIFFITH, Lord of Half Edeirnion, second son of OWEN BROGYNTYN, Lord of Edeirnion, Dinmael, and Abertarrad. The male line terminated with DAVID AP GWYN LLOYD, Baron of Hendwyr, who left three daus. and co-heiresses). Ar. on a chev. gu. three fleurs-de-lis or.

Lloyd (Tyfos-yn-Edeirnion, co. Merioneth; derived from THOMAS AP IEVAN, AP GWYN LLOYD, Baron of Hendwr). Same *Arms*.

Lloyd (Aston, co. Salop; derived, through RICHARD EVAN LLOYD, of Park Promise, second son of MEREDITH AP HOWELL, of Glascoed, from EINION EFELL, Lord of Cynllaeth). *Arms*, those of EINION EFELL, viz., Per fess sa. and ar. a lion ramp. counterchanged, armed and langued gu.

Lloyd (Cwm Bychan). See LLWYD, of Cwm Bychan.

Lloyd (Plas Enion, derived through ROGER LLOYD, of Brynglas Lloyd, second son of DAVID AP ELLIS, of Plas-yn-Yale, co. Denbigh, from OSBORNE FITZGERALD, Lord of Ynys-y-Maengwyn). *Arms*, those of OSBORNE FITZGERALD, viz., Erm. a saltire gu.

Lloyd (Carrog; derived, through GRIFFITH LLOYD, sixth son of DAVID AP ELLIS, of Plas-yn-Yale, from OSBORNE FITZGERALD). Same *Arms*.

Lloyd (Bodidris-yn-Yale, co. Denbigh, bart., extinct 1700: derived, through LLEWELYN AP YNYR, of Yale, from SANDDE HARDD, Lord of Burton, MARGARET, dau. and heiress of Sir EVAN LLOYD, the last bart., *m.* RICHARD VAUGHAN, Esq., of Cors-y-Gedol, co. Merioneth). Quarterly, 1st and 4th, paly of eight ar. and gu.; 2nd, az. a lion ramp. ar.; 3rd, erm. a lion ramp. az. crowned or.

Lloyd (Llyn, co. Carnarvon; derived from Sir GRIFFITH LLOYD, a chieftain of Carnarvonshire, who is said to have conveyed to Edward I. the intelligence of the birth of his son, created Prince of Wales, and to have received the honour of knighthood in consequence from the King). Gu. a chev. or, a chief erm.

Lloyd (Rhiwaedog, co. Merioneth; derived, through WILLIAM LLWYD, of Rhiwaedog, eldest son of MORYS AP JOHN, of Rhiwaedog, of Clennenneu, co. Carnarvon, and of Park, co. Merioneth, from RODERICK, Lord of Anglesey, son of OWEN GWYNEDD, Prince of North Wales. The direct male line of this family terminated with WILLIAM LLOYD, Esq., of Rhiwaedog, whose sister was mother of WILLIAM LLOYD DOLBEN, Esq., of Rhiwaedog). *Arms*, those of OWEN GWYNEDD, viz., Vert three eagles displ. in fess or.

614

Lloyd (Plas-yn-dre, co. Merioneth; GEORGE PRICE LLOYD Esq., of that place, High Sheriff, co. Merioneth 1840, was fifth in descent from SIMON LLOYD, Esq., of Plas-yn-dre, second son of LEWIS LLOYD, Esq., of Rhiwaedog, living in 1650). Same *Arms*. *Crest*—An eagle, as in the *Arms*.

Lloyd (Llanllyr; derived from CADIVOR AP DYFNWAL. BRIDGET, dau. and heiress of THOMAS LLOYD, Esq., of Llanllyr, *m.* RICHARD VAUGHAN, second *Earl of Carbery*, but left no surviving issue. Sa. three scaling ladders ar. between the two upper ones a spear head of the last, point imbrued ppr. on a chief gu. a tower triple-towered of the second, being the coat of arms granted to CADIVOR AP DYFNWAL, ninth in descent from Roderic the Great, Prince of Wales, by his cousin, the great *Lord Rhys* for taking the castle of Cardigan, by escalade, from the *Earl of Clare* and the Flemings in 1164.

Lloyd (Wernwylyg, co. Cardigan; derived from CADIVOR AP DYFNWAL. ELIZABETH, dau. and heiress of THOMAS LLOYD, Esq., of Wernwylyg, *m.* JOHN LLOYD, Esq., of Ffoes-y-Bleiddiod). Same *Arms* as the preceding.

Lloyd (Millfield, co. Cardigan, Bart., extinct 1750; derived from CADIVOR AP DYFNWAL. The baronetcy became extinct in 1750, on the death *s. p.* of Sir LUCIUS CHRISTIANUS LLOYD, Bart.). Same *Arms*.

Lloyd (Ffoes-y-Bleiddiod; derived from CADIVOR AP DYFN-WAL, represented by LLOYD-PHILLIPS, of Dale Castle, co. Pembroke). Same *Arms*.

Lloyd (Pound, co. Devon; derived from CADIVOR AP DYFN-WAL). Same *Arms* as the preceding.

Lloyd (Danryallt, co. Carmarthen; descended from LLOYD, of Ffoes-y-Bleiddiod, co. Cardigan). Same *Arms*. *Crests*—1st: A wolf ramp. ar. a spear's head imbrued betw. his paws and piercing the dexter paw, underneath three drops of blood: 2nd: a lion ramp. reguard. sa. *Motto*—Heb Dduw heb ddim, a Duw a digon.

Lloyd (Esclusham, and Dulaseu; derived from DAVID GOCH AP DAVID, Lord of Penmachno, whose estates passed to co-heiresses). *Arms*, those of DAVID GOCH, Lord of Penmachno, viz., Sa. a lion ramp. ar. a bordure engr. or.

Lloyd (Marrington, Martin, and Stockton, all in the parish of Chirbury, co. Salop; Sheriff co. Montgomery, 1616; represented by Rev. WILLIAM VALENTINE LLOYD, R.N., F.R.G.S., Incumbent of Marton in 1857, *m.* 1850, the Hon. CAROLINE AMELIA SOPHIA AYLMER, only sister of UDOLPHUS, seventh *Baron Aylmer*). Sa. three nags' heads ar. Quarterings entered in Visit. Salop, 1584 and 1623 : 1st, gu. a griffin segreant or, LLOWDDEN; 2nd ; sa. a chev. betw. three owls, ar., BROUGHTON; 3rd gu. three snakes nowed in a triangular knot ar., EDNOWAIN AP BRADWEN; 4th, ar. on a bend vert three wolves' heads erased of the field, RIRID MIDDLETON; 5th, vert a chev. betw. three wolves' heads erased ar., RIRID FLAIDD, *i.e.*, WOLF; 6th gu. on a bend or, three lions pass. sa., MIDDLETON, of Middleton, Chirbury: 7th, ar. two Cornish Choughs in pale ppr., DE BOULERS or BOWDLER. *Crest*—A nag's head erased ar. *Motto*—Frangas non flectes.

Lloyd (Wygfair, co. Flint; derived from EDNOWAIN BENDEW founder of the XIII. Noble Tribe of North Wales and Powys). *Arms*, those of EDNOWAIN BENDEW, viz., Ar. a chev. betw. three boars' heads couped sa.

Lloyd (Bank House, co. Salop; granted to JOHN LLOYD, Esq.). Per pale gu. and sa. on a fesse engr. betw. three greyhounds current ar. collared or, as many boars' heads erased of the second. *Crest*—On a mount vert amidst heath ppr. a greyhound current ar. collared or.

Lloyd (Welcombe, co Warwick, London, Acombe and Coatham, co. York; presumed to derive from the LLOYD, of Llanynys, co. Denbigh, and descended immediately from GAMALIEL LLOYD, Esq., of Mattersey, co. Nottingham, *d.* in 1661). Ar. three lions dormant in pale sa., quartering CARTE, ar. a stag. trippant gu. *Crest* (of CARTE) borne by the family —A dexter cubit arm in scale armour ppr. cuff. ar. grasping a lizard sinisterways vert.

Lloyd (Gwyrch, co. Denbigh; the heiress, FRANCES LLOYD, of Gwyrch Castle, *m.* 1785, ROBERT BAMFORD HESKETH, Esq., of Bamford Hall, co. Lancaster, and Upton, co. Chester). Sa. three roses ar.

Lloyd (Glansevin, co. Carmarthen; descended from IDIO WYLLT, son of SUTHRIE, Lord of Desmond, in Ireland, by NEST, his wife, dau. of TEWDWR MAWR, Prince of South Wales. Having come to Wales to assist his uncle, RHYS AP TEWDWR MAWR, against Bernard Newmarch, about 1090, he received the lordship of Llywel, in Brecon). Ar. a lion ramp. sa. the tail introverted, the head, paws and brush of the tail of the field.

Lloyd (Ithagatt, co. Merioneth, Berth, co. Denbigh, &c., derived from the stock of TUDOR TREVOR, Lord of the Marches of Wales). Per bend sinister erm. and ermines, over all a lion ramp. ar.

Lloyd (Cefndyrrys; Gen. Sir EVAN LLOYD, of Ferney Hall, co. Salop, K.C.H., son and heir of the late EVAN LLOYD, Esq., derived from ELYSTAN GLODRYDD). Quarterly, 1st and 4th, gu. a lion ramp. reguard. or; 2nd and 3rd, az. three boars' heads couped sa. *Crest*—Out of a ducal coronet or, a griffin's head vert. *Motto*—Gwell angau neu cywilydd.

Lloyd (Havod-Dinas, co. Denbigh; represented by CLOUGH, of Estyn). Sa. a hart trippant ar. attired or. *Crest*—A hart trippant ar. Attired or, with a snake in the mouth vert.

Lloyd (Bronwydd, co. Cardigan, bart. ; descended from the ancient Lords of Dyfed). Az. a wolf ramp. ar. a bordure erm. *Crest*—In front of a holly tree ppr. a boar pass. ar. semée of estoiles az. collared and chained to the tree or. *Motto*—Iddow Bŏr diolch—in English, To God be thanks.

Lloyd (co. Cardigan). Per bend sinister ar. and az. semée of erm. spots or, over all a lion ramp. of the last, armed and langued gu.

Lloyd (Cynfell, co. Merioneth; granted 1784). Sa. a lion ramp. per fesse ar. and erminois.

Lloyd (Laques, co. Carmarthen). Quarterly, 1st, gu. on a bend betw. three daggers ar. a lion pass. sa.; 2nd, ar. on a chev. gu. three garbs or ; 3rd, ar. two lions reguard. sa. ; 4th, sa. an eagle with two heads displ. or. *Crest*—An eagle preying on a bird.

Lloyd (Tralwyn, co. Carnarvon). Az. on a chev. or, betw. three spear heads ar. a torteau betw. two bulls' heads caboshed sa. *Crest*—A lion ramp. ar. guttée de sang surmounting two spears in saltire ppr. *Motto*—Instanta perfectus.

Lloyd (Cilcen Hall, and Plas-yn-Clan, co. Flint). Gu. a Saracen's head erased at the neck ppr. wreathed about the temples sa. and ar. *Crest*—A Saracen's head, as in the arms, ar. *Motto*—Dial Gwaed Cymro.

Lloyd (Dinas, co. Brecon). Sa. a lion ramp. reguard. or. *Crest*—A lion, as in the arms.

Lloyd (Clochfaen Llangurig, co. Montgomery). Quarterly, 1st and 4th, erm. a lion ramp. sa. armed gu. a border of the last, charged with eight annulets ar. ; 2nd and 3rd, per bend sinister erm. and ermines, a lion ramp, or, for TUDOR. *Crests* —1st: A lion ramp. gu.; 2nd: Out of a ducal coronet or, a demi lion ramp. sa. over it the motto, "Heb Dduw heb Ddim, a Duw y Digon." *Motto*—In te, Domine, speravi.

Lloyd (Nantgwillt, co. Radnor). Quarterly, 1st and 4th, ar. an eagle displ. gu. ; 2nd and 3rd, a lion ramp. or. *Crest*—On a cap of maintenance an heraldic tiger statant.

Lloyd (Pale, co. Merioneth). Sa. a stag trippant ar. attired or. *Crest*—A stag ar.

Lloyd (WILLIAM LLOYD, D.D., Bishop of Worcester, 1700-17, son of Rev. RICHARD LLOYD, Rector of Tilehurst, co. Berks, and grandson of DAVID LLYWD, of Henblâs, Anglesea). Ar. a chev. betw. three crows sa. in each of their bills an erm. spot.

Lloyd (confirmed by PORTER. Visit. Worcester, 1684). Vert a chev. betw. three wolves' heads erased ar.

Lloyd (co. Pembroke). Sa. three foxes' heads erased ar.

Lloyd (Crickadarn, co. Brecon). Az. a wolf ramp. ar.

Lloyd (Leaton Knolls, co. Salop; descended from MADOC LLOYD, "Lord of Chirk Land," North Wales, a scion of the stock of TUDOR TREVOR). Per bend sinister erm. and erminois, a lion ramp. or, with a bordure gu. *Crest*—A demi lion ramp. or.

Lloyd (Coedmore, co. Cardigan). Quarterly, 1st and 4th, sa. a spearhead ar. erect embrued ppr. betw. three scaling ladders in bend of the second ; 2nd and 3rd, quarterly, 1st and 4th, ar. a lion ramp. gu., 2nd and 3rd, az. a lion ramp. within an orle of quatrefoils ar. *Crest*—A lion ramp. ar. *Motto*—Fide et fortitudine.

Lloyd (Bryneston, near Wrexham, co. Denbigh ; RICHARD MIDDLETON MASSIE LLOYD, Esq., of Plas Madoc and Bry-nestyn, fifth son of THOMAS LLOYD, Esq., of Plas Madoc and Wrexham, grandson of the Rev. THOMAS LLOYD, of Plas Power, co. Denbigh, derived in a direct line from IORWERTH, surnamed PENWYN, ninth in descent from MARCHUDD AF CYNAN, Founder of the VIII. Noble Tribe of North Wales). Gu. three boars' heads erased in pale ar.

Lloyd (confirmed, 1838, to Major Sir WILLIAM LLOYD, Knt., of Bryneston, son of RICHARD MIDDLETON MASSIE LLOYD, Esq., of that place, in consideration of his services in India). Gu. three boars' heads erased in pale ar. on a chief embattled of the last a representation of the fortress of Seetabuldee, extending to the village of Telpoorce on the sinister all ppr. superinscribed with the word "Seetabuldee" in letters all sa. *Crest*—A boar's head erased ar. in front of two flagstaves in saltire ppr. flowing from that on the dexter a banner tenné, inscribed " Nagpoor " in letters of gold, and

615

from that on the sinister a banner vert, inscribed "Muckee" in letters also of gold. *Mottoes*—Below the shield: Heb Dduw heb Ddim ; above the crest : Jure non dono. The arms borne by Sir WILLIAM LLOYD's father were simply—Gu. three boars' heads erased in pale ar.

Lloyd (Lancing, co. Sussex, bart., extinct). Per bend sinister erm. and pean, a lion ramp. or, gorged with a wreath of oak vert, and supporting in the dexter forepaw a sword erect ppr. pommel and hilt gold. *Crest*—A lion's head erased per bend sinister erm. and pean, gorged with a wreath of oak vert.

Lloyd (Bradenham House, near Wycomb, co. Bucks). Quarterly, or and az. four roebucks trippant counterchanged. *Crest*—A lion pass. gu. charged with two characters of the planet Venus, viz., on the shoulder one thus ♀, and on the hip another thus ⚗.

Lloyd (Clockfaen, co. Montgomery). Vert three goats pass. in pale ppr.

Lloyd (co. Denbigh). Quarterly, or and az. four lions pass. counterchanged.

Lloyd (cos. Denbigh and Kent). Or, three men's heads ppr. in armour ar. garnished of the field. *Crest*—A man's head ppr. in armour ar. garnished or, on a label issuing from his mouth, and proceeding over the head, these words, " Avonno div dervid."

Lloyd (co. Gloucester). Ar. a quiver gu. banded and replenished with arrows or, betw. three pheons sa.

Lloyd (Holyrood and Whitnester, co. Gloucester, and Cheame, co. Surrey). Quarterly, or and az. five roebucks counterchanged. *Crest*—A stag's head erased sa. charged on the neck with a crescent erm.

Lloyd (co. Hants). Az. a lion ramp. or. *Crest*—On a mount vert a lion sejant guard. gu.

Lloyd (co. Hereford). Sa. three nags' heads erased ar. *Crest* —A nag's head erased ar.

Lloyd (WILLIAM LLOYD, Bishop of St. Asaph, 1680-92, of Lichfield and Coventry, 1692-99, and of Worcester, 1700-17). Ar. a chev. betw. three crowns sa. each bearing in the beak an erm. spot.

Lloyd (London and Wales; granted 1578). Ar. a griffin segreant vert. *Crest*—Out of a ducal coronet or, a cock's head betw. two wings gu. combed, beaked, and wattled of the first.

Lloyd (co. Montgomery). Gyronny of four, in the first quarter or, a lion pass. sa. ; 2nd, purp. three falcons or; 3rd, gu. three horses' heads erased ar. ; 4th, purp. a falcon or. *Crest*—A horse's head erased sa. maned or.

Lloyd (co. Pembroke). Sa. three nags' heads erased ar.

Lloyd (Garth, co. Montgomery, bart., extinct 1743). Same *Arms.*

Lloyd (Woking, co. Surrey, bart., extinct 1674 ; descended from LLOYD, of Forest, co. Carmarthen). Gu. a lion ramp . ar. a border dancettée of the last.

Lloyd (Flaxley Grange, co. Gloucester ; granted to JOSEPH SKIPP LLOYD, Esq., M.A., Oxford, Barrister-at-law, formerly Clerk of the Cheque and Adjutant of H.M. Body Guard of Gentlemen-at-Arms, eldest son of JOSEPH LLOYD, Esq., of Abinghall, co. Gloucester, by PENELOPE SKIPP, his wife, dau. and co-heir of GEORGE SKIPP, Esq., of Flaxley Grange, who was a descendant of JOHN SKIPP, Bishop of Hereford, 1539-52, Lord Almoner to Queen Anna Boleyn). Quarterly, 1st and 4th, or, a griffin segreant vert betw. three roses gu. barbed and seeded ppr., for LLOYD; 2nd and 3rd, az. on a chev. betw. three estoiles or, two roses gu. barbed and seeded ppr. branched chevronwise vert, for SKIPP. *Crest*—A cock's head couped ar. combed and wattled gu. charged on the neck with two estoiles in pale az. betw. two wings erect vair. *Motto*—Virtus rosâ suavior stellâ clarior.

Lloyd (JOHN LLOYD, Bishop of St. David's, 1686, d. 13 Feb. 1687). Gu. a lion ramp. reguard. or, armed and langued az.

Lloyd (Hardwicke, co. Salop). Ar. an eagle with two heads gu. a bordure of the last.

Lloyd (Ludlow, co. Salop). Gu. a lion ramp. reguard. or, quartering ar. three boars' heads couped sa.

Lloyd (Oswestry, co. Salop). Per fesse sa. and ar. a lion ramp. counterchanged. *Crest*—Out of a five-leaved coronet or, a demi lion ramp. or.

Lloyd (Swan Hill, co. Salop). Quarterly, or and gu. four lions pass. counterchanged. *Crest*—A lion ramp. gu.

Lloyd (Heightley, co. Salop; THOMAS LLOYD, Esq., was Sheriff, 1736). Ar. on a bend sa. three leopards' faces of the first.

Lloyd (Whittington, co. Salop). Vert a chev. betw. three wolves' heads erased erm. (another, ar.).

Lloyd (Ipswich, co. Suffolk). Per fesse ar. and sa. a lion ramp. counterchanged.

Lloyd (Forest, co. Carmarthen). Gu. a lion ramp. ar. a border dancettée of the last.

Lloyd (Wales and Maryland). Az. a lion ramp. or. *Crest*—A demi lion ramp. guard. or, supporting in the paws an arrow in pale ar.

Lloyd (Manor of Queen's Village, Lloyd's Neck, Long Island, New York; descended from JAMES LLOYD, of Lloyd's Neck, who emigrated from England about 1660, *m.* a dau. of Sir JOHN LEVERETT, Governor of Massachusetts; the heiress of this family *m.* LEONARD VASSALL BORLAND, Esq., of Boston). Gu. a lion ramp. or. *Crest*—A bird rising or. *Another Crest*, borne by the Hon. JAMES LLOYD, United States Senator from Massachusetts—A pelican feeding its young ppr.

Lloyd. Sa. a chev. betw. three spears' heads ar. embrued gu. *Crest*—A stag's head couped ar.

Lloyd. Or, three lions dormant in pale sa. *Crest*—An arm in armour, the hand grasping a lizard all ppr.

Lloyd (quartered by CRAWLEY and CRAWLEY-BOEVEY, bart.). Erm. on a saltire gu. betw. two boars' heads erased in pale sa. a crescent or.

Lloyd (Fun. Ent. Ulster's Office, 1597, EDWARD LLOYD). Vert a chev. erm. betw. three griffins' heads erased ar. a label of three points gu.

Lloyd (Reg. Ulster's Office). Gu. a chev. erm. a chief or.

Lloyd (Reg. Ulster's Office). Ar. a quiver gu. arrows feathered or, betw. three pheons sa.

Lloyd (Gloster, King's co.; descended from TREVOR LLOYD, younger son of EVAN LLOYD, Esq., of Bodidris-yn-Yale; Colonel HARDRESS LLOYD, M.P. King's co. 1807-16, the last male heir of the family, *d. unm.* 1860, when the representation of the family devolved on VAUGHAN, of Golden Grove, King's co.). Same *Arms* as LLOYD, Bart., of Bodidris. *Crest*—A lion ramp. ar. holding in the dexter paw a snake ppr. *Motto*—Respice prospice.

Lloyd-Vaughan (representing LLOYD, of Gloster). See HUTCHINSON-LLOYD-VAUGHAN, of Golden Grove. SAMUEL DAWSON HUTCHINSON, Esq., of Mount Heaton, *m.* MARY LLOYD, only dau. and heir of JOHN LLOYD, Esq., last surviving brother of Colonel HARDRESS LLOYD, of Gloster, and assumed thereupon the additional surnames of LLOYD and VAUGHAN.

Lloyd (Croghan, co. Roscommon; derived from HEDD MOLWYNOG, Lord of Uwch Aled, founder of the IX. Noble Tribe of North Wales and Powys). Quarterly, 1st and 4th, gu. a chev. or, on a chief erm. a canton ar. charged with an eagle displ. with two heads sa. The canton which the LLOYDS of Croghan bear as an augmentation were the arms achieved by Meuric Llwyd, of Llwyn-y-maen, "a valiant captain under the Earl of Arundel." 2nd and 3rd, ar. a bend sa. within a bordure engr. of the second. *Crests*—A stag's head couped ppr. the neck surcharged with a laurel chaplet; and on a ducal coronet or, an eagle displ. with two heads sa. *Mottoes*—Over the stag's head: Spectemur agendo; and above the eagle: Eo altius quo profundius.

Lloyd (Rockville, co. Roscommon; allowed by Betham, Ulster, 1813, to OWEN LLOYD, Esq., of Rockville, Lieut.-Colonel Roscommon Militia). Az. a chev. or, a chief erminois, quartering, per pale dancettée or and az. a lion pass. guard. counterchanged, a crescent for diff. *Crest*—An eagle displ. with two heads sa. armed gu.

Lloyd (Strancally Castle, co. Waterford). Ar. three lions dormant in pale sa. *Crest*—A cubit arm vested sa. cuffed ar. holding in the hand ppr. a lizard vert.

Lloyd (Stockton Hall, co. York; descended from the preceding). Same *Arms, Crest*, and *Motto.*

Lloyd (Cowsby Hall, co. York; descended from the same family). Same *Arms, Crest*, and *Motto.*

Lloyd (Lloydsboro', co. Tipperary). Paly of eight or and ar. *Crest*—A lion ramp. ar. holding in the dexter paw a snake ppr. *Motto*—Ynir o yale.

Lloyd (Lisheen). As preceding.

Lloyd-Flood. See FLOOD.

Lloyde. Az. a boar ar. betw. ten trefoils slipped of the second.

Lluellin (co. Hertford). Gu. three chev. ar. *Crest*—A paschal lamb ppr.

Lluellyn (South Withiam, co. Lincoln, 1654; originally of ancient Welsh descent, represented by Colonel RICHARD LLUELLYN, C.B., only son of the late RICHARD LLUELLYN, Esq., Deputy-Lieutenant of co. Lincoln, by MARGARET, his wife, dau. of WARREN MAUDE, Esq., of Sunnyside). Ar. a lion ramp. sa. ducally crowned or. *Crest*—On a rock ppr. a Cornish chough also ppr. *Motto*—Mors mihi lucrum.

Llwyd (Cwm Bychan, co. Merioneth; derived through MEURIC, Lord of Nannau, co. Merioneth, from CADWGAN,

Lord of Nannau). *Arms*, those of CADWGAN, Lord of Nannau, viz., Or, a lion ramp. az.

Llwyd (Caerwys, co. Flint; derived through the LLWYDS of Cwm Bychan, from CADWGAN, Lord of Nannau; Miss ANGHARAD LLWYD, of Caerwys, eminent for her research in Welsh literature and antiquities, descended from this family). Same *Arms*.

Llwyd (Llwyn-Maen, co. Salop; derived from HEDD MOLWYNOG, founder of the IX. Noble Tribe of North Wales and Powys). Ar. an eagle displ. with two heads.

Llyddocka. Az. a lion ramp. per fesse or and ar. within a bordure of the last charged with eight pellets.

Loader. Ar. a pale gu. over all a lion pass. sa. *Crest*—On a chapeau gu. two lions ramp. supporting a garb gu.

Loader. Six mullets, three, two, and one. *Crest*—A dragon pass. ppr.

Loades (London; granted 30 July, 1687). Sa. a wolf saliant reguard. or. *Crest*—On a wreath a mural coronet ar. therefrom an arm issuing, habited sa. cuff of the first, the hand ppr. holding a key or. *Motto*—Obey and rule.

Loadsman (North Shields, co. Northumberland). Ar. on a bend engr. sa. three annulets of the field.

Loane (co. Kent). Az. a lion (another, an antelope; another, a tiger) pass. or. *Crest*—A demi lion ramp. sa. brandishing a scymitar ppr.

Loat. Bendy of six vert and ar. a chief erm. *Crest*—A spur rowel betw. two wings ppr.

Loban. Gu. a lion pass. or, on a canton ar. a key paleways sa. *Crest*—A dexter arm in armour embowed, holding a tilting spear ppr.

Lobb. Ar. two lions combatant gu. *Crest*—A lion's head erased collared gu.

Lobenham. Gu. a chev. engr. or, betw. three owls of the last.

Lobert, or Loberd (co. Leicester). Gu. a fesse dancettée or, an annulet of the second (another, a bezant). *Crest*—A dexter arm embowed, vested az. holding in the hand ppr. a hunting spear point downwards sa. headed ar.

Lobert (co. Leicester). Gu. a fesse indented betw. eight bezants, four and four.

Lobley. Sa. a chev. or, betw. three apes ar. chained of the second.

Locard. Ar. a saltire within a bordure az.

Locavell. Gu. three sails ar.

Loch (Drylaw, co. Edinburgh). Or, a saltire engr. sa. betw. two swans naiant in fesse in a loch ppr. *Crest*—A swan with wings endorsed devouring a perch both ppr. *Motto*—Assiduitate, non desidiâ.

Loch (Scotland, 16th century). Az. a saltire engr. betw. three swans naiant in lochs ppr. two in the flanks and one in base.

Lochard (The Byletts, co. Hereford, 17th century; quartered by CONINGSBY). Sa. three loaches naiant in pale ar.

Locherd, or Louchard. Ar. a saltire engr. az. within a bordure or.

Lochore (Scotland). Ar. three piles in point sa.

Lochrayn. Ar. a fesse wavy betw. two cotises az. depressed by a lion pass. gu.

Lock (London). Per fesse az. and or, in chief three falcons volant of the second. *Crest*—A hand ppr. holding up a cushion or.

Lock (Warnford, co. Southampton; THOMAS LOCK, Esq., Clarenceux King of Arms, 1784; granted 1767). Per fesse az. and or, a pale counterchanged, on the first three falcons rising of the second, collared gu. *Crest*—A falcon, as in the arms, in the beak a padlock pendent sa.

Lock (Mildenhall, co. Suffolk; granted 8 Dec. 1770). Same *Arms*, falcons ducally crowned az. *Crest*—A falcon rising or, ducally crowned ar. in the beak a padlock pendent sa.

Lock (Norbury Park, co. Surrey). Per fesse az. and or, a pale and three falcons, two and one, with wings addorsed and belled, each holding in the beak a padlock all counterchanged *Crest*—A falcon as in the arms.

Lock (London; Sir WILLIAM LOCK, Knt., Alderman, Visit. London, 1563; his dau. DOROTHY, *m.* JOHN COSWORTH, Esq., heir presumptive to his nephew, JOHN COSWORTH, Esq., of Cosworth, co. Cornwall). Per fess az. and or, a pale counterchanged, three falcons rising, each holding in their beaks a padlock of the second.

Lockard. Ar. a saltire engr. az. within a bordure engr. or.

Locke (JOSEPH LOCKE, Esq., of Lowndes Square, London, Lord of the Manor of Honiton). Az. three piles, two issuing from the chief and one from the base or, each charged with a falcon belled, rising, of the field. *Crest*—A falcon belled or, wings elevated chequy of the last and az. and resting the dexter claw upon a padlock sa. *Motto*—Mente non marte.

Locke (Ashton Gifford, co. Wilts, and Stourcliffe, co. Hants; granted 5 July, 2 Philip and Mary). Per fesse az. and or, a pale counterchanged, three hawks with wings endorsed of the last. *Crest*—A hawk with wings endorsed holding in the beak a padlock or.

Locke (confirmed by St. George, Ulster, 1675, to Lieut. RICHARD LOCKE, J.P., co. Kildare, descended from the LOCKES, of the Isle of Wight). Per pale ar. and gu. on a saltire five roundles all counterchanged. *Crest*—An eagle's head ppr. beaked or.

Locker. Quarterly, 1st and 4th, ar. a chev. betw. three dragons' heads erased gu.; 2nd and 3rd, ar. a fesse betw. three lozenges az. *Crest*—A buck's head erased ppr.

Lockerby (that Ilk). Gu. a chev. ar. betw. three roses or.

Lockett (Clouterbrook, co. Chester, West Houghton, and Liverpool, co. Lancaster, and of the town of Derby). Or, a chev. gu. betw. three stags' heads couped ppr. *Crest*—A stag's head, as in the arms.

Lockey (Homes, co. Hertford, cos. Essex, Hereford, and York). Ar. a bend betw. two water bouges sa. *Crest*—An ostrich's head couped at the neck ar. holding in the beak a key sa.

Lockey. Ar. a chev. betw. three cinquefoils az.

Lockhart (Lee, co. Lanark). *Old Arms*—Az. three boars' hands erased or. As recorded 1735—Ar. a man's heart ppr. within a fetterlock sa. on a chief az. three boars' heads erased of the first. *Crest*—A boars' head erased ar. *Supporters*—Dexter, a man completely armed, the visor of his helmet open, a spear in his dexter hand, and pendent from his neck by a gold chain a heart ppr. *Motto*—Corda serrata pando.

Lockhart (*Count Lockhart-Wishart*, 1780). Ar. a heart gu. within a fetterlock sa. on a chief ar. three boars' heads erased of the first within a bordure of the fourth, charged with five mullets of six points or. *Crests*—1st: In the centre, two flags parted per fesse ar. and gu. flotant to the dexter and sinister, placed behind a boars' head erased ppr.; 2nd: On the dexter, on a ducal coronet an eagle displ. reguard.; 3rd: On the sinister, out of a ducal coronet a demi lion holding in the dexter paw a sword. *Supporters*—As preceding. *Motto*—Corda serrata pando.

Lockhart (Carnwath, co. Lanark, 1733). Ar. a man's head ppr. within a fetterlock sa. on a chief az. a boar's head erased of the first, all within a bordure of the fourth, charged with five stars of the field. *Crest*—A dexter hand ppr. holding a banner az. charged with a saltire ar. *Mottoes* (above the crest)—Quid non pro patria; (below the shield) Corda serrata.

Lockhart (MACDONALD-LOCKHART, of Lee and Carnwath, bart., 1806). Quarterly, 1st and 4th, ar. a man's heart gu. within a fetterlock sa. on a chief az. three boars' heads erased of the first, for LOCKHART; 2nd and 3rd grand quarterings, quarterly, 1st, or, a lion ramp. gu., 2nd, or, a naked arm issuing from the sinister side in fesse ppr. holding a cross crosslet fitchée gu., 3rd, ar. a galley, her oars in action in saltire sa. ensigned gu., 4th, vert a salmon in fesse ar., for MACDONALD. *Crest*—A boar's head erased ar. *Supporters*—Dexter, a chevalier armed at all points, his visor up, holding a spear in his hand, a sword by his side, and a gold chain about his neck, thereat a man's heart pendent gu. ensigned with an imperial crown or, and on his helmet a plume of feathers, the centre gu. the other ar. ; sinister, a buck ppr. *Mottoes*—1st, LOCKHART: Corda serrata pando; 2nd, MACDONALD: Semper paratus pugnare pro patriâ.

Lockhart (Barr, co. Dumfries). Ar. on a bend sa. three fetterlocks or.

Lockhart (nephew of Barr, 1672). Gu. on a fesse betw. three boars' heads erased ar. a heart of the field within a fetterlock sa. *Crest*—A dexter hand holding forth a key bendways ppr. *Motto*—Corda serrata pando.

Lockhart (Cleghorn, co. Lanark). Az. three boars' heads erased ar. *Crest*-- A boar's head erased ar. *Supporters*—Two wild harts ppr. *Motto* Sine labe fides.

Lockhart (Birkhill, co. Lanark). Ar. on a bend betw. three boars' heads erased az. a man's heart ppr. within a fetterlock or. *Crest*—A boar's head erased ar. *Motto*—Eeroci fortior.

Lockhart (Kirktoun, co. Lanark). Ar. on a chev. betw. three boars' heads erased ar. a man's heart within a fetterlock or. *Crest*—A dexter hand holding a boar's head erased ppr. *Motto*—Feroci fortior.

617

Lockhart (Sir WILLIAM LOCKHART, Solicitor-General, 1610). Quarterly, 1st, az. three boars' heads erased ar., for LOCKHART; 2nd, ar. a chev. sa. betw. three boars' heads erased of the first within a bordure gu., for ELPHINSTONE, of Calderhall; 3rd, per pale indented sa. and ar. on a chief of the second a crescent vert betw. two erm. spots, for HENDERSON, of Fordel; 4th, ar. a cross betw. four mullets az., for BANNATYNE, of Corehouse. *Crest*—A dexter hand holding up a boar's head erased ppr. *Motto*—Sine labe fides.

Locksmith. Ar. a chev. betw. three horseshoes sa. a chief gu. *Crest*—Out of a mural crown or, a griffin's head ppr.

Lockton (Swinsted, co. Lincoln). Ar. a chev. az. *Crest* – Out of a ducal coronet or, a griffin's head az.

Lockton (co. Lincoln). Ar. a chief az.

Lockton (co. York). Ar. on a chev. az. a martlet of the first within a bordure engr. of the second.

Locktou. Ar. a chev. az. a bordure engr. of the last, charged with eight mullets or.

Lockwood (Lockwood, co. Stafford : ANNE LOCKWOOD, the heiress of the family, *temp*. Edward IV., *m*. JOHN COLCLOUGH, Esq., of Bluerton and Ingleton, in same co., whose grandson, Sir ANTHONY COLCLOUGH, obtained a grant of Tintern Abbey, co. Wexford, from Queen Elizabeth. Visit. London, 1563). Sa. a fess betw. three martlets ar. *Crest*—A camel's head couped sa.

Lockwood (Dewes Hall, co. Essex, and Gayton, co. Northampton; descended from Rev. RICHARD LOCKWOOD, Rector of Dingley, co. Northampton, in 1530). Quarterly, 1st and 4th, ar. a fesse betw. three martlets sa., for LOCKWOOD ; 2nd and 3rd, a erm. on a bend engr. sa. three plates, for CUTTS. *Crest*—On the stump of an oak tree erased ppr. a martlet sa.

Lockwood (Dews Hall). See WOOD.

Lockyer (Plymouth, co. Devon); confirmed to Rev. EDMUND LEOPOLD LOCKYER, M.A., son of EDMUND LOCKYER, M.D., by ELIZA, his wife, dau. and co-heir of Captain THOMAS PATRICKSON BRAITHWAITE, R N.). Az. on a chev. ar. betw. three lions ramp. or, as many ants fesseways ppr. *Crest*—On the sea a ship under sail, her three topsails hoisted ppr. the main topsail charged with a lion ramp. gu. the fore and mizen topsails charged each with an ant, as in the arms, a red ensign flying and a pennant ar. at the maintop-gallant masthead, charged with a cross az. *Motto*—Sedule et secunde.

Lockyer (1672). Az. a fesse or, betw. three daggers' heads of the last.

Locock (Speldhurst, co. Kent, and Hertford Street, Mayfair, bart). Az. a gauntlet or, in chief three mullets ar. *Crest*—On a mount vert a cock ar. guttée de sang, the dexter foot resting on a gauntlet gold. *Motto*—Victoria.

Locres. Ar. (another, or) a fesse gu.

Lodbroc (THOMAS DE LODBROC, of Ladbroke, 24 Edward III., eleventh in descent from WILLIAM DE LODBROC, 11 Henry II. Visit. Warwick, Dugdale). Az. a chev. erm.

Lodbrooke (Lodbrooke, co. Warwick). Az. a chev. erm. (another, ar.). *Crest*—A unicorn ramp.

Lodbrooke. Erm. a cross gu.

Lodder (granted to WILLIAM PHILIP JAMES LODDER, Esq., of Southampton, some time Captain in the 6th Regt. of Foot). Ar. on a chev. engr. az. betw. three swords erect ppr. pommels and hilts or, as many gryphons' heads erased of the last. *Crest*—A demi gryphon or, charged with a chev. az. and supporting a passion cross in bend also az. *Motto*—In Deo confiteor.

Loder. Erm. on a fesse three escallops. *Crest*—A stag's head couped at the neck, betw. the horns a cross crosslet.

Loder. Sa. six annulets, three and three in pale ar.

Leder. Sa. ten bezants, four, three, two, and one.

Lodge (Sir THOMAS LODGE, Lord Mayor of London, 1562). Az. a lion ramp. ar. crusily fitchée gu. within a bordure flory of the second. *Crest*—A demi lion ramp. couped sa. holding in the paws a cross pattée fitchée gu.

Lodge (London). Ar. a lion ramp. ar. crusily gu. within a tressure of demi fleurs-de-lis and a bordure of the second.

Lodge (co. Salop). Gu. a lion ramp. ar. within a bordure flory or.

Lodge (Nettlested, co. Suffolk). Az. a lion ramp. within a double tressure flory counterflory or. *Crest*—A lion double queued az.

Lodge (Leeds, co. York). Per fesse gu. and sa. a lion ramp. ar. semée of crosses crosslet of the first.

Lodge. Per bend sinister sa. and ar. crusily and a lion ramp. all counterchanged.

Lodge (Bodsilin, co. Carnarvon ; as borne by ADAM LODGE, Esq., Barrister-at-law, whose poetic works are well known).

Az. a lion ramp. ar. semée of crosses pattée fitchée gu. within a bordure of the second charged with eight fleurs-de-lis of the third. *Crest*—A demi lion erased sa. semée of fleurs-de-lis or, supporting a cross pattée fitchée gu.

Lodge (Fun. Ent. Ulster's Office, 1607, JOAN, dau. of GEORGE LODGE, and wife of RALPH GRIMESDICH, Farmer of the Customs of the port of Dublin). Per bend sinister ar. and sa. crusillée fitchée a lion ramp. counterchanged, armed and langued gu.

Lodham. Ar. on a bend az. seven crosses crosslet or.

Lodington (Weldingworth, co. Lincoln). Paly of six ar. and az. on a chief gu. a lion pass. guard. or. *Crest*—A demi lady richly attired az. in her dexter hand a garland of laurel vert.

Lodwick. Gu. a chev. betw. three cocks ar. *Crest*—A cock ppr.

Lodyngton (London). Ar. three palets az. on a chief gu. a lion pass. guard. or.

Loe. Az. a wolf pass. ar. *Crest*—A wolf's head couped ar. collared gu. charged with three bezants.

Loffroy. See LEFROY.

Lofft (Troston, co. Suffolk). Gu. a chev. engr. erm. betw. three trefoils slipped ar. *Crest*—A demi lion ramp. holding in his paws a cross crosslet fitchée. *Motto*—Fide et fortitudine.

Lofft. See MOSELY.

Lofft (Glemham House, co. Suffolk; granted to HENRY CAPEL LOFFT, Esq.). Gu. two chevronels erm. betw. three trefoils in chief and another in base ar. *Crest*—A boar's head couped and erect ar. in the mouth a cross crosslet fitchy gu. betw. two branches of oak fructed ppr. *Motto*—Fide et fortitudine.

Loft (Healing, co. Lincoln). Erm. on a bend gu. a pheon in canton or. *Crest*—A wolf's head couped gu. charged on the neck with a pheon transfixed through the mouth by a broken spear fesseways or, the head of the spear embrued ppr.

Lofthouse. Sa. a chev. engr. betw. three trefoils slipped ar. *Crest*—A spur betw. two wings ppr.

Loftie (Tandcragee, co. Armagh, formerly of Smeeth, co. Kent; settled at Westwell, co. Kent, cir. 1495; arms on a monument, 1678, in Smeeth Church). Sa. a chev. (another, engr.) erm. betw. three trefoils slipped ar. *Crest*—A boar's head erect and erased ar. tusked or. *Mottoes*—Prend moy tel que je suis; and, Loyal au mort.

Loftus (Swineshead, co. York; EDWARD LOFTUS, Esq., of that place, temp. Henry VIII., had two sons, ROBERT, ancestor of *Viscount Loftus*, of Elye, and ADAM LOFTUS, ancestor of *Viscount Lisburne, Earl* and *Marquis of Ely.* Sa. a chev. engr. betw. three trefoils slipped ar.

Loftus (*Viscount Loftus*, of Eyle, extinct 1725; descended from ROBERT LOFTUS, eldest son of EDWARD LOFTUS, of Swineshead, whose eldest son, ADAM LOFTUS, Esq., of Monasterevan, Queen's co., was appointed Lord Chancellor of Ireland 1619, and created a peer 1622; JANE, dau. and heiress of the last viscount, m. CHARLES, *Lord Moore*, eldest son of HENRY, third *Earl of Drogheda*, and her son, HENRY, fourth *Earl of Drogheda*, inherited Monasterevan and the other Loftus estates). Sa. a chev. erm. betw. three trefoils slipped ar. *Crest*—A boar's head erect and erased ar. armed or, langued gu. *Supporters*—Two bucks erm. attired or. *Motto*—Loyal au mort.

Loftus (ADAM LOFTUS, Archbishop of Dublin, Lord Chancellor of Ireland, and one of the Lords Justices, second son of EDWARD LOFTUS, Esq., of Swineshead, co. York, buried at St. Sepulcre's, Dublin, 5 April, 1605. Fun. Ent. Ulster's Office). Quarterly, 1st and 4th, per chev. ar. and sa. a chev. erm. betw. three trefoils slipped counterchanged; 2nd and 3rd, gyronny of eight, a saltire engr. betw. four fleurs-de-lis, the stems converging towards the centre all counterchanged.

Loftus (EDWARD LOFTUS, the Queen's Serjeant, eldest son of ADAM LOFTUS, Archbishop of Dublin and Lord Chancellor of Ireland, buried at St. Patrick's Cathedral, 5 Sept. 1602, Fun. Ent. Ulster's Office). Per chev. ar. and sa. a chev. erm. betw. three trefoils slipped counterchanged, a label of three points gu.

Loftus (Sir DUDLEY LOFTUS, Knt., of Rathfarnham, co. Dublin, second but eldest surviving son of ADAM LOFTUS, Archbishop of Dublin and Lord Chancellor, knighted by Sir WILLIAM FITZWILLIAM, Lord Deputy, 2 Dec. 1593). Gyronny of eight ar. and sa. a saltire engr. betw. four fleurs-de-lis, the stems converging towards the centre all counterchanged.

Loftus (*Viscount Lisburne*, extinct 1691; descended from Sir ADAM LOFTUS, Knt., of Rathfarnham, eldest son of Sir DUDLEY LOFTUS, of same place; LUCIA, dau. and heiress of *Viscount Lisburne*, m. THOMAS, first *Marquess of Wharton*,

618

her son PHILIP, *Duke of Wharton*, inherited the estates). Quarterly, 1st and 4th, sa. a chev. erm. betw. three trefoils slipped ar.; 2nd and 3rd, gyronny of eight ar. and sa. a saltire engr. counterchanged. *Crest*—A boar's head erased and erect ar. *Supporters*—Two eagles, wings inverted ar. each charged on the breast with a trefoil slipped vert. *Motto*—Prend moi tel que je suis.

Loftus (confirmed by Carney, Ulster, to DUDLEY LOFTUS, LL.D., Vice-Treasurer, Ireland, second son of Sir ADAM LOFTUS, Knt., of Rathfarnham, and to his wife, FRANCES NANGLE, granddaughter and heiress of THOMAS NANGLE, *Baron of Navan*). Quarterly, 1st, sa. a chev. engr. erm. betw. three trefoils slipped ar.; 2nd, or, on a fess az. three harps of the first stringed ar.; 3rd, az. three fusils conjoined in fess or; 4th, gyronny of eight a saltire engr. betw. four fleurs-de-lis, their stems converging towards the centre all counterchanged. *Crest*—A boar's head erased and erect ar. armed or. *Motto*—Sempre in un modo.

Loftus (*Earl of Ely*, extinct 1783; descended from NICHOLAS LOFTUS, Esq., of Fethard, co. Wexford, second son of Sir DUDLEY LOFTUS, Knt., of Rathfarnham; HENRY, last *Earl of Ely*, left three sisters, his co-heiresses: 1st, MARY, m. WILLIAM ALCOCK, Esq., of Wilton, co. Wexford; 2nd, ANNE, m. CHARLES TOTTENHAM, Esq., of New Ross, second son of CHARLES TOTTENHAM, Esq., of Tottenham Green, co. Wexford; 3rd, ELIZABETH, m. Sir JOHN TOTTENHAM, Bart., eldest son of CHARLES TOTTENHAM, Esq., of Tottenham Green; from their son, Sir CHARLES TOTTENHAM, who was testamentary heir of his uncle, the last *Earl of Ely*, descends the *Marquess of Ely*). Sa. a chev. engr. erm. betw. three trefoils slipped ar. *Crest*—A boar's head erased and erect ar. langued gu. *Supporters*—Two eagles, wings inverted ar. each charged on the breast with a trefoil slipped vert. *Motto*—Prend moi tel que je suis. N.B. NICHOLAS, first *Baron Loftus*, of Loftus Hall, and *Viscount Ely*, the father of the first *Earl of Ely*, bore the same arms as ADAM LOFTUS, Archbishop of Dublin, and for *Supporters*, two eagles ppr. charged with a trefoil also ppr.

Loftus-Hume (exemplified by Hawkins, Ulster, 1736, to NICHOLAS LOFTUS, Esq., of Loftus Hall, co. Wexford, afterwards second *Viscount Loftus* and *Earl of Ely*, upon his assuming the additional surname of HUME, in accordance with the testamentary injunction of his wife's father, Sir GUSTAVUS HUME, third bart. of Castle Hume, co. Fermanagh). Quarterly, 1st, vert a lion ramp. ar., for HUME; 2nd, sa. a chev. engr. erm. between three trefoils slipped ar., for LOFTUS; 3rd, gyronny of eight ar. and sa. a saltire engr. betw. four fleurs-de-lis, the stems converging towards the centre all counterchanged, also for LOFTUS; 4th, or, a chev. gu. betw. three buglehorns sa. stringed az., for CREWKERNE. Same *Crest* and *Motto* as the last.

Loftus (Ballinermine and Oldtown, co. Dublin; Col. WILLIAM JAMES LOFTUS is male representative of the noble house of LOFTUS, descended from Sir THOMAS LOFTUS, Knt., of Killyon, co. Meath, third son of ADAM LOFTUS, Archbishop of Dublin). Quarterly, 1st and 4th, sa. a chev. engr. erm. betw. three trefoils slipped ar.; 2nd, gyronny of eight ar. and sa. a saltire engr. betw. four fleurs-de-lis, the stems converging towards the centre all counterchanged; 3rd, az. a cross or, guttée de sang betw. four pelicans of the second. *Crest*—A boar's head couped and erect ar. langued gu., motto over, Loyal au mort. *Motto*—Prend mois tel que je suis.

Loftus (*Marquess of Ely*; descended from Sir JOHN TOTTENHAM, Bart., of Tottenham Green, co. Wexford, by Hon. ELIZABETH LOFTUS, his wife, sister of the last *Earl of Ely*, their son, Sir CHARLES TOTTENHAM, having inherited Loftus Hall and other estates, assumed the surname of LOFTUS, was raised to the peerage 1785, and finally created *Marquess of Ely* 1800). Sa. a chev. engr. erm. betw. three trefoils slipped ar. *Crest*—A boar's head erased and erect ar. *Supporters*—Two eagles, wings inverted ar. beaked and legged ar, each charged on the breast with a trefoil slipped vert. *Mottoes*—Under the arms : Prends moi tel que je suis ; over the crest: Loyal a mort.

Logan (that Ilk). Or, three passion nails in point piercing a man's heart gu. *Crest*—A passion nail piercing a man's heart ppr. *Motto*—Hoc majorum virtus.

Logan (Restalrig, co. Edinburgh). Or, three passion nails sa. conjoined in point, piercing a man's heart in base gu. ; otherwise—quarterly, 1st and 4th, or, three piles conjoined in point sa., for LOGAN; 2nd and 3rd, ar. an eagle displ. with two heads sa. beaked and membered gu., for RAMSAY. *Crest*—A buglehorn stringed ppr.

Logat. Erm. a lion ramp. gu.

Loges (RICHARD DE LOGES, of Chesterton, co. Warwick; temp. Edward I., Dugdale). Ar. three piles gu. on a canton az. a buck trippant or.

Loges. Ar. three piles in point az. on a canton gu. a lion ramp. of the first. *Crest*—A swan collared and lined ppr.

Loggan, or Logan (Staverton, co. Berks, and co. Bucks). Or, a lion pass. sa. in chief three Roman piles of the second. *Crest*—A stag's head erased gu. attired, collared, and lined or.

Loghlan, or Lauchlan (Scotland). Az. two bars wavy ar. betw. as many crosses crosslet fitchée or, in chief and a swan in base ppr. *Crest*—A swan ppr. *Motto*—Divina sibi canit.

Logie (that Ilk, co. Perth; the family to which David II's second Queen, or at least her first husband, belonged, ended in the 15th century in an heiress, who *m.* THOMAS HAY, younger son of the *Earl of Errol*). Ar. two chevronels sa. betw. three roses gu.; otherwise, Sa. three bars wavy or.

Logie (Boddam, co. Aberdeen, 1734). Sa. three bars wavy or, within a bordure of the last. *Crest*—A dexter hand pointing with two fingers ppr. *Motto*—Tam marte quam arte.

Login (Sir J. S. LOGIN, of Southend, Orkney, 1855). Az. three tilting spears conjoined, two in saltire and one in pale ppr. standing on a mount in base vert, each having a pennon ar. bearing a cross pattée gu. around the middle of the spear a celestial crown or, all within a bordure of the last, charged with four leopards' faces, two in pale and two in fess sa. *Crest*—A dexter arm in armour embowed and gauntleted ppr. garnished or, holding erect a tilting spear as the former with pennon gu. and a cross pattée or. *Motto*—By the grace of God.

Lokard (Reg. Ulster's Office). Gu. three wolves' heads couped fessways ar.

Loke (London). Or, on a chief az. three falcons jessed and belled or.

Loke, or Locke. Or, three pales az., on a chev. of the last a pair of wings conjoined of the first.

Loker. Gu. three wolves' heads couped ar.

Loketon. Ar. on a chev. az. a mullet of the first within a bordure engr. of the second.

Lokyer (Idbury, co. Oxford, and co. Salop). Az. a lion ramp. ar. maned or, collared sa.

Lokyer (Much Wenlock). Az. a lion ramp. ar. collared sa.

Lomas. Ar. betw. two palets gu. three fleurs-de-lis in pale sa. a chief az. *Crest*—On a chapeau a pelican vulning herself ppr.

Lomax (St. George's, Hanover Square, Westminster). Erm. a greyhound courant sa. betw. three escallops gu. *Crest*—A dexter hand issuing from a heart brandishing a scymitar all ppr.

Lomax (Parkhurst, co. Surrey). Ar. a greyhound courant betw. three escallops sa. *Crest*—A demi greyhound ar. collared gu.

Lomax (Clayton Hall, co. Lancaster). Quarterly, 1st and 4th, per pale or and sa. on a bend cotised erm. three escallops gu., for LOMAX; 2nd, ar. a griffin segreant sa. armed or, for GRIMSHAW; 3rd, ar. a cross sa. betw. four bezants, for CLAYTON. *Crest*—Out of a mural crown a demi lion gu. collared and holding an escallop. *Motto*—Fato prudentia major.

Lomax (co. Hertford). Erm. a greyhound courant sa., betw. three escallops gu., quartering as. three fleurs for KAYE. *Crest*—Out of a ducal coronet or, a demi lion gu. holding an escallop or.

Lomax (granted to RICHARD LOMAX, Esq., Inner Temple, London). Or, on a bend betw. two fleurs-de-lis gu. an annulet betw. two escallops of the field. *Crest*—A demi lion erased per bend or and gu. charged with two fleurs-de-lis counterchanged, and holding betw. the paws an escallop gu. within an annulet or. *Motto*—Nil nisi de jure.

Lombard, or Lombart (Ireland). Per pale, the dexter or, a demi eagle imperial sa., the sinister fusily or and sa.

Lombe (Melton, co. Norfolk, bart.; JOHN HASE, Esq., assumed by Act of Parliament, 1762, the surname and arms of LOMBE, was created a bart. 1783, with special remainder to the male descendants of his niece VIRTUE, dau. of EDWARD HASE, Esq., of Sale, co. Norfolk, and wife of RICHARD PAUL JODRELL, Esq., of Duffield, co. Derby. See JODRELL, Bart.). Az. two combs in fesse betw. a broken lance barways or, one piece in chief, the head respecting the dexter, the other half towards the dexter base.

Lombe (Bylaugh and Great Melton, co. Norfolk; exemplified to Rev. HENRY EVANS, of Bylaugh Hall, third son of THOMAS BROWNE EVANS, Esq., of North Tuddenham, same co., upon his assuming by royal licence, 1862, the surname of LOMBE, under the will of Sir JOHN LOMBE, Bart.).

Az. two combs in fesse betw. a broken tilting spear barways or, one piece in chief, the head towards the dexter, the other half in base, a canton ar. *Crest*—Two tilting spears in saltire or, each having a pendent gu. *Motto*—Justitæ tenax.

Lomber. Ar. on a fesse betw. three lions' heads erased az. as many lozenges of the field.

Lomneir, Lomnyer, or Lomener (co. Norfolk.) Sa. on a bend ar. cotised erm. three escallops gu. *Crest*—A unicorn's head sa. armed and crined or, betw. two wings ar. *Another Crest*—A unicorn's head sa. winged ar. horned or, in the mouth a rose ppr.

Lomond (co. Lincoln). Az. a fret ar. within a bordure or.

Londey (co. Northumberland). Az. fretty ar. within a bordure or.

Londham (co. Norfolk). Ar. three inescutcheons sa. a label of as many points gu.

Londham, or Lowdham (cos. Norfolk and Suffolk). Ar. a bend az. crusily or. *Crest*—On a chapeau ppr. an escallop sa.

London, See of. Gu. two swords in saltire ar. hilts and pommels or.

London, University of. Ar. the cross of St. George, thereon the Union rose irradiated and ensigned with the imperial crown ppr. a chief az. thereon an open book also ppr. clasps gold.

London, City of. Ar. a cross gu. on the dexter chief quarter a sword erect (by some called a dagger) of the second. *Crest*—A dragon sinister, wings expanded ar. charged with a cross gu. *Supporters*—Two dragons with wings expanded ar. charged on the wings with a cross gu. *Motto*—Domine dirige nos.

London, Twelve First, or Principal Corporate Companies of.

MERCERS (incorporated 1394; confirmed by St. George, Richmond Herald, 1634). Gu. a demi virgin couped below the shoulders, issuing from clouds all ppr. vested or, crowned with an Eastern crown of the last, her hair dishevelled, and wreathed round the temples with roses of the second, all within an orle of clouds ppr. *Motto*—Honor Deo.

GROCERS (granted 23 Henry VIII.). Ar. a chev. gu. betw. nine cloves sa. three, three, and three. *Crest*—A camel pass. ppr. bridled gu. on his back a bale ar. corded gu. *Supporters*—Two griffins per fesse gu. and or. *Motto*—God grant grace.

DRAPERS (incorporated 17 Henry VI.). Az. three clouds ppr. radiated in base or, each surmounted with a triple crown or, caps gu. *Crest*—A mount vert, thereon a ram couchant or, attired sa. *Supporters*—Two lions ar. pellettée. *Motto* —Unto God only be honour and glory.

FISHMONGERS. Az. three dolphins naiant in pale ar. finned and ducally crowned or, betw. two pairs of lucies in saltire (the sinister surmounting the dexter) ppr. over the nose of each lucy a ducal crown of the third, on a chief gu. three pairs of keys endorsed in saltire or. *Crest*—Two cubit arms erect, the dexter vested or, the sinister az. both cuffed ar. holding in the hands ppr. a regal crown of the last. *Supporters*—Dexter, a merman ppr. on his head a helmet, the body only covered in armour, in his dexter hand a sabre, all of the first; sinister, a mermaid ppr. crined or, in her sinister hand a mirror of the last. *Motto*—All worship be to God only.

GOLDSMITHS (incorporated 1327). Quarterly, gu. and az. in the 1st and 4th a leopard's head or, in the 2nd and 3rd a covered cup, and in chief two round buckles, the tongues fesseways, points to the dexter, all of the third. *Crest*—A demi lady, her arms extended ppr. issuing out of clouds of the last, vested gu. garnished or, cuff ar. round her neck a ruff of the last, in her dexter hand a pair of scales of the third, in her sinister hand a touchstone sa. *Supporters*—Two unicorns or, armed, crined, and hoofed ar. *Motto*—Justitia virtutum regina. *Another Motto* occasionally used by the Company was—To God only be all glory. *Note*—The crest is vested in the dress of the reign of Elizabeth.

SKINNERS (incorporated 1 Edward III.). Erm. on a chief gu. three princes' crowns composed of crosses pattée and fleurs-de-lis or, with caps of the first tasselled of the third. *Crest*—A lizard ppr. wreathed about the neck with laurel leaves vert, purfled or. *Supporters*—Dexter, a lizard, or short-tailed wild cat of Norway, ramp. guard. ppr.; sinister, a martin sa. each gorged with a wreath of laurel leaves vert, purfled or. *Motto*—To God only be all glory.

MERCHANT-TAYLORS, anciently denominated TAYLORS and LINEN ARMOURERS (incorporated 1466). Ar. a royal tent betw. two parliament robes gu. lined erm. the tent garnished or, tentstaff and pennant of the last, on a chief az. a lion pass. guard. or. *Crest*—A mount vert, thereon a lamb pass.

ar. holding the banner of the last, staff ppr. on the banner a cross pattée gu. all within a glory of the third. *Supporters* —Two camels or. *Motto*—Concordia parvæ res crescunt.

HABERDASHERS, anciently called HURRERS and MILLENERS (incorporated 26 Henry VI.). Barry nebulée of six ar. and az. on a bend gu. a lion pass. guard. or. *Crest*—Two arms embowed ppr. issuing from clouds of the last, holding a chaplet of laurel vert. *Supporters*—Two Indian goats ar. attired and unguled or. *Motto*—Serve and obey.

SALTERS (incorporated 22 Henry VIII.). Per chev. az. and gu. three covered salts or sprinkling salts (*i.e.* covered cups) ar. *Crest*—A cubit arm erect issuing from clouds all ppr. holding a covered salt or sprinkling salt ar. *Supporters*—Two otters sa. bezantée, ducally collared and chained or. *Motto*—Sal sapit omnia.

IRONMONGERS (incorporated 3 Edward IV.). Ar. on a chev. gu. three swivels or (the middle one paleways, the other two with the line of the chev.) betw. three steel gads az. *Crest*—Two scaly lizards erect on their hind feet combatant ppr. (*i.e.* vert) each gorged with a plain collar or, the collars chained together, a chain with a ring at the end pendent betw. the two lizards of the last. *Motto*, anciently: Assher dure ; at present : God is our strength.

VINTNERS (incorporated 15 Henry VI.). Sa. a chev. betw. three tuns ar.

CLOTHWORKERS (incorporated 1482). Sa. a chev. erm. betw. two habicks in chief ar. and a tezel in base slipped or. *Crest*—A mount vert, thereon a ram statant or. *Supporters* —Two griffins or, pellettée. *Motto*—My trust is in God alone.

London-Braziers, Company of (as impaled by the Armourers' Company, since the incorporation of the two Companies). Az. on a chev. or, betw. two ewers (*i.e.* beakers) in chief, and a three-legged pot with two handles in base of the second, three roses gu. seeded or, barbed vert. *Crest*— A demi man in armour couped at the middle of the thighs all ppr. garnished or, the beaver up, on the head a plume of three feathers, two ar. and one gu. round his waist a sash of the last, fringed of the second, holding in his dexter hand a sword erect of the first, hilt and pommel or. *Supporters*— Two men ppr. in complete armour, the dexter of the first, garnished or, the sinister all of the last, on their heads plumes of feathers, round their waists a sash, and each holding in his exterior hand a sword as the crest. *Motto*— We are one.

London: For the other Corporate Companies of, see their *respective names.*

London (Albye, co. Norfolk; granted 10 Feb. 1664). Ar. three crosses crosslet betw. two bendlets gu.

London. Ar. a fesse erm. betw. three towers sa. port gu. *Crest*—Out of a tower a demi man in armour sidefaced, holding in the dexter hand a sword by the blade in pale.

London (Tinsley, near Rotherham). Az. a lion ramp. ar. a border erm.

London (quartered by MITFORD, through OSBALDESTON, WENTWORTH, and HOTON). Az. a lion ramp. or, within a bordure erm.

Londonderry, Marquess of. See STEWART.

Londonderry, Port and Harbour Commissioners. Or, on a cross gu. a tower ppr. on a chief ar. the representation of the entrance to a harbour, and a ship with three masts sailing in, all also ppr. *Crest*—A lighthouse standing on a rock ppr. *Supporters*—Two dragons with wings expanded ppr. each charged on the shoulder with a tower also ppr. *Motto*—In portu quies.

Londonderry, City of (granted by Molyneux, Ulster, 1623, at the request of JOHN ROWLEY, past Mayor of the city, and the Commonalty thereof). A skeleton of human bones sitting on a stone, leaning the dexter elbow on the knee, and resting the head on the hand, the sinister hand resting on the hip ppr. in the dexter chief a tower, in chief the arms of the City of London. *Legend*—Vita veritas victoria.

Londonderry, City Seal of. Same *Arms* on an escutcheon, surrounded by the legend, all within a circle circumscribed "Civitas de Londonderry."

Londons. Quarterly, or and az. in chief two cantons, in base a chev. counterchanged, over all an inescutcheon ar. all within a bordure of the last.

Londres. Per pale ar. and sa. a chev. gu. (another, counterchanged).

Londres, or Lendres. Per pale sa. and ar. a chev. per pale or and gu.

Londres. Sa. a lion ramp. or, a bordure erm.

Londres. Or, six annulets az. three, two, and one.

Lone' (co. Kent, Warlingham and Ellour, co. Suffolk). Az. a tiger pass. or. *Crest*—A demi buck saliant ar. attired or.

620

Lone (London). Ar. an heraldic tiger statant gu. on a bordure sa. eight fleurs-de-lis. *Crest*—A demi buck saliant. *Motto*—I am lone.

Lonell. Or, two bars nebulée gu. over all a bend az.

Lonesby. Gu. three rabbits ar. within a bordure engr. sa. *Crest*—A rabbit ar.

Loney. Per chev. engr. sa. and erm. *Crest*—An arm from the elbow, vested componée or and gu. holding an anchor ppr. ringed sa.

Loney. Ar. on three piles engr. sa. three crosses fitchée of the first.

Long (Draycot, co. Wilts, and Wanstead, co. Essex ; settled at a very remote period at Wraxall, and afterwards at Draycot, by marriage with the heiress of Cerne ; KATHERINE LONG, eldest dau. and heiress of Sir JAMES TILNEY LONG, Bart., *d.* 1805, *m.* the Hon. WILLIAM WELLESLEY POLE, only son of *Lord Maryborough*). Sa. semée of crosses crosslet, a lion ramp. ar., quartering POPHAM, SEYMOUR, and CHILD. This coat bears a strong resemblance to that of the PREUX family, "sa. semée of crosses crosslet or, three lioncels ramp. ar. ; " and supports in some degree the tradition mentioned by Camden, of the origin of the LONGS, from a younger son of the house of PREUX, which was seated at Gidley Castle, co. Devon, soon after the Conquest, and of which was WILLIAM LE PREUX, M.P. for Wilton, co. Wilts, 28 Edward I. *Crest*—Out of a ducal coronet or, a demi lion ramp. ar. Another *Crest* was granted by Henry VIII. to Sir HENRY LONG, of Wraxall and Draycot, for his gallantry at Therouenne, viz., a lion's head ar. in its mouth a hand erased gu.

Long (Potterne, Little Cheverell, Melksam, and Collingbourne Kingston, co. Wilts ; derived, it is presumed, from a younger son of the Wraxall family ; THOMAS LONG, Esq., of Little Cheverell and Potterne, High Sheriff of co. Wilts in 1652, left four sons : I. JOHN, who *d. s. p.* ; II. RICHARD, who *m.* ELIZABETH, sister and heiress of HENRY LONG, Esq., of Rowde Ashton, and was ancestor of LONG, now of Rowde Ashton, co. Wilts ; III. THOMAS, ancestor of LONG, now of Preshaw, co. Hants ; and IV. WILLIAM, ancestor of LONG, of Baynton). Same *Arms*. *Crest*—Out of a ducal coronet or, a demi lion ramp. ar. *Motto*—Pieux quoique preux.

Long (Rood Ashton, co. Wilts ; descended from LONG, of Potterne). Same *Arms*, *Crest*, and *Motto*.

Long (Preshaw, co. Southampton ; descended also from LONG, of Potterne). Same *Arms*, *Crest*, and *Motto*.

Long (Monkton, Farleigh, and Baynton, co. Wilts ; descended from LONG, of Rood Ashton). Same *Arms*, *Crest*, and *Motto*.

Long (Whaddon, co. Wilts, bart., extinct 1710 ; supposed to descend from LONG, of Wraxall). Same *Arms*.

Long (Westminster, bart., extinct 1805 ; descended from LONG, of Draycot ; Sir JAMES TYLNEY-LONG, eighth and last bart., *d. s. p.,* when his estates devolved on his sister, KATHERINE TYLNEY-LONG, wife of WILLIAM, fourth *Earl of Mornington*). Same *Arms*.

Long (granted in 1589, to GIFFORD LONG, Esq., of Rowde Ashton, Sheriff of co. Wilts in 1624, whose granddaughter, ELIZABETH, *m.* RICHARD LONG, Esq., of Collingbourne Kingston). Sa. a lion pass. ar. on a chief of the second three crosses crosslet of the first. *Crest*—Out of a ducal coronet a lion's head erased sa. guttée d'eau.

Long (Longville, Jamaica, and Hampton Lodge, co. Surrey ; descended from JOHN LONG, of Netheravon, co. Wilts, *d.* 1630 ; SAMUEL LONG, his grandson, having participated in the conquest of Jamaica by Penn and Venables, became a person of great consideration in that island, where his great-grandson, EDWARD LONG, Esq., filled the office of Chief Justice of the Vice-Admiralty Court). Sa. a lion pass. ar. holding in the dexter paw a cross crosslet fitchée or, on a chief of the second three crosses crosslet of the field, quartering TATE, ZOUCHE, and ST. MAUR. *Crest*—Out of a ducal coronet or, a lion's head ar. guttée de sang. *Motto*— Pieux quoique preux.

Long (*Baron Farnborough*, extinct 1838). Same *Arms* and *Crest*. *Supporters*—Two lions reguard. ar. guttée de sang, each gorged with a ducal coronet or, thereto pendent an escutcheon sa. charged with a cross crosslet ar. *Motto*— Ingenuas suscipit artes.

Long (Trowbridge, co. Wilts ; granted, 1561, to THOMAS LONG, Esq., of Trowbridge, a descendant of the LONGS, of Wraxall, and borne by LONG, of Whaddon and Beckington). Sa. semée of crosses crosslet a lion ramp. ar. all betw. two flaunches erm. *Crest*—Out of a crescent or, a demi lion sa. guttée d'eau.

Long (co. Gloucester ; WALTER LONG, son of WALTER LONG, living *temp.* Henry VIII., the grandson of ROBERT LONG, a younger son of LONG, of the co. Wilts. Visit. Devon, 1620).

Sa. semée of crosses pattée a lion ramp. ar. on the breast a mullet for diff.

Long (North Molton, co. Devon; THOMAS LONG, second son of WALTER LONG, temp. Henry VIII. Visit. Devon, 1620). Same Arms.

Long (Isle of Wight; SIMON LONG; his dau. MARY, m. Sir WILLIAM ALLEN, Knt., Mayor of London in 1572. Visit. London, 1563). Sa. semée of crosses crosslet a lion ramp. ar. a border engr. or.

Long (Souldan, co. Hertford, and Barrow, co. Suffolk). Gu. a saltire engr. or, on a chief of the last three crosses crosslet of the first. Crest—A lion ramp. gu. holding a saltire engr. or.

Long (Spixworth Park, co. Norfolk). Quarterly, 1st and 4th, gu. a saltire engr. or, on a chief of the last three cross crosslets of the 1st; 2nd and 3rd, or, two leopards' faces in pale betw. two flaunches gu. Crest—A lion sejant ramp. gu. supporting a saltire gu. engr. or.

Long (West Hackney, co. Middlesex). Or, a lion ramp. betw. three escutcheons sa. each charged with a quatrefoil of the first. Crest—Upon a mount in front of a tree ppr. a wyvern couchant vert. Motto—Confide recte agens.

Long (Reg. Ulster's Office). Sa. semée of crosses crosslet and a lion ramp. ar. langued and armed gu. Crest—Out of a ducal coronet or, a lion's head gu.

Long (Reg. Ulster's Office for one of Oliver Cromwell's colonels, sent to Ireland 1649). Sa. a lion ramp. ar. armed and langued gu. betw. two flanges erm.

Long (Clerkenwell, London). Per bend sinister ar. and sa. a lion ramp. of the field crusily counterchanged. Crest—A lion's head erased per pale ar. and sa. charged with three guttées counterchanged, two and one.

Long (London). Or, crusily a lion ramp. gu. Crest—A lion's head erased gu. Motto—Iram leonis noli timere.

Long (Swinthorpe, co. Norfolk). Or, crusily a lion ramp. Crest—On a mount vert a greyhound courant sa. collared and lined erm.

Long. Sa. semée of crosses crosslet a lion ramp. ar. within a bordure chequy or and gu. Crest—Out of a five-leaved coronet or, a demi lion ramp ar.

Long. Gu. semée of annulets or, a lion ramp ar.

Long. Vert three lions ramp. or.

Longaspee, or Longsparde. Az. six lions ramp. or, three, two, and one.

Longayne. Barry of six or and az. on a bend gu. three cinquefoils of the first.

Longbet. Lozengy az. and or.

Long Bowstring Makers Company (London). Az. a hank or knot of bowstrings in pale or, on a chief ar. three bows. Crest—A man vested ppr. shooting with a bow and arrow of the last. Motto—Nec habeo, nec careo, nec curo.

Longchampe (Wilton, co. Hereford, temp. Henry I.). Or, on three crescents gu. as many mullets ar.

Longchampe, or Longchamp. Ar. three crescents gu. each charged with a plate. Crest—A tower triple-towered ppr.

Longchampe. Ar. three crescents gu. each charged with a mullet of the field.

Longchampe. Gu. an annulet betw. three crescents or, within a bordure erm.

Longchampe. Vair two palets or.

Longcroft (co. Worcester). Gu. on two bars ar. six martlets sa. Crest—A bull's head couped.

Longcroft (CHARLES BEARE LONGCROFT, Esq., of Hall Place, Havant). Per fess nebuly gu. and sa. a lion ramp. ar. betw. six cross crosslets botonnée fitchée in pale or. Crest—A demi lion ramp. ar. holding betw. the paws three annulets interlaced or, and charged on the shoulder with a saltire gu. Motto—Nunc ut olim.

Longden (Bramcote Hills, co. Nottingham; as borne by JOHN SHERWIN LONGDEN, Esq., of Bramcote Hills, who assumed the name and arms of SHERWIN in 1818, under a provision in his father's will, and who subsequently assumed the name of GREGORY only, and the arms of GREGORY in 1860, upon succeeding to the estates of the family of GREGORY, of Harlaxton, co. Lincoln). Ar. on a bend engr. az. betw. two bucks' heads cabossed sa. an eagle's head erased betw. two escallops or. Crest—An eagle with wings expanded ppr. charged on the breast and on either wing with an escallop az. supporting with the dexter claw a buck's head cabossed also ppr.

Longden. Az. three bars dancettée or. Crest—On a chapeau gu. turned up or, a dove with wings endorsed az.

Longe (Spixworth Park, co. Norfolk; FRANCIS LONGE, Esq., Recorder of Yarmouth, purchased the estate of Spixworth

sometime towards the close of the seventeenth century). Gu. a saltire engr. or, on a chief of the last three crosses crosslet of the first. Crest—A lion sejant gu. holding a saltire engr. or. Motto—Pro fide ac patriæ.

Longe (Calais). Sa. on two pales betw. three leopards' heads or, six crosses crosslet gu.

Longe (co. Gloucester). Gu. a saltire engr. or. Crest—Out of a ducal coronet a phœnix in flames ppr.

Longe (Fun. Ent. Ulster's Office, 1610). Sa. three greyhounds courant in pale ar. collared vert, a mullet or, for diff.

Longe (New Ross, co. Wexford; THOMAS LONGE, of Dublin, merchant, 1607, was son of JOHN LONGE, burgess of New Ross, who was great-grand-son of THOMAS LONGE, also a burgess of New Ross. Visit. Dublin, 1607). Ar. a lion ramp. sa. armed and langued gu. betw. five crosses crosslet of the second, a lion ramp. of the third. Crest—Out of a ducal coronet or, a lion ramp. sa. armed and langued gu.

Longe (RICHARD LONGE, Clerk of the Court of Chancery, Ireland; Fun. Ent. Ulster's Office, of his dau., d. 20 Feb. 1624). Sa. three greyhounds courant in pale ar. collared gemels of the first.

Longeford, or Longford. Az. a chev. betw. three boars' heads ar.

Longespee. Gu. three swords in pale ar.

Longespee (Reg. Ulster's Office). Or, three chevronels gu. in chief two lions ramp. sa.

Longespee (Earl of Salisbury, extinct 41 Henry III., A.D. 1256. See DEVEREUX, Earl of Salisbury. WILLIAM, illegitimate son of Henry II., surnamed, from the long sword he carried, "Longespee," m. EVA, dau. and heir of WILLIAM DE EVEREUX, second Earl of Salisbury, of the creation of the Empress Maud, and became, jure uxoris, third Earl of Salisbury). Az. six lions ramp. or, three, two, and one.

Longevile. Sa. a hawk's lure ar.

Longfield (Kilbride, co. Meath; confirmed by Hawkins, Ulster, 1714, to WILLIAM LONGFIELD, son of ROBERT LONGFIELD, ancestor of LONGFIELD, co. Cork). Gu. a chev. erm. betw. seven crosses crosslet fitchée, three in chief and four in base ar. Crest—Out of a ducal coronet or, a demi lion ramp. gu. Motto—Parcere subjectis.

Longfield (Longueville; descended from JOHN LONGFIELD, younger brother of ROBERT LONGFIELD, Esq., of Kilbride, co. Meath). Same Arms, Crest, and Motto.

Longfield (Viscount Longueville, extinct 1811; RICHARD LONGFIELD, Esq., of Longueville, was created a baron 1795, and raised to a viscounty 1800, d.s.p., when the estates devolved on his cousin and heir male, JOHN LONGFIELD, Esq.). Same Arms, Crest, and Motto.

Longfield (Waterloo House, co. Cork). Same Arms, Crest, and Motto.

Longfield (Castle Mary, co. Cork). Same Arms, Crest, and Motto.

Longford, Earl of. See PAKENHAM.

Longford (Longford, co. Derby. Visit. Notts, 1614). Paly of six or and gu. a bend az., quartering, 1st, paly of six or and gu. on a chief az. a bar dancettée of the first; 2nd, ar. a fess dancettée betw. ten billets sa. a label az.; 3rd, quarterly ar. and gu.

Longford (Mansfield and Sutton, co. Nottingham; ROGER LONGFORD, of the former, and THOMAS LONGFORD, of the latter, sons of THOMAS LONGFORD, Esq., of Mansfield, the grandson of GEORGE LONGFORD, a younger son of LONGFORD, of Longford. Visit. Notts, 1569). Same Arms, a crescent for diff.

Longford (The Hough, co. Lancaster). Same Arms, &c.

Longford (co. Leicester). Paly of six ar. and gu. a bend of the first.

Longford, or Langford. Per pale ar. and gu. three mullets counterchanged. Crest—A boar's head erased az.

Longford. Az. a sheldrake az.

Longforde. Ar. a fesse indented betw. six crosses crosslet fitchée gu.

Longhurst. Sa. five bendlets ar. over all a chev. gu. Crest—In a ducal coronet or, a griffin's head holding in the beak a key ppr.

Longland (Toymoke, co. Buckingham). Ar. on a chev. gu. betw. three pellets as many escallops of the first. Crest—On a mount vert a garb or.

Longland. Ar. a chev. gu. betw. three pellets, on a chief az. a cock betw. two crosses fitchée ar. Crest—An arm couped or, pellettée, hand ppr. holding a crosslet fitchée gu.

Longland. Ar. on a chev. gu. betw. three pellets a cock of the first. Crest—On the stump of a tree eradicated and couped or, a dove ar.

Longland (JOHN LONGLAND, Bishop of Lincoln, 1521-47;

arms in the Hall of New College, Oxford. Visit. Oxon, 1566).
Ar. on a chev. gu. betw. three pellets a cock of the field, on
a fillet in chief vert a rose or, betw. two leopards' faces of
the first.

Longlevers, Longwers, or Longvillers (co. York).
Sa. a bend betw. six crosses crosslet ar.

Longley (Rev. CHARLES T. LONGLEY, late Head Master of
Harrow School, consecrated Bishop of Ripon, 1836. Quarterly, per fesse indented or and az., quartering BOND, ar. on
a chev. sa. three bezants. *Crest*—A lion sejant ar. *Motto*—
Esse quam videri.

Longley (co. Kent). Per pale and per fesse indented or
and az.

Longley. Paly of six ar. and vert, per fesse counterchanged. *Crest*—An arm couped at the shoulder resting
on the elbow, and holding a sword in pale enfiled with a
savage's head, couped ppr.

Longman. Az. a rose or. *Crest*—A dexter hand in
fesse holding an anchor in pale environed with clouds
all ppr.

Longman (co. Somerset, and London). Gu. three lozenge
shaped buckles or. *Crest*—A lion ramp. az.

Longman (granted to WILLIAM CHURCHILL LONGMAN, Esq.).
Per saltire gu. and or, in pale two trefoils and in fesse as
many roses counterchanged. *Crest*—In front of an oak tree
ppr. a greyhound sejant erm. holding in the mouth a trefoil
or, and resting the dexter forepaw on a rose gu.

Longmore (The Myths, Tewkesbury). Erm. on a chev.
az. three cross crosslets betw. two leopards' heads and a
lion pass.

Longmore (HUMPHREY LONGMORE, Mayor of Worcester,
1663; impaled in St. Andrew's Church, Worcester, by
EDWARD COOKSEY, who d. 1692-3, in right of his wife,
JANE, dau. of GEORGE LONGMORE, of Upper Arley). Sa. a
chev. or, and a canton erm. *Crest*—Two spears or.

Longridge. (Wallbottle). Per pale ar. and gu. three fleurs-
de-lis counterchanged. *Crest*—An arm embowed, vested,
holding a garb.

Longsdon (Little Longsdon, co. Derby, *temp.* Edward I.).
An eagle displ. with two heads.

Longshare. Ar. two serpents erect and endorsed or.

Longspeare. Sa. three palets or, on the first and third
three crosses gu., on the second as many leopards' heads.
Crest—A talbot's head couped, paly of four or and gu.
holding in the mouth a demi hare erased ar.

Longspee. Az. three lions ramp. or. *Crest*—On a pellet,
winged or, an eagle, wings displ. ppr.

Longspee (Normandy). Gu. two leopards pass. guard. in
pale or.

Longspee. Gu. two lions pass. guard. or, depressed by a
sword erect in pale ar. hilted or.

Longstaff. Or, a bend sa. fimbriated ar. betw. three pheons
of the second, on a chief gu. a bezant betw. two fleurs-de-
lis of the field. *Crest*—A stag standing at gaze under a
tree ppr.

Longstaff. Az. a chev. betw. three quarter-staffs ar. *Crest*
—A demi lion ramp. holding betw. the paws a quarter-staff
all ppr.

Longstoder, or Longstrother. Ar. a chev. gu. betw.
three escallops sa.

Longueville (Wolverton, co. Buckingham; descended from
HENRY DE LONGUEVILLE, of Overton Longueville, *temp.*
Henry I., son of WALTENUS, Lord of Overton, at the Conquest). Gu. a fesse dancettée erm. betw. six crosses crosslet
ar. *Crest*—A talbot's head gu. eared ar. gorged with a
collar dancettée of the second.

Longueville (Penlyn, co. Salop). Gu. a fesse dancettée
erm. betw. six crosses crosslet ar. *Crest*—A talbot's head gu.
eared ar. gorged with a collar dancettée of the second.
Motto—Till then thus.

Longvale. Gu. three bends vair.

Longvile (Wolverton, co. Bucks; Fun. Ent. Ulster's Office,
1626. KATHERINE, dau. of Sir EDWARD LONGVILE, Knt.,
and wife of Sir ROGER JONES, Vice-President of Connaught).
Gu. a fess dancettée betw. three crosses crosslet fitchée
or.

Longvyle (JOHN LONGVYLE, *temp.* Richard II.). Gu.
crusily or, a fesse dancettée ar.

Longville. Gu. crusily or, a fess dancettée ar.

Longvilliers (co. Northampton, *temp.* Edward I.). Sa. a
bend betw. six crosses crosslet or.

Longvilliers (*Baron Longvilliers*, extinct 1374; THOMAS
DE LONGVILLIERS, son of JOHN DE LONGVILLIERS, who was
seized of the manors of Cokesford, co. Nottingham, and
Gloseborne, co. Yorks; was summoned to Parliament 1342,
but never after). Sa. a bend betw. six crosses crosslet ar.

Longworth (Longworth, co. Lancaster). Ar. three

dragons' heads couped sa. *Crest*—A boar's head couped
holding in the mouth a sword ppr.

Longworth (co. Gloucester; as borne by FRANCIS LONG-
WORTH, Esq., of Cotswold House, near Cheltenham). Ar.
three dragons' heads erased sa.

Longworth (Upper Rawcliffe, co. Lancaster, 1664). Ar.
three wolves' heads erased sa.

Lonisington, or Loinsington. Sa. three boars' heads
couped close ar. tusked or.

Lonsdale, Earl of. See LOWTHER.

Lonsdale (co. York). Quarterly, vert and ar. in the
2nd and 3rd a buglehorn stringed, over all, on a bend
engr. or, three annulets, quartering GILBY, FITZWILLIAMS,
&c. *Crest*—A demi stag saliant erased gu. charged on the
body with a crescent sa. attired, ungualed, and collared of the
last, the collar charged with three crescents.

Lonsdale. Gyronny of eight gu. and or, an annulet
counterchanged. *Crest*—A bull pass. gu.

Lony (co. Lincoln). Chequy ar. and az. on a chief gu. three
mullets or.

Lonyson (London; granted 20 June, 1575). Or, a cross
gu. *Crest*—A swan issuant ppr. betw. two ostrich feathers
or.

Looker. Ar. a pale gu. charged with a cross or. *Crest*—A
pillar ensigned with a heart gu.

Lopes (Maristow, co. Devon, bart.). Quarterly, 1st and 4th,
az. on a chev. betw. three eagles rising or, as many bars
gemelle gu. on a chief of the second five lozenges of the first,
for LOPES; 2nd and 3rd, in a landscape field a fountain, thereout issuing a palm tree all ppr., for FRANCO. *Crests*—1st,
LOPES: A lion sejant erminois, gorged with a bar gemelle,
as in the arms, reposing the dexter paw on a lozenge az.;
2nd, FRANCO: A dexter arm couped and embowed, habited
purp. purfled and diapered or, the cuff ar. holding in the
hand ppr. a palm branch vert. *Mottoes*—LOPES: Quod tibi,
id alii; FRANCO: Sub pace copia.

Loraigne. Ar. on a fesse wavy az. a lion pass. or.

Lorain (Angelraw, co. Berwick, 1774). Or, on a bend gu.
betw. two lions ramp. vert three allerions in bend ar. *Crest*
—An armed dexter arm from the elbow, holding a branch of
laurel ppr. *Crests*—Lauro resurgo.

Loraine (Kirk-Harle, co. Northumberland, bart.). Ar. five
lozenges conjoined in pale az. in the dexter chief point an
escutcheon of the last. *Crest*—A palm tree ppr. hanging to
the dexter side thereof by a belt gu. an escutcheon az.
Motto—Lauro scutoque resurgo.

Loraine (Lumley Park, co. Durham). Same *Arms*, *Crest*,
and *Motto*, with a crescent for diff.

Lorance (St. Ives, co. Huntingdon. Visit. 1575). Ar. a
cross raguly gu. on a chief of the last a lion pass. guard. or,
langued az. *Crest*—An antelope's head erased ppr. horned
or, and ducally gorged ar.

Lorand. Ar. a cross wavy gu. *Crest*—On a tower ar. a
martlet sa.

Lorayne. Or, a bend gu. betw. three bats sa.

Lord (London). Ar. on a fesse betw. three cinquefoils az. two
pheons of the field. *Crest*—A dexter arm, hands clenched
ppr. in a maunch az. cuffed or.

Lord (assigned by Carney, Ulster, 1684, to Rev. DANIEL LORD,
M.A., Trin. Coll. Dublin, Rector of Marragh, co. Cork, and
Prebendary of St. Finbar's Cathedral, son of RICHARD LORD,
of Dublin). Ar. on a fess gu. betw. three roses az. seeded
and barbed or, two pheons of the first. *Crest*—A dove or,
holding an olive branch ppr.

Lordell. Ar. a fesse gu. in chief a label of three points az.

Lorimer (England). Ar. a chev. sa. betw. three spur-rowels
az. *Crest*—An arm couped at the shoulder in a maunch,
embowed and resting the elbow on the wreath.

Lorimer (Edinburgh, 1794). Ar. a sprig of laurel ppr.
betw. two roses gu. *Crest*—A horse courant ar. *Motto*—
Virtutis gloria merces.

Lorimer (Kellyfield, co. Forfar, 1859). Per chev. gu. and
or, two spurs paleways, rowels downwards, buckled and
strapped in chief of the second, in base a horse courant at
liberty sa. *Crest*—Two eagles, wings conjoined and expanded ppr. surmounted of a cross crosslet fitchée gu.
Mottoes—On the crest: Upward; below the shield:
Onward.

Loriners, or Bit Makers, Company of (London).
Az. on a chev. ar. betw. three manage bits or, as many
bosses sa.

Loring, or Loringe (co. Suffolk). Quarterly, ar. and gu.
a bend engr. of the second.

Loringe (co. Bedford). Same *Arms*, bend lozengy.

Loringe (Sir NIGEL or NELE LOBINGE, son and heir of ROGER
LORYNG, of Chalgrave, co. Bedford, by CASSANDRA, his wife,
dau. of REGINALD PERROTT, was one of the Founder Knights

of the Garter, 1344, *d.* 18 March, 1386; Garter plate remaining in his stall, the tenth on the Princes' side). Quarterly, ar. and gu. a bend engr. sa. *Crest*—The leaves of a plant issuant from a flower-pot.

Loringe. Same *Arms.* *Crest*—Out of a bowl or, five quills erect ar.

Loringe, or Loring. Quarterly, ar. and gu. a bend of the second. *Crest*—A hand holding a millrind.

Lorkin (Reg. Ulster's Office). Erm. three leopards' faces sa.

Lorks. Az. a bend double dancettée ar.

Lorrane (Harwood, Scotland). Ar. three laurel leaves vert.

Lorsor, or Lovsor (Kellow, co. Durham). Sa. on a chev. engr. or, betw. three leopards' heads ar. as many annulets of the first. *Crest*—A wolf sejant ppr. holding in the mouth an arrow in pale or, barbed and feathered ar.

Lort (Stackpoole Court, co. Pembroke, bart., extinct 1698; the heiress, ELIZABETH LORT, *m.* Sir ALEXANDER CAMPBELL, ancestor of the *Earl of Cawdor*). Gu. a cross or. *Crest*—An Ionic pillar and base ar.

L'Orti (*Baron L'Orti;* abeyance *temp.* Edward III. ; HENRY D'ORTRAI, *temp.* Henry III., *d.* 1241, leaving a son, HENRY L'ORTI, summoned to Parliament 1299). Vert a pale or.

Lorton, Viscount. See KING.

Lorty (cos. Leicester and Somerset). Az. a cross or.

Lorty (co. Dorset). Same *Arms,* a martlet for diff.

Lorty (co. Somerset). Per pale wavy az. and ar. a lion ramp. per pale wavy or and gu.

Losack. Ar. two bars sa. betw. as many crosses crosslet fitchée in chief and an anchor in base of the last. *Crest*—A dexter hand issuing from a cloud, holding an anchor in pale all ppr.

Loscombe (Bristol ; granted 1762). Ar. on a fesse az. betw. three leopards' faces ppr. a cross moline betw. two crosses crosslet or. *Crest*—A demi leopard ppr. collared gu. holding in the dexter paw a cross moline, as in the arms.

Losh. Or, a boar's head erased gu. *Crest*—A cubit arm ppr. holding up a crescent or.

Lospital. Gu. (another, az.) a cock ar.

Losse (Stanmore, co. Middlesex). Gyronny of eight ar. and sa. a saltire betw. four fleurs de-lis counterchanged. *Crest*— A lion's head erased per saltire ar. and sa. charged with four guttées counterchanged.

Losse (Cobdock, co. Suffolk). Quarterly, ar. and sa. a saltire per saltire betw. four fleurs-de-lis all counterchanged. *Crest*—A cubit arm erect, vested gu. holding in the hand ppr. a fleur-de-lis per pale ar. and sa.

Lostock (Sir GEORGE HOLFORD, *temp.* Henry VIII. Sir Peter Leycester says he bore LOSTOCK'S coat). Ar. a grey-hound pass. sa.

Loften (St. James's, Westminster, co. Middlesex, originally of Flanders ; granted 1765). Quarterly, 1st and 4th, or, a sprig with three gillyflowers in bud vert, for LOTEN; 2nd and 3rd, vert a swan naiant in water ppr. beaked or, for VAN JUCHEN. *Crest*—A gillyflower ppr. betw. two wings erect, the dexter or, the sinister vert.

Loth, or Lothe. Az. an eagle displ. with two heads or, (another, field or, eagle purp.). *Crest*—An arrow and a bent bow in saltire ppr.

Lotham. Sa. three pheons ar. edge engr.

Lother. Sa. six annulets, three and three, in pale or.

Lotherington, or Lotherton. Ar. a fesse gu. in chief two crescents of the last.

Lothian, Marquess of. See KERR.

Lothian (Edinburgh, 1673, and Overgogar, co. Edinburgh, 1837). Ar. on a mount in base a pine-tree vert, a talbot tied thereto ppr. on the branches a bugle, garnished or, stringed az. pendent, all within a bordure of the second. *Crest*—A bugle, as in the arms. *Motto*—Non dormit qui custodit.

Lothian (Kingsbarns, co. Fife). As the last, but the bordure invecked az.

Lothume, Lowtham, or Lovayne (co. Essex). Gu. billettée a fesse or.

Lott (Honiton, co. Devon). Ar. a double-headed eagle displ. sa. *Crest*—A talbot's head couped.

Lotysham (Chiph and Fornington, co. Somerset). Sa. a chev. vairé or and gu. betw. three otters pass. of the second. *Crest*—On a ducal coronet gu. an otter's head erased or, in the mouth a fish ppr.

Lou. Gu. two wolves pass. ar.

Louche, or Lowche. Ar. two bars gu. in chief a lion pass. of the second.

Loudham (cos. Nottingham and Derby). Ar. a bend az. crusily or.

Loudham (Sir JOHN DE LOUDHAM, Knt., one of the knights of cos. Derby and Nottingham, *temp.* Edward I. Visit.

Notts, 1614). Ar. on a bend az. three crosses crosslet or.

Loudham (Lowdham, co Suffolk, *temp.* Edward III.). Ar. three escutcheons sa.

Loudham. Ar. on a bend gu. three (another, five) crosses crosslet or.

Loudoun (that Ilk, co. Ayr ; heiress, in 13th century, *m.* Sir REGINALD CRAWFORD). Ar. three inescutcheons sa.

Loudoun, Earl of. See HASTINGS.

Loughor (Tythegston, co. Glamorgan). Three chev.

Loughnan (granted by Betham, Ulster, to FRANCIS LOUGH-NAN, Esq., Lieut. 50th N. I. Madras, son of ANDREW LOUGHNAN, of London ; descended from the Sept of O'LACHT-NAN). Vert a dexter hand couped apaumée, and in chief an arrow fessways ar. *Crest*—A demi wolf ramp. sa.

Louis (Chelston, co. Devon, bart.). Az. a lion ramp. ar. charged on the shoulder with an eagle displ. sa. on a chief wavy erm. an anchor erect of the third, the shank surrounded with a naval crown, the rim az. stern and sails ppr. *Crest*—A griffin's head erased az. betw. two wings elevated or, in the beak a fleur-de-lis, and on the breast a trident erect gold. *Supporters*—Dexter, a British sailor habited ppr. his exterior hand supporting a staff, thereon hoisted a flag ar. charged with a cross gu. surmounted by a pair of wings or, and inscribed with the words "St. Domingo" in base sa. ; sinister, an allegorical figure, representing the Nile, the head and upper part of the face concealed by a veil ar. the mantle vert, inscribed with hieroglyphics, wreathed about the waist with bulrushes ppr. and in the exterior hand the ancient rudder or. *Motto*—In Canopo ut ad Canopum.

Louis (Merchiston, Scotland). Or, three laurel leaves vert. *Crest*—A dexter hand holding a lance in bend ppr. *Motto*—Nos aspera juvant.

Louis. Sa. a wolf ramp. ar. *Crest*—A wolf, as in the arms.

Louis (GEORGE LOUIS, Esq., of Colyton House, co. Devon, representative of a family, originally DE GREILLET, from Provence, in France). Gu. on a bend engr. ar. a grass-hopper sa. *Crest*—In front of clouds ppr. a decrescent or. *Motto*—Doucement mais fermement.

Lound (co. Lincoln, 1640). Ar. a fret of eight pieces sa. on a canton gu. a lion's head erased or.

Loumeau (extinct in Guernsey). Gu. on a fesse ar. three greyhounds' heads couped sa.

Lounders. Per pale sa. and ar. a chev. per pale or and gu.

Loundres. Sa. a lion ramp. or, a bordure engr. erm.

Loundres (*Baron of Naas.* Reg. Ulster's Office). Az. a lion ramp. or, a border erm.

Lourie (Scotland). Sa. out of a cup ar. a garland of laurel betw. two trefoils slipped of the last.

Louris, or Lowrs (Ogbery, Beardon, and Trantock, co. Cornwall, and co. Devon). Or, a chev. engr. gu. betw. three shovellers ppr. *Crest*—A bear ramp. sa. muzzled and lined ar.

Lousada (*Duke de Losada y Lousada,* in the Kingdom of Spain). Ar. three doves reguard. ar. wings expanded or, in their beaks a sprig of olive ppr. *Crest*—On a mount vert a dove, as in the arms, a sprig of olive in its beak ppr. *Supporters*—Two angels ppr. the exterior hand of each supporting a standard gu. charged with an Eastern crown or.

Lousada (Peak House, co. Devon). Az. on a chev. betw. three doves reguard. ar. wings expanded or, two sugar canes of the last sprigged vert. *Crest*—On a mount vert a dove, as in the arms, charged on the neck with a bar gemelle or, a sprig in its beak ppr. *Motto*—Honneur me guide.

Louth, Baron of. See PLUNKETT.

Louth, or Lowth (co. Lincoln). Or, a wolf saliant sa. armed gu. (another, armed or).

Louthe. Per pale indented or and gu.

Louther. See LOWTHER.

Louvain, or Lovain. Or, a lion ramp. az. *Crest*—On a chapeau gu. lined erm. a lion pass. az. tail extended.

Lovaine (co. Essex). Gu. a fesse (another, ar.) betw. ten billets or, three, two, three, and two.

Lovat, Baron. See FRASER.

Lovatt (Clayton Hall, co. Stafford ; a younger branch of LOVETT, of Astwell, co. Northampton, and descended of the Norman race of DE LOUET; MARY, only dau. and heiress of HUGH BOOTH, co. Chester, m. his wife, dau. and heiress of THOMAS LOVATT, Esq., *m.* JOHN AYSHFORD WISE, Esq.). Ar. three wolves pass. sa. *Crest*—A demi wolf ramp. sa.

Lovayne (Brabant). Or, a lion ramp. az.

Lovayne (co. Kent). Sa. on a bend ar. cotised or, three saltires gu.

Lovayne (co. Suffolk). Gu. billettée a fesse ar. *Crest*—A cross crosslet fitchée or.

Love (Basing, co. Hants. Visit. 1634. The heiress, SUSANNA, only child of RICHARD LOVE, Esq., of Basing, *m.* FRANCIS BECKFORD, Esq.; her son and heir, FRANCIS LOVE BECKFORD, *s.* to the estates). Ar. three bars gu. in chief as many lions' heads erased of the last. *Crest*—On a cross formée fitchée gu. a bird ar.

Love (Norton and Goudhurst, co. Hants, and co. Oxford). Vert a lion ramp. ar. charged on the shoulder with a cross pattée gu. *Crest*—Out of a ducal coronet or, a cross formée gu. thereon a bird ar.

Love (Sevenoaks, co. Kent). Az. a tiger pass. or. *Crest*—A demi buck.

Love (Kirksted, co. Norfolk ; granted 10 Dec. 1663). Vert an heraldic tiger pass. or, mane and tuft of the tail ar. *Crest*—An heraldic tiger's head erased vert, maned ar.

Love (Aynho, co. Northampton; EDWARD LOVE, second son of GILES LOVE, Captain of Dover Castle ; his dau. ELIZABETH, *m.* SIMON PERROTE, of Oxford. Visit. Oxon, 1574). Vert a lion ramp. reguard. or. *Crest*—A demi greyhound ramp. ar. collared and lined sa. end of line coiled.

Love (Broughton, co. Oxford ; GILES LOVE, second son of EDWARD LOVE, of Aynho. Visit. Oxon, 1574). Vert a lion ramp. or, charged on the breast with a cross pattée gu. Same *Crest.*

Love (co. Suffolk ; Rev. EDWARD M. LOVE, A.M., Rector of Somerleyton). Same *Arms* and *Crest.*

Love. Az. a lion ramp. ar. *Crest*—A hand holding an annulet ppr.

Love (quartered by ALCHORNE. Visit. Kent, 1619). Vert a lion ramp. guard. ar. *Crest*—On a chapeau gu. turned up erm. a lion pass. ar.

Love. Or, on a chev. betw. three lions' heads erased gu. as many bezants.

Loveband (from Penn MS.). Gu. on a bend betw. three martlets ar. a lion's head erased of the field.

Loveburie (co. Chester). Ar. on a bend sa. three chess-rooks of the field.

Loveburie (co. Chester). Erm. on a bend engr. vert three mullets or.

Lovedale. Sa. a buglehorn stringed ar. on a chief of the second a lion pass. guard. gu.

Loveday (co. Essex). Az. three fleurs-de-lis or.

Loveday (co. Leicester). Barry of six dancettée or and az.

Loveday (co. Norfolk, and Cheston, co. Suffolk). Per pale ar. and sa. an eagle displ. with two necks counterchanged, gorged with a ducal coronet or (another, crowned). *Crest*—A squirrel ppr.

Loveday. Sa. guttée de sang, on a chief ar. three grey-hounds' heads erased sa. collared or.

Loveday. Per pale or and sa. an eagle displ. with two heads counterchanged, gorged with a ducal coronet of the first.

Loveday (Williamscote, co. Oxford). Quarterly, 1st and 4th, per pale ar. and sa. an eagle displ. with two heads counterchanged, armed, membered, and ducally gorged or ; 2nd and 3rd, erm. on a chief indented sa. three escallops ar. *Crest*—An eagle displ. with two heads, as in the arms. *Motto*—Cum prima luce.

Loveden (Fyfield and Buscot, co. Berks ; granted 1589, 32 Queen Elizabeth, and exemplified, August 1, 1772, to EDWARD LOVEDEN TOWNSHEND, Esq., on his assuming the surname of LOVEDEN). Gu. a bend betw. four sinister hands couped ar. *Crest*—A leopard sejant or, ducally gorged ar. *Motto*—Manus juxta nardus.

Lovedon. Gu. a bend betw. three dexter hands couped ar.

Lovegrove. Ar. three anchors sa. a chief az. *Crest*—A staff raguly, surmounted by an eagle displ. ppr.

Lovein. Sa. on a bend ar. cotised or, three saltires hu-mettée gu.

Loveis (Hennock, co. Devon ; six descents recorded in Visit. 1620). Or, a chev. engr. gu. betw. three ducks ppr. *Crest*—A bear sejant sa.

Lovejoy. Gyronny of twelve gu. and or. *Crest*—An arm from the elbow in armour, holding a galtrap.

Lovejoy (Caleys Grange or Callis Court, Thanet, co. Kent). Az. three bars dancettée or.

Lovekin, or Lewkyn (Lord Mayor of London, 1348, 1358, 1365, and 1366). Gu. on a chev. ar. three escallops sa. betw. as many eagles rising or.

Lovel (*Baron Lovel*, of Kary ; barony passed to ST. MAUR, 1351; RALPH LOVEL, second son of WILLIAM DE PERCEVAL, *Earl of Yvery* in Normandy, surnamed "LUPELLUS, LUPEL, LOVEL," or, the Wolf, assumed the surname of LOVEL, and was ancestor of Sir RICHARD LOVEL, summoned to Parliament 1348 to 1350). Or, semée of crosses crosslet a lion ramp. az.

624

Lovel (*Baron Lovel*, of Tichmarsh, and *Viscount Lovel*, attainted after the battle of Bosworth ; WILLIAM LOVEL, fourth son of WILLIAM DE PERCEVAL, surnamed "LUPELLUS," &c., was ancestor of Sir JOHN LOVEL, summoned to Parliament 1299 to 1311). Barry nebulée of six or and gu.

Lovel (Tickwell). Same *Arms*, a bend az. for diff.

Lovel (Tarrant Rawston, co. Dorset). Quarterly, barry nebulée of six or and gu. ; 2nd, ar. a chev. gu. betw. three ermines ; 3rd, erm. a chev. sa. ; 4th, erm. on a chief in dented gu. three ducks ar. *Crest*—A fox az. bezantée, collared with a coronet or.

Lovelace, Earl of. See KING.

Lovelace (Hurley, co. Berks, Lovelace and Canterbury, co. Kent). Gu. on a chief indented ar. three martlets sa. *Crest*—On a staff raguly vert an eagle displ. ar.

Lovelace (*Baron Lovelace*, extinct 1736; Sir RICHARD LOVELACE, Knt., son of RICHARD LOVELACE, Esq., of Hurley, was so created 1627. MARGARET LOVELACE, dau. of JOHN, second *Lord Lovelace*, by Lady ANNE WENTWORTH, dau. of THOMAS, *Earl of Cleveland, Baroness Wentworth* in her own right, *m.* Sir WILLIAM NOEL, Bart., of Kirby Malory, and was ancestress of the *Earl of Lovelace* and of *Lord* ... *Worth*). Quarterly, 1st and 4th, gu. on a chief inden ... ar. three martlets sa., for LOVELACE; 2nd, az. on a saltire engr. ar. five martlets sa., for HENGHAM; 3rd, gu. on a saltire ar. a rose of Lancaster, for NEVILLE. *Crest*—On the trunk of a tree vert an eagle displ. ar. *Supporters*—Two pegasi purp.

Lovelace. Per fesse indented sa. and gu. in chief three martlets ar.

Lovelace. Paly of six engr. gu. and ar.

Lovelace (Sir WILLIAM LOVELACE, knighted by ROBERT, *Earl of Essex*, Lord Lieutenant of Ireland, 30 July, 1599). Gu. on a chief indented sa. a mullet ar.

Loveland (co. Norfolk). Sa. three boars' heads couped or. *Crest*—A boar's head and neck couped ar.

Lovelas. Az. on a saltire engr. ar. five martlets sa.

Loveles (co. Berks). Sa. three bars indented or.

Loveless. Or, three laurel leaves vert. *Crest*—A demi talbot ppr.

Loveley (cos. Northampton and Norfolk). Gu. on a fesse betw. three popinjays ar. as many mullets sa. *Crest*—An estoile pierced or.

Lovell, or Lovet (co. Buckingham). Sa. three square padlocks ar.

Lovell (London ; THOMAS LOVELL, one of the Queen's Customers for Wool, Visit. London, 1563, son of HENRY LOVELL, Esq., of Skelton, co. York). Ar. a chev. sa. betw. three foxes' heads erased gu.

Lovell (co. Dorset ; WILLIAM LOVELL, *temp.* Henry VII. , his dau. ELIZABETH, *m.* WILLIAM BAMFIELD, of Turnworth, co. Dorset; their dau. and heir, MARY BAMFIELD, *m.* WILLIAM FRERE, J.P., of Oxford, and *d.* 1568. Visit. Oxon, 1634). Barry nebulée of six or and gu. in chief three bezants.

Lovell (co. Worcester; Penn MS.). Ar. a chev. az. betw. three squirrels sejant gu. *Crest*—A garb vert, banded or.

Lovell (Terant, co. Dorset). Barry nebulée of six or and gu. on the second five bezants *Crest*—A wolf pass. az. bezantée collared and lined or.

Lovell (Barton and Harling, co. Norfolk). Ar. a chev. az. betw. three squirrels sejant gu. *Crest*—A peacock's tail erect ppr. banded with a belt sa. rimmed and buckled ar. the end pendent. *Another Crest*—A squirrel sejant, cracking a nut.

Lovell (Chilcote Manor, and Dinder). Ar. a chev. sa. betw. three wolves' heads erased gu. *Crest*—A talbot courant az.

Lovell (co. Oxford). Ar. a lion ramp. az. within an orle of eight crosses crosslet fitchée of the second.

Lovell (Ballumbie, co. Forfar). Ar. three piles sa. surmounted of a fesse wavy gu.

Lovell (co. Somerset). Barry wavy of six ar. and gu.

Lovell, or Luvel (co. Somerset). Or, crusily a lion ramp. az.

Lovell (Laxfield, co. Suffolk ; granted 25 June, 1579). Barry nebulée of six or and gu. a bordure az. charged with ten trefoils slipped ar. *Crest*—A greyhound' pass. sa. collared, ringed, and lined or, a cubit arm erect ppr. habited purp. holding the line.

Lovell (Cole Park, Malmesbury, co. Wilts). Ar. a chev. az. betw. three squirrels gu. each cracking a nut ppr. *Crest*—A squirrel sejant, cracking a nut ppr.

Lovell (Skelton, co. York. Visit. 1665 ; Dugdale). Ar. a chev. sa. betw. three wolves' heads erased gu. *Crest*—A talbot courant ar.

Lovell (co. York). Ar. a chev. sa. betw. three lions' heads gu.

Lovell (Harleston, co. Northampton, now of cos. Lincoln and Bucks, MARY LOVELL, only dau. and heiress of Capt. SAMUEL LOVELL, grandson of Sir SALATHIEL LOVELL, one of the Barons of the Exchequer, 1708, m. 1742, her cousin, RICHARD LOVELL-BADCOCK, Esq., of Twickenham, and was grandmother of Col. BENJAMIN LOVELL-BADCOCK, K.H., 15th Dragoons, and of Capt. WILLIAM STANHOPE-BADCOCK, who both assumed by sign manual in 1840, the name of LOVELL only). Or, three bars nebulée gu. *Crest*—A talbot pass. ar. *Motto*—Tempus omnia monstrat.

Lovell. Az. a lion ramp. within an orle of fleurs-de-lis or.

Lovell. Ar. a lion ramp. sa. crowned or, a bordure az.

Lovell. Az. on a fesse betw. three crescents ar. a mullet sa.

Lovell. Or (another, ar.) a wolf saliant az. within a bordure engr. sa.

Lovelock. Vert a lion ramp. within an orle ar. *Crest*—A greyhound pass. sa.

Lovely. Ar. on a chev. az. three leopards' faces or.

Loveney. Or, on a fesse betw. three cocks gu. as many mullets of the field. *Crest*—A griffin sejant, wings endorsed ppr.

Loveney. Ar. a fesse betw. three cocks gu.

Lovenham. Quarterly, per fesse indented gu. and vert a swan with wings displ. ar.

Loverdaw (co. Cornwall). Sa. three covers for cups ar.

Lovet, or Lovett (Codnor, co. Derby, Tavistock, co. Devon, and cos. Essex and Huntingdon). Ar. three wolves pass. in pale sa. *Crests*—1st: A wolf's head erased sa.; 2nd: A wolf pass.; 3rd: A demi wolf ramp. sa. pierced through the breast with an arrow or, flighted ar.

Lovet (Astwell, co. Northants; THOMAS LOVETT, Esq.; his dau. ELIZABETH, m. Sir WILLIAM CHESTER, Knt., Mayor of London, 1560. Visit. London, 1563). Same *Arms*.

Lovet (Stanton, co. Leicester). Ar. three wolves pass. gu.

Lovet (co. Derby; descended from LOVET, of Stanton). Same *Arms*. *Crest*—A wolf's head erased sa.

Lovet (co. Northampton). Quarterly, 1st and 4th, ar. three greyhounds courant sa.; 2nd and 3rd, erm. all within a bordure of the second platée.

Lovetoft, Lovetot, or Livetot (co. Huntingdon, and Worksop, co. Nottingham, temp. Henry I.). Ar. a lion ramp. per fesse gu. and sa.

Lovett (co. Hants). Same *Arms*. *Crest*—A griffin segreant ppr.

Lovett. Sa. three padlocks ar.

Lovett (Liscombe, co. Bucks, bart., extinct 1812; descended from WILLIAM LOVETT, "filius RICARDI DE LOUET de Normannia, temp. Conquestoris," who was appointed Master of the Wolf Hounds, and in consequence, took for his arms ar. three wolves pass. in pale sa. The male heir, Sir JONATHAN LOVETT, of Liscombe, was created a baronet in 1781, but d. s. p. m., when the title became extinct. The Liscombe estates devolved on Sir JONATHAN's daus. ELIZABETH and LETITIA, and passed at their decease to their kinsman, PHILLIPS COSBY LOVETT, Esq.). Quarterly, 1st and 4th, sa. three wolves' heads or, for LOVETT, of Normandy; 2nd and 3rd, ar. three wolves pass. in pale sa., for LOVETT, of England. *Crest*—A wolf's head erased sa.

Lovett (Fun. Ent. Ulster's Office, 1679, CHRISTOPHER LOVETT, Alderman of Dublin). Ar. three wolves courant in pale sa.

Lovett (Elmley Lovett, Hampton Lovett, &c., co. Worcester; Sir JOHN LOVETT, Lord of Elmley, left two daus. who d. s. p.). Sa. three wolves' heads erased or.

Lovett (Belmont, co. Salop). Ar. three wolves pass. in pale sa. *Crest*—A wolf pass. ppr.

Lovett (Fernhill). Same *Arms*, &c.

Loveyne, or Lovinge (co. Lincoln). Chequy ar. and az. on a chief gu. two mullets or.

Loveyne. Gu. a fesse ar. betw. seven billets or, four and three.

Loveys (Berdon, co. Cornwall; ROBERT LOVEYS, grandson of LEONARD LOVEYS, Esq., of Ogbeare, same co., the son of HUMPHRY LOVES, by JANE, dau. of HATCH, of co. Devon. Visit. Cornwall, 1620). Or, a chev. engr. sa. betw. three sea pies ppr.

Lovibond (Hatfield Peverell, co. Essex; GEORGE BRUDENELL MICHELSEN LOVIBOND, son and heir of GEORGE LOVIBOND, Esq., and his wife, MARTHA, dau. of Sir ELIJAH IMPEY). Ar. a boar's head couped and erect gu. betw. three roundles per fesse or and of the second. *Crest*—A boar's head, as in the arms.

Lovibond (IMPEY-LOVIBOND; exemplified to ARCHIBALD IMPEY, Esq., Ireton House, Cheltenham, co. Gloucester, upon his taking the name of LOVIBOND in addition to and after that of IMPEY, by royal licence, 1872). Quarterly, 1st and

4th, ar. a boar's head erect and couped within an crle gu. the whole betw. three torteaux, for LOVIBOND; 2nd and 3rd, gu. on. a chev. betw. three leopards' faces or, as many pallets sa. each charged with a crescent of the second, on a chief erm. a sword fessewise ppr. pommel and hilt gold, for IMPEY. *Crests*—1st, LOVIBOND : Upon a rock ppr. a boar's head erect and couped gu. within a chain in arch or; 2nd, IMPEY : A leopard's face or, in front of a sword in pale, point downwards ppr. pommel and hilt or, betw. two wings sa. *Motto* —Leges juraque servo.

Lovinge, or Levinge (co. Derby, and Colsell, co. Warwick). Vert a chev. or, in chief three escallops ar.

Lovingham, or Lovenham. Quarterly, indented gu. and vert, a goose rising ar.

Lovyck, or Lowyke. Sa. a saltire ar. on a chief of the second three bulls' heads cabossed of the first.

Lovys, or Luvys (co. Cornwall). Ar. three lizards in pale vert.

Low (co. Lancaster). Ar. an eagle displ. with two heads vert.

Low (London, 1684). Quarterly, 1st and 4th. gu, a wolf pass. ar. ; 2nd, ar. a hunting horn stringed sa. betw. three crescents of the last; 3rd, ar. on a fesse betw. three crescents gu. as many mullets or.

Low. Gu. two wolves pass. ar. *Crest*—A wolf pass. ar.

Low. Ar. three leaves vert. *Crest*—A falcon reguard. holding in the dexter claw a laurel crown ppr.

Low. Erm. on a bend (another, engr.) az. three cinquefoils or.

Low (confirmed by Fortescue, Ulster, to SIMON Low, Esq., of Galbally, co. Limerick). Ar. on a bend vert three wolves' heads erased or, each charged with an annulet gu. *Crest*—A wolf's head, as in the arms. *Motto*—Facta non verba.

Low (Aberdeen, Scotland). Ar. three leaves vert within a bordure wavy gu. *Crest*—A leaf betw. two thistles stalked and leaved ppr. *Motto*—Aspera me juvant.

Lowde (Kirkham, co. Lancaster, 1664). Ar. three buglehorns sa. stringed or. *Crest*—A buglehorn of the arms.

Lowde. Ar. a lion ramp. sa. a chief lozengy or and gu.

Lowdell. Per pale ar. and sa. a chev. betw. three millrinds counterchanged. *Crest*—A sphinx couchant guard. wings endorsed.

Lowden. Az. three bars dancettée or.

Lowden. Sa. three poleaxes ar.

Lowder. Or, six annulets gu. two, two, and two. *Crest*— Out of a mural coronet seven halberts facing outwarde ppr.

Lowders. Paly of six engr. ar. and gu.

Lowdes (of the North). Ar. six annulets sa. three, two, and one. *Crest*—A wivern ar.

Lowdham (co. Derby). Ar. on a bend az. three crosses crosslet or.

Lowdham (co. Suffolk). Ar. three escutcheons sa. *Crest*— an escallop betw. two palm branches ppr.

Lowe (Lowe, co. Worcester; THOMAS LOWE, Esq., of Lowe, was chief of his family temp. Queen Elizabeth). Or, on a bend cotised sa. three wolves' heads erased of the field. *Crest*—A demi griffin ramp. or. *Motto*—Spero meliora.

Lowe (Bromsgrove, co. Worcester; Very Rev. THOMAS HILL PEREGRINE FURYE LOWE, Dean of Exeter, descended from Lowe, of Lowe). Same *Arms, Crest*, and *Motto*, quartering FURYE.

Lowe (Highfield, co. Nottingham; a branch of LOWE, of La Lowe, co. Chester, formerly seated at the Hulse, in that co., now represented by EDWARD JOSEPH LOWE, Esq., of Highfield, J.P. and D.L., F.R.S., whose great-grandfather, JOSEPH LOWE, Esq., of Highfield, m. SARAH, dau. and heir of JAMES HURST, Esq., of Hurst, co. Lancaster, by ELIZABETH, his wife, sister and co-heir of JOSEPH WILSON, Esq., of Rivington Hall, and heiress, through her mother, MARGARET, of BENJAMIN SMYTH, of Ashton, temp. Charles I.). Ar. on a bend engr. az. three wolves' heads erased of the first, within a bordure also engr. of the second. *Crest*—A wolf pass. ar. collared and chained gu. reflexed over the back. *Motto*—Innocentia quamvis in agro sanguinis.

Lowe (Southm'',t, co. Bedford; Her. Off.) Ar. on a bend az. three wolves' heads erased of the field. *Crest*—Out of a mural crown gu. a wolf's head ar. transfixed with a spear or, armed of the second.

Lowe (Clifton-Reynes, co. Bucks). Same *Arms*. *Crest*—A wolf's head erased ar.

Lowe (co. Derby). Gu. a hart trippant ar. *Crest*—A wolf pass. ar.

Lowe (Walden, co. Essex; descended from Lowe, co. Worcester). Gu. two wolves pass. ar. *Crest*—An ermine ppr. collared, ringed, and lined gu. *Another Crest*—A wolf's head couped ppr. collared and ringed or.

Lowe (Bromley, co. Kent; and Lord Mayor of London, 1604). Erm. on a bend engr. az. (another, sa.) three cinquefoils or. *Crest*—A falcon with wings expanded or.

Lowe (co. Stafford; granted by Cooke, Clarenceux, 1592). Ar. on a bend cotised az. three lions' heads erased of the field. *Crest*—A demi griffin segreant erased ar.

Lowe (Shrewsbury, co. Salop, and Calne, co. Wilts). Gu. a wolf pass. ar. *Crest*—An ermine pass. ppr. collared or, lined and ringed gu.

Lowe (Westminster; granted 1694). Quarterly, erm. and or, over all an eagle displ. with two heads vert. *Crest*—Two keys in saltire or, interlaced with a chaplet ppr.

Lowe (New Sarum, co. Wilts). Gu. a wolf preyant ar. *Crest* —A wolf's head couped ar. collared or.

Lowe (co. Worcester). Erm. on a bend az. three cinquefoils or.

Lowe (Denby and Locko, co. Derby, originally from co. Chester; descended from the marriage, *temp.* Henry VI., of LAWRENCE LOWE, Serjeant-at-law, with the heiress of ROSELL, of Denby. The last male heir, RICHARD LOWE, Esq., of Locko, *d.* in 1785, having bequeathed his estates to his kinsman, WILLIAM DRURY, Esq., who assumed in consequence, in 1791, the additional name and arms of LOWE). Az. a hart trippant ar. *Crest*—A wolf pass. ar. The *Arms* of DRURY, borne quarterly, are—Ar. on a chief vert two mullets or, each charged with an annulet az. *Crest* of DRURY—A greyhound courant sa. gorged with a plain collar or, and charged with two mullets of the last.

Lowe (Alderwasley, co. Derby; a younger branch of LOWE, of Denby, descended from THOMAS LOWE, who *m. temp.* Henry VII. the heiress of FOWNE, of Alderwasley. The heiress of LOWE, of Alderwasley, *m.* HURT). Same *Arms* and *Crest*.

Lowe (Court of Hill, co. Salop). Quarterly, 1st and 4th, ar. on a bend sinister cotised sa. three wolves' heads erased of the field, for LOWE, of Bromsgrove; 2nd and 3rd, erm. on a fesse sa. a castle triple-towered ar., for HILL, of Court of Hill. *Crest*—A demi griffin ramp. or. *Motto*—Spero meliora.

Lowe. Gu. a fesse erm. betw. two wolves pass. ar.

Lowe. Ar. on a bend engr. az. three wolves' heads erased of the first, a bordure also engr. of the second.

Lowe (Stopford, or Stockport, co. Chester; quartered by STARKEY). Gu. a wolf pass. ar. on a bend sa. three wolves' head erased of the first.

Lowe, alias Fifield (THOMAS LOWE, Alderman of London, Visit. 1568, fourth in descent from JOHN FIFIELD, *alias* LOWE). Per fess vert and ar. a pale counterchanged three acorns or.

Lowe (GEORGE LOWE, Registrar of the Prerogative Court, Ireland : Fun. Ent. Ulster's Office, of his wife, *d.* 16 Nov. 1623). Ar. on a bend az. three griffins' heads erased of the field, an annulet for diff.

Lowell (Quarlewood, Scotland). Gu. three mascles or.

Lowen (London; JOHN LOWEN, draper, son of JOHN LOWEN, Esq., of Gerpins, *alias* Gerbeviles. Visit London, 1563). Quarterly, per fess embattled or and az. three stags' heads cabossed counterchanged, quartering Per chev. flory counter-flory ar. and gu. three martlets counterchanged. *Crest*—A stag statant quarterly per pale indented or and az. the sinister horn of the first, the dexter of the last.

Lower (St. Winnow Barton, Polmawgan, Tremeere, and Lezant, co. Cornwall; thirteen generations in Visit. 1620). Sa. a chev. betw. three roses ar. *Crest*—A unicorn's head erased quarterly ar. and sa. *Another Crest*—A unicorn's head erased ar.

Lower (St. Tudy, co. Cornwall). Same *Arms*. *Crest*—A unicorn's head erased ar. crined and armed or.

Lower (Trelaske, co. Cornwall; THOMAS LOWER, son of PETER LOWER, and grandson of THOMAS LOWER, all of same place. Visit. Cornwall, 1620). Sa. a chev. betw. three roses ar. (another, field az. chev. engr. roses or). *Crest*—A unicorn's head erased ar.

Lower (co. Devon). Sa. three oak leaves ar.

Lowes (Ridley Hall, co. Northumberland). Gu. a wolf pass. ar. *Crest*—A wolf pass. ar. collared and lined or. *Motto*—Dulces ante omnia musæ.

Lowfield. Per fesse vert and or, a pale counterchanged, in chief a bull's head couped sa. in base two garbs of the last. *Crest*—A bull's head couped sa.

Lowis (Lowis, co. Nottingham). Per pale or and sa. a chev. betw. three escallops counterchanged.

Lowis (co. Devon; HUMPHREY LOWIS, Visit. Devon, 1620, grandson of LEONARD LOWIS, of Ugbart, co. Cornwall). Ar. a chev. gu. betw. three shovellers sa. breasted of the field. *Crest*—A bear sejant sa. collared, lined, and muzzled ar.

Lowis (Merchistoun, Scotland). Or, three laurel leaves vert. *Crest*—A dexter hand holding a lance in bend ppr. *Motto* —Non aspera juvant.

626

Lowis. Ar. three bears in pale sa.

Lowis (Manor, co. Peebles). Ar. a mullet az. betw. three laurel leaves vert.

Lowle (co. Somerset, and Yardley, co. Worcester). Sa. a hand couped at the wrist grasping three darts, one in pale and two in saltire ar. *Crest*—A stag's head cabossed or, betw. the attires a pheon az.

Lowles. Paly of six engr. ar. and gu.

Lowman (Whitstone and Brokeland, co. Devon; JAMES LOWMAN, Visit. Devon, 1620, grandson of JOHN LOWMAN, of Brokeland). Ar. three escutcheons sa. each charged with a dexter gauntlet or, back affrontée. *Crest*—A lion's gamb erect and erased sa. holding a battle axe or.

Lowman (co. Somerset). Same *Arms* and *Crest*. *Motto*—Par sit fortune labori.

Lowmer (co. Norfolk). Sa. on a bend engr. cotised erm. three escallops gu.

Lownde (Jekesford, co. Cambridge). Per chev. flory counterflory or and gu. three lions pass. counterchanged. *Crest*—On a mount vert a griffin sejant, wings endorsed or.

Lownde (cos. Sussex and York). Az. a fret ar. *Crest*—A hind reguard. ppr. collared gu. resting the dexter paw on a beehive ppr.

Lownde (co. Lincoln; granted 1596). Same *Arms*, a bordure or. *Crest*—Out of a ducal coronet or, a hawk close gold, beaked and legged ar.

Lowndes (Hassall Hall, co. Chester). Ar. fretty az. on a canton gu. a lion's head erased or. *Crest*—A lion's head erased or.

Lowndes (co. Oxford; originally from co. Chester; settled at Winslow, co. Bucks, early in the 15th century. WILLIAM LOWNDES, Esq., of Winslow, Secretary of the Treasury, and Chairman of the Committee of Ways and Means, *temp.* Queen Anne and George 1., obtained a confirmation of his armorial ensigns in 1704; he was ancestor of LOWNDES, of Chesham, Whaddon Hall, and Astwood, co. Buckingham, of Brightwell, co. Oxford, and of Rose Hill, Dorking, co. Surrey). Ar. fretty az. the interlacings each charged with a bezant, on a canton gu. a leopard's head erased at the neck or. *Crest*—A leopard's head, as in the arms, gorged with a laurel branch ppr.

Lowndes (The Bury, Chesham, co. Bucks; a branch of LOWNDES, of Winslow). Same *Arms*, quartering SHALES, BARRINGTON, POLE, and PLANTAGENET. *Crest*—A leopard's head, as in the arms, gorged with a laurel branch ppr. *Motto*—Ways and means.

Lowndes (Palterton, co. Derby). Ar. fretty az. a canton gu. thereon a lion's head erased or, quartering GORST. *Crest*—A lion's head erased or, gorged with a wreath of laurel vert.

Lowndes (Barrington Hall, co. Essex). Quarterly, 1st and 4th, LOWNDES, ar. fretty az. on a canton sa. a lion's head erased or; 2nd and 3rd, CLAYTON, ar. a cross engr. sa. betw. four torteaux. *Crests*—1st, LOWNDES: A lion's head erased or; 2nd, CLAYTON: A dexter arm embowed, the hand grasping a dagger, the point to the dexter all ar.

Lowndes (Lostock Hall, co. Lancaster). Quarterly, 1st and 4th, LOWNDES, ar. fretty az. a canton gu. thereon a lion's head erased or; 2nd and 3rd, CLAYTON. *Crest* of LOWNDES—A lion's head erased or, gorged with a wreath of laurel vert, and the crest of CLAYTON.

Lowndes (STONE-LOWNDES, Brightwell Park, co. Oxford). Ar. fretty az. on a canton gu. a lion's head erased or, quartering STONE, viz., Ar. three cinquefoils sa. a chief of the second. *Crest*—A lion's head erased or, gorged with a chaplet vert. *Motto*—Mediocria firma.

Lowndes (Mordon, co. Surrey). Or, two lions pass. in pale betw. three crosses crosslet fitchée sa. a canton gu. for diff. *Crest*—A goat ar. armed, hoofed, collared, and line reflexed over the back or, charged on the shoulder with a rose gu. for diff.

Lownes. Quarterly, or and sa. on the 1st and 4th quarters a cinquefoil gu. *Crest*—A hydra ppr.

Lownsford (co. Suffolk). Or, on a fesse az. three boars' heads couped of the field.

Lowrde (London). Erm. on a bend engr. az. three cinquefoils or.

Lowry (Pomeroy House, co. Tyrone; descended from ROBERT LOWRY, Esq., of Ahenis, in the same county, grandfather of the first *Earl of Belmore*). Sa. a cup ar. with a garland of laurel betw. two branches of the same, all issuing thereout ppr. *Crest*—Two laurel branches interfretted ppr. motto over, Floreant Lauri. *Motto*—Virtus semper viridis.

Lowry (Rockdale, co. Tyrone; descended from LOWRY, of Pomeroy House). Same *Arms*, *Crest*, and *Mottoes*.

Lowry (Crosby, near Carlisle). Same *Arms*. *Crest*—Two sprigs of laurel in orle ppr.

Lowry-Corry, *Earl of Belmore.* See CORRY.

Lowten (Manley, co. Chester; confirmed 2 Aug. 1814). Ar. on a fesse engr. sa. plain cotised gu. betw. three crosses crosslet fitchée az as many cinquefoils or. *Crest*—A demi griffin per fesse indented erminois and erm. wings elevated sa. in the dexter claw a cross crosslet fitchée az.

Lowth. See LOUTH.

Lowther (*Earl of Lonsdale*). Or, six annulets, three, two, and one, sa. *Crest*—A dragon pass. ar. *Supporters*—Two horses ar. each gorged with a wreath of laurel vert. *Motto* —Magistratus indicat virum.

Lowther (Whitehaven, bart., extinct 1755). Same *Arms, Crest,* and *Motto.*

Lowther (Marske, co. York, bart., extinct 1753). Same *Arms, Crest,* and *Motto.*

Lowther (Swillington, co. York, bart., extinct 1763). Same *Arms, Crest,* and *Motto.*

Lowther (Ireland). Same *Arms. Crest*—A dexter hand ppr. holding up an escallop or.

Lowther (Sir GERRARD LOWTHER, Judge of the Common Pleas in Ireland; Fun. Ent. Ulster's Office, 1624). Same *Arms,* a crescent for diff.

Lowther (Captain HUGH LOWTHER, third son of Sir RICHARD LOWTHER, Knt., co. Westmorland; Fun. Ent. Ulster's Office, 1628). Same *Arms,* a mullet for diff.

Lowther (Kilrue, co. Meath). Same *Arms. Crest*—A dragon pass. ar. *Motto*—Magistratus indicat virum.

Lowther (Shrigley Park). Same *Arms,* &c.

Lowther (co. Northumberland). Sa. six annulets in pale or, three and three.

Lowthwick. Paly of four erm. and vert, two lions pass. gu.

Lowyn (Upminster, co. Essex). Ar. a fesse engr. betw. three hinds' heads couped sa. a bordure of the last.

Lowyn (cos. Hertford and Kent). Per pale gu. and az. three bucks' heads couped or. *Crest*—A crab sa.

Loxam. Ar. a bend gu. betw. eight guttées de sang, four and four. *Crest*—A stork's head couped ar. holding in his beak an escallop sa.

Loxdale (Ryton Grove, co. Salop). Erm. on a chief sa. three lions ramp. or. *Crest*—A bull's head couped ppr.

Loxly (co. Stafford). Az. a lion ramp. within an orle of eight crosses crosslet ar.

Loxton (co. Worcester). Ar. a chev. chequy erm and sa. betw. three griffins' heads erased of the last, guttée d'or.

Lloyd (Havering, co. Essex). Ar. an eagle displ. with two heads sa. beaked and legged gu. *Crest*—A stag's head couped ppr. attired or, gorged with a chaplet of laurel vert.

Loyd, or Lloyd (Keyswin, co. Merioneth, Marington, co. Salop, and co. Stafford). Or, a lion ramp. reguard. sa. *Crest*—A demi lion ramp.

Loyd (Wales). Ar. an eagle displ. with two heads sa. beaked gu. *Crest*—A stag's head erased ppr. attired or.

Loyd (*Baron Overstone*). Per bend sinister erm. and ar. an eagle with two heads displ. sa. a bordure of the last bezantée. *Crest*—A buck's head ppr. attired or, erased sa. charged on the neck with a fesse engr. of the third, thereon three bezants. *Supporters*—Dexter, a stag ppr. attired, ducally gorged, and chain reflexed over the back, and charged on the shoulder with a cross clechée or; sinister, an eagle, wings elevated sa. beaked and membered or, ducally gorged, chain reflexed over the back, and charged on the breast with a cross clechée voided also or. *Motto*—Non mihi, sed patriæ.

Loyd (Wigorn and co. Salop). Ar. a quiver gu. banded and replenished with arrows or, betw. three pheons sa.

Loyd. Gu. a lion ramp. reguard. ar. *Crest*—A lion ramp. holding betw. the forepaws a boar's head couped.

Loyd. Az. a lion ramp. betw. eight cinquefoils or.

Lozenge. Lozengy ar. and gu.

Luard (Blyborough Hall, co. Lincoln). Sa. a lion ramp. ar. holding betw. the forepaws a cinquefoil of the last. *Crest*— A heart gu. charged with a rose ppr. *Motto*—Prospice.

Luard (the Lodge, Witham). Same *Arms, Crest,* and *Motto.*

Lubbock (Lamas, co. Norfolk, bart.). Ar. on a mount vert a stork close erm. on a chief gu. three estoiles of the field. *Crest*—A stork, wings elevated erm. resting the dexter claw on an antique shield az. bordured or, charged with a lion ramp. guard. ar. *Motto*—Auctor pretiosa facit.

Lubé (ROCKLIFF-LUBÉ; exemplified to WILLIAM ROCKLIFF, of Liverpool, on his assuming, by royal licence, 1862, the additional surname and arms of LUBÉ). Quarterly, 1st and 4th, ar. on oak tree eradicated and fructed ppr. betw. two mullets in fess gu., for LUBÉ; 2nd and 3rd, per pale ar. and gu. on a chev. betw. three lions' heads erased a crescent all

627

counterchanged, for ROCKLIFF. *Crests*—1st, LUBÉ: A dexter arm embowed in armour ppr. charged with two mullets in pale gu. grasping in the hand a sword encircled by a wreath of oak fructed all ppr.; 2nd, ROCKLIFF: A bull's head erased per pale ar. and gu. gorged with a mural crown ppr. *Motto* —Virtus propter se.

Lucan, Earl of. See BINGHAM.

Lucar (Madenbrook, co. Somerset). Ar. a chev. sa. betw. three nags' heads erased gu. bridled or. *Crest*—A cubit arm erect, vested per pale ar. and gu. cuffed ar. holding in the hand a hawk's lure ppr.

Lucar (Bridgewater, co. Somerset). Ar. a fesse nebulée az. betw. three mascles gu. betw. the two in chief a lion's head erased of the second. *Crest,* as the last.

Lucar (co. Somerset). Ar. on a fesse wavy betw. three lions' heads erased az. as many mascles of the field.

Lucar (London; EDWARD LUCAR, Esq. Visit. London, 1563). Ar. a chev. sa. betw. three nags' heads erased gu. bridled or, quartering, Ar. a fess nebulée az. in chief a lion's head erased of the last betw. two mascles in chief and one in base gu. *Crest*—A dexter arm couped at the elbow, vested per pale az. and gu. holding in the hand ppr. a lure ar. stringed of the second, ringed and knotted or.

Lucas (*Baron Lucas,* of Shenfield, co. Essex, extinct 1705; Sir JOHN LUCAS, Knt., a zealous supporter of Charles I., was created a Peer with remainder, in default of his own male issue, to his brother, Sir CHARLES LUCAS, Knt., an eminent Royalist, shot by order of Oliver Cromwell, 1648, and also with a special remainder over, in default of the male issue of the said Sir CHARLES LUCAS, to Sir THOMAS LUCAS, his illegitimate brother, born before the marriage of his father). Ar. a fess betw. six annulets gu. *Crest*—Out of a ducal coronet or, a dragon's head and shoulders, wings erect gu. *Supporters*—Two dragons ar. wings elevated gu. ducally gorged or.

Lucas (*Baroness Lucas,* of Crudwell, co. Wilts; vested in ANNE FLORENCE, *Dowager Countess of Cowper;* MARY LUCAS, only dau. and heir of JOHN, first *Lord Lucas,* was so created with special remainder to her descendants, male and female, 1663). Same *Arms. Arms* borne by ANNE FLORENCE, Countess of Cowper, now *Baroness Lucas*—Quarterly, 1st and 4th, barry of six ar. and az., for DE GREY; 2nd and 3rd, vert a chev. betw. three stags at gaze or, for ROBINSON. *Supporters*—Two dragons, wings erect or.

Lucas (Filby, co. Norfolk). Ar. a fesse betw. six annulets gu.

Lucas (Berwick-on-Tweed). Ar. a fesse betw. six annulets gu. *Crest*—Out of a ducal coronet or, a demi griffin wings expanded gu.

Lucas (granted to MATTHIAS PRIME LUCAS, Esq., of Wateringbury, co. Kent, Lord Mayor of London in 1827). Erm. a fesse engr. az. betw. six annulets gu. *Crest*—Out of a crown vallery or, a dragon's head az. gorged with a collar ar. charged with three annulets, as in the arms, wings elevated of the third.

Lucas (Halden: JOHN LUCAS, Visit. London, 1563; his dau. MARGARET, *m.* ROBERT BROWNE, of London, gent.). Ar. a fess betw. six annulets sa.

Lucas (Fenton, co. Lincoln, bart., extinct 1668). Ar. a chev. gu. betw. three pellets, on a chief az. a moorcock of the field betw. two crosses crosslet fitchée or.

Lucas (co. Cornwall). Ar. on a canton sa. a ducal coronet or. *Crest*—A sword erect ar. hilt and pommel or, betw. two wings expanded gu.

Lucas (co. Cornwall). Erm. two lions ramp. combatant gu. *Crest*—A lamp or, lighted ppr.

Lucas (co. Suffolk). Same *Arms,* field ar.

Lucas (co. Durham). Or, a fesse betw. six annulets sa.

Lucas (co. Kent; granted 8 Nov. 1571). Ar. a fesse erm. betw. six annulets sa. *Crest*—A cameleopard pass. sa. attired or.

Lucas (Hasland, co. Derby; descended from THOMAS LUCAS, who purchased that estate *temp.* Queen Anne). Erm. a chev. engr. gu. betw. three annulets sa. on a chief az. a moorcock betw. two crosses crosslet or. *Crest*—Out of battlements or, a dexter arm embowed ppr. charged on the elbow with five annulets in cross sa. holding in the hand a cross crosslet gu.

Lucas (Newark). Vert on a chev. or, betw. three talbots pass. ar. as many torteaux, on a chief ar. three lions' heads erased sa.

Lucas (Castle Shane, co. Monaghan; EDWARD LUCAS, Esq., of Castle Shane, was for some time M.P. for the county of Monaghan, and Under Secretary of State for Ireland). Ar. a fesse betw. six annulets gu. three in chief and as many in base. *Crest*—Out of a ducal coronet or, a demi griffin wings expanded gu.

Lucas (Rathealy and Rickfordstown, co. Cork). Same *Arms,* field ar. *Crest*—Out of a ducal coronet or, a wyvern's head gu.

2 S 2

Lucas. Ar. & chev. gu. betw. three hurts; another, Ar. two lions ramp. endorsed, first az. second gu.; another, Az. a fesse dancettée ar.; another, Erm. on two bars sa. three combs ar.; another, Az. three bars ar.

Lucas-Clement. See CLEMENT.

Luce. Az. a crescent ar. *Crest*—An eagle reguard. wings displ. holding in the dexter claw a sword erect.

Luce (Jersey). Same *Arms*.

Lucels (co. Leicester). Ar. a pale fusily gu.

Lucie (Egremont and Cockermouth, co. Cumberland, *temp.* Richard I.). Qu. three lucies haurient ar.

Lucie (London). Az. a crescent ar. *Crest*—A crescent ar.

Lucie (co. Kent). Gu. three lucies haurient or, betw. the two in chief a cross crosslet of the second.

Lucien. Ar. a lion ramp. gu.

Lucinge. Quarterly, per fesse indented erm. and az.

Lucion. Ar. a lion ramp. gu. over all a bend gobonated or and of the second.

Luck (Rotherfield, co. Sussex; confirmed by Segar, Garter). Erm. five mascles in fesse betw. three greyhounds' heads erased sa. *Crest*—A pelican wings elevated endorsed sa. betw. the circumference of two branches vert.

Luck. Az. three mural crowns or. *Crest*—A hawk hooded and belled, perched on the stump of a tree all ppr.

Luckin (Malden, Deverell, and Waltham, co. Essex). Sa. a fesse indented betw. two leopards' faces or. *Crest*—A demi griffin or, issuing out of a tower paly of six of the last and sa.

Luckyn (Waltham, co. Essex; created a bart. in 1629. Sir CAPEL LUCKYN, second bart., *m.* MARY, dau. of Sir HARBOTTLE GRIMSTON, second bart. of Bradfield. Sir WILLIAM LUCKYN, fifth bart., having *s.* 1703, to the Grimston estates, assumed that surname, was created *Viscount Grimston,* and was ancestor of the *Earl of Verulam*). Sa. a fesse dancettée betw. two leopards' faces or.

Lucombe (Bodmin and Heligan, co. Cornwall; carved on the crosses in the roof of Bodmin Church, and on the drop end of the wood moulding of the tower door at St. Maben; quartered by FLAMANK and HILL, 1470). Ar. a saltire betw. four estoiles gu.

Lucon. Vert an eagle displ. with two heads or.

Lucree. Ar. an orle sa.

Lucy (Charlecote, co. Warwick; the original surname of the LUCYS was CHARLECOTE, derived from the village of that name, co. Warwick, conferred by Henry de Montfort upon, and confirmed by Richard I. to Sir WALTER DE CHARLECOTE. His son and heir was called Sir WILLIAM DE LUCY; Dugdale supposes his mother might have been an heir of some branch of the feudal house of LUCY; from that period it has been known as LUCY of Charlecote, and has always enjoyed an eminent station amongst the gentry of England). Gu. semée of crosses crosslet three lucies haurient ar. *Ancient Arms*— Vair three lucies haurient ar. *Crest*—Out of a ducal coronet gu. a boar's head erect ar. guttée de poix betw. two wings erect sa. billettée or. *Motto*—By truth and diligence.

Lucy (*Baron Lucy;* vested since the death of MAUDE, *Countess of Northumberland, temp.* Henry IV.,dau. of THOMAS, second *Baron Lucy,* in the descendant, if any, of JOANE, dau. of ANTHONY, first baron, and her husband, Sir WILLIAM MELTON, Knt. ANTHONY LUCY, descended from RICHARD DE LUCIE, Governor of Faleis, Normandy, *temp.* King Stephen, was summoned to Parliament, 1320). Gu. three lucies haurient ar.

Lucy (Broxbourne, co. Herts, bart., extinct 1759; RICHARD LUCY, second son of Sir THOMAS LUCY, Knt., of Charlecote, *m.* ELIZABETH, dau. and co-heir of Sir HENRY COCK, Knt., of Broxbourne, and was created a bart. 1618). Gu. three lucies haurient ar.

Lucy (granted to WILLIAM LUCY, Esq., Mayor of Birmingham). Erm. on a pile betw. two pikes haurient in base gu. a pike also haurient betw. three cross crosslets ar. *Crest*—On a mount vert a boar's head gu. issuant from a wreath of oak ppr. betw. two wings barry of six ar. and gu. *Motto*—En avant.

Lucy (London, formerly of Antwerp). Az. a crescent ar. *Crest*—A crescent, as in the arms.

Lucy (co. Dorset). Gu. a pike haurient or.

Lucy (co. Kent). Gu. semée of crosses crosslet three lucies haurient or.

Lucy. Gu. three lucies haurient ar. *Crest*—Out of a ducal coronet a boar erm. armed or.

Lucy. Gu. three lucies haurient ar. betw. nine crosslets or. *Crest*—Out of a ducal coronet or, a boar's head betw. two wings sa. billettée of the first.

Lucy. Az. (another, gu.) crusily or, three lions ramp. ar.

Lucy. Ar. a lion ramp. gu. betw. three trefoils slipped vert.

Lucy. Gu. three pikes naiant in pale ar. (another adds, a bordure of the last).

Lucy. Gu. three pikes haurient, a bordure engr. ar.

Lucy. Gu. three pikes haurient inverted betw. seven crosses crosslet or, three, two, and one.

Lucyng. Quarterly, indented erm. and az.

Ludbrough. Gu. a chev. ar. betw. three leopards' faces or.

Luddington (London; NICHOLAS LUDDINGTON, citizen of London, son and heir of HENRY LUDDINGTON. Visit. London, 1563). Paly of six ar. and gu. on a chief of the last a lion pass. guard. of the first.

Ludford (Ansley, co. Warwick; confirmed by the Deputies of Camden, Clarenceux, to GEORGE LUDFORD. Visit. Warwick). Az. a chev. betw. three boars' heads erased or.

Ludford (exemplified, 1808, to JOHN LUDFORD, Esq., of Ansley Hall, co. Warwick, who by sign manual assumed the name of NEWDIGATE before that of LUDFORD, son and heir of JOHN LUDFORD, Esq., of the same place, by JULIANA, his wife, third dau. of Sir RICHARD NEWDIGATE, bart.). Quarterly, 1st and 4th, az. on a chev. betw. three boars' heads couped or, as many fleurs-de-lis gu., for LUDFORD; 2nd and 3rd, gu. three lions' gambs erased, two and one ar., for NEWDIGATE. *Crests*—1st, LUDFORD: A boar's head couped erminois, in the mouth a cross pattée gu.; 2nd, NEWDIGATE: A fleur-de-lis ar.

Ludgate. Az. a portcullis or.

Ludgater (granted to JAMES LUDGATER, Esq., of Eltham, co. Kent). Gu. on a pile engr. or, betw. in base two fleurs-de-lis ar. three estoiles, two and one az. *Crest*—A demi greyhound couped sa. gorged with a collar or, pendent therefrom an escutcheon gold, charged with a leopard's face jessant-de-lis az.

Ludham (London; granted 1726). Per pale or and az. on a chev. three martlets all counterchanged. *Crest*— A demi dragon erm. wings elevated, holding betw. the paws a key or, charged on the shoulder with a cinquefoil gu.

Ludham. Sa., on a bend ar. cotised or, three escallops gu.

Ludham. Ar. on a bend az. three crosses crosslet or.

Ludham. Ar. three escutcheons sa. on each nine bezants, three, three, two, and one.

Ludington (Shrawley, co. Worcester). Quarterly, 1st and 4th, paly of six ar. and az. on a chief gu. a lion pass. guard. or, for LUDINGTON; 2nd and 3rd, sa. a fess nebuly ar. guttée de sang betw. three elephants' heads couped or, for SUCKLING. *Crest*—A swan sejant in the beak a branch ppr.

Ludington (co. Lincoln). Paly of six ar. and az. on a chief gu. a lion pass. guard. or. *Crest*—A palmer's staff erect sa.

Ludkin (Ipswich, co. Suffolk). Gu. a chev. betw. three birds, wings expanded az. *Crest*—A bird, as in the arms, az. beaked and legged or.

Ludlow (*Earl of Ludlow,* extinct 1842). Quarterly, 1st and 4th, ar. a chev. betw. three foxes' heads erased sa., for LUDLOW; 2nd and 3rd, sa. on a chief sa. three crescents of the first, for PRESTON. *Crest*—A lion ramp. sa. bezantée. *Supporters*—Two stags reguard. ppr. *Motto*—Spero infestis metuo secundis.

Ludlow (co. Gloucester). Or, on a fesse sa. betw. three mullets gu. as many crosses crosslet of the field.

Ludlow (Morehouse, co. Salop). Or, a lion ramp. (another, pass.) sa. armed and langued gu.

Ludlow (co. Salop). Az. three lions pass. in pale ar. (another, two lions pass. guard. ar.).

Ludlow (Wales). Or, a lion ramp. sa. betw. three torteaux.

Ludlow (Hill Deverill, co. Wilts). Ar. a chev. betw. three bears' heads erased sa. *Crest*—A demi bear ramp. sa.

Ludlow (Heywood House, co. Wilts). Same *Arms. Crest*— A lion ramp. *Another Crest*—A dexter arm embowed in armour, holding in the hand a battle axe all ppr. *Motto*— Nec temere, nec timide.

Ludlow (co. Wilts). Ar. a fesse betw three horses' heads erased sa.

Ludlow. Or, three lions pass. reguard. az. (another, sa.; another, tinctures reversed).

Ludlow. Az. three lions ramp. guard. in pale ar.; another, Ar. a lion ramp. sa. on the shoulder a guttée d'or; another, Ar. a lion ramp. in the dexter paw a torteau; another, Gu. a lion pass. and bordure engr. ar.

Ludlow. See LODELOW.

Ludlow, Town of (co Salop). Az. a lion couchant betw. three roses ar.

Luffyngcotte. Ar. guttée de sang an eagle displ. ss.

Luffull. Gu. three helmets ar.

Lufkyn. Sa. on a chev. betw. three eagles displ. or, as many mullets of the first.

Lugg (co. Gloucester). Gu. on a bend betw. two cotises ar. a bendlet wavy az. *Crest*—Out of a ducal coronet or, a pelican's head vulning betw. two wings ppr.

Luggar (Bodmin, co. Cornwall; granted 20 Dec. 1602). Gu. three leopards' faces in fess within two barrulets or, betw. as many ostrich feathers erect ar.

Luggershall, Town of (co. Wilts). Az. a castle ppr.

Lughborough, or Lughteburgh. Gu. a chev. ar. guttée de sang betw. three leopards' faces of the second.

Luke (Copley, co. Bedford, Paxton, co. Durham, and co. Huntingdon). Ar. a buglehorn sa. stringed gu. *Crest*—A bull's head az. attired or, betw. two wings endorsed gold.

Luke (Woodend, co. Bedford). Same *Arms* and *Crest*.

Luke (co. Cornwall). Gu. on a chief sa. three martlets ar. *Crest*—An escallop ppr.

Luke (Glasgow and Greenfield, Scotland; granted 1749). Ar. on a bend az. surmounted by a buglehorn sa. three buckles or, on a chief paly of three of the first and second, in the centre as many bells of the fourth, on the dexter and sinister a saltire engr. of the third betw. four mullets gu. *Crest*—A bull's head ppr. winged or. *Motto*—Strenue insequor.

Luke. Quarterly, 1st and 4th, ar. a buglehorn sa. stringed vert; 2nd and 3rd, gu. a fleur-de-lis ar. *Crest*—An archer shooting with a bow ppr.

Luke (Luke, co. Nottingham). Sa. nine annulets or, four, three, two, and one.

Luke (Screveton, co. Nottingham). Ar. on a saltire engr. sa. nine annulets or, within a bordure also engr. of the second, charged with eight crosses pattée of the third.

Luker (Drangan, co. Tipperary). Marcus Luker, Lord of that Manor, *d.* 1530, was son of William Luker, settled in Ireland *temp.* Henry VI., second son of Luke or Lucar, of Exmoor, co. Somerset; allowed by Hawkins, Ulster, 1769, to Edward John Luker, Colonel in the service of France). Ar. a chev. sa. betw. three nags' heads erased gu. bridled or. *Crest*—An arm erect couped at the elbow, vested per pale az. and gu. cuffed ar. holding a hawk's lure ppr.

Luker (another coat, Reg. Ulster's Office to same family). Ar. three horses pass. ar. a crescent for diff. *Crest*—Out of a ducal coronet or, a demi horse ramp. gu.

Luker (Reg. Ulster's Office). Sa. two hinds in fess ar. the dexter pass. the sinister counter-pass.

Lukie (co. Cornwall; the heiress *m.* Polwhele). Az. three goats' heads erased ar.

Lukin (co. Lincoln). Ar. a lion ramp. gu. over all a bendlet gobony or and az. *Crest*—A demi lion gu. collared gobony or and az.

Lukin (city of Oxford; Thomas Lukin, Visit. Oxon, 1634, descended from Lukin, of Barking, co. Essex). Ar. a lion ramp. gu. debruised by a bend gobony or and az. *Crest*—A demi lion ramp. gu. collared chequy or and az.

Lukin (Oxford; Har. MSS. 1480). Sa. a fess dancettée betw. two lions' faces or. *Crest*—Out of a tower a dragon issuant.

Lukin (Dunmow, co. Essex; descended from Lionel Lukin, Esq., of Hythe, co. Kent). Same *Arms* and *Crest*.

Lukis (Guernsey). Az. a chev. erm. betw. two annulets in chief and in base a bow lying fesseways ar. crossed by two arrows in saltire, points downwards or, feathered of the third, on a chief of the second a Cornish chough ppr. betw. two crosses crosslet fitchy gu. *Crest*—A cubit arm vested gu. cuffed vert, garnished gold, holding a sprig of three holly leaves ppr. betw. two wings or, each charged with a cross crosslet az. *Motto*—Esse quam videri.

Luknor. Az. three chevronels ar.

Lulle. Az. a bend or, betw. six bezants.

Luls. Per fesse sa. and or, a lion ramp. counterchanged.

Lum (co. York). Or, three mullets sa. *Crest*—A Moor's head in profile ppr. wreathed about the temples or and sa.

Lumb. Gu. a fesse betw. three eagles' heads erased ar. *Crest*—A sceptre erect or.

Lumb (Brigham Hall, co. Cumberland). Or, three escutcheons sa. each charged with a mullet pierced of the first. *Crest*—A blackamoor's head in profile, couped at the shoulders ppr. wreathed about the temples or and sa. and charged on the neck with a mullet of six points gold, within a wreath in arch or and sa. *Motto*—Respice finem.

Lumley (Lumley Castle, co. Durham). Gu. six martlets ar.

Lumley (Baron *Lumley*, under attainder since 1537; Sir Ralph de Lumley was summoned to Parliament 1384). Gu. six martlets ar., original arms, and after the marriage of Sir Robert de Lumley, *temp.* Edward II., with Lucia, sister and co-heir of William de Thweng, *Baron Thweng*, of Kilton Castle, co. York, the arms of that family, viz., Or, a fess gu. betw. three parrots ppr. collared of the second.

Lumley (*Earl of Scarborough*). Ar. a fesse gu. betw. three parrots vert, collared of the second. *Crest*—A pelican in her piety ppr. *Supporters*—Two parrots, wings inverted vert. *Motto*—Murus aëneus conscientia sana.

Lumley (Great Bradfield, co. Essex, bart., extinct 1771; of Italian descent). Or, a chief gu. *Crest*—An eagle displ. sa. crowned or.

Lumley (cos. Middlesex and York). Ar. a fesse gu. betw. three parrots ppr. gorged with collars of the second. *Crest* —A pelican in her piety ppr.

Lumley (Harbling, co. Lincoln). Gu. a fesse betw. three pigeons ar. *Crest*—A pigeon ar. in the beak a laurel sprig vert.

Lumley (co. Worcester). Ar. a fess gu. betw. three pansy flowers ppr.

Lumley (Lord Mayor of London). Ar. a chief vert.

Lumley (Clipston, co. Northampton). Gu. on a fesse betw. three popinjays ar. as many mullets sa.

Lumm (confirmed by Fortescue, Ulster, to Col. Charles Lumm, and the descendants of Elnathan Lumm, Esq.). Ar. a trefoil slipped vert betw. three mullets sa. *Crest*—A Moor's head in profile ppr. wreathed about the temples or and vert. *Motto*—Vita potior libertas.

Lumsdaine (Lumsdaine). See Sandys-Lumsdaine.

Lumsden (that Ilk and Blanearn, co. Berwick). Az. on a chev. betw. three mullets or, a buckle of the first; or (after the marriage with the heiress of Blanearn, of that Ilk), Az. on a chev. ar. betw. two mullets in chief and an earn perching on a salmon in base or, a buckle of the first.

Lumsden (Cushnie, co. Aberdeen). Az. a buckle or, betw. two wolves' heads in chief and an escallop in base ar. *Crest* —A naked arm grasping a sword ppr. *Motto*—Dei dono sum quod sum.

Lumsden (Innergelly, co. Fife). Az. a chev. or, betw. a wolf's head couped and a buckle in chief and an escallop in base ar. *Crest*—A heron devouring a salmon ppr. *Motto*— Beware in time.

Lumsden (brother of Innergelly, 1672). Same *Arms*, within a bordure engr. or. Same *Crest* and *Motto*.

Lumsden (Conland, co. Fife). Ar. a chev. sa. betw. two otters' heads couped in chief gu. and an escallop in base vert.

Lumsden (Glasgow, 1863). Az. a chev. or, betw. two wolves' heads erased ar. in chief and an escallop in base of the third. *Crest*—A hand grasping a sword in bend sinister ppr. *Motto*—Dei dono sum quod sum.

Lumsden (Glasgow, 1871). Same *Arms*, within a bordure or. Same *Crest* and *Motto*.

Lund (Parson's Green, Fulham, co. Middlesex, and co. York). Per chev. or and gu. three lions pass. counter-changed.

Lund (Shelford, co. Cambridge, and co. York). Gyronny of eight ar. and az. on a bordure engr. sa. as many plates.

Lund (Lovely Hall, Blackburn, co. Lancaster; granted to Thomas Lund, Esq., Mayor of Blackburn, 1863-4). Gyronny of eight ar. and gu. three covered cups or, a chief indented sa. charged with annulets of the third and bezants alternately. *Crest*—A demi lion ramp. gu. charged with two covered cups in pale, as in the arms, and holding betw. the paws a plate, thereon a cross pattée throughout also gu. *Motto*—Semper fidelis.

Lunderthorp. Gu. three lions ramp. erm.

Lundin (that Ilk, co. Fife). Or, a lion ramp. gu. within the royal tressure flory and counterflory of the last, all within a bordure gobonated az. and ar. *Crest*—Out of an antique crown or, a lion issuing affrontée gu. holding in the dexter paw a sword erect, and in the sinister a thistle slipped all ppr. *Supporters* — Two lions guard. gu. having collars or, charged with three thistles vert. *Motto*—Dei dono sum quod sum.

Lundin (Baldester, co. Fife). Quarterly, 1st and 4th, as Lundin, of that Ilk ; 2nd and 3rd, paly of six ar. and gu. on a bend az. three cushions of the first, the whole within a bordure az. *Crest*—An open hand charged in the palm with an eye ppr. *Motto*—Certior dum cerno.

Lundin (Balgony, co. Fife). Quarterly, 1st and 4th, paly of six ar. and gu. on a bend az. three cushions of the first; 2nd and 3rd, ar. a cross moline square pierced gu., for Sibbald.

Lundin (Auchtermarnie, co. Fife). Paly of six ar. and gu. a bend az. charged with three cushions or, all within a bordure indented of the third. *Crest*—A hand ppr. holding a cushion in pale ar. *Motto*—Tam genus, quam virtus.

Lunel. Az. a fesse ar. betw. three crescents or.

Lunsford (confirmed by the Deputies of Camden, Clarenceux, to John Lunsford, of Hoterley, co. Warwick, third in descent from John Lunsford, co. Sussex. Visit. Warwick). Az. a chev. betw. three boars' heads or, couped gu. *Crest*— A boar's head or, couped gu.

Luntley (co. Stafford). Ar. a fesse betw. three martlets vert.

Luntley. Az. on a chev. ar. betw. three lions' heads erased or, as many martlets sa. *Crest*—A lion's head or, charged with a martlet sa.

Luppingcote (co. Devon). Per fesse embattled gu. and sa. three cats pass. ar. (another, leopards spotted of the second).

Lupton (Thame, co. Oxford). Ar. a chev. sa. charged with three white lilies leaved vert betw. as many wolves' heads erased of the second, langued gu. on a chief of the last a Tau of St. Anthony betw. two escallops or. *Crest*—A wolf's head erased sa.

Lupton (co. York; granted *temp.* Henry VII.). Same *Arms* and *Crest.*

Lupus (*Earl of Chester;* created 1070, passed to DE MES-CHINES). See ABRINCES, *Earl of Chester.*

Lupus (Sir CHARLES LUPUS, *temp.* Edward III.; his dau. *m.* JOHN DURANT, of Cottesmore and Borough, co. Rutland. Visit. Rutland, 1619). Az. a wolf's head erased ar.

Lurgan, Baron. See BROWNLOW.

Lurkin (Hunston, co. Suffolk, settled there 1600; the heiress, MARY LURKIN *m.* JOHN HEIGHAM, and *d.* 1718). Ar. a lion ramp. gu. over all a bendlet gobony or and az.

Lusada, or Losada (descended from the same family as the Duc de Losada, Chamberlain to Charles, King of Spain, and a Grandee of the first class). Az. on a chev. betw. three doves reguard. ar. wings expanded or, two sugar canes of the last, sprigged vert. *Crest*—On a mount vert a dove, as in the arms, charged on the neck with a bar gemelle or, a sprig in the beak ppr. *Motto*—Honneur me guide.

Luscombe (granted to JOHN HENRY LUSCOMBE, Esq., of Havelock House, Lewisham). Or, a saltire engr. betw. two crosses patonce in pale az. and as many leopards' faces in fesse ppr. *Crest*—A demi leopard ppr. semée of estoiles az. and holding betw. the paws an escutcheon charged with a cross, as in the arms. *Motto*—Mors omnibus communis.

Luscombe (Comb Royal, co. Devon). Ar. on a pile az. a lion ramp. guard. crowned or. *Crest*—A demi lion ramp. guard. crowned or.

Luscombe (Totness, co. Devon; confirmed to TOOKE CUM-MING LUSCOMBE, Esq., of Miltown Castle, co. Dublin, son of THOMAS POPHAM LUSCOMBE, Esq., of Gayfield House, co. Dublin, Commissary-General, by CATHERINE, his wife, dau. of WILLIAM TOOKE ROBINSON, Esq., of Walthamstow, co. Essex). Ar. on a pile az. betw. two stags' heads cabossed in base ppr. a lion ramp. guard. crowned or. *Crest*—A demi lion ramp. crowned or, collared az. pierced through the neck with an arrow ppr. charged on the shoulder with a cinquefoil gu. *Motto*—Deo duce ferro comitante.

Lushel, or Lusells (co. Worcester). Ar. a pale fusily gu. a bordure az. bezantée.

Lusher (London). Gu. a lion pass. betw. three gauntlets, their backs affrontée or. *Crest*—A demi lion gu. resting the paws on a gauntlet or.

Lusher (London, Putney, Sholand, and Starland, co. Surrey). Gu. three martlets or, on a chief of the second as many mullets az. *Crest*—A martlet or.

Lushill (co. Wilts). Ar. a pale fusily gu. within a bordure az. bezantée.

Lushill. Ar. five fusils in fess gu. a bordure az. bezantée.

Lushington (South Hill Park, co. Berks, bart.). Or, on a fesse wavy betw. three lions' heads erased vert, langued gu. as many erm. spots of the field. *Crest*—A lion's head erased vert, charged on the erasure with three erm. spots or, ducally gorged or.

Lushington (Park House, co. Kent). Same *Arms* and *Crest. Motto*—Fides nudaque veritas.

Lushington (WILDMAN-LUSHINGTON, Norton Court, Faversham, co. Kent). Quarterly, 1st and 4th, or, on a fess wavy betw. three lions' heads erased vert as many erm. spots gold, for LUSHINGTON; 2nd and 3rd, az. on a chev. betw. two eagles displ. in chief and a lion pass. in base or, two erm. spots betw. three estoiles of the field, for WILDMAN. *Crests*—1st, LUSHINGTON: A lion's head erased vert, ducally gorged or; 2nd, WILDMAN: Out of a mural coronet chequy or and az. a demi lion ramp. ar. supporting a battle axe gold, blade ppr. distilling drops of blood. *Motto*—Prudens qui patiens.

Lusk (Sheriff of London, 1860-61). Az. a lymphad ppr., quartering, Gu. on a chev. ar. three mullets of the first, on a canton of the second a pellet. *Crest*—A lymphad, as in the arms. *Motto*—Laus Deo.

Lusk (Colney Park, co. Hereford, bart.). Az. an ancient ship with three masts, sails furled ppr. colours flying gu. on a

chief ar. a woolpack sa. betw. two mullets gu. *Crest*—An ancient ship, as in the arms, surmounted by a rainbow ppr. *Motto*—Laus Deo.

Luswell, or Ruswell (Fun. Ent. Ulster's Office). Or, a chev. az. betw. three roses gu. leaved vert.

Lutburgh. Gu. a chev. ar. guttée de poix betw. three leopards' faces sa.

Lutefoot (Orchill, co. Perth). Ar. a chev. gu. betw. two crescents in chief az. and a martlet in base sa. *Crest*—A swan ppr. on the head a crescent montant. *Motto*—Addicunt aves.

Luteral (cos. Derby and Nottingham, *temp.* Richard 1.). Or, a bend betw. six martlets gu.

Luther (Myles's, co. Essex; established in England *temp.* Henry VIII. and said to have been allied to the Reformer MARTIN LUTHER. The last male heir of this family, JOHN LUTHER, Esq., of Myles's, M.P. co. Essex, *d. s. p.* leaving two sisters and co-heirs—CHARLOTTE, *m.* HENRY FANE, Esq., of Wormsley, brother of the *Earl of Westmorland,* and REBECCA, *m.* JOHN TAYLOR, Esq.). Ar. two bars sa. in chief three round buckles az. *Crest*—Two arms embowed in armour ppr. holding in the hands a round buckle or. Granted in 1614.

Luther. Same *Arms. Crest*—A hand armed with a gauntlet az. holding a sword in pale, hilt and pommel or.

Luther (Fun. Ent. Ulster's Office, 1678). Barry of six az. and ar. in chief three round buckles of the last.

Luthum. Gu. semée of billets a fesse or.

Lutley (Bromscroft Castle, co. Salop; quartered by JOHN HABINGDON BARNEBY-LUTLEY, of Brockhampton, co. Hereford). Quarterly, or and az. four lions ramp. counterchanged.

Lutley (Lawton and Bromscroft, co. Salop; descended from Sir WILLIAM LUTLEY, Knt., of Munslow Hall, same co.). Quarterly, or and az. four lions ramp. counterchanged.

Lutley (BARNEBY-LUTLEY, Brockhampton, co. Hereford). Quarterly, 1st and 4th, sa. a lion pass. guard. betw. three escallops ar., for BARNEBY; 2nd and 3rd, quarterly, or and az. four lions ramp. counterchanged, for LUTLEY, together with upwards of fifty-four quarterings, chiefly brought in by HABINGDON and SHIRLEY. *Crest*—A lion couchant guard. sa. *Motto*—Virtute non vi.

Lutman (Bentley, co. Hants, and Langley, co. Sussex; granted 1738). Az. four lions ramp. two in chief, and as many in base or. *Crest*—Out of a mural crown ar. a demi lion ramp. az. holding betw. the paws a mullets or.

Luton, or Lucon. Vert an imperial eagle or, membered gu.

Lutteley (Bromscroft, co. Salop, and co. Worcester). Quarterly, or and az. four lions ramp. counterchanged. *Crest* —On a plate an eagle displ. sa.

Lutterell (Hartland Abbey, co. Devon, and Dunster Castle, co. Somerset). See LUTTRELL.

Lutterell. Or, six martlets sa. three, two, and one; another, Az. a fesse betw. six mullets ar.; another, Gu. two bars or, in chief a bezant.

Lutterford (Lutterford, co. Stafford). Gu. on a bend ar. betw. two escallops or, a greyhound courant sa. all within a bordure engr. of the third. *Crest*—A spear or, embrued gu. betw. two wings expanded sa.

Lutton (Cofford, co. Devon; EMANUEL LUTTON, Visit. Devon, 1620, descended from RICHARD LOTYN, who made a grant of Cofford to his son, THOMAS LOTYN, dated 1 Aug. 10 Henry V. 1422). Vert an eagle displ. with two heads within an orle of trefoils or.

Lutton (Knapton, co. York. Visit. Dugdale, 1665). Gu. a chev. ar. betw. three crosses formée or. *Crest*—On the stump of a tree eradicated or, a peacock close ppr.

Lutton (co. York). Ar. three bends wavy gu.

Lutton. Sa. on a bend ar. three escallops gu.

Luttrell, or Loterel (*Baron Luttrell,* passed in 1417 to the HILTONS, and from them through the ARUNDELS, of Wardour, to the CLIFFORDS. Sir ROBERT DE LUTRRELL, of Hooton Pagnel, co. York, was summoned to Parliament as a baron in 1295). Or, a bend betw. six martlets sa.

Luttrell (Dunster Castle, co. Somerset; the parent stock of LUTTRELL, of Luttrellstown, co. Dublin, LUTTRELL, of Hartland, Honnebere, Sandon Court, and Chelsea; descended from JOHN LUTTRELL, of Chilton, M.P. for Devon, 37 Edward III., youngest son of ANDREW LUTTRELL, of East Quantoxhead, *temp.* Edward I. MARGARET, only dau. and heir of ALEX-ANDER LUTTRELL, Esq., of Dunster Castle, *m.* HENRY FOWNES, Esq., of Nethway House, co. Devon, who assumed in consequence the name and arms of LUTTRELL). Quarterly, 1st and 4th, or, a bend betw. six martlets sa., for LUTTRELL; 2nd and 3rd, az. two eagles displ. in fesse and a mullet in base ar., for FOWNES. *Crest*—Out of a ducal coronet or, a plume of five feathers ar. *Motto*—Quæsita marte tuenda arte.

Luttrell (Hanbury, co Somerset, and of Hartland Abbey, co. Devon; NICHOLAS LUTTRELL, Visit. Devon, 1620, sixth in descent from Sir JOHN LUTTRELL, living temp. Henry VI., who took the Queen of Scotland prisoner on the field of battle, and then bore a coronet for his crest; he subsequently took an earl prisoner in France, and thenceforth bore for his crest a swan chained and collared; he was eighth in descent from Sir JOHN LUTTRELL, Knt., temp. King John). Or, a bend betw. six martlets sa. Crest—A boar pass. ar. bristled or, charged on the shoulder with a rose gold.

Luttrell (Luttrellstown, Ireland). Ar. a fesse sa. betw three otters of the last, in the mouth of each a fish ppr. Crest —An otter pass. sa. in the mouth a fish ppr. Motto—En Dieu est ma fiance.

Luttrell-Olmius (Earl of Carhampton ; extinct 1829). Per fesse az. and ar. a fesse counter-embattled or, in chief a mullet of six points of the second, in base on a mount vert an elm tree ppr. Crest—A demi Moor habited in armour ppr. garnished or, betw. two laurel branches vert, a wreath round the temples ar. and gu. and on the breast a fesse, as in the arms. Supporters—Dexter, an ancient warrior ppr. arms and thighs vested in mail of the last, body habited crimson, round the waist a sword-belt or, across the body from the dexter shoulder a sash az. from the middle of the thighs to the knees a vest vert tied with bows, face, hands, and legs ppr. in the right hand a bow, at the back a quiver of arrows, at the side a sword, hilt and pommel gold, shoes ar. his helmet adorned with feathers of the last; sinister, a female representing Plenty, under robe white, the upper robe flowing, crimson, in her left hand a cornucopia with fruit, all ppr. Motto—En Dieu est ma fiance.

Luttrell (Four Oaks, co. Warwick). Ar. a fesse betw. three otters sa. Crest—An otter sa. in the mouth a fish ppr.

Luttrington. Gu. on a bend or, three bears statant sa.

Lutwich (co. Salop). Ar. on a fesse engr. az. three garbs or.

Lutwidge (Holme Rook, co. Cumberland). Az. three morions or steel caps or, turned up erm. Crest—A lion ramp. gu. Motto—Deo patriæ amicis.

Lutwidge. Gu. a demi lion ramp. erased ar. Crest— Betw. two branches of laurel in orle a hand holding a scroll of parchment all ppr.

Lutwyche (Lutwych, co. Salop). Or, a tiger pass. gu. Crest—A tiger's head erased gu. tufted and maned or.

Lutwyche, or Lutwich. Same Arms. Crest—An arm in armour brandishing a sword all ppr.

Luward (co. York). Az. a cross pattée or.

Luveine, or Lovaine (Eystaines, co. Essex, temp. Henry III.). Gu. a fesse ar. betw. ten billets or.

Luxford (Wartling, co. Sussex). Or, on a pile az. three boars' heads couped of the field. Crest—A boar's head ar. erased at the neck gu. holding in the mouth a spear or, headed of the first. Another Crest—A wolf ramp. supporting an arrow paleways, point downwards or, flighted ar.

Luxford (Higham, co. Sussex). Same Arms and Crest.

Luxford. Az. a demi lion ramp. three boars' heads couped or. Crest—A boar's head, as in the arms.

Luxmoore (Keralake, co. Devon). Ar. a chev. sa. betw. three moorcocks ppr. Crest—A battle axe erect ppr. Motto —Securis fecit securum.

Luxmoore (Southweek, co. Devon). Az. a chev. betw. three moorhens ppr.

Lyal (Scotland). Or, a cross betw. four crosses pattée fitchée gu. all within a bordure engr. az. Crest—A swallow flying ppr. Motto—Sedulo et honeste.

Lyall (Hedley, co. Surrey). Quarterly, 1st and 4th, az. a bend betw. six cross crosslets fitchée or; 2nd and 3rd, gu. fretty or. Crest—A cock or, crested gu. Motto—An I may.

Lyarde, Lyarte, or Lyharte (Bishop of Norwich, 1446). Ar. a bull pass. sa. attired or, a bordure of the second bezantée.

Lyband. Az. a lion pass. ar.

Lybb (co. Oxford). Erm. a bend betw. two lions pass. reguard. gu. Crest—A naked arm erect holding an oak branch fructed all ppr.

Lybbe (Hardwick, co. Oxford; RICHARD LYBBE, son and heir of RICHARD LYBBE, Lord of the Manor of Hardwick, buried there 21 Aug. 1599, son and heir of RICHARD LYBBE, Esq., of Checkenden, co. Oxford, son and heir of RICHARD LYBBE, Esq., of Taston, co. Devon. Visits. Oxon, 1574 and 1634). Erm. a bend betw. two lions ramp. gu. Crest—An arm embowed in mail, holding a halbert ppr.

Lychefield. Per chev. sa. and ar. in chief three leopards' faces or. Crest—An arm embowed, vested ar. holding in the hand ppr. a bow or, strung gu.

631

Lychfield (co. Salop). Same Arms (another, the heads ar.). Crest—A boar's head couped az.

Lychford (Charlwood, co. Surrey). Sa. a chev. betw. three leopards' faces ar. Crest—A leopard's face per pale ar. and sa. betw. two wings counterchanged.

Lycke (JOHN LYCKE, Esq., of London). Gu. a lion ramp. ar. Crest—A demi lion ppr. holding a broken spear, point downwards or.

Lydall, or Lyddall (Sunning and Didcot, co. Berks, Ipsden and Uxmore, co. Oxford). Az. a saltire or, over all on a fesse of the last three pellets. Crest—Out of a mural coronet chequy or and az. a heron's head erased of the first, in the beak a scroll, inscribed "Et patribus, et posteritati."

Lydcotte (co. Buckingham, Woodhurcot, co. Northampton, and Surrey). Or, two bars vairé ar. and sa. Crest—On a ducal coronet or, a boar's head couped of the last.

Lydcotte (Chickendon, co. Oxford). Vairé ar. and sa. two bars or, on a chief of the last three dovecotes gu.

Lydd, Town of (co. Kent). Az. the base wavy of six of the last and ar. on the base a castle with tower and spire, near the centre of the field, all on the dexter side, a ship on the sinister with one mast, as if passing by the castle of the second, sail furled of the last, on the stern a man blowing a horn all or, the mast, round tops, and rigging, all of the last on a canton gold, a cross betw. four lions ramp. gu.

Lyde. Or, on a fess betw. two chevronels sa. three cinqua foils ar.

Lyde (Ayot St. Lawrence, co. Hertford, bart., extinct 1791 descended from CORNELIUS LYDE, Esq., of Stanton Wick, co Somerset, b. in 1641; the last male heir, Sir LYONEL LYDE, of Ayot St. Lawrence, was created a bart. in 1772. The manor of Ayot St. Lawrence eventually vested in the family of AMES). Az. an eagle displ. with two heads erminois, for LYDE, quartering the arms of SAGE, PAYNE, and MORTIMER. Crest—A buck's head erased erminois. Motto—Non sibi.

Lyde (AMES-LYDE; exemplified to LIONEL NEVILLE FREDERICK AMES, Esq., of Ayot St. Lawrence and The Hyde, co. Hertford, and Thornham Hall, Brancaster, co. Norfolk, upon his assuming, by royal licence, 1874, the additional surname of LYDE). Quarterly, 1st and 4th, az. an eagle with two heads displ. erminois, for LYDE; 2nd and 3rd, ar. on a bend cotised betw. two annulets sa. a quatrefoil betw. two roses of the field, for AMES. Crests—1st, LYDE : A buck's head erased erminois, attired or; 2nd, AMES: A rose ar. slipped and leaved ppr. in front thereof an annulet or. Motto— Non sibi.

Lydeate (co. Worcester). Ar. three bars vairé or and gu. in chief as many annulets sa.

Lydnor. Az. a fesse nebulée ar. in chief a crescent surmounted by a fleur-de-lis or, quartered by AMHURST through EVERING.

Lye (cos. Wilts and Hereford). Or, three lions couchant gu. Crest—An eagle displ. ar. beaked and legged gu.

Lye. Per pale gu. and az. two wings conjoined ar.; another, Ar. a fesse fusily sa. betw. three crescents gu.; another, Ar. a bend fusily sa. betw. six crescents gu.; another, Ar. a fleurde-lis sa.

Lyell (Murthill, co. Aberdeen). Or, a cross az. betw. four crosses pattée fitchée gu. Crest—A dexter hand holding a sword erect ppr. Motto—Forti non ignavo.

Lyell (Woodhead, 1680). As the last, within a bordure engr. az. Crest—A swallow volant ppr. Motto—Sedule et honeste.

Lyell (Dysart, 1680). Or, a cross az. betw. four cross crosslets fitchée gu. Crest—A dexter hand holding a sword erect all ppr. Motto—Tutela.

Lyell (Kinnordy, co. Forfar, bart., 1864, extinct 1875). Or, a cross parted and fretty az. betw. four crosses pattée gu. a bordure engr. of the last. Crest—Upon a rock a dexter cubit arm erect in armour ppr. charged with a cross parted and fretty gu. the hand grasping a sword also ppr. Motto —Forti non ignavo.

Lyfe. Quarterly, or and az., in the 1st and 4th an eagle displ. gu. ; in the 2nd and 3rd an eagle displ. of the first.

Lyfield (Stoke Dabernon. co. Surrey; granted May, 10 Queen Elizabeth, A.D. 1567). Or, on a chev. betw. three demi lions ramp. gu. as many trefoils slipped ar. Crest—A bull's head cabossed ar. charged with three guttées sa.

Lyford. Or, three bendlets az. an inescutcheon chequy or and gu. Crest—A fox's head erased or.

Lygon (Earl Beauchamp). Ar. two lions pass. in pale gu. Crest—A savage's head affrontee couped at the shoulders ppr. Supporters—Dexter, a bear ppr. muzzled, collared, and chained or; sinister, a swan ar. wings elevated gu. beaked and legged sa. gorged with a ducal coronet and lined or, on the breast of each supporter, suspended from the collar and coronet, a shield gu. charged with a fesse betw. six martlets gold. *Motto*—Ex fide fortis.

Lygon (Madresfield and Warndon, co. Worcester; extinct in the male line, represented in the female by *Earl Beauchamp*). Ar. two lions pass. in pale double queued gu. armed and langued az. *Crest*—A Saracen's head affrontée couped at the shoulders ppr. wreathed about the temples ar. and gu.

Lyle, De (*Lord Lyle*). Quarterly, 1st and 4th, az. a bend betw. six crosses crosslet fitchée or, for MAR; 2nd and 3rd, gu. fretty or, for LYLE. *Crest*—A cock or, crested gu. *Supporters*—Two cats ppr. *Motto*—An I may.

Lyle (co. Hants). Or, a chev. betw. three holly leaves gu.

Lyle (Bournehide). Quarterly, 1st and 4th, per pale ar. and sa. three piles counterchanged; 2nd and 3rd, ar. three crosses pattée gu.

Lyle, or L'Isle. Gu. fretty or (another, gu. a fret or).

Lyle (Stonypath, Scotland). Gu. fretty of six or, with a mullet of the last in chief for diff.

Lyle, or Lyell (Woodhead, Scotland). Or, a cross az. betw. four crosses pattée fitchée gu. within a bordure engr. of the second. *Crest*—A swallow volant ppr. *Motto*—Sedulo et honeste.

Lyley (Fulham, co. Middlesex). Quarterly, 1st and 4th, gu. a lion pass. guard. ar. ducally crowned or, in chief three mullets of the second, pierced of the field, for LYLEY; 2nd and 3rd, or, a bend vair betw. three hurts, for PITT. *Crest* A cubit arm in armour, the hand within a gauntlet grasping a war mace all ppr. from the handle of the mace a chain pendent encircling the arm or.

Lylgrave. Or, on a chev. sa. betw. three water bougets gu. as many estoiles of the first, a bordure engr. az. *Crest* —A peacock's head couped at the neck gobonated or and az. in the beak a lily ar.

Lyly (London). Gu. three lilies ar. stalked and leaved vert, a bordure of the second and a crescent for diff.

Lymber, or Lymbury. Ar. three cinquefoils gu. pierced or. *Crest*—A dexter hand ppr. holding a trident sa.

Lyminge (co. Leicester). Gu. three birds ar.

Lymington, Town of (co. Hants). The seal represents on the sea an antique ship with one mast, her sail furled, on the sinister side of the mast an escutcheon of the arms of COURTNEY, viz., Or, three torteaux with a label of three points az.

Lymme, afterwards Leigh (Lymm, co. Chester). Gu. a pale lozengy ar. *Crest*—A lion's head couped per pale indented ar. and gu.

Lymon, or Lynam. Per chev. gu. and ar. in base an annulet of the first.

Lynacre, or Lynaker (co. Derby). Sa. a chev. betw. three escallops ar. on a chief or, as many greyhounds' heads erased of the field. *Crest*—A greyhound's head erased ar.

Lynaker. Ar. on a cross az. five mullets or.

Lynaker. Ar. on a bend engr. sa. three buglehorns of the field, stringed vert.

Lynam (St. Kew, co. Cornwall; RICHARD LYNAM, Visit. Cornwall, 1620, son of JOHN LYNAM, and grandson of ROBERT LYNAM, all of same place). Ar. a chev. gu. betw. three boars pass. sa.

Lynch (Galway, Ireland; a family of great antiquity in Connaught, one of "The Tribes of Galway." WILLIAM LE PETIT is stated, in an old MS. in Ulster's Office, to have been the progenitor of all the LYNCHES in Ireland). Az. a chev. betw. three trefoils slipped or. *Crest*—A lynx pass. az. collared or.

Lynch-Blosse (Castle Carra, co. Mayo, bart.; descended from NICHOLAS LYNCH, Mayor of Galway, *temp*. James 1., who had twelve sons. HENRY LYNCH, the eldest, was created a bart. 1622. Sir ROBERT LYNCH, sixth bart., assumed the additional surname of BLOSSE). Same *Arms*. *Crest*—A lynx pass. cowarded ar. *Motto*—Nec temere nec timide.

Lynch (Partry House, co. Mayo). Same *Arms* and *Crest*, without the mullet. *Motto*—Semper constans et fidelis.

Lynch (Clough Ballymore Castle, co. Galway). Same *Arms* and *Crest*.

Lynch (Ballinafad, co. Galway). Same *Arms* and *Crest*.

Lynch (Peterborough, Lancaster, Barna, Loberry, and Lavally, all co. Galway). Same *Arms* and *Crest*.

Lynch (Clydagh House and Duras Park; confirmed by GEORGE STAUNTON LYNCH, Esq., of Clydagh House, co. Galway, eldest son of MARK LYNCH, Esq., of Duras Park, same co., and their descendants). Az. on a chev. betw. three trefoils slipped or, a mullet gu. *Crest*—A lynx pass. ppr. charged on the shoulder with a mullet gu. *Motto*—Semper fidelis.

Lynch (Clogher House, co. Mayo). Quarterly, 1st and 4th, az. a chev. betw. three trefoils slipped or, for LYNCH; 2nd and 3rd, a wolf saliant betw. three hearts, for CREAN. *Crests*—1st: A lynx pass. guard. ppr., for LYNCH; 2nd: A demi wolf, holding betw. the paws a heart, for CREAN. *Motto*—Cor mundum crea in me Deus.

Lynch (Fun. Ent. Ulster's Office, 1613, CHRISTOPHER LYNCH, Esq., of Croboy, Recorder of Drogheda). Ar. a cross sa. betw. four lions ramp. gu. armed and langued az.

Lynch (Fun. Ent. Ulster's Office, 1615, RICHARD LYNCH, Somonister in the Exchequer, Ireland). Az. on a chev. betw. three trefoils slipped or, a lozenge gu.

Lynch (Groves, co. Kent, and Rixton Hall, co. Lancaster). Sa. three leopards ramp. ar. spotted of the field.

Lynch (Teddington, co. Middlesex). Az. a chev. betw. three trefoils slipped or, on a chief ar. as many roses gu. seeded and barbed vert. *Crest*—A lynx pass. guard. ppr.

Lynch (Southampton). Az. a chev. betw. three quatrefoils or. *Crest*—A fox saliant ppr.

Lynch. Sa. three lynxes pass. guard. ar. *Crest*—On a ducal coronet or, a lynx, as in the arms.

Lynch-Power. See POWER.

Lynde, or Lynne (co. Cambridge, and London). Gu. a demi lion ramp. or (another, ar.) a bordure sa. bezantée.

Lynde (arms in a window in Christ's Church, Oxford. Visit. Oxon, 1564). Sa. a pelican in her piety ppr.

Lynde. Ar. two bars sa. a bend gu.

Lynde. Gu. three bucks' heads couped ar.

Lyndey, or Lynd (co. Dorset). Sa. a pelican in her piety ar. vulned gu. nest or.

Lyndey (co. Surrey). Ar. a cross engr. gu.

Lyndford. Gu. a fret engr. erm.

Lyndford. Ar. a cross gu.

Lyndhurst, Baron. See COPLEY.

Lyndley (Lyndley, co. York; WILLIAM LYNDLEY, eldest son of PERCIVAL LYNDLEY, *temp*. Henry VI., left two daus. his co-heirs. Visit. Notts, 1614). Ar. on a chief sa. three griffins' heads erased of the field. *Crest*—A griffin's head ar. gorged with a bar gemel sa.

Lyndley (Skegby, co. Nottingham; FRANCIS LYNDLEY, Visit. Notts, 1614, great-grandson of THOMAS LYNDLEY, second son of PERCEVAL LYNDLEY, Esq., of Lyndley, *temp*. Henry VI.). Same *Arms* and *Crest*.

Lyndley (co. Kent). Same *Arms*.

Lyndon (Carrickfergus, co. Antrim; confirmed by Preston, Ulster, 1639, to ROGER LYNDON, Mayor of that Town, second son of ROBERT LYNDON, co. Somerset). Sa. a mural crown or, betw. three leopards' faces ar. *Crest*—A sea dragon volant vert, armed and langued gu. murally gorged or.

Lyndon (co. Somerset). Sa. three leopards' faces or, (another, ar.). *Crest*—Five arrows, one in pale and four in saltire, banded and buckled ppr.

Lyndon. Az. a mural crown betw. three leopards' faces ar.

Lyndonne, or Lyndowne. Sa. three leopards' faces ar.

Lyndown. Or, three leopards' faces sa. *Crest*—On a pillar a man's heart ppr.

Lyndowne. Gu. a chev. ar. betw. three crescents or.

Lyndsay (the Mount, co. Fife; Sir DAVID LYNDSAY, Lord Lion King at Arms, created by James V. 1530). Gu. a fesse chequy ar. and az. betw. three stars (or mullets) in chief and a man's heart in base ar. *Crest*—Amidst flames a heart transfixed by a dart all ppr. *Supporters*—Faith and Hope.

Lyndsey (co. Huntingdon). Gu. an inescutcheon vair bordured az. within an orle of eight crosses crosslet or.

Lyndsey (co. Kent). Or, an eagle displ. sa. on the breast a mullet of the first a bordure gu. charged with eight cinquefoils ar.

Lyndsey (co. Lancaster). Gu. an orle ar.

Lyndsey (London, and Bucksted, co. Sussex). Or an eagle displ. sa. armed az. a chief vair. *Crest*—An eagle displ. sa. beaked and legged or, charged on the breast with a cross pattée of the last.

Lyndsey (Colby, co. Norfolk). Or, an eagle displ. gu. *Crest*—A unicorn sejant reguard. or, armed, hoofed, maned, and ducally gorged ar.

Lyndsey (Gunton, co. Norfolk). Same *Arms*, a bordure of the last charged with ten cinquefoils ar.

Lyndsey (co. Northumberland). Or, an eagle displ. vert.

Lyndsey, or Lymesey (co. Warwick). Gu. an eagle displ. or.

Lyndsey. Or, an eagle displ. sa. on the breast nine plates in cross.

Lyndsey. Ar. a lion ramp. gu. betw. three trefoils vert.

Lyndsey, or Lyndesey. Per fesse sa. and ar. a bear ramp. counterchanged, muzzled gu. *Crest*—A demi bear ramp. sa.

Lyndsey. Gu. an orle vair betw. twelve crosses crosslet or.

Lyndwood. Ar. a fease crenellée betw. three fleurs-de-lis sa. *Crest*—A fleur-de-lis per pale ar. and sa.

Lyne (Chichester and Ringwood, co. Hants; granted, 2 Philip and Mary, to RICHARD LYNE). Gu. three bucks' heads couped ar. on a chief of the second two griffins' heads erased sa. *Crest*—A griffin's head erased sa.

Lyne (co. Cornwall). Ar. a chev. betw. three roses gu. Same *Crest* as the last.

Lyne-Stephens (exemplified, 1826, to CHARLES LYNE, Esq., of Devonshire Place, and of Weymouth, upon his assuming, by royal licence, the surname of STEPHENS). Quarterly, 1st and 4th, or, on a chev. gu. betw. three demi lions ramp. sa. a cross crosslet ar. betw. two towers of the field, for STEPHENS; 2nd and 3rd, gu. three bucks' heads erased ar. each charged on the neck with an erm. spot, sa. on a chief of the second a cross crosslet az. betw. two griffins' head erased sa., for LYNE. *Crests*—1st, STEPHENS: In front of a raven's head couped erm. beaked az. betw. two wings or, a tower gold; 2nd, LYNE: A griffin's head erased sa. charged on the neck with an erm. spot ar. surmounting a cross crosslet in bend sinister or. *Motto*—Recte et suaviter.

Lynedock, Baron. See GRAHAM.

Lyneham (Fun. Ent. Ulster's Office, 1619, KATHERINE, wife of JOHN LYNEHAM). Ar. a chev. gu. betw. three boars pass. sa. langued of the second.

Lynell, or Lineall (cos. Salop and Chester; Har. MSS. 2163). Az. on a bend ar. three crosses crosslet sa. on a chief or, a trefoil betw. two garbs of the field. *Crest*—A garb or, betw. two trefoils ar.

Lynes. Vert on a fesse ar. three garbs gu. *Crest*—An elephant's head erased purp.

Lynes (Tooley Park, co. Leicester, and Hatton, co. Warwick; descended from JOHN LYNES, Esq., of Corley and Kirkby Mallory). Ar. on a bend az. betw. two lions ramp. gu. a fleur-de-lis betw. two griffins' heads erased or. *Crest*—In front of a fleur-de-lis ar. a lion ramp. gu. *Motto*—Foi, Roi, Droit.

Lynesholme. Ar. a fleur-de-lis sa.

Lyngarde, or Linger (co. Lancaster). Barry of six or and az. on a bend sa. three escallops ar.

Lyngarde (Crudworth, co. Warwick). Same *Arms.* Crest—A tiger's head maned and tufted all sa.

Lyngayne. Barry of six or and az. on a bend gu. three plates (another, cinquefoils or).

Lyngharde, or Lyngard (Willinburgh, co. Northampton). Barry of six or and az. on a bend gu. a lion pass. betw. two roses all of the first (another, ar.). *Crest*—A lion sejant guard. sa. holding in the dexter paw a key erect or. *Another Crest*—A lion's gamb erect and erased ar. holding in the paw three roses gu. stalked and leaved vert.

Lynn (Bassingbourne, co. Cambridge; WILLIAM LYNN, of that place, and JOHN LYNN, of Exeter, co. Devon, his brother, sons of JOHN LYNN, the son of THOMAS LYNN, and grandson of JOHN LYNN, all of Bassingbourne. Visit. Devon, 1620). Gu. a demi lion ramp. ar. a border sa. bezantée.

Lynn (Parliament Street, Westminster, and Clapham, co. Surrey). Same *Arms.* *Crest*—A lion's head erased ar.

Lynn (Woodbridge, co. Suffolk). Gyronny of eight or and gu. a demi lion ramp. erm. charged on the shoulder with a martlet gu. within an orle of eight annulets counterchanged. *Crest*—A demi eagle erm. wings addorsed and erect az. bezantée, charged on the breast with a martlet gu. and holding in the beak an annulet also of the last.

Lynn (Southwick Hall, co. Northants). Same *Arms.* *Crest*—A lion's head erminois erased gu. ducally crowned or, and gorged with a collar sa. charged with four bezants.

Lynne (co. York). Az. three crosses crosslet fitchée in fesse betw. as many eagles displ. or. *Crest*—A squirrel sejant ppr. supporting a cross crosslet fitchée gu.

Lynnington (co. Leicester). Gu. a chev. or, voided and engr. sa. betw. three lapwings ar.

Lynol, or Lynell (co. Worcester; impaled by EDMUND WYATT, Mayor of Worcester, 1695). Gu. on a bend ar. three crosses bottony sa. on a chief or, a trefoil betw. two garbs of the third.

Lynsey (London). Or, an eagle displ. sa. a chief vair. *Crest*—A cat's head ar. spotted, collared, and studded or.

Lynsey. Ar. on a fesse sa. three falcons' heads erased of the first.

Lynsey. Per fesse sa. and ar. a bear ramp. counterchanged, muzzled gu.

633

Lyon (Glamis, co. Forfar, now LYON-BOWES, *Earl of Strathmore*). Ar. a lion ramp. az. armed and langued, within a double tressure flory counterflory gu., now borne quarterly with, erm. three bows strung in pale ppr., for BOWES. *Crest*—Within two branches of laurel a lady to the girdle habited and holding in her right hand the royal thistle all ppr., commemorative of the alliance with the royal house of STEWART. *Supporters*—Dexter, a unicorn ar. armed and unguled or; sinister, a lion per fess or and gu. *Motto*—In te, Domine, speravi.

Lyon (Rev. RALPH LYON, D.D., Rector of Bishop's Caudle, co. Dorset). Erm. a lion ramp. within an orle flory within az. and charged with eight crosses pattée ar. *Crest*—A lion ramp. az. charged on the body with three crosses pattée ar. and resting the sinister forepaw upon a cross moline or. *Motto*—Innixus vero validus.

Lyon (Appleton Hall, co. Chester; descended from THOMAS LYON, of ancient Scottish descent, *b.* about the year 1626, who served in the Scots Greys, and settled eventually at Warrington, co. Lancaster). Ar. a lion ramp. vert. *Crest*—A lion's head erased ppr. *Motto*—Pro rege et patriâ.

Lyon (granted to Lieut.-General Sir JAMES LYON, K.C.B., 1815). Ar. a lion ramp. az. betw. three cinquefoils gu. all within a double tressure flory counterflory of the last. *Crest*—A demi lady ppr. attired or and az. holding in the dexter hand a thistle, and in the sinister a chaplet of laurel ppr., motto over: Lauro redimita quiescam. *Motto*—Speravi.

Lyon (co. Hereford, London, and West Twyford, co. Middlesex). Az. on a fesse or, betw. three plates, each charged with a griffin's head erased sa. a lion pass. betw. two cinquefoils gu. *Crest*—On a pink flowered gu. leaved vert a lion's head erased paly quarterly erm. and ermines.

Lyon-Office, or Office of Arms at Edinburgh. Ar. a lion sejant guard. gu. armed and langued az. holding in his dexter paw a thistle ppr. and in his sinister a shield of the second sa. on a chief az. a St. Andrew's cross of the first; the seal of office is the above betw. two palm branches, the whole encircled with the inscription, Sigillum officii leonis regis armorum.

Lyons (*Baron Lyons*). Sa. on a chev. betw. three lions sejant guard. ar. as many castles triple-towered of the field. *Crest*—On a chapeau gu. turned up erm. a sea lion's head erased ar. gorged with a naval crown az. holding in the mouth a flag staff in bend sinister ppr. therefrom flowing a banner az., having inscribed thereon "Marack" in letters of gold. *Supporters*—On either side a lion guard. sa. charged on the shoulder with a castle triple-towered ar. *Motto*—Noli irritare leones.

Lyons (Island of Antigua). Sa. a chev. betw. three lions sejant guard. ar. *Crest*—On a chapeau gu. turned up erm. a lion's head erased ar. *Motto*—Noli irritare leones.

Lyons (quartered by RAYNESFORD, of Great Lew, co. Oxford. Visit. Oxon, 1574). Per pale or and az. a chev. erm.

Lyons (quartered by WOODHULL, of Mollington, co. Oxford. Visit. Oxon, 1574). Ar. a lion ramp. gu.

Lyons. Ar. a chev. sa. betw. three lions dormant cowarded gu.

Lyons. Purp. a lion ramp. ar. (another, ar. a lion ramp. vert).

Lyons (Old Park, co. Antrim; granted by Betham, Ulster, to WILLIAM LYONS, Esq., of Old Park, near Belfast, grandson of DAVID LYONS, of Belfast, and to their descendants). Per fess or and gu. a lion ramp. within a tressure flory counterchanged, holding in the paws an annulet az. and in chief two trefoils vert. *Crest*—A demi lion ramp. az. holding in the paws an annulet or, thereon a trefoil vert. *Motto*—In te, Domine, speravi.

Lyons (granted by Betham, Ulster, to Sir WILLIAM LYONS, Mayor of Cork, knighted on the occasion of Her Majesty's visit to that city). Ar. a royal crown ppr. betw. two lions pass. guard. in chief sa. and in base an ancient ship of three masts of the second betw. two flowers gu. being part of the arms of the city of Cork. *Crest*—A demi lion ramp. sa. *Motto*—Virtute et fidelitate.

Lyons (Ledestown, co. Westmeath). Sa. a chev. erm. betw. three lions sejant guard. ar. *Crest*—On a chapeau gu. turned up erm. a lion's head erased ar. *Motto*—Noli irritare leones.

Lyons (exemplified by Betham, Ulster, to CHARLES CONNELL, Esq., of Cork, on his taking by royal licence, 1814, the surname of LYONS, in remembrance of his maternal uncle, JAMES LYONS, Esq., of Cork). Ar. on a bend betw. two lions ramp. gu. three trefoils slipped or, on a chief az. a bezant between two woolpacks of the field. *Crest*—A woolpack ar. thereon a lion pass. gu.

Lyons-Montgomery. See MONTGOMERY.

Lyose, or Lyosey. Az. a saltire or, betw. four billets ar.

Lys, or Lysse (co. Hants; a French refugee family.)

Paly of six ar. and az. a fesse or.   *Crest*—A fleur-de-lis or, betw. two palm branches vert.

Lysaght (*Born Lisle*).   Ar. three spears erect in fesse gu. on a chief az. a lion of England.   *Crest*—A dexter arm embowed in armour, the hand brandishing a dagger all ppr.   *Supporters*—Two lions or.   *Motto*—Bella! horrida bella!

Lysers, or Lysours (co. Lincoln).   Or, a chief az.

Lysers. Paly of six gu. and or, a fesse az.   *Crest*—An anchor sa. betw. two wings or.

Lysle (Cambridge, Compton Davrill, co. Somerset, and co. Sussex).   Or, a fesse betw. two chev. sa.   *Crest*—On a chapeau gu. turned up erm. a millstone ar. charged with a millrind or.

Lysle, or Lysley. Or, on a fesse betw. two chev. sa. three roses of the first.

Lysle, or Lysley. Sa. a fesse betw. two chev. or.

Lysley, or Lisle (originally of Harewood, Lyley Kirkheaton, Rothwell, and Warmfield, co. York, Mimwood, co. Herts, and Pewsham, co. Wilts).   Quarterly, 1st, gu. a lion pass. guard. ar. ducally crowned or; 2nd and 3rd, or, a fesse betw. two chev. sa.; 4th, same as the first, three mullets ar. pierced of the field in chief.   *Crests*—1st: On a chapeau gu. turned up erm. a millstone ar. charged with a millrind or; 2nd: A cubit arm in armour, the hand in a gauntlet grasping a war mace all ppr. from the handle of the mace a chain pendent encircling the arm or.

Lysons (Hempsted Court, co. Gloucester; established in that co. for three centuries; of this family was the late Rev. DANIEL LYSONS, M.A., F.R.S., and F.A.S., the antiquary and topographer).   Gu. a chief nebulée ar. issuant therefrom the rays of the sun ppr.   *Crest*—The sun rising out of a bank of clouds ppr.   *Motto*—Valebit.

Lysons (THOMAS LYSONS, Mayor of Worcester, 1651).   Gu. a chief nebuly ar. issuant therefrom rays of the sun ppr.

Lysores. Az. two chevronels in dexter chief a martlet or.

Lyster (Rowton Castle, co. Salop; descended from WILLIAM LYSTER, of Rowton Castle, living in 1451, with whom the Her. Visit. commences).   Erm. on a fesse sa. three mullets ar.   *Crest*—A stag's head erased ppr.   *Motto*—Loyal au mort.

Lyster (exemplified by Fortescue, Ulster, to JAMES WEST, Esq., of Fort William, co. Roscommon, on his assuming, by royal licence, 1805, the surname of LYSTER, in lieu of WEST).   Erm. on a fess sa. three mullets ar.   *Crest*—A stag's head erased ppr.

Lytcott (co. Buckingham, Stratford-Langthorne, co. Essex, and Maulsey, co. Surrey).   Or, two bars vairé ar. and sa.

Lyte (Lytescary, co. Somerset).   Gu. a chev. betw. three swans ar.   *Crest*—A demi swan ar. wings expanded gu. in front of a plume of three feathers, the middle one of the first, the other two of the second.

Lyte. Same *Arms*.   *Crest*—A bear ramp. sa. muzzled gu. supporting a staff.

Lythegraynes (JOHN LYTHEGRAYNES, *temp.* Richard II.).   Gu. an orle ar. over all a bend or.

Lyttel (Reg. Ulster's Office).   Az. a saltire engr. or, in chief a mullet and in base a crescent both of the last.   *Crest*—A pot of flowers ppr.   *Motto*—Magnum in parvo.

Lyttelton (*Baron Lyttelton*; Sir THOMAS LYTTLETON, Knt., of Frankley, Judge of Common Pleas, author of "The Treatise on Tenures," *d.* 1481, leaving three sons: I. Sir WILLIAM LYTTLETON, Knt., of Frankley, ancestor of the *Lords Lyttelton*; II. RICHARD LYTTLETON, ancestor of LITTLETON, Bart., of Pillaton, extinct, and *Lord Hatherton*; III. THOMAS LYTTLETON, Esq., of Spetchley, ancestor of LITTLETON, Bart., of Stoke Milburgh, extinct, and *Lord Littleton*, of Mounslow, extinct).   Ar. a chev. betw. three escallops sa. This family bears the following quarterings: 1st, ar. a bend cotised sa. a bordure engr. gu. bezantée, for WESTCOTE; 2nd, gu. a lion ramp. and a bordure engr. or, for TALBOT; 3rd, ar. six fleurs-de-lis, three, two, and one, and a chief indented gu. for PASTON; 4th, France and England quarterly, within a bordure gobony ar. and az., for BEAUFORT.   *Crest*—A Moor's head in profile couped at the shoulders ppr. wreathed about the temples ar. and sa.   *Supporters*—On either side a merman ppr. in the exterior hand of each a trident or.   *Motto*—Ung Dieu, ung roy.

Lyttelton (Naunton-Beauchamp, Groveley, and Halesowen, co. Worcester, and Studley, co. Warwick).   Same *Arms, &c.*

Lyttelton (*Baron Lyttelton*, of Mounslow, extinct 1645; descended from THOMAS LYTTLETON, third son of Sir THOMAS LYTTLETON, Knt., of Frankley).   Ar. a chev. betw. three escallops sa. a mullet for diff.

Lytton (Lytton, co. Derby, *temp.* Henry III., and Knebworth, co. Herts, *temp.* Henry VII.; descended from Sir ROBERT DE LYTTON, K.B., of Lytton, Under Treasurer to

634

Henry VII., who purchased Knebworth 7th of that reign; the eventual heiress, ELIZABETH BARBARA, only child of RICHARD WARBURTON LYTTON, Esq., of Knebworth, *m.* General WILLIAM EARLE BULWER, of Heydon, in Norfolk).   Erm. on a chief indented az. three ducal crowns or.   *Crest*—A bittern in flags seeded all ppr.

Lytton-Bulwer (*Lord Dalling and Bulwer*, extinct 1872).   Quarterly, 1st and 4th, same *Arms*; 2nd and 3rd, or three mullets sa. pierced gu. on a chief wavy az. a dove reguard. or, in the beak an olive branch vert.   *Crests*—1st: A horned wolf's head erased erm. crined and armed or; 2nd: A dove reguard. ar. in the beak an olive branch vert.   *Supporters*—Dexter, a dragon vert semée of crosses pattée or; sinister, a lion reguard. ppr. gorged with a plain collar or, therefrom pendent an escutcheon ar. charged with a boar's head erased sa.   *Motto*—Adversis major par secundis.

Lytton (BULWER-LYTTON, *Baron Lytton*).   Quarterly, 1st, erm. on a chief dancettée az. three ducal coronets or, for LYTTON; 2nd, gu. on a chev. ar. betw. three eaglets reguard. or, as many cinquefoils sa., for BULWER; 3rd, az. a fess double cotised or, for EARLE; 4th, quarterly ar. and gu. on a fess az. a crescent or, in the 2nd and 3rd quarters a fret of the last, for NORREYS.   *Crests*—1st, LYTTON: A bittern in flags all ppr.; 2nd, BULWER: A wolf's head erased erm. crined and horned or.   *Motto*—Hoc virtutis opus.

Lyversage (Whelock, co. Chester; confirmed 24 Sept. 1580).   Ar. a chev. betw. three laver-cutters (or ploughshares) sa.

M

MABBALL, or MABBATT. Erm. six lions ramp. sa. three, two, and one.   *Crest*—A wivern vert, on the point of the tail another head, each vomiting flames ppr.

Mabbe (London; JOHN MABBE, eldest son of JOHN MABBE, Goldsmith, the son of JOHN MABBE, Esq., of Clayton, co. Sussex. Visit. London, 1568).   Per pale gu. and az. a tiger pass. ar.   *Crest*—A wyvern, wings endorsed or, pellettée.

Mabbe (Chamberlain of the city of London, *temp.* Queen Elizabeth).   Same *Arms* and Crest.

Mabbs (Bynham and Wallingham, co. Norfolk).   Vert a cross patonce erm. betw. four birds ar.

Maben. Az. a fetterlock and key ar.

Maberley, or Maberly. Quarterly, ar. and gu. in the 1st and 4th quarter a martlet of the second.   *Crest*—Out of a ducal coronet or, a demi lion gu.

Mablethorpe (co. Nottingham, 1462).   Gu. a chev. or, betw. three crosses botonnée ar. in chief a lion pass. guard. of the last.

Mablethorpe. Az. a chev. betw. three crosses crosslet ar. in chief (another, on a chief gu.) a lion pass. or.

Mablethorpe. Az. a chev. betw. three crosses crosslet ar.

Mablethorpe. Gu. a chev. betw. a lion pass. in chief, and three crosses crosslet in base or (another, crosses crosslet ar.).

Mablethorpe. Ar. a chev. betw. three crosses crosslet sa. a bordure of the last charged with eight bezants.

Mablethorpe. Lozengy gu. and ar.

M'Aben (Knockdolian, Scotland).   Az. on a rock ppr. a castle ar.   *Crest*—A swallow ppr.   *Motto*—Nulli præda.

M'Adam (Waterhead, in the Stewartry of Kirkcudbright, and Ballochmorrie, co. Ayr).   Vert three arrows paleways, points downwards, barbed and feathered ar.   *Crest*—The head of a red deer erased ppr.   *Motto*—Under the arms: Crux mihi grata quies; over the crest: Calm. (The ancient *Arms*, as found on the Old Tower, over the gate of the family burial ground, tombstones, &c., were—Vert an arrow ar. point upwards.)

M'Adam (Craigengillan, co. Ayr).   Gu. a fesse chequy or and az. betw. three arrows, points upward, of the second.   *Crest*—A stag's head erased ppr.   *Motto*—Steady.

M'Adam-Steuart (Glenormiston).   See STEUART.

Mac Adam (confirmed to THOMAS STANNARD MAC ADAM, Esq., of Blackwater, co. Clare, and to the descendants of his grandfather, THOMAS MAC ADAM, of Churchland, and afterwards of Spring Hill, co. Clare).   Vert a cross calvary, in the dexter chief a mullet, and in the sinister a crescent all or.   *Crest*—On a mount vert a cock ppr. in the bill a cross, as in the arms.   *Motto*—In hoc signo vinces.

Macalister (Loup and Kennox, Scotland; derived from ALEXANDER, eldest son of ANGUS MOR, of the Isles).   Or, an eagle displ. gu. armed sa. surmounted on the breast of a galley of the first within a bordure of the third, charged with six cross crosslets fitchée ar.   *Crest*—A dexter arm in armour erect, the hand holding a dagger in pale all ppr.   *Supporters*—Dexter, a bear, pierced in the back with an arrow; sinister. an eagle all **ppr.** *Mottoes*—Above the crest: Fortiter; below the shield : Per mare per terras.

Mac Alpine (confirmed by Betham, Ulster, to Lieut.-Col. James Mac Alpine, 15th Hussars; descended from a Scotch family of Mac Gregor, or Clan Alpine, which settled in the north of Ireland, *temp.* James I.). Quarterly, 1st and 4th, ar. on a mount vert a fir tree ppr. surmounted by a Highland broadsword, or claymore, on the point of which in dexter fess point a royal crown of Scotland all ppr. on a canton az. a trefoil slipped or, for Mac Alpine; 2nd and 3rd, ar. a shakefork gu. betw. a trefoil slipped vert in chief, and in fess two mullets sa., for Cunningham. *Crest*—Out of a ducal coronet or, a thistle erect, flowered and leaved ppr. *Motto*—E'en do bide spare not.

M'Anaspog (Anglice, the Bishop's son; Reg. Ulster's Office). Per fess or and erm. a fess az. betw. in chief a bishop's hat vert, and in base two gem rings of the first, gemmed of the third. *Crest*—Out of a ducal coronet or, a rock ppr.

M'Andrew (London, 1785). Sa. an eagle displ. or, in the dexter talon a dagger ppr. a bordure ar. charged with six stars gu. *Crest*—A galley, oars erected in saltire sa. and flags gu. *Motto*—Fortuna juvat.

M'Andrew (Ceylon, 1850). Sa. an eagle displ. or, in the dexter talon a dagger ppr. a bordure ar. charged with three lozenges gu. on a chief of the fourth in saltire a sword in bend az. hilted and pommelled of the second, supporting on its point an antique crown of the second, and an oak tree eradicated in bend sinister ppr. *Crest*—A lion's head erased ppr. crowned with an antique crown or. *Motto*—Righ gu brath.

M'Ara (Col. Robert M'Ara, 42nd Regiment, 1814). Erm. a tree eradicated in bend ppr. surmounted of a sword in bend sinister also ppr. hilted and pommelled or, ensigned on the point with an imperial crown also ppr. *Crest*—A thistle, stalked and leaved, in front of a dexter arm from the elbow, holding a sword in bend sinister all ppr.

Mac Artain (Reg. Ulster's Office). Vert a lion ramp. or, on a chief ar. a dexter hand couped at the wrist gu. betw. in the dexter a crescent of the last, and in the sinister a mullet sa. *Crest*—A bear ramp. sa. muzzled or.

M'Arthur (Scotland). Az. a cross moline ar. betw. three antique crowns or. *Crest*—Two laurel branches in orle. *Motto*—Fide et opera.

M'Arthur-Stewart (Miltoun and Ascog, co. Bute). Quarterly, 1st and 4th, az. a Maltese cross betw. three antique crowns or; 2nd and 3rd, or, a fesse chequy az. and ar. within a bordure sa. charged with eight mascles of the third. *Crest*—A greyhound couchant within two branches of bay ppr. *Motto*—Fide et opera.

Macartney (confirmed by St. George, Ulster, 1678, to George Macartney, Esq., of Belfast; descended from Auchinleck, in Scotland, whose arms were certified by Erskine, Lord Lyon of that kingdom). Or, a buck trippant gu. attired and unguled ar. a border of the second. *Crest*—An arm erect couped below the elbow ppr. holding a rose branch vert, flowered gu. *Motto*—Stimulat sed ornat.

Macartney (co. Antrim; Fun. Ent. Ulster's Office, 1684, Frances, wife of James Macartney, eldest son of George Macartney, late of Auchinleck, in Scotland, High Sheriff and J.P. co. Antrim, and nine times Mayor of Belfast). Ar. a stag trippant gu. attired and unguled or, a border of the second, over all a label of three points.

Macartney (*Earl Macartney*, extinct 1806). Or, a stag trippant gu. attired ar. a border of the second. *Crest*—A naked arm couped below the elbow, holding a branch of roses all ppr. *Supporters*—Dexter, a horse ar. hoofed or, bridled and charged on the body with three roses gu. leaved vert, seeded gold; sinister, a buck ar. attired and unguled or, collared chequy of the first and az. charged on the body with three trefoils slipped vert, and holding in the mouth a thistle slipped ppr. *Motto*—Mens conscia recti.

Macartney (Lish, co. Armagh, bart.). Same *Arms*. *Crest* —A hand holding a slip of a rose tree with three roses thereon all ppr. *Motto*—Mens conscia recti.

Macartney (Lissanoure, co. Antrim; exemplified to George Hume, Esq., of Dublin, on his assuming, by royal licence, 1814, the surname of Macartney only, under the will of his maternal grand-uncle, George, *Earl Macartney*). Or, a buck trippant gu. attired ar. a bordure of the second. *Crest*—A cubit arm erect, the hand grasping a rose branch in flower all ppr. *Motto*—Mens conscia recti.

Macartney (Ellison-Macartney; exemplified to John William Ellison, Esq., of The Palace, Clogher, co. Tyrone, only son of Rev. Thomas Ellison, by Catherine, his wife, second dau. of Arthur Chichester Macartney, Esq., on his assuming, by royal licence 1859. the additional surname and arms of Macartney). Quarterly, 1st and 4th, or, a

buck trippant gu. a bordure of the last, for Macartney; 2nd and 3rd, gu. on a chev. betw. three eagles' heads erased ar. a trefoil slipped vert, for Ellison. *Crests*—1st, Macartney: A cubit arm erect, the hand grasping a rose branch flowered all ppr.; motto over, Stimulat sed ornat. 2nd, Ellison: A buck's head erased ppr. charged on the neck with a trefoil slipped vert. *Motto*—Spe gaudeo.

Macartney (Mickle Leathes, Auchinleck, and Blacket, co Kirkcudbright; derived, it is affirmed, from Daniel Macarthy, who went from Ireland to North Britain, and founded the family of Macartney). Or, a buck trippant gu. attired ar. within a bordure of the second. The *Crest* of the Auchinleck branch was, a dexter hand holding a slip of a rose bush ppr. *Motto*—Stimulat sed ornat.

Macaulay (Ardincaple, co. Argyll). Gu. two arrows in saltire ar. surmounted of a fess chequy of the second and first betw. three buckles or.

Macaulay (Edinburgh, 1672). The same, within a bordure indented or. *Crest*—A boot couped at the ankle, thereon a spur all ppr. *Motto*—Dulce periculum.

Macaulay (*Baron Macaulay ;* extinct 1859). Gu. two arrows in saltire, points downward ar. surmounted by as many barrulets compony or and az. betw. two buckles in pale of the third, a bordure engr. also of the third. *Crest* —Upon a rock a boot ppr. thereon a spur or. *Supporters*— Two herons ppr. *Motto*—Dulce periculum.

M'Auliffe (an ancient Sept in the province of Munster, of the same race as McCarthy. Reg. Ulster's Office). Ar. three mermaids with combs and mirrors in fess az. betw. as many mullets of the last. *Crest*—A boar's head couped or.

Mac Awley (an Irish Sept; descended from Nial, of the Nine Hostages, Monarch of Ireland, 375; Reg. Ulster's Office). Ar. a lion ramp. gu. armed and langued az. in chief two dexter hands couped at the wrist of the second. *Crest*—A demi lion ramp. gu.

Mac Awley, or Magawley (Williamstown, co. Westmeath: Fun. Ent. Ulster's Office, 1638, Mortogh McAwley or Magawley, gent.). Same *Arms* and *Crest*, a crescent for diff.

M'Barnet (Torridon, co. Ross, 1865). Az. a hart's head cabossed, attired with ten tynes ar. a chief embattled of the last. *Crest*—A hand grasping a sword in bend ppr. *Motto*— Sic ad astra.

M'Bean (Inverness, Scotland, 1672). Quarterly, 1st, or, a lion ramp. gu.; 2nd, ar. a dexter hand couped apaumée gu.; 3rd, ar. a sword in pale within a bordure indented gu.; 4th, or, a lymphad, her oars in saltire sa. *Crest*—A cat sejant ppr. *Motto*—Touch not a cat, but a glove.

M'Beath (Scotland). Gu. a dexter arm issuing from the base, holding a sword erect, and on the point thereof a wivern all ar.

M'Beath (Scotland). Az. a chev. betw. two mullets in chief and a crescent in base ar.

M'Beth (London; descended of Scotland, 1678). Gu. a dexter hand issuing from the base, holding on the point of a sword in pale ppr. a dragon reguard. or, all within a bordure of the last. *Crest*—A serpent's head couped ppr. *Motto*— Conjuncta virtuti fortuna.

M'Blane (co. Wigton). Ar. on a fess sa. a mullet betw. two crescents of the first, in base a rose gu.

Mac Brady (Toneymore, co. Cavan; an ancient Irish family, formerly Barons of Lurgtee, same co.). Sa. in the sinister base a dexter hand couped at the wrist ppr. pointing with the index finger to the sun in splendour in the dexter chief or.

Mac Brady (allowed by Hawkins, Ulster, 1766, to James Bernard Mac Brady, Count of the Holy Roman Empire, Knight of the Order of Maria Theresa). Same *Arms*. *Crest* —A cherub ppr. wings or. *Motto*—Claritate dextra.

M'Braid. Ar. on a fesse gu. three mullets of the field. *Crest*—A dexter hand gu. holding a bible ar.

M'Braire (Netherwood, co. Dumfries). Ar. a fesse gu. betw. three stars in chief and a lion ramp. in base of the last. *Crest*—A lion ramp. gu. *Motto*—In defiance.

M'Brayne (Glasgow, 1773). Gu. two lions pass. guard. in pale per pale or and ar. *Crest*—A dexter arm issuing out of a ducal coronet grasping a sword all ppr. *Motto*— Fortis ceu leo fidus.

M'Brayne (Glenbranter, co. Argyll, 1871). Same *Arms*, quartered with M'Nachten, of that Ilk. Same *Crest* and *Motto*.

M'Brayne (Summerlee, co. Lanark, 1791). As M'Brayne, of Glasgow, within a bordure ar. charged in the flanks with two cross crosslets fitchée az. and as many saltires couped in chief and base vert. *Crest*—A demi lion ramp. or, issuing from a ducal coronet ppr. *Mottoes*—Over the crest. I hope in God; below the shield: The righteous are bold as a lion.

Mac Bride (*Earl of Angus*). Gu. a cinquefoil or.

Macbride (England). Gu. three chevronels betw. as many escallops ar. *Crest*—On a chapeau a salamander in flames ppr.

Macbride (J. D. MACBRIDE, D.C.L., Principal of Magdalen Hall, Oxford). Ar. on a chev. betw. three fishes gu. a rose of the field in chief chequy of the first and second.

M'Call (Scotland). Ar. two mullets in chief gu. and a pheon in base az.

M'Call (Daldowie, co. Lanark). Gu. two arrows in saltire ar. surmounted by a fess chequy of the second and sa. betw. three buckles also of the second, all within a bordure engr. or. *Crest*—A leg in armour, couped at the calf ppr. and spurred or. *Motto*—Dulce periculum.

M'Callum, or Malcolm (Scotland). Ar. a saltire az. betw. four bucks' heads couped gu.

M'Callum (KELLIE-MCCALLUM, of Braco, co. Perth). Quarterly, 1st and 4th, ar. on a saltire az. betw. a stag's head erased in chief gu. and an oak tree eradicated and lying fessways in base vert five mullets or; 2nd and 3rd, or, a saltire sa. in chief a fleur-de-lis az., for KELLIE. *Crest*—A tower or, masoned sa. *Motto*—In ardua tendit.

M'Callum (England). Az. three cinquefoils ar. *Crest*—A tower ppr. cupola and flag gu.

Mac Can (Lords of Clanbrassel, co. Armagh; descended from CANA, Lord of Clanbrassel, younger son of MAHON, Lord of Oriel, ancestor of MAC MAHON, co. Monaghan; Reg. Ulster's Office). Az. fretty or, on a fess ar. a boar pass. gu. *Crest*—A salmon naiant ppr. *Motto*—Crescit sub pondere virtus.

Mac Cartan (Chiefs of Kinelarty or Mac Cartan's country, co. Down; ANTHONY MAC CARTAN followed James II. to France, and became Captain in the Irish Brigade there; Reg. Ulster's Office). Vert a lion ramp. or, on a chief ar. a crescent betw. two dexter hands couped at the wrist gu. *Crest*—A lance erect or, headed ar. entwined with a snake descending vert. *Motto*—Buailim se: I strike him.

McCarthy (Chiefs of Carbery and Muskerry, co. Cork, a powerful Irish Sept, descended from CARTACH, King of Desmond prior to the English invasion, the Chief of which was styled THE MCCARTHY MORE). Ar. a stag trippant, attired and unguled or.

McCarthy (*Earl of Clancare* and *Viscount Valentia*, extinct; DONOGH MCCARTHY MORE, seventh in descent from CORMAC MORE MCCARTHY, was so created 1556, *d. s. p. m.*). Ar. a stag trippant gu. attired and unguled or.

McCarthy (*Earl of Clancarty and Viscount Muskerry*, attainted 1690; CORMAC OGE MCCARTHY, of Blarney, descended from DERMOT MCCARTY, second son of CORMAC MORE MCCARTHY, was created a viscount, 1628; his son, second viscount, was created an earl, 1658). Same Arms. *Crest*—A dexter arm in armour ppr. cuffed ar. erect and couped at the wrist, holding in the hand a lizard both also ppr. *Supporters*—Two angels ppr. vested ar. habited gu. winged or, each holding in the exterior hand a shield, thereon a human head affrontée erased. *Motto*—Forti et fideli nihil difficile. *Another Motto*, borne by DERMOT MCCARTHY, *Viscount Muskerry*—Ex arduis perpetuum nomen.

McCarthy (Carrignavar, co. Cork; the present male representative of the Clan CARTHY descended from DONEL MCCARTHY, who built Carrignavar, brother of CORMAC OGE MCCARTHY, father of the first Viscount Muskerry). Same Arms. *Crest*—A dexter arm in mail ar. holding in the hand a lizard both ppr.

McCarthy (MCCARTHY-REAGH, the second Sept in order of the Clan CARTY, descended from DONEL MORE MCCARTHY, second son of DONEL MORE MCCARTHY, THE MCCARTHY MORE. The Chief of this Sept was known as THE MCCARTHY REAGH). Same Arms. *Crest*—A dexter arm erect, couped at the elbow, vested az. cuffed ar. holding in the hand ppr. a lizard vert. *Motto*—Fortis ferox et celer.

McCarthy (Springhouse, co. Tipperary; descended from THE MCCARTHY REAGH; allowed by Hawkins, Ulster, 1772). Same Arms. *Crest*—A dexter arm erect, couped at the elbow, vested az. cuffed ar. holding in the hand a lizard both ppr. *Motto*—Fortis ferox et celer.

McCarthy (Kilbrittain and Rupella, co. Cork; allowed by Hawkins, Ulster, 1767, to CHARLES MCCARTHY, Knt. of St. Louis, Captain in the French Navy, descended from THE MCCARTHY REAGH). Same Arms and Crest.

Mac Carthy Glas (Gleannacroim, co. Cork, "the Slught Ferlimy," or race of Felim, descended from CORMAC DONN, younger son of DONAL CAOMH, Chief of Carbery, A.D. 1311; of the family MAC CARTHY GLAS was the late Sir CHARLES MAC CARTHY, Governor of Ceylon, and to it belongs the

present FLORENCE MAC CARTHY, Esq., of West Down House, North Devon). Same Arms, &c.

Mac Carthy (MAC CARTHY LERAGH; allowed by Betham, Ulster, to Lieut.-Col. CHARLES MAC CARTHY, Lieut.-Governor of the Island of Senegal, 1812; descended from DONEL MAC CARTHY LERAGH, Esq., of Manshie, temp. James I.). Erm. a stag trippant gu. attired and unguled or. *Crest*—Out of a ducal coronet or, an arm embowed, vested az. cuffed ar. the hand holding a lizard ppr. *Motto*—Lamh laidir a-buagh.

McCartron (Reg. Ulster's Office). Ar. a lion ramp. gu. armed and langued az. in chief two dexter hands couped at the wrist of the second.

M'Casland (Newlandmuir, co. Lanark, 1863). Or, a lion ramp. sa. holding in his dexter paw a scymitar in bend ppr. betw. two mullets of the third pierced of the field in chief and a pheon pointing upwards az. in base. *Crest*—A dexter hand erect ppr. holding up a ducal cap tufted on the top with a rose gu. within two branches of laurel disposed orleways also ppr. *Motto*—Audaces juvo.

Mac Causland (Fruithill, co. Londonderry; confirmed to MARCUS MAC CAUSLAND, Esq., third son of CONOLLY MAC CAUSLAND, of Fruithill). Or, a boar's head erased betw. three boars pass. az. *Crest*—A boar's head erased az. armed or, langued gu. and charged with a crescent of the second. *Motto*—Virtus sola nobilitat.

Mac Causland (Bessbrooke, co. Londonderry). Same Arms and Motto. *Crest*—On a chapeau gu. turned up erm. a boar's head erased, as in the arms.

Mac Causland (Strahane, co. Tyrone). Or, a lion ramp. sa. holding in the dexter paw a sabre ppr. within a double tressure flory counterflory of the second. *Crest*—A hand couped, holding a duke's coronet or cap of maintenance surrounded with two laurel branches wreathed all ppr., motto over, Audaces Juvo. *Motto*—Clarior hinc honos.

Macclesfield (Staveley or Stayley, co. Chester). Gu. a cross engr. erm.

Macclesfield (Maer, co. Stafford). Same Arms. *Crest*—Out of a ducal coronet or, a goat's head ar. armed gold, holding in the mouth a sprig of rose-tree vert.

Macclesfield, Earl of. See PARKER.

Macclesfield, Abbey of (co. Chester). Gu. a mitre betw. three garbs or.

M'Chlery (Kildrochit, co. Wigtown, and London, 1840). Az. on a chev. ar. betw. a ship in full sail or, placed betw. a cross crosslet fitchée and a palm tree eradicated fessways in chief of the second, and in base the figure of Commerce of the third, three roses gu. *Crest*—A thistle ppr. *Motto*—Labore et honore.

Mac Chlery (Gardin, Scotland). Or, a chev. az. betw. three roses gu.

M'Cleish (Maryfield, co. Edinburgh). Ar. within an orle gu. a lion ramp. az. betw. three crosses crosslet fitchée of the second. *Crest*—A cross crosslet fitchée gu. *Motto*—Love.

McClelland (Reg. Ulster's Office). Or, two chevronels gu. a border engr. of the last. *Crest*—An arm in armour embowed, the hand holding a sword piercing a negro's head couped all ppr. *Motto*—Think on.

McClintock (Trintagh, co. Donegal, Londonderry, and co. Tyrone; allowed by Betham, Ulster). Per pale gu. and az. a chev. erm. betw. three escallops, that in the dexter chief or, in the sinister ar. and in the base per pale of the fourth and last. *Crest*—A lion pass. ar. *Motto*—Virtute et labore.

McClintock (Baron *Rathdonnell*). Per pale gu. and az. a chev. erm. betw. three escallops ar. *Crest*—A lion pass. ppr. *Supporters*—Dexter, a lion; and sinister, a leopard, both ppr. each gorged with a collar erm. and charged on the shoulder with an escallop ar. *Motto*—Virtute et labore.

McClintock (Hampstead Hall, co. Londonderry). Per pale gu. and az. a chev. erm. betw. three escallops ar. *Crest*—A lion pass. ppr. *Motto*—Virtute et labore.

McClintock-Bunbury. See BUNBURY.

M'Clure (Belmont and Dundela, co. Down, bart.). Ar. on a chev. engr. az. betw. two roses in chief gu. and a sword point downwards in base of the second, a mullet or. *Crest*—A tower domed ppr. from the top a flag ar. thereon a rose gu. *Motto*—Spectemur agendo.

Mac Cochlan (JOHN OGE MAC COCHLAN, Chief of his Sept; Reg. Ulster's Office). Ar. three lions pass. guard. gu. crowned or. *Motto*—Ceart na suas.

Mac Cochlan (Reg. Ulster's Office). Quarterly, sa. and as four nags' heads couped counterchanged.

McCoghlan (Cloghan, King's co.; Fun. Ent. Ulster's Office, 1629, GARRETT MCCOGHLAN, son and heir of Sir JOHN MCCOGHLAN, Knt.). Gu. three lions pass. guard. in pale ar.

Crest—A dexter arm embowed, vested gu. holding in the hand a sword both ppr.

Mac Colgan (confirmed by Hawkins, Ulster, to JOHN MAC COLGAN, Esq., descended from an ancient family of that name, seated at Kilcoglan, in the King's co.). Az. a lion ramp. or, betw. three pheons, points down ar. *Crest*—A dexter arm embowed in armour, the hand grasping a spear thrust through a stag's head couped all ppr.

Mac Colgan, or Cologan (Island of Teneriffe; allowed by Hawkins, Ulster, 1773, to THOMAS and FRANCIS XAVERIA COLOGAN, *alias* MAC COLGAN, sons of JOHN COLOGAN, *alias* MAC COLGAN, of same place, and grandsons of DENIS MAC COLGAN, Esq., of Loughlinstown, co. Meath, descended from Kilcolgan). Same *Arms* and *Crest*. *Motto*—Virtus probata florescit.

Mac Concaled (Ireland). Per fesse wavy ar. and vert, in chief three crosses crosslet gu. and in base a salmon naiant of the first. *Crest*—Two trees couped and raguled in saltire ppr. bound by a garland of leaves vert.

M'Connell (Kintyre, co. Argyll). Quarterly, 1st, az. a lion ramp. ar.; 2nd, or, a dexter hand gu. grasping a cross crosslet fitchée az.; 3rd, or, a lymphad sa.; 4th, per pale ar. and az. a rock gu.

M'Connell (Carsriggan, co. Wigtown, and Cressbrook, co. Derby, 1860). Or, in dexter chief a dexter arm couped in fess gu. the hand holding a cross crosslet fitchée erect sa. in sinister chief a galley, her sails furled and oars in action of the third, flagged of the second, and in base a lion ramp. also of the second, on a chief of the second three trefoils slipped of the first. *Crest*—A stag's head erased gu. charged in the neck with a trefoil slipped or. *Motto*—Victor in arduis.

M'Connell (Manchester, 1860). As the last, with the chief engr. Same *Crest* and *Motto*.

M'Connell (Queensland, 1860). As the last, with the chief invected. Same *Crest* and *Motto*.

McConnell (co. Dublin). Per fess ar. and vert a stag trippant ppr. betw. three trefoils slipped counterchanged. *Crest*—A stag's head erased ar. charged on the neck with a trefoil slipped vert.

M'Cormack (Scotland). Ar. a fesse dancettée betw. three eagles displ. gu.

M'Cormick (Ireland). Ar. a fesse dancettée gu. betw. three eagles displ. az. a bordure engr. sa. *Crest*—A dexter hand holding a spear in pale ppr.

M'Corquodell (that Ilk and Phantillans, co. Argyll). Ar. a demi stag gu. naissant out of a fesse tortille of the second and first. *Crest*—A stag standing at gaze, attired gu. *Motto*—Vivat rex.

Mac Costello (Reg. Ulster's Office). Or, three fusils az. *Crest*—A falcon ppr. belled and jessed or.

Mac Cullen (co. Donegal; Reg. Ulster's Office). Ar. a chev. betw. three ravens sa. beaked and legged az.

M'Culloch (Myrtoun, co. Wigton, bart.). Erm. fretty gu. *Crest*—A hand throwing a dart ppr. *Motto*—Vi et animo.

M'Culloch (Muill, co. Wigton). Erm. fretty gu. within a bordure indented of the second.

M'Culloch (Barholm, co. Kirkcudbright; in 1814, representative of Myrtoun and of Muill). Erm. a fret engr. gu. on an escutcheon az. three wolves' heads erased or. *Crest*—A hand throwing a dart ppr. *Supporters*—Two men in armour, each holding a spear all ppr. *Motto*—Vi et animo.

M'Culloch (Drummoral, co. Wigton). Erm. fretty gu. a bordure engr. of the second. *Motto*—Verus et sedulus.

M'Culloch (Piltoun, co. Edinburgh). Erm. a fret engr. gu. *Crest*—An ermine ppr. *Motto*—Sine maculâ.

M'Cullock (England). Ar. a saltire engr. gu. in chief a boar's head erased az. *Crest*—A triangular harrow gu.

McCurten (Reg. Ulster's Office; HUGH BUIDHE McCURTEN, Chief of his Sept, published an Irish dictionary in Paris, 1732). Vert in front of a lance in pale or, a stag trippant ar. attired gold, betw. three crosses crosslet of the second, two and one, and as many trefoils slipped of the third, one and two. *Crest*—In front of two lances in saltire ar. headed or, an Irish harp sa.

Mac Daniel (Reg. Ulster's Office). Az. a lion ramp. or.

Mac Daniel. See McDONNELL.

Mac Deargan (Reg. Ulster's Office). Vert a griffin segreant or. *Crest*—A pewit or plover ppr.

Macdiarmid (Glenlyon, co. Perth). Gu. three boars' heads couped in fess ar. betw. as many crosses crosslet fitchée of the last. *Crest*—A lion ramp. ar. betw. the paws a garland of flowers ppr. *Motto*—Non immemor beneficii.

McDiarmot (Reg. Ulster's Office). Az. three boars' heads couped ar. langued gu. betw. two crosses crosslet in chief and one in base or. *Crest*—A lion ramp. ar. holding a sceptre or.

Mac Dermot (Chiefs of Moylurg, co. Roscommon; an ancient Irish Sept, descended from MAOLROONA, second son of TEIGE, King of Connaught in the 7th century). Ar. on a chev. gu. betw. three boars' heads erased az. tusked and bristled or, as many cross crosslets or. *Crest*—A demi lion ramp. az. holding in the dexter paw a sceptre crowned or. motto over, Honor et virtus. *Motto*—Honor probataque virtus.

McDermot (Coolavin, co. Sligo, commonly called *Prince of Coolavin*, representative of the chiefs of Moylurg). Same *Arms* and *Crest*. *Motto*—Honore et virtute.

McDermot (MAC DERMOTT ROE; Alderford, co. Roscommon). *Arms, Crest,* and *Motto,* same as MAC DERMOT, of Moylurg.

Mac Dermot (Carrig, co. Roscommon; Fun. Ent. Ulster's Office, 1637, BRIAN MAC DERMOT, eldest son of BRYAN MAC DERMOT, of same place). Ar. three boars pass. az. armed and bristled or. *Crest*—A boar's head erased az.

Mac Dermot (granted by Carney, Ulster, 1690, to TERENCE MAC DERMOT, Esq., Lord Mayor of Dublin, descended from MAC DERMOT, of Carrig, co. Roscommon). Ar. on a chev. engr. gu. betw. three boars pass. az. armed and bristled or, as many bezants. *Crest*—A demi lion az. holding betw. the paws a tower ar. *Motto*—Honor virtutis præmium.

Mac Dermot (Rostaley, co. Fermanagh; Reg. Ulster's Office). Ar. a fess gu. betw. three boars pass. az. armed and bristled or.

McDermott (granted by Betham, Ulster, to ANDREW McDERMOTT, Esq., of Liverpool, son of JOHN MAC DERMOTT, Esq., of Toomavarra, co. Tipperary, who resumed the ancient family surname of MAC DERMOTT instead of that of DERMODY, which his ancestor had adopted). Or, on a chev. az. betw. three boars' heads erased az. as many cross crosslets of the field. *Crest*—A demi lion ramp. gu. holding in the dexter paw a sceptre or. *Motto*—Honor et virtus.

McDermott (confirmed to JOHN JOSEPH McDERMOTT, M.D., F.R.C.S.I., Surgeon-Major Bengal Medical Service, third son of WILLIAM McDERMOTT, of Dublin; descended from the co. Roscommon family of McDERMOTT). Ar. on a chev. gu. betw. three boars' heads erased az. armed and bristled or, an eastern crown betw. two crosses crosslet of the last. *Crest*—Out of an eastern crown or, a demi lion ramp. az. charged on the shoulder with a cross crosslet of the first, and holding betw. the paws a sceptre erect, surmounted by a regal crown all ppr. *Motto*—Honore et virtute.

McDonagh (Ballylowy, co. Carlow; impalement Fun. Ent. Ulster's Office, 1619, REDMOND KEATING, of Clonogh, in same co. whose wife was ELIZABETH, dau. of MORTAGH McDONAGH). Ar. a lion pass. gu. betw. in chief a mullet sa. and in base two crescents of the second.

Macdonald (ancient Lords of the Isles). Or, an eagle displ. with two heads az. (some have the eagle with only one head) surmounted by a lymphad sa. in the dexter chief point a dexter hand couped gu. *Crest*—A raven sa. standing on a rock az.

Macdonald (Slate, Isle of Skye, bart., 1625). Quarterly, 1st and 4th, ar. a lion ramp. gu.; 2nd, or, a dexter arm in armour couped in fess ppr. the hand holding a cross crosslet fitchée gu.; 3rd, or, a lymphad, oars and sails sa. flags flying gu.; 4th, vert a salmon naiant ppr.

Macdonald (BOSVILLE-MACDONALD, *Baron Macdonald*, of Slate, co. Antrim). Quarterly, 1st and 4th, counter-quartered, as the last; 2nd and 3rd, ar. five fusils in fess gu. in chief three boars' heads sa., for BOSVILLE. *Crest*—A dexter arm in armour couped in fess ppr. the hand also ppr. holding a cross crosslet fitchée gu. *Supporters*—Two leopards ppr. collared or. *Motto*—Per mare, per terras.

Macdonald (East Sheen, co. Surrey, bart.). Quarterly, 1st, ar. a lion ramp. gu.; 2nd, or, a hand in armour holding a cross crosslet fitchée gu.; 3rd, a row-galley, the sails furled sa.; 4th, ar. a salmon naiant in fesse ppr. *Crest*—A hand in armour holding a cross crosslet fitchée gu. *Motto*—Per mare, per terras.

Macdonald (Moydart, Scotland, Captain of Clanranald). Quarterly, 1st, ar. a lion ramp. gu. armed or; 2nd, or, a dexter hand couped fessways, holding a cross crosslet fitchée gu.; 3rd, or, a lymphad, oars in saltire sa. and in base a salmon naiant in a sea vert; 4th, ar. an oak tree vert surmounted by an eagle or. *Crest*—A castle triple-towered ar. masoned sa. and issuing from the centre tower a dexter arm in armour embowed, grasping a sword all ppr. *Mottoes*—Over the crest: My hope is constant in thee, below the shield: Dhandeon co Heiragha.

Macdonald (Largie; heiress *m.* LOCKHART, of Carnwath).

Quarterly, 1st, or, a lion ramp. gu.; 2nd, or, a dexter hand issuing from the left of the shield ppr. holding a cross crosslet fitchée gu.; 3rd, ar. a lymphad, sails furled and oars in saltire sa.; 4th, vert a salmon naiant in fess ppr. *Crest*—A dexter arm from the shoulder ppr. holding a dagger in pale ppr. *Mottoes*—Over the crest: Semper pugnare paratus; below the shield: Pro patria.

Macdonald (Sir JOHN MACDONALD, K.C.B., 1818). As Slate, within a canton gu. charged with a mural crown or, in the first quarter. *Crest*—Out of an eastern crown or, a cubit arm erect ppr. encircled by a laurel wreath vert, in the hand a dagger erect also ppr. hilted and pommelled or.

Macdonald (General Sir JOHN MACDONALD, G.C.B., 1849). Quarterly, as Slate, within a bordure gu. *Crest and Motto*, as *Lord Macdonald*.

Macdonald (St. Martin's, co. Perth, 1849). Quarterly, as Slate, within a bordure az. charged with two mascles in chief ar. and a boar's head erased in base or. *Crest*—A demi lion gu. holding in his dexter paw a hand ppr. *Motto* —Per mare, per terras.

Macdonald (FOOTE-MACDONALD, heir of line of Knoydart, 1850). Quarterly, as Slate, within a bordure gu. charged with three antique crowns or. *Crest and Motto*, as *Lord Macdonald*.

Macdonald (Craig-na-Gower, co. Argyll, 1875). Quarterly, 1st, or, a lion ramp. gu.; 2nd, or, a dexter hand fessways couped at the wrist, holding a cross crosslet fitchée gu.; 3rd, or, a lymphad, sails furled sa.; 4th, per fess ar. and vert a salmon naiant ppr. *Crest*—A dexter arm in armour fessways couped below the elbow ppr. the hand holding a cross crosslet fitchée gu. *Motto*—Per mare, per terras.

Macdonald-Bowie (Holland. 1685). Quarterly, 1st, ar. a lion ramp. gu.; 2nd, az. a dexter hand couped fessways, holding a cross crosslet fitchée ar.; 3rd, or, a galley, oars in saltire sa.; 4th, per fess wavy ar. and vert, in base a fish naiant of the first, all within a bordure quarterly gu. and ar. *Crest*—The Holy Bible expanded ppr. *Motto*—Cœlestia sequor.

Macdonald-Lockhart. See LOCKHART.

Macdonald-Steuart. See STEUART.

Macdonell (Glengarry; descended from REGINALD, of Glengarry, son of JOHN, Lord of the Isles, *temp.* David Bruce; arms confirmed, 1870, to the heir male, ÆNEAS RANALD WESTROP MACDONELL). Or, an eagle displ. gu. surmounted by a lymphad sa. sails furled and rigged ppr. in the dexter chief a dexter hand couped of the second, in the sinister a cross crosslet fitchée of the third. *Crest*—A raven ppr. perched on a rock az., motto over, Cragan an Fhithich. *Supporters*—Two bears, each having an arrow pierced through the body all ppr. *Motto*—Per mare, per terras.

Macdonell (*Lord Macdonell and Arross*). As Glengarry.

Macdonell (Sir JOHN MACDONELL, G.C.B., brother of Glengarry, 1856). As Glengarry, within a bordure gu. Same *Crest* and *Motto*.

Macdonell (Morar, co. Inverness, 1860). Per chev. or and vert, in dexter chief a dexter hand fessways couped at the wrist gu. in sinister chief a cross crosslet fitchée of the third, and in base a two-headed eagle also of the first, surmounted of a galley also of the first, sails furled and rigged sa. *Crest*—A raven perching on a rock ppr. *Mottoes*—Over the crest: Faicilleach; below the shield: Per mare, per terras.

McDonnell (*Earl of Antrim*). Quarterly, 1st and 4th, McDONNELL, quarterly, 1st, or, a lion ramp. gu., 2nd, or, a dexter arm issuant from the sinister fess point out of a cloud ppr. in the hand a cross crosslet fitchée erect az., 3rd, ar. a lymphad, sails furled sa., 4th, per fesse az. and vert a dolphin naiant in fess ppr.; 2nd and 3rd, KERR, quarterly, 1st and 4th, az. a sun in splendour or, 2nd, gu. on a chev. ar. three unicorns' heads ar. as many mullets of the field, 3rd, sa. on a chev. betw. three unicorns' heads ar. as many mullets of the field. *Crests*—1st, McDONNELL: A dexter arm embowed fessways, couped at the shoulder. vested or, cuff ar. holding in the hand a cross crosslet fitchée erect az.; 2nd, KERR: A sun in splendour or. *Supporters* —Dexter, a savage wreathed about the temples and loins with ivy all ppr.; sinister, a falcon, wings inverted ppr. beaked, membered, and belled or. *Motto*—Sero sed serio.

McDonnell (Murlough and Kilmore, in Glens of Antrim. of the Clan IAN VOHR; descended from COLL KITTAGH, Chief of the Clan IAN VOHR, put to death by Argyll in 1647). Quarterly, 1st, or, a lion ramp. gu.; 2nd, or, a dexter arm issuant from the sinister fesse point out of a cloud ppr. in the hand a cross crosslet fitchée erect az.; 3rd, ar. a lymphad, sails furled sa.; 4th, per fesse az. and vert a dolphin naiant ppr. *Crest*—A dexter arm embowed fessewise, couped at the shoulder, vested or, cuff ar. holding in the

hand a cross crosslet fitchée erect az. *Motto*—Toujours prêt.

Mac Donnell (Moye, co. Antrim, bart., forfeited 1690; ALEXANDER MAC DONNELL, ninth son of Sir JAMES McGORLEY BOYE MAC DONNELL, brother of RANDAL, first *Earl of Antrim*, was created a bart. 1687; Sir RANDAL MAC DONNELL, third bart., adhered to James II., and was attainted). Or, a lion ramp. gu.

McDonnell (Dublin, bart., extinct 1875; Right Hon. ALEXANDER McDONNELL, Q.C., of the Murlough family, was created a bart. 1872, in consideration of his long and distinguished career in the public service, *d. s. p.*). Quarterly, 1st, or, a lion ramp. gu.; 2nd, or, a dexter arm issuant from the sinister fesse point out of a cloud ppr. in the hand a cross crosslet fitchée erect az.; 3rd, ar. a lymphad sails furled sa.; 4th, per fesse az. and vert a dolphin naiant ppr. on the centre point over all a trefoil slipped also ppr. *Crest*—A dexter arm embowed fesseways, vested or, cuffed ar. the hand holding a cross crosslet fitchée erect az. the arm charged with a trefoil slipped ppr. *Motto*—Toujours pret.

Mac Donnell (Connaught; arms from a monument in MACDONNELL'S Chapel, Ross Abbey, co. Galway). Az. an ancient galley, sails set and flags flying ar. betw. in chief a cross calvary on three grieces or, betw. in the dexter an increscent of the second, and in the sinister a dexter hand couped at the wrist apaumée ppr. and in base a salmon naiant also of the second. *Crest*—A unicorn pass. gu. *Motto*—His vinces.

Mac Donnell (confirmed to Rev. RICHARD MAC DONNELL, D.D., Provost of Trinity College, Dublin, and the descendants of his grandfather, RICHARD MAC DONNELL, of Peacockstown, co. Meath). Quarterly, 1st, or, a lion ramp. gu.; 2nd, or, a dexter arm issuant from the sinister fess point out of a cloud ppr. in the hand a cross crosslet fitchée erect az.; 3rd, ar. a lymphad sails furled sa.; 4th, per fess az. and vert a dolphin naiant in fess ppr. in the centre point over all a cross pattée per fess gu. and erminois. *Crest*—A dexter arm embowed fessways, vested or, cuffed ar. the hand holding a cross crosslet fitchée erect az. the arm charged with a cross pattée gu *Motto*—Toujours pret.

Mac Donnell (ARMSTRONG-MAC DONNELL; exemplified to WILLIAM EDWARD ARMSTRONG, of New Hall and Kilkee, co. Clare, J.P., D.L., third son of WILLIAM HENRY ARMSTRONG, M.P., of Mount Heaton, King's co., by BRIDGET, his wife, only dau. of Col. CHARLES MAC DONNELL, M.P., of New Hall and Kilkee, on his assuming by royal licence, 1858, the additional surname and arms of MAC DONNELL). Quarterly, 1st and 4th grand quarters, for MAC DONNELL, 1st and 4th, or, a lion ramp. gu., 2nd, or, a dexter arm issuant from the sinister fess point out of a cloud ppr. in the hand a cross crosslet fitchée erect az., 3rd, ar. a lymphad, sails furled sa., 4th, per fess az. and vert a fish naiant in fess ppr. on the centre point a crescent gu.; 2nd and 3rd grand quarters, for ARMSTRONG, gu. three dexter arms vambraced and embowed ppr. hands clenched also ppr. in the centre chief point a mullet or. *Crests*—1st, MAC DONNELL: A dexter arm embowed fessways, vested or, cuffed ar. the hand holding a cross crosslet fitchée erect az. the arm charged with a crescent gu.; 2nd, ARMSTRONG: A dexter arm vambraced fessways and embowed ppr. charged with a mullet gu. the hand grasping an armed leg couped at the thigh and bleeding also ppr. *Motto*—Toujours prêt.

Mac Donogh (Annagh, co. Sligo: descended from MAC DONOGH, of Craoghane, co. Roscommon; Fun Ent. Ulster's Office, 1630, CONNOR MAC DONOGH, eldest son and heir of MEANUS MAC DONOGH). Per chev. invected or and vert, in chief two lions pass. guard. gu. in base a boar pass. ar. armed and bristled of the first, langued of the third. *Crest*— A dexter arm erect, couped at the elbow, vested az. cuffed ar. (another, the arm in armour embowed ppr.) holding in the hand a sword erect, entwined with a lizard all ppr. *Motto*—Virtutis gloria merces.

M'Dougal (Lorn; represented by Dunolly, co. Argyll). Quarterly, 1st and 4th, az. a lion ramp. ar.; 2nd and 3rd, or, a lymphad sa. with a flame of fire ppr. issuing from the topmast. *Crest*—An arm in armour embowed ppr. holding a cross crosslet fitchée gu. *Motto*—Vincere vel mori.

Mac Dougall (Makerston, co. Roxburgh; ANN MARIA HAY MAKDOUGAL, eldest dau. and heiress of Sir HENRY HAY MAKDOUGAL, Bart., of Makerston, *m.* General Sir THOMAS BRISBANE, Bart.: the prior heiress of the MAC DOUGALS, BARBARA, only child of HENRY MAC DOUGAL, of Makerston, *m.* Sir GEORGE HAY, Bart., of Alderston, who, in consequence, assumed the additional surname of MAC DOUGAL, and was grandfather, by the said BARBARA, of Lady BRISBANE). *L L* a lion ramp. ar. crowned with an antique crown or, armed and langued gu. within a border of the second, charged with six frasiers of the first. *Crest*—A lion issuing guard. ppr. holding in his dexter paw a cross crosslet fitchée gu. *Motto*—Fear God.

M'Dowall (Garthland, co. Wigton). Az. a lion ramp. ar. crowned or. *Crest*—A lion's paw erased and erect ppr. *Motto*—Vincere vel mori.

M'Dowall (Castle Semple, co. Renfrew, and Garthland, cadet of the last). As the last, with a crescent of the second in chief for diff. *Crest*—A lion's paw erased and erect, and holding a dagger ppr. *Motto*—Fortis in arduis.

M'Dowall (London and Scotland, 1680). Az. a lion ramp. ar. crowned with an antique crown or, within a bordure chequy of the first and second. *Crest*—A lion's gamb erect and erased ppr. holding an olive branch vert. *Motto*—Vincam vel moriar.

M'Dowall (Logan, co. Wigton). Az. a lion ramp. ar. gorged with an antique crown or. *Crest*—A tiger's head erased, crowned with an imperial crown, with a lion's paw issuing from a cloud grasping the crown from the tiger's head ppr. *Supporters*—Two lions crowned with antique crowns ppr. *Mottoes*—Above the crest: Usurpari nolo; below the shield: Victoria.

M'Dowall (Portugal, 1767). Az. a lion ramp. ar. gorged with an antique crown or, a bordure counter-compony gu. and of the last. *Crest*—A lion ramp. holding in his paw a sword erect ppr. *Motto*—Sic itur ad astra.

M'Dowall (Neilsland, Scotland). Per fesse wavy az. and or, on the first a lion ramp. ar. gorged with an antique crown vert.

M'Dowall (Freugh, co. Wigton). Az. a lion ramp. ar. gorged with an antique crown and imperially crowned or. *Crest*—A lion's gamb erect and erased. *Supporters*—Two wild men wreathed about the head and middle with laurel, holding in their hands flaming daggers pointing upward all ppr. *Mottoes*—Over the crest: Vincet vel mori; under the arms: Pro Deo, Rege, et Patria.

M'Dowall (Crichen, co. Wigton). Az. a lion ramp. ar. gorged with an antique crown or, on a canton ar. a hart's head cabossed gu. *Crest* and *Motto*, as of Logan.

M'Dowall (Culgroat, co. Wigton). Az. a lion ramp. ar. gorged with an antique crown or, within a bordure of the second charged with eight sinister hands couped gu. *Crest*, as M'Dowall, of Logan.

M'Dowall (Stodrig, co. Roxburgh). Az. a lion ramp. ar. gorged with an open crown or, holding betw. the paws a man's heart ppr. *Crest*—A lion's gamb. *Motto*—Vincere vel mori.

M'Dowall (Edinburgh). Az. a lion ramp. ar. ducally crowned or, on a canton of the second three piles gu. *Crest*—A demi lion ar. royally crowned or. *Motto*—Vincere vel mori.

Mac Dowell (an Irish Sept in Ulster, descended of the race of Mac Donnel; Reg. Ulster's Office). Az. a lion ramp, ar. crowned or, ducally gorged gu. *Crest*—A lion ramp. or, crowned gu.

M'Duff (*Earl of Fife*). Or, a lion ramp. gu. *Crest*—A demi lion ramp. gu.

Mace (Exeter, co. Devon; William Mace, Visit. Devon, 1620, son of Roger Mace, and grandson of William Mace, who was born in Normandy, came to England *temp*. Henry VIII., and settled at Chard, co. Somerset). Az. a chev. ar. betw. in chief two mullets or, and in base a dexter gauntlet lying fessways of the second, holding a mace erect of the third.

Mace (Tenterden, co. Kent). Same *Arms*. *Crest*—An arm in armour ppr. holding in the hand a mace erect or.

Mac Egan (Bally-mac-Egan, co. Tipperary; confirmed by Hawkins, Ulster, 1715, to Darby Egan, Esq., Barrister-at-law, son of John Egan, Esq., of Uskean, grandson of Constance Egan, Esq., of Killnelagh, and great-grandson of Daniel Mac Egan, Esq., of Bally-mac-Egan). Quarterly, 1st, gu. a tower ar. supported on either side by a man in complete armour, each holding in the interior hand a battle axe all ppr. in chief a snake fessways or; 2nd and 3rd, or, on a bend vert three plates; 4th, gu. a tower betw. two men in complete armour, as in the 1st quarter, on the tower a swan ppr. *Crest*—A tower ar. issuant from the top a demi man in armour couped at the knees, holding in the dexter hand a battle axe all ppr. *Motto*—Fortitude et prudentiâ.

Maceldon, or Malcedon. Gu. an eagle displ. with two heads ar.

Mac Eligot (co. Kerry; Reg. Ulster's Office). Az. a tower triple-towered ar.

Mac Eniery (Reg. Ulster's Office). Ar. an eagle displ. vert. *Crest*—A falcon close belled ppr.

Mac Evoy (Tobertinan, co. Meath : an ancient Irish Sept of the Clan Colla, commemorated by O'Heidhrin in his topographical poems of Ireland, formerly chiefs of the territory of Hy-Mac-Vais, co. Westmeath, now known as the barony of Moygoish : they also ruled over a territory in the present barony of Stradbally, in the Queen's co.; Edward McEvoy, Esq., J.P., of Tobertinan, late M.P. for co. Meath, is eldest son of the late James McEvoy, Esq., and Theresa Meredith, his wife, dau. and co-heir of Sir Joshua Colles Meredyth, eighth bart. of Greenhills). Per fess az. and per pale or and erm. a fess gu. issuant therefrom a demi lion ar. in the dexter base a dexter hand couped at the wrist of the fourth. *Crest*—A cubit arm erect, vested gu. cuffed erminois, in the hand a sword ppr. *Motto*—Bear and forbear.

MacEvoy-Netterville. See Netterville.

Macey. Az. a chev. ar. betw. two mullets pierced or, in chief and a dexter gauntlet supporting a mace in base of the last.

M'Ewan (Muckly, co. Argyll). Per fess az. and or, in chief a lion ramp. ar. gorged with an antique crown vert, in base a garb of the first.

M'Ewan (Glenboig, co. Stirling, 1796). Ar. four roses in saltire gu. in the centre of the field a sheaf of five arrows ppr. banded az. *Crest*—A dexter arm couped at the shoulder, the elbow resting on the wreath and grasping a scynitar all ppr. *Motto*—Pervicax recte.

M'Ewan (Glasgow, 1847). Az. on a fess ar. betw. a lion ramp. in chief of the second and a garb in base or, a ship in full sail on the sea betw. a thistle and a stalk of sugarcane, both slipped ppr. a bordure gyronny of eight of the third and sa. *Crest*—The trunk of an oak tree with a branch sprouting forth on either side ppr. *Motto*—Reviresco.

Macfarlan (that Ilk, and Arroquhar, co. Dumbarton). Ar. a saltire wavy (recorded in 1780 as engr.) betw. four roses gu. *Crest*—A demi savage grasping in his dexter hand a sheaf of arrows, and pointing with the sinister to an imperial crown or. *Supporters*—Two Highlandmen in belted plaids, with broadswords, and bows and arrows in full draught ppr. and on a compartment wavy the word " Lochsloy." *Motto*—This I'll defend.

M'Farlane (Keithtoun, Scotland). Ar. on a saltire wavy betw. four roses gu. a crescent of the field. *Crest*—A naked man holding forth a sheaf of arrows ppr. a crown or, standing by it. *Motto*—This I'll defend.

M'Farlane (Gartartan, co. Stirling, 1814). Ar. a saltire engr. gu. charged with an urcheon or. *Crest* and *Motto*, as Macfarlane, of that Ilk.

Macfie (Langhouse, co. Renfrew, and Airds, co. Argyll). Per fess wavy az. and or, in chief a sword ar. point downwards, hilted and pommelled of the second, and in base a lymphad sa. under sail of the third. *Crest*—A demi lion ramp. sa. *Motto*—Pro rege.

Macfie (Dreghorn, co. Edinburgh). Per fess nebuly az. and or, in chief a sword ar. point downwards, hilted and pommelled of the second, and in base a lymphad sa. under sail of the third. *Crest*—A demi lion ramp. ppr. *Motto*—Pro rege.

Mac Fingah (Reg. Ulster's Office). Erm. a lion pass. guard. or, on a chief az. a crescent betw. two roses of the second. *Crest*—An arm embowed in armour, the hand grasping a tilting spear all ppr.

Mac Garry (an Irish Sept of the same race as Mac Hugh; Reg. Ulster's Office). Ar. a lion ramp. betw. four trefoils slipped vert, in chief a lizard pass. of the last. *Crest*—A fox's head couped gu. holding in the mouth a snake ppr. *Motto*—Fear garbh ar mait.

M'Geachen (Dalquhat, Scotland). Or, a dexter hand gu.

Mac Gees. Gu. two swords chevronways, points meeting ppr. pommel and hilt or, betw. three boars' heads couped ar.

McGenis (ancient territorial Lords of Iveagh, in Dalraida (the present co. Down), who ranked as head of the Clanna Rory. In 1314, when Edward II. sought the aid of the Irish chieftains, he directed a letter to "Admilis Mac Anegus, Duci Hibernicorum de Onenagh," he being then The McGenis; Art McGenis, Lord of Iveagh, was treacherously taken prisoner, 1380, by Edmund Mortimer, *Earl of March*), Vert a lion ramp. or, on a chief ar. a dexter hand erect, couped at the wrist gu.

McGenis, or Magenis (*Viscount Iveagh*, extinct 1693; Sir Arthur Mc Genis, Knt., of Rathfriland, co. Down, was so created 1623). Same *Arms*. *Crest*—A boar pass. ppr. langued gu. armed and hoofed or. *Supporters*--Two bucks gu. langued az. crined, unguled, and gorged with collars gemel or. *Motto*—Sola salus servire Deo.

McGenis (Tollymore, co. Down: Phelim McGenis, *temp*. Charles II., whose dau. and heiress, Eleanor, m. William

HAMILTON, Esq., of Erenagh, co. Down, the great-grand-daughter of which marriage, Lady ANNE HAMILTON, sister and heiress of JAMES, last *Earl of Clanbrassil*, m. ROBERT, first *Earl of Roden;* Fun. Ent. Ulster's Office, WILLIAM HAMILTON, d. 26 Feb. 1686). Same *Arms*.

McGenis (Castle Wellan, co. Down; EVER McGENIS, Esq., *temp*. James I., whose descendant sold his estate to the ancestor of the *Earl Annesley*). Same *Arms*.

Mac Geoghegan (Moycashell, co. Westmeath; ROSS MAC GEOGHEGAN, chief of his name, forfeited his estates 1641;. Reg. Ulster's Office). Ar. a lion ramp. betw. three dexter hands couped at the wrist gu. *Crest*—A greyhound statant ar. *Motto*—Semper patriæ servire presto.

Mac Geoghegan (Ballymac-Hugh, Kilbeggan, and Tyrrels-pass, co. Westmeath; descended from ROSS MAC GEOGHEGAN, brother of CONNOR MAC GEOGHEGAN, chief of his name, *temp*. Henry VIII.; Reg. Ulster's Office). Same *Arms* and *Crest.*

Mac Geoghegan (Castletown, co. Westmeath: impalement Fun. Ent. Ulster's Office. 1614, Sir FRANCIS SHAEN, whose wife was MARY, dau. of CONLIE MAC GEOGHEGAN). Ar. a lion ramp. gu. armed and langued az. betw. three dexter hands couped at the wrist of the second.

Mac Geoghegan (Athboy, co. Meath; Fun. Ent. Ulster's Office, 1619, MARY, wife of THOMAS MAC GEOGHEGAN). Ar. a lion ramp. gu. armed and langued az. in chief two dexter hands couped at the wrist of the second.

Mac George (confirmed to ANDREW MAC GEORGE, of Glenarm, co. Dumbarton; descended from the BERMINGHAMS, *Barons of Athenry*). Per pale indented or and gu. in the centre point a crescent erm. *Crest*—An antelope's head erased ar. attired or, gorged with a collar dancettée gu. *Motto*—Pro veritate.

Macgeorge (confirmed to WILLIAM MACGEORGE, Esq., Lieut.-Col. Indian Army; descended from the BERMINGHAMS, *Barons of Athenry*). Per pale indented or and gu. in chief two mullets counterchanged. *Crest*—A dexter cubit arm, the hand grasping a sabre all ppr. and charged with a rose indented az. *Motto*—Dread God.

McGeough (Drumsill, co. Armagh; WALTER McGEOUGH, Esq., of that place, assumed the additional surname of BOND, by royal licence, 1824. See BOND). Per bend sa. and or, three leopards' faces counterchanged. *Crest*—A naked arm embowed, the hand holding a scymitar all ppr.

Mac Geraghty (an Irish Sept of the same race as the O'CONORS; descended from CAHIR, or CHARLES, King of Connaught; Reg. Ulster's Office). Ar. on a mount vert an oak tree ppr. in chief two falcons volant gu. *Crest*—On a mount vert an oak tree ppr. bent towards the dexter.

Mac Ghie (Balmaghie, co. Kirkcudbright). Sa. three leopards' faces or.

M'Gilchrist (Northbarr, 1672). Gu. a lion ramp. ar. within a bordure invecked of the second. *Crest*—A lion's paw in bend ar. *Motto*—Cogit in hostem.

M'Gill, or Makgill (Rankeillour, co. Fife). Gu. three. martlets ar. *Crest*—A martlet ar. *Motto*—In Domino confido.

M'Gill (Kemback, co. Fife, 1676). Gu. three martlets ar. within a bordure indented of the last. *Crest*—A martlet rising ppr. *Motto*—In Deo confido.

M'Gill (Kemback, 1771, as heir male of Rankeillour). Quarter-ly, 1st and 4th, gu. three martlets ar.; 2nd and 3rd, ar. an eagle displ. sa. beaked, langued. and membered gu. charged with another eagle displ. or, for RAMSAY, of Brakmouth. *Crest* —A martlet ar. *Supporters*—Dexter, a horse ar. maned, hoofed, and tailed or, gorged with a collar, whereto a chain is affixed passing betw. his forelegs and reflexed over his back of the last; sinister, a buck sa. armed, unguled, and tailed or, gorged and chained as the other. *Motto*—In Domino confido.

M'Gill (*Viscount of Oxenford*). Gu. three martlets or. *Crest*—A phœnix in flames ppr. *Supporters*—Dexter, a horse at liberty ar. maned and hoofed or, gorged with a viscount's coronet, thereto a chain attached of the last; sinister, a bull sa. collared and chained as the other. *Motto*—Sine fine.

M'Gill (Ballynester, Ireland, cadet of Oxenford). Gu. three martlets or, within a bordure ar. *Crest*—A phœnix in flames ppr. *Motto*—Sine sine.

M'Gill (Rumgally, co. Fife). Gu. three martlets ar. within a bordure engr. of the last. *Crest*—A martlet rising ppr. *Motto*—In Deo confido.

Mac Gill (Fun. Ent. Ulster's Office, 1677). Az. three doves ar.

Mac Gillafoyle. Az. two bars ar. *Crest*—A demi lion ramp. ar. holding betw. the paws a battle axe erect gu. blade also ar.

Mac Gilla-Patrick (an ancient Irish Sept who possessed

and held regal sway over the territory of Upper Ossory, in the present Queen's co., from whom descended the name and family of FITZ PATRICK, extinct *Barons* and *Earls of Upper Ossory*, and *Barons of Gowran*. DONEL MAC GILLA-PATRICK, Chief of Upper Ossory, submitted to Henry II. Reg. Ulster's Office). Sa. a saltire az. on a chief az. three fleurs-de-lis or.

Mac Gilleoun (Scotland). See M'LEAN.

Mac Gillicuddy (MAC GILLICUDDY of the Reeks, an ancient Irish Sept in co. Kerry; descended from the Sept of O'SULLIVAN MORE; granted by Carney, Ulster, 1688, to DONOUGH MAC GILLICUDDY, eldest son and heir of CONNOR MAC GILLICUDDY, MAC GILLICUDDY of the Reeks, Chief of his name). Gu. a wyvern or. *Crest*—A representation of Mac Gillicuddy's Reeks, co. Kerry, ppr. *Motto*—Sursum corda.

McGillikelly (Reg. Ulster's Office). Vert two lions sup-porting a tower triple-towered or, betw. two crescents in chief and one in base ar. *Crest*—An arm in armour holding in the hand a spear all ppr. headed or (another, the hand holding a sword ppr.).

M'Gillivray (the naturalist and traveller). Quarterly, 1st, or, a cat sejant ppr. (tabby); 2nd, erm. a glove lying fesse-wise apaumée, and tasselled of a brown or tan colour; 3rd, ar. in water in base ppr. a fish naiant vert, finned gu.; 4th, az. a galley or, flags and oars gu. on a chief of the second a mullet pierced betw. two crosses crosslet fitchée also of the second, the whole within a bordure per pale ar. and of the second on a chief of augmentation, with a representation of sky and water, a canoe with a flag at the end gu. and the character N W in gold, six Canadians rowing, another person seated in the centre, in the naval uniform of England. *Crest*—On a mount vert, by the brink of a river, a beaver in the act of gnawing a tree by the roots, represented as nearly falling, the branches entwined with an escroll, bearing the motto, Perseverance, all ppr. *Motto*—Under the arms: Touch not the cat, but a glove.

M'Gillivray (Montreal). Az. a lymphad. sails furled and oars in action or, flagged gu. within a bordure ar. on a chief of the second a buck's head cabossed sa. attired of the third, betw. two cross crosslets fitchée of the last. *Crest*—A buck's head and neck ppr. attired or. *Motto*—Be mindful.

M'Gouan (Skeoch, co. Wigton). Ar. a lion ramp. gu. betw. three cinquefoils vert, on a chief of the last a boar's head couped betw. two fleurs-de-lis or. *Crest*—A thistle ppr. *Motto*—Juncta arma decori.

M'Goun (Scotland). Ar. a lion ramp. gu. betw. two cinque-foils vert.

M'Grath (co. Kirkcudbright). Per pale and per chev. ar. and gu.

McGrath (impalement Fun. Ent. Ulster's Office). Quarterly, 1st, ar. three lions pass. gu.; 2nd, or, a dexter hand lying fessways, couped at the wrist ppr. holding a cross formée fitchée az.; 3rd, gu. a dexter hand lying fessways, couped at the wrist ppr. holding a battle axe or; 4th, ar. an antelope trippant sa. attired or.

M'Gregor (Glengyle, co. Perth). Ar. a fir tree growing out of a mount in base vert, surmounted of a sword bendways supporting on its point, in the dexter canton, an imperial crown ppr.

M'Gregor (Lanrick and Balquhidder, co. Perth, bart., 1795). Ar. an oak tree eradicated in bend sinister ppr. surmounted of a sword in bend supporting on its point, in the dexter canton, an antique crown gu. *Crest*—A lion's head erased crowned with an antique crown ppr. *Supporters*—Dexter, a unicorn ar. crowned and horned or; sinister, a deer ppr. tyned az. *Mottoes*—Srioghal mo dhream; and Ard cheille.

M'Gregor, or Murray (Napier Ruskie, co. Perth). Quarterly, 1st and 4th, as the last; 2nd and 3rd, MACDONALD, of Slate. Same *Crest*. *Motto*—E'en do, and spare not.

M'Gregor-Skinner, now M'Gregor (Belfast, and Carsbank, Isle of Wight). Quarterly, 1st and 4th, as Lanrick; 2nd and 3rd, sa. a chev. betw. three griffins' heads erased er, for SKINNER. *Crest*—As Lanrick. *Mottoes*—E'en do, and spare not; and, Nunquam non paratus.

M'Gregor (Capt. R. F. H. M'GREGOR, 1872). Quarterly, as the last, with a crescent az. in the centre of the quarters. *Crest* and *Mottoes*—As the last.

M'Gregor (Raigmore, 1782). Ar. a fir tree growing out of a mount in base ppr. surmounted of a sword in bend also ppr. hilted and pommelled or, in chief two crowns gu. a bordure engr. of the last. *Crest*—A hand holding a dagger in pale ppr. *Motto*—E'en do, and spare not.

M'Gregor (bart., 1828). Ar. from a mount in base an oak tree surmounted by a sword in bend ppr. and in chief two Eastern crowns gu. all within a bordure engr. of the last.

Crest—A human hand couped at the wrist, and holding a dagger erect ppr. pommel and hilt gold. *Motto*—Over the crest: Ein do, and spare not.

M'Gregor (Camden Hill, Middlesex, bart., 1831). Ar. a fir-tree growing out of a mount in base vert, surmounted of a sword in bend az. hilted and pommelled or, supporting on its point an antique crown gu. on a chief az. a tower or, betw. a representation of the badge of the Royal Portuguese Order of the Tower and Sword, and a representation of the badge of the Imperial Ottoman Order of the Crescent both ppr. *Crest*—A lion's head erased ppr. crowned with an antique crown or. *Motto*—Srioghal mo dhream.

M'Gregor (Brediland, co. Renfrew, 1870). Ar. a pine tree eradicated in bend sinister, surmounted of a sword in bend, the sword ensigned with an antique crown all ppr. in base a garb vert. *Crest*—A pine tree eradicated ppr. *Motto*—Ardchoille.

Mac Guarie (that Ilk, Isle of Ulva; descended from Donald Mac Gowrie, whom Douglas derives from Gorbredus, grandson of Alphine Ruodh, King of Scotland in 830, from a younger son of the Mac Guaries, of that Ilk, derived the Mac Guires, of Ireland, *Earls of Enniskillen*). Quarterly, 1st and 4th, vert three towers embattled in chief ar.; 2nd and 3rd, ar. three crosses crosslet fitchée. *Crest*—Out of an antique crown an arm in armour embowed, grasping a dagger all ppr. *Motto*—Turris fortis mihi Deus.

M'Guarie (Ormaig, isle of Ulva; descended from Hector Macguarie, second son of Donald Macguarie, of that Ilk). Same *Arms*, with a crescent in the centre. *Crest*—A nag's head couped ar. bridled gu. *Motto*—Be true.

M'Guffie (Crosshill, Cumberland, 1874). Ar. two crosiers in saltire sa. betw. a man's heart in chief and two boars' heads couped of the second in base. *Crest*—A boar's head, as in the arms. *Motto*—Arma parato fero.

M'Guffock (Rusco, co. Kirkcudbright). Ar. two crosiers in saltire az. betw. a man's heart in chief ppr. and three stars in base of the second. *Crest*—A dove ppr. *Motto*—Industria et labore.

McGuire (Lord of Fermanagh; an ancient Irish Sept; descended from Uidhir, Lord of Fermanagh, ninth in descent from Colla da Chrioch, grandson of Cormac Ulfadha, Monarch of Ireland, from whom the Sept took their surname of Mac Wire, McGuire, and Maguire; Thomas Mor McGuire, The McGuire, Lord of Fermanagh, 1400, *d.* 1430, leaving four sons: I. Philip; II. Thomas Oge: III. Hugh; who were the ancestors of the three principal lines of the Sept, and IV. Rory, Bishop of Clogher, 1449-83). Vert a white horse fully caparisoned, thereon a knight in complete armour, on his helmet a plume of ostrich feathers, and his right hand brandishing a sword all ppr.

McGuire (Tempo, co. Fermanagh; Chief of McGuire; descended from Philip McGuire, The McGuire, eldest son of Thomas Mor McGuire, Lord of Fermanagh, 1400; the last known chief of this line, the celebrated Captain Brian McGuire, *d.* 1835, leaving one son, Charles McGuire, of whom nothing has been since known). Same *Arms*. *Crest*—On a ducal coronet or, a stag at gaze ppr. collared and lined gold. *Motto*—Justitia et fortitudo invincibilia sunt.

McGuire (Knockaninny, co. Fermanagh; descended from Thomas Oge McGuire, second son of Thomas Mor McGuire, Lord of Fermanagh, through his eldest son, Edmond McGuire; Captain Brian McGuire, of Knockaninny, *d. temp.* William III., leaving Edmond McGuire, his heir, *d.* 1736, and two other sons. Part of the property is still in possession of John McGuire, one of the descendants). Same *Arms*, *Crest*, and *Motto*.

McGuire (*Baron Enniskillen*, attainted 1690; descended from Thomas Oge McGuire, second son of Thomas Mor McGuire, Lord of Fermanagh, through his second son, Connor Mor McGuire; Sir Brian McGuire, Knt., was created a Peer by the title of Lord McGuire, Baron of Enniskillen, 1627; the last known male descendant, Alexander McGuire, commonly called Lord Enniskillen, settled in France 1719). Same *Arms*. *Crest*—A cubit dexter arm embowed in complete armour, grasping in the gauntlet a sword all ppr. *Supporters*—Two knights in complete armour, swords by their sides and targets on their shoulders all ppr. *Motto*—Marte et arte.

McGuire (Carrigbawn, Rostrevor, co. Down; descended from Hugh McGuire, third son of Thomas Mor McGuire, Lord of Fermanagh, 1400; the present William Richard Bermingham McGuire, and Edward Thomas St. Lawrence McGuire, Lieut.-Col. 1st Royals, are sons of the late William John McGuire, Esq., of Carrigbawn, by Lady Mary Annesley, his wife, and dau. of William Richard, third *Earl Annesley*, by his first wife, Lady Isabella St. Lawrence, dau. of William, second *Earl of Howth*, and

641

co-heir of her mother, Lady Mary Bermingham, dau. and co-heir of Thomas, twenty-second *Lord Athenry* and *Earl of Louth ;* Reg. Ulster's Office). Same *Arms*. *Crest*—On a ducal coronet or, a stag at gaze ppr. collared and lined gold. *Motto*—Justitia et fortitudo invincibilia sunt.

McGuire (Clonea House, co. Waterford; Samuel Edward McGuire, Esq., High Sheriff of the co. 1869; descended from Carrigbawn; Reg. Ulster's Office). Same *Arms* and *Crest*, motto over, Fortitudo et justicia. *Motto*—Virtus et fortitudo invincibilia sunt.

McGuire, or Maguire (Gortoral House, co. Fermanagh; represented by Hugh Maguire, son of Edward Maguire, Esq., of Gortoral, J.P. and D.L., High Sheriff co. Leitrim, who *d.* 1874; claiming descent from the McGuires, of Tempo). Same *Arms* and *Crest*, motto over, Marte et arte. *Motto*—Fortitudo et justicia invictæ sunt.

Machado (Roger Machado, Clarenceux King of Arms, *temp.* Henry VIII., *d.* 1516). Gu. five battle axes, two, one and two.

Macham. Ar. a chev. gu. betw. three greyhounds courant sa. *Crest*—A greyhound courant sa.

M'Han (Scotland). Az. a chev. betw. three cinquefoils ar.

Machell, Mauchael, or Mauchel (Crakenthorpe Hall, co. Westmoreland ; of Saxon origin ; seated at Crakenthorpe at the Domesday survey, afterwards of Beverley, co. York). Sa. three greyhounds courant in pale ar. collared or. *Crest*—A stag's head erased ppr. ducally gorged or; the more ancient crest of the family was a fleur-de-lis.

Machell (Wendover, co. Buckingham), Same *Arms*, a bordure ar. *Crest*—A camel's head erased or, ducally gorged ar.

Machell (Penny Bridge, co. Lancaster; a younger branch of Machell, of Crakenthorpe). Quarterly, 1st and 4th, sa. three greyhounds courant in pale ar. collared or; 2nd and 3rd, az. five fleurs-de-lis or. *Crest*—A stag's head erased ducally gorged ppr. *Motto*—Mauvais chiens.

Machell (Swaley, co. Lincoln). Sa. three greyhounds courant in pale ar. collared gu. a bordure engr. or.

Machen (Eastbach Court and Whitemead Park, co. Gloucester; descended from Thomas Machin, three times Mayor of Gloucester, buried in that city in 1614; granted to Richard Machen, co. Gloucester, 1615 ; the present representative is Rev. Edward Machen, of Eastbach Court and Whitemead Park). Gu. a fesse vair betw. three pelicans' heads erased or, vulning themselves ppr. *Crest*—A pelican's head erased or.

Machen, Machin, or Machon. Same *Arms*. *Crest*—A lion's head erased sa. on the head a cap of maintenance or.

Mac Henry. See Mac Eniery.

Machet (co. Surrey; confirmed by Segar, Garter, to John Machet, Rector of Lambeth, 5 July, 1526). Per saltire or and az. on a fess gu. three fleurs-de-lis ar. *Crest*—A demi lion ramp. or, on a collar gu. three fleurs-de-lis ar.

Machet (cos. Norfolk and Suffolk). Per saltire or and vert, on a fesse gu. three fleurs-de-lis ar. Same *Crest* as the last.

Machon (Machon Bank, near Sheffield; removed to Durham). Gu. a fess vair betw. three swans' heads erased ar. and a canton of the last.

Machon (Sherburn House, Durham). Same *Arms*.

Machon (co. York). Gu. a fess vair betw. three pelicans' heads ar. vulning themselves ppr. a canton ar.

Machonchy (granted 1741, to George Machonchy, of the City of Dublin, M.D., descended of an ancient family of that name in North Britain). Per saltire gu. and erm. on a fess or, three thistles slipped ppr. *Crest*—A demi swan, wings expanded ppr.

Mac Hugh (an Irish Sept of the same race as O'Quin, of Munster; Reg. Ulster's Office). Vert a lion ramp. or, in chief a fleur-de-lis betw. two annulets ar. *Crest*—A greyhound's head couped ar.

Mac Hugh (an Irish Sept of the same race as O'Flaherty; Reg. Ulster's Office). Ar. a saltire vert betw. a dexter hand couped at the wrist in chief gu. two trefoils slipped of the second in fess, and a boat with oars ppr. in base.

M'Ilvain (Grimmet, Scotland). Gu. two covered cups or, in the middle chief point a star ar.

McInroy (Sheirglass, co. Perth, 1828). Ar. three wolves' heads erased gu. and betw. two mullets sa. on a pile per pale or and of the last a mullet counterchanged. *Crest*—A lymphad in full sail sa. *Motto*—Sequor.

M'Intire (England). Quarterly, 1st and 4th, or, an eagle displ. gu. ; 2nd and 3rd, ar. a galley, her sails furled sa. flags gu. *Crest*—Out of a tower a demi greyhound ramp. ppr.

M'Intyre (Glenoe, Scotland). Quarterly, 1st and 4th, or, an eagle displ. gu. armed and langued sa; 2nd and 3rd, ar. a galley, her sails furled sa. flags gu. ; 3rd, ar. a sinister hand couped fesseways gu. holding a cross crosslet fitchée sa. *Crest*—A

2 T

dexter hand holding a dagger in pale both ppr. *Motto*—Per ardua.

M'Iver (Asknish, co. Argyll). Quarterly, or and gu. a bend sa. *Crest*—A boar's head couped or. *Motto*—Nunquam obliviscar.

M'Iver Campbell (Asknish). Quarterly, 1st, gyronny of eight or and sa. ; 2nd, ar. a dexter hand couped fesseways, grasping a dagger in pale gu. ; 3rd, ar. a galley, her sails furled and oars in action sa.; 4th, quarterly, or and gu. a bend sa. *Crest and Motto*, as above.

Mack. Ar. a fesse gu. charged with a mullet of the field, in base a chev. of the second.

Mack (Scotland). Paly of eight or and gu. a bend sinister az. charged with a martlet betw. two mullets of the first.

Mack. Ar. a fesse enhanced and a chev. gu. *Crest*—A heart gu. thrust through with an arrow in bend sinister ar. *Motto*—Above it: Et domi, et foras; and below the arms; Cor vulneretum.

M'Kaile (Aberdeen, 1672). Gu. two dirks in saltire ar. points downward, hilted and pommelled or, in base a lancet open, point upward ppr. *Crest*—A cancer ppr. *Motto*—Nec ferro, nec igne.

Mackay (*Baron Reay*) Az. on a chev. or, betw. three bears' heads couped ar. muzzled gu. a roebuck's head erased betw. two hands issuant from the ends of the chev. each holding a dagger all ppr. *Crest*—A dexter arm from the elbow erect, holding a dagger in pale all ppr. pommel and hilt or. *Supporters*—A pikeman armed at all points, and a musketeer both ppr. *Motto*—Manu forti.

Mackay (Hon. Gen. ALEXANDER MACKAY, 1773). As Lord *Reay*, within a bordure gu.

Mackay (Holland, 1765). ancestor of the tenth and eleventh *Lords Reay*). As Lord *Reay*, within a bordure engr. or. Same *Crest* and *Motto*.

Mackay (London, 1750). As Lord *Reay*, but the chev. wavy for diff. Same *Crest* and *Motto*.

Macked (co. Kent). Erm. on a canton gu. a stag pass. or.

M'Kellar (England). Gu. a boar's head erased ar. *Crest*—Out of a castle triple-towered a demi lion ramp.

Mac Kenna (Trough, co. Monaghan; the Sept of MAC CIONAITH). Vert a fess ar. betw. three lions' heads affrontée or. *Crest*—A salmon naiant ppr.

Mackennal (Cloverbank, now of Merk). Az. a chev. or, betw. two swords, blades wavy, paleways in chief and a castle in base ar. *Crest*—An eagle's head erased ppr. *Motto* —Intrepidus et benignus.

McKenny (granted by Betham, Ulster, to THOMAS McKENNY, Alderman of Dublin). Or, a fleur-de-lis betw. three crescents az. on a chief vert a greyhound pursuing a stag ar. attired gold. *Crest*—A cubit arm in armour ppr. garnished or, the gauntlet grasping a scroll ar. *Motto*— Vincit veritas.

McKenny (Dublin, bart., extinct 1866). Same *Arms, Crest*, and *Motto*.

Mackenzie (*Earl of Seaforth*; "Chief of Kintail "). Az. a stag's head cabossed or. *Crest*—A mountain in flames ppr. *Supporters*—Two savages wreathed about the temples and loins with laurel, each holding in the exterior hand a baton erect, with fire issuing out of the top all ppr. *Motto*—Luceo non uro.

Mackenzie (STEWART-MACKENZIE, of Seaforth). As *Earl of Seaforth*, quarterly with the arms of STEWART, *Earl of Galloway* (q.v.).

M'Kenzie (Allangrange, 1817 ; heir male of Seaforth). Quarterly, 1st and 4th, az. a stag's head cabossed or ; 2nd and 3rd, az. a falcon displ. ar. charged on the breast with a man's heart gu. all betw. three mullets of the second. *Crest* —A mountain in flames ppr. *Supporters*—Two savages wreathed about the head and middle with laurel, and holding in their exterior hands clubs erect flaming at the top all ppr. *Mottoes*—Over the crest: Luceo non uro; below the arms: Vive ut vivas.

Mackenzie (Rosehaugh, co. Ross; from the fifth son of the first *Lord Mackenzie*, of Kintail, *Marquess of Bute*, the heir of line; the property has gone to younger branches of the BUTE family). Az. a stag's head cabossed or, within two laurel branches disposed in orle of the last. *Crest*—An eagle rising from a rock ppr. *Motto*—Firma et ardua.

Mackenzie (Tarbet, co. Cromarty, bart., 1628 ; *Earl of Cromartie;* granddau. and heiress m. *Duke of Sutherland*, and was made *Countess of Oromartie*). Quarterly, 1st or, a rock in flames ppr., for MACLEOD, of Lewis; 2nd, az. a stag's head cabossed or, for MACKENZIE; 3rd, gu. three human legs armed ppr. conjoined in the centre at the upper part of the thigh, flexed in triangle, garnished and spurred or, for the Isle of Man; 4th, ar. on a pale sa. an imperial crown within a double tressure flory and counterflory with fleurs-de-lis gu.,

642

for ERSKINE, of Innerteil. *Crest*—The sun in his splendour ppr. *Supporters*—Two savages wreathed about the middle with laurel, holding batons over their shoulders ppr. *Motto* —Luceo non uro.

Mac Kenzie (*Viscount Fortrose* and *Earl of Seaforth*, in the Peerage of Ireland, extinct 1781 ; KENNETH MAC KENZIE, son and heir of KENNETH, *Lord Fortrose*, eldest son of WILLIAM, fifth *Earl of Seaforth*, in the Peerage of Scotland, attainted 1715, was raised to the Peerage in Ireland, 1766, when the following arms were recorded in Ulster's Office). Quarterly, 1st and 4th, sa. a stag's head cabossed or, for MAC KENZIE; 2nd and 3rd, quarterly, or and gu. a label of three points, each point charged with as many bezants, for HUNTINGFIELD. *Crest*—A mountain in flames ppr. *Supporters*—Dexter, a white greyhound ppr.; sinister, a savage wreathed about the temples and loins with ivy, and holding over the left shoulder a club all ppr. *Motto*—Fide parta, fide aucta.

Mackenzie (Scatwell, co. Ross, bart., 1703; from a younger brother of Sir JOHN MACKENZIE, of Tarbet, first bart.). Quarterly, 1st grand quarter, counter-quartered, 1st, az. a stag's head cabossed or, for MACKENZIE, 2nd, or, a rock in flames ppr., 3rd, az. three legs of man armed ppr. conjoined in the centre at the upper part of the thighs, flexed in triangle, garnished and spurred or, for MACLEOD, of Lewis, 4th, az. a stag's head cabossed or, within a bordure of the second, charged with eight crescents of the first, for MACKENZIE, of Findon; 2nd and 3rd grand quarters, az. a stag's head attired with ten tynes or, within a bordure embattled of the second, for MACKENZIE, of Suddie. *Crests*—1st, SCATWELL : The sun in splendour ppr.; 2nd, SUDDY: A dexter hand grasping a sword in bend ppr. *Supporters*—Two stags ppr. *Mottoes*—Above the crest: Sine maculâ; under the arms: Sic itur ad astra.

Mackenzie (Scotsburn, a second son of Scatwell, 1733). Quarterly, 1st and 4th, az. a stag's head cabossed or ; 2nd, MACLEOD, as in the last; 3rd, MAN, as in the last, in the centre of the quarters a crescent ar. *Crest*—The sun in his splendour ppr. *Motto*—Sans tache.

Mackenzie (Kilcoy, co. Ross, bart., 1836; from a younger brother of the first *Lord Mackenzie*, of Kintail). Quarterly, 1st and 4th grand quarters, az. a stag's head cabossed surmounted of a mullet betw. the attires or, for MACKENZIE; 2nd grand quarter, quarterly, 1st and 4th, az. three cinquefoils ar. two and one, 2nd and 3rd, or, three antique crowns, two and one gu. ; 3rd grand quarter, quarterly, 1st and 4th, az. three garbs, two and one or, 2nd and 3rd, quarterly, 1st and 4th, ar. a pale sa.; 2nd and 3rd, az. a bend betw. six crosses crosslet, two and one, and one and two, or, all for the earldom of BUCHAN. *Crests*—1st : A dexter arm embowed couped at the shoulder, in chain mail, holding a broadsword in bend all ppr.; 2nd : A stag's head cabossed or, pierced with an arrow ppr. *Mottoes*—Above the crests : Fide parta, fide aucta; below the arms : Dia's-mo-Dhuthaich ; equivalent to, Pro Deo et patria.

Mackenzie (Findon, co. Ross; the dau. and heiress of Sir RODERICK MACKENZIE, of Findon, nephew of *Lord Mackenzie*, of Kintail, m. Sir KENNETH MACKENZIE, Bart., of Scatwell). Az. a deer's head cabossed or, within a bordure of the last charged with eight crescents of the first. *Crest*— A crescent ar. *Motto*—Crescitque virtute.

M'Kenzie (Applecross, co. Ross; as recorded 1756; descended from RODERICK MACKENZIE, eldest son of ALEXANDER MACKENZIE, first *Baron of Coull*). Quarterly, 1st and 4th, az. a stag's head cabossed or; 2nd and 3rd, ar. a lion ramp. gu., now borne, in consequence of two descents through females, within a bordure or. *Crest*—A lion couchant guard. ppr. *Mottoes*—Over the crest: Insult me not; below the arms: Fide parta, fide aucta.

Mackenzie (Coull, co. Ross, bart., 1673; from the second son of ALEXANDER MACKENZIE, of Applecross and Coull, nephew of the first *Lord Mackenzie*, of Kintail). Quarterly, 1st and 4th, az. a stag's head cabossed or, for MACKENZIE; 2nd and 3rd, gu. a boar's head couped ar., for CHRISHOLM. *Crest*—A boar's head erect or, betw. the attires of a stag, fixed to a scalp sa. *Supporters*—Dexter, an armed Highlander in full costume ppr.; sinister, a roebuck ppr. *Motto* —Pulchrior ex arduis.

Mackenzie (SHAW-MACKENZIE, of Newhall, co. Cromarty, 1857). Quarterly, 1st and 4th, az. a stag's head cabossed or, in chief three boars' heads couped of the second ; 2nd and 3rd, az. a fess chequy ar. and of the first betw. three covered cups of the second, for SHAW. *Crests*—1st, MACKENZIE: A stag's head affrontée and neck couped ppr.; 2nd, SHAW : A dexter hand holding a covered cup ar. *Mottoes*—Perseverando, for MACKENZIE; I mean well, for SHAW.

Mackenzie (MUIR-MACKENZIE, of Delvine, co. Perth, cadet

of Coull, bart., 1805). Quarterly, 1st and 4th, ar. on a fesse az. three stars or, for MUIR, of Cassencarrie; 2nd and 3rd, az. a stag's head cabossed or, all within a bordure nebulée quarterly gu. and ar. *Crests*—1st: A palm branch in bend, surmounted by a sword saltireways all ppr.; 2nd: A dexter hand grasping a dart ppr. *Supporters*—Dexter, a Highlander attired with sword pointing to the ground; sinister, a husbandman resting on a sword both ppr. *Motto*—In utrumque paratus.

Mackenzie (Redcastle, co. Ross; from an uncle of the first Lord Mackenzie, of Kintail). Az. a stag's head cabossed or, within a bordure chequy of the second and first. *Crest*—A man's heart in flames within two palm branches in orle all ppr. *Motto*—Ferendum et sperandum.

Mackenzie (Lechwards, co. Ayr; descended from Davochmaluak, 1835). Az. a stag's head cabossed or, within a bordure of the second, charged with three mullets sa. *Crest*—A dexter arm embowed, holding a sword in bend all ppr. *Motto*—Fide parta, fide aucta.

M'Kenzie (Lieut.-Col. M'KENZIE, 52nd Foot, 1805; descended of Achilty). Quarterly, 1st and 4th, az. a stag's head cabossed or; 2nd and 3rd, quarterly, 1st and 4th, az. three cinquefoils ar., 2nd and 3rd, gu. three antique crowns or, all within a bordure gu. charged with three mullets ar. *Crest*—A lady from the middle, holding in the dexter hand a cinquefoil ppr. *Motto*—Amore vici.

M'Kenzie (Ardross, co. Ross). Az. a stag's head cabossed or, betw. the attires a spur-rowel erm. *Crest*—A rugged rock ppr. *Motto*—Truth will prevail.

Mackenzie (Fairburn, co. Ross). Az. a deer's head cabossed or, within a bordure embattled ar. *Crest*—A mountain in flames ppr. *Motto*—Fide parta, fide aucta.

Mackenzie (Suddie, co. Ross; the heiress m. Sir JAMES WEMYSS MACKENZIE, Bart., of Scatwell). Az. a deer's head cabossed or, within a bordure embattled of the last. *Crest*—A dexter hand grasping a sword in bend ppr. *Motto*—Sic itur ad astra.

Mackenzie (Gairloch, co. Ross, bart.). Quarterly, 1st and 4th, az. a stag's head cabossed or; 2nd and 3rd, az. three frases ar. *Crest*—A dexter arm holding a garland of laurel ppr. *Motto*—Virtute et valore.

M'Kenzie (Portmore, co. Peebles, cadet of Gairloch). Quarterly, 1st and 4th, az. a stag's head cabossed or; 2nd and 3rd, az. three frases or; over all, in the centre of the quarters, a wolf's head erased or. *Crest*—A dexter arm from the elbow, holding a wreath of laurel ppr. *Motto*—Virtute et valore.

Mackenzie (COLIN MACKÉNZIE, Deputy Keeper of the Great Seal, 1874). As the last, within a bordure per pale or and ar. Same *Crest* and *Motto*.

M'Kenzie (Hiltoun, co. Inverness; derived from DUNCAN, second son of ALEXANDER, seventh *Baron of Kintail*). Az. a stag's head cabossed or, betw. the attires a dirk point downwards ar. hilted of the second. *Crest*—Two hands holding a two-handed sword in bend ppr. *Motto*—Always faithful.

M'Kenzie (England). Az. a stag's head cabossed or, betw. three fleurs-de-lis ar. one in chief and two in base.

Mac Keogh (co. Roscommon; descended from the Sept of O'KELLY, Reg. Ulster's Office). Ar. a lion ramp. gu. in dexter chief a dexter hand couped at the wrist, and in the sinister a crescent, both of the second. *Crest*—A boar pass. az.

McKeown (Reg. Ulster's Office). Ar. two lions ramp. combatant sa. supporting a dexter hand couped at the wrist gu. in chief four mullets of eight points of the last, in base waves of the sea, therein a salmon naiant all ppr. *Crest*—An arm embowed in chain armour, the hand holding a sword, blade wavy all ppr.

Mac Kerell (Norwich, co. Norfolk; granted in 1718). Per fess az. and vert three mackerels naiant in pale ppr. *Crest*—A horseman's spear erected in pale ppr. behind two mackerels saltireways, heads upwards ppr.

Mac Kerell (Ringland, co. Norfolk). Same *Arms*.

M'Kerrell (Hillhouse, co. Ayr). Az. on a fess or, three lozenges gu. a bordure engr. ar. *Crest*—A Roman soldier on his march, with a standard and utensils all ppr. *Motto*—Dulcis pro patriâ labor.

Mackesy (granted to THOMAS LEWIS MACKESY, M.D., of Aughmacart, Queen's co., and Dunkitt, co. Kilkenny, Mayor of Waterford, 1841-2). Ar. a dexter arm couped in fess from the sinister side ppr. sleeved gu. cuffed az. holding a sword entwined with a snake also ppr. all betw. two flaunches of the fourth, each charged with a demi eagle displ. couped or. *Crest*—Out of a mural crown ppr. a demi eagle or, charged on the breast with a sword entwined with a snake in pale, as in the arms. *Motto*—In Deo manuque fides.

Mackey (confirmed to Sir JAMES WILLIAM MACKEY, Knt., of Clonsilla House, co. Dublin, Lord Mayor of Dublin 1873).

Az. on a chev. or, betw. in chief two bears' heads couped ar. muzzled gu. and in base a civic crown of the second, a roe buck's head erased betw. two hands couped at the wrist, each holding a dagger all ppr. *Crest*—Out of a mural crown a dexter hand grasping a dagger all ppr. *Motto*—Manu forti.

Mackie (Bargally, co. Kirkcudbright). Ar. in chief a lion pass. az. and in base two ravens pendent from an arrow fesseways sa. *Crest*—A raven ppr. *Motto*—Labora.

Mackie (Dowloch, Scotland). As the last, within a bordure engr. az. Same *Crest* and *Motto*.

Mackie (Auchencairn, co. Kirkcudbright). Ar. on a chev. betw. a lion pass. az. in chief and a raven in base of the second a tower of the first. *Crest*—A hand holding a dagger ppr. *Motto*—Labore.

Mackie (Larg, co. Kirkcudbright). Ar. a lion ramp. gu.

Mackillop, or M'Killop (England). Sa. a stag's head cabossed ar. *Crest*—A demi eagle reguard. ppr.

Mackinnon (Portswood Park, co. Hants, chief of the clan MACKINNON). Quarterly, 1st, vert a boar's head couped, holding in the mouth a shin-bone ar.; 2nd, az. a tower triple-towered ar.; 3rd, or, a galley gu.; 4th, ar. a man's arm couped below the wrist from the sinister ppr. grasping a cross crosslet fitchée sa. all within a bordure gu. *Crest*—A boar's head erased holding in the mouth the shin-bone of a deer all ppr. *Supporters*—Dexter, a lion; sinister, a leopard, both ppr. *Motto*—Audentes fortuna juvat.

Mackinnon (Rev. JOHN MACKINNON, of Kilmodan, 1802). Ar. a dog in chase of a deer in full speed ppr. on ground in base vert, a bordure az. *Crest*, as the last.

Mackintosh (that Ilk, and Tor Castle, co. Inverness; claims to be chief of the Clan Chattan; Sir ÆNEAS MACKINTOSH, of Mackintosh, created a bart. in 1812, d. s. p. in 1820). Quarterly, 1st, or, a lion ramp. gu.; 2nd, ar. a dexter hand fesseways couped at the wrist and holding a human heart gu.; 3rd, az. a boar's head couped or; 4th, or, a lymphad, her oars in saltire sa. *Crest*—A cat-a-mountain saliant guard. ppr. *Supporters*—Two cats ppr. *Motto*—Over the crest: Touch not the cat, but a glove.

Mackintosh (Kellachie, co. Inverness; Sir JAMES MACKINTOSH, the distinguished orator and statesman, was representative of this branch). Quarterly, 1st and 4th, or, a lion ramp. gu.; 2nd and 3rd, or, a dexter hand couped fesseways, holding a dagger paleways in chief gu. and a galley, her oars saltireways in base sa. all within a bordure gu. *Crest* and *Motto*, as MACKINTOSH, of that Ilk.

Mackintosh (Connadge, co. Inverness). The same quartered coat, within a bordure vair. *Crest* and *Motto*, as the former.

Mackintosh (Kinrara, co. Inverness). Quarterly, 1st and 4th, or, a lion ramp. gu.; 2nd, or, a chev. sa. betw. a dexter hand couped fesseways, grasping a man's heart paleways gu. and a lymphad, her oars erect in saltire of the second; 3rd, az. a boar's head couped or. *Crest* and *Motto*, as the former.

Mackintosh (Aberarder, co. Inverness). The same *Arms* as MACKINTOSH, of that Ilk, all within a bordure gu. charged with eight annulets or. *Crest*—A cat courant and guard. ppr. *Motto*, as above.

Macklow (co. Worcester). Gyronny of eight or and az. a lion ramp. of the first guttée de sang. *Crest*—A sinister arm holding a bow strung.

Macklow, or Mucklowe. Gyronny of eight or and az. a lion ramp. erm. (another, counterchanged) on a chief ar. an escallop betw. two fleurs-de-lis sa. *Crest*—A dragon's head per pale indented gu. and ar. guttée counterchanged, in the mouth an eagle's leg erased or.

McKirdy (Birkwood, co. Lanark, 1856). Per fess or and sa. in chief a martlet of the second, and in base a fir-tree growing out of a mount, surmounted of a sword in bend, supporting on the point an antique crown or. *Crest*—A demi wivern displ. ppr. *Motto*—Dieu et mon pays.

Macklesfield, or Maxfield. Gu. a cross engr. erm.

Macklethorp. Az. a chev. betw. three crosses crosslet or

Mackley (Leckonfield). Az. three wolves' heads erased ar.

Macknight-Crawfurd. See CRAWFURD.

Mackworth (Mackworth Castle, co. Derby; THOMAS MACKWORTH, of Mackworth, having m. ALICE, sister and heiress of Sir JOHN DE BASINGS, of Normanton, co. Rutland, made that seat his place of residence, and was ancestor of the MACKWORTHS, of Normanton, whose chief, Sir THOMAS MACKWORTH, temp. James I., was created a bart. JOHN MACKWORTH and JAMES MACKWORTH, "valiant men," were granted by John Touchet, Lord Audley, 1404, son-in-law and eventually successor of James de Audley, Lord Audley, "A part of the arms of AUDLEY, for the services rendered by them and their ancestors to the Audley family, especially at the battle of Poictiers"). Per pale indented sa. and erm. a chev. gu. fretly or. *Crest*—A wing per pale indented, as in the arms.

Mackworth (Normanton, co. Rutland, bart., extinct 1803 ; THOMAS MACKWORTH, Esq., of Normanton, descended from MACKWORTH, of Mackworth, was created a bart. 1619). Same *Arms*. *Crest*—A wing per pale indented sa. and erm.

Mackworth (Glen Uske, co. Monmouth, bart., formerly of Gnoll Castle, co. Glamorgan). Quarterly, 1st and 4th, per pale indented sa. and erm. on a chev. gu. five crosses pattée or, for MACKWORTH; 2nd, gu. three chevronels ar., for EVANS, of Gnoll Castle (being the arms of JESTIN AP GWRGAN, Prince of Glamorgan); 3rd, ar. a wyvern's head erased vert, holding in the mouth a sinister hand couped at the wrist gu., for MORGAN, of Pencrug. *Crest*—A cock ppr. *Motto*—Gwell angau na cywilydd.

Mackworth (Betton Grange, in the parish of Meole Bruce, co. Salop). Per pale indented sa. and erm. on a chev. gu. five crosses pattée or. *Crest*—A cock gu. beaked, legged, combed, and wattled or.

Mackworth. Per pale indented erm. and sa. on a chief gu. a lion pass. guard. or.

Mackworth-Praed. See PRAED.

Macky (Scotland). Paly of eight or and gu. over all a bend sinister az. charged with a crescent ar. betw. two stars of the first.

Maclachlan (that Ilk, co. Argyll). Quarterly, 1st, or a lion ramp. gu. ; 2nd, a dexter hand couped fessways, holding a cross pattée paleways gu. ; 3rd, or, a galley, her oars in saltire sa. placed on the sea ppr. ; 4th, ar. on a base undée vert a salmon naiant ppr. *Crest*—A castle on a rock ppr. *Supporters*—Two roebucks ppr. *Motto*—Fortis et fidus.

M'Lachlan (Kilchoan, co. Argyll). Quarterly, 1st, or, a lion ramp. gu. ; 2nd, ar. a dexter arm fesseways couped gu. holding a cross pattée sa. ; 3rd, ar. a lymphad sa. sails furled and streamers flying in the sea ppr. ; 4th, or, in base a salmon naiant ppr. *Crest*—Out of a ducal coronet or, a lion's head erased ppr. *Motto*—Fortis et fidus.

M'Lachlan (Trinidad ; granted 1787). Quarterly, 1st, or, a lion ramp. gu. ; 2nd, ar. a dexter hand couped fesseways gu. holding a cross formée fitchée az. ; 3rd, ar. in base the sea ppr. thereon a galley, oars in action and sails furled sa. flags gu. ; 4th, per fesse ar. and az. a fish naiant in base or ; over all, dividing the quarters, a leopard's face gold. *Crest*—A leopard's face ppr. *Motto*—Fortiter.

M'Lagan (Scotland). Or, two chev. sa. a bordure of the last. *Crest*—A mortar piece or. *Motto*—Superba franga.

Maclagan (Edinburgh). Ar. two chevronels sa. on a bordure vert three martlets or. *Crest*—A beaver statant ppr. *Motto*—Principiis obsta.

M'Lannahan (co. Edinburgh, 1876). Ar. a rock gu. issuing from the base and in chief a dexter hand couped below the elbow ppr. holding in the hand a cross crosslet fitchée az. *Crest*—A tower gu. *Motto*—Virtue is my honour.

Maclaine (Kington House, Thornbury, co. Gloucester). Quarterly, 1st, ar. a lion ramp. gu. ; 2nd, az. a tower ar. ; 3rd, or, a dexter hand couped in fesse gu. holding a cross crosslet fitchée az. ; 4th, ar. a lymphad ppr. her sails furled, in base a salmon naiant ppr. *Crest*—A Lochaber axe erect betw. two branches of laurel and cypress all ppr. *Motto*—Vincere vel mori.

M'Larty (Jamaica and Kilcolmkill, co. Argyll, 1819). Quarterly, 1st, ar. a dexter hand spaumée couped gu. ; 2nd, az. the east end of a cathedral church ppr. ; 3rd, az. two estoiles in fesse ar. ; 4th, ar. a galley, sails furled sa. flags gu. in the topmast a beacon ppr. all surmounted by an eagle displ. of the third. *Crest*—A dexter hand ppr. holding up a cross crosslet fitchée in pale gu. *Motto*—In te fido.

McLaughlin (Reg. Ulster's Office). Quarterly, 1st, or, a lion ramp. gu. ; 2nd, ar. a dexter hand couped at the wrist ppr. lying fessways and grasping a cross pattée fitchée az. ; 3rd, or, on waves of the sea in base ppr. a galley, sails furled sa. pennon flying ppr. ; 4th, ar. in waves of the sea in base a salmon naiant all ppr. *Crest*—Out of a ducal coronet or, a lion's head gu. *Motto*—Fortis et fidus.

M'Laurin (Dreghorn, co. Edinburgh, 1781). Ar. a shepherd's crook in pale sa. *Crest*—The Virgin and Child ppr. vested vert. *Supporters*—Two tritons ppr. *Motto*—Bi se macant Slaurie.

Maclaurin (London, 1866). Or, two chevronels gu. in base a lymphad sa. sails furled, flags flying, and oars in action, a bordure nebuly of the second. *Crest*—A lion's head erased ppr. on it an antique crown or, all betw. two branches of laurel issuing from the wreath ppr. *Mottoes*—Dalriada ; and, Aborigine fidus.

Maclay (co. York). Az. three wolves' heads ar. langued gu.

M'Lea (Russia ; granted 1806). Quarterly, 1st and 4th, ar. three cinquefoils gu. ; 2nd and 3rd, ar. a chev. embattled sa. betw. three boars' heads erased gu. all within a bordure dovetailed gu., for ELPHINSTONE. *Crest*—Two arms, dexter and sinister, from the shoulder extended in saltire, the

dexter holding a pair of compasses extended, and the sinister a sword erect all ppr. *Motto*—Tam arte quam marte.

Maclean (Dowart, afterwards Morvaren, bart., 1632). Quarterly, 1st, ar. a rock gu. ; 2nd, ar. a dexter hand fesseways couped gu. holding a cross crosslet fitchée in pale az. ; 3rd, or, a lymphad sa. ; 4th, ar. a salmon naiant ppr. and in chief two eagles' heads erased affrontée gu. *Crest*—A tower embattled ar. *Supporters*—Two seals ppr. *Motto*—Virtue mine honour.

Maclean (Sir JOHN MACLEAN, K.C.B., 1814). Quarterly, as the last, a chief gu. thereon pendent from the middle chief point a representation of the gold cross commemorative of his services, in the dexter chief point the badge of the Portuguese Military Order of the Tower and Sword, and in dexter chief the badge of the Ottoman Order of the Crescent. *Crest*—A battle axe erect in pale, crowned by a branch of laurel and of cypress in saltire all ppr. *Motto*—Virtue mine honour.

Maclean (Sir GEORGE MACLEAN, K.C.B., 1856). Quarterly, as Dowart, within a bordure gu. charged with two antique crowns in fess and a mullet in chief and in base or. *Crest*, as the last. *Motto*—Altera merces.

M'Lean (Coll ; derived from JOHN GARVE MACLEAN, son of LAUCHLAN BRONACH MACLEAN, of Dowart). Quarterly, 1st, ar. a hill issuing vert ; 2nd ar. a dexter arm issuing from the sinister in fesse gu. holding a cross crosslet fitchée in pale az. ; 3rd, az. a galley, her oars erect in saltire, and sails furled sa. flags displ. gu. ; 4th, per fesse or and az. in chief two hawks' heads couped affrontée gu. and in base a salmon naiant ppr. *Crest*, as the last. *Supporters*—Dexter, a greyhound ppr. collared and leashed gu. ; sinister, an ostrich ppr. in its beak a horseshoe az. *Mottoes*—Over the crest: Altera merces ; and below the arms : Virtus durissima ferit.

Maclean (Haremere Hall, co. Sussex). Quarterly, 1st, or, a rock ppr. ; 2nd, ar. a dexter hand couped in fesse ppr. holding a cross crosslet fitchée gu. ; 3rd, az. a galley, sails furled and a flag gu. ; 4th, in chief two eagles' heads erased gu. in base az. a salmon naiant ar. *Crest*—A Lochaber axe in pale, crossed by a branch of laurel and cypress—" Altera Merces.' *Motto*—Virtus durissima ferit.

M'Leay (Keiss, co. Caithness). Ar. on a chev. gu. betw. three bucks' heads couped of the last, armed or, a hawk's head erased of the last. two salmons erect ppr. on a chief az. an anchor betw. two garbs or. *Crest*—A buck's head erased ppr. *Motto*—Spes anchora vitæ.

M'Leish (Scotland). Or, two chev. gu. a canton sa. *Crest*—A demi lion ramp. guard. or.

Maclellan (Bomby ; Lord Kirkcudbright, dormant since 1832). Or, two chev. sa. *Crest*—A naked arm supporting on the point of a sword a Moor's head. *Supporters*—Dexter, a man armed at all points, holding in his hand a baton ppr. ; sinister, a horse ar. furnished gu. *Motto*—Think on (and at other times, for *Crest*, a mortar-piece ppr., with the *Motto*, Superba frango).

Maclellan (Barclay, Scotland, 1719). Or, two chev. within a bordure engr. gu. *Crest* and *Motto*, as the last.

Maclellan (Edinburgh, 1685). Ar. two chev. sa. each charged with a plate *Crest*—A Moor's head and neck ppr. *Motto*—Sapit qui reputat.

Macleod (that Ilk, and Dunvegan, Isle of Skye). Az. a castle triple-towered and embattled ar. masoned sa. windows and porch gu. *Crest*—A bull's head cabossed betw. two flags gu. *Supporters*—Two lions reguard. gu. each holding a dagger ppr. *Motto*—Murus aheneus.

Macleod (Talisker, Skye). Same *Arms*, within a bordure ar. Same *Crest* and *Motto*.

Macleod (Muiravonside ; descended from Sir NORMAN MACLEOD, of Bernera, third son of MACLEOD, of that Ilk). Quarterly, 1st and 4th, as MACLEOD, of that Ilk ; 2nd, gu. three legs in armour conjoined at the upper part of the thigh ppr. placed in triangle and garnished and spurred or, the arms of the Isle of Man ; 3rd, az. a deer's head cabossed or. *Crest*—A lion's head erased gu. *Motto*—Murus aheneus.

Macleod (Sir CHARLES MACLEOD, K.C.B., and issue of his brother, Sir JOHN MACLEOD, C.B., K.H.). As Muiravonside, within a bordure ar. charged with four antique crowns gu. *Crest*—As MACLEOD, of that Ilk. *Mottoes*—Hold fast ; and, Hic murus aheneus.

Macleod (Arley Castle, co. Stafford, 1844). Quarterly, 1st and 4th, as MACLEOD, of that Ilk ; 2nd and 3rd, the arms of the Isle of Man, as above, all within a bordure embattled or. *Crest* and *Mottoes*, as the last.

Macleod-Annesley. See ANNESLEY, of Arley Castle.

Macleod (Lord of Lewis). Or, a mountain az. inflamed ppr. *Crest*—The sun in his splendour ppr. *Supporters*—Two savages with flames of fire on their heads and hands, each issuing out of a burning hillock all ppr.

Macleod (Colbecks, 1762). Or, on a pedestal a mountain vert inflamed ppr. in a canton the arms of the Isle of Man. *Crest*—An eagle displ. in the midst of flames of fire ppr. *Supporters*—Two eagles ppr. *Mottoes*—Luceo non uro; and, I ruke while I see.

Macleod (Rasay, 1772). Or, a burning mountain ppr. in the dexter and sinister chief points two crosses pattée fitchée gu. *Crest and Supporters*, as Lewis. *Motto*—Luceo non uro.

Macleod (Cadboll, co. Ross, 1725). Quarterly, 1st, as MACLEOD, of Lewis; 2nd, Isle of Man; 3rd, or, a lymphad sa. flags gu.; 4th, az. a castle triple-towered and embattled ar. masoned sa. windows and portcullis gu. *Crest*—The sun in his splendour ppr. *Mottoes*—Loisgim agus soilleirighim; and, Quocunque jeceris stabit; on a compartment below the shield an antique crown or.

M'Liver (Bristol, 1867; heir male of *Lord Clyde*). Or, on a fess betw. two crosses pattée fitchée of the second in chief and a salmon naiant ppr. in base, a mural crown of the first. *Crest*—Issuing out of a mural crown or, a swan sa. collared, lined, and crowned with an eastern crown also or. *Motto*—Be mindful.

MacLochlin (an Irish Sept descended of the same line as MACSWINY; Reg. Ulster's Office). Per fess az. and gu. in chief a lion ramp. or, betw. two swords erect ar. pommel and hilt of the third, in base three crescents of the fourth, two and one. *Motto*—Cuimhnig do geallamhnaca.

McLoskie (arms from a seal in 1678, Reg. Ulster's Office). Ar. issuant from the dexter side of the shield a sinister arm fessways holding an oak tree all ppr. *Crest*—A dexter hand couped at the wrist holding a dagger all ppr.

McLoskey (confirmed to PATRICK McLOSKEY, M.D., of Rothwell, co. Northampton, son of EDWARD McLOSKEY, of Killunaght, co. Londonderry). Gu. a dexter cubit arm issuing from the sinister side vested ar. cuffed erm. in the hand ppr. a chalice or, in chief two trefoils slipped of the last. *Crest*—In front of two crosses crosslet fitchée in saltire sa. a dexter cubit arm erect, vested ar. cuffed erm. the hand grasping a dagger ppr. point downwards. *Motto*—Sica inimicis.

Mac Mahon (of the same Sept as O'BRIEN, *Earls of Thomond and Inchiquin*, anciently Kings of Thomond; TURLOUGH MAC MAHON, of Clonderlaw, co. Clare, Reg. Ulster's Office as chief of his Sept in 1472). Ar. three lions pass. reguard. in pale gu. armed and langued az. *Crest*—A dexter arm in armour embowed ppr. garnished or, holding in the hand a sword both ar. pommel and hilt gold. *Motto*—Sic nos sic sacra tuemur.

Mac Mahon (Coagy and Tuagh, co. Clare; descended from MAC MAHON, of Clonderlaw; allowed by Mac Cullogh, Ulster, 1764). Same *Arms, Crest*, and *Motto*.

Mac Mahon (Leadmore, co. Clare; descended from MAC MAHON, of Coagy; allowed by Mac Cullogh, Ulster, 1764). Same *Arms, Crest*, and *Motto*.

Mac Mahon (CORNELIUS MACMAHON, Count of the Holy Roman Empire, descended from MAC MAHON, of Clonderlaw, through MACMAHON, of Coagy, co. Clare, Tuagh, and Ballykielty, co. Limerick; allowed by Bryan, Deputy Ulster, 1770). Same *Arms, Crest*, and *Motto*.

Mac Mahon (MARIE EDME PATRICE MAURICE MAC MAHON, *Duke of Magenta*, Marshal of France, President of the French Republic; allowed by Hawkins, Ulster, 1750, to the Marshal's ancestor, JOHN BAPTIST MAC MAHON, *Count of Eguilly*, son of PATRICK MAC MAHON, Esq., of Torrodile, co. Limerick, descended from DONOGH MAC MAHON, Lord of Finish and Reynana, son of TURLOUGH MAC MAHON, Lord of Clonderlaw, and chief of his Sept, 1472. The head of the MAC MAHONS, of France, is the *Marquis de Mac Mahon*, of Sully, near Autun). Same *Arms, Crest*, and *Motto*, as Clonderlaw.

Mac Mahon (Clenagh, Ballylean, &c., co. Clare, of the ancient Sept of the MAC MAHONS, of Clare; JANE McMAHON, sister and heir of Rev. DONAT McMAHON, of Clenagh, *m.* WILLIAM COPPINGER, Esq., of Barryscourt, co. Cork, and *d.* 1833, leaving, with two sons, who *d. s. p.*, an elder dau., ELIZABETH COPPINGER, who *m.*, 1806, JOHN O'CONNELL, Esq., of Grenagh, co. Kerry, and had, with other issue, an elder son, MORGAN JOHN O'CONNELL, M.P., co. Kerry, who *m.*, 1865, MARY ANNE, only dau. of CHARLES BIANCONI, Esq., of Longfield, co. Tipperary, and *d.* 1875, leaving JOHN CHARLES COPPINGER O'CONNELL, Esq., *b.* 1871, the present representative of this line). Same *Arms*. *Crest*—A naked arm embowed holding a sword the blade entwined with a serpent all ppr. *Motto*—Sic nos sic sacra tuemur.

Mac Mahon (Portugal; allowed by Hawkins, Ulster, 1749, to MAURICE MAC MAHON, Major in the service of the King of Portugal, descended from DONOGH MACMAHON, younger son of TERENCE MAC MAHON, of Clonderlaw, chief of his Sept 1472). Same *Arms* and *Crest*.

Mac Mahon (co. Monaghan; impalement Fun. Ent. Ulster's Office, 1628, Capt. HUGH REILLY, of Lecanon, co. Cavan, whose wife was KATHERINE, dau. of Sir BRIAN McMAHON, Knt.). Ar. an ostrich sa. holding in the beak a horseshoe or.

McMahon (Hollymount, co. Carlow). Quarterly, 1st and 4th, or, a lion ramp. gu.; 2nd, gu. a sinister arm in armour embowed, holding in the hand a sword bendwise, hilted or; 3rd, az. a sinister hand and arm couped at the elbow, holding a sword erect wavy with a snake entwined thereon all ppr. *Crest*—A demi griffin segreant ar.

Mac Mahon (Dublin, bart.; granted by Betham, Ulster, to Right Hon. WILLIAM MACMAHON, Master of the Rolls, Ireland, created a bart. 1815). Per saltire or and erm. a lion pass. az. betw. two lions pass. reguard. gu. all in pale. *Crest*—Behind a portcullis gu. chained or, an armed arm embowed ppr. the hand grasping a sword wavy ppr. hilted and pommelled of the second. *Motto*—Sic nos sic sacra tuemur.

McMahon (London, bart.; Right Hon. JOHN McMAHON, elder brother of Sir WILLIAM MAC MAHON, Bart., Master of the Rolls, was created a bart., with special remainder to his brother, THOMAS McMAHON, 1817). Same *Arms, Crest*, and *Motto*.

Mac Manus (co. Fermanagh, a branch of McGUIRE, Lord of Fermanagh; Reg. Ulster's Office). Vert a griffin segreant or, in chief three crescents ar. *Crest*—A hand and arm couped below the elbow erect, holding a long cross ppr.

MacManus (co. Antrim; Reg. Ulster's Office). Or, a fess gu. in chief a boar pass. sa. *Crest*—A dexter hand apaumée couped at the wrist gu.

McManus (confirmed by Betham, Ulster, to ALEXANDER McMANUS, Esq., of Mount Davis, co. Antrim). Same *Arms* and *Crest*. *Motto*—Cor et manus.

Mac Marhoo (also borne by GRANE; Reg. Ulster's Office). Gu. a lion ramp. ar.

M'Mathan (co. Ross). Ar. three dexter hands couped erect gu.

Mac Michael (Scotland). Sa. a fesse betw. three crescents or.

Macmillan (Scotland). Ar. a lion pass. betw. two barrulets gu. in chief three stars az.

Mac Millan (Dunmore, 1672). Or, a lion ramp. sa. in chief three mullets az. *Crest*—A dexter and sinister hand issuing from the wreath, brandishing a two-handed sword ppr. *Motto*—Miseris succurrere disco.

M'Millan (clan BUCHANAN). Or, a lion ramp. sa. on a chief per fesse of the first and gu. three mullets ar.

M'Millan (England). Ar. a chev. betw. three mullets sa. *Crest*—A yew tree ppr.

Mac Millan (Reg. Ulster's Office). Ar. on a chev. sa. betw. three mullets gu. as many bezants, a border of the third. *Crest*—A naked arm erect couped below the elbow, holding a sword all ppr.

Macmillan-Scott. See SCOTT.

M'Moran (Glaspine, co. Kirkcudbright). Az. betw. two mullets or, a sword in pale ar. bearing on the point a dexter hand couped gu.; otherwise, ar. three Moors' heads ppr. banded of the field.

Mac Moran (Edinburgh, 1672). Az. a sword in pale ar. bearing on the point a dexter hand couped gu. betw. a crescent on the dexter and a mullet on the sinister in fesse or, within a bordure indented of the second. *Crest*—A dexter hand couped gu. *Motto*—Virtus virtutis præmium.

Mac More (Reg. Ulster's Office). Ar. a lion ramp. purp.

Mac Moresh (Reg. Ulster's Office). Ar. a saltire gu. betw. twenty lozenges sa.

Mac Morogh (King of Leinster; DERMOT MACMOROGH, King of Leinster, surrendered his sovereignty to Henry II., 1172; from him descended the KAVANAGHS, and KINSELAGHS, and from him brother, MOROGH NA GAOIDHEAL, descended O'MORECHOE, or MURPHY, MAC DAVIE MORE, and MAC VADOCK, co. Wexford, all known as the Clan MAC MOROGH). Sa. three garbs or. *Crest*—Out of clouds a hand erect holding a crown betw. two swords in bend and bend sinister, points upwards all ppr.

Mac Morogh (Reg. Ulster's Office). Gu. a lion ramp. ar.

McMurray (confirmed to ROBERT McMURRAY, Esq., of Roxborough House, Limerick, and Patrickswell, co. Limerick). Ar. a lion ramp. az. on a chief of the second three mullets pierced of the field. *Crest*—A demi lion ramp. guard. gu. holding a Lochaber axe, and charged on the shoulder with a rose ar. *Motto*—Virtute fideque.

Mac Murrogh (cos. Carlow and Wexford; Reg. Ulster's Office, branches of the Sept of KAVANAGH). Ar. a lion ramp. holding betw. the paws a battle axe gu. *Crest*—Out of the horns of a crescent or, a garb issuant gu.

M'Nab (that Ilk; a family of great antiquity in the Highlands of Scotland, whose chief, JOHN MACNAB, of that Ilk, a distinguished royalist, joined Montrose with his whole clan, and fought gallantly at Kilsyth; he was subsequently besieged in his Castle of Kincardine, by General Leslie, and eventually slain at the Battle of Worcester. The cadets of MACNAB, of that Ilk, were MACNAB, of Acharne, MACNAB, of Newton, MACNAB, of Cowel, MACNAB, of Jamaica, MACNAB, of Inchewen, &c.). Sa. on a chev. ar, three crescents vert, in base an open boat, oars in action, in a sea ppr. *Crest*—A savage's head erased ppr. *Motto*—Timor omnis abesto.

M'Nab (Sir A. NAPIER M'NAB, of Dundurn) As the last, within a bordure engr. or. *Crest*—As the last. *Mottoes*—Timor omnis abesto; and, Gun eagal.

Macnaghten (Bushmills, co. Antrim, and Mahan, co. Armagh, Ireland, bart.). Quarterly, 1st and 4th, ar. a hand issuing from the sinister ppr. holding a cross crosslet fitchée az.; 2nd and 3rd, or, a tower embattled gu. all within a bordure erm., quartering WORKMAN, Or, three martlets sa. betw. two bars wavy gu. in chief three crescents, and in base a portcullis of the second. *Crests*—1st: A tower gu., for MACNAGHTEN; 2nd: Out of a crescent quarterly ar. and sa. a lictor's fasces ppr., for WORKMAN. *Supporters*—Two roebucks ppr. *Mottoes*—I hope in God; and, over the crests: Non pas l'ouvrage mais l'ouvrier.

M'Nair. Or, a lion ramp. gu. betw. three pheons az. *Crest*—A mermaid ppr. holding in her dexter hand a mirror, and in the sinister a comb.

M'Nair (Glasgow, 1761). Quarterly, 1st and 4th, ar. in a sea a ship in full sail ppr.; 2nd, gu. a close helmet ar.; 3rd, az. an anchor in pale or, charged with a cross crosslet fitchée az. *Crest*—A demi negro holding a sugar cane over the dexter shoulder, and in the sinister hand a bunch of tobacco leaves all ppr. *Motto*—Labor omnia vincit.

Mac Nally (Reg. Ulster's Office). Ar. an arm in armour couped at the shoulder in fess, holding in the hand a battle axe all ppr. betw. six martlets sa. three and three, paleways, in dexter chief an ancient Irish crown gu. *Crest*—A naked arm couped below the shoulder erect, holding a dagger also erect all ppr.

Macnamara (co. Clare; an ancient Irish Sept, descended from DOMHNAL, d. A.D. 1099, son of CUMARA, Chief of Maghadhair, co. Clare, from whom the surname of MAC CONMARA, or MACNAMARA, is derived; JOHN MACNAMARA FIONN, chief of his name, was restored to his estate 1655, and left an only dau. and heir; his brother, DONOUGH, had two sons, DONOUGH and MICHAEL, who were living in France, 1714). Gu. a lion ramp. ar. in chief two spear heads or.

Macnamara (Doolen, and Ennistymon House, co. Clare; descended from DONOUGH MACNAMARA, of Moyrisk, co. Clare, brother of JOHN MACCON MACNAMARA FIONN, Chieftain, 1602, whose grandson, DONAL OGE MACNAMARA, of Ballynacraige, was grandfather of BARTHOLOMEW MACNAMARA, of Muraghin, same co., b. 1685, whose late representative was Lieut.-Col. FRANCIS MACNAMARA, of Doolen, M.P. for Ennis). Same *Arms*. *Crest*—A naked arm embowed grasping a scymitar all ppr. *Motto*—Virtute et armis.

Macnamara (Ayle, and Ranna Castle, co. Clare, and co. Dublin; descended from FINGHEN MACNAMARA, of Rosroe, co. Clare, brother of MACCON MACNAMARA, Chieftain, 1426; DILLON MACNAMARA, Esq., of Birchfield, co. Dublin, representative of this branch, d. 1838, leaving two sons: I. CONNELL WILKINS, m. and had a son, RICHARD FRANCIS; and II. PATRICK JAMES DILLON, of Ayle, J.P.). Same *Arms*. *Crest*, as on the family vault in Quin Abbey, same as the last, issuing out of a ducal coronet or. *Motto*—Firmitas in cœlo.

Macnamara (Kilgurtin, co. Clare, and France; descended from TEIGE, brother of STODHA CAM MACNAMARA, Chieftain, 1402; allowed, 1733, to JAMES and FRANCIS MACNAMARA, then of France, sons of DENIS, third son of JOHN MACNAMARA, of Kilgurtin). Same *Arms* and *Crest*, without the coronet, a crescent for diff. *Motto*—Firmitas in cœlo.

M'Naught (Kilquharity, co. Kirkcudbright). Sa. an escutcheon chequy ar. and az. betw. three lions' heads erased of the second. *Crest*—A lion's head, as in the arms. *Motto*—Omnia fortunæ committo.

MacNaughten (that Ilk, Scotland). Quarterly, 1st and 4th, ar. a dexter hand couped fessways ppr. holding a cross crosslet fitchée az.; 2nd and 3rd, ar. a tower gu. *Crest*—A tower, as in the arms. *Supporters*—Two roebucks ppr. *Motto*—I hope in God.

Mac Neil, or Macneill (Barra, co. Inverness; chief of the MACNEILLS, an ancient clan of the Western Isles, in ancient times enrolled under the standards of the Lords of the Isles; now represented by Colonel RODERICK MACNEILL, of Barra). Quarterly, 1st, vert a lion ramp. or; 2nd, ar.

in base the sea with a castle above the sea ppr.; 3rd, or, a lymphad sa. sails furled; 4th, or, a dexter hand erect, couped gu. within an orle of nine fetterlocks gu. *Crest*—A rock ppr. *Supporters*—Two lions ramp. ppr. *Motto*—Vincere vel mori.

M'Neill (Gigha, co. Argyll). Quarterly, 1st and 4th, az. a lion ramp. ar.; 2nd, ar. a sinister hand couped fessways in chief gu. and in base wavy az. a salmon naiant of the first; 3rd, or, a galley, her oars in saltire gu. on a chief of the last three mullets of the first. *Crest*—An armed man, from the shoulder issuing, holding a dagger point upwards all ppr. *Motto*—Vincere vel mori.

M'Neill (*Baron Colonsay*). As the last, within a bordure erm. *Crest*—A mailed arm and hand holding a dagger ppr. *Supporters*—Two Highland deerhounds ppr. *Motto*—Vincere aut mori.

M'Neill (Sir JOHN M'NEIL, G.C.B., 1857). As Gigha, within a bordure gu. *Crest* and *Motto*, as *Lord Colonsay*. *Supporters*—Two Persian lions without manes ppr.

Macneill (Reg. Ulster's Office to Sir JOHN MACNEILL, Knt., Professor of Practical Engineering, Trinity College, Dublin, on whom the *Earl de Grey* conferred the honour of knighthood at the opening of the Dublin and Drogheda Railway, 1844). Per fess in chief per pale az. and ar. the base or, in dexter chief a lion ramp. of the second, in sinister chief a dexter hand couped at the wrist, lying fessway, and a salmon naiant in waves of the sea all ppr. in base a lymphad gu. oars in action of the last, on a chief also of the last three mullets of the third. *Crest*—An arm in armour embowed, the hand holding a sword all ppr. *Motto*—Vincere vel mori.

McNeil (Reg. Ulster's Office). Quarterly, 1st, az. a lion ramp. ar.; 2nd, or, a dexter arm couped below the elbow lying fessways gu. the hand grasping a cross crosslet fitchée az.; 3rd, or, a lymphad sa.; 4th, ar. out of waves of the sea in base ppr. a rock issuant gu. *Crest*—A rock gu. *Motto*—Per virtutem scientamque.

Mac Neill (confirmed by Betham, Ulster, to Sir JOHN MAC NEILL, Knt., D.C.L., F.R.S., son of TORQUIL PARKES MAC NEILL, Esq., of Mount Pleasant, co. Louth, and grandson of JOHN MAC NEILL, of Lower Fanchard, co. Louth, descended from a Highland family of MAC NEILL, of Gaya and Fearfergus, co. Argyll). Per fess gu. and or, in chief three mullets of the second, in base a lymphad with sails furled and oars of the first, over all on a fess per pale az. and ar. dexter a lion ramp. of the last, sinister a dexter hand fessways, and in base a salmon naiant in the sea all ppr. *Crest*—A dexter arm embowed in armour, in the hand a dagger all ppr. *Motto*—Vincere aut mori.

M'Neish (Scotland). Az. a chev. betw. two mullets in chief and a crescent in base ar.

McNevins (Reg. Ulster's Office). Az. a fess ar. betw. in chief a crescent and a crescent inverted, and in base a palm branch all of the last. *Crest*—A palm branch vert. *Motto*—Vivis sperandum.

Maconochie (Meadowbank, co. Edinburgh, 1819). Az. three dexter hands couped fessways in chief, each holding a bunch of arrows ppr. and in base a royal crown gold, all within a bordure gyronny of eight or and sa. *Crest*—A demi Highlandman holding in the dexter hand a bunch of arrows all ppr. above an imperial crown. *Supporters*—Two Highlanders, each holding in the exterior hand a bow and arrow, and having a quiver on his back all ppr. *Motto*—His nitimur et munitur.

Maconochie-Wellwood. See WELLWOOD.

M'Ostrich (confirmed as a quartering to JOHN CARMICHAEL M'OSTRICH, of Cork, upon his assuming by royal licence, 1861, the surname of CARMICHAEL). Per fess gu. and az. three fishes haurient ar. betw. eight crosses crosslet fitchée of the last. *Crest*—Out of a mural crown ppr. an ostrich's head az. holding in the beak a horse shoe or, and charged on the neck with a cross crosslet fitchée gold.

Mac Pherson (Cluny, co. Inverness; chief of the Clan MACPHERSONS, claims to be chief of Clan Chattan). Per fesse or and az. a lymphad of the first, with her sails furled, oars in action, and mast and tackling all ppr. flags flying gu. in the dexter chief point a hand couped grasping a dagger, point upwards gu. in the sinister chief a cross crosslet fitchée of the last. *Crest*—A cat sejant ppr. *Supporters*—Two Highlandmen in short tartan jackets and hose, with steel helmets on their heads, thighs bare, their shirt tied between them, and round targets on their arms all ppr. *Motto*—Touch not the cat, but a glove.

Mac Pherson (Invereshie, co. Inverness; derived from GILLIES MACPHERSON, third son of EWAN BAWN MACPHERSON). Same *Arms*, within a bordure gu. *Crest*—A cat sejant with her forefeet erect guard. ppr. *Motto*—As Cluny.

Mac Pherson (Pitmean, co. Inverness; derived from JOHN MACPHERSON, second son of EWAN BAWN MACPHERSON). Same *Arms* as of Cluny, per fesse invecked. *Crest* and *Motto*, as Cluny.

M'Pherson, or Macpherson (England). Per fesse or and az. a galley, her oars in action and sails furled, betw. two lions' heads erased in chief all counterchanged. *Crest*— A cat's paw issuing sa. holding up a crescent or.

Macpherson (Calcutta, bart., extinct 1821; Sir JOHN MACPHERSON, Governor-General of Bengal, 1784, afterwards M.P. for Horsham, was so created 1784, *d. s. p.*). Per fess or and az. a lymphad, sails furled, oars in action of the first, in the dexter chief a hand fessways couped, grasping a dagger erect gu. in the sinister chief a cross crosslet fitchée of the last.

Mac Quay, McQuay, or Maquay (Dublin; allowed by Betham, Ulster, 1813). Ar. three wolves' heads erased sa. langued gu. collared and chained or. *Crest*—Two swords in saltire, points down ppr. pommels and hilts or. *Motto*— Licentiam refrœna.

Macqueen (Corrybrough, co. Inverness, known in the Highlands as the Clan Revan). Ar. three wolves' heads couped sa. *Crest*—An heraldic tiger ramp. erm. holding an arrow, point downwards ar. pheoned gu. *Supporters*—Two heraldic tigers ar. *Motto*—Constant and faithful.

Macqueen (THOMAS POTTER MACQUEEN, Esq., of Ridgmount House, co. Bedford, formerly M.P. for that shire). Vert a pegasus saliant ar. a chief or, quartering POTTER, viz., Sa. a fesse erm. betw. three cinquefoils ar. *Crest*—A wolf's head erased ppr. *Motto*—Quæ sursum volo videre.

M'Quhan (Scotland). Ar. three were-wolves' heads couped sa.

Macrae, or Macraigh (Scotland). Ar. a fess betw. three stars in chief and a lion ramp. in base gu.

Macrae (Orangefield, 1736). Ar. a fess betw. three mullets in chief and a lion ramp. in base gu. *Crest*—A hand grasping a scymitar ppr. *Motto* — Malim esse quam videri.

Mac Ranell (co. Leitrim; ancestor of REYNOLDS; Reg. Ulster's Office). Vert a lion ramp. betw. three escallops all ppr. *Crest*—On a mount a stag couchant all ppr.

Macrath (Fallbower, co. Mayo; confirmed, 1742, to FERGUS MACRATH, Esq.). Az. a fess betw. a star of eight rays in chief and a lion ramp. in base or. *Crest*—A naked arm couped below the elbow, holding in the hand the upper part of a broken lance all ppr. headed or.

Macreadie (Pearston, co. Ayr). Ar. a fesse quarterly sa. and or, betw. three trefoils vert. *Crest*—A dexter hand grasping a sword ppr. *Motto*—Semper paratus.

Mac Rery (Reg. Ulster's Office). Ar. a lion ramp. az. crowned or, holding in the dexter paw a sword ppr. pommel and hilt of the third. *Crest*—A demi lion ramp. az. crowned or, holding in the dexter paw a sword ppr. pommel and hilt gold.

Mac Shanly (a Sept possessed of Corcachlan, co. Roscommon. The Four Masters record, under the year 1254, that SITRIG MAC SEANLAOIGH was taken prisoner by Felim, son of Cathal Crovdearg O'Conor, and under the year 1404, that DONOGH, son of MOROGH MAC SHANLY, a landed proprietor of Corcachlan, the intimate friend of RODERICK O'CONOR, King of Connaught, died). Ar. a lion pass. or, in chief three estoiles of the last. *Crest*—A gauntlet erect grasping a broken sword ppr.

Mac Sheehy (Reg. Ulster's Office). Quarterly, 1st az. a lion pass. guard. ar.; 2nd, ar. three lizards vert; 3rd, az. three pole-axes in fess or; 4th, ar. a ship with three masts sa. *Crest*—An arm in armour, couped below the elbow and erect, holding in the hand a sword, the blade entwined with a serpent all ppr.

Mac Surtaine, alias Yorden, or Jordan (Lord of the Dessen, in Connaught; Reg. Ulster's Office). Ar. a fess sa. in base a lion pass. of the last (another coat bears three mullets sa. in chief).

Mac Sween (Granada, 1773). Per pale ar. and sa. a saltire, and in base a crescent all counterchanged. *Crest*—A broadsword and bow in saltire ppr. *Motto*—By the providence of God.

Mac Sweeney (an Irish Sept possessed of a territory in co. Donegal, of the race of O'NEILL, and claiming descent from SUIBHNE MENN, or SWEENEY *the Renowned*, who was monarch of Ireland A.D. 616-28; MACSWEENEY FANAIT was chief of this Sept., while St. Kevin was at Glen-da-loch, Reg. Ulster's Office). Or, on a fess vert three boars pass. sa. a lizard ar. *Crest*—An arm in armour embowed, holding a battle axe all ppr.

Mac Sweeney (MACSWEENEY NA TUADH, *i.e.*, of the axes). Az. two boars ramp. combatant or, in chief two battle axes

647

in saltire of the last. *Crest*—A demi griffin ramp. or, holding in the claws a lizard ppr.

Mac Sweeney (Rynedwocharrigy, co. Donegal; Fun. Ent. Ulster's Office, 1638, Captain DANIEL GORME MAC SWEENEY, son and heir of DANIEL MAC SWEENEY). Same *Arms* and *Crest*.

Mac Sweeney (Duagh, co. Donegal). Or, two boars ramp. combatant sa. on a chief of the second two battle axes in saltire of the first, blades ar. *Crest*—A boar pass. sa.

Mac Sweeney (Reg. Ulster's Office). Ar. a fess betw. three boars pass. sa. armed and bristled or. *Crest*—A boar pass. sa. bristled or.

Mac Sweeney (co. Donegal, MORAGH MOR MAC SWEENEY, Chieftain, 1267; Reg. Ulster's Office). Ar. a lion in chief and a boar in base both pass. gu.

Mac Swiney (confirmed to Alderman PETER PAUL MAC SWINEY, Lord Mayor of Dublin 1864 and 1875). Ar. on a fess az. betw. in chief a lion pass. gu. and in base a boar pass. sa. two battle axes in saltire or. *Crest*—A demi griffin segreant or, holding a lizard ppr. and charged on the breast with two battle axes in saltire sa. *Motto*—Tuagha tulaig abu.

Mac Swyny, and Mac Swyne. Same as MAC SWEENEY.

M'Taggart (London, from Scotland, 1796). Ar. a bend sa. betw. two owls ppr. *Crest*—An owl ppr. *Motto*—Ratione non vi.

M'Taggart (Madras, 1842). Ar. a fess gu. betw. three trefoils slipped vert, on a chief erm. a lion ramp. of the second betw. two cinquefoils of the third. *Crest*—A lion's head erased ppr. *Motto*—Ditat Deus.

M'Tavish (Dunarday, Scotland, 1793). Quarterly, 1st and 4th, gyronny of eight sa. and ar.; 2nd and 3rd, ar. a buck's head cabossed gu. attired or, on a chief engr. az. a cross crosslet fitchée betw. two mullets of the third. *Crest*—A boar's head erased or. *Motto*—Non oblitus.

M'Tavish (Gartbeg, Scotland, 1793). Quarterly, as the last, within a bordure or. Same *Crest* and *Motto*.

Mac Tiernan (a branch of O'ROURKE). Erm. two lions pass. gu. *Crest*—A griffin statant gu. wings erect vert.

M'Turk (Stenhouse, co. Dumfries). Ar. a chev. az. betw. two hunting horns vert, garnished and stringed gu. in chief, and in base a burning mount ppr. *Crest*—A ram's head cabossed or. *Motto*—Pace vel bello.

Mac Vais (an Irish Sept of the same race as O'FLYNN, from which descends the Sept of MAC EVOY; Reg. Ulster's Office). Az. a wolf pass. ar. in chief three bezants. *Crest*—A hand couped at the wrist erect, grasping a snake all ppr.

McVeagh (Lurgan, co. Armagh; confirmed, 1782, to Captain JOSEPH McVEAGH, 101st Regt. of Foot, son of SIMON McVEAGH, and grandson of FERDINAND McVEAGH, Esq., of Lurgan). Erm. a lion pass. guard. or, on a chief az. a crescent betw. two roses gold. *Crest*—An arm embowed in armour, holding in the hand a tilting spear all ppr. *Motto*— Per ardua.

M'Vicar-Affleck (Edinghame, Scotland, 1777). Quarterly, 1st and 4th, ar. a galley, her oars in action and sails furled sa. a flame of fire on the masthead ppr. betw. an eagle's head erased of the last in the dexter, and a cross crosslet fitchée gu. in the sinister chief points, for VICAR; 2nd and 3rd, ar. three bars sa. within a bordure gu., for AFFLECK. *Crest*—A green branch growing out of the trunk of an oak tree ppr. *Motto*—Tandem.

M'Whirter (Dr. JOHN M'WHIRTER, East India Company's Service, 1824). Per fesse or and sa. a lion ramp. counterchanged, armed and langued gu. on a canton of the last an Esculapius's rod paleways with serpents entwined ar. *Crest* —An antique Scottish harp or, with nine strings ar. *Motto* —Te Deum laudamus.

Mac Williams (co. Gloucester; WILLIAM MAC WILLIAMS; his dau. and heir, ISABEL, *m.* Sir JOHN SEYMOUR, Knt., of Hache, High Sheriff co. Southampton, 9 Henry VI., A.D. 1434. Visit. Oxon, 1566). Per bend ar. and gu. three roses bendways counterchanged.

Mac Worth (Reg. Ulster's Office). Per pale indented erm. and sa. a chev. company counter-compony or and gu.

Madacres, or Maders. Erm. on a fesse gu. three annulets or.

Madden. See O'MADDEN.

Madden (confirmed by Roberts, Ulster, 1647, as the ancient coat armour of his ancestors differenced, to Lieutenant HUGH MADDEN, descended from an ancient family of that name, co. Galway, who served Charles I. under Lord *Dockwro*). Sa. a falcon seizing a duck ar. on a chief or, a cross crosslet gu. *Crest*—A wolf saliant gu. *Motto*—Christo duce vincamus.

Madden (Bloxham Beauchamp, co. Oxford, Baggots Rath, co. Dublin, Manor Waterhouse, co. Fermanagh, and now of Hilton Park, co. Monaghan; Fun. Ent. Ulster's Office, 1671,

ELIZABETH, dau. and co-heir of CHARLES WATERHOUSE, Esq., of Manor Waterhouse, and wife of JOHN MADDEN, Esq., of Maddenton, co. Kildare, eldest son of THOMAS MADDEN, Esq., of Baggots Rath, who was eldest son of JOHN MADDEN, Esq., of Bloxham Beauchamp, the son of HUGH MADDEN, Esq., of same place). Same Arms, the cross botonnée. Crest—Out of a ducal coronet gu. a falcon rising or, holding in the beak a cross crosslet fitchée also gu. Another Crest (Fun. Ent.)—A falcon, wings expanded ar. membered or, holding in the dexter paw a cross botonnée gu. Motto—Fortior qui se vincit.

Madden (Roslea Manor, co. Fermanagh). Same Arms, Crest, and Motto, a crescent for diff.

Madden (Inch House, co. Dublin). Same Arms, Crest, and Motto, a mullet for diff.

Madden (Meadesbrook; descended from ROBERT MADDEN, Esq. of Dunmore, co. Dublin, d. 1635, second son of THOMAS MADDEN; Fun. Ent. Ulster's Office, JANE, dau. of said ROBERT MADDEN, m. Rev. JOHN GOLDSMITH, Parson of Newtown, co. Meath, ancestor of OLIVER GOLDSMITH, the Poet). Same Arms.

Madden (granted by Betham, Ulster, to Sir FREDERICK MADDEN, K.A., Gentleman of the Privy Chamber, son of WILLIAM JOHN MADDEN, Esq., of Portsmouth, and grandson of JAMES MADDEN, of Cole Hill House, Fulham, Middlesex, and to their descendants). Sa. a falcon or, belled gu. preying on a mallard ar. on a chief indented of the second a cross botonnée of the third. Crest—Out of a ducal coronet gu. a falcon rising or, holding in the beak a cross botonnée, as in the arms. Motto—Propria virtute audax.

Madder (co. Stafford). Erm. on a fesse wavy az. three lions ramp. or. Crest—On the trunk of a tree lying fesseways vert a lion sejant or.

Madder, or Mather (Scotland). Az. two bars ar. on a chief of the last an escallop betw. two mullets of the first.

Maddersfield (co. Worcester; temp. Charles II.). Az. on a bend or, three bars dancettée gu.

Maddersfield (co. Worcester). Az. on a bend cotised or, three bars dancettée gu.

Maddersfield (co. Worcester). Az. on a bend double cotised or, three bars dancettée gu.

Maddestock (co. Warwick). Ar. on a chief az. two mullets or.

Maddison (Unthank, co. Durham. Visit. 1575). Quarterly, 1st and 4th, ar. on a chev. betw. three martlets sa. as many mullets or, for MARLEY; 2nd, ar. three bars gu. a bordure sa.; 3rd, sa. a fleur-de-lis ar. Crest—A dexter arm erect vested erminois, hand ppr. grasping a battle axe sa. WILLIAM MADDISON, of Ellergill, having married the heiress of MARLEY, of Unthank, bore the MARLEY arms till 1635, when Sir LIONELL MADDISON, Knt., of Newcastle, descended of the MADDISONS, of Ellergill, in the bishopric of Durham, obtained a grant, 6 June, 1635, from Le Neve, Norroy, of the following arms—Quarterly, 1st and 4th, ar. two battle axes in saltire sa.; 2nd and 3rd, ar. on a chev. sa. betw. three martlets of the second, a mullet or, for MARLEY. Crest—An armed arm with a gauntlet ppr. garnished gold, issuing out of a crown flory, and holding a battle axe ppr. charged with a cross gu. the staff sa.

Maddison (Partney Hall, co. Lincoln). Quarterly, 1st and 4th, ar. two battle axes in saltire sa., for MADDISON; 2nd and 3rd, ar. a chev. sa. charged with a mullet or, betw. three martlets of the second, for MARLEY. Crest—Out of a crown flory or, a cubit arm in armour ppr. grasping a battle axe sa. Motto—Væ timido.

Maddock. Per pale az. and gu. two lions pass. or.

Maddock (Naseby, co. Northants). See ASHBY, of Naseby.

Maddocks. Per pale gu. and az. two lions pass. in fesse or. Crest—An elephant's head erased gu.

Maddox (Wormley, co. Herts, bart., extinct 1716; Sir BENJAMIN MADDOX m. DOROTHY, dau. and heir of Sir WILLIAM GLASCOKE, Knt., of Wormley, was so created, 1676, d. s. p. m.). Per pale az. and gu. two lions pass. in pale or. Crest—A Bengal tiger pass. guard. ducally gorged ppr.

Maddox (ISAAC MADDOX, Bishop of St. Asaph, 1736-43, and of Worcester, 1743-59). Same Arms.

Maddy (co. Gloucester). Az. a fesse betw. a fleece in chief and a wolf pass. in base or. Crest—A garb vert, charged with a fleece, as in the arms.

Madelley (St. Pancras, co. Middlesex, and co. Salop). As. on a fesse embattled counter-embattled betw. six martlets or, a lion pass. reguard. betw. two crosses crosslet fitchée sa. Crest—A hawk ppr. preying on a martlet sa.

Madeson (arms in the Chapel, University College, Oxford. Visit. Oxon, 1574). Ar. a chev. betw. three martlets sa.

648

Madeston (granted 1587). Ar. on a chev. betw. three martlets sa. as many mullets or. Crest—A cubit arm erect in armour per pale crenellée or and ar. holding in the gauntlet a halbert headed and garnished of the last.

Madeston. Gu. three maidens' heads couped ar. crined or.

Madeston, or Madesson. Barry of four az. and ar. in chief a lion ramp. or. Crest—An ostrich reguard. sa. ducally crowned or, resting the dexter foot on a pellet.

Madley (co. Somerset). Barry wavy of six erm. and gu. on a chev. az. three fleurs-de-lis or.

Madoc (Llanfryneich, co. Brecon). Sa. a chev. betw. three spears' heads ar. embrued gu.

Madoc. Gu. a lion ramp. or, a bordure engr. of the last.

Madoc (DAVID AP MADOC AP LLEWELLYN VYCHAN AP LLEWELLYN AP MADOC VAEL, which latter is buried in Marchwiel Church). Erm. a lion ramp. az.

Madoc (Hendower, co. Merioneth). Ar. on a chev. gu. three fleurs-de-lis or.

Madoc (Prince of Lower Powys). Ar. a lion ramp. sa.

Madoc Goch (Mawddwy, co. Merioneth). Or, a lion sa. a bordure go.

Madoc ap Raen. Sa. a chev. betw. three hawks' lures, stringed or.

Madock (Hartbury, co. Gloucester). Az. a bend or, in chief three boys' heads couped at the shoulders ar. each enwrapped about the neck with a snake ppr. in base as many griffins' heads erased of the third. Crest—A lion's head erased or, pierced through the neck with a sword in pale, the point coming out at the top of the head embrued ppr. hilted and pommelled of the first.

Madock. Same Arms. Crest—An engle displ. holding in the dexter claw a sword, and in the sinister a pistol all ppr.

Madock (Reg. Ulster's Office). Ar. on a fesse betw. three crosses crosslet fitchée sa. as many cinquefoils of the field. Crest—A demi wolf reguard. ar. vulned on the shoulder ppr.

Madocke (co. Suffolk). Or, fretty sa.

Madocks (co. Middlesex; confirmed 26 March, 1592). Ar. a chev. betw. three castles sa. flammant gu.

Madocks (Vron-Yw and Glanywern, North Wales; descended from Sir ROBERT PENDERLING, Knt., Constable of Diserth Castle, temp. Henry II.). Quarterly, 1st and 4th, ar. a butterfly gu. paleways betw. three roses of the last, in the centre chief, betw. the two upper roses, and over the head of the butterfly a crown or, for Sir ROBERT PENDERLING: 2nd and 3rd, gu. a lion ramp. ar. armed az., for WILLIAMS, of Vron Iw. Crest—A demi lion ramp.

Madox (London, and Masterley, co. Salop). Per pale gu. and az. two lions pass. or. Crest—A lion sejant or, in the dexter paw a sword ar. hilt and pomnel of the first.

Madox. Same Arms. Crest—A lion's paw erased, holding a dagger both ppr.

Madras, See of. Ar. on a mount vert, in front of a banyan tree, a kid on the dexter couchant looking towards the sinister, and on the sinister a leopard couchant guard. all ppr. a chief az. thereon a dove rising, in the beak an olive branch also ppr. betw. two crosses pattée or.

Madreston. Gu. an eagle displ. erm. armed or. - Crest—An acorn or (sometimes, a torteau charged with a sun or).

Madworth (co. Lincoln). Ar. on a bend sa. three pheons of the field.

Mady. Az. a chev. erm. betw. three pheons ar.

Madyson (co. Durham, Fonby, co. Lincoln, Newcastle-on-Tyne, co. Northumberland). Ar. a chev. betw. three martlets sa. Crest—A cubit arm erminois, holding in the hand ppr. a battle axe sa.

Mael ap Cadvael (Lord of Melienydd; derived from CADELH AP RHODRI MAWR, King of Wales; descendants: I. GETHINS, of Masebrook; II. EVANS, of Llandrino; III. BOWEN, of Llandrino, and Brithdir, in Gilsfield; IV. MORRIS, of Gallt Vawr, in Myvod). Or, a cross moline pierced or the field betw. four lozenges az.

Maelawg Crwm (Lord of Llechwedd Isa, co. Carnarvon; descendants; CHALONER, of Lloran, Ganol, Denbigh, and Chester). Ar. a chev. sa. betw. three cherubs' heads or.

Maelor Crwm (Lord of Llechuidd-isaf and Creuddyn, co. Carnarvon; Founder of the VII. Noble Tribe of North Wales and Powys; from MAELOR derived the CHALONERS, of Gisborough, co. York). Ar. on a chev. sa. three angels or.

Maesmor (Maesmor, in Dinmael, co. Denbigh; derived, through GRIFFITH, of Maesmor, second son of RHYS AP DAVID, Baron of Rûg in Edeirnion, from OWEN BROGYNTYN, Lord of Edeirnion, Dinmael, and Abertanat; CATHERINE, dau. and heiress of ROBERT MAESMOR, Esq., of Maesmor, m. JOHN MORRIS, Esq., of Hafod-y-Maedd). Ar. a lion ramp. sa. armed and langued gu.

Magan (Emoe, co. Westmeath; descended from RICHARD MAGAN, Esq., of Emoe, one of the Jacobite officers included within the Articles of Limerick, whose father, RICHARD MAGAN, was elder brother of THOMAS MAGAN, ancestor of MAGAN, of Clonearl; FRANCIS MAGAN, Esq., of Emoe, d. 1841, leaving three daus. his co-heirs, I. MARY, m. JOHN FRANCIS LENTAIGNE, Esq., C.B., of Tallaght, co. Dublin; II. MARGARET, m. MICHAEL CAHILL, Esq., of Ballyconra, co. Kilkenny; III. ANNA MARIA, m. MICHAEL CORCORAN, Esq., Barrister-at-law). Ar. a chev. betw. three boars erms. az. tusked, hoofed, and bristled or. Crest—A boar's head erased az. tusked and bristled or. Motto—Virtute probitate.

Magan (Clonearl, King's co., and Togherstown, co. Meath; descended from MORGAN MAGAN, Esq., brother of THOMAS MAGAN, Esq., ancestor of MAGAN, of Emoe; confirmed by Hawkins, Ulster, 1705, to THOMAS MAGAN, Esq., of Togherstown, Sheriff co. Westmeath, and MORGAN MAGAN, his brother, and their descendants; represented by Capt. THOMAS TILSON SHAW MAGAN, Madras Army). Same Arms, &c.

Magawly-Cerati(VALERIO, Count Magawly-Cerati, a Count of the Holy Roman Empire, representative of a very ancient Irish family, the chiefs of which were styled Princes of Calry, in the county of Westmeath; the title of Count was conferred in 1631 on Field-Marshal PHILIP HENRY MAGAWLY, by the Emperor Charles VI.). Ar. a lion ramp. gu. in the dexter and sinister chief points a dexter hand of the last. Crest— A demi lion ramp. gu. Supporters—The black eagles of Austria. Motto—Laimh deargh aboo.

Magawley (Ireland). See McGAWLEY.

Magdalen College (Oxford; founded in the year 1456 by WILLIAM PATTEN, or, as he was otherwise called from the place of his nativity, WILLIAM OF WAINFLEET, Bishop of Winchester). Lozengy erm. and sa. on a chief of the last three lilies slipped ar.

Magdalen College (Cambridge; founded in 1541 by THOMAS AUDLEY, Baron Walden, and Lord Chancellor of England). Quarterly, per pale indented or and az. in the 2nd and 3rd quarters an eagle displ. of the first, on a bend of the second a fret betw. two martlets of the first.

Magee (Most Rev. WILLIAM MAGEE, Bishop of Raphoe 1819, Archbishop of Dublin 1822, d. 1831). Sa. three leopards' faces ar.

Magee (Right Rev. WILLIAM CONNOR MAGEE, Bishop of Peterborough 1868, son of Rev. JOHN MAGEE, Vicar of Drogheda, and grandson of the Archbishop of Dublin). Same Arms.

Magens (MAGENS DORRIEN MAGENS, Esq., of Hammerwood Lodge, East Grinstead, co. Sussex, and London). Quarterly, 1st and 4th, az. a cross hameçon ar.; 2nd and 3rd, ar. on a mount in base three trefoils issuing vert, in chief a gem ring or, stoned az. Crest—An arm erect ppr. holding three trefoils vert.

Magenis (Ireland). See McGENIS.

Magenis (Waringstown, co. Devon; confirmed by Betham, Ulster, to RICHARD MAGENIS, Esq., of that place). Vert a lion ramp. or, on a chief ar. a dexter hand couped gu. Crest—A boar pass. ppr. Motto—Sola salus vertere Deo.

Mageoghegan (Ireland). Ar. a lion ramp. betw. three dexter hands couped at the wrist gu. Crest—A bloodhound pass. collared indented ppr.

Maggot (co. Kent). Ar. on a canton gu. a round buckle of the field.

Maghull (Lords of the Manor of Maghull, co. Chester, temp. King John, in which place RICHARD MAGHULL, Esq., of Maghull, was living, 1639). Ar. a swepe (or balista) az. charged with a stone or. "This was an engine of war in fashion seeming like to that which the brewers use to draw water withal, and therefore we call it a swepe as they do. With this engine they used to throw great stones into the towns and fortifications of the enemy."—Guillim.

Magill. See MAC GILL.

Magill. Ar. three doves az. Crest—A savage's head couped ppr.

Magill (exemplified to JOHN HAWKINS, Esq., eldest son of JOHN HAWKINS, Esq., of Rathfriland, co. Down, upon his assuming, 1701, the name of MAGILL, in compliance with the will of his maternal uncle, Sir JOHN MAGILL, Bart.). Quarterly, 1st and 4th, az. three pewits ar., for MAGILL; 2nd and 3rd, per chev. ar. and vert three stags trippant ppr., for HAWKINS. Crest—A falcon standing on a hawk's lure both ppr. lined ar. and vert.

Magin (England). Ar. two palets sa. a chief gu. Crest—A demi wivern vert.

Maginn (Ireland). Sa. two palets ar. a chief or. Crest—A cockatrice displ. vert.

Magnall (Manchester and London; granted 1765). Ar. on a mount vert a swepe (or balista) az. charged with a stone

ppr. a chief per fesse embattled or and gu. Crest—On a mount vert an eagle rising ppr. crowned with an Eastern coronet or.

Magnay (Postford House, co. Surrey, bart.). Erm. fretty gu. on a chief per pale of the second and az. a sword ppr. pommel and hilt or, surmounting a key saltirewise, the ward upwards gold, interlaced with the collar of the Lord Mayor of the city of London, betw. two leopards' faces erminois. Crest—A lion ramp. sa. billety erminois murally crowned, gorged with a chain reflexed over the back, and holding betw. the forepaws a leopard's face or. Motto—Magna est veritas.

Magnes. Barry of six vert and gu. on a bend or, a lion pass. betw. two cinquefoils purp.

Magnus (co. York). Barry of six vert and gu. on a fesse or, a lion pass. guard. betw. two cinquefoils purp. Crest—A lion's gamb erased or.

Magor (Penventon House, Redruth, co. Cornwall). Gu. an anchor ppr. on a chief ar. three roses of the first. Crest—A greyhound's head erased and collared.

Magrath (Ireland). See McGRATH.

Magrath (Lambeth, London). Quarterly, 1st, vert three lions pass. in pale ar.; 2nd, gu. an arm fesseways, couped ppr. the hand holding a cross crosslet fitchée or; 3rd, gu. an arm erect, the hand holding a battle axe in bend sinister; 4th, vert a buck saliant or. Crest—An arm fesseways couped ppr. Motto—Salus in fide.

Magrath-FitzGerald. See FITZGERALD.

Maguire. See McGUIRE.

Maguire (Linea Antiqua, Ulster's Office). Gu. a salmon naiant in fess ar. in chief a dexter hand apaumée of the last. Another Coat—Gu. a salmon naiant ppr. on a chief ar. a dexter hand apaumée of the first.

Mahend. Per fesse ar. and gu. a cross moline counterchanged.

Maher (Ballinkeele, co. Wexford; confirmed to JOHN MAHER, Esq., and to the descendants of his grandfather, JOHN MAHER, Esq., of Tully-mac-James, co. Tipperary). Az. two lions ramp. combatant or, supporting a sword in pale ppr. in base two crescents of the second. Crest—On a mount vert a hawk rising, belled and hooded ppr. on each wing a crescent or. Motto—In periculis audax.

Maher (Woodlands, co. Somerset). Same Arms. Crest— An eagle with wings expanded preying.

Mahewe, alias Heller, or Mayow (Lostwithiel, co. Cornwall). Gu. a chev. vair betw. three ducal crowns or. Crest—A Cornish chough erm. Another Crest—An eagle with wings expanded or, preying on a snake nowed ppr.

Mahewe (co. Essex). Same Arms, field az. and a bordure engr. gu.

Mahewe, or Mathew (Clipsby and Byllockegsby, co. Norfolk). Same Arms, the bordure engr. or. Crest—A unicorn's head erased ar. maned gu. the horn twisted of the first and second, charged on the neck with a chev. vair.

Mahewe. Az. a fesse erm. betw. six eagles' heads erased ar.

Mahewe. Az. a chev. vairé ar. and gu. within a bordure engr. of the last.

Mahewe, or Mahuys. Erm. on a fesse gu. three palets or.

Mahewe, or Mahuys. Erm. a fesse counter-componée or and gu.

Mahomud (NOWAB ALI MAHOMUD KHAN BAHADOOR, Her Majesty's Justice of the Peace, Bombay, a Jagheerdar of His Highness the Nizam's Court, in the Deccan, and Consul-General of the Sublime Porte at Bombay, East Indies, bears the following armorial bearings, under the authority of the College of Arms, London). Quarterly, az. and gu. on a bend engr. or, betw. a horse's head erased in the 2nd quarter, and in the 3rd a dexter hand couped and erect ar. an arrow point upwards sa. on a chief of the third a ship in full sail on waves of the sea ppr. Crest—A demi lion ppr. charged with two bars or, holding in the dexter paw a sword also ppr. and resting the sinister upon an escutcheon az. charged with the sun in splendour gold. Motto—Nil desperandum.

Mahon (Ireland). Or, a lion ramp. az. Crest—A demi husbandman holding over the dexter shoulder an ox-yoke ppr.

Mahon (Baron Hartland, extinct 1845). Or, a lion ramp. az. armed and langued gu. Crest—An heraldic tiger statant, holding in the dexter paw a broken tilting spear all ppr. Supporters—Dexter, a lion guard. az.; sinister, a stag ppr. ducally gorged and chained or. Motto—Periculum fortitudine evasi.

Mahon (PAKENHAM-MAHON; exemplified to HENRY SANDFORD PAKENHAM, Esq., who m. GRACE, dau. and heiress of

Denis Mahon, Esq., of Strokestown, co. Roscommon, upon his assuming, by royal licence, 1847, the additional surname and arms of **Mahon**). Quarterly, 1st and 4th, or, a lion ramp. az. armed and langued gu., for **Mahon**; 2nd and 3rd, quarterly, or and gu., in the 1st quarter an eagle displ. vert, a martlet for diff., for **Pakenham**. *Crest*—An heraldic tiger pass. holding in the dexter paw a broken tilting spear ppr. *Motto*—Periculum fortitudine evasi.

Mahon (Castlegar, co. Galway, bart.). Per fesse sa. and ar. an ostrich counterchanged. *Crest*—A dexter arm in armour embowed ppr. garnished or, holding in the hand a dagger also ppr. pommel and hilt gold. *Motto*—Moniti meliora sequamur.

Mahon. Gu. out of a maunch erm. a hand ppr. holding a fleur-de-lis or.

Mahony (Dunloe Castle, co. Kerry; allowed by Fortescue, Ulster, 1792, as the arms of **Daniel Mahony**, Esq., of Dunloe, descended from O'Mahony, of Castle O'Mahony, co. Cork). Quarterly, 1st and 4th, or, a lion ramp. az.; 2nd, per pale ar. and gu. a lion ramp. counterchanged; 3rd, ar. a chev. gu. betw. three lizards in pale sa. *Crest*—A naked arm embowed, the hand grasping a sword flammant all ppr. *Another Crest*—An arm in armour embowed, holding a sword all ppr. run through a fleur-de lis or. *Motto*—Lasair romhuin a buadh.

Mahony (allowed by Fortescue, Ulster, 1792, to **William Mahony**, Knight of the Order of Maria Theresa, an officer in the Austrian Service, second son of **John Mahony**, Esq., of Dunloe Castle). Same *Arms* and *Motto*. *Crest*—Out of a foreign coronet or, with nine silver balls on the rim, an arm in armour embowed, holding a sword all ppr. run through a fleur-de-lis gold.

Mahony (exemplified by Betham, Ulster, to **John Hickson**, a minor, second son of **John Hickson**, Esq., of Dingle, co. Kerry, on his assuming, by royal licence, 1827, the surname of **Mahony** only, in memory of his maternal uncle, **Richard Mahony**, Esq., of Dromore, co. Kerry). Quarterly, 1st and 4th, or, a lion ramp. az.; 2nd, per pale ar. and gu. a lion ramp. counterchanged; 3rd. ar. a chev. gu. betw. three snakes wavy in pale sa. *Crest*—Out of the coronet of a count of France, a dexter arm armed, embowed ppr. the hand bare, grasping a sword ppr. hilt and pommel or, run through a fleur-de-lis of the last. *Motto*—Lasair romhuin a buadh.

Maideston (in Ulcombe Church, Kent). Sa. a chev. betw. three covered cups ar. crowned or.

Maidestone (co. Lincoln). Erm. two battleaxes in saltire sa.

Maidman (Isle of Portsea, co. Southampton; granted 1765). Az. on a chev. or, betw. three doves ppr. as many laurel slips vert. *Crest*—A dexter arm embowed per pale indented az. and or, cuffed ar. the hand ppr. grasping a dove, as in the arms.

Maidman. Same *Arms*. *Crest*—A leopard's head erased and guard. ducally gorged.

Maidstone (Boxsted, co. Essex; granted 1614). Or, two battleaxes in saltire sa. headed ar.

Maidstone, Town of (co. Kent). Ar. a fesse wavy az. betw. three torteaux, on a chief gu. a lion pass. guard. or.

Main (co. Buckingham). Erm. on a bend sa. three dexter hands or.

Main (England). Gu. on a bend ar. three cinquefoils of the field. *Crest*—A leopard ramp. ppr.

Main (Scotland). Ar. a chev. cotised betw. three pheons gu. *Crest*—An escallop or, charged with a mullet gu.

Main (Easter House). Ar. a chev. cotised betw. two pheons in chief and a unicorn's head erased in base of the last.

Main (Lochwood, co. Stirling). Ar. a chev. gu. voided of the field betw. two pheons in chief and a unicorn's head erased in base sa. *Crest*—A hand throwing a dart ppr. *Motto*—Projeci.

Main (Edinburgh, 1685). Ar. on a chev. voided gu. betw. two fleurs-de-lis in chief and a unicorn's head couped in base a pheon sa. *Crest*—A dexter hand holding an annulet or, stoned az. *Motto*—Virtute et labore.

Mainard (co. Devon). Ar. a chev. betw. three sinister hands gu.

Maine (granted 1765). Erm. on a chev. gu. an escallop betw. a sinister and dexter hand couped in bend ar. on a canton az. a covered cup with handles or. *Crest*—Out of a mural coronet per pale gu. and erm. a dexter arm erased, garnished or, grasping a spear, point downwards ppr. *Motto*—Vincit pericula virtus.

Maingy, Maingay, or Mainguy (Guernsey). Erm. three eagles' legs erased sa. *Crest*—A wolf's head erased erminois.

Mainstone, alias Mayneston (Urchingfield, co.
650

Hereford, and London, *temp.* Edward III.). Az. a chev. betw. three hedgehogs ar. *Crest*—A hedgehog ar.

Mainstone. Or, on a chev. gu. a hand extended fesseways ar.

Mainwaring (Over Peover, co. Chester; founded by **Ranulphus**, who accompanied the Conqueror to England, and received the grant of fifteen lordships in co. Chester, including Peuer, now Over Peover). Ar. two bars gu. *Ancient Coat*—Ar. two bars gu. on a chief of the second a lion pass. guard. or. *Crest*—Out of a ducal coronet or, an ass's head in a hempen halter ppr. *Motto*—Devant si je puis.

Mainwaring (Over Peover, co. Chester, bart., extinct 1797; Sir **Henry Mainwaring**, the fourth and last bart., was the son of **Henry Mainwaring**, brother of Sir **Thomas Mainwaring**, the third bart., by **Diana**, his wife, dau. of **William Blackett**, Esq.; she *m.* secondly, Rev. **Thomas Wetenhall**, Rector of Walthamstow, co. Essex, and had by him a son, **Thomas Wetenhall**, to whom the last bart. bequeathed the family estates, whereupon he assumed the name of **Mainwaring**, and had a son, **Henry Mainwaring**, created a bart. 1804). Ar. two bars gu., quartering az. three garbs or, for **Hugh Kevelioc**, *Earl of Chester, temp.* Henry II. *Crest*—Out of a ducal coronet or, an ass's head ppr. *Motto*—Devant si je puis.

Mainwaring (Whitmore, co. Stafford; descended from **Edward Mainwaring**, Esq., of Whitmore, a younger son of Sir **John Mainwaring**, of Over Peover, co. Chester, knighted in France in 1513). Same *Arms* as **Mainwaring**, of Over Peover.

Mainwaring (Exeter, co. **Devon**; **Christopher Mainwaring**, Visit. Devon, 1620, sixth son of **George Mainwaring**, the third son of **William Mainwaring**, Esq., of Namptwich, who was third son of **Randle Mainwaring**, Esq., of Kermincham, Namptwich, third son of **Randle Mainwaring**, Esq., of Over Peover, all in co. Chester). Same *Arms*, a border gobony or and sa. *Crest*—An ass's head erased ar. haltered and maned or.

Mainwaring (Ightfield, co. Salop; descended from **William**, second son of **Randle Mainwaring**, of Over Peover, who *d.* in 1546). Same *Arms*, &c., as **Mainwaring**, of Over Peover.

Mainwaring, or Manwaring (Kermincham, co. Chester; derived from **Ralph Mainwaring**, third son of **Randle Mainwaring**, Esq., of Over Peover, *d.* 1546; **Roger Manwaring Parker**, third son of **John Robert Parker**, Esq., of Green Park, co. Cork, by **Catherine**, his wife, dau. of **John Uniacke**, Esq., of Cottage, and **Frances**, his wife, dau. of **Roger Manwaring** of Kermincham, assumed in 1809 the surname and arms of **Manwaring**). Same *Arms*, &c., as **Mainwaring**, of Over Peover.

Mainwaring (Oteley Park, co. Salop; descended from **Randle**, third son of **Edward Mainwaring**, of Whitmore). Same *Arms* as **Mainwaring**, of Over Peover.

Mainwaring (Nantwich, co. Chester, 1613). Ar. two bars gu. betw. six martlets vert, three in chief, two in fesse, and one in base.

Mainwaring (Warmincham, co. Chester). Same *Arms* as **Mainwaring**, of Peover, without the hempen collar in the crest.

Mainwaring (**Milman-Mainwaring**; exemplified to **Charles Egerton Forbes Milman**, Esq., only son of Major-Gen. **Egerton Charles William Miles Milman**, upon his assuming, by royal licence, the additional name of **Mainwaring**). Quarterly, 1st and 4th, ar. two bars gu., for **Mainwaring**; 2nd and 3rd, az. a snake nowed or, betw. three dexter gauntlets open ar., for **Milman**. *Crests*—1st, **Mainwaring**: An ass's head erased ppr. haltered ar.; 2nd, **Milman**: A hart lodged per pale erm. and erminois, attired or, charged on the body with two hurts fessways.

Mainwaring (**Massey-Mainwaring**, Knaresborough, co. York; exemplified to Hon. **William Frederick Barton Massey**, fifth son of **Eyre**, third *Lord Clarina*, and to his wife, **Isabella Anne**, only dau. and heir of **Benjamin Lee Mainwaring**, Esq., of Knaresborough, and widow of Major-Gen. **Egerton Charles William Miles Milman**, upon their assuming, by royal licence, 8 May, 1874, the additional surname of **Mainwaring**). Quarterly, 1st and 4th, ar. two bars gu., and, for distinction, a canton of the last, for **Mainwaring**; 2nd and 3rd, ar. on a chev. betw. three lozenges sa. a lion pass. or, for **Massey**. *Crests*—1st, **Mainwaring**: An ass's head erased ppr. haltered ar. charged on the neck for distinction with a cross crosslet or; 2nd, **Massey**: Out of a ducal coronet or, a bull's head gu. armed sa.

Mainwaring (Over Peover, co. Chester, bart., formerly **Wetenhall**, created 1804). Ar. two bars gu., quartering the arms of **Hugh Kyvelioc**, *Earl of Chester*, being, az. six

garbs or. *Crest*—Out of a ducal coronet an ass's head or.
Motto Devant si je puis.

Mainwaring (Croxton, co. Chester; HUGH MAINWARING, illegitimate son of RANDLE MAINWARING, Esq., of Peover, *temp.* Henry VI., by EMMA DE FARINGTON, *m.* MARGARET, sister and heiress of RALPH CROXTON, Esq., of Croxton). Same *Arms* as MAINWARING, of Peover, within a bordure componée sa. and ar. *Crest*—An ass's head ppr.

Mainwaring (Newton, co. Kildare; Fun. Ent. Ulster's Office, RICHARD MAINWARING, *d.* 1622, *m.* ELEANOR, dau. of MICHAEL DELAHIDE, and left RICHARD and MARGARET MAINWARING). Ar. two bars gu. a mullet for diff.

Mainwaring (Kilkenny; HENRY MAINWARING, one of the Masters in Chancery in Ireland; Fun. Ent. Ulster's Office, of his son, THOMAS MAINWARING, *d.* 1623). Ar. two bars gu. betw. six martlets, three, two, and one.

Mair (W. MAIR, Esq., of Glassels). Or, three bars dancettée gu. the first charged with a crescent and estoile ar.

Mair (England). Barry of six indented or and gu. *Crest*—A demi pegasus issuing ar. enfiled round the waist with a ducal coronet gu.

Mair (Scotland). Ar. on a bend az. three eaglets displ. or.

Mair (Aberdeen, 1776). Or, three bars indented gu. that in chief charged with a crescent and a star of six points ar. *Crest*—A lion's head erased ar. *Motto*—Spes et fortitudo.

Mair (London, from co. Ayr, 1784). Or, three bars counter-indented gu. on the uppermost a crescent and a spur-rowel ar. a bordure az. *Crest*—A swan ppr. *Motto*—Candidior.

Maire (Hardwick, co. Durham, and Lartington, co. York; derived from JOHN MAIRE, of the city of Durham, who descended from the MAIRES of Meire, co. Chester). Ar. on waves ppr. a three-masted galley sa.

Maire. Ar. a spaniel dog pass. ppr. on a chief embattled az. a key paleways, the wards upwards, betw. two crosses crosslet or.

Maires (descended from POICTON, in France). Gu. a fesse erm. betw. three water bougets ar.

Mairis (Marston, co. Wilts; descended of an ancient baronial family, DE MAREYS, or DE MARISCO, lost their estates by the Wars of the Roses, originally seated at Huntspill, and Camely, co. Somerset). Quarterly, or and az. a cross quarterly gu. and ar. betw. an eagle displ. in the 1st and 4th quarters, and a water bouget in the 2nd and 3rd, counterchanged of the field. *Crest*—A mount vert, thereon a peacock in his pride or, from the beak issuant an escroll inscribed "Esse quam videri," the dexter foot resting on an escutcheon az. charged with a cross pattée fitchée gold. *Motto*—Si Deus nobiscum, quis contra nos?

Mairstoun (Park). Quarterly, 1st and 4th, ar. a chev. gu. a chief az.; 2nd and 3rd, ar. an eagle displ. sa.

Maison (Scotland). Ar. a bend wavy az. betw. two mullets in chief and a fleurs-de-lis in base gu.

Maister (Wood Hall, in Holderness, co. York; formerly of Winistead and Hull). Az. a fesse embattled betw. three griffins' heads erased or. *Crest*—Out of a mural crown or, a unicorn's head az. armed and crined gold. *Motto*—Vix ea nostra voco.

Maister (Beverley, co. York). Same *Arms* and *Crest.*

Maisterson (Nantwich, co. Chester, *temp.* Edward I.). See MASTERSON.

Maitland (Lethington and Thirlstane, co. Berwick). Or, a lion ramp. dechaussée gu.

Maitland (*Earl of Lauderdale*). Or, a lion ramp. dechaussé gu. within ¦a double tressure flory counterflory az. *Crest*—A lion sejant affrontée gu. ducally crowned, holding in the dexter paw a sword ppr. pommel and hilt or, in the sinister a fleur-de-lis az. *Supporters*—Two eagles, wings expanded ppr. *Motto*—Consilio et animis.

Maitland (RAMSAY-GIBSON-MAITLAND, of Clifton Hall, co. Mid-Lothian, bart.). Quarterly, 1st and 4th, or, a lion ramp. déchaussée gu. within a double tressure flory counterflory az., for MAITLAND; 2nd, quarterly, 1st and 4th, az. three keys fesseways in pale, wards downwards or, for GIBSON, 2nd and 3rd, az. a chev. betw. three battle axes ar. within a bordure of the last, for WRIGHT; 3rd, ar. an eagle displ. sa. within a bordure of the last bezanty, on a chief gu. two cinquefoils erm., for RAMSAY. *Crest and Motto*, as the last.

Maitland (Kilmaron, co. Fife, 1811). As *Earl of Lauderdale*, within a bordure embattled az. Same *Crest and Motto.*

Maitland (Eccles, co. Berwick; a cadet of Lethington). Or, a lion ramp. gu. dechaussée of the first, within a bordure az. *Crest*—A demi lion'ramp. gu. couped as in the arms, issuing out of water ppr. *Motto*—Luctor at emergam.

Maitland (Pittrichie, co. Aberdeen, bart., title extinct; descended from ROBERT, a younger son of ROBERT MAITLAND, of Thirlstane, *temp.* Robert III.). Same *Arms*, within a ¦

651

bordure chequy az. and ar. *Crest*—A lion's head erased gu. *Motto*—Paix et peu.

Maitland (Lieutenant of the Bass, Scotland, 1080). Same *Arms* as MAITLAND, of Lethington, within a bordure wavy az. *Crest*—A rock placed in the sea ppr. *Motto*—Non fluctuo fluctia.

Maitland (Scotland, 1685). Same *Arms*, charging the bordure with eight granadoes of the first. *Crest*, as the last. *Motto*—Attamen tranquillus.

Maitland (Dundrennan, co. Kirkcudbright). Quarterly, 1st and 4th, or, a lion ramp. déchaussée, within a bordure embattled gu.; 2nd and 3rd, ar. the ruins of an old abbey on a piece of ground ppr. *Crest*—A demi monk vested grey, holding in the dexter hand a crucifix ar. in the sinister a rosary ppr. *Motto*—Esse quam videri.

Maitland (Auchlane, co. Kirkcudbright, 1818). Or, a lion ramp. gu. within a bordure embattled of the last, on a chief sa. a rose ar. Same *Crest* and *Motto* as the *Earl of Lauderdale.*

Maitland (GAMMIE-MAITLAND, Shotover House, co. Oxford). Or, a lion ramp. gu. couped in all the joints of the first within a bordure az. *Crest*—A demi lion ramp. gu. couped as in the arms, issuing out of water ppr. *Motto*—Luctor ut emergam.

Majendie (Castle-Hedingham, co. Essex). Or, on a mount in base vert a tree betw. a serpent erect on the dexter, and a dove close on the sinister all ppr. *Crest*—An arm embowed in armour, the hand holding a scymitar all ppr.

Major, or Mager (Southampton and the Isle of Wight; Reg. Her. Off.). Gu. an anchor ar. on a chief or, three roses of the first. *Crest*—A greyhound's head gu. collared or.

Major (co. Leicester; arms confirmed and crest granted to JOHN MAJOR, gent., of Leicester, 15 May, 1646). Ar. two bars sa. in chief three mullets of the last pierced. *Crest*—A demi greyhound sa. collared ar. thereon three martlets of the first.

Major (Brampston, co. Nottingham). Same *Arms.* *Crest*—A greyhound ramp. sa. collared ar. thereon three mullets of the first.

Major (Worlingworth Hall, co. Suffolk; granted 1765). Az. three pillars of the Corinthian order, two and one, on the top of each a ball or. *Crest*—A dexter arm embowed, habited az. cuff ar. charged on the arm with a plate, in the hand ppr. a baton or.

Major-Henniker (*Baron Henniker*). See HENNIKER-MAJOR.

Major (HENNIKER-MAJOR, Stratford-upon-Slaney, co. Wicklow, bart.). Quarterly, 1st and 4th, or, on a chev. gu. betw. two crescents in chief, and in base an escallop az. three estoiles ar., for HENNIKER; 2nd and 3rd, az. three columns or pillars of the Corinthian order, two and one, on the top of each a ball or, for MAJOR. *Crests*—1st, HENNIKER: An escallop or, charged with an estoile gu.; 2nd, MAJOR: A dexter arm embowed, habited az. cuff ar. and charged on the elbow with a plate, holding in the hand ppr. a baton or. *Supporters*—Dexter, a stag ar. attired and unguled or, gorged with a chaplet of oak ppr. fructed gold, therefrom pendent a shield az. charged with the crest of HENNIKER; sinister, an otter ar. ducally gorged or, pendent therefrom a shield of the arms of MAJOR. *Motto*—Deus major columna.

Makareth (co. Lancaster). Gu. three cinquefoils or, a chief of the second. *Crest*—A dexter arm embowed in armour, holding in the hand a broken tilting spear all ppr.

Makelfeld (Bolton, co. York). Ar. on a chev. betw. three garbs or. banded or, as many buckles of the last.

Makepeace (Pensham Court, co. Worcester, Middle Temple, London, and co. Warwick; granted by Anstis, Garter, 1724, to WILLIAM MAKEPEACE, and the descendants of his father, WILLIAM MAKEPEACE, of co. Warwick). Az. on a fesse betw. two leopards pass. or, three crosses crosslet fitchée gu. *Crest*—A leopard pass. reguard. or, resting the dexter foot on a shield gu. charged with a cross crosslet fitchée gold.

Makepeace (London, and Warfield, co. Berks). Same *Arms* and *Crest.*

Makepeace. Same *Arms.* *Crest*—A unicorn's head ar. betw. two laurel branches orleways vert.

Makepeace. Az. on a fesse betw. two leopards pass. or, three crosses crosslet gu. *Crest*—A dove holding in the beak an olive branch all ppr.

Makerell. Az. three mackerels haurient ar.

Makingfield (co. York). Ar. on a bend·sa. three bezants.

Makins (Craven Hill, co. Middlesex). Ar. on a fesse embattled counter-embattled sa. betw. in chief two leopards ppr. belled or, and in base a lion's face of the second, an annulet gold betw. two bezants. *Crest*—A dexter arm embowed in armour ppr. encircled by an annulet or, and holding a flagstaff ppr. therefrom flowing a banner ar. charged with a lion's face gu. *Motto*—In lumine luce.

Malabasee. Or, three chevronels sa. bezantée.

Malabassell. Ar. (another, or) three chevronels sa. on each five plates.

Malbanc (Wick-Malbanc and Nantwich, co. Chester). Quarterly, or and gu. a bendlet sa.

Malbank (co. Dorset). Ar. four bars wavy az. over all a saltire ar.

Malbanke (co. Dorset). Barry wavy of eight ar. and gu. a saltire or. *Crest*—On a tortoise an eagle perched ppr.

Malbanke (co. Lancaster). Paly of six ar. and gu. a bend erm. on a canton or, a lion's head erased of the second. *Crest*—A lion's head erased gu. charged with a bend erm.

Malbanke (co. Stafford). Or, fretty gu. on a canton az. a cross patonce ar. (another, field ar. cross pattée or).

Malbech, Malbesh, or Malbish. Gu. a chev. or, betw. three hinds' heads erased ar.

Malbise. Ar. a chev. betw. two closets gu.

Malbone. Quarterly, or and gu. a bend sa.

Malbone. Or, two bends gobonated ar. and gu.

Malbourne (confirmed June, 1615). Az. three escallops ar. a border engr. of the last charged with eleven crosses crosslet fitchée gu.

Malby (co. Norfolk). Az. a cross formée or.

Malby, or Maltby. Ar. on a bend gu. three garbs or. *Crest*—An Indian goat pass. or.

Malby (Sir NICHOLAS MALBY, Chief Commissioner of Connaught, knighted at Athlone, by Sir HENRY SYDNEY, Lord Deputy of Ireland, 7 Oct. 1576). Ar. on a bend betw. two cotises gu. three garbs or.

Malbys. Ar. a chev. betw. three hinds' heads erased gu.

Malcake. Vert a saltire lozengy or.

Malcasty. Barry of eight ar. and gu. a bend sinister az. three bezants.

Malcher. Ar. on a bend engr. betw. two lions ramp. sa. three bezants.

Malcolm (Paltalloch, co. Argyll). Ar. on a saltire az. betw. four bucks' heads couped gu. five mullets or. *Crest*—A tower ar. *Supporters*—On either side a stag at gaze ppr. chain reflexed over the back or. *Motto*—In ardua petit.

Malcolm (Jamaica, 1773). As the last, with a galley or, in fess point for diff. Same *Crest* and *Motto*.

Malcolm (Balbeadie and Grange, co. Fife, bart., 1665). Or, a saltire az. betw. three stags' heads couped gu. *Crest*—A pyramid encircled by a laurel wreath ppr. *Motto*—Ardua tendo.

Malcolm (Col. HENRY MALCOLM, 1797). Or, a saltire az. betw. a lion ramp. gu. having on his head an engineer's helmet ppr. and three bucks' heads erased in flanks and base of the third. *Crest*—A castle ar. masoned sa. windows and portcullis gu. *Motto*—In ardua tendit.

Malcolm (Sir JAMES MALCOLM, K.C.B., second son of GEORGE MALCOLM, of Burnfoot, co. Dumfries, 1815). Or, on a saltire sa. betw. four harts' heads erased gu. five crescents of the field, on a canton gu. betw. two branches of laurel an anchor erect, the stem charged with a mural crown, and pendent therefrom a representation of the gold medal presented to him for his services at the capture of Washington. *Crest*—On a mount vert a tower ar. masoned sa. *Motto*—In ardua tendit.

Malcolm (Admiral Sir PULTENEY MALCOLM, G.C.B., third son of GEORGE MALCOLM, of Burnfoot, 1815). Or, on a saltire az. betw. four harts' heads erased gu. five crescents of the field, on a canton az. a naval crown or, and pendent therefrom a representation of the gold medal presented to Sir PULTENEY by his Majesty's command, for his meritorious services in the memorable action with the French fleet off St. Domingo on 6 Feb. 1806. *Crest*—On a mount vert a tower ar. masoned sa. *Supporters*—Dexter, a stag reguard. ppr. gorged with a naval crown or; sinister, a seahorse also ppr. gorged as the dexter. *Motto*—In ardua tendit.

Malcolm (Sir JOHN MALCOLM, G.C.B., 1815, fourth son of GEORGE MALCOLM, of Burnfoot). Or, on a saltire az. betw. four harts' heads erased gu. five crescents of the field, on a chief vert the badge of the Persian Order of the Lion and Sun betw. two antique crowns or. *Crest*—On a mount vert a tower ar. masoned sa. ensigned by the aforesaid Order of the Lion and Sun. *Motto*—In ardua tendit.

Malcolm (Glenmorag, co. Argyll, 1864). Or, on a saltire az. betw. two harts' heads erased of the field and base gu. and as many cross croslets fitchée in flank sa. a fusil of the field. *Crest*—A tower embattled ar. masoned sa. windows and port gu. *Motto*—In ardua tendit.

Maldock (co. Suffolk). Or, fretty sa.

Maldon, Town of (co. Essex). Az. three lions pass. reguard. in pale or, on the reverse of the Corporation seal a

ship of one mast on the sea, sail furled, in the stern a castle, thereon a flag of the before-mentioned arms. *Legend*—Sigillum commune Corp. villæ de Maldon.

Malebar (co. Derby; originally from France). Or, two axes erect endorsed, handles az. blades sa. on a chief gu. a lion pass. guard. of the first.

Malefaunt. Gu. three bars gemelles ar. on a chief or, a lion pass. sa.

Malefont, or Malefant. Barry of ten gu. and ar. on a chief or, a lion pass. sa.

Malefont. Gu. on a chev. or, a lion pass. sa. crowned of the second.

Malefont, or Malesaunts. Per chev. or and gu. in chief a lion pass. sa. in base a fret ar.

Maleock (Wales). Ar. on a chev. sa. three angels kneeling, habited in long robes, close girt, their hands conjoined, elevated upon their breasts, wings displ. or.

Malephant (co. Louth; Reg. Ulster's Office). Barry of ten gu. and ar. a chief or.

Malet (Wilbury House, co. Wilts, bart.). Az. three escallops or, quartering, 1st, FITCHETT; 2nd, HULL; 3rd, CLIFFE; 4th, VALETORT; 5th, HATCHE; 6th, WILRINGTON; 7th, ALEIGH; 8th, MORDAKE; 9th, AUDLEY; 10th, DURWYN; 11th, CRESSY; 12th, MARKHAM; 13th, ESSE. *Crest*—Out of a ducal coronet or, an heraldic tiger's head erm. *Motto*—Ma force d'en haut.

Malet (*ancient*). Gu. a lion ramp. or, debruised with a bendlet erm.

Malet (Ash, in Iddesleigh, co. Devon; descended from Sir BALDWIN MALET, Knt., of Enemer, temp. Henry III. Visit. Devon, 1620). Same *Arms* as MALET, Bart. *Crest*—A hind's, a tiger's, and an antelope's head ar. have been borne by different branches of the family.

Malet (co. Nottingham). Gu. a fesse erm. betw. six square buckles or.

Malfit. Or, on a chief gu. a label of five points of the field. *Crest*—A dexter arm in armour holding a scymitar erect all ppr.

Malford. Sa. three lions pass. in pale or.

Malford. Sa. a fesse erm. betw. three ducks ar.

Malham (impalement Fun. Ent. Ulster's Office, 1628, Sir LAWRENCE PARSONS, Baron of the Exchequer in Ireland, whose wife was ANNE MALHAM, co. York). Gu. three chevronels interlaced ar. on a chief or, a lion pass. az.

Malham (Elsack, co. York). Gu. three chev. in base ar. on a chief or, a lion pass. guard az. a fleur-de-lis for diff., quartering, 1st, RADCLIFFE, ar. a bend engr. sa. charged with an annulet or, and in the sinister chief point an escallop sa.; 2nd, DAWTREY, az. five fusils in fess ar. surmounted by a bendlet gu.; 3rd, HEWICK, gu. a lion ramp. within an orle of roundlets ar.

Malherbe (Fenyton, co. Devon, 1580; the heiress *m.* FERRERS; quartered by COTTELL, of Yeambridge. Visit. Devon, 1620). Or, a chev. gu. betw. three nettle leaves vert. *Crest*—On a tree ar. and sa. a demi naked man, a wreath about his head, in his hand an oak branch all ppr. acorned or.

Malherbe. Gu. a chev. betw. three sprigs of mallow leaves ar.

Maling. Gu. a crescent ar. on a chief or, three goats' heads erased sa. *Crest*—Out of a ducal coronet or, a plume of ostrich feathers in a case ppr.

Maling (Scarborough and Sunderland). Erm. on a chev. vert betw. three hawks ppr. as many roses ar.

Malins (originally settled in co. Warwick, afterwards resident at Birmingham). Sa. on a fess or, two palets gu. *Crest*—An arm in armour erect ppr. couped at the elbow, grasping a crescent or. *Motto*—Adjuvante Deo.

Malins (cos. Warwick and Worcester; borne by Sir RICHARD MALINS, Vice-Chancellor). Sa. on a fess or, two palets gu. *Crest*—An arm in armour ppr. grasping a crescent or. *Motto*—Post prœlia prœmia.

Malivorer (Allerton, co. York; MS. Names and Arms of Yorkshire Gentry, 1616). Gu. three greyhounds courant ar. collared or.

Mall (Fun. Ent. Ulster's Office, 1671, THOMAS MALL, of Dublin). Gu. six escallops, three, two, and one ar. an inescutcheon per pale or and of the second.

Mallac (co. Devon). Gu. a chev. betw. three fleurs-de-lis or.

Mallack (co. Devon; impalement Fun. Ent. Ulster's Office, 1670, RICHARD, fourth *Lord Blayney*, whose wife was dau. of JOHN MALLACK, co. Devon). Per chev. engr. or and sa. in chief two pellets, each charged with a fleur-de-lis of the first, and in base a bezant charged with a fleur-de-lis of the second.

Mallagyn. Sa. a covered cup ar.

Mallake (Axmouth, co. Devon). Per chev. engr. or and

sa. in chief two pellets, each charged with a fleur-de-lis of the first, in base a bezant charged with a fleur-de-lis of the second. *Crest*—A cubit arm erect, vested or, thereon two bends wavy sa. in the hand ppr. a mallet of the first.

Mallam. Ar. two bars az. in chief three mullets pierced sa. *Crest*—A dolphin naiant or.

Mallard. Vert on a bend ar. three crescents sa. *Crest*—On a chapeau gu. a stag trippant ppr.

Mallard. Vert a chev. betw. three rams statant ar.

Maller. Ar. a bend sa.

Mallerby (co. Devon). Or (another, ar.) a bunch of nettles vert.

Mallere. Erm. a chev. gu. a bordure engr. sa.

Mallet (Ash, co. Devon). Az three escallops or. *Crest*—A hind's head ar. ducally gorged or. *Motto*—Ma force d'en haut.

Mallet, or Malet (cos. Cornwall, Devon, and Somerset, *temp.* William the Conqueror). Az. three escallops or. *Crest*—A hind's head ar. ducally gorged or. *Another Crest*—Out of a ducal coronet or, a tiger's head erm. (another, Out of a ducal coronet or, an antelope's head ar.).

Mallet, or Martell (co. Berks). Gu. three mallets ar.

Mallet (co. Buckingham). Sa. a chev. between three chaplets ar.

Mallet (co. Buckingham, and Normanton, co. York). Sa. a chev. betw. three round buckles ar. (another, tinctures reversed).

Mallet (co. Derby). Gu. a fesse erm. betw. three (another, six) buckles or (another, fess dancettée and buckles ar.).

Mallet, or Martell (Normanton, co. Nottingham). Gu. a fesse betw. six mallets or (another, three mallets ar.).

Mallet (co. Derby). Gu. a fesse erm. betw. six round buckles or.

Mallet (Enmore, co. Somerset; ancient). Paly of six gu. and or, a lion statant guard. ar.

Mallet. Gu. a fesse nebulée or

Mallet (Jersey). Erm. a fleur-de-lis gu. over all a label of three points gobonated ar. and az. (another, gu. three buckles or, a crescent for diff.). *Crest*—On a wreath (another, out of a ducal coronet) a cock statant ppr. *Motto*—In cruce salus (another, En Dieu affie).

Mallett (Sir THOMAS MALLETT, one of the Knights of the co. Notts, *temp.* Edward I. Visit. Notts, 1614). Gu. a fess erm. betw. six oval buckles or.

Mallett (Willoughby, co. Notts; ROBERT MALLETT, Esq., of Willoughby; *temp.* Edward IV. whose dau. and heiress *m.* THOMAS HATFIELD. Whalley Ped. Visit. Notts, 1614). Or, a saltire gu. betw. four eaglets displ. az.

Malley. Ar. a bend sa. *Crest* A goat's head erased sa. bezantée.

Mallock (Cockington, formerly of Rouse Down, co. Devon, seated at the former place since 1654). Per chev. engr. or and sa. in chief two pellets, each charged with a fleur-de-lis of the first, in base a bezant charged with a fleur-de-lis of the second. *Crest*—A cubit arm erect, vested or, thereon two bends wavy sa. in the hand ppr. a mallet of the first.

Mallom (Walter-Acton, co. Norfolk; granted 4 May, 1685). Ar. three chev. braced in base gu. on a chief of the second a lion pass. betw. two mullets of the first. *Crest*—A dexter arm erect, habited vert, the cuff turned up erm. the hand ppr. holding a lure feathered ar. garnished or, stringed and tasselled gu.

Mallorey (co. Warwick; confirmed by the Deputies of Camden, Clarenceux, to ROBERT MALLOREY, fifth in descent from Sir GILBERT MALLOREY, Knt. Visit. Warwick). Erm. a chev. gu. a border engr. sa.

Mallory, or Mallorie (Papworth, co. Cambridge, and Kirkbie-Mallorie, co. Leicester). Or, a lion ramp. gu.

Mallory (Studley, co. York; Sir WILLIAM MALLORY, knighted at Oxford, 1642). Or, a lion ramp. gu. collared ar. *Crest*—A nag's head couped gu.

Mallory (Mobberley, co. Chester, *temp.* James I.; granted 1663; descended from Rev. THOMAS MALLORY, Dean of Chester, a younger son of Sir WILLIAM MALLORY, Knt., of Studley. Rev. JOHN HOLDSWORTH MALLORY, Rector of Mobberley, left an only dau. and heiress, JULIA, *m.* Rev. GEORGE LEIGH, who assumed the surname of MALLORY). Same *Arms* and *Crest*, a canton az.

Mallory (Sir WILLIAM MALLORY, Knt., of Kirkby-Mallory, co. Leicester, *temp.* Henry III.; MARY, dau. and co-heir of his great-grandson, Sir ANTIKELL MALLORY (*d.* 17 Richard II., A.D. 1393), *m.* Sir ROBERT MOTON, Knt., of Pickleton, same co. Visit. Leicester, 1619). Or, a lion ramp. gu. double queued.

Mallory (Walton, co. Leicester; THOMAS MALLORY, Lord of Walton, *temp.* Henry II., Har. MSS., 1400. Visit. Notts,

653

1569; his granddaughter and co-heir *m.* JOHN FENTON, Esq., of Fenton, same co.). Or, a lion ramp. gu. collared ar.

Mallory (Sir RICHARD MALLORY, Lord Mayor of London, *temp.* Queen Elizabeth; his eldest dau. and co-heir *m.* ROBERT SHARPE, of London, merchant. Visit. Devon, 1620). Or, a lion ramp. gu. collared ar. a crescent for diff.

Mallory (Woodford, co. Northampton). Or, a lion ramp. double queued gu. collared ar. on the shoulder a fleur-de-lis of the first. *Crest*—A nag's head gu. crined or, charged with a fleur-de-lis of the last.

Mallory (co. Northampton). Purp. a lion ramp. or, collared gu. *Crest*—A nag's head or.

Mallory (Wooderson, co. York). Sa. three greyhounds courant ar. collared gu.

Mallory. Or, three lions ramp. sa. a bordure engr. az.

Mallory. Gu. two bars ar. in chief three mullets pierced of the second.

Mallory (co. Cork; Fun. Ent. Ulster's Office, 1625, RICHARD MALLORY, son of ANTHONY MALLORY). Or, a demi lion ramp. gu. charged on the shoulder with a crescent ar. thereon a mullet sa.

Mallow. Az. a fesse engr. or, betw. three boys' heads couped ar. *Crest*—On a chapeau gu. turned up erm. two sceptres in saltire or.

Malluvel (Rampton, co. Nottingham). Vert three greyhounds courant in pale or.

Mallworth. Az. a dolphin naiant ar.

Mallyng (co. Cornwall). Gu. three goats pass. ar. attired or.

Malmains. Sa. a bend lozengy ar.; another, Ar. a bend lozengy purp.; another, Az. (another, gu.) three sinister hands couped ar. *Crest*—A lamb supporting a banner ar.

Malmaynes. Same *Arms*. *Crest*—An arm embowed in armour, hand apaumée ppr.

Malmaynes. Erm. on a chev. (another, on a chief) gu. three sinister hands couped ar.

Malmaynes. Gu. three sinister hands couped ar. guttée de poix.

Malmaynes. Gu. three dexter hands couped and erect ar.

Malmaynes. Ar. a chev. gu. betw. ten crosses crosslet sa.

Malmeis. Ar. a bend engr. vert.

Malmesbury, Earl of. See HARRIS.

Malmesbury, Corporation of the Town of. The seal represents a castle with an embattled tower at each end, on the centre a tower domed, thereon a pennon: on each side of the castle three ears of wheat on one stalk; in chief, on the dexter side, a mullet of six points, and on the sinister an increscent; again, on the sinister side three balls, one near the dome of the upper tower, and the other two near the battlements of the sinister tower, the base of the escutcheon water.

Malmesbury-Abbey (co. Wilts). Gu. two lions pass. guard. in pale or, on a chief ar. a mitre betw. two crosiers az.

Malone (Ballynahowne, co. Westmeath; Fun. Ent. Ulster's Office, 1686, ANNE, wife of EDMOND MALONE, son of EDMOND MALONE, grandson of EDMOND MALONE, and great-grandson of EDMOND MALONE, all of the same place). Vert a lion ramp. betw. three mullets ar.

Malone (*Baron Sunderlin*, extinct 1816; RICHARD MALONE, Esq., son of EDMOND MALONE, the second son of RICHARD MALONE, Esq., of Baronstown, co. Westmeath, descended from EDMOND MALONE, Esq., of Ballinahown, same co., *temp.* Queen Elizabeth, of an ancient Irish Sept of the same race as O'CONOR, King of Connaught, was so created 1785, and *d. s. p.*). Quarterly, 1st and 4th, vert, a lion ramp. or, betw. three mullets ar.; 2nd and 3rd, ar. on a chev. az. betw. three demi unicorns ramp. gu. as many acorns or. *Crest*—A man in complete armour holding in the dexter hand a lance, and on the sinister arm a shield all ppr. *Supporters*—Dexter, a unicorn; sinister, a pegasus, both ar. collared and chained az. *Motto*—Fidelis ad urnam.

Malone (Dublin; EDMOND MALONE, Sheriff of Dublin, 1604, son of JOHN MALONE, Sheriff of Dublin, 1581, of the Sept of O'MALONE, co. Westmeath. Visit. city of Dublin, 1607). Or, on a bend az. three crosses pattée ar.

Malone (co. Wexford; Reg. Ulster's Office). Vert a lion ramp. or, betw. three mullets ar. *Crest*—A man standing in complete armour, a pike in the right hand all ppr. on the left a shield or.

Malone. See O'MALONE.

Maloques. Paly of ten or and gu. a bordure ar.

Malory (co. Leicester). Or, a lion ramp. tail forchée gu.

Malory (co. Cambridge, and London). Same *Arms*, a bordure gu.

Malory (Draughton, co. Northampton). Or, three lions pass. guard. in pale sa.

Malory (co. York). Or, a lion ramp. gu. collared of the first.

Malorye (co. Stafford). Per pale indented ar. and sa.

Maloure (co. Leicester, *temp.* Edward I.). Or, three lions pass. guard. in pale sa.

Malovell (quartered by SKEFFINGTON, of Skeffington, co. Leicester. Visit. Leicester, 1619). Vert three greyhounds courant in pale or.

Maloysell. Ar. on a bend sa. three martlets or.

Malpas (feudal Barons of Malpas, co. Chester). Ar. a cross flory az.

Malpas (Hampton and Bickerton, co. Chester, *temp.* Henry VI.). Gu. a chev. betw. three pheons ar.

Malpas (Bickley, co. Chester). Sa. a fesse betw. three pheons ar. *Crest*—On a ducal coronet a wivern vomiting flames at both ends ppr.

Malpas. A cross patonce (another, pattée) az.

Malpas (Dublin and Dundalk; ROBERT MALPAS, merchant, son of WALTER MALPAS, and grandson of THOMAS MALPAS, both of Dundalk). Gu. a chev. betw. three pheons, points down ar. a border of the last, charged with twelve roses of the first, a crescent for diff. *Crest* (confirmed to his descendant, JOHN MALPAS, Esq., of Rochestown, co. Dublin)—A demi lion ramp. gu. holding in the dexter paw a pheon point upwards ar.

Malson, or Mallesome. Per pale az. and gu. three crescents ar.

Malston (Malston and East Ogwell, co. Devon; arms from the seal of ROBERT DE MALSTON, Lord of those Manors, affixed to a deed dated "the feast of the Exaltation of the Holy Cross," 9 Edward II., A.D. 1315. Visit. Devon, 1620). Az. a fess engr. ar.

Malston (co. Devon). Az. on a fesse engr. or, three lozenges gu.

Malston (co. Devon). Ar. a fox (another, a wolf) sa. enraged gu.

Malt (co. Somerset; Har. MSS., 1404). Gu. a horse armed or, bridled and saddled of the first, with a plume on his head, and trappings, and on his shoulder a cinquefoil of the last, on his hip an escutcheon charged with a cross all betw. three garbs of the second.

Maltby (Maltby, Cleveland, co. York). Ar. on a bend gu. three garbs or. *Crest*—A garb or, banded gu.

Maltby (EDWARD MALTBY, Bishop of Chichester, 1831, and of Durham, 1836-56). Ar. on a bend gu. betw. a lion ramp. and a cross pattée of the second three garbs or.

Malterstone (Scotland). Ar. a chev. gu. on a chief of the last a crescent or.

Maltiward (Rougham, co. Suffolk). Sa. on a saltire ar. a griffin's head erased of the first. *Crest*—A demi griffin ar. holding betw. the claws a saltire sa.

Malton Priory. Barry of six ar. and gu. over all in bend sinister a palmer's staff or.

Malton, or Melton (South Hayne, co. Devon, and co. York). Az. a cross flory voided ar. *Crest*—A snake nowed and erect in pale ppr. ducally gorged or.

Malton, or Melton (co. Lancaster). Ar. a cross pattée voided gu. *Crest*—A dolphin haurient devouring a fish ppr.

Malton, or Melton (co. Middlesex). Ar. a cross flory az. voided of the field, charged with a bezant (another, the field erm. cross gu.).

Malton, or Melton. Az. a cross patonce or, charged with another of the field.

Malton. Sa. (another, az.) a lion ramp. ar. crowned or, betw. three (another, two) annulets of the second.

Malton. Ar. a cross patonce purp. voided of the field, a bordure sa. charged with eight trefoils slipped of the first.

Malton. Sa. a lion ramp. ar. crowned or, on a bordure of the second eight annulets of the first.

Maltravers (Baron Maltravers, summoned to Parliament 1330, barony passed to FITZ-ALAN, *Earl of Arundel*, and through that to HOWARD, *Duke of Norfolk*, in which noble house it was settled by Act of Parliament 3 Charles I., 1627). Sa. a fret or, and a label of three points erm.

Maltravers (cos. Leicester and Dorset). Same *Arms*, the label of four points erm. (another, without the label).

Malveysin (cos. Stafford and Lancaster; the elder co-heir of the family of MALVEYSIN, or MAUVEYSIN, of Mayvesin-Rideway, co. Stafford, ELIZABETH MALVEYSIN, dau. of Sir ROBERT MAUVEYSIN, Knt., *m.* first, *temp.* Richard II., ROGER DE CHETWYND, *d. s. p.*; second, Sir JOHN CAWARDEN, Knt., co. Chester). Gu. three bendlets ar. *Crest*—A talbot's head gu.

654

Malwyn. Or, a cross moline az.

Maly (co. Kent). Gu. a fesse cotised ar. betw. eight billets of the last, three and two in chief, and two and one in base. *Crest*—An arm embowed, holding an anchor by the middle in pale, the bottom of it resting on the wreath.

Malyn. Gu. a fess cotised ar. betw. six billets of the second. *Crest*—An arm embowed, vested sa. holding an anchor or, the hand ppr.

Malyn. Erm. a fess paly of six or and gu.

Malyn. Erm. on a chev. vert betw. three falcons ppr. belled or, as many crosses moline of the last.

Malyart. Ar. on a fesse sa. three escallops of the first, in chief as many pellets, each charged with a fleur-de-lis or.

Malynes (co. Kent). Ar. a bend engr. purp.

Malynes. Erm. a fesse gu. in chief three palets of the second. *Crest*—A reindeer's head cabossed ppr.

Malynes. Or, three palets gu. on an escutcheon ar. an imperial eagle sa.

Malyns (arms over the belfry, Churchill Church, co. Oxford. Visit. Oxon, 1574). Erm. on a fess gu. three billets or.

Malyns (arms in Hasley Church, co. Oxford. Visit. Oxon, 1574). Erm. on a fess gu. three bucks' heads cabossed or.

Malyns (arms in Chyner Church, co. Oxford; REGINALD DE MALYNS, *d.* 1430. Visit. Oxon, 1574). Erm. a fess paly or and gu.

Man (co. Lancaster). Per fesse embattled ar. and az. three goats pass. counterchanged, attired or.

Man (Long Sutton, co. Lincoln). Or, three chevronels sa. in chief as many pellets.

Man (Bullinbrooke, co. Lincoln). Per fesse embattled ar. and gu. three goats pass. counterchanged.

Man (Newcastle). Sa. on a fesse betw. three goats pass. ar. as many pellets.

Man, or Mann (Ipswich, co. Suffolk; granted 2 March, 1692). Sa. on a fesse counter-embattled betw. three goats pass. ar. as many pellets. *Crest*—A demi dragon with wings endorsed ar. guttée de poix.

Man (London). Az. on a fesse counter-batelly betw. three goats pass. ar. as many pellets. *Crest*—A dragon's head betw. two dragons' wings expanded gu. guttée d'or.

Man. Or, a fesse cotised az.

Man, Isle of. Gu. three legs conjoined in the fesse point in armour ppr. garnished and spurred or.

Manaton, or Mannington (Manaton, Southill, co. Cornwall). Ar. on a bend sa. three mullets pierced of the field. *Crest*—A demi unicorn ramp. sa.

Manbucker, or Montbucher. Ar. three pots gu. a bordure sa. bezantée.

Manby (Elsham, co. Lincoln, and London; Reg. Her. Office). Ar. a lion ramp. sa. an orle of eight escallops gu. *Crest*—An arm couped at the elbow erect, vested per pale crenellée or and ar. holding in the gauntlet a sword pommelled of the first.

Manby (Downsall Hall, co. Essex; represented by COLEGRAVE, of Ellingham). Same *Arms* and *Crest*. *Motto*—Pro patria mori.

Manby. Az. a lion ramp. or, on a chief sa. three martlets ar.

Manby. Ar. a lion ramp. az. on a chief sa. three martlets of the first.

Manby (Capt. G. W. MANBY, F.R.S., Great Yarmouth, co. Norfolk, *d.* 1854, inventor of the plan for throwing a rope over stranded vessels and hauling the crew on shore by means of a cradle). Ar. a lion ramp. sa. within an orle of escallops gu. a canton of the last. *Crest*—A head affrontée couped at the shoulders ppr. habited gu. collar or, on the head a plain cap az. band or. *Motto*—Pro patria.

Manby. Ar. three (another, two) bars sa. over all a maunch gu.

Manby (Rear-Admiral THOMAS MANBY, son of M. P. MANBY, Esq., of Woodhall, co. Norfolk). Ar. a lion ramp. within an orle of lilies gu. a canton of the last. *Crest*—A Moor's head affrontée, couped below the shoulders ppr. vested gu. trimmed or, on the head a cap gold.

Mancester, or Manchester (co. Warwick). Vairé ar. and sa. on a bend gu. an eagle or (another, three eagles).

Mancester (co. Warwick). Vair a bend gu.

Manchell. Ar. three greyhounds courant in pale sa. collared or.

Manchenhall. Ar. a bend engr. or.

Manchester, Duke of. See MONTAGUE.

Manchester, Town of. Gu. three bendlets enhanced or.

Manchester, See of. Or, on a pale engr. gu. three mitres labelled gold, on a canton of the second three bendlets enhanced ar.

Manchester (co. Stafford). Potent counterpotent ar. and sa. over all a bend gu.

Manchester. See MANCESTER.

Mancestre (co. Warwick; Sir EDMUND DE MANCESTRE, seventh in descent from WALKELINUS DE MANCESTRE, temp. King Stephen; Dugdale's Warwick). Vairé ar. and sa. a bend engr. gu.

Manchinghall. Gu. a bend engr. or, a label ar.

Mancourt. Ar. on a bend sa. three eagles displ. or.

Mancy. Ar. three chevronels sa.

Mandatt. Gu. three bendlets dancettée or.

Manderne (Penzance, co. Cornwall). Az. a lion ramp. or, guttée de sang, crowned of the second. Crest—A lion ramp. or, guttée de sang, crowned of the first.

Manders (Brackdenstown, co. Dublin; allowed, 1811, by Betham, Ulster, to Alderman RICHARD MANDERS, High Sheriff of the city of Dublin 1794, and of the co. 1807, Lord Mayor 1801, son of JOHN MANDERS, of Marmin, Queen's co., and grandson of RICHARD MANDERS, who settled in Ireland temp. William III., and was at the siege of Derry). Erm. on a saltire gu. five bezants. Crest—A plover ppr. beaked and legged gu. holding in the beak a slip of oak leaved vert, acorned or. Motto—Pro omnibus laus Deo.

Manderson (England). Ar. a pale vairé or and az. Crest—An antelope pass. ar. collared gu.

Mandevile (co. Essex). Az. three wolves pass. or.

Mandevile (co. Warwick). Or, a fret az. (another, tinctures reversed).

Mandevile (co. Wilts). Quarterly, vert and gu. a fesse wavy betw. three trefoils counterchanged.

Mandevile. Quarterly, vair and gu. Crest—Two dexter hands conjoined supporting a scymitar in pale all ppr.

Mandevile. Vairé ar. and gu.

Mandevile. Gyronny of eight gu. and ar. an escarbuncle sa.

Mandevile. Or, on a chief indented gu. three trefoils ar.

Mandevile. Vert three wolves pass. in pale or.

Mandevile (Reg. Ulster's Office). Or, two bars sa.

Mandevile (Clonmel, co. Tipperary ; confirmed, 1759, as the arms of THEOBALD MANDEVILE, Esq., of Clonmel, whose dau. and heiress, MARY, m. PIERS BUTLER, son of EDMUND BUTLER, Esq., of Edmundsbury, Queen's co., of the house of Galmoye). Quarterly, or and gu. an escarbuncle sa.

Mandeville (Earl of Essex ; GEOFFREY DE MANDEVILLE was so created by special charter of King Stephen ; his descendant, WILLIAM DE MANDEVILLE, sixth Earl of Essex, d. s. p. 1227, when the earldom passed, through his sister, MAUD, wife of ROBERT DE BOHUN, Earl of Hereford, to that family). Quarterly, or and gu.

Mandeville (second Earl of Essex, temp. King John). Quarterly, or and gu.

Mandeville (fifth Earl of Essex). Quarterly, or and gu. a bordure vair.

Mandeville (Earl of Essex). Per pale or and gu. the regalia sa.

Mandeville (co. Dorset). Gu. three lions pass. in pale ar. over all a bendlet az.

Mandeville (Nottley, co. Essex). Ar. on a chief indented gu. three martlets or.

Mandeville (co. Bucks). Same Arms.

Mandeville. Gu. an escarbuncle nowed and flowered or.

Mandeville (granted to Very Rev. CHARLES MANDEVILLE, D.D., Dean of Peterborough, 1722). Per saltire or and gu. an escarbuncle nowed and flowered sa. Crest—A mural crown ar. charged with an escarbuncle, as in the arms.

Mandeville. Or, three bars az. ; another, Quarterly, or and az. four sinister wings displ. counterchanged ; another, Az. fretty or, a fesse gu. ; another, Gu. a lion ramp. ar.

Mandeville-Power. See POWER.

Mandeyet. Paly wavy of six gu. and or.

Mandit (Great Stretton, co. Lincoln). Per pale wavy or and gu. over all on a bend ar. three torteaux.

Mandit, or Manduyt. Chequy or and az. a bordure gu. Crest—A garland of laurel leaves vert.

Mandley (Poulton, co. Chester, temp. Henry VIII.). Ar. a dexter hand couped and erect within a border engr. sa.

Mandrey (co. Essex). Ar. a demi lion within an orle of fleurs-de-lis gu.

Mandut (co. Lincoln). Ar. three palets dancettée ar.

Mandut (co. Wilts). Same Arms, palets or.

Mandut, or Manduyt (cos. Northumberland and Stafford). Erm. two bars gu.

Mandut, or Manduyt. Gu. three bars dancettée or. Crest—A plate charged with a stag standing on a mount ppr.

655

Manelson (co. Lincoln). Az. in a crescent ar. a sun or.

Maneward (quartered by NOAH TOOKEY, Esq., of South Luffenham, co. Rutland. Visit. Rutland, 1618). Quarterly, ar. and gu. a bend sa.

Maney (Linton, co. Kent). Per pale ar. and sa. three chevronels betw. as many cinquefoils all counterchanged. Crest—An arm couped at the elbow and erect, habited per pale ar. and sa. the cuff counterchanged, holding in the hand ppr. a battle axe of the last.

Maney (Sir ANTHONY MANEY, of Biddenden, co. Kent, knighted by Sir WILLIAM FITZ-WILLIAM, Lord Deputy of Ireland, 17 Jan. 1594). Same Arms.

Maney (co. Kent). Or, two bars sa. on a chief of the second three cinquefoils of the first.

Maney. Ar. three inescutcheons gu.

Maney, or Maynoye. Gu. a fesse betw. three martlets ar.

Manfeld (Skirpenbeck, co. York; confirmed 20 Sept. 1563). Gu. a bend cotised ar. between six crosses crosslet or.

Manfeld (Hutton-on-Derwent, co. York). Same Arms.

Manfeld. Ar. two bars sa. on the uppermost a wivern, volant, tail extended of the field.

Manfield, or Mansfield (co. Buckingham). Sa. three sinister hands couped at the wrist ar. Crest—A tiger sejant or, ducally gorged gu.

Manfield (West Leake, co. Nottingham). Ar. a chev. betw. three maunches sa. Crest—A griffin's head erased.

Manfield. Ar. a cross engr. sa.

Manfold, or Manyfold (co. Cornwall). Ar. a chev. wavy betw. three roses gu.

Manford. Or, a fesse betw. three fleurs-de-lis gu. Crest—Three annulets interlaced or.

Manford, Mounford, or Mondeford. Or, three fleurs-de-lis gu.

Manger (Jersey and Guernsey). Gu. an anchor erect in pale or, on a chief of the second three roses of the first. Crest—A greyhound's head erased gu. collared and ringed or.

Mangfield. Ar. three lions' heads erased sa.

Mangles (Woodbridge, co. Surrey). Or, a bend vair betw. two crosses verdée, voided sa. Crest—An arm embowed in armour ppr. charged with two roses gu. grasping in the hand a scymitar all ppr.

Manick (arms impaled with THROGMORTON, St. Mary's Church, Oxford. Visit. Oxon, 1574). Az. a fess betw. three maidens' heads couped at the breast or, crined ar.

Manigford. Ar. a chev. engr. between three roses gu.

Manigham. Ar. on a chev. betw. three wrens gu. as many mullets of the first.

Maningham (Fendrayton, co. Cambridge, and co. Kent). Sa. a fesse erm. in chief three griffins' heads erased or. Crest—Out of a ducal coronet ar. a talbot's head or, collared and lined gu. at the end of the line a bow-knot.

Maningham. Or, a water bouget sa. in chief three pellets.

Maningham. Ar. a chev. sa. betw. three moorcocks az.

Manington (Manington and Combeshed, co. Cornwall ; SAMPSON MANINGTON, Esq., of Manington, son of PETER MANINGTON, of same place, and PIERSE MANINGTON, Esq., of Combershed, son of SAMPSON MANINGTON, which PETER MANINGTON and the last named SAMPSON MANINGTON, were sons of EDWARD MANINGTON, Esq., of Manington, eighth in descent from ADAM MANINGTON, temp. Edward II. Visit. Cornwall, 1620). Ar. on a bend sa. three mullets pierced of the field. Crest—A demi unicorn sa. crined and unguled ar. charged on the shoulder with a crescent or, for diff.

Manington (co. Devon). Ar. on a bend sa. three mullets or (another, three cinquefoils of the field).

Maniot. Barry of six or and sa. on a canton of the last a fleur-de-lis of the first. Crest—A Saracen's head affrontée ppr. wreathed about the temples ar. and sa.

Manlery. Sa. on a chief ar. a demi lion ramp. issuant of the first.

Manley (Manley, co. Chester, and Erbistock, co. Denbigh ; derived from one of the companions in arms of the Conqueror, whose name appears on the Battell Abbey Roll). Ar. a dexter hand couped and erect sa. a bordure engr. of the last. Crest—A Saracen's head affrontée ppr. wreathed about the temples ar. and sa. Motto—Manus hæc inimica tyrannis.

Manley. Or, on a bend. sa. three eagles displ. ar. Crest—A cross pattée az.

Manley. Or, on a bend sa. three dolphins ar. ; another, Purp. a sinister hand couped and erect ar.; another, Vair a maunch gu.

Manlove (co. Stafford). Gu. a chev. erm. betw. three anchors or.

Manlove (Ashborne, co. Derby, originally from co. Stafford). Az. a chev. betw. three anchors erm. *Crest*— Out of a mural coronet gu. a cubit arm erect, vested erminois, cuffed ar. grasping in the hand ppr. a flaming sword of the third.

Manlovell. Vert three wolves pass. in pale or. *Crest*— Five bellflowers erect ppr. leaved vert.

Manly. Or, a bend engr. sa. *Crest*—A cross pattée or.

Manmaker (Middleburgh, Zealand). Gu. three acorns or. *Crest*—Two wings displ. gu.

Mann (Linton, co. Kent, bart., extinct 1814: descended from EDWARD MANN, Esq., of Ipswich, co. Suffolk, *temp.* Charles I.). Sa. on a fesse embattled counter-embattled betw. three goats pass. ar. as many pellets. *Crest*—A demi dragon, wings endorsed sa. guttée d'eau, inside of wings and talons ppr. *Motto*—Per ardua stabilis.

Mann (Norwich, co. Norfolk). Same *Arms*.

Mann (Broadoak, co. Essex). Or, a chev. ermines betw. three lions ramp. sa. *Crest*—A tower or, issuant from the top five tilting spears ppr. *Motto*—Virtus vincet invidiam.

Mann (Ireland; Reg. Ulster's Office). Same *Arms, Crest,* and *Motto.*

Mann (Dunmyle and Corvey, co. Tyrone; confirmed to DEANE MANN, Esq., of Dunmoyle, and the descendants of his grandfather, HENRY MANN). Or, on a chev. engr. ermines betw. three lions ramp. sa. a trefoil of the first. *Crest*—A tower or, charged with a trefoil vert issuant from the battlements five spears ppr. *Motto*—Virtus vincit invidiam.

Mann (*Earl of Cornwallis.* See CORNWALLIS, *Marquis* and *Earl of Cornwallis,* extinct 1852. JAMES CORNWALLIS assumed, 1814, by royal licence, the surname of his mother's family, KATHARINE, sister of Sir HORATIO MANN, last bart. of Linton, when the following coat was exemplified to him; he *s.* as fifth *Earl of Cornwallis,* 1824). Quarterly, 1st and 4th, sa. on a fesse counter-embattled betw. three goats pass. ar. as many pellets, for MANN; 2nd and 3rd, sa. guttée d'eau on a fesse ar. three Cornish choughs ppr., for CORNWALLIS. *Crests*—1st: A demi dragon sa. guttée d'eau, for MANN; 2nd, on a mount vert a stag lodged reguard. ar. attired and unguled or, gorged with a chaplet of laurel vert, vulned in the shoulder ppr., for CORNWALLIS.

Mann. Ar. three antique boots sa. spurs or. *Crest*—A demi man ppr. wreathed about the temples and loins vert, holding over the dexter shoulder an arrow ppr.

Mannel (Jersey). Gu. a hand ppr. winged at the wrist or, holding a sword in pale ar. pommelled of the third, the whole within a bordure of the last.

Manners (Ethale, or Etall, co. Northumberland). Or, two bars az. a chief gu. *Crest*—A bull's head erased gu. ducally gorged and chained or. In the time of Henry VIII., a honourable augmentation was granted to THOMAS MANNERS, of Etall and Belvoir, Lord Ros, created *Earl of Rutland* in 1525, viz., a chief quarterly, az. and gu., on the 1st and 4th, two fleurs-de-lis or; on the 2nd and 3rd, a lion of England.

Manners (*Duke of Rutland*). Or, two bars az. a chief quarterly of the last and gu. in the 1st and 4th, two fleurs-de-lis, and in the 2nd and 3rd, a lion pass. guard. all or. This chief was anciently gu., the alteration being an honorary augmentation, showing a descent from the blood-royal of King Edward IV. *Crest*—On a chapeau gu. turned up erm. a peacock in its pride ppr. *Supporters*—Two unicorns ar. armed, maned, tufted, and unguled or. *Motto*—Pour y parvenir.

Manners-Sutton (*Viscount Canterbury*). See SUTTON.

Manners-Sutton (*Baron Manners*). See SUTTON.

Manners (Long Framlingham, co. Northumberland; represented by FENWICKE, of that place; descended from JAMES FENWICKE, Esq., of Longwitton Hall, co. Northumberland, by JANE, his wife, dau. and heir of JOHN FENWICKE, Esq., of Long Framlington). Same *Arms, &c.,* as MANNERS, of Etall.

Manners (Hanby Hall, co. Lincoln, and Buckminster, co. Leicester, bart.; WILLIAM MANNERS, eldest son of JOHN MANNERS, Esq., of Grantham Grange, co. Lincoln. by Lady LOUISA TOLLEMACHE, his wife, who *s.* her brother WILBRAHAM, fifth *Earl of Dysart,* 1821, as *Countess of Dysart* in her own right, was created a bart. 1793, assumed the name of TOLLEMACHE, and *d.* 1833, when his eldest son *s.* as second bart. of Hanby, and at the death of his grandmother, 1840, *s.* as sixth *Earl of Dysart*). Or, two bars az. a chief quarterly of the second and gu. in the 1st and 4th quarters two fleurs-de-lis, in the 2nd and 3rd, a lion pass. guard. all or, a bordure wavy gobony ar. and sa. *Crest*—On a chapeau gu. turned up erm. a peacock in pride ppr. each charged with a bendlet sinister wavy gobony or and sa,.

Manney. Or, three chevronels sa.

656

Manning (Cholmondley, co. Chester). Gu. a cross patonce betw. four trefoils slipped or.

Manning (Stanbury in Shorwinstow, co. Cornwall). Per pale gu. (sometimes az.) and or, a lion ramp. counterchanged.

Manning (Codham, co. Kent; granted 1577). Gu. a cross patonce betw. four cinquefoils or. *Crest*—Out of a ducal crown or, an eagle's head sa. beaked gold, betw. two ostrich feathers ar.

Manning (Eversfield, co. Devon). Same *Arms. Crest*— Out of a ducal coronet or, a griffin's head sa. betw. two feathers ppr. *Motto*—Esse quam videri.

Manning (Downe, co. Kent; confirmed by Dethick, 20 April, 1577). Gu. a cross flory betw. four trefoils slipped or. *Crest*—Out of a ducal coronet or, an eagle's head sa. beaked or, betw. two ostrich feathers ar.

Manning (Diss, co. Norfolk). Quarterly, gu. and az. a cross flory betw. four cinquefoils pierced or. *Crest*—Out of a ducal coronet or, an eagle's head sa. beaked gold, betw. two ostrich feathers ar.

Manning (co. Sussex). Gu. a cross patonce betw. four trefoils or. *Crest*—Out of a ducal coronet or, an eagle's head ar. betw. two wings sa.

Manning. Ar. a chev. betw. three quatrefoils gu.

Manning (London; ISAAC MANNING, *temp.* James I.; his dau. and heir, ELIZABETH, *m.* HUMPHREY CLERK, Esq., of Edmonton, co. Middlesex. Visit. Middlesex, 1663). Gu. three crosses botonnée or.

Manning (Reg. Ulster's Office). Gu. three crescents ar. a border erm. (another, the border of the second).

Manning (Fun. Ent. Ulster's Office, 1617, GRACE MANNING). Gu. three crescents or, a border ar.

Manningham (co. Kent). Sa. a fesse erm. in chief three griffins' heads erased or. *Crest*—Out of a ducal coronet or, a talbot's head gu. collared gold, lined sa.

Manningham. Ar. a chev. sa. betw. three peacocks az.

Manningham-Buller, Bart. See BULLER.

Mannington. Ar. on a bend sa. three mullets or.

Mannock (Gifford's Hall, co. Suffolk, bart., extinct 1787; descended from ROBERT MANNOCK, of Stoke-juxta-Neyland, same co., *temp.* Edward III.). Sa. a cross flory ar. *Crest*— An heraldic tiger's head erased quarterly ar. and gu.

Mannock (co. Essex). Sa. a cross flory or.

Mannors (co. Cambridge). Ar. a saltire engr. sa. (another, the saltire charged with five bezants).

Mannours (Sir MICHAEL MANNOURS, Knt., d. 30 Henry III., Ped. Pierpoint. Visit. Notts, 1628). Ar. six annulets, two, two, and two sa.

Manny (*Baron Manny,* extinct 1391; WALTER DE MANNY was summoned to Parliament 1347, and *d.* 1372, when the barony devolved on his dau. MARY, wife of JOHN DE HASTINGS, second *Earl of Pembroke,* and passed to her son, JOHN, third *Earl of Pembroke,* who *d. s. p.*). Sa. a cross voided ar.

Manny. Or, two chev. sa.

Manny. Or, three chevronels sa. on the uppermost a lion pass. reguard. of the field.

Mannyfold, or Manyfold. Ar. a chev. wavy betw. three roses gu.

Mannyford (co. Dorset). Ar. a chev. engr. betw. three roses gu.

Mannyngge. Gu. a cross patonce or, charged with a pellet, in the dexter chief a trefoil slipped of the second. *Crest*—Out of a ducal coronet or, an eagle's head sa. beaked gold, betw. two ostrich feathers ar.

Mansbridge (London; JOHN MANSBRIDGE, citizen and draper. Visit. London, 1568). Quarterly, ar. and vert four eagles displ. counterchanged.

Mansbridge (London). Quarterly, ar. and or, four eagles displ. with two heads vert. *Crest*—A dexter arm erect, habited az. cuffed ar. holding in the hand ppr. a demi eagle displ. with two heads gu. ducally gorged or.

Manse (Suffolk, *temp.* Edward III.). Ar. a lion ramp. within an orle of escallops gu.

Mansel (Margam, co. Glamorgan, bart., extinct 1750; PHILIP DE MANSEL came to England with William I.; his descendant, Sir EDWARD MANSEL, knighted 1572, had two sons, Sir THOMAS MANSEL, Bart., of Margam, created 1611, and Sir FRANCIS MANSEL, Bart., of Muddlescombe, created 1621). Ar. a chev. betw. three maunches sa. *Crest*—A chapeau enflamed on the top all ppr. *Motto*—Quod vult valde vult.

Mansel (*Baron Mansel,* extinct 1750; Sir THOMAS MANSEL, fourth bart. of Margam, was so created 1712). Same *Arms. Crest*—A chapeau gu. turned up. erm. enflamed at the top ppr. (another, A falcon rising or; another, A griffin's head erased per pale indented ar. and gu.). *Supporters*—Dexter, a falcon, wings expanded and belled or; sinister, a griffin, wings expanded per pale indented ar. and gu. *Motto*—Quod vult valde vult.

Mansel (now TALBOT, of Margam). See TALBOT.

Mansel (Muddlescombe, co. Carmarthen, bart.; Sir FRANCIS MANSEL, brother of Sir THOMAS MANSEL, first bart. of Margam, was so created 1621). Same *Arms, Crest,* and *Motto.*

Mansel (Trimsaran, co. Carmarthen, bart., extinct 1798; descended from JOHN MANSEL, eldest son of Sir FRANCIS MANSEL, first bart, of Muddlescombe, by his second wife). Same *Arms, Crest,* and *Motto.*

Mansel (Cosgrave Hall, co. Northampton). Ar. three maunches sa. *Crest*—On a chapeau gu. turned up erm. a falcon rising ppr. *Motto*—Quod vult valde vult.

Mansel (Smedmore and Longthorns, co. Dorset). Ar. a chev. betw. three maunches ar. *Crest*—A cap of maintenance enflamed on the top ppr. *Motto*—Quod vult valde vult.

Mansel (co. Dorset). Sa. a chev. betw. three mullets ar.

Mansell (co. Gloucester). Gu. a fesse ar. a label of the second.

Mansell (Guildford, co. Surrey; granted by Walker, Garter). Or, three maunches sa. on a chief gu. a lion pass. guard. or.

Mansell. Sa. a chev. betw. three maunches ar. *Crest*—On a chapeau gu. turned up erm. a flame of fire ppr.

Mansell, or Maunsell. Or, on a fesse dancettée gu. three lions ramp. or.

Manser (Lampits, Hoddesdon, co. Herts). Gu. on a bend invected betw. two stags statant ar. an arrow, point to the dexter ppr. *Crest*—In front of three arrows ppr. one in pale, the others in saltire, a leopard's head erased also ppr. *Motto* —Dum spiro spero.

Manser (Penryn, co. Cornwall; granted to WILLIAM MANSER, Esq.). Gu. on a bend invected ar. betw. two stags statant or, an arrow, point upwards ppr. *Crest*—A leopard's head erased in front of three arrows, points upwards, one in pale and two in saltire all ppr. *Motto*—Dum spiro spero.

Mansbergh (Berwick Hall, co. Westmoreland). Ar. a bend raguly betw. three arrows gu. feathered and barbed or. *Crest* —A demi lion ramp. ar. gorged with a collar raguly gu. holding in the dexter paw an arrow of the last feathered and barbed or.

Mansfield, Earl of. See MURRAY.

Mansfield (*Baron Sandhurst*). Ar. on a chev. embattled az. betw. three maunches sa. an eastern crown or, on a chief engr. of the third a lion of the fourth combatant with a tiger cowed ppr. *Crest*—Out of an eastern crown ar. a gryphon's head sa. beaked or, betw. two branches of laurel ppr. *Supporters*—Dexter, a horse ar. mane and tail sa. charged on the shoulder with a rose gu. barbed and seeded ppr. holding in the mouth a branch of laurel vert; sinister, a tiger cowed ppr. gorged with a collar and chain reflexed over the back sa. *Motto*—Steadfast.

Mansfield (co. Nottingham, *temp.* James I.). Ar. a chev. betw. three maunches sa.

Mansfield (West Leake, co. Nottingham). Ar. on a chev. betw. three maunches sa. as many bezants.

Mansfield (Birstall House, co. Leicester). Erm. on a fesse wavy az. a leopard's face ar. betw. two bezants. *Crest*—An eagle rising, wings expanded, in the beak an estoile ar.

Mansfield (London). Ar. three lions' heads erased sa. *Crest*—A cross pattée fitchée erm.

Mansfield. Quarterly, or and az. four trefoils reversed, slipped, and counterchanged.

Mansfield. Gu. a bend cotised betw. six crosses crosslet fitchée ar. (another, crosslets or).

Mansfield (Reg. Ulster's Office). Ar. three bars sa. that in chief charged with a wyvern of the first.

Mansfield (Ballynamultinagh, co. Waterford, afterwards of Yeomanstown and Morristown Lattin, co. Kildare; allowed by Betham, Ulster, 1813, to JOHN MANSFIELD, Esq., of Yeomanstown, sixth in descent from WALTER MANSFIELD, Esq., of Ballynamultinagh, *d.* 1600). Quarterly, 1st, ar. three bars sa. that in chief charged with a wyvern of the first, for MANSFIELD; 2nd, gu. a saltire or, for EUSTACE; 3rd, per fess ar. and gu. in chief on a mount vert a wolf pass. in front of an oak tree ppr., for WOULFE; 4th, ar. a chief indented sa., for POWER. *Crest*—A dexter arm embowed in armour ppr. garnished or, the hand holding a sword both also ppr. pommel and hilt gold. *Motto*—Turris fortitudinis.

Mansham. Ar. a fesse humettée gu. betw. two lions pass. sa. *Crest*—A griffin's head erased or, betw. two wings gu.

Manson (England). Per chev. ar. and gu. in chief three crescents of the last. *Crest*—On a chapeau ppr. a garb or.

Manson (Scotland, 16th century). Ar. a cross calvary betw. two mullets gu.

Manson (Holland, from Scotland, 1672). Ar. a lion saliant ar. armed and langued vert, holding in his dexter paw a sword erected of the second within an orle of eight crescents or. *Crest*—A dexter hand holding a thistle ppr. *Motto*—Mea memor originis.

Manson. Sa. a chev. betw. three annulets ar.

Mansted. Gu. a fesse erm. betw. three mullets pierced or. *Crest*—An arm in armour holding a holly branch fructed ppr.

Mansted. Gu. a fesse erm. betw. three mullets ar.

Mansted, or Maunsted. Gu. a fesse engr. erm. betw. three mullets or.

Manston (Manston, co. Dorset). Or, three martlets sa.

Manston (Manston Court, co. Kent, Sheriff of Kent, *temp.* Henry VI.). Gu. a fesse erm. betw. three mullets ar.

Manston (co. Kent). Gu. a fesse betw. three crescents ar.

Manston. Sa. a bend indented ar.

Manston. Ar. a fesse gu. betw. three eagles displ. sa.

Manston, or Maunston. Gu. on a fesse betw. three mullets pierced ar. as many annulets of the field.

Manston. Quarterly, or and gu. a lion ramp. counterchanged.

Manston, or Maston. Sa. a bend counter-embattled ar. *Crest*—A harp or.

Mansuer, or Mansuen (co. Norfolk, and Mansuer, co. Westmoreland). Vair a bend gu. (another, the field vairé ar. and sa.). *Crest*—A pelican in her piety ppr. nest or.

Mant. Sa. three annulets in pale betw. two palets or, a chief ar. *Crest*—An antelope pass. or.

Mant (Ipswich). Per pale gu. and sa. a lion ramp. counterchanged. *Crest*—A demi lion ramp. ar.

Mantaby. Az. three bendlets or.

Mantebey (granted 1612). Erm. on a bend gu. betw. two cotises engr. of the second three garbs or. *Crest*—A boar's head bendways ar. armed or, with flames of fire issuing from the mouth ppr.

Mantell (co. Kent and Heyford, co. Northampton). Ar. a cross engr. betw. four martlets sa. *Crest*—A stag's head couped at the neck guard. ar. (another, erm.).

Mantell (Lewes, co, Sussex; derived from THOMAS MANTELL, Head Burgess of that town in 1562). Same *Arms, &c.*

Manthelby. Gu. a serpent nowed or.

Manthey, or Maby. Az. a cross or.

Manton. Ar. on a cross engr. az. five garbs or. *Crest*—A unicorn sejant or, resting the dexter paw against a tree vert.

Mantory, or Mantres. Sa. on a chief or, a demi lion ramp. of the field (another, az.).

Mantua, Mantue, or Manton. Ar. a cross gu. betw. four eagles displ. sa.

Manvers, Earl. See PIERREPONT.

Manvers (Holme Pierrepont, co. Nottingham). Ar. six annulets sa. two, two, and two.

Manvers. Ar. six annulets sa. three, two, and one.

Manvoysin, or Mansyne. Or, two bars gu.

Manwairing. See MAINWARING.

Manwell. Gu. three hands couped in fesse ar. *Crest*—A ram pass. gu.

Manwike. Sa. an eagle displ. or, in chief two bezants. *Crest*—On a hurt an estoile or.

Manwike. Sa. an eagle displ. or.

Manwood (Bramfield, co. Essex, and co. Kent). Sa. two palets or, on a chief of the second a demi lion issuant ramp. of the first. *Crest*—On a ducal coronet a lion's head guard. or.

Manyngham. Gu. a chev. ar. betw. three martlets or. *Crest*—An ostrich, wings endorsed, in the beak a horseshoe all ppr.

Manyngton. Ar. on a bend sa. three mullets of the first.

Mape (Reg. Ulster's Office). Ar. an eagle displ. per pale gu. and vert.

Mapes (Feltham and Rollesby, co. Norfolk). Sa. four lozenges in fesse or. *Crest*—An arm embowed in armour or, holding in the gauntlet a spur ar. leathered sa.

Maples. Per pale az. and or, three boars' heads in bend counterchanged. *Crest*—A tower or.

Maplesden (co. Kent). Sa. a cross formée fitchée ar. *Crest*—Out of a mural crown az. two arms embowed in armour ppr. sustaining a flag gu. flotant to the sinister, staff or.

Mapletoft (co. Lincoln). Az. a chev. betw. three crosses crosslet or, on a chief ar. a lion pass. gu.

Mapowder (Holsworthy and Pyeworthy, co. Devon. Visit.

1620). Barry gu. and ar. on a **chief of** the second a grey-hound courant sa.

Mapperley (Mapperley, co. Nottingham). Sa. a bend betw. six crosses crosslet ar.

Mappin (Sheffield; arms in a window in the parish church, Sheffield). Az. on a bend betw. two boars' heads fesswise ar. three lozenges of the first.

Mappin (Birchlands, Sheffield, co York; granted, July, 1857, to JOHN NEWTON MAPPIN, Esq.). Az. on a bend engr. betw. two boars' heads erased ar. three lozenges of the field. *Crest*—A boar sa. charged with a pale or, and resting the dexter foot upon a spur fessewise gold. *Motto*—Cor forte suum calcar est.

Mar (*Earl of Mar*). Ar. a cross betw. six crosses crosslet fitchée gu.

Mar, Earl of. See DOUGLAS and ERSKINE.

Marblers, Company of (London). Gu. a chev. ar. betw. two chipping axes in chief of the last, and a mullet in base or. *Crest*—An arm embowed, vested az. cuffed ar. holding in the hand ppr. an engraving chisel of the last. *Motto*—Grind well.

Marbury (Marbury, co. Chester, temp. Edward II.). Sa. a cross engr. ar. betw. four pheons (sometimes crosses tau) of the second. *Crest*—On a chapeau gu. turned up ar. and semée of plates, a Saracen's head in profile couped ppr. crined and bearded sa. wreathed about the temples ar.

Marbury, or Merbury (Walton, co. Chester, temp. Edward III.). Ar. on a fesse engr. az. three garbs or. *Crest*—A mermaid ppr. holding in the dexter hand a mirror, and in the sinister a comb or.

Marbury (co. Northumberland). Sa. a cross betw. four nails ar.

Marbury (Gresby, co. Lincoln). Ar. on a fesse engr. gu. three garbs or.

Marbury. Gu. two bars or, on a chief of the second a lion pass. of the first.

Marbury (Marbury). Or, on a fess engr. az. three garbs of the first.

Marbury (Fun. Ent. Ulster's Office, 1619, ANNE MARBURY, wife of Sir RICHARD HANSARD, Knt.). Sa. a cross engr. betw. four spear heads erect ar.

Marbury. Sa. a fesse engr. betw. three nails ar.

Marbury (London; THOMAS MARBURY, citizen and haber-dasher of London. Visit. London, 1568). Sa. a cross engr. betw. four pheons ar. *Crest*—A seahorse assurgent per pale or and az. crined gu.

Marbury (Lambeth, co. Surrey; confirmed by Segar, Garter, 10 May, 1616). Same *Arms*.

March (Redworth, co. Durham). Sa. a fesse counter-componée or and gu. in chief a cross crosslet fitchée of the second betw. two lions' heads erased ar. in base a lion's head erased of the last betw. two crosses crosslet fitchée of the second.

March (Isle of Wight, co. Hants). Sa. on a cross or, betw. four lions' heads erased ar. as many crescents gu. *Crest*—A cubit arm erect, vested barry wavy of six or and gu. cuffed ar. holding in the hand a battle axe in bend sinister ppr. headed of the third.

March (London). Same *Arms*, the cross fretty az.

March. Sa. a cross patonce betw. four lions' heads erased ar. *Crest*—A demi lion ramp. ar.

March. Or, a lion ramp. gu. over all a bendlet gobony of the second and first.

March. Gu. a lion ramp. ar. a bordure of the last charged with eight roses of the field.

March. Sa. a cross betw. four lions' heads erased ar. a crescent for diff. *Crest*—An arm bendy wavy sinister or and purp. hand ppr. holding a flower gu. leaved vert, on the top a goldfinch volant ppr.

March (Willesly Park, co. Cambridge, and More Critchell, co. Dorset; THOMAS MARCH, Esq., of More Critchell, assumed, 1777, on succeeding to the estates of Garendon and Gracedieu, in co. Leicester, the name and arms of PHILLIPPS). Quarterly, gu. and az. a cross erm. betw. four lions' heads erased or. *Crest*—A demi lion ramp. ar. holding a Maltese cross or.

March-Phillipps (Garendon). See DE LISLE, of Garendon and Grace Dieu Manor.

Marchall. Gu. a bend engr. or, over all a label ar. *Crest*—A mullet or, betw. two palm branches vert.

Marchand (co. Buckingham; granted 1582). Sa. a bend cotised betw. two griffins segreant or.

Marchant (co. Devon). Or, three anchors sa.

Marchant. Az. a hare ramp. or, betw. three mullets of the last. *Crest*—Out of a ducal coronet or, a nag's head az.

Marche (Isle of Ely, co. Cambridge. Visit. 1574 and 1619. The eventual heiress, DOROTHY, only child of THOMAS

658

MARCHE, Esq., of the Isle of Ely, m. JOHN NORTON, Esq., of Rotherfield, Hants, d. s. p. in 1703). Or, three palets az. on a chief gu. three talbots' heads erased of the first. *Crest*—On a ducal coronet or, a water spaniel (sometimes a wolf) pass. az. langued or.

Marche (Haddenham, co. Cambridge. Visit. 1684; de-scended from MARCHE, of the Isle of Ely; the eventual heiress, SARAH ROWLANDS MARCHE, last surviving child of RALPH MARCHE, Esq., of Haddenham, m. first, PELL GAT-WARD, Esq., who d. s. p. 1741, and second, Sir ISAAC WOLLASTON, Bart., of Loseby). Paly of six or and az. on a chief gu. three talbots' heads erased of the first. *Crest*—On a ducal coronet or, a wolf pass. ar. langued gold.

Marche (London; granted 1585). Gu. a horse's head couped betw. three crosses crosslet fitchée ar. *Crest*—A griffin's head erased az. holding in the beak a rose gu. stalked and leaved vert.

Marche. Ar. on a bend sa. three covered cups or.

Marche. Sa. a lion ramp. ar. depressed by a bend gobonated of the second and az.

Marchington. Ar. three crescents sa. flammant ppr.

Marchington. Or, a fret and canton gu.

Marchington. Ar. fretty sa. on a canton gu. a martlet of the first.

Marchudd-ap-Cynan (Lord of Abergelleu; Founder of the VIII. Noble Tribe of North Wales and Powys, co-temporary with Rhodri Mawr, King of Wales, who s. to the throne in 843, and d. 847. Descendants: I. EDNYFED VYCHAN, Lord of Brynffenigl. II. WYNNS, of Kilgwyn. III. WYNNS, of Coed Coch and Treforth. IV. PUGHS, of Crenddyn. V. MORRIS, of Bryn-yr-Odyn. VI. EDNOWAIN-AP-BRADWEN, Lord of Llys Bradwen, Founder of the XV. Noble Tribe of North Wales and Powys. VII. GRONO LLWYD-Y-PENWYN. VIII. ROBERTS, of Gwysaney. IX. VAUGHANS, of Hen Blas. X. WYNNS, of Abergelleu. XI. WYNNS, of Llanolian. XII. RHYS-AP-EDRID. XIII. FOULKES, of Eriviatt). Gu. a Saracen's head erased at the neck ppr. wreathed about the temples as. and ar.

Marchweithian (Is-ALED DENBIGH-LAND-MARCHWEITHIAN was lord of his tribe, and held his court at Lleweny. De-scendants: I. PRICE, of Giler, &c. II. WYNNS, of Voelas, &c. III. GETHINS, of Crinioge. IV. VAUGHANS, of Pant Glas. V. PARRYS, of Twysog. VI. DAVIES, of Llathwryd. VII. LLOYDS, of Comb. VIII. WILLIAMS, of Llanstyndwy. IX. FOULKS, of Llys Llywarch, and others). Gu. a lion ramp. ar. armed and langued az.

Marckby, or Markby (co. Worcester). Sa. two lions' gambs ar.

Marckner. Gu. an eagle displ. ar. crowned or.

Marckwick (co. Sussex). Per pale ar. and az. a saltire wavy counterchanged. *Crest*—A boar pass. per pale or and az. charged with a saltire counterchanged.

Marcon (Yaxham, Edgfield, co. Norfolk; borne by Col. JOHN MARCH, J.P., of Wallington Hall, co. Norfolk). Per fesse or and az. a demi lion in chief issuant gu. all within a bordure ar. *Crest*—A lion sejant, winged, and supporting a lyre with the dexter foot, behind the lion's head the sun in splendour all gold.

Marcury. Az. a cross flory betw. four cinquefoils or.

Mardake. Or, a fret sa. *Crest*—An eagle displ. or, en-vironed by a serpent vert, the head turned to the dexter over the eagle's head.

Mardakes, or Murdakes. Gu. three bendlets or.

Marden (Marden, co. Hereford, and London). Gu. a bend ar. in the dexter point a Cornish chough ppr. *Crest*—Out of a ducal coronet or, a unicorn's head sa. armed and maned gold.

Marden (London). Or, a bend gu. in the sinister chief point a Cornish chough ppr.

Marden, or Morden (co. Warwick). Erm. on a chief sa. a talbot pass. or, an annulet gu. for diff.

Mardeston. Ar. two bars az. on a chief of the second a lion pass. or.

Mardet. Gu. three palets wavy or.

Mardewike. Vert three lions ramp. ar. crowned or.

Mardock (co. Hertford). Az. a chev. quarterly or and ar. betw. three fleurs-de-lis of the second.

Mardock (Owlton, co. Norfolk). Or, fretty vert, on a chief of the second three annulets of the first.

Mare (*Baron De la Mare*, extinct 1316; JOHN DE LA MARE was summoned to Parliament 1299, but neither he or his descendants afterwards). Gu. two lions pass. in pale ar.

Mare (Blackheath. co. Chester). Gu. two leopards pass. in pale ar. spotted sa. *Crest*—A demi leopard saliant, spotted as in the arms.

Mare. Gu. two chev. or. *Crest*—A hand apaumée gu.

Mare, or De la Mare. Or, three bars dancettée gu.

Mareli. Or, a cross gu. fretty ar. betw. four eagles displ. az.

Mares. Barry nebulée of six erm. and ar.

Mareschall (Hengham, co. Norfolk, *temp.* Henry III.). Gu. a bend lozengy or.

Marett (La Haule, Jersey). Ar. three bars gu. *Crest—A* talbot ppr.

Mareward. Vert a fesse ar. betw. three cinquefoils or.

Marewood, or Marwood. Vert a fesse betw. three trefoils pierced ar. *Crest*—Out of a mural crown or, a beacon fired ppr. betw. two wings ar.

Margaret. Az. a fesse (another, engr.) erm. betw. three eagles displ. ar.

Margaret. Az. a fesse erm. in chief an eagle displ. ar.

Margary (Kensington, co. Middlesex; granted to JOSHUA JOHN LLOYD MARGARY, Esq., of Kensington, of an ancient family, DE MARGUERIE, *Marquis de Vassy*, in Normandy, one of whom, escaping the persecution of the Protestants in France, landed in Guernsey, and afterwards settled in the county of Devon). Per fesse az. and ar. a pale counterchanged, three daisies slipped, two and one of the second. *Crest*—Upon a mount vert an arm in bend ppr. holding a daisy slipped ar. *Motto*—Cherche qui n'a.

Margate, Margat, or Margott (Tournay). Gu. semée-de-lis ar. (another, or).

Margeron. Gyronny of six or and sa.

Margerison (Bradford, co. York; granted to JOHN LISTER. Esq.). Per chev. or and az. in chief two gryphons segreant and in base semée of mullets counterchanged. *Crest*—A gryphon statant az. semée of mullets or, and resting the dexter claw upon a millrind also or. *Motto*—Industria et probitate.

Margesson (Offington, co. Sussex, originally of co. York, where the family held lands *temp.* Richard II.; descended from RICHARD MARGETSON, Esq., of Rotheram, son of JOHN MARGETSON, or MARGESSON, Esq., of Wakefield, co. York, living in 1400). Sa. a lion pass. guard. ar. a chief engr. or, quartering for WHITEBREAD, ar. a chev. sa. betw. three hinds' heads erased ppr. *Crest*—On a ducal coronet or, a lion pass. guard. sa. gorged with a ducal coronet gold. *Motto*—Loyalté me lie.

Margetson (JAMES MARGETSON, D.D., Archbishop of Dublin, 1661-63, Archbishop of Armagh and Lord Primate, 1663-78; confirmed by Roberts, Ulster, 1647). Sa. a lion pass. ar. armed and langued gu. a chief engr. or. *Crest*—On a ducal coronet or, a lion pass. guard. sa. ducally gorged gold. *Another Crest* (Reg. Ulster's Office)—A demi lion ramp. ar. the dexter paw resting on an estoile of eight points gu. *Motto*—Par Dieu est mon tout.

Marines (co. Kent). Or, a cross engr. gu.

Marjerolles. Gu. ten cross crosslets, four, three, two, and one ar., quartered by MITFORD through OSBALDESTON, WENTWORTH, HOTON, and LONDON.

Mariot. Barry of eight ar. and sa. a bend erm.

Mariott (cos. Warwick and Gloucester). Barry of six or and sa.

Marjoribanks (Balbeardie, co. Linlithgow). Ar. a mullet gu. on a chief sa. a cushion or. *Crest*—A demi griffin or. *Motto*—Et custos et pugnax.

Marjoribanks (Lees, co. Berwick, and of Hallyards, Mid-Lothian, bart., 1814, representative of Leuchie). Ar. on a chief gu. a cushion betw. two spur-rowels of the field. *Crest*—A lion's gamb erect and erased grasping a tilting lance in bend sinister, point downwards ppr. *Supporters*—Dexter, a lion guard. gu.; sinister, a horse reguard. ar. furnished ppr. *Motto*—Advance with courage.

Marjoribanks (Guisachan, co. Inverness, bart., 1866). As Lees, but without the supporters.

Marjoribanks (Marjoribanks). Ar. a mullet gu. on a chief sa. a cushion or. *Crest*—A demi griffin ppr. *Motto*—Custos et pugnax.

Marke (Liscard, co. Cornwall; JAMES MARKE, son of JOHN MARKE, and grandson of WILLIAM MARKE, all of same place. Visit. Cornwall, 1620). Gu. a lion ramp. within an orle of eight fleurs-de-lis or, a canton erm.

Marke (Woodhill, co. Cornwall). Same *Arms*. *Crest*—A demi lion holding a fleur-de-lis in his dexter paw.

Marke. Per pale erm. and az. a lion ramp. counterchanged. *Crest*—A lion's gamb sa. holding a battle axe or.

Marke. Same *Arms*, a bordure sa. bezantée.

Marke. Ar. on a cross gu. five cinquefoils or.

Marke. Per pale ar. and gu. a pile counterchanged.

Markeby. Sa. two lions' gambs couped and erect in pale ar.

Markeby. Sa. two lions' gambs chevronways, meeting foot to foot ar. betw. three annulets or.

Markenfield (co. York). Ar. on a bend sa. three bezants.

Marker (Uffculme, co. Devon). Per pale ar. and gu. a pale

659

counterchanged. *Crest*—A greyhound statant per pale ar. and sa.

Marker. Quarterly, nebulée or and sa. four martlets counterchanged. *Crest*—An eagle with wings expanded, resting the dexter paw on a mount ppr.

Marker (exemplified to Rev. GEORGE TOWNSEND SMITH, Rector of Uffculme, co. Devon, upon his assuming, by royal licence, the surname of MARKER only). Per pale dovetail ar. and gu. a pale counterchanged, on a canton of the second a saltire couped of the first. *Crest*—A greyhound per pale ar. and sa. resting the dexter paw upon a saltire gu. *Motto* —Festina lente.

Markes (co. Essex). Gu. a lion pass. ar. a bordure engr. of the last.

Markes (co. Essex). Ar. a chev. betw. three trefoils vert.

Markes. Gu. a lion ramp. within an orle of fleurs-de-lis or, a canton erm.

Markey (Alton Court, co. Hereford; JOHN MARKEY, Esq., son of WILLIAM MARKEY, of Alton Court, gent., by SIBEL, dau. of ROBERT KYRLE, Esq., m. in 1635, BENEDICTA, sister of Sir BENNETT HOSKYNS, Bart., of Harewood). Vert a fesse ar. betw. three mallets or.

Markham (Markham, co. Nottingham; descended from Sir ALEXANDER DE MARKHAM, Constable of the Castle of Nottingham, *temp.* Henry III., from whom descended Sir JOHN MARKHAM, Knt., Judge of the Common Pleas from 20 Richard II. to 9 Henry IV., 1396-1407, who had two sons, I. Sir ROBERT MARKHAM, ancestor of MARKHAM, of Coatham and Allerton, co. Nottingham; and II. Sir JOHN MARKHAM, Lord Chief Justice of the King's Bench, *temp.* Henry VI. and Edward IV.). Az. on a chief or, a demi lion ramp. issuant gu. *Crest*—A lion of St. Mark sejant guard. winged or, circled round the head ar. supporting a harp or lyre of the first.

Markham (Sedgebrooke, co. Nottingham, bart., extinct 1779; descended from Sir JOHN MARKHAM, Lord Chief Justice of the King's Bench, *temp.* Henry VI. and Edward IV.). Same *Arms*. *Crest*—A lion of St. Mark sejant guard. resting the dexter forepaw on a shield ar.

Markham (Ollerton, co. Nottingham; a branch of Sedgebrooke). Same *Arms*, with a bordure ar. *Crest*—A lion of St. Mark sejant guard. winged or, circled round the head ar. supporting a harp or lyre of the first.

Markham (WILLIAM MARKHAM, Bishop of Chester, 1771-77; Archbishop of York, 1777-1807, stated to have descended from MARKHAM, of Coatham). Same *Arms*, as MARKHAM, of Sedgebrooke.

Markham (Cufforth Hall, co. York; descended from WILLIAM MARKHAM, Archbishop of York). Same *Arms*. *Crest*— A lion of St. Mark sejant guard. resting the dexter paw on a pair of hames or. *Motto*—Mitis et audax.

Markham (Becca Hall, co. York, formerly of Coatham, co. Nottingham; descended from WILLIAM MARKHAM, Archbishop of York, 1777-1807; WILLIAM MARKHAM, Esq., of Becca Hall, eldest son and heir of WILLIAM MARKHAM, Private Secretary to Warren Hastings, settled at Becca Hall, was grandson of the Archbishop of York). Same *Arms*, &c.

Markham. Az. on a chief or, a lion pass. sa.

Markham. Ar. on a cross patoncée az. five escallops or.

Markham (Dublin; confirmed by Roberts, Ulster, 1644, to WILLIAM MARKHAM, of that city, gent.). Az. a saltire engr. or, on a chief of the last a lion ramp. issuant of the first. *Crest*—A lion's head erased erm.

Markingfield (co. York). Ar. on a bend sa. three bezants.

Markington (co. York). Gu. an orle ar. over all a bend ermines.

Markington. Per bend indented sa. and ar. (another, or and az.).

Markland. Ar. a chev. betw. three martlets sa. *Crest*—A lion's head erased.

Markoe. Gu. a lion ramp. ar. *Crest*—A demi lion gu. ducally gorged or (another, ducally gorged ar.).

Marks (Steeple-Ashton and Salisbury, co. Wilts, and Pancras, co. Middlesex). Gu. semée-de-lis a lion ramp. or. *Crest*—A demi lion ramp. erm. holding a fleur-de-lis or.

Marks, or Markes (co. Suffolk). Gu. semée-de-lis or, a lion ramp. and canton erm. *Crest*—A demi lion ramp. erm. holding a fleur-de-lis or.

Marks. Gu. a lion ramp. ar. a bordure engr. or.

Marland (co. Kent). Gu. three bars wavy ar. (another, or), on each as many martlets sa.

Marland. Barry nebulée of six gu. and ar. seven martlets sa. three, three, and one, on a chief or, three pellets.

Marlay. Vairé ar. and gu. a bordure az. bezantée.

Marlay (THOMAS MARLAY, Lord Chief Baron of Exchequer in Ireland, 1733; Reg. Ulster's Office). Quarterly, 1st and 4th, barry of eight or and gu. on an orle az. eight martlets of the first; 2nd, a chev. betw. three martlets sa.; 3rd, ar. three bars sa. *Crest*—An eagle displ. ppr.   *Motto*—Nulli præda sumus.

Marlay (Belvedere, co. Westmeath). Barry of eight or and gu. on a bordure az. eight martlets of the field. *Crest*—An eagle displ. ppr.   *Motto*—Nulli præda sumus.

Marlborough, Duke of. See CHURCHILL.

Marlborough, Town of (co. Wilts). Per saltire gu. and az. in chief a bull pass. ar. armed or, in fesse two cocks of the third, in base three greyhounds courant in pale of the last, on a chief or, a pale betw. two roses gu. thereon a tower triple-towered of the fourth. *Crest*—A tower ar. *Supporters*—Two hounds. The original arms of Marlborough, as entered in the Visitation of Wilts, 1565, were, Az. a tower triple-towered ar.

Marle. Sa. a saltire betw. four martlets ar.

Marler, or Marley (Knavestock, co. Essex, and Crayford, co. Kent). Ar. a chev. purp. in the dexter canton an escallop sa.

Marler (co. Kent). Or, a chev. az. (another, field or, chev. gu.).

Marler (London; granted 1583). Ar. a chev. purp. *Crest*—On a chapeau ppr. turned up erm. an eagle, wings endorsed or, ducally gorged, beaked, and legged gu.

Marlere. Az. a bend engr. or.

Marleton (co. Worcester). Ar. on a pale az. (another, sa.) three martlets or.

Marleton. Erm. on a pale az. three martlets or. *Crest*—On a tower ar. a lion ramp. ppr.

Marletoys (co. Worcester). Erm. **on a pale sa.** three martlets or.

Marley. Ar. two bars wavy gu.

Marley (co. Durham). Ar. a chev. betw. three martlets sa.

Marley. Or, on a bend sa. three dolphins naiant embowed ar.

Marlion. Vert on an inescutcheon erm. a chev. gu. an orle of martlets ar. *Crest*—An ostrich's neck gu. and wings endorsed ar. and az. in the mouth a horseshoe of the second.

Marlott (Mundham, co. Sussex). Gu. three mullets ar. *Crest*—A demi heraldic tiger ramp. ar. erased gu.

Marlow. Ar. on a fesse per fesse indented az. and purp. betw. three pinks vert, flowered or, as many trefoils of the first.

Marlow, or Marley. Or, a bend sa. *Crest*—A cross moline pierced erm.

Marlow, or Marlowe. Quarterly, az. and or, three bendlets gu.

Marlow (borne by Rev. MICHAEL MARLOW, D.D., Prebendary of Canterbury, and President of St. John's College, Oxford). Quarterly, or and az. three bendlets gu. quartering KENT, viz., Az. a lion pass. guard. or, a chief erm.

Marlowe (Lord Mayor of London, 1409 and 1417). Quarterly, gu. and az. an orle of martlets or.

Marlowe. Ar. a fesse vairé or and gu. betw. three billets of the last.

Marlton. Erm. on a pale sa. three martlets or.

Marlyn. Ar. two bars gu. *Crest*—A tower ar. masoned sa. on the top a cupola or.

Marlyn. Az. an inescutcheon per chev. erm. and gu. eight martlets in orle ar.

Marlyon. Vert on an inescutcheon erm. a chev. gu.

Marmabell (Gernock). Gu. on a bend or, betw. two cotises indented of the last three mullets of the first.

Marmaduke (from the seal of RICHARD MARMADUC, 1318). Ar. a fesse gu. betw. three parrots vert. *Crest*—Three mullets in chev. ar.

Marmaduke. Gu. a fesse betw. three ringdoves ar. beaked, legged, and collared or.

Marmaduke. Vairé ar. and gu. a bordure az. bezantée.

Marmyon (*Baron Marmyon;* ROBERT DE MARMYON, Lord of Fontney, in Normandy, was granted the Castle of Tamworth, co. Warwick, by William I.; his grandson, ROBERT DE MARMYON, feudal Baron of Tamworth, 1184–1217, had three sons, I. ROBERT DE MARMYON; II. ROBERT MARMYON, jun., ancestor of *Baron Marmyon,* of Wetrington; and III. WILLIAM MARMYON, *Baron Marmyon,* of Torrington; PHILIP DE MARMYON, son of ROBERT DE MARMYON, the eldest of the above sons of ROBERT MARMYON, feudal Baron of Tamworth, 1184–1217, was summoned to Parliament 1260; *d. temp.* Henry III., leaving three daus. his co-heirs; the barony being deemed a feudal one only, has never since been revived; the descendant of his youngest dau. and co-heir is DYMOKE, of Scrivelsby, in right of that manor, *The Hon. the Queen's Champion.* Vair a fess gu.

Marmyon (*Baron Marmyon,* of Wetrington, in abeyance

660

since the death of the third baron; JOHN DE MARMYON, grandson of ROBERT DE MARMYON, jun., second son of ROBERT DE MARMYON, feudal Baron of Tamworth, 1184–1217, was summoned to Parliament, 1294; the third baron left two sisters, co-heirs, JOANE, *m.* Sir JOHN BERNACK; and AVICE, *m.,* as second wife, JOHN, second *Lord Grey,* of Rotherfield). Same *Arms.*

Marmyon (*Baron Marmyon,* of Torrington, extinct; WILLIAM DE MARMYON, third son of ROBERT DE MARMYON, feudal Lord of Tamworth, 1184–1217, was summoned to Parliament 1264, but appears to have *d. s. p.*). Same *Arms.*

Marmyon (co. Notts; HENRY MARMYON, *temp.* Henry VIII., whose dau., BRIDGET, *m.* JOHN TRUSSELL, Esq., of Cosshall, second son of WILLIAM TRUSSELL, Esq., of Billesley, same co.; Trussell Ped. Visit. Notts, 1614). Same *Arms.*

Marmyon (burial escutcheons, Christ Church, Oxford. Visit. Oxon, 1574). Vair three lozenges gu.

Marmyon (co. Gloucester). Gu. a lion ramp. vair. *Crest*—A tent az. garnished or.

Marmyon (co. Leicester). Same *Arms,* lion crowned or. *Crest*—A rose gu. barbed vert.

Marmyon. Gu. a lion ramp. or, fretty az.; another, Ar. three lions ramp. sa. crowned or.; another, Vair a fess or (another, same field, a canton gu.); another, same field, three fusils or mascles gu.).

Marnell. Az. a demi lion ramp. or, an orle of fleurs-de-lis of the last. *Crest*—A stag trippant or.

Marnell. Or, a cross engr. az.

Marner. Or, on a bend sa. three crosses crosslet fitchée ar. *Crest*—Out of a ducal coronet or, a mullet az. betw. two laurel branches vert.

Marner. Az. a fesse gu. betw. six lions ramp. ar.

Marnes. Or, a cross engr. gu.

Marney (*Baron Marney,* extinct 1525; Sir HENRY MARNEY, K.G., Privy Councillor to Henry VII. and Henry VIII., descended from ROBERT DE MARNEY, *temp.* Edward III., was so created 1523; JOHN, second *Lord Marney,* left two daus. co-heirs). Gu. a lion ramp. guard. ar.

Marney (co. Cornwall). Gu. a lion ramp. guard. ar. *Crest*—A chapeau sa. turned up erm. betw. a pair of wings elevated ar.

Marney (co. Essex). Gu. a leopard ramp. ar.

Marney (co. Norfolk). Gu. a lion ramp. guard. ar.

Marney. Or, a cross engr. gu. *Crest*—A granade inflamed ppr.

Marney. Gu. a lion pass. vair crowned or.

Marnham. Gu. a lion ramp. ar. crowned az. *Crest*—Betw. two stalks of wheat in orle or, a cross moline gu.

Marnham. Vair a fesse or, fretty gu. (another, e' fretty gu.).

Maroley (co. York; *temp.* Edward I.). Or, on a bend sa. three clusters of grapes ar.

Marow (Berkeswell, co. Warwick, bart., extinct 1714; descended from WILLIAM MAROW, Lord Mayor of London, 35 Henry VI., 1455). Az. a fesse engr. betw. three maidens' heads couped at the shoulders ar. hair dishevelled or.

Marple (Bonsal, co. Derby). Sa. semée of crosses crosslet fitchée ar. a griffin segreant or.

Marple (Edenstoure, co. Derby; confirmed 20 Sept. 1574). Sa. semée of crosses crosslet fitchée a griffin segreant wings endorsed or.

Marr (Colchester, co. Essex). Ar. a fret sa. on a canton of the last a dexter gauntlet or. *Crest*—Two lions' gambs erased in saltire or, in each a battle-axe, handles gu. blades ar.

Marr (England). Chequy or and ar. **a fesse gu.** *Crest*—A horse's head erased and bridled ppr.

Marrable (Sir THOMAS MARRABLE, Knt., Secretary to the Board of Green Cloth, in the Lord Steward's Department of the Royal Household, second son of JOHN MARRABLE, Esq., of the city of Canterbury). Quarterly, or and gu. a fess erm. in the 1st quarter a canton az. charged with a ring jewelled of the first, in the 2nd and 3rd quarters a lion pass. guard. the dexter forepaw resting on two keys in saltire, the wards downwards gold. *Crest*—A lion ramp. guard. or, holding betw. the paws a chaplet of oak vert, encircling a key in bend sinister, the wards upwards gold, surmounted by a staff ar. *Motto*—Integritate sola.

Marr (Scotland). See MAR.

Marrant (London). Gu. a chev. ar. betw. three talbots courant or. *Crest*—A crane, wings endorsed reguard. ar. resting the foot on a pellet.

Marriot. Ar. three bars sa. on a canton gu. a fleur-de-lis or. *Crest*—Out of a ducal coronet or, a ram's head ar. attired gold.

Marriott. Same *Arms* and *Crest* as MARYET, or MARYOTT.

Marriott (Cotesbach, co. Leicester). **Ar.** three bars az. on a canton sa. a fleur-de-lis of the first, quartering, vert a cross raguly betw. four leopards' faces or. *Crest*—Out of a ducal coronet or, a ram's head ppr. *Motto*—Sursum.

Marriott (co. Northampton). Barry of six or and sa. *Crest*—A talbot pass. sa. collared and chained or.

Marriott (co. Derby). Same *Arms*. *Crest*—A ram's head ar.

Marriott (Avonbank, co. Worcester, formerly of The Leases, co. York; descended from AUGUSTINE MARRIOT, citizen of London, living in 1689). Same *Arms*. *Crest*—A talbot pass. sa. collared and chained or. *Motto*—Virtute et fide.

Marriott. Barry of six or and sa. on a canton az. a boar pass. or. *Crest*—A talbot pass. collared and lined.

Marriott (SMITH-MARRIOTT, Sydling St. Nicholas, co. Dorset, bart.). Quarterly, 1st and 4th, ba?ry of six or and sa. and in chief two escallops gu., for MARRIOTT; 2nd and 3rd, sa. a fesse erminois cotised or, betw. three martlets of the last, each charged with an erm. spot, for SMITH. *Crests* —1st, MARRIOTT: A mount vert, thereon a talbot pass. sa. guttée d'eau, collared and a line reflexed over the back or; 2nd, SMITH: A greyhound sejant gu. collared and a line reflexed over the back or, charged on the shoulder with a mascle ar. *Motto*—Semper fidelis.

Marrow. Or, billettée sa. a fesse of the last. *Crest*—A pillar ar. base az.

Marrow (confirmed by Carney, Ulster, 1656, to WILLIAM MARROW, of the Ordnance, who came to Ireland with Oliver Cromwell, 1649). Az. on a fess engr. or, betw. three maidens' heads ppr. a mullet sa. betw +wo pellets. *Crest*— A maiden's head ppr.

Marris (Barton, co. York). Gu. a saltire engr. ar. *Crest*— A castle ppr.

Marryatt. Paly of six ar. and sa. a bend erm. *Crest*—A lion ramp. double queued ppr.

Marsden (Manchester, and Chelmorton, co. Derby; Rev. WILLIAM MARSDEN, Vicar of Eccles, co. Lancaster, was of this family; granted 1733). Gu. on a bend ar. three baldcoots sa. beaked and legged of the first, in the sinister chief a unicorn's head erased of the second. *Crest*—A unicorn's head erased ar. guttée de sang, gorged with a ducal coronet az. *Motto*—Mars denique victor est.

Marsden (WILLIAM MARSDEN, Esq., Secretary to the Admiralty *temp.* George III., and ALEXANDER MARSDEN, Esq., Under Secretary of Ireland; descended from MARSDEN, of Manchester and Chelmorton). Same *Arms*, and, for distinction, a sprig of shamrock ppr. in the unicorn's mouth, and a key with a sprig of shamrock in the dexter chief of the shield.

Marsh (co. Cambridge) Paly of six ar. and az. on a chief gu. three talbots' heads erased or.

Marsh, or Marshe (co. Huntingdon). Paly of six or and az. on a chief gu. three talbots' heads erased or.

Marsh (Marton in Langden, co. Kent; confirmed 1602). Quarterly, gu. and ar. in the dexter chief quarter a horse's head couped of the second. *Crest*—Out of a mural crown gu. a horse's head ar. ducally gorged or.

Marsh (Marton, near East Langton, co. Kent; granted 16 June, 1616). Same *Arms*. *Crest*—A ram's head ar. attired and crowned or.

Marsh (Snave Manor and Ivy Church, co. Kent). Same *Arms* and *Crest*.

Marsh (Gaynes Park, co. Essex). Quarterly, 1st and 4th, same *Arms*, for MARSH; 2nd and 3rd, ar. three crosses crosslet fitchée gu. a bordure engr. of the last, for CHISENHALE. *Crests*—1st, MARSH: Out of a mural crown gu. a horse's head ar. ducally gorged or; 2nd, CHISENHALE: A griffin pass. gu. collared and lined or, the collar charged with three cross crosslets gu.

Marsh (Edmonton, co. Middlesex, Fincham, co. Bucks, and London; ROBERT MARSH, gent., of Edmonton, Visit. Middlesex, 1663, and Rev. SAMUEL MARSH, D.D., sons of SAMUEL MARSH, gent., of Fincham, 1633, and grandsons of ROBERT MARSH, of London, *d.* 7 Oct. 1602). Ar. on a bend gu. three lozenges of the first, in chief a trefoil of the second. *Crest*—A demi leopard ramp. ppr. pellettée, ducally gorged or.

Marsh (co. Middlesex). Barry of eight ar. and az. a lion ramp. gu. ducally crowned or.

Marsh (Ramridge, co. Hants). Or, three birds az. on a chief of the last the sun of the first. *Crest*—A lion's head erased or.

Marsh (London, formerly Dorking, co. Surrey; quartered by ADAMS, of Dummer, co. Hants). Per fesse dancettée gu. and ar. a pale counterchanged, three horses' heads couped of the second.

Marsh (Darks, co. Middlesex). Same *Arms*. *Crest*—A

demi lion ramp. erased sa. bezantée, gorged with a duca¹ coronet ar.

Marsh (The Lloyd, co. Stafford). Gu. a horse's head couped betw. three crosses crosslet ar.

Marsh (London, merchant, *d.* in Dublin, 1661; Fun. Ent. Ulster's Office). Sa. a cross ar. fretty of the first betw. four lions' heads erased of the second.

Marsh (Springmount, Queen's co.). Gu. a horse's head couped or, betw. two trefoils in chief and a fleur-de-lis in base ar. *Crest*—A griffin's head couped az. gorged with a ducal coronet or, in the beak a rose ar. seeded or, slipped, leaved, and beaked vert. *Motto*—Nolo servile capistrum.

Marsh (bart., extinct 1868; confirmed to HENRY MARSH, M.D., of Dublin, Physician-in-Ordinary to the Queen in Ireland, created a bart. 1839, great-great-grandson of FRANCIS MARSH, Archbishop of Dublin, by his wife, MARY, dau. and co-heir of JEREMY TAYLOR, D.D., Bishop of Down and Connor). Quarterly, 1st and 4th, gu. a horse's head couped or, betw. two trefoils slipped in chief and in base a fleur-de-lis ar., for MARSH; 2nd and 3rd, erm. a bishop's mitre az. on a chief indented gu. three escallops ar., for TAYLOR. *Crest*—A griffin's head couped az. ducally gorged or, holding in the beak a rose ar. seeded gold, slipped, barbed, and leaved vert. *Motto*—Nolo servile capistrum.

Marshal (*Baron Marshal*, barony passed to WILLIAM, third Lord Morley, whose mother was HAWISE, sister and heir of JOHN, second Lord Marshal; WILLIAM MARSHAL, descended from JOHN MARSHAL, who sided with the Empress Maud against King Stephen, and was Marshal of the Realm 10 Henry II., was summoned to Parliament 1309). Gu. a bend fusilly or.

Marshal (*Earl of Pembroke*, extinct 1245; WILLIAM MARSHAL, Marshal to Henry II., a member of the foregoing family, *m.* ISABEL DE CLARE, only dau. and heir of RICHARD, *Earl of Pembroke*, the celebrated Strongbow, and acquired that earldom in her right, in which rank he carried the golden sceptre, surmounted by the cross, at the coronation of Richard I.). Same *Arms*, but after he became Marshal of the Realm he bore, Per pale or and vert a lion ramp. gu. armed and langued az.

Marshall (Blowbery and Windsor, co. Berks). Or, two bars gemelles sa. in chief a chessrook betw. two mullets of the last. *Crest*—A griffin's head erased or, charged on the neck with a chessrook betw. two mullets sa.

Marshall (Fremington, co. Devon). Or, a millrind sa. on a chief gu. three antelopes' heads erased or.

Marshall (Woodwalton, co. Huntingdon). Paly of six erm. and gu. on a chief az. three eagles' heads erased ar. *Crest*—An arrow ar. headed and feathered az. enfiled with a ducal coronet or.

Marshall (Abbotts Anne, co. Hants. Visit. 1575). Sa. three bars ar. a canton or. *Crest*—Out of a ducal coronet a stag's head all or. *Another Crest*—Out of a ducal coronet a bull's head all or.

Marshall (Much-Haddon. co. Herts). Gu. on a fesse ar. betw. three mascles or, as many lions' heads erased az.

Marshall (granted to Col. HUBERT MARSHALL). Barry of six ar. and sa. on a chev. engr. gu. three pheons or. *Crest*— A demi heraldic tiger sa. guttée d'or, armed, crined, tufted, and gorged with a collar gemel also or, resting the sinister paw upon an escocheon gu. charged with a pheon gold. *Motto*—Ducit amor patriæ.

Marshall (Marston, co. Lincoln, and Fiskerton, Doncaster, &c.; granted, 1 June, 1562, to HENRY MARSHALL, Esq., of Carleton). Sa. three bars ar. a canton erm. *Crest*—A man of arms from the waist upwards, armed in armour ppr. garnished or, beaver open, with a plume of feathers of divers colours on the helm, wearing a scarf gu. bawdric-wise, with a staff gold in his hand.

Marshall (Patterdale, co. Westmoreland). Same *Arms* and *Crest*. *Motto*—Nec cito nec tarde.

Marshall (Cookridge, co. York). Same *Arms* and *Crest*.

Marshall (Mark Coniston, co. York). Same *Arms* and *Crest*.

Marshall (Weetwood Hall, co. York). Same *Arms* and *Crest*.

Marshall (Aislabie Grange, co. York, Theddlethorpe, co. Lincoln, and London). Barry of six ar. and sa. a canton erm. *Crest*—A man in armour ppr. in his dexter hand a baton or, over his armour a sash gu.

Marshall (London). Ar. on a chev. engr. gu. betw. three spearheads sa. as many bezants, a chief paly of six gu. and az. thereon an antelope courant or.

Marshall (JOHN MARSHALL, Alderman of London, 1548). Per pale or and sa. three greyhounds courant counterchanged, collared gold. *Crest*—A camel's head or, gorged with a coronet.

Marshall. Ar. a chev. embattled counter-embattled per fess gu. and sa. betw. three eagles' heads erased of the last. *Crest*—A beehive with bees volant about it ppr.

Marshall (Sellaby, co. Durham, and Chelsea, co. Middlesex). Ar. a chev. betw. three crescents gu.

Marshall (Pickering and Aislaby, co. York; descended from co. Notts). Same *Arms. Crest*—A man in armour ppr. holding in the dexter hand a truncheon or, over his armour a sash gu.

Marshall (Carleton, co. Notts; HUMPHREY MARSHALL, Visit. Notts, 1614, descended from JOHN MARSHALL, of that place, *temp.* Edward I.; Harl. MSS., 1400; granted by Harvey, Norroy, 1562, to HENRY MARSHALL, Esq., of Carleton). Sa. three bars ar. a canton erm. *Crest*—A demi man in armour ppr. holding in the dexter hand a baton, over the shoulder a sash az. tied at the shoulder with a ribbon gu.

Marshall (co. Northumberland). Ar. a chev. vert betw. three crescents gu.

Marshall (Ivythorne, co. Somerset; granted 1573). Ar. on a fesse betw. three chessrooks sa. as many mullets of the first. *Crest*—A dexter arm embowed in armour ppr. garnished or, a scarf of the last and az. holding in the hand ppr. a broken tilting-spear of the second.

Marshall (Southwark; granted, 1611, by Camden). Ar. a chev. cotised sa. betw. three bucks' heads cabossed gu. *Crest*—A greyhound sejant ar. gorged with a collar gu. ringed or, resting the dexter foot on a buck's head cabossed of the second.

Marshall (Broadwater, co. Surrey, formerly of co. Sussex; THOMAS MARSHALL, son of THOMAS MARSHALL, Esq., of Eastbourne, left the county, and m. in the year 1743, MARY, the only dau. of WILLIAM BRYANT, of Haslemere, co. Surrey). Az. on a pile betw. two anchors in base or, an arrow. *Crest*—A crested female figure vested ar. the right hand pointing to a rainbow above her head ppr. and with the left supporting an anchor in front sa. *Motto*—Spes mea in cœlo.

Marshall (Diceworth, co. Leicester). Ar. a chev. vert betw. three crescents gu.

Marshall (Milford, co. Wilts. Visit. Wilts, 1677). Gu. five swords in saltire, points upwards ar.

Marshall (Bescott and Walsall, co. Stafford, and Ward End, co. Warwick). Barry of six erm. and az. a horseshoe or, betw. three bezants. *Crest*—A bezant charged with a shoeshoe az. betw. two wings barry of six erm. and az. *Motto*—Vi martiali Deo adjuvante.

Marshall (Alderman Sir CHAPMAN MARSHALL, Knt., Lord Mayor of London in 1840). Paly of six erm. and gu. on a chief az. three griffins' heads erased or. *Crest*—An arrow erect or, flighted and barbed az. and enfiled in the centre with a ducal coronet or.

Marshall (Michelham and Lewes, co. Sussex). Barry of six ar. and sa. on a canton erm. an escutcheon of the second. *Crest*—A demi man in armour ppr. in his dexter hand a baton or, tipped sa. a sash az.

Marshall (co. Wilts). Or, a fer-de-moline gu.

Marshall (co. York). Sa. on a fesse engr. or, betw. three garbs ar. a bird betw. two guttées gu.

Marshall. Ar. a saltire az. betw. four laurel leaves vert, on a bordure gu. eight annulets or. *Crest*—A dove with an olive branch in the beak all ppr. *Motto*—Virtute tutus.

Marshall. Ar. on a chev. engr. gu. betw. three lozenges sa. as many plates, a chief paly of four gu. and az. thereon an antelope courant or. *Crest*—A demi antelope with wings endorsed per pale.

Marshall. Gu. two leopards pass. in pale or (another, ar.)

Marshall. Paly of four ar. and vert (another, or and vert).

Marshall. Ar. a fesse betw. six annulets sa. (another, the fess az. and three annulets).

Marshall. Quarterly, sa. and ar. four mullets counterchanged.

Marshall. Ar. a bend raguly vert betw. two crescents gu.

Marshall. Or, an ink-moline sa. on a chief gu. three tigers' heads erased of the field.

Marshall. Ar. on a chief az. three crosses formée fitchée of the first.

Marshall. Ar. on a fesse gu. three guttees erm.

Marshall. Vert a fesse betw. three martlets ar.

Marshall (JOHN WILLIAM PHILLIPS MARSHALL, Esq., of Rochester, co. Kent). Or, on a chev. az. betw. three lions ramp. gu. an anchor of the first surmounting a sword saltireways ppr. pommel and hilt gold, a chief wavy of the second, thereon a naval crown or, betw. a representation of the cross of the Imperial Russian Military Order of St. George on the dexter,

662

and a like representation of the cross of the Royal Swedish Military Order of the Sword on the sinister, each pendent from the respective ribbons of the said orders all ppr. *Crest*—Upon a mount vert, in front of a Newfoundland dog sejant reguard. ppr. an escutcheon ar. thereon in base waves of the sea, and floating therein a naked man, the sinister arm elevated also ppr.

Marshall (Treworgy House, co. Cornwall; WILLIAM MARSHALL, Esq., of that place, inherited the seat and estate from the family of Connock, whose residence it was in the reign of Henry VIII.; he descended paternally from the co. Devon). Or, a millrind sa. on a chief gu. three antelopes' heads of the field. *Crest*—An antelope's head erased or.

Marshall (The Priory, Totnes, co. Devon). Same *Arms* and *Crest. Motto*—Ordine Colloco.

Marshall (Ardwick and Penwortham Lodge, co. Lancaster, and Taunton, co. Somerset). Quarterly, 1st and 4th, gu. two bars ar. betw. as many flanches erm. on each a cross crosslet of the field, for MARSHALL; 2nd and 3rd, or, a heron sa. a chief of the last, thereon three annulets gold, for EARNSHAW. *Crest*—A man habited as a pikeman of the seventeenth century, and in a corslet, holding in the dexter hand a cross crosslet fitchée or, on the head in profile a morion ppr. plumed gu. *Motto*—Utilem pete finem.

Marshall, alias Bury (Visit. Warwick, 1619). Ar. a chev. sa. betw. three squirrels ppr.

Marshall (Ward End House, co. Warwick; granted 1867). Barry of six erm. and az. a horseshoe or, betw. three bezants. *Crest*—A bezant charged with a horseshoe az. betw. two wings barry of six erm. and az. *Motto*—Vi martiali Deo adjuvante.

Marshall, alias Lokesmyth. Ar. a chev. betw. three horseshoes sa. a chief gu. *Crest*—Out of a mural crown ar. an eagle's head ppr.

Marshall (Church Aston, co. Salop, 1769). Az. a saltire ar. on a chief of the second three edock leaves slipped vert. *Crest*—A buck couchant ppr. *Motto*—Virtus semper virescit.

Marshall (Queensborough). Ar. a saltire couped az. betw. three edock leaves slipped vert. *Crest*—A trefoil slipped ppr. *Motto*—Semper virescit virtus.

Marshall (Hillcairney, co. Fife, 1792). Ar. a saltire az. betw. three edock leaves slipped in chief and flanks ppr. and a heart in base sa. all within a bordure of the last. *Crest*—A dove with an olive branch in its beak ppr. *Motto*—Virtute tutus.

Marshall (Luncarty, co. Perth, 1872). Ar. on a saltire az. betw. three edock leaves slipped ppr. in chief and flank, and a hunting horn sa. stringed gu. in base, a cross crosslet fitchée of the field. *Crest* and *Motto* as the last.

Marshall (HUNTER-MARSHALL, of Callendar, co. Perth, 1872). Quarterly, 1st and 4th, ar. a saltire az. betw. four laurel leaves slipped vert, a bordure sa., for MARSHALL; 2nd and 3rd, gu. a hunting horn stringed or, on a chief engr. of the second three mullets of the first. *Crest*—A dove with an olive branch in its beak ppr. *Motto*—Decerpta dabunt odores.

Marshall (Curriehill, co. Edinburgh, 1873). Ar. a saltire sa. betw. three edock leaves slipped vert in chief, and a bell of the second in base, a bordure gu. *Crest*—A dove ppr. *Motto*—Alta petit.

Marshall (Dublin; Fun. Ent. Ulster's Office, 1597, JOHN MARSHALL, formerly Sheriff of the city). Gu. a bend lozengy ar. a crescent for diff.

Marshall (Reg. Ulster's Office). Gu. a cross betw. four crescents ar.

Marshall (Carrigonnon, co. Cork; crest granted 16 May, 1608, to ROBERT MARSHALL, of the Castle of Carrigonnon, co. Cork, and to his brother, Sir GEORGE MARSHALL, Equerry to James I.). Barry of six ar. and sa. a canton erm. *Crest*—A lion ramp. holding a cross pattée fitchée.

Marshall (granted by Betham, Ulster, to JOHN MARKHAM MARSHALL, Esq., of Ballymacanam, co. Cork, son of RALPH MARSHALL, Esq., by JANE, his wife, dau. and heir of JOHN MARKHAM, Esq., of Brewsterfield, same co.). Barry of six ar. and sa. on a canton erm. an inescutcheon of the second, charged with a trefoil slipped or. *Crest*—A demi man in armour affrontée ppr. girded round the loins with a sash gu. holding a baton sa. tipped or, and charged on the breast with a red rose ppr.

Marshall (exemplified to RICHARD JOHN LEESON, Esq., on his assuming, by royal licence, 1852, the surname of MARSHALL, instead of that of LEESON, in compliance with the testamentary injunction of his maternal uncle, JOHN MARKHAM MARSHALL, Esq., of Callinferry, co. Kerry). Quarterly, 1st and 4th, barry of six ar. and sa. on a canton erm. an escatcheon of the second, charged with a trefoil slipped or, crescent gu. for diff., for MARSHALL; 2nd, gu. a chief nebuly ar. the rays of the sun issuing therefrom or, for LEESON; 3rd, or, on a chief az. a demi lion ar. holding betw. the paws a harp of the first, for MARKHAM. Crests—1st: A demi man in armour affrontée ppr. holding in the dexter hand a baton sa. tipped or, charged on the breast with a rose gu. girded with a sash also gu. a crescent as in the arms for diff., for MARSHALL; 2nd: A demi lion ramp. gu. holding in the paws a sun or, partially eclipsed by clouds ppr. for LEESON; 3rd: A winged lion sejant guard. ar. wings addorsed holding betw. the forepaws a harp or, the head encircled with a plain glory of the last, for MARKHAM. Motto—Sapere aude.

Marsham (Stratton Strawless, co. Norfolk; settled there since Henry I.). Ar. crusily fitchée sa. a lion pass. gu. in bend betw. two bendlets az. each charged with three crosses crosslet or. Crest—A lion's head erased gu. charged with three crosses crosslet or, one and two. Motto—Quod adest.

Marsham (Earl of Romney). Ar. a lion pass. in bend gu. betw. two bendlets az. Crest—A lion's head erased gu. Supporters—Two lions az. semée of crosses crosslet or, each gorged with a naval coronet of the last. Motto—Non sibi sed patriæ.

Marsham. Or, a fesse humettée gu. betw. two lions pass. sa.; another, Ar. on a bend betw. three crosses formée gu. a lion pass. or; another, Ar. a lion pass. gu. betw. two bendlets az. on each three crosslets or. Crest—A falcon rising or, winged az.

Marshe (Dunstable). Per pale gu. and az. a horse's head couped ar. betw. three quatrefoils (another, trefoils) ar. Crest—Out of a mural crown az. a horse's head ar. gorged with a chaplet of laurel vert.

Marshe (Waresley, co. Huntingdon). Gu. a nag's head couped betw. three crosses crosslet fitchée or. Crest—A griffin's head sa. ducally gorged and lined or, in the beak a rose gu. stalked and leaved vert. Another Crest—A griffin's head sa. in the beak a rose gu. leaved vert.

Marshe (co. Kent). Sa. a cross ar. fretty of the first, betw. four lions' heads erased of the second.

Marshe, or Marsh (co. Lincoln). Ar. two bars sa. on a canton of the last a mascle of the first.

Marshe (London, and co. Worcester). Sa. a cross betw. four lions' heads erased ar. (another, or).

Marshe (Darks, South Mims, co. Middlesex). Gu. a horse's head couped betw. three crosses botonée fitchée ar.

Marshe, or Marsh (Wales). Ar. a lion ramp. reguard. ermines a chief vert.

Marshe. Barry ar. and az. six lions ramp. gu.

Marshe. Sa. a lion ramp. ar. depressed with a bend gobonated or and gu.

Marshe. Erm. on a bend sa. three goats' heads erased ar. attired or.

Marske (co. York). Gu. on a chev. ar. betw. three crosses crosslet or, as many cinquefoils az. Crest—A lion's head erased az. charged with a cinquefoil or.

Marson (Hadham, co. Hertford; ROGER MARSON, Esq., of Hadham, temp. James I. Visit. London, 1568). Ar. three bucks' heads cabossed sa. a bordure gu.

Marston (Hawston, co. Leicester; WILLIAM MARSTON, aged 26 years, son of WILLIAM MARSTON, Esq., of Marston at Visit. Leicester, 1619, the grandson of WILLIAM MARSTON, of same place, temp. Henry VII.). Sa. a fess indented erm. betw. three fleurs-de-lis ar.

Marston (Eastcot and Heyton, co. Salop). Same Arms. Crest—A demi greyhound sa. gorged with a collar dancettée erm.

Marston (Hall Green, co. Worcester. Visit. Worcester, 1682). Same Arms and Crest.

Marston. Sa. a fesse double cotised dancettée erm. betw. three fleurs-de-lis ar. Crest—The sail of a ship ppr.

Marson. Gu. three swords in triangle, hilts inwards ar. betw. a fleur-de-lis ar. and a mullet in each flank of the last. Crest—A portcullis az.

Martale (Reg. Ulster's Office). Az. on a bend ar. three hammers gu.

Martell (Chelwell, co. Notts; PETER MARTELL, temp. Henry IV., his dau. and heir, MARGARET, m. Sir WILLIAM BABINGTON, K.B., at the Coronation of Henry VI., Justice of the Common Pleas. Visit. Oxon, 1566). Sa. three martlets ar.

Martell (co. Lincoln). Gu. three hammers or (another, ar.).

Martell. Or, three mallets gu.; another, Ar. a cross engr. betw. four martlets sa.; another, Or, three Danish axes gu.

Marten (Bildeston, co. Suffolk; granted 1600). Or, on an inescutcheon az. a chev. betw. three lions ramp. of the first. Crest—An eagle's head betw. two wings issuing out of a ducal coronet or.

Marten (Marshals Wick, co. Hertford, Radford and Rowsham, co. Oxford, and Old Bond Street, London; descended

663

from JOHN MARTEN, of Rowsham, 1550). Sa. three oval buckles fesseways, two and one, ar. Crest—A martin sa. holding in the beak a buckle, as in the arms.

Marten (co. Sussex; descended from Aquitaine, in France, anno 1386). Ar. a foil sa. on a chief indented gu. three escallops or.

Martham. Gu. a bend wavy betw. three dolphins ar. Crest—A demi lion holding betw. the paws a bomb fired, issuing from a tower all ppr.

Martham. Gu. on a bend wavy ar. three dolphins sa.; another, Gu. a bend betw. six lions ramp. ar.

Martheby. Ar. three squirrels sejant cracking nuts gu.

Martiall (London, 1696). Ar. a chev. within two couple closes betw. three stags' heads cabossed sa. Crest—A greyhound saliant ppr.

Martin (Baron Martin, abeyance 1325; WILLIAM MARTIN, descended from ROBERT MARTIN, temp. Henry I., son of MARTIN DE TOURS, a Norman, was summoned to Parliament, 1295). Ar. two bars gu.

Martin (Lockynge, co. Berks, bart.). Gu. on a chev. betw. three crescents ar. an anchor erect and cable ppr. Crest—A dexter hand brandishing a sabre ppr. pommel and hilt or. Motto—Auxilium ab alto.

Martin (Long Melford, co. Suffolk, also of Burnham, co. Norfolk, bart., extinct). Ar. on a chev. betw. three mascles sa. a bordure engr. gu. Crest—A cockatrice's head betw. two wings. Another Crest—A martin pass. ppr. Motto—Initium sapientiæ, est timor Domini.

Martin (Plymouth, co. Devon; JOHN MARTIN, aged 70, Visit. Devon, 1620, "who went round about the world with Sir FRANCIS DRAKE, anno 1577," fourth in descent from WILLIAM MARTIN, fourth son of RICHARD MARTIN, Esq., of Poulehurst, co. Kent; arms confirmed by Dethick, Garter, 24 Queen Elizabeth, anno 1581). Gu. on a chev. or, three bloodhounds pass. sa. Crest—On a celestial globe sans frame an eagle ppr. wings displ. or, ducally gorged gold.

Martin (Exeter, co. Devon; NICHOLAS MARTIN, Visit. Devon, 1620, son of RICHARD MARTIN, and grandson of Sir WILLIAM MABTIN, Knt., by CHRISTIAN PAULET, his wife, dau. of Sir WILLIAM PAULET, Knt., of Hinton St. George, co. Somerset, temp. Henry VI., ancestor of the Earl of Powlett, the Marquis of Winchester, and Lord Bolton). Ar. two bars gu. a crescent for diff. Crest—An estoile gu.

Martin (co. Durham). Ar. two bars gu. on a canton of the second an inescutcheon of the first. Crest—A demi ostrich erased ar. wings elevated gu. and in the mouth a horse shoe.

Martin, or Martain (Bowton, co. Cambridge, 1604). Az. on a bend or, three fleurs-de-lis of the first, on a chief of the second two eagles displ. of the field. Crest—A tower triple-towered chequy or and az.

Martin (Bodmin, co. Cornwall; the co-heirs m. TREFUSIS and WINTER, temp. Henry IV.). Ar. three bars gu.

Martin (Athelhampston, co. Dorset). Ar. two bars gu.

Martin, or Martyn (Exeter, co. Devon; a branch of MARTIN, of Athelampston; the last male heir, WILLIAM CLIFFORD MARTIN, Esq., d. in 1769). Same Arms. Crest—On the trunk of a tree ar. a bear sejant ppr. chained of the first holding a mirror or.

Martin (East Court, co. Kent). Vert a chev. ar. betw. three doves of.

Martin (co. Leicester; ROBERT MARTIN, of an old family of the county, acquired the estate of Anstey Pastures, in the 16th century). Per saltire ar. and or, three martlets betw. two bars gu., quartering the arms of RICHARDS, of Normanton, viz., Ar. a chev. invected betw. two escallops in chief and a cross pattée in base gu. Crest—A talbot's head erased ar. crusily eared and langued gu. gorged with a collar vert. Motto—Sure and stedfast.

Martin (Whatton House, co. Leicester). Same Arms, Crest, and Motto.

Martin (Wilderness, co. Surrey, and Stonefield, co. Cumberland). Paly of six or and gu. on a chev. ar. an anchor erect sa. on a chief of the second three martlets of the first, quartering HUTCHINSON, RICHMOND, VAUX, of Catterlen, VAUX, of Tryermayne, DELAMERE, and LEYBOURNE. Crest—In front of a garb or, a martin cat statant ppr. Motto—Fide et clementia.

Martin (FRANCIS MARTIN, Bluemantle, 1796, afterwards Norroy and Clarenceux King of Arms). 1st and 4th, Ar. two bars engr. gu. in chief a mantle betw. two roses; 2nd and 3rd, quarterly, or and az. on a fesse erm. betw. three pelicans vulning three annulets.

Martin (co. Dorset). Ar. two bars gu. each charged with an annulet or.

Martin (Leeds Castle, co. Kent: GENERAL PHILIP MARTIN, the last male heir, d. s. p.). Gu. a lion ramp. within an orle of **crosses** crosslet and mullets alternately or. *Crest*—A martin entwined by a serpent ppr. in the **beak a cross** crosslet fitchée or.

Martin (WYKEHAM-MARTIN, Chacombe Priory, co. Northants, and Leeds Castle, co. Kent; FIENNES WYKEHAM, *s.* his kinsman Gen. PHILIP MARTIN, in the family estates, and assumed the additional surname of MARTIN; he was son of Rev. RICHARD WYKEHAM, by MARY FOX, his wife, dau. and heir of CHARLES FOX, Esq., of Chacombe Priory, who was the great grand daughter of JOSEPH MARTIN, Esq., of Ripe, co. Sussex). Quarterly, 1st and 4th, gu. a lion ramp. or, an orle of crosses crosslet and mullets alternately of the last, for MARTIN; 2nd and 3rd, ar. two chevronels betw. three roses gu., for WYKEHAM. *Crest*—A bull's head erased sa. charged with two chevronels ar.

Martin (cos. Somerset and Devon; borne by RICHARD MARTIN, of Old Quebec Street). Ar. on two bars gu. three crosses formée or, two and one. *Crest*—An eagle's head betw. two wings issuant from a ducal coronet all ppr. *Motto*—Accendit cantu.

Martin (cos. Kent and York). Or, three bars gu. in the dexter corner an escutcheon erm. *Crest*—A stag's head sa.

Martin (London; granted Aug. 1615). Az. three bends ar. a chief erm. *Crest*—A wood martin ppr. collared ar.

Martin (Exeter, and Kemys, co. Pembroke; *temp.* Henry I.). Ar. two bars gu. *Crest*—An estoile gu. *Another Crest*—A leopard's head erased ppr.

Martin (founder of Martin College, Oxford). Or, three chevronels per pale az. and gu.

Martin (Bangor, co. Carnarvon, and London, 1634). Ar. two bars gu. in chief three estoiles sa. *Crest*—A martlet rising, ar. charged on the breast with an estoile sa.

Martin (co. York). Ar. two bars gu. each charged with three bezants. *Crest*—An eagle displ. or.

Martin (co. York). Az. three bars nebulée ar.

Martin. Gu. a chev. betw. three crescents ar. *Crest*—A cubit arm erect ppr. brandishing a scymitar, blade ppr. hilt and pommel or.

Martin. Gu. a chev. betw. three martlets in chief and a crescent in base ar. *Crest*—A dexter arm erect ppr. holding a scymitar of the last, hilt and pommel or.

Martin. Ar. three nags' heads erased gu. *Crest*—A greyhound's head erased ar. collared sa.

Martin (Hemingston, co. Suffolk, and Colston Bassett, co. Nottingham). Ar. two bars gu. *Crest*—An ape admiring himself in a looking-glass ppr. *Motto*—Sans tache.

Martin (Worsboro', co. York). Same *Arms, Crest,* and *Motto.*

Martin (Admiral Sir THOMAS BYAM MARTIN, G.C.B. and Knt. T.S.). Gu. on a chev. betw. three mullets in chief and a crescent in base ar. an anchor sa., for MARTIN. *Crest*—A cubit arm erect grasping a faulchion all ppr. *Supporters*—On the dexter an eagle with wings expanded and invected ar. and on the sinister a sea horse with wings expanded and invected ar. tail ppr. *Motto*—Auxilio ab alto.

Martin (Saffron Walden, co. Essex). Or, three palets az. on a chief gu. as many martlets or. *Crest*—A marten-cat pass. ppr.

Martin (granted, 1722, to MATTHEW MARTIN, Capt. H.E.I. Naval Service, of Wivenhoe, co. Essex, *d.* 1749. The patent recites that he was descended from the family of MARTIN, of Saffron Walden, and that the augmentation of the medal, &c., was given to Capt. MARTIN, Commander of the Marlborough, "with this jewel and £1,000 sterling, for defending his ship in India three days successively against three French ships of war, and bringing her safe to Fort St. George"). Or, three palets gu. on a chief az. as many martlets of the first, on a canton gu. suspended from a knot an oval medal with the arms of the East India Company. *Crest*—A martin salient against a cannon erect.

Martin. Or, a tree vert, betw. two crescents az.

Martin. Az. two bars or, in chief a rose betw. **two bugle-**horns of the first.

Martin (Guernsey). Ar. two palets az. on a chief invecked gu. three martlets of the first. *Crest*—A marten-cat pass. ppr.

Martin (Galway; impalement Fun. Ent. Ulster's Office, 1636, of MARTIN DARCY, whose wife was CHRISTICK, dau. of RICHARD MARTIN, Alderman of Galway). Az. a cross calvary on three grieces at the dexter arm terminating in a sun in splendour or, the sinister in a decrescent of the second. *Crest* (Reg. Ulster's Office)—An estoile or. *Motto*—Auxilium meum a Domino.

Martin (Tullyra, co. Galway; RICHARD MARTIN, Esq., of that place, *temp.* William III.; Reg. Ulster's Office). Same *Arms* and *Crest*. *Motto*—Spes mea in cruce unica.

664

Martin (Doebeg, **co. Sligo**; **descended** from OLIVER MARTIN, Esq., of Doebeg, 1709, **son** of RICHARD MARTIN, Esq., of Tullyra. Reg. Ulster's Office). Same *Arms, Crest,* and *Motto.*

Martin (allowed by Fortescue, Ulster, 1805, to Lieut.-Col. THOMAS MARTIN, Major ROBERT MARTIN, and Capt. PETER MARTIN, all of the Austrian service, sons of JOHN MARTIN, Esq., of Doebeg). Same *Arms, Crest,* and *Motto.*

Martin (Martinique, West Indies; allowed by Hawkins, Ulster, 1735, to ANDREW MARTIN, Knt. of the Order of St. Louis, in France, and Governor of Martinique for the King of France). Same *Arms*. *Crest*—A star of six points or. *Motto*—Auxilium meum a Domino.

Martin (Elphin, co. Roscommon; Reg. Ulster's Office). Same *Arms, Crest,* and *Motto.*

Martin (Montserrat, and the Island of Grand Terre, America; allowed by Hawkins, Ulster, 1772, to PAUL MARTIN, Major-General of Horse at Grand Terre, grandson of PAUL MARTIN, Esq., of Elphin, who settled at Montserrat). Same *Arms, Crest,* and *Motto.*

Martin, or Martyn (Tullyra Castle, co. Galway). Same *Arms* and *Crest*. *Motto*—Sic itur ad astra.

Martin (exemplified to ARTHUR GONNE-BELL, Esq., of Brook Lodge, co. Mayo, and his wife, MARY LETITIA, only dau. and heiress of THOMAS BARNEWALL MARTIN, Esq., of Ballinahiuch Castle, co. Galway, on their assuming, by royal licence, 1847, the surname of MARTIN in lieu of BELL). Same *Arms*. *Crest*—An estoile of eight points or. *Motto*—Auxilium meum a Domino.

Martin (impalement Fun. Ent. Ulster's Office, 1625, PATRICK BROWNE, of Irishtown, Dublin, whose wife was ANNABELLA MARTIN). Gu. a chev. ar. betw. three mascles or.

Martin (Kells, co. Meath; Fun. Ent. Ulster's Office, 1639, ELIZABETH, dau. of THOMAS MARTIN, of Kells, Merchant, and wife of JOHN FLEMING, of Dublin, Merchant). Sa. a bend engr. ar. surmounted of another az. charged with three pheons points down of the second.

Martin (Drogheda, co. Louth; Fun. Ent. Ulster's Office, 1666, EDWARD MARTIN, of that place). Erm. three bars gu. each charged with as many plates.

Martin (Dublin; Fun. Ent. Ulster's Office, 1671, HENRY MARTIN, *m.* MARGERY, dau. of Sir ANTHONY BRABAZON, Knt., of Tallaghstown, co. Louth). Or, two bars gu. on the upper one an inescutcheon erm.

Martin (Dublin; Fun. Ent. Ulster's Office, 1685, MARY, wife of SAMUEL MARTIN, Merchant, and dau. of Sir Richard Carney, Ulster King of Arms). Or, on a chev. gu. three talbots pass. ar.

Martin (Bloomfield and Cleveragh, co. Sligo; confirmed to ABRAHAM MARTIN, Esq., of Cleveragh, and the descendants of his grandfather, ABRAHAM MARTIN, Esq., of Bloomfield). Sa. on a chev. betw. three crescents ar. a thistle ppr. *Crest*—A lion ramp. holding in the dexter paw a crescent or, and charged on the shoulder with a thistle ppr. *Motto*—Hinc fortior et clarior.

Martin (WOOD-MARTIN; exemplified to Mrs. ANNE WOOD, widow of JAMES WOOD, of Woodville, co. Sligo, and eldest dau. of ABRAHAM MARTIN, Esq., of Cleveragh, co. Sligo, on her assuming by royal licence, 1874, the additional surname and arms of MARTIN, in compliance with the will of her brother, JAMES WOOD, Esq., of Bloomfield and Cleveragh). Quarterly, 1st and 4th, sa. a chev. betw. three crescents ar., for MARTIN; 2nd and 3rd, ar. an oak tree fructed, growing out of a mound in base all ppr., in the dexter chief point a crescent gu., for WOOD, and for her descendants. *Crests*—1st: A lion ramp. ppr. holding in the dexter paw a crescent or, for MARTIN: 2nd: A demi savage ppr. wreathed about the temples and loins vert, and charged on the breast with a crescent gu., in his dexter hand an oak tree fructed, and in his sinister a club resting on his shoulder, all also ppr., for WOOD. *Mottoes*—Under the arms: Hinc fortior et clarior; Above: Fructu cognoscitur arbor.

Martin (Midhope, co. Linlithgow). Sa. a chev. betw. three crescents ar.

Martin (Edinburgh, 1672). Sa. on a chev. betw. three crescents ar. a mascle of the field. *Crest*—A lion holding in the dexter paw a crescent all or. *Motto*—Hinc fortior et clarior.

Martin (Anstruther, Scotland, 1672). Sa. a chev. invecked betw. three crescents ar. *Motto*—Auxilium cedest Divinum.

Martin (Gibliston, co. Fife). Sa. a chev. vair betw three crescents ar. *Crest*—An adder, with young ones bursting through the side of her ppr. *Motto*—Ingratis servire nefas.

Martin (Islay Herald, 1725). Sa. on a chev. betw. three crescents ar. a saltire gu. all within a bordure of the second. *Crest*—A lion ramp. holding in his dexter paw a sabre ppr., and in his sinister a thistle ppr. slipped vert. *Motto*—Hinc fortior et clarior.

Martin (Liverpool, from Scotland, 1859). Sa. on a chev. wavy betw. three crescents ar. as many mullets az. *Crest*— A dexter arm erect, couped at the elbow ppr. the hand holding a crescent ar. *Motto*—Sans tâche.

Martin (Auchendennan, co. Dumbarton, 1868). Per chev. sa. and gu. on a chev. betw. three crescents ar. a dexter hand couped of the first. *Crest*—A dexter hand sa. holding a crescent ar. *Motto*—Hinc fortior et clarior.

Martin-Edmunds. See EDMUNDS.

Martin-Abbey (co. Surrey). Or, fretty az. on each point an eagle displ. ar.

Martinal (Nowesley, co. Leicester). Ar. a cinquefoil sa. *Crest*—Three organ pipes, two in saltire and one in pale ppr.

Martindale. Ar. two bars gu. over all a bend az. *Crest*— A wolf courant ppr.

Martine. Or, six lions ramp. sa. on a chief gu. three cinquefoils of the first.

Martineau (Basing Park, co. Hants, and Stamford Hill, co. Middlesex). Paly of six or and gu. on a fesse of the last three roses ar. *Crest*– A martin pass. ppr.

Martineau. Per fess paly of six or and gu. counterchanged on a fesse of the second three roses ar.

Martineau. Ar. a fesse betw. three pairs of wings conjoined az. *Crest*—A ram's head erased gu.

Martineaux. Ar. a cinquefoil gu.

Martingdale (Arcleby, co. Cumberland). Barry of six ar. and gu. a bend sa.

Martinson (Newcastle-on-Tyne). Ar. a chev. betw. three martins sa. *Crest*—Out of a ducal coronet or, a plume of five ostrich feathers ar. thereon a martlet, wings expanded ppr. *Motto*—We rise.

Martivall (Nowesley, co. Leicester; NICHOLAS DE MARTIVAL, Lord of Nowesley, 17 Edward I., A.D. 1288; son of THOMAS MARTIVAL, the great grandson of ANKETINUS DE MARTIVALL, Lord of Nowesley, *temp*. King Stephen. Visit. Leices. 1619). Ar. a cinquefoil gu.

Marton (Capernwray Hall, co. Lancaster. Quarterly, 1st and 4th, or, three bars gu. in the dexter chief point an escutcheon erm.; 2nd, ar. on a cross gu. five escallops of the field, a bordure vert; 3rd, ar. two chevronels the lowermost rompu sa. betw. three chaplets gu *Crest*—A stag's head couped ppr. attired sa. *Motto*—Dieu et ma patrie.

Marton-Priory, or Abbey (co. York). Gu. billettée a lion ramp. or; another, Ar. a fret betw. four eagles displ. gu.

Martoset. Sa. on a mount in base vert a buck salient or, on a chief or, a heathcock ppr.

Martyen. Ar. an eagle displ. az. within a double tressure flory sa.

Martyn, alias Dukenfield (city of Chester, 1603). Ar. a cross voided pointed sa.

Martyn (co. Berks). Sa. three buckles ar. garnished or.

Martyn (Okingham, co. Berks). Ar. on a bend sa. three cinquefoils or. *Crest*—Out of a ducal coronet or, a falcon's head az. beaked gold.

Martyn (co. Buckingham). Sa. a chev. betw. three buckles ar.

Martyn (Staplemorden, co. Cambridge). Erm. an eagle displ. gu. *Crest*—A griffin segreant per fesse erm. and or, wings gold.

Martyn (co. Cambridge). Ar. two bars gu. bezantée.

Martyn (St. Dominic, co. Cornwall. Visit. Cornwall, 1620). Ar. two bars gu.

Martyn (Parkpale, co. Dorset, and Saberow, co. Somerset). Or, three bars gu. on each three bezants, a crescent for diff. *Crest*—On the stump of a tree couped and eradicated ar. a monkey sejant ppr. collared and lined or, looking in a mirror framed of the last.

Martyn (Oxton, co. Devon). Same *Arms*. *Crest*—An estoile of sixteen points gu.

Martyn (Totness, co. Devon). Ar. on two bars gu. three crosses formée or. *Crest*—Out of a ducal coronet or, an eagle's head ar. betw. two wings expanded gu.

Martyn (co. Devon). Ar. three bends sa.

Martyn (co. Devon). Ar. two bars gu. a bordure engr. sa.

Martyn (city of Durham). Ar. two bars gu. on a canton of the last an escutcheon of the first. *Crest*—An ostrich head ar. betw. two wings expanded gu. in the beak a horseshoe or.

Martyn (Woodford, co. Essex, co. Lancaster, and London). Az. three bendlets ar. a chief erm. *Crest*—A wood martin ppr. collared ar.

665

Martyn (co. Gloucester). Ar. on two bars gu. three bezants two and one (another, on each bar three bezants).

Martyn (co. Hertford). Ar. two bars gu., on the first an escutcheon erm.

Martyn (Lord Mayor of London, 1492). Same *Arms*, the field or.

Martyn (co. Kent). Ar. on a chev. gu. three talbots pass. or (another, of the field).

Martyn (co. Kent). Ar. three greyhounds courant in pale gu.

Martyn (Long Milford, co. Suffolk. Visit. London, 1568). Quarterly, 1st and 4th, ar. a chev. betw. three mascles sa. a border engr. gu.; 2nd and 3rd, gu. a fess engr. betw. three swans' heads erased ar. *Crest*—A cockatrice's head or, beaked and wattled gu. betw. two wings expanded vert.

Martyn (Sir ROGER MARTYN, Knt., Lord Mayor of London, 1568, son of LAWRENCE MARTYN, second son of RICHARD MARTYN, Esq., of Long Milford, co. Suffolk. Visit. London, 1568). Same *Arms* and *Crest*, a crescent for diff.

Martyn (London; granted 10 Jan. 1572). Paly of six or and az., on a chief gu. three martlets of the first. *Crest*—A martin pass. ppr.

Martyn (London). Or, six lions ramp. sa. three, two, and one, on a chief of the last three cinquefoils of the first.

Martyn (London). Ar. an eagle displ. gu. within a double tressure sa. *Crest*—An eagle displ. gu.

Martyn (Stanton, co. Suffolk, and co. York). Az. three bars wavy ar.

Martyn. Per pale gu. and az. three eagles displ. ar.; another, Ar. on a chief indented az. three martlets or; another, Ar. a fesse betw. three martlets sa.; another, Ar. an eagle displ. within an orle of crosses flory gu. (another, an orle of fleurs-de-lis sa.); another, Ar. three lozenges in bend ar.; another, Ar. a crescent betw. three martlets sa. on a chief of the second as many escallops of the first.

Martyn. See MARTIN.

Martyne (Crekars, co. Bedford). Per pale gu. and ar. on a chev. betw. three mullets as many talbots all counterchanged.

Martyr. Ar. an eagle displ. within a double tressure flory counterflory gu., on a chief quarterly, or and of the second, a rose betw. two lions ramp. in fesse counterchanged. *Crest*—A griffin segreant or, wings endorsed az. supporting a rose gu. stalked and leaved vert.

Martyre. Chequy gu. and ar. a bend wavy or. *Crest*—A demi lion ramp. ppr.

Marvel (ANDREW MARVEL, the patriotic Member of Parliament, *temp*. Charles I. and II.). Or, a chev. engr. betw. three leopards' faces sa. *Crest*—Out of a ducal coronet or, a plume of feathers ar.

Marvyle. Or, a cross lozengy gu.

Marward (co. Dorset). Gu. a fesse erm. betw. three martlets or.

Marward. Vert (another, az.) a fesse betw. six (another three) cinquefoils ar. (another, cinquefoils or).

Marward (*Baron of Skreen*, co. Meath; Reg. Ulster's Office). Vert a fesse betw. three cinquefoils or.

Marward, or Maurward (Reg. Ulster's Office). Az. a fess betw. three cinquefoils ar.

Marwick. Per pale ar. and az. a saltire wavy counterchanged. *Crest*—A boar pass. per pale ar and az. charged with a saltire wavy counterchanged.

Marwood (West Marwood, co. Devon; resident there from *temp*. Henry III. to Queen Elizabeth, when two of the coheiresses m. CHICHESTER and WINCHALSE). Gu. a chev. ar. betw. three goats' heads erased erm. attired or. *Crest*—A goat's head erased ar. attired or, charged with a chev. gu.

Marwood (Widworthy, co. Devon; descended from MARWOOD of Marwood, co. Devon). Gu. a chev. betw. three goats' heads erased ar. *Crest*—On a mount vert a ram couchant ppr. attired or.

Marwood (Plymouth, co. Devon and Worcester; granted 1596). Az. a chev. betw. three goats' heads erased ar. attired or. *Crest*—A goat's head erased ar. attired or, charged on the neck with a chev. gu.

Marwood, or Morwood (Little Busby, and Northallerton, co. York, bart.; extinct 1740. Dugdale's Visit. 1665; exemplified to WILLIAM METCALFE, Esq., of Northallerton, when he took the surname of MARWOOD). Gu. a chev. erm. betw. three goats' heads erased ar. *Crest*—On a mount vert a ram couchant ar. horned and hoofed or. See METCALFE.

Marwood. Gu. a chev. engr. betw. three goats' heads erased ar. armed or, a bordure engr. of the second.

Marwood-Elton, Bart. See ELTON.

Maryborough, Baron. See WELLESLEY-POLE.

Maryborough, Borough of (Queen's co.; incorporated

by Mary I., 1551, confirmed by Carney, Ulster. Visit. 1656). Per fess gu. and az. in chief two lions pass. guard. in pale and in fess as many fleurs-de-lis fess ways all or.

Maryet, or Maryot (co. Berks.; Preston, co. Gloucester; Bredfield, co. Suffolk; and Whitchurch, co. Warwick). Barry of six, or and sa. *Crest*—A talbot pass. sa. collared and lined or, the line coiled at the end.

Mascall (co. Kent). Barry of eight, or and az. three inescutcheons erm. *Crest*—A lion's head erased ppr. ducally crowned or.

Mascall (co. Durham). Sa. six fleurs-de-lis, three, two, and one or, a bordure engr. ar. *Crest*—An elephant ppr.

Mascall (East Mascall and Lewes, co. Sussex). Same *Arms*.

Maseley (London). Sa. a chev. betw. three halberts ar.

Masham (High Lever, co. Essex; bart. extinct 1776). Or, a fess humettée gu. betw. two lions pass. sa.

Masham (*Baron Masham*, created 1712; extinct 1776; Sir SAMUEL MASHAM, fourth bart. of High Lever, whose wife, a near relation of SARAH JENNINGS, wife of JOHN, first *Duke of Marlborough*, was the favourite of Queen Anne; SAMUEL, second *Lord Masham d. s. p.*). Same *Arms*. *Crest*—A griffin's head couped or, between two wings erect gu. *Supporters*—Dexter, a lion sa.; sinister, a leopard guard. ppr., both crowned with an eastern crown or. *Motto*—Mihi jussa capessere.

Masham (co. Suffolk). Same *Arms*. *Crest*—A griffin's head per pale or and gu. betw. two wings az.

Mashiter (Priests, co. Essex). Gu. on a cross erm. an anchor sa. betw. four leopards' faces az. *Crest*—On a mount vert a talbot pass. erm. collared and chained or, resting the fore paw on an escutcheon az. charged with a leopard's face ar. *Motto*—Spero et vivo.

Masingham (Reg. Ulster's Office). Gu. on a bend or, three escallops az.

Maskelyne (Greenwich; borne by the Rev. NEVIL MASKELYNE, D.D., F.R.S., for 46 years Astronomer Royal, d. 9 Feb. 1811, aged 79). Sa. a fesse engr. or, betw. three escallops ar. *Crest*—A demi lion ramp. holding betw. the paws an escallop.

Maskney. Sa. three pairs of keys ar.

Mason (Grade, co. Cornwall). Az. a fesse embattled betw. three griffins' heads erased or.

Mason (Hemingford and Cuckney, co. Huntingdon). Or, a lion ramp. az. *Crest*—A mermaid with comb and glass ppr.

Mason (Sion, co. Middlesex). Same *Arms* and *Crest*. Motto—Dum spiro spero.

Mason (Aldenham Lodge, co. Hertford). Per fesse erm. and az. a lion ramp. with two heads counterchanged. *Crest*—A mermaid per fesse wavy ar. and az. the upper part guttée de larmes, holding in her dexter hand a comb, and in the sinister a mirror, frame and hair sa.

Mason (Greenwich, co. Kent; granted 1739). Same *Arms* and *Crest*.

Mason (London, 1634). Ar. a fesse az. in chief two lions' heads couped or the last. *Crest*—A lion's head az. betw. two wings ar. on the arms and crest a mullet for diff.

Mason (Inner Temple, London, and Stratford-upon-Avon, co. Warwick). Az. on a point with three battlements ar. as many fleurs-de-lis gu. on the middle battlement a dove, wings displ. ppr.

Mason (Didlebury and Minton, co. Salop). Vert two lions combatant or. *Crest*—A mermaid ppr.

Mason (co. Warwick). Per fesse embattled az. and ar. on the embattlement a dove, wings expanded ar. beaked and legged gu. in base three fleurs-de-lis of the last, two and one. *Crest*—A talbot pass. reguard. ar. eared sa. holding in the mouth a hart's horn or.

Mason (co. York). Quarterly, 1st and 4th, per fesse or and gu. a lion ramp. counterchanged; 2nd, or, a lion ramp. with two heads az.; 3rd, ar. a chev. gu. betw. three snails sa.

Mason (Beel House, near Amersham, co. Bucks). Az. a lion ramp. with two heads ar. holding betw. the paws a crescent or, quartering POMEROY, viz., Ar. a lion ramp. sa. a bordure engr. gu. *Crest*—A demi lion ramp. ar. holding a crescent or.

Mason. Per pale ar. and sa. a chev. betw. three masons' squares all counterchanged. *Crest*—A stag's head erased sa. attired or, ducally gorged gold.

Mason. Ar. guttée de sang a lion ramp. with two heads az.

Mason (Necton Hall, co. Norfolk; descended from PAUL MILLER MASON, citizen of London, who first built, and fixed his family at Necton, *temp.* Henry VII.; GEORGE MASON, Esq., second son of WILLIAM MASON, Esq., of Necton, and grandson of WILLIAM MASON, Esq., of Necton, by ELIZABETH, his wife, dau. of FRANCIS BLOMEFIELD, assumed the name

of BLOMEFIELD, s. his eldest brother, WILLIAM MASON, Esq., of Necton, 1865, and d. 1871, when the estates devolved on his eldest sister, ELIZABETH MASON, of Necton). Ar. a fesse az. two lions' heads in chief of the second. *Crest*—A lion's head winged az. *Motto*—God my trust.

Mason (Ireland). Ar. a lion ramp. with two heads az. *Crest:*—Three Moors' heads conjoined in one neck, wreathed round the temples vert.

Mason (granted by Carney, Ulster, 1697, to ROBERT MASON, of the City of Dublin). Quarterly, or and erm. a lion ramp. az. *Crest*—A tower triple-towered gu. within a chaplet or. *Motto*—Sola virtus munimentum.

Mason (Masonbrook, co. Galway; confirmed, 1711, to ROBERT MASON, Esq., of Masonbrook, son of ROBERT MASON, Esq., of same place, and grandson of Captain CHRISTOPHER MASON, descended from MASON, of Sion, co. Middlesex; of this family were JOHN MONCK MASON, and his brothers WILLIAM, HENRY, and THOMAS, sons of Lieut.-Col. HENRY MONCK MASON). Or, a lion ramp. with two heads gu. *Crest*—A mermaid with comb and mirror all ppr.

Mason (Ayr and Rosebank, Scotland). Ar. a bend wavy az. betw. two spur-rowels in chief and a fleur-de-lis in base gu. *Crest*—A tower ppr. masoned sa. *Motto*—Demeure par la verité.

Mason (Mordun, co. Edinburgh, 1795). Ar. a bend wavy betw. two mullets in chief az. and a fleur-de-lis in base gu. *Crest*—A fortified house ppr. *Motto*—Arte firmus.

Mason (Inveresk, co. Edinburgh). Ar. a bend wavy az. betw. two spur-rowels in chief and a fleur-de-lis in base gu. within a bordure engr. of the second. *Crest*—A house ppr. ensigned on the top with a crescent ar. *Motto*—Dominus providebit.

Masons, Company of (London). Sa. on a chev. betw. three towers ar. a pair of compasses of the first. *Crest*—A castle, as in the arms. *Motto*—In the Lord is all our trust.

Masons, Company of (Edinburgh). Ar. on a chev. az. betw. three castles ppr. masoned sa. a pair of compasses or.

Masquenay, or Makenay. Sa. three pairs of keys endorsed, the bows interlaced ar.

Massam (confirmed by Roberts, Ulster, 1648, to DE RINZY MASSAM, son and heir of WILLIAM MASSAM, who was son and heir of WILLIAM MASSAM, Receiver General of the Revenue in Ireland, descended from a "right noble and most ancient family"). Gu. a fess humettée or, betw. two lions pass. guard. ar. armed and langued az. *Crest*—Out of a ducal coronet or, a demi griffin, wings expanded, and holding a pole-axe gu. *Motto*—Qui constans fortis.

Massareene, Viscount. See SKEFFINGTON-FOSTER.

Massenden, or Missenden (Helme, co. Lincoln). Or, a cross engr. gu. in the dexter chief quarter a Cornish chough ppr. *Crest*—A Cornish chough sa. beaked and legged gu. in the beak a laurel sprig vert.

Masser. Sa. a cinquefoil or.

Massey (Baron of Dunham Massey, co. Chester, Baronn under HUGH LUPUS, or DE ABRINCIS, *Earl of Chester, temp.* William I.). Quarterly, gu. and or, in the 1st quarter a lion pass. ar.

Massey (Coddington, co. Chester; HUGH MASSEY, m. AGNES, dau. and heir of NICHOLAS BOLD; his son WILLIAM MASSEY, purchased the manor of Coddington, *temp.* Henry VI.). Quarterly, gu. and or, in the 1st and 4th quarters three fleurs-de-lis ar., a canton ar. for diff. *Crest*—A demi pegasus with wings displ. quarterly or and gu.

Massey (Pool Hall, co. Chester; descended from MASSEY, of Coddington, same co.; REV. WILLIAM MASSEY, rector of Ditchingham, co. Norfolk, grandson of ROGER MASSEY, second son of ROGER MASSEY, Esq., of Coddington, m. ELIZABETH, dau. and heiress of FRANCIS ELCOCKE, of Whitepool, co. Chester; their second son, WILLIAM MASSEY, inherited his mother's property, and was father of FRANCIS ELCOCKE MASSEY, Esq., of Pool Hall). *Arms* and *Crest*, same as MASSEY, of Coddington, quartering ELCOCKE, viz., Gu. a saltire vair betw. four cocks statant ar.

Massey (Sale, co. Chester). Ar. a chev. betw. three lozenges sa. *Crest*—Out of a ducal coronet or, a bull's head erased az. armed gold.

Massey (Broxton, co. Chester). Same *Arms*, a crescent for diff. *Crest*—A demi pegasus ramp. wings elevated per pale gu. and or, the wings counterchanged.

Massey (Grafton). Quarterly, gu. and or, in the 1st quarter a lion pass. ar. in the centre point a trefoil slipped vert.

Massey (Tatton, co. Chester). Quarterly, gu. and or.

Massey (Rixton, co. Lancaster; descended from HAMON MASSEY, second son of ROBERT MASSEY, Esq., of Tatton, co. Chester, who m. 16 Edward III., the dau. and sole heiress of ALAN DE RIXTON, fifth Lord of Rixton of that name;

Francis Massey, seventeenth in descent from Hamon, above-named, Lord of the Manors of Rixton and Glazebrook, d. unm. 1748, when the family became extinct). 1st, ar. on a bend sa. three covered cups of the field, for Rixton; 2nd, quarterly, gu. and ar. in the 2nd quarter a mullet sa., for Massey, of Rixton; 3rd, vert a fesse or, betw. three parrots ar., for Penington; 4th, ar. a squirrel sejant gu., for Horton. Crest—A covered cup ar.

Massey (Timperley). Quarterly ar. and gu. over all a bend az.

Massey (Podington, po. Chester). Quarterly, gu. and or, in the 1st and 4th quarters, three fleurs-de-lis ar. Crest—A lion's head erased.

Massey (Cringleford, co. Norfolk). Same Arms. Crest—A demi pegasus ar.

Massey (Isle of Ely, co. Cambridge, and Podington, co. Chester). Same Arms. Crest—An owl ar.

Massey (Hoo, co. Chester). Ar. on a chev. sa. three crescents of the first.

Massey (Winsham, co. Chester). Ar. a chev. betw. three lozenges (another, mascles) sa.

Massey (co. Chester). Ar. on a chev. betw. three lozenges sa. a lion pass. or. Crest—On a ducal coronet or, a bull's head gu. attired sa.

Massey (Renton, co. Lancaster). Quarterly, gu. and ar. in the sinister chief quarter a mullet sa.

Massey (London). Ar. a pale, quarterly, gu. and or, in the dexter chief quarter a lion pass. ar. Crest—On a mount vert, a lion couchant ar. interlaced with two trees of the first.

Massey (Wrenton, co. Somerset; granted 1760). Quarterly, ar. and gu. in the 1st and 4th quarters, a mullet sa.

Massey (Springfield). Gu. three fleurs-de-lis ar.

Massey (Audlem, co. Chester). Quarterly, gu. and or, in the 1st and 4th quarters three escallops ar. Crest—A heath-cock statant sa. legged, combed, and wattled gu.

Massey (Oliver-Massey; Denfield and Dunham Massey, co. Chester; derived in a direct line from Hamon Massey, first baron of Dunham Massey, temp. William the Conqueror; Magaret-Elizabeth, only child and heiress of the Rev. Millington Massey-Jackson, M.A., of Dunham Massey and Baguley Hall, co. Chester, Vicar of Warminster, Wilts, and Rector of Kingston Deverill, m. Richard Mansel Oliver, Esq., of Melton Lodge, co. Leicester, who assumed by royal licence, 1844, the additional surname of Massey). Quarterly, 1st and 4th, quarterly gu. and or, in the 1st and 4th, quarters three escallops ar. for distinction a canton of the second, for Massey; 2nd and 3rd, per saltire or and erm. on a chief per pale gu. and sa. three lions ramp. ar. collared of the first, for Oliver. Crest—1st, Massey: A moorcock sa. combed and wattled gu. charged on the breast for distinction with a cross crosslet or; 2nd, Oliver: A lion's gamb erased grasping a branch of olive ppr. and a chain therefrom pendent a bugle or. Mottoes—Massey: Pro libertate patriæ; 2nd, Oliver: Nunquam fallentis termes Olivæ.

Massey (Grafton, co. Chester). See Milneton.

Massey (Baron Clarina). Ar. on a chev. betw. three lozenges sa. a lion pass. or. Crest—Out of a ducal coronet or, a bull's head gu. armed sa. Supporters—Two grenadier soldiers in the uniform of the 27th foot, ppr. each holding in his exterior hand a sword also ppr. Motto—Pro libertate patriæ.

Massey-Mainwaring. See Mainwaring.

Massie. Quarterly, az. and ar. in the 1st and 4th quarter a mullet or. Crest—A horned owl ppr.

Massie. Ar. a pale, quarterly gu. and or, on the 1st quarter a lion pass. of the field. Crest—Betw. two trees ppr. a lion salient ar.

Massie (quartered by Birde, of Yowley, co. Chester, and London. Visit. London, 1568). Quarterly, gu. and or, in the 1st and 4th quarters, three fleurs-de-lis ar. over all a trefoil slipped vert. Crest—A griffin's head erased bendy of six sa. and ar.

Massicks (The Oaks, Millom, co. Cumberland; granted to Thomas Massicks, Esq., of that place). Per pale or and az. on a fesse betw. four leopards' faces jessant-de-lis, three in chief and one in base, two quatrefoils all counterchanged. Crest—A cross pattée az. surmounted by a leopard's face jessant-de-lis or. Motto—Vestigia nulla retrorsum.

Massingberd (Braytoft Hall, co. Lincoln, bart., extinct 1723, originally Massingbergh, or Massyngberd; Lambert Massingberd was living temp. Edward I.). Az. three quatre-foils or, in chief a boar pass. of the last charged on the shoulder with a cross pattée gu.

Massingberd (co. Lincoln; Thomas Massingberd, Esq., of Braytoft Hall, 6 Edward VI., was the last Member who represented Calais; his direct descendant and male repre-

sentative was the Rev. Francis Charles Massingberd, Rector of Ormsby, co. Lincoln). Quarterly, 1st and 4th. az. three quatrefoils, two and one, and in chief a boar pass. or, charged with a cross pattée gu.; 2nd and 3rd, quarterly, or and ar. on a cross humettée gu. betw. four lions ramp. sa. two escallops of the first. Crests—1st: A dragon's head erased quarterly or and gu. betw. two wings az.; 2nd: A lion's head erased az. charged on the neck with two arrows in saltire ar. betw. four guttées d'or. Motto—Est meruisse satis.

Massingberd (Gunby, co. Lincoln; Elizabeth Mary Anne Massingberd, heiress of the family, m. 1802, Peregrine Langton, second son of Bennet Langton, Esq., of Langton). Az. three trefoils slipped or, in chief a boar of the second charged with a fleur-de-lis gu. Crest—A lion's head erased az. charged with two arrows in saltire betw. four guttes or.

Massingberd (Gunby, co. Lincoln; exemplified to Peregrine Langton, who assumed the name of Massingberd). Quarterly, 1st and 4th, az. three quatrefoils, two and one, and in chief a boar statant or, charged on the shoulder with a cross pattée gu., for Massingberd; 2nd and 3rd, quarterly, or and ar. on a cross-humettée gu. betw. four lions ramp. sa. two escallops of the first, for Langton. Crests—1st: A dragon's head erased, quarterly or and gu. betw. two wings az.; 2nd: A lion's head erased, charged with two broad arrows in saltire ar. barbed or, betw. four gouttes d'eau. Motto—Est meruisse satis.

Massingberd (co. Lincoln). Az. in chief three cinquefoils ar. Crest—A laurel branch fructed ppr.

Massingberd (co. Lincoln). Quarterly, or and ar. four lions ramp. and an escallop sa.

Massingberd. Erm. on a fesse sa. three escallops or.

Massingberd-Mundy. Quarterly, 1st and 4th, per pale gu. and sa. on a cross engr. ar. five lozenges purp. on a chief or, three eagles' legs erased az., for Mundy; 2nd, az. three quatrefoils, two and one or, in chief a boar statant of the last charged with a plain cross gu., for Massingberd; 3rd, quarterly, or and ar. on a cross couped betw. four lions ramp. sa. five escallops of the first, also for Massingberd. Crests—1st, Mundy: A panther's head erased sa. bezantée; 2nd, Massingberd: A lion's head erased az. charged with two arrows saltirewise betw. four gouttes ar.

Massinger, or Messenger (co. Gloucester). Ar. a chev. betw. three close helmets sa.

Massingham (co. Norfolk). Ar. on a chev. gu. betw. three martlets sa. as many fleurs-de-lis of the first, a bordure engr. of the third bezantée.

Massue (Earl of Galway, extinct 1720: Henry de Massue, de Ruvigny, a native of France, who served under William III., and gained distinction at the battle of Aughrim, was elevated to the Peerage of Ireland, as Viscount Galway, 1692, and was raised to the earldom, 1697, d. s. p.). Quarterly, 1st and 4th, ar. a fess gu. in chief three martlets sa. on a canton or, a battle axe of the third; 2nd, gu. a chaplet of laurel ppr., a chief chequy ar. and az.; 3rd, ar. three martlets gu. Crest—A demi savage crowned and girt with laurel, holding with both hands a club all ppr. Supporters—Two savages, crowned and girt with laurel, each, holding in the exterior hand a club, and on the same arm a shield with the arms of Ireland all ppr. Motto—Duce Deo.

Massy (Alford, co. Chester; quarterly, gu. and or, in the first quarter a lion pass. ar. a bordure gobony of the last and az. Crest—An owl sa. gorged with a collar gobony ar.

Massy (Allerborough, co. Chester). Quarterly, gu. and or, in the 1st and 4th quarters a lion pass. ar.; in the 2nd and 3rd, a mullet sa. Crest—A lion's head erased ar.

Massy (co. Lancaster). Ar. on a bend sa. three covered cups of the field.

Massy. Ar. a bend gu. betw. three wiverns' heads erased sa.

Massy. Or, a bend gu. betw. three wolves' heads' erased sa.

Massy. Ar. a chev. (another, a fesse) betw. three crescents sa.

Massy (Ireland; ancestor of Lords Massy, Lords Clarina, the barts. of Doonas, &c.; certified by Roberts, Ulster, 1648, to Hugh Massy, descended from an ancient family of that name in co. Chester, who came to Ireland as captain of a troop of horse, under command of Col. Chidley Coote). Ar. on a chev. betw. three lozenges sa. a lion pass. or. Crest—Out of a ducal coronet or, a bull's head gu. armed sa.

Massy (Baron Massy). Ar. on a chev. betw. three lozenges sa. a lion pass. or. Crest—Out of a ducal coronet or, a bull's head gu. armed sa. Supporters—Dexter, a lion; sinister, a

leopard reguard. both ppr. and collared and chained or.
Motto—Pro libertate patriæ.

Massy (Bart., of Doonas, co. Clare, extinct 1870). Same *Arms, Crest*, and *Motto.*

Massy (Kingswell House, co. Tipperary). Same *Arms, Crest,* and *Motto.*

Massy (BOLTON-MASSY; exemplified to JOHN MASSY BOLTON, of Brazil, co. Dublin, and of Ballywire, co. Tipperary, on his assuming, by royal licence, 1842, the additional surname and arms of MASSY, in memory of his grand-uncle, Hon. JOHN MASSY, of Massy Park, co. Limerick). Quarterly, 1st and 4th, ar. on a chev. betw. three fusils sa. a lion pass. or, a mullet for diff., for MASSY; 2nd, az. on bend engr. or, three martlets gu., a crescent for diff., for DAWSON; 3rd, or, on a chev. gu. three lions couchant of the first, a crescent for diff., for BOLTON. *Crests*—1st: Out of a ducal coronet or, a bull's head gu. armed sa., for MASSY; 2nd: A falcon belled ppr. jessed az., for BOLTON. *Motto*—Pro libertate patriæ.

Massy-Richardson. See RICHARDSON.

Massy-Beresford. See BERESFORD.

Massy. See MASSEY.

Massyngberd, or Massingbird (the ancient arms of the family). Quarterly, or and sa. on a cross betw. four lions ramp. five escallops all counterchanged.

Masted, or Mesteed. Gu. a fesse engr. erm. betw. three mullets or.

Master (East Langdon, co. Kent; descended from Sir EDWARD MASTER, Knt., of Ospringe, co. Kent, and ETHELBREDA, his wife, dau. and co-heir of ROBERT STREYNSHAM, Esq., the daus. and co-heirs of JAMES MASTER, Esq., of East Langdon, who d. 1702, were MARGARET, m. GEORGE, first *Viscount Torrington;* JOYCE, m. Rev. THOMAS POCOCK, D.D., father of Sir GEORGE POCOCK, K.B., the gallant naval Commander; and ISABELLA, m. JOHN BRAMSTON, Esq.). Az. a fesse embattled betw. three griffins' heads erased or. *Crest*—Out of a mural crown or, a unicorn's head ar. crined and armed gu., granted 2 May, 1608.

Master (Codnor Castle, co. Derby; descended from Sir STREYNSHAM MASTER, Knt., Governor of Fort St. George, in the East Indies, younger son of RICHARD MASTER, Esq., of Langdon, co. Kent). Same *Arms* and *Crest. Motto*—Non minor est virtus quam quærere parta tueri.

Master (Croston, co. Lancaster; descended from Rev. ROBERT MASTER, younger brother of LEIGH MASTER, Esq., of Newhall). Same *Arms* and *Crest.*

Master (Cirencester, and Knole Park, co. Gloucester, originally of Kent; descended from Sir WILLIAM MASTER, Knt., of Cirencester, M.P., a distinguished royalist, son of GEORGE MASTER, Esq., of Cirencester, by BRIDGET, his wife, dau. and heir of JOHN CORNWALL, Esq.). Gu. a lion ramp. guard. or, tail forked supporting betw. the paws a united rose of Lancaster and York, stalked and leaved vert. *Crest* —Within a ring or, gemmed ppr. two snakes entwined erect on their tails and endorsed az. *Motto*—Virtute et ingenio.

Master (Willesborough, co. Kent). Gu. a lion ramp. guard. or, tail double queued. *Crest*—In a gem ring or, two snakes entwined and nowed ppr.

Master (co. Oxford). Same *Arms.*

Master, or Measter (co. Wilts). Sa. on a fesse or, betw. three honeysuckles ar. two lions pass. az. *Crest*—An arm couped at the elbow and erect, vested gu. puffed ar. holding in the hand a bunch of honeysuckles all ppr.

Master (Bapchild, co. Kent). Ar. on a bend cotised sa. a lion pass. guard. of the first crowned or.

Master (Barrow Green House, co. Surrey). Az. a fesse embattled betw. three griffins' heads erased or. *Crest*—In a mural crown or, a unicorn's head ar. crined and armed gold. *Motto*—Non minor est virtus quam quærere, parta tueri.

Masterman (Riccal, co. York). Gu. three fleurs-de-lis ar. *Crest*—A Moor's head sidefaced ppr. wreathed about the temples ar. and gu.

Masterman. Paly of six ar. and az. three crescents or.

Masters (Ewdon, co. Salop). Gu. two chevronels betw. two falcons belled, rising in chief or, each charged on the breast with a cross pattée fitchée az. and in base a cross pattée fitchée of the second. *Crest*—A cock's head erased ar. combed and wattled gu. in the beak an ear of wheat slipped or, betw. two wings az. semée of estoiles gold.

Masters. Or, on a fesse betw. three pheons gu. two lions pass. of the field. *Crest*—An arrow in pale sa. barbed and feathered ar. enfiled with a leopard's face or.

Masters. Sa. on a chief ar. a demi lion ramp. of the field.

Masters. Sa. on a fesse or, betw. three flowers ar. leaved of

the second two lions pass. az. *Crest*—An arm gu. holding two branches flowered ar. leaved vert.

Masterson (Nantwich, co. Chester; THOMAS MASTERSON, of this place, was taken prisoner at Flodden). Erm. a chev. az. betw. three garbs or. *Crest*—An heraldic tiger pass. ar.

Masterson (Ferns Castle, co. Wexford; Sir THOMAS MASTERSON, Seneschal of co. Wexford, knighted in 1588, second son of THOMAS MASTERSON, Esq., of Nantwich, taken prisoner at Flodden; his eldest son, Sir RICHARD MASTERSON, Knt., of Ferns, left four daus. his co-heiresses, viz., MABEL, m. NICHOLAS DEVEREUX, Esq., of Balmagir, co. Wexford; KATHERINE, m. EDWARD BUTLER, Baron of the Kayre, in same co.; MARGARET, m. ROBERT SHEE, Esq., of Upper Court, co. Kilkenny; and MARY, m. WALTER SYNOTT, Esq., of Ballybrennan, co. Wexford. Visit. Wexford, 1618). Same *Arms,* a crescent for diff. *Crest*—A garb or, banded vert.

Masterson (Moneyseed and Castletown, co. Wexford; descended from the second son of Sir THOMAS MASTERSON, Knt., of Ferns, Seneschal of Wexford, of whom male descendants still continue in the co.). Same *Arms* and *Crest.*

Masterson (Sir THOMAS MASTERSON, Knt.). Ar. two bars gu. betw. six martlets, three two and one vert.

Masterton (Parkmilne and Gogar, co. Perth). Ar. a chev. gu. and chief az. *Crest*—A stag courant bearing on the attires an oaken slip fructed all ppr. *Motto*—Per ardua.

Masterton (Grange, co. Perth). Ar. a chev. betw. two crescents in chief and a mullet in base gu., on a chief az. an eagle displ. or. *Crest*—A dexter hand holding a scymetar ppr. *Motto*—Pro Deo et rege.

Maston (co. Kent). Gu. a fesse betw. three crescents ar.

Maston, or Marston (co. Kent). Gu. on a fesse erm. betw. three mullets ar. as many annulets of the first. *Crest* —The sail of a ship ppr.

Maston. Ar. a fesse gu. betw. three eagles displ. sa.

Maston. Per bend ar. and gu. five roses, two, two, and one, counterchanged (another, three roses two and one).

Maston. Sa. a bend embattled counter-embattled (another, ragulée) ar.

Maston. Gu. a fesse erm. betw. three annulets or.

Matcham. Vert on a fesse or, betw. three bundles of arrows of the second a greyhound courant az. pellettée. *Crest* —An arm erect habited vert cuffed ar. holding in the hand three ears of wheat ppr.

Matcham. Vert on a fesse betw. three bundles of wheat (or barley) each consisting of as many stalks, one erect and two in saltire or, a greyhound courant az. pied ppr.

Matchet, or Matcheton. Az. on a fesse wavy or, a cross pattée fitchée gu., on a chief of the second two estoiles of the third. *Crest*—A cross pattée fitchée gu.

Matchett. Per saltire or and vert on a fesse gu. three fleurs-de-lis or.

Mateos (granted to ANTHONY MATEOS, Esq., of Gibraltar). Ar. on a bend engr. gu. a serpent nowed betw. two lions' faces or. *Crest*—A lion's face or, encircled by two serpents ppr. *Motto*—Perseverantia Vincit.

Matford (co. Devon). Ar. a chev. gu. betw. three quatrefoils slipped vert.

Mathadarda (co. Cornwall; the heiress m. BEVILLE). Gu. three bars wavy or, on each three martlets sa.

Mather (Seacroft, co. York; granted 11 Feb. 1575). Erm. a fesse embattled gu.

Mather (England). Barry of six az. and ar. on a chief of the last three mullets of the first. *Crest*—A hand erect issuing from a cloud holding an arrow point downwards all ppr.

Mather (Lanton, co. Roxburgh). Az. two bars or, on a chief of the last an escallop betw. two mullets of the field. *Crest*—An eagle displ. ppr. *Motto*—Fortiter et celeriter.

Mather (Maytone, co. Armagh, Twyford, co. Derby, and New Orleans, in the United States of America). Erm. a fesse embattled gu. *Crest*—A hand erect issuing from a cloud holding an arrow point downwards all ppr.

Matheson (Colonel GEORGE MATHESON, Scotland, 1639). Gyronny of eight sa. and gu. a lion ramp. or, armed ar. all within a bordure of the third, charged with eight crosses pattée gu. *Crest*—An armed hand holding a naked sword ppr. *Motto*—Heart in hand.

Matheson (Ardentoul, co. Ross, 1841). Ar. three dexter hands couped erect, within a bordure of the last. *Crest*—A hand holding a scymitar in fess all ppr. *Motto*—Fac et spera.

Matheson (the Lews, co. Ross, bart.). Gyronny of eight

pieces sa. and gu. a lion ramp. or, armed and langued az. all within a bordure of the third charged with three bears' heads, two in chief and one in base, couped az. muzzled ar. and two hands fessewaysin fesse holding daggers erect gu. *Crest*—A dexter arm in armour erect the hand holding a scymitar in fesse ppr. *Motto*—Heart and Hand.

Matheson (Bennetsfield). Ar. two Lochaber axes in saltire heads to the chief betw. a cock in chief and a rose in base. *Crest*—A dexter hand brandishing a scymitar ppr. *Motto*—Fac et spera.

Matheson (Balmaçara). Gyronny of eight sa. and gu. a lion ramp. ar. on a bordure of the last eight crosses crosslet of the second. *Crest* and *Motto*, as the last.

Mathew (co. Glamorgan; descended from Yvorc, Lord of Torkelyn in Anglesey, who accompanied Einion to the assistance of Jystyn ap Gurgant, Prince of Glamorgan, and received large grants of land in that county. From Sir David Mathew, of Llandaff, Grand Standard bearer to Henry VI., whose fine monument is extant in Llandaff Cathedral, derived the following families: I. Mathew, of Llandaff Court, believed to have become extinct at the decease, at Bath, in 1823, of Captain Thomas Mathews, grandson of the ill-used Admiral Mathew, M.P. co. Glamorgan; II. Mathew, of Radyr, descended from Sir William Mathew, second son of Sir David Mathew, who was made a knight banneret on Bosworth Field by Henry VII., George Mathew, eldest son of Edmond Mathew, of Radyr, High Sheriff co. Glamorgan in 1592, *m.* Elizabeth, Viscountess Thurles, mother of James, Duke of Ormonde; his descendant, James Mathew, of Thomastown and Thurles, was created *Earl of Llandaff* in Ireland; III. Mathew, of Dodbroke, co. Devon, and of Tresunger and Pennytenny, co. Cornwall). Or, a lion ramp. sa. *Crest*—On a mount vert a moorcock ppr.

Mathew (*Earl of Llandaff*, extinct 1833. The direct ancestor of this family in Ireland, George Mathew, m. Elizabeth, dau. of Sir John Pointz, Knt., of Acton, co. Gloucester, and widow of Thomas Butler, *Viscount Thurles*, eldest son of Walter, eleventh *Earl of Ormonde and Ossory*, and father of James, first *Duke of Ormonde*). Same *Arms* and *Crest*. *Supporters*—Two unicorns ar. horned, maned, tufted, hoofed, plain collared and chained or. *Motto*—Y fyn Duw a fydd.

Mathew (Castle-Menych; descended from Robert Mathew, next brother to Sir David Mathew, of Llandaff). Sa. a lion ramp. ar. *Crest*—An eagle displ. per fesse ar. and gu.

Mathew (Stanstead, co. Sussex; descended from Thomas Mathew, of Castle-Menych, Knight Harbinger to Henry VIII. on the Field of the Cloth of Gold). Same *Arms* and *Crest*.

Mathew (Dodbroke, co. Devon). Sa. a stork ppr, legged and beaked gu.

Mathew (Tresunger and Pennytenny, co. Cornwall. The descent of Mathew, cos. Devon and Cornwall, is given in the Heralds' Visitations from Jenkyn Mathew, of Glamorgan (third son of Sir David Mathew, of Llandaff, who changed his coat of arms on marrying Lucia, dau. and heir of William Starkie, brother to Sir Humphrey Starkie, Chief Baron of the Exchequer. The representative of the Cornish family is George Buckley-Mathew, Esq., C.B., H.M.S. Envoy Extraordinary and Min. Plenipo. at the Court of Brazil). Sa. a stork ppr. legged and beaked gu. a bordure ar. *Crest*—On a mount vert a stork, as in the arms. *Motto*—Æquam servare mentem.

Mathew (Milton, and co. Cornwall. Visit. Cornw. 1620). Sa. a stork close ar.

Mathew (St. Kew, co. Cornwall. Visit. Cornw. 1620). Same *Arms*, a border of the last for diff.

Mathew (Lyth, co. Salop). Same *Arms*.

Mathew (Coggeshall, co. Essex). Az. three lions ramp. ar. on a chief of the last as many crosses crosslet sa. *Crest*—A lion's gamb erect, holding a cross crosslet in pale sa. *Motto over*—Cruce non leone fides.

Mathew (Pentloe Hall, co. Essex). Same *Arms*, *Crest*, and *Motto*.

Mathew (Bradden, co. Northampton; descended from Sir John Mathew, Lord Mayor of London, 1 Richard III.). Gyronny of eight sa. and gu. over all a lion ramp. or, a bordure az. semée of cross crosslets or.

Mathew (Thornborough, co. Bucks). Same *Arms*.

Mathew (Felix Hall, co. Essex). Sa. a stork ppr. a border ar. *Crest*—On a mount vert a heathcock ppr.

Mathew (Clonville, co. Hants; Brownlow Bertie Mathew, Esq., son of General Edward Mathew, younger brother to Daniel, of Felix Hall, assumed the name and arms of Bertie, in compliance with the will of his maternal uncle,

Brownlow, last *Duke of Ancaster* and *Marquess of Lindsey*). Same *Arms*, *Crest*, and *Motto*.

Mathew (Billokesby, co. Norfolk). Az. a chev. vairé ar. and gu. betw. three ducal coronets of the second a bordure engr. or. *Crest*—A unicorn's head erased ar. armed and maned gu. charged on the neck with a chev. vairé of the first and second.

Mathews (England). Gu. three chevronels or. *Crest*—On an escallop gu. betw. two wings az. a cross flory or.

Mathias (Lamphey Court and Llangwarren, co. Pembroke). Gu. three dice ar. two and one, on each die six spots in front, two at top, and three on the sinister side sa. *Crest*—A stag trippant ppr. armed or.

Mathias. Same *Arms*. *Crest*—Out of a ducal coronet a broken battle axe.

Matoke, or Mattick (cos. Hertford and York). Az. a chev. quarterly, or and ar. betw. three fleurs-de-lis of the second. *Crest*—A bear salient per bend ar. and sa.

Maton. Gu. three tuns in pale ar. *Crest*—A sheaf of seven arrows sa. enfiled by a mural crown or.

Matran (co. Devon). Or, on a bend sa. three mullets of the field. *Crest*—A sinister arm the hand clenched ppr.

Matravers. Same as Maltravers. *Crest*—Two halberts endorsed entwined with a serpent ppr.

Matres. Sa. on a chief ar. a lion ramp. naissant of the field.

Matrevers (co. Suffolk). Same as Maltravers. *Crest*—A stag's head cabossed or.

Matrevers. Same *Arms*, on a canton gu. three leopards pass. ar.

Matson (co. Lancaster). Sa. a cross formée voided or.

Matson. Ar. three cinquefoils chevronways sa. *Crest*—On a rock a fort in flames ppr.

Matsteed. Gu. a fesse engr. betw. three mullets or.

Matthew (Stansted, co. Sussex). Sa. a lion ramp. ar. *Crest*—An eagle displ. per fesse ar. and gu.

Matthew. Az. an eagle displ. or; another, Sa. a chev. betw. three escallops ar.; another, Quarterly, ar. and sa. in the 1st quarter a rock ppr. in the 2nd a lozenge of the first; another, Ar. on a fesse sa. betw. three lions ramp. gu. as many mullets of the field; another, Ar. on a chev. gu. three quatrefoils of the first; another, Ar. a fesse betw. three birds sa.; another, Az. an eagle displ. with two heads ar.

Matthews (co. Hereford). Quarterly, 1st, or, a lion ramp. reguard. betw. two flaunches sa. each charged with a mullet ar.; 2nd, per pale az. and gu. a chev. betw. three lions ramp. or; 3rd, ar. on a chev. sa. five erm. spots, in the dexter chief point a mullet of the second; 4th, gu. three stirrups leathered and buckled or; 5th, or, a cross pattée fitchée gu.; 6th, gu. three lions pass. ar. *Crest*—On a mount vert a moorcock with a sprig of heath in the mouth all ppr.

Matthews (Great Gobions, co. Essex, and Edmonton, co. Middlesex, bart.; extinct 1708). Gu. three catharine wheels ar. on a chief of the second a bull's head couped sa. *Crest*—A bull's head couped sa. betw. two wings endorsed ar. *Motto*—Omne solum viro patria est.

Matthews (Swansea, co. Glamorgan). Gu. three chev. or.

Matthews (London). Gu. three chev. or.

Matthews (Scotland). Gyronny of eight gu. and sa. a chief or. *Crest*—A cross crosslet fitchée az. and palm branch in saltire vert.

Maturin (confirmed by Hawkins, Ulster, 1728, to Very Rev. Peter Maturin, LL.D., Dean of Killala, 1724-41, son of Rev. Gabriel Maturin; descended from Maturin, of Mont Auriol in Guienne). Ar. a chev. betw. two martlets in chief gu. and a mount in base ppr. *Crest*—A horse in full speed ar. *Motto*—Minatur.

Maturin-Baird. See Baird.

Mauburney. Lozengy gu. and erm. on a quarter az. a cross recercelée or.

Maucel (Guernsey). Ar. a tower sa. surmounted by a scaling ladder in bend or.

Maud (Hargood Hill, co. York). Barry of six ar. and sa. a lion ramp. gu.

Maude (West Riddlesden, Halling Hall, Woodhouse, Staynland, Alverthorpe, &c., &c., formerly Montalt, co. York. Visit. 1585). Ar. three bars gemelles sa. over all a lion ramp. gu. charged on the shoulder with a cross crosslet fitchée or. *Crest*—A lion's head couped gu. charged with a cross crosslet fitchée or. *Motto*—De Monte Alto.

Maude (Kendal, co. Westmoreland, and Blawith, co. Lancaster; descended from West Riddlesden). Ar. three bars gemelles sa. over all a lion ramp. gu. charged on the shoulder with a cross crosslet fitchée or. *Crest*—A lion's head couped gu. charged with a cross crosslet fitchée or. Motto—De Monte Alto.

Maude (*Viscount Hawarden*). Quarterly, 1st and 4th, az. a lion ramp. ar.; 2nd and 3rd, ar.; three bars gemelles sa. over all a lion ramp. gu. charged on the shoulder with a cross crosslet, fitchée or. *Crest*—A lion's gamb erased and erect ppr. holding an oak branch slipped, vert, acorned or. *Supporters*—Two lions ramp. each charged on the breast with a cross crosslet fitchée or. *Motto*—Virtute securus.

Maudele, or Mawdley (Wells, co. Somerset). Ar. a chev. az. three fleurs-de-lis or, a bordure engr. sa. *Crest*— Out of a ducal coronet or, an eagle's head ar.

Maudinne (Reg. Ulster's Office). Ar. on a chief gu. three martlets or.

Maudley (Nunneys, co. Somerset; granted 1537). Ar. on a chev. az. betw. three lozenges gu. as many fleurs-de-lis or, a bordure engr. sa. *Crest*—Out of a ducal coronet ar. a falcon's head of the last.

Maudley (Poulton). Ar. a dexter hand couped and erect within a bordure engr. sa.

Mauduit (*Earl of Warwick*, extinct 1267; WILLIAM MAU-DUIT, feudal *Baron of Hanslape*, great-grandson of WILLIAM MAUDUIT, Chamberlain to Henry I. m. ALICE DE NEWBURGH, dau. of WALERAN, fourth *Earl of Warwick*, of that family; his son WILLIAM MAUDUIT, having become heir to his mother's family, was summoned, 47 Henry III., 1262, as *Earl of Warwick* to attend the King at Worcester to march against the Welsh, *d. s. p.*). Ar. two bars gu.

Mauduit (*Baron Mauduit*, extinct 1347; JOHN MAUDUIT of the same family, as the *Earl of Warwick*, was summoned to Parliament 1342, but the summons was not continued to his son or any of his descendants). Same *Arms.*

Mauduit. Paly wavy of six or and sa.

Maul (Fun. Ent. Ulster's Office, 1667). Ar. three bars sa. over all a lion ramp. gu.

Maule (Panmure, co. Forfar, *Earl of Panmure*, attainted after 1715). Per pale ar. and gu. a bordure charged with eight escallops all counterchanged. *Crest*—A dragon sa. from the mouth and tail fire issuing ppr. *Supporters*—Two greyhounds ar. collared gu. the collars charged with escallops ar. *Motto*—Clementia et animis; afterwards: In est clementia forti.

Maule (*Baron Panmure*, extinct 1874. The second baron *s.* to the Earldom of Dalhousie in 1860). Quarterly, 1st and 4th, per pale ar. and gu. on a bordure eight escallops all counterchanged, for MAULE; 2nd, ar. three pallets wavy gu., for DE VALONIIS; 3rd, quarterly, 1st and 4th, az. a chev. betw. three crosses pattée or, for BARCLAY of Brechin; 2nd and 3rd, ar. three piles issuing from the chief conjoined by points gu., for WISHART of Brechin. *Crest*—A wivern vert, spouting fire before and behind. *Supporters*—Two grey-hounds ppr. each gorged with a collar gu. charged with three escallops ar. *Motto*—Clementiâ et animis.

Maule (*Earl of Panmure*, in the peerage of Ireland; extinct 1782; WILLIAM MAULE, Esq., of Kelly, eldest son of Hon. HARRY MAULE, brother of JAMES, fourth *Earl of Panmure*, in peerage of Scotland, attainted 1715, became eventually heir male of the family, and was raised to the peerage 1743 ; *d. unm.*). Per pale ar. and gu. a border charged with eight escallops all counterchanged. *Crest*—A dragon vert spouting fire at both ends ppr. *Supporters*—Two greyhounds ar. each gorged with a collar gu. charged with three escallops of the first. *Motto*—In est clementia forti.

Maule (Ballumbie, co. Forfar; second son of second *Earl of Panmure*, who afterwards succeeded as fourth earl). As *Earl of Panmure*, with a crescent ar. in the fesse point for diff. *Crest*—A wivern vert with two heads vomiting fire at both ends ppr. charged with a crescent ar. *Motto*—Clementia tecta rigore.

Maule (Kellie; third son of the second *Earl of Panmure*). As *Earl of Panmure*, with a mullet ar. in the fess point for diff. *Crest*—A wivern vert with two heads vomiting fire at both ends ppr. charged with a mullet ar. Same *Motto.*

Maule (Inverkeillor ; younger son of the last, 1744). Quarterly, as *Baron Panmure*, within a bordure az. *Crest*—A dragon vert spouting fire before and behind. *Motto*—In est clementia forti.

Maule (Dr. THOMAS MAULE, 1672). Per pale wavy, on a bordure eight escallops all counterchanged. *Crest —A* phœnix ...sing ppr. *Motto*—Vivit post funera virtus.

Maule (Rev. GEORGE MAULE, S.T.B., Rector of Vange, co. Essex, *d.* 1667). Ar. on a bend sa. three dolphins naiant embowed or, in chief a crescent for diff. *Crest*—On a chapeau gu. turned up erm. a demi peacock, wings displ. ar.

Mauleverer (Arncliffe, co. York; descended from Sir

RICHARD MAULEVERER, Knt., *temp.* William I.; TIMOTHI MAULEVERER, Esq., of Arncliffe, *d.* 1784, leaving four daus. his co-heirs; of these, ANNE *m.* CLOTWORTHY GOWAN, Esq., and her son, WILLIAM GOWAN, having inherited the estates in 1833, assumed the name and arms of MAULEVERER). Gu. three greyhounds courant in pale ar. collared or. *Crest*—A maple branch sprouting from the trunk of a tree all ppr. *Motto*—En Dieu ma foy.

Mauleverer (Allerton-Mauleverer, co. York, bart., ex-tinct 1713 ; descended from Sir THOMAS MAULEVERER, Knt., of Allerton-Mauleverer, *temp.* Henry VII.). Same *Arms.*

Mauley (*Baron de Mauley*, in abeyance 1415; EDWARD DE MAULEY was summoned to Parliament 1295; PETER, fourth *Lord de Mauley*, *d. s. p.*, when his sisters, CONSTANCE, wife of JOHN BIGOT, and ELIZABETH, wife of JOHN SALVIN, became his co-heirs; Lady BARBARA ASHLEY COOPER, dau. and heir of ANTHONY, fifth *Earl of Shaftesbury*, co-heir, through her mother, of JOHN SALVIN and ELIZABETH DE MAULEY, his wife, *m.* 1814, Hon. WILLIAM FRANCIS SPENCER-PONSONBY, who was created *Lord de Mauley* 1838). Or, a head sa.

Mauley. Vair out of a maunch gu. a hand ppr. holding a fleur-de-lis or

Mauley. Or, on a bend sa. three dolphins naiant (another, three eagles displ.) ar.

Maunby. Ar. three bars sa. over all a maunch gu.

Maund (Oxford, 1660). Az. on a bend ar. betw. two eagles displ. or, three mascles of the field.

Maundrell (co. Wilts). Ar. a demi lion betw. eight fleurs-de-lis gu. *Crest*—A dexter arm embowed fesseways couped vested ar. holding in the hand ppr. a cross crosslet fitchéo sa.

Maundrell (granted to the Rev. HERBERT MAUNDRELL). Ar. on a pile az. betw. two doves, in the beak of each an olive branch, in base all ppr. a cherub's head, wings elevated or. *Crest*—In front of three palm branches slipped, one in pale and two in saltire vert, an escallop or. *Motto*—Patior potior.

Maundy (Sandwich, co. Kent). Ar. three bars gu. betw. ten heads, three, three, three, and one, pass. sa. *Motto*—Pour quoy non.

Maunsel (Plassy and Bank Hall, co. Limerick; a younger branch of MANSEL, of Margam). Ar. a chev. betw. three maunches sa. *Crest*—A cap of maintenance inflamed at the top ppr.

Maunsell (Ballywilliam, co. Limerick; descended from RICHARD MAUNSELL, Esq., of Ballywilliam, younger brother of THOMAS MAUNSELL, LL.D., M.P., ancestor of the MAUN-SELLS of Plassy; the present representative is GEORGE MEARES MAUNSELL, Esq., of Ballywilliam, co. Limerick, High Sheriff 1835). Same *Arms. Crest*—A hawk rising ppr. *Motto*—Honorantes me honorabo.

Maunsell (ROBERT MAUNSELL, Esq., of Merrion Square, Dublin, fifth son of the late DANIEL MAUNSELL, Esq., of Ballywilliam). Same *Arms, Crest,* and *Motto.*

Maunsell (Oakley Park, co. Kildare ; a younger branch of the MAUNSELLS of Ballywilliam). Same *Arms, Crest,* and *Motto.*

Maunsell (Thorpe Malsor, co. Northampton). Ar. a chev. betw. three maunches sa. *Crest*—A falcon rising ppr. *Motto*—Honorantes me honorabo.

Maunsell. Sa. a chev. betw. three mullets pierced ar.

Mauntell (Heyford, co. Northants). Ar. a cross engr. betw. four martlets sa. *Crest*—A stag's head couped erm.

Maurice (Brynygwalie, co. Denbigh, and Bodynfol, co. Montgomery; descended, through LLEWELYN VOELGRWN, Lord of Main, from BLEDDYN AP CYNFYN, Prince of Powys; the only dau. and heir of the late Rev. RICHARD MAURICE, of Brynygwalie, *m.* JOHN BONNER, Esq., and their son, ROBERT MAURICE BONNER MAURICE, Esq., purchased the estate of Bodynfol, co. Montgomery). Quarterly, 1st and 4th, az. on a bend ar. three escallops gu.; 2nd and 3rd, ar. a lion pass. sa. a bordure indented gu. *Crests*—1st: A unicorn's head erased sa. winged ar. horned, maned, and bearded or, holding in the mouth a shamrock ppr.; 2nd : A lion pass. sa., as in the arms.

Maurice (Lloran, co. Denbigh, and Pentrekenrick, co. Salop; descended from EINION EFELL, one of the sons of MADOC AP MEREDYDD AP BLEDDYN AP CYNFYN, Prince of Powys. The Rev. THOMAS MAURICE, the learned author of "Indian Antiquities," &c., was of the Pentrekenrick family). Per fesse sa. and ar. a lion ramp. counterchanged of the field, armed and langued gu.

Maurice (Astrad, co. Denbigh; descended from RIRID FLAIDD, Lord of Penllyn, North Wales). Ar. a chev. betw. three wolves' heads erased sa.

Maurice (Myrod Llanhassaph, co. Flint). Sa. three roses ar.

Maurice. Gu. a lion ramp. reguard. or. *Crest*—A hawk perching upon the stump of a tree or, armed and belled gu.

Maurice. Gu. three roses ar.

Maurice (Fun. Ent. Ulster's Office, 1620, JASPER MAURICE). A chev. removed betw. three bucks' heads cabossed.

Maurice. See BONNER-MAURICE.

Mautbey (co. Norfolk, 1373). Az. a cross or.

Mautby (granted May, 1612). Erm. on a bend betw. two cotises engr. gu. three garbs or.

Maver. Ar. three bars voided sa. over all a lion ramp. gu. *Crest*—On a rock an eagle standing ppr.

Maveson (Maveson, co. Salop). Ar. a chev. engr. betw. three mullets sa.

Maw (cos. Lancaster and Suffolk). Az. two bars erm. betw. six martlets or. *Crest*—On a mount vert a camel couchant ar. the hump on the back and end of the tail or.

Mawbey (Mawtby, co. Norfolk; SIMON DE MAWTBY was tenant of that place, 10 Richard I., A.D. 1198; Sir JOHN DE MAWTBY, his descendant, *d.* 1403, leaving two sons, I. Sir JOHN DE MAWTBY, whose dau. and heir, ALIANORA DE MAWTBY *m.* Sir WILLIAM CALTHORPE; II. Sir ROBERT DE MAWTBY, made a settlement of his estates, 1413, and left two sons: 1. JOHN DE MAWTBY, whose dau. and heir *m.* JOHN PASTON, ancestor of the extinct *Earl of Yarmouth;* 2. THOMAS MAWTBY, Esq., of Sparham). Or, a cross gu. fretty of the field betw. four eagles displ. az. each charged on the breast with a bezant.

Mawbey (Botleys, co. Surrey, bart., extinct 1817; descended from THOMAS MAWTBY, Esq., of Sparham, younger son of Sir ROBERT DE MAWTBY, who settled his estates 1413). Same *Arms*. *Crest*—An eagle displ. az. charged on the breast with a bezant. *Mottoes*—Auriga virtutum prudentia; and, Always for liberty.

Mawbey (Kennington, co. Surrey; granted 1757). Or, a cross gu. fretty of the field betw. four eagles displ. az. each charged on the breast with a bezant. *Crest*—An eagle displ. az. charged on the breast with a bezant.

Mawddwy (co. Merioneth, FOULK, son of JOHN-AP-WIL-LIAM, Lord of Mawdwy, was great-grandson of GRIFFITH-AP-GWENWYNWYN, Prince of Powis Wenwynwyn; ELIZABETH, sister and heiress of FOULK, *m.* Sir HUGH DE BURGH, Knt., a descendant of the Justiciar, HUBERT DE BURGH, and was mother of Sir JOHN DE BURGH, Knt., in her right Lord of the Barony of Mawddwy, who had four daus. and co-heirs. The second of those daus., ELEANOR, conveyed Mawddwy in marriage to THOMAS MYTTON, Esq., with whose descendants it remained until alienated by the late JOHN MYTTON, Esq., of Halston). *Arms*, those of GWEN-WYNWYN, Prince of Powis, viz., Or, a lion ramp. gu.

Mawddwy (Merioneth; MADOC, younger son of GWEN-WYNWYN, Prince of Powis Wenwynwyn, derived from BLEDDYN AP CYNFYN, Prince of Powys; EVA, dau. and heiress of MADOC, *m.* IORWERTH, eldest son of OWEN BROGYN-TYN, Lord of Edeirnion, Dinmael, and Abertanat, living A.D. 1166, son of MADOC, last Prince of Powys, and was mother of GRIFFITH AP IORWERTH, living *temp.* Edward I., from whose grandson and heir, LLEWELYN DDU, Baron of Kymmer-yn-Edeirnion, derived the HUGHES's, of Gwerclas, Barons of Kymmer-yn-Edeirnion). *Arms*, those of his father, GWEN-WYNWYN, Prince of Powis, Or, a lion ramp. gu., quartering, ar. three boars' heads couped sa. langued gu. tusked or, for ATHELYSTAN GLODRYDD, Lord of Ferlys; and per bend erm. and ermines a lion ramp. or, for TUDOR TREVOR, Lord of Whittington.

Mawdesley (Mawdesley, co. Lancaster, 1664). Sa. a chev. betw. three pickaxes or. *Crest*—An eagle displ. sa.

Mawdesley (Leyland, co. Lancaster, 1664). Sa. on a chev. betw three pickaxes ar. as many annulets of the first. *Crest* —An eagle displ. sa. charged on the breast with an annulet or.

Mawedby. Az. a cross or.

Mawer. Ar. three martlets vert, beaked gu. on a chief indented sa. (another, gu.) as many mullets ar. (another, or). *Crest*—A lion's gamb issuing sa. resting on an escutcheon erm.

Mawey (co. Worcester). Gu. a fesse betw. five martlets ar.

Mawes, St., Town of (co. Cornwall). Az. a bend lozengy or, betw. a tower in the sinister chief ar. and a ship with three masts, the sails furled, in the dexter base of the second.

Mawgan (co. Cornwall). Ar. two bars, and in chief two mullets sa.

Mawhood (certified at the College of Arms, London, May, 1779). Or, three bars gemelles sa. over all a lion ramp. gu. charged on the shoulder with a cross crosslet fitchée or. *Crest*—A lion's head erased ar. gorged with a collar gu. rimmed, studded, and ringed or, charged on the neck with a cross crosslet fitchée also gu.

Mawle (co. Suffolk). Or, on a bend sa. three dolphins embowed or, in chief a crescent gu. *Crest*—On a chapeau gu. turned up erm a demi peacock displ. ar.

Mawley (co. Chester). Ar. a sinister hand and bordure engr. sa.

Mawley (co. York). Ar. on a bend sa. three eagles displ. of the first. *Crest*—A cross crosslet fitchée gu. and palm branch ppr. both in saltire.

Mawley (co. York). Or, on a bend sa. three dolphins ar.

Mawley. Vair a maunch gu.

Mawley, or Malo Lacu (1328). Or, a bend sa.

Mawnell. Or, on a fesse dancettée gu. three lions ramp. ar.

Mawrice. Az. on a chief gu. three bendlets ar.

Mawson (London; granted 1692). Per fesse erm. and ermines a pale counterchanged, over all a lion saliant or. *Crest*—A lion's head or, collared gobony erm. and ermines. *Another Crest*—A greyhound ar. passing a tree vert.

Maxey (Higham Ferrers, co. Northants, and Halothen and Courtnoll, co. Notts; JOHN MAXEY, Bishop of Elphin, HENRY MAXEY, of the latter place, and LAWRENCE MAXEY, of Halo-then, sons of HENRY MAXEY, of the first place. Visit. Notts, 1614). Ar. a chev. betw. three crescents gu.

Maxey, or Maxie (Bradwell, co. Essex, and Shotley, co. Suffolk). Gu. a fesse ar. betw. three talbots' heads erased of the second. *Crest*—A talbot's head erased ar. collared and ringed gu.

Maxey (Medley, co. Huntingdon). Gu. a chev. or, betw. three crescents ar. (another, the crescents of the second).

Maxey (Saylin, co. Essex; impalement Fun. Ent. Ulster's Office, 1687, WALTER WARNEFORD, whose wife was FRANCES, dau. of Sir WILLIAM MAXEY, Knt., of Saylin). Gu. a fess betw. three talbots' heads erased ar.

Maxfield (co. Chester). Gu. a cross engr. erm. *Crest*— On a ducal coronet a dolphin naiant.

Maxfield (Macclesfield Priory). Gu. a mitre betw. two garbs or.

Maxlird. Gu. three plates.

Maxtoke-Priory (co. Warwick). Ar. on a chief az. two mullets or, pierced gu.

Maxtone (Cultoquhey, co. Perth). Or, a chev. gu. betw. three crosses crosslet fitchée az. *Crest*—A bee ppr. *Motto* —Providus esto.

Maxtone-Graham (Cultoquhey and Redgorton, co. Perth). Quarterly, 1st and 4th, as the last; 2nd and 3rd, or, three piles sa. within a double tressure flory counterflory gu. on a chief of the second a rose betw. two escallops of the first, for GRAHAM. *Crest* and *Motto*, for MAXTONE, as the last. For GRAHAM: *Crest*—A dove ppr. *Motto*—Candide ut secure.

Maxwell (*Lord Maxwell*, 15th and 16th centuries). Ar. a saltire sa. sometimes borne on the breast of a two-headed eagle sa.

Maxwell (*Earl of Morton;* title conferred on the tenth Lord Maxwell). Quarterly, 1st, ar. a saltire sa.; 2nd, ar. a two-headed eagle displ. sa. beaked and membered gu.; 3rd, ar. three urcheons sa., for HERRIES; 4th, gu. a cross or, for CORSBIE; en surtout, ar, on a chief gu. two stars of the field, for DOUGLAS, of Dalkeith. *Crest*—A stag couchant under a holly bush ppr. *Supporters*—Two stags ppr.

Maxwell (*Earl of Nithsdale;* arms borne by first and second earls). Ar. a two-headed eagle displ. sa. beaked and membered gu. on his breast an escutcheon of the first charged with a saltire of the second. *Crest*—A stag ppr. attired or, lodged before a holly bush also ppr. *Supporters*—Two stags ppr. attired or. *Motto*—Reviresco; sometimes—I bide ye fair.

Maxwell (*Lord Herries*, of Terregles; from a younger son of the third Lord Maxwell and the heiress of HERRIES, Lord Herries). Quarterly, 1st and 4th, ar. a saltire sa. in chief a label of three points gu., for MAXWELL; 2nd and 3rd, ar. three urcheons sa., for HERRIES. *Crest*—A stag's head or. *Supporters*—Two savages, wreathed head and middle with ivy ppr. *Motto*—Dominus dedit.

Maxwell (*Earls of Nithsdale*, of the HERRIES branch; the seventh Lord Herries became third Earl of Nithsdale). Quarterly, 1st and 4th, grand quarters, ar. a two-headed eagle sa. beaked and membered gu. on his breast an escut-cheon of the first charged with a saltire of the second, surcharged with an urcheon or; 2nd and 3rd grand quarters, counterquartered, 1st and 4th, ar. a saltire sa. in chief a label of three points gu., 2nd and 3rd, ar. three urcheons sa. *Crest*—A stag's head ppr. attired sa. *Supporters*—Two stags ppr. attired or. *Motto*—Reviresco.

Maxwell (CONSTABLE-MAXWELL, *Lord Herries*, as now borne). Quarterly, 1st, ar. an eagle displ. with two heads sa. beaked and membered gu. on his breast an escutcheon of the first charged with a saltire of the second, and surcharged with an urcheon or, for MAXWELL; 2nd, quarterly, 1st and 4th, or, a saltire sa., 2nd and 3rd, ar. three urcheons sa., for HERRIES; 3rd, quarterly, gu. and vair, a bend or, for CONSTABLE; 4th, az. on a bend cotised ar. three billets sa., for HAGGERSTON. *Crest*—A stag's head couped or. *Supporters*—Two savages wreathed head and middle with laurel, and holding clubs ppr. *Motto*—Dominus dedit.

Maxwell (CONSTABLE-MAXWELL, of Terregles, 1875). Quarterly, as the last, with a crescent sa. in the centre of the quarters. *Crest*—A stag lodged in front of a holly tree ppr. *Motto*—Reviresco.

Maxwell-Constable-Stuart (Traquair). See STUART.

Maxwell (Munches and Terraughty, co. Dumfries, paternally JOHNSTONE, 1868). Quarterly, 1st and 4th grand quarters, ar. a two-headed eagle displ. sa. beaked and membered gu. on its breast an escutcheon of the first charged with a saltire of the second, for MAXWELL; 2nd grand quarter, ar. three urcheons sa., for HERRIES; 3rd grand quarter, counter-quartered, 1st and 4th, ar. a saltire sa. a bordure of the second charged with eight lozenges of the first, for MAXWELL, of Barncleugh, 2nd and 3rd, ar. a saltire invecked sa. betw. two pellets in flank, on a chief gu. three cushions or, for JOHNSTONE, of Clauchrie. *Crest*—A stag lodged in front of a holly bush ppr. *Motto*—Reviresco.

Maxwell (GEORGE MAXWELL, of Carruchan, co. Kirkcudbright, heir male of the MAXWELL family in 1815, *d. s. p.* 1848). *Arms, Crest, Supporters,* and *Motto,* of first and second *Earls of Nithsdale.*

Maxwell (Spottis and Orchardton, bart., 1663; title dormant since 1786). Ar. a saltire sa. betw. an urcheon of the last in chief and a lion's head couped . . . in base.

Maxwell (Breoch, co. Kirkcudbright). **Ar. a saltire sa.** betw. nine mullets, three, three, and three, az.

Maxwell (Cowhill, co. Dumfries, now Drumpark, co. Kirkcudbright ; from the second son of the third *Lord Maxwell*). Ar. a saltire sa. in base a holly leaf vert. *Crest*—A stag ppr. attired of ten tynes ar. lodged before a holly bush also ppr. *Motto*—Reviresco.

Maxwell (Broomholm, co. Dumfries, cadet of Cowhill, 1759). Quarterly, 1st and 4th, ar. on a saltire sa. a crescent or; 2nd and 3rd, ar. a lion ramp. az., for CRICHTON. *Crest* —A hart courant ppr. *Mottoes*—Over the crest : Virtutem sic et culpam ; below the arms : Peto ac fagio.

Maxwell (Hills, co. Kirkcudbright). Ar. a saltire sa. betw. a mullet in chief and a crescent in base gu.

Maxwell (Kirkconnell, co. Kirkcudbright; from younger son of the second *Lord Maxwell,* who m. the heiress of Kirkconnell; heiress m. 1844, ROBERT S. J. WITHAM). Quarterly, 1st and 4th, ar. an eagle displ. sa. beaked and membered gu. on its breast an escutcheon of the first charged with a saltire of the second; 2nd and 3rd, az. two croziers in saltire addossée and in chief a mitre or, for KIRKCONNELL, of that Ilk. *Crest*—A demi eagle rising ppr. *Motto*—Spero meliora.

Maxwell (Col. THOMAS MAXWELL, cadet of Kirkconnell, 1690). Ar. a saltire sa. within a bordure embattled gu. *Crest*—A stag lodged under a bush of holly ppr. *Motto*— Non dormio.

Maxwell (Barncleugh, co. Kirkcudbright, cadet of Kirkconnell, 1672; for arms of their heir of line and representative, see *supra,* under Munches and Terraughty). Ar. a saltire sa. a bordure of the last charged with eight lozenges of the first.

Maxwell (HYSLOP-MAXWELL, of Glengaber, co. Dumfries, 1867). Quarterly, 1st and 4th, ar. a saltire sa. on a bordure engr. of the second eight lozenges of the first; 2nd and 3rd, ar. on a mount vert a stag lodged in front of a holly bush ppr. on a chief invecked of the second three mullets of the first, for HYSLOP. *Crest*—A stag lodged between two branches of holly issuing from the wreath all ppr. *Motto*— Curo dum quiesco.

Maxwell (Tinwald, co. Dumfries, from the second son of the first *Lord Maxwell*). Ar. a saltire sa. in chief a rose gu.

Maxwell (Monreith, co. Wigtoun, cadet of Tinwald, bart., 1681). Ar. a two-headed eagle displ. sa. beaked and membered gu. on his breast an escutcheon of the first charged with a saltire of the second, surcharged with an urcheon or

a bordure of the third. *Crest*—An eagle rising ppr. *Motto* —Reviresco.

Maxwell (Carnsalloch, co. Dumfries; from a younger son of the first *Lord Maxwell*). Ar. a saltire sa. a bordure of the second charged with eight crescents or. *Crest*—A stag rising from a holly bush ppr. *Motto*—Viresco et surgo.

Maxwell (Tealing, co. Forfar; from a brother of the first *Lord Maxwell*). Ar. on a saltire sa. a man's heart or. *Crest*—A falcon looking to the sinister ppr. *Motto*—I'll byde Broad Albion.

Maxwell (Lackiebank, cadet of Tealing, 1676). Ar. on a saltire sa. betw. two stars in chief and base az. a man's heart or. *Crest*—A falcon looking to the sinister ppr. *Motto*—Tendit ad astra.

Maxwell (Brediland, co. Renfrew, 1789). Ar. on a saltire sa. a martlet on, a bordure engr. gu. *Crest*—A buck's head couped ppr. attired gu. *Motto*—Spero meliora.

Maxwell (GRAHAM-MAXWELL, of Merksworth, 1858). Quarterly, 1st and 4th, ar. on a saltire sa. a martlet or, a bordure invecked gu., for MAXWELL, of Merksworth; 2nd, or, on a chief ermines three escallops of the first, for GRAHAM; 3rd, ar. on a saltire sa. an annulet or, stoned az. a bordure of the second, for MAXWELL, of Williamwood. *Crest*—A buck's head couped ppr. attired or. *Motto*—Spero meliora.

Maxwell (Pollok, co. Renfrew, bart., 1633, 1682, 1707). Ar. on a saltire sa. an annulet or, stoned az. *Crest*—A stag's head erased az. *Supporters*—Two apes ppr. (on a seal of 1400 are two lions). *Motto*—I am ready. These arms are now quartered with STIRLING, of Keir, by Sir WILLIAM STIRLING-MAXWELL, Bart, K.T., who s. his maternal uncle in the baronetcy in 1865, under the limitation of the patent of 1707.

Maxwell (Springkell, co. Dumfries, bart., 1683). Ar. on a saltire sa. an annulet or, stoned az. in base a crescent of the second, all within a bordure gu. charged with eight bezants. *Crest*—A dexter hand ppr. holding the head of a double eagle erased sa. *Motto*—Revirescat.

Maxwell (Dalswinton, co. Dumfries). As Pollok, with a heart gu. in base for diff.

Maxwell (Williamwood, co. Renfrew; MAXWELL, of Merksworth, heir of line of this branch, see *supra*). As Pollok, within a bordure sa.

Maxwell (Calderwood, co. Lanark, cadet of Pollok, bart., 1627). Quarterly, 1st and 4th, ar. a saltire sa. within a bordure counter-compony of the last and first; 2nd and 3rd, ar. a bend az., for DENNISTOUN. *Crest*—A man's head looking "foreright" ppr. *Supporters*—An ape chained, and a stag, both ppr. *Motto*—Think on.

Maxwell (*Lord Farnham,* cadet of Calderwood). Quarterly, 1st and 4th, ar. a saltire sa. on a chief of the first three pellets of the second; 2nd and 3rd, barry of six ar. and gu. *Crest*—A buck's head erased ppr. *Supporters*—Two bucks ppr. *Motto*—Je suis prêt.

Maxwell (Cardoness, co. Kirkcudbright, cadet of Calderwood, bart., 1804). Quarterly, 1st, ar. an eagle displ. ppr.; 2nd, az. a gable end of a church, with a cross at the top and Gothic window ar., as patron of ANWORTH; 3rd, ar. a saltire sa. within a bordure counter-compony of the second and first; 4th, ar. a saltire sa.; the whole within a bordure embattled gu. *Crest*—A man's head looking "foreright," within two branches of laurel disposed in orle all ppr. *Supporters* —A lion and a stag, both ppr. *Motto*—Think on.

Maxwell (Dargavel, co. Renfrew). Ar. a saltire sa. in base a stag's head ppr.

Maxwell (Birdstown, co. Donegal; exemplified to RICHARD CHARLETON, Esq., upon his assuming, by royal licence, 1790, the name of MAXWELL instead of CHARLETON, in compliance with the testamentary injunction of his maternal uncle, WILLIAM MAXWELL, Esq., of Birdstown). Ar. an eagle with two heads displ. sa. beaked and membered gu. surmounted of a shield of the first charged with a saltire of the second, thereon a hedgehog or. *Crest*—On a mount vert a holly bush, in front thereof a stag lodged all ppr. *Motto*—Reviresco.

Maxwell (WARING-MAXWELL, Finnebrogue, co. Down; exemplified to DOROTHEA, only dau. and heiress of ROBERT MAXWELL, Esq., of Finnebrogue, and widow of JOHN WARING, of Belvedere Place, Dublin, and to her issue, on their assuming, by royal licence, 1803, the additional surname and arms of MAXWELL). Quarterly, 1st and 4th, ar. on a bend sa. three mascles of the first, for WARING; 2nd and 3rd, ar. a saltire sa. on a chief of the first three palets of the second, for MAXWELL. *Crest*—A stork's head couped ar. *Motto*—Nec vi nec Astutia.

Maxwell (PERCEVAL-MAXWELL; exemplified to ROBERT PER-

CEVAL, of Kilmore Hill, co. Waterford, on his assuming, by royal licence, 1839, the additional surname and arms of MAXWELL, in compliance with the desire of his maternal uncle, JOHN WARING-MAXWELL, Esq., of Finnebrogue, co. Down). Quarterly, 1st and 4th, ar. a saltire sa. on a chief of the last three pallets of the first, for MAXWELL; 2nd and 3rd, ar. on a chief indented gu. three crosses pattée of the first, for PERCEVAL. Crest—A stag's head and neck erased ppr. Motto—Je suis prêt.

May (Faunt, co. Sussex; THOMAS MAY, temp. Edward IV. Visit. Leicester, 1619). Gu. a fess betw. eight billets or. Crest—Out of a ducal coronet or, a leopard's head gu.

May (Sutton Cheyney, co. Leicester; GEOFFREY MAY, aged 70, Visit. Leicester, 1619, son of RICHARD MAY, who removed from co. Sussex to co. Leicester, second son of THOMAS MAY, Esq., of Faunt, temp. Edward IV.). Same Arms and Crest, each charged with a crescent for diff.

May (Breamore, co. Hants). Same Arms and Crest.

May (Paskley, co. Sussex). Same Arms and Crest, the leopard's head bezantée.

May (London; RICHARD MAY, citizen of London, temp. James I., and Sir HUMPHREY MAY, Master of the Rolls, 1629; granted 1573). Same Arms. Crest—Out of a ducal coronet or, a lion's head gu.

May (Rawmere, co. Sussex; descended from JOHN MAY, younger son of RICHARD MAY, citizen of London, temp. James I.; THOMAS BROADNAX, son of WILLIAM BROADNAX, Esq., of Godmersham, co. Kent, by ANNE MAY, his wife, dau. and heir of CHRISTOPHER MAY, Esq., of Rawmere, assumed the surname of MAY, by Act of Parliament, 1738). Same Arms and Crest.

May (co. Essex). Gu. a fess betw. six billets or.

May (Oxney, co. Kent). Gu. a fess or, betw. eight billets ar. Crest—Out of a ducal coronet or, a leopard's head and neck ppr.

May (Highcross, in St. Austell, co. Cornwall). Gu. a chev. vair betw. three ducal coronets or.

May (Stoke, co. Suffolk; granted 4 June, 1687-8). Gu. two barrulets erm. betw. six billets or. Crest—Out of a mural coronet ar. a leopard's head gu. billettée or.

May (co. Wilts). Ar. on a bend vert betw. two bucks' heads cabossed sa. three roses of the first.

May. Az. three fishes naiant in pale ar. Crest—A dexter arm embowed in mail armour, in the hand all ppr. a truncheon or, tipped sa.

May. Ar. a chev. sa. betw. three roses or, a chief of the last. Crest—A leopard's head ppr.

May (allowed as an impalement by Cooke, Clarenceux, 1590, to JOHN TEDEASCASTLE, of London, m. ELIZABETH MAY). Vert a chev. betw. three roses or, a chief indented erm.

May. Vert a chev. betw. three crosses crosslet fitchée ar.

May (Fun. Ent. Ulster's Office, 1616, KATHERINE, dau. of PATRICK MAY, and wife, first of JOHN USHER, Sheriff of Dublin, and second, of Alderman THOMAS BISHOP, Mayor of Dublin). Ar. on a chev. gu. betw. three ancient galleys with three masts, sails furled, flags flying sa. a lion ramp. or, armed and langued az.

May (Fun. Ent. Ulster's Office, FRANCES, dau. of Sir THADY DUFFE, Knt., of Dublin, and wife of JAMES MAY, of Dublin, merchant, d. 1635, leaving two sons, BARTHOLOMEW MAY and MATHEW MAY). Ar. on a chev. az. betw. three ancient galleys, with three masts, sails furled ppr. flags flowing gu. a lion ramp. of the first.

May (Dublin; Fun. Ent. Ulster's Office, 1640, EDWARD MAY, second son of Sir THOMAS MAY, Knt., of Mayfield, co. Sussex). Gu. a fess betw. eight billets or, a crescent on a crescent for diff.

May (Mayfield, co. Waterford, bart., extinct). Gu. a fess betw. eight billets or. Crest—Out of a ducal coronet a leopard's head couped ppr.

May (granted by Betham, Ulster, to Sir STEPHEN MAY, Knt., of Belfast). Az. a fess indented ar. betw. ten billets or. Crest—On a ducal coronet or, a leopard's head and neck gu. charged with a billet gold.

Maybank. Az. a chev. betw. three tents ar.

Mayce. Or, three tigers' faces vert. Crest—A swan, wings endorsed ar. ducally gorged and lined sa. Another Crest—A pestle and mortar ppr.

Maycock. Per fesse embattled ar. and gu. two cocks counterchanged.

Maycote, alias Mackwith (Reculver, co. Kent; confirmed Nov. 1604). Erm. on a canton gu. a buck pass. or. Crest—Out of a mural coronet gu. a buck's head or.

Maydeley. Ar. on a chev. az. three fleurs-de-lis or, a bordure engr. sa.

Maydeley. Az. on a fesse counter-embattled ar. semée of

crosses crosslet sa. betw. six martlets or, a lion pass. guard. of the third.

Maydenwell (Nether-Teynton, co. Lincoln). Ar. on an inescutcheon betw. eight martlets sa. a cinquefoil or.

Maydeston, or Maydston (co. Lincoln). Erm. two halberts in saltire sa.

Maydestone. Ar. three bars az. on the second two annulets interlaced or.

Maydestone. Gu. three women's heads couped at the shoulders ar. hair dishevelled or.

Maydstone (co. Kent). Az. a chev. betw. three fleurs-de-lis ar.

Maydwell (co. Northampton, and London; granted 1634). Or, on an inescutcheon gu. a crescent ar. within an orle of eight martlets of the second. Crest—Out of a ducal coronet or, a pyramid of laurel leaves vert.

Maydwell (granted to HENRY LAWRENCE MAYDWELL, Esq., of the 82nd Regiment of Foot). Per pale erm. and or, an inescutcheon within an orle of martlets gu. Crest—Out of a crown vallery or, the rim charged with two cinquefoils gu. ten bay leaves, four, three, two, and one, vert.

Maye (co. Kent). Az. three plates in fess betw. as many crosses crosslet ar.

Mayell. Ar. on a chev. sa. three cinquefoils of the field.

Mayer, or Mayor (Island of Jersey; granted temp. Henry VII.). Gu. an anchor erect in pale or, on a chief of the second three roses of the field. Crest—A demi lion ramp. reguard. holding a sword in the dexter paw ppr. hilt and pommel or.

Mayer. Ar. a Moor, the sinister hand touching the head sa. bound round the temples, and holding in the dexter hand a sword blade wavy or, vested round the waist chequy of the last and of the second, fringed gold. Crest—An eagle, wings endorsed ppr.

Mayern (London). Sa. two bends or, on a chief of the last an eagle displ. of the first.

Mayew (RICHARD MAYEW, Bishop of Hereford, 1504-16; arms in St. Mary's Church, Oxford. Visit. Oxon, 1574). Ar. on a fess az. betw. three roses gu. a lily of the first.

Mayffe (Tatton, co. Chester). Quarterly, or and gu.

Mayfield (Cambridge; granted 9 Oct. 1684). Gu. a cross engr. erm. in chief two mayflowers slipped or. Crest—A lion's head couped gu. holding in the mouth a mayflower or.

Mayger. Or, a fesse az. betw. in chief a pellet charged with a portcullis of the first betw. two demi roses per pale gu. and ar., and in base a fleur-de-lis betw. two swans close ar.

Mayhew (Hemington, co. Suffolk). Gu. a chev. vair betw. three ducal coronets or. Crest—A unicorn's head erased gu. armed and maned or, charged on the neck with a chev. vair.

Mayhew (Woodlands, co. Lancaster). Same Arms and Crest. Motto—Sola in Deo salus.

Mayhew (Clippesby, co. Norfolk; confirmed 9 Nov. 1503). Az. a chev. vairé ar. and gu. betw. three ducal coronets or, a bordure engr. of the last. Crest—A unicorn's head erased ar. charged with a chev. vair or and gu.

Mayhugh. Sa. on a chev. betw. three bucks' heads cabossed ar. as many buglehorns stringed of the first.

Mayland. Paly of eight ar. and gu. a lion ramp. sa.

Mayn. Ar. on a bend sa. three dexter hands of the first. Crest—An oak tree ppr.

Maynard (Baron Maynard, of Wicklow and Estaines, extinct 1775; Sir HENRY MAYNARD, High Sheriff of co. Essex, 1602, had two sons, 1. Sir WILLIAM MAYNARD, created a bart. 1611, and Viscount Maynard 1620; II. CHARLES MAYNARD, ancestor of Viscount Maynard; Sir CHARLES, fifth bart. and fifth Viscount Maynard, was created Viscount Maynard, of Easton, with special remainder to male descendants of his kinsman, Sir WILLIAM MAYNARD, fourth bart. of Walton). Ar. a chev. betw. three sinister hands couped at the wrist gu. Crest—A stag trippant ppr. attired and unguled or. Supporters—Dexter, a stag ppr.; sinister, a talbot ar. pied sa. gorged with a plain collar gu. Motto—Manus justa nardus.

Maynard (Viscount Maynard, extinct 1865; SIR CHARLES MAYNARD, fifth bart. of Walton, s. his kinsman as second viscount 1775: the third viscount d. s. p. m.). Same Arms and Motto. Crest—A stag statant or. Supporters—Dexter, a stag ppr. attired or; sinister, a talbot ar. pied sa. gorged with a plain collar gu.

Maynard (Sherford, co. Devon; NICHOLAS, THOMAS, and JOHN MAYNARD, Visit. Devon, 1620, sons of JOHN MAYNARD, grandsons of THOMAS MAYNARD, the son of THOMAS MAYNARD, all of Sherford). Ar. three sinister hands couped at the wrist gu. Crest—A stag trippant ar. attired or.

Maynard (Milton, co. Cornwall. Visit. Cornwall, 1620) Same Arms.

Maynard (Chesterfield, co, Derby; JOHN CHARLES MAYNARD, Esq., of Harsley Hall, co. York, grandson of SARAH JEFFERSON, and her husband, JOHN LAX, Esq., of Eryholme, same co., which SARAH was great-granddaughter, through his daughter JANE, of JOHN MAYNARD, Esq., of Kirklevington, co. York, and having inherited the MAYNARD estates, she assumed, by sign manual, in 1784, for herself and her issue, the surname and arms of MAYNARD). Quarterly, 1st and 4th, ar. on a chev. vert betw. three sinister hands erect gu. five erm. spots or, for MAYNARD; 2nd and 3rd, barry of six erm. and gu. on a chief az. three catherine wheels or, for LAX. Crests—1st, MAYNARD: A buck pass. or, gorged with a collar invecked ar. fimbriated sa.; 2nd, LAX: A mount vert, thereon a catherine wheel, as in the arms. Motto—Manus justa narùus.

Maynard (St. Alban's, co. Hertford). Ar. a chev. quarterly gu. and az. betw. three sinister hands couped of the second. Crest—A buck ppr.

Maynard (co. Kent). Ar. a chev. sa. betw. three sinister hands couped at the wrist gu.

Maynard (Hammersmith, co. Middlesex). Ar. a chev. betw. three dexter hands couped and erect gu. a crescent for diff.

Maynard (Mosely, co. Leicester; exemplified 28 March, 1770, to THOMAS HASILRIDGE, upon his taking, by royal licence, the name and arms of MAYNARD). Same Arms. Crest—A stag or, attired ppr.

Maynard. Sa. three sinister hands erased ar.

Maynard (Carriglas, co. Longford; confirmed by Hawkins, Ulster, 1714, to WILLIAM MAYNARD, Esq., M.P. for Tullow, co. Waterford, great-grandson of Sir WILLIAM MAYNARD, Knt., the son of WILLIAM MAYNARD, Esq., of Fulham and London, by ANGEL, his wife, dau. and co-heir of Alderman HUMPHREY BASKERVILE, of London). Quarterly, 1st and 4th, or, a chev. gu. cotised az. betw. three dexter hands couped at the wrist and erect sa., for MAYNARD; 2nd and 3rd, ar. a chev. gu. betw. three torteaux, for BASKERVILE. Crest—A wolf's head erased, holding in the mouth a broken spear all ppr. Motto—Tam corde quam manu.

Mayne (Farley Hill, co. Berks). Ar. two chevronels betw. as many pheons in chief sa. and a fleur-de-lis in base within a bordure engr. of the last. Crest—A cubit arm erect in armour, holding in the hand ppr. a cross flory ar.

Mayne. Same Arms. Crest—A cubit arm erect ppr. habited sa. cuffed ar. holding a cross crosslet gu.

Mayne (Creslow, co. Bucks; granted June, 1604). Erm. on a bend sa. three dexter hands couped ar. Crest—A dexter hand ppr. betw. two wings erm.

Mayne (Teffont Ewyas, co. Wilts; descended from JOEL DE MAINE, of Kings Nymet, temp. Henry 1.). Ar. on a bend engr. sa. three dexter hands couped at the wrist of the first. Crest—Out of a mural coronet or, a dragon's head erm. Motto, ancient—Await the day; modern—Virtuti fortuna comes.

Mayne (Littington, co. Devon, and London). Sa. a chev. betw. three sinister hands couped and erect ar. Crest—A cubit arm vested az. in the palm of the hand an eye all ppr.

Mayne (co. Essex). Per pale ar. and sa. three chevronels betw. as many cinquefoils counterchanged.

Mayne (Bornington, co. Hertford). Ar. on a bend sa. three sinister hands couped at the wrist of the first.

Mayne (co. Warwick, and Rowston, co. York). Ar. on a bend sa. three dexter hands couped of the field. Crest—Out of a ducal coronet or, a dragon's head erm.

Mayne. Ar. three chevronels sa. each charged with an escallop the first, on a chief of the second three mullets of the field.

Mayne (Powis and Logie, co. Clackmannan; derived from the MAINS, of Lochwood, co. Stirling). Ar. a chev. gu. voided of the field betw. two pheons in chief sa. and a fleur-de-lis in base az. a bordure wavy of the last. Crest—A dexter hand holding a plain cross gu. Motto—Virtuti fortuna comes.

Mayne (Baron Newhaven, extinct 1794; Sir WILLIAM MAYNE, descended from MAYNE, of Logie, was so created 1776, d. s. p.). Ar. a chev. gu. voided of the field betw. two pheons in chief sa. and a fleur-de-lis in base az. a border wavy of the last. Crest—An arm erect couped below the elbow, habited az. cuffed ar. holding in the hand ppr. a cross in pale az. Supporters—Dexter, a tiger ramp. guard. tenné armed gu. collared or; sinister, a talbot sa. armed and langued gu. collared or. Motto—Virtuti fortuna comes.

Maynehell. Sa. three dexter hands couped ar.

Maynell (co. Lancaster). Or, on a fesse dancettée gu. three lions ramp. ar.

Maynell, Meynell, and Menell. Vairé ar. and sa.

674

Crest—A demi savage holding in the dexter hand a dagger and in the sinister a key all ppr.

Maynell. Ar. on a chev. sa. three cinquefoils of the first.

Mayner. Gu. a fesse ar. betw. three plates. Crest—A hand erect ppr. holding a lion's gamb erased ar.

Maynes. Gu. a chev. betw. three horseshoes ar.

Mayney (Linton, co. Kent, bart., extinct 1706; descended from Sir WALTER DE MAYNEY, temp. Edward III.). Per pale ar. and sa. three chevronels betw. as many cinquefoils all counterchanged. Crest—An arm armed quarterly ar. and sa. holding a battle axe of the second, staff or.

Maynselyne. Or, on a chief gu. a sinister hand couped at the wrist ar.

Maynsling, or Mainstone. Ar. on a chief gu. a dexter hand extended and borne traversed of the field.

Maynstone (Langaran, co. Gloucester, and co. Hereford). Vert a chev. betw. three hedgehogs or. Crest—A reindeer pass. ppr.

Maynwaring. Ar. on two bars gu. three mullets of the first.

Mayo, Earl of. See BOURKE.

Mayo (co. Dorset). Gu. a chev. vair betw. three ducal coronets or. Crest—Out of a ducal coronet or, a sinister hand ppr. betw. two wings ar.

Mayo (Tottenham High Cross, co. Middlesex; JAMES MAYO, gent., son of RICHARD MAYO, Esq., of Much Marcle, co. Hereford. Visit. Middlesex, 1663). Sa. a chev. betw. three roses ar. a chief or.

Mayo. Ar. a woodman wreathed about the head and hips walking upon a mount betw. two trees with a club over the dexter shoulder all ppr.

Mayo. Sa. a fesse ar. betw. two lions pass. reguard or. (another coat has a canton ar.)

Mayor. Gu. a fesse betw. three daggers, points upwards or. Crest—On a chapeau gu. turned up erm. an escallop gu. betw. two wings or.

Mayor (granted to Rev. CHARLES MAYOR, of Rugby). Gu. an anchor ar. on a chief or, three roses of the first. Crest—A greyhound's head couped gu. collared or. Motto—Mea anchora Christus.

Mayow (Dinton, co. Wilts). Ar. (another, or) on a chev. sa. betw. three birds of the last five lozenges of the field.

Mayow (Lowe and Bray, co. Cornwall; PHILIP MAYOW, Esq., of Bray, son of JOHN MAYOW, grandson of PHILIP MAYOW, and great-grandson of PHILIP MAYOW, all of Lowe. Visit. Cornwall, 1620). Gu. a chev. vair betw. three ducal coronets or. Crest—A falcon erm. devouring a snake ppr.

Mayow. See WYNELL-MAYOW.

Maypowder (Halesworthy, co. Devon; TRISTRAM MAYPOWDER, grandson and heir of THOMAS MAYPOWDER, and grandson of RICHARD MAYPOWDER, all of same place. Visit. Devon, 1620). Barruly gu. and ar. on a chief of the second a greyhound courant sa.

Maypowder (Killinboy, co. Roscommon; impalement Fun. Ent. Ulster's Office, 1634, Sir MATHEW DE RENZI, Knt., whose wife was MARY, dau. of RICHARD MAYPOWDER). Sa. a griffin pass. wings elevated ar. betw. three escallop or.

Mayre (Lartington Hall, co. York). Ar. on the sea in base ppr. a ship of three masts with sails furled sa.

Mayroll. Chequy or and az. a chev. gu.

Maysmor (RICHARD POWELL MAYSMOR, Esq., Surgeon Extraordinary to William IV.; a descendant of the MAKSMORS, of Maesmor). Ar. a lion ramp. sa. armed and langued gu.

Maze. Gu. a fesse betw. three cinquefoils or. Crest—A lion's head erased az. crowned with cap of dignity or.

Maze (co. Somerset; granted to PETER MAZE, Esq., Sheriff of Bristol). Or. on a bend engr. betw. two eagles displ. az. another bend plain or, charged with three lions pass. ppr. Crest—An eagle displ. erm. charged on the breast and on either wing with a cinquefoil gu. Motto—Garde ta bien aimée.

Maze (BLACKBURNE-MAZE, Boundes Park, Tunbridge Wells, co. Kent). Quarterly, 1st and 4th, erm. on a bend engr. betw. two eagles displ. az. another bend plain or, thereon three lions pass. ppr. a canton gu. for diff., for MAZE; 2nd and 3rd, az. a fess nebulée betw. three mullets sa., for BLACKBURNE. Crests—1st, MAZE: An eagle displ. erminois, charged on the breast and wings with a cinquefoil gu. plain collared az.; 2nd, BLACKBURNE: On a mount vert a trumpet or, thereon a cock gu. beaked, wattled, armed, and charged on the breast with a cinquefoil gold.

Maziere (PETER DE LA MAZIERE, Esq., of Cork). Gu. a fesse erm. A lion's head erased ppr.

Mazzinghi (London; originally from Germany, settled in the 10th century in Tuscany, at Campi and Florence; represented by JOSEPH, Count Maz:inghi, a lineal descendant from DOMENICO, created Count by Pope Eugene IV.). Az.

three clubs ar. with wriststraps gu. *Crest*—A demi lion ppr. holding a club ar. *Supporters*—A bear ppr. with chequered mantle, hawk* and dogs ppr. and a lion also ppr. with cap **gu.** holding a fleur-de-lis gu. *Motto*—Chi la fa l'aspetti.

* The hawk and the German descent are thus alluded to by Verini, *de Illustratione Florentiæ*:

"Pistorium accipitrem dedit annua dona vetustis, Mazzinghis civesque suos ab origine credit, Hos sub Othone tamen Thuscis Germania misit."

Meacham. Az. on a fesse or, betw. three lions' heads erased ar. as many escallops of the field. *Crest*—A falcon, wings expanded ppr. belled or.

Mead. Sa. a chev. erminois betw. three pelicans or, vulning themselves ppr.

Mead (arms confirmed and crest granted by Hawkins, Ulster, 1706, to BENJAMIN MEAD, of Meath Street, Dublin, Proctor in the Bishop's Court). Sa. on a chev. betw. pelicans vulning themselves or, as many martlets of the field. *Crest*—A pelican in her piety ppr.

Mead. Gu. a chev. betw. three trefoils slipped ar. *Crest*—A reindeer trippant vert.

Meade (Fun. Ent. Ulster's Office, 1626, Sir JOHN MEADE, Knt., who *m.* KATHERINE SARSFIELD, dau. of DOMINICK, *Viscount Kilmallock*, and was ancestor of the *Earl of Clanwilliam*). Gu. a chev. erm. betw. three trefoils slipped ar.

Meade (*Earl of Clanwilliam*). Az. a chev. erm. betw. three trefoils slipped ar. *Crest*—An eagle displ. with two heads as. armed or. *Supporters*—Dexter, an eagle close sa.; sinister, a falcon close ppr. beaked and legged or, each collared and chained gold. *Motto*—Toujours prêt.

Meade (Ballintobber and Ballymartle, co. Cork). Gu. a chev. erm. betw. three trefoils slipped ar. *Crest*—An eagle displ. with two heads sa. armed or. *Motto*—Toujours prest.

Meade (cos. Cambridge and Somerset). Gu. a chev. erm. betw. three trefoils slipped ar.

Meade (co. Essex). Sa. a chev. betw. three pelicans or, vulned gu. *Crest*—An eagle displ. or.

Meade (London; THOMAS MEADE, Draper, Visit. London, 1568; his dau. KATHERINE, *m.* THOMAS RICH, Mercer, of London, *b.* 1591). Sa. a chev. betw. three pelicans or, vulning themselves ppr.

Meade (Northborowe, co. Leicester; HENRY MEADE, Visit. Leicester, 1619, eldest son of JAMES MEADE, Esq., of Northborowe, who was grandson of WILLIAM MEADE, Esq., of Gretton, co. Stafford). Sa. a chev. betw. three pelicans, wings endorsed or, vulning themselves ppr.

Meades (London). Sa. on a chev. ar. betw. three pelicans vulning themselves or, as many anchors of the first.

Meadowcroft (Smethurst, co. Lancaster, 1664). Ar. on a saltire sa. five fleurs-de-lis of the first.

Meadows, or Medows (Witnesham Hall and Great Bealings, co. Suffolk; *Earl Manvers* represents the *younger* branch of the MEADOWS family). Gu. a chev. erm. betw. three pelicans vulning themselves ppr. (granted as an augmentation) on a canton az. a lion sejant, and in chief a label of three points, quartering BREWSTER, of Wrentham Hall, co. Suffolk, sa. a chev erm. betw. three estoiles ar. *Crest*—A pelican vulning itself ppr. *Motto*—Mea dos virtus.

Meadows. Az. a chev. erm. betw. three pelicans, wings endorsed or, vulned ppr. on a canton of the third an inescutcheon gu. charged with a lion pass. guard. or. *Crest*—Out of a ducal coronet or, a demi eagle, wings expanded sa.

Meager. Ar. a lion pass. az. on a chief of the second seven plates, four and three. *Crest*—A buffalo's head erased or.

Meakin (granted to Rev. JAMES MEAKIN, A.M., Prebendary of Worcester). Per chev. nebulée or and az. in chief two estoiles and in base a garb all counterchanged. *Crest*—A unicorn's head erased.

Meales (co. Lancaster). Ar. three torteaux in fesse, a bordure gu. *Crest*—A stag standing at gaze sa.

Meara (Reg. Ulster's Office). Gu. three lions pass. guard. per pale ar. and or, a border az. charged with eight crescents of the third. *Crest*—A pelican displ. ar. membered and beaked gu. vulning the breast guttée de sang, surmounted by a lozenge vert. *Motto*—Virescit vultiere virtus.

Meares (BEATRIX MEARES, *temp.* Edward I., *m.* Sir MAIOR STAUNTON, Lord of Staunton, co. Notts. Visit. Notts, 1614). Gu. a fess betw. three water bougets erm.

Meares (co. Lancaster). Same *Arms.*

Meares (Corsley, co. Wilts; **settled** there 1341). Ar. a ship with three masts, sails furled and shrouded sa.

Meares (Meares Court, co. Westmeath; descended from LEWIS MEARES, *b.* 1625, youngest son of JOHN MEARES, Esq., of Corsley; JOHN MEARES, Esq., of Meares Court, grandson of JOHN MEARES, Esq., of Meares Court, *temp.* Queen Anne **and** George I., *d. s. p.* 1790, and bequeathed the **estates to**

675

his nephew, WILLIAM DEVENISH, son of his sister, KATHERINE MEARES, and her husband, JOHN DEVENISH, Esq., of Pattick, when the male representation of the family devolved on GEORGE GALBRAITH MEARES, grandson of Rev. ROBERT MEARES, the brother of JOHN MEARES, Esq., of Meares Court, *temp.* Queen Anne, and is now vested in GEORGE GERALD MEARES, Esq.). Same *Arms.* *Crest*—A kingfisher ppr. *Motto*—Omnia providentiæ committo.

Meares (Fun. Ent. Ulster's Office, 1654, MARGARET, dau. and heir of Major WILLIAM MEARES, Corporal of the Field, and wife of JOHN KENNEDY, Esq., of Mullagh, co. Longford). Ar. three ancient galleys sa.

Mearing, or Meering (co. Nottingham). Ar. on a chev. sa. three escallops or. *Crest*—On a ducal coronet or, a griffin segreant gu.

Mearns (Scotland). Or, three piles gu.

Mearns (Scotland). Or, three piles vert, on a canton sa. a lion pass. ar.

Mears. Lozengy sa. and or, a chief erm. *Crest*—A cock's head ppr.

Meath, Earl of. See BRABAZON.

Meath, See of. Sa. three mitres ar.

Meath (arms of the ancient Kingdom of Meath; Reg. Ulster's Office). Az. a king sitting on a throne, the dexter hand and arm extended, the sinister holding a sceptre all ppr.

Meautys (West Ham, co. Essex). Az. a unicorn saliant erminois armed or. *Crest*—A unicorn sejant erminois.

Meaux, or Meux (Kingston, Isle of Wight, bart., extinct 1706; descended from LUDOVICK MEUX, grandson of Sir WALTER MEUX, Knt., of London, *m.* ALICE, dau. and heir of WILLIAM DREW, of Kingston; Sir JOHN MEUX, of Kingston, was created a bart. 11 Dec. 1641, but the title expired with his grandson, Sir WILLIAM MEUX, who *d. unm.* in 1706, leaving his sisters his co-heirs; the eldest, ELIZABETH, *m.* Sir JOHN MILLER, Bart., of Froyle, and had an only dau. and heiress, ELIZABETH, *m.* to Sir EDWARD WORSLEY, of Gatcombe. The present Sir HENRY MEUX, Bart., of Theobald's Park, descends from a younger branch of the Kingston family). Paly of six or and az. on a chief gu. three crosses pattée of the first. *Crest*—Two wings endorsed, the points downwards ar. tied together with a cord or.

Meaux, or Melsa-Abbey (co. York). Gu. a cross patonce vair betw. four martlets ar.

Meawlys. Az. a unicorn saliant ar.

Meayes. Ar. on a fesse gu. three mullets pierced of the field.

Medcalf (Askrigh, Berepark, and Reddall, co. York). Ar. three calves pass. sa. *Crest*—A talbot sejant ppr. reposing his foot on an escutcheon ar.

Mecham (Garrycastle, co. Westmeath; granted by Betham, Ulster, to GEORGE MECHAM, Esq., son of GEORGE MECHAM, Esq., of Athlone, and to their descendants). Or, a fess dancettée az. in chief two human hearts gu. *Crest*—A dexter cubit arm erect, grasping a dagger transfixed through a human heart, emitting drops of blood, all ppr. *Motto*—Animi fortitudo.

Medcroft. Paly of six ar. and az. a canton gu. ; another, Ar. on a saltire sa. five fleurs-de-lis or (another, ar.).

Meddew (Great Yarmouth). Bendy of six or and az. on a chief of the second two crosses pattée of the first.

Meddowes. Sa. a chev. erm. betw. three pelicans' wings inverted or.

Meddus, or Medowes (co. Chester). Bendy of six or and az. on a chief of the second two crosses formée of the first. *Crest*—A cross formée or, entwined with a snake ppr.

Mede, or Meade (cos. Cambridge and Cornwall; brass of Sir PHILIP MEDE, St. Mary Radcliff, Bristol). Gu. a chev. erm. betw. three trefoils (another, cinquefoils) ar.

Medford. Per fesse az. and erm. in chief two martlets or. *Crest*—A deer lodged ar.

Medhall. Ar. on a fesse betw. two chevronels gu. three escallops of the field.

Medhop (Medhop Hall, co. York; arms borne by ROGER MEDHOP, son and heir of HENRY DE MEDHOP, 1219, as they appeared in the second book of the Abbey of Furnes, co. Lancaster, in the custody of Auditor Fanshaw, in 1613, and allowed by St. George, Norroy, that year). Erm. a lion ramp. az. crowned or.

Medhop (EDMOND MEDHOP, Clerk of the Common Pleas of Exchequer in Ireland, late of Lincoln's Inn, London, son and heir of THOMAS MEDHOP, formerly of Aston, co. Oxford, who was fourth son of ROGER MEDHOP, Esq., of Medhop Hall, co. Oxford; confirmed by St. George Norroy, 1613; Fun. Ent. Ulster's Office, 1621, of his wife ELIZABETH, dau. of Sir JOHN PICTON, Bart., of Picton Castle, co. Pembroke). Same *Arms,* with ppr. diff. *Crest*—A demi lion ramp. az. holding a crown or.

2 x 2

Medhop (Trenant, co. Cornwall). Same *Arms.*

Medhurst (Kippax Hall, co. York). Quarterly, 1st and 4th, paly of six gu. and ar. on a canton or, a martlet of the second; 2nd and 3rd, vert on a fesse or, three lions ramp. of the first. *Crest*—A martlet charged with a fleur-de-lis holding in the beak, an acorn and an oak leaf ppr. *Motto*—Adversa virtute repello.

Medland (Launceston, co. Cornwall; granted 17th May, 1730). Gu. a fesse wavy ar. betw. three sea-gulls ppr. a crescent for diff. *Crest*—A sea-gull rising ppr. charged on the breast with a crescent for diff.

Medley (Buxted, co. Sussex; descended from BENEDICT MEDLEY, Clerk of the Signet to Henry VIII.; the eventual heiress, JULIA ANNABELLA, only dau. of JAMES EVELYN, Esq., of Fellbridge, co. Surrey, by ANNABELLA, his wife, sister of GEORGE MEDLEY, Esq., of Buxted, m. Sir GEORGE AUGUSTUS WILLIAM SHUCKBURGH, Bart.). Ar. two bars gemelles sa. in chief three mullets pierced of the last. *Crest*—A tiger sejant vert, tufted and maned or. *Motto*—In Deo fides.

Medley (Iver, co. Bucks; descended from MEDLEY, of Buxted, co. Sussex). Same *Arms, Crest*, and *Motto.*

Medley (co. Warwick). Sa. two bars gemelles ar. on a chief of the last three mullets of the first.

Medlicott (Modelicote, co. Salop; an ancient family in that co., descended from LLEWELLIN DE MODELICOTE, of Modelicote, *temp.* Henry III.). Quarterly, per fess indented gu. and az. three lions ramp. ar.

Medlicott (Pontesbury, co. Salop, Abingdon, co. Berks, and St. Clement Danes, co. Middlesex. Visit. London). Same *Arms.*

Medlicott (Dunmurry, co. Kildare; JAMES EDWARD MEDLICOTT, Esq., of Dunmurry, J.P., representative in the male line of MEDLICOTT, of Pontesbury and Abingdon). Same *Arms. Crest*—Out of a mural crown gu. a demi eagle displ. or. *Motto*—Dat cura quietem.

Medlycott (Rocketts Castle, co. Waterford; Rev. JOHN THOMAS MEDLYCOTT, descended from THOMAS MEDLICOTT, Esq., of Binfield, co. Berks, youngest son of THOMAS MEDLICOTT, Esq., of Abingdon, M.P. for that place 1668). Same *Arms, Crest*, and *Motto.*

Medlycott (Ven House, co. Somerset, bart.; descended maternally from JAMES MEDLICOTT, eldest son of THOMAS MEDLICOTT, Esq., of Abingdon, M.P., 1668, whose eldest dau., ELIZABETH MEDLICOTT, m. JAMES HUTCHINGS, Esq., and her son, THOMAS HUTCHINGS, assumed the surname of MEDLYCOTT). Same *Arms, Crest*, and *Motto.*

Medlycott (Cottingham, co. Northampton; granted 24 Dec. 1801). Quarterly, az. and ar. per fess embattled three lions ramp. counterchanged.

Mednerst. Paly of six ar. and az. on a canton of the second a martlet of the first.

Medville, or Midville. Sa. a chev. betw. three fishing hooks ar.

Medwel (co. Northampton). Or, an escutcheon betw. eight martlets or.

Mee (East Retford, co. Nottingham). Az. a chev. erm. betw. three roses or, on a chief dancettée ar. three crosses crosslet fitchée of the field. *Crest*—A stag's head erased betw. two sprigs of oak ppr.

Mee (St. Bennet's Fink, London). Gu. a chev. betw. three boars' heads erased ar.

Mee. Per pale gu. and sa. three chevronels ar. *Crest*—A ram's head erased ar. armed or.

Meech. Ar. on a canton gu. a lion's head erased or. *Crest*—A greyhound courant ar.

Meek. Ar. three water bougets sa. a chief of the last. *Crest*—A demi wolf ducally gorged and lined, holding betw. the paws a mullet of six points.

Meek. Gu. three chevronels ar. *Crest*—A demi lion ramp. holding over the head a scymitar. *Motto*—Pro recto.

Meeke (co. Essex). Gu. a lion ramp. ar. a bordure indented or. *Crest*—A lion, as in the arms.

Meelop (Wales). Per fesse sa. and erm.

Meer (Sherborn, co. Dorset). Az. a chev. betw. three mullets of six points or. *Crest*—An eagle's head couped or, the mouth embrued gu.

Meer (co. Dorset and Durham). Sa. a chev. or, betw. three water bo igets erm. *Crest*—A demi dogfish.

Meere (Chaldon Boys, co. Dorset). Sa. a chev. or, cotised erm. betw. three water bougets of the last.

Meere (co. Wilts). Ar. a chev. sa. betw. three lions ramp. gu.

Meerehurst (Warpleston, co. Surrey). Per pale az. and gu. three roses ar. on a chief or, a lion pass. guard. of the second. *Crest*—A rose ar. barbed vert betw. two dragons' wings gu.

Meeres (Meeres, co. Lancaster). Ar. a fesse ermines betw. three water bougets gu.

Meeres (Awber, co. Lincoln). Gu. a fesse engr. betw. three water bougets erm.

Meeres (Houghton, co. Lincoln). Same *Arms. Crest*—A peacock's tail erect ppr.

Meeres (Branckoser, co. Norfolk). Same *Arms*, a bordure of the last.

Meeres (Holland, co. Lincoln). Gu. a fesse erm. betw. three water bougets ar.

Meetkerke (Julians, co. Herts). Gu. two swords in saltire or. *Crest*—A unicorn's head, horned, crined, and maned or, langued gu.

Meggison (Whalton, near Morpeth, co. Northumberland, and Ashford Ford, co. Middlesex; descended from LAUNCELOT MEGATSON, Esq., of Deane House, Whalton, *b.* 1567). Ar. on a chief gu. three chaplets of roses ppr.

Meggison. Ar. a lion sejant sa. *Crest*—On a mountain a dove all ppr.

Meggott. Erminois three leopards' heads sa. collared ar.

Meggs (co. Kent). Or, a chev. sa. betw. three mascles gu. a chief ar.

Meggs (Whitechapel, co. Middlesex; Rev. JAMES MEGGS, D.D., and WILLIAM MEGGS, Esq., sons of WILLIAM MEGGS, gent., of same place, and grandsons of WILLIAM MEGGS, gent., of London. Visit. Middlesex, 1663; granted by Cooke, Clarenceux, 1579). Or, a chev. engr. az. betw. three mascles gu. on a chief sa. a greyhound courant ar. *Crest*—A griffin sejant per bend gu. and or, ducally gorged gold.

Meggs (cos. Cambridge and Kent). Or, a chev. betw. three mascles gu. on a chief of the second a wolf ar. *Crest*—A greyhound's head sa. eared ar. charged on the neck with a bar gemel or, betw. three bezants, one and two, issuing out of his head three oak branches ppr.

Meggs (Bradford Peverel, co. Dorset). Or, a chev. betw. three mascles az. on a chief gu. a wolf pass. ar. *Crest*—A talbot's head erased sa.

Meggs (co. Warwick). Or, on a chief sa. a lion pass. ar.

Meigh (granted in 1840 to JOB MEIGH, Esq., of Ash Hall, co. Stafford). Gu. on a cross engr. betw. four boars' heads erased ar. three blackbirds in fesse ppr. and two crosses pattée fitched at the foot az. *Crest*—A lion ramp. or, holding in the dexter paw a cross pattée, as in the arms, the sinister paw resting on an anchor ppr. pendent therefrom by a chain or, an escutcheon gu. charged with a boar's head erased ar. *Motto*—Benigno Numine.

Meighan (allowed by Hawkins, Ulster, 1769, to CHRISTOPHER MEIGHAN, of Normandy, grandson of CHRISTOPHER O'MEIGHAN, an officer in the army of James II., who fell at the Battle of the Boyne; descended from O'MEIGHAN, of Bally O'Meighan, co. Leitrim). Gu. on a chev. ar. three bucks' heads erased of the field, attired or, in base a demi lion ramp. of the second. *Crest*—A griffin's head erased, wings endorsed or.

Meighan. See O'MEIGHAN.

Meighe (Reg. Ulster's Office). Ar. a fess dancettée az.

Meik (Scotland). Ar. a duck swimming in a loch in base ppr. on a chief indented gu. a boar's head couped betw. two stars of the first.

Meik (Leidcassie, Scotland, 1680). Ar. a duck ppr. on a chief dancettée gu. a boar's head couped betw. two crescents of the first. *Crest*—An increscent and decrescent respecting and joining one to the other. *Motto*—Jungor ut implear.

Meiller (Reg. Ulster's Office). Per fess vert and ar.

Mein (England). Az. a cross crosslet or. *Crest*—A hand holding a vine branch ppr.

Meinill (*Baron Meinill*, extinct 1322; NICHOLAS DE MEINILL, descended from ROBERT DE MEINILL, *temp.* Hen.y I., was summoned to Parliament, 1295). Az. three bars gemel or, a chief of the last.

Meirion Goch (Llyn, Wales. Descendants: JONES, of Castellnarch, in Llynn). Ar. a chev. betw. three horses' heads erased sa.

Mekelfeld (Bolton, co. York). Ar. on a chev. betw. three garbs gu. banded or, as many buckles of the last.

Mekelfeld, or Mekilfeld. Ar. a cross engr. sa. guttée d'or (another, the field or).

Mekton. Sa. a lion ramp. ar. crowned or, an orle of annulets of the second.

Mekton (*temp.* Richard II.). Sa. a lion ramp. ar. crowned or, armed gu. within an orle of martlets of the second.

Melborne (London). Quarterly, or and gu. a fesse betw. three leopards' faces counterchanged.

Melborne (granted 1615). Az. three escallops ar. a bordure of the second, charged with eight crosses crosslet fitchée gu.

Melborne. Sa. on an inescutcheon ar. a crescent of the first.

Melborne. Az. fretty erm.

Melbourne. Ar. a crescent and a bordure sa.

Melbourne. Ar. a cross moline sa. quarter pierced of the field.

Melbourne. Gu. a chev. betw. three escallops ar.

Melbourne (University of, Australia). Az. a figure intended to represent Victory, robed and attired ppr. the dexter hand extended, holding a wreath of laurel or, betw. four stars of eight points, two in pale and two in fesse ar. *Motto*—Postera crescam lande.

Meldert. Or, on a chief erm. three palets gu. *Crest*—A dexter gauntlet apaumée az.

Meldon (confirmed to CHARLES HENRY MELDON, Esq., of 25, Rutland Square, and of Newtown House, Blackrock, co. Dublin, M.P., and the descendants of his grandfather, ANTHONY DILLON MULDOON, of Fore, co. Westmeath, of Celtic origin). Vert a dexter hand couped ar. betw. three crescents or, issuant therefrom as many estoiles of the second. *Crest*—A dexter hand ppr. surmounted by a crescent or, therefrom issuant an estoile ar. *Motto*—Pro fide et patria.

Meldrum (that Ilk, co. Aberdeen; now represented by the URQUHARTS of Meldrum as heirs of line). Ar. a demi otter issuing out of a bar wavy sa.

Meldrum (Fyvie, co. Aberdeen). Quarterly, 1st and 4th, as the last; 2nd and 3rd, ar. three unicorns' heads erased sa., for PRESTON.

Meldrum (Crombie, co. Banff). Quarterly, as the last, within a bordure engr. sa. *Crest*—A dexter hand holding a book ppr. *Motto*—Mens immota manet.

Meldrum (Dumbreck, co. Aberdeen). Quarterly, as Fyvie, with a crescent sa. in the centre of the quarters for diff.

Meldrum (Segie, co. Fife). Ar. three otters' heads comped sa.

Mele (co. Kent). Az. on a bend or, three lozenges gu. (another, sa.).

Meles (Meles, co. Lancaster). Ar. three torteaux in fesse, a bordure gu. *Crest*—On the stump of a tree a martlet ppr.

Melford. Ar. a fesse betw. three mullets sa.

Melhuish (Taunton, co. Somerset, and co. Devon). Ar. on a bend engr. sa. three fleurs-de-lis of the field. *Crest*—A naked arm couped below the elbow, holding a pheon erect.

Melhuish. Ar. a martlet sa. in the middle chief point a dagger paleways az. hilted or.

Mell. Or, a fret gu. *Crest*—On a chapeau az. turned up or, a martlet with wings endorsed sa.

Mell (co. Suffolk). Same *Arms*, a border of the second bezantée and an annulet az.

Mellent. Lozengy or and az. (another, with a bordure gu.).

Mellent, or Mellert. Or, two bars sa. betw. six crosses crosslet gu. three, two, and one.

Meller (Middle Temple, London; granted 1719). Ar. three martlets sa. beaked or, a chief dancettée of the second.

Meller (ROBERT MELLER, Doctor of Physic; descended from Sir ROBERT MELLER, Knt., of Bredy, co. Dorset; Fun. Ent. Ulster's Office, 1684, of ELIZABETH, his wife, dau. of WILLIAM FREEMAN, Esq., of Leigh, co. Surrey). Az. four mascles in cross or. *Crest*—A demi lion az. holding a mascle or.

Meller (Reg. Ulster's Office). Gu. a lion ramp. ar. betw. four annulets of the last.

Mellers, or Meller (Laiston, co. Suffolk). Az. a fesse ar. fretty gu. betw. three crowns or, a bordure wavy of the second. *Crest*—A greyhound pass. sa. collared or, resting the dexter paw on an escutcheon az.

Melliar (FOSTER-MELLIAR, North Aston Hall, Oxon). Ar. three martlets gu. on a chief dancettée az. an annulet or, betw. two fleurs-de-lis of the field. *Crest*—In front of a lion's gamb erect and couped or, holding a branch of myrtle ppr. two mascles interlaced fessways az. *Motto*—Cupio meliora.

Mellis (Scotland). Per fesse ar. and vert a pale counterchanged, three cinquefoils of the second. *Crest*—The sun in splendour or.

Mellish, or Melish (London, Ragnold, co. Nottingham, and Sandersted, co. Surrey). Az. two swans in pale betw. as many flaunches erm. *Crest*—Out of a ducal coronet or, a swan's head and neck ar.

Mellish (Blythe, co. Nottingham). Az. two swans in pale ar. betw. as many flaunches erm. quartering qu. a fesse betw. three crosses crosslet fitchée or, for GORE, of Bush Hill Park. *Crest*—A swan's head and neck erased ar. ducally gorged or.

Mellish (Hamels, co. Hertford). Same *Arms*.

Mello. Az. three boars' heads erased in bend ar. *Crest*—A mullet ar.

Mello. Ar. a bend betw. two lions' heads erased sa.

Mellor (co. Derby). Ar. three blackbirds ppr. *Crest*—A demi leopard issuant or, supporting an anchor sa.

Mellor (The Hon. Sir JOHN MELLOR, Knt., a Judge of the High Court of Justice in England, *b.* 1809, was called to the Bar by the Inner Temple, 1832, and went the Midland Circuit; became a Q.C. 1851; was formerly Recorder of Warwick, afterwards of Leicester, 1855–61; was M.P. for Great Yarmouth, 1857–9, for Nottingham, from 1859 till he was raised to the Bench in Nov. 1861; *m.*, 1832, ELIZABETH, dau. of W. MOSELEY, Esq.). Ar. three blackbirds ppr. *Crest* —A blackbird, as in the arms. *Motto*—Semper constans et fidelis.

Mellor (Ideridgehay and Derby). Ar. three blackbirds ppr. a chief dancettée sa. *Crest*—A bull's head erased ppr. ducally gorged or, holding in the mouth the upper end of a broken lance gold.

Melsanby. Sa. two bars gemel and a chief ar.

Melton (Tottenham High Cross, co. Middlesex; granted 1 Sept. 1626). Az. a cross voided ar. in the centre a bezant.

Melton (co. York). Ar. a cross patonce voided az.

Melton. Az. a cross patonce ar. surmounted of another of the first bend. four cinquefoils or. *Crest*—A lion's head erased az. guttée d'or, ducally gorged gold.

Melvehouse, or Melnehouse. Ar. on a bend engr. sa. three fleurs-de-lis of the field.

Melveton (co. Chester). Az. three plates, on each an inkmoline sa.

Melveton. Az. three plates. *Crest*—A lion's paw gu. holding a key az.

Melville, Viscount. See DUNDAS.

Melville (England). Ar. a fesse betw. three mascles gu. *Crest*—A talbot's head or.

Melville (that Ilk, co. Edinburgh; the heiress, in 15th century, *m.* Sir JOHN ROSS, of Halkhead). Gu. three crescents ar. a bordure of the last, charged with eight roses of the first.

Melville (Glenbervie, co. Kincardine; heiress, in 15th century, *m.* Sir JOHN AUCHINLECK). Ar. a fess betw. three crescents gu.

Melville (Raith, co. Fife). Ar. a fess gu.

Melville (*Earl of Melville*). Quarterly, 1st and 4th, gu. three crescents ar. within a bordure of the last, charged with eight roses of the first; 2nd and 3rd, ar. a fess gu. *Crest*— A ratchhound's head erased ppr. collared gu. *Supporters*— Dexter, an eagle volant ppr.; sinister, a ratchhound ppr. collared gu. *Motto*—Denique cœlum.

Melville (LESLIE-MELVILLE, *Earl of Leven and Melville*). See LESLIE.

Melville (Cassingray, co. Fife). Quarterly, as *Earl of Melville*, within a bordure or. *Crest*—A ratchhound's head erased ppr. collared gu. the collar charged with a crescent ar. *Motto*—Denique cœlo fruar.

Melville (Murdocairnie, co. Fife, 1672). Gu. a sun betw. three crescents ar. within a bordure of the second, charged with eight roses of the first. *Crest*—A crescent ar. *Motto*— Denique cœlum.

Melville (Auchmoor, co. Fife). Ar. on a fesse waved on the upper and engr. on the under side gu. three crescents of the field. *Crest*—A sleuth-hound's head couped ppr. *Motto*— Denique cœlum.

Melville (Carnbee, co. Fife). Or, three cushions gu. on each a crescent of the field, all within a bordure of the second. *Crest*—An eagle rising ppr. *Motto*—Ultra aspicio.

Melville (Strathkinness, co. Fife, 1773). Gu. three crescents ar. within a bordure of the last, charged with eight roses of the first, a small crescent of the second in chief for diff. *Crest*—A crescent ar. *Motto*—Denique cœlum.

Melville-Whyte (Bennochy and Strathkinness, co. Fife). Quarterly, 1st and 4th, ar. a martlet displ. betw. three quatrefoils, two and one sa. on a chief of the last as many quatrefoils of the first, for WHYTE; 2nd and 3rd, gu. three crescents ar. within a bordure of the last charged with eight roses of the field, a crescent for diff., for MELVILLE. *Crests*— 1st, WHYTE: A dexter arm embowed holding up a wreath of laurel all ppr.; 2nd, MELVILLE: A crescent ar. *Supporters*— Two eagles sa. beaked, membered, collared, and chained or, thereon three quatrefoils sa. *Mottoes*—Virtute parta; over the second crest: Denique cœlum.

Melville (Scotland, 1672). Gu. three crescents ar. a bordure invecked of the last, charged with eight roses of the first. *Crest*—Two eagles' wings conjoined ppr. *Motto*—Denique sursum.

Melville (Sir JOHN MELVILLE, Lord Provost of Edinburgh, 1854). Ar. a fess gu. betw. two hearts in chief of the second and a salmon naiant in base az. *Crest*—An eagle rising ppr. *Motto*—Ad altiora tendo.

Melward (RICHARD MELWARD, great-grandson of SYMON MELWARD, d. temp. Edward III. ; AGNES, dau. and heiress of the said RICHARD, m. JOHN JEFFERAY, Esq., of Chittingly Manor, co. Sussex). Ar. a cross moline sa. betw. four crescents gu.

Memes, or Mennys (cō. Kent, and London; granted 1616). Gu. a chev. vair betw. three leopards' faces or. Crest—An antelope's head gu. tufted and armed or, issuing out of rays of the last.

Menadarva, or Mathadarva (Menadarva, Cambourne, co. Cornwall). Gu. three fesses wavy sa. on each as many birds ar.

Mencaster (co. Essex). Ar. three bars gu. on a bend sa. as many escallops gu.

Mence (co. Worcester; BENJAMIN MENCE, Mayor of that city in 1714). Az. six griffins segreant, three, two, and one or. These arms appear on the monument of Sir GODFREY DE MENS, who took part in the tournament at Stepney, 2 Edward II. JOHN MENCE, of Hanbury, disclaimed at the Visit. of 1682.

Mence, or Mens. Paly of six ar. and az. on a chief gu. three crescents (another, crosses formée) of the first.

Mendez (London). Gu. six broken shinbones, the joints almost meeting, barways, two, two, and two ar. a canton erm.

Menell. See MEYNELL.

Menersh. Gu. a fesse dancettée or.

Menet, or Menett. Barry of six or and sa. Crest—A demi lion ramp. az.

Menhall, Or, on a fesse betw. two chevronels gu. three escallops of the first.

Menis. Ar. on a fesse gu. three mullets pierced of the field.

Menles, or Melles. Ar. two bars gu. in chief three escallops of the second (another, torteaux). Crest—A portcullis sa. chains or.

Menles, or Mens. Az. six griffins segreant (another, pass.) or, three, two, and one.

Menmarch. Gu. a fesse engr. or.

Menne. Or, a chief az.

Mennell (Malton, co. York). Az. three bars gemel and a chief or, over all a bend gu.

Mennell. Paly of six gu. and or, on a bend sa. three horseshoes ar.

Mennes, or Menns (Inner Temple, London; granted 1616). Gu. a chev. vairé or and az. betw. three leopards' faces of the second.

Mennicone (Paris and Sunbury, co. Middlesex). Or, a bend az. betw two mullets gu.

Menteath (Earl of Menteath). Or, a bend chequy az. and sa.

Menteath (Kerse, co. Stirling). Quarterly, 1st and 4th, as the last; 2nd and 3rd, az. three buckles or, for STIRLING.

Menteath (Closeburn, co. Dumfries, bart.). Quarterly, as the last, all within a bordure gu. Crest—A lymphad ppr. with flags gu. thereon a canton ar. with the cross of St. Andrew az. Motto—Dum vivo spero.

Menteath (Auldcathie, co. Linlithgow, 1672). Or, a bend chequy sa. and ar. on a canton of the second a lion's head erased of the first. Crest—An eagle rising ppr. looking up to the sun in his glory. Motto—Sub sole nihil.

Menvile. Or, on a bend sa. three cinquefoils ar ; another, Vert a lion ramp. ar. crowned gu.

Menwynick, or Menwinnick (Menwynick, co. Cornwall, temp. Henry IV.; WILLIAM MENWYNICK, fourth in descent from ROGER MENWYNICK, of same place. Visit. Cornwall, 1620. The heiress m. COPLESTONE). Sa. a chev. betw. three falcons, wings expanded ar.

Menyll. Paly of six gu. and or, on a bend sa. three horseshoes of the second.

Menyll. Vairé ar. and sa.

Menzies (Castle Menzies, co. Perth, bart.). Ar. a chief gu. Crest—A savage's head erased ppr. Supporters—Two savages wreathed round the head and loins with laurel all ppr. Motto—Vill God, I sall.

Menzies (Professor JOHN MENZIES, Aberdeen, 1672). Erm. on a chief az. a cherub's head ar. Crest—A cherub with wings expanded ppr. Motto—Scopus vitæ Christus.

Menzies (Edinburgh, 1695). Per pale ar. and or, three crescents gu. a chief of the last. Crest—A crescent ppr. Motto—Ut crescit clarescit.

Menzies (Pitfoddel, co. Aberdeen). Erm. a chief gu. Crest—A demi eagle with wings expanded ppr. Supporters—Two greyhounds ar. collared gu. Motto—Malo mori quam fœdari.

Menzies (Culdares, co. Perth). Ar. a sword in pale ppr. hilted and pommelled or, a chief gu. Crest—A demi lion holding in the dexter paw a baton ppr. Motto—Fortem fors juvat.

Menzies (Shian, co. Perth). Ar. a chief gu. a bordure chequy az. and of the first. Crest—A book expanded ppr. Motto—Spero.

Meoles (co. Chester). Ar. a bend betw. two lions' heads sa. langued gu. Crest—A lion's head erased sa. winged or.

Mepertshall. Ar. fretty sa. on a chief gu. a lion pass. or.

Mepham (STEPHEN DE MEPHAM, Archbishop of Canterbury, 1328-33, temp. Edward I.). Az. three bendlets or.

Merary. Az. a cross flory betw. four cinquefoils or.

Merbroke. Bendy of six az. and or, a bordure gu.

Merbury (co. Chester). Or, on a fesse engr. az. three garbs of the first. Crest—A camel's head sa. ducally gorged or.

Merbury (Reg. Ulster's Office). Ar. a cross engr. betw. four spearheads sa.

Merbury (Walton, co. Chester). Same Arms. Crest—A mermaid ppr. holding in the dexter hand a mirror, and in the sinister a comb.

Mercaunt (Seamer, co. Suffolk). Ar. a fret sa. on a canton or, a gauntlet of the second. Crest—Two lions' gambs erased in saltire or, each holding a battle axe ar. handled gu.

Mercer (Aldie, co. Berks). Sa. on a fesse betw. three chessrooks or, as many martlets of the first.

Mercer (Aldie, co. Kinross; represented by the Marchioness of Lansdowne as heir of line). Or, on a fess betw. three crosses pattée gu. in chief and a mullet az. in base as many bezants. Crest—A cross or. Motto—Crux Christi nostra corona.

Mercer (Salineshaw, co. Fife, 1680). As Aldie, within a bordure indented gu. Crest—A cross fitchée gu. Motto—Crux Christi mea corona.

Mercer (Easter Newton, co. Perth, 1676). As Aldie, within a bordure gu. charged with eight annulets or. Crest—A dexter hand holding a Bible expanded ppr. Motto—Jehova portio mea.

Mercer (Huntingtower, co. Perth, 1864). As Aldie, with a canton gu. charged with a boar's head couped or. Crest—The head and neck of a stork, holding in his beak a serpent writhing ppr. Mottoes—Over the crest: Ye great pule; below the arms: Crux Christi nostra corona.

Mercer (Fordel, co. Fife, 1853). Or, on a fess betw. three crosses pattée gu. in chief and a star of six points az. in base as many bezants, all within a bordure of the third, Crest—The head and neck of a heron erased, holding in its beak an eel seizing the neck of the former all ppr. Motto —The grit pool.

Mercer (Balleif, co. Perth). Or, on a fess betw. three crosses pattée gu. as many bezants.

Merchand, or Merchant (co. Buckingham). Sa. a bend cotised betw. two griffins segreant or. Crest—On a mount vert a moorcock ppr.

Merchant Taylors, Company of (London). See LONDON, principal Companies of.

Merchants, Company of (Exeter; incorporated 4 May, 3 Mary I., 1556). Az. a tower triple-towered or, standing on the waves of the sea in base ppr. in chief two ducal coronets of the second. Motto—Deo duce fortuna comitante.

Mercia. Sa. an eagle displ. or.

Mercier (co. Northumberland). Or, a fesse chequy az. and ar. betw. two boars' heads in chief sa. and a crescent in base gu. a bordure engr. of the last. Crest—A demi huntsman winding a horn ppr. vested az., motto over, Blow shrill. Motto—Toujours fidèle.

Mercury. Az. a cross flory betw. four cinquefoils or.

Mercy (Northall, co. Essex, and co. Hereford). Gu. on a fesse engr. ar. betw. three water bougets or, a cross formée sa. bezantée betw. two cloves of the last.

Mercy. Ar. on a bend gu. three lozenges of the field.

Mere (Mere, co. Chester). Ar. an ancient three-masted vessel, sails furled sa. Crest—A mermaid ppr. tail vert, crined or, in the right hand a comb, and in the left a mirror ppr. the frame and handle gold.

Meredith (Henbury, co. Chester). Gu. a lion ramp. reguard. or. Crest—A demi lion ramp. sa. collared and chained, reflexed over the back or.

Meredith (Stansley, co. Denbigh, bart., extinct 1739, and Leeds Abbey, co. Kent). Az. a lion ramp. or. Crest—A lion's head erased ppr. Another Crest—An Eastern coronet or, thereon a dragon pass. wings expanded gu.

Meredith (Prince of Wales). Or, a lion's gamb erased in bend gu.

Meredith ap Conan (Lord of Rhiwhirieth, Coel Tabog, and Neuadd Wenn, North Wales. Descendants: I. ROBERTS, near Lhain Wenn; II. OLIVER, of Neuadd Wenn and Llanervil; III. WILLIAMS, of Dolanog; IV. LLOYD, of Mairdre in

Edeirnion, and Randir; V. HANMER, of Hanmer; VI. BRA-
DENHEATH, of Penley, Bittifield, Halghton, Llai, Fens, Pentre
David, Maesbrook, and Bryn; also of Buryrigg, in Yorkshire; VII. OVERTON, of Overton Maddock. MEREDITH was
brother of GRIFFITH AP CONAN, Prince of North Wales).
Quarterly, ar. and gu. four lions pass. counterchanged of the
field.

Meredith (Pentrebychan, co. Denbigh; derived from HUGH
MEREDITH, Esq., of Wrexham and Pentrebychan, temp.
Elizabeth, younger brother of Sir WILLIAM MEREDITH,
Knt., of Stansly. Az. a lion ramp. or. Crest—A lion's
head or. Motto—Heb Dduw heb ddim, a Duw a digon:
With God everything, without Him nothing.

Meredith (Upper Weld, co. Buckingham). Per pale or and
ar. a lion ramp. sa. Crest—A demi lion ramp. per pale or
and ar. collared and lined sa.

Meredith (Crediton, co. Devon). Ar. a lion ramp. reguard.
sa. Crest—A demi lion ramp. sa. ducally gorged and
chained or.

Meredith (Oswestry, co. Salop). A lion ramp. sa. over all
a bend sinister or.

Meredith (Radnor, Wales; granted 1574). Ar. a lion
ramp. sa. gorged with a collar and chain affixed thereto,
reflexed over the back or. Crest—A demi lion ramp. sa.
collared and chained or.

Meredith. Ar. three nags' heads erased sa.

Meredith (Cloonamahon, co. Sligo). Az. a lion ramp. ar.
Crest—On an Eastern crown or, a griffin gu. Motto—Heb
Dduw heb ddim, a Duw a digon.

Meredyth. Per chev. ar. and or, a lion ramp. sa. a canton
gu. Crest—A yew tree ppr.

Meredyth (Greenhills, co. Kildare, bart.). Ar. a lion ramp.
sa. collared and chained or. Crest—A demi lion ramp.
collared and chained, as in the arms. Motto—Heb Dduw
heb ddim, a Duw a digon: Without God there is nothing,
with God enough.

Meredyth (Carlandstown, co. Meath, bart.). Same Arms
and Crest, a crescent for diff. Crest—Fiat Dei voluntas.

Merefield (St. Columb, co. Cornwall). Ar. a chev. sa. betw.
three (another, five) Cornish choughs ppr.

Merefield (co. Devon and Crewkerne, co. Somerset). Or,
on a fesse cotised az. betw. three crescents sa. as many
roses ar.

Merefield (London). Sa. five garbs in cross or. Crest—A
garb or, banded sa.

Merefield. Vert two lions ramp. (another, pass.) ar.
crowned or; another, Ar. a chev. betw. three martlets
(another, crows) sa.; another, Vert three lions pass. guard.
ar.; another, Vert six lions ramp. ar.; another, Sa. six lions
ramp. or; another, Or, on a fesse az. betw. three crescents
gu. as many roses ar.

Mereford, or Meriford (London). Gu. a lion ramp.
erm.

Meremond. Ar. two bars sa. in chief a mullet of six points
pierced gu.

Meres (co. Lincoln). Gu. a fesse betw. three water bougets
erm. Crest—A dexter hand holding a sword in bend ppr.
Motto—Sine metu.

Meres, Meeres, Mere, Meare, or Meyres (co.
Cambridge, Meare, co. Chester, Bewbridge, co. Salop,
and co. Wilts). Ar. a ship with three masts, sails furled,
shrouded sa. Crest—A mermaid ppr. hair or.

Meres, or Meros. Paly of six or and az. on a chief gu.
three crosses formée of the first.

Meres, or Mareys. Gu. a fesse erm. betw. three water
bougets ar.

Mereson, or Meresen. Ar. three bucks' heads cabossed
sa.

Merevale Abbey (co. Warwick). Vairé or and gu.

Merevall. Az. semée-de-lis or, a demi lion ramp. ar.

Merewether (HENRY ALLWORTH MEREWETHER, Serjeant-
at-Law, of Castlefield, Calne, co. Wilts, and Whitehall,
London; and Very Rev. JOHN MEREWETHER, D.D., Dean of
Hereford). Or, three martlets sa. Crest—Out of a chief
az. a sun in splendour ppr., for MEREWETHER (quartering
ALLWORTH), or, a saltire engr. betw. twelve billets sa.). Crest
—An arm embowed in armour garnished or, holding in the
hand ppr. a sword of the last, hilt and pommel or, entwined round the blade with a snake ppr. Motto—Vi et
consilio.

Merewether (Bowden Hill, co. Wilts). Same Arms, Crest,
and Motto.

Mereworth, or Merworth. Ar. (another, or), a chev.
gu. betw. ten crosses crosslet sa.

Merfyn, or Mervyn (co. Kent). Or, on a chev. sa. a
mullet (another, three crescents) ar.

Merfyn. See MORFIN.

679

Mergith (Wales). Gu. a Saracen's head erased at the neck
ar. environed about the temples with a wreath of the last
and sa.

Mergrant. Ar. a chief indented gu.

Merick, or Meyrick (London and Wales; granted 24
Oct. 1601). Az. a fesse wavy ar. in chief two mullets pierced
or. Crest—A sea horse ppr. maned or, holding in the paws
a mullet pierced az. Another Crest—A cat's face sa.

Merick (Norcott, co. Middlesex, 1663). Same Arms, &c.

Merick (West Camel, co. Somerset; granted 1589). Paly
of six or and az. on a fesse gu. three mullets ar. (another,
or). Crest—A water spaniel pass. ar.

Mericke (Wigmore Castle, Hereford, temp. Queen Elizabeth).
Gu. two porcupines in pale ar.

Mericke (cos. Hereford and Radnor). Same Arms.

Mericks (Wales). Ar. on a cross sa. five crescents of the
field, in the 1st quarter a spear's head gu.

Merill. Or, on a bend gu. a crescent ar. in base a cross
crosslet of the second.

Mering (Mering, co. Notts; Sir WILLIAM MERING, Knt., of
Mering; temp. Henry VIII., nineteenth in descent from Sir
GILBERT MERING, Knt. Visit. Notts, 1569). Ar. on a chev.
sa. three escallops or. Crest—A horse's head erased sa. be
zantée, in the nostrils an annulet or.

Mering (co. York). Or, on a chev. sa. three escallops ar.

Merison. Ar. three bucks' heads sa.

Meriton. Az. on a chev. ar. three roses vert, a canton
erm.

Meritt (co. Wilts). Barry of six or and sa. a bend erm.

Merks (co. Essex). Gu. a lion ramp. ar. a bordure engr.
or. Crest—An otter's head and neck erased sa.

Merland. Az. a bend raguly ar. in sinister chief a ducal
coronet or.

Merlawe, or Marls (Carnllwyd, co. Glamorgan). Paly
of six ar. and az.

Merlay. Sa. a bend erm. cotised ar. betw. six martlets or.
Crest—A hind's head or, gorged with a collar sa. charged
with three bezants.

Merley (Newminster and Morpeth, co. Northumberland,
temp. Henry III.). Barry of ten ar. and gu. on a bordure
az. eight martlets or.

Merlin (EDWARD MERLIN, Portcullis Pursuivant at Arms,
temp. Queen Elizabeth, 1559). Az. a bend raguled, in the
sinister chief a ducal coronet or.

Merling. Or, three billets gu. Crest—A lion's head erased
gu.

Merling. Quarterly, 1st and 4th, or, three billets gu.; 2nd
and 3rd, per bend wavy gu. and sa.

Merlington. Or, three martlets gu.

Merlowe. Quarterly, sa. and gu. eight martlets in orle or.

Merlyon. Gu. a chev. vair betw. three eagles displ. or.
Crest—An eagle's head or, betw. two wings vair.

Mermes. Or, three piles gu. on a canton sa. a lion pass.
ar.

Merrett (London; granted 13 July, 1666). Barry of six ar.
and sa. a bend erm.

Merrey, or Mery (Renburne and Barton, co. Derby).
Erm. three lions ramp. gu. crowned or. Crest—Out of a
ducal coronet or, a demi lion gu. ducally crowned gold.

Merrey. Gu. three cinquefoils pierced or. Crest—A thistle
and rose stalked and leaved in saltire ppr.

Merrey. Ar. on a bend gu. three lozenges of the field.

Merrick (Wales). See MEYNIK.

Merrick (Norcote, co. Middlesex, and London; CHRISTOPHER
MERRICK, gent., of Norcote, and JOHN and ROBERT MERRICK,
of London, sons of CHRISTOPHER MERRICK, Esq., of Norcote,
the son of RICHARD MERRICK, co. Gloucester. Visit. Middlesex, 1663). Az. a fess wavy or, in chief two mullets of the
last, quartering, 1st, erm. on a chev. az. three lions ramp.
ar.; 2nd, per bend az. and sa. three bezants. Crest—A sea
lion couchant or, betw. the fins a mullet az.

Merrick (Bollitree, co. Hereford). Gu. a fesse wavy or, in
chief two mullets ar.

Merrick (Sir FRANCIS MERRICK, knighted at Dublin by
ROBERT, Earl of Essex, Lord Lieutenant, 5 Aug. 1599). Per
fess or and sa. two palets counterchanged, on a fess gu.
three mullets of the first.

Merrifield. Erm. on a fesse betw. six annulets az. three
mullets ar. Crest—A sun rising ppr.

Merrifield. Ar. a chev. betw. three martlets sa. Same
Crest.

Merrifield. Or, three roses in fess az. enclosed by two bars
of the second betw. three crescents sa.

Merrike. Gu. three palets vair, on a chief or, a label of as
many points of the first.

Merrill. Or, a pale engr. gu. voided of the field, betw. two
fleurs-de-lis az. Crest—A peacock's head erased ppr.

Merriman. Lozengy sa. and ar. a chief erm. *Crest*—A boar pass. collared and bristled vert.

Merriman (confirmed, 21 Dec. 1833, to SAMUEL MERRIMAN, Esq., M.D., of Rodbourne Cheney, co. Wilts, and to the descendants of his grandfather, NATHANIEL MERRIMAN, Esq., of Marlborough). Ar. on a chev. cotised sa. betw. three Cornish choughs ppr. as many crescents of the field. *Crest* —A serpent nowed, therefrom issuant a dexter arm embowed in armour ppr. garnished or, the hand grasping a short sword also ppr. pommel and hilt gold. *Motto*—Terar dum prosim.

Merry (Barton, co. Derby; the heiress *m.* SIMPSON). Erm. three lions ramp. gu. crowned or, a canton of the second. *Crest*—A demi lion ramp. erm. crowned or, issuing out of a ducal coronet of the second.

Merry (Herringfleet Hall, near Yarmouth, co. Norfolk). Gu. on a fesse engr. betw. three water bougets ar. a cross formée sa. charged with five bezants betw. two cloves of the second. *Crest*—A mast of a ship, rompu and erect, thereto a yard with sail furled in bend sinister, above it a round top, three arrows issuing therefrom on each side saltireways, points upward all ppr.

Merry (Highlandus, co. Berks). Erm. on a fesse engr. az. betw. three lions ramp. gu. a water bouget betw. two crosses pattée or. *Crest*—Out of a mural crown ar. a demi lion ramp. gu. ducally crowned or, charged on the shoulder with a cross pattée of the first, and holding betw. the paws a water bouget, as in the arms. *Motto*—Persto et spero.

Merry (impaled by MYLLES, of London. Visit. London, 1568). Gu. on a fesse engr. betw. three water bougets erminois as many crosses pattée sa.

Merry (Waterford, co. Sevillu, in Spain; allowed by Fortescue, Ulster, to JOSEPH MERRY, of Seville, and his brothers, JOHN, FRANCIS, RALPHAEL, and ANTHONY MERRY, sons of JOSEPH MERRY, of Waterford, *d.* 1804, who was fourth in descent from RICHARD MERRY, of same place). Ar. on a bend gu. three lozenges or. *Crest*—An arm in armour embowed, the hand brandishing a scymitar all ppr. *Motto*— Suprema manus validior.

Merry. Gu. three cinquefoils or.

Merry (Belladrum, co. Inverness, 1863). Gu. three lions ramp. or, on a chief ar. three stars of the field. *Crest*—A demi lion ramp. gu. crowned with an antique crown or. *Motto*—Persto et spero.

Merrye. Erm. a pellet betw. three lions ramp. gu. crowned or.

Merryton. Az. on a chev. ar. three roses vert. *Crest*—Two wings erect ar.

Merser (Lincoln). Gu. a fesse wavy ar. betw. three plates, on a chief or, a lion pass. guard. of the first. *Crest*—Out of a mural coronet gu. a demi lion or, holding a battle axe ar. handle of the first.

Mertens (London, originally from Germany). Erm. two chev. engr. az. betw. three storks sa., quartering DIRS, Ar. on a chev. vert betw. three lions ramp. gu. a pair of wings conjoined in lure betw. two mullets of six points or. *Crest* —A demi stork, wings expanded sa. in its beak a key, as in the arms.

Merting, Mertigny, or Mertygne. Gu. five fusils in bend or.

Mertingham (Frocester, co. Gloucester). Ar. on a chev. betw. three stags' heads couped sa. as many buglehorns stringed of the first.

Mertins (Lord Mayor of London, 1725). Az. two bars or, in chief a catharine wheel betw. as many buglehorns ar.

Merton (Merton, co. Devon; MARGERY MERTON, of Merton, *m.* WILLIAM DE MOYNE, living 11 Edward III., A.D. 1330; quartered by HOLLAND, *Earl of Kent* and *Duke of Exeter*. Visit. Devon, 1620). Az. three bends ar.

Merton (co. Lancaster). Same *Arms.*

Merton (Merton Sands, co. Chester; the heiress *m.* GLEGG). Same *Arms.*

Merton. Same *Arms*, tinctures reversed.

Merton. Ar. three chevronels per pale az. and gu. *Crest* —A demi Moor brandishing a scymitar ppr.

Merton. Barry of six az. and or; another, Ar. three heathcocks sa. beaked and legged gu.

Merton (WALTER MERTON, Lord Chancellor of England, *temp.* Henry III., Bishop of Rochester, 1274-77, founder of Merton College, Oxford, 1274; arms in Merton College. Visit. Oxon 1574). Or, three chevronels per pale az. and gu.

Merton-College (Oxford; founded, 1274, by WALTER DE MERTON, first Lord Chancellor of England, and afterwards Bishop of Rochester). Or, three chevronels per pale, the first and third az. and gu. the second gu. and az.

Mertoun (that Ilk). Ar. a chev. sa. betw. three torteaux.

Mervin (co. Cambridge). Ar. a demi lion ramp. sa. *Crest*— An escutcheon per cross or and gu.

Mervin (Pertood, co. Wilts). Same *Arms*, a fleur-de-lis for diff.

Mervis, or Mervisse (co. Suffolk). Az. three oak leaves or.

Mervyn (Fonthill Giffard, co. Wilts). Sa. three lions pass. guard. per pale or and ar. The funeral certificate of Sir JOHN MERVYN, who was of this family, *d.* 1566, as well as the pedigrees in the College of Arms, gives the above arms as the coat of MERVYN, of Fonthill Giffard. *Crest*—A squirrel sejant ppr. cracking a nut or, a plain collar of the last, charged with three torteaux. *Motto*—De Dieu tout. (One of the descendants of this Sir JOHN MERVYN settled at Marwood, co. Devon, and the last male heir of that branch *d.* 1756, leaving two daus., one of whom *d. unm.*, and the other, who eventually became sole heiress, *m.* CHARLES NEWELL CUTCLIFFE, Esq., of Damage, co. Devon).

Mervyn (Pertwood, co. Wilts, and co. Devon. Visit. Wilts, 1565). Ar. a demi lion ramp. sa. charged with a fleur-de-lis or.

Mervyn (Trellick Castle, co. Tyrone; descended from Sir AUDLEY MERVYN, M.P. for the county of Tyrone, and Speaker of the Irish House of Commons, son of Sir HENRY MERVYN, descended from co. Wilts, by the Lady CHRISTIANA, his wife, dau. of GEORGE, *Earl of Castlehaven*). Or, a chev. sa.

Mervyn-D'Arcy-Irvine. See IRVINE.

Mervyn Vrych (Lord of Anglesey). Gu. three crowns in bend or; another, Ar. three fusils conjoined in fesse gu. each charged with an eagle displ. or.

Mervyn (impalement Fun. Ent. Ulster's Office, 1621, Sir RICHARD ALDWORTH, Knt., of Newmarket, co. Cork, who *m.* ANNE MERVYN, *d. s. p.*). Per fess sa. and ar. a lion ramp. counterchanged.

Mervyn (Fun. Ent. Ulster's Office, 1632, EDITH MERVYN, *m.* 1st, Sir MORRIS GRIFFITH, Knt., and 2nd, Lieut. GLINN). Ar. a demi lion ramp. sa. armed and langued gu.

Mervyn (Fun. Ent. Ulster's Office, 1675, AUDLEY MERVYN). Or, a chev. sa.

Mervyn (Durford Abbey, co. Sussex). As MERVYN, of Fonthill Giffard.

Mervyn. Ar. a demi lion ramp. sa.

Merwood (impalement Fun. Ent. Ulster's Office, 1615, Mrs. ELENOR MERWOOD, *alias* PLUNKETT). Gu. a chev. betw. three goats' heads erased ar.

Mery, or Merrey (co. Hertford, and Barton, co. Derby). Gu. on a fesse engr. ar. betw. three water bougets or, as many crosses pattée sa.

Merydale (Great Brickhill, and Salbury, co. Bucks). Erm. on a cross gu. five eagles' heads erased ar. *Crest*—An eagle's head erased per fesse gu. and ar.

Meryet. Barry of six or and gu. a bend erm. *Crest*—A porcupine's head issuing sa.

Meryett. Ar. three bars sa. on a canton of the second a fleur-de-lis or.

Meryfeld. Ar. two lions pass. vert.

Meryng (co. Nottingham). Ar. on a chev. sa. three escallops or. *Crest*—A nag's head erased sa. bezantée, in the mouth an annulet or.

Meryton (Castle Leventon, co. York, 1665). Sa. on a chev. or, three roses gu. a canton erm.

Meryott (co. Somerset). Barry of six or and sa.

Meryweather (Barfraystones, co. Kent). See MEREWETHER.

Meschines (*Earl of Chester;* granted *temp.* Henry I., extinct 1231). The first earl bore, Or, a lion ramp. gu. The third earl bore, Az. six garbs or, three, two, and one. The last earl bore, Az. three garbs or, two and one.

Meschines. Or, three bars gu. *Crest*—A rose ar. surmounted by a thistle ppr.

Mescow, or Mestow. Ar. three bucks' heads cabossed sa. *Crest*—A buck's head erased sa. attired or.

Mesham (co. Flint; granted to ARTHUR MESHAM, Esq., of Pontryffydd, Bodvari, of Ewloe, co. Flint, and of Plas Bennett, Llandyrnog, co. Denbigh). Per pale or and az. two stags trippant betw. as many stars of eight points in fesse all counterchanged. *Crest*—A lion guard. ppr. charged on the body with a star of eight points, and supporting with the dexter forepaw a stag's attires or. *Motto*—Duty.

Mesnill, or Meignill. Az. three bars gemel and a chief or.

Messarmy. Or, a chev. per pale ar. and vert betw. three apples gu.

Messenger, Messanger, or Massinger. Ar. a chev. betw. three esquires' helmets ar. *Crest*—A pegasus courant ar. ducally gorged and chained or.

Messewy. Or, a chev. vert betw. three apples gu. stalked of the second.

Messewy (Attorney General of Jersey, 1685). Or, three cherries gu. stalked vert. *Crest*—A cherry tree ppr. *Motto* —Au valeureux cœur rien impossible.

Messing. Gu. three dolphins haurian*t* or. *Crest*—An eagle displ. gu.

Messingham (Reg. Ulster's Office). Gu. on a border or, three escallops az.

Mested (Sir ANDREW MESTED, *temp.* Edward II.; his dau. and heir, ELLINOR MESTED, *m.* 24 Edward III., 1350, JOHN HOLLAND, fourth son of Sir ROBERT HOLLAND, first *Lord Holland*, summoned to Parliament 1314. Visit. Devon, 1620). Quarterly, gu. and or, four escallops counterchanged.

Metcalf (THOMAS METCALF, Citizen and Goldsmith, of London. Visit. London, 1568). Ar. on a fess vert betw. three calves pass. sa. a leopard's face betw. two annulets or. *Crest*—A demi sea calf purfled or.

Metcalfe (Murton and Seatonville, co. Northumberland). Per fesse or and sa. in chief two calves and in base a dove volant counterchanged.

Metcalfe (Fern Hill, co. Berks, bart.). Ar. on a fesse wavy gu. betw. three calves pass. sa. a sword fesseways, point to the sinister ppr. pommel and hilt or. *Crest*—A talbot sejant sa. the dexter paw supporting an escutcheon or, charged with a hand issuing from clouds on the sinister holding a pen all ppr. *Motto*—Conquiesco.

Metcalfe (*Baron Metcalfe*, extinct 1846; Sir CHARLES THEOPHILUS METCALFE, third bart. of Fern Hill, Governor-General of Canada, was created a peer 1845, *d. s. p.*). Quarterly, 1st and 4th, same *Arms*, for METCALFE; 2nd and 3rd, per fesse gu. and az. on a fesse betw. a castle in chief and a lion ramp. in base or, three mullets of six points of the first, for DEBONNAIRE. *Crest*—A talbot sejant sa. the dexter paw supporting an escutcheon or, charged with a hand issuant from clouds on the sinister and holding a pen all ppr. *Supporters*—Dexter, a moonshee of Bengal habited ppr.; sinister, a soldier of the Bengal Native Infantry equipped and armed ppr. *Motto*—Conquiesco.

Metcalfe (Nappa Hall, Wensleydale, co. York; descended from THOMAS METCALFE, of Nappa, Chancellor of the Duchy of Lancaster, 1483). Ar. three calves pass. sa.

Metcalfe (Beare Park, Bedale, and Bellerby, co. York, and Louth Park, co. Lincoln, a branch of METCALFE, of Nappa). Same *Arms*. *Crest* (granted by Cooke, Clarenceux, 29 Sept. 1581, to MATTHEW METCALFE, of Bellerby)—A hound sejant ppr. posing the forefoot on an escutcheon or.

Metcalfe (Northallerton, co. York; a branch of METCALFE, of Nappa; as borne by Capt. WILLIAM MARWOOD METCALFE, grandson of THOMAS METCALFE, Esq., of Lincoln's Inn, and by JOHN HENRY METCALFE, grandson of Rev. FRANCIS METCALFE, M.A., Rector of Kirkbride, who represent the two younger branches of the METCALFES of Northallerton, descendants of WILLIAM METCALFE, of that place, and ANNA, his wife, daughter of Sir GEORGE MARWOOD, Bart., of Little Busby, co. York). Ar. three calves pass. sa. a canton az. for diff. (Visit. of Yorkshire, 1665—6). *Crest* (as entered in the Harleian MSS., 1487)—A satyr affronté ppr. with a girdle of oak leaves round his loins vert, holding in the dexter hand, over the right shoulder, a spiked club or morning star or.

Metcalfe (Thornborough Hall, Romanby, near Northallerton, co. York; a branch of METCALFE, of Nappa). Ar. three calves pass. sa. a canton az. for diff. (confirmed by Dugdale, Norroy. Visit. Yorkshire).

Metcalfe (Epping, Essex; descended from METCALFE, of Nappa, and now borne by WALTER CHARLES METCALFE, Esq., F.S.A., of Epping). Ar. three calves pass. sa. in chief a martlet gu. for diff.

Metcalfe. See *Supplement.*

Metcalfe (Fun. Ent. Ulster's Office, 1632, JAMES METCALFE, Doctor of Physic, whose wife was ELIZABETH METCALFE, of co. York). Ar. three calves pass. sa. each holding in the mouth a trefoil slipped vert.

Mete (co. Kent). Az. on a bend or, three fusils gu.

Mete. Gu. on a bend or, three lozenges az. (another, the field az. and the bend charged with three mascles gu.).

Meteau (co. Devon). Or, on a bend sa. three mullets of the first.

Metford. Or, a fesse gu. betw. three martlets sa. *Crest*— A lion ramp. gu. supporting with the forepaws a garb ppr.

Metford. Sa. a lion ramp. double queued ar. betw. the double queue a fleur-de-lis of the last.

Metford. Ar. a fesse betw. three hedgehogs sa.

Metge (Athlumney, co. Meath). Ar. three fleurs-de-lis az. *Motto*—Hoc age.

Metham (Bollington, co. Lincoln). Quarterly, ar. and az. in the sinister chief quarter a fleur-de-lis or. *Crest*—A bull's head barry of ten ar. and sa. attired sa.

681

Metham (Metham, co. York. Visit. York, 1530). Quarterly, az. and ar. in the dexter chief quarter a fleur-de-lis or. Same *Crest.*

Metham. Same *Arms. Crest*—A bull's head barry of six ar. and az.

Metham (Barwell, co. Leicester). Same *Arms*, quartering ASHBY, of Quenby, a martlet for diff.

Methley (Estley, co. Notts; List of Knights, *temp.* Edward I. and II.; ELIZABETH, dau. and heiress of BARTHOLOMEW METHLEY, *temp.* Henry IV., *m.* JOHN LASCELLS, third son of GEORGE LASCELLS, Esq., of Sturton. LASCELLS Ped., Visit. Notts, 1614). Barry of six sa. and ar. on a chief of the last three mullets pierced of the first.

Methoulde, or Methwold (Longford and Ringworth, co. Norfolk). Az. six escallops or (another, seven; another, eight). *Crest*—A goat's head erased ar. attired and bearded sa. (another, or).

Methuen (*Baron Methuen*, of Corsham, co. Wilts.) Ar. three wolves' heads erased ppr. borne on the breast of an imperial eagle. *Crest*—A wolf's head couped ppr. *Supporters*—Two fiery lynxes reguard. ppr. collared and chained or. *Motto*—Virtus invidiæ scopus.

Methven (Craigtown, co. Fife, 1672). Ar. on a chev. sa. ensigned on the top with a cross pattée gu. a crescent of the field, in base a heart of the third. *Crest*—A cross pattée or, within a crescent ar. *Motto*—Marte et clypeo.

Methwold. Az. nine escallops or, three, three, two, and one. *Crest*—A goat's head erased ar

Methwold (Sir WILLIAM METHWOLD, Lord Chief Baron of Exchequer, Ireland; Fun. Ent. Ulster's Office, 1619). Az. six escallops or, three, two, and one, a crescent for diff.

Metivier (Guernsey). Az. two scythes in saltire betw. as many mullets ar. in chief a crescent of the last and in base a garb or. *Crest*—Over a French count's coronet a demi lion reguard. ar. *Supporters*—Two lions reguard. ar. *Motto*—Virtute.

Metley (co. Warwick). Gu. a fret or, a chief ar. *Crest*— A mermaid ppr.

Metringham. Vert a chev. betw. three horse-pickers ar.

Metsted (co. Devon). Quarterly, or and gu. four escallops counterchanged.

Metsteed. Gu. a fesse erm. betw. three mullets or.

Mettingham Monastery (co. Suffolk). Per pale az. and gu. a lion ramp. ar.

Metz. Az. on a bend or, three mascles gu.

Meune. Or, a chief az.

Meurs. Or, a fesse sa. *Crest*—A demi savage, over the shoulder a club, entwined round the sinister arm and wreathed round the middle with leaves all ppr.

Meus. Az. six griffins segreant or.

Meus. Paly of six ar. and az. on a chief gu. three crescents of the first.

Meuter, or Mouter. Sa. four martlets ar. two and two.

Meux (Kingston, Isle of Wight, bart., extinct 1706). Paly six or and az. on a chief gu. three crosses pattée of the first.

Meux (Theobald's Park, co. Hertford, bart.). Paly of six or and az. on a chief gu. three crosses pattée of the first. *Crest* —Two wings inverted and indorsed ar. conjoined by a cord with tassels or.

Meverell (Tidswell, co. Derby). Ar. a griffin segreant gu. *Crest*—A gauntlet grasping a dagger all ppr.

Meverell (co. Derby). Or, three piles gu. on a canton ar. a lion ramp. sa.

Meverell (Throwley, co. Stafford, and Tidswell, co. Derby; the last male heir, ROBERT MEVERELL, Esq., *d.* in 1626; his dau. and heiress, ELIZABETH, *m.* THOS. CROMWELL, *Earl of Ardglass*). Or (another, ar.) a griffin segreant sa. beaked and legged gu. *Crest*—A demi griffin segreant sa. beaked and legged gu.

Meverell (Chertsey, co. Surrey). Ar. a griffin segreant sa. beaked and legged gu.

Meverell. Az. semée-de-lis or, a lion ramp. ar.

Meverell, and Mevill. Or, on a bend sa. three cinquefoils ar.

Meversh. Gu. a fesse dancettée or.

Mewee, or Mewis (Holdenby, co. Northampton, and Bishopton, co. Wilts). Az. four palets or, on a chief gu. three crosses formée ar.

Meweham, Mewham, and Mewtham. Az. an estoile or.

Mewes. Paly of six or and az. on a chief gu. three crosses pattée of the first.

Mewes (The Low Country, Flanders; Fun. Ent. Ulster's Office, 1598, Mrs. MEWES, a Dutch woman, widow of Capt. ANTHONY HAWES). Ar. three bars gu.

Mewes, Mewsse, or Mowse (Woburn, co. Bedford). Or, a chief erm. over all an eagle displ. sa. *Crest*—A demi eagle displ. or, ducally gorged gu. beaked az.

Mewis. Az. six griffins segreant (another, eagles) or, three, two, and one. *Crest*—A dexter hand couped fesseways, charged with an eye ppr.

Mewy (Merry, co. Devon). Gu. three sea mews ar. beaks and legs or.

Mewy (quartered by HALS, of Beauford and Hardwick, co. Devon. Visit. Devon, 1620). Ar. a fess betw. three sea mews sa.

Mewys. Az. four palets or, on a chief gu. three crosses formée ar.

Mexborough, Earl of. See SAVILLE.

Mey (Houldham Abbey, co. Norfolk). Vert a chev. betw. three crosses crosslet fitchée or, on a chief of the last as many roses gu. *Crest*—A demi savage wreathed round the middle with leaves and holding a club over the dexter shoulder ppr. having a serpent entwined round the sinister arm vert.

Meyde. Sa. three lions' heads erased or, a chief ar.

Meyer (London). Ar. on a mount a savage in a walking position, wreathed about the head and waist with oak leaves, in the dexter hand a club resting on the shoulder, the sinister on his hip betw. two oak trees all ppr.

Meyler (co. Wexford, an Anglo-Norman family; arms confirmed to GEORGE MEYLER, Esq., fourth son of WALTER MEYLER, by ANNE FEWTRELL, his second wife, and grandson of THOMAS MEYLER, Esq., of Tincurry, co. Wexford). Ar. a chief vert. *Crest*—A demi lion ramp. gu. holding in the forepaw an annulet er. *Motto*—*Amor patriæ vincit.*

Meymott (granted, 1835, to the descendants of Rev. SAMUEL MEYMOTT, Rector of North Chapel, co. Sussex, *b.* 11 Feb. 1691). Or, three demi lions couped in bend az. each charged with a mullet ar. *Crest*—Three mullets fesseways gu. in front of a dexter arm embowed in armour ppr. in the hand also ppr. a wreath of laurel or.

Meyne (co, Lincoln). Sa. a fess dancettée betw. six annulets ar.

Meynell (North-Kilvington, co. York; descended from HUGH DE MENELL, of Hilton, living in 1203, second son of WALTER DE MAINILL, represented by MEYNELL, of North Kilvington, and the Fryerage, near Yarm. Visit. York, 1665). Az. three bars gemel and a chief or. *Crest*—A savage's head ppr. couped at the shoulders and wreathed round the temples or and az. *Motto*—*Deus non reliquit memoriam humilium.*

Meynell (Langley, co. Derby). Vairé ar. and sa. *Crest*—A horse's head erased ar. *Motto*—Virtute vici.

Meynell (Bradley, co. Derby; descended from FRANCIS MEYNELL, Sheriff and Alderman of London, who purchased the Manor of Bradley, and *d.* 1666; his son, GODFREY MEYNELL, Esq., of Bradley, High Sheriff co. Derby, 1681, was father of HUGO MEYNELL. Esq., of Bradley, High Sheriff of the co. 1758, and M.P. for Lichfield, whose grandson, HUGO CHARLES IRVINE MEYNELL, Esq., of Bradley, and Hoar Cross, co. Stafford, was Sheriff of co. Derby, 1826). Same *Arms, Crest,* and *Motto.*

Meynell-Ingram (Hoar Cross Hall, co. Stafford). Quarterly, 1st and 4th, erm. on a fesse gu. three escallops or, for INGRAM; 2nd and 3rd, vairé ar. and sa., for MEYNELL. *Crests* —1st, INGRAM: A cock or; 2nd, MEYNELL: A horse's head erased ar. *Motto*—Virtute vici.

Meynell, or Menell (cos. Cambridge, Cornwall, and Norfolk). Vairé ar. and sa.

Meynell, or Menell (co. York). Az. four (another, six) bars gemel and a chief or.

Meynell, or Mennell. Paly of six gu. and or, on a bend sa. three horseshoes or.

Meynton. Ar. a fesse betw. six quatrefoils gu.

Meyny. Or, a cross engr. sa. a bendlet gu.

Meyric, or Meyrick (Bôdorgan, co. Anglesey; descended from the marriage of EINIAWN SAIS AP DAVID, Usher of the Palace at Sheen, *temp.* Henry V. and Henry VI., with EVA, dau. and heiress of MEREDYDD AP CADWGAN, of Bôdorgan; EINIAWN SAIS, who derived his descent from CADAVAL YNAD, Judge of the Court of Powis, *temp.* King John, obtained an augmentation to his arms for his services in France; represented by MEYRICK, of Bôdorgan). Sa. on a chev. ar. betw. three staves raguly or, inflamed ppr. a fleur-de-lis az. betw two Cornish choughs ppr. *Crest*—On a tower or, a Cornish chough ppr. holding in the dexter claw a fleur-de-lis az.

Meyric (Prince of Cardigan). Sa. a lion ramp. ar.

Meyrick. See TAPPS-GERVIS-MEYRICK, Bart.

Meyrick (co. Hereford; descended from ROWLAND MEYRICK, Bishop of Bangor, 1559 66, second son of MEURIC AP

682

LLEWELYN, of Bôdorgan, Esquire of the Body to Henry VII.). Az. a fesse wavy erminois betw. three mullets pierced or. *Crest*—A tower per pale ar. and erminois. *Motto*—Stemmata quid faciunt.

Meyrick (Bush, co. Pembroke; descended from Sir FRANCIS METRICK, Knt., of Monkton, co. Pembroke, second son of ROWLAND MEYRICK, Bishop of Bangor). Sa. on a chev. ar. betw. three staves raguly of the last inflamed ppr. a fleur-de-lis betw. two Cornish choughs gu. (another, the fleur-de-lis and choughs sa.).

Meyrick (Woodlands, co. Wilts). Sa. on a chev. betw. three staves raguly ar. fired at the top ppr. a fleur-de-lis gu. betw. two Cornish choughs ppr. *Crest*—On a tower ar. a Cornish chough ppr. the dexter claw supporting a fleur-de-lis gu.

Meyrig Lloyd (Uwch Aled, derived from Hedd Molwynog. Descendants: I. LLOYD, of Llwyn y Mean Llanvorda; II. LLOYD, of Dre Newydd, in Whittington parish; these two families being, according to John Reynolds, the Oswestry Antiquary, the most ancient of the name of LLOYD in North Wales). Ar. an eagle displ. with two necks sa. beaked and armed or.

Meysey (co. Worcester). Ar. a fess betw. three cinquefoils pierced sa. *Crest*—A dragon's head quarterly or and az.

Meysey (Shakenhurst, co. Worcester. Visit. of that co., exemplified by patent, by Benolte, Clarenceux, to JOHN MEYSEY). Same *Arms,* a mullet for diff. *Crest*—A dragon's head quarterly or and az.

Meysey-Thompson, Bart. See THOMPSON.

Meytam. Quarterly, az. and ar. in the 1st quarter a fleur-de-lis or.

Michaell. Gu. a chief indented erm.

Michaelson. Quarterly, sa. and gu. the sun in splendour or.

Michall, or Michell (Old Windsor, co. Berks). Az. three leopards' heads erased or, a chief embattled erm. *Crest*—A leopard's face per pale or and az.

Miche (Kepleton, co. Dorset). Sa. a chev. betw. three escallops ar.

Micheall. Sa. an escallop betw. three swans' head erased ar.

Michel (Kingston Russell, co. Dorset; descended from JOHN MICHEL, resident *temp* Elizabeth at Dalwood, in Stockland parish, in the chapel of which place the arms still borne by the family appear). Per chev. ar. and sa. three herons' heads erased counterchanged. *Crest*—A dexter hand holding a heron's head erased all ppr.

Michel (Dewlish, co. Dorset; descended from MICHEL, of Kingston Russell, branches of which became allied with the BEAUCHAMPS, POLES, and other honourable houses in the West of England. The present representative is the Right Hon. Sir JOHN MICHEL, G.C.B., General commanding the Forces in Ireland). Quarterly, 1st, per chev. ar. and sa. three herons' heads erased counterchanged, for MICHEL; 2nd, az. a bend cotised betw. six crosses pattée or, for BINGHAM; 3rd, per pale ar. and az. in the dexter three palets sa., for TRENCHARD; 4th, gu. a maunch erm. *Crest*—A dexter cubit arm, vested, holding a crane's head erased all ppr. *Motto*—Nil conscire sibi.

Michelborne (Bradhurst and Stanmore, co. Sussex. Sir RICHARD MICHELBORNE, Knt., of Bradhurst and Stanmer, was Sheriff co. Surrey and Sussex 1620. His fourth son, ABRAHAM MICHELBORNE, Esq., settled at Kilcandra, co. Wicklow, and was father of Colonel JOHN MICHELBORNE, Governor of Londonderry, *d.* 1721). Or, a cross betw. four eagles displ. sa. *Crest*—A tiger or, mouth embrued ppr.

Michelborne (Ballyarthur, co. Wicklow; descended from ABRAHAM MICHELBORNE, Esq., of Kilcandra, same co., fourth son of Sir RICHARD MICHELBORNE, Knt., of Bradhurst, 1620. His son, Col. JOHN MICHELBORNE, *d.* 1721, was Governor of Londonderry; RACHAEL MICHELBORNE, sister and heir of RICHARD MICHELBORNE, Esq., of Ballyarthur, *m.* 1684, RICHARD SANDHAM, Esq., of Rushamore, co. Louth, and had two daus. co-heirs, viz., ELIZABETH SANDHAM, *m.* Rev. MICHAEL SYMES, Rector of Kilcommon, co. Wicklow; his heir general is EDWARD SYMES BAYLEY, Esq., of Ballyarthur; and MARY SANDHAM *m.* JOHN SYMES, Esq., of Hillbrook, brother of Rev. MICHAEL SYMES; his male representative is JOSEPH GLASCOTT SYMES, only son of the late JAMES SYMES, Esq., M.D., Kilkenny Fusiliers). Same *Arms* and *Crest,* a crescent for diff.

Michelborne (Sir EDWARD MICHELBORNE, knighted at Dublin by ROBERT, Earl of Essex, Lord Lieutenant, 5 Aug. 1599). Same *Arms* and *Crest.*

Michelfield. Ar. a cross engr. sa. guttée d'or.

Michelgood. Sa. a fesse betw. three dolphins naiant ar.

Michelgrove (co. Sussex). Quarterly, or and az. a falcon volant ar. *Crest*—A unicorn's head erased ar.

Michelgrove. Az. a goshawk ar.

Michell (Codicote and Standon, co. Hertford; the dau. of EDWARD MICHELL *m.* EDWARD GYLL, Esq., of Ansley, co. Hertford). Sa. a chev. ar. betw. three escallops ppr.

Michell (Truro and St. Columb, co. Cornwall; JOHN MICHELL and JAMES MICHELL, Visit. Cornw. 1620, sons of JAMES MICHELL, Esq., of Truro, the great-grandson of WILLIAM MICHELL, Esq., of St. Columb). Sa. an escallop betw. three birds' heads erased or.

Michell (Bodmin, co. Cornwall; PHILIP MICHELL, Visit. Cornw. 1620, son of GILBERT MICHELL, and grandson of RALPH MICHELL, both of same place). Sa. a falcon close in fess or, betw. two barrulets ar. in chief two falcons close of the second.

Michell (Truro, co. Cornwall). Ar. a chev. sa. betw. seven dragons' heads erased close to the head and erect vert, four in chief and three in base, in the mouth of each a cross crosslet fitchée gu. *Crest*—An arm in armour embowed, holding in the hand a sword with drops of blood falling from the blade all ppr.

Michell (Calne, co. Wilts). Ar. a chev. purp. betw. seven dragons' heads erased close to the head and erect vert, in each mouth a cross crosslet fitchée gu. four in chief and three in base. *Crest*—An arm couped at the elbow and erect ppr. holding in the hand a sword ar. hilt and pommel or, seven flames of fire issuing from the blade ppr. three from each side and one from the point. *Motto*—Crescat amicitia.

Michell (co. Wilts). Gu. on a chev. betw. three wings or, as many griffins' heads erased of the field. *Crest*—A dexter arm embowed in armour ppr. garnished or, grasping a broken spear gold.

Michell (Harlyn, co. Cornwall; acquired *temp.* Henry VII., by marriage with the heiress of Tregoyes; ELIZABETH, only dau. and heiress of HENRY MICHELL, Esq., of Harlyn, *m.* THOMAS PETER). Sa. an escallop betw. three griffins' heads or, erased gu. *Crest*—A pegasus flying.

Michell (Old Windsor, co. Berks; confirmed 7 April, 1581). Az. three leopards' faces or, langued gu. a chief embattled erm.

Michell (Lord Mayor of London, 1424 and 1436). Sa. a chev. or, betw. three escallops ar.

Michell, or Mihill (Hamworth and Hawston, co. Norfolk). Sa. a fesse betw. three lozenges erm. *Crest*—An arm embowed, habited in mail, holding in the hand all ppr. a cutlass ar. on the edge of the blade three spikes, hilt and pommel or.

Michell (Cannington, co. Somerset). Per chev. sa. and gu. a chev. betw. three swans ar.

Michell (Salcombe Regis and Seaside House, in Branscombe, co. Devon; Sir ISAAC HEARD, Garter King of Arms, *temp.* George III., was its representative). Same *Arms*.

Michell (Garmstreet, co. Somerset). Gu. a chev. betw. three swans ar.

Michell (Scotland). Sa. a fesse betw. three mascles or.

Michell (Stamerham and Horsham, co. Sussex; MARY CATHARINE, dau. and heiress of Rev. THEOBALD MICHELL, of Horsham, *m.* Sir BYSSHE SHELLEY, Bart.). Sa. a chev. betw. three escallops ar.

Michell (Houghton, co. Sussex). Same *Arms*, a mullet for diff.

Michell. Az. on a bend ar. a cross crosslet sa. on a chief of the second three escallops gu.; another, Az. a leopard's head erased or; another, Per pale ar. and sa. a fesse and in chief three trefoils slipped all counterchanged; another, Per pale az. and or, a lion ramp. counterchanged; another, Per chev. sa. and gu. three swans ar.; another, Az. a chev. betw. three merlions or; another, Sa. three greyhounds courant in pale ar. collared or.

Michell (Glassell, co. Kincardine, and Forcett Hall, co. York). Per chev. gu. and sa. a chev. betw. three swans ar. *Crest*—On a mount ppr. a swan ar. *Motto*—Ferar unus et idem.

Michelson. Quarterly, az. and gu. over all the sun in splendour or.

Michelstan, Michelston, or Michelstane. Sa. three annulets ar.

Michelston, or Michelstone. Gu. (another, sa.) three annulets ar.

Michelstowe (Michelstowe, co. Cornwall, extinct; the co-heiresses *m.* TREFFRY, of Fowey, and WALLACOMBE, of Devon). Sa. three wings ar. *Crest*—A banner displ. ar. thereon a cross gu. betw. four torteaux.

Mickerton. Az. three mitres or.

Micklethwait (*Viscount Micklethwait*, extinct 1733; descended from MICKLETHWAIT, of Ingbirchworth and Kim-

berworth, co. York). Chequy ar. and gu. a chief indented az. *Crest*—A griffin's head erased ppr. *Supporters*—Two horses erm. *Motto*—Favente Numine.

Micklethwait (Beeston and Faverham, co. Norfolk, and Iridge Place, co. Sussex; descended from JOHN MICKLE-THWAIT, Esq., of Beeston, sixth in descent from Sir WILLIAM MICKLETHWAIT, Knt., of Ingbirchworth and Kimberworth, co. York, ancestor of *Viscount Micklethwait*). Chequy ar. and gu. a chief indented az. *Crest*—A griffin's head ar. erased gu. gorged with a collar componée of the second and first. *Motto*—Favente Numine.

Micklethwait (PECKHAM-MICKLETHWAIT, Iridge Place, co. Sussex, bart., extinct 1853; SOTHERTON BRANTHWAYT MICKLETHWAIT, second son of NATHANIEL MICKLETHWAIT, Esq., of Beeston, assumed the additional surname of PECK-HAM by royal licence, 1824, and was created a bart., 1838, *d. s. p.*). Quarterly, 1st and 4th, chequy ar. and gu. a chief indented az. a crescent for diff., for MICKLETHWAIT; 2nd and 3rd, erm. a chief potent quarterly or and gu., for PECKHAM. *Crests*—1st, MICKLETHWAIT: A griffin's head ar. erased gu. gorged with a collar componée of the second and first; 2nd, PECKHAM: On a mount betw. two palm branches vert an ostrich or, in the beak a horseshoe az. *Motto*—Favente Numine, Regina servatur.

Micklethwait (Ardsley and Thornville, co. York; descended from BENJAMIN MICKLETHWAIT, Esq., of Ardsley, second son of WILLIAM MICKLETHWAIT, Esq., of Ingbirchworth and Kimberworth, 1655). Chequy ar. and gu. a chief indented az. *Crest*—A griffin's head ar. erased gu. gorged with a collar componée of the second and first.

Micklethwayt, or Micklethwaite (Swayne, co. York, and co. Lincoln; granted 1666). Same *Arms* and *Crest*. *Motto*—In cœlo spes mea est.

Mickleton (Crook Hall, co. Durham). Vert on a chev. ar. three trefoils slipped of the first.

Mico (London). Or, three Moors' heads couped in profile sa. wreathed round the temples ar. *Crest*—A hand issuing out of the clouds holding a sword erect ppr. hilt and pommel or, charged on the blade with a Moor's head ppr. the point embrued of the last.

Middlecote (co. Lincoln). Az. an eagle displ. erm. on a chief gu. three escallops or. *Crest*—A demi eagle displ. erm. ducally gorged or, holding in the beak an escallop gold.

Middlehurst (Middlehurst-in-Appleton, co. Chester, 1718; settled at Middlehurst before 1402). Ar. a pale potent betw. three mullets sa. *Crest*—A wolf's head erased ar.

Middlemore (Edgbaston, co. Warwick; the heiress of ROBERT MIDDLEMORE, Esq., of Edgbaston, *m.* 1719, JOHN GAGE, Esq., of Firle, co. Sussex). Per chev. ar. and sa. in chief two moorcocks ppr. *Crest*—In grass and flags a moor-cock all ppr.

Middlemore (Hazlewell and Hawkesley House, co. Worcester; a branch of MIDDLEMORE, of Edgbaston, descended from THOMAS MIDDLEMORE, Esq., of Hawkesley House during the civil war). Same *Arms*, &c.

Middlemore (Enfield, co. Middlesex). Ar. a chev. betw. three moorcocks sa. beaked and membered gu. *Crest*—A moorcock ppr. in grass and reeds.

Middlemore (arms impaled with THROGMORTON in a glass window in the Manor House of Chastleton, co. Oxford; Visit. Oxon, 1634). Per chev. ar. and sa. in chief two peacocks of the last.

Middleton (Middleton Hall, co. Westmorland; descended from THOMAS MIDDLETON, Esq., of Middleton Hall, *temp.* Edward III. The last male heir in the direct line, JOHN MIDDLETON, Esq., of Middleton, *temp.* Charles II., left two daus. his co-heiresses; BRIDGET, *m.* JOSHUA HEBLETHWAITE, Esq., of Dent, and MARY, *m.* JAMES CRAGG, Esq., of Dent. See MOORE, of Grimeshill). Ar. a saltire engr. sa. *Crest*—A hawk's head ar. beaked or.

Middleton (Leighton Hall, co. Lancaster, bart., extinct 1673; descended from Sir JEFFREY MIDDLETON, Knt., third son of JOHN MIDDLETON, Esq., of Middleton, *temp.* Richard II.; Sir GEORGE MIDDLETON, Knt., of Leighton, a distinguished partisan of Charles I., was created a bart. in 1642; his dau. and heiress, MARY, *m.* SOMERFORD OLD-FIELD, Esq., of Somerford, co. Chester). Same *Arms*, a mullet for diff.

Middleton (Warton, co. Lancaster; descended from ROBERT MIDDLETON, younger brother of Sir THOMAS MIDDLETON, of Leighton, first bart., who *m.* JANE, dau. and co-heiress of THOMAS KITSON, of Warton). Same *Arms*.

Middleton (Durham and Wintertown, co. Lincoln). Same *Arms*. *Crest*—A monkey pass. ringed round the loins or, on the trunk of a tree raguled all ppr.

Middleton, Baron. See WILLOUGHBY.

Middleton (Crowfield Hall, and Shrubland Hall, co. Suffolk, bart.). Ar. fretty sa. on a canton per chev. of the second and or, a unicorn's head likewise per chev. gu. and or, the horn of the last and sa. *Crest*—A garb or, banded vert betw. two wings sa. *Motto*—Regardez mon droit.

Middleton (co. Cambridge, and Stockeld, co. York). **Ar.** fretty sa. a canton of the last. *Crest*—A garb or, betw. two wings erect ar.

Middleton (Silksworth, co. Durham. Visit. 1615). Quarterly, gu. and or, in the 1st quarter a cross flory ar.

Middleton (Seaton, co. Durham. Visit. 1615). Same *Arms*, a mullet for diff.

Middleton (Unthank, co. Durham). Quarterly, or and gu. in the 1st quarter a cross crosslet of the second.

Middleton (Stansted, Mountiltchet, co. Essex, and Middleton, co. Salop). Same *Arms. Crest*—A wolf's head erased ppr.

Middleton (co. Essex). Ar. on a pile vert three wolves' heads couped of the field.

Middleton (co. Essex). Per fesse or and gu. a lion ramp. and a bordure indented all counterchanged.

Middleton (Belsay Castle, co. Northumberland; created a bart. 24 Oct. 1662). Quarterly, gu. and or, in the 1st quarter a cross patonce ar. *Crest*—A savage, in the dexter hand an oak tree erased and fructed all ppr. *Motto*—Lesses dire.

Middleton (Westerham, co. Kent; descended from MIDDLETON, of Belsay Castle, co. Northumberland; confirmed to DAVID MIDDLETON, Esq., of Westerham, co. Kent, by Segar, Garter, 17 Dec. 8 James I.). Quarterly, gu. and or, in the 1st quarter a cross patonce ar. *Crest*—A savage man wreathed about the head with leaves all ppr. in the dexter hand, extended on a scroll the motto, Servire Deo regnare est ; and resting the sinister hand on a club inverted or.

Middleton (co. Lancaster). Ar. on a saltire sa. a tower triple-towered of the field.

Middleton (Middleton Hall, co. Lancaster). Quarterly, gu. and or, a cross flory in the dexter quarter ar.

Middleton (Lord Mayor of London, 1613). Ar. on a bend vert three griffins' heads erased of the first.

Middleton (Abbot of Midgeley). Sa. three baskets full of bread ar.

Middleton (Middleton, co. Salop). Az. a buck's head cabossed or.

Middleton (Mendham, co. Suffolk). Sa. a fesse erm. betw. three crosses botonnée or.

Middleton (co. Suffolk). Ar. on a cross engr. sa. five garbs or,

Middleton (Newington, co. Surrey). Ar. on a saltire engr. sa. a tower triple-towered of the field. *Crest*—A monkey pass. ppr. ringed and lined or.

Middleton (Horsham and Boxgrove, co. Sussex. Visit. 1634). Ar. a saltire engr. sa. in chief a cinquefoil gu.

Middleton (co. York). Quarterly, gu. and or, in the dexter quarter a cross ar.

Middleton (co. York). Az. a fesse lozengy or, betw. three garbs ar.

Middleton (Leam, co. Derby; MARMADUKE MIDDLETON CARVER, of Leam, High Sheriff, 1808, assumed the name and arms of MIDDLETON, 1792). Erm. on a saltire engr. sa. an eagle's head erased or, quartering CARVER, viz., or upon a chev. betw. three crosses clechée sa. a fleur-de-lis betw. two stags' heads cabossed of the first. *Crests*—1st, for MIDDLETON: An eagle's head erased ar. charged on the neck with a saltire, as in the arms; 2nd, for CARVER: A mount vert, thereon a cross clechée or, charged in the centre with a fleur-de-lis sa. *Motto*—Conjunctio firmat. JOHN CARVER, eldest son of MARMADUKE-MIDDLETON CARVER, Esq., of Leam, by MARY ANNE, his wife, dau. of ROBERT ATHORPE, Esq., of Dini agton, co. York, assumed the name and arms of ATHORPE, and bore the following *Arms*: Quarterly, 1st and 4th, per pale nebulée az. and az. two mullets in fesse counterchanged, for ATHORPE; 2nd, MIDDLETON: 3rd, CARVER. *Crest*—Of ATHORPE: A falcon ppr. belled or, the dexter claw resting on an escutcheon per pale nebulée, and two mullets in fesse as in the arms; of MIDDLETON; and of CARVER.

Middleton (The Grove, co. Leicester). Ar. fretty sa. a canton of the second. *Crest*—A garb or, betw. two wings expanded sa.

Middleton (The Grove, Norwich; registered in the Herald's College to GEORGE MIDDLETON, Esq.). Ar. fretty az. on a pale of the last a garb betw. two wings erect ar. *Crest*—A garb surmounted by an estoile or, betw. two wings ar. fretty az. *Motto*—Meret qui laborat.

Middleton (BROKE-MIDDLETON, Bart., Broke Hall, co. Suffolk). Quarterly, 1st and 4th, ar. fretty sa. on a canton
684

per chev. of the second and or, a unicorn's head, likewise per chev. gu. and gold, the horn of the last and sa., for MIDDLETON; 2nd and 3rd, or, a cross engr. party per pale sa. and gu., for BROKE. *Crests*—1st, MIDDLETON: A garb erminois, banded vert, betw. two wings sa.; 2nd, BROKE, of honourable augmentation: Out of a naval crown or, a dexter arm embowed, encircled with a wreath of laurel ppr. and grasping a trident of the first; 3rd, BROKE (family): A brock or badger pass. ppr. *Motto*—Sævumque tridentem servamus.

Middleton-Wybrants. See WYBRANTS.

Middleton (Killhill, co. Kincardine). Per fesse or and gu. a lion ramp. counterchanged.

Middleton (*Earl of Middleton*, Scotland). Per fesse or and a lion gu. ramp. within a double tressure flory counterflory all counterchanged. *Crest*—Issuing out of a tower sa. a lion ramp. gu. *Supporters*—Two eagles volant sa. armed and beaked or. *Motto*—Fortis in arduis.

Middleton (Rector of Cricksey, co. Essex, 1672). Per fess or and gu. a lion ramp. of the first within a bordure indented of the second. *Crest*—A lion's paw grasping a branch of palm ppr. *Motto*—Sobrie, pie, juste.

Middleton (Seaton, co. Aberdeen, 1737). Per fess or and gu. a lion ramp. holding in his dexter paw a shakefork within a double tressure flory counterflory all counterchanged. *Crest*—Issuing out of a tower embattled sa. a lion ramp. ppr. *Mottoes*—Fortis in arduis ; and, Je n'oublierai pas.

Middleton (London, 1740). Per fess or and gu. a lion ramp. within a bordure engr. counterchanged. *Crest*—A falcon or, on a perch ppr. *Motto*—Diis bene juvantibus.

Middleton (Dr. PETER MIDDLETON, 1768). Per fess wavy or and gu. a lion ramp. within a bordure nebuly counterchanged. *Crest*—Issuing out of a tower sa. a demi lion gu. holding in his dexter paw a scymitar ppr. *Motto*—Fortis et fidus.

Middleton (Capt. ROBERT MIDDLETON, 1672). Per fess or and gu. a lion ramp. and a border embattled all counterchanged. *Crest*—A boar's head erect and erased az. *Motto*—Guard yourself.

Middleton (Clerkhill, Scotland). Same *Arms*, border nebulée. *Crest*—An ape sitting on the top of a tree all ppr. *Motto*—Arte et marte.

Middleton (Fraserburgh, co. Aberdeen, 1672). Per fess or and gu. a lion ramp. counterchanged, holding in the dexter paw an astrolabe ppr. *Motto*—My hope is in God.

Middleton (Glasgow, 1864). Per fess or and gu. a lion ramp. counterchanged within a bordure az. *Crest*—Issuing out of a tower sa. a lion ramp. gu. *Motto*—Fortis in arduis.

Middleton (granted by Carney, Principal Herald of Ireland during the usurpation of Oliver Cromwell, to HUGH MIDDLETON, commander of the "Ship Guist" under the Commonwealth, who was engaged at the sea fight off Dungeness, and twenty-three single fights against the Dutch, French, and Spaniards). Ar. on a chev. wavy az. betw. three lions' heads erased gu. a star or. *Crest*—Out of a naval crown or, a dexter hand ppr. pointing at a star gold.

Mideleho. Ar. a lion ramp. sa. a fesse counter-embattled az. and a border engr. gu.

Midelton, or Middleton (Stockeld, co. York ; descended from Sir PETER DE MIDELTON, Knt., *temp.* Edward II., son of WILLIAM DE MIDELTON, and AGNES, his wife, dau. of NIGEL BOTELER. The heiress, ELIZABETH, sister of WILLIAM MIDELTON, Esq., of Stockeld, who *d. s. p.* in 1763, *m.* Sir CARNABY HAGGERSTON, Bart. Visit. York, 1665). Ar. fretty sa. a canton of the second. *Crest*—A garb or, betw. two wings ar.

Midford (co. Durham). Ar. a fesse betw. three moles sa. *Crest*—An owl ar.

Midgeley (Midgeley and Clayton, co. York). Sa. two bars gemel or, on a chief of the second three caltraps of the first. *Crest*—Two keys in saltire az. wards down.

Midgley (Rochdale, co. Lancaster). Same *Arms. Crest*—a tiger sejant ppr. holding in his dexter paw a caltrap sa.

Midgley (Scholes Moor, Bradford, co. Lancaster; arms on a monument in Bradford Church). Same *Arms*.

Midlame. Ar. a lion ramp sa. crowned gu.

Midland. Bendy of six gu. and or.

Midleham. Or, a chief indented az. *Crest*—On a chepeau vert, turned up or, a wivern, wings expanded ar.

Midleham. Or, on a chief indented az. a lion pass. of the field.

Midlemore. Az. on a chev. engr. or, betw. three fleurs-delis ar. as many rooks sa.

Midlemore. Erm. on a canton sa. a pheon ar.

Midlesive. Ar. a lion ramp. sa. crowned or, over all a fesse counter-componée of the third and az.

Midleton, Viscount. See BRODRICK.

Midleton (co. Denbigh). Ar. on a bend vert three wolves' heads erased of the field.

Midleton (Barnard Castle, co. Durham. Visit. 1615). Ar. a saltire engr. sa. an annulet for diff.

Midleton (co. Kent). Az. three cinquefoils **ar. a bordure of** the last.

Midleton (co. Salop). Vert a chev. betw. **three wolves'** heads erased ar.

Midleton. Az. a buck's head cabossed or.

Midleton. Erm! on a canton gu. a chev. or.

Midwinter (co Devon). Per fesse indented or and sa. three martlets counterchanged. *Crest*—A dexter arm embowed per pale sa. and or, holding in the hand ppr. a plume of feathers, two sa. one or.

Might (Fun. Ent. Ulster's Office, 1621, the wife of HENRY MIGHT, Esq.). Az. two annulets in fess interlaced or, betw. three eagles' legs erased **à** la quise of the last.

Mignot (granted to DAVID MIGNOT, M.D., of Kensington Crescent). Or, a chev. betw. nine links of a chain, each division consisting of three links sa. on a chief gu. a large diamond set in the midst of a triangle within a double row of brilliants ppr. *Crest*—A diamond set triangularly, as in the arms.

Mihil (Reg. Ulster's Office). Az. a lion's head cabossed or.

Mikieson (Hill, Scotland, 1693). Ar. a duck ppr. on a chief dancettée gu. a boar's head couped betw. two crescents or. *Crest*—A decrescent ppr. *Motto*—Ut implear.

Milbanke (Halnaby, co. York, bart.). Gu. a bend erm. on a canton or, a lion's head erased of the first. *Crest*—A lion's head erased gu. charged with a bend erm. *Motto*—Resolute and firm.

Milbanke (Thorp Perrow, co. York; descended from JOHN MILBANKE, Esq., of Thorpe Perrow, fourth son of Sir MARK MILBANKE, of Halnaby). Same *Arms, Crest,* and *Motto*.

Milbanke-Huskisson, Bart. See HUSKISSON.

Milbanke (*Baron Wentworth*). Quarterly, 1st and 4th, gu. a bend erm. on a canton or, a lion's head erased of the first, for MILBANKE; 2nd and 3rd, sa. three spears' heads erect ar. imbrued ppr. on a chief or, three poleaxes az., for KING. *Crests*—1st, MILBANKE: A lion's head couped gu. charged with a bend erm.; 2nd, KING: A dexter arm couped, vested az. cuff sa. the arm charged with three arm. spots in fesse or, in the hand a truncheon sa. headed ar. *Supporters*—On either side a gryphon ar. gorged with a collar per pale gu. and az. *Motto*—Pensez à bien.

Milborne (co. Derby, Dunmow and Markes, **co.** Essex, Tylington, co. Hereford, and co. Stafford). **Gu. a** chev. betw. three escallops ar.

Milborne (Lord Mayor of London, 1521). Sa. on a bend betw. two leopards' faces or, three crosses formée of the field, on a chief of the second as many escallops of the first.

Milborne (London). Sa. two leopards' faces in bend ar. betw. three crosses formée az. on a chief or, as many escallops gu.

Milborne (Alderman of London, 1535; Founder of the Almshouses in Crutched Friars). Sa. on a bend betw. two leopards' faces or, three crosses pattée sa. on a chief ar. as many escallops of the field.

Milborne (Suffolk). Same *Arms* and *Crest*.

Milborne, or Milbourne. Per pale or and gu. a fesse betw. three leopards' faces all counterchanged.

Milborne. Ar. a crescent sa. a bordure of the last; another, Quarterly, or and gu. a fesse betw. three leopards' faces all counterchanged; another, Az. a fret erm.; another, Ar. a fer-de-moline sa.; another, Ar. a cross moline pierced gu.; another, Az. two shin bones in saltire ar.; another, Ar. a cross moline pierced quatrefoil-like sa.; another, Gu. a chev. erm. betw. three escallops ar.

Milbourne (Armathwaite Castle, co. Cumberland). Sa. a chev. betw. three escallops ar. *Crest*—A griffin's head erased.

Milbourneport, Town of (co. Somerset). A lion pass. guard.

Milburn (co. Lancaster). Quarterly, or and gu. in the 1st and 4th quarters a crescent **sa.** *Crest*—A bear's head erased sa. muzzled or.

Milford. Or, an orle gu.

Milcham (co. Norfolk). Erm. on a chief **az.** three trefoils slipped or. *Crest*—A griffin's head ppr.

Milcombe. Or (another, ar.) a fret sa. (another, fretty of six), on a chief of the second a fess gold.

Milde (co. Suffolk). Ar. a lion ramp. sa. a fesse counter-componée or and az.

Mildmar. Az. (another, sa.) three lions ramp. ar. enraged **gu.**

685

Mildmar. Ar. three lions ramp. az.

Mildmay (Moulsham Hall, co. Essex, bart., extinct 1626). Ar. three lions ramp. az. armed and langued gu. *Crest*—A lion ramp. guard. az. armed and langued gu.

Mildmay (*Earl and Baron Fitz Walter ;* earldom extinct 1756, barony in abeyance; Sir THOMAS MILDMAY, Knt., of Moulsham, m. Lady FRANCES RATCLIFFE, dau. of HENRY, third *Lord Fitz Walter,* and second *Earl of Sussex ;* the great-grandson of this marriage was summoned to Parliament in the barony of FITZ-WALTER, 1670). Same *Arms,* quartering, ar. a bend engr. sa., for RATCLIFFE. *Crest*—A lion ramp. guard. az. *Supporters*—Two lions guard. az. each crowned with a chapeau gu. turned up erm. *Motto*—Alla ta hara.

Mildmay (The Graces, co. Essex). Same *Arms. Crest*—A lion ramp. guard. az.

Mildmay (Danbury, co. Essex, and Apthorp, co. Northampton). Same *Arms. Crest*—A leopard's head erased or, ducally gorged gu. ringed and lined of the last, on the neck beneath the coronet three pellets.

Mildmay (ST. JOHN-MILDMAY, Moulsham Hall, Essex, bart. ; Sir HENRY PAULET ST. JOHN, Bart., m. JANE, dau. and co-heir of CAREN MILDMAY, Esq., and assumed the surname and arms of MILDMAY). Quarterly, 1st and 4th, ar. three lions ramp. az. armed and langued gu., for MILDMAY; 2nd and 2nd, ar. on a chief gu. two mullets or. *Crest*—A lion ramp. guard. az. armed and langued gu. *Supporters*—Dexter, a greyhound ar. ducally gorged and chained or; sinister, a falcon, wings expanded or, ducally gorged and belled gu. *Motto*—Alla ta hara.

Mildmay (Shoreham Place, co. Kent). Same *Arms, Crest,* and *Motto.*

Mildmay (co. Essex; granted 20 May, 1552). Az. on a bend ar. a pegasus sa. in full speed. *Crest*—A demi stag saliant ppr. attired and collared or, wings endorsed ar.

Mildmay (co. Essex). Per fesse nebulée ar. and sa. three greyhounds' heads couped counterchanged, collared gu. studded or.

Mildred. Sa. a chev. wavy erm. betw. three mullets pierced or. *Crest*—A bear pass. struck through with the head of a broken spear in bend ppr.

Mileham (Burmingham, co. Norfolk). Sa. a fesse betw. three griffins' heads erased or. *Crest* A griffin's head erased or.

Miles (Narborough, co. Leicester). Az. on a chev. engr. betw. three knights' helmets or, as many millrinds sa. *Crest* —An eagle rising erminois collared, therefrom a chain reflexed over the back, and charged on the breast with a millrind sa.

Miles (Leigh Court, co. Somerset, bart.). Az. a chev. erm. betw. three mascles, ar. each charged with a fleur-de-lis **sa.** *Crest*—A dexter arm embowed in armour ppr. garnished or, supporting with the hand an anchor also ppr.

Miles (Cuddington). Erm. a millrind sa. a chief vert.

Miles. Gu. two bends or. *Crest*—A demi lion supporting an anchor all ppr.

Miles (Kingsweston, co. Gloucester). Az. a chev. erm. betw. three mascles ar. each charged with a fleur-de-lis sa. *Crest* —A dexter arm embowed in armour ppr. garnished or, supporting with the hand an anchor also ppr.

Miles (granted by Betham, Ulster, to Lieut.-Col. EDWARD MILES, C.B., son of EDWARD MILES, of Rochestown and Ballylaffin, co. Tipperary). Gu. betw. two bendlets erminois a sword ppr. the hilt in chief or. *Crest*—Out of a ducal coronet or, charged on the rim with three bombs fired ppr. a lion's head az. ensigned with a mural crown ar. and gorged with a laurel wreath gold. *Motto*—Sola virtus invicta.

Mileson (Esthathesley, co. York). Ar. on an inescutcheon sa. betw. three crosses formée fitchée of the last, each pointing to the centre of the field a cross or. *Crest*—A tiger's head sa. tufted, tusked, collared, and lined or.

Milford (Wickington, co. Devon; settled there long before Visit. 1620). Ar. there oak leaves in pale all ppr.

Milford (SAMUEL FREDERICK MILFORD, Esq.). Gu. an inescutcheon ar. a border of the last. *Crest*—A griffin sejant, wings elevated.

Milford. Same *Arms. Crest*—A lion's gamb holding a trefoil ppr.

Military Society. Gu. a regal crown ppr. on a chief ar. the cross of St. George of the first. *Crest*—On a prince's coronet or, a dexter arm in armour erect, holding in the gauntlet a tilting spear, thereon a banner charged with the motto "Ich dien," all ppr. fringed, lined, and tasselled of the first. *Supporters*—Two war horses completely accoutred, on the head a skull plate, with a spike in each armour for the neck, &c., all ppr. on each head a plume of three feathers.

Militon (Pengersick, co. Cornwall descended from co.

Devon, extinct *temp.* Queen Elizabeth; the co-heiresses *m.* I. ERISEY and PARKER; II. LANYON; III. TREFUSIS and TREGO-DICK; IV. TRENWITH, ARUNDELL and HEARLE; V. BONITHON; and VI. ABBOT). Gu. a chev. or, betw. three fishes naiant ar.

Milketfield. Ar. a cross engr. gu. (another, sa.) guttée d'or.

Mill (Camois Court, co. Essex, and Mottisfont, co. Hants, bart., extinct 1835). Per fesse ar. and sa. a pale counterchanged, three bears saliant of the second, muzzled and chained or. *Crest*—A demi bear, as in the arms. *Motto*—Aides Dieu.

Mill (Mottisfont, co. Hants, bart., extinct 1860; Rev. JOHN BARKER, son of JOHN BARKER, Esq., of Wareham, co. Dorset, by MARY MILL, his wife, only sister of Sir CHARLES MILL, tenth and last bart. of Camois Court, assumed the surname and arms of MILL by royal licence, 1835, and was created a bart. 1636). Same *Arms, Crest,* and *Motto.*

Mill (Hampton, co. Kent; granted 25 Henry VIII.). Per fesse sa. and ar. a pale counterchanged, three bears ramp. of the second, muzzled, ringed, and lined or, betw. as many foxes' heads erased ppr. *Crest*—A demi bear saliant sa. muzzled, ringed, and lined or, charged on the shoulder with three gouttes d'or.

Mill, or Milles (cos. Gloucester and Surrey). Erm. an ink moline sa.

Mill (Pulberche, co. Sussex). Per fesse sa. and ar. a pale counterchanged, three bears ramp. of the second, muzzled, ringed, and lined or, collared gu. *Crest*—A demi bear saliant sa. muzzled, ringed, and lined or.

Mill (granted 3 July, 1684). Ar. a chev. betw. three crosses moline sa. *Crest*—An eagle's head erased gu. beaked or, holding a cross moline erect sa.

Mill. Or, a cross moline betw. three mullets sa. *Crest*—A greyhound's head erased.

Mill (HUMPHREY MILL, of the city of Dublin, lieut. of a troop of horse, third son of EDWARD MILL, Esq., of Hascombe Court, co. Gloucester; descended from a very ancient family of that name; confirmed by Roberts, Ulster, 1647). Erm. a fer-de-moline pierced sa. in the dexter chief point a swan of the last. *Crest*—A demi lion ramp. guard. gu. holding in the dexter paw an arming sword ppr. *Motto*—Gladium musarum nutrix.

Mill (Fun. Ent. Ulster's Office, 1687, MARY, wife of STANHOPE MILL, Esq.). Erm. a millrind pierced paleways sa.

Mill (Scotland). See MILNE.

Millais (Jersey, and Cromwell Place, South Kensington). Per bend or and az. a star of eight points counterchanged. *Crest*—A hand gauntleted and apaumée in pale gu.

Millais (Kingston, co. Surrey). Same *Arms,* quartering, 1st, az. a passion cross ar. surmounted of an eastern crown or, for LE JARDERAY; 2nd, or, an orle az., for BERTRAM: 3rd, ar. a palm tree ppr., for PALLOT; 4th, ar. a cock statant ppr., for FAULTRART; 5th, ar. a cross sa. betw. a Maltese cross gu. in the 1st and 4th quarters, and a tent of the same in the 2nd and 3rd, for BAUDOUIN; 6th, ar. on a chev. sa. betw. three mullets gu. four eagles of the field, for MORICE DE LA RIPANDIERE; 7th, erm. a lion ramp. gu., for LE GRYT. *Crest*—A hand gauntleted and apaumée in pale gu.

Millar. Ar. a cross moline gu. *Crest*—Three ears of wheat issuing or. *Another Crest*—A dexter hand holding an open book ppr. *Motto*—Felicem reddet religio.

Millar (JAMES OGILVY MILLAR, LL.D., Vicar of Cirencester, 1873). Ar. a cross moline gu. in chief a lion ramp. guard. of the second, imperially crowned or, betw. two lozenges also of the second. *Crest*—The half-length figure of a lady affrontée, vested az. holding before her a portcullis gu. *Motto*—Keep tryst and trust.

Millard (co. Hants, 1634). Az. four mascles in cross or. *Crest*—A demi lion ramp. az. holding betw. the paws a mascle or.

Millard. Sa. two chevronels erm. *Crest*—On a mount vert a stag browsing ppr.

Millbank. Gu. a bend erm. on a canton or, a lion's head erased sa. *Crest*—A mount vert.

Millburn. Quarterly, or and gu. a fesse betw. three leopards' faces all counterchanged. *Crest*—Out of a ducal coronet a demi lion all ppr.

Mille. Paly of six ar. and az. three bars sa.

Millecent (Barkham Hall, co. Cambridge). Or, a chev. sa. betw. three fleurs-de-lis az.

Millenchop (impalement Fun. Ent. Ulster's Office, 1637, JANE, dau. of JOHN MILLES, Sheriff of Dublin, *m.* first, BLIKE; second, MILLENCHOP; and third, ARDAGH). Ar. a fret gu. on a chief sa. a lion pass. guard. or.

Millenton. Az. on three millstones ar. as many millrinds sa.

Miller (Chichester, co. Sussex, bart.; granted by Dugdale, Garter, 1684). Ar. a fesse wavy az. betw. three wolves' heads erased gu. *Crest*—A wolf's head erased ar. gorged with a collar wavy az.

Miller (Plumpton, co. Cumberland). Erm. three wolves' heads erased az. vulned gu. *Crest*—A caltrap or, the upper point embrued ppr.

Miller (Dunstable, co. Bedford; granted 1765). Per fesse ar. and az. in chief two wolves' heads erased purp. collared or, in base a lion pass. of the last. *Crest*—A wolf's head erased per pale erm. and purp. collared or.

Miller (Collier's Wood, co. Surrey; BOYD DARBY, Esq., assumed the surname of MILLER by royal licence, 1800). Same *Arms, Crest,* and *Motto.*

Miller (co. Surrey; allowed at the Visit. of that co., 1662, and borne by JOHN FRANCIS MILLER, Esq., of Timberham, in the parish of Charlwood, and afterwards of Werndean Hall, Norwood). Erm. a fess gu. betw. three wolves' heads erased az. *Crest*—A wolf's head erased az. collared erm. *Motto*—Mea spes est in Deo.

Miller (co. Devon, and Islington, co. Middlesex), Az. an escutcheon betw. four mascles or. *Crest*—A demi lion ramp. guard. az. holding a mascle or.

Miller (Preston, co. Lancaster; granted to THOMAS MILLER, Esq., of Winckley Square, in that town). Per pale or and gu. a fess dancettée betw. three wolves' heads erased counterchanged. *Crest*—A wolf's head erased bendy or and gu. in the mouth a ragged staff sa. *Motto*—Sibimet merces industria.

Miller (Cawne, Frome, Kingston, and Leigh, co. Dorset, and co. Hants). Az. four mascles in cross or. *Crest*—A demi lion az. holding betw. the paws a mascle or.

Miller (Radway, co. Warwick). Same *Arms* and *Crest.*

Miller (co. Dorset). Vert a chev. betw. three rams ar.

Miller (Oxenhoath, co. Kent, bart., extinct 1714; descended from NICHOLAS MILLER, Esq., of Horsnells Crouch in Wrotham, Sheriff of Kent, 8 Charles I.). Erm. a fesse az. betw. three wolves' heads erased az. *Crest*—A wolf's head erased az. collared erm.

Miller (London). Az. a cross ar. betw. four mascles or.

Miller (granted 16 May, 1672). Ar. a double tressure flory counterflory, over all a fesse embattled counter-embattled gu.

Miller (granted by Camden). Erm. three wolves' heads erased az.

Miller. Per fesse ar. and az. in chief two wolves' heads erased purp. collared or, and in base a lion pass. of the last. *Crest*—A wolf's head erased per pale or and purp. collared gold.

Miller. Erm. three wolves' heads erased gu. *Crest*—A cheval-trap or, the uppermost point embrued gu.

Miller (granted in 1821 to THOMAS MILLER, Esq., of Preston, co. Lancaster, Mayor of that borough in 1827). Az. on a fesse ar. betw. two bees volant in chief ppr. and in base a wolf's head couped or, a wheelshuttle in fesse also ppr. *Crest*—A demi wolf erm. gorged with a collar gobony ar. and az. supporting with the paw a spindle erect ppr.

Miller (Ballycasey, co. Clare). Ar. a fesse wavy az. betw. three griffins' heads erased gu. *Crest*—A griffin's head erased ar. ducally gorged and chained az.

Miller (Downpatrick, co. Down; confirmed to ALEXANDER MILLER, Esq., grandson of ROBERT MILLER, Esq., of Coleraine, by MARY ANNE, his wife, dau. and co-heiress of WILLIAM GAMBLE, Esq., of Derry, and their descendants). Quarterly, 1st and 4th, erm. a tower ppr. betw. three wolves' heads erased az., for MILLER; 2nd and 3rd, gu. a fleur-de-lis or, on a chief ar. three roses of the field stalked and leaved vert, for GAMBLE. *Crest*—A wolf's head erased az. charged with a rose or. *Motto*—Nil conscire sibi.

Miller (BOWEN-MILLER, Milford, co. Mayo; exemplified to CROASDAILE BOWEN, Esq., on his assuming, by royal licence, 1812, the additional surname and arms of MILLER, in compliance with the will of his maternal uncle, Brig.-Gen. CHARLES MILLER, of Milford). Quarterly, 1st and 4th, erm. three wolves' heads erased az.; 2nd and 3rd, gu. a stag trippant ar. pierced in the back with an arrow and attired or. *Crests*—1st: A wolf's head erased as in the arms, for MILLER; 2nd: A falcon, wings close ppr. belled or, for BOWEN. *Motto*—Esse quam videri.

Miller (Scotland). Ar. a cross moline az.; another, Ar. a cross moline betw. four hearts gu.

Miller (Gourlebank, Scotland). Ar. a cross moline az. placed in a loch ppr. and in chief two mullets of the second. *Crest*—Two arms, their hands joined ppr. *Motto*—Unione augetur.

Miller (Glenlee, co. Kirkcudbright, bart., 1788). Ar. a cross moline az. the base wavy vert, in chief a lozenge betw two mullets of the second. *Crest*—A dexter hand with the first and second fingers pointing upwards ppr. *Supporters*—Two roebucks ppr. *Motto*—Manent optima cœlo.

Miller (Manchester, from Scotland, 1784). Ar. a cross moline betw. three stars az. a bordure gu. *Crest*—A dexter hand with the forefinger pointing upwards ppr. *Motto*—Manent optima cœlo.

Miller (Minister of Cumnock, 1814). Sa. a cross moline ar. a chief of the last. *Crest*—A dexter hand with the first and second fingers pointing upwards ppr. *Motto*—Spei bonæ atque animæ.

Miller (Manderston, co. Berwick, bart., 1854). Ar. a cross moline az. square pieced of the field, on a chief gu. a garb betw. two mullets or. *Crest*—A dexter hand erect with the first and second fingers pointing upwards issuing out of a cloud ppr. *Motto*—Omne bonum superne.

Miller (St. Petersburgh, 1853). Or, a cross moline az. square pierced of the field, a bordure gu. on a chief of the last a garb betw. two mullets or. *Crest and Motto*, as the last.

Miller (Leith, 1853). Or, a cross moline az. square pierced of the field, a bordure engr. erm. on a chief gu. a garb betw. two mullets or. Same *Crest and Motto*.

Miller (Craigentinny, co. Edinburgh, 1859). Ar. a cross moline az. charged with five lozenges or. *Crest*—A dexter hand erect holding an open book ppr. *Motto*—Manent optima cœlo.

Miller (CHRYSTIE-MILLER, of Cragentinny, 1868). Quarterly, 1st and 4th grand quarters counter-quartered, 1st and 4th, ar. a cross moline az., for MILLER, 2nd, ar. a mullet pierced az. betw. three cross crosslets fitchée gu., for ADAM, 3rd, per fess az. and sa. a castle with four towers ar. porch open and windows of the second, for RAWSON; 2nd and 3rd grand quarters, or, a saltire engr. betw. two mullets in chief and base and two roses in flank sa., for CHRYSTIE. *Crest and Motto*, for MILLER, as the last; for CHRYSTIE: A holly stump withered sprouting out leaves ppr. *Motto*—Sic viresco.

Miller (Leithen, co. Peebles, 1864). Ar. a cross moline az. square pieced of the field betw. four hearts gu. *Crest*—A dexter hand with one finger pointing upwards ppr. *Motto*—In cœlo spero.

Miller (Pittendreich, co. Forfar, 1864). Ar. a cross moline square pieced of the field betw. two helmets ppr. in chief and as many cross crosslets of the second in base. *Crest*—A dexter hand with one finger pointing upwards ppr. *Motto*—Manent optima cœlo.

Millerd (Rathcormuck, co. Cork; descended from Rev. JOHN MILLERD, who removed into that kingdom from co. Hereford in 1654, at the special invitation of Cromwell's Commissioners, and became Rector of Passage, co. Waterford; confirmed to CHARLES HUGH MILLERD, Esq., of Rathcormuck, co. Cork, and the descendants of his grandfather, Rev. THOMAS MILLERD, of Glintown, co. Cork). Erm. a fess az. betw. three wolfs' heads erased sa. *Crest*—Out of a baron's coronet ppr. a griffin's head couped gu. holding in the mouth a rose branch ppr. *Motto*—Per mille ardua.

Millerd (Glintown, co. Cork and Monard, same co.; allowed and Ped. Reg. by Betham, Ulster, 1815). Quarterly, 1st and 4th, same *Arms*; 2nd and 3rd, sa. a cinquefoil ar. betw. three leopards' heads erased and affrontée or. *Crest*—Out of a baron's coronet ppr. a griffin's head gu. holding in the beak a rose branch all ppr. *Motto*—Per mille ardua.

Milles (*Baron Sondes*). Erm. a fer-de-moline betw. two martlets in pale sa. on a chief engr. az. two marlions' wings conjoined or. *Crest*—A lion ramp. erminois, holding betw. the paws a fer-de-moline, as in the arms. *Supporters*—Dexter, a griffin ar. ducally gorged or; sinister, a bear ppr. collared with a belt, buckled, the strap pendent ar. charged with two crescents or, the buckle and edges of the last. *Motto*—Esto quod esse videris.

Milles, or Mills (Shelford, co. Cambridge). Barry of ten or and az.

Milles (co. Cornwall). Per fesse sa. and ar. a pale and six bars counterchanged.

Milles (Duloe, co. Cornwall, and Exeter). Ar. a chev. betw. three millrinds sa.

Milles (Nackington, co. Kent, and North Elmham, co. Norfolk). Erm. a millrind sa. betw. two martlets in pale gu. on a chief az. two wings conjoined and expanded or. *Crest*—A lion ramp. or, holding in the paws a millrind sa.

Milles (co. Suffolk). Ar. a chev. betw. three millrinds sa. *Crest*—A hare sejant ppr. in the mouth three ears of wheat or.

Milles. Paly of eight ar. and sa. *Crest*—A bear pass. sa. muzzled and chained or.

Milles. Barry of ten ar. and vert, over all six escutcheons gu. three, two, and one. *Crest*—A cat sejant ppr.

Milles (Clondalkin, co. Dublin; Fun. Ent. 1675, JOHN MILLES). Erm. a pale masculy sa.

Milles. Az. two ducks in pale ar. betw. as many flaunches erm.

Milles. Per fesse ar. and az. on a pale counterchanged three bears ramp. sa. muzzled, collared, and lined or, as many falcons of the last, collared gu. *Crest*—A demi bear sa. muzzled, collared, and stringed or.

Milles (Fun. Ent. Ulster's Office, 1601, JOHN MILLES, Sheriff of Dublin, buried in Christ's Church). Gu. on a bend ar. a millrind sa. betw. two roses of the first.

Milles (THOMAS MILLES, Bishop of Waterford and Lismore, 1710). Ar. a chev. betw. three millrinds sa.

Millet. Gu. a cinquefoil pierced ar.

Milleton (co. Cornwall). Gu. a chev. betw. three salmons naiant ar.

Millett (Denham, co. Buckingham, and co. Middlesex). Ar. a fesse gu. betw. three dragons' heads erased vert. *Crest*—Out of a mural coronet an arm in pale, habited or, grasping in a glove ar. a dragon's head erased vert.

Millett (Hayes Court, co. Kent). Az. a fess dancettée (another, a lion pass. guard.) betw. three birds or.

Milley (Rev. NICHOLAS MILLEY, Vicar of Dunleckney and Agha, co. Carlow, formerly Chaplain of a regt. of dragoons commanded by RICHARD, second *Viscount Molesworth*, son of THOMAS MILLEY, who came from France; confirmed by Hawkins, Ulster, 1733). Az. a chev. or, surmounted of another gu. betw. three estoiles of the second. *Crest* (granted at same time)—The Holy Bible az. charged on the cover with a fleur-de-lis ar.

Millicent. Or, a chev. sa. betw. three fleurs-de-lis az.

Millicent (Linton, co. Cambridge; JOHN, son and heir of THOMAS MYLSENT, m. ELIZABETH, eldest dau. of JOHN GYLL, Esq., of Wyddial, co. Hertford). Or, a chev. sa. betw. three fleurs-de-lis az.

Milliken (that Ilk, co. Renfrew, Scotland; heiress m. Gen. WILLIAM NAPIER, of Culcreuch). Ar. three demi lions ramp. gu. issuing out of two bars wavy az. two out of the upper and one out of the under bar. *Crest*—A demi lion ramp. gu. *Motto*—Regarde bien.

Millington (Millington, co. Chester; the heiress m. Sir JOHN THOROLD, Bart., 1796). Quarterly, 1st and 4th, az. three millstones ar.; 2nd and 3rd, an eagle displ. az.

Millington (co. Essex). Ar. an eagle displ. with two heads sa.

Millington (co. Chester). Ar. on a cross engr. az. five garbs or.

Millington (co. Devon). Gu. a chev. betw. there fishes naiant ar.

Millington (co. Dorset). Gu. a chev. betw. three mullets ar. (another, or).

Millington (co. Suffolk). Ar. a fesse betw. two chevronels gu.

Millington. Sa. a cross patonce betw. four escallops ar. *Crest*—An ass's head ppr.

Millman. Az. three sinister gauntlets ar. *Crest*—A sinister gauntlet or.

Millman. Same *Arms*. *Crest*—A stag lodged per pale ar. and or, attired and hoofed of the last, charged on the body with two hurts in fesse.

Millner (Nun-Appleton, co. York). Per pale or and sa. a chev. betw. three bits counterchanged. *Crest*—A horse's head sa. crined and bridled or, charged on the neck with a bezant.

Millot (Whitehill, co. Durham. Visit. 1615). Ar. three billets in fess betw. two bars gu. *Crest*—A dexter arm embowed in armour, gauntleted all ppr. grasping a billet sa.

Millot (co. Durham). Ar. three billets sa. in fess betw. two bars gemels gu.

Millot (co. Chester). Az. three billets in fesse betw. two bars gemels ar.

Mills (Bisterne, co. Hants). Gyronny of six ar. and az. a millrind sa. *Crest*—A demi lion reguard. or, gorged with a collar gemel az. betw. the paws a millrind sa. *Motto*—Nil conscire sibi.

Mills (Hillingdon Court, and Camelford House, Park Lane, London, bart.). Gyronny of six ar. and az. a millrind sa. *Crest*—A demi lion reguard. or, gorged with a collar gemel az. betw. the paws a millrind sa. *Motto*—Nil conscire sibi.

Mills (Casnalbery, co. Hertford, and co. Bedford; granted Nov. 1613). Barry of ten ar. and vert, over all six escutcheons gu. three, two, and one. *Crest*—A wing barry of ten ar. and vert.

Mills, or Mylles (Knightington, co. Berks). Erm. a millrind sa. a chief or. *Crest*—A lion ramp. or, holding in the mouth a sinister hand gu.

Mills (Lexden Park, Colchester, co. Essex; granted 4 Jan.

1800). Az. a cross pattée betw. four mullets or, each charged with a pellet. *Crest*—A hurt charged with an estoile or.

Mills (co. Essex). Gyronny of eight ar. and az. a millrind sa. *Crest*—A demi lion ramp. reguard. or, holding betw. the paws a millrind sa.

Mills (Saxham Hall, co. Suffolk). Erm. a fer-de-moline sa. *Crest*—A lion ramp. or. *Motto*—Confido.

Mills (Harscomb, co. Gloucester, and Croydon, co. Surrey). Erm. a millrind sa. *Crest*—A lion ramp. or.

Mills. Same *Arms*. *Crest*—A demi lion ramp. or, holding in the paws a millrind sa.

Mills (Bitterne, co. Hants, *temp.* Queen Elizabeth). Paly of six ar. and sa. over all on a fesse gu. three mullets or. *Crest*—On a mural coronet gu. an escallop ar.

Mills (Tolmers, co. Herts). Erm. a millrind sa., quartering 1st, ar. six lions, three, two, and one sa.; 2nd, az. a mullet pierced ar.; 3rd, per chev. or and az. three mullets counterchanged. *Crest*—A lion ramp. or. *Motto*—Deo adjuvante.

Mills (Norton Court, co. Kent). Erm. a millrind sa. on a chief az. two marlions' wings or. *Crest*—On a chapeau gu. turned up erm. a millrind sa. betw. two marlions' wings of the second.

Mills (co. Middlesex). Erm. a millrind sa. *Crest*—On a ducal coronet a lion ramp. gu. *Motto*—Honor virtutis pretium.

Mills (Clermont Lodge, co. Norfolk). Erm. a millrind in pale sa. *Crest*—A lion ramp. or. *Motto*—Deo adjuvante.

Mills (London; descended from co. Cornwall). Az. a millrind in fesse or. *Crest*—A paschal lamb pass. ar. unguled or, bearing on the dexter shoulder a banner of St. George double pennoned.

Mills (co. Suffolk). Paly of six ar. and sa. *Crest*—A demi bear ramp. sa. muzzled, collared, and chained or.

Mills (Reg. Ulster's Office). Az. two swans in pale ar. betw. as many flaunches erm.

Mills. Az. a cross pattée pierced betw. two mullets pierced or. *Crest*—On a hurt an estoile pierced or.

Mills. Erm. a millrind sa. pierced of the field. *Crest*—On a ducal coronet or, a lion ramp. gu.

Mills, or Meyles. Ar. a bend betw. two lions' heads erased sa.

Milltown, Earl of. See LEESON.

Millward. Or, on a pale sa. betw. two pellets in chief an eagle displ. of the field. *Crest*—A dexter arm in armour embowed, brandishing a sabre ppr.

Milman (Levaton, co. Devon, bart.). Az. a snake nowed or, betw. three dexter gauntlets open ar. *Crest*—A hart lodged per pale erm. and erminois, attired and unguled or, charged on the body with two hurts fesseways. *Motto*—Deus nobiscum quis contra?

Milman-Mainwaring. See MAINWARING.

Milne (bart.; Sir ALEXANDER MILNE, G.C.B., Admiral R.N., was created a bart. 1876). Erminois a cross moline quarterly pierced or, betw. three mullets az. a chief of honourable augmentation wavy ar. thereon a fortified circular lighthouse with a red flag flying, flanked on the dexter by a hexagon battery of three tiers of guns with a like flag flying, and on the sinister by another battery of two tiers of guns connected by a wall with the lighthouse all ppr., the whole intended to represent that part of the works defending the town and port of Algiers to which His Majesty's ship "Impregnable," which bore the flag of the Admiral, was opposed in the memorable attack on the 27th day of August, 1816. *Crest*—Out of a naval crown or, a dexter cubit arm vested az. the hand ppr. grasping a flagstaff, therefrom flying the flag of a Rear-Admiral of the Blue, inscribed with the word "Impregnable" in letters of gold. *Supporters*—Dexter, a figure designed to represent a Christian slave, holding in his hand a passion cross or, and in his sinister hand his fetters broken ppr.: sinister, a sailor habited and armed with cutlass and pistols ppr. holding in the exterior hand a flagstaff, therefrom flowing to the dexter a banner az. in canton the Union. *Motto*—Tam marte quam arte.

Milne (Balfarg, co. Fife; His Majesty's Master Mason, 1672; confirmed 1767, to ROBERT MYLNE, architect, London). Or, a cross moline az. square pierced of the field betw. three mullets of the second. *Crest*—Pallas's head couped at the shoulders ppr. vested about the neck vert. on the head a helmet az. beaver turned up, on the top a plume of feathers gu. *Motto*—Tam arte quam marte.

Milne (Balwyllo, co. Forfar, 1680). Or, a cross moline engr. az. betw. three mullets of the last. *Crest*—A cross moline sa. in the sea ppr. betw. two stalks of wheat orleways also ppr. *Motto*—Clarum reddit industria.

Milne (Blairtoun and Aberdeen, 1692). Or, a cross moline

az. pierced ovalways of the field betw. three mullets sa. all within a bordure wavy of the second. *Crest*—A galley with oars erect in saltire ppr. *Motto*—Dat cura com modum.

Milne (Edinburgh, 1672). Or, a cross moline pierced lozengeways betw. three mullets az. within a bordure nebulée of the second. *Crest*—A martlet volant ar. *Motto*—Ex industria.

Milne (Muretoun, Scotland, 1672). Or, a cross moline pierced lozengeways of the field betw. three mullets az. within a bordure invecked sa. *Crest*—A dexter hand holding a folded book ppr. *Motto*—Efficiunt clarum studia.

Milne. Ar. a cross patonce pierced az. betw. three mullets sa.

Milne (Melgum, co. Aberdeen, 1867). Or, a cross moline pierced az. on a chief gu. a stag at gaze betw. two cross crosslets ar. *Crest*—A galley, sails furled and oars in saltire ppr. flagged gu. *Motto*—Suum cuique.

Milne (STOTT-MILNE, Rochdale, co. Lancaster; exemplified to JAMES STOTT, Esq., upon his assuming, by royal licence, the additional surname of MILNE). Quarterly, 1st and 4th, sa. a millrind ar. betw. two flaunches or, each charged with a lion ramp. of the field, for MILNE; 2nd and 3rd, az. in base the tower of a belfry thereon a spire ppr. surmounted by a vane or, on a chief of the last three pellets gu. the centre charged with a heart also or, and the 1st and 3rd with a bezant, for STOTT. *Crests*—1st, MILNE: In front of two palm trees a lamb couchant ppr. holding with the dexter foot a pennon ar. charged with a cross crosslet gu. 2nd, STOTT: A cross pattée sa. therefrom rising a moorcock holding in the beak a sprig of heath ppr. *Motto*—Prudenter qui sedulo.

Milnel, or Milvel. Az. three bars gemel or.

Milner (Nun-Appleton Hall, co. York, bart.). Per pale or and sa. a chev. betw. three horses' bits counterchanged. *Crest*—A horse's head couped ar. bridled and maned or, charged on the neck with a bezant betw. two wings gold. *Motto*—Addit frena feris.

Milner (confirmed June, 1772). Same *Arms*. *Crest*—A horse's head sa. bridled or, betw. two wings elevated of the last.

Milner (cos. Cornwall and York; granted by Camden). Erm. three wolves' heads ppr. couped gu. *Crest*—A wolf's head ppr. couped gu. pierced through the neck with a broken sword, the point in front of the neck and the wound guttée de sang, pommel or.

Milner (Lylliston Green, co. Middlesex; JOHN MILNER, of Lincoln's Inn, son of JOHN MILNER, Esq., of Gray's Inn, and grandson of RICHARD MILNER, all of Lylliston. Visit. 1663). Ermines three wolves' heads erased or. *Crest*—A wolf's head pierced through with a sword all ppr.

Milner (co. Lincoln). Sa. a chev. betw. three snaffle-bits or.

Milner (Pudsey, co. York). Sa. three snaffle-bits or.

Milner (co. York). Sa. a chev. betw. three snaffle-bits or. *Crest*—A horse's head erased sa. bridled or, charged on the neck with a bezant.

Milner. Quarterly, 1st and 4th, ar. three lozenges conjoined in fesse sa. each charged with a bezant, for WHEELER, 2nd and 3rd, gu. three catharine wheels ar., for WHEELER. *Crests*—1st, MILNER: A greyhound courant sa. collared and ringed or; 2nd, WHEELER: A lion's head couped ar. charged on the breast with a catharine wheel gu.

Milner (co. Nottingham). Ar. a fesse dancettée gu. in chief a crescent sa.

Milnes (Aldercar, Dunston, and Cromford, co. Derby; descended from WILLIAM MILNES, Esq., of Ashford, within the hundred of High Peak, *temp.* Queen Elizabeth. From his eldest son, RICHARD MILNES, Alderman of Chesterfield, derived the MILNES of Dunston and Aldercar Park; his dau. and heir m. ROBERT MOWER, Esq.; his brother, WILLIAM MILNES, Esq., acquired the estate of Cromford in marriage with the heiress of SORESBY, and was Sheriff co. Derby, 1771 ; in 1795 he obtained a confirmatory grant of arms, and d. in 1797, leaving three daus. his co-heirs, of whom the youngest m. GELL, of Hopton). Or, a bear ramp. sa. muzzled, collared, and lined gu. *Crest*—A bear's head couped at the neck sa. charged with a millrind or.

Milnes (Alton Manor, co. Derby). Erm. a millrind paleways betw. two flaunches sa. *Crest*—A garb erminois betw. two trefoils vert. *Motto*—Non sine labore.

Milnes (Tapton Hall, co. Derby; descended from JAMES MILNES, fourth son of WILLIAM MILNES, Esq., of Ashford, *temp.* Queen Elizabeth. His son, RICHARD, d. in 1706, leaving five sons: I. RICHARD, whose line is extinct. II. ROBERT, of Wakefield, ancestor of *Lord Houghton*, and MILNER of Galfrey, bart., extinct, of Sir ROBERT SHORE MILNES,

Bart., and great-grandfather of ROBERT PEMBERTON MILNES, of Fryston Hall, and Bawtry Hall, both in the co. of York. III. JAMES, of Chesterfield, represented by LOWNDES, Esq., of Hampstead. IV. JOHN, represented by GASKELL, of Thornes House, Lupset Hall, near Wakefield. V. WILLIAM, whose line is extinct). Az. a chev. betw. three windmill sails crossways or. *Crest*—A garb or, banded by a fess dancettée az. charged with three mullets pierced gold. *Motto*—Scio cui credidi.

Milnes (*Baron Houghton*). Az. a chev. betw. three windmill sails or. *Crest*—A garb or, charged with a fess dancettée az. thereon three mullets ar. *Supporters*—On either side a pegasus ar. gorged with a collar dancettée az. thereon three mullets ar. in the mouth a branch of laurel ppr. *Motto*—Scio cui credidi.

Milnes (Galfrey, co. Leicester, bart., extinct; Sir ROBERT SHORE MILNES, Lieut.-Governor of Lower Canada, was so created 21 March, 1801). Same *Arms. Crest*—A garb or, banded by a fess dancettée az. charged with three mullets pierced gold.

Milnes (North Shorbury, co. Essex). Gu. a cross pattée betw. three mullets pierced ar.

Milnes (Stubbing Edge, co. Derby). Erm. a millrind sa. *Crest*—A demi lion ramp. or, holding in the paws a millrind sa.

Milnes (Beckingham Hall, co. Nottingham). Quarterly, 1st and 4th, az. on a chev. ar. three millrinds sa. on a canton or, a trefoil slipped of the third, for MILNES; 2nd, gu. on a fesse engr. ar. betw. three leopards' faces or, two escallops az., for WRIGHT; 3rd, gu. two bars ar. each charged with three mascles of the field, on a canton or, a hurt. *Crest*—An elephant's head erased ppr. gorged with a ducal coronet or.

Milnes (SMITH-MILNES, Dunston Hall, Chesterfield, co. Derby; exemplified to WILLIAM BROUGHTON SMITH, upon his assuming, by royal licence, 1873, the additional surname of MILNES). Quarterly, 1st and 4th, erm. a bear ramp. sa. muzzled and gorged with a collar or, therefrom a line reflexed over the back gu., for MILNES; 2nd and 3rd, ar. on a bend engr. az. betw. two unicorns' heads erased gu. three fleurs-de-lis or, for SMITH.

Milnes (Stirling, 1814). Ar. a cross moline az. on a canton gyronny of eight or and sa. a bordure embattled gu. and a chief of the third charged with three pallets of the fifth. *Crest*—Out of a mural crown or, an eagle's head sa. gorged with a collar or, charged with three pallets gu. *Motto*—In cruce salus.

Milneton (Grafton, co. Chester; founded by PAGAN DE MILNETON, illegitimate son of HUGH KEVELIOK, *Earl of Chester.* RALPH DE MYLNETON *m. temp.* Henry IV. or V., dau. and heir of WILLIAM DE GRAFTON, co. Chester; MARGARET MILNETON, dau. and co-heir of WILLIAM DE MYLNETON, *m.* JOHN MASSEY, *temp.* Henry VI., and her son, WILLIAM MASSEY, had the lands of Grafton). Ar. on a cross engr. az. five garbs or, for MILNETON; quartering MASSEY, of Dunham, with a trefoil slipped vert in the centre.

Milnston (co. Chester). Az. three millstones ar. each charged with a millrind sa.

Milroy (Rev. A. WALLACE MILROY, Forthside, co. Stirling, and London, 1876). Per fess, in chief chequy or and vert in base gu. the latter charged with a lion ramp. ar. on a canton of the fourth a rose of the third barbed of the second. *Crest*—An ostrich ppr. *Motto*—Espérance.

Miltecombe. Or, fretty sa. on a chief of the last a lion pass. guard. of the first.

Milton (London, 1634). Ar. a cross flory betw. four caltraps az. *Crest*—A dexter arm in armour ppr. scarfed az. grasping a broken spear gu. headed ar.

Milton (co. Salop). Per pale gu. and az. an eagle displ. or.

Milton. Ar. three pomeis, on each two bendlets wavy of the field; another, Az. a cross flory ar.; another, Ar. three chaplets gu.; another, Az. a cross patonce voided ar.

Milton (Milton, near Thame, co. Oxford; of this family was JOHN MILTON, the Poet). Ar. an eagle displ. with two heads gu. beaked and legged sa. *Crest*—A lion's gamb erect ar. grasping an eagle's head erased gu.

Milton-Abbey (co. Dorset). Sa. three baskets of bread (or wastell cakes) ar.

Milveton (co. Chester). Az. three plates, on each an inkmoline sa.

Milveton. Az. three millstones ar.; another, Ar. on a saltire engr. az. five garbs or.

Milward (Wollescote and Alvechurch, co. Worcester; THOMAS MILWARD, Esq., of Wollescote, was party to a deed, 1566; THOMAS MILWARD, of same place, *m.* MARTHA, dau. of Rev. SIMON FORD, D.D., Rector of Oldswinford, and *d.* 1734). 689

leaving THOMAS MILWARD his successor, who left two daus. his co-heirs. During the Civil Wars, *temp.* Charles I., Prince Rupert made Wollescote House, the residence of THOMAS MILWARD, Esq., his head quarters for a considerable time. When the Prince broke up his quarters at Wollescote, he presented Mr. MILWARD with a signet ring, which he took off his own finger, and told him, though he could not recompense him for his loyalty, that when the King's affairs turned out prosperously he should be rewarded on presenting that ring). Erm. on a fess gu. three bezants.

Milward (Ballyharran, co. Wexford, and Tullogher, co. Kilkenny; CLEMENT MILWARD, Esq., Q.C., Alice Holt, co. Surrey, eldest surviving son of the late Admiral CLEMENT MILWARD, R.N., of Tullogher, the great-grandson of THOMAS MILWARD, Esq., of Ballyharran, whose father, CLEMENT MILWARD, held the lands of Hillfields, in the Manor of Alehurst, under the Bishop of Gloucester, and settled at Enniscorthy, co. Wexford, 1696). Erm. on a fess gu. three plates. *Crest*—A dragon's head couped vert betw. two wings gu.

Milward (SAYER-MILWARD, St. Leonard's, Wallingford, co. Berks; exemplified, 1856, to SAYER, on assuming, by royal licence, the surname of MILWARD). Quarterly, 1st and 4th, MILWARD, erm. on a fesse gu. fimbriated or, three bezants, each charged with a chevronel of the second; 2nd and 3rd, SAYER, per chev. gu. and sa. a chev. erm. betw. three sea mews ar. *Crests*—1st, MILWARD: Out of a wreath of oak or, a bear's paw erect sa. holding a sceptre in pale and charged with a bar gold; 2nd, SAYER: A mount vert, thereon out of rays of the sun a dexter arm embowed in armour ppr. the hand also ppr. grasping a dragon's head at the neck also vert. *Motto*—Bear and forbear.

Milward (co. Bedford). Ar. a cross moline sa. betw. four crescents gu.

Milward (Braxted, co. Essex). Erm. on a fesse gu. a fleur-de-lis ar. betw. two bezants. *Crest*—Out of a palisado coronet or, a lion's gamb sa. grasping a sceptre gold (another bears the crest without the coronet).

Milward (Eaton Dovedale, co. Derby: six descents in Visit. 1611: the heiress *m.* CLARKE, of Somersall. A younger branch became extinct in the male line at the decease, 1670, of JOHN MILWARD Esq., of Snitterton in Darley; his co-heiresses *m.* BOOTHBY, JENNENS, and ADDERLEY). Erm. on a fesse gu. three plates. *Crest*—A lion's paw issuing out of a wreath sa. grasping a sceptre or.

Milward (Thurgarton Priory, co. Notts). Erm. on a fesse gu. three bezants. *Crest*—A lion's paw issuing sa. grasping a sceptre or. *Motto*—Nec temere nec timide.

Milward (London). Sa. a millrind betw. three leopards' faces ar.

Milward (Batcomb, co. Somerset). Ar. a millrind sa. betw. four crescents gu.

Milward (Manor House, Lechlade, co. Gloucester). Erm. a cross moline sa. betw. three torteaux, two and one, each charged with a crescent or. *Crest*—Betw. two wings az. a bear's paw erased sa. claws or, holding a sceptre in bend sinister gold, entwined by a sprig of oak ppr. *Motto*—Nec temere, nec timide.

Milwater (Stoke Edith, co. Hereford, *temp.* Henry VII.). Ar. on a chev. betw. three fleurs-de-lis sa. as many water bougets or. (Harl. MSS. 615).

Minchin. Ar. three chev. betw. as many fleurs-de-lis az. *Crest*—A lion's tail erased ppr.

Minchin (Busherstown, Ballynakill, co. Tipperary; confirmed by Hawkins, Ulster, 1720, to HUMPHREY MINCHIN, Esq., J.P., of that place). Erm. a chev. with two couple-closes gu. betw. three fleurs-de-lis az. *Crest*—A naked arm embowed ppr. grasping a baton or. *Motto*—Regarde à la mort.

Minchin (Rathclough, co. Tipperary). Same *Arms, Crest,* and *Motto.*

Mineral and Battery Works, Society of (London; incorporated 1568). Az. on a mount vert a square brazen pillar, supported on the dexter by a lion ramp. reguard. and on the sinister by a dragon segreant, both or, in chief, on the top of the pillar a bundle of wire tied and bound together of the last, betw. a bezant on the dexter side and a plate on the sinister. *Crest*—Two arms embowed ppr. both hands holding a calamine stone ar. spotted with red, yellow, and blue. *Supporters*—Two emblematical figures, viz., the dexter a female ppr. representing Science, vested in a short bodice, coat, ruff, &c. ar. (being the dress of the ladies in the reign of Elizabeth), in her dexter hand a pair of compasses, and on her head a crescent both or, crined of the last; the sinister figure, an old man ppr. representing Labour, vested in a long frock, turned up over his elbows ar. in his sinister hand a hammer or.

Miners Royal, or Mine Adventurers Company (London; incorporated 1568). Ar. a mine open, of earth colour, the upper part variegated with various shrubs vert, within the mine a miner ppr. vested sa. on his head a cap ar. round his body a belt of the last, and in the attitude of working the dexter sides of the mine with two hammers, on the sinister side a candle ar. lighted ppr. in a candlestick az. fixed in the mine, on a chief brown, a square plate or, betw. a bezant on the dexter and a plate on the sinister. *Crest*—A demi miner ppr. vested and capped, as in the arms, holding in his dexter hand a pointed spade erect ar. betw. two hammers in saltire, and in his sinister hand a compass. *Supporters*—The dexter, a miner, his face, legs, and arms of a brownish colour, vested in a frock ar. tied above his knees as at work, cap and shoes of the last, holding in his dexter hand erect a hammer az. handled ppr.; the sinister supporter, another miner ppr. cap, frock, and shoes ar. the frock loose and down to his ankles, in his sinister hand a fork az. handled ppr.

Minett. Ar. in base on the sea ppr. three persons in military costume seated in an open boat, rowed by two sailors all ppr. in fesse three erm. spots, on a chief or, a mount vert, thereon an oak tree ppr. fructed or. *Crest*—A wing erect ar. charged with three bars gu. *Motto*—Quantam est in rebus inane.

Mingay, or Mingey (Gymingham, co. Norfolk; granted by Cooke, Clarenceux, 1580). Or, on a bend az. three leopards' faces ar. (another, or). *Crest*—A lance or, headed ar. environed with a laurel branch vert.

Mingey (Armingall, co. Norfolk). Or, on a canton sa. a leopard's face of the first. Same *Crest* as the last.

Miniett. Ar. three helmets, beavers open sa. *Crest*—An eagle volant over a ruined castle ppr.

Minifie (Honiton, co. Devon, and Sarum, co. Wilts). Vert on a chev. betw. three martlets ar. as many eagles displ. of the first.

Miniott. Gu. three helmets ar. crested or.

Minne (co. Rutland). Sa. a fesse dancettée paly of eight gu. and erm. betw. six crosses crosslet ar. *Crest*—A heathcock ppr.

Minne, or Myn (Reg. Ulster's Office). Sa. a fess gobony erm. and gu. betw. five crosses crosslet fitchée ar. three in chief and two in base.

Minnes (cos. Kent and Middlesex; granted July, 1616). Gu. a chev. vairé or and az. betw. three leopards' faces or.

Minnett. Quarterly, erminois and ar. three bars gu.

Minnitt (Knygh Castle, co. Tipperary; founded in Ireland by Captain John Minnitt, of ancient English descent, represented in the female line by Atkins, of Firville, co. Cork, through Mary, dau. and co-heiress of John Minnitt, Esq., the last of that branch). Gu. three helmets ppr. garnished or. *Crest*—A helmet as in the arms. *Motto*—Virtute et armis.

Minnitt (Blackfort, co. Tipperary; represented in the female line by FitzGerald, of Ardival, co. Kerry, through Anne, only dau. and heiress of Rev. Robert Minnitt, of Blackfort, Rector of Tulla, co. Clare). Same *Arms, Crest,* and *Motto*.

Minnitt (Annabeg, co. Tipperary; male heir of the family descended from Joshua Minnitt, Esq., of Annabeg, youngest brother of Rev. Robert Minnitt, of Blackfort, Rector of Tulla). Same *Arms, Crest,* and *Motto*.

Minnoch (Glasgow, 1875). Or, a fess wavy az. betw. two crosses flory sa. in chief and a lion ramp. of the third in base. *Crest*—An owl ppr. *Motto*—Je pense plus.

Minns (co. Gloucester). Gu. on a chev. engr. betw. three fleurs-de-lis ar. as many chessrooks sa.

Minors (co. Hertford, London, and co. Stafford). Gu. a fess ar. betw. three plates. *Crest*—A dexter cubit arm, naked, the hand holding a lion's gamb erased all ppr.

Minors. Same *Arms*. *Crest*—A wolf's head erased sa. devouring a sinister hand ppr.

Minors (London). Sa. an eagle displ. or, on a chief az. bordured ar. a chev. betw. two crescents in chief and a rose in base of the second.

Minors. Per pale gu. and az. an eagle displ. or; another, Ar. a fesse gu. betw. three torteaux.

Minors. See Mynors.

Minshaw. Bendy of eight ar. and gu. *Crest*—A dexter hand ppr. holding up a cup or.

Minshull (cos. Chester, Buckingham, Devon, Suffolk, and Portslade, co. Sussex). Az. an estoile of six points issuing from a crescent ar. *Crest*—A Turk kneeling on one knee, habited gu. legs and arms in mail ppr. at the side a scymitar sa. hilted or, on the head a turban, with a crescent and feather ar. holding in the dexter hand a crescent of the last. Crest was granted by Sir William Le Neve in 1642 to

690

Sir Robert Minshull, instead of the original one, viz., the lion's paws holding a crescent.

Minshull (Hampton, co. Chester; descended from Randle Minshull, son of John Minshull, Esq., and Elizabeth, his wife, dau. of William Leycester, Esq., of Worleston, now represented by the descendants of the daus. and co-heirs of John Minshull, Esq., Ann, m. Lynde Walter, Esq., of Boston, United States, and Mary, m. D. Anthony Mazzinghi, Esq.). Az. an estoile of six points issuing from a crescent ar. *Crest*—Two lions' gambs gu. supporting a crescent ar. *Motto*—In hoc plenius redibo.

Minshull (Erdswick Hall, co. Chester. Visit. Chester by Dugdale, who allowed no crest). Same *Arms*.

Minshull (Exeter, co. Devon; Thomas Minshull, second son of John Minshull, of Nantwich, co. Chester, the great-grandson of Nicholas Minshull, a younger son of Minshull, co. Chester. Visit. Devon, 1620). Same *Arms*, an annulet or, for diff.

Minshull (Woodnorton, co. Norfolk). Az. a crescent betw. two estoiles in pale or.

Minshull. Az. a crescent betw. three estoiles or.

Minshull. Az. a chev. betw. three crescents, out of each an estoile issuing all ar.

Minsterchamber (Godmanchester, co. Huntingdon, and Stuston, co. Suffolk). Ar. a fesse betw. three millrinds sa.

Minterne, or Minterin (Batcombe, co. Dorset, and Thorpe, co. Surrey). Az. two bars ar. betw. three lions pass. in pale or. *Crest*—A bull's head gu. ducally gorged and armed or.

Minto, Earl of. See Elliot.

Minton (Stoke-upon-Trent, co. Stafford). Vert three garbs or, within two bars erm. betw. two heraldic tigers pass. one in chief and another in base of the second. *Crest*—Upon a mount vert an heraldic tiger as in the arms, the dexter paw resting on a garb erect ppr. *Motto*—Pro Deo et patriâ.

Mirehouse (Brownslade, co. Pembroke; descended from Mirehouse, of Miresike, co. Cumberland). Gu. a bend ar. billettée of the field. *Crest*—An arm embowed in armour holding a sword all ppr. *Motto*—Qualis ab incepto.

Mirehouse (Hambrook Grove, co. Gloucester, and Colsterworth, co. Lincoln; descended from Mirehouse, of Miresike, co. Cumberland, which property is stated to have been in the possession of the family from the time of Edward the Confessor. The Rev. John Mirehouse, of Hambrook Grove and Colsterworth, Rector of Colsterworth, is the son and heir of the late Rev. Wm. Mirehouse, of Hambrook Grove, Rector of Colsterworth, Chaplain to H.R.H. the Princess Sophia, J.P. for the cos. of Pembroke and Gloucester, by Eliza Brunetta, his wife, only dau. of the late George Arthur Herbert, Esq., of Glanafrew, co. Montgomery, J.P., D.L., and High Sheriff of that county, by Mary, sister of the late Sir John Edwards, Bart., M.P., of Garth and Machynlleth, co. Montgomery, who was the son of the Rev. Thomas Mirehouse, Canon of Peterborough, Rector of Elton, and Rector of Wilford, who was the second son of John Myrehouse, Esq., of Miresike). Gu. a bend ar. billettée sa. *Crest*—An arm embowed in armour holding a sword all ppr. *Motto*—Qualis ab incepto.

Mirfield. Ar. two lions pass. guard. in pale vert.

Mirfin (Lord Mayor of London, 1518). Or, on a chev. sa. a mullet ar. *Crest*—A demi lion ppr. supporting a flag ar. charged with a saltire sa. See Mervyn.

Mirnor. Vair a canton gu.

Mirrie. Ar. on a bend az. a crescent betw. two mullets of the first, in the sinister chief point three roses gu. growing out of one stalk vert, the same in the dexter base point.

Mirry, or Mirrie. Ar. three lions ramp. gu. *Crest*—Out of a ducal coronet or, a demi lion gu.

Mirtle. Per fesse wavy gu. and ar. in chief a lion pass. guard. erminois, in base on a mount vert a fir tree ppr. *Crest*—An arm erect couped at the elbow ppr. encircled with a myrtle chaplet vert, in the hand a scymitar ar. hilt and pommel or, on the blade a shackle severed sa.

Missenden-Monastery (co. Berks). Erm. two bars wavy sa. over all a crosier in bend or. *Another Coat*—Ar. a chev. sa. betw. three cocks gu. on a chief az. a greyhound courant ar.

Missenden. See Mussenden.

Misserinen. Ar. a tree eradicated vert, on a canton gu. two battle axes endorsed ppr. *Crest*—A battle axe in pale ppr.

Misset (Ireland, 1213; Reg. Ulster's Office). Ar. on a chief sa. three lozenges erm.

Missett (Dowdingstown, co. Dublin; Fun. Ent. Ulster's Office, 1619, Gerald Missett, Esq., of that place). Ar. three lions ramp. per fess gu. and sa. a crescent for diff.

Misted. Gu. a fesse engr. erm. betw. three mullets or.

Misterton. Gu. a unicorn pass. ar. armed or, guttée de sang, a chief of the second.

Mitchell (Bodmin, co. Cornwall). Sa. a falcon close in fesse betw. two barrulets ar. in chief two falcons close or.

Mitchell (Truro, co. Cornwall). Sa. an escallop betw. three birds' heads erased or. Crest—A demi pegasus or, winged az. charged on the shoulder with a demi rose gu. divided fesseways rays issuing from the division pendent ar.

Mitchell (Stapleton Mitchell, co. Dorset, and co. York). Sa. a chev. or, betw. three escallops ar.

Mitchell (Deptford, co. Kent). Az. a chev. betw. three swans ar. Crest—A swan ppr. Motto—Moriendo modulor.

Mitchell (Enderby Hall, co. Leicester). Or, a chev. engr. betw. two mascles in chief and a ducal crown in base gu. Crest—A garb or, banded gu. pendent therefrom an escutcheon az. charged with three slips of laurel vert.

Mitchell (Llanfretcha Grange, co. Monmouth). Sa. a chev. betw. three escallops or. Crest—A garb of bearded wheat or.

Mitchell. Ar. a chev. purp. betw. seven heraldic tigers' or dragons' heads erect and erased vert, each devouring a cross crosslet fitchée gu. Crest—An arm embowed clothed in leaves vert, the hand ppr. holding a sword ar. hilt and pommel or, the point embrued and dropping with blood. Another Crest—A dexter arm erect holding a sword, rays of fire issuing from each side thereof all ppr.

Mitchell. Sa. a fesse betw. three mascles or. Crest—St. Michael, the archangel, in armour ppr. face, neck, arms, and legs bare, wings ar. hair auburn, in the dexter hand a spear of the first.

Mitchell. Per pale sa. and ar. three cranes' heads erased counterchanged. Crest—An arm erect couped at the elbow, vested gu. cuffed ar. grasping a crane's head erased ppr.

Mitchell. Ar. a chev. gu. surmounted by another erm. betw. two mascles in chief az. and a laurel branch slipped in base vert. Crest—A garb vert.

Mitchell (confirmed by Hawkins, Ulster, 1724, to PATRICK MITCHELL, Doctor of Physic, descended from the co. Aberdeen, in Scotland). Sa. on a fess wavy betw. three mascles or, a crescent betw. two estoiles gu. Crest—An angel kneeling in a praying posture ppr.

Mitchell (Mount Mitchell, co. Leitrim; allowed by Mac Culloch, Ulster, 1760, to PATRICK MITCHELL, of Bordeaux, in the Kingdom of France, merchant, great-grandson of LAWRENCE MITCHELL, Esq., of Fingal, co. Meath, who was ninth in descent from AMBROSE MITCHELL, Esq., of Mount Mitchell, temp. Edward III.). Az. a chev. betw. three leopards' faces or. Crest—A dexter arm embowed in armour, holding in the hand a sword all ppr. pommel and hilt or, pierced through a leopard's face gold. Motto—Sola virtus nobilitat.

Mitchell (granted by Betham, Deputy Ulster, to PIERREPOINT OLIVER MITCHELL, co. Cork, and the descendants of HUGH HENRY MITCHELL, his grandfather). Sa. on a fess betw. three mascles or, as many trefoils vert. Crest—An angel in armour, holding in the dexter hand a spear ppr. Motto—Tout jour pret.

Mitchell (granted by Betham, Ulster, to FANNY, only child of THOMAS WILLIAM O'BRIEN MITCHELL, Esq., of Aghadda, co. Cork, and wife of ROBERT PLAMPIN, Esq.). Ar. three trefoils slipped chevronways vert within two chevrons betw. as many mascles az.

Mitchell (that Ilk, and Craigend, Scotland). Sa. a fesse betw. three mascles or, in the middle chief a dagger erect, point upwards ppr. handle of the second, all within a bordure ar. charged with eight cinquefoils gu. Crest—A hand holding a writing pen ppr. Motto—Favente Deo supero.

Mitchell (Tillygreig, Aberdeen, 1672). Sa. a fesse wavy betw. three mascles or. Motto—Secura frugalitas.

Mitchell (Landath, Scotland, 1672). Sa. a fesse engr. betw. three mascles or. Motto—Labor improbus omnia vincit.

Mitchell (Wester New Birny, Scotland, 1672). Sa. a fesse invecked betw. three mascles or. Motto—Omnia superat diligentia.

Mitchell (Thainston, co. Aberdeen; as borne by DUNCAN FORBES MITCHELL, Esq., of Thainston, grandson of DUNCAN FORBES MITCHELL, Esq., second son of Sir ARTHUR FORBES, fourth bart. of Craigievar). Quarterly, 1st and 4th, FORBES, of Craigievar ; 2nd and 3rd, sa. a fess.

Mitchell (Berry and Westshore, Zetland, bart. 1724, extinct 1783). Sa. a fesse betw. three mascles or, a bordure chequy of the second and first. Crest—Three ears of barley conjoined in the stalk ppr. Motto—Sapiens qui assiduus.

Mitchell (Alderston, co. Edinburgh, 1722). Sa. a chev. betw. three mascles or. Crest—A stalk of wheat bladed and erected in pale ppr. Motto—Cresco.

Mitchell (Thainston, co. Aberdeen, 1766). Sa. a fess wavy betw. three mascles or. Crest—A phœnix in flames ppr. Motto—Nulla pallesare culpa.

Mitchell (Admiral WILLIAM MITCHELL, 1814). Sa. a fess wavy erminois, in chief a naval crown or, betw. three mascles ar. and in base an anchor in pale of the third. Crest— Betw. two ears of wheat or, an arm erect, vested az. cuff or, the hand ppr. grasping an anchor in bend sinister ppr. Motto —Omnia superat virtus.

Mitchell (SCOTT-MITCHELL, New South Wales, 1860). Sa. on a bend betw. three mascles or, a dove with an olive branch in its beak ppr. betw. a mullet and a crescent az. Crest—A dexter hand erect, holding a garland of laurel ppr. Mottoes— Over the crest: Deo favente; below the shield : Ευρηκα. Motto—Deo favente.

Mitchell (Stow, co. Edinburgh, 1866). Quarterly, 1st and 4th, sa. on a fess betw. three mascles or, a star wavy az., for MITCHELL; 2nd and 3rd, ar. a chev. wavy betw. three stars of six points wavy az., for INNES. Crest—A dexter hand holding a garland of laurel ppr. Motto—Deo favente.

Mitchell-Innes. See INNES.

Mitchelson (Middleton, co. Edinburgh). Ar. a demi lion ramp. naissant out of the base gu. on a chief indented sa. a star betw. two crescents of the first. Crest—An increscent ar. Motto—Crescam ut prosim.

Mitchener. Erm. a fesse betw. three hunting-horns sa. stringed gu. Crest—A dove ar.

Mitchenson, or Michenson. Ar. a lion ramp. az.

Mitford (Mitford, co. Northumberland; an old baronial family, settled at Mitford, temp. William I.). Ar. a fesse betw. three moles sa. Crest—A dexter and sinister hand couped ppr. supporting a sword in pale ar. pommelled or, pierced through a boar's head sa. tusked gold, couped gu.

Mitford (descended from MITFORD, of Mitford, co. Northumberland, temp. William I. The eldest line merged in an heiress, MARGARET SUSAN, only child of the late Admiral ROBERT MITFORD, of Mitford and Hunmanby, co. York, and wife of WILLIAM AMHURST TYSSEN-AMHURST, Esq., of Didlington Hull, co. Norfolk). Ar. a fesse betw. three moles sa., quartering WHARTON, KIRKBY, ASHTON, BARTON, OSBALDESTON, MOLYNEUX, KYVERDALE, DARWENT, BALDERSTON, WENTWORTH, WODEHOUSE, POLLINGTON, HOTON, TYNNESLOW, LONDON, MARGEROLLES, WHITBY, DOWNES, MALTBY, FOUNTAINE, WALSHE, DOUNE, STOUNHOUSE, MONCKTON, MORTON, BOSVILE, and OLDFIELD.

Mitford (Exbury, co. Hants, and Newton Park, co. Northumberland; descended from MITFORD, of Mitford : JOHN MITFORD, Esq., of Lincoln's Inn, Barrister-at-law, grandson of JOHN MITFORD, Esq., of London, third son of ROBERT MITFORD, Esq., of Mitford Castle, m. in 1749, PHILADELPHIA, dau. and eventual heiress of WILLY REVELEY, Esq., of Newton Underwood, co. Northumberland, and was father of JOHN, first Baron Redesdale ; and an elder son, his heir, WILLIAM MITFORD, Esq., of Exbury, the eminent historian of Greece). Same Arms and Crest as MITFORD, of Mitford, quartering REVELEY.

Mitford (FREEMAN-MITFORD, Earl of Redesdale). Quarterly, 1st and 4th, ar. a fesse betw. three moledewarps sa., for MITFORD; 2nd and 3rd, az. three fusils in fesse or, for distinction a canton erm., for FREEMAN. Crests—1st, MITFORD: Two hands couped at the wrist ppr. grasping a sword erect ar. the point and hilt or, the blade enfiled with a boar's head erased sa.; 2nd, FREEMAN: A demi wolf ar. supporting betw. the paws a fusil or, for distinction gorged with a collar dancettée gu. Supporters—Two eagles rising sa. each gorged with a wreath of shamrock ppr. and each beaked, membered, and charged on the breast with a fusil or. Motto—Æquabiliter et diligenter.

Mitford (MARY RUSSELL MITFORD, the author of "Our Village," only surviving child of the Rev. GEORGE MITFORD, a descendant of MITFORD, of Mitford Castle). Same Arms as MITFORD, of Mitford.

Mitford (Pits Hill, co. Sussex; descended from MITFORD, of Mitford Castle, co. Northumberland), Same Arms and Crest as MITFORD, of Mitford). Motto—God carryeth for us.

Mithorpe. Erm. a lion ramp. az. crowned or.

Mitton, or Mylton (co. Oxford). Ar. an eagle displ. with two heads gu. Crest—A lion's gamb couped and erect ar. grasping an eagle's head erased gu.

Mitton (co. Salop). Per pale gu. and az. an eagle displ. with two heads or, a bordure counterchanged. Crest— A demi eagle displ. with two heads per pale or and az.

Mitton (co. Stafford). Per pale az. and gu. (another, purp.) an eagle displ. with two heads ar. Crest—A bull's head sa. armed or, charged with three annulets of the last.

Mitton (Mitton, co. York). Same Arms and Crest.

Mixfine (co. Cambridge). Ar. on a chev. sa. a mullet of the field.

Mobberley. Ar. two bars gu. on a canton of the last a cross crosslet fitchée of the field.

Mobbs (Houghton, co. Norfolk). Vert a cross pattée betw. four doves ar.

Moberley, or Mobdurley. Ar. two chevronels gu. on a canton of the second a cross crosslet fitchée of the first. *Crest*—A demi lady in the character of Justice, holding in the dexter hand a pair of scales.

Mocket (co. Kent). Or, on a chief az. three cinquefoils of the first. *Crest*—A tiger sejant az. collared ar.

Mocklow (Broughton Soulney, co. Nottingham). Gyronny of eight or and az. a lion ramp. erm. on a chief ar. an escallop betw. two fleurs-de-lis sa. a canton gu. *Crest*—A griffin's head per pale indented ar. and gu. guttée de larmes, in the beak a buck's foot of the first.

Mocklow, or Mucklaw (co. Worcester). Gyronny of twelve gu. and az. a lion ramp. erm. tail forked, on a chief ar. an escallop betw. two fleurs-de-lis sa. *Crest*—A griffin's head per pale indented gu. and ar. in the beak an eagle's leg erased or.

Modder (co. Stafford). Erm. on a fesse wavy az. three lions ramp. or. *Crest*—On a staff couped and raguly lying fesseways vert a lion sejant or.

Moderby (cos. Berks and Gloucester). Az. fretty or (another, ar.).

Moderby. Sa. a bend or, on a chief ar. three escallops gu. *Crest*—A hand and thunderbolt ppr.

Moderby. Sa. on a chief ar. three chaplets gu. (another adds, a bordure or).

Modey. Gu. a chev. erm. betw. three trefoils or. *Crest*—Out of a ducal coronet, a demi eagle, wings displ. gu.

Modlicote (Whitley Hall, co. Salop). Sa. a lion ramp. ar.

Modyford (Chiswick and London, bart., extinct 1675; Sir JAMES MODYFORD, Lieut.-Governor of Jamaica, was created a bart. in 1661. By ELIZABETH, his wife, dau. and heir of the famed Cavalier commander, Sir NICHOLAS SLANNING, Knt., of Maristow, co. Devon, he left an only child, GRACE MODYFORD, m. PETER HEYWOOD, Esq.). Erm. on a bend az. a mullet ar. betw. two garbs or. *Crest*—A garb erect or.

Modyford (Lincoln's Inn, bart., extinct 1703. Sir THOMAS MODYFORD, a brother of Sir JAMES MODYFORD, Bart., of Chiswick and London, Governor of Jamaica, was also Governor of that island, and was created a bart. 1664). Same *Arms* and Crest.

Moels (Baron Moels, abeyance 1337; JOHN DE MOELS was summoned to Parliament 1299; the fourth baron left two daus. co-heirs, m. COURTENAY and BOTREAUX). Ar. two bars gu. in chief three torteaux. *Crest*—A mule pass. ppr.

Moels, or Mules (Emsborough, co. Devon). See MULES.

Moffat (that Ilk, Annandale). Sa. a saltire and chief ar. (sometimes, a saltire az. and chief gu.).

Moffatt (Goodrich Court, co. Hereford). Ar. a saltire gu. and a chief az. *Crest*—The sun in splendour ppr.

Moffatt (Lauder, co. Hertford). Ar. a lion ramp. sa. betw. eight escallops in orle gu.

Moffett (Chipping Barnet, co. Hertford; granted 10 May, 1585). Same *Arms*, a rose or, for diff.

Mogg (Farrington Gurney, co. Somerset; there seated for a considerable period; JOHN MOGG, Esq., was High Sheriff of the county in 1703). Ar. a fesse pean betw. six erm. spots, five in chief and one in base, surmounted by a crescent gu. *Crest*—A cock ppr. pendent from the neck by a chain or, a shield ar. charged with a crescent as in the arms. *Motto*—Cura pii Diis sunt.

Mogg (REES-MOGG, Cholwell House, co. Somerset; exemplified to Rev. JOHN REES, Prebendary of Tytherington, on his assuming by royal licence, 1805, the additional surname and arms of MOGG, in pursuance of the will of the maternal grandfather of his wife, SARAH HODGES, only child and heir of JACOB MOGG, Esq., of High Littleton House, co. Somerset, who was the fourth son of JACOB MOGG, Esq., brother of JOHN MOGG, Esq., of Cholwell). Quarterly, 1st and 4th, ar. on a fesse pean betw. six erm. spots, five in chief and one in base, surmounted by a crescent gu. a cock or, for MOGG; 2nd and 3rd, gu. a chev. erminois betw. three swans ar. wings elevated or, for REES. *Crests*—1st, MOGG: Betw. two spearheads erect sa. a cock ppr. 2nd, REES: A swan ar. wings elevated or, holding in the beak a water lily slipped ppr. *Motto*—Cura pii Diis sunt.

Mogridge. Per pale or and az. three eagles displ. with two heads counterchanged.

Mohant. Az. a lion ramp. ar.

Mohant, or Mohan. Gu. a chev. ar. betw. three talbots pass. or.

Mohamud (ALI-MOHAMUD, of Bombay, J.P.). Quarterly, az. and gu. on a bend engr. or, betw. a horse's head erased

in the 2nd quarter, and in the 3rd a dexter hand couped and erect ar. an arrow point upwards sa. on a chief of the third a ship in full sail on waves of the sea ppr. *Crest*—A demi lion ppr. charged with two bars or, holding in the dexter paw a sword also ppr. and resting the sinister paw on an escutcheon az. charged with the sun in splendour gold. *Motto*—Nil desperandum.

Mohun (Baron Mohun, of Dunster Castle, co. Somerset; summoned to Parliament 1299, barony passed to STRANGE). Or, a cross argt. sa.

Mohun (Boconock Hall, co. Cornwall, and Oakhampton, co. Devon, bart., extinct 1712; descended from REGINALD DE MOHUN, younger son of JOHN, first Lord Mohun, of Dunster; Sir REGINALD MOHUN, Knt., of Boconock, was created a bart. 1612). Or, a cross engr. sa. *Crest*—A maunch erm. holding in the hand ppr. a fleur-de-lis ar.

Mohun (Baron Mohun, of Oakhampton, extinct 1712; Sir JOHN MOHUN, second bart. of Boconock, was so created 1628; the fifth baron fell in a duel with the fourth Duke of Hamilton, when both combatants were slain). Same *Arms*. *Crest*—A maunch erm. therein a hand ppr. holding a fleur-de-lis or. *Supporters*—Two lions guard. ar. ducally crowned or.

Mohun (cos. Devon, Somerset, Warwick, and Wilts, temp. William I.). Gu. a maunch erm. the hand ppr. holding a fleur-de-lis ar.

Mohun (Fleet, co. Dorset, and Aldenham, co. Hertford). Gu. a dexter arm habited with a maunch erm. in the hand ppr. a fleur-de-lis or. *Crest*—An arm, as in the arms.

Mohun. Or, a crescent sa.

Mohun (Reg. Ulster's Office). Gu. issuing from the sinister side of the shield an arm vested erm. holding in the hand ppr. a fleur-de-lis in pale or.

Moigne (co. Huntingdon). Az. a fesse indented or, betw. six crosses crosslet ar.

Moigne (co. Leicester). A semée of crosses crosslet ar. a fesse rompu erm.

Moigne, or Moine (co. Suffolk). Or, a saltire engr. gu. (another, sa.).

Moigne. Ar. two bars and a chief gu.

Moigne, or Moygne. Or, three bars vert.

Moigne (THOMAS MOIGNE, Bishop of Meath, 1612-28; Fun. Ent. Ulster's Office). Sa. a fess dancettée betw. three mullets in chief, two and one, and as many in base also two and one all ar. a crescent for diff.

Moigne, or Moyne. Ar. two bars and three mullets in chief sa.

Moigne, or Moin. Ar. a cross flory gu.

Moigne, or Moine. Az. a fesse indented betw. ten crosses crosslet ar. three, two, three, and two.

Moilliet (Abberley Hall, co. Worcester, and Cheyney Court, co. Hereford). Gu. a swan ar. swimming in water in base ppr. in chief three estoiles or, quartering, ar. on a cross engr. sa. betw. four roses gu. barbed vert, seeded or, three lozenges in pale gold. *Crest*—A swan ar. *Motto*—Gaudet in luce veritas.

Moir (Abergeldie and Otterburn, Scotland). Ar. three Negroes' heads couped ppr. a bordure counter-indented sa. and or. *Crest*—A Negro's head couped ppr. *Motto*—Mediocriter.

Moir (Hilton, co. Aberdeen). Ar. three Moors' heads couped, distilling drops of blood ppr. wreathed about with bay leaves vert. *Crest*—A dexter arm from the shoulder issuing out of a cloud, holding a branch of laurel slipped ppr. *Motto*—Virtute non aliter.

Moir (Scotstoun, co. Aberdeen). Ar. three Negroes' heads couped ppr. banded of the first. *Crest*—A morthead with two leg-bones in saltire ppr. *Motto*—Non sibi sed cunctis.

Moir (Stoneywood, co. Aberdeen). Ar. three Moors' heads couped, distilling drops of blood ppr. *Crest*—A Moor's head couped, as in the arms. *Motto*—Major opima ferat.

Moir (Invernettie, co. Aberdeen, 1792). Ar. three Moors' heads couped, each wreathed with laurel and distilling drops of blood, in chief a dexter hand pointing with the forefinger towards the base all ppr. *Crest*—An eye ppr. *Motto*—Deus dedit.

Moir (Leckie, co. Stirling, paternally GRAHAM, 1796). Quarterly, 1st and 4th, ar. three Moors' heads couped and distilling three drops of blood ppr. banded of the first; 2nd, ar. a man's heart crowned ppr. on a chief sa. three escallops or, for GRAHAM; 3rd, quarterly, for STEWART; 3rd and 4th, or, a fess chequy az. and ar., 2nd and 3rd, ar. a lymphad, sails furled and oars in action sa. *Crest*—A falcon ppr. armed and belled or, perched on a heron lying on its back ppr. beaked and membered gu. *Motto*—Ne oublie.

Moises (Newcastle-on-Tyne). Gu. a fesse erminois betw. three bulls' heads couped ar.

Moland (co. Stafford). Ar. on a chief gu. a lion pass. or.

Molant. Ar. a lion ramp. sa. tail queued or. *Crest*—A demi mule ramp. gu.

Moldford. Ar. a fesse erm. betw. three swans ppr. *Crest*—A buck's head gu.

Moldworth, or Mudeworth (co. Chester). Ar. on a bend engr. sa. three pheons of the first.

Mole (Tringeg, co. Bedford, and co. Northampton). Ar. two bars gu. in chief three torteaux. *Crest*—Out of clouds ppr. a cubit arm erect, vested gu. the hand apaumée also ppr.

Mole (Molton, co. Devon; granted 1592). Barry wavy of four ar. and az. on a chief sa. a lion pass. guard. of the first. *Crest*—Out of a ducal coronet or, a snake, the head erect and body entwined ppr.

Mole, De. Or, a fesse az. betw. two chevronels gu.

Moleins (co. Dorset). Erm. an ink-moline az. (another, sa.).

Molenick (Molenick, St. German's, co. Cornwall). Ar. a chev. sa. betw. three goldfinches ppr.

Molenick (co. Cornwall). Ar. a chev. az. betw. three falcons close of the second.

Molens. Or, three palets wavy gu.

Moles. Ar. a bend sa. betw. two lions' heads erased of the last.

Molesworth (*Viscount Molesworth*). Vair a bordure gu. charged with eight crosses crosslet or. *Crest*—A dexter arm embowed in armour ppr. holding a cross crosslet or. *Supporters*—Dexter, a pegasus ar. wings elevated **or**; sinister, a pegasus, wings elevated gu. semée of crosses crosslet gold. *Motto*—Vincit amor patriæ.

Molesworth (Pencarrow, co. Cornwall, bart.). Gu. an escutcheon vair betw. eight crosses crosslet ar. *Crest*—An armed arm embowed ppr. holding a cross crosslet or. *Motto*—Sic fidem teneo.

Molesworth (Pencarrow; brass in Minster Church, co. Cornwall, before 1620). Gu. a cross crosslet within an orle of crosses crosslet ar. a border vair.

Molesworth (Rochdale, co. Lancaster). *Arms, Crest*, and *Motto*, as *Viscount Molesworth*, from whose family they are descended.

Molesworth (Spring Garden, Jamaica). Gu. an inescutcheon vair betw. eight crosses crosslet ar.

Molford (Southmolton, and Cadburie, co. Devon; JOHN and THOMAS MOLFORD, sons of ROGER MOLFORD, by AMY, his wife, dau. and heiress of CADBURIE, of Cadburie. Visit. Devon, 1620). Sa. fess erm. betw. three swans ar. *Crest*—Out of a ducal coronet or, a demi swan, wings expanded ar. beaked gu.

Molfyn, or Molfin. Or, a lion ramp. gu. an orle of eight mullets az.

Molin (Bretaign). Az. three heads of lances within an annulet ar.

Moline De (Ambassador from the Doge of Venice, *temp.* James I.). Az. the wheel of a watermill or, on a canton of augmentation ar. the royal badge of England and Scotland, viz.: the rose and thistle conjoined paleways ppr.

Molines (*Baron Molines*; barony passed to HUNGERFORD, 1423; JAMES DE MOLINES was summoned to Parliament, 1347). Paly wavy of six or and gu.

Molines. Sa. on a chief ar. three lozenges of the field (another, gu.).

Molines. Erm. a fer-de-moline az.

Molineux (Cranbourne, co. Dorset). Quarterly, 1st and 4th, az. a cross or, pierced sa.; 2nd and 3rd, ar. three wolves' heads erased az.

Molineux (co. Dorset, and Yalcus, co. Lancaster). Erm. a fer-de-moline az.

Molineux (Crosby, co. Lancaster). Az. a cross moline or, in the chief point a ducal coronet of the last.

Molineux (Hawkley, co. Lancaster). Az. a cross moline or. *Crest*—A beaver pass. ppr.

Molineux (Knerdale, co. Lancaster). Az. a cross moline quarter pierced or, in the dexter canton a fleur-de-lis ar.

Molineux (Woodhouse, co. Lancaster). Az. a cross moline ar.

Molineux (New Hall, co. Lancaster, 1664). Az. a cross moline or, a canton ar.

Molineux (co. Lancaster, *temp.* Richard II.). Az. a cross moline pierced lozengeways or. *Crest*—Out of a chapeau gu. turned up erm. a peacock's tail ppr.

Molineux (co. Nottingham). Az. a cross moline or, a bordure ar.

Molineux (co. Stafford; descended from Sir THOMAS MOLYNEUX, of Haughton, co. Notts, Knight Bannéret, second son of Sir RICHARD MOLYNEUX, of Sefton, brother of RICHARD,

ancestor of the *Earl of Sefton*). Az. a cross moline quarter pierced or. *Crest*—A hand issuing from flames grasping an eagle's leg all ppr.. *Motto*—En droyt devant.

Molington. Sa. a cross moline (another, a cross pattée throughout) erm.

Molins (HENRY MOLINS, son of JOHN MOLINS, and grandson of WILLIAM MOLINS, by ELIZABETH, his wife, dau. and co-heir of WILLIAM MONTACUTE (the other dau. and co-heir m. JAMES DE PORTE, of Shepshed, co. Leicester). Visit. Leicester, 1619). Or, a cross moline sa. on a chief of the last three leopards' faces of the first.

Molins (London). Erm. a fer-de-moline az. pierced of the field. *Crest*—A water wheel or.

Molins (Sir MICHAEL MOLINS, knighted by Sir William Fitz-William, Lord Deputy of Ireland, Feb. 1592). Az. a cross moline ar. quarter pierced of the field, on a chief or, three lions' heads erased sa., quartering 1st, ar. three crescents or, and 2nd, ar. a bend engr. gu.

Mölle (Fun. Ent. Ulster's Office, 1596, ANNE MOLLE, wife of THOMAS SMYTH, of Dublin). Az. a cross patonce or, fretty gu. in the dexter chief a plate, thereon a mole pass. sa.

Moller (D'OSTEN-MÖLLER; exemplified to CHARLES CHAMPION MÖLLER, Esq., son of ANDREW MÖLLER, Esq., of Booterstown, co. Dublin, and grandson of Rev. OLANS V. MÖLLER, of Dublin, on his assuming by royal licence, 1857, the prefix surname of D'OSTEN, in addition to and before that of MÖLLER). Quarterly, 1st and 4th, or, a mill wheel sa., for MÖLLER; 2nd and 3rd, per pale ar. and gu. the dexter half charged with three bends sinister wavy az. and the sinister half with a key in pale or, for D'OSTEN. *Crests*—1st, MÖLLER: On a Danish baron's coronet a fleur-de-lis or; 2nd, D'OSTEN: In front of three peacock feathers erect ppr. two keys in saltire or, betw. as many eagles' wings ar. *Motto*—Die moller salich ihm.

Molleson (Lachintilly, co. Aberdeen, 1672). Or, two crosses crosslet fitchée in chief and the attires of a stag affixed to the scalp gu. a chief chequy of the second and ar. *Crest*—A hart's head cabossed ppr. attired with ten tynes or. *Motto*—Fax mentis honestæ gloria.

Molleson (Aberdeen, 1672). As the last, within a bordure gu. *Crest*—A Saracen's head erased and distilling drops of blood ppr. Same *Motto*.

Molling, or Molyng. Sa. three mullets or. *Crest*—On a rock a martlet sa.

Mollington (co. Suffolk). Ar. a fesse betw. two chevronels gu. (another, az.).

Mollington. Same *Arms*. *Crest*—A demi man shooting an arrow from a bow ppr.

Mollington. Sa. a cross sarcelly erm.

Mollins (Watterton, co. Hants). Or, a cross moline sa. in chief three goats' heads erased of the last.

Mollins (quartered by RAYNESFORD, of Great Tewe, and by ASHFIELD, of Ewelme, co. Oxford. Visit. Oxon 1566). Sa. on a chief ar. three lozenges gu.

Molloy. See O'MULLOY.

Molloy (Drynaunly, King's co.; Fun. Ent. Ulster's Office, 1639, Rev. NEALE MOLLOY, Rector of Lynally, in same co., second son of COSNY MOLLOY, of Drynaunly). Ar. a lion ramp. sa. armed and langued gu. betw. three trefoils slipped of the last.

Molloy (St. Mary-le-bone, co. Middlesex). Ar. a lion ramp. sa. betw. three trefoils slipped gu. *Crest*—A greyhound courant ar. in front of a tree vert.

Moloney. See O'MULLOWNEY.

Molony (Kiltanon, co. Clare; descended from the ancient Irish Sept of O'MULLOWNEY, *which see*). Az. on the dexter a quiver with three arrows, on the sinister a bow erect all or, quartering, gu. two griffins segreant respecting each other and grasping a staff erect all ar. *Crest*—A dexter arm embowed in armour, the hand in a gauntlet holding a dagger all ppr. *Motto*—In Domino et non in arcu sperabo.

Molony (Granahan, and Six Mile Bridge House, co. Clare; descended from CROASDAILE MOLONY, second son of JAMES MOLONY, Esq., of Kiltanon). Same *Arms, Crest*, and *Motto*.

Molsford (co. Devon). Sa. a fesse erm. betw. three swans ar.

Molson. Per pale az. and gu. three crescents ar. *Crest*—A crescent ar. betw. two wings expanded ppr.

Molston. Gu. two bars ar. in chief three plates.

Molte (co. Stafford). Or, fretty gu.

Molton (Francton). Gu. three bars ar. in chief as many crescents or.

Molton (co. Kent). Or, three bars vert.

Molton (co. Lincoln). Chequy or and gu. (another, or and sa.).

Molton, or **Moulton** (Plympton and Collumpton, co. Devon; William Molton, of the former place, and his nephew, John Molton, of the latter, Visit. Devon, 1620); descended from Edward Moulton, of Plympton, and his wife, the heiress of Quick). Per pale ar. and erm. three bars gu. quartering Quick, viz., Az. a bend wavy betw. two moles ar. Crest—A cubit arm erect vested gu. cuffed erm. holding in the hand ppr. a chaplet of roses also gu. leaved vert.

Molton (co. Norfolk). Ar. three bars gu. in chief as many martlets az. Crest—A shark's head reguard. issuing, swallowing a blackamoor.

Molton (Pinho, co. Devon; the heiress m. Strechie). Chequy or and sa.

Molton. Per chev. or and sa. (another, or and gu.); another, Az. a cross bottonée or; another, Az. a cross or, fretty gu.; another, Gu. a chev. betw. three mullets ar.; another, Ar. three bars gu. a canton erm.; another, Or, a chief gu.; another, Ar. two bars gu. a bend sa.; another, Sa. semée of annulets a lion ramp. ar.; another, Gu. three bars ar.; another, Ar. a cross formée elongated at the foot and pierced gu ; another, Sa. a lion ramp. and an orle of eight annulets ar.

Molwynog (Uwch-Alid, Wales). Sa. a stag statant ar. armed or.

Molyne (co. Leicester). Or, a cross moline sa. on a chief of the last three leopards' faces of the first.

Molyne. Sa. three mullets ar.

Molynes (Chapcot and Wallingford, co. Berks, and co. Leicester). Or, a cross moline sa. in chief three leopards' heads erased of the last. Crest—A falcon's head with wings expanded ppr.

Molynes. Same Arms. Crest—A savage's head couped ppr.

Molynes. Sa. on a chief or, three lozenges gu.

Molynes, Molins, or Molense. Paly wavy of six or and gu.

Molyneux (Earl of Sefton). Az. a cross moline or. Crest—A chapeau gu. turned up erm. adorned with a plume of peacock's feathers ppr. Supporters—Two lions az. Motto—Vivere sat vincere.

Molyneux (Teversal, co. Nottingham, bart., extinct 1812; descended from Sir Thomas Molyneux, of Haughton, made a Knight Banneret by Richard, Duke of Gloucester, at Berwick, in 1482, second son of Richard Molyneux, one of the heroes of Azincourt, and brother of Richard Molyneux, ancestor of the Earl of Sefton. Visit. Notts, 1614. Sir Francis Molyneux, seventh bart., d. s. p. in 1812, when the baronetcy expired, the estates passing to his nephew, the late Lord Henry Thomas Molyneux Howard, second son of Henry Howard, Esq., of Glossop, by Juliana, his wife, dau. of Sir William Molyneux, Bart.). Az. a cross moline quarter pierced or. Crest—On a chapeau gu. turned up erm. a plume of peacock's feathers ppr.

Molyneux (Loseley, co. Surrey; Sir Thomas Molyneux, Knt., m. Margaret, dau. of Rev. Nicholas More, and niece and heir of Sir Peynings More, Bart., of Loseley). Same Arms, quartering More, of Loseley.

Molyneux. Az. a chev. betw. three crosses moline ar. Crest—A cock's head betw. two wings ppr.

Molyneux (Daniel Molyneux, Ulster King of Arms, 1597; from his Fun. Ent. Ulster's Office; d. 13 June, 1632). Az. a cross moline or, quarter pierced of the field, in dexter chief a fleur-de-lis of the second. Crest—An heraldic tiger pass. ar. holding in the dexter paw a cross moline or.

Molyneux (Castle Dillon, co. Armagh, bart.; descended from Daniel Molyneux, Ulster King of Arms). Same Arms and Crest. Motto—Stat fortuna domus virtute.

Molyneux (quartered by Mitford, through Osbaldeston. Visit. York, 1666). Same Arms.

Molyns (Sandell, co. Hants, and co. Somerset). Erm. a cross moline sa. in chief three leopards' heads erased of the last.

Molyns. Sa. on a chief ar. (another, or) three lozenges gu.

Molyns, or Molyner. Az. six bezants, three, two, and one, on a chief or, a demi lion ramp. gu.

Mompesson (co. Norfolk). Ar. a lion ramp. sa. on the shoulder a dolphin or. Crest—A plume of ostrich feathers ar. Motto—Ma foi en Dieu seulement.

Mompesson (Bathampton, co. Wilts). Ar. a lion ramp. sa. charged on the shoulder with a martlet of the field. Crest—A jug or, with a string az. tasselled of the first. Another Crest—A plume of ostrich feathers ar. the centre one sa. all turned up or. Same Motto as the last.

Mompesson (Durnford). Same Arms.

Mompesson (Eatening, co. Nottingham). Same Arms.

Mompesson (Az. twelve pigeons ar. (another, the tinctures reversed).

Monahan, or **Monaghan.** See O'Monaghan.

Monamy (extinct in Guernsey). Per bend or and gu. a crescent counterchanged.

Monbocher (Gamston, co. Nottingham; Sir George Monbocher, temp. Henry V., son of Bertram Monbocher, and grandson of Bertram Monbocher, by Margaret, his wife, dau. and heir of Sir Richard Sutton, Knt., of Sutton-upon-Trent; Joane, dau. of said Sir George Monbocher, m. Edmond Pierpoynt. Visit. Notts, 1614). Ar. three covered cups gu. a border sa. bezantée.

Monbocher. Ar. three fusils in fesse gu. a border sa. bezantée.

Monburnay. Lozengy gu. and erm. on a canton az. a cross moline or.

Moncaster, or Molcaster (co. York). Barry of six ar. and gu. a bend sa. (another, az.). Crest—An old man's head affrontée ppr. ducally crowned or.

Moncaster. Barry of ten or and gu. on a bend sa. three escallops of the first.

Moncaster. Or, a chev. az. betw. three pairs of annulets conjoined gu.

Monceaux (Hammond Monceaux, Sheriff of co. Cumberland, temp. Richard II.). Gu. a cross recercellé, and in dexter chief an escallop or.

Monceup. Sa. a bend ar.

Monceux. Or (another, ar.) a bend sa.; another, Gu. a maunch or; another, Or, a saltire gu. on a chief of the second three escallops ar.; another, Gu. a fesse betw. three trefoils ar.

Monchensey. Ar. a chev. betw. three billets sa.; another, Ar. on a chev. sa. three boars' heads or, in the dexter chief a trefoil slipped gu.

Monchensy. Or, three escutcheons barry of six vair and gu.

Monchensy. Barruly ar. and az.

Monches. Or, on a fesse per fesse gu. and az. three buckles ar.

Monck, Monk, or Le Moyne (Potheridge, co. Devon; traced in Visit. Devon, 1620, seven generations before the reign of Edward I., and assigned a coat of eighty-eight quarterings; William Le Moyne, Esq., of Potheridge, living 3 Henry VI., 1424, had two sons, I. John Le Moyne, his successor, and II. Robert Le Moyne, from whom Viscount Monck, &c., in Ireland. The representation of this distinguished family, into which had married heiresses of Tilley, Estcott, Rishford, Trenchard, Crukerne, Grant, Champernowne, Wood, and Plantagenet, devolved, at the decease of Sir Thomas Monk, of Potheridge, upon his brother, George Monck, the celebrated Duke of Albemarle). Gu. a chev. betw. three lions' heads erased ar. Crest—A cockatrice ar.

Monck (Duke of Albemarle, extinct 1687; George Monck, or Monk, second son of Sir Thomas Monk, Knt., of Potheridge, was, for his exertions in bringing about the Restoration of Charles II., raised to the Peerage 1670). Same Arms. Crest—On a chapeau gu. turned up. erm. a cat-a-mountain statant guard. per pale sa. and ar. betw. two branches of olive vert. Supporters—Dexter, a lion ar.; sinister, a dragon ar. each supporting in the exterior paw a branch of olive vert. Motto—Fortiter, fideliter, feliciter.

Monck (Charleville, co. Wicklow; Charles Monck, Esq., of Grange Gorman, co. Dublin, descended from Robert Le Moyne, second son of William Le Moyne, Esq., of Potheridge, 1424, m. 1705, Agneta, sister and heir of John Stephens, alias Hitchcock, Esq., of Charleville, and grand-dau. of Sir John Stephens, Knt., of Finglas, co. Dublin, and Charleville, and was father of a son and a dau., viz.: Henry Monck, Esq., of Charleville, whose only dau. and heir, Elizabeth, m. George, first Marquess of Waterford; and Anne, m. Henry Quin, Esq., M.D., and had a dau., Ann Quin, m. her cousin, Charles Stanley Monck, afterwards first Viscount Monck). Same Arms. Crest—A dragon, wings elevated sa. Motto, same as last.

Monck (Viscount Monck ; Charles Stanley Monck, Esq. cousin and heir male of Henry Monck, Esq., of Charleville, was created, 1797, Baron Monck, and was raised to a Viscounty 1800. Same Arms and Crest. Supporters—Dexter, a dragon; sinister, a lion, both ar. gorged with an oak branch ppr. Motto—Fortiter, fideliter, feliciter.

Monck (Earl of Rathdown, extinct 1848; Henry Stanley, second Viscount Monck, was created an earl 1822, d. s. p. m.). Same Arms, Crest, Supporters, and Motto.

Monck (Coley Park, co. Berks; descended from William Monck, brother of Charles Monck, Esq., of Charleville, 1705). Same Arms, Crest, and Motto.

Monck (Belsay Castle, co. Northumberland, bart.; Sir William Middleton, fifth bart. of Belsay, m. Jane, dau. and heir of LAWRENCE MONCK, Esq., of Caenby, co. Lincoln; their son, the sixth bart., assumed the name and arms of MONCK, 1799). Ar. a chev. chequy or and sa. betw. three leopards' heads erased az. collared and lined gold. *Crest*—Upon a mount vert a demi griffin couchant couped ar.

Monck (Newcastle-on-Tyne). Az. a lion ramp. erm.

Moncke (Newton, near Drogheda, co. Louth; Fun. Ent. Ulster's Office, 1620, EDWARD MONCKE, Esq., of that place). Gu. a chev. betw. three lions' heads erased ar. a martlet for diff.

Monckton, or Monketon (co. Lincoln, Egham, co. Surrey, and Cavill, co. York; represented by *Viscount Galway*). Sa. on a chev. betw. three martlets or, as many mullets of the field. *Crest*—A martlet or.

Monckton-Arundel (*Viscount Galway*). See ARUNDEL.

Monckton (quartered by MITFORD, through OSBALDESTON and FOUNTAINE). Same *Arms*.

Monckton, or Mongton (co. York). Az. a fesse dancettée or.

Monckton, Mongton, or Mongdene (co. York). Per fesse indented gu. and ar. three annulets counterchanged.

Monckton, Mongton, Monkton, or Mongdene. Same *Arms*. *Crest*—Two arms in armour embowed placing a Saracen's head affrontée on the point of a spear all ppr.

Monckton (Somerford Hall, co. Stafford). Gu. on a chev. betw. three martlets or, as many mullets of the field. *Crest*—A martlet or. *Motto*—Famam extendere factis.

Mon.kton (Fineshade Abbey, co. Northampton). Same *Arms*, *Crest*, and *Motto*.

Monckton. Az. a griffin segreant or.

Monglas. Ar. two bars gu. in chief three martlets of the second.

Moncreiff-Wellwood (Tullibole, co. Kinross, originally MONCREIFF, of that Ilk, bart., 1626). Quarterly, 1st and 4th, ar. a lion ramp. gu. a chief erm.; 2nd and 3rd, ar. an oak issuing out of a well in base ppr. *Crest*—A demi lion ramp. as in the arms. *Supporters*—Two men armed cap-à-pie bearing picks upon their shoulders ppr. *Motto*—Sur esperance.

Moncreiff (*Baron Moncreiff*). Same *Arms*, *Crest*, and *Motto*. *Supporters*—On either side a man in armour holding in the exterior hand a spear resting on the shoulder all ppr. the breast-plate charged with a crescent gu.

Moncreiff (Boghall, Scotland). Ar. a lion ramp. gu. a chief erm. a bordure invecked of the second charged with six crescents of the field. *Motto*—Firma spes.

Moncreiff (France, 1672). Ar. a lion ramp. gu. on a chief erm. a martlet of the second. *Crest*—A demi lion ramp. gu. *Motto*—Sur esperance.

Moncreiff (Readie, co. Fife). Ar. a lion ramp. gu. on a chief erm. a rose of the second. *Crest*—A demi lion ramp. gu. *Motto*—Sur esperance.

Moncreiff (Murnipay, co. Fife). Same *Arms*, with a crescent for diff. *Crest*—A demi lion ramp. gu. *Motto*, as the last.

Moncreiff (Sauchope, co. Fife). Or, a lion ramp. gu. a chief erm. and a bordure indented of the second, charged with eight bezants. *Crest*—Three ears of rye banded together ppr.

Moncrieff (Culfargie, co. Perth; now represented by Major ALEXANDER MONCREIFF, the inventor of the Moncrieff gun). Ar. a lion ramp. gu. a chief erm. all within a bordure engr. az. charged with six stars or. *Crest*—A lion's head erased gu.

Moncrieff (SCOTT-MONCRIEFF, of Coats and Rynd, 1771). Quarterly, 1st and 4th, ar. a pheon az. betw. three lions' heads erased gu.; 2nd and 3rd, ar. a lion ramp. gu. a chief erm. all within a bordure engr. az. *Crest*—Three stalks of wheat growing out of the ground ppr. *Motto*—Inde spes.

Moncreiffe (that Ilk, co. Perth, bart., 1685). Ar. a lion ramp. betw. two mullets gu. a chief erm. *Crest*—A demi lion ramp. gu. *Motto*—Sur esperance.

Moncreiffe (DAVID STEWART MONCREIFFE, 1768). Quarterly, 1st and 4th grand quarters counterquartered, 1st and 4th, or, a fess chequy az. and ar., 2nd and 3rd, ar. a galley, sails furled and oars in action sa.; 2nd and 3rd grand quarters, ar. a lion ramp. gu. a chief erm. and crescent az. in fess, for MONCREIFFE. *Crest*—A unicorn's head and neck ar. maned or, and horned gu. *Mottoes*—Over the crest: Quidder will zie; below the arms: Sur espérance.

Moncur (that Ilk, co. Kincardine). Or, a fess betw. three inescutcheons gu.

Moncur (Scotland). Gu. on a chief ar. three hearts of the first.

Moncur (Slains, co. Aberdeen). Gu. a chevalier mounted and armed at all points, with sword erect ar.

Mondeford (co. Norfolk). Or, three fleurs-de-lis gu.

Monderell (co. Warwick). Az. fretty ar. (another, or).

Monderell. Gu. a fleur-de-lis ar.

Mone (co. Cornwall). Or, a cross engr. sa. a label of three points gu. each charged with as many bezants.

Mone (Mone Hall, Sheffield, and Burgthorpe, co. Hereford; GEORGE MONE, Esq. Visit. Hereford, 1634). Paly of six sa. and ar. a bend gu., quartering BRIGHTOMLEY, az. a chev. betw. three fleurs-de-lis ar.

Money, Moneye, and Morney. Chequy ar. and gu. *Crest*—An eagle's head erased, in the beak three roses stalked all ppr.

Money-Kyrle (Much Marcle, co. Hereford, Whetham, co. Wilts, and Pitsford, co. Northampton, bart., representative of the WASHBOURNES, of Washbourne, the EBNLES, of Ernle, the STOUGHTONS, of Stoughton, and the KYRLES, of Walford). Quarterly, 1st and 4th, chequy ar. and gu. on a chief sa. three eagles displ. or, for MONEY; 2nd and 3rd, vert a chev. betw. three fleurs-de-lis or, for KYRLE; quartering in addition the names of thirty-one ancient families, among which are WASHBOURNE, DABITOT, ERNLE, MALWYN, FINAMORE, KYRLE, SCUDAMORE, GIFFORD, TREGOZ, EWYAS, WINDSOR, STOUGHTON, THOROLD, RICHMOND, &c. *Crests*—1st, MONEY: An eagle's head sa. erased ar, collared gemelle, and holding in the beak a fleur-de-lis or; 2nd, KYRLE: On a mount vert a hedgehog or. *Motto*—Nil moror ictus.

Money (Walthamstow, co. Essex; confirmed to Rev. WILLIAM MONEY, and the other descendants of the late WILLIAM TAYLOR MONEY, Esq., of Walthamstow, K.H., Consul-General at Venice and Milan). Or, on a pile az. ten bezants, four, three, two, and one, on a chief erm. a lion pass. of the second, langued gu. *Crest*—A bezant betw. two wings az. each wing a semée-de-lis or. *Motto*—Factis non verbis.

Monfichett (co. Essex). Gu. three chevronels or.

Mongredien (Liverpool). Or, on a pale az. a dexter hand couped at the wrist erect ar. in chief three estoiles of the first. *Crest*—On a mount vert an eagle's head erased or, betw. two palm branches ppr. *Motto*—Sursum.

Monhalt. Az. a lion ramp. ar. *Crest*—A lion's gamb erased ar. holding a branch of oak fructed or, leaved vert.

Monhault (co. Lancaster). Az. a lion ramp. ar. tail double queued.

Monhault (co. Lancaster). Ar. three bars gemel az.

Monhault (West Riddlesden, co. York. Glover's Visit. See MAUDE, co. York). Az. three bars gemel sa. over all a lion ramp. gu. *Crest*—A lion's head gu. charged with a cross crosslet fitchée or.

Monhault. Az. a lion ramp, ar. a border or.

Monie (Sir EDWARD MONIE, knighted by Sir William Russell, Lord Deputy of Ireland, 20 April, 1595). Gu. three crescents or.

Monings. Or, three crescents gu.

Monings. Gu. a cross humettée ar. betw. four birds of the last.

Monington (co. Cornwall). Ar. on a bend sa. three mullets of six points of the first. *Crest*—A savage's head in profile ppr.

Monington (Sarnesfield Court, co. Hereford; THOMAS MONINGTON, Esq., of that place, was High Sheriff co. Hereford, 1837). Ar. a chev. betw. three unicorns saliant sa.

Monins (Waldershare and Dover, co. Kent, bart., extinct 1678; descended, according to a pedigree among Hasted's MSS. British Museum, from Sir SIMON DE MONINS, Knt., who came to England with William I.). Gu. three crescents or. *Crest*—An increscent or.

Monins (Waldershare, co. Kent; WILLIAM MONINS, Esq., Lieut.-Col. East Kent Militia, and a Deputy Lieutenant of the co. of Kent, was son of JOHN MONINS, Esq., of the Palace, Canterbury, and grandson of Rev. RICHARD MONINS, M.A., Prebendary of Bristol, representative of Dover and Canterbury, representing the ancient family of MONYN, of co. Kent, the senior line of which were the extinct barts. of Waldershare). Same *Arms* and *Crest*. *Motto*—Mediocria maxima.

Monjoye (Yeldersley, co. Derby; the heiress m. IRELAND, temp. Edward III.). Az. three escutcheons or.

Monk. See MONCK.

Monk (LINGARD-MONK, Broome House, co. Lancaster; exemplified to RICHARD BOUGHEY MONK LINGARD, Esq., of Heaton Norris, co. Lancaster, eldest son of ROGER ROWSON LINGARD, of the latter place, and of Milgate, co. Chester, by MARY MONK, his second wife, dau. of Rev. GEORGE MONK, of St. Paul's, Liverpool, and sister and heir of Rev. JOHN BOUGHEY MONK, Fellow of Trin. Coll., Cam., upon his assuming, by royal licence, 1875, the additional surname of MONK) Quarterly, 1st and 6th, MONK and LINGARD, quarterly, 1st and 4th, MONK, gu. a chev. dove-

tailed betw **our** lions' heads erased, three in chief and one
in base ar., 2nd and 3rd, LINGARD, barry of six or and
vair, on a bend engr. sa. four escallops ar.; 2nd, ROWSON,
quarterly, az. and sa. a quadrangular castle with four
towers ppr. betw. two flaunches ar. each charged with an
annulet gu.; 3rd, MONK, gu. a chev. dovetailed betw. four
lions' heads erased, three in chief and one in base ar.; 4th,
BOUGHEY, erm. three crosses pattée chevronwise gu. betw.
as many stags' heads erased and affrontée sa.; 5th, JENNINGS,
or, a chev. az. betw. in chief two plummets of the last
and in base a saltire gu. Crests—1st, MONK: A dragon sa.
charged on the wing with a cross pattée or, resting the
dexter claw on an escocheon gu. thereon a lion's head erased
gold; 2nd, LINGARD: A wolf's head erased sa. charged with
an escallop or, holding in the mouth three cinquefoils
slipped vert. Motto—Tout d'en haut.
Monk-Breton Priory (co. York). Sa. in chief two
covered cups ar. in base a cross pattée of the last.
Monkhouse (Newcastle-on-Tyne). Per fesse purp. and vert,
on a fesse ar. a monastery with two wings, in base three
monks, the centre one affrontée, the other two confronting
him, habited all ppr. Crest—Out of a tower ppr. masoned
sa. an arm in armour embowed wielding a sword also ppr.
Motto—Monachus salvabor.
Monkhouse. Vair in point gu. and ar. Crest—A church
ppr.
Monleret. Ar. a lion ramp. double queued sa.
Monmouth (Monmouth Castle, temp. Henry III.). Ar. two
bars gemel sa. over all a lion saliant gu. armed and langued
as.
Monmouth. Az. a cinquefoil betw. two demi lions pass.
guard. in pale or, betw. as many flaunches ar. each charged
with a griffin segreant of the first. Crest—A hawk's head
erased vert, charged on the neck with a chev. or, in the
mouth a trefoil of the first.
Monmouth (London). Same Arms.
Monmouth, or Mounmouth. Same Arms. Crest—
An eagle's head erased or, on the neck a chev. and in the
mouth a trefoil or.
Monmouth, Town of (co. Monmouth). Az. three chevronels or, over all a fesse gu.
Monnoux (Wotton, co. Bedford, bart., extinct 1814). Ar.
on a chev. sa. betw. three oak leaves vert as many bezants.
Crest—A turtle-dove az. winged or, membered and beaked
purp. holding in the beak an oak branch vert acorned gold.
Monnox, or Monnoux (co. Bedford, and London). Ar.
on a chev. sa. betw. three oak leaves vert as many bezants
(another, annulets or), on a chief gu. a martlet betw. **two**
anchors of the first.
Monnox. Ar. a cross sarcelly gu. a bend az.
Monnter. Sa. four martlets ar.
Monnyngs (co. Suffolk). Or, on a pile az. betw. an increscent in dexter and decrescent in sinister base gu. a
crescent or. Crest—Three crescents interwoven or.
Monox (co. Nottingham; List of Knts. co. Notts, temp.
Edward I. and II. Visit. Notts, 1614). Az. on a chev. embattled counter-embattled or, betw. three herons ar. a
leopard's face betw. two fleurs-de-lis gu. Crest—A demi
heron ar. wings gu. in the mouth a flower or, slipped and
leaved vert.
Monox (co. Huntingdon). Same Arms.
Monox (Walthamstow, co. Essex; granted 10 June, 1561).
Ar. on a chev. sa. betw. three oak leaves vert as many
bezants, on a chief gu. a dove betw. two anchors of the first.
Crest—A dove ar. holding in the beak three acorns vert
fructed or.
Monox, or Monnox (Chorley Woods, co. Herts). Same
Arms.
Monpesare (France). Or, three bends gu. on a chief az.
as many mullets of the field.
Monre, De La, or Monrey. Ar. six martlets in orle sa.
Monro (Bearcrofts, Scotland). Or, an eagle's head erased gu.
holding in the beak a laurel branch vert. Crest—An eagle
perching or. Motto—Non inferiora.
Monro (Craiglockhart, co. Edinburgh). Or, an eagle's head
erased gu. holding in beak a laurel branch vert, in dexter
chief a sinister hand erect and couped of the second, a bordure engr. az. Crest—An eagle rising ppr. Motto—Non
inferiora.
Monro (Pitlundie, Scotland). Or, an eagle's head erased gu.
holding in its beak an olive branch vert. Crest—An eagle
looking up to the sun in his glory ppr. Motto—Non inferiora.
Monro (Dr. ALEXANDER MONRO, Principal of Edinburgh
College, 1687). Or, an eagle's head erased within a bordure
wavy gu. Crest—An eagle rising with a sword ppr. Motto—
Alis et animo.

696

Monro (Coull, co. Ross, 1680). Or, an eagle's head erased
gu. within a bordure of the last. Crest—An eagle perching
ppr. Motto—Time Deum.
Monro. See MUNRO.
Monsder, or Monster (co. Derby). Gu. a chev. betw.
three leopards' faces or.
Monsell (Baron Emly). Ar. on a chev. betw. three mullets
sa. a trefoil slipped or. Crest—A lion ramp. ppr. holding
betw. the paws a mullet sa. Supporters—On either side a
lion ppr. gorged with a collar vair, therefrom pendent an
escutcheon of the arms. Motto—Mone sale.
Monson (Baron Monson). Or, two chevronels gu. Crest—
A lion ramp. ppr. supporting a column or. Supporters—
Dexter, a lion or, gorged with a collar and having a line
reflexed over the back az. the collar charged with three
crescents of the first; sinister, a griffin, wings elevated ar.
beaked and membered az. collared and lined as the dexter.
Motto—Prest pour mon pais.
Monson (Viscount Castlemaine ; Sir WILLIAM MONSON,
second son of Sir THOMAS MONSON, Bart., of Carleton, co
Lincoln, ancestor of Baron Monson, was so created 1628,
and degraded from his honours 12 July, 1661, having been
a regicide). Same Arms and Crest.
Monsterberge. Per pale or and ar. an eagle displ. with
two necks gu. armed az. (another, sa.).
Monstrell. Az. a chief ar. (another, the tinctures re-
versed).
Montabien. Gu. six mascles or, three, two, and one.
Montaby. Az. a cross or, fretty gu.
Montacute (founded in England by DROGO DE MONTE
ACUTO, who came to England with William I. in the train
of ROBERT, Earl of Moreton ; he appears by Domesday
Book to have held under the Earl the manors of Shipton
Montacute and Sutton Montacute ; from him descend all the
noble families of MONTACUTE and MONTAGU ; his great-
grandson, temp. Henry III., DRU DE MONTACUTE, had
two sons: I. DRU DE MONTACUTE, whose son, WILLIAM DE
MONTACUTE, left two daus. co-heirs, MARGARET, wife of
WILLIAM DE ECHINGHAM, and ISABEL, wife of THOMAS DE
AUDHAM; II. WILLIAM DE MONTACUTE, who continued the
male line). Ar. three lozenges in fess gu.
Montacute (Earl of Salisbury and Baron Montacute ;
passed to the NEVILLS, and through them to PLANTAGENET.
MARGARET PLANTAGENET, Countess of Salisbury, last of the
PLANTAGENETS, was beheaded and attainted, 1541; SIMON
DE MONTACUTE descended from WILLIAM DE MONTACUTE,
second son of DRU DE MONTACUTE, temp. Henry III., was
summoned to Parliament 1300; WILLIAM, third Baron
Montacute, was created Earl of Salisbury by charter, 1337).
Same Arms. Crest, from the Garter plate of WILLIAM,
second Earl of Salisbury, K.G., one of the Founder Knights
—Out of a ducal coronet gu. a griffin's head betw. two wings
ar.
Montacute (Baron Montacute ; Sir EDWARD DE MONTA-
CUTE, youngest brother of WILLIAM, first Earl of Salis-
bury, was summoned to Parliament 1342, d. 1361, when the
barony devolved on his only dau. and heir, JOANE DE
MONTACUTE, wife of WILLIAM DE UFFORD, second Earl of
Suffolk, who d. s. p.). Same Arms, each lozenge charged
with an eagle displ. a label of three points.
Montagu (Duke and Earl of Montagu, extinct 1749; descended from Sir EDWARD MONTAGU, Knt., of Boughton
Castle, co. Northampton, son of Sir EDWARD MONTAGU, Lord
Chief Justice of England, 30 Henry VIII., 1538). Quarterly,
1st and 4th, ar. three lozenges conjoined in fess gu. a border
sa., for MONTAGU ; 2nd and 3rd, or, an eagle displ. vert,
beaked and membered gu., for MONTHERMER. Crest—A
griffin's head couped or, wings endorsed and beaked sa.
Supporters—Two griffins or, winged, beaked, and membered
sa. Motto—Æquitas actionum regula.
Montagu (Duke and Earl of Manchester ; descended from
Sir HENRY MONTAGU, Lord Chief Justice of England, 1616,
fourth son of Sir EDWARD MONTAGU, Knt., of Boughton,
ancestor of the Dukes of Montagu). Quarterly, 1st and
4th, ar. three lozenges conjoined in fesse gu. a border
sa., for MONTAGU ; 2nd and 3rd, or, an eagle displ. vert,
beaked and membered gu., for MONTHERMER. Crest—A
griffin's head couped, wings elevated or, gorged with a
collar ar. charged with three lozenges gu. Supporters—
Dexter, an heraldic antelope or, armed, tufted, and hoofed
ar.; sinister, a griffin or, gorged with a collar as in the
crest. Motto—Disponendo me, non mutando me.
Montagu (Earl of Halifax, extinct 1772; descended from
Hon. GEORGE MONTAGU, son of HENRY, first Earl of Manchester, by his second wife, MARGARET CROUCH). Ar. three
lozenges in fess gu. a border sa. a mullet for diff.,
quartering MONTHERMER. Crest—A griffin's head couped

or, beaked, winged, and charged on the neck with a portcullis sa. *Supporters*—Two griffins ar. guttée de sang, beaked, membered, and wings expanded gu. each charged on the breast with a portcullis sa. *Motto*—Otium cum dignitate.

Montagu (*Earl of Sandwich*; descended from Sir SIDNEY MONTAGU, Master of the Court of Requests to Charles I., seventh son of Sir EDWARD MONTAGU, Knt., of Boughton, ancestor of the *Dukes of Manchester*). Quarterly, 1st and 4th, ar. three lozenges conjoined in fesse gu. within a border sa., for MONTAGU; 2nd and 3rd, or, an eagle displ. vert, beaked and membered gu., for MONTHERMER. *Crest*—A griffin's head couped or, beaked sa. wings endorsed of the last. *Supporters*—Dexter, a triton holding over the right shoulder a trident all ppr. crowned with an eastern crown or; sinister, an eagle, wings endorsed vert. *Motto*—Post tot naufragia portus.

Montagu (BRUDENELL-MONTAGU, *Duke of Montagu*, extinct 1790; GEORGE, fourth *Earl of Cardigan*, *m.* Lady MARY MONTAGU, dau. and co-heir of JOHN, second *Duke of Montagu*, of the MONTAGU family, who *d.* 1749; assumed the name of MONTAGU, and was created, 1766, *Duke of Montagu*, and further created, 1781, *Baron Montagu*, of Boughton, with special remainder to his grandson, Lord HENRY JAMES SCOTT, second son of his dau., Lady ELIZABETH MONTAGU, wife of HENRY, third *Duke of Buccleugh and Queensberry*, *d. s. p. m.* surviving, 1790). Quarterly, 1st and 4th, same as MONTAGU, *Duke of Montagu;* 2nd and 3rd, sa. a lion ramp. ar. on a canton of the last a cross gu., for CHURCHILL. *Crest*—A griffin's head couped or, beaked, winged, and fore-legged sa.; sinister, a wyvern, wings expanded gu. collared or, pendent therefrom an oval shield az. thereon the cross of St. Andrew ar. *Motto*—Spectemur agendo.

Montagu (BRUDENELL - MONTAGU, *Baron Montagu*, of Boughton, extinct 1770; JOHN, *Lord Brudenell*, eldest son and heir-apparent of GEORGE, fourth *Earl of Cardigan*, was so created 1762, before his father's elevation to the Dukedom of Montagu, *d. umn. vita patris*). Same *Arms*, *Crest*, *Supporters* and *Motto* as his father bore as *Duke of Montagu*.

Montagu-Scott (*Baron Montagu*, of Boughton, extinct 1845; Lord HENRY SCOTT, second son of HENRY, third *Duke of Buccleugh and Queensberry*, by Lady ELIZABETH BRUDENELL MONTAGU, dau. and co-heir of GEORGE, *Duke of Montagu* under the creation of 1766, *s.* his maternal grandfather as *Baron Montagu* under a special remainder in the patent of 1781, and assumed the name of MONTAGU, *d. s. p. m.*). Quarterly, 1st and 4th grand quarters, quarterly, 1st and 4th, France and England quarterly, 2nd, Scotland, 3rd, Ireland, over all a sinister baton ar., for FITZROY; 2nd grand quarter, or, a bend az. charged with a star of six points betw. two crescents of the field, for SCOTT; 3rd grand quarter, quarterly, 1st and 4th, ar. three lozenges conjoined in fesse gu. within a border sa., for MONTAGU; 2nd and 3rd, or, an eagle displ. vert, beaked and membered gu., for MONTHERMER. *Crest*—A griffin's head or. *Supporters*—Dexter, a unicorn ar. armed, maned, and unguled or; sinister, a griffin or, beaked and winged sa. *Motto*—Spectemur agendo.

Montagu (Lackham, co. Wilts; descended from Hon. JAMES MONTAGU, third son of HENRY, first *Earl of Manchester*, *m.* MARY, dau. and heiress of Sir ROBERT BAYNARD, of Lackham). Same *Arms*, *Crest*, and *Motto* as the *Duke of Manchester*.

Montagu (*Baron Rokeby;* MATTHEW ROBINSON, brother of MORRIS, third *Lord Rokeby*, assumed the name and arms of MONTAGU, 1776, and *s.* his brother as *Lord Rokeby*,1829). Quarterly, 1st and 4th, ar. three lozenges conjoined in fesse gu. within a border sa. a mullet for diff., for MONTAGU; 2nd and 3rd, or, an eagle displ. vert, for MONTHERMER. *Crest*—A griffin's head couped or, beaked and wings elevated sa. a mullet for diff. *Supporters*—On either side a roebuck ppr. ducally gorged and chained or, the dexter charged on the shoulder with a mullet ar. the sinister charged on the shoulder with a quatrefoil gu. *Motto*—Solo Deo salus.

Montagu-Douglas-Scott (*Duke of Buccleugh and Queensberry*). See SCOTT.

Montagu (POLLOCK-MONTAGU, Bart.). See POLLOCK.

Montagu (Montreal, Canada). Ar. three lozenges conjoined in fesse gu. on a border az. four fleurs-de-lis or, and as many roses alternately of the first, barbed and seeded ppr. *Crest*—A griffin's head couped at the neck or, elevated sa. betw. two fleurs-de-lis also sa.

Montagu (Boveney and Dorney, co. Buckingham). Ar. three fusils in fesse gu. betw. as many pellets.

Montague (co. Dorset). Az. a griffin segreant or.

Montague (JAMES MONTAGUE, Bishop of Bath and Wells, 1608-16, and of Winchester, 1616-18). Ar. three fusils in fesse gu. a border sa. *Crest*—A griffin's head or, wings endorsed sa. beaked of the last.

Montague. Sa. two talbots pass. in pale ar. (another, az. a griffin pass. or).

Montague (*temp.* Richard II.). Az. a griffin segreant **or.**

Montague (granted to Rev. HORATIO MONTAGUE). Per pale ar. and gu. four lozenges conjoined in fesse and counterchanged. *Crest*—A griffin's head couped erminois, wings endorsed and elevated pean, collared of the last. *Motto*—Spectemur agendo.

Montague. Az. a chev. or, betw. three mullets ar. on a chief gu. a lion pass. guard. of the third (another, the lion pass. or); another, Ar. three torteaux in fesse; another, Ar. (another, erm.) three fusils in fesse gu.

Montalt (*Baron Montalt*, extinct 1329; summoned to Parliament 1295; descended from ROBERT DE MONTALT, a baron to the *Earl of Chester*, *temp.* Henry II., who assumed his name from Montalt Castle, co. Flint). Az. a lion ramp. ar. *Crest*—A dexter arm embowed issuing from the wreath and throwing a dart ppr.

Montbernay. Lozengy gu. and erm. on a canton az. a cross sarcelly or.

Montberney. Ar. a fesse lozengy gu. on a canton az. a cross sarcelly or.

Montbéry (quartered by POLE, of Colcombe, co. Devon. Visit. Devon, 1620). Sa. a maunch or.

Montbliard Az. billettée and a lion ramp. crowned or.

Montbocher. Ar. three fleshpots gu. (another, has a border sa. bezantée).

Montchansey. Or, an inescutcheon gu. charged with three bars vair.

Montchansey, or Montchancy. Or, three escutcheons barry of six vair and gu. *Crest*—A ship sailing in the sea all ppr.

Montchansey, or Mountchansey (co. Suffolk). Barry of twelve ar. and az. *Crest*—A hand holding a scymitar in pale ppr.

Monteaders (co. Suffolk). Sa. fretty or.

Monteagh. Or, two bars gu. a chief indented of the last.

Monteagle, Baron. See RICE.

Monteath (granted to Lieut.-Colonel THOMAS MONTEATH). Or, a bend chequy az. and ar. a bordure gu. a chief embattled of the last, thereon an Eastern crown of the third, the rim inscribed "Ghuznée" in letters sa. betw. on the dexter, pendent by a riband per pale vert and of the fourth a representation of the badge of the third class of the Order of the Dooranée empire, and on the sinister, pendent from the like riband, a representation of the gold medal presented to Col. MONTEATH by the King of Affghanistan for his services at the siege and capture of the fort of Ghuznée, on 23 July, 1839. *Crest*—Out of an Eastern crown or, the rim charged with three bombs fired, an oak tree, the stem transfixed by a sword in fesse, the pommel and hilt to the dexter, all ppr.

Montefelant. Gu. six fleurs-de-lis or, three, two, and one.

Montefiore (granted to Rev. THOMAS LAW MONTEFIORE, M.A., Trinity College, Cambridge, Rector of Catherston Leweston, co. Dorset, second surviving son of the late JOHN MONTEFIORE, Esq., West India merchant, of London, and of "Neil's Estate," in the Island of Barbadoes, *m.* KATHERINE, only surviving child of Rev. EDWARD COWELL BRICE, Incumbent of Newnham, co. Gloucester, descended from JOHN BRICE, Esq., Bluemantle, *temp.* Richard III. and Henry VII.) Per pale gu. and az. on a chev. betw. three demi lions or, as many crosses moline of the first. *Crest*—On a mount vert three fleurs-de-lis az. in front of a demi lion or, holding betw. the paws a cross moline, as in the arms. *Motto*—Video meliora.

Montefiore (East Cliffe Lodge, Isle of Thanet, co. Kent, bart.). Ar. a cedar tree betw. two mounts of flowers ppr. on a chief az. a dagger erect ppr. pommel and hilt or, betw. two mullets of six points gold. *Crests*—1st: An Eastern crown or, the rim charged with two roses gu; 2nd: Two mounts, as in the arms, therefrom issuant a demi lion or, supporting a flag-staff ppr. thereon hoisted a forked pendant flying towards the sinister az. inscribed "Jerusalem" in Hebrew characters gold. *Supporters*—Dexter, a lion guard. or; sinister, a stag ppr. each supporting a flag-staff, therefrom flowing a banner to the dexter az. inscribed "Jerusalem" in Hebrew characters gold. *Motto*—Think and thank.

Monteique (George Monteique, Bishop of Lincoln 1617, London 1621, Durham 1628, and Archbishop of York 1628; granted 1613). Barry lozengy or and az. on a chief gu. three crosses crosslet of the first. *Crest*—Issuing out of flames ppr. a crane's head or.

Monteith. See Menteath.

Montenake. Vert a lion ramp. or.

Monteney. Paly of six or and gu. on a chief ar. a mullet sa. in the dexter chief.

Monteney. Gu. a bend cotised betw. six mullets or.

Monter. Sa. four martlets ar. two and two.

Montermer. Az. on an escutcheon betw. eight lions pass. guard. or, an eagle displ. vert.

Montesey, or Montisey. Gu. a chev. betw. three billets or. *Crest*—A sea lion holding in the paws an anchor all ppr.

Montessey. Gu. a chev. or, betw. three delves of the second.

Montferant. Or, an eagle displ. with two heads sa.

Montfichett (Stansted-Montfichett, co. Essex, *temp.* Henry II.). Gu. three chevronels or.

Montforant. Paly of six sa. and or, on a chief of the first three bezants.

Montford. See Mountfort.

Montford (granted 1342). Erm.

Montford (co. Leicester). Gu. a lion ramp. double queued ar.

Montford (London). Ar. semée of crosses crosslet gu. a lion ramp. az.

Montford (Kylnhurst, co. York). Ar. semée of crosses crosslet fitchée gu. a lion ramp. az. a bordure ermines. *Crest* —A talbot's head sa. eared or, gorged with a ducal coronet gold.

Montford. Az. four bendlets or.

Montfort, or De Dreux (*Duke of Brittany, Earl of Montfort,* and *Earl of Richmond ;* the heiress m. Louis XII. of France). Chequy or and az. a bordure gu. semée of lions of England, a canton erm.

Montfort, Lord. See Bromley.

Montfort (*Earl of Leicester,* extinct 1264 ; Simon de Montfort was so created by King John, 1206). Gu. a lion ramp. queue fourchée ar.

Montfort (*Baron Montfort,* abeyance 1367, summoned to Parliament 1295; descended from Thurstan de Montfort, of Beldesert Castle, co. Warwick, *temp.* Henry II.). Bendy of ten or and az.

Montfort (Tamworth, co. Warwick). Same *Arms,* a border of the first.

Montfort. Per pale indented ar. and gu.

Montgomerie (*Earl of Eglinton* and *Winton*). Quarterly, 1st and 4th, az. three fleurs-de-lis or, for Montgomerie; 2nd and 3rd, gu. three annulets or, stoned az., for Eglinton; all within a bordure or, charged with a double tressure flory counterflory gu., for Seton. *Crest*—A female figure ppr. anciently attired az. holding in the dexter hand an anchor or, and in the sinister the head of a savage couped of the first. *Supporters*—Two wiverns vert vomiting fire ppr. *Motto*—Gardez bien.

Montgomerie (Coylsfield, co. Ayr ; younger son of sixth *Earl of Eglinton,* whose grandson s. as twelfth earl). As the last, with a crescent in the centre of the quarterings for diff.

Montgomery (Hessilhead, co. Ayr). Gu. two spears crossing each other saltireways betw. three fleurs-de-lis in chief and fess, and as many annulets in base stoned az.

Montgomery (Skelmorlie, co. Ayr., bart. ; from whom the *Earl of Eglinton* descends through an heiress). Quarterly, 1st and 4th, az. three fleurs-de-lis or, for Montgomery; 2nd and 3rd, gu. three rings or, gemmed az., for Eglinton ; over all in the centre a two-handed sword in pale ppr. *Crest*—A man's heart surmounted of an eye ppr. *Supporters*—Two unicorns ar. armed, maned, and unguled or. *Motto*—Tout bien ou rien.

Montgomery (Kirktonholme, cadet of Skelmorlie, 1732). As the last, with a bordure ar. charged with mullets and ravens alternately sa. Same *Crest* and *Motto.*

Montgomery (Broomlands, co. Ayr). Quarterly, 1st and 4th, az. a branch of palm betw. three fleurs-de-lis or; 2nd and 3rd, Eglinton. *Crest*—A palm branch ppr. *Motto*—Procedamus in pace.

Montgomery (Scotston). Quarterly, 1st and 4th, Montgomery; 2nd and 3rd, Eglinton, en surtout, a hart's head cabossed gu.

Montgomery (Giffen, co. Ayr). Quarterly, 1st and 4th, Montgomery; 2nd and 3rd, Eglinton, over all, dividing the quarters, a cross wavy or.

Montgomery (Magbie Hill, co. Peebles, bart., extinct 1831). As the last, with a rose gu. in the centre for diff.

Montgomery (Graham-Montgomery, Stanhope, co. Peebles, bart., 1801). Quarterly, 1st and 4th, counter-quartered, Montgomerie and Eglinton, over all a cross wavy or, charged with a star betw. four crescents az. ; 2nd and 3rd, ar. a man's heart crowned ppr. on a chief sa. three escallops or, a bordure erm., for Graham. *Crest* and *Motto,* for Montgomery, as *Earl of Eglinton.* *Crest,* for Graham—An escallop or. *Motto*—Spero meliora.

Montgomery (Newton, co. Ayr, 1774). As Giffen, the cross charged with three cinquefoils in fess for diff. *Crest*—A dexter hand holding a sword indented on the back like a saw ppr. *Motto*—Fideliter.

Montgomery (Lanishaw, co. Ayr). Quarterly, 1st and 4th grand quarters, 1st and 4th, az. a bend betw. six cross crosslets fitchée or, for Mar, 2nd and 3rd, gu. a fret or, for Lyle; 2nd and 3rd grand quarters, ar. on a fess az. three stars of the first, for Mure, of Skeldon; en surtout, quarterly, 1st and 4th, az. three fleurs-de-lis or, for Montgomery; 2nd and 3rd, gu. three rings or, gemmed az., for Eglinton. *Crest*—A cock rising ppr. *Motto*—An I may.

Montgomery (Paris; descended from Lanishaw, 1860). Quarterly, 1st and 4th, counter-quartered, Montgomery and Eglinton, with a mullet or, in the centre and a bordure engr. or; 2nd and 3rd, counter-quartered, 1st and 4th, gu. a fret or, for Lyle, 2nd and 3rd, az. a bend betw. six cross crosslets fitchée or, for Mar. *Crest* and *Motto,* as *Earl of Eglinton.*

Montgomery (Braidstane, co. Ayr; descended from a second brother of the third *Lord Montgomerie*). Quarterly, 1st and 4th, Montgomery; 2nd and 3rd, Eglinton; en surtout, ar. a boar's head couped gu.

Montgomery, Town of. On the Corporation seal are two keys in saltire and endorsed; by some the *Arms* of the town are presumed to be, az. a lion ramp. or, within a border of the last.

Montgomery (Sir William de Montgomery, one of the knts. of the co. Derby, *temp.* Edward I. Visit. Notts. 1614). Or, an eagle displ. az.

Montgomery (*Baron Montgomery*; John de Montgomery was summoned to Parliament 1342, but never afterwards; he was appointed Captain of Calais and Admiral of the King's whole Fleet, 21 Edward III., A.D. 1237). Same *Arms.*

Montgomery (Sir Thomas Montgomery, K.G., 4 Nov. 1476, d. 11 Jan. 1495). Gu. a chev. erm. betw. three fleurs-de-lis or.

Montgomery (Hanby, co. Rutland ; quartered by Overton, of Morecote, in some co.; Jane, dau. and co-heir of John Montgomery, *temp.* Henry VIII., m. Bartholomew Overton. Visit. Rutland, 1618). Or, an eagle displ. az. armed and beaked gu.

Montgomery (co. Stafford). Erm. on a border gu. eight horseshoes or.

Montgomery. Ar. a cross engr. betw. four mullets gu. *Crest*—A mermaid ppr. holding a target or.

Montgomery. Gu. a lion ramp. or, a border of the last.

Montgomery (borne by the late Rev. G. Augustus Montgomery, Rector of Bishopstone, Salisbury). Az. in chief two fleurs-de-lis and in base a mullet, a bordure engr. or. *Crest* —A lion couchant ar. semée-de-lis az. gorged with a collar or, fimbriated of the second.

Montgomery (*Earl of Mount Alexander,* extinct 1757). Quarterly, 1st and 4th, az. three fleurs-de-lis or, for Montgomery; 2nd and 3rd, gu. three annulets or, gemmed az., for Eglinton, all within a bordure gold, charged with a double tressure flory counterflory gu. on a surcoat of the last a sword and sceptre saltireways ppr. *Crest*—On a cap of maintenance a dexter gauntlet erect holding a dagger all ppr. *Supporters*—Dexter, a wivern vert, gorged with a viscount's coronet or; sinister, an angel vested az. girded or, crined and winged of the last, over the shoulder a belt gu. a sword pendent ar. pommel and hilt gold. *Motto*—Honneur sans repos.

Montgomery (George Montgomery, Bishop of Meath, 1611-21, brother of Sir Hugh Montgomery, first *Viscount Montgomery,* grandfather of Hugh, first *Earl of Mount Alexander.* Fun. Ent. Ulster's Office). Per pale gu. and az. a tilting spear or, and a sword point upwards ar. pommel and hilt gold in saltire betw. a fleur-de-lis in chief, two others in fess all of the third, and three gem rings in base, one and two of the last, gemmed of the fourth.

Montgomery (Reg. Ulster's Office). Erm. a border gu. charged with six horseshoes and as many mullets alternately or.

Montgomery (Reg. Ulster's Office). Quarterly, 1st and 4th, erm. on a border gu. eight horseshoes ar.; 2nd and 3rd, az. an eagle displ. or.

Montgomery (The Hall, co. Donegal, bart.; confirmed by

Fortescue, Ulster, to HENRY CONYNGHAM MONTGOMERY, Esq., son of ALEXANDER MONTGOMERY, and their descendants). Quarterly, 1st and 4th, az. three fleurs-de-lis or; 2nd and 3rd, gu. three annulets or, gemmed az. all within a bordure ar. charged with shamrocks vert, on an escutcheon ar. a tilting spear and sword in saltire ppr. Crest—On a chapeau gu. turned up erm. a cubit arm armed, grasping a broken tilting spear ppr. Motto—Gardez bien.

Montgomery (Belhavel, co. Leitrim). Quarterly, 1st and 4th grand quarters, quarterly, 1st and 4th, az. three fleurs-de-lis or, 2nd and 3rd, gu. three gemmed rings or, gemmed az., over all an escutcheon ar. charged with a trefoil slipped vert, for MONTGOMERY; 2nd, az. three battle axes erect ar., for BATTEN; 3rd, per fesse or and az. three lions ramp. all within a tressure flory counterchanged, for LYONS. Crest A cubit arm erect vested gu. cuffed ar. grasping a broken tilting spear, the point falling downwards ppr. Motto—Patriæ infelici fidelis.

Montgomery (Convoy House, co. Donegal). Quarterly, 1st and 4th, az. three fleurs-de-lis or, for MONTGOMERY; 2nd and 3rd, gu. three annulets or, gemmed az., for EGLINTON. Crest—An arm embowed in armour, the hand grasping a broken spear head drooping all ppr. Motto—Patriæ infelici fidelis.

Montgomery (Grey Abbey, co. Down). Quarterly, 1st and 4th, az. three fleurs-de-lis or, for MONTGOMERY; 2nd and 3rd, gu. three annulets or, gemmed az., for EGLINTON; all within a bordure or, charged with a double tressure flory counterfiory gu.; on an escutcheon ar. a sword and sceptre saltirewise ppr. Crest—Out of a cap of maintenance an arm in armour erect, grasping a sword.

Montgomery (confirmed to Maj.-Gen. GEORGE SAMUEL MONTGOMERY, C.S.I.). Gu. two spears in saltire betw. three fleurs-de-lis in chief and as many annulets in base or, stoned az., quartering COLE, MONTGOMERY, of Mount Alexander, TIPPING, TICHBORNE, BYSSE, &c. Crest—A dexter arm in armour embowed, the hand grasping a broken spear all ppr. Motto—Patriæ infelice fidelis.

Montgomery (Beaulieu, co. Louth). Quarterly, 1st and 4th, as preceding, for MONTGOMERY; 2nd and 3rd, gu. three annulets or, stoned az., for EGLINTON; all within a border of the second, charged with a double tressure of the third. Crest—MONTGOMERY: An arm embowed in armour, the hand grasping a broken spear, head drooping, all ppr. The quarterings of TICHBORNE, of Beaulieu, are ten in number, in addition to TICHBORNE. Motto—Patriæ infelici fidelis.

Montgomery (exemplified to CONWAY HEATLEY, Esq., eldest son of WILLIAM HEATLEY, Esq., by his wife, ANNA HELENA, dau. of WILLIAM MONTGOMERY, of Rosemount, co. Down, descended from a younger branch of MONTGOMERY, Earl of Mount Alexander, on his assuming, by royal licence, 1820, the surname of MONTGOMERY only). Quarterly, 1st and 4th, az. three fleurs-de-lis or; 2nd and 3rd, gu. three gem rings or, stoned az. on an inescutcheon gu. a sword and sceptre in saltire ppr. The whole within a border of the second, a double tressure flory counterflory gu. Crest—On a chapeau gu. turned up erm. a dexter gauntlet erect holding a dagger ppr. Motto—Honneur sans repos.

Montgomery. See MONTGOMERIE.

Montgommere (co. Derby). Ar. an eagle displ. az. armed gu.

Monthalt (co. Lincoln). Ar. three bars gemelles sa. over all a lion ramp. gu.

Monthermer (Earl of Gloucester and Hereford, Baron Monthermer, earldom extinct 1340, barony passed to MONTACUTE, Earl of Salisbury, through MARGARET, only dau. and heiress of THOMAS, second Lord Monthermer and Earl of Gloucester and Hereford, who m. Sir JOHN DE MONTACUTE, second son of WILLIAM, first Earl of Salisbury, whose son JOHN DE MONTACUTE, Lord Monthermer, jure matris, succeeded as third Earl of Salisbury). Or, an eagle displ. vert, beaked and beaked gu.

Monthermer. Or, an eagle displ. vert. Crest—A griffin's head betw. two wings ppr.

Monthermer (Stockenham). Or, an eagle displ. vert, beaked and membered gu.

Monthermer. Same Arms, a bordure gu. charged with eight lions pass. guard. of the first.

Montjoy. Vairé ar. and sa. a bend gu.

Montlaby. Az. a cross ar. fretty gu. Crest—A demi fleur-de-lis issuing.

Montmorency (France: "le premier Baron Chrestien"). Or, a cross gu. betw. four eagles displ. sa. This was the original coat; but MATHIEU DE MONTMORENCY, Constable of France under Philip Augustus, having gallantly distinguished himself at the battle of Bovines, added twelve

699

eagles to his arms in commemoration of the capture of that number of Imperial Standards. Crest—A dog courant ppr. Supporters—Two angels ppr. Motto—Dieu ayde au premier Baron Chrestien.

Montmorency (Ireland; by royal licence, dated 17 June, 1815, the family of MORRES, of co. Tipperary, was allowed to take the surname and arms of DE MONTMORENCY). Or, a cross gu. betw. four eagles displ. az. Crest—On a ducal coronet or, a peacock in its pride ppr. Motto—Dieu ayde.

Montmorency (Viscount Frankfort and Viscount Mount Morres). See DE MONTMORENCY.

Montolieu (Marseilles, Languedoc, France; borne in virtue of a diploma granted by the Emperor Joseph, in 1706, to DAVID DE MONTOLIEU, and his heirs for ever, Baron de Saint Hippolite, of the Holy Roman Empire, a general in the British army, who d. in 1761, whose great-granddaughter, representative and eldest co-heir, MARIA GEORGIANA, m. HUGH HAMMERSLEY, Esq.). Az. a fleur-de-lis or, betw. three crescents in chief and as many mullets in base ar. Crest—A fleur-de-lis or, betw. two wings erect sa. Supporters—Two eagles reguard. wings expanded and invected ppr. Motto—Deo et Principi.

Montpinson, or Mountpinzo (co. Norfolk, temp. Edward III.). Ar. a lion ramp. sa. on the shoulder a dolphin embowed naiant or.

Montresor (Denne Hill, co. Kent). Az. two arms mailed ppr. holding each a sword erect, on a plate in chief a cross couped gu. Crest—A royal helmet or. Motto—Mon Trésor.

Montrollier. Or, fretty az. on an inescutcheon gu. a demi lion erased ar.

Montrose, Duke of. See GRAHAM.

Montveron. Az. three dolphins naiant ar.

Montwellet. Or, a fret gu. a canton az.

Monypenny (Pitmilly, co. Fife). Quarterly, 1st and 4th, ar. a dolphin naiant az., for MONYPENNY; 2nd and 3rd, az. three crosses crosslet fitchée issuing out of as many crescents ar., for CATHCART. Crest—Neptune bestriding a dolphin naiant in waves of the sea, holding with his dexter hand the reins, and in his sinister the trident all ppr. Motto—Imperat æquor.

Moodie, or Mudie (Melsetter, in the Orkney Isles, now of the Cape of Good Hope). Quarterly, 1st and 4th, az. three ships in full sail ar. on a chief wavy gu. a beacon or; 2nd and 3rd, az. a chev. erm. betw. three pheons ar. in chief a hunting-horn ppr. Crest—On a naval coronet a lion pass. holding a flag, on a scroll above the same, "The reward of valour." The ancient motto of the family was, "God with us." The 2nd and 3rd quarters are the ancient coat of MOODIE, or MUDIE, of Melsetter; the 1st and 4th quarters being an augmentation granted by Queen Anne.

Moodie (England). Ar. a chev. betw. three trefoils sa. a chief of the last. Crest—A demi pegasus, wings endorsed, body enfiled with a ducal coronet.

Moodie. Az. a chev. erm. betw. three pheons ar.

Moody (Aspley, co. Bedford; EDMUND Moody, Esq., of Southampton, m. URSULA, sister and co-heir of RICHARD VERNON SADLEIR, Esq., of Aspley Guise, a descendant of Sir RALPH SADLEIR, temp. Henry VIII., Edward VI., Mary I., and Queen Elizabeth). Per pale az. and ar. a chev. engr. betw. three trefoils slipped, a chief per pale thereon three fusils all counterchanged, quartering SADLEIR, CHUTE, TROTT, and A'LEIGH. Crest—Two falchions in saltire ppr. pommels and hilts or, surmounted by a wolf's head erased per pale ar. and az.

Moody. Ar. on a fesse sa. betw. three trefoils slipped az. as many mascles or, on a chief of the third two hands in fesse issuant from clouds on the dexter and sinister sides ppr. holding a rose gu. Crest—Two arms embowed and crossed in saltire near the wrist, the dexter vested gu. surmounted of the sinister vested vert, cuffs ar. each holding in the hand a falchion ppr. pommels and hilts or, the blades saltireways.

Moody, or Moodye (Garesdon, co. Wilts, bart., unclaimed since 1662). Vert a fesse engr. ar. surmounted of another gu. betw. three harpies of the second crined or. Crest—A wolf's head erased ppr.

Moodye (Ipswich, co. Suffolk). Ar. on a chev. engr. sa. betw. three trefoils slipped vert as many lozenges or, on a chief az. two arms issuing from clouds ppr. vested bendy or and gu. holding in the hands a rose of the last. Crest—Tw arms embowed in saltire, the dexter vested gu. the sinister vert, each holding a cutlass ar. hilted or

Mooke (co. Devon). Ar. three leopards' faces gu. (another sa.).

Moole (co. Stafford). Or, fretty gu. an annulet ar.

Moon (Portman Square, London, bart.). Ar. an eagle displ. gu. charged on the breast with two swords in saltire ppr. on a chief nebuly az. a fasces erect or, betw. two crescents ar. *Crest*—A crescent ar. in front of a fasces in bend or, surmounting a sword in bend sinister ppr. *Motto*—Æquam servare mentem.

Moone (Ash, co. Devon). Ar. an eagle displ. sa. beaked and legged or, on a chief of the second three crescents erm.

Moone (co Devon). Per fesse gu. and az. three crescents ar.

Moone, Moun, or Moyne. Ar. a cross engr. sa. *Crest*—A bear ramp. supporting a staff in pale ppr.

Moone. Or, a cross engr. sa. a label or, semée of hurts. *Crest*—An arm erm. holding a fleur-de-lis or.

Moone. Gu. a maunch erm. charged with a cinque-foil or.

Mooney (Garris and Ringelstown, co. Meath; Fun. Ent. Ulster's Office, 1638, THOMAS MOONEY, Esq., of Garris, descended from MOONEY, of Ballagh Mooney, in the King's co., who were a branch of the Sept of O'CONOR FAILY). Ar. a holly tree eradicated vert, thereon a lizard pass. or, a border compony counter-compony of the first and second.

Moonson (co. Lincoln). Az. out of a crescent ar. a sun or.

Moor (East Grinstead, co. Sussex; granted to HENRY ISAAC MOOR, Esq., of Greenwich, Lord of the Manor of Otterham, co. Kent, Lieutenant R.N. and Captain E.I.C.'s Naval Service). Az. two greyhounds courant in pale ar. on a chief or, an anchor sa. surmounted by a sword in saltire ppr. pommel and hilt of the third betw. two Moors' heads couped also ppr. wreathed about the temples of the second and vert. *Crest*—The bust of a Moorish king ppr. vested gu. wreathed about the temples ar. and vert, on the head an Eastern crown or, surmounting an anchor in bend sinister *Motto*—In Deo confido.

Moor (Bank Hall, in Kirkdale, co. Lancaster, 1567). Ar. three greyhounds courant sa. collared or. *Crest*—A moorcock ar. guttée de poix, membered and wattled gu. holding in the beak a branch of carnation ppr.

Moorcroft. Sa. an ass. ar. saddled, bridled, and caparisoned gu. betw. three marigolds or.

Moore (Fawley, co. Berks, bart., extinct 1807 ; Sir FRANCIS MOORE, an eminent person temp. Queen Elizabeth, M.P. for Oxford, fifth in descent from ROGER MOORE, temp. Henry VI., d. 1621, leaving a son and heir, HENRY MOORE, Esq., of Fawley, created a bart. 1627). Ar. a moorcock sa. combed and wattled gu. *Crest*—On a tuft of grass vert a moorcock sa. combed and wattled gu. *Motto*—Nihil utile quod non honestum.

Moore (Appleby-Parva, cos. Leicester and Derby, a manor purchased temp. Elizabeth, by CHARLES MOORE, of Stretton, from Sir Edward Griffin, Knt.). Erm. three greyhounds courant sa. collared gu. on a canton of the last a lion pass. or. *Crest*—A moorcock sa. guttée d'or, the beak, comb, wattles, and legs gu. holding in the beak a branch of heath ppr. *Motto*—Non civium ardor.

Moore (Grimeshill, co. Westmoreland; WILLIAM MOORE, Esq., was the only son of Lieut.-Col. JOHN MOORE, by ELIZA, his wife, second dau. and co-heir of RICHARD GATHORNE, Esq., of Kirkby Lonsdale, and fourth in descent from GILES MOORE, Esq., of Grimeshill, a Deputy Lieutenant for co. Westmoreland, who m. MARY, second dau. and co-heir of JAMES CRAGG, Esq., of Dent, by MARY, his wife, second dau. and co-heir of JOHN MIDDLETON, Esq., the last male descendant of the very ancient family of MIDDLETON, of Middleton). Or, on a chev. pean betw. three Moors' heads in profile couped at the neck ppr. wreathed about the temples ar. and sa. a pheon of the field, quartering CRAGG, MIDDLETON, BINDLOSSE, and GATHORNE. *Crest*—A swan, wings elevated ar. charged on the breast with a pheon sa. in front of bullrushes ppr. *Motto*—Animum rege.

Moore (Apsley Guise, co. Bedford). Sa. a swan, wings expanded ar. membered or, within a bordure engr. of the third. *Crest*—An eagle ar. preying on a hare sa.

Moore (Cookham, co. Berks, and Corbet, co. Salop). Sa. a swan, wings expanded ar. membered or, a bordure engr. of the third. *Crest*—An eagle ar. preying on a hare sa.

Moore (cos. Devon, Hants, and Surrey). Sa. a swan close ar. a bordure engr. or. *Crest*—Out of a ducal coronet az. a swan's neck ar. beaked gu.

Moore (Blandford Forum, co. Dorset). Or, three roses in chev. gu. barbed and seeded ppr. betw. as many moorcocks also ppr. *Crest*—A staff raguly fessways or, thereon a moorcock ppr. charged on the breast with a trefoil gold. *Motto*—Amore floresco.

Moore (Northanton, co. Oxford; WILLIAM MOORE, alias

MEREDITH, second son of JOHN MOORE, Esq., of Upperwyld, co. Bucks, temp. Queen Elizabeth. Visit. Oxon, 1566). Per pale or and ar. a lion ramp. sa. *Crest*—A demi lion ramp. couped per pale or and ar. collared and lined sa.

Moore, alias Meredith (co. Bedford). Same *Arms*.

Moore (Looseley; Sheriff of Surrey, temp. Henry VIII.). Az. on a cross ar. five martlets sa.

Moore (co. Somerset; sometime lords of the manor of Greinton and Mere). Ar. two bars engr. vert betw. nine martlets gu. each bar charged with a spear head erect ar.

Moore (Langley Lodge, Gerard's Cross, co. Bucks, and Liverpool). Ar. on a cross ar. betw. in the 1st and 4th quarters a negro's head in profile ppr. and in the 2nd and 3rd a mullet go. a bee volant or. *Crest*—On a mount vert a moorcock sa. in the beak a sprig of bramble slipped ppr. *Motto*—Æquabiliter et diligenter.

Moore (Thelwall, co. Chester, 1636). Sa. a cross ar. *Crest*—A Moor's head couped ppr. with a cap gu. turned up erm.

Moore (Stockwell, co. Surrey). Ar. a chev. engr. betw. three moorcocks sa. combs, wattles, and legs gu. *Crest*—A Moor's head affrontée ppr. wreathed round the temples az. and or, a jewel pendent in the ears az. *Motto*—Resolve well, persevere.

Moore (Frampton Hall, co. Lincoln). Quarterly, 1st, ar. a chev. engr. sa. betw. three moorcocks ppr.; 2nd, ar. on a chev. betw. three unicorns' heads erased sa. as many bezants; 3rd, or, three lions ramp. gu., for CRESACRE; 4th, per chev. sa. and or, three elephants' heads erased counterchanged, for SAUNDERS; 5th, erm. on a chev. sa. betw. two dragons' heads erased ppr. in chief and a bugle-horn of the second stringed gu. in base a griffin's head couped betw. two buglehorns stringed or, for TUNNARD (modern); 6th, az. a chev. betw. three demi griffins or, for TUNNARD (ancient); 7th, sa. on a fesse cotised or, betw. three coneys courant ar. as many escallops of the field, for CONEY; 8th, vert three escutcheons ar. each charged with a border engr. or, for BURRELL. *Crest*—A Moor's head affrontée ppr. wreathed round the temples az. and or, a jewel pendent in the ears ar. *Motto*—Disce mori mundo.

Moore (Pendridge, co. Dorset). Ar. on a fesse betw. three moorcocks sa. as many mullets or.

Moore (Canterbury). Ar. a chev. betw. three moorcocks sa. *Crest*—A Moor's head sidefaced ppr. wreathed about the temples or and sa. on the neck a crescent for diff.

Moore (Wollington, co. Hereford). Sa. a chev. betw. three fleurs-de-lis ar. a crescent for diff.

Moore (Sandon and Haddon, co. Hertford, and London). Ar. guttée de sang two chevronels gu. *Crest*—A demi lion ramp. guard. or, issuing out of a demi castle ar. holding a banner of the arms, the staff sa. (another bears the crest issuing out of a ducal coronet gu.).

Moore (co. Kent). Per fesse indented or and az. three mullets in chief gu.

Moore, or More (co. Kent). Az. on a chief indented or, three mullets pierced gu. *Crest*—Out of a ducal coronet or, a Moor's head ppr. filleted round the temples az. and or, a jewel pendent in the ears ar.

Moore (Bankill, co. Lancaster). Vert ten trefoils ar. four, three, two, and one.

Moore (Grantham, co. Lincoln; granted 1635). Gu. on a chief indented ar. three mullets sa. *Crest*—A lion pass. guard. gu. ducally gorged and chained ar.

Moore (co. Lincoln). Vairé gu. and erm.

Moore (Lord Mayor of London, 1682). Erm. three greyhounds courant sa. and for augmentation, on a canton gu. a lion of England.

Moore (Inner Temple, London; granted 28 April, 1569). Same *Arms* and *Crest* as MOOR, Bart., of Fawley, co. Berks.

Moore (JOHN MOORE, Bishop of Norwich, 1691-1707, and Bishop of Ely, 1707-14). Erm. on a chev. three cinquefoils ar.

Moore (co. Oxford). Ar. a fesse indented componée sa. and gu. betw. three mullets of the last.

Moore (The Moore, co. Salop). Per pale az. and ar. barry of twelve counterchanged.

Moore (Ipswich, co. Suffolk). Ar. a fesse betw. three mullets az. *Crest*—A stag pass sa. platée, attired or.

Moore (borne by the late Sir JOHN MOORE, K.B., the hero of Corunna; by JAMES CARRICK-MOORE, Esq., of Corswall, co. Wigton; by Admiral Sir GRAHAM MOORE, K.C.B.; by CHARLES MOORE, Esq., Barrister-at-law; and by FRANCIS MOORE, Esq., formerly Under Secretary at War; sons of JOHN MOORE, of Dovehill, M.D., the author of "Zeluco"). Ar. on a fesse engr. az. three mullets of the field, in chief a sphinx ppr. a bordure engr. gu. *Crest*—A Moor's head couped at the neck, turban ppr.

Moore (EDMUND F. MOORE, Esq., of Lincoln's Inn, Barrister-at-law). Ar. two greyhounds courant in pale sa. on a chief **as.** three estoiles or, quartering sa. two pallets ar. on a fesse **gu.** three fleurs-de-lis or. *Crest*—A blackamoor's head in profile ppr. the head encircled with a wreath ar. and az. and crowned with an Eastern coronet of six points, gold earrings, and vested in a white drapery fastened with a gold buckle on the shoulder. *Motto*—In Deo confido.

Moore (Moorehayes, in Cullompton, co. Devon, *temp.* Henry III.; the last male heir, GEORGE MOORE, Esq., *d.* in 1711; the heiress *m.* BLACKMORE). Erm. on a chev. az. three cinquefoils or. *Crest*—A dexter arm embowed ppr. holding a sword ar.

Moore (Wichford, co. Hants. Visit. 1634). Ar. two bars vert betw. nine martlets gu. three, three, and three. *Crest*—A mermaid ppr. hair, mirror, and comb or.

Moore (Newington, co. Surrey, 1576). Az. on a chev. betw. three lions' heads erased or, as many martlets sa. *Crest*—A demi bull saliant erminois, attired sa.

Moore (co. Wilts). Az. three leopards' faces or.

Moore (Barwick, St. John, co. Wilts). Erm. on a chev. betw. three Moors' heads couped sa. two swords in saltire ar.

Moore (granted to WILLIAM CAMERON MOORE, Esq., of Manchester, and of Bamford, co. Derby). Az. a swan ar. wings elevated or, a border nebuly of the last. on a chief of the second a lion pass. of the first betw. two flowers of the cotton tree slipped ppr. *Crest*—A swan ar. wings elevated barry of six or and az. holding in the beak a flower of the cotton tree, as in the arms. *Motto*—Mores hoc mutato.

Moore. Az. on a chief indented or, three mullets pierced gu. *Crest*—On a human heart gu. an eagle's leg erased at the thigh sa. *Another Crest*—Out of a ducal coronet or, a Moor's head and shoulders in profile sa. wreathed about the temples.

Moore. Ar. three Moors' heads couped at the shoulders ppr. wreathed about the temples of the field. *Crest*—A Moor's head, as in the arms.

Moore. Ar. a chev. sa. betw. **three fleurs-de-lis** gu. a pile of the second.

Moore (Rev. WALTER MOORE). Ar. three greyhounds courant in pale sa. collared or. *Crest*—A moorcock ppr. *Motto*—Dum spiro spero.

Moore. Gu. a fesse betw. three boars' heads sa.; another, Ar. two bars az. betw. nine martlets vert, three, two, and one; another, Ar. ten martlets sa.; another, Gu. three text S's or; another, Ar. a fleur-de-lis betw. three Moors' heads sa.; another, Sa. a swan ar. within a bordure engr. or; another, Ar. a fesse gu. betw. six moorcocks sa. beaked and legged of the second; another, Erm. on a chev. az. three cinquefoils or.

Moore. Az. on a chev. betw. three lions' heads erased or, as many martlets sa. *Crest*—A demi bull erm. armed or.

Moore. Ar. on a chev. sa. betw. three blackamoors' heads in profile, couped of the second, clothed on the shoulder gu. two swords, the points crossing each other of the first, hilts and pommels or.

Moore. Ar. three Moors' heads in profile couped sa. a fleur-de-lis in chief. *Crest*—A naked man sa. holding a dart or.

Moore, or O'More (Chieftains of the territory of Leix, now the Queen's co.). See O'MORE.

Moore, or More (Balyna, co. Kildare; descended from O'MORE; LETITIA, dau. and heir of JAMES MOORE, Esq., of Balyna, *m.* RICHARD O'FERRALL, Esq., of Ballyree, co. Longford, and *d.* 1778). Vert a lion ramp. or, in chief three mullets of the last. *Crest*—A hand lying fessways, couped at the wrist, holding a sword erect, impaling three gory heads all ppr. *Mottoes*—Conlan a-bu; and, Spea mea Deus.

Moore (Cremorgan, in the Queen's co.; descended from MORTOGH OGE O'MORE, of Cremorgan, *d.* 1580). Same *Arms* and *Crest*. *Motto*—Semper fidelis et audax.

Moore (granted to JOHN MULCAIL, Esq., of the city of Dublin, by Hawkins, Ulster, 1770, upon his taking the surname of MOORE, on a claim that he was descended from JOHN MOORE, or MORE, son of RORY O'MORE, last Lord of Leix, who was called MULCAUGHO, and whose descendants called themselves MULCAIL). Same *Arms*.

Moore (Moore Place, and Benenden, co. Kent; descended from THOMAS DE LA MORE, who held the manor of Moore Place, or Moore Court, in Ivy Church, co. Kent, *temp.* Henry II.; his representative, *temp.* Henry VIII., JOHN MOORE, Esq., of Benenden, co. Kent, *m.* MARGARET, dau. of JOHN BRENT, and cousin and heir of ROBERT BRENT, Esq., of Wellsborough, and had six sons, viz., I. OWEN, *d. s. p.*; II. Sir EDWARD, ancestor of the *Marquess of Drogheda*; III. GEORGE, *d. s. p.*; IV. Sir THOMAS, ancestor of MOORE, of Croghan, and the extinct *Earl of Charleville*; V. NICHOLAS;

701

VI. BRENT, ancestor of MOORE, of co. Louth). Az. on a chief indented or, three mullets pierced gu.

Moore (*Earl and Marquess of Drogheda*; descended from Sir EDWARD MOORE, Knt., eldest surviving son of JOHN MOORE, Esq., of Benenden). Same *Arms*. *Crest*—Out of a ducal coronet or, a Moor's head ppr. wreathed about the temples ar. and az. *Supporters*—Two greyhounds ar. *Motto*—Fortis cadere cedere non potest.

Moore (Ballyhale, co. Kilkenny, Moorfield, co. Kildare, &c.; descended from Hon. PONSONBY MOORE, second son of EDWARD, fifth *Earl of Drogheda*). Same *Arms Crest*, and *Motto*.

Moore (Kersant, co. Berks, bart., extinct; Admiral Sir JOHN MOORE, son of Hon. and Rev. HENRY MOORE, third son of HENRY, third *Earl of Drogheda*, was created a bart. 1766, and a Knight of the Bath 25 June, 1772, *d. s. p. m.*). Same *Arms, Crest*, and *Motto*. *Supporters*—Two greyhounds reguard. ar. each supporting with the exterior foot an anchor sa.

Moore (Croghan, King's co.; descended from Sir THOMAS MOORE, Knt., second surviving son of JOHN MOORE, Esq., of Moore Place, and Benenden, co. Kent; Fun. Ent. Ulster's Office, 1633, Sir JOHN MOORE, Knt., of Croghan). Same *Arms* and *Crest*, a crescent for diff.

Moore (*Earl of Charleville*, extinct 1764; JOHN MOORE, Esq., of Croghan, was created *Baron Tullamore*, 1715; his son and successor was raised to an earldom 1758). Same *Arms* and *Crest*, a crescent for diff. *Supporters*—Two blackamoors attired az. wreathed about the temples of the last and or, each holding in the exterior hand a dart ppr. *Motto*—Fortis cadere cedere non potest.

Moore (co. Louth; descended from BRENT MOORE, sixth son of JOHN MOORE, Esq., of Benenden, co. Kent; Fun. Ent. Ulster's Office, 1684, THOMAS MOORE, eldest son of Col. BRENT MOORE). Same *Arms*, a crescent for diff.

Moore (Ross Carbery, co. Cork, bart.). Same *Arms*. *Crest* —Out of a ducal coronet a Moor's head in profile all ppr. *Motto*—Fortis cadere cedere non potest.

Moore (Tara House, co. Meath, and Tullyhallen, co. Louth; descended from JOHN MOORE, of Dublin, who purchased land in co. Louth 1721). Same *Arms* and *Crest*. *Motto*— Durum patientia frango.

Moore-Brabazon (Tara House). See BRABAZON.

Moore (*Earl of Mountcashell*; descended from STEPHEN MOORE, Esq., of Kilworth, eldest son of RICHARD MOORE, Esq., co. Salop, who settled at Clonmell, *temp.* James I.). Sa. a swan ar. membered and beaked or, a border engr. of the last. *Crest*—A goshawk, wings addorsed, preying on a coney all ppr. *Supporters*—Dexter, a leopard; sinister, a rhinoceros, both ppr. collared and chained or. *Motto*—Vis unita fortior.

Moore (Barne, co. Tipperary; descended from THOMAS MOORE, second son of RICHARD MOORE, Esq., co. Salop). Same *Arms, Crest*, and *Motto*, a crescent for diff.

Moore (Mooresfort, co. Tipperary; EMILY, dau. and heiress of MAURICE CROSBIE MOORE, Esq., of Mooresfort, *m.* 1841, Lord CECIL GORDON, fifth son of GEORGE, ninth *Marquess of Huntley*). Ar. a chev. engr. betw. three moorcocks sa. *Crest*—A Moor's head and shoulders in profile ppr. wreathed about the temples ar. and az.

Moore (GORDON-MOORE; exemplified to Lord CECIL GORDON and EMILY MOORE, his wife, dau. of MAURICE CROSBIE MOORE, Esq., of Mooresfort, co. Tipperary, on their assuming, by royal licence, 1850, the additional surname and arms of MOORE). Quarterly, 1st and 4th, ar. a chev. engr. betw. three moorcocks sa., for MOORE; 2nd and 3rd, az. three boars' heads couped, two and one or, for GORDON. *Crests*—1st: A Moor's head and shoulders in profile ppr. wreathed about the temples ar. and az., for MOORE; 2nd: A stag's head couped ppr. corned or, for GORDON. *Motto*—Audaces fortuna juvat.

Moore (Ballina, co. Mayo, and Alicante, in Spain; allowed by Hawkins, Ulster, 1773, to GEORGE MOORE, of Alicante, greatgrandson of GEORGE MOORE, Esq., of Ballina, who was son of THOMAS MOORE, Esq., of Barenburgh, co. York). Ar. a chev. gu. betw. three moorcocks ppr. *Crest*—On a ducal coronet or, a moorcock ppr. *Motto*—Fortis cadere cedere non potest.

Moore (Moore Hall, co. Mayo). Or, a chev. engr. betw. three moorcocks sa. *Crest*—A Moor's head and shoulders ppr. in the ear a ring or. *Motto*—Fortis cadere cedere non potest.

Moore (Moigne Hall, co. Cavan; Reg. Ulster's Office, to NICHOLAS MOORE, captain in the regiment of Col. Robert Tothill, sent to Ireland by the Parliament, 1649). Az. on a chief indented or, three mullets gu. pierced ar. a border indented erm. *Crest*—An eagle's leg erased a la quise sa. grasping a human heart gu.

Moore (Col. MOORE, one of the officers sent to Ireland by the Parliament, 1649). Vert ten trefoils slipped ar. four, three, two, and one.

Moore (Rosscarberry, co. Cork). Ar. two bars sa. betw. nine martlets gu. *Crest*—An heraldic tiger's head couped ar. pierced through with a broken spear ppr.

Moore (Drogheda; Reg. Ulster's Office). Barry of six ar. and sa. a lion ramp. gu.

Moore (Barmeath and Carblagh, co. Meath; Fun. Ent. Ulster's Office, 1614, PATRICK MOORE, of the latter place, son of BARTHOLOMEW MOORE, who was second son of MOORE, of Barmeath). Sa. two bars ar..

Moore (impalement Fun. Ent. 1667, Ulster's Office). Ar. a chev. betw. three Moor's heads in profile couped at the neck sa.

Moore (certified to JOHN MOORE, Esq., of Bristol, son of JOHN MOORE, of Bristol and of Ireland). Ar. two bars engr. vert, each charged with a spear's head or, betw. nine martlets, three, three, and three gu. *Crest*—A tiger's head erased or, thrust through the neck with a broken spear ar. *Motto*—Fortis cadere cedere non potest.

Moore (Moore Fort, co. Antrim; confirmed to WILLIAM MOORE, Esq., and to the descendants of his grandfather). Az. on a chief engr. or, an annulet betw. two mullets gu. *Crest*—Out of a mural crown ppr. charged with an annulet gu. a Moor's head in profile also ppr. the temples encircled with a wreath ar. and az. *Motto*—Fortis cadere cedere non potest.

Moore (granted to CHARLES MOORE, Esq., of Coogee, Sydney, New South Wales, Mayor of that city, 1867-9, son of JAMES MOORE, of Ballymacarue, co. Cavan). Az. a cross crosslet or, on a canton ar. a kangaroo ppr. *Crest*—Out of a mural crown gu. a Moor's head couped at the shoulders ppr. on the neck a cross crosslet gold, and round the temples a wreath or and az. *Motto*—Perseverando et cavendo.

Moore (granted to CHARLES MOORE, Esq., of Mooresfort, co. Tipperary). Az. on a chief engr. or, a rose gu. barbed and seeded ppr. betw. two mullets pierced of the third. *Crest*—Out of a mural crown ppr. a Moor's head also ppr. wreathed about the temples ar. and az. and charged on the neck with a rose gu. barbed vert. *Motto*—Fortis cadere cedere non potest.

Moores. Az. on a saltire or, betw. four annulets of the second five pallets gu. *Crest*—An eagle rising ppr. *Motto*—Juravi et adjuravi.

Moorhouse (co. York). Or, a saltire gobony sa. and ar. *Crest*—A pelican vulning herself ppr.

Mooris. Sa. on a saltire ar. an escutcheon gu. charged with a cross or.

Moorle. Ar. fretty gu. semée of lions pass. guard. of the second.

Moorman. Or, a cross engr. chequy gu. and ar. *Crest*—A hand holding four arrows points downward all ppr.

Moorside. Quarterly, 1st and 4th, ar. a bull pass. sa. on a border of the second eight bezants; 2nd and 3rd, or, on a chev. az. betw. three boars' heads erased sa. as many mullets pierced ar. *Crests*—1st: A demi dragon vert, holding in the paw an arrow point downwards sa.; 2nd: A tree vert. *Motto*—Insiste firmiter.

Moorsom. Erminois on a chev. az. betw. two moorcocks in chief and a galley in base ppr. three estoiles of six points ar. *Crest*—On a mount vert a moorcock in front of a banner erect ppr. *Motto*—Ad astra.

Moorton, or Moreton (Moorton, co. Stafford). Ar. a chev. gu. betw. three square buckles sa. tongues paleways.

Moran (granted to PATRICK O'ROURKE MORAN, Esq., of Ballinamore, co. Leitrim, son of JOHN MORAN, of Ballinamore, by MARY, his wife, dau. and heiress of OWEN O'ROURKE, also of Ballinamore). Quarterly, 1st and 4th, az. on a mount ppr. two lions combatant or, supporting a flag staff also ppr. therefrom a flag ar., for MORAN; 2nd and 3rd, or, two lions pass. in pale sa. on a canton gu. an ancient Irish crown of the first, for O'ROURKE. *Crests*—1st, MORAN: Out of a mural crown a demi Saracen, head in profile all ppr.; 2nd, O'ROURKE: Out of an ancient Irish crown or, a cubit arm in armour holding a scymitar all ppr. *Motto*—Fides non timet.

Morant (Brockenhurst Park, co. Hants). Gu. a fesse ar. fretty az. betw. three talbots sejant of the second. *Crest*—A dove, in the beak an olive branch all ppr.

Morant (Shirley House, co. Monaghan). Same *Arms* and *Crest*.

Morant (co. Essex). Gu. on a chev. ar. three talbots sa.

Morant, Mordant, or Morhant. Gu. a chev. ar. betw. three talbots courant or.

Morant (Great Yarmouth). Sa. a saltire engr. ar. *Crest*—A lion ramp. or, charged on the breast with a cross sa.

Morar (London). Erm. a fesse bendy of ten or and az. *Crest*—A lion's head erased erm. collared bendy or and az.

Moray, Earl of. See STUART.

Moray (Abercairney, co. Perth; generally considered the chief of the ancient family of MORAY or MURRAY; arms as recorded 1725). Quarterly, 1st and 4th, az. three stars ar. within a double tressure flory counterflory or, for MORAY; 2nd and 3rd, or, two chev. gu., for STRATHEARN. *Crest*—An earl's coronet surmounted of a star of twelve rays ar. *Supporters*—Two eagles ppr. *Mottoes*—Sans tâche; and, Tanti talem genuere parent· s.

Moray (HOME-DRUMMOND-MORAY, of Abercairney). Quarterly, 1st and 4th, counterquartered, MORAY and STRATHEARN, as above; 2nd, or, three bars wavy gu. each charged with an escallop of the field, for DRUMMOND; 3rd, the quartered coat of HOME, of Kames (q. v.). *Crest* and *Mottoes*, as the last.

Moray (Ogilface, co. Stirling, a cadet of Abercairney). Az. a fess betw. three stars ar.

Morby. Ar. on a bend az. three mullets of six points pierced or. *Crest*—An eagle displ. or.

Morcombe, or Morconds (co. Suffolk). Gu. a bend ar. guttée de poix.

Morcraft. Az. a horse ar. bridled gu. betw. three wheels or. *Crest*—A bull's head sa. attired or, issuing out of a ducal coronet gold.

Mordant (Ricklemarsh, co. Kent). Ar. a fleur-de-lis gu.

Mordant. Ar. a chev. sa.; another, Ar. a chev. betw. three spears sa. points az.; another, Purp. an eagle displ. with two heads on, a chief ar.; another, Quarterly, per pale indented gu. and or, in the 1st and 4th quarters five lozenges conjoined in cross of the second.

Mordaunt (Turvey, co. Beds; descended from Sir OSBORNE LE MORDAUNT, temp. William I., whose grandson, EUSTACH LE MORDAUNT, m. ALICE DE ALUETO, eldest dau. and co-heir of Sir WILLIAM DE ALUETO, Knt., of Turvey). Ar. a chev. betw. three estoiles sa.

Mordaunt (*Earl of Peterborough* and *Baron Mordaunt;* earldom extinct 1814; barony passed to the *Duke of Gordon*, d. s. p. 1836; since in abeyance. Sir JOHN MORDAUNT, Knt., of Turvey, grandson of WILLIAM MORDAUNT, Esq., of Turvey, temp. Edward IV., was summoned to Parliament 1532. JOHN, fifth *Lord Mordaunt*, was created *Earl of Peterborough* 1628). Same *Arms*. *Crest*—A blackamoor's head affrontée couped at the shoulders ppr. banded with a wreath round the temples or and gu. and ribands of the same. *Supporters*—Two eagles, wings expanded ar. *Motto*—Nec placido contenta quiete est.

Mordaunt (*Earl of Monmouth*, merged in the Earldom of *Peterborough* 1697. Hon. JOHN MORDAUNT, second son of first *Earl of Peterborough*, was created *Viscount Mordaunt* 1659; his son, the second *Viscount*, was created *Earl of Monmouth* 1689, and s. as third *Earl of Peterborough* 1697). Same *Arms* and *Crest*. *Supporters*—Two lions ar. each charged on the shoulder with three estoiles barways sa.

Mordaunt (Massingham, co. Norfolk, bart.; descended from WILLIAM MORDAUNT, second son of WILLIAM MORDAUNT, Esq., of Turvey, temp. Edward IV.). Same *Arms* and *Crest*. *Motto*—Ferro comite.

Mordaunt (Carrick, co. Clare; Fun. Ent. Ulster's Office, 1623, Sir NICHOLAS MORDAUNT, Knt., of Carrick). Sa. a chev. betw. three mullets ar.

Mordeil. Vair three pallets gu.

Mordel (co. Rutland). Or, a fret sa.

Morden (Wricklesmarsh, co. Kent, bart., extinct 1708; Sir JOHN MORDEN was created a bart. in 1688; he was a great Turkey merchant, and founded at Blackheath a college for decayed merchants). Ar. a fleur-de-lis gu.

Morden College, or Hospital (Blackheath). Ar. a fleur-de-lis gu. on a canton ar. a sinister hand couped of the second, for the distinction of baronet, impaling az. two swords in saltire ar. hilt and pommel or, within a border engr. of the third. *Crest*—A lion ramp. gu.

Morden (co. Kent). Ar. on a fesse gu. betw. three otters sa. as many crosses crosslet or. *Crest*—A hawk, wings endorsed ar. beaked or, preying on a partridge ppr.

Morden. See MERDEN.

Mordey (Sunderland, co. Durham). Ar. a fleur-de-lis gu. *Crest*—A demi lion ramp. gu. langued or. *Motto*—l'ie repone te.

Mordock (co. Norfolk). Or, fretty sa.

Mordon (Lord Mayor of London, 1368). Ar. a fleur-de-lis gu.

Mordon. Ar. a fleur-de-lis sa. (another, field or, fleur-de-lis gu.).

More (co. Bedford). Per saltire or and ar. in pale two moorcocks, in fesse as many escallops sa.

More (cos. Bedford and Kent). Ar. a fesse dancettée paly of six sa. and gu. betw. three mullets of the second.

More (co. Bedford). Ar. two bars betw. nine martlets gu.

More (More Hall and Bank Hall, co. Lancaster, bart., extinct 1810: a family of great antiquity, of which was Sir WILLIAM DE LA MORE, made a knight banneret by the Black Prince at Poictiers. Sir EDWARD MORE, of More Hall, was created a bart. in 1675, a title which expired in 1810 with his grandson, Sir WILLIAM MORE, whose only dau. and heir, ELIZABETH, m. in 1795, CHARLES BROWNING, Esq., of Horton Lodge, co. Surrey). Ar. three greyhounds courant in pale sa. collared or. Crest—A partridge, wings expanded ppr. in the mouth a stalk of wheat the last. Motto—Comme je fus.

More (Sir THOMAS MORE, the eminent Lord Chancellor, temp. Henry VIII.; his only son, JOHN MORE, was ancestor of the MORES, of Barnborough, co. York; his dau. MARGARET, m. WILLIAM ROPER, Esq., of Eltham, co. Kent). Ar. a chev. engr. betw. three moorcocks sa. combs, wattles, and legs gu., quartering ar. on a chev. betw. three unicorns' heads erased sa. as many bezants. Crest—A Moor's head affrontée sa.

More (co. Cambridge). Gu. a cross pattée ar. in chief an escallop of the second.

More (co. Chester). Erm. a fesse gu. betw. five (another, six) moorcocks ppr.; another, Ar. a fleur-de-lis betw. three Moors' heads couped ppr.; another, Ar. a Moor's head couped betw. three fleurs-de-lis sa.

More (co. Derby). Ar. a chev. betw. three Moors' heads couped sa.

More (Broadclist, co. Devon; Rev. JOHN MORE, a minister, son of JOHN MORE, who came to England 1561, and d. 1591, claimed and registered a descent from the Irish Sept of MACMURROGH. Visit. Devon, 1620). Sa. three garbs ar. a border gobony or and gu. Crest—A demi lion ramp. guard. az. holding betw. the paws a garb vert banded gu.

More, or Moore (St. Colis More, co. Devon; descended from JOHN MORE, to whom the Vicar of Broadwoodwiger made a deed of release 7 Henry VII., 1491. Visit. Devon, 1620). Ar. a chev. betw. three moorcocks sa. crested gu.

More, or Moring (Mooretown and Little Torrington, co. Devon; ANTHONY DE LA MORE, alias MORING, b. 1590, descended from THOMAS DE LA MORE, grantor in a deed dated at La More, Wednesday next before the feast of St. Agatha the Virgin, 12 Edward II., 1318. Visit. Devon, 1620). Ar. six martlets sa. three, two, and one.

More, or Moore (Moore Hayes, co. Devon; JOHN MORE, son of HUMPHRY MORE, by MARY, his wife, dau. of RICHARD BAMFYLDE, Esq., of Poltimore, same co., the sixth in descent from JOHN MORE, or MOORE, of Moore Hayes. Visit. Devon, 1620). Erm. on a chev. az. three cinquefoils or. Crest—An arm embowed holding in the hand a sword all ppr. pommel and hilt or.

More (co. Devon). Sa. a swan ar. membered gu. a border engr. of the second; another, Ar. two chev. gu.; another, Erm. on a chev. gu. three cinquefoils or; another, Ar. a fesse dancettée gobony sa. and gu. betw. three mullets of the third.

More, De La (co. Oxford; arms in Brampton Church. Visit. Oxon, 1574). Ar. a fess dancettée gobony gu. and sa. betw. three mullets of the second (another, in Bicester Church, sa.).

More, or Moore, or Atmore (Braye, co. Oxford, temp. Edward III.; quartered by the descendants of THOMAS PURY, servant to Henry IV., who m. MAUD, dau. of WILLIAM ATMORE. Visit. Oxon, 1566). Or, a chev. gu. betw. three martlets sa.

More (Burfield, co. Oxford; RICHARD MORE, temp. Henry VIII., whose dau. and heir m. JOHN DOYLEY, Esq., of Stodhampton, same co. Visit. Oxon, 1634). Ar. a moorcock sa. combed and wattled gu.

More, or Moore (Brodclift, co. Dorset). Sa. three garbs ar. two and one, a border gobony or and gu.¹ Crest—A demi lion ramp. guard. az. holding betw. the paws a garb vert banded gu.

More (Barking, co. Essex). Ar. a cock gu. armed, jelloped, and membered or.

More (co. Essex). Ar. a fesse sa.

More (cos. Essex, Lincoln, and Stafford, and London; confirmed 14 July, 1593). Ar. two greyhounds courant sa. on a chief az. three estoiles or. Crest—A Moor's head ppr. wreathed ar. and sa.

More (France). Or, a saltire betw. four martlets gu.

More (co. Hants). Ar. on a fesse betw. three moorcocks sa. as many mullets or, an annulet of the last.

More (cos. Hants and Somerset). Ar. two bars vert betw.

nine martlets gu. three, three, and three. Crest—A mermaid ppr.

More (co. Lancaster). Ar. ten trefoils slipped gu. (another, sa.) four, three, two, and one; another, Vairé erm. and gu.; another, Ar. three greyhounds courant in pale sa. collared or.

More, or Moore (Buckhall, co. Lancaster). Ar. ten trefoils slipped vert, four, three, two, and one (another, a canton gu.) Crest—A moorcock ar. wings expanded guttée de poix, combed and wattled gu. in the beak an ear of wheat or.

More, or De la More (co. Leicester). Sa. a cross ar.

More (co. Leicester). Or, a fesse dancettée gu. in chief three martlets sa.

More (Sixill, co. Lincoln). Ar. a fesse dancettée betw. three mullets sa.

More (Lord Mayor of London, 1395). Ar. a fesse dancettée paly of six gu. and sa. betw. three estoiles pierced of the third.

More (London, 1634). Vert ten trefoils slipped, four, three, two, and one, ar. a border of the last. Crest—A moorcock ar. guttée de poix, beaked and legged gu.

More (London). Ar. a fesse dancettée gobony gu. and sa. betw. three estoiles pierced of the third.

More (London). Az. on a chev. engr. or, three martlets sa. in chief a lion's head erased of the second.

More (London). Ar. a chev. engr. betw. three moorcocks sa.

More (co. Norfolk). Ar. a bend engr. gu. cotised sa.

More (Wallerton, co. Norfolk). Gu. a fesse betw. three boars heads couped ar.

More (Norwich). Gu. a fesse betw. three boars' heads couped ar. armed or, each having in the mouth a bezant.

More (Kittington, co. Nottingham). Sa. a cross ar. Crest—A Moor's head in profile ppr. on the head a chapeau gu. turned up erm.

More (Larden Hall, co. Salop; descended from RICHARD DE MORE, of More, co. Salop, temp. King John). Sa. a swan close ar. a border engr. or. Crest—An eagle ar. preying on a hare sa.

More (Linley, co. Salop; descended from Larden; ROBERT BRIDGEMAN MORE, Esq., of Linley, Sheriff co. Salop, 1822, was eldest son of ROBERT MORE, Esq., of Linley, the second son of ROBERT MORE, Esq., M.P., of Larden). Same Arms, &c.

More (co. Salop). Paly of six or and sa. over all a bend gu.

More (Loseley, co. Surrey, bart., extinct 1684, originally from co. Derby; descended from Sir CHRISTOPHER MORE, Knt., King's Remembrancer in the Exchequer, who purchased the manor of Loseley, and d. in 1549. Sir POYNINGS MORE, M.P., of Loseley Hall, was created a baronet in 1642, but his son, Sir WILLIAM MORE, of Loseley, dying s. p. in 1684, the title became extinct. The heiress of the family, MARGARET, sister and heiress of ROBERT MORE, Esq., of Loseley, nephew of the first baronet, m. Sir THOMAS MOLYNEUX, Knt.). Az. on a cross ar. five martlets sa. Crest—On a ducal coronet ar. an antelope of the last.

More (Taunton, co. Somerset, and Heytesbury, co. Wilts). Ar. two bars engr. az. betw. nine martlets gu. three, three, and three. Crest—A tiger's head erased ar. pierced through the neck with a broken spear or, headed of the first.

More (co. Somerset). Ar. two bars az. on each as many martlets of the first.

More (co. Suffolk). Or, a chev. engr. ermines betw. three Moors' heads couped at the shoulders sa. wreathed about the temples ar. and az. the ends of the wreath tied in knots. Crest—A wolf's head erased sa. gorged with a collar dancettée or.

More (co. Suffolk). Or, a chev. engr. ermines, in chief a Moor's head full-faced, couped at the shoulders sa.

More (co. Suffolk). Ar. a fesse az. in chief a mullet of the second.

More (co. Suffolk). Ar. two bars engr. the first sa. the second az. betw. nine martlets gu. three, three, and three.

More (The Priory, Taunton, co. Somerset; in 1550, Henry VIII. granted the Priory of Taunton to MATHEW COLTHURST, who sold it to THOMAS MORE, Esq., descended from MORE, of Bagborough. In the chancel of St. Mary Magdalene is a table monument to his memory, with this inscription :— " THOMAS MORE, of the Pryory of Taunton, Esquyer, hear lying, departed this lyfe the 28th day of March, Anno D'ni 1596, and had two wyfes; by the first he left lyving ROBERT, GEFREY, FRANCIS, JOHAN, by the second JESPER and FLORENCE, and blest them all "). Ar. two bars engr. az. betw. nine martlets gu. three, three, and three. Crest—A tiger's head erased ar. pierced through the neck with a broken spear or, headed of the first.

More (Newington, co. Surrey). Az. on a chev. ar. three martlets sa. in chief a lion's head erased or.

More (Morehouse, co. Sussex). A bend betw. two bucks' heads cabossed.

More (co. York). Erm. on a chev. betw. three Moors' heads couped sa. two swords conjoined in point ar. hilts or. *Crest*—A demi Moor ppr. holding with both hands a sword ar. hilt or, reclining over the sinister shoulder.

More (Angram Grange, co. York, 1665). Ar. a chev. sa. betw. three heathcocks of the second, crested and wattled gu. *Crest*—A Moor's head in profile sa. wreathed round the temples gu. and ar.

More (co. York). Ar. a fesse dancettée gobony gu. and sa. betw. three mullets of the third.

More (co. York). Ar. a cross az. betw. four Moors' heads couped sa. *Crest*—On a tower triple-towered or, a Moor's head in profile ppr.

More. Gu. a maunch erm.; another, Ar. two bars betw. nine martlets vert, three, three, and three.

More. Per chev. or and sa. a chev. engr. erm. in chief a moor's head full-faced couped of the second, wreathed about the head ar.

More. Ar. a chev. betw. three unicorns' heads erased sa. in chief as many hurts; another, Or, three palets gu.; another, Sa. on a cross ar. five negroes' heads couped ppr.

More. Az. three leopards' faces or; another, Ar. a chev. and pile sa. counterchanged of the field betw. three fleurs-de-lis of the second; another, Ar. a bend engr. gu. cotised sa.

More. Gu. on a chief dancettée ar. three mullets sa. *Crest*—A lion pass. reguard. gu. ducally gorged and lined ar.

More (Chieftain of Leix, now the Queen's co.). See O'MORE.

More (Ballina). See MOORE.

More (Reg. Ulster's Office). Ar. a fess sa.

More-Gordon (Charlton). See GORDON.

Moreau (confirmed, 1770, to DAVID MOREAU, Esq.). Gu. a leopard ramp. reguard. ar. pierced in the side with an arrow in bend sinister of the last, on a chief or, three Moors' heads in profile erased at the neck ppr. *Crest*—Out of a coronet composed of fleurs-de-lis or, a dexter arm embowed in armour ppr. holding in the gauntlet a scymitar ar. hilt and pommel gold.

Moreau (Jersey). Gu. a sword in pale ar. pommel and hilt or, point in base.

Morecrofte (Kinkham, co Oxford; GEORGE MORECROFTE, Prebend of Oxford, 1634, son of EDWARD MORECROFTE, Prebend of Windsor. Visit. Oxon, 1634). Az. a mule pass. ar. betw. three marygolds or.

Morecroft (Churchill, co. Oxford). Same *Arms*.

Morehead (Herbertshire, co. Stirling, 1718). Ar. on a bend az. three acorns or, in chief a man's heart ppr. within a fetterlock sa. *Crest*—Two hands conjoined grasping a two-handed sword ppr. *Motto*—Auxilio Dei.

Moreiddig (Warwyn, co. Brecon). Sa. three boys' heads couped at the shoulders ppr. having snakes wreathed about their necks vert. *Crest*—A boy's head as in the arms (another, crined or).

Moreland, or Mereland. Az. a griffin segreant or.

Moreland. Sa. a lion pass. guard. in chief or, in base a leopard's face jessant-de-lis of the last. *Crest*—A ship in full sail ppr.

Moreland (co. Kent). Gu. on three bars nebulée ar. ten martlets sa. four, four, and two.

Morell. Gu. a bend or.

Moresby (Moresby, co. Cumberland; extinct before 1500; the heiress *m*. PICKERING). Sa. a cross ar. in the 1st quarter a cinquefoil or.

Moresby (granted to Rear-Admiral Sir FAIRFAX MORESBY, K.C.B.). Sa. a cross parted and fretty betw. in dexter chief an anchor erect and in sinister base a cinquefoil or. *Crest*—An heraldic antelope ramp. gu. navally gorged and with chain reflexed over the back or, supporting a tilting spear erect sa. *Motto*—Je le feray durant ma vie.

Moreswith, or Moresworth. Sa. a pale erm.

Moret. Bendy of six ar. and gu. on a bend or, a lozenge of the second. *Crest*—A demi griffin gu. collared or, sustaining an anchor az.

Moreton, or De Burgo (*Earl of Cornwall*, forfeited; ROBERT DE MORETON, *Earl of Moreton*, in Normandy, son of HARLOWEN DE BURGO by ARLOTTA, his wife, mother of William I., was created *Earl of Cornwall* 1068; WILLIAM, second *Earl of Cornwall*, having been taken prisoner at the Battle of Tenerchebray, was sent to England, where Henry I. had his eyes put out and imprisoned him for life, when his earldom became forfeited). Erm. a chief indented gu.

Moreton (Great Moreton, co. Chester; founded by ALEXANDER MORETON, *temp*. King John, *m*. AGNES, dau. and co-heir of GILBERT CROSLEY, Esq., of Crosley in Buglawton, co. Chester; AGNES, sister of THOMAS DE MORETON, *temp*. Richard II., *m*. ALEXANDER DENNIS, and had the lands of Crosley; from her descend the MASSIES of Crosley; KATHERINE, dau. and ultimately sole heiress of the said THOMAS DE MORETON, *m*. JOHN BELLET, or BELLOT, heir male of WILLIAM BELLET, of Gayton, co. Norfolk). Ar. on a bend sa. three round buckles of the field.

Moreton (co. Chester; the heiress of MORETON *m*. *temp*. Henry III. Sir GRALAM DE LOSTOCK, Knt.; her grandson assumed the surname of MORETON; from him descended WILLIAM MORETON, Esq., of Moreton, living *temp*. Henry VIII., mentioned as arbitrator, who decided a dispute between two co. Chester gentlemen, namely, "which should sit highest in the churche, and foremost goe in procession, by awarding the honour to him, that may dispends in lands by title of inheritance ten marks, or above, more than the other." His grandson, JOHN MORETON, *m*. ANNE DAVENPORT, co-heir of her mother, JANE, daughter and heiress of RICHARD MASSEY, Esq., of Tatton; his last male descendant, Sir WILLIAM MORETON, Recorder of the City of London, *d*. 1763, when the property devolved upon his nephew, the Rev. RICHARD TAYLOR, who assumed the surname of MORETON, and was father of the Rev. WILLIAM MORETON MORETON, of Little Moreton, co. Chester). Ar. a greyhound courant sa. *Crest*—A wolf's head couped ar.

Moreton (REYNOLD-MORETON, *Earl of Ducie*). Quarterly, 1st and 4th, ar. a chev. gu. betw. three square buckles sa.; 2nd and 3rd, or, two lions pass. gu. *Crest*—A peacock's head or, combed and wattled gu. betw. two wings az. *Supporters*—Two unicorns ar. armed, maned, tufted, and unguled or, each gorged with a ducal coronet per pale gold and gu. *Motto*—Perseverando.

Moreton (co. Bedford). Erm. a chief dancettée gu.

Moreton (co. York). Sa. an ink-moline or, pierced sa.

Moreton (Wybaston, Fordhouses, and Moseley Court, Bushbury, co. Stafford; granted to JOHN MORETON, Esq., J.P.). Per fesse dancettée ar. and gu. a pale with three buckles, the tongues erect, two and one, and as many wings, one and two, all counterchanged. *Crest*—A buckle, the tongue erect gu. betw. two wings vair. *Motto*—By perseverance.

Moreton (Moreton, co. Nottingham). Quarterly, gu. and erm. in the 1st and 4th quarters a goat's head erased ar. attired or.

Moreton (co. Kent). Same *Arms*.

Moreton. Ar. a chev. betw. three square buckles sa. tongues pendent. *Crest*—A demi moorcock displ. sa. combed and wattled gu., over it, on a scroll, this *Motto*—Perseverando.

Moreton. Quarterly, 1st and 4th, az. a chev. betw. three trefoils slipped sa.; 2nd and 3rd, gu. a cock or. *Crest*—A cock's head or, wings expanded az. collared with a fess cotised gu. combed of the last, in the bill a trefoil slipped of the third.

Moreton. Ar. a chev. betw. three trefoils slipped sa.; another, Gu. two bars vair; another, Erm. a chief indented gu.

Moreton. Quarterly, gu. and or, in the 1st quarter a goat's head erased ar. on a chief of the last three torteaux, each charged with an escallop of the second.

Moreton. See MORTON.

Moreville. Az. a lion ramp. ar. crowned or.

Morewell. Az. a fess betw. two chevronels or.

Morwick (cos. Durham and Northumberland, *temp*. Henry II.). Gu. a saltire vairé ar. and sa.

Morewood (Hallowes, co. Derby). Ar. an oak tree fructed ppr. *Crest*—Two arms embowed in armour ppr. holding a chaplet or.

Morewood (Alfreton, co. Derby; resident at Staden in Bakewell previous to the reign of Henry VIII., when ROWLAND MOREWOOD *m*. a co-heir of STAFFORD, of Eyam. The last male heir, GEORGE MOREWOOD, Esq., of Alfreton, *d.s.p.* in 1792; his widow, HELEN, dau. of RICHARD GOODWIN, of Ashbourne, *m*. Rev. HENRY CASE, Rector of Ladbrooke, co. Warwick). Vert an oak tree ar. fructed or. *Crest*—A dexter and sinister arm armed ppr. supporting a chaplet of oak branches vert, acorned or.

Morewood (Alfreton; exemplified to Rev. HENRY CASE, Rector of Ladbrook, co. Warwick, upon his assuming, by royal licence, 1793, the additional name of MOREWOOD). Quarterly, 1st and 4th, same *Arms*, for MOREWOOD; 2nd and 3rd, or, on a bend invecked az. double cotised gu. three square buckles of the first, for CASE. *Crests*—1st, MOREWOOD: As the preceding; 2nd, CASE: A cubit arm armed, in the hand ppr. a buglehorn sa. stringed gu. betw. two oak branches ppr. fructed or,

Morewood (Alfreton; WILLIAM PALMER, Esq., son and heir of the late CHARLES PALMER, Esq., of Ludbroke, co. Warwick, by JANE, his wife, dau. of RICHARD GOODWIN, Esq., of Ashbourne, and sister of HELEN, wife first of GEORGE MOREWOOD, Esq., of Alfreton, assumed the additional name of MOREWOOD). Quarterly, 1st and 4th, MOREWOOD; 2nd and 3rd, ar. on two bars sa. three trefoils of the first, in chief a greyhound courant of the second, for PALMER. Crests—1st, MOREWOOD; 2nd, PALMER: A greyhound sejant sa. collared or.

Morewood (co. York; JOHN MOREWOOD, Esq.; Fun. Ent. Ulster's Office, 1660, of his dau. ELLENOR MOREWOOD, wife of JAMES STOPFORD, Esq., of Saltersford, co. Chester, and New Hall, co. Meath, ancestor of the Earl of Courtown). Ar. three oak trees eradicated vert.

Moreyne, or Moryne (co. Essex). Ar. a chev. sa. betw. three fleurs-de-lis gu.

Moreyne (co. Suffolk). Az. three mulberry leaves or.

Moreyns. Gu. on a bend ar. seven billets sa. one, two, one, two, and one.

Morffin. Or, on a chev. sa. three crescents ar.

Morfin. Sa. on a fess engr. or, betw. three garbs ar. a martlet enclosed by two guttées of the second.

Morfyn, or Murfyn (cos. Essex and Kent). Or, a chev. sa. in the dexter chief a mullet pierced of the second. Crest —A blackamoor's head couped at the shoulders habited paly of six erm. and ermines, pendents in his ears or, wreathed on the forehead, bats' wings to his head sa. expanded on each side.

Morgaine, or Morgan (Weston-under-Witherley, co. Warwick). Ar. on a bend sa. three cinquefoils of the field, on a chief az. a cross crosslet betw. two fleurs-de-lis or.

Morgal (Registrar of the Bishop's Court, Chester, temp. Charles I.). Ar. on a bend engr. gu. three cinquefoils pierced erm. on a chief az. three fleurs-de-lis or.

Morgan ap Meredith (Lord of Tredegar, co. Monmouth; the heiress, ANGHARAD, conveyed Tredegar to her husband, LLEWELLIN AP IVOR, Lord of St. Clere, ancestor of MORGAN, of Tredegar). Ar. a lion ramp. gu. incensed az.

Morgan (Baron Tredegar). Quarterly, 1st and 4th, MORGAN, or, a gryphon segreant sa.; 2nd and 3rd, GOULD, or, on a chev. betw. three roses az. as many thistles slipped of the field. Crest—A reindeer's head couped or, attired gu. Supporters—Dexter, a lion sa. charged on the shoulder with a thistle slipped or; sinister, a gryphon sa. charged in like manner with a thistle slipped or.

Morgan (Llantarnam Abbey, co. Monmouth, bart., extinct 1681; descended from WILLIAM MORGAN, Esq., of Llantarnam, High Sheriff of the county in 1567, and M.P. in 1571, son of JOHN MORGAN, Esq., of Caerleon, and grandson of Sir THOMAS MORGAN, Knt., of Pencoed, who was son of MORGAN AP JENKIN, of Langston. Sir EDWARD MORGAN, Knt., of Llantarnam, was created a bart. 1642; his grandson, Sir EDWARD MORGAN, third and last bart., left two daus. his co-heirs; ANNE, d. unm., FRANCES, m. EDMUND BRAY, Esq.). Ar. a griffin segreant sa.

Morgan (Tredunnock, co. Monmouth; descended from JOHN MORGAN, Esq., of Tredunnock, son of MORGAN AP JENKIN, of Langston, by his third wife; represented by HAWKINS, of Tredunnock). Or, a griffin segreant sa. Crest —A reindeer's head couped or, attired gu.

Morgan (Penllyne, co. Monmouth). Same Arms.

Morgan (Lansore, co. Monmouth). Ar. three bulls' heads cabossed ar., quartering, Sa. a cross engr. ar. betw. four spearheads of the last, points embrued, for PROSSER, of Lansore. Crest—A reindeer's head couped or, attired gu. Motto—Y Droddefodd y orfy; and, Vincet qui patitur.

Morgan (Pencrüg, co. Monmouth; represented by MACKWORTH, Bart., of Glen Usk). Ar. a wivern's head erased vert, holding in the mouth a hand couped gu. Crest—A demi eagle displ. or, charged on the body with a fess wavy sa.

Morgan (Llangattock, co. Monmouth. bart., extinct 1767; Sir THOMAS MORGAN, of Llangattock, a celebrated parliamentary leader, was created a bart. 1661; he and Sir HENRY MORGAN, Governor of Jamaica (better known as Captain MORGAN, the Buccaneer) were sons of LEWIS MORGAN, Esq., of Llangattock, who descended, from a common ancestor with MORGAN, of Tredegar. Sir JOHN MORGAN, second bart., left three daus. his co-heirs; HESTER m. JOHN WALSHAM, Esq., of Knill Court, co. Hereford; DELARIVIERE d. unm., and ANNABETA m. THOMAS CLUTTON, Esq., of Pensax, co. Worcester). Ar. three bulls' heads cabossed sa.

Morgan (Langston, co. Monmouth; descended from PHILIP MORGAN, second son of MORGAN AP LLEWELLIN, Lord of St.

705

Clere and Tredegar, who m. the dau. and heir of Sir JOHN NORRIS, Knt., of l'enline Castle). Ar. a lion ramp. guard. sa. on a dexter canton or, a griffin segreant sa., on a sinister canton ar. three bulls' heads cabossed sa. armed gold.

Morgan (co. Monmouth). Vert a lion ramp. or.

Morgan (Rev. HECTOR DAVIES MORGAN, A.M., of Plas Aberforth, co. Cardigan, maternally descended from the BLACKSTONES, ABBOTTS, and ASHBYS, of Harefield, co. Middlesex). Or, three bucks' heads couped sa., for MORGAN; quartering, Gu. three snakes nowed in triangle ar., for EDNOWAIN AP BRADWEN. Crest—A lion ramp. sa.

Morgan (Draws Vynnydd; derived. through ITHEL, of Draws Vynnydd, second son of IORWERTH AP EINION, of Ynys-y-Maengwyn, from OSBORNE FITZGERALD, Lord of Ynys-y-Maengwyn). Arms, those of OSBORNE FITZGERALD, viz., Erm. a saltire gu.

Morgan (Golden Grove, co. Flint; derived from BLETHIN AP GWILLIM, fifth in descent from EDNYFED VYCHAN, Lord of Brynffenigl (see that name). Quarterly, 1st and 4th, gu. a chev. erm. betw. three Englishmen's heads couped in profile ppr.; 2nd, ar. a pelican sa. feeding her young; 3rd, ar. a chev. betw. three boars' heads sa. Crests—1st: An Englishman's head, as in the arms; 2nd: A Cornish chough ppr. Motto—Heb Dduw Heb ddim, a Dduw Digon.

Morgan (Abercothy, co. Carmarthen, and Biddlesden Park, co. Northampton). Sa. a lion ramp. reguard. ar. Crest— A demi lion ramp. reguard. as in the arms.

Morgan (Langeney, co. Brecon). Ar. a dragon's head and neck erased vert, holding in the mouth a bloody hand ppr.

Morgan (Penderin, co. Brecon). Az. three cocks gu. combed and wattled or.

Morgan (Ashtowne, Wales). Per pale az. and gu. three lions ramp. double queued ar.

Morgan (co. Devon, and Hambury, co. Worcester). Ar. on a bend cotised sa. a fleur-de-lis betw. two cinquefoils of the first (another, or). Crest—A tiger sejant sa. crined and tufted or, holding in the dexter paw a battle-axe erect ppr.

Morgan (South Maplerton, co. Dorset). Ar. on a bend cotised sa. a fleur-de-lis betw. two cinquefoils of the first, on a chief az. a cross patonce betw. two arrows or. Crest—A griffin's head erased or, charged with two bends sa.

Morgan (Mellhouse, co. Durham. Visit. 1615). Gu. a lion ramp. ar. crowned or. Crest—Out of a ducal coronet or, a demi eagle displ. with two heads gu.

Morgan (co. Essex). Ar. a fesse betw. three martlets gu. on a chief az. three wolves' heads erased of the first.

Morgan (Little Hallingbury, co. Essex; granted in 1588 to HUGH MORGAN, Esq., of London, and confirmed in 1613 to ROBERT MORGAN, Esq., of Little Hallingbury). Or, a fesse wavy sa. in chief two eagles displ. of the last. Crest—A demi eagle displ. or, charged on the body with a fesse wavy sa.

Morgan (Bardfield, co. Essex, confirmed 1588, by Dethick, Garter, and again 1613, by Camden, Clarenceux). Or, a fess wavy sa. in chief two eagles displ. of the last, quartering for COPCOTT, barry of twelve or and az. Crest—An eagle displ. or, charged on the breast with a fess wavy sa.

Morgan (Barfold, co. Suffolk). Same Arms and Crest.

Morgan (Blackmore, co. Hereford; granted 27 May, 1602). Ar. a lion ramp. sa. ducally crowned or.

Morgan (Bushy Hall, co. Hertford, and Wales). Or, a griffin segreant sa. on the breast a rose ar.

Morgan (co. Kent). Ar. on a bend sa. three cinquefoils of the first, on a chief az. a cross crosslet betw. two fleurs-de-lis or.

Morgan (co. Kent, and Wales). Sa. a chev. betw. three spearheads ar. points embrued ppr.

Morgan (Kingsthorp, co. Notts, co. Lincoln, and Middle Temple, London). Ar. on a bend engr. sa. three cinquefoils of the first, on a chief az. a cross flory betw. two fleurs-de-lis or.

Morgan (St. Bennet Finck, London, author of the "Sphere of Gentry," d. 27 March, 1693). Ar. a lion ramp. sa. ducally crowned or.

Morgan (Burnham Norton, co. Norfolk, and Chalworth, co. Surrey). Ar. a griffin segreant sa. Crest—A reindeer's head or. Another Crest—The head sa. attired or, and charged on the neck with a mullet.

Morgan (Henfield, co. Sussex; granted to NELSON SMITH MORGAN, Esq.). Or, a griffon segreant sa. in chief two mullets of six points gu. pierced of the field. Crest—A fer de moulin fesseways sa. thereon a griffin's head erased ppr.

Morgan (granted to FRANCIS MORGAN, Judge of the King's

Bench, by Hervey, Clarenceux, 1558). Ar. on a bend engr. sa. three cinquefoils pierced erm. on a chief az. a cross flory betw. two fleurs-de-lis or. Crest—A dragon's head erased gu. langued az. collared or, betw. two bars gemells wavy ar.

Morgan (Little Comberton and Hanbury, co. Worcester. Visit. 1569). Ar. on a bend cotised sa. a fleur-de-lis betw. two cinquefoils of the field. Crest—A tiger sejant sa. crined and tufted or, holding in the dexter paw a battle axe erect headed gold.

Morgan (Dudelston, co. Salop). Ar. a lion ramp. sa.

Morgan (Eston, co. Somerset; granted 1591). Sa. three crosses bottonnée in bend ar. Crest—A demi griffin segreant erased sa.

Morgan (Arkston, co. Stafford). Ar. a lion ramp. sa. ducally crowned or.

Morgan. Ar. a fesse betw. three martlets gu. on a chief az. three griffins' heads erased of the first. Crest—On a mount an oak tree fructed or, against it a wolf pass. ppr.

Morgan. Ar. on a cross flory gu. five roses of the field.

Morgan. Gu. three towers ar.

Morgan. Ar. a cross patonce betw. four escallops sa.

Morgan. Ar. on a bend betw. two cotises sa. three fleurs-de-lis of the first.

Morgan. Quarterly, gu. and az. a lion (another, three lions) ramp. ar.

Morgan. Quarterly, ar. and sa. a cross flory counterchanged.

Morgan. Ar. on a cross patonce gu. five roses of the first a bordure engr. sa.

Morgan (Sir RICHARD MORGAN, knighted at Dublin by Robert, Earl of Essex, Lord Lieutenant, 5 Aug. 1599). Sa. a chev. ar. betw. three spear heads of the last, points upwards, embrued gu.

Morgan (Dublin; Fun. Ent. Ulster's Office, 1619, GEORGE MORGAN, of that city). Ar. a griffin segreant sa. armed, beaked, and forelegged gu. a border of the second.

Morgan (confirmed by St. George, Ulster, 1680, to that family, then settled in Ireland). Or, a griffin segreant sa. Crest—A stag's head cabossed ppr. attired or.

Morgan (Cottlestown, co. Sligo; descended from ROBERT MORGAN, Esq., who settled in Ireland, temp. Charles I., and who is stated to have been a younger son of Sir THOMAS MORGAN, Knt., of Langston. Colonel HUGH MORGAN, of Cottlestown, d. 1761, leaving an only dau. and heir, KATHERINE, m. ROBERT STEARNE TIGHE, Esq., of Mitchelstown, co. Westmeath). Same Arms. Crest—A reindeer's head erased.

Morgan (Waterford; SAMUEL MORGAN, Esq., Mayor of Waterford, son of WILLIAM MORGAN, Esq., also Mayor of the same, by SARAH GROGAN, his wife, dau. of JOHN GROGAN, Esq., of Johnstown, co. Wexford, d. s. p., and bequeathed his estates, 1826, to HAMILTON KNOX GROGAN, Esq., of Johnstown, greatgrandson of CORNELIUS GROGAN, Esq., of Johnstown, the brother of said SARAH GROGAN, upon condition of his taking the additional surname of MORGAN). Same Arms. Crest—A reindeer's head cabossed or. Motto—Fidus et audax.

Morgan. See GROGAN-MORGAN.

Morgan (DEANE-MORGAN; exemplified to Hon. ROBERT FITZMAURICE TILSON DEANE, of Springfield Castle, co. Limerick, and ELIZABETH GERALDINE GROGAN-MORGAN, his wife, dau. of HAMILTON KNOX GROGAN-MORGAN, Esq., of Johnstown Castle, co. Wexford, on their assuming, by royal licence, 1854, the additional surname and arms of MORGAN). Quarterly, 1st and 4th, or, a griffin segreant sa. a mullet az. for diff., for MORGAN; 2nd and 3rd, ar. two bars gu., for DEANE. Crests—1st, MORGAN: A reindeer's head cabossed or, charged with a mullet az. for diff.; 2nd, DEANE: Out of a ducal coronet or, a demi sea-otter ppr. In a scroll above the crests the motto, Honor et virtus. Motto—Under the arms: Forti et fideli nihil difficile.

Morgan (DEANE-MORGAN, Baron Muskerry). Quarterly, 1st grand quarter, quarterly, 1st and 4th, or, a griffin segreant sa. in the dexter chief point a mullet az., for MORGAN, 2nd and 3rd, ar. two bars gu., for DEANE; 2nd grand quarter, ar. two bars gu., for DEANE; 3rd grand quarter, sa. on a bend betw. two cinquefoils or, three bears' heads couped of the first, muzzled, for BRETTRIGE; 4th grand quarter, ar. a saltire gu. and a chief erm. a crescent for diff., for FITZMAURICE. Crests—1st, MORGAN: A reindeer's head cabossed or, charged with a mullet az.; 2nd, DEANE: Out of a ducal coronet or, a demi sea otter ppr. Mottoes—Above MORGAN crest: Honor et virtus; under the arms: Forti et fideli nihil difficile. Supporters—Two angels habited and winged az. holding in their exterior hands medallions ppr.

706

Morgan (FORBES-MORGAN, Countess of Granard; exemplified to JANE COLCLOUGH, Countess of Granard, wife of GEORGE ARTHUR HASTINGS, seventh Earl of Granard, K.P., and dau. and co-heiress of HAMILTON KNOX GROGAN-MORGAN, Esq., of Johnstown Castle, co. Wexford on her assuming, by royal licence, 1859, the additional surname and arms of MORGAN). Az. three bears' heads couped ar. muzzled gu., an escutcheon of pretence for MORGAN, or, a griffin segreant sa. langued gu.

Moriarty. See O'MORIARTIE.

Moriarty. Ar. an eagle displ. sa. Crest—An arm embowed in armour holding a dagger, the blade environed with a serpent.

Morice (Clennenu, co. Carnarvon; descended through ELLIS, of Clennenu, second son of MORYS AP JOHN, of Rhiwaedog, Clennenu, and Park; from RODERICK, Lord of Anglesey, son of OWEN GWYNEDD, Prince of North Wales; Sir WILLIAM MORICE, Knt., of Clennenu, m. the heiress of LACON, of Llanddyn and Porkington; and the heiress of the three houses m. JOHN OWEN, Esq., fourth son of JOHN OWEN, of Bodsilin (Secretary to the Minister, Walsingham), the eldest son of which marriage was the memorable Sir JOHN OWEN, of Porkington, Llanddyn, and Clennenu; the representation eventually vested in Mrs. ORMSBY-GORE, mother of Lord Harlech). Arms, those of OWEN GWYNEDD, viz., Vert three eagles displ. in fess ar.

Morice (Werrington, co. Devon, bart., extinct 1750; descended from IEVAN MORICE, LL.D., Chancellor of Exeter in 1594, younger brother of Captain WILLIAM MORYS, ancestor of MORICE, of Betshanger. Sir WILLIAM MORICE, of Werrington, son of Sir WILLIAM MORICE, Knt., M.P., Secretary of State temp. Charles II., was created a bart. in 1661; his granddaughters, heiresses to their brother, Sir WILLIAM MORICE, the last bart., KATHERINE m. Sir JOHN ST. AUBYN, Bart., and BARBARA m. Sir JOHN MOLESWORTH, Bart.). Gu. a lion ramp. reguard. or.

Moriens (co. Suffolk). Az. three Moors' heads couped or; another, Az. a water leaf ar.

Morieux (co. Suffolk). Az. a bend ar. billettée sa.

Morieux (THOMAS MORIEUX, Sheriff of Norfolk, 1354). Gu. on a bend ar. seven billets sa.

Morin (Car Colston, co. Nottingham). Quarterly, 1st and 4th, per pale indented ar. and az.; 2nd and 3rd, ar. a fleur-de-lis az.

Morin. Ar. a chev. sa. betw. three fleurs-de-lis gu.

Morin (Bailly of Jersey, 1467). Ar. on the waves of the sea a dolphin embowed all ppr. Crest—On a cap of maintenance a dolphin, as in the arms, all ppr. Motto—Fortune le veut.

Moriner. Az. three fusils in fesse or.

Moring, or De la More (Moretion, co. Devon). Ar. six martlets sa. three, two, and one. Crest—A greyhound statant.

Morins (co. Kent). Gu. a cross humettée betw. four birds ar.

Morion (co. Norfolk). Gu. a bend ar. guttée de poix.

Moris (co. Suffolk). Vert a buck pass. or. Crest—A talbot gu. collared and lined or.

Moris. Sa. three bears' heads erased ar. muzzled gu. on a canton of the third a crown or.

Morisby, or Morison. Sa. a cross ar. in the 1st quarter a cinquefoil pierced or.

Moriskines. Barry wavy of six ar. and az. on a chief or, three swallows, wings expanded sa. Crest—A stork or, legged and beaked sa.

Morison (Cashiobury, co. Herts, bart., extinct). See MORISON.

Morison (Standon, co. Herts, and Cadby, co. Lincoln). Or, on a cross sa. five fleurs-de-lis of the field. Crest—Out of a ducal coronet or, an eagle's head betw. two wings endorsed ar.

Morison (London). Per saltire or and gu. in pale two pelicans of the first, in fess as many leopards' faces of the second, on a chief or, three chaplets gu.

Morison (Dairsie, co. Fife, Scotland). Az. three Saracens' heads erased, conjoined in one neck, and wreathed with laurel ppr. the faces looking to the chief, dexter, and sinister sides of the shield.

Morison (Edinburgh, cadet of Dairsie, 1672). The same, betw. two falcons' heads couped az. Crest—A serpent ppr. Motto—Prætio prudentia præstat.

Morison (Bognie, co. Aberdeen). Az. three Saracens' heads erased, conjoined in one neck, the faces looking to the chief, dexter, and sinister sides, the uppermost head affixed by a wreath to the other two. Motto—Sunt tria hæc unum.

Morison (Prestongrange, co. Edinburgh). Ar. three Moors' heads couped sa. two and one, banded of the first. Crest

—Three Saracens' heads conjoined in one neck, their faces looking to the chief, dexter, and sinister sides ppr.

Morison. Ar. on a chief gu. three estoiles or.

Morison. Ar. three bucks' heads sa.

Morison (Major ALEXANDER MORISON, H.E.I.C.S., 1806). Erm. an eagle displ. sa. betw. three Moors' heads of the last banded or. Crest—Three Saracens' heads erased, conjoined in one neck, and wreathed with laurel ppr. the faces looking to the chief, dexter, and sinister. Motto—Pretio prudentia præstat.

Morison (DUNCAN-MORISON, of Naughton, co. Fife, 1853). Quarterly, 1st and 4th, ar. a saltire couped sa. charged with a man's heart or, betw. three Moors' heads couped of the second, banded of the third, for MORISON; 2nd, gu. a chev. or, betw. two cinquefoils in chief ar. and a huntinghorn in base of the last garnished az. all within a bordure of the second, for DUNCAN; 3rd, the quartered coat of HALDANE, of Gleneagles [which see] within a bordure gu. Crests—1st: Three Saracens' heads conjoined in one neck, erased and wreathed with laurel ppr. looking to the chief dexter, and sinister sides; 2nd: A ship in distress in the sea ppr.; 3rd: An eagle's head erased or. Mottoes—Pretio prudentia præstat: Disce pati; and, Suffer.

Morison (WALKER-MORISON, of Falfield, co. Fife, 1854). Quarterly, 1st and 4th, ar. a lion ramp. gu. betw. three Moors' heads couped sa. banded or, for MORISON; 2nd and 3rd, or, three pallets gu. surmounted of a saltire wavy ar. on a chief az. a demi lion holding betw. his paws a fleur-de-lis of the third betw. two cushions of the field. Crests—Three Saracens' heads conjoined in one neck ppr. their faces looking to the chief, dexter, and sinister, a serpent ppr., for MORISON; a greyhound courant ppr., for WALKER. Mottoes—Prætio prudentia præstat, for MORISON; Fac et spera, for WALKER.

Morison (Touch House, Stirling, 1851). Ar. three Saracens' heads couped sa. banded of the first, within a bordure engr. az. charged with three fleurs-de-lis or. Crest—Three Saracens' heads conjoined in one neck ppr. their heads looking to the chief, dexter, and sinister. Motto—In Deo confido.

Morison (BROWN-MORISON, of Finderlie, co. Kinross, and Coupar Grange, co. Fife, 1866). Quarterly, 1st and 4th, ar. a fess sa. betw. three Moors' heads couped ppr. banded or, for MORISON; 2nd and 3rd, gu. a chev. betw. fleurs-de-lis ar., for BROWN. Crests—Three Saracens' heads conjoined in one neck ppr. banded or, the faces looking to the chief, dexter, and sinister, for MORISON; A lion ramp. ppr. holding in its dexter fore paw a fleur-de-lis ar., for BROWN. Mottoes—Prudentia præstet, for MORISON; Floreat majestas, for BROWN.

Morivale (quartered by HASELRIGG, of Castle Dorrington. Visit. Notts, 1614). Ar. a cinquefoil az.

Morland (Southamstede Banaster, co. Berks, bart., extinct 1716; granted by Walker, Garter, to Sir SAMUEL MORLAND, alias MORLEY, created a bart., 18 July, 1660. Visit. Middlesex, 1663). Sa. a leopard's face jessant-de-lis or. Crest—A lion's head betw. two wings ar.

Morland (Lee, co. Kent). Same Arms, on a chief of the second a lion pass. guard. gu. Crest—A leopard's face jessant-de-lis or, betw. two wings erm.

Morland (Kimble, co. Bucks, and Westminster). Az. semée of leopards' heads jessant-de-lis, a griffin segreant or. Crest—A griffin's head, wings endorsed az. semée-de-lis and crosses crosslet or.

Morland (Court Lodge, Lamberhurst, co. Kent). Az. a griffin segreant or. Crest—A falcon ppr. belled or.

Morland (Capplethwaite, co. Westmoreland). Same Arms and Crest.

Morland. Gu. three bars wavy or, each charged with as many martlets. Crest—A camel's head erased, charged with three bars wavy.

Morland. Ar. on a chev. betw. three lions ramp. sa. the two in chief respecting each other, as many bezants.

Morland. Sa. a lion pass. guard. in chief, and in base a leopard's face jessant-de-lis or. Crest—A dove or, in the beak an olive branch ppr.

Morland (BERNARD-MORLAND, Nettleham, co. Lincoln, bart.). Quarterly, 1st and 4th, az. semée of leopards' faces jessant-de-lis, a griffin segreant or, for MORLAND; 2nd and 3rd, ar. a bear ramp. sa. muzzled and collared or, for BERNARD. Crests—1st, MORLAND: A griffin's head, wings endorsed az. semée of fleurs-de-lis and cross crosslets alternately or; 2nd, BERNARD: A demi bear sa. muzzled and collared or. Motto—Bear and forbear.

Morleigh (co. Lancaster). Ar. fretty gu. a chief az. Crest—A unicorn's head erased or.

Morlent. Sa. a lion ramp. double queued or.

707

Morles (co. Somerset). Ar. two bars gu. in chief three torteaux.

Morleton. Ar. a chev. sa. fretty of the first, betw. three mullets of the second.

Morley, Earl of. See PARKER.

Morley (Morley, co. Lancaster; descended from RICHARD MORLEY, Esq., of Morley, temp. Edward III., who m. MARGARET, dau. and heir of GILBERT WINNINGTON). Sa. three leopards' faces or, jessant-de-lis ar. Crest—A man in complete armour ppr. garnished or, in the dexter hand a baton gold, across his body a sash az.

Morley (Glynde, co. Sussex; descended from NICHOLAS MORLEY, second son of FRANCIS MORLEY, Esq., of Morley, co. Lancaster, who m. the dau. and co-heir of Sir JOHN WALLEYS, Knt., of Glynde). Same Arms and Crest.

Morley (Marrick Park, co. York). Sa. a leopard's face or, jessant-de-lis ar. Crests—1st: A leopard's face jessant-de-lis or; 2nd: Out of a ducal coronet or, a griffin's head betw. two wings expanded, all ar. Motto—S'ils te mordent, mord les.

Morley (East Lavant, co. Sussex). Same Arms. Crest—A griffin's head betw. two wings expanded, issuing out of a ducal coronet all ar.

Morley (Halnaker, co. Sussex; descended from JOHN MORLEY of Saxham, who purchased Halnaker, temp. James I.). Sa. a leopard's head ar. jessant-de-lis or. Crest—On a chapeau gu. turned up. erm. a leopard's face ar. jessant-de-lis or.

Morley (co. Hants; granted, in 1575, to JOHN MORLEY, of Barnes, co. Southampton). Same Arms. Crest—Out of a ducal coronet a demi talbot or.

Morley. Same Arms, a bordure engr. or, semée of torteaux. Crest—A talbot ermines pass. reguard. collared or.

Morley. Per pale gu. and az. a leopard's face jessant-de-lis or. Crest—Out of a mural coronet a griffin's head betw. two wings.

Morley, or Merley (France). Or, two bars gu. an orle of martlets of the last.

Morley (co. Norfolk). Ar. a lion ramp. sa. crowned or (another, the tail double queued).

Morley (Morley, co. Derby). Same Arms, a fleur-de-lis for diff.

Morley (Norwich, co. Norfolk). Barry of six az. and or, on a chief ar. three lions' heads erased sa. Crest—A wolf sejant sa. maned, tufted, collared, and lined or.

Morley (Halsted, co. Essex; granted by Anstis, Garter). Vert three leopards' faces in pale jessant-de-lis or. Crest—A demi man ppr. habited az. holding a poleaxe bendways or, on his head a steel cap with three feathers gu., or, and az. Motto—Nec errat nec assat.

Morley. (Craven, co. York). Sa. a leopard's face or, jessant-de-lis ar.

Morley (Hackney, co. Middlesex; granted to JOHN MORLEY, Esq., of that place, and the other descendants of his father, SAMUEL MORLEY, Esq., of Honiton, co. Notts). Az. a leopard's face jessant-de-lis sa. betw. three griffins' heads erased gu. Crest—A demi griffin ar. wings elevated erm. holding betw. the claws a leopard's face jessant-de-lis, as in the arms. Motto—Tenax propositi.

Morlosht, or Mortoft. Sa. a buck lodged or, betw. the attires a heathcock volant of the second.

Mornell. Az. three demi lions within an orle of fleurs-de-lis or. Crest—Out of a mural coronet az. a dragon's head issuing flames ppr.

Mornsell. Sa. a cross sarcelly, quarterly or and ar.

Moroney (co. Clare; Reg. Ulster's Office, 23 April, 1780, to JOHN MORONEY, Esq., of Dunahain, and THOMAS MORONEY, Esq., of Milltown, barrister-at-law, sons of EDMOND MORONEY, Esq., of Kilmacduagh, all in co. Clare). Az. three crosses crosslet or, betw. as many boars' heads, couped above the shoulders ar. langued gu. Crest—A lion ramp. ar. holding a sceptre or.

Morow. Gu. a bend az. Crest—Out of a ducal coronet or, an eagle's head betw. two wings ppr.

Morpeth, Town of (co. Northumberland). Ar. three bars gu. over all a tower triple towered ar. on a bordure az. eight doves or.

Morrall (Plas Yolyn, co. Salop; descended from JOHN MORRALL, Esq., of Plas Yolyn, who m. 1669, JUDITH, dau. and heir of THOMAS EDWARDES, Esq., of Kilhendre, eighteenth in descent from TUDOR TREVOR). Ar. on a fesse embattled gu. betw. six Cornish choughs ppr. three palm branches of the first; quartering, for EDWARDES, Gu. a chev. engr. betw. three boars' heads erased ar. Crest—A demi griffin. Motto—Norma tuta veritas.

Morrell. Az. on a cross ar. a lion ramp. gu. Crest—The horns of a bull adhering to the scalp ppr.

Morrell (Headington Hill. co. Oxford). Or, a bend gu. in

MOR   THE GENERAL ARMORY.   MOR

base a cross crosslet of the last. *Crest*—A demi lion ramp. reguard. *Motto*—Bono animo esto.

Morrell (Wallingford, co. Berks, and Forthampton, co. Gloucester; descended from JEREMIAH MORELL, Esq., of Wallingford, *d.* 1766). Same *Arms*. *Crest*—A demi lion ramp. guard. per pale ar. and sa. holding in the dexter paw a sprig of three roses gu. *Motto*—Bono anima esto.

Morres (Kilkreen, co. Kilkenny, bart., extinct). Ar. a fesse sa. dancettée in chief a crescent, and in base a lion ramp. gu. *Crest*—A demi lion ramp. ppr. *Motto*—Deus nobis quis contra.

Morrey (co. Sussex). Sa. three leopards' faces jessant-de-lis or.

Morrey (Yoxall, co. Stafford; arms from a window in Foxall Church). Ar. two bars gu. each charged with three martlets or, in chief a cross flory betw. two fleurs-de-lis az.

Morrice (Werington, co. Devon). See MORICE.

Morrice (Chipping Ongar, co. Essex). Az. on a fess ar. betw. three boars' heads couped at the shoulders, environed round the neck with a snake ppr. a cock gu. beaked and legged or, betw. two pheons of the fourth. *Crest*—A cock gu. beaked, combed, and wattled or, environed round the neck with a snake ppr.

Morrice, or Morys (London). Gu. on a lion ramp. or, a pellet, a border indented of the second pellettée. *Crest*—A lion ramp. or, collared gu. holding a pellet.

Morrice (*temp.* Henry VII.). Ar. on a saltire engr. sa. an escutcheon or, charged with a cross gu. *Crest*—A lion ramp. or, charged on the shoulder with a cross gu.

Morrice. Gu. a lion ramp. reguard. or. *Crest*—A hawk ppr. belled and jessed or.

Morrice (Betshanger, co. Kent; descended, through MORTS AP MORGAN, from ETHELYSTAN GLODRYDD, Prince of Ferlys, Founder of the IV. Royal Tribe of North Wales and Powys; ADMIRAL SALMON MORRICE, a distinguished naval officer, purchased Betshanger in 1712). Quarterly, 1st, gu. a lion ramp. reguard. or, for MORRICE; 2nd, per bend sinister erm. and ermines, a lion ramp. or, for TUDOR TREVOR; 3rd, ar. three boars' heads couped sa., for CADWGAN; 4th, gu. an escutcheon within an orle of martlets ar., for CHADWICK, *Crest* --On a rest, a falcon ppr. beaked and belled or.

Morries, or Morrys. Ar. on a chev. vert three crescents or.

Morris (Clasemount, co. Glamorgan, bart.). Sa. on a saltire engr. erm. a bezant charged with a cross couped gu. *Crest*—A lion ramp. or, charged on the shoulder with a cross couped gu. within a chain in the form of an arch gold. *Motto*—Scuto fidei.

Morris, or Mores (Coxwell, co. Berks). Or, on a fesse humettée betw. three moorcocks ppr. a garb of the field. *Crest*—A Moor's head erased erminois in profile, wreathed round the temples or and az.

Morris (Pale-yn-Edeirnion, co. Merioneth; descended from ELLIS, of Pale, second son of HOWEL, of Crogen-yn-Edeirnion and Pale, son of GRIFFITH, of Crogen and Branas, second son of RHYS AP IEVAN, Baron of Kymmer-yn-Edeirnion, ancestor of HUGHES, of Gwerclas, Baron of Kymmer-yn-Edeirnion; ANGHARAD, dau. and heir of MORRIS AP JOHN, of Pale, *m.* IEVAN LLOYD, gent.). *Arms*, those of HUGHES, of Gwerclas, viz., Ar. a lion ramp. sa. armed and langued gu.

Morris (Wanstead, co. Essex; granted by St. George, Clarenceux). Sa. on a cross patonce betw. twelve billets ar. five torteaux. *Crest*—A lion ramp. sa. bezantée, ducally gorged or.

Morris (co. Gloucester). Ar. on a chief gu. three bezants.

Morris (quartered by AMHURST through EVERING. Visit. Kent, 1619). Ar. an eagle displ. sa. beaked and legged or.

Morris (Wingfield House Bath, co. Somerset, 1770). Sa. a saltire engr. ar. on an inescutcheon or, a cross gu. *Crest*—A lion ramp. or.

Morris (Peckham, co. Surrey). Per fesse or and gu. a lion ramp. betw. three quatrefoils within a border indented charged with eight annulets all counterchanged. *Crest*—Upon a mount vert a lion ramp. or, semée of quatrefoils and holding in the dexter paw an annulet gu. *Motto*—Pro rege semper.

Morris (granted to Capt. RICHARD MORRIS, 10th April, 1677). Gu. a saltire engr. ar. guttée de sang. *Crest*—A lion's head ar. guttée de sang. *Motto*—Virtute et fortitudine.

Morris (Netherby, co. York; represented by the Rev. FRANCIS ORPEN MORRIS, B.A., Worcester Coll., Oxford. Chaplain to the *Duke of Cleveland*, and Rector of Nunburnholme, and a magistrate for the East Riding of co. York, a distinguished naturalist, of ancient Welsh ancestry, his family being one of those which claim descent from ELYSTAN GLODRYDD, Prince of Ferlys). Quarterly, 1st and 4th, gu. a lion ramp. reguard. or; 2nd and 3rd, ar. three boars' heads couped sa.

708

Crest—A lion ramp. reguard. or. *Motto*—Marte et mare faventibus; and, over the arms, Gwell Angau na Chwilydd.

Morris (co. Hereford). Ar. six cocks sa. three, two, and one, crested and jelloped gu.

Morris (co. Hertford). Sa. three bears' heads erased ar. on a canton gu. a ducal crown or.

Morris (Broadfield House, near Devizes, co. Wilts). Sa. a saltire engr. ar. *Crest*—A lion ramp. or, charged on the shoulder with a cross gu.

Morris (co. Cardigan). Sa. a lion pass. or, betw. three scaling ladders ar.

Morris (co. Carnarvon). Sa. a stag standing at gaze or.

Morris. Az. a cross engr. ar. *Crest*—A stag pass. ppr.

Morris. Sa. a cross engr. ar. *Crest*—A lion ramp. gu.

Morris. Ar. three lions' gambs couped ppr. *Crest*—A fox's head couped ppr.

Morris. Gu. a lion ramp. or, charged on the breast with a plate. *Crest*—A demi lion ramp. or, holding betw. the paws a plate.

Morris. Az. two battle axes in saltire ppr. *Crest*—A tower ppr. inflamed of the last.

Morris. Sa. a lion pass. betw. three scaling ladders ar. *Crest*—A castle, domed ar.

Morris. Ar. a fesse betw. three martlets gu. on a chief sa. as many wolves' heads erased of the field.

Morris (The Hurst, co. Salop). Ar. an eagle displ. with two heads sa. *Crest*—An eagle displ. sa.

Morris ap Griffith. Sa. the tops of three broken spears erect or, pointed ar. betw. as many crescents of the second.

Morris. Az. a battle axe in bend sinister surmounted of a tilting spear in bend dexter or, betw. four cannons of the same, on a chief of the second a fleur-de-lis of the first, enclosed by a demi rose gu. the other half radiated like the rays of the sun or, and the stump of a tree eradicated and couped at the top gu. *Crest*—A tower or, inflamed gu.

Morris (Ystradmeuric, co. Cardigan). Ar. on a bend sa. three leopards' heads erased of the field. *Crest*—A naked arm erect holding an open Bible ppr. inscribed with the Welsh word " Bibl." *Motto*—A Gair Duw yn uchaf.

Morris (Barnwood, co. Gloucester; granted, 1795, to ROBERT MORRIS, Esq.). Vert a cross flory ar. betw. four garbs or, on a chief of the second a lion ramp. gu. *Crest*—A demi lion ramp. or, charged on the shoulder with a cross flory sa. and holding in the paws an ear of wheat ppr.

Morris (North Elmsall, co. York, 1660). Az. three eaglets displ. or, on a canton ar. a castle gu. (the canton alluding to the seizure of Pontefract Castle by JOHN MORRIS during the civil war).

Morris. Ar. a fess betw. three lions couchant gu.; another, Az. (another, sa.) billettée and a cross ar.; another, Erm. three bars wavy ar.; another, Az. a fess gu. a chief ar. fretty az.; another, Barry wavy of six ermines and ar.; another, Barry wavy of six ar. and sa. the last guttée d'eau; another, Vert a stag or; another, Bendy of six or and gu. an estoile of sixteen points az.; another, Ar. an eagle displ. with two heads sa. armed or; another, Ar. two chevronels sa. on each three roses or; another, Ar. on a chev. vert three crescents or; another, Ar. a fess betw. three lions dormant sa.

Morris (POLLOK-MORRIS, of Craig, co. Ayr, 1863). Quarterly, 1st and 4th, ar. on a chev. az. betw. three Moors' heads couped sa. banded or, three crescents of the last, for MORRIS; 2nd and 3rd, vert on a saltire ar. betw. three hunting horns in flank and base of the second, viroled and stringed gu. a lion ramp. sa., for POLLOK. *Crests*—A lion ramp. ppr., for MORRIS; a wild boar pierced with a dart ppr., for POLLOK. *Mottoes*—Fide et fortitudine, for MORRIS ; Audacter et strenue, for POLLOK.

Morris (Templemore, co. Tipperary; Impalement Fun. Ent. Ulster's Office, 1629; THOMAS PURCELL, Esq., of Borris-o-Leagh, same co., *m.* ELEANOR, dau. of REDMOND MORRIS, Esq., of Templemore). Or, a fesse dancetté betw. in chief a crescent and in base a lion ramp. sa.

Morris, or Morech (co. Galway; Reg. Ulster's Office, Az. a halbert surmounted by a lance in saltire betw. four culverines fesseways or, on a chief ar. a fleur-de-lis betw. two trunks of trees couped and eradicated sa. *Crest*—A fleur-de-lis or.

Morris (Impalement Fun. Ent. Ulster's Office, 1660). Ar. on a chev. sa. three roses or.

Morris (Capt. RICHARD MORRIS, of His Majesty's Regt. of Guards in Ireland ; granted by St. George, Ulster, 1677). Gu. a saltire engr. ar. guttée de sang. *Crest*—A lion's head erased ar. guttée de sang.

Morris (Reg. Ulster's Office). Gu. a fess or, in base a pike fish naiant ar.

Morris (Ferns, co. Wexford; allowed by Hawkins, Ulster, 1746, to AUGUSTUS MORRIS, of Rotherhithe, London, great grandson of JOHN MORRIS, Esq., of Ferns). Or, a fesse dancettée sa. in base a lion ramp. of the last armed and langued gu. *Crest*—A demi lion erased guttée de sang langued gu.

Morrison (Cashiobury, co. Hertford, bart., extinct 1628; descended from WILLIAM MORYSON, of Chardwell, co. York, *temp.* Henry VI.; Sir CHARLES MORRISON, K.B., was created a bart. 1611, his only dau. and heir, ELIZABETH MORRISON, *m.* ARTHUR, *Lord Capel*, and was mother of ARTHUR, first *Earl of Essex*, who inherited Cashiobury). Or, on a chief gu. three chaplets of the first.

Morrison (co. Lancaster). Or, on a cross sa. five fleurs-de-lis ar. *Crest*—Out a ducal coronet or, an eagle's head and neck betw. two wings displ. ar.

Morrison. Or, on a cross sa. five fleurs-de-lis of the field. *Crest*—A cubit arm in armour holding a branch of oak all ppr.

Morrison (Sir RICHARD MORRISON, knighted at Dublin by Robert, *Earl of Essex*, Lord-Lieutenant, 5 Aug., 1599). Ar. on a cross sa. five fleurs-de-lis or, in the dexter quarter a martlet az.

Morrison (Coolegegan, in the King's co.; confirmed to RICHARD FIELDING MORRISON, Esq., and the descendants of his grandfather, Sir RICHARD MORRISON, Vice-Pres. Royal Institute of Architects of Ireland). Or, on a cross per cross sa. and gu. four fleurs-de-lis ar. in the first quarter a crescent of the third. *Crest*—On a mural crown gu. an eagle's head and neck betw. two wings displ. ar. the neck and each wing charged with a fleur-de-lis sa. *Motto*—Utile et dulce.

Morrit. Sa. a cross ar. on a chief of the last a rose gu. betw. two fleurs-de-lis of the first. *Crest*—A griffin's head erased holding in the beak a rose branch ppr.

Morritt (Rokeby Park, Barnard Castle). Ar. a cross az. betw. four billets sa. on a chief of the second a rose of the first barbed or, betw. two fleurs-de-lis of the last, quartering SAWREY. *Crest*—A griffin's head erased ppr. holding in the beak a rose gu. barbed and slipped vert.

Morritt. Ar. a cross az. betw. four billets sa. on a chief f the second a rose of the first barbed or, betw. two fleurs-de-lis of the last. *Crest*—A griffin's head erased ppr. holding in the beak a rose gu. barbed and slipped vert.

Morrogh (co. Limerick; Reg. Ulster's Office). Vert three escallops or. *Crest*—A hand couped at the wrist and erect, holding a sword in pale all ppr.

Morrogh (confirmed to JAMES MORROGH, Esq., of Old Court, Doneraile, co. Cork, son of EDWARD MORROGH, of Glanmire House, same co.). Az. a harp or, stringed ar. betw. three escallops of the second. *Crest*—A staff ppr. with a flag attached az. charged with a harp as in the arms. *Motto*—Virtus invicta.

Morse. Ar. a battle axe in pale gu. betw. three pellets. *Crest*—A lion ramp. supporting a plumb rule. *Another Crest*—Two battle axes in saltire ppr. banded with a chaplet of roses of the last.

Morse-Boycott. See BOYCOTT.

Morser (co. York). Az. on a chev. ar. betw. three birds of the last, beaked and legged gu. as many talbots' heads sa. collared or.

Morshead (Trenant Park, co. Cornwall, bart.). Az. a cross crosslet ar. betw. four martlets or, on a chief of the second, three escallops gu. *Crest*—A demi wyvern ramp. reguard. vert collared or, supporting an escutcheon ar. charged with a bezant.

Morshead (Widey, co. Kent). Same *Arms* and *Crest*.

Morshead (Lavethan, co. Cornwall). Same *Arms*, a bordure wavy erminois. *Crest*—A demi dragon reguard. vert, debruised by a bendlet wavy, collared or, holding betw. the paws an escutcheon sa. charged with a bezant.

Morskin (co. Kent). Az. three bars wavy ar. on a chief or, three falcons rising ppr.

Morskin (London. The sole heiress *m.* ROGER JAMES before 1580. Visit. Kent, 1619). Barry wavy of six az. and ar. on a chief or, three swallows volant ppr. *Crest*—A stork or, beaked and legged sa.

Mortagh, or Morchearty (a branch of the O'BRIENS, of Thomond, Reg. Ulster's Office). Ar. three lions pass. guard. in pale gu.

Morsley. Ar. a saltire sa. in chief a cinquefoil gu.

Morson (London; descended from Norwich; granted 1723). Per fesse erm. and gu. a pale counterchanged out of all a lion ramp. reguard. or (another has, on a chief sa. three covered cups gu). *Crest*—A lion's head erased per fesse erm. and gu. debruised with a pale counterchanged.

Morson. Sa. on a fesse or, a martlet gu. betw. two gouttes de poix.

Morston. Ar. on a chief gu. three martlets or.

Mort (Astley, co. Lancaster). Ar. on a bend gu. four (another, three) lozenges of the field. *Crest*—A phœnix in flames ppr.

Mortaigne. Or, six lions ramp. sa. three, two, and one.

Mortaine (co. Leicester). Or, three lions ramp. double queued sa.

Mortaine. Per fesse az. and ar. a fesse gu. three mullets in chief or.

Mortein, or Morteign. Ar. six lions ramp. az.

Mortein (Sir ROGER MORTEIN, Lord of Dunesley, *temp.* Edward II.; his dau. ISABEL MORTEIN, *m.* Sir RICHARD WILLOUGHBY, Knt., of Willoughby-upon-Wold, co. Notts, Judge of the Common Pleas. Visit. Notts, 1614). Or, six lioncels ramp. sa.

Mortemer. Gu. two bars vair.

Mortemer. Gu. two bars ar. in chief three fleurs-de-lis of the second.

Morteyn. Ar. a fesse gu. on a chief az. two mullets of the first.

Morteyne (Eyam and Risley, co. Derby; the heiress *m.* WILLOUGHBY, *temp.* Edward III.). Erm. a chief gu.

Morth, or Murth (Talland, co. Cornwall). Ar. a lion ramp. betw. three fleurs-de-lis gu.

Mortier. Chequy or (another, az.) and ar.

Mortimer (*Baron Mortimer* of Wigmore, and *Earl of March*; earldom extinct 1424; barony merged in the Crown upon the accession of Edward IV., descended from RALPH DE MORTIME, who accompanied William I. to England, and had a grant of Wigmore Castle; Sir EDMUND MORTIMER, Lord of Wigmore, fourth in descent from HUGH DE MORTIMER, first feudal Lord of Wigmore, the eldest son of the grantee, was summoned to Parliament, 1294. The second baron, ROGER MORTIMER, one of the Founder Knights of the Garter, was created *Earl of March* by charter, 1328. EDMUND, third *Earl of March*, *m.* the Lady PHILIPPA PLANTAGENET, only dau. and heir of LIONEL, *Duke of Clarence*, second son of Edward III.; his son ROGER, fourth *Earl of March*, was declared by Parliament, 9 Richard II., 1285, "Heir presumptive to the Crown." Lady ANNE MORTIMER, only dau. of the fourth earl, and sister and heir of the fifth and last earl, *m.* RICHARD PLANTAGENET, *Earl of Cambridge*, and her grandson, EDWARD, *Duke of York*, ascended the throne as Edward IV., when the honours of the MORTIMERS merged in the Crown). Barry of six or and az. on a chief of the first two pallets betw. two base esquierres of the second, over all an inescutcheon ar. The seal of EDMUND, fifth *Earl of March*, exhibits the same arms quarterly with DE BURGH, *Earl of Ulster*, viz., Or, a cross gu. *Crest*—Out of a ducal coronet a plume of feathers. *Supporters*—Two lions guard.

Mortimer (*Baron Mortimer*, of Chirke. ROGER MORTIMER, second son of ROGER MORTIMER, fifth feudal Lord of Wigmore, was summoned to Parliament, 1307, but none of his descendants were subsequently summoned). Same *Arms*, with due diff.

Mortimer (*Baron Mortimer*, of Richards Castle, abeyance 1304; descended from ROBERT MORTIMER, younger brother of HUGH MORTIMER, first feudal Lord of Wigmore). Same *Arms*, a bend gu. for diff.

Mortimer (Cheshunt, co. Herts; granted 14 June, 1688). Or, ten fleurs-de-lis, four, three, two, and one sa. a chief az.

Mortimer (London). Same *Arms.* *Crest*—A torteau betw. two wings or.

Mortimer (London). Or, guttée de sang a lion ramp. az. *Crest*—A buck's head erased quarterly or and gu. *Motto*—Press forward.

Mortimer (Kingston Manor, co. Cambridge; CONSTANTINE MORTIMER, *temp.* Richard II.). Or, three fleurs-de-lis sa.

Mortimer (Chelmarsh). Barry of six or and gu. an inescutcheon ar. on a chief of the first three pallets betw. two esquierres of the second.

Mortimer (co. Norfolk). Or, semée-de-lis sa. *Crest*—A buck's head quarterly or and gu. attired of the first.

Mortimer. Barry of six or and vert sixteen fleurs-de-lis counterchanged, three, three, three, three, three, and one.

Mortimer. Or, six fleurs-de-lis az. (another, sa.); another, Ar. semée of crosses crosslet sa. three fleurs-de-lis of the last; another, Az. semée-de-lis ar.; another, Gu. two bars ar. in chief three mullets pierced of the second; another, Erm. on a fess az. three crosses crosslet or; another, Ar. on a cross az. five fleurs-de-lis (another, escallops) or.

Mortimer (Reg. Ulster's Office). Or, six fleurs-de-lis sa. three, two, and one.

Mortimer (Craigievar, co. Aberdeen). Or, a lion ramp. sa. guttée d'or.

Mortimer (Auchenbody, Scotland). Paly of six ar. and az. a lion ramp sa. guttée d'eau. *Crest*—A bulls' head cabossed sa. *Motto*—Acquirit qui tuetur.

Mortimer (Fonthill Park, co.Wilts, from Scotland, 1827). Or, a lion ramp. sa. guttée of the field betw. three sinister hands couped paleways gu. *Crest*—A stag's head affrontée erased ppr. attired or. *Motto*—Acquirit qui tuetur.

Mortinall (Nowesley, co. Leicester). Ar. a cinquefoil pierced sa.

Mortlake (co. Surrey). Gu. a lion ramp. or, a bordure indented of the last. *Crest*—A lion sejant or, holding in the dexter paw a cross pattée fitchée az., on it a scroll with this motto—Hic labor, and resting the sinister paw on a cone ar., and on that another scroll with the motto—Hoc opus.

Mortlock (Abington Hall, co. Cambridge; granted to THOMAS MORTLOCK, Esq., High Sheriff co. Cambridge, 1840, and his brother, Sir JOHN CHEETHAM MORTLOCK, Commissioner of Excise). Gu. a lion ramp. or, a border indented of the last. *Crest*—A greyhound's head on a cross pattée fitchée az. *Motto*—Hic labor hoc opus.

Mortlock (co. Norfolk). Erm. a fret az. on a chief engr. gu. three fleurs-de-lis or.

Mortlock. Ar. three lozenges gu. *Crest*—A lion's head erased sa.

Mortlyne. Erm. on a chev. sa. a crescent or, a chief of the second.

Mortoft (Iringham, co. Norfolk; confirmed Oct. 1606). Sa. on a mount ppr. a stag lodged or, on a chief of the third a moorcock of the second. *Crest*—A stag's head erased sa. the nose ar. attired or, gorged with a ducal coronet gold.

Morton, or Morteyne (co. Bedford). Erm. a chief indented gu.

Morton (co. Chester). Ar. a greyhound courant sa. collared vert, rimmed gold. *Crest*—A greyhound's head ar. collared vert, rimmed gold.

Morton (granted to THOMAS MORTON, Esq., of Lechlade, 15 May, 1515, by Wriothesley, Garter). Quarterly, gu. and erm. in dexter chief and sinister base a goat's head erased ar. attired or, in the centre point a fleur-de-lis within a crescent of the last.

Morton (co. Cornwall). Ar. a chev. betw. three moorcocks sa.

Morton (co. Essex). Ar. three lions' heads erased sa.

Morton (Erbeck, co. Hereford). Quarterly, gu. and or, in the 1st quarter a goat's head erased ar. on a chief of the second three torteaux, each charged with an escallop gold. *Crest*—An eagle, wings expanded erm.

Morton (co. Kent, and Croydon, co. Surrey; JOHN MORTON, Archbishop of Canterbury 1486, *d.* 1500). Quarterly, gu. and erm. in the dexter chief and sinister base a goat's head erased ar. attired or. *Crest*—A goat's head erased ar. attired or.

Morton (co. Kent). Gu. a fesse chequy or and sa.

Morton (Morton and Ingleton, co. Stafford). Ar. on a chev. gu. betw. three demi buckles tongues pendent sa. a mullet or. *Crest*—A cock's head or, betw. two wings expanded az.

Morton (Sutton, co. Leicester ; THOMAS MORTON, grandson of ROBERT MORTON, Esq., of Sutton, the eldest son of WILLIAM MORTON, Esq., of Bosworth, in same co., descended from MORTON, of Morton, co. Stafford. Visit. Leicester, 1619). Same *Arms*.

Morton (Bosworth, co. Leicester ; ROBERT MORTON, Visit. Leicester, 1619, grandson of NICHOLAS MORTON, younger son of the above WILLIAM MORTON, Esq., of Bosworth). Same *Arms*, a crescent for diff.

Morton (Potters Cotten, co. Warwick, North Kilworth and Quarenden, co. Leicester ; descended from younger sons of the above WILLIAM MORTON, Esq., of Bosworth. Visit. Leicester, 1619). Same *Arms*.

Morton, or Morkton (co. Lincoln). Sa. on a chev. betw. three martlets or, as many mullets of the field.

Morton (Houghton, co. Salop). Ar. a chev. betw. three buckles sa.

Morton (co. Salop). Ar. a chev. betw. three trefoils slipped sa. *Crest*—A cock's head or, betw. two wings expanded az.

Morton (co. Sussex). Ar. three leopards' heads erased sa.

Morton (co. York). Ar. a chev. betw. three lozenges sa.

Morton. Ar. a chev. gu. betw. three square buckles sa. tongues pendent. *Crest*—A demi moorcock displ. sa. combed and wattled gu., motto over, Perseverando.

Morton. Ar. a greyhound in full course sa. collared gu. *Crest*—A wolf's head ar.

Morton, or Moreton (Milbourne St. Andrew, co. Dorset, bart., extinct 1699; descended from WILLIAM MORTON, younger

710

son of CHARLES MORTON, Esq., of Morton, co. York; of this family was JOHN MORTON, the celebrated Cardinal MORTON, Archbishop of Canterbury and Lord Chancellor of England, *temp.* Henry VII.; Sir GEORGE MORTON, of Milbourne St. Andrew, was created a bart. in 1619. His son and successor, Sir JOHN MORTON, of Milbourne St. Andrew, *d.* 1698, leaving a dau. and heiress, ANNE, *m.* EDMUND PLEYDELL, Esq., of Midgehall, co. Wilts, M.P.). Quarterly, gu. and erm. in the sinister chief and dexter base a goat's head erased ar. attired or.

Morton (Cardinal JOHN MORTON, Bishop of Ely, 1479-86, Archbishop of Canterbury 1486-1500. Arms in the Divinity School, Oxford. Visit. Oxon, 1574). Same *Arms*.

Morton (THOMAS MORTON, nephew to Cardinal MORTON, Archbishop of Canterbury, *d.* 8 Henry VIII. Visit. Leicester, 1619). Quarterly, erm. and gu. in the 2nd and 3rd quarters a goat's head erased ar. attired or.

Morton (Wrath House, co. York, 1666). Ar. three ravens sa. a border az. in chief a trefoil vert.

Morton (Whitehorse, Croydon, co. Surrey; arms of Sir ROBERT MORTON). Quarterly, 1st and 4th, quarterly, gu. and or, in the dexter chief and sinister base a goat's head erased ar. attired of the second, on a chief az. three bezants, each charged with an escallop of the first; 2nd and 3rd, ar. a chev. betw. three lapwings rising sa., for TWINIHO.

Morton. Ar. a chev. betw. three cushions erm. ; another, Quarterly, sa. and erm. in the dexter chief and sinister base a buck's head erased ar. ; another, Ar. six lions ramp. sa. tails double queued, three, two, and one (another, field or, lions az.); another, Or (another, ar.) a raven sa. ; another, Per fess ar. and gu. (another, or) six fleurs-de-lis sa. three, two, and one; another, Gu. two bars vair ; another, Erm. a chev. engr. gu. ; another, Or, a cinquefoil az. ; another, Ar. three bends az. (another, the field or).

Morton (Fun. Ent. Ulster's Office, 1655, BRIDGET MORTON, wife of JOHN PEPYS, whose father was Lord Chief Justice of Ireland). Quarterly, gu. and erm. in the 1st and 4th quarters a goat's head erased ar.

Morton (Greenock, 1857). Ar. on a fess az. betw. three roses gu. barbed vert a shakefork betw. two mullets of the field. *Crest*—A unicorn's head erased ar. armed, maned, and tufted or. *Motto*—Perseverando.

Morton (Belmont, Scotland, 1863). Ar. on a chev. sa. betw. three roses in chief gu. barbed vert, and in base two writing pens in saltire of the third, a raven ar. betw. two lions' heads erased of the first. *Crest*—A wolf's head couped ppr. *Motto*—Virtutis præmium.

Morton, Earl of. See DOUGLAS.

Mortymer (Attleburgh, co. Norfolk). Or, semée-de-lis sa. *Crest*—A buck's head erased quarterly or and gu.

Mortymer (co. Northampton). Erm. on a fesse az. three crosses sarcelly or.

Mortymer. See MORTIMER.

Morvile, or Morenill (France). Az. semée-de-lis or, a demi lion ramp. of the second (another, ar.).

Morvile. Az. semée-de-lis or. *Crest*—A cat's head guard. gu.

Morvile. Gu. a fret or.

Morvill (co. Cumberland, *temp.* Henry II.). Az. an eagle displ. barry gu. and ar. (another, ar. and gu.).

Morvill (co. Chester). Or, three boars' heads az. tusked ar.; another, Ar. three tigers' heads az.

Morvill (quartered by HARINGTON, Bart., of Ridlington, co. Rutland. Visit. Rutland, 1618). Az. semée-de-lis and fretty or. N.B. ADA, dau. and heir of HUGH DE MORVILL, *m.* THOMAS DE MULTON, Sheriff of Lincoln, 15 King John, A.D. 1228.

Morwell. Az. (another, gu.) a fesse betw. two chevronels or.

Morwen. Ar. six moorcocks sa. three, two, and one.

Morwick (Visit. Durham, 1615). Gu. a saltire vairé ar. and sa.

Moryn. Ar. a chev. sa. betw. three fleurs-de-lis gu.

Moryne. Gu. three lions pass. guard. ar. betw. two bends gobony of the last and az.

Morys. Per fesse ar. and az. a fesse gu. in chief fretty of the second, in base a dolphin naiant of the first.

Mose. Erm. a cross pattée sa.

Mosel (co. Norfolk). Ar. a chev. betw. three boars' heads couped sa.

Moseley (Moseley and Bilston, co. Stafford; descended from JOHN MOSELEY, Esq., of Moseley, *m.* PHILLIS, sister and heir of ROBERT SCHAMPION. Visit. co. Lancaster). Sa. on a chev. betw. three millpicks ar. three mullets gu., quartering Ar. on a fesse sa. three escallops or, for SCHAMPION.

Moseley (Owsden, co. Suffolk; descended from JOHN MOSELEY, Esq., of Wittington, grandson of JOHN MOSELEY, second son of JOHN MOSELEY, Esq., of Moseley. He purchased, 1512, from his wife's brother, HENRY LONGMORE, the estate of the Mere, Anville, co. Stafford). Sa. a chev. betw. three millpicks or. Crest—Out of a mural crown chequy or and sa. a demi lion holding in the dexter paw a millpick ar. Motto—Incrementum dat Deus.

Moseley, or Mosley (Mere, co. Stafford; descended from MICHAEL MOSELEY, of London, younger brother of HUMPHREY MOSELEY, Esq., of Owsden; WALTER MOSELEY, Esq., of the Mere, m., temp. Queen Anne, JANE, dau. and heiress of WILLIAM ACTON, son of Sir EDWARD ACTON, Bart., of Aldenham). Sa. a chev. betw. three millpicks ar. Crest—An eagle displ. erm.

Moseley (LOFFT-MOSELEY, Glemham House, co. Suffolk; exemplified to HENRY CAPEL LOFFT, Esq., upon his assuming, by royal licence, the additional surname of MOSELEY). Quarterly, 1st and 4th, sa. a chev. betw. three millpicks ar., for MOSELEY; 2nd and 3rd, LOFFT, of Glemham House, [which see]. Crests—1st, MOSELEY: Out of a mural crown chequy ar. and sa. a demi lion or, holding in the dexter paw a pickaxe ppr.; 2nd : LOFFT, of Glemham.

Moses. Gu. a chev. betw. three cocks or.

Mosleton. Or, three pallets az. betw. two flaunches gu.

Mosley (Houghend, co. Lancaster; descended from OSWALD MOSELEY, second son of ERNOLD DE MOSELEY, Lord of Moseley, temp. King John; EDWARD MOSLEY, Esq., of Houghend, temp. Henry VI., had three sons: I. OSWALD, his heir; II. Sir NICHOLAS, Lord Mayor of London; and III. ANTHONY, ancestor of MOSLEY, Bart., of Rolleston). Sa. a chev. betw. three millpicks ar.

Mosley (Hough, co. Stafford, bart., extinct 1665; descended from Sir NICHOLAS MOSLEY, Lord Mayor of London, 1599, second son of EDWARD MOSLEY, Esq., of Houghend, temp. Henry VI.). Same Arms, a crescent for diff., quartering Or, a fess betw. three eaglets displ. sa.

Mosley (Rolleston, co. Stafford, bart., extinct 1779; descended from ANTHONY OSWALD, third son of EDWARD OSWALD, Esq., of Houghend, temp. Henry VI.). Quarterly, 1st and 4th, same Arms; 2nd and 3rd, or, a fesse betw. three eagles displ. sa. Crest—An eagle displ. erm. Motto—Mos legem regit.

Mosley (Ancoats, co. Lancaster, bart.; descended from NICHOLAS MOSLEY, brother of Sir OSWALD MOSLEY, first bart. of Rolleston). Quarterly, 1st and 4th, same Arms; 2nd and 3rd, or, a fesse betw. three eagles displ. sa. Crest—An eagle displ. erm. Motto—Mos legem regit.

Mosley (Burnaston House, co. Derby; descended from ASHTON NICHOLAS MOSLEY, Esq., of Park Hill, co. Derby, third son of Sir JOHN PARKER MOSLEY, first bart. of Ancoats). Same Arms and Crest.

Mosley (Sir NICHOLAS MOSLEY, Lord Mayor of London, 1599, and co. Lancaster). Same Arms, an estoile for diff.

Mosley (Newcastle-on-Tyne). Sa. on a chev. betw. three millpicks ar. as many mullets gu. Crest—An eagle displ. erm. Motto—Mos legem regit.

Mosley. Ar. a chev. betw. three lozenges sa.

Moss (EDWARDS-MOSS, Roby Hall, co. Lancaster, bart.). Quarterly, 1st and 4th, quarterly, erm. and erminois, a cross pattée az. betw. six billets, three in chief and three in base gu., for MOSS; 2nd and 3rd, ar. a lion ramp. guard. sa. on a chief of the last two eagles displ. of the first, for EDWARDS. Crests—1st : Issuant from the battlements of a tower or, charged with a rose gu. slipped ppr. a griffin's head erm. on the neck a cross pattée az., for MOSS; 2nd : A rock ppr. therefrom rising a dove ar. holding in the beak an olive branch and surmounted of a rainbow ppr., for EDWARDS. Motto—En la rose je fleurie.

Moss (granted to SAUL MOSS, of Kingston, Jamaica, R.A.). Ar. on a chev. az. betw. three pineapples ppr. as many horses' heads couped also ppr. Crest—A demi seahorse ppr. collared vair, and resting the sinister foot on an escutcheon ar. charged with a pineapple ppr. Motto—Non nobis solum.

Mosse (Horton Regis, co. Bedford). Erm. on a cross formée sa. a bezant. Crest—Out of a mural coronet or, a griffin's head erm. charged on the neck with a bezant.

Mosseley. Az. a crescent betw. three fleurs-de-lis or.

Mossman (Auchtyfardell, co. Lanark). Az. a chev. betw. three oak trees or. Crest—A hand erect holding a closed book ppr. Motto—Me meliora manent.

Moston (co. Northumberland). Sa. three bars ar. in chief as many plates.

Moston (quartered by MITFORD, through OSBALDESTON, FOUNTAINE, and MONCKTON). Ar. a chev. betw. three crosses patonée sa.

Moston. Sa. three bars ar. in chief as many annulets of the second. Crest—A lion's head gu.; another, Sa. two bars ar.

in chief an annulet of the second; another, Gu. on a fesse erm. betw. three mullets ar. as many annulets gu.; another, Ar. a chev. sa. betw. three crosses patoncé of the last.

Mostyn (Mostyn Hall, co. Flint, bart., extinct 1831; ELIZA BETH MOSTYN, eldest surviving sister and co-heir of Sir THOMAS MOSTYN, sixth and last bart., m. Sir EDWARD PRYCE LLOYD, Bart., created Lord Mostyn 1831). Per bend sinister erm. and ermines a lion ramp. or. Crest—A lion ramp. or. Motto—Auxilium meum a Domino.

Mostyn (Pengwern, Llanwanda, North Wales; descended from the principal line of MOSTYN, of Mostyn). Same Arms, &c.

Mostyn (Kilken, co. Flint; the heiress, CHARLOTTE MOSTYN, m. EDWARDS, of Pentre, co. Montgomery). Same Arms, &c.

Mostyn (Bodscallan, co. Anglesey; the heiress, MARGARET, dau. of RICHARD MOSTYN, Esq., second son of THOMAS AP RICHARD AP HOWEL, m. GRIFFITH WYNN, second son of JOHN WYNN AP MEREDITH, of Gwydir, co. Carnarvon). Same Arms, &c.

Mostyn (Talacre, co. Flint, bart.). Same Arms, Crest, and Motto.

Mostyn (Baron Vaux). Quarterly, 1st and 4th, MOSTYN, per bend sinister erm. and ermines a lion ramp. or; 2nd and 3rd, VAUX, chequy or and gu. on a chev. az. three roses gold. Crest—An eagle's head sa. beaked or. Supporters—Dexter, a griffin sa. langued gu. beaked and membered or; sinister, a buck or. Motto—Hodie non cras.

Mostyn (LLOYD-MOSTYN, Baron Mostyn). Gu. a Saracen's head erased at the neck ppr. wreathed about the temples sa. and ar. Crest—A stag trippant ppr. Supporters—Dexter, a stag ppr. attired or, charged on the shoulder with an escocheon gu. thereon a chev. ar. betw. three men's heads couped in profile ppr.; sinister, a lion or, charged on the shoulder with an escutcheon ar. thereon a cross engr. and fleurettée sa. betw. four Cornish choughs ppr. Motto—Heb Dduw heb ddym, a Duw a dygon.

Moteyns. Erm. a chief gu.

Motham (Drinkston, co. Suffolk). Sa. a cross indented erm. Crest—On a mount vert a talbot couchant erm.

Moton (Pickleton and Stapleton, co. Leicester; descended from ALEXANDER MOTON, of Pickleton, temp. King John; the heiress, ELIZABETH, dau. of Sir ROBERT MOTON, Knt., of Pickleton, who d. 13 Henry VII., A.D. 1497, m. Sir JOHN HARINGTON, Knt., of Exton, ancestor of Sir JOHN EDWARD HARINGTON, Bart., of Ridlington, co. Rutland. Visit. Leicester, 1619). Ar. a cinquefoil az.

Mott (Braintree, co. Essex, and Kedington, co. Suffolk). Sa. a crescent ar. Crest—An estoile of eight points ar.

Mott. Az. five lozenges conjoined in fess or, each charged with an escallop gu. on a chief of the second a griffin's head erased betw. two fleurs-de-lis of the first.

Mott (Barningham Hall, co. Norfolk; exemplified to THOMAS VERTUE, Esq., who assumed the name and arms of MOTT, in accordance with the testamentary injunction of JOHN THURSTON, M.D., of Market Weston, co. Suffolk). Sa. a crescent ar. Crest—An estoile of eight points ar. Motto—Spectemur agendo.

Motte. Az. on a bend betw. three leopards' faces or, as many martlets gu.

Mottershed. Sa. on a chev. ar. betw. three crosses crosslet or, as many quatrefoils gu. Crest—The stump of a tree ppr. s branch vert issuing from the dexter side.

Motteux (Beechamwell, co. Norfolk ; of French extraction, settled in England at the Revocation of the Edict of Nantes). Or, three lions pass. guard. in pale towards the sinister gu. Crest—A lion pass. guard. to the sinister gu. ducally crowned or. Motto—Quid vult, valde vult.

Motton (co. Leicester). Ar. a cinquefoil pierced az.

Motton. Ar. three bars gu. a canton ermines. Crest—A stag statant wounded with an arrow all ppr.

Mottram, alias Mottvane (Bishopdike Hall, co. York. Visit. Dugdale, 1665). Sa. on a chev. ar. betw. three crosses crosslet or, as many cinquefoils gu.

Mouat (England). Az. a tower ar. Crest—A lion pass. guard. ppr.

Moubray (Barnbougle, co. Edinburgh; descended from a common ancestor with MOWBRAY, ancestors in the female line of Dukes of Norfolk). Gu. a lion ramp. ar. crowned with a ducal crown or. Crest—A demi lion ramp. gu. Motto—Fortitudine.

Moubray (Cockairny, co. Fife; now representative of Barnbougle). As Barnbougle. Crest—A demi lion ramp. ar. Supporters—Dexter, a man in court dress; sinister, a woman habited ppr. Mottoes—Over the crest : Fortitudine; under the arms : Let the deed shaw.

Moubray (GEORGE MOUBRAY, H.E.I.C.S., 1793). Gu. a

lion ramp. ar. crowned with an antique crown or, betw. three bears' heads couped of the last, muzzled ar. *Crest*—The figure of Fortune holding in her dexter hand an escroll with the motto, Suivez moi, and in his sinister a cornucopia all ppr.

Mouchet. Gu. a long sword erect ppr. hilted and pommelled or. *Crest*—A dexter arm embowed vambraced, the hand raised holding a sword in bend dexter, the point downwards ppr. hilt and pomel or.

Mould (Appleby, co. Liecester; represented by the Rev. JOHN MOULD, M.A., of Appleby). Ar. two bars sa. in chief three torteaux. *Crest*—A dexter arm erect ppr.

Mould (co. York, 1665). Sa. two bars wavy ar. in chief a lion pass. guard. of the last. *Crest*—A demi lion ramp. guard. or.

Moulden (Stalenborough House, co. Kent, and co. Lancaster). Or, three bars guttée a canton ermines. *Crest*—A griffin's head erased.

Moule (co. Bedford). Ar. a trefoil slipped sa. two bars gu. in chief three torteaux. *Crest*—A cubit arm issuing out of clouds ppr. habited gu. cuffed ar. the hand open and erect. gu.

Moule (co. Northampton). Barry of four gu. and ar. *Crest*—A lion ramp. supporting a broad arrow point downwards all ppr.

Moulent. Sa. a lion ramp. double queued ar.

Moullin (Guernsey). Ar. a cross moline sa. charged with an escallop or.

Moulso. Per chev. gu. and sa. a fleur-de-lis erm.

Moulso. Or, a chev. per chev. gu. and sa. betw. three fleurs-de-lis ermines.

Moulson (Lord Mayor of London, 1634). Gu. a chev. componée or and sa. betw. three mullets of the second.

Moulson. Gu. a chev. ar. fretty sa. betw. three mullets or. *Crest*—A lion's head erased per pale embattled or and sa. *Another Crest*, borne by RICHARD MOULSON, M.D.—A griffin pass. resting the forepaw on an estoile or. *Another Crest*—An elephant ar. lifting with the proboscis a laurel branch vert. *Motto*—Regi fidelis.

Moulson. Az. an estoile of eight points or, out of a crescent ar.

Moult (co. Nottingham; granted 1686). Az. three bars wavy ar. in chief as many fleur-de-lis or. *Crest*—A mound or, thereon a pelican ar. wings expanded, beaked and legged sa. vulning her breast gu.

Moult. Same *Arms*. *Crest*—A fish naiant sa. spotted or.

Moulton (Plympton, co. Devon; four descents given in Visit. 1620). Per pale ar. and erm. three bars gu. *Crest*—A cubit arm erect, vested gu. cuffed erm. holding in the hand ppr. a chaplet of roses of the first, leaved vert.

Moulton (cos. Gloucester, Kent, and York, and London; granted 1571). Ar. three bars gu. betw. eight escallops sa. three, two, two, and one. *Crest*—On a pellet a falcon rising ar.

Moulton (Wicklewood, co. Norfolk). Gyronny of six or and az. four martlets counterchanged.

Moulton (co. Norfolk). Barry of six gu. and ar. on a chief of the second three martlets az.

Moulton, or Moulson (London). Gu. (another, sa.). a chev. ar. fretty sa. betw. three mullets or. *Crest*—A griffin pass. per pale gu. and az. resting the dexter foot on a mullet or.

Moulton. Gu. a chev. ar. fretty sa. betw. three mullets pierced or (another, the mullets of the second pierced of the third); another, Barry of six gu. and ar. a border sa.; another, Az. a chev. ar. fretty gu. betw. three annulets of the second; another, Ar. two bars gu.; another, Chequy or and gu. a bend sa.; another, Sa. three bars in chief as many annulets of the second.

Moultrie (Aston, co. Salop). Az. on a chev. betw. three escallops ar. a boar's head erased sa. langued gu. betw. two estoiles of the last.

Mounboucher (quartered by HARBOTTELL, of Harbottell, Basingthorpe, co. Lincoln, and Eglington, co. Rutland; THOMAS MOUNBOUCHER, *temp.* Henry IV.; his dau. and heir, GRACE, *m.* Sir RALPH HARBOTTLE. Visit. Rutland, 1618). Ar. three water-pots covered gu.

Mounchensey. Or, three escutcheons vairé ar. and gu. (another, or and gu.).

Moundeford. Ar. three fleurs-de-lis gu.

Mounderby (co. Berks). Az. fretty or.

Moune (co. Devon). Gu. a maunch erm.

Mounsack. Gu. a cross moline ar.

Mounsel. Ar. a chev. betw. three maunches sa.

Mounser (co. Derby). Gu. a chev. betw. three leopards' faces or.

Mounserant. Paly of six ar. and sa. on a chief gu. three sixfoils or.

712

Mounsey (Castletown, near Carlisle). Chequy or and gu. on a chev. erm. two lions pass. counter-pass. az. *Crest*—A demi griffin gorged with a wreath of oak, and holding betw. the claws a banner erect. *Motto*—Semper paratus.

Mounsey (Killilung, co. Renfrew, 1763). Chequy or and gu. on a chief of the second three mullets of the first. *Crest*—On a mount an eagle looking at the setting sun ppr. *Motto*—Decor integer.

Mounsor (Carleton, co. Lincoln). Or, two chev. gu.

Mountstaby. Az. a cross ar. fretty gu.

Mount (co. Kent). Ar. on a mount vert a lion ramp. gu. crowned or. *Crest*—A fox saliant supporting the trunk of a tree ragulée ppr.

Mount. Same *Arms*. *Crest*—A demi man in armour brandishing a scymitar ppr.

Mount. Or, on a mount vert a lion ramp. gu. crowned of the field; another, Sa. four martlets ar.

Mountague (Bourney, co. Buckingham). Ar. three fusils in fesse gu. betw. as many pellets.

Mountague. Ar. three fusils in fesse gu. a border sa. *Crest*—A griffin's head betw. two wings endorsed ppr.

Mountaine (Westminster; granted 1613). Barry lozengy or and az. on a chief gu. three crosses crosslet of the first. *Crest*—A stork's head issuing out of rays or.

Mountain, or Montaigne (The Heath, co. Hertford; descended from the ancient house of MONTAIGNE, of which was the celebrated MICHEL DE MONTAIGNE, and established in England at the Revocation of the Edict of Nantes). Quarterly, 1st and 4th, erm. on a chev. az. betw. three lions ramp. guard. sa. each supporting betw. the forepaws an escallop erect gu. a mitre or, enclosed by two crosses crosslet fitchée ar., for MOUNTAIN, or MONTAIGNE; 2nd and 3rd, ar. on a cross sa. five lions ramp. or, for WALE. *Crest*—A demi lion ramp. guard. per fess wavy ar. and sa. supporting betw. the paws an escallop gu. on the breast a cross crosslet fitchée of the second. *Motto*—Cum cruce salus.

Mountboucher. Ar. three fleshpots gu. a bordure engr. sa. bezantée.

Mountcashell, Earl of. See MOORE.

Mount-Edgecumbe, Earl of. See EDGECUMBE.

Mountfitchet. Gu. three chevronels gu.

Mountford, or Mountfort (Fuwell, co. Norfolk). Ar. three fleurs-de-lis gu. *Crest*—A fleur-de-lis gu.

Mountford (London; allowed at Visit. 1568). Same *Arms*, a martlet for diff.

Mountford (co. Norfolk). Ar. on a chief az. two fleurs-de-lis of the first; another, Or, three garbs gu.; another, Gu. three garbs ar.

Mountford (Radwinter, co. Stafford, and co. Warwick). Bendy of ten or and az. *Crest*—A lion's head couped az.

Mountford (co. Sussex). Or, four bendlets az.

Mountford (co. Warwick). Bendy of six or and az. a border gu.

Mountford (co. Warwick). Ar. two bars gu. a bend az.

Mountford (quartered by WILLOUGHBY, of Willoughby-upon-Wold, Risley and Wollaton, co. Notts. Visit. Notts, 1614). Bendy of eight or and az.

Mountford (Kelnhurst, co. York). Ar. a lion ramp. az. betw. ten crosses crosslet fitchée gu. a bordure erm. *Crest*—A talbot's head sa. ducally gorged and eared or.

Mountford (co. York; granted 18 Feb. 1602). Ar. a lion ramp. tail double queued az. an orle of crosses crosslet gu. *Crest*—A talbot's head sa. ducally gorged or.

Mountford. Ar. a lion ramp. gu. tail queued; another, Ar. crusily a lion ramp. sa. a chief gu.; another, Barry of twelve or and az.; annulets, Ar. on a chief az. three fleurs-de-lis or; another, Sa. three fleurs-de-lis ar.

Mountfort (Beamhurst Hall, co. Stafford; claiming descent from SIMON DE MONTFORT, *Earl of Leicester*). Bendy or and az. *Crest*—A plume of five feathers.

Mountfort (Sapworth). Same *Arms*, a border gu.

Mountfort. See MOUNTFORD.

Mountfort. See MOUNTFORD.

Mounthermer. Or, an eagle displ. vert, armed az. a border of the third charged with eight lions pass. guard. of the field.

Mountjoy. Or, a castle sa. *Crest*—A demi sportsman firing his piece ppr.

Mountjoy (co. Devon). Barry nebulée of six or and sa.

Mountjoy. Gu. three escutcheons or; another, Ar. semée-de-lis gu.; another, Or, three bars wavy sa.; another, Barry wavy of six or and sa.

Mountmorres, Viscount. See DE MONTMORENCY.

Mountney (cos. Essex and Leicester, and Gestwick, co. Norfolk). Az. a bend betw. six martlets or. *Crest*—A wolf sejant ar. collared and lined gu.

Mountney (co. Essex). Gu. a bend cotised betw. six martlets (another, mullets) or.

Mountney (Newland-Verdon, co. Leicester). Az. a bend ar. betw. three martlets or. *Crest*—A greyhound sejant collared and lined.

Mountney (Cowley, co. York). Or, a bend betw. six martlets gu.

Mountney. Gu. a bend betw. six martlets ar. (another, or); another, Gu. a bend cotised betw. six martlets (another, mullets) or; another, Paly of six or and gu. on a chief sa. three bezants (another, the chief ar.).

Mountpinson. Or, three bends gu. on a chief az. as many mullets of the field.

Mountroye. Barry nebulée of six or and gu.

Mount St. Bernard's, Abbey of (co. Leicester; founded by the PHILLIPS DE LISLE family). Or, a pastoral staff in pale with regillium dependent therefrom sa. on a chief az. three lions ramp. of the field.

Mountsey. Gu. a fesse betw. three cinquefoils ar.

Mountstephen, or Mountsteven (Cullompton, co. Devon, and Petersborough, co. Northampton). Gyronny of eight or and az. on an inescutcheon sa. a lion ramp. ar. *Crest*—A demi griffin saliant, wings endorsed sa. armed or.

Mountsword. Gu. a fesse engr. betw. three cinquefoils pierced or.

Moushall (co. Lancaster). Ar. three bars gemelles gu.

Mouthwey. Ar. a lion ramp. gu. a border engr. sa. *Crest*—A Doric pillar entwined with ivy, and on the top a flame of fire all ppr.

Moultrie (Seafield and Rescobie, Scotland). Az. on a chev. betw. three escallops ar. a boar's head couped sa. betw. two spur-rowels gu. *Crest*—A mermaid ppr. *Motto*—Nunquam non fidelis.

Mow (that Ilk; represented, 1672, by Mow, of East Mains, co. Berwick). Az. a boar's head erased ar. armed gu. betw. three mullets of the second. *Crest*—A phœnix rising out of flames. *Motto*—Post funera fœnus.

Mowat (Balquhollie, co. Aberdeen; the name was anciently written DE MONTE ALTO, and is thus written in a perambulation of the lands of Cleish, in Fifeshire: "Per Michaelem De Monte Alto et Philippum de Melgedrum, tunc Justiciarios Scotiæ, anno 1252"). Ar. a lion ramp. sa.

Mowat (Capt. GEORGE MOWAT, R.N., 1811, representative of Balquhollie). Same *Arms*. *Crest*—The battlement of a castle or, issuant therefrom a demi warrior, armed and accoutred ppr. holding in his dexter hand a sword also ppr. hilted and pommelled or, and in his sinister a flagstaff, thereon twisted a banner vert, fringed and charged with an antique crown or. *Supporters*—Two savages wreathed head and middle with oak ppr. each holding in his exterior hand a trident or. *Mottoes*—Over the crest: Monte alto; below the shield: Commit thy work to God.

Mowat (Inglistoun, Scotland, bart., 1664). Same *Arms* as the preceding, within a bordure of the second. *Crest*—An oak tree growing out of a rock ppr. *Motto*—Monte alto.

Mowatt. Sa. a tower triple towered ar. *Crest*—A demi lion or.

Mowbray (*Duke of Norfolk, Earl of Nottingham, Earl of Warren and Surrey, Earl Marshal* of England, and *Baron Mowbray;* dukedom and earldoms extinct 1475, when the barony fell into abeyance. The MOWBRAYS descended from ROGER DE MOWBRAY, son of NIGEL DE ALBINI, who, possessing the lands of MOWBRAY, assumed that surname by command of Henry I., his descendant, ROGER DE MOWBRAY, was summoned to Parliament 1295, the fifth baron was created *Earl of Nottingham,* 1377, *d. s. p.,* his brother, the sixth Baron, was re-created *Earl of Nottingham,* 1383, constituted *Earl Marshal,* and created *Duke of Norfolk,* 1396, the fourth Duke was created *Earl of Warren and Surrey, vitâ patris,* and. d. without surviving issue, when all his honours became extinct except the barony, which fell into abeyance among the descendants of the daus. of the first Duke, of whom Lady ISABEL is represented by the *Earl of Berkeley,* and Lady MARGARET by the *Lords Stourton and Petre,* as heirs general, and by the *Duke of Norfolk,* as heir male). Gu. a lion ramp. ar. *Crest*—A leopard or, ducally gorged ar.; granted by patent to the first duke, 17 Richard II., which acknowledges his right to bear for his crest "a golden leopard with a white label," the crest of his maternal ancestor, THOMAS PLANTAGENET, *Earl of Norfolk,* and grants the coronet instead of the label, which would of right belong to the King's son.

Mowbray (co. York). Same *Arms*, a border of the last.

Mowbray (co. York). Same *Arms*, a border gobony or and sa.

713

Mowbray (Grangewood House, co. Leicester; male representative of MOWBRAY, of Bishopwearmouth). Quarterly, 1st and 8th, MOWBRAY, gu. a lion ramp. betw. two flaunches or, each charged with three billets az.; 2nd, READ, or, on a chev. betw. three garbs gu. three ears of wheat stalked and leaved ar.; 3rd, SHIPPERDSON, sa. on a bend ar. three lozenges az. each charged with a planetary sun in his glory; 4th, COGHILL, erm. a chev. betw. three cocks gu.; 5th, COGHILL, gu. on a chev. ar. three pellets, a chief sa.; 6th, CRAMER, or, on a chief indented az. three fleurs-de-lis of the field; 7th, HOLLAND, az. a lion ramp. guard. betw. eight fleurs-de-lis ar. *Crest*—An oak tree or, therefrom pendent an escutcheon gu. charged with a lion's head erased ar. *Motto*—Suo stat robore virtus.

Mowbray (Bishopwearmouth, co. Durham; exemplified to Right Hon. JOHN ROBERT MOWBRAY, D.L., M.P. for the city of Durham, Judge Advocate General, only son of ROBERT STRIBLING CORNISH, Esq., of the city of Exeter, upon his assuming by royal licence, 1847, the surname of MOWBRAY only, upon his marriage with ELIZABETH GRAY, only child of GEORGE ISAAC MOWBRAY, Esq., of Bishopwearmouth, co. Durham, and Mortimer, co. Berks). Quarterly, 1st and 4th, MOWBRAY, gu. a lion ramp. erm. two flaunches or, each charged with three billets in pale az. and in the centre chief point a cross crosslet of the third; 2nd and 3rd, CORNISH, per pale az. and sa. a chev. embattled betw. in chief two roses and in base a cross pattée or. On an escutcheon of pretence: 1st and 8th, MOWBRAY; 2nd, READ, or, a chev. betw. three garbs gu. three ears of wheat stalked and leaved ar.; 3rd, SHIPPERDSON, sa. on a bend ar. three lozenges az. each charged with a planetary sun in his glory; 4th, COGHILL, erm. a chev. betw. three cocks gu.; 5th, COGHILL, gu. on a chev. ar. three pellets, a chief sa.; 6th, CRAMER, or, on a chief indented az. three fleurs-de-lis of the field; 7th, HOLLAND, az. a lion ramp. guard. betw. eight fleurs-de-lis ar. *Crests*—1st, MOWBRAY: An oak tree or, therefrom pendent an escutcheon gu. charged with a lion's head erased ar.; 2nd, CORNISH: Betw. two branches of laurel in saltire a Cornish chough rising ppr. charged on the breast with a cross pattée or. *Mottoes*—Suo stat robore virtus, for MOWBRAY; and, Deu pascit corvos, for CORNISH.

Mowbray. Gu. a lion pass. ar. *Crest*—On a chapeau gu. lined erm. a lion pass. ar. betw. a pair of stags' attires or.

Mowbricke (Mowbricke, co. Lancaster). Or, three garbs vert.

Mower (Woodseats, co. Derby, *temp.* Henry VI.; represented, when Lysons wrote, by GEORGE MOWER, Esq., of Holt House, in Darley). Erm. on a chev. az. three roses ar.

Mower (co. Devon). Ar. two chev. gu. *Crest*—A dove with an olive branch in the beak ppr.

Mowgre, or Mowgrey. Ar. on a bend az. six fleurs-de-lis or, two, two, and two (another, bears the field or).

Mowgrill, or Mowgrale. Per fesse gu. and az. a lion ramp. or.

Mowin. Or, three cinquefoils gu. a canton of the last.

Mowlder. Ar. a fesse betw. three bunches of grapes sa.

Mowlsey. Per chev. gu. and sa. a fleur-de-lis erm.

Mowlton (co. Kent). Barry of six or and vert.

Mownbowchier. See MOUNBOWCHIER.

Mowne (co. Devon). Per fesse gu. and ar. three crescents ar. *Crest*—Two arms in armour embowed ppr. sustaining a ball sa.

Mowne (co. Devon). Per pale gu. and ar. three crescents countercnanged.

Mowne. Or, a cross engr. sa. a bendlet gu.

Mownes. Or, three bars az. a lion ramp. gu.

Mowrand, or Mowron. Ar. on a fesse sa. three cinquefoils or, in chief a lion pass. gu.

Moxon. Per fesse gu. and az. a fesse or, betw. a mullet in chief and a crescent in base ar. *Crest*—A demi eagle displ. az.

Moy (France). Or, a saltire betw. four martlets gu.

Moyer (Petsey Hall, co. Essex, bart., extinct 1716; Sir SAMUEL MOYER, an opulent Turkey merchant, was created a bart. in 1701). Ar. two chevronels az.

Moyes (Canons, co. Surrey). Erm. on a pale betw. two roses gu. a cross calvary or. *Crest*—A dove ar. in the beak a laurel sprig vert.

Moygne. Barry of six or and vert.

Moyle (Bake, co. Cornwall; JOHN MOYLE, Esq., of Bake, Visit. Cornwall, 1620, descended from ROGER MOYLE, living 29 Edward I., anno. 1300, the grandson of ROBERT MOYLE, *temp.* King John). Gu. a mule pass. ar.

Moyle (St. Austel, co. Cornwall; RICHARD MOYLE, Visit.

Cornwall, 1620, son of RICHARD MOYLE, Esq., of St. Austel, descended from MOYLE, of Bake). Same *Arms*, a mullet for diff. *Crest*—Two demi dragons sans wings addorsed, the necks entwined, the dexter gu. sinister ar.

Moyle (co. Kent). Same *Arms*.

Moyle (Wye, co. Kent). Same *Arms*, a border of the last.

Moyle (Bowerhall and Lymby, co. Notts; JOHN MOYLE, of the latter place, son of THOMAS MOYLE, grandson of RALPH MOYLE, Esq., of the former place, and great-grandson of THOMAS MOYLE and AMY, his wife, dau. and heir of LANG-STON, of Langston. Visit. Notts, 1614). Same *Arms*, in dexter chief a mullet ar, for diff. *Crest*—Two demi dragons addorsed, necks entwined, dexter gu. sinister or. *Motto*—Dieu garda Le Moyle.

Moyle. Same *Arms*, adding a chief of the second. *Crest*—A wivern, wings expanded gu. platée.

Moyle (co. Chester). Ar. a greyhound courant sa. betw. two bars gu. in chief three torteaux.

Moyne, or Moon (co. Cornwall). Or, a cross engr. sa. a label of three points ar. each charged with a torteaux.

Moyne, or Moigne (cos. Essex and Norfolk). Az. a chev. betw. three crescents or, each charged with a pellet.

Moyne (Charter House, Hinton, and Mendip, co. Somerset). Sa. a chev. betw. three roses ar. *Crest*—Out of a ducal coronet a tiger's head.

Moyne (co. Suffolk). Ar. a saltire engr. sa.

Moyne. Ar. two bars sa. in chief three mullets (another, estoiles) of the second; another, Or, crusily sa. a cross pattée of the last.

Moyne, or Moone. Gu. a cross betw. eight crosses formée ar.; another, Az. on a chief gu. three crescents ar.

Moyne. See MOIGNE and MOONE.

Moyne, Le. See MONCK.

Moynes (co. Huntingdon). Az. a fesse dancettée or, betw. six crosses crosslet ar. *Crest*—A lion ramp. holding in the dexter paw a battle axe all ppr.

Moynes (co. Suffolk). Ar. a saltire engr. gu.

Moynes. Ar. two bars sa. a chief gu. ; another, Az. a fesse dancettée ar. ; another, Az. crusily a fesse dancettée ar.

Moynes, or Moune. Or, a cross engr. sa. a label of five points gobonated gu. and ar.

Moynes, or Mohun. Ar. a cross engr. sa.

Moynley. Ar. a dexter hand couped sa. *Crest*—A hind's head couped.

Moyone (co. Suffolk). Or, a saltire engr. gu.

Moyre. Ar. a canton gu.

Moyry (granted by Betham, Ulster, to the descendants of PETER MOYRY, Esq., of Waterford). Ar. a shamrock vert betw. three mullets az. a bordure wavy gu.

Moyse. Erminois on a pale gu. a cross calvary with three grieces or; another, Erm. on a pale betw. two roses gu. a cross calvary ar. *Crest*—A leopard ramp. ppr.

Moyser (Farlington, co. York). Az. on a chev. betw. three hawks close ar. belled and jessed or, as many talbots' heads erased sa. collared of the third. *Crest*—A demi horse ramp. erminois, bridled or.

Moysey (Henton, co. Somerset; granted 1765). Or, on a fesse sa. betw. three cinquefoils vert a cross flory of the field. *Crest*—A dragon's head vert charged on the neck with a cross flory or.

Moyshole, Moyshold, or Moysholl. Ar. on a cross az. five leopards' faces or.

Moyt. Or, a lion ramp. reguard. sa.

Muckle (Scotland). Ar. three martlets gu. *Crest*—A lion pass. gu.

Muckleston (Merrington, co. Salop; descended from HOCSKYN MUCCLESTON, b. 1345, m. GERTRUDE, dau. of HUGH KYNASTON. The estate of Merrington came to MUCKLESTON through EDWARD MUCKLESTON, Esq., of Pen-y-lan, Recorder of Oswestry, m. 1615, MARY, dau. and heir of THOMAS CORBET, Esq., whose wife was sister and heir of THOMAS COLEFOXE, Esq., of Merrington). Quarterly, 1st, vert on a fesse betw. three greyhounds' heads erased ar. three crosses pattée gu., for MUCKLESTON; 2nd, or, two ravens sa., for CORBET; 3rd, ar. a cross engr. sa. betw. four pellets, each charged with a pheon of the field, for FLETCHER; 4th, sa. two shinbones in saltire, three surmounted of the dexter ar. *Crest*—A greyhound's head erased ppr. collared gu. *Motto*—Fideliter.

Mucklewaite. Chequy ar. and gu. a chief indented az. *Crest*—A griffin's head erased ppr.

Mucklow (Broughton Sulney, co. Nottingham). Gyronny of six or and az. a lion ramp. erm. on a chief of the first an escallop betw. two fleurs-de-lis sa. a canton gu. *Crest*—A griffin's head couped per pale indented ar. guttée de larmes

714

and gu. holding in the beak an eagle's leg erased à la cuisse or.

Mudals. Ar. fretty sa.

Muddiford. Ermines on a bend ar. betw. two garbs or, a mullet az.

Mudehall, or Muderall. Ar. a saltire engr. vert.

Muden. Or, two staves ragulée in saltire gu. betw. four escallops az.

Mudenale, or Mudevall. Ar. a saltire engr. vert.

Mudgan (Mudgan, co. Cornwall; the heiress m. CHYNOWETH). Vert a chev. erm. betw. three escallops or.

Mudge (Sydney, co. Devon). Ar. a chev. betw. three cockatrices gu. *Crest*—A cockatrice, as in the arms. *Motto*—All's well.

Mudge. Ar. a fesse betw. three cinquefoils gu.

Mudie (Arbeckie, Scotland). Az. a chev. erm. betw. three pheons ar. a border of the last. *Crest*—A pheon ar. *Motto*—Defensio non offensio.

Mudie. See MOODIE.

Mugge, or Mudge (Guildford, co. Surrey; WALTER, son of THOMAS MUGGE, made his will 9 Feb. 1495, which was proved 1 April same year; he directed that his arms should be engraved on his tomb). Ar. three cockatrices sa.

Muggeridge (granted to HENRY MUGGERIDGE, Esq., of Streatham, Surrey, and of the City of London, Alderman of the Ward of Castle Baynard). Per chev. engr. ar. and az. in chief two griffins segreant of the second, and in base a garb or. *Crest*—Upon a mount vert a buck's head erased ppr. charged with two chevronels az. betw. four stalks of oats in full grain (two on either side). *Motto*—Dat Deus incrementum.

Muhant. Az. a lion ramp. ar. *Crest*—A bouchier's knot sa.

Muilman (London, and Debden Hall, co. Essex; granted 8 Nov. 1772). Az. a chev. betw. three mullets of six points or, quartering MULENCAR, of Amsterdam). *Crest*—A mullet of six points or, betw. two wings expanded ar.

Muir (Cassencarry, Scotland, 1773, now represented by MUIR-MACKENZIE, of Dublin, bart.). Quarterly, 1st and 4th, ar. on fess az. three mullets or; 2nd, az. three garbs or; 3rd, ar. a shakefork, and in chief a star or.

Muir (Ardenvohr, co. Dumbarton, 1872). Per fess ar. and or, on a fess cotised az. three mullets of the first. *Crest*—A Saracen's head wreathed with laurel ppr. *Motto*—Duris non frangor.

Muir. See MURE.

Muirhead (Lauchop, Scotland). Ar. on a bend az. three acorns or. *Crest*—Two hands supporting a sword erect in pale ppr. *Motto*—Auxilio Dei.

Muirhead (Bredisholm, co. Lanark). Same *Arms*, with a crescent betw. the acorns.

Muirhead (DU VERNET-GROSSETT-MUIRHEAD, of Bredisholm; his dau. and heir m. ROBERT STEUART, of the family of Alderston). Quarterly, 1st and 4th, as the last; 2nd, az. three stars in fess ar. and as many bezants in fess or, below the middle of the shield, in chief an acorn of the second, for GROSSETT; 3rd, az. a chev. betw. two mullets in chief or, and a unicorn ramp. in base ar., for DU VERNET. *Crest*—A demi unicorn ramp. ar. *Motto*—Pro patria auxilio Dei.

Mulbery, or Mulbury. Per pale gu. and sa. a lion ramp. ar. *Crest*—A lion pass. sa. holding a crescent or.

Mulcaster (Carlisle, co. Cumberland; descended from Sir RICHARD MULCASTER, Knt., Lord of Taperham, temp. WILLIAM II.). Ar. four bars gu. over all a bend az. *Crest*—A lion ramp. az. ducally gorged or, holding a sword erect ar. pommel and hilt of the second, the point embrued gu.

Mulcaster (Charlwood, co. Surrey, Visit. 1662, descended from GEORGE MULCASTER, a younger son of WILLIAM MULCASTER, Esq., of Carlisle. Major-Gen. FREDERICK GEORGE MULCASTER, Col. Royal Engineers, a descendant of this line, d. 1797, leaving three sons: Gen. FREDERICK WILLIAM MULCASTER, of Charlton Place, near Canterbury; Sir WILLIAM HOWE MULCASTER, C.B., Captain R.N.; and Captain EDMUND ROBERT MULCASTER, slain at Badajoz). Same *Arms* and *Crest*.

Mulcaster (Barham, co. Kent). Barry pf ten or and sa. a bend erminois, a canton gu. *Crest*—A lion ramp. erminois, in the dexter forepaw a sword erect, the dexter hind foot resting upon a bomb fired ppr.

Mulencar (Amsterdam). Gu. on a sinister hand couped and erect ppr. a human heart of the field, charged with a cross ar.

Mules (JOHN MULES, living temp. Richard II.; his sister and heir, MARY MULES, m. JOHN UPTON, Esq., of Upton, co. Cornwall. Visit. Devon, 1620). Ar. two bars gu. in chief three torteaux.

Mules (Honiton, co. Devon). Same *Arms.* *Crest*—A mule ppr. *Motto*—Misericordia temperet gladium.

Mules. Same *Arms.* *Crest*—An arm in armour embowed ppr., wielding a scymitar ppr. hilted or. Same *Motto.*

Mules (Ernsborough in Swimbridge, co. Devon, and Cadbury, co. Somerset; descended from the ancient baronial family of MOELS). Ar. two bars gu. in chief three torteaux. *Crest* —A mule pass. ppr.

Mules (Ilminster, co. Somerset, and Barn Park, Marwood, co. Devon; a branch of MULES, of Swimbridge and Cadbury). Same *Arms* and *Crest.*

Mulgrave. Per pale ar. and gu. a quatrefoil counterchanged.

Mulhall (allowed by Hawkins, Ulster, 1767, to THOMAS MULHALL, of the city of Dublin, and JOHN MULHALL, Knight of St. Louis, Captain in the legion of John Charles, third Duke of Fitz-James, in the kingdom of France, sons of WILLIAM MULHALL, Esq., the grandson of JOHN O'MORE, who adopted the name of MULCOHALL, descended from O'MORE, Lord of Leix). Same *Arms* as O'MORE, viz., Vert a lion ramp. or, in chief three mullets of the last. *Crest*—On an ancient Irish crown or, a dexter hand couped at the wrist, lying fessways, holding a sword erect, impaling three gory heads all ppr.

Mulholland (Springvale, co. Down; confirmed by Betham, Ulster, to ANDREW MULHOLLAND, Esq., of Springvale, co. Down). Az. a stag's head erased ar. betw. three escallops or. *Crest*—An escallop gu. *Motto*—Semper prœcinctus.

Mulholland (Ballywater Park, co. Down). Same *Arms, Crest,* and *Motto.*

Mulholland (Eglantine, co. Down). Same *Arms, Crest,* and *Motto.*

Muliens. Az. a chev. betw. three mullets or.

Mulle. Ar. a cross moline quarter, pierced sa. a border engr. of the last.

Mulledy (Robertstown, co. Meath; granted by St. George, Ulster, 1679, to ANTHONY MULLEDY, Resident for Philip IV., King of Spain, to Charles II. after the Restoration, nephew and heir of Sir PATRICK MULLEDY, Knt., of Robertstown). The family of MULLEDY, or, anciently, MAOIL O'NEADY, or the bald-headed, being a branch of O'FERRAL, Ulster granted the arms of O'FERRAL with an addition, viz., Vert a lion ramp. or, on a chief ar. a bald head betw. two ducal helmets crowned ppr. *Crest*—On a ducal coronet or, a greyhound courant sa.

Muller. Az. a pile or, surmounted by a chev. ar. charged with a cinquefoil of the field. *Crest*—A swan ppr.

Muller. Az. an antique bow in fesse and arrow in pale ar.

Mulleswell. Ar. on a chev. engr. betw. three crosses crosslet sa. as many crescents or; another, Gu. on a chev. engr. or, betw. three crescents of the second as many crosslets sa.

Mullett. Sa. three quatrefoils or, a border of the last.

Mulling (co. Cornwall). Ar. three goats sa.

Mulling, or Mullinge (Thingden, co. Northampton, and co. Northumberland). Sa. three goats pass. in pale ar.

Mullins (EVELEIGH-DE MOLEYNS, *Lord Ventry*). See DE MOLEYNS, *Baron Ventry.*

Mullins, or Mulliens. Az. a chev. betw. three mullets or.

Mulloy (Standard Bearer to the Crown of England in Ireland). See O'MULLOY.

Mulloy (Oak Port, co. Roscommon; descended from WILLIAM MOLLOY, of Oak Port, youngest son of COOTE MULLOY, Esq., of Hughstown). Ar. a lion ramp. sa. betw. three trefoils gu. *Crest*—In front of a tree a greyhound courant all ppr. ducally gorged or. *Motto*—Malo mori quam fœdari.

Mulock (granted by Betham, Ulster, to THOMAS MOLLOYS, Esq., of Bellair, King's co., on his taking by royal licence, 1843, the names of HOMAN-MULOCK, in compliance with the desire of his maternal uncle, THOMAS HOMAN MULOCK, Esq., of Bellair). Quarterly, 1st and 4th, az. a cross moline quarter pierced, in the dexter chief a fetterlock ar., for MULOCK; 2nd and 3rd, vert on a chev. ar. betw. three pheons, points downwards or, as many trefoils slipped ppr., for HOMAN. *Crest*—A lion pass. az. in the dexter paw a crosslet fitchée gu. *Motto*—In hoc signo vinces.

Mulrian. See O'MULRIAN.

Mulsho, or Mulso. Ar. on a bend sa. three goats' heads erased of the first, horned or.

Mulshoe, or Mulsho (Gothurst, co. Buckingham; granted 10 Dec. 1587; Sheriff of Norfolk, *temp.* Richard II.). Erm. on a bend sa. three goats' heads erased ar. *Crest*—A griffin sejant, wings endorsed gu. armed or.

715

Mulso. Ar. a chev. per chev. or and sa. betw. three fleurde-lis ermines.

Mulswell. Sa. on a chev. engr. betw. three crescents or, as many crosses crosslet of the first (another, the tinctures reversed).

Multon (*Baron Multon,* of Egremont, in abeyance since 1334; THOMAS DE MULTON, descended from THOMAS DE MULTON, of Multon, co. Lincoln, *temp.* Henry I., was summoned to Parliament 1297; the second baron *d. s. p.,* leaving his sisters his co-heirs). Ar. three bars gu.

Multon (*Baron Multon,* of Gillesland; barony passed to DACRE; THOMAS DE MULTON, descended from THOMAS DE MULTON, feudal Baron of Multon, *temp.* King John and Henry III., ancestor of the *Barons Multon,* of Egremont, was summoned to Parliament 1307, *d.* 1313, leaving an only dau. and heir, MARGARET MULTON, *m.* RANULPH, *Lord Dacre,* of the North). Same *Arms.*

Multon (St. Clare's, co. Kent). Or, three bars vert.

Multon, or Moulton. Same *Arms.* *Crest*—A savage's head couped, wreathed about the temples with laurel ppr.

Multon. Ar. three bars gu. a bend sa.; another, Barry of six ar. and gu.; another, Sa. three bars ar. in chief as many annulets of the second (another, the bars or); another, Ar. three bars gu. a canton of the last.

Mulenee. Sa. on a chief ar. three chaplets gu.

Mulvihill (Knockanira, co. Clare; granted by Betham, Ulster, to CHARLES MULVIHILL, Esq., and the descendants of his grandfather, LAWRENCE MULVIHILL, Esq.). Per fess ar. and gu. in chief a salmon naiant ppr. betw. two lions ramp. combatant az. supporting a dexter hand of the second, in base a harp or, betw. two battle axes in pale, the blades turned outwards ppr. *Crest*—A dexter cubit arm in pale ppr. grasping two battle axes in saltire ppr. the blades outwards. *Motto*—Pro aris et focis.

Mumby (co. Lincoln). Or, fretty az. on a canton gu. a cross pattée ar. *Crest*—On a ducal coronet a lion sejant all ppr.

Mumford (Burport, co. Dorset). Bendy of ten az. and or.

Mumford. Or, a lion saliant az. *Crest*—A demi cat ramp. guard. ppr.

Mun (co. Essex, Finchley and Hackney, co. Middlesex; granted to JOHN MUN, Esq., of Hackney, 1562, by Hervey, Clarenceux). Per chev. flory counterflory sa. and or, in chief three bezants, in base a tower of the first. *Crest*— A cubit arm in armour grasping a lion's gamb erased gu.

Muncaster, Baron. See PENNINGTON.

Munchensi (*Baron Munchensi;* HUBERT DE MUNCHENSI made grants of lands in cos. Suffolk and Norfolk to the Monks of Eye and Thetford, *temp.* William I.; his descendant, WILLIAM DE MUNCHENSI, was summoned to Parliament 1264, *d.* 1289, leaving an only dau. and heir, DYONISIA DE MUNCHENSI, who *m.* HUGH DE VERE, third son of ROBERT, fifth *Earl of Oxford,* who was summoned to Parliament 1299, and *d. s. p.* 1313). Or, three escutcheons barry of six vair and gu.

Munday (Rialton, co. Cornwall; THOMAS MUNDAY, son of WILLIAM MUNDAY, and grandson of JOHN MUNDAY, a younger son of MUNDAY, of co. Derby, and brother of THOMAS MUNDAY, Prior of Bodmin, *temp.* Henry VIII., who settled in co. Cornwall about 1540, under the auspices of his brother, the Prior. Visit. Cornwall, 1620). Quarterly, gu. and sa. on a cross engr. ar. five lozenges az. on a chief or, three eagles' legs erased a-la-quise of the fourth.

Mundell (Glasgow). A ducal coronet betw. two mullets in chief and a crescent in base, a canton.

Munden. Gu. on a cross engr. or, five lozenges sa. on a chief of the second three eagles' legs erased a-la-quise of the third, on a canton erm. an anchor az.

Munden (Chelsea, co. Middlesex; granted, 1680, to the widow of Sir RICHARD MUNDEN, Knt., R.N., her children, and her husband's brother, Sir JOHN MUNDEN, Knt., Rear-Admiral of the King's Fleet). Per pale gu. and sa. on a cross engr. ar. five lozenges az. on a chief or, three eagles' legs erased a-la-quise of the second, on a canton erm. an anchor or. *Crest*—On a rostral crown or, a leopard's head sa. bezantée.

Mundevill (cos. Northampton and Suffolk). Az. a fret or.

Mundevill. Quarterly vair and gu.

Munds, Mouns, or Muns (cos. Cambridge, Essex, Middlesex, and Maidstone, co. Kent). Per chev. flory counterflory sa. and ar. (another, or) in chief three bezants, in base a tower triple towered of the first. *Crest*—An armed arm ppr. couped at the elbow and erect, grasping a lion's gamb erased or.

Mundy (Markeaton, co. Derby; Sir JOHN MUNDY, Knt., of Chekenden, co. Oxford, Knt., Lord Mayor of London, 1522-3, descended from JOHN MUNDY, *temp.* Edward I., *d.* 1538, seised of Markeaton and other manors, co. Derby). Per pale gu. and sa. on a cross engr. ar. five lozenges purp. on a chief or, three eagles' legs erased a-la-quise az. *Crest*— A wolf's head erased sa. bezantée, fire issuing from the mouth ppr. *Motto*—Deus providebit.

Mundy (Burton Hall, co. Leicester). Same *Arms, Crest,* and *Motto.*

Mundy (Shipley Hall, co. Derby; descended from GILBERT MUNDY, Esq., High Sheriff co. Derby, 1697, younger son of JOHN MUNDY, Esq., of Markeaton). Per pale gu. and sa. on a cross engr. ar. five lozenges az. on a chief or, three eagles' legs erased a-la-quise of the fourth. *Crest*—A wolf's head erased sa. bezantée, fire issuing from the mouth ppr.

Mundy (co. Buckingham). Per pale ar. and sa. on a cross gu. five fusils or, on a chief az. three eagles' legs erased a-la-quise ar.

Mundy (London). Sa. on a cross engr. ar. five lozenges purp. on a chief of the second three eagles' legs erased a-la-quise az. *Crest*—A leopard's head erased sa. bezantée, fire issuing from the mouth ppr.

Muned, or Mynd (co. Salop). Ar. on a chev. gu. betw. three lions' heads erased sa. as many gadbees volant of the field.

Munn. Per chev. sa. and or, in chief three bezants, and in base a castle triple-towered of the first. *Crest*—A dexter arm in armour holding a lion's paw erased ppr. *Motto*—Omnia vincit veritas.

Munn. Per chev. sa. and or, two bezants in chief and a castle triple-towered in base of the first. *Crest*—A lion's head erased erm.

Munro (Foulis, co. Ross, N.S., bart., 1634). Or, an eagle's head erased gu. *Crest*—An eagle perching ppr. *Supporters* —Two eagles, wings expanded ppr. *Motto*—Dread God.

Munro (GUN-MUNRO, of Poyntzfield, co. Cromarty). Quarterly, 1st and 4th, or, an eagle's head erased gu. beaked and langued az.; 2nd, ar. a three-masted ship in the sea ppr. flagged gu. on a chief of the last three legs in armour conjoined at the thigh and flexed in triangle ppr. betw. two mullets or, for GUN; 3rd, barry of eight or and gu., for POYNTZ. *Crest*—An eagle rising ppr. *Motto*—Dread God.

Munro (Major-Gen. Sir HECTOR MUNRO, installed Knight of the Bath, 19 May, 1779, *d.* 1806). Or, an eagle's head erased gu. *Crest*—An eagle close ppr., motto over it, Dread God. *Supporters*—Dexter, a tiger ppr. murally gorged and chained or; sinister, an eagle ppr. murally gorged or.

Munro (Sir THOMAS MUNRO, Bart., 1823). Or, an eagle's head erased gu. encircled by a branch of laurel on the dexter and of oak on the sinister side, on a chief ar. the representation of an Indian hill-fort, and beneath, in letters of gold, the word "Badamy," on a canton gu. a representation of a silver medal presented by the E. I. Co. to the first baronet for his services in Seringapatam in 1799. *Crest*—An eagle close ppr. having a representation of the medal above-mentioned pendent from its neck by a ribbon, the dexter claw resting on an escutcheon gu. charged with a representation of the first, of BADAMY, as in the arms, and in the beak a sprig of laurel.

Munro. Or, an eagle's head erased gu. murally crowned ar. *Crest*—On a mural coronet ar. an eagle close or.

Munsemberg. Ar. a chief gu.

Munster, Earl of. See FITZCLARENCE.

Munster, Province of (Reg. Ulster's Office). **Az. three** eastern crowns ppr.

Munt (Cheshunt, co. Hertford). Az. on a fesse betw. three bears' heads couped ar. muzzled gu. a cross crosslet of the last. *Crest*—A bear's head, as in the arms, within a chain in arch or.

Munt. Ar. three peacocks in their pride ppr. *Crest*—A savage's head couped, distilling drops of blood all ppr.

Munton. Gu. three chev. interlaced or, a chief ar. *Crest* —A cannon mounted ppr.

Muntz (Umberslade, co. Warwick). Or, a swan, wings extended ppr. *Crest*—A demi swan, as in the arms. *Motto* —Fortiter sed suaviter.

Munyard (Camden Town, co. Middlesex; granted to JOSEPH MUNYARD, Esq.). Erminois a-la-in ramp. sa. betw. three fleurs-de-lis az. on a chief indented of the last three sinister hands erect and couped or. *Crest*—A mount vert, issuant therefrom in front of a branch of oak in bend sinister ppr. a demi lion erm. holding in the dexter paw a sinister hand erased also ppr. the sinister paw resting on a fleur-de-lis gu.

Murchison (Tarradale, co. Ross; lately represented by Sir

716

RODERICK IMPEY MURCHISON, the geologist). Or, a lion ramp sa. betw. two pine-apples in chief vert and an escallop in base az. *Crest*—A dexter hand holding a ducal coronet of three leaves ppr. *Motto*—Impavido pectore.

Murdall. Or, a fret sa.; another, Ar. a fret sa.; another, Ar. fretty sa.

Murden (Morten Morrell, co. Warwick; confirmed Dec. 1618). Erm. on a chief sa. a talbot pass. ar. an annulet gu. for diff. *Crest*—A leopard ramp. guard. ppr.

Murdoch (Rosshall, co. Renfrew, 1779). Ar. a fesse chequy az. and of the field, over all two crows sa. pendent on an arrow fesseways ppr. *Crest*—A lion's head erased gu. *Motto*—Omine secundo.

Murdoch. Or, on a chev. gu. three mascles ar. *Crest*—A sword in pale enfiled with a savage's head couped ppr.

Murdocke (co. Northumberland). Or, fretty sa.

Mure (co. Lincoln). Sa. four hawks volant or.

Mure (Rowallan, co. Ayr). Quarterly, 1st and 4th, ar. on a fess az. three mullets or, for MURE; 2nd and 3rd, az. three garbs or, for CUMMING.

Mure (Caldwell, co. Renfrew). Ar. on a fesse az. three stars or, within a bordure engr. gu. *Crest*—A Saracen's head ppr. *Motto*—Duris non frangor.

Mure (London, 1868). As Caldwell, in the honour point a crescent az. for diff. Same *Crest* and *Motto.*

Mure (Glanderston). As Caldwell, with a crescent in base gu. for diff.

Mure (Herringswell House, co. Suffolk). Ar. on a fesse az. three mullets of the field, a border engr. gu. *Crest*—A Saracen's head ppr. *Motto*—Duris non frangor.

Mure (Parson of Philorth, Scotland, 1672). Ar. on a fesse az. three mullets or, and in base a book expanded ppr. *Motto*— Ora et labora.

Mure (Riccartoun, Scotland). Ar. on a fesse engr. az. three mullets or, within a bordure also engr. gu. *Crest*—A savage's head and neck from the shoulders, wreathed round the temples with palm ppr. *Motto*—Duris non frangor.

Mure. Sa. four martlets (another, volant) ar. beaked and legged or.

Murgatroid (MICHAEL MURGATROID, Secretary to Archbishop Whitgift). Ar. three crosses pattée flory gu. each charged with five bezants, on a canton of the second a conger's head couped in pale or, derived from the coats of his two patrons, Whitgift and Gascoigne.

Murhall (Bagnall, co. Stafford). Ar. three boars' heads couped sa.

Muriell (London). Sa. a dexter wing betw. three birds ar. *Crest*—A lion pass. guard. tail extended ppr.

Muriell. Sa. on a fesse wavy or, betw. three martlets ar. as many wings gu. a border engr. of the second. *Crest*—A demi cat per pale ar. and sa. holding in the claws a branch of roses of the first, leaved vert, gorged with a fesse counterchanged.

Murison (Anchorfield, Scotland, 1791). Ar. three Moors' heads couped sa. banded az. a border engr. gu. *Crest*— Three Moors' heads conjoined on one neck ppr. *Motto*— Mediocriter.

Murmyon (co. Oxford). Vair three mascles gu.

Murphy (Oulartleigh, co. Wexford). See O'MORCHOE.

Murphy. See O'MURPHY.

Murphy (Dublin; Fun. Ent. Ulster's Office, 1603, JOHN MURPHY, Surgeon). Quarterly, ar. and gu. four lions ramp. counterchanged, on a fess sa. three garbs or.

Murphy (city of Kilkenny; Fun. Ent. Ulster's Office, 1666, AUSTACE MURPHY, dau. of ANDREW MURPHY, granddau. of PATRICK MURPHY, of Kilkenny, and wife of LUKE HORE, of Waterford). Same *Arms.*

Murphy (Graignamanagh, co. Kilkenny, and Malaga, in Spain; allowed by Hawkins, Ulster, 1787, to JOHN MURPHY, Esq., of Malaga, grandson of FRANCIS MURPHY, Esq., of Waterford, who was the grandson of TIMOTHY MURPHY, Esq., of Graignamanagh). Same *Arms.*

Murphy (Kilbrew, co. Meath; granted to WILLIAM MURPHY, Esq., and the descendants of his grandfather, WILLIAM MURPHY, of Mount Merrion, co. Dublin). Per pale or and gu. on a fess engr. betw. four lions ramp. two garbs all counterchanged. *Crest*—On a mount vert a lion ramp. gu. bezantée, holding in the forepaws a garb or.

Murrant (London; granted 1575). Gu. a chev. ar. betw. three talbots pass. or. *Crest*—A Moor's head ppr. betw. two dragons' wings or, wreathed round the temples ar. and gu.

Murray (Bothwell, co. Lanark). Az. three stars or.

Murray (Touchadam and Polmaise, co. Stirling). Az. three stars ar. within a double tressure flory counterflory or. *Crest*—A mermaid with a mirror in her dexter and a comb in her sinister hand ppr. *Motto*—Tout prêt.

Murray (Tullibardine, *Earl of Athole*, as borne in 17th century). Quarterly, 1st and 4th grand quarters, counterquartered, 1st and 4th, paly of six or and sa., for ATHOLE, 2nd and 3rd, or, a fess chequy az. and ar., for STEWART; 2nd and 3rd grand quarters, az. three stars ar. within a double tressure flory counterflory or, for MURRAY. *Crest*—A demi savage ppr. in his dexter hand a sword erect also ppr., in his sinister a key or. *Supporters*—A savage holding a chain in his dexter hand ppr., and a lion gu. gorged with a collar az. charged with three stars ar. *Motto* —Furth fortune and fill the fetters.

Murray (*Duke of Athole*, as now borne). Quarterly, 1st grand quarter, 1st and 4th. paly of six or and sa., for the ancient Earldom of Athole, 2nd and 3rd, or, a fesse chequy az. and ar., for STEWART; 2nd grand quarter, az. three mullets ar. within a double tressure flory counterflory or, for MURRAY; 3rd grand quarter, 1st, ar. on a bend az. three bucks' heads cabossed or, for STANLEY, 2nd, gu. three legs in armour ppr. garnished and spurred or, conjoined in triangle at the upper part of the thigh, for the Isle of Man, as lords thereof, 3rd, or, on a chief indented az., three plates, for LATHAM, 4th, gu. two lions pass. in pale ar., for STRANGE; 4th grand quarter, 1st and 4th, or, a lion ramp. az., 2nd and 3rd, az. five fusils in fesse or, both for PERCY. *Crest*--A demi savage ppr. holding in his right hand a dagger ppr. pommel and hilt or, and in his left hand a key of the last. *Supporters*—Dexter, a savage ppr. wreathed about the head and waist vert, his feet in fetters of iron, the chain held up by his right hand also ppr.; sinister, a lion gu. gorged with a plain collar az. thereon three mullets ar. *Motto*—Furth fortune and fill the fetters.

Murray (*Earl of Dunmore*). Quarterly, 1st, az. three mullets ar. within a double tressure flory counterflory or, for MURRAY; 2nd, or, a fesse chequy ar. and az., for STEWART; 3rd, paly of six or and sa., for ATHOLE; 4th, ar. on a bend az. three stags' heads cabossed or, for STANLEY; 5th, gu. three legs in armour, spurred and garnished or, conjoined in triangle at the thigh, for the Isle of Man; 6th, gu. two lions pass. in pale ar., for STRANGE. *Crest*—A demi savage wreathed about the head and loins with oak, holding in the dexter hand a sword erect ppr. pommel and hilt or, and in the sinister a key of the last. *Supporters*—Dexter, a lion gu. gorged with a collar az. charged with three mullets ar.; sinister, a savage wreathed as the crest ppr. *Motto*— Furth fortune and fill the fetters.

Murray (Capt. JOHN MURRAY; descended of Tullibardine, 1672). Az. three stars ar. within a double tressure flory counterflory or, in fess point a thistle ppr. *Crest*—A lion's paw holding a sword ppr. *Motto*—Fortes fortuna adjuvat.

Murray (*Viscount Stormont, Earl of Mansfield*). Quarterly, 1st and 4th, az. three stars within a double tressure flory counterflory with fleurs-de-lis or, for MURRAY; 2nd and 3rd, gu. three crosses pattée or, two and one, for BARCLAY of Balvaird. *Crest*—A buck's head couped or, with a cross pattée betw. his antlers ar. *Supporters*—Two lions gu. armed or. *Mottoes*—Uni æquus virtuti ; and, Spero meliora.

_**Murray** (GRAHAM-MURRAY, of Murrayshall, co. Perth). Quarterly, 1st and 4th, or, three piles sa. within a double tressure flory counterflory gu. on a chief of the second a crescent betw. two escallops of the first, for GRAHAM; 2nd and 3rd, az. a cross pattée betw. three stars ar. within a double tressure flory counterflory or, for MURRAY. *Crests*— 1st: A dove ppr., for GRAHAM; 2nd: A buck's head couped ppr., for MURRAY. *Mottoes*—Candide et secure, for GRAHAM; Macte virtute, for MURRAY.

Murray (Drumcairn, co. Perth, 1672) Az. a cross pattée betw. three stars ar. *Crest*—A swan's head couped ppr. *Motto*—Mali mori quam fœdari.

Murray (Strowan, co. Perth, 1672). Az. three stars ar. in middle chief a crescent or.

Murray (Lochland, 1672). Az. a falcon's head erased betw. three stars ar. *Crest*—A greyhound courant ppr. *Motto*— Gloria non præda.

Murray (Ochtertyre, co. Perth, bart., 1673). Az. three stars ar. in the centre a cross of the second surmounted of a saltire gu. *Crest*—An olive branch ppr. *Motto*—Ex bello quies.

Murray (Gen. Sir GEORGE MURRAY, G.C.B., G.C.H., second son of Sir WILLIAM MURRAY, of Ochtertyre, fifth bart.). Same *Arms*, with a crescent for diff. *Crest*—A laurel branch erect vert, over it, Paritur bello. *Supporters*—Dexter, a lion ramp. gu. gorged with a collar az. thereon three mullets ar.; sinister, a man wreathed about the loins, having fetters on the ankles, the chain from which he holds in the sinister hand all ppr. ; both supporters charged on the breast with a cross surmounted by a saltire, as in the arms. *Motto*—Furth fortune and fill the fetters.

717

Murray (Lintrose, co. Perth, 1803). Same *Arms*, with a crescent or, in chief for diff.

Murray (DAVID MURRAY, third brother of MURRAY of Dollarie, co. Perth, 1673). As Ochtertyre, with a crescent surmounted of a mullet or, in dexter chief. *Motto*—A rore colorem.

Murray (Glendoick, bart., 1678). Az. a cross pattée betw. three mullets ar. a double tressure flory counterflory or. *Crest* —A dexter hand holding a mirror ppr. *Motto*—Nosce teipsum. See also HEPBURN, co. Blackcastle.

Murray (*Earl of Dysart*). Az. an imperial crown ppr. betw. three stars ar. a double tressure flory counterflory or. *Crest*— A mermaid holding in her dexter hand a mirror, and in her sinister a comb ppr. *Supporters*—Two lions gu. collared az. the collar charged with three stars ar. *Motto*—Tout prest.

Murray (Falahill, co. Edinburgh, and Philiphaugh, co. Selkirk). Ar. a hunting horn sa. garnished and stringed gu. on a chief az. three stars of the first. *Crest*—A demi man winding a horn ppr. *Motto*—Hinc usque superna venabor.

Murray (Deuchar, co. Selkirk). Same *Arms*, within a bordure gu. *Crest*—An escallop gu. *Motto*—Fidei signum.

Murray (Melgund, co. Forfar, bart., 1704). Ar. a hunting horn sa. garnished and stringed gu. on a chief wavy az. three stars of the first. *Crest*—A burning lamp ppr. *Motto* —Placeam dum peream.

Murray (Pilkeirie, co. Fife, 1672). As Philiphaugh, with a mullet surmounted by a crescent in fess point for diff. *Crest* —A ship under sail ppr. *Motto*—Tutum te littore sistam.

Murray (Stanhope, co. Peebles, bart., 1665). Quarterly, 1st and 4th, as MURRAY, of Philiphaugh; 2nd, az. three frases ar. ; 3rd, ar. on a chief gu. three cushions or. *Crest*— A dove with an olive branch in its beak ppr. *Motto*—Pacis nuncia.

Murray (Cockpool, co. Dumfries). Ar. a saltire engr. az. on a chief of the last three stars of the field.

Murray (*Earl of Annandale*). Az. a crescent betw. three stars ar. a tressure flory counterflory of the last, on a canton of the last a thistle vert, crowned or. *Crest*—An angel ppr. *Motto*—Noclesque diesque præsto.

Murray (Broughton, co. Wigtoun). Quarterly, 1st and **4th**, az. three stars ar. ; 2nd and 3rd, counterquartered, 1st and 4th, ar. a saltire cantoned with four roses gu., 2nd and 3rd, or, a fess chequy az. and ar. *Crest*—A griffin saliant ppr. *Motto*—Impero.

Murray (Murraythwaite, co. Dumfries). Quarterly, 1st and 4th, az. a crescent betw. three stars ar. a double tressure flory counterflory of the last, all within a bordure or, for MURRAY; 2nd and 3rd, or, on a saltire az. nine lozenges of the field, all within a bordure engr. gu., for DALRYMPLE. *Crest*—A cherub ppr. winged or. *Motto*—Noctesque diesque præsto.

Murray (Blackbarony, co. Peebles, bart., 1628). Or, a fetterlock az. on a chief of the second three stars az. *Crest* —A dexter hand holding a scroll fessways ppr. *Motto*— Deum time.

Murray (Cringletie, co. Peebles, 1777). As the last, within a bordure gu. Same *Crest* and *Motto*.

Murray (Henderland and Murrayfield). Ar. a martlet az. in a fetterlock sa. within a bordure gu. on a chief of the second three stars of the field. Same *Crest* and *Motto*.

Murray (*Lord Elibank*, as borne by the first lord). Az. a martlet betw. three stars ar. all within a double tressure flory counterflory or. *Crest*—A lion ramp. gu. holding a battle axe ppr. *Supporters*—Two horses ar. furnished gu. *Motto*—Virtute fideque.

Murray (*Lord Elibank*, as now borne). Quarterly, 1st and 4th, or, a fetterlock az. on a chief of the last three stars ar., for MURRAY; 2nd and 3rd, for BLACKBARONY; 2nd, gu. a chev. betw. three crescents ar., for OLIPHANT; 3rd, az. three stars within a double tressure flory counterflory or, and in the centre a martlet or, being his lordship's paternal arms. *Crest*—A lion ramp. gu. holding betw. the paws a battle axe ppr. *Supporters*—Two horses ar. bridled gu. *Motto*—Virtute fideque.

Murray (Spott and Longhermandston, co. Haddington). Az. a martlet betw. three stars ar. all within a double tressure flory counterflory or, a bordure per pale of the first and second. *Crest*—A horse ar. furnished gu. *Motto*— Virtute fideque.

Murray (Col. GEORGE MURRAY, fourth son of first *Lord Elibank*). Az. a martlet betw. three stars ar. within a double tressure flory counterflory or, a bordure embattled ar. *Crest*—A horse saliant ar. furnished gu. *Motto*—Juncta virtuti fides.

Murray (Simprim, co. Forfar; from a natural son of the first *Lord Elibank*; line ended in daus , one of whom m. *Lord Talbot de Malahide*). Az. a martlet or, betw. three stars ar. a double tressure flory counterflory of the second, all within a bordure compony of the third and gu. *Crest*—A demi lion gu. holding a Lochaber axe ppr. betw. his paws. *Motto*—Virtute fideque.

Murray (Clermont, co. Fife, bart., 1626). Or, a fetterlock az. within a bordure embattled gu. on a chief of the second three mullets ar. *Crest*—A dexter hand brandishing a flaming sword ppr. *Motto*, over crest—Deum time.

Murray (Pennyland, co. Caithness; heiress *m.* STUART THREIPLAND, of Fingask). Az. a bezant betw. three stars ar. *Crest*—A mermaid holding a sword in her dexter hand ppr. *Motto*—In utrumque paratus.

Murray (Capt. JAMES MURRAY, R.N., 1812). Az. a martlet or, betw. three stars ar. a bordure of the second, on a canton erm. a sword ppr. surmounted by a trident saltireways sa. *Crest*—A lion ramp. guard. gu. collared and chained, supporting an anchor erect or. *Motto*—They by permission shine.

Murray (Vice-Admiral GEORGE MURRAY, 1814). Az. an anchor erect or, betw. three estoiles ar. all within a double tressure flory counterflory of the second. *Crest*—A demi savage ppr. wreathed head and middle vert, in his dexter hand a dagger ppr. pommel and hilt or, in his sinister an anchor of the last.

Murray (Birmingham). Ar. a hunting horn sa. stringed gu. a bordure of the second charged with three escallops or, on a chief az. as many stars of the field. *Crest*—A telescope on a stand or. *Motto*—They by permission shine.

Murray (Danesfield, co. Bucks). Quarterly, 1st and 4th, ar. a buglehorn ppr. stringed gu. on a chief az. three mullets of the first, for MURRAY, of Philiphaugh; 2nd and 3rd, or, on a bend az. an estoile betw. two crescents and on a border engr. sa. eight escallops of the first, for SCOTT. *Crests*—A demi savage wreathed about the temples and loins, holding a buglehorn all ppr., for MURRAY; a stag trippant, for SCOTT. *Motto*—Hinc usque superna venabor.

Murray-Stewart. See STEWART.

Murray (GOSTLING-MURRAY; Col. CHARLES EDWARD MURRAY, J.P. and D.L., of Whitton Park, Twickenham, assumed by royal licence, 1875, the surname and arms of MURRAY in addition to GOSTLING). 1st and 4th, MURRAY (see *Duke of Athole*); 2nd and 3rd, GOSTLING.

Murray (Castle Murray, co. Donegal; exemplified to ALEXANDER MURRAY, Esq., upon his assuming by royal licence, 1812, the surname of MURRAY, in compliance with the will of JAMES MURRAY, Esq., of Broughton). Az. three stars ar. *Crest*—A griffin segreant ppr. *Motto*—Imperio.

Murray (granted to GEORGE MOORE MURRAY, of Mexico). Az. a chaplet of oak or, betw. three mullets ar. within a bordure nebulée of the second *Crest*—Out of a crescent or, a demi savage affrontée ppr. wreathed about the temples or and az. holding in the dexter hand a sword erect also ppr. and in the sinister a key, the ward upwards, gold.

Murrill. Or, a bend gu. in base a cross crosslet of the last. *Crest*—A demi lion ramp. per pale ar. and sa. collared, counterchanged, holding in the dexter paw a bunch of flowers of the first stalked vert.

Murthe (Murthe and Taland, co. Cornwall; JOHN MURTHE, Esq., of Taland, Visit. Cornw. 1620; eighth in descent from RICHARD MURTHE, Esq., of Murthe, *temp.* Richard II.). Ar. a lion ramp. betw. three fleurs-de-lis gu.

Muryell. Sa. on a fesse wavy betw. two martlets ar. as many mascles gu.

Musard (Stavely, co. Derby). Or, two chevronels az. a bordure of the last.

Musard (cos. Derby and Devon; the heiress *m.* FLECHVILLE). Gu. three plates. *Crest*—A savage's head couped and distilling drops of blood ppr.

Musard (co. Devon). Gu. a lion ramp. ar. crowned or.

Musard (London). Ar. a bend gu. a border engr. of the last.

Musard. Az. a fesse ar. betw. three cinquefoils or.

Muschamp (Feudal *Barons of Wooler*, co. Northumberland; descended from ROBERT DE MUSCHAMP, who obtained divers lordships from Henry I., left an only dau. and heir, CICELY MUSCHAMP, *m.* Sir STEPHEN DE BULMER, second son of BULMER, of Sheriff Hutton, co. York, and her doscendants assumed the name of MUSCHAMP; ROBERT DE MUSCHAMP, *Baron of Wooler*, great-grandson of Sir STEPHEN and CICELY, d. 1249, leaving three co-heiresses: CICELY, *m.* ODINEL DE FORD; MARY, *m.* VALISE, *Earl of Strathearn*, in Scotland; and ISABELLA, *m.* WILLIAM DE HUNTERCOMBE). A deed of ROBERT DE MUSCHAMP's, ratifying certain grants of land in Howburn to the monks of Durham, bears his seal, " or, three bars gu. ;" but the more ancient ensigns of the family were: Ar. a chev vert betw. three flies ppr. The charges in the arms are in some authorities called bees, in others butterflies or beetles, but they are obviously " flies," allusive to the presumed derivation of the name from " musca."

718

Muschamp (Barmoor, co. Northumberland; descended from Sir WILLIAM DE MUSCHAMP, Knt., of Barmoor, 1267, son of STEPHEN DE MUSCHAMP, third son of THOMAS DE MUSCHAMP, *Baron of Wooler*, and grandson of Sir STEPHEN BULMER by CICELY MUSCHAMP, his wife). Or, three bars gu. *Crest*—A mastiff dog ppr. collared ar.

Muschamp (Brotherlee, co. Durham; descended from JOHN MUSCHAMP, fifth son of GEORGE MUSCHAMP, Esq., of Barmoor, High Sheriff co. Northumberland, 1596). Ar. a chev. vert betw. three flies ppr. *Crest*—A lion ramp. gu. holding in the dexter paw on a banner az. a crescent or. *Motto*—Vulneror non vincor.

Muschamp (Camberwell, co. Surrey; allowed at Visit. London, 1568, to THOMAS MUSCHAMP, goldsmith, of London, son of WILLIAM MUSCHAMP, Esq., of Camberwell). Or, three bars gu. a martlet for diff. *Crest*—A mountain cat ppr. tied round the neck with a scarf ar. charged on the breast with a martlet for diff.

Muschamp (Horsley, co. Surrey). Or, three bars gu. *Crest*—A mastiff dog ppr. collared or.

Muschamp (Dublin and Cork; granted by Carney, Ulster, 1685, to DENNY MUSCHAMP, Esq., of the city of Dublin, Muster Master General of Ireland, son of Major AGMONDISHAM MUSCHAMP, of the city of Cork, who was second son of Sir AGMONDISHAM MUSCHAMP, Knt., of Robarnes, co. Surrey. The eventual heiress of the family, MARY KUSCHAMP, dau. of the Muster Master General, *m.* Right Rev. Sir THOMAS VESEY, Bishop of Ossory, ancestor of *Viscount De Vesci*.) Or, three bars gu. on a canton az. a harvest fly displ. of the first. *Crest*—On a cannon royal mounted or, a cat-a-mountain pass. guard. ppr. *Motto*—Quid gens sine mente.

Muschamp (Fun. Ent. Ulster's Office, 1661, WILLIAM MUSCHAMP, Esq., descended from MUSCHAMP, of Barmoore. co. Northumberland). Sa. three flies ar. quartering ar. three boars pass. sa. armed and hoofed or, for SWYNE, and az. a chief indented or, for DUNHAM.

Muschamp. Az. a fesse engr. or, betw. three talbots' heads erased ar.

Muschamp. Az. three butterflies volant or.

Muschampe. Or, a chief az.; another, Or, three bends gu.; another, Gu. two bars or, a crescent in chief of the last.

Muscote (Barton and Welby, co. Northampton). Gu. on a cross engr. ar. five roses of the first.

Musenburgh. Ar. a cross gu.

Musgrave (*Baron Musgrave*: Sir ADAM MUSGRAVE, *temp.* King John, whose ancestor came to England with William I., was ancestor of Sir THOMAS MUSGRAVE, a commander in the English army, 20 Edward III., 1346, which defeated David II. of Scotland at Durham. He was summoned to Parliament 1350, but the writ was not renewed to any of his descendants). Gu. six annulets or. *Crest*—Two arms in armour embowed ppr. the gauntlets grasping an annulet or. The following tradition has been handed down as the origin of the arms of the family :—The Emperor of Germany had two generals, who both wooed his daughter at the same time. Having had experience of the good services of each, he did not care to prefer one to the other, but, to decide the matter, ordered the rival generals and lovers to " run at the ring "—a favourite feat then—for his daughter. MUSGRAVE, a Lord Marcher, one of the Rivals, had the fortune to pierce the ring with the point of his spear, and as a reward of his dexterity and valour obtained the lady as his bride, and had " six annulets or " given him for his coat of arms, and " two arms in armour holding an annulet " for his coat.

Musgrave (Edenhall, co. Cumberland, bart.; descended from *Baron Musgrave*). Same *Arms* and *Crest*. *Motto*—Sans changer.

Musgrave (Hayton, bart.; descended from Edenhall). Same *Arms*. *Crest*—Two arms in armour embowed sustaining the sun ppr.

Musgrave (Tourin, co. Waterford, bart.). Same *Arms* and *Crest*. *Motto*—Sans changer.

Musgrave (Ashby Musgrave, co. Westmoreland). Same *Arms*. *Crest*—Two arms in armour embowed ppr. grasping an annulet or.

Musgrave (Hartley Castle, co. Westmoreland). Same *Arms* and *Crest*.

Musgrave (Borden, co. Kent, and Shillington Manor, co. Bedford). Same *Arms* and *Crest*.

Musgrave (Fairbank, or Musgrave Hall). Same *Arms* and *Crest*.

Musgrave (Crookdale, co. Cumberland). Same *Arms* and *Crest*.

Musgrave (SAGAR-MUSGRAVE, Sandford House, Leeds, co. York; exemplified to JOHN MUSGRAVE SAGAR, Esq., upon nis taking the additional surname of MUSGRAVE). Quarterly, 1st and 4th, ar. on a pile per pale az. and gu. six annulets, or, for MUSGRAVE; 2nd and 3rd, per bend or and az. a cross moline counterchanged, a chief paly of six of the first and gu., for SAGAR. Crests—1st, MUSGRAVE: Two arms embowed ppr. holding an annulet or, encircling a tilting spear erect also ppr.; 2nd, SAGAR: Upon a rock ppr. an eagle reguard. or, each wing charged with three bendlets gu. resting the dexter claw upon a cross moline az. Motto—Valde et sapienter.

Musgrove (Speldhurst, co. Kent, bart.). Ar. two bendlets engr. az. betw. three lozenges, one and two, of the last, each charged with a fleur-de-lis or. Crest—A demi lion ppr. gorged with a double collar gemelle sa. and holding betw. the paws a lozenge az. charged with a cross crosslet or. Motto—Nil desperandum.

Mushat, or Mushet (England). Or, a fesse betw. three crescents az. Crest—A mount vert semée of strawberries ppr.

Musheleener. Az. a chev. betw. three acorns or, husked and slipped vert.

Mushet (that Ilk, co. Perth; originally DE MONTE FIXO). Erm. three chevronels gu.

Mushet (Craighead). Erm. two chevronels gu. a border az.

Mushet (Holland). Same Arms, the border charged with eight crescents ar. Crest—A twig of rose blooming ppr. Motto—Dabunt aspera rosas.

Musicians, Society of (London; incorporated 1604). Az. a swan, wings expanded ar. a double tressure flory counterflory or, on a chief gu. a pale betw. two lions pass. guard. of the third, thereon a rose of the fourth, seeded gold, barbed vert. Crest—A lyre or.

Musis, or Le Musis. Gu. a bend betw. six roses ar. seeded or.

Muskeham. Ar. a chev. betw. three flies sa.

Muskerry, Baron. See DEANE and MORGAN.

Muskett (co. Suffolk). Ar. two bars betw. six lions' heads cabossed gu. Crest—Out of a ducal coronet or, a demi antelope sa. chained and ringed gold.

Muskett (Intwood Hall, co. Norfolk; descended from a family which possessed landed property in the parish of Haughleigh, co. Suffolk, temp. Henry VIII.). Same Arms and Crest.

Muskett (Clippersby House, co. Norfolk). Same Arms and Crest.

Musner. Az. a fesse betw. three cinquefoils or. Crest—Out of a ducal coronet or, a camel's head sa.

Musner. Az. a fesse betw. three roses or.

Mussard (co. Devon). Gu. three plates.

Musselburgh, Town of (Scotland). Az. three anchors in pale, one in chief and two in flanks or, accompanied by as many mussels, two in the dexter and sinister chief points, and the third in base ppr. Motto—Honesty.

Mussell (Staple Langford, co. Wilts). Sa. a fesse or, betw. five plates, two in chief and three in base. Crest—A wolf saliant sa.

Mussenden (Heling, co. Lincoln). Or, a cross engr. gu. in the dexter quarter a Cornish chough sa. beaked and legged of the second. Crest—A Cornish chough ppr. in the beak a laurel sprig vert.

Mussenden (Larchfield, Lisburn, co. Antrim). Same Arms and Crest. Motto—J'aime la liberté.

Mussenden. See LEATHES.

Musters (Syrston, co. Notts; HENRY MUSTERS, temp. Edward III., his dau. and heir, JOANE MUSTERS, m. ROBERT SUTTON, Esq., of Averham, co. Notts, Inq. Post. Mort. 50 Edward III., A.D. 1376, Visit. Notts, 1614). Ar. a bend gu. a border of the last.

Musters (Colwick, Annesley and Wiverton, co. Notts; descended from Sir JOHN MUSTERS, Knt., who purchased the Colwick estate temp. Charles II., and whose descendant, JOHN MUSTERS, Esq., of Colwick, m. MARY ANNE, dau. and heir of GEORGE CHAWORTH, Esq., of Annesley). Ar. on a bend gu. a lion pass. guard. or, a border engr. of the second. Crest—A lion sejant guard. or, supporting in the forepaws a shield of the arms.

Musterton. Gu. a unicorn pass. ar. armed and unguled or (another adds, guttée de sang).

Mustian. Or, three bars gu.

Mustion (Reg. Ulster's Office). Or, three bars gu.

Muston (Gotham and Callis, co. Notts; List of Knights, temp. Edward II.; ANNE, dau. and heir of WILLIAM MUSTON, Esq., of Callis, temp. Henry VIII., m. THOMAS MARSHALL, Esq., of Carlton, same co. Visit. Notts, 1614). Ar. a chev. betw. three swords erect gu. (another coat has the field or).

Muston. Ar. a chev. betw. three crosses flory sa. Crest—On a chapeau gu. turned up. erm. a garb or.

Musward. Az. a fesse betw. three cinquefoils ar.

Muswell (quartered by LOVELL). Vert two chevronels ar. each charged with three cinquefoils gu.

Muswell (East Herling, co. Norfolk). Same Arms.

Mutas, Mutts, or Muteize (co. Middlesex). Az. a unicorn saliant erminois.

Muter (Scotland). Gu. a fesse betw. three shields or.

Muterer (Scotland). Gu. a fesse betw. three inescutcheons or. Crest—A castle triple-towered ppr. door and windows gu. Motto—Patience and resolution.

Mutlow (cos. Gloucester and Worcester). Gyronny of six or and az. over all a lion ramp. erm. on a chief ar. an escallop betw. two fleurs-de-lis sa. Crest—A griffin's head couped per pale indented ar. and gu. guttée counterchanged, holding in the beak a buck's foot erased and erect or.

Mutter (Governor of Cape Coast Castle, 1767). Gu. a fess betw. three inescutcheons or. Crest—A castle ppr. Motto—Patience and resolution.

Muttes (co. Middlesex). Az. a unicorn pass. or.

Muttlebury (Jordaine, co. Somerset). Erm. on a bend gu. three round buckles or, a border of the second. Crest—A hare courant ar.

Muttlebury. Sa. two barrulets betw. three martlets or.

Mutton (Sir EVERARD DE MUTTON, Knt., of Halston. Descendants: I. MYTTON, of Halston; II. MYTTON, by change of name THORNYCROFT, of Thornycroft; III. MYTTON, of Garth and Pen-y-lan, originally of Pont-ys-Cowryd; IV. MUTTON, of Llanerch Park; V. MYTTON, of Weston). Quarterly, 1st and 4th, per pale az. and gu. an eagle displ. with two heads or, a border engr. of the last; 2nd and 3rd, ar. a cinquefoil az.

Mutton (Llanerch Park, co. Denbigh; Sir PETER MUTTON, Chief Justice of North Wales, descended from JENKIN MUTTON, third son of RICHARD MYTTON, Esq., ancestor of MYTTON, of Halston, left two daus., his co-heirs: I. ANNE, m. ROBERT DAVIES, Esq., of Gwysaney, co, Flint, ancestor of DAVIES, of Gwysaney; DAVIES, of Eton House, co. Kent; and DAVIES, of Marrington Hall; II. ELEANOR, m. KENRICK EYTON, Esq., of Eyton). Same Arms.

Mutton (Pickleton, co. Leicester). Ar. a cinquefoil pierced az. Crest—A unicorn ramp.

Myall. Az. on a chev. engr. betw. three knights' helmets or, as many millrinds sa. Crest—An eagle, wings endorsed erminois, collared, chained, and charged on the breast with a millrind sa.

Mychell. Sa. a chev. betw. three eagles displ. ar.

Mychell. Sa. three greyhounds courant in pale ar. a bordure gobony or and gu.

Mychell. Per pale ar. and sa. on a chief three trefoils slipped all counterchanged.

Mychell. Per pale ar. and sa. a fesse betw. three trefoils all counterchanged.

Mychell. Az. a leopard's head erased guard. or.

Mychell. Ar. a fesse erm. betw. three lozenges of the last.

Mychestainy (co. Cornwall). Sa. three wings elevated ar.

Myddelton (Gwaynynog, co. Denbigh; the parent stock of the MYDDELTONS, of Chirk Castle and Ruthyn, descended from DAVID MYDDELTON, Esq., of Gwaynynog, Receiver of North Wales, temp. Edward IV.). Ar. on a bend vert three wolves' heads erased of the field. Crest—Out of a ducal coronet or, a dexter hand ppr.

Myddelton (Chirk Castle, co. Denbigh, bart., extinct 1718; descended from Sir THOMAS MYDDELTON, Knt. of Chirk, Lord Mayor of London 1613, eldest son of RICHARD MYDDELTON, Esq., Governor of Denbigh Castle, temp. Edward VI., who was son of FULKE MYDDELTON, Esq., of Denbigh, a younger son of DAVID MYDDELTON, Esq., of Gwaynynog, Receiver of North Wales, temp. Edward IV. THOMAS MYDDELTON, Esq., of Chirk Castle, was created a bart. in 1660, the title became extinct at the decease of Sir WILLIAM MYDDELTON, fourth bart., when the estates passed to the heir male of the family, ROBERT MYDDELTON, Esq., of Lysfasi, and from him to his brother, JOHN MYDDELTON, Esq., whose grandson, RICHARD MYDDELTON, Esq., d. unm. in 1796, leaving his three sisters his co-heirs; of those ladies, CHARLOTTE m. ROBERT BIDDULPH, Esq., and had a son, ROBERT MYDDELTON BIDDULPH, Esq., of Chirk Castle, see BIDDULPH; and MARIA m. the Hon. FREDERICK WEST). Same Arms and Crest.

Myddelton, or Middelton (Ruthyn, co. Denbigh, bart., dormant since 1675; descended from the celebrated projector of the New River, Sir HUGH MYDDELTON, bart., sixth son of RICHARD MYDDELTON, Governor of Denbigh Castle).

719

Ar. on a pile vert three wolves' heads erased of the field. The pile was substituted for the bend by Camden, on the application of Sir Hugh). Same *Crest* as last.

Myddelton (Hackney, co. Middlesex, bart., extinct; Hugh Myddelton, grandson of Sir Hugh Myddelton, first bart. of Ruthyn, was created a bart. 1660, and *d. s. p. m.*). Same *Arms* and *Crest.*

Myddleton (Har. MS. 1241; Sir Alexander Myddleton, Governor of Montgomery Castle, *temp.* Richard II.). Gu. on a bend or, three lions pass. sa. armed and langued of the first.

Myddleton (Offerton, co. Durham; Elizabeth, only dau. and heiress of Christopher Wharton, Esq., of Offerton, *m.* George Myddleton, Esq., of Silksworth, a lineal descendant of Sir John Myddleton, Knt., of Belsay Castle; his grandson, Richard Myddleton, Esq., of Offerton, left two daus., his co-heirs, 1st, Katherine, *m.* Cuthbert Heron, whose son, Sir Thomas Heron, assumed the name of Myddleton, but *d. s. p.* 1801; 2nd, Mary, *m.* to Robert Wharton, Esq., by whom she was grandmother of Robert Wharton-Myddleton, Esq., of Old Park, co. Durham, and Grinkle Park, co. York). Quarterly, gu. and or, in the 1st quarter a cross patonce ar. *Crest*—A savage man wreathed about the head with leaves, in the dexter hand and supporting on the shoulder an oak tree erased and fructed all ppr.

Mydhope (co. York). Erm. a lion ramp. az. crowned or. *Crest*—A demi lion ramp. az. holding a ducal coronet or.

Myers (Gristhorpe Filey, co. York). Ar. a lymphad sa.

Myers (Whitehaven, co. Cumberland, and Monkstown, co. Dublin, bart., extinct 1811; Gen. William Myers, third son of Christopher Myers, Esq., of Monkstown, was Col. 2nd West India Regt., Governor of Tobago, Commander-in-Chief of the Southern District of Ireland, and of H.M. Forces in the Leeward Isles, he was created a bart. 1804; Sir William Myers, second bart., fell at the battle of Albuera, 1811). Ar. on the sea ppr. an ancient ship at anchor with three masts, on each a single yard across, sails furled sa. colours flying gu. and az. An honourable augmentation granted to Gen. Sir William Myers, 12 June, 1804, to be borne by him and his descendants, and also by the descendants of his late brothers, Graham Myers and John Myers, with due diff.: on a canton of three a last a baton or, and a sword also ppr. pommel and hilt gold, in saltire, encircled by a mural crown of the field. *Crest*—A mermaid ppr. the waist encircled by a mural crown or. *Motto*—Non dormiat qui custodit.

Myers (Waskett-Myers, Pentlow Hall, co. Essex, and Chester Street, London; exemplified to Sir Francis Waskett, K.C.S., upon his assuming by royal licence, 1818, the additional surname of Myers). Quarterly, 1st and 4th, ar. on the sea ppr. an ancient ship at anchor with three masts, on each a single yard across, the sails furled sa. colours flying gu. on a canton of the last a baton or, a sword also ppr. pommel and hilt gold, in saltire, encircled by a mural crown ar., and for distinction, pendent from the mainmast an inescutcheon of the field charged with a mullet of eight points az., Myers; 2nd and 3rd, or, a bend cotised betw. a lion ramp. in chief and two lions combatant in base gu., Waskett; the whole charged with an escutcheon of pretence, Myers, as above, without the inescutcheon for distinction of blood. *Crests*—1st.: A mermaid ppr. her waist also encircled by a mural crown or, and for distinction charged on the breast with a cross pattée az., Myers; 2nd.: A lion ramp. gu. gorged with a collar flory counterflory or, holding betw. the paws a mullet of eight points az., Waskett. *Motto*—Non dormiat qui custodit.

Mykeley, or Milkeley (co. Hereford). Gu. three chevronels ar.

Mykelfeld. Ar. a cross engr. sa. guttée d'or.

Mylbourne. Sa. on a bend ar. betw. two leopards' faces of the second three crosses pattée az. on a chief or, as many escallops gu. *Crest*—A leopard's face per pale ar. and sa.

Myld. Ar. a lion ramp. az. crowned or.

Mylde, alias Burley. See Burley, *alias* Mylde.

Myldred. Sa. three mullets or, a chief embattled (another, nebulée) erm.

Mylecut (co. York). Ar. an escutcheon sa. charged with a cross or, betw. three crosses formée, each pointing towards the centre of the shield of the second. *Crest*—A dragon's head sa. collared and chained or, issuing out of an antique crown or.

Myles (Dartford, co. Kent). Gu. a chev. ar. betw. three organ-rests ppr. *Crest*—A buzzard ppr.

Mylles (London. Visit. London, 1568). Erm. a millrind sa. *Crest*—A lion ramp. or.

720

Mylles (co. Hants). Sa. a bear erect ar. chained and muzzled or.

Mylne (London, from Scotland). See Milne, of Balfarg.

Mylne (Sir John Mylne, Bart., extinct, Lieut.-Governor of Guernsey, 1759). Or, a cross moline az. pierced lozengeways of the field betw. three mullets of the second. *Crest*—A hand grasping by the middle a baton ppr. *Motto*—Prudentia et mars.

Mymyng, or Mynors. Gu. on a chev. engr. or, betw. three fleurs-de-lis ar. as many rooks sa. (another, three cocks sa).

Mymyng, Mynors, or Mynos. Gu. a chev. engr. or, betw. three fleurs-de-lis ar.

Myn (Myn, co. Salop). Ar. a fesse dancettée paly of six erm. and gu. betw. six crosses crosslet sa.

Mynde, or Mynds (Mynde Town, co. Salop). Ar. on a chev. gu. betw. three lions' heads erased sa. as many bees volant of the first. *Crest*—A heathcock ppr.

Myne (co. Kent). Per pale ar. and sa. three chevronels betw. as many cinquefoils all counterchanged.

Mynell. Or, three bars gemelles az.

Myners (Blackvole, co. Stafford). Gu. a fesse ar. betw. three plates.

Mynn (Sir William Mynn, Woodcote, co. Surrey). Sa. a fess dancettée paly of six ar. and az.

Myngham (co. Kent). Az. four lozenges conjoined in 'ss or, betw. three griffins' heads erased ar.

Mynn (Cratfield, co. Suffolk). Ar. on a chev. betw. couple closes sa. three leopards' faces or. *Crest*—A demi pegasus issuing or.

Mynnes (co. Kent, *temp.* Charles I.). Gu. a chev. vairé or and az. betw. three leopards' faces of the second.

Mynors (Treago, co. Hereford; there since the Conquest, and descended from one of the companions in arms of William I., whose name appears on the roll of Battle Abbey. In 16 Henry III., John de Minors, of Treago, was Sheriff co. Hereford, and was appointed by Edward II. Keeper of the Castle of St. Briavel, and of the forest of Dene, now represented by Rickards-Mynors, of Treago, co. Hereford, and Evenjobb House, co. Radnor). Sa. an eagle displ. or, on a chief az. bordured ar. a chev. betw. two crescents in chief and a rose in base of the second. *Crest*—A naked arm embowed, the hand holding an eagle's leg erased at the thigh all ppr. *Motto*—Spero ut fidelis.

Mynors (co. Hereford). Az. an eagle displ. or, a chief ar. *Crest*—A naked arm couped at the elbow ppr. holding in the hand a lion's gamb erased sa.

Mynors (co. Stafford). Gu. a fesse ar. betw. three plates.

Mynors (Weatheroak Hill, co. Worcester). Same *Arms. Crest*—A dexter cubit arm in armour, the hand holding a lion's paw erased all ppr. *Motto*—Fac et spera.

Mynshull (Wistaston, co. Chester). Az. a crescent ar. issuant from the horns thereof an estoile of the last.

Mynshull (Manchester, co. Lancaster, 1664; descended from Mynshull, of Wistaston, co. Chester). Same *Arms.*

Mynshull. See Minshull.

Mynter, or Myntur. Or, a pillar sa. encircled with an adder ar.

Mynyot, or Mynyett. Ar. three helmets open sa.

Myrton (Cambo, co. Fife, Scotland). Ar. a chev. sa. betw. three torteaux.

Myrton (Scotland, 1696). Or, three torteaux within a bordure wavy and parted per pale sa. and ar. *Crest*—Two arms issuing from a cloud and drawing up an anchor out of the water ppr. *Motto*—Undique fulsus.

Myrton (Gogar, co. Edinburgh, bart., 1701). Ar. a chev. sa. betw. three pellets. *Crest*—A pinetree fructuating ppr. *Motto*—Virtutis præmium.

Mysters (Charterhouse Square, London). Sa. two bars gemelles or, in chief three griffins' heads erased of the second. *Crest*—A griffin's head erased sa. charged with two bars gemelles or.

Myte (Gunthorpe). Az. on a bend or, three mascles gu.

Myterton. Az. three mitres or.

Myttecomb. Sa. fretty or, in chief a lion pass. guard. of the last.

Mytton (Halston, co. Salop; descended from Sir Everard de Mutton, Knt.). Quarterly, 1st and 4th, per pale az. and gu. an eagle displ. with two heads or, within a border engr. of the last; 2nd and 3rd, ar. a cinquefoil az. *Crest*—A ram's head couped ar. horned or.

Mytton (Weston-under-Lizard, co. Salop; descended from Sir Richard Mutton, Knt., of Weston, son of Reginald de Mutton, M.P. for Shrewsbury, 1373. The male line terminated with William Mytton, Esq., of Weston, *d. s. p.*), leaving his two sisters and co-heirs: I. Constance, who *m.* Thomas Phillips, Esq., of Netley, co. Salop; II. Joyce, *m.* John

HARPSFIELD, Esq., London, mother of EDWARD HARPSFIELD, Esq., who assumed the surname of MYTTON only, 4 Edward VI.; from him descended EDWARD MYTTON, Esq., of Weston, whose dau. and heir, ELIZABETH MYTTON, of Weston, m. Sir THOMAS WILBRAHAM, Bart., of Woodhey, co. Chester). Same *Arms* and *Crest.*

Mytton, by change of name **Thornycroft.** See THORNYCROFT.

Mytton (Garth and Pen-y-lan, co. Montgomery; descended from JOHN, second son of RICHARD MYTTON, Esq., of Salop, by his first wife, ANNE, dau. of Sir EDWARD GREY, of Enville, Knt., represented by RICHARD HERBERT MYTTON, Esq., of Garth). Same *Arms.*

Mytton (Cleobury North, co. Salop). Quarterly, 1st and 4th, per pale az. and gu. an eagle displ. with two heads or, a border engr. of the last; 2nd and 3rd, ar. a chev. sa. betw. three birds ppr. *Crest*—A bull's head charged with three annulets. *Motto*—Interno robore.

Mytton (Shipton Hall, co. Salop). Per pale az. and gu. an eagle displ. with two heads or, a border engr. of the last. *Crest*—A bull's head erased bezantée.

Mytton (Shrewsbury, co. Salop). Same *Arms.* *Crest*—An arm in armour embowed holding by the blade a sword point downwards ppr.

N

NABBS (co. Stafford). Ar. on a bend cotised gu. three escallops or.

Nadal. Az. the sun in his glory.

Nadeston (Reg. Ulster's Office). Quarterly, or and gu. four escallops counterchanged.

Naftel (Guernsey). Erm. a lion ramp. gu. on a chief az. three fleurs-de-lis or.

Nagle (Mount Nagle, Annakissey, and Nagle's Borough, co. Cork; Reg. Ulster's Office). Erm. on a fess az. three lozenges or. *Crest*—A nightingale or.

Nagle (allowed by Hawkins, Ulster, 1770, to GARRETT NAGLE, Knight of the Military Order of St. Louis, and Captain in the service of the King of France, seventh son of JAMES NAGLE, Esq., of Annakissey, co. Cork). Same *Arms* and *Crest.*

Nagle (confirmed to Sir RICHARD NAGLE, Attorney-General for Ireland, *temp.* James II.). Same *Arms* and *Crest.*

Nagle (James-Town House, co. Westmeath, bart., extinct). Same *Arms* and *Crest.* *Motto*—Non vox sed votum.

Nagle (granted by Betham, Ulster, to Vice-Admiral Sir EDMUND NAGLE, Knt., and the descendants of his grandfather, PATRICK NAGLE, Esq., of Ballyduff, co. Cork). Erm. on a fess wavy az. cotised gu. three mascles or, over all on a bend of the third a sword ar. the hilt enriched with diamonds ppr. being a representation of the sword presented to him by the Prince Regent. *Crest*—A naval crown or, thereon a falcon with wings expanded ppr. belled and jessed or, resting his dexter claw on an anchor sa. *Motto*—Gratitude and loyalty.

Nagle (Calverleigh Court, co. Devon; exemplified to JOSEPH CHICHESTER, Esq., son of CHARLES JOSEPH CHICHESTER, Esq., of Calverleigh, who assumed the surname of NAGLE by royal licence, on inheriting the estates of his maternal grand-uncle, JOSEPH NAGLE, Esq., of Calverleigh, co. Devon, and Ballygriffin, co. Cork). Quarterly, 1st and 4th, quarterly, 1st and 4th, erm. on a fesse az. three fusils or, 2nd and 3rd, ar. a lion ramp. betw. three dexter hands couped at the wrist gu., for NAGLE; 2nd and 3rd, chequy or and gu. a chief vair, for CHICHESTER; 2nd, CHICHESTER: A heron rising with an eel in the beak ppr. *Motto*—Non vox sed votum.

Nagle (granted to Lieut.-Colonel JAMES NAGLE). Erm. on a fesse az. three lozenges or, a chief embattled vert, thereon a sword ppr. pommel and hilt gold, surmounted in saltire by a branch of laurel, ensigned by an Eastern crown, and on a canton of the last an elephant ppr. with the word "ASSAYE," sa. *Crest*—An Eastern crown gu. thereon a nightingale or, gorged with a wreath of laurel vert, the dexter paw supporting a banner of the second, with the word "ASSAYE" inscribed thereon sa.

Nagle. Sa. a fesse betw. three towers ar. *Crest*—A unicorn's head sa.

Nail. Ar. a round buckle gu. *Crest*—A round buckle gu. betw. two wings, the dexter ar. the sinister of the first.

Nailer. Ar. on a bend sa. three covered cups or.

Nairn (St. Fort, or Sandford, co. Fife). Per pale ar. and sa. on a chaplet four mullets counterchanged. *Crest*—A celestial sphere or and az. standing on a foot gu. *Mottoes:* over it—Spes ultra; and below the arms—L'espérance me comfort.

Nairn (Langside, Scotland). Per pale sa. and ar. on a chaplet four mullets, in the centre a crescent all counterchanged. *Crest* and *Motto,* as of St. Fort.

Nairn (Seggieden, co. Perth; represented by HAY, of Seggieden, as heir of line). Per pale sa. and ar. on a chaplet four quatrefoils counterchanged, a martlet for diff. *Crest*—The trunk of an oak tree sprouting out leaves ppr. *Motto*—Sero, sed serio.

Nairn (*Lord Nairn;* the title is now held by Baroness Nairn, Dowager Marchioness of Lansdowne). Quarterly, 1st and 4th, per pale sa. and ar. on a chaplet four quatrefoils all counterchanged, for NAIRN; 2nd, az. three mullets ar. within a double tressure flory counterflory or, for MURRAY; 3rd, quarterly, 1st and 4th, paly of six or and sa., for ATHOLL; 2nd and 3rd, or, a fesse chequy az. and ar., for STEWART. *Crest*—A sphere, and above it, Plus ultra. *Supporters*—Two talbots, or ratch hounds, ppr. *Motto*—L'espérance me comfort.

Nairn (Kirkhill, Scotland). Per pale ar. and sa. on a chaplet four mullets pierced counterchanged. *Crest* and *Motto,* as St. Fort.

Nairn (cos. Kent and Sussex). Paly of three sa. and ar. a chaplet of four roses leaved ppr.

Nairne (Dunsinnane, co. Perth, bart., 1704). Per pale sa. and ar. on a chaplet four mullets all counterchanged. *Crest*—A celestial globe on a stand ppr. *Mottoes*—Over the crest: Spes ultra; and below the arms: L'espérance me comfort.

Nairne (England). Per pale sa. and ar. on a chaplet betw. three cinquefoils four roundles all counterchanged. *Crest*—The sun in splendour or.

Naish. Az. on a chev. ar. within two couple closes or, betw. three doves' heads erased ppr. a pellet enclosed by four crosses crosslet sa. *Crest*—A dexter hand holding a sword in pale ppr.

Naish (Ballycullen, co. Limerick). Az. three doves ar. membered or, each holding in the beak on olive branch ppr. *Crest*—A greyhound sejant ppr. collared ar. *Motto*—Omnia vincit veritas.

Naizon. Ar. a chev. betw. three annulets sa. on a chief of the last as many estoiles of the first.

Nalder (Reading, co. Berks, 1787). Ar. on a saltire engr. az. betw. four griffins' heads erased per pale gu. and vert, as many lozenges or. *Crest*—A griffin's head erased.

Nalingest, or **Nallinghurst** (co. Essex). Gu. a cross engr. or (another, the field semée-de-lis or).

Nanby. Ar. a chev. gu. on a chief sa. two swords in saltire of the first, pommels and hilts or. *Crest*—A lion's paw sa. holding an ostrich's feather ar.

Nancarrow (Nancarrow, co. Cornwall). Ar. a chev. betw. three stags, attires sa.

Nance, alias Trengove (Nance, co. Cornwall). See TRENGOVE, of Nance.

Nancothan (Redriff, co. Cornwall). Ar. three moles sa.

Nandike (Elstone, co. York). Ar. a pale betw. two crosses pattée sa. *Crest*—A demi griffin, wings endorsed ar. supporting a spear sa. headed of the first.

Nanfan. Sa. a chev. betw. three gem rings ar.

Nanfan (Nanfan, co. Cornwall). Sa. a chev. erm. betw. three wings inverted ar.

Nanfan (Trethewell in St. Kew, co. Cornwall; descended from NANFAN, of Nanfan; JANE, dau. and co-heir of JACOB NANFAN, Esq., of Trethewell, m. JOHN TRENOWITH, Esq. of Fentongollan). Same *Arms.*

Nanfan (Birtsmorton Court, Berrow and Pendock, co. Worcester; the last male heir, BRIDGES NANFAN, Esq., of Birtsmorton Court, had an only dau. and heiress, KATHERINE, m. RICHARD COOTE, *Earl of Bellamont.* Visit. Worcester). Same *Arms.* *Crest*—A water spaniel pass. ar.

Nanfant. Ar. three wolves pass. in pale ar. *Crest*—Three pruning-hooks, two in saltire and one in pale or, environed in the middle with a wreath.

Nanfant. Sa. a chev. erm. betw. three wings ar. *Crests* 1st: A spaniel dog ar.; 2nd: Three vine-hooks or pruning-hooks crossing ar. one erect and two in saltire.

Nanfant (impalement Fun. Ent. Ulster's Office, 1676, RICHARD NEWCOMEN, Esq., of Dalkey, co. Dublin, whose wife's name was NANFANT). Sa. a chev. erm. betw. three sinister wings inverted ar.

Nangle (Feudal Baron of Navan, co. Meath; impalement Fun. Ent. Ulster's Office, 1619, CHRISTOPHER BARNEWALL, Esq., of Newton, whose wife was AGNES, dau. of MARTIN NANGLE, Baron of Navan). Az. three fusils conjoined in fess or. *Crest*—A falcon close sa. jessed and belled or.

Nangle (Kildalkie, co. Meath; Fun. Ent. Ulster's Office, 1836, MABLE, dau. of WALTER NANGLE, Esq., of Kildalkie, and wife of NICHOLAS FITZ WILLIAM, Esq., of Ballydongan).

Az. three fusils conjoined in fess or, a crescent on a crescent for diff.

Nangle, alias McCostello (Reg. Ulster's Office). Or, three lozenges az. (another, the field ar. and the lozenges sa.). *Crest*—A falcon close sa. jessed and belled or.

Nangothan, or Nangotham (Scotland). Ar. three moles sa. their snouts and feet gu. *Crest*—A polecat ar.

Nankevill (St. Wenn, *alias* Colomb Major, co. Cornwall; JOHN NANKEVILL, *alias* TIPETT, Esq., of St. Wenn, Visit. Cornwall, 1620, son and heir of RICHARD NANKEVILL, Esq., of same place, fourth in descent from TIPETT NANKEVILL, of same place). Ar. a cross humettée voided sa.

Nannau (co. Merioneth, feudal Barons; descendants, and representatives of CADWGAN, Lord of Nannau, younger son of BLEDDYN AP CYNFYN, King of Powys). Or, a lion ramp. az., being the arms of CADWGAN, Lord of Nannau.

Nanney (Nannau, ço. Merioneth; descended from MEURIC, Lord of Nannau, brother and heir male of HOWEL, Lord of Nannau, JANET, dau. of HUGH NANNEY, Esq., of Nannau, m. ROBERT VAUGHAN, Esq., of Hengwrt and Wengraig, co. Merioneth, from whom descend VAUGHAN, Bart., of Nannau). Same *Arms*.

Nanney (Cefndeuddwr and Gwynfryn; descended from CADWGAN, Lord of Nannau, son of BLEDDYN AP CYNFYN, Prince of Powys. OWEN JONES ELLIS NANNEY, Esq., of Gwynfryn, co. Canarvon, son of JOHN JONES, Esq., of Brynhir, by ELIZABETH, his wife, dau. of the Rev. RICHARD ELLIS, of Gwynfryn, by CATHERINE, his wife, sister and heir of the Rev. RICHARD NANNEY, of Cefndeuddwr, assumed the name of NANNEY). Same *Arms*, or, a lion ramp. az. *Arms* of ELLIS —Gu. a chev. betw. three lions ramp. or (as descended from Sir HOWELL-Y-PEDOLAU, foster brother of Edward II., by whom he was knighted).

Nanney (Maes-y-Neuadd, co. Merioneth; descended from MAURICE WYNN, Esq., second son of WILLIAM WYNN, Esq., of Glynn, co. Merioneth, who was descended from OSBORNE FITZGERALD, Lord of Ynys y-Maengwyn). Quarterly, 1st and 4th, or, a lion ramp. az., for NANNEY; 2nd and 3rd, erm. on a saltire gu. a crescent or, for WYNN. *Crest*—A lion ramp. az.

Nanphan (Birts Morton, co. Worcester; descended from co. Cornwall). Sa. a chev. erm. betw. three dexter wings ar. *Crest*—A water spaniel pass. ar.

Nanphan, or Nanfan. Same *Arms*. *Crest*—Two dolphins endorsed az.

Nanphant (co. Cornwall). Ar. three wolves courant in pale az.

Nanscawen (co. Cornwall). Gu. on a cross or, four escallops of the first.

Nanscours (co. Cornwall). Sa. three bucks' heads cabossed ar. attired or.

Nansegles (co. Cornwall). Ar. three ravens sa.

Nansladron, or Lansladron (*temp.* Edward I.). Sa. three chevronels ar.

Nansolyn. Az. three bezants. *Crest*—A cross pattée fitchée az.

Nanson, or Nanfan. Sa. a chev. betw. three annulets ar.

Nansperian (co. Cornwall). Ar. three lozenges sa

Nanspian (Garlyn, and Crowen, co. Cornwall; JAMES NANSPIAN, Esq., of Garlyn, and HENRY NANSPIAN, Esq., of Crowen, Visit. Cornw. 1620, sons of JOHN NANSPYAN, by JANE, his wife, dau. and heir of THOMAS TREGOZE). Ar. three lozenges in fess sa. a chief of the last.

Nanstalen. Or, a chev. betw. three saltorels sa.

Nantian (quartered by BEVILLE). Or (another, ar.) a fesse gu. in chief two mullets of the last.

Nanton (co. Suffolk). Sa. three martlets ar. *Crest*—A cockatrice close ppr. wings sa.

Nants, alias Trengrove. Ar. a cross humettée sa. *Crest*—An estoile of eight points or.

Nanture. Or, a saltire gu.

Nantwich Priory (co. Chester). Per pale az. and gu. two croziers (palmers' staves) in saltire or.

Nantyon. Ar. a fesse gu. in chief two estoiles of the last.

Nanvers. Ar. two bars gu. in chief three crescents of the last.

Naper, Napper, or Napier (Hallywell, co. Oxford; EDMUND NAPPER, Visit. Oxon, 1634, son of WILLIAM NAPPER, who was son of EDWARD NAPER, or NAPIER, of Swyre, co. Dorset). Ar. a saltire betw. four roses gu.

Naper, or Napper (co. Oxford; Har. MSS., No. 1480). Ar. a saltire engr. gu. betw. four cinquefoils of the last. *Crest*—A demi antelope ramp. or.

Naper, or Napper (Fun. Ent. Ulster's Office, 1676, Colonel JAMES NAPPER). Ar. a saltire engr. gu. betw. four roses of the last seeded or, leaved vert. *Crest*—A dexter arm erect couped below the elbow, the hand ppr. grasping a crescent ar.

Naper, or Napper (confirmed *temp.* Charles II. to Colonel THOMAS NAPER, who raised a regiment of foot in Ireland). Ar. a saltire sa. betw. four cinquefoils pierced gu. a canton of the last. *Crest*—A phœnix ppr.

Naper, or Napper (Reg. Ulster's Office, Sir ROBERT NAPER, Chief Baron of the Exchequer in Ireland, *d.* 1615, second son of JAMES NAPER, or NAPIER, Esq., of Middlemershall and Punknoll, co. Dorset). Ar. a saltire engr. betw four roses gu.

Naper, or Napper (Bawnmore, New Ross, co. Wexford, descended from JOHN NAPER, or NAPPER, Esq., of Kilscanlon, same co., *d.* 1699, third son of Sir NATHANIEL NAPER, Knt., of Middlemershall and Morecritchell, who was son of Sir ROBERT NAPER, of same place, Chief Baron of Exchequer, represented in the male line by Colonel ROBERT ALEXANDER NAPPER, Bengal Staff Corps). Same *Arms*. *Crest*—A dexter arm couped at the elbow, vested gu. turned up ar. grasping a crescent also gu. *Motto*—Sans tache.

Naper (Loughcrew, co. Meath; descended from JAMES NAPER, fourth son of Sir NATHANIEL NAPER, Knt., of Middlemershall and More Critchell; his son, JAMES NAPER, Esq., of Loughcrew, *m.* ANNE, dau. and eventual co-heir of Sir RALPH, DUTTON, Bart., of Sherborne, and had a son, JAMES LENNOX NAPER, who assumed the name of DUTTON, and was father of JAMES DUTTON, created *Lord Sherborne* 1784, and of WILLIAM NAPER, ESQ., of Loughcrew, grandfather of the present JAMES LENOX NAPIER, Esq., of Loughcrew). Same *Arms* and *Crest*.

Naper. See NAPIER.

Naper (Devon; granted 1 Aug. 1577). Ar. a saltire engr. betw. four cinquefoils gu. *Crest*—A demi antelope erased or, attired ar.

Naper, alias Sandey, alias Tandy (Reg. Ulster's Office). Gu. a saltire engr. betw. four roses or (another, the field ar. and the roses gu).

Napier (Murchiston, co. Edinburgh). Ar. a saltire engr. betw. four roses gu. barbed vert.

Napier (*Baron Napier and Ettrick*). Quarterly, 1st and 4th, ar. a saltire engr. betw. four roses gu. barbed vert, for NAPIER; 2nd and 3rd, or, on a bend az. a mull pierced betw. two crescents of the field within a double tressure flory counterflory of the second, for SCOTT, of Thirlestane. *Crest* —1st: A dexter arm erect couped below the elbow ppr. grasping a crescent ar., over it the motto, Sans tache; 2nd: The top of an embattled tower ar. masoned sa. issuing therefrom six lances disposed saltireways, three and three, with pennons az., for SCOTT. *Supporters*—Dexter, an eagle, wings expanded ppr.; sinister, a chevalier in a coat of mail with a steel cap all ppr. holding in the exterior hand a spear with a pennon az. *Motto*—Ready, aye ready.

Napier (Napier, co. Haddington, bart.). Quarterly, 1st and 4th, ar. a saltire engr. betw. four roses gu. the roses barbed vert, for NAPIER, of Merchistoun; 2nd, az. a lion ramp. ar. crowned or, for MACDOWALL, of Garthland ; 3rd, ar. a fesse az. voided of the field betw. three demi lions crowned gu., of MILLIKEN. *Crests*—1st: An arm grasping an eagle's leg ppr., for NAPIER; 2nd: A demi lion ramp. gu. holding in his dexter forepaw a dagger or, for MILLIKEN. *Supporters*—Two eagles with their wings closed ppr. *Mottoes*—Sans tache; and Regarde bien.

Napier (Culcreuch, co. Stirling). Ar. on a saltire engr. betw. four roses gu. five mullets of the field. *Crest*—A hand holding an eagle's leg erased ppr. the talons expanded gu. *Motto*—Fides servata secundat.

Napier (Balwhapple, co. Dumbarton). Ar. a saltire engr. betw. four roses gu. with a mullet for diff. *Crest*—An eagle's leg erased in bend ppr. armed gu. *Motto*—Usque fidelis.

Napier (Falside, co. Fife). Ar. a saltire engr. betw. four roses gu. within a bordure indented of the last. *Crest*—Two hands conjoined, and both grasping a cutlass ppr. *Motto*—Absque dedecore.

Napier (Harviestoun, co. Clackmannan). Same *Arms*, the bordure charged with eight crescents ar.

Napier (Tayock, Scotland). Ar. a saltire engr. betw. four roses gu. within a bordure indented of the last, charged with eight martlets of the field. *Motto*—Patientia vincit.

Napier (Blackstone, co. Renfrew). Ar. on a saltire engr. gu. betw. four roses of the second a fleur-de-lis of the first. *Crest*—A dexter arm holding up a crescent. *Motto*—Sans tache.

Napier (Ballikinrain, co. Dumbarton). Ar. a saltire engr. betw. four roses gu. within a bordure of the last. *Crest*—A dexter hand holding an eagle's leg erased in bend ppr. armed gu. *Motto*—Nil veretur veritas.

Napier (Ballichearne, co. Dumbarton). Same *Arms*, the bordure charged with eight crescents ar. *Crest*—An eagle's leg erased ppr. armed gu. disposed fesseways. *Motto*—Vincit veritas.

Napier (Craigannet, co. Stirling). Ar. on a saltire engr. betw. four roses gu. a mullet sa. *Crest*—A hand holding a couteau sword ppr. *Motto*—Sans tache.

Napier (Kilmachew, co. Dumbarton). Gu. on a bend ar. three crescents az. and in the sinister chief point a spur-rowel of the second. *Crest*—A man's head adorned with laurel ppr. *Motto*—Virtute gloria parta.

Napier (Wright's Houses, co. Edinburgh). Or, on a bend az. a crescent betw. two spur-rowels of the first.

Napier (West Shandon, co. Dumbarton, 1869). Per fess gu. and sa. on a bend ar. three crescents az. *Crest*—A man's head in profile, wreathed with laurel ppr. *Motto*—Virtutis gloria parta.

Napier (Luton-Hoo, co. Bedford, and Halliwell, co. Oxford, bart., extinct 1747). Ar. a saltire engr. betw. four cinque-foils (another, roses) gu. *Crest*—A greyhound sejant gu. collared and lined or. *Supporters*—Dexter, an eagle ppr. beaked or; sinister, a greyhound gu. collared and lined or.

Napier (Middlemershall and Morecritchell, co. Dorset, bart., extinct 1765; GERARD NAPIER, eldest son of Sir NATHANIEL NAPIER, Knt., of Morecritchell, and grandson of Sir ROBERT NAPER, NAPPER, or NAPIER, Chief Baron of Exchequer in Ireland, was created a bart. 1641). Same *Arms*.

Napier (Puncknoll, co. Dorset, bart., extinct 1743; descended from ROBERT NAPIER, second son of Sir NATHANIEL NAPIER, Knt., of Morecritchell). Same *Arms*.

Napier (*Lord Napier of Magdala*). Gu. on a saltire betw. two mural crowns in pale and as many lions pass. in fess or, a rose of the field. *Crest*—On a mount vert a lion pass. or, gorged with a collar gu. and a broken chain reflexed over the back gold, supporting with the dexter forepaw a flagstaff in bend sinister ppr. therefrom flowing a banner ar. charged with a cross couped gu. *Supporters*—Dexter, a soldier of the Royal Engineers; sinister, a Sikh sirdar, both habited, and each holding in his exterior hand a musket all ppr. *Motto*—Tu vincula frange.

Napier (Pennard House, co. Somerset). Quarterly, 1st and 4th, ar. a saltire engr. betw. four roses gu., for NAPIER; 2nd and 3rd, or, on a bend az. a mullet betw. two crescents of the field, within a double tressure flory counterflory of the second, for SCOTT, of Thirlestane. *Crest*—A dexter arm erect, couped below the elbow ppr. grasping a crescent. *Motto*—Fato providentia major.

Napier (Rt. Hon. Sir JOSEPH NAPIER, Bart., late Lord Chancellor of Ireland, and now Vice-Chancellor of Trinity College, Dublin). Ar. on a saltire engr. betw. four roses gu. five escallops or. *Crest*—A dexter cubit arm erect ppr. the hand grasping a crescent ar. the arm charged with a rose as in the arms. *Motto*—Sans tache.

Napleton. Or, a squirrel sejant gu. holding a sprig ppr.

Napps, or Nap (Needham). Or, a lion pass. betw. three helmets sa.

Napton (co. Stafford). Or, on a fesse sa. three escallops ar.

Napton (co. Warwick). Ar. a lion ramp. gu. crowned or. *Crest*—A lion pass. tail extended ppr.

Narbon. Ar. three demi garters couped in fesse az. buckled and garnished or. *Crest*—A dove volant, in the beak an olive branch all ppr.

Narbone (Narbone and Colne, co. Wilts; confirmed 14 July, 1660). Erm. a fesse nebulée gu. on a canton of the second a ducal coronet or.

Narboon, or Narboone. Or, three demi garters nowed az. garnished of the field. *Crest*—A fleece or, banded az.

Narborough, Narburgh, or Newborough (co. Norfolk). Gu. a chief erm.

Nares (Biddenden, co. Kent). Gu. on a fesse or, three spear heads ppr. *Crest*—Two spears in saltire ppr. banded az. (another, gu.).

Narford. Gu. a fesse ar. *Crest*—Out of a cloud a dexter hand fesseways ppr. holding a cross crosslet fitcheé gu.

Narstaffe (co. Essex). Sa. billettée ar. a lion ramp. or.

Narstoft, Nartoft, or Nartost (cos. Devon and Essex). Sa. a lion ramp. or.

Nary. Gu. on a fesse ar. three spearheads of the first, in chief as many annulets or.

Nash (Woodstock, co. Oxford; MICHAEL NASH, Esq., of Old Woodstock, Visit. Oxon, 1574, son of JOHN NASH; arms on a stone in Bicester Church). Az. on a chev. betw. three eagles' heads erased ar. a pellet betw. four crosses crosslet sa.

Nash (Martley, Claines, and Droitwich, co. Worcester. Visit. 1634. Dr. TREADWAY RUSSELL NASH, the historian of co. Worcester, succeeded to the representation of the family at the death of his elder brother, RICHARD NASH, D.D., and

d. 1811; his only dau. and heiress, MARGARET, *m.* JOHN, first *Earl Somers. Arms* recorded in Visit. of 1634). Sa. on a chev. betw. three greyhounds statant ar. as many sprigs of ash slipped vert; as generally borne: Vert a chev. betw. three greyhounds courant ar. *Crest*—A greyhound courant ar.

Nash (The Noak, Martley, co. Worcester; confirmed, 1841, to JAMES NASH, M.D., of the Noak, great-grandson of JAMES NASH, Esq., of Bedford Court, of the family of RICHARD NASH, the historian of co. Worcester). Per fesse vert and sa. in chief a chev. betw. three greyhounds courant, and in base on a chev. betw. as many greyhounds statant ar. a like number of sprigs of ash ppr. *Crest*—Upon a mount vert a greyhound courant ar. charged on the body with an erm. spot sa. in the mouth a sprig of ash ppr. *Motto*—In utroque fidelis.

Nash (Lord Mayor of London, 1772). Az. on a chev. betw. three ravens' heads erased ar. a pellet betw. four crosses crosslet sa. *Crest*—An arm erect, couped at the elbow, vested az. cuffed ar. holding in the hand ppr. an acorn branch vert fructed ppr.

Nash (Reg. Ulster's Office). Gu. three doves ar. membered or, each holding in the beak an olive branch vert.

Nash (Reg. Ulster's Office, as the arms of WILLIAM NASH, Esq., *temp.* Charles II., whose dau., PHILLIS NASH, *m.* JOHN MACNAMARA, Esq., of Kilkeshan, co. Clare). Or, a tricorporate lion ramp. issuing out of the dexter and sinister chief points and the base, all meeting under one head in the fess point sa.

Nashe. Sa. on a chev. betw. three greyhounds courant ar. as many sprigs of ashen leaves ppr.

Nashe. Or, a tricorporated lion issuing out of three corners of the escutcheon, all meeting under one head in the fess point az.

Nasmyth (Posso, co. Peebles, bart., 1706). Quarterly, 1st and 4th, gu. a dexter hand couped ppr. holding a sword paleways ar. betw. two broken hammers or, for NASMYTH; 2nd and 3rd, az. on a fesse ar. betw. three mullets in chief and a sanglier pass. in base of the second, a boar's head couped gu., for BAIRD, of Posso. *Crest*—A hand holding a hammer, as in the arms. *Motto*—Non arte sed marte.

Nason. Az. three rams' heads couped or.

Nassau (*Prince of Orange*). Az. billettée a lion ramp. or. *Crest*—Out of a ducal coronet or, the attires of a buck gu.

Nassau (*Earl of Rochford*, extinct 1830; FREDERICK DE NASSAU, illegitimate son of HENRY FREDERICK DE NASSAU, *Prince of Orange*, the grandfather of William III., was father of WILLIAM HENRY DE ZUYLESTON, the confidential friend of William III., who raised him to the Peerage of England, 1695). Quarterly, 1st, az. billettée or, a lion ramp. of the second, for NASSAU; 2nd, or, a lion ramp. gu. ducally crowned az., for DIETZ; 3rd, gu. a fesse ar., for VIANDEN; 4th, gu two lions pass. guard. in pale or, for CATZNELLOGEN; over all in an escutcheon gu. three zules ar. in chief a label of three points of the last, for ZUYLESTON. *Crest*—Out of a coronet composed of fleurs-de-lis and strawberry leaves or, two single attires of a stag gu. *Supporters*—Two lions erminois, each ducally crowned az. *Motto*—Ne supra modum sapere. *Another Motto*—Spes durat avorum.

Nassau (*Earl of Grantham*, extinct 1754; HENRY DE NASSAU, Lord of Auverquerque, in Holland, *d.* 1668; his youngest son, HENRY DE NASSAU, came to England with William III. "Who, on his deathbed strained his feeble voice to thank Nassau for his affectionate and loyal service of thirty years;" Nassau fell in the campaign of 1708: his son had been raised to the Peerage 1698). Quarterly, 1st, az. billettée a lion ramp. or; 2nd, or, a lion ramp. couped. gu. ducally crowned az.; 3rd, gu. a fesse ar., for VIANDEN; 4th, gu. two lions pass. guard. in pale or, over all in an escutcheon az. a lion ramp. sa. *Crest*—On a chapeau az. turned up erminois a lion ramp. guard. gu. ducally crowned az. *Supporters*—Dexter, an eagle reguard. wings disclosed sa. beaked, membered, and ducally crowned or; sinister, a lion guard. or. *Motto*—Je m'en souviendray.

Nassouille. Az. three bezants.

Nastadran (co. Cornwall). Sa. three chevronels ar.

Natal, Cape of Good Hope, See of. Gu. a saltire and in chief a star of six points ar.

Nathaley, Natheley, or Nathiley. Gu. an adder nowed or. *Crest*—Out of a ducal coronet or, a demi swan sa. wings displ.

Nathan. Or, a fesse within two barrulets sa. betw. three carpenters' compasses extended az. *Crest*—A human heart gu. pierced with an arrow in bend sinister sa.

Natovillet, or Natvillet. Ar. a fret sa. a canton of the second.

Natterville. Erm. three savages' heads erased affrontée sa.

Naughton. Sa. three martlets ar. *Crest*—A demi lion ramp. guard. holding in the dexter paw a fleur-de-lis.

Naughton. See O'NAUGHTON.

Naugles. Ar. four lozenges in fesse sa.

Naunton. Sa. a lion ramp. or, ducally crowned ar. betw. three crosses crosslet of the second. *Crest*—An ostrich's head ar. ducally gorged az.

Naunton (BARTHOLOMEW DE NAUNTON, *temp.* Richard II.). Sa. three martlets ar.

Navan, Town of (co. Meath; Reg. Ulster's Office). Az. out of clouds in base a naked arm couped at the elbow erect in pale, holding in the hand a human heart all ppr. betw. on the dexter an Irish harp or, and on the sinister a rose ar. slipped and leaved vert, both in fess, in chief the royal crown gold.

Navy Office. The seal represents an anchor in pale betw. two small anchors erect, within the beam and fluke, with this *Motto*—Sigillum Officii Navalis.

Nawghley. Ar. three fusils in fesse sa.

Naxton (co. Essex). Or, on a fesse az. three escallops ar.

Nayler (Sir GEORGE NAYLER, Garter King of Arms). Or, a pale betw. two lions ramp. sa. on a canton gu. a rose ar.

Naylinghurst (co. Essex). Gu. a cross engr. or.

Naylor (Wakefield, co. York). Sa. three covered cups in pale or, betw. two palets ar. *Crest*—A lark volant or.

Naylor. Ar. on a chev. gu. betw. three lozenges sa. as many martlets or.

Naylor (London; granted, 1564, by Harvey, Clarenceux). Or, a pale betw. two lions ramp. sa. *Crest*—A lion's head couped sa. charged on the neck with a saltire humettée or.

Naylor (Newland, co. Gloucester). Or, on a bend cotised sa. three covered cups of the first. *Crest*—A goat's head or, attired sa. in the mouth a laurel sprig vert.

Naylor (Leighton Hall, co. Montgomery). Per pale or and ar. a pale sa. fretty gold betw. two lions ramp. of the third. *Crest*—A lion pass. sa. charged on the body with two saltires or, resting the forepaw upon a shield charged with the arms. *Motto*—Hoc age.

Naylor (Hooton Hall, co. Chester). Same *Arms, &c.*

Naylour, or Naylor (co. Durham, and Offord-Darcy, co. Huntingdon). Or, a pale betw. two lions ramp. sa. *Crest*—A lion's head erased sa. charged on the neck with a saltire or.

Naylour (RICHARD NAYLOUR, of London, Visit. 1586, son and heir of WILLIAM NAYLOUR, Esq., one of the Six Clerks in Chancery). Same *Arms* and *Crest.*

Naylour (co. Kent). Ar. on a bend sa. three covered cups of the field. *Crest*—On a mount vert an eagle rising ppr.

Neafe (Methie). Az. a man in armour, on horseback ar. advancing his sword, in the sinister chief a left hand of the third.

Neal (Yeovil, co. Somerset). Paly of six ar. and az. on a bend gu. a greyhound's head erased betw. two dexter hands couped at the wrist ar. *Crest*—Out of a wreath of oak or, a dexter cubit arm in armour, in the gauntlet ppr. a sword erect also ppr. pommel and hilt gold, transfixing a greyhound's head, as in the arms.

Neale, or Nele (co. Buckingham). Paly of six ar. and gu. on a bend of the second three mullets ar.

Neale (Deane, co. Bedford, and Ellenborough, co. Berks; THOMAS NEALE, Esq., of Deane, 1543, grandson of THOMAS NEALE, Esq., of Ellenborough). Per pale sa. and gu. a lion pass. guard. ar. *Crest*—Out of a mural crown or, a demi lion ramp. per fess erm. and gu. charged with an escallop counterchanged.

Neale (co. Wexford; CONSTANTINE NEALE, great-grandson of THOMAS NEALE, Esq., of Deane, in 1543, was High Sheriff co. Wexford, 1672; his son, Ven. BENJAMIN NEALE, Archdeacon of Leighlin, left two daus. his co-heirs: I. DEBORAH, m. JOHN BAYLEY, Esq., of Debsborough; II. MARTHA, m. JOHN STRATFORD, Esq., of Belan, co. Kildare, first *Earl of Aldborough*). Same *Arms* and *Crest.*

Neale (Walhampton, co. Hants). Az. a lion pass. betw. three estoiles ar. *Crest*—A dexter arm embowed, couped at the elbow, brandishing a sword ppr.

Neale, Neal, or Neyll (Yelden, co. Bedford, co. Essex, Wollaston and Hanging Houghton, co. Northampton). Per pale sa. and gu. a lion pass. guard. ar. *Crest*—A griffin's head erased ar.

Neale, Nele, or Fitz-Nele (co. Buckingham). Paly of six ar. and gu.

Neale (Warnford, co. Hants; granted 1579). Ar. a fesse gu. in chief two crescents of the second, in base a buglehorn of the last, stringed vert. *Crest*—Out of a ducal coronet or, a chaplet of laurel vert.

724

Neale, or Neele (Lynn-Magna, co. Leicester, 20 Henry VI.). Gu. three greyhounds' heads erased ar. collared sa. ringed or.

Neale (Allesley Park, co. Warwick; exemplified to Rev. EDWARD VANSITTART, Rector of Taplow, second son of GEORGE VANSITTART, Esq., M.P., of Bisham Abbey, co. Berks, by SARAH, his wife, dau. of Sir JAMES STONEHOUSE, Bart., and ANNE, his wife, eldest dau. of JOHN NEALE, of Allesley, M.P. Coventry, who assumed the name of NEALE, by royal licence, 1805). Quarterly, 1st and 4th, per pale sa. and gu. a lion pass. guard. ar., for NEALE; 2nd and 3rd, erm. an eagle displ. sa. on a chief gu. a ducal coronet betw. two crosses pattée ar., for VANSITTART. *Crests*—1st, NEALE: Out of a mural crown or, a demi lion ramp. per fesse erm. and gu. charged on the shoulder with an escallop counterchanged; 2nd, VANSITTART: On two crosses pattée ar. a demi eagle displ. sa.

Neale (Daventry, co. Northampton). Gu. an annulet or, betw. three greyhounds' heads erased ar. collared sa. ringed of the second.

Neale (Westminster; granted Nov. 1612). Gu. a lion ramp. betw. three dexter hands couped gu. *Crest*—A dragon's head or, vulned in the neck gu.

Neale. Gu. two bars gemel ar. on a chief of the last five trefoils az. three and two. *Crest*—A tower gu. out of the battlements a pelican rising, wings displ. or, vulning herself ppr.

Neale (impalement Fun. Ent. Ulster's Office, 1617, EDWARD KENNY, whose wife was dau. of WILLIAM NEALE). Ar. an oak tree eradicated vert, acorned or, over all a fess wavy az.

Neale, Nell, or Nele. Gu. semée of trefoils and two dolphins endorsed ar. *Crest*—A fret az.

Neale. Gu. three lions pass. guard. ar.; another, Ar. on a bend sa. three greyhounds courant or; another, Per pale gu. and ermines, a lion pass. guard.

Neale, or Nell. Ar. on a bend sa. three greyhounds courant of the field.

Neale, alias Nigill. Or, a lion ramp. purp.

Nealewell. Ar. on a chev. gu. three bezants.

Nearn (Reg. Ulster's Office). Az. a griffin ramp. holding in each paw a key all or *Crest*—A lion's head or.

Nearne (co. Kent). Quarterly or and az. four lions' heads erased counterchanged.

Neast (Chaseley, co. Worcester. Visit. 1634). Ar. two lions' gambs erased in saltire gu.

Neate (London, and Swindon, co. Wilts). Ar. a chev. betw. two trefoils in chief vert and a bull's head couped at the neck in base gu. horned and crined or. *Crest*—A bull's head couped at the neck gu. armed and crined ar. betw. two dragons' wings expanded vert.

Neave (Dagnam Park, co. Essex, bart.). Ar. on a cross sa. five fleurs-de-lis or. *Crest*—Out of a ducal coronet or, a lily stalked and leaved vert, flowered and seeded gold. *Motto* —Sola proba quæ honesta.

Neave (London; granted 1763). Ar. on a cross sa. five fleurs-de-lis of the field, in the 1st and 4th quarters a leopard pass. guard. ppr. *Crest*—A demi leopard ramp. guard. ppr. supporting an anchor or. *Motto*—Industria permanente.

Neaves (Hon. CHARLES NEAVES, Judge of the Court of Session, 1869). Per fess erm. and sa. a chev. wavy or. *Crest*—A demi lion guard. gu. supporting an anchor or. *Motto*—Spe et industria.

Neborgy. Or, three bendlets az. a border engr. gu.

Nedeham. Ar. a bend engr. az. betw. two bulls' heads cabossed or.

Nedham (Wimeley, co. Hertford). Az. on a chev. betw. three escallops ar. as many acorns ppr. slipped vert, on a chief crenellée or, three martlets gu. *Crest*—A dolphin naiant or.

Nedham (Wymondesley, co. Hertford; confirmed 18 Feb. 1586). Ar. on a bend engr. az. betw. two bucks' heads cabossed sa. attired or, an escallop of the last.

Nedham (co. Hertford; granted 1586). Same *Arms.* *Crest*—Out of a pallisado coronet or, a buck's head attired of the first.

Nedham (Litchborough, co. Northampton). Same *Arms.* *Crest*—Out of a pallisado coronet or, a buck's head sa. attired of the first.

Need (Fountain Dale, co. Notts). Per chev. or and erm. in chief two griffins' heads erased ppr. *Crest*—Out of an eastern coronet or, a griffin's head ppr.

Need (Blidworth, co. Notts). Per chev. or and erm. in chief two griffins' heads erased sa. *Crest*—An eastern coronet or, thereout a griffin's head issuing sa. charged with an estoile gold.

Needham, or Nedham (Nedham in the Peak, co. Derby,

1 Henry II.; CHRISTOPHER NEEDHAM, of Thornsett, sixth in descent from THOMAS NEEDHAM, Esq., of Needham, and MAUD his wife, dau. of ROGER MELLURE, of Thornsett, was ancestor of NEEDHAM, of Needham, Thornsett, Snitterton, and Cowley (Visit. Derby, 1611), and NEEDHAM, cos. Suffolk, Hertford, and Leicester). Ar. a bend engr. az. betw. two bucks' heads cabossed sa. attired or. Crest—A phœnix in flames ppr. Another Crest—On a mount vert a stag lodged sa. attired or; Another Crest—Out of a coronet formed of pallisades a buck's head sa.

Needham (Alexton and Gadesby, co. Leicester, and Belton, co. Rutland; FRANCIS NEEDHAM, Esq., of Gadesby. Visits. Rutland, 1618, and Leicester, 1619, grandson of THOMAS NEEDHAM, Esq., of Bolton, the eldest son of THOMAS NEEDHAM, Esq., of Alexton). Same Arms. Crest—On a mount vert a stag lodged sa. attired or.

Needham (Ilston, co. Leicester; JOHN NEEDHAM, Esq., of Ilston, son of FRANCIS NEEDHAM, who was younger son of THOMAS NEEDHAM, Esq., of Alexton. Visit. Leicester, 1619). Same Arms and Crest, a crescent for diff.

Needham (Sir ROBERT NEEDHAM, knighted by Sir William Russell, Lord Deputy of Ireland, Sept. 1594). Ar. a bend betw. three bucks' heads cabossed ar.

Needham (Earl of Kilmorey). Ar. a bend engr. az. b tw. two bucks' heads cabossed sa. Crest—A demi phœnix i flames ppr. Supporters—Dexter, a horse ar.; sinister, a stag ppr. Motto—Nunc aut nunquam.

Needham (Lenton, co. Nottingham, and The Varteg, co Monmouth). Ar. a bend engr. az. betw. three bucks' heads cabossed sa. Crest—A demi eagle displ. issuing out of flames all ppr. Motto—Soyez ferme.

Needham (Kynoleton, co. Derby). Ar. a bend engr. az. betw. two bucks' heads cabossed sa. a canton or. Crest—A phœnix ppr. charged on the breast with a trefoil slipped or.

Needle-Makers, Company of (London; incorporated 1656). Vert three needles in fesse ar. each ducally crowned or. Crest—Originally a tree ppr., now a Moor's head couped at the shoulders in profile ppr., wreathed about the temples ar. and gu. vested round the shoulder ar. in his ear a pearl. Supporters—Dexter, a man; sinister, a woman, both ppr. each wreathed round the waist with leaves of the last, in the woman's dexter hand a needle ar. The supporters are commonly called Adam and Eve. Motto—"They sewed fig leaves together and made themselves aprons."

Needs (THOMAS NEEDS, gent., of Great Queen Street, London, 1770, m. MARY, dau. of BENJAMIN GRAZEBROOK, Esq., of Bisley, co. Gloucester, by whom he had two daus. his co-heir esses, MARY-ANNE m. MICHAEL GRAZEBROOK, Esq., of Audnam, co. Stafford, d. 1846, leaving issue; and CHARLOTTE, m. 1795, THOMAS VERE Fox, Esq., of London, who d. s. p. 6 Feb. 1797 ; quartered by GRAZEBROOK). Ar. on a bend engr. vert betw. two bucks' heads cabossed sa. attired or, three bezants, a canton erminois.

Neefield, or Nerfield. Ar. a cinquefoil gu. Crest—Two anchors in saltire az.

Neefield, Neefeld, or Neerfield. Ar. three cinquefoils gu.

Neel (Jersey). Gu. semée-de-lis and crosses crosslet alternately or, two pikes in pale embowed and addorsed ar. Crest—A lion's head affrontee ppr. Motto—Nostre roy et nostre foy.

Neele (Prestwood, co. Leicester; FRANCIS NEELE, Esq., of Prestwood. Visit. Leicester, 1619, third in descent from RICHARD NEELE, Judge of Common Pleas, 1 Henry VII., 1485; FRANCIS NEELE, left two daus. his co-heirs: I. m. HALL, of Gratford, co. Lincoln; II. MARY, m. first, EVERARD DIGBY, Esq., of Tilton, and second, SAMPSON ERDESWICK, Esq., of London). Quarterly, 1st and 4th, gu. three greyhounds' heads erased or collared or; 2nd and 3rd, or, a lion ramp. double queued vert.

Neeld (Grittleton House, co. Wilts, bart.). Per pale ar. and az. a lion pass. betw. three greyhounds' heads erased counterchanged. Crest—On a mount vert a wolf's head erased sa. betw. two branches of palm ppr. Motto—Nomen extendere factis.

Nefield, or Nesfield (co. York). Ar. a chev. betw. three mullets sa. Crest—A pillar ar. supported by two lions' paws ppr.

Nefydd Hardd (Lord of Nant Conway, Founder of the VI. Noble Tribe of North Wales and Powys ; from him descended Dr. WILLIAM MORGAN, Bishop of St. Asaph, the translator of the Bible into Welsh). Ar. three spears' heads embrued sa. pointed upwards.

Negus (co. Norfolk). Erm. on a chief nebulée az. three escallops or.

Negus (co. Bedford). Ar. on a chief indented sa. three escallops of the field.

725

Negus (Brome, co. Suffolk). Erm. on a chief nebulée az. three escallops or.

Neham, or Nehun. Chequy ar. and gu. a chief or.

Neil (England). Or, a galley, sails furled and oars in action sa. in chief a dexter hand couped fesseways gu. holding a dagger point downwards az. betw. two crosses crosslet fitchée of the third. Crest—A unicorn's head erased gu.

Neill. Purp. three griffins' heads ar.

Neild (England). Per pale sa. and az. a lion pass. guard. or. Crest—A hand issuing from a cloud, holding a club all ppr.

Neill. See O'NEILL.

Neilson (Corsock, co. Wigtoun). Az. two hammers in saltire or, in the dexter flank a crescent and in base a star ar. Crest—A demi man issuing, holding over his shoulder a hammer all ppr. Motto—Præsto pro patria.

Neilson (Craigcaffie, Scotland). Per chev. ar. and or, in chief two sinister hands couped and erect gu. in base a dagger in pale, point downwards ppr. Crest—A dexter hand holding a lance erect all ppr. Motto—His Regi servitium.

Neilson (Maxwood, Scotland). Same Arms, with a man's heart ppr. in the centre point for diff. Crest—A dexter hand holding a dagger ppr. Motto—Virtute et votis.

Neilson (Craigo, Scotland). Ar. three sinister hands bend sinisterways couped gu. two and one.

Neirford, or Neereford (co. Norfolk). Gu. a lion ramp. erm. (another, the tail queued).

Neke. Ar. a chev. betw. three leopards' faces gu. Crest—A lion's gamb az. holding a lozenge in pale ar. charged with a cross crosslet sa.

Nele (Reg. Ulster's Office). Ar. two bars gu. on a chief of the last a lion pass. of the first.

Nele. Gu. two fishes addorsed ar.

Nelme. Az. a saltire or, on a chief of the last a cross crosslet fitchée gu. Crest—Out of a ducal coronet or, a demi dragon gold, wings inverted az. holding betw. the claws a cross crosslet fitchée gu.

Nelson (Earl Nelson). Or, a cross flory sa. a bend gu. surmounted by another engr. of the field, charged with three bombs fired ppr. on a chief (of honourable augmentation) undulated ar. waves of the sea, from which a palm tree issuant betw. a disabled ship on the dexter, and a battery in ruins on the sinister all ppr. Crests—On the dexter (as a crest of honourable augmentation), on a naval crown or, the chelengk, or plume of triumph, presented to HORATIO, Viscount Nelson, by the Grand Signior, or Sultan, Selim III.; and on the sinister the family crest, viz., on a wreath of the colours, upon waves of the sea, the stern of a Spanish man-of war all ppr., thereon inscribed "San Joseff." Supporters—Dexter, a sailor armed with a cutlass and a pair of pistols in his belt ppr. the right hand supporting a staff, thereon hoisted a commodore's flag gu. and in his left a palm branch ppr.; sinister, a lion ramp. reguard. in his mouth two broken flag-staffs ppr. flowing from one a Spanish flag or and gu. and from the other a tri-coloured flag, in his dexter paw a palm branch ppr. Motto—Palmam qui meruit ferat.

Nelson (Chaddleworth, co. Berks, 1576; ANNE, eldest dau. and co-heir of THOMAS NELSON, Esq., of Chaddleworth, m. RICHARD WALTER, Esq., her son, RICHARD WALTER, succeeding, on the decease of his aunts, to his grandfather's property, assumed the name and arms of NELSON, but dying unm. in 1805, he devised the Chaddleworth estate to the youngest son of his only sister, MARY WALTER, by her husband, JOHN KERR, Esq., GEORGE KERR, Esq., who assumed the additional name and arms of NELSON). Paly of six ar. and gu. a bend vairé or and sa.

Nelson (Mandesley and Fairhurst, co. Lancaster, 1664). Ar. a cross flory sa. over all a bend gu.

Nelson (Lord Mayor of London, 1766). Gu. on a bend az. a cross formée ar.

Nelson (Bedale, co. York; ABRAHAM NELSON, Esq., of Gray's Inn, one of the Cursitors in Chancery, and a Gentleman of the Privy Chamber to Charles II., son of WILLIAM NELSON, gent., of Chancery Lane, also one of the Cursitors in Chancery, and grandson of WILLIAM NELSON, gent., of Bedale. Visit. Middlesex, 1663). Per pale ar. and sa. a chev. betw. three fleurs-de-lis counterchanged.

Nelson (Plymouth Dock). Same Arms. Crest—A dexter arm in armour, couped and erect ppr. holding a fleur-de-lis, as in the arms.

Nelson (Secretary of the Navy Office, d. 1820). Per chev. ar. and or, in chief two sinister hands couped at the wrist gu. and in base a sword in pale ppr. point downwards, hilt and pommel or. Crest—A dexter arm erect holding a tilting spear all ppr.

Nel.on. Same Arms. Crest—A dexter hand erect ppr. the

first finger and thumb pointing to a crescent or, the others clenched.

Nelson (Grimston, co. York). Per pale ar. and sa. a chev. betw. three fleurs-de-lis all counterchanged. *Crest*—A cubit arm quarterly ar. and sa. holding in the hand ppr. a fleur-de-lis per pale ar. and sa.

Nelson. Or, a cross patonce sa. betw. four mullets gu. a bendlet of the last. *Crest*—A lion's gamb erect ppr. holding an escutcheon sa. thereon a cross patonce or.

Nelson, or Nealson (THOMAS NELSON, or NEALSON, Clerk of the Council Chamber of Munster; impalement Fun. Ent. Ulster's Office, 1632, of his son-in-law, MICHAEL BROWNE, Sheriff of Dublin). Quarterly, ar. and sa. three fleurs-de-lis counterchanged.

Nelson, New Zealand, See of. Or, a calvary cross az. on a canton of the second three stars of six points ar.

Nelson (Edinburgh, 1872). Ar. two sinister hands couped gu. in chief, and a dagger, point downwards, hilted and pommelled or, in base. *Crest*—A dexter arm in armour embowed ppr. the hand grasping a dagger erect also ppr. hilted and pommelled or. *Motto*—Virtute et votis.

Nelson (Edinburgh, 1872). As the last, within a bordure az. Same *Crest* and *Motto.*

Nelston (Mawdisley, co. Lancaster, 1587). Or, a cross flory sa. a bendlet gu.

Nelthorpe (Gray's Inn, co. Middlesex, and Sealby, co. Lincoln, bart., extinct). Ar. on a pale sa. a sword erect of the first, pommel and hilt or. *Crest*—Out of clouds an arm couped ppr. lying fesseways, holding in the hand a sword erect ar. pommel and hilt or.

Nelthorpe (Leggesby, co. Lincoln). Same *Arms* and *Crest.*

Nemarch. Gu. a fesse engr. or.

Nemarke, or Newmarke. Az. three bars gemel ar. as many lions' heads erased in chief of the last.

Nembhard, or Nemphartz (from the German Nemp and Hartz, *i.e.,* a stealer of hearts). Ar. a chev. gu. betw. three human hearts ppr. *Crest*—A demi lamb salient, bearing over the dexter shoulder the holy banner of the cross all ppr. *Motto*—Pax potior bello.

Nemle. Gu. a fesse dancettée ar. a border indented of the last.

Nemle. Paly of six or and az. on a chief gu. three escallops of the second.

Nepean (Botherhampton, co. Dorset, bart.). Gu. a fesse wavy erminois betw. three mullets ar. *Crest*—On a mount vert a goat pass. sa. charged on the side with two erm. spots in fesse or, collared and horned gold. *Motto*—Respice.

Nerberye. Ar. a bend sa. on a chief gu. two barrulets of the first.

Nerborough, or Newborough (co. Wilts). Or, three bends az. a border gu.

Nerborough. Erm. a fesse chequy or and az. on a chief sa. three roses ar. seeded gu.

Nerbury (co. Derby). Ar. a bend sa. on a chief gu. two bars or. *Crest*—Three organ pipes, two in saltire and one in pale or, banded with leaves vert.

Nerbury (co. Derby). Same *Arms,* a border vairé or and gu.

Nereford (co. Norfolk; ROBERT DE NEREFORD was Governor of Dover Castle, 1 Henry III., A.D. 1216). Gu. a lion ramp. erm.

Nereford (*Baron Nereford;* WILLIAM DE NEREFORD, son of the Governor of Dover Castle, was summoned to Parliament 1297; his line failed with his grandson, Sir JOHN DE NEREFORD, who fell in the wars in France 38 Edward III., leaving an only dau., MARY DE NEREFORD, who *d. s. p.*). Gu. a lion ramp. erm.

Nermont, or Nernewte. Gu. a lion ramp. ar. a border gobony of the last and sa. (another, the lion or).

Nerncrote. Sa. a lion ramp. ar. a border gobony of the second and first.

Neroys (co. Chester). Gu. a fesse ar. in chief three plates.

Nersfield. Ar. three cinquefoils gu.

Nertost (co. Essex, *temp.* Edward I.). Or, a lion ramp. sa.

Nesfield. See NEFIELD.

Nesham (Stockton, co. Durham). Az. on a fess ar. three crosses crosslet gu. *Crest*—A demi lion ramp. ppr. holding in the dexter paw a cross crosslet gu. *Motto*—Spes salus decus.

Netby (Netby, co. Lancaster). Sa. a chev. ar. betw. two escallops in chief and a boar's head in base of the second. *Crest*—A lion's paw holding a bird-bolt sa.

Nethercoat (Moulton Grange, co. Northampton). Per pale or and ar. on a chev. az. betw. three boars' heads sa. three bezants. *Crest*—A wolf's head erased.

726

Nethercoats (co. Lincoln). Erm. a bend wavy gu. a chief az.

Nethermill (co. Warwick). Ar. a chev. betw. three crescents az.

Nethersall, Nethersole, or Neithershall (Wingham Would, co. Kent; granted 10 May, 1578). Per pale gu. and az. three griffins segreant or. *Crest*—On a dexter arm embowed in armour ppr. a scarf flotant vert, holding within the gauntlet a broken tilting-spear or.

Netter. Or, a tower triple-towered gu. a chief of the second. *Crest*—A unicorn's head erased gu. ducally gorged, armed, and maned or.

Netterville (*Viscount Netterville*). Ar. a cross gu. fretty or. *Crest*—A demi lion ramp. gu. bezantée. *Supporters*—Dexter, a sea horse per fesse gu. and ppr. mane, legs, fins, and tip of the tail or; sinister, a lion guard. gu. bezantée. *Motto*—Cruci dum spiro spero.

Netterville (exemplified to JOSHUA JAMES McEVOY, Esq., J.P., second son of the late JAMES McEVOY, Esq., of Tobertinan, co. Meath, and Frankfort, co. Longford, and to his wife, Hon. MARY NETTERVILLE, dau. and co-heiress of JAMES, seventh *Viscount Netterville,* on their assuming, by royal licence, 1865, the surname of NETTERVILLE, in lieu of that of McEvoy). Quarterly, 1st and 4th, ar. a cross gu. fretty or, in the 1st quarter a lozenge of the second for diff., for NETTERVILLE; 2nd and 3rd, per fess az. and per pale or and erm. a fess gu. issuant therefrom a demi lion ar. in the dexter base a dexter hand couped at the wrist of the fourth, for McEvoy. *Crests*—1st, NETTERVILLE: A demi lion ramp. guard. gu. bezantée and charged with a lozenge or, for diff.. 2nd, McEvoy: A cubit arm erect, vested gu. cuffed erminois, in the hand a sword ppr. *Motto*—Cruci dum spiro fido.

Netterville (Castletown, co. Meath; Fun. Ent. Ulster's Office, 1633, ALSON, dau. of JOHN NETTERVILLE, Esq., of Castletown, and wife of Sir WALTER TALBOT, Bart., of Carton). Ar. a cross gu. fretty or, a crescent for diff.

Nettlefold. Per pale and per saltire erm. and or, a water bouget sa. *Crest*—A water bouget gu.

Nettles (Nettleville and Beareforest, co. Cork, and Toureen, co. Waterford; first settled in Ireland about 1620). Or, a chev. gu. betw. three nettle leaves ppr. *Crest*—A stag statant under a tree ppr. *Motto*—Nemo me impune lacessit.

Nettleship (Grocers' Hall). Az. on a fesse betw. three fleurs-de-lis or, a lion pass. gu. betw. two buckles of the field. *Crest*—A lion pass. per pale erm. and az. holding in the dexter paw a buckle or.

Nettleship. Per pale or and sa. six mascles counterchanged. *Crest*—A demi bear ramp. ar. muzzled or.

Nettleship. Same *Arms.* *Crest*—A dexter hand ppr. holding a nettle branch vert.

Nettleton (Nettleton, co. York). Sa. two serpents entwined in saltire ar. the heads respecting each other.

Nettleton (Thornhill Lees, co. York; York Peds. Ulster's Office). Az. two snakes in pale knotted and entwined ar. the heads respecting each other.

Nettleton (impalement Fun. Ent. Ulster's Office, 1640, Sir RICHARD OSBALDESTON, Attorney-General for Ireland, whose second wife was MARY, dau. of THOMAS NETTLE-TON, Esq., of Nettleton Hall, co. York). Az. two snakes in pale, knotted and entwined vert, the heads respecting each other.

Nettleton (Fun. Ent. Ulster's Office, 1640, GEORGE NETTLE-TON, second son of THOMAS NETTLETON, Esq., of Thornhill Lees, co. York). Same *Arms* as the last, with a crescent for diff.

Netwold (co. Kent). Erm. a cross engr. gu. in dexter chief a wolf's head erased of the second.

Neunchan (cos. Sussex and Surrey). Ar a cross gu. a bend az.

Neve. Gu. a trout in bend ar.

Neve (Rev. FREDERICK NEVE, Vicar of Old Warden, co. Bedford, son of the late Dr. TIMOTHY NEVE, D.D.). Ar. on a cross az. five fleurs-de-lis of the field. *Crest*—Out of a ducal coronet or, a lily ar. stalked and leaved vert, bladed and seeded gold. *Motto*—Aιεν αυιενειν.

Neve, Le (Aslactum and Tivetishall, co. Norfolk, and London; originally of France). Ar. on a cross sa. five fleurs-de-lis of the field. *Crest*—Out of a ducal coronet or, a lily ar. leaved vert.

Nevele. Gu. a fesse dancettée ar. in chief three moles or.

Nevers (co. Norfolk). Vairé ar. and gu.

Nevers. Ar. two bars gu. in chief three crescents of the second.

Nevesfeld, or Nevestfeld. Vert an eagle displ. or membered sa.

Nevill, (NEVILE or NEVILLE Raby, co. Durham; one of the most illustrious families in European genealogy. RANULPH DE NEVILL, of Raby, was summoned to Parliament as a baron, 8 June, 1294, and his great-grandson, RALPH DE NEVILL, fourth *Lord Nevill,* of Baby, was created *Earl of Westmorland,* 1397). Gu. a saltire ar.

Nevill (*Earl of Westmorland;* RALPH DE NEVILL, fourth *Lord Nevill,* of Raby, was created *Earl of Westmorland* 1397; title attainted 13 Elizabeth, A.D. 1545). Same *Arms* as last. *Crest*—Out of a ducal coronet or, a bull's head pied. The seal of RALPH, fourth *Lord Nevill,* of Raby, and first *Earl of Westmorland,* exhibits the shield, Gu. a saltire ar. the crest of the pied bull, and for supporters two greyhounds collared.

Nevill (*Earl of Warwick and Salisbury;* Sir RICHARD NEVILL, K.G., eldest son of RALPH, first *Earl of Westmorland,* by his second wife, JOAN DE BEAUFORT, dau. of JOHN OF GAUNT, *Duke of Lancaster,* m. Lady ALICE MONTACUTE, dau. and heiress of THOMAS, fourth *Earl of Salisbury,* and had the Earldom of *Salisbury* renewed in his person; his son and heir, RICHARD, second *Earl of Salisbury,* K.G., who m. Lady ANNE BEAUCHAMP, heiress of her niece, ANNE, *Countess of Warwick,* thenceforward was known as *Earl of Warwick.* This was the famous King Maker: his seal as *Earl of Warwick,* attached to a deed, 4 Edward IV., during the lifetime of his father, shows a quartered shield: 1st grand quarter, BEAUCHAMP and CLARE quarterly; 2nd grand quarter, MONTACUTE and MONTHERMER quarterly; 3rd grand quarter, NEVILL, differenced by a label of three points; 4th grand quarter, WARWICK and LE DESPENCER. *Supporters*—Dexter, a bear muzzled and chained; sinister, a griffin. *Crests*—1st: Out of a ducal coronet a swan's head and neck; 2nd: On a ducal coronet a griffin sejant with this legend, "Sigillum ricardi nevill comitis warrewici domini de bergevenny." The daus. and co-heirs of RICHARD NEVILL, *Earl of Warwick,* the King Maker, were ISABEL, wife of GEORGE PLANTAGENET, *Duke of Clarence,* and ANNE, m. first, EDWARD, *Prince of Wales,* and secondly, RICHARD, *Duke of Gloucester,* afterwards Richard III.). Same *Arms* and *Crest.*

Nevill (*Earl of Northumberland, Marquess of Montacute,* and *Duke of Bedford*). Gu. a saltire ar. a label gobony ar. and az. a crescent for diff.

Nevill (*Baron Fauconberg* and *Earl of Kent,* earldom extinct, 1463; Sir WILLIAM NEVILL, Knt., second son of RALPH, first *Earl of Westmorland,* by JOAN DE BEAUFORT, his second wife, m. JOAN DE FAUCONBERG, and was summoned to Parliament, *jure uxoris,* 1429). Gu. a saltire ar. a mullet sa. for diff.

Nevill (*Baron Latimer;* Sir GEORGE NEVILL, third son of RALPH, first *Earl of Westmorland,* by JOAN DE BEAUFORT, his second wife, was summoned to Parliament as *Baron Latimer,* 1432, title in abeyance). Gu. a saltire ar. an annulet sa. for diff.

Nevill (*Lord Bergavenny, Earl* and *Marquess of Abergavenny;* EDWARD NEVILL, fourth son of RALPH, first *Earl of Westmorland,* by JOAN BEAUFORT, his second wife, m. Lady ELIZABETH BEAUCHAMP, of Bergavenny, and was summoned to Parliament as *Baron Bergavenny* in 1450; the fifteenth Baron was created *Earl of Abergavenny* 1784, and the fifth Earl, *Marquess of Abergavenny,* 1876). Quarterly, 1st and 4th, gu. on a saltire ar. a rose of the field barbed and seeded ppr. for NEVILL, of Raby (the red rose used for diff. is commemorative of the marriage of RALPH, first *Earl of Westmorland,* with JOAN, dau. of JOHN OF GAUNT, *Duke of Lancaster*); 2nd and 3rd, or, fretty gu. on a canton, per pale erm. and gold, a galley sa., for NEVILLE, of Bulmer. *Crest*—A bull ar. pied sa. armed gold, and charged on the neck with a rose barbed and seeded ppr. *Supporters* — Two bulls ar. pied sa., armed, unguled, collared and chained, and at the end of the chain two staples or. *Badges*—On the dexter, a rose gu. seeded or, barbed vert; on the sinister, a portcullis or. *Motto*—Ne vile velis.

Nevill (Bentworth, Hants; Fun. Ent. Ulster's Office, 1640, of the eldest son of FRANCIS NEVILL, the second son of the fifth *Lord Bergavenny*). Same *Arms. Crest,* and *Motto.*

Nevill (Mereworth, co. Kent; Sir THOMAS NEVILL, Knt., of Mereworth, Secretary of State to Henry VIII., and afterwards Speaker of the House of Commons, younger son of GEORGE, second *Lord Bergavenny,* left an only dau. and heiress, MARGARET, m. Sir ROBERT SOUTHWELL, Master of the Rolls). His *Arms* appear on a brass in Mereworth Church, viz., Quarterly, 1st, gu. a saltire ar. thereon a red rose; 2nd, chequy or and az.; 3rd, quarterly, 1st and 4th, two chevronels gu., 2nd and 3rd, quarterly, ar. and gu., in the 2nd and 3rd quarters, a fret or, over all a bend sa.; 4th, gu. on a fess betw. six cross crosslets or, a crescent sa.

727

Nevill (*Baron Furnival;* THOMAS NEVILL, brother of RALPH, first *Earl of Westmorland,* m. JOANE, dau. and heiress of WILLIAM DE FURNIVAL, fourth *Lord Furnival,* and was summoned to Parliament 1383; co-heirs of the barony, now in abeyance, are the Lords Stourton and Petre). Gu. a saltire ar. differenced by a martlet sa.

Nevill (Ragnall, afterwards Grove, co. Nottingham, bart., extinct 1686; descended from the marriage of GEORGE NEVILL, Esq., of Ragnall, who m. BARBARA, sister and co-heir of Sir JOHN HERCY, Knt., of Grove. Visit. Notts, 1614. The last male heir in the direct line, EDWARD NEVILL, Esq., of Grove, was created a bart. in 1674, but *d. s. p.* 1686). Gu. a saltire ar. *Crests*—1st: Out of a ducal coronet a bull's head pied; 2nd: On a chapeau gu. turned up erm. a ship with sails furled or, of Grove. *Motto*—Ne vile.

Nevill, or Nevile (Thorney, co. Nottingham; descended from GEORGE NEVILL, Esq., of Thorney, second son of GEORGE NEVILL, Esq., of Grove, by BARBARA HERCY, his wife). Quarterly, 1st and 4th, gu. a saltire ar., for the Lords of Raby; 2nd and 3rd, or, fretty gu. on a canton per pale erm. and or, a ship with sails furled sa. *Crests and Motto,* same as NEVILL, of Grove.

Nevill, or Nevile (Wellingore, co. Lincoln; a branch of NEVILL, of Thorney; CHRISTOPHER HENRY NEVILL, of Wellingore, took the surname of NOEL, his only dau. and heir, SOPHIA MARY, m. Col. F. W. ALLIX, of Willoughby Hall, co. Lincoln). Same *Arms* and *Crest.*

Nevill (Walcot and Wellingore; descended from the Rev. HENRY NEVILL, Rector of Cottesmore, second son of CHRISTOPHER NEVILL, Esq., of Wellingore). Same *Arms* and *Crest.*

Nevill, or Nevile (Stubton, co. Notts). Same *Arms* and *Crest.*

Nevill (Chevet, co. York; granted 1513). Ar. a saltire gu. a mullet and label of three points vert. *Crest*—A greyhound's head erased or, charged on the neck with a label of three points vert, betw. as many pellets, one and two

Nevill (Badsworth, co. York; derived from DYONISIUS, fifth son of GEORGE NEVILL, Esq., of Grove, by BARBARA HERCY, his wife). Same *Arms,* &c., as NEVILL, of Grove.

Nevill (Holt, co. Leicester; Sir THOMAS NEVILL, Knt., of Holt, living 1564, ninth in descent from SOLOMON NEVILL, Lord of Holt, second son of GEOFFREY NEVILL, of Raby, co. Durham, and brother of ROBERT NEVILL, Lord of Raby, ancestor of the extinct *Earls of Westmorland* and the *Marquis of Abergavenny.* Visit. Leicester, 1619). Gu. a saltire erm., quartering, Or, fretty gu. on a canton per pale ar. and erm. a lymphad sa. *Crest*—Out of a ducal coronet or, a bull's head erm. armed of the first.

Nevill (Billingbeare, co. Berks, and Kent. Same *Arms. Crest*—A bull pass. pied, collared, lined, and armed or.

Nevill (co. Essex). Sa. a lion ramp. ar. guttée de sang. *Crest*—A demi lion ramp. ar. guttée de sang, holding a sword of the first erect, hilt and pommel or.

Nevill (cos. Essex and Nottingham). Az. a lion ramp. or.

Nevill (cos. Huntingdon and Lincoln). Or, a fesse dancettée gu. a bend sa.

Nevill (Llangenneck Park, co. Carmarthen). Gu. on a saltire indented or, a crescent betw. four roses of the field barbed and seeded ppr. *Crest*—A pied bull armed and gorged with a collar and line reflexed over the back or, and supporting with the dexter foot an escutcheon of the last, charged with an anchor erect sa.

Nevill (Reresby, co. Leicester). Erm. a chief indented az.

Nevill (co. Leicester). Gu. four fusils in fesse or, a border of the last; another, Gu. crusily fitchée, three leopards' faces jessant-de-lis ar. (another, or); another, Gu. a fesse indented ar.; another, Gu. a fess dancettée ar in chief three mullets or.

Nevill (Rolleston, co. Notts). Gu. a saltire erm.

Nevill (Scotton, co. Lincoln). Gu. three fusils in fesse ar. a border engr. or; another, or, a bend indented gu. a chief vert. *Crest*—A tiger sejant erm.

Nevill (Faldingworth, co. Lincoln). Or, a chief indented vert, a bend gu.

Nevill (co. Nottingham). Az. three bustards rising or.

Nevill (Shenstone Park, co. Stafford). Gu. on a saltire ar. a crescent sa. *Crest*—A griffin pass. or, charged on the breast with a crescent sa.

Nevill (co. Sussex). Gu. two trumpets in saltire betw. nine crosses crosslet fitchée or.

Nevill (Thornton Brigg, co. York). Gu. on a saltire ar. a mullet pierced sa.

Nevill (Ven. HENRY RALPH NEVILL, M.A., Archdeacon of Norfolk). Gu. on a saltire engr or. a crescent betw. four roses of the field. *Crest*—A bull collared and line reflexed over the back, resting dexter foot on an escutcheon charged with an anchor. *Motto*—Ne vile velis.

Nevill. Gu. fretty or, a quarter per pale erm. and of the second.

Nevill. Gu. a fret of six ar. over all a bend vairé or and of the first.

Nevill. Or, fretty gu. a canton erm. (another, the canton per pale erm. and of the first charged with a slip sa.; another, has the canton erm. charged with a buglehorn sa.).

Nevill. Gu. a fesse dancettée ar. in chief two (another, three) mullets or; another, Ar. a fesse dancettée sa.; another, Or, five lozenges in fesse gu.; another, Four lozenges sa. a border of the last bezantée.

Nevill. Az. two bars gemelles ar. a chief of the last; another, Gu. five mascles in fesse ar. a border engr. or; another, Gu. crusily ar. three fleurs-de-lis of the last; another, Az. three roses ar. (another, cinquefoils); another, Gu. three leopards' faces ar.; another, Or, on a fesse dancettée gu. a chev. sa.; another, Erm. a chief indented sa.; another, Paly of six or and az. on a chief gu. three escallops ar.

Nevill (Feudal *Baron of Rossgarland*, co. Wexford; THOMAS NYVELL was of Old Ross, same co. 1303; SIMON NEVILL, *Baron of Rossgarland*, was fined 38 Edward III., 1363, for not attending with men, arms, and horses, at the Duffrey in that co. in obedience to his summons; arms Reg. Ulster's Office. DAVID NEVILL, *Baron of Rossgarland*, was attainted *temp.* Edward VI.). Barry of four ar. and az. on a chief gu. a saltire of the first.

Nevill (Nevill's Court, Tullacanna, Ambrosetown, New Ross, &c., co. Wexford, branches of Rossgarland). Same *Arms.*

Nevill (Phornauts, or Furness, co. Kildare; descended from RICHARD NEVILLE, Esq., of Great Phremagin, in same co. *m.* MARGARET, dau. of Sir WILLIAM USHER, Knt. of Bridgefoot Street, Dublin, and *d.* 13 Sept. 1682; *Fun. Ent.* Ulster's Office; RICHARD's eldest son, also named RICHARD, left an only dau. and heir, MARY, wife of Colonel RICHARD EDWARD JONES, who took the name of NEVILLE, and was grandfather of the late RICHARD NEVILLE, Esq., of Furness, M.P., whose eldest dau. and co-heir, HENRIETTA, *m.* first, EDWARD DERING, Esq., and secondly, Sir WILLIAM GEARY, Bart.). Same *Arms* as NEVILL, feudal Baron of Rossgarland, co. Wexford.

Nevill (Annamult and Marymount, co. Kilkenny; a branch of NEVILL, of Furness). Same *Arms* as NEVILL, of Furness.

Nevill (granted by Roberts, Ulster, 1644, to JOHN NEVILL, Surgeon-Major of the regiment under command of PHILIP, *Earl of Leicester*). Or, on a bend gu. a harp gold, on a chief of the second a saltire of the first. *Crest*—A greyhound's head erased sa. collared gu. studded with harps or.

Nevill (impalement *Fun. Ent.* Ulster's Office, WILLIAM, Sir JOHN BINGLEY, a Privy Councillor in Ireland). Gu. on a saltire ar. a rose of the first.

Nevill (*Fun. Ent.* Ulster's Office, RICHARD NEVILL, of Dublin, buried in St. Werburgh's Church, 7 May, 1617). Barry of four ar. and sa. on a chief gu. a saltire of the first.

Neville (*Baron Braybrooke*; Quarterly, 1st and 4th, sa. a griffin segreant ar. beaked and forelegged or, for GRIFFIN; 2nd and 3rd, gu. on a saltire ar. a rose of the field seeded and barbed ppr., for NEVILLE. *Crests*—1st, GRIFFIN: A talbot's head erased sa.; 2nd, NEVILLE: A bull statant ar. spotted of a liver colour, collared and chained or. *Supporters*—Two lions ramp. reguard. ar. maned and tufted sa. gorged with a chaplet of olive vert. *Motto*—Ne vile velis.

Neville. Gu. semée of crosses crosslet ar. three leopards' faces jessant-de-lis of the last. *Crest*—Out of a cloud a hand holding up a wheat-sheaf by the band all ppr.

Neville (Ileacham Hall, co. Norfolk. See ROLFE). Gu. five fusils conjoined in fesse or, each charged with an erm. spot, a border nebulée ar. *Crest*—A mount vert, thereon issuant out of a crescent gu. a rose ar. slipped vert.

Neville (Haselour, co. Stafford). Gu. on a saltire ar. a rose of the first. *Crest*—Out of a ducal coronet or, a bull's head pled ppr. *Motto*—Ne vile velis.

Neville (Bawnmore House, co. Kilkenny). Gu. a saltire ar. *Crest*—Out of a ducal coronet or, a bull's head pied, attired of the first. *Motto*—Ne vile velis.

Nevins (confirmed to WILLIS NEVINS, Esq., son of Rev. WILLIAM NEVINS, Rector of Miningsbye, co. Lincoln, and grandson of JOHN JOWITT NEVINS, Esq., of Clevedale, co. Gloucester, a native of Ireland, and their descendants). Az. on a fess betw. an increscent and a decrescent in chief and in base a palm branch ar. a crescent of the first. *Crest*—On a mount a palm branch vert. *Motto*—Nil desperandum.

Nevinson, or Nevison (Estrey, co. Kent; granted 1570). Ar. a chev. betw. three eagles displ. az. beaked and legged gu. *Crest*—A wolf pass. ar. pellettée, collared, lined, and ringed or.

Nevoy (that Ilk). Sa. a chevalier armed at all points, on horseback, brandishing a scymitar ar.

Nevoy (Sir DAVID NEVOY, a Lord of Session in Scotland). Same *Arms*, a bordure ar. *Crest*—A pegasus ppr. *Motto*—Marte et arte.

New. Per saltire or and gu. four chaplets counterchanged. *Crest*—A dexter arm ppr. vested per chev. or and gu. holding a roll of parchment ar.

Newall (Hare Hill, and Town House, Littleborough, Rochdale, co. Lancaster). Per pale gu. and az. three covered cups within an orle or, quartering KYRKESHAH: Or, on a chief per pale gu. and sa. three bezants; and LITHOLMES : Sa. a lion ramp. or, semée of caltraps sa. *Crest*—A Saracen's head affrontée ppr. wreathed round the temples or and gu. suspended from the mouth by a ribbon of the last a shield paly indented of four also or and gu.

Newall. Az. three plates, on each an erm. spot sa. *Crest*—A cross crosslet fitchée az.

Newall (Barskeoch, co. Wigtoun, 1677). Per saltire gu. and or, three bustards rising counterchanged. *Crest*—A bustard holding in the foot a writing pen ppr. *Motto*—Diligentia ditat.

Newark, Town of (co. Nottingham; granted by Dethick, Garter, 1561). Barry wavy of six ar. and az. on a chief gu. a peacock in pride ppr. betw. a fleur-de-lis on the dexter and a lion pass. guard. on the sinister or. *Crest*—A sea gull ppr. holding in the beak an eel ar. *Supporters*—On the dexter an otter, on the sinister a beaver.

Newarke (Akham, co. York). Az. two bars gemelle ar. in chief three lions' heads erased of the last (another, or). *Crest*—A savage's head in profile, looking upright ppr.

Newarke (co. York). Ar. (another, erm.) three saltires engr. sa. two and one.

Newarke. Az. three lions' heads erased in fesse betw. two bars gemelles ar.; another, Az. a fesse erm. betw. three leopards' faces per pale or and ar.; another, Erm. three saltires engr. ermines; another, Barry of eight ar. and az. on a chief of the second three lions' heads erased of the first; another, Sa. three saltires engr. ar.

Newbald. Barry of six ar. and az.; another, Az. two bends (another, bars) ar. a chief of the last.

Newbery. Sa. three pallets erm. on a canton ar. a demi lion az. *Crest*—A dexter arm ppr. vested az. cuffed or, holding a truncheon gu. tipped gold.

Newbery (London). Ar. three bars az. a chief gu. *Crest*—A Moor's head in profile ppr.

Newbery (Reg. Ulster's Office). Ar. a chev. gu. betw. three bunches of strawberries slipped ppr.

Newbigging (Dr. WILLIAM NEWBIGGIN, Scotland, 1829). Ar. on a fess gu. three escallops of the first. *Crest*—An eagle rising ppr. *Motto*—I'll try.

Newbold, or Newbald (co. Derby, and London). Az. two bends ar. a chief of the last. *Crest*—A cross flory fitchée az.

Newbold (co. York). Ar. three boars pass. in pale sa. *Crest*—A boar's head and neck couped, holding in the mouth a broken spear in bend ppr.

Newbold. Ar. three griffins' heads erased in fesse gu.

Newbold. Az. two bars ar. a chief of the last.

Newborough, Baron. See WYNN.

Newborough (London). Erm. a fesse chequy or and az. on a chief sa. three roses ar. barbed of the second.

Newborougn (Berkeley, co. Somerset, and co. Wilts). Or, three bends az. a border engr. gu.

Newborough (co. Warwick). Lozengy or and az. a border gu. bezantée.

Newborough. Gu. a cinquefoil erm.; another, Gu. a chief erm.; another, Az. three bars or, a border gu.; another, Bendy of six or and az. a border gu.

Newborough. Or, a bendlet ar. a border engr. gu. *Crest*—A blackamoor's head sidefaced sa.

Newbottle, Newbottell, or Newbottel. Per fesse fesse ar. and gu. an eagle displ. with two heads counterchanged.

Newburgh, Countess of. See GIUSTINIANI.

Newburgh. See LIVINGSTONE.

Newburgh (co. Dorset). Bendy of eight or and a... a bordure engr. gu.

Newburgh Abbey (co. York). Gu. a lion ramp. or, surmounted by a pilgrim's crutch in bend sinister of the last.

Newburgh (*Earl of Warwick*, extinct 1267; HENRY DE NEWBURGH, was so created by William I.; THOMAS, sixth

Earl of Warwick, *d. s. p.* 1242, leaving his sister Lady MARGERY, wife of JOHN MARESCHAL, his heir, who *d. s. p.* 1243, WILLIAM MAUDUIT, son of WILLIAM, *Baron of Hanslape*, by ALICE DE NEWBURGH, his wife, dau. of WALERAN, *Earl of Warwick*, was summoned to attend the King at Worcester, as *Earl of Warwick*, 47 Henry III., but *d. s. p.* 1267, leaving his sister his heir, viz., ISABEL MAUDUIT, wife of WILLIAM BEAUCHAMP, of Elmeley, and thus conveyed the earldom first to that family). Lozengy or and az. on a border gu. eight plates. *Arms* of MAUDUIT—Ar. two bars gu.

Newburgh (quartered by REGINALD, Cardinal POLE; arms in a coat in Magdalen College, Oxford. Visit. Oxon, 1566). Chequy ar. and az. a chev. erm.

Newburgh (Warmwell and Berkeley, co. Somerset). Or, three bendlets az. a border gu.

Newburgh. Bendy of six or and az. a border engr. gu.

Newbury (co. Berks). Sa. three palets erm. on a canton ar. a lion ramp. az. *Crest*—A demi eagle displ. or.

Newbury, Town of (co. Berks). The Corporation seal is —On a mount a castle with three domed towers on each a pennon. *Legend*—Burgus Newberie.

Newby (Northfenton, co. York). Ar. two stilts in saltire sa. garnished or.

Newby (JOHN DE NEWBY, *temp.* Richard II.). Ar. a fess betw. three roses gu. *Crest*—An arm in armour, brandishing a sword all ppr.

Newby (Hooton, co. York). Ar. a chev. betw. three crosses pattée gu.

Newcastle, Duke of. See CLINTON.

Newcastle-upon-Tyne, Town of. Gu. three towers triple-towered ar. *Crest*—A tower ar. thereon a demi lion issuant ramp. guard. or, holding a split banner gu. ensigned with the arms of St. George. *Supporters*—Two sea-horses ar. crined and finned or. *Motto*—Fortiter defendit triumphans.

Newce (Haddam, Bradborne, and Raynthorp Hall, co. Herts). Sa. two palets ar. on a canton erm. a mascle gu. *Crest*—On a mount vert a garb or, banded gu.

Newce (Much-Haddam, co. Herts, and Ditchingham, co. Norfolk; granted 1575). Sa. two palets ar. a canton erm. *Crest*—On a mount vert a garb or.

Newce, or Newes (co. Oxford). Gyronny of four gu. and or, as many chaplets counterchanged.

Newce (Serjeant-at-Arms of Munster, Fun. Ent. Ulster's Office, 1625, of his dau., the wife of PETER PALMER, a judge of Common Pleas). Paly of four ar. and sa. a canton erm.

Newce, or Nuce (Newmarket, co. Cork; Fun. Ent. Ulster's Office, 1634, Captain SAMUEL NEWCE, or NUCE). Sa. two palets ar. a canton erm. a martlet for diff.

New-College (Oxford; founded in 1379 by WILLIAM DE WYKEHAM, Bishop of Winchester and Lord Chancellor of England). Ar. two chevronels sa. betw. three roses gu. seeded or, barbed vert, impaled with the arms of the see, encircled with the Garter, and ensigned with an episcopal mitre, in allusion to the Bishops of Winchester always being prelates of the order of the Garter. *Motto*—Manners makyth man.

Newcom (co. Chester). Ar. a cross flory sa.

Newcombe (Stanton Drew and Exeter, co. Devon. Visit. 1620). Ar. a fesse embattled betw. two escallops in pale sa. *Crest*—A demi horse ar. gorged with a chaplet vert. *Another Crest*—On a mural coronet or, a falcon rising ppr.

Newcome (Upper Wimpole Street, London). Ar. a fesse embattled sa. betw. two escallops in pale of the last. *Crest*—Out of a mural coronet or, a Cornish chough, wings extended ppr.

Newcome (Shenley, co. Herts). Ar. a lion's head erased sa. betw. three crescents gu. *Crest*—A lion's gamb erect and erased gu. armed gu.

Newcombe (Reg. Ulster's Office). Ar. a fess embattled betw. two escallops sa. *Crest*—On a mural crown or, a chough, wings displ. sa.

Newcomen (Saltfleetby, co. Lincoln; descended from HUGH NEWCOMEN, of that place, living *temp.* Richard I.). Ar. a lion's head erased sa. langued gu. betw. three crescents of the last. *Crest*—A lion's gamb erased and erect sa. armed gu.

Newcomen (Nether Taynton, co. Lincoln; RICHARD NEWCOMEN, son of WILLIAM NEWCOMEN, of Soleby, second son of MARTIN NEWCOMEN, of Saltfleetby, *temp.* Henry VII., *m.* MARGARET, dau. and heir of THOMAS MAYDENWELL, of Nether Taynton). Same *Arms* and *Crest*.

Newcomen (Renagh, co. Longford, bart., extinct 1789; Sir ROBERT NEWCOMEN, knighted by Sir Arthur Chichester, Lord Deputy of Ireland, 1605, was created a bart., 1625). Same *Arms* and *Crest*.

729

Newcomen (*Viscount Newcomen*, extinct 1825. KATHERINE NEWCOMEN, only dau. of CHARLES NEWCOMEN, Esq., of Carrickglas, co. Longford, and granddau. of CHARLES NEWCOMEN, Esq., of Droming, youngest son of Sir THOMAS NEWCOMEN, fifth bart., *m.* WILLIAM GLEADOWE, Esq., of Killester, co. Dublin. She was created a Baroness 1800, and a Viscountess 1803, and *d.* 1817, when she was *s.* by her son, THOMAS, *Viscount Newcomen*, *d. s. p.*). Quarterly, 1st and 4th, az. three lozenges conjoined in fess ar., for GLEADOWE; 2nd and 3rd, ar. a lion's head erased sa. langued gu. betw. three crescents of the second. *Crest*—A cock or. *Supporters*—Dexter, a brown horse; sinister, a talbot, both ppr. and semée of crescents gu. *Motto*—Vigilant.

Newcomen (GLEADOWE-NEWCOMEN, Killester, co. Dublin, bart., extinct 1825; exemplified to WILLIAM GLEADOWE, Esq., of Killester, who *m.* KATHERINE, only dau. and heir of CHARLES NEWCOMEN, Esq., of Carrickglas, afterwards *Viscountess Newcomen*, when he assumed the name of NEWCOMEN; he was created a bart. 1781). *Arms*, *Crest*, and *Motto* same as the last, the shield charged with an escutcheon of pretence of the NEWCOMEN arms.

Newcomen (Sutton, co. Dublin; granted, 1712, to BRABAZON NEWCOMEN, Esq., of Sutton, son of Sir THOMAS NEWCOMEN, Knt., who was an illegitimate son of Sir BEVERLEY NEWCOMEN, second bart., of Kenagh). Ar. a lion's head erased sa. langued gu. betw. three crescents of the last, a border of the second. *Crest*—A lion's gamb erect and erased sa. armed gu. the paw holding a crescent ar.

Newcourt (Pickwell, Halesworthy, and Georgeham, co. Devon; TOBY NEWCOURT, Esq., of Pickwell, and JOHN NEWCOURT, Esq., of Georgeham, sons of JOHN NEWCOURT, Esq., of Pickswell, *d.* 1612, eldest son of JOHN NEWCOURT, of same place. Visit. Devon, 1620). Sa. a bend erm. betw. two eagles with two heads displ. or, quartering, for FLOYER: Sa. a chev. betw. three arrows, points down ar. *Crest*—A demi griffin ramp. gu. guttée d'or, beaked gold.

Newcourt (Tiverton, co. Devon; PHIL'P NEWCOURT, younger son of JOHN NEWCOURT, Esq., of Pickswell, and brother of JOHN NEWCOURT, of same place, who *d.* 1612. Visit. Devon, 1620). Same *Arms* and *Crest*.

Newdich, or Newdick (co. Worcester; granted 1 Dec. 1580). Paly of four ar. and sa. on a bend gu. five bezants. *Crest*—Out of a mural coronet or, a lion's head gu.

Newdegate (Newdegate, co. Surrey; THOMAS NEWDEGATE, Esq., of Newdigate, *temp.* Charles I., left two daus. his co-heirs: MARY, *m.* WILLIAM STEPER, and ANNE, *m.* WILLIAM SMITHYMAN). Gu. three lions' gambs erased ar. *Crest*—A fleur-de-lis ar. *Another Crest*—A lion's gamb erased ar. *Another Crest*—A swan ar. beaked and membered gu. gorged with a ducal coronet or, thereto a chain affixed, and reflexed over the back vert. *Another Crest*—A horse courant az. flames of fire issuing from his nostrils ppr. *Motto*—Confide recte agens.

Newdegate (Harefield, co. Middlesex; Sir JOHN NEWDEGATE, Knt., second son of JOHN NEWDIGATE, Esq., of Newdigate, *m.* JOAN, sister and co-heir of WILLIAM SWAN LAND, Esq., of Harefield). Same *Arms*, *Crests*, and *Motto*.

Newdegate (Arbury, co. Warwick, bart., extinct 1800; RICHARD NEWDEGATE, grandson of JOHN NEWDIGATE, who was created a bart. 1677). Same *Arms*. *Crest*—A fleur-de-lis ar. *Motto*—Confide recte agens.

Newdegate (Kirk Hallam, co. Derby; FRANCIS PARKER, Esq., of Kirk Hallam, second son of WILLIAM PARKER, Esq., of Salford Priors, co. Warwick, by MILLICENT NEWDEGATE, his wife, only dau. of FRANCIS NEWDEGATE, the second son of Sir RICHARD NEWDEGATE, second bart. of Arbury, assumed the surname of NEWDEGATE). Same *Arms* and *Crest*.

Newdegate (Arbury and Astley Castle, co. Warwick, and Harefield Place, co. Middlesex; CHARLES NEWDIGATE PARKER, Esq., son of CHARLES PARKER, Esq., of Harefield, third son of WILLIAM PARKER, Esq., of Salford Priors, by MILLICENT NEWDEGATE, his wife, only dau. of FRANCIS NEWDEGATE, the second son of Sir RICHARD NEWDEGATE, second bart. of Arbury, assumed the surname of NEWDEGATE; his son, CHARLES-NEWDIGATE NEWDEGATE, Esq., M.P. co. Warwick, eventually *s.* to the estates of Sir ROGER NEWDEGATE, last bart. of Arbury). Same *Arms*, *Crest*, and *Motto*.

Neweke (Ar. three talbots' heads erased sa. *Crest*—A mullet az. betw. two quills ar.

Neweke. Ar. three covered cups sa.

Newell (Adwell, co. Oxford; granted 1755). Ar. on a chev. engr. az. betw. three wells ppr. as many cinquefoils of the field. *Crest*—An Italian greyhound ppr. collared, dovetailed or, charged on the shoulder with a cinquefoil ar.

Newell (England). Same *Arms.* *Crest*—Out of a mural coronet az. a lion's head or.

Newell. Gu. two hautboys in saltire, the sinister surmounted of the dexter betw. four crosses crosslet, all or.

Newell. Ar. three bars gu. over all a bend engr. sa.

Newenham (Everdon, co. Northampton, and co. Nottingham). Az. three demi lions ramp. ar. each charged on the shoulder with as many gouttes de sang. *Crest*—A demi lion ramp. ar. charged on the shoulder with three gouttes de sang. betw two wings expanded gu.

Newenham (Northaw, co. Herts). Ar. a cross sa. over all a bend vert. *Crest*—A demi lion ramp. ar. charged with a bend vert.

Newenham (Thenford, co. Northampton; ANNE, dau. and co-heir of WILLIAM NEWENHAM, of that place, m. FOULK WODEHULL, or WAHULL, d. 24 Henry VII. A.D. 1504; the descendant and representative of THOMAS DE WAHULL, summoned to Parliament 1297. Visit. Oxon, 1574). Ar. a cross gu. a bend az.

Newenham, or Nevenham (cos. Suffolk, Sussex, and Surrey). Same *Arms.* *Crest*—A pegasus courant ppr.

Newenham. Ar. three eagles displ. gu.

Nevenson (Rainthorp Hall, and Haddam, co. Herts, and Eastry, co. Kent). See NEVINSON.

Newent. Sa. on a cross ar. five eagles displ. of the field (another, gu.).

Newenton (co. Essex). Ar. a chev. betw. three crows' heads erased sa.

Newenton, Newington, or Newerton (Kingston-Bousey, co. Sussex, and co. Essex). Az. six eagles displ. ar. three, two, and one. *Crest*—On a chapeau az. turned up erm. a demi eagle displ. ar.

Newenton (co. Norfolk). Vairé ar. and gu.

Newenton. Ar. a chev. betw. three eagles' heads erased gu. *Crest*—A sea lion ramp. or.

Newers (ROGER NEWERS, living *temp.* Richard II.). Az. a fess ar. betw. three garbs or.

Newfoundland, See of. Ar. on a cross betw. four crosses pattée gu. an imperial crown ppr. a chief az. thereon a paschal lamb also ppr.

Newfoundland, Company of (London). Quarterly, gu. and az. a cross ar. in the 1st and 4th quarters a lion pass. guard. regally crowned or; in the 2nd and 3rd quarters an unicorn pass. of the third, armed, maned, and hoofed of the fourth, gorged with a prince's coronet, thereto a chain affixed and reflected over his back and here. h:s hind legs of the last. *Crest*—A reindeer trippant. *Supporters*—Two Newfoundland men, in the habits of that country all ppr. viz. the body covered with skins to the middle of the thigh, round the neck and breast two rows of pearl shells, and round the body two rows. At the back shields made of skins, and in their exterior hands bows, each supporter charged on the breast with a mascle or.

Newgent (Reg. Ulster's Office). Gu. a fess betw. three crescents ar. (another, or).

Newhouse (co. Lancaster). Vert a chev. ar. betw. two garbs in chief or, and a house in base ppr. *Crest*—An arm erect ppr. grasping a banner az. *Another Crest*—A squirrel sejant gu.

Newike. Ar. three covered cups sa.

Newike, Nowike, or Nonwike. Sa. an eagle displ. or.

Newington. Az. six eagles displ. ar. three, two, and one. *Crest*—A reindeer's head cabossed sa. attired or.

Newington (co. Sussex). Same *Arms.* *Crest*—On a chapeau az. turned up ar. a demi eagle, wings elevated of the last. *Motto*—Pac justa.

Newinton. Az. three eagles displ. ar.

Newland (Totnes, co. Devon). Ar. on chev. the upper part terminating in a cross formée gu. three bezants. *Crest*—A lion's gamb erect ar. holding a cross formée fitchée gu. charged with three bezants.

Newland (descended from ROGER NEWLAND, Esq., of Newlands, co. Southampton, who, having failed in the attempt to effect the escape of Charles I. from Carisbroke Castle, suffered death on the scaffold, exclaiming, "Deprived of my life and my property, I leave to my posterity, Le nom, les armes, la loyauté," which has since been retained as the motto of the family). Ar. on a chev. the upper part terminating in a cross pattée fitchée gu. three bezants. *Crest*—A wolf's head couped ppr. collared or. *Motto*—Le nom, les armes, la loyauté.

Newland (co. Essex). Ar. on a chev. sa. an escallop or.

Newland (co. Hertford; granted 1693). Ar. on a chev. sa. betw. three lions ramp. double queued sa. crowned or, as many crescents of the first. *Crest*—A tiger's head erased ar. maned and tufted or, gorged with a collar sa. charged

730

with three crescents of the first, holding in the mouth a broken spear embrued ppr.

Newland. Ar. on a chev. betw. three lions ramp. sa. as many escallops of the field.

Newlands (Edinburgh). Ar. three covered cups sa.

Newlands (Scotland). Ar. on a chev. betw. three lions ramp. sa. as many crescents of the first. *Crest*—A demi lion ramp. *Motto*—Pro patria.

Newle. Gu. a chev. betw. three hearts ar. each pierced through with a dagger ppr.

Newling (Rev. JOHN NEWLING, B.D., Canon Residentiary of Lichfield). Ar. on a chev. pattée at the point gu. three bezants. *Crest*—A lion's gamb erased ar. holding a cross pattée fitchée gu. *Motto*—In hoc signo vinces.

Newman (co. Berks). Sa. three mullets ar. *Crest*—A swallow volant ppr.

Newman (Fifehead Magdale, co. Dorset, bart., extinct 1747; and Thornbury Park, co. Gloucester; ANNE, dau. of RICHARD NEWMAN, Esq., of Evercreech Park, co. Somerset, m. ASHBURNHAM TOLL, Esq., of Graywell, co. Hants, and was grandmother of the Rev. ASHBURNHAM PHILIP TOLL, Prebendary of York). Quarterly, sa. and ar. in the 1st and 4th quarters three mullets of the second, in the centre an inescutcheon gu. charged with a portcullis imperially crowned or, an augmentation granted by Charles II. to Colonel NEWMAN, for his distinguished conduct at the battle of Worcester. *Crest*—A swallow rising ppr. *Motto*—Lux mea Christus.

Newman (St. Giles's, co. Middlesex; OSBASTON NEWMAN, aged 19 at Visit. Middlesex, 1663, only surviving son of ARTHUR NEWMAN, gent., and grandson of ARTHUR NEWMAN, gent., of Rickmansworth, co. Hertford). Az. a chev. wavy betw. three griffins segreant or. *Crest*—Out of a plume of feathers three az. two or and az. a griffin's head gold.

Newman (Gunston, co. Stafford). Az. a fess wavy betw. six dolphins ar.

Newman (Mamhead, co. Devon, bart.). Sa. three demi lions ramp. ar. langued gu. *Crest*—A lion ramp. ar. *Motto*—Ubi amor ibi fides.

Newman (Ludgvan and Gluvias, co. Cornwall). Az. three demi lions ramp. ar. guttée de sang. *Crest*—A demi lion, as in the arms, betw. two wings expanded gu.

Newman (Crediton, co. Devon). Sa. three demi lions ramp. erm.

Newman (co. Devon). Ar. three eagles displ. gu. crowned or.

Newman (Eastwood, co. Essex). Ar. a fesse dancettée gu. betw. three eagles displ. sa.

Newman (co. Kent). Per pale gu. and vert, three eagles displ. or.

Newman (London; granted 15 Feb. 1663-4). Or, a fesse dancettée betw. three hearts gu.

Newman (London, 1610). Az. a chev. wavy betw. three griffins segreant or. *Crest*—On a plume of five feathers, three az. two or, a griffin's head of the last.

Newman (London). Erm. on a chief sa. three crosses pattée or. *Crest*—On a mount vert a man, jacket az. breeches sa. on the head ppr. a cap gu. on a ladder lighting a beacon all ppr.

Newman (granted 1611). Or, a fesse indented gu. betw. three eagles displ. sa. *Crest*—A mermaid in the sea ppr. hair or.

Newman. Gu. a portcullis crowned or.

Newman. Erm. on a chief sa. three crosses pattée ar.

Newman. Or, three bars az. a canton erm.

Newman (granted to WILLIAM ABIAH NEWMAN, D.D.). Per chev. ar. and az. in chief three crosses pattée of the second, and in base an heraldic antelope statant of the first. *Crest*—A lion ramp. ar. holding in the dexter paw an anchor or, and resting the sinister upon a shield az. charged with a star of eight points also ar. *Motto*—Firmiter et fideliter.

Newman (WILLIAM NEWMAN, Mayor of Dublin; Fun. Ent. Ulster's Office, 1597, of his son, WILLIAM NEWMAN). Ar. a lion ramp. gu. charged on the shoulder with three escallops or, two and one.

Newman (JACOB NEWMAN, Clerk in the Master of the Rolls Office, Ireland, Fun. Ent. 1651, of his dau. ELIZABETH, wife of Sir JAMES WARE, Auditor-General of Ireland). Az. three demi lions ramp. ar. guttée de sang. *Crest*—A demi lion ramp., as in the arms, betw. two wings erect sa.

Newman (Drommaneene, co. Cork; granted by St. George, Ulster, 1674, to RICHARD NEWMAN, a Justice of the Peace for that co., descended from NEWMAN, of co. Somerset). Ar. a chev. betw. three demi lions pass. gu. a chief az. *Crest*—An eagle's head erased az. charged on the neck with an escallop or.

Newman (Reg. Ulster's Office). Sa. a chev. betw. three escallops ar.

Newmarch (co. Brecknock, Wales, which estate was acquired by BERNARD DE NEWMARCH, *temp.* William I.). Gu. five fusils conjoined in fesse or.

Newmarch (*Baron Newmarch;* ADAM DE NEWMARCH joined the Baronial Standard *temp.* Henry III., and was summoned to Parliament by the rebellious lords after the battle of Lewes, but the writ was not renewed to any of his descendants). Gu. five lozenges conjoined in fess or.

Newmarch (Sir THOMAS DE NEWMARCH, Roll of Knights in cos. Derby and Notts, *temp.* Edward I.). Ar. a fess indented gu.

Newmarch (Sir JOHN DE NEWMARCH, Roll of Knights in cos. Derby and Notts, *temp.* Edward I.). Same *Arms*, tinctures reversed.

Newmarch (co. Nottingham). Ar. five fusils conjoined in fesse gu. on a border sa. eight crosses crosslet of the field.

Newmarch (co. York). Gu. a fess indented or. *Crest*—A dove, holding in the beak an olive branch all ppr.

Newmarch (Newcastle-on-Tyne). Gu. on a fess or, five fusils sa. *Crest*—A demi griffin ppr.

Newmarch. Gu. a fesse dancettée ar. *Crest*—On the sea an anchor in pale ensigned with a dove and olive branch all ppr.

Newmarch. Or, five fusils in fesse gu. on each an escallop of the field; another, Ar. a fess fusily gu. on the centre one an escallop or; another, Gu. five fusils in bend ar.; another, Ar. five fusils in fess gu. on each an escallop or; another, Ar. three chevronels sa.; another, Ar. a fess fusily gu. on a border sa. eight martlets of the first; another, Sa. on an inescutcheon ar. a fesse lozengy gu.

Newmarche (co. Derby). Gu. five fusils in fess engr. or.

Newmarche (co. Nottingham). Ar. four (another, five) fusils in fess gu. *Crest*—A tower, triple-towered ppr.

Newnam. Ar. three eagles displ. gu.

Newnham. Ar. a cross sa. a bend vert.

Newnton. Sa. three martlets ar.

Newport (co. Salop; descended from JOHN DE NEWPORT, *temp.* Edward I.). Ar. a chev. gu. betw. three leopards' faces sa. *Crest*—A unicorn's head ar. armed and crined or, erased gu. *Another Crest*—A unicorn's head erased ar. ducally gorged or.

Newport (*Earl of Bradford,* extinct 1762; Sir RICHARD NEWPORT, Knt., of High Ercall, descended from THOMAS NEWPORT, Esq., and ANNE ERCALL, his wife, dau. and co-heir of JOHN ERCALL, Esq., of High Ercall, co. Salop, was created *Baron Newport* 1642, his son, FRANCIS, second *Baron Newport,* was created, 1694, *Earl of Bradford.* Lady ANNE NEWPORT, eldest sister of THOMAS, fifth and last *Earl of Bradford, m.* Sir ORLANDO BRIDGEMAN, Bart., of Great Lever, co. Lancaster, in whose descendants the title was revived). Same *Arms,* quartering ERCALL, GREY, of Codnor, BURGH, MOUTHWEY, and BROMLEY. *Crest*—A unicorn's head ar. erased gu. armed and ducally gorged or. *Supporters*—Two leopards guard. ppr. *Motto*—Ne supra modum sapere.

Newport (New Park, co. Kilkenny, bart., extinct 1862). Or, a chev. gu. betw. three leopards' faces sa. *Crest*—A unicorn's head erased ar. armed, maned, bearded, and ducally gorged or. *Motto*—Ne supra modum sapere.

Newport (co. Hertford, and Welton, co. Northampton). Ar. (another, or) a fess betw. three crescents sa. *Crest*—A buck statant gu. attired, gorged, and chained or.

Newport (co. Huntingdon). Ar. a fesse dancettée gu. a bend sa.

Newport (co. Stafford). Gu. on a canton ar. a fleur-de-lis sa.

Newport (Hanley Court, co. Worcester). Ar. a fess betw. three crescents sa. *Crest*—A fleur-de-lis or.

Newport. Az. on a bend betw. three frets ar. as many bugle horns of the first. *Crest*—A dexter arm embowed in armour garnished or, holding in the hand ppr. a sword ar. hilt and pommel gold.

Newport. Quarterly, gu. and az. a lion ramp. ar. (another, or); another, Gu. six annulets or (another, tinctures reversed); another, Sa. on a chev. betw. three pheons ar. as many mullets of the field; another, Sa. a chev. betw. three pheons ar.; another, Gu, three wings elevated ar.; another, Per pale gu. and az. a lion ramp. ar.; another, Paly of six or and az., on a chief gu. three escallops ar.

Newport. Ar. on a bend sa. betw. two lions of the second a wivern extended of the field.

News (co. Oxford). Per saltire ar. and gu. four chaplets counterchanged. *Crest*—A demi lion ppr. holding a branch of laurel vert.

Newsam, or Newson (co. Lancaster, 1567). Az. on a fess ar. three crosses crosslet gu.

731

Newsam (co. Warwick). Ar. on a fess sa. three crosses crosslet of the field. *Crest*—A lion's gamb gu. holding a crescent or.

Newsam (co. York). Sa. on a fesse ar. three crosses patonce of the first, on a canton of the second a spearhead gu. *Crest*—A sword erect ar. enfiled with a thistle ppr.

Newsam (confirmed by Roberts, Ulster, 1647, to EDWARD NEWSAM, fourth Captain in the regiment under command of Colonel JAMES CASTELL; descended from the co. York). Sa. on a fess ar. three crosses patonce of the first, on a canton of the second a spearhead gu. *Crest*—A sword erect enfiled with a thistle ppr.

Newsham (Knighton, co. Worcester, and Chadshunt, co. Warwick; Herald's Visit.). Sa. on a fess ar. three crosses crosslet of the field.

Newsham (co. Lancaster; originally from co. Warwick). Az. on a fesse ar. three crosses crosslet gu. *Crest*—A boar's head erased or, charged on the cheek with a crosslet gu. Some branches of the family, and also the co. Warwick family, have borne ar. on a fess sa. three crosslets of the field.

Newsome (Major NEWSOME, R.E.). Az. on a fess ar. cotised or, three crosses crosslet of the field. *Crest*—A sword erect pierced through a thistle ppr.

Newson. Sa. on a fess ar. cotised or, three crosses crosslet gu.

Newstead Priory (co. Nottingham). Az. three lions pass. guard. in pale or, on a chief gu. the Virgin and Child of the second.

Newte (Tiverton, co. Devon; traced to *temp.* Queen Elizabeth). Gu. a chev. betw. three human hearts ar. each pierced through with a sword in bend sinister ppr. hilt and pommel in chief or. *Crest*—A newt ppr.

Newthall (Catteshall, co. Chester). Ar. an ox yoke sa.

Newton (Crabaton, co. Devon; JOHN NEWTON, aged 36, 1620, son and heir of WILLIAM NEWTON, who came from co. Somerset. Visit. Devon, 1620. The heiress, ELIZABETH NEWTON, *m.* in 1729, JOHN FOWELL, Esq., of Blackhall and Diptford, co. Devon). Vert two shinbones in saltire, the sinister surmounted of the dexter ar. *Crest*—An eastern prince crowned or, kneeling and delivering up his sword, blade ppr. hilt or, granted, says family tradition, to an ancestor of the NEWTONS, who overcame and took prisoner an eastern prince at the battle of Ascalon.

Newton (Horsley and Mickle-Over, co. Derby; descended from NEWTON, of Newton, co. Chester, settled at Horsley about A.D. 1500. The senior line, NEWTON, of Duffield, became extinct at the decease of TIMOTHY NEWTON, Esq., whose heiress *m.* HANCOCK, of Brampton; but the male line was continued by NEWTON, of Mickle-Over, until the death of ROBERT NEWTON, of that place, 1789, when the estates and representation of the family devolved on JOHN LEAPER, who assumed by sign manual the additional name and arms of NEWTON). Sa. two human shinbones in saltire the sinister surmounted of the dexter ar. *Crest*—A naked man kneeling on his sinister knee and holding a sword ppr. the point downward, hilt and pommel or. *Motto*—Huic habeo non tibi.

Newton (Duffield, co. Derby, Hader, co. Lincoln, and Thorpe, co. York). Sa. two shinbones in saltire, the sinister surmounted of the dexter ar. *Crest*—A lion ramp. ar. *Another Crest*—An eastern prince kneeling on the sinister knee, and presenting a sword all ppr.

Newton (Barr's Court, co. Gloucester, bart., extinct 1743, and co. Somerset; descended from Sir RICHARD CRADOCK, Chief Justice of England, through his second son, Sir THOMAS NEWTON, *temp.* Edward IV.; his descendant, Sir JOHN NEWTON, of Barr's Court, was created a baronet in 1660). Quarterly, 1st and 4th, sa. two shinbones saltireways, the sinister surmounted of the dexter ar., for NEWTON; 2nd and 3rd, ar. on a chev. az. three garbs or, for CRADOCK. *Crest*—Same as NEWTON, of Duffield.

Newton (Newton, co. Chester). Vert a lion or; sometimes, Ar. a lion ramp. sa. charged on the shoulder with a cross pattée or. *Crest*—A lion's gamb sa. holding a key or, to which is a chain dependent, fastened to a ring of the last.

Newton (Cheadle Heath, co. Chester; descended from NEWTON, of Newton). Gu. a cross erm. flory or, betw. four lions' gambs of the last. *Crest*—A lion ramp. per fesse erm. and gu. collared also gu. holding betw. the paws a cross, as in the arms. *Motto*—Faveat fortuna.

Newton (Badenham, co. Bedford, Lavendon, co. Buckingham, and Exmouth, co. Devon). Ar. three lozenges conjoined in fesse az. each charged with a garb or. *Crest*—Two arms counter-embowed dexter and sinister, vested az. holding up in the hands ppr. a garb or.

Newton (co. Cambridge). Sa. two shinbones in saltire, the dexter surmounted of the sinister ar.

Newton (co. Chester). Ar. three eagles displ. az.

Newton (cos. Chester, Gloucester, Norfolk, and Somerset; Sir JOHN NEWTON, KNT., of Harptre, in the latter co., 1567). Ar. on a chev. az. three garbs or.

Newton (co. Oxford). Ar.-a lion ramp. double queued sa. armed and langued gu.

Newton (Highley, co. Salop). Ar. a cross flory sa. the ends or. *Crest*—An eagle's leg erased at the thigh sa. environed with a snake or.

Newton (Bagdale Hall, co. York). Sa. three pairs of shinbones in saltire ar. a martlet for diff.

Newton (co. Durham. Visit. 1615). Az. on a chev. or, three garbs sa.

Newton (co. Essex). Sa. a bend sinister surmounted of another dexter or (another, ar.).

Newton (Charlton, co. Kent, and Priory, co. Warwick, bart., extinct 1700). Az. two ostrich feathers in saltire betw. three boars' heads couped at the neck ar. bristled and tusked or. *Crest*—Out of a ducal coronet or, a boar's head betw. two ostrich feathers ar.

Newton (Next Trent, co. Lincoln; granted 14 June, 1660). Vert a cross ragulée betw. four leopards' faces ar.

Newton (London, cos. Somerset, Suffolk, Sussex, and Wilts). Ar. a lion ramp. sa. armed gu. tail double queued, charged on the shoulder with a cross pattée of the field. *Crest*—A lion's gamb erect holding a key or.

Newton. Ar. a lion ramp. double queued sa. gorged with a chaplet or. *Crest*—A lion's gamb erect gu. grasping a key affixed to a chain or.

Newton (Newcastle-on-Tyne). Az, two shinbones in saltire, the sinister surmounted of the dexter or, a crescent for diff. *Crest*—An arm embowed, habited, holding a shinbone.

Newton (co. Salop). Per fesse vert and gu. a pale counterchanged, three leopards' faces or.

Newton (co. Suffolk). Ar. a lion ramp. tail double queued sa. on the shoulder a cross crosslet or.

Newton (co. Sussex, 1633). Gu. a Saracen's head couped at the neck ppr. wreathed round the temples ar. and az. betw. three eagles' claws issuing out of the three points of the escutcheon ar.

Newton (Richmond Castle, co. Somerset; granted 12 Dec. 10 Elizabeth). Ar. on a chev. az. three garbs or, quartering CRADOCK, *alias* NEWTON, SHERBORNE, ANGELL, PIROT, HARVY, SHEDDER, HAMPTON, BITTON, FURNEAUX, GAWDESCOT, GURNEY, and HAWTREY.

Newton (Croxton Park, co. Cambridge). A chev. sa. betw. three eagles' legs erased, each entwined by a snake. *Crest*—an eagle's leg erased entwined by a snake.

Newton. Az. three eagles displ. ar.; another, Ar. two chev. reversed gu.; another, Az. a boar's head couped, surmounted by a knot within a garter all or; another, Gu. twelve plates, four, four, three, and one; another, Vert a lion ramp. or, armed and langued gu.; another, Ar. fretty az. on a fess gu. three mullets or.

Newton. Ar. on a chev. az. three garbs or. *Crest*—A bear's head couped ar. muzzled gu.

Newton, Town of (co. Lancaster). Has only a *Crest*, viz.—Out of a ducal coronet a ram's head, holding in the mouth a sprig of laurel.

Newton (Reg. Ulster's Office; descended out of co. York). Sa. a Saracen's head couped at the neck ar. betw. three lion's gambs issuant from the dexter chief, sinister chief, and base points or.

Newton (Carrickfergus, co. Antrim; confirmed to ANDREW NEWTON, Esq., of Dungannon, co. Tyrone, descended from RICHARD NEWTON, who settled at Carrickfergus before 1595). Ar. in chief two lions' gambs sa. each grasping a key ppr. and in base a lion ramp. gu. charged on the breast with a cross pattée of the field. *Crest*—A martlet sa. charged on the breast with a cross pattée ar. *Motto*—Faveat fortuna.

Newton (Hillmount, co. Londonderry). Same *Arms*, *Crest*, and *Motto*.

Newton (Dunleckney, co. Carlow; confirmed to PHILIP JOCELYN NEWTON, Esq., of Dunleckney, and the descendants of his grandfather). Az. two ostrich feathers in saltire betw. three boars' heads erased, two in fess and one in base ar. tusked or, and in the centre chief point a cross crosslet of the last. *Crest*—Out of a ducal coronet or, a boar's head betw. two ostrich feathers ar. the neck charged with a cross crosslet az. *Motto*—Pro patriâ.

Newton (Newton, co. Haddington). The last male heir, Sir RICHARD NEWTON, Bart., of Newton, settled his estate, by entail dated 18 June, 1724, on RICHARD HAY, fourth son of Lord WILLIAM HAY). Vert a lion ramp. or, on a chief of the last three roses gu. *Crest*—A demi lion or, holding in the dexter paw a scymitar all ppr. *Motto*—Pro patriâ. The

old arms of the family seem to have been, Ar. three boars' heads couped az.

Newton (HAY-NEWTON, of Newton), See HAY.

Newton (Dalcoif, co. Berwick). Per fesse az. and gu. on the first two stars, on the second a lion pass. ar.

Newtown, or Franville, Town of (co. Hants). Has no armorial ensign; the seal, which is very ancient, represents an antique ship on the sea with one mast, sail furled and pennon flying; on the ship a lion pass. guard. in chief, on the dexter a mullet, on the sinister a crescent in fesse, on the sinister side an escutcheon of St. George.

Neylan. See O'NEYLAN.

Nibbs (granted 13 Oct. 1759). Az. a chev. engr. erm. on a chief ar. two bucks' heads cabossed gu. *Crest*—A buck's head cabossed gu. pierced through with an arrow or, feathered ar.

Niblett (Haresfield Court, co. Gloucester). Az. on a chev. ar. betw. three eagles rising or, as many bars gemelles gu. *Crest*—An eagle rising, quarterly or and ar.

Nich, alias Nye (co. Sussex). Paly of six ar. and sa. per fesse counterchanged.

Nichell. Az. on a chev. or, betw. two eagles displ. in chief and in base a lion pass. of the last, a hart charged with a leopard's face. inclosed by two torteaux, each charged with an escallop of the third. *Crest*—A demi griffin az. in the mouth a pink, flowered gu. leaved vert.

Nichell. Az. a chev. betw. three eagles displ. or.

Nichells (JOAN, dau. and sole heir of JOHN NICHELLS, m. Sir THOMAS OFFLEY, Knt., who *d.* 29 Aug. 1582. Visit. London, 1586). Quarterly, 1st and 4th, az. on a chev. or, betw. two eagles displ. in chief and in base a lion pass. of the last a hart charged with a leopard's face ar. inclosed by two torteaux, each charged with an escallop of the third; 2nd and 3rd, ar. a chev. gu. betw. four tassels sa.

Nicholas (France). Gyronny of eight ar. and gu. in chief an eagle displ. sa.

Nicholas (Winterborne Earls, co. Wilts, cos. Devon and Somerset; granted 1612). Ar. on a fess sa. betw. three ravens ppr. as many lions ramp. of the first. *Crest*—A raven, wings elevated sa. perched on the battlements of a tower ar.

Nicholas (granted, 1649, to Sir EDWARD NICHOLAS, Secretary to Charles II.). Quarterly, 1st and 4th, az. on a cross gu. an imperial crown or; 2nd and 3rd, ar. a fess wa———twwtw. three ravens sa. *Crest*—A lion pass. az. semée of ———toiles or.

Nicholas, or Nicholls (Prestbury, co. Gloucester, Allcannings and Roundway, co. Wilts). Or, on a chev. betw. three ravens sa. two lions combatant ar. *Crest*—A quatrefoil on a stalk ragulée or, charged with a martlet sa.

Nicholas (London). Az. on a chev. betw. two eagles displ. in chief and a lion pass. in base or, three torteaux, the middle one charged with a leopard's face, and the other two with an escallop all ar.

Nicholas (London). Or, three fleurs-de-lis az. on a chief gu. a lion pass. of the field.

Nicholas (London). Az. on a chev. betw. two eagles displ. or, a lion pass. of the field.

Nicholas (London, and Ashton Keynes and Roundway, co. Wilts). Az. a chev. engr. betw. three owls or. *Crest*—On a chapeau az. (another, gu.) turned up erm. an owl, wings expanded or.

Nicholas (co. Middlesex). Az. on a chev. betw. two eagles displ. in chief and a lion pass. in base or, a torteau charged with an escallop ar.

Nicholas (co. Worcester). Ar. a fess betw. six holly (another, oak) leaves vert.

Nicholas. Ar. on a cross gu. a crown or. *Crest*—A lion pass. az. semée of estoiles or.

Nicholas. Ar. on a cross gu. a rose or. *Crest*—A lion statant or, semée of estoiles or.

Nicholas. Ar. on a chev. az. betw. three tigers' heads erased sa. as many crescents erm.

Nicholas. Per pale ar. and sa. six crescents counterchanged, two, two, and two.

Nicholl (co. Cornwall). Sa. a pheon ar. *Crest*—A cubit arm holding a bow all ppr.

Nicholl (Penros, co. Cornwall; HUMPHREY NICHOLL, Esq., of Penros, Visit. Cornwall 1620, son and heir of HUMPHREY NICHOLL, of the same, was father of ANTHONY NICHOLL, aged 9 years at Visit.). Sa. a pheon ar. *Crest*- A Cornish chough ppr.

Nicholl (Llantwitt-Major, co. Glamorgan). Sa. three pheons ar. *Crest*—A Cornish chough, wings elevated ppr. perched on the battlements of a tower ar.

Nicholl (The Ham, co. Glamorgan). Same *Arms* and *Crest*.

Nicholl (Tredunnock, co. Monmouth). Same *Arms* and *Crest*.

Nicholl (Dimlands, co. Glamorgan). Same *Arms* and *Crest*. *Motto*—Duw a digon.

Nicholl (Penlline, co. Glamorgan). Same *Arms* and *Crest*.

Nicholl (Llanmaes, co. Glamorgan). Same *Arms* and *Crest*.

Nicholl (Merthyr Mawr, co. Glamorgan). Same *Arms* and *Crest*.

Nicholl, or Nicol (Penrose, co. Cornwall, originally of Guernsey: settled at Penrose in the sixteenth century). Same *Arms*. *Crest*—A cubit arm ppr. holding a bow or, stringed ar.

Nicholl (Greenhill Grove, co. Hereford). Az. two bars erm. in chief three suns or.

Nicholl (borne by JOHN NICHOLL, Esq., of Islington, co. Middlesex, son of JOHN NICHOLL, by MARY his wife, dau. of MATTHIAS MILLER, of Epping, and grandson of JOSEPH NICHOLL, Esq., of Hadham). Ar. on a chev. az. betw. three wolves' heads erased sa. as many crescents erm. on a canton of the third a pheon of the field. *Crest*—A squirrel sa. holding a pheon ar.

Nicholl (granted to JOHN NICHOLL, Esq., F.S.A., of Theydon Gernon, co. Essex, and Canonbury Place, Islington). Quarterly, sa. and gu. a pheon ar., in the first quarter a falcon belled of the third. *Crest*—A demi lion ramp. guard. ar. guttée de poix, holding in the dexter paw a lily ppr. *Motto* —Fort Fahren und Verharren.

Nicholls (Islip Willen, co. Buckingham). Az. semée of crosses crosslet fitchée or, three eagles displ. in bend betw. two cotises engr. of the last. *Crest*—An eagle rising or, sustaining a cross crosslet fitchée of the last.

Nicholls (Trewane, co. Cornwall; JOHN NICHOLLS. Visit. Cornwall, 1620, son and heir of JOHN NICHOLLS, and grandson of JOHN NICHOLLS, all of same place, *m.* ELIZABETH, dau. of EDMUND FORTESCUE, Esq., of Fallopit, and had as son and heir, JOHN NICHOLLS, aged seven years at Visit.). Sa. three pheons or.

Nicholls (co. Cornwall, confirmed by Camden, Clarenceux). Same *Arms*. *Crest*—A hand couped above the wrist, lying fesseways holding a bow, strung, and across it an arrow all ppr.

Nicholls (Hardwick, co. Northampton, bart., extinct 1717; FRANCIS NICHOLLS, Esq., of Hardwick, son and heir of THOMAS NICHOLLS, Esq., of Pickley, in same co., who *d.* 1568, son of NICHOLLS, of Ecton, in same co., *temp.* Edward IV. Visit. Leicester, 1619). Same *Arms*.

Nicholls (Faxton, co. Leicester; AUGUSTINE NICHOLLS, of that place, one of the Justices of the Common Pleas, second son of THOMAS NICHOLLS, Esq., of Pickley, *d.* 1617, leaving his nephew, FRANCIS NICHOLLS, Esq., of Hardwick, his heir. Visit. Leicester, 1619). Same *Arms*, a crescent for diff.

Nicholls (Tilton, co. Leicester; WILLIAM NICHOLLS, Esq., of Tilton, third son of THOMAS NICHOLLS, Esq., of Pickley. Visit. Leicester, 1619). Same *Arms*, a mullet for diff.

Nicholls (Saffron-Walden, co. Essex). Ar. on a chev. az. betw. three wolves' heads erased sa. as many crescents erm. on a canton of the third a pheon or. *Crest*—A squirrel ppr.

Nicholls (co. Essex). Sa. a pheon ar. on a canton of the second an owl ppr.

Nicholls (Boycote, co. Salop). Sa. a pheon ar. a crescent for diff. *Crest*—A Cornish chough.

Nicholls (Bowells, co. Salop). Sa. three pheons ar. a canton of the last.

Nicholls (Culverlands, co. Berks). Sa. three pheons ar. *Crest*—A cubit arm ppr. holding a bow or, stringed ar. *Motto*—Fide sed cui vide.

Nicholls (JOHN NICHOLLS, Controller of the Works at London Bridge. Visit. London, 1586). Az. a fess betw. three lions' heads erased or. *Crest*—A tiger sejant erm.

Nicholls (Trewane, in St. Kew, co. Cornwall; confirmed by Camden, Clarenceux; extinct when JOHN NICHOLLS, Esq. *d.* 1709; the heiress *m.* GLYNN, of Glynn). Sa. three pheons ar. *Crest*—A hand couped above the wrist lying fesseways ppr. holding a bow or, stringed ar.

Nicholls (granted to BENJAMIN NICHOLLS, Esq., Mayor of Manchester). Per chev. or and az. a castle betw. three pheons counterchanged. *Crest*—Two battle axes in saltire in front of a castle surmounted of a Cornish chough all ppr. the dexter paw resting on a pheon sa. *Motto*—Semper fidelis.

Nicholls (Treriefe, in Madron, co. Cornwall; *temp.* Elizabeth). Same *Arms*.

Nicholls (Swafield, co. Lincoln). Az. a fess betw. three lions' heads erased or.

Nicholls (Baynham, co. Suffolk). Gu. a chev. ar. betw. three trefoils stalked or.

733

Nicholls, or Nycolls. Quarterly, or and gu. a bend sa.

Nicholls (Whitgreave, co. Stafford; granted by Cooke, Clarenceux). Sa. three pheons ar. a canton of the last. *Crest*—A wolf's head erased sa.

Nicholls (Drogheda, co. Louth; Fun. Ent. Ulster's Office, 1677, EDWARD NICHOLLS, Alderman of Drogheda). Gu. on a chev. betw. three griffins' heads erased ar. as many crescents of the first.

Nichols. Az. two bars erm. in chief three suns or. *Crest*— Out of a ducal coronet or, a demi lion ramp. ar.

Nichols (co. Norfolk). Ar. on a chev. betw. three foxes' heads erased sa. as many crescents erm. a canton of the second. *Crest*—A fox's head erased ppr.

Nichols (Lawford Hall, co. Essex). Same *Arms*, *Crest*, and *Motto*.

Nichols (granted 23 March, 1861, to JOHN BOWYER NICHOLS, Esq., of Hanger Vale, Ealing, F.S.A., grandfather of JOHN BRUCE NICHOLS, Esq., of Holmwood, co. Surrey). Az. on a fesse humettée betw. three lions' heads erased or, two eagles rising of the field. *Crest*— A lion's head erased az. gorged with a collar gemel or, betw. two wings, paly of six or and az. *Motto*—Labor ipso voluptas.

Nicholson (cos. Lancaster and Cumberland, and London). Az. two bars erm. on a chief ar. three suns ppr. *Crest*— A lion's head erased gu. ducally gorged or; granted 27 Queen Elizabeth, by Dethick, Garter, to THOMAS, son of WILLIAM NICHOLSON, of co. Lancaster, an Examiner in Chancery, and confirmed by Sir William Dethick to OTHO NICHOLSON, of London, gent., son of THOMAS, son of WILLIAM, son of NICHOLAS NICHOLSON, of Cumberland. *Motto*—Per castra ad astra.

Nicholson (Thelwall Hall, co. Chester). Az. two bars erm. in chief three suns or. *Crest*—Out of a ducal coronet gu. a lion's head erm. *Motto*—Per castra ad astra.

Nicholson (Waverley Abbey, co. Surrey). Per pale dovetailed az. and gu. two bars ar. guttée de sang in chief two suns in glory ar. *Crest*—A lion's head erased in front of rays.

Nicholson (Rounday Park, co. York). Barry of six erminois and gu. on a chief az. a cross pattée ar. betw. two suns in splendour or. *Crest*—On a branch of a tree fesseways ppr. a lion's head erased at the neck or, and charged with a cross pattée gu. *Motto*—Providentiâ Dei.

Nicholson (ALEXANDER NICHOLSON, Esq., late M'INNES, of East Court, Charlton-Kings, co. Gloucester, formerly a capt. in the 2nd Regiment of Life Guards, by royal sign manual, in 1821, assumed the surname and arms of NICHOLSON, out of respect to the memory of his late maternal uncle, General ROBERT NICHOLSON). Quarterly, 1st and 4th, or, on a chev. embattled az. betw. three eagles' heads erased gu. an Eastern crown betw. two wreaths of laurel of the field, for NICHOLSON; 2nd and 3rd, gu. two estoiles in chief ar. and a lion pass, in base or, on a chief of the second two swords in saltire ppr. pommels and hilts gold, the blades encircled by a wreath of laurel vert, in the centre chief point pendent from a ribbon of the first fimbriated az. a representation of the medal presented to him by command of his Majesty, for his services at the Battle of Waterloo, ppr. circumscribed " Waterloo," in letters of gold, for M'INNES. *Crests*—A demi lion erased, charged with a bomb fired ppr. supporting a flagstaff also encircled by an Eastern crown or, therefrom flowing towards the sinister a banner gu. inscribed " Barvach," in letters of gold, in commemoration of the services of his late uncle, Lieut.-General ROBERT NICHOLSON, at the siege of that fortress in the East Indies, for NICHOLSON; 2nd, out of a mural crown ppr. inscribed " Vittoria," a dexter arm embowed, vested gu. entwined by a thistle ppr. the hand in a glove ar. grasping a sword all ppr. pendent from the guard the Waterloo medal, as in the arms, for M'INNES. *Mottoes*— Generositate, for NICHOLSON; and, Post Prœlia premier, for M'INNES.

Nicholson (Sydney and Luddenham, Australia, bart.). Az. two bars nebuly ar. in chief a sun in splendour ppr. betw. two stars of eight points or. *Crest*—On a rock ppr. a lion's head az. charged with a star, as in the arms. *Motto* —Virtus sola nobilitas.

Nicholson (cos. Cumberland and Lancaster). Az. two bars erm., in chief three suns in splendour or. *Crest*— Out of a ducal coronet gu. a lion's head erm.

Nicholson (London; confirmed 1596). Same *Arms* and *Crest*.

Nicholson (granted to PATRICK CHARLES NICHOLSON, Esq., of Ashton-under-Lyne, co. Lancaster). Sa. two bars chequy or and az. in chief a stag's head caboshed betw. two suns in splendour of the second. *Crest*—A lion's head erased erm.

charged on the neck with a burning heart gu. within two branches of palm ppr.

Nicholson (Virginia; FRANCIS NICHOLSON, Captain-General and Governor of South Carolina, granted 1693-4). Az. on a cross ar. betw. four suns in splendour or, a cathedral church gu. Crest—A demi man habited in a close coat az. the buttons and cuffs of the sleeves turned up or, his face and hands ppr. armed with a head-piece and gorget ar. the beaver open, holding in the dexter hand a sword erect ppr. hilt and pommel of the second, and in the sinister hand a Bible open, clasps ar. Motto—Deus mihi sol.

Nicholson. Erm. on a pale sa. three martlets ar.

Nicholson. Per pale wavy or and gu. six martlets, two, two, and two, respecting each other, and counterchanged.

Nicholson (Dublin, Reg. Ulster's Office). Erm. on a pale sa. three martlets in pale ar. Crest—A pelican in her piety ppr.

Nicholson (Ballow, co. Down; granted by Betham, Ulster, to ROBERT NICHOLSON, Esq.) Gu. two bars erm. in chief three suns in splendour or. Crest—Out of a ducal coronet or, a lion's head erminois. Motto—Deus mihi sol.

Nicholson (Roe Park, co. Londonderry; confirmed to HARVEY NICHOLSON, Esq., son of JOHN NICHOLSON, Town Mayor and Alderman of Derry). Per chev. engr. or and gu. three hawks' heads erased counterchanged. Crest—Out of a mural crown a demi lion ramp. all ppr. Motto—Generositate.

Nicholson (exemplified to JAMES CUSTIS, of Glasnevin Lodge, co. Dublin, surgeon, son of Rev. EDMUND CUSTIS, Rector of Saul, co. Down, by ELIZABETH, his wife, sister and heir of JAMES NICHOLSON, Esq., of Iceford, co. Sligo, on his assuming, by royal licence, 1861, the surname and arms of NICHOLSON). Az. on a cross engr. betw. four suns in splendour or, a wolf's head erased ppr. Crest—A wolf's head erased ppr. gorged with a collar engr. gu. and charged on the neck with a sun as in the arms.

Nicklin. Sa. three boars' heads couped in fesse ar. Crest —A griffin's head erased ar.

Nickson (Coolattin, Munny, and Killinure, co. Wicklow, and Ballymur, co. Carlow; CHRISTIANA, dau. of LORENZO NICKSON, Esq., of Munny, m. Right Hon. JOHN HELY-HUTCHINSON, and was created Baroness Donoughmore 1783, and her son, RICHARD, Baron Donoughmore, was created Earl of Donoughmore 1801; Reg. Ulster's Office). Az. a garb in fess betw. three tigers' heads erased ar. armed or, collared gu. Crest—A tiger's head or, pierced through the jaw with a dart ppr. feathered ar.

Nicol (Alloa, co. Clackmannan, 1733). Az. on a fess ar. three mascles of the first, in chief a ship with sails furled and rays across the mast of the second, in base a globe ppr. and two anchors in saltire ar. Crest—A dexter hand holding a quadrant ppr. Motto—Sedulitate.

Nicol (Lord Provost of Aberdeen, 1872). Per pale invecked az. and ar. a fess betw. four mascles counterchanged. Crest—A demi lion ramp. az. Motto—Nil sistere contra.

Nicol (Ballogie, co. Aberdeen, 1875). Az. a fess ar. betw. three mascles or. Crest—A greyhound's head ppr. Motto —Sedulitate.

Nicolas (co. Cornwall; descended from NICOLAS, of Brittany, in France, and established in England immediately after the revocation of the Edict of Nantes, by ABEL NICOLAS, son of JEAN NICOLAS, Chevalier des Champs Gérault, who with his brother, GERMAIN NICOLAS, Seigneur de Claye, was on the "Reformation de la Noblesse" of Brittany, 20 August, 1669, recognised as noblesse of ancient extraction. The ancient Arms of the family of NICOLAS, Seigneurs de Claye, de Champs Gérault, &c., are—Gu. on a fesse ar. betw. three wolves' heads erased ar, three martlets sa. Crest—A wolf's head erased or, issuing from a coronet. Supporters—Dexter, a lion reguard. or, langued gu.; sinister, a syren ppr. Motto—En bon espoir. In 1816, Captain JOHN HARRIS NICOLAS, of East Looe, in Cornwall, the representative of the family in England, received a grant of arms from the Heralds' College, as follows:—Gyronny of eight ar. and az. an eagle displ. erminois, on a chief wavy (in allusion to the services of Capt. NICOLAS, and of his eldest son, Capt. TOUP NICOLAS, C.B.) erm. a trident or, surmounting in saltire a flagstaff ppr. thereon hoisted a pennant gu. both passing through a chaplet of laurel vert. Crest—A demi eagle sa. wings elevated erminois, each charged with a cross couped gu. issuing from a naval crown or. An l on 16 October, 1816, Capt. TOUP NICOLAS received the following augmentation, to the above crest: the word "Pilot" inscribed on the rim of the naval crown, "in commemoration of his distinguished services in H.M. sloop 'Pilot' on the east and west coasts of Calabria, during the years 1810, 1811, and 1812; and also

734

in allusion to the gallant action fought near Toulon, between H.M. said sloop and the French national ship 'La Legére,' of 28 guns and 300 men on June the 17th, 1815." Motto—Patria cara carior fides.

Nicolas (allowed 1832 to Sir NICHOLAS HARRIS NICOLAS, Chancellor and Knight Grand Cross of the Order of St. Michael and St. George, fourth son of Captain JOHN HARRIS NICOLAS, R.N., of East Looe). Ar. a fess engr. and in chief three eagles displ. gu. Crest—A fetterlock or, the fetter passing through a plume of five ostrich feathers alternately ar. and gu. Supporters (as G.C.M.G., granted 1 Dec. 1840)—On either side the Sept Insular lion, viz., a lion guard. with wings elevated, holding in the forepaw a book and seven arrows, with a glory round the head, all or. Motto—Patria cara carior fides.

Nicolas (co. Huntingdon). Ar. three fleurs-de-lis gu. on a chief az. a lion pass. guard. or.

Nicolas (Brittany). Gu. on a fesse ar. betw. three wolves' heads erased or, as many martlets sa. Crest—A wolf's head issuing from the coronet of a count all ppr.

Nicolas. Ar. a fesse wavy sa. betw. three ravens ppr.; another, Or, on a cross gu. a ducal crown or.

Nicolets (The Hill, Eastham, co. Worcester, and Hopton, Solers, co. Hereford). Ar. on a bend sa. three cinquefoils of the first.

Nicoll (Henden Place, co. Middlesex). Az. on a fess betw. three lions' heads erased ar. as many birds ppr.

Nicoll (London; granted to DONALD NICOLL, Esq., Sheriff of London, of Oldfields, Acton, Middlesex). Az. a fess betw. in chief three mascles or, and in base a sword erect ppr. within an oak wreath gu. Crest—A greyhound's head erased sa. charged with a mascle or, and in the mouth a thistle slipped ppr. Motto—Deo duce comite industria.

Nicoll. Sa. a pheon ar. Crest—A sparrow-hawk sa. beaked and legged gu.

Nicoll. Gu. a chev. ar. betw. three trefoils, stalked, couped, and ragulée or.

Nicoll. Az. on a fess betw. three lions' heads erased ar. as many martlets sa. Crest—A lion's head erased az. collared ar. thereon three martlets sa.

Nicolle (Jersey, Guernsey, and Penrose, co. Cornwall). Sa. a pheon ar. Crest—A cubit arm ppr. holding a bow or, stringed ar.

Nicolle (Jersey). Az. three crescents or. Crest—A falcon rising belled ppr. Motto—Essorant victorieux.

Nicolls, or Nycolls (London). Sa. two palets engr. ar. on a chief or, three Cornish choughs ppr. Crest—A demi Cornish chough ppr. holding in the beak an ear of wheat or.

Nicolls, or Nicoll (Colneyhatch, co. Middlesex; granted 7 Feb. 1722). Sa. three pheons shafted rompu ar. Crest—A wolf's head sa. charged with five erm. spots in fesse or.

Nicolls (Mershland, co. Norfolk). Ar. on a chev. az. betw. three lynxes' heads erased sa. as many crescents erm. Crest —A squirrel sejant sa. collared or, holding betw. the fore legs a water bouget ar.

Nicolls (Tilney, co. Norfolk). Ar. on a chev. az. betw. three griffins' heads erased sa. as many crescents erm.

Nicolls (Hardwick, co. Northampton; of which family were Sir FRANCIS NICHOLLS, of Hardwick, Bart., extinct, and his uncle, Sir AUGUSTINE NICOLLS, of Faxton, one of the Judges of the Common Pleas, temp. James I.). Sa. three pheons ar., these were the arms borne by WILLIAM NICHOLLS, Esq., of Hardwicke, temp. Edward IV., but his grandson, FRANCIS NICHOLLS, Esq., of the same place, had a confirmation of the coat with the addition of "a canton ar." Crest —A wolf's head erased sa.

Nicolls (Garisker, co. Kildare). Az. three pheons ar. points down, on a chief of the last a thistle ppr. betw. two trefoils slipped vert. Crest—A naked arm couped at the elbow and erect ppr. charged with a pheon sa. and holding in the hand a bow or, stringed ar. Motto—As an arrow true.

Nicolson (Nicolson and Lasswade, co. Edinburgh, bart., 1629). Or, three falcons' heads erased gu. beaked or. Crest —A demi lion ramp. or. Supporters—Two eagles or, armed gu. Motto—Generositate.

Nicolson (Clunie, afterwards Kemnay, co. Aberdeen, and Glenbervie, co. Kincardine, bart., 1700). Or, three eagles' heads erased gu. Crest—A lion's head erased or. Motto, as the last.

Nicolson (Carnock and Tillicoultry, bart., 1637). Or, a lion's head betw. three falcons' heads erased gu. a border of the last.

Nicolson (Carnock, paternally STEWART, 1807). Or, three hawks' heads erased gu. a bordure az. Crest—A lion's head erased gu. *Supporters*—Two eagles reguard. ppr. wings endorsed and inverted. *Motto*—Nil sistere contra.

Nicolson (Cockburnspath, co. Berwick). Gu. a lion's head erased betw. three hawks' heads erased or, a bordure engr. of the last.

Nicolson (cos. Kent, Lancaster, and Middlesex). Or, a fesse wavy az. betw. four lions' gambs issuing out of each corner of the escutcheon gu. on a chief of the second a vessel of the first betw. two bezants. *Crest*—A lion's gamb embowed gu. holding an anchor or.

Nicolson (London, 1588). Erm. on a pale sa. three martlets or (another, ar.). *Crest*—On a mount vert a leopard sejant ar. spotted sa. pierced through the breast with a lance ppr. the wound guttée de sang.

Niddrie (Scotland). Az. a fesse or, betw. three mullets of the last pierced of the field.

Niffield (co. York). Or, a bend wavy betw. two cotises sa.

Nigel. Gu. a pale fusily or.

Nigell (Baron of Halton, co. Chester). **Gu. a pale of five** lozenges or. *Crest*—An oak tree vert.

Nightingale (Kneesworth Hall, co. Cambridge, bart.). Per pale erm. and gu. a rose counterchanged. *Crest*—An ibex sejant ar. tufted, armed, and maned or.

Nightingale (Newportpond, co. Essex). Same *Arms* and *Crest*.

Nightingale (Neale, co. Essex). Per pale sa. and gu. a rose counterchanged, barbed vert, seeded or.

Nightingale (Lichfield, London, and co. Warwick; granted 1593). Erm. a rose gu. seeded or, barbed vert, a crescent for diff. *Crest*—A greyhound courant erm. charged with a crescent for diff.

Nightingale (Ballygran, co. Wexford; Fun. Ent. Ulster's Office, 1632, of ISABEL, wife of LUKE NIGHTINGALE, Esq.. of Ballygran). Per pale ar. and gu. three roses counterchanged, leaved vert, seeded or.

Nightingall (Brome Hall, co. Norfolk). Erm. a rose gu. on a chief embattled or, two banners in saltire, the staves enfiled by a wreath of laurel ppr. a canton gu. charged with the representation of a medal. *Crest*—On a mural crown or, an ibex ar. horned, maned, and tufted or, gorged with a wreath of laurel vert.

Nightingall. Erm. a rose gu. *Crest*—An ibex ppr.

Nihell (Reg. Ulster's Office). Gu. a man in complete armour, the beaver of the helmet close, brandishing a sword over the head all ppr. on a chief az. three mullets of six points ar. *Crest*—A greyhound ar. collared gu. *Motto*—Vi et fide vivo.

Nilson. Az. on a cross or, quarter pierced of the field a ducal crown of the second betw. four lions ramp. ar.

Nimmo, or Nemmock (Scotland). Or, on a saltire gu. betw. four crescents of the last as many cinquefoils of the first.

Nind (Reading, and Hawthorns Harchatch, co. Berks). Ar. a chev. betw. three dragons' heads gu. *Crest*—Out of a mural crown ar. a dragon's head gu. *Motto*—Fortis et fidelis.

Nind. Or, three crosses crosslet fitchée in fesse gu. betw. six mullets az. *Crest*—A torteau charged with a pale indented ar.

Nisbet (Dean, Mid-Lothian, bart.). Ar. a chev. gu. betw. three boars' heads erased sa. *Crest*—An eagle. displ. ppr. *Supporters*—Dexter, a savage holding a club over his shoulder and wreathed about the loins and head ppr.; sinister, a greyhound ppr. *Motto*—Non obest virtute sors.

Nisbet (that Ilk, co. Berwick). Ar. three boars' heads erased sa. *Crest*—A boar pass. sa. *Motto*—I byde it.

Nisbet (Craigentinny, co. Edinburgh). Ar. on a chev. gu. betw. three boars' heads erased sa. as many cinquefoils of the first. *Crest*—A boar pass. sa. *Motto*—I byde it.

Nisbet (Dirleton, co. Haddington). Same *Arms* as the last, the chev. ensigned on the top with a thistle ppr. *Crest*—A dexter hand issuant out of a cloud, and holding a balance and scales all ppr. *Motto*—Discite justitiam.

Nisbet (HAMILTON-NISBET, of Dirleton and Belhaven, 1801). Quarterly, 1st and 4th, as the last; 2nd and 3rd, gu. a sword paleways ar. hilted and pommelled or, betw. three cinquefoils of the second, for HAMILTON. *Crest* and *Motto* as above. *Supporters*—Two horses ar. bridled gu. *Additional Motto*—Ride through. See also *under* HAMILTON.

Nisbet (Greenholm, co. Ayr, and Carphin). Ar. three boars' heads erased, within a bordure sa. *Crest*—A boar's head as in the arms. *Motto*—His fortibus arma.

Nisbet (Southbroome House, co. Wilts). Ar. three boars' heads erased sa. a border invected gu. *Crest*—A boar's head, as in the arms. *Motto*—Vis fortibus arma.

Nisbet (Bordeaux, 1681). Ar. on a chev. indented gu. betw. three goats' heads erased sa. as many cinquefoils of the first.

735

Crest—A castle sa. and growing beside it a thistle ppr. *Motto* —Hinc ducitur honos.

Niven (Shousburgh and Windhouse, in Zetland). Az. a fesse betw. an increscent and decrescent in chief ar. and in base a branch of palm slipped or. *Crest*—A branch of palm vert. *Motto*—Vivis sperandum.

Niven (Peebles and Thornton, co. Aberdeen, 1796). Ar. a tower embattled gu. betw. an increscent and a decrescent in chief az. and a branch of palm in base ppr. *Crest*— A pegasus courant ar. crowned and winged or. *Motto* over the crest: I hope in God; below the shield: Marto et arte.

Niven (Kirkbride, co. Ayr, 1842). Az. on a fess betw. an increscent and a decrescent in chief ar. and in base a branch of palm slipped of the last, three spear heads in pale gu. *Crest*—A branch of palm vert. *Motto*—Vivis sperandum.

Niven (England). Az. a fesse betw. an increscent and a decrescent in chief, and a crescent in base ar. *Crest*—A holly branch vert.

Nix. Or, a chev. betw three leopards' faces gu. *Crest*—On a mount a stag lodged ppr.

Nixon (Blechingdon, co. Oxford). Or, on a chev. betw. three leopards' faces gu. as many suns in splendour ppr. *Crest*—A leopard ramp. guard. ppr.

Nixon (co. Fermanagh; confirmed to BRINSLEY DE COURCY NIXON, Esq., and the descendants of his grandfather, Rev. BRINSLEY NIXON, rector of Puinstown, co. Meath). Sa. five bezants, two, two, and one, on a chief engr. ar. a battle axe in fess of the field. *Crest*—A gamecock ppr. charged on the breast with a bezant. *Motto*—Toujours prêt.

Nixon. Sa. six plates and a chief ar. *Crest*—A dexter hand holding a sword ppr.; another, Ar. on a cross patonce gu. five escallops or.

Noads (Shepalbury, co. Herts; granted 10 Feb. 1634). Sa. on a pile ar. three trefoils slipped of the first.

Nobbes (Houghton, co. Norfolk). Vert a cross patonce erm. betw. three birds ar. *Crest*—On a chapeau gu. turned up erm. an eagle's head az.

Noble (co. Cornwall, Belson and Bishops' Tentor, co. Devon, and Barming, near Maidstone, co. Kent). Or, two lions pass. guard. in pale az. betw. as many flaunches of the last, on a fesse gu. three bezants. *Crest*—A lion pass. az.

Noble (co. Berwick). Erm. three leopards' faces sa. ducally crowned gu.

Noble (Fairnell, co. Stafford). Or, on a fess gu. three bezants betw. two lions pass. az.

Noble (Reresby, co. Leicester; THOMAS NOBLE, b. 1574, grandson of WILLIAM NOBLE, Esq., of Rushington, in same co. Visit. Leicester, 1619). Ar. on a chief gu. a lion pass. or. *Crest*—An eagle displ. or. *Motto*—Fide et fortitudine.

Noble (co. Stafford). Ar. on a fesse gu. betw. two lions pass. guard. sa. three bezants.

Noble. Erm. three leopards' faces sa. ducally crowned or; another, Or, on a fesse gu. betw. two lions pass. sa. three bezants.

Noble (RICHARD NOBLE, *temp.* Queen Elizabeth, Fun. Ent. Ulster's Office, 1604, of his wife, MARY, dau. of JAMES RYAN, Sheriff of Dublin). Sa. a chev. ar. betw. three leopards' faces or.

Noble (Fun. Ent. Ulster's Office, 1660). Or, two lions pass. in pale az. betw. as many flaunches of the last, on a fess gu. three bezants.

Noble (Allerstown, co. Meath; granted by Betham, Ulster, to Rev. MUNGO HENRY NOBLE). Vert on a fess or, betw. three leopards' faces ar. a fleur-de-lis betw. two annulets sa. *Crest*—A dove ar. holding in the beak a ring or, gemmed az.

Noble (Ardmore and Ardarden-Noble, co. Dumbarton). Gu. a chev. erm. betw. three bay leaves slipped or. *Crest*—A dexter hand holding a dagger all ppr. *Motto*—Virtute et valore.

Nock. Az. a bend betw. three annulets or. *Crest*—A dexter hand brandishing a scymitar ppr.

Nock. Per bend sinister az. and or, three annulets bend-ways counterchanged.

Nocourt. Gu. a cross engr. ar.

Nodegate. Per pale ar. and gu. three lions' gambs in verted and erased counterchanged.

Nodes. Sa. on a pile ar. three trefoils slipped of the first. *Crest*—Two lions' gambs. sa. holding a garb or.

Nodin Erm. a chev. gu. in base three piles issuing from the chev. sa. *Crest*—A stag's head couped gu,

Noel (Ellenhall, co. Stafford, an ancient family of Norman extraction; ROBERT NOEL was Lord of Ellenhall *temp.* Henry I. and Henry II., and had two sons; I, THOMAS NOEL, Sheriff co. Stafford *temp.* Henry II. and Richard I., who left two daus., his co-heirs, viz., ALICE, *m.* WILLIAM HARCOURT, of Staunton Harcourt, and JOAN, *m.* WILLIAM DE DUSTON, of Northamptonshire; II. PHILIP NOEL, ancestor of NOEL, of Hilcote, co. Stafford. Or, fretty gu. a canton erm.

Noel (Hilcote, co. Stafford, now of Bell Hall, Belbroughton, co. Worcester. This is the only remaining branch in the male line of the very ancient family of NOEL, of which the *Earls of Gainsborough* represented a junior branch. The Hilcote estate remained with them until recent times. WALTER NOEL, Esq. (son of WALTER NOEL, Esq., of Hilcote, by ELIZABETH, dau. of PAUL FOLEY, of Preestwood, co. Stafford, acquired Bell Hall and extensive estates in the neighbourhood, in marriage, in 1764, with CATHERINE, dau. and heir of JOHN PERROTT, Esq., of Bell Hall. He was the grandfather of CHARLES NOEL, Esq., of Bell Hall, High Sheriff of co. Worcester in 1853). Or, fretty gu. a canton erm. quartering, for PERROTT, Gu. three pears or, on a chief ar. a demi lion issuant sa. armed and langued of the field. *Crest*—A buck at gaze ar. attired or. *Motto*—Jus suum cuique.

Noel (Dalby, co. Leicester, bart., extinct; descended from NOEL, of Hilcote. Or, fretty gu. a canton erm. *Crest*—A buck at gaze ar. attired or.

Noel (*Earl of Gainsborough*, extinct 1798; Sir EDWARD NOEL, bart., of Dalby, was created, 1617, *Baron Noel*, of Ridlington, co. Rutland; his son BAPTIST became *Viscount Campden*, and was father of EDWARD, *Viscount Campden*, created *Earl of Gainsborough*, 1682; on the extinction of the Peerage the estates devolved on GERARD NOEL EDWARDS, Esq., who assumed the surname of NOEL, and had a son, CHARLES NOEL, created *Earl of Gainsborough*). Or, fretty gu. a canton erm. *Crest*—A buck at gaze ar. attired or. *Supporters*—Two bulls ar. armed and hoofed ppr. *Motto*—Tout bien ou rien.

Noel (*Earl of Gainsborough*). Or, fretty gu. a canton erm. *Crest*—A buck at gaze ar. attired or. *Supporters*—On either side a bull ar. armed and unguled ppr. gorged with a naval crown az. therefrom a chain reflexed over the back gold, pendent from the crown an escutcheon also az. charged with an anchor erect encircled by a wreath of laurel or. *Motto*—Tout bien ou rien.

Noel (Kirkby Mallory, co. Leicester; *Viscount Wentworth*, created 1762, extinct 1815; descended from JOHN NOEL, younger son of ANDREW NOEL, of Dalby, ancestor of the *Earls of Gainsborough*. The last male heir of the Kirkby line, Sir THOMAS NOEL, Bart., *Viscount Wentworth*, d. s.p. in 1815, leaving his sister, JUDITH, wife of Sir RALPH MILBANKE, Bart., and his nephew, NATHANIEL, *Lord Scarsdale*, co-heirs to the barony of Wentworth. *Lord Scarsdale* d. unm. 1856, when his niece, ANNE ISABELLA, widow of GEORGE GORDON, sixth *Lord Byron*, the poet, only child of Lady MILBANKE, became *Baroness Wentworth*, she d. 1860, and was s. by her grandson, RALPH GORDON NOEL MILBANKE, *Lord Wentworth*, only surviving son of WILLIAM, *Earl of Lovelace*, by his first wife, Hon. AUGUSTA ADA BYRON. *Arms* and *Crest*, same as preceding. *Supporters of Viscount Wentworth*—Two griffins ar. collared or. *Motto*—Pensez à bien.

Noel (KING-NOEL, *Earl of Lovelace*). Quarterly, 1st and 4th, NOEL, or, fretty gu. a canton erm.; 2nd and 3rd, KING, sa. three spears' heads erect ar. the points sanguine, on a chief or, three pole-axes az., their edges to the sinister. *Crests*—1st, NOEL: A buck at gaze ar. attired or; 2nd, KING: A dexter arm erect couped at the elbow vested sa., adorned with three ermine spots in fesse or, the cuff turned up, grasping a truncheon of a spear, the head silver. *Supporters*—On either side a mastiff dog reguard. ppr. collared gu. *Motto*—Pensez à bien.

Noel (Walcot, co. Lincoln; CHRISTOPHER HENRY NEVILE, Esq., of Wellingore, co. Lincoln, eldest son of CHRISTOPHER NEVILE, Esq., of Wellingore, by Lady SOPHIA NOEL, his wife, youngest dau. of BAPTISTE, fourth *Earl of Gainsborough*, assumed the surname of NOEL). Or, fretty gu. a canton erm. *Crest*—A buck at gaze ar. attired or.

Noel-Hill (*Lord Berwick*). See HILL.

Noel (Newbole, co. Stafford, *temp.* Edward III.). Ar. fretty sa. a canton erm.

Noel (Moxhull Park, co. Warwick). Same *Arms* as NOEL, of Kirkby Mallory. *Crest*—A buck at gaze ar. attired or. *Motto*—Tout bien ou rien.

Noel (Persall, co. Stafford). Or, fretty gu. on a canton ar. a mullet sa.

Noke (Stottesbrook, co. Bucks). Or, on a fess sa. betw. three leopards' faces gu. as many crowns of the field; another, A dulcipher betw. two crowns or. on the fess.

Nolan (co. Galway; Reg. Ulster's Office). Ar. on a cross

gu. betw. four swords erect of the last, pommels and hilts sa., a lion pass. betw. four martlets of the first. *Crest*—On a mount vert a falcon close ppr.

Nolan (Ballinderry and Portacarron, co. Galway; descended from the ancient Irish Sept of O'NOWLAN or O'NOLAN. PATRICK NOLAN, Esq., of Ballinderry, had several grants of land in cos. Mayo and Galway, *temp.* Charles II.; his representative, JOHN PHILIP NOLAN, Esq., of Ballinderry, is M.P. co. Galway, since 1874). Gu. on a cross or, betw. four swords erect ar. pommels and hilts of the second, a lion pass. of the first betw. four martlets sa. *Crest*—A demi lion ramp. gu. *Motto*—Cor unum via una.

Nolan (Bedford Square, London). Az. on a bend betw. two fleurs-de-lis or, a lion pass. guard. gu. holding in the dexter forepaw a fleur-de-lis of the first. *Crest*—A demi lion ramp. gu. holding a fleur-de-lis or.

Nolan. See O'NOWLAN.

Nomure, or Nowers. Vairé ar. and gu.

Nonant (*Baron of Totnes*; heiress *m.* BEAUCHAMP). Ar. a lion ramp. gu.

None (co. Leicester). Ar. a chev. betw. three millrinds fesseways sa.

Nones, Noone, or Noves (Shelfhamer, co. Norfolk). Or, a cross engr. vert.

Nones. Per pale gu. and ar. a fess az.

Nonwers, or Nowers. Ar. two bars gu. in chief as many crescents of the second.

Nonwike. Sa. an eagle displ. or. *Crest*—A demi griffin ppr. issuing from a plume of ostrich feathers ar.

Nonycke. Gu. a fesse dancettée ar. in chief three mullets or.

Noone (Swaffham, co. Norfolk, and Tostock, co. Suffolk). Sa. a saltire betw. four lions' gambs erased or. *Crest*—A bull's head erased per fesse ar. and gu. attired of the last.

Noone (co. Norfolk). Or, a cross engr. vert. *Crest*—An eagle displ. vert.

Noone (Walton, co. Leicester; confirmed by Camden, Clarenceux, 1611; FRANCIS NOONE, Esq., of Walton, *b.* 1587, eldest son of ROBERT NOONE, Esq., of Walton, who was great-grandson of JOHN NOONE, of same place. Visit. Leicester, 1619). Or, on a cross engr. vert a crescent of the field. *Crest*—An eagle displ. with two heads or, wings vert.

Noone. Paly of six ar. and sa.

Noonwers. Ar. two bars gu. in chief three crescents of the last.

Noor (co. Kent). Az. on a chief indented or, three mullets gu.

Noores. Az. a chev. betw. three rams' heads erased sa.

Nooth (co. Dorset; borne by Major HENRY NOOTH, 4th Dragoons, who assumed the name of VAVASOUR in 1791). Or, a demi lion ramp. couped gu. armed az.

Norbery (co. Chester). Ar. on a chev. engr. sa. betw. three bulls' heads of the second a fleur-de-lis of the first.

Norbery (co. Derby). Ar. a bend sa. on a chief gu. a barrulet wavy or.

Norbery, Norberry, or Norbury. Ar. a bend sa. a chief vairé or and gu. *Crest*—A dove or.

Norbery. See NORBURY.

Norborne (Bremhill, co. Wilts). Erm. a fesse nebulée gu. on a canton of the last a ducal coronet or. *Crest*—A demi lion erm. holding betw. the paws a ducal coronet or.

Norburgh. Gu. a chief erm.

Norbury, Earl of. See TOLER.

Norbury (Norbury, co. Chester; originally BULKELEY; descended from ROGER BULKELEY, of Norbury, third son of WILLIAM BULKELEY, of Bulkeley. Of this branch was Sir JOHN NORBURY, Lord Treasurer of England, *temp.* Henry IV.). Sa. a chev. betw. three bulls' heads cabossed ar. *Crest*—Out of a ducal coronet or, a bull's head sa.

Norbury (Droitwich and Sherridge, co. Worcester; THOMAS JONES, Esq., of Sherridge, who *m.* MARY ANNE, dau. and heiress of CONINGSBY NORBURY, Esq., of Droitwich, assumed, together with his wife, by royal licence in 1840, the surname and arms of NORBURY only). Sa. a chev. indented erm. betw. three bulls' heads cabossed ar. armed or. *Crest*—Out of a crown vallery or, a bull's head sa. armed gold, in the mouth a trefoil vert.

Norbury (co. Chester). Sa. a chev. engr. betw. three bulls' heads cabossed ar. *Crest*—Out of a ducal coronet or, a bull's head sa.

Norbury, or Norberrey (Norberrey, co. Derby). Ar. a bend sa. a chief vairé or and gu.

Norbury (Fun. Ent. Ulster's Office, 1682, JOHN NORBURY). Ar. a chev. engr. betw. three bulls' heads cabossed ar. armed or, a mullet for diff.

Norcambrowe, Norchambrowe, or Norcham-Derone. Gu. a cinquefoil (another, three) or, betw. nine crosses crosslet ar.

Norcliffe (Langton Hall, co. York). Az. five mascles voided in cross or, a chief erm. *Crest*—A greyhound sejant or, collared az. sustaining with the right fore-foot a mascle ar. *Motto*—Sine maculâ.

Norcop (RADFORD-NORCOP, Betton Hall, co. Salop). Quarterly, 1st, sa. three ostrich feathers chevronways within two chevronels, betw. three boars' heads erased or, for NORCOP; 2nd, ar. a fess engr. az. fretty or, betw. two chev. vair, for RADFORD; 3rd, ar. on a fess engr. gu. betw. three greyhounds' heads erased sa. collared or, as many bezants, for CHURCH; 4th, sa. a chev. betw. three boys' heads couped at the shoulders ar. crined or, each enwrapped about the neck with a snake ppr., for VAUGHAN. *Crests*—1st: Upon a mount vert, a boar's head erased sa. in front of two ostrich feathers or, for NORCOP; 2nd: A fret or, thereon a partridge ppr. *Motto*—Possunt quia posse videntur.

Norden (Easthill, co. Kent). Ar. on a fess gu. betw. three beavers pass. sa. as many crosses crosslet fitchée or. *Crest* —A hawk ar. belled or, preying on a partridge also ar. beaked gold.

Norden (London; granted 1771). Ar. on a mount vert, a palm tree of the last, thereon pendent a shield az. charged with three mullets of the first, pierced of the third, on a chief of the last a sun ppr. betw. two rings or, each adorned with a diamond ppr. *Crest*—An arm couped and erect habited az. cuffed ar. in the hand ppr. an escarbuncle or. *Motto*—Providentia tutamur.

Norden (co. Kent). Ar. on a fess gu. betw. three beavers or sea-horses pass. sa. langued or, a crosslet fitchée betw. two trefoils of the last. *Crest*—A demi beaver sa. holding in the mouth a branch of five leaves vert.

Nordet. Az. an eagle displ. with two heads or, a chief ar. *Crest*—A torteaux betw. two wings ppr.

Norfolk, Duke of. See HOWARD.

Norgat (co. Norfolk). Gu. two gauntlets in saltire ar. garnished or.

Norgate (Rev. THOMAS STARLING NORGATE, of Sparham, co. Norfolk). Same *Arms*. *Crest*—A demi wolf ramp. ar. armed and langued gu. charged on the breast with an estoile for diff. *Motto*—Virtus constat in actione.

Norham. Per pale gu. and az. a chev. erm. betw. three escallops ar.; another, Per chev. gu. and az. three escallops erm.; another, Per chev. ar. and az. a fesse erm. betw. three escallops counterchanged.

Norhope (cos. Kent and Nottingham). Quarterly, ar. and vert, a cross counter-componée of the same. *Crest*—A cubit arm vested per pale ar. and vert, holding in the hand ppr. a garland of the second

Norie, or Norrie. Gu. a fesse ar. *Crest*—A wolf's head erased sa.

Norie (Noristone, co. Stirling, 1678). Per pale ar. and sa. an orle engr. on both sides and charged with four quatrefoils within a bordure all counterchanged of the same. *Crest*— On a pheon a negro's head couped betw. two arms vambraced in orle all ppr. *Motto*—Domi ac foris.

Norington, or Norwington. Ar. a saltire gu.

Norland (co. Kent). Ar. on a chev. betw. three lions ramp. sa. as many bezants; another, Gu. on a chev. ar. betw. three lions ramp. or, three pellets.

Norleighe. Ar. a chev. sa. betw. three roses gu.

Norley (Norley, co. Chester). Gu. a cross engr. ar.

Norley (co. Devon). Ar. a chev. betw. three roses gu.

Normall (Reg. Ulster's Office). Or, on a chief indented gu. three lions ramp. ar.

Norman (Dencombe, co. Sussex). Quarterly, 1st and 4th, ar. on a bend gu. three bucks' heads cabossed of the field; 2nd and 3rd, gu. on waves of the sea, a ship of three masts ppr. in chief three mullets ar. *Crest*—A sea-horse sejant, resting the dexter paw on an anchor all ppr. *Motto*—Deus dabit vela.

Norman (Slaugham Park, co Sussex). Gu. on waves of the sea, a ship of three masts ppr. in chief three mullets ar. *Motto*—Deus dabit vela.

Norman (Claverham House, co. Somerset). Barry nebulée of eight ar. and gu. on a bend sa. three escallops ppr. *Crest*—A cubit arm embowed in armour ppr. pommelled and hilted or. *Motto*—Pro fide strictus.

Norman (originally of Shepton Mallet, co. Somerset; JAMES NORMAN, Esq., Captain R.N., who left three daus. and co-heiresses: I. ELIZA; II. ANN, *m.* first to JAMES BREMER, Esq., lieut. R.N., by whom she had a son, Sir JAMES JOHN GORDON BREMER, Captain R.N., K.C.B., and K.C.H., of the Priory, co. Devon, and secondly to Colonel ROBY; III.

HARRIET, who *m.* THOMAS ELPHINSTONE, Esq., Captain R N., son of Rear-Admiral ELPHINSTONE, and *d. s. p.*). Barry of six or and gu. on a chief ar. three fleurs-de-lis sa. *Crest*—A demi lion ramp. holding betw. the paws a fleur-de-lis, as in the arms.

Norman (England). Sa. a lion ramp. or. *Crest*—A spear issuing in pale, thrust through a savage's head couped ppr.

Norman (co. Kent). Ar. on a chev. sa. three boars' heads couped or.

Norman (Lord Mayor of London, 1250). Ar. on a chief sa. three leopards' faces or.

Norman (Lord Mayor of London, 1453). Or, three bars gu. on a chief ar. as many fleurs-de-lis sa.

Norman (Honyngham, co. Norfolk). Ar. a chev. betw. three birds sa.

Norman (co. Somerset). Ar. a chev. betw. three leopards' faces sa.

Norman. Barry of eight ar. and gu. in chief three fleurs-de-lis sa.; another, Or, three bars gu. on a chief of the last three fleurs-de-lis of the field; another, Bendy of six or and gu. a chief per chief sa. and erm. in chief three fleurs-de-lis ar.; another, Ar. on a fesse double cotised gu. three fleurs-de-lis of the first.

Norman. Ar. on a chev. sa. three leopards' faces or; another, Barry of six or and gu. on a chief ar. three fleurs-de-lis sa.; another, Or, three bars gu. on a chief of the last three bucks' heads cabossed of the field (another, heads or); another, Per chev. gu. and az. three escallops erm.

Norman (co. Stafford). Ar. three horses' heads erased sa

Norman (LEE-NORMAN, Corballis, co. Louth; exemplified to THOMAS LEE, Esq., on his assuming, by royal licence, the additional surname and arms of NORMAN, 1817, in compliance with the will of his maternal grandfather, Rev. THOMAS NORMAN, of Lagore, co. Meath). Quarterly, 1st and 4th, or, a chev. betw. three lions' faces gu., for NORMAN; 2nd and 3rd, ar. a chev. gu. betw. three leopards' faces ppr., for LEE. *Crests*—1st, NORMAN: A lion pass. guard. ppr.; 2nd, LEE: A demi lion ramp. grasping a sceptre all ppr.

Norman (LEE-NORMAN; exemplified to LUKE ALEXANDER NORMAN, Esq., of 26, Rutland Square, Dublin, son of ALEXANDER NORMAN, Esq., Q.C., on his assuming, by royal licence, 1876, the additional surname and arms of LEE). Same *Arms* and *Crests* as preceding. *Motto*—Honor virtutis præmium.

Normanby, Marquess of. See PHIPPS.

Normand (Scotland). Sa. a lion ramp. or, on a chief of the last seven billets az. *Crest*—A paschal lamb ppr. *Motto*—Auxilium ab alto.

Normansell, or Normanvile (cos. Stafford and York). Ar. on a fess betw. two cotises az. three fleurs-de-lis or.

Normanton, Earl of. See AGAR.

Normanton. Ar. a saltire gu.

Normanton. Ar. three cinquefoils gu. (another adds, a label sa.).

Normanton. Ar. on a saltire gu. a mullet of the first.

Normanvile (co. York). Ar. on a fess cotised gu. three fleurs-de-lis of the field.

Normanvile. Ar. a fess betw. two barrulets gu. on a canton or, a fess lozengy of the second; another, Gu. a fess cotised ar.

Normanvill (Kilwick, co. York). Ar. on a fess betw. four barrulets gu. three fleurs-de-lis of the first, a bend sinister az.

Normanvill. Ar. on a fess betw. two bars gemels gu. (another, az.) three fleurs-de-lis of the first.

Normanville (Gargunnock, Scotland). See NORVILLE.

Normecott (Croston, co. Salop). Sa. a fess or, betw. three escallops ar.

Normeston (co. Buckingham). Az. two lions pass. guard. ar.

Norres (West Derby, co. Lancaster, 1664). Quarterly, ar. and gu., in 2nd and 3rd quarters a fret or, on a fess az. three mullets of the third.

Norres (Tarlton, co. Lancaster, 1664). Same *Arms*.

Norres (Middleforth, co. Lancaster, 1664). Same *Arms*, the fess charged with three bezants instead of mullets.

Norreys (Speke, co. Lancaster; an ancient family in that co., descended from WILLIAM NORREYS, Esq., of Sutton, who *m.* JOAN, heiress of SPEKE, dau. of Sir JOHN MOLYNEUX, Knt., of Sefton. The eventual heiress, MARY, only child of THOMAS NORREYS, Esq., of Speke, M.P. for Liverpool, *m.* Lord SYDNEY BEAUCLERK. The families of NORREYS of Bray, Lords NORREYS of Rycote, NORREYS of Fifield, and NORREYS of Davyhulme, all descended from younger sons of the house of Speke. Of the house of Speke were the NORREYS of Bray, co. Berks, who eventually became *Barons Norreys*). Quarterly, ar. and gu., in the 2nd and 3rd quarters a fret or, over all a fesse az. The original crest of the family appears, by a copy from a window in Childwall Church, co. Lancaster (Harl. MSS. 1997), to have been a woman's head couped at the breasts, but on the marriage of Sir HENRY NORREYS, *temp.* Henry V., with the dau. and heir of ROGER ERNEIS, of Chester, the ERNEIS' bearing was taken for a crest, viz., An eagle as. rising from a mount vert.

Norreys (*Earl of Berkshire* and *Baron Norreys*, of Rycote, earldom extinct 1623; barony vested in the *Earl of Abingdon*). Quarterly, ar. and gu. in the 2nd and 3rd quarters a fret or, over all a bend az. *Supporters*—Two monkeys collared and chained ppr.

Norreys (bart. extinct; Sir WILLIAM NORREYS, M.P. for Liverpool, brother of THOMAS NORREYS, Esq., of Speke, was created a bart. 1698, and *d. s. p.*). Same *Arms* and Crest.

Norreys (Davyhulme Hall, co. Lancaster; a branch of NORREYS, of Speke; HENRY NORRIS, Esq., of Davyhulme Hall, left an only dau. and heiress, MARY NORRIS, of Davyhulme, *m.* 1809, ROBERT JOSIAS JACKSON HARRIS, Esq., who assumed the name and arms of NORRIS). Quarterly, ar. and gu. in the 2nd and 3rd quarters a fret or, over all on a fess az. three bezants. *Crest*—On a mount vert an eagle, sa.

Norreys (co. Gloucester). Sa. semée of billets ar. a cross flory at the top only of the second.

Norreys (Cockwells, co. Berks). Ar. a chev. sa. betw. three ravens' heads erased of the last. *Crest*—An eagle (or raven) sa. *Motto*—Feythfully serve.

Norreys (Weston-on-the-Green, co. Oxford; Sir FRANCIS NORREYS, Knt., of Weston. Visit. Oxon 1634, *d.* July, 1669). Quarterly, ar. and gu., in the 2nd and 3rd quarters a fret or, a fess az. *Crest*—A raven's wings elevated sa. collared or.

Norreys (quartered by REGINALD, Cardinal POLE, in a coat in Magdalen College, Oxford. Visit. Oxon, 1566). Quarterly, ar. and gu., a bend sa.

Norreys (Sir THOMAS NORREYS, knighted at Christ Church Cathedral, Dublin, by Sir WILLIAM FITZWILLIAM, Lord-Deputy, 1588; he was afterwards, 1597, Lord-Deputy of Ireland) Quarterly, ar. and gu., a fess az., in the 2nd and 3rd quarters a fret or, an annulet for diff. *Crest*—A falcon rising sa.

Norreys (JEPHSON-NORREYS, Mallow, co. Cork, bart.). Quarterly, 1st and 4th, quarterly, ar. and gu., in the 2nd and 3rd quarters ar, over all a fesse az., for NORREYS; 2nd and 3rd, ar. on a chev. sa. a sun in glory or, betw. three lions' heads bezantée gu., for JEPHSON. *Crest*—On a mount vert a raven rising ppr. *Motto*—Loyalement je sers.

Norrington. Erm. three bars or. *Crest*—A bat displ. ppr.

Norris (Norris, co. Devon; the heiress *m.* FORTESCUE). Quarterly, gu. and ar., the 1st and 4th quarters fretty or.

Norris, or Norreys (Penlyne, co. Glamorgan; Harl. MSS. 1366). Sa. billettée ar. a cross flory of the last. *Crest*—A demi stag ar. attired sa. pierced through the body with an arrow of the last, headed and feathered of the first.

Norris (Wychingham, co. Norfolk, 1766). Quarterly, ar, and gu., in the 2nd and 3rd a fret or, over all a fess az.

Norris (arms in Raynesford Manor House, co. Oxford. Visit. Oxon, 1566). Quarterly, gu. and ar. in the 1st and 4th quarters a fret of the second, over all on a fess az. two mullets also of the second.

Norris (co. Hants). Ar. a chev. betw. three pelicans' heads erased sa.

Norris (Swalcliffe Park, co. Norfolk). Sa. billettée ar. a cross flory of the last. *Crest*—A demi stag ar. attired sa. pierced through the body with an arrow of the last, feathered of the first.

Norris (Guist and Woodnorton, co. Norfolk). Sa. a cross flory fitchée betw. twelve billets ar. *Crest*—A talbot sejant gu. collared and ringed or.

Norris. Sa. billettée ar. a cross patonce of the last. *Crest*—A demi buck ar. attired and unguled sa. vulned in the shoulder with an arrow of the last, feathered of the first.

Norris, or Norreys (JOHN NORREYS, second son of Sir WILLIAM NORREYS, of Speke, who *m.* the dau. and heir of RAVENSCROFT, of Cotton, and assumed the arms of that family). Ar. a chev. betw three ravens' heads erased sa.

Norris. Per pale ar. and sa. three reindeers' heads cabossed and counterchanged.

Norris, alias Banks, alias Bank. Ar. a chev. betw. three falcons' heads erased sa.

738

Norris (Fun. Ent. Ulster's Office, 1642; LETTICE, wife of TOBIAS NORRIS, merchant, Dublin). Ar. a cross betw. four billets sa. on a chief of the second a fleur-de-lis of the first.

Norris (Fun. Ent. Ulster's Office, 1662, RICHARD NORRIS, Esq.). Quarterly, gu. and ar. on a fess az. a cross moline or, in the 1st and 4th quarter a fret of the second.

Norris, or Nores (Reg. Ulster's Office). Az. two organ pipes in saltire ar. the dexter surmounted of the sinister.

North (*Earl of Guilford*). Az. a lion pass. or, betw. three fleurs-de-lis ar. *Crest*—A dragon's head erased sa. ducally gorged and chained ar. *Supporters*—Two mastiffs ppr. *Mottoes*—La vertu est la seule noblesse. Animo et fide.

North (*Baroness North*). Az. a lion pass. betw. three fleurs-de-lis or. *Supporters*—Two dragons, wings elevated sa. ducally gorged and chained or.

North (Mildenhall, co. Suffolk, bart., extinct 1695; descended from Sir HENRY NORTH, Knt., of Mildenhall, second son of ROGER, second *Lord North*). Same *Arms.*

North (co. Cambridge). Per pale or and az. a lion pass. guard. betw. three fleurs-de-lis counterchanged.

North (co. Hants). Per pale az. and gu. three pheasants close or. *Crest*—A stag's head erased ar. attired or, pierced by an arrow gold, flighted ar. holding in the mouth a slip of olive vert.

North (Feltham, co. Middlesex). Az. on a chev. ar. betw. three crosses pattée fitchée or, a cinquefoil betw. two escallops gu., on a chief of the third a greyhound courant sa. betw. two pellets. *Crest*—A cock's head couped, winged or, each wing charged with two chevronels sa. collared, holding in the beak a branch of holly leaved vert, fructed gu.

North (Docker, parish of Whittington, co. Lancaster). Quarterly, or and az. in the 1st quarter a crescent of the last. *Motto*—Animo et fide.

North (Cubley, co. Derby; granted by Dugdale, Garter, 1676). Az. a lion pass. or, on a chief of the last three fleurs-de-lis of the first. *Crest*—A swan ppr. gorged with a ducal coronet, and chained gu.

North (Walkeringham, co. Nottingham, and Huddersfield, co. York; granted 1600). Ar. two chevrons betw. three mullets sa. *Crest*—A lion's head erased ar. collared vair, or, and az.

North (Rougham, co. Norfolk). Az. a lion pass. or, betw. three fleurs-de-lis ar. *Crest*—A dragon's head erased sa. ducally gorged and chained or. *Motto*—Animo et fide.

North. Az. a lion pass. betw. three fleurs-de-lis ar.; another, Az. a lion pass. or, betw. three crowns ar.; another, Sa. a lion pass. or, betw. three fleurs-de-lis ar.

Northage (Upper Gower Street, London). Ar. on a bend sa. three martlets or. *Crest*—A stag's head and neck affrontée ppr.

Northall. Vert three dexter hands couped or.

Northam. Per pale gu. and az. a lion ramp. ar. crowned or. *Crest*—A demi wolf gu.

North American Colonial Association. See under ASSOCIATIONS.

Northampton, Marquess of. See COMPTON.

Northampton (Lord Mayor of London, 1381 and 1382). Gu. two lions ramp. guard. with one head or, crowned az. tails coward.

Northampton, or Norshampton. Ar. on a fess az. betw. three crescents gu. as many fleurs-de-lis or.

Northampton, Town of. Gu. on a mount vert, a tower triple-towered, supported by two lions ramp. guard. or, in the port a portcullis.

North-Bomford. See BOMFORD.

Northbrook, Earl of. See BARING.

Northcote (co. Devon; allowed by Cooke, Clarenceux). Ar. three crosses crosslet in bend sa.

Northcote (Hayne, co. Devon, bart.; descended from a family of great antiquity which derived, at a very early period, its name from Northcote, in the parish of East Down). Quarterly, 1st and 4th, ar. a fess betw. three crosses moline sa.; 2nd and 3rd, ar. three crosses crosslet in bend sa. *Crest*—On a chapeau gu. turned up erm. a stag trippant ar. *Motto*—Christi crux est mea lux.

Northcote (Crediton and Yewton, co. Devon; JOHN NORTHCOTE, Esq., of Yewton, second, but eldest surviving son of JOHN NORTHCOTE, Esq., of Crediton, who was son of WALTER NORTHCOTE, and grandson of JOHN NORTHCOTE, of same place. Visit. Devon, 1620). Ar. three crosses crosslet in bend sa. *Crest*, as NORTHCOTE, of Hayne.

Northcote (co. Devon, 1671). Or, a pale bendy of six ar. and sa. *Crest*—A demi unicorn ramp. erased ar. armed and maned or.

Northcote (Feniton Court, co. Devon, Somerset Court, co. Somerset). Or, a pale engr. bendy of six, ar. and az. betw.

four crosses botonnée of the last. *Crest*—A stag ar. charged on the body with two crosses botonnée gu. and resting the dexter fore foot on an escutcheon or, charged with a pale, as in the arms. *Motto*—Cito non temere.

Northe. Az. on a saltire betw. four crosses crosslet fitchée ar. five annulets gu. a border of the last; another, Gu. two chev. ar. betw. three mullets of the same; another, Quarterly, per fess indented ar. and sa., in the 1st quarter a buglehorn of the last.

Northen (co. Essex). Az. a chev. erm. voided or, betw. three martlets of the third. *Crest*—Out of a mural coronet a dragon's head vomiting flames ppr.

Northesk, Earl of. See CARNEGIE.

Northey (co. Wilts; an ancient county family, of which was Sir EDWARD NORTHEY, Knt., of Epsom, co. Surrey, Attorney-General to Queen Anne, whose son and heir, WILLIAM NORTHEY, Esq., of Ivey House, co. Wilts, Groom of the Chamber to George III., a distinguished senator, *m.* ANNE, dau. of the Right Hon. EDWARD HOPKINS, Secretary of State for Ireland, and left three sons : WILLIAM, of Box, co. Wilts, M.P., *d. s. p.* ; EDWARD, Canon of Windsor ; and General RICHARD NORTHEY-HOPKINS, of Oving House, co. Buckingham). Or, on a fess az. betw. three panthers statant ppr., semée of estoiles ar. two lilies of the last, with a rose in the centre gold, stem vert. *Crest*—A cockatrice, flames issuant from the mouth ppr.

Northey (Epsom, co. Surrey). Or, on a fess az. betw. three panthers statant ppr. semée of estoiles ar. a pansey of the first betw. two lilies of the third. *Crest*—A cockatrice, flames issuing from the mouth ppr. *Motto*—Steady.

Northey (Bocking, co. Essex). Or, on a fess az. betw. three panthers pass. ppr. a pansey of the first betw. two lilies ar.

Northfolke, or Norfolk. Gu. a fess betw. two chevronels ar. *Crest*—A lion ramp. sa.

Northie. Quarterly, ar. and az.

Northin (London). Az. three bars gemelles or, in chief as many lions of the last. *Crest*—On a ducal coronet or, a talbot pass. az. collared of the last.

Northleigh (Northleigh, co. Devon; WILLIAM NORTHLEIGH, Esq., of Northleigh, *d. ante* 1620, leaving two daus. co-heirs, MARY, *m.* GRIFFIN TRIVETT, and EGLERIA, *m.* HENRY DREWE; he was eldest son of RAYMOND NORTHLEIGH, of the same place, who was seventh in descent from ROBERT DE NORTHLEIGH. Visit. Devon, 1620). Ar. a chev. sa. betw. three roses gu. *Crest*—Three savages' heads conjoined in one neck, one looking to the dexter, one to the sinister, and one upwards.

Northleigh (Matford, co. Devon; ROBERT NORTHLEIGH. Visit. Devon, 1620; grandson of RICHARD NORTHLEIGH, younger brother of RAYMOND NORTHLEIGH, Esq., of Northleigh). Same *Arms* and *Crest*.

Northmore (Cleve House, Exeter). Gu. a lion ramp. or, langued and armed az. crowned with an Eastern crown az. *Crest*—A lion's head erased gu. crowned as above, and charged on the neck with a rose ar. bearded and seeded ppr. *Motto*—Nec elata, nec dejecta.

Northover (Allersome and Alercourt, co. Somerset; granted 1614). Or, five lozenges in saltire betw. four crosses crosslet az. *Crest*—A lion's gamb ar. supporting a lozenge az. charged with a cross crosslet or.

Northumberland, Duke of. See PERCY.
Northumberland, Earl of. See COSPATRICK.
Northumberland, Earl of. See COMYN.

Northumborow. Az. three cinquefoils or, betw. nine crosses crosslet ar.

Northwick, Baron. See RUSHOUT.

Northwode (*Baron Northwode;* in abeyance since 1416, descended from Sir ROGER DE NORTHWODE, Sheriff of co. Kent, 42 Henry III.; Sir JOHN DE NORTHWODE, his son, was summoned to Parliament 1313 ; JOHN, sixth Baron, *d. s. p.* leaving his sisters his co-heirs. The arms are on a brass in Minster Church, Sheppy, to Sir JOHN DE NORTHWODE). Erm. a cross engr. gu.

Northwood, or Norwood. Erm. a cross engr. gu. in the 1st quarter a wolf's head couped.

Nortoft (co. Essex). Sa. a lion ramp. or.

Norton (*Lord Grantley*). Az. a maunch erm. a bend gu. *Crest*—A Moor's head affrontée couped at the shoulders ppr. wreathed round the temples with laurel, and round the neck a torse ar. and az. *Supporters*—Dexter, a lion ar. gorged with a ducal coronet gold, pendant thereto by a riband gu. an escocheon of the arms of Norton; sinister, a griffin ar. gorged as the dexter. *Motto*—Avi numerantur avorum.

Norton (cos. Bedford and Buckingham, and Mark-Atcell, co. Hertford). Gu. a fret ar. a bend vair; another, Vairé or

and gu. *Crest*—A griffin sejant ppr. winged gu. beak and fore legs or.

Norton (co. Berks). Gu. three pheons in pale, the middlemost point downwards ar.

Norton (Charlton, co. Berks, co. Kent, and Fulham, co. Middlesex). Ar. a chev. betw. three crescents az. *Crest*—Out of a ducal coronet az. a demi lion ramp. double queued ar.

Norton (Ixworth, co. Suffolk). Az. three swords in triangle, pommel to pommel ar. hilts or, on a chief gu. a lion pass. betw. two maunches of the second. *Crest*—A demi lion ramp. gu. *Another Coat*—Vert a lion ramp. or. *Crest* - A man's head affrontée ppr. bound about the forehead with a fillet wreathed and tied in a knot ar. az. and gu. *Motto*—Confide recte agens.

Norton (Sir SAMPSON NORTON, Knt., Master of the Ordnance of War to Henry VIII.). Gu. three swords ar. pommels meeting in fess point or, on a chief or, a lion pass. gu. betw. two maunches erm. *Crest*—A demi dragon holding a sword.

Norton (King's Norton, co. Worcester, Sherington, co. Buckingham, and Hinxton, co. Cambridge; Visit. Bucks, Harl. MSS. 1533, and Visit. Camb., Harl. MSS. 1043). Ar. on a bend betw. two lions ramp. sa. three escallops of the first. *Crest*—A greyhound's head or, gorged with a fess engr. betw. two bars gu. the fess ringed behind of the first.

Norton (co. Devon; quartered by PROUZ, of Shagford, in same co.; Visit. Devon, 1620). Ar. a bar dancettée gu. in chief two martlets sa.

Norton (co. Gloucester). Az. three swords in triangle, pommel to pommel, ar. hilts gu. on a chief or, a lion pass. of the third betw. two maunches erm.

Norton (Rotherfield, co. Hants, bart., extinct 1652; RICHARD NORTON, living 10 Henry VII., 1494, *m.* ELIZABETH, dau. and heir of Sir WILLIAM ROTHERFIELD, Knt., of Rotherfield their descendant, Sir RICHARD NORTON, of Rotherfield, was created a bart. 23 May, 1622; his only dau. and heiress, ELIZABETH, *m.* FRANCIS PAULET, Esq., of Amport). Quarterly, 1st and 4th, vert a lion ramp. or; 2nd, az. on a fess betw. six crosses crosslet or, three escallops gu. ; 3rd, az. a fess nebulée betw. three crescents or. *Crest*—A Moor's head couped ppr. wreathed about the temples ar. az. and gu.

Norton (Southwick, co. Hants; a younger branch of NORTON, of Rotherfield). Same *Arms, &c.*

Norton (ROBERT DE NORTON, Sheriff of Norfolk, 1269). Vert a lion ramp. or.

Norton (Church Stretton, co. Salop; BONHAM NORTON, Esq., High Sheriff, *temp.* James I., 1611). Or, two bars gu. on a chief az. an inescutcheon erm.

Norton (Sir NICHOLAS NORTON). Az. a maunch erm. a bend or, a canton gu. *Crests*—1st: A buck's head cabossed or; 2nd: A maiden's head ppr. wreathed vert.

Norton (Canterbury, co. Kent). Ar. on a bend cotised betw. two lions ramp. sa. three escallops or.

Norton (Northwood, co. Kent). Gu. a cross potent erm. *Crest*—A wolf's head erased.

Norton (co. Kent). Ar. on a chev. betw. three lions ramp. sa. as many bezants.

Norton (co. Kent). Gu. on a chev. erm. (another, ar.) three crescents sa.

Norton (London and Coventry, co. Warwick). Ar. a chev. betw. three crescents az.

Norton (London, 1611). Or, two bars gu. on a chief az. an inescutcheon erm. *Crest*—A wreath of laurel vert, tied with a ribbon gu. betw. two wings expanded or.

Norton (North Elmham, Toftwood, East Dereham, co. Norfolk, and Rickinghall, co. Suffolk). Az. three swords, one in pale, point upwards, surmounted of the other two in saltire, points downwards ar. *Crest*—A halbert ppr. *Motto*—Dieu et mon espée. (On a wood carving of great antiquity, which has been in the family for upwards of two hundred years, the arms are : Three tilting spears, one in pale, point upwards, surmounted of the other two in saltire points downwards).

Norton (Southcreak, co. Norfolk). Sa. three covered cups or, a border gold.

Norton (co. Northumberland). Az. a maunch erm.

Norton-Priory (co. Chester). Gu. a pale fusily or, on a border az. eight mitres labelled of the second.

Norton (co. Somerset). Ar. on a bend cotised betw. six lions ramp. sa. three escallops of the field; another, three lions, the escallops or.

Norton (co. Suffolk). Ar. on a chev. engr. gu. betw. three fleurs-de-lis az. as many erm. spots or, on a chief of the third two swords in saltire of the first betw. as many maunches erm. *Crest* — A hare sejant gu. in grass vert.

Norton (cos. Suffolk and York). Az. a maunch erm. a bend gu. *Crest*—A Moor's head couped at the shoulder ppr.

Norton (Birlingham, co. Worcester). Az. a maunch erm. on a chief or, a lion pass. sa. *Crest*—A tiger's head erased or, in the mouth a broken spear of the last.

Norton, alias Conyers (co. York). Az. a maunch erm. a bendlet gu.

Norton. Vert a lion ramp. or, a border engr. of the last. *Crest*—A griffin's head or.

Norton. Gu. a cross formée erm.; another, Gu. a chev. betw. three crosses crosslet or.

Norton. Ar. a chev. gu betw. three crows' heads erased sa.; another, Ar. a chev. gu. betw. three tuns sa. hooped or; another, Gu. three fleurs-de-lis or; another, Ar. a chev. betw. three cushions sa.

Norton. Az. on a fesse betw. three (another, six) crosses crosslet or, as many escallops gu.; another, Gu. a fret ar. over all a bend vair; another, Gu. on a fesse erm. betw. three buglehorns stringed ar. as many boars' heads erased az.; another, Ar. a chev. betw. three hinds sa.; another, Erm. on a chief indented gu. three ducal crowns or, a bordure sa.

Norton. Or, a pile triple pointed flory sa. issuing from the dexter chief bendways.

Norton. Quarterly, 1st and 4th, sa. a pile triple-pointed flory ar. issuing out of the sinister base bendways; 2nd and 3rd, ar.

Norton (impalement Fun. Ent. Ulster's Office, 1615, RICHARD BROWNE, Sheriff of Dublin). Per pale gu. and az. three swords ar. in triangle, meeting at the pommels, pommels and hilts or.

Norton (Sir DUDLEY NORTON, Knt., Principal Secretary of State in Ireland, *temp.* Charles I., Fun. Ent. Ulster's Office, 1634). Ar. a fess betw. three crescents az. a crescent for diff.

Norton (Fun. Ent. Ulster's Office, 1677). Ar. on a bend betw. two lions ramp. sa. three escallops of the first.

Nortost (co. Norfolk). Sa. a stag lodged reguard. or, betw. the attires a bird of the last.

Nortost. Sa. a lion ramp. or.

Norvel (that Ilk). Sa. on a bend ar. three martlets of the first.

Norvel, or Normanville (Gargunnock, Scotland). Ar. on a bend sa. voided of the first, three martlets of the second beaked gu.

Norvill (Boghall, Scotland, 1682). Sa. on a bend betw. two cotises or, three martlets az. *Crest*—A martlet rising ppr. *Motto*—Spem renovant alæ.

Norvill, or Norvyle. Gu. fretty ar. a bend vairé or and of the first.

Norway. Sa. a chev. betw. three bulls' heads cabossed ar.

Norwey. Gu. a lion ramp. supporting betw. the paws a curtal ax or, a border of the last.

Norwich (cos. Essex, Norfolk, Northampton, and Suffolk; *temp.* Edward II.). Per pale gu. and az. a lion ramp. erm. *Crest*—On a mount vert a cock ar. combed, legged, and wattled gu. By some families of the name the field of the arms has been borne variously, per pale ar. and gu. and per pale sa. and purp. and the lion ar.

Norwich (*Baron Norwich*, extinct 1374; Sir JOHN DE NORWICH descended from GEOFFREY DE NORWICH, *temp.* King John, was summoned to Parliament 1342). Per pale gu. and az. a lion ramp. erm.

Norwich (Brampton, co. Northants, bart., extinct 1742). Per pale gu. and az. a lion ramp. erm.

Norwich (co. Norfolk). Erm. a fesse engr. az. (another, gu.).

Norwich. Sa. an eagle displ. or.

Norwich, See of. Az. three mitres labelled or.

Norwich Monastery (co. Norfolk). Ar. a cross sa.

Norwich, Deanery of. Same *Arms.*

Norwich, City of (confirmed by Harvey, Clarenceux). Gu. a castle surmounted with a tower ar. in base a lion pass. guard. or.

Norwold, or Narwold (co. Kent). Erm. a cross engr. gu. in the dexter chief canton a griffin's head couped sa.

Norwood (co. Bedford, Tulsey and Leckhampton, co. Gloucester). Erm. a cross engr. gu.

Norwood, or Northwood (cos. Buckingham and Norfolk; granted 1585). Same *Arms,* a crescent for diff. *Crest* —A demi lion ramp. erased ar. ducally crowned or, holding in the gamba a palm branch vert.

Norwood (cos. Devon and Gloucester). Erm. a cross engr. sa.

740

Norwood (arms in Throgmorton Manor House, co. Oxford. Visit. Oxon, 1566. Impalement KATHERINE, dau. of HENRY NORWOOD). Erm. a cross engr. gu.

Norwood, or Northwood (Dean Court, co. Kent). Same *Arms,* in the dexter chief quarter a wolf's head couped (another, erased) gu. *Crest*—Out of a ducal coronet a boar's head and neck all or.

Norwood. Ar. on a chev. gu. three crosses crosslet of the field.

Norwood (Ashford, Kent). Erm. a cross engr. gu. *Crest*— On waves of the sea ppr. a lion sejant, holding betw. the paws an anchor, fluxes upwards. *Motto*—Sub cruce vinces.

Noseworth. Ar. a pile sa. over all a chev. counterchanged. *Crest*—Out of a ducal coronet or, a unicorn's head sa. armed and crined ar.

Noseworthy. Gu. a pile and chev. or, counterchanged of the field.

Nostel, or Nostle-Priory (co. York). Gu. a cross betw. four lions ramp. or.

Nosworthy (Ince Castle, co. Cornwall). Per pale gu. and or, a chev. and a pile conjoined in point at the top of the chev. all counterchanged.

Notbeene, or Notbone. Gu. a fess wavy erm.

Notingham (co. Gloucester, *temp.* Edward IV.). Ar. a fess engr. betw. three pheons sa.

Notingham. Ar. an orle sa. on a chief of the last three annulets of the first.

Notley (Combe Sydenham, co. Somerset). Quarterly, 1st and 4th, or, on a bend cotised az. three bezants, for NOTLEY; 2nd and 3rd, gu. a chev. erm. betw. three goats' heads erased ar., for MARWOOD. *Crest*—Out of a mural crown a lion's head. *Motto*—Noli mentiri.

Notman. Or, a fess betw. three fusils sa. *Crest*—An eagle rising ppr. sustaining a flag gu. staff sa.

Noton. Per saltire sa. and ar. four mullets counterchanged. *Crest*—A hind's head or.

Nott (Kent and London; Lord Mayor of London, 1363; crest granted 1587). Az. on a bend betw. three leopards' faces or, as many martlets gu. *Crest*—A martlet ar. ducally crowned or, in the beak an olive branch ppr.

Nott, or Notte (London, and Shelsley Beauchamp, co. Worcester). Az. a bend betw. three leopards' faces or. *Crest*—A talbot sejant erm. collared or. *Motto*—Solus mihi invidus obstat.

Nott. Same *Arms. Crest*—A stag's head issuing ppr.

Nott (PYKE-NOTT, Parracombe, Devon: exemplified to JOHN NOTT-PYKE, Esq., on his assuming, by royal licence, 1863, the additional surname and arms of NOTT). Quarterly, 1st and 4th, gu. on a bend engr. or, betw. four leopards faces, two and two ar. an estoile of eight points betw. two martlets of the field, for NOTT; 2nd and 3rd, quarterly, or and gu. on a chev. barry wavy of four ar. and az. betw. two trefoils in chief and another in base counterchanged a pike naiant ppr., for PYKE. *Crests*—1st, NOTT: Two mascles fessewise interlaced ar. thereon a martlet gu. ducally gorged gold, in the beak a sprig of laurel ppr.; 2nd, PYKE: On a mount vert a demi pike hauriant ppr. betw. two wings gu. each charged with a trefoil or.

Nott (South Molton, Devon; exemplified to late Rev. RICHARD HARDING, on his assuming, by royal licence, the surname of NOTT). Quarterly, 1st and 4th, gu. on a bend engr. or, betw. four leopards' faces, two and two ar. an estoile of eight points betw. two martlets of the field, for NOTT; 2nd and 3rd, or, three martlets in bend betw. two bendlets, all betw. two crosses pattée az., for HARDING. *Crests*—1st, NOTT: Two mascles fessewise interlaced or, thereon a martlet gu. ducally gorged gold, in the beak a sprig of laurel ppr.; 2nd, HARDING: On a rock a Cornish chough ppr. collared or, resting the dexter claw on a cross pattée also or. *Motto*—Pax vobiscum.

Nottage. Ar. five lozenges in cross conjoined gu. *Crest* —A seax (a kind of scymitar notched on the back, from which the word "Saxon" is derived) ppr.

Nottidge (Rev. EDWARD NOTTIDGE, Rector of Black Notley, co. Essex). Az. a chev. betw. two garbs in chief and a fleece in base or. *Crest*—A boar's head couped gu. armed and tusked or, collared erminois. *Motto*—Peace and plenty.

Nottingham (England). Sa. an inescutcheon betw. three annulets or. *Crest*—A dexter hand ppr. holding an annulet or.

Nottingham. Same *Arms,* a border of the second.

Nottingham, Town of. Gu. two staves ragulée couped, one in pale, surmounted by the other in fess vert, betw. two ducal coronets in chief or, the bottom part of the staff in pale, enfiled with a ducal coronet of the last. *Motto* —Vivat post funera virtus.

Nottingham (Seal of the Corporation. Visit. Notts, 1614). The seal exhibits a fort or castle, composed of four square towers joined together by curtain walls, all within a circular wall with a gateway, in dexter chief a crescent, and in the sinister an estoile, around the whole the words: S: COMVNÆ : VILLA : DE : NOTTINGHAM : ✠

Nottingham. Sa. an inescutcheon or, in chief three annulets and a border of the last; another, Az. on a bend cotised ar. betw. six lions or, three mullets pierced gu.; another, Gu. a lion ramp. ar.

Nottingham. Ar. a chev. engr. sa. guttée d'or (another, d'eau).

Nottingham (Reg. Ulster's Office). Gu. a fess betw. three escallops or.

Nottingham (Reg. Ulster's Office). Gu. on a bend or, three escallops az.

Noune, or Nunne (Tostock, co. Norfolk). Sa. a saltire betw. four lions' gambs erased or. *Crest*—A bull's head erased per fess ar. and gu. attired of the last.

Nourse (Milton, co. Bucks; co. Essex; Chilling Place and Wood Eaton, co. Oxford). Gu. a fess betw. two chevronels ar. *Crest*—An arm embowed, vested az. cuffed ar. the hand ppr. holding a snake vert, entwined round the arm.

Nourse (Woodeaton, co. Oxford; RICHARD NOURSE, *b.* 1601, son of JOHN NOURSE, Esq., of Chilling Place, same co., and grandson of JOHN NOURSE, Esq., of Milton, co. Bucks. Visit. Oxon, 1634). Same *Arms*. *Crest*—An arm embowed, vested az. cuffed ar. the hand ppr. holding a snake vert, entwined round the arm.

Nourse. Same *Arms*. *Crest*—A stag's head or.

Novant (co. Devon). Ar. a lion ramp. tail double queued gu.

Nove (co. Leicester, 1611). Or, a cross engr. vert, charged in the centre with a crescent of the first. *Crest*—An eagle displ. vert.

Novell (London, 1652). Or, fretty gu. a canton erm. *Crest*—A buck trippant ar.

Novembe. Or, fretty gu. a canton of the second.

Novers (co. Norfolk). Vairé ar. and gu.

Novike. Gu. a fess dancettée ar. (another, or), in chief three mullets ar.

Novike. Gu. five fusils in fess ar. in chief three mullets pierced or.

Now. Sa. a chev. betw. three pheons ar.

Nowbery (Reg. Ulster's Office). Erm. a chev. gu.

Noweford, or Neirford. Gu. a lion ramp. erm.

Nowell (cos. Kent, Lancaster, and Sussex). Ar. three covered cups sa. *Crest*—An arm embowed in armour ppr. garnished or, holding in the hand a fireball also ppr.

Nowell, or Noell (Merley, co. Lancaster). Paly of six ar. and gu.

Nowell, Novelle, or Novell (co. Stafford). Gu. fretty ar. a bend vairé of the second and first (another, or and gu.).

Nowell (Edmonton, co. Middlesex). Ar. three covered cups sa. a crescent for diff. *Crest*—A cubit arm erect ppr. grasping a snake or, environed round the arm.

Nowell (Netheride and Linton, co. York; formerly of Reade, co. Lancaster, 1613 and 1664). Ar. three covered cups sa. *Crest*—An arm embowed in armour, in the hand a flaming bomb all ppr.

Nowell (Little Merley, co. Lancaster, 1567). Ar. three covered cups sa. garnished or, quartering, Gu. a pelican in her piety or, foliage vert, nest of the second, for GASGYLL.

Nowell (Great Merley, co. Lancaster, 1567). Same *Arms*, without the quartering.

Nowell. See FITZ NEEL and NOEL.

Nowell, or Novelle. Or, a fret gu. a chief az.; another, Gu. fretty or, a canton ar.

Nowenham. Az. three demi lions ramp. ar. guttée de sang. *Crest*—A sturgeon ppr.

Nowers, Norwers, Nonwers, or De la Nouers (Gothurst, co. Buckingham, *temp.* Henry III.). Ar. two bars gu. in chief three crescents of the last. *Crest*—A pestle and mortar ppr.

Nowers (Knossington, co. Leicester; RALPH DE NOWERS, living 2 Edward II., 1317; left a dau. and heir, MARGARET, *m.* WILLIAM WILCOCKS. RALPH DE NOWERS was son of ROBERT DE NOWERS, who was son of Sir ROBERT DE NOWERS, Knt., of Knossington, *temp.* King John. Visit. Leicester, 1619). Per fess chequy or, gu. and erm.

Nowers (arms in Aylsworth Manor House, Tackley, co. Oxford. Visit. Oxon, 1566). Az. a fess ar. betw. three garbs or.

Nowers. Barry nebulée of six gu. and erm.; another, Sa. three garbs or, banded ar.; another, Vairé ar. and gu.; another, Ar. a fess betw four crescents gu. three in chief and one in base.

741

Nowlan. See O'NOWLAN.

Nowland (Nowland's Fort, co. Carlow; Reg. Ulster's Office). Az. on a bend betw. two fleurs-de-lis ar. a lion pass. gu.

Nowmery. Sa. on an inescutcheon, within an orle of martlets or, five lozenges gu.

Nowne (co. Suffolk). Or, a cross engr. gu. *Crest*—A lion ramp. or, charged on the shoulder with a crescent gu.

Nowport. Ar. on a fess betw. three crescents sa. as many crescents of the field.

Noxe. Gu. three escutcheons or, on each a leaf vert.

Noy, or Noye. Ar. three bendlets sa. on a canton of the last a cross of the first.

Noybers, or Noyers. Az. a fess ar.

Noyce. Ar. three carnations gu. stalked and leaved vert.

Noye (Pendrea in St. Burian, or Burryan, co. Cornwall; WILLIAM NOYE, of that place, *m.* PHILIPPA LENEYNE, of Gwynier, in same co., and had three sons—I. EDWARD, whose son, WILLIAM NOYE, was Attorney-General, *temp.* Charles I.; II. JOHN; III. WILLIAM, aged 56 years in 1620. Visit. Cornwall, 1620). Az. three crosses crosslet in bend ar. *Crest*—On a chapeau gu. turned up erm. a falcon close ar., in the beak a laurel branch vert. *Another Crest*—A dove or, in the beak a sprig of laurel vert.

Noye. Az. three bendlets sa. on a canton of the last a cross of the first. *Crest*—On a chapeau gu. turned up erm. a falcon wings expanded ppr. in the beak a laurel branch vert.

Noyes (East Mascalls, co. Sussex). Az. three crosses crosslet, in bend ar. *Crest*—On a chapeau gu. turned up erm. a dove, holding in the beak an olive branch ppr. *Motto*—Nuncia pacis oliva.

Nuce (Hadham, co. Hertford). Sa. two pallets ar. a canton erm.

Nugent (co. Westmeath; descended from HUGH DE NUGENT, who went to Ireland, *temp.* Henry II., with his cousins, HUGH DE LACY and GILBERT and RICHARD DE NUGENT. He got a grant of Bracklyn, and was direct ancestor of NICHOLAS NUGENT, of Bracklyn, in 1391, who had two sons, viz.—I. THOMAS NUGENT, of Bracklyn, whose descendant, EDWARD NUGENT of Bracklyn, *temp.* Charles II., left a dau. and heiress, ELLINOR NUGENT, *m.* JAMES NUGENT, Esq., of Dromeng; II. Sir WILLIAM NUGENT, *m.* KATHERINE, dau. and sole heir of JOHN FITZJOHN, eighth *Baron of Delvin*, and was ancestor of the noble house of NUGENT, *Baron Delvin* and *Earl of Westmeath*). Erm. two bars gu.

Nugent (*Earl of Westmeath* and *Baron Delvin*). Erm. two bars gu. (In a funeral entry preserved in Ulster's Office, 1620, the arms of the fourteenth *Baron Delvin* are thus marshalled:—Quarterly, 1st, NUGENT: Erm. two bars gu.; 2nd, NUGENT: Quarterly, or and gu. a bordure vair; 3rd, DRAKE: Ar. a wyvern, tail nowed gu.; 4th, ar. a chev. sa. betw. three daws close az.; 5th, gu. seven mascles conjoined, three, three, and one or; 6th, or, a fret gu.). *Crest*—A cockatrice wings elevated vert, tail nowed, combed and wattled gu. *Supporters*—Two cockatrices, wings elevated and endorsed vert, tails nowed, combed and wattled gu. *Motto*—Decrevi.

Nugent (Pallas, co. Galway; *Baron Riverstoun;* Hon. THOMAS NUGENT, of Pallas, Lord Chief Justice of the King's Bench, Ireland, second son of RICHARD, second *Earl of Westmeath*, was created *Baron Riverstown*, 1689, by James II., after his abdication; his representative, ANTHONY FRANCIS NUGENT, of Pallas, sixth inheritor of the Riverstown patent of 1689, *s.* 1871, GEORGE THOMAS, eighth *Earl* and first *Marquess of Westmeath* as ninth *Earl of Westmeath*, and twenty-fourth *Baron Delvin*). Same *Arms* and *Crest*, a crescent for diff. This difference is, of course, omitted since the accession of NUGENT, of Pallas, to the earldom of Westmeath. *Supporters*—Two griffins vert, beaked, forelegged, and wings inverted or, armed and langued gu. *Motto*—Decrevi.

Nugent (*Marquess of Westmeath*, extinct 1871; GEORGE THOMAS, eighth *Earl of Westmeath*, was created a *Marquess* 1822; he left an only dau. and heiress, Lady ROSA EMILY MARY ANNE NUGENT, *m.* Col. FULKE SOUTHWELL GREVILLE, who assumed the additional surname of NUGENT, and was created *Lord Greville*, of Clonyn). Same *Arms*, *Crest*, *Supporters*, and *Motto* as the *Earl of Westmeath*.

Nugent (GREVILLE-NUGENT, *Lord Greville*). Quarterly, 1st and 4th, erm. two bars gu. and a canton of the last for diff., for NUGENT; 2nd and 3rd, sa. on a cross within a border, both engr. or, five pellets, for GREVILLE. *Crests*—1st: A cockatrice ppr. wings elevated and charged on the breast with a pellet for diff., for NUGENT, motto over, Decrevi; 2nd : Out of a ducal coronet gu. a demi swan with wings expanded and elevated ar., for GREVILLE. *Supporters*—Dexter a swan, wings inverted ar. ducally gorged gu. charged on the breast with a pellet; sinister, a cockatrice, wings elevated and endorsed vert, gorged with an antique Irish crown or, combed and wattled gu. *Motto*—Vix ea nostra voco.

Nugent (Dromeng; descended from Hon. JOHN NUGENT, third son of RICHARD, first *Earl of Westmeath*, whose son, JAMES NUGENT, *m.* ELEANOR, dau. and heir of EDWARD NUGENT, Esq., of Bracklyn, and was ancestor of LAVALL NUGENT, K.C.B., *Count Nugent*, a magnate of Hungary, a Roman Prince, Field Marshal in the service of the Emperor of Austria, &c., &c., who *m.* JANE, Duchess of Riario Sforza, only dau. and heir of RAPHAEL, Duke of Riario Sforza, descended from EDWARD, Duke of Bavaria, Count Palatine of the Rhine, K.G., fourth son of Frederick V., King of Bohemia, and his Queen, the Princess Elizabeth, only dau. of James I. Field Marshal Count Nugent *d.* 1862, leaving, with other issue, a son and heir, ALBERT, *Count Nugent*). Same *Arms* and *Quarterings, Crest, Motto,* and *Supporters* as the *Earl of Westmeath.*

Nugent (Killasonna, co. Longford; Count Nugent, descended from Hon. WILLIAM NUGENT, sixth son of CHRISTOPHER, fourteenth *Lord Delvin*). Erm. two bars gu. *Crest*—A cockatrice, wings elevated vert, tail nowed combed and wattled gu. *Motto*—Decrevi.

Nugent (Coolamber, co. Westmeath; Count of Valdesoto descended from JAMES NUGENT, Esq., of Coolamber, second son of Hon. Sir CHRISTOPHER NUGENT, and brother of RICHARD, twelfth *Lord Delvin*. Fun. Ent. Ulster's Office, 1620, of CONNALL O'FERRALL, Esq., of Tenelick, co. Longford, whose wife was KATHERINE, dau. of JAMES NUGENT, Esq., of Coolamber). Erm. two bars gu. a crescent for diff.

Nugent (Ballina ; descended from OLIVER NUGENT, third son of Hon. Sir CHRISTOPHER NUGENT, through his eldest son JAMES NUGENT). Erm. two bars gu.

Nugent (Farren-Connell, co. Cavan; descended from OLIVER NUGENT, third son of Hon. Sir CHRISTOPHER NUGENT, through his younger son WILLIAM NUGENT). Erm. two bars gu. *Crest*—A cockatrice, wings expanded vert, tail nowed, combed, and wattled gu. *Motto*—Decrevi.

Nugent (*Viscount Clare* and *Earl Nugent; viscounty* extinct 1788, earldom vested in the *Duke of Buckingham* and *Chandos.* ROBERT NUGENT, Esq., of Carlanstown, descended from Sir THOMAS NUGENT, Knt., of Carlanstown, second son of RICHARD, seventh *Lord Delvin*, was created a viscount 1767, and advanced to an earldom 1776, with special remainder to GEORGE, *Marquess of Buckingham*, K.G., the husband of his eldest dau. and co-heir, Lady MARY ELIZABETH NUGENT). Erm. two bars gu. a crescent for diff. *Crest*—A cockatrice, wings expanded vert, combed and wattled gu. charged on the breast with a crescent for diff. *Supporters*—Two cockatrices, wings elevated vert, combed and wattled gu. each ducally gorged and chained or. *Motto* —Decrevi.

Nugent-Temple (*Baroness Nugent*, of Carlanstown, extinct 1850. MARY ELIZABETH, *Marchioness of Buckingham*, eldest dau. and co-heir of ROBERT, *Earl Nugent*, was so created 1800, with special remainder to her second son, Lord GEORGE NUGENT-GRENVILLE, who *s.* as *Baron Nugent* at her decease, 1812, and *d. s. p.*). Quarterly, 1st and 4th, erm. two bars gu., for NUGENT ; 2nd, ar. a wyvern, wings expanded gu. ; 3rd, az. a chev. engr. or, betw. three falcons close ar. beaked and belled or. *Supporters*—Dexter, a lion per fess embattled or and gu. ; sinister, a horse ar. semée of eaglets displ. sa., both collared erm. rimmed gu.

Nugent (Drumcree, co. Westmeath, and New Haggard, co. Meath ; descended from ROBERT NUGENT, second son of Hon. JAMES NUGENT, brother of the eleventh *Lord Delvin*). Erm. two bars gu. *Crest*—A cockatrice, wings elevated vert, tail nowed, combed and wattled gu. *Motto*—Decrevi.

Nugent (Dysert and Tulloughan, co. Westmeath ; descended from Hon. LAVALIN NUGENT, third son of JAMES, third *Lord Delvin* ; allowed by Fortescue, 1793.). Erm. two bars gu. *Crest*—A cockatrice ppr. *Motto*—Decrevi.

Nugent (Portaferry, co. Down; ANDREW NUGENT, Esq., of Dysert, *m.* Lady KATHERINE NUGENT, dau. and co-heir of THOMAS, fourth *Earl of Westmeath*, his eldest dau. and eventual co-heir, MARGARET NUGENT, *m.* ANDREW SAVAGE, Esq., of Portaferry, and her grandson, ANDREW SAVAGE, assumed the surname of NUGENT, 1812, when the following arms, &c., were exemplified). Erm. two bars gu. *Crest*—A cockatrice, wings expanded vert, tail nowed, combed and wattled gu. *Motto*—Decrevi.

Nugent (Ballinlough Castle, co. Westmeath, bart. ; *Count Nugent*, of the Holy Roman Empire; ANDREW NUGENT, Esq., of Dysert, *m.* Lady KATHERINE NUGENT, dau. and co-heir of THOMAS, fourth *Earl of Westmeath*, his youngest dau. and eventual co-heir, BARBARA NUGENT, *m.* JAMES O'REILLY, Esq., of Ballinlough, and her son, HUGH O'REILLY, was created a bart. 1795, and assumed the surname of NUGENT on the death of his maternal uncle, JOHN NUGENT). Erm. two bars gu. *Crest*—A cockatrice ppr. *Motto*—Decrevi.

Nugent (Ballynacorr ; descended from CHRISTOPHER NUGENT, second son of ANDREW NUGENT, Esq., of Dysert; EDMUND NUGENT, Esq., of Ballynacorr, *m.* 1741, ELIZABETH, sister of CHRISTOPHER D'ALTON, a Count of the Holy Roman Empire). Erm. two bars gu. *Crest*—A cockatrice rising ppr. *Motto*—Decrevi.

Nugent (Donore, co. Westmeath, bart., extinct 1797; descended from WALTER NUGENT, eldest son of ANDREW NUGENT, brother of CHRISTOPHER, eleventh *Lord Delvin*). Erm. two bars gu.

Nugent (formerly FITZ-GERALD, Donore, bart.; PERCY FITZ-GERALD, eldest son of Capt. THOMAS FITZ-GERALD, R.N., and grandson of PIERCE FITZ-GERALD, Esq., of Baltinoran, by CHRISTIANA NUGENT, his wife, sister of Sir PETER NUGENT, first bart., of Donore, was created a bart. 1831, and assumed the surname of NUGENT, by royal licence, same year, when the following coat was exemplified to him). Erm. two bars gu. *Crest*—A cockatrice wings elevated, vert, tail nowed, combed and wattled gu. *Motto*—Decrevi.

Nugent (Clonlost, co. Westmeath; descended from ANDREW NUGENT, second son of ANDREW NUGENT, brother of CHRISTOPHER, eleventh *Lord Delvin*). Erm. two bars gu. *Crest*—A cockatrice, wings elevated vert tail nowed, combed and wattled gu. *Motto*—Decrevi.

Nugent (Cloncoskraine, co. Waterford; descended from EDWARD NUGENT, second son of RICHARD, tenth *Lord Delvin*, who *m.* JOAN, dau. and heir of RICHARD BUTLER, Esq., of Cloncoskraine: the heiress *m.* CHARLES HUMBLE, Esq., whose son, JOHN NUGENT HUMBLE, was created a bart. 1831; Arms allowed by Hawkins, Ulster, 1729). Erm. two bars gu. *Crest*—A cockatrice, wings elevated vert, tail nowed, combed, and wattled gu.

Nugent (Moyrath, co. Westmeath, bart., forfeited ; THOMAS NUGENT, Esq., of Moyrath, descended from Sir WILLIAM OGE NUGENT, of same place, second son of WILLIAM, first *Lord Delvin*, was created a bart. 1621 ; the third bart. sided with James II. and was attainted). Erm. two bars gu.

Nugent (Dardistown, co. Meath; descended from FRANCIS NUGENT, Esq., of Dardistown, second son of the first bart. of Moyrath). Erm. two bars gu.

Nugent (Ballybrannough, *alias* Walshestown; Fun. Ent. Ulster's Office, 1620 ; Sir ROBERT NUGENT, Knt., of that place). Erm. two bars gu. a crescent for diff.

Nugent (Fun. Ent. Ulster's Office, 1621 ; RICHARD NUGENT, of Dublin, merchant). Erm. two bars gu., on the upper one a lozenge ar. charged with another sa.

Nugent (Waddesdon, co. Berks, bart. ; Sir GEORGE NUGENT, G.C.B., reputed son of Hon. EDMUND NUGENT, Lieut.-Col. 1st Regt. Foot Guards, son of *Earl Nugent*, was created a bart. 1806). Erm. two bars within a border engr. gu., on a canton of the last a dagger erect ppr. pommel and hilt or. *Crest*—A cockatrice vert gorged with a plain collar or, pendent therefrom an escutcheon gu. charged with a dagger erect. as in the arms. *Supporters*—Two cockatrices vert, wings endorsed, collared or, pendent therefrom a shield gu., charged with a dagger, as in the arms. *Motto*—Decrevi.

Nun. Ar. a saltire gu. betw. four lions' gambs erect ppr. *Crest*—A bull's head erased per fesse vert and or.

Nune (Thorp, co. Northampton). Gu. three chev. ar.

Nunn (cos. Essex, Suffolk, and Norfolk). Sa. a saltire betw. four lions' gambs or. *Crest*—A bull's head erased per fess ar. and gu. armed and crined of the last.

Nunn (St. Margarets, co. Wexford; descended from JOSHUA NUNN, Esq., of St. Margaret's, High Sheriff, co. Wexford, 1709, eldest son of RICHARD NUNN, a Captain in Ireton's Regt., 1649, who settled in Ireland, and was High Sheriff, co. Wexford, 1676). Same *Arms* and *Crest. Motto*—Suaviter in modo, fortiter in re.

Nunn (Hill Castle, co. Wexford; descended from RICHARD NUNN, second son of RICHARD NUNN, Captain in Ireton's Regt., 1649 ; JOSEPH NUNN, Esq., of Hill Castle, *d.* 1804, leaving two daus. his co-heirs, the eldest of whom, FRANCES NUNN, *m.* 1787, JOSHUA NUNN, Esq., of St. Margaret's, and thus united both branches). Same *Arms, Crest,* and *Motto,* a crescent for diff.

Nunn (ELIAS SHIRLEY NUNN, Esq., of Bury St. Edmunds, co. Suffolk). Az. a saltire erm. betw. two bulls' heads erased in pale, and as many lions' gambs erased in fesse **or.**

Crest—Upon a mount vert in front of an oak tree ppr. a beehive or.

Nunsegles (Visit. Durham, 1615). Ar. on a chev. az. betw. three eagles displ. sa. as many estoiles or.

Nunwicke. Sa. an eagle displ. or.

Nurse (Scotland). Gu. a fess or, betw. a chev. in chief and a cinquefoil in base ar. a border of the second. *Crest* —A pair of balances ppr. *Motto*—Justitia.

Nurse (cos. Oxford and Gloucester, now Middlesex). Sa. on a saltire ar. a fleur-de-lis of the first.

Nuse. Ar. a chev. betw. three annulets sa. a chief of the last.

Nusham (Nusham Hall, co. York). Sa. on a fess ar. three crosses crosslet gu. *Crest*—A monster, with a lion's head, fish's body, and bird's feet ppr.

Nuswell. Vert two chev. ar. each charged with three cinquefoils gu.

Nutbrowne (Barking, co. Essex; granted 1588). Erm. on a chief sa. three lions' heads erased or. *Crest*—A lion sejant sa. holding in the forepaws a sword ar. hilt of the first, pommel and gripe of the second.

Nutcombe (co. Wilts). Or, a fess embattled betw. two escallops gu. *Crest*—on a mural coronet or, a falcon close ppr. beaked and belled or.

Nuthal (Cattenal, co. Chester). Quarterly, 1st and 4th, ar. a shackbolt sa., for NUTHAL; 2nd, ar. a griffin segreant sa. armed or., for GRIFFIN; 3rd, sa. a buck's head cabossed ar. attired or, for HORTON. *Crest*—A falcon rising ar. beaked and ducally gorged or.

Nuthoobhoy (Sirguam House, Bombay). Ar. a sheaf of rice ppr. banded gu. encircled by two sickles also ppr., on a chief dancettée az. a mullet or, betw. two bezants. *Crest*— Upon a mount vert an elephant ppr. charged on the body with two mullets or, holding in the trunk a branch of palm also ppr. *Motto*—Wisdom above riches.

Nuthurst. Ar. a chev. gu. betw. three nut-hooks sa.

Nutshall (Nutshall, co. Lancaster). Ar. a squirrel sejant gu. supporting a hazel branch vert fructed or.

Nutt (Tewkesbury, co. Gloucester, and Mayes, co. Sussex). Per fess az. and erm. a pale counterchanged three pheons ar. *Crest*—On a chapeau gu. turned up erm. a pheon or, betw. two wings expanded ar. *Another Crest*—A pheon ar. betw. two wings vert. *Another Crest*—On a chapeau gu. turned up erm. a cock crowing ppr.

Nutt (co. Kent). Az. a pheon or.

Nuttall (Nuttall Hall, anciently Nothogh, within the Chase of Holcome, co. Lancaster; represented, in the female line, by FORMBY, of Formby). Ar. a shacklebolt sa. *Crest*—A talbot statant ar. chained and collared sa.

Nuttall (Tottington Hall, co. Lancaster; represented, in the female line, by RADCLYFFE, of Foxdenton). Same *Arms* and *Crest*.

Nuttall (Walmersley, co. Lancaster; a branch of the Nuttall Hall family, *temp.* Henry VII., represented, in the female line, by ORMEROD, of Tyldesly). Same *Arms* and *Crest*.

Nuttall (Kempsey, co. Worcester). Same *Arms*. *Crest*— On a chapeau sa. turned up erm. a martlet sa. *Motto*—Serva jugum.

Nuttall. Gu. six cocks ar.

Nutter. Ar. a boar pass. sa. betw. three crescents gu. *Crest*—A dolphin naiant or.

Nyssell (co. Kent). Ar. a saltire engr. betw. four laurel leaves sa. *Crest*—A lion ramp. per fesse ar. and az. holding in the dexter paw a fleur-de-lis or.

O

OAK (cos. Somerset and Wilts). Sa. on a fess ar. betw. six acorns or, a cross crosslet fitchée betw. two oak leaves slipped vert. *Crest*—A demi leopard ramp. gorged with an antique crown, holding in the dexter paw an acorn branch fructed all ppr., and supporting with the sinister a cross crosslet, as in the arms. *Motto*—Persevere.

Oakden (Ladham House, co. Kent). Gyronny of eight ar. and gu. the dexter charged with an oak branch fructed ppr. *Crest*—A wolf ramp. ar. against an oak tree fructed ppr. *Motto*—Et si ostendo non jacto.

Oakeley (Oakeley, co. Salop; an ancient family in that co.). Ar. on a fess betw. three crescents gu. as many fleurs-de-lis or. *Crest*—A dexter arm embowed in armour ppr. in the hand a scymitar also ppr. pommel and hilt gold.

Oakeley (Plas Tan-y-Bwlch, co. Merioneth; descended from WILLIAM OAKELEY, Esq., grandson of WILLIAM OAKELEY, third son of WILLIAM OAKELEY, Esq., of Oakeley, M.P. for Bishop's Castle, 1660, who *m.* MARGARET only dau. and

heir of EVAN GRYFFYDD, Esq., of Plas Tan-y-Bwlch). Same *Arms* and *Crest*, quartering GRYFFYDD.

Oakeley (Shrewsbury, co. Salop, bart.; descended from CHARLES OAKELEY, second son of Rev. WILLIAM OAKELEY, Rector of Forton, co. Stafford, and brother of WILLIAM OAKELEY, who *m.* the heiress of Plas Tan-y-Bwlch). Ar. on a fess betw. three crescents gu. as many fleurs-de-lis or, for OAKELEY; the family quarters, Az. a stag trippant or, for STRAHAN. *Crest*—A dexter arm embowed in armour ppr. charged with two fleurs-de-lis or, each in a crescent gu., in the hand a scymitar also ppr. pommel and hilt gold; the present baronet, and those preceding him, have taken a second crest, viz., A stag's head erased or, for STRAHAN. *Motto*—Non timeo sed caveo.

Oakes (Mitcham Hall, co. Surrey, bart.). Ar. on a chev. engr. sa. betw. three sprigs of oak fructed ppr. a cross of eight points of the field, on a canton gu. a mullet of as many points within an increscent of the first. *Crest*—Out of a mural crown gu. a buck's head erased ppr. gorged with a collar embattled, counter-embattled or. *Motto*— Persevere.

Oakes, or Okes (Oundle, co. Northampton). Gu. two lions combatant ar. a chief of the last, quartering, Sa. a fesse betw. six acorns or. *Crest*—An oak tree vert fructed or, supported by two lions ramp. ar.

Oakes (Newton Court, co. Suffolk). Sa. on a fess engr. betw. six slips of oak fructed or, three oak leaves vert. *Crest* —An oak tree ppr. fructed or, encircled with pallisades. *Motto*—Quercus robur salus patriæ.

Oakhampton, Town of (co. Devon). Chequy or and az. two bars ar. *Crest*—A castle.

Oates (Perran Zabuloe, and St. Agnes, co. Cornwall). Az. a chev. engr. or, betw. two plates.

Oates. Ar. a bear ramp. sa. muzzled gu. *Crest*—A boar's head erased ar.

O'Beirne (a Sept in Connaught, chiefs of Hy-Briuin-Na-Sinna, co. Roscommon, deriving their name from BEIRN, who was of the race of O'CONOR, of Magh Naoi). Ar. an oak tree eradicated and fructed ppr. in base a lizard vert, in the dexter base point a saltire couped gu. on a chief az. the sun in his splendour or, and a crescent of the first. *Crest*—A dexter arm in armour embowed, the hand grasping a sword all ppr.

O'Beirne (allowed by Mac Cullogh, Ulster, 1761, as the arms of HENRY O'BEIRNE, an officer in the service of the King of Spain, whose only dau. MARIA THERESA O'BEIRNE, Maid of Honour to the Queen of Spain, *m.* PHILIP, *Duke of Wharton*, and *d.* 1777). Same *Arms* and *Crest*. *Motto*—Fuimus.

O'Beirne (allowed by Mac Cullogh, Ulster, 1761, to THADDEUS O'BEIRNE, an officer in the service of the King of Spain, son of MICHAEL O'BEIRNE, and cousin germain of MARIA THERESA O'BEIRNE, *Duchess of Wharton*). Same *Arms*, *Crest*, and *Motto*.

Obert. Ar. a fess betw. two barrulets wavy gu.

O'Boyle (a sept in Ulster of the race of CINEL CONAILL, deriving their name from BAOIGHILL, chief of the Barony of Boylagh, co. Donegal). Or, an oak tree eradicated vert. *Crest*—A sword point upwards ppr. and a passion cross or, in saltire surmounted of a heart gu.

O'Brenan (Ossory, in Leinster; a numerous Sept in Ossory, formerly O'BRAONAIN, the last recognized chief of which was Doctor JOHN BRENNAN, of Dublin). Gu. two lions ramp. combatant supporting a garb all or, in chief three swords, two in saltire, points upwards, and one fesswaye, point to the dexter ar. pommels and hilts gold. *Crest*—An arm embowed in armour grasping a sword all ppr.

O'Brenan (Cloncen and Moneenroe, co. Kilkenny, and Malaga; allowed by Fortescue, Ulster, 1789, to JOHN O'BRENAN, of Malaga, in Spain, son of EDMUND O'BRENAN, Esq., of Moneenroe, who was great-grandson of PATRICK O'BRENAN, of Cloncen). Same *Arms* and *Crest*. *Motto*—Sub hoc signo vinces.

O'Brenon (the Sept of O'BRAONAN, or O'BRAONAIN, of Ulster and Connaught). Ar. a lion ramp. az. in chief two dexter hands couped at the wrist apaumée gu. *Crest*—Out of a ducal coronet or, a plume of five ostrich feathers alternately az. and gold.

O'Brien (descended from BRIEN BORUMHA, King of Munster, and MONARCH OF ALL IRELAND, A.D. 1002, who fell at the Battle of Clontarf, A.D. 1014). Gu. three lions pass. guard. in pale per pale or and ar.

O'Brien (*Earl of Thomond*, dormant since 1741; CONOR O'BRIEN, the descendant of BRIEN BOROIMHE, Monarch of Ireland, was inaugurated King of Thomond, 1528, and *d.* 1540, leaving a son DONOUGH O'BRIEN, who was deposed by his uncle, MURROUGH O'BRIEN, he then usurped the sceptre of Thomond and resigned the royalty to Henry VIII., when he was created, 1543, *Earl of Thomond* for life, with remainder to his deposed nephew, DONOUGH O'BRIEN; HENRY, eighth *Earl of Thomond*, *d. s. p.* 1741, when the earldom devolved on CHARLES O'BRIEN, sixth *Viscount Clare*, Marshal THOMOND, of the French service, whose grandfather, DANIEL, third *Viscount Clare*, was outlawed 1690). Quarterly, 1st and 4th, gu. three lions pass. guard. in pale per pale or and ar.; 2nd, ar. three piles meeting in point gu.; 3rd, or, a pheon az. *Crest*—A dexter arm embowed issuing out of a cloud and brandishing a sword all ppr. *Supporters*—Two lions guard. per fess or and ar. *Mottoes*—Ancient: Lamh laidir an nachtar (the strong hand from above); modern: Vigueur de dessus.

O'Brien (*Viscount Clare*, attainted 1690; Sir DANIEL O'BRIEN, third son of CONNOR, third *Earl of Thomond*, was created, 1662, *Viscount O'Brien of Clare*; his grandson, DANIEL, third *Viscount Clare*, was outlawed 1690, for his adhesion to James II.; the outlawed Viscount's grandson, CHARLES, sixth *Viscount Clare*, became, in 1741, heir to the earldom of *Thomond*, on the death of HENRY, eighth *Earl of Thomond*, and assumed the title. This was the famous Lord Clare, of the Irish Brigade, afterwards Marshal Thomond, of the French service, so distinguished at Fontenoy and Laffeldt. He *d.* 1761, leaving a son and heir, CHARLES O'BRIEN, *d. s. p.* 1764, and a dau. ANTOINETTE CHARLOTTE MARIE SEPTIMANIE, *m.* the Duke de Choiseul-Praslin, and her descendant the present Duke de Choiseul-Praslin, is heir general of the *Viscounts Clare* and the *Earls of Thomond*). Gu. three lions pass. guard. in pale per pale or and ar. *Crest*—A dexter arm embowed vested gu. brandishing a sword ppr. pommel and hilt or. *Supporters*—Two lions guard. per fess or and ar. armed and langued gu. *Motto*—Lamh laidir an nachtar.

O'Brien (*Baron Inchiquin*; MURROGH O'BRIEN, who usurped the sovereignty of Thomond, 1540, on the death of his brother, CONOR, King of Thomond, and resigned the same to Henry VIII., was created, as above, *Earl of Thomond*, with remainder to his deposed nephew, DONOUGH O'BRIEN, and was created, at same time, *Baron Inchiquin*, with remainder to the heirs male of his body). Quarterly, 1st and 4th, gu. three lions pass. guard. in pale per pale or and ar., for O'BRIEN; 2nd, ar. three piles meeting in point issuing from the chief gu.; 3rd, or, a pheon az. *Crest*—Issuing from a cloud an arm embowed ppr. brandishing a sword ar. pommel and hilt or, motto over: Lamh laidir an nachtar. *Supporters* —Two lions guard. per fesse or and ar. *Motto*—Vigueur de dessus.

O'Brien (*Earl of Inchiquin*, and *Marquis of Thomond*, extinct 1855; MURROGH, fifth *Baron Inchiquin*, was raised to an earldom 1654; MURROGH, fifth earl, was raised to the marquisate of *Thomond* 1800, the third Marquis *d. s. p.*; when Sir LUCIUS O'BRIEN, fifth bart. of Dromoland, succeeded to the Barony of Inchiquin, as thirteenth baron). Same *Arms, Crest, Supporters,* and *Mottoes.*

O'Brien (Dromoland, co. Clare, bart., now *Baron Inchiquin*; DONOUGH O'BRIEN, fourth in descent from DONOUGH O'BRIEN, third son of MURROUGH, first *Baron Inchiquin*, was created a bart. 1686, the fifth bart. *s.* 1855, as thirteenth *Baron Inchiquin*, on the failure of the senior line). Gu. three lions pass. guard. in pale per pale or and ar. *Crest*, same as the last. *Motto*—Lamh laidir an nachtar (the strong hand uppermost).

O'Brien (WYNDHAM-O'BRIEN, *Earl of Thomond*, extinct 1774; HENRY, eighth *Earl of Thomond*, bequeathed his estates to PERCY WYNDHAM, Esq., brother of CHARLES, first *Earl of Egremont*, who thereupon assumed the additional surname and arms of O'BRIEN, and was raised to the peerage 1756, *d. s. p.*). Quarterly, 1st and 4th, same as O'BRIEN, *Earl of Thomond;* 2nd and 3rd, az. a chev. betw. three lions' heads erased or, for WYNDHAM. *Crest*—A naked arm embowed, holding a sword all ppr. *Supporters*—Two lions guard. per fess or and ar.

O'Brien (Sir TIRLOGH O'BRIEN, uncle to the then *Earl of Thomond*, was knighted 14 March, 1601, by Charles, *Lord Mountjoy*, Lord Lieutenant of Ireland). Gu. three lions pass. guard. in pale ar.

O'Brien (Carrigogoinell, co. Limerick, Curryglass and Mogeely, co. Cork, and France; allowed by Hawkins, Ulster, 1758, to Col. JAMES DANIEL O'BRIEN, of the French service, sixth in descent from TORLOGH O'BRIEN, of Curryglass and Mogeely, who was fifth in descent from CONOR O'BRIEN, of Carrigogoinell, second son of MAHON O'BRIEN, King of Thomond, ancestor of *Lord Inchiquin*). Same *Arms* as the *Earls of Thomond* and *Inchiquin*. *Crest*—A dexter arm embowed, vested gu. holding in the hand a sword ppr. pommel and hilt or. *Motto*—Lamh laidir an nachtar.

O'Brien (Ballynalacken, co. Clare; of this family is the Hon.

744

JAMES O'BRIEN, one of the Judges of the Court of Queen's Bench in Ireland). Gu. three lions pass. guard. in pale per pale or and ar. *Crest*—An arm embowed, brandishing a sword ar. pommeled and hilted or. *Motto*—Vigueur de dessus.

O'Brien (Borris, in Ossory, Queen's co. bart.; granted by Betham, Ulster, to TIMOTHY O'BRIEN, Esq., Lord Mayor of Dublin, 1839, created a bart. that year on Her Majesty's first visit to Ireland). Ar. three lions pass. guard. per pale gu. and az. armed or, all within a border vert. *Crest*—From a castle ar. in flames, a naked arm embowed, grasping a sword ppr. *Motto*—Lamh laidhir an nachtar.

O'Byrne (Glenmalure, co. Wicklow, of the same race as O'TOOLE, deriving their surname from BRAN, BROIN, or BIRN, Chief of the Sept. FIAGH MAC HUGH O'BYRNE, of Glenmalure, Chief of this great and historic Sept, having been in rebellion, submitted to Queen Elizabeth, 1595. His son, PHELIM MAC FIAGH O'BYRNE got a re-grant of his lands 1606, and *d.* 1630). Gu. a chev. betw. three dexter hands couped at the wrist ar. *Crest*—A mermaid with comb and mirror all ppr.

O'Byrne (Timogue, Queen's co., bart., confirmed by St. George, Ulster, 1664, to DANIEL BYRNE, of Dublin, descended from the O'BYRNES, of co. Wicklow: his eldest son, Sir GREGORY BYRNE, was created a bart. 1671, and is now represented by GEORGE, *Lord de Tabley*. See LEICESTER, *Lord de Tabley*). Same *Arms*, with a border of the second for diff. *Crest*—A mermaid with comb and mirror all ppr. *Motto*— Certavi et vici.

O'Byrne (Cabinteely, co. Dublin; WILLIAM RICHARD O'BYRNE, Esq., of Cabinteely, M.P. co. Wicklow, is descended from JOHN BYRNE, Esq., High Sheriff, co. Wicklow, 1675, younger son of DANIEL BYRNE, of Dublin, ancestor of *Lord de Tabley*). Same *Arms* and *Crest*. *Motto*—Certavi et vici.

O'Byrne Brany (Reg. Ped. Ulster's Office; SHILIE, dau. of LOUGHLIN O'BYRNE BRANY, *m.* CHRISTOPHER MAC AWLEY). Ar. a lion ramp. gu. armed and langued az. on a chief or, two dexter hands couped at the wrist of the second.

O'Cahan (Chiefs of Limavady and the Rout, co. Londonderry, descended from the race of O'NEILL, and deriving their surname from CAHAN, Chief of the Sept. Tenth in descent from him was MANUS O'CAHAN, Chief of the Sept. killed at the battle of Down, A.D. 1260. His descendant, Sir DONAL O'CAHAN, Chief of his Sept, was knighted by Sir ARTHUR CHICHESTER, Lord Deputy of Ireland, 28 June, 1607). Az. on a fess per pale gu. and ar. betw. in chief out of the horns of a crescent, a dexter hand couped at the wrist and apaumée, surmounted by an estoile betw. on the dexter a horse counter-saliant, and on the sinister a lion ramp. e.t.n also surmounted by an estoile, and in base a salmon na.ai all ar. on the dexter side three lizards pass. bend sinisterw..ys gu. and on the dexter an oak tree eradicated vert, over all an escutcheon ar. charged with a cross calvary on three grieces ppr. *Crest*—A cat-a-mountain ramp. ppr. *Motto*— Felis demulcta mitis.

O'Cahan (Ballynaclosky, co. Londonderry; QUOY BALLACU O'CAHAN, *d.* 1637, grandson of DONELL O'CAHAN, of C: ryan, same co., third son of SHANE O'CAHAN, Chief of Sept). Gu. three salmon haurient, two and one or. *Crest*— A mountain cat saliant ppr. *Motto*—Inclytus virtute.

O'Cahill (a Sept who possessed Corca Thine, now Corkahinny, or the parish of Templemore, co. Tipperary; they descend from and derive their name from CATHAL, brother of CONOR-NA-LUINGE CUAITHE, ancestor of O'CONOR, of Corcomroe). Ar. a whale spouting in the sea ppr. *Crest*—An anchor erect, cable twined around the stock all ppr.

O'Callan, or O'Cuillean. Or, on a bend gu. three martlets ar. *Crest*—A demi griffin ramp. gu.

O'Callaghan (a Sept of the same race as MACCARTHY, who possessed a territory in the barony of Duhallow, co. Cork, and derived their surname from CEALLACHAIN, a Chieftain of the Sept. The Chief of this Sept was transplanted into co. Clare by Oliver Cromwell). Ar. in base a mount vert, on the dexter side a hurst of oak trees, therefrom issuant a wolf pass. towards the sinister all ppr.

O'Callaghan (Clonmyn, co. Cork; Fun. Ent. Ulster's Office; CALLAGHAN O'CALLAGHAN, *d.* 1631). Same *Arms.*

O'Callaghan (*Viscount Lismore*). Same *Arms*. *Crest*—A naked dexter arm embowed, holding bendwise a sword entwined with a snake all ppr. *Supporters*—Two stags ppr. *Motto*—Fidus et audax.

O'Callaghan (Cadogan, co. Cork). Same *Arms, Crest,* and *Motto.*

O'Callaghan (Baden-Baden; allowed by Hawkins, Ulster, 1765, to JAMES LOUIS O'CALLAGHAN, of that place, son of JOHN O'CALLAGHAN, a Captain in O'Brien's regiment in the service of France, *d.* 1712, descended from CAHIR O'CAL-

LAGHAN, of Dromine, co. Cork, *temp.* Queen Elizabeth). Same *Arms, Crest,* and *Motto.*

O'Carrie, or O'Carry (a Sept of the Clan CATHAIL, of the race of CATHAIL, second son of MUIREADHACH MUIL-LIETHAN, King of Connaught, *d.* A.D. 701). Az. a lion pass. guard. or. *Crest*—An arm in armour embowed, holding a spear, point downwards, shaft couped all ppr.

O'Carroll (Lord of Ely, or the territory of Eile, extending over part of the King's co. and co. Tipperary; descended from EILE, seventh in descent from CIAN, son of OLIOL OLLUM, King of Munster; Sir WILLIAM O'CARROLL, Chief of his name, was knighted at Limerick, 30 March, 1567, by Sir Henry Sydney, Lord Deputy of Ireland). Sa. two lions ramp. combatant or, armed and langued gu. supporting a sword, point upwards ppr. pommel and hilt gold.

O'Carroll (Lord of Ely O'Carroll; Sir MAOLROONA O'CARROLL, Chief of his name, was knighted at Dublin by Sir George Cary, Lord Deputy, 25 July, 1603. He was son of Sir WILLIAM O'CARROLL ODHAR, Lord of Ely, the brother of TEIGE O'CARROLL, of Ely O'Carroll, Chief of his Sept, who is styled by Sir James Ware, "Petty King of Ely "). Ar. two lions ramp. combatant gu. supporting a sword point upwards of the last, pommel and hilt or.

O'Carroll (Carrollstown, Maryland, U.S. America; descended from CHARLES O'CARROLL, Attorney-General for Maryland, where he got a grant of 60,000 acres, the son of ROGER and grandson of Sir MAOLROONA O'CARROLL, knighted 1 March, 1608. MARY, dau. and heir of CHARLES CARROLL, of Carrollstown, one of those who signed the Declaration of American Independence, *m.* RICHARD CATON, Esq., Maryland, and had three daus. co-heirs: I. MARY ANNE, *m.* first, ROBERT PATERSON, Esq., and, secondly, 1835, RICHARD, *Marquess Wellesley ;* II. ELIZABETH, *m.,* 1836, GEORGE WILLIAM, Lord *Stafford ;* III. LOUISA, *m.,* first, 1817, Sir FELTON HERVEY BATHURST, Bart. ; and, secondly, FRANCIS GODOLPHIN, seventh *Duke of Leeds*). Gu. two lions ramp. combatant ar. supporting a sword point upwards ppr. pommel and hilt or. This coat was exemplified by Betham, Ulster, 12 July, 1826, to MARY ANNE, *Marchioness Wellesley. Crest*—On the stump of an oak-tree sprouting, a hawk rising all ppr. belled or.

O'Carroll (Maryland, U.S. America, a branch of O'CARROLL, of Ely O'Carroll, descended from RONEY O'CARROLL and JAMES O'CARROLL, nephews of Sir DANIEL O'CARROLL, Knt., of St. Jago, in Spain, who emigrated to St. Kitts, West Indies, *temp.* Queen Anne). Same *Arms* and *Crest.*

O'Carroll (Ardagh, co. Galway, also Dunmore, in same co., and Avondale, Blackrock, co. Dublin; descended from REDMOND or REMY O'CARROLL, Esq., of Ardagh, *d.* 1755, brother of Sir DANIEL O'CARROLL, Knt., of St. Jago, in Spain, now represented by Rev. JOHN JAMES O'CARROLL, of the Oratory, Brompton, London. Reg. Ulster's Office). Same *Arms. Crest*—On the stump of an oak tree sprouting new branches a hawk rising all ppr. belled or. *Motto*—In fide et in bello forte.

Ochterlony (Guynd, co. Forfar). Az. a lion ramp. ar. within a bordure gu. charged with eight buckles and escallops alternately or. *Crest*—An eagle displ. az. *Motto* —Deus mihi adjutor.

Ochterlony (That Ilk, and Kelly, co. Forfar). Az. a lion ramp. on a border ar. eight buckles of the first.

Ochterlony (bart. 1823, extinct). Az. A lion ramp. ar. holding in the paws a trident erect or, and charged on the shoulder with a key, the wards upwards, of the field, all within a bordure wavy of the second, charged with four buckles gu. *Crest*—A swan, wings elevated ar. ducally collared and chained or, the breast charged with a buckle gu. and the wings and body debruised by a bendlet sinister wavy az. *Motto*—Spes labor levis.

Ochterlony (certified at the College of Arms, London, 1779). Az. a lion ramp. ar. charged on the side with a key in pale of the field, and holding in the dexter paw a trident or. *Crest*—A swan rousant ar. ducally crowned or, collared and chained of the last, charged on the breast with a rose gu.

Ochterlony (Minister of Aberlemno, co. Forfar, 1672). Az. a lion ramp. ar. in base the Holy Bible expanded ppr. a bordure gu. charged with eight buckles or. *Motto*—Sic itur ad astra.

O'Cinsallagh (a Sept descended from ENNA CINSALLAGH, son of DERMOT McMURROGH, last King of Leinster, *d.* 1171, and brother of DONEL CAOMHNAGH, ancestor of the KAVA-NAGHS. This Sept possessed a territory in the north of the co. Wexford, known as Hy Cinsallagh, extending from the bounds of the county at Wicklow to The O'Morchoes' territory). Ar. a fess gu. betw. in chief two garbs of the last, and in base a lion pass. sa.

745

Ockleshaw (co. Lancaster). Per fess embattled ar. and gu. two arrows fessways counterchanged, plumed az *Crest*—A flaming sword erect in pale or.

O'Clancy (Downmacfelimy, co. Clare, and Newtown, co. Galway, *temp.* James I.). Ar. two lions pass. guard. in pale gu. *Crest*—A dexter hand couped at the wrist erect, holding a sword in pale, pierced through a boar's head couped all ppr.

O'Clary. Per pale indented or and gu. two lions ramp. combatant counterchanged. *Crest*—An arm in armour embowed, the hand grasping a sword all ppr.

O'Clery (The Sept of O'CLEIRIGH, inhabiting the territory of O'Fiachrach, Aidhne, co. Galway, who were dispersed after the English invasion, 1172). Or, three nettle leaves vert.

O'Coffey (co. Cork; the Sept of O'COBHTHAIGH, who possessed Tricha chéd medhonach, *i.e.,* "the central cantred," identical with the present Barony of Barry Roe, where the Sept had seven castles, viz., Dundeedy, Dunowen, Dunore, Duneen, Dunacowig, Dunworley, and Dungorley). Vert a fess erm. betw. three corns or Irish cups or. *Crest*—A man riding on a dolphin ppr.

O'Collins (the Sept of O'COILEN, of the same race as O'Donovan : they inhabited the district of Hy Conaill, co. Limerick, but were driven out of their country by the Geraldines). Ar. two lions ramp. combatant ppr. *Crest*— A pelican vulning herself, wings elevated all ppr.

O'Concanon (a Sept descended from CUCENAIND, of the race of MAC DERMOT, of Moylurg, who were Chiefs of Corcamoe, co. Galway. The Chief of the Sept resided at Kiltullagh, in the present parish of Corcamoe). Ar. on a mount in base ppr. an oak tree vert, perched on the top thereof a falcon of the second, two crosses crosslet fitchée in fess az. *Crest*—An elephant sa. tusked or. *Motto* —Con can an.

O'Concannon (a Sept descended from CONGHAILE, Chief of Magh O'gCoinchinn, now Mugunihy, a territory forming the eastern portion of the co. Kerry. The O'Donoghoes, shortly before the Norman Conquest, invaded this territory, and drove the O'CONNELLS out of Mugunihy westward into Iveragh, where they settled at Ballycarbery as Castellans to MacCarthy More. The Chief of this Sept was transplanted by Oliver Cromwell to Brenter, near Callan Hill, co. Clare). Per fess ar. and vert a stag trippant ppr. betw. three trefoils slipped counterchanged.

O'Connell (Darrinane Abbey, co. Kerry; descended from DANIEL O'CONNELL, Esq., of Aghavore, in the Barony of Iveragh ; DANIEL O'CONNELL, of Darrinane Abbey, Q.C., M.P., who *d.* at Genoa, 1847, is represented by his grandson, DANIEL O'CONNELL, Esq., of Darrinane Abbey, J.P., D.L.). Same *Arms. Crest*—A stag's head erased ar. charged with a trefoil slipped vert. *Motto*—Ciall agus neart.

O'Connell (Ballyhean Lodge, co. Clare ; descended from JOHN O'CONNELL, Esq., of Greenagh, brother of the late DANIEL O'CONNELL, Esq., M.P., of Darrinane Abbey; his eldest son, MORGAN JOHN O'CONNELL, M.P., *m.,* 1865, MARY ANNE, only dau. of CHARLES BIANCONI, Esq., of Longfield, co. Tipperary, and *d.* 1875, leaving an only son, JOHN CHARLES COPPINGER O'CONNELL). Same *Arms, Crest,* and *Motto.* See MacMAHON.

O'Connell (Lake View, co. Kerry, bart.; descended from Sir JAMES O'CONNELL, created a bart., 1869, brother of the late DANIEL O'CONNELL, Esq., M.P., of Darrinane Abbey). Same *Arms, Crest,* and *Motto.*

O'Connell (Castle Connell, co. Limerick ; allowed by Hawkins, Ulster, 1755, to JAMES O'CONNELL, son of MICHAEL O'CONNELL, of London, and grandson of HUGH O'CONNELL, Captain of Horse to James II. Same *Arms. Crest*—A stag's head erased ppr. *Motto*—Victor in arduis.

O'Connell. Ar. a lion ramp. sa. holding in the dexter paw a trefoil slipped vert, on a chief az. three mullets or. *Crest* —A buck statant ppr.

O'Connor Kerry (a Sept descended from MATHGAMHAN O'CONCHOBHAIR, King of Cairraighe, 1138, *i.e.,* that part of the present co. Kerry extending from the Strand of Tralee to the River Shannon). Vert a lion ramp. double queued and crowned or. *Crest*—A dexter arm embowed in mail garnished or, the hand grasping a sword erect ppr. pommel and hilt gold. *Motto*—Nec timeo, nec sperno.

O'Connor (co. Kerry; THOMAS O'CONNOR, Esq., The Spa, Tralee, co. Kerry, 1846, and his brother, Rev. CHARLES JAMES O'CONNOR, Glancullen, co. Dublin). Same *Arms, Crest,* and *Motto.*

O'Connor (Carrigfoile, co. Kerry ; Fun. Ent. Ulster's Office, 1639, JOHN O'CONNOR, of that place, who had four daus. his co-heirs, the third of whom, MARY O'CONNOR, *m.* CONNOR O'CONNOR, of Kariragh, in same co., heir to the lands of his father-in-law). Same *Arms, Crest,* and *Motto.*

O'Connor Failghe (a Sept in Leinster, who were descended from ROSSA FAILGHE, son of CATHAOIR MOR, Monarch of Ireland, and possessed the territory of Hy Failghe, extending over the baronies of Offaley, co. Kildare, and portions of the King's and Queen's cos. This Sept was the parent stock of O'DOINN and O'DEMPSEY). Ar. on a mount in base vert an oak tree acorned ppr.

O'Connor (Gortnamona, or Mount Pleasant, King's co.; descended from O'CONNOR FAILGHE. The representative, MAURICE NUGENT O'CONNOR, Esq., of Mount Pleasant, d. 1818, leaving four daus., his co-heirs, viz., CATHERINE, Countess of Desart; MARY, Mrs. TUITE, of Sonna; JULIA, who d. unm. ; and ELIZABETH, who m. 1822, Rev. BENJAMIN MORRIS). Same Arms.

O'Connor (Corcomroe; a Sept which held considerable estates in the co. Clare down to 1584). Vert a stag trippant ar. Crest—A hand in a gauntlet erect holding a broken dart all ppr.

O'Connor (Glean-Geimhin and Cianachta, now the Barony of Keenaght, co. Londonderry; a Sept of the same race as O'CARROLL, who were driven out of their territory by the O'CAHANS before the English invasion). Ar. on a mount in base an oak tree all ppr.

O'Connor (Newtown, King's co.; Fun. Ent. Ulster's Office, 1675, DONOUGH O'CONNOR, son of JOHN O'CONNOR, of same place, was buried with his father at Killihie, in same co., leaving an only son, JOHN O'CONNOR). Ar. an oak tree eradicated ppr.

O'Connor (Derrymolin, King's co.; impalement Fun. Ent. Ulster's Office, 1640, WILLIAM FITZGERALD, Esq., of Rahannan, co. Kerry, whose wife was MARY O'CONNOR, dau. of CHARLES O'CONNOR, Esq., of Derrymolin). Ar. an oak tree eradicated vert fructed and charged with a lizard pass. or, a crescent for diff.

O'Conor (Kings of Connaught; RODERICK O'CONOR, King of Connaught, was elected Monarch of Ireland, and resigned the sovereignty to Henry II., d. in the Monastery of Cong, A.D. 1198). Ar. an oak tree eradicated ppr.

O'Conor Don (descended from CHARLES or CHARLES O'CONOR (Crobhderg), King of Connaught, d. 1224, brother of RODE- RICK O'CONOR, last Monarch of Ireland. Sir HUGH O'CONOR DON was knighted at Meath, 24 July, 1599, by ROBERT, Earl of Essex, Lord-Lieutenant of Ireland. O'CONOR DON, M.P., co. Roscommon, is Chief of the House of O'CONOR). Ar. an oak tree vert, surmounted by a crown. Crest—An arm embowed in armour holding a short sword entwined with a serpent all ppr. Motto—O Dhia gach an cabhair.

O'Conor (Mount Druid, co. Roscommon). Same Arms and Crest.

O'Conor (Dundermott, co. Roscommon). Same Arms and Crest.

O'Conor (Milton, co. Roscommon). Same Arms and Crest.

O'Conor Roe (TEIGE O'CONOR; the representative of this line was a Colonel in the French Army in 1700). Erm. an oak tree eradicated and acorned ppr.

O'Conor Sligo (descended from BRIAN O'CONOR, younger brother of RODERICK O'CONOR, last Monarch of Ireland; Sir DANIEL O'CONOR SLIGO was knighted by Sir Henry Sydney, Lord-Deputy of Ireland, 1567). Per pale vert and ar. in the dexter a lion ramp. to the sinister, in the sinister on a mount in base vert an oak tree ppr. Crest—An arm in armour embowed holding a sword all ppr.

O'Conor (a branch of O'CONOR ROE). Ar. an oak tree eradicated and acorned ppr. over all on a fess wavy az. a unicorn's head erased betw. two salmon naiant of the first.

O'Conor, alias Lee (the Sept of O'LAODHOG, or O'LEE, hereditary physicians to O'CONOR, King of Connaught. LEE, or O'CONOR, a professor of physic, was buried in Dublin, 20 Dec. 1595,. Ar. an oak tree eradicated ppr. on a fess wavy az. a fox's head erased of the first betw. two fish naiant or.

O'Conry (a Sept of the same race as MAC COCHLAN, inhabiting part of the King's co.). Quarterly, 1st, vert three goats pass. ar.; 2nd, ar. a lion ramp. gu.: 3rd, gu. three escallops ar.; 4th, vert a cock statant ppr. Crest—A blackamoor's head in profile couped at the shoulders sa. and bound round the temples with a ribbon ar.

O'Conry (Dungarvan, co. Waterford, and Seville, in the Kingdom of Spain; allowed by Hawkins, Ulster, 1782, to PHILIP FERDINAND O'CONRY, of the latter place, fourth in descent f om PATRICK O'CONRY, of the former). Same Arms and Crest. Motto—Vincit omnia.

O'Cornyn (a Sept claiming descent from DUAGH, second son of LUGHAIDH McCON, Monarch of Ireland). Per fess ar. and erm. a fess gu. in chief a demi lion ramp. sa. Crest —A sagittarius ppr.

746

O'Corrigan (an ancient Sept of the same descent as McGUIRE, descended from COLLA DA CHRIOCH). Or, a chev. betw. two trefoils slipped in chief and a lizard pass. in base vert. Crest—Two battle axes in saltire in front of a sword ppr. point downwards, pommel and hilt or.

O'Corrigan. See CORRIGAN, Bart.

O'Crean (O'CRAIDHEN, cos. Mayo and Sligo). Ar. a wolf ramp. sa. betw. three human hearts gu. Crest—A demi wolf ramp. sa. holding betw. the paws a human heart or. Motto—Cor mundum crea in me, Deus.

O'Crean. See LYNCH, of Clogher.

O'Crouley, O'Crowly, and O'Croly (a Sept in Connaught, deriving their name from DERMOT, called CRUATH LOCHA, the Hardy Champion, who was descended from McDERMOT, of Moylurg). Az. a boar pass. betw. three crosses crosslet or. Crest—An arm erect couped below the elbow, vested gu. holding in the hand ppr. a spear, bend sinisterways, point upwards, also ppr.

O'Crouley (Chiefs of Kilshallow, a territory west of Bandon, co. Cork; descended from Connaught). Ar. a boar pass. az. betw. three crosses crosslet gu.

O'Crouley (City of Limerick, and Cadiz, in Spain; allowed by Hawkins, Ulster, 1771, to PETER ALPHONSO O'CROULEY, of the latter place, son of JEREMIAH O'CROULEY, of Limerick, who emigrated to Cadiz; descended from CORMICK O'CROULEY, of Carbery, co. Cork). Same Arms. Crest—A naked arm erect couped below the elbow gu. holding a spear in bend, point upwards, ppr. Motto—Spero in Deo.

O'Crouley (Tome, in the Barony of Carbery, co. Cork; Fun. Ent. Ulster's Office, 1637, ELLICE, dau. of DERMOT MAC TEIGE O'CROULEY, of that place, m. DONOUGH O'LEARY, of Dromcar, co. Cork). Same Arms.

O'Cullen (the Sept of O'CUILLEN). Gu. on a chev. betw. three dexter hands erect couped at the wrist ar. a garb betw. two trefoils slipped vert. Crest—A mermaid with comb and mirror all ppr.

O'Cullen (Ballydonoghragh, co. Wicklow; Fun. Ent. Ulster's Office, 1622, the wife of MORTOGH O'CULLEN, of that place). Same Arms.

O'Curnin. Sa. a chev. betw. two sheep statant or. Crest— A sheep statant or.

O'Daly (Chiefs of Corca Adhamh, a territory in the present Barony of Magheradernon, co. Westmeath; descended from and deriving their surname from DALAIGH, Chief of the Sept, claiming descent from NIALL, of the Nine Hostages; this Sept were scattered after the invasion of 1172). Per fess ar. and or, a lion ramp. per fess sa. and gu. in chief two dexter hands couped at the wrist of the last.

O'Daly (Finnvara, co. Clare; descended from DONOUGH MOR O'DALY, a famous poet; they removed to Hy Maine temp. Henry VI. and Edward IV., where they acquired property after the revolution of 1688). Same Arms.

O'Daly (Killymore, co. Galway; now represented by Lord Dunsandle and Clan-Conal. See DALY). Same Arms. Crest—In front of an oak tree ppr. a greyhound courant sa. Motto—Deo fidelis et regi.

O'Daly (Killeleigh, co. Westmeath). Same Arms.

O'Davoren (Cahirmacneaghty, co. Clare; where CONSTANCE O'DAVOREN d. 1634, son of GILLENEAF O'DAVOREN, and grandson of GILLENEAF O'DAVOREN, who was son of HUGH O'DAVOREN, and grandson of MANUS O'DAVOREN). Ar. a sword erect in pale distilling drops of blood ppr. pommel and hilt or. Crest—A hind statant ppr.

Oddeston (co. Leicester). Or, fretty gu. a canton sa.

Oddeworth, or Utworth (co. Surrey; the heiress m. SANDERS, of Charlewood,t emp. Richard II.). Ar. on a cross gu. five lioncels ramp. or.

Oddie (HENRY HOYLE ODDIE, Esq., of Colney House, co. Herts, son and heir of the late HENRY HOYLE ODDIE, Esq., and grandson of JOHN ODDIE, of Storkhouse and Gisburne, co. York, by SARAH, his wife, dau. and heir of EDWARD HOYLE, Esq., who was great-grandson of the Rev. HENRY HOYLE, M.A., presented to the Vicarage of Gisburne in 1602). Ar. a fess per fess indented vert and sa. betw. three plain cotises of the last. Crest—A brock coming out of a rock ppr.

Oddy. Az. a saltire ar. Crest—A goat's head per pale or and az. counterchanged.

O'Dea (anciently O'DEADHAIGH, of Tully-O'Dea, and Disert-Tola, a district on the west side of the River Fergus, co. Clare). Ar. a dexter hand lying fessways, couped at the wrist, cuffed indented az. holding a sword in pale all ppr. in chief two snakes embowed vert.

Odehame. Sa. on a fess ar. two water bougets of the field.

Odell, or Odehull. Ar. three crescents gu. Crest—An eagle displ. gu.

Odell (Carriglea, co. Waterford; confirmed to JOHN ODELL, Esq., of that place). Or, a trefoil slipped vert betw. three crescents, two and one, gu. *Crest*—A dexter arm embowed, armed, the hand grasping a naked sword, the blade passing through a chaplet of red roses and trefoils all ppr.

Odell (Kilcleagh Park, co. Westmeath; confirmed to THOMAS SCRUTON ODELL, Esq., of that place, and the descendants of his grandfather, Lieut. JOHN ODELL, R.N.). Per chev. or and ar. three crescents gu. *Crest*—A demi lion ramp. in armour, the hand holding a sword all ppr. the arm charged with two crescents in pale gu. *Motto*—Pro patriâ invictus.

O'Dempsey (Chief of the Clann Maoi Lurghra, whose territory lay on both sides of the River Barrow, in the present King's and Queen's co., of the same race as O'CONOR FAILGHE, or FALEY and O'DOINN, and deriving their surname from DIOMASAIGH, Chief of the Sept. The Four Masters record the death, 1193, of DERMOD, son of CONBROGHDA O'DIOMASAIGH, a long time Chief of Clann Maoi Lurghra). Gu. a lion ramp. ar. armed and langued az. betw. two swords, points upwards of the second, pommels and hilts or, one in bend dexter, the other in bend sinister.

O'Dempsey (*Viscount Glenmalier*, dormant since 1714; Sir TERENCE O'DEMPSEY, *The O'Dempsey*, was knighted by ROBERT, *Earl of Essex*, at Kiltenan, or Kiltannan, co. Limerick, 22 May, 1599, and was created a viscount 1631; the third viscount *d. s. p.*; since his death the title has been unclaimed). Same *Arms*. *Crest*—A demi lion ramp. gu. langued az. supporting in the dexter paw a sword ar. pommel and hilt or. *Supporters*—Two knights in complete armour chained together by the left and right leg all ppr. *Motto*—Elatum a Deo non deprimat.

O'Dempsey (Bishops Court, co. Kildare; forfeited *temp.* James II.). Same *Arms*, *Crest*, and *Motto*.

O'Dempsey (Kilnecourt, in the Queen's co.; HUGH O'DEMPSEY was deprived of his estate by Oliver Cromwell). Same *Arms*, *Crest*, and *Motto*.

Odiard. Sa. a chev. betw. three covered cups or. *Crest*—An arm embowed in armour ppr. garnished or, holding in the gauntlet a covered cup or.

Odin (co. Kent; ODIN, of Boston, United States, America). Gu. a lion ramp. ar. debruised with a crozier in bend sinister or. *Crest*—A horse ramp. ar.

Odingleigh. Ar. a fess gu. in chief a mullet pierced az.

Odingsell, or Odingells (Eperston, co. Nottingham). Ar. a fess gu. in the dexter chief point a mullet of the second. *Crest*—A wolf pass. gu.

Odingsell. Ar. on a fess sa. betw. three mullets gu. as many escallops or.

Odingsell. Ar. on a fess gu. three escallops or, in chief two mullets of the second.

Odingsells (Trusley, co. Derby, *temp.* Edward I.; one of the co-heiresses, ELIZABETH, *m.* THOMAS COKE, Esq., and was ancestor of COKE, of Trusley; the other *m.* RICHARD PIPER). Ar. a fess gu. in chief three mullets sa.

Odingsells (co. Warwick; confirmed to WILLIAM ODINGSELLS, of Long Itchington, thirteenth in descent from Sir EVERARD ODINGSELLS, *temp.* Henry II.). Ar. a fess gu. in chief two mullets of the last. *Crest*—A naked arm erect, holding in the hand ppr. a mullet gu. *Another Crest*—A wolf pass. or, guttée on the neck gu.

Odingsells. Ar. a fess gu. in the dexter chief a mullet of the second. *Crest*—A wolf pass. or, guttée on the neck gu.

Odo (*Earl of Kent*, extinct 1099; ODO, Bishop of Bayeux, in Normandy, half brother of William I., was so created by the Conqueror, 1067). Gu. a lion ramp. ar. debruised with a crosier staff gu.

O'Dogherty (a Sept of Ulster, of the same race as O'BOYLE, deriving their name from DOCHARTAIGH, Chief of the territory of Cinel-Edna and Ard-Miodhair, co. Donegal; BRIEN DUFF O'DOGHERTY, was Lord of Ennishowen, same co., 1440; Sir CAHIR O'DOGHERTY, Lord of Ennishowen, was killed in rebellion 1608, when all his lands were forfeited). Ar. a stag springing gu. on a chief vert three mullets of the first. *Crest*—A hand couped at the wrist erect grasping a sword all ppr. *Another Crest*—A greyhound courant ar. holding in the mouth a hare ppr. *Motto*—Ar nDuthchas. For my inheritance.

O'Dogherty (co. Leitrim, and Spain; allowed by Fortescue, Ulster, 1790, to HENRY, JOHN, and CLINTON-DILLON, O'DOGHERTY, then residing in the Kingdom of Spain, sons of OWEN O'DOGHERTY, *d.* 1784, descended from JOHN O'DOGHERTY, *d.* 1630, second son of Sir JOHN O'DOGHERTY, knt., of Ennishowen, Chief of his Sept, and brother of Sir

COLIN O'DOGHERTY, killed in rebellion 1608). Ar. a chev. engr. betw. three trefoils slipped vert. *Crest*—An arm in armour embowed, holding a scymitar all ppr. *Motto*—Arn Duthchas.

O'Doinn (Chiefs of Hy Regain, in the present Queen's co., a very ancient Sept in Leinster, of the same race as O'CONOR FAILGHE, or FALEY, and O'DEMPSEY; RORIE O'DOINN, Chief of Hy Regain, *d.*, according to the Four Masters, 1427; TEIGE O'DOINN, *The O'Doinn*, *temp.* Queen Elizabeth, made a settlement of his estates on his sons, with remainders over to collateral relations, by deed of 17 April, 1593; from this line descend DOYNE, of Wells, co. Wexford; DUNNE, of Brittas, in the Queen's co.; DUNNE, of Ards, in same co.). Az. an eagle displ. or. *Crest*—In front of a holly bush ppr. a lizard pass. or. *Motto*—Mullach a-bu, the ancient war cry or call to arms of the Sept.

O'Donagan (a Sept who possessed the territory of Ara, co. Tipperary; they were of the Ulster race of Clanna Rory, descended from FERGUS MAC ROIGH, King of Ulster; the name has been corrupted to PONEGAN). Ar. three ermine spots in pale sa. betw. four lions ramp., those in dexter chief and sinister base gu., and those in sinister chief and dexter base of the second. *Crest*—A greyhound's head couped sa. charged on the neck with an erm. spot ar.

O'Donelan (Ross-I-Donelan, co. Roscommon; Fun. Ent. Ulster's Office, 1638, MELAUGHLIN O'DONELAN, of that place). Ar. an oak tree eradicated vert, fructed and charged with a crescent or.

O'Donellan (a Sept in Connaught, deriving their name from DONELAN, Lord of the territory of Clann-Breasail, lying between Ballinasloe and Loughrea, co. Galway, descended from the race of O'CONOR, of Magh Naoi). Ar. an oak tree eradicated ppr. on the sinister side a slave sa. chained to the stem gu. *Crest*—On a mount ppr. a lion ramp. or. *Motto*—Omni violentia major.

O'Donlevy (a Sept of the Clanna Rory, in Ulster, seated in co. Down; the Sept lost their ancient rank shortly after the invasion of 1172, and removed into Tirconnell, where they became hereditary physicians to O'DONNELL. The original name, O'DUINNSLEIBHE, is derived from DUN, "a fortress," and SLEIBHE, "the mountain," one of their chieftains having his fortress in the Mourne mountains. The Four Masters record, under the year 1199, that RORY O'DUNSLEVE joined a party of the English of Meath, and plundered the monastery of SS. Peter and Paul, at Armagh). Ar. on a mount in base ppr. a lion gu. and a buck of the second ramp. combatant supporting a dexter hand couped at the wrist of the third. *Crest*—A lion ramp. gu.

O'Donnell, O'Donel, or O'Donell. The origin of the arms of this historic family is of remarkable interest and of great antiquity. CONNELL, son of NIAL, "of the Nine Hostages" (Rex. Hib. 375-402) is recorded, in two of the Lives of St. Patrick, to have been converted to Christianity by that saint, who, to reward him for his singular zeal, marked on his shield the sign of the Cross, directing him and his descendants ever afterwards to bear it as the emblem of victory. The incident is thus related in the Sept. Vita (Tripartite) cap. xcv. : " Et mox cum baculo suo, qui baculus-Jesu dicebatur, Crucis Signum ejus Scuto impressit, asserens neminem de stirpe ejus in bello vincendum qui signum illud in suo scuto impressum gestaret." There can be no doubt that this sign or symbol was borne by his descendants, the Chiefs of Tirconnell, as their emblem, down to the introduction of Heraldry as a science. When HUGH O'DONEL, Chief of Tirconnell (thirty-third in descent from CONNELL) made his submission to the English Government in 1567, and was knighted by Sir HENRY SIDNEY, the Lord Deputy, his arms were thus recorded : *Arms* of Sir HUGH O'DONNELL, *Lord of Tirconnell*, A.D. 1567—Or, issuing from the sinister side of the shield an arm fessways vested az. cuffed ar. holding in the hand ppr. a cross crosslet fitchée gu. *Arms* of RODERICK, *Earl of Tirconnell*, *d.* in Rome 1608, as carved upon his tomb in the church of San Pietro in Montorio—Ar. issuing from the dexter side an arm sleeved az. holding palewise a passion cross gu. shield surmounted by a ducal coronet. *Motto*—In hoc signo vinces. *Supporters*—Dexter, a lion or; sinister, a bull of the same, both guard. *Arms* of his son, HUGH ALBERT, titular *Earl of Tirconnell*, were precisely the same, as appears by his seal on numerous original letters preserved in the church of San Isidore, Rome. This line of the family became extinct. The elder branch, *i.e.*, the sons of CON, son of CALVAGH, Chief 1565, have transmitted the descent and the arms to the present day. His three sons who left issue were: I. Sir NIAL GARVE, last inaugurated Chief, who *d.* a prisoner in the Tower of London, 1626, from whom descended General Count MANUS O'DONEL, and O'DONELL, Bart., of Newport. *Arms* of Count

MANUS O'DONNELL, *d.* 1793, as inscribed on his tomb in Strade Abbey, Mayo—Ar. issuing from the sinister side an arm sleeved holding a passion cross. *Crest*—Two arms armed, bent and counter crossed, each holding a sword, that on the dexter side transfixing a boar's head, the other a heart. Same *Motto*. *Arms* of O'DONNELL, of Newport, bart.—Gu. issuing from the sinister side a cubit sinister arm vested az. cuffed or, the hand ppr. grasping a cross fitchée of the third. In the crest the right hand grasps a scymitar and the left holds a heart. Same *Motto*. II. HUGH BOY, *d.* 1649, from whom descended the famous "Ball-dearg" of the wars of James II., and through his brother CONNELL the present family of Larkfield, co. Leitrim, represented by the Rev. CONSTANTINE O'DONEL, A.B., Vicar of St. Peter's, Allenheads, Northumberland. To this branch also belonged Field-Marshal CONNELL O'DONNELL, in the service of Maria Teresa. *Arms* of the O'DONNELLS, of Larkfield, same as those of Newport. III. CONOGE, killed at the siege of Donegal Castle, 1601, from whom are descended three branches: 1. The Irish branch, represented by CHARLES J. O'DONEL, Esq., Dublin; 2. The Spanish branch, represented by his Excellency, Don CARLOS O'DONEL, *Duke of Tetuan*, Spanish Minister at Vienna, nephew and heir of the late Marshal LEOPOLD O'DONEL, *Duke of Tetuan*, who *d.* in 1869; 3. The Austrian branch, represented by General MAXIMILIAN, *Count O'Donell*, who has the distinguished honour of impaling with his family shield the Imperial arms of Austria. These three branches bear the Spanish colours on the shield. *Arms* of the descendants of CON OGE—Per saltire or and gu. issuing from the dexter side in fess an arm sleeved of the first, with the hand ppr. in the centre, holding in pale a passion cross of the second. *Crest*—Same as described *infra*. Same *Motto*. In addition to these family arms, the present Emperor of Austria, in reward for having saved His Majesty's life from assassination at the peril of his own, by patent, dated the 28th July, 1853, conferred on General MAXIMILIAN, *Count O'Donell* (forty-third in descent from CONNELL) and his heirs, the right of impaling the Imperial arms on his shield, emblazoned as follows—"A shield divided per pale, the dexter field or, contains the Austrian double eagle sa. armed or, langued gu., on each head a hoop-crown or, and suspended above the Imperial crown, the eagle carries, as the escutcheon of our house, on a breast-shield gu. a bar ar. whereon the Imperial initials F.J. appear in golden capitals. The sinister field divided per saltire, or and gu. displays a passion cross gu. held in the centre palewise by an arm sleeved with cloth of gold, with naked hand issuing from the pale. On the shield a count's coronet, over which a tilting helm, with hoops or, and jewelled border or, on the dexter side sa., on the sinister gu., surrounded with helm ornaments or, arranged into the beaver. A leaf-crown or, adorns the helmet, upon which two arms embowed and counterly crossed, each in golden edged armour with hand ppr.; that on the dexter side holding a heart gu., that on the sinister grasping by the hilt or, a glittering short sword pointing upwards. Under the shield is the *Motto*—In hoc signo vinces, in capitals or, on a scroll gu. upon which stand the *Supporters*, viz., dexter, a lion or, langued gu. guard.; sinister, a bull sa. reguard."

O'Donnell (allowed by Hawkins, Ulster, 1772, to JAMES BRAND O'DONNELL, Esq., son of RICHARD O'DONNELL, Esq., by ALICE TAYLOR, his wife, dau. of JOHN TAYLOR, Esq., of Swords, co. Dublin, descended from HUGH O'DONNELL, second son of RODERICK O'DONNELL, 1603). Sa. two lions ramp. combatant ar. armed and langued gu. in chief a dexter hand couped erect betw. two mullets, and in base another mullet all of the second. *Crest*—Out of a ducal coronet or, a naked arm embowed grasping a dart all ppr. *Motto*—In hoc signo vinces.

O'Donnell (allowed by Hawkins, Ulster, 1777, to JOHN O'DONNELL, lieut.-gen. in the service of the Emperor of Germany; descended from O'DONNELL, *Earl of Tyrconnell*). Same *Arms*, *Crest*, and *Motto*.

O'Donnell (confirmed by Fortescue, Ulster, to JOHN O'DONNELL, Esq., of the city of Dublin). Sa. two lions ramp. combatant, and in chief a hand betw. two mullets and one in base ar. *Crest*—Out of a ducal coronet or, a naked arm bent at the elbow holding a spear, the point down all ppr. *Motto*—In hoc signo vinces.

O'Donnelly (granted by Betham, Ulster, to Vice-Admiral Sir Ross DONNELLY, K.C.B.; descended from the Sept of O'DONNELLY, of Gortcherran, co. Tyrone, a branch of O'NIELL, Monarchs of Ireland). Ar. two lions ramp. combatant supporting a dexter hand couped at the wrist gu. and in base a salmon naiant in the sea all ppr. on a chief as. a naval crown or, betw. two mullets ar. *Crest*—Out of

a naval crown or, charged on the circlet with the words "1 June, 1794," sa. an armed arm embowed, grasping a sword wavy ppr. thereon a wreath of laurel vert, over the crest in a scroll the motto, Justitia tandem. *Motto*—Lamh dearg eirin.

O'Donoghoe (*O'Donoghoe Mor*, Lough Lein, co. Kerry; a Sept deriving their name from DONNCHADHA, Chief of the Sept, A.D. 1030. The chief of the Sept, O'DONOGHOE-MOR, lived at Ross Castle, in the Lakes of Killarney, up to the reign of Queen Elizabeth). Vert two foxes ramp. combatant ar. on a chief of the last an eagle volant sa. *Crest*—An arm in armour embowed holding a sword, the blade entwined with a serpent all ppr.

O'Donoghoe (*O'Donoghoe of the Glens*, Glen Flesk; the second branch of O'DONOGHOE. O'DONOGHOE of the Glens is M.P. for Tralee). Same *Arms* and *Crest*. Another Crest (Reg. Ulster's Office)—A pelican in her piety ppr.

O'Donovan (*The O'Donovan*; HENRY WINTHROP O'DONOVAN, of Lissard, co. Cork, Chief of Clan Cathal, a Sept who in ancient times ruled over Hy Fidhgeinte, a territory extending along the banks of the River Maigue, co. Limerick, on which stood the Castle of Crom. Driven from their territory by the Fitzgeralds and De Burghos after the invasion of 1172, they settled in the Barony of Carbery, co. Cork, where the estates of the present chieftain are situate. CATHAL, Chief of Hy Fidhgeinte, was slain by Callaghan Cashel, King of Munster, A.D. 964, and was s. by his son, DONOVAN, who ruled as Chief 977, from him the Sept took their tribe name; seventh in descent from DONOVAN was CROM O'DONOVAN, *The O'Donovan*, slain 1254, leaving three sons :— I. CATHAL O'DONOVAN, *O'Donovan*, ancestor of the subsequent chieftains; II. ANESLIS O'DONOVAN, ancestor of *O'Donovan*, Mac Aneslis; III. LOUGHLIN O'DONOVAN, ancestor of *The O'Donovan*, of Clan Loughlin; from these three sons descend the whole family of O'DONOVAN and DONOVAN. DONEL O'DONOVAN, *The O'Donovan*, *s.* his father 1584, and had seven sons :—I. DONEL, ancestor of the succeeding chieftains, whose male line became extinct, 1829, on the death of RICHARD O'DONOVAN, *The O'Donovan*, General in the Army; II. TEIGE, ancestor of the present chieftain; III. MOROGH, ancestor of O'DONOVAN, of Malaga, in Spain ; IV. DONOUGH, ancestor of O'DONOVAN, of Cooldurragh; V. DERMOT; VI. RICHARD, ancestor of O'DONOVAN, of O'Donovan Street, Cork; VII. KEADAGH, ancestor of O'DONOVAN, Clan Keady, from whom descend the branches of Lisheens and Ardahill). Ar. issuing from the sinister side of the shield a cubit dexter arm vested gu. cuffed of the first, the hand grasping a skein or old Irish sword in pale, the blade entwined with a serpent all ppr. *Crest*—On a chapeau gu. turned up erm. a falcon alighting ar. tips of wings and tail sa. *Motto*—Vir super hostem, a translation of the ancient slogan, or call to war, of the Sept, viz., Giolla ar a-namhuid a-bu.

O'Donovan (O'DONOVAN MAC ANESLIS; descended from ANESLIS O'DONOVAN, second son of CROM O'DONOVAN, *The O'Donovan*, 1254, who possessed a territory about Macroom, co. Cork. The only known member of this branch is WILLIAM O'DONOVAN RICKARD, now resident in America). Same *Arms*, *Crest*, and *Motto*, with the ppr. diff.

O'Donovan (O'DONOVAN, of CLAN LOUGHLIN; descended from LOUGHLIN O'DONOVAN, third son of CROM O'DONOVAN, *The O'Donovan*, 1254; DONEL OGE NA CARTAN O'DONOVAN, Chief of Clan Loughlin, *d.* 1629, leaving two sons :—I. MORTOGH McDONEL OGE NA CARTAN O'DONOVAN, ancestor of the present chief of this line, JEREMIAH ALEXANDER O'DONOVAN, and of DONOVAN, of Squince, co. Cork; II. RICHARD NA CARTAN O'DONOVAN, whose grandson, RICKARD DONOVAN, settled in the co. Wexford, and was ancestor of DONOVAN, of Ballymore, in that co. See DONOVAN, of Ballymore). Same *Arms*, *Crest*, and *Motto* as *O'Donovan*, with the ppr. diff.

O'Donovan (Malaga, in the kingdom of Spain; allowed and pedigree registered by Hawkins, Ulster, 1771, to JOHN O'DONOVAN, of that place, fourth in descent from MOROGH O'DONOVAN, Esq., of Castle Ire, co. Cork, third son of DONEL O'DONOVAN, *The O'Donovan*, 1584). Ar. a dexter arm couped below the elbow, lying fessways, vested gu. cuffed of the first, holding in the hand a sword in pale entwine with a serpent descending all ppr. *Crest*—An eagle alighting or.

O'Donovan (O'Donovan Street, in the city of Cork; descended from RICHARD O'DONOVAN, sixth son of DONEL O'DONOVAN, *The O'Donovan*, 1584. This coat is taken from an ancient parchment pedigree which was in the possession of PHILIP O'DONOVAN, Esq., Lieut. R.N., of O'Donovan Street *temp.* George IV.). Ar. issuing from the sinister side of the shield a cubit dexter arm naked, the hand grasping a sword in pale entwined with a lizard betw. three golden balls all ppr. *Crest*—A white falcon alighting. *Motto*—Crom a-boo.

O'Donovan (O'Donovan's Cove, co. Cork; descended from TEIGE O'DONOVAN, of Gorteenithir, co. Cork, a near kinsman of TEIGE O'DONOVAN, *The O'Donovan, temp.* Henry VII.). Ar. issuing from the sinister side of the shield a cubit dexter arm vested gu. cuffed of the first, the hand grasping a skein, or old Irish sword in pale, entwined with a lizard all ppr. *Crest* and *Motto*, same as *O'Donovan*.

O'Donovan. See DONOVAN, of Ballymore, &c.

O'Dorken. Ar. a saltire sa. betw. two nettle leaves in chief and one in base vert.

O'Dowde (anciently O'DUBHDA, Chiefs of Hy Fiuchrach, in Briefne, tributary to O'ROURKE). Vert a saltire or, in chief two swords in saltire, points upwards, the dexter surmounted of the sinister ar. pommels and hilts gold.

O'Dowling (Reg. Ulster's Office, to MURTOGH O'DOWLING, of co. Kilkenny). Ar. a holly tree eradicated ppr. on a chief az. a lion pass. betw. two trefoils slipped or. *Crest*—A lion's head erased az. collared gemelles or.

O'Driscoll (a Sept possessed of Bearra, now the Barony of Beare, co. Cork, from which they were driven by the O'Sullivans; they derive their surname from EIDERSCEOIL, Chief of Bearra; thirteenth in descent from him was Sir FINGHEEN O'HEEIDERSCEOIL MOR, who founded the Franciscan Abbey on Iniskeen Island, 1460. The Four Masters record that O'DRISCOLL MOR was slain by the crew of a merchant vessel in Cork, 1414). Ar. a ship or ancient galley, sails furled sa. *Crest*—A cormorant ppr.

O'Driscoll (Baltimore, co. Cork; CHRISTOPHER O'DRISCOLL, of that place, *temp.* Queen Elizabeth). Same *Arms*.

O'Driscoll (Reg. Ulster's Office). Ar. a ship of three masts, sails set sa. *Crest*—A tower ppr.

O'Dron (an ancient Irish Sept). Ar. a serpent enwrapped vert.

Odron. Ar. a cross gu. betw. four lions pass. respecting each other sa.

O'Duana (Duanahagh, co. Sligo; a Sept of the same race as O'HARA and O'GARA). Erm. a fox pass. sa. in chief two crescents of the last. *Crest*—A fox's head couped sa.

O'Duffy (Ballyduffy, co. Monaghan; HUGH O'DUFFY, of that place, buried at Clontibret, same co., Jan. 1636, was son of GILLA-PATRICK, son of CORMACK, son of OWEN MORE O'DUFFY, all of same place, descended from the Sept of O'ROURKE). Vert a lion ramp. or.

O'Dugenan (a Sept in Ulster, descended from the race of O'NEILL). Ar. on a mount in base vert an oak tree, the stem entwined with two serpents interwoven and erect respecting each other all ppr. *Crest*—An owl at gaze ppr.

O'Dwyer (a Sept seated at Muintir-Duibhidhir, a district in the present Barony of Kilnamanagh, co. Tipperary, deriving their name from DUIBHIDHIR, Chief of the Sept. The Four Masters record that THOMAS O'DWYER, son of CONOR, son of THOMAS O'DWYER, of Ormonde, was slain by the O'Kennedys, 1473). Ar. a lion ramp. gu. betw. three erm. spots. *Crest*—A hand couped at the wrist and erect, grasping a sword all ppr.

O'Dwyer (Cadiz, in Spain; allowed by Hawkins, Ulster, 1776, to ANTHONY O'DWYER, of that place, son of DERMOT O'DWYER, Captain of Grenadiers in the Irish Brigade in the service of Spain, who was fourth in descent from EDMOND O'DWYER, second son of ANTHONY O'DWYER, of Kilnamanagh, Chief of the Sept, 1567). Same *Arms* and *Crest*. *Motto*—Virtus sola nobilitas.

O'Dwyer (Clonyhorpa, co. Tipperary, Fun. Ent. Ulster's Office, 1629, DABBY O'DWYER, Esq., of that place. Same *Arms*.

O'Dwyer (Drumdromy, co. Tipperary; Fun. Ent. Ulster's Office, 1627, JOHN O'DWYER, Esq., of that place). Same *Arms*, a crescent for diff.

Odwyn (King of Cardigan). Sa. a lion ramp. ar.

Odyearne. Sa. a chev. betw. three covered cups or. *Crest* —An arm in armour ppr. garnished or, couped at the shoulder, lying fessways, the hand erect from the elbow also ppr. holding a covered cup gold.

Oeils (London). Ar. a fess sa. a demi lion ramp. issuant gu. in base three mullets or six points az.

O'Faelan (a Sept in Munster, derived from FAELAN, chief of North Decies). Ar. four lozenges in bend conjoined az. betw. two cotises in base on a chief gu. three fleurs-de-lis of the first.

O'Fahy, or O'Fay (a Sept of the race of O'CONOR, King of Connaught). Az. a hand couped at the wrist fessways in chief ppr. holding a sword paleways ar. pommel and hilt or, point downwards, pierced through a boar's head erased of

749

the last. *Crest*—A naked arm erect, couped below the elbow, holding a broken spear all ppr. point downwards or.

O'Fallon (a Sept in Connaught, deriving their name from FALLAMHAIN, chief of the territory of Clann Uadach, in the parishes of Camma and Dysart, co. Roscommon; of the race of O'CONOR, of Magh Naoi). See FALLON. Gu. a greyhound ramp. ar. holding betw. the fore paws a tilting spear, point to the dexter or. *Crest*—A demi greyhound saliant ar.

O'Farrell, or O'Ferrall (Clarendon MSS., 4639, British Museum). Vert a lion ramp. or, armed and langued gu. *Crest*—A greyhound in full course ppr.

O'Farrell (Glin and Killindowde, co. Longford; allowed by Hawkins, Ulster, 1775, to RICHARD O'FARRELL, of Havanna, in the West Indies, descended from O'FARRELL, of Killindowde, a branch of O'FARRELL, of Glin). Same *Arms*. *Crest*—A greyhound springing ar. collared gu. *Motto*— Cu reubha.

O'Farrell (Dalyston, co. Galway; exemplified to CHARLES CARROLL, Esq., J.P., of Dalyston, maternally a descendant of O'FARRELL, of Mornyng and Bawn, co. Longford, of the Clanna Boy, upon his succeeding to the estates of his maternal uncle, the late CHARLES FARRELL, Esq., M.D., of Dalyston, and assuming, by royal licence, 1855, the surname and arms of O'FARRELL, in lieu of those of CARROLL). Per fess or and vert a lion ramp. counterchanged, on a canton gu. an Irish harp of the first. *Crest*—On an Eastern crown or, a greyhound courant per pale ar. and sa. gorged with a collar gu. therefrom a broken chain of the last. *Motto*—Cu reubha.

O'Feargus (Reg. Ulster's Office). Az. a fess betw. a star of eight rays in chief and a lion ramp. in base all or. *Crest*— A lance in pale broken ppr. the head hanging down or, ferrule gold.

O'Ferrall Buoy (Lords of Annaly, formerly Anghaile, co. Longford; descended from FEARGHAIL, Chief of the Sept, who fell at the Battle of Clontarf, A.D. 1014). Vert a lion ramp. or. *Crest*—On a ducal coronet or, a greyhound springing sa. *Motto*—Cu reubha (I have broken my hold).

O'Ferrall (Ballintobber, co. Longford; descended from O'FERRALL BUOY). Same *Arms, Crest,* and *Motto*.

O'Ferrall (Tenelick, co. Longford; Fun. Ent. Ulster's Office, 1620, CONNALL O'FERRAL, of that place). Same *Arms*, quartering, 1st, az. a talbot pass. ar. collared and langued gu.; 2nd, az. a griffin segreant ar.; 3rd, ar. a lizard displ. vert. Same *Crest* and *Motto*.

O'Ferrall Bane (Bawne, co. Longford; descended from the same Sept as O'FERRALL, of Tenelick). Same *Arms*, *Crest,* and *Motto*, without the quarterings.

O'Ferrall (Mornin, co. Longford, and Conskeagh, co. Roscommon; Fun. Ent. Ulster's Office, 1640, EDMUND O'FERRALL, of the latter, son of IRIAL O'FERRALL, of the former, who was son and heir of FAGHNY O'FERRALL, and grandson of BRIAN FERRALL, both of Mornin). Same *Arms*.

O'Ferrall (Balyna, co. Kildare). Quarterly, 1st and 4th, vert a lion ramp. or, for O'FERRALL; 2nd and 3rd, vert a lion ramp. or, on a chief az. three mullets of the second, for O'MORE. *Crest*—On a ducal coronet or, a greyhound springing sa.

Offerton. Gu. on a chief or, three annulets of the field.

Offewell (co. Devon; quartered by DRAKE, of Otterton and Ashe, and by POLE, of Colcombe, same co. Visit. Devon, 1620). Erm. three bars az.

Offield, or Ofield. Ar. a cross gu. (another, tinctures reversed).

Offington. Az. a saltire engr. ar. (another, or).

Offley (co. Gloucester). Ar. on a cross flory betw. four Cornish choughs sa. beaked and legged gu. a lion pass. guard. or. *Crest*—A demi lion ramp. per pale or and az. collared per pale counterchanged, and holding a branch of laurel ppr.

Offley (Lord Mayor of London, 1556. Visit. London, 1568). Same *Arms* and *Crest*.

Offley (London, and Putney, co. Surrey; granted 5 Sept. 1588). Ar. a cross flory az. betw. four Cornish choughs ppr. *Crest*—A demi lion ramp. or, collared gu. holding in the paws an olive branch stalked and leaved vert, fructed of the first.

Offley (Norton Hall, co. Derby; EDMUND OFFLEY, Esq., of Norton Hall, great-grandson of STEPHEN OFFLEY, Esq., of Norton Hall, High Sheriff of the county in 1716, d. unm. in 1745, leaving his sisters, m. to SHORE and EDMUNDS, his co-heirs). Same *Arms*, and *Crest*.

Offley (Madeley, co. Stafford). Ar. on a cross pattée flory az. a lion pass. guard. or, betw. four Cornish choughs ppr. *Crest*—A demi lion per pale or and az. collared and lined, holding a pink ppr. stalked and leaved vert.

Offley. Ar. three lions' heads erased sa. a border engr. of the last. *Crest*—Out of a ducal coronet or, the attires of a stag affixed to the scalp sa.

Offord. Barry of six (another, of eight) ar. and az. on a bend gu. three mullets of the first, a border or.

Offspring. See OXSPRING.

O'Fienella. Az. two swords in saltire, points upwards ar. pommels and hilts or, betw. two crosses crosslet in pale and as many escallops in fess of the last. *Crest*—An escallop or, surmounted by a cross crosslet az.

O'Finnegan (one of the Tribes of Hy Maine, in Connaught, formerly MAC GIOLLA FIONNAGAIN; they possessed the territory of Clan Fhlaitheamhain, in the present Barony of Moycarnon, co. Roscommon; the name is sometimes modernised into FINUCANE). Gu. two lions ramp. combatant ar. supporting a sword in pale, blade wavy, point upwards ppr. *Crest*—A falcon alighting ppr.

O'Flaherty (a Sept who ruled over Iar Connaught, or West Connaught, deriving their surname from FLAITHBHEARTAIGH, Chieftain of the Sept, A.D. 970). Ar. two lions ramp. combatant, supporting a dexter hand couped at the wrist all gu. in base a boat with eight oars sa.

O'Flaherty (Ballynahinch and Bunowen, co. Galway; MOROGH NA MOR O'FLAHERTY, of these places, was Chief of the Sept *temp.* Queen Elizabeth; he was ninth in descent from HUGH O'FLAHERTY, who built the Church of Anaghdun, co. Galway, A.D. 1400, the eldest son of DONALD O'FLAHERTY). Same *Arms*. *Crest*—A lizard pass. vert. *Motto*—Fortuna faveat.

O'Flaherty (Lemonfield, co. Galway; descended from MOROGH NA DOE O'FLAHERTY, of Augnenure, or Lemonfield, who was one of the Irish chieftains who sat in Sir John Perrott's Parliament, 1585; he was ninth in descent from BRIAN O'FLAHERTY, brother of HUGH O'FLAHERTY, who built Anaghdun Church, A.D. 1400). Same *Arms*. *Crest*—A lizard pass. ppr. *Motto*—Fortuna favit fortibus.

O'Flaherty (Moycullen, co. Galway; descended from GILLDUFF O'FLAHERTY, younger son of BRIAN O'FLAHERTY, the ancestor of O'FLAHERTY, of Lemonfield; ROGER O'FLAHERTY, b. 1629, chief of this branch, was the author of "The Ogygia"). Same *Arms*, &c.

O'Flanagan (a Sept in Connaught, of the same race as O'DONELLAN, deriving their name from FLANNAGAIN, who ruled over the territory of Magh Aoi, co. Roscommon; this Sept enjoyed the hereditary office of Stewards to the Kings of Connaught). Ar. out of a mount in base vert an oak tree ppr. a border of the second. *Crest*—A dexter cubit arm in armour ppr. garnished or and gu. holding a flaming sword az. pommel and hilt gold. *Motto*—Certavi et vici.

O'Flanagan (Cinel Farga, now Kinelargy, a territory in ancient Ely O'Carroll, corresponding with the Barony of Ballybrit, in the King's co.; a Sept of the same race as O'CARROLL, who derived their name from FLANNAGAIN, one of their ancestors). Ar. on a mount in base an oak tree ppr. a border vert.

O'Flynn (a Sept in Munster, deriving their name from FLOINN; descended from the ancient Kings of Connaught; the Chieftain of the Sept lived at Ardagh Castle, in a territory between Skibbereen and Baltimore, co. Cork). Az. a wolf pass. ar. in chief three bezants. *Crest*—A dexter hand erect, couped, holding a serpent, tail embowed, head to the sinister all ppr.

O'Flynn. Ar. a dexter arm couped betw. two swords in pale all ppr.

O'Flynn (PHELIM FLYNN). Quarterly, ar. and gu. four dexter hands couped at the wrist counterchanged. *Crest*—An arm erect issuing out of a cloud ppr. holding a newt ar.

O'Flynn (NEIL FLYNN). Per fess ar. and gu. a sword in pale betw. two dexter hands couped at the wrist, one in chief the other in base counterchanged.

O'Fogarty (a Sept who possessed the territory of Eile-Hy-Fhogartaigh, now the Barony of Eliogarty, co. Tipperary, deriving their name from their Chieftain, FHOGARTAIGH). Az. two lions ramp. combatant supporting a garb all or, in dexter base a crescent ar. and in sinister base a harp of the second, stringed of the third. *Motto*—Fleadh agus failte (A banquet and a welcome).

O'Fogarty (Castle Fogarty, co. Tipperary; the senior line of the Sept of O'FOGARTY, extinct in the male line *temp.* George II.). Same *Arms*, &c.

O'Friell (Killmacrenan, co. Donegal; allowed by Hawkins, Ulster, 1750, to JAMES O'FRIELL, Esq.). Gu. in dexter fess a garb or, in sinister fess a dexter hand couped at the wrist fessways ppr. grasping a cross calvary on three grieces ar. in chief three mullets of the second. *Crest*—A garb or.

Ofspring (London, 1633). Ar. on a fess betw. three bells gu. as many crosses crosslet ar.

750

Ofwell. See OFFEWELL.

O'Gallagher (a Sept who possessed a territory in the Baronies of Raphoe and Tirhugh, co. Donegal, and held the Castles of Lifford and Ballyshannon, deriving their surname from GALLCHOBHAIR, a warrior of the Sept, who lived A.D. 950). Ar. a lion ramp. sa. treading on a serpent in fess ppr. betw. eight trefoils vert. *Crest*—A crescent gu. out of the horns a serpent erect ppr.

Ogan, Ougan, or Hogan. Sa. on a chief or, three annulets of the field (another, the tinctures reversed).

O'Gara (Coolavin, co. Sligo; an Irish Sept which possessed a tract of land in the Barony of Coolavin prior to the invasion of 1172; descended from GADHRA, Chief of Coolavin and Sliabh Lugha; they were dispossessed in 1648). Ar. three lions ramp. az. on a chief gu. a demi lion ramp. or. *Crest*—A demi lion ramp. erm. holding betw. the paws a wreath of oak vert, acorned or. *Motto*—Fortiter et fideliter.

O'Gara (allowed by Hawkins, Ulster, 1756, to CHARLES O'GARA). Same *Arms*, *Crest*, and *Motto*.

O'Gara (allowed by Mac Cullogh, Ulster, 1776, to CHARLES O'GARA, son of Captain OLIVER O'GARA). Same *Arms*, *Crest*, and *Motto*.

Ogarde, or Ogard. Az. an estoile of six (another, of eight; another, sixteen) points ar.

Ogden. Sa. on a fess ar. betw. six acorns or, three oak leaves vert. *Crest*—A stag's head cabossed ppr. attired or, betw. two oak branches in orle, leaves ppr. acorned gold.

Ogden. Same *Arms*. *Crest*—A griffin's head erased, holding in the beak an oak branch acorned ppr.

Ogden (granted, *temp.* Charles II., to JOHN OODEN, for his faithful services to the King). Gyronny of eight ar. and gu. in dexter chief an oak branch fructed ppr. *Crest*—An oak tree ppr. a lion ramp. against it. *Motto*—Et si ostendo non jacto.

Ogden (arms on the monument of GEORGE OGDEN, 1788, in the Cathedral of Chester). Sa. on a fess or, betw. six acorns of the last, slipped and leaved ppr. three oak leaves vert. *Crest*—A boar pass. sa. betw. two branches of oak ppr. fructed or.

Ogden (The Laurels, Iron Acton, co. Gloucester; exemplified to PETER HASSELL, Esq., on his assuming, by royal licence, the surname of OGDEN). Quarterly, 1st and 4th, or, on a fess dancettée sa. betw. three oak leaves vert as many acorns of the field, for OGDEN; 2nd and 3rd, erm. a fess vairé ar. and sa. betw. three pheons az., for HASSELL. *Crests*—1st, OGDEN: A griffin's head erased sa. in the beak an acorn ppr. and charged on the breast with a cross pattée or; 2nd, HASSELL: A pheon az. betw. two branches of hazel ppr. *Motto*—Ilias in nuce.

Ogie. Ar. on a chief az. three crosses pattée fitchée. *Crest*—A human heart gu. pierced with a passion nail in bend sinister az.

Ogilby (Pollipar House, co. Londonderry; granted by Betham, Ulster, to ROBERT OGILBY, Esq., of that place). Ar. a lion pass. guard. gu. betw. two crescents, one in chief and one in base az. *Crest*—A lion ramp. gu. armed and langued az. supporting a tilting spear entwined with a string of trefoils ppr.

Ogill (Poppill, co. Haddington). Ar. on a fess az. three cocks of the first, in chief a crescent of the second.

Ogill (Hartramwood, Scotland). Ar. on a fess az. three bitterns of the field.

Ogilvie (that Ilk, and Easter Powrie, co. Forfar). Ar. a lion pass. guard. gu. crowned or.

Ogilvie (Auchterhouse, co. Forfar; heiress *m.* JAMES STEWART, afterwards *Earl of Buchan*). Quarterly, 1st and 4th, as the last; 2nd and 3rd, ar. an eagle displ. sa. beaked and membered gu., for RAMSAY.

Ogilvie (*Earl of Airlie*, Innerquharity, &c.). See OGILVY.

Ogilvie (*Earl of Findlater*). Quarterly, 1st and 4th, ar. a lion pass. guard. gu. crowned or; 2nd and 3rd, ar. a cross engr. sa., for SINCLAIR. *Crest*—A lion ramp. gu. holding in his paws a plummet or. *Supporters*—Two lions ramp. or. *Motto*—Tout jour.

Ogilvie (GRANT-OGILVIE, *Earl of Seafield*). Quarterly, 1st and 4th grand quarters, quarterly, 1st and 4th, ar. a lion pass. guard. gu. imperially crowned ppr., for OGILVIE, 2nd and 3rd, ar. a cross engr. sa., for SINCLAIR; 2nd and 3rd grand quarters, gu. three antique crowns or, for GRANT. *Crests*—1st: A lion ramp. gu. holding betw. the paws a plumb-rule erect ppr., for OGILVIE; 2nd: A mountain in flames ppr., for GRANT. *Supporters*—Dexter, a lion guard. or; sinister, a naked man ppr. wreathed about the head and middle with laurel, and in his exterior hand a club. *Mottoes*—Over 1st crest: Tout jour; over 2nd crest: Craigellachie.

Ogilvie (Miltoun, co Banff, 1779). Quarterly 1st and 4th, ar. a lion pass. guard. gu. crowned or; 2nd, per fess or and az. a lymphad of the first, the masts, sails, and tacklings ppr. in the dexter chief point a dexter hand couped in fess, holding a dagger in pale az. in the sinister chief a cross pattée fitchée of the last, for McPHERSON, of Pettyown; 3rd, ar. a cross engr. sa., for SINCLAIR. *Crest*—A lion ramp. ppr. in his dexter paw a rose gu. stalked and leaved ppr. *Supporters*—Dexter, a lion ramp. or; sinister, a Highlander, a broadsword by his side, a pair of pistols in his belt, and a target on his sinister arm all ppr. *Motto*—Fortiter et suaviter.

Ogilvie (Auchiries, co. Aberdeen). Quarterly, as *Earl of Findlater*, within a bordure az. *Crest*—As *Earl of Findlater*. *Motto*—Tout jour fidèle.

Ogilvie (Glasshaugh, co. Banff). Ar. a lion pass. guard. gu. crowned or, standing on a mound az.

Ogilvie (Boyne, co. Banff, bart.). Quarterly, 1st and 4th, ar. a lion pass. guard. gu.; 2nd and 3rd, or, three crescents gu., for EDMONDSTONE; over all, dividing the quarters, a cross engr. sa., for SINCLAIR. *Crest*—A dexter hand holding a sword ppr. *Motto*—Pro patria.

Ogilvie (Raggell, co. Banff). As Boyne, within a bordure engr. az. *Crest*—A sword in bend ppr. *Motto*—Pugna pro patria.

Ogilvie (Jamaica, 1772). Quarterly, 1st and 4th, ar. a lion pass. guard. gu. betw. two escallops in chief and a spur-rowel in base az. a bordure indented of the second; 2nd and 3rd, ar. three crescents gu. *Crest*—A hand holding a plummet ppr. *Motto*—Tout jour.

Ogilvie (*Lord Banff*). Quarterly, 1st and 4th, ar. a lion pass. guard. gu. imperially crowned or; 2nd and 3rd, az. three papingoes vert, beaked and membered gu. *Crest*—A lion's head erased gu. *Supporters*—Dexter, a man in armour with a target ppr.; sinister, a lion ramp. gu. *Motto*—Fideliter.

Ogilvie (Carnousie, co. Banff, bart., 1626). Quarterly, as the last, with a crescent in the centre for diff.

Ogilvie (Birnes, co. Aberdeen). Quarterly, as *Lord Banff*, with, en surtout, or, a lion ramp. gu. debruised with a ribbon sa., for ABERNETHY.

Ogilvie (Hartwoodmyres, co. Selkirk, 1778). Ar. on a pale sa. a cross crosslet fitchée or, surmounted of a lion ramp. guard. gu. imperially crowned ppr. *Crest*—A talbot's head and neck ar. *Motto*—Ad funem spera.

Ogilvie (Edinburgh, 1672). Ar. a lion pass. guard. gu. imperially crowned or, betw. three primroses of the second. *Crest*—A lady's hand with a bracelet round the wrist ppr. *Motto*—Pro saluta.

Ogilvie (Provost of Banff, 1672). Ar. a lion pass. guard. betw. two crescents in chief and a cinquefoil in base gu. *Crest*—A dexter hand holding a branch of palm ppr. *Motto*—Secundat vera fides.

Ogilvie (*Earl of Airlie*). Ar. a lion pass. guard. gu. crowned with an imperial crown and collared with an open one or. *Supporters*—Two bulls sa. unguled and horned vert, with a garland of flowers about their necks. *Crest*—A lady from the waist upwards ppr. holding a portcullis gu. *Motto*—A fin.

Ogilvy (Cove, co. Dumfries). Quarterly, 1st and 4th, ar. a lion pass. guard. gu. imperially crowned ppr. within a bordure invecked of the second; 2nd and 3rd, quarterly, as SETON, of Pitmedden (*q. v.*), with a crescent az. in the centre of the quarters. *Crest*—A demi lion ramp. az. holding in his dexter paw a garb or. *Motto*--Quæ moderata firma.

Ogilvy (Pitmouies, co. Forfar). Ar. a lion pass. guard. gu. imperially crowned or, within a bordure engr. of the second. *Crest*—A lion guard. gu. standing on a garb lying fessways or. *Motto*—Quæ moderata firma.

Ogilvy (New Grange, 1672). As the last, but the bordure indented. *Crest*—A demi lion ramp. az. grasping in his dexter paw a garb ppr. *Motto*—Marte et industria.

Ogilvy (Cluny, co. Perth). As Pitmouies. *Crest*—A bull issuant collared with a garland of roses ppr. *Motto*—Industria.

Ogilvy (Logie, descended of Balfour, co. Forfar, 1672). Ar. a lion pass. guard. gu. imperially crowned or, within a bordure of the second charged with four crescents of the first. *Crest*—A demi lion ramp. holding betw. the forepaws a sword in pale ppr. *Motto*—Ex armis honos.

Ogilvy (Innerquharity, co. Forfar, bart.. 1626). Quarterly, 1st and 4th, ar. a lion pass. guard. gu. gorged with an open crown and crowned with a close imperial one or, for OGILVY; 2nd and 3rd, ar. an eagle displ. sa. beaked and membered gu., for RAMSAY, of Auchterhouse. *Crest*—A demi lion ramp. gu. armed az. *Mottoes*—Over the crest: Forward; under the shield: Terrena pericula sperno.

Ogilvy (Balbegno, co. Forfar). Quarterly, as the last, within a bordure az. *Crest*—A sunflower ppr. *Motto*—Qua duxeris adsum.

751

Ogilvy (Ruthven, co. Forfar; heiress m. 1811, PETER, second son of JAMES WEDDERBURN, of Inveresk). Ar. a lion pass. guard. gu. collared and imperially crowned or, betw. two chess-rooks in chief sa. and a flaming cup in base all within a border az. *Crest*—A lion ramp. guard. ppr. *Motto*—Nil desperandum.

Ogilvy (Barras, co. Kincardine, bart.). Ar. a lion pass. guard. gu. holding in the dexter paw a sword ppr. defending a thistle ensigned with a crown or, in the dexter chief point. *Crest*—A demi man in armour holding forth his dexter hand ppr. *Motto*—Præclarum regi et regno servitium.

Oglander (Nunwell, Isle of Wight, also of Parnham, co. Dorset, bart., created 1665, extinct 1874). Az. a stork betw. three crosses crosslet fitchée or. *Crest*—A bear's head couped or, the mouth embrued gu. *Motto*—Servare munia vitæ.

Oglander. Same *Arms*. *Crest*—A boar's head couped lying fesseways.

Ogle (Ogle Castle, co. Northumberland; descended from the marriage of Sir ROBERT OGLE, son of ROBERT OGLE, of Ogle, living *temp*. Edward III., with HELEN, dau. and heiress of Sir ROBERT BERTRAM, Knt., feudal baron of Bothall). Ar. a fess betw. three crescents gu. quartering az. an orle az., for BERTRAM. *Crest*—An antelope's head erased ar. tufted, maned, and horned or. *Another Crest*, for BERTRAM—A bull's head or, armed az. ducally gorged gu.

Ogle (*Baron Ogle*, in abeyance since 1691; Sir ROBERT OGLE, Knt., of Ogle Castle, Sheriff co. Northumberland, 16 Henry VI., 1437, was summoned to Parliament 1461. CUTHBERT, sixth *Baron Ogle*, d. 1560, leaving: JOAN; m. EDWARD, eighth *Earl of Shrewsbury*, d. s. p. 1627; and KATHERINE, m. Sir CHARLES CAVENDISH, Knt., of Welbeck, she s. as *Baroness Ogle* 1627; her grandson, HENRY CAVENDISH, *Baron Ogle* and second *Duke of Newcastle*, d. s. p., when the title fell into abeyance). Ar. a fess betw. three crescents gu.

Ogle (Cawsey Park, co. Northumberland; descended from Sir WILLIAM OGLE, of Cockle Park, second son of RALPH, third *Lord Ogle*). Same *Arms*, &c., as OGLE, of Ogle Castle.

Ogle (Kirkley Hall, co. Northumberland; descended from JOHN OGLE, third son of RALPH, third *Lord Ogle*, who d. in 1512). Same *Arms*, &c. *Motto*—Prenez en gré.

Ogle (Worthy, co. Hants, bart.). Ar. a fess betw. three crescents gu. a mullet for diff. *Crest*—An heraldic antelope's head erased ar. tufted, maned, and horned gu. *Motto*—Prenez en gré.

Ogle (Eglingham, co. Northumberland; descended from MARK OGLE, of Eglingham, who had a grant of arms in 1535). Quarterly, 1st and 4th, ar. a fess betw. three crescents gu.; 2nd and 3rd, or, an escutcheon az. on a chief of the last six annulets or. *Crest*—An arm armed in mail, issuing from a circle of gold, holding in the hand a sword broken in the middle, the edge bloody, hilted and pommelled or; granted to MARK OGLE, of Eglingham, Esq., for "services done in Scotland against the King our sovereign lord's enemies, there manly and valiantly using himself, for the which good service, Norroy King of Arms, seeing such qualities of vertue, did grant the said arms."

Ogle (Pinchbeck, co. Lincoln; seal of THOMAS OGLE, 1568). Ar. a fess betw. three crescents gu. issuant from each a fleur-de-lis of the second. *Crest*—A bull's head erased or, armed gu. gorged with a chaplet vert.

Ogle (Whiston, co. Lancaster, 1664). Ar. a fess betw. three crescents gu. *Crest*—A bull's head erased sa. horned or.

Ogle (cos. Northampton and Northumberland). Ar. a fess betw. three crescents gu. *Crest*—Out of a ducal coronet a bull's head ppr.

Ogle (Birchgrove, co. Wexford; descended from SAMUEL OGLE, a Commissioner in Ireland, temp. Charles II., son of LUKE OGLE, of Berwick-on-Tweed; Right Hon. GEORGE OGLE, M.P., co. Wexford, his grandson, by his second wife, URSULA, Dowager Lady Altham, d. s. p. 1815, when his cousin, RICHARD DONOVAN, Esq., of Ballymore, became his heir-at-law; he was son of EDWARD DONOVAN, Esq., of Ballymore, by MARY BROUGHTON, his wife, dau. of Captain JOHN BROUGHTON, of Maidstone, co. Kent, by MARY OGLE, his wife, only dau. of the above SAMUEL OGLE, by his first wife, ELIZABETH DAWSON). Ar. a fess betw. three crescents gu.

Ogle. Ar. on a fess betw. three crescents gu. a lion pass. or. *Crest*—A demi lion or, holding in the dexter paw a truncheon gu.; another, Ar. three greyhounds courant sa.; another, Erm. a fesse betw. three crescents gu.

Ogle (Oglethorpe, co. York). Ar. a chev. embattled betw. three boars' heads sa.

Oglethorpe (Rawdon, co. York). Same *Arms*.

Oglethorpe (Thorpe Arch, co. York). Same *Arms*.

Oglethorpe (Brandesley, co. York, 1666). Same *Arms*.

Oglethorpe (Kynnalton, co. Nottingham. Visit. Notts.). Ar. on a fess dancettée betw. three boars' heads sa. a mascle or. *Crest*—A boar's head ar. couped and vulned gu. pierced with a broken spear, the staff or, point ar. and charged on the neck with a mascle sa.

Oglethorpe (Newington, co. Oxford; descended from JOHN OGLETHORPE, Esq., co. York, temp. Edward IV. Visit. Oxon, 1566). Ar. a chev. vairé or and vert betw. three boars' heads sa. couped gu. a label of as many points az. *Crest*—A boar's head couped gu. in the mouth an acorn branch vert, fructed or.

Oglethorpe. Ar. five fusils in fess sa. in chief three boars' heads couped of the last.

Oglethorpe (Sir ROBERT OGLETHORPE, Baron of the Exchequer in Ireland, was knighted in the Presence-chamber, Dublin Castle, 6 Jan. 1608, by Sir Arthur Chichester, Lord Deputy of Ireland). Quarterly, 1st, ar. a fess dancettée betw. three boars' heads couped sa. armed, langued, and couped gu.; 2nd, ar. a fess betw. three mullets pierced sa.; 3rd, ar. a lion ramp. gu. armed and langued az. over all a fess sa.; 4th, ar. a chev. betw. three crosses crosslet fitchée sa. over all a crescent az. for diff. *Crest*—A lion ramp. gu. armed and langued az. supporting a cross crosslet fitchée ar.

Ognal. Per saltire or and gu. two eagles displ. in pale of the first.

Ognell (Ognell Hall, co. Lancaster, and Baddesley Clinton, co. Warwick). Per saltire or and gu. two eagles in pale of the first. *Crest*—A lion's head erased or, guttée sa.

Ognies (France). Vert a fess erm.

O'Gorman (a Sept derived from CATHAIR MOR, King of Leinster, who inhabited the territory of Hy Bairche, in the Queen's co. and co. Carlow, from which they were driven after the invasion of 1172, and settled under the O'Briens in the Barony of Ibrickan, in Thomond; they derived their surname from GORMAIN, Chief of the Sept). Az. a lion pass. betw. three swords erect ar. *Crest*—An arm embowed in armour, grasping in the hand a sword, blade wavy, all ppr. *Mottoes*—Tosach catha agus deineadh air; and, Primi et ultimi in bello.

O'Gorman (Cahir-Morrughu, co. Clare; allowed by Mac Culloch, Ulster, 1763, to THOMAS O'GORMAN, Esq., fourth in descent from MAHON O'GORMAN, of Cahir-Morrughu, descended from COIEBHA MOR O'GORMAN, Chief of Clahanes and Monemore, co. Clare). Same *Arms*, *Crest*, and *Mottoes*.

O'Gorman (London; allowed by Mac Culloch, Ulster, 1763, to THOMAS O'GORMAN, of that place, fourth in descent from DENIS O'GORMAN, brother of CAHIR O'GORMAN, of Cahir-Morrughu). Same *Arms*, *Crest*, and *Mottoes*.

O'Gorman (confirmed to TIMOTHY ELLIS O'GORMAN, Esq., Chef d'Escadron aux Lanciers du Prince de Schwarzenberg; and his brothers, REGINALD O'GORMAN, Esq., Chef d'Escadron aux Dragons de Ficquelmont, and FERDINAND O'GORMAN, Esq., resident at Nancy). Gu. a lion pass. or, betw. three swords erect ar. pommelled and hilted of the second.

O'Gormley (a Sept deriving their name from GAIRM LADHAIGHS, a Chieftain who ruled over a territory in the co. Donegal, identical with the present Barony of Raphoe, from which they were driven by the O'Donells, when they settled on the east side of the River Foyle, and retained a considerable estate there until the plantation of Ulster, 1609). Or, three martlets gu. *Crest*—A martlet az.

O'Gowan, or Mac-an-Gabhan. See SMITH.

O'Grady (*The O'Grady*, Kilballyowen, co. Limerick, formerly Chiefs of Cinel-Dunghaile, a district comprising the present parishes of Tomgraney, co. Clare, and Iniscaltra and Clonrush, co. Galway; the Four Masters record, under A.D. 1184, that CENFAOLADH O'GRADA, of Tuaim Grene, died; DONALD O'GRADY, The O'Grady, fell in battle A.D. 1309, leaving a son, HUGH O'GRADY, The O'Grady, who obtained the lands of Kilballyowen that year in marriage with the dau. and heiress of O'KERWICK, Chief of Aniah Cliah, which has continued the residence of the chieftain ever since; THOMAS DE COURCY O'GRADY, The O'Grady s. his father as Chieftain 1873). Per pale gu. and sa. three lions pass. per pale ar. and or. *Crest*—A horse's head erased ar. *Motto*—Vulneratus non victus.

O'Grady (*Viscount Guillamore;* Right Hon. STANDISH O'GRADY, Lord Chief Baron of the Exchequer in Ireland, great-grandson of JOHN O'GRADY, The O'Grady, temp. William III. and Queen Anne, through his second son, was so created 1831). Per pale gu. and sa. three lions pass. guard. per pale ar. and or, the centre lion charged on the side with a portcullis az. *Crest*—A horse's head erased ar. charged with a portcullis az. *Supporters*—Two lions guard. per

fesse ar. and or, each charged on the shoulder with a portcullis az. *Motto*—Vulneratus non victus.

O'Grady (The Grange). See CROKER.

Ogston (that Ilk, co. Aberdeen). Ar. three mascles sa. on a chief of the second two lions pass. (another, ramp.) of the field.

Ogston (Fettercairn, co. Kincardine; the heiress *m.* 1479, DOUGLAS, of Tilquhilly). Ar. three mascles sa. on a chief of the second as many lions pass. guard. of the first.

Ogston (Ardoe, co. Aberdeen, 1876). Ar. three mascles sa. on a chief of the second two lions pass. of the field. *Crest*—A lion pass. ar. *Motto*—Vi et anime.

Ogston (Norwood, co. Aberdeen, 1876). As the last with a crescent ar. in middle chief for diff. Same *Crest* and *Motto*.

Ogston (Dr. Francis, Aberdeen, 1876). As OGSTON of Ardoe, within a bordure gu. Same *Crest* and *Motto*.

Ogye. Ar. on a chief az. three crosses formée fitchée of the field.

O'Hagan (Chiefs of Tullahogue, in the Barony of Dungannon, co. Tyrone, and Brehons to O'NEILL, Prince of Tyrone. The clan of O'HAGAN (O'HAEDHAGAIN) had their seat in ancient times at Tullahogue, in the county of Tyrone, and in this fortress, according to Dr. O'Donovan, in his "Tribes and Customs of Hy Fiachrach," the Kings of Ulster were solemnly inaugurated into the style and authority of O'NEILL, by O'HAGAN, Chieftain of Tullahogue, in whom vested the hereditary right to perform the ceremony). Quarterly, ar and az. in 1st quarter a shoe ppr. on a canton per chev. gu. and erm. three covered cups or; in 2nd quarter a flag of the first charged with a dexter hand of the fourth; in 3rd quarter a lion ramp. of the sixth; and in 4th quarter a fish naiant ppr. *Crest*—A cubit arm vested gu. cuffed erm. the hand holding a dagger erect both also ppr. *Motto*—Vincere aut mori.

O'Hagan (*Baron O'Hagan*, of Tullahogue; Right Hon. THOMAS O'HAGAN, Lord Chancellor of Ireland, 1868-74, was so created 1870). Quarterly, ar and az. in the 1st quarter a shoe ppr. and on a canton per chev. gu. and erm. three covered cups or; in the 2nd quarter a flag of the first charged with a dexter hand of the fourth; in the 3rd quarter a lion ramp. of the sixth, and in the 4th quarter a fish naiant ppr. *Crest*—On a Roman fasces lying fessewise ppr. a cubit arm vested gu. cuffed erm. the hand holding a dagger erect both ppr. *Supporters*—Two lions or, collared sa. each holding a banner ar. charged with a dexter hand gu. *Motto*—Buadh no bas (Victory or death).

O'Halloran (Chiefs of Clan Fergaill, a large territory near Lough Corrib, co. Galway). Gu. a horse pass. ar. saddled and bridled ppr. on a chief of the second three mullets az. *Crest*—A lizard or. *Motto*—Clan-Fergail a-bu.

O'Halloran. Az. a boat with mast and sail spread or, in dexter chief an estoile of the last, on a chief ar. a stag in full course gu. pursued and seized in the shoulder by a greyhound sa. *Crest*—A sword erect distilling drops of blood all ppr.

O'Halloran (granted by Betham, Ulster, to Sir JOSEPH O'HALLORAN, G.C.B., a distinguished Indian military officer). Quarterly, 1st and 4th, az. a castle of two towers with a curtain wall and portal approached by three steps ar. standing on a mound vert, on which is inscribed the word "HURREHURPORE," gold, in chief a sword and an Indian sabre in saltire ppr. pommels and hilts or. surmounted by an Eastern crown of the last, for O'HALLORAN; 2nd and 3rd, gu. a horse pass. ar. on grass ppr. caparisoned az. bridled and saddled or, on a chief of the second three mullets pierced of the third, for O'HALLORAN (ancient), over all a cross of pearls ppr. *Crests*—1st, for augmentation: Out of an Eastern crown or, an arm in armour ppr. garnished gold, the hand in a gauntlet also ppr. grasping a flagstaff, therefrom flowing a standard az. charged with a monkey statant also or, motto over, PURSWARRIE; 2nd, O'HALLORAN (ancient): A lizard pass. or, motto over, Clan-Fergail a-boo. *Motto*—Lothim agus marbhaim (I wound and I kill).

O'Haly. Per fess or and vert in chief an estoile az. *Crest*—An estoile or.

O'Hamlin. Vert a horse pass. erm.

O'Hanlon (a Sept of the race of COLLA DA CHRIOCH, descended and deriving their surname from HANLUAN, Chief of Hy-Reith-Thire, now the Barony of Orior, co. Armagh). Vert on a mount in base ppr. a boar pass. erm. *Crest*—A lizard displ. vert. *Another Coat*—Ar. on a mount vert a boar pass. ppr. armed or.

O'Hanly (a Sept who possessed Cinel-Dobhtha, now Doohy-Hanly, a territory extending along the River Shannon, in co. Roscommon). Vert a boar pass. ar. armed, hoofed, and bristled or, betw. two arrows barways of the second, headed of the third, that in chief pointing to the dexter, and that in base to the sinister. *Crest*—Three arrows sa. flighted ar. pointed or, one in pale, the other two barways, the upper one pointing to the dexter, the lower to the sinister. *Motto*—Saigeadoir collach a-buadh (The valiant archer for ever).

O'Hanraghan (a Sept formerly of note in co. Tipperary, deriving their surname from ANRACHANA, Chief of the Sept). Gu. a lizard pass. in fess or, in chief a trefoil slipped betw. two holly leaves ar. in base a garb of the second. *Crest*—An arm erect, couped below the elbow, vested vert, cuffed ar. holding in the hand ppr. a holly leaf vert. *Motto* —An uachtar.

O'Hanratty (co. Monaghan; a Sept formerly O'HENRAGHTY or O'H INNREACHTAIGH, descended from an Irish Chieftain, IONEACHTAGH, a descendant of COLLA DA CHRIOCH, of the same race as McGUIRE). Az. a griffin pass. wings elevated or. *Crest*—On a helmet in profile, visor closed, a dolphin naiant all ppr.

O'Hara (a Sept of the Clanna Ceirs, descended from CIAN, son of OLIOLL OLLUM, King of Munster; they derive their surname from H'EAGHRA, Chief of Luighne, now the Barony of Leyney, co. Sligo). Vert on a pale radiant or, a lion ramp. sa.

O'Hara (Nymphsfield, co. Sligo, formerly of Coolany, in same co.; allowed by Fortescue, Ulster, 1794, to CHARLES O'HARA, Esq., of Nymphsfield, M.P. for co. Sligo, and one of the governors of the co., descended from CORMAC O'HARA, Esq., of Coolany, *d.* 1612). Same *Arms*. *Crest*—A demi lion ramp. erm. holding betw. the paws a chaplet of oak leaves ppr. *Motto*—Virtute et claritate.

O'Hara (Annaghmore and Cooper's Hill, co. Sligo; exemplified to CHARLES WILLIAM COOPER, Esq., of Cooper's Hill, co. Sligo, M.P., on his assuming, by royal licence, 1860, the surname of O'HARA in lieu of COOPER). Quarterly, 1st and 4th, vert on a pale radiant or, a lion ramp. sa., for O'HARA; 2nd and 3rd, gu. on a bend betw. six lions ramp. or, a crescent sa., for COOPER. *Crests*—1st: A demi lion ramp. erm. holding betw. the paws a chaplet of oak leaves ppr., for O'HARA; 2nd: A man's bust in profile couped at the shoulders ppr. on the head an Irish crown or, and charged on the neck with a crescent sa. over the crest on an escroll, "Vincit amor patriæ," for COOPER. *Motto*—Virtute et claritate.

O'Hara (Ballyhara, Cursailagh, and Mollane, co. Sligo; allowed by Fortescue, Ulster, 1795, to ANTHONY MARIA MAR-CELLUS O'HARA, Knt. of the Order of Malta, and St. Vladimir of Russia, a Lieut.-Col. in the service of the Empress of Russia, grandson of RODERICK O'HARA, Esq., of Ballyhara, who was great-grandson of CORMICK O'HARA, Esq., second son of CORMICK O'HARA, of Coolany, same co.). Same *Arms*. *Crest*—A demi lion ramp. ar. holding betw. the paws a chaplet of oak leaves ppr. *Motto*—Virtute et claritate.

O'Hara (*Baron Tyrawley and Kilmaine*, extinct 1774; Sir CHARLES O'HARA, a native of co. Mayo, was *Baron Tyrawley*, created 1706; his son and successor was created *Baron Kilmaine*, 1721, and *d. s. p.*, when both titles became extinct). Vert on a pale radiant or, a lion ramp. sa. *Crest* —A demi lion ramp. erm. holding betw. the paws a wreath of oak leaves ppr. *Supporters*—Dexter, a lion pean gorged with a collar radiant or; sinister, a lion erm. gorged with a garland of oak leaves and laurel fructed ppr. *Motto*—Try.

O'Hara (O'Hara Brook, co. Antrim). Vert on a pale radiant or, a lion ramp. sa. *Crest*—A demi lion ramp. pean, holding betw. his paws a chaplet of oak leaves vert, acorned ppr.

O'Hart (a Sept of the same race as O'CONOR, settled in co. Sligo; they derive their surname from AIRT, Chief of the Sept). Gu. a lion pass. guard. or, in base a human heart ar. *Crest* —A naked arm couped below the elbow and erect, grasping a sword flammant all ppr. *Motto*—Fortiter et fideliter.

O'Hartagan (Az. a lion ramp. or, holding in each forepaw a dagger az. pommels and hilts gold. *Crest*—A gauntlet erect, grasping a sword ppr. pommel and hilt or.

O'Haugherne (Carrigery, co. Clare; allowed by Hawkins, Ulster, 1775, to SIMON O'HAUGHERNE, son of WILLIAM O'HAUGHERNE, Esq., of Carrigery). Vert three herons close or. *Crest*—A pelican in her piety or, nest ppr. *Motto*—Per ardua surgo.

O'Haydon, or O'Heydon (Munster; "Ped. of McGUIRE," by Chas. Linegar, 1731). Or, a cross humettée betw. four fleurs-de-lis gu.

O'Hea (the Sept of O'H-AODHA, who inhabited Muscraighe Luachra, a territory extending on both sides of the River Blackwater, co. Cork, near its source). Ar. a dexter arm lying fessways, couped below the elbow, vested ar. turned up of the first, grasping in the hand a sword in pale entwined with a serpent descending all ppr.

O'Heffernan (a Sept of the same race as MACCOCULAN, located in cos. Limerick and Tipperary, deriving their name from IFEARNAN, one of the ancestors of the Sept). Per fess vert and gu. on a fess or, a lion pass. guard. az. in chief three crescents of the third.

O'Hegarty (originally of Magherabegin and Clonsillagh, co. Donegal; allowed by Hawkins, Ulster, 1744, to DOMINICK O'HEGARTY, Esq., second son of DANIEL O'HEGARTY, Capt. in the regiment of Col. Charles O'Neill, and brother of PATRICK O'HEGARTY, Knt. of St. Louis, Capt. in Dillon's regiment, PETER O'HEGARTY, Governor of the Isle of Bourbon, and FRANCIS O'HEGARTY, also a Capt. in Dillon's regiment). Ar. an oak tree eradicated ppr. on a chief gu. three birds ar. beaked and legged sa. *Crest*—An arm in armour embowed, the hand grasping a scymitar all ppr. *Motto*—Nec flectitur nec mutant.

O'Hennessy (a Sept whose tribe name was Clan Colgain, possessed of a district adjoining the hill of Croghan, Barony of Lower Philipstown, King's co., deriving their surname from AENGHUS, an ancestor who flourished in the 8th century). Vert a stag trippant az. betw. six arrows, two, two, and two, saltireways ar. *Crest*—Betw. the attires of a stag affixed to the scalp or, an arrow, point downwards gu. headed and flighted ar.

O'Hennessy, or Hennessy (Ballyhenness, co. Kerry, and Ballymacreedy, co. Cork). Gu. a boar pass. ppr. *Crest* —An arm in armour embowed holding a battle axe all ppr. *Motto*—Vi vivo et armis.

O'Heron (the Sept of O'HAUGHERNE, co. Kerry). Vert three herons ar. *Crest*—A pelican in her piety ppr. *Motto* —Per ardua surgo.

O'Heyne (a Sept who possessed the territory of Hy-Fiachrach-Aidhne, now the diocese of Kilmacduagh, co. Galway, of the race of GUAIRE AIDHNE, "The Hospitable" King of Connaught. The Four Masters record, under A.D. 1180, that MAURICE O'HEIDHIN, Lord of Hy Fiachrach Aidhne, was slain by the men of Munster). Per pale indented or and gu. two lions ramp. combatant counterchanged. *Crest*—A dexter arm armed, embowed, the hand grasping a sword all ppr.

O'Hickey (a Sept derived from IOCAIGH, Chieftain of his Sept, from whom the name O'H-IOCAIGH). Az. a lion pass. guard. or, on a chief erm. a bend sa. *Crest*—A hand in a gauntlet erect, holding a baton all ppr.

O'Higgin (a Sept located in Connaught, a branch of which settled in co. Westmeath; TEIGE O'HIGGIN, of Kilbeg, in that co., *d.* Jan. 1633, Fun. Ent. Ulster's Office; the name is derived from one of their chiefs, UIGIN, from whence the name O'HUIGIN). Ar. guttée de poix on a fess az. three towers of the first. *Crest*—A tower sa. issuant from the battlements a demi griffin, wings elevated ar. holding in the dexter claw a sword ppr.

O'Higgins (Ballynary, co. Sligo, and Spain; allowed by Fortescue, Ulster, 1788, to Don AMBROSE O'HIGGINS, Brigadier-General and Commandant of the King of Spain's Forces in Chili, great-grandson of SHANE DUFF O'HIGGINS, of Ballynary). Same *Arms* and *Crest*. *Motto*—Pro patria.

Ohmann (Dublin, from Hamburgh). Ar. in pale erect affrontée, Hercules girdled round the middle, his club held over the dexter shoulder, its apex showing above the other shoulder, the sinister hand resting on the groin ppr. *Crest*— A globe, thereon represented Dame Fortune standing on her dexter foot, the sinister thrown back, her arms both in bend sinister holding a scarf arched overhead.

O'Horan (a Sept settled in co. Galway). Vert three lions ramp. two and one, or. *Crest*—A demi lion ramp.

O'Houlaghan (a Sept formerly in the province of Munster, deriving their surname from H-ULLACHAIN, Chief of the Sept; they were driven into Connaught by Oliver Cromwell). Az. a tower or, supported by two lions ramp. ar. in base two crescents of the last, on a chief of the third three annulets gu.

O'Kane. See O'CAHAN.

Oke. Sa. on a fess betw. six acorns or, as many oak leaves bendways vert.

O'Kearin (a Sept residing in Thomond, co. Clare; TEIGE O'KEARIN was buried at Ennis in that co. 1634. He was sixth in descent from DERMOT O'KEARIN, who first settled there. THOMAS KEARIN or KEIRAN, Alderman of Dublin, had a grant of Ballymore, Ferns, &c., co. Wexford, and *d.* 1694, leaving his estate to his nephew, MORTOGH DONOVAN, eldest son of RICKARD DONOVAN, Esq., of Clonmore, in same co., by BRIDGET KEIRAN, sister of Alderman KEIRAN, whose descendant, RICHARD DONOVAN, Esq., of Ballymore. D.L., possesses the estate). Vert on a chev ar. three leopards' faces gu. *Crest*—A demi lion ramp. sa. holding in the dexter paw a sword erect ar. pommel and hilt or. *Motto*—Fidens et constans.

O'Kearney (a Sept descended from CATHARNAIGH, Chief of Teffia, in the ancient kingdom of Meath. The Four Masters record that GIOLLA-CHRIOST O'CEARNAIGH was appointed Abbot of Derry Columkille by the chiefs and clergy of the North of Ireland, A.D. 1198). Ar. three lions ramp. gu. on a chief az. betw. two pheons of the first a gauntleted hand fessways or, holding a dagger erect ppr. pommel and hilt gold. *Crest*—A gauntleted hand holding a dagger, as in the arms.

O'Kearney. See KEARNEY.

Okeborne. Ar. on a pale gu. a crescent or.

Okeborne, or Okeburne. Ar. a pale gu.

Okebourn. Ar. on a pale gu. a crescent or. *Crest*—An eagle rising from a globe winged all ppr.

Okeden (Ellingham, co. Hants. Visit. 1634). Sa. on a fess ar. betw. three acorns or, as many oak leaves vert. *Crest*—A buck's head cabossed betw. two oak branches in orle all ppr.

Okeden (Turnworth, co. Dorset). Same *Arms*. *Crest*—A bear's paw sa. grasping an oak branch ppr. fructed or.

O'Keefe (a Sept who originally possessed the southern half of ancient Feara Maighe, now Fermoy, co. Cork, from which they were driven after the English invasion, when they settled at Duhallow, same co., in the district known as Pobble O'Keefe. The name is derived from CAOIMH or KEEVE, Chief of the Sept., who lived A.D. 950). Vert a lion ramp. or, in chief two dexter hands couped at the wrist erect and apaumée of the last. *Crest*—A griffin pass. or, holding in the dexter claw a sword ppr.

O'Keefe (Ballymaguirk, co. Cork; descended from ART MAC DONEL O'KEEFE, chief of his name *temp.* Queen Elizabeth; DANIEL O'KEEFE, of Ballymaguirk, was killed at the battle of Aughrim on the side of James II., leaving three sons who settled in France; allowed by Fortescue, Ulster, 1797). Az. on a mount in base ppr. a lion ramp. or. *Crest*—A griffin pass. or, holding in the dexter claw a sword ppr. *Motto*—Forti et fideli nihil difficile.

O'Keegan. Gu. a lion ramp. ar. holding in the dexter paw a crescent of the last, in chief a ducal coronet or.

O'Keevan (a Sept of the same race as O'DOWD, who possessed Moylena, a district in co. Tyrone, afterwards called The Closach, deriving their surname from CAOMHAN, Chief of the Sept A.D. 876). Vert a saltire or, betw. in chief and in base a lizard pass. of the last, and in fess two daggers erect ar. pommels and hilts gold. *Crest*—A dagger erect ar. pommel and hilt or, the blade impaling a lizard vert.

Okeham (Upminster, co. Essex). Gu. a fess betw. three crescents ar. (another, or).

Okehampton (co. Devon). Chequy or and az. two bars ar.

Okeley (quartered by WOODHULL, of Mollington. Visit. Oxon, 1566). Sa. fretty or, a fess erm. on a chief ar. three leopards' faces gu.

Okeley. Or, on a fess betw. three lozenges gu. as many plates.

O'Keggan (co. Westmeath; confirmed by Roberts, Ulster, to CORNELIUS KEGGAN, Captain in Colonel William Warren's regiment). Gu. a lion ramp. ar. holding in the dexter paw a crescent of the last, in the middle chief a ducal coronet or.

Okeley. Or, on a fess betw. three lozenges gu. as many plates.

O'Kelly (a Sept of the race of COLLA DA CHRIOCH, Chiefs of Hy Maine, in the cos. of Galway and Roscommon, deriving their surname from CEALLAIGH, Chief of Hy Maine, A.D. 874). Az. a tower triple-towered supported by two lions ramp. ar. as many chains descending from the battlements betw. the lions' legs or. *Crest*—On a ducal coronet or, an enfield vert. N.B.—This animal is supposed to be composed as follows: the head of a fox, the chest of an elephant, the mane of a horse, the forelegs of an eagle, the body and hind legs of a greyhound, and the tail of a lion. *Motto*—Turris fortis mihi Deus.

O'Kelly (Aughrane, Castle Kelly, and Screen, co. Roscommon; descended from MANUS O'KELY, second son of BRYAN O'KELLY, Tanist of Hy Maine). Same *Arms*. *Crest*—An enfield statant vert. *Motto*—Turris fortis mihi Deus.

O'Kelly (Clonlyon, co. Galway; descended from O'KELLY, of Screen; allowed by Hawkins, Ulster, 1755, to Captain DENNIS O'KELLY, of Clonlyon; from the Clonlyon line descend the Counts O'Kelly, of Montauban, in France). Same *Arms*, *Crest*, and *Motto*.

O'Kelly (Aughrim, co. Galway; JAMES O'KELLY, Esq., of Aughrim, descended from FEIGH O'KELLY, Chief of his Sept at the invasion of 1172, was killed at the battle of Aughrim, 1691, leaving a son, Counsellor JOHN O'KELLY, of Keenagh, co. Roscommon; allowed by Fortescue, Ulster, 1803). Same *Arms*, *Crest*, and *Motto*.

O'Kelly (Gallagh, co. Galway; *Count O'Kelly*, of the Holy Roman Empire; allowed by Hawkins, Ulster, 1782, as the arms of CONNOR O'KELLY, *Count O'Kelly*, great-grandson of DENIS O'KELLY, Esq., of Gallagh). Same *Arms*, *Crest*, and *Motto*.

O'Kelly (Tycooly, co. Galway; allowed by Hawkins, Ulster, 1767, to DILLON JOHN O'KELLY, Captain in the service of the Empress Maria Theresa, son of FESTUS O'KELLY, Esq., of Tycooly, who was grandson of Col. THADDEUS O'KELLY, of Gallagh, in same co.). Same *Arms*, *Crest*, and *Motto*.

O'Kelly (allowed by Hawkins, Ulster, 1757, to Major-General WILLIAM O'KELLY, descended from co. Galway). Same *Arms*, *Crest*, and *Motto*.

O'Kelly (Killahan and Gort, co. Roscommon; Reg. Ulster's Office as the arms of MATTHEW O'KELLY, of those places, *temp.* Charles II.). Same *Arms*, *Crest*, and *Motto*.

O'Kelly (Barretstown, co. Kildare). Gu. on a mount or rock ppr., a tower supported by two lions ramp. ar., the lions ducally crowned or. *Crest*—An enfield. *Motto*—Turris fortis mihi Deus.

O'Kennedy (a Sept descended from DONNCHUAN, brother of BRIEN BOROIMHA, King of Thomond, who inhabited the territory of Gleann Omra, now known as Killo-Kennedy, co. Clare, and derived their name from CINNEIDIGH, the son of DONNCHUAN). Sa. three helmets in profile ppr. *Crest*—An arm embowed vested az. holding a scymitar all ppr.

O'Kennelly. Ar. a lion pass. sa. in the dexter chief point a cushion gu. thereon an imperial crown or. *Crest*—An arm in armour embowed, holding a sword, blade wavy all ppr.

Okenton. Gyronny of eight or and az. a canton erm.

Okeover (Okeover, co. Stafford; settled there for upwards of 700 years). Erm. on a chief gu. three bezants. *Crest*—Out of a ducal coronet or, a demi dragon erm.

Okeover (London; ROWLAND OKEOVER, merchant, third son of PHILIP OKEOVER. Visit. London, 1508). Erm. on a chief gu. three bezants, the centre one charged with a mullet sa. *Crest*—An oak tree vert, acorned or.

Okeover (arms in a window in Queen's College, Oxford. Visit. Oxon, 1566). Erm. on a chief gu. three bezants.

Okes. Ar. three hearts betw. two bendlets sa. *Crest*—A cockatrice sa.

Okested, or Okesteed. Gu. an oak branch slipped and acorned ppr.

Okestede (co. Kent). Ar. an oak slip gu. acorned or.

Oketon, or Okton. Gyronny of eight az. and or, a canton erm. *Crest*—A fleur-de-lis or.

Okewold, or Ockwold (Odington, co. Gloucester). Vair on a pale gu. three leopards' faces or. *Crest*—A leopard's head erased or, betw. two wings expanded vert.

O'Kinealy (the Sept of O'CINNFHAELADH, who inhabited the territory of Eoghancht-Gabhra, or Hy Conaill Gabhra, now the Barony of Conello, co. Limerick). Gu. a stag statant gu. *Crest*—An arm in armour embowed, holding a sword fessways the blade flammant all ppr.

O'Kyan. See O'CAHAN.

Oldagh (Fun. Ent. Ulster's Office, 1599). Az. fretty or.

Oldbeife (WILLIAM OLDBEIFE, *temp.* Henry V.; his dau. and heir, MARGARET, *m.* JOHN SKEFFINGTON, Esq., of Skeffington. Visit. Leicester, 1619). Az. a bend or, cotised ar. betw. six mullets of the second. *Crest*—A spread eagle sa.

Oldbury. Ar. a fess gu.

Oldcastle (co. Kent). Ar. a tower triple-towered sa. chained transverse, the port or.

Olde (ROBERT OLDE, Corporal of the Field, slain in the streets of Dublin by Edward Fitz-Henry; Fun. Ent. Ulster's Office, 1602). Sa. a cross betw. four martlets ar. a border of the last charged with eight hurts.

Oldehall. Gu. a lion ramp. erm.

Oldenby, or Olenby. Az. five cinquefoils in saltire ar.

Oldenham. See OLDHAM.

Olderbury (London). Sa. a fess ar. *Crest*—Out of an antique crown or, a demi lion ramp. az.

Olderdon (co. York). Sa. three water bougets sa.

Oldershaw (Kegworth, and Loughborough Old Parks, co. Leicester, settled at Kegworth prior to A.D. 1497). Az. three annulets or. *Crest*—A snake twisted betw. three arrows, one erect and two in saltire. *Motto*—Certanti dabitur.

Oldes. Gu. on a mount in base vert a lion sejant guard, or. *Crest*—A lion sejant guard. ppr. supporting an antique shield gu. charged with a fesse or.

Oldesworth (Poulton's Court, co. Gloucester; granted 1569). Gu. on a fess ar. three lions pass. guard. purp. *Crest*—A lion ramp. sejant gu. holding in the paws a scroll or.

Oldfield (Oldfield, co. Chester, where the family was seated above 400 years). Ar. on a bend gu. three crosses pattée fitchée of the field. *Crest*—Out of a ducal coronet or, a demi wivern, wings displ. ar. *Motto*—In cruce vincam.

Oldfield (Bradfield, co. Chester; confirmed **7 Feb. 1578**). Same *Arms*. *Crest*—A demi eagle displ. ar.

Oldfield (cos. Leicester and Oxford). Or, on a pile vert three garbs of the field. *Crest*—On a garb or, a dove ar. beaked and legged gu. holding in the beak an ear of wheat gold.

Oldfield (Spalding, co. Lincoln, bart., extinct *temp*. Queen Anne, created 1660; ELIZABETH, dau. and co-heir of Sir JOHN OLDFIELD, Bart., of Spalding, *m*. JOHN WINGFIELD, Esq., of Ti·kencote). Same *Arms* and *Crest*.

Oldfield (Durington, co. Lincoln). Vairé erm. and sa. *Crest*—A dove close ar. holding in the beak an ear of wheat or.

Oldfield. Vairé ar. and sa. (another, sa. and or).

Oldgate. Or, a bend betw. two bulls' heads couped sa. *Crest*—Out of a mural coronet or, a bull's head sa.

Oldgrave (co. Chester; Lord Mayor of London, 1467). Az. a fess engr. erm. betw. three owls or.

Oldgrove, or Oldgreen. Az. a fess engr. betw. three owls or.

Oldhall. Per pale az. (another, gu.) and purp. a lion ramp. erm.

Oldham (Oldham, co. Lancaster). Sa. a chev. or, betw. three owls ar. on a chief of the second as many roses gu. *Crest*—An owl ppr.

Oldham (Manchester, co. Lancaster, 1664). Same *Arms*. *Crest*—An owl ar. in front of a holly bush vert.

Oldham (Cainham Court, co. Salop ; JOSEPH OLDHAM, Esq., was High Sheriff of the co. 1789). Same *Arms*, &c.

Oldham (HUGH OLDHAM, Bishop of Exeter, 1505-19 ; arms in the Hall of Corpus Christi College, Oxford. Visit. Oxon, 1566). Sa. a chev. or, betw. three owls ar. on a chief of the second as many roses gu.

Oldham (Hatherleigh, co. Devon). Quarterly, 1st and 4th, sa. a pale ar. over all a chev. betw. three owls counterchanged, a chief erminois, thereon three roses gu. barbed and seeded ppr., for OLDHAM; 2nd and 3rd, per fess or and ar. three piles in point, each charged with a thistle stalked and leaved of the first, for LAING. *Crests*—1st, OLDHAM: On a mount vert in front of a tree an owl all ppr.; 2nd, LAING: A mount vert, thereon a cock, the dexter claw resting on a thistle ppr.

Oldhaugh (Oldhaugh, co. Chester; the heiress m. SMITH). Az. a fret or.

Oldington, or Olton. Quarterly, vert and gu. a lion ramp. ar.

Oldmixon (Oldmixon, co. Somerset). Sa. a battle axe in pale or, headed ar. *Crest*—A battle axe erect or, headed ar. in the middle of the handle a ribbon tied az.

Oldmixon. Az. a battle axe or, headed ar. the edge to the sinister.

Oldon (Exeter). Az. a chev. or, betw. three owls ar. on a chief of the second as many roses gu.

Oldon, or Olton. Or, on a mount vert a boar pass. sa.

Oldston. See OLLASTON.

Oldsworth (Pulton's Court, co. Gloucester: granted 15 June, 1569). Gu. on a fess betw. three billets ar. as many lions pass. guard. of the first. *Crest*—A lion sejant guard. gu. resting the forepaw on a carved shield or.

Oldsworth. Gu. on a fess or, three lions pass. guard. az.

Oldton, or Olton. Per pale gu. and az. a lion ramp. ar.

O'Learie. Ar. a lion pass. in base gu. in chief a ship of three masts sa. sails set ppr. from the stern the flag of St. George flotant. *Crest*—Out of a ducal coronet or, an arm in armour embowed, holding a sword ppr. pommel and hilt gold. *Motto*—Laidir isé lear Righ (Strong is the King of the Sea, or LEARIE is powerful). *Another Motto*—Fortis undis et armis.

O'Leary (Dromcar, co. Cork; Fun. Ent. Ulster's Office, 1637, DONOGH O'LEARY, gen.). Per fess ar. and vert, in chief a talbot pass. gu. and in base a boar pass. of the first. *Crest*—An arm erect couped below the elbow, vested az. the hand holding a sword impaling an evet or lizard all ppr.

O'Leaury. Ar. a falcon rising within an ivy branch in orle all ppr. *Crest*—An arm in armour couped below the elbow and erect, grasping a dagger all ppr.

Oliffe. Az. a wolf ramp. ar.

Oliph (London; JOHN OLIPH, Esq., of FOXGRAVE, co. Kent, Alderman of London; JOAN, his dau. and heiress, m. JOHN LEIGH, Esq., of Addington, co. Surrey). Per pale and chev. or and sa. three greyhounds' heads erased counterchanged, collared ar. *Crest*—A cockatrice's head erased quarterly ar. and sa. beaked, combed, and wattled or.

Oliphant (Lord *Oliphant*, Scotland). Gu. three crescents ar. *Crest*—A unicorn's head couped ar. maned and horned or. *Supporters*—Two elephants ppr. *Motto*—Tout pour-voir.

Oliphant (Gask, co. Perth; understood to have been re-presentative of the family on the death of the eleventh lord; the last of this branch *d*. 1847, and the present KINGTON-OLIPHANT, of Gask, is his heir of line). As *Lord Oliphant*, with a crescent or, in fess for diff.

Oliphant (Condie, co. Perth). Gu. three crescents ar. within a bordure counter-componée of the second and first. *Crest*—A falcon volant ppr. *Motto*—Altiora peto.

Oliphant (Bachiltoun, co. Perth). Gu. a chev. betw. three crescents ar. *Crest*—A crescent or. *Motto*—What was, may be.

Oliphant (Clashbainy, co. Perth). Same *Arms*, with the chev. crenellée. *Crest*—The sun in his glory ppr. *Motto*—Hinc illuminabimur.

Oliphant (Culquhir, co. Perth). Gu. a cinquefoil slipped betw. three crescents ar. *Crest* — An elephant's trunk ppr.

Oliphant (Kelly, co. Fife). Gu. three crescents within a bordure engr. ar.

Oliphant (Kinnedder, co. Fife). Gu. three crescents ar. within a bordure chequy of the second and first. *Motto*—Honesta peto.

Oliphant (Prinlis, co. Fife). Gu. a saltire engr. betw. three crescents, one in chief and two in the flanks ar. *Crest*—A hand pointing to the clouds ppr. *Motto*—I'll hope, and not rue.

Oliphant (Rossie, co. Perth). Gu. an estoile betw. three crescents ar. *Crest*—An eagle reguard. with wings expanded ppr. *Motto*—Altiora peto.

Oliphant (Carpow, co. Fife). Gu. three crescents within a bordure ar. *Crest*—A unicorn's head couped ar. *Motto*—Tout pourvoir.

Oliphant (FERGUSON-OLIPHANT, Broadfield House, co. Cumberland). Quarterly, 1st and 4th, gu. an elephant's head couped betw. three crescents ar, for OLIPHANT; 2nd and 3rd, per chev. dovetailed or and az. three boars' heads couped counterchanged, within a bordure ar. charged with six buckles, for FERGUSON. *Crests*—An elephant statant semée of crescents, holding in the trunk a fer de moline or, for OLIPHANT; a demi lion ramp. per chev. or and az. the dexter paw holding a thistle, and the sinister resting on a boar's head couped az., for FERGUSON.

Olive (Hayley). Ar. on a fess sa. three mullets or.

Oliver (Cornwall). Ar. on a mount vert an oak tree ppr. fructed or. *Crest*—An arm embowed in armour, holding in the hand a sprig of oak ppr. fructed or.

Oliver (Exeter, co. Devon). Erm. on a chief sa. three lions ramp. ar. *Crest*—A lion's head erased ermines, collared and ringed ar.

Oliver (Musbury, co. Devon, Bristol, and Wollescote Hall, Stourbridge, co. Worcester). Erm. on a chief sa. three lions ramp. ar. *Crest*—A demi lion ramp. gu. *Motto*—Dieu mon appui.

Oliver (Croomhill, co. Kent). Erm. on a chief gu. three lions ramp. or. *Crest*—A lion's head erased gu. *Motto*—Non sine.

Oliver (Lewes, co. Sussex). Ar. a hand and arm issuing from out of clouds on the sinister side fessways, and grasping a dexter hand couped at the wrist all ppr. *Crest*—A martlet ar. in the beak a sprig vert.

Oliver. Ar. a mullet betw. three crescents ar.

Oliver. Sa. a chev. erm. betw. three millrinds or, on a chief ar. a lion pass. gu.

Oliver (Kingsbridge, co. Devon). Az. a dexter hand and arm issuing from the sinister side fessways, grasping a sinister hand couped at the wrist ppr.

Olivier (Potterne Manor, co. Wilts, and Clifton, co. Bedford). Ar. on a mount in base an olive tree ppr. *Crest*—An esquire's helmet ppr. *Motto*—Sicut oliva virens lætor in æde Dei.

Oliver (Castle Oliver, co. Limerick; granted by Betham, Ulster, to RICHARD OLIVER, Esq., of that place, and the other descendants of his ancestor, ROBERT OLIVER, Esq., of Clonodfoy, same co.). Or, a chev. sa. betw. two pellets in chief, and in base a salmon naiant gu. *Crest*—A cubit arm erect vested gu. cuffed ar. the hand grasping an olive branch ppr.

Oliver (confirmed by Betham, Ulster, to THOMAS OLIVER, son of ROBERT OLIVER, of the North of Ireland, afterwards of U.S. America). Quarterly, 1st and 4th, ar. a hand and arm issuant from clouds on the sinister side fessways and grasping a dexter hand couped at the wrist all ppr., for OLIVER; 2nd and 3rd, erm. on a fess sa. three crescents ar., for CRAIG: in the centre fess point a trefoil for diff. *Crest*—A martlet ar. in the beak a sprig vert. *Motto*—Ad fuedera cresco.

Oliver (Cloughanadfoy, co. Limerick). Or, a chev. sa. betw.

two pellets in chief and a mullet naiant in base gu. Crest—A cubit arm vested gu. cuffed ar. hand ppr. holding a branch of olive also ppr.

Oliver (Cherrymount, co. Wicklow). Same Arms and Crest.

Oliver (Edinburgh, 1771, afterwards OLIVER-RUTHERFORD, of Edgerston, co. Roxburgh). Ar. two chev. gu. betw. three martlets sa. in chief and a heart crowned in base ppr. Crest—A dexter arm ppr. vested ar. turned up gu. grasping an olive branch fructed ppr. Motto—Ad fœdera cresco.

Oliver-Gascoigne. See GASCOIGNE.

Oliverson (RICHARD OLIVERSON, Esq., of Middle Temple, London). Per fess gu. and vair, in chief three lions ramp. ar. Crest—Three pheons az. thereon a lion's head erased or. Motto—Dum spiro spero.

Ollaston, or Oldston. Ar. two chevronels gu. on a canton of the last a lion ramp. or.

Olley (London, and co. Norfolk). Gu. on a fess embattled ar. two fleurs-de-lis sa.

Olliffe (Sir FRANCIS JOSEPH OLLIFFE, Knt., M.D., Physician to the British Embassy at Paris). Ar. a chev. engr. vert betw. three olive branches slipped and fructed ppr. Crest—On a millrind sa. a dove, wings elevated ar. in the beak a sprig of olive ppr. Motto—Est voluntas Dei.

Ollivier (Alderney). Erm. on a chief sa. three lions ramp. ar.

Ollington. Or, a lion ramp. az. a border engr. of the last.

Olmeridge. Chequy or and sa.

Olmebrige, or Ellinbridge. Chequy ar. and sa.

Olmius (London). Per fess az. and ar. a fess counter-embattled or, in chief a mullet of six points of the second, in base on a mount vert an elm tree ppr. Crest—A demi Moor habited in armour ppr. garnished or, betw. two laurel branches vert, wreathed round the temples ar. and gu. on the breast a fess counter-embattled, as in the arms.

Olmius (Baron Waltham, extinct 1787). Same Arms and Crest. Supporters—Dexter, a goat ar. horned and hoofed or; sinister, a hind az. ducally crowned ar. Motto—Meritez.

Olnden. Ar. a fess dancettée betw. three buglehorns stringed or.

Olnehor. Ar. a tree vert.

Olney (co. Bucks). Az. a fess betw. six crosses crosslet ar.

Olney (Lord Mayor of London, 1446). Gu. five bezants in saltire betw. two flaunches ar. each charged with a lion ramp. reguard. sa.

Olney, Oneley, or Onley (Catesby and Staverton, co. Northampton). Or, three piles in base gu. on a canton ar. a mullet sa. Crest—Out of a ducal coronet or, a phœnix ppr. in the beak a sprig vert.

Olney, or Oneley (Tachbrook, co. Warwick). Sa. a chev. betw. three pikes naiant ar.

Olney (co. Warwick). Ar. a fess embattled betw. six crosses crosslet fitchée gu.

Olney (ROBERT OLNEY, temp. Henry VI.; his dau. and heir m. Sir ROBERT THROCKMORTON, Knt., of Coughton, co. Warwick, who d. 24 Henry VII., A.D. 1408. Visit. Oxon, 1574). Ar. on a fess embattled betw. six crosses crosslet fitchée gu. three crescents of the field.

Olney. Ar. on a fess betw. three crosses crosslet fitchée sa. as many crescents of the field; another, Per pale sa. and ar. a (another, three) bull's head counterchanged; another, Barry of six ar. and az. a border engr. gu.; another, Ar. on a fess crenellée betw. six crosses crosslet fitchée gu. three plates.

O'Lonargan (Chiefs and owners of Cahir and the surrounding districts till dispossessed by the Butlers, of Ormonde, in the 14th century; the Four Masters record, under the year 1215, that DIONISIUS O'LONARGAN, Archbishop of Cashel, d. at Rome). Ar. on a chev. az. three estoiles or, in chief two arrows in saltire, points downwards ar. Crest—An arrow in pale, point downwards, distilling drops of blood all ppr.

O'Loughlin (a Sept in Connaught deriving their name from LOCHLAINN, their Chieftain, who ruled over Boirinn, now the Barony of Burren, co. Clare: they were of the race of O'CONOR, of Corcamroe). Gu. a man in complete armour facing the sinister, shooting an arrow from a bow all ppr. Crest—An anchor entwined with a cable ppr. Motto—Anchora salutis.

O'Loughlin (Newtown, descended from the above). Same Arms, Crest, and Motto.

O'Loghlen (bart.). Same Arms. Crest—On a ducal coronet or, an anchor erect entwined with a cable ppr. Motto—Anchora salutis.

Olton. Quarterly, gu. and ar. a lion ramp. or.

Olveston Priory (co. Leicester). Ar. three bars az. a border gu.

Olyet (London). Ar. on a chev. sa. betw. three suns gu. as many bucks' heads cabossed of the first.

Olyff. Ar. on a chev. gu. betw. three estoiles or, as many bucks' heads cabossed.

Olyffe (East Wickham, co. Kent). Per pale and per chev. or and sa. three greyhounds' heads crowned counterchanged.

O'Madden (Chief of Siol Anmchadha, a territory extending over the present Barony of Longford, co. Galway, and along the east side of the Shannon in the King's co.; the Sept derive their surname from MADAGHAN, Chief of Siol Annchadha, A.D. 1009; DONEL O'MADDEN, Chieftain, temp. Queen Elizabeth, was appointed Captain of his nation by letters patent, dated 20 June, 1567; he settled his property in the Barony of Longford on his sons, according to English law, by deed, dated 8 March, 1611; his grandson, JOHN O'MADDEN, was dispossessed by Oliver Cromwell, but got back a portion of his estates by patent, 6 Aug. 1677). Sa. a falcon volant seizing a mallard ar.

O'Mahony (a Sept possessing the territory of Hy Eathach, or Ivaugh, co. Cork, deriving their name from MATHGHAMHNA, Chief of the Sept, 1014). Quarterly, 1st and 4th, or, a lion ramp. az.; 2nd, per pale ar. and gu. a lion ramp. counterchanged; 3rd, ar. a chev. gu. betw. three snakes torqued ppr. Crest—Out of a viscount's coronet or, an arm in armour embowed, holding a sword ppr. pommel and hilt or, pierced through a fleur-de-lis az.

O'Mahony (allowed by Hawkins, Ulster, 1712, to JOHN MAHONY, Captain of a regiment in the service of the Emperor of Germany, son of JEREMIAH MAHONY, Colonel in the army of James II., descended from the O'MAHONYS, co. Cork). Same Arms and Crest.

O'Malley (a Sept which ruled over the territory of the two Umhalls, or Owles, now the Baronies of Murrisk and Burrishoole, co. Mayo, deriving their surname from MAILLE, Chief of the Sept; the O'MALLEYS are celebrated in Irish minstrelsy as expert seamen, and called the MANANNANS, or Sea Gods of the Western Ocean. GRACE O'MALLEY, dau. of OWEN O'MALLEY, Chief of the Sept, temp. Queen Elizabeth, was the famous GRAN UAILE, who visited England, and was presented to the Queen by the Lord Deputy). Or, a boar ramp. gu. Crest—A ship with three masts, sails set, all ppr.

O'Malley (Snugborough, co. Mayo; allowed by Hawkins, Ulster, 1775, to GEORGE O'MALLEY, Esq., of that place, descended from O'MALLEY, of Bellclare, same co.). Same Arms. Crest—A horse ramp. ar.

O'Malley (Rosehill, co. Mayo, bart.; descended from OWEN O'MALLEY, Esq., of Burrishoole, same co., whose ancestor, BRYAN McCORMAC O'MALLEY, held the Castle of Moriske and Manor of Strode, temp. Queen Elizabeth, which were granted to his father, CORMAC O'MALLEY, who d. abroad in Her Majesty's service, 1582). Ar. a boar ramp. gu. bristled or, betw. three long-bows charged with arrows and bent, pointing in centre, one in chief, and a skiff with oars sa. betw. the two in base. Crest—A horse in full speed ar. Motto—Terra marique potens.

O'Malley (Newcastle, co. Mayo; descended from PATRICK O'MALLEY, second son of OWEN O'MALLEY, Esq., of Burrishoole, the ancestor of O'MALLEY, Bart.). Same Arms, Crest, and Motto as O'MALLEY, Bart.

O'Mallun (Baron Glen-O'Mallun, extinct; Sir DERMOT O'MALLUN was created by patent, dated 5 Oct. 1622, Baron of Glen-O'Mallun, of co. Clare, for life, with remainder to ALBERT O'MALLUN and the heirs male of his body). Ar. a bend vert. Crest—Out of a basket ppr. a greyhound's head and neck affrontée ar. collared or, the collar adorned with spikes. Supporters—Two greyhounds ar. armed and langued gu. clothed vert fretty rimmed and studded or, each supporting betw. the forepaws a spear ppr. headed gold with a banner of the arms. Motto—Gaudet patentia duris.

O'Malone (a Sept deriving their name from MAOILEOIN, nephew of RODERICK O'CONOR, last Monarch of Ireland of the Milesian line; EDMOND O'MALONE, of Kilgarvan, co. Westmeath, was Chief of the Sept, temp. Henry VII. and Henry VIII.; EDMOND MALONE, Esq., of Ba__ehowna, same co., s. his uncle as Chieftain, 1758, now rep___ __ted by his descendant, JOHN MALONE, Esq., of Bacons___ ___, same co.). Ar. a lion ramp. or, betw. three mullets ar. Crest—A man in complete armour, in the dexter hand a spear resting on the ground all ppr. Motto—Fidelis ad urnam.

O'Mannis. Vert a griffin segreant, wings elevated or, in chief three crescents ar. Crest—A hand couped at the wrist erect ppr. holding a long cross gu.

O'Meagher (a Sept whose Chief ruled over Hy-Cairin, now

the Barony of Skerr, in co. Tipperary; descended from MEACHAR, one of their Chieftains, from whence O'MEAGHER. AZ. two lions ramp. combatant or, supporting a sword ar. pommel and hilt of the second, in base two crescents of the third. *Crest*—A falcon ar. belled or, lighting on a helmet ppr.

O'Meara (the Sept of O'MEARADHAIGH, whose Chief ruled over the territory of Hy-Fathaidh, now the Barony of Iffa and Offa, co. Tipperary). Gu. three lions pass. guard. in pale per pale or and ar. a border az. charged with eight escallops of the last. *Crest*—A pelican vulning herself ppr. *Motto*—Opima spolia.

O'Meara (Lishenuske, co. Tipperary; Fun. Ent. Ulster's Office, 1636, TEIGE O'MEARA, son and heir of WILLIAM O'MEARA, both of same place). Gu. three lions pass. guard. in pale per pale ar. and or, armed and langued az. a border of the last, semée of crescents of the third.

O'Meara (Dublin; arms confirmed and crest granted to JEREMIAH O'MEARA, 1775). Same *Arms*. *Crest*—Out of a ducal coronet or, a lion's head az.

O'Meighan (Ballaghmeighan, co. Leitrim; a Sept who possessed Beallach, now the parish of Ballymeehan, deriving their surname from MIADHACHAIN, Chief of the Sept. The *Four Masters* record that EDRU O'MIADHACHAIN, Bishop of Clonard, d. A.D. 1173. A curious relic, consisting of a metal box, which contained the gospel of St. Molaisc, of Devenish, a celebrated saint of the 6th century, is still in the possession of the family, the Sept having preserved it for more than 1200 years; CHRISTOPHER O'MEIGHAN, an officer in the army of James II., fell at the battle of the Boyne. Reg. Ulster's Office). Gu. on a chev. ar. three bucks' heads erased of the field, attired or, in base a demi lion ramp. of the second. *Crest*—A griffin's head erased, wings endorsed or.

O'Melaghlin (hereditary Kings of Meath, and frequently Monarch of Ireland. See BURKE's "Vicissitudes of Families"; deriving their surname from MAELSEACHLAINN, King of Meath, d. 1022). Per fess, the chief two coats, 1st, ar three dexter hands couped at the wrist gu.; 2nd, ar. a lion ramp. gu. armed and langued az., the base wavy az. and ar. a salmon naiant ppr. O'Ferrall's Linea Antiqua, gives for the bearings of O'MELAGHLIN, the same *Arms*, with the difference that the lion ramp. is placed in the first coat of this chief, the hands are omitted, and the second coat of the chief is, ar. a ship under full sail. See also McLAUGHLIN.

O'Melaghlin (Ballinderry, co. Westmeath; allowed by Hawkins, Ulster, 1712, to ART O'MELAGHLIN, Esq., of that place, descended from the ancient Sept of O'MAELSEACHLAINN). Same *Arms*. *Crest*—A swan, wings expanded ar. membered gu. *Motto*—Scuto amoris divini.

Omer. Az. on a fess betw. three crescents or, as many pellets. *Crest*—A dove holding in the beak an olive branch ppr.

Omfield (co. Lincoln). Ar. three lions pass. guard. gu.

Ommaney (borne by Rear-Admiral Sir JOHN ACWORTH OMMANEY, K.C.B., eldest son of Admiral CORNTHWAITE OMMANEY, and brother of Sir FRANCIS MOLINEUX OMMANEY, Knt.). Per pale ar. and sa. three chev. betw. as many cinquefoils counterchanged. *Crest*—A cubit arm erect per pale ar. and sa. cuffed of the first, the hand holding a battle axe in bend sinister ppr.

O'Moledy (a Sept descended from MAOL-AN-EDY, brother of FEARGHAIL, ancestor of O'FERRALL. Sir PATRICK MOLEDY, Knt., travelled in Germany when a young man, became tutor to the Archduke of Austria, and was afterwards Ambassador to England, *temp.* Charles II.; in his old age he returned to Ireland and purchased an estate there, which he, for want of issue, bequeathed to his nephews, Sir ANTHONY MOLEDY, Knt., of Robertstown; REDMOND MOLEDY, Esq., of Rathwire; and Major HUGH MOLEDY). Vert a lion ramp. double queued and crowned or, betw. three close helmets in profile ar.

O'Molloy (Ballyduff, King's co.; Fun. Ent. Ulster's Office, 1636, HUGH O'MOLLOY, eldest son of JOHN O'MOLLOY, of same place). Ar. a lion ramp. sa. armed and langued gu. betw. three trefoils slipped gu. a crescent for diff.

O'Molloy. See O'MULLOY.

O'Monaghan (Chiefs of Hy Briuin-na-Sinna, a district between Elphin and Jamestown, co. Roscommon; the Chief had his seat at Lisadorn in 1249, this became the lordship of the O'BEIRNES, when O'MONAGHAN became Chief of the three Tuathas in the same co. The Four Masters record that GIOLLA-NA-NOGE O'MANNACHAIN, Lord of the three Tuathas, d. 1287). Az. a chev. betw. three mullets ar. *Crest*—A knight in complete armour, resting the sinister hand on the hip, and holding in the dexter a tilting spear,

757

thereon a forked pennon ar. charged with an escutcheon of the arms.

O'Moran (a Sept in Leinster, deriving their name from MURCHADHAIN, their Chief, who ruled over Magh Aoife, or Mayiffy, a district in Offaly). Sa. three stars rayed or. *Crest*—A star rayed or. *Motto*—Lucent in tenebris.

O'Morchoe (a Sept of the tribe of MAC MURCHADHA, or MAC MOROGH, of Leinster, descended from MUCHADHA NA NGAOIDHEAL, or MOROGH, "The Irishman," brother of DERMOT MAC MOROGH, King of Leinster, who surrendered his sovereignty to Henry II., 1172; the Sept possessed the territory of "The Murrows," now comprising the Baronies of Ballagh-keen, North and South, co. Wexford, and their chief residences at Tubberlimnagh and Oulartleigh. MORTOGH O'MORCHOE, Chief of the Sept, had a charter, 1 Edward IV., 1461, to entitle him to use English law among his Sept. The subsequent chiefs retained their gallowglasses, or armed soldiers, down to the sixteenth century. CONAL O'MORCHOE, of Tubberlimnagh, *The O'Morchoe* (son of DONEL, son of ART, son of DONEL, son of ART, son of TEIGE, *The O'Morchoe*), d. Oct. 1634, leaving four sons: I. TEIGE, who forfeited his estate 1641; II. PHELIM, d. unm.; III. PIERS; IV. DANIEL. Fun. Ent. Ulster's Office). Ar. an apple tree eradicated fructed ppr. on a chief vert a lion pass. or. *Crest*—On a chapeau gu. turned up erm. a lion ramp. also gu. holding betw. the paws a garb or.

O'Morchoe, now Murphy (Oulartleigh, co. Wexford; represented by ARTHUR MAC MOROGH MURPHY, Esq., only son of the late ARTHUR MURPHY, Esq., of Oulartleigh, d. 1867; descended from ARTHUR MURPHY, alias O'MORCHOE, eldest son of DANIEL O'MORCHOE, Esq., of Outlartleigh, and great grandson of BRAIN McHUGH BALLAGH O'MORCHOE, who was granted Oulartleigh 1618). Same *Arms*. *Crest*—On a chapeau gu. turned up erm. a lion ramp. also gu. holding betw. the paws a garb or, motto over, Vincere vel mori. *Motto*—Fortis et hospitalis.

O'More (*The O'More*, Lord of Laoighis, or Leix, an extensive territory comprising the eastern and southern baronies of the present Queen's co.; the territory was so called from the tribe designation of the Sept, MAC LAOIGHIS, a name derived from their ancestor, LAOISEACH, son of CONAL CEARNACH, Chief of the Craebhruadh, or Red Branch of Ulster; MORDHA, the descendant of LAOISEACH, was Lord of Laoighis, and from him derived the surname O'MORE. RORY O'MORE, Lord of Leix, *temp.* Queen Elizabeth, waged war against Her Majesty, and was slain in rebellion, 1578. ANTHONY, or OWNY, O'MORE, his son, s. as Lord of Leix, but was slain in rebellion, 1601, when all the estates were forfeited and the Sept scattered). Vert a lion ramp. or, in chief three mullets of the last. *Crest*—A dexter hand lying fessways, couped at the wrist, holding a sword in pale, pierced through three gory heads all ppr. *Motto*—Conlan-a-bu.

O'More (Balyna, co. Kildare, now represented by MORE O'FERRALL; descended from O'MORE, Lord of Leix. JAMES O'MORE, Esq., of Balyna, d. 1778, leaving an only dau. and heiress, MARY, wife of RICHARD O'FERRALL, Esq.). Same *Arms*. *Crest*—Out of a ducal coronet or, a dexter hand erect appaumée ppr.

O'More (Cremorgan, Queen's co.; descended from O'MORE, Lord of Leix. MORTOGE OGE O'MORE, of Cremorgan, d. 1580, leaving a son and heir, LYSAGH O'MORE, of Cremorgan, who left a son, PATRICK O'MORE, his heir, in 1591). Same *Arms* and *Crest* as O'MORE, Lord of Leix. *Motto*—Semper fidelis et audax.

O'More (Ballynakill and Stradbally, Queen's co., and Lorraine; allowed by Hawkins, Ulster, 1774, to CHARLES O'MORE, Lord of Valmont, in Lorraine, son of MORTOGH O'MORE, Captain of Horse in the service of the Duke of Lorraine; descended from EDMOND O'MORE, younger son of O'MORE, Lord of Leix). Same *Arms* and *Crest*.

O'Moriartie (the Sept of O'MUIRCHEARTAIGH possessing the "Flock-abounding Plain," of Aos Aisde, on the River Mang, co. Kerry). Ar. an eagle displ. sa. *Crest*—An arm in armour embowed, holding a sword fessways entwined with a serpent all ppr.

O'Moriarty (the Sept of O'MORCHEARTAIGH). Ar. three lions pass. guard. gu.

O'Mullan (a Sept in Connaught, deriving their name from MULLAN, of the race of O'CONCANON, and MAC GERACHTY). Ar. a dexter hand couped at the wrist in fess gu. holding a dagger in pale ppr. betw. three crescents of the second. *Crest*—Out of a crescent gu. a dagger erect ppr.

O'Mullowney, or O'Moloney (a Sept whose Chief ruled over Cuiltenan, now the parish of Kiltonanlea, Barony of Tulla, co. Clare; descended, according to O'Halloran's History of Ireland, from the same race as O'QUIN, O'GRADY,

McENEIRY, &c., &c., of the line of CORMAC CAS, Monarch of Ireland; MOLONY, of Kiltanon, is the Chief of this Sept). Az. on the dexter side a quiver with three arrows, on the sinister a bow erect all or.

O'Mulloy (Standard Bearer to the Sovereign in Ireland, a Sept descended from FIACHADA, third son of NIALL, of the Nine Hostages, Monarch of Ireland, A.D. 371, deriving their name from MAOLMHUAIDH, Chief of the territory of Feara Ceall, in the King's co., who was slain 1019, and enjoying the hereditary office of Standard Bearer to the Sovereign. The Four Masters record that GIOLLA COLUIM O'MAOLMHUAIDH, Lord of Fercall, was slain 1177; CONAL O'MOLLOY, Chief of his Sept, surrendered his estates to the Crown, and had a re-grant of them, 32 Queen Elizabeth, A.D. 1590). Ar. a lion ramp. sa. betw. three trefoils slipped gu. *Crest*—In front of an oak tree growing out of a mount all ppr. a greyhound springing sa. collared or. *Motto*—Gearaigh agus dogh buadh (Cut and burn away). A record by Preston, Ulster, 1634, preserved in Ulster's Office, has the following entry: "This Coat-Armour belongeth to the MULLOYS, Standarts Bearers to the Crowne of England, in this Kingdome of Ireland," viz.: Ar. a brown horse in full speed ppr. bridled, saddled, and caparisoned gu. fringed or, thereon a knight in complete armour also ppr. on the left arm a shield, thereon the arms of O'MULLOY, and holding in the right hand a spear, thereon a scarlet pennon, forked, the part adjoining the staff ar. charged with the cross of St. George.

O'Mulloy (Ughterthiery, Lachan, and Hughstown. co, Roscommon; Captain ANTHONY O'MULLOY, commonly called "The Green Mulloy," eighth in descent from CULLEN O'MULLOY, younger son of HUGH OGE O'MULLOY, The O'Mulloy, Lord of Fercall, settled in co. Roscommon, temp. Queen Elizabeth, and d. 1603; his direct descendant is Rev. COOTE CHARLES MULLOY, of Hughstown). Ar. a lion ramp. sa. betw. three trefoils slipped gu. *Crest*—In front of an oak tree ppr. a greyhound courant sa. collared or. *Motto*—Malo mori quam fœdari.

O'Mulloy (Aghadonagh, King's co., formerly of Kilmanaghan, in same co.; descended from JOHN O'MULLOY, of Aghadonagh, d. 1634 (Fun. Ent. Ulster's Office) fourth in descent from COSNYAGH O'MULLOY, the second son of DONOUGH O'MULLOY, ancestor of O'MULLOY, of Ughterthiera). Same *Arms* and *Crest*.

O'Mulloy (Drynaunly, King's co.; Fun. Ent. Ulster's Office, of Rev. NEAL MULLOY, d. 1639, son of COSNYAGH O'MULLOY, of Drynaunly). Same *Arms*, the lion charged on the shoulder with a crescent of the field for diff.

O'Mulloy (Ballyduffe, King's co.; Fun. Ent. Ulster's Office, HUGH O'MULLOY, d. 1635, eldest son of JOHN O'MULLOY, both of that place). Same *Arms*, in chief a crescent of the second for diff.

O'Mulrian (Owney, co. Tipperary, now RYAN, a Sept claiming descent from CATHAOIR MOR, King of Leinster). Gu. three griffins' heads erased ar. *Crest*—A griffin segreant gu. holding in the sinister claw a dagger ppr.

O'Mulrony (a Sept inhabiting Crumhthan, now Craffon, a territory in co. Galway, comprising the present Barony of Killyan, deriving their surname from MAOILRUANAIDH, Chief of the Sept). Ar. a dexter hand couped at the wrist and erect gu. a border az. charged in the dexter chief with an open book ppr.

O'Mulvihill (Knockanira, and Kilglassy, co. Clare; a Sept descended from MAOILMHICHILL, Chief of Corcaseashnail, co. Roscommon. The Four Masters record that GIOLLA-NA-NAOMH, son of GIOLLA-COMAIN, son of MUIREADHACH BAN O'MAOLMHICHIL, was one of a party who slew O'CONOR, King of Connaught, A.D. 1189). Per fess ar. and gu. in chief two lions ramp. combatant az. supporting a dexter hand couped at the wrist of the second, and in base a salmon naiant ppr. in base an Irish harp or, stringed of the first, betw. two battle axes of the last. *Crest*—A dexter arm couped below the elbow and erect holding two battleaxes in saltire ppr.

O'Murphy (a Sept settled in Muskerry, co. Cork, descended from FEIDHLIME, younger son of ENNA CINSEALAGH, King of Leinster, they formerly possessed a territory in co. Carlow, known as Hy Felimy). Quarterly, ar. and gu. on a fess sa. betw. four lions ramp. counterchanged three garbs ar.

O'Murphy (The island of Teneriffe; allowed by Hawkins, Ulster, 1736, to Captain DENIS O'MURPHY, of that place, fifth in descent from DONEL EVALA O'MURPHY, by MARY, his wife, dau. of JAMES O'CONOR, of the House of O'CONOR, Sligo). Same *Arms*. *Crest*—A lion pass. gu. resting the dexter paw on a garb or.

O'Murphy (Dondown, co. Waterford, Armaloghan, co. Meath, and Nantes, in France; allowed by Hawkins, Ulster,

1765, to MICHAEL and PATRICK O'MURPHY, of the latter place, sons of JOHN O'MURPHY, who was descended from CHARLES O'MURPHY, of Dondown). Same *Arms*. *Crest*—A demi lion ramp. gu. holding betw. the paws a garb or. *Motto*—Fortis et hospitalis.

O'Murphy (Paris; allowed by Hawkins, Ulster, 1772, to MARY-LOUISA, and MARY BRIDGET O'MURPHY, as the coat of their father DANIEL O'MURPHY, of Paris, d. 1753, who was grandson of DENIS O'MURPHY, of Beard, co. Kerry). Same *Arms*, *Crest* and *Motto*.

O'Naghten (Chiefs of Maenmbagh, in Hy Maine, of the same race as O'MADDEN, deriving their surname from NEACHTAIN, Chief of the Sept). Quarterly, 1st and 4th, gu. three falcons close ppr.; 2nd and 3rd, vert three swords ar. pommels and hilts or, one in pale, point downwards, the others in saltire, points upwards. *Crest*—A falcon close ppr.

O'Naghten (Thomastown, co. Roscommon, and France; allowed by Fortescue, Ulster, 1738, to JOHN O'NAGHTEN, Captain in the Spanish service, grandson of Captain THOMAS O'NAGHTEN, of Thomastown, Governor of co. Roscommon, 1688). Same *Arms* and *Crest*. *Motto*—Sagax et audax.

Onbey (co. Northampton). Az. five cinquefoils in saltire, pierced az.

Onebye (Onebye, co. Leicester, granted 7 August, 1680, to JOHN ONEBYE, Esq.). Or, a chev. vert betw. three towers gu. *Crest*—A bear's head couped per pale ar. and gu.

Onedert. Quarterly, az. and gu. an escarbuncle of eight staves or.

O'Neill (Prince of Tyrone, Kings of Ulster, and several times Monarchs of Ireland, descended from NIALL GLANDUBH, Monarch of Ireland, slain by the Danes of Dublin, A.D. 946, from whom the surname is derived; DONEL O'NEILL, surnamed ARDMACHA, 46th Monarch of Ireland, of the race of Hy Neale, d. at Armagh, A.D. 987. His descendant, HUGH MACCAONEH O'NEILL, Prince of Tyrone, had two sons: I. NIAL ROE O'NEILL, ancestor to the subsequent Princes of Tyrone; II. HUGH DUBH O'NEILL, d. 1230, ancestor of O'NEILL, of Claneboy, O'NEILL, Earl d'Neill, &c., CON O'NEILL, Prince of Tyrone, direct descendant and representative of NIALL ROE O'NEILL, founded the Franciscan Monastery of Ballynasagart, co. Tyrone, 1489, and was murdered by his brother HENRY O'NEILL, 1493). Ar. a sinister hand couped at the wrist affrontée gu.

O'Neill (Earl of Tyrone, created 1542, attainted. CONN-BACCOGH O'NEILL, eldest son of CON O'NEILL, Prince of Tyrone, renounced the title of O'NEILL; had a re-grant of his lands by patent, dated 1 October, 34 Henry VIII., and was created same day Earl of Tyrone for life, with remainder to his illegitimate son, MATHEW O'NEILL, called "Feardoragh," although he had two legitimate sons, SHANE A DIAMUS O'NEILL and PHELIM CAOCH O'NEILL, both of whom left descendants. He d. 1559, when the earldom passed according to the limitation). Quarterly, 1st and 4th, ar. a sinister hand couped at the wrist gu.; 2nd and 3rd, the arms of Ulster, viz., Or, a cross gu. *Supporters*—Two lions gu. langued az. *Motto*—Lamb dearg Eirin.

O'Neill (The O'Neill, of Tyrone, descended from SHANE A DIAMUS O'NEILL, or JOHN, the proud O'NEILL, the eldest legitimate son of CON BACCAGH O'NEILL, first Earl of Tyrone, who waged war against Queen Elizabeth, and visited the queen at her Court to arrange terms of peace, when he astonished the citizens of London by marching through the streets of the city as chieftain at the head of his gallowglasses, or armed guards, with unshaven beards, flowing hair, and saffron-dyed mantles; he was slain 1567, by MAC DONELL, leaving four sons, I. JOHN; II. HENRY; III. CON; IV. ART. CON O'NEILL, the third son, was hanged 1590, by order of HUGH, Earl of Tyrone, the son of his father's illegitimate brother, Lord Dungannon, leaving a son, ART OGE O'NEILL, father of CON ROE O'NEILL, who had two sons: I. ART, who had a son, CON; and II. Colonel JOHN O'NEILL, who were the last known members of this senior line of O'NEILL). Ar. two lions ramp. combatant gu. armed and langued az. supporting a sinister hand couped at the wrist of the second.

O'Neill (Baron Dungannon, afterwards Earl of Tyrone, MATHEW, or FEARDERAGH O'NEILL, illegitimate son of CON BACCOGH O'NEILL, first Earl of Tyrone, was created Baron Dungannon by patent dated 1 October, 1542. He was slain by his father's legitimate son and heir, SHANE A DIAMUS O'NEILL, The O'Neill, 1558, when he was s. by his son HUGH O'NEILL, as Baron Dungannon, who became Earl of Tyrone 1559). Ar. two lions ramp. combatant gu. armed and langued az. supporting a sinister hand couped at the wrist of the second, over all a sinister bendlet sa.

O'Neill (The Fews, co. Armagh, descended from HUGH O'NEILL of the Fews, second son of OWEN O'NEILL. Prince of

Tyrone, who d. 1436, Sir TIRLOGH O'NEILL, Knt., of the Fews, was knighted by Sir George Cary, Lord Deputy of Ireland, 17 April, 1604, and d. 24 February, 1639, Fun. Ent. Ulster's Office; his great grandson CON O'NEILL, of the Fews, was transplanted to Connaught by Oliver Cromwell. Per fess wavy the chief ar. and the base representing waves of the sea, in chief a dexter hand couped at the wrist gu. in base a salmon naiant ppr. Crest—An arm embowed in armour, the hand grasping a sword all ppr.

O'Neill (Newcastle, Foxford, and Carrowry, co. Mayo, Cloon, co. Leitrim, and Spain; allowed by Fortescue, Ulster, 1803, to ARTHUR O'NEILL, Governor of Yeucatan, in South America, Lieut.-Gen. and Counsellor of the Supreme Council of War in Spain, fourth in descent from CON O'NEILL, of the Fews, who was transplanted into Connaught by Oliver Cromwell). Same Arms. Crest—A naked arm embowed, brandishing a sword all ppr. Motto—Hœc manus pro patriæ pugando vulnera passa.

O'Neill (Fassagh and Killebane, co. Armagh; descended from ART O'NEILL, second son of Sir TIRLOGH O'NEILL, Knt., of the Fews, d. 1639). Same Arms and Crest as O'NEILL, of the Fews.

O'Neill (Claneboy or Clan Aedh Buidhe; descended from HUGH DUBH O'NEILL, d. 1230, second son of HUGH MACCONEH O'NEILL, Prince of Tyrone, and brother of NIAL ROE O'NEILL, Prince of Tyrone, ancestor of O'NEILL, Earl of Tyrone, from HUGH BUIDHE O'NEILL, grandson of HUGH DUBH O'NEILL. This line were designated the Claneboy O'NEILLS. They had their chief seat at Edenduffcarrick, now Shanes Castle, co. Antrim. JOHN O'NEILL, Esq., of Shane's Castle, ninth in descent from HUGH BUIDHE O'NEILL, d. 1617, leaving four sons, viz., I. Sir HENRY O'NEILL, Knt., of Shane's Castle, whose only dau. and heiress ROSE O'NEILL, m. RANDALL, Marquess of Antrim, and d. 1707; II. ARTHUR O'NEILL, whose male line failed with his grandsons; III. PHELIM DUBH O'NEILL, ancestor of the Earl O'Neill; IV. SHANE OGE O'NEILL, ancestor of O'NEILL, of Ballybollen). Per fess wavy the chief ar. the base representing waves of the sea, in chief a dexter hand couped at the wrist gu. in base a salmon naiant ppr. Crest—An arm in armour embowed the hand grasping a sword all ppr. Motto—Lamb dearg Eirin.

O'Neill (Earl O'Neill, extinct 1841, and Viscount O'Neill, extinct 1855; descended from PHELIM DUBH O'NEILL, third son of JOHN O'NEILL, Esq., of Shane's Castle, whose grandson JOHN O'NEILL, known as French John, s. to Shane's Castle on the extinction of the male issue of the elder brothers of his father, and d. 1739, leaving three sons, I. HENRY O'NEILL, whose only dau. and heiress, MARY O'NEILL, m. Rev. ARTHUR CHICHESTER, great grandfather of the present Lord O'Neill; II. CHARLES O'NEILL, whose son, JOHN O'NEILL, was raised to the peerage 1793; III. CLOTWORTHY O'NEILL, d. unm.). Same Arms, Crest and Motto. Supporters—Two lions gu. armed and langued az. each gorged with an eastern crown and chained or.

O'Neill (Baron O'Neill, descended maternally from HENRY O'NEILL, Esq., of Shane's Castle, eldest son of JOHN O'NEILL, French John, of Shane's Castle, through his only dau. MARY O'NEILL, wife of Rev. ARTHUR CHICHESTER; her great-grandson, Rev. WILLIAM CHICHESTER, having s. to Shane's Castle and the O'NEILL estates by the will of his kinsman, JOHN BRUCE RICHARD, third Viscount O'Neill, 1855, assumed by royal licence the surname and arms of O'NEILL, and was raised to the Peerage 1868). Quarterly, 1st and 4th, same as the last, for O'NEILL; 2nd and 3rd, chequy or and gu. a chief vair, for CHICHESTER. Crests—1st, O'NEILL: An arm embowed in armour, the hand grasping a sword all ppr.; 2nd, CHICHESTER: A stork rising with a snake in its beak all ppr., motto over, Invitum sequitur honos. Supporters —Two lions gu. each gorged with an eastern crown ar. pendent therefrom by a gold chain, an escutcheon, that on the dexter charged with the arms of O'NEILL, and that on the sinister with those of CHICHESTER. Motto—Lamb dearg Eirin.

O'Neill (Flowerfield, co. Londonderry; descended from ARTHUR O'NEILL, Esq., of Neillsbrooke, second son of PHELIM DUBH O'NEILL, the ancestor of the Earl O'Neill). Same Arms, Crest and Motto as the Earl O'Neill.

O'Neill (Ballybollen, co. Antrim; descended from SHANE OGE O'NEILL, fourth son of JOHN O'NEILL, Esq., of Shane's Castle, who d. 1617 AMBROSE O'NEILL, the great grandson of SHANE OGE, d. 1753, leaving an only dau. and heiress, SARAH O'NEILL, m. DANIEL O'ROURKE, Esq.). Same Arms, Crest, and Motto.

O'Neill (Upper Claneboys, bart., dormant since 1799; descended from HENRY CALCH O'NEILL, second son of BRIAN BALLAGH O'NEILL, Chief of Claneboy, who was fourth in

759

descent from HUGH BUIDHE O'NEILL, from whom the design nation of Claneboy was derived, Colonel BRIAN O'NEILL, seventh in descent from HENRY CALCH O'NEILL, was created a Baronet of England, 13 November, 1643, by Charles I., in recompense for his services in the royal cause, especially for his bravery at the battle of Edge Hill, 22 August, 1642. Sir FRANCIS O'NEILL, sixth bart., who lived at Slane, co. Meath, d. 1799, leaving four sons, I. HENRY, went to Spain and has not been heard of since 1798; II. FRANCIS, of Drogheda; III. JAMES, of Dublin; and IV. BRIAN, Sergeant-Major, 88th Connaught Rangers, whose male descendants are still living. Since the decease of the sixth bart., the title has been unclaimed. See BURKE'S " Vicissitudes of Families "). Ar. two lions ramp. combatant gu. supporting a sinister hand couped at the wrist of the last, in chief three mullets of the second, and in base a salmon naiant ppr. Crest—An arm embowed in antique chain armour holding in the gauntlet a sword all ppr.

O'Neill (Killeleagh, bart. extinct; descended from HUGH McPHELIM BACCOGH O'NEILL, younger brother of BRIAN O'NEILL, of Shane's Castle, temp. Queen Elizabeth; HENRY O'NEILL, of Killyleagh, the great grandson of HUGH McPHELIM, was created a bart. 1666, and had two sons, who both d. s. p. m.). Ar. two lions ramp. combatant gu. supporting a dexter hand couped at the wrist of the last, in chief three estoiles az. in base waves of the sea therein naiant a salmon all ppr. Crest—An arm couped below the elbow erect gu. embued with a ducal coronet or, and holding in the hand a sword ppr. pommel and hilt gold.

O'Neill (Mullaghgane in the Feevagh, co. Antrim, and Athboy, co. Meath; descended from BRIAN O'NEILL, of that place, of the Clandeboy line of O'NEILL; PATRICK FRANCIS O'NEILL, Esq., of Athboy, d. 1741, leaving a son, JOHN O'NEILL, b. 1740, who was Catholic Delegate for Athboy 1792, m. 1768, MARY, only dau. and heiress of WALTER PLUNKETT, Esq., of Rathmore, and d. 1803; his dau. and eventual heiress, MARY THERESA O'NEILL, m. BENJAMIN LENTAIGNE, Esq., M.D., and d. 1820, leaving an elder son and heir, JOHN FRANCIS LENTAIGNE, Esq., of Tallaght). Ar. two lions ramp. combatant gu. supporting a dexter hand couped at the wrist of the last, in chief three estoiles of the second, in base waves of the sea, therein naiant a salmon all ppr. Crest—An arm in armour embowed grasping a sword all ppr. Motto—Pro fide rege et patriâ pugno.

O'Neill (Bunowen Castle, co. Galway; exemplified by JOHN GEOGHEGAN, Esq., of that place, on his assuming, by royal licence, 1807, the surname of O'NEILL in lieu of GEOGHEGAN). Erm. a dexter hand gu. supported by two lions ramp. az. and in base a salmon naiant in the sea ppr. Crest—A sinister arm embowed in armour, grasping a sword all ppr.

O'Neylan (a Sept settled in Ulster, deriving their surname from a chieftain, NILLAN, a descendant of COLLA DA CRIOCH, of the same race as McGUIRE). Sa. two unicorns pass. in pale ar. horned and hoofed or. Crest—A dexter hand erect, couped at the wrist, grasping a dagger all ppr.

O'Neylan. Ar. a dragon pass. wings elevated ppr. Crest —A hand couped at the wrist holding a sword erect, the point pierced through a boar's head couped fessways all ppr.

Ongawyn. Or, on a chief sa. three martlets of the field.

Ongham. Per fess or and sa. a pile (another, a pale) counterchanged.

Ongley (Baron Ongley, extinct 1877). Quarterly, 1st and 4th, ar. a fess gu.; 2nd and 3rd, ar. in chief three piles gu. in base a mount vert, on a canton az. a sun or. Crest—A phœnix, holding in the beak a fireball all ppr. Supporters —Two griffins ar. collared gu. chained or. Motto—Mihi cura futuri.

Onington. Gu. on a bend ar. three mallets sa.

Onion. Gu. a chev. erm. betw. three millrinds or. Crest— A dexter hand gu. holding a spear or.

Onley (Catesby and Pulborough, co. Northampton). Or, three piles in point gu. on a canton ar. a mullet pierced sa. Crest, granted by Dethick, Garter, 1597—In a ducal coronet or, a phœnix head in flames ppr. holding in the beak a laurel branch vert.

Onley (Bransford, co. Worcester, claiming descent from ONLEY, of Catesby). Same Arms and Crest.

Onley (Stisted Hall, co. Essex). Quarterly, 1st and 4th, per pale or and gu. three piles meeting in point counterchanged, on a canton ar. a mullet pierced sa., for ONLEY; 2nd, ar. on a bend sa. cotised gu. three owls of the field, for SAVILL; 3rd, erm. on a chief indented gu. three crescents ar., for HARVEY. Crest—1st: Out of a crown valory or, an eagle's head issuing from flames ppr. holding in the beak a sprig of laurel also ppr., for ONLEY; 2nd: On a mount vert an owl ar. charged on the body with three mullets in bend gu., for SAVILL; 3rd: A dexter cubit arm ppr. apaumée also ppr. charged from the wrist with a pile gu. above the fingers a crescent reversed ar., for HARVEY. *Motto* — Alteri si tibi.

O'Nowlan (Chiefs of Fotharta-Tea, now the Barony of Forth, co. Carlow, a Sept of the same race as O'MORE, of Leix, deriving their surname from NUALLAIN, Chief of the Sept). Ar. on a cross gu. a lion pass. betw. four martlets of the first, in each quarter a sword erect of the second. *Crest* —A martlet ar. *Another Coat* bears the swords points down, and the hilt of each surmounted with a martlet. See NOLAN.

Onscott. Or, on a bend sa. three martlets ar.

Onsley (Courtenhall, co. Northampton, and Onslow, **co.** Salop). Gu. crusily ar. on a bend of the second a mullet sa.

Onslow (*Earl of Onslow*). Ar. a fess gu. betw. six Cornish choughs ppr. *Crest*—An eagle sa. preying upon a partridge or, motto over, Semper fidelis. *Supporters*—Two falcons close ppr. belled or. *Motto*—Festina lente.

Onslow (Hengar House, Cornwall, bart.). Quarterly, 1st and 4th, ar. a fess gu. betw. six Cornish choughs ppr.; 2nd and 3rd, ar. on a bend az. three martlets or, with a double crescent for diff. *Crest*—An eagle sa. preying upon a partridge or. *Motto*—Festina lente.

Onslow (Staughton House, co. Hunts). Ar. a fess gu. betw. six Cornish choughs ppr. *Crest*—An eagle sa. preying upon a partridge or. *Motto*—Festina lente.

Onslow (Stoke Park, co. Surrey). Ar. a fess gu. betw. six Cornish choughs ppr. *Crest*—An eagle sa. preying upon a partridge or, motto over, Semper fidelis. *Motto*—Festina lente.

Onslow (MAINWARING-ELLERKER-ONSLOW; exemplified to GUILDFORD JAMES HILLIER ONSLOW, Esq., of Risby Park, co. York, on his assuming the surnames of MAINWARING and ELLERKER before his patronymic by royal licence in 1861). Quarterly, 1st and 4th, ar. a fess gu. between six Cornish choughs ppr., for ONSLOW; 2nd, az. a fret and chief ar. a canton of the last, for ELLERKER; 3rd, ar. two bars gu., for MAINWARING. *Crests*—1st, ONSLOW: In the centre; 2nd, ELLERKER: On the dexter side; 3rd, MAINWARING: On the sinister, *Motto*—Festina lente.

Onslow (West Clandon, co. Surrey). Ar. a fess gu. betw. six Cornish choughs ppr. *Crest*—A falcon ppr. legged and belled or, preying on a partridge of the first.

Onslow (Rev. RICHARD FRANCIS ONSLOW, of Newent, Rector of Stoke Edith, Ledbury, co. Hereford). *Arms, Crest,* and *Motto,* as Lord Onslow.

Opall, or Opull. Per pale or and az. an eagle displ. per pale sa. and of the first.

Ophane (co. Kent). Sa. on a fess or, two water bougets of the field.

Opie (Plymouth, co. Devon; SARAH, dau. of NICHOLAS OPIE, *m.* CHRISTOPHER WARREN, of London. Visit. Devon, 1620). Sa. on a chev. or, betw. three garbs ar. as many hurts.

Opie (Pawton, in St. Breock, co. Cornwall; extinct about the middle of the 18th century, a younger branch was of St. Erme. The celebrated painter, OPIE, is said to have been descended from a younger son of this line). Sa. on a chev. betw. three garbs or, as many hurts. *Crest*—A demi stag erm. attired or, pierced through the neck with an arrow sa. feathered and headed ar. the wound and head of the arrow guttée de sang.

Opie (Penhargard, co. Cornwall). Same *Arms.*

Ople. Vair a bend gu., over all a label ar.

Oppeshall, or Oppsall. Ar. a cross. sa. fretty or.

Oppin (Saxony). Az. a saltire ar. charged in the centre with a double rose gu.

Opsate. Ar. a cross sa.

Opton, or Oxton (co. Gloucester). Gu. a lion ramp. within an orle of crosses crosslet or.

Opull. See OPALL.

O'Quigley. Gu. an orle ar., over all a bend erminois. *Crest*—An estoile ar.

O'Quin (formerly O'CUINN, Chiefs of Muintir-Ifearnain, a territory extending around Corofin, in the barony of Inchiquin, co. Clare. The Chief of the Sept had his seat at Inchiquin, but was driven out by the O'BRIENS; the tribe name of Ifearnain is derived from IFEARNAIN, son of CORC, one of the Dalcassian Septs. The Four Masters record that EDAVIN, dau. of O'QUIN, Lady of Munster, *d.* 1188 while on a pilgrimage at Derry. Of this ancient Irish Sept the *Earl of Dunraven* is a descendant). Gu. a hand couped below the wrist grasping a sword all ppr. betw. in chief two crescents ar. and in base as many serpents erect and re-

760

specting each other, tails nowed or. *Crest*—A boar's head erased and erect ar. langued gu.

O'Quin (WYNDHAM-QUIN, *Earl of Dunraven and Mount Earl*). Quarterly, 1st and 4th, same as the last, for O'QUIN, of Muintir-Ifearnain; 2nd and 3rd, az. a chev. betw. three lions' heads erased or, langued gu. a mullet ar. for diff., for WYNDHAM. *Crests*—1st, O'QUIN: A wolf's head erased ar.; 2nd, WYNDHAM: A lion's head erased or, within a fetterlock and chain gold. *Supporters*—Two ravens' wings elevated ppr. collared and chained or. *Motto*—Quæ sursum volo videre.

O'Quin (formerly O'CUINN, Chiefs of Muintir-Gillagan, a territory extending over the present baronies of Ardagh, Moydon, and Shrule, co. Longford, which they were dispossessed of by the O'Ferralls *temp.* Edward II. and Edward III., the Chief of the Sept had his residence at Rathcline, in Anally. The Four Masters record, under the year 1171, that Tiernan O'Rourk, at the head of the men of Breffney, made an attack on Miles de Cogan and his knights, but was defeated with great loss; among the slain was the grandson of DERMOD O'CUINN). Vert a pegasus pass. wings elevated ar. a chief or.

O'Quin (Galway, Longford, and Bordeaux; allowed by Hawkins, Ulster, 1775, to PATRICK O'QUIN, of Galway, son of JOHN VALENTINE O'QUIN, of Bordeaux, who was descended from THOMAS O'QUIN, of co. Longford, A.D. 1387). Same *Arms. Crest*—A wolf's head erased erm. *Motto*—Quo sursum volo videre.

O'Quin. See QUIN.

O'Quinlevan (a Sept located on the borders of the Kings co. and co. Tipperary, formerly the CLANN COINLEGHAIN). Per pale erm. and or, two lions ramp. combatant betw. in chief a mullet surmounted of a crescent and in base a dexter hand couped at the wrist and erect all gu.; another, Gu. three lizards pass. in pale or.

Oram. Lozengy ar. and sa. two chev. or. *Crest*—A hurt charged with a stag standing on a mount all ppr.

Orange (Foscott and Mells, co. Somerset; JAMES ORANGE, Esq., of Foscott, Visit. Somerset, 1623, son of WILLIAM ORANGE, Esq., of Mells; granted to JOHN ORANGE, Esq., of the Middle Temple, by Cooke, Clarenceux, 35 Queen Elizabeth). Ar. three pairs of barnacles open in pale gu. *Crest*—A demi talbot erased or.

Orange (France). Or, a buglehorn stringed and viroled gu.

Oranmore and Browne, Baron. See BROWNE and GUTHRIE.

Oray, or Oyry. Barry of six or and ar. *Crest*—A pennon per fess gu. and or, a staff in bend counterchanged.

Orbaston. Ar. a bend and chev. gu., on a canton of the second a lion pass. (another, ramp.) of the first.

Orby (Gosworth, co. Chester). Ar. two chev. gu., a canton of the last.

Orby (Croyland Abbey, co. Lincoln, bart., **extinct**; Sir THOMAS ORBY, of Croyland, was created a baronet in 1658. His grandson, Sir THOMAS ORBY, third baronet, left an only dau. and heir, ELIZABETH, *m.* first, to Lord John Hay, and secondly to General ROBERT HUNTER, Governor of Jamaica. By the latter she was ancestor of ORBY-HUNTER, of Croyland Abbey). Erm. three chev. gu., on a canton of the second a lion pass. guard. or.

Orby, or Orreby (co. Lincoln). Erm. three chev. sa., on a canton gu. a lion pass. guard. or.

Orby, or Orreby (co. Chester). Gu. two lions pass. ar. a label of three points or. *Crest*—On a chapeau gu. turned up erm. a ram's head ppr.

Orby. Gu. two lions ramp. in fess or.

Orchard (co. Devon; CHRISTIAN ORCHARD, heiress of the family *temp.* Henry VI., *m.* Sir PHILIP CARY, ancestor of CARY, of Cloveland, in same co. Visit. Devon, 1620). Az. a chev. az. betw. three pears pendant or. *Crest*—A crow sa.

Orchard (Hartland Abbey, co. Devon; the sisters and coheirs of PAUL ORCHARD, Esq., who *d.* in 1812, *m.* MORRISON and BUCK). Same *Arms. Crest*—Out of a mural crown ppr. a dexter arm couped at the elbow, vested az. adorned with three fleurs-de-lis or, one and two, the cuff turned up erm. holding in the hand also ppr. a pear as in the arms.

Orcharton. Ar. a chev. sa. a label gu.

Ord (Sands, co. Durham; descended from LIONEL OURD, Esq., of Fishburne, living 9 James I.). Sa. three salmons haurient ar. a canton of the second.

Ord (Fornham House, co. Suffolk). Same *Arms,* quartering HUTCHINSON and CRAVEN. *Crest*—An elk's head ppr. *Motto*—Mitis et fortis.

Ord (Whitfield Hall, co. Northumberland). Sa. three salmon haurient ar. quartering DILLINGHAM, viz., Gu. a fess betw. three martlets ar. *Crest*—An elk's head ppr.

Ord (Edge Hill, near Derby; descended from ORD, of Whitfield). Same *Arms* and *Crest*.

Ord (Captain WILLIAM REDMAN ORD, Royal Engineers). Quarterly, 1st, sa. three salmon haurient ar. a mullet for diff., for ORD; 2nd, gu. three cushions erm. tasselled or, for REDMAN; 3rd, per pale gu. and az. a lion ramp. betw. eight crosses crosslet or, for HUTCHINSON; 4th, quarterly 1st and 4th, ar. a fesse betw. six crosses crosslets fitchée gu., 2nd and 3rd, or, five fleurs-de-lis in cross sa. a chief wavy gu., for CRAVEN. *Crests*—1st, ORD: An elk's head couped ppr.; 2nd, CRAVEN,: On a chapeau purp. turned up erm. a griffin statant, wings elevated and endorsed erm. beak or.

Ord (Scotland). Ar. a chev. az. betw. a crescent betw. two mullets in chief of the last, and a demi otter issuing out of water in base ppr.

Orde (East Orde, co. Durham, and Morpeth, co. Northumberland; descended from SIMON ORDE, *d.* 1362. From this family descend, through junior branches, the Lords Bolton, and the Baronets Orde; the senior branch is represented by ORDE, of Nunny Kirk and Morpeth). Sa. three fishes (supposed to be salmon, the word signifying a salmon weir) haurient in fesse ar.

Orde (Nunny Kirke, co. Northumberland). Same *Arms*, quartering for WARD, Ar. a cross crosslet or. *Crest*—An elk's head ppr. *Motto*—Mitis et fortis.

Orde (Westwood Hall, co. Northumberland). Same *Arms* and *Crest*.

Orde-Powlett (*Baron Bolton*). See POWLETT.

Orde (Morpeth, co. Northumberland, bart.). Sa. three salmons haurient ar. *Crest*—An elk's head or, charged with a collar invecked sa.

Orde. Gu. a cross moline or.

Ordeit. Quarterly, az. and gu. an escarbuncle or.

Orden. Erm. a bend engr. az.

Ordnance Office. Az. three field-pieces on their carriages in pale or, on a chief ar. as many cannon-balls sa.

Ordre. Per pale ar. and or, a cross moline gu.

Ordway. Per pale ar. and or, on a chief indented vert a crescent betw. two mullets of the second. *Crest*—Two wings displ. each charged with a mullet pierced.

Ordway. Ar. on a chief vert a crescent of the first betw. two mullets or, pierced gu.

Ore, or **Oare** (Oare, co. Sussex). Ar. a bend tortile az. and or.

Ore (co. Kent). Ar. a cross gu. fretty or, betw. four buds sa.

O'Reardan. See O'RIORDAN.

O'Reilly (Princes of East Breifne, a territory comprising a portion of the present cos. of Cavan and Leitrim, descended from RAGHALLAIGH, Prince of Breifne, who s. his father A.D. 981; Sir JOHN O'REILLY, Prince of Breifne, entered into certain articles of agreement with Sir John Perrott, Lord Deputy of Ireland, under which he surrendered the principality of Breifne to Queen Elizabeth, and got a re-grant of the same to hold in capite of the Crown, his direct descendant and representative, EDMUND O'REILLY, Knt., of St. Louis, and Lieut.-Col. in Dillon's Regiment, was resident in Paris at the beginning of the French Revolution; Fun. Ent. Ulster's Office, 1636, of MULMORE MAC HUGH CONOLAGH O'REILLY, of Camett, co. Cavan, chief of his name, son of HUGH CONOLAGH O'REILLY, and grandson of MULMORE MAC SHANE MAC CAHILL O'REILLY). Vert two lions ramp. combatant or, supporting a dexter hand couped at the wrist erect and apaumée bloody ppr.

O'Reilly (Heath House, Queen's co.; descended from EDMUND O'REILLY, Esq., of Kilnacrott, brother of Sir JOHN O'REILLY, Prince of Breifne, *temp.* Queen Elizabeth, who *s.* his brother as chief according to the law of tanistry). Quarterly, 1st and 4th, same *Arms*; 2nd and 3rd, ar. on a mount an oak tree a snake descending the trunk all ppr. supported by two lions ramp. gu. *Crests*—1st: An oak tree with a snake entwined descendant ppr. issuing out of a ducal coronet or; 2nd: An arm mailed in armour, couped at the elbow the gauntlet grasping a dagger all ppr. *Motto*—Fortitudine et prudentia.

O'Reilly (Knock Abbey Castle, co. Louth; MYLES WILLIAM PATRICK O'REILLY, J.P. and D.L., M.P. co. Longford, 1862, descended from O'REILLY, of Heath House). Same *Arms*, *Crest*, and *Motto*.

OReilly (Baltrasna, co. Meath). Same *Arms*, *Crest*, and *Motto*.

O'Reilly (Scarvagh, co. Down; descended from TORLOGH O'REILLY, youngest son of EDMOND O'REILLY, of Kilnacrott, ancestor of O'REILLY, of Heath House). Same *Arms*, *Crest*, and *Motto*.

O'Reilly (allowed by Hawkins, Ulster, 1752, to ALEXANDER O'REILLY, an officer in the army of the King of Spain, son of

THOMAS O'REILLY, Esq., co. Meath, descended from EDMOND O'REILLY, Esq., co. Cavan). Same *Arms*, *Crest*, and *Motto*.

O'Reilly (Scarborough, co. York; confirmed to FRANCIS GAMMEL O'REILLY, Esq., of that place, claiming descent from O'REILLY, of East Breifne, son of EDWARD O'REILLY, Esq., by ELIZABETH, his wife, sister of Sir FRANCIS WOOD, first bart. of Barnsley). Vert two lions combatant or, supporting a dexter hand ppr. in base a rose ar. seeded and barbed of the second. *Crest*—Out of an antique Irish crown or, a tree therefrom a serpent descending entwined round the stem both ppr. *Motto*—Fortitudine et prudentia.

O'Reilly (Ballinlough, co. Westmeath, bart.; confirmed by Fortescue, Ulster, 1795, to Sir HUGH O'REILLY, first bart., who afterwards assumed the name of NUGENT). Ar. upon a meunt vert two lions ramp. combatant gu. surmounting the trunk entwined with a serpent descending all ppr. *Crest*—An arm in armour embowed, grasping a falchion ot scymitar all ppr.

O'Reilly (allowed by Hawkins, Ulster, 1774, to HUGH O'REILLY, ANDREW O'REILLY, Captain in the Austrian service, and JAMES O'REILLY, Captain in the same service, sons of JAMES O'REILLY, who was great-grandson of HUGH O'REILLY, Esq., of Ballinlough). Same *Arms* and *Crest*. *Motto*—Fortitudine et prudentia.

Orenge. See ORANGE.

Orfeur (High-Close and Plumbland Hall, co. Cumberland; granted 1685. The ORFEURS, of High-Close, traceable to the reign of Edward II., became extinct by the decease of Major-General ORFEUR in 1741; of the co-heirs, one *m.* YATES, and another PATTENSON). Sa. a cross ar. *Crest*—A woman's head couped at the breast all ppr. on her head a cross pattée fitchée or.

Orford, Earl of. See WALPOLE.

Orford, Town of (co. Suffolk). On a mount a tower, supported by two lions ramp. beneath them a date, viz. 1579, as on the present Seal of the Corporation, which is thus circumscribed—"Sigillum officii majoris burgi OREFORD."

Orgaine (Lambrooke, co. Berks, and co. Wilts; granted by Camden, Clarenceux). Per saltire or and erm. a cross couped gu. *Crest*—Three organ pipes, two in saltire and one in pale ar. entwined with a chaplet of laurel vert.

Orgill (Beccles, co. Suffolk). Ar. a fesse betw. three crescents, each surmounted by a fleur-de-lis gu. *Crest*—A buffalo's head sa. gorged with a wreath of roses ppr.

O'Riordan, or **O'Rearden** (a Sept of note in Muskerr/, co. Cork; distinguished as military chiefs). Quarterly, 1st and 4th, gu. out of clouds in the sinister side a dexter arm fessways ppr. holding a dagger in pale ar. pommel and hilt or; 2nd and 3rd, ar. a lion ramp. gu. against a tree in the dexter couped ppr. *Crest*—A fleur-de-lis gu. *Motto*—Pro Deo et patriâ.

O'Riordan (Derryroe, co. Cork, and Nantes, in the Kingdom of France; allowed by Hawkins, Ulster, 1751, to STEPHEN O'RIORDAN, of the latter place, son of ROBERT O'RIORDAN, by ANASTACIA CREAGH, his wife, dau. of STEPHEN CREAGH, Esq., of Limerick, and descended from RIORDAN, of Derryroe). Same *Arms*, *Crest*, and *Motto*.

Oriel College (Oxford; founded 1323, by Adam le Brome, Confessor to Edward II.). Gu. three lions pass. guard. in pale or, a border engr. ar.

Orion, or **Orren** (Rochester, co. Kent). Ar. three torteaux, in bend betw. two cotises gu. a chief sa.

Orkeley, or **Orkesley.** Erm. on a chief indented az. three lions ramp. or.

Orker (co. Dorset). Erm. on a chief gu. three bezants.

Orkesley, or **Okesley.** Erm. a chief sa.

Orkney, Earl of. See FITZMAURICE.

Orkney, See of. Ar. St. Magnus vested in royal robes, on his head an antique crown in his dexter hand a sceptre all ppr.

Orlebar (Hinwick House, co. Bedford; GEORGE ORLEBAR, *temp.* Queen Elizabeth, *m.* MARGARET, only dau. and heiress of RICHARD CHILD, of Poddington, co. Bedford, and heir of WILLIAM PAYNE, lord of the manor of Poddington. His great-grandson, RICHARD ORLEBAR, built Hinwick House on that estate). Ar. two bars gu. charged the upper with two roses and the lower with one of the field, barbed vert, seeded or. *Crest*—An eagle's head betw. two wings erect ar. charged on the neck with two barrulets gu. *Motto*—Ora et labora.

Orleston. Or, two chev. gu. on a canton of the second a lion pass. ar.

Orleston. Ar. fretty gu.

Orleton (Orlton, co. Salop). Ar. a bend double cotised sa. in chief a martlet of the last.

Orly (France). Sa. a bear ramp. or.

Orlyans. Az. four bars dancettée or (another, tinctures reversed).

Orme (co. Northampton). Ar. a chev. betw. three escallops gu. *Crest*—A dolphin embowed ar. fins, tail, and tusk or.

Orme (Hanch Hall, co. Stafford; granted by Dugdale). Az. an eagle displ. betw. three poleaxes or. *Crest*—A dolphin az. finned or, in mouth a spear.

Orme (Abbeytown, co. Mayo; confirmed by Betham, Ulster, to WILLIAM HENRY ORME, Esq., of that place). Az. an eagle displ. betw. three poleaxes erect or. *Crest*—A dolphin embowed az. fins and tail or, surmounted by a poleaxe in bend, as in the arms. *Motto*—Fortis et fidelis.

Orme (Glenmore, co. Mayo). Same *Arms, Crest,* and *Motto*—A crescent for diff.

Orme (Owenmore, co. Mayo). Same *Arms, Crest,* and *Motto.*

Orme (Ballycorroon, co Mayo). Same *Arms, Crest,* and *Motto.*

Ormer, or Ormers. Vert six eagles displ. or.

Ormerod (Ormerod, co. Lancaster; CHARLOTTE ANNE, only dau. and heiress of LAWRENCE ORMEROD, Esq., of Ormerod, the then representative of that ancient family, who *d.* in 1773, *m.* JOHN HARGREAVES, Esq., and conveyed Ormerod to her husband; she had two daus., her co-heiresses; ELEANOR MARY HARGREAVES *m.* Rev. WILLIAM THURSBY, and CHARLOTTE ANNE HARGREAVES *m.* Hon. J. YORKE SCARLETT. Arms allowed by the Deputies of Camden, Visit. Somerset, 1623, to a younger branch settled at Huntspill, and confirmed in 1818, amongst other quarterings, to Colonel HARGREAVES of Ormerod). Or, three bars and a lion pass. in chief gu.

Ormerod (Chorlton, co. Chester). Or, three bars and a lion pass. in chief gu.

Ormerod (Tyldesley, co. Lancaster, and Sedbury Park, co. Gloucester; descended from the youngest son of PETER ORMEROD, Esq., of Ormerod, *b.* 1588). Same *Arms,* quartering JOHNSON, of Tyldesley, WAREING, of Walmersley, CROMPTON, of Hacking Hall, and NUTTALL, of Walmersley. *Crest*—A wolf's head couped, barry of four pieces or and gu. in the mouth an ostrich feather erect ppr. This crest is that of WAREING, duly confirmed to the Tyldesley branch of ORMEROD. The previous crest, used after the alliance with HAYDOCK, was a fleur-de-lis gu.

Ormesby (None Ormesby and Louth, co. Lincoln). Gu. a bend betw. six crosses crosslet fitchée or (another, ar.). *Crest*—An arm couped at the elbow vested sa. holding in the hand a leg in armour, couped at the thigh all ppr.

Ormesby (co. Lincoln). Sa. three chessrooks or, a chief of the last, quartering, gu. a bendlet betw. six crosses crosslet fitchée or. *Crest*—An arm embowed vested sa. cuffed or, holding in the hand ppr. a leg in armour couped at the thigh of the last garnished gold.

Ormesby (co. York). Az. a bend betw. six crosses crosslet fitchée or.

Ormesby. Gu. a bend counter-componée or and az.

Ormesby. Gu. a cross ar. over all a bend componée or and az.

Ormesby (co. Roscommon; Fun. Ent. Ulster's Office, 1630, ANTHONY ORMESBY, Esq., of that place). Gu. a bend betw. six crosses crosslet fitchée or, a crescent on a crescent for diff.

Ormesby (Sligo; Fun. Ent. Ulster's Office, 1662, THOMAS ORMESBY, buried at St. John's, Sligo). Quarterly, 1st and 3rd, az. semée of crosses crosslet a lion ramp. ar., for ORMESBY; 2nd and 3rd, az. semée of crosses crosslet a lion ramp. ar., for KINARDSLEY; 4th, sa. three chessrooks ar. a chief or, for WERDAN.

Ormesley (co. Lancaster). Sa. a. chev. gu. three leopards' faces in chief of the last.

Ormesley. Erm. on a chief dancettée az. three lions ramp. or.

Ormeston, or Orneston (co. Essex). Sa. a chev. betw. three spearheads ar. a border gu.

Ormeston (Ormston, co. Lancaster. The heiress *m.* HYDE). Ar. a squirrel pass. sa.

Ormestone. Ar. fretty gu. on a chief az. a lion pass or.

Ormeston (that Ilk, co. Haddington). Ar. three pelicans vulning themselves sa.

Ormiston (London, 1693). Same *Arms,* a border wavy vert. *Crest*—An anchor ppr. *Motto*—Felicior quo certior.

Ormonde, Marquess of. See BUTLER.

Ormsby (Ireland; descended from HENRY ORMSBY, or ORMESBY, of the Lincolnshire family, who settled in Ireland *temp.* Elizabeth, and left, by SUSANNAH KELK, his first wife, three sons, ANTHONY ORMSBY, ancestor of ORMSBY, of Rathlec, EDWARD ORMSBY, ancestor of ORMSBY, of Tobbervaddy, and MALLEY ORMSBY, ancestor of ORMSBY of Cloghan; and by his second wife, ELIZABETH, three other sons, from whom descend ORMSBY, of Moryvilla, Annagh, Comyn, and Willowbrook). Gu. a bend betw. six crosses crosslet fitchée or.

Ormsby (Willowbrook, co. Sligo; MARY JANE ORMSBY, only child and heiress of OWEN ORMSBY, Esq., of Willowbrook, by MARGARET, eldest dau. and eventually heiress of WILLIAM OWEN, Esq., of Porkington, co. Salop, *m.* in 1815, WILLIAM GORE, Esq., M.P., who assumed the prefix surname of ORMSBY: the eldest surviving son of this marriage is WILLIAM RICHARD, *Lord Harlech*). Same *Arms,* without the quarterings, &c. *Crest*—A dexter arm embowed in armour ppr. charged with a rose gu. holding in the hand a man's leg also in armour couped at the thigh.

Ormsby (Cloghan, co. Mayo, bart., extinct 1833; Sir CHARLES MONTAGU ORMSBY, K.C., was created a bart. 1812). Gu. a bend betw. six crosses crosslet or. *Crest*—A dexter armed arm embowed, the hand grasping a leg in armour couped above the knee all ppr. *Motto*—Fortis qui prudens.

Ormsby (Ballinamore House, co. Mayo). Same *Arms. Crest*—A dexter arm embowed in armour ppr. charged with a rose gu. holding in the hand a man's leg also in armour couped at the thigh.

Ormsby (Gortner Abbey, co. Mayo). Same *Arms,* &c.

Ormsby (co. Norfolk). Gu. crusily ar. a bend chequy or and az. *Crest*—A falcon rising or.

Ornell, or Arnell (Scotland). Ar. two eels paleways wavy betw. two stars in the flanks az.

Ornell (co. Lancaster). Ar. three torteaux in bend betw. two cotises gu. a chief sa.

O'Rorke (a Sept who were Chiefs of West Breifne, now comprised in the counties of Cavan and Leitrim, deriving their surname from RUAIRE, a chieftain, *d.* A.D. 893. Three of this Sept were kings of Connaught, of whom the most distinguished was ART O'RORKE, King of Connaught, slain A.D. 1046). Or, two lions pass. in pale sa. *Crest*—Out of an ancient Irish crown or, an arm in armour erect, grasping a sword ppr. pommel and hilt gold, motto over, Buagh, *i.e.,* Victory. *Motto*—Serviendo guberno.

O'Rorke (Sir BRIAN O'RORKE, knighted at Dublin 3 May, 1579, by Sir Henry Sydney, Lord Deputy of Ireland). Or, two lions pass. in pale sa.

O'Rorke (Sir TEIGE O'RORKE, knighted by Sir George Cary, Lord Deputy of Ireland, 17 April, 1604). Quarterly, 1st and 4th, or, two lions pass. in pale sa.; 2nd and 3rd, ar. two boars pass. in pale gu.

O'Rorke (Cloncorick, co. Leitrim; Fun. Ent. Ulster's Office, 1637, SHANE OGE MAC SHANE O'RORKE, son of SHANE O'RORKE, grandson of LOUGHLIN O'RORKE, and great-grandson of OWEN O'RORKE, all of same place). Same *Arms* and *Crest,* without the quartering.

O'Rorke, or O'Rourke (Nantes, France; allowed by Hawkins, Ulster, 1770, to EDMOND ROCH O'ROURKE, of that place, descended from THADY O'RORKE, Lord of Breifne, co. Leitrim, 1470, by AGNES, his wife, dau. of HUGH McGUIRE, Lord of Fermanagh). Same *Arms. Crest*—Out of a crown or, an arm in armour erect grasping a sword ppr. *Motto*—Victorious.

O'Rourke (Count O'Rourke, in the Kingdom of France; allowed by Bryan, Deputy Ulster, 1782, to JOHN O'ROURKE, Count O'Rourke, who was born in the parish of Oghteragh, in Breifne, emigrated to France, served as captain of the Royal Scotch in that kingdom, major of horse in the service of Russia, afterwards colonel of horse in France, created a count by the King of France, 1771). Per pale or and az., on the dexter side three lions pass. sa. on the sinister in chief a tabby cat couchant guard. to the sinister side of the shield ppr. supporting in a bend a flagstaff or, thereon a pennon gu. inscribed with the word " buadh," letters gold, in base a boar pass. of the fourth. *Crest*—Out of a royal crown a naked arm erect, holding a scymitar all ppr. *Motto*—Victorious.

Orpen (Killowen, co. Kerry; ROBERT ORPEN settled in Ireland, *temp.* Charles I. His male representative *is* JOHN HERBERT ORPEN, Esq., LL.D., Stephen's Green, Dublin, Barrister-at-law, *m.* 1840, ELLEN SUSAN GERTRUDE, dau. of Rev. JOHN RICHARDS, of Grange, co. Wexford, and has with other issue a son and heir, JOHN RICHARDS ORPEN). Per pale az. and or, a lion ramp. counterchanged. *Crest*—A demi lion ramp. or. *Motto*—Veritas vincet.

Orpen (Ardtully, co. Kerry; confirmed to Sir RICHARD JOHN THEODORE ORPEN, Knt., of Ardtully, President of the Society of Attorneys in Ireland, son of Rev. FRANCIS ORPEN, Incumbent of Douglas, co. Cork, by SUSANNA, his wife, dau. and co-heiress of HUGH MILLERD, of Monard, an Alderman of Cork). Quarterly, 1st and 4th, per pale az. and or, a lion ramp. counterchanged, in the dexter chief point a cross crosslet of the second, for ORPEN; 2nd and 3rd, erm. a fess az. betw. three wolves' heads erased sa., for MILLERD. *Crest* —A demi lion ramp. or, charged on the shoulder with a cross crosslet sa. *Motto*—Veritas vincet.

Orpen (Killaha Castle). Same *Arms*, &c.

Orpie (THOMAS ORPIE, Sheriff of Dublin; Fun. Ent. Ulster's Office, 1635, ELINOR ORPIE, his wife). Per fess ar. and sa. a pale counterchanged, three crescents of the second issuant from the horns of each an estoile gu., an annulet for diff.

Jrpwood (Abingdon, co. Berks; confirmed Oct. 1600). Vert three crosses formée ar. on a chief of the last as many boars' heads sa. tusked or, langued gu. *Crest*—A boar pass. quarterly erm. and ermines, armed, bristled, and hoofed or.

Orr (England). Gu. three hinds' heads erased ar. *Crest*— A lion pass. ppr. resting the dexter paw on a torteau.

Orr (Barrowfield, Scotland). Gu. three piles in point ar. on a chief or, a torteau betw. two crosses crosslet fitchée of the field. *Crest*—A cornucopia ppr. *Motto*—Bonis omnia bona.

Orr (Edinburgh, 1768). Gu. three piles in point ar. a bordure of the last, on a chief or, a torteau betw. two crosses crosslet az. *Crest*, as the last. *Motto*—Virtuti fortuna comes.

Orr (Ralston, co. Renfrew, 1802). Gu. three piles in point within a bordure engr. erminois, on a chief or, three torteaux az. *Crest*—A dexter hand holding a tree ppr. *Motto*—Ego accedo.

Orr (Harvieston and Castle Campbell, co. Clackmannan, 1863). Gu. three piles erm. on a chief or, three cinquefoils of the first. *Crest*—A tower ppr. *Motto*—Fortis et vigilans.

Orr-Ewing. See EWING.

Orr (Belfast; granted to JAMES ORR, Esq., of the Villa Antoinette, Cannes, Alpes Maritimes, France, second son of JAMES ORR, Esq., of Ballygowan, afterwards of Holywood House, co. Down, and of Belfast, banker, by JANE STEWART, his wife, of the family of STEWART, of Ballintoy, co. Antrim, and grandson of ALEXANDER ORR, of Belfast, and to their descendants). Gu. three piles in point ar. the centre pile charged with a trefoil slipped vert, on a chief or, a torteau betw. two cross crosslets fitchée of the field. *Crest*—A cornucopia ppr. charged with a trefoil slipped, as in the arms. *Motto*— Bonis omnia bona.

Orre. Gu. a bend ar. fretty az.

Orreby (co. Chester). Erm. three chev. gu. on a canton of the second a lion ramp. or.

Orreby (Gawsworth, co. Chester). *Ancient*—Erm. five chevronels gu. on a canton of the second a lion pass. or. *Modern*— Ar. two chevronels a canton gu.

Orreby (Dalby, Lord of Fulk, Stapleford, co. Chester, after their alliance with STRANGE). Gu. two lions pass. in pale ar. a label of the second.

Orreby (Hagneby, co. Lincoln, *temp.* Henry II.). Erm. five chevronels gu. on a canton of the second a lion pass. or.

Orred (Tranmere Weston, and Runcorn, co. Chester). Quarterly, 1st and 4th, gu. a fess dancettée ar.. for ORRED; 2nd, sa. a cross engr. ar. betw. four plates each charged with a pheon of the field, for FLETCHER; 3rd, ar. a cross engr. sa., for MIDDLETON. *Crest*—A hare saliant ppr. in the mouth three ears of corn or.

Orrel (Orrell-in-the-Moors, co. Lancaster; an ancient family. Visit. 1613). Ar. three torteaux in bend betw. two bendlets gu.

Orrell (Turton, co. Lancaster; descended from WILLIAM ORRELL second son of NICHOLAS ORRELL, Esq., of Orrell). Same *Arms*, a chief sa. *Crest*—A lion's head erased ar. ducally gorged gu. semée of torteaux.

Orrell (Blackbrooke, co. Lancaster; descended from ORRELL, of Turton). Same *Arms* and *Crest*.

Orrell (Isle of Ely, co. Chester). Ar. three torteaux betw. two bendlets gu. a chief sa. *Crest*—A lion's head erased ar. powdered with torteaux and ducally gorged gu.

Orrell (Slaugham, co. Sussex). Same *Arms*, the chief gu.

Orrell, Orwell, or Ornell (co. Kent). Sa. a fess or (another, ar.).

Orrell. Ar. a semée of cinquefoils gu. a lion ramp. sa.

Orrock (that Ilk, co. Fife). Sa. on a chev. betw. three mullets ar. as many chessrooks of the first. *Crest*—A falcon perched ppr. *Motto*—Solus Christus mea rupes.

Orrock (Steward Clerk of St. Andrew's 1672). Sa. on a chev. engr. or, betw. three mullets ar. as many chessrooks of the first. *Crest*—A writing pen thrust through a man's heart ppr. *Motto*—Arte fideque.

Orrock (Provost Marshall of the Netherlands, 1690). Sa. on a chev. waved on the upper and embattled on the lower side or, betw. three mullets ar. as many chessrooks of the first. *Crest*—A hawk perching ppr. *Motto*—Christus mea rupes.

Orseys (co. Worcester). Per fess or and az. three annulets counterchanged.

Orton (Orton, cc. Cumberland; the heiress *m.* SKELTON). Vert a lion ramp. ar. crowned and armed gu.

Orton, or Ortun (Lea, co. Leicester). Ar. a bend sa. betw. a rose in chief and a fleur-de-lis in base gu. *Crest*—A tower ppr. cupola and flags gu.

Orton (co. Kent). Or, a squirrel sejant gu. cracking a nut ppr.

Orton (Frense, co. Norfolk). Ar. a lion ramp. guard. vert, crowned or.

Orton. Az. a lion ramp. or; another, Az. a leopard ramp. ar. crowned or.

Orway. Erm. on a chief indented sa. three crosses pattée fitchée or.

Orwell (Isle of Ely). Az. a chev. erm. betw. three lions ramp. or.

Orwell (co. Kent). Sa. on a fess or, an annulet of the field.

Orwell. Sa. a fess ar.

Orwell. Az. a fess ar. a border engr. or.

Orwey (Orwey, co. Devon, *temp.* Henry III.; ELIZABETH, dau. and heir of ROBERT DE ORWEY, *temp.* Edward III., *m.* ROBERT OAKBEARE; she was sixth in descent from ROBERT DE ORWEY, *temp.* King John. Visit. Devon, 1620). Ar. on a fess indented sa. three crosses crosslet fitchée or.

Ory. Az. a chameleon on sandy ground ppr. in chief a sun or. *Crest*—An armed arm holding a sword all ppr.

Osan. Per chev. engr. purp. and az. three fleurs-de-lis or.

Osan, or Osanne. Purp. a chev. engr. betw. three fleurs-de-lis or.

O'Ryan. See O'MULRIAN.

Osbaldeston (Osbaldeston, co. Lancaster). Ar. a mascle sa. betw. three pellets. *Crest*—1st: A stag's head erased per pale ar. and sa. guttée counterchanged attired or; 2nd: A man in armour on horseback all ppr. in the dexter hand a sword ar. hilt or.

Osbaldeston (Hunmanby, co. York; descended from a second son of OSBALDESTON, of Osbaldeston, co. Lancaster; Sir RICHARD OSBALDESTON, Knt., of Hunmanby, Attorney-General for Ireland, was knighted in Dublin 9 April, 1637, by the *Earl of Strafford*. His great grandson, RICHARD OSBALDESTON, Bishop of London, *d. s. p.* 1764. His lordship's sisters, who became eventually co-heirs of their brothers, were THEODOSIA, wife of ROBERT POCKLEY, Esq., of Brayton; ELIZABETH, wife of JOHN HEALY, Esq.; and MARY, wife of ROBERT MITFORD, Esq., of Mitford Castle. See FIRMAN and MITFORD, pages 351 and 691, and also Fun. Ent. Ulster's Office). Same *Arms*, a martlet for diff.

Osbaldeston (Sunderland, co. Lancaster, 1664). Same *Arms* as OSBALDESTON, of Osbaldeston, with a canton gu.

Osbaldeston (Chadlington, co. Oxford; a family of great antiquity, descended from OSWALD DE STONE, who came to England with William I.; JOHN OSBALDESTON, of that place, Visit. Oxon, 1574, fifth in descent from Sir JOHN OSBALDESTON, Knt., of Chadlington, *temp.* Henry IV.). Quarterly, ar. and sa. four leopards' faces counterchanged.

Osbaldeston (Chadlington, co. Oxford, bart., extinct; LITTLETON OSBALDESTON, Esq., of Chalington, son of JOHN OSBALDESTON, and grandson of HERCULES OSBALDESTON, who was the son of ARTHUR OSBALDESTON, the last named in Visit. Oxon, was created a bart. 1664, since which period the family bore the following arms). Ar. a mascle sa. betw. three pellets. *Crest*—A knight in complete armour on a white horse, on his shield the family arms. *Motto*—Constance et ferme.

Osbaldeston (Hutton-Bushel, and Ebberstone Lodge, co. York; the present representative is GEORGE OSBALDESTON, Esq.). Same *Arms* and *Crest*.

Osbaldeston (Hunmanby, co. York, 1665). Ar. a mascle sa. betw. three pellets, a canton gu. *Crest*—A knight on horseback in armour.

Osber. Ar. on a bend betw. three cats salient sa. as many buckles or.

Osbert. Ar. on a chief az. three crosses formée fitchée of the field.

Osbert. Ar. a lion ramp. gu. crowned or, a border engr. sa.

Osbert. Ar. two palets ge on each four bezants.

Osborn (Chicksand Priory, co. Bedford, bart.). Ar. a bend betw. two lions ramp. sa. *Crest*—A lion's head ppr. ducally crowned or. *Motto*—Quantum in rebus inane.

Osborn. Ar. a bend betw. three lions ramp. sa. *Crest*—A lion's head erased ar. ducally crowned or.

Osborn Wyddel (claiming descent from a younger son of the House of DESMOND, said to have settled in Wales, *circa*

1237, *temp.* Llewelyn the Great; he founded several of the most distinguished families in co. Merioneth, among others, VAUGHAN, of Corsygedol; WYNNE, of Ynysmaengwyn, and Maesynewadd, now extinct, and WYNNE, of Peniarth). Erm. on a saltire gu. a crescent or. *Crest*—On a chapeau gu. turned up erm. a boar pass. ar. fretty gu.

Osborn (Peppermilne, co. Edinburgh, 1672). Gu. a bend surmounted by a fess ar. *Crest*—A sword in pale ppr. *Motto*—Je gagne.

Osborne (*Duke of Leeds*). Quarterly, 1st and 4th, quarterly, erm. and az. a cross or, for OSBORNE; 2nd and 3rd, az. semée of crosses crosslet and three cinquefoils ar., for D'ARCY, all over the imperial eagle. *Crests*—1st: An heraldic tiger pass. or, tufted and maned sa., for OSBORNE; 2nd: A dolphin embowed sa., for GODOLPHIN; 3rd: On a chapeau gu. turned up erm. a bull sa. armed or, for D'ARCY. *Supporters*—Dexter, A griffin or; sinister, an heraldic tiger ar. each gorged with a ducal coronet az. *Motto*—Pax in bello.

Osborne (Hartlip Place, co. Kent, *temp.* Edward IV.; ELIZABETH, dau. of THOMAS OSBORNE, Esq., of Place House, Hartlip, and co-heiress of her brothers, *m.* 1810, RICHARD TYEDEN, of Milsted, in the same co., and devised her whole property at her decease, 1766, to her two daus., MARY and PHILLIPPA, the former of whom *m.* Rev. THOMAS BLAND, M.A., Vicar of Sittingbourne. At the death of WILLIAM BLAND, his cousin, Rev. HENRY GODFREY FAUSSET, *s.* to Hartlip, and took the name of OSBORNE). Quarterly, ar. and az. on a cross or, five annulets sa. in the 1st and 4th quarters an erm. spot. *Crest*—A demi ounce ramp. erm. pellettée, collared and lined.

Osborne (Osborne House, Spondon, co. Derby). Ar. a bend sa. betw. two lions ramp. gu. *Crest*—A demi lion ramp. gu.

Osborne (co. Derby). Or, on a bend betw. two wolves' heads erased sa. three dolphins of the first. *Crest*—A pelican in her nest feeding her young or.

Osborne (Cleby, co. Essex, and Kirkby Bydon, co. Norfolk). Ar. on a bend betw. two tigers salient sa. three dolphins or. *Crest*—Out of a ducal coronet or, a tiger's head sa. armed and crined of the first.

Osborne (co. Kent and London). Quarterly, erm. and gu. a cross or.

Osborne (Ashford, Kens, London, and Keyton, co. Notts; Lord Mayor of London, 1583; *Visit.* London, 1568, and *Visit.* Notts). Quarterly, erm. and az. a cross or. *Crest*—An heraldic tiger pass. or, tufted and maned sa. charged with a pellet.

Osborne (Kelmarsh, co. Northampton; of this family was Sir ROBERT OSBORNE, of Kilmarsh, an eminent lawyer, *temp.* Charles I.). Quarterly, erm. and az. a cross engr. or. *Crest*—A tiger pass. ar. crested and tufted sa. *Motto*—Pax in bello.

Osborne (St. Ives, co. Huntingdon; a branch of OSBORNE, of Kelmarsh). Same *Arms*, *Crest*, and *Motto*.

Osborne (London). Ar. a bend ermines betw. two lions ramp. sa. *Crest*—A lion's head erased ar. ducally crowned or.

Osborne (co. Norfolk). Ar. a bend betw. two tigers sa.

Osborne (Debenham, co. Suffolk). Sa. a griffin segreant betw. ten billets or. *Crest*—A unicorn pass. or, ducally gorged, ringed, lined, armed, and crined sa.

Osborne (London, *temp.* Henry VI.). Ar. on a bend cotised sa. three trouts or; another, Quarterly, ar. and az. in the 1st and 4th an erm. spot, in the 2nd and 3rd a cross or, charged with five annulets sa.; another, Az. a chev. erm. betw. three pelicans or, vulned gu.

Osborne. Gu. three dolphins or; another, Ar. on a bend betw. two tigers sa. armed and langued gu. three dolphins or; another, Gu. a bend betw. three dolphins or; another, Ar. on a bend cotised sa. three fishes of the field; another, Quarterly, ar. and az., the 1st and 4th quarters charged with an erm. spot, on a cross erminois five annulets gu.; another, Erm. two bars gu. on a chief of the last a lion pass. guard. or.

Osborne (Sir HEWET OSBORNE, knighted by ROBERT, *Earl of Essex*, Lord-Lieutenant of Ireland, in co. Meath, 23 July, 1599). Quarterly, erm. and az. a cross or.

Osborne (Fun. Ent. Ulster's Office, 1615, KATHERINE OSBORNE, wife of GEORGE SEXTON, Secretary to the Lord-Deputy of Ireland, Sir Arthur Chichester). Gu. on a fess ar. betw. two barrulets or, as many fountains, over all a bendlet of the second.

Osborne (Kiveton, co. York; impalement Fun. Ent. Ulster's Office, 1641, Right Hon. CHRISTOPHER WANDESFORD, Lord-Deputy of Ireland, whose second wife was ALICE, dau. of Sir HEWET OSBORNE, Knt., of Kiveton). Quarterly, erm. and az. on a cross or, five pellets.

Osborne (Beechwood, co. Tipperary). Gu. on a fess cotised or, two fountains, bend ar. *Crest*—A sea lion holding a trident. *Motto*—Pax in bello.

Osborne (BERNAL-OSBORNE, Newtown-Anner, co. Tipperary; KATHERINE ISABELLA OSBORNE, only dau. and heiress of Sir THOMAS OSBORNE, eighth bart. of Newtown-Anner, *m.* 1844, RALPH BERNAL, Esq., M.P., who assumed, by royal licence, 1844, the additional surname of OSBORNE). Quarterly, 1st and 4th, gu. on a fess or, cotised ar. two fountains, over all a bend of the third charged for diff. with a cross crosslet az., for OSBORNE; 2nd and 3rd, vair three chevronels or, on a canton gu. a tower ar., for BERNAL. *Crests*—1st, OSBORNE: A sea lion sejant ppr. supporting with the dexter paw a trident sa. headed or, and charged for diff. on the shoulder with a cross crosslet az.; 2nd, BERNAL: A demi lion per fess gu. and vair, langued az. holding a torch or, fired ppr. *Motto*—Pax.

O'Shanly. See MAC SHANLY.

O'Shaughnessy (a tribe who possessed a territory comprising the eastern half of the diocese of Kilmacduagh, co. Galway, deriving their name from SEACHNASACH, Chief of the Sept, A.D. 1100). Vert a tower triple-towered ar. from each tower a pennant flotant gu. supported by two lions ramp. combattant or. *Crest*—An arm in chain armour embowed, the hand grasping a spear shaft broken, all ppr.

O'Shaughnessy (Sir ROGER, or RORY, O'SHAUGHNESSY, Chief of his Sept, son of DERMOT REAGH O'SHAUGHNESSY, and grandson of GIRDUFF O'SHAUGHNESSY, was knighted, 1567, by Sir Henry Sydney, Lord-Deputy of Ireland). Same *Arms* and *Crest*.

O'Shea, or O'Shee (a Sept of the same race as O'CONNELL, who formerly possessed Hy-Rathach, now the barony of Iveragh, co. Kerry, and deriving their name from SEAGHA, Chief of the Sept; they afterwards branched into the cos. Tipperary, Kilkenny, and Waterford). Per bend indented az. and or, two fleurs-de-lis counterchanged. *Crest*—A swan rousant sa. beaked and legged gu.

O'Shee (Sheestown, co. Kilkenny, and Garden Morres, co. Waterford; Reg. Ulster's Office). Quarterly, 1st and 8th, per bend indented az. and or, two fleurs-de-lis counter changed; 2nd, gu. three swords fessways in pale ar. pommels and hilts or, the centre one pointing to the dexter, the other two to the sinister; 3rd, sa. three pheons ar. points down; 4th, gu. three swords ar. pommels and hilts or, two in saltire, points down, surmounted of the third in pale, point upwards; 5th, ar. a chev. erm. betw. three pheons sa. points down; 6th, per pale indented or and gu.; 7th, ar. three bars gu. a bend sa. *Crest*—A swan rousant sa. beaked and legged gu. *Motto*—Vincit veritas.

O'Shee (Paris; allowed by Fortescue, Ulster, 1790, to HENRY O'SHEE, Knt., of St. Louis, and Colonel of Horse, in the kingdom of France, descended from O'SHEE, of Sheestown). Quarterly, 1st and 6th, per bend indented az. and or, two fleurs-de-lis counterchanged, with the same quarterings as O'SHEE, of Sheestown). Same *Crest* and *Motto*.

O'Shee (Brussels; allowed by Fortescue, Ulster, 1793, to JOHN O'SHEE, Esq., then living at Brussels, fifth in descent from RICHARD O'SHEE, of Kilkenny, and ROSE, his wife, dau. of PETER ROTH). Per bend indented az. and or, two fleurs-de-lis counterchanged, quartering, 1st, gu. three swords barways in pale ar. pommels and hilts or, the centre one pointing to the dexter, the others to the sinister; 2nd, sa. three pheons, points down, ar.; 3rd, gu. three swords ar. pommels and hilts or, one in pale, point upwards, the others in saltire, points down. Same *Crest* and *Motto*.

O'Shee (Courtstown, co. Kilkenny; WILLIAM O'SHEE, Esq., of that place, A.D. 1600, descended from Sheestown, Reg. Ulster's Office). Per bend indented az. and or, two fleurs-de-lis counterchanged.

O'Sheehan (the Sept of O'SHIGHAN). Az. on a mount in base vert a dove ar. holding in the beak an olive branch ppr. *Crest*—A dove ar. holding in the beak an olive branch ppr.

O'Sheil (Castle Burg, co. Galway, and of Nantes, in the kingdom of France; allowed by Hawkins, Ulster, 1754, to LUKE O'SHEIL, of Nantes, great-great-grandson of LUKE O'SHEIL, Esq., of Castle Burg, who was great grandson of EDWARD O'SHEIL, Esq., of Draward, co. Tyrone). Same *Arms*. *Crest*—An arm erect couped at the wrist gu. enfiled with a ducal coronet or, and grasping a sword ppr. pommel and hilt gold. *Motto*—Omne solum forti patria.

O'Sheill (co. Tyrone; a Sept said to be of the line of O'NEILL, possessing a territory in co. Antrim: they derived their surname from SIAGHAIL, Chief of the Sept. The Four Masters record, under the year 1548, that "the only son of O'SIAGHAIL, *i.e.* MURTOGH, the best physician of his age in the surrounding neighbourhood," was slain by Mac Coghlan). Ar. a lion ramp. betw. two dexter hands couped at the wrist erect apaumée in chief and a mullet in base a l gu. *Crest*—Out of a ducal coronet or, an arm erect vested gu. holding a sword ppr. *Motto*—Omne solum forti patria.

Osmond (Coventry, and Barkeswell, co. Warwick). Or, on a pile az. an eagle displ. in chief of the field a fesse dancettée erm. *Crest*—Out of a mount vert a perch sa. thereon an eagl. displ. erm.

Osmond (Exeter, co. Devon). Sa. a fess dancettée erm. betw. two eagles displ. ar. a crescent for diff. *Crest*—An eagle or.

Osmond (Thorpe). Per pale az. and gu. three crescents ar.

Osmunderley, or Osmotherley (Langrigg, co. Cumberland; settled in the parish of Bromfield, *temp.* Edward I., and possessed of Langrigg since the time of Richard II. The last of the family, the Rev. SALKELD OSMUNDERLEY, sold the estate of Langrigg 1735). Ar. a fess betw. three martlets sa.

Osmond (Stagmill, co. Devon; HENRY OSMOND, grandson of THOMAS OSMOND, of Stagmill, left two daus. and co-heirs: ANNE, *m.* JOHN FOXWELL, of Exeter, and HESTER, *m.* JOHN FOXWELL, of Combralye. Visit. Devon, 1620). Sa. a fess dancettée erm. in chief an eagle displ. ar.

Osmond (Exeter, co. Devon; CHRISTOPHER OSMOND, aged 39, Visit. 1620, grandson of MICHAEL OSMOND, the second son of THOMAS OSMOND, of Stagmill). Same *Arms*, a crescent for diff.

Osney-Abbey (co. Oxford). Az. two bends or.

Osney (Louth, co. Lincoln). Az. a lion ramp. guard. within an orle of bells ar.

Osney (co. Worcester). Sa. a fess embattled ar.

Ospringe. Ar. on a fess betw. three bells gu. as many crosses crosslet of the first.

Ossam. Purp. a chev. (another, engr.) betw. three fleurs-de-lis or.

Ossory, See of. *Ancient*—Az. a bishop in his pontificals standing betw. two pillars ar. a mitre on his head, in dexter hand a crozier, and in sinister a Bible closed, all or. *Modern*—Gu. a covered cup, on the top thereof a cross pattée betw. five crosses pattée fitchée or.

Ostost, or Ostoft. Sa. three fishes' heads erased ar.

Ostotevill, or Ostotenvyll. Barry of ten ar. and gu. a lion ramp. sa.

Ostreete. Gu. a fess or.

Ostrehan (Rev. J. DUNCAN OSTREHAN, B.A., of Worcester College, Oxford). Ar. on a chev. gu. three hunters' horns or, betw. three lions ramp. gu.

Ostrich, or Austry (co. Hereford). Barry wavy of six ar. and az., on a chief gu. three plates.

Ostrich, or Ostreche (London). Gu. three fishes in pale betw. ten crosses crosslet fitchée ar. (another, crosses botonnée).

Ostrich. Barry wavy of six ar. and az., on a chief gu. three bezants.

Ostrich. Gu. three fishes haurient ar. betw. nine crosses crosslet fitchée of the second. *Crest*—An ostrich's head erased az. in his mouth a horseshoe or.

O'Sullivan (a Sept who originally possessed a territory in the co. Tipperary, but were driven out by the De Burghos, and settled in cos. Cork and Kerry; the name is derived from SCILLEABHRA, a Chieftain who flourished A.D. 950). Per fess the base per pale in chief or, a dexter hand couped at the wrist grasping a sword erect, pommel and hilt gu., the guard entwined with a serpent ppr. betw. two lions ramp. respecting each other of the second on the dexter base vert a stag trippant gold, on the sinister base per pale ar. and sa. a boar pass. counterchanged.

O'Sullivan Mor (the Chief of the senior line of the Sept was known as O'SULLIVAN MOR). Same *Arms*. *Crest*—On a ducal coronet or, a robin redbreast holding in the beak a sprig of laurel all ppr. *Motto*—Lamh foistenach abu (the open hand defying).

O'Sullivan Beare (the second branch of the Sept, settled at Bearra, co. Cork, now Bearhaven; their Chieftain was known as O'SULLIVAN BEARE). Per pale sa. and ar. a fess betw. in chief a boar pass. and in base another counterpass. all counterchanged; armed, hoofed, and bristled or. *Crest*—On a lizard vert a robin redbreast ppr.

O'Sullivan (Dunkerron, co. Kerry; Impalement Fun. Ent. Ulster's Office, 1639. JOHN O'CONNOR, Esq., of Carrigfoyle, in same co., whose wife was SHEELY O'SULLIVAN, dau. of OWEN O'SULLIVAN, of Dunkerron). Same *Arms*. *Crest*—Out a ducal coronet or, a lion's head ar. langued gu. *Motto*—Nec timeo nec sperno.

765

Oswald (England). Az. a cross bet ꝑ. four lions ramp. or. *Crest*—On a mount a stag lodged under a holly bush all ppr.

Oswald (Fingalton. co. Renfrew, 1672). Az. a savage wreathed head and middle with bay leaves, having a sheaf. of arrows hanging by his side, and bearing a bow in the sinister hand all ppr. and pointing with the other to a comet placed in the dexter chief point or. *Crest*—A dexter hand issuing out of a cloud and pointing to a star of eight rays ppr. *Motto*—Forti favet cœlum.

Oswald (Scotstown, co. Renfrew, 1764). As the last, within a bordure erm. *Crest*—A ship under sail ppr. *Motto*—Non mihi commodus uni.

Oswald (GORDON-OSWALD, Scotstown, 1865). Quarterly, 1st and 4th, as the last : 2nd, az. three boars' heads couped or, within a bordure per fesse ar. and of the second, and charged with three cushions gu., for GORDON; 3rd, quarterly, as HALDANE, of Gleneagles (*which see*), a bordure wavy ar. *Crest and Motto*, for OSWALD, as above. For GORDON, a dagger erect piercing a boar's head erased ppr. *Motto*—Non astutia.

Oswald (Auchincruive, co. Ayr, 1770). As Fingalton, within a bordure engr. or. *Crest*—A dexter hand issuing out of a cloud and pointing to a star ppr. *Motto*—Sequamur.

Oswald (HALDANE-OSWALD, of Auchincruive, 1861). Quarterly, 1st, as the last; 2nd, gu. three leopards in pale pass. guard. ar., for HALDANE, of that Ilk; 3rd, ar. a saltire engr. betw. four roses gu.; 4th, or, a bend chequy sa. and ar. *Additional Crest*—An eagle's head erased ppr. *Additional Motto*—Suffer. *Supporters*—Two eagles ppr. beaked and membered or.

Oswald (Dunnikier, co, Fife). Az. a savage ppr. wreathed with laurel, bearing in his sinister hand a baton erected on his shoulder vert, and in his dexter hand a cross staff, and pointing to a star placed in dexter chief or. *Crest*—A star of six points wavy ar. *Motto*—Monstrant viam.

Oswald (Dalderne, co. Sterling). Az. a savage ppr. wreathed with laurel bearing in his sinister hand a baton erected on his shoulder vert, and pointing with the dexter to a comet or, placed in dexter chief. *Crest*—A comet or. *Motto*—Monstrant astra viam.

Oswalde. Az. a cross flory or, betw. four lions ramp. ar.

Oswaldkirke. Ar. two lions pass. guard. sa.

Oswalstre. Ar. a lion ramp. gu., over all a bend of the first charged with three mullets sa.

Oswynde, or Oswyn. Gu. three ducal coronets or.

Oswell (co. Devon; the dau. and heir *m.* ORWET). Erm. three bars az.

Oteley. Ar. on a bend az. three oat sheaves or.

Otes (Shipdon). Az. a saltire ar. betw. four crosses crosslet fitchée or.

O'Toole (a Sept possessed of a territory in the southern half of the co. Kildare, called Hy Muireadhaigh, or Hy Muirthi, from which they were driven shortly after the invasion of 1172, into Imail, in the present co. Wicklow, and afterwards into Feara Cualann, in same co. ; the residences of the chiefs were O'Toole's Castle, now Talbots Town in Imail, and Powerscourt, in Feara Cuallann. They derived their surname from Tuathal, King of Leinster, at. A.D. 950. Of this Sept was ST. LAWRENCE O'TOOLE, Archbishop of Dublin, d. in Normandy 1180, son of MORTOGH O'TOOLE, Chief of Imail). Gu. a lion pass. ar. *Crest*—A boar pass. ppr.

O'Toole (Wicklow, afterwards of Edermine and Curracloe, co. Wexford; Reg. Ulster's Office). Same *Arms*. *Crest*—A lion ramp. ar. holding a forked pennon gu. *Motto*—Spero.

O'Toole (Buckstown, co. Wexford; now represented by HALL, of Hollybush, co. Derby, of this line was JOHN, Count O'Toole *m.* Lady KATHERINE ANNESLEY, dau. of RICHARD, 6th *Earl of Anglesey*). Same *Arms*, &c. See HALL, of Hollybush.

Otgher. Az. a fesse embattled betw. three martlets ar. *Crest*—A martlet, wings expanded ar.

Otoft, or Otost. Az. a chev. or, betw. three bezants.

Ottarburn. Gu. a crescent or.

Otteby (co. Lincoln.). Gu. two bars ar. betw. three plates.

Otteby, or Ottsby. Purp. two bars ar. in chief three plates.

Otteley (Lord Mayor of London, 1434). Ar. three lions' heads erased sa. a bordure engr. of the last.

Otteley, or Oteley (co. Suffolk). Ar. three lion's heads erased sa. (another, az.); another, Same *Arms*. within a border sa.

Ottenbury (co. York). Gu. (another, az.) on an escallop or, a cock of the second.

Otter (co. Huntingdon). Or on a bend gu. three crescents of the first. *Crest*—A crescent or.

Otter (Welham, co. Nottingham; represented by Rev. GEORGE OTTER, M.A., vicar of Hucknall Forkard, co. Nottingham, nephew of Right Rev. WILLIAM OTTER, D.D., *Bishop of Chichester*, 1837). Same *Arms*. *Crest*— A crescent or. *Motto*—Watch.

Otterborne (co. York). Ar. on a chief engr. gu. three crosses crosslet fitchée or; another, Gu. a crescent or.

Otterburn (Red Hall, Scotland). Ar. guttée sa. a chev. betw. three otters' heads couped of the last, on a chief az. a crescent or.

Otterbury. Az. a dunghill cock perched upon an escallop or.

Otterby, Otby, and Otteby (co. Lincoln). Gu. two bars ar. in chief three plates.

Otterington (Dublin; confirmed to Alderman JOHN OTTERINGTON, of that city, 1684). Per pale or and az. a chev. betw. three annulets, all counterchanged. *Crest*—On a tun lying fessways or, an otter pass. sa.

Ottetez, or Ottys. Az. a saltire engr. ar. betw. four crosses crosslet fitchée or.

Ottewell, or Ottiwell. Ar. three magpies ppr.

Ottley (Ottley, co. Salop; the heiress, ELIZABETH, dau. of RICHARD OTTLEY, Esq., of Ottley, *m.* HUMPHREY KYNASTON, of Stoke, 2 Henry V.). Ar. on a bend az. three oat sheaves or. *Crest*—An oat sheaf or, banded vert.

Ottley (Pichford, co. Salop; ADAM OTLEY, Esq., of Pichford, the last male heir, *d.* 1807. Visit. Salop). Same *Arms* and *Crest*.

Ottley. Ar. on a cross flory az. a lion pass. guard. or. *Crest*—A demi lion or, holding a branch vert.

Ottley (St. Christopher's, St. Vincent's, and Antigua in the West Indies, descended from OTTLEY, of Pitchford, co. Salop. DREWRY OTTLEY, Esq., of ARTHUR OTTLEY, who was *b.* 1648, and *d.* 1705, was Treasurer of the Island of St. Christopher and, in 1714 a Member of the House of Assembly; from him descend the existing branches). Per bend or and ar. on a bend nebulée betw. two cross crosslets az. three garbs bendways of the first. *Crest*—In front of a garb or, three arrows, two in saltire, one in pale, points downwards sa. *Motto*—Dat Deus incrementum.

Ottley (Delaford, co. Dublin; descended from DREWRY OTTLEY, Treasurer of St. Christophers). Same *Arms*, *Crest*, and *Motto*.

Ottys. Az. a cross engr. ar. betw. four crosslets fitchée or.

Ottys. Ar. a saltire engr. betw. four crosses crosslets fitchée az.

Otway (Ingmire Hall and Middleton, co. Westmoreland; Sir JOHN OTWAY, Knt., of Ingmire, *b.* 1618; a Bencher of Gray's Inn, Vice-Chancellor and Attorney General of the co. Palatine of Lancaster, was knighted at Whitehall 20 June, 1673, and *d.* without surviving male issue 1697; his elder dau. ANNE OTWAY, *m.* 1st, JOHN WARDEN, Esq., of Burnchurch, co. Kilkenny; and 2nd, AGMONDESHAM CUFFE, Esq., of Desart, same co., by whom she had JOHN, first *Lord Desart;* the youngest dau. KATHERINE OTWAY, *m.* WILLIAM UPTON, Esq., of Upton, ancestor of UPTON of Ingmire Hall). Ar. a pile sa. over all a chev. counterchanged. *Crest*—Out of a ducal coronet or, two wings expanded sa.

Otway (Cloghonan, afterwards Castle Otway, co. Tipperary; JOHN OTWAY, Esq., had a grant of that place 1665, and *m.* PHŒBE, dau. of NICHOLAS LOFTUS, Esq., of Fethard, co. Wexford; his eldest surviving son, THOMAS OTWAY, Esq., of Lisson Hall, was grandfather of COOKE OTWAY, Esq., of Castle Otway, whose son and heir, HENRY OTWAY, Esq., of Castle Otway, *m.* SARAH, dau. and heiress of Sir THOMAS CAVE, 6th bart., of Stamford, afterwards *Baroness Braye* in her own right, and was father of Hon. ROBERT OTWAY-CAVE, M.P., co. Tipperary, who *d. s. p.* 1844). Ar. a pile az. over all a chev. sa. counterchanged of the field. *Crest*—Out of a ducal coronet or, two wings expanded sa. *Motto*—Si Deus nobiscum quis contra nos.

Otway (Brighthelmstone, co. Sussex, bart.; heir male of OTWAY, of Castle Otway. Admiral Sir ROBERT OTWAY, G.C.B., second son of COOKE OTWAY, Esq., of Castle Otway, was created a bart. 1831). Ar. a pile sa. a chev. counterchanged. *Crest*—Out of a ducal coronet or, two wings erect sa. *Supporters*—(granted to the first bart. by royal licence 16 June, 1845, to descend with the baronetcy). On either side a triton blowing his shell ppr. navally crowned or, across the shoulder a wreath of red coral, and holding in the exterior hand a trident points downwards sa. *Motto*—Si Deus nobiscum quis contra nos.

766

Otway (Castle Otway; ROBERT JOCELYN OTWAY, Capt. R.N., second son of Rev. SAMUEL JOCELYN OTWAY, who was third son of COOKE OTWAY, Esq., of Castle Otway, *s.* to that estate under the will of the widow of Hon. ROBERT OTWAY-CAVE, 1849). Ar. a pile az. over all a chev. sa. counterchanged of the field. *Crest* and *Motto* same as the last.

Otway (Kilnacarr, Rapla, and Nenagh, co. Tipperary; descended from JAMES OTWAY, Esq., of Kilnacarr, youngest son of JOHN OTWAY, Esq., of Cloghonan, by PHŒBE LOFTUS, his wife, now represented by JOHN HASTINGS OTWAY, Esq., Q.C., Chairman of Quarter Sessions, co. Antrim, and Recorder of Belfast, eldest son of the late Rev. CÆSAR OTWAY by FRANCES HASTINGS, his wife, sister, and in her issue heiress of Rev. ANTHONY HASTINGS, of Lurgvall, co. Donegal, J.P.). Same *Arms*, *Crest*, and *Motto*, quartering, Ar. a maunch sa., for HASTINGS.

Otway (Otway Towers, co. Herts; exemplified to WILLIAM-JOHN-MAJORIBANKS HUGHES, Esq., of Cumberland Street, London, who *m.* 1837, GEORGIANA FRANCES, only dau. of Gen. Sir LOFTUS WILLIAM OTWAY, K.C.B., and who assumed by royal licence, 1873, the surname of OTWAY). Quarterly, 1st and 4th, ar. a pile sa. over all a chev. counterchanged and for distinction in the centre chief point a cross crosslet of the first, for OTWAY; 2nd and 3rd, gu. a chev. or, betw. in chief two morions and in base as many swords saltirewise points upwards ppr. pomels and hilts gold, for HUGHES. *Crests*— 1st, OTWAY: Out of a ducal coronet a passion cross or, betw. two wings sa. each charged for distinction with a cross crosslet ar.; 2nd, HUGHES: Upon the battlements of a tower an arm in armour fesswise couped holding in the hand a sword erect betw. two branches of oak all ppr. *Motto*— Semper viligans.

Otway (confirmed by Fortescue, Ulster, to Capt. WILLIAM ALBANY OTWAY, R.N.). Ar. on a pile az. charged with a naval crown or, a chev. counterchanged ar. and sa. *Crest*— Out of a ducal coronet or, two wings expanded sa. *Motto*— Si Deus nobiscum quis contra nos.

Ouge. Or, a chev. vert.

Oughton (Scotland; as borne by Sir ADOLPHUS OUGHTON, installed Knight of the Bath 19 May, 1779). Per pale gu. and az. over all a lion ramp. or, guttée de sang. *Crest*—A tower, the sinister side battlement broken all ppr. thereout a sprig of laurel vert the tower charged on the centre with a grenade sa. fired ppr. *Supporters*—Two lions or, guttée de sang, each gorged with a plain collar pean. *Motto*—Nescit abolere vetustas.

Oughton. Per pale gu. and az. a lion ramp. or. *Crest*—An eagle's head or.

Oughton. Same *Arms*. *Crest*—A tower ruined in the sinister top, and therefrom issuing a branch of laurel ppr. *Motto*—Nescit abolere vetustas.

Oughtred. Or, on a cross patonce gu. five escallops of the first (another, tinctures reversed).

Oulane (co. York). Ar. a chev. sa. betw. three pellets.

Ouldesworth. Gu. on a fess cotised ar. three lions pass. purp. *Crest*—A lion sejant gu. resting the forepaw on a shield or.

Ouldfield (co. Lincoln). Or, on a pile vert three garbs of the first. *Crest*—On a garb or, a dove ar. in the beak an ear of wheat of the first.

Ouldfield. Gu. a lion ramp. ar. on a bend sa. three crosses potent fitchée of the first.

Ouldgrent, or Ouldgrove. Az. a fess engr. erm. betw. three owls ar. membered or.

Ouldhaugh. Ar. a fret or.

Ouldsworth (co. Gloucester). Gu. on a fess betw. three billets ar. as many lions pass. guard. of the first. *Crest*— A lion sejant gu. resting the forepaw on a carved shield or.

Ouldsworth (Poulton, co. Gloucester). Gu. on a fess betw. three fleurs-de-lis ar. as many lions pass. guard. of the first.

Ouldsworth (Wotton, co. Gloucester). Gu. on a fess betw. three billets ar. as many lions pass of the first. *Crest* —Out of a ducal coronet a plume of ostrich feathers ppr.

Oulond, Ouland, or Olound. Or, six annulets sa. two, two, and two.

Oulry. Or, three owls in fess sa. *Crest*—An owl sa. betw. two wings endorsed, the dexter or, the sinister of the first.

Oulton (Oulton, co. Chester). Quarterly, az. and gu. a lion ramp. ar.

Oulton (co. Chester). Quarterly, vert and gu. (another, vert and or) a lion ramp. ar.

Oulton, or Owlton. Per pale az. and gu. a lion ramp. or. *Crest*—A martlet ar.

Ounell. Ar. three mullets gu., a label of as many points az.

Ourry. Az. upon a mount in base ppr. a chameleon **statant** or, in chief the sun in splendour of the second.

Oursone, or Ourston (co. Norfolk). Ar. **a bend gu.** bezantée.

Ousefoot. Az. on a bend ar. three mullets gu.

Ouseley (Courteen Hall, co. Northampton; descended from co. Salop). Or, a chev. sa. betw. three holly leaves vert a chief sa. Crest, same as the last.

Ouseley (Claremont, co. Herts, bart.; descended from Sir JOHN OUSELEY, of Courteen Hall, co. Northampton, who fell at the siege of Breda, in 1624). Same Arms. Crest—Out of a ducal coronet or, a wolf's head erased sa., holding in the mouth a bleeding hand gu. couped at the wrist. Supporters (borne by Sir GEORGE GORE OUSELEY, first bart. as a G.C.B.)—Two Indian warriors ppr. Motto—Mors lupi agnis vita.

Ouseley (Sir JOHN OUSELEY, knighted at Reban, co. Kildare, 24 March, 1604, by Sir George Cary, Lord Deputy of Ireland). Or, a chev. sa. betw. three holly leaves vert a chief of the second. Crest—Out of a ducal coronet or, a wolf's head ar.

Ousley (co. Stafford). Ar. a talbot pass. gu.

Ouston (Scotland). Gu. a crescent betw. two stars barways in chief, and three stars barways in base ar.

Outhred. Ar. on a cross pattée gu. five mullets pierced or.

Outlawe (Little Wichingham, co. Norfolk; assigned June, 1613). Ar. a saltire gu. betw. four wolves' heads couped ppr. Crest —A demi wolf ppr. pierced through the side with an arrow or, feathered and headed ar. the arrow lying bend sinisterways.

Outram (Edinburgh, bart.). Or, on a chev. embattled betw. three crosses flory gu. five escallops of the first. Crest—Out of an eastern crown a demi lion or, gorged with a wreath of laurel ppr. holding betw. the paws a cross flory gu. Supporters—On either side a royal Bengal tiger guard. ppr. gorged with a wreath of laurel vert, and on the head an eastern crown or ; granted to Sir JAMES OUTRAM, first bart., created G.C.B., 1857, d. 1863. Motto—Mutare fidem nescio.

Ouvry (a noble refugee French family, from Picardy, in Normandy, represented by Rev. PETER THOMAS OUVRY, rector of Grove, and vicar of Wing, co. Bucks). Quarterly, 1st and 4th, ar. a lion ramp. sa. crowned, armed, and langued gu., for OUVRY; 2nd and 3rd, per pale or and az. barry of six, on a chief a pale betw. two esquires all counterchanged, over all an inescutcheon ar., for GARNAULT.

Ovedale (co. Hants). Az. fretty or.

Over. Or, on a bend az. a fret of the first. Crest—A bird rising or, beaked and membered gu. holding in the beak an olive branch vert fructed or.

Overbury, or Overbery (Aston-Underedge, co. Gloucester). Sa. three mullets betw. two bendlets ar. Crest —A lion's gamb erect ar. encircled in a ducal coronet or.

Overend. Ar. on a chev. gu. betw. three pheons sa. as many frogs or.

Overman (co. Norfolk). Az. on a bend or, two fleurs-de-lis of the field, on a chief of the second a lion pass. gu. Crest— A leopard sejant ppr. holding in the dexter paw a fleur-de-lis or.

Overman (Southwark, co. Surrey). Az. a chev. betw. three fleurs-de-lis or, on a chief of the last a lion pass. guard. gu. Crest—A leopard sejant ppr. holding in the paw a fleur-de-lis or.

Overton (Somersham, co. Huntington, cos. Warwick and Lincoln. Visit. Warwick, 1619). Az. a chev. erm. betw. three unicorns' heads erased ar. armed and crined or.

Overton (Lea, co. Leicester). Ar. a bend az. betw. a rose in chief and a fleur-de-lis in base gu.

Overton (Morecot, co. Rutland. Visit. 1618). Ar. a cross formée gu. Crest—A maiden's head ppr. vested gu. crined or.

Overton (co. Westmorland). Az. a bend or, a border ar.

Overton (co. York). Az. a fess wavy gu. betw. three magpies ppr.

Overton. Ar. a bend sa. in chief a rose gu. in base a fleur-de-lis of the last; another, Az. a bend or, a border of the last. Crest—On a chapeau gu. turned up erm. a martlet sa.

Overton. Lozengy ar and az. on a chief ar. a saltire gu. charged with five bezants betw. two mullets in pale of the fourth; another, Sa. a chev. betw. three peacocks' heads erased ar.; another, Ar. on a bend sa. three crosses crosslet or.

Overy. Or, three martlets az. Crest—A bull's head az.

Ovingham, or Owingham. Per chev. sa. and erm. in chief two covered cups ar. (another, or.)

Ovington (co. Kent). Sa. three cocks or, membered gu.

Ovington. Gu. on a bend ar. three mullets (another, martlets) sa.

Owen Gwynedd (Prince of North Wales, d. Dec. 1169, son of GRIFFITH AP CYNAN, Prince of North Wales, descended from ÍVARAWD, King of North Wales, eldest son of RHODRI MAWR, King of Wales). Vert, three eagles displ. in fess or.

Owen Tudor (son of MEREDITH AP TUDOR, and grandson of Sir TUDOR AP GRONO, Knt., descended from GRONO, Lord of Trefgastell in Anglesey, eldest son of EDNYFED VYCHAN, Lord of Brynffenigl, representative of MARCHUDD AP CONAN, Founder of the VIII. Noble Tribe of North Wales and Powys; OWEN TUDOR was ancestor of the Royal House of TUDOR). Gu. a chev. erm. betw. three esquires' helmets ar.

Owen (Orielton, co. Pembroke, bart. ; descended from HWFA-AP-CYNDDELW, Lord of Llys, Llifon, co. Anglesey, Steward to OWEN GWYNEDD, Prince of North Wales). Gu. a chev. betw. three lions ramp. or. Crest—A lion ramp. or. Motto— Honestas optima politia.

Owen Brogyntyn (Lord of Edeirnion, Dinmael, and Abertanat, in Powys-Fadoc, younger son of MADOC AP MEREDITH, last Prince of Powys-Fadoc. OWEN BROGYNTYN was one of the most distinguished warriors of his age. Entering with his brothers into an alliance with OWEN GWYNEDD, Prince of North Wales, and RHYS AP TEWDWR, Prince of South Wales, to resist the renewed attempt of Henry II. of England on the principality, contributed materially to the victory obtained over the English in 1165, at the battle of Crogen. "Beneath Castelh Crogen," the present Chirk Castle, whence the battle field is still called "Adwyr Beddall," or the Pass of the Graves, OWEN BROGYNTYN made a grant to God, St. Mary, and the monks of Basing Werk Abbey, of a "certain water in Penthlinn, called Tehlentegil, or Pemblemere, (Bala Lake in Merioneth) and all the pasture of the said land of Penthlinn." From this chieftain derived: I. The HUGHES's, of Gwerclas, Barons of Kymmer-yn-Edeirnion; II. LLOYDS, of Dolyglessyn ; III. LLOYDS, of Crogen; IV. MORRIS, of Pale; V. BRANAS, of Branas; VI. FOULKS, of Cilan; VII. OWENS, of Plas-Isaa; VIII. The Barons of Cryniarth; IX. The Barons of Crogen and Branas; X. The Barons of Hendwr; XI. LLOYDS, of Tyfos; XII. RHYS's, Barons of Rûg; XIII. MAESMORES, of Maesmor; XIV. WYNNS, of Pentre Morgan; XV. VAUGHANS, of Duddleston; XVI. LLOYDS, of Ebnal). Arms, those of his father, MADOC AP MEREDITH, viz. Ar. a lion ramp. sa. armed and langued gu.

Owen ap Griffith Vychan (Lord of Glyndwrdwy in Merioneth, the OWEN GLENDOWER, of English writers; representative of GRIFFITH MAELOR, Lord of Bromfield, eldest son of MADOC, last Prince of Powys-Fadoc, he had five daughters, viz. I. ISABEL, m. ADDA AP IORWORTH; II. ELIZABETH, m. Sir JOHN SCUDAMORE, Knt., of Ewyas, Holme Lacy, and Kent Church, co. Hereford; III. JANET, m. JOHN CROFT, of Croft Castle, co. Hereford; IV. JANE, m. HUMPHREY, Lord Ruthyn ; V. MARGARET, m. ROGER MORNINGTON, of Mornington, co. Hereford). The hereditary Arms of OWEN GLENDOWER, were those of GRIFFITH MAELOR, viz., Paly of eight ar. and gu. a lion ramp. sa., but he assumed, with the claim to and title of King of Wales, the arms of LLEWELYN AP GRIFFITH, Prince of North Wales, as appears by his privy seal presented to the Cymwradorion Society by Sir Samuel Rush Meyrick, viz., Quarterly or and gu. four lions pass. counterchanged.

Owen ap Griffith (last Prince of Powys-Wenwynwyn; descended from GRIFFITH, second son of MEREDITH AP BLEDDYN, Prince of Powys; HAWYS GADARN, his dau. and heir m. JOHN DE CHERLTON, eldest son of Sir ALLAN CHERLTON, of Apley Castle, co. Salop, was summoned, 26 July, 1313, to Parliament as Baron Charlton). Arms, those of BLEDDYN AP CYNFIN, King of Powys, viz., Or, a lion ramp. gu. armed and langued az.

Owen (Plas-Issa in Edeirnion, co. Merioneth; descended from OWEN AP ROBERT, second son of ROBERT AP REINALLT, of Branas-yn-Edeirnion, who was the descendant of RHYS AP IEVAN, Baron of Kynmer, Crogen, and Branas, ancestor of the HUGHES's of Gwerclas, Barons of Kymmer-yn-Edeirnion. The male line terminated with ROBERT WYNN, Esq., of Plas-Issa, who left two sisters and co-heirs, I. REBECCA, m. JOHN LLOYD, Esq., of Pontriffith, co. Flint, and from this marriage descends Lord Mostyn; II. ELIZABETH, m. JOHN LLOYD, Esq., of Forest). Arms, those of HUGHES, of Gwerclas, viz., Ar. a lion ramp. sa. armed and langued gu.

Owen (Cevn Havod and Glansevern, co. Montgomery; descended from KADIVOR AP DYNIAWAL, the captor of Cardigan Castle, 1164, descended from RHODRI MAWR, King of Wales. The representative of this family, WILLIAM OWEN, Esq., of Glan Severn, third son of

·Owen Owen, Esq., of Cevn Hafod, and brother of Sir Arthur Davies Owen, Knt., of Glan Severn, bequeathed his property, 1837, to his widow, Anne-Warburton, only child of Captain Thomas Slaughter). Sa. a tilting spear erect or, the head ppr. embrued gu. betw. three scaling ladders ar. on a chief erm. a fort triple-towered also ppr., quartering 1st, erm. a lion ramp. sa. within a bordure gu. semée of mulletsar. for the heiress of Cefn Havod, derived from Madoc Danwr ; 2nd, az. a lion ramp. guard. or, for Evans, of Rhyd y Carw ; 3rd, sa. three nags' heads erased ar., for Davies, of Llivor. Crest—A wolf salient ppr. supporting a ladder of the arms. Motto—Frangi non flecti.

Owen (Humphreys-Owen, Glansevern, co. Montgomery). Sa. a tilting spear erect or, the head ppr. imbrued gu. betw. three scaling ladders ar. on a chief erm. a fort triple-towered also ppr. Crest—A wolf salient ppr. supporting a scaling ladder as in the arms. Motto—Frangi non flecti.

Owen (Rhin Saeson, co. Montgomery ; descended from Ethelystan Glodrydd, Prince of Ferlys, whose heiress, Anne, sister of Corbet Owen, Esq., marrying Price Maurice, Esq., of Lloran, was mother of Edward Maurice, of Ynysymaengwyn. Arms, those of Ethelystan Glodrydd, viz., Per bend sinister erm. and ermines a lion ramp. or.

Owen (Glynafon, co. Anglesey ; descended from Llywarch ap Bran Lord of Menai, founder of the II. Noble Tribe of North Wales, and Powys, who was descended from Rhodri Mawr, King of all Wales, a.d. 843). Ar. a chev. sa. betw. three ravens ppr. with bait in their beaks. Crest—A raven ppr. with bait in the beak. Motto—Deus pascit corvos.

Owen (Bodsilin, Malldraeth, co. Anglesey). Quarterly, 1st and 4th, gu. a chev. betw. three lions ramp. or; 2nd, gu. a chev. erm. betw. three human heads in profile couped ar. hair and beard sa. ; 3rd, gu. a chev. betw. three stags' heads cabossed ar. attired or.

Owen (Clenneney, co. Carnarvon, and Porkington, co. Salop; descended from Sir John Owen, Knt., of Clenneney, Colonel in the Army, and Vice-Admiral of North Wales, son of John Owen, Esq., secretary to Lord Walsingham; the eventual heiress, Margaret Owen, dau. of William Owen, Esq., of Porkington, m. 1777, Owen Ormsby, Esq., of Willowbrook, co. Sligo, and left at her decease, in 1806, an only dau. Mary Jane Ormsby, m. 1815, William Gore, Esq., who assumed the additional surname of Ormsby, and was mother of Lord Harlech). Gu. a chev. betw. three lions ramp. or.

Owen (Llunllo, co. Montgomery ; an ancient Welsh family, descended from Grono ap Owen, second son of Owen ap Howell Dda, King of South Wales ; Rowland Owen, Esq., of Llunllo, High Sheriff co. Montgomery, 1611, was the first of this family who assumed the surname of Owen, he was son and heir of Owen ap John, who was grandson of David Lloyd ap Owen, the eldest son of Owen ap Griffith, of Llunllo ; Thomas Owen, Esq., of Llunllo, the great-grandson of Rowland Owen, the Sheriff in 1611, was succeeded by his eldest son, Thomas Owen, Esq., of Llunllo, whose male line failed, and his grand-dau. and heir m. John Herbert, Esq., of Dolvorgan, in same co.). Ar. a lion ramp. sa. a canton of the last.

Owen (Bettws, co. Montgomery ; descended from William Owen, Esq., of Bettws, second son of Thomas Owen, Esq., of Llunllo, and brother of Thomas Owen, Esq., of same place, 1611, whose male line failed ; Hugh Darby Owen, Esq., of Bettws, is the male heir and representative of Owen of Llunllo). Ar. a lion ramp. sa. a canton of the last, quartering, ar. a cross flory engr. sa. betw. four Cornish choughs ppr. on a chief az. a boar's head couped of the first tusked or, langued gu. Crests—1st : A Cornish chough ppr. holding in the dexter claw a fleur-de-lis ar.; 2nd : Two eagles' heads conjoined and erased per fess or and gu. membered also gu.

Owen (Tedsmore, co. Salop, extinct in the male line; Hugh Owen, Esq., of Tedsmore, b. 1706, third son of Thomas Owen, Llunllo, d. s. p. 1764, and bequeathed Tedsmore to his sister, Sarah, wife of Richard Bulkeley Hatchett, whose second son, Hugh Hatchett, assumed the surname of Owen). Quarterly, 1st and 4th, ar. a cross flory engr. sa. betw. four Cornish choughs ppr. on a chief az. a boar's head couped of the first, tusked or, langued gu., quartering, Ar. a lion ramp. sa. a canton of the last, for Owen ; 2nd and 3rd, sa. a chev. betw. three bulls' heads cabossed ar., for Bulkeley. Crest—Out of a ducal coronet or, a bull's head ar. armed gold. Motto—Ceidw Owain a Gafodd; also, Nec temere nec timide.

Owen (Woodhouse, co. Salop, extinct in the male line; descended from Howell ap Owen, second son of Owen ap Griffith, of Llunllo ; John Owen, Esq., of Woodhouse, d.

1737, leaving two daus. co-heirs, who both d. s. p., the estates eventually devolved on William Mostyn, who assumed the surname of Owen; he was grandson of William Mostyn, by Mary Kynaston, his wife, only dau. and heir of Humphrey Kynaston, Esq., of Bryngwyn, and Martha Owen, his wife, sister of the last John Owen, Esq., of Woodhouse). Ar. a lion ramp. sa. a canton of the last. Crest—Two eagles' heads conjoined and erased per fess or and gu. membered also gu.

Owen (Condover, co. Salop, extinct in the male line; descended from Richard ap Owen, third son of Owen ap Griffith, of Llunllo ; Thomas Owen, Esq., of Condover, the last male descendant of this line, d. unm. 1731, leaving his sister, Letitia Owen, his heir, who m. Richard Mytton, Esq., and had a dau., Anna Maria Mytton, m. Sir Charlton Leighton, third bart. of Loton, and had, inter alios, a dau. Anna Maria Leighton, to whom her grandmother bequeathed Condover. She m. Nicholas Smythe, Esq., and had, with other issue, Nicholas Smythe, who assumed the surname of Owen, d. s. p., and Caroline Elizabeth, m. Charles Cholmondeley, brother of the first Lord Delamere ; her grandson, Reginald Cholmondeley, Esq., of Condover, enjoys the estates). Ar. a lion ramp. sa. a canton of the last. Crest—Two eagles' heads conjoined and erased or, membered gu.

Owen-ap-Madoc (Wales). Ar. three ravens' legs erased sa. meeting in the fess point, talons gu. extended in the dexter chief, sinister chief, and centre base points of the escutcheon.

Owen-ap-Meredith. Gu. a chev. erm. betw. three helmets ar.

Owen (Garth Angharad, Caerbellan, &c., co. Merioneth ; descended from Lewis Owen, Esq., one of the Barons of the Welsh Exchequer, and Vice-Chamberlain of Wales, who was murdered near Dinas Mawddwy, co. Merioneth, on Christmas Eve, 1554). Quarterly, 1st and 4th, az. a chev. betw. three cocks ar. armed, crested, and jelloped or ; 2nd and 3rd, gu. three snakes nowed az. Crest—A cock's head erased ar. holding a snake az. in his mouth.

Owen. Ar. a lion ramp. sa. ducally crowned gu. Crest—An eagle's head erased at the neck or ; another, Gu. a cross or ; another, Or, a cross gu.; another, Barry of six or and gu.; another, Gu. a cross ar. in the dexter quarter an inescutcheon or, charged with three chev. of the first : another, Gu. a chev. erm. betw. three men's heads erased ar. each guttée de sang ; another, Gu. a chev. erm. betw. three heads in profile in helmets ar.; another, Per chev. or and az. three roses in chief gu. stalked and slipped ppr.; another, Az. semée of roses, a lion ramp. or; another, Per pale ar. and gu. a lion ramp. sa.

Owen. Or, an anchor in fess sa. betw. two lions pass. gu. Crest—An anchor sa. on the base thereof a lion ..... nt gu.

Owen (Godstone, co. Oxford; Richard Owen, Visit. 1566, eldest son of George Owen, of same place. William Owen, of Oxford city, second son of the same). Ar. a chev. erm. betw. three Cornish choughs sa. quartering per chev. or and az. in chief two roses gu. slipped and leaved vert, in base a feather erect ar. Crest—An arm erect couped below the elbow, vested gu. cuffed erm. holding a wreath of laurel vert.

Owen (co. Salop). Vert a chev. betw. three wolves' heads erased ar. Crest—A wolf pass. ar.

Owen (Shrewsbury, co. Salop). Sa. three nags' heads erased ar.

Owen (Wales). Per bend ar. and sa. a lion ramp. counterchanged.

Owen (Wrexham, co. Denbigh ; quartered by Rogers-Harrison). Az. a lion ramp. double queued sa. a canton az. thereon a rose of the first, slipped ppr.

Owen (John Owen, Esq., banker, of Worcester). Ar. a chev. betw. three ravens' legs erased à la quise sa. Crest—An eagle's neck with two heads couped ppr.

Owen (co. Gloucester). Per pale az. and sa. a chev. betw. three fleurs-de-lis or. Crest—Out of a mural coronet or, a lion's gamb. sa. holding a fleur-de-lis of the first.

Owen (co. Kent, London, and co. Salop). Ar. a lion ramp. sa. a canton of the second. Crest—An eagle's head erased at the neck or.

Owen (co. Oxford). Ar. a chev. erm. betw. three Cornish choughs sa. Crest—A cubic arm erect. vested az. cuffed erm. holding in the hand ppr. a chaplet vert.

Owen (co. Oxford). Per chev. or and az. in chief three roses gu. stalked vert, in base a feather ar.

Owen (Adbrightly, co. Salop). Or. a lion ramp. gu. Crest—A demi dragon gu. winged or.

Owen (co. Pembroke). Gu. a boar ar. armed, bristled, collared, and chained or, tied to a holly bush on a mount in base, both ppr. *Crest*—An eagle's head erased at the neck or.

Owen (Dublin, originally from co. Merioneth; granted by Betham, Ulster, to Jacob Owen, Esq., of Dublin, Architect to H.M. Board of Works in Ireland). Az. on a mount vert an Ionic pillar ar. base and capital or, supported by two lions counter-ramp. of the last. *Crest*—A demi lion ramp. gu. armed and langued az. supporting an Ionic pillar as in the arms. *Motto*—Firmitas in cœlo.

Owendelle, or Owyndale. Ar. two bars sa. on a chief vair (another, vert) three crosses pattée or.

Owens. Gu. six pineapples or. *Crest*—Out of a ducal coronet sa. a beech tree vert.

Owens (Holestone, co. Antrim; granted by Betham, Ulster, to James Owens, Esq., of Holestone). Gu. on a mount in base vert a boar pass. ar. armed, collared, and chained or, to a hollybush ppr. on a canton of the third three ravens' legs erased meeting in the fess point sa. *Crest*—A boar pass. ppr. collared and chained or, as in the arms. *Motto*—Inutilis vis est.

Owgan, or Ougan (co. Pembroke). Or, on a chief sa. three martlets of the field.

Owgan (Sir John Owgan, knighted by Sir John Perrott, Lord Deputy of Ireland, 1588). Or, on a chief sa. three martlets of the field. *Crest*—A cockatrice close gu. legged and beaked sa. crested or.

Owle (Visit. Notts; quartered by Flower). Or, three owls sa.

Owslett. Or, on a bend sa. three mullets of the field.

Owthred (co. York). Or, on a cross pattée gu. five mullets of the field.

Owtred. Ar. on a cross flory gu. four mullets (another, pierced) or.

Owtred. Gu. on a cross patonce or, five mullets of the first.

Owtred. Gu. a saltire ar.

Owyngham. Per chev. sa. and erm. in chief two covered cups or.

Oxburgh, or Oxborough (King's Lynn and Emneth, co. Norfolk). Or, two bars az. a lion ramp. guard. gu. *Crest*—On a mount vert a lion ramp. or, holding up a spear gu. headed ar. under the head two ribbons flotant, one gold, the other az.

Oxburgh, or Oxborough. Same *Arms*. *Crest*—On the point of a sword in pale ppr. a cross pattée sa.

Oxcliffe. Or (another, ar.) an ox's head cabossed sa. *Crest*—On a mount vert a bull pass. sa.

Oxcliffe. Ar. three ox heads cabossed sa. (another, couped at the shoulders sa.).

Oxenbridge (co. Hants. Visit. 1634). Gu. a lion ramp. ar. tail double queued vert, on a border of the last eight escallops or. *Crest*—A demi lion ramp. tail double queued ar. langued and armed gu. holding in the dexter paw an escallop or.

Oxenbridge. Gu. a lion ramp. ar. a border vert.

Oxenbrig. Gu. a lion ramp. ar. ducally crowned or, on a border vert eight escallops of the second.

Oxenden (Dene, co. Kent, bart.; confirmed 24 Henry VI.). Ar. a chev. gu. betw. three oxen sa. *Crest*—Out of a ducal coronet gu. a lion's head affrontée or.

Oxenden (Brook, co. Kent). Same *Arms*.

Oxenford. Quarterly, gu. and or, a fess ar.

Oxenham (Oxenham, South Tawton, co. Devon: the last male heir, William Long Oxenham, Esq., d. in 1814; the heiress m. Arthur Acland, Esq.). Gu. a fess betw. three mullets or.

Oxensey (co. Essex). Per fess sa. and ar. a bull's head counterchanged, horned or.

Oxford, Earl of. See Harley.

Oxford, See of. Sa. a fess ar. in chief three ladies from the waist, heads affrontée, arrayed and veiled ar. crowned or, in base an ox of the second, passing over a ford ppr.

Oxford, City of. Ar. an ox gu. armed and unguled or, passing a ford of water in base ppr. *Crest*—A demi lion ramp. guard. or, regally crowned of the first, holding betw. his paws a rose ar. charged with another gu. *Supporters*—On the dexter an elephant erm. eared, collared, and lined ar. armed or; sinister, a beaver ppr. ducally collared and lined or. *Motto*—Fortis est veritas. Some authorities give, Bendy wavy ar. and az. an ox gu. passing over a ford ppr. as the arms of the City of Oxford.

Oxford. See University.

Oxford (co. Oxford). Paly of six ar. and az. on a bend gu. three mullets of the first, a border or.

Oxford. Az. three bars or, on a chief ar. a lion pass. guard. gu.

Oxley. Az. three peacocks' heads erased or. *Crest*—Out of a ducal coronet or, a peacock ppr.

Oxley (Ripon, co. York). Ar. a fess gu. betw. three oxen sa. *Crest*—An ox's head couped sa. charged with three erm. spots or. *Motto*—Tam aris quam aratris.

Oxley (co. York). Ar. on a fess gu. betw. three church bells az. as many crosses pattée of the field.

Oxman (co. Rutland). Erm. a lion ramp. reguard. gu. *Crest*—A demi lion ramp. reguard. gu.

Oxnam (St. Newlyn and Penzance, co. Cornwall). Ar. a fess betw. three oxen sa. *Crest*—An ox sa.

Oxney. Sa. three oxen's heads cabossed ar. (another, or), counterchanged, armed or.

Oxney. Per fess sa. and ar. an ox's head cabossed and counterchanged, armed or.

Oxon. Barry of six ar. and sa.

Oxspringe (co. York). Ar. on a fess betw. three church bells gu. as many crosses crosslet of the field.

Oxtoby. Ar. a bend sa. betw. three torteaux. *Crest*—A dexter hand brandishing a sword all ppr.

Oxton (co. Devon). Barry of six az. and or, a saltire gu. a border engr. of the last.

Oxton. Gu. semée of crosses crosslet a lion ramp. or.

Oyke (co. Norfolk). Gu. on a fess ar. betw. six acorns or, three oak leaves vert. *Crest*—An ox yoke in pale sa. bows or.

Oyry, or Oyrey. Az. three lucies haurient ar. betw. as many crosses crosslet (another, frets) or, one and two.

Oyry (Fulke de Oyry). Barry of six or and az.

Ozanne (The Landes, in the Island of Guernsey; descended from Richard Ozanne, son of James Ozanne, both of the Landes; granted to Richard Mansell Ozanne, and his descendants, and the descendants of his uncle, Peter Ozanne). Purp. on a chev. engr. betw. three fleurs-de-lis or, a helmet ppr. betw. two crosses crosslet fitchée gu. *Crest*—A demi lion purp. holding in the dexter paw a cross crosslet fitchée or, and resting the sinister upon a helmet ppr.

P.

PABENHAM. Or, a cross gu. a label of three points az. flory of the field.

Pabenhem. Barry of six ar. and az. on a bend gu. three mullets of the first (another, or).

Pace (Ingleton). Purp. three bezants.

Pace. Or, on a cross quarterly az. and gu. a bird betw. a lion pass. in chief, two squirrels sejant in fess, and an annulet in base, all of the first. *Crest*—A boar's head couped and erect sa. eared or, charged with an anchor of the last.

Pace. Ar. a chev. sa. betw. three gillyflowers ppr.

Paceford, or Paciford. Gu. on a chief or, a lion pass. az.

Pack, or Packe. Quarterly, ar. and erm. in the first quarter a cinquefoil or. *Crest*—A leg in armour, couped and bent at the knee, spurred all ppr.

Pack. Ar. on a chief az. three anchors or.

Pack (Avisford, co. Sussex; as borne by Colonel Arthur John Reynell-Pack, C.B., of Avisford, elder son of Major-General Sir Denis Pack, K.C.B., who assumed the prefix surname of Reynell, 1857). Same *Arms*, quartering Reynell. *Crest*—A mural crown ar. issuing therefrom a lion's head gu. gorged with a wreath or. *Motto*—Fidus confido.

Pack (granted by Betham, Ulster, to Major-General Sir Denis Pack, K.C.B., K.T.S., son of Very Rev. Thomas Pack, D.D., Dean of Ossory, and grandson of Thomas Pack, Esq., of Ballynakill, Queen's co., and to their descendants). Quarterly, sa. and erminois, in the 1st quarter a sword in bend sinister ar. hilted and pommelled or, the hilt encircled by a wreath of the last; in the 4th quarter a cinquefoil of the third; pendent from a crimson ribbon, bordered blue, in the centre chief a representation of golden cross and clasps presented to Major-General Denis Pack by George III., for his services in the Peninsula. *Crest*—A mural coronet ar. issuant therefrom a lion's head gu. gorged with a wreath or. *Motto*—Fidus confido.

Pack-Beresford (Fenagh, co. Carlow). See Beresford.

Packam (co. Kent). Sa. a chev. betw. three crosses crosslet fitchée or.

Packe (Prestwold, co. Leicester; Sir Christopher Packe, knighted by Cromwell, and made a member of the Usurper's Upper House, as Lord Packe, Lord Mayor of London, 1654-5). Quarterly, sa. and or, in the first quarter a cinquefoil ar. with an erm. spot on each leaf. *Crest*—A lion's head or, collared sa. on the collar three cinquefoils with an erm. spot on each leaf. *Motto*—Libertas sub Rege pio.

Packe (Harlestone Park, co. Northampton). Quarterly, sa. and or, in the first quarter a cinquefoil ar. *Crest*—A lion's head erased or, collared sa. thereon three mullets ar.

Packenham (co. Hants). Quarterly, or and gu. in the first canton an eagle displ. az. *Crest*—A leopard couchant ppr.

Packenham (North Witham, co. Lincoln; Fun. Ent. Ulster's Office, 1683, PHILIP PACKENHAM, son of ROBERT PACKENHAM, Esq., of North Witham; certificate attested by ROBERT PACKENHAM, Esq., of Bracklyn, co. Westmeath). Quarterly, or and az. in the first quarter an eagle displ. vert.

Packenham (Tullenally, co. Westmeath; descended of an ancient family of that surname of North Wytham, co. Lincoln; arms confirmed and crest granted by St. George, Ulster, in 1665). Quarterly, or and gu. in the first quarter an eagle displ. vert. *Crest*—A demi eagle displ. gu. armed or, issuing out of a crown mural gold.

Packer (Bucklebury, co. Berks). Gu. a cross lozengy betw. four roses ar. *Crest*—A Moor's head couped sa. wreathed about the temples or and gu.

Packer (Baddow, co. Essex). Same *Arms*. *Crest*—A pelican in her piety ar.

Packer (Alston, co. Gloucester, and Groombridge, co. Kent). Same *Arms*.

Packington (co. Bedford). Per chev. or and ar. in chief three mullets sa. in base as many garbs gu. *Crest*—A demi hare az. charged with three bezants.

Packington (Edgeworth, co. Middlesex, and co. Surrey; Her. Off. Vincent's Surrey). Sa. on a bend ar. three garbs gu. *Crest*—A demi lion az. holding in the dexter paw a dagger ar.

Packington. Ar. a cinquefoil sa. on a chief gu. a lion pass. of the field.

Packington. Per chev. sa. and ar. in chief three mullets of the second.

Packwood (co. Warwick). Quarterly, 1st and 4th, az. three pickaxes or, for PACKWOOD; 2nd and 3rd, sa. three bells ar. a canton erm., for PORTER. *Crest*—A demi lion ramp. ar. holding in the dexter and supporting with the sinister paw a bell sa. with a canton erm. as in the arms. *Motto*—None is truly great but he that is truly good.

Paddesley (Lord Mayor of London, 1440). Ar. three fleurs-de-lis az. on each an annulet or.

Paddon (Henton Deweney, co. Hants; granted 1590). Ar. a bend betw. three crescents sa. flammant ppr. *Crest*—A tower or, flammant ppr. *Another Crest*—A dexter hand ppr. holding up a covered cup or.

Paddy (NICHOLAS PADDY, Lancaster Herald, *temp.* Queen Elizabeth; granted 1591). Sa. an inescutcheon erm. betw. four lions ramp. ar. *Crest*—On a chapeau gu. turned up erm. a lion pass. ar.

Padenham. Gu. a chev. betw. three crosses pommettée fitchée ar.

Paderday. Ar. on a bend sa. three quatrefoils slipped and leaved of the first.

Padmore (Ireland; Fun. Ent. Ulster's Office, 1661, Mrs. COREY, *alias* PADMORE). Az. on a bend ar. cotised or, a lion pass. sa. armed and langued gu.

Pagan (Scotland). Bendy of six or and az. on a chief erm. a label gu., a bordure of the first charged with three fleurs-de-lis of the second. *Crest*—Out of a mural coronet a demi eagle displ. all ppr.

Pagan (England). Az. three fleurs-de-lis or, a bordure engr. of the last. *Crest*—A dexter hand holding a dagger erect ppr. *Motto*—Nec timeo nec sperno.

Paganell. Gu. a cinquefoil pierced ar.

Paganell, Paganel, or Painell (Bahuntune, *temp.* Henry II.). Or, two lions pass. az.

Paganell, or Pagnell (*temp.* Henry I.). Gu. a cinquefoil erm. charged in the middle with a crescent sa. *Crest*—A column sa. in the sea ppr.

Paganell, or Pagnell. Vert a maunch or.

Page (granted to PETER PAGE, Esq., J.P., of East Sheen, co. Surrey). Sa. a fess betw. three doves ar. beaked and armed gu. *Crest*—Out of a ducal coronet a demi griffin, wings elevated, both per pale or and gu. counterchanged. *Motto*—Spe labor levis.

Page (Donnington, co. Sussex, A.D. 1591). Gu. on a chev. betw. three doves ar. as many pheons sa.

Page (Berry Hall, co. Bedford, and Blackheath, co. Kent). Or, a fess indented betw. three martlets az. *Crest*—A demi horse per pale dancettée or and az.

Page (Wemley, co. Middlesex). Or, a fess dancettée betw. three martlets az. a border of like.

Page (co. Cambridge). Or, a fess dancettée betw. three martlets ar. on a border engr. of the last eight bezants. *Crest*—A demi griffin holding a ducal coronet or.

770

Page, or Paige (co. Devon). Ar. a bend betw. three eagles displ. sa. *Crest*—An eagle displ. erm.

Page (granted to JOSEPH PAGE, Esq., of Little Bromley, co. Essex). Per fess ar. and gu. an eagle displ. within an orle of four anchors and as many crosses moline alternately all counterchanged. *Crest*—A demi gryphon ar. supporting an anchor ppr. and charged on the wing with a cross moline gu. *Motto*—Crux mihi anchora.

Page (Holebrook, co. Somerset; ROBERT PAGE, Esq., of Holbrook, was son and eventual heir of Sir THOMAS HYDE PAGE, Knt., R.E., F.R.S., by MARY WOODWARD, his wife, granddau. of RICHARD WOODWARD, Esq., of Little Ealing, Middlesex, by MARY, his wife, dau. and heir of LEONARD HANCOCK, Esq., J.P., of Theobald's Park, Herts). Quarterly, 1st and 4th, az. a chev. betw. three lozenges or, for PAGE, of Middlesex; 2nd, az. a chev. betw. three lozenges or, for HYDE, of Chester; 3rd, barry of six or and sa. on a canton gu. a demi woodman with a club on his shoulder of the first, for WOODWARD, co. Stafford; 4th, gu. a dexter hand couped and erect ar. on a chief of the second three cocks of the first, for HANCOCK, Twining, co. Gloucester. *Crest*—A demi griffin gu. *Motto*—Honneur pour objet.

Page (Rev. THOMAS DOUGLAS PAGE, M.A., Rector of Sibstone, co. Leicester, youngest son of ROBERT PAGE, Esq., of Holebrooke). Same *Arms*, &c.

Page (GRESHAM PAGE, Esq., of Saxthorpe, High Sheriff co. Norfolk, 1722). Or, a chev. betw. three martlets az. quartering Ar. a chev. ermines betw. three mullets pierced sa., GRESHAM.

Page (Hesset, &c., co. Suffolk; granted 1552). Or, on a fess engr. ermines betw. three seamews sa. membered gu. as many martlets of the first.

Page (Gosport, co. Hants). Az. a fess dancettée betw. three martlets ar. *Crest*—A demi seahorse assurgent.

Page (co. Kent). Ar. on a bend sa. three doves of the field, membered gu. *Crest*—A demi griffin erm. beaked and legged gu.

Page (co. Middlesex). Gu. a chev. vair betw. three lions' heads erased or. *Crest*—Out of a mural coronet gu. a lion's head or.

Page (granted 1 Feb. 1530). Sa. a fess betw. three doves ar. membered gu. *Crest*—Out of a ducal coronet per pale or and gu. (another, gu. and or) a demi griffin salient per pale, counterchanged, beaked of the second.

Page (Eardshaw, co. Chester). Sa. a fess ar. betw. three birds of the second.

Page. Gu. on a chev. betw. three martlets ar. as many pheons sa. *Crest*—Out of a mural coronet or, a demi griffin gu. (another, out of a ducal coronet).

Page (co. Surrey). Gu. a fess engr. erm. betw. three doves ar. beaked and membered of the field, a border engr. of the second.

Page (Easthatch, co. Wilts). Sa. a fess betw. three doves ar. a border engr. erm.

Page (London; WILLIAM PAGE, of Shorne, and his brother, EDMUND PAGE, of London, great-grandsons of EDMUND PAGE, gent., of Pipe Place, co. Kent. Visit. Middlesex, 1663). Ar. on a bend sa. three doves close or. *Crest*—A demi griffin erm.

Page. Ar. two bends sa. on each three plates.

Page. Per saltire or and gu. a griffin's head counterchanged.

Page (City of Chester, 1711). Gu. a fess ar. betw. three birds of the second. *Crest*—An eagle displ. or.

Page-Turner, Bart. See TURNER.

Page (granted by Roberts, Ulster, 1647, to ROBERT PAGE, Captain of the ship called the "Exchange of London;" descended from the family of PAGE, co. Gloucester). Sa. on a chev. or, betw. three doves ar. as many cinquefoils ppr. *Crest*—A demi lion ramp. gu. holding betw. the paws a pine ppr.

Page (Newhall, co. Kildare; Fun. Ent. Ulster's Office, 1640, JOHN PAGE, Esq., of that place, third son of PAGE, of Clebroke, co. Leicester). Gu. a chev. betw. three doves ar. beaked and legged sa., a mullet on a crescent for diff.

Pagenham. Quarterly, or and gu. in the 1st quarter an eagle displ. vert. *Crest*—Out of a mural coronet or, a demi eagle gu. armed of the first.

Paget (*Marquess of Anglesey*). Sa. on a cross engr. betw. four eagles displ. ar. five lions pass. guard. of the field. *Crest*—A demi heraldic tiger sa. maned, ducally gorged, and tufted ar. *Supporters*—Two heraldic tigers sa. ducally gorged, tufted, and maned ar. *Motto*—Per il suo contrario.

Paget (Harewood Place, London, bart.). Sa. on a cross engr. betw., in the 1st and 4th quarters an eagle displ., and in the 2nd and 3rd an heraldic tiger pass. ar. an escallop of the first. *Crest*—An heraldic tiger pass. ar. gorged with a collar, and charged with two escallops sa. *Motto*—Labor ipsa voluptas.

Paget (Cranmore Hall, co. Somerset). Sa. on a cross engr. betw. four eagles displ. ar. five lions pass. guard. of the field, quartering MOORE, BRADFORD, BOLESWORTH, and SNOW. *Crest*—A demi tiger ramp. sa. tufted and maned ar. ducally gorged or. *Motto*—Diciendo y haciendo.

Paget (Chipping Norton, co. Oxford, and the Sneyd, co. Worcester). Sa. á cross engr. ar. in the 1st quarter an escallop of the last. *Crest*—A cubit arm erect habited sa. cuffed ar. holding a scroll of the second, bearing the inscription " Deo pagit." *Motto*—Post spinas palma.

Paget (Ruddington Grange, co. Notts). Sa. a cross engr. ar. in the dexter quarter an escallop of the last. *Crest*—A lion ramp. ppr. *Motto*—Honestas.

Paget (Ibstock and Humberstone, co. Leicester). Sa. a cross engr. ar. in the dexter chief an escallop of the second, a crescent for diff. *Crest*—A lion ramp. ppr. resting his sinister paw on an escutcheon. *Motto*—Espere et persevere.

Paget (Thorp Satchville, co. Leicester). Same *Arms*, *Crest*, and *Motto*.

Paget. Sa. a cross engr. ar.

Paget (granted to ROBERT PAGET, Sheriff of London, 1536, father of JAMES PAGET, Sheriff co. Hants, 1580). Ar. a chev. vair betw. three talbots pass. sa.

Paggin (Wandsworth, co. Surrey). Vert a fess embattled betw. three ragged staves erect ar. *Crest*—Two ragged staves in saltire ar. chained sa.

Pagit (Gray's Inn, London, and Hadley, co. Middlesex, and Crayneford, Barton Segrave, and Hanned, near Kettering, co. Northampton; allowed at Visit. Middlesex, 1663, to JUSTINIAN PAGITT, of Hadley, Custos Brevium and Recorder of the King's Bench, son of JAMES PAGITT, Baron of the Court of Exchequer, who was great grandson of THOMAS PAGITT, Esq., of Burton-Segrave, and Handred, co. Northants). Sa. a cross engr. ar. in the dexter quarter an escallop of the last. *Crest*—A cubit arm erect, habited sa. cuffed ar. holding in the hand ppr. a scroll of the second, thereon the words " Deo Pagit," a seal affixed hereto pendent gu.

Pagitt (Middle Temple, London; confirmed 24 Feb. 1575). Same *Arms* and *Crest*.

Pain. Paly of six ar. and vert, on a chief az. three garbs or. *Crest*—A lion ramp. ppr. supporting a wheat sheaf or.

Paine (Ireland; Fun. Ent. Ulster's Office, 1652, the wife of Captain PAINE, b. at St. Patrick's, Dublin). Per saltire ar. and sa. a lion ramp. counterchanged, quartering Ar. a chev. betw. three martlets sa., for MADESON.

Painter Stainers, Company of (London). Quarterly, 1st and 4th, az. three escutcheons ar. ; 2nd and 3rd, az. a chev. betw. three phœnix heads erased or. *Crest*—A phœnix close or, in flames ppr. *Supporters*—Two leopards ar. spotted with various colours, ducally crowned, collared and chained or. *Motto*—Amor et obedientia.

Painter Stainers (Gateshead-on-Tyne, 1671). Az. a chev. betw. three phœnix heads erased or. *Crest*—A phœnix close or, in flames ppr. *Supporters*—Two leopards ar. spotted sa. ducally crowned, collared and chained or. *Motto*—Amor et obedientia.

Painters, Company of (Exeter). *Arms* and *Crest*, same as PAINTER STAINERS of London. *Motto*—Amor et obedientia.

Pakeman. Or, on a chief sa. three martlets of the first, *Crest*—A cockatrice close gu. combed, beaked, and wattled or.

Pakeman. Ar. two bars gu. on a canton of the second a boar's head couped or (another, or).

Pakeman. Gu. a boar's head couped ar. betw. three crosses crosslet botonnée of the second.

Pakeman. Ar. two bars gu. in chief as many pellets of the second, on a canton sa. a boar's head couped of the first.

Pakeman. Gu. a chev. ar. betw. three crosses botonnée fitchée of the last.

Pakenham (co. Suffolk). Quarterly, or and gu. in the first quarter an eagle displ. of the second. *Crest*—A griffin segreant, holding an escarbuncle all ppr.

Pakenham. Same *Arms*. *Crest*—A hand holding three arrows, points downward, all ppr.

Pakenham (co. Bedford). Barry of six az. and ar. (another, sa. and or) on a bend gu. three mullets or,

Pakenham. Barry of six or and sa. on a bend gu. three eagles displ. or.

777

Pakenham. Ar. two bars gu. in chief a pile of the last charged with a boar's head couped of the field.

Pakenham (*Earl of Longford*). Quarterly, 1st, quarterly, or and gu. in the first quarter an eagle displ. vert, for PAKENHAM; 2nd, ar. on a bend indented sa. cotised az. three fleurs-de-lis of the field, each cotise charged with three bezants, for CUFF; 3rd, erm. a griffin segreant az., for AUNGIER; 4th, per bend crenellé ar. and gu., for BOYLE. *Crest*—Out of a mural crown or, a demi eagle displ. gu. beaked gold. *Supporters*—Dexter, a lion az. charged on the shoulder with an escarbuncle or; sinister, a griffin az. beak, forelegs, and wings or. *Motto*—Gloria virtutis umbra.

Pakenham (granted as an honourable augmentation to the family arms by Chichester Fortescue, Ulster, 1795, to Hon. THOMAS PAKENHAM, second son of THOMAS, first Lord Longford, afterwards Admiral of the Red and G.C.B., father of EDWARD MICHAEL CONOLLY, Esq., of Castletown, co. Kildare, M.P.). Quarterly, or and gu. in the first quarter an eagle displ. sa.; for honourable augmentation, on a chief, the sea, and on the stern of an antique ship riding thereon, Britannia standing, Victory alighting on the prow, and placing a wreath of laurel on her, Britannia's, head, all ppr., being the device on the medal emblematic of the glorious sea fight of June 1, 1794, wherein the said Captain Hon. THOMAS PAKENHAM commanded H.M.S. " Invincible," 74 guns, which captured " Le Juste," 80 guns, one of the enemy's ships. *Crest*—Out of a mural crown or, a demi eagle displ. gu. beaked gold.

Pakenham-Mahon. See MAHON.

Pakington (Aylesbury and Westwood, co. Bucks, bart., extinct, 1830; originally, so far back as the reign of Henry I., of Packington, co. Stafford. At the decease of Sir JOHN PAKINGTON, eighth bart., the estates devolved on JOHN SOMERSET RUSSELL, Esq., son of ELIZABETH, Sir JOHN PAKINGTON's eldest sister, who assumed the name and arms of PAKINGTON, was created a bart. 1846, and a peer as Baron Hampton in 1874). Per chev. sa. and ar. in chief three mullets ar. in base as many garbs gu. *Crest*—An elephant pass. or, armed gu.

Pakington (*Baron Hampton*). Per chev. sa. and ar. in chief three mullets or, pierced of the first, in base as many garbs, one and two, gu. banded of the third. *Crests*—1st: An elephant pass. or, tusked gu.; 2nd : A demi hare az. charged on the shoulder with four bezants, one, two, and one. *Supporters*—Dexter, an elephant or; sinister, a talbot ar. both charged on the shoulder with a mullet pierced sa. *Mottoes*—For PAKINGTON: Par viribus virtus; for RUSSELL: Fidelis et audax.

Pakington. Ar. a cinquefoil sa. on a chief gu. a lion pass. guard. or.

Pakington. Per chev. sa. and ar. in chief three mullets of the second. *Crest*—A demi squirrel erased gu.

Pakisworth. Or, three dragons' heads erased gu.

Palavicini (an Italian family settled in co. Cambridge). Or, a cross quarter pierced az. on a chief of the first a ragged staff fessways sa.

Paletoot (Sir JOHN DE PALETOOT, 1361). Paly of six or and vert, a chief indented of the second.

Palgrave (Norwood Barningham, co. Norfolk). Az. a lion ramp. ar. *Crest*—A lion's head erased ar.

Palk (Haldon House, co. Devon, bart.). Sa. an eagle displ. ar. beaked and legged or, a border engr. of the second. *Crest*—On a semi terrestrial globe of the northern hemisphere ppr. an eagle rising ar. beaked and membered or.

Palingham. Ar. a bend gobony gu. and or, on the chief point of the bend a lion pass. of the last.

Palfrey (Ireland; Fun. Ent. Ulster's Office, 1653). Sa. a chev. betw. three horses at full speed or.

Pallant (THOMAS PALLANT, Esq., of Redgrave, co. Suffolk). Barry of six ar. and erminois. *Crest*—An escutcheon of the arms betw. two wings erect ppr.

Palles (Dublin; Fun. Ent. Ulster's Office, 1603, Alderman ALEXANDER PALLES). Az. three bendlets ragulée ar. on a fess gu. a bezant betw. two crosses pattée fitchée or.

Palles (Mount Palles, co. Cavan, of Italian origin, being descended from the DEL PALATIOS, confirmed to ANDREW CHRISTOPHER PALLES, Esq., father of the Right Hon. CHRISTOPHER PALLES, now Lord Chief Baron of the Court of Exchequer, in Ireland, only child of the late ANDREW PALLES, Esq., of Mount Palles, by ELIZABETH, his wife, daughter of RICHARD O'FERRALL, Esq., of Balyna, co. Kildare, and grandson of ANDREW PALLES, Esq., of Mount Palles, by JANE, his wife, daughter and co-heiress of NICHOLAS READ, Esq., of Dunboyne, co. Meath). Quarterly, 1st and 4th az. three bendlets raguly ar on a fess gu. a cross pattée fitchée betw. two annulets or, for PALLES; 2nd, erm.

3 D 2

two bars gu. an annulet for diff., for NUGENT; 3rd, az. a griffin segreant or, for READ. *Crest*—A lion sejant az. bezantée holding betw. the paws a cross pattée fitchée or. *Motto*—Deo duce comite fortunâ.

Palley. Or, three lions ramp. gu. a bend az. *Crest*—A camel's head sa.

Palley. Gu. on a bend or, betw. three lions ramp. ar. as many mullets az.

Palley. Gu. three lions pass. in pale ar. on a bend az. as many mullets or.

Pallingham. Ar. on a bend gu. (another, az.) a lion ramp. or.

Palliser (Great Island and Portobello, co. Wexford; descended from JOHN PALLISER, Esq., of Newby-Super-Wisk, co. York, whose grandson, JOHN PALLISER, b. 1639, m. URSULA, dau. of Sir HUGH BETHELL, Knt., of Ellerton, co. York, and had with other issue, two sons, I. THOMAS, of Portobello, colonel in the army, whose grandson, PHILIP PALLISER, d. s. p. when his estates devolved on the descendants of his sister, KATHERINE PALLISER, wife of JOHN WILSON, Esq., of Scarr, same co.; II. HUGH, of North Deighton, co. York, ancestor of PALLISER, Bart.). Per pale sa. and ar. three lions ramp. counterchanged.

Palliser (WILLIAM PALLISER, Bishop of Cloyne, 1692-94, Archbishop of Cashel 1694-1726, brother of JOHN PALLISER, the ancestor of PALLISER, co. Wexford, and grandson of JOHN PALLISER, Esq., of Newby-Super-Wisk; Fun. Ent. Ulster's Office, 1683, of ELIZABETH HALE his wife; his only son, WILLIAM PALLISER, d. s. p. 1769, and his dau. and eventual heiress, JANE PALLISER, m. JOHN BURY, Esq., of Shannon Grove, and had two sons, I. WILLIAM BURY, ancestor of the extinct *Earls of Charleville*; II. JOHN BURY, of Comragh, co. Waterford). Same *Arms*.

Palliser (Castletown, co. Wexford, bart., extinct 1868; HUGH PALLISER, Esq., of North Deighton, co. York, second son of JOHN PALLISER, ancestor of PALLISER, co. Wexford, had one son, HUGH PALLISER, Esq., of The Vatch, co. Bucks, who was created a bart. 1773, with special remainder to his nephew, GEORGE ROBINSON WALTERS, son of Major WILLIAM WALTERS, by REBECCA PALLISER, his sister, d. unm. 1796, and was s. by his grand-nephew, Sir HUGH PALLISER WALTERS, who assumed the surname and arms of PALLISER by royal licence, 1798, and was father of the last bart. who d. unm.) Same *Arms*. *Crest* (granted 8 Oct. 1773, to Sir HUGH PALLISER, first bart.)—Out of a ducal coronet gu. a demi eagle, wings elevated or.

Palliser (granted to GEORGE THOMAS, The Vatch, co. Buckingham, illegitimate son of Sir HUGH PALLISER, first bart. of Castletown, who s. to The Vatch under the baronet's will, and assumed the name of PALLISER). Per pale sa. and ar. three lions ramp. counterchanged, two and one, a bordure per pale of the second and az. *Crest*—Out of a ducal coronet gu. a demi eagle or, wings displ. erminois, and charged on the breast with an anchor in pale az.

Palmer (Carlton, co. Northampton, bart.). Sa. a chev. or, betw. three crescents ar. *Crest*—A wyvern or, armed and langued gu. *Motto*—Par sit fortuna labori.

Palmer (Marston, co. Stafford; descended from PALMER, co. York; JOHN PALMER, Esq., living 1566, had two sons, I. ROBERT, his heir, whose representative, WILLIAM PALMER, assumed the surname of MOREWOOD (see MOREWOOD); II. WILLIAM, whose great grandson, ARCHDALE PALMER, had, with other issue, two sons, I. HENRY, whose dau. and eventual heir, KATHERINE SUSAN, m. 1766, Sir CHARLES GRAVE HUDSON, first bart. of Wanlip, whose son, Sir CHARLES THOMAS HUDSON, second bart., assumed the surname of PALMER, by royal licence, 1813; II. THOMAS, father of WILLIAM PALMER, Esq., of Nazing Park). Ar. on two bars sa. three trefoils slipped the first, in chief a greyhound courant of the first, collared or. *Crest*—A greyhound sejant sa. *Motto*—Palma virtute.

Palmer (Nazing Park, co. Essex; WILLIAM PALMER, Esq., of Nazing Park, had, with other issue, I. GEORGE, M.P. co. Essex, his successor; II. Rev. WILLIAM, B.D., Rector of Mixbury and Finmore, co. Oxford, whose second son, Sir ROUNDELL PALMER, Lord High Chancellor of England, was created, 1872, *Lord Selborne*). Same *Arms*, *Crest*, and *Motto*.

Palmer (*Baron Selborne*). Ar. on two bars sa. three trefoils slipped of the first, in chief a greyhound courant of the second, collared or. *Crest*—A greyhound sejant sa. collared or, and charged on the shoulder with a trefoil slipped ar. *Supporters*—On either side a greyhound sa. collared and charged on the shoulder with a trefoil slipped ar. *Motto*—Palma virtuti.

Palmer (Wanlip, co. Leicester, bart.; Sir CHARLES GRAVE HUDSON assumed, 1813, by royal licence, the surname and

arms of PALMER). Quarterly, 1st and 4th, ar. two bars sa. charged with three trefoils slipped of the field, in chief a greyhound courant of the second, collared or; 2nd and 3rd, per chev. embattled erm. and az. three martlets counterchanged. *Crest*—On a mount vert a greyhound sejant sa. gorged with a collar or, rimmed gu. and charged on the shoulder with a trefoil slipped vert.

Palmer-Morewood (Ladbroke, co. Warwick, and Alfreton Hall, co. Derby). See MOREWOOD.

Palmer (King's Messenger, temp. Queen Anne. The coheiresses, JANE, m. THOMAS DRURY, Esq., and DOROTHY, m. THOMAS KIRKLAND, M.D., of Ashby de la Zouch, co. Leicester). Ar. on a bend sa. betw. two oyresses three trefoils slipped of the field. *Crest*—A cubit arm in armour, grasping a trefoil slipped vert.

Palmer (confirmed to EMMANUEL PALMER, captain of horse in Col. CHUDLEIGH COOTE's regiment). Chequy ar. and az. on a chief gu. a ducal crown or. *Crest*—A lion pass. sa. armed and langued, holding in his dexter paw a dagger gu.

Palmer (Wingham, co. Kent, and Dorney Court, co. Buckingham, bart., extinct). Or, two bars gu. each charged with three trefoils ar. in chief a greyhound courant sa. *Crest*—A demi panther ramp. issuing flames out of its mouth and ears, holding in the paws a holly branch, with leaves and berries all ppr. *Motto*—Palma virtuti.

Palmer (Hill, co. Bedford). Ar. two bars gu. on each three escallops or. *Crest*—A greyhound courant sa.

Palmer (Walden Street, co. Bedford, and Ladbrooke, co. Warwick). Ar. two bars sa. charged with three trefoils slipped of the field, in chief a greyhound courant of the second.

Palmer (Cheam Park, co. Surrey). Same *Arms*. *Crest*—A greyhound sejant sa. collared or, charged on the shoulder with a trefoil slipped ar.

Palmer (Great Yarmouth and Loddon, co. Norfolk; descended from WILLIAM PALMER, b. 1672) Or, two bars gu. each charged with three trefoils of the field, in chief a lion pass. ppr. *Crest*—A demi panther ramp. guard. issuant flames from his mouth and ears all ppr. holding a branch vert fructed gu. *Motto*—Palma virtuti.

Palmer (co. Bedford). Ar. two bars gu. on each three cinquefoils or. *Crest*—A greyhound courant sa.

Palmer (Wadesden, co. Buckingham, and Stockdale, co. Northampton; granted 22 Elizabeth). Az. a chev. engr. betw. three crescents ar. *Crest*—A cubit arm erect in mall ppr. holding a halbert sa. headed ar. *Another Crest*—A griffin's head ar. issuing out of rays ppr.

Palmer (Dorrington and Lymington, co. Gloucester, and co. Warwick). Ar. on a chief sa. three cinquefoils of the field.

Palmer (Linche, co. Hertford). Az. in chief a fleur-de-lis or, in base two trefoils slipped ar. a border engr. of the second. *Crest*—A wivern's head or, collared gu. wings expanded vert, fretty and semée of trefoils slipped ar.

Palmer (Upton Snodsbury, co. Worcester; EDWARD PALMER, of that place, was High Sheriff 6 Queen Anne). Same *Arms* and *Crest*.

Palmer (Hartlip, co. Kent; granted 19 Queen Elizabeth). Sa. a fess betw. three lions ramp. or. *Crest*—An ostrich volant ar.

Palmer (Howlets, co. Kent, 1586). Ar. a chev. betw. three palmers' scrips sa. the tassels and buckles or.

Palmer (Wood Court, co. Somerset). Same *Arms*. *Crest*—A hand grasping a palmer's staff. *Motto*—Palma virtuti.

Palmer (co. Kent). Barry of ten ar. and az. a griffin segreant or.

Palmer (granted to CHARLES MARK PALMER, Esq., of Grinkle Park, Easington, co. York). Sa. on a chev. betw. three crescents in chief and a lion pass. in base ar. two tilting spears chevronwise ppr. *Crest*—In front of a tilting spear erect ppr. a wyvern or, resting the dexter foot on a crescent ar. *Motto*—Par sit fortuna labori.

Palmer (Withcote Hall, co. Leicester). Sa. a chev. or, betw. three crescents ar. *Crest*—A wyvern or, armed and langued gu. *Motto*—Par sit fortuna labori.

Palmer (Bosworth and Duddington, co. Leicester, and Kentish Town, co. Middlesex). Az. three fleurs-de-lis ar. a border engr. or.

Palmer (co. Leicester). Az. a fleur-de-lis erm.

Palmer (co. Leicester). Ar. on a bend sa. five bezants.

Palmer (Winthorp, co. Lincoln). Ar. three palmers' staves sa. the heads, ends, and rests or. *Crest*—A cubit arm erect, habited az. cuffed ar. grasping in the hand ppr. a palmer's staff.

Palmer (London, 1634). Ar. a lion ramp. betw. three palmers' staves sa. heads, ends, and rests or. *Crest*—A lion ramp. or, grasping a palmer's staff, as in the arms.

Palmer (Stepney, co. Middlesex, co. Northampton, and Kingston-upon-Hull; confirmed 3 May, 1670). Or, on a chev. gu. five acorns of the field.

Palmer (Stokedale, co. Northampton). Sa. a chev. engr. betw. three crescents ar. *Crest*—A cubit arm erect in coat of mail ppr. holding in the hand of the last a halbert sa. headed ar.

Palmer (co. Sussex). Or, two bars gu. each charged with three trefoils slipped ar. in chief a greyhound courant sa. *Crest*—A demi panther ramp. guard. issuing flames from his ears and mouth ppr. holding a branch vert, fructed gu.

Palmer (Parham, co. Sussex, and Fairfield, co. Somerset). Same *Arms*. *Crest*—A demi panther guard. ar. spotted gu. vert, or, and az. alternately, flames issuant from the mouth and ears, holding a palm branch ppr. *Motto*—Palma virtuti.

Palmer (Barton, co. Warwick, and co. York). Chequy ar. and az. a chief gu. (another, chequy or and az.). *Crest*—A griffin sejant.

Palmer (co. Warwick). Gu. five cinquefoils (another, quatrefoils) in saltire ar.

Palmer. Chequy ar. and az. a chief gu. *Crest*—Out of a ducal coronet or, an elephant's head sa.

Palmer (Holme Park, co. Berks). Chequy or and sa. on a chief gu. two mullets of the first. *Crest*—A talbot sejant erminois.

Palmer. Ar. three palmers' staves sa. heads, rests, and ends or, on a chief of the second as many escallops of the first. *Crest*—An escallop ar. betw. two laurel branches vert.

Palmer. Az. a fleur-de-lis in chief and two trefoils slipped in fess ar. a border engr. or. *Crest*—A dragon's head couped or, collared and winged vert, on the collar three plates, the breast guttée de poix, the wings fretty ar. betw. the fret trefoils of the last.

Palmer. Sa. three fleurs-de-lis betw. seven crosslets ar. a canton erm.

Palmer (*Earl of Castlemaine*, a branch of PALMER, of Wingham, extinct 1705). Or, two bars gu. each charged with three trefoils ar. in chief a greyhound courant sa. *Crest*—Same as PALMER, of Wingham. *Supporters*—Two lions guard. ar. *Crest*—Palma virtuti.

Palmer (Rahan House, King's co.). Az. a chev. or, betw. three palmers' staves and scrips sa. *Crest*—An arm in armour embowed ppr. garnished or, the hand grasping a spear also ppr. *Motto*—Honor virtutis præmium.

Palmer (Castle Lacken, co. Mayo, bart.). Quarterly, 1st and 4th, ar. a chev. vert betw. three palmers' staves and scrips sa. garnished gu.; 2nd and 3rd, chequy ar. and az. on a chief gu. three annulets or. *Crests*—1st : An arm embowed vested az. cuffed or, grasping a tilting-spear ppr.; 2nd : A griffin sejant ar. wings addorsed gu. charged with three annulets of the second beaked and membered or. *Motto*—Sic bene merenti palma.

Palmer (Dublin; confirmed by Carney, Ulster, 1683, as the arms of ELINOR, wife of ABEL RAM, Esq., of Ramsfort, co. Wexford, Alderman of Dublin, and daughter of STEPHEN PALMER, of Dublin). Ar. a chev. betw. three palmers' scrips sa. tassels and buckles or.

Palmer (Fun. Ent. Ulster's Office, 1621, PETER PALMER, one of the Justices of the Common Pleas in Ireland). Sa. a chev. betw. three crescents ar.

Palmer (granted by Betham, Ulster, to WILLIAM PALMER, Esq., of Hyderabad). Az. on a fess or, betw. in chief a greyhound courant and in base a pelican in her piety ar., two trefoils slipped vert. *Crest*—An eagle volant rising from a mount with a palm branch in his beak, all ppr., motto over, "It shall flourish." *Motto*—Deeds not words.

Palmerston, Viscount. See TEMPLE.

Palmes (Naburn, co. York). Gu. three fleurs-de-lis ar. a chief vair, quartering CHARLTON, STAPLETON, and PLUMPTON. *Crest*—A hand holding a palm branch all ppr. *Motto*—Ut palma justus.

Palshed, or Polshed. Ar. on a bend gu. betw. two mullets of the last, three trefoils slipped of the first, on a chief az. an eagle, wings expanded, betw. two cinquefoils stalked and leaved or. *Crest*—An arm embowed, vested bendy of eight ar. and gu. in the hand ppr. three flowers az. stalked and leaved vert.

Paltock (Kingston-upon-Thames, co. Surrey; confirmed 1612). Az. an inescutcheon betw. eight cinquefoils in orle or. *Crest*—On a mount vert a greyhound sejant sa. spotted ar. collared or.

Palton (co. Devon). Ar. six roses gu. seeded or, three, two, and one.

Palyard. Ar. a cross sa. fretty or.

Pamping, or Pampynge. Sa. a dolphin in fess betw. three escallops ar.

Pamsey, or Paunsey. Sa. a pair of wings conjoined ar. a border engr. of the second.

Pamure. Az. on a chev. ar. betw. two roses in chief, and an acorn stalked and leaved or, in base, two palm branches vert. *Crest*—A demi lion ramp. az. holding in the dexter paw a rose, stalked and leaved as in the arms.

Panbridge. Or, three bars az.

Paneler. Gu. on a bend betw. as many mullets or, three leopards' faces ar.

Panell. Ar. two bars sa. betw. eight martlets gu. three, two and three.

Panell (Sir WALTER PANELL, K.G., 1348). Barry of six or and az. a bend ar. (another coat az. a cross patonce or).

Panell. Ar. two bars vert, betw. nine martlets gu. three, three, and three.

Panell. Az. two lions pass. reguard. or.

Panfull. Erm. a lion ramp. purp. crowned or.

Panill. Az. on a fess betw. six martlets ar. two martlets of the first.

Pankhurst, or Penckhurst (Mayfield, co. Sussex). Ar. a fess ermines betw. six mullets sa.

Panley (co. Oxford). Barry nebulée of six or and sa.

Panmure, Baron. See MAULE.

Pannal, Pannel, or Pannell (co. Lincoln, and Pannall, co. York). Ar. a bend sa.

Pannell (co. Norfolk). Gu. two chev. ar. (another adds, a border engr. of the second).

Pannell (co. York). Ar. two lions pass. guard. gu. crowned az.

Pannell. Or, a maunch vert.

Pannell. Gu. a cross ar.

Pannell. Gu. a cross moline erm.

Pannell. Az. a cross or, on a chief ar. five fleurs-de-lis sa. three and two.

Pannerton (co. Stafford). Gu. two bars ar. over all an ink moline erm.

Panther (that Ilk). Ar. on a fess az. betw. three spur-rowels in chief gu. and a rose in base of the last, three helmets of the field.

Panther (Pitmedden, co. Aberdeen). Or, an eagle displ. sa.

Panther (Newmains, Scotland). Ar. on a fess az. betw. two spur-rowels in chief gu. and a rose in base of the last, three garbs or.

Panting (Dublin; Fun. Ent. Ulster's Office, 1600, ROBERT PANTING, Alderman and Sheriff of Dublin). Az. a leopard's face jessant-de-lis ar. *Crest*—A dexter hand ar. betw. two wings az. guttée d'eau.

Panton (Bishopwearmouth, co. Durham). Gu. two bars erm. on a canton sa. a fer-de-moline ar. *Crest*—A sword ppr. hilt and pommel or, enfiled with a leopard's face of the last. *Motto*—Semper eadem.

Panton (co. Denbigh, North Wales). Same *Arms* (another, the fer-de-moline erm.) and *Crest*.

Panton (cos. Lincoln and Stafford). Gu. two bars ar. in the dexter chief point a fer-de-moline erm.

Panton (Blackhouse, Scotland). Or, an eagle displ. sa. in chief a rose gu. betw. two mullets of the second. *Motto*—Sine pondere sursum.

Panton (Captain GEORGE PANTON, 1672). As the last, a border gu. *Crest*—A spear head ppr. *Motto*—Firmius, et pugnan.

Panton (Sussex; granted, 1615). Gu. two bars or. on a canton az. a dolphin embowed or. *Crest*—A dolphin haurient or, betw. two wings gu. each charged with as many bars ar.

Panton. Per chev. gu. and or, in chief two towers ar. and in base a lion ramp. az. *Crest*—A lion couchant, the tail betw. the hind legs az. bezantée.

Panton. Gu. two bars erm. on a canton of the last a cross of the field.

Panton. Barry of ten ar. and gu. a canton of the second.

Panton. Gu. a chev. vair, a chief or.

Panton. Sa. a cross engr. or, in the dexter chief point a mullet ar.

Pantulf (Baron of Weme, co. Salop, the dau. and heir m. temp. Henry III., RALPH BOTELER, of Oversley, co. Hereford, and who became, jure uxoris, Baron of Weme). Gu. two bars erm.

Panture. Ar. three bars gemelles and a canton gu.

Pape. Gu. a bend chequy or and az. *Crest*—A dexter hand ppr. holding up a clam shell or.

Papillion (Crowhurst Park, co. Sussex, formerly of Acrise, co. Kent). Az. on a chev. betw. three butterflies ar. *Crest*— A crescent ar. *Motto*—Ditat servata fides.

Paprell (co. Cornwall). Ar. a chev. gu. betw. three pine-apples vert.

Papworth (cos. Cambridge, Dorset, Devon, and Hunting-don). Gu. a fess dancettée ar. *Crest*—A fox's head erased gu.

Paradis, or De Paradis (Youghal; originally from Lyons, Huguenot settlers in Ireland). Az. a cross or, betw. four birds of Paradise ppr. *Crest*—A bird of Paradise ppr.

Paramour (Paramour, co. Kent; granted 1616). Az.a fess counter-embattled betw. three estoiles or. *Crest*—Two arms embowed vested az. holding betw. the hands ppr. an estoile or.

Paramour (co. Leicester, and Shipton, co. Salop). Ar. on a fess az. three crescents of the field. *Crest*—An antelope sejant or, attired, maned, armed, and tufted sa.

Paramour (St. Nicholas, in the Isle of Thanet,; assigned by Cooke, Clarenceux, 1585). Az. a fess embattled betw. three estoiles or. *Crest*—A cubit arm erect, vested az. cuffed ar. holding in the hand ppr. an estoile or.

Parbo (Sandwich, co. Kent, and co. Chester). Vert semée of fleurs-de-lis and fretty or, a chief erm.

Paravicin, or Palavicini (Sir PETER PARAVICIN, knighted 1687). Az. a swan ar. *Crest*—A swan's head betw. two wings. Sir PETER appeared at the Visit. of London, 1687, and entered a pedigree of three descents. The arms he produced (as above) were taken from an old seal, and it was admitted that the colours were "the Painter's fancy." Le Neve (Ped. of Knights) ascribes to him: Az. an eagle displ. ar.; and in Add. M.S. British Museum 14,832, the arms of PARAVICIN, of London, are given as: Gu. a swan ar. beaked and membered or.

Parbury (of ancient German origin; descended, in the female line, from the POLLENS, of Little Bookham, co. Surrey; represented by GEORGE PARBURY, Esq., of Mansfield House, Russell Square, London). Or, on a bend engr. cotised, also engr. az. betw. six torteaux five escallops ar. *Crest*—Two branches of laurel in saltire ppr. surmounted by a pelican or, semée of torteaux in her nest ppr. feeding her young, gold. *Motto*—Cras mihi.

Pardoe (Park House, Bewdley, co. Worcester). Ar. a chev. betw. three crosses crosslet fitchée sa. quartering, for ACTON of Wolverton, Gu. a chev. betw. three cinquefoils ar. *Crest* —Two vultures' heads and necks conjoined ppr.

Pardoe (Hailes Park, co. Worcester). Or, on a chev. em-battled betw. three towers gu. from the portal of each a doe issuant ppr. three cinquefoils of the field. *Crest*—A tower with a doe issuant ppr.

Pardoe (Nash Court, co. Salop). Ar. a cross counter-com-ponée or and gu. betw. in the 1st quarter, a water bouget, in the 2nd an eagle displ., in the 3rd a swan, and in the 4th an escallop all sa., on a chief az. a lion pass. guard. of the first. *Crest*—A lion pass. guard. *Another Crest*—A demi lion ramp. guard. ar. holding an escallop sa.

Pardoe. Same *Arms*. *Crest*—A griffin sejant az. winged, legged and beaked or.

Pardoe (Welwyn, co. Herts). Ar. on a chev. embattled counter-embattled betw. three castles sa. as many bombs of the field fired ppr. a chief az. *Crest*—A tower ar.

Pardoe (Leyton, co. Essex). Same *Arms* and *Crest*.

Pardy (that Ilk). Or, a chev. az. betw. three stars of sixteen points.

Pare (West Leake, co. Nottingham). Ar. a chev. betw. three crosses crosslet sa.

Pares (Hopwell Hall, co. Derby, and Kirby Frith, co. Leicester; settled in the latter county since the time of Queen Elizabeth). Sa. a chev. ar. in the dexter chief quarter a cross crosslet of the second. *Crest*—A demi griffin or. *Motto*— Pares cum paribus.

Parent. Ar. three martlets gu.

Pares. Sa. a chev. betw. three crosses crosslet ar. *Crest*—A greyhound courant gu.

Parfitt (Bruton, co. Somerset; long settled in that county. The late JOHN PARFITT, of Bruton, left four sons and three daus. The eldest son, the Very Rev. CHARLES PARFITT, of Cottles, co. Wilts, is Canon of Clifton, and Chamberlain of Honour to H.H. the Pope). Quarterly, 1st and 4th, az. a cross lozengy or, in the sinister chief and dexter base points an estoile ar. over all a bend erm. charged with a trefoil vert; 2nd and 3rd, sa. on a chev. engr. betw. three pistols or, as many roses gu. barbed vert. *Crest*—A falcon rising

774

ar. winged, beaked, and legged or, on the breast a trefoil, as in the arms, and in the beak an ear of wheat vert. *Motto* En tout parfait.

Pargiter (Barking, co. Essex, London, and Chipping Nor-ton, co. Oxford). Az. a fess indented betw. three pigeons or.

Pargiter (Lord Mayor of London, 1530). Az. a fess dan-cettée betw. three hawks or.

Pargiter (London). Barry of four ar. and sa. three mascles counterchanged.

Pargiter (Greetworth, co. Northampton). Barry of four or and sa. three mascles counterchanged. *Crest*—A dexter arm embowed ppr. vested ar. holding np a covered cup or.

Parham. Ar. on a chev. engr. gu. three lions' gambs erased or, betw. as many mallets ppr. a border engr. sa. bezantée.

Paringham. Az. a lion salient guard. or.

Paris (Little Linton, co. Cambridge, and Poding-Norton, co. Norfolk). Gu. three unicorns' heads couped or.

Paris (Hitchin, co. Herts, and Stone, co. Huntingdon; granted 15 June, 1573). Gu. a fess wavy betw. three unicorns' heads couped or. *Crest*—A sphinx couchant gu. face and breast ppr. wings endorsed or, crined of the last.

Paris (co. Huntingdon). Same *Arms* and *Crest*, the sphinx or, face and breast ppr.

Paris (co. Lincoln). Sa. a chev. betw. three (another, ten) crosses crosslet ar.

Paris. Gu. three unicorns' heads couped or, a border engr. of the last.

Paris. Gu. a saltire betw. four lions ramp. or.

Paris. Ar. a chev. betw. ten crosses crosslet sa.

Paris, or Parris. Ar. a bend gobony az. and gu.

Paris (Scotland). Gu. a ship in full sail or, masts and sails ar. betw. three fleurs-de-lis of the second. *Crest*—A quill in pale ppr.

Parish. Gu. three unicorns' heads couped ar. *Crest*—A unicorn's head erased ar.

Parish Clerks, Company of (London). Az. a fleur-de-lis or, on a chief gu. a leopard's face betw. two song books (shut) of the second, stringed vert. *Crest*—A cubit arm erect, vested az. cuffed erm. holding in the hand ppr. a music book (open) of the last, garnished or, stringed vert. *Motto*—Unitas societatis stabilitas.

Park (Holland; descended from Scotland). Az. a fess chequy ar. and gu. betw. three cinquefoils in chief of the second, and a buck's head cabossed or, in base. *Crest*—A sinister hand holding up an open book ppr. *Motto*— Sapienter et pie.

Park (that Ilk). Or, a fess chequy ar. and az. betw. three stags' heads couped gu.

Park (Fulfordlees, co. Berwick). Or, a fesse chequy gu. and ar. betw. three bucks' heads cabossed, all within a bordure of the second. *Motto*—Providentiæ me committo.

Park (Scotland, 1672). Az. a fesse chequy gu. and ar. betw. three frases of the second. *Crest*—A dexter hand holding up a shut book ppr. *Motto*—Graviter et pie.

Parke (*Lord Wensleydale*, extinct 1868; Right Hon. JAMES PARKE, a Baron of the Court of Exchequer, was created *Baron Wensleydale*, 1856, he d. without male issue, when the title became extinct). Gu. on a pale engr. betw. two palets three stags' heads cabossed of the field, attired or. *Crest*—A talbot's head couped gu. eared and gorged with a collar gemel or, and pierced in the breast with a pheon gold. *Supporters*—On either side a stag gu. attired and gorged with a collar or, pendent therefrom a portcullis gold. *Motto* —Justitiæ tenax.

Parke (originally of co. Cumberland, afterwards of Henbury House, Sturminster Marshall, co. Dorset). Az. on a fess engr. betw. three hinds trippant or, as many torteaux, each charged with a pheon of the third. *Crest*—A stag's head couped sa. holding in the mouth a key or. *Motto*—True and Fast.

Parke (Wisbeach, in the Isle of Ely, co. Cambridge; granted 1618). Gu. on a pale ar. three bucks' heads cabossed of the first. *Crest*—A talbot's head gu. pierced in the breast with a pheon or.

Parke (co. Kent and London). Sa. on a fess engr. ar. betw. three hinds trippant or, as many torteaux each charged with a pheon of the second.

Parke. Ar. on a pale az. three bucks' heads cabossed of the field. *Crest*—A talbot's head erased ar. pierced through with an arrow barways ppr.

Parke. Az. an eagle displ. ar. armed or.

Parke. Sa. an eagle displ. ar. a border of the last.

Parke. Ar. on a fess sa. three escallops of the first, a canton erm.

Parke (Sligo and Leitrim). Ar. on a fess sa. three bezants. *Crest*—A wing az. semée of estoiles or.

Parke. Same *Arms*. *Crest*—On a mount vert paled in ar. a fox paly of four or and az.

Parkeley. Chequy gu. and ar. on a bend az. three billets or.

Parker (Norton Lees, co. Derby, *temp.* Richard II. ; the heiress *m.* BARKER). Gu. a chev. betw. three leopards' faces or. *Crest*—A leopard's head affrontée erased or, ducally gorged gu.

Parker (Park Hall, co. Stafford; a younger branch of the Norton Lees family and the senior line of the noble house of MACCLESFIELD). Same *Arms* and *Crest*.

Parker (*Earl of Macclesfield*). Same *Arms* and *Crest*. *Supporters*—Two leopards reguard. ppr. each gorged with a ducal coronet gu. *Motto*—Sapere aude.

Parker (*Baron Morley and Monteagle; b*aronies in abeyance since *temp.* James II. between the representatives of the daus. of WILLIAM PARKER, 4th *Lord Morley and Monteagle*, viz., CATHERINE, wife of JOHN SAVAGE, *Earl Rivers*, and ELIZABETH, wife of EDWARD CRANFIELD, Esq.). Az. betw. two bars. sa. charged with three bezants a lion pass. gu. in chief three bucks' heads cabossed of the second. *Crest*—An heraldic antelope statant or, ducally gorged and chained az. *Supporters*—Dexter, an heraldic antelope or, hoofed sa. ducally gorged and chained az.; sinister, a griffin or, ducally gorged and chained az.

Parker (*Earl of Morley*). Sa. a stag's head caboshed betw. two flaunches ar. *Crest*—A cubit arm erect couped below the elbow sleeved az. cuffed and slashed ar. in the hand a stag's attire gu. *Supporters*—Dexter, a stag ar. collared or, therefrom suspended an escocheon vert charged with a horse's head couped ar. bridled or; sinister, a greyhound sa. collared or, therefrom suspended an escocheon gu. charged with a ducal coronet or. *Motto*—Fideli certa merces.

Parker (Melford Hall, Suffolk, bart.). 1st and 4th, **sa. a** buck's head caboshed betw. two. flaunches ar., for PARKER; 2nd and 3rd, az. a chev. betw. three lozenges or, for HYDE. To these, the coat as generally borne, further belong the quarterings of ar. a chev. sa. betw. three bulls' heads caboshed gu., for NORBURY; and ar. a tiger looking down in a glass reguard. gu., for SYBELL. *Crest*—A dexter arm erect vested az. slashed and cuffed ar. holding in the hand ppr. an attire of a stag or.

Parker (Bassingbourn, co. Essex, bart., extinct). Gu. on a chev. betw. three keys erect ar. as many fleurs-de-lis of the field. *Crest*—An elephant's head couped ar. collared gu. charged with three fleurs-de-lis or. *Motto*—Try.

Parker (Harburn, co. Warwick, bart.). Erm. an anchor erect az. betw. three escallops gu., on a chief wavy of the second a naval crown or, sterns and sails ar. *Crest*—On a naval crown az. the sterns and sails ppr. a hart at gaze ar. in front of a slip of oak erect and issuant vert.

Parker (Shenstone Lodge, Lichfield, bart.). Gu. a chev. betw. three leopards' faces or. *Crest*—A leopard's head erased affrontée or, ducally gorged gu.

Parker (granted to JOHN PARKER, R.N.). Az. a chev. betw. two leopards' faces in chief and in base the stern of a ship or. *Crest*—Out of a naval crown az. a demi stag or, supporting between the paws an anchor erect sa. encircled by a wreath of laurel ppr.

Parker (co. Chester). Ar. a chev. embattled sa. betw. three bucks' heads cabossed gu. *Crest*—On a mount vert a talbot sejant collared or, resting the dexter paw on a buck's head cabossed gu.

Parker (co. Chester). Vert a buck ramp. ppr. *Crest*—A buck's head erased ppr.

Parker (co. Cornwall). Az. fretty ar. a fess or.

Parker (co. Cambridge). Az. a buck trippant or, betw. three pheons ar. a border engr. of the second hurtée.

Parker (co. Derby). Ar. on a chev. gu. three bucks' heads cabossed or, in chief as many mullets az.

Parker (co. Derby, and Whitley Hall, co. Lincoln). Gu. a chev. engr. betw. three leopards' faces or. *Crest*—A leopard's head erased guard. or, ducally gorged gu.

Parker (cos. Derby and Lancaster). Ar. a chev. gu. betw. three mullets pierced sa., on a chief az. as many bucks' heads cabossed or.

Parker (Whiteway, co. Devon). Sa. a stag's head cabossed betw. two flaunches ar. *Crest*—An arm erect, vested az. cuffed ar. the hand holding the attire of a stag ppr. *Motto*—Fideli certa merces.

Parker (Plympton, St. Mary's, co. Devon, and Honington, co. Warwick). Sa. a buck's head cabossed betw. two flaunches or. *Crest*—A cubit arm erect, vested sa. cuffed ar. the hand ppr. grasping a stag's horn gu.

775

Parker (Fryth Hall, co. Essex; granted 21 Feb. 1557). Or, three escutcheons sa. each charged with a broad arrowhead of the field. *Crest*—A lion's gamb erased or, grasping an arrow gu. headed and feathered ar.

Parker (Northleach, co. Gloucester). Sa. a buck pass. ar. betw. three pheons or, a border engr. of the second, pellettée.

Parker (Finglesham. co. Kent). Ar. a chev. ermines betw. three mascles az. *Crest*—Out of a mural coronet or, a horse's head gu. maned gold.

Parker (co. Kent). Az. a chev. erm. betw. three mascles or. Same *Crest*, as the last.

Parker (Northfleet, co. Kent). Erm. a buck's head cabossed gu. *Crest*—Out of a ducal coronet gu. a bull's head or, armed ar.

Parker (Sandwich, co. Kent, and Margate, in the Isle of Thanet; granted by Sir John Borough, Garter King of Arms). Gu. on a chev. betw. three keys erect, wards upward ar. as many fleurs-de-lis of the first. *Crest*—An elephant's head couped ar. gorged with a collar gu. charged with three fleurs-de-lis or.

Parker (Syberswold, co. Kent; confirmed 6 May, 1588). Erm. six escallops gu. three, two, and one. *Crest*—A talbot pass. ar. against an oak tree ppr. fructed or.

Parker (Bradkirke, co. Lancaster, 1664). Ar. a chev. gu. betw. three mullets sa. on a chief az. three stags' heads cabossed or. *Crest*—A stag's head couped or.

Parker (Haling, co. Surrey). Or, a buck trippant gu. on a canton of the first a ship az.

Parker (co. Kent). Erm. ten escallops gu. four, three, two, and one. *Crest*—A cubit arm erect, in coat of mail or, holding in the hand ppr. a falchion ar. hilt and pommel gold.

Parker (co. Kent). Gu. on a chev. betw. three keys or, (sometimes, ar.) as many estoiles (sometimes, mullets) sa.

Parker (Aldborough, co. Norfolk). Ar. a chev. betw. three mascles sa. *Crest*—A demi cock, wings endorsed gu. combed and wattled ar.

Parker (co. Norfolk). Ar. on a fess sa. three bezants.

Parker (co. Norfolk). Or, a chev. sa. betw. three mascles az. *Crest*—A demi cock wings expanded gu. beaked, combed, and wattled ar.

Parker (co. Norfolk). Or, a chev. sa. betw. three fusils az.

Parker (co. Stafford). Gu. a chev. betw. three leopards' faces or.

Parker (Willows, Suffolk, 1609; Her. Office, m. 14). Erm. on a chief vert, three bucks' heads cabossed or. *Crest*—A talbot pass. ar. resting the dexter paw on a buck's head cabossed or.

Parker (Hanthorpe House, co. Lincoln). Per fess gu. and ar. a pale counterchanged, a chev. erm. betw. three leopards' faces or. *Crest*—betw. two oak branches ppr. a leopard's face or, over which a mullet of six points. *Motto*—Auctor pretiosa facit.

Parker (Hurstmonceux, co. Sussex). Ar. betw. two bars sa. (another az.) charged with three bezants a lion pass. gu. in chief as many bucks' heads cabossed of the third. *Crest*—Out of a ducal coronet or, a bear's head sa. muzzled gold.

Parker (Ratton, co. Sussex; bart., extinct 1750; descended from GEOFFREY PARKER, of Bexley, *temp.* Edward I. ; the last male heir, Sir WALTER PARKER, of Ratton, third bart. *d. unm.* in 1750, when the CHALVINGTON property passed to the FULLERS; THOMAS FULLER, Esq., fourth son of THOMAS FULLER, of Rose Hill and Waldron, co. Sussex, having *m.* ELINOR, dau. of JOHN LIDGITER, Esq., which lady was heiress both to the TRAYTONS and PARKERS). Az. fretty or, over all a fess of the second. *Crest*—On a chapeau az. turned up erm. a greyhound or.

Parker (London). Same *Arms*. *Crest*—On a chapeau az. a greyhound pass. or, collared ringed, and lined ar.

Parker (Wales). Az. a chev. erm. betw. three acorns slipped or. *Crest*—A lion ramp. or.

Parker (Cuerden and Extwistle, co. Lancaster: seated at the latter place in the time of Richard II.). Gu. a chev. betw. three leopards' faces or, in the mouth of each an arrow fessways ar., quartering TOWNLEY of Royle, and BANASTER of Bank (*which see*). *Crest*—A buck trippant ppr. transpierced through the body with an arrow paleways point downwards ar.

Parker (THOMAS PARKER, Esq., of Warwick Hall, near Carlisle). Az. two bars gemelles ar. betw. three bucks' heads erased or, all betw. two flaunches of the last. *Crest*s—A cubit arm vested vert cuffed ar. holding in each hand the attire of a stag and a bow and arrow saltirewise all ppr.

Parker (CHRISTOPHER PARKER, Esq., of Petterell Green, co. Cumberland). Same *Arms* and *Crest*. *Motto*—Virtutis alimentum honos.

Parker (Blisland and Trengoffe, near Cornwall). Ar. a chev. betw. three mascles az.

Parker (Woodthorpe, co.York; descended from JOHN PARKER, of Little Norton, co. Derby, temp. Queen ELIZABETH, represented by the Right Hon. JOHN PARKER, of Onslow Squnre, London, formerly M.P. for Sheffield). Ar a chev. pean betw. three mullets sa. on a chief az. as many bucks' heads cabossed or. Crest—A talbot's head couped ar. ears and tongue gu. gorged with a collar pean.

Parker (St. James's, Westminster; confirmed 1769). Ar. a leopard's face gu. betw. three escutcheons sa. each charged with a pheon or. Crest—A stag pass. ppr.

Parker (confirmed 20 April, 1563). Per pale or and sa. on a chev. betw. three annulets as many bucks' heads all counterchanged.

Parker (granted 1772). Gu. on a chev. ar. betw. three keys erect wards upward or, as many fleurs-de-lis az. Crest—An elephant's head ar. trunk and tusks or, ears gu.

Parker (The Ould, co. Warwick). Or, on two bars gu. three leopards' faces of the field. Crest—Out of a ducal coronet or, a plume of five feathers sa.

Parker. Sa. a buck's heads cabossed betw. two flaunches ar. Crest—An arm erect vested az. cuffed and puffed ar. holding in the hand ppr. an attire of a stag gu.

Parker. Ar. a stag pass. gu. on a canton az. a galley or. Crest—A stag's head couped ppr.

Parker. Ar. a chev. pean betw. three mullets sa. on a chief az. three bucks' heads cabossed or. Crest—A talbot's head ar. collared pean, eared gu.

Parker (Arwerton, co. Suffolk, Sheriff of the co. temp. Queen Elizabeth). Ar. a lion pass. gu. betw. two bars sa. charged with three bezants, two and one, in chief as many bucks' heads of the third Crest—On a mount vert a stag trippant ppr.

Parker (co. Gloucester). Ar. a chev. betw. three bucks' heads gu. attired or.

Parker. Az. a buck ar. betw. three pheons or, a border engr. of the last, charged with eight hurts. Crest—A buck's head couped ar. attired or, with an arrow through the horns of the first.

Parker. Az. a chev. or, betw. three cotton hanks lying fessways ar. Crest—A horse's head couped per pale indented ar. and az.

Parker. Erm. seven escallops gu. four, two, and one. Crest—A hand or, holding a falchion, blade ar. hilt gold.

Parker. Erm. on a fess sa. three bezants.

Parker. Ar. a chev. sa. betw. three mascles az. Crest—A cock's head gu. wings tawny, bill ar.

Parker (Sweeney, co. Salop). Sa. on a fess ar. betw. three pheons, points downwards or, a buck's head cabossed of the field betw. two pellets. Crest—A buck's head cabossed sa.

Parker (Upton Cheney, co. Gloucester). Ar. three bucks trippant ppr. a chief az. Crest—A buck's head, in the mouth an acorn leaved all ppr.

Parker (Browsholme and Newton, co. York). Vert a chev. betw. three stags' heads cabossed or. Crest—On a chapeau gu. turned up erm. a stag trippant ppr. Motto—Non fluctu nec flatu movetur.

Parker (Copenhall, co. Chester). Ar. a chev. sa. betw. three stag's heads cabossed gu.

Parker (Lambeth, co. Surrey; granted by Dethick, 1559, to MATTHEW PARKER, Archbishop of Canterbury). Gu. on a chev. betw. three keys ar. (for an augmentation) three estoiles or. Same Arms confirmed (without the estoiles and the following crest; granted by Cooke, Clarenceux, to JOHN PARKER, son of the Archbishop). An elephant's head couped or, tusked gu.

Parker (JOHN PARKER, Archbishop of Tuam, 1667-79, and of Dublin, 1679-82. Fun. Ent. Ulster's Office, 1669, of his dau.). Ar. a lion pass. gu. betw. two bars sa. the upper charged with two and the lower with one bezant.

Parker (Castle Lough). See Supplement.

Parkes. Gu. on a pale ar. three bucks' heads caboshed of the field. Crest—A talbot's head erased gu. charged on the breast with a pheon or.

Parkes (Willingsworth and Wednesbury, co. Stafford; granted to RICHARD PARKES, 4 Feb. 1615; the grand dau. of RICHARD PARKES carried the property at the above places in marriage to WILLIAM, younger son of HUMBLE, Lord Ward). Sa. a fess erm. betw. three bucks' heads couped or. Crest—An oak tree flourishing with leaves and acorns thereon a squirrel all ppr.

Parkes (Fun. Ent. Ulster's Office, 1671). Ar on a fess sa. three bezants, quartering, for JONES, Gu. on a cross betw. four mullets pierced or, a pheon staff broken point down.

Parkhill (Scotland). Ar. a stag trippant ppr. attired and unguled or.

776

Parkhill (Scotland; Capt. DAVID PARKHILL, 1803). Quarterly, 1st and 4th, ar. on a hillock ppr. a stag trippant attired and unguled gu. within a bordure az.; 2nd and 3rd, gu. an. inescutcheon erm. betw. three pikes' heads couped or, in chief a mullet ar. Crest—A cornucopia or, filled with fruit and grain ppr. Motto—Capta majora.

Parkhouse (Eastfield Lodge, co. Hants). Per chev. embattled vert and ar. in chief two bucks trippant ppr. gorged with a collar or, in base a cross flory of the first. Crest—A buck ppr. charged on the body with three mullets az. the dexter foreleg resting on a cross fiory as in the arms. Motto—The Cross our stay.

Parkhurst (London). Ar. a cross erm. betw. four bucks trippant ppr. Crest—Out of a pallisado coronet or, a buck's head erased ar. attired of the first.

Parkhurst (Ripple, co. Worcester; FLEETWOOD PARKHURST, of that place, was High Sheriff co. Worcester in 1792). Same Arms and Crest.

Parkhurst. Same Arms. Crest—A griffin ramp. per fess or and gu.

Parkhurst (Lord Mayor of London, 1635). Same Arms, on a chief gu. three crescents or.

Parkhurst (Hall, co. Norfolk; granted 2 Elizabeth). Same Arms and Crest.

Parkhurst (Guildford, co. Surrey). Same Arms. Crest—A demi griffin, wings endorsed sa. holding in the dexter paw a cutlass ar. hilt and pommel or.

Parkin. Ar. a fess gu. betw. three axes az. hafted sa. Crest—A fox sejant ppr.

Parkinges. Gu. two chev. betw. three escallops ar.

Parkins (London; granted 1589). Or, on a fess dancettée sa. betw. ten billets erm. a sun betw. two crosses crosslet fitchée of the field. Crest—A bull pass. az. wings endorsed or, ducally gorged gold.

Parkins. Gu. two chev. betw. three escallops ar.

Parkins. Az. a chev. embattled or, betw. three crosses crosslet fitchée of the last.

Parkinson (Falsnape, co. Lancaster, 1613). Gu. on a chev. betw. three ostrich feathers ar. as many mullets sa. Crest—A cubit arm vested or, charged with five erm. spots in saltire sa. cuffed ar. the hand ppr. holding an ostrich feather gu.

Parkinson (Kinnersley Castle, co. Hereford). Gu. on a chev. betw. three ostrich feathers erect ar. as many mullets sa. Crest—A cubit arm erect vested erminois cuff ar. holding in the hand ppr. an ostrich feather also erect gu.

Parkinson. Gu. on a chev. betw. two ostrich feathers adossé in chief and a saltire couped in base ar. three torteaux. Crest—A griffin's head erased, holding in the beak a sword ppr.

Parkinson (East Ravendale, co. Lincoln). Gu. on a chev. engr. betw. three ostrich feathers erect ar. a fleur-de-lis az. betw. two pellets. Crest—An antelope trippant ppr. in the mouth two ostrich feathers ar.

Parkinson (granted to Rev. JOHN POSTHUMUS WILSON, M.A., Fellow of Magdalen College, Oxford, on his marriage with MARY, dau. and heiress of Rev. Dr. PARKINSON, of East Ravendale, upon his assuming, by royal licence, the surname of PARKINSON). Gu. on a chev. engr. betw. three ostrich feathers erect ar. a fleur-de-lis az. betw. two pellets, a canton or, for distinction. Crest—An antelope trippant ppr. in the mouth two ostrich feathers ar. charged on the shoulder with a pellet for distinction.

Parkinson - Fortescue. (Baron Carlingford). See FORTESCUE.

Parkville, or Pierrepoint. Ar. semée de cinquefoils gu. a lion ramp. sa.

Parkyns (Baron Rancliffe, extinct 1 Nov. 1850; Ruddington Manor, Notts, bart.). Ar. an eagle displ. sa. on a canton or, a fess dancettée betw. seven billets erm. Crest—Out of a ducal coronet or, a fir cone (apple of the pine tree) ppr. Motto—Honeste audax. A second crest and supporters were granted to Lord Rancliffe and his descendants, viz.: Crest—Out of a ducal coronet or, a demi-eagle displ. az. billeteé erm. Supporters—Two pegasi ar. billettée erm. wings endorsed ducally gorged and chained or.

Parkyns. Or, on a fess dancettée sa. ten billets ar.

Parlar (Westminster). Three lions pass in pale ar. over all on a bend sa. three mullets or. Crest—A Cornish chough sa. beaked and legged gu.

Parlby (Manadon, co. Devon). Quarterly, 1st and 4th, ar. a parrot vert, for PARLBY; 2nd and 3rd, ar. a cross gu. three talbots' heads erased of the last, for HALL. Crests—1st: Out of a ducal coronet a peacock's head erased on the beak a serpent, for PARLBY; 2nd: A talbot's head erased gu., for HALL. Motto—Parle bien.

Parler (co. Lancaster). Vair on a cross gu. a lion's head erased or.

Parleys, or Parlys. Per pale indented or and az.

Parmiger (cos. Kent and Hants. Visit. of the latter county, 1634). Gu. a fesse vairé or and az. betw. three doves of the second. *Crest*—Out of a ducal coronet or, a stag's head gu. attired gold transpierced through the neck by an arrow in bend sinister ppr. headed and flighted ar.

Parminster (Tockington, co Gloucester, *temp.* Henry III., and Watermouth, co. Devon, *temp.* Henry VII.). Ar. a saltire betw. four lozenges voided gu. on a chief az. a demi two-headed eagle displ. or. *Crest*—A dexter arm in armour embowed, the mailed hand grasping above the hilt a sword, the point broken off. *Motto*—Deo favente.

Parnell (*Baron Congleton*). Gu. two chevronels, and in chief three escallops ar. *Crest*—A boar's head erased or, betw. two wings gu. each charged with two chevronels ar. *Supporters*—Dexter, an angel vested ar. wings gold, and radiated of the same; sinister, a hermit vested ppr. a staff in his exterior hand, and an escallop or, in his hat. *Motto*—Te digna sequere.

Parnell. Gu. two chev. ar. a bend sa. *Crest*—As the last.

Parnell. Gu. two chev. ar. a bend sa. and a bordure or (another, ar.).

Parnell. Ar. an estoile sa.

Parner. Gu. a chev. or, betw. three crescents ar.

Parnham. Ar. a chev. az. betw. three pears gu. *Crest*—A leopard's head erased ar.

Parnther. Sa. three chev. ar. on a chief of the second as many crosses crosslet of the first. *Crest*—A dexter arm in armour ppr. holding a cross crosslet fitchée in pale or.

Parott. Ar. (another, erm.) on a bend sinister gu. three escallops or.

Parr (Parr, co. Lancaster). Ar. two bars az. a bordure engr. sa. *Crest*—A female's head full-faced, couped below the shoulders ppr. habited az. on her head a wreath of roses, alternately ar. and gu.

Parr (Kendal, co. Westmorland; borne by WILLIAM PARR, *Marquess of Northampton;* extinct 1571, derived from the marriage of Sir WILLIAM PARR, of Parre, co. Lancaster, Knt., with ELIZABETH DE Roos, granddau. and heiress of Sir THOMAS DE Roos, Baron of Kendal. The younger branches were the PARRS, Barons Parr, of Horton, co. Northampton, the PARRS of cos. Derby and Leicester, the PARRS of Kempnall, the PARRS of Backford, the PARRS of Eccleston, the PARRS of Lythwood, &c.). Ar. two bars az. within a bordure engr. sa. Coat of Augmentation granted by King Henry VIII. to the family of his Queen, Katherine Parr: Or, on a pile gu. betw. six roses of Lancaster three roses of York. *Crest*—As PARR of Parr, except that some authorities vest the crest erm. instead of az. and others place a crown on the female's head, instead of a wreath: some give both, the crown above the wreath. *Supporters*—Dexter, a stag or; sinister, a wivern ar. *Motto*—Amour avecque loiaulté. *Badges and Crests* of the time of Henry VIII.: PARE (PARR) a maiden's head full-faced ppr. vested gu. crined or. (This, issuant out of a red and white rose, was the badge of Queen Katherine Parr. *Collectanea Genealogica et Topographica*, vol. iii. p. 74). Sir William Segar, in his MSS. in Coll. of Arms, states the Crest, a maiden's head, to be the Crest of Roos; yet it appears certain that the PARRS bore arms before their alliance with the heiress of Roos, as ROBERT DE PARR and HENRY DE PARR were among the gentlemen of coat armour who gave evidence on the Scrope and Grosvenor trial in 1386; ELIZABETH DE Roos was not married till 1390.

Parr (coat of augmentation, granted by Henry VIII. to his Queen Katherine, dau. of Sir THOMAS PARR, of Kendal). Or, on a pile gu. betw. six roses of the last three roses ar.

Parr (Kempnall, co. Lancaster; represented by STARKIE, of Huntroyd. Her. Visit. 1567). Ar. two bars az. within a bordure engr. sa. *Crest*—A horse's head gu. maned or.

Parr (Backford, co. Chester; seated at Backford for four generations, till ROBERT PARR sold the estate to THOMAS ALDERSEY, about 1580: he *d. s. p.* 1582). Ar. two bars az. within a bordure engr. sa. bezantée. *Crest*—A demi bear ramp. az. bristled or, charged with a bend gu. thereon three lozenges or.

Parr (Stonelands, co. Devon). Ar. two bars az. within a bordure engr. sa., quartering CODRINGTON, viz., Ar. a fesse embattled counter-embattled betw. three lions pass. sa. *Crest*—Out of a ducal coronet or, a dragon's head gu. betw. two wings chequy or and az. being the Crest of CODRINGTON.

Parr (granted in 1590, to JOHN PARR, of London, Embroiderer to Queen Elizabeth, son of THURSTAN PARR, of Parwich, near Warrington, co. Lancaster). Ar. two bars az. a bordure engr. sa. charged with eight escallops of the field, borne with several quarterings. *Crest*—A female's head ppr.

vested az. charged on the breast with three escallops barwise ar.

Parr (granted to the Rev. JOHN LYNES, LL.B., of Tooley Park, in behalf of his wife, CAROLINE SOBIESKI, and to her sister, AUGUSTA ELIZA WYNNE, the wife of Captain Sir JOHN MARSHALL, R.N., C.B., and K.C.H., as the two representatives of the Rev. Dr. SAMUEL PARR, Prebendary of St. Paul's). Erm. two bars az. each charged with as many crosses pattée or, a bordure engr. sa. thereon four escallops and as many roses alternately ar. *Crest*—A mount vert therefrom issuing in front of a pear tree fructed ppr. a rose tree vert bearing five roses gu. barbed and seeded also ppr.

Parr (Lythwood, co. Salop; derived from a younger branch of the family of PARR of Kendal. The late THOMAS PARR, Esq., of Lythwood, one of the most eminent merchants of Liverpool, was fourth son of JOHN PARR, Esq., of Liverpool, and of Elm House, West Derby). Ar. two bars az. a bordure engr. sa. a crescent for diff. *Crest*—A female's head couped below the shoulders full faced ppr. habited az. on her head a wreath of roses alternately ar. and gu. *Motto*—Amour avec loiaulté.

Parr (Rev. HENRY PARR, Vicar of Yoxford, co. Suffolk, only surviving son of the late THOMAS PARR, Esq., of Lythwood (*see preceding article*). Same *Arms*, &c.

Parr (Grappenhall Heyes, co. Chester; derived from JOHN PARR, Esq., the descendant of an ancient Lancaster family, which was possessed of estates in the parish of Ormskirk). Ar. two bars az. a bordure engr. sa. charged with eight escallops of the field. *Crest*—A female's head couped below the shoulders ppr. habited az. the vest charged with three escallops ar. the centre one suspended by a chain round the neck. *Motto*—Faire sans dire.

Parram (co. Wilts, *temp.* Richard II.). Ar. on a chev. engr. betw. three mullets gu. within a bordure engr. sa. bezantée as many lions' paws erased of the second. *Crest*—A lion's paw erased or, holding a mallet erect gu.

Parre (co. Devon). Erm. on a chev. gu. three martlets or.

Parre. Or, on a pale betw. six roses gu. three of the same ar.

Parrock (Parrock, co. Kent). Erm. a chief quarterly, or and gu. in the first quarter a chessrook sa.

Parrot, or Parrott. Gu. on orle ar. in chief three mascles or. *Crest*—A parrot gu.

Parry (JONES-PARRY, Madryn Castle, co. Carnarvon). Quarterly, 1st and 4th, ar. a fesse betw. three lozenges az., for PARRY; 2nd and 3rd, quarterly, 1st and 4th, erm. a lion ramp. sa., for JONES, 2nd and 3rd, per bend sinister erm. and ermines a lion ramp. or, armed and langued az., for TUDOR TREVOR. *Crests*—1st: Three battle axes erect staves gu. headed or, for PARRY; 2nd: On a chapeau gu. turned up erm. a demi lion ramp. or, for JONES; 3rd: A stag trippant ar. attired and unguled or; 4th: A nag's head and neck erased ar. maned or. *Mottoes*—Gofal Dyn Duw .ai gwerid; A prudent man God will guard. Over the battle axes, Heb Dduw heb Ddym, Duw a Dygon; over the stag, Nil desperandum.

Parry (JONES-PARRY, Llwyn Onn, co. Denbigh). Same *Arms*, &c.

Parry (Hamsted Marshall, co. Berks). Sa. a chev. betw. three boys' heads couped at the shoulders ppr. crined or, round each neck a snake tied vert. *Crest*—A cubit arm ppr. grasping a snake vert biting the hand.

Parry (Twysog, co. Denbigh; exemplified to EDWARD WILLIAM GRAINGER, Esq., resident in Bavaria, only son and heir of the late EDWARD WILLIAM GRAINGER, and grandson of EDWARD FRANCIS GRAINGER, Esq., who was son of WILLIAM GRAINGER, Esq., of Causestown, co. Meath. The first-named EDWARD WILLIAM GRAINGER, Esq., and the other descendants of his grandfather, EDWARD FRANCIS GRAINGER, by ROSE PARRY, his wife were authorised by royal licence, 1864, to take the surname and arms of PARRY in lieu of GRAINGER). Gu. a lion ramp. ar. *Crest*—A demi lion ramp. ar. charged on the shoulder with a cross gu. *Motto*—Si Deus nobiscum.

Parry (Exeter, Old Court, and Wormbridge, co. Hereford, and co. Warwick; Reg. Her. Coll.). Ar. a fesse betw. three lozenges sa.

Parry (SEGAR-PARRY, Little Haddam, co. Hertford). Quarterly, 1st and 4th, PARRY. ar. a fesse betw. three lozenges az.; 2nd and 3rd, SEGAR, az. a cross moline ar. *Crests*—1st, PARRY: A buck's head couped ar. holding in the mouth a sprig ppr.; 2nd, SEGAR: On a ducal coronet or, two snakes vert, entwined round a sceptre of the first, betw. two wings, the dexter or, the other ar.

Parry (co. Hereford). Ar. a fesse betw. three lozenges az.

within a bordure of the last. *Crest*—Three battle axes erect ppr.

Parry (Highnam Court, co. Gloucester). Ar. a fesse betw. three lozenges sa. *Crest*—Three battle axes erect ppr. *Motto*—Tu ne cede malis.

Parry (Lord Mayor of London, 1739). Quarterly, or and sa. on a bend gu. cotised erm. three lions pass. ar.

Parry. Ar. on a chev. betw. three lions ramp. az. as many garbs or. *Crest*—A demi lion ramp. az. on the head a garb as in the arms.

Parry. Ar. a fesse betw. three lozenges sa. *Crest*—A lamb ar. bearing a banner or.

Parry. Ar. three boars' heads cabossed sa.

Parry. Sa. a fesse betw. two bars dancettée ar.

Parry (Noyadd, co. Cardigan; descended from the ancient Lords of Cardigan). Sa. a spear's head ar. embrued gu. betw. three scaling ladders of the second, two and one, on a chief gu. a castle triple-towered ppr.

Parry (Trevor Issa, near Llangollen, descended from OWEN, of Treveilir, who derived from Gwalchmai ap Meilir, Lord of Treveilir, co. Anglesey, in 1170). Ar. three saddles sa. stirrups and leathers or.

Parry (JOHN PARRY, Bishop of Ossory, 1672-77; Fun. Ent. Ulster's Office). Az. a cinquefoil ar. betw. three ducal coronets or.

Parscoe. Gyronny of eight sa. and ar. eight mullets counterchanged. *Crest*—A castle triple-towered ppr. from the middle tower a demi lion ramp. az.

Parsons (*Viscount and Earl of Rosse*, extinct 1764; confirmed by St. George, Ulster, 1682, to Sir RICHARD PARSONS, created 1718, *Baron of Oxmantown*, and *Viscount Rosse*). Gu. three leopards' faces or. *Crest*—A halbert's head or, embrued gu. *Supporters*—Two leopards ar. spotted sa. collared gu.

Parsons (*Earl of Rosse*). Gu. three leopards' faces ar. *Crest*—Out of a ducal coronet or, a cubit arm holding a sprig of roses all ppr. *Supporters*—Two leopards ar. pellettée each gorged with a collar gu. charged with four bezants. *Motto*—Pro Deo et rege.

Parsons (co. Buckingham). Az. on a chev. ar. betw. three oak leaves or, as many crosses gu. *Crest*—On a chapeau az. turned up erm. an eagle's head erased ar. ducally crowned or, charged on the neck with a cross gu.

Parsons (Hemerton, co. Gloucester). Az. a chev. erm. betw. three trefoils ar.

Parsons (co. Hereford). Gu. a leopard's face betw. three crosses pattée fitchée at the foot ar. *Crest*—A halbert headed ar. embrued gu.

Parsons (Sir JOHN PARSONS, Lord Mayor of London in 1704, and HUMPHREY PARSONS, Lord Mayor in 1731). Gu. two chevronels erm. betw. three eagles displ. or. *Crest*—An eagle's leg erased at the thigh or, standing on a leopard's face gu.

Parsons (Island of Barbadoes; borne by the Rev. JOHN PARSONS, M.A., of Begbrook House, co. Gloucester, Vicar of Marden, co. Wilts, son of the late DANIEL PARSONS, Esq., M.D., of Barbadoes, in which island the family, a branch of that of Great Milton, co. Oxford, has long been settled). Gu. two chevronels erm. betw. three eagles displ. or. *Crest*—A demi griffin segreant ar. beaked and armed gu.

Parsons (Steyning, co. Sussex; granted 23 April, 1661). Per fesse az. and sa. three suns or. *Crest*—A garb of quatrefoils vert, banded or.

Parsons. Per fesse sa. and az. three suns or. *Crest*—A garb of trefoils vert, banded or.

Parsons. Az. two swords in saltire blades ar. hilts and pomels or, pierced through a human heart ppr. in chief a cinquefoil az. *Crest*—A tower ar.

Parsons. Gu. a leopard's face betw. three crosses pattée fitchée ar.

Parsons (Clanclewedog, co. Radnor). Quarterly, 1st, or, a chev. betw. four crosses crosslet fitchée gu., for PARSONS; 2nd, ar. two lions pass. guard. az. armed and langued gu., for HANMER; 3rd, erm. a lion ramp. sa. armed and langued gu. a canton chequey or and gu., for JEFFREYS; 4th, gu., three owls ar., for MORGAN. *Crest*—A demi lion ramp. gu. *Motto*—Quid retribuam.

Parsons (Langley, co. Buckingham, Epsom, co. Surrey, and Stanton-on-the-Wolds, co. Nottingham, bart., extinct 1812; this family obtained a baronetcy in 1661, and became extinct in the male line on the death of Sir MARK PARSONS, fourth and last bart.). Ar. a chev. betw. three holly leaves vert. *Crest*—Upon a chapeau gu. turned up erm. a griffin's head erased ar. beaked also gu.

Partheriche, or Parthericke (co. Middlesex). Vairé az. and ar. on a chief of the last three cinquefoils gu. *Crest*—A dexter arm in armour embowed and couped, holding a scymitar ppr.

778

Partington. Or, three pheons gu. *Crest*—An arm ppr. vested ar. holding an anchor also ppr.

Partington. Gu. on a fesse ar. three Cornish choughs sa. *Crest*—A hawk wings expanded ppr.

Partington. Ar. a fesse gu. betw. three mullets pierced az.

Partney. Barruly ar. and az. a bend gu.

Partrich (Long Sutton, co. Lincoln). Gu. a fesse or, betw. three partridges volant ar.

Partrich (London). Gu. a fesse vairé or and az. betw. three bezants, on each a partridge of the field.

Partrich. Sa. a fesse cotised between three partridges volant or. *Crest*—A partridge volant or.

Partrich. Ar. on an inescutcheon within an orle of martlets gu. a lion ramp. or.

Partrich. Ar. fretty gu.

Partrich. Gu. three roundles vair, on a chief or, a lion pass. sa.

Partrickson (co. Cumberland; granted 1592). Or, a greyhound courant sa. *Crest*—On a mount vert a stag courant reguard. ppr. attired and unguled or.

Partrickson. See PATRICKSON.

Partridge (co. Kent). Chequy ar. and sa. a bend gu.

Partridge (Cirencester and Wishanger, co. Gloucester, and Finbarrow, co. Suffolk). Chequy ar. and sa. on a bend gu. three escallops ar. *Crest*—A horse's head sa. crined or, erased per fesse gu. *Another Crest*—Out of a ducal coronet or, a horse's head sa.

Partridge (Bishop's Wood, cos. Gloucester and Hereford). Same as Wishanger.

Partridge (co. Kent; 4 March, 1630). Vairé ar. and sa. on a chief of the last three roses of the first seeded or, barbed vert. *Crest*—An arm embowed, tied round the elbow with a ribbon, holding in the hand ppr. a fireball of the last.

Partridge (Breakspeares, co. Middlesex). Quarterly, 1st and 4th, gu. on a fesse engr. cotised or, betw. three partridges rising of the last as many torteaux, for PARTRIDGE; 2nd and 3rd, az. a chev. or, betw. three eagles displ. with two heads ar., for ASHBY. *Crest*—A partridge rising with an ear of wheat in the mouth all ppr.

Partridge (co. Stafford). Gu. a scythe in pale ar.

Partridge. Gu. on a fesse ar. betw. three lions ramp. or, as many partridges ppr. *Crest*—A demi lion ramp. or, collared gu. garnished of the first.

Partridge. Vert a chev. erm. betw. three partridges rising or. *Crest*—A partridge rising or, in the beak an ear of wheat ppr.

Partridge (Horsenden House, co. Bucks). Az. on a bend engr. or, three partridges ppr. *Crest*—An etoile or. *Motto*—Esse quam videri.

Partridge. Gu. a fesse vairé or, and az. betw. three bezants each charged with a partridge of the field a bordure of the second, billettée sa. *Crest*—A demi leopard ramp. guard. sa. bezantée, gorged with a collar gu. charged with three plates.

Partridge. Chequy ar. and sa. on a bend gu. three martlets or.

Partridge, or Partrich. Gu. on a bend ar. betw. two lions ramp. or, three parrots vert. *Crest*—Out of a rose gu. stalked and leaved vert, a lion's head or.

Partridge, or Partrich. Gu. on a fesse betw. two cotises and three partridges volant or, as many torteaux, each charged with a demi rose of the second.

Partridge (Northwold, co. Norfolk, and Hockham Hall, Thetford, co. Norfolk; descended from HENRY PARTRIDGE, Esq., Alderman of London, who *d.* in 1666). Gu. on a fesse cotised or, betw. three partridges with wings displ. of the last, as many torteaux. *Crest*—A partridge as in the arms. *Motto*—Dum spiro spero.

Partyn (cos. Salop and Stafford). Vert a lion ramp. grasping a halbert ar.

Paruck (Bombay; granted to CURSETJEE FURDOONJEE PARUCK, merchant and Justice of the Peace of the city of Bombay). Ar. a chev. gu. betw. three lymphads with sails furled sa., on a chief of the second a sun in splendour betw. two estoiles or. *Crest*—On a mount vert in front of a palm tree ppr. a winged lion pass. or, charged on the shoulder with an estoile gu. *Motto*—A good conscience is a sure defence.

Parvies, or Parneys (Lord Mayor of London, 1432). Or, a fesse vert, over all a saltire gu.

Parvis (co. Surrey; granted 12 Jan. 24 Queen Elizabeth, and afterwards, by another patent, 3 Dec. 1597). Sa. on a chev. ar. three Cornish choughs ppr. on a canton of the second a demi lion ramp. of the first.

Parvise (Unsted, co. Surrey). Sa. on a chev. ar. three Cornish choughs ppr. a canton of the second charged with a demi lion ramp. of the first. *Crest*—A Cornish chough ppr.

Pascall, or Paschall (Much-Badowe and Springfield, co. Essex ; granted 1556). Ar. on a cross gu. betw. in the first and fourth quarters a lion pass. guard. sa. armed or, in the second and third quarters an eagle volant of the second armed of the fourth, a paschal lamb couchant of the first, glory gold, banner gu. *Crest*—A demi man couped at the breast, habited ppr. lined erm., head, hair and beard of the first.

Pascall (co. Hants). Ar. a cross flory sa. betw. two eagles displ. and as many dolphins az.

Paschall (Eastwood, co. Nottingham). Ar. on a bend gu. three hedgehogs or. *Crest*—On a mount a holy lamb ppr. the flag sa.

Pashley (co. Berks). Ar. three bars gu. ꞁ

Pashley, or Pasley (cos. Lincoln and York). Ar. a chev. betw. three mullets pierced sa.

Pashley. Purp. a lion ramp. or; another crowned ar.

Paske. Quarterly, ar. and sa. ; in the second and third quarters three fleurs-de-lis in pale of the first. *Crest*—A lion ramp. ar. sustaining a cross pattée fitchée sa.

Paske. Ar. a lion ramp. sa.

Paskin. Gu. on a bend or, three pansy flowers ppr. stalked and leaved vert.

Pasleire. Ar. a chev. betw. three mullets az.

Paslew (co. Durham). Ar. a fesse betw. three mullets pierced az.

Paslew (cos. Suffolk and York). Same *Arms*. *Crest*—A lion ramp. gu.

Paslew (co. York). Gu. a lion ramp. ar. crowned or.

Pasley (Craig, co. Dumfries, bart.). Az. on a chev. ar. betw. three roses in chief of the last, and in base an anchor or, three thistles slipped ppr. *Crest*—Out of a naval coronet gold a sinister arm in armour ppr. grasping in the hand a staff, thereon a flag ar. charged with a cross gu., and on a canton az. a human leg erect, couped above the knee or. *Motto*—Pro rege et patriâ pugnans.

Pasley (co. Kent). Gu. a lion ramp. tail double queued ar.

Pasley (co. York). Ar. a chev. betw. three mullets pierced sa.

Pasmore (Maidenhead, co. Berks). Or, a fesse betw. three escutcheons gu. on each a bend vair betw. two cinquefoils of the first all within a bordure az. bezantée. *Crest*—A demi sea-wolf ppr.

Pasmore. Az. in chief a cinquefoil or. *Crest*—Out of a mural coronet seven Lochaber axes adossée ppr.

Passeburie (Visit. Devon, 1620). Ar. on a fesse az. a lion pass. or.

Passelon, or Passelton (co. Essex). Bendy of ten or and az. on a canton ar. a lion pass. guard. gu.

Passmere (Passemerehayes, and Swetton, co. Devon. Visit. 1620). Or, a fesse betw. three escutcheons gu. each charged with a bend vair betw. two cinquefoils of the first all within a bordure az. bezantée. *Crest*—A semi sea-dog az. finned ar.

Passmore. Ar. three water bougets gu. *Crest*—A stag standing at gaze ar.

Paston (Paston, co. Norfolk; settled there soon after the Conquest; *Earl of Yarmouth*, extinct 1732. In 1642, Sir WILLIAM PASTON, of Paston and Oxhead, was created a bart., and in 1673 his son, Sir ROBERT PASTON, was elevated to the peerage as *Viscount Yarmouth*, and subsequently made *Earl of Yarmouth*). Ar. six fleurs-de-lis three, two, and one. a chief indented or, quartering, WALCOTE, MAULTBY, SHERBORNE, GOURNAY, HEINGRANE, BITTON, FURNEAUX. *Crest*—A griffin sejant, wings endorsed or, collared gu. *Supporters*—Dexter a bear sa. muzzled, collared, and chained or; sinister, an ostrich ar. holding in the mouth a horseshoe or. *Motto*—De mieulx je pense en mieulx.

Paston (co. Norfolk). Or, six fleurs-de-lis az. three, two, and one, a chief indented ar.

Paston (Horton, co. Gloucester). Ar. six fleurs-de-lis, az., three, two, and one. *Crest*—A griffin pass. or, collared ar. lined az.

Paston. Gu. a chev. engr. betw. three eagles displ. ar.

Paston-Bedingfeld, Bart. See BEDINGFELD.

Pasture (France; an ancient family of the noblesse of the Boulonnais, derived from JEAN DE LA PASTURE, who received, in 1457, from the Duke of Burgundy, a grant of armorial ensigns. The present representative is HENRY, COUNT DE LA PASTURE, one of the 18th Hussars, British Service). Ar. on a bend sa. six lozenges or. *Supporters* —Two lions reguard. ar.

Patch (co. Devon). Ar. in chief three oak leaves vert, and in base a buglehorn stringed sa. *Crest*—A dexter arm in
779

armour fesseways couped ppr. holding a cross crosslet fitchée sa.

Patch (Tiverton, co. Devon; FREDERICK OWEN PATCH, Esq., of that place). Or, semée of oak leaves vert a lion ramp. az. a canton gu. thereon a buglehorn stringed of the first. *Crest*—A cubit arm erect vested az. cuffed ar. surmounting two crosses crosslet fitchée in saltire sa. the hand grasping a flagstaff ppr. therefrom a flag per pale ar. and or, the dexter side charged with a cross sa.

Pate (co. Essex). Ar. on a chev. engr. gu. three crosses formée of the field.

Pate (Cheltenham and Masterden, co. Gloucester). Ar. a chev. sa. betw. three pellets, on a chief of the second as many crosses crosslet fitchée of the first. *Crest*—A demi lion ramp. vair crowned or.

Pate (Brin, co. Leicester). Ar. three Roman text R's sa. *Crest*—A stag's head cabossed ar. attired or, betw. the attires a raven wings expanded sa.

Pate (Sysonby, co. Leicester, bart. extinct 1652, a branch of PATE, of Brin). Same *Arms*, &c.

Pate (ROBERT FRANCIS PATE, Esq., of Wisbeach, Isle of Ely). Ar. a lion pass. guard. az. betw. three Roman text **R**'s. *Crest*—A stag's head cabossed or, betw. the attires a Roman text **R**.

Pate (granted by Roberts, Ulster, in 1643, to Captain PATE, employed in command of a troop of dragoons in Ireland). Gu. two poleaxes ar. on a chief of the second three crosses pattée of the first. *Crest*—A lion's paw or, holding a wolf's head erased gu.

Pater. Ar. three bends wavy gu. *Crest*—A leopard's head and neck erased guard. sa.

Paterda (Paterda in St. Germains, co. Cornwall; quartered by TRELAWNY). Sa. three lions' tails erased or, two and one.

Paternoster (co. Salop). Ar. a chev. gu. betw. three saltorels engr. sa.

Paterson (Dalkeith, co. Edinburgh). Ar. three pelicans gu. feeding their young in nests vert on a chief az. three mullets of the field.

Paterson (Dunmure, co. Fife). Ar. three pelicans feeding their young or, in nests vert. *Crest*—A dexter hand issuing out of a cloud holding a branch of laurel ppr. *Motto*—Huc tendimus omnes.

Paterson (Capt. ROBERT PATERSON, brother of Dunmure, 1672). The same with a crescent for diff. *Crest*—A branch of palm ppr. *Motto*—Virtute viresco.

Paterson (Bannockburn, co. Stirling, bart. 1686). Ar. three pelicans vulned gu. on a chief embattled az. as many mullets of the field. *Crest*—A dexter hand holding a quill ppr. *Motto*—Hinc orior.

Paterson-Wallace. See WALLACE.

Paterson (JOHN PATERSON, Bishop of Ross, and his eldest son JOHN, Bishop of Galloway, 1664). Ar. three pelicans feeding their young or, in nests vert, on a chief az. as many mullets of the field. *Motto*—Pro rege et grege.

Paterson (Seafield; second son of the Bishop of Ross, 1672). Ar. three pelicans feeding their young or, in nests vert, on a chief az. a mitre of the second betw. two mullets of the first. *Crest*—A hand grasping a sword erected ppr. *Motto*—Pro rege et grege.

Paterson (Aberdeen; fourth son of the Bishop of Ross, 1672). Ar. three pelicans feeding their young or, in nests vert, in the centre a mitre az. on a chief of the fourth as many mullets of the first. *Crest*—A pelican's head couped ppr. *Motto*—Pro rege et grege.

Paterson (Castle Huntly, co. Perth). Ar. three pelicans feeding their young in nests ppr. on a chief embattled az. a bezant betw. two stars of the field. *Crest*—A pelican feeding her young in a nest ppr. *Motto*—Over the crest, Merui ; below the shield, Je meurs pour ceux que j'aime.

Paterson (London, 1812). Ar. three pelicans ppr. vulned gu. on a chief embattled az. a bear's head erased or, betw. two mullets of the first. *Crest*—On a mural crown or, a stag's head erased ppr. attired gu. gorged with a collar az. and pendent therefrom a man's heart gu. *Motto*—Hinc orior.

Paterson (Kinnettles, co. Forfar, 1867). Az. a fess betw. two pelicans in their nests feeding their young in chief, and a pot of lilies in base all ar. *Crest*—A pelican as in the arms. *Motto*—Pro rege et patria.

Paterson-Balfour-Hay. See HAY.

Pates (co. Gloucester). Ar. a chev. sa. betw. three pellets in chief as many crosses pattée fitchée of the second. *Crest*—A lion vairé sa. and ar. crowned or.

Pateshall (Allensmore, co. Hereford). Az. on a chev. betw. three hearts or, as many escallops gu. *Crest*—Out of a ducal coronet or, a pelican ar. vulning itself ppr.

Pateshall (Layford, co. Hereford). Gu. on a chev. ar. betw. three hearts or, as many escallops of the first. *Crest*—A demi griffin ar.

Pateshall. Sa. on a fesse ar. betw. three plates, each charged with a crescent gu. as many lions' heads erased az. *Crest*—A demi peacock's head sa. betw. two wings expanded or, beaked of the last, on the neck three bends ar.

Pateshall. Ar. a fesse wavy sa. betw. three crescents gu.

Pateshall. Ar. a fesse nebulée sa. betw. three crescents gu.

Pateshull (*Baron Pateshull* by writ, 1342, extinct 1360). Ar. a fesse sa. betw. three crescents gu.

Pateshull. Az. on a chev. ar. betw. three hearts or, as many escallops gu.

Patesley. Or, three fleurs-de-lis az.

Patesole. Paly of six or and gu. a chief ar.

Patford. Gu. on a chief or, a lion pass. az.

Patishall (co. Devon; Reg. Her. Office). Paly of six ar. and gu. a chief of the first.

Patishall, or Pateshall (co. Essex). Ar. a fesse sa. betw. three mullets gu.

Patishall. Erm. a lion ramp. gu. (another purp.) crowned or.

Patisley (London). Or, three fleurs-de-lis az. on each an annulet of the field.

Patissolle (co. Devon). Paly of six or and gu. a chev. ar.

Patmer (co. York). Ar. a bend vert betw. three inescutcheons gu. *Crest*—A hand holding an imperial crown ppr.

Patmer (co. York). Ar. three inescutcheons gu. on each a bend vair betw. two cinquefoils ar.

Patmer. Same *Arms*, a bordure engr. az. bezantée.

Patmyne, or Patman. Erm. three chev. gu.

Patman. Sa. a stork ar. within an orle of eight crosses crosslet fitchée of the last.

Paton (Scotland, 16th century). Az. a fleur-de-lis or, betw. three crescents ar.

Paton (Kinaldy, co. Aberdeen). Az. a sword in pale ar. hilted and pommelled or, betw. three crescents of the second. *Crest*—A sparrow hawk perched ppr. *Motto*—Virtus laudando.

Paton (Ferrochie, now Grandholm, co. Aberdeen). Az. three crescents ar. *Crest*—A sparrow-hawk, with wings expanded ppr. *Motto*—Virtute adepta.

Paton (Sir JOSEPH NOEL PATON, H.M. Limner for Scotland, 1869). Az. a wolf's head erased ar. betw. two crescents in chief gu. and a fleur-de-lis in base or. *Crest*—Betw. two doves' wings expanded ppr. a cubit arm erect also ppr. charged on the palm with a passion cross gu. *Motto*—Do right and fear nocht.

Patour (Richmond, co. Surrey; granted June, 1772). Az. a sword erect ppr. hilt and pommel or, betw. two crescents in chief ar. and a bezant in base. *Crest*—A sparrow hawk close ppr. charged on the breast with a trefoil slipped or.

Patrick (Lord of Malpas, co. Chester). Gu. three mullets of six points ar. (ERDISWICK). On the seal of WILLIAM PATRICK, father of WILLIAM PATRICK, who *m.* BEATRIX DE MALPAS, three pheons.

Patrick (Durham City). Gu. a lion ramp. ar. within a bordure of the last, charged with eight cinquefoils of the first. *Crest*—An arm in armour embowed ppr.

Patrick (RALSTON-PATRICK, of Roughwood, co. Ayr, 1861). Quarterly, 1st and 4th, ar. a saltire sa. on a chief of the second two roses of the first, all within a bordure gu., for PATRICK; 2nd and 3rd, ar. on a bend az. three acorns or, for RALSTON. *Crests*—A dexter hand erect, holding a saltire sa., for PATRICK; A falcon looking to the sinister ppr., for RALSTON. *Motto*—Ora et labora, for PATRICK; Fide et Marte, for RALSTON.

Patrick (Crowneast, near Worcester). Gu. three mullets or. *Crest*—A dexter hand ppr. holding a cross crosslet.

Patrickson (Stockhow, Caswell-How, and Calder-Abbey, co. Cumberland, a very ancient family; Visit. Cumberland, 1615). Or, a fesse betw. three greyhounds courant sa. *Crest*—On a mount vert a stag courant reguard. ppr. hoofed and attired or; granted 1592.

Patris. Ar. fretty gu.

Patshull (Bletsho, co. Bedford; *temp.* Henry III.). Ar. a fesse betw. three crescents gu.

Patshull, or Pateshall. Az. on a fesse ar. betw. three plates, each charged with a crescent gu. as many lions' heads erased of the first.

Patte. Az. two bars or, over all a bend of the second. *Crest*—A lion ramp. az.

Patten (cos. Essex and Lancaster, traceable back to the year

780

1119. To this ancient house, the chief seat of which was at Dagenham, belonged WILLIAM PATTEN, alias WAYNFLETE' Bishop of Winchester, Lord High Chancellor of England' and Founder of Magdalen Coll. Oxford. The present male representative is *Lord Winmarleigh*). Fusilly erm. and sa.

Patten (WILSON PATTEN, *Baron Winmarleigh*). Quarterly, 1st and 4th, fusilly erm. and sa. a canton gu., for PATTEN; 2nd and 3rd, sa. a wolf ramp. or, in chief three estoiles of the second, for WILSON. *Crests*—1st: A griffin's head erased vert, beaked or, for PATTEN; 2nd, A demi wolf ramp. or, for WILSON. *Supporters*—Dexter, a griffin vert, beaked or, charged on the shoulder with a lozenge erm.; sinister, a wolf or, charged on the shoulder with an etoile sa. *Mottoes*—For PATTEN: "Nullâ pallescere culpâ;" for WILSON: "Virtus ad sidera tollit."

Patten (MERCURY PATTEN, Bluemantle Pursuivant of Arms, *temp.* James I.). Fusilly sa. and erm.

Patten. Fusilly erm. and sa. on a chief of the first three lilies ar.

Patten-Makers, Company of (London). Gu. on a chev. ar. betw. three pattens or, tied of the second, the ties lined az. two cutting knives conjoined sa. *Crest*—A patten, as in the arms. *Motto*—Recipiunt fœminæ sustentacula nobis.

Pattenson (Chery Burton, co York). Ar. on a fesse sa. three fleurs-de-lis or. *Crest*—Out of a ducal coronet a camel's head.

Pattenson (Melmerby Hall, co. Cumberland). Same *Arms*.

Pattenson (Ibornden, co. Kent). Ar. on a fesse sa. a bugle horn stringed of the field betw. two fleurs-de-lis or, quartering TYLDEN. *Crest*—A camel's head erased sa. bezantée. *Motto*—Finem respice.

Patters. Ar. three peacocks' heads erased gu. *Crest*—A cross crosslet fitchée or, and palm branch vert in saltire.

Pattinson (granted to HUGH LEE PATTINSON, Esq., of West Bolden, co. Durham, and his nephew, WILLIAM WATSON PATTINSON, Esq., of Felling House, near Gateshead). Sa. semée of drops of silver, issuant from the base flames of fire ppr. *Crest*—In front of flames of fire, a dexter hand bendwise, holding an ingot of silver, all ppr. *Motto*—Ex vile pretiosa; granted in allusion to the discovery by HUGH LEE PATTINSON of a process for the separation of silver from lead.

Pattison (England). Ar. guttée de sang a lion ramp. gu. on a chief of the last three escallops or. *Crest*—A hind's head couped or.

Pattison (Kelvin Grove, co. Lanark). Ar. guttée de sang a lion ramp. sa. guttée d'or, on a chief az. three escallops of the field. *Crest*—A camel's head ar. guttée sa. issuing from a ducal coronet or, crowned with an antique crown of the last, collared az. charged with three escallops of the first. *Motto*—Hostis honori invidia.

Pattle. Or, five lozenges conjoined in fesse az. *Crest*—An eagle displ. ppr. (another, or).

Patton (Glenalmond, co. Perth, 1809). Quarterly, 1st and 4th, az. a fleur-de-lis betw. three crescents or; 2nd and 3rd, ar. a saltire az. betw. three edock leaves in chief and flanks vert, all within a bordure engr. gu. *Crest*—A sparrow-hawk rising ppr. *Motto*—Virtute adepta.

Patton (Cairnies). Az. a fleur-de-lis betw. three crescents or, on a chief of the second a cross pattée gu. Same *Crest* and *Motto* as PATTEN, of Glenalmond.

Patton. Per pale gu. and az. three crescents counterchanged. *Crest*—On a rock a swan close ppr.

Patton (Bishops Hall and Stoke Court, Taunton). Az. a sword ar. hilted or, betw. three crescents of the second. *Crest*—A hawk ar. *Motto*—Virtute adepta.

Patwarden. Gu. two lions pass. or.

Patynson. Ar. on a fesse sa. three fleurs-de-lis or.

Paul (High Grove, co. Gloucester). Ar. on a fesse az. betw. six erm. spots three crosses crosslet, or. *Crest*—A leopard's head erased per pale or and az. on the neck a cross crosslet counterchanged.

Paul (Rodburgh, co. Gloucester, bart.). Ar. on a fesse az. three cross crosslets or, in base as many erm. spots sa. *Crest*—An ounce's head ppr. erased gu. *Motto*—Pro rege et republicâ.

Paul, St., Bart. See ST. PAUL.

Paul (King's Stanley, co. Gloucester). Ar. on a fesse az. three crosses crosslet or.

Paul (Woodchester, co. Gloucester, 1761, Reg. Her. Off.). Ar. on a fesse az. three crosses crosslet or, in base as many erm. spots. *Crest*—A leopard's head ppr. erased gu. *Motto*—Pro rege et republicâ.

Paul (St. Andrew's, Holborn, co. Middlesex; granted 1758). Or, a lion ramp. double queued, ducally crowned, brandishing in the dexter paw a falchion, all gu. *Crest*—An elephant ar. on the back a castle gu. tied under the belly, on the point of his trunk a falchion erect of the last.

Paul, or Paule (Norfolk, and Lambeth, co. Surrey). Ar. two bars az. a canton sa. *Crest*—On the trunk of a tree raguly lying fesseways, sprigged and leaved vert, a bird close ar. *Another Crest*—A garb vert banded ar.

Paul (Paulville, co. Carlow, and Ballyglan, co. Waterford, bart.; confirmed by Fortescue, Ulster, to Joshua Paul, Esq., of Paulville, co. Carlow). Az. a sword erect ar. pommel and hilt or, betw. four crosses pattée fitchée of the second. *Crest*—A cross pattée fitchée or, betw. two swords erect in saltire ar. pommels and hilts gold. *Motto*—Vana spes vitæ.

Paul (Silverspring, co. Wexford; descended from Paul, of Paulville; Mary, dau. and heir of Jeffrey Paul, Esq., of Silverspring, m. 1799, Right Hon. Thomas Lefroy, Lord Chief Justice of Ireland). Same *Arms, Crest*, and *Motto*.

Paul (Scotland). Ar. a martlet sa. a chief gu. *Crest*— Two arms in armour, placing a Saracen's head affrontée on a pheon.

Paule (co. York). Ar. on a fesse az. three crosses crosslet or.

Paule. Erm. on a fesse az. three mullets or.

Paulet (*Marquess of Winchester and Duke of Belton;* Charles Paulet, sixth *Marquess of Winchester*, was created *Duke of Bolton* 1689; dukedom extinct 1794). Sa. three swords in pile, points in base ar. pommels and hilts or. *Crest*—A falcon, wings displ. or, belled of the same, and gorged with a ducal coronet gu. *Supporters*—Two hinds purp. semée of estoiles and ducally gorged or. *Motto*— Aymez loyaulté.

Paulet (West Hill Lodge, co. Hants, bart.). Sa. three swords in pile, points downwards ppr. pommels and hilts or. *Crest*—A falcon, wings displ. or, belled of the same and ducally collared gu. *Motto*—Aimez loyaulté.

Paulet (Leigh Paulet, co. Devon, and Thornbury, co. Gloucester). Sa. three swords in pile ar. hilts and pommels or. *Crest*—An armed arm embowed holding a sword all ppr.

Paulin (Odcombe, co. Stafford, 22 Edward III.). On a chev. betw. three cinquefoils as many darts' heads broken at the shaft.

Paulin. Az. on a bend betw. six lozenges or, each charged with an escallop az. four escallops of the last.

Paulsworth, or Pilsworth. Gu. a chev. ar. betw. three St. Paul's heads ppr.

Pauly. Or, four bars nebulée az.

Paulmier (co. Devon). Az. on a chev. ar. betw. two roses in chief of the last, and an ananas in base, leaved or, two palm branches vert. *Crest*—A hawk's leg erased, jessed and belled ppr.

Pauncefoot, or Pauncefoote (cos. Hants and Somerset). Per fesse az. and gu. three fleurs-de-lis or.

Pauncefoot, or Pauncefort (co. Somerset). Per fesse gu. and az. a crescent ar. betw. three fleurs-de-lis seeded or.

Pauncefort-Duncombe, Bart. See Duncombe.

Pauncefote (Hasfield, co. Gloucester; possessed, according to Camden, of lands in that county, *temp.* Conquestoris: Sir George Smith, Bart., of East Stoke, descended maternally from the Pauncefotes, assumed by royal licence, 1803, the surname and arms of Pauncefote, which he afterwards changed for those of Bromley). Gu. three lions ramp. ar. *Crest*—A lion ramp. ar. ducally crowned or. *Motto*—Pensez forte.

Pauncefote (Preston Court, co. Gloucester; descended from Pauncefote, of Hasfield). Same *Arms*, &c., as Pauncefote, of Hasfield.

Paunton. Gu. a chev. vair, a chief or.

Paveley (Lord of Westbury, co. Wilts. *temp.* Edward III.). Az. a cross patonce or. *Crest*—An anchor and sword in saltire ppr.

Paveley (Paulerspury, co. Northants). Erm. on a fesse az. three crosses moline (sometimes pattée) or.

Paveley. Barry nebulée of six, or and sa. a hendlet ar.

Pavell. Az. two wolves pass. reguard. cowarded or.

Pavell. Az. two lions pass. reguard. or.

Pavely (co. Oxford). Barry wavy of eight, or and sa.

Pavent. Ar. on a bend gu. three eagles displ. or.

Paver. Ar. three fusils in fesse az. a chief chequy or and gu.

Pavey (co. Norfolk). Sa. a fesse crenellée ar. betw. three eagles displ. or. *Crest*—A lion ramp. guard. sa.

Pavey, Pavie, or Pavy. Erm. on a fesse gu. three martlets or.

Pavier. Or, a chev. gu. a bordure sa. bezantée.

Pavier (Russell-Pavier, exemplified to William Adey Russell, Esq., of Heaton Moor, Heaton Norris, co. Lancaster, and Hammerwich, co. Stafford, upon his assuming, by royal

781

licence, 1874, the additional surname of Pavier). 1st and 4th, sa. three fusils in fesse or, betw. two flaunches of the last, each charged with a mallet of the first a chief chequey of the second and gu., for Pavier; 2nd and 3rd, ar. a fesse dancettée erm. betw. three crosses crosslet fitchée in chief, and two in base sa., for Russell. *Crests*—1st, Pavier: Two arms embowed ppr. rested above the elbow ar., that on the dexter holding a chisel, and that on the sinister a mallet also ppr.; 2nd, Russell: In front of two palm branches saltirewise vert a fret or, thereon a martlet sa. *Motto*—Quo fata vocant.

Paviours, Company of (London). Ar. a chev. betw. three flagstones sa. *Crest*—An arm embowed, vested az. cuff. ar. holding in the hand ppr. a pickaxe of the last. *Motto*—God can raise to Abraham children of stones.

Pavyn, or Pavys. Gu. two halberts in pale, addorsed or.

Paw. Gu. crusily fitchée or, a griffin salient of the last.

Pawle. Erm. on a fesse az. three crosses crosslet fitchée or. *Crest*—A leopard's head erased ppr.

Pawlet. See Poulett.

Pawleter (Wimondley, co. Herts). Ar. a bend voided sa.

Pawlett (Willesden, co. Middlesex; John Pawlett, gent., son of John Pawlett, gent., and grandson of John Paw-lett, gent., all of Willsdon, Visit. Middlesex 1663). Sa. three swords in pile points in base ar. pommelled and hilted or, betw. two flanges of the last pellettée. *Crest*—On a mount a falcon rising or, pellettée, belled gold.

Pawlett (St. James's, Westminster; granted 1737). Sa. three swords in pile, points in base ar. hilts and pommels or, betw. two flaunches of the third, each charged with a demi spear erect rompu az. fringed gu. *Crest*—A terrestrial orb or, thereon a falcon rising ppr. collared and belled of the first.

Pawley (Gunwin in Lelant, co. Cornwall). Ar. a lion ramp. sa. on a chief dancettée of the last three mullets of the first.

Pawne. Ar. three peacocks in their pride ppr.

Pawne. Ar. three peacocks in pride az. within a bordure engr. gu.

Pawne, or Paun. Sa. a hawk's lure within a bordure engr. ar.

Pawson (co. York; *temp.* Henry IV. The senior branch was that of Allerton Gledhow, near Leeds. The next that of Shawdon, co. Northumberland). Erm. two chev. betw. three lions' gambs erased and erect or, for Pawson; quartering, for Hargrave, Quarterly, indented az. and gu. on a fesse ar. betw. three stags courant or, as many mascles of the first betw. four erm. spots. *Crests*—1st: On a mount vert, the sun in splendour or, for Pawson; 2nd: A buck's head erased, quarterly, indented ar. and gu. attired sa., for Hargrave. *Motto*—Favente Deo.

Pawson (Leeds, co. York). Gu. a chev. betw. three lions pass. or.

Pawson. Az. a cross or, fretty gu. betw. four annulets of the second. *Crest*—A griffin's head or.

Paxston. Or, two chev. sa. betw. three mullets in pale gu.

Paxton (Cholderton, co. Wilts, Watford, co. Herts, and Middleton Hall, co. Carmarthen; granted 13 May, 1806). Erm. two chev. the one sa. the other az. three mullets in pale of the last. *Crest*—An eagle's head erased az. charged on the neck with two chev. or, betw. a pair of wings ar. semée of mullets gu.

Payen. Ar. three pellets, two and one, that in the dexter chief charged with a rose of the field.

Payferer, or Peyferer (co. Kent). Ar. six fleurs-de-lis sa. (another, az.) three, two, and one.

Payler (co. York; confirmed 20 Oct. 1585). Gu. three lions pass. guard. ar. over all on a bend sa. as many mullets of six points pierced or.

Payler (Thoralby, co. York, bart. extinct 1706; Sir Edward Payler, of Thoralby, was created a baronet in 1642, and dying about 1649, was s. by his grandson, Sir Watkinson Payler, second bart., who *d. s. p.* in 1706; shortly after, Thomas Turner, Esq., of Kent, assumed the surname of Payler; and had, besides a dau., Margaret, wife of the Rev. Edward Taylor, of Bifrons, a son, the late Thomas Watkinson Payler, Esq., of Heden). Gu. three lions pass. guard ar. debruised by a bend or, charged with three mullets of six points sa.

Paylow. Purp. a lion ramp. or.

Payn, alias Gybon (confirmed 24 Nov. 1570). Gu. a lion ramp. or, debruised by a bend ar. charged with three crosses flory sa.

Payn. Ar. three trefoils slipped sa.

Payn. Ar. on a cross wavy vert five plates.

Payn (Seigneurs of Oulande, la Godelière, Samarés, Ponterrin, Montfort, Dielament, le Chaslelet, Payn, Grainville, Quctivel, la Fosse, les Niesmez, &c., Jersey; descended from THIBAULT PAYEN, Count of Gisors, whose son, HUGH PAYEN, gave by Charter, *circa.* 1200, the original of which now exists in the departmental Archives at St. Lo, Normandy, six quarters of wheat rent, derived from his lands in Jersey, to the Abbot of Saint Mary, near Cherbourg. From this HUGH PAYEN, who was Valvasor of the king of England, and jurat of his royal court there, scarcely a generation of the family has existed without having a representative on the local bench. At the period of the Great Rebellion, ABRAHAM and STEPHEN PAYN VEL PAYNE, being ardent Royalists, migrated to co. Devon, and founded families still existing in England). Ar. three trefoils slipped sa. *Crest*—A woman's head couped below the shoulders, vested az. turned up ar. face ppr. hair or, on her head an antique crown of the last. *Motto*—Playsyr vaut Payn *Supporters*—Two angels ppr.

Payne (*Baron Lavington;* extinct 1807). Gu. a fess betw. two lions pass. ar. *Crest*—A lion's gamb erased ar. grasping a broken tilting lance gu. *Supporters*—Dexter, Fortitude: represented by a woman ppr. vested in yellow, over which a loose robe purp. with a red scarf depending from her waist, sandals on her feet az. fastened or, holding in her sinister hand an oak branch, the arm resting on a column ppr.; sinister, Justice, vested az. robed gu. sandals as before, holding in her dexter hand a pair of scales or, in the sinister a sword erect ppr. hilt and pommel of the third. *Motto*—Malo mori quam fœdari.

Payne-Gallwey (Bart.). See GALLWEY.

Payne (St. Christopher's and Blunham House, co. Bedford, bart.). Gu. a fesse betw. two lions pass. ar. *Crest*—A lion's gamb erased and erect ar. grasping a broken tilting spear gu. *Motto*—Malo mori quam fœdari.

Payne (Wallingford, co. Berks; confirmed 12 Jan. 1586, and of London). Or, on a bend engr. betw. two cotises sa. three roses of the first. *Crest*—A demi ostrich wings endorsed ar. in the beak a key or.

Payne (Tempsford House, South Kensington, co. Middlesex; borne by Colonel J. BERTRAND PAYEN-PAYNE, descended from STEPHEN PAYN VEL PAYNE, a colonel of horse, in the service of Charles I. and II., who, with his elder brother ABRAHAM, migrated from Jersey to co. Devon at the period of the Great Rebellion). Gu. on a fesse betw. two lions pass. ar. *Crest*—A lion's gamb couped ar. grasping a broken tilting lance, the spear end pendent gu. *Motto*—Malo mori quam fœdari. Quartering, PAYN, of JERSEY, PAYEN, of Normandy, DE BARENTINE, DE CARTERET, D'ALBINI, DE ST. MARTIN, SPARK, SARRE, LEMPRIERE, BRAS-DE-FER, LE ROULX, MORIN, LE FEBVRE, and LANGLOIS.

Payne (co. Denbigh, and Westbrooke, co. Dorset). Per bend or and az. six roundles counterchanged, two, two, and two. *Crest*—A leopard's head or, gorged with a collar az. rimmed gold, charged with three escallops.

Payne (Mayor of Norwich, granted 1 Sept. 1660, by Walker, Garter). Sa. a fess ragulée betw. three lions' gambs erased or, armed gu. *Crest*—A lion's gamb or, holding a baton ragulée or.

Payne (co. Dorset, and Medborne, co. Leicester). Paly of six or and az. a chief erm. *Crest*—Out of a ducal coronet or, a woman's head couped below the shoulders ppr. vested erm. her hair dishevelled of the first, on her head a chapeau az.

Payne (co. Hereford). Paly of eight or and az. a chief erm.

Payne (Midlow, St. Neot's, co. Huntington). Az. a bend ragulée betw. six estoiles or. *Crest*—In grass vert, an otter pass. or, in the mouth a fish ar.

Payne (Great Marlow, co. Huntington). Or, on a chief indented sa. three cinquefoils of the first.

Payne (Market Bosworth, co. Leicester, and Paine, co. Suffolk). Ar. on a fesse engr. gu. betw. three martlets sa. as many mascles or, all within a bordure engr. of the second, bezantée. *Crest*—A wolf's head erased az. charged with five bezants saltireways.

Payne (cos. Lincoln and Stafford). Gyronny of four ar. and sa. four lions ramp. counterchanged.

Payne (London, and co. Berks; confirmed by Cooke, Clarenceux, 1586). Sa. a fesse betw. three leopards' faces or. *Crest*—A dexter arm embowed in armour ar. holding a sword ppr. hilt and pommel or, enfiled with a boar's head sa. vulned gu.

Payne (London). Ar. a chev. gu. betw. three griffins's head erased sa.

Payne (St. Mary-le-bone, co. Middlesex; granted 1770). Gu. a fesse betw. two lions pass. ar., quartering, Az. a cross sarcely or, betw. four crosses crosslet fitchée ar., for CAR-

782

LISLE. *Crest*—A lion's gamb erect and erased ar. holding a tilting spear rompu gu. *Motto*—Malo mori quam fœdari.

Payne (Fulham, co. Middlesex). Ar. on a fesse engr. betw. three martlets sa. as many cinquefoils of the first. *Crest*—A griffin pass. wings endorsed, or.

Payne, or Paine (Dunham, co. Norfolk). Vert, a fesse betw. three leopards' faces or. *Crest*—An ostrich's head or, issuing out of a plume of feathers ar.

Payne (Ittringham, co. Norfolk). Ar. a chev. vair, betw. three lions ramp. az. *Crest*—An ostrich's head erased or, betw. two wings expanded sa. in the beak a horseshoe of the last.

Payne (Sulby Hall, co. Northampton). Same *Arms*, &c.

Payne (granted 1826 to HENRY PAYNE, Esq., Newark, co. Leicester). Ermines on a pile or, three martlets sa. over all a fesse engr. gu. charged with as many mascles of the second. *Crest*—An heraldic tiger sejant per pale engr. az. and erm. surmounting a branch of oak fructed ppr. the dexter forepaw resting on a mascle gu.

Payne (Rowdham, co. Norfolk). Ar. on a fesse gu. betw. three martlets sa. as many mascles or.

Payne (co. Somerset). Gu. three crosses botonnée ar. on a chief az. two escallops or.

Payne (Stoke Neyland, co. Suffolk). Sa. a fesse chequy or and az. betw. three leopards' faces of the second. *Crest*—An armed arm embowed and gauntleted or, holding a leopard's face of the last.

Payne (East Grinstead, and of Newick, co. Sussex; granted 25 Feb. 1661). Per fesse sa. and ar. two lions pass. counterchanged, armed and langued gu. *Crest*—A lion's head erased per fesse sa. and ar.

Payne (Petworth, co. Sussex). Ar. on a fesse engr. gu. betw. three martlets sa. as many roses erm. *Crest*—A griffin pass. wings endorsed per pale or and az.

Payne (granted 19 May, 1575). Per bend or and az. three (another, six) roundles counterchanged, two and one. *Crest* —A lion's head erased ppr. ducally gorged, lined, and ringed or, holding in the mouth a sprig of laurel vert.

Payne. Gu. a lion ramp. or, debruised by a bend ar. charged with three crosses pattée sa. *Crest*—A lion's gamb holding a cross pattée sa.

Payne. Or, three hurts, on a chief embattled az. as many bezants. *Crest*—An ostrich head couped or, betw. two wings sa.

Payne. Ar. on a bend gu. betw. a lion's head cabossed in chief and an eagle's leg couped a-la-quise holding a torteau in base ppr. three arrows or. *Crest*—A demi man couped at the loins in profile holding in the dexter hand an arrow.

Payne. Vert, a fesse betw. three leopards' faces or. *Crest* —Out of a plume of ostrich feathers a leopard's head or.

Payne. Per saltire ar. and sa. a lion ramp. counterchanged; another, Per bend or and sa. eight plates in orle, each charged with a torteau; another, Ar. a bend az. (another, sa.); another, Ar. a chev. barruly az. and of the first, betw. three lions ramp. of the second; another, Quarterly, az. and gu., in the first a lion ramp. ar. tail forked, on the second a cross flory or; another, Or, a chev. vair betw. three lions ramp. az.

Paynell (*Baron Paynell,* of Drax, co. York). Or, two bars az. within an orle of eight martlets gu.

Paynell (co. Hants). Or, two bars az. within an orle of eight martlets gu.

Paynell (co. Sussex). Or, two bars sa. within an orle of six martlets gu.

Paynell (Boothby, co. Lincoln). Gu. two chev. ar. *Crest*— An ostrich's head ppr.

Paynell (Sir JOHN PAYNELL, Roll of Arms, co. Leicester, Cotton MSS.). Ar. a bend sa.

Paynell. Gu. two chev. ar. a bordure of the last, over all a bend sa. *Crest*—A lion ramp. vert.

Paynell. Or, two bars az. betw. three martlets gu.; another, Barry of eight ar. and az. in chief three martlets gu.; another, Az. two wolves (another, lions) pass. coward or; another, Gu. two chev. ar. a bordure engr. ar. of the last; another, Gu. a cross pattée (another, sarcelly) ar.

Paynes. Ar. ten roses gu. four, three, two, and one.

Payntell (London, 1611). Barry lozengy ar. and gu. on a chief az. three estoiles or. *Crest*—An arm in pale habited gu. cuff ar. holding in the hand ppr. three lillies or, leaved vert.

Paynter (Twidall, co. Kent). Gu. a chev. betw. three griffins' heads erased or, on a chief of the second a close helmet sa. betw. two pellets. *Crest*—On the stump of a tree eradicated ppr. a wivern, sans wings, vert, the tail entwined round the tree.

Paynter (Sprote, co. Norfolk). Ar. three books closed gu. leaved, clasped and garnished or. *Crest*—A lapwing ar. environed with two branches vert whose tops close in saltire.

Paynter. Gu. a chev. betw. three griffins' heads erased or, on a chief ar. three pellets. *Crest*—An old man's head couped at the shoulders ppr. vested gu. on his head a long cap az.

Paynter (Boskenna, co. Cornwall). Az. three billets ar. each charged with an annulet sa. *Crest*—Three broken broad arrows or, knit with a lace and mantlet gu. doubled ar.

Paytefin, Poytevin, or Pictavensis (Headingley, co. York). Erm. three chevronels gu.

Payton (Sutton Coldfield, co. Warwick; confirmed by Lennard and Vincent to WALTER PAYTON, of Sutton Coldfield, fifth in descent from JOHN PEITON, of Peiton Hall). Sa. a cross engr. or. *Crest*—A griffin sejant or.

Payton. See PEYTON.

Payzant. Or, a pale vert, on a chief gu. a pheasant ar. all within a bordure az. charged with eight estoiles of the first.

Peace. Vert a fesse betw. three doves wings expanded ar. *Crest*—A dove wings expanded ar. holding in the beak an olive branch vert.

Peacer. Quarterly, sa. and az. three bezants, two and one.

Peach (Rooksmore, co. Gloucester; granted 8 Nov. 1769). Gu. three martlets betw. two chev. ar. *Crest*—A demi lion ramp. per fesse erm. and gu. ducally crowned or.

Peach (KEIGHLY-PEACH, Idlicote House, Shipton-on-Stour, co. Warwick). Quarterly, 1st and 4th, for PEACH, gu. betw. two chev. ar. three martlets of the second; 2nd and 3rd, for KEIGHLY, per bend engr. sa. and ar. a fesse charged with two mullets, all counterchanged. *Crests*—1st: A demi lion ramp. erm. and gu. crowned or, clawed az., for PEACH; 2nd: A griffin's head sa. langued gu. charged with three mullets or, for KEIGHLY. *Motto*, for PEACH—Quicquid dignum sapiente bonoque est.

Peache (co. Worcester). Gu. a fesse betw. six cross crosslets ar.

Peache, or Peche. Erm. in chief two chaplets gu. in base a rose of the last.

Peachey (*Baron Selsey*; extinct 1838). Az. a lion ramp. double queued erm. on a canton ar. a mullet pierced gu. *Crest*—A demi lion double queued erm. holding in the dexter paw a mullet pierced gu. *Supporters*—Two female figures faces ppr. crined or, habited of a brown colour, holding in their exterior hands branches of laurel also ppr. and on each of their heads a plume of three ostrich feathers ar. *Motto* —Memor et fidelis.

Peachey (North Bersted, Rumbolds Wyke, and South Mundham, co. Sussex; descended from JOHN PEACHEY, Esq., of Shripney, same co., 1614). Az. a lion ramp. erm. ducally crowned or, a canton of the last charged with a mullet pierced gu.

Peacock (Slyne, co. Lancaster; settled there 1713). Gu. on a fesse engr. ar. betw. three bezants each charged with a mascle sa. as many peacocks' heads erased az. *Crest*—A peacock's head erased az.

Peacock (granted to MARK BEAUCHAMP PEACOCK, Esq.). Per fesse or and az. a pale three eagles displ. one in chief and two in base, and three roundles, two in chief and one in base, each charged with a cross crosslet all counterchanged. *Crest*—A mount vert thereon an eagle displ. erminois, in the beak a cross crosslet fitchée gu. the dexter claw supporting a hurt charged with a cross crosslet or.

Peacock (Cowley, co. Berks; granted 27 June, 1640). Gu. a fesse ar. betw. three plates each charged with a lozenge sa.

Peacock (Burnhall, co. Durham; granted by Norroy, 1688). Sa. three peacocks in their pride ar. a chief embattled or. *Crest*—A peacock's head erased az. gorged with a mural coronet or.

Peacock (London; Lord Mayor, 1532). Gu. on a fesse engr. ar. betw. three bezants, each charged with a peacock's head erased az. as many mascles sa. *Crest*—A peacock's head and neck or, wings expanded az. and a snake entwined about the neck of the last.

Peacock (London). Gu. a chev. betw. three peacocks in their pride ar.

Peacock (South Rauceby, co. Lincoln). See WILLSON.

Peacock (Stone Hall, co. Pembroke; borne by Rev. EDWARD PEACOCK, M.A., of Stone Hall, eldest son of Rev. EDWARD PEACOCK, Vicar of Fifehead-Magdalen, co. Dorset, of an old and respectable family long possessed of the Manor of Potterhanworth). Gu. on a fesse engr. ar. betw. three mascles, each within an annulet or, as many peacocks'

783

heads erased ppr. *Crest*—A peacock's head erased ppr. gorged with a mural crown or, holding in the beak a rose gu. leaved and slipped ppr. *Motto*—Be just and fear not.

Peacock (London). Quarterly, or and az. four lozenges conjoined in cross betw. as many annulets counterchanged.

Peacock (London). Az. a fesse engr. gu. betw. three bezants.

Peacock (Finchley, co. Middlesex). Sa. three peacocks close ar. two and one.

Peacock (co. Down). Gu. on a fesse engr. ar. betw. three bezants as many mascles sa. in the centre chief point a peacock holding in the beak a thistle leaved ppr. *Crest*—A peacock's head erased, holding in the beak a thistle leaved all ppr.

Peacock (Bridge-end, Scotland). Ar. three peacocks in their pride ppr.

Peacock (Scotland, 15th century). Ar. three peacocks in their pride ppr. betw. as many stars gu.

Peacock-Yate. See YATE.

Peacocke (Efford Hall, Hants). Quarterly, or and az. four lozenges conjoined in cross betw. as many annulets all counterchanged. *Crest*—A cockatrice wings erect vert. *Motto*—Vincit veritas.

Peacocke (Barntic, co. Clare, bart., extinct 1876). Quarterly, or and az. four lozenges conjoined in cross betw. as many annulets all counterchanged. *Crest*—A cockatrice vert. *Motto*—Vincit veritas.

Peacocke. See SANDFORD.

Peak (co. Lincoln, and Achurch, co. Northampton; borne by Sir WILLIAM PEAK, Lord Mayor of London in 1668). Vert on a chev. betw. three lions' heads erased or, as many crosses crosslet az. *Crest*—A lion's head or, pierced through the side of the head with an arrow in fesse, the point coming out at the mouth of the first, feathered and headed ar.

Peak. Ar. a saltire gu. in chief a billet of the last. *Crest*— A lion's head issuing or.

Peake (Sandwich, co. Kent). Az. three talbots pass. or. *Crest*—A cockatrice volant or, beaked, combed, legged and wattled gu.

Peake (Bilton, co. Lincoln). Vert on a chev. betw. three lions' heads erased or, as many crosses crosslet gu.

Peake (Lutterworth, co. Leicester, and London; granted 13 Dec. 1598). Sa. three crosses pattée, two and one, betw. nine fleurs-de-lis or. *Crest*—A human heart gu. betw. a pair of wings expanded ar. (another, erm.).

Peake (London). Az. semée-de-lis or, three crosses formée ar. two and one. *Crest*—A human heart gu. winged ar.

Peake (Foxton, co. Middlesex). Az. an eagle displ. betw. three fleurs-de-lis or.

Peake (Llweny, Wales). Chequy or and gu. a saltire erm. *Crest*—A leopard's face gu. in the mouth an arrow ppr. flighted or. *Motto*—Heb Dduw, heb ddim: Without God, without everything.

Peake, or Peke (co. York). Ar. on a chev. engr. gu. three crosses crosslet (another, crosses formée) of the field.

Peake, or Peke. Gyronny of four ar. and gu. a griffin's head erased, counterchanged.

Peake (Mr. Serjeant PEAKE). Chequy, or and gu. a saltire erm. *Crest*—A leopard's face gu. in the mouth an arrow ppr. headed and flighted or.

Peakeney (co. Northumberland). Or, five fusils gu.

Pearce (Penzance, co. Cornwall). Az. on a fesse ar. three pellets betw. as many pelicans or. *Crest*—An arm embowed in armour holding an arrow in pale the shaft resting on the wreath.

Pearce (Dr. PEARCE, Dean of Ely and Master of Jesus College, Cambridge). Quarterly, 1st and 4th, ar. on a mount vert three heraldic roses gu. stalked and leaved ppr.; 2nd and 3rd, ar. three Cornish choughs sa. beaked and membered gu. *Crest*—A Cornish chough, as in the arms.

Pearce, or Pearse (co. Kent). Sa. a chev. wavy ar. between two unicorns' heads erased or.

Pearce (Parson's Green, Fulham, co. Middlesex. EDWARD PEARCE, Visit. Middlesex, 1663, grandson of JOHN PEARCE, Esq., of Glyn, co. Sussex). Vert on a bend cotised er, an annulet sa. *Crest*—A demi pelican or, vulning herself ppr. crowned gu.

Pearce (Withingham, co. Norfolk; granted 20 Oct. 1715). Vert on a bend betw. two cotises or, an annulet sa. *Crest*—A demi pelican rising or, vulned in the breast ppr. crowned gu.

Pearce. Erm. a leopard ramp. guard. ppr., in chief three bees volant sa. *Crest*—A leopard sejant guard. ppr. the forepaw reposing on an escutcheon ar. charged with a bee volant sa.

Pearce. Erm. a leopard ramp. reguard. ppr. in chief three bees volant also ppr. *Crest*—A dexter arm embowed in armour holding a lance, point to the dexter.

Pearce (ZACHARY PEARCE, Bishop of Bangor 1747, translated to Rochester 1756, *d.* 1774). Erm. a leopard ramp. reguard. and in chief three bees all ppr.

Pearce (co. York). Az. a ducal coronet betw. three crosses crosslet fitchée or, two and one. *Crest*—A cross crosslet, as in the arms, crowned with a mural coronet gu.

Pearce. Gu. on a bend betw. two cotlises or, an annulet sa.

Pearce (Ffrwdgreech, co. Brecon). Az. a mural crown betw. two lions pass. in chief and as many cross crosslets fitchée in base or. *Crest*—On rocks ppr. a cross crosslet fitchée or, transpiercing a mural crown az. *Motto*—Celer et audax.

Pearche. Gu. a fesse betw. three crosses botonnée ar.

Peard (co. Devon; OLIVER PEARD was Mayor of Barnstaple in 1575; the heiress *m.* DICKINSON). Or, two wolves pass. in pale sa. their mouths embrued gu. *Crest*—A tiger's head or, pierced through the neck with a broken spear ppr. headed ar. the wound embrued gu.

Peard. Same *Arms.* *Crest*—A demi lion ramp. erm. collared sa.

Peareth (Usworth House, Gateshead, co. Durham). Gu. a chev. ar. between three pears or. *Crest*—A leopard's head and neck erased ppr. holding in the mouth a cross-crosslet fitchée. *Motto*—Verax et fidelis.

Pearle (co. Hereford). Gu. on a chev. betw. three leopards' faces or, as many mullets sa.

Pearle. Sa. two broad arrows in saltire ar. betw. four plates. *Crest*—A hand holding a thistle ppr.

Pearle. Sa. five pheons in saltire ar. headed and feathered or.

Pearle. Sa. two broad arrows in saltire ar.

Pearley. Per pale ar. and gu. a lion pass. or.

Pearmain. Or, on a chev. gu. betw. three escallops az. as many crosses crosslet of the first. *Crest*—A demi lion ramp.

Pearne. Ar. a chev. az. betw. three pears vert.

Pears - Archbold (exemplified *to* JAMES ARCHBOLD PEARS, Esq., of Fenham Hall, co. Northumberland, on his assuming the additional name of ARCHBOLD by royal license, dated 1 Feb. 1870). Quarterly, 1st and 4th, ar. a lion ramp. sa. holding betw. the paws a fret az. in base a fleur-de-lis of the last, on a chief also az. two fleurs-de-lis, for ARCHBOLD ; 2nd and 3rd, gu. two bendlets nebuly or, betw. two unicorns' heads erased of the last, each charged with an estoile of the first, for PEARS. *Crest*—1st, ARCHBOLD : Two lion's gambs erased, each encircled with a wreath of oak ppr. holding an escocheon az. charged with a fleur-de-lis az.; 2nd, PEARS : Upon a rock ppr. a wyvern vert gorged with a collar gemel or, supporting with the dexter claw an escocheon gold, charged with an estoile gu. *Motto*—Vi et virtute.

Pearsall (Willsbridge, co. Gloucester). Ar. a cross fleurettée betw. two wolves' heads erased in bend sa. *Crest*—A boar's head erased gu. crined and tusked and charged with a cross fleurettée or.

Pearsall. Ar. three piles and a bordure az. *Crest*—A lion's head erased or.

Pearsall. Az. on a fess betw. two chev. ar. as many pellets.

Pearse (Court, co. Devon ; granted 12 Aug. 1641). Ar. two bars sa. betw. six estoiles gu. three, two and one. *Crest*—A dexter arm embowed in armour, holding in the hand a lance by the middle, point to the dexter, ppr. *Motto*—Cadenti porrigo dextram.

Pearse (cos. Middlesex and Norfolk). Vert a bend cotised or.

Pearse (Bradninch, co. Devon). Gu. a bend embattled betw. two unicorns' heads erased or. *Crest*—A wivern gu. wings displ. ar.

Pearse (Dulverton, co. Somerset). Same *Arms*, &c., as of co. Devon.

Pearse (Northwold, co. Norfolk). Sa. a chev. erm. betw. three dragons' heads erased ar.

Pearse (co. Suffolk). Vert a bend cotised ar.

Pearse (granted to ELIAS PEARSE, Esq., of Thurles, co. Tipperary, third son of DANIEL PEARSE, of the city of Cork). Vert a bend nebulée plain cotised or, a canton erm. thereon a trefoil of the field. *Crest*—A fern brake, thereon a pelican in her piety, wings elevated ppr. charged on the breast with a trefoil vert. *Motto*—Nihil amanti durum.

Pearse. Erm. a leopard ramp. in chief three bees volant sa. *Crest*—A seax az. hilt and pommel or.

Pearse. Or, on a cross pierced az. four mascles of the field.

Pearse, or Peeres. Ar. two bars gemelles az.

Pearse, or Peeres. Quarterly, ar. and sa. in the first quarter a mullet of six points (another, pierced) gu.

Pearse (Harlington, co. Beds). Sa. a chev. erm. betw. three lions' heads erased ar., quarterly with TREED. *Crest*—A lion's head erased ar. *Motto*—Vi diviná.

Pearson (co. Lancaster). Az. five fusils in fesse or, within a double tressure flory counterflory ar.

Pearson, or Pierson (London). Per fesse embattled az. and gu. three suns or.

Pearson, or Pierson. Same *Arms.* *Crest*—Three savages' heads conjoined in one neck, one looking to the dexter, one to the sinister, and one upwards.

Pearson (Storrs Hall, co. Lancaster). Az. five fusils in fesse or, within a double tressure flory counterflory ar.

Pearson (granted, 1714, to HUGH PEARSON, son of MATTHEW PEARSON, son of DANIEL PEARSON, descended from a family of PEARSON, of Wisbeach, Isle of Ely, Cambridge). Per fess embattled az. and gu. three suns in splendour or. *Crest*—On a mural crown or, a paroquet vert, beaked and legged gu.

Pearson (co. Northampton). Erm. on two bars gu. three bezants two and one.

Pearson (Tankerton, and Maize Hill, Greenwich, co. Kent ; descended from THOMAS PEARSON, of Spratton, co. Northampton, living *temp.* Richard III.). Erm. on two bars gu. three bezants. *Crest*—A boar's head couped sa. in his mouth an acorn or, leaved vert. *Motto*—Perduret probitas.

Pearson (Tyers Hill, co. York). Az. betw. two pallets wavy erm. three suns or. *Crest*—A sun ppr. issuing out of a cloud.

Pearson (Lowthorpe, co. York, 1665). Per fesse embattled gu. and az. three suns in splendour or, a canton ar.

Pearson (York, 1715). Ar. a chev. betw. three roses gu.

Pearson (Upper Gloucester Place, London). Ar. billety az. on a pile of the last three horses' heads erased of the field. *Crest*—A horse's head erased sa. billety and gorged with a mural crown or.

Pearson, or Pierson (Westminster). Ar. two chev. sa. on a canton of the second an eagle displ. or.

Pearson (registered, 1698, to Lieut.-Col. JOHN PEARSON). Quarterly, 1st and 4th, per fess embattled az. and or, in chief two suns in splendour of the last, and in base a sun in splendour gu.; 2nd and 3rd, gu. a chev. erm. betw. three oak leaves or. *Crest*—A demi griffin segreant az. beaked or, and charged on the shoulder with a sun of the arms.

Pearson (co. Chester). Ar. a chev. erm. betw. three laurel leaves ppr.

Pearson (New Sleaford, co. Lincoln, and Tunbridge Hall, near Godstone, co. Surrey). Or, on a pale az. betw. two lions ramp. respecting each other gu. a sun in splendour of the field. *Crest*—A cock's head erased az. combed and wattled gu. betw. two palm branches vert, holding in the beak a heartsease or pansey ppr. and charged on the neck with a sun in splendour or.

Pearson, or Pierson (Balmadies, co. Forfar). Ar. two swords chevronways az. piercing a man's heart in chief ppr. in base a cinquefoil of the second. *Crest*—A dove holding an olive branch in her beak ppr. *Motto*—Dum spiro spero.

Pearson (Kippenross, co. Stirling). Ar. two daggers in bend and bend sinister, conjoined in point az. piercing a man's heart in base ppr. in the honour point a cinquefoil sa. *Crest*—A tower ppr. *Motto*—Rather die than disloyal.

Pearson (Westhall, co. Forfar, 1672). Ar. two swords chevronways az. hilted and pommelled or, piercing a heart gu. betw. two crescents in chief and a cinquefoil in base of the second.

Pearson (Bielside, co. Haddington, 1856). Ar. on a fess gu. a saltire of the first, over all two swords chevronways az. hilted and pommelled or, piercing a heart in chief of the second, in base a cinquefoil az. *Crest* and *Motto*—As Balmadies.

Peart, or Pert (cos. Essex, Middlesex and Norfolk). Ar. on a bend gu. three mascles or (another, ar.).

Peart (arms on the monument of ROBERT PEART, of the city of Lincoln, *d.* 1732, St. Mary, Wigford, Lincoln). Ar. on a bend az. three mascles or. *Crest*—A crane betw. reeds ppr.

Peart (co. York). Ar. on a bend gu. within a bordure gobony or and az. three mascles or.

Peart. Quarterly az. and gu. four leopards pass. ar.

Peart, or Pert. Quarterly az. and gu. four leopards pass. or, on a chief of the third a pellet.

Peart, or Pert. Az. two lances in saltire betw. four harts or, on a chief of the second a hand sa.

Peart. Quarterly gu. and az. four lions ramp. or. *Crest*—A lion ramp. as in the arms.

Pearton (co. Stafford). Ar. on a chev. betw. three pears gu. as many bezants.

Pease (Hesslewood House, co. York). Vert a chev. betw. three stags trippant or, in the centre chief point a bezant, on a chief per fesse gu. and ar. an eagle displ. counterchanged. *Crest*—An eagle's head erased ar. holding in the beak or, a peascod vert. *Motto*—Confide recte agens.

Pease (Ottery St. Mary, co. Devon). Gu. a saltire ar. betw. four plates, each charged with a leopard's face ppr. *Crest*—A leopard's head guard. couped at the neck, holding in the mouth a sword barways ppr. collared az.

Pease (Darlington, co. Durham). Per pale gu. and vert a fesse indented erm. betw. three lambs pass. ar. *Crest*—On a mount vert a dove rising ar. holding in the beak gu. a pea stalk, the blossom and pods ppr. the legs as the beak.

Pease (JOSEPH WHITWELL PEASE, Esq., M.P. for South Durham, eldest son of JOSEPH PEASE, Esq., of Darlington, by EMMA, his wife, youngest dau. and co-heiress of the late JOSEPH GURNEY, Esq., of Lakenham Grove, Norwich). Same *Arms*, quartering, GURNEY, Ar. a cross engr. gu.

Pease (London; granted 1763). Per pale gu. and vert a fesse indented erminois betw. three lambs pass. ar. *Crest*—On a mount vert a dove rising ar. holding in the beak gu. a pea-stalk, the blossoms and pods ppr. the legs as the beak.

Peasley. See PRISLEY.

Peast. Ar. a fesse sa. betw. three lions ramp. gu.

Peat (Sevenoaks, co. Kent). Ar. on a bend engr. gu. betw. two escallops az. three mascles or. *Crest*—On a mount of bulrushes ppr. a stork ar. beaked and legged gu. in front of mount two mascles interlaced fesseways az. *Motto*—Ardens.

Peat (England). Gyronny of twelve sa. and or. *Crest*—A hand holding a fish ppr.

Pech, or Peach. Sa. a falcon rising or.

Pecham, or Peckham (Chichester and Franfield, co. Sussex). Erm. a chief quarterly or and gu.

Pecham. Az. six annulets or, three, two, and one.

Pechand. Az. six eagles or, three, two, and one.

Peche (*Baron Peche*, of Brunne, co. Cambridge, *temp.* Edward I.; descended from HAMON PECHE, Sheriff co. Cambridge, 1155-65, *m.* ALICE, dau. and co-heir of PAIN PEVERELL, Lord of Brunne, co. Cambridge; the great-grandson of this marriage, GILBERT PECHE, was summoned to Parliament 1229, but the writ was not continued to his descendants). Ar. a fesse betw. two chev. gu.

Peche (*Baron Peche*, of Wormleighton, co. Warwick, *temp.* Edward II.; Sir JOHN PECHE, son and heir of RICHARD PECHE, Lord of Wormleighton, co. Warwick, in right of his mother, PETRONEL, dau. and heir of RICHARD WALSH, was summoned to Parliament 1321, but the writ was not continued to his descendants). Gu. a fesse betw. six crosses crosslet ar., in chief a label of three points.

Peche (ROBERT PECHE, Bishop of Lichfield and Coventry, 1121-26, and RICHARD PECHE, Bishop of same diocese, 1161-82). Same *Arms*.

Peche, or Pechy (co. Cambridge). Az. an eagle displ. or, crowned gu. on the breast a maunch of the third.

Peche (Sherowall, co. Derby, and co. Lancaster). Az. a lion ramp. double queued erm. crowned or, on a canton of the third a mullet gu.

Peche (Lullingstone, co. Kent). Az. a lion ramp. tail forked erm. crowned or, a mullet pierced gu.

Peche (Lord Mayor of London, 1361). Gu. a fesse betw. six crosses crosslet ar.

Peche, or Pechey (co. Oxford). Az. an eagle displ. ar. on his breast a maunch gu.

Peche, or Pechey (co. Suffolk). Ar. a fesse betw. two chev. gu. (another, sa.).

Peche, or Pechey. Ar. a fesse betw. two chev. az. *Crest*—An astrolabe or.

Peche, or Pechey. Sa. an eagle displ. ar. armed and crowned or; another, Erm. two roses gu.; another, Gu. a crescent or, on a chief ar. three mullets with six points of the field; another, Sa. three eagles displ. ar.; another, Erm. a cross gu.

Pechell (BROOKE-PECHELL, Pagglesham, co. Essex, bart.). Gu. a lion ramp. or, out of a chief of the second three laurel slips issuant ppr., quarterly with BROOKE, Or, a cross engr. per pale sa. and gu. *Crest*—A lark ppr. charged with two fleurs-de-lis or. *Crest of* PECHELL—A brock or badger pass. ppr. *Motto*—Vix ea nostra voco.

Pechein. Per pale az. and ar. a cross moline gu.

Pechey (co. Cornwall). Az. a lion ramp. within an orle of trefoils ar.

785

Pechey, or Peach (co. Kent). Az. a lion ramp. erm. crowned or. *Crest*—A lion's head erm. crowned or.

Pechey (co. Suffolk). Ar. the field replenished with martlets sa. a fesse betw. two chev. gu.

Pechey, or Peache (Chichester, co. Sussex). Az. a lion ramp. ar. tail forked, armed, and crowned or. *Crest*—A lion's head erased ar. ducally crowned or.

Pechey. Per pale or or (another, or and gu.); another, Ar. a chev. gu. within a bordure sa. bezantée; another, Ar. a fesse betw. two chev. sa. a label az. bezantée; another, Gu. crusily a fesse ar.

Pechey, or Pech. Gu. a fesse betw. six crosses crosslet ar.

Peck (co. Derby, and Wakefield, co. York). Ar. on a chev. gu. three crosses formée of the field.

Peck (Samford Hill, co. Essex, and Wood-Pelling and Methwould, co. Norfolk, *temp.* Charles II.). Or, on a chev. gu. three crosses formée of the field. *Crest*—Two lances or, in saltire, headed ar. pennons hanging to them gold, each charged with a cross formée gu. the spears enfiled with a chaplet vert.

Peck (cos. Leicester and Lincoln). Ar. on a chev. engr. gu. three crosses formée of the field.

Peck (Cornish Hall, co. Denbigh). Quarterly, 1st and 4th, ar. on a chev. engr. gu. three crosses formée of the field, for PECK; 2nd and 3rd, gu. a cross flory or, on a chief az. three round buckles of the second, for HASELDEN. *Crest*—Out of a ducal coronet or, a cubit arm erect, vested and cuffed, the hand ppr. holding a sprig of three roses. *Motto*—Crux Christi salus mea.

Peck (London). Az. a fesse embattled ar. in chief three anchors or. *Crest*—A demi lion ramp. ppr. holding an anchor or.

Peckam (cos. Buckingham and Kent). Sa. a chev. or, betw. ten crosses crosslet fitchée ar.

Peckam (co. Kent). Sa. a chev. or, betw. three crosses botonnée fitchée ar.

Peckam. Gu. a chev. betw. three crosses crosslet fitchée ar. *Crest*—A hand holding a scroll of paper ppr.

Pecke (co. Berks). Lozengy or and gu. a saltire erm.

Pecke (Winchilsea and Lewes, co. Sussex). Az. a fesse betw. three horses in full speed ar. *Crest*—A helmet in profile close plumed sa.

Pecke. Ar. a buck's head gu.

Peckham (Swaffham, co. Norfolk). Chequy or and sa. a fesse erm.

Peckham (co. Suffolk). Sa. a chev. or, betw. three crosses crosslet fitchée ar.

Peckham (co. Kent, and Little Green, Upmarden, and Lordington, co. Sussex; the dau. and heir, SARAH PECKHAM, *m.* THOMAS PHIPPS, Esq., of Heywood House, co. Wilts). Erm. a chief quarterly gu. and or.

Peckham (Nyton, co. Sussex; claiming descent from the PECKHAMS of Kent; the heiress, MARY, *m.* CHARLES HEWITT SMITH, Esq., of Ashling Lodge, co. Sussex, and left one son, CHARLES PECKHAM SMITH, Esq., of Nyton, who assumed, in 1820, the name and arms of PECKHAM only). Erm. a chief quarterly or and gu. *Crest*—An ostrich ppr. *Motto*—Tentanda via est.

Peckham. Sa. a chev. ar. betw. three crosses crosslet ar.

Peckham. Az. a cross terminated with four leopards' heads or.

Peckham. Erm. on a chief per pale or and az. a crescent gu.

Peckingham. Az. a lion ramp. ar. supporting with the forepaw a cross formée fitchée or.

Peckitt (Thirsk, co. York). Az. two bars or, and in chief three bezants. *Motto*—Ductore Deo.

Pecksall (Westminster). Ar. a cross patonce engr. betw. four Cornish choughs sa. *Crest*—A Moor's head couped ppr.

Pecksall. Ar. a cross formée flory sa. on a canton gu. a lion's head erased of the field, crowned or.

Pedder. Per pale and per chev. ar. and az. counterchanged. *Crest*—Two branches of palm in orle vert.

Pedder (Ashton Lodge, co. Lancaster). Quarterly, sa. and gu. on a bend betw. two escallops or, a greyhound courant betw. two quatrefoils of the second. *Crest*—Betw. two branches of olive ppr. as many lions' heads erased at the neck and addorsed erminois, gorged with one collar gu. *Motto*—Je dis la verité.

Peddie (Raehill, co. Dumfries, 1721). Ar. three papingoes vert within a bordure gu. *Crest*—A papingo holding in his beak an arrow ppr. *Motto*—Consulto.

Pede (Bury, co. Suffolk). Az. on a bend or, three shambrogues gu. *Crest*—A chapeau gu. turned up erm. with two

3 S

ostrich feathers, one stuck on each side, the dexter or, the sinister az.

Pedecrew. Ar. a chev. betw. three falcons' legs couped gu.

Pedell (co. Huntingdon). Gu. a chev. engr. betw. three escallops ar.

Pederton (cos. Cornwall and Somerset). Ar. a bend gu. betw. three lions' heads erased sa. crowned of the second (another, crowned or).

Pederton. Quarterly, 1st and 4th, gu. semée of crosses crosslet a lion pass. guard. ar.; 2nd and 3rd, or, semée of crosses crosslet a lion ramp. az.

Pedigrew (co. Cornwall). Ar. a chev. sa. betw. three eagles' legs couped gu.

Pedler (granted to Lieut.-Colonel PHILIP WARREN PEDLER, of Mutley House, near Plymouth, an officer of the East India Company's Service, and distinguished as having formed, disciplined, and commanded the cavalry of the Rajah of Nagpore). Sa. three lozenges ar. on a chief embattled of the last, an oriental crown betw. two fleurs-de-lis az. Crest—A demi lion ramp. sa. crowned with an oriental crown or, holding betw. the forepaws a lozenge ar. charged with a fleur-de-lis az. and bearing in its mouth a red flag. Motto—Animo non astutiâ.

Pedley (Tetworth and Abbotsley, co. Hunts). Sa. three lozenges ar. on a chief or, as many fleurs-de-lis gu. Crest—A demi lion ramp. ar. holding in the paws a lozenge or, charged with a fleur-de-lis gu.

Pedley. Same Arms. Crest—A lion's head gu.

Pedley, or Petley. Sa. three lozenges ar. a chief or.

Pedocrew. Az. three eagles displ. with two heads or.

Pedwarden (co. Hereford). Gu. two lions pass. in pale or.

Pedwardyn. Or, two (another, three) lions pass. gu. betw. three popinjays ppr.

Peebles (Dewsbury, co. York). Ar. a chev. engr. sa.

Peebles (Scotland). Ar. a chev. engr. sa. betw. three popinjays vert membered gu.

Peek (Rousden, co. Devon, bart.).—Az. an estoile ar. in chief three bezants of the last. Crest—Two hazel nuts slipped ppr. Motto—Le maitre vient.

Peek (Hazelwood, near Kingsbridge, co. Devon; granted in 1832 to JOHN PEEK, Esq., of that place). Gu. on a chev. ar. betw. three chaplets of hazel in chief or, and a plough in base ppr. three shakeforks sa. Crest—Two hazel nuts slipped ppr.

Peel (Peele Fold, co. Lancaster, and Trenant Park, co. Cornwall; ROBERT PEELE, a member of a family previously resident at Craven, co. York, settled at Hole House, near Blackburn, co. Lancaster, and d. 1608; his great-grandson, ROBERT PEEL, Esq., of Peele Fold, had seven sons, viz.: I. WILLIAM, ancestor of PEEL, of Peele Fold and Trenant Park, and PEEL, of Taliaris; II. EDMUND, left two daus. co-heirs; III. Sir ROBERT, of Drayton Manor, created a bart. 1800; IV. JONATHAN, ancestor of PEEL, of Accrington and Knowlmere; V. LAWRENCE, ancestor of PEEL, of Stone Hall and Aylesmore; VI. JOSEPH, of Bowes, near London; VII. JOHN, of Burton-on-Trent, co. Stafford). Ar. three sheaves of as many arrows ppr. banded gu. on a chief az. a bee volant or. Crest—A demi lion ramp. or. gorged with a collar az. charged with three bezants, holding betw. the paws a shuttle or. Motto—Industria.

Peel (Taliaris Park, co. Caermarthen). Same Arms, &c.

Peel (Drayton Manor, co. Stafford, bart.). Ar. three sheaves of as many arrows ppr. two and one, banded gu. on a chief az. a bee volant or. Crest—A demi lion ramp. or. gorged with a collar az. charged with three bezants holding betw. the paws a shuttle or. Supporters—Two lions guard. ar. each gorged with a collar az. thereon three bezants and each charged on the shoulder with a trefoil vert. Motto—Industria.

Peel (Bryn-y-pys, co. Flint; exemplified to EDMUND ETHEL-STON, Esq., of Bryn-y-pys, co. Flint, on his assuming, by royal licence, the surname of PEEL). Quarterly, 1st and 4th, ar. three sheaves of as many arrows ppr. banded gu. on a chief az. a bee volant or, for PEEL; 2nd and 3rd. az. on pile betw. two crosses crosslet in base ar. an eagle displ. purp., for ETHELSTON. Crests—A demi lion ramp. ar. gorged with a collar az. charged with three bezants holding betw. the paws a shuttle or, for PEEL; A ram's head couped sa. charged with three crosses crosslet or. Motto—Industria.

Peel (Knowlmere Manor, co. York). Arms, &c., as PEEL, of Peele Fold.

Peel (Stone Hall, co. Pembroke). Arms, &c., as PEEL, of Peele Fold.

Peel (Aylesmore, co. Gloucester). Arms, &c., as PEEL, of Peele Fold.

786

Peel (Singleton Brook, co. Lancaster; a younger branch of PEEL, of Peele Fold). Ar. three sheaves of as many arrows ppr. banded gu. on a chief az. a bee volant or. Crest—A demi lion ramp. ar. gorged with a collar az. charged with three bezants, holding betw. the paws a shuttle or. Motto—Industria.

Peel (Brookfield, co. Chester; descended from WILLIAM PEEL, Esq., of Oswaldwistle, co. Lancaster, grandfather of the first Sir ROBERT PEEL, Bart.). Arms, &c., same as the preceding.

Peel (WILLIAM PEEL, Esq., Ackworth Park, co. York, only son of SAMUEL PEEL, Esq., of Carrwood House, co. York). Erm. a sheaf of three arrows ppr. banded az. betw. two flaunches of the last, each charged with a bee volant or. Crest—A lion couchant ar. charged on the shoulder with a sheaf of arrows ppr. banded az. and resting the dexter paw upon an escocheon also az. charged with a bee volant or. Motto—Meret qui laborat.

Peele (co. Chester). Ar. a bend betw. two mullets (another, pierced) sa.

Peele, or Pill (co. Devon). Ar. a bend erm. betw. two mullets sa.

Peer (granted to LOTT PEER, Esq., of co. Cork, by Preston, Ulster, 13 Dec. 1634). Az. three piles wavy or, charged with a fleur-de-lis of the first. Crest—A mermaid ppr. holding in her right hand a pile wavy or, and in her left a fleur-de-lis az.

Peeres (co. Essex). Vert a bend ar. cotised or.

Peeres, or Perse (Westdown, co. Kent). Sa. a bend wavy ar. betw. two unicorns' heads erased or. Crest—A sphere or, at the north and south pole an estoile of the last.

Peeres. See PEERS.

Peeres. Az. a pelican with wings displ. feeding her young, crowned or, sitting on her nest vert.

Peeres. Sa. a chev. erm. betw. three lions' heads erased ar. (another adds, a chief or).

Peerman. Gu. a stag trippant or, on a chief of the second three crescents of the first. Crest—A stag's head couped or, collared sa.

Peers (Lord Mayor of London, 1716). Sa. a chev. betw. three lions' heads erased ar. a chief or.

Peers (Alveston, co. Warwick; granted by Cooke, Clarenceux, and confirmed by Camden, to EDMUND PEERS, Esq., of that place). Az. on a fesse ar. betw. three pelicans or, vulning themselves gu. as many pellets. Crest—Out of clouds ar. a dexter arm embowed in armour ppr. garnished or, tied round above the elbow with a ribbon in a bow gu. holding in the gauntlet a spear headed with a pheon gold.

Peers (arms on the monument of JOHN CONSETT PEERS, Capt R.N., 1798, in Eglosshayle Church, co. Cornwall). Quarterly, ar. and az. four pheons counterchanged. Crest—A crossbow.

Peers. Sa. a chev. betw. three lions' heads erased ar. Crest—On a chapeau ppr. a lion's head per chev. or and az.

Peers. Vert a bend ar. cotised or.

Peers (Chislehampton, co. Oxford; descended from Sir CHARLES PEERS, Knt., Alderman of London, and Lord Mayor in 1715. The quartering is derived from the marriage of CHARLES PEERS, Esq., of Chislehampton, with KATHERINE, dau. of JOHN KNAPP, Esq.). Quarterly, 1st and 4th, sa. a chev. betw. three lions' heads erased ar. a chief or, for PEERS; 2nd and 3rd, or, a lion pass. in base, and in chief three esquires' helmets sa., for KNAPP. Crest—A demi griffin segreant wings addorsed ar.

Peerson (Wisbeach, Isle of Ely, and London). Per fesse embattled gu. and az. three suns or. Crest—A parrot ppr.

Peerson (granted 1616). Per fesse az. and gu. three suns or. Crest—Out of a mural coronet chequy ar. and az. a parrot's head vert.

Pegge (Yeldersley and Beauchieff Abbey, co. Derby, and Osmaston, same co. See BURNELL). Ar. a chev. betw. three wedges sa. Crest—The sun rising in splendour, the rays alternately sa., or, and ar.

Peirce (Canterbury, co. Kent). Az. a bend wavy or, betw. two unicorns' heads erased ar. maned gold. Crest—A unicorn's head couped ar. armed and maned or.

Peirce (London). Ar. a fesse humettée gu. betw. three ravens rising sa.

Peirce. Sa. a bend raguly betw. two unicorns' heads erased or. Crest—A griffin pass. or.

Peires (co. Cambridge). Gu. a chev. erm. betw. three dragons' heads erased ar.

Peirs. Az. a pelican crowned or, vulned ppr.

Peirse (Bedale, co. York). Az. a ducal coronet betw. three crosses crosslet fitchée or. *Crest*—A cross crosslet fitchée or, surmounted with a mural coronet.

Peirse (BERESFORD-PEIRSE, bart.). Quarterly, 1st and 4th, az. a ducal coronet betw. three cross crosslets fitchée or, for PEIRSE; 2nd and 3rd, ar. semée of crosses crosslet fitchée three fleurs-de-lis, two and one sa. within a bordure wavy erm., for BERESFORD. *Crests*—1st: A cross crosslet fitchée or, surmounted with a mural crown gu., for PEIRSE; 2nd: Out of a naval crown or, a dragon's head per fess wavy ar. and gu. the lower part of the neck transfixed by a broken tilting spear, and in the mouth the remaining part of the spear point upwards, gold, for BERESFORD. *Motto*—Non sine pulvere palma.

Peirse (Lazenby, co. York, 1666). Gu. a ducal coronet betw. three cross crosslets or.

Peirse. Az. a bend ar. cotised or, betw. six martlets of the third.

Peirson. Az. three shuttles or, quills ar. *Crest*—A deer's head issuing or.

Peisley, or Peasley (Punchestown, co. Kildare; granted by Preston, Ulster, 1638, to BARTHOLOMEW PEISLY, of that place, Comptroller to Thomas, *Viscount Wentworth*, Lord Deputy of Ireland, son of GEORGE PEISLEY, Esq., of Ascot, co. Oxford. See VAUGHAN, of Golden Grove, King's co.). Gu. a lion ramp. double queued, crowned or, armed and langued az. in the dexter chief point a cross crosslet fitchée ar. *Crest*—A dragon sejant vert, advancing a spear or, the head az. embrued with blood, and garnished gu. *Motto*—Periculum fortitudine evasi.

Peiton. See PAYTON.

Peke (Sandwich, co. Kent). Az. three talbots pass. or.

Peke (Horncastle, co. Lincoln). Vert on a chev. ar. betw. three lions' heads erased or, as many crosses crosslet az. *Crest*—A lion's head erased or, guttée de sang, pierced through the side of the head with an arrow of the first headed and feathered ar. the arrow coming through the mouth, vulned gu.

Pelasham. Sa. three shovellers ar.

Pelborough (London). Per bend sa. and gu. on a fesse betw. three mullets or, a lion ramp. az.

Pelborough. Per bend sa. and gu. on a fesse betw. three annulets ar. a lion ramp. of the first.

Pelcot. Paly of six or and vert, a chief of the second.

Peleford (cos. Lancaster and York). Sa. three crosses formée a.

Pelham-Holles (*Duke of Newcastle*, extinct 1768). See HOLLES.

Pelham (*Earl of Chichester*). Quarterly, 1st and 4th, az. three pelicans ar. vulning themselves ppr.; 2nd and 3rd, gu. two pieces of belts with buckles erect in pale, the buckles upwards ar. *Crest*—A peacock in pride ar. *Supporters*—Dexter, a horse of a mouse colour; sinister, a bear ppr. each collared with a belt ar. buckle and pendant or. *Motto*—Vincit amor patriæ.

Pelham (ANDERSON-PELHAM, *Earl of Yarborough*). Quarterly, 1st and 4th grand quarters, the two coats of PELHAM, viz., quarterly, 1st and 4th, az. three pelicans ar. vulning themselves ppr., 2nd and 3rd, gu. two pieces of belts with buckles erect in pale, the buckles upwards ar.; 2nd and 3rd grand quarters, ar. a chev. betw. three crosses flory sa., for ANDERSON. *Crests*—1st: A peacock in pride ar., for PELHAM; 2nd: A water-spaniel dog ar, for ANDERSON. *Supporters*—Dexter, a bay horse reguard. charged on the body with three antique buckles in bend sinister or ; sinister, a water-spaniel dog reguard. or, charged on the body with three crosses flory in bend sa. *Motto*—Vincit amor patriæ.

Pelham (Compton-Valence, co. Dorset; descended from ANTHONY PELHAM, Esq., of Buxted, a younger son of the ancestor of the *Earl of Chichester*, represented by THISTLE-THWAYTE, of Southwick Park, Hants, co. Somerset, and Laughton, co. Sussex). Az. three pelicans ar. vulning themselves ppr. *Crest*—A peacock in pride ar.

Pelham (Sir WILLIAM PELHAM, Knt., *circa*. 1580, Ulster's Office). Az. three pelicans vulning themselves or.

Pelham (Cound Hall, co. Salop). Quarterly, 1st and 4th, PELHAM, quarterly, 1st and 4th, az. three pelicans ar. vulning themselves ppr.; 2nd and 3rd, gu. two belts in pale, issuing from the base ar. with buckles and studs or; 2nd and 3rd, THURSBY, ar. a chev. betw. three lions ramp. sa. *Crests*—A peacock in his pride ar., for PELHAM; A curlew with wings expanded ar. the beak and legs ppr., for THURSBY. *Mottoes*—Vincit amor patriæ, for PELHAM; In silentio fortitudo, for THURSBY.

Pelham. Gu. two pieces of belts with buckles erect in fesse ar. the buckles in chief.

787

Pelham (Sir EDMOND PELHAM, Lord Chief Baron of the Exchequer in Ireland, the first who had the title of Lord Chief Baron in Ireland; Fun. Ent. Ulster's Office, 1609, his dau. PHILIPPA, wife of ROGER DOUNTIN, Clerk of the Pipe). Az. three pelicans vulning themselves or.

Pelingard (Pelingard, co. Lancaster). Sa. three crosses pattée ar.

Pelissier (granted, 1741, to Rev. JOHN PELISSIER, D.D., Senior Fellow Trinity College, Dublin, son of Capt. ABEL PELISSIER, of Castres, Languedoc, France, who went to Ireland with William III. in 1690). Ar. on a cross az. a bezant betw. four fleurs-de-lis or, on a chief gu. a lion pass. guard. of the third. *Crest*—A fleur-de-lis or, surmounting a bezant betw. a pair of falcon's wings per fess ar. and az. *Motto*—Victrix fortunæ sapientia.

Pell (Dimblesby, co. Lincoln, and Dersingham, co. Norfolk; granted 19 Oct. 1594). Erm. on a canton az. a pelican or, vulning herself gu. *Crest*—On a chaplet vert flowered or, a pelican gold, vulning herself gu.

Pell (co. Hants). Sa. a chev. or, betw. three bezants.

Pell. Ar. a bend betw. two mullets sa. *Crest*—On a mural coronet or, a mullet pierced sa. *Another Crest*—A pelican wings endorsed ar. vulning herself ppr.

Pell (Sir ALBERT PELL, serjeant-at-law). Same *Arms*, the mullets in the arms and crest pierced.

Pellett. Az. a chev. betw. three covered cups or.

Pellew (*Viscount Exmouth*). Gu. a lion pass. guard. and in chief two chaplets of laurel or, on a chief of augmentation, wavy ar. a representation of Algiers with a British man-of-war before it, all ppr. *Crest*—Upon waves of the sea the wreck of the "Dutton," East Indiaman, upon a rocky shore off Plymouth garrison, all ppr., motto over, Deo adjuvante. *Supporters*—Dexter, a lion ramp. guard. or, navally crowned az. resting the dexter paw upon a decrescent ar.; sinister, a male figure representing slavery, trousers ar. striped az. the upper part of the body naked, holding in the dexter hand broken chains ppr. the sinister arm elevated and holding a cross or. *Motto*—Algiers.

Pellew (Treverry, co. Cornwall, 1876). Ar. a chev. gu. in base an oak wreath vert tied az. on a chief of the second three mascles of the first. *Crest*—A ship in distress on a rock ppr. *Mottoes*—Over the crest in a scroll, Deo juvante ; and under the arms, Deo non fortuna.

Fellew. Ar. a chev. gu. on a chief of the last three mascles of the first.

Pelley. Or, on a bend engr. vert three martlets ar. in chief a trefoil of the second. *Crest*—Out of a ducal coronet or, an elephant's head ar.

Pelley. Barry wavy of six or and az. a bend ar.

Pelliford (co. Lancaster). Sa. a cross formée ar.

Pelligrey. Or, a wivern volant sa.

Pellot, Pellat, or Pellet (Bignall Park and Bolney, co. Sussex). Ar. two bars sa. on the first a bezant. *Crest*—A lion pass. ar. guttée de poix, in the dexter paw an acorn slipped vert, fructed or.

Pellot. Sa. a fesse or, in chief three covered cups of the second.

Pellouer (co. Cornwall). Sa. a chev. or, betw. three bezants.

Pelly (Upton, co. Essex, bart.). Or, on a bend engr. az. betw. two trefoils slipped vert three martlets of the first. *Crest*—Out of a naval crown an elephant's head. *Motto*—Deo ducente nil nocet.

Pelmore. Or, nine crosses crosslet az.; another, Az. nine crosses crosslet or, three, three, two, and one.

Pelsant, alias Buswell (Clipston, co. Northampton, bart. extinct). Quarterly, 1st and 4th, gu. a bend raguly betw. two crosses crosslet ar.; 2nd and 3rd, sa. a fesse betw. three pelicans ar. *Crest*—A lion's head erased gu. langued az. gorged with a collar raguly ar.

Pelsett (Milton, co. Cambridge, and Itham, co. Kent). Gu. a bend raguly betw. two crosses crosslet ar.

Pelstone. Sa. three lions pass. ar.

Pelton (co. Northampton). Or, on a fesse betw. three mullets sa. as many bezants.

Pelton, or Polton. Ar. three mullets sa. *Crest*—A hand holding a swan's head and neck erased all ppr.

Pelton. Or, six starlings betw. three mullets sa. each charged with a bezant.

Peltot (London). Paly of six or and vert, a chief indented of the second.

Peltot (*temp.* Edward I.). Paly of six or and sa. a chief indented vert; another, Paly of six ar. and sa. (another, or and sa.); another, Paly of six or and vert, on a chief of the second a mullet of the first.

Pelytoe. Paly of six or and az. a chief indented vert.

Pelytot (Woodhall, co. Hertford; the heiress of Sir PHILIP PELYTOT m., *temp.* Edward III., RALPH LE BOTELER, of Pulre-

3 E 2

bach and Norbury, and brought the Manor of Woodhall into his family. Paly of six or and az. a chief indented vert.

Pemarthe (co. Cornwall). Ar. a chev. betw. three bears' heads erased sa. muzzled gu.

Pemberton (St. Alban's, co. Herts). Ar. three buckets sa. hoops and handles or. *Crest*—A dragon's head erased sa.

Pemberton (Pemberton, co. Lancaster). Ar. a chev. vert betw. three buckets sa. hoops and handles or.

Pemberton (co. Lancaster). Ar. a chev. betw. three buckets sa. *Crest*—An eagle ppr. preying on a coney ar.

Pemberton (Lord Mayor of London, 1611, and of Rushdon, co. Northampton). Ar. a chev. betw. three buckets sa. hoops or. *Crest*—A dragon's head vert couped gu.

Pemberton (co. York). Ar. three buckets sa. hoops and handles or.

Pemberton (Aislaby, co. Durham, A.D. 1595; descended from JOHN PEMBERTON, of Stanhope, living in 1400). Ar. a chev. ermines betw. three griffins' heads couped sa. *Crest* —A griffin's head couped and gorged with a ducal coronet all ppr.

Pemberton (Bainbridge Holme and Barnes, co. Durham; descended from JOHN PEMBERTON, Esq., of Hilton, a scion of PEMBERTON, of Aislaby). Same *Arms* and *Crest*. *Motto* —Labore et honore.

Pemberton (Torry Hill, near Sittingbourne). Erm. an estoile or, betw. three buckets sa. hoops and handles or. *Crest*—A dragon's head erm. erased gu. ducally gorged or, and transfixed by an arrow fessewise ppr. *Motto*—Ut tibi sic alteri.

Pemberton-Leigh (*Baron Kingsdown*). See LEIGH.

Pemberton (Milton, co. Northampton). Quarterly, 1st and 4th, ar. a chev. betw. three buckets sa. with hoops and handles or; 2nd and 3rd, ar. three dragons' heads erect sa. couped and langued gu. *Crest*—A dragon's head erect sa. couped and langued gu.

Pemberton (CHILDE-PEMBERTON, Millichope Park, co. Salop). Quarterly, 1st and 4th, PEMBERTON, or, two chevronels betw. three buckets sa.; 2nd, CHILDE, gu. a chev. erm. betw. three eagles close ar.; 3rd, BALDWYN, ar. a saltire sa. a crescent for diff. *Crests*—1st, CHILDE: An eagle with wings expanded ar. enveloped with a snake ppr.; 2nd, PEMBERTON: A griffin's head couped sa. in the front a crescent or; 3rd, BALDWYN: On a mount vert a cockatrice ar. wattled, combed, and beaked or, ducally gorged and lined gold, a crescent for diff. *Motto*—Per Deum meum, transilio murum.

Pemberton. Ar. a chev. vert betw. three well buckets sa.; another, Ar. a water bucket sa. hoops and handle or.

Pembridge (co. Chester). Ar. a bend engr. gu. a chief az. *Crest*—A bull's head sa. betw. two wings or.

Pembridge (co. Chester). Ar. five fuzils in bend gu. a chief az.

Pembridge (Mansell Gamage, co. Hereford). Barry of six or and sa., on a bend gu. three mullets ar.

Pembridge, or Pembruge (co. Leicester). Barry of six or and sa.

Pembridge (co. Salop). Or, three bars az.

Pembridge (Mansellgamel, Wales). Barry of six or and az. on a bend gu. three mullets ar.; another, Ar. a chief az. a bordure engr. gu.; another, Or, a fesse cotised az. a bend gu.; another, Or, four bars az.

Pembroke, Earl of. See HERBERT.

Pembroke, Earl of. See CLARE.

Pembroke (St. Alban's, co. Herts, and Chertsey, co. Surrey; confirmed by patent. dated 7 Feb. 1771, to GEORGE PEMBROKE, Esq., of St. Albans, and the descendants of his father JOSHUA PEMBROKE, Esq., of the same place, and of Lincoln's Inn, and to those of his uncle, NATHANIEL PEMBROKE, of Chertsey, co. Surrey. WM. PEMBROKE, of St. Albans, only surviving son of the said GEORGE, and CHARLES PEMBROKE, of Chertsey, grandson of the said NATHANIEL, were respectively Esquires to Sir Robert Keith Murray, K.P., 1772, and to Sir Philip Francis, K.P., 1812. The pedigree is traced to WM. PEMBROKE, Burgess of Bristol, who died in 1417. Quarterly, 1st and 4th, or, on a bend gu. two lions ramp. sa. a dragon pass. wings elevated, of the first, for PEMBROKE; 2nd and 3rd, ar. a wolf statant gu. on a chief indented of the last three fleurs-de-lis of the first, for FLINDELL. *Crest*—A wolf's head gu. issuing out of a ducal coronet or. *Motto*—Rebus in arduis constans.

Pembroke, Town of. The Corporation seal represents a castle embattled and towered in the middle, the exterior towers domed, and on each a flag.

Pembroke College (Oxford; founded in 1620 by the joint benefactions of THOMAS TESDALE, Esq., of Glympton, co. Oxford, and RICHARD WHITWICK, B.A., Rector of Ilsley,

788

co. Berks; originally it was called Broadgate Hall, famous for the study of the civil law, and obtained the name of Pembroke College from the Earl of Pembroke, who was Chancellor of the University when the college was founded). Per pale az. and gu. three lions ramp. two and one ar., a chief per pale or and ar., charged on the dexter side with a rose gu. and on the sinister with a thistle vert.

Pembroke Hall (Cambridge; founded in 1343 by MARY, dau. of GUY DE CHASTILLION, *Compte de St. Paul*, in France, and wife of AYMER DE VALENCE, *Earl of Pembroke*). The dexter half of the coat of VALENCE, impaled with the sinister half of the coat of GUY DE CHASTILLION, *Compte de St. Paul*, which at that time was the usual method of impaling the arms of baron and feme, and was called dimidiating. It has long been disused in England, but it is still continued by the French heralds. The arms of VALANCE are—Barry of ten ar. and az. over all ten martlets in orle gu. Those of GUY DE CHASTILLION—Vair, three pallets gu. on a chief or, a label of three points throughout az.

Pembrooke (co. Lancaster). Barruly ar. and az. an orle of martlets gu.

Pembrooke. Per pale ar. and or, a chev. betw. three crescents gu. *Crest*—A heart gu. charged with a rose ar.

Pembruge. See PEMBRIDGE.

Pemerton (Ireland, Fun. Ent. Ulster's Office, 1651; Captain PEMERTON, buried in Christ Church). Ar. on a chev. betw. three baskets sa. a mullet or.

Pempans. Gu. three greyhounds courant ar., a bezant in chief.

Pempens (co. Cornwall). Sa. a cross crosslet or, betw. three lions pass. guard. ar.

Pemperde. Per saltire or and az.

Pempons (co. Cornwall). Sa. a fret or, betw. four lions pass. (another, ramp.) ar.

Pencester (co. Sussex). Gu. a cross or.

Pencoler. Ar. a bend vairé or and gu.

Pendarves (Pendarves, co. Cornwall; EDWARD WILLIAM WYNNE-PENDARVES, Esq., of that place, M.P. for Cornwall, assumed the name of WYNNE, in lieu of his patronymic STACKHOUSE, 4 Jan. 1815, and on 28 Feb. following added that of PENDARVES). Quarterly, 1st and 4th, sa. a falcon betw. three mullets or, for PENDARVES; 2nd and 3rd, gu. a chev. betw. three lions ramp. or, for WYNNE; quartering, WILLIAMS, COURTENAY, ABRINCIS, AVENEL, ST. AUBYN, CARMINOW. *Crests*—1st: A lion ramp. reguard. or; 2nd: A demi bear erm. muzzled, lined, and ringed or; 3rd: A saltire raguly or.

Pender (co. Cornwall). Ar. on a bend per bend az. and gu. three fleurs-de-lis of the first.

Pender (Scotland). Gu. on a bend ar. two lions' heads erased of the first. *Crest*—A demi lion or, holding a sabre ppr.

Penderell. Ar. on a mount an oak tree ppr. over all a fess sa. charged with three regal crowns also ppr. *Crest*—A sword and sceptre in saltire, surmounted of a regal crown ppr. Of the honourable augmentations granted by Charles II. to the devoted partisans who loyally protected him after the battle of Worcester, we may mention those of LANE, CARLOS and PENDERELL. The first-named family received the additional crest of "a strawberry roan horse salient couped at the flanks, bridled sa. bitted and garnished or, supporting betw. the feet an imperial crown ppr." To the PENDERELLS, the humble but no less faithful protectors of the fugitive prince, were assigned the arms and identical bearings, differing in tincture only, as were given to Col. CARLOS.

Pendle. Sa. a lion ramp. ar.

Pendleton (co. Lancaster). Az. on a fesse gu. three garbs or, a chief gu. *Crest*—A lion's paw sa. holding a battle axe or.

Pendleton (Norwich). Gu. an inescutcheon ar. betw. four escallops in saltire or. *Crest*—On a chapeau gu. turned up erm. a demi dragon, wings inverted or, holding an escallop ar.

Pendleton (Fun. Ent. Ulster's Office, 1625, MARGARET PENDLETON, wife of RICHARD WIGGATT, Alderman and Mayor of Dublin). Az. a cross moline ar. surmounted of a similar cross gu.

Pendleton (confirmed to ALAN O'BRYEN GEORGE WILLIAM PENDLETON, Esq., eldest surviving son of HENRY LATHAM PENDLETON, Esq., of Pollon, co. Louth, and grandson of PHILIP PENDLETON, Esq., of Moorton, co. Meath, and to their descendants). Gu. a garb betw. four escallops in saltire or. *Crest*—A lion's gamb erased sa. charged with an escallop or, and grasping a battle axe gold. *Motto*— Audaces fortuna juvat.

Pendock (Tollerton). Gu. four bars gemelles ar. on a chief of the last five trefoils az. three and two. *Crest*—On the top of a tower gu. a demi pelican with wings endorsed or, vulning her breast of the first.

Pendred (co. Northampton; Broghillstown, co. Carlow; and Barraderry, co. Wicklow; this family, after the loss of their English estate, settled in Ireland; GEORGE PENDRED, Esq., of Broghillstown, m. CORDELIA, dau. and heiress of MORLEY SAUNDERS, Esq., of Saunders Grove, co. Wicklow, LL.D., Prime Serjeant, and had a son, MORLEY PENDRED, Esq., who eventually inherited Saunders Grove). Sa. on a chev. ar. three fleurs-de-lis of the first. *Crest*—A helmet, the vizor up. *Motto*—Nosce teipsum.

Pendreth (co. Kent; granted 1586). Paly of six ar. and sa. (another, az.) on a chief or, a griffin segreant of the second. *Crest*—A tiger sejant erm. tufted, maned, and ducally crowned or.

Penell (Woodstone in Lindridge, co. Worcester. Visit. 1634). Ar. on a fesse gu. three garbs or.

Penell. Ar. on a saltire sa. five mullets or.

Penelton. Gu. four leopards' faces jessant-de-lis or, a canton erm.

Peneway, or Penway. Barry of four gu. and or, on a chief ar. three mullets pierced az.

Peneystone (Leigh, co. Sussex; originally of co. Cornwall, bart., extinct 1705; Sir THOMAS PENEYSTONE, first bart., was Sheriff co. Oxford, *temp.* Charles I.). Ar. three Cornish choughs ppr. *Crest*—A griffin pass. sa. armed ar.

Penfold. Gu. a chev. betw. three carpenter's axes or, hafted ar. *Crest*—A lion ramp. double queued or.

Penfold (Cissbury, co. Sussex). Az. a chev. or, surmounted by another couped sa. betw. three wood pigeons ppr. each charged on the breast with a pellet. *Crest*—Out of park pales alternately ar. and sa. charged with three escallops in fesse or, a pine tree fructed ppr.

Penford (co. Cambridge). Gu. a bend embattled counter-embattled or.

Penford (co. Cumberland). Vert a bend embattled ar.

Penfound (Penfound in Poundstock, co. Cornwall; traced eight generations before 1620). Ar. a chev. betw. three pewits sa. membered and wattled gu.

Pengeley (co. Cornwall). Gu. a lion ramp. within an orle of trefoils ar. *Crest*—A lion's paw holding a palm branch all ppr.

Pengelley (co. Cornwall). Gu. the field replenished with acorns or, a lion ramp. ar.

Pengelly (co. Cornwall). Or, on a fesse per pale az. and gu. three lions ramp. ar. *Crest*—A wivern, wings inverted vert, devouring a dexter arm ppr.

Pengelly (Pengelly, co. Cornwall; the heiress m. BEARE). Or, a chev. betw. three griffins pass. wings elevated and inverted gu.

Pengelly (Sortridge, in Whitchurch, co. Devon). Gu. a lion ramp. ar. betw. six trefoils slipped of the second.

Penhallow (Penhallow, co. Cornwall; living there time Edward III.). Vert a coney ar. *Crest*—A goat pass. az. hoofed and attired or.

Penhellege (co. Cornwall). Sa. three bird bolts ar.

Penhellicke, or Penhellirke (Penhelleek, co. Cornwall). Sa. three butterflies volant ar. *Crest*—A Saracen's head ppr.

Penhergard (co. Cornwall). Ar. a saltire engr. ermines; another, Sa. a saltire erm.

Penherst, or Penhurst. Sa. a mullet ar.

Penken (co. Worcester). Ar. an eagle displ. sa. on a canton of the last a fesse dancettée or. *Crest*—An antelope sejant sa. tufted, attired, and maned ar.

Penkerch, or Penkerth (co. Lincoln). Ar. a fesse sa. betw. three fish-hooks gu.

Penkeridge. Ar. a fesse betw. three flesh-hooks sa.

Penketh (Penketh, co. Lancaster; the heiress m. ASHTON). Ar. three kingfishers az.

Penketh (co. Lancaster). Ar. a chev. gu. betw. three mullets sa. on a chief of the last as many bucks' heads cabossed or.

Penkevell, or Penkevill (Penkevell, co. Cornwall, *temp.* Edward II.). Ar. three chev. gu. in chief a lion pass. of the second. *Crest*—On a mount vert a lion couchant ppr.

Penleaze (High Cliff, Christchurch, co. Hants). Gu. semée of crosses crosslet a lion ramp. ar. *Crest*—A wivern, wings elevated ppr.

Penley. Sa. a chief or. *Crest*—A lion's head erased gu. ducally crowned or.

Penley, or Penlay. Sa. a chief ar.; another, Ar. (an-

789

other, or) a chief sa.; another, Sa. a chev. ar.; another, Barry wavy of six or and az. a bend ar.

Penman (Gibraltar, 1743). Az. on a chev. ar. ensigned with a thistle or, betw. three pens in full feather of the second as many crescents of the first. *Crest*—A dexter hand and arm issuing out of the clouds, holding a hammer over an anvil, all ppr. *Motto*—Inexpugnabilis.

Penmarch. Az. a horse's head couped ar. bridled gu. *Crest*—An ostrich reguard. murally crowned and resting the dexter paw on an escallop ppr.

Penmarche. Erm. on a fesse az. three crosses moline or.

Penn (Stoke Pogeis, co. Buckingham; settled at an early period at Minety, co. Gloucester, and at Penn's Lodge, co. Wilts; descended from WILLIAM PENN, founder of the Province of Pennsylvania, North America). Ar. on a fesse sa. three plates. *Crest*— A demi lion ramp. ar. gorged with a collar sa. charged with three plates. *Motto*—Dum clarum rectum teneam.

Penn-Gaskell (Shanagarry, co. Cork). Quarterly, 1st and 4th, or, three bars engr. vert in chief a rose gu. barbed and seeded ppr. betw. two trefoils slipped of the second, for GASKELL; 2nd and 3rd, the arms of PENN, viz., on a fesse sa. three plates a canton gu. thereon a crown ppr. representing the royal crown of King Charles II. *Crests*—1st, GASKELL: A sinister arm embowed in armour ppr. the hand supporting an escocheon or, charged with an anchor erect with cable sa., motto over, Spes; 2nd, PENN: A demi lion ar. gorged with a collar sa. charged with three plates, motto over, Pennsylvania.

Penn (co. Buckingham). Ar. on a chev. sa. three fleurs-de-lis or.

Penn (Harborough Hall, Churchill, near Stourbridge). Ar. on a fesse sa. three plates, in chief a lion pass. gu.

Penn (co. Oxford). Ar. on a fesse gu. three plates.

Penn. Sa. six fleurs-de-lis ar.

Pennant (Downing and Bychton, co. Flint; hence descended the PENNANTS of Bagilt, the PENNANTS of Jamaica, of which were the late *Lord Penrhyn*, DAWKINS-PENNANT, of Penrhyn Castle, and the PENNANTS of Holywell). *Arms*, those of TUDOR TREVOR, viz. Per bend sinister erm. and ermines, a lion ramp. or armed and langued gu. *Crest*—Out of a ducal coronet ar. an heraldic antelope's head of the last, maned, tufted, armed, and crined or; recorded *Coll. of Arms*, 2 May, 1580.

Pennant (*Baron Penrhyn*, created 1783, extinct 1808). *Arms* and *Crest* same as PENNANT, of Downing. *Supporters* —Two antelopes ppr. and chained or, the dexter charged with a canton pendent to the collar gu. thereon a man's head couped ar. *Motto*—Æquo animo.

Pennant (DAWKINS-PENNANT, of Penrhyn Castle, co. Carnarvon; GEORGE HAY DAWKINS-PENNANT, Esq., of Penrhyn Castle, left at his decease, 17 Dec. 1840, several daus. his co-heiresses; the eldest, JULIANA ISABELLA MARY, m. Lieut.-Colonel the Hon. EDWARD GORDON DOUGLAS, brother of the *Earl of Morton*, who assumed the additional name of PENNANT, and was created *Baron Penrhyn* in 1866. Quarterly, 1st and 4th, per bend sinister erm. and ermines, a lion ramp. or, armed and langued gu., for PENNANT; 2nd and 3rd, gu. a lion pass. guard. or, betw. two roses in pale ar. the whole betw. as many flaunches of the second, each charged with a lion ramp. sa., for DAWKINS; quartering, 1st, ar. three bars wavy az. the one in fesse charged with three cheldrakes of the field, for YSWITTAN WYDDELL; 2nd, az. three boars pass. in pale ar., for PHILIP PHICHDAN; 3rd, ar. on a bend az. three fleurs-de-lis of the field, for GRUFFYD LLOYD. *Crests*—1st, Out of a ducal coronet ar. an heraldic antelope's head of the last, tufted, horned, and crined or, for PENNANT; 2nd, A dexter arm embowed ppr. ensigned with a crescent gu. for diff. holding a battle-axe ppr. blade ar. charged with a rose gu., for DAWKINS.

Pennant (DOUGLAS-PENNANT, *Baron Penrhyn*). Quarterly, 1st and 4th, per bend sinister erm. and ermines, a lion ramp. or, for PENNANT; 2nd and 3rd quarterly, 1st and 4th ar. a human heart gu. ensigned with a crown or, on a chief az. three mullets of the field; 2nd and 3rd ar. three piles gu. and in chief two mullets of the field for DOUGLAS. *Crests*— 1st, PENNANT: Out of a ducal coronet an antelope's head ar. maned and tufted or. 2nd, DOUGLAS: A sanglier sticking betw. the cleft of an oak tree fructed, with a lock holding the clefts together, all ppr. *Supporters*—On either side an antelope ppr. collared and chained or, the dexter having suspended from the collar an escocheon gu. charged with a man's head couped and affrontée ppr. *Motto*—Æquo animo.

Pennant (Lord Mayor of London, 1750). Ar. three bars wavy az., on the middle one as many martlets or.

Pennant. Erm. two bars sa. charged with three plates, two and one. *Crest*—A lion pass. guard. gu.

Pennarth (from GUILLIM). Ar. a chev. betw. three bears' heads erased sa. muzzled or.

Penne (Toller Welma). Gu. six fleurs-de-lis or, three, two, and one.

Penne (Fun. Ent. Ulster's Office, 1596; quartered on the coat of THOMAS SMYTH, Alderman of Dublin). Sa. six fleurs-de-lis, three, two, and one, ar.

Penneck (co. Cornwall; granted 2 Aug. 1712). Ar. on a chev. gu. betw. three wrens' heads erased ppr. as many escallops or. *Crest*—A dexter arm embowed, sleeved gu. cuffed or, the hand holding a wren ppr.

Pennefather. See PENYFATHER.

Pennefather (Newpark, co. Tipperary; descended from MATTHEW PENNEFATHER, Quartermaster of the *Earl of Desmond's* Regiment of Horse, 1662, who got grants of land in co. Tipperary, 1666, great-grandson of WILLIAM PENY-FATHER, younger brother of JOHN PENYFATHER, of Barton-under-Needwood. Ped. and arms Reg. Ulster's Office). Per fesse or and gu. a bend erm. *Crest*—A lion sejant ar. sustaining an oval shield, per fesse or and gu. charged with a bend erm. *Motto*—I abyde my tyme.

Pennel, or Pennell. Erm. a bend gu. surmounted by a fesse or. *Crest*—An arm in armour, couped at the shoulder, embowed, and resting the elbow on the wreath, holding a scimetar all ppr.

Pennell (borne by WILLIAM PENNELL, Esq., Consul-General in Brazil). Ar. on a saltire engr. sa. five mullets or. *Crest*—A griffin sejant.

Pennell (co. Chester). Ar. on a fesse gu. three garbs or; another, Gu. two chev. ar. *Crest*—An ostrich's head, couped.

Penner. Gu. a chev. erm. betw. three pine apples ar. (another, or).

Pennerton (arms of Sir THOMAS PENNERTON, Knt., and Commander of the Mount of St. Johns. Visitation of York by Tong and Hervey in 1530 and 1552). Quarterly, 1st and 4th, ar. a chev. betw. three snakes' heads erect ppr.; 2nd and 3rd, ar. a fess. betw. three buckets sa.

Penneston (Halsted, co. Kent). Ar. three Cornish choughs ppr.

Penney (Bedford and Coddicot, co. Hertford). Ar. on a fesse gu. betw. three lapwings az. a lion pass. guard. or, betw. two combs of the first. *Crest*—A demi lion ramp. gu. holding a comb. ppr.

Penney, or Penny. Sa. six fleurs-de-lis ar. three, two, and one. *Crest*—A demi lion ramp. ar. collared sa.

Penniles (Lupton, co. Devon). Ar. on a chev. az. three fishes or.

Penning. Gu. three bucks' heads erased ar., a chief indented of the last.

Penning (Ipswich, co. Suffolk; granted 1594). Gu. three bucks' heads cabossed ar., a chief indented erm. *Crest*—A buck's head erased per fesse indented ar. and gu. attired of the last.

Pennington (Pennington, co. Lancaster, 1664). Or, five fusils conjoined in fess az.

Pennington (*Baron Muncaster*). Or, five fusils in fess az. *Crest*—A mountain cat pass. guard. ppr. *Supporters*—Dexter, a lion reguard. ppr. charged on the breast with an oak branch vert; sinister, a horse reguard. ppr. bridled or. *Mottoes*—Vincit amor patriæ. Over the crest, Firm, vigilant, active.

Pennington (Thorley, co. Herts). Same *Arms*, &c.

Pennington (Thickthorn, co. Warwick). Same *Arms*. *Crest*—A leopard pass. guard. *Motto*—Vincit amor patriæ.

Pennington (Wigan, co. Lancaster, 1664). Same *Arms*, with a canton gu.

Pennington (Thorncomb, co. Devon). Or, five fusils in fesse az. each charged with a cinquefoil ar. *Crest*—A man's head couped below the shoulders in armour front face ppr. betw. two wings.

Pennington (co. Lancaster). Az. three falcons or; another, Az. three falcons ar. belled, beaked and legged or.

Pennoyre (co. Brecknock). Ar. on a bend sa. three pears ppr.

Penny, or Penne (Peterborough, co. Northampton; granted 1574). Erm. two greyhounds courant, per pale gu and sa. (another, the greyhounds reguard.). *Crest*—On a ducal coronet ar. a lynx or.

Penny. Per pale ar. and sa. an eagle displ. counter-changed.

Penny (Higher Nutwell House, co. Devon; granted to ROBERT PENNY GREENWOOD PENNY, Esq.). Per saltire erminois and erm. two greyhounds courant reguard. gu. *Crest*—Upon a

790

crown vallery gu. a lynx statant or, holding in the mouth a fleur-de-lis az.

Penny. Ar. five fusils in fesse sa.

Pennycook (that Ilk, co. Edinburgh). Ar. a bend az. betw. three hunting horns stringed sa.

Pennycook (Newhall, co. Edinburgh, 1672). Or, a fesse sa. betw. three hunting horns of the last garnished and stringed gu. *Crest*—A stag lodged under an oak tree ppr. *Motto*—Ut resurgam.

Pennyman (Ormsby, co. York, bart. extinct; granted 1559). Gu. a chev. erm. betw. three half spears, broken staves or, headed ar. *Crest*—Out of a mural crown gu. a lion's head erased or, pierced through the neck with a broken spear, as in the arms. *Motto*—Fortiter et fideliter.

Pennystone, Penyston, Pennistone, or Penniston. Sa. three Cornish choughs ar. membered gu.

Pennythorne. Sa. on a fesse betw. three owls ar. as many crosses crosslet of the first.

Penpons (Penpons, in St. Kew, co. Cornwall; the heiress m. ARUNDELL, of Tolverne). Ar. three wolves pass. in pale sa.

Penpons (Treswithan, co. Cornwall). Ar. three wolves courant in pale az.

Penrell. Az. three garbs ar. a chief or; another, Vairé or and az. a bend ar.; another, Vairé or and vert.

Penreth. Ar. on a chev. sa. betw. three popinjays vert, beaked, legged, and collared gu. as many pears pendent or.

Penrey (co. Norfolk). Or, two bars sa. on the uppermost a mullet of the first.

Penrey. Ar. on a chev. az. (another, gu.) three fleurs-de-lis or; another, Or, two bends gu. a label az.

Penrhyn, Lord. See PENNANT.

Penrice (Penrice Castle, co. Glamorgan; the heiress m. Sir HUGH MANSEL, Knt.). Per pale indented ar. and gu.

Penrice (Crowe, co. Worcester. Visit. 1634). Per pale indented gu. and ar.

Penrice. Per pale or and az.

Penrice (Great Yarmouth, co. Norfolk; Witton House, co. Norfolk; Kilvrough House, co. Glamorgan; Plumpstead Hall, co. Norfolk; confirmed in College of Arms). Per pale indented ar. and gu. in dexter chief a wolf's head couped at the neck sa. *Crest*—A wing elevated, surmounting another, ar., the former charged with two mullets of six points in pale gu. *Mottoes*—Above the crest; Tuto et celeriter; under the arms: Justus et propositi tenax.

Penrise. Or, three bars gu.

Penrith (co. Cumberland). Ar. a chev. sa. betw. three bears' heads erased of the second, muzzled gu.

Penrith. Ar. a chev. sa. betw. three mullets (another, martlets) vert.

Penrose (co. Cornwall). Erm. on a bend az. three roses or.

Penrose (Penrose, in Sithney, co. Cornwall). *Arms* as given in the Visit. 1531, were, Erm. on a bend az. three roses or; but the family bore subsequently, ar. three bends sa. each charged with as many roses of the field. *Crest*—A trout naiant or.

Penrose (Tregethow, in Manaccan, co. Cornwall; a branch of PENROSE, of Penrose). Ar. three bends sa. each charged with as many roses of the first. *Crest*—A trout naiant or.

Penrose (granted to Sir GEORGE DEVONSHER PENROSE, Knt., Mayor of Cork, in 1876). Per bend or and ar. on a bend az. betw. three roses gu. barbed and seeded vert a civic crown of the first. *Crest*—A lion's head erased or, gorged with a chaplet of red roses, and crowned with a civic wreath both ppr. *Motto*—Rosa sine spina.

Penruddocke (Arcleby, co. Cumberland; *temp.* Queen Elizabeth). Gu. a bend raguly sr. *Crest*—A demi dragon sans wings ramp. vert betw. two eagles' wings expanded or.

Penruddocke (Compton Chamberlayne, co. Wilts; derived from the PENRUDDOCKES, of Arcleby). Same *Arms*, &c.

Penruddocke. Same *Arms*. *Crest*—A ram's head erased sa. armed or.

Penruddocke. Gu. the trunk of a tree raguly and trunked in bend ar.

Penryn (Torwerth, Wales). Gu. three boars' heads erased in pale ar.

Penryn, Town of (co. Cornwall). The Corporation seal is very ancient, and has on it a shield, thereon a bust of a man in profile, couped at the breast, vested over the shoulder, and wreathed above the temples with laurel, tied behind with two ribbons flotant.

Penshurt. Gu. a mullet ar.

Penson (WILLIAM PENSON, *Lancaster Herald, temp.* Charles I.). Gyronny of eight sa. and gu. on a fesse ar. three cinquefoils az. seeded or, betw. as many eagles displ. of the third.

Penteny (Castletown Jarvagh, Barony of Skrine, co. Meath,

and of The Cabragh, co. Louth). Sa. a chev. erm. betw. three spearheads ar. a bordure of the last semée of hurts. *Crest* On a mount vert an oak tree ppr. *Motto*—Malo mori quam fœdari.

Penthar. Ar. a cross flory gu. in the sinister quarter an escutcheon sa. charged with a cross of the field.

Pentheny. See PENTONEY.

Pentire (Pentire, co. Cornwall). Two coats—1st, Ar. a chev. sa. betw. three seapies ppr. ; 2nd, Per fesse or and ar. a lion ramp. per fesse sa. and gu.

Pentland (that Ilk, co. Edinburgh). Ar. a fesse az. betw. three lions' heads erased in chief and as many crescents in base gu. *Crest*—A lion's head erased gu. gorged with a collar ar. charged with three crescents of the first. *Motto* —Virtute et operâ.

Pentney Priory (co. Norfolk). Gu. three covered baskets or.

Pentolph (co. Salop). Gu. two bars erm. over all a bend engr. sa.

Penton (Pentonville). Per chev. gu. and or, in chief two castles ar. in base a lion ramp. az. *Crest*—A lion couchant guard. double queued az. bezantée.

Penton. Same *Arms*. *Crest*—A lion's paw erased.

Pentoney (Dublin, Fun. Ent. Ulster's Office, 1599, WILLIAM PENTONEY, of that city). Sa. a chev. erm. betw. three spear heads ar. a border engr. of the last semée of hurts.

Penury (West Yoke, Ash, co. Kent). Sa. a cross or, on a chief ar. three eagles displ. az.

Penwallis. Ar. on a chev. az. three brushes of the field ; another, Ar. on a chev. az. three fleurs-de-lis of the field.

Penwarn (Penwarn and Mullyton, co. Cornwall). Sa. a chev. or, betw. three fleurs-de-lis ar. *Crest*—A demi lion ramp. supporting in both paws the helm of a ship.

Penwortham Priory (co. Lancaster). Ar. on a chev. betw. three water bougets gu. two pair of keys in saltire or.

Penwyn (co. Cornwall). Gu. three boars' heads erased in pale ar. *Crest*—A stag's head couped per fesse indented ar. and gu.

Penyfather (Barton-under Needwood, co. Stafford, *temp.* Queen Elizabeth). Per fesse or and gu. a bend erm. *Crest* —A lion sejant ar. sustaining an oval shield per fesse or and gu. charged with a bend erm.

Penyfather (London ; confirmed by Camden, Clarenceux, 1603, to WILLIAM PENYFATHER, Sheriff of London, younger son of JOHN PENYFATHER, Esq., of Barton-under-Needwood). Same *Arms* and *Crest*, a mullet for diff.

Penyng (Kettleborough and Ipswich, co. Suffolk). Gu. three bucks' heads cabossed ar. a chief indented erm. *Crest*—A buck's head erased per fesse indented ar. and gu. attired of the last.

Penyston (co. Bucks, and Leigh, co. Sussex ; granted 12 May, 1564). Ar. three Cornish choughs ppr. *Crest*—A griffin pass. ar. armed or.

Penyston (co. Norfolk). Gu. three leopards' faces reversed ar. jessant-de-lis sa. *Crest*—Two lion's gambs erased ar. supporting a cone gu. standing on the point.

Penyston (Cornwell, co. Oxford ; exemplified to JOHN FRANCIS PARTRIDGE, Esq., upon his assuming, by royal licence, the surname of PENYSTON). Ar. three Cornish choughs ppr., and for distinction in the centre chief point a cross crosslet gu. *Crest*—A gryphon statant sa. charged, for distinction, with a cross crosslet ar. *Motto*—Virtus invicta vigit.

Penythorne. Sa. on a fesse betw. three owls ar. as many crosses crosslet of the field.

Pepdie (Dunglass, co. Berwick ; heiress *m.* in 14th century, Sir THOMAS HUME, of that Ilk, whose descendants have since quartered that coat). Ar. three popinjays vert, beaked and membered gu.

Pepdie (quartered by HUME, Bart., of Castle Hume, co. Fermanagh, extinct ; Fun. Ent. Ulster's Office, 1685). Ar. three popinjays vert, beaked and legged gu.

Pepe, or Pape (Holland). Or, three palets az. on a chief gu. a saltire of the field. *Crest*—A falcon with wings expanded ppr.

Penenrell, Popenrill, or Perperell (co. Cornwall). Ar. a chev. gu. betw. three pine apples vert stalked or.

Peper. Ar. on a chev. gu. three fleurs-de-lis or.

Peper (Canterbury, co. Kent ; the co-heirs *m.* ROUTHLAND and TWINE. Visit. Hants, 1634). Ar. a fesse embattled sa. in chief two estoiles of the last. *Crest*—A cubit arm erect, holding in the hand ppr. two snakes, heads contrariwise, tails entwined and knotted round the arm az.

Peperde. Ar. two bars az. on a canton of the last a cinque foil of the first.

791

Peperell (Massachussetts Bay, New England, bart., extinct). Ar. a chev gu. betw. three pine apples vert, on a canton of the second a fleur-de-lis of the first. *Crest*—Out of a mural coronet or, an armed arm embowed betw. two laurel branches issuing from the coronet ppr. grasping a staff thereon a flag ar. *Mottoes*—Over the crest, Peperi ; and under the arms, Fortiter et fideliter.

Peperell. Gyronny of twelve ar. and gu. a bordure sa bezantée.

Peperell. Ar. a chev. gu. betw. three cinquefoils vert.

Peple (co. Devon). Ar. on a bend sa. betw. two bendlets dancettée gu. three eagles displ. of the first. *Crest*—An eagle's head couped ar.

Peploe. Az. a chev. embattled counter-embattled betw. three bugle horns or. *Crest*—Out of a ducal coronet or, a reindeer's head of the last.

Peploe (co. Salop). Same *Arms*, &c.

Peploe (Garnstone Castle, co. Hereford). Az. on a chev. embattled counter-embattled betw. three bugle horns stringed or, a mitre with labels of the field, on a canton erm. a crozier or, and a sword gu. in saltire, the former surmounted by the latter. *Crest*—A ducal coronet or, thereon a reindeer's head gu. antlered or, charged on the neck with a human eye shedding drops of tears ppr.

Peploe (now of Garnstone ; exemplified to JOHN BIRCH PEPLOE WEBB, Esq., upon his assuming, by royal licence, the surname of PEPLOE). Quarterly, 1st and 4th, az. on a chev. embattled counter-embattled ar. betw. three bugle horns stringed or, a mitre with labels of the field, on a canton erm. a crozier or, and a sword in saltire gu. the former surmounted by the latter, for PEPLOE ; 2nd and 3rd, or, a cross paly sa. and az. in the 1st and 4th quarters an eagle displ. of the second, for WEBB. *Crests*—PEPLOE : A ducal coronet or, issuant therefrom a reindeer's head gu. attired gold, charged on the neck with a human eye shedding tears ppr. ; WEBB : An eagle displ. sa. semée de fleurs-de-lis or, and in the mouth a trefoil vert.

Peppard (Fun. Ent. Ulster's Office, 1597, ELIZABETH PEPPARD, *m.* 1st, JOHN EUSTACE, Esq., of Castlemarten ; 2nd, Captain THOMAS LEA). Ar. two bars az. the upper charged with three fleurs-de-lis and the lower with as many martlets, all of the first, on a canton of the second a cinquefoil pierced of the field.

Peppard (Drogheda ; Fun Ent. Ulster's Office, 1676, Alderman GEORGE PEPPARD). Ar. two bars az. on a canton of the second a cinquefoil pierced of the field.

Peppard (Cappagh House, co. Limerick). Az. two bars or, the upper charged with three fleurs-de-lis, the under with as many martlets gu. on a canton of the third a cinquefoil ar. *Crest*—In front of three ostrich feathers ar. and az. a greyhound courant ppr. *Motto*.—Virtute et valore.

Pepper (Thurmarston, co. Leicester, and co. York). Gu. on a chev. ar. betw. three demi lions ramp. or, as many sickles sa. *Crest*—A demi lion ramp. or.

Pepper (Thorlesby, co. Lincoln). Gu. a griffin segreant or, over all a bendlet ar. *Crest*—A stag trippant ar.

Pepper (Norfolk). Ar. two bars gu. on a canton az. a rose or.

Pepper (Ballygarth, co. Meath ; granted by Betham, Ulster, to THOMAS PEPPER, Esq., of that place, and the descendants of his great great grandfather). Gu. on a chev. ar. betw. three demi lions ramp. or, as many grains of pepper ppr. and in chief a trefoil slipped of the second. *Crest*—A demi lion ramp. or. *Motto*—Semper erectus.

Pepper (Lisanisky, co. Tipperary). Same *Arms*, &c.

Peppercorne (granted to JAMES PEPPERCORNE, Esq.). Per chev. gu. and az. on a chev. engr. ar. betw. two bezants in chief and a fleur-de-lis in base of the third, a lion pass. ppr. betw. two crosses crosslet sa. *Crest*—On a mount vert a horse's head erased sa. surmounted of two branches of palm in saltire or, tied with a riband of the last.

Pepperell (London). Ar. a chev. gu. betw. three pinecones vert, on a canton az. a fleur-de-lis or. *Crest*—Out of a mural crown ar. with three laurel leaves ppr. in the embrasures an armed arm embowed holding a banner ar. *Motto*—Peperi.

Peppin (granted 1757). Vert a cross avellane ar. *Crest*— A pegasus courant with wings endorsed ar. charged on the shoulder with a cross as in the arms, vert.

Pepplesham (co. Sussex ; *temp.* Edward III.). Sa. three ducks or.

Pepsall (co. Hants, 1571. Visit. Hants, 1654). Ar. on a cross engr. flory sa. four popinjays ppr. collared ar. beaked and membered gu. an escallop or.

Pepwell (Bristol and co. Gloucester). Or, on a chev. az. betw. three carnations ar. stalked and leaved vert as many lions' heads erased of the first. *Crest*—A hawk close betw. two carnations all ppr.

Pepys (*Earl of Cottenham*). Sa. on a bend or, betw. two horses' heads erased ar. three fleurs-de-lis of the field. *Crest*—A camel's head erased or, bridled and gorged with a ducal coronet sa. *Supporters*—On either side a horse ar. bridled and gorged with a ducal coronet sa. pendant therefrom an escutcheon or, charged with a fleur-de-lis of the second. *Motto*—Mens cujusque is est quisque.

Pepys (London, and Ridley Hall, co. Chester, bart., extinct 1849). Sa. on a bend or, betw. two horses' heads erased ar. three fleurs-de-lis of the field. *Crest*—A camel's head erased or, bridled, lined, ringed, and gorged with a ducal coronet sa. *Motto*—Mens cujusque is est quisque.

Pepys, or Pipis (Cottenham, and Brampton, co. Hunts). Same *Arms* and *Crest*. Another *Crest*—A camel's head erased ppr. ducally gorged and lined or.

Pepys (Ashop, co. Essex, and Southcreak, co. Norfolk). Same *Arms*.

Perbo (Lincoln's Inn, co. Middlesex; descended from co. Chester; granted 1620). Vert, semée-de-lis and fretty of eight or, a chief erm. *Crest*—A tiger's head ar. maned and langued or, collared vert, thereon three fleurs-de-lis of the last.

Perbut, or Perbutt. Or (another ar.), ten pellets, four, three, two, and one.

Percehay (Ryton, co. York). Ar. a cross flory gu. *Crest*—A bull's head az. horns per fesse, of the same and or.

Percehay. Ar. a cross pattée gu. (another adds, in the first quarter a lozenge of the last; another, a border of the last).

Percehay. Or, five lozenges in fesse sa.

Percher. Quarterly, sa. and az., in the 1st and 4th quarters three bezants, in the 2nd and 3rd a pile wavy in point or; another, Sa. three bezants.

Perceval (*Earl of Egmont*). Quarterly, 1st and 4th, ar. on a chief indented gu. three crosses pattée of the field for PER-CEVAL; 2nd and 3rd, barry nebulé of six or and gu., for LOVEL of Tichmersh. *Crest*—A thistle erect, leaved ppr. *Supporters*—Dexter, an antelope ar. attired and unguled or, ducally gorged and chained of the last; sinister, a stag sa. attired and unguled or, ducally gorged and chained of the last, each holding in the mouth a thistle ppr. *Motto*—Sub cruce candidâ. (It appears from ancient documents that the family of PERCEVAL, of the house of Weston, co. Somerset, of which line the *Earl of Egmont* is the chief, have borne and used, as supporters to their arms, two eagles sa. as depicted and blazoned in a book remaining in the *College of Arms London*, marked 3d D, 141, p. 182 and 186, from the time of Edward I. Confirmed 16 April 1740, by Charles Greene, Lancaster, and Richard Mawson, Portcullis, Officers at Arms).

Perceval (assigned 1770 to Right Hon. CATHERINE, *Countess of Egmont*, second wife of JOHN *Earl of Egmont* and dau. of the Hon. CHARLES COMPTON, on her creation as *Baroness Arden*). Ar. on a chief indented gu. three crosses pattée of the field. *Crest*—Out of a ducal coronet or, a bear's head sa. muzzled gold. *Supporters*—Two griffins az. semée-de-lis or, beaked, ducally gorged and chained gold. *Motto*—Sub cruce candidâ.

Perceval (Temple House, co. Sligo; descended from GEORGE, second son of Sir PHILIP PERCEVAL, Knt., ancestors of the *Earls of Egmont*). Ar. on a chief indented gu. three crosses pattée of the field. *Crest*—A thistle erect leaved ppr. *Mottoes*—Over the crest: Yvery; under the shield: Sub cruce candidâ.

Perceval (Cappaheaden, co. Kilkenny, and Kilmon Hill, co. Waterford, and Annefield, co. Dublin). Same *Arms*, &c.

Perceval (Royton and Manchester, co. Lancaster; cadet of the house of EGMONT). Same *Arms*, &c.

Perceval (Barntown, co. Wexford). Ar. on a chief indented gu. three crosses pattée or. *Crest*—A thistle erect leaved ppr.

Perceval (Gortnadroma, co. Clare; Fun. Ent. Ulster's Office, 1683, HUGH PERCEVAL, of that place). Sa. a horse pass. ar. the foreleg attached to the hind leg on the near side by a fetterlock.

Percham. Per pale az. and ar. a cross sarcelly gu.

Perchard (Jersey and Guernsey; Lord Mayor of London, 1804). Ar. five lozenges conjoined in fesse sa. *Crest*—On a mount vert a pheasant ppr. *Motto*—En faizant bien.

Perchford. Chequy or and az. on a fesse ar. three lions ramp. gu.

Percival (Ireland; CHRISTOPHER PERCIVAL, whose dau. ELIZABETH, m. Rev. LUKE CALIONER, D.D., who was very active in the building and founding of Trinity College, Dublin, and was buried there 1613; Fun. Ent. Ulster's Office). Sa. a chev. erm. betw. three mullets ar.

Percival (Dublin; Fun. Ent. Ulster's Office, 1652, ELIZA-BETH, dau. of DOMINIC PERCIVAL, of that city, and wife of

792

THOMAS RICHARDSON, Auditor of Public Accounts in Ireland). Same *Arms*.

Percival-Maxwell. See MAXWELL.

Percival (Newport-Pagnel, co. Buckingham; granted 1745). Vert a saltire invecked erminois betw. two pheons in pale or, and as many swans in fesse ar. a chief of the second.

Percival (granted to WILLIAM PERCIVAL, Esq., of Moorlands House, Kirkby Stephen, co. Westmorland, and of Bolton, same co.). Gu. a cross parted and fretty betw. in the 1st and 4th quarters, a bull's head couped, and in the 2nd and 3rd, a cross pattée ar. *Crest*—A bull's head couped ar. charged with a cross pattée gu. the neck encircled by an annulet gold. *Motto*—Sub cruce vinces.

Percival (Lord Mayor of London, 1498). Per chev. az. and gu. three greyhounds' heads ar. collared or.

Percival. Or, a bend sa. on a chief az. three griffins' heads erased of the field. *Crest*—A thistle slipped and leaved.

Percival. Per chev. ar. and az. three greyhounds' heads erased counterchanged.

Percival (formerly LOCKWOOD; Lambourne Hall, co. Essex). Sa. a horse pass. ar. spancelled in both legs, on the near side gu. *Crest*—A nag's head couped ar., also the crest of LOCKWOOD.

Percivall (co. Hants). Sa. a horse pass. ar. spancelled in both legs, on the near side gu. *Crest*—A demi lion ramp. or (another, a nag's head ar.).

Percivall. Per chev. gu. and az. three greyhounds' heads erased ar. collared of the first. *Crest*—A demi lion gu.; another, Or, a fesse sa. on a chief of the second three griffins' heads erased of the first; another, Or, two lions pass. in pale az.; another, Purp. semée of crosses or; another, Purp. eight crosses crosslet or, on a canton ar. (another, erm.) an estoile sa.; another, Az. two lions pass. ar. (another, or).

Percy (*Baron Percy* by tenure; descended from WILLIAM DE PERCY, who accompanied William I. from Normandy, 1066; JOSCELINE, of Louvaine, brother of Queen Adeliza, second wife of Henry I., and son of GODFREY BARBATUS, *Duke of Brabant*, m. AGNES DE PERCY, dau., and eventually sole heiress, of WILLIAM, third *Lord Percy* by tenure, and assumed the surname of PERCY. From this marriage sprang the Lords Percy, of Alnwick, and the other branches of the great and historic house of PERCY, of Northumberland). Az. five fusils conjoined in fess or.

Percy (*Baron Percy* by writ, and *Earl of Northumberland*). Quarterly, 1st and 4th grand quarters, 1st and 4th, or, a lion ramp. az., 2nd and 3rd, gu. three lucies or pikes haurient ar.; 2nd and 3rd grand quarters, az. five fusils conjoined in fesse or. *Crest*—On a chapeau gu. turned up erm. a lion statant, the tail extended az. *Supporters*—Dexter, a lion ramp. az.; sinister, a lion ramp. guard. or, ducally crowned of the last, gorged with a collar gobony az. and az. *Motto*—Espérance en Dieu. *Badge*—A crescent ar. within the horns per pale sa. and gu. charged with a double manacle fesswaye or.

Percy (*Duke of Northumberland*). Same *Arms*, &c., as last.

Percy (*Baron Prudhoe*, extinct 1865). Same *Arms* and *Crest* as the last, with a crescent in the arms for diff. *Supporters*—Dexter, a lion az. charged on the shoulder with an anchor; sinister, a lion guard. ducally drowned or, collared gobony ar. and az.; on the shoulder a crescent of the third. *Motto*—Espérance en Dieu. (Succeeded as fourth *Duke of Northumberland*, and *d. s. p.* 1865, when the Dukedom devolved on the *Earl of Beverley*).

Percy (*Earl of Beverley*, merged in the Dukedom; GEORGE, second *Earl of Beverley*, *s.* as fifth *Duke of Northumberland*). Same *Arms*, *Crest*, and *Motto*, as the last. *Supporters*—Dexter, a lion az. charged on the shoulder with a crescent ar.; sinister, a unicorn ar. armed, unguled, maned, tufted, and ducally gorged, or; on the shoulder a double shackle fessceways gold.

Percy (*Earl of Worcester*; Sir THOMAS PERCY, a younger brother of HENRY, first *Earl of Northumberland*, was created 1397, beheaded 1402, *s. p.*). Same as *Earl of Northumberland*.

Percy (Hon. CHARLES GREATHEED BERTIE PERCY, of Guy's Cliff, co. Warwick, youngest son of ALGERNON, first *Earl of Beverley*). Quarterly of four grand quarters, 1st and 4th, quarterly of four, 1st and 4th, or, a lion ramp az., 2nd and 3rd, gu. three lucies, or pikes, haurient, two and one, ar.; 2nd and 3rd, az. five fusils in fesse or, the centre point charged with a crescent ar. thereon a fleur-de-lis gu.; quartering, in the 2nd and 3rd principal quarters, GREAT-HEED and BERTIE. *Crest* of PERCY, as the *Earl of Beverley's*, with due distinction, with *Crests* of GREATHEED and BERTIE. *Motto*—Espérance en Dieu. See GREATHEED.

Percy (Shaftesbury, Bushton, and Manston, co. Dorset). Or, a fesse humettée gu. betw. three birds, wings expanded sa. *Crest*—A demi lion ramp. az. collared or, holding in the dexter paw a spear of the last.

Percy (Islington, co. Middlesex). Az. three fusils in fesse, within a double tressure flory counterflory or.

Percy (Ardingworth, co. Northampton). Ar. four fusils in fesse sa.

Percy (Hodnet). See HEBER-PERCY.

Percy (Sir RICHARD PERCY, knighted in Christchurch, Dublin, 13 Sept. 1598). Quarterly, 1st and 4th, or, a lion ramp. az.; 2nd and 3rd, gu. three fishes haurient ar. a crescent for diff.

Percy (co. Northampton). Or, four fusils in fesse sa.

Percy (Holderness, co. York). Or, a lion ramp. az. a bordure gobony ar. and gu.

Percy (Scotton, co. York). Per fesse ar. and gu. a lion ramp. per fesse sa. and of the first.

Percy. Same *Arms*, the lion collared and chained or.

Percy. Or, a fusil in pale engr. sa.; another, Ar. five fusils in fesse sa. on each three palets or; another, Az. a fesse indented ar.; another, Ar. three fusils in fesse sa. on each a bezant; another, Ar. on a fesse betw. six martlets sa. three mullets of the field; another, Ar. a cross flory gu.; another, Quarterly, or and gu. on a bend sa. three lions pass. ar.

Percy (granted by Betham, Ulster, to JOHN PERCY, Esq., of Ballintemple, King's co.). Quarterly, 1st and 4th, or, a lion ramp. az. betw. three trefoils slipped vert; 2nd and 3rd, az. three fusils in fess or, betw. two trefoils slipped ar., all within a bordure gobony gu. and ar. *Crest*—On a chapeau gu. turned up erm. a lion pass. tail extended az. holding in the dexter forepaw a trefoil slipped or. *Motto*—Espérance en Dieu.

Pereley. Per pale ar. and gu. a lion pass. counterchanged.

Periam (Fulford, co. Devon). Gu. a chev. engr. betw. three leopards' faces or.

Pericot, or Percot. Az. two bars or, in chief three bezants.

Perient. Ar. three bendlets az. a bordure gu. bezantée.

Perient. Gu. three crescents ar.

Periers (co. Cornwall). Per pale indented or and gu.

Periers, or Perers. Quarterly, ar. and sa.; in the first quarter a mullet of six points pierced gu.

Perike, or Perke. Or, on a cross pierced az. four mascles of the first.

Perike, or Perke. Ar. a buck's head cabossed gu.

Perin. Ar. on a chev. betw. three escallops sa. as many crosses pattée or. *Crest*—Out of a ducal coronet or, a peacock's head ppr.

Perin. Ar. a chev. betw. three escallops gu.

Periond. Ar. on a fesse sa. three lamps ar.

Perire. Ar. on a bend sa. three pears or.

Perisey. Ar. a cross flowery gu.

Periton, or Pertree. Vert a, fret or.

Perk. Ar. on a bend gu. three mascles or.

Perke. Or, on a cross quarterly pierced az. four mascles of the field.

Perke. Lozengy or and gu. a saltire lozengy erm. and ermines.

Perke. Sa. two broad arrows in saltire ar. betw. nine plates.

Perkens. Or, a fesse indented betw. eight billets ermines.

Perkin (co. Worcester, Harl. MSS.). Ar. an eagle displ. sa. on a canton of the last a fess dancettée or. *Crest*—An antelope sejant sa. tufted, armed, and maned ar. *Motto*—A spe in spem.

Perkin. Erm. on a fesse gu. three annulets or. *Crest*—A stag lodged ppr.

Perkins (Upton Court, co. Berks, Teddington, co. Middlesex). Or, a fesse dancettée betw. six billets ermines. *Crest*—A pineapple ppr. stalked and leaved vert.

Perkins (Orton Hall, co. Leicester, and Sutton Coldfield, co. Warwick). Sa. an eagle displ. ppr. on a canton ar. a fesse dancettée of the first. *Crest*—A unicorn's head issuing out of a ducal coronet. *Motto*—Toujours juste.

Perkins (co. Lincoln). Vert a chev. betw. three ostrich feathers ar. a bordure or.

Perkins (co. Lincoln). Ar. (another, or) a fesse dancettée betw. ten billets ermines, four, three, two, and one.

Perkins (Bunney, co. Nottingham). Ar. an eagle displ. sa. on a canton or, a fesse dancettée between six billets ermines. *Crest*—A pineapple ppr. stalked and leaved vert.

Perkins (Nuneaton, co. Warwick). Ar. a lion pass. sa. betw. three fleurs-de-lis gu. *Crest*—A lion pass. sa. holding in the paw a fleur-de-lis gu. *Motto*—Simplex vigilum veri.

Perkins (Marston, co. Warwick). Gu. two chev. betw.

three escallops ar. *Crest*—Out of a ducal coronet o°, a unicorn's head erm. maned and horned gold.

Perkins (granted by Roberts, Ulster, 1646, to RICHARD PERKINS, J.P. co Donegal, son and heir of THOMAS PERKINS, Esq., also J.P. of same co.). Ar. an eagle displ· sa. membered and beaked gu. on a canton of the second a fess indented or, a crescent for diff. *Crest*—A demi eagle displ. sa. *Motto*—Ne nimis altus.

Perkinson. Or, on a chev. gu. betw. three pellets, as many ostrich feathers ar. *Crest*—A unicorn's head erased ar.

Perkinson, alias Fetherston (co. Durham). Gu. on a chev. betw. three ostrich feathers ar. as many pellets. *Crest*—A falcon ppr.

Perkinson (Beaumondhill, co. Durham). Same *Arms* and *Crest*.

Perks. Or, three organ rests gu. *Crest*—A lion's head erased or.

Pern (co. Cambridge; granted 1575). Or, on a chev. betw. three pelicans' heads erased at the neck az. vulning themselves gu. a mullet of six points pierced of the field. *Crest*—Out of a ducal coronet ar. a pelican's head or, vulned gu.

Perne (Ely, co. Cambridge; granted 15 June, 1575). Ar. on a chev. betw. three pelicans' heads erased az. vulned gu. an estoile or. Same *Crest* as the last.

Perneys, or Pernys. Ar. a chev. betw. three pears az. (another, vert).

Peron (Quarley, co. Wilts). Quarterly, or and az. a cross moline gu.

Perot, and Perott. See PERROTT.

Perpound, Peirepont, or Pierrepoint. Ar. a lion ramp. sa. betw. six cinquefoils gu. *Crest*—A lion's gamb erased sa. holding a cinquefoil gu.

Perraro. Ar. on a mount vert a lion pass. gu. against a tree ppr.

Perreau (London). Gu. on a chev. or, betw. three leopards' faces ar. as many fleurs-de-lis az. *Crest*—Out of a ducal coronet or, a leopard's head guard. couped at the neck ar.

Perring (bart.). Ar. on a chev. engr. sa. betw. three fir-cones pendent vert, as many leopards' faces of the field. *Crest*—On a mount ppr. a fir cone vert. *Motto*—Impavidum feriunt ruinæ.

Perrin (Jersey and Guernsey). Gu. three greyhounds courant in pale ar.

Perrin (Hall Car, Sheffield, and Salop). Ar. on a chev. betw. three fir-apples pendent vert, as many leopards' faces of the field.

Perrings. Ar. three stags' heads erased gu. *Crest*—Three organ pipes, two in saltire surmounted by one in pale az. banded vert.

Perris (London). Ar. on a chev. betw. three pheons gu. as many tigers' heads erased of the first. *Crest*—A demi tiger reguard. per chev. gu. and ar. holding in the dexter paw an arrow also ar.

Perrier (Lota Park, co. Cork; confirmed to ANTHONY PERRIER, Esq., of Lota, third son of Sir ANTHONY PERRIER, of Carrigmore, same co., Lord Mayor of Cork, 1820-1, and grandson of ANTHONY PERRIER, High Sheriff of Dublin, and to their descendants). Ar. a lion ramp. gu. debruised by a bend or, on a chief az. a lion's head couped of the first. *Crest*—A lion's head ppr. issuant from a French ducal coronet or. *Motto*—Consilio et vi.

Perrott (Ystington, Haroldston, and Carew Castle, co. Pembroke, a very ancient family of Norman origin; the name appears on Hollingshed's Roll of Battel Abbey. Sir STEPHEN PERROTT, *temp.* Henry I., *m.* HELEN, dau. of MARCHION-AP-RICE, *Prince of South Wales*, and obtained with her the Lordship of Ystington: their descendant, PETER PERROTT, *temp.* Edward III., *m.* ALICE, dau. and heir of Sir RICHARD HAROLD, Knt., of Haroldston, same co.: seventh in descent from this marriage was Sir JOHN PERROTT, K.B., appointed by Queen Elizabeth Governor and Keeper of Carew Castle, co. Pembroke, Lord Deputy of Ireland 1583-88. Immediately on his appointment as Lord Deputy he made a Deed of Settlement entailing his estates on his sons and their male descendants, and in default of such, on his cousin, THOMAS PERROTT, of Broke, co. Carmarthen. He *d.* 1599: his only legitimate son, Sir THOMAS PERROTT, Knt., of Haroldston, *m.* 1583, Lady DOROTHY DEVEREUX, dau. of WALTER, first *Earl of Essex*, and sister of ROBERT, second *Earl of Essex*, the favourite of Queen Elizabeth, and by her (who *m.* secondly, HENRY, ninth *Earl of Northumberland*) he had a dau. and heir, PENELOPE PERROTT, *m.* first, WILLIAM LOWER, Esq., and secondly, Sir ROBERT NAUNTON, Secretary of State to James I., author of "Fragmenta Regalia," who *d.* 1635). Gu. three pears or, on a chief ar. a demi lion issuant sa. armed and langued of the field. *Crest*—A parrot vert holding in the dexter claw a pear or, leaved ppr. *Supporters*—Dexter, an Ancient Briton armed and blazoned ppr.; sinister, a dragon gu. *Motto*—Amo ut invenio.

Perrott (Haroldston, co. Pembroke, formerly of Morton-on-Lug, co. Hereford; Sir HERBERT PERROTT, Knt., son and heir of ROBERT PERROTT, Esq., of Morton, and grandson of RICHARD PERROTT, of same place, who was son of THOMAS PERROTT, Esq., of Broke, eventually *s.* to the estates of the Lord Deputy PERROTT: his only dau. and heiress, HESTER PERROTT, *m.* Sir JOHN PAKINGTON, fourth bart. of Ailesbury, co. Bucks, ancestor of Sir JOHN SOMERSET PAKINGTON, created 1874 *Lord Hampton*). Same *Arms*, *Crest*, and *Motto.*

Perrott (Coolfinn, Queen's co.; ROBERT PERROTT, descended from the foregoing, obtained grants of land at Coolfinn, and at Loughboy, Welland Park, &c., in co. Kilkenny, under the Act of Settlement, *temp.* Charles II.; his dau. ANNE PERROTT, co-heir of her brother, RICHARD PERROTT, Esq., of Dartmouth, co. Devon, *m.*, 1680, JOHN GLASCOTT, Esq., of Aldertown, co. Wexford, whose son, GEORGE GLASCOTT, Esq., of Aldertown, *d.* 1755, inherited the PERROTT estates, co. Kilkenny, and bequeathed them to his second son, GEORGE GLASCOTT, Esq., *d.* 1788; his son, JOHN GLASCOTT, Esq., of Killowen, *d.* 1841, was grandfather of JOHN H. GLASCOTT, Esq., J.P., co. Wexford. See GLASCOTT, of Aldertown and Killowen). Same *Arms* and *Crest.*

Perrott (Northleigh, co. Oxford, EDWARD PERROTT, Esq., of Northleigh, at Visit. Oxon, 1634, grandson of SIMON PERROTT, of same place, Visit. Oxon, 1574, who was grandson of GEORGE PERROTT, of Haverford West, son of OWEN PERROTT, a third son of PERROTT, of Haroldston; confirmed by Dethick, Garter). Same *Arms* and *Crest*, a mullet for diff.

Perrott (Drayton, co. Oxford, and Amersham, co. Bucks; LEONARD PERROTT, younger brother of SIMON PERROTT, Esq., of Northleigh. Visit. Oxon, 1574). Same *Arms* and *Crest*, a mullet charged with a crescent for diff., confirmed by Bysshe, 1664.

Perrott (Bell Hall, in Belbroughton, formerly of Wollaston, both in co. Worcester. HUMPHREY PERROTT, of Wollaston, admitted a student of the Inner Temple, 1582, purchased the estate in Belbroughton; JOHN PERROTT, Esq., of Bell Hall, High Sheriff, co. Worcester, 1738, left an only dau. and heir KATHERINE, *m.* WALTER NOEL, Esq., of Hilcote, co. Stafford). Same *Arms* and *Crest.*

Perrott (Ballyhaise and Dromahart, co. Cavan; descended from Bell Hall; confirmed by St. George, Ulster, 1661, to HUMPHREY PERROTT, High Sheriff, co. Cavan, 1661 and 1681, who *m.* ELIZABETH, dau. and co-heir of BROCKHILL TAYLOR, Esq., of Ballyhaise). Same *Arms* and *Crest*, a crescent for diff. *Motto*—Amo ut invenio.

Perrott (Llandegveth, and Bedwelty, co. Monmouth; JANE PERROTT, dau. of Rev. GREGORY PERROTT, rector of Gellygare, co. Glamorgan, and sister and heir of WILLIAM PERROTT, Esq., of Llandegveth *m.* WILLIAM NICHOLL, Esq., of Tynmawr, High Sheriff, co. Monmouth, 1775). Same *Arms* and *Crest.*

Perrott (co. Bedford; RALPH PERROTT, of that co. from a roll of arms, *temp.* Edward III.). Quarterly, per fess indented or and az.

Perrott. Erm. on a bend cotised gu. three escallops or; another, Az. a bend lozengy (another fusily), betw. six martlets or; another, Ar. five mullets pierced in cross sa., with crest, A bull's head couped sa. armed or, gorged on the neck with two bars gold; another, Ar. a boar pass. sa. enraged and unguled gu.

Perry (Turville, co. Buckingham). Per chev. ar. and az. three mullets counterchanged.

Perry (co. Cornwall). Per pale indented or and gu.

Perry, or Pery (Walter, co. Devon). Quarterly, gu. and or, on a bend ar. three lions pass. az. *Crest*—A hind's head erased or, holding in the mouth a sprig of pear tree vert, fructed gold.

Perry (Wotton-Underedge, co. Gloucester). Ar. on a chev. az. betw. three lions ramp. gu. as many buglehorns or. *Crest*—A stag's head ppr. pierced through the neck with an arrow or, feathered ar. headed sa.

Perry (co. Gloucester). Quarterly, ar. and vert, in the first quarter a mullet gu.

Perry (London; granted 8 March, 1700). Quarterly, or and sa. on a bend gu. cotised erm. three lions pass. guard. ar. *Crest*—A hind's head erased ppr. gorged with a ducal coronet or, holding in the mouth a pear tree branch vert, fructed gold.

Perry (co. Worcester). Ar. on a bend sa. three pears or.

Crest—A cubit arm in armour ppr. grasping in the gauntlet a sword ar. hilt and pommel or, strings and tassels flowing from the pommel ga.

Perry (Bitham House, co. Warwick). Ar. on a pile vert three pears stalked and leaved or. *Crest*—A gryphon sejant, wings elevated or, the wings fretty vert and resting, the dexter claw upon a mascle gold. *Motto*—Recte agens confido.

Perry. Az. a fesse embattled or. betw. three pears or. *Crest*—An arm armed and erect ppr. issuing out of the top of a tower gu. holding in the hand a dagger sa.

Perry. Vert a fesse embattled betw. three pears or. *Crest*—A castle ar. masoned sa.

Perry. Or, a fesse engr. az.; another, Quarterly, sa. and ar.; another, Ar. three fusils sa., two and one, on each a bezant.

Perry. Quarterly, 1st and 4th, quarterly, gu. and or, on a bend ar. three lions pass. ppr., for PERRY; 2nd and 3rd, barry of six ar. and sa. on a chief gu. a saltire or, for WATLINGTON. *Crest*—A lion's head erased ppr. ducally crowned or.

Perry (co. Clare; descended from Capt. GEORGE PERRY, who went to Ireland, 1639, son of JAMES PERRY, Esq., co. Gloucester; allowed by Hawkins, Ulster, 1773). Quarterly, gu. and or, on a bend ar. three lions pass. guard. sa. *Crest*—A hind's head couped ar. holding in the mouth a pear branch fructed ppr.

Perryman (London; granted 25 March, 1710). Or, on a pile vert a chev. engr. betw. three leopards' faces of the field. *Crest*—Two arms issuing out of clouds ppr. habited vert, cuffed ar. holding a leopard's face or.

Perryman, or Perriman. Same *Arms*. *Crest*—A wolf pass. sa.

Perryn (cos. Derby and Gloucester, Ashby, co. Leicester, Acton, co. Middlesex, and Brockton, co. Salop). Ar. on a chev. sa. betw. three pine-apples vert, as many leopards' faces of the first. *Crest*—A pineapple or, stalked and leaved vert.

Perryn. Ar. a fesse betw. three pineapples az.

Persall. Paly of ten or and az. a bordure erm.

Persall. Quarterly, or and erm. three palets az. a border of the last bezantée.

Persall. Az. a fesse betw. two chevronels erm. (another adds, a canton gu.).

Persall. Az. a fesse betw. two chevronels erm. in chief two pellets.

Persam. Az. semée of estoiles or, a bend of the last.

Perse, or Peeres (West Down, co. Kent). Sa. a fesse wavy betw. two unicorns' heads ar. *Crest*—A sphere or, at the north and south pole an estoile gold.

Perse, or Peerse Vert a sceptre surmounted of another, in saltire or.

Persey. Az. a fesse fusily within a tressure of demi fleurs-delis or.

Persfret. Ar. three fleurs-de-lis sa.

Pershall (Bromley, co. Kent). Ar. a plain cross flory sa. on a canton of the last a wolf's head erased of the field.

Pershall, or Peshall (Doynton, co. Lincoln, and Horsley, co. Stafford; seal *temp.* Richard II.). Ar. a cross patée flory sa. on a canton gu. a wolf's head erased of the field. *Crest*—A wolf's head sa. holding in the mouth a marigold ppr.

Pershall. Gu. a lion ramp. ar. crowned or.

Pershouse (Reynolds Hall and Sedgley, co. Stafford, originally of Pershouse Hall; confirmed by St. George, Norroy. Visit. Stafford, 1614). Or, on a pile az. a stag's head caboshed gold, quartering purp. a lion ramp. ar. a mullet in the dexter chief or. *Crest*—A mastiff dog sejant sa. collared or, resting the dexter paw on a caltrap ar.

Pershouse (Penn Hall, co. Stafford, now extinct). Quarterly, 1st and 4th, or, three pales gu.; 2nd and 3rd, erm. all within a bordure sa.

Person. Erm. on a fesse az. three lions ramp. ar.

Person (FELIX PERSON, Esq., of Westminster). Per fesse invected az. and erm. a pale also invected counterchanged, and three suns in splendour or. *Crest*—A mount vert thereon a saltire engr. gu. charged in the centre with a sun, as in the arms.

Person (Fun. Ent. Ulster's Office, 1668, Lady PERSON). Ar. a chev. engr. betw. three oak leaves vert.

Pert (co. Essex). Gu. on a bend ar. three mascles of the first.

Pert (Arnold, co. Essex). Ar. on a bend gu. three mascles or. *Crest*—A stork ppr. beaked or, standing among bulrushes of the last leaved vert, bearing cats' tails sa.

Pert (Fryarne, co. Middlesex). Same *Arms*. *Crest*—A

ram's head erased ar. armed or, charged on the neck with three bars gemelles gu.

Pert. Quarterly, az. and gu. four lions pass. guard. or, on a chief dancettée ar. three pellets.

Perth and Melfort, Earl of. See DRUMMOND.

Perth, Town of (Scotland). Gu. a holy lamb pass. reguard. staff and cross ar. with a banner of St. Andrew ppr. all within a double tressure flory counterflory of the second, the escutcheon being placed on the breast of an eagle displ. with two heads or. *Motto*—Pro rege, lege, et grege.

Perth, See of (Western Australia). Az. two croziers in saltire ar. crooks or, betw. four mullets pierced and radiated gold.

Perthey. Ar. a cross flory gu. (another, within a bordure engr. of the second).

Pertney. Per pale az. and or, barry of six counterchanged, an inescutcheon ar. on a chief of the second a palet of the first betw. two cantons, the dexter per bend az. and gold, sinister, per bend sinister, as the dexter.

Perton (Barndsley, co. Salop). Ar. on a chev. gu. three pears or. *Crest*—On a mount vert a pear tree fructed ppr.

Perton. Sa. a hound salient within a bordure engr. ar.

Perton, or Periton. Or, a pear tree vert fructed ppr.

Pertond. Sa. a cross engr. or.

Pertricke (co. Suffolk). Chequy ar. and sa. on a bend or, three escallops of the second (another, the bend gu.).

Pertt. Ar. on a bend gu. three mascles or.

Pertwell. Sa. a fret betw. two pheons in pale or.

Pervis. Quarterly, ar. and sa., in the first quarter a crescent gu.

Perwiche (co. Leicester, and Blisworth, co. Northampton). Gu. a cross moline or.

Perwiche. Per pale or and gu. three crescents counterchanged. *Crest*—A crescent per pale or and gu.

Perwing, or Perwinke. Sa. three mullets ar. (another, or), within a bordure engr. or.

Pery (*Viscount Pery*, of Newtown Pery, co. Limerick, created 1785, extinct 1806). Quarterly, gu. and or, on a bend ar. three lions pass. sa. *Crest*—A fawn's head erased ppr. *Supporters*—Two fawns ppr. *Motto*—Virtute non astutiâ.

Pery (*Earl of Limerick*). Quarterly, 1st and 4th, quarterly, gu. and or, on a bend ar., three lions pass. sa., for PERY; 2nd and 3rd, per chev. engr. or and sa. in chief three pellets and in base a stag pass. of the first, for SEXTON. *Crests*—1st: A hind's head erased ppr., for PERY; 2nd: A demi-Saracen supporting on the dexter shoulder a sword, the point resting on the palm of the hand, the sinister arm extended holding a battle axe all ppr., for SEXTON. *Supporters*—Dexter, a lion erm.; sinister, a fawn ppr. ducally collared and chained or. *Motto*—Virtute non astutiâ.

Pery (West Waters, co. Devon). Quarterly, gu. and or, on a bend of the first three lions pass. az.

Pery. Ar. on a bend sa. three pears or; another, Ar. three lozenges sa. each charged with a bezant (another, three rustres sa.).

Peryam. Gu. a chev. engr. betw. three leopards' faces or.

Peryent, or Peryan (Digswell, co. Hertford). Gu. three crescents ar. *Crest*—A lion ramp. ar. guttée de sang. *Another Crest*—A griffin's head erased gu. charged with three crescents in pale ar.

Pescod (Newton Valence, co. Hants; Visit. 1634). Ermines on a chief ar, three griffins segreant sa. *Crest*—A griffin sejant ar. the dexter claw raised, beaked and membered or.

Pesemarsh. Per bend sa. and ar. an eagle displ. counterchanged crowned or.

Peshall (co. Chester). Ar. a cross pattée gu., on a quarter of the second a wolf's head erased of the field.

Peshall (co. Salop). Ar. a cross formée flory sa., on a canton gu. a lion's (another, a griffin's) head erased of the first crowned or.

Peshall (Eccleshall, co. Stafford). Ar. a cross flory sa., on a dexter canton az. a wolf's head erased of the first, on a sinister canton ar. a lion ramp. double queued gu. ducally crowned or. *Crest*—A boar's head couped at the neck gu. tusked and crined or.

Peshall (Horsley, co. Stafford, bart., extinct 1712). Ar. a cross formée florettée sa. on a canton gu. a wolf's head of the first.

Peshall. Or, a cross pattée engr. sa.

Pesmarsh, or Pesmersh (co. Essex). Per pale sa. and ar. an eagle displ. counterchanged crowned gu.

Pesmede (Sherborne St. John, co. Hants; Visit. 1634). Ar. a millrind gu. a bordure engr. of the last.

Pessamarche, or Pessmarch (Essex). Per bend sa. and ar. an eagle displ. counterchanged, crowned and armed gu.

795

Pessun (co. Kent). Erm. a fess az.

Pestell (co. Leicester). Or, a chev. engr. betw. three stags' heads erased gu.

Pestell (confirmed 1648, to WILLIAM PESTELL, mate to Captain Jones in a ship of war, "descended from an ancient family in the county of Leicester"). Or, a chev. engr. sa. betw. three stags' heads couped gu. *Crest*—A demi stag sa. attired ppr.

Peter (Bowhay, co. Devon. Visit. Devon, 1620; descended from WILLIAM PETER, younger brother of JOHN PETRE, of Torr Newton, ancestor of the *Lords Petre*, of Writtle; JOHN PETER, Esq., the last of the Bowhay branch, *d.* in 1643, leaving an only dau. and heir, *m.* to Sir ALLEN APSLEY, ancestor in the female line of *Earl Bathurst*). Gu. on a bend or, betw. two escallops ar. a Cornish chough ppr. enclosed by as many cinquefoils az. *Crest*—Two lions' heads erased and endorsed, the dexter or, the sinister az. gorged with a plain collar, counterchanged. *Mottoes*—Sans Dieu rien; and, Sub libertate quietem.

Peter (Chyverton and Harlyn, co. Cornwall; descended from the marriage of THOMAS PETER, third son of JOHN PETER, Esq., of Bowhay, M.P. for Exeter, *temp.* Mary I., with ELIZABETH, only dau. and heir of HENRY MITCHELL, Esq.). *Arms*, &c., same as preceding.

Peter, or Peter (co. Essex). Gu. on a bend (sometimes a chev.) or, betw. two escallops ar. a Cornish chough ppr. enclosed by as many cinquefoils az. on a chief of the second a rose betw. two fleurs-de-lis of the first, seeded or, barbed and leaved vert. *Crest*—Two lions' heads erased, conjoined and endorsed, the dexter or, the sinister az. collared and ringed, counterchanged.

Peter. Gu. on a bend or, a martlet sa. on a chief of the second a rose betw. two cinquefoils az. Same *Crest* as the last.

Peter (Ingatestone, co. Essex). Gu. on a bend or, betw. two escallops ar. a Cornish chough ppr. betw. as many cinquefoils az. a chief of the second charged with a cross betw. two demi fleurs-de-lis of the first.

Peter. Ar. a chev. gu. betw. three leopards' faces of the second; another, Gu. a bend or, betw. two escallops ar.

Peter (Brigadier-General THOMAS PETER, of Corsbasket, co. Forfar, 1806). Vert a crescent betw. three pairs of keys in saltire or. *Crest*—Out of a mural crown ar. masoned sa. a dexter arm in armour vambraced, grasping a scymitar ppr. *Motto*—Pour mon Dieu.

Peterborough, City and See of (co. Northampton). Gu. two keys endorsed in saltire betw. four crosses crosslet fitchée or.

Peterborough, Abbey of (co. Northampton). Gu. two keys in saltire betw. four crosses formée fitchée or.

Peter House, or St. Peter's College (Cambridge; founded in 1256 by HUGH DE BALESHAM, or BALSHAM, Bishop of Ely). Or, three palets gu. a bordure of the last charged with eight ducal coronets of the first.

Peters (Platbridge, co. Lancaster). Gu. a bend or, betw. two escallops ar. *Crest*—Two lions' heads erased and addorsed, the dexter or, the sinister az. each gorged with a plain collar counterchanged. *Motto*—Sans Dieu rien.

Peters (Black Friars, Canterbury, co. Kent). Or, three roses gu. *Crest*—An arm holding a rose sprig ppr.

Peters (London; granted 1748). Or, a lion ramp. sa. on a chief of the last three mascles of the first. *Crest*—A swan, reguard. ppr. gorged with a ducal coronet sa. reposing the dexter foot on a mascle or.

Peters (London). Gu. on a bend or, betw. two escallops ar. a Cornish chough ppr. enclosed by as many cinquefoils az.

Peters (Newcastle-on-Tyne). Sa. on a bend erm. cotised engr. or, betw. two cinquefoils of the last a hurt enclosed by as many escallops az. *Crest*—A lion's head erased erm. charged with a bend engr. betw. two escallops az. *Motto*—Absque Deo nihil.

Peters (London). Gu. a bend ar. betw. two escallops or, on a chief of the last a cinquefoil enclosed by as many fleurs-de-lis az. *Crest*—A buckle ar.

Peters (London; JAMES PETERS, Esq., of Park Street, Grosvenor Square). Or, a lion ramp. sa. on a chief of the second three mascles of the field. *Crest*—A swan, wings endorsed reguard. ar. ducally gorged or, reposing the dexter foot on a mascle sa. *Motto*—Invidiâ major.

Peters (Rev. MICHAEL NOWELL PETERS, Vicar of Madron, co. Cornwall). Gu. on a bend or, betw. two escallops ar. a Cornish chough ppr. enclosed by as many cinquefoils az. *Crest*—Two lions' heads erased and addorsed, the dexter or, the sinister az.

Peters (PARSONS-PETERS; WILLIAM PARSONS-PETERS, Esq., Yeabridge, co. Somerset). Az. on a fesse betw. five escallops, three in chief, and two in base ar. as many lozenges conjoined of the first. *Crest*—A horse's head ar. crusily az. holding in the mouth a cinquefoil slipped vert. *Motto*—Fidelitas et veritas.

Peters (Kilburn, and Westbourne Terrace, Bayswater). Quarterly, 1st and 4th, or, a lion ramp. sa., on a chief of the second three mascles of the first; 2nd and 3rd, ar. a bugle-horn stringed betw. three double attires all sa., for WINPENNY. *Crests*—PETERS: A swan reguard. ppr. resting the dexter foot on a mascle or; WINPENNY: A griffin's head couped ppr. holding by the string a buglehorn az.

Peters (arms entered and crest granted in Ulster's Office, 1704, to NICHOLAS PETERS, Usher of the Exchequer, son of JOHN PETERS, of Cologne, Germany, by ELEANOR, his wife, dau. and heiress of ALEXANDER PLUNKETT, Esq., of Castle Kerron, co. Meath). Quarterly, 1st and 4th, az. an eagle displ. with two heads or, for PETERS; 2nd and 3rd, sa. a bend ar. in sinister chief a tower triple-towered of the last, for PLUNKETT. *Crest*—An eagle's head erased sa. holding in the mouth a key, wards downwards, ppr.

Petersfield, Town of (co. Hants). Ar. on a rose gu. barbed vert an escutcheon of the first, charged with an annulet sa. betw. four pellets.

Peterson. Sa. on a cross betw. four lions ramp. ar. five eagles displ. of the field. *Crest*—A dexter hand brandishing a sabre ppr.

Peterson. Sa. on a cross betw. four talbots' heads erased ar. five eagles of the field.

Peterson (London). Gu. on a fesse ar. three greyhounds' heads couped sa. collared or, a bordure of the last.

Peterson (London). Sa. on a cross betw. four lions' heads erased ar. five eagles displ. of the field.

Peterson (Scotland). Same *Arms*. *Crest*—A pelican ppr. *Motto*—Nihil sine Deo.

Petersone (Scotland). Az. a fesse betw. three bears' heads of the last muzzled gu.

Peterster. Ar. a cross sa. betw. four Cornish choughs ppr.

Peterstrey. Ar. a cross betw. four mullets sa.

Petfyn. Az. a bend betw. three swans ar. crowned or (another adds, collared and chained of the last).

Petham. Az. six annulets or, three, two, and one.

Pether. Ar. on a cross flory az. a fleur-de-lis or. *Crest*—A rose gu. barbed vert, seeded or.

Petit (co. Cornwall; Sir JOHN PETIT, cousin and heir to Sir OTES PETIT and Dame ELIZABETH LE BLANCHE, his wife, *temp.* Henry III., *m.* ALICE, dau. of Sir MICHAEL BEAUCHAMP. Visit. Cornwall: his descendant, THOMAS PETIT, of Trelowyth and Goviley, co. Cornwall, had an only dau. and heiress, ALICE, wife of JAMES TRESAHER, of Budock, *temp.* Queen Elizabeth). Ar. a lion ramp. gu.

Petit (Ardevora, in Filleigh, co. Cornwall; traceable for seven descents *m.* ARUNDEL of Trerice, SAYER, and KILLIGREW). Ar. a lion pass. gu.

Petit, or Pettyt (Dente de Lion, co. Kent). Ar. on a chev. gu. betw. three lions' heads erased sa. crowned or, as many bezants. *Crest*—A lion's gamb erased and erect or, holding a pellet.

Petit (Hexstall, co. Stafford; granted 1583). Ar. a chev. gu. betw. three buglehorns sa. stringed of the second. *Crest*—A demi wolf salient ppr.

Petit. Ar. a chev. engr. gu. betw. three hunting-horns sa. stringed or. *Crest*—A hand holding a hunting-horn ar.

Petit. Gu. a fesse betw. three annulets or.

Petite. Ar. a fesse sa.

Petiver. Gu. a fesse betw. three dexter (another, sinister) hands or.

Petley (Riverhead and Filson, co. Kent). Ar. two bends engr. sa. a canton of the last. *Crest*—A cubit arm in armour erect ppr. garnished or, grasping a scymitar by the blade also ppr. hilted gold.

Petmore. Or, semée of crosses crosslet az.

Petmyn, or Petoryn. Erm. three chev. gu.

Petnall. Erm. on a chief gu. three bezants.

Peto (Somerleyton Hall, co. Suffolk, bart.). Per pale indented or and gu. barry of six two annulets in fesse all counterchanged. *Crest*—On a rock ppr. a sinister wing or, thereon three annulets gu. *Motto*—Ad finem fidelis.

Petoe (co. Suffolk). Ar. a chev. gu., in chief three mascles of the second.

Petoe, or Peyto (Chesterton, co. Warwick; allowed by the Deputies of Camden, Clarenceux). Per pale indented ar. and gu. barry of six counterchanged. *Crest*—A sinister wing or. *Another Crest*—Two wings addorsed ar.

Petre (*Baron Petre*). Gu. a bend or, betw. two escallops ar. *Original Arms*—Az. on a bend betw. two escallops or, a Cornish chough sa. enclosed by as many cinquefoils gu. *Crest*—Two lions' heads erased and addorsed, the dexter or,

the sinister az., collared, counterchanged. *Supporters*—Dexter, a lion reguard. or, collared az.; sinister, a lion reguard. az. collared or. *Motto*—Sans Dieu rien.

Petre (Knt., *d.* 1572). Same *Arms*, on a chief of the second a rose betw. two dimidiated fleurs-de-lis of the fourth.

Petre (Fidlers, co. Essex; JOHN PETRE, Esq., of Fidlers, great-grandson of the Hon. JOHN PETRE, of the same place, son of the second *Lord Petre*, left an only dau. and eventually heiress, MARY PETRE, who *m.* FRANCIS CANNING, of Foxcote, co. Warwick). Same *Arms*, &c., as Lord *Petre*.

Petro. Az. a bird's leg couped at the thigh or, conjoined to a savage's head ar. hair sa.

Petree. Az. a bend betw. a deer's head erased in chief and three crosses crosslet fitchée in base ar. *Crest*—An anchor in pale sa. *Motto*—Spem fortuna alit.

Petree. Same *Arms*. *Crest*—A cross crosslet sa. *Motto*—Fides.

Petrie (Lewisham, co. Kent). Az. a bend betw. a buck's head couped in chief, and a cross crosslet in base ar., on a chief of the second three escallops gu.

Petrie (Portlethen, co. Kincardine, 1672). Az. a bend betw. a stag's head couped in chief, and three crosses crosslet fitchée in base ar., on a chief of the last as many escallops gu. *Crest*—An eagle soaring aloft ppr. looking up to the sun in his glory or. *Motto*—Fide sed vide.

Pett (Chatham, co. Kent). Or, on a fesse gu. betw. three pellets a lion pass. of the field. *Crest*—Out of a ducal coronet or, a demi pelican, wings expanded ar.

Pett (London, and Walworth, co. Surrey). Ar. (another, or) a fesse chequy or and az. betw. three pellets, on each a martlet of the first, a bordure gu. charged with escallops and martlets alternately gold. *Crest*—A demi greyhound sa. collared and charged on the body with two bendlets or, betw. as many fern branches vert.

Pettegrew (Scotland). Gu. an increscent betw. three mullets or. *Crest*—An increscent gu. *Motto*—Sine sole nihil.

Pettet (Shalmisford, co. Kent). Gu. a chev. betw. three leopards' faces ar. *Crest*—A leopard pass. ppr.

Pettet. Gu. a dexter arm in fesse issuing from clouds on the sinister side of the shield holding a battle axe all ar. in chief two mullets of the last.

Pettet. Az. on a chev. or, betw. three leopards' faces ar. as many cinquefoils vert.

Pettigrew (Scotland). Gu. a crescent betw. three stars ar.

Pettit (co. Cornwall). Ar. a lion saliant gu.

Pettit (co. Kent). Az. on a chev. or, betw. three leopards' faces ar. as many cinquefoils pierced gu.

Pettit (co. Kent). Gu. a chev. betw. three wolves' heads erased ar.

Pettit (confirmed 1722, Ulster's Office, to JAMES PETTIT, of the house of Baltrasny, in Meath, a cavalry officer in the service of Spain). Ar. a lion ramp. gu. and in the dexter chief point a spear head sa. *Crest*—A raven ppr.

Pettiward (Finborough Hall, co. Suffolk). Ar. on a cross ragulée sa. five estoiles of the first. *Crest*—A cross, as in the arms.

Pettus (Rackheath, co. Norfolk, bart., extinct 1772). Gu. a fesse ar. betw. three annulets or. *Crest*—Out of a ducal coronet or, a demi lion erm. vulned and holding erect a piece of a broken tilting spear ppr.

Pettus, or Pettous (Norwich). Same *Arms*. *Crest*—A hammer erect ar. handle or. *Another Crest*—Out of a ducal coronet or, a demi lion ar. holding a spear gu. headed of the first.

Petty (granted by Carney, Ulster, 20 March, 1656, to WILLIAM PETTY, M.D., son of ANTHONY PETTY, of Rumsey, co. Hants. This WILLIAM PETTY became Physician-General to the army in Ireland, and was Surveyor-General of that kingdom; he was knighted in 1661, and founded the noble house of PETTY, *Barons and Earls of Shelburne*). Erm. on a bend az. a magnetic needle ppr. pointing at the pole star or. *Crest*—A beehive and bees ppr. *Motto*—Ut apes geometriam.

Sir W. PETTY's explanation of his coat of arms:

Cœruleus candore color mea scuta decoret,
    Non atrum aut fulvum, nec cruor horrificet.
Stellam ut spectat avis, positoque timore quiescit,
    Sic mens quæ spectat sola quieta Deum.
Mella ut apes condunt sic scire Geometra quærit;
    Utile quærere apum est, scire geometriæ.
Sedulus ergo ut apes feci geometriam ut inde
    Utile cum dulci scire et habere queam.
At si perdam ut apes quæ per geometriam habebam
    Heu! "Vos non vobis mellificatis apes."

Petty (*Earls of Shelburne*). *Arms, Crest,* and *Motto,* as the preceding. *Supporters*—Two pegasuses erm. bridled, maned, tailed, winged, and hoofed or, each charged on the shoulder with a fleur-de-lis az.

Petty-Fitzmaurice (*Marquess of Lansdowne*). See FITZ-MAURICE.

Petty (Ilmington, co. Warwick, *Harl. MSS.*). Quarterly, or and az. on a bend vert three martlets of the first. *Crest*—Out of a ducal coronet or, an elephant's head ar. tusked and eared gu.

Petty (Stoke-Talmach, co. Oxford; MARY, dau. of JOHN PETTY, Esq., of that place, *m.* Sir JAMES LEY, Chief Justice of the King's Bench in Ireland, *temp.* James I., Reg. Ulster's Office). Quarterly, or and az., on a bend vert three martlets of the first.

Pettyward (London; granted 16 July, 1660). Ar. on a cross ragulée sa. five billets of the field.

Pettyward. Ar. on a cross ragulée sa. five estoiles of the field. *Crest*—Out of a ducal coronet or, a demi pelican, wings expanded ar.

Petwarden (co. Lincoln). Gu. two lions pass. in pale or.

Petye, Pettie, or Petty (Tetsworth and Henley, co. Oxford, and Ilmington, co. Warwick). Quarterly, or and az. on a bend vert three martlets of the first. *Crest*—Out of a ducal coronet or, an elephant's head ar. armed and eared gu.

Petyt (Ackworth Park; confirmed in 1810 to JOHN PETYT, Esq., of co. York). Erm. a lion ramp. gu. armed and langued az. on a canton of the last a pheon or. *Crest*—A crane erm. holding in the dexter claw a pebble sa. *Motto*—Qui s'estime Petyt deviendra grand.

Petyt (co. Cornwall; Middle Temple, London, and co. York). Ar. a lion ramp. gu. in the dexter chief point a pheon sa.

Petyt, or Petit (co. Cornwall). Ar. a lion ramp. gu. *Crest*—A bishop's mitre gu.

Petyt (London; granted 1688). Ar. a lion ramp. gu. on a canton az. a pheon or. *Crest*—A crane holding with the dexter foot a pebble stone ppr.

Petyt. Or, a fesse sa.; another, Sa. three lions ramp. in fesse betw. two bars dancettée ar.

Petytt (Shep Meadow, co. Suffolk). Erm. a chev. gu. betw. three cock pheasants' heads couped az. *Crest*—A demi swan displ. ar. beaked gu. betw. two battle axes vert.

Peusay (descended from Preston, co. Lancaster). Az. three estoiles or. *Crest*—A pelican's head vulning herself ppr.

Pevelesdon. Az. an eagle displ. or, a bordure engr. of the second. *Crest*—A stag's head erased ppr.

Pevensey (co. Lincoln). Ar. a chev. engr. az. betw. three martlets sa. *Crest*—A demi Moor sa. holding in the dexter hand a broken tilting spear or.

Pevensey. Barruly of fourteen ar. and gu. an orle of martlets sa. *Crest*—Out of a castle ar. six laurel leaves vert.

Pevensey. Az. a chev. or, fretty gu. betw. three crosses patonce ar.

Pevensey. Or, an eagle displ. gu. armed az.; another, Gu. an eagle displ. or, armed sa.

Pever (co. Bedford). Ar. on a chev. gu. three fleurs-de-lis or.

Pever (co. Norfolk). Or, two bars sa.

Pever, or Piner (co. Norfolk). Or, two bars sa. on the uppermost a mullet pierced ar.

Pever. Ar. two bars sa. on the uppermost a mullet pierced or.

Pever. Or, on a chev. az. three swans ppr.

Peverell (co. Cornwall). Ar. a chev. betw. three trefoils vert.

Peverell (Sir HUGH PEVERELL and JAMES PEVERELL, his son, co. Cornwall, *temp.* Edward II.; quartered by FLAMANK, of Buscave, co. Cornwall. Visit. Cornwall, 1620). Az. three garbs ar., a chief or.

Peverell (Sampford-Peverell, co. Devon; the co-heirs *m.* COTTLE, WROKESHALL, and RIVERS). Az. three garbs ar.

Peverell (Bradford-Peverell, co. Dorset, *temp.* Edward I.). Gyronny of eight ar. and gu.

Peverell (co. Hants). Gyronny of twelve ar. and gu. a bordure sa. bezantée. *Crest*—A hand holding a dagger point downwards ppr. *Motto*—Hinc nihil salus.

Peverell (co. Leicester). Gu. a fesse ar. betw. six (another, nine) crosses pattée (another, crosses crosslet) or.

Peverell (founder of Linton Abbey). Vairé az. and or.

Peverell (co. Norfolk). Ar. on a saltire gu. five mullets or.

Peverell, or Peverel (co. Nottingham, *temp.* William I.). Quarterly gu. and vairé or and az. a lion ramp. ar.

Peverell (co. Somerset). Ar. on a cross wavy five bezants (another, five plates).

797

Peverell (co. Worcester). Ar. on a bend az. three garbs or.

Peverell. Az. on a chief gu. three crescents ar.

Peverell. Gyronny of eight or and gu. *Crest*—A plume of four ostrich feathers two gu and two az. enfiled with a ducal coronet or.

Peverell (Park in Egloshayle, co. Cornwall, settled in that county, *temp.* Richard I.). Gu. a fesse ar. betw. six crosses patée or.

Peverell (Ermington, co. Devon; the heiress *m.* CAREW). Or, an eagle displ. az.

Peverell (KATHERINE, dau. and co-heir of THOMAS PEVERELL, *m.* Sir WALTER HUNGERFORD, Baron Hungerford, temp. Henry VI.). Gu. three garbs ar. banded of the field a chief or.

Peverell. Vairé or and gu.; another, Quarterly, vair and gu. three bars or, over all a lion ramp. az.; another, Quarterly, vert and or, a bend ar.; another, Quarterly, gu. and vert, two bars wavy ar.; another, Vairé gu. and ar. three bars or, over all a lion ramp. of the second; another, Gu. two bars or, over all a lion ramp. ar.; another, Gu. three lions ramp. or, a bordure engr. ar.; another, Gyronny of eight vair and gu. (another, gu. and vair); another, Ar. on a saltire sa. five mullets pierced or; another, Ar. on a saltire sa. four mullets or; another, Ar. on a cross sa. five mullets or; another, Ar. a cross engr. az.; another, Ar. on a fesse az. three garbs or, banded gu.; another, Az. on a fesse or, three garbs gu.; another, Az. three owls' heads erased ar. a chief or; another, Ar. on a chev. az. three fleurs-de-lis or.

Peveris. Quarterly, ar. and sa.

Pewley. Barry nebulée of six or and az. over all a bend ar.

Pewlle. Ar. a star of six points sa. pierced or, betw. four pellets.

Pewterer, or Pewterwre. Paly of four ar. and sa. three eagles counterchanged.

Pewterers, Company of (London). Az. on a chev. or, betw. three antique limbecks ar. as many roses gu. seeded of the second barbed vert. *Crest*—A mount vert, thereon two arms embowed ppr. vested ar. cuffed gu. holding in both hands erect a dish of the third. *Supporters*—Two seahorses or, their tails ppr. *Motto*—In God is all my trust.

Pewterers (Gateshead-on-Tyne, 1671). Az. on a chev. or, betw. three antique limbecks ar. as many roses gu. *Crest*—Two arms embowed ppr. holding in both hands erect a dish ar. *Supporters*—Two sea horses or, their tails ppr. *Motto*—In God is all my trust.

Pexall (co. Buckingham). Or, a cross flory engr. sa. betw. four martlets az.

Pexall (co. Hants). Ar. on a cross flory engr. sa. betw. four birds az. membered gu. with rings about their necks or (another, az.) an escallop of the last.

Pexall. Or, on a cross fitchée engr. sa. betw. four birds az. collared ar. an escallop of the first.

Peyce (London). Or, ten billets gu. four, three, two and one.

Peyforer (co. Kent). Ar. six fleurs-de-lis az. (another, sa.).

Peyforer (co. Kent). Ar. a fess gu. betw. six fleurs-de-lis sa.

Peyner. Ar. on a chev. gu. three fleurs-de-lis or.

Peyrse (Northwold, co. Norfolk). Sa. a chev. erm. betw. three dragons' heads erased ar. *Crest*—A pelican, wings endorsed ar. vulning her breast ppr.

Peyte. Gu. a fesse betw. three hounds or.

Peytener. Gu. a fesse betw. three dexter hands ar.

Peyting (co. Lincoln). Ar. three chev. gu.

Peyto. Per pale ar. and gu. barry of six counterchanged.

Peytoe (Chesterton, co. Warwick). Per pale indented ar. and gu. barry of six counterchanged.

Peyton (Isleham, co. Cambridge; created a bart., 1611, dormant 1815; MARTHA, dau. and eventual heiress of Sir JOHN PEYTON, third bart., *m.* GEORGE DUNCOMBE, Esq., of Shalford, co. Surrey). Sa. a cross engr. or. *Crest*—A griffin sejant or. *Motto*—Patior, potior.

Peyton (Virginia, America; claiming to be descended from, and entitled to the baronetcy of PEYTON, of Isleham). Same *Arms, &c.*

Peyton (Knowlton, co. Kent; bart., extinct 1683). Same as PEYTON, of Isleham.

Peyton (Doddington, co. Cambridge, bart.). Sa. a cross engr. or, in the first quarter a mullet ar. *Crest*—A griffin sejant or. *Motto*—Patior, potior.

Peyton (Wakehurst Place, co. Sussex; borne by JOSEPH JOHN WAKEHURST PEYTON, Esq., of Wakehurst Place, son

of the late JOHN RITTSON PEYTON, Esq., Captain R.N., grandson of Admiral JOSEPH PEYTON, and great-grandson, by KATHERINE STRUTT, his wife, of Admiral JOSEPH PEYTON, who inherited the estate of Wakehurst from his maternal ancestors, the LYDDELLS). Sa. a cross engr. or, in the second quarter a mullet ar. *Crest*—A griffin sejant or. *Motto*— Patior, potior.

Peyton (Commodore Sir JOHN STRUTT PEYTON, K.C.H., of Yealmpton, co. Devon, knighted in 1837, son of WILLIAM PEYTON, a younger son of Admiral JOSEPH PEYTON, by KATHERINE STRUTT, his wife). *Arms*, &c., as the preceding.

Peyton (granted 24 July, 1641). Same *Arms*, a bordure erm.

Peyton (co. Lancaster). Ar. three magpies ppr.

Peyton (co. Brecknock). Vert a hind couchant ar.

Peyton (Sutton Coldfield, co. Warwick. Visit. 1619). Sa. a cross. engr. or, a mullet ar.

Peyton (Fun. Ent. Ulster's Office, 1612, CHRISTOPHER PEYTON, Auditor at War and of the Revenue). Sa. a cross engr. or, in the first quarter a mullet ar.

Peyton (Laheen, co. Leitrim). Same *Arms*. *Crest*—A griffin sejant or. *Motto*—Pator, potior.

Peyton (Driney House, Drumcong, co. Leitrim). Same *Arms* and *Crest*.

Phaire (Killoughram, co. Wexford; descended from Colonel ROBERT PHAIRE, of the Grange, co. Cork, governor of the city of Cork under Oliver Cromwell, to whom, and Col. Francis Hacker, and Col. Hunkes, the Regicides directed their warrant for the murder of Charles I.). Gu. a cross moline ar. surmounted of a bend az. *Crest*—Out of a ducal coronet or, a falcon rising ppr.

Phayre (granted to Sir ARTHUR PURVES PHAYRE, K.C.S.I., C.B., late Chief Commissioner in British Burmah, second son of RICHARD PHAYRE, Esq., H.E.I.C.S.). Gu. a cross moline ar. surmounted of a bend az. in the sinister chief point an Eastern crown or, all within a bordure of the last. *Crest*—A dove ppr. gorged with an Eastern crown or, in the beak an olive branch vert. *Motto*—Virtute tutus.

Phelan (Ireland). See O'FAELAN.

Phelip (Donnyton, co. Worcester). Quarterly, gu. and ar. in the 1st quarter an eagle displ. or, on the breast an annulet sa.

Phelips (Montacute, co. Somerset, settled there for many centuries; descended from Sir EDWARD PHELIPS, Knt., Master of the Rolls, and Speaker of the House of Commons, *temp.* Queen Elizabeth, fourth son of THOMAS PHELIPS, Esq., of Barrington, who built the present mansion at Montacute, and *d.* 1588; Sir EDWARD's son and heir, ROBERT PHELIPS, was M.P. co. Somerset in many Parliaments, *temp.* James I., and Charles I., and a distinguished and active member of the popular party). Ar. a chev. gu. betw. three roses of the last, seeded and leaved ppr. *Crest*—A square beacon, or chest, on two wheels or, filled with fire ppr. *Motto*—Pro aris et focis.

Phelips (Corfe Mullen, co. Dorset; the senior line of the PHELIPS, of Barrington and Corfe Mullen; the heiress, JANE PHELIPS, *m.* the Rev. Sir JAMES HANHAM, Bart.). Same *Arms*, &c.

Phelips (Barrington, bart., extinct 1690). Same *Arms*, &c.

Phelips (Briggins Park, co. Hertford; the Rev. CHARLES PHELIPS, fourth son of EDWARD PHELIPS, Esq., of Montacute, descended from Sir EDWARD PHELIPS, Knt., Master of the Rolls, *temp.* Elizabeth, *m.* in 1792, MARY, dau. of THOMAS BLACKMORE, Esq., of Briggins Park, by MARY, his wife, sister of JOHN OLD GOODFORD, Esq.). Same *Arms*, &c.

Phelps (Russell Square, London). Per pale or and ar. a wolf salient az. betw. eight crosses crosslet fitchée gu. *Crest*— A wolf's head erased az. collared or, thereon a martlet sa.

Phelps. Ar. a lion ramp. sa. betw. six crosses crosslet fitchée gu.

Phelps (Salisbury, co. Wilts). Sa. a wolf salient betw. two cross crosslets fitchée in chief, as many in base, and two fleurs-de-lis in fess ar. *Crest*—A demi lion erased sa. charged on the shoulder with a chev. ar. holding in the dexter paw a tilting spear ppr. and resting the left on a cross pattée also sa. *Motto*—Toujours prêt.

Phelps (Dursley, co. Gloucester). Per pale or and ar. semée of cross crosslets fitchée gu. a wolf saliant az. *Crest*—A wolf's head az. langued and erased gu. gorged with a collar or, thereon a martlet sa.

Phesant (London, 1634). Per fesse or and az. a fesse per fesse dancettée counterchanged. *Crest*—A pheasant close or, in the beak a gillyflower ppr.

798

Phesant (Tottenham, co. Middlesex). Per pale or and az. a fesse per fesse dancettée counterchanged. *Crest*—A pheasant close or.

Phesant. Gu. on a fesse or, betw. two chev. engr. of the last, three roses of the first. *Crest*—A pheasant ppr. holding in the beak a rose gu. stalked and leaved vert.

Phesant (quartered by GROSVENOR, *Duke of Westminster*; JOAN, dau. and co-heir of Sir WILLIAM PHESANT, co. Stafford, *m.* Sir WILLIAM GROSVENOR, Knt.). Az. three pheasants or.

Phesant. Gu. on a fesse engr. betw. two chevronels or, three roses of the first.

Phesant (Baggott Rath, co. Dublin; Fun. Ent. Ulster's Office, 1622, AMY, wife of THOMAS PHESANT, of that place). Per fess or and az. a fess point in point of the second and first.

Phesant (Donnybrook, co. Dublin; Fun. Ent. Ulster's Office, 1633, MARY, wife of THOMAS PHESANT, of that place). Same *Arms*, a crescent for diff.

Phetiplace. See FETTIPLACE.

Philibert, De St. (co. Norfolk; JOHN DE ST. PHILIBERT, *temp.* Edward III.). Bendy of six az. and ar.

Philip-ap-Uchdryd. Az. three cocks ar. armed, crested, and jelloped or.

Philip-ap-Ivor (*Lord of Iscoed*). Az. an eagle displ. or.

Philip, or Philips (London, and co. Suffolk, late of Jamaica). Quarterly, gu. and ar. in the dexter chief quarter an eagle displ. or, armed of the field. *Crest*—Out of a ducal coronet az. three ostrich feathers ar.

Philip. Per bend ar. and or, a lion ramp. sa. a bordure gobony of the first and az.; another, Per bend or and ar. a lion ramp. sa. within a bordure gobony of the second and purp.; another, Sa. a lion ramp. crowned or, betw. eight fleurs-de-lis ar.

Philip (Ormistone, co. Haddington, 1685). Az. on a chev. betw. three talbots' heads erased ar. two lozenges of the first. *Crest*—A talbot ppr. *Motto*—Vivis sperandum.

Philip (Over Carnble, co. Fife, 1672). Az. a chev. invecked betw. three talbots' heads erased or. *Motto*—Sors omnia versat.

Philip (Amrecloss, co. Forfar). Az. a chev. betw. three talbots' heads couped ar. *Motto*—Non dormit qui custodit.

Philipot (Folkestone, co. Kent). Gu. a cross betw. four swords ar. hilts or.

Philipot (Tunbridge, co. Kent). Sa. a bend erm.

Philipps (Picton Castle, co. Pembroke; *Baron Milford*, extinct 1823; derived from CADIVOR VAWR; Sir JOHN PHILIPPS, of Picton Castle, was created a bart. 1621; Sir RICHARD PHILIPPS, seventh bart., was elevated to the peerage of Ireland 1776, *d. s. p.* in 1823, when the estate of Picton Castle passed under his will to his cousin, RICHARD BULKELEY PHILIPPE GRANT, created a bart. in 1828; the ancient baronetcy devolved on the male heir of the family). Ar. a lion ramp. sa. ducally gorged and chained or. *Crest*—A lion, as in the arms. *Supporters*—Two horses ar.

Philipps (Picton Castle, co. Pembroke, bart.). Ar. a lion ramp. sa. ducally gorged and chained or. *Crest*—A lion, as in the arms. *Motto*—Ducit amor patriæ.

Philipps (*Baron Milford*, extinct 1857; RICHARD BULKELEY GRANT, Esq., who *s.* to the estates of the PHILIPPS family under the will of *Lord Milford*, assumed the surname of PHILIPPS 1824, was created a bart. 1828, and a peer 1847, *d. s. p.*). Same *Arms* and *Crest*. *Supporters*—Two horses ar. *Motto*—Ducit amor patriæ.

Philipps (Aberglasney, co. Caermarthen). Quarterly, 1st and 4th, or, a lion ramp. sa. two fleurs-de-lis in chief az. and a stag's head erased in base gu., for PHILIPPS: 2nd and 3rd, gu. three snakes interlaced betw. two spear heads erect in chief, and a rose in base ar. barbed and seeded ppr., for WALTERS. *Crests*—1st, PHILIPPS: A lion ramp. sa. holding betw. the forepaws an escutcheon or, thereon three snakes interlaced ppr. the dexter hind-paw on a fleur-de-lis also or; 2nd, WALTERS: An eagle displ. erm. the body entwined by two snakes respecting each other ppr. and holding in each claw a rose gu. slipped and leaved vert. *Motto*—Fÿ Nuw a Chymry.

Philipps (LLOYD-PHILIPPS, Penty Park, co. Pembroke, and Dale Castle, co. Pembroke, and Mabws, co. Caermarthen; JOHN LLOYD, of Foes-y-Bleiddiad, *m.* MARY, dau. of JAMES PHILIPPS, Esq., of Penty Park, co. Pembroke, and was grandfather of JOHN LLOYD, of Foes-y-Bleiddiad, who dying in 1820, was *s.* by his grandson, JOHN PHILIPPS-ALLEN-LLOYD, Esq., of Dale Castle, and Mabws, who assumed the name of PHILIPPS, under the will of JAMES PHILIPPS, of Penty Park). Ar. a lion ramp. sa. ducally gorged gu. and chained or. *Crest*—A lion, as in the arms. *Motto*—Ducit amor patriæ.

Philips (Weston, co. Warwick, bart.). Per pale az. and sa.

within an orle of fleurs-de-lis ar. a lion ramp. erminois, ducally crowned and holding betw. the paws a mascle or, a canton erm). *Crest*—A demi lion ramp. erminois, collared sa. ducally crowned or, holding between the paws a fleur-de-lis az. within a mascle gold. *Motto*—Nil nisi honestum.

Philips (Yarpole, co. Hereford; granted 14 June, 1579). Az. a fess betw. three falcons close ar. beaked and legged or.

Philips (Leominster, co. Hereford). Or, on a chev. gu. three falcons' heads erased ar.

Philips (Tenterden, co. Kent). Per fess gu. and az. a lion ramp. or, within a bordure of the last. *Crest*—On a mount vert a stag sejant erm. attired or.

Philips (Inner Temple, London). Az. a chev. betw. three falcons ar.

Philips (co. Lancaster). Sa. a lion ramp. ar. (another, erm.) betw. ten fleurs-de-lis ar.

Philips, or Phillips (London; descended out of co. Dorset; confirmed 10 Dec. 1633). Or, on a chev. engr. sa. three eagles' heads erased ar. *Crest*—A rose branch vert, bearing three roses gu. betw. two wings ar.

Philips, or Phillips (Barnstaple, co. Devon). Same *Arms.*

Philips (co. Salop). Vert three cinquefoils betw. two flaunches ar.

Philips. Same *Arms*. *Crest*—A horse pass. with a wreath of laurel encircling the neck.

Philips (Tamworth, co. Warwick). Or, a lion ramp. sa. a chief of the second. *Crest*—A leopard sejant or.

Philips (co. Worcester). Az. a lion ramp. ar. a chief erm. *Crest*—On a chapeau az. turned up erm. a demi lion ramp. guard. ar.

Philips. Barry wavy of six az. and ar. on a chief or, a lion pass. sa.

Philips. Ar. on a pile issuing out of the dexter chief of the escutcheon sa. a lion ramp. of the field.

Philips. Sa. a bend erm.

Philips (Heath House, co. Stafford; descended from FRANCIS PHYLYPPE, of Neyther Teyne, *d.* 6 Edward VI.; his great-grandson, RICHARD PHILIPS, Esq., *m.* CHRISTOBEL, second dau. and co-heir of ROBERT WHETALL, Esq., of Bignoll Hill, co. Stafford, and was father of NATHANIEL PHILIPS, Esq., of Heath House, *b.* 1659). Per pale az. and sa. within an orle of fleurs-de-lis ar. a lion ramp. erminois, ducally crowned and holding betw. the paws a mascle or, a canton erm *Crest*—A demi lion ramp. erminois, collared sa. ducally crowned or, holding betw. the paws a fleur-de-lis ar. within a mascle gold. *Motto*—Simplex munditiis.

Philips (Rev. GILBERT HENDERSON PHILIPS, Vicar of Brodsworth, co. York, of the family of PHILIPS, of Heath House). Quarterly, 1st, per pale az. and sa. within an orle of fleurs-de-lis ar. a lion ramp. erminois, ducally crowned and holding betw. the paws a mascle or, a canton erm., for PHILIPS; 2nd, gu. on a bend ar. with cotises engr. erm. betw. two pheons of the second three stags' heads caboshed of the field, for STUBBS; 3rd, ar. a crescent within an orle of estoiles gu. a bordure engr. of the last, for BURTON; 4th, gu. three piles issuant from the sinister within a bordure or, on a chief erm. a crescent az., for HENDERSON. *Crest*—A demi lion ramp. erminois, collared sa. ducally crowned or, holding betw. the paws a fleur-de-lis az. within a mascle also or. *Motto*—Simplex munditiis.

Philips (Bank Hall, co. Lancaster, and Welcombe, co. Radnor; descended from NATHANIEL PHILIPS, Esq., of Manchester, third son of NATHANIEL PHILIPS, Esq., of Heath House, by ELIZABETH, his wife, dau. and co-heir of JOHN STUBBS, Esq., of The Shaw, whose youngest son, JOHN PHILIPS, Esq., by ELIZABETH, his wife, eldest dau. and co-heir of JOHN BURTON, Esq., of Derby, purchased, in 1777, the estate of Bank Hall, and which he devised at his death to his fourth son, FRANCIS PHILIPS). Same *Arms*, &c.

Philips (The Park, Prestwich, co. Lancaster, and Welcombe, co. Warwick; borne by MARK PHILIPS, Esq., of The Park, grandson of NATHANIEL PHILIPS, Esq., of Stand, in Prestwich, who was second son of JOHN PHILIPS, Esq., of Heath House, by SUSANNA, youngest dau. and co-heir of JOHN BURTON, Esq., of Derby). *Arms*, &c., as PHILIPS, of Heath House.

Philipse (Philipsburg, America). Az. a lion ramp. or. *Crest*—Out of a ducal coronet a demi lion ramp. *Motto*—Quod tibi vis fieri facias.

Philipson (Swadderden Hall, co. Westmoreland). Gu. a chev. betw. three boars' heads couped erm. all within a bordure engr. ar. *Crest*—Out of a mural coronet or, a plume of seven feathers, four ar. and three gu.

Philliebert (co. Oxford). Bendy of six ar. and sa.

Philler. Sa. three cinquefoils ar.

799

Philler, or Philer. Sa. three cinquefoils betw. nine crosses crosslet ar.

Phillimore (Kendall's, co Herts). Sa. three bars or, and in chief as many cinquefoils of the last. *Crest*—On a tower a falcon, wings elevated all ppr. *Motto*—Fortem posce animum.

Phillimore (Shiplake House, co. Oxford). Same *Arms* *Crest*—On a tower a falcon, wings elevated all ppr. *Motto*—Fortem posce animum.

Phillimore. Sa. three bars ar. in chief as many cinquefoils of the last. *Crest*—An eagle displ. gu.

Phillimore. Upon monuments of the PHILLIMORE family at Cam Church, co. Gloucester, are these *Arms:* Sa. three bars or, in chief as many cinquefoils ar; and upon a monument in the church of King's Stanley, in the same county, and likewise belonging to the PHILLIMORE family, are these *Arms:* Gu. three bars or, in chief as many cinquefoils of the last. *Crest*—On a castle a cock, wings expanded. *Another Crest*—A dexter arm habited and cuffed, couped below the elbow, the hand holding a strawberry twig in flower.

Phillip (Donynton, co. Suffolk; Sir JOHN PHILLIP was father of Sir WILLIAM PHILLIP, elected K.G. 1418, *m.* JOAN, dau., and co-heir of THOMAS, fifth *Lord Bardolf*, and is said to have been created *Lord Bardolf* by patent, but was never summoned, *d.* 6 June, 1441, leaving an only dau. *Elizabeth*, *m.* JOHN, first *Viscount Beaumont*). Quarterly, gu. and or, in the first quarter an eagle displ. of the second.

Phillip (Lord Mayor of London, 1463). Sa. semée-de-lis or, a lion ramp. erm. crowned of the second.

Phillip (Scotland). Az. a chev. betw. three talbots' heads couped ar. *Crest*—A bear's head erased sa.

Phillip. Per bend or and ar. a lion ramp. sa. a bordure gobony of the second and purp. *Crest*—Out of a flower ar. stalked and leaved vert, a greyhound's head issuing of the first, collared or.

Phillip. Per fess indented or and ar. a lion ramp. sa. on a bordure gu. eight plates. *Crest*—A lion's gamb sa. holding three branches of flowers az. leaved vert.

Phillip. Quarterly, gu. and ar., in the 1st quarter an eagle displ. or. *Crest*—Out of a ducal coronet or, a pyramid ar.

Phillip. Sa. a lion ramp. erm. crowned or, within an orle of fleurs-de-lis of the third.

Phillip. Ar. on a chev. betw. three roses gu. a mullet of the field.

Phillip. Paly of six or and gu. on a chief of the last a lion pass. ar.

Phillipps (Eaton Bishop, co. Hereford; descended, according to tradition, from a junior branch of the family of PHILIPPS, of Picton Castle; the first settler in co. He eford, OWEN PHILLIPPS, younger brother of JOHN PHILLIPPS, of Kilgainvin in Disserth, co. Radnor, was living 1595). Quarterly, 1st and 4th, or, a lion ramp. sa. collared and chained of the first, on a bordure of the second eight cross crosslets gold, for PHILLIPPS; 2nd and 3rd, erm. three ravens ppr. each standing on a mount vert, for RAVENHILL. *Crest*—A demi lion sa. collared and chained, holding betw. the paws a leopard's face jessant-de-lis or.

Phillipps (Longworth, co. Hereford; descended from PHILLIPPS, of Eaton). Same *Arms* and *Crest*.

Phillipps (Bryngwyn, co. Hereford; descended from PHILLIPPS, of Eaton). Same *Arms* and *Crest*.

Phillipps (Middle Hill, co. Worcester, bart., extinct). The *Arms* granted to Sir THOMAS PHILLIPPS, F.R.S. and F.S.A., on the creation of the baronetcy were: Sa. flory or, a lion ramp. ar. ducally crowned gold, and holding in dexter forepaw a sword erect ppr. all within a bordure wavy of the second. *Crest*—On a mount vert a lion ramp. sa. semée-de-lis or, charged with a bendlet wavy erm. and holding in dexter forepaw a sword, as in the arms. Sir THOMAS PHILLIPPS subsequently obtained a fresh grant, viz., Ar. a lion ramp. sa. flory and collared and chained or, in dexter paw a sword erect ppr. in a bordure wavy of the second. *Motto*—Deus, patria, rex.

Phillipps (exemplified to JAMES ORCHARD HALLIWELL, Esq., now of Middle Hill, co. Worcester, on his assuming, by royal licence, 1872, the surname of PHILLIPPS only, in right of his wife, HENRIETTA ELIZABETH MOLYNEUX, eldest dau. of the late Sir THOMAS PHILLIPPS, Bart., of Middle Hill). Ar. a lion ramp. sa. ducally gorged with chain reflexed over the back or, holding in the dexter paw a sword erect ppr. a canton (for distinction) of the second. *Crest*—On a mount vert a lion ramp. sa. ducally gorged and chain reflexed over the back or, holding in the dexter paw a sword erect ppr. charged on the shoulder (for distinction) with a cross crosslet gold.

Phillipps (Garendon Park and Grace Dieu Manor, co. Leicester; CHARLES MARCH PHILLIPPS, Esq., of Garendon Park, High Sheriff in 1825, and formerly M.P. co. Leicester, was son and heir of the late THOMAS MARCH, Esq., of More Critchell, co. Dorset, who took the surname and arms of PHILLIPPS, and subsequently assumed the arms and crest of LISLE, in right of his mother, SUSAN LISLE, dau. and co-heiress of CHARLES LISLE, Esq., whose family Mr. MARCH PHILLIPPS represented. See DE LISLE). Quarterly, 1st, az. a chev. betw. three mullets ar., for PHILLIPPS; 2nd, quarterly, gu. and az. a cross erm. betw. four lions' heads erased or, for MARCH; 3rd, or, on a chief az. three lions ramp. of the field, for LISLE; 4th, ar. a chev. betw. three martlets sa., for COLLUMBERS; 5th, gu. and az. a chev. betw. three roses or, for CORMAILLES; 6th, or, three torteaux, for COURTENAY. Crests—1st: A demi griffin ppr. gorged or, holding a shield az. charged with a lion ramp. gold, for PHILLIPPS; 2nd: A demi lion ramp. ar. holding a Maltese cross or, for MARCH; 3rd: A stag trippant ppr., for LISLE. Motto—Quod justum non quod utile.

Phillips (Coventry; EDWARD PHILLIPS, Esq., of Whitmore Hall, Whitmore Park, near that city). Erm. a lion ramp. sa. on a chief engr. vert a stag's head cabossed betw. two garbs or. Crest—A garb fesseways or, thereon a leopard sejant ppr. in the mouth a trefoil slipped vert. Motto—Mens conscia recti.

Phillips (Newport House, co. Cornwall). Or, a lion ramp. sa. chained of the first. Crest—A lion, as in the arms.

Phillips (Tredrea, co. Cornwall). Az. on a cross engr. or, a torteau betw. four crosses crosslet fitchée gu.

Phillips (Sir THOMAS PHILLIPS, Knt., Q.C.). Sa. a chev. betw. three spear heads ar. Crest—A dragon's head erased. Motto—Cwell angau neu chivilydo.

Phillips (Winterdyne House, Bewdley, and Hanbury, co. Worcester, and Edstone, co. Warwick; granted, 1825, by Nayler, Garter, to JOHN PHILLIPS, Esq., of Hanbury, High Sheriff of co. Worcester 1803). Erminois a lion ramp. sa. ducally gorged and chained or, betw. two cross crosslets fitchée in chief and an escallop in base gu. Crest—On a garb. lying fessways or, a lion ramp. sa. ducally gorged and chained of the first, holding betw. the forepaws a cross crosslet gold.

Phillips (Lawrenny, co. Pembroke). Ar. a lion ramp. sa. ducally gorged and chained or, quartering LORT. Crest —A lion, as in the arms. Motto—Animo et fide.

Phillips (Witston House, co. Monmouth). Quarterly, 1st and 4th, gu. three boars' heads or; 2nd and 3rd, az. a cross betw. four pheons or. Crest—A boar's head sa. langued gu. ringed or. Motto—Spero meliora.

Phillips (London, 1634). Ar. a lion ramp. sa. collared, chained, and ducally crowned or.

Phillips. Az. a chev. or, betw. three falcons close ar. belled of the first.

Phillips (Chelmicke, co. Salop). Or, on a chev. gu. three cocks' heads erased ar. combed and wattled of the first. Crest—An eagle's head erased az.

Phillips (Netley, co. Salop). Ar. a lion ramp. sa. collared and chained or. Crest—A lion ramp. as in the arms.

Phillips (co. Salop). Ar. a cross engr. flory sa. betw. four Cornish choughs ppr   Crest—The trunk of a tree lying fesseways and sprouting at the dexter end vert, thereon a Cornish chough ppr.

Phillips (Yeovil, co. Somerset). Ar. a lion ramp. sa. collared and lined or. Crest—A lion sejant sa. collared and lined or.

Phillips. Az. a lion ramp. sa. ducally gorged and chained or. Crest—A lion, as in the arms. Motto—Ducit amor patriæ.

Phillips. Az. a chev. ar. betw. three falcons ppr. ducally gorged, beaked, and membered or. Crest—Out of a ducal coronet or, an arm embowed in armour, the hand holding a broken spear ppr. powdered with fleurs-de-lis gold.

Phillips. Sa. semée-de-lis or, a lion ramp. ar. ducally crowned of the second a canton erm. Crest—A demi lion crowned as in the arms, holding a fleur-de-lis or.

Phillips. Vert three roses in pale ar. betw. two flaunches of the last. Crest—A horse pass. erm. gorged with a chaplet vert.

Phillips. Ar. a chev. betw. three roses gu.

Phillips (Ireland; granted in 1600). Barry wavy of six. az. and ar. on a chief of the last a lion pass. sa. collared or. Crest—An arm embowed in armour ppr. charged with a fleur-de-lis gold, purfled or, grasping a broken spear also ppr.

Phillips (Mount Rivers, co. Tipperary; confirmed by Betham, Ulster, to RICHARD EDWARD PHILLIPS, Esq.). Quarterly, 1st

and 4th, ar. three bars wavy az. in chief a lion pass. sa., for PHILLIPS; 2nd, ar. three fleurs-de-lis sa., for STUMBLES; 3rd, erm. three battle axes sa., for WEEKES. Crests—1st: An arm embowed in armour, garnished or, grasping a broken tilting spear ppr.; 2nd: A cock grouse rising ppr. Motto—Pro Deo et rege.

Phillipson, alias Thelwall (Crook Hall and Colegarth co. Westmoreland). Gu. a chev. betw. three boars' heads couped erm. tusked or. Crest—Out of a mural coronet or a plume of seven feathers, four ar. and three gu.

Phillipson (of the North). Gu. a chev. betw. three boars heads couped erm. a bordure or. Crest—Out of a mural coronet or, a plume of feathers gu.

Phillipson. Sa. a chev. erm. betw. three bats displ. or. Crest—A greyhound's head couped vert, in the mouth a laurel branch of the last.

Phillipson. Sa. a chev. erm. betw. three bats displ. ar. Crest—A camel's head couped, in the mouth an oak branch with three acorns ppr.

Phillipson (BURTON-PHILLIPSON). Quarterly, 1st and 4th, sa. a chev. betw. three bats displ. or; 2nd and 3rd, sa. a chev. betw. three owls ar. crowned or.

Philpot (cos. Hereford and Salop). Gu. a fess or, betw. three swans close ar.

Phillpotts, or Philpot (granted by Richard II. to JOHN PHILPOT, Alderman of London). Gu. a cross ar. betw. four swords erect of the last, pommels and hilts or. Crest— A dexter arm embowed in armour, holding in the hand a sword all ppr.

Phillpotts (Porthgwidden, near Truro). Gu. a cross betw. four swords erect ar. pommels and hilts or. Crest—A dexter arm embowed in armour, holding in the hand a sword all ppr. Motto—Semper paratus.

Philosophy School (Cambridge). The arms of the See of Lincoln, impaling, Ar. a cross moline sa., being the arms of WILLIAM ALNWICK, Bishop of Lincoln.

Philpot (Apstone Hall, co. Herts). Gu. a cross betw. four swords ar. pommels and hilts or. Crest—A porcupine pass. or.

Philpot (Compton and Thaxton, co. Hants; Fun. Ent. Ulster's Office, 1640, ELIZABETH, dau. of Sir JOHN PHILPOT, and wife of Capt. JAMES MERVYN). Sa. a bend erm.

Philpot (Wood Hall, co. Hants; and Lord Mayor of London, 1378). Same Arms.

Philpot (Faversham, co. Kent, and London). Sa. a bend erm. in chief a lion's head erased ar. Crest—A lion's head erased ar. betw. two wings sa. each charged with a bend erm.

Philpot. Sa. on a bend erm. an annulet gu. in chief a lion pass. guard. ar. Crest—A porcupine or, charged with an annulet for diff.

Philpot. Az. (another, sa.) a bend erm.; another, Sa. a chev. betw. three tuns ar.; another, Gu. a cross ar. betw. four swords erect of the second, hilted or.

Phin (Whitehill, Scotland, 1672). Gu. a crane without a head ar. in chief two mullets of the last. Crest—A crane's head couped ppr. Motto—Vigilanti securitas.

Phippen. See FITZ-PAU.

Phippen (Truro, co. Cornwall). Ar. two bars sa. in chief three escallops of the second.

Phippes (London; granted 22 July, 1656). Ar. on a pile issuing from the dexter chief to the sinister base sa. a lion ramp. of the first. Crest—A demi lion ramp. ar. holding in both paws a palm branch vert.

Phipps (Marquess of Normanby). Quarterly, 1st and 4th, sa. a trefoil slipped betw. eight mullets ar., for PHIPPS; 2nd (by grant from James II. to his illegitimate dau. Lady CATHERINE DARNLEY), the royal arms of England, temp. JAMES II., a bordure compony ar. and az.; 3rd, paly of six ar. and az. a bend gu., for ANNESLEY. Crest—A lion's gamb erect sa. holding a trefoil slipped ar. Supporters—Dexter, a unicorn erm.; sinister, a goat erm. each armed and unguled or, gorged with a chaplet of roses ppr. Motto— Virtute quies.

Phipps (Selsey, co. Sussex). Sa. a trefoil within an orle of mullets ar. Crest—A lion's gamb sa. holding a trefoil ar.

Phipps (granted 1767). Same Arms. Crest—A lion's gamb erect and erased sa. holding erect a trefoil slipped ar.

Phipps. Same Arms. Crest—Two laurel branches issuing from the wreath ppr.

Phipps (Heywood House, Westbury, co. Wilts; derived from NICHOLAS, eldest son of NICHOLAS PHIPPS, of Westbury, living in 1568). Sa. a trefoil slipped betw. eight mullets ar. Crest—A lion's gamb erect sa. holding a trefoil slipped ar.

Phipps (Leighton House, co. Wilts; descended from THOMAS, second son of NICHOLAS PHIPPS, of Westbury, living in 1568). Same *Arms*, &c.

Phipps (granted by Betham, Ulster, to Dame ANNE CATHERINE PREVOST, widow of Lieut.-Gen. Sir GEORGE PREVOST, Bart., and dau. of Major-Gen. JOHN PHIPPS, and her issue). Per pale sa. and az. a trefoil slipped ar. within an orle of eight mullets or.

Phipson (Selley Hall, near Birmingham, co. Warwick). Sa. a chev. erm. betw. three bats displ. ar. *Crest*—A plume of seven feathers alternately ar. and gu.

Phipson-Wybrants. See WYBRANTS.

Phorpe (co. Gloucester). Az. a chev. betw. three doves ar.

Physic-School (Cambridge). Az. a fess erm. betw. three lozenges or, on a chief gu. a lion pass. guard. of the third, charged on the side with the text letter **M** sa.

Physicians, College of (incorporated by Henry VIII. A.D. 1523). Sa. a hand ppr. vested ar. issuing out of clouds in chief of the second rayonnée or, feeling the pulse of an arm ppr. issuing from the sinister side of the shield vested ar. in base a pomegranate or, betw. five demi fleurs-de-lis bordering the edge of the escutcheon of the last.

Physicians, College of (Dublin; College constituted by Charles II., and arms granted by St. George, Ulster, 1667). Per fess ar. and az. in the middle of the chief a celestrial hand issuing out of a cloud feeling the pulse of a terrestrial hand all ppr. and in base the royal harp of Ireland, as a distinction from the arms of the like College in England. *Motto*—Ratione et experientiâ.

Physicians, King and Queen's College of (Ireland; College reconstituted 29 Sept. 1692, and arms regranted by Burke, Ulster, 1863). Per fess erm. and az. a dexter celestial hand issuing out of clouds in chief ppr. and in base the harp of Ireland ensigned with the royal crown, all also ppr. *Motto*—Ratione et experientiâ.

Picard. Ar. two bars az. on a canton of the last a cinquefoil or. *Crest*—A dexter hand holding a sword in pale ppr.

Pichard (co. Brecknock). Az. a fess erm. betw. three pilchers or.

Pichford. Chequy or and az. on a fess ar. three lions pass. gu.

Pichford. Chequy or and az. on a fess of the first a lion pass. of the second.

Pichford, or Pitchford (Lee Brockhurst, co. Salop; allowed by Cooke, Clarenceux, *temp.* Elizabeth). Az. a cinquefoil betw. six martlets or. *Crest*—An ostrich ar. beaked and ducally gorged or.

Pickard, or Picard (Lord Mayor of London, 1356). Gyronny of eight az. and ar. on a canton gu. a fleur-de-lis or. *Crest*—A lion sejant ar. resting the dexter paw on a shield gu. charged with a fleur-de-lis, within a bordure or.

Pickard. Gyronny of eight ar. and az. on a canton gu. a fleur-de-lis or. *Crest*—A lion sejant ar. supporting an antique shield charged with a canton.

Pickas. Ar. on a chev. betw. three demi lions ramp. gu. two spears in saltire ar. *Crest*—A demi lion ramp. gu. holding in the paws a spear ar. headed and garnished or.

Pickborne. Ar. a fess engr. sa. betw. three magpies ppr.

Picke (co. Westmorland). Gu. a saltire engr. betw. four mullets or, pierced of the field.

Pickerell (London). Az. a swan close ar. a chief erm.

Pickering (Tichmarsh, co. Northampton, bart.; GILBERT PICKERING, Esq., purchased the manor of Tichmarsh, *temp.* Queen Elizabeth, from WILLIAM, *Earl of Worcester;* GILBERT PICKERING, son of JOHN PICKERING, Esq., of Gretton, and grandson by MARGARET, his wife, dau. and heir of LASCELLS, of Escrick, co. York, of JAMES PICKERING, of Winderwath, co. Westmorland, was greatgrandfather of Sir GILBERT PICKERING, of Tichmarsh, created a Baronet of Nova Scotia; Sir EDWARD PICKERING, of Duncannon Fort, co. Wexford, the last who bore the title, *m.* 1770, ELIZABETH, dau. of GEORGE GLASCOTT, Esq., of Aldertown, but *d. s. p.* 1803). Quarterly, 1st and 4th, erm. a lion ramp. az. crowned or, for PICKERING; 2nd and 3rd, ar. three chaplets gu., for LASCELLS. *Crest*—A lion's gamb erect and erased az. armed or.

Pickering (Old Lodge and Clapham, co. Surrey; borne by EDWARD ROWLAND PICKERING, Esq., of Old Lodge, son of EDWARD LAKE PICKERING, Esq., of the Exchequer Office, Temple, by MARY, his wife, only dau. and heir of WILLIAM UMFREVILLE, Esq.). Erm. a lion ramp. az. armed gu. crowned or. *Crest*—A lion's gamb erect and erased az.

Pickering (Paxton, co. Huntingdon). Same *Arms* and *Crest.*

Pickering (Tablehurst and East Grinstead, co. Sussex). Same *Arms* and *Crest*, a crescent on a crescent for diff.

Pickering (Whaddon, co. Cambridge, bart., extinct 1705; Sir HENRY PICKERING purchased the manor of Whaddon in 1648, and was created a baronet 2 Jan. 1660-1). Same *Arms* and *Crest.*

Pickering (Wallford, co. Chester). Erm. a lion ramp. az. crowned or, on a bordure of the second eight plates. *Crest* —A lion's gamb erect and erased az. enfiled with a ducal coronet or.

Pickering (co. Nottingham). Gu. on a chev. ar. betw. three fleurs-de-lis or, as many hurts. *Crest*—A leopard's head couped or, semée of hurts.

Pickering (cos. Chester and York). Gu. a fesse ar. fretty az. betw. six annulets or.

Pickering (Alkmonberry, co. Huntingdon). Gu. a pike or lucie naiant in fesse betw. three annulets ar.

Pickering (co. Northampton). Or, a fesse per fesse crenellée gu. and az. betw. three cocks' heads erased vert, combed and wattled of the second.

Pickering (cos. Nottingham and York). Gu. on a chev. ar. betw. three fleurs-de-lis or, as many pellets (another, hurts). *Crest*—A leopard's face or.

Pickering (Thorpe's Lodge, co. York). Erm. a lion ramp. az. crowned or. *Crest*—A lion's gamb erased and erect az. armed or.

Pickering. Or (another, ar.) a lion ramp. sa. a bordure gu. bezantée.

Pickering (Threlkeld, co. Cumberland). Erm. a lion ramp. az.

Pickering (Hartford, co. Chester). Erm. a lion ramp. az. ducally crowned or. *Crest*—A demi griffin sa. beaked and membered ar. grasping a wheatsheaf or.

Pickering (Coram, in Coverdale, co. York). Gu. on a chev. betw. three fleurs-de-lis az. as many annulets sa. *Crest*—A lion's gamb erect and erased az.

Pickering. Ar. a lion ramp. az. ducally crowned or. *Crest* —A sword erect ppr. hilt and pommel or, within two branches of laurel disposed in orle vert.

Pickering. Gu. a fess ar. betw. six annulets or (another adds, on the fesse a pellet).

Pickering. Chequy ar. and gu. a bend sa.

Pickernell. Per chev. sa. and ar. in base a demi lion couped gu. *Crest*—A lion's head erased gu.

Pickersgill (Blendon Hall, co. Kent). Ar. three eagles, wings elevated sa. on a chief gu. as many fountains. *Crest*—On a rock ppr. an eagle, wings elevated sa. bezantée, and holding in the beak a cross crosslet fitchée or. *Motto*— Quæ recta sequor.

Pickersgill (WILLIAM HENRY PICKERSOILL, Esq., of Stratford Place). Or, a fesse indented sa. betw. three magpies ppr. a bordure nebulée of the second. *Crest*—Upon a rock a magpie holding in the beak an acorn slipped ppr. *Motto*—Labore et ingenio.

Pickett. Sa. three pickaxes ar. *Crest*—A dexter arm embowed, vested ar. cuffed vert, charged with two bars wavy of the last, holding a pickaxe ppr.

Pickeworth, or Pickworth. Gu. a bend betw. six pickaxes ar.

Pickford. Chequy or and az. on a fess gu. three lions ramp. of the first. *Crest*—A lion's head erased.

Pickford. Az. three endorses and as many barrulets in cross fretty ar. a chief dovetailed or. *Crest*—An arm embowed grasping an arrow ppr.

Pickingham. Az. a lion ramp. or.

Pickman. Gu. two poleaxes in saltire or, betw. four martlets ar.

Pickup (WILLIAM PICKUP, formerly BROUGHTON, Esq., of Spring Hill, Accrington, co. Lancaster). Az. three catharine wheels within two bendlets, all betw. two stags' heads erased or, a bordure wavy of the last. *Crest*—A stag's head couped ppr. in front thereof a demi catharine wheel az. *Motto*— Candide et constanter.

Pickwick (WILLIAM ELEAZAR PICKWICK, Esq., of Bathford, co. Somerset). Per fess embattled gu. and az. in chief two pickaxes and in base a cross moline or. *Crest*—A hart's head couped erm. attired or, gorged with a collar gu. therefrom a chain reflexed over the neck gold, betw. two wings az.

Pickworth. Ar. three millpicks (another, pickaxes) gu.

Picton (Wyvill Court, co. Berks, and co. Chester). Sa. guttée d'or, a lion ramp. gold. *Crest*—A demi lion ramp. gu.

Picton (Picton Castle, co. Pembroke; Sir JOHN AP WILLIAM AP THOMAS AP Sir WILLIAM PICTON, Knt., had an only dau. and heir, ALICE; *m.* Sir THOMAS PERROTT, Knt., of

Haroldston, co. Pembroke, who d. 1461). Gu. three pikes naiant in pale ar.

Picton (JOHN PICTON, Esq., of Isceod, co. Carmarthen). Gu. three pikes in pale ppr. on a canton ar. a mount vert, thereon the section of a castle, intended to represent that of Badajos, surmounted by a scaling ladder ppr. *Crest*—Out of a mural crown gu. betw. two branches of laurel ppr. a mullet or, charged with a pellet.

Pidocock (originally of co. Derby, and afterwards of cos. Stafford and Worcester). Per pale sa. and gu. a pied cock per fess or and ar. betw. three acorns of the third. *Crest*—A bar shot ppr. thereon a griffin segreant sa. holding within its claws a grenade fired also ppr. *Motto*—Seigneur, je te prie, garde ma vie.

Piddle (Athelhampton). Quarterly ar. and sa. four hawks' heads counterchanged. *Crest*—A hawk's head ar.

Piddock (Brisingham, co. Norfolk). Chequy or and az. on a pale sa. a woman's breast distilling drops of milk ppr.

Pierce (Liverpool; Reg. Her. Coll. to HUGH PIERCE, Esq., of Liverpool). Erm. on a chev. az. betw. in chief two dragons' heads erased gu. and in base upon a mount vert a cross calvary of the third, a buglehorn stringed ar. *Crest*—The battlements of a tower, therefrom issuant a dexter arm embowed in armour, grasping a tilting spear palewise all ppr. in front of the battlements a buglehorn stringed gu. *Motto* —Sub cruce salus.

Pierce (co. Meath; Fun. Ent. Ulster's Office, 1655, Captain EDWARD PIERCE, of that co., buried 22 March, 1655, in Christ's Church Cathedral). Ar. a chev. sa. betw. three boars' heads couped of the last, armed, langued, and vulned gu.

Pierie. Ar. a saltire engr. gu. in each flank a buglehorn sa. all within a bordure az. *Crest*—A huntinghorn az. garnished or, stringed gu. *Motto*—Vespere et mane.

Pierpoint (co. Sussex). Az. a chief chequy ar. and gu.

Pierpoint (co. York). Az. a chief chequy or and gu.

Pierpoint. Chequy or and gu. a chief az. (another, Gu. three crescents ar.)

Pierpont. Sa. semée of cinquefoils a lion ramp. ar.

Pierpont. Ar. a lion ramp. within an orle of roses sa. (another, the roses gu.).

Pierreford. Gu. a fess betw. six pears or.

Pierrepont (Holme Pierrepont, co. Nottingham; *Earls* and *Duke of Kingston*, extinct 1773; descended from the marriage, *temp.* Edward I., of Sir HENRY PIERRE-PONT, son of ROBERT DE PIERREPONT, a stanch adherent of Henry III. during the baronial wars, with ANNORA, sister and heir of LIONEL DE MANVERS, of Holme; the representative of the family, *temp.* Charles I., ROBERT PIERREPONT, Esq., of Holme Pierrepont, was created *Earl of Kingston* in 1628, and, as such, became a distinguished cavalier commander. His lordship's last male descendant, EVELYN PIERREPONT, second *Duke of Kingston*, d. in 1773, when his honours became extinct, and his estates devolved on his nephew, CHARLES MEADOWS, Esq., who assumed the surname of PIERREPONT, and was created *Earl Manvers*). Ar. semée of cinquefoils gu. a lion ramp. sa. *Crest*—A lion, as in the arms, betw. two wings erect ar. *Another Crest*—A fox pass. ppr. *Supporters* of the *Dukes of Kingston*—Two lions sa. armed and langued gu. *Motto*—Pie repone te.

Pierrepont (*Earl Manvers*). Ar. semée of mullets gu. a lion ramp. sa. *Crest*—A lion ramp. sa. betw. two wings erect ar. *Supporters*—Two lions sa. armed and langued gu. *Motto*—Pie repone te.

Piers (Fun. Ent. Ulster's Office, 1595, Captain HENRY PIERS, buried in Christ Church, 4 Aug. that year, leaving a son, WILLIAM PIERS). Az. three lions pass. guard. in fess ar. betw. two bars gemellée of the last.

Piers (Tristernagh Abbey, co. Westmeath, bart.). Az. three lions pass. guard. in fess betw. two double cotises ar. *Crest* —An arm embowed vested az. cuffed ar. the hand holding a flag erect per fess of the last and of the first, in chief two torteaux, and in base a plate. *Motto*—Nobilis est ira leonis.

Piers. Sa. a bend wavy ar. betw. two unicorns' heads erased or. *Crest*—A griffin or, winged ar.

Piers. Sa. a chev. erm. betw. three lions' heads erased ar.; another, Vert six eagles displ. or.

Piers (Archbishop of York, 1588). Az. a pelican in her piety ppr.

Pierse (Alsten, co. Warwick; granted 10 June, 1605). Az. on a fess ar. three pellets betw. as many pelicans or, vulning themselves gu.

Pierse. Purp. a chev. engr. or.

Pierse (Ballynagaragh, co. Kerry; Reg. Ulster's Office, 1750, to JANE WORTH, widow of JAMES PIERSE, Esq., son of

RICHARD PIERSE, Esq., of Ballynagaragh). Ar. a saltire gu. a chief erm., a crescent of the second for diff., on an escutcheon of pretence ar. a cross ragulée sa.

Pierson (co. Bedford). Per fess embattled gu. and az. three suns or.

Pierson (co. Devon). Per fess embattled gu. and az. three suns in splendour or. *Crest*—Out of a mural coronet chequy or and az. a parrot's head ppr.

Pierson (cos. Gloucester and Hertford, and Westminster; granted 1577; borne by PIERSON, of Hitchin, co. Hertford). Ar. two chev. sa. on a canton of the last an eagle displ. of the first. *Crest*—Out of a ducal coronet or, an ostrich's head betw. two ostrich feathers ar.

Pierson (Dean of Salisbury). Per fess az. and gu. three suns or. *Crest*—A demi lion ppr. holding in the dexter paw a sun or.

Pierson. Sa. three suns in pale or, betw. two palets erminois.

Pierson (granted by Segar, Garter, to RICHARD, son of THOMAS PIERSON, of Olney, co. Bucks). Ar. two chevronels az. betw. three leaves vert. *Crest*—A hind's head couped ar. charged with two chevronels az.

Pierson (confirmed to THOMAS PIERSON, 21 Oct. 1577). Ar. two chev. sa. betw. three oak leaves erect ppr.

Pierson (Visit. London 1634, borne by HENRY PIERSON, then residing at Benenden, co. Kent). Same *Arms*. *Crest*—An ounce sejant az. armed and langued gu.

Pierson (London). Ar. two chev. az. betw. three leaves erect vert. *Crest*—A doe or hind's head couped ar. charged with two chev. az.

Pierson (Scotland). See PEARSON.

Piett (granted Feb. 1611, to RICHARD PIETT, Sheriff of London). Az. on a fess or, a lion pass. gu. in chief three bezants.

Pig. Gu. seven mascles or, three, three, and one.

Pigeon (Deptford, co. Kent). Ar. on a bend sa. three doves close of the first. *Crest*—A demi griffin erm. beaked and legged or.

Pigeon (Hampton-upon-Thames, co. Middlesex, and co. Hants). Or, three inescutcheons az. each charged with a lion ramp. of the first. *Crest*—On a chapeau gu. turned up erm. a buck's head ppr.

Pigeon (Beckham and Yockthorpe, co. Norfolk). Sa. a chev. engr. or, betw. three pigeons' heads erased ar. *Crest* —An elephant's head erased gu. eared, tusked, collared, lined, and ringed or.

Piget (co. Kent). Sa. a cross engr. ar. in the dexter chief quarter an escallop of the second.

Piget. Or, a cross moline gu.

Pigg. Ar. a chev. betw. three boars' heads couped sa. *Crest*—A demi lion purp.

Piggott (co. Denbigh; Fun. Ent. Ulster's Office, 1626, ANNE, dau. of RICHARD PIGGOTT, and wife of RICHARD DUTTON, Usher of the Exchequer). Erm. three fusils conjoined in fess sa.

Pigmeyne, or Pigveney. Ar. two bars gu. a bordure of the second.

Pigon (co. Warwick). Ar. two lions pass. gu.

Pigot (Patshull, co. Stafford, bart.). Erm. three pikeheads in fess sa. *Crest*—A wolf's head erased ar. *Motto*—Tout foys prest.

Pigot (co. Derby). Gu. a bend fusily betw. six martlets or.

Pigot (co. Norfolk). Ar. on a bend betw. two cotises engr. sa. three mullets of the field.

Pigot (London). Gu. a fess engr. ar. betw. three bezants.

Pigot (Dodington, co. York). Az. two bars or, in chief three bezants.

Pigot (co. York). Or, on a cross gu. five escallops ar.

Pigot (Radcliffe-upon-Soar, co. Nottingham). Az. a bend fusily betw. six martlets or.

Pigot (Preston, co. Lancaster, 1664). Erm. three fusils conjoined in fess sa. *Crest*—A wolf's head erased ar.

Pigot, or Pickett. Ar. three mullets betw. two bends engr. sa. *Crest*—A martlet gu.

Pigot. Quarterly, gu. and sa. a cross ar.; another, Quarterly, az. and gu. four lions ramp. counterchanged; another, Ar. three martlets in bend sa. betw. two bendlets engr. gu.; another, Sa. a saltire patonce ar. betw. four lions pass. or; another, Az. a bend fusily betw. six martlets or.

Pigot (*Baron Pigot*, of Patshull, co. Dublin; created 1766, extinct 1777). Ar. three fusils in fess sa. *Crest*—A wolf's head erased sa. *Supporters*—Two leopards guard. ppr.

Pigott (Chetwynd, co. Salop; derived from the marriage of RICHARD PIGOTT, co. Chester, with the dau. and co-heir of Sir RICHARD DE PESHALL, Knt., of Chetwynd; the grand son of this alliance, ROBERT PIGOTT, of Chetwynd, Sheriff co. Salop, 1517, bore for *Arms*, az. a chev. betw. three mullets or, on a chief erm. three fusils sa.; represented by PIGOTT, of Edgmond, co. Salop). Erm. three fusils conjoined in fess sa. Crest—A wolf's head erased ar. langued gu.

Pigott (Edgmond, co. Salop). Same Arms. Crest—A wolf's head erased ar. langued gu. Motto—Toute foys preste.

Pigott (Doddershall Park, co. Buckingham; a younger branch of PIGOTT, of Chetwynd, descended from co. Salop. Rev. WILLIAM PIGOTT, Rector of Edgmond and Chetwynd, a younger son of ROBERT PIGOTT, Esq., of Chetwynd, Sheriff co. Salop, 1697). Same Arms, &c., as PIGOTT, of Chetwynd.

Pigott (SMYTH-PIGOTT, Brockley, co. Somerset). Quarterly, 1st and 4th, erm. three fusils conjoined in fess sa.; 2nd and 3rd, gu. on a chev. betw. three cinquefoils ar. as many leopards' faces sa. Crests—1st: A wolf's head erased sa. gorged with a collar ar. charged with three torteaux; 2nd: A griffin's head erased gu. charged on the neck with a bar gemel, beaked and eared or.

Pigott (Willaston, co. Salop). Erm. three fusils in fesse sa.

Pigott (Bedford, Marsham, co. Berks, Bechampton, co. Buckingham, and Weston, co. Nottingham). Sa. three pickaxes ar. a bordure of the second. Crest—A greyhound pass. sa.

Pigott (Abington-Pigotts, co. Cambridge). Same Arms, with a canton az. Same Crest as the last.

Pigott (GRAHAM FOSTER PIGOTT, Abington-Pigotts, Royston, co. Cambridge). Quarterly, 1st and 4th, sa. three pickaxes, two and one, within a bordure ar. a canton az. for distinction, for PIGOTT; 2nd, per pale ar. and sa. a chev. per pale of the second and or, betw. three buglehorns stringed, counterchanged of the field, and, for distinction, the chev. charged with two escallops counterchanged thereof, for FOSTER; 3rd, ar. a human heart gu. ensigned with an imperial crown or, on a chief sa. three escallops or, for GRAHAM. Crests—1st: A mount vert, thereon in front of a pickaxe or, a greyhound pass. sa. gorged for distinction with a collar or, for PIGOTT; 2nd: In front of a stag's head couped ar, attired sa. gorged for distinction with a mural crown gu. a buglehorn also sa. garnished or, for FOSTER; 3rd, an escallop or, with the words "Spero meliora" above it, for GRAHAM. Motto—Hoc age.

Pigott (co. Bedford). Ar. a bend betw. six pickaxes sa.

Pigott (co. Bedford). Gu. a fess chequy ar. and az. betw. three pickaxes of the second.

Pigott (Dodershall, co. Bucks, and Braytoft, co. Lincoln). Sa. three pickaxes ar. Crest—A greyhound couchant, collared ar. charged on the breast with three millpicks sa.

Pigott (Archer Lodge, co. Hants: granted in 1775 to FRANCIS PIGOTT, Esq., Barrister-at-law, impropriator of Banbury, Oxon). Per fess erm. and sa. three pickaxes counterchanged. Crest—A greyhound statant per pale sa. and erm. These same arms were allowed to Mr. PAYTON PIGOTT, when he took the surnames and arms of STAINSBY-CONANT, and he bore them quarterly, with the arms of STAINSBY and CONANT, thus: 1st and 4th, CONANT; 2nd, STAINSBY; 3rd, PIGOTT. The crest of STAINSBY is a mount vert, thereon a lion ramp. erm., holding betw. the forepaws a fleur-de-lis az. the dexter hindpaw resting on a millrind sa. Mottoes—Labore et virtute; and Conanti dabitur.

Pigott (co. Norfolk). Ar. two bends engr. gu.

Pigott (co. Nottingham). Sa. three pickaxes or. Crest—A greyhound sejant sa. collared and ringed or.

Pigott (Sir ROBERT PIGOTT, of Dysert in Leix, knighted Sept. 1609; Ulster's Office; the heiress, ANNE, dau. of Rev. RICHARD PIGOTT, D.D., m. ROBERT SHAPLAND CAREW, Esq.). Erm. three fusils conjoined in fess sa. on the centre one a crescent or. Crest—A wolf's head erased ar. charged with a crescent gu.

Pigott (Knapton, Queen's co., bart.). Erm. three fusils in fess sa. a crescent for diff. Crest—A wolf's head erased ppr. collared or.

Pigott (Eagle Hill, co. Galway). Erm. three fusils conjoined in fess sa. Crest—A wolf's head erased ppr. Motto—Crescit sub pondere virtus.

Pigou, or Pigott. Or, three spearheads in fess ppr. Crest—A dove with an olive branch ppr.

Pigou (London; originally of Normandy). Or, three spearheads gu. two and one.

Pigou. Same Arms. Crest—A lion's head erased ppr.

Pike (co. Devon). Per pale ar. and gu. a chev. az. betw. three trefoils, slipped and counterchanged.

Pike (co. Essex). Sa. on a pale ar. three crosses formée gu. a bordure engr. of the second.

Pike (London). Gu. three pikes naiant wavy ar. a bordure engr. of the second.

Pike (Gottenburgh, Sweden; granted 1751). Sa. three pikes staves ar. two and one, on the top of each an annulet or. Crest—A demi Moor ppr. in the ears rings and drops ar. holding in the dexter hand a like pikestaff as in the arms.

Pike (Livericks, co. Kent). Az. three talbots or.

Pike. Per pale or and gu. a chev. az. betw. three trefoils slipped and counterchanged. Crest—A pike naiant or.

Pike (Glendarary, co. Mayo; confirmed to WILLIAM PIKE, Esq., of that place, J.P., Barrister-at-law, son of the late JONATHAN PIKE, of Beechgrove, co. Tyrone, and grandson of RICHARD PIKE, of Summerhill, co. Cork, and Fuller's Court, co. Kildare, and to their descendants). Per pale or and ar. on a chev. az. betw. three trefoils slipped vert an escallop of the second. Crest—An arm embowed in armour, the hand gauntleted grasping a broken spear all ppr. and charged on the elbow with an escallop az. Motto—Vrai à la fin.

Pikeman (Dublin; Fun. Ent. Ulster's Office, 1636, Captain JOHN PIKEMAN, formerly captain in the town of Berwick-on-Tweed, and afterwards in Queen Elizabeth's service in Ireland). Per pale ar. and gu. on a chief indented sa. a mullet or, betw. two annulets of the first, on a canton of the second a tilting spear of the third, with a pennon striped vert and of the first in bend sinister surmounted of a sword ppr. pommel and hilt gold in bend dexter, encircled with a chaplet of laurel also ppr.

Pikenham. Az. a lion ramp. ar.; another, Az. a lion saliant or, a bordure engr. gu.; another, Or, a lion ramp. sa.

Pikton. Sa. a lion ramp. or.

Pikworth. Gu. a bend betw. six pickaxes or.

Pikworth, or Pitworth. Ar. three pikes naiant gu.

Pilborough (co. Essex). Per fess sa. and gu. an eagle displ. ar.

Pilborough (co. Essex). Per bend sa. and gu. three mullets or, on a chief ar. a griffin pass. az.

Pilcher. Or, three chev. interlaced gu. a chief of the last. Crest—On a chapeau gu. turned up erm. a cockatrice, wings expanded vert, and crowned with a ducal coronet or.

Pile (Compton-Beauchamp, co. Berks, bart., extinct 1761; Sir FRANCIS PILE, of Compton-Beauchamp, was created a baronet in 1628). Ar. a cross betw. four nails gu.

Pilesburgh, or Pilesborough (co. Essex). Per fess sa. and az. on an eagle displ. ar. three griffins' heads erased of the second.

Pilesdon (quartered by HORNE, of Stoke, co. Warwick). Sa. three mullets ar.

Pilgrim. Or, three pilgrims' staves sa. Crest—A dexter arm embowed in armour ppr. garnished or, holding in the hand a cutlass also ppr. hilt and pommel gold.

Pilgrim, or Pilgrime. Az. three pilgrims' staves or. Crest—An escallop or.

Pilkington (Rivington, co. Lancaster; Fuller styles the PILKINGTONS, "a right ancient family," and relates that they were gentlemen of repute in the co. before the Conquest, at which period the chief of the house being sought after by the Norman soldiers, was fain to disguise himself as a thrasher in a barn; from which circumstance, partly alluding to the head of the flail falling sometimes on the one and sometimes on the other side, and occasionally on himself, he took for motto, "Now thus! now thus!"). Ar. a cross patonce voided gu. Crest—A mower ppr. Motto—Now thus! now thus!

Pilkington (co. Lancaster). Ar. a cross patonce voided gu. on a chief vert three suns in their splendour or.

Pilkington (JAMES PILKINGTON, Bishop of Durham, 1561-76; granted by Sir Gilbert Dethick, Garter, 1551). Ar. a cross patonce voided gu. on a chief vert three suns or.

Pilkington (Park Lane Hall, co. York). A cross patonce gu. voided of the field. Crest—A mower of party colours ar. and gu. Motto—Now thus! now thus!

Pilkington (Chevet Hall, co. York, bart.). Quarterly, 1st and 4th, PILKINGTON, ar. a cross flory voided gu.; 2nd, SWINNERTON, ar. a cross formée fleurettée sa. surmounted by a bend engr. gu.; 3rd, MILBORNE, per pale ar. and gu. a cross patonce betw. in the sinister chief and dexter base two leopards' faces counterchanged. Crests—1st, PILKINGTON: A mower with his scythe ppr. habited per pale ar. and sa.; 2nd, SWINNERTON: On a mount vert a boar pass. ar. charged with a cross formée fleurettée sa.; 3rd, MILBORNE: A demi lion per fess ar. and gu. holding betw. the paws a leopard's face of the first. Motto—Honestæ gloria fax mentis.

Pilkington (Halliwell Hill, co. Lancaster). Same Arms, &c.

Pilkington (Stanton, co. Derby). Az. a cross pattée voidec. ar.

Pilkington (cos. Durham and Lancaster, and Worthington,

co. Leicester). Ar. a cross patonce voided gu. *Crest*—A mower with his scythe ppr. habited quarterly ar. and gu.

Pilkington (co. Lincoln, and Wastell and Pennyless-Pery, co. Northampton). Ar. a cross flory voided gu. a mullet for diff. Same *Crest* as the last.

Pilkington (granted 10 Feb. 1560). Ar. a cross patonce voided gu. on a chief vert three suns or.

Pilkington. Paly of six ar. and gu. on a bend sa. three mullets or.

Pilkington (Rev. CHARLES PILKINGTON, of Stockton Rectory, co. Warwick). Ar. a cross patonce voided gu. in the dexter chief on a mullet sa. a crescent of the field for diff. *Crest*—A mower habited sa. holding in his hands a scythe ppr. charged on the breast with a mullet and crescent, as in the arms, the mullet sa. *Motto*—Now thus! now thus!

Pilkington (Bolton, co. Lancaster). Ar. a cross patonce voided gu. quartering, Ar.a chev. betw. three lozenges erm. *Crest*—A mower with his scythe ppr. the pole or, habited quarterly gu. and ar. his cap per pale of the last and third. *Motto*—Now thus! now thus!

Pilkington (Tore, co. Westmeath; descended from PILKINGTON, of Rivington, co. Lancaster, and now represented by HENRY MULOCK PILKINGTON, Esq., Q.C., of Tore). Ar. a cross patonce gu. voided of the field. *Crest*—A mower with his scythe in front, habited as follows: A high-crowned hat with flap, the crown party per pale, flap the same, counterchanged, coat buttoned in the middle, with his scythe in bend ppr. habited throughout, quarterly and counterchanged ar. and gu., motto over, Now thus! now thus! *Motto*—"Pilkyngton Pailedowne—The master mows the meadows."

Pilland (co. Devon). Ar. two chev. wavy betw. three fleurs-de-lis sa. (another, the chev. gu.).

Pilland. Ar. a chev. gu. betw. three garbs vert. *Crest*—On a chapeau gu. turned up erm. a garb or.

Pillans (Leith, Scotland). Ar. three piles issuing from the chief az. surmounted by a chev. gu. charged with as many plates. *Crest*—A hand holding a sword ppr. *Motto*—Virtute et robore.

Pillans. Same *Arms*, the chev. charged with bezants. *Crest*—A dexter hand holding a dagger, point upwards, all ppr. *Motto*—As the last.

Pillans (England). Ar. three piles az. over all on a chev. counterchanged as many pellets.

Pillard (co. Kent). Ar. two chev. wavy betw. three fleurs-de-lis sa.

Pillesden. Ar. on a bend sa. betw. four lions' heads erased gu. three estoiles or.

Pillesdon (co. Chester). Sa. three mullets ar.

Pillett (co. Lincoln). Az. a chev. betw. three covered cups or.

Pillett, or Pillott. Ar. two bars sa. *Crest*—A lion sejant gu. holding betw. the paws an escutcheon of the arms.

Pillett. Sa. a chev. ar. betw. three covered cups or.

Pillett, or Pillott. Ar. two bars sa. on the first a bezant.

Pilling-Taylor. See TAYLOR.

Pillond (Pillond, co. Devon; the heiress *m.* BRETT). Sa. an eagle displ. ar.

Pilmure (Coupar Angus, Scotland, 1672). Ar. on a bend betw. a martlet in chief az. and a bugle in base sa. stringed of the second, two crescents of the first. *Crest*—A martlet volant az. *Motto*—Honeste vivo.

Pilsworth (WILLIAM PILSWORTH, Bishop of Kildare, 1604-35; impalement Fun. Ent. Ulster's Office, 1639, Rev. NEALE MOLLOY, of Lynally, King's co., whose wife, MARY PILSWORTH, was the bishop's dau.). Or, three dragons' heads couped gu. langued az.

Pimpe (co. Kent). Barry of six ar. and gu. a chief vair; another, Ar. two bars gemelles gu. on a chief sa. a bar nebulée of the first.

Pimpard (1240). Gyronny of four or and sa.

Pincerna, alias Panherne (co. Cornwall). Gu. on a bend sa. three covered cups ar.

Pincerna. Az. three covered cups or.

Pinchbeck (Pinchbeck, co. Lincoln). Ar. on a bend sa. a bezant.

Pincheon (Writtle, co. Essex). Sa. six plates, three, two, and one.

Pinchpowle, or Pincepole. Ar. a bugle-horn stringed betw. three trefoils slipped sa.

Pinchyon (Writtle, co. Essex). Per bend ar. and sa. three roundles within a bordure engr. counterchanged. *Crest*—A tiger's head erased ar.

Pinckard (GEORGE PINCKARD, M.D., Bloomsbury-square,

London). Ar. on a fess betw. three bulls' heads erased sa. armed and ringed or, a fret betw. two doves of the first. *Crest*—A dexter arm embowed ppr. vested az. charged with two bars ar. cuffed of the last, holding a sword ppr. the point resting on the wreath, hilt and pommel or.

Pinckney (cos. Northampton and Northumberland). Or, five fusils in fess gu.

Pinckney (co. Rutland). Ar. five fusils in fesse gu.

Pinckney, or Pynkenny (Sutton-Pagnell, co. York). Or, a bend lozengy gu.

Pinckny, or Pynkenny. Ar. five fusils in cross sa. a bordure engr. of the last.

Pindar, or Pyndar (*Earl Beauchamp*; Hon. JOHN BEAUCHAMP LYGON, assumed the surname of PYNDAR 1813, and *s.* his brother as third *Earl Beauchamp* 1823, *d. s. p.* 1853. See LYGON, *Earl Beauchamp*). Gu. a chev. engr. erminois betw. three lions' heads erased erm. ducally crowned gold. *Crest*—A lion's head as in the arms. *Supporters*—Dexter, a bear ppr. muzzled, collared, and chained or; sinister, a swan ar. wings elevated gu. beaked and legged sa. gorged with a ducal coronet, and lined or, on the breast of each supporter, suspended from the collar and coronet, a shield gu. charged with a fesse betw. six martlets gold. *Motto*—Ex fide fortis.

Pindar (Idenshaw, co. Chester, bart., extinct 1705; Sir PETER PINDAR was created a bart. in 1662). *Arms* (disallowed by Sir William Dugdale in the Visit. of 1663)—Az. three lions' heads erased erm. crowned or.

Pindar (Duffield, co. Derby, afterwards of Kempley, co. Gloucester). Az. a chev. ar. betw. three lions' heads erased erm. ducally crowned or. *Crest*—A lion's head erased erm.

Pindar. Az. a fess betw. three lions' heads erased erm. crowned or.

Pinder (co. Lincoln; granted 1538). Az. a chev. betw. three lions' heads erased ar. guttee de poix ducally crowned or. *Crest*—A lion's head erased or, ducally crowned ar.

Pine. See PYNE.

Pine (co. Cornwall). Ar. a bend gu. betw. six mullets sa.

Pine. Ar. on a mount in base a pine tree fructed all ppr.

Pine-Coffin (Portledge). See PYNE and COFFIN.

Pine, or Pyne. Gu. a chev. erm. betw. three pine apples or.

Pine. Ar. three holly leaves pendent vert.

Pine (Dublin; Fun. Ent. Ulster's Office, 1677, Mrs. PINE, *alias* NORTON, wife of Counsellor RICHARD PINE). Gu. a chev. erm. betw. three pine apples or.

Pinel (Seigneur of Melesches, Jersey, *temp.* King John). Per pale ar. and or, an eagle displ. standing on a billet raguly az.

Pinell. Ar. on a chev. engr. gu. a lion ramp. crowned or.

Pinfold (Dunstable, co. Bedford; granted 18 Oct. 1501). Az. a chev. or, surmounted of another of the field betw. three doves ppr. *Crest*—A pine tree or, leaved vert, fructed ppr. enclosed with pales ar. and sa.

Pinfold (Walton Hall, co. Bucks; FANNY MARIA PINFOLD, only child of the late Rev. CHARLES JOHN PINFOLD, Rector of Bramshall, co. Stafford, by ANNA MARIA, his only dau. of the Rev. JOHN SEAGRAVE, Rector of Castle Ashby, co. Northampton, succeeded to the representation of the family of PINFOLD, of Walton Hall, at the death of her grandfather, CHARLES PINFOLD, Esq., of Walton Hall, 28 Aug. 1857). Az. on a chev. or, surmounted of another of the field betw. three doves ppr. as many plates.

Pink, or Pinck (co. Oxford). Ar. five lozenges in pale gu. on a bordure az. eight crosses pattée fitchée or. *Crest*—A cubit arm erect, vested az. cuffed ar. holding in the hand ppr. a cross pattée fitchée in pale or.

Pink, or Pinck. Same *Arms*. *Crest*—A mullet of six points or.

Pinkeney (co. Rutland). Ar. five fusils in fess gu.

Pinker (Dinder, co. Somerset). Sa. a bend cotised betw. two griffins ar. *Crest*—On a mount vert a heathcock rising ppr.

Pinkerton (London, from Scotland, 1781). Or, a chev. vert. *Crest*—A rose gu. stalked and leaved vert. *Motto*—Post nubila sol.

Pinkney, or Pincheni (*Baron Pinkeny*, of Weedon, co. Northampton, extinct *temp.* Edward I.). Or, four fusils in fess gu.

Pinkney (Upper Sheen, co. Surrey). Or, five lozenges in fess gu. *Crest*—Out of a ducal coronet or, a griffin's head ppr.

Pinmakers, Company of (London; incorporated 1636). Vert a demi virgin couped at the waist ppr. mantled gu. turned down erm. her hair dishevelled, on her head an Eastern crown or; an ancient seal of the company represented a demi queen couped below the waist, and vested in royal robes, on her head a crown composed of fleurs-de-lis, and the *Motto*—Virginitas et unitas nostra fraternitas.

Pinner (London; granted 12 Aug. 1577). Az. a chev. ar. betw. three lions' heads erased erm. ducally crowned or. *Crest*—A stork pass. ar. ducally gorged or.

Pinner (Bury St. Edmund's, co. Suffolk, and co. Sussex; granted 2 May, 1612). Gu. two bars or, on each as many leopards' faces sa.

Pinney (Somerton Erleigh, co. Somerset). Quarterly, 1st and 4th, gu. three crescents or, issuing from each a cross crosslet fitchee ar,, for PINNEY; 2nd and 3rd, or, an eagle displ. with two heads vert, beaked and membered gu., for PRETOR. *Crest*—An armed hand and arm ppr. holding a cross crosslet fitchée ar., for PINNEY; An eagle's head couped or, wings expanded sa. gorged with a collar ar., for PRETOR. *Motto*—Amor patriæ.

Pinoke, or Pinnock. Sa. a lion pass. or.

Pinnock (impalement Fun. Ent. Ulster's Office, 1668). Per. saltire gu. and sa. on a chev. betw. three lions' heads erased, from the mouth of each issuant a cross crosslet fessways issuant all or, as many cinquefoils az.

Pinson (London). Gu. a chev. engr. betw. three estoiles of six points ar.

Pinson. Gyronny of eight gu. and az. a fesse engr. betw. three eagles ar.

Pipard (Larkbear, co. Devon; the heiress *m.* DE LISLE). Ar. three bars gemelles az.

Pipard, or Pypard (*Baron Pipard*, extinct 1309). Ar. two bars az. a canton of the last. *Crest*—A lion sejant ppr. supporting an escutcheon of the arms.

Pipard. Per saltire ar. and az. (another, or and sa.).

Pipard. Quarterly az. and ar. four lions ramp. counter-changed.

Pipard, or Pipart. Ar. two bars sa. on a canton of the second a cinquefoil pierced or; another, Ar. a chev. gu. betw. three Cornish choughs sa. ; another, Az. two bars or; another, Ar. three bars gu. on a canton az. a cinquefoil or.

Pipe (Cottenham, co. Cambridge). Sa. on a bend or, betw. two nags' heads erased ar. three fleurs-de-lis of the first. *Crest*—A camel's head erased or, bridled and ducally gorged sa.

Pipe (co. Essex). Az. a fess cotised or, betw. six crosses crosslet ar.

Pipe (Lord Mayor of London, 1578). Az. crusily or, a chev. betw. two organ pipes of the last.

Pipe (co. Stafford). Ar. two organ pipes conjoined in chev. gu. betw. ten crosses crosslet sa.; another, Vert crusily two fifes or sackbuts or.

Pipe (*temp.* Edward III.). Or, a fess betw. six crosses crosslet az.

Pipe. Az. a fess ar. betw. six crosses crosslet of the second; another, Or, a chev. gu. a canton vert; another, Ar. on a fess wavy betw. three leopards' faces az. as many crescents of the field, a chief vair; another, Az. two lions pass. guard. or.

Piper (Culliton, co. Devon; originally from Holstein, in Saxony; borne by Lieut.-Colonel JOHN PIPER, C.B., by SAMUEL AIRAULT PIPER, M.D., Surgeon of the 30th Regiment, and by ROBERT SLOPER PIPER, Esq., Major Royal Engineers, sons of Captain JOHN PIPER, of Culliton House, descended from MAGNUS PIPER, of Nieustadt, in Holstein). Quarterly, embattled or and erm. over all an eagle displ. sa. quartering Az. two chev. or, for AIRAULT. *Crest*—A cubit arm encircled by a wreath of laurel ppr. grasping a boar's head fessways sa. *Motto*—Feroci fortior.

Piper (Tresmarrow, co. Cornwall; the heiress *m.* VYVYAN). Ar. a chev. betw. three magpies sa. *Another Coat*—Gyronny of four or and az. *Crest*—A magpie sa.

Piper (Ridgewell, co. Essex). Paly of four or and gu. on a chief az. a garb erect of the first betw. two escallops ar. *Crest*—Out of an Eastern crown or, a demi dove ar. wings endorsed.

Piper (Ashen, co. Essex; granted 23 July, 1723, to JOHN PIPER, Esq., of Ashen, son of JOHN PIPER, of Cornard Magna, and grandson of JOHN PIPER, also of Cornard Magna, co. Suffolk, and to the descendants of his said grandfather; MARY PIPER, the heiress, *m.* HENRY SPERLING, Esq., of Dynes Hall, co. Essex). Gu. a chev. embattled ar. betw. two falcons belled in chief or, and a dexter gauntlet in base barwise, holding a sword erect all ppr. *Crest*—A demi griffin reguard. ppr. supporting an antique shield charged with a gauntlet and sword, as in the arms.

Piper, or Pyper. Ar. a saltire az. betw. four oak leaves vert. *Crest*—A unicorn's head ar.

Piper. Sa. three organ pipes ar.

Piper. Ar. two bars az. on a canton of the last a cinquefoil or.

800

Pipewell, Abbey of (co. Northampton). Ar. three crescents gu. impaling az. a crosier in pale or.

Pipho (Hollywood, co. Dublin; Fun. Ent. Ulster's Office, 1610, ROBERT PIPHO). Ar. on a fess wavy betw. three leopards' faces az. as many crescents of the field, a chief vair.

Piree (Warberton, co. Chester). Ar. two chev. gu. on a quarter of the second a mullet or.

Pirie (granted to Sir JOHN PIRIE, Lord Mayor of London). Ar. on a saltire gu. betw. four buglehorns stringed sa. three ostrich feathers erect of the field. *Crest*—An eagle's head erased sa. in the beak an ostrich feather ar.

Pipon (Noirmont Manor, Jersey). Per chev. gu. and or, in chief two mullets ar. *Crest*—A demi lion holding betw. the paws a mullet or ; another, A squirrel sejant ppr.

Pirot. Ar. a boar pass. sa.

Pirry (co. Dorset). Ar. on a fesse barry sa. and of the first betw. three martlets of the second, as many mullets pierced or.

Pirry. Ar. a fess betw. six martlets sa. three mullets of the field.

Piry (co. Worcester). Ar. on a bend sa. three pears or.

Pisseford (Langwada, co. Northampton). Gu. three bends vair, a label of five points or.

Pisseford (co. Oxon). Same *Arms*.

Pister (Metheringham, co. Lincoln, and Ryegate, co. Surrey). Ar. on a baker's peal sa. three plates. *Crest*—A cubit arm erect vested sa. and cuffed ar. holding in the hand ppr. a baker's peal sa. thereon three plates.

Pitblado (that Ilk). Vert a boar's head erased ar.

Pitcairn (that Ilk, afterwards Forthar, co. Fife). Quarterly, 1st and 4th, ar. three lozenges gu. ; 2nd and 3rd, ar. an eagle displ. sa., for RAMSAY. *Crest*—A moon in her com plement ppr. *Motto*—Plena refulget.

Pitcairn (Pitcairn, co. Fife, 1672, a younger branch of the last). Same *Arms*, within a bordure engr. gu. Same *Crest* and *Motto*.

Pitcairn (Pitfour, co. Fife). Quarterly, 1st and 4th, ar. three lozenges gu.; 2nd and 3rd, az. a chev. betw. three crescents ar., for DURIE. *Crest*—An anchor in pale az. *Motto*—Sperabo.

Pitcairn (Pitcairn, co. Perth, 1808). Ar. an anchor in pale az. betw. three lozenges gu. *Crest*—The sun in his splendour or. *Motto*—Spes lucis æternæ.

Pitcairn (JAMES PITCAIRN, Surgeon to the Forces, 1803). Ar. three lozenges gu. within a bordure az. *Crest*—A moon in her complement ppr. *Motto*—Plena refulget.

Pitcairn (Dreghorn, Scotland). Ar. three lozenges within a bordure gu. *Crest*—A star of six points wavy, with straight rays betw. each point, within a circle of clouds. *Motto*—Spes lucis æternæ.

Pitcairn (Pont's MS.). Ar. three mascles gu.

Pitcher (JOHN SOUTHERBY PITCHER, Esq., of London). Per chev. erm. and az., in chief two slips of oak vert, fructed ppr., in base a state barge floating in water of the last. *Crest*—A griffin's head couped, gorged with a wreath of oak ppr., betw. two wings on each a roundell. *Motto*—Perseverentia et labore. (An older coat : three ewers or jugs, one and two, surmounted by a bend, over all a scymitar paleways, point upwards. Crest as before, minus the wreath and roundels).

Pitcher. Or, a bend gu. surmounted by another az. *Crest*—A demi man in a military habit, holding a flag displ. az.

Pitches. Ar. two chev. gu. betw. three gouttes de poix.

Pitchford (Lee Brockhurst, co. Salop; allowed at the Visit. 1584). Az. a cinquefoil vert. six martlets or. *Crest*—An ostrich ar. beaked and ducally crowned ppr.

Pitchford (Pitchford, co. Salop; descended from RANULPH DE PYCHEFORD, *temp.* Henry I.). Or, a lion pass. az. armed and langued gu.

Pite. Per pale ar. and or, an eagle displ. with two heads gu.

Pitesdon (Wales). Ar. on a bend sa. betw. four lions' heads erased gu. three estoiles or.

Pitfield (Hoxton, co. Middlesex; CHARLES PITFIELD, Esq., J.P., of Hoxton, son of JOHN PITFIELD, seventh son of ROBERT PITFIELD, Esq., of Arlington, co. Dorset. Visit. Middlesex, 1663; certified by Norgate, Windsor Herald). Az. a bend engr. betw. two swans ar. ducally gorged and chained or.

Pitfield (Seymonsbury, co. Dorset). Same *Arms*.

Pitis, or Pitts (co. Kent). Ar. a chev. gu. betw. three peacocks' heads erased az.

Pitman (Dunchideock, co. Devon; settled there for several generations). Quarterly, ar. and or, an eagle displ. with two heads gu. *Crest*—A martlet upon a shell.

Pitman (Oulton Hall, co. Norfolk). Same *Arms* and *Crest*.

Pitman (Woodbridge, co. Suffolk). Gu. two poleaxes in saltire or, headed ar. betw. four mullets of the last. *Crest*—A Moor's arm ppr. escarroned (chequy) gu. and or, advancing a poleaxe, handle or, headed ar.

Pitson (Guildford, co. Surrey). Erm. a chev. betw. three peacocks' heads erased az. *Crest*—A peacock's head erased az.

Pitt (Boconnock, co. Cornwall ; *Baron Camelford*, extinct 1804 ; THOMAS PITT, Esq., of Boconnock, son of THOMAS PITT, Esq., of Boconnock, elder brother of WILLIAM, first *Earl of Chatham*, was created *Baron Camelford*, 1784). Sa. a fess chequy ar. and az. betw. three bezants. *Crest*—A stork ar. *Supporters*—Two Cornish choughs reguard. wings elevated ppr. *Motto*—Per ardua liberi.

Pitt (*Earl of Chatham*, extinct 1835). Sa. a fess chequy ar. and az. betw. three bezants. *Crest*—A stork ppr. beaked and membered or, resting the dexter claw on an anchor erect, cabled of the last. *Supporters*—Dexter, a lion ramp. guard. ppr. charged on the right shoulder with an acorn or, slipped and leaved vert; sinister, a buck ppr. attired, collared, and chained or. *Motto*—Benigno numine.

Pitt (*Earl of Londonderry;* Col. THOMAS PITT, M.P., of the same family as PITT, *Earl of Chatham*, m. Lady FRANCES RIDGEWAY, dau. and co-heiress of ROBERT, *Earl of Londonderry*, and was created *Earl of Londonderry* in 1726 ; title extinct, 1764). Quarterly, 1st and 4th, sa. a fess chequy ar. and az. betw. three bezants : 2nd and 3rd, sa. two wings conjoined ar. *Crest*—A stork ar. beaked and membered or, holding up its dexter foot. *Supporters*—Two falcons sa. beaked, membered, and belled or, each gorged with a chaplet of red roses, barbed and seeded ppr. *Motto*—Amitié.

Pitt (*Baron Rivers*). See RIVERS.

Pitt (Churwiard; Sir EDWARD PITT, Sheriff co. Worcester, *temp.* James I.). Az. three bars ar. in chief as many estoiles or.

Pitt (Ewern-Stepleton, co. Dorset; granted 1604 to WILLIAM PITT, Esq., of that place). Same *Arms*. *Crest*—A stork ar. beaked and legged ppr.

Pitt (East Mount, near Cirencester, co. Gloucester). Same *Arms*. *Crest*—A stork ppr.

Pitt (Priorsley and Shiffnall, co. Salop; granted, 1758, to HUMPHREY PITT, Esq.). Gu. an elephant erminois, on a chief or, a human heart ppr. betw. two horseshoes az. *Crest*—A cubit arm erect ppr. erased at the elbow gu. holding a banner or, charged with a human heart also ppr.

Pitt, or Pytts (Kyre-Ward, cos. Salop and Worcester). Barry of six or and az. on a chief of the second three estoiles pierced of the first. *Crest*—A dove, wings expanded ar. beaked and legged gu. betw. two ears of wheat or.

Pitt (Cricket-Malherby, co. Somerset). Gu. a fess gobony counter-gobony or and az. betw. three bezants. *Crest*—A stork ppr. resting the dexter claw on a bezant.

Pitt (Causeway and Melcombe Regis, co. Dorset, and North Crickett, co. Somerset). Barry of ten or and az. over all an escutcheon ar.

Pitt (co. Worcester). Barry of ten or and az. eight inescutcheons, three, two, two, and one, ar. *Crest*—On a trunk of a tree, lying fessways and raguly, vert, a stag ppr. attired or, betw. two acorn branches, sprouting from the tree ppr. fructed gold.

Pitt. Erm. on a buck's head a cross formée fitchée gu.

Pitt (Goldhall, co. York; quartered by LYSLEY). Or, a bend vair betw. three hurts.

Pitt (Dublin; Fun Ent. Ulster's Office, 1622, JOHN PITT, Collector of the Customs). Az. three bars ar. in chief as many estoiles of the last, a crescent for diff.

Pittendreich (that Ilk). Ar. a saltire az. betw. four roses gu.

Pittenween, Town of (Scotland). Az. in the sea a galley, her oars in action ar. and thereon standing the figure of St. Adrian, with long garments, close girt, and a mitre on his head ppr. holding in his sinister hand a crozier or, in the stern a flag disveloped or, charged with the arms of Scotland. *Motto*—Deo duce.

Pitter (Croydon, co. Surrey). Ar. a chev. gu. betw. three bees volant ppr. on a chief az. a rose of the field, seeded or, barbed vert, betw. two billets erect gold. *Crest*—On two billets erect, as in the arms, a stag's head erased and attired, ppr. gorged with a collar and chain or.

Pittlesdon. Ar. a fess sa. betw. three pellicans az. vulning themselves gu.

Pittman (East India House, London). Gu. two poleaxes in saltire ar. headed ar. betw. four mullets of the last. *Crest*

—A Moor's arm ppr. escarroned gu. and or, advancing a poleaxe, the handle or, headed ar.

Pitts (co. Bedford). Per pale ar. and gu. a chev. betw. three trefoils counterchanged.

Pitts (London, and co. Somerset). Gu. a fess counter-componée or and az. betw. three bezants. *Crest*—A stork ar. beaked and legged gu. resting the dexter claw on a bezant.

Pitts, or Pytts (co. Worcester). Az. three bars or, in chief as many estoiles of the last. *Crest*—A dove ppr. enclosed by a wreath of wheat or.

Piver. Or, two bars sa. on the uppermost a mullet pierced ar.

Piverne. Gu. on a chev. betw. three leopards' faces ar. as many escallops az. *Crest*—A cubit arm habited gu. cuffed ar. holding in the hand ppr. a sword in pale enfiled with a leopard's head of the second, hilt and pommel or, point guttée de sang.

Pix (Crayford, co. Kent). Az. a chev. betw. three crosses crosslet fitchée or. *Crest*—On a chapeau gu. turned up erm. a cross crosslet fitchée ar. betw. two wings expanded az.

Pix. Same *Arms*. *Crest*—A tree vert.

Pix. Az. a fess or, betw. three crosses crosslet fitchée ar.

Pixt (Hawkhurst, co. Kent). Az. a fess betw. three crosses crosslet fitchée or. *Crest*—On a chapeau gu. turned up erm. a cross crosslet fitchée or, betw. two wings expanded az.

Pixton. Gu. three piles engr. ar. meeting in point, each charged with as many pellets.

Pixwell. Ar. a chev. betw. three fleurs-de-lis sa.

Place (Dinsdale, co. Durham; descended from ROBERT PLAYSE, and KATHERINE his wife, dau. and heir of HALNATH of Halnaby). Per pale or and gu. a lion pass. guard. counterchanged. *Crest*—Out of a ducal coronet or, a dexter arm embowed in armour, holding in the hand a battle axe, all ppr.

Place (Weddington Hall, co. Warwick; descended from PLACE, of Dinsdale). Same *Arms*, &c.

Plaisterers, Company of (London ; incorporated 1501, granted by Hawley, Clarenceux, 37 Henry VIII.). Az. on a chev. engr. or, betw. two plaisterers' hammers and a trowel ar. in chief, hammers handled of the second, and a treble flat brush in base of the third, handled of the fourth, a rose gu. seeded or, barbed vert, betw. two fleurs-de-lis of the first. *Crest*—A dexter arm embowed, habited or, charged with a bend gu. cuffed of the last, holding in the hand ppr. a hammer az. handled or. *Supporters*—Two opinici vert, purfled or, beaked sa. wings. gu. *Motto*—Factum est. *Another Motto*, sometimes used—Let brotherly love continue.

Planche (co. Bucks.). Ar. billettée sa. a lion ramp. of the last, crowned or.

Planche (co. Leicester). Same *Arms*.

Planges, or Plaunches (co. Worcester). Same *Arms*.

Plank (co. Essex). Sa. a lion ramp. ar.

Planke, or Plank. Or, on a fess az. three hawks' bells of the field. *Crest*—An olive branch ppr.

Plant. Ar. a label in bend az. in chief a rose gu. *Crest*—A stag trippant gu.

Planta (The Right. Hon. JOSEPH PLANTA, of Fairlight Place, co. Sussex, son of the late JOSEPH PLANTA, Esq., F.R.S., a native of Switzerland, for many years principal librarian at the British Museum). Ar. a black bear's dexter hind leg erect, couped at the thigh, showing the bottom of the foot all ppr. *Crest*—Out of a marquess' coronet or, a bear's hind leg, as in the arms.

Plantagenet (founded by GEOFFREY, Count of Anjou, who, it is said by some writers, derived the name, afterwards so illustrious in his royal descendants, from the full blossomed branch of the yellow broom (*planta-genistæ*), which he wore by way of plume in his helm. Rapin ascribes, however, the assumption of PLANTAGENET to FULK, the great Count of Anjou, who, "being stung with remorse for some wicked action, in order to atone for it went a pilgrimage to Jerusalem, and before the Holy Sepulchre was scourged with broom twigs, which grew in great plenty there." GEOFFREY, Count of Anjou, m. 1127, MATILDA, or MAUD, widow of the Emperor Henry V., of Germany, and dau. and heiress of Henry I., King of England, and had by her a son and successor, HENRY, who ascended the English throne as second of his name, and founded the PLANTAGENET dynasty). Gu. three lions pass. guard. or, were borne by King Henry II., after his marriage with ELEANOR of Aquitaine. The royal shield had previously exhibited simply two lions. The royal arms thus continued unaltered till the time of Edward III., who assumed, in right of his mother, ISABELLA, dau of PHILIP the Fair, the fleurs-de-lis of France. Edward III. was the first English monarch who bore a crest, and the one he took was, A lion pass. guard. crowned or, on a chapeau. His shield was, 1st and 4th, az. semée of fleurs-de-lis or; 2nd and 3rd, gu. three lions pass. guard. or. Henry V. adopted, however, the alteration introduced by the French King, and limited the number of fleurs-de-lis to three. The eventual heiress of the house of PLANTAGENET was the Princess Elizabeth of York, dau. of Edward IV., and Queen Consort of Henry VII.; the representative and heir general of her eldest dau. MARGARET, wife of James IV. of Scotland, is MARIA THERESA, Archduchess of Austria, wife of LOUIS, Prince of Bavaria: the senior co-heir-general and co-representative of her second dau. MARY TUDOR, wife of CHARLES BRANDON, Duke of Suffolk, is RICHARD PLANTAGENET CAMPBELL, Duke of Buckingham and Chandos, while the Earl of Jersey is the senior co-heir of Lady ELEANOR BRANDON, second dau. of the Princess MARY TUDOR.

Plantagenet (*Duke of Clarence*, borne by LIONEL PLANTAGENET, called of Antwerp, *Earl of Ulster and Duke of Clarence*, K.G., third son of Edward III. direct ancestor of Her Majesty Queen VICTORIA; LIONEL was elected in the room of JOHN, *Lord Beauchamp*, one of the Founder Knights, 1363). Quarterly, 1st and 4th, az. semée of fleurs-de-lis or, for FRANCE; 2nd and 3rd, gu. three lions pass. guard. or, for ENGLAND; a label of three points ar. each point charged with a canton gu. N.B. The distinction represents the ancient bearing of CLARE, the heiress of which the Duke married, viz., Ar. a canton gu.

Plantagenet (*Duke of Lancaster;* the arms of JOHN of GAUNT, *Duke of Lancaster*, fourth son of Edward III.). FRANCE and ENGLAND, as the preceding, a label of three points erm.

Plantaganet (*Duke of York;* borne by EDMOND, of Langley, fifth son of Edward III.). Same as preceding, a label of three points ar. charged with as many torteaux.

Plantagenet (*Duke of Clarence*, as borne by / GEORGE PLANTAGENET, son of RICHARD, *Duke of York*, and brother of Edward IV. He m. ISABEL, dau. and co-heir of RICHARD NEVILLE, *Earl of Salisbury and Warwick*, and was put to death 1477. His only son, EDWARD, *Earl of Warwick*, last male PLANTAGENET, was executed 1499 s. p.; his sister and heiress, MARGARET PLANTAGENET, *Countess of Salisbury*, m. Sir RICHARD POLE, K.G., and her senior heirs-general are the *Earl of Loudoun*, nephew of HENRY WEYSFORD CHARLES PLANTAGENET, fourth and last *Marquess of Hastings*, and his aunts, the daus. and co-heirs of GEORGE AUGUSTUS FRANCIS, second *Marquess of Hastings*). Quarterly, 1st and 4th, FRANCE: Az. three fleurs-de-lis or; 2nd and 3rd, ENGLAND: A label of three points ar. each charged with a canton gu.

Plantagenet (*Duke of Gloucester;* borne by THOMAS, of Woodstock, *Duke of Gloucester*, sixth son of Edward III.). Same as preceding, without the label, but with a bordure gr.

Plantagenet (*Earl of Norfolk;* borne by THOMAS, of Brotherton, *Earl of Norfolk*, second son of Edward I.). ENGLAND: Gu. three lions pass. guard. or, a label of three points ar.

Plantagenet (*Earl of Kent;* borne by EDMUND, of Woodstock, *Earl of Kent*, sixth son of Edward I.). ENGLAND, a bordure ar.

Plantagenet (*Earl of Lancaster;* borne by EDMUND, *Earl of Lancaster*, second son of Henry III.). ENGLAND, with a label of three points ar. each charged with as many fleurs-de-lis or.

Plantagenet (*Viscount L'Isle*, extinct 1541; ARTHUR PLANTAGENET, K.G., illegitimate son of Edward IV., was so created by Henry VIII., 1533; he left three daus. his co-heirs, I. BRIDGET, m. Sir WILLIAM CARDEN, Knt. II. FRANCES, m. first, JOHN BASSET, Esq., of Umberleigh, co. Devon, and second, THOMAS MONCK, Esq., of Potheridge, same co., ancestor of the *Duke of Albemarle*. III. ELIZABETH, m. Sir FRANCIS JOBSON, Lieutenant of the Tower). Quarterly, 1st and 4th, FRANCE and ENGLAND, quarterly, the arms of EDWARD IV.; 2nd, a cross gu., for ULSTER; 3rd, barry of six or and az. on a chief of the first two palets betw. as many base esquirres of the second, over all a sinister baton gu.

Plantayne. Per saltire ar. and sa. in chief and in base a cross pattée of the second.

Plantney (Wolverhampton, co. Stafford; granted 1583). Sa. a lion ramp. betw. eight trefoils slipped ar. *Crest*—A tiger's head erased or, tufted and maned gu.

Plaskett. Az. a bend erm. in chief three bezants fessways. *Crest*—A swan ar.

Platt (Plastow, co. Essex; granted 6 Feb. 21 Elizabeth). Ar. on a bend betw. three escallops az. a bezant. *Crest*—A shoveller, wings expanded ppr.

Platt (Wigan, co. Lancaster). Az. on a chev. betw. three escallops ar. as many leopards' faces gu.

Platt. Same *Arms*. *Crest*—A bird volant az. wings ar. and sa. holding in the beak an escallop of the first.

Platt (London and Kentish Town, co. Middlesex; granted by Camden, Clarenceux, to RICHARD PLATT, of London, brewer). Or, fretty sa. on each joint a plate. *Crest*—A demi lion ramp. ppr. holding in the paws a plate.

Platt. Same *Arms*. *Crest*—A garb or, banded vert.

Platt. Vert three quatrefoils ar. each charged with a lion's head erased sa.

Platt (Deanwater, co. Chester; granted to ROBERT PLATT, Esq., of that place, son and heir of GEORGE PLATT, of Stalybridge, Stockport). Per fess dancettée ar. and gu. a pale and three frets, one and two, counterchanged. *Crest*—A demi wolf gu. semée of plates, armed and langued az. holding in the dexter paw a wreath ar. and gu. *Motto*—Labitur et labetur.

Plaudell (co. Norfolk). Ar. a bend gu. guttée d'eau betw. two martlets sa. a chief counter-componée or and sa.

Playce (Hanlaby, co. Durham). Az. on a chief ar. three torteaux, on each a cinquefoil or.

Playce (cos. Oxford and Salop). Ar. six annulets gu. three, two, and one.

Player (Hackney, co. Middlesex). Az. a pale or, guttée de sang. *Crest*—An arm in armour fessways holding a broken lance all ppr. *Motto*—Servitute clarior.

Player. Az. a pale erm. *Crest*—An armed arm in bend couped below the elbow, the hand supporting a broken spear erect all ppr.

Playfair (England). Ar. a cross betw. four mullets sa. *Crest*—On a chapeau gu. turned up erm. a pelican vulning herself ppr.

Playford (cos. Kent, Norfolk, and Suffolk). Vert a lion ramp. ar. on a chief gu. a fleur-de-lis ar. betw. two castles of the second. *Crest*—A leopard sejant ppr.

Playford. Gu. a fleur-de-lis or.

Playne (co. Kent). Ar. a cross pattée fitchée sa. on a chief of the second three fleurs-de-lis of the first.

Playne (Sudbury, co. Suffolk). Or, on a pile sa. three mullets of the field. *Crest*—A dead tree erased at the root and erect ppr.

Playse (co. Kent). Gu. a fleur-de-lis or.

Playse, or Plaiz (Tofte, co. Norfolk). Per pale or and gu. a lion pass. ar. *Crest*—A lion's head erased issuing flames of fire ppr.

Playse. Az. on a fess ar. three chaplets gu.; another, Per pale ar. and gu. a lion pass. or; another, Az. a pale ar. billettée sa.; another, Ar. a chev. sa. betw. three pellets; another, Az. on a chief ar. three escallops az.

Playses. Az. a pale or, guttée de sang. *Crest*—A gauntlet lying fessways ppr. holding erect a broken tilting-spear or, the top hanging down headed ar.

Playses. Az. on a pale ar. eight billets sa.

Playsted (cos. Suffolk and Sussex). Ar. three boars' heads couped gu.

Playstow. Gu. a lion ramp. ar. betw. two cotises or. *Crest*—Out of a ducal coronet or, a griffin's head ppr.

Player, or Playtor. Ar. three bendlets wavy az.

Player, or Platt (co. Norfolk). Gu. a lion pass. ar.

Playter (co. Kent). Gu. a fleur-de-lis or.

Players, or Plater (Sotterley, co. Suffolk, bart., extinct 1832; descended from THOMAS PLAYTERS, of Thornden and Sotterley, d. 1479, buried in Sotterley Church; Sir THOMAS PLAYTERS, of Sotterley, High Sheriff of Suffolk in 1605, was created a bart. in 1623). Bendy wavy of six ar. and az. *Crest*—A hawk regard. or, winged az. belled gold.

Playz (*Baron Playz;* summoned to Parliament 1287, in abeyance since 1359; the heiress, MARGARET, m. Sir JOHN HOWARD). Per pale or and gu. a lion pass. ar.

Pleasance (Tudenham, co. Suffolk). Sa. a cross erm. betw. four escallops ar. *Crest*—A griffin sejant wings expanded erm.

Pleckford. Chequy or and vert. *Crest*—A demi swan rising ar. wings addorsed ducally gorged or.

Plecy. See PLESSETS.

Pledger (Bottlesham, co. Cambridge; *temp.* Queen Elizabeth). Sa. a fess engr. betw. three bucks trippant or, pellettée. *Crest*—A buck's head erased or, holding in the mouth a sprig of oak ppr. acorned of the first.

Pledged (Bosthum, co. Cambridge). Sa. on a fess engr. betw. three bucks trippant or, as many laurel leaves vert. *Crest*—A stag's head erased or, in the mouth an acorn branch vert fructed gold.

Plenderleith (Blyth, Scotland, 1693). Vert a chev. betw. two trefoils slipped in chief, and a fleur-de-lis in base ar.

Crest—A hand holding a scroll of paper ppr. *Motto*—Prompte et consulto.

Plessets, or Plessetis (*Earl of Warwick and Baron Plessets;* JOHN DE PLESSETS was styled in a licence of Henry III., *Earl of Warwick,* his grandson, HUGH DE PLESSETS, not being considered an earl, was summoned to Parliament as a baron 1299, of whom there is no further account). Ar. six annulets gu. a chief chequy or and sa.

Plessett (Milton, co. Cambridge). Gu. a bend ragulée betw. two crosses crosslet ar.

Plessetts. Ar. a chev. betw. three mullets gu.

Plessey, or Plessis (co. Oxford). Ar. six annulets gu. three, two, and one.

Plessington (Demples, co. Lancaster). Az. a cross patonce (another, flory) betw. four martlets ar.

Plesstis, or Plecy (Upwinborne Plecy, co. Dorset, *temp.* Edward I.). Ar. six annulets gu. a chief chequy or and sa.

Plett (London). Lozengy or and sa. seven torteaux.

Plette, or Plettey (London). Or, on a fret sa. nine plates.

Pleydell (Midgehill, co Wilts, and Milbourne St. Andrew, co. Dorset; descended from GABRIEL PLEYDELL, second son of WILLIAM PLEYDELL, Esq., of Coleshill; EDMUND PLEYDELL, Esq., M.P., grandson of Sir CHARLES PLEYDELL, Knt., of Midgehill, *m.* ANNE, dau. and heir of Sir JOHN MORTON, Bart., of Milbourne St. Andrew, co. Dorset). Ar. a bend gu. guttée d'eau betw. two Cornish choughs sa. a chief chequy or and of the last. *Crest*—A panther's head erased sa. bezantée, swallowing a cross pattée fitchée gu.

Pleydell (Coleshill, and Shrivenham, co. Berks, and Cricklade, co. Wilts; Sir MARK STUART PLEYDELL, of Coleshill and Shrivenham, was created a Baronet in 1732; his only dau. and heir, HARRIET, *m.* WILLIAM BOUVERIE, first *Earl of Radnor*). Same *Arms. Crest*—A panther's head erased sa. bezantée, swallowing a cross pattée fitchée gu.

Pleydell (Whatcombe, co. Dorset). Quarterly, 1st and 4th, ar. a bend gu. guttée of the field betw. two choughs of the second, a chief chequy or and sa., for PLEYDELL; 2nd and 3rd, quarterly, gu. and erm., 1st and 4th, a goat's head erased or, for MORTON. *Crest*—A panther's head erased sa. bezantée, swallowing a cross pattée fitchée gu. *Motto*—Imitari quam invidere.

Pleydell (MANSEL-PLEYDELL, now of Whatcombe). PLEYDELL, as before, quartering MANSEL, of Smedmore. See p. 657. *Crests*—1st: PLEYDELL; 2nd: MANSEL. *Motto*—Imitari quam invidere.

Plimpton, Monastery of (co. Devon). Gu. two keys addorsed in bend or, interlaced with a sword in bend sinister ar. hilt and pommel of the second.

Plomer (co. Bedford, and Radwell, co. Herts). Vert a chev. betw. three lions' heads erased or, on each as many gouttes gu. (another, four billets).

Plomer (Inner Temple, London, bart., extinct 1697; WALTER PLOMER, Esq., was created a Baronet 1660-1). Per chev. flory counterflory ar. and sa. three martlets counterchanged.

Plomer (Mayfield and Pettingho, co. Sussex). Per chev. flory counterflory ar. and gu. three martlets counterchanged. *Crest*—A demi lion ramp. gu. holding a garb or.

Plomer. Az. on a chev. betw. three lions' heads erased or, as many martlets of the field. *Crest*—A demi lion ramp. ar. holding in the dexter paw a sprig vert.

Plomley (Dartmouth, co. Devon). Erm a bend lozengy gu.

Plompsted (Hatfield, co. Lancaster). Erm. a chev. sa.

Plompton (cos. Essex and Hertford). Az. three lozenges in fess or, each charged with an escallop gu.

Plompton (co. Lancaster). Az. a bend betw. six lozenges or.

Plompton (co. Lincoln). Same *Arms,* within a bordure ar.

Plompton, or Plumpton (co. York). Az. five lozenges in fess or, each charged with an escallop gu.; another, Az. on a fess lozengy or, five escallops gu.

Plompton. Erm. three water bougets gu. *Crest*—A buck's head couped ar. attired or; another, Erm. three mullets (another, escallops; another, crescents) gu.; another, Ar. four fusils in fess az.

Plomsted (Plomsted, co. Norfolk). Erm. three chevronels sa. on the uppermost as many annulets ar. *Crest*—Out of a ducal coronet or, a griffin's head ar. eared sa. beaked or (another coat, the tinctures reversed).

Plomton. Az. on a fess engr. or, five mullets gu.

Plonket. Ar. a bend gu. cotised, indented sa.

Plonkett, or Plonket. Erm. a bend fusily gu. *Crest*—A stag's head affrontée, gorged with a ducal coronet or.

Plott (Sparsholt, co. Berks). Vert three quatrefoils ar. each charged with a lion's head erased sa.

Plott, or Plot (Sutton Barne, Borden, co. Kent; Mowbray Herald Extraordinary, *d.* 30 April, 1626). Same *Arms.*

Plott (cos. Devon and Hereford, descended from co. Kent; granted 1587). Vert three quatrefoils or, each charged with a lion's head erased sa. *Crest*—A dexter arm armed or, purfled sa. holding a falchion ar. hilt and pommel gold, a scarf flotant from the hilt, enfiling the wrist, and tied in a knot of the first and second.

Plowden (Plowden, co. Salop; of this ancient family was the learned Serjeant EDMUND PLOWDEN, of Plowden, so eminent as a lawyer, *temp.* Mary I. and Queen Elizabeth). Az. a fess dancettée, the two upper points terminating in fleurs-de-lis or. *Crest*—On a mount vert a buck pass. sa. attired or.

Plowden (Ewhurst Park, co. Hants). Az. a fess dancettée or, the two upper points terminating in fleurs-de-lis ar. *Crest*—A buck statant sa. on a mount vert. *Motto*—Quod tibi hoc alteri.

Plower. Or, a cross flory sa.

Plowman. Vert a cross voided ar. *Crest*—A demi savage wreathed about the middle, holding over the shoulder a club, and round the sinister arm a serpent entwined all ppr.

Pluckley (co. Kent). Ar. a fleur-de-lis sa.

Plugenet (Lambourne, co. Berks; HUGH DE PLUGENET had lands in co. Oxford, *temp.* Henry II., and afterwards at Lambourne). Erm. a bend engr. gu.

Plugenet (*Baron Plugenet,* extinct 1327; Sir ALAN DE PLUGENET was summoned to Parliament as a Baron, 1295; his son *d. s. p.*). Same *Arms.*

Plukenett. Erm. six (another, five) fusils in bend gu.

Plucknett (The Manor House, Finchley, co. Middlesex). Or, five lozenges betw. two bendlets gu. all betw. two martlets sa. *Crest*—The battlements of a tower ppr. issuant therefrom a demi eagle reguard. wings expanded or, charged on the breast with a lozenge gu. *Motto*—In Deo fides.

Plum (Maldon, co. Essex). Ar. a bend vairé or and gu. betw. two bendlets vert. *Crest*—A talbot sejant gu. collared and lined or.

Plum, or Plume. Same *Arms. Crest*—Out of a ducal coronet or, a plume of ostrich feathers ppr.

Plumbe (co. Kent, Marston, co. Leicester, and co. Norfolk; granted 10 June. 1563). Erm. a bend vair cotised sa. *Crest*—A greyhound (another, an otter hound; another, a talbot) sejant ar. collared gu.

Plumbe (Prescott, co. Lancaster; descended from the PLUMBES of co. Leicester; JOHN PLUMBE, Esq., of Tong, son and heir of THOMAS PLUMBE, Esq., of Aughton, by ELIZABETH, his wife, dau. of JOHN TEMPEST, Esq., and cousin and heir of Sir HENRY TEMPEST, fourth and last bart. of Thorpe House, assumed, by royal licence, 1824, the surname of TEMPEST). Same *Arms,* &c.

Plumbers, Company of (London; incorporated 1612). Or, on a chev. sa. betw. a cross staff fesseways of the last, enclosed by two plummets az. all in chief, and a level reversed in base of the second, two soldering irons in saltire betw. a cutting knife on the dexter, and a shave-hook on the sinister ar. *Crest*—A triple fountain or, issuing water ppr. on the top an angel of the last, vested an ducally crowned and winged of the first, holding in the dexter hand a sword, and in the sinister a pair of scales, both or. *Mottoes*—Over the crest: Justitia et pax; under the arms: In God is all our hope.

Plumbers (Gateshead-on-Tyne, 1671). Ar. on a chev. sa. betw. a cross staff fesseways of the same, enclosed by two plummets az. all in chief, and a level reversed in base of the second, two soldering irons in saltire or, betw. a cutting knife on the dexter and a shave-hook on the sinister ar. *Crest*—A triple fountain ar. issuing water ppr. on the top an angel holding in the dexter hand a sword and in the sinister a pair of scales, all or.

Plues (SAMUEL SWIRE PLUES, Esq., Attorney-General for Honduras). Erm. on a pale engr. az. a fasces erect or. *Crest*—On a mount vert a mahogany tree ppr. therefrom pendent by a riband a fasces in bend or. *Motto*—Fiat justitia.

Plumerage. Az. on a chev. ar. betw. three doves of the second, beaked and legged gu. as many fleurs-de-lis of the last. *Crest*—A demi lion ramp. az. holding betw. the paws a fleur-de-lis gu.

Plumerdon, or Plurendon. Per fess sa. and ar. in chief two mullets of the second, in base a magpie ppr. *Crest*—A magpie ppr.

Plumleigh, or Plumley (Dartmouth, co. Devon). Erm. a bend fusily gu. *Crest*—An arm embowed, vested gu. cuffed ar. holding in the hand ppr. an arrow of the first, sans feathers, headed of the second.

Plummer (Middlestead, co. Selkirk, 1698). Quarterly, 1st and 4th, az. on a chev. betw. three lions' heads erased ar. guttée de sang, as many mullets of the field, for PLUMMER; 2nd and 3rd, gu. on a chev. ar. three mullets of the first, in base a stag's head erased or, guttée de sang, for KARR, of Zair. *Crest*—A dexter hand issuing out of a cloud and holding a plumb rule within a garland all ppr. *Motto*—Jus dicere decus.

Plummer (son of PLUMMER, of Middlestead, 1695). Az. on a chev. wavy betw. three lions' heads erased or, guttée de sang, as many mullets of the field. *Crest*—A demi lion ar. holding in its dexter paw a branch of palm ppr. *Motto*—Consulto et audacter.

Plumpton (Plumpton, co. York, 1665). Az. five fusils in fess or, each charged with an escallop gu.

Plumpton (co. Lancaster). Az. a bend betw. six lozenges or.

Plumpton (Darley, co. Derby, descended from co. York; the co-heirs of Sir WILLIAM PLUMPTON, who *d.* in 1480, *m.* SOTEHILL and ROCLIFFE). Ar. five fusils in fess sa. each charged with an escallop of the first.

Plumptre (cos. Nottingham and Kent; settled in the former co., *temp.* Edward I.; JOHN DE PLUMPTRE was M.P. for the town of Nottingham, *temp.* Richard II.; another JOHN PLUMPTRE was M.P. for same, *temp.* Queen Anne). Ar. a chev. betw. two mullets pierced in chief, and an annulet in base sa. *Crest*—A phœnix or, out of flames ppr. *Motto*—Sufficit meruisse. *Another Motto*—Turpi secernare honestum.

Plumptre (Fredville, co. Kent). Same *Arms, Crest,* and *Motto.*

Plumptre (arms from a list of Knights of cos. Derby and Notts, *temp.* Edward I.). Ar. on a saltire sa. five fleurs-de-lis or.

Plumridge (Sir JAMES HANWAY PLUMRIDGE, K.C.B., of Hopton Hall, co. Suffolk). Gu. a chev. engr. betw. two boars' heads couped in chief and an anchor erect in base or. *Crest*—Upon a mount vert a boar's head couped or, in front of a flagstaff erect ppr., therefrom flowing to the dexter a flag gu. charged with a naval crown gold.

Plumstead (Plumstead, co. Norfolk; granted by Cooke, Clarenceux, 3 August, 15 Elizabeth). Erm. three chev. sa. each charged with as many annulets ar. *Crest*—Out of a coronet or, a griffin's head ar.

Plumstead (co. Norfolk). Sa. an eagle displ. wings inverted ar.

Plumstead. Gu. a fleur-de-lis or, a label of three points ar.

Plumstock. Az. a chev. betw. three goats' heads ar. armed or. *Crest*—On a goat's head erased ar. attired or, a chev. gu.

Plumton. Az. on a fess dancettée or, six mullets gu. three and three.

Plunket (*Baron Plunket*). Sa. a bend betw. a castle in chief and a portcullis in base ar. *Crest*—A horse pass. ar. charged on the shoulder with a portcullis sa. *Supporters*—Dexter, an antelope ppr.; sinister, a horse ar. both charged on the shoulder with a portcullis sa. *Motto*—Festina lente.

Plunkett (Beaulieu or Bewley, co. Louth; JOHN PLUNKETT *d.* there 3 August, 1082. His descendant, JOHN PLUNKETT, *temp.* Henry III., had two sons, I. JOHN, whose descendant, Sir OLIVER PLUNKETT, was created *Baron of Louth*, 1541; II. RICHARD, whose grandson, Sir CHRISTOPHER PLUNKETT, *m.* 1403, JOAN, dau. and heir of Sir LUCAS CUSACK, *Lord of Killeen*, co. Meath, and became in her right *Lord of Killeen;* from him descend the *Earls of Fingal*, the *Earls of Killeen*, PLUNKETT, of Rathmore, PLUNKETT, of Dunsoghley, &c. &c.). Sa. a bend ar. in sinister chief a tower triple-towered of the last.

Plunkett (*Baron of Louth*). Sa. a bend ar. in sinister chief a tower triple-towered of the last. *Crest*—A horse pass. ar. *Supporters*—Dexter, a pegasus per fess or and ar.; sinister, an heraldic antelope ar. *Motto*—Festina lente.

Plunkett (Bewley, co. Louth; descended from Sir JOHN PLUNKETT, brother of Sir OLIVER PLUNKETT, first *Lord Louth.* WILLIAM PLUNKETT, Esq., the representative of this line, *s.* his father 1621, being then three years old; was a Captain in the Irish army in the rebellion of 1641. Fun. Ent. Ulster's Office). Same *Arms,* &c.

Plunkett (*Earl of Fingall ;* LUCAS, tenth *Lord Killeen,* was so created 1628). Sa. a bend ar. in the sinister chief a tower triple-towered of the second. *Crest*—A horse pass. ar. Sup-

809

porters—Dexter, a pegasus per fess or and ar.; sinister, an antelope ar. horned, unguled, gorged with a plain collar, and chained or. *Motto*—Festina lente.

Plunkett (*Baron Dunsany*, descended from CHRISTOPHER PLUNKETT, second son of Sir CHRISTOPHER PLUNKETT, first *Lord Killeen*). Sa. a bend ar. in the sinister point a tower triple-towered of the last. *Crest*—A horse pass. ar. *Supporters*—Dexter, a pegasus per fesse or and ar.; sinister, an antelope ar. collared, chained, armed, and hoofed or. *Motto*—Festina lente.

Plunkett (Clonbreny, co. Meath; Fun. Ent. Ulster's Office, 1641, THOMAS PLUNKETT, Esq., of that place, descended from NICHOLAS PLUNKETT, of same place, *temp.* Edward IV., second son of JOHN, third *Lord Dunsany*). Same *Arms*, a crescent for diff.

Plunkett (Loughcrew, co. Meath, and Portmarnock, co. Dublin; descended from JOHN PLUNKETT, second son of the house of Dunsany; Fun. Ent. Ulster's Office, 1595. Visit. Dublin, 1606. Of this branch was the Most Rev. OLIVER PLUNKETT, R.C. Primate of Ireland, beheaded at Tyburn 1681). Same *Arms,* a crescent for diff.

Plunkett (Rathmore, co. Meath; descended from Sir THOMAS PLUNKETT, Lord Chief Justice of Ireland, *d.* 1471, third son of Sir CHRISTOPHER PLUNKETT, first *Lord Killeen,* who became *Lord of Rathmore* in right of his wife MARIAN, dau. of Sir CHRISTOPHER CRUISE; his descendant, WALTER PLUNKETT Esq., of Rathmore, 1680, had three sons, viz., I. THOMAS, whose male descendants settled in France, Austria, and Portugal; II. WALTER, whose dau. and heir, MARY PLUNKETT, *b.* 1747, *m.* JOHN O'NEILL, Esq., and had an only dau. and eventual heiress, MARY, who *m.* 1799, BENJAMIN LENTAIGNE, Esq., and was mother of JOHN LENTAIGNE, Esq., of Tallaght, C.B.; III. OLIVER, whose dau., SUSAN, *m.* 1740, GERALD RICHARD DEASE, Esq., of Turbotstown). Same *Arms* as the *Earl of Fingall.*

Plunkett (Gibstown and Possextown, co. Meath; descended from JOHN PLUNKETT, fourth son of Sir ALEXANDER PLUNKETT, Knt., of Rathmore, Lord Chancellor of Ireland). Same *Arms.*

Plunkett (Dunsoghley, co. Dublin; descended from ROWLAND PLUNKETT, fourth son of Sir CHRISTOPHER PLUNKETT, first *Lord Killeen.* Sir CHRISTOPHER PLUNKETT, of Dunsoghley, was knighted at his Manor House by *Lord Burgh,* of Gainsborough, Lord Lieutenant, 1597; represented by FRANCIS PLUNKETT DUNNE, Esq., of Brittas, whose great grandfather, FRANCIS DUNNE, Esq., of Brittas, *m.* 1760, MARGARET PLUNKETT, dau. and co-heir of NICHOLAS PLUNKETT, Esq., of Dunsoghley Castle. ALICE, dau. of Sir JOHN PLUNKETT, *m.* RICHARD NETTERVILLE, of Corballis, who *d.* 1607. Fun Ent. Ulster's Office). Same *Arms,* an annulet for diff.

Plunkett (Talgharogue, co. Meath; Fun. Ent. Ulster's Office, 1616, RICHARD PLUNKETT, of that place). Same *Arms.*

Plunkett (The Deenes, co. Meath; Fun. Ent. Ulster's Office, 1619, JOHN PLUNKETT, Esq., of that place). Same *Arms,* a mullet for diff.

Plunkett (Athboy, co. Meath; Fun. Ent. Ulster's Office, 1620, RICHARD PLUNKETT, Esq., of that place). Same *Arms,* a mullet for diff.

Plunkett (Tullinoge, co. Meath; Fun. Ent. Ulster's Office, 1622, RICHARD PLUNKETT, of that place). Same *Arms,* a crescent for diff.

Plunkett (Dublin; HENRY PLUNKETT, Alderman and Mayor of the city, son of RICHARD PLUNKETT, the illegitimate son of Sir ALEXANDER PLUNKETT, Knt., of Rathmore. Visit. Dublin, 1568; Fun. Ent. Ulster's Office, 1623, ALICE, dau. of Alderman HENRY PLUNKETT). Same *Arms,* within a border gu.

Plunkett (exemplified, 1704, to PLUNKETT STOWELL, Esq., son and heir of WILLIAM STOWELL, Alderman of Dublin, on his assuming the surname of PLUNKETT, under the will of Right Hon. Sir WALTER PLUNKETT, who *d. s. p.* 1702). Quarterly, 1st and 4th, sa. a bend ar. in the sinister point a tower triple-towered of the last, PLUNKETT : 2nd and 3rd, gu. a cross lozengy ar., STOWELL. *Crest*—A dove ar. in the mouth an olive branch ppr. This exemplification was incorrect. Sir WALTER PLUNKETT was descended from RICHARD PLUNKETT, natural son of Sir ALEXANDER PLUNKETT, Knt., of Rathmore, *temp.* Henry VIII. The PLUNKETT coat should consequently be within a bordure gu.

Plymouth, Earl of. See WINDSOR.

Plymouth, Town of. Ar. a saltire vert betw. four castles sa. over the arms a coronet composed of eight fleurs-de-lis or. *Supporters*—Two lions ramp. guard. or. *Motto*—Turris fortissima est nomen Jehovah. (In a manuscript in the British Museum there is a more ancient coat for this town, viz. Gu. a ship with three masts, sans sails and yard-arms, all or, on the round top a fire beacon ppr. the base of the shield barry wavy of six ar. and az. as also the first blazoned arms).

Pocell. Gu. three pales vair, a chief or (another adds, on the chief a lion pass. of the first).

Pochen, or Poching (Barklay, co. Leicester). Ar. a chev. gu. betw. three horseshoes sa. *Crest*—A harpy ppr. wings endorsed or.

Pochin (Barkby Hall, co. Leicester; descended from RICHARD POCHIN, who m. ALICE, granddau. and eventual heiress of ANNE, only dau. and heiress of WALTER POWER, Esq., of Barkby). Or, a chev. gu. betw. three horseshoes sa. *Crest* —A harpy, wings ppr. full-faced, and tail twisted round the leg.

Pochin (Edmonthorpe Hall, co. Leicester). Same *Arms* and *Crest.*

Pockeswell (co. Dorset). Sa. a chev. betw. three estoiles or.

Pockley (Thorp Willoughby, co. York. Dugdale's Visit. 1665). Gu. a bend ar. cotised or, betw. two covered cups of the second. *Crest*—A dove, wings displ. ar. in her beak an oak branch slipped vert.

Pocklington, or Pollington (co. York). Paly of six ar. and gu. a bend counterchanged.

Pocklington (granted 22 June, 1761). Erm. three bendlets az. on a chief or, as many martlets sa. *Crest*—A demi leopard ramp. ppr. holding in the dexter paw an ostrich feather ar.

Pocklington (Muskham House, co. Nottingham, and Barrow House, co. Cumberland). Erm. three bends az. on a chief or, three martlets sa. *Crest*—A demi leopard ppr. issuing, holding in the dexter paw an ostrich feather ar.

Pocklington (Chelsworth Hall, co. Suffolk). Same *Arms* and *Crest.*

Pocklington. See SENHOUSE.

Pocock (Hart, co. Durham, bart.). Chequy ar. and gu. a lion ramp. guard. or, and for honourable augmentation, a chief wavy az. thereon a sea horse ppr. betw. two Eastern crowns or, and above, the word "Havannah," in letters of gold. *Crest*—An antelope's head ppr. attired or, issuing out of a naval crown gold. *Supporters* (granted pursuant to royal warrant, dated 15 Dec. 1821)—Two sea horses, each resting the exterior paw on an anchor all ppr. *Motto*—Regi regnoque fidelis.

Pode (Slade, co. Devon). Az. on a chev. or, betw. two eagles displ. in chief ar. and a lion's head erased of the second, in base three estoiles gu. *Crest*—Issuant from clouds ppr. a demi eagle az. collared or, wings elevated ar. on the breast and each wing an estoile counterchanged. *Motto*—Altiora sequimur.

Podenham. Az. an eagle displ. ar. within a bordure of the last.

Podmore (granted, 1683, by Carney, Ulster, to ARTHUR PODMORE, of the city of Dublin, Chief Clerk to the Lord Lieutenant's Principal Secretary and Secretary at War, Keeper of the Records in the Bermingham Tower). Vert a pile wavy erm. charged with a Moor's head couped sa. *Crest*—Out of a mural crown ar. a cubit arm ppr. holding a record (roll of parchment) of the first.

Poe (LEONARD POE, M.D. to Queen Elizabeth, James I., and Charles I.). Ar. a fess betw. three crescents az. issuing flames ppr.

Poer, Le (Curraghmore, co. Waterford; descended from Sir ROGER LE POER, who accompanied Strongbow to Ireland. His descendant, 13 Sept. 1535, *Lord Le Poer*). Ar. a chief indented sa. See POWER, *Earl of Tyrone*, and POWER, now DE LA POER, of Gurtcen La Poer.

Poer (Belleville Park, co. Waterford). Quarterly, 1st and 4th, ar. a saltire gu. on a chief the last three escallops of the field; 2nd and 3rd, sa. on a bend double cotised ar. three lions pass. guard. of the first. *Crest*—Same as POWER, *Earl of Tyrone. Motto*—Per crucem ad coronam.

Poer, or Power (co. Devon). Per pale wavy or and az.

Poger. Ar. on a saltire gu. the sun or, cantoned in chief by a heart of the second, and in the flanks and base a cross crosslet fitchée sa. on a chief of the field a double-headed eagle of the fourth betw. two lions ramp. both facing the centre of the last. *Crest*—A demi double-headed eagle sa. collared or.

Poger, or Pogey (co. Bucks). Gu. masculy ar.

Poher (co. Cornwall). Ar. two bars nebulée sa. over all a bend gu.

Poher (Wichenford, co. Worcester; in the 43rd of Edward III. JOHN LE POHER is styled Lord of the Manor of Wichenford; the heiress of the family, MARGARET, only child of JOHN POHER, Esq., of Wichenford, m. JOHN WASHBOURNE,

of Washbourne, now represented by MONEY, of cos. Hereford and Wilts). Gu. a fess or, in chief two mullets ar.

Poictevin (West Riding, co. York). Paly of eight gu. and ar.

Poierd. Az. a bend or, cotised indented ar.

Poingdestre (Jersey). Per fess az. and or, in chief a dexter hand clenched ppr. cuffed of the second, in base a mullet of the first. *Crest*—An esquire's helmet ppr. *Motto*—Nemo me impune lacessit.

Pointington, or Pontington (Pennycott, co. Devon, *temp.* Edward III.). Ar. a bend gu. betw. six fleurs-de-lis vert.

Pointrill. Quarterly, per fess indented ar. and gu.

Pointz (*Baron Pointz* by writ, 1295, in abeyance). Barry of eight or and gu.

Poissy. Or, an eagle displ. sa. armed az.

Pokeswell. Or, a buck's head cabossed gu. betw. the horns a fleur-de-lis of the last.

Pokesworth. Or, three dragons' heads erased gu.

Poking, or Porkins (co. Kent). Ar. on a fess betw. three talbots courant gu. as many mascles or.

Poldegrew, or Pollicrew. Gu. a lion ramp. guard. or, a bend az.

Poldegrew. Gu. a lion ramp. guard. or, collared ar. depressed by a bend az.

Pole, or De la Pole (*Baron de la Pole, Earl of Pembroke*, and *Duke of Suffolk*, forfeited 1513; derived from MICHAEL DE LA POLE, an opulent merchant at Kingston-upon-Hull, *temp.* Edward III.; RICHARD DE LA POLE, the last male heir of this gallant race, son of JOHN DE LA POLE, *Duke of Suffolk*, by the Lady ELIZABETH PLANTAGENET, his wife, sister of King Edward IV., was slain at the battle of Pavia in 1524, when the Duke of Bourbon honoured his remains with splendid obsequies). Quarterly, 1st and 4th, az. a fess betw. three leopards' faces or; 2nd and 3rd, per fess gu. and ar. a lion ramp. or, *Crest*—A savage man's head couped at the shoulders ppr. banded or, studded az.

Pole (*Baron Montagu*, attainted 1539, restored 1 Mary I., now in abeyance between the *Earl of Loudoun* and his aunts, LOWNDES, of Chesham, SELBY-LOWNDES, of Whaddon, and others; Sir RICHARD POLE, K.G., summoned to Parliament 1553, *m.* Lady MARGARET PLANTAGENET, dau. of GEORGE, *Duke of Clarence*, and left issue four sons and one dau., viz., I. HENRY, second *Baron Montagu*, whose daus. and co-heirs were, KATHERINE, wife of FRANCIS, second *Earl of Huntingdon*, and WINIFRED, *m.* first to Sir THOMAS HASTINGS, and secondly to Sir THOMAS BARRINGTON; II. GEFFERY, Sir; III. ARTHUR; IV. REGINALD, the celebrated Cardinal POLE; and, V. URSULA, *m.* to HENRY, *Lord Stafford*). Quarterly, 1st, or, a lion ramp. gu. a label of three points az.; 2nd, per pale or and sa. a saltire engr. counterchanged; 3rd, quarterly, 1st and 4th, az. three fleurs-de-lis or, 2nd and 3rd, gu. three lions pass guard. in pale or, a label of three points ar. each point charged with a canton gu., being the arms of GEORGE PLANTAGENET, *Duke of Clarence*; 4th, gu. a saltire ar. a label of three points componée of the last and az. *Crest*—An eagle or, preying on a fish ppr. *Supporters*—Two griffins or, each standing on a mount ppr.

Pole (WELLESLEY-POLE, *Baron Maryborough*, extinct 1863; Hon. WILLIAM WELLESLEY, second son of GARRETT, first *Earl of Mornington*, and brother of ARTHUR, first *Duke of Wellington*, assumed the additional surname of POLE, and was created *Lord Maryborough* 1821; he *s.* as third *Earl of Mornington* 1842; his grandson *d. s. p.* 1863, when the barony became extinct, and the carldom passed to the *Duke of Wellington*). Quarterly, 1st and 4th, az. semée-de-lis or, a lion ramp. ar., for POLE; 2nd, gu. a cross ar. betw. five plates in each quarter saltireways, for WELLESLEY; 3rd, or, a lion ramp. gu., for COLLEY. *Crests*—1st: A lion's gamb erect and erased gu. armed or, for POLE; 2nd: Out of a ducal coronet or, a demi lion ramp. holding a forked pennon gu. flowing to the sinister, one third per pale from the staff ar. charged with a cross of St. George, for WELLESLEY; 3rd: A cubit arm erect vested gu. cuffed ar. holding in the hand a scymitar ppr. pommel and hilt or, the arm enfiled with a ducal coronet gold. *Supporters*—Two lions gu. each gorged with an Eastern crown and chained or. *Motto*—Pollet virtus.

Pole (Shute House, co. Devon, bart.). Az. semée-de-lis a lion ramp. ar. *Crest*—A lion's gamb gu. armed or. *Supporters* —Dexter, a stag gu. attired and unguled or; sinister, a griffin az. gorged with a ducal coronet ppr. armed and beaked or. *Motto*—Pollet virtus.

Pole (Aldenham Abbey, co. Hertford, bart., extinct 1830; Admiral Sir CHARLES MORRICE POLE, K.C.B., second son of REGINALD POLE, Esq., of Stoke Damarel, co. Devon, and grandson of the Rev. CAROLUS POLE, who was third son of Sir JOHN POLE, third bart. of Shute, was created a bart. 1801, d. 1830, leaving two daus. his co-heirs, of whom the elder, HENRIETTA MARIA SARAH, m. WILLIAM STUART, Esq., of Tempsford Hall, co. Bedford). Same *Arms*, a crescent for diff. *Crest*—A lion's gamb gu. armed or. *Supporters*—Dexter, a stag gu. attired or; sinister, a griffin az. legged and ducally gorged or. *Motto*—Pollet virtus.

Pole (VAN NOTTEN-POLE, Todenham House, co. Gloucester, bart.). Quarterly, 1st and 4th, ar. a chev. betw. three crescents gu. a mullet for diff., for POLE; 2nd and 3rd, quarterly, 1st and 4th, ar. four palets az., 2nd, a snake in pale wavy, the upper half az., the lower sa., 3rd, or, three crescents gu., for VAN NOTTEN. *Crest*—A falcon rising ppr. charged with a mullet for diff., for POLE, *Motto* over—Pollet virtus. A snake in pale wavy, the upper half az., the lower sa., betw. two wings per fesse az. and ar. counterchanged, for VAN NOTTEN; *Motto* over—Prudens sicut serpens. *Supporters*—On either side a lion reguard. ppr., being the supporters of his Serene Highness William, Landgrave of Hesse Cassel, each differenced by a pale of three colours, which were confirmed to the first bart. and the heirs male of his body, by royal warrant dated 18 Jan. 1794, the same having been conferred on him by his Serene Highness as a mark of his acknowledgment of the great service rendered by Sir CHARLES POLE'S family to his Serene Highness's ancestors, and also as a proof of his Serene Highness's own esteem for him.

Pole (CHANDOS-POLE, Radbourn, co. Derby, formerly of co. Stafford; descended from PETER DE LA POLE, M.P. co. Derby, 2 Henry IV., who m. ELIZABETH, only dau. and heir of Sir JOHN LAWTON, by ALIANORE, his wife, sister, and at length sole heir, of Sir JOHN CHANDOS, one of the Founder Knights of the Garter, Lord of St. Saviours le Viscount, 10 Edward III.; PETER DE LA POLE was son of Sir JOHN DE LA POLE, of Newborough, co. Stafford, by CECILIA, his wife, sister and heir of Sir WILLIAM DE WAKEBRIDGE, Knt.; SACHEVERELL POLE, Esq., of Radbourn, assumed, by royal licence, 1807, the surname of CHANDOS, in addition to and before his patronymic, as representative of Sir JOHN CHANDOS, K.G.). Ar. a chev. betw. three crescents gu., quartering WAKEBRIDGE, CHANDOS, FITZ-WALKELYN, TWYFORD, BRAILSFORD, BASSET, COLVILE, MOTON, &c. *Crest*—A hawk rising ppr. belled and jessed or.

Pole-Gell (Hopton Hall, co. Derby; HENRY CHANDOS POLE, Esq., second son of the late EDWARD SACHEVERELL CHANDOS-POLE, Esq., of Radbourn, assumed the additional surname of GELL, by royal licence, 1863). Same *Arms* and *Crest* for POLE, quarterly with GELL.

Pole (Wakebridge, co. Derby; a younger branch of POLE, of Radbourn; a cadet of POLE, of Wakebridge, was seated at Park Hall, in Barlborough). Same *Arms*, &c., as POLE, of Radbourn, with the addition of "a canton az."

Pole (Henge, co. Derby; the co-heiresses m. FRITH and CHAWORTH). Same *Arms*, &c.

Pole (Rochester, co. Kent; ALICE, dau. of WALTER POLE, Esq., of that place, m. ROBERT BOWEN, Esq., Provost Marshal of Leinster, who d. 31 July, 1621; Fun. Ent. Ulster's Office). Erm. a fess nebulée betw. three bucks' heads cabossed az.

Pole, or Pale (co. Norfolk). Or, two bars wavy az.

Pole (co. Sussex). Or, a hart's head cabossed gu.

Pole. Ar. a buck's head gu.; another, Ar. three bars sa. on the uppermost as many roses of the field; another, Az. two bars ar. and a bend or.

Pole, or De la Pole. Or (another, ar.) a saltire gu. a bordure sa. charged with twelve bezants.

Poleford. Sa. a cross pattée (another, flory) ar.

Polesworth, Monastery of (co. Warwick). **Az. a fess** cotised ar. betw. six crosses crosslet or.

Poley (Boxted Hall, co. Suffolk, removed from Poley, co. Hertford, to Boxted and Badley, co. Suffolk, *temp.* Edward III. or Richard II.). Or, a lion ramp. sa. *Crest*—A lion ramp. as in the arms, collared and chained or. Sir HUMPHREY DE POLEY, who lived 7 Henry I. bore, as appears from a manuscript, " De Nobilitate," formerly in the possession of Sir Symonds D'Ewes, " ar. on a bend gu. three crosses crosslet or," to which was afterwards added "on a canton or, a lion ramp. sa." The ancient bearing was subsequently discontinued, and the canton assumed as the coat, but not without dispute, for an authentic record intimates that, " this being noticed as the ancient coat of the Earls of Flanders, by Count Maurice of Nassau, Prince of Orange, and Henry, Earl of Northumberland, being then also present in the Netherland army, who pretended to descend from the Earls of Flanders, they had some discourse and question

with Sir JOHN POLEY, who gave so good satisfaction that it did rightly belong to him, as that they never after made scruple touching the same."

Poleyne. Or, a bend nebulée gu.; another, Or, a fess gu. over all a bendlet sa.

Polgreen (Polgreen, near Fowey, co. Cornwall). Ar. two chev. az. each charged with as many palets or.

Polhey (co. Essex). Or, on a bend gu. three escallops ar.

Polhill (cos. Kent, Sussex, and Bedford; descended from JOHN POLHILL, *alias* POLLEY, of Detling, near Hollingbourne, in the first-named county, *b.* about 1420, who *m.* ALICE, dau. and heir of THOMAS DE BUCKLAND, of Bokeland and Preston). Or, on a bend gu. three crosses crosslet of the first, quartering, Ar. an eagle sa. beaked and unguled or, for DE BUCKLAND. *Crest*—Out of a mural crown or, a hind's head ppr. betw. two acorn branches vert, fructed gold.

Polhill (Howbury Hall, co. Beds). Same *Arms* and *Crest*.

Polimore (Polimore, co. Devon). Sa. a lion ramp. ar.

Polington. Ar. three piles (another, pales) gu. a bend counterchanged.

Polives. Ar. a chev. sa. betw. three roses gu.

Polkinghorne (Polkinghorne, co. Cornwall; settled there A.D. 1299; the heiress of the elder branch *m. circa* 1500, WILLIAMS, who took the name and arms of POLKINGHORNE, and was ancestor of OTHO POLKINGHORNE, whose dau. and heir, MARY, *m.* THOMAS GLYNN, Esq., of Helston, represented by the GRYLLS, of Helston). Ar. three bars sa. *Crest*—An arm in armour embowed, holding a battle axe all ppr.

Polkington (Bolton, co. Lancaster). Ar. a cross patonce voided gu., quartering ar. a chev. betw. three lozenges ermines. *Crest*—A mower with his scythe ppr.

Polland. Ar. an eagle displ. sa. armed or.

Pollard (Trelligh, co. Cornwall; Weye and Horwood, co. Devon; cos. Oxford and Worcester. Visit. Devon, 1620). Ar. a chev. sa. betw. three escallops gu. *Crest*—A stag trippant ar. attired or.

Pollard (King's Nympton, co. Devon, bart., extinct 1693; descended from Sir LEWIS POLLARD, Knt., Judge of the Common Pleas, son of ROBERT POLLARD, second son of JOHN POLLARD, of Way; LEWIS POLLARD, of King's Nympton, was created a bart. in 1627). Same *Arms*.

Pollard (Pollard Hall, co. Durham, and Brunton and Bierley, co. York). Erm. a cross engr. sa. *Crest*—A falchion erect ar. gripe vert, hilt or.

Pollard (Poulton, co. Lancaster, originally from Bierley, co. York; represented by POLLARD, of Parson Drove, co. Cambridge). Erm. a cross engr. sa. *Crest*—A falchion erect ar. pommel and hilt or.

Pollard (co. Devon). Ar. a chev. sa. (another, az.) betw. three mullets gu.

Pollard (Kelve, co. Somerset). Ar. a chev. sa. betw. three crescents gu.

Pollard (co. York). Vert a boar pass. ar.

Pollard (Hundhill, Pontefract, co. York). Ar. a chev. sa. betw. three mullets pierced gu. *Crest*—A stag trippant ar. attired or.

Pollard. Ar. on a fess betw. three mullets sa. as many bezants.

Pollard. Ar. a chev. az. betw. three escallops gu. *Crest*—A stag trippant ar.

Pollard (Castle Pollard, co. Westmeath; exemplified to CHARLES HAMPSON, Esq., of Aghacrevy, co. Cavan, and LETTICE, his wife, only child of Capt. WALTER POLLARD, of Castle Pollard, on their assuming the surname of POLLARD, 1718). Quarterly, 1st and 4th, ar. a chev. betw. three escallops az., for POLLARD; 2nd and 3rd, ar. three hempbrakes sa., for HAMPSON. *Crest*—Out of a mural crown ppr. a greyhound's head sa. collared ar. rimmed or.

Pollard-Urquhart. See URQUHART.

Pollardby. Per bend sinister wavy ar. and az. three annulets counterchanged.

Pollen (Redenham, co. Hants, bart.). Az. on a bend cotised or, betw. six lozenges ar. each charged with an escallop sa. five escallops of the field. *Crest*—A pelican, wings expanded, in her nest per pale or and az. vulning herself and feeding her young ppr. charged on the wing with a lozenge ar. thereon an escallop sa.

Pollen (BOILEAU-POLLEN, Little Bookham, co. Surrey; descended from the same ancestor as POLLEN, Bart., of Redenham. EDWARD POLLEN, Esq., eldest son and heir of JOHN PAULYN, Esq., M.P. for Andover, was father of BENJAMIN POLLEN, who inherited, through his mother, the manor of Little Bookham; his dau. and heiress d. *s.p.* in 1764, when she bequeathed her estates to her stepmother, with remainder to her half-uncle, and then to her cousin, Rev. GEORGE POLLEN, Rector of Bookham, whose eldest dau. m

JOHN PETER BOILEAU, Esq., and was mother of Rev. GEORGE POLLEN BOILEAU, of Little Bookham, who assumed the surname of POLLEN upon succeeding his maternal grandfather in 1812). Az. on a bend cotised or, betw. six lozenges ar. each charged with an escallop sa. six escallops vert, quarterly, with BOILEAU. *Crest*—A pelican with wings expanded, in her nest per pale or and az. vulning herself ppr. charged on the wing with a lozenge ar. thereon an escallop sa. *Motto*—De tout mon cœur.

Pollen. Az. a bend betw. six lozenges or, each charged with an escallop sa. *Crest*—A pelican or, in her piety ppr.; another, Vert a chev. or, betw. three plates.

Pollexfen (Kitley, co. Devon; four descents given in Visit. 1620; the heiress *m.* WILLIAM BASTARD, Esq.). Quarterly, ar. and az., in the 1st and 4th a lion ramp. gu.

Pollexfen (JOHN JAMES POLLEXFEN, Capt. 15th Bombay Native Infantry). Quarterly, or and gu. a cross parted and fretty counterchanged betw. in the 1st and 4th quarters a lion of the second, and in the 2nd and 3rd a sword erect ppr. *Crest*—Upon a mount vert two swords in saltire ppr. in front of a quiver erect or, filled with arrows ar. *Motto*—Semper fidelis.

Pollexfen (Ireland ; Fun. Ent. Ulster's Office, 1662. EDWARD POLLEXFEN, buried at St. Nicholas Church, Dublin). Or, a trefoil slipped gu. betw. three battle axes sa., quartering FISHER, viz.: Ar. on a chev. betw. three demi lions ramp. couped gu. as many bezants.

Polley (co. Cambridge). Or, a lion ramp. sa. on the shoulder a martlet ar.

Polley, or Pooley. Or, a fleur-de-lis betw. three (another, two) stags' heads cabossed gu.

Polleyne (King's Weston, co. Gloucester). Or, a bend sa. over all a fess gu. *Crest*—A hound couchant or. *Another Crest*—On a mount vert a hound courant ar. collared and lined, the end tied in a knot sa.

Polleyne. Ar. a fess and bend gu.

Polleyne. Az. a griffin pass. or.

Polliard. Ar. a cross sa. fretty or.

Pollington. Per pale or and gu. a bend counterchanged.

Pollington. Sa. a chev. betw. three leopards' faces or.

Pollington (quartered by MITFORD, through OSBALDESTON and WENTWORTH). Paly of six ar. and gu. a bend counterchanged.

Pollock (Temple Hatton, co. Middlesex, bart., 1866). Az. three fleurs-de-lis within a bordure engr. or, a canton erm. thereon a portcullis of the second. *Crest*—A boar pass. quartered or and vert, pierced through the sinister shoulder with an arrow ppr. *Supporters*—On either side a talbot sa. gorged with a collar and therefrom pendent a portcullis or. *Motto*—Over the crest: Audacter et strenue.

Pollock-Morris. See MORRIS.

Pollock (MONTAGU-POLLOCK, bart., 1872). Quarterly, 1st and 4th, az. three fleurs-de-lis within a bordure embattled or, and for an honourable augmentation in respect of the late baronet's distinguished services in the Affghan war, on a chief of the second an Eastern crown gu. superscribed " Khyber," and on a canton erm. three cannons issuing in pale sa.; 2nd and 3rd, per pale ar. and gu. four lozenges conjoined in fess counterchanged. *Crests*—1st : A lion ramp. guard. ar. adorned with an Eastern crown or, holding in his dexter paw in bend an Affghan banner displ. gu. bordered or and vert, the staff broken in two, and in his sinister paw a part of the broken staff, and in an escroll over the same this motto, " Affghanistan "; 2nd : A boar pass. quartered, embattled or and vert, pierced through the sinister shoulder with an arrow ppr. and in an escroll over the same this motto, " Audacter et strenue "; 3rd : A griffin's head couped erminois, wings endorsed and collared erminois, and in an escroll over the same this motto, " Spectemur agendo."

Pollok (Overpollock, co. Renfrew, 1672). Vert a saltire or, betw. three hunting horns in fess and base ar. garnished gu. *Crest*—A boar pass. shot through with a dart ppr. *Motto*—Audacter et strenue.

Pollok (CRAWFORD-POLLOK, of Pollok, bart.). See CRAWFORD.

Pollymore. Or, a lion ramp. vert.

Polmervy. Ar. three bars wavy gu.

Polshed. Ar. on a bend betw. two mullets gu. three trefoils of the first, on a chief sa. a pelican betw. two trefoils or.

Polstrod, or Polstodd (Westeley and Albury, co. Surrey). Ar. fretty sa. *Crest*—Out of a ducal coronet or, a boar's head and neck sa.

Poltesmore (co. Devon). Or, a cross engr. gu. over all a bend gobony of the field and az. (another, ar. and az.).

Poltimore (Poltimore, co. Devon; the heiress *m.* JEWE) Az. a griffin segreant or.

Poltimore, Baron. See BAMPFYLDE.

Poltock (co. Surrey). Az. an inescutcheon within an orle of eight cinquefoils or.

Polton (co. Hants). Ar. a fess betw. three mullets sa. (another, the fess charged with three bezants).

Polwarth, Baron. See SCOTT.

Polwarth (that Ilk). Ar. three piles engr. gu. conjoined in point (sometimes, the field gu. the piles indented ar.).

Polwhele (Polwhele, co. Cornwall; descended from JOHN POLWHYLL, of Polwhyll, *temp.* Henry V. (a lineal descendant of DROGO DE POLWHEILE, Chamberlain to the Empress Matilda), whose great-grandson, JOHN POLWHEILE, of Polwheile, *m.* the dau. and heiress of JOHN TRESAWELL, Esq., of Tresawell; his grandson, DIGORY POLWHELE, Esq., acquired Treworgan with his wife, CATHERINE, dau. and co-heir of ROBERT TRENCREEK, Esq., of that place, the first Recorder of Truro, and became of Polwhele and Treworgan). Quarterly, 1st and 6th, sa. a saltire engr. erm.; 2nd, az. three goats' heads erased ar. attired or, for LUKIE (ALICIA, dau. and heir of OTHO LUKIE, *m. temp.* Henry VI., JOHN POLWHYLE, of Polwhyle); 3rd, ar. an eagle displ. with two heads sa. a bordure of the second bezantée, for KILLEGREW of Arwenick (MARY, dau. and heir of WALTER KILLEGREW, *m. temp.* Edward IV., OTHO POLWHEILE, of Polwheile); 4th, ar. on a a bend or, cotised sa. three mullets gu., for TRESAWELL, of Tresawell Probus (the only dau. and heir of JOHN TRESAWELL, *m.* in the 16th century, JOHN POLWHEILE, of Polwheile); 5th, ar. a chev. with a cross pattée issuing from its point sa., for TRENCREEK, of Trencreek. *Crests*—1st : A Black-amoor's head with an olive branch in his mouth ; 2nd : A bull gu. with horns or. *Motto*—Karenza wheelas Karenza.

Pomell. Ermines three bezants.

Pomerai (Berie-Pomerai, co. Devon, *temp.* Henry I.). Or, a lion ramp. guard. gu. armed and langued az. a bordure indented sa.

Pomeris, or Pomise. Barry of six ar. and az. on a bordure gu. eight apples or.

Pomeroy (Chalfont, St. Giles, co. Bucks). Ar. a lion ramp. sa. a bordure invecked gu. *Crest*—A fir-cone vert charged with a bezant.

Pomeroy (Berry-Pomeroy, co. Devon. Visit. Devon, 1620). Or, a lion ramp. and a bordure engr. gu. *Crest*—A lion sejant or, holding in the dexter forepaw an apple vert.

Pomeroy (cos. Devon and Worcester). Or, a lion ramp. gu. within a bordure engr. sa.

Pomeroy (*Viscount Harberton*). Or, a lion ramp. gu. holding betw. the paws an apple ppr. *Crest*—A lion ramp. gu. holding betw. the paws an apple ppr. *Supporters*—Two wolves, the dexter ppr., sinister ar., both plain collared and chained or. *Motto*—Virtutis fortuna comes.

Pomeroy. Chequy gu. and ar. on a chev. sa. three annulets or. *Crest*—A lion's head erased gu. charged with four bezants and crowned with a ducal coronet gu.

Pomeroy (granted to JAMES POMEROY, Esq., of Epping). Or, a lion ramp. gu. a bordure engr. sa. charged with eight crosses pattée or. *Crest*—A fir cone erect ppr. charged with a fret or, betw. two fir-sprigs also ppr.

Pomeroy (granted 14 Oct. 1841, to JAMES POMEROY, and without the crest, to EMILY POMEROY POMEROY, formerly WAKE-FIELD, the children of ROBERT WAKEFIELD, of Clapton, in the parish of Hackney, Middlesex, gentleman, by MARY, his wife, dau. and co-heir of THOMAS POMEROY, Esq., late of Epping). Or, a lion ramp. gu. a bordure engr. sa. *Crest*—A lion sejant gu. holding in his dexter paw an apple or.

Pomery, or Pomeroy (St. Collumb, co. Cornwall, and co. Devon). Or, a lion ramp. a bordure engr. gu. a crescent for diff. *Crest*—Out of a ducal coronet or, a lion's head guard. gu.

Pomery (Tregny, co. Cornwall). Or, a lion ramp. gu. a bordure engr. sa. *Crest*—A lion sejant gu. holding in the dexter paw an apple or.

Pomesworth. Per pale ar. and az. a pale counterchanged.

Pomfret (Butbery, co. Essex). Quarterly, ar. and gu. a bend sa.

Pomfret. Ar. three cocks sa. armed or.

Pomfrett (Dewlish, co. Dorset). Quarterly, ar. and gu. over all a bend sinister sa. in chief a label of five points of the last.

Pomfret (co. Essex). Ar. a cross patonce gu.

Ponchardon (Sa. ten (another, fifteen) plates, four, three, two, and one. *Crest*—A unicorn's head erased gu. bezantée, armed or.

Ponde (Somerset Herald, *temp.* Henry VIII.). Ar. a fess gu. betw. two boars' heads in chief erased sa. and a cross pattée in base of the second.

Poneley. Barry wavy or and sa.

Ponepot (co. Suffolk). Ar. seven torteaux, two, two, two, and one.

Ponet. Per bend dancettée or and az. two pelicans vulning themselves, wings expanded, betw. four fleurs-de-lis all counterchanged.

Pongton (co. York). Or, five lozenges in fess az. a label of three points gu.

Ponnsdon (co. Hereford). Quarterly, or and az. in the 1st quarter a lion pass. gu.

Ponpons. Ar. three wolves pass. in pale az. *Crest*—Three pruning-hooks, two in saltire and one in pale or, environed in the middle by a wreath.

Ponsbury. Per saltire erm. and az. in the fess point a leopard's face or.

Ponseigne. Quarterly, ar. and az., in the 1st quarter a lion saliant gu.

Ponseyn (co. Hereford). Quarterly, az. and ar. in the 1st quarter a lion of the second (another, tinctures reversed).

Ponsford (Exeter; granted 20 May, 1710). Ar. three escallops in fess sa. betw. as many lions ramp. gu. *Crest*—A lion sejant reguard. gu. crowned ar. on the neck three escallops or, holding betw. the forepaws an anchor of the last.

Ponsonby (Hale Hall, Haugh, co. Cumberland; originally of Ponsonby, same co., *temp.* Edward II.; from a branch of this family descend the *Earls of Bessborough*). Gu. a chev. betw. three combs ar. *Crest*—On a ducal coronet or, three arrows, one in pale and two in saltire, the points downwards, shafts gold, feathered and pointed ar. entwined by a serpent ppr. *Motto*—Pro rege, lege, grege.

Ponsonby (confirmed by Roberts, Ulster, 1647, to Col. JOHN PONSONBY, son and heir of HENRY PONSONBY, Esq., late of Ponsonby, co. Cumberland). Gu. a chev. betw. three combs ar. *Crest*—On a ducal coronet or, a serpent ppr. pierced through with five darts fretty gu. *Motto*—Pro rege, lege, grege.

Ponsonby (*Earl of Bessborough*). Gu. a chev. betw. three combs ar. *Crest*—On a ducal coronet or, three arrows, one in pale and two in saltire, points downward, shafts gold, feathered and pointed ar. entwined by a snake ppr. *Supporters*—Two lions reguard. ppr. *Motto*—Pro rege, lege, grege.

Ponsonby (*Viscount and Baron Ponsonby*, of Imokilly, extinct 1866). Same *Arms*, &c.

Ponsonby (*Baron De Mauley*). Same *Arms*, *Crest*, and *Motto*. *Supporters*—Dexter, a lion reguard. ppr.; sinister, a bull sa. armed, unguled, and gorged with a ducal coronet or.

Ponsonby (Crotto, co. Kerry; a branch of PONSONBY, of Hale). Same *Arms*.

Ponsonby-Barker (Kilcooly). See BARKER.

Ponsonby (TALBOT-PONSONBY, Inchiquin, co. Cork; exemplified to CHARLES WILLIAM TALBOT, Esq., Lieut. R.N., eldest son of Adm. Sir CHARLES TALBOT, K.C.B., of Southsea, co. Hants, by Hon. CHARLOTTE GEORGINA TALBOT, his wife, sister of WILLIAM, third *Lord Ponsonby*, of Imokilly, co. Cork, on his assuming, by royal licence, 1866, the additional surname of PONSONBY). Quarterly, 1st and 4th, gu. a chev. betw. three combs ar., for PONSONBY; 2nd and 3rd, gu. a lion ramp. within a bordure engr. or, for TALBOT. *Crests*—1st: On a ducal coronet or, three arrows, points downwards, one in pale and two in saltire, shafts gold, feathered and pointed ar. entwined by a serpent ppr., for PONSONBY; 2nd: On a cap of maintenance gu. turned up erm. a lion statant, tail extended ar., for TALBOT. *Motto*—Pro rege, lege, grege.

Pont (Shyr's Mill, Scotland). Ar. three rainbows ppr. betw. two stars in chief gu. and a galley in base sa. *Crest*—A sphere az. beautified with six celestial signs, environing the terrestrial globe, all ppr. *Motto*—Perenne sub polo nihil.

Pont. Ar. a rainbow ppr.

Pont (Godmanchester, cos. Huntingdon and Cambridge. Visit. Huntingdon, 1684). Gu. two wings conjoined ar. within a bordure engr. or.

Pontefract, Town of (co. York). Sa. a quadrangular tower with four towers in perspective ar. masoned ppr. the base of the escutcheon water of the last.

Pontefract, Priory of (co. York). Quarterly, or and gu. a bend sa. over all a label of five points throughout ar.

Ponthieu. Or, three bendlets az. a bordure gu.

Pontifex. Ar. two palets az. betw. three mullets in chief of the last, a chief gu. *Crest*—A tower ensigned with a crescent gu.

813

Pontifex (Bath, co. Somerset; granted to EDMUND PONTIFEX, Esq.). Az. in base barry wavy of four ar. and of the field a bridge of three arches embattled ppr. a chief of the second, thereon two pallets betw. as many mullets of the field. *Crest*—A tower ppr. charged with a cross moline az. and surmounted by a rainbow also ppr. *Motto*—In hoc signo vinces.

Ponton (Scotland). Az. a lion ramp. and a chief or.

Ponton. Az. a lion ramp. ar. betw. three escallops or.

Pontrell. Or, on a bend az. three fleurs-de-lis ar.; another, Ar. a fess betw. three roses gu.

Pool (co. Chester). Az. semée-de-lis or, a lion ramp. of the last, on a canton ar. a ship in full sail ppr. *Crest*—A mermaid in profile ppr. holding in her hands a Saxon coronet or.

Pool (New Shoreham, co. Sussex; granted 1648). Az. semée-de-lis or, a lion ramp. guard. of the second, on a canton ar. a ship in full sail ppr. Same *Crest*.

Pool. See POLE.

Poole (Poole, co. Chester; bart., extinct 1801: descended from ROBERT PULL, *alias* POOLE, Lord of Barretspoole, 8 Edward I.; Sir JAMES POOLE, of Poole, was created a bart. in 1677; CHARLOTTE ELIZABETH, dau. and co-heir of Sir HENRY POOLE, the fifth bart., m. ROBERT WILLIS BLENCOWE, Esq.). Az. semée of fleurs-de-lis or, a lion ramp. ar. *Crest*—Out of a ducal coronet or, a griffin's head ar. *Another Crest* (granted by Wrottesley, Garter)—A bull's head cabossed gu. attired barry of five az. and or, sinister horn counterchanged. *Motto*—Pollet virtus.

Poole (DAVID POOLE, Bishop of Peterborough, 1556; granted by Hawley, Clarenceux, 15 June, 3 and 4 Mary I.). Ar. on a chev. engr. betw. three heathcocks az. as many cinquefoils of the field, on a canton per pale or and sa. a saltire couped counterchanged.

Poole (co. Bristol). Per pale or and gu. a saltire betw. two mascles in pale and as many leopards' faces jessant-de-lis in fess, all counterchanged.

Poole, or Pooley (co. Chester). Or, a lion ramp. gu. over all a bend sa.

Poole (co. Chester). Az. semée-de-lis or, a lion ramp. of the last, on a canton ar. a ship in full sail ppr. *Crest*—A mermaid ppr. crined or, holding in both hands a naval crown gold.

Poole (co. Derby). Gu. a chev. betw. three crescents ar.

Poole (co. Derby). Or, two bars az.

Poole (co. Devon). Or (another, ar.) a buck's head gu.

Poole (co. Devon, Saperton, co. Gloucester, and Oakley, co. Wilts). Az. a lion ramp. ar. betw. eight fleurs-de-lis or. *Crest*—A stag's head cabossed gu. the attires barry of six or and az.

Poole (Waltham, co. Essex; granted 7 May, 1569). Az. a fess erm. betw. three lions pass. or. *Crest*—A unicorn pass. az. tufted, maned, and armed or, ducally gorged ar.

Poole (co. Norfolk). Or, two bars wavy az.

Poole (co. Oxford). Or, four barrulets wavy sa. a bend ar.

Poole, or Pooley (co. Suffolk). Az. a fess betw. three leopards' faces or.

Poole (co. York). Same *Arms*, leopards' faces ar.

Poole. Per pale or and sa. a saltire counterchanged (another, the saltire engr.).

Poole. Ar. a chev. betw. three crescents gu. over all a bendlet sinister.

Poole (confirmed by Roberts, Ulster, 1648, to RICHARD POOLE, captain of a ship of war in the service of King Charles I., second son of THOMAS POOLE, only son and heir of Captain RICHARD POOLE, co. Sussex, descended from an ancient family in co. Chester). Az. semée-de-lis or, a lion ramp. guard. of the last, on a canton ar. a ship with her mainsail furled ppr. *Crest*—A mermaid ppr. holding betwixt her hands a naval crown or.

Poole (Sir JAMES POOLE, knighted at Dublin Castle, 1603; Ulster's Office). Quarterly, 1st and 4th, ar. a chev. betw. three crescents gu; 2nd and 3rd, az. a fess betw. three leopards' faces or. *Crest*—A falcon rising ar.

Poole (Geraldstown, co. Meath; Fun. Ent. Ulster's Office, 1685, NATHANIEL POOLE, Serjeant-at-Arms, son of PERIAM POOLE, Esq., of Southcutsheyes, co. Devon). Az. semée-de-lis or, a lion ramp. ar.

Pooler (Tyross, co. Armagh; confirmed to Rev. JAMES GALBRAITH POOLER, Incumbent of Newtownards, co. Down, and to the descendants of his grandfather, ROBERT POOLER, Esq., of Tyross, co. Armagh). Per pale or and ar. a fess az. betw. two lions' heads erased in chief gu. and a crescent in base of the third. *Crest*—A falcon rising ppr. belled or, and charged on the breast with a lozenge gu. *Motto*—Vi et virtute.

Poole, Town of (co. Dorset). Gu. three bars wavy or, over all a dolphin embowed naiant ar. in chief three escallops of the second. *Crest*—A mermaid ppr. holding in her dexter hand an anchor in pale, cabled without a beam, her sinister hand extended, holding a ball all ppr. *Motto*—Admorem villæ de Poole.

Pooley (cos. Chester and Suffolk). Or, a lion ramp. sa. on the shoulder a crescent ar. *Crest*—A lion ramp. sa. collared and lined or. *Another Crest*—A lion ramp. or, collared and lined sa.

Pooley (co. Gloucester). Ar. a lion ramp. sa. a bordure engr. gu.

Pooley. Or, a hart's head gu.; another, Ar. on a bend gu. three crosses crosslet or; another, Ar. three bars sa. on the first bar as many roses of the field.

Pooll (Frome, co. Somerset; granted to ROBERT POOK POOLL, Esq.). Ar. a lion ramp. betw. two fleurs-de-lis in pale az. and as many fountains in fess, the lion charged with a battle axe erect ppr. *Crest*—In front of a gryphon's head erased erm. charged with a fountain, a battle axe fessewise, the head to the dexter ppr. *Motto*—Confide recte agens.

Pooly (Sir JOHN POOLY, knighted at Dublin, 1599 ; Ulster's Office). Or, a lion ramp. sa. *Crest*—A lion ramp. sa. collared or.

Poor (Darrington, co. Wilts). Ar. a fess az. betw. three mullets gu. *Crest*—A tower sa. masoned ar.

Poore (Rushall, co. Wilts, bart.). Ar. a fess az. betw. three mullets gu. *Crest*—A cubit arm erect, vested sa. slashed ar. cuffed erm. charged with two mullets in fess or, grasping in the hand an arrow ppr. *Motto*—Pauper non in spe.

Poore. See POER and POWER.

Poore (co. Oxford). Ar. three bars nebulée sa. over all a bend or.

Pope (Hendall, co. Sussex; descended from EDMOND POPE, Esq., of Hendall, *d.* 1550, great-grandson of THOMAS POPE, of the Privy Chamber to Henry VI., by JOAN his wife, dau. and heir of WILLIAM WESTON, of Bucksted, co. Sussex). Or, two chev. gu. on a canton of the second a mullet of the first. *Crest*—On a chapeau gu. turned up erm. a tiger statant ar. tufted, maned, collared, ringed, and lined or.

Pope. Same *Arms*. *Crest*—A demi lion vert.

Pope (Marnehull, co. Devon, and co. Dorset). Ar. two chevronels gu. on a chief of the last an escallop or, a bordure of the second.

Pope (London). Ar. two chev. gu. on a canton of the last a mullet or.

Pope. Ar. a fess chequy ar. and az. betw. three bells of the last.

Pope (Wilcote, Wroxton, and Dedington, co. Oxford, and Tittenhanger, co. Herts). Per pale or and az. on a chev. betw. three griffins' heads erased four fleurs-de-lis all counterchanged. *Crest*—Two griffins' heads erased addorsed or and az. ducally collared, counterchanged.

Pope (*Earl of Downe*, extinct 1668; Sir WILLIAM POPE, only son of JOHN POPE, Esq., of Wroxton, and grandson of WILLIAM POPE, Esq., of Deelington, was created a bart. 1611, and *Earl of Downe* 1628; THOMAS, last *Earl of Downe, d. unm.* in 1668, leaving his sisters his co-heirs, viz., ANNE, *m.* to Sir EDWARD BOUGHTON, Bart.; BEATA. *m.* to Sir WILLIAM SOAMES, Bart.; FRANCES, *m.* to Sir FRANCIS NORTH, the celebrated Lord Keeper; and FINETTA, *m.* to ROBERT HYDE, Esq.). Same *Arms* and *Crest*. *Supporters*—Two griffins, the dexter az. ducally gorged or, the sinister or, ducally gorged az.

Pope (co. Salop). Or, two chev. gu. a canton az. *Crest*—A cubit arm erect, habited gu. cuffed ar. holding in the hand ppr. a pair of scales or. *Motto*—Mihi tibi.

Pope (co. Cornwall). Az. three griffins' heads erased or. *Crest*—A griffin pass. ar. collared gu.

Pope. Ar. two chev. gu. on a chief of the second an escallop or; another, Ar. a bend and chev. gu. on a canton of the second a mullet pierced or; another, Sa. two keys in saltire or, in chief three talbots' heads couped ar.

Pope (General GEORGE POPE, C.B., 1862). Gu. an antique crown within two branches of laurel in saltire betw. three mullets or, on a chief erm. a key sa. surmounting a sword ppr. in saltire. *Crest*—A demi lion ramp. gu. gorged with an antique crown or, and holding in the dexter paw a key in bend of the last. *Motto*—Fideliter et fortiter.

Popelley. Ar. on a bend sa. three eagles displ. of the field.

Popelley. Ar. a bend betw. three eagles displ. sa.

Popenham. Barry of six ar. and az. on a bend gu. three mullets pierced of the first.

Popham (Popham, co. Hants, *temp.* King John; the last male heir of the chief line, Sir STEPHEN POPHAM, Knt., of Popham, left four daus. his co-heirs, viz., MARGERY, *m.*

THOMAS HAMPDEN, Esq.; ELEANOR, *m.* JOHN BARENTINE, Esq.; ELIZABETH, *m.* JOHN WADHAM, Esq.; and ALICE, *m.* HUMPHREY FOSTER, Esq.). Ar. on a chief gu. two bucks' heads cabossed ppr. *Crest*—A buck's head erased ppr.

Popham (Huntworth, co. Somerset; descended from Sir HUGH POPHAM, Knt., of Huntworth, second son of ROBERT POPHAM, Esq., of Popham, *m.* JOAN, dau. and heiress of Sir STEPHEN DE KENTISBURY, Knt.). Same *Arms* and *Crest.*

Popham (Bagborough, co. Somerset; originally, from the time of Edward III., of Huntworth). Same *Arms* and *Crest.*

Popham (Littlecott, co. Wilts; descended from Sir JOHN POPHAM, Lord Chief Justice of England *temp.* Queen ELIZABETH, second son of ALEXANDER POPHAM, Esq., of Huntworth; the last male representative of POPHAM, of Littlecott, FRANCIS POPHAM, Esq., of Littlecott, *d. s. p.* 1780, having devised his estates to (the son of his sister ANNE, *m.* to WILLIAM LEYBORNE LEYBORNE, Esq.) his nephew, EDWARD WILLIAM LEYBORNE, who took the name and arms of POPHAM, and became General LEYBORNE POPHAM, of Littlecott). Same *Arms* and *Crest*, quartering LEYBORNE, Az. six lions ramp. ar. *Motto*—Mens pristina mansit.

Popham (Shanklin, Isle of Wight; descended from GEORGE POPHAM, Esq., of Barwick Bassett, younger son of ALEXANDER POPHAM, Esq., of Littlecott, M.P. co. Somerset, and one of the Protector's Upper House; MARY, dau. and heir of JOHN POPHAM, Esq., of Shanklin and Kitehill, *m.* the Rev. RICHARD WALTON WHITE, and their son, FRANCIS WHITE, Esq., assumed by royal licence 1853, the additional surname of POPHAM). Same *Arms*, &c., as POPHAM, of Popham.

Popham (Lynton, co. Devon. Visit. Devon, 1620). Same *Arms.*

Popham. Ar. a fesse gu. two bucks' heads in chief of the last; another, Ar. on a fess gu. two bucks' heads or; another, Gu. a fess betw. two bucks' heads ar.

Popingay (Portsmouth). Paly of six or and vert, on a chief gu. a greyhound courant erm. *Crest*—A lion's head per pale or and az. ducally crowned and powdered with roundles all counterchanged.

Popingay (Ireland, Ulster's Office). Ar. three popinjays ppr.

Popington (co. York). Or, five lozenges in fess az. a label gu.

Popkin (co. Glamorgan). Gu. a buck trippant ar.

Popkin (Scotland). Same *Arms.* *Crest*—A hand holding a writing pen ppr.

Pople (cos. Wilts and York). Ar. on a bend sa. betw. two bendlets dancettée gu. three eagles displ. of the first.

Popler. Sa. a shoveller ar.

Poplesham (co. Worcester). Sa. three cranes or; another, Sa. a chev. erm. betw. three shovellers ar.

Poplewell. Or, on a chev. az. betw. three gillyflowers ppr. as many lions' heads of the field.

Popley (Bristol; granted 24 Charles II.). Or, on a bend sa. betw. two cotises dancettée gu. three eagles displ. of the first.

Popley (Sarum, co. Wilts). Ar. on a bend betw. two bendlets dancettée sa. three eagles displ. or.

Popley (Morehouse, co. York). Ar. on a bend cotised sa. three eagles displ. of the first.

Popley. Ar. a bend betw. three eagles displ. sa.

Popplewell. Gyronny of eight vert and or, on each a trefoil slipped counterchanged. *Crest*—A demi lion ramp. ppr.

Popplewell. Or, on a chev. az. betw. three gillyflowers ppr. as many lions' heads erased of the field. *Crest*—A falcon belled vert betw. two gillyflowers ppr.

Porch (Edgarley, near Glastonbury, co. Somerset). Ar. on a chev. engr. gu. surmounted by another chev. plain or, charged with a battle axe erect betw. two bows stringed, each surmounting two arrows in saltire, points downwards sa. three wolves' heads erased of the field, quartering REEVES. *Crest*—A mount vert, thereon a wolf pass. in the mouth an arrow, the barb downwards, the dexter forepaw holding a bolt stringed all ppr. *Motto*—Cordi dat robora virtus.

Porcher (Snare Hill, co. Norfolk, Borough Green, co. Cambridge). Per pale ar. and gu. barry of eight counterchanged a cinquefoil erm. *Crest*—A lion ramp. or, charged with three bars gu. holding betw. the paws a cinquefoil as in the arms. *Motto*—Pro rege.

Porcher (Clyffe, co. Dorset). Same *Arms*, *Crest*, and *Motto.*

Porcher. Ar. a cinquefoil gu.

Porches (London). Or, a lion ramp. az. on a fess sa. three bezants.

Porches. Or, a lion ramp. sa. on a fess az. three bezants.

Porchester. Barry of fourteen az. and or (another, or and az.).

Pordage (Sandwich, co. Kent). Ar. a fess chequy or and gu. betw. three crosses crosslet sa. *Crest*—A dragon's head erased or, vomiting flames of fire ppr.

Pordage (co. Kent). Ar. a fess chequy or and gu. in chief three crosses botonnée sa.

Pordage. Ar. a fess chequy or and gu. in chief three cross crosslets fitchée of the last.

Pordon. See PURDON.

Porgyes, or Pogers (co. Buckingham). Gu. masculy ar.

Poringe. Ar. two bars betw. nine martlets gu. three in chief, three in fess, and three in base.

Porkeswell. Or, a hart's head cabossed, betw. the attires a fleur-de lis gu.

Porman. Or, a bend sa. in chief a martlet vert.

Pormort (Saltfleetby and Kenington, co. Lincoln). Ar. on a chev. betw. three leopards' faces sa. as many mullets of the field.

Pormorth (Todlethorp, co. Lincoln). Ar. on a chev. betw. three leopards' faces sa. as many crosses formée fitchée of the field.

Porquyn (co. Cornwall). Ar. a stag lodged gu.

Porritt (Armley, co. York; WILLIAM HENRY PORRITT, Esq., of that place, son of DAVID WRIGHT PORRITT, Esq.). Or, on a bend nebuly betw. two lions' heads erased ga. three bezants. *Crest*—A demi heraldic antelope gu. plain collared or, resting the sinister paw on a shield gold, charged with a lion's head of the arms. *Motto*—Fortiter et sapienter ferre.

Pors. Gu. fretty or, on a canton of the first an estoile of six points of the second.

Porsey. Gu. three piles or, on a canton sa. a mullet ar.

Port, or Porte (Etwall, co. Derby, Sir JOHN PORT, Knt., of Etwall, son of Sir JOHN PORT, Judge of the King's Bench, by his wife, the heiress of FITZHERBERT, of Etwall, left three daus. his co-heirs, ELIZABETH, m. Sir THOMAS GERARD, Knt., of Bryn, Sheriff co. Lancaster, 1558; DOROTHY, m GEORGE, fourth *Earl of Huntingdon;* and MARGARET, m. Sir THOMAS STANHOPE, Knt., Shelford, M.P.). Az. a fess engr. betw. three pigeons, each having in the beak a cross formée fitchée, all or.

Port, or Porte (co. Derby). Az. a fess engr. cotised betw. three pigeons, each having in the beak a cross formée fitchée, all or.

Port (Poole, co. Dorset). Gu. on a chev. betw. three portcullises or, five roses of the first.

Port (Basing, co. Hants, *temp.* William I.). Barry of six az. and ar. (another, or and az.) a saltire gu.

Port (Eardisley Castle, co. Hereford, *temp.* Henry II.). Ar. a chev. az. on a chief of the second three estoiles or.

Port, or De Port (Sheepshead, co. Leicester). Ar. two bars az. over all a saltire gu.

Port, or Porte (co. Stafford). Same *Arms. Crest*—A hand erect holding a pistol ppr.

Port (Ilam, co. Stafford). Vert a fess engr. ar. cotised of the last betw. three pigeons, each holding in the beak a cross formée fitchée or.

Port (co. Stafford). Az. a fess engr. or, betw. three pigeons, each bearing in the beak a cross pattée fitchée ar.

Port. Az. a fess engr. betw. three eagles close holding in the beak a cross pattée fitchée or. *Crest*—An eagle's head erased, holding in the beak a cross as in the arms.

Port. Az. two dolphins addorsed ar. betw. seven crosses crosslet (another, fitchée) or, on a chief gu. three leopards' faces of the third.

Portal (Freefolk House, co. Hants). Per saltire az. and gu. a castellated portal flanked by two towers ar. on a chief erm. a crescent of the first betw. two mullets of the second. *Crest*—A portal as in the arms, each tower charged with a fleur-de-lis in chief az. and a wreath of laurel in base vert.

Portal (Laverstoke, co. Hants). Ar. a lion ramp. sa. on a chief az. six mullets or, three and three. *Crest*—A portal flanked by two towers ar. each tower charged with a fleur-de-lis az. *Supporters*—Dexter, a lion; sinister, a savage bearing a club on his shoulder. *Motto*—Armet nos ultio regna. This motto was first borne by RAYMOND DE PORTAL, to whom it was, it is stated, assigned, in 1336, by Charles V. of France, in honour of his being one of the four hundred knights of Toulouse who volunteered to accompany Bertrand du Guesclin on his expedition into Spain to avenge the death of Blanche of Bourbon, Queen of Castile, and sister of the

815

Queen of France, who had been poisoned by her husband, Peter the Cruel. RAYMOND DE PORTAL distinguished himself in this expedition, and was celebrated in a poem (which is still extant) dedicated to Clemence-Isaure, by a troubadour of that day.

Portal. Gyronny of eight ar. and gu. on each a quatrefoil counterchanged. *Crest*—A lion's head erased or.

Portal (Ash Park, Overton, co. Hants). Ar. a castle gu. on a chief az. a crescent betw. two mullets of the field. *Crest*—A castle ar.

Portarlington, Earl of. See DAWSON.

Portayne, or Porteyne. Gu. three pales vair, in chief a lion pass. or.

Porte. Gu. on a chev. betw. three portcullises or, five roses of the field.

Porteen. Gu. a bend or. *Crest*—A pair of wings expanded, the dexter or, sinister gu.

Porteous (Craig Lockhart, co. Edinburgh, 1672). Az. a thistle betw. three bucks' heads erased or. *Crest*—A turtle dove with an olive branch in her beak all ppr. *Motto*—I wait my time.

Porteous (Halkshaw, Scotland, 16th century). Az. three stag's heads couped ar. attired with ten tynes or.

Porter (co. Lancaster, 1664). Sa. three bells ar. a canton or.

Porter (Alwardby, or Allerby, co. Cumberland). Gu. on a fess or, three church bells az. a border engr. ar.

Porter (Weary Hall, co. Cumberland; a younger branch of PORTER, of Allerby). Sa. three church bells ar.

Porter (The Close, co. Cumberland; presumed to derive from the PORTERS, of Weary Hall; of this branch of the family was JOHN PORTER, D.D., Bishop of Clogher, 1798-1819). Same *Arms.*

Porter (co. Buckingham). Gu. three church bells or.

Porter (St. Stephen's, co. Cornwall, and co. Lincoln, 1640). Sa. three church bells ar. a canton erm.

Porter (Launcells, co. Cornwall; the heiress m. HELE). Gu. on a fess ar. betw. three falcons' wings of the last a bezant charged with a lion pass. of the field. *Crest*—A demi goat erect.

Porter (Shield Row, co. Durham; the heiress, JANE PORTER, m. NICHOLAS BLAKISTON). Gu. on a fess or (sometimes engr.) three bells sa. a bordure engr. ar. charged with eight pellets.

Porter (Newark, co. Gloucester). Gu. five marlions' wings in saltire ar.

Porter (co. Gloucester). Gu. on a fess betw. five falcons' wings or, three hurts.

Porter (Aston, co. Warwick). Sa. three church bells ar. *Crest*—Betw. two pillars roofed and spired or, a church bell ar.

Porter (Isle of Wight). Ar. three dragons' heads couped gu. *Crest*—A dragon's head couped gu.

Porter (co. Lancaster). Barry of six or and az. on a bend gu. three escallops of the first.

Porter (cos. Lincoln and Kent). Sa. three church bells ar. a canton erm. *Crest*—A portcullis ar. chained or.

Porter (Wadhurst and Seaford, co. Sussex). Same *Arms* and *Crest,* a crescent for diff.

Porter (co. Lincoln, and St. Margaret's-in-Southernam, co. Suffolk). Sa. three church bells ar. a chief erm. *Crest*—A portcullis ar. nailed and chained or, the chains cast over in fret.

Porter (EDWARD ROBERT PORTER, Esq., of London). Per chev. sa. and ar. in chief three church bells of the second, each charged with an erm. spot counterchanged. *Crest*—An heraldic antelope's head erased ar. attired or, gorged with a collar gu. therefrom, on the centre of the neck, a bell pendent sa. charged with an erm. spot of the first.

Porter (London). Ar. a fess engr. sa. (another, vert) fretty or, in chief three church bells of the second.

Porter (London). Az. two dolphins in pale, embowed and addorsed ar. betw. six crosses crosslet fitchée or, on a chief gu. three leopards' faces of the third.

Porter (co. Warwick). Ar. a bull's head couped gu. armed or.

Porter (Etington, co. Warwick). Sa. three bells ar. a canton erm. *Crest*—A portcullis ar. chained or.

Porter (Claines, co. Worcester. Visit. 1634). Ar. a fess engr. vert, fretty or, in chief three bells sa. *Crest*—A squirrel sejant, holding a bell sa. garnished gold.

Porter. Same *Arms. Crest*—A demi squirrel or, semée of hurts, holding an acorn branch vert, acorned of the first.

Porter. Gu. on a fess or, a torteau charged with a lion pass. guard. of the second (another, betw. three wings gold). *Crest*—A demi antelope or, spotted, collared, and attired gu.

Porter, alias Gloucester. Gu. on a fess or, three hurts, the middle one charged with a lion pass. the other with a fleur-de-lis betw. three wings all of the second. *Crest*—A stag's head erased ar. attired and ducally gorged or, betw. two laurel branches vert.

Porter. Gu. on a fess betw. three wings or, an annulet of the first.

Porter. Ar. on the trunk of a tree raguly vert an eagle, wings expanded gu.

Porter. Gu. on a fess betw. an eagle in chief, wings close, and two bucks' heads erased in base all ar. three cinquefoils of the field.

Porter (Alfarthing, co. Surrey; descended from ENDYMION PORTER, Groom of the Bedchamber to Charles I., a celebrated courtier of the period, who was descended from ROBERT PORTER, brother of Sir WILLIAM PORTER, Knt., *temp.* Henry V. ELEANOR, dau. of JOHN PORTER, Esq., of Alfarthing, m. PIERCE WALSH, Esq., co. Waterford, and her son, PIERCE WALSH, inherited the property of his maternal uncle). Sa. three bells ar. a canton erm.

Porter. Az. a fess ar. fretty vert.

Porter. Gu. on a fess betw. a falcon in chief and two bucks' heads couped in base ar. three roses of the field.

Porter (Kingston, co. Meath; Fun. Ent. Ulster's Office, 1623, WILLIAM PORTER, of that place). Gu. three church bells ar.

Porter (Oldbridge, co. Meath; Fun. Ent. Ulster's Office, 1623, MAUDE, wife of WILLIAM PORTER, of that place). Same *Arms*, a crescent for diff.

Porter (Reg. Ulster's Office). Sa. three church bells ar. a canton erm. *Crest*—A cubit arm, habited az. cuffed ar. grasping in the hand ppr. a battle axe also ppr.

Porter (Waterford; confirmed by Hawkins, Ulster, 1717, to NICHOLAS PORTER, son of JOHN PORTER, Esq., of Waterford, by his wife, MARY HOARE, of Shandon). Sa. three bells ar. a canton erm. *Crest*—A stag's head couped sa. attired or.

Porter (exemplified to THOMAS STEWART ELLISON-MACARTNEY, Lieutenant R.N., son of JOHN WILLIAM ELLISON-MACARTNEY, Esq., of the Palace, Clogher, co. Tyrone, M.P., by ELIZABETH PHŒBE his wife, dau. of Rev. JOHN GREY PORTER, of Kilskeery, co. Tyrone, on his assuming, by royal licence, 1875, the surname and arms of PORTER, in lieu of those of ELLISON-MACARTNEY). Sa. three bells ar. a canton of the last charged with a portcullis ppr. *Crest*—A portcullis ppr. therefrom pendent by a chain or, a shield of the arms. *Motto*—Et fide et virtute.

Porter (exemplified to JOHN PORTER ARCHDALL, of Caius College, Cambridge, son of NICHOLAS MONTGOMERY ARCHDALL, Esq., of Crockmacrieve, co. Fermanagh, by ADELAIDE MARY, his wife, dau. of Rev. JOHN GREY PORTER, of Kilskeery, co. Tyrone, on his assuming, by royal licence, 1876, the surname and arms of PORTER, in lieu of ARCHDALL). *Arms*, *Crest*, and *Motto*, as preceding.

Porter (Troquain, co. Kirkcudbright; granted 1804). Quarterly, 1st, ar. a dexter arm embowed and erased ppr. holding a key az.; 2nd and 3rd, gu. a mastiff dog sejant, holding in the forepaws a Lochaber axe ppr.; 4th, ar. a church bell az. tongued or. *Crest*—A dexter arm in armour embowed, grasping a sword all ppr. *Motto*—Vigilantiâ et virtute.

Porterfield (that Ilk, co. Renfrew). Or, a bendlet betw. a stag's head erased in chief and a hunting-horn in base sa. garnished gu. *Crest*—A branch of palm ppr. *Motto*—Sub pondere sursum.

Portester, or Potester (co. York). Ar. a cross betw. four martlets sa.

Portington (cos. Lincoln and York). Gu. on a bend ar. three martlets sa. *Crest*—A dexter hand holding a dart, point downwards ppr.

Portington (Barnby-Dun, co. York). Gu. on a bend ar. three martlets sa. *Crest*—A goat's head couped or.

Portington (Malton, co. York. Visit. Dugdale). Gu. on a bend ar. three martlets sa.

Portland, Duke of. See BENTINCK.

Portman (Bryanston, co. Dorset, and Orchard Portman, co. Somerset, bart., extinct 1695; a family of great distinction and antiquity, co. Somerset; descended from WALTER PORTMAN, son of WILLIAM PORTMAN, of Taunton, *temp.* Henry IV., a lineal descendant of THOMAS PORTMAN, *temp.* Edward I.). Or, a fleur-de-lis az. *Crest*—A talbot sejant or.

Portman (BERKELEY-PORTMAN, Orchard-Portman, co. Somerset; Sir WILLIAM PORTMAN, fifth bart. of Orchard Portman, settled his estates on his next heirs in the female line; they eventually devolved on WILLIAM BERKELEY, Esq., of Pylle, who assumed the surname of PORTMAN; his great-grandson, EDWARD BERKELEY PORTMAN, was created, 1837, Baron Portman, and 1873, Viscount Portman). Quarterly, 1st and 4th, 816

same as the last, for PORTMAN; 2nd and 3rd, gu. a chev. erm. betw. ten crosses pattée or, for BERKELEY. *Crests*—1st, PORTMAN: Same as the last; 2nd, BERKELEY: A unicorn gu.

Portman (*Baron Portman*). Same *Arms* and *Crest* as the preceding. *Supporters*—Dexter, a savage wreathed about the head and waist with ivy, in his dexter hand a club resting on the shoulder ppr.; sinister, a talbot or. *Motto*—Make a clean heart and a cheerful spirit.

Portnew. Gu. a gate or; another, Three goats pass. or.

Portour (Alwamby, co. Cumberland). Gu. on a fess or, three bells az. within a bordure engr. ar.

Port Pigham, alias West Lowe (co. Cornwall). Has no armorial ensign. The seal is very ancient, and represents a man habited as an Indian, on his head a cap, in his dexter hand a long bow, in his sinister an arrow.

Portrea (Barnstaple, co. Devon). Az. three sceptres in bend or.

Portridge (cos. Suffolk and Salop). Chequy ar. and sa. on a bend gu. three escallops or.

Ports, Le. Az. three towers with cupolas or, ports sa.

Portsmouth, Earl of. See WALLOP.

Portsmouth, Town of. Az. a crescent or, surmounted by an estoile of eight points of the last.

Porwings. Sa. three mullets within a bordure engr. or.

Posingworth, Possingworth, or Posynworth. Paly of six argled, the angles in bend dexter ar. and az. *Crest*—Out of a ducal coronet or, a plume of ostrich feathers ppr.

Posingworth. Paly of six ar. and az.; another, Same *Arms*, per fess counterchanged.

Posingworth. Per pale ar. and az. a pale counterchanged.

Possall. Ar. a cross flory sa. in the 1st quarter an inescutcheon gu. charged with a lion ramp. or (another, the lion ar.).

Posselow. Bendy of ten az. and or, on a canton ar. a lion pass. guard. gu.

Posthall. Ar. a cross flory sa.

Postlethwaite (The Oaks, co. Cumberland). Ar. a chev. betw. three boars heads couped sa. *Crest*—Out of a ducal coronet or, a boar's head sa. *Motto*—Semper paratus.

Postlethwaite. Ar. a bugle-horn sa. stringed gu. in base a chev. of the second, a chief indented of the third.

Postmer. Sa. a chev. betw. three eagles displ. or.

Poston. Ar. on a fess betw. three arches gu. a lion pass. or, within two bezants. *Crest*—A demi lion or, supporting an arch gu.

Postred. Erm. three chevronels sa. (another, ermines).

Potale. Vert on a chev. engr. ar. betw. three magpies ppr. as many pellets.

Pote (Cloughton, co. Devon. Visit. Devon, 1620). Az. a chev. engr. cotised ar. betw. three doves of the second.

Potersten. Ar. a cross betw. four martlets sa.

Potesford, or Putford (Church Putford, co. Devon; the co-heiresses m. STOCKHEY and POLLARD). Ar. a plain cross fitchée in base gu.

Potetort. Or, on a saltire engr. sa. a cinquefoil of the first.

Potey. Ar. on a bend gu. three crosses crosslet or.

Potkin (Cambridge, Rickmansworth, co. Herts, and Sevenoaks, co. Kent; granted 1517). Ar. on a fess betw. three talbots gu. as many lozenges or. *Crest*—A stag's head erased sa. attired or, the nose ar.

Potman (co. Kent). Paly of six or and sa. on a chief of the second three cinquefoils of the first.

Potrister. Ar. a cross betw. four eagles sa.

Pott (Stancliff, co. Derby, and co. Chester). Barry of ten ar. and sa. on a bend az. three trefoils slipped or. *Crest*—On a mount vert a greyhound couchant gu. collared and ringed or.

Pott, or Potts (London, and co. Norfolk). Az. two bars or, over all a bend of the last. *Crest*, granted 1583—A leopard, or ounce, sejant ppr. collared, lined, and ringed az. *Another Crest*—On a mount vert an ounce sejant ppr. collared and chained or.

Pott (Pott Hall, co. Chester). Same *Arms*. *Crest*—A wild cat sejant, collared and chained or.

Pott (Bentham Hill, co. Kent). Az. two bars debruised by a bendlet or. *Crest*—On a mount vert a leopard sejant ppr. collared and chained or. *Motto*—Fortis et astutus.

Potte (impalement Fun. Ent. Ulster's Office, 1617, ROBERT FITZ SYMON, whose wife was ANNE POTTE). Barry of six az. and or, a bend of the last.

Pottenhall. Or, on a fess az. three increscents of the first.

Potter (co. Chester). Ar. a chev. gu. betw. three erm. spots.

Potter (cos. Devon, Kent, Oxford, Leicester, and Somerset). Sa. a fess erm. betw. three cinquefoils ar. (another, or). *Crest*—A seahorse or (another, ppr.).

Potter (CHRISTOPHER POTTER, D.D., Provost of Queen's College, Oxford, and Dean of Worcester, d. 3 March, 1645). Ar. on a pale az. three pairs of wings conjoined and elevated of the first.

Potter (Buile Hill, near Manchester; Sir JOHN POTTER, Knt., J.P. for that city and co. Lancaster, son of Sir THOMAS POTTER, the first Mayor of Manchester, received knighthood on the Queen's visit to that city in 1851). Sa. on a fess erm. betw. in chief two cinquefoils pierced or, and in base a knight's helmet ppr. a terrestrial globe also ppr. betw. two garbs of the third. *Crest*—On a mount vert a seahorse erect ppr. gorged with a collar gemel sa. and supporting a rudder or.

Potter. Ar. on a castle az. three wings conjoined of the first. *Crest*—A star of twelve rays or, betw. a pair of wings ar.

Potter. Ar. on a chief az. two fleshpots ar.

Potter (WILLIAM POTTER, Esq., of Liverpool). Az. a fess vairé or and gu. cotised engr. betw. three cinquefoils of the second. *Crest*—A seahorse or, in front of a cross crosslet fitchée gu.

Potter (co. Norfolk). Sa. a fess betw. three mullets ar. *Crest*—An elephant's head erased ar. guttée de sang.

Potter (co. Kent). Per saltire az. and gu. a griffin pass. betw. five fleurs-de-lis, two in chief and three in base or.

Pottinger (Mount Pottinger, co. Devon). Vert an Eastern crown or, betw. three pelicans in their piety ppr. on a canton ar. a cross gu. *Crest*—A dexter arm embowed in armour grasping a sword all ppr. surmounted by an Eastern crown gu. *Motto*—Virtus in ardua.

Pottinger (bart., Sir HENRY POTTINGER, G.C.B., fifth son of ELDRED CURWEN POTTINGER, Esq., of Mount Pottinger, was created a bart. 1839). Vert an Eastern crown or, betw. three pelicans in their piety ppr. a canton or. charged with a cross gu. *Crest*—A dexter arm embowed in armour ppr. garnished or, the hand gauntleted and grasping a sword also ppr. hilted and pommelled gold, the arm encircled by an Eastern crown gu. *Supporters* (granted to the first bart. as a G.C.B.)—Dexter, a Chinese mandarin habited ppr. holding a scroll; sinister, a Scinde soldier habited and equipped ppr. in his exterior hand a Scinde firelock ppr. *Motto*—Virtus in ardua.

Pottman. Per bend embattled or and az. *Crest*—A fleur-de-lis gu.

Potton (co. Hants). Ar. on a fess betw. three mullets sa. as many bezants.

Potts (South Shields, co. Durham). Az. two bars or, over all a bend of the last. *Crest*—On a mount vert an ounce sejant ppr. collared and chained or.

Potts. Ar. a bend sa.

Potts (Mannington, co. Norfolk, bart., extinct; descended from JOHN POT, grandson of Sir WILLIAM POT, 1583. Sir JOHN POTTS, of Mannington, M.P. for Norfolk, was created a bart. 14 Aug. 1641; arms granted 1583). Az. two bars or, over all a bend of the last. *Crest*—A leopard sejant ppr. collared and lined or.

Potts. See POTT.

Potyn (co. Kent; SYMOND POTYN, Esq., was M.P. in several Parliaments for the city of Rochester, and the benevolent founder of the hospital called The Hospital of St. Catherine of Rochester). Ar. semée-de-lis az.

Poulain (Jersey). Ar. a holly bush vert, on a canton gu. a cross engr. ar.

Poulden. Ar. a Negro's head couped sa. *Crest*—A hand issuing from a cloud, holding a book expanded all ppr.

Poullett (*Earl Poulett*, chief of the ancient and noble family of POLLETT, POWLETT, and PAULETT, whose junior branches were ennobled under the titles of *Marquess of Winchester*, extant, and *Duke of Bolton*, extinct). Sa. three swords in pile, points in base ar. pommels and hilts or. *Crest*—An arm embowed in armour, holding in the hand a sword all ppr. *Supporters*—Dexter, a savage man; sinister, a woman, both ppr. wreathed about their temples and loins with leaves vert. *Motto*—Gardez la foi.

Pouley (co. Essex). Or, three eagles displ. az. *Crest*—An eagle displ. az. within an annulet or.

Poulteney (co. Warwick). Ar. two bars gu. in chief three leopards' faces sa.

Poulter (co. Essex). Ar. two bendlets sa.

Poulter. Ar. two bendlets sa. betw. as many Cornish choughs ppr. *Crest*—A ship in full sail ppr.

Poulter. Ar. three mullets sa. a chief gu.

Poulterers, Company of (London; incorporated 1504). Ar. on a chev. betw. three storks gu. as many swans ppr.

817

Crest—On a mural coronet sa. a stork with **wings expanded** gu. *Supporters*—Two pelicans or, with **wings indorsed,** vulning their breasts ppr.

Poultney (Miserton, co. Leicester, and co. York). Ar. a fess dancettée gu. in chief three leopards' faces sa. *Crest*—A leopard's head guard. erased at the neck sa. gorged with a ducal coronet or. *Another Crest*, without the coronet.

Poultney-Priory. Gu. three covered cups or, betw. as many gouttes of the last.

Poulton (Disborough, co. Northampton). Ar. a fess betw. three mullets sa. (another, on the fess three bezants).

Pounces. Sa. three dexter hands clenched ar.

Pouncey. See POUNSE.

Pound (Drayton, co. Hants). Ar. on a fess gu. betw. two dragons' heads couped sa. in chief, and in base a cross formée fitchée of the last, three mullets of the field. *Crest*—A castle ppr.

Pound, or De la Pound. Az. fretty ar. on a chief of the last three torteaux.

Pound. Ar. on a fess gu. betw. two boars' heads couped sa. and a cross pattée fitchée of the third, three mullets of the first.

Poune (co. Hertford). Ar. on a saltire per saltire vert and gu. five crescents or, betw. four eagles' heads erased sa.

Pounse, or Pouncy (co. Dorset and London). Sa. two wings conjoined ar. a bordure engr. of the last.

Pount (co. Lincoln, 1640). Gu. two wings conjoined in fesse ar. a bordure engr. or, a crescent for diff.

Pount, or Point. Az. a bridge of two arches ar.

Pourdon. Erm. a chev. sa. on a chief of the last a leopard's face or.

Povey (*temp.* Charles II.; confirmed 12 May, 1588). Sa. a bend engr. betw. six cinquefoils or.

Povey (London; granted Nov. 1614). Sa. on a bend engr. betw. six cinquefoils or, an annulet of the field. *Crest*—Out of a mural crown or, a griffin's head ppr. an annulet for diff.

Povey. Sa. a bend engr. ar. betw. six cinquefoils or. *Crest*—A buglehorn sa. viroled or, stringed gu.

Povey (Sir JOHN POVEY, Lord Chief Justice of the King's Bench in Ireland; Fun. Ent. Ulster's Office, 1677, of Lady POVEY). Sa. a bend engr. betw. six cinquefoils or.

Powcher. Ar. a cinquefoil gu.

Powcher. Per pale ar. and or, a cinquefoil gu.

Powcher. Gu. a cinquefoil per pale ar. and or.

Powderell, Powndrell, or Powtrell. Or, on a bend engr. az. three fleurs-de-lis of the first.

Powe. Ar. a fess betw. three crescents az. issuing flames ppr. *Crest*—A crescent az.

Powel, or Powell. Sa. an escutcheon betw. three roses ar. *Crest*—A demi savage holding a club ppr.

Powell (Penkelly, co. Carmarthen). Or, two chev. betw. three lions' gambs erased gu.

Powell (Nanteos, co. Cardigan; descended from Sir THOMAS POWELL, a learned judge *temp.* William III.). Ar. a cross flory engr. sa. betw. four Cornish choughs ppr. on a chief az. a boar's head couped ar. tusked or, langued gu. *Crest*—A talbot's head couped ppr. *Motto*—Inter hestas et hostes.

Powell (co. Brecknock). Az. a stag pass. ar. attired or, betw. the attires a regal crown ppr.

Powell (cos. Chester and Hertford). Sa. three roses ar. seeded or.

Powell (Llwydarth, Lanharen, and Maesteg, co. Glamorgan). Sa. a chev. betw. three fleurs-de-lis ar. *Crest*—A boar's head cabossed.

Powell (Penkelly, co. Hereford). Or, a chev. betw. three lions' gambs couped or. *Crest*—A lion's gamb erased or.

Powell (St. Alban's, co. Herts). Sa. three roses ar. slipped vert. *Crest*—Out of a ducal coronet or, a demi griffin sa. beaked and legged gold.

Powell (Horton Old Hall, Bradford, co. York). Sa. three escocheons ar. each charged with a boar's **head** erased **of the field,** a bordure or. *Crest*—A lion ramp. sa. **sa.** gorged with a double chain or, therefrom pendent a pheon ar. and resting the sinister forepaw upon a shield gold, charged with an eagle's head erased az. *Motto*—Omne bonum, Dei donum.

Powell (Sir JOHN POWELL, Judge of the King's Bench *temp.* William III.). Per pale az. and gu. three lioncels ramp. ar.

Powell (Fellow of Jesus College, d. 6 Feb. 1685). Ar. a lion ramp. sa. crowned or.

Powell (Boughton Monchensy, co. Kent, Ednop and Newton, co. Salop, and Ewhurst, co. Sussex; descended from ETHELYSTAN GLODRYDD, Prince of Ferlys; of this family was RICHARD POWELL, of Ednor, author of the "Pentarchia," a short history of the royal tribes of Wales and their descendants, written about the year 1020; Sir NATHANIEL POWELL, of Ewhurst and Boughton-Monchensy, son of

MEREDITH POWELL, of Brampton Ralf, co. Somerset, and grandson of JOHN-AP-HOWELL, of Ednop, co. Salop, was created a bart. in 1661). Gu. a lion ramp. reguard. or, quartering, Ar. three boars' heads couped sa.

Powell (Sandford, co. Oxford). Or, a lion ramp. sa. a fess gu.

Powell (co. Oxford). Or, on two chev. betw. three wells az. as many lions' gambs erased ar.

Powell (Park, co. Salop). Per fess or and ar. a lion ramp. gu.

Powell (Worthen and All-Stretton, co. Salop). Ar. three boars' heads couped sa.

Powell (Parkhall, co. Salop). Az. on a chief or, a lion ramp. issuant gu.

Powell (Bruton, co. Somerset; granted 1584). Per pale gu. and az. crusily fitchée or, a lion ramp. of the last. Crest— A lion pass. resting the dexter paw on a broken tilting-spear ar.

Powell (Pengethley, co. Hereford, bart., extinct 1653; Sir EDWARD POWELL was created a bart. 1622, but the title expired. See HINSON). Or, a chev. betw. three lions' gambs erased gu.

Powell (Fulham, co. Middlesex, and St. James, Clerkenwell; RICHARD POWELL, Esq., of the latter place, Visit. Middlesex, 1663, son of EDWARD POWELL, Esq., of the former place, descended from POWELL, of Pengethley, co. Hereford). Same Arms. Crest—A lion's gamb erased gu.

Powell (Hinton, co. Hereford). Ar. a chev. betw. three roses gu. seeded or, barbed vert. Crest—Out of a ducal coronet or, a demi griffin sa. beaked and legged gold.

Powell (Castle Madoc, co. Brecknock; descended through LLEWELLYN-AP-EINION SAIS, brother of the renowned DAVID GAM, from BLEDDYN-AP-MAENYRCH, Lord of Brecon, temp. William II.; HUGH PRICE, Esq., of Castle Madoc, High Sheriff, of the co. in 1815, was great-grandson of ROGER PRICE, Esq., of Maes-yr-onn, by PENELOPE, his wife, dau. of HUGH HOWELL POWELL, Esq., of Castle Madoc, who d. 1749). Sa. a chev. betw. three spearheads or, embrued gu.

Powell (Stanage Park, co. Radnor; descended through WALTER POWELL, of Bucknell, co. Salop, living temp. Queen Elizabeth, from RHYS-AP-TUDOR, King of South Wales). Quarterly, 1st and 4th, gu. a lion ramp. or, a bordure engr. of the last, a mullet within an annulet gold for diff.; 2nd and 3rd, gu. a bend betw. six lions' heads erased ar., for SKULL.

Powell (Brandlesome Hall, co. Lancaster; HENRY FOLLIOTT POWELL, Esq., of Brandlesome Hall, son of SAMUEL POWELL, Esq., of Hammerton Hall, co. York, and Brandlesome Hall, co. Lancaster, and great-great-grandson of SAMUEL POWELL, Esq., of Stanage Park, by the Hon. ELIZABETH FOLLIOTT, his wife, sister and co-heir of HENRY, Lord Folliott, became representative of the ancient family of POWELL, of Stanage). Quarterly, 1st and 4th, gu. a lion ramp. within a bordure engr. or, for POWELL; 2nd, gu. a bend betw. six lions' heads erased ar., for SKULL; 3rd, ar. a lion ramp. double queued purp. ducally crowned or, for FOLLIOTT. Crest—A lion's head erased ar. gorged with a collar flory counterflory gu. Motto—Anima in amicis una.

Powell (Hurdcott House, co. Wilts; a branch of Penkelly, co. Hereford, which settled in co. Wilts temp. Charles I.; Sir ALEXANDER POWELL, of New Sarum, knighted in 1702, Recorder for that city, was grandson of JOHN POWELL, Esq., of New Sarum, was father of FRANCIS POWELL, Esq., of Hurdcott House, whose son, ALEXANDER POWELL, Esq., of Hurdcott House, was M.P. for the borough of Downton). Or, a chev. betw. three lions' gambs erect and erased gu. Crest—A lion's gamb, as in the arms. Motto—Spes mea, Christus erit.

Powell (Filworth, co. Surrey). Ar. a lion ramp. sa. a fess engr. gu.

Powell (Horsley, co. Denbigh, bart., extinct temp. William III.; descended through IORWERTH VYCHAN, fourth son of IORWERTH AP DAVID, from SANDDE HARDD, Lord of Burton). Sa. an escutcheon betw. three roses ar.

Powell (co. Surrey). Ar. a chev. gu. betw. three garbs vert. Crest—A lion ramp. ar. holding a garb vert.

Powell (Newicke, co. Sussex). Per fess or and ar. a lion ramp. guard. gu. Crest—A lion pass. or, holding in the dexter paw the broken shaft of a spear erect ppr.

Powell (Wales). Per fess ar. and sa. a lion ramp. counterchanged.

Powell. Per fess or and ar. a lion ramp. gu. Crest—Two broken spears in saltire ppr. (the dexter the top, and the sinister the bottom of the spear, resting on the wreath), the whole within two branches of laurel disposed orleways vert.

Powell. Az. a lion ramp. guard. ar. Crest—A boar pass. sa. collared and lined or; another, Ar. three boars' heads bendways couped sa.; another, Ar. a lion ramp. sa.

crowned gu.; another, Or, a lion ramp. gu. a canton of the last; another, Ar. a cross botonnée engr. az. betw four birds gu. on a canton sa. a chev. betw. three spear-heads of the first.

Powell (JEFFREYS-POWELL, of Broynllis, co. Brecon; exemplified to DAVID JEFFREYS upon his assuming, by royal licence, the additional surname of POWELL). Quarterly, 1st and 4th, ar. on a chev. gu. betw. in chief two garbs vert and in base a boar's head erased sa. three pallets of the field, for POWELL; 2nd and 3rd, sa. a chev. embattled chequy or and az. betw. in chief two spearheads imbrued ppr. and in base a garb of the second, for JEFFREYS. Crests—1st, POWELL: A lion ramp. ar. holding betw. the paws a garb vert and supporting with the dexter hind paw an escocheon sa. charged with a boar's head erased ar.; 2nd, JEFFREYS: Upon the stump of a tree betw. two palm branches ppr. a heron ar. holding in the beak a spearhead ppr. Motto—Labore et scientiâ.

Powell (Banlahan, co. Cork; confirmed to HENRY CLARING-BOLD POWELL, Esq., J.P., Colonel in the Army, second, but eldest surviving, son of the late EDWARD POWELL, Esq., Major in the Army; traditionally descended from the ancient Welsh family of POWELL, or AP HOWELL, of Penkelly). Or, two chevronels betw. three lions' gambs erased gu. in the centre chief point a trefoil slipped vert. Crest—Out of a ducal coronet or, a demi griffin vert, charged on the shoulder with a trefoil slipped gold. Motto—Edrych i fynw.

Powell (SWEETMAN-POWELL; exemplified to JOHN MICHAEL SWEETMAN, Esq., son and heir of the late MICHAEL JAMES SWEETMAN, Esq., of Lamberton Park, Queen's co., and of MARY MARGARET, his wife, only child of MICHAEL POWELL, Esq., of Fitzwilliam Square, Dublin, on his assuming, by royal licence, 1874, the additional surname and arms of POWELL, in compliance with the will of his maternal grandfather). Quarterly, 1st and 4th, ar. on a chev. gu. betw. three garbs vert as many cross crosslets or, for POWELL; 2nd and 3rd, per pale gu. and chequy az. and ar. on the dexter an eagle displ. dimidiated or, in the dexter chief point a mullet of the last, for SWEETMAN. Crests—1st: A lion ramp. ar. charged with a cross crosslet gu. and holding betw. the paws a garb vert, for POWELL; 2nd: Out of an antique crown or, a griffin's head gu. charged with a mullet gold, for SWEETMAN. Motto—Vi et virtute; and over the second crest—Spera in Deo.

Power, formerly Le Poer (co. Waterford; founded in Ireland by Sir ROGER LE POER, a valiant knight, who went to Ireland with Strongbow, 1172. Concerning him Giraldus says, "though young and beardless, he showed himself such a lusty, valiant, and courageous gentleman, and grew into such good credit, that he was appointed to the government of the country about Leighlin and Ossory." Sir ROGER m. a niece of Sir ARMORICUS TRISTRAM, ancestor of the Earls of Howth, and was slain 1188). Ar. a chief indented sa.

Power (Baron of Donhill, co. Waterford, A.D. 1273). Ar. on a chief indented sa. three lions ramp. of the first.

Power (Kilmeadon, co. Waterford; descended from POWER, of Donhill; Fun. Ent. Ulster's Office, 1677, Colonel MILES, or MILO POWER, grandson of JOHN POWER, Esq., of Kilmeadon, temp. Queen Elizabeth). Ar. a bend engr. gu. on a chief of the last three escallops of the field.

Power (Kilbolane, co. Cork; transplanted to Connaught by Oliver Cromwell; descended from Sir WILLIAM POWER b. 1545, knighted by Sir Arthur Chichester, Lord Deputy of Ireland, eldest of JOHN POWER, Esq., of Kilmeadon, temp. Queen Elizabeth, 24 March, 1609, d. 1649, aged 105 years). Same Arms. Crest—A stag's head couped sa.

Power (Corheen, co. Galway; descended from Kilbolane, the representative, DAVID POWER, Esq., of Corheen, co. Galway, b. 1685, left an only dau. and heiress, FRANCES POWER, m. RICHARD TRENCH, Esq., of Garbally, and had a son, WILLIAM POWER KEATING TRENCH, first Earl of Clancarty. Arms confirmed by Fortescue, Ulster, to DAVID POWER, Esq., of Corheen, co. Galway). Ar. a chief indented sa. Crest—A buck's head cabossed ar. attired or, betw. the attires a crucifix ppr.

Power (Rosskeen, co. Cork; descended through POWER, of Carrialyne and Kilbolane, from POWER, of Kilmeadon). Ar. on a chief indented sa. three escallops of the field. Crest—A buck's head cabossed ar. attired or, betw. the attires or, a crucifix ppr. Motto—Per crucem ad coronam.

Power (Baron Power, of Curraghmore, and Earl of Tyrone; barony dormant, earldom extinct 1704; Sir RICHARD POWER, of Curraghmore, was created Baron Power, of Curraghmore, by patent, 13 Sept. 1535, with remainder to the heirs male of his body; his descendant, RICHARD, sixth Lord Power, was created, 1673, *Earl of Tyrone:* JAMES, third Earl, *d. s. p. m.* 1704, when the earldom became extinct, and the barony reverted to the male heir of the body of the grantee, who was then Col. JOHN POWER of James II.'s army, attainted after the battle of the Boyne; his only son, HENRY POWER, called *Lord Power,* petitioned for the Curraghmore estates in 1717, and *d s. p.* 1742; EDMOND POWER, or DE LA POER, of Gurteen, now Gurteen La Poer, *Count De la Poer,* claims to be the heir male of the body of RICHARD LE POER, the patentee in 1535). Same *Arms.* *Crest*—A stag's head cabossed ppr. attired or, betw. the attires a crucifix ppr. *Supporters*—Two angels ppr. vested ar. crined and winged or, each holding in the exterior hand a sword also ppr. pommels and hilts gold.

Power (Gurteen La Poer, co. Waterford; FRANCES, widow of JOHN POWER, Esq., of Gurteen, and mother of EDMOND POWER, Esq., of Gurteen La Poer, *Count De la Poer,* was authorised, for herself and her issue, by royal licence, 1863, to take the name of DE LA POER, instead of POWER, *Count De la Poer* is the male heir and representative of JOHN POWER FITZ-EDMOND, Esq., of Grange, co. Galway, who became "nearest heir male" of HENRY POWER, called *Lord Power,* the heir male of the third and last *Earl of Tyrone*). Same *Arms* and *Crest,* a mullet for diff. *Motto*—Per crucem ad coronam.

Power (Clashmore, co. Waterford; RICHARD POWER, Esq., the male representative of this line, *m.* DOROTHEA, sister of ROBERT SHAPLAND, first *Lord Carew,* and left an only dau. and heiress, ELIZABETH ANNE POWER, *m.* 1835, FRANCIS THEOPHILUS HENRY, twelfth *Earl of Huntingdon,* and *d.* 1857). Same *Arms* and *Crest.*

Power (Gardenmorres, co. Waterford; ELIZABETH POWER, dau. and heir of RICHARD POWER, Esq., of Gardenmorres, *m.* JOHN O'SHEE, Esq., of Sheestown, and was grandmother of NICHOLAS POWER O'SHEE, Esq., now of Gardenmorres and Sheestown). Same *Arms.*

Power (Kilfane, co. Kilkenny, bart.). Ar. a bend engr. gu. betw. two foxes' heads erased ppr. on a chief of the second three escallops of the field. *Crest*—A stag's head erased ppr. *Motto*—Pro patriâ semper.

Power (Edermine, co. Wexford, bart.; granted by Betham, Ulster, to JOHN POWER, Esq., of Roebuck House, co. Dublin, and Sampton, co. Wexford; created a bart. 1841). Per saltire or and ar. three lions ramp. az. armed and langued gu. in the centre chief section an open helmet affronted, unbarred ppr. on a chief gu. three escallops ar. *Crest*—A buck's head caboshed quarterly gu. and or, betw. the horns counterchanged a cross calvary erect gu. *Motto*—Per crucem ad coronam.

Power (The Hill Court, near Ross, co. Hereford; granted by Betham, Ulster, to Major-Gen. Sir MANLEY POWER, K.C.B., grandson of THOMAS POWER, Esq., some time Captain of the Battle Axe Guards). Gu. a sword in bend sinister ppr. hilted and pommelled or, the point elevated, and blade encompassed with a laurel wreath of the last, on a chief ar. betw. two mullets sa. pierced of the field, in the centre chief point, pendent from a riband gu. fimbriated az. a representation of the golden cross and clasp presented to Sir MANLEY POWER for his services in the Peninsula. *Crest* —Issuant from a mural crown or, a stag's head sa. gorged with a laurel wreath and attired gold. *Motto*—Angelis suis præcipiet de te.

Power (MANDEVILLE-POWER; exemplified to FRANCIS MAN-DEVILLE, Esq., of Wilmar, co. Tipperary, on his assuming, by royal licence, 1814, the additional surname and arms of POWER, pursuant to the will of his maternal uncle, WILLIAM POWER, of Ballydine, co. Tipperary). Quarterly, 1st and 4th, ar. a bend engr. gu. on a chief of the last three escallops of the first, for POWER; 2nd and 3rd, quarterly, or and gu. over all an escarbuncle sa., for MANDEVILLE. *Crest*—A stag's head cabossed ar. attired or, betw. the attires a calvary cross of the first, thereon a representation of the crucifixion ppr. *Motto*—Per crucem ad coronam.

Power (LYNCH-POWER; exemplified to EDMOND LYNCH, Esq., of Dublin, on his assuming, by royal licence, 1814, the additional surname and arms of POWER, pursuant to the will of his maternal uncle, WILLIAM POWER, Esq., of Ballydine). Quarterly, 1st and 4th, POWER, as the last; 2nd and 3rd, LYNCH, az. a chev. betw. three trefoils slipped or. Same *Crest* and *Motto* as the last.

Power-Lalor. See LALOR.

Power (Powershayes, co. Devon; ROGER POWER, Esq., of Powershayes, *temp.* Henry IV., had an only dau. and heir, CICKLY POWER, *m.* DUKE, of co. Devon; the descendant of this marriage, Sir HENRY DUKE, of Castle Jordan, co. Meath, was knighted by Sir William Fitz-William, **Lord Deputy of** Ireland, 1588). Per pale wavy az. and or.

Power (*Viscount Valentia,* extinct 1642; Sir HENRY POWER, Knt., of Bersham, co. Denbigh, Knight Mareschal of Ireland, and Constable of the Castle of Maryborough, was so created 1620, and *d. s. p.*). Gu. on a chief ar. three mullets pierced sa. *Crest*—A demi stag salient sa. attired and unguled or. *Supporters*—Two angels ppr. vested ar. winged and girdle round the waist or, from the latter a short petticoat az. under petticoat sa. each holding in the exterior hand a sword also ppr. pommel and hilt gold. *Motto*—Angelis suis præcipiet de te.

Power (co. Cornwall). Vert a bend betw. two cotises dancettée or; another, Gu. a fess ar. betw. three mullets of the second pierced sa.; another (co. Devon), Az. a bend cotised indented or.

Power (co. Norfolk). Quarterly, gu. and or, a bordure az.; another, Quarterly, az. and erm. in the 1st quarter a leopard's face or.

Power (Bletchington, co. Surrey; granted 8 June, 1601). Ar. two bars nebulée sa. a mullet or.

Power (Stanton, co. Wilts). Per pale gu. and az. on a chief ar. three mullets sa.

Power (co. Worcester). Gu. a fess ar. in chief two mullets of the last.

Power. Erm. three lions ramp. gu. on a chief sa. as many escallops ar. each charged with a cross of the second. *Crest* —A buck's head cabossed ppr. betw. the attires a cross gu. surmounting an escallop ar.

Power. Ar. three lions ramp. gu. on a chief az. as many escallops of the first. *Crest*—A stag's head cabossed ppr. attired or, on the top of the scalp a cross botonnée gu.

Power. Gu. a fess ar. on a chief of the second two mullets sa.; another. Ar. a fess az. betw. three mullets gu.

Powerdon (co. Derby). Erm. a chev. sa. on a chief of the second three leopards' faces or.

Powers. Per fess vert and ar. a stag trippant betw. three trefoils counterchanged. *Crest*—A stag's head couped ppr. charged on the neck with a trefoil vert.

Powerscourt, Viscount. See WINGFIELD.

Powerton (co. Essex). Erm. on a chev. az. three leopards' faces or; another, Sa. a greyhound salient ar.; another, Ar. three pheons sa. on a chief of the second a greyhound pass. of the first, collared or. *Crest*—A hand ppr. holding a spur or.

Powges. Ar. masculy sa.

Powhill (co. Cornwall). Sa. a saltire engr. erm. a pile in chief or.

Powis, Earl of. See HERBERT.

Powis (Sutton, co. Salop). Or, a lion ramp. gu. a canton of the second. *Crest*—A lion's gamb erased gu. grasping a sceptre or, on the top a fleur-de-lis gold.

Powis (Moreton, co. Chester). Or, a lion's gamb erased in bend betw. two crosses crosslet fitchée gu.

Powis. Or, a lion ramp. within a bordure engr. or (another, ar.); another, Or, a lion ramp. (another, tail forked) gu.; another, Or, a lion's gamb in bend erased gu.

Powkeswell. Sa. a chev. ar. betw. three estoiles or.

Powlbes. Ar. two bends sa. in the sinister chief point a Cornish chough ppr.

Powle (Alford, co. Essex). Az. a fess engr. erm. betw. three lions pass. or. *Crest*—A unicorn pass. az. horned and maned or.

Powle (London; granted 7 May, 1769, to THOMAS POWLE, Esq., Clerk of the Crown, one of the six Clerks of the Court of Chancery, Comptroller of the Haniper, Clerk of the Forest of Waltham, and High Steward to Queen Elizabeth of all her manors in the co. of Essex, *d.* 1601). Same *Arms,* quartering MERTON, or MARTON. *Crest*—A unicorn pass. az. horned, tufted, and hoofed or.

Powle. Gu. three pales vair, on a chief or, an eagle displ. sa. *Crest*—A demi savage brandishing a sabre ppr.

Powle. Az. a chev. erm. betw. six lions ramp. or.

Powles (Eversley, co. Hants). Per pale ar. and az. three mascles counterchanged.

Powlett. See POULETT and PAULETT.

Powlett (*Duke of Cleveland, Earl of Darlington,* and *Baron Barnard;* Lord HARRY GEORGE VANE, third son of WILLIAM HENRY, first *Duke of Cleveland,* by Lady KATHERINE MARGARET POWLETT, his wife, dau. and coheir of HENRY, sixth and last *Duke of Bolton, s.* as third *Duke of Cleveland,* and assumed, 1864, the surname and arms of POWLETT, by royal licence). Quarterly, 1st and 4th, sa. three swords in pile, points to the base ppr., for POWLETT; 2nd, az. three sinister gauntlets or, for VANE; 3rd, quarterly, 1st and 4th, quarterly, FRANCE and ENGLAND, 2nd, SCOT-LAND, 3rd, IRELAND (being the arms of Charles II.), a sinister baton erm., for FITZROY, *Duke of Cleveland.* *Crest*—A falcon rising or, belled gold, and ducally gorged gu. *Supporters* —Dexter, a lion guard. or, ducally crowned az. and gorged with a collar company erm. and az.; sinister, a grey-hound ar. gorged with a collar, as the dexter. *Motto*—Aymes loyaulté.

Powlett-Townshend (*Baron Bayning*, extinct 1866; Hon. WILLIAM TOWNSHEND, second son of CHARLES, second *Viscount Townshend*, *m.* 1725, HENRIETTA, only dau. and heir of Lord WILLIAM POWLETT, and was created *Baron Bayning* 1797; his son, HENRY, third *Lord Bayning*, assumed the surname of POWLETT, 1823). Az. a chev. erm. betw. three escallops ar. a mullet for diff. *Crest*—A buck statant sa. attired or, charged on the body with a mullet ar. for diff. *Supporters*—Dexter, a buck sa. attired, collared, and lined or, the collar charged with three mullets az.; sinister, a leopard ar. pellettée, ducally gorged and lined or, therefrom a shield pendent ar. charged with two bars sa. thereon four escallops gold. *Motto*—Stare super vias antiquas.

Powlett (Legh Powlet, co. Devon). Sa. three swords in pile ar. points to the base, hilts or.

Powlett (co. Hants). Sa. three swords in pile ar. points meeting in base. *Crest*—A sphinx statant, wings expanded ppr.

Powlett (Llandisil, co. Cardigan; exemplified to BARTON WILLIAM POWLETT WALLOP, Esq., upon his assuming, by royal licence, the surname of POWLETT). Sa. three swords in pile, points to the base ppr. pommels and hilts or. *Crest*—A falcon rising or, belled gold, ducally gorged gu.

Powlett (ORDE-POWLETT, *Baron Bolton;* Right Hon. THOMAS ORDE, Secretary to the Treasury, 1782, and Secretary to the Duke of Rutland, Lord Lieutenant of Ireland, and Privy Councillor of Ireland, *m.* JANE MARY PAULETT, illegitimate dau. of CHARLES, fifth *Duke of Bolton*, and having succeeded to the Bolton estates, 1795, assumed the additional surname of POWLETT, and was created *Lord Bolton* 1797). Sa. three swords in pile, points to the base ar. pommels and hilts or, on a canton of the second an escocheon of the field charged with a salmon haurient ppr. *Crest*—A falcon rising or, charged on the breast with an estoile gu. gorged with a ducal coronet az. and holding in the beak a salmon ppr. *Supporters*—Dexter, a hind ppr. gorged with a ducal coronet or, and charged on the shoulder with a rose ar. barbed vert, seeded gold; sinister, a Cornish chough ppr. charged with a rose, as the dexter. *Motto*—Aymez loyauté.

Powley (Radley, co. Suffolk). Or, a lion ramp. sa.

Powlyard. Per pale ar. and vert a lion ramp. gu.

Powmale. Ar. a cross pomelle sa.

Powna (co. Cornwall; the elder line became extinct *temp.* Henry VI.; a co-heir *m.* TRELAWNY). Erm. on a chev. gu. three (sometimes five) oak leaves ar.

Pownall (Pownall, co. Chester; originally, according to Brooke, Somerset Herald, Paynel, or Paganell: "It appears," says that authority, "that members of this family were Chamberlaynes to the Kings, as Earls of Chester, and on that account, in allusion to their office and their name, they bore for crest, a lion's paw holding a golden key." The last male heir, ROBERT DE POWNALL, *d.* 1328, leaving an only dau. and heir, MARGERY, *m.* HUGH FITTON, second son of JOHN FITTON, feudal Lord of Bollyn). Ar. a lion ramp. sa. charged on the breast with a cross pattée az. *Crest*—A lion's gamb erect and erased ppr. grasping a key or, a chain reflexed gold.

Pownall (Barnton, co. Chester; a branch of POWNALL, of Pownall, from which descended the late THOMAS POWNALL, Governor of New Jersey, *d.* 1805; and Sir GEORGE POWNALL, Knt., Provost Marshal General of the Leeward Islands, *d.* 1834). Same *Arms*, &c.

Pownall (Liverpool; claiming descent from POWNALL, of Pownall). Gu. a lion ramp. erm. gorged with a collar gemel az. therefrom pendent an escutcheon of the last charged with a mullet ar. *Crest*—A lion's gamb erased ppr. charged with two mullets in pale ar. in the paw a key in bend sinister or, affixed thereto a chain entwined about the gamb gold. *Motto*—Officium præsto.

Pownall (granted to the descendants of the late THOMAS POWNALL, Esq., of the parish of St. Paul, Covent Garden, London). Or, a lion ramp. sa. charged on the shoulder with a cross pattée of the first, a chief wavy az. thereon a dolphin embowed of the field betw. two crescents ar. *Crest*—A lion's gamb sa. erased and charged with two roses in pale ar. in the paw a key and chain entwined about the gamb affixed thereto in bend sinister, the ward downwards or.

Pownall (Woodlands Lodge, co. Hants). Same *Arms* and *Crest*. *Motto*—Grace me guide.

Pownall. Ar. a saltire gu. a chief vert. *Crest*—A unicorn's head erm.

Powney (Old Windsor, co. Berks; granted 31 May, 1661) Sa. a fess ar. in chief three mascles of the last. *Crest*—A demi eagle, wings expanded sa. charged on the breast with a mascle ar.

820

Pownse. Sa. a hand cienched ar.

Powrie (Woodcocksholme, Scotland). Ar. a saltire engr. gu. charged with another or, betw. four hunting horns sa. *Crest*—A hunting horn az. garnished gu. *Motto*—Vespere et mane.

Powrie (Roswallie, co. Forfar, 1856). Ar. a saltire engr. gu. charged with another or, betw. a hunting horn in chief, two crescents in flanks, and a garb in base all sa. the last banded of the third. *Crest*—A hunting horn az. garnished and stringed gu. *Motto*—Vespere et mane.

Powtrell (West Hallam, co. Derby; originally of Thrumpton, co. Nottingham, where eight generations had resided previously to the reign of Henry V.). Ar. a fess betw. three cinquefoils gu. *Crest*—A hedgehog gu. collared, chained, and quilled or.

Powtrell, or Poundrell (co. Derby). Or (another, ar.) on a bend az. three fleurs-de-lis of the first.

Powtrell. Ar. a fess betw. three roses gu. *Crest*—A Saracen's head issuing ppr.

Powtrell, or Powntrell. Or, on a bend engr. az. three fleurs-de-lis ar. (another, within a bordure gu.).

Powys-Wenwynwyn, Princes of (derived through GWENWYNWYN, Prince of Powys-Wenwynwyn, from GRIFFITH AP MEREDITH, Lord of Mawddwy, second son of MEREDITH AP BLEDDYN, Prince of Powys. The male line terminated with OWEN AP GRIFFITH, last Prince of Powys Wenwynwyn, whose dau. and heir, HAWISE, *m.* Sir JOHN CHARLTON, Knt., summoned to Parliament, 26 July, 1313, as *Baron Charlton* of Powys. GWENWYNWYN had a younger son, MADOC GOCH, Lord of Mawddwy in Merioneth, whose dau. and heir, EFA, *m.* IORWERTH, Lord of Half Edeirnion, eldest son of OWEN BROGYNTYN, Lord of Edeirnion, and from this alliance descended HUGHES, of Gwerclas). *Arms*, those of BLEDDYN AP CYNFYN, King of Powys, viz., Or, a lion ramp. gu. armed and langued az.

Powys (*Baron Lilford*). Or, a lion's gamb erased in bend dexter betw. two crosses crosslet fitchée in bend sinister gu. These arms have been substituted for the former ensigns of the family, viz., Quarterly, 1st and 4th, ar. a lion pass. sa. a bordure indented gu., for LLEWELYN VOELGRWN, seventh Baron of Main-yn-Meifod; 2nd ar, a lion ramp. sa. armed and langued gu., for MEREDITH AP BLEDDYN, Prince of Powys; 3rd, or, a lion ramp. gu. armed and langued az., for BLEDDYN AP CYNFYN, King of Powys. *Crest*—A bear's gamb erased and erect gu. holding a sceptre in bend sinister, headed with a fleur-de-lis or. *Supporters*—Dexter, a reaper, with ears of corn round his hat, a reap-hook in his exterior hand, and a garb erect lying at his feet, all ppr.; sinister, a soldier of the Northampton Yeomanry Cavalry, habited vert, turned up buff, booted, his exterior hand resting upon his sword, the point on the ground all ppr. *Motto*—Parta tueri.

Powys (Berwick, co. Salop; descended from JOHN POWYS, Esq., of Brindrinoke, younger brother of THOMAS POWYS, Esq., of Snitton, *b.* in 1559, ancestor of the *Lords Lilford;* THOMAS JELF POWYS, Esq., of Berwick, had three daus. his co-heirs: I. ANNE CATHERINE, *m.* 1791, WILLIAM ROBERT, Viscount *Feilding;* her second son, the Hon. HENRY WENTWORTH FEILDING, assumed by royal licence, 1832, the surname of POWYS upon succeeding to the estates of Berwick; II. HARRIETT, *m.* JOHN, *Lord Tara*, of Ireland; and III. EMILY LISSEY, *m.* Sir FRANCIS BRIAN HILL, Knt., of Preston Montford). Same *Arms* and *Crest* as POWYS, *Lord Lilford*.

Powys (Westwood, co. Stafford; a branch of POWYS, of Berwick, descended from EDWARD POWYS, Esq., of Westwood, younger brother of THOMAS JELF POWYS, Esq., of Berwick). Same *Arms* and *Crest* as *Lord Lilford*.

Powys (Hardwick House, co. Oxford). Or, a lion's gamb in bend erased gu. betw. two crosses crosslet of the last. *Crest*—A lion's gamb erased gu. grasping a sceptre or.

Powys-Keck (Staughton Grange, co. Leicester). See KECK.

Poxwell (co. Cornwall). Sa. a chev. betw. three estoiles or.

Poxwell (Stroud, co. Dorset). Sa. a chev. ar. betw. three mullets of six points pierced or.

Poyle (Castlezance, co. Cornwall). Ar. a pair of barnacles sa. *Crest*—A hemp-hackle or.

Poyle. Gu. a saltire ar. on a bordure of the second eight hurts.

Poyle. Ar. a saltire gu. a bordure sa. bezantée.

Poyly. Gu. a bend betw. six crosses crosslet ar.

Poynder (Montague Place, Russell Square, London). Sa. two piles issuing out of the base, the points of each ending in a cross pattée counterchanged, in chief a tower ar. in base two martlets of the field. *Crest*—Out of a demi tower ar charged with a cross patonce gu. a cubit arm erect, habited sa. cuffed or, the hand ppr. holding a cross pattée fitchée also ar.

Poynder. Pily counterpily of four traits or and sa. the points ending in crosses formée, two in chief and one in base, in the centre chief point a castle of the second, and in base two martlets of the first, on a chief az. a key erect, wards upwards and to the sinister gold, betw. a rose on the dexter side and a fleur-de-lis on the sinister ar. *Crest*—Issuant out of the battlements of a castle ar. charged with a cross flory gu. a dexter cubit arm vested sa. charged with a key as in the arms, cuffed or, the hand ppr. holding a cross pattée fitchée in bend also ar. The key was granted to Mr. POYNDER, Treasurer of Christ's Hospital.

Poyner (Beslow and Shrewsbury, co. Salop). Or, a parrot close vert, legged gu. *Crest*—A demi buck ramp. ppr. attired or, holding in his feet a chaplet of laurel vert.

Poynes (North Okingdon, co. Essex, and Alderley, co. Gloucester). Barry of eight or and gu. *Crest*—A hand issuing out of clouds ppr.

Poynes (co. Devon). Paly of ten or and gu.

Poynes (co. Sussex). Barry of six or and vert, on a bend gu. three martlets of the first (another, three mullets).

Poynes. Az. a bend or, cotised ar. *Crest*—A demi leopard ducally gorged ppr.

Poynings (*Baron Poynings;* barony passed to PERCY, *Earl of Northumberland, temp.* Henry VI., summoned to Parliament 23 April, 1337). Barry of six or and vert, a bendlet gu., quartering FITZ-PAYN. *Crest*—A dragon's head, wings displ. *Badges*—A key erect, with handle uppermost, surmounted by an antique crown and a unicorn statant.

Poynings (*Baron St. John,* of Basing, abeyance since temp. Henry VI.; LUCAS DE POYNINGS, youngest son of THOMAS, first *Lord Poynings, m.* ISABEL, dau. of HUGH, *Lord St. John,* of Basing, and was summoned to Parliament 1368). Same *Arms.*

Poynings (*Baron Poynings,* extinct 1545; ROBERT DE POYNINGS, second son of ROBERT, fifth *Lord Poynings,* by writ of 1337, was father of Sir EDWARD POYNINGS, an active adherent of Henry VII., whose illegitimate son, Sir THOMAS POYNINGS, was created *Lord Poynings* by patent 1545, *d. s. p.* same year). Same *Arms.*

Poynings. Same *Arms. Crest*—A pomegranate ppr. *Another Crest*—A key ar. crowned or.

Poyntell (London; granted June, 1611). Barry lozengy ar. and gu. on a chief az. three estoiles or.

Poynter (co. Chester). Sa. three piles, the points ending in crosses formée, two in base and one in chief or. *Crest*—An arm bendways, vested sa. cuffed or, pointing with the forefinger ppr.

Poynter, alias Kidley (co. Devon). Gu. three pales or, on a chief of the second as many pellets.

Poynter (Lincoln's Inn, co. Middlesex; granted 1694). Pily counterpily or and sa. the points ending in crosses formée, three in chief and two in base. *Crest*—A hand and arm couped at the elbow, habited sa. cuffed ar. holding in the hand ppr. a baton bendways, ensigned with a cross formée or.

Poyntingdon (Pennicott, co. Devon. Visit. 1620). **Ar.** a bend gu. betw. six fleurs-de-lis vert.

Poynton (co. Chester). Chequy or and az. on a canton gu. a lion ramp. ar.

Poynton (co. York). Or, four lozenges in fess gu. a label of the second.

Poynton. Erm. five fusils in fess sa. betw. three crosses fitchée of the last. *Crest*—A stag's head vert; another, Erm. on a fess fusily sa. three crosses crosslet or; another, Ar. a fess fusily betw. six crosses crosslet sa.; another, Ar. a lion ramp. sa. a bordure of the second semée of bezants; another, Ar. a lion ramp. sa. within an orle of torteaux; another, Quarterly, per fess indented gu. and ar.

Poyntz (Iron Acton, co. Gloucester, Midgham, co. Berks, and Cowdray, co. Sussex ; Sir HUGH POYNTZ had summons to Parliament as a baron in 1295, but the barony fell into abeyance between the daus. of NICHOLAS, the fourth baron, at his decease. A younger branch, descended from the first baron, terminated with Sir JOHN POYNTZ, of Iron Acton, 1680: a junior line continued through the descendants of JOHN POYNTZ, son of ROBERT POYNTZ, of Iron Acton, Sheriff co. Gloucester in 1491; his younger son, WILLIAM POYNTZ, of Ryegate, co. Surrey, was great-great-grandfather of the Right Hon. STEPHEN POYNTZ, of Midgham, co. Berks, Ambassador to Sweden in 1728, grandfather of WILLIAM STEPHEN POYNTZ, Esq., of Midgham House and Cowdray Park, who d. 1840, leaving three daus. his co-heirs, viz. : FRANCES SELINA, *Lady Clinton;* ELIZABETH GEORGIANA, *Countess Spencer;* and ISABELLA, *Marchioness of Exeter*).

Barry of eight or and gu. Visit. Gloucester, 1623. It appears from the Roll of the Siege of Karlaveroc in 1300, that there had been a controversy between Fitz-Alan and Poyntz, respecting this bearing. *Crest*—A cubit arm, the fist clenched ppr. vested in a shirt sleeve ar.

Poyntz (Havant and Bedhampton, co. Northampton; claiming descent from the family of POYNTZ, of Iron Acton). Barry of eight or and gu. a bordure az. a chief wavy of the last, on the dexter a representation of the ship "Solebay," and on the sinister four French ships, all ppr. *Crest*—Out of a naval crown ar. a cubit arm, the hand grasping two flag staffs in saltire ppr. flowing from either a French tricoloured flag, that on the dexter inscribed "Tiburon," and that on the sinister "Impeteaux" in letters of gold.

Poyntz (co. Essex; MARGARET, dau. of JOHN POYNTZ, *temp.* Henry VI., m. RICHARD GLASCOTT, co. Essex. Visit. Essex, 1614). Barry of eight gu. and or, a mullet for diff.

Poyntz (Acton, co. Armagh; a branch of POYNTZ, of Iron Acton; SIR CHARLES POYNTZ, knighted 1630, was father of Sir TOBY POYNTZ, M.P., whose daus. and co-heirs were SARAH, wife of Col. CHARLES STEWART, of Ballintoy, and CHRISTIAN, wife of ROGER HALL, Esq., of Narrow Water, co. Down; from the last named co-heiress descends the family of ORR, of Ballygowan). Barry of eight gu. and or. *Crest*—A cubit arm erect, the fist clenched ppr. vested in a shirt sleeve ar.

Poyntz, or Poynes. Barry of eight gu. and or. *Crest*—A cubit arm erect, the fist clenched ppr. vested in a shirt sleeve ar.; another, Barry of six az. and ar. *Crest*—A sword in pale ppr.

Poyser (London; granted 1772). Az. a fess erminois betw. two lions pass. and counterpass. ar. each crowned with an Eastern coronet or. *Crest*—A stag's head erased gu. attired or, in the mouth an olive branch fructed ppr. charged on the neck with an Eastern crown gold.

Praed (Trevethow, in Lelant, co. Cornwall, *temp.* James I. To WILLIAM PRAED, who d. 1620, a fine monument was erected in Lelant Church, bearing a shield of the *Arms.* The last male heir, JOHN PRAED, Esq., of Trevethow, M.P. for St. Ives in 1708 and 1710, d. in 1717, leaving a dau. and heir, MARTHA PRAED, m. WILLIAM MACKWORTH, Esq., third son of Sir HUMPHREY MACKWORTH, Knt.). Az. six mullets ar. three, two, and one. *Crest*—Out of a five-leaved ducal coronet or, a unicorn's head ar. maned and horned gold.

Praed (MACKWORTH-PRAED, Bitton, Dallamore, and Halwell, co. Devon, and Ousden Hall, co. Suffolk). Quarterly, 1st and 4th, as PRAED, 2nd and 3rd, MACKWORTH, per pale indented sa. and erm. on a chev. gu. five crosses pattée or.

Praed. Az. a lozenge throughout or, charged with a crescent gu. *Crest*—A demi lion az.

Praers (Barthomley, co. Chester). Gu. a scythe ar.

Praers (Stoke, co. Chester). Per chev. vert and erm. a chev. engr. counterchanged.

Prale, or Prall. Sa. two lions combatant ar. crowned or.

Pranes (Westbury, co. Buckingham). Or, a lion ramp. az. on a chief of the second three ostrich feathers ar.

Prannell, or Pranell (Martin Wothy, co. Hants, and London; granted 1584). Or, three bars vert, an eagle displ. sa. *Crest*—An eagle's head sa. issuing out of rays ppr.

Prannell (Rudsmill, co. Hertford). Same *Arms,* the eagle gu. *Crest*—An eagle's head or, issuing out of rays of the last.

Prater (Eton-Water, co. Wilts). Sa. three wolves' heads erased ar. on a chief or, a lion pass. of the first. *Crest*—A pegasus courant sa. ducally gorged or.

Pratt (*Marquess of Camden*). Quarterly, 1st and 4th, sa. on a fess betw. three elephants' heads erased ar. as many mullets of the first, for PRATT; 2nd and 3rd, sa. a chev. betw. three spears' heads ar. the points embrued, for JEFFREYS. *Crests*—1st, PRATT : An elephant's head erased ar.; 2nd : A dragon's head erased vert, holding in the mouth a sinister hand couped at the wrist gu. and about the neck a chain, and pendent therefrom a portcullis or. *Supporters* —Dexter, a griffin sa. beak and claws gu.; sinister, a lion ramp. or, each gorged with a collar ar. charged with three mullets sa. *Motto*—Judicium parium aut lex terræ.

Pratt (Ryston Hall, co. Norfolk; descended from EDMUND PRATT, Esq., Lord of the Manor of Carles in Hockwold, *temp.* Henry VIII.). Ar. on a chev. sa. betw. two pellets, each charged with a martlet of the first in chief, and another pellet in base, charged with a trefoil slipped ar. three mascles or, quartering GYLOUR, viz., Sa. on a chev. betw. three pewits' heads erased erm. beaked gu. as many annulets of the field. *Crest*—Betw. a branch of oak and another of pine ppr. each fructed or, a wolf's head per pale ar. and sa. gorged with a collar, charged with three roundles, all counterchanged, langued and erased gu. *Motto*—Rident florentia prata.

Pratt (Hathern, co. Leicester, and Southwark, co. Surrey; granted 23 August, 1601). Az. three bezants, each charged with a martlet of the first, a chief or. *Crest*— A demi unicorn salient or, holding in the paws a mascle az.

Pratt (co. Leicster). Sa. a chev. or, in base three bezants, each charged with a martlet az. *Crest*—A demi unicorn or, holding a lozenge az.

Pratt (co. Norfolk). Ar. on a chev. sa. betw. three pellets, each charged with a martlet of the field, as many mascles or. *Crest*—A wolf's head per pale ar. and sa. *Another Crest*—A lion's head couped sa. pierced in bend sinister by a broken spear or.

Pratt (London). Ar. on a fess az. three mascles or, betw. as many pellets, on each an annulet of the first.

Pratt (co. Suffolk). Ar. on a chev. sa. betw. three pellets each charged with an escallop or, as many mascles of the third. *Crest*—A lizard vert, ducally gorged and lined or.

Pratt. Ar. on a chev. sa. betw. three pellets as many mascles or. *Crest*—A wolf's head erased quarterly ar. and sa.

Pratt (co. Meath ; JOSEPH PRATT, Esq., *temp.* Charles II.; Fun. Ent. Ulster's Office, 1680, his wife LYDIA, dau. of ABRAHAM CLEMENT, of Killenacrate, co. Cavan). Ar. on a chev. betw. three pellets, each charged with a martlet of the field, as many mascles of the last. *Crest*—A falcon ppr. belled and jessed or.

Pratt (Youghal and Castlemartyr, co. Cork; granted by Betham, Ulster, to Lieut.-General JOHN PRATT, Rev. JAMES PRATT, Rector of Kilnglory, co. Cork, Colonel CHARLES PRATT, and the descendants of their grandfather, JAMES PRATT, Esq., of Youghal). Gu. on a fess or, three mullets sa. betw. as many elephants' heads erased of the second, tusked ar. *Crest*—An elephant's head erased sa. tusked or.

Pratt (Cabra Castle, co. Cavan; confirmed by Betham, Ulster, to Rev. JOSEPH PRATT, of that place). Quarterly, 1st and 4th, ar. on a chev. sa. betw. three pellets, each charged with a martlet of the first, as many mascles of the field, for PRATT; 2nd and 3rd, or, an adder curling and erected on its tail sa., for COACH. *Crest*—A lion's head erased gu. pierced through the back of the neck with a broken spear ppr. *Motto*—Virtute et armis.

Prattenton (Clareland and Hartlebury, co. Worcester. In Hartlebury Church there is a brass plate recording the death of WILLIAM PRATTENTON, 1627. WILLIAM PRATTENTON, Esq., of Clareland, *d. s. p.* 1864, and bequeathed his estate to his grandnephew, Rev. GEORGE DEAKIN ONLEY, who then assumed the surname of PRATTENTON). Gu. on a bend or, three Cornish choughs ppr. *Crest*—A goat's head erased or.

Prattinton (Bewdley, co. Worcester; descended from PRATTENTON, of Clareland. ADAM PRATTINTON was Bailiff or Mayor of Bewdley, 1726; PETER PRATTINTON, M.B., son of WILLIAM PRATTINTON, of Bewdley. was the well-known antiquary of co. Worcester; he *d. s.p.* 1848, and was s. in the representation of this branch by his nephew, WILLIAM PRATTENTON, who also *d. s. p.*, when this branch became extinct). Same *Arms* and *Crest*. *Motto*—Vim vi repellere licet.

Prayers, or Preeres (co. Essex). Gu. a fess (another, a bend) cotised ar. (another, cotises or).

Prayers, or Pryers (co. Rutland). Gu. three escallops or.

Prayes. Gu. a scythe in fess, blade upwards ar.

Preacher. Sa. a chev. ar.

Prelate (Cirencester, co. Gloucester, A.D. 1462). Ar. an escallop gu.

Prendergast (England). Ar. a saltire az. betw. four trefoils vert. *Crest*—A man's head couped at the neck ppr.

Prendergast (The Gurteen, co. Wexford; an Anglo-Norman family, dispossessed by Oliver Cromwell; MAURICE PRENDERGAST, or PRENDLEGAST, an Anglo-Norman knight, accompanied Fitz-Stephen to the conquest of Ireland, and landed at Bag-an-Bon, co. Wexford, 2 May, 1170, with two ships bringing ten knights and a great number of archers; JASPER PRENDERGAST, living 1618, proved five descents at Visit. Wexford, 1618). Vair on a chief or, three oak leaves vert.

Prendergast (Newcastle, co. Tipperary; confirmed by Carney, Ulster, 1697, to Col. THOMAS PRENDERGAST, of Newcastle Prendergast, co. Tipperary, as his ancient bearing;

822

EDMUND PRENDERGAST, Esq., of Newcastle, was confirmed in that Manor, 1639 ; his eldest son, JEFFREY PRENDERGAST, had issue who followed James II. to France, and his younger son, THOMAS PRENDERGAST, was father of Sir THOMAS PRENDERGAST, first bart. of Gort, and of JEFFREY PRENDERGAST, Esq., of Crohane). Gu. a saltire vairé or and az. *Crest*—At heraldic antelope trippant ppr. attired and unguled or. *Motto*—Vincit veritas.

Prendergast (Gort, co. Galway, bart., extinct 1760; ELIZABETH, sister of Sir THOMAS PRENDERGAST, second and last bart., *m.* CHARLES SMYTH, Esq., M.P., Limerick, and her son, JOHN SMYTH, assumed, 1760, the surname of PRENDERGAST, and was created *Viscount Gort* 1816, with special remainder to CHARLES VEREKER, eldest son of his sister JULIANA, who *m.* THOMAS VEREKER, Esq., of Roxborough, co. Limerick). Same *Arms*, *Crest*, and *Motto*.

Prendergast (Crohane, co. Tipperary; descended from JEFFREY PRENDERGAST, brother of Sir THOMAS PRENDERGAST, first bart. of Gort). Same *Arms*, *Crest*, and *Motto*.

Prene, or Prenue. Sa. a chev. or, betw. three hawks' lures ar.

Prenne. Sa. a lion ramp. ar. within an orle of bezants.

Prenne. Sa. a chev. or, betw. three leopards' faces ar.

Prentice. Gyronny of eight az. and or, on a chief ar. a fleur-de-lis betw. two crescents gu. *Crest*—An eagle displ. holding in the dexter claw a dagger, and in the sinister a pistol all ppr.

Prentisse. Az. a chev. betw. three roses ar.

Prenton (Prenton, co. York). Ar. a chev. betw. three annulets gu.

Prentys (Wygenhall and Burston, co. Norfolk). Per chev. or and sa. three greyhounds courant counterchanged, collared gu. *Crest*—A demi greyhound ramp. or, collared, ringed, and lined sa. the line coiled in a knot at the end.

Prescop. Or, on a chief sa. three crosses tau of the field. *Crest*—A horse's head or.

Prescot (Prescot, co. Devon; the heiress seems to have *m.* ALMESCOMBE, who took the name, &c.). Erm. a chev. sa. on a chief or, two leopards' faces gu.

Prescot (Derby, co. Lincoln). Erm. a chev. sa. on a chief of the second two leopards' faces or. *Crest*—Out of a ducal coronet or, a boar's head and neck ar. bristled gold.

Prescot. Per chev. ar. and erm. a chev. and two leopards' faces in chief gu.

Prescott (Theobald's Park, co. Hertford, bart.). Sa. a chev. betw. three owls ar. *Crest*—A cubit arm erect, vested gu. cuff erm. holding in the hand a pitch-pot (or hand beacon) sa. fired ppr. *Motto*—Lux mihi Deus.

Prescott (London, and cos. Lancaster and York, 1627). Same *Arms* and *Crest*.

Prescott (co. Hants). Same *Arms*. *Crest*—On a mural coronet a buck sejant.

Presland, or Prestland (Thoby, co. Essex). Sa. a lion ramp. ar. debruised by a bend gobony or and gu.

Prest (granted in 1823 to EDWARD PREST, Esq., of the city of York). Per bend sinister erminois and sa. on a fess cotised betw. three martlets two mullets all counterchanged. *Crest* —A semi terrestrial globe ppr. thereon a demi pegasus reguard. erm. semée of mullets gu. supporting an anchor erect sa.

Prestland (Prestland and Wardle, co. Chester). *Ancient*— Ar. a chev. betw. three bulls' heads cabossed sa. *Modern*— Sa. a lion ramp. ar. debruised by a bend componée or and gu.

Prestley (co. Hertford and London). See PRIESTLEY.

Preston (Preston Richard, Preston Patrick, Nether Levens, co. Westmoreland, and of the Manor and Abbey of Furness, co. Lancaster). Ar. two bars gu. on a canton of the last a cinquefoil or. *Crests*—1st: On a ruined tower ar. a falcon volant of the same, beaked, legged, and belled or; 2nd: On a chapeau gu. turned up erm. a wolf or. *Motto*—Si Dieu veult.

Preston (Furness Abbey, co. Lancaster, bart., extinct *temp.* Anne). Same *Arms*.

Preston (Holker, co. Lancaster, 1613 and 1664). Ar. two bars gu. on a canton of the second a cinquefoil or. *Crest*—On a tower ar. a stork rising of the last, beaked or.

Preston (Up-Ottery, co. Devon; descended from co. Lancaster). Same *Arms*. *Crest*—On a chapeau gu. turned up erm. a wolf or.

Preston (Flasby Hall, Gargrave, co. York). Same *Arms*. *Crest*—On a ruined tower a falcon rising ar. beaked, legged, and belled or. *Motto*—Si Dieu veult.

Preston (Moreby, near York). Same *Arms*, *Crest*, and *Motto*.

Preston (Askham Bryan Hall, co. York). Same *Arms*, *Crest*, and *Motto*.

Preston (co. Bedford, and Chilwick, co. Hertford; granted 1629). Ar. two bars gu. on a bordure sa. eight cinquefoils or. *Crest*—Out of a mural crown or, a demi fox ramp. sa. gorged with a collar erm.

Preston (co. Cumberland). Ar. (another, erm.) two bars gu. on a canton of the second a cinquefoil or.

Preston (Preston in Amounderness, co. Lancaster, 1613). Or, on a chief sa. (gu. in Visit. of 1664), three crescents of the first. *Crest*, 1664—A wolf pass. ppr.

Preston (Beeston, St. Lawrence, co. Norfolk, bart.). Erm. on a chief sa. three crescents or. *Crest*—A crescent or. *Motto*—Pristinum spero lumen.

Preston (Stanfield Hall, co. Norfolk). Erm. on a chief indented sa. three crescents or.

Preston (Yarmouth). Erm. on a chief sa. three crescents or. *Crest*—A crescent or, betw. two wings sa.

Preston (Dalby Park, Spilsby, co. Lincoln). Or, on a chief sa. three crescents ar. *Crest*—On a chapeau gu. turned up erm. a wolf ppr.

Preston (co. Chester). Ar. a chev. engr. betw. three annulets gu.

Preston (Bawton, co. Suffolk). Sa. a chev. or, fretty gu. betw. three garbs ar.

Preston (Crickett, co. Somerset). Az. ten bezants, four, three, two, and one, on a chief ar. two lions pass. counterpass. sa.

Preston (co. Suffolk). Erm. on a chief sa. three crescents or. *Crest*—A crescent or, betw. two wings az.

Preston (Melton, co. Leicester). Erm. a talbot pass. sa.

Preston (co. Leicester). Ar. on a bend sa. betw. six crosses crosslet fitchée gu. three bezants.

Preston (co. Lincoln). Or, three garbs gu. banded ar.

Preston (*Viscount Gormanston*, Premier Viscount in the Peerage of Ireland, and *Baron Gormanston* of Whitewood, co. Meath, in the Peerage of the United Kingdom; descended from ROGER DE PRESTON, Justice of the Common Pleas in Ireland, 1 Edward III., A.D. 1327, fourth in descent from the Chief Justice, Sir ROBERT PRESTON, Lord Deputy of Ireland, A.D. 1478, was created same year *Viscount Gormanston*). Or, on a chief sa. three crescents of the first. *Crest*—On a chapeau gu. turned up erm. a fox statant ppr. *Supporters*—Dexter, a fox ppr.; sinister, a lion or. *Motto*—Sans tache.

Preston (*Viscount Tara*, extinct 1647; Hon. THOMAS PRESTON, second son of CHRISTOPHER, fourth *Viscount Gormanston*, a General in the Army of the Confederate Catholics of Ireland, 1642, was so created 1650). Same *Arms*, a crescent for diff.

Preston (Ballymadun; ELENOR, dau. of ROBERT PRESTON, of that place, *m.* Alderman NICHOLAS ALCOCK, of Drogheda, who *d.* 18 June, 1616. Fun. Ent. Ulster's Office). Same *Arms*.

Preston (The Ninch. co. Meath; Fun. Ent. Ulster's Office, 1617, WILLIAM PRESTON, of that place, some time Sheriff of Dublin, nephew and heir of JOHN PRESTON, of Ninch). Same *Arms*, a crescent on a crescent for diff.

Preston (Mayor of Dublin, 1654; Fun. Ent. Ulster's Office, 1686, Alderman JOHN PRESTON, of Dublin, son of HUGH PRESTON, of Bolton, co. Lancaster; arms granted by St. George, Ulster, 1665). Ermines on a chief ar. three crescents gu.

Preston (Ardsallagh, co. Meath; descended from beforementioned Alderman JOHN PRESTON, of Dublin). Same *Arms*. *Crest*—A crescent or, betw. two wings inverted az. *Motto*—Sui ipsius præmium.

Preston (Bellinter, co. Meath; descended from Ardsallagh). Same *Arms* and *Crest*. *Motto*—Virtus sui ipsius præmium.

Preston (*Baron Tara*, extinct 1821; JOHN PRESTON, Esq., of Bellinter, was so created 1800, and *d. s. p.*, when his estates passed to his brother, Rev. JOSEPH PRESTON). Same *Arms*, &c.

Preston (Swainston, co. Meath). Same *Arms*, &c.

Preston (THOMAS PRESTON, Ulster King of Arms, 1633-42). Same *Arms*. *Crest*—A crescent or, betw. two wings az.

Preston (that Ilk, and Craigmillar, co. Edinburgh). Ar. three unicorns' heads erased sa. *Crest*—A good angel ppr. *Motto*—Præsto ut præstem.

Preston (Cousland Whitehill, Scotland). Same *Arms*, within a bordure engr. of the last.

Preston (Valleyfield House, co. Perth, bart.). Ar. three unicorns' heads erased sa. a bordure az. *Crest*—Out of a ducal coronet or, a unicorn's head ppr. *Motto*—Præsto ut præstem.

Preston (*Lord Dingwall*). Ar. three unicorns' heads erased sa. *Crest*—Out of a ducal coronet or, a unicorn's head sa. *Supporters*—Two lions gu. *Motto*—Pour bien fort.

Preston (Airdrie). Same *Arms*, a border vairé ar. and gu

Preston. Quarterly, or and gu. on a chief sa. three crescents of the first; another, Gu. a bend betw. six crosses crosslet fitchée at the foot (another, pattée fitchée) or; another, Sa. a cross erm. betw. four leopards' faces or; another, Ar. on a cross gu. five escallops of the field, a bordure vert; another, Gu. six crosses crosslet fitchée, three, two, and one, a bordure or; another, Per pale indented or and gu. a bordure vert platée; another, Ar. on a cross gu. five escallops or, a bordure vert; another, Gu. two bars fusily ar.; another, Gu. three garbs or; another, Az. a chev. or, betw. three garbs ar.; another, Gu. eight mascles or, five and three; another, Gu. eight mascles ar. four and four; another, Gu. eight lozenges ar. four, three, and one; another, Quarterly, ar. and az. a bend gu.

Preston, Town of (co. Lancaster). Az. a paschal lamb couchant, with the banner all ar. round the head a nimbus or, in base the letters P. P. of the last.

Prestwich (Prestwich, co. Lancaster). Erm. on a chev. gu. three leopards' faces or, on a chief of the third a wolf pass. sa. betw. two fleurs-de-lis of the second.

Prestwich (Holme, co. Lancaster, bart., extinct 1689; granted by Barker, Garter. The daus. and co-heiresses of Sir THOMAS PRESTWICH, Bart., were ARABELLA, *m.* MATTHEW DUCIE, *Baron Moreton*; PROCELLA; and MARGARET, *m.* RICHARD RINGROSE, Esq., of Barnaboy, Moynoe, co. Clare). Gu. (another, vert) a mermaid ar. comb and glass or. *Crest*—A porcupine ppr. *Motto*—In te Domine speravi.

Prestwich (Holme, co. Lancaster). Erm. on a chev. gu. a bezant betw. two leopards' faces or, on a chief of the last a wolf pass. sa. betw. two fleurs-de-lis of the second.

Prestwich (Holme, co. Lancaster). Erm. on a chev. gu. three bezants, a chief or, charged with a wolf pass. betw. two fleurs-de-lis sa.

Prestwich. Same *Arms*. *Crest*—A leopard's face jessant-de-lis or.

Prestwich (London). Erm. on a chev. gu. three leopards' faces or.

Prestwold (co. Worcester). Sa. a lion ramp. or, betw. two flaunches ar.

Prestwold (co. Leicester). Sa. (another, az.) a chev. or, fretty gu. betw. three garbs ar. *Crest*—A demi lion ramp. ducally gorged ppr.

Prestwood (Prestwood, co. Salop). Ar. a chev. gu. betw. three cinquefoils of the field.

Prestwood (Boterford, in North Huish, co. Devon, *temp.* Queen Elizabeth). Sa. a lion ramp. betw. two flaunches or. *Crest*—A griffin's head sa. with wings endorsed or, pelletée, beaked of the last.

Prestwood (co. Stafford, *temp.* Henry IV.). Ar. a chev. gu. betw. three cinquefoils sa.

Prestwood. Ar. on a chev. gu. betw. three cinquefoils az. as many plates.

Pretor (SAMUEL PRETOR, Esq., J.P., formerly of Sherborne House, and afterwards of Wyke House, near Weymouth). Gu. on a saltire ar. betw. four bezants two fasces in saltire. *Crest*—A dexter arm fessways, couped, habited, charged with two roundles, holding in the hand a fasces. *Motto*—Amor patriæ.

Prettyjohn. Gu. a lion pass. guard. betw. three mullets ar.

Prettyman (co. Norfolk, and Bawton, co. Suffolk; granted by Segar, 1599; confirmed by Camden, Clarenceux, 1607). Gu. a lion pass. betw. three mullets or. *Crest*—Two lions' gambs erased or, holding a mullet of the first.

Prettyman. Same *Arms* and *Crest*, the field az.

Prettyman. Same *Arms*, the lion pass. guard.

Preuze. Sa. three lions ramp. ar. betw. nine crosses crosslet or.

Prevost (Belmont, co. Hants, bart.) Az. a dexter arm in fesse issuing from a cloud in the sinister fesse point, the hand grasping a sword erect ppr. pommel and hilt or, in chief two mullets ar. *Crest*—A demi lion ramp. az. charged on the shoulder with a mural crown or, the sinister paw grasping a sword erect, as in the arms. *Supporters*—Two grenadiers of the 16th (or Bedfordshire) regt. of infantry, each supporting with the exterior hand a flag gu. that on the dexter flowing towards the sinister, inscribed "WEST INDIES," and that on the sinister flowing towards the dexter, inscribed "CANADA." *Motto*—Servatum cineri. The supporters, and the motto, "Servatum cineri," were granted in 1817, by royal warrants, under sign manual. The old motto was "J'ai bien servi."

Prevost. See PHIPPS.

Prewert, Az. a chev. betw. three lions ramp. or.

Prewes. Per saltire az. and gu. a cross potent or.

Preys. Paly of six or and gu. on a chief of the last a lion pass. guard ar.

Priaulx (Guernsey). Gu. an eagle displ. or. *Crest*—An eagle, as in the arms. *Motto*—César Auguste.

Pribecke. Ar. on a cross pierced az. four mascles of the field.

Price (Rhiwlas, co. Merioneth; descended from MARCH-WITHIAN, a chieftian of North Wales, who served under Prince Gruffydd ap Cynan at the close of the 11th century). Gu. a lion ramp. ar. armed and langued az. *Crest*—A lion ramp. ar. holding a rose sprig in the right paw. *Motto* —Vita brevis gloria æterna.

Price (Gilir, co. Merioneth; descended from Rhiwlas. Of this family was ROBERT PRICE, M.P., Baron of the Exchequer). Same *Arms*.

Price (Bryn-y-Pys, co. Flint; FRANCIS PRICE, Esq., of Bryn-y-Pys, and Castle Lyons, Ireland, *m.* ALICE, dau. and eventually heiress of JOHN CLEVELAND, of Birkenhead, co. Chester, and had a son, RICHARD PRICE, Esq., who assumed the name of PARRY, in consequence of a bequest by the Right Hon. BENJAMIN PARRY). Az. on a chev. ar. betw. three leopards' heads erased or, three spearheads sa.

Price (Glangwilly, co. Carmarthen; descended from the LLOYDS of that place, and the LLOYDS of Crynfryn and Olmarch, co. Cardigan). Quarterly, 1st, ar. a lion ramp. reguard. sa. langued gu.; 2nd, sa. semée of trefoils or; 3rd, sa. a boar pass ar.; 4th, az. a wolf ramp. ar. armed and langued gu.; 5th, sa. three scaling ladders, betw. the upper ones a spear's head ar. the point embrued ppr. on a chief gu. a tower triple-towered of the second; 6th, gu. a chev. betw. three roses ar. *Crest*—A wolf ramp. ar. langued gu. *Motto*—Spes tutissima cœlis.

Price (Plas Cadnant, co. Anglesey). Or, a falcon rising az. *Crest*—A falcon, as in the arms. *Motto*—Na fynw Duw ni fydd.

Price (Foxley, co. Hereford, bart., extinct 1857). Gu. a lion ramp. ar. *Crest*—A lion, as in the arms, holding in the dexter forepaw a rose slipped ppr. *Motto*—Auxilium meum a Domino.

Price (RUGGE-PRICE, Spring Grove, co. Surrey, bart.). Quarterly, 1st and 4th, gu. a lion ramp. ar., for PRICE; 2nd and 3rd, sa. on a chev. invected ar. betw. three mullets or, pierced of the field, a unicorn's head erased of the first, for RUGGE. *Crests*—1st: A lion ramp. ar. in the dexter paw a rose slipped ppr., for PRICE; 2nd: A talbot pass. ar. gorged with a collar or, and pendent therefrom an escocheon sa. charged with the head of an ibex couped also ar., for RUGGE. *Motto*—Vive ut vivas.

Price (Trengwainton, co. Cornwall, bart.). Sa. a chev. erminois betw. three spears' heads ar. embrued at the points ppr. *Crest*—A dragon's head vert erased gu. holding in the mouth a sinister hand couped at the wrist dropping blood all ppr.

Price (The Priory and Fonmon, co. Brecknock). Sa. a chev. betw. three spearheads ar. embrued gu.

Price (Castle Madoc, co. Brecknock). Quarterly, 1st, sa. a chev. betw. spearheads or, embrued gu.; 2nd, gu. a lion ramp. reguard. or; 3rd, ar. a dragon's head erased, holding in the mouth a hand gu.; 4th, gu. a chev. erm.; 5th, per pale gu. and sa. three fleurs-de-lis or; 6th, sa. a fesse betw. three swords erect ar. pommels and hilts or. *Crests*—1st: A dragon's head erased ppr. bearing in the mouth a sinister hand couped gu. dropping blood; 2nd: A boar's head erased.

Price (co. Brecknock). Or, a chev. betw. three spearheads sa.

Price (Westbury, co. Buckingham). Ar. three Cornish choughs sa. beaked and legged gu. *Crest*—A leopard's head or.

Price (co. Carnarvon). Or, a lion ramp. reguard. sa.

Price (co. Denbigh). Gu. a lion ramp. ar. (another, or). *Crest*—A lion ramp. or, holding a rose gu. stalked and leaved vert.

Price (GREEN-PRICE, Norton Manor, co. Radnor, bart.). Sa. a chev. invected ar. betw. three escutcheons of the last, each charged with a spearhead of the first embrued ppr. *Crest*—In front of a dragon's head erased vert, holding in the mouth a dexter hand couped at the wrist gu. three escallops ar. *Motto*—Vive hodie.

Price (co. Chester). Ar. three torteaux in bend betw. two cotises sa.

Price (Barton-Regis, co. Gloucester; granted 8 April, 1573). Ar. a cross betw. four pheons az. *Crest*—Out of a mural coronet or, a lion's head ppr

Price (co. Hereford). Sa. a chev. betw. three leopards' faces

or, on a chief ar. as many spearheads of the first embrued gu.

Price (Washingley, co. Huntingdon). Sa. three spears ar.

Price (London). Ar. a chev. betw. three pheons sa. *Crest*— A griffin's head erased ar. in the beak a thistle gu. stalked and leaved vert, all betw. two wings ppr. *Motto*—Virtus præ numina.

Price (London). Ar. a cock sa. *Crest*—A horse's head couped gu. in the mouth a spear ar.

Price (Jesus' College, Oxford). Az. three stags trippant ar.

Price (Kingston-upon-Thames, co. Surrey; confirmed 1602). Or, a lion ramp. reguard. sa. on a canton of the second a garb of the first. *Crest*—On a mural coronet or, a lion ramp. reguard. sa. holding in the forefeet a fleur-de-lis gold.

Price (quartered by FOUNTAINE, of Nasford Hall, co. Norfolk, and Reg. in Coll. of Arms). Or, guttée de poix a lion ramp. reguard. sa. gorged with a chain gold, pendent therefrom an escocheon of the first charged with an elephant's head erased sa.

Price (Wales). Ar. three cocks gu. armed, crested, and jelloped or; another, Ar. a lion pass. gu. betw. three fleurs-de-lis az.; another, Gu. a griffin segreant or, collared az. betw. three fleurs-de-lis ar.; another, Ar. a chev. betw. three spearheads a.

Price. See PRYCE.

Price (Keenagh, co. Longford; Fun. Ent. Ulster's Office, 1642, CHRISTOPHER PRICE, Gentleman of the Ordnance in Ireland, son of Captain SAMUEL PRICE, of Keenagh, and grandson of PETER PRICE, of Whitford, co. Flint). Ar. a chev. betw. three boars' heads couped sa. langued, vulned, and distilling drops of blood gu.

Price (confirmed by Carney, Ulster, 1686, to JOHN PRICE, Esq., His Majesty's Receiver-General and Treasurer at War in Ireland). Az. on a chev. ar. betw. three leopards' heads erased affrontée or, as many spearheads sa. embrued gu. *Crest*—A cock gu. holding in the mouth a peascod ppr. *Motto*—In vigila sic vinces.

Price (Saintfield, co. Down; exemplified to JAMES BLACK-WOOD, Esq., of that place, on his assuming, by royal licence, 1847, the surname of PRICE, in lieu of BLACKWOOD, in compliance with an injunction in a deed made by NICHOLAS PRICE, Esq., of Saintfield House). Az. three lions' heads erased or, a bordure of the last. *Crest*—A lion's head, as in the arms. *Motto*—Quis timet.

Prices (Abertreweren, co. Brecknock). Ar. three bulls' heads cabossed sa.

Prichard (Preston and Chorley, co. Lancaster). Ar. a dragon's head erased at the neck vert, holding in the mouth a sinister hand erased gu. issuing from it guttée de sang. *Crest*—A dragon's head, as in the arms.

Prichard (London; Sir WILLIAM PRICHARD, Knt., Alderman, and Lord Mayor of London, *d.* 18 Feb. 1705, aged 73). Erm. a lion ramp. sa. a bordure az. *Crest* (1705)—A horse's head erm. erased gu.

Prichard, or Prichar. Gu. a fess or, betw. three escallops ar.

Prickett (Allerthorpe and Octon Lodge, co. York). Or, on a cross az. quarter pierced of the field four mascles of the first.

Prickett (Bridlington, co. York; descended from PRICKETT, of Allerthorpe). Same *Arms*. *Crest*—A hind trippant ppr. *Motto*—Auxilium ab alto.

Prickett. Vairé or and gu. *Crest*—A heart gu. within a fetterlock az.

Prickly, alias Harris. Or, a chev. erm. betw. three nails az. *Crest*—On a chapeau gu. turned up erm. a mural crown az. thereon an arm embowed in armour ppr. vambraced or, holding a battle axe also ppr. headed sa.

Priddle. Gu. on a chev. betw. three griffins' heads ar. a cinquefoil vert. *Crest*—A demi lion or.

Pride (Shrewsbury, co. Salop). Sa. three preeds or small lampreys haurient in fess ar.

Prideaux (Prideaux Castle, co. Cornwall; PAGANUS DE PRIDEAUX was seized of that castle, *temp.* William I.; his grandson, NICHOLAS, Lord of Prideaux, *d.* 1169, leaving twin sons: I. RICHARD, his successor, whose male line terminated with RICHARD PRIDEAUX, *d.* 11 Richard II., A.D. 1387, leaving an only dau. and heir, JANE PRIDEAUX, *m.* PHILIP ARVES, whose only son, RICHARD ARVES, Lord of Prideaux, *temp.* Henry VI., left an only dau. and heir, JANE, *m.* THOMAS HERLE, Esq., of West Herle, co. Northumberland, who carried the lordship of Prideaux into that family; II. HERDEN, *m.* the dau. of RALPH ORCHARTON, of Orcharton, co. Devon, and was ancestor of PRIDEAUX, of Orcharton, PRIDEAUX, of Soldon, PRIDEAUX-BRUNE, of Prideaux Place, PRIDEAUX, of Netherton, bart., extinct, PRIDEAUX, of Luson, &c., &c.). Per pale ar and gu. three towers triple-towered counterchanged.

Prideaux (Orcharton, co. Devon; descended from HERDEN PRIDEAUX, who *m.* the heiress of Orcharton, and adopted the arms of her family). Ar. a chev. sa. a label of three points gu.

Prideaux (Soldon, co. Devon; descended from PRIDEAUX, of Orcharton. ROGER PRIDEAUX, Esq., of Soldon, High Sheriff co. Devon, 1578, had two sons: I. NICHOLAS, ancestor of PRIDEAUX-BRUNE; II. EDMUND, ancestor of PRIDEAUX, Bart., of Netherton, extinct). Same *Arms*, quartering PRIDEAUX, of Prideaux.

Prideaux-Brune (Prideaux Place, co. Cornwall; descended from PRIDEAUX, of Soldon). Quarterly, 1st and 4th, ar. a chev. sa. in chief a label of three points gu., adopted by the PRIDEAUXS after the marriage with the heiress of Orcharton; 2nd and 3rd, per pale ar. and gu. three castles counterchanged, being the ancient arms of PRIDEAUX, of Prideaux. *Crest*—A Saracen's head in profile couped at the shoulders, on the head a chapeau az. turned up ar.

Prideaux (Netherton, co. Devon, bart., extinct 1875; descended from PRIDEAUX, of Soldon). Ar. a chev. sa. in chief a label of three points gu. *Crest*—A man's head in profile couped at the shoulders, on the head a chapeau az. turned up ar. *Supporters*—Two Knights Templars in complete armour, each holding in the exterior hand a staff with the cross of St. John of Jerusalem. *Motto*—Deus providebit.

Prideaux (Luson, co. Devon; descended from PRIDEAUX, of Orcharton). Same *Arms* and *Crest*.

Prideaux (Notewell, co. Devon). Ar. on a chev. sa. four bars wavy of the field, in chief a label gu.

Prideokis (co. Cornwall). Ar. a cross flory gu. over all a bendlet az.

Pridham (Ottery and Plymouth, co. Devon). Az. on a pile or, three lions' heads erased of the first. *Crest*—A lion's gamb erased az. grasping a fetterlock or. *Motto*—Prudhomme et loyal.

Pridham. Ar. two bars gu. in chief three crescents of the last. *Crest*—A hand ppr. holding a chapeau az. turned up erm. all betw. two branches of laurel in orle vert.

Pridmore (co. Dorset). Per fess nebulée az. and or, three suns counterchanged.

Prierse. Ar. two bars sa. betw. six estoiles gu. *Crest*—A unicorn's head gu. collared vert.

Priest. Sa. on a chief ar. three estoiles gu. *Crest*—A martlet sa.

Priestley (Whitewindows, Sowerby, co. York; WILLIAM PRIESTLEY, resident at York temp. Edward I., occurs as a juryman in a writ of enquiry respecting the fishery on the river Ouse; and another WILLIAM PRIESTLEY was living in Sowerby 22 Henry VIII.). Gu. on a chev. betw. three towers ar. issuing out of each a demi lion ramp. or, as many grappling-irons sa. *Crest*—A cockatrice ar. standing on the lower part of a broken spear lying fessways or, in the mouth the other portion. *Motto*—Respice finem.

Priestley (Lightcliffe, afterwards Thorparch, co. York; descended from PRIESTLEY, of Whitewindows). Same *Arms, Crest,* and *Motto.*

Priestley. Gu. a fess erm. *Crest*—A demi lion sa.

Prifet, and Prosett. Erm. on a chief gu. three taus or.

Prigion (co. Lincoln). Malo three roses in bend two bendlets ar. *Crest*—A greyhound's head erased sa. gorged with three roses in fesse betw. two bars ar.

Prike, or Prykke. Or, on a cross pierced gu. four mascles of the field.

Prime (Walberton House, co. Sussex). Ar. a human leg erased at the thigh in pale sa. *Crest*—An owl ppr. gorged with a collar or, charged with two mullets sa. and issuing from the mouth a scroll with this *Motto*—Nil invita Minerva.

Prime. Same *Arms.* *Crest*—Out of a ducal coronet or, a lion's gamb holding a tilting spear ppr.

Prime. Ar. an eagle's leg erased a-la-quise sa. armed or.

Primouth, or Primout (co. Surrey). Per bend sinister ar. and chequy or and az. in the dexter chief point a demi buck sa. *Crest*—A demi buck sa. attired or.

Primrose (Scotland, 16th century). Az. a chev. or, betw. three primroses slipped ppr.

Primrose (Earl of Rosebery). Quarterly, 1st and 4th, vert three primroses within a double tressure flory counterflory or, for PRIMROSE; 2nd and 3rd, ar. a lion ramp. double-queued sa., for CRESSY. *Crest*—A demi lion gu. holding in the dexter paw a primrose, as in the arms. *Supporters*—Two lions or. *Motto*—Fide et fiducia.

826

Prin. Or, a fess az. betw. three escallops gu. *Crest* – Out of a ducal coronet or, a demi eagle volant sa.

Prince (Shrewsbury and Abbey Foregate, co. Salop; grantee 1584). Gu. a saltire or, surmounted of a cross engr. erm *Crest*—Out of a ducal coronet or, a cubit arm habited gu. cuffed erm. holding in the hand ppr. three pine apples gold, stalked and leaved vert.

Princep. Sa. three piles issuing out of the base in bend sinister flory at the points or. *Crest*—An eagle's head erased ppr.

Princeps. Or, a lion's paw erased in bend gu.

Pring. Vert on a pale betw. two annulets or, three cinquefoils of the field. *Crest*—A dagger in pale ppr.

Pringle (Galashiels, co. Selkirk). Ar. on a saltire engr. sa. five escallops or.

Pringle (Whytbank and Yair, co. Selkirk, representative of Galashiels). Same *Arms.* *Crest*—A man's heart ppr. winged or. *Supporters*—Two pilgrims habited ppr. *Motto* —Sursum.

Pringle (Torwoodle, co. Selkirk). Ar. on a saltire engr. az. five escallops of the first. *Crest*—A serpent nowed ppr. *Motto*—Nosce teipsum.

Pringle (Clifton, co. Roxburgh). Az. on a chev. ar. three escallops of the field. *Crest*—An escallop within two branches of palm in orle ppr. *Motto* -Spero et progredior.

Pringle (Haining, co. Selkirk). Az. on a chev. erm. three escallops of the field. *Crest*—An escallop demi expanded, and therein a pearl ppr. *Motto*—Præmium virtutis.

Pringle (Crichton). Az. on a chev. ar. three escallops of the field, in base a mullet or. *Crest*—A saltire ar. *Motto*— Spero et progredior.

Pringle (Stichill, co. Roxburgh, bart., 1683). Az. three escallops or. *Crest*—A saltire ar. within a garland of bay leaves ppr. *Motto*—Coronat fides.

Pringle (Sir JOHN PRINGLE, physician to George III., bart., extinct 1782). Az. three escallops ar. a mullet of the last in the fess point for diff. *Crest and Motto*, as Stichill.

Pringle (Greenknowe). Az. three escallops or, a bordure engr. of the last. *Crest*—An anchor within a garland of bay leaves ppr. *Motto*—Semper spero meliora.

Pringle (Newhall, co. Selkirk). Az. a bezant betw. three escallops or. *Crest*—A saltire ar. within a garland of bay leaves ppr. *Motto*—Coronat fides.

Pringle (Barnhouse). Ar. on a bend sa. three escallops ar.

Pringle (Torsonce). Ar. on a bend sa. three escallops or.

Pringle (Caledon, co. Tyrone; granted by Betham, Ulster, to JOHN PRINGLE, Esq., of that place, Deputy Governor of cos. Armagh and Tyrone). Erm. on a bend sa. three escallops erminois. *Crest*—An escallop, as in the arms. *Motto*—Amicitia reddit honores.

Prinne (co. Worcester, and Allington, co. Wilts.; granted 1588). Or, a fess engr. az. betw. three escallops gu. *Crest*—Out of a ducal coronet or, a demi eagle displ. ppr. beaked sa.

Prior (Roding, co. Essex, subsequently settled in the counties of Oxford, Lancaster, and Cambridge; a descendant of the family, THOMAS PRIOR, Esq., of Rathdowney, Queens' co., the celebrated Founder of the Royal Dublin Society, *d.* in 1751, having devised his property to his cousin, JOHN MURRAY, only son of the Rev. THOMAS MURRAY, by MARY, his wife, dau. of Captain THOMAS PRIOR, the first settler in Ireland). Sa. on a bend erm. betw. four stars of eight points wavy or, three chevronels gu. *Crest*—A star, as in the arms. *Motto* —Malo mori quam fœdari.

Prior (Paragon House, Blackheath, co. Kent). Gu. three escallops ar. *Crest*—An escallop ar. *Motto*—Speriamo.

Prior. Vert a bend cotised or. *Crest*—A dexter hand holding a crosier ppr.; another, Gu. on a bend erm. three chev. of the first.

Prior, Pryor, or Pryer. Gu. three escallops ar. *Crest* —An escallop ar.

Prior (granted by Betham, Ulster, to THOMAS YOUNG PRIOR, Esq., of the Middle Temple, Barrister-at-law, youngest son of Rev. THOMAS PRIOR, D.D., Senior Fellow, and sometime Vice-Provost of Trinity College, Dublin, descended from a family long seated in the cos. of Essex and Cambridge). Quarterly, 1st and 4th, vert on a bend erm. three chevronels gu., for PRIOR; 2nd and 3rd, per bend or and ar. a fess gu, in chief a lion pass. az., for WALLIS; surmounted by an inescutcheon erm. a lion ramp. gu. in chiefthree escallops sa., for RUSSELL. *Crest*—1st: An estoile vert; 2nd: A talbot's head erased ar. charged on the breast with a trefoil slipped ppr. *Motto*—Quis audeat luci aggredi.

Priory of Dunmow (co. Essex). Sa. a cross ar. betw. four mullets or.

Priory of Kenilworth (co. Warwick). Ar. on a chief az. two mullets or, pierced gu.

Priory of Kirkeby-Beler (co. Leicester). Per pale sa. and or, a lion ramp. ar.

Priory of Kirkham (co. York). Gu. three water bougets or, two and one, in pale a pilgrim's staff of the last enfiled with the water bouget in the base.

Priory of Laiton, or Latton (co. Essex). Gu. five mullets or, two, two, and one, on a canton of the second a griffin segreant sa.

Priory of Llandaff (co. Glamorgan). Sa. two crosiers in saltire, the dexter or, the sinister ar. on a chief az. three mitres labelled of the second.

Priory of Lande, or Launde (co. Leicester). Or, three pales gu. a bordure az. bezantée; another, Az. on a bend gu. cotised or, betw. two mullets ar. pierced of the field, three escallop shells of the third.

Priory of Lanecroft (co. Cumberland). Or, two flaunches gu.

Priory of Laneguest, or Vale of Laneguest. Gu. on a lion ramp. betw. three crosses crosslet ar. as many bars sa.

Priory of Langdone (co. Kent). Az. two crosiers in saltire ar. the dexter crook or, the sinister sa.

Priory of Malton (co. York). Ar. three bars gu. over all a pilgrim's crutch in bend sinister of the first.

Priscle. Erm. on a fess gu. three castles ar.

Priset. Or, in chief three Taus gu.

Prisett, or Prosset (co. Salop). Gu. on a chief ar. three Taus sa. *Crest*—A hand gu. holding a torteau.

Priske (Helston, co. Cornwall; the co-heirs *m.* TREWREN, PENROSE, and PENNECK). Or, on a bend sa. three horse-shoes ar.

Prislet, or Prisley. Gu. on a chev. betw. three castles ar. each charged with a demi lion issuant or, as many grapers sa.

Prisott, or Prysett. Gu. on a chief ar. three crosses pattée sa.

Pristow. Erminois a chev. betw. three mullets ar.

Pritchard (Campston, co. Monmouth). Barry of six or and az. on a chief of the first three palets betw. two base esquirres, dexter and sinister of the second, an inescutcheon ar.

Pritchard (Swansea; originally of Campston Hall, co. Monmouth). Erm. a lion ramp. sa. *Crest*—A lion ramp. as in the arms.

Pritchard. Same *Arms*, with a bordure az. *Crest*—A dexter arm ppr. holding a battle-axe, handle gu.

Pritchard (Tresgawen, Anglesey). Vert three eagles displ. in fess or.

Pritchard (Broseley, co. Salop). Ar. on a fess betw. three escallops sa. a buck's head cabossed betw. two buckles or. *Crest*—A dragon's head erased ar. in the mouth an escallop sa. the neck charged with two buckles in fess betw. as many barrulets az. *Motto*—Labore et fide.

Prittie (granted to HENRY PRITTIE, Esq., of Kilboy, co. Tipperary, by Fortescue, Ulster, 1800). Per pale ar. and gu. three wolves' heads erased and counterchanged. *Crest*—A wolf's head erased ar. *Motto*—In omnis paratus.

Prittie (*Baron Dunalley*). Same *Arms*. *Crest*—A wolf's head erased ar. *Supporters*—Dexter, a man in complete armour holding in the exterior hand a tilting spear all ppr.; sinister, a stag ppr. armed, hoofed, ducally collared and chained or. *Motto*—In omnia paratus.

Pritty (registered to PRITTY, Major of Horse). Per pale ar. and gu. three wolves' heads counterchanged. *Crest*—A wolf's head erased per pale ar. and gu.

Pritwell. Az. (another, sa.) a fess ar. betw. three bucks' heads (another, heads cabossed) or.

Pritzler. Per fess az. and sa. in chief two arrows in saltire ppr. surmounted by a heart gu. ducally crowned az. and in base an anchor with chain, &c., all or.

Privy-Council Office. The seal of office represents a rose and a thistle, each stalked, leaved, and conjoined to one stem in base betw. the royal supporters of England; the lion holding the rose betw. his forefeet, and the unicorn the thistle. The supporters standing on a scroll, with the words "Sigill. Priv. Council;" over the rose and thistle the regal crown of England.

Probert. Per pale az. and sa. three fleurs-de-lis or.

Proby, or Ap Robin (West Chester, and Elton Hall, co. Huntingdon, and co. Salop; granted 1586). Erm. on a fess gu. a lion pass. or. *Crest*—An ostrich's head erased ar. ducally gorged or, in the mouth a key of the last.

Proby (*Earl of Carysfort*). Quarterly, 1st and 4th, erm. on a fess gu. a lion pass. or, for PROBY; 2nd and 3rd, ar. two bars wavy and a plain chief az. on the latter an estoile betw.

826

two escallops or, for ALLEN. *Crest*—An ostrich's head erased ppr. ducally gorged or, in the beak a key of the last. *Supporters*—Dexter, an ostrich ppr. ducally gorged or, in the beak a key of the last; sinister, a talbot sa. *Motto*—Manus hæc inimica tyrannis.

Probyn (as borne by the Rev. JOHN PROBYN, Archdeacon of Llandaff). Same *Arms* and *Crest* as PROBY, or AP ROBIN.

Probyn (Longhope, co. Gloucester). Same *Arms*, &c.

Proctor (Wisbeach, co. Cambridge, and co. Middlesex). Or, three nails sa. *Crest*—A martlet gu.

Proctor (co. Middlesex, granted 1761; and London). Ar. a chev. sa. betw. three martlets gu. *Crest*—On a mount vert a greyhound sejant ar. spotted brown, collared or.

Proctor (Thorpe-upon-the-Hill, and Springfield House, co. York). Ar. a chev. betw. ten crosses crosslet, six in chief and four in base gu.

Proctor-Beauchamp, Bart. See BEAUCHAMP.

Prodgers (Ayot Bury, Welwyn, co. Herts, and Broomfield, co. Salop). Per pale gu. and az. three lions ramp. two and one ar. betw. three crosses pattée fitched in the foot, one and two, erminois. *Crest*—In front of a cross calvary or, a wivern with wings endorsed vert, in the mouth a sinister hand couped at the wrist gu. gorged with a collar and line and reflexed over the back gold, the dexter claw resting on a cross pattée of the last. *Motto*—Devouement sans bornes.

Prodney. Ar. a chev. sa.

Progers, or Ap Roger (Gwarindee, or Werndu, co. Monmouth; descended from JENKIN AP GWILLIM, eldest son of WILLIAM AP JENKIN, alias HERBERT, Lord of Gwarindee, *temp.* Edward III., who was, through his younger sons, ancestor of the HERBERTS, of Llanarth and Clytha; the HERBERTS, *Barons Herbert* by writ, 1461, represented by the *Duke of Beaufort*; the senior line of the *Earls of Pembroke* and the *Earl of Huntingdon*, extinct *temp.* Henry VII.; the *Lords Herbert*, of Chirbury, extinct 1691; the HERBERTS, *Marquesses of Powis*, extinct; and the HERBERTS, of Mucross). Per pale az. and gu. three lions ramp. ar.

Prosser (Belmont, co. Hereford). See WEGG-PROSSER.

Prosser. Erm. on a chief vert three wheatsheaves ar. *Crest*—On a mount a horse bridled at full speed all ppr.

Prother. Az. on a chief ar. three fetterlocks of the field. *Crest*—On a tower sa. a crescent or.

Prothero. Chequy az. and or, an annulet gu. *Crest*—A bird flying purp.

Protheroe, Prytherch, or ap Rhydderch (Dolwilym, and Plas Landra, co. Carmarthen, and of Bristol). Ar. a lion ramp. guard. sa.

Protheroe, Prytherch, or ap Rhydderch (Hawksbrook and Llaugharne, co. Carmarthen, extinct; quartered by DAVIS, of Cwm, co. Carmarthen, and others). Ar. a chev. sa. betw. three ravens ppr. This coat has also been borne by PROTHEROE, of Dolwilym. *Crest*—A raven ppr. *Motto*—Deus pascit corvos.

Protheroe (derived from a younger branch of PROTHEROE or PRITHERCH, of Egermond, co. Carmarthen, a scion of PROTHEROE (AP RHYDDERCH) of Dolwilym, in the same county, sprung from CADIVOR VAWR, Lord of Blaen Cuch, in Dyved (West South Wales), *d.* 1089, the common ancestor also of the PHILIPPS of Picton, MORGANS of Tredegar, Llantarnum, &c., LEWISES of St. Pierre, LLOYDS of Llanstephan, Lakes, and Llanllawddog). Ar. a lion ramp. guard. sa.

Protheroe (North Wales and co. Norfolk. Visit. Norfolk). Gu. a chev. betw. three stags ar. It is the coat of SARDDUS, a North Welsh chief.

Proud (co. Salop and Westminster, 1605). Or, on a chev. gu. three bars ar. *Crest*—A cross formée fitchée or, charged with five pellets, a chaplet of laurel entwined round the cross vert. *Another Crest*—A buffalo's head erased vair.

Proude (Egston, co. Kent). Az. three otters pass. in pale or, each holding in the mouth a fish ar. *Crest*—An otter's head erased or, holding in the mouth a fish ar.

Proudfonte. Gu. a fess or, fretty of the first platée at the joints.

Proudfoot (Proudfootstown, co. Meath; JOHN PROUDFOOT, son of ROBERT PROUDFOOT, of same place, buried in the church of Dowth, 2 Feb. 1634). Vert a leg in armour embowed and couped at the thigh ppr. under the foot a bezant charged with a cross moline. *Crest*—An arm embowed in armour ppr. holding in the hand an arrow of the last.

Proudfoot (Dublin; Fun. Ent. Ulster's Office, 1622, SUSAN, dau. of RICHARD PROUDFOOT, merchant, and wife of NATHANIEL HAMMOND, of same place). Same *Arms*, a crescent for diff.

Prous, or Prowze (Gidley Castle, co. Devon, *temp.*

Henry II., and Way, in Chagford, same co. Visit. Devon, 1620; the heiress of the senior line *m.* MOELS or MULES. There were younger branches of this ancient family at Withecomb, Barnstaple, Tiverton, Crediton, &c.). Sa. three lions ramp. ar.

Prous, or Prowze (granted 1589). Ermines three lions ramp. ar. *Crest*—An ibex sejant or, armed, tufted, and maned ar.

Prouse, or Prouze. Quarterly, sa. and ar. a bend or. *Crest*—A demi lion or.

Prout (WILLIAM PROUT, M.D., F.R.S., of Sackville Street, St. James's). Az. a lion pass. guard. betw. two roses in pale ar. *Crest*—Issuant from grass ppr. a lion ramp. guard. ar. collared and ringed or, holding in the paws a lighted taper ppr.

Prout (Foscot, co. Somerset). Quarterly, sa. and ar. a bend or.

Provender (Allington, co. Wilts). Gu. a fess vair betw. three dragons' heads erased or. *Crest*—A squirrel courant, quarterly or and gu. (another, or and sa.).

Provis (co. Somerset). Az. a chief ar. *Crest*—On a rock a wild duck ppr.

Provost. Sa. three round buckles or, on a chief of the second a demi lion ramp. gu. *Crest*—A buckle or.

Prow (co. Essex). Gu. a chev. ar. betw. three pineapples or.

Prow. Az. a chev. ar.

Prowdfoote. Gu. a fess or, fretty of the field, on each knot a plate.

Prowes. Per saltire gu. and ar. over all a cross crosslet or.

Prowse (co. Cornwall). Sa. three roebucks' heads cabossed or. *Crest*—A golden fleece ppr.

Prowse (Oldcliffe, co. Somerset). Sa. three lions ramp. ar. a bordure or. *Crest*—An ibex's head erased sa. eared or, armed, collared, and lined gold.

Prowse (Wicklow, co. Northampton). Same *Arms. Crest*—Out of a ducal coronet ar. a demi lion ramp. guard. also ar. collared and winged or.

Prowst. Az. a chev. or.

Prowze. Quarterly, sa. and ar. a bend or. *Crest*—A dexter hand throwing a dart ppr.

Prudhoe, Baron. See PERCY.

Prudhome (co. Devon; the heiress of the chief line, PRUDHOME, of Upton Prudhome, *m.* and conveyed considerable estates into the family of WHITING; and more recently, JOAN, daughter of WILLIAM PRUDHOME, *m.* WILLIAM FEILDING, ancestor to the *Earl of Denbigh*). Az. three lions' heads erased or. *Crest*—A lion's gamb erased ppr.

Prue, or Prew. Or, two bars gu. betw. eight escallops az.

Pruen (Cheltenham, co. Gloucester). Per pale gu. and az. on a fess ar. be'w. three eagles displ. erminois as many crosses pattée sa., quartering, for ELBOROUGH, Erminois on a fess couped vert betw. two talbots pass. in pale sa. a rose ar. barbed and seeded ppr. *Crest*— A demi eagle displ. sa. charged on the breast with a fess ar. thereon three crosses pattée gu. in the beak a sprig of olive ppr.

Prujean. Gu. three roses in bend betw. two cotises ar. *Crest*—A greyhound's head erased sa. charged on the neck with three roses betw. two cotises collarways ar. *Another Crest*—A griffin's head erased sa.

Prunes (Westbury, co. Bucks). Or, a lion ramp. az. on a chief of the last an ostrich's feather of the first betw. two others ar.

Prust (Gorven and Hartland, co. Devon; fifteen descents traced in Visit. 1620). Gu. on a chief ar. two estoiles sa.

Pruteston (Pruteston, now Preston, co. Devon; the heiress *m.* FORTESCUE, of Wimpston). Or, on a bend az. three crosses formée fitchée az.

Prutin. Per pale gu. and az. a fess betw. two chev. ar.

Pryce (St. John's College, Cambridge). Or, a lion ramp. reguard. holding betw. the forepaws a fleur-de-lis gu. *Crest* —A lion, as in the arms.

Pryce, or Price (Wrotham, co. Herts). Sa. on a chev. betw. three leopards' faces ar. as many spearheads of the first, a chief of the second, charged with three cocks gu. combed, wattled, and legged or. *Crest*—A cock gu. combed, wattled, and legged or, holding in the beak a violet az. stalked and leaved vert.

Pryce (Gunley, co. Montgomery; derived from EINION AP SITSYLLT, Lord of Mathafarn, in Cyveiliog, tenth in descent from GWYDDNO GARANHIR, Prince or Lord of Cantref Gwaelod). Ar. a lion pass. sa. betw. three fleurs-de-lis gu., quartering, 1st, az. on a bend sa. betw. two crescents gu. three annulets

827

or, for IEVAN AP RYS; 2nd, sa. three nags' heads erased ar., for DAVID LLOYD AP GRIFFITH AP BIRID, of Gunley; 3rd, ar. three boars' heads couped sa. langued gu. tusked or, for EVAN AP RHYS AP HUGH, of Rhiwhirieth. *Crest*— A demi lion ramp. sa. holding betw. the paws a fleur-de-lis of the arms.

Pryce (Newtown, co. Montgomery, bart., extinct; descended from REES AP DAVID LLOYD, Esquire of the Body to Edward IV., who was descended from ETHELYSTAN GLODRYDD, Prince of Ferlys). Gu. a lion ramp. reguard. or. *Crest*—A lion, as in the arms. *Motto*—Avi numerantur avorum.

Pryce (Mansriefed, co. Cardigan; descended from PRYCE, of Newtown). Same *Arms,* quartering, ar. three boars' heads couped ppr. *Crest*—A lion, as in the arms. *Motto*—Avi numerantur avorum.

Pryce (Bodfach, co. Montgomery; descended from PRYCE, of Newtown; the heiress *m.* BELL LLOYD). Same *Arms.*

Pryce (Glan Miheli; descended from PRYCE, of Newtown). Same *Arms.*

Pryce (Gunley, co. Montgomery). Ar. a lion pass. sa. betw. three fleurs-de-lis gu. the lion armed and langued of the last.

Pryce (BRUCE-PRYCE, Dyffryn, co. Glamorgan; JOHN BRUCE-PRYCE, Esq., assumed the name of KNIGHT, on coming of age, and the additional surname of PRYCE, in 1837, at the decease of his cousin, the Hon. Mrs. BOOTH GREY; he was son of JOHN KNIGHT, Esq., by MARGARET, his wife, dau. of WILLIAM BRUCE, Esq., of Llanblethian). Quarterly, 1st, gu. three chevronels ar. a crescent for diff., for PRYCE; 2nd, or, a saltire gu. on a chief of the last a martlet gold, for BRUCE; 3rd, paly of six ar. and az. on a canton of the last a spur or, for KNIGHT; 4th, quarterly, 1st, sa. a lion ramp. ar., 2nd, sa. a chev. betw. three spears' heads ar., 3rd, sa. a chev. betw. three fleurs-de-lis or, 4th, or, on a canton gu. two lions pass. of the first, for LEWIS, of Llanishen. *Crests*—1st: A paschal lamb ppr., for PRYCE; 2nd: A dexter arm in armour ppr. in bend grasping a sceptre, for BRUCE; 3rd: On a spur lying fesseways feathered or, a falcon, wings expanded erm., for KNIGHT. *Mottoes*—Over the crest of BRUCE: Fuimus; under the arms: Duw ar fy rhan; in English: God for my portion.

Pryce. Ar. a chev. betw. three spearheads sa. ; another, Sa. three spearheads ar.

Prydeux (co. Cornwall). Per pale ar. and gu. three castles counterchanged.

Prydeux (co. Cornwall). Ar. a cross pattée gu. over all a bend az.

Prydeux (Nutwell, co. Devon; granted 16 May, 1558). Ar. on a chev. sa. betw. three eagles' legs couped gu. a book or, purfled vert, betw. two bow-knots of the first. *Crest*—A dove volant ar. membered and beaked gu.

Prydeux. Per pale ar. and gu. a cross pattée counterchanged, a bend of the first; another, Per pale ar. and gu. a cross pattée of the second, a bend az.; another, Sa. a saltire engr. ar. *Crest*—A dexter arm from the elbow ppr. holding a billet in pale az.

Prye (Horwell, co. Devon; five descents given in Visit. 1620). Erm. a chev. gu. (sometimes, sa.) a chief az. fretty or.

Pryer (France). Or, on two bars gu. eight escallops ar. a bordure vert.

Pryer (High Elms, Baldock, co. Herts). Ar. three bars wavy sa. on a chief gu. a saltire or. *Crest*—A demi lion ramp.

Prykele, Prykke, or Prikkes (Bury St. Edmunds, co. Suffolk). Or, on a cross quarterly pierced az. four mascles of the first.

Prynn, or Resprynn. Ar. a chev. gu. betw. three boars' heads sa.

Prynne (co. Salop; granted by Dethick, Garter, 1588, to EDWARD PRYNNE, of co. Salop; Harl. MSS. 1069). Or, a fess engr. az. betw. three escallops gu. *Crest*—Out of a ducal coronet or, an eagle displ. ppr. beaked sa.

Prynne (Chaddesley Corbet, co. Worcester). Same *Arms.*

Prys (Rev. EDMUND PRYS, Rector of Maentwrog, co. Merioneth, and Archdeacon of Merioneth, author of the "Metrical Version of the Welsh Psalms;" derived from MARCHUDD AP CYNAN). *Arms* of MARCHUDD AP CYNAN, viz., Gu. a Saracen's head erased at the neck ppr. wreathed about the temples sa. and ar.

Pryse (Gogerddan, co. Cardigan; descended, through the celebrated Welsh poet, RHYDDERCH AP IEVAN LLOYD, of Gogerddan, from GWAETH VOED, Lord of Cardigan, at the commencement of the 12th century. The eventual heiress, *m.* EDWARD LOVEDEN LOVEDEN, Esq., of Buscot. co. Berks). Or, a lion ramp. reguard. sa. quartering LOVEDEN. *Crest*—A lion, as in the arms, holding in the paws a fleur-de-lis or. *Motto*—Duw Ar bendithio; "God with us."

Prytherch (Abergole, co. Carmarthen; originally AP RHYDDERCH; descended, through JAMES PRYDDERCH, Esq., High Sheriff co. Carmarthen 1599, from RHYDDERCH AP GWILYN, of the line of CRADOC AP GWILYN, Lord of Tallyn). Quarterly, 1st and 4th, az. a stag trippant ar. collared and lined or, betw. the attires an imperial crown ppr.; 2nd and 3rd, gu. on a chev. betw. three men's heads couped in profile ar. five gouttes de sang. Crest—A stag's head cabossed, betw. the attires an imperial crown, as in the arms. Motto —Duw a digon; God and enough.

Pstrelle (co. Nottingham). Paly of six ar. and az.

Puckering (Weston, co. Hertford, and co. Warwick). Sa. a bend fusily cotised ar. Crest—A buck ramp. (another, courant) or.

Puckering (Flamborough, co. York; confirmed 26 June, 1579). Sa. five fusils in bend cotised ar.

Puckle (co. Sussex). Gu. three dexter hands couped ar. the fingers towards the nombril point. Crest—On a dexter hand couped erect ar. a rose ppr.

Pudley. Az. a chev. engr. erm.

Pudlicott (co. Oxford). Gu. nine lozenges pierced or, conjoined in threes, six in chief and three in base.

Pudsey (Stonefield, co. Bedford, co. Lancaster, Ellesfield, co. Oxford, cos. Stafford and York). Vert a chev. betw. three mullets or. Crest—A cat (or leopard) pass. ppr.

Pudsey (co. Northumberland; HUGH PUDSEY, E'shop of Durham, temp. Richard I., 1153-95). Per saltire or and ar. a cross formée az.

Pudsey (co. Oxford, and Langley, co. Warwick. Visit. Warwick and Oxford, and monument, Sutton Coldfield Church). Vert a chev. betw. three mullets or. Crest—A cat pass. ppr.

Pudsey (Bolton, near Richmond, co. York). Vert a chev. betw. three mullets or.

Pudsey (Lawfield, co. York, 1665). Vert a chev. betw. three mullets or, a canton ar.

Pudsey (Seisdon Hall, co. Stafford). Vert a chev. betw. three mullets or, on a canton ar. a lozenge sa. Crest—A mountain cat pass. guard. charged on the shoulder with a lozenge or, for distinction. Motto—Fortunâ favente.

Pudsey, or Puddesey (Barford, co. York). Vert a chev. betw. three mullets or.

Pueray. Or, two bars sa.

Pugeis, or Pugiers. Lozengy gu. and ar.

Puges. Gu. a mascle ar.

Puget. Az. a chev. wavy betw. three mullets ar. Crest —A dove holding an olive branch and flying over the sea all ppr.

Puget. Az. a saltire or, in chief the sun in splendour ppr.

Pugges. Gu. three lozenges ar. Crest—A dexter hand ppr. holding up a covered cup or.

Pugh (Llanerchydol, co. Montgomery; descended from CADWALLADER, of Llanerchydol). Quarterly, 1st and 4th, ar. a lion pass. guard. sa. crowned or, betw. three fleurs-de-lis gu.; 2nd and 3rd, sa. three greyhounds courant ar. Crest—A lion, as in the arms, holding a fleur-de-lis gu. Motto —Qui invidet minor est.

Pugh. Ar. a lion pass. sa. betw/ three fleurs-de-lis gu. Crest —A dolphin embowed ppr.

Pugh (Manoravon, near Llandilo, co. Carmarthen). Gu. a lion pass. betw. three fleurs-de-lis or. Motto—Sic itur ad astra.

Pughe (Ty Gwyn). Ar. a lion pass. gu. betw. three fleurs-de-lis sa. Crest—A lion's head erased, in the mouth a trefoil slipped ppr. Motto—Nid meddyg ond meddyg eniad.

Pujolas (St. Marylebone, co. Middlesex; granted 1762). Per fesse wavy az. and ar. in chief three doves ppr. in base on a mount vert a ram couchant sa. horned and hoofed or. Crest—A hind at gaze ppr. about the neck a buglehorn or, the string gu.

Pukenham. Az. a lion ramp. or, a bordure engr. gu.

Pulderfield (co. Devon). Sa. a cross voided or.

Pulesborough, or Pullebrough (London). Per fess sa. and gu. an eagle displ. ar.

Pulesden. Ar. three mullets sa.

Pulesdon, Pullesdon, Pulleston, or Puleston (cos. Chester, Flint and Salop; granted 1582). Sa. three mullets ar. Crest—A buck pass. ppr. attired or.

Pulesdon, Pulisdon, Puliston, or Puleston (co. Flint, and Wales; granted 1583). Ar. on a fess betw. three pelicans sa. as many hawks' lures or. Crest—A stag pass. ppr.

Puleston, or Pulesden. Ar. on a bend sa. three mullets of the field.

Puleston (Havod y Werne, co. Denbigh). Quarterly, 1st and

828

4th, ar. on a bend sa. three mullets of the field, 2nd, sa three lions pass. ar. armed and langued gu., for HWFA at JORWETH; 3rd, SANDDE HARDD.

Puleston (Emral, co. Flint, bart.). Sa. three mullets ar. Crests—1st: An oak tree ppr. pendent therefrom by a band az. an escutcheon gu. charged with three ostrich feathers, in commemoration of Sir RICHARD PULESTON's having had the honour of introducing the Prince of Wales, 9th Sept. 1806, into the Principality; 2nd: On a chapeau gu. turned up erm. a buck statant ppr. attired or. Motto—Clariores a tenebris.

Puleyne, or Pullen (Fun. Ent. Ulster's Office, 1668, Mrs. ABBEY, alias PULEYNE or PULLEN). Az. on a bend betw. six lozenges or, each charged with an escallop sa. five escallops of the last.

Pulford (Pulford, co. Chester; descended from ROBERT DE PULFORD, temp. King John). Sa. a cross patonce ar.

Pulford (co. Westmorland). Sa. a cross sarcelly ar.

Pullein (Killinghall, Carleton Hall, and Crake Hall, co. York; descended from RICHARD PULLEINE, of Killinghall, living at the commencement of the sixteenth century; MARY WINIFRED, only dau. and heir of THOMAS BABINGTON PULLEINE, Esq., of Carleton Hall, m. WALTER SPENCER STANHOPE, Esq., of Cannon Hall). Az. on a bend cotised ar. three escallops gu. on a chief or, as many martlets sa. Crest—A pelican on her nest all or. Motto—Nulla pallescere culpa.

Pullein (Fun. Ent. Ulster's Office, 1677, the wife of Mr. HUNT). Az. a bend betw. six lozenges or.

Pullen (co. York). Az. on a bend cotised ar. three escallops gu. on a chief or, as many martlets sa.

Puller (Sir CHRISTOPHER PULLER, Knt., Lord Chief Justice of Bengal, d. 1824). Az. a bend cotised betw. three escallops or, on a chief of the last as many escallops of the first. Crest—On a chapeau gu. turned up erm. a dove ppr. in the beak a branch of laurel vert.

Puller. Az. a lion ramp. ar. betw. six escallops or, three, two, and one. Crest—A dexter hand holding a trident in bend.

Pulley (Leigh, co. Essex). Or, three eagles displ. az.

Pulley. Per saltire or and sa. Crest—A palm tree vert.

Pulleyn (Scotton, co. York). Az. on a bend or, betw. six lozenges of the second, each charged with an escallop sa. five escallops of the last. Crest—A pelican on her nest all or.

Pulling (Mr. Serjeant PULLING, late of Newark Park, co. Gloucester, now Redcliffe Gardens, South Kensington). Az. on a bend or, betw. six lozenges of the second, each charged with an escallop sa. five escallops of the last. Crest—A pelican in her nest vulning herself ppr.

Pulling. Or, three eagles displ. gu. on a chief wavy az. three fleurs-de-lis ar. Crest—A demi eagle displ. gu. charged on each wing with a cross pattée fitchée or, and on the breast with a millrind gold.

Pullyn (Great Yarmouth). Quarterly, 1st and 4th, or a lion ramp. sa.; 2nd and 3rd, ar. a chev. betw. three garbs sa. Crest—A lion ramp. sa.

Pulsdon, or Pulston. Ar. on a bend sa. three mullets of the first.

Pulse (St. Anne's, Westminster). Gu. three eagles' heads erased ar. beaked or, on a chief of the second three trefoils slipped ppr. Crest—An eagle's head erased ar. in the beak a trefoil slipped.

Pulteney (Earl of Bath, extinct 1764; WILLIAM PULTENEY, orator and statesman, grandson of WILLIAM PULTENEY, Esq., of Misterton, co. Leicester, was so created 1742, d. s. p.). Ar. a fess indented gu. in chief three leopards' faces sa. Crest—A leopard's head affrontée and erased sa. ducally gorged or. Supporters—Dexter a leopard; sinister, a tiger, both guard. ar. guttée de poix, and gorged with a bar dancettée gu. Motto—Quo virtus.

Pulteney (Countess of Bath, extinct 1808; HENRIETTA LAURA JOHNSTONE, wife of Sir WILLIAM JOHNSTONE, Bart., of Westerhall, and dau. and heir of HENRY PULTENEY, brother of WILLIAM, Earl of Bath, having s. to the estates of the earl, assumed the surname of PULTENEY, and was created Baroness Bath 1792, and Countess of Bath 1803, d. s. p.). Same Arms and Supporters.

Pulteney (Northerwood, Hants). Ar. a fess indented gu. in chief three leopards' faces sa. on a canton of the second an estoile of the first. Crest—A leopard's head erased sa. gorged with a ducal coronet or, and charged with a cross crosslet. Motto—Vis unita fortior.

Pulter (Bradfield-Wimondley, co. Hertford). Ar. two bendlets sa. in the sinister chief a Cornish chough of the last.

Pultison (London). Per pale ar. and sa. three lions ramp. counterchanged.

Pulton. Ar. a fess dancettée sa. betw. three leopards faces az.

Pulton, Abbey of (co. Chester). Az. three garbs or, in pale a crozier of the last.

Pults. Gu. three eagles' heads erased ar. beaks or, on a chief of the second as many trefoils vert. *Crest*—An eagle's head erased, as in the arms, holding a trefoil vert.

Pulverston (Bromsford, co. Lancaster). Ar. three covered cups sa.

Pulvertoft (Spalding, co. Lincoln). Ar. a mullet betw. eight fleurs-de-lis gu.

Pulvertoft (Whaplod, co. Lancaster). Ar. three fleurs-de-lis, two and one, betw. as many annulets, one and two sa.

Pulvertoft (co. Lincoln, 1640). Or, a mullet pierced gu. an orle of fleur-de-lis az.

Pulyne (co. Cornwall). Gu. semée of crosses crosslet a saltire vair.

Pumfrey (Scotland, 16th century). Az. a chev. ar. betw. three garbs or.

Puminge. Or, three bars vert, a bend gu.

Pumise, or Puynse. Or, an eagle displ. gu.

Punchardon (Punchardon in Kentisbear, and Heanton Punchardon, co. Devon; the co-heiresses *m.* BEAUMONT, RALEGH, and BEAUPLE). Ar. a cross sarcelly voided gu.

Punchardon. Ar. a fess gu. on a bordure of the last eight escallops of the first.

Puncheon. Per pale ar. and sa. three roundles counterchanged.

Punshon (West Herrington, co. Durham; granted to WILLIAM PUNSHON, of West Herrington, in 1575, by Flower, Norroy). Az. a fess crenellée betw. three lambs' heads erased ar.

Punshon (Killingworth Cottage, co. Northumberland; granted 1823). Az. a fess embattled counter-embattled betw. three lambs' heads erased ar. a bordure wavy erm. *Crest*—A lamb pass. erm. charged with a palet wavy az. betw. two oval buckles or, tongues pointing upward.

Purbutt. Ar. (another, or) ten pellets, four, three, two, and one.

Purcell (*Baron of Loughmoe;* so created by the *Earl of Ormonde*, as Palatine of Tipperary; impalement Fun. Ent. Ulster's Office, 1626, PEIRCE BUTLER, Esq., of Nodstown, whose wife was ELLEN, dau. of THOMAS PURCELL, *Baron of Loughmoe*). Or, a saltire betw. four boars' heads couped sa. *Crest*—A cubit arm erect ppr. habited az. cuffed ar. grasping a sword also ppr. pommel and hilt or, piercing through the jaw a boar's head couped sa. vulned and distilling drops of blood. *Motto*—Aut vincam aut periam.

Purcell (Borris-o-leagh, co. Tipperary; Fun. Ent. Ulster's Office, 1629, THOMAS PURCELL, of that place, gentleman). Same *Arms*, a crescent for diff.

Purcell (Foulkes Rath, co. Kilkenny; Fun. Ent. Ulster's Office, 1637; ROBNETT PURCELL, of that place, descended from GEOFFREY PURCELL, second son of PURCELL, *Baron of Loughmoe*). Same *Arms*.

Purcell (Croagh, co. Limerick; Fun. Ent. Ulster's Office, 1638, PIERCE PURCELL, of that place, descended from a second brother of PURCELL, of Loughmoe). Ar. a boar pass. gu. tusked, hoofed, and bristled or, langued az. on a chief of the last three plates, a crescent for diff.

Purcell (Crumlin, co. Dublin; a branch of PURCELL, of Croagh, co. Limerick, lineally descended from EDMUND PURCELL, Sheriff of Dublin in 1598, *d.* 1612, whose grandson, EDMUND PURCELL, brother of General PATRICK PURCELL, was put to death by Ireton; arms allowed by Hawkins, Ulster, 1715). Ar. a boar pass. gu. armed and bristled or, on a chief az. three plates. *Crest*—A hand couped above the wrist erect, holding a sword ppr. pommelled and hilted or, pierced through the jaw of a boar's head couped sa. vulned and distilling drops of blood, the sleeve az. turned up ar.

Purcell (Rorestown, co. Tipperary; confirmed by Hawkins, Ulster, 1757, to Captain JOHN EDMUND PURCELL, son of Major THEOBALD PURCELL, of Ballymartin, co. Kilkenny, whose sister, ANNA, was wife of EDMUND BUTLER, *Viscount Mountganet*). Same *Arms* and *Crest*.

Purcell (co. Cork; descendant and representative of PURCELL, of Croagh Purcell, co. Limerick. The principal seats of the PURCELLS of the county of Cork are, Temple-Mary, now the property of the co-heiresses of the late RICHARD PURCELL, Esq.; Burton House and Highfort, the residences of the Rev. MATTHEW PURCELL, and of his brother, RICHARD PURCELL, M.D.; Altamira, the seat of PIERCE PURCELL, Esq.; and Annabella, of RICHARD HARRIS PURCELL, Esq.). Barry wavy of six ar. and gu. on a bend sa. three boars' heads of the first. *Crest*—A hand couped above the wrist

829

erect, holding a sword ppr. pommelled and hilted or, pierced through the jaws of a boar's head also couped sa. vulned and distilling drops of blood, the sleeve az. turned up ar.

Purcell (Burton House, co. Cork). Or, a saltire betw. four boars' heads couped sa. Some branches of the family bear, Barry wavy of six ar. and gu. on a bend sa. three boars' heads of the first. Same *Crest*.

Purcell (Fun. Ent. Ulster's Office, 1616, NICHOLAS PURCELL, Sheriff of Dublin). Ar. a boar pass. gu. tusked, hoofed, and bristled or, langued az. on a chief of the last three plates.

Purcell (granted by Betham, Ulster, to JOHN PURCELL, Esq., son of JOHN PURCELL, of Dublin, M.D.). Ar. a saltire gu. betw. four boars' heads couped sa. armed or. and langued gu. *Crest*—A dexter arm couped at the elbow ppr. the sleeve gu. with an indented cuff erm. the hand grasping a sword ppr. hilted and guarded or, pierced through the jaws of a wolf's head couped sa. vulned ppr. *Motto*—Humani nihil alienum.

Purcell (Ouneslow, co. Salop; granted April, 1597). Barry nebulée of six ar. and gu. on a bend sa. three boars' heads of the first. *Crest*—Out of a ducal coronet or, a boar's head ar. guttée de sang.

Purcell (co. Salop). Barry wavy of six ar. and az. on a bend sa. three boars' heads couped of the first. *Crest*—A boar's head erased lying fessways ar.

Purcell (Westminster). Barry wavy of six ar. and az. on a bend sa. three boars' heads erased or.

Purcell. Vairé ar. and gu. on a bend sa. three boars heads couped or.

Purcell. Ar. three torteaux.

Purcell. See FITZGERALD.

Purchas (co. York). Ar. a lion ramp. sa. debruised by a fesse az. charged with three bezants. *Crest*—A dexter hand ppr. holding up a cushion sa. tasselled or.

Purchas (cos. Essex and Monmouth; descended from Sir WILLIAM PURCHAS, Lord Mayor of London, 1494 and 1498). Ar. a lion ramp. az. debruised by a fess sa. charged with three bezants. *Crest*—A demi lion ramp. az. holding a bezant in the dexter paw. *Motto*—Semper paratus.

Purchon (THOMAS PURCHON, Esq., of York House, Leeds). Vert a chev. erm. betw. in chief two fleeces ar. banded, and in base a portcullis or, on a bordure of the last eight escallops gu. *Crest*—In front of a demi woman habited az. mantle flowing over the left shoulder gu. in her right hand a palm branch ppr. two anchors in saltire or. *Motto*—Prudentiâ et vigilantiâ.

Purde. Ar. a cross componée or and az., in the 1st quarter a water bouget, in the 2nd an eagle displ., in the 3rd a swan close, in the 4th an escallop, all sa. on a chief az. a lion pass. guard. or.

Purdew. Ar. a fess chequy or and sa.

Purdey (London). Ar. a fess chequy or and gu.

Purdon (co. Cumberland). Ar. a leopard's face gu. betw. a chief and a chev. sa. *Crest*—A dexter arm in armour, the hand ppr. holding a banner gu. fringed or, charged with a leopard's face ar. the staff broken above the hand.

Purdon (Tinerana, co. Clare; originally settled at Kirklington, co. Cumberland, and established in Ireland, *temp.* Henry VIII., by JAMES PURDON, Esq., of Kirklington; confirmed by Usher, Ulster, 1588, to GILBERT PURDON, Esq., of Dublin, son of JAMES PURDON, of Kirklington). Quarterly, 1st and 4th, ar. a leopard's face betw. a chief and a chev. sa.; 2nd, or, a lion ramp. sa. over all on a fess gu. three mullets of the field, for CASAURON; 3rd, or, a cross gu. in the 1st quarter a dexter hand sa., for BURKE. *Crest*—A dexter arm embowed ppr. holding a banner gu. fringed or, charged with a leopard's face ar. the staff broken above the hand. *Motto*—Pro aris et focis.

Purdon (Curristown, co. Westmeath). Ar. a chev. sa. in centre chief point a leopard's face of the last. *Crest*—A dexter arm embowed ppr. holding a banner gu. fringed or, charged with a leopard's face ar. the staff broken above the hand. *Motto*—Pro aris et focis.

Purdon (Lisnabin, co. Westmeath). Same *Arms*, &c.

Purdon (Lurgan Race, co. Louth; Fun. Ent. Ulster's Office, 1595, JANE, dau. of ADAM PURDON, Esq., and wife of ADAM LOFTUS, Archbishop of Dublin and Lord Chancellor of Ireland). Ar. a chev. sa. in chief a leopard's face gu. a chief of the second.

Purdon (Tallaght, co. Dublin; Fun. Ent. Ulster's Office, 1612, ISABEL, dau. of SIMON PURDON, of that place, and wife of WILLIAM CONWAY). Same *Arms*.

Purefoy (co. Leicester). Gu. a saltire engr. ar betw. four mullets or.

Purefoy. Sa. three pairs of dexter hands conjoined or, ruffled ar. *Crest*—A demi talbot ramp. sa. ducally gorged or.

Purefoy (Shadlestone, co. Bucks). Gu. three pairs of hands addorsed ar.

Purefoy (Misterton and Drayton, co. Leicester; seated at the former place 1277, and at the latter 1397. The branches were PUREFOY, of Barwell, Wolvershill, Shalleston, Wadley, &c.). Sa. six armed hands in pairs embracing, two and one ar. *Crest*—A dexter gauntlet or, the inside az. fingers grasping a broken tilting-spear of the second.

Purefoy (Caldecote, co. Warwick; confirmed by Camden, Clarenceux, to WILLIAM PUREFOY, Esq., of Caldecote, tenth in descent from PHILIP PUREFOY, Esq., of Newnham, same co.). Sa. six armed hands in pairs embracing, two and one ar. *Crest*—In a dexter gauntlet ar. a broken tilting-spear or.

Purefoy (co. Tipperary; descended from MICHAEL PUREFOY, Esq., of Caldecote, co. Warwick, escheater for that county, *temp.* Mary I., second son of THOMAS PUREFOY, Esq., of Drayton.) Same *Arms* and *Crest.*

Purefoy. Gu. three pairs of hands couped hand in hand ar.

Purefoy, or Purfoy. Gu. two arms issuing from the sides of the escutcheon, hand in hand ar. betw. three human hearts or (another adds, a crescent in fess).

Purefoy, or Purferoy (co. Kent). Sa. six armed hands clasped ar. *Crest*—A dexter hand holding a garland of flowers ppr.

Purefoy (BAGWELL-PUREFOY, Greenfield, co. Tipperary; exemplified to EDWARD BAGWELL, Esq., Lieut. 3rd Dragoon Guards, on his assuming, by royal licence, 1847, the additional surname of PUREFOY, in compliance with the will of WILLIAM PUREFOY, Esq., of Greenfield). Quarterly, 1st and 4th, sa. three pairs of hands conjoined, one and two or, ruffled ar., for PUREFOY; 2nd and 3rd, paly of six ar. and az. on a chief gu. a lion of the pass. of the first, for BAGWELL. *Crest*—A hand in armour grasping a broken lance all ppr. *Motto*—En bonne foy.

Purkis. Quarterly, ar. and gu., in the 1st and 4th quarters a bee volant sa. *Crest*—Out of a ducal coronet or, a greyhound's head ppr.

Purland (East Walton, co. Norfolk). Sa. five wings in saltire or. *Crest*—A demi eagle with wings displ.

Purley. Chequy ar. and sa.

Purling (Hatton Garden, London; granted 1759). Az. a lion ramp. or, crowned with a naval crown ar. on a chief of the second two crescents of the first. *Crest*—A lion sejant or, crowned with a naval coronet ar. holding in the dexter paw an anchor sa. *Another Crest*—A dexter hand holding a grenade fired ppr.

Purling. Az. a lion ramp. or, crowned with an Eastern coronet, on a chief of the last two crescents gu. *Crest*—A lion sejant or, crowned as in the arms, reposing the dexter paw on an anchor sa.

Purllysden. Ar. on a fess sa. betw. three pelicans az. vulned gu. as many hawks' lures or.

Purnell (Dursley, Forward, Stancombe, and Wickselm, co. Gloucester; granted 1768). Ar. on a fess sa. betw. three lozenges gu. as many cinquefoils of the first. *Crest*—Out of a mural coronet ar. (another, or) a demi griffin segreant erminois, in the dexter claw a thunderbolt ppr.

Purnell (Wickwar, co. Gloucester). Ar. on a fess betw. three mascles az. as many cinquefoils of the field.

Purnell (Stancombe Park, co. Gloucester; exemplified to PURNELL BRANSBY COOPER, Esq., of Kingshill, near Dursley, co. Warwick, on assuming, by royal licence, 1805, the name of PURNELL). Ar. on a fess sa. betw. three lozenges gu. as many cinquefoils of the first, for PURNELL, quartering, COOPER, BRANSBY, and PASTON. *Crests*—1st, PURNELL: Out of a mural crown ar. a demi griffin segreant erminois, holding in the dexter claw a thunderbolt ppr.; 2nd, COOPER: Out of a mural coronet ar. a demi-spear erect ppr. fringed or, and surmounted by two palm branches in saltire vert. *Motto*—Fide et virtute.

Purnell (Boddington Manor, co. Gloucester). Erminois on a fess betw. three lozenges gu. as many cinquefoils ar. *Crest*—Issuant from a mural crown ar. charged with three lozenges fessways gu. a demi falcon rising ppr. holding in the beak a cinquefoil slipped vert.

Purrier. Ar. a chev. vert betw. two spears in chief of the last, and in base on a mount of the second a pear tree ppr. fructed or, a chief erm. *Crest*—A dolphin embowed sa. under a pear tree ppr. fructed or.

Purse. Gu. six trefoils slipped ar. *Crest*—A demi bull per fess or and gu.

Purser. Gu. three clawed wrights' hammers ar. *Crest*—A fox's head erased or.

830

Pursey. Per pale ar. and gu. a lion ramp. counterchanged.

Purslow (Sudbury and Hoxstow, co. Salop). Ar. a cross patonce (another, flory) engr. sa. a bordure engr. gu. bezantée. *Crest*—A hare sejant erm.

Purslow (co. Worcester). Ar. a cross moline engr. bordure sa. bezantée.

Purslow. Quarterly, per fess indented gu. and erm.

Pursthall. Ar. fretty sa. on a chief gu. a lion pass. guard. or.

Purton (Faintree, co. Salop; descended from Sir JOHN DE PURTON, Knt., of Purton, co. Stafford, who was in high estimation with Edward III., and served as Sheriff co. Stafford, 38th, 44th, and 45th years of that reign. WILLIAM PURTON, Esq., *m.* HESTER MARIA, dau. and heir of THOMAS PARDOE, Esq., of Faintree, High Sheriff co. Salop 1791, and thereby acquired that estate). Ar. on a chev. gu. three pears or, quartering, ar. a cross componée or and gu. in the 1st quarter a water bouget, in the 2nd an eagle displ., in the 3rd a swan, in the 4th an escallop, all sa. on a chief az. a lion ramp. gu. of the second. *Motto*—Fructu arbor cognoscitur.

Purton. Quarterly, ar. and sa., in the 1st quarter a fleur-de-lis gu. *Crest*—An eagle displ. gu.

Purves (that Ilk, co. Berwick, bart.), 1655; now HUME CAMPBELL, which see). Az. on a fess betw. three mascles ar. as many cinquefoils of the first. *Crest*—The sun rising out of a cloud ppr. *Supporters*—Two lynxes ppr. *Motto*—Clarior e tenebris.

Purvis (Kinaldy, co. Fife, 1868). Az. on a chev. ar. betw. three mascles or, as many cinquefoils vert. *Crest*—A dexter hand pointing upwards to the sun in his splendour ppr. *Motto*—Per vias rectas.

Purvis (Darsham, co. Suffolk; descended from GEORGE PURVIS, Esq., of Darsham, Comptroller of the Navy, 1735, descended from a common ancestor with the Baronets PURVES, represented by Sir WILLIAM PURVES-HUME-CAMPBELL). Az. on a fess ar. betw. three mascles or, as many cinquefoils of the field. *Crest*—The sun in splendour rising from clouds all ppr. *Motto* over—Clarior e tenebris.

Purvis. Az. on a chev. betw. three mascles ar. as many cinquefoils of the first (another, gu.). *Crest*, as the last, *Motto* over—Post nubila Phœbus.

Pury (Drayton and Barwell, co. Leicester). Ar. on a fess betw. six martlets sa. three mullets of the field. *Crest*—On a ducal coronet or, a martlet gu.

Pury (co. Oxford). Ar. on a fess betw. three martlets sa. as many mullets of the field.

Pury, or Pyry (co. Wilts). Ar. on a bend cotised betw. three martlets sa. as many mullets or.

Pusey (Pusey, co. Berks; traditionally stated to have been settled at Pusey prior to the Conquest, and to have held that estate by cornage, or the service of a horn, under a grant of Canute. CHARLES PUSEY, the last direct male heir, *d.* 1710, and bequeathed the manor to his nephew, JOHN ALLEN, Esq., who thereupon assumed the surname of PUSEY, and *m.* a dau. of Sir WILLIAM BOUVERIE, Bart., grandfather of the first Earl of Radnor, but *d. s. p.*, when the estate was further entailed upon Mr. PUSEY's sisters and nieces, the ALLENS, which ladies alternately inherited it, and joined in settling it upon the Hon. PHILIP BOUVERIE, nephew of Mr. JOHN ALLEN PUSEY's wife, who also assumed the surname of PUSEY). Gu. three bars ar., now quartering BOUVERIE. *Crest*—A cat pass. ar.

Put. Ar. on a lozenge sa. a lion ramp. of the first. *Crest*—A demi lion ramp. ar. holding a mascle sa.

Putman, or Putnam (co. Sussex). Sa. a martlet betw. six crosses crosslet ar.

Putnam. Sa. a bend betw. six crosses crosslet ar. three, two, and one.

Putt (Coombe, co. Devon, bart., extinct 1721; descended from NICHOLAS PUTT, Esq., who purchased the manor of Combe Gillingham from Sir Henry Beaumont in 1615. His grandson, Sir THOMAS PUTT, was created a bart. in 1666; Sir THOMAS PUTT, second bart., *d. s. p.* 1721, when the estate of Combe passed to his cousin, the heir male of the family, RAYMUND PUTT, Esq.). Ar. within a mascle sa. a lion ramp. of the last. *Crest*—Out of a mural coronet a leopard's head ducally gorged all ppr.

Puttenham (Sherfield, co. Hants. Visit. 1634. RICHARD PUTTENHAM, Esq., of Sherfield, grandson of Sir GEORGE PUTTENHAM, Knt., of Sherfield, left an only dau. and heir, ANNE, wife of FRANCIS MORRIS, of Copwell). Ar. crusily fitchée sa. a stork of the last. *Crest*—A wolf's head couped gu.

Puttenham, or Putnam (co. Beds, and Penn, co. Bucks). Sa. crusily fitchée ar. a stork of the last, beaked and legged gu. *Crest*—A wolf's head couped gu.

Putter. Or, three lozenges (another, fusils) az.

Puxley (Dunboy Castle, co. Cork; granted to HENRY LAVALLIN PUXLEY, Esq., of that place, J.P., and to the descendants of his grandfather). Quarterly, 1st and 4th, gu. on a bend cotised ar. five lozenges conjoined of the first, in the sinister chief point an annulet or, for PUXLEY; 2nd and 3rd, ar. a fleur-de-lis sa. a chief engr. az., for LAVALLIN. *Crest*—An arm in armour embowed ppr. charged with a lozenge betw. two annulets in pale gu. the hand grasping a dagger also ppr. *Motto*—Pro libertate patriæ.

Puxty (co. York). Quarterly, ar. and gu. on a bend sa. three fleurs-de-lis or. *Crest*—A pelican's head vulned ppr.

Pybus (Greenhill Grove, near Barnet, co. Herts; granted 1768). Ar. on a chev. gu. three cinnamon leaves of the field, in chief two cinnamon trees eradicated vert, in base a negro girt round the waist with blue and white striped linen, carrying with a yoke of bamboo cane two bundles of cinnamon all ppr. *Crest*—An elephant carrying in his trunk some sugar canes all ppr.

Pychar. Ar. three lozenges sa. a label of five points gu.

Pychard (cos. Hereford and Salop). Gu. a fess or, betw. three escallops ar.

Pychard, or Pychow. Quarterly, or and az. *Crest*— A hand holding a club erect ppr.; another, Ar. three lozenges sa. (another, gu.); another, Or, two bends gu.

Pycroft. Sa. a cross flory or. *Crest*—A hand couped in fess apaumée, charged with an eye ppr.

Pycroft (Swanton Abbot). Sa. a cross flory or, a bordure engr. ar.

Pye (co. Hertford). Vert three fleurs-de-lis stalked and slipped or.

Pye (London; granted 2 May, 1634). Or, on a pile az. three escallops of the first. *Crest*—A demi lion ramp. az. gorged with a ducal coronet or, holding an escallop of the last.

Pye (Nansarth, afterwards of Bodenneck, in St. Stephen's, Brannell, co. Cornwall). Ar. on a fess az. three escallops of the field.

Pye (The Mynde, co. Hereford; derived from HUGH PYE, or AP HUGH, Lord of Kilpec Castle, *temp.* Henry I.; Sir WALTER PYE, Knt., Visit. Berks, 1664, son of Sir WALTER PYE, Knt., eldest son of ROGER PYE, Esq., of The Mynde, *temp.* Queen Elizabeth). Erm. a bend fusily gu. *Crest*—A cross crosslet fitchée gu. betw. two wings displ. ar.

Pye (Faringdon, co. Berks, afterwards of Clifton Hall, co. Stafford; descended from Sir ROBERT PYE, Knt., Auditor of the Receipt of the Exchequer to James I. and Charles I., second son of ROGER PYE, Esq., of the Mynde, *temp.* Queen Elizabeth. Visit. Middlesex, 1663). Same *Arms*, quartering, 1st, sa. a lion pass. ar.; 2nd, per pale ar. and sa. a lion ramp. counterchanged supporting with the forepaws a tree eradicated vert; 3rd, gu. three stirrups with leathers or; 4th, ar. on a chev. engr. betw. three birds sa. as many escallops or. *Crest*—A cross crosslet fitchée gu. betw. two wings displ. ar. *Motto*—In cruce salus.

Pye (Hone, co. Derby, bart., extinct 1734; descended from Sir JOHN PYE, Knt., of Hone, second son of Sir ROBERT PYE, Knt., of Faringdon, Auditor of the Receipt of the Exchequer). Same *Arms*, &c.

Pye (Rosehall, co. Lanark; descended from a younger branch of PYE, of Faringdon). Same *Arms*, &c.

Pye (Stoke Damerell, co. Devon). Ar. on a fess per pale az and gu. a talbot's head couped betw. two escallops of the field, a bordure wavy of the second. *Crest*—Upon a mount vert a talbot's head couped ar. charged with a saltire wavy az. *Motto*—Pietatis causa.

Pyell. Ar. a bend betw. two mullets sa.

Pyemont (Lofthouse, co. York). Ar. on a chev. gu. betw. three pickaxes sa. as many clusters of grapes or. *Crest*— On a mount a knight in armour on his knees praying.

Pyennes. Az. a fess betw. six billets or.

Pygott (Gravenhurst, Stratton, and Holme, co. Bedford). Sa. three pickaxes ar. *Crest*—A cubit arm vested bendy of six ar. and vert, in the hand ppr. a pickaxe of the first.

Pykard. Gu. a fess or, betw. three escallops ar.

Pyke, or Pikey (co. Devon). Per pale or and gu. on a chev. az. betw. three trefoils counterchanged, a pike ar.

Pyke (*temp.* Henry VI.). Az. semée of crosses crosslet or, two shepherds' pipes chevronways of the second.

Pyke (co. Somerset). Sa. three pitchforks paleways in fess ar. *Crest*—A boar pass. ar. gorged with a garland of laurel vert.

Pyke (co. Essex). Az. three pikes naiant or.

Pyke-Nott (Parracombe, co. Devon). Quarterly, 1st and 4th, gu. on a bend engr. or, betw. four leopards' faces, two and two ar. an estoile of eight points enclosed by two martlets of the field, for NOTT; 2nd and 3rd, quarterly, or

and gu. on a chev. barry wavy of four ar. and az. betw. two trefoils in chief and another in base counterchanged, a pike naiant ppr., for PYKE. *Crests*—1st: Two mascles fesswise, interlaced or, thereon a martlet gu. ducally gorged gold, in the beak a sprig of laurel ppr.; 2nd: On a mount vert a demi pike haurient ppr. betw. two wings gu. each charged with a trefoil or.

Pykelworthe. Ar. three pickaxes gu.

Pykin, or Pynkney. Ar. a chev. betw. three hounds courant gu. *Crest*—A savage's head couped sa.

Pykingham. Az. a lion ramp. or, holding a battle axe ar.

Pyland. Ar. a chev. gu. betw. three garbs vert.

Pyland. Gu. a fess or, betw. three escallops ar.

Pylborow, or Pilborow. Per bend sa. and gu. on a fesse between three mullets or, a griffin pass. az. *Crest*—An eagle's head erased bendy of six ar. and az. five bezants thereon, holding in the beak a branch of three roses gu. leaved vert.

Pyle (confirmed 1 Jan. 1650). Az. three piles or, on a canton gu. a leopard's face of the second.

Pym (Brymmore, co. Somerset, bart., extinct 1688; JOHN PYM, the celebrated patriot, left an only surviving son, Sir CHARLES PYM, who was created a bart. in 1663. His only dau. MARY, heiress of her brother, Sir CHARLES PYM, second and last bart., m. Sir THOMAS HALES, Bart., of Beaksbourne). Sa. a bull's head couped ar. enclosed in a wreath or and az. *Crest*—A lion's gamb holding up a human heart ppr.

Pym (arms in Norton Church, co. Hereford). Sa. on a fess ar. betw. three owls ar. as many crosses crosslet of the field, a bordure of the second.

Pym (the Hasells, co. Beds). Sa. on a fess betw. three owls or, as many crosses crosslet of the first. *Crest*—A hind's head erased or, gorged with a collar flory counterflory az. and holding in the mouth trefoil slipped ppr.

Pym (Sidford, co. Devon). Ar. an annulet sa.

Pymar (Endsbury, co. Dorset). Gu. on a pile betw. two crosses crosslet ar. a cross crosslet of the field. *Crest*—A rock, thereon a seapye, in the beak a sprig of laver all ppr.

Pyme, or Pyne (co. Cornwall). Ar. a bend gu. betw. six mullets sa.

Pymme (Wycombe, co. Bucks). Gu. on a fess betw. three owls as many crosses patonce sa. a bordure of the second.

Pyncepole (co. Essex). Ar. a buglehorn betw. three trefoils sa.

Pyncester. Gu. a cross or.

Pyncherdon. Ar. a cross sa.

Pyncombe (South Moulton and East Buckland, co. Devon; granted 18 July, 1616). Per pale gu. and az. three close helmets ar. garnished or. *Crest*—An armed arm embowed ppr. purfled or, holding in the hand a Poland mace ar. fastened to the arm with a scarf gu.

Pyndar (Kempley, co. Gloucester; granted by Dugdale and St. George, 1682, to REGINALD PYNDAR, Esq., of Kempley, and borne by his descendant, Rev. REGINALD PYNDAR, of Ledbury, co. Hereford, Rector of Madresfield, co. Worcester). Gu. a chev. ar. betw. three lions' heads erased erminois, crowned of the second. *Crest*—A lion's head erased erminois, crowned ar.

Pynde. Az. fretty ar. on a chief or, three torteaux. *Crest*—A lion's gamb erased ar. holding three pines or, fructed vert.

Pyne, or Pine (Ham, co. Cornwall, and East Downe, co. Devon; descended from OLIVER PYNE, Esq., of Ham, 1296, who m. the heiress of DOWNE, of East Downe, co. Devon; Rev. JOHN PINE assumed the additional name and arms of COFFIN, 1797, on succeeding to the estate of Portledge). Gu. a chev. erm. betw. three pineapples or. *Crest*—A pine branch with three pineapples or, leaved vert. *Another Crest*—A pine- tree ppr.

Pyne (co. Cornwall). Ar. a bend betw. six mullets gu.

Pyne (Merriott and Currymallet, co. Somerset; a family described by Cooke, Clarenceux, in 1573, as ancient and honourable, long time bearing arms). Az. a fess betw. three escallops or. *Crest*—An antelope's head couped or, horned and maned sa.

Pyne (Lord Chief Justice of Ireland, A.D. 1702). Gu. a chev. erm. betw. three pineapples or. *Crest*—A pine tree fructed ppr. growing on a mount vert.

Pynell. Az. an eagle displ. with two heads or. *Crest*—A demi eagle displ. with two heads gu. winged or.

Pynell. Per pale or and ar. an eagle displ. perched on a ragged staff sa.; another, Ar. on a chev. engr. sa. two griffins combatant of the first; another, Ar. on a chev. engr. gu. a lion ramp. crowned or.

Pynk. Ar. two chevronels sa. betw. three roses gu. seeded or, barbed vert.

Pynk. Erm. two bendlets gu.

Pynkeney. Ar. a pale fusily sa. a bordure engr. of the last.

Pynnoke. Per saltire sa. and gu. on a fess betw. three lions' heads erased or, as many cinquefoils az.

Pynnoke (co. Kent). Per saltire sa. and gu. on a fess or, betw. three lions' heads erased reguard. ar. each holding a cross crosslet of the third, as many cinquefoils az.

Pynock (France). Or (another, ar.) a lion pass. sa.

Pynoke. Gyronny of six gu. and sa. on a fess betw. three cinquefoils or, as many lions' heads erased az.

Pynon. Vair two bars gu. a canton or.

Pynsent (Carleton Curlieu, co. Leicester, and Urchfont, co. Wilts). Gu. a chev. betw. three mullets (another, estoiles) ar.

Pynson (co. Middlesex). Gyronny of eight sa. and gu. a fess engr. ar. betw. three eagles displ. or.

Pynson (co. York). Per pale ar. and sa. three roundles counterchanged. Crest—On a chapeau az. turned up or, an eagle, wings expanded ppr.

Pynson. Gyronny of eight gu. and sa. on a fess betw. three eagles ar. (another, or) as many cinquefoils gu. (another, az.) Crest—A demi eagle displ. holding in the beak a branch of pineapples fructed or, leaved vert.

Pynson. Gu. a chev. engr. ar. betw. three pineapples pendent of the second, on a chief az. as many estoiles or. Crest—Three leaves or, issuing from an estoile of sixteen points gu.

Pyntrell, or Pintrell. Ar. a fess betw. three cinquefoils gu.

Pyntrell. Ar. a fess betw. three crosses crosslet gu.

Pynyll. Az. an eagle displ. per pale or and ar. armed gu. standing on a piece of a tree raguly per pale of the third and second.

Pyot (co. Stafford). Az. on a fess or, a lion pass. guard gu. in chief three bezants. Crest—A demi lion gu. charged on the shoulder with three bezants, two and one.

Pyot (Richard Pyot, Alderman of London 1611). Az. on a fess or, a lion pass. sa. in chief three bezants.

Pypard (co. Cornwall). Ar. a chev. gu. betw. three pears ppr.

Pypard (co. Gloucester, temp. Henry II.). Ar. two bars gu. on a canton az. a cinquefoil or.

Pypard (co. Worcester). Ar. two bars az. on a canton sa. a cinquefoil or.

Pyrke (Deane Hall, co. Gloucester). Ar. on a fess sa. three mullets of the field, a canton ermines. Crest—A cock pheasant with a wheat ear ppr.

Pyrley. Per pale ar. and or, over all a lion ramp. sa.

Pyrot (Knowlton, co. Kent; Richard Pyrot, Alderman of London). Ar. a fess, in chief three escallops sa.

Pyrry (Baynton, co. Wilts). Ar. on a fess cotised sa. betw. three martlets of the last, as many mullets or. Crest- A stag's head erased ar. attired or, in the mouth a pear branch vert, fructed of the second.

Pyrs (Shrewsbury, co. Salop). Quarterly, or and az. four pheons counterchanged.

Pyrton (co. Essex). Erm. on a chev. engr. az. three leo pards' faces or. Crest—On a chapeau az. (another, gu.) turned up erm. a wivern, wings expanded vert.

Pyrton, Pirion, or Pirren (co. Hertford). Gu. three crescents ar.

Pyrton. Ar. on a chev. az. three leopards' faces or.

Pyrton. Ar. (another, or) on a mount in base vert a pear tree fructed ppr.

Pysent. Az. a chevronel engr. betw. three mullets ar.

Pytis. Erm. a chev. gu. betw. three griffins' heads az. beaked or.

Pytts (Kyre, co. Worcester. Visit. 1634. Catherine Pitts, the heiress, m. William Lacon Childe, Esq., of Kinlet, co. Salop). Az. three bars ar. in chief as many estoiles or. Crest—Within a circular wreath of wheat or, a dove with wings displ. ar. beaked and legged gu.

Pyxe (Thomas Pyxe, temp. Richard II.). Az. a fess betw. six crosses crosslet fitchée or.

832

Q

QUADERING, or Quadring (Irisby, co. Lincoln). Erm. a fess engr. gu. Crest—A Moor's head full faced ppr. couped below the shoulders, and wreathed about the temples ar. and gu.

Quadring. Ar. a chev. betw. three hares sa.

Quaile. Erm. on a canton vert a cross calvary on three grieces or.

Quaile (co. Worcester). Vert three quails ppr.

Quain (Richard Quain, Esq., of Cavendish Square, co. Middlesex, F.R.S., and F.R.G.S.). Ar. three acorns chevronways ppr. within two chevronels az. betw. in chief two fers-de-moline, and in base on a mount an oak tree of the second. Crest—An oak tree, the trunk entwined with a serpent all ppr. and charged with an escutcheon ar. thereon a fer-de-moline sa. Motto—Je ne plie ni ne romps.

Quain (Sir John Richard Quain, LL.B., Justice of the Court of Queen's Bench, England). Same Arms, Crest, and Motto.

Quantock (Norton House, Ilminster, co. Somerset). Az. an eagle displ. with two heads erminois, in chief three estoiles ar. Crest—Out of the battlements of a tower gu. charged with two annulets or, a demi eagle with two heads and wings issuant per pale erminois and erm. Motto—Non immemor beneficii.

Quaplade (arms in the Library of Balliol Coll., Oxford. Visit. Oxon, 1566). Barry of six or and az. a bendlet gu. Crest—On a mount vert a boar pass. ppr.

Quardeby. Ar. a saltire engr. sa. on a chief of the last two mullets of the first.

Quarles (co. Bedford). Or, a fess dancettée ermines betw. three sea-pewits vert. Crest—Out of a ducal coronet or, a demi eagle displ. vert.

Quarles (Romford, co. Essex). Same Arms.

Quarles (Ufford, co. Northampton, and London, temp. Henry VII.). Same Arms.

Quarles (Haddam, co. Hertford). Same Arms.

Quarles (London; confirmed 15 Feb. 1577). Or, a fess dancettée betw. three eagles close vert.

Quarles (co. Northampton). Or, a fess dancettée ermines, in chief a sea-pewit vert, beaked and legged gu.

Quarles. Or, a fess dancettée ermines, over all a bend vert.

Quarles (Ireland; Fun. Ent. Ulster's Office, 1616, Jonas Quarles). Vert a fess dancettée erm. betw. four sea-pewits or.

Quarlton. Ar. a leopard pass. gu.

Quarm (Nancor, co. Cornwall; originally of Dartmouth, co. Devon). Barry lozengy ar. and gu. counterchanged.

Quarme (Woodhouse, co. Devon, afterwards of St. Keverne, co. Cornwall; Robert Quarme, of the latter place, Visit. Cornwall, 1620, son of Robert Quarme, of the former, who was son of Roger, and grandson of Roger Quarme, both of same place). Barry lozengy ar. and gu. counterchanged.

Quarrell. Ar. a chev. betw. three oak leaves sa. Crest —A wolf courant ppr.

Quart (co. Bucks). Gu. nine lozenges pierced or, conjoined in threes, two and one.

Quarton. Sa. a maunch ar. Crest—A hand ppr. in a maunch ppr.

Quarton. Sa. a chev. betw. three peacocks' (another, griffins') heads erased ar.

Quash (Exeter, co. Devon). Ar. on a fesse sa. three escallops or, in chief a lion pass. of the second. Crest—A demi griffin or, wings endorsed sa. legged of the last, holding betw. the paws a fleur-de-lis gold.

Quatermain (quartered by Lyttelton, of Frankley, co. Worcester; Sir Thomas de Luttelton, Knt., of Frankley, Esquire of the Body to Richard II., Henry IV., and Henry V., m. the dau. and heir of Quatermain, and d. 1422, leaving an only dau. and heir, Elizabeth de Luttelton, m. Thomas Westcote, Esq., ancestor of the Lords Lyttelton. Visit. Devon, 1620). Ar. a fess engr. gu. betw. four dexter hands couped at the wrist and erect az.

Quatermaines (Dublin; Fun. Ent. Ulster's Office, 1599, William Quatermaines, merchant). Gu. on a fess betw. three dexter hands couped at the wrist and erect or, as many martlets sa.

Quatermains (Weston, co. Oxford; Maud, dau. of Thomas Quatermains, Esq., of that place, m. John, son and heir of William Braley, Esq., of Waterstoke, same co. Visit. Oxford, 1566. Arms impaled with Braley in a window in Waterstoke Church). Gu. a fess betw. four dexter hands couped and erect or. Crest—A hand holding a sickle ppr.

Quatermars (co. Leicester). Or, nine mascles in cross gu.

Quatermayne. Ar. a fesse sa. betw. four dexter hands couped gu.

Quatermaynes. Ar. a fesse betw. four sinister hands couped and erect gu.

Quatermaynes. Gu. a fesse betw. three sinister hands couped ar.

Quatrod (Dublin; Fun. Ent. Ulster's Office, 1599, James Quatrod, merchant). Ar. fretty gu. on a canton of the first two bars az. betw. nine martlets, three, three, and three sa.,

Quayle (Crogga, near Douglas, Isle of Man). Ar. a chev. sa. guttée d'eau betw. three quails ppr. Crest—A quail ppr. Motto—Qualis ero spero.

Quebec, See of. Gu. a lion of England holding in the dexter fore-paw a key erect ar. on a chief wavy az. an open book with clasps also ppr. surmounted of a crosier gold, a canton of the second charged with the cross of St. George betw. four crosses pattée fitchée sa.

Quatherine, or Queatherine (co. Lincoln). Erm. a fesse engr. gu. Crest—A ship in full sail ppr. flagged gu. Motto—Ad littora tendit.

Queenborough, Corporation of (co. Kent). The seal is very ancient, and represents a quadrangular castle surmounted with another, over the battlements the bust of a woman, her hair dishevelled and ducally crowned.

Queensberry, Marquess of. See Douglas.

Queen's College (Oxford; founded in [1]1340 by Robert Eglesfield, Confessor to Queen Philippa, wife of Edward III.). Ar. three eagles displ. gu. beaked and legged or. The seal of the College represents an eagle reguard. with wings expanded, resting the dexter claw on a carved shield bearing the arms of the founder, viz., Az. three leopards' faces or, a chief embattled erm.; round the seal the words, "The Common Seal of Mitchel's Visitors;" and on the exergue, "Queen's College, Oxon."

Queen's College (Cambridge; founded in 1441 by Margaret of Anjou, Queen of Henry VI.). Quarterly of six, 1st, barry of eight ar. and gu.; 2nd, az. semée-de-lis or, a label of three points throughout gu.; 3rd, az. a cross potent cantoned with four crosses or; 4th, az. semée-de-lis gu. a bordure of the last; 5th, az. semée of crosses crosslet or, two barbels haurient and endorsed of the last; 6th, or, on a bend gu. three allerions displ. ar. the whole within a bordure vert, being the arms of Margaret of Anjou. Crest—In a coronet of gold an eagle rousant sa. wings or. These arms and crest were granted to the College in 1576.

Queensferry, Town of (Scotland). Ar. in the sea az. a galley with sails braced up sa. in the middle Queen Margaret of Scotland standing richly apparelled and crowned ppr. holding in her dexter hand a sceptre ensigned with a fleur-de-lis or, and in her sinister, lying on her breast, a book folded purp.

Queenstown, Town Commissioners of (co. Cork; granted 1870). Ar. a ship of war in full sail, from the masthead the royal standard of the United Kingdom of Great Britain and Ireland all ppr. in chief a harp ensigned with the imperial crown also ppr. betw. two trefoils slipped vert. Motto—Nomine Reginæ statio fidissima classi.

Queen's University (Ireland; granted by Betham, Ulster, 1851). Ar. a saltire gu. charged with a royal crown of England betw. an open ancient book in chief and the harp in base all ppr.

Quelch (Wallingford, co. Berks). Gu. on a bend ar. betw. two elephants' heads erased or, three pellets. Crest—An elephant's head erased az. charged with a castle ar. fired ppr.

Quelch. Same Arms. Crest—A stag's head at gaze erased ppr.

Quelch (Reg. Ulster's Office). Gu. on a bend ar. betw. two elephants' heads erased or, three pellets. Crest—An elephant's head erased az. charged with a castle of two towers ar.

Quelly. Ar. a chev. betw. three mullets sa.

Quelpdale (arms in the Library of Balliol Coll., Oxford. Visit. Oxon, 1566). Ar. three greyhounds courant gu. on the shoulder of the first a mullet or.

Quenkyn. Erm. three bends gu.

Quennell (Chittingfold, co. Surrey). Az. a cross ar. betw. two roses in chief or, and as many fleurs-de-lis in base of the second.

Querey, or Quaera. Per pale or and az. a cross moline gu.

Querion, or Querryn. Az. a lion ramp. or, a chief gu.

Querleton. Ar. a lion pass. guard. gu. Crest—An acorn stalked and leaved ppr.

Querouaille (Duchess of Portsmouth, extinct 1734; Louisa Renée de Perrencourt de Querouaille, a Frenchwoman who came to England in the train of Henrietta, Duchess of Orleans, the king's sister, was mother, by Charles II., of Charles Lennox, ancestor of the Duke of Richmond, Lennox, and Gordon; she was created a duchess in the Peerage of England, 1673, for life, and was also created by Louis XIV. of France, Duchess of Aubigny in that kingdom, a peerage still enjoyed by the Duke of Richmond). Az. three bars ar.

Querouaille. Barry of eight az. and ar. Crest—A dagger and sword in saltire ppr.

Quesnes. Ar. a lion pass. gu.

Questred. Gu. on a chev. ar. three garbs of the first. Crest—Out of a mural coronet a garb, thereon a blackbird all ppr.

Quewne, or Coyghney (Wedgnock, co. Warwick; confirmed by the Deputies of Camden, Clarenceux). Or, on a bend sa. three cinquefoils slipped ar.

Quicke, or Quick (Westwanke, co. Buckingham, West Monkton, co. Somerset, and Newton St. Cyres, co. Devon, 1623). Sa. a chev. vairé or and of the first betw. three griffins' heads erased of the second. Crest—A demi antelope ar. armed, attired, tufted, and maned gu. collared sa. lined or.

Quicke (co. Devon). Az. a bend wavy betw. three moles ar.

Quicke (Reg. Ulster's Office). Ar. a bend wavy sa. betw. two cocks gu. combed and wattled or, on a canton per pale nebulée of the last and az. a swan ar.

Quicke (co. Devon). Sa. a chev. chequy or and az. betw. three griffins' heads erased ar. Crest—A tent ar. flag gu.

Quickerell. Ar. a buck's head cabossed gu. attired or, betw. the horns a cross pattée fitchée of the second, a bordure gobony or and az.

Quigley (Kildarry, co. Donegal; Reg. Ulster's Office). Gu. an orle ar. over all a bend erm. Crest—An estoile ar.

Quilter (Staple, co. Kent; granted 12 June, 1551). Ar. a bend sa. betw. three Cornish choughs ppr. Crest—An arm embowed in armour holding a battle axe all ppr. a scarf round the wrist ar.

Quin. See O'Quin.

Quin (granted by Carney, Ulster, 1688, to Thady Quin, Esq., of Adare, J.P. co. Limerick, descended from an ancient and honourable family of that surname). Vert a pegasus erm. a chief or. Crest—A wolf's head erased erm. Motto—Quæ sursum volo videre.

Quin (Wyndham-Quin, Earl of Dunraven and Mountearl). Quarterly, 1st and 4th, gu. a hand couped below the wrist grasping a sword ppr. on each side a serpent, tail nowed, the heads respecting each other or, in chief two crescents ar., for O'Quin, of Munster; 2nd and 3rd, az. a chev. betw. three lions' heads erased or, with a mullet for diff., for Wyndham. The Earl of Dunraven wishing to perpetuate the more ancient arms of his ancestors, the O'Quins, of Munster, obtained from the present Ulster King of Arms the right to bear them, instead of those assigned to his ancestor, Thady Quin, Esq., of Adare, by Carney, Ulster, 29 Nov. 1688. Crests—1st, Quin: A wolf's head erased ar.; 2nd, Wyndham: A lion's head erased within a fetterlock and chain or. Supporters—Two ravens with wings elevated ppr. collared and chained or. Motto—Quæ sursum volo videre.

Quin (Quinsborough, co. Clare; exemplified to Lord George Taylor, second son of Thomas, first Marquess of Headfort, by Mary Quin, his wife, only dau. and heir of George Quin, Esq., of Quinsborough, upon his assuming, by royal licence, 1813, the surname of Quin). Vert a pegasus courant, wings endorsed erm. a chief or, a crescent for diff. Crest—A wolf's head erased erm. Motto—Quæ sursum volo videre.

Quin (confirmed by Carney, Ulster, 1690, to Thomas Quin, Captain in the Dublin Militia, and High Sheriff of the city). Per pale or and az. a pegasus erm. rising from a mount ppr. Crest—A wolf's head erased gu. charged with a cinquefoil or.

Quin (co. Galway; Reg. Ulster's Office). Vert a pegasus erm. Crest—A demi pegasus erm.

Quin (Dublin; Fun. Ent. Ulster's Office, 1620, Elinor, dau. of John Quin, and wife of Robert Barnewall). Vert a pegasus pass. erm. wings elevated gu.

Quinan (granted by Betham, Ulster, 1833, to Thomas Quinan, Esq., Leeson Street, Dublin, son of Michael Quinan, M.D., and grandson of Michael Cahan, who claimed descent from the Sept of O'Cahan). Quarterly, 1st, barry of four ar. and gu. in chief three estoiles az.; 2nd, out of a crescent a dexter hand betw. a horse counter-ramp. and a lion ramp. all of the first; 3rd, in dexter three lizards in bend sinister, and in sinister an oak tree eradicated vert; 4th, in base a salmon naiant ppr. Crest—A squirrel holding in the paws an oak tree fructed all ppr. Motto—Qui non patriam amat.

Quinborough (co. Norfolk). Per fess indented ar. and sa. three bears pass. counterchanged.

Quincey (co. Lincoln). Gu. seven mascles conjoined or, three, three, and one.

Quincey. Gu. six mascles or, three, two, and one; another, Gu. five cinquefoils ar. two, two, and one; another, Az. six cinquefoils pierced ar. three, two, and one; another,

Gu. **six** cinquefoils pierced or, three, two, and **one**; another, Gu. a cinquefoil pierced or (another, ar.).

Quincey (Scotland). Gu. three mascles or.

Quincy (*Earl of Winchester*, extinct 1264; SAIER DE QUINCY, *temp.* Henry II., had a grant of the Manor of Bushby, co. Northampton, his son, SAIER DE QUINCY, was created *Earl of Winchester* by King John, and had two sons, ROBERT, second earl, *d. s. p. m.* in the Holy Land, and ROGER, third earl, *d. s. p. m.* 1264). Borne by ROBERT DE QUINCY—Or, a fess gu. a label of twelve points az.; borne by ROGER DE QUINCY—Gu. seven mascles conjoined or, three, three, and one.

Quiney, or Quyney (Shottery, co. Warwick, from London). Or, on a bend sa. three trefoils slipped ar. *Crest*—A cubit arm vested or, cuffed and slashed ar. hand ppr. holding a scymitar ar. imbrued gu. the hilt and pommel gold.

Quiney (Stratford-upon-Avon, co. **Warwick. Visit. 1682**). Same *Arms*.

Quiney. Ar. a fret gu. on a chief az. three fleurs-de-lis or.

Quinlan (Reg. Ulster's Office). Per pale erm. and or, two lions ramp. combatant betw. a mullet surmounted of a crescent in chief and a dexter hand couped at the wrist and erect in base all gu. *Crest*—A stork az. pierced through the body with an arrow ar. *Motto*—True to the end.

Quinlan. See O'QUINLEVAN.

Quintin (co. Wilts). Erm. on a chief gu. three lions ramp. or.

Quintin (arms from the seal of Sir JOHN DE ST. QUINTIN, A.D. 1311). Or, a chev. gu. a chief vair. *Crest*—Out of a ducal coronet or, a lion's paw sa. holding a cross crosslet fitchée gold.

Quintin. Or, three chev. gu. a chief vair.

Quinton, alias Oliver (Heyborne and Leyborne, co. Kent, and Boulton, co. Wilts). Erm. on a chief gu. three lions ramp. or.

Quinton, or Quintin. Gu. on a bend ar. three martlets sa.

Quinton. Same *Arms*, a bordure gobony of the second and third.

Quintridge. Ar. a fret gu. a canton of the last.

Quintwell, or Quittwell (Filmington, co. Norfolk). Gu. a cross pattée (another, flory) ar.

Quivill (PETER QUIVILL, Bishop of Exeter, 1280-91). Az. a cross flory ar. betw. two roses in chief and as many fleurs-de-lis in base or.

Quixley. Gu. three greyhounds courant ar. collared sa. studded or.

Quixley. Gu. three greyhounds courant ar. collared chequy or and sa. each charged on shoulder with an escallop sa.

Quose, or Quoys (North Kendon, co. Essex). Sa. on a chev. betw. three spearheads ar. as many crosses crosslet of of the first.

Quynborow (co. Norfolk). Per fesse indented ar. and sa. three bears muzzled countercharged.

Quynell (Compton, near Guildford, co. Surrey). Az. a cross betw. two roses in chief or, and as many fleurs-de-lis in base ar.

Quytre, or Quytrick. Ar. a fret and canton gu.

Quytricke (*temp.* Richard II.). Ar. a fret and quarter gu.

Quyxley, or Quixley. Gu. an inescutcheon ar. over all a bend sa. *Crest*—An antelope's head erased gu.

Quyxley. Gu. an orle ar. over all a bend erm.

B

RABAN. Ar. a chev. chequy or and az. betw. three boars' heads erased sa. on a chief erminois a mount vert, thereon a raven sa. a canton gu. charged with a sword or. *Crest*—On a mural coronet or, charged with three fireballs sa. a boar's head erased, lying fessways, also sa. holding in the mouth a sword in pale ppr.

Rabett (Dunwich and Bramfield Hall, co. Suffolk; JOHN RABETT was Bailiff of Dunwich, co. Suffolk, 1453; WILLIAM RABETT, Esq., of Bramfield and Dunwich, was M.P. for Dunwich, 8 Edward IV., 1468; REGINALD RABETT, Esq., of Bramfield Hall, *m.* MARY, sister of General Sir EDWARD KERRISON, Bart., M.P., *d.* 1810, left two sons and a dau., viz., Rev. REGINALD RABETT, A.M., of Bramfield Hall, Vicar of Thornton-cum-Bagworth, co. Leicester; GEORGE WILLIAM RABETT, Commander R.N.; and MARY, *m.* HENRY, *Viscount Maynard*). Ar. a chev. sa. charged with five gouttes d'or, betw. three rabbits' heads couped of the second,

each charged on the breast with a goutte d'or. *Crest*—A demi rabbit ramp. sa. guttée d'or. *Motto*—Superabit omnia virtus.

Rabbitt (co. Nottingham). **Ar. a** chev. betw. three rabbits' heads couped sa.

Rabon (JOYCE, dau. of HUGH RABON, *temp.* Queen Elizabeth, *m.* JOHN FENTON, Esq., of Fenton. co. Nottingham. Visit. Notts, 1614). Gu. three wolves pass. counter-pass. pale or.

Raby (Raby, co. Durham; ROBERT, Lord of Raby, *m.* ISABEL, dau. of GEOFFREY DE NEVILL, who became heiress of her brother, HENRY DE NEVILL, 1227; their son, GEOFFREY, assumed his mother's surname, and had two sons, ROBERT, ancestor of the *Lords Nevill*, of Raby, *Earls of Westmorland*, &c., and JOLANUS, ancestor of NEVILL, of Holt, co. Leicester. Visit. Leicester, 1619). Gu. a saltire erm.

Raby, or Rabey. Gu. crusily or, a bend vair.

Rackley, or Rakeley. Lozengy or and gu. a fess sa.

Rackleworth. Gu. three eagles displ. or, armed ar.

Racy (co. Suffolk). Quarterly, or and sa on a bend gu. three martlets of the first, in chief a label of five points erm.

Radbard (Lambroke, co. Somerset). Or, a chev. betw. three bulls sa. horned ar.

Radborne. Ar. a boar's head couped sa. crowned or, betw. three crosses crosslet fitchée of the second, a bordure gu. *Crest*—A horse's head betw. two wings ar.

Radborne. Ar. a boar's head couped betw. three crosses crosslet sa.

Radcliff (co. Chester, Mulgrave and Newton, co. Durham, co. Oxford, and Standish, co. Warwick). Ar. a bend engr. sa. a mullet for diff.

Radcliff (co. Leicester). Ar. on a bend engr. sa. an annulet or, for diff.

Radcliff (Stepney). Ar. a bend engr. sa. a crescent gu. charged with a mullet or, for diff.

Radcliff. Ar. a cross crosslet gu. betw. two bendlets engr. sa. *Crest*—A bull's head erased gu. gorged with a ducal coronet or.

Radcliff. Az. a chev. or, betw. three lions ramp. ar.

Radcliff. Ar. on a bend engr. sa. an escallop gu. *Crest*—A dragon sans legs and wings az.

Radcliffe (Radcliffe Tower, co. Lancaster; decended from WILLIAM RADCLIFFE, Sheriff co. Lancaster 1194; his great-grandson, RICHARD RADCLIFFE, Esq., of Radcliffe Tower, obtained from Edward I., 1303, a charter of free warren and chase in all his demesne lands at Radcliffe; he left three sons: I. ROBERT, ancestor of RADCLIFFE, of Southills and Tingrave; II. WILLIAM, ancestor of the *Earls of Derwentwater*, RATCLIFFE, *Earls of Sussex*, and RATCLIFFE, of Langley; III. Sir JOHN, Knt., of Ordshall, co. Lancaster). Ar. two bendlets engr. sa. *Crest*—A bull's head erased sa. ducally gorged and lined or.

Radcliffe (*Earl of Derwentwater*, attainted 1715; Sir FRANCIS RADCLIFFE, Knt., of Dilston, co. Northumberland, was so created 1688; his grandson, JAMES, third *Earl of Derwentwater*, was beheaded on Tower Hill for participation in the rising in 1715). Ar. a bend engr. sa. *Crest*—Out of a ducal coronet a bull's head sa. armed or. *Supporters*—Two bulls pean gorged with ducal coronets, armed and chained ar.

Radcliffe (*Earl of Newburgh;* JAMES BARTHOLOMEW RADCLIFFE, eldest son of Hon. CHARLES RADCLIFFE, the brother of the attainted *Earl of Derwentwater*, by his wife, CHARLOTTE MARIA, *Countess of Newburgh* in her own right, *s.* his brother as third *Earl of Newburgh* 1755; earldom, now vested in the Princess GIUSTINIANI, *Countess of Newburgh* in her own right). Ar' on a bend betw. two acorns slipped gu. an anchor of the first, a double tressure flory counterflory vert.

Radcliffe (*Earl of Sussex*, extinct 1641). See RATCLIFFE.

Radcliffe (Langley, co. York; descended from RADCLIFFE, of Ordshall). Ar. a bend engr. sa. charged with a crescent of the field for diff. *Crest*—A bull's head erased sa. horned ar. tipped or, gorged with a ducal coronet of the second. *Motto*—Virtus propter se.

Radcliffe (Milnsbridge House, co. York, and Caverswall Castle, co. Stafford, bart.; descended from JOSEPH PICKFORD, Esq., of Althill, co. Lancaster, who *m.* MARY, sister and heir of WILLIAM RADCLIFFE, Esq., of Milnsbridge, and had a son, JOSEPH PICKFORD, assumed the name of RADCLIFFE, and was created a bart. 1813). Ar. a bend engr. sa. charged with a crescent of the field for diff. *Crest*—A bull's head erased sa. horns ar. tipped or, gorged with a ducal coronet of the second. *Motto*—Virtus propter se.

Radcliffe (Hockworthy, co. Devon). Ar. a bend engr. sa. on a canton of the first a horse's head couped of the second. *Crest*—Out of a mural crown ar. a bull's head sa. horned or.

Radcliffe (Mellor, co. Derby; a younger branch of

Lightning Source UK Ltd.
Milton Keynes UK
UKOW031812100512

192333UK00011B/23/P